A CLASSIFIED
SHAKESPEARE BIBLIOGRAPHY

A
CLASSIFIED
SHAKESPEARE
BIBLIOGRAPHY
1936-1958

by
GORDON ROSS SMITH

1963
THE PENNSYLVANIA STATE UNIVERSITY PRESS
University Park, Pennsylvania

Copyright© 1963 by The Pennsylvania State University

Library of Congress Catalog Card Number 63-17265

Manufactured in the United States of America

Designed by Marilyn E. Shobaken

CONDENSED
TABLE OF CONTENTS

Complete table of contents begins on page vii.
Page references below refer to the complete table.

A. GENERAL

B.   THE WORKS OF SHAKESPEARE EXAMINED INDIVIDUALLY

TABLE OF CONTENTS

Classes are generally continued from the Ebisch and Schücking Shakespeare Bibliographies of 1931 and 1937. The numbers in parentheses following various classes below indicate the page numbers of equivalent classes in the Ebisch and Schücking bibliographies; semi-colons separate page numbers of the bibliography of 1931 from those of the compilation of 1937. Present amalgamations of Ebisch and Schücking classes are indicated by the doubling of such numbers; present omissions are noted here and in the text. Classes without any Ebisch and Schücking page numbers are newly added.

A. GENERAL

          (c)   England in General A4543

          (d)   Shakespeare A4559

   c. Influence of French Literature (72;27) A4563

      (1) General (72;-) A4563

      (2) Individual French Authors (73;27)   .   .   .   A4569

          (a)   Belleforest A4569

          (b)   Froissart A4571

          (c)   Garnier A4574

          (d)   Montaigne A4577

          (e)   Others A4602

   d. Influence of Spanish Literature (74;27) A4604

      (1) General (74;-) A4604

      (2) Individual Spanish and Portuguese Authors (74;27)   .   .   A4612

          (a)   Cervantes A4612

          (b)   F. de Rojas A4616

          (c)   Gil Vicente A4620

          (d)   Others A4622

   e. Influence of Germanic Literature (75;28)   .   .   .   A4630

      (1) General (75;-) A4630

      (2) Individual Germanic Authors (75;28)   .   .   A4636

          (a)   Erasmus A4636

          (b)   Gnaphaeus A4646

4. Influence of Contemporaneous English Nondramatic Literature (75;28)   .   A4649

   a. General Studies of Various Sources A4649

   b. Chronicles and Histories A4669

      (1) Tudor Principles A4669

      (2) History and Literature A4676

          (a)   Geoffrey of Monmouth   .   .   .   A4684

          (b)   T. More A4687

          (c)   Polydore Vergil A4690

          (d)   Hall and Holinshed   .   .   .   A4695

   c. Prose Fiction Generally A4712

   d. Individual Writers A4719

      (1) Beverley A4719

      (2) Bright A4721

      (3) Brooke A4723

      (4) Buchanan A4725

      (5) Daniel A4727

      (6) Deloney A4735

      (7) Sylvester's DuBartas A4738

      (8) J. Eliot A4740

      (9) T. Elyot A4742

    (10) Gascoigne A4750

    (11) Greene A4752

    (12) Harsnett A4754

    (13) Lewkenor A4757

    (14) Lodge A4759

    (15) Nashe A4761

    (16) Rich A4770

    (17) The School of Night   .   .   .   A4787

    (18) Sidney A4790

    (19) Spenser A4807

    (20) Geo. Wilkins A4821

    (21) Wilson A4825

    (22) Others A4827

5. Influence of Contemporaneous English Dramatists (76;28)   .   .   A4856

   a. Collaboration and Other Problems of Authorship (18;4,5)   .   .   A4856

ACKNOWLEDGMENTS

My obligations are many. I am most indebted to Dr. Frederick R. Matson, Assistant Dean for Research of the College of the Liberal Arts, The Pennsylvania State University, and to the Central Fund for Research of the same institution. Without their support over some seven years, this bibliography simply would not have reached publication. I am also indebted to Prof. Henry W. Sams, Chairman of the Department of English, who assigned me graduate assistants.

I wish to thank Dr. James G. McManaway of the Folger Shakespeare Library for his encouragement and many helpful suggestions, and Dr. Louis B. Wright of that institution for a Folger fellowship in 1958. I am grateful to the staffs of the New York Public Library, the Library of Congress, the libraries of Columbia University, and especially to the librarians of the Pattee Library of The Pennsylvania State University.

I want to thank Dr. Levin L. Schücking and the Clarendon Press for permission to use and adapt the Ebisch and Schücking system of classification, Dr. James G. McManaway and Mrs. Donald F. Hyde of The Shakespeare Association of America for permission to use the bibliographies of SQ and SAB, Prof. Dougald MacMillan and the University of North Carolina for permission to use the bibliographies of SP, and Prof. William Wells for the loan of a twenty-year file of the SP bibliographies.

For aid in classifying items in Slavic languages I am indebted to Professors Peter Rudy of Northwestern University, Edgar Lehrman of Emory University, William Edgerton of Indiana University, William Harkins of Columbia University, and Thomas Magner of The Pennsylvania State University. For various degrees of help with Scandinavian, Dutch, Italian and Spanish, I am indebted to Professors Helen Adolf, Dagobert de Levie, Alfred Triolo, and Donald Bleznick, respectively, all of The Pennsylvania State University.

Finally, I am indebted to a number of graduate assistants, chiefly Mr. Kevin Thomas, who prepared the list of abbreviations, Miss Alyce Sands, Mr. Donald Wineke, and Mr. Alan Rosen, but also to Miss Nylda Rivera, Mr. Harvey Haldeman, Mr. K. S. Narayana Rao, Mr. Dyson Shultz, Miss Harriet Gould, and Mr. Paul Norton.

FOREWORD

Scope of this Compilation

THE best argument for so comprehensive a bibliography as this is that no two judgments are alike, that one does not and should not rely on the infallibility of a single source, and therefore that any user of a selective bibliography is likely to be haunted by the fear and perhaps the likelihood that something particularly relevant to his study has been missed. For these reasons I have, within the chronological limits of this bibliography, included everything in the sources listed below.

Nevertheless this is not a comprehensive bibliography, even within the years which set its limits. If it were possible to achieve such a bibliography, there would not at present be any way whatever of knowing when one had arrived. My objective therefore has been more limited. Although I should have liked a comprehensive bibliography, this is strictly speaking only a bibliography of everything on Shakespeare that has appeared in certain standard bibliographies, mostly annuals, listed below. My purpose has been to provide a bibliography that scholars and students might use with the confidence that they would not also have to consult the bibliographies from which this one has been compiled. They may thereby be saved countless hours of poring over annual bibliographies which, however repetitious, nevertheless always contain some items not in the others. For the same reason I have included everything in the specified dissertation bibliographies not already in one of the Ebisch and Schücking bibliographies. The user of this bibliography should examine the following list of sources to see exactly what he may hope to dispense with. Dates given here are for the years covered by the bibliographies, not for the years of publication.

ANNUAL SHAKESPEARE BIBLIOGRAPHIES:

SQ, 1949-1958. All listed items and some of the annotations.

SAB, 1936-1948. All Shakespeare items, but not those on other dramatists or poets. Items listed by Dr. Tannenbaum under specific plays have always been continued under the same plays in this compilation, although they may appear elsewhere also. Since in his bibliographies Dr. Tannenbaum changed the titles of articles, including his own, at will, some of his modified titles may have slipped in here, although I corrected all that I encountered.

SJ, 1936-1943, 1947-1958. *SJ* published no bibliographies for the years 1944-1946. Items classified under specific plays have been included under the same plays in this compilation.

PMLA, 1936-1958.   Shakespeare section, including all cross-referenced items.

SP, 1936-1958.   All of the Shakespeare sections, including cross-referenced items; all items in the drama sections having to do with Shakespeare, including cross-references; occasional annotations from the foregoing; a selection of items from the "General" and "English History, Manners, and Customs" sections having to do with categories of subjects already among the Ebisch and Schücking classes, e.g., philosophical, ethical, religious, scientific, social and political thought, printing customs, translations, etc.   The *SP* bibliographies are not exhaustive in these subjects, and listings here are therefore a further critical selection.

Literature and Psychology, Quarterly News Letter of General Topics 10, MLA, 1951-1958.   All Shakespeare items from the current and retrospective bibliographies unless already in one of the Ebisch and Schücking bibliographies.

MHRA, 1936-1954.   Shakespeare sections.   Items classified under specific plays have been continued there.

YWES, 1936-1954.   Shakespeare chapters.

DISSERTATION BIBLIOGRAPHIES.   Only dissertations relevant to Shakespeare have been culled; many series were not yet available through 1958 when this compilation was closed; I hope that in a later supplement they may be caught up with.

AMERICAN:

Gilchrist, Donald B., et al.   *Doctoral Dissertations Accepted by American Universities.* New York: H. W. Wilson Co., Nos. 3-22, 1935-36 to 1954-55 inclusive. "Literature and Art" sections and "Humanities" sections.

DA and *Microfilm Abstracts*.   Vols. 1-20, 1938-1957.   Literature, drama, and speech sections.

Association of Research Libraries.   *Index to American Doctoral Dissertations.*   (Combination and continuation of the above two series.)   Vols. 16-18, 1955-56 to 1957-58 inclusive.

BRITISH:

Record, P. D., and Magda Whitrow.   *Index to Theses Accepted for Higher Degrees in the Universities of Great Britain and Ireland.*   London: Aslib.   Vols. 1-7, 1950-51 to 1956-57 inclusive.

London University.   *Subjects of Dissertations, Theses, and Published Works Presented by Successful Candidates at Examinations for Higher Degrees.*   London: University of London.   1937 to 1955-56 inclusive.

Cambridge University.   *Abstracts of Dissertations Approved for the Ph. D., M. Sc. and M. Litt. Degrees in the University of Cambridge.*   Cambridge: Cambridge University Press.   1935-36 to 1954-55 inclusive.

Oxford University Committee for Advanced Studies.   *Abstracts of Dissertations for the Degree of Doctor of Philosophy.*   Oxford: Clarendon Press.   Vols. 1-13, 1925-28 to 1940 inclusive.

Oxford University Committee for Advanced Study.   *Successful Candidates for the Degrees of S. Phil., B. Litt., and B. Sc., with Titles of Their Theses.*   Oxford: University Press.   Vols. 1-7, 1940-49 to 1954-55 inclusive.

University of Edinburgh.   *List of Theses Accepted for Doctorates.*   1933-34 to 1950-51 inclusive.

Aberdeen University. *Abstracts of Theses.* 1931-32 to 1936-37 inclusive.

University of Durham. *Abstracts of Theses for Doctorates.* 1931-32 to 1938-39 inclusive.

University of Leeds. *Publications and Abstracts of Theses by Members of the University.* 1927-28 to 1937-38 inclusive.

CANADIAN, SOUTH AFRICAN, etc.

Canadian Graduate Theses in the Humanities and Social Sciences, 1921-1946. Ottawa: Printer to the King, 1951. Pp. 194. Contains many masters' theses. Everything on Shakespeare has been included.

Robinson, Anthony Meredith Lewin. *Catalogue of Theses and Dissertations Accepted for Degrees by the South African Universities.* Cape Town, 1943. Pp. 155.

Jenkins, D. *Union List of Theses of the University of New Zealand, 1910-1954.* Wellington: Library Association, 1956.

FRENCH:

Ministère de l'Éducation Nationale. *Catalogue des Thèses et Écrits Académiques.* Paris. 1936-1956 inclusive.

BELGIAN:

Université Catholique de Louvain. *Bibliographie Académique.* Vol. 7, 1934-1954 inclusive.

SWISS:

Blanc, Hermann. *Catalogue des Ouvrages, Articles, et Mémoires Publiés par les Professeurs . . . de l'Université de Genève . . . et des Thèses Présentées . . . pour l'Obtention de Grades Universitaires.* 1938-1952 inclusive.

Jahresverzeichnis der Schweizerischen Hochschulschriften. Basel: Verlag der Universitätsbibliothek. For the universities of Basel, Bern, Freiburg, Geneva, Lausanne, Neuchâtel, and Zürich and the Technische Hochschule Zürich. 1935-36 to 1956 inclusive.

GERMAN:

Mummendey, Richard. *Language and Literature of the Anglo-Saxon Nations as Presented in German Doctoral Dissertations, 1885-1950.* Bonn, Charlottesville, 1954. All dissertations having to do with Shakespeare not already in the Ebisch and Schücking bibliographies have been included, whatever their dates.

Jahresverzeichnis der deutschen Hochschulschriften. Bearbeitet von der Deutschen Bücherei. Leipzig: Verlag für Buch- und Bibliothekswesen. 1951-1953 inclusive.

AUSTRIAN:

Alker, Lisl. *Verzeichnis der an der Universität Wien Approbierten Dissertationen, 1937-1944.* Vienna: O. Kerry, 1954.

Alker, Lisl. *Verzeichnis der an der Universität Wien Approbierten Dissertationen, 1945-1949.* Vienna: O. Kerry, 1952.

Österreichische Bibliographie; Verzeichnis der Österreichischer Neuerscheinungen. Bearbeitet von der Österreichischen Nationalbibliothek Wien. 1950-1956 inclusive.

DUTCH:

Nederlandsche Vereeniging van Bibliothecarissen. *Catalogus van academische Geschriften in Nederland en Nederlandsch Indie verschenen.* 1936-1951 inclusive.

SWEDISH:

Uppsala Universitet Bibliotek. *Scripta Academica. Écrits Académiques et Thèses.* 1939-40 to 1956-57 inclusive.

Tuneld, John. *Akademiska Avhandlingar vid Sveriges Universitet och Högskolor, Läsåren 1910/11-1939/40.* Lund: Ohlsson, 1945. Pp. 336.

Lunds Universitets Bibliografi, Lund. Sometimes *Envoi de la Bibliothèque de l'Université Royale de Lund.* 1923-24 to 1955-56 inclusive.

NORWEGIAN:

Norske Bokhandlerforening. *Årskatalog over Norsk Litteratur.* Oslo. 1936-37 to 1956 inclusive.

DANISH:

Université de Copenhague. *Année Académique . . . Liste des Thèses et d'Écrits Académiques.* 1928 to 1956 inclusive.

FINNISH:

Universität Helsinki. *Verzeichnis der im Studienjahre 1935-36* [or subsequent years] *erschienenen akademischen Schriften der Universität Helsinki.* Sometimes *List of Academical Publications Issued at the University of Helsinki in the Academic Year* . . . Helsinki. 1935-36 to 1955-56 inclusive.

SPANISH:

Madrid, Universidad. *Catálogo de las Tesis Doctorales Manuscritas Existentes en la Universidad de Madrid.* Madrid: Gráficas González, 1952.

Madrid, Universidad. Facultad de Filosofía y Letras. *Sumarios y Extractos de las Tesis Doctorales, Leídas desde 1940 a 1950 en las Secciones de Filosofía y Pedagogía.* Madrid, 1953.

MEXICAN:

Chávez, Tobías. *Notas para la Bibliografía de las Obras Editadas o Patrocinadas por la Universidad Nacional Autónoma de México.* Contiene además las notas bibliográficas de las tesis presentadas por los graduados, durante los años de 1937 a 1942. México: Imprenta Universitaria, 1943.

Mexico City College. *A Descriptive List of Research Papers and Theses Accepted by the Graduate School of Mexico City College,* 1947-1954. Mexico City College Press, 1954.

JAPANESE:

Union of Japanese Societies of Literature, Philosophy and History. *The Japan Science Review: Literature, Philosophy and History.* Vols. 1-9, 1950-1958 inclusive.

Method of Compilation

To reduce the incidence of error attendant upon repeated transcription, photographic copies were made of all the annual bibliographies of *SQ, SJ,* and the drama sections of *SP* which covered publications of the years 1936-1958 inclusive. Every item in these three series was mounted with its annotation and previous class designation, if any, on a 4 x 6 card. These cards were then collated with the Shakespeare sections of the annual bibliographies of *PMLA, MHRA, YWES* and *SAB* for the same years. Typed cards were made of the considerable yield of items from these four series. To all these were added the numerous European and American dissertations culled from the various dissertation bibliographies listed above.

Use of the Ebisch and Schücking Classification System

An unavoidable problem with a classified bibliography of this size is that there are either a great multiplicity of classes or else classes of such size that they cease to be classes. Rather than institute still another system of classification, the present bibliography employs the system set up by Ebisch and Schücking in their bibliography of 1930. Since that bibliography contains only about 3,800 items, and this one over 20,000, it has been necessary to establish many new classes. These have been determined more by the nature of the material than by a logical expansion where the latter would have been irrelevant to the existing material. A study of these logical lacunae will indicate much more work to be done. Duplicated classes in Ebisch and Schücking, such as theatre audience, ghosts, madmen, dictionaries of quotations, etc., have been combined. The whole of section XIII, "Civilization in Shakespeare's England," has been combined with section IV, "Shakespeare's Personality," because essentially the same subjects are involved in both sections and because it is impossible in practice to separate discussions of the contemporaneous climate of opinion on these matters from discussions of Shakespeare's probable attitudes, or discussions of these from discussions of the plays themselves. All but part 6 of section II, "Elizabethan Literature," has been omitted because of restrictions upon the sources of this compilation, and part 6 has been transferred to the section called "The Influence of Contemporary English Dramatists."

Method of Classification

The guiding principle has been to examine all books, before classifying them, all available dissertations, and all articles whenever the annotation and classification in the source bibliography and the title and length were still not sufficient evidence to be certain of the contents. These good intentions were not always possible to realize, making the following modifications of the initial principle necessary.

Except for trade editions of Shakespeare, all books in English have been examined before classification. Most books in French, Italian, German, Dutch, or Scandinavian languages which were not translations of English texts have also been examined. Those few which were not looked at are books mostly of the late 1930's and early 1940's not in the libraries where I worked and not generally available in America. Russian and Japanese books when accessible have been classified with the help of persons who read those languages. They have also been collected in their respective national sections.

All dissertations available from University Microfilms have also been examined before classification. Dissertations not on microfilm have been classified from the published abstracts if any existed. Where neither existed, they have been entered by title alone. Where title was also uncertain evidence, they have been deposited in a special section at the end of the bibliography.

Thousands of articles have been examined because title, length, and source annotation and class failed to indicate their contents. The doubtful articles inaccessible to me form the bulk of the unclassified section at the end of the bibliography; that section also contains a few articles erroneously included in some standard Shakespeare bibliographies but not relevant to Shakespeare or any general class in this compilation. Other thousands of articles have been classified on the evidences already mentioned.

Items have been put into two or more different classes chiefly where it seemed that a searcher might otherwise miss them. For example, an article or book which discusses both *The Book of Sir Thomas More* and "The Phoenix and the Turtle" will be listed in both sections, since it is not to be supposed that a researcher would normally look for material on either in the other class. The only exceptions to this principle are books and articles of such singular importance that they should not by any means be missed, and these will appear in related as well as in dissimilar classes.

Festschriften and other collections of essays have been grouped together for reference purposes and for review listings. Articles from Festschriften may be listed elsewhere as merely in "the Doe Festschrift," and one should turn to the Festschriften section for further necessary information.

Within most classes listing is chronological by year and alphabetical by author's surname within each year. A few classes such as "Shakespeare's Philosophical Ideas" and "Aesthetic Criticism" are alphabetical by author's surname only. Such arrangement has been made on the assumption that valid contributions are more independent of date in these classes than in most others. Anti-Stratfordian sections are also alphabetically arranged but on the conviction that the material is *sui generis* and independent of any evidence. Some other classes seemed to fall into a natural progression by content, and these have been so arranged, usually with a prefatory note at the head of the class about the type of arrangement.

When the entire bibliography had been arranged, but before the editing of cards took place, the first 10,000 items were numbered and given a prefatory letter A. The second 10,000 were given a B, and the third 10,000 were begun with C. Such a system of numbering can go to 260,000 but remain at a letter and four numbers the whole way. Should a supplement to this bibliography seem desirable, numbering could start with D1, and if it contained less than 20,000 numbered items, a second supplement might begin with F1, and so forth. Even supposing a doubling of the volume of Shakespearean scholarship and publication between now and the end of this century—perhaps a total of 100,000 items—this numbering method is adequate, and the use of the letter, number, and author's surname (e.g., B1748 Harbage), would be sufficient to identify the bibliography, the volume it is listed in, and the book or article itself. The advantages of a comprehensive and continuing compilation with a uniform system of classification and designation hardly need be expatiated upon.

Style of Entry

In general the style of entry follows the MLA Style Sheet of 1951. The chief exception is the substitution of Arabic for Roman volume numbers from 80 onward. Roman numbers frequently get cumbersome beyond XXXV, and I submit that no one can distinguish the *SJ* volume numbers LXXXIV/LXXXVI and LXXXVII/LXXXVIII from each other or LXXXIX from LXXIX so readily as he can read 84/86, 87/88, 89 or 79. Volume numbers therefore appear in both Roman and Arabic styles, and Arabic volume numbers are to be identified by their place, i.e., before the date instead of afterwards, as with page numbers. Roman numbers have been discontinued after LXXIX. Many reviews which contain the volume number in Roman figures are not accompanied with their dates. It seemed unnecessary always to include the date for each separate review when so often many were of the same year. The rule therefore is that all undated reviews are the same year as the last preceding review for which the date is supplied. The user who wants to know the date of an undated review should look *backwards* to the last preceding dated review and *not* forwards to the next dated review from which he subtracts one year because in a batch of many reviews of a single year the date is sometimes reinserted along the middle somewhere in order to spare the user too long a trek backwards. Moreover, there may also be a belated review which came out two years after the last preceding one, in which event the user would again calculate the wrong year. Apart from chronological order by year of appearance, the reviews are in no particular order, since almost all but those from *MHRA* were edited from photographic copy, and different sources adhered to different systems, or none. For the same reason—photographic copy—it did not seem worthwhile to expand commonplace German abbreviations known to all readers of German, or to expand "Shakspere" to "Shakespeare."

The Use of this Bibliography

Accomplished scholars should have little difficulty in using this bibliography, but beginning students might profit from the following suggestions.

First, if one looks in only two or three classes of this bibliography, he is using it improperly. The bibliography is divided into two main parts, the general section and the section on the individual plays, and one should always look in both. Moreover, most of the Ebisch and Schücking classes have new subdivisions which include both general and specific sections, and one should always look in both types. Finally, large quantities of material usually defy any system of classification and flow from class to class, and any effort to classify must be to some degree arbitrary. So is it here, and the serious student should consult every related class he can find.

The second suggestion would seem too obvious to mention were it not for the tendency of people in the 1940's to treat the Ebisch and Schücking bibliographies as if they were the last word. It is that the student should not rely on this bibliography alone. He should consult not only the Ebisch and Schücking bibliographies but also the *CBEL*, the issues of *SP*, *MHRA*, *YWES*, *PMLA*, *SJ*, and *SAB* before 1936, and the annual bibliographies since 1958.

Students not looking for specific items but wishing merely to understand Shakespeare and his times might do well to begin with the sections on the Thought of the Times, A3741-A4013, Shakespeare's Personality, A864-A2637, the sections on Tragedy, History, and Comedy, B4936-B5300, and that on Aesthetic Criticism, A8072-A8446.

GORDON ROSS SMITH

The Pennsylvania State University
University Park, Pennsylvania
1963

ABBREVIATIONS

The journal abbreviations employed by *SP*, *SQ*, *SJ*, and *SAB*, from 1936 through 1958 have been compiled and compared. Wherever all four used a common abbreviation, that one has been used here. Where there was hopeless divergence, the abbreviation for that journal which was listed in the *PMLA* bibliography of 1958 has been employed. Where the journal was defunct by 1958, the *SJ* abbreviation has been preferred for German journals and the *SP* abbreviation for others. Books and articles which appeared only in the *MHRA*, *PMLA*, or *YWES* bibliographies, or in some other, have had their abbreviations altered to conform to this list. Thus some journals with standard abbreviations, such as *SAQ*, are not so abbreviated here because none of the editors of *SP*, *SQ*, *SJ*, and *SAB* for these 23 years saw fit to include *SAQ* (or any other than those here) in their annual lists of abbreviations.

JOURNAL ABBREVIATIONS

ADA	Anzeiger für dts. Altertum
AglGR	Anglo-German Review
AHR	American Historical Review
AJP	American Journal of Philology
AMS	Joseph Quincy Adams Memorial Studies
Archiv	Archiv für das Studium der neuren Sprachen
Archiv. rom.	Archivum Romanicum
Archiv. stor.	Archivo storico
Ba	Baconiana
Beiblatt	Beiblatt zur Anglia
BH	Bulletin Hispanique
BHR	Bibliothèque d'Humanisme et Renaissance
BHS	Bulletin of Hispanic Studies
Biblio.	Bibliofilia
BJRL	Bulletin of the John Rylands Library
BSS	Bulletin of Spanish Studies
Cam Abs.	Cambridge Abstracts
CamJ	Cambridge Journal
CamR	Cambridge Review

CE	College English
CL	Comparative Literature
CM	Cornhill Magazine
ConR	Contemporary Review
CR	Classical Review
CS	Cahiers du Sud
DA	Dissertation Abstracts
DDHS	Dts. Höhere Schule
DL	Die Literatur
DLZ	Deutsche Literaturzeitung
DNL	Die Neue Literatur
DUJ	Durham University Journal
DuV	Dichtung und Volkstum
DVLG	Deutsche Vierteljahrsschrift für Literaturwissenschaft und Geistesgeschichte
DW	Die Weltliteratur
DWD	Dts. Wissenschaftlicher Dienst
DWEV	Dts. Wissenschaft, Erziehung und Volksbildung
EA	Etudes Anglaises
EdR	Edinburgh Review
EHR	English Historical Review
EI	Etudes Italiennes
EIC	Essays in Criticism
EIE	English Institute Essays
EL	Europäische Literatur
ELH	ELH. A Journal of English Literary History
EngR	English Review
Eng. Studn.	Englische Studien
ES	English Studies
ETJ	Educational Theatre Journal
EWD	Europäischer Wissenschaftsdienst
Expl.	Explicator
FortnR	Fortnightly Review
FuF	Forschungen und Fortschritte
GA	Geistige Arbeit
GQ	Germanic Quarterly
GR	Germanic Review
GRM	Germanisch-Romanische Monatsschrift
GSLI	Giornale Storico della Letteratura Italiana
HAHR	Hispanic American Historical Review
Hel.	Helicon. Zeitschrift für Grundfragen der Literaturwissenschaft

Hisp.	Hispania
HLQ	Huntington Library Quarterly
HR	Hispanic Review
H & R	Humanisme et Renaissance
HZ	Historische Zeitschrift
ICS	Italia che Scrive
Ital.	Italica
JAAC	Journal of Aesthetics and Art Criticism
Jb. f. niederdt. Spr.	Jahrbuch für niederdeutsche Sprachforschung
Jb. u. Ersch. ger. Lit.	Jahresberichte über die Erscheinungen auf dem Gebiete der germanischen Literaturgeschichte
JEGP	Journal of English and Germanic Philology
JHI	Journal of the History of Ideas
JMH	Journal of Modern History
JWCI	Journal of the Warburg and Courtauld Institutes
KR	Kenyon Review
LanM	Les Langues Modernes
Lbl	Literaturblatt für germanische und romanische Philologie
LNN	Leipziger Neueste Nachrichten
LT	Levende Talen
LZ	Literarisches Zentralblatt
MdF	Mercure de France
MDG	Monatsschrift f. dts. Geistesleben
MDtShG	Mitteilungen der Deutschen Shakespeare-Gesellschaft
MGW	Manchester Guardian Weekly
MLJ	Modern Language Journal
MLN	Modern Language Notes
MLQ	Modern Language Quarterly
MLR	Modern Language Review
MNN	Münchener Neueste Nachrichten
Monatshefte	Monatshefte für den deutschen Unterricht
MP	Modern Philology
MSR	Malone Society Reprints
NA	Nuova Antologia
Neophil	Neophilologus
N. Mitt.	Neuphilologische Mitteilungen
N. Mon.	Neuphilologische Monatsschrift
N & Q	Notes and Queries
NR	New Republic
NRF	Nouvelle Revue Française
NRFH	Nueva revista de filología hispánica

NS	Die Neuren Sprachen
NstN	New Statesman and Nation
NYHTBR	New York Herald-Tribune Book Review
NYTBR	New York Times Book Review
Obs.	The Observer
OxAbs	Oxford Abstracts
PMLA	PMLA. Publications of the Modern Language Association
PQ	Philological Quarterly
QJS	Quarterly Journal of Speech
QQ	Queen's Quarterly
QR	Quarterly Review
RAA	Revue Anglo-Américaine
RBPH	Revue belge de philologie et d'histoire
RCHL	Revue critique d'Histoire et de Littérature
RCC	Revue des Cours et Conférences
RddxM	Revue des deux Mondes
RES	Review of English Studies
RFE	Revista de filología española
RFH	Revista de filología hispánica
RG	Revue Germanique
RH	Revue Historique
RHM	Revista Hispánica Moderna
RHE	Revue d'Histoire Ecclésiastique
RHL	Revue d'Histoire Littéraire de la France
RHT	Revue d'Histoire du Théâtre
RLC	Revue de Littérature Comparée
RN	Renaissance News
Rom	Romania
RR	Romanic Review
RUnBrux	Revue de l'Université de Bruxelles
SAB	Shakespeare Association Bulletin
SatR	Saturday Review
SB	Studies in Bibliography
SCN	Seventeenth Century News
ShN	Shakespeare Newsletter
ShS	Shakespeare Survey
SJ	Shakespeare-Jahrbuch
SN	Studia Neophilologica
SP	Studies in Philology
SQ	Shakespeare Quarterly
SR	Sewanee Review

SRL	Saturday Review of Literature
SS	Scandinavian Studies
TAr	Theatre Arts
TC	Twentieth Century
TLS	The Times Literary Supplement
TLZ	Theologische Literaturzeitung
TN	Theatre Notebook
TRSC	Transactions of the Royal Society of Canada
TxSE	Texas Studies in English
TZ	Theologische Zeitschrift
UTQ	University of Toronto Quarterly
VB (B)	Völkischer Beobachter (Berlin)
VB (Mü)	Völkischer Beobachter (Munich)
VQR	Virginia Quarterly Review
YR	Yale Review
YWES	Year's Work in English Studies
ZAA	Zeitschrift für Anglistik und Amerikanistik
ZAAK	Zeitschrift für Aesthetik und Allgem. Kunstwissenschaft
Zbl. f. Bibl.	Zentralblatt für Bibliothekswesen
ZDA	Zeitschrift für Dts. Altertum u. Dts. Literatur
ZDB	Zeitschrift für Deutsche Bildung
ZDG	Zeitschrift für Deutsche Geisteswissenschaft
ZDK	Zeitschrift für Deutschkunde
ZDP	Zeitschrift für Deutsche Philologie
ZDWDU	Zeitschrift für Deutschwissenschaft und Deutschunterricht
ZfSchKg	Zeitschrift für Schweizerische Kirchengeschichte
ZNS	Zeitschrift für Neure Sprachen
ZNU	Zeitschrift für neusprachlichen Unterricht
ZRG	Zeitschrift für Religions- und Geistesgeschichte
ZRP	Zeitschrift für romanische Philologie

OTHER ABBREVIATIONS

Abstr.	Abstract
Assoc.	Association
Bul. & Bull.	Bulletin
DD	Doctoral Dissertation
Ed.	Editor, editors, edition, editions
Eng.	English, Englisch
Grad.	Graduate

Hist.	History, Historical
Jour.	Journal
Lib.	Library
Philos.	Philosophy
Publ.	Published, Publication
Quar.	Quarterly
Rec.	Record
Rev	Review, Reviews
rev.	revised
Ser.	Series
Soc.	Society
Stud.	Studies
Tr.	Translated, translator, translation
Trans.	Transactions
Univ.	University
Ztg.	Zeitung

A CLASSIFIED
SHAKESPEARE BIBLIOGRAPHY

A. GENERAL

GENERAL BIBLIOGRAPHY

A1   Bohatta, H., Franz Hodes, and W. Funke. *International Bibliographie der Bibliographie: Ein Nachschlagewerk.* Parts 1-8. Frankfurt: Klostermann, 1939-1950. Pp. 652.
      Rev: by James B. Childs, *Papers Bibl. Soc. Amer.*, XLV (1951), 180-181.

A2   Linder, LeRoy Harold. *The Rise of Current Complete National Bibliography in England, France, Germany, and the United States, 1564 to 1939.* DD, Univ. of Chicago, 1958.

A3   Bateson, F. W., ed. *Cambridge Bibliography of English Literature.* I: A.D. 600-1660; II: 1660-1800; III: 1800-1900; IV: Index. Cambridge Univ. Press; New York: Macmillan, 1941. Pp. xl, 912; xx, 1003; xxii, 1098; 287.
      Rev: by Michael Sadleir, *Nineteenth Century*, 130 (1941), 53-60; *N & Q*, 180 (1941), 89-90; by Davidson Cook, *TLS*, June 14, 1941, p. 292; by E. E. Kellett, *NstN*, March 8, 1941, p. 254; by M. F. Ashley Montagu, *Isis*, XXXIII, 550-551; by N. I. White, *South Atlantic Quar.*, XI, 298-300; by G. L. M., *Papers Bibl. Soc. Amer.*, XXXV, 163-165; by Arthur Friedman, *Lib. Quar.*, XI, 521-524; by H. W., *Lib. Assoc. Rec.*, XLIII, 18; by Christian Gauss, *SRL*, Apr. 19, 1941, p. 7; by D. A. Roberts, *Nation* (New York), 153 (1941), 76-77; by H. S. V. J., *JEGP*, XI, 564-566; by A. B. Shepperson, "The Wages of Literature," *VQR*, XVII, 597-600; by L. N. Broughton, *MLN*, LVII (1942), 285-288; by F. C. Francis, *Library*, NS, XXII, 250-255; by René Wellek, *PQ*, XXI, 251-256; by D. F. Bond, *MP*, XXXIX, 303-312; by J. R. Sutherland, *RES*, XVII, 490-494; by Hardin Craig, *CE*, III, 422-424.

A4   Bateson, F. W., and George Watson, eds. *Cambridge Bibliography of English Literature.* V: Supplement 600-1900. Cambridge Univ. Press, 1957. Pp. xiv, 710.
      Rev: *TLS*, Oct. 4, 1957, p. 600; by George L. McKay, *Papers Bibl. Soc. Amer.*, LII (1958), 68-70; by John Hayward, *Book Collector*, VII, 82, 85; by L. W. Hanson, *Library*, 5th Series, XIII, 208-210; by L. Bonnerot, *EA*, XI, 155.

A4a   Watson, George, ed. *Concise Cambridge Bibliography of English Literature.* Cambridge Univ. Press, 1958. Pp. xi, 271.

A5   Cross, Tom Peete, ed. *Bibliographical Guide to English Studies.* 7th ed. rev. and enlarged. Univ. Chicago Press, 1938. Pp. viii, 123. 8th ed., 1943; 9th ed., 1947.
      Rev: by T. G. Ehrsam, *Lib. Quar.*, IX (1938), 235-261; by T. G. Ehrsam, *Lib. Quar.*, XIV (1944), 174-175; by J. H. P. Pafford, *Library*, 4th Series, XXV (1944-45), 193.

A6   Kennedy, Arthur G. *A Concise Bibliography for Students of English.* Stanford Univ. Press. 1st ed., 1940; 2nd ed., 1945; 3rd ed., 1954.

A7   Spargo, John W. *A Bibliographical Manual for Students of the Language and Literature of England and the United States. A Short-title List.* 2nd ed., Chicago: Packard & Co., 1941. Pp. x, 260. 3rd ed., New York: Hendricks House, 1956. Pp. x, 285.
      Rev: by R. C. Bald, *MLN*, LVIII (1943), 234-235.

A8   *Doctoral Dissertations Accepted by American Universities.* Compiled for the Assoc. of Research Libraries. New York: H. W. Wilson Co. Began 1933-34, Nos. 1-6 ed., Donald B. Gilchrist; 7-11 ed., Edward A. Henry; 12-15 ed., Arnold H. Trotier; 16-22 ed., Arnold H. Trotier and Marian Harman. Supplanted by *Dissertation Abstracts*, 1955-1956, et seq.

A9   Knower, Franklin H. "Graduate Theses; An Index of Graduate Work in Theatre." *ETJ*, May, 1951, and each May thereafter through 1958. Formerly in *Speech Monographs*, II (1935), et seq., until 1951.

A10   Peddie, R. A. *Subject Index of Books: Published Up To and Including 1880.* New Series, A-Z. London: Grafton & Co., 1948. Pp. viii, 872.
    Constitutes a supplement to its three predecessors, 1933, 1935, and 1939 respectively.
      Rev: *TLS*, Aug. 7, 1948, p. 448.

BIBLIOGRAPHIES ON SPECIFIC SUBJECTS

A11   Bergier, Jean-François. "Bibliographie des Articles Relatifs à l'Histoire de l'Humanisme et de la Renaissance, 1956 et 1957." *BHR*, XX (1958), 607-627.

A12   Milne, Alexander Taylor. *Writings on British History, 1934: A Bibliography of Books and Articles on the History of Great Britain from about 450 A.D. to 1914.* London: Cape, 1937. Pp. 427.
Rev: *TLS*, Feb. 19, 1938, p. 121; *AHR*, XLIII, 669-700.

A13   Massie, Joseph, ed. *Bibliography of the Collections of Books and Tracts on Commerce, Currency, and Poor Law (1557-1763).* Transcribed from Lansdowne MS MXLIX with hist. and bibl. Intro. by William A. Shaw. London: George Harding's Bookshop, Ltd., 1937. Pp. xlii, 173.
Rev: by F. A. Hayek, *Economica*, V (1938), 363-364; by H. Higgs, *EHR*, LIII, 731-732.

A14   Schücking, Levin L., and W. Ebisch. "Bibliographie zur Geschichte des literarischen Geschmacks in England." *Anglia*, LXIII (1939), 1-64.

A15   Peery, William, ed. "Renaissance Books of 1953, A Bibliographical Supplement." *Studies in the Renaissance* (Univ. Texas Press), I (1954), 157-179.

A16   Taylor, Archer. *Renaissance Reference Books: A Checklist of Some Bibliographies Printed Before 1700.* Issued under the Auspices of the Committee on Renaissance Studies of the American Council of Learned Societies. Renaissance Bibliographies and Checklists, I. Univ. Calif. Press, 1941. Pp. 24.

A17   Christensen, Niels. *Renaissance and Reformation. Books for Libraries, Scholars and Booklovers.* Bloomfield, New Jersey, 1946. Pp. 217.

A18   Harbage, Alfred. *Annals of English Drama, 975-1700: An Analytical Record of All Plays, Extant or Lost, Chronologically Arranged and Indexed by Authors, Titles, Dramatic Companies, etc.* Univ. Pa. Press, 1940. Pp. 264.
Rev: A2923.

A19   Eccles, M. "A Biographical Dictionary of Elizabethan Authors." *HLQ*, V (1942), 281-302.

A20   Jayne, Sears. *Library Catalogues of the English Renaissance.* Berkeley, 1956.
Rev: by D. C. Allen, *MLN*, LXXII (1957), 387-388; by Rudolf Hirsch, *RN*, X, 202-204; by Howard W. Winger, *Lib. Quar.*, XXVII, 210-211; *TLS*, Nov. 8, 1957, p. 680.

A21   *The Player's Library.* Catalogue of the Library of the British Drama League. London: Faber and Faber, 1950.
Supplements issued 1951, 1954.

A22   Lowenberg, Alfred. *The Theatre of the British Isles Excluding London.* Soc. for Theatrical Research, First Annual Publ., 1948-9. London: The Soc., 1950. Pp. xi, 75.
Rev: by J. H. McDowell, *QJS*, XXXVI (1950), 425-426; K. A. M., *Lib. Assoc. Record*, LII, 216-217.

A23   Clunes, Alec. *British Theatre History.* Reader's Guides, Second Series III. Published for the National Book League. Cambridge Univ. Press, 1955.
Rev: by Hermann Heuer, *SJ*, 92 (1956), 356-357.

A24   Wood, F. T. "The Attack on the Stage in the Eighteenth Century: A Bibliography." *N &Q*, 173 (1937), 218-222.

A25   Wheat, Cathleen Hayhurst. *Tudor Poetry and Drama Reprinted in England between 1800 and 1835: A Bibliography with Introduction and Notes.* DD, University of California, Los Angeles, 1945.

A26   Vowles, Richard B. "Dramatic Theory: A Bibliography." *Bulletin of the New York Public Library*, LIV (1955), 412-429; 464-482; 525-534; 578-585.
Rev: by Alan S. Downer, *QJS*, XLII (1956), 311-312.

A27   Baker, Blanch Merritt. *Theatre and Applied Arts: A Guide to Books Dealing with the History, Criticism, and Technic of the Drama and Theatre.* New York: Wilson, 1952. Pp. xiii, 536. Shak., pp. 57-70.

A28   Ogden, Henry V., and Margaret S. Ogden. "A Bibliography of Seventeenth-Century Writings on the Pictorial Arts in English." *Art Bulletin*, XXIX (1947), 196-201.

A29   Osborne, Mary Tom. *Advice-to-a-Painter Poems, 1633-1856: An Annotated Finding List.* Univ. Texas Press, 1949. Pp. 92.
Rev: *N &Q*, 195 (1950), 373.

A30   Brown, H. "The Classical Tradition in English Literature: A Bibliography." *Harvard Studies and Notes in Philology*, Cambridge, Mass., 1935, pp. 7-46.

A31   Schnapper, Edith B., ed. *The British Union-Catalogue of Early Music Printed before the Year 1801.* 2 vols. London: Butterworth, 1958. Pp. 583, 593.
Rev: *TLS*, July 4, 1958, p. 384.

A32   Dudley, Fred A., Norbert Fuerst, Francis R. Johnson, and Hyatt H. Waggoner. *The Relations of Literature and Science: A Selected Bibliography, 1930-1949.* Publ. for "General Topics VII" of MLA by the Dept. of English, State College of Washington, Pullman, Wash., 1949. Pp. 59.
Rev: by H. Dingle, *MLR*, XLV (1950), 425.

A33   Coleman, Edward D. "The Jew in English Drama: An Annotated Bibliography." *Bul. New York Public Lib.*, XLII (1938), 827-850, 919-932; XLIII (1939), 45-52, 374-378; XLIV (1940), 361-372, 429-444, 495-504, 543-558, 620-634, 675-698, 777-788, 843-866.

A34   Walbridge, Earle F. "Drames à Clef. A List of Plays with Characters Based on Real People." *Bul. New York Public Lib.*, LX (1956), 156-174.
See pp. 161-166 for list of Elizabethan plays.

A35 Schwanbeck, Gisela. *Bibliographie der deutschsprachigen Hochschulschriften zur Theaterwissenschaft von 1885 bis 1955*. Berlin: Ges. f. Theatergesch., 1956. Pp. XIV, 563. Typewritten.

A36 Greenough, Chester Noyes. *A Bibliography of the Theophrastian Character in English*. Prepared for pub. by J. Milton French. Harvard Univ. Press, 1947. Pp. xii, 347.
Rev: "The Theophrastians," *TLS*, July 12, 1947, p. 351; by D. C. A., *MLN*, LXIII (1948), 211-212; by B. Boyce, *JEGP*, XLVII, 92-94; by H. Macdonald, *RES*, XXIV, 255-256; by V. B. Heltzel, *PQ*, XXVII, 285-288; by Jean Robertson, *MLR*, XLIII, 11-12.

A37 Matthews, William. *British Diaries: An Annotated Bibliography of British Diaries Written between 1442 and 1942*. Univ. Calif. Press, 1950. Pp. xxiv, 339.
Rev: *N&Q*, 195 (1950), 417; by A. Esdaile, *English*, VIII, 148-149; by R. Halsband, *SRL*, June 3, 1950, pp. 20-21.

A38 Noyes, Gertrude E. *Bibliography of Courtesy and Conduct Books in Seventeenth-Century England* New Haven: Tuttle, Morehouse and Taylor, 1937. Pp. iv, 111.
Rev: A4537.

A39 Mish, C. C. *English Prose Fiction 1600-1640; 1641-1660*. Charlottesville, Va.: Bibl. Soc. Univ. Va., 1952. Pp. v, 34; iii, 21.

A40 Herr, A. F. "The Elizabethan Sermon: A Survey & Bibliography." DD, University of Pennsylvania, 1940.

A41 "Bibliographical Notes." *Papers Bibl. Soc. Amer.*, XXXIV (1940) to LIII (1959). Various pages. Contains sections on incunabula and on English Books (1475-1800).
For bibliographies of individual scholars, see Tributes, B3936-B4003, and Festschriften, B4396-B4495.

I. SHAKESPEARE BIBLIOGRAPHY (1,2;1)
1. ANNUALS
a. SHAKESPEARE ASSOCIATION BULLETIN

A42 Tannenbaum, Samuel A. "Shakespeare and His Contemporaries in the Literature of 1934: A Classified Bibliography." *SAB*, X (1935), 3-30, 95-105.

A43 Ditto for 1935, XI (1936), 3-32, 107-117.

A44 Ditto for 1936, XII (1937), 2-34, 109-117.

A45 Ditto for 1937, XIII (1938), 2-29; "Index of Names and Subjects" compiled by R. W. Babcock, 99-107.

A46 Ditto for 1938, XIV (1939), 2-26; "Index of Names and Subjects" compiled by R. W. Babcock, 101-107.

A47 Ditto for 1939, XV (1940), 2-22; "Index of Names and Subjects" compiled by Ralph P. Rosenberg, 95-102.

A48 Ditto for 1940, XVI (1941), 2-16; "Index of Names and Subjects" compiled by Ralph P. Rosenberg, 17-24.

A49 Ditto for 1941, XVII (1942), 2-17; "Index of Names and Subjects" compiled by Ralph P. Rosenberg, 18-24.

A50 Ditto for 1942, XVIII (1943), 2-14; "Index of Names and Subjects" compiled by Ralph P. Rosenberg, 15-21.

A51 Ditto for 1943, XIX (1944), 2-13; "Index of Names and Subjects" by Ralph P. Rosenberg, 14-19.

A52 Tannenbaum, Samuel A., and Dorothy R. Tannenbaum. "Shakspere and His Contemporaries: A Classified Bibliography for 1944." *SAB*, XX (1945), 2-14; "Index of Names and Subjects," 15-21.

A53 Ditto for 1945, XXI (1946), 3-17; "Index," 18-24.

A54 Ditto for 1946, XXII (1947), 3-29.

A55 Ditto for 1947, XXIII (1948), 24-50.

A56 Tannenbaum, Dorothy R. "Shakespeare and His Contemporaries: A Classified Bibliography for 1948." *SAB*, XXIV (1949), 136-175.
Last of this series; unclassified annual bibliography continued by *SQ*.

b. SHAKESPEARE QUARTERLY

A57 Thomas, Sidney, ed. "Shakespeare: An Annotated Bibliography for 1949." *SQ*, I (1950), 97-120.

A58 Ditto for 1950, II (1951), 145-169.

A59 Ditto for 1951, III (1952), 149-184.

A60 Ditto for 1952, IV (1953), 219-254.

A61 Ditto for 1953, V (1954), 219-245.

A62 Jorgensen, Paul A., et al. "Shakespeare: An Annotated Bibliography for 1954." *SQ*, VI (1955), 201-245.

A63 Ditto for 1955, VII (1956), 291-345.

A64   Ditto for 1956, VIII (1957), 247-301.
A65   Ditto for 1957, IX (1958), 217-286.

c. SHAKESPEARE-JAHRBUCH

A66   Preis, Anton. "Shakespeare-Bibliographie für 1936 mit Nachtrag aus früheren Jahren." *SJ*, LXXIII (1937), 200-220.
A67   Ditto for 1937, LXXIV (1938), 223-250.
A68   Ditto for 1938, LXXV (1939), 199-229.
A69   Ditto for 1939, 1940, and 1941, LXXVIII-LXXIX (1943), 138-188.
A70   Ditto for 1942 and 1943, 80/81 (1946), 122-138.
          For years 1944-1946 inclusive, see A144.
A71   Kindervater, Jos. Wilh., and Erich Thurmann. "Shakespeare-Bibliographie für 1947 und 1948." *SJ*, 89 (1953), 249-304.
A72   Ditto for 1949 and 1950, 90 (1954), 370-435.
A73   Ditto for 1951 and 1952, 91 (1955), 372-435.
A74   Ditto for 1953 and 1954, 92 (1956), 464-531.
A75   Ditto for 1955 and 1956, 93 (1957), 292-365.
A76   Ditto for 1957, 94 (1958), 316-361.

d. STUDIES IN PHILOLOGY

A77   Craig, Hardin, D. Patrick, and W. Wells. "Recent Literature of the English Renaissance." *SP*, XXXIII (1936), 283-396.
A78   Ditto, XXXIV (1937), 260-382.
A79   Ditto, XXXV (1938), 274-403.
A80   Ditto, XXXVI (1939), 253-432.
A81   Ditto, XXXVII (1940), 283-460.
A82   Ditto, XXXVIII (1941), 271-426.
A83   Ditto, XXXIX (1942), 332-486.
A84   Ditto, XL (1943), 257-366.
A85   Ditto, XLI (1944), 265-369.
A86   Ditto, XLII (1945), 269-377.
A87   Ditto, XLIII (1946), 273-460.
A88   Ditto, XLIV (1947), 265-452.
A89   Ditto, XLV (1948), 236-417.
A90   Ditto, XLVI (1949), 204-386.
              Rev: by M. A. Shaaber, *RN*, II (1949), 41-43.
A91   Ditto, XLVII (1950), 243-449.
A92   Ditto, XLVIII (1951), 267-450.
              Rev: by R. Fratt., *Accademie e Biblioteche d'Italia*, XX (1952), 774.
A93   Ditto, XLIX (1952), 264-324.
A94   Ditto, L (1953), 231-435.
A95   Ditto, LI (1954), 215-424.
A96   Ditto, LII (1955), 213-432.
A97   Ditto, LIII (1956), 239-427.
A98   Ditto, LIV (1957), 185-386.
A99   Ditto, LV (1958), 219-422.

e. PMLA

A100   Baugh, Albert C., et al. "American Bibliography for 1936." *PMLA*, LI (1936), 1209-1293.
A100a   Henshaw, Millett, et al. "American Bibliography for 1937." *PMLA*, LII (1937), 1215-1319.
A100b   Ditto for 1938, LIII (1938), 1213-1312.
A100c   Ditto for 1939, LIV (1939), 1199-1313.
A100d   Ditto for 1940, LV (1940), 1215-1328.
A101   Ditto for 1941, LVI (1941), 1201-1323.
A102   Ditto for 1942, LVII (1942), 1207-1329.
A103   Ditto for 1943, LVIII (1943), 1181-1292.
A104   Ditto for 1944, LIX (1944), 1173-1279.
A105   Ditto for 1945, LX (1945), 1181-1289.
A106   Ditto for 1946, LXI (1946), 1213-1314.

A107   Ditto for 1947, LXIII (1948), Suppl., Part 2, 1-121.

A108   Ditto for 1948, LXIV (May, 1949), 3-75.

A109   Ditto for 1949, LXV (April, 1950), 21-122.

A110   Ditto for 1950, LXVI (April, 1951), 35-137.

A111   Brown, Paul A., ed. "1951 American Bibliography." *PMLA*, LXVII (April, 1952), 1-114.

A112   1952 ditto. LXVIII (April, 1953), 81-207.

A113   1953 ditto. LXIX (April, 1954), 69-201.

A114   1954 ditto. LXX (April, 1955), 103-259.

A115   1955 ditto. LXXI (April, 1956), 103-266.

A116   Brown, Paul A. "1956 Annual Bibliography." *PMLA*, LXXII (April, 1957), 134-402.
        (No longer exclusively American).

A117   1957 ditto. LXXIII (April, 1958), 97-364.

A118   Various compilers. "Research in Progress in the Modern Languages and Literatures." *PMLA*.
        Various issues, sometimes annual, sometimes biannual, now discontinued.

f. MODERN HUMANITIES RESEARCH ASSOCIATION

A119   Serjeantson, Mary S., and Leslie N. Broughton. *Annual Bibliography of English Language and
        Literature*. Ed. for the Modern Humanities Research Assoc., XV, 1934. Cambridge: Bowes
        and Bowes, 1935. Pp. x, 296.
        Rev: by A. Digeon, *RAA*, XIII (1936), 432; by Hermann M. Flasdieck, *Beiblatt*, XLVII,
        214-215; by C. J. Sisson, *MLR*, XXXII (1937), 136.

A120   Serjeantson, Mary S., and Leslie N. Broughton. *Annual Bibliography of English Language
        and Literature*. Ed. for the Modern Humanities Research Assoc., XVI, 1935. Cambridge:
        Bowes and Bowes, 1936. Pp. xii, 279.
        Rev: by A. E., *Library Assoc. Record*, XXXIX (1937), 141.

A121   Serjeantson, Mary S., and L. N. Broughton. *Annual Bibliography of English Language and
        Literature*. Ed. for the Modern Humanities Research Assoc., XVII, 1936. Cambridge Univ.
        Press, 1938. Pp. xii, 279.
        Rev: by A. Digeon, *EA*, II (1938), 390-391; by C. J. Sisson, *MLR*, XXXIV (1939), 126-127.

A122   Sergeantson, Mary S., and Leslie N. Broughton. *Annual Bibliography of English Language and
        Literature*. Ed. for the Modern Humanities Research Assoc., XVIII, 1937. Cambridge Univ.
        Press, 1939.
        Rev: by R. D. H., *MLN*, LV (1940), 239-240.

A123   Macdonald, Angus, and L. N. Broughton. *Annual Bibliography of English Language and
        Literature*. Ed. for the Modern Humanities Research Assoc., XIX, 1938. Cambridge Univ.
        Press, 1940. Pp. xii, 284.

A124   Macdonald, Angus, and L. N. Broughton, eds. *Annual Bibliography of English Language and
        Literature*. XX, 1939. Cambridge Univ. Press, 1948. Pp. xii, 292.
        Rev: by A. F. Allison, *Library*, III (1948), 72-74.

A125   Macdonald, Angus, and Leslie N. Broughton, eds. *Annual Bibliography of English Language and
        Literature*. XXI, 1940. Cambridge Univ. Press, 1950. Pp. 287.

A126   Macdonald, Angus, and Leslie Broughton, eds. *Annual Bibliography of English Language and
        Literature*. XXII, 1941. Cambridge Univ. Press, 1952. Pp. xvi, 154.

A127   Macdonald, Angus, and Henry J. Pettit, Jr., eds. *Annual Bibliography of English Language and
        Literature*. XXIII, 1942. Cambridge Univ. Press, 1952. Pp. xvi, 154.

A128   Macdonald, Angus, and Henry J. Pettit, Jr., eds. *Annual Bibliography of English Language and
        Literature*. XXIV, 1943-1944. Cambridge Univ. Press, 1956.

A129   Macdonald, Angus, and Henry J. Pettit, Jr., eds. *Annual Bibliography of English Language and
        Literature*. XXV, 1945. Cambridge Univ. Press, 1956.
        Rev: by J. R. Brown, *MLR*, LII (1957), 578-579.

A130   Macdonald, Angus, and Henry J. Pettit, Jr., eds. *Annual Bibliography of English Language and
        Literature*. XXVI, 1946. Cambridge Univ. Press, 1958. Pp. 130. Paperbound.
        Rev: *TLS*, May 9, 1958, p. 259; by Hermann Heuer, *SJ*, 94 (1958), 256-257.

A131   Pettit, Henry J., Jr., and Angus Macdonald, eds. *Annual Bibliography of English Language and
        Literature*. XXVII, 1947. Cambridge Univ. Press, in association with the Univ. of Colorado
        Press, 1956.
        Rev: by J. R. Brown, *MLR*, LII (1957), 578-579.

A132   Pettit, Henry J., Jr., and Angus Macdonald, eds. *Annual Bibliography of English Language and
        Literature*. XXVIII, 1948. Cambridge Univ. Press, in association with the Univ. of Colorado
        Press, 1957. Pp. xiii, 259.

A132a   Pettit, Henry J., Jr., and Angus Macdonald. *Annual Bibliography of English Language and
        Literature*. XXIX, 1949. Cambridge Univ. Press, in association with the Univ. of Colorado
        Press, 1957. Pp. xiv, 293.

g. STUDIES IN BIBLIOGRAPHY

A133 Hirsch, Rudolf, Lucy Clark, and Fredson Bowers. "A Selective Check List of Bibliographical Scholarship for 1949." *SB*, III (1950), 292-302. The first of the series.

A134 Hirsch, Rudolf, and Howell J. Heaney. "A Selective Check List of Bibliographical Scholarship for 1950." *SB*, IV (1951), 317-335.

A135 Hirsch, Rudolph, and Howell J. Heaney. "A Selective Check List of Bibliographical Scholarship for 1951." *SB*, V (1952), 211-228.

A136 Ditto for 1952, VI (1954), 266-286.

A137 Ditto for 1953, VII (1955), 219-240.

A137a Ditto for 1954, VIII (1956), 250-270.

A138 *A Selective Check List of Bibliographical Scholarship, 1949-1955.* Univ. of Virginia Press, 1958. Pp. 192. Reprint of previous volumes' bibliographies. "Decennial Extra Volume" of *SB*. Only new contents is bibliography for 1955.

A139 Hirsch, Rudolf, and Howell J. Heaney. "A Selective Check List of Bibliographical Scholarship for 1956 Series B." *SB*, XI (1958), 269-290.
Series B is first issue after Vol. x, the collection, A138.

h. JOURNAL OF ENGLISH AND GERMANIC PHILOLOGY

A140 Pochmann, Henry A. "Anglo-German Bibliography for 1935." *JEGP*, XXXV (1936), 271 ff.

A141 Pochmann, Henry A. "Anglo-German Bibliography for 1936." *JEGP*, XXXVI (1937), 246-262.

A142 Pochmann, Henry A. "Anglo-German Bibliography for 1937." *JEGP*, XXXVII (1938), 267-284. No further issues reported in sources, but nevertheless subsequently continued.

i. ARCHIV

A143 Horn, Wilhelm, and Gerhard Rohlfs, eds. "Bibliographie: Englisch." *Archiv*, 185 (1948), 142-152.

A143a Ditto, 186 (1949), 158-159.

A144 Lüdeke, H. "Shakespeare-Bibliographie für die Kriegsjahre 1939-1946 (England und Amerika)." *Archiv*, 187 (1950), 25-36.

A144a Lüdeke, H. "Shakespeare-Bibliographie für die Kreigsjahre 1939-1946 (England und Amerika)." *Archiv*, 188 (1951), 8-40.

A145 "Bibliographie der anglistischen Neuerscheinungen für die Jahre 1949 und 1950." *Archiv*, 189 (1953), 337-355.

A146 "Englisch Bibliographie der anglistischen Neuerscheinungen für die Jahre 1950 und 1951 mit Nachträgen für 1949 (Folge II)." *Archiv*, 190 (1953), 105-131.

A147 "Englisch Bibliographie der anglistischen Neuerscheinungen für das Jahr 1952 mit Nachträgen für 1951 (Folge III)." *Archiv*, 190 (1954), 332-339.

A148 "Englisch Bibliographie der anglistischen Neuerscheinungen für das Jahr 1952 mit Nachträgen für 1951 (Folge IV)." *Archiv*, 191 (1954), 73-86.

A149 "Englisch Bibliographie der anglistischen Neuerscheinungen für das Jahr 1953 mit Nachträgen für 1952 (Folge V)." *Archiv*, 191 (1955), 339-359.

A150 Fricker, Robert. "Ausgewählte Bibliographie von Neuerscheinungen auf dem Gebiet der neueren englischen Literaturgeschichte für 1954." *Archiv*, 192 (1956), 313-336.

A151 Senn, Gustav Theodore. Ditto for 1955, 193 (1956/57), 310-333.

A152 Ditto for 1956, 194 (1958), 316-319.

A153 Ditto for 1957, 195 (1958/59), 341-354.

2. INDIVIDUAL
a. GENERAL

A154 Ebisch, Walter, and Levin L. Schücking. *Supplement for the Years 1930-1935 to A Shakespeare Bibliography.* Oxford: Clarendon Press, 1937. Pp. 104.
Rev: *N &Q*, 172 (1937), 288; by S. C. Chew, *NYHTBR*, Apr. 4, 1937, p. 37; by H. S., *Library*, NS, XVIII, 119; by I. A. Williams, *London Mercury*, XXXV, 506; by W. Keller, *SJ*, LXXIII (1937), 171; by Peter Alexander, *MLR*, XXXIII (1938), 581-582; by H. S., *MLN*, LIII, 77.

A155 The Rosenbach Company. *English Plays to 1700, including an Unique Shakespeare Collection.* Philadelphia and New York: The Rosenbach Company, 1940. Pp. 104.

A156 Ford, H. L. *Shakespeare, 1700-1740: A Collation of the Editions and Separate Plays with Some Account of T. Johnson and R. Walker.* Oxford Univ. Press, 1935. Pp. viii, 145.
Rev: A3079.

A157 Bibliothèque Nationale. *Catalogue des ouvrages de William Shakespeare Conservés au Département des Imprimés.* Paris, 1948. Pp. vii, 424 columns.

A158 Mummendey, Richard. *Language and Literature of the Anglo-Saxon Nations as Presented in German Doctoral Dissertations 1885-1950.* Bonn, Germany: H. Vouvier; Charlottesville, Virginia: Bibliographical Society of the University of Virginia, 1954. Pp. xvi, 200.
Rev: by G. Jacob, *Archiv*, 191 (1955), 361-362; by R. Juchhoff, *Zs. f. Bibliotheksw. u.*

Bibliogr., II (1955), 135; by H. M. Flasdieck, *Anglia*, LXXIII (1955/56), 365-366; comments by Mummendey and Flasdieck, *Anglia*, LXXIV (1956/57), 278-280; by M. Baacke, *JEGP*, LV (1956), 286-287; by J. H. P. Pafford, *MLR*, LI (1956), 137-138; by B. von Lindheim, *RES*, VIII (1957), 276-278; briefly by James G. McManaway, *SQ*, VIII (1957), 126.

A159 Sisson, Charles J. *Shakespeare*. British Council Series Writers and Their Work, no. 58. London: Longmans, 1955. Pp. 50.
Contains a "Select Bibliography" by J. R. Brown, pp. 33-50.
Rev: *TLS*, May 27, 1955, p. 290; *MdF*, 323 (1955), 721; by A. H. R. Fairchild, *SQ*, VI, 463-465; *ES*, XXXVI, 94; by G. Lambin, *LanM*, XLIX, 78; by H. Heuer, *SJ*, 92 (1956), 365-366; by L. L. Schücking, *GRM*, XXXVII, 87.

A160 Cordasco, Francesco, and Kenneth W. Scott. *A Brief Shakespeare Bibliography for the Use of Students*. New Orleans and New York: Phoenix Press, 1950. Pp. 26.

A161 Worth, Katherine J., ed. *Shakespeare* (National Book League, Second Series). Cambridge Univ. Press for the National Book League, 1952. Pp. 31.
Rev: briefly by J. C. Maxwell, *RES*, IV (1953), 404-405; by J. G. McManaway, *SQ*, IV, 360.

A162 British Drama. *History and Criticism*. National Book League Book List. Cambridge Univ. Press, 1950. Pp. 33. Shak., pp. 24-28.

A163 Scopin, G. A. *William Shakespeare: A Short Bibliography*. For the 325th anniversary of his death. The Fundamental Library of the Tatar Autonomous Soviet Socialist Republic at the Kazan State University, 1941. Pp. 30.

A164 White, William. "Shakespeare Dissertations and Work in Progress." *ShN*, IV (1954), 5.

A165 Oyama, Toshikazu. *Saikinno Shakespeare Kenkyuho* (A Bibliographical Approach to Recent Shakespeare Studies). Tokyo: Shinozaki Shorin, 1956. Pp. iv, 242, ix.

A166 Chambers, Sir Edmund K. *Sources for a Biography of Shakespeare*. Oxford: Clarendon Press, 1946. Pp. 80.
Rev: A395.

A167 Feldman, A. Bronson, ed. "Fifty Years of the Psychoanalysis of Literature: 1900-1951." *Literature and Psychology*, Aug., 1955.

A168 Walcutt, Charles C., et al. "A Check List of Explication." *Expl.*, XIII (1955), Index.

A169 Smith, Gordon Ross. "Shakespeare Bibliography." *ShN*, VII (1957), 36.
A note upon this project.

b. OF SEPARATE WORKS

A170 Raven, Anton A. *Hamlet Bibliography and Reference Guide, 1877-1935*. Univ. of Chicago Press, 1936. Pp. xvi, 292.
Rev: by James Southall Wilson, *VQR*, XII (1936), 636-640; *Library Quar.*, VI, 448-449; by Wolfgang Keller, *SJ*, LXXII, 148; *TLS*, Dec. 26, 1936, p. 1070; by B. M., *PQ*, XVI (1937), 89-90; by F. Delattre, *RBPH*, XVI, 987-988; by Hazelton Spencer, *MLN*, LII, 437-442; by Levin L. Schücking, *RES*, XIII, 484-485; by W. Fischer, *Beiblatt*, XLVIII, 105-107; by Robert M. Smith, *SAB*, XII, 35-40; by Enid Welsford, *MLR*, XXXIII (1938), 122.

A170a Smith, Robert M. "A Bibliography of Hamlet." *SAB*, XII (1937), 35-40.
A review article of Anton A. Raven's *A Hamlet Bibliography and Reference Guide, 1877-1935*. Contains a list of omitted items.

A171 Tannenbaum, Samuel A. *Shakespeare's The Merchant of Venice: A Concise Bibliography*. (Elizabethan Bibliographies, No. 17). New York, 1941. Pp. 150.

A172 Tannenbaum, Samuel A. *Shakespeare's King Lear: A Concise Bibliography*. (Elizabethan Bibliographies, No. 16). New York, 1940. Pp. x, 101.

A173 Tannenbaum, Samuel A. *Shakespeare's Sonnets: A Concise Bibliography*. (Elizabethan Bibliographies, No. 11). New York, 1940. Pp. xii, 88.

A174 Tannenbaum, Samuel A. *Shakespeare's Macbeth: A Concise Bibliography*. (Elizabethan Bibliographies, No. 11). New York, 1940. Pp. x, 165.

A175 Tannenbaum, Samuel A. *Shakespeare's Othello: A Concise Bibliography*. (Elizabethan Bibliographies, No. 28). New York, 1943. Pp. x, 132.

A176 Tannenbaum, Samuel A. *Shakespeare's Troilus and Cressida: A Concise Bibliography*. (Elizabethan Bibliographies, No. 29). New York: Samuel A. Tannenbaum, 1943. Pp. 54.

A177 Tannenbaum, Samuel A. *Anthony Mundy. Including the Play of Sir Thomas Moore: A concise Bibliography*. (Elizabethan Bibliographies, No. 27). New York: Samuel A. Tannenbaum, 1942. Pp. viii, 36.

A178 Tannenbaum, Samuel A., and D. R. *Shakespeare's Romeo and Juliet: A Concise Bibliography*. (Elizabethan Bibliographies, No. 41). New York, 1950. Pp. 133.

c. SPECIAL ASPECTS OF SHAKESPEARE
(1) GENERAL

A179 Guttman, Selma. *The Foreign Sources of Shakespeare's Works: An Annotated Bibliography of the Commentary on this Subject between 1904 and 1940, Together with Lists of Certain Translations Available to Shakespeare*. DD, Columbia University, 1946. New York: King's Crown Press, 1947. Pp. xxii, 168.

A Compilation of previous discoveries, mention and reference only; evidence not repeated.
Rev: briefly, *TLS*, Mar. 27, 1948, p. 182; by H. W. Herrington, *Symposium*, II, 300-302; by Fernand Baldensperger, *RLC*, XXII, 589-591; by E. E. Willoughby, *SAB*, XXIII, 204-205; by P. Reyher, *LanM*, XLII, 296; by R. T. H., *Books Abroad*, XXIII (1949), 79; by A. M. C. Latham, *RES*, NS, I (1950), 91.

A180   Clendenning, Logan. "A Bibliographic Account of the Bacon-Shakespeare Controversy." *Colophon*, New Graphic Ser., No. 3, 1939.
Rev: *TLS*, Jan. 6, 1940, p. 12.

A181   Galland, Joseph S. *Digesta Anti-Shakespeareana*. DD, University of Wisconsin, 1914. Pp. 1667. Mic A48-384. *Microf. Ab.*, IX (1949), 199. Publication No. 1175.
Not a doctoral dissertation in its present form. Introduction dated Dec., 1948, and signed by Galland's son-in-law, Burton A. Milligan. An annotated bibliography.

A182   Butler, E. H. "Shakespeare through the Imaginative Writers." *Eng. Jour.*, XXX (1941), 749-753.
A 3-page bibliog. of comments by famous writers upon Shak.; suitable for schools.

A183   Stone, M. W. "Shakespeare and the Juvenile Drama." *TN*, VIII (1954), 65-66.
A list of the juvenile dramas adapted from Shakespeare, with their publishers and dates.
See also B4186-B4395.

A184   Redi, Riccardo, and Roberto Chiti. "Shakespeare e il cinema. Contributo a una bibliografia." *Bianco e nero* (Rome), XVIII, i (1957), 89-91.

(2)   SHAKESPEARE IN NON-ENGLISH-SPEAKING COUNTRIES
See also Shakespeare's Influence, A8701, ff.,
and Translations, B262, ff.

A185   "Shakespeare in Greek and Latin." *N &Q*, 175 (1938), 389-390, 409, 464.
Letters by Demetrius Caclamanos, C. Kessary, William Jaggard, Paul Morgan, and L. G. H. Horton-Smith.

A186   Heun, Hans Georg. "Probleme der Shakespeare-Übersetzüngen. Eine Bibliographie." *SJ*, 92 (1956), 450-463.

A187   *Mitteilungen der Deutschen Shakespeare-Gesellschaft*, I, Bochum, Germany, August, 1949. Pp. 12. Information bulletin of the German Shakespeare Association. Contains a bibliography of German editions of Shak. since 1945.

A188   Molin, Nils. "Shakespeare Translated into Swedish." *SJ*, 92 (1956), 232-243.
Includes a bibliography of Swedish Shak. translations.

A189   Goldberg, M. J. "List of Hebrew Translations of Shakespeare in the Library of Congress." *Chavrutha* (Hebrew), Feb. 27, 1945, pp. 26-28.

A189a   Fucilla, Joseph G. "Shakespeare in Italian Criticism: A Supplement to the Bibliographies Compiled by Ebisch and Schücking." *PQ*, XX (1941), 559-572.

A190   Travers, Seymour. *Catalogue of Nineteenth Century French Theatrical Parodies: A Compilation of the Parodies Between 1789 and 1914 of Which Any Record Was Found*. DD, Columbia University, 1942. New York: King's Crown Press, 1942. Pp. 130. Shak., pp. 96-97.

A191   Coe, Ada M. *Catálogo bibliográfico y crítico de las comedias anunciadas en los periódicos de Madrid desde 1661 hasta 1819*. Johns Hopkins Studies in Romance Literatures and Languages. Extra Vol. IX. Baltimore: Johns Hopkins Press, 1935. Pp. xii, 270.
Rev: by G. T. Northrup, *MP*, XXXIV (1936/37), 98-99; by A. Hâmel, *Lbl*, LVIII (1937), 272; by W. C. Atkinson, *MLR*, XXXII, 315-316.

A192   Lehrman, Edgar H. *Soviet Shakespeare Appreciation (1917-1952)*. DD, Columbia University, 1954. Pp. 465. Mic A54-2072. *DA*, XIV (1954), 1413.
In microfilm edition, various bibliographies are on pp. 356-456 and total 1177 items.

A193   Toyoda, Minoru. *Shakespeare in Japan: An Historical Survey*. Tokyo: The Iwanami Shoten, 1940. Pp. xi, 139 (in English). An outline history of Shak. studies in Japan, with "A Japanese Shakespeare-Bibliography," pp. 121-139.

II.   SURVEYS OF SCHOLARSHIP
1.   RENAISSANCE IN GENERAL

A194   Wright, Louis B. "Introduction to a Survey of Renaissance Studies." *MLQ*, II (1941), 355-362.

A195   Committee on Renaissance Studies. *Surveys of Recent Scholarship in the Period of Renaissance*. Compiled for the Committee of Renaissance Studies of the American Council of Learned Societies. First Series, 1945. (Not paged consecutively; reprints.)
Rev: by A. Bergstraesser, *MP*, XLIV (1946), 55-57; by Don Cameron Allen, *MLN*, LXI, 71; by O. H. Green, *HR*, XIV, 279-280; by F. P. Wilson, *RES*, XXIII (1947), 276-277.

A196   Thomson, S. Harrison. *Progress of Medieval and Renaissance Studies in the United States and Canada*. Univ. of Colorado, 1940. Pp. 85.
Rev: by James F. Kenney, *AHR*, XLVI, 197.

A197   Thomson, S. Harrison, ed. *Progress of Medieval and Renaissance Studies in the United States and Canada*. Bul. No. 17. Boulder, Colo.: Univ. of Colorado, 1942. Pp. 131.

A198   Thomson, S. Harrison, ed. *Progress of Medieval and Renaissance Studies in the United States and Canada.* Bul. No. 18. Univ. of Colorado, 1944. Pp. 125.

A199   Thomson, S. Harrison, ed. *Progress of Medieval and Renaissance Studies in the United States and Canada.* Bul. No. 19. Univ. of Colorado, 1947. Pp. 187.

A200   Thomson, S. Harrison, ed. *Progress in Medieval and Renaissance Studies in the United States and Canada.* Bulletins 20, 21. Univ. of Colorado, 1949, 1951. Pp. 142, 176.
        Rev: by R. F. Treharne, *History*, XXXVII (1952), 241-242.

A201   Thomson, S. Harrison, ed. *Progress of Medieval and Renaissance Studies in the United States and Canada.* Bul. No. 22. Univ. of Colorado, 1953. Pp. 142.

A202   Ditto Bul. No. 23, Univ. of Colorado, 1955. Pp. 142.

A203   Ditto Bul. No. 24, Univ. of Colorado, 1957. Pp. 123.

2. SHAKESPEARE
a. THE SHAKESPEARE SURVEY

A204   Empson, William, and George Garrett. *Shakespeare Survey.* London: Brendin Publ. Co., 1937. Pp. 68.
        A separate, earlier volume, not part of a series and not to be confused with subsequent numbered *Shakespeare Surveys.*

A205   Nicoll, Allardyce, ed. *Shakespeare Survey I: An Annual Survey of Shakespearian Study and Production.* Cambridge Univ. Press, 1948. Pp. x, 144.
        Rev: "Live-long Monument," *TLS*, Apr. 24, 1948, p. 233; by H. B. C., *MGW*, June 10, 1948, p. 10; by John Garrett, *Spectator*, June 11, 1948, p. 712; by M. C. Bradbrook, *CamJ*, I, 701-702; by M. St. Clare Byrne, *English*, VII, 145-146; by H. Lüdeke, *ES*, XXIX, 152-156; *N&Q*, 193 (1948), 308; by H. K. Fisher, *Life and Letters*, LVIII, 65; by J. M., *Listy z Teatru* (Cracow), No. 24, pp. 20-29; by R. M. Smith, *SAB*, XXIII, 136-137; by J. Gassner, *TAr*, XXXIII (1949), 4; by Harry Levin, *NYTBR*, Aug.7, 1949, p. 5; by Geoffrey Bullough, *MLR*, XLIV, 108; by André Koszul, *LanM*, V, 65; by J. M. Nosworthy, *RES*, NS, I (1950), 70-72; by R. Flatter, *SJ*, 87/88 (1952), 227-230.

A206   Nicoll, Allardyce, ed. *Shakespeare Survey, II.* Cambridge Univ. Press, 1949. Pp. viii, 164.
        Rev: by S. R. Littlewood, *English*, VII (1949), 239-240; briefly by Robert Halsband, *SRL*, Sept. 3, 1949, p. 12; by G. B. Harrison, *Commonweal*, L, 398; *N&Q*, 194 (1949), 573; by R. G. Cox, *Scrutiny*, XVI (1949), 335-339; by Harry Levin, *NYTBR*, Aug. 7, 1949, p. 5; *TLS*, July 8, 1949, p. 446; by André Koszul, *LanM*, XLIV (1950), 121-122; by R. V. Bannon, *Dalhousie Rev.*, XXIX (1950), 454-455; by J. S. Wilson, *VQR*, XXVI, 317; by Geoffrey Bullough, *MLR*, XLVI (1951), 87; by J. M. Nosworthy, *RES*, NS, II, 174-175; by Karl J. Holzknecht, *MLQ*, XIII (1952), 101-103.

A207   Nicoll, Allardyce, ed. *Shakespeare Survey, III.* Cambridge Univ. Press, 1950. Pp. viii, 167.
        Rev: *TLS*, June 9, 1950, p. 352; *Listener*, XLIX, 513, 515; by H. Popkin, *TAr*, XXXIV (August, 1950), 6, 8; by A. C. Partridge, *ConR*, LXXII (1950/51), 82; by M. C. Bradbrook, *MLR*, XLVI (1951), 262-263; by T. G. Herring, *Southerly*, XII, 165-166; by Frank Kermode, *RES*, NS, III (1952), 171-173; by William Peery, *MLQ*, XIV (1953), 121-122.

A208   Nicoll, Allardyce, ed. *Shakespeare Survey, IV.* Cambridge Univ. Press, 1951. Pp. ix, 176.
        Rev: *TLS*, May 4, 1951, p. 274; (see letters in *TLS*, 1951, relating to Mr. Wilson's art. noted below: by Janet Spens, June 15, p. 373; by Mr. Wilson, June 29, p. 405; and by Miss Spens, July 20, p. 453); by Hugh Dick, *SQ*, II, 263-265; by Roy Walker, *Theatre Newsletter*, Apr. 28, p. 6; by H. Lüdeke, *ES*, XXXII, 172-176 (incl. also notice of *2,3*); by H. S. Wilson, *UTQ*, XXI, 83-88 (incl. also notice of *1, 2, 3*); by H. B. Charlton, *MGW*, June 14, 1951, p. 11; by Julian Hall, *English*, VIII, 257; *Adelphi*, XXVIII, 454-455; by F. S. Boas, *YWES*, XXX, 119-120; by G. Banyard, *Fortnightly*, 170 (1951), 449; *Listener*, XLV, 848; *N&Q*, 196 (1951), 395.

A209   Nicoll, Allardyce, ed. *Shakespeare Survey, V.* Cambridge Univ. Press, 1952. Pp. viii, 164.
        Rev: *TLS*, June 27, 1952, p. 422; by Oliver Warner, *Time and Tide*, Apr. 26, 1952, p. 426; by John Bryson, *Spectator*, May 9, 1952, p. 622, 624; by G. B. Harrison, *SatR*, June 14, 1952, pp. 28-29; by Philip Williams, *SQ*, III, 273-275; by Frank Kermode, *RES*, NS, IV (1953), 161-162; by A. Koszul, *EA*, VI, 151-152.

A210   Nicoll, Allardyce, ed. *Shakespeare Survey, VI.* Cambridge Univ. Press, 1953. Pp. viii, 185.
        Rev: *TLS*, May 8, 1953, p. 303; by J. Vallette, *MdF*, 318 (1953), 339-340; by S. F. Johnson, *SQ*, IV, 181-185; *Listener*, May 14, 1953, pp. 809, 811; by H. B. Charlton, *MGW*, May 14, 1953, p. 10; *N&Q*, 198 (1953), 319; by G. B. Harrison, *SatR*, Oct. 10, 1953, p. 19; *Adelphi*, XXIX, 256-258; by Donald C. Baker, *Books Abroad*, XXVII, 437; by D. M. S., *English*, IX, 230-231; by William Angus, *QQ*, LX (1953/54), 448-451; by Frank Kermode, *RES*, NS, V (1954), 186-188; by Oscar James Campbell, *RN*, VII, 30-31; by G. Lambin, *LanM*, XLVIII (1954), 84-85; by Nelson Magill, *QJS*, XL, 88; by H. Lüdeke, *ES*, XXXVI (1955), 170-171.

A211   Nicoll, Allardyce, ed. *Shakespeare Survey, VII.* Cambridge Univ. Press, 1954. Pp. vii, 168.
        Rev: *TLS*, June 4, 1954, p. 363; by David Hardman, *John o'London's Weekly*, LXIII, 414; by Thom Gunn, *Spectator*, July 2, 1954, pp. 32-33; by G. B. Harrison, *SatR*, Sept. 25, 1954, p. 22; by Oscar J. Campbell, *RN*, VII, 30-31; *N&Q*, 199 (1954), 457; by J. Vallette, *MdF*, 321 (1954), 728-729; by Irving Ribner, *ShN*, IV, 23; by James L. Jackson, *QJS*, XL, 455-456;

by A. Koszul, *EA*, VII, 323; by William Blissett, *QQ*, LXI, 412-413; by B. Ifor Evans, *MGW*, July 7, 1954, p. 11; *N &Q*, NS, I, 457; by G. Lambin, *LanM*, XLIX (1955), 269-270; by Robert G. Shedd, *MLN*, LXX, 138-141; by Madeleine Doran, *SQ*, VI, 90-96; by J. M. Nosworthy, *RES*, NS, VI, 196-197; *CE*, XVI, 200; by Aerol Arnold, *Personalist*, XXXVI, 211-212; by William T. Hastings, *SQ*, VI, 112; by H. Lüdeke, *ES*, XXXVII (1956), 81-83.

A212   Nicoll, Allardyce, ed. *Shakespeare Survey, VIII.* Cambridge Univ. Press, 1955. Pp. viii, 171.
Rev: *CE*, XVII (1955), 63; by Robertson Davies, *Saturday Night*, June 11, 1955; *N &Q*, NS, II, 320; *TLS*, May 27, 1955, p. 286; by E. C. Pettet, *English*, X, 189; by Albert Gilman, *QJS*, XLI, 318-319; *NstN*, June 4, 1955, p. 793; by G. Lambin, *LanM*, XLIX, (1955) 461-462; by J. Vallette, *MdF*, 324 (1955), 533-534; by Oscar James Campbell, *RN*, IX (1956), 21-25; by Robert G. Shedd, *MLN*, LXXI, 301-306; by M. C. Bradbrook, *MLR*, LI, 98-99; *VQR*, XXXII, xlviii; *ShN*, VI, 3; by R. E. Davril, *SQ*, VII, 250-252; by C. G. Thayer, *Books Abroad*, XXX, 95; by Aerol Arnold, *Personalist*, XXXVII, 415-416; by A. Koszul, *EA*, IX, 154-156; by Marion B. Smith, *QQ*, LXII, 634-635; by Alice Walker, *RES*, NS, VIII (1957), 63-64.

A213   Nicoll, Allardyce, ed. *Shakespeare Survey, IX.* Cambridge Univ. Press, 1956. Pp. viii, 168.
Rev: by Kenneth O. Myrick, *SQ*, VII (1956), 252-256; *VQR*, XXXII, no. 3, xcv; by Hermann Peschmann, *English*, XI, 69; *N &Q*, NS, III, 365-366; by M. St. Claire Byrne, *TN*, XI, no. 1, 32-34; by G. Lambin, *LanM*, L, 359; by J. Vallette, *MdF*, 327 (1956), 363-366, 530-531; by Albert Gilman, *QJS*, XLIII (1957), 88-89; by S. F. Johnson, *RN*, X, 40-41; by M. C. Bradbrook, *MLR*, LII, 255-256; by Robert G. Shedd, *MLN*, LXXII, 369-373; by Joseph H. Marshburn, *Books Abroad*, XXXI, 310; by J. W. Saunders, *EIC*, VII, 282-294; by René Pruvost, *EA*, X, 253-254; *ShN*, VII, 46; by Alice Walker, *RES*, NS, IX (1958), 318-319.

A214   Nicoll, Allardyce, ed. *Shakespeare Survey, X.* Cambridge Univ. Press, 1957. Pp. viii, 171.
Rev: *ConR*, July, 1957, p. 63; *VQR*, XXXIII, lxxxviii; by Margaret Willy, *English*, XI, 189-191; by Richard Findlater, *Drama*, Summer, 1957, pp. 37-39; by Frank Granville-Barker, *Plays and Players*, Sept. 1957, p. 17; *N &Q*, NS, IV, 363; by Wallace A. Bacon, *QJS*, XLIII, 309-310; by G. Lambin, *LanM*, LI, 609; by J. Vallette, *MdF*, 330 (1957), 712-713; by H. Lüdeke, *ES*, XXXVIII, 216-220; *ShN*, VIII (1958), 14; by M. C. Bradbrook, *MLR*, LIII, 241-242; by Mark Eccles, *SQ*, IX, 193-194; by Robert G. Shedd, *MLN*, LXXIII, 121-125.

A215   Nicoll, Allardyce, ed. *Shakespeare Survey, XI.* Cambridge Univ. Press, 1958. Pp. 222.
Rev: *TLS*, May 30, 1958, p. 303; by Margaret Willy, *English*, XII, 62-63; by Ivor Brown, *Drama*, Autumn, 1958, p. 39; by Gösta Langenfelt, *Moderna språk*, LII, 329-330; by William A. Armstrong, *TN*, XIII, i, 28-30; by C. G. Thayer, *Books Abroad*, XXXII, 452; by Rudolf Stamm, *SQ*, IX, 568-569; by G. Lambin, *LanM*, Dec., 1958, pp. 62-63; by J. Vallette, *MdF*, 334 (1958), 141-142; *SCN*, XVI, 20-21; by Eric Gillett, *National and English Rev.*, June, 254; *N &Q*, NS, V, 498-499.

(1) YEAR'S CONTRIBUTIONS

A216   Ellis-Fermor, Una. "The Year's Contribution to Shakespearian Study: 1. Critical Studies." *ShS*, I (1948), 118-122.

A217   Ditto, II (1949), 132-141.

A218   Ditto, III (1950), 130-137.

A219   Stewart, J. I. M. "The Year's Contributions to Shakespearian Study: Critical Studies." *ShS*, IV (1951), 139-147.

A220   Ditto, V (1952), 129-137.

A221   Bradbrook, M. C. "The Year's Contributions to Shakespearian Study: Critical Studies." *ShS*, VI (1953), 147-154.

A222   Leech, Clifford. "The Year's Contributions to Shakespearian Study: 1. Critical Studies." *ShS*, VII (1954), 128-138.

A223   Ditto, VIII (1955), 139-146.

A224   Muir, Kenneth. "The Year's Contributions to Shakespearian Study: 1. Critical Studies." *ShS*, IX (1956), 132-140.

A225   Ditto, X (1957), 135-143.

A226   Ditto, XI (1958), 136-142.

A227   Leech, Clifford. "The Year's Contributions to Shakespearian Study: 2. Shakespeare's Life and Times." *ShS*, I (1948), 122-127.

A228   Gordon, D. J. "The Year's Contributions to Shakespearian Study: Shakespeare's Life and Times." *ShS*, II (1949), 141-144.

A229   Leech, Clifford. "The Year's Contributions to Shakespearian Study: Shakespeare's Life and Times." *ShS*, III (1950), 138-142.

A230   Ditto, IV (1951), 148-153.

A231   Ditto, V (1952), 137-144.

A232   Ditto, VI (1953), 154-163.

A233   Jenkins, Harold. "The Year's Contributions to Shakespearian Study: 2. Shakespeare's Life, Times, and Stage." *ShS*, VII (1954), 138-146.

A234   Shapiro, I. A. "The Year's Contributions to Shakespearian Study: 2. Shakespeare's Life, Times and Stage." *ShS*, VIII (1955), 146-153.
A235   Foakes, R. A. "The Year's Contributions to Shakespearian Study: 2. Shakespeare's Life, Times, and Stage." *ShS*, IX (1956), 141-148.
A236   Ditto, X (1957), 143-150.
A237   Ditto, XI (1958), 142-149.
A238   McManaway, James G. "The Year's Contributions to Shakespearian Study: 3. Textual Studies." *ShS*, I (1948), 127-131.
A239   Ditto, II (1949), 145-153.
A240   Ditto, III (1950), 143-152.
A241   Ditto, IV (1951), 153-163.
A242   Ditto, V (1952), 144-152.
A243   Ditto, VI (1953), 163-172.
A244   Ditto, VII (1954), 147-153.
A245   Ditto, VIII (1955), 153-159.
A246   Ditto, IX (1956), 148-156.
A247   Ditto, X (1957), 151-158.
A248   Ditto, XI (1958), 149-155.

(2) SPECIAL TOPICS

A249   Nicoll, Allardyce. "Studies in the Elizabethan Stage Since 1900." *ShS*, I (1948), 1-16.
A250   Craig, Hardin. "Trend of Shakespeare Scholarship." *ShS*, II (1949), 107-114.
A251   Sisson, Charles J. "Studies in the Life and Environment of Shakespeare Since 1900." *ShS*, III (1950), 1-12.
A252   McManaway, James G. "Recent Studies in Shakespeare's Chronology." *ShS*, III (1950), 22-33.
A253   Muir, Kenneth. "Fifty Years of Shakespearian Criticism: 1900-1950." *ShS*, IV (1951), 1-25.
A254   Bradbrook, M. C. "Fifty Years of the Criticism of Shakespeare's Style." *ShS*, VII (1954), 1-11.
A255   Brown, John Russell. "The Interpretation of Shakespeare's Comedies." *ShS*, VIII (1955), 1-12.
A256   Leech, Clifford. "Studies in *Hamlet*, 1901-1955." *ShS*, IX (1956), 1-15.
A257   Maxwell, J. C. "Shakespeare's Roman Plays: 1900-1956." *ShS*, X (1957), 1-11.
A258   Edwards, Philip. "Shakespeare's Romances: 1900-1957." *ShS*, XI (1958), 1-18.
A259   "International News," *ShS*, 1948-1950.
A260   "International Notes," *ShS*, 1951-1958.
       Annual reports from correspondents upon books and performances in various countries.

b. SHAKESPEARE QUARTERLY

(The American *Shakespeare Quarterly*, running from 1950 to beyond the terminal date of this bibliography, should not be confused with an earlier journal of the same title, edited by Richard Flatter and limited to one issue dated London, Summer, 1947.)
A261   Campbell, Oscar James. "A Review of Recent Shakespeare Scholarship." *SQ*, II (1951), 103-110.
A262   Law, R. A. "Some Products of Shakespeare Scholarship in 1951." *SQ*, III (1952), 83-90.
A263   Craig, Hardin. "Review of Shakespeare Scholarship in 1952." *SQ*, IV (1953), 115-124.
A264   Price, Hereward T. "A Survey of Shakespeare Scholarship in 1953." *SQ*, V (1954), 109-128.
A265   Hastings, William T. "A Survey of Shakespeare Scholarship in 1954." *SQ*, VI (1955), 109-134.
A265a "Mr. Anonymous." "Editing Shakespeare." *TLS*, June 8, 1956, p. 345.
       Disputes a remark concerning C. J. Sisson's edition made in A265, pp. 114-115.
A266   Brennecke, Ernest. "All Kinds of Shakespeares." *SQ*, I (1950), 272-280.
       Discusses recent biographies of Shakespeare.

c. SHAKESPEARE NEWSLETTER

A267   Marder, Louis, ed. *The Shakespeare Newsletter*, I, No. 1-7, 1951.
A268   Ditto, II, No. 1-8 (3 and 4 a double number), 1952.
A269   Ditto, III, No. 1-6, 1953.
A270   Ditto, IV, No. 1-6, 1954.
A271   Ditto, V, No. 1-6, 1955.
A272   Ditto, VI, No. 1-6, 1956.
A273   Ditto, VII, No. 1-6, 1957.
A274   Ditto, VIII, No. 1-6, 1958.

d. SHAKESPEARE-JAHRBUCH

A275 Stoll, E. E. "Recent Shakespeare Criticism." *SJ*, LXXIV (1938), 50-81.

A276 Stamm, Rudolf. "Dramenforschung." *SJ*, 91 (1955), 121-135.

A277 Otto, Teo. "Shakespeare-Aufführungen und Bühnenbild." *SJ*, 93 (1957), 141-144.

A278 Besides preceding: Annual surveys of books, articles, and productions by W. Keller, Kurt Schrey, Karl Wentersdorf, Robert Fricker, Richard Flatter, Hermann Heuer, Karl Brinkmann, and others.

e. YEAR'S WORK IN ENGLISH STUDIES

A279 *The Year's Work in English Studies.* Ed. for the Eng. Assoc. by F. S. Boas and Mary S. Serjeantson. XIV, 1933. Oxford Univ. Press, 1935.

A280 Ditto, XV, 1934. Oxford Univ. Press, 1936.

A281 Ditto, XVI, 1935. Oxford Univ. Press, 1937.
Rev: *London Mercury*, XXXVI (1937), 408; *TLS*, Sept. 18, 1937, p. 677; *N &Q*, 173 (1937), 17-18; by W. Fischer, *Beiblatt*, XLVIII, 304; by C. J. Sisson, *MLR*, XXXIII (1938), 620-621; by Reinald Hoops, *Eng. Studn.*, LXXIII, 155-156; by A. Brandl, *Archiv*, 174 (1938), 110-112.

A282 Ditto, XVII, 1936. Oxford Univ. Press, 1938.
Rev: by W. Fischer, *Beiblatt*, XLIX (1938), 347-348; by A. Brandl, *Archiv*, 174 (1938), 250-251.

A283 Ditto, XVIII, 1937. Oxford Univ. Press, 1939.
Rev: by A. Brandl, *Archiv*, 176 (1940), 81-82.

A284 Ditto, XIX, 1938. Oxford Univ. Press, 1940.
Rev: *N &Q*, 179 (1940), 269-270; *TLS*, Oct. 12, 1940, p. 522; by C. J. Sisson, *MLR*, XXX (1941), 279; by Don Cameron Allen, *MLQ*, IV (1943), 112-113.

A285 Ditto, XX, 1939. Oxford Univ. Press, 1941.

A286 Ditto, XXI, 1940. Oxford Univ. Press, 1942.
Rev: *TLS*, Jan. 23, 1943, p. 46; by C. J. Sisson, *MLR*, XXXVIII, 165-166; *N &Q*, 185 (1943), 59; by B. L. Conway, *Catholic World*, 158 (1943), 102.

A287 Ditto, XXII, 1941. Oxford Univ. Press, 1944.
Rev: *N &Q*, 187 (1944), 88.

A288 Ditto, XXIII, 1942. Oxford Univ. Press, 1945.
Rev: *TLS*, Apr. 21, 1945, p. 188; *N &Q*, 188 (1945), 176; by C. J. Sisson, *MLR*, XL, 220.

A289 Ditto, XXIV, 1943. Oxford Univ. Press, 1945.
Rev: *TLS*, Apr. 20, 1946, p. 189; by C. J. Sisson, *MLR*, XLI, 343.

A290 Ditto, XXV, 1944. Oxford Univ. Press, 1946.
Rev: by A. Macdonald, *RES*, XXIV (1948), 75-77.

A291 Ditto, XXVI, 1945. Oxford Univ. Press, 1947.
Rev: Brief mention, *TLS*, Jan. 10, 1948, p. 27; by A. Macdonald, *RES*, XXV (1949), 182-183.

A292 Ditto, XXVII, 1946. Oxford Univ. Press, 1948.
Rev: by C. J. Sisson, *MLR*, XLIV (1949), 589; *TLS*, Jan. 22, 1949, p. 62.

A293 Ditto, XXVIII, 1947. Oxford Univ. Press, 1949.
Rev: by C. J. Sisson, *MLR*, XLV (1950), 420-421; *TLS*, Jan. 27, 1950, p. 62; by A. Macdonald, *RES*, II (1951), 97-100.

A294 Ditto, XXIX, 1948. Oxford Univ. Press, 1950.
Rev: *Modern Quarterly*, 196 (1951), 175; briefly by C. J. Sisson, *MLR*, XLVI (1951), 299.

A295 Ditto, XXX, 1949. Oxford Univ. Press, 1951.
Rev: *N &Q*, 197 (1951), 154; briefly by C. J. Sisson, *MLR*, XLVII (1952), 420.

A296 Ditto, XXXI, 1950. Oxford Univ. Press, 1952.
Rev: *TLS*, Dec. 12, 1952, p. 826.

A297 Ditto, XXXII, 1951. Oxford Univ. Press, 1953.

A298 Ditto, XXXIII, 1952. Oxford Univ. Press, 1954.

A299 Ditto, XXXIV, 1953. Oxford Univ. Press, 1955.
Rev: by Hermann Heuer, *SJ*, 92 (1956), 356; by Paul A. Jorgensen, *SQ*, VIII (1957), 124-125; by L. Bonnerot, *EA*, XI (1958), 83.

A300 Ditto, Ed. by Beatrice White. XXXV, 1954. Oxford Univ. Press, 1956.
Rev: *TLS*, Jan. 11, 1957, p. 26; by C. J. Sisson, *MLR*, LII (1957), 623; by Paul A. Jorgensen, *SQ*, IX (1958), 578-579.

A301 Ditto, XXXVI, 1955. Oxford Univ. Press, 1957.
Rev: briefly, *TLS*, Jan. 3, 1958, p. 11.

A302 Ditto, XXXVII, 1956. Oxford Univ. Press, 1958.

f. SCATTERED SURVEYS
(According to accessibility rather than subject matter. See also "Shakespeare's Influence Through the Centuries," XIII.)

(1) UNITED KINGDOM

A303 Entwistle, William J., L. W. Tancock, A. Gillies, S. C. Aston, L. T. Topsfield, eds. *Year's Work in Modern Language Studies*, Vols. 6-19 (1936-1958). Cambridge Univ. Press.

A304 The Times Literary Supplement. "Shakespeare Scholars at Work: An Age of Discovery and Advance." *TLS*, May 1, 1937, pp. 334-335.
A survey of Shakespeare scholarship from 1837 to 1937.

A305 Ellis-Fermor, Una. *Some Recent Research in Shakespeare's Imagery*. Oxford Univ. Press, 1937. Pp. 39.
Rev: A5630.

A306 Husbands, H. Winifred. "Summary of Periodical Literature." *RES*, XII (1936), 117 ff.; 247 ff.; 377 ff.; 495 ff.

A307 Husbands, H. Winifred. "Summary of Periodical Literature." *RES*, XIII (1937), 118-128; 247-256; 378-384; 496-506.

A308 Dowling, Margaret. "Summary of Periodical Literature." *RES*, XIV (1938), 121-128; 249-256; 377-384; 499-506.

A309 Wilson, F. P. "Shakespeare and the New Bibliography." *The Bibliographical Society, 1892-1942. Studies in Retrospect* (ed. by F. C. Francis, London: Bibl. Soc., 1945), pp. 76-135.

A310 Wilson, F. P. "Shakespeare Today." *Britain Today*, 131 (1947), 25-29.

A311 Parrott, Thomas M. "Shakespeare and the New Bibliography." *Library*, III (1948), 63-65.
Comments upon A309.

A312 Isaacs, J. "New Light on Shakespeare." *Listener*, XLII (July 7, 1949), 17-19.

A313 Ellis-Fermor, Una. "Shakespeare and His World: The Poet's Imagery." *Listener*, XLII (July 28, 1949), 157-158.

A314 Wilson, J. Dover. "Shakespeare and His World: The Text of the Plays." *Listener*, XLII (Aug. 18, 1949), 262-264.

A315 Fluchère, Henri. "Shakespeare in France: 1900-1948." *ShS*, II (1949), 115-124.

A316 Henriques, Alf. "Shakespeare and Denmark: 1900-1949." *ShS*, III (1950), 107-115.

A317 Simko, Jàn. "Shakespeare in Slovakia." *ShS*, IV (1951), 109-116.

A318 McManaway, James G. "Bibliography." *Literature and Science* (Proceedings of the Sixth Triennial Congress, Oxford, 1954), pp. 27-35. Oxford: Basil Blackwell (for the International Federation for Modern Languages and Literatures), 1955.

A319 Ellis-Fermor, Una. "English and American Shakespeare Studies 1937-1952." *Anglia*, LXXI (1952), 1-49.

(2) UNITED STATES AND CANADA

A320 Law, R. A. "Recent Books Reviewed." *MLN*, LII (1937), 526-530.

A321 Coffman, George R. "Some Trends in English Literary Scholarship, with Special Reference to Mediaeval Backgrounds." *SP*, XXXV (1938), 500-514.

A322 Knox, R. S. "Shakespeare: A Diversity of Doctrine." *UTQ*, VII (1938), 249-261.

A323 Tuve, Rosemond. "A Critical Survey of Scholarship in the Field of English Literature of the Renaissance." *SP*, XL (1943), 204-255.

A324 Craig, Hardin. "Recent Scholarship of the English Renaissance: A Brief Survey." *SP*, XLII (1945), 498-529.

A325 Law, Robert A. "Shakespeare and American Scholarship." *Twentieth Century English*, ed. by W. S. Knickerbocker. New York: Philosophical Library, 1946, pp. 425-431.

A326 Bush, Douglas. "Surveys of Recent Scholarship in the Period of the Renaissance." *Comparative Literature Newsletter*, IV (1946), 17-18.

A327 Wilson, John Dover. "New Ideas and Discoveries About Shakespeare." *VQR*, XXIII (1947), 537-542.

A328 Bradner, Leicester. "The Renaissance: 1939-1945." *Medievalia et Humanistica*, V (1948), 62-72.

A329 Law, Robert Adger. "Is English Literary Scholarship Advancing?" *TxSE*, XXVIII (1949), 271-284.

A330 Orsini, N. "Shakespeare in Italy." *Comparative Literature*, III (1951), 178-179.

A331 Johnson, S. F. "Shakespearean Acting and Production." *ShN*, II (1952), 5.

A332 Babcock, R. W. "Historical Criticism of Shakespeare." *MLQ*, XIII (1952), 6-20.

A333 Williams, Philip. "Recent Shakespeare Scholarship." *South Atlantic Quar.*, LIII (1954), 268-274.

A334 Harrison, G. B. "The Bardic Bookshelf." *SatR*, Sept. 25, 1954, pp. 22 ff.

A335 Dace, William. "A Survey of Opera in Modern Translation, with Short Production Notes." *Educational Theatre Journal*, VIII (1956), 229-245.

A336 Harrison, G. B. "The Bard at Mid-Century." *SatR*, Aug. 3, 1957, pp. 17, 28.

A337 Bryant, J. A., Jr. "Elizabethan Drama: 1956." *SR*, LXV (1957), 152-160.

A338   Bentley, G. E. "Shakespeare and His Times." *Contemporary Literary Scholarship: A Critical Review*, ed. by Lewis Leary. New York: Appleton-Century-Crofts, 1958, pp. 53-65.

(3) GERMANY

A339   Ra. "Shakespeare-Forschung in England." *VB*, Sept. 25, 1938, p. 18.

A340   Müller, J. "Shakespeare im Deutschunterricht." *ZDK*, LIII (1939), 497-517.

A341   Keller, W. "Deutschlands Arbeit an Shakespeare." *DWD*, I (1940), Heft 21, pp. 4-5.

A342   Kalthoff, W. "Neue Shakespeare-Literatur." *GA*, VII (1940), Heft 21, p. 8.

A343   Holzer, Gustav. *Shakespeare im Lichte der neuesten Forschung. Eine Studie.* Karlsruhe i. B: Gutsch., 1942. Pp. 33.

A344   Schmitt, Saladin. "Das Shakespeare-Bild unserer Tage." *Theater-Almanach*, I (1946/47), 144-159.

A345   Gütlinger, F. "Shakespeare-Forschung." *Das Buch*, I (1947), 21-22.

A346   Bab, Julius. "Shakespeare in Amerika." *SJ*, 82/83 (1949), 164-174.

A347   "Deutsche Veröffentlichungen über Shakespeare seit 1945. Bearb. v. d. Stadtbücherei Bochum." *MDtShG*, II (1950), 3-5.

A348   Ellis-Fermor, U. M. "English and American Shakespeare Studies 1937-1952." *Anglia*, LXXI (1952), 1-49.

A349   Sehrt, Ernst Th. "Die Shakespeareforschung 1937-1952 in Deutschland und in der Schweiz." *Anglia*, LXXI (1952), 50-81.

A350   Stamm, Rudolf. *Die moderne Shakespeareforschung und das lebende Theater in England.* Thalwil: Schweizer Gesellschaft für Theaterkultur, 1954. Also in *Neue Schweizer Rundschau*, neue Folge, XXII (1954), 112-122.

A351   Cancelled.

A352   Oppel, Horst. " 'One of the Least Typical of all Elizabethans': Probleme und Perspektiven der Shakespeare-Forschung." *Anglia*, LXXIV, (1956/57), 16-65.

A353   Oppel, Horst. "Stand und Aufgaben der deutschen Shakespeare-Forschung (1952-1957)." *DVLG*, XXXII, No. 1 (1958), 113-171.

(4) SCANDINAVIA

A354   Ottosen, J. "Nyere engelsk Shakespeare Forskning." *Tilskueren* (Copenhagen), LI, ii, 50-58.

A355   Spencer, J. W. "Some Trends in Modern Shakespeare Criticism." *Meddelelser fra Engelsklaererforeningen* (Copenhagen), III (1950), 1-14.

A356   Gyller, Harald. "Shakespeare Litteratur." *Bokvännen* (Stockholm), VI (1951), 259-262.

A357   Nixon, Ingeborg, and Kirsten L. Røder. "Realisme og idealisme. Skiftende syn paa Shakespeare." *Gads Danske Magasin*, XLVI (1952), 331-352.

A358   Hallberg, P. "Hamlet." *Edda*, LII (1952), 233-250.

A359   Molin, Nils. "Modern Shakespeareforskning." *Göteborgsstudier i litteraturhistoria tillägnade Sverker Ek* (Göteborg), 1954, pp. 10-25.

(5) HOLLAND

A360   Kranendonk, Anthon. Gerardus van. "Nieuwe Shakespeare Studien." *De Stem. Critisch Bulletin* (Arnhem), XVII (1938), 641-644.

A361   Gutteling, J. F. C. "Modern Hamlet-Criticism." *Neophil*, XXV (1941), 276-285.

A362   Malone, Kemp. "Anglistics in the United States During the War Years." *ES*, XXVIII (1947), 129-143.

A363   Westerlinck, A. "Shakespeare studie. Kroniek." *Dietsche Warande en Belfort*, 1948, pp. 246-247.

A364   Schrickx, W. "Aspecten van het Shakespeare probleem. Enkele recente gegevens." *Vlaamse Gids*, XXXV (1951), 615-620.

A365   Zandvoort, R. W. *Shakespeare in de Twintigste Eeuw.* Groningen: J. B. Wolters, 1952. Pp. 19.
        Rev: by P. H. Breitenstein, *LT*, 1952, p. 495; by F. Mossé, *EA*, VI (1953), 153; by Harry R. Hoppe, *SQ*, V (1954), 327.

A366   Bachrach, A. G. H. *Naar Het Hem Leek. Een Inleiding tot Shakespeare in Vijf Brieven.* The Hague: Bert Bakker/Daamen; Antwerp: De Sikkel, 1957. Pp. 272.
        Rev: R. W. Zandvoort, *ES*, XXXIX (1958), 92.

(6) FRANCE

A367   Lemonnier, Léon. "Du Nouveau sur Shakespeare." *NRF*, XXX (1942), 424-435.

A368   Simon, Irène. *Les Progrès de la critique Shakespearienne au XXe siècle.* Brussels: M. Didier, 1950. Pp. 30. Also published in *Revue des langues vivantes*, XVI (1950), 303-330.

A369   Paris, Jean. "Nouveaux Essais sur Shakespeare." *Rivista di Letterature Moderne*, Vols. 15-16 (1954), 80-98.

A370 Vallette, Jacques. "Shakespeariana." *MdF*, 318 (1953), 336-341; 321 (1954), 727-733.

A371 Ditto, 324 (1955), 530-535; 327 (1956), 526-531.

A372 Ditto, 330 (1957), 710-714.

A373 Vallette, Jacques. "Autour de Shakespeare." *MdF*, 330 (1957), 158-160.

(7) ITALY

A374 Orsini, N. "Shakespeare in Italy." *Comparative Literature*, III (1951), 178-180. An account of the work of Italian scholars.

A375 Orsini, N. "Stato attuale della filologia shakespeariana." *Paideia*, VIII (1953), 153-176.

A376 Praz, Mario. "Shakespeariana." *Paragone* (Florence), June, 1953, pp. 74-80.

A377 Baldini, Gabriele. "Riletture shakespeariane." *Nuova Antologia*, July, 1954, pp. 353-368.

(8) SLAVIC COUNTRIES

A378 Zabludovsky, M. "New Books on Shakespeare (in England and America)." *International Literature* (USSR), V (1941), 190-197.

A379 Morozov, Mikhail M. "Shakespeare v zrcalu literarne kritike." *Slovenski prevod v Gledališkem listu Akademije za igralsko umetnost. št.*, I (1946).

A380 Krzyżanowski, Juliusz. "Szekspirologia wojenna i powojenna." *Nauka i sztuka* (Wrocław [Breslau]), I (1948), 17-58.

A381 Frühling, Jacek. "Szekspir v sosie anglo-amerykańskim." *Teatr* (Warsaw) No. 6 (1952), 26.

(9) JAPAN

A382 Oyama, Toshikazu. *Saikinno Shakespeare Kenkyuho* (A Bibliographical Approach to Recent Shakespeare Studies). Tokyo: Shinozaki Shorin, 1956. Pp. iv, 242, ix.

A383 The Theatre Arts Society of Japan, ed. *Studies in Shakespeare*, with a list of performances of Shakespeare's plays in Japan (*Journal of Theatre Arts*, II, No. 1). Tokyo: Chuokoron-sha, 1951. (In Japanese.)

A384 Toyoda, Minoru. *Shakespeare in Japan: An Historical Survey*. Tokyo: The Iwanami Shoten, 1940. Pp. xi, 139. (In English.)
An outline history of Shak. studies in Japan, from the origins up to the date of publication, with "A Japanese Shakespeare-Bibliography," pp. 121-139.

II. ELIZABETHAN LITERATURE (2;1)
(Omitted except for section entitled "The Elizabethan Dramatists and their Mutual Relations," which is transferred to "Influence of Contemporary English Dramatists," VI,5)

III. SHAKESPEARE'S LIFE (23;7)
1. DOCUMENTARY EVIDENCE (23;7)

A385 Osborn, James M. "The Search for English Literary Documents." *EIE, 1939*. New York: Columbia Univ. Press, 1940, pp. 31-55.

A386 Tate, W. E. *The Parish Chest*. Cambridge Univ. Press, 1946. Pp. 346.
A guide to the contents of English parish registers and other local records.
Rev: *TLS*, Nov. 16, 1946, p. 560; by H. C. Johnson, *Bul. Inst. Hist. Research*, XXI (1946), 77-78; *MGW*, Jan. 2, 1947, p. 11; *N &Q*, 92 (1947), 264; by J. C. Russell, *AHR*, LII, 777; by W. S. Hudson, *Church Hist.*, XVI, 115-116; by Hilda Hulme, *MLR*, XLII, 370-371; by C. C. R., *Anglican Theol. Rev.*, XXIX, 119-120; by Edward Miller, *Church Quar. Rev.*, 143 (1947), 256-258; by P. M. Dawley, *Christendom*, XII, 408-409; by Helen W. Carr, *Economic Hist. Rev.*, XVII, 152-154; by C. M. Sage, *Catholic Hist. Rev.*, XXXIII, 112-113; by Charles Johnson, *History*, XXXII, 136-137.

A387 de Chambrun, Clara Longworth. *Essential Documents . . . in the Shakespearean Case*. Bordeaux: Delmas, 1935.
Rev: by G. Connes, *RAA*, XII (1934/35), 430-432.

A388 Tannenbaum, Samuel A. "The Mystery of the Shakspere Manuscripts." *SAB*, XIV (1939), 190-191.

A389 Lewis, Benjamin Roland. *The Shakespeare Documents. Facsimiles, Transliterations, Translations & Commentary*. Stanford Univ. Press, 1940. Pp. xxiv, 324; xii, 325-631.
Rev: by Samuel A. Tannenbaum, "Raw Materials for a Shakspere Biography," *SAB*, XVI (1941), 104-117; by John Corbin, *NYTBR*, Aug. 24, 1941, pp. 9, 22; by T. W. Baldwin, *MLN*, LVII (1942), 364-373; *TLS*, Aug. 22, 1942, p. 420; see also editorial comment, ibid., Aug. 22, 1942, p. 415; by B. E. Boothe, "The Life of Shakespeare," *CE*, III (1943), 686-687; by J. G. McManaway, *JEGP*, XLIV (1945), 100-105.

A390 Tannenbaum, Samuel A. "Shakespeare's Will." *SAB*, XV (1940), 126-127.

A391 Stalker, A. "Is Shakespeare's Will a Forgery?" *QR*, 274 (1940), 248-262.

A392 Brooke, T. "The License for Shakespeare's Marriage." *MLN*, LVII (1942), 687-688; reply by James G. McManaway, ibid., 688-689.

A393   Wigmore, J. H. "Shakespeare's Legal Documents." *American Bar Association Jour.*, XXVIII (1942), 134.

A394   A., H. "Shakespeare's Will." *N &Q*, 188 (1945), 127; Wm. Jaggard, ibid., 174.

A395   Chambers, Sir Edmund K. *Sources for a Biography of Shakespeare.* Oxford: Clarendon Press, 1946. Pp. 80.
Rev: *TLS*, June 15, 1946, p. 285; by H. B. Charlton, *MGW*, LV, 34; by J. M. S. Tompkins, *RES*, XXIII (1947), 162-163; *TAr*, XXXI, 79; by C. J. Sisson, *MLR*, XLII, 152; by T. W. Baldwin, *JEGP*, XLVI, 310-312; by R. S. Knox, *UTQ*, XVII, 99-100; by J. G. McManaway, *MLQ*, IX (1948), 106-107.

A396   Brown, Arthur. "Shakespeare's Deposition in the Belott-Mountjoy Suit." *ShS*, III (1950), 13.

A397   Fox, Levi. "An Early Copy of Shakespeare's Will." *ShS*, IV (1951), 69-77.

A398   Austin, Warren B. *New Light on Shakespeare: From Documents in the Nashe-Harvey Controversy.* DD, Columbia University, 1953.

A399   Frye, Roland M. "Shakespeare's 'Second Best Bed' and a Contemporary Parallel." *N & Q*, NS, I (1954), 468-469. Comment by K. B. Danks, ibid., NS, II (1955), 227.

A400   Hill, R. H. "Shakespeare's Will." *TLS*, July 15, 1955, p. 397. See also *TLS*, July 22, p. 413, and July 29, p. 429.

A401   Schwarzstein, Leonard. "Knight, Ireland, Steevens, and the Shakespeare Testament." *N &Q*, NS, II (1955), 76-78.

A402   Broadbent, C. "Shakespeare and Shakeshaft." *N &Q*, NS, III (1956), 154-157.

A403   Isham, Sir Gyles. "Bernard or Barnard." *N &Q*, NS, IV (1957), 338-339.
There is only a remote possibility that any Shak. papers which might have been in the possession of Sir John Bernard's family have survived.

2.   SHAKESPEARE'S HANDWRITING (24;8)

A404   Baker, H. Kendra. "Variations in Spelling One's Own Name." *N &Q*, 172 (1937), 178-179. Cf. W. Jaggard, ibid., 229-230.

A405   Carter, G. E. L. "A Shakespearean Holograph." *Library Assoc. Record*, XXXVIII (1936), 424-426.

A406   Jackson, H. E. "An Alleged Shakespeare Signature at Stanford University." *Christian Science Monitor*, Apr. 14, 1937, p. 4.

A407   Tannenbaum, Samuel A. "New Shakespeare Signatures." *SAB*, XIII (1938), 63-64.

A408   "Another Signature by Bard Reported." *New York Times*, January 20, 1939.

A409   Marks, Seymour. "Signatures of Shakespeare." *TLS*, June 10, 1939, p. 341.

A410   Tannenbaum, Samuel A. "The Mystery of the Shakspere Manuscripts." *SAB*, XIV (1939), 190-191.

A411   Adams, Joseph Quincy. "A New Signature of Shakespeare?" *BJRL*, XXVII (1943), 256-259. Concerns a signature found in a copy of Lambarde's *Archaionomia*, 1568, now owned by the Folger Shakespeare Library.
See also "One of Shakespeare's Books?" *TLS*, May 1, 1943, p. 216; C. L. Ewen, "A New Shakespeare Signature," *N &Q*, 185 (1943), 196; Ambrose Heal, ibid., 263; R. L. Eagle, ibid.; William Jaggard, ibid.

A412   Caldiero, Frank. "Shakespeare's Signature in Lambarde's APXAIONOMIA." *N &Q*, 188 (1945), 162-163.
Believes the evidence supports the authenticity of the signature.

A413   Otsuka, Takanobu. *A Study of Shakespeare's Handwriting* (Shakespeare Studies Series). Tokyo: Sogen-sha, 1949. Pp. 138 + 22 (in Japanese). New edition: Tokyo: Shinozaki Shorin, 1952. Pp. 167, 17 plates.

a.   THE ANNOTATOR
The busy graduate student with much of value to catch up on will do well to pass over this Annotator controversy completely.

A414   Chambrun, Clara Longworth de. "The Book Shakespeare Used." *Scribner's*, 100 (1936), 28-34.
See comments by Samuel A. Tannenbaum, *SAB*, XI, (1936) 187.
Describes a copy of Holinshed's *Chronicles* (apparently the second edition), now the property of Mr. William Jaggard. In the text of this copy passages used by Shakespeare in several of his history plays have been marked with a pen.

A415   Chambrun, Clara Longworth, Comtesse de. *Shakespeare Rediscovered by Means of Public Records, Secret Reports and Private Correspondence Newly Set Forth as Evidence on his Life and Work.* Preface by G. B. Harrison. New York: Scribner's, 1938. Pp. xii, 323.
Rev: A509.

A416   Keen, Alan. "A Short Account of the Recently Discovered Copy of Edward Hall's *Union of the Noble Houses of Lancaster and York*, Notable for Its Manuscript Additions." *BJRL*, XXIV (1940), 255-262.

A417   Rossiter, A. P. "Prognosis on a Shakespearian Problem." *DUJ*, XXXIII (1940), 126-139.

A418 Fletcher, R. F. W. "Annotations by Shakespeare?" *TLS*, Sept. 14, 1940, p. 471. Cf. ibid., Aug. 29, p. 5. Further correspondence from W. W. Greg, ibid., Sept. 28, p. 500. Reply from Alan Keen, ibid., Oct. 12, p. 519.

A419 Wadman, H. "Who Wrote in the Margin (of a copy of Hall's *Chronicle*, 1550)?" *Picture Post*, Apr. 26, 1941, pp. 27-29.

A420 Tannenbaum, Samuel A. "Self-Deception, Hoax or Fraud?" (Supposed Shakespeare autograph). *SAB*, XVI (1941), 254-255.

A421 Keen, Alan. "Hall and Shakespeare." *TLS*, April 26, 1947, p. 197.
      See letters by John Crow, ibid., May 10, 1947, p. 225; by W. J. F. Hutcheson, ibid., May 24, p. 253; by A. P. Rossiter, ibid., May 31, p. 267; by Denys Hay, ibid., May 17; by Mr. Keen, ibid., Nov. 29, p. 615; by A. P. Rossiter, ibid., Jan. 10, 1948, p. 23; by Martin R. Holmes, ibid., Jan. 24, p. 51; by Annie Brière, *Nouvelles littéraires*, XXX (1951), 1.

A422 McLaren, Moray. *"By Me:" A Report Upon the Apparent Discovery of Some Working Notes of William Shakespeare in a Sixteenth Century Book.* London: John Redington, 1949. Pp. 67.
      Rev: "Not Proven," *TLS*, Sept. 2, 1949, p. 569; by A. Koszul, *LanM*, XLIV (1950), 122-123.

A423 Keen, Alan. "A Shakespearian Riddle." *TLS*, April 21, 1950, p. 252.
      See the letter by C. G. Gray, ibid., April 28, 1950, p. 261; by A. R. Wagner, ibid., May 5, 1950, p. 277; by G. Slevin, idem; by R. F. Rattray, ibid., May 19, 1950, p. 309; by W. J. Hemp, ibid., June 2, 1950, p. 341; by A. Keen, ibid., June 30, 1950, p. 405.
      Mr. Keen points to Shakespeare's possible link with a "Shropshire Circle" as an indication of how the poet may have obtained the annotated copy of Hall's *Chronicle* in which Mr. Keen has been interested; Messrs. Gray, Wagner, Slevin, and Hemp urge caution in using Mr. Keen's genealogical information.

A423a Shield, H. A. "Links with Shakespeare. VII." *N&Q*, 195 (1950), 385-386.
      Comment by Cecil G. Gray and reply by H. A. Shield, ibid., 558-560.

A424 Partridge, A. C. "The Fabulous Find." *Rand Daily Mail*, Apr. 5, 1951, p. 6.

A425 Keen, Alan, and Roger Lubbock. *The Annotator: The Pursuit of an Elizabethan Reader of Halle's "Chronicle" Involving Some Surmises About the Early Life of William Shakespeare.* London: Putnam, 1954. Pp. xiii, 216.
      Rev: by Christopher Devlin, *Month*, XI (1954), 307-308; *TLS*, Mar. 26, p. 198; by David Hardman, *John o' London's Weekly*, LXIII, 290; by Anthony Thwaite, *Spectator*, May 28, p. 656; by Milton Crane, *Chicago Sunday Tribune*, Sept. 5, p. 8; by J. F. Sullivan, *Commonweal*, LX, 585; *Kirkus*, XXII, 375; by H. B. Charlton, *MGW*, Apr. 20, p. 4; by J. I. M. Stewart, *NstN*, XLVII, 326; *New Yorker*, Sept. 25, p. 143; by J. H. Jackson, *San Francisco Chronicle*, Aug. 19, p. 15; by G. B. Harrison, *SatR*, Sept. 25, pp. 22, 32; by P. A. Duhamel, *America*, 92 (1954), 18-19; by Ivor Brown, *Obs.*, Mar. 7, p. 9; by G. Lambin, *LanM*, XLVII, 71; by A. Günther, *Dt. Ztg. u. Wirtschaftsztg.*, IX, No. 101, 24; *Listener*, LI, 793; by A. Günther, *Neue Züricher Ztg.*, Fernausg. No. 165 (June 18, 1955), p. 8; by Alice Griffin, *TAr*, XXXIX (Apr.), 7; by Alfred Harbage, *YR*, XLIV, 443-446; by H. C. Kiefer, *Arizona Quarterly*, XI, 183-184; by Clifford Leech, *DUJ*, XLVII (Mar.), 90; *CE*, XVI, 521-522; by G. W. Williams, *SQ*, VII (1956), 131-132.

A426 "Case of a Vexatious Man." *Time*, LXIII (Apr. 5, 1954), 49-52.

A427 Law, Robert Adger. "Hall's *Chronicle* and Its Annotator." *Lib. Chron. Univ. Texas*, V (1956), 3-7.
      Finds no significant relationship between Shak.'s plays and the annotations (in a 1550 Hall's *Chronicle*) discovered by Alan Keen.

A428 Law, Robert Adger. "Guessing About the Youthful Shakespeare." *University of Texas Studies in English*, XXXIV (1955), 43-50.

A429 Frost, William. "Shakespeare His Own Granpaw." *CE*, XVII (1956), 219-222.

b. THE BOOK OF SIR THOMAS MORE

A430 Flatter, Richard. "Eine Szene in Shakespeares Handschrift." *Neue Auslese*, II, No. 6 (1947), 61-66. Also *Neues Abendland*, III (1948), 59.

A431 Bald, R. C. *"The Booke of Sir Thomas More* and Its Problems." *ShS*, II (1949), 44-65.

A432 Nosworthy, J. M. "Hand B in *Sir Thomas More*." *Library*, 5th Series, XI (1956), 47-50.

c. OTHER

A433 Ewen, C. L'Estrange. *What Shakespeare Signatures Reveal: A Chapter from an Unpublished Book.* Paignton: Author, 1940. Pp. 6.
      Rev: Briefly, *TLS*, Jan. 25, 1941, p. 47.

A434 Beaumont, C. "Shakespeare's Handwriting." *Ba*, XXXII (1948), 156-160.

A435 Ashe, Geoffrey. "Shakespeare's First Manuscript?" *The Month*, VI (1951), 236-240.

A436 Everitt, E. B. *The Young Shakespeare: Studies in Documentary Evidence.* Vol. II: *Anglistica*. Copenhagen: Rosenkilde and Bagger, 1954. Pp. 188.
      Rev: A2449.

A437 "Stolen Books with Value of $16,000 Found." *Chicago Tribune*, Aug. 1, 1958, pp. 1, 8.

Still unfound, according to owner John Sisto, was a 50-page MS of *Hamlet*, in the handwriting of Shak., worth $25,000.

d. SUPPLEMENT: SHAKESPEARE FORGERIES (24;8)
(1) IRELAND (24;8)

A438   Mair, John. *The Fourth Forger: William Ireland and the Shakespeare Paper.* London: Cobden-Sanderson, 1938. Pp. xv, 244.
        Rev: by John Carter, *Spectator*, Aug. 19, 1938, p. 310; *MGW*, Aug. 26, 1938, p. 175; by Trevor James, *Life and Letters*, XIX, No. 14, 124-125; by Sylva Norman, *London Mercury*, XXXVIII, 465-466; by W. Stonier, *NstN*, NS, XVI, 286; *TLS*, Aug. 6, 1938, p. 515; by William T. Hastings, *SAB*, XIV (1939), 248-251; by W. T. Hastings, *SRL*, XX, 16; by P. Hutchison, *NYTBR*, June 4, p. 2; by E. W. Bowen, *Virginia Journal of Education*, XXXIII (1939/40), 201-204; by T. W. Baldwin, *MLN*, LV (1940), 458.

A439   Hastings, William T. *Shakespeare, Ireland's First Folio.* Ltd. ed. (Friends' Bulletin, Books at Brown, Vol. II, No. 3). Providence, Rhode Island: Brown Univ. Lib., 1940. Also in *Colophon*, New Graphic Series, I, No. 4 (1940), 75-86.

A440   Hare, K. "A Forger of Shakespeare: W. H. Ireland." *Chambers' Journal*, March, 1945, pp. 119-121.

A441   Hyde, Mary Crapo. "Shakespeare, Jr." Ed. by Percy E. Lawler, John Fleming, and Edwin Wolf. *To Doctor R.: Essays Here Collected and Published in Honor of the Seventieth Birthday of Dr. A. S. W. Rosenbach.* Philadelphia: Privately printed, 1946, pp. 85-96.

A442   Heltzel, Virgil. *Fair Rosamond: A Study of the Development of a Literary Theme.* Northwestern Univ. Studies in the Humanities, No. 16. Northwestern Univ. Press, 1947. Pp. viii, 135. Ireland, pp. 79-82.
        Rev: Brief mention, *TLS*, Feb. 7, 1948, p. 83; by Mary O. Cowper, *South Atlantic Quar.*, XLVII, 610-611; by J. F. Kermode, *RES*, XXIV, 355-356; by F. W. S., *N&Q*, 193 (1948), 69-70; by J. Gerritsen, *ES*, XXIX, 93; by G. Bullough, *MLR*, XLIV (1949), 119-120; by G. B. Parks, *MLN*, LXIV, 143; by B. P. Millar, *MLQ*, X, 532-533.

A443   Cancelled.

A444   Schwarzstein, Leonard. "Knight, Ireland, Steevens, and the Shakespeare Testament." *N&Q*, NS, II (1955), 76-78.

A445   Hammond, Muriel E. "The Great Shakespeare Mystery." *Chambers' Journal*, Oct., 1955, pp. 597, 599.

A446   Ireland, W. H. "Boy Who Wrote a Play by Shakespeare; Excerpts from 'Confession'." *Grand Deception; the World's Most Spectacular and Successful Hoaxes, Impostures, Ruses and Frauds.* New York: Lippincott, 1955, pp. 117-125.

(2) COLLIER (25;8)

A447   Swander, Homer. "Biographies in Brief: John Payne Collier." *ShN*, VI (1956), 24.

A448   Tillotson, Kathleen. "Another Collier Forgery." *TLS*, July 11, 1936, p. 576.

A449   Ringler, William. "Another Collier Forgery." *TLS*, Oct. 29, 1938, p. 693.

A450   Gorrell, Robert Mark. "John Payne Collier and *The Murder of Iohn Brewen*." *MLN*, LVII (1942), 441-444.

A451   E., S. Y. "A Shakespeare MS?" *N&Q*, 189 (1945), 193; Wm. Jaggard, ibid., 263; James G. McManaway, ibid., 284; Jaggard, ibid., 190 (1946), 65; S. Y. E., ibid., 191 (1946), 85; S. Y. E., ibid., 192 (1947), 218; S. Y. E., ibid., 193 (1948), 388; James G. McManaway, ibid., 525; S. Y. E., ibid., 547, and 194 (1949), 19.

A452   Nosworthy, J. M. "*Macbeth* at the Globe." *Library*, II (1947), 108-118.

A453   Wilson, J. Dover, and R. W. Hunt. "The Authenticity of Simon Forman's *Bocke of Plaies*." *RES*, XXIII (1947), 193-208.

A454   Hotson, Leslie. "Manningham's 'Mid . . .'." *TLS*, Sept. 9, 1949, p. 585.

A455   Race, Sidney. "John Payne Collier." *N&Q*, 195 (1950), 21.

A456   Race, Sidney. "Collier's 'History of English Dramatic Poetry'." *N&Q*, 195 (1950), 33-35.
        See also Sidney Race, "Manningham's Diary." *N&Q*, 195 (1950), 218.

A457   Race, Sidney. "J. P. Collier and the Dulwich Papers." *N&Q*, 195 (1950), 112-114.

A458   Race, Sydney. "J. P. Collier's Fabrications." *N&Q*, 195 (1950), 345-346, 501-502.
        See letter by Sir William Foster, ibid., 414-415; by S. Race, ibid., 480-481.

A459   Muir, Kenneth. "A Chapman Masque?" *TLS*, Dec. 15, 1950, p. 801.
        See letters by Margaret Dean-Smith, ibid., Dec. 29, 1950, p. 827; ibid., Jan. 26, 1951, p. 53.

A460   Schrickx, W. "Notes on the So-called Collier Forgery of the Dedication to Chapman's *All Fools*." *RBPH*, XXVIII (1950), 142-146.

A461   Evans, G. Blakemore. "The Authenticity of Keeling's Journal Entries on *Hamlet* and *Richard II*." *N&Q*, 196 (1951), 313-315.
        See comment by Sidney Race, ibid., 513-515.

A462   Evans, G. Blakemore. "The Authenticity of the Keeling Journal Entries Reasserted." *N&Q*, 197 (1952), 127-128.

See letters referring to Mr. Sidney Race's charge of forgery by Mr. J. C. Maxwell, *TLS*, Feb. 22, 1952, p. 141, and by F. S. Boas, *TLS*, Mar. 7, 1952, p. 173; and Mr. Race's restatement of the case, *N &Q*, 197 (1952), 181-182.

A463   Race, Sydney. "John Payne Collier and His Fabrications." *N &Q*, 197 (1952), 54-56.

A464   Race, Sydney. "Simon Forman's *Bocke of Plaies*: Ms. Ashmole 208." *N &Q*, 197 (1952), 116-117.

A465   Amneus, Daniel A. *A Textual Study of "Macbeth."* DD, University of Southern California, 1953.
        Discusses authenticity of Forman's *Bocke of Plaies*.

A466   Race, Sydney. "The Masques of the Twelve Months and the Four Seasons." *N &Q*, 197 (1952), 347-349; 525.
        See letter by Mr. Ralph C. Elsey, ibid., p. 402.

A467   Race, Sidney. " 'The Marriage of Wit and Wisdom'." *N &Q*, 198 (1953), 18-20.

A468   Race, Sidney. "The Moral Play of Wit and Science." *N &Q*, 198 (1953), 96-99.

A469   Race, Sydney, "J. P. Collier and his Fabrications: Early Poetical Miscellanies and Shakespeare Papers." *N &Q*, 198, No. 9 (Sept., 1953), 391-395; No. 12 (Dec.), 531-534.

A470   Race, Sydney. "Manningham's Diary: The Case for Re-examination." *N &Q*, 199, No. 9 (Sept., 1954), 380-383.

A471   Race, Sydney. "John Payne Collier and the Stationers' Registers." *N &Q*, NS, II (1955), 492-495.

A472   Race, Sydney. "John Payne Collier and the Stationers' Registers." *N &Q*, NS, III (1956), 120-122.

A473   Race, Sydney. "John Payne Collier and the Essex Papers." *N &Q*, NS, III (1956), 218-219.

A474   Race, Sydney. "Manningham and Marston." *N &Q*, NS, IV (1957), 69, 147.

A475   Jenkins, Gladys. "Manningham, Marston and Alderman More's Wife's Daughter." *N &Q*, NS, IV (1957), 243-244.

A476   Race, Sydney. "John Payne Collier and his Fabrications." *N &Q*, NS, IV (1957), 309-312.

A477   Race, Sydney. "John Payne Collier and the Percy Society." *N &Q*, NS, IV (1957), 395-397.

A478   Race, Sydney. "Simon Forman's *Bocke of Plaies* Examined." *N &Q*, NS, V (1958), 9-14.
        Concludes that the *Bocke of Plaies* is a Collier forgery.

A479   Race, Sydney. "J. O. Halliwell and Simon Forman." *N &Q*, NS, V (1958), 315-320.

(3) CUNNINGHAM FORGERIES (26;9)
Omitted

(4) FENTON

A480   Field, Arthur. *Recent Discoveries Relating to the Life and Works of William Shakespeare.* New ed. Southampton: Roy Davis, privately printed, 1953. Pp. i, 103. Typescript. Subsequently published in London: Mitre Press, 1954. Pp. 84.
        Rev: *TLS*, Oct. 15, 1954, p. 654; letter by C. A. O. Fox, *TLS*, Oct. 29, p. 696.

A481   "Richard Fenton and His 'Quizzing Age'." *TLS*, Oct. 28, 1955, 648.

3. SHAKESPEARE'S NAME (26;9)

A482   Ewen, C. L'Estrange. "The Name 'Shakespeare'." *N &Q*, 171 (1936), 187-188; 281-282.

A483   Welby, A. "The Name 'Shakespeare': Saxby." *N &Q*, 171 (1936), 230-231.

A484   Baker, H. K. "Variations in Spelling One's Own Name." *N &Q*, 172 (1937), 178-179.
        See also Wm. Jaggard, ibid., 229-230.

A485   Weekley, Ernest. *Surnames.* New York: Dutton & Co., 1937. Pp. xxii, 360.
        "The Shakespearian Type of Surname," pp. 252-277.
        Rev: by A. Taylor, *MP*, XXXV (1937/38), 217-219.

A486   Ewen, C. L'Estrange. "Shakespeare of Nottinghamshire." *N &Q*, 174 (1938), 100-101.
        See letter by F. Williamson, *N &Q*, ibid., 134.

A487   Radice, S. "The Spelling of 'Shakespeare'." *N &Q*, 178 (1940), 191; M. H. Dodds and A. J. H., ibid., 304-305; C. L'Estrange Ewen and A. C. C., ibid., 358-359; Wm. Jaggard and James Seton-Anderson, ibid., 392-393; F. C. White, ibid., 412; C. L'Estrange Ewen, ibid., 448.

A488   to 490 Cancelled.

A491   Wachler, E. "Sind Shakespeare und Shaksper die gleiche Persönlichkeit?" *Darmstädter Tageblatt*, June 6, 1939.

A492   Hoops, Johannes. "Shakespeare's Name and Origin." *Studies for William A Read, A Miscellany Presented by Some of His Colleagues and Friends*, pp. 67-87.

A493   Lewis, Benjamin Roland. *The Shakespeare Documents: Facsimiles, Transliterations, Translations and Commentary.* Stanford Univ. Press, 1940. Pp. xxiv, 324; xii, 325-631.
        Rev: A389.

A494   Hoops, J. "Schreibung und Aussprache des Namens Shakespeares." *FuF*, XVII (1941), 303-305.

A495   Hoops, J. "Spelling and Pronunciation of the Name of Shakespeare." *Research and Progress* (Leipzig), VIII (1941), 203. English version of A494.

A496   Hoops, J. "Bedeutung und Ursprung des Namens Shakespeares." *FuF*, XVII (1941), 337-340.

A497   Hoops, J. "Meaning and origin of the name of Shakespeare." *Research and Progress* (Leipzig), VIII (1941), 265-274. English version of A496.

A498   Hoops, J. *Shakespeares Name und Herkunft.* (Sitzungsberichte der Heidelberger Akademie der Wissenschaften, XXX, v.) Heidelberg: Winter, 1941. Pp. 56.
        Rev: by W. Keller, *SJ*, LXXVII (1941) 198-199; by W. Ebisch, *Beiblatt*, LIII (1942), 115-117; *LZ*, 93 (1942), 532; by H. Marcus, *DDHS*, X (1943), 97; by E. Eckhardt, *Eng. Studn.*, LXXV (1943), 232-236; by Eilert Ekwall, *ES*, XXV, 25-27; by Karl Brunner, *Lbl*, LXIV (1943), 94-95.

A499   Troubridge, St. Vincent. "Spelling of Shakespeare's Name." *N &Q*, 180 (1941), 323.

A500   Robb, J. D. "The N. E. D. and the Spelling of Shakespeare's Name." *TLS*, Aug. 3, 1946, p. 285.

A501   Horn, Wilhelm. "Der Name Shakespeare." *Archiv*, 185 (1949), 26-35.

A502   "Hyphenating Shakespeare." *ShN*, VII (1957), 36.

4. THE MOST IMPORTANT BIOGRAPHIES (27;9)
(including general studies of Shakespeare's life and works)
(See also Short Introductions, XII, 9.)

a. ENGLISH AND AMERICAN
(1) BOOKS

A503   Aubrey, John. *Aubrey's Brief Lives.* Ed. by Oliver Lawson Dick. London: Secker & Warburg, 1949. Pp. cxiv, 408.
        Rev: by V. de S. Pinto, *English*, VIII (1950), 89-91; *TLS*, Jan. 27, 1950, p. 59 (see Mr. Dick's answer, ibid., Feb. 24, 1950, p. 121); by B. R. Redman, *SRL*, May 27, 1950, p. 41; *NstN*, Jan. 21, 1950, p. 80; by John Arlott, *FortnR*, Apr., 1950, pp. 276-277; by James R. Newman, *NR*, Jan. 8, 1951, pp. 19-20.

A503a   Aubrey, John. *Brief Lives and Other Selected Writings.* Ed. with Introd. and Notes by Anthony Powell. Cresset Lib. London: Cresset Press, 1949. Pp. xxv, 410.
        Rev: "The Note-Takers," *TLS*, Aug. 26, 1949, p. 553; *MGW*, Sept. 15, 1949, p. 11; by Sir John Squire, *Illustrated London News*, 125 (1949), 808.

A503b   Powell, Anthony. *John Aubrey and His Friends.* London: Eyre and Spottiswoode; New York: Scribner's, 1949. Pp. 335.
        Rev: by V. de S. Pinto, *English*, VII (1949), 242-243; by James Stern, *NYTBR*, May 15, 1949, p. 5; *MGW*, Sept. 15, 1949, p. 11; by H. R. Trevor-Roper, *NstN*, XXXVII, 15-16.

A504   Adams, Joseph Quincy. *A Life of William Shakespeare.* New York: Houghton Mifflin, 1923. Student's ed. London: Constable, 1947. Pp. 360.
        Rev: by C. F. Tucker Brooke, "A New Life of Shakespeare." *Essays on Shakespeare and Other Elizabethans*, 1948, pp. 108-114.

A505   Alexander, Peter. *Shakespeare's Life and Art.* London: Nisbet, 1938. Pp. vi, 248.
        Rev: by H. B. Charlton, *MGW*, Feb. 3, 1939, p. 94; by Kenneth Muir, *Spectator*, Mar. 3, 1939, pp. 359-360; by F. C. Danchin, *EA*, III, 378; *TLS*, Feb. 25, p. 122; *Ba*, XXIV, 93-100; by Rudolf Stamm, *SJ*, 84/86 (1951), 245-249.

A506   Brahms, C., and S. J. Simon. *No Bed for Bacon.* London, 1941; New York: Crowell, 1950. Pp. 241.
        Rev: by E. Brennecke, *SQ*, I (1950), 280; by L. Rogow, *SRL*, XXXIII, 16.

A507   Brown, Ivor. *Shakespeare.* London: Collins; New York: Doubleday & Co., 1949. Pp. 306; 237. Tr. by Ernst Eduard Stein as *Shakespeare: Der Mensch, der Dichter, seine Zeit.* Zürich: Manesse-Verlag, 1950. Excerpt publ. in *Neue Schweizer Rundschau*, XVIII (1950), 473-479. Paperback ed., London: Collins, 1957. Pp. 254. Revised and abridged for inclusion in Comet Books.
        Rev: *TLS*, Aug. 12, 1949, p. 516; by Kenneth Muir, *Spectator*, July 29, 1949, p. 146; by Maurice Evans, *NYTBR*, July 24, p. 3; by H. B. Charlton, *MGW*, July 28, p. 10; by Margaret Webster, *NYHTBR*, July 24, p. 5; by D. S. White, *English*, VII 294-295; by Eric Gillett, *FortnR*, 166 (1949), 351-352; by J. I. M. Stewart, *NstN*, XXXVIII, 200; by O. J. Campbell, *SRL*, XXXII, 10-11; by C. de Groot, *Nieuwe Eeuw*, Nov. 19; *Listener*, XLII, 159; *Elseviers Weekblad*, Dec. 3; by Paul V. Rubow, *Berlingske Aften* (Copenhagen), Oct. 12; *Ottawa Journal*, Oct. 1; *Calgary Herald*, Aug. 27; by J. B. Priestley, *NstN*, XXXVIII, 12; briefly in *American Mercury*, LXIX, 505; by Charles Sisson, *Sunday Times*, July 17, p. 3; by J. B. Fort, *LanM*, XLIV (1950), 38-41, 414-415; by Douglas Bush, *NR*, Apr. 24, 1950, pp. 20-21; by James Southall Wilson, *VQR*, XXVI, 316-320; by Hamilton Basso, *New Yorker*, Apr. 8, pp. 113-114; by R. Flatter, *SJ*, 88 (1950), 239-240; *TLS*, June 28, 1957, p. 402.

A508   Chambers, Sir E. K. *A Short Life of Shakespeare, with the Sources.* Abridged from the author's *William Shakespeare . . .* by Charles Williams. Oxford, 1933.
        Rev: by H. de Groot, *ES*, XX (1938), 223-225.

A509   Chambrun, Clara Longworth, Comtesse de. *Shakespeare Rediscovered by Means of Public Records,*

Secret Reports and Private Correspondence Newly Set Forth as Evidence on his Life and Work. Preface by G. B. Harrison. New York: Scribner's, 1938. Pp. xii, 323.
    Rev: by Hyder Rollins, *JEGP*, xxxvII (1938), 432-437; *London Mercury*, xxxvIII, 97-98; by Tucker Brooke, *SRL*, Apr. 23, 1938, p. 17; *More Books*, xIII, 196-197; by Mark Van Doren, *Nation* (N. Y.), 146 (1938), 728; *TLS*, June 4, p. 388; by C. J. McCole, *Catholic World*, 147 (1938), 379-380; by W. J. Lawrence, *Spectator*, May 27, 1938, p. 974; by H. B. Charlton, *MGW*, May 20, p. 394; by Floris Delattre, *EA*, II, 393-396; by H. Scherman, *Book-of-the-Month Club News*, Apr., 1938, p. 9; by H. Strode, *NYTBR*, Mar. 27, pp. 4, 20; *Ba*, xxIII, 134-142; by Louis Gillet, *RddxM*, 108, 47 (1938), 443-457; by Jac. Overmans, S. J., *Stimmen der Zeit*, 136 (1939), 324; by B. T. Spencer, *SR*, xLVII, 294-305; by C. J. Sisson, *MLR*, xxxIV, 90-91; by Alice Walker, *RES*, xv, 215-216; by A., *Polybiblion*, 195 (1939), 364-366.

A510   Chambrun, Clara Longworth, Comtesse de. *Shakespeare retrouvé: sa vie, son œuvre*. Paris: Larousse-Plon, 1947. Pp. 494.
    Rev: by William John Tucker, *Thought*, xxII (1947), 719-721; by W. Weidlé, *Critique*, Oct., 1947; by F. Delattre, *LanM*, xLI, 549-556; by G. Connes, ibid., 601-604; by A. Foerster, *Paru*, Aug., 1947, pp. 58-59; by Joseph H. Marshburn, *Books Abroad*, xxII (1948), 373-374; by H. Roddier, *RLC*, xxII, 594-596.

A510a   Chambrun, Clara Longworth, Comtesse de. *Shakespeare: A Portrait Restored*. London: Hollis & Carter, 1957. Pp. 406. Translation of A510.
    Rev: by James Laver, *Month*, xvIII (1957), 343-348; by Paul E. McLane, *America*, Nov. 16, 1957, pp. 219-221; *San Francisco Chronicle*, Nov. 24, p. 15; *New York Times*, Jan. 12, 1958, Sec. vIII, p. 33; by E. V. Wyatt, *Catholic World*, Feb., 1958, p. v; by George Freedly, *Library Journal*, 83 (1958), 94; *Kirkus*, xxv, 344; *Players Magazine*, xxxIV, 126; *Dublin Magazine*, Apr.-June, p. 54; briefly by Albert Howard Carter, *SQ*, IX, 579.

A511   Chute, Marchette. *Shakespeare of London*. New York: E. P. Dutton, 1949. Pp. xii, 397. Paperback ed., 1957.
    Rev: *CE*, xI (1950), 470-471; by Clorinda Clarke, *Catholic World*, 172 (1950), 77; by R. A. Law, *Southwest Rev.*, xxxv, 291-292; by Harry Levin, *NYTBR*, Mar. 26, p. 7; by Margaret Webster, *NYHTBR*, Mar. 26, p. 1; by O. J. Campbell, *SRL*, Apr. 1, pp. 13-14; by Alfred Harbage, *Nation*, 170 (1950), 378-379; by Douglas Bush, *NR*, Apr. 24, pp. 20-21; by Hallett Smith, *YR*, xxxIX, 743-746; by James Southall Wilson, *VQR*, xxvI, 316-320; by Robert Adger Law, *SR*, xxxv, 291-292; by Hamilton Basso, *New Yorker*, Apr. 8, pp. 114, 117; by E. Brennecke, *SQ*, I, 274; by H. Popkin, *TAr*, xxxIV, 9-10; by I. B. Clemeshaw, *Theosophical Forum*, xxvIII, 421-426; *TLS*, June 8, 1951, p. 354; by Kenneth Young, *Spectator*, May 11, p. 624; by J. I. M. Stewart, *NstN*, May 19, p. 573; *Adelphi*, xxvII, 361-362; by Ivor Brown, *Obs.*, July 8, p. 7; by Roy Walker, *Theatre Newsletter*, Apr. 28, p. 6.
    See also Marchette Chute, "Shakespeare of London." *Horn Book Magazine*, xxxI (1955), 28-35. Informal comments on research and writing methods for her book.

A512   Dawson, Giles E. *The Life of Shakespeare* (Folger Booklets on Tudor and Stuart Civilization). Washington, D. C.: The Folger Shakespeare Library, 1958. Pp. 34.

A513   Dobbs, Leonard. *Shakespeare Revealed*. London: Skeffington and Son, 1948. Pp. 222.
    Sees the plays as revelations of his personality and symbolic presentations of his life and his relations with his fellow dramatists.
    Rev: by G. Lambin, *LanM*, xLIII (1949), 334; by E. Brennecke, *SQ*, I (1950), 278-279; by Karl J. Holzknecht, *SQ*, II (1951), 364-366.

A514   Fripp, Edgar I. *Shakespeare, Man and Artist*. Ed. by F. C. Wellstood. 2 Vols., Oxford Univ. Press, 1938. Pp. xxii, 464; xii, 474.
    Rev: by W. J. Lawrence, *London Mercury*, xxxvIII (1938), 280-281; *TLS*, July 30, p. 506; by J. S. Wilson, *VQR*, xIV, 637-640; *N &Q*, 175 (1938), 35-36; by W. A. Neilson, *SRL*, Dec. 3, p. 40; by Edwin H. Zeydel, *MLJ*, xxIII, 231-232; by W. Keller, *SJ*, LxxIV, 173-174; by F. E. C. H., *Ba*, xxIII (Oct., 1938), 188-198; by P. M. Jack, *NYTBR*, Aug. 28, p. 3; by B. R. Lewis, *SAB*, xIV (1939), 37-45; by Alois Brandl, *DLZ*, Lx, 1061-64; by B. T. Spencer, *SR*, xLVII, 294-305; by C. J. Sisson, *MLR*, xxxIV, 433-434; by Alice Walker, *RES*, xv, 213-215.

A515   Halliday, Frank Ernest. *Shakespeare: A Pictorial Biography*. London: Thames & Hudson, 1956. Pp. 147; illus. 151.
    Rev: A774.

A516   Hill, Frank Ernest. *To Meet Will Shakespeare*. New York: Dodd, Mead & Co., 1949. Pp. xii, 481.
    A popular fictionalized treatment of the life and works.
    Rev: by Charles Norman, *NYTBR*, Oct. 16, 1949, p. 34; by Alfred Harbage, *NYHTBR*, Dec. 4, p. 44; by O. J. Campbell, *SRL*, xxxII, p. 36; by E. Brennecke, *SQ*, I (1950), 279-280.

A517   Norman, Charles. *So Worthy a Friend: William Shakespeare*. New York: Rinehart, 1947. Pp. xv, 316.
    Rev: by F. S. Tupper, *QJS*, xxxIV (1947), 241-242; by William John Tucker, *Catholic World*, 166 (1947), 572; by O. Prescott, *New York Times*, Dec. 2, p. 27; by W. McFee, *New York Sun*, Dec. 10; by W. B. C. Watkins, *NYTBR*, Dec. 14, p. 18; by S. C. Chew, *NYHTBR*, Dec. 21, p. 8; by E. Brennecke, *SQ*, I (1950), 273-274.

A518   Ottosen, Ingemann. *Shakespeare Under Elizabeth*. Copenhagen: Nyt Nordisk Forlag, Arnold Busck, 1948. Pp. 278.

Rev: by Paul V. Rubow, *Spraget og Stillen*, 1949, pp. 109-115; by P. Krüger, *Orbis*, VII, 305-308; by Hans Brix, *Analyser og Problemer*, VI (1950), 315-316.

A519   Pearson, Hesketh. *A Life of Shakespeare*. London: Carroll & Nicholson, 1949.   Pp. 240. A revised edition of an earlier work.   Includes anthology of Shak.'s poetry.
Rev: by R. L. Eagle, *Ba*, XXVI (1942), 161-165; *Ottawa Journal*, Sept. 24, 1949; by K. Muir, *Spectator*, 6318 (1949), p. 146; by E. Brennecke, *SQ*, I (1950), 274-275.

A520   Reese, M. M. *Shakespeare: His World and His Work*. London, 1953.
Rev: A871.

A521   Ridley, M. R. *William Shakespeare: A Commentary*. The New Temple Shakespeare. London, 1936.
Rev: A8345.

A522   Spencer, Hazelton. *The Art and Life of William Shakespeare*. New York: Harcourt, Brace, 1940; London: Bell, 1947.   Pp. xx, 495.
Rev: by C. J. Sisson, *MLN*, LV (1940), 534-536; *TLS*, June 15, 1940, p. 294; by William Allan Neilson, *SRL*, XXI, No. 20, 5-6; by Edgar C. Knowlton, *South Atlantic Quar.*, XXXIX, 478; by Helen Andrews Kahin, *MLQ*, I, 248-249; by R. G. Berkelman, *SR*, XLVIII, 284-286; by C. Donahue, *Commonweal*, XXXI, 456-457; by J. Corbin, *NYTBR*, Mar. 3, p. 2; by A. G. van Kranendonk, *ES*, XXII, 150-151; *Eng. Jour.*, XXIX, 343; by Garland Greever, *Personalist*, XXI, 428-429; by Peter Alexander, *MLR*, XXXVI (1941), 122-124; by E. K. Chambers, *RES*, XVII, 345-346; by G. C. Taylor, *YR*, XXX, 418-421; by R. A. Law, *JEGP*, XL, 152-153; see note by James J. Lynch, *MLN*, LVI, 603-604, and reply by Mr. Spencer, ibid., LVI, 604; by E. C. Pettet, *English*, VII (1948/49), 33-34; by R. F. Rattray, *QR*, 287 (1949), 320-335; *TLS*, Feb. 17, 1949, p. 107; by Richard Flatter, *SJ*, 88 (1952), 227.

A523   Smith, Robert M. "An Agnostic Life of Shakespeare." *SAB*, XV (1940), 75-87. A review article of A522.

A524   De Vocht, Henry. *Shakespeare: His Life, Work and Afterlife*. A Lecture. Turnhout: Brepols, 1945.   Pp. 40.

A525   Williams, Charles. *A Short Life of Shakespeare with the Sources*. Oxford, 1933.
Rev: by H. de Groot, *ES*, XX (1938), 223-225.

(a) JUVENILES

A526   Godwin, Edward F., and S. A. *The Greenwood Tree: A Portrait of William Shakespeare*. New York: Dutton, 1950.   Pp. 178.

A527   White, A. T. *Will Shakespeare and the Globe Theater*. New York: Random House, 1955.
Rev: B4229.
See also A8626-A8651.

(2) ESSAYS

A528   Bax, C. "Portrait of Mr. W. S., or 'Gulielmo Scespiro'." *New English Rev.*, XI (1945), 60-69.

A529   Brennecke, Ernest. "All Kinds of Shakespeares." *SQ*, I (1950), 272-280.

A530   Gour, Sir Harry Singh. "Shakespeare: His Life and Work." *Calcutta Rev.*, Ser. 3, 86 (Jan.-Mar., 1943), 21-30.

A531   Morozov, M. "Of Shakespeare's Life." *Literary Critic* (USSR), I (1940), 181-190.

A532   Phelps, William L. "Notes on Shakespeare." *Proc. Amer. Philos. Soc.*, 81 (1939), 573-579.

A533   Phelps, William L. "More Notes on Shakespeare." *Proc. Amer. Philos. Soc.*, 83 (1940), 493-502.

A534   Ray, P. C. "The Shakespearian Puzzle." *Calcutta Rev.*, LXXIII (Nov., 1939), 129-139; (Dec.), 247-256; LXXIV (Jan., 1940), 1-13; (Feb.), 103-112; (Mar.), 231-237; LXXV (April, 1940), 1-12; (May), 91-100; LXXVI (July, 1940), 1-8; (Aug.), 115-124; LXXVII (Oct., 1940), 1-10; LXXVIII (Jan., 1941), 1-7; (Feb.), 87-92; (Mar.), 207-213; LXXIX (April, 1941), 1-5.

A535   Spencer, Benjamin T. "The Man Who Was Shakespeare." *SR*, XLVII (1939), 294-305.

A536   Williams, C. "William Shakespeare." *Stories of Great Names*, London, 1937, pp. 112-140.

b. GERMAN
(1) BOOKS

A537   Brandl, Alois. *Shakespeare: Leben, Umwelt, Kunst*. Berlin: Grotesche Verlagsbuchhandlung, 1937.   Pp. xii, 521.   A new edition of his *Shakespeare* published in 1922.
Rev: *TLS*, June 12, 1937, p. 447; by W. Keller, *SJ*, LXXIII, 157-158; by Hans Marcus, *DLZ*, LVIII, 1585-90; by Muth-Klingenbrun, *VB*(Mü), May 9, 1937; by Walter Rumpf, *Die Bücherei*, IV, 439; by A. Eichler, *Eng. Studn.*, LXXII (1938), 405-406; by Wolfg. Goetz, *Archiv*, 173 (1938), 229-232; by Ernst Weigelin, *DDHS*, VI (1939), 38; by Gabriele Reuter, *NYTBR*, Oct. 8, 1939, p. 8.

A538   Brunner, Karl. *William Shakespeare*. Tübingen, 1957.
Rev: briefly by R. W. Zandvoort, *ES*, XXXIX (1958), 92; by Hermann Heuer, *SJ*, 94 (1958), 266-267.

A539   Gregor, Joseph. *Shakespeare: Der Aufbau eines Zeitalters*. Vienna, 1935.   2 ed. Munich: Piper, 1942.   3rd ed., 1948.

Rev: by Gustav Mueller, *Books Abroad*, x (1936), 295; *TAr*, xx, 244; by Wolfgang Keller, *SJ*, LXXII, 138-139; by L. Stettner, *Neue Jahrbücher für Wissenschaft und Jugendbildung*, XII, 375; by F. Knorr, *DNL*, XXXVII, 534-535; by H. Wyneken, *DL*, XXXVIII, 92-93; by Hans Bŭtow, "Shakespeare und das Theater," *Frankf. Ztg., Lbl*, Nr. 9, June 21, 1943; by Joachim Müller, *ZDK*, LVII (1943), 39.

A540   Gundolf, Friedrich. *Shakespeare: Sein Wesen und Werk*. 2nd ed. Vols. I and II. Berlin: Küpper, 1949.

A541   Holm, Hans. *Der Schwan von Avon*. Vienna: Amandus, 1948. Pp. 264.

A542   Meissner, Paul. *Shakespeare*. "Sammlung Göschen:" Band 1142. Berlin: de Gruyter, 1940. Pp. 115. 2nd ed., revised by Martin Lehnert. Berlin: de Gruyter, 1954. Pp. 136.
     Rev: by Willy Casper, *ZNU*, XXXIX (1940), 281-283; by W. Keller, *SJ*, LXXVI, 204-205; by Kurt Wittig, *Eng. Studn.*, LXXIV (1940/41), 371-372; by E. F. W. Behl, *DL*, XLIII (1940/41), 146; by R. W. Zandvoort, *ES*, XXIII (1941), 93; *Archiv*, 180 (1941), 55; by R. W. Zandvoort, *Beiblatt*, LII (1941), 110-115; by Hans Knudsen, *DNL*, XLII, 182; by L. Meyn, *NS*, XLIX, 129-130; by W. Kalthoff, *GA*, VIII, xii (1941), 8; by Walter Hübner, *N. Mon.*, XII, 120; by Jewel Wurtzbaugh, *Books Abroad*, XVI (1942), 304; by H. Marcus, *DLZ*, LXIII (1942), 539-541; *GRM*, XXX, 147; *De Weegschaal*, VIII, Heft 6. Of 2nd edition by Fernand Mossé, *EA*, VIII (1955), 69; by R. Fricker, *Archiv*, 193 (1957), 331.

A543   Schilling, Kurt. *Shakespeare: Die Idee des Menschseins in seinen Werken*. 1953.
     Rev: A6473.

A544   Schmidt-Hidding, Wolfgang. *William Shakespeare*. Kevelaer: Butzow & Berker, 1950. Pp. 31.

(2) ESSAYS

A545   Bowra. "Shakespeares letzte Jahre." *Frankf. Ztg.*, (1936), No. 591/2.

A546   Murry, J. M. "Shakespeares Ebenbild." *Die Neue Rundschau*, XLVIII (1937), Bd. 1, 604-620.

A547   Schmidt, Wolfgang. "Shakespeares Leben und der Sinn der Tragödien." *NS*, XLVI (1938), 339-353.

c. SCANDINAVIAN

A548   Fredén, Gustaf. *William Shakespeare*. Stockholm: Natur och Kultur, 1958. Pp. 106.
Includes biographical material, treatment of dramatic tradition, and analysis of separate works.
     Rev: by Allan Fagerström, *Aftonbladet* (Stockholm), Feb. 10, 1958; by Bernt Eklundh, *Göteborgstidningen* (Göteborg), Mar. 2; by Lennart Josephson, *Sydsvenska Dagbladet* (Malmö), Feb. 5; by Sig. Möhlenbrock, *Norrköpings tidningar* (Norrköping), May 10.

A549   Meurling, Per. *Shakespeare*. Stockholm: Wahlström & Widstrand, 1952. Pp. 255.
     Rev: Alan S. Downer, *SQ*, VII (1956), 115-116.

A550   Rubow, Paul V. "Digternes Ansigter." *Smaa kritiske Breve*, Copenhagen: Levin and Munksgaard, 1936, pp. 51-63. An essay criticizing the attempts of Shakespearian biography to reconstruct the poet's personality.

A551   Segerström, Sigurd. *Shakespeares Liv och Författarskap*. Stockholm: Bonnier, 1950. Pp. 10.

d. DUTCH

A552   Kranendonk, A. G. van. *Shakespeare en zijn Tijd*. Amsterdam: Querido, 1938. Pp. 321 Republished Amsterdam, 1947. Pp. 275.
     Rev: *Socialistische Gids.*, 1938, pp. 344-348; by Jos. Panhuysen, *Boekenshouw.*, XXXIII (1939), 6-11; by H. Folmer, *JMH*, XXII (1950), 85.

A553   Monteyne, Lode. *Over Shakespeare. Zijn tijd, zijn leven, zijn werk*. Turnhout, Belgium: J. van Mierlo-Proost, 1941. Pp. 48.

e. FRENCH

A554   Baldensperger, Fernand. *La Vie et l'œuvre de William Shakespeare*. Montréal: Édit. de l'Arbre, 1945. Pp. 261.
     Rev: by Robert Adger Law, *Books Abroad*, xx (1946), 43; by M. Rudwin, *Le Jour*, Jan. 5, 1946, p. 6; by R. H. Perkinson, *Theatre*, XXIII (1948), 343-344; by H. Roddier, *RLC*, XXII, 594-596.

A555   Gillet, L. *Shakespeare*. Paris: Flammarion, 1937. Pp. 128.

A556   Lemonnier, Léon. *Shakespeare*. Paris: Tallandier, 1943. Pp. 316.
     Rev: by H. Effelberger, *ZNS*, (1944), p. 38; by M. Poirier, *LanM*, XLII (1948), 296-297.

f. ITALIAN

A557   Apollonio, Mario. *Shakespeare*. Brescia: Morcelliana, 1941. Pp. 201. Repr. 1947. Pp. 184.
     Rev: by Salvatore Rosati, *L'Italia che Scrive*, XXIV (1941), 235-236.

A558   Baldini, Gabriele. *Le Tragedie di Shakespeare*. Turin: Editrice ERI. Edizioni Radio Italiana (Tip. Iltet), 1957. Pp. 199, with portrait.

A559   Biancotti, Angiolo. *Guglielmo Shakespeare*. Turin: Società Editrice Internazionale, 1957. Pp. viii, 307 con dodici tavole.

A560 Borsa, Mario. *Shakespeare*. Milan: Ed. Genio, 1947. Pp. 133.

A561 Cinti, Decio. *Guglielmo Shakespeare*. *La vita e le opere*. (Gli uomini illustri.) Milan: Sonzogno, 1941. Pp. 63

A562 Parodi, M. *Shakespeare e le sue opere*. Milan: Cavallotti, 1947. Pp. 134.

A563 Rebora, Piero. *Shakespeare*. Milan: Mondadori, 1947. Pp. 360. Republished Milan, 1958. Pp. 347.

g. SPANISH

A564 Bula Pérez, Roberto. *William Shakespeare*. Montevideo: Avecedo, 1952.

A565 Hugo, Victor. *Vida de Shakespeare*. Versión castellana de Edmundo E. Barthelemy. Buenos Aires: Edit. Claridad, 1941. Pp. 334.

h. SLAVIC LANGUAGES

A566 Chudoba, Frant. *Kniha o Shakespearovi*. *The Book of Shakespeare*. First Part. Environment and Life of Shakespeare. Prague: J. Laichter, 1941. Pp. 815.

A567 Helsztyński, Stanislaw. *Wizerunek William Szekspira* (Literatura europejska w okresie Renesansu i i Baroku obejmuje Nastepujace zeszyty, no. 13). Warsaw, 1947. Pp. 59.

A568 Mincoff, Marco. *Shakespeare, epoha i tvorčestvo* (Shakespeare, His Times and Works). Sofia: Duržavno Izdatelstvo, 1946. Pp. 229.

A569 Morozov, M. *Shekspir (1564-1616)*. Moscow: Mol. gvardiia, 1947. 280 s. s ill. I-1. portr. (Zhizn' zamechatel'nykh liudei).
Rev: Lozinskaia L. "Neudavshaiasia populiarizatsiia." *Izvestiia*, 13 iiunia.
Tr: Morozov, M., *Shakespeare (1564-1616)*. Moscow: Moladaia gvardiia, 1947. Pp. 280, with illustration and 1 portrait. (Lives of Remarkable People series).
Rev: by L. Lozinskaia. "Unsuccessful popularization," *Izvestiia*, June 13, 1948.

A570 Morozov, Mikhail M. *Szekspir*. Warszawa: Czytelnik, 1950. Pp. 222.
Rev: by Z. Hierowski, *Swiat i życie*, 1952, Nr. 8, p. 2. Polish tr.

A571 Morozov, Mikhail M. *W. Shekspir*. Tr. Radovan Teodorovič. Beograd-Zagreb: Kultura, 1948. Pp. 137. Serbo-Croatian tr.

A572 Pokorný, Jaroslav. *W. Shakespeare, jeho doba a divadlo*. Prague: Státni pedag. nakl., 1952. Pp. 84. Typewritten. Subsequently *Shakespeareova doba a divadlo*. Prague: Českosl. Akad., 1955. Pp. 199.

5. SHAKESPEARE—ACTOR AND MAN OF THE THEATRE (29;-)
a. GENERAL

A573 Harrison, G. B. *Shakespeare at Work, 1592-1603*. London: Routledge, 1933. Pp. 325. Published in USA as *Shakespeare Under Elizabeth*, New York: Henry Holt, 1933.
Rev: by W. Keller, *SJ*, LXXIII (1937), 156-157.

A574 Lewis, Benjamin Roland. *Ths Shakespeare Documents. Facsimiles, Transliterations, Translations & Commentary*. Stanford Univ. Press, 1940. Pp. xxiv, 324; xii, 325-631.
Rev: A389.

A575 Fleming, Edith Alice. *Shakespeare's Recurring Ideas*. MA thesis, University of Alberta, 1941. Pp. 314.

A576 Gray, Henry David. "Shakespeare, Southampton and Avisa." *Stanford Studies in Language and Literature* (Stanford Univ. Press, 1941), pp. 143-151.

A577 Harbage, Alfred. "A Contemporary Attack Upon Shakspere?" *SAB*, XVI (1941), 42-48.

A578 Lemonnier, Léon. "Du Nouveau Sur Shakespeare." *NRF*, LVII (1942), 425-435.

A579 Chambers, Sir E. K. *Shakespearean Gleanings*. Oxford Univ. Press, 1944.
Rev: B4466.

A580 Q., D. "Shakespeare, Oxford, and an Oxford Inn." *N &Q*, 193 (1948), 70.

A581 Chute, Marchette. "The Bubble, Reputation." *VQR*, XXV (1949), 575-584.

A582 Günther, Alfred. *Der junge Shakespeare*. Stuttgart: Deutsche Verlagsanstalt, 1947; Zürich: Ex-Libris Verlag, 1949. Pp. 249.
Rev: A2441.

A583 Leishman, J. B., ed. *The Three Parnassus Plays*. London: Nicholson, 1949.
Rev: A7549.

A584 Rattray, R. F. "Shakespeare As Seen To-Day." *QR*, July, 1950, pp. 320-335.

A585 Fort, Joseph B. "Quelques Problèmes Shakespeariens: l'Homme, le Texte, la Sagesse Pourpre." *LanM*, XLIV (1950), 414-417.

A586 Gaillard, Ottofritz. "Die 'Zurücknahme' Shakespeares." *Theater d. Zeit*, Oct. 5, 1950, pp. 4-5.

A587 Savage, D. S. *Hamlet and the Pirates*. London: Eyre and Spottiswoode, 1950. Pp. 115.
Rev: A2768.

A588 Shapiro, I. A. "The 'Mermaid Club'." *MLR*, XLV (1950), 6-18. Also, Percy Simpson, and I. A. Shapiro, " 'The Mermaid Club': An Answer and a Rejoinder." *MLR*, XLVI (1951), 58-63.

A589   Howarth, R. G. *Literature of the Theatre: Marlowe to Shirley*. Sydney, N.S.W., 1953. Pp. 14.

A590   Jenkins, Harold. "The Year's Contributions to Shakespearian Study. 2. Shakespeare's Life, Times, and Stage." *ShS*, VII (1954), 138-146.

A591   Montgomery, Roy F. "A Fair House Built on Another Man's Ground." *SQ*, V (1954), 207-208.

A592   Keen, Alan. "Shakespeare's Northern Apprenticeship." *TLS*, Nov. 18, 1955, p. 689.
See also Keen's letter of Dec. 16, *TLS*, p. 761, in which he claims identification of the famous bear Sackerson in *The Merry Wives*, and his "Shakespeare and the Chester Players," *TLS*, Mar. 30, 1956, p. 195.

A593   Fadiman, C. "Party of One." *Holiday*, April, 1956, p. 8 ff.

A594   Halliday, F. E. *Shakespeare in his Age*. London: Duckworth, 1956. Pp. xvi, 362.
Rev: *NstN*, Sept. 15, 1956, p. 321; by John Bayley, *Spectator*, Sept. 28, pp. 421-422; by Hermann Heuer, *SJ*, 93 (1957), 253; by J. B. Fort, *EA*, X, 444-445; by Horst Oppel, *DLZ*, LXXVIII, 895-896; by Donald FitzJohn, *Drama*, Spring, pp. 38-39; by G. Lambin, *LanM*, LI, 98-99; by J. Vallette, *MdF*, 329 (1957), 333-334; 330 (1957), 158; by Anna Maria Crinò, *SQ*, IX (1958), 569-572.

b. SHAKESPEARE AS AN ACTOR

A595   Lewes, G. H. "Shakespeare: Actor and Critic." *Theatre Workshop*, Oct., 1936, pp. 41-50. (Repr. from *On Actors & the Art of Acting*).

A596   Herrmann, B. *War Shakespeare ein Schauspieler?* Würzburg: Triltsch, 1937. Pp. 12.
Rev: Karl Brunner, *Lbl*, LIX (1938), 24.

A597   Lawson, R. "When Shakespeare was an Actor." *Theatre World*, XXVII (1937), 256, 262.

A598   Everett, A. L. "Shakespeare in 1596." *SAB*, XIV (1939), 144-157.

A599   Millenkovich-Morold, Max von. "Shakespeare, der Schauspieler." *Neues Wiener Tagblatt*, No. 14, 1939.

A600   Hart, Alfred. "Did Shakespeare Produce his own Plays?" *MLR*, XXXVI (1941), 173-183.

A601   Taylor, George C. "Did Shakespeare, Actor, Improvise in *Every Man in his Humour?*" *AMS*, pp. 21-32.

A602   Chute, Marchette. "World Playbill No. 1." *SRL*, July 23, 1949, pp. 9-11, 30-32.

A603   Flatter, Richard. "Shakespeare, Der Schauspieler." *SJ*, 89 (1953), 35-50.
Repr. in Flatter: *Triumph der Gnade. Shakespeare Essays*. Vienna, Munich: Kurt Desch, 1956, pp. 27-45.
Rev: by H. T. Price, *SQ*, V (1954), 117.

A604   Isaacs, J. *Shakespeare's Earliest Years in the Theatre*. Annual Shakespeare Lecture of the British Academy, 1953. *Proceedings of the British Academy*, XXXIX. London: Cumberlege, 1955.
Rev: *TLS*, May 13, 1955, p. 258; by P. Alexander, *RES*, VII (1956), 329; by Harold Wilson, *SQ*, VIII (1957), 399.

A605   Ramage, David. "Sir Andrew Shakeface." *N &Q*, NS, III (1956), 508.

c. GREENE'S ATTACK

A606   McNeal, Thomas H. "The Tyger's Heart Wrapt in a Player's Hide." *SAB*, XIII (1938), 30-39.

A607   Pruvost, René. *Robert Greene et ses Romans (1558-1592)*. Contribution à l'histoire de la Renaissance en Angleterre. Publications de la Faculté des Lettres d'Alger. 2e Ser. Tome 11. Paris: Les Belles Lettres, 1938. Pp. 650. Shak. passim.

A608   Thomas, Sidney. "The Meaning of Greene's Attack on Shakespeare." *MLN*, LXVI (1951), 483-484.

A609   Walker, Roy. "'The Upstart Crow'." *TLS*, August 10, 1951, p. 501.

A610   Wilson, J. Dover. "Malone and the Upstart Crow." *ShS*, IV (1951), 56-58.
Comment by Janet Spens in *TLS*, June 15, p. 373. Reply to J. Dover Wilson, June 29, p. 405. Further comment by Janet Spens, July 20, p. 453. Comment by Roy Walker, Aug. 10, p. 501; by C. A. C. Davis, Aug. 17, p. 517.

A611   Austin, Warren B. "A Supposed Contemporary Allusion to Shakespeare as a Plagiarist." *SQ*, VI (1955), 373-380.

A612   Okubo, Junichiro. "Robert Greene and Shakespeare." (Japanese) *Kanazawa English Studies*, Kanazawa Univ., January, 1956.

d. RELATIONS WITH OTHER FELLOW DRAMATISTS

A613   Henderson, Philip. *And Morning in His Eyes. A Study of Christopher Marlowe*. London: Boriswood, 1937. Pp. 352.
Rev: *TLS*, Oct. 2, 1937, p. 710; see letter by Mr. Henderson, ibid., Oct. 9, 1937, p. 735; reply by the reviewer, ibid., Oct. 16, p. 759; *National Rev.*, 109 (1937), 683-684; by Kenneth Muir, *Spectator*, Feb. 11, 1938, p. 234; by E. Eckhardt, *Eng. Studn.*, LXXIII, 92-94.

A614   Keller, Wolfgang. "Ben Jonson und Shakespeare." *SJ*, LXXIII (1937), 31-52.

A615   Murry, John Middleton. "Chapman the Rival Poet." *TLS*, June 4, 1938, pp. 385-386.
See letters by G. G. Loane and Alfred Douglas, *TLS*, June 11, 1938, p. 402.

A616   Norman, Charles. *The Muses' Darling: The Life of Christopher Marlowe.* New York: Rinehart
        & Co., 1946. Pp. xvi, 272.
             Rev: by Alexander Cowie, *NYTBR*, Oct. 13, 1946, p. 14; by B. R. Redman, *SRL*, Nov. 2,
             p. 19; by J. M. Nosworthy, *Life & Letters*, LVII (1948), 159-160; by F. S. Boas, *English*, VII,
             75-76; by John Le Maistre, *Adelphi*, XXIV, 256.

A617   Feldman, Abraham. "Shakespeare and the Scholars." *N &Q*, 194 (1949), 556. Also Howard
        Parsons, ibid., 195 (1950), 283-284.
             See letter by J. C. Maxwell, *N &Q*, 195 (1950), 349; by H. Parsons, ibid., pp. 569-570.

A618   Jacquot, Jean. *George Chapman (1559-1634). Sa vie, sa poésie, son théâtre, sa pensée.* Annales de
        l'Université de Lyon, Lettres, 3ᵐᵉ Serie, Fasc. 19. Paris: Société d'Edition Les Belles Lettres,
        1951. Pp. iv, 308.
             Rev: by Franck L. Schoell, *EA*, V (1952), 223-226; by T. M. Parrott, *JEGP*, LI, 422-425; by
             Harold Jenkins, *RES*, IV (1953), 169-171; by Phyllis Bartlett, *MLN*, LXVIII, 129-131; by
             Ernest A. Strathmann, *SQ*, IV, 192-194; by Lilian Haddakin, *MLR*, XLVIII, 459-460; by
             Jean Robertson, *BHR*, XVII (1955), 460-462; by Marcello Pagnini, *Riv. di lett. mod. e comp.*,
             VI, 128-130.

A619   Chute, Marchette. *Ben Jonson of Westminster.* New York: E. P. Dutton & Co., 1953. Pp. 380.
             Rev: by Alfred Harbage, *NYTBR*, Oct. 18, 1953, pp. 3, 38; by Joseph Wood Krutch, *SatR*,
             Oct. 17, pp. 13-14; by Samuel C. Chew, *NYHTBR*, Oct. 18, pp. 1, 13; by Charles Tyler
             Prouty, *YR*, XLIII (1954), 471-473; *Nation*, Jan. 9, p. 37; by George Burke Johnson, *SQ*, V,
             422-423; *TLS*, Dec. 31, p. 851; by E. D. O'Brien, *Illus. London News*, Jan. 8, 1955, p. 96; by
             Hermann Heuer, *SJ*, 91 (1955), 317-318; by M. Poirier, *EA*, VIII, 339-340; by J. C. Trewin,
             Books of the Month, Jan., pp. 22, 28.

A620   Legman, G. " 'Ever or Never'." *N &Q*, NS, II (1955), 361.

A621   Schrickx, W. "Nashe, Greene and Shakespeare in 1592." *Revue des Langues Vivantes* (Brussels),
        XXII, No. 1 (1956).

A622   Schrickx, W. *Shakespeare's Early Contemporaries. The Background of the Harvey-Nashe Polemic
        and "Love's Labour's Lost."* Antwerp: De Nederlandsche Boekhandel, 1956. Pp. viii, 291.
             Rev: by Albert Gérard, *Rev. des Langues Vivantes*, XXII (1956), 573-577; by S. K. Heninger,
             Jr., *MLN*, LXXII (1957), 437-439; *TLS*, June 28, p. 392; *ShN*, VII, 46; by G. D. Willcock,
             MLR, LIII (1958), 234-236; by Rupert Taylor, *SQ*, IX, 70-72.

A623   Musgrove, S. *Shakespeare and Jonson.* Bulletin No. 51, English Series No. 9. Auckland, N. Z.:
        Auckland Univ. College, 1957. Pp. 55. Paperbound.
             Rev: *TLS*, Feb. 14, 1958, p. 91; by G. E. Bentley, *SQ*, IX, 575.

6. SHAKESPEARE'S FAMILY AND PRIVATE LIFE (29;10)

a. FOREBEARS

See also H. A. Shield's "Links with Shakespeare," A709-A718.

A624   Kimball, Elisabeth G. "The Shakespeares in Warwickshire." *TLS*, May 9, 1936, p. 400.

A625   Ewen, C. L'Estrange. "Shakespeare of Olditch in Balsall." *N &Q*, 172 (1937), 259-260.

A626   Ewen, C. L'Estrange. "Shakespere of Nottinghamshire." *N &Q*, 174 (1938), 100-101;
        see also F. Williamson, ibid., 134.

A627   Cancelled.

A628   Healy, T. F. "Shakespeare Was an Irishman." *American Mercury*, LI (1941), 24-32. Also
        "Shakespeare als Ire." *Monatshefte für auswärtige Politik*, VIII (1941), 117. Nonsense.

A629   Hoops, Johannes. "Shakespeare's Name and Origin." *Studies for William A. Read*, pp. 67-87.

A630   Taylor, Rupert. "John Shakespeare, Corviser, of Stratford-on-Avon and the Balsall Shake-
        speares." *PMLA*, LV (1940), 721-726.

A631   Hoops, J. *Shakespeares Name und Herkunft.* Heidelberg: Winter, 1941. Pp. 56.
             Rev: A498.

A632   Taylor, Rupert. "Shakespeare's Cousin, Thomas Greene, and his Kin: Possible Light on the
        Shakespeare Family Background." *PMLA*, LX (1945), 81-94.

A633   de Groot, John Henry. *The Shakespeares and "The Old Faith."* New York: King's Crown
        Press, 1946. Pp. x, 258.
             Rev: by W. J. Tucker, *Catholic World*, 193 (1946), 378; by S. C. Chew, *NYHTBR*, May 19,
             1946, p. 26; by Richard Perinson, *Theatre*, XXI, 722-723; by T. P. Harrison, Jr., *MLQ*, VIII
             (1947), 253-254; by E. K. Chambers, *RES*, XXIII, 161-162; by R. W. Loew, *Luthern Church
             Quar.*, XX, 450-451; by Ephrim Everitt, *SAB*, XXIII (1948), 114-118.

A634   Graham, N. H. "The Puttenham Family." *N &Q*, NS, I (1954), 100-101. See letter by
        K. B. Danks, ibid., p. 362.

b. PRIVATE LIFE

Arranged by chronological order of events in his life.

A635   Lewis, Benjamin Roland. *The Shakespeare Documents. Facsimiles, Transliterations, Translations*

       & Commentary. Stanford Univ. Press, 1940. Pp. xxiv, 324; xii, 325-631.
       Rev: A389.

A636   Wollenberg, Robert. *Shakespeare, Persönliches aus Welt und Werk.* Abhandlungen zur Geschichte der Medizin und der Naturwissenschaften, 31. Berlin: Ebering, 1939. Pp. 139.
       Rev: A865.

A637   *Anecdotes, Traditionary, of Shakespeare Collected in Warwickshire in the Year 1693, Now First Publ. from the Original MS.* London: T. Rodd, 1938. Pp. 20.

A638   J., W. H. "Shakespeare in the Stocks." *N &Q*, 173 (1937), 47.

A639   Bolitho, Hector. "Shakespeare: A Fantastic Document." *John o'London's Weekly*, LXIII (1954), 405.
       See comment by R. L. Eagle in *John o'London's Weekly*, LXIII, 469.

A640   Brooke, C. F. Tucker. "Shakespeare Remembers His Youth in Stratford." *Essays on Shakespeare and Other Elizabethans.* Yale Univ. Press, 1948, pp. 32-36. Also in *Essays and Studies in Honor of Carleton Brown*, New York Univ. Press, 1940.

A641   McManaway, James G. "The License for Shakespeare's Marriage." *MLN*, LVII (1942), 450-451.

A642   Brooke, C. F. Tucker. "The License for Shakespeare's Marriage." *MLN*, LVII (1942), 687-688; reply by James G. McManaway, ibid., pp. 688-689.

A643   Langdale, A. Barnett. "Phineas Fletcher's Marriage: A Parallel to the Shakespeare Marriage Records." *N &Q*, 177 (1939), 327-328.

A644   Bayley, A. R. "Christian Name Hamnet." *N &Q*, 171 (1936), 428.

A645   B., St. C. "Christian Name 'Hamnet'." *N &Q*, 172 (1937), 11.

A646   Chute, Marchette. "Shakespeare: Husband, Actor." *Wisdom*, Jan., 1956, pp. 20-23.

A647   Eagle, R. L. "Agnes or Anne Hathaway?" *N &Q*, NS, III (1956), 504.

A648   Halpert, Herbert. "Shakespeare, Abelard, and The Unquiet Grave." *Journal of American Folklore*, LXIX (1956), 74-75.

A649   Feldman, A. Bronson. "Shakespeare's Early Errors." *International Journal of Psycho-Analysis*, XXXVI (1955), 114-133. Farfetched.

A650   Baker, Oliver. *In Shakespeare's Warwickshire and the Unknown Years.* London, 1937.
       Rev: A811.

A651   Neilson, Francis (Rhadamanthus, pseudonym). *Shakespeare and the Tempest.* New Hampshire: Richard R. Smith, 1956.
       Rev: B9830.

A652   Gray, Cecil G. "Shakespeare's Lost Years." *John o'London's Weekly*, LIX (1951), 249-250.

A653   Johnston, D. R. Lukin. "Var Shakespeare en Revisor?" *Revision og Regnskabsvaesen* (Copenhagen), XXIV (1955), 501-506. Radio talk.

A654   Angell, P. K. "Light on the Dark Lady: A Study of Some Elizabethan Libels." *PMLA*, LII (1937), 652-674.

A655   Mackenzie, Barbara A. *Shakespeare's Sonnets: Their Relation to his Life.* Cape Town: Maskew Miller, 1946. Pp. x, 82.
       Rev: B9965.

A656   Sisson, C. J. *The Mythical Sorrows of Shakespeare.* Oxford Univ. Press, 1934.
       Rev: A7937.

A657   Huebner, F. M. "Stratford und Shakespeares tragische Ehe." *Theater der Welt*, II (1938), 3.

A658   Troni, A. "Sfortuna di Shakespeare." *Colloqui col tempo.* Palermo: I quaderni de la Sinossi, 1935, pp. 23-28.

A659   Castelain, M. "L'Enigme d'Hamlet." *Université de Poitiers, Mélanges littéraires et historiques publiés à l'occasion du centenaire de sa restauration en 1845.* Paris: Belles-Lettres, 1946, pp. 20-36.

A660   Bing, Just. "Veien til Hamlet." *Edda* (Oslo), L (1950), 39-55.

A661   Gray, Cecil G. "Shakespeare's Co-Plaintiffs in the Blackfriars Lawsuit of 1615." *N &Q*, 196 (1951), 490-491.

A662   Hotson, Leslie. *I, William Shakespeare, do Appoint Thomas Russell, Esquire . . .* London: Cape, 1937. Pp. 296, il.
       Rev: by A. L. Rowse, *Spectator*, Dec. 10, 1937, pp. 1066, 1068; *TLS*, Dec. 4, 1937, p. 925; by Hazelton Spencer, *MLN*, LIII (1938), 450-453; by David Garnett, *NstN*, NS, XIV, 1066; by W. J. Lawrence, *London Mercury*, XXXVII, 338-339; by Esther C. Dunn, *SRL*, Mar. 5, 1938, p. 11; *More Books*, XIII, 196; by Mark Van Doren, *Nation* (N. Y.), 146 (1938), 728; by Tucker Brooke, *YR*, XXVII, 810, 811; by Bernard Blackstone, *Criterion*, XVII, 540-542; by Clara Longworth, Comtesse de Chambrun, *EA*, II (1938), 158-159; by J. S. Wilson, "Shakespeare and His Friends," *VQR*, XIV, 637-640; by S. C. Chew, *NYHTBR*, Mar. 6, p. 21X; by B. T. Spencer, *SR*, XLVII (1939), 294-305.

A663   Hill, R. H. "Shakespeare's Will." *TLS*, July 15, 1955, p. 397.
    See letter by M. D. H. Parker, *TLS*, July 22, p. 413.

A664   Clarkson, Paul S., and Clyde T. Warren. *The Law of Property in Shakespeare and the Elizabethan Drama*. Johns Hopkins Press, 1942. Pp. xxvii, 346.
        Rev: A2000.

A665   Frye, Roland Mushat. "Shakespeare's 'Second Best Bed' and a Contemporary Parallel." *N &Q*, NS, I (1954), 468-469.

A666   Danks, K. B. "Shakespeare's Second Best Bed." *N &Q*, NS, II (1955), 227.

c. DESCENDANTS

A667   Gray, Arthur. *Shakespeare's Son-in-Law, John Hall*. Cambridge: Heffer, 1939.
        Rev: *TLS*, Aug. 5, 1939, p. 470.

A668   Olybrius. "Edward Nash, Descendant of Shakespeare." *N &Q*, 180 (1941), 134; Wm. Jaggard, ibid., p. 176.

A669   Inquirer. "John Shakespeare." *N &Q*, 184 (1943), 47-48; A. R. Bayley, ibid., p. 113; A. J. H., and C. L'Estrange Ewen, ibid., p. 145.

A670   *The Victoria History of the County of Warwick*. London: Oxford Univ. Press for Univ. London, Institute Hist. Research.
        Vol. I.   Ed. H. Arthur Doubleday and William Page, London, 1904. Pp. xxii, 415.
        Vol. II.   Ed. William Page, London, 1908. Pp. xv, 468.
        Vol. III.   Gen. Ed. L. F. Salzman; Local Ed. Philip Styles, London, 1945. Pp. xv, 288.
        Vol. IV.   Ed. L. F. Salzman, London, 1947. Pp. xiii, 263.
        Vol. V.   Ed. L. F. Salzman, London, 1949. Pp. xiii, 224.
        Vol. VI.   Ed. L. F. Salzman, London, 1951. Pp. xiii, 287.
        Index to Vols. I-VI. Ed. R. B. Pugh, London, 1955. Pp. xii, 142. Shak. and family referred to in Vols. II-V incl.; Stratford, in all six, but especially III, 221-282.
        Rev: A813.

A671   Mitchell, C. Martin. *The Shakespeare Circle: A Life of Dr. John Hall, Shakespeare's Son-in-law*. Birmingham: Cornish Brothers, 1947. Pp. 116.
        Rev: Brief mention, *TLS*, Dec. 6, 1947, p. 635; by Ivor Brown, *Obs.*, Jan. 4, 1948, p. 3.

A672   Race, Sydney. "Sir John Bernard's Descendants." *N &Q*, NS, IV (1957), 26-27.

A673   Race, Sydney. "Sir John Bernard's Descendants." *N &Q*, NS, IV (1957), 225.

A674   Isham, Sir Gyles. "Bernard or Barnard." *N &Q*, NS, IV (1957), 338-339.

7. SHAKESPEARE'S SOCIAL ENVIRONMENT (30;10)
a. FRIENDS AND ACQUAINTANCES (30;10)
(1) JONSON

A675   Hennecke, Hans. "Ben Jonson, Shakespeares Freund und Berufsgenosse. Zur 300 Wieder-kehr seines Todestages." *Berliner Tageblatt*, 1937, No. 371.

A676   Bentley, Gerald Eades. *The Swan of Avon and the Bricklayer of Westminster*. Inaugural Lecture in Princeton Univ., March 15, 1946. Princeton Univ. Press, 1948. Pp. 18.

A677   Müllertz, Mogens. "De Fire Shakespeare Folioer." *Bogvennen* (Copenhagen), New Vol., Part 4 (1949), 1-59.

A678   Shapiro, I. A. "The 'Mermaid Club'." *MLR*, XLV (1950), 6-18.

A679   Simpson, Percy, and I. A. Shapiro. " 'The Mermaid Club': An Answer and a Rejoinder." *MLR*, XLVI (1951), 58-63.

A680   Race, Sydney. "Harleian MS. 6395 and Its Editor." *N &Q*, NS, IV (1957), 77-79.

(2) STRACHEY

A681   Sanders, Charles Richard. "William Strachey, the Virginia Colony and Shakespeare." *Virginia Magazine of History and Biography*, LVII (1949), 115-132.

A682   Ashe, Geoffrey. "William Strachey." *N &Q*, 195 (1950), 508-511.
        Replies by R. L. Eagle, ibid., p. 196 (1951), 19; by Kenneth Muir, ibid., pp. 19-20; by Herbert H. Huxley, ibid., pp. 85-86.

(3) OTHERS

A683   "One of Shakespeare's Books?" *TLS*, May 1, 1943, p. 216.

A684   Ashe, Geoffrey. "Shakespeare and a Catholic Exile." *The Month*, V (1951), 207-214.

A685   Brennecke, Ernest, Jr. "Shakespeare's Musical Collaboration with Morley." *PMLA*, LIV (1939), 139-149.
        See also "A Reply and a Symposium" by Robert Moore, ibid., pp. 149-152, and "Postscript" by author, ibid., p. 152.

A686   Brooke, C. F. Tucker. "Willobie's *Avisa*." *Essays on Shakespeare and Other Elizabethans*. Yale Univ. Press, 1948, pp. 167-178. Also in *Essays in Honor of Albert Feuillerat, Yale Romanic Studies*, XXII, Yale Univ. Press, 1943.

A687   Brown, Arthur. "Shakespeare's Deposition in the Belott-Mountjoy Suit." *ShS*, III (1950), 13.

A688   Crundell, H. W. "Shakespeare and Clement Swallow." *N&Q*, 189 (1945), 271-272.

A689   Douglas, Lord Alfred. "Shakespeare and Will Hughes." *TLS*, May 21, 1938, p. 353.
        See letters by Lord Alfred Douglas and A. R. Cripps, *TLS*, May 28, 1938, p. 370; by A. J. A.
        Symons, ibid., June 18, 1938, p. 417; by J. Middleton Murry, ibid., June 4, pp. 385-386; by
        G. G. Loane and Douglas, ibid., Nov. 6, p. 402.

A690   Graham, Norman H. "The Puttenham Family." *N&Q*, NS, I (1954), 100-101. See also
        K. B. Danks, ibid., p. 362.

A691   Graham, Norman H. "The Puttenham Family." (Part II) *N&Q*, NS, IV (1958), 424-431.

A692   Gray, Cecil G. "The 16th-Century Burbages of Stratford-on-Avon." *N&Q*, 196 (1951), 490.

A693   Gray, H. David, and Percy Simpson. "Shakespeare or Heminge? A Rejoinder and a Surre-
        joinder." *MLR*, XLV (1950), 148-152.

A694   Gray, Cecil G. "Mary Fitton and Sir Richard Leveson." *N&Q*, 197 (1952), 74-75.

A695   Hotson, Leslie. "Maypoles and Puritans." *SQ*, I (1950), 205-207.

A696   Hotson, Leslie. *Shakespeare's Sonnets Dated, and Other Essays.* London: Rupert Hart-Davis;
        Toronto: Clarke, Irwin & Co., 1949. Pp. 244.
            Rev: C21.

A697   James, Wilfred P. *The Life and Work of Richard Barnfield: A Critical Study.* DD, Northwestern
        University, 1952. Abstr. publ. in Northwestern Univ. *Summaries of Doctoral Dissertations, 1952,*
        Vol. 20, Chicago and Evanston, 1953, pp. 14-18.

A698   Kane, Robert J. " 'Richard du Champ' in *Cymbeline*." *SQ*, IV (1953), 206-207.

A699   Keen, Alan. "A Shakespearian Riddle." *TLS*, April 21, 1950, p. 252.
        Comment by C. G. Gray, Apr. 28, p. 261; by Anthony R. Wagner and Gerard Slevin, May 5,
        p. 277; by R. F. Rattray, May 19, p. 309; by W. J. Hemp, June 2, p. 341; by Alan Keen,
        June 30, p. 405.

A700   Keen, Alan. " 'In the Quick Forge and Working-House of Thought . . .' Lancashire and
        Shropshire and the Young Shakespeare." *BJRL*, XXXIII (1951), 256-270.

A701   Keen, Alan. "Shakespeare's Northern Apprenticeship." *TLS*, Nov. 18, 1955, p. 689;
        Dec. 16, p. 761.

A702   Keen, Alan. "Shakespeare and the Chester Players." *TLS*, March 30, 1956, p. 195.

A703   Lambin, G. "Shakespeare était-il essexien?" *LanM*, XLII (1948), fasc. A, A14-A22.

A704   Lewis, Benjamin Roland. *The Shakespeare Documents. Facsimiles, Transliterations, Translations
        & Commentary.* Stanford Univ. Press, 1940. Pp. xxiv, 324; xii, 325-631.
            Rev: A389.

A705   McManaway, Mary R. "Poets in the Parish of St. Giles, Cripplegate." *SQ*, IX (1958), 561-562.

A706   McNeal, T. H. "Studies in the Greene-Shakespeare Relationship." *SAB*, XV (1940), 210-218.

A707   Patterson, Remington. "Shakespearian Connexions." *TLS*, Dec. 23, 1955, p. 777.
        New light on Thomas Newman and Robert Withens, against whom William Gardiner brought
        suit in 1594 (Hotson, *Shakespeare versus Shallow*, 264-282).

A708   Shanker, S. "Shakespeare Pays Some Compliments." *MLN*, LXIII (1948), 540-541.

A709   Shield, H. A. "Links with Shakespeare." *N&Q*, 191 (1946), 112-114.

A710   Shield, H. A. "Links with Shakespeare." *N&Q*, 195 (1950), 114-115, 205-206, 385-386.
        See also "Shakespeare Link with Shropshire," by Cecil G. Gray and H. A. Shield, ibid.,
        pp. 558-560.

A711   Shield, H. A. "Links with Shakespeare." *N&Q*, 194 (1949), 30-32, 320, 536-537.
        Genealogical details on some families remotely and indirectly associated with Shak.

A712   Shield, H. A. "Links with Shakespeare. VIII." *N&Q*, 196 (1951), 250-252.
        Traces the family connections of Agnes Bennet, adopted godmother of Augustine Phillips.

A713   Shield, H. A. "Links with Shakespeare." *N&Q*, 197 (1952), 156-157; 387-389. See also
        Wm. Kent, ibid., p. 438.
        Identifies the dark lady with the daughter of Thomas Spencer, Jane Spencer Harsnape, who
        bore Robert Hesketh five illegitimate children and became his third wife in 1617, and who,
        upon his death, was married to Sir Richard Houghton. The second article deals with Thomas
        Thorpe.

A714   Shield, H. A. "Links with Shakespeare." *N&Q*, 198 (1953), 280-282.
        See correction by Mr. Shield, pp. 405-406. On genealogical evidence supports Grosart's
        identification of the author of *Love's Martyr* with Robert Chester of Royston, "until some
        definite Robert Chester of Denbighshire can be produced."

A715   Shield, H. A. "Links with Shakespeare." *N&Q*, NS, II (1955), 94-97, 513-514.

A716   Shield, H. A. "Links with Shakespeare." *N&Q*, NS, III (1956), 423-424.

A717   Shield, H. A. "Links with Shakespeare." *N&Q*, NS, IV (1957), 522-523.

A718   Shield, H. A. "Links with Shakespeare." *N&Q*, NS, V (1958), 526-527.
        Biographical matter concerning John Nicholas, son and heir of Sir Ambrose Nicholas, and
        brother of David Nicholas, the friend of Shakespeare.

A719   Stevenson, Robert. "Shakespeare's Interest in Harsnet's *Declaration*." *PMLA*, LXVII (1952), 898-902.

A720   Walker, Roy. " 'The Upstart Crow'." *TLS*, August 10, 1951, p. 501. C. A. C. Davis, ibid., August 17, 1951, p. 517.

A721   Whitebrook, J. C. "Fynes Moryson, Giordano Bruno and William Shakespeare." *N &Q*, 171 (1936), 255-260.
See also section on Philip Henslowe, IX, 1,a,(1),(b).

b. COURT AND PATRONS (31;11)

A722   Short, Raymond W. *The Patronage of Poetry under James the First*. DD, Cornell University, 1936.

A723   Draper, John W. *King James and Shakespeare's Literary Style*. *Archiv*, 171 (1937), 36-48.

A724   Hinman, Charlton. "The Pronunciation of Wriothesley." *TLS*, Oct. 2, 1937, p. 715.
For a reply by A. F. Pollard, see *TLS*, Oct. 9, 1937, p. 735.

A725   Steeholm, C. & H. *James I of England*. New York: Covici-Friede, 1938. Pp. 502.
    Rev: by P. Hutchinson, *NYTBR*, May 15, 1938, p. 5.

A726   Blair, Thomas Marshall Howe, ed. *The Unhappy Favorite, or, The Earl of Essex*. Columbia Univ. Press, 1939. Pp. xii, 144.
    Rev: A8937.

A727   Wollenberg, Robert. "Shakespeare, Essex und andere Beziehungen." *FuF*, XVI (1940), 93-95.

A728   Heuer, Hermann. "Shakespeares Verhältnis zu König Jakob I." *Anglia*, LXVI (1943), 223-227.

A729   Wilson, Elkin Calhoun. *Prince Henry and English Literature*. Cornell Univ. Press, 1946. Pp. xi, 187.
    Rev: *TLS*, Aug. 31, 1946, p. 414; by Baldwin Maxwell, *PQ*, XXV, 192; by H. S. W., *UTQ*, XVI, 105-106; by M. M., *QQ*, LIII, 275-276; by Leicester Bradner, *MLN*, LXII (1947), 69-70; by D. H. Willson, *South Atlantic Quar.*, XLVI, 143-144; by A. H. Carter, *MP*, XLV, 64-65; by J. L. Lievsay, *MLQ*, VIII, 498-499.

A730   Heltzel, Virgil B. "Sir Thomas Egerton as Patron." *HLQ*, XI (1948), 105-127.

A731   Wilson, F. P. "Some Notes on Authors and Patrons in Tudor and Stuart Times." *AMS*, pp. 553-561.

A732   Daniel, Samuel. *The Tragedy of Philotas*. Ed. by Laurence Michel. Yale Studies in Eng., 110. Yale Univ. Press, 1949. Pp. x, 183.
    Rev: *TLS*, Dec. 30, 1949, p. 860; by H. Jenkins, *MLR*, XLV (1950), 243-244; by M. A. Shaaber, *MLN*, LXV, 494-495; by Peter Ure, *RES*, II, 72-73.

A733   Thomson, Patricia. "The Patronage of Letters under Elizabeth and James I." *English*, VII (1949), 278-282.

A734   Thomson, Patricia. "The Literature of Patronage, 1580-1630." *EIC*, II (1952), 267-284.

A735   Kerr, S. Parnell. "Shakespeare's Patron." *TLS*, Mar. 13, 1953, p. 169.
A further note by the author, Apr. 3, p. 228, reveals that the name is Uvedale.

A736   Rosenberg, Eleanor. *Maecenas in England: The Earl of Leicester as Patron of Literature and Propaganda, 1559-1588*. DD, Columbia University, 1953. Publ. as *Leicester, Patron of Letters*. New York: Columbia Univ. Press, 1955. Pp. xx, 395.
    Rev: briefly by I. Willis Russell, *SQ*, IX (1958), 77-78.

A737   Morgan, Florence H. *A Biography of Lucy, Countess of Bedford, the Last Great Literary Patroness* DD, University of Southern California, 1956(?).

A738   Mithal, H. S. D. " 'Will, my Lord of Leicester's Jesting Player'." *N &Q*, NS, V (1958), 427-429.

A739   Cancelled.

c. LONDON AND SHAKESPEARE'S HOME (31;11)

A740   Kashiwakura, Shunzo. *Shakespeare and His Environs*. Tokyo: Kenkyusha, 1954. Pp. 250.

(1) LONDON (180;63)
(a) PHYSICAL FEATURES

A741   Staley, Wren. *St. Paul's Cathedral in English Life and Literature Circa 607-1666*. DD, Northwestern University, 1937. Abstr. publ. in *Summaries of Doctoral Dissertations, 1937*, Vol. 5, Chicago & Evanston: Northwestern Univ., 1937, pp. 25-28.

A742   Williams, Franklin B., Jr. *Elizabethan England*. Reconstructing the past. Illustrative set, No. 1, Museum Extension Publications. Boston: Museum of Fine Arts, 1939 (40 plates, with a 32-page booklet for each plate). Loose leaf portfolio.
    Rev: by R. B. McKerrow, *RES*, XVI (1940), 87-89.

A743   Richards, Gertrude R. B. "John Stow's 'Survey of London'." *More Books*, XX (1945), 27-28.

A744   Sutton, Vivian Ryan. *Inns and Taverns and English Literature, 1558-1642*. DD, Bryn Mawr College, 1942. Pp. 223. Mic A44-3353. *Microf. Ab.*, VI (1945), 80. Publication No. 669.

A745   C., T. C. "London Place-Names and Men of Letters." *N &Q*, 190 (1946), 12-13.

A746   Ball, Sir William Valentine. *Lincoln's Inn: Its History and Tradition.* Inns of Court, No. 1. London: Stevens, 1947. Pp. 285.

A747   Gardner, Eric. "Speed's *Theatre.*" *TLS*, Dec. 6, 1947, p. 629.

A748   Kirby, Thomas A. "*The Triple Tun.*" *MLN*, LXII (1947), 191-192. See also Kirby's " *The Triple Tun* Again." *MLN*, LXIII (1948), 56-57.

A749   Roberts, Sir James Reginald Howard, and Walter H. Godfrey, eds. *London City Council Survey of London. XXII: Bankside (the Parishes of St. Saviour and Christchurch, Southwark)* London: City Council, 1950. Pp. 152, pl. 92.
        Rev: *TLS*, May 19, 1950, p. 306. See the letters concerning the state of the 1618 map of Bankside and the location of documents by H. V. Smith, ibid., July 7, 1950, p. 421; by Ida Darlington, ibid., July 21, 1950, p. 453; by W. S. Samuel, idem.

A750   *An Atlas of Tudor England and Wales.* Forty plates from John Speed's Pocket Atlas of 1627. Introduced and described by E. G. R. Taylor. London: Penguin Books, 1951. Pp. 32.

A751   Cook, G. H. *Old St. Paul's.* London: Phoenix House, 1955.
        Rev: *QR*, 294 (1956), 134-135.

A752   *The Site of the Office of the Times, 1276-1956.* London: Privately printed, 1956.
        History of the site of the Blackfriars playhouse and of the Gatehouse property bought by Shak. Maps and drawings.

(b) COMMUNITIES

A753   Scouloudi, Irene. *Alien Immigration into, and Alien Communities in, London, 1558-1640.* Thesis, abstracted in *Bul. Inst. Hist. Research*, XVI (1939), 193-195.
        Compare Miss Scouloudi's paper with the same title published in *Pro. Huguenot Soc. London*, XVI (1939), 49-51.

A754   Sisson, C. J. "A Colony of Jews in Shakespeare's London." *Essays and Studies by Members of the English Association*, XXIV. Oxford: Clarendon Press, 1939.

A755   Whitebrook, J. C. "Huguenots of Blackfriars, and Its Neighbourhood, in Shakespearian Days." *N &Q*, 181 (1941), 226-228, 242-244, 254-256.

A756   Wilson, W. G. "Welshmen in Elizabethan London." *Life and Letters*, XLI (1944), 177-186.

A757   Heine, Arthur. "The Influence of Environment." *SAB*, XX (1945), 77-81.
        Southwark as a part of the setting in *Measure for Measure* and *The Tempest*.

A758   Esdaile, Katharine. "Some Fellow-Citizens of Shakespeare in Southwark." *Essays & Studies*, V (1952), 26-31.

(c) MISCELLANEOUS

A759   Broadbridge, G. T. "Shakespeare and London." *Stratford Herald*, April 30, 1937, p. 4.

A760   Smith, Hubert L. *The History of East London from the Earliest Times to the End of the Eighteenth Century.* London: Macmillan, 1939. Pp. 340.
        Rev: *TLS*, Sept. 2, 1939, p. 517.

A761   Short, E. "A Shakespeare Walk in London." *Ba*, XXXII (1948), 104-108.

A762   Wildi, Max. "London in Zeitalter Shakespeare." *Hesperia* (Zürich), III (1952), 117-128.

A763   Borinski, Ludwig. "Die Bedeutung Londons für die englische Literatur." *Studium Generale*, VIII (1955), 88-97.

A764   Wilson, E. "To Keep the Memory of So Worthy a Friend: First Shakespeare Folios." *Reporter*, Dec. 13, 1956, pp. 35-36.

(2) STRATFORD AND ITS NEIGHBORHOOD (180;-)
(a) THE BIRTHPLACE

A765   Wellstood, Frederick C. "Shakespeare's Birthplace Library and Repository, Stratford-upon-Avon." *Bul. of the Institute of Hist. Research*, XII (1936), 210-211.

A766   Wellstood, F. C. (comp.). *Catalogue of the Books, Manuscripts . . . Relics . . . in Shakespeare's Birthplace.* Stratford, 1937. Pp. 180.

A767   Brown, Ivor, and George Fearon. *The Shakespeares and the Birthplace.* Stratford-on-Avon: Edward Fox and Son, 1939.

A768   Eagle, R. L. "Shakespeare's Birthplace." *N &Q*, 176 (1939), 368.

A769   Mansinha, M. "At the Birthplace of Shakespeare." *The Modern Review* (Calcutta), LXIV (1939), 677.

A770   Brooke, Tucker. "Shakespeare's Dove-House." *MLN*, LIX (1944), 160-161. Repr. in *Essays on Shakespeare and Other Elizabethans*.

A771   Fox, Levi. "The Heritage of Shakespeare's Birthplace." *ShS*, I (1948), 79-88.

A772   Fox, Levi. "The Stratford Collections." *TN*, VI (1951/52), 60-62.

A773   Fox, Levi. *Shakespeare's Birthplace: A History and Descriptions* (Cotman Photo Books Series). Norwich: Jarrold, 1954. Pp. 22.

A774 Halliday, F. E. *Shakespeare: A Pictorial Biography*. London: Thames and Hudson, 1956. Pp. 148.
    Rev: briefly, *TLS*, Dec. 7, 1956, p. 738; by Donald FitzJohn, *Drama*, Spring, 1957, pp. 38-39; briefly by G. B. Harrison, *SatR*, Aug. 3, p. 17; by Wallace A. Bacon, *QJS*, XLIII, 307-308; by James G. McManaway, *SQ*, VIII, 397; *ShN*, VII, 22; by René Pruvost, *EA*, X, 252; by Henrik Sjögren, *Kvällsposten* (Malmö), Apr. 2; by H. Heuer, *SJ*, 93 (1957), 252-253; by G. Lambin, *LanM*, LI, 609; by J. Vallette, *MdF*, 330 (1957), 158; *Players Magazine*, XXXIV (1958), 126; *VQR*, XXXIV, No. 2, lx.

A775 Kaiser, Henry. "Noget Om Shakespeares By Og Lidt Om Hans Hoved." *Vendyssel Tidende* (Hjörring), June 15, 1958.

A776 *Annual Report and Statement of Accounts*. Trustees and Guardians of Shakespeare's Birthplace. Stratford-upon-Avon, 1958.

(b) NEW PLACE

A777 Simpson, Frank. "New Place: The Only Representation of Shakespeare's House, from an Unpublished Manuscript." *ShS*, V (1952), 55-57.

A778 Fox, Levi. *The Shakespearean Gardens* (Magna Colour Books). Norwich, England: Jarrolds, 1954. Pp. 28.

A779 "New Place, Stratford-upon-Avon and the Old Grammar School, on Either Side of the Guild Chapel." *Illustrated London News*, May 5, 1956, pp. 458-459.
Drawings by D. Flanders.

(c) THE TOWN

A780 Ramsay, R. E. "The Annual Shakespeare Sermon." *Stratford Herald*, Apr. 30, 1937, p. 3.

A781 Houghton, Arthur A. "A Letter." *SAB*, XIII (1938), 255-256.

A782 Bidou, H. "La Visite à Shakespeare." *L'Europe Nouvelle*, Aug. 26, 1939, pp. 941-942.

A783 Bradbrooke, William. "Shakespeare's Grave Opened." *N &Q*, 176 (1939), 31-32; Wm. Jaggard, ibid., p. 32; P. M., ibid., p. 32.

A784 Rickett, Edmond W. "Bombs and Mr. Shakespeare." *SRL*, XXII, No. 24 (Oct. 5, 1940), 9.

A785 Jaggard, W. "Graveyard Monuments at Stratford." *N &Q*, 187 (1944), 303.

A786 Garrett, J. "Shakespeare and Stratford." *NstN*, XXX (1945), 295.

A787 Styles, Philip, and J. W. Bloe. *The Borough of Stratford-upon-Avon and the Parish of Alveston*. Oxford Univ. Press, 1946. Pp. 72, pl. 10. Repr. from *The Victoria History of the County of Warwick*, A813.

A788 Swinyard, Lawrence. *Shakespeare's Stratford-on-Avon*. London: Charles F. Kimble & Sons, 1946. Pp. 21.

A789 Massingham, Harold John. "The Roots of Shakespeare." *Country Life*, 101 (1947), 382-383.

A790 Monselet, Charles. "Visite à Shakespeare." *Revue de la Pensée Française*, VIII (Aug., 1947), 74-78.

A791 Thorndike, Russell. *In the Steps of Shakespeare*. London: Rich and Cowan, 1948. Pp. 308.
    Rev: briefly, *TLS*, Apr. 24, 1948, p. 239; *SRL*, June 3, 1950, p. 20.

A792 Fox, Levi. *Stratford-upon-Avon* (Garland of England, No. 3). Bristol: Garland Press, 1949. Pp. 60.

A793 Fox, Levi. *Shakespeare's Town, Stratford-upon-Avon*. Coventry: H. & J. Busst, 1949. Pp. 40.

A794 Garwood, H. P. "Shakespeare's Church." *NstN*, XXXVII (1949), 182. Discussed on pp. 206, 230, 254.

A795 Trewin, John Courtenay. *The Story of Stratford-upon-Avon*. London: Staples Press, 1950. Pp. 80.
    Rev: *Spectator*, No. 6393 (1951), p. 26.

A796 *Stratford-upon-Avon Scene*. (Monthly) Published in Stratford. Vols. I-III (Nos. 1-30) Sept., 1946-Oct., 1950.

A797 Dobie, J. Frank. "Shakespeare's Home Town." *Holiday*, July, 1951, pp. 94-99, 125-126.

A798 Larbaud, Valéry. "Au Tombeau de Shakespeare." *Le Figaro Littéraire*, VI, No. 267 (1951), 1, 5.

A799 Eagle, R. L. "Shakespeare's Monument at Stratford." *N &Q*, 197 (1952), 325-326. See also Frank Simpson, p. 394; Wm. Kent, pp. 479-481; R. L. Eagle, p. 548.

A800 Fox, Levi. "Some New Sidelights on Stratford-upon-Avon's Medieval Guild Buildings." *Transactions of the Birmingham Archeological Society*, LXX (1952), 48-59.

A801 Fox, Levi. *The Borough Town of Stratford-on-Avon*. Corporation of Stratford-upon-Avon, 1953. Pp. 168.
    Rev: *N & Q*, 198 (1953), 547-548; by Philip Styles, *SQ*, V (1954), 415-417.

A802 Pellezzi, Camillo. "La Città di Shakespeare." *L'Illustrazione Italiana*, No. 9, 1953.

A803 Watkins, Leslie. *The Story of Shakespeare's School, 1553-1953*. Stratford-upon-Avon: The Herald Press and Edward Fox & Sons, 1953. Pp. viii, 72. Illus.

A803a Watkins, Leslie. *The Story of Shakespeare's School, 1853-1953*. Stratford-upon-Avon: The Herald Press and Edward Fox & Sons, 1955. Pp. xii, 60. Illustrated.

Survey, by the headmaster, of the past century of the Stratford-upon-Avon Grammar School.
Rev: *TLS*, Mar. 25, 1955, p. 186; by Hermann Heuer, *SJ*, 91 (1955), 315; by J. H. Walter, *SQ*, VIII (1957), 400.

A804   Fenton, E. W. *Map of Stratford-upon-Avon.* London: Newman Neame, 1954.

A804a Kirsanova, T. "In the Native Land of Shakespeare: On the Occasion of the 390th Anniversary of his Birth." *Voknug Sveta*, No. 4 (1954), 20-23.

A805   Trewin, John Courtenay. *The Pictorial History of William Shakespeare and Stratford-upon-Avon.* London: Pitkin, 1954. Pp. 24.

A806   Veerman, J. W. "Verslag van een bedevaart (naar Stratford-upon-Avon)." *Ontmoeting* (Amsterdam), IX (1956), 24-26.

A807   *Shakespeare's Stratford.* Color filmstrip, 73 frames, with 33⅓ record. Narration by Frank Titus. Literary Backgrounds, 44 Turney Road, Fairfield, Conn., 1957.
Rev: briefly by Stephen Dunning, *English Journal*, XLVI (1957), 595.

(d) THE NEIGHBORHOOD

A808   Heidrich, Hans. *John Davies of Hereford, 1565(?)-1618, und sein Bild von Shakespeares Umgebung.* DD, Berlin, Humboldt Univ., 1932. Pp. vi, 124. Publ. *Palaestra*, 143.

A809   Gover, J. E. B., A. Mawer, F. M. Stenton, and F. T. S. Houghton. *The Place-Names of Warr.* Cambridge Univ. Press, 1936. Pp. xii, 410.

A810   Mee, Arthur. *Warwickshire: Shakespeare's Country.* (King's England Series). London: Hodder, 1936. Pp. 319.

A811   Baker, Oliver. *In Shakespeare's Warwickshire and the Unknown Years.* London: Simpkin Marshall, 1937. Pp. 327, pl.
Rev: by A. L. Rowse, *Spectator*, Dec. 10, 1937, pp. 1066, 1068; by Bernard Blackstone, *Criterion*, XVII, 540-542; by Beatrice White, *National Rev.*, 110 (1937), 401-404; *TLS*, Dec. 18, 1937, p. 961; by B. T. Spencer, *SR*, XLVII (1939), 294-305.

A812   Russell, John. *Shakespeare's Country.* 4th ed., London: Batsford, 1942. Pp. vii, 152.
Rev: *TLS*, May 16, 1942, p. 248.

A813   *The Victoria History of the County of Warwick.* London: Oxford Univ. Press for Univ. London, Institute Hist. Research.
Vol. I.   Ed. H. Arthur Doubleday and Wm. Page, London, 1904. Pp. xxii, 415.
Vol. II. Ed. Wm. Page, London, 1908. Pp. xv, 468.
Vol. III. Gen. Ed. L. F. Salzman; Local Ed. Philip Styles, London, 1945. Pp. xv, 288.
Vol. IV. Ed. L. F. Salzman, London, 1947. Pp. xiii, 263.
Vol. V. Ed. L. F. Salzman, London, 1949. Pp. xiii, 224.
Vol. VI. Ed. L. F. Salzman, London, 1951. Pp. xiii, 287.
Index to Vols. I-VI. Ed. R. B. Pugh, London, 1955. Pp. xii, 142. Shak. and family referred to in Vols. II-V incl.; Stratford, in all 6, but especially III, 221-282.
Rev: Of III: "Shakespeare's County," *TLS*, Apr. 27, 1946, p. 193; by J. C. Russell, *AHR*, LII (1946), 171. Of V: *TLS*, Feb. 24, 1950, p. 124; by H. M. C., *EHR*, LXV, 538-539.

A814   "Library Notes and News." *BJRL*, XXIX (1945), 22-23.

A815   Schofield, M. "Avon and Severn in Shakespeare's Day." *Chambers' Journal*, 1947, pp. 461-463.

A816   Q., D. "Shakespeare Oxford, and an Oxford Inn." *N &Q*, 193 (1948), 70.

A817   Cash, J. Allan. *Shakespeare's Avon.* London: Chapman & Hall, 1949. Pp. lxxx, 46.

A817a Hohoff, Curt. "In Shakespeares Stadt." *Rhein. Merkur*, V, No. 20 (1950), 5.

A818   Cleave, Philip. *Shakespeare's County in Pictures.* Foreword by J. C. Trewin. London: Odhams Press, 1951. Pp. 128.
Rev: by T. Roscoe, *ConR*, 181 (1952), 256.

A819   "Shakespeare Country." British Information Series, 1951. Cited in *Filmstrip Guide*, 1954, p. 350.
A black and white filmstrip on Shak.'s countryside.

A820   Massingham, H. J. *The Shakespeare Country; Incl. the Peak and the Cotswolds.* Photographed by Alfred Furness. London: Allen & Unwin, 1952. Pp. xvi, 90.
Rev: briefly, *TLS*, Mar. 28, 1952, p. 227; by W. R. N. Payne, *SQ*, IV (1953), 196-197.

A821   Austin, E. W. *The Shakespeare Tour, from London to Warwick, Stratford, and Oxford* (Master Guides). London: J. C. Henderson, 1953. Pp. 89.

A822   Fox, Levi. *Shakespeare's Country: An Appreciation* (Magna Crome Books). Norwich: Jarrold, 1953. Pp. 32, illus.

A823   Francis, Raymond. "Shakespeare Country." *Looking for Elizabethan England.* London: Macdonald, 1954, pp. 108-124.

A824   Schulz, Herbert. "A Shakespeare Haunt in Bucks?" *SQ*, V (1954), 177-178.

A825   Trewin, J. C. *Shakespeare's Country in Pictures.* Transatlantic Arts, Inc., 1955.

A826   Moore, John. "The Shakespeare Country." *London Calling*, Apr., 1957, pp. 14-15.

A827   Nicolai, C. L. R. (i.e. Colin Clair). *Shakespeare's England.* Watford (Herts.): Bruce & Gawthorn, 1957. Pp. 64.

A828   *The Shakespeare Country* (Slidebooks, Beautiful Britain Series). London: Educational Publications in Collaboration with British Travel and Holidays Association, 1957. Pp. 24.

A829   Fairfax-Lucy, Alice. *Charlecote and the Lucys.* Oxford: Univ. Press, 1958. Pp. 327.
        Rev: *TLS*, Oct. 17, 1958, p. 590.

8. SHAKESPEARE ICONOGRAPHY (31;11)
a. PORTRAITS AND BUSTS (31;11)
(1) PORTRAITS

A830   Dawson, Giles E. "A Note on the Arlaud-Duchange Portrait of Shakespeare." *Library*, NS, XVIII (1937), 342-344.

A831   Carter, A. C. R. "Spielmann's Work on Shakespeare's Portraits Sold to G. Wells." London: *Daily Telegraph*, Mar. 15, 1937.

A832   Barrell, Charles W. "Identifying *Shakespeare*." *Scientific American*, 162 (1939), 4-8; 43-45. See also C. W. Barrell, "Shakespeare's Portraits." New York *Times*, Dec. 24, 1939, Sec. 4, p. 9.

A833   Campbell, Oscar James. "Shakespeare Himself." *Harper's Mag.*, July, 1940, pp. 172-185.

A834   Tannenbaum, Samuel A. "Editorial Notes and Comments." *SAB*, XVII (1942), 112.

A835   Hussey, Richard. "Arnold on Shakespeare." *N &Q*, 182 (1942), 221.
        See letters by Wm. Jaggard and by W. H. J., ibid., 276; by Mr. Hussey, ibid., 348.

A836   G., W. W. "Shakespeare Portraits." *N &Q*, 187 (1944), 299.

A837   Jarratt, J. Ernest. "The Grafton Portrait." *BJRL*, XXIX (1945), 225-229.

A838   Sainte-Croix, A. "Un Nouveau Portrait de Shakespeare." *Le Jour* (Montreal), Feb. 9, 1946, p. 6.

A839   Shearer, J. A., and Ed Shearer. "Shakespeare Portraits." *N &Q*, 193 (1948), 238; M. H. Dodds, ibid., p. 349; J. G. M., ibid., p. 455; S. R., ibid., pp. 547-548.

A840   Lamborn, E. A. Greening. "Great Tew and the Chandos Portrait." *N &Q*, 194 (1949), 71-72.

A841   Manggold, Walter. "Der wahre Shakespeare? Zu (4) Shakespeare-Bildern." *Die Erzählung*, IV, Issue 8 (1950), 50-51.

A842   Kliegman, Benjamin. "A 'Jonson-Shakespeare' Portrait." *ShN*, II (1952), 35.

A843   Knight, G. Wilson. "Life Portrait of Shakespeare?" *Listener*, Oct. 2, 1952, p. 535.

A844   Gildersleeve, Virginia C. "Literary Expeditions." *Many a Good Crusade*. New York: Macmillan, 1954, pp. 230-246.

A845   Waterford, William. "The Lost Shakespeare?" *This Week Magazine*, May 30, 1954, pp. 12-13.

A846   Maker, H. J. "Lord St. Leonard's Portrait of William Shakespeare." *Hobbies*, LIX (Dec., 1954), 105-107.

A847   Fedde, Ove. "Ett porträtt av Shakespeare." *Karlstadstidningen* (Karlstad, Sweden), Mar. 6, 1957, p. 13.

A848   Pohl, Frederick J. "Is This the Face of Shakespeare?" *The Pictou Advocate* (Nova Scotia), Oct. 17, 1957, pp. 7-8.

A849   Fedde, Ove. "Ett porträtt av Shakespeare." *Västerviktidningen* (Västervik, Sweden), Mar. 5, 1958.

(2) THE BUST

A850   Esdaile, Katharine. "Some Fellow-Citizens of Shakespeare in Southwark." *Essays and Studies*, NS, V (1952), 26-31.

A851   Eagle, R. L. "Shakespeare's Monument." *N &Q*, 197 (1952), 325-326.
        See letters by Frank Simpson, ibid., p. 394; William Kent, pp. 479-481; and Mr. Eagle, p. 548.

A852   Schücking, L. L. "Shakespeare's Stratforder Epitaph." *Vermeil-Festschr.*, 1952.

A853   Kaiser, Henry. "Noget Om Shakespeares By Og Lidt Om Hans Hoved." *Vendyssel Tidende* (Hjörring), June 15, 1958.

(3) RELICS, ETC.

A854   Lee, A. "Ceramic Shakespeareana." *Antiques*, XXXI (1937), 176-179.

A855   Esdaile, Katharine Ada. *Shakespeare's Verses in Tong Church.* Shrewsburg: Brown & Brinnard, Claremont Street, 1939. See letter by E. B. Goodacre, "Shakespeare and the Tong Epitaph," *N &Q*, 178 (1940), 96-97; and reply by Wm. Jaggard, ibid., pp. 178-179.

A856   Payr, Bernhard. *Französische und angelsächsische Miniaturen* [pp. 166-169: "Shak. in Stromlinie"]. Oldenburg i./O. u. B.: Gerh. Stalling, 1939.

A857   "A Goblet Made from Shakespeare's Mulberry Tree Offered for Sale for £95." Catalogue No. 41, C. J. Sawyer, London, 1938, pp. 20-21.

A858   Roe, Fred R. I., and F. Gordon Roe. "Shakespeare's Chair?" *Connoisseur*, 106 (1941), 10-12, 19.

A859   Horsley, Phyllis M. "George Keate and the Voltaire-Shakespeare Controversy." *Comp. Lit. Studies*, XVI (1945), 5-8.

A860   Palmer, Arnold. "Mistakes Cut in Marble." *TLS*, Feb. 5, 1949, p. 89.
A861   Holmes, Martin. "Portrait of a Celebrity." *TN*, XI (1956/57), 53-55.
        Comments by Brian Manvell, "Kemble Statuette," p. 108; Raymond Mander and Joe Mitchenson, "Further Notes on the Porcelain Statuette of Richard III," pp. 128-130.
A862   Mander, Raymond, and Joe Mitchenson. "The China Statuettes of Quin as Falstaff." *TN*, XII (1958), 54-58. See also Raymond Mander, and Joe Mitchenson, "Hamlet Costumes: A Correction." *ShS*, XI (1958), 123-124.

b. THE DEATH MASK (32;-)

A863   Fuchs, Georg. "Die Totenmaske Shakespeares." *VB* (Mü), May 14, 1939, p. 9.

IV. SHAKESPEARE'S PERSONALITY AND ATTITUDES OF HIS TIMES (32,173;12,60)

1. GENERAL ACCOUNT OF SHAKESPEARE'S CHARACTER (32;12)

a. BOOKS

A864   Muir, Kenneth, and Sean O'Loughlin. *The Voyage to Illyria.* A New Study of Shakespeare. London: Methuen, 1937. Pp. 242.
        Rev: A8307.
A865   Wollenberg, Robert. *Shakespeare, Persönliches aus Welt und Werk.* Abhandlungen zur Geschichte der Medizin und der Naturwissenschaften, 31. Berlin: Ebering, 1939. Pp. 139.
        Rev: by van Kranendonk, *De Weegschaal*, VI, No. 10 (1939); by W. Keller, *SJ*, LXXV (1939), 150-151; by Wolfgang Schmidt, *Beiblatt*, LI (1940), 137-139; by T. W. Baldwin, *MLN*, LV, 458; by W. S., *GRM*, XXIX (1941), 74.
A866   Wolff, Emil. *Gedanken über das Shakespeare-Problem.* Hamburg: Hoffman and Campe-Verlag, 1946. Pp. 51.
        Rev: by K. Wentersdorf, *SJ*, 82/83 (1946/47), 209-211.
        Argentine tr.: Emil Wolff, *Shakespeare: El problema de su personalidad y su obra.* Mendoza: Universidad Nacional de Cuyo, 1950. Pp. 58.
        Rev: by John Jean Lievsay, *SQ*, III (1952), 278.
A867   Wormhoudt, Arthur. *The Demon Lover.* New York: Exposition Press, 1949.
A868   Dobbs, Leonard. *Shakespeare Revealed.* London: Skeffington and Son, 1951. Pp. 222.
        Rev: A513.
A869   Emde Boas, Conrad van. "The Connection Between Shakespeare's Sonnets and his 'Travesti-Double' Plays." *International Journal of Sexology*, Nov., 1950.
        See A870.
A870   Emde Boas, C. van. *Shakespeares Sonnetten en Hun Verband met de "Travesti-Double" Spelen. Een Medesch-Psychologische Studie.* Amsterdam, 1951. Pp. 520.
        Rev: by H. deVries, *Critisch Bulletin*, XVIII (1951), 449-457; by J. Meyer, *Groene Amsterdammer*, Oct. 27; by H. Furstner, *LT*, 1952, pp. 115-116; by P. J. Meertens, *Vlam*, Jan. 5; by S. M. Hilge, *De Periscoop*, Mar., 1952.
A871   Reese, M. M. *Shakespeare: His World and His Work.* New York: St. Martin's Press, 1953. Pp. xiii, 589.
        Rev: by Kenneth Muir, *Spectator*, May 8, 1953, pp. 577-578; *TLS*, July 3, p. 428; by H. B. Charlton, *MGW*, May 28, p. 10; by John Wain, *TC*, 154 (1953), 141-143; by Edgar Johnson, *SatR*, Oct. 10, pp. 38-39; *NstN*, May 2, p. 526; Samuel C. Chew, *NYHTBR*, Dec. 27, p. 5; by R. A. Foakes, *English*, IX, 220-221; *Listener*, L, 112; by J. Vallette, *MdF*, 318 (1953), 720; by D. J. Gordon, *MLR*, XLIX (1954), 226-227; by J. B. Fort, *EA*, VII, 112-114; by Harold Jenkins, *ShS*, VII, 138; by Raymond Chapman, *CamJ*, VII, 310-311; by Karl J. Holzknecht, *SQ*, V, 418-419; by H. Heuer, *SJ*, 90 (1954), 335-337; by H. T. Price, *SQ*, V, 109-110; by G. Lambin, *LanM*, XLIX (1955), 462-463.
A872   McCurdy, Harold Grier. *The Personality of Shakespeare: A Venture in Psychological Method.* Yale Univ. Press, 1953. Pp. vii, 243.
        Rev: by G. B. Harrison, *SatR*, Sept. 25, 1954, p. 32; by Irving M. Copi, *JAAC*, XIII, 271-272; by I. A. Shapiro, *ShS*, VIII (1955), 148-149.
A873   Powys, John Cowper. *Visions and Revisions: A Book of Literary Devotions.* London: Macdonald, 1955. Pp. 221. Shak., pp. 49-62.
        Rev: *TLS*, Dec. 2, 1955, p. 720; *Listener*, LV (1956), 771.

b. ARTICLES

(1) NEGATIVE CAPABILITY

A874   Wigod, Jacob. D. "Negative Capability and Wise Passiveness." *PMLA*, LXVII (1952), 383-390.
A875   Hardy, Barbara. "Keats, Coleridge and Negative Capability." *N &Q*, 197 (1952), 299-300.
A876   Eastman, Arthur M. "Shakespeare's Negative Capability." *Papers of the Michigan Academy of Science, Arts, and Letters*, XLII (1957), 339-347.

(2) AS A MAN OF HIS TIME

A877   Uhler, John E. "Shakespeare's Melancholy." *Studies for William A Read*, 1940, pp. 201-206.
A878   Nakano, Yoshio. "Shakespeare: A Man of Renaissance." *Kaizo* (Japan), 1947, No. 2.
A879   Borinski, Ludwig. "Die Tragische Periode der Englischen Literatur." *NS*, NS, IV (1955), 289-307.
A880   Hart, Jeffrey P. [That Shakespeare was not a Renaissance Man. Too English.] *Boston University Studies in English*, II (1956).
A881   Oppel, Horst. " 'One of the Least Typical of All Elizabethans'." *Anglia*, LXXIV (1956), 16-65.

(3) AS A MAN OF FEELING

A882   Collier, D. W. "Shakespeare the Man and the Poet: His Want of Human Sympathy." *Birmingham Post*, April 24, 1936, p. 14.
A883   Rokotov, T. "The Great Brotherly Soul." *International Literature* (U.S.S.R.), 1939, pp. 3-4, 262-270.
A884   Wilson, J. D. "Shakespeare and Humanity." *LanM*, XLI (1947), 264-270.
A885   Hahn, Herbert. "Über die Menschlichkeit bei Shakespeare." *Die Kommenden* (Freiburg), III, No. 4 (1949), 6.
A886   Rattray, R. F. "Cruelty to Animals." *QR*, 296 (1958), 257-267.

(4) MISCELLANEOUS

A887   Rank, O. "Shakespeares Vaterkomplex." *Das Inzest-Motiv in Dichtung und Sage*, Leipzig, 1912, pp. 204-233.
A888   Rubow, Paul V. "Digternes Ansigter." *Smaa kritiske Breve*, Copenhagen: Levin and Munksgaard, pp. 51-63.
A889   Hiebel, Friedrich. "Shakespeare und der Beginn des neuzeitlichen Selbstbewusstseins." *Das Goetheanum*, XV (1936), 412-414. See also Frederick Hiebel. *Shakespeare and the Awakening of Modern Consciousness*. New York: Anthroposophic Press, 1940. Pp. 47.
A890   Kittredge, G. L. "The Man Shakespeare." *SAB*, XI (1936), 171-174.
A891   Hiebel, Friedrich. "Das Licht des neuzeitlichen Ichbewusstseins in Shakespeares Schaffen." *Das Goetheanum*, XVI (1937), 20-21, 29-30.
A892   Hiebel, Friedrich. "Höllenfahrt und Erlösung in Shakespeares Bewusstseinserleben." *Das Goetheanum*, XVI (1937), 168-170.
A893   "Shakespeare Self-Introduced." *TLS*, Dec. 3, 1939, p. 701.
A894   Deutschbein, Max. "Shakespeares Persönliche und Literarische Sonette I." *SJ*, LXXVII (1941), 151-188. See also LXXVIII/LXXIX (1943), 105-127.
A895   Kingsmill, H. "The 'Who' and the 'What'." *New English Review*, XI (1945), 558-561.
A896   "Library Notes and News." *BJRL*, XXIX (1946), 244-247.
A897   Brooke, C. F. Tucker. "Shakespeare Apart." *Essays on Shakespeare and Other Elizabethans*, Yale Univ. Press, 1948, pp. 16-31.
A898   Croce, Benedetto. *Filosofia-Poesia-Storia*. Pagine tratte di tutte le Opere dell'autore. Naples: Ricciardi, 1951. Contains: "Shakespeare: I. Persona pratica e persona poetica; II. La tragedia della volontà (*Antonio e Cleopatra*)," pp. 788-801.
A899   Smith, Hallet. "In Search of the Real Shakespeare." *YR*, XL (1951), 483.
A900   Josten, Walter. "Shakespeares Persönlichkeit in seinen Werken." *Begegnung* (Cologne), VI (1951), 252-253. Also in *Die Pforte* (Stuttgart), IV (1952), 98-101.
A901   Guttmann, Bernhard. "Shakespeare im Selbstgespräch." Guttmann's *Das alte Ohr*. Frankfurt a.M., 1955, pp. 123-139.
A902   Quennell, Peter. "Odi et Amo: A Note on the Origins of the Literary Temperament." *London Magazine*, IV, x (1957), 36-46. Speculations on Shakespeare's character, pp. 43-45.
A903   Reynolds, George F. "The Voice of Shakespeare." *Univ. of Colorado Studies in Language and Literature*, No. 6 (1957), pp. 1-12.
A904   Lenormand, Henri-René. "L'homme Shakespeare." *Revue théâtrale*, No. 38 (1958), pp. 5-9.

2. SHAKESPEARE'S CONCEPTION OF LIFE AND THE WORLD (33;12)

a. SHAKESPEARE'S PHILOSOPHICAL AND ETHICAL IDEAS IN GENERAL (33;12)

A905   Allen, Don Cameron. "Shakespeare and the Doctrine of Cosmic Identities." *SAB*, XIV (1939), 182-189.
A906   Anderson, Ruth L. "As Heart Can Think." *SAB*, XII (1937), 246-251.
A907   Bald, R. C. " 'Thou, Nature, Art My Goddess': Edmund and Renaissance Free-Thought." *AMS*, pp. 337-349.
A908   Baldwin, T. W. "Shakspere's Aphthonian Man." *MLN*, LXV (1950), 111-112.

A909 Baten, Anderson M. *The Philosophy of Shakespeare.* Kingsport, Tenn.: Kingsport Press, 1937. Pp. 618.
Rev: by Samuel A. Tannenbaum, *SAB*, XII (1937), 192.

A910 Baum, Bernard. *"Tempest* and *Hairy Ape*: The Literary Incarnation of Mythos." *MLQ*, XIV (1953), 258-273.

A911 Bentley, Eric. *The Playwright as Thinker.* New York: Reynal and Hitchcock, 1946. Pp. 382. See also B. Deming, "The Playwright as Playwright." *Chimera*, V (1946), 19-30.

A912 Bentley, Eric. *What Is Theatre?* A Query in Chronicle Form. London: Dennis Dobson, 1957. Pp. x, 273.
Rev: *TLS*, Oct. 4, 1957, p. 595; by E. J. West, *ETJ*, IX, 258-260.

A913 Bernad, Miguel A. "The Paradox of Shakespeare's Golden World." *Philippine Stud.*, IV (1956), 441-458.

A914 Bethell, S. L. *The Cultural Revolution of the Seventeenth Century.* London: Dobson, 1952. Pp. 161.
Rev: A3963.

A915 Bickersteth, G. L. "The Philosophy of Shakespeare." *Aberdeen University Review*, XXVIII (April, 1941), 84-92; (July), 173-183.

A916 Blackett, Douglas. "Shakespeare's Views on the Ethical Foundations of Society." *Studien aus dem Inst. f. natur- und geisteswiss. Anthropologie Berlin-Dahlem*, II (1952), 96-107.

A917 Brandt, William Jeans. *The Continental Origins of English Renaissance Conceptions of the Nature of Man.* DD, University of California, Berkeley, 1957.

A918 Brock, F. H. Cecil. "Oedipus, Macbeth and the Christian Tradition." *ConR*, March, 1950, pp. 176-181.

A919 Bruers, Antonio. "La Dottrina Sociale di Shakespeare." *Osservatore Romano*, 91 (1951), 3.

A920 Bush, G. D. *The Idea of Nature in Shakespeare's Four Principal Tragedies.* B. Litt. thesis, Oxford, 1952.

A921 Bush, Geoffrey. *Shakespeare and the Natural Condition.* Harvard Univ. Press, 1956. Pp. 140.
Rev: briefly, *Essential Books*, June, 1956, p. 34; *Hist. Ideas News Letter*, III (1957), 2, 17-18; by Irving Ribner, *MLN*, LXXII, 288-289; by R. J. Kaufmann, *Nation*, Apr. 27, pp. 367-370; by Pat M. Ryan, Jr., *QJS*, XLIII, 204-205; by R. A. Foakes, *English*, XI, 150-151; by Peter Alexander, *SQ*, VIII, 385-387; by J. A. Bryant, Jr., *SR*, LXV, 152-160; by Winifred M. T. Nowottny, *MLR*, LIII (1958), 239-240; by L. C. Knights, *RES*, NS, IX, 316-317; by Michel Poirier, *EA*, XI, 248.

A922 Cadoux, A. T. *Shakespearean Selves.* London: Lincoln Library, Epworth Press, 1938. Pp. 176.
Rev: *TLS*, August 20, 1938, p. 542; *London Quar. and Holborn Rev.*, Jan., 1939, pp. 132-133.

A923 Carr, G. "Shakespere, Browning and the Self." *The Personalist*, XXIX (1948), 391-395.

A924 Cetrangolo, G. *L'Universo Dantesco e la Terra di Shakespeare.* Rome: Edit. Opere Nuove, 1953.

A925 Craig, Hardin. "An Aspect of Shakespearean Study." *SAB*, XXIV (1949), 247-257.

A926 Craig, Hardin. "A Cutpurse of the Empire: On Shakespeare Cosmology." *A Tribute to George Coffin Taylor.* Univ. North Carolina Press, 1952, pp. 3-16.

A927 Craig, Hardin. "Shakespeare and His World: Shakespeare as an Elizabethan." *Listener*, XLII (July 21, 1949), 99-100.

A928 Craig, Hardin. "Shakespeare and the Here and Now." *PMLA*, LXVII (1952), 87-94.

A929 Craig, Hardin. *Shakespeare and the Normal World.* Rice Inst. Pamphlet (Houston, Texas), XXXI, No. 1 (1944). Pp. vi, 49.
Rev: by H. M. Jarrell, *South Atlantic Bull.*, XI (Apr., 1945), 6-7; by J. H. Walter, *MLR*, XL, 230.

A930 Crocker, Lester G. "Hamlet, Don Quijote, La vida es sueño: The Quest for Values." *PMLA*, LXIX (1954), 278-313.

A931 Curry, Walter Clyde. *Shakespeare's Philosophical Patterns.* Louisiana State Univ. Press, 1937. Pp. xii, 244.
Rev: *TLS*, Sept. 4, 1937, p. 637; *NYTBR*, Dec. 5, 1937, p. 34; *QR*, 269 (1937), 368; by M. Y. Hughes, *MLN*, LIII (1938), 448-450; by E. O. Sisson, *MLR*, XXXIII, 429-430; by Hardin Craig, *PQ*, XVII, 319-320; by G. R. Coffman, *SP*, XXXV, 509-511; by Mark Van Doren, *Nation* (N. Y.), 146 (1938), 728; by R. C. Bald, *RES*, XIV, 496; by L. C. Knights, *Criterion*, XVII, 574-579; by Alois Brandl, *Archiv*, 172 (1938), 249; by Eduard Eckhardt, *Eng. Studn.*, LXXII, 407-410; by R. G. Cox, *Scrutiny*, VI, 348-350; by R. M. Smith, *SAB*, XIII, 184-187; by W. Keller, *SJ*, LXXIV, 185-186; by Friedrich Brie, *ES*, XXI (1939), 82-83; by Georges Connes, *EA*, III, 104; by J. C. Ransom, *KR*, I, 75-80; by T. W. Baldwin, *JEGP*, XXXIX (1940), 402-404; by P. Wheelwright, *Philosophical Rev.*, XLIX (1940), 80-81.

A932 Cysarz, Herbert. "Zur 'Weltanschauung' Shakespeares." In Cysarz's *Welträtsel im Wort*, Vienna, 1948, pp. 58-91.

A933 Daiches, David. "Guilt and Justice in Shakespeare." *Literary Essays*, Edinburgh: Oliver and Boyd, 1956, pp. 1-25.

A934 Danby, John F. *Shakespeare's Doctrine of Nature: A Study of "King Lear."* London: Faber & Faber, 1949. Pp. 234.

Rev: *TLS*, May 6, 1949, p. 298; *DUJ*, x, 114-116; by E. M. W. Tillyard, *CamJ*, II, 760-762; by H. B. Charlton, *MGW*, April 28, 1949, p. 10; *Dublin Mag.*, XXIV, 3, 61-62; by D. S. White, *English*, VII, 294-295; by L. C. Knights, *Scrutiny*, XVI, 157-162, 325; by J. B. Fort, *LanM*, XLIV (1950), 417; by G. I. Duthie, *RES*, NS, II (1951), 78-81; *The Hindustan Review*, Oct., 1949.

A935   Daniels, R. Balfour. "Shakspere and the Puritans." *SAB*, XIII (1938), 40-53.

A936   Dean, Leonard F. "Shakespeare's Treatment of Conventional Ideas." *SR*, LII (1944), 414-423.

A937   Deutschberger, Paul. "Shakspere on Degree: A Study in Backgrounds." *SAB*, XVII (1942), 200-207.

A938   Dinsmore, Charles Allen. *The Great Poets and the Meaning of Life.* Boston: Houghton Mifflin, 1937. Pp. ix, 250.

A939   Doran, Madeleine. *Endeavors of Art: A Study of Form in Elizabethan Drama.* Madison: Univ. of Wisconsin Press, 1953. Pp. xv, 482.
        Rev: A7827.

A940   Duthie, G. I. *Shakespeare.* London: Hutchinson's University Library, 1951. Pp. 206.
        Rev: A8162.

A941   Eckhoff, Lorentz. *Shakespeare: Spokesman of the Third Estate.* Oslo Studies in English, No. 3. Tr. by R. I. Christophersen. Oslo, Norway: Akademisk Forlag; Oxford: Basil Blackwell, 1954. Pp. xiv, 201.
        English transl. of the 2nd ed. of *William Shakespeare*, which was published in Norwegian in 1948. First edition, Oslo and Copenhagen: Gyldendal, 1939. Pp. 224. Presented to Dr. Eckhoff on his 70th birthday by colleagues, students, and friends.
        Rev: by Frederik Schyberg, *Digteren, Elskeren og den Afsindige, Litterare Kroniker*, pp. 7-26, (Copenhagen: Thaning og Appel, 1947. Pp. 272); by P. Legouis, *EA*, VIII (1955), 259-260; by Kenneth Muir, *RES*, NS, VII (1956), 420-421; *ShN*, VII (1957), 14.

A942   Eckhoff, Lorentz. "Stoicism in Shakespeare . . . and Elsewhere." *Wiener Beiträge zur Englischen Philologie*, LXV (1957), 32-43. In Brunner *Festschrift*, B4400.

A943   Ellis-Fermor, Una. "Die Spätwerke grosser Dramatiker." *DVLG*, XXIV (1950), 423-439.

A944   Elton, William. "Timothy Bright and Shakespeare's Seeds of Nature." *MLN*, LXV (1950), 196-197.

A945   Emery, Léon. *La Vision Shakespearienne du Monde et de l'Homme.* Lyon: Cahiers Libres, 1957. Pp. 150.

A946   Fitch, R. E. "Shakespeare and Redemptive Love." *Religion in Life*, XX (1951), 374-383.

A947   Flatter, Richard. "Shakespeares Weg vom Recht zur Gnade." In Flatter: *Triumph der Gnade. Shakespeare Essays.* Vienna and Munich. Kurt Desch, 1956, pp. 139-157.

A948   Flint, Robert W. "The Tragedy of Hamlet." *Union Seminary Quarterly Review*, II, iii (1947), 20-25.

A949   Fluchère, H. *Shakespeare: Dramaturge Elizabéthain.* Marseille, 1948.
        Rev: A8187.

A950   Fluchère, Henri. *Shakespeare.* London: Longmans, Green, 1953. Pp. x, 272.
        A translation by Guy Hamilton of A949. Foreword by T. S. Eliot.
        Rev: A8188.

A951   Fort, Joseph B. "Quelques Problèmes Shakespeariens: L'Homme, Le Texte, La 'Sagesse Pourpre'." *LanM*, Nov., 1950, pp. 38-41.

A952   Fredén, Gustaf. "En strand där timjan blommar vild. En studie i Shakespeare-dramats bakgrund." *Orestes och försoningen*, Lund, 1955, pp. 85-108.

A953   Fredén, G. "Shakespeare och hans Världsbild (Shakespeare's World Picture)." *Studiekamraten*, No. 12 (1952), pp. 275-280.

A954   Freund, John Richard. *Dualism in Richard II: A Study in Thematic Structure.* DD, Indiana University, 1955. Pp. 249. Mic A55-1843. *DA*, XV (1955), 1397. Publication No. 12,827.

A955   Gallagher, Ligera Cécile. *Shakespeare and the Aristotelian Ethical Tradition.* DD, Stanford University, 1956. Pp. 338. Mic 56-3017. *DA*, XVI (1956), 1898. Publication No. 17,720.

A956   Gardner, Helen. *The Noble Moor.* Annual Shakespeare Lecture of the British Academy, 1955. In *Proceedings of the Brit. Acad.*, XLI (1955), 189-205.
        Rev: by W. W. Robson, *EIC*, VII (1957), 303-317; by M. R. Ridley, *RES*, NS, IX (1958), 344.

A957   Goddard, Harold C. *The Meaning of Shakespeare.* Univ. Chicago Press, 1951. Pp. xii, 691.
        Rev: A8199.

A958   Hankins, John Erskine. *The Character of Hamlet and Other Essays.* Univ. North Carolina Press, 1941. Pp. xii, 264.
        Rev: B7664.

A959   Harbage, Alfred. *As They Liked It: An Essay on Shakespeare and Morality.* New York: Macmillan, 1947. Pp. xiii, 238.
        Rev: by Rufus Putney, *PQ*, XXV (1946), 384; by R. S. Knox, *Canadian Forum*, XXVII (1947), 70-71; by E. H. Harbison, *JMH*, XIX, 159-160; by Milton Crane, *NYTBR*, Mar 16, 1947, p. 41; by John Garrett, *Spectator*, Nov. 7, 1947, pp. 600-602; "Shakespeare's Secret," *TLS*,

Nov. 22, 1947, p. 603; *TLS*, July 26, p. 383; *TAr*, XXXI, 78-79; by J. V. Moldenhawer, *Religion in Life*, XVII (1948), 135-136; by K. O. Myrick, *MLN*, LXIII, 277-280; by B. Jessup, *JAAC*, VI, 279-281; by E. Hubler, *JEGP*, XLVII, 95-96; by B. M., *Dalhousie Rev.*, XXVIII, 104; by G. B. H., *QQ*, LV, 225-226; by J. C. Maxwell, *RES*, XXIV, 250-251; by R. S. Knox, *UTQ*, XVIII, 99-100; by Peter Alexander, *MLR*, XLIII, 257-258; by E. A. Taylor, *MLQ*, X (1949), 111-112.

A960   Harbage, Alfred. *Shakespeare and the Rival Traditions.* New York: Macmillan, 1952. Pp. xviii, 393.
        Rev: A7708.

A961   Harbage, Alfred. "Shakespeare's Ideal Man." *AMS*, pp. 65-80.

A962   Harding, Davis P. "Elizabethan Betrothals and *Measure for Measure.*" *JEGP*, XLIX (1950), 139-158.

A963   Harrison, Charles T. "The Poet as Witness." *SR*, LXIII (1955), 539-550.

A964   Haydn, Hiram. *The Counter-Renaissance.* New York: Charles Scribner's Sons, 1950. Pp. xvii, 705.
        Rev: A3836.

A965   Heilman, R. B. *This Great Stage: Image and Structure in "King Lear."* Louisiana State Univ. Press, 1948.
        Rev: B8892.

A966   Henn, T. R. *The Harvest of Tragedy.* London: Methuen, 1956. Pp. xv, 304.
        Rev: A6912.

A967   Heuer, Hermann. "Der Geist und seine Ordnung bei Shakespeare." *SJ*, 84/86 (1951), 40-63.

A968   Honeyford, Bruce N. M. *Problems of Good and Evil in Jacobean Tragedy.* DD, University of Toronto, 1952.

A969   Howse, Ernest Marshall. *Spiritual Values in Shakespeare.* New York: Abington Press, 1955. Pp. 158.
        Rev: by Fred Eastman, *Religion in Life*, XXIV (1955), 632-633; by W. S. Handley Jones, *London Quar. & Holborn Rev.*, July, 234-235; *English Journal*, XLIV, 366; by Robertson Davies, *Saturday Night*, June 11; by Roy W. Battenhouse, *SQ*, VI, 354-355; by A. Parker, *Christian Century*, LXXII, 657 (reply by L. L. Strayer, LXXII, 734 and 846); by E. Winston Jones, *QJS*, XLII (1956), 93-94; by Aerol Arnold, *Personalist*, XXXVII, 310; by H. S. Wilson, *UTQ*, XXV, 341.

A970   Hubler, Edward. "Three Shakespearean Myths: Mutability, Plenitude, and Reputation." *EIE, 1948.* New York: Columbia Univ. Press, 1949, pp. 95-119.

A971   Hunter, Edwin R. *Shakespeare and Common Sense.* Boston: The Christopher Publishing House, 1954. Pp. 312.
        Rev: by Ray Irwin, *QJS*, XLI (1955), 317-318; *CE*, XVI, 392; by W. Gordon Zeeveld, *SQ*, VI, 470-471.

A972   James, D. G. *The Dream of Learning: An Essay on "The Advancement of Learning," "Hamlet," and "King Lear."* Oxford: Clarendon Press, 1951. Pp. 126.
        Rev: A3959.

A973   Jarratt, Louise Paschal. *A Study of Death in English Renaissance Tragedy.* Master's thesis, North Carolina, 1943. Abstr. publ. in *University of North Carolina Record, Research in Progress*, Grad. School Series, No. 50, 1946, pp. 156-157.

A974   Jepsen, Laura P. *Ethos in Classical and Shakespearean Tragedy.* DD, State University of Iowa, 1946. Abstr. publ. by State University of Iowa in *Doctoral Dissertations: Abstracts & References* (1942 through 1948), VI (1943), 418-425.

A975   Jepsen, Laura. *Ethical Aspects of Tragedy.* Gainesville: Univ. of Florida Press, 1953. Pp. ix, 130.
        Rev: by William T. Hastings, *SQ*, V (1954), 323-327; by Clifford Leech, *RES*, NS, V, 287-288; by Hans Galinsky, *Archiv*, 191 (1955), 231-232.

A976   Jones, D. E. *The Development of the Story of Troilus and Cressida as Reflecting the Change from Medieval to Renaissance Sensibility.* MA thesis, Wales, 1953.

A977   Kerl, Willi. *Fortuna und Natura in ihrem Verhältnis zum Menschen in Shakespeares Barockdramen.* DD, Marburg, 1949. Pp. ix, 187. Typewritten.

A978   Keunen, J. "Het shakespeareaansche pessimisme en de verklaring ervan door B. Shaw." *Dietsche Warande*, 1939, pp. 837-848.

A979   Kirschbaum, Leo. "Shakespeare's 'Good' and 'Bad'." *RES*, XXI (1945), 136-142.

A980   Klitscher, Hermann. *Dämonie und Willensfreiheit in Shakespeares Gestalten.* DD, Marburg, 1924. Pp. 147. Typewritten.

A981   Knights, Lionel Charles. "On the Background of Shakespeare's Use of Nature in *Macbeth.*" *SR*, LXIV (1956), 207-217.

A982   Knowlton, Edgar. "Nature and Shakespeare." *PMLA*, LI (1936), 719-744.

A983   Knox, R. S. "Shakespeare and the Nature of Man." *UTQ*, XIII (1944), 241-245.

A984   Koenigsberger, Hannelore. *The Untuned String: Shakespeare's Concept of Chaos.* DD, Columbia University, 1951. Pp. 222. *DA*, XII (1952), 66. Publication No. 3353.

A985   Koldewey, E. *Über die Willensfreiheit im älteren englischen Drama.* DD, Berlin, 1937. Wurzburg: Triltsch, 1937. Pp. 98.

Rev: by W. Héraucourt, *Eng. Studn.*, LXXIII (1939), 383-385; by Wolfgang Keller, *SJ*, LXXV, 156-157; by W. Héraucourt, *Lbl*, LX, 477-480.

A986   Lacy, E. W. "Justice in Shakespeare." (Abstract of thesis). *Bul. of Vanderbilt Univ.*, XXXVII (1937), 42.

A987   Langenfelt, Gösta. " 'The Noble Savage' until Shakespeare." *ES*, XXXVI (1955), 222-227.

A988   Leech, Clifford. "The 'Meaning' of *Measure for Measure*." *ShS*, III (1950), 66-73.

A989   Lindemann, R. "Shakespeares Weltbild." *Hochland*, XXXVIII (1941), 335-340.

A990   Lloyd, Roger. "The Rack of This Tough World." *QR*, 285 (1947), 530-540.

A991   Luce, Morton. *Man and Nature*. London: Bell, 1935. Pp. 283. Chap. V: "Spencer and Shakespeare."

A992   McAvoy, William Charles. *Shakespeare's Use of the Laus of Apthonius*. DD, University of Illinois, 1952. Pp. 225. Mic A53-237. *DA*, XIII (1953), 97. Publication No. 4464.

A993   Martin, L. C. "Shakespeare, Lucretius, and the Commonplaces." *RES*, XXI (1945), 174-182.

A994   Maxwell, J. C., and Clifford Leech. [Comments in] "The Critical Forum: The Presuppositions of Tragedy." *EIC*, V (1955), 175-180.

A995   Mayer, Frederick. "Invitation to Understanding." *Wisdom*, July, 1956, p. 5.

A996   Messiaen, Pierre. "La Période Pessimiste et la Conversion de Shakespeare." *La Vie Intellectuelle*, Oct., 1938, pp. 302-318.

A997   Messiaen, Pierre. "Thèmes Moraux et Sentimentaux dans Shakespeare." *Revue Universitaire*, 1936, pp. 420-427.

A998   Moldenhawer, J. V. "Shakespeare's Creed." *The Voice of Books*, 1940, pp. 26-40.

A999   Morgan, Roberta. "Some Stoic Lines in *Hamlet* and the Problem of Interpretation." *PQ*, XX (1941), 549-558.

A1000   Morozov, M. M. "Humanism in Shakespeare's Works." *SAB*, XVIII (1943), 51-61.

A1001   Muir, Kenneth, and Sean O'Loughlin. *The Voyage to Illyria*. A New Study of Shakespeare. London: Methuen, 1937. Pp. 242.
        Rev: A8307.

A1002   Muller, Herbert J. *The Spirit of Tragedy*. New York: Knopf, 1956. Pp. ix, 335.
        Rev: A6914.

A1003   Murphy, George H. "Reflections on the Tragedies of Shakespeare." *Dalhousie Review*, XXXVI (1956), 266-274.

A1004   Murry, John Middleton. *Heaven—and Earth*. London: Cape, 1938. Pp. 318.

A1004a Niederstenbruch, Alex. "Gedanken zum Begriff des Sittlichen bei Shakespeare." *ZNU*, XL (1941), 225-227.

A1005   O'Brien, Gordon Worth. *Renaissance Poetics and the Problem of Power*. Publication No. 2 of Institute of Elizabethan Studies, 1956. Pp. 127.
        Rev: A1726.

A1006   O'Donnell, Joseph Leo. *Ethical Principles of the Christian Middle Ages in Shakespeare*. MA thesis, University of Western Ontario, 1941. Pp. 206.

A1007   Ornstein, Robert. *The Ethics of Jacobean Tragedy, A Study of the Influence of Renaissance Free Thought*. DD, University of Wisconsin, 1954. Abstr. publ. in *Summaries of Doctoral Dissertations*, 1953/54, Vol. 15, Madison: Univ. of Wisconsin Press, 1955, pp. 622-624.

A1008   Pace, Caroline J. *The Anatomy of Justice in Shakespeare's Plays*. DD, University of North Carolina, 1950. Abstr. publ. in *Univ. of North Carolina Record, Research in Progress*, January-December, 1949, Grad. School Series, No. 58, pp. 111-112.

A1009   Pack, Robert. "Macbeth: The Anatomy of Loss." *YR*, Summer, 1956, pp. 533-548.

A1010   Parkes, H. B. "Nature's Diverse Laws: The Double Vision of the Elizabethans." *SR*, LVIII (1950), 402-418.

A1011   Pearce, Josephine Anna. *The Manipulations of Time in Shakespeare's English History Plays*. DD, University of Missouri, 1955. Pp. 236. Mic 55-1110. *DA*, XV (1955), 2192. Publication No. 14,618.

A1012   Pogrell, Nancy von. *Die Philosophisch-poetische Entwicklung George Chapmans. Ein Versuch zur Interpretation seines Werkes*. Hamburg: Friederichsen, de Gruyter & Co., 1939. Pp. 171. Shak. passim.

A1013   Presson, Robert K. "The Structural Use of a Traditional Theme in *Troilus and Cressida*." *PQ*, XXXI (1952), 180-188.

A1014   Prior, Moody. "The Thought of *Hamlet* and the Modern Temper." *ELH*, XV (1948), 261-285.

A1015   Prym-von Becherer, Gisela. *Das Weltbild der Shakespearezeit mit besonderer Berücksichtigung von Shakespeares "Hamlet."* DD, Marburg, 1946. Pp. xviii, 159, 8. Typewritten.

A1016   Quadri, G. *Guglielmo Shakespeare e la Maturità della Coscienza Tragica*. Florence: La Nuova Italia, 1947. Pp. 110.
        Rev: by R. N. Bower, "An Existentialist Shakespeare," *N &Q*, 198 (1953), 22-23.

A1017   Rebora, Piero. "Espressioni sulla vita in Dante e in Shakespeare." *Studi Urbinati* (Urbino), XXIX (1955), 23-35.

A1018 Reeg, Ludwig. *Shakespeare und die Weltordnung.* Stuttgart: Schröder, 1950. Pp. 151.

A1019 Reese, M. M. *Shakespeare: His World and His Work.* New York: St. Martin's Press, 1953. Pp. xiii, 589.
Rev: A871.

A1020 Renner, Ida. *Der Ordnungsgedanke bei Shakespeare mit besonderem Hinblick auf "King Lear."* DD, Münster, 1948. Pp. 114. Typewritten.

A1021 Reyher, P. *Essai sur les Idées dans l'Œuvre de Shakespeare.* Paris, 1947. Pp. xxx, 662.
Rev: by D. J. Gordon, *MLR*, XLIV (1949), 109; by S. L. Bethell, *RES*, XXV, 167-168; by R. E. Davril, *MLN*, LXIV, 122-124; by T. W. Baldwin, *JEGP*, XLVIII, 400-404; by F. S. Boas, *English*, VII, 234-236; by L. Noldus, *RBPH*, XXVII, 1186-88; by A. Koszul, *LanM*, V, 62-63; by A. G. van Kranendonk, *ES*, XXX, 136-138.

A1022 Rogers, Carmen. "Heavenly Justice in the Tragedies of Shakespeare." Matthews and Emery, eds., *Studies in Shakespeare*, pp. 116-128.

A1023 Röhrman, H. *Marlowe and Shakespeare: A Thematic Exposition of Some of their Plays.* Arnhem: van Loghum Slaterus, 1952. Pp. x, 109.
Rev: *TLS*, Feb. 27, 1953, p. 142 (see letter by the author, Mar. 27, p. 205); by C. G. Thayer, *Books Abroad*, XXVII, 433; by B. Stroman, *Critisch Bulletin*, XX, 275-278; by J. Meyer, *Gids*, 116 (1953), 138; by P. H. Breitenstein, *LT*, 1953, p. 83; by J. R. Brown, *MLR*, XLIX (1954), 112-113; by Clifford Leech, *ShS*, VII, 132; by Paul H. Kocher, *SQ*, V, 86-88; by H. W. Donner, *Studier i Modern Språkvetenskap* (Stockholm), XLVII (1954), 312-313.

A1024 Rowe, Kenneth. "Values for the War in *Hamlet, Othello, King Lear*, and *The Tempest.*" *CE*, V (1944), 207-213.

A1025 Savithri, R. Sethu. "Good and Evil in Shakespeare." *The Literary Criterion* (India), I (1952).

A1026 Schilling, Kurt. *Shakespeare. Die Idee des Menschseins in seinen Werken.* Munich, Basel: Reinhardt, 1953. Pp. 294.
Rev: by L. Bergel, *Books Abroad*, XXVII (1953), 402; by K. Brunner, *SJ*, 89 (1953), 197-200; by H. Reitz, *Welt und Wort*, VIII, 27; by M. Lüthi, *GRM*, XXXV (1954), 76-77; by S. F. Johnson, *JAAC*, XII, 527, 528; by H. T. Price, *SQ*, V, 110 and VI (1955), 188-189.

A1027 Schücking, Levin L. "Die Persönlichkeitsidee bei Shakespeare." *Politische Erziehung. Höhere Schule. Beilage zu der dts. Erzieher*, VII (1939), 88. Also in B4487.

A1028 Sears, Lloyd C. *Shakespeare and the Problem of Evil.* DD, University of Chicago, 1936.

A1029 Sears, Lloyd C. *The Problem of Evil in Shakespeare.* Chicago, 1941. Part of A1028.

A1030 Sehrt, Ernst Th. "Der Gedanke der Vergebung bei Shakespeare." *Die Sammlung*, Mar., April and May, 1949.

A1031 Siegel, Paul N. "Adversity and the Miracle of Love in *King Lear.*" *SQ*, VI (1955), 325-336.

A1032 Smirnov, A. *Shekspir. Renessans i barokko (k voprosu o prirode i razvitii shekspirovskogo gumanizma).* Vestnik Leningradskogo universiteta, 1946. No. 1, pp. 96-112. Title tr.: *Shakespeare: Renaissance and Baroque (On the question of the Nature and Development of Shakespeare's Humanism).*

A1032a Smith, Gordon Ross. *Good in Evil in Shakespearean Tragedy.* DD, The Pennsylvania State University, 1956. Pp. 446. Mic 57-568. *DA*, XVII (1957), 358. Publication No. 19,323.

A1033 Smith, Robert M. "Shakespeare's Philosophical Patterns." *SAB*, XIII (1938), 184-187.

A1034 Spalding, Kenneth Jay. *The Philosophy of Shakespeare.* New York: Philosophical Library; Oxford: George Ronald; Toronto: Copp, 1953. Pp. 191.
Rev: *TLS*, July 3, 1953, p. 428; *QR*, 291 (1953), 554-555; by H. B. Charlton, *MGW*,, Sept. 15, p. 4, and Sept. 24, pp. 10, 11; by Kay Burton, *Church Quar. Rev.*, 154 (1953), 494-496; *NstN*, Aug. 15, p. 188; by Edwin Muir, *Obs.*, June 7, p. 9; by Charles T. Harrison, *SR*, LXII (1954), 163-164; by Michel Poirier, *EA*, VII, 320; by Kenneth Muir, *MLN*, LXIX, 433-435; by W. H. Davenport, *Personalist*, XXXVII, 431-432; by H. T. Price, *SQ*, V, 111; by Melvin T. Solve, *Arizona Quarterly*, X, 167-169; *Christian Century*, LXX, 1454; by Dorothy Hewlett, *Aryan Path*, XXIV, 512-513; by Hermann Heuer, *SJ*, 90 (1954), 337-338.

A1035 Speaight, Robert. *Nature in Shakespearean Tragedy.* London: Hollis and Carter, 1955. Pp. viii, 179.
Rev: *TLS*, July 1, 1955, p. 367; by Philip Henderson, *Time and Tide*, XXXVI, 843-844; by J. Wain, *Spectator*, 195 (1955), 100; *MdF*, 315 (1955), 153; *Times of India* (Bombay), Sept. 18, p. 6; by Christopher Devlin, *Month*, NS, XIV, 372-374; by F. S. Boas, *ConR*, 188 (1955), 281-283; by John Jones, *NstN*, July 30, p. 140; by H. Dinwiddy, *Tablet*, 206 (1955), 108-109; by Hermann Heuer, *SJ*, 92 (1956), 369-371; by L. G. Salingar, *Universities Quarterly*, X, 199-204; briefly, *VQR*, XXXII, cxiv; briefly, *Lib. Jour.*, 81 (1956), 1203; *TAr*, Oct., p. 11; *ShN*, VI, 25; by Dom Raphael Appleby, *Downside Rev.*, LXXIV, 181; by T. S. Dorsch, *YWES*, XXXV (1954), 101; by John V. Curry, S. J., *Thought*, XXXII (1957), 144-145; by Pat M. Ryan, Jr., *QJS*, XLIII, 204-205; by L. Bonnerot, *EA*, X, 53-54; by G. Greever, *Personalist*, XXXVII, 212; by Lorenz Eckhoff, *SQ*, VIII, 112-115; by K. Muir, *ShS*, X, 137-138.

A1036 Speaight, Robert. "Nature and Grace in *Macbeth.*" *Essays by Divers Hands, Being the Transactions of the Royal Society of Literature*, NS, XXVII (1955), 89-109.

A1037 Speaight, Robert. "Nature and Grace in *The Tempest.*" *Dublin Review*, No. 459 (1953), pp. 28-51.

A1038 Speaight, Robert. "La Nature et la Grâce dans l'Univers Shakespearien." *Laval Théologique et Philosophique*, VI (1950), 63-127.

A1039 Speaight, Robert. *Nature et Grâce dans les Tragédies de Shakespeare.* Tr. by Henri Lemaître. Paris: Editions du Cerf, 1957. Pp. 228.
Rev: by R. Lalou, *LanM*, LI (1957), 610.

A1040 Spencer, Benjamin T. "*King Lear*: A Prophetic Tragedy." *CE*, V (1944), 302-308.

A1041 Spencer, Benjamin T. "This Elizabethan Shakespeare." *SR*, XLIX (1941), 536-552.

A1042 Spencer, Theodore. "Appearance and Reality in Shakespeare's Last Plays." *MP*, XXXIX (1942), 265-274.

A1043 Spencer, Theodore. *Death and Elizabethan Tragedy.* A Study of Convention and Opinion on the Elizabethan Drama. Harvard Univ. Press, 1936. Pp. xiii, 288.
Rev: A6823.

A1044 Spencer, Theodore. *Shakespeare and the Nature of Man.* Lowell Lectures, 1942. New York: Macmillan, 1942. Pp. xiii, 233. Second ed., 1949.
Rev: by W. A. Neilson, *SRL*, Dec. 12, 1942, p. 6; by S. C. Chew, *NYHTBR*, Jan. 10, 1943, p. viii, 3; by W. J. Grace, *Theatre*, XVIII (1943), 531-532; by E. C. Knowlton, *South Atlantic Quar.*, XLII, 304-305; by Arnold Stein, *KR*, V, 448-451; by Medford Evans, *SR*, LI, 435-439; by Tucker Brooke, *YR*, XXXII, 581-583; by William Troy, *NR*, 108 (1943), 324-325; by William Phillips, *Nation*, 156 (Jan. 23), 136-137; by E. G. Clark, *Catholic World*, 157 (1943), 435-437; by James Southall Wilson, *VQR*, XIX, 476-480; by Dudley Wynn, *New Mexico Quar.*, XIII, 104-106; by Ernest E. Cox, *MLQ*, V (1944), 494-495; by Peter Alexander, *MLR*, XXXIX, 406-408; *TLS*, Jan. 29, p. 54; by H. McC., *More Books*, XVIII, 74; by Alfred Harbage, *MLN*, LIX, 131-132; by L. C. Knights, *Scrutiny*, XII, 146-152; by J. V. Moldenhawer, *Anglican Theol. Rev.*, XXVII (1945), 79-85; by Hermann Heuer, *SJ*, 84/86 (1951), 249-250; by Michel Poirier, *EA*, VII (1954), 229-230.

A1045 Spira, Theodor. "Shakespeares Dichtung und die Welt der Geschichte." *SJ*, 91 (1955), 65-86.

A1046 Stauffer, Donald A. *Shakespeare's World of Images: The Development of His Moral Ideas.* New York: W. W. Norton, 1949. Pp. 393.
Rev: by Harry Levin, *NYTBR*, Oct. 30, 1949, p. 5; by Douglas Bush, *NR*, 121 (1949), 28-29; by G. B. Harrison, *Commonweal*, LI, 274-275; by H. Smith, *YR*, XXXIX (1950), 743-746; by B. E. Jessup, *JAAC*, VIII, 270; by S. C. Chew, *NYHTBR*, Jan. 8, 1950, p. 6; by W. I. Brewster, *SQ*, I, 177-182; by J. S. Wilson, *VQR*, XXVI, 318-320; by O. J. Campbell, *SRL*, Jan. 28, 1950, p. 16; by R. A. Law, *Southwest Rev.*, XXXV, 74-75; by Henry Popkin, *TAr*, March, pp. 4-5; by Howard Nemerov, *SR*, LIX (1951), 161-167; by Hermann Heuer, *SJ*, 87/88 (1952), 256.

A1047 Stirling, Brents. *Unity in Shakespearean Tragedy. The Interplay of Theme and Character.* New York: Columbia Univ. Press, 1956. Pp. viii, 212.
Rev: B5018.

A1048 Stoll, Elmer Edgar. " 'Multi-Consciousness' in the Theatre." *PQ*, XXIX (1950), 1-14.

A1049 Straumann, Heinrich. *Phönix und Taube: Zur Interpretation von Shakespeares Gedankenwelt.* Zurich, 1953.
Rev: C267.

A1050 Stříbrný, Zdeněk. "K Otázce Shakespearova světového nazoru." *Časopis pro Moderní Filologii* (Československá Akademie Věd), XXXVII, Nos. 2-3 (1955), 96-104.

A1051 Taylor, George Coffin. "Shakespeare's Use of the Idea of the Beast in Man." *SP*, XLII (1945), 530-543.

A1052 Taylor, George Coffin. "Two Notes on Shakespeare." *Renaissance Studies in Honor of Hardin Craig*, (Stanford Univ. Press, 1941), pp. 179-184; also *PQ*, XX (1941), 371-376.

A1053 Thiess, Frank. *Shakespeare und die Idee der Unsterblichkeit.* Dortmund: Schwalvenberg, 1947. Pp. 37. Also in Thiess's *Vulkanische Zeit. Vorträge, Reden, Aufsätze.* Neustadt/Haardt: Corona-Verl., 1949, pp. 411-441.
Rev: by H. Oppel, *Literatur d. Gegenwart*, I (1948), 41-43.

A1054 Traversi, Derek. *Shakespeare: The Last Phase.* London: Hollis & Carter, 1954. Pp. vii, 272.
Rev: B5262.

A1055 Trnka, Bohumil. "Shakespearova filosofie." *Časopis pro Moderní Filologii* (Československá Akademie Věd), XXXVII, Nos. 2-3 (1955), 73-82.

A1056 Tyler, Parker. "Phaethon: The Metaphysical Tension Between the Ego and the Universe in English Poetry." *Accent*, XVI (Winter, 1956), 29-44.

A1057 Vorwahl, H. "Shakespeares Weltanschauung: Nordisch oder Christlich?" *Protestantenblatt*, LXXII (1939 ?), 418.

A1058 Walker, Roy. "The Problem of Free Will in Shakespeare." *Aryan Path*, XXV (1954), 3-7.

A1059 Wark, R. "What Did Shakespeare Say?" *Literary Guide*, Nov., 1941, pp. 116-117.

A1060 Watkins, W. B. C. *Shakespeare and Spenser.* Princeton Univ. Press, 1950. Pp. ix, 339.
Rev: A8549.

A1061 Watkins, W. B. C. "The Two Techniques in *King Lear*." *RES*, XVIII (1942), 1-26.

A1062   Wiese, Benno von. "Gestaltungen des Bösen in Shakespeares dramatischen Werk." *SJ*, 89 (1953), 51-71.
        Rev: by H. T. Price, *SQ*, v (1954), 117-118.

A1063   Weller, Earl F. *Una Comparación de la Filosofía de Shakespeare con la de Cervantes.* MAE thesis, Mexico, 1942. Pp. 117. Typewritten.

A1064   Whitaker, Virgil K. "Philosophy and Romance in Shakespeare's 'Problem' Comedies." *The Seventeenth Century: Studies in the History of English Thought and Literature from Bacon to Pope* (Jones Festschrift), pp. 339-354.

A1065   Wilson, H. S. *On the Design of Shakespearean Tragedy.* Univ. of Toronto Press, 1957. Pp. 256.
        Rev: A6073.

A1066   Wilson, John Dover. "Shakespeare e l'Umanità." *Minerva* (Rome), LXIV (1954), 4-7.

A1067   Woesler, Richard. "Das Bild des Menschen in der englischen Sprache der älteren Zeit." *N. Mon.*, VII (1936), 321-336, 383-397.

A1068   Yates, Frances A. "Shakespeare and the Platonic Tradition." *Univ. of Edin. Jour.*, XII (1942), 2-12.

b. PSYCHOLOGY (34;12)
(1) REPRINTS OF CONTEMPORANEOUS WORKS

A1069   Bright, Timothy. *A Treatise on Melancholie.* Reproduced from the 1586 ed. printed by Thomas Vautrollier, with an Intro. by Hardin Craig. Columbia Univ. Press, 1940. Pp. 284. See also A1168.
        Rev: *TLS*, June 29, 1940, p. 319; *N &Q*, 179 (1940), 162; by R. T. F., *Personalist*, XXII (1941), 84-85; by G. B. Harrison, *RES*, XVII, 250.

(2) GENERAL COMMENTARY

A1070   Forrest, Louise C. Turner. "A Caveat for Critics against Invoking Elizabethan Psychology." *PMLA*, LXI (1946), 651-672.

A1071   Babb, Lawrence. "On the Nature of Elizabethan Psychological Literature." *AMS*, pp. 509-522. Professor Babb points out that there is no agreement about such fundamental matters as the classification of the passions, or the number of spirits in the body.

A1072   Craig, Hardin. "Shakespeare and Elizabethan Psychology: Status of the Subject." *Shakespeare-Studien, Festschrift für Heinrich Mutschmann*, pp. 48-55.

A1073   Griffin, William T. "The Uses and Abuses of Psychoanalysis in the Study of Literature." *Literature and Psychology*, I, Nos. 5 and 6 (1951).

A1074   Foakes, R. A. "The Player's Passion: Some Notes on Elizabethan Psychology and Acting." *Essays and Studies*, VII (1954), 62-77.
        A warning for critics who make excessive use of the approach to Shak. through Elizabethan psychology. Elizabethan acting was thought at the time to be lifelike.

A1075   Crockett, Campbell. "Psychoanalysis in Art Criticism." *JAAC*, XVII (1958), 34-44.

(a) WORKS ON 16th AND 17th CENTURY PSYCHOLOGIES

A1076   Campbell, Lily Bess. *Shakespeare's Tragic Heroes: Slaves of Passion.* New York: Barnes & Noble. Reprint 1952. First publ. in 1930.
        In Ebisch and Schücking Supplement, pp. 12 and 37.
        Rev: *Bulletin of Bibliography*, XX, 230.

A1077   Kreider, Paul V. *Elizabethan Comic Character Conventions as Revealed in the Comedies of George Chapman.* Univ. of Michigan Press, 1935. Pp. xi, 206.
        Much, *i.a.*, on Shak. and on Eliz. psychology.
        Rev: A6543.

A1078   Walker, Albert L. *Conventions in Shakespeare's Dramatic Poetry.* DD, State University of Iowa, 1935. Abstract in Univ. of Iowa *Programs Announcing Candidates for Higher Degrees . . .* , no pagination.

A1079   Babb, Lawrence. "The Cave of Spleen." *RES*, XII (1936), 165-176.
        Traces the descent of 18th-century spleen from the hypochondriacal melancholy of an earlier time.

A1080   Camden, Carroll, Jr. "Shakespeare on Sleep and Dreams." *Rice Institute Pamphlet*, XXIII (1936), 106-133.

A1081   Craig, Hardin. *The Enchanted Glass. The Elizabethan Mind in Literature.* Oxford Univ. Press, 1936. Pp. ix, 293. Psychological approaches, pp. 233-237 and elsewhere.
        Rev: A3857.

A1082   Miller, Joseph L. "A Discussion of Burton's *Anatomy of Melancholy*." *Annals of Medical History*, VIII (1936), 44-53.

A1083   Pomeranz, Herman. *Medicine in the Shakespearean Plays and Dickens's Doctors.* New York: Powell Publications, 1936. Pp. 410.
        Sect. VIII, pp. 238-291, "Nervous and Mental Diseases."

A1084 Anderson, Ruth L. " 'As Heart Can Think'." *SAB*, XII (1937), 246-251.

A1085 Hankiss, M. J. "Les Périodes Littéraires et la Psychologie Collective." *Bul. of the International Committee of Hist. Sciences*, IX (1937), 280-286.

A1086 Spearman, C. *Psychology Down the Ages.* 2 vols. London: Macmillan, 1937. Pp. xi, 454; vii, 355.

A1087 Stahl, William Harrison. "Moon Madness." *Annals of Medical History*, NS, IX (1937), 248-263.

A1088 Dietz, P. A. "De Psychologie van de Misdaad bij Shakespeare." *Haagsch Maandblad*, I (1938), 260-268.

A1089 Draper, John W. "The Melancholy Duke Orsino." *Bul. Inst. Hist. Medicine*, VI (1938), 1020-29.

A1090 Silvette, Herbert. "On Insanity in Seventeenth Century England." *Bulletin of the Institute of Medicine*, VI (1938), 22-33.

A1091 Walker, Albert L. "Convention in Shakespeare's Description of Emotion." *PQ*, XVII (1938), 26-66.

A1092 Anderson, Ruth L. "The Mirror Concept and Its Relation to the Drama of the Renaissance." *Northwest Missouri State Teachers College Studies*, III i (1939), 1-30.

A1093 Camden, C. C., Jr. "Memory, the Warder of the Brain." *PQ*, XVIII (1939), 52-72.

A1094 Draper, John W. "Kate the Curst." *Journal of Nervous and Mental Diseases*, 89 (1939), 757-764. Explanation in terms of humors.

A1095 Draper, J. W. "Coriolanus: A Study in Renaissance Psychology." *West Virginia University Bulletin*, III (1939), 22-36.

A1096 Ewing, S. B., Jr. "Burton, Ford, and *Andromana*." *PMLA*, LIV (1939), 1007-17.

A1097 Hoche, A. C. "Geisteskranke bei Shakespeare." *Kölnische Ztg.*, No. 407-408, 1939.

A1098 Legouis, Émile. "La Psychologie dans le Songe d'une Nuit d'Été." *EA*, III (1939), 113-117.

A1099 McCullen, Joseph Thomas, Jr. *The Use of Madness in Shakespearean Tragedy for Characterization and for Protection in Satire.* Master's thesis, North Carolina, 1939. Abstr. publ. in *Univ. of North Carolina Record, Research in Progress*, Grad. School Series, No. 36, 1939, p. 81.

A1100 Ewing, S. Blaine. *Burtonian Melancholy in the Plays of John Ford.* Princeton Univ. Press, 1940. Pp. x, 132.
Rev: by H. S., *MLN*, LVI (1941), 482-483; by G. F. Sensabaugh, *JEGP*, XL, 412-415.

A1101 Uhler, J. E. "Shakespeare's Melancholy." *Studies for William A. Read, a Miscellany*, 1940.

A1102 Babb, Lawrence. "Melancholy and the Elizabethan Man of Letters." *HLQ*, IV (1941), 247-261.

A1103 Camden, Carroll. "The Mind's Construction in the Face." *Renaissance Studies in Honor of Hardin Craig* (Stanford Univ. Press, 1941), pp. 208-220; also *PQ*, XX (1941), 400-412.

A1104 Draper, John W. "Lady Macbeth." *Psychoanalytic Rev.*, XXVIII (1941), 479-486.

A1105 Jacobi, Walter. "Falstaff, Eine Psychologisch-ästhetische Studie." *SJ*, LXXVII (1941), 2-48.

A1106 Siegel, Paul N. *Studies in Elizabethan Melancholy.* DD, Harvard University, 1941. Abstr. publ. in Harvard University *Summaries of Theses, 1941.* Cambridge: Harvard Univ. Press, 1945, pp. 341-344.

A1107 Smith, M. Ellwood. "The Lunatic, The Lover and The Poet." *SAB*, XVI (1941), 77-88.

A1108 Thomas, Sidney. "The Elizabethan Idea of Melancholy." *MLN*, LVI (1941), 261-263.
A passage in a treatise of William Perkins, the eminent Puritan divine, may reflect more exactly the average Elizabethan's conception of melancholy than does Timothy Bright's famous treatise, so often read in interpreting such characters as Hamlet and Jacques.

A1109 Zilboorg, Gregory, and George H. Henry. *A History of Medical Psychology.* New York: Norton, 1941. Pp. 606.
Rev: by Adolph Meyer, *YR*, XXXI (1942), 621-623; by M. F. Ashley Montagu, *Isis*, XXXIV, 189-190.

A1110 Deutschbein, Max. "Die Bedeutung von 'Mind' im 16. Jahrhundert. Eine Vorstudie zu Shakespeares *Hamlet*." *Anglia*, LXVI (1942), 169-222.

A1111 Duffy, Philip Howlett. *The Theory and Practice of Medicine in Elizabethan England as Illustrated by Certain Dramatic Texts.* DD, Harvard University, 1942. Abstr. publ. in *Summaries of Ph.D. Theses, 1942.* Cambridge: Harvard Univ. Press, 1946, pp. 268-271.

A1112 Floyd, John Paul. *The Convention of Melancholy in the Plays of Marston and Shakespeare.* DD, Harvard University, 1942. Abstr. publ. in *Summaries of Ph.D. Theses, 1942.* Cambridge: Harvard Univ. Press, 1946, pp. 271-272.
Asserts observation was replacing theory; that Elizabethan "melancholy" is modern "maladjustment."

A1113 Stewart, Bain T. *The Renaissance Interpretation of Dreams and their Use in Elizabethan Drama.* DD, Northwestern, 1942. Abstr. publ. in *Summaries of Doctoral Dissertations* (Northwestern Univ.), X (1942), 33-36.

A1114 Watkins, W. B. C. "The Two Techniques in *King Lear*." *RES*, XVIII (1942), 1-26.
The two techniques: psychological realism and symbolical stylization.

A1115 Babb, Lawrence. "Scientific Theories of Grief in Some Elizabethan Plays." *SP*, XL (1943), 502-519.

A1116 Babb, Lawrence. "Sorrow and Love on the Elizabethan Stage." *SAB*, XVIII (1943), 137-142.

A1117 Sarton, George. "Remarks on the Theory of Temperaments With a German 'Temperament' Text of c. 1480." *Isis*, XXXIV (1943), 205-208.

A1118 Wittlake, Käthe. *Die Bedeutung von 'Wit' bei Shakespeare.* DD, Marburg, 1943. Pp. 138.

A1119 Babb, Lawrence. "Hamlet, Melancholy, and the Devil." *MLN*, LIX (1944), 120-122.

A1120 Evans, Bergen, in consultation with George J. Mohn. *The Psychiatry of Robert Burton.* Columbia Univ. Press, 1944. Pp. ix, 129.
       Rev: by O. Temkin, *Bul. Hist. Medicine*, XVI (1944), 518-519; by Helge Lundholm, *South Atlantic Quar.*, XLIV, 115; by Wendell Johnson, *PQ*, XXIV, 282-283.

A1121 Shen, Yao. *Some Chapters on Shakespearean Criticism: Coleridge, Hazlitt and Stoll.* DD, University of Michigan, 1944. Pp. 306. Mic A47-33. *Microf. Ab.*, VII (1947), 91. Publication No. 825.
       Assails Stoll's attacks upon Coleridge and Hazlitt.

A1122 Stearns, Marshall W. "Robert Henryson and the Aristotelian Tradition of Psychology." *SP*, LIX (1944), 492-500.

A1123 Draper, John W. *The Humors and Shakespeare's Characters.* Duke Univ. Press, 1945. Pp. vii, 126. Sanguine, Phlegmatic, Choleric, Melancholy, Balanced and Mercurial, Counterfeit, and Changing.
       Rev: A6527.

A1124 Higgins, M. H. "'Senecal Man': A Study in Jacobean Psychology." *RES*, XXI (1945), 183-191.

A1125 Hunt, F. C. "Shakespeare's Delineation of the Passion of Anger." *Ba*, XXIX (1945), 135-141.

A1126 Armstrong, Edward A. *Shakespeare's Imagination.* London: Lindsay Drummond, 1946. Pp. 191. Discusses "characteristic image-clusters" in Shak.
       Rev: A5647.

A1127 Draper, John W. "Shakespeare's Attitude Toward Old Age." *Jour. Gerontology*, I (1946), 118-126.

A1128 Bauer, Robert V. *The Use of Humors in Comedy by Ben Jonson and his Contemporaries.* DD, University of Illinois, 1947.

A1129 Nakano, Yoshio. "Shakespeare's Psychological Techniques." *Rising Generation* (Japan), 93, No. 1 (1947).

A1130 Ribner, Irving. "Lear's Madness in the Nineteenth Century." *SAB*, XXII (1947), 117-129.

A1131 Camden, Carroll. "The Suffocation of the Mother." *MLN*, LXIII (1948), 390-393.
       On the medical background of the well-known passage in *Lear*.

A1132 McCullen, Joseph T., Jr. *The Functions or Uses of Madness in Elizabethan Drama Between 1590 and 1638.* DD, University of North Carolina, 1948. Abstr. publ. in *Univ. of North Carolina Record, Research in Progress, 1945-1948*, Grad. School Ser., No. 56, 1949, pp. 193-194.

A1133 Schücking, Levin L. "Shakespeares Persönlichkeitsideal." *Essays über Shakespeare, Pepys, Rossetti, Shaw und Anderes.* Wiesbaden: Dietrich, 1948, pp. 175-197.

A1134 Heuer, Hermann. "Der Geist und seine Ordnung bei Shakespeare." *SJ*, 84/86 (1950), 40-63.

A1135 Johnson, Francis R. "Elizabethan Drama and the Elizabethan Science of Psychology." *English Studies Today*, ed. by C. L. Wrenn and G. Bullough. London: Oxford Univ. Press, 1951, pp. 111-119.

A1136 Reed, Robert R., Jr. "A Factual Interpretation of 'The Changeling's' Madhouse Scenes." *N &Q*, 195 (1950), 247-248.

A1137 Bowden, W. R. *The English Dramatic Lyric, 1603-1642.* Yale Univ. Press, 1951.
       Rev: A6142.

A1138 Carrère, Félix. "Le Théâtre de Shakespeare: Reflet du Monde Platonicien." *LanM*, November, 1951, pp. 24-33.

A1139 Cruttwell, Patrick. "Physiology and Psychology in Shakespeare's Age." *JHI*, XII (1951), 75-89.
       Investigation of the ideas of Shakespeare's time based on Vicary and Boorde.

A1140 Knights, L. C. "*Troilus and Cressida* Again." *Scrutiny*, XVIII (1951), 144-157.

A1141 Koenigsberger, Hannelore. *The Untuned String: Shakespeare's Concept of Chaos.* DD, Columbia University, 1951. Pp. 222. *DA*, XII (1952), 66. Publication No. 3353.

A1142 McCullen, Joseph T., Jr. "Madness and the Isolation of Characters in Elizabethan and Early Stuart Drama." *SP*, XLVIII (1951), 206-218.

A1143 Sewell, Arthur. *Character and Society in Shakespeare.* Oxford: Clarendon Press, 1951. Pp. 149.
       Rev: A6522.

A1144 Trienens, Roger. *The Green-eyed Monster: A Study of Sexual Jealousy in the Literature of the English Renaissance.* DD, Northwestern University, 1951. Abstr. publ. in *Summaries of*

Doctoral Dissertations, 1951, Vol. 19, Chicago & Evanston: Northwestern Univ., 1952, pp. 45-49.

A1145   Bamborough, J. B. *The Little World of Man*. London: Longmans, Greene, 1952. Pp. 187.
Rev: by J. I. M. Stewart, *NstN*, Nov. 29, 1952, p. 658; by R. A. Foakes, *English*, IX (1952/53), 141-142; by J. C. Maxwell, *CamJ*, VI, 764-766; by M. Poirier, *EA*, VI (1953), 152-153.

A1146   Eickhoff, Louise F. W. "Lear and Cordelia." *TLS*, December 12, 1952, p. 819.
See letters by O. H. T. Dudley and John W. Harvey, *TLS*, Dec. 5, 1952, p. 797; by J. Lloyd, ibid., Dec. 12, 1952, p. 819.

A1147   Jansen, Bernhard. "Die Scholastische Psychologie vom 16. bis 18. Jahrhundert." *Scholastik*, XXVI (1952), 342-363.

A1148   McCullen, J. T., Jr. "The Functions of Songs Aroused by Madness in Elizabethan Drama." *A Tribute to George Coffin Taylor*, ed. by Arnold Williams. Univ. of North Carolina Press, 1952, pp. 185-196.

A1149   Melián Lafinur, Luis. "El 'humour', la fantasía, la pasión, el crimen y la virtud en Shakespeare." *Revista nacional* (Montevideo), LVI, No. 163 (1952), 128-145.

A1150   Rogers, Carmen. "English Renaissance Melancholy: A Prologue of Men and Manners." *Florida State Univ. Studies*, V (1952), 45-66.

A1151   Schoff, Francis G. *Aspects of Shakespearean Criticism, 1914-1950: A Commentary Centered on British and American Criticism of "Hamlet."* DD, University of Minnesota, 1952. Pp. 504. Mic A53-430. *DA*, XIII (1953), 230. Publication No. 4877.
Chap. V: "Elizabethan Psychology," pp. 68-98.

A1152   Oppel, Horst. "Zur Problematik des Willenskampfes bei Shakespeare." *SJ*, 89 (1953), 72-105.
Rev: by H. T. Price, *SQ*, V (1954), 118-119.

A1153   Rossky, William. *The Theory of Imagination in Elizabethan Literature: Psychology, Rhetoric and Poetic*. DD, New York University, 1953.

A1154   Hennings, Elsa. *Hamlet: Shakespeares "Faust"-Tragödie*. Bonn: H. Bouvier & Co., 1954. Pp. 296. "Literarische Kritik contra Psychiatrie," pp. 106-123.
Rev: A8574.

A1155   Kocher, Paul. "Lady Macbeth and the Doctor." *SQ*, V (1954), 341-349.

A1156   Milunas, Joseph George, S. J. *Shakespeare and the Christian View of Man*. DD, Stanford University, 1954. Pp. 378. Mic A54-749. *DA*, XIV (1954), 526-527. Publication No. 7500.

A1157   Soellner, Rolf H. *Anima and Affectus: Theories of the Emotions in Sixteenth Century Grammar Schools and Their Reflections in the Works of Shakspere*. DD, University of Illinois, 1954. Pp. 275. Mic A54-489. *DA*, XIV (1954), 351. Publication No. 6983.

A1158   Barnet, Sylvan. "Some Limitations of a Christian Approach to Shakespeare." *ELH*, XXII (1955), 81-92.

A1159   Campbell, Lily B. *Shakespeare's Tragic Heroes*. A reprint. New York: Barnes & Noble, 1955. Pp. xii, 296.
Rev: B5002.

A1160   Chandler, Simon B. "Shakespeare and Sleep." *Bulletin of the History of Medicine*, XXIX (1955), 255-260.

A1161   Stewart, Bain T. "The Misunderstood Dreams in the Plays of Shakespeare and His Contemporaries." *Essays in Honor of W. C. Curry*, pp. 197-206.

A1162   Lange-Eichbaum, Wilhelm. *Genie, Irrsinn und Ruhm*. Eine Pathographie d. Genies. Munich: Reinhardt, 1956. Pp. 628. Shak., pp. 24, 168, 330, 428, 566.

A1163   Natanson, W. "Psychologiczne Problemy Otella." *Teatr* (Warsaw), August 11, 1956, pp. 13-14.

A1164   Thompson, Marvin Orville. *Uses of Music and Reflections of Current Theories of the Psychology of Music in the Plays of Shakespeare, Jonson, and Beaumont and Fletcher*. DD, University of Minnesota, 1956. Pp. 272. Mic 56-3899. *DA*, XVI (1956), 2448. Publication No. 18,954.

A1165   Dillingham, William B. "Antonio and Black Bile." *N &Q*, NS, IV (1957), 419.

A1166   Kahn, Sholom J. " 'Enter Lear Mad'." *SQ*, VIII (1957), 311-329.

A1167   Riesenfeld, Kurt. "Timothy Bright und Shakespeare." *Sudhoffs Archiv f. Geschichte d. Medizin u. d. Naturwiss.*, XLI (1957), 244-254.

A1168   Winny, James, ed. *The Frame of Order. An Outline of Elizabethan Belief Taken from Treatises of the Late Sixteenth Century*. London: Allen & Unwin, 1957. Pp. 224.
Rev: by H. Gardner, *London Magazine*, Dec. 4, 1957, pp. 73-78; by J. I. M. Stewart, *NstN*, LIV (1957), 93; by Katharine Koller, *SQ*, IX (1958), 411-412.

A1169   Rossky, William. "Imagination in the English Renaissance: Psychology and Poetic." *Studies in the Renaissance* (Ren. Soc. Amer.), V (1958), 49-73.

A1170   Soellner, Rolf. "The Four Primary Passions: A Renaissance Theory Reflected in the Works of Shakespeare." *SP*, LV (1958), 549-567.

(b) PSYCHOANALYTIC DISCUSSIONS AND OTHER
APPLICATIONS OF MODERN KNOWLEDGE

The following items published before 1936 were not in either Ebisch and Schücking Shakespeare bibliography but did appear in the sources from which this bibliography is compiled and are therefore included here. This list by no means includes all items upon this subject published before 1936. Interested persons should consult the bibliography in Adnès, A1237, below.

A1171 Menninger, C. F. "Insanity of Hamlet." *Journal of Kansas Medical Society* (Topeka), xxxv (Sept., 1934), 334-338. (First delivered in 1890.)

A1172 Régis, E. "Le Personnage d'Hamlet et son Interprétation par Mme Sarah Bernhardt." *Revue Philomatique de Bordeaux et du Sud-Ouest*, ii (1899), 469-480. Reproduit dans *Revue de Psychologie Clinique et Thérapeutique* (Paris), iii (1899), 336-344. Analysé [La Folie d'Hamlet] dans *Le Gaulois*, Paris, 17 Decembre 1899.

A1173 Singer, S. "Über die physiologischen Grundlagen der Shakespeareschen Psychologie." *SJ*, xxxvi (1900), 65-94.

A1174 Bettencourt-Ferreira, J. "La Folie au Théâtre. Quelques Considérations sur l'Etat Morbide Représénte dans *Hamlet*." *Revue de Psychologie Clinique et Thérapeutique* (Paris), iv (1900), 108-114.

A1175 Freud, Sigmund. *The Interpretation of Dreams* (First Part). *The Standard Edition of the Complete Psychological Works*. Translated from the German under the General Editorship of James Strachey in Collaboration with Anna Freud. London: The Hogarth Press and The Institute of Psycho-Analysis, 1953. Freud's famous discussion of *Hamlet*, subsequently expanded by Ernest Jones, appears on pages 264-266. (First published in 1900.)

A1176 Halleck, Reuben P. *Education of the Central Nervous System*. New York, 1902. Fifty-five pages on Shak.

A1177 Freud, Sigmund. "Psychopathic Characters on the Stage." *Psychoanalytic Quar.*, xi (1942), 459-464. (Tr. H. A. Bunker).
A paper originally written in 1904, the MS of which was supplied by Max Graf; comments on Ajax, Philoctetes, Hamlet, and others. *Standard Edition*, vii (1953), 305-310. (Tr. James Strachey).

A1178 S., E. F. "The Insanity of Ophelia." *The Sketch*, London, April 26, 1905, pp. 46.

A1179 Freud, S. "Contributions to the Psychology of Love." *Collected Papers*, iv, Chap. XI, 192-202. A mere line (p. 201) on why Macduff knew no fear (Caesarian operation left no birth-trauma). First published 1910.

A1180 Palmer, J. F. "Macbeth: A Study in Monomania." *The Medical Magazine* (London), xix (1910), 577-584.

A1181 Rahner, Rich. *Ophelia in Shakespeares 'Hamlet'*. Eine psychologisch-psychiatrische Studie. Leipzig: Xenien-Verlag, 1910. Diognosis of Mania.

A1182 Lloyd, James Hendrie. "The So-called Oedipus-complex in *Hamlet*." *Journal of the American Medical Association*, lvi (1911), 1377-79.

A1183 Palmer, J. F. "*Hamlet*: A Study in Melancholia." *The Medical Magazine* (London), xx (1911), 396-411.

A1184 Rank, Otto. "Ein Beispiel von poetischer Verwertung des Versprechens." *Zentralblatt für Psychoanalyse*, i (1911), 109-110.
Reappears in Brill's translation of Freud's *Psychopathology of Everyday Life*, Chapter V, "Mistakes in Speech."

A1185 Palmer, J. F. "Ophelia: A Short Study in Acute Delirious Mania." *The Medical Magazine* (London), xxi (1912), 448-453.

A1186 Rank, O. "Shakespeares Vaterkomplex." *Das Inzest-Motiv in Dichtung und Sage*, Leipzig, 1912, pp. 204-233.
Deals with Richard III, Brutus, Caesar, Macbeth, Hamlet, and Coriolanus (Mutterkomplex).

A1187 von Winterstein, Alfred Freiherr. "Zur Psychoanalyse des Reisens." *Imago*, i (1912), 497.

A1188 Freud, Sigmund. "Das Motiv der Kästchenwahl." *Imago*, (Leipzig and Vienna), ii (1913), 257-266. Translated as "The Theme of the Three Caskets," *Collected Papers*, International Psycho-Analytic Library, London, Hogarth Press, 1950, iv, pp. 244-256. Also in *Standard Edition*, xii (1958), 289-301.

A1189 Juliusburger, O. "Shakespeares Hamlet ein Sexualproblem." *Die neue Generation*, ix (1913). Restated by Hanns Sachs, *Bericht über die Fortschritte der Psychoanalyse in den Jahren 1914-1919*. Leipzig: Internationaler Psychoanalytischer Verlag, 1921, p. 239.

A1190 Coriat, I. H. "Psychoanalyse der Lady Macbeth." *Zentralblatt für Psychoanalyse*, iv (1914), 384.

A1191 Eisler, Robert. "Der Fisch als Sexualsymbol." *Imago*, iii (1914), 165-196. Caliban is fishy, therefore sexual symbol and phallic demon.

A1192 Mallinckrodt, Frieda. "Zur Psychoanalyse der Lady Macbeth." *Int. Zeitschrift für Psychoanalyse*, iv (Aug., 1914), 612-613.

A1193 Oczeret, Herbert. "Das Hamlet-Problem und die Psychoanalyse." *Frankfurter Zeitung*, Frankfurt a. M., No. 65 (erstes Morgenblatt), March 6, 1914.

A1194 Sadger, I. *Über Nachtwandeln und Mondsucht*. Eine medizinisch-literarische Studie (*Macbeth*, pp. 143-169). Leipzig and Vienna: F. Deuticke, 1914. Tr. by Louise Brink as *Sleep Walking and Moon Walking.* A medico-literary study. New York and Washington: Nervous and Mental Disease Publishing Co., 1920.

A1195 Dees. "Timon von Athen, Drama von Shakespeare, nach psychopathologischen Gesichtspunkten erklärt." *Zeitschrift für die gesamte Neurologie und Psychiatrie* (Berlin and Leipzig), XXVIII (1915), 50-64.

A1196 Rank, O. "Das Schauspiel in *Hamlet.*" *Imago,* 1915, pp. 41-51.

A1197 Freud, S. "Einige Charaktertypen aus der psychoanalyt. Arbeit." *Imago,* IV (1916), 317, and *Sammlg. kl. Schr. z. Neur.,* IV (1918), Folge. 521. Tr. by E. Colburn Mayne as "Some Charactertypes Met with in Psychoanalytic Work." Freud's *Collected Papers,* IV, 323-333. Also in the *Standard Edition* of the Complete Psychological Works, tr. James Strachey and others, XIV (1957), 309-333.

A1198 Jekels, Ludwig. "Shakespeares *Macbeth.*" *Imago,* V (1918), 170. Translated as "The Riddle of Shakespeare's Macbeth." *Psychoanalytic Review,* XXX (1943), 361-385. Also in Jekels' *Selected Papers.* New York and London, 1953.

A1199 Cancelled.

A1200 MacCurdy, John T. "Concerning Hamlet and Orestes." *Journal of Abnormal Psychology,* XIII (1918), 250-260.
Draws on Gilbert Murray's *Hamlet and Orestes.* Both heroes are associated with death and madness; both are winter figures.

A1201 Sachs, Hanns. "Der 'Sturm'." *Imago,* V (1918), 203.

A1202 Vigouroux, A. "La Pathologie mentale dans les drames de Shakespeare." *Annales médico-psychologiques,* X (1918), 152-172, 225-251.

A1203 Delgado, Honorio F. "El enigma psicológico de Hamlet." *La Crónica Médica* (Lima), XXXVII (1920), 158-162.
Repeats the Freud-Jones view.

A1204 Coriat, Isidore H. "Anal-Erotic Character Traits in Shylock." *International Journal of Psycho-Analysis,* II (1921), 354-360.

A1205 Sachs, Hanns. "Aesthetics and Psychology of the Artist." *International Journal of Psycho-Analysis,* II (1921), 94-100.

A1206 Towne, Jackson Edmund. "A Psychoanalytic Study of Shakespeare's *Coriolanus.*" *Psychoanalytic Review,* VIII (1921), 84-91.

A1207 Clutton-Brock, Arthur. *Shakespeare's Hamlet.* London: Methuen, 1922.
Rev: by Ernest Jones, *International Journal of Psycho-Analysis,* III (1922), 495-497.

A1208 Jones, Ernest. "The Madonna's Conception Through the Ear." *Selected Essays in Applied Psycho-Analysis.* International Psycho-Analytical Library, No. 5. London: International Psycho-Analytical Press, 1923, pp. 261-359.
Dream, II.i.128-132.

A1209 Sachs, Hanns. "*The Tempest.*" *International Journal of Psycho-Analysis,* IV (1923), 43-88.

A1210 Allen, L. H. "The Hypnosis Scene in *The Tempest.*" *Australasian Journal of Psychology and Philosophy,* IV (1926), 110-118.

A1211 Jekels, Ludwig. "On the Psychology of Comedy." *Imago,* XII (1926); Jekels' *Selected Papers,* New York: International Universities Press, 1952, pp. 97-104; *The Tulane Drama Review,* II (1958), 55-61.

A1212 Taylor, M. P. "A Father Pleads for the Death of His Son." *International Journal of Psycho-Analysis,* VIII (1927), 53-55. In Richard II.

A1213 Price, George E. "Shakespeare as a Neuropsychiatrist." *Annals of Medical History* (New York), X (1928), 159-164.

A1214 Symons, Norman J. "The Graveyard Scene in *Hamlet.*" *International Journal of Psycho-Analysis,* IX (1928), 96-119.

A1215 Whitmire, C. L. "Psychoses of Shakespearean Characters." *Illinois Medical Journal,* LIII (1928), 64-72.

A1216 Ewer, Bernard C. *Social Psychology.* New York: The Macmillan Co., 1929.
Julius Caesar, pp. 255-256.

A1217 Sharpe, Ella Freeman. "The Impatience of Hamlet." *International Journal of Psycho-Analysis,* X (1929), 270-279. Published as "Hamlets Ungeduld." *Internationale Zeitschrift für Individualpsychologie,* VII (1929), 329-339. Also in her *Collected Papers,* London: Hogarth Press, 1950, pp. 203-213.

A1218 Libby, W. "Shakespeare as a Psychologist." *Archeion* (Rome), XII (1930), 282-295.

A1219 Mairet, P. "Hamlet der Neurotiker." *Internationale Zeitschrift für Individualpsychologie,* IX (1931), 424-437.

A1220 Rinaker, Clarissa. "Some Unconscious Factors in the Sonnet as a Poetic Form." *International Journal of Psycho-Analysis,* XII (1931), 167-187.

A1221 Rank, Otto. *Art and Artist.* Tr. by Charles F. Atkinson, New York: Knopf, 1932. Pp. xxvii, 431, xii.
Shak. passim.

A1222 Alexander, Franz. "A Note on Falstaff." *Psychoanalytic Quar.*, II (1933), 592-606.

A1223 Jekels, Ludwig. "The Problem of the Duplicated Expression of Psychic Themes." *International Journal of Psycho-Analysis*, XIV (1933), 300-309. Also in his *Selected Papers*, New York: International Universities Press, 1952, pp. 131-141.

A1224 Pauncz, Arpad. "Der Learkomplex, die Kehrseite des Oedipuskomplexes." *Zeitschrift für die gesamte Neurologie und Psychiatrie*, 143 (1933), 294-332.

A1225 Bodkin, Maud. *Archetypal Patterns in Poetry.* Oxford Univ. Press, 1934. Pp. xiv, 340. Shak., pp. 217-224, 280-285, 332-334.
       Rev: A8096.

A1226 Bransom, James S. H. *The Tragedy of King Lear.* Oxford: B. Blackwell, 1934.

A1227 Ewing, Fayette C. *Hamlet: An Analytic and Psychologic Study.* Boston: Stratford Co., 1934. Pp. 32.

A1228 Hoche, Alfred. *Jahresringe. Innenansicht eines Menschenlebens.* Munich: J. F. Lehmann, 1934. Pp. 298.
       Rev: by H. Tjost, *SJ*, LXXI (1935), 112-113.

A1229 Ross, T. A. "A Note on *The Merchant of Venice.*" *British Journal of Medical Psychology*, XIV (1934), 303-311.

A1230 Sachs, Wulf. *Psychoanalysis: Its Meaning and Practical Applications.* London: Cassell, 1934. Essay based on Jones's *Hamlet*, pp. 197-212.

A1231 Edgar, Irving I. "Shakespeare's Medical Knowledge, with Particular Reference to his Delineation of Madness." *Annals of Medical History*, VI (1935), 150-168.

A1232 Edgar, Irving I. "Shakespeare's Psychopathological Knowledge: A Study in Criticism and Interpretation." *Jour. of Abnormal and Social Psychology*, XXX (1935), 70-83.

A1233 Granville-Barker, Harley. *Study of Drama.* Cambridge Univ. Press, 1934. Section (F), "Freudianism in Literature," pp. 53-56.
       Calls it all "dirty nonsense." "I do not use the word 'dirty' abusively, but to connote the more material side of our nature, which was formed, as we know, out of the dust of the earth."
       Rev: by L. Cazamian, *RAA*, XII (1934/35), 352-353; by K. Arns, *Eng. Studn.*, LXXI (1936/37), 288.

A1234 Adnès, André. *Shakespeare et la Pathologie Mentale.* Paris: Librairie Maloine, 1935. Pp. 247.
       Rev: by W. Keller, *SJ*, LXXI (1935), 113-114.

A1235 Bacon, L. "Analytical Psychology and Poetry." *Die Kulturellebedeutung d. Komplexen Psychologie* (Berlin), 1935, pp. 365-369.

A1236 Adler, Charles A. "Richard III—His Significance as a Study in Criminal Life-Style." *International Journal of Individual Psychology*, II (1936), 55-60.

A1237 Adnès, André. *Shakespeare et la Folie.* Étude Médico-Psychologique. DD, Paris, 1935. Paris: Librairie Maloine, 1936. Pp. 315.
       Rev: by Floris Delattre, *EA*, I (1937), 138-139.

A1238 Babb, Lawrence. "Abnormal Psychology in John Ford's *Perkin Warbeck.*" *MLN*, LI (1936), 234-237.

A1239 Clark, Cumberland. *Shakespeare and Psychology.* London: Williams & Norgate, 1936. Pp. 192.

A1240 March, Richard. "Psychology and Criticism." *Scrutiny*, V (1936), 32-43; cf. D. W. Harding, ibid., V, 44-47.

A1241 Lukas, G. "The Intellectual Physiognomy of Literary Characters." Tr. by L. E. Mins. *International Literature*, 1936, pp. 55-83.

A1242 Plewa, Franz. "Shakespeare und die Macht." *Internationale Zeitschrift für Individualpsychologie*, XIV (1936), 26-36.

A1243 Vessie, P. R. "Psychiatry Catches Up with Shakespeare." *Medical Record*, 144 (1936), 141-145.

A1244 Young, H. McClure. *The Sonnets of Shakespeare: A Psycho-Sexual Analysis.* Menasha, Wisconsin, 1936.
       Rev: C51.

A1245 Brock, J. H. E. *Iago and Some Shakespearean Villains.* Cambridge: W. Heffer and Sons, 1937. Pp. viii, 48.
       Rev: by Samuel A. Tannenbaum, *SAB*, XII (1937), 260.

A1246 Cazamian, Louis. *Essais en Deux Langues.* Paris: Didier, 1938. Pp. xv, 318.
       Contains essay entitled "La Psychanalyse et la Critique Littéraire."

A1247 Hinrichsen, O. "Is the Problem of Hamlet's Insanity Solved?" *Psychiatr.-Neurol.-Wochenschrift*, XXXIX (1937), 36-40.

A1248 Pastor, José Francisco. "Zur Problematik der Anwendung der psychoanalystischen Methode auf literarhistorischen Gebiet." *Neophil*, XXII (1937), 205-209.

A1249 Sachs, Wulf. *Black Hamlet.* London: Bles, 1937; Boston: Little, Brown, 1947. Tr. by H. Claireau, "Un Hamlet Noir." *Revue de Paris*, Feb. 15, 1939, pp. 39-69; Mar. 1, pp. 51-82; Mar. 15, pp. 336-373; Apr. 1, pp. 619-651.
       Hamlet, pp. 170-174, Boston edition. Cited in *ShS*, IX (1956), 13.

A1250 Tannenbaum, Samuel A. "Freudism and Shakespeare." *SAB*, XII (1937), 260.

A1251   Vessie, P. R. "Interpretation of Shakespeare's Sex Play." *Medical Record*, 146 (July 7, 1937), 14-16.

A1252   Iwakura, Tomahide. "Psychosexuale Analyse von Shakespeares 'Sonetten'." *Tokyo Zeitschrift für Psychoanalyse*, VI (May, 1938).

A1253   Lundholm, H. "Antony's Speech and the Psychology of Persuasion." *Character and Personality*, VI (1938), 293-305.

A1254   Menon, C. Narayana. *Shakespeare Criticism: An Essay in Synthesis*. Oxford Univ. Press, 1938. Pp. 276.
        Attack on psychoanalysis, pp. 37-41.
        Recurrently incredible; e.g., "Following the advice of Ezhuthachan, Melpattur Bhattathiri cured himself of leprosy by composing a poem on the life of Krishna," p. 41.

A1255   Oktski, Kenji. "Analytische Würdigung von Shakespeares Hamlet." *Tokyo Zeitschrift für Psychoanalyse*, 1938.

A1256   Wile, Ira S. "Love at First Sight as Manifest in *The Tempest*." *American Journal of Orthopsychiatry*, VIII (1938), 341-356.

A1257   Adler, Alfred. *Social Interest: A Challenge to Mankind*. Tr. by Linton and Vaughan. New York: Putnam, 1939. Hamlet note, pp. 106-107.

A1258   Goll, J. A. "Criminal Types in Shakespeare." *Journal of Criminal Law and Criminology* (Chicago), XXIX (1939), 492-516, 645-667.

A1259   Goll, A. (tr. J. Moritzen). "Iago, the Criminal Type." *Journal of Criminal Law and Criminology*, XXX (1939), 35-51.

A1260   Goll, A. (tr. J. Moritzen). "Richard III as the Criminal Type." *Journal of Criminal Law and Criminology*, XXX (1939), 22-35.

A1261   Goll, A. (tr. J. Moritzen). "Lady Macbeth as a Criminal Type." *Case and Comment*, XLV (July, 1939), 5-11.

A1262   Goll, A. "*Coriolan*, Shakespeare's Tragedy." *Gads Danske Magasin* (Copenhagen), XXVIII (1939), 333-368.

A1263   Skinner, B. F. "The Alliteration in Shakespeare's Sonnets: A Study in Literary Behavior." *Psychological Record*, III (1939), 186-192.
        Answered by E. E. Stoll, *MLN*, LV (1939), 388-390.

A1264   Turel, A. "*King Lear*." *Bachofen-Freud: Zur Emanzipation d. Mannes vom Reich d. Mütter*. Bern: H. Huber, 1939, pp. 61-74.

A1265   Wollenberg, Robert. *Shakespeare, Persönliches aus Welt und Werk*. Eine psychologische Studie. Berlin, 1939.
        Rev: A865.

A1266   Lee, Harry B. "A Theory Concerning Free Creation in the Inventive Arts." *Psychiatry*, III (1940), 292.

A1267   Phillips, Daniel Edward. *The Human Element in Literature*. New York: Fortuny, 1940. Pp. 230.

A1268   Reik, Theodore. "The Way of All Flesh." *From Thirty Years with Freud*. Tr. Richard Winston, New York: Farrar and Rinehart, Inc., 1940, pp. 197-212.

A1269   Sterba, Richard. "The Problem of Art in Freud's Writings." *Psychoanalytic Quarterly*, IX (1940), 256-268.

A1269a Trilling, Lionel. "II. Literary and Aesthetic." [Part of a symposium entitled "The Legacy of Sigmund Freud: An Appraisal."] *KR*, II (1940), 152-173. See also A1301 and A1334.

A1269b Burke, Kenneth. "Freud—and the Analysis of Poetry." *The Philosophy of Literary Form*. Louisiana State Univ. Press, 1941; New York: Vintage Press, 1957.

A1270   Gutteling, J. F. C. "Modern Hamlet-Criticism." *Neophil*, XXV (1941), 276-285.
        Reviews Jones (pp. 278-279) and finds him plausible. Examines Stoll and finds him very wanting. Notices C. M. Lewis' *Genesis of Hamlet* (1907), A. J. A. Waldock's *Hamlet: A Study in Critical Method* (which he calls fine), Dover Wilson, and J. Draper.

A1271   Hendrick, Ives. *Facts and Theories of Psychoanalysis*. New York: Knopf, 1941.
        Repeats Freud-Jones view.

A1272   Wertham, Frederic. *Dark Legend*. New York: Duell, Sloan, and Pearce, 1941.
        A case history of a boy comparable to the Jones interpretation of Hamlet, but differing in that Wertham's emphasis is on Hamlet's hostility to his mother.
        Rev: by G. W. Stonier, "The Dark Passage," *NstN*, XXXIV (1947), 454 (favorable); by Clifford Leech, *ShS*, IX (1956), 13 (favorable).

A1273   Wertham, Frederic. "The Matricidal Impulse: Critique of Freud's Interpretation of Hamlet." *Journal of Criminal Psychopathology*, II (1941), 455-464.

A1274   Campbell, Oscar J. "What's the Matter with Hamlet?" *YR*, XXXII (1942), 309-322.
        Critique of Freud-Jones view. Suggests Hamlet is the victim of cycles like those of a manic depressive which always give him the wrong emotion at the wrong time.

A1275   Davie, T. M. "Hamlet's 'Madness'." *Journal of Mental Science*, 88 (1942), 449-450.

A1276   Lewis, C. S. "Psycho-Analysis and Literary Criticism." *Essays and Studies by Members of the English Association*, XXVII (1941). Oxford: Clarendon Press, 1942, pp. 7-21.

A1277   Lewis, C. S. *Hamlet: The Prince or the Poem.* Annual Shakespeare Lecture of the British Academy. London, 1942. Pp. 18.
Comments on *Merch & Much.* Against concern with motives and character of Hamlet.

A1278   Sachs, Hanns. "The Unconscious in Shakespeare's *Tempest*, Analytical Considerations." *The Creative Unconscious*, Cambridge (Mass.): Sci-Art, 1942, pp. 289-323. 2nd edition, 1951.

A1279   Sachs, Hanns. "What Would Have Happened if . . . ?" *The Creative Unconscious*, Cambridge (Mass.): Sci-Art, 1942, pp. 339-340. 2nd edition, 1951.

A1280   Sachs, Hanns. "The Measure in *Measure for Measure.*" *The Creative Unconscious*, Cambridge (Mass.): Sci-Art, 1942, pp. 63-99. 2nd edition, 1951.

A1281   Stern, E. S., and W. H. Whiles. "Three Ganser States and *Hamlet.*" *Journal of Mental Science*, 88 (1942), 134-141.
Answered by T. M. Davie, "Hamlet's Madness," ibid., 449-450.

A1282   Foulds, Elizabeth. "Enter Ophelia, Distracted." *Life and Letters Today*, XXXVI (1943), 36-41.

A1283   Stocker, A. "La Prière du Grand Will—Etude Psychologique de Quelques Sonnets de Shakespeare." *Des Hommes Qui Racontent leur Ame*, St. Maurice, Switzerland: Editions St. Augustin, 1943, pp. 203-273.

A1284   Bunker, H. Alden. "Mother-Murder in Myth and Legend." *Psychoanalytic Quarterly*, XIII (1944), 198-207.
Considers Hamlet more like Orestes than Oedipus.

A1285   Kris, Ernst. "Approaches to Art." *Psychoanalysis Today*, ed. by Sandor Lorand. New York: International Universities Press, 1944, pp. 354-370.

A1286   Reik, Theodore. *A Psychologist Looks at Love.* New York: Farrar and Rinehart, 1944.

A1287   Wittels, Fritz. "Psychoanalysis and Literature." *Psychoanalysis Today*, ed. by Sandor Lorand. New York: International Universities Press, 1944, pp. 371-380. Supports Jones on *Hamlet.*

A1288   Abenheimer, K. M. "On Narcissism—Including an Analysis of Shakespeare's *King Lear.*" *British Journal of Medical Psychology*, XX (1945), 322-329.

A1289   Hoffman, Frederick J. "Psychology and Literature." *Freudianism and the Literary Mind.* 2nd edition. Baton Rouge: Louisiana State Univ. Press, 1945 and 1957. New York: Grove Press, 1959.

A1290   Abenheimer, K. M. "Shakespeare's *Tempest*, A Psychological Analysis." *Psychoanalytic Review*, XXXIII (1946), 399-415.

A1291   Armstrong, Edward A. *Shakespeare's Imagination.* London: Lindsay Drummond, 1946. Pp. 191.
Discusses "characteristic image-clusters" in Shak.
Rev: A5647.

A1292   Brunot, Henriette. "Hamlet de Shakespeare, traduction d'André Gide." *Psyché*, I (1946), 229-232.

A1293   Lindbåck, Erland. "Hamlet i Psykoanalytisk Belysning." *Studier tillägnade Anton Blanck den 29. Dec. 1946*, pp. 61-79.

A1294   Sharpe, Ella Freeman. "From *King Lear* to *The Tempest.*" *International Journal of Psycho-Analysis*, XXVII (1946), 19-30. Reprinted in her *Collected Papers*, pp. 214-241.

A1295   Sypher, Wylie. "Hamlet: The Existential Madness." *Nation*, June 21, 1946.

A1296   Tissi, Silvio. *Al Microscopio Psicanalitico. Pirandello, Ibsen, Shakespeare, Tolstoi, Shaw, Bourget, Gide.* 4th ed., Milan: Hoepli, 1946. Pp. xxx, 540.

A1297   Bergler, E. "Psychoanalysis of Writers and of Literary Productivity." *Psychoanalysis and the Social Sciences*, I (1947), 247-296.

A1298   Shakespeare, William. *Hamlet: With a Psycho-Analytic Study by Ernest Jones, M. D.* Drawings by F. Roberts Johnson. London: Vision Press, 1947. Pp. 180, pl. 8.
Rev: by H. B. Charlton, *MGW*, March 4, 1948, p. 11; by A. P. Rossiter, *CamJ*, I, 638-639; by Desmond MacCarthy, *Sunday Times*, Feb. 15, 1948, p. 3; brief mention, *TLS*, Jan. 31, 1948, p. 71; by F. W. Dupee, *Partisan Review*, XV, 1136-39; *TAr*, XXXII, 102.

A1299   Ribner, J. "Lear's Madness in the Nineteenth Century." *SAB*, XXII (1947), 117-129.

A1300   Röling, B. V. A. *De Criminologische Betekenis van Shakespeares Macbeth.* Nijmegen: Dekker & Van de Vegt, 1947. Pp. xvi, 143.

A1301   Trilling, Lionel. "Freud and Literature." *Horizon*, XVI (1947), 182-200.
Merits and limitations of Freudian approach to literature. Also discusses A1188 and A1222 above, and earlier version of A1314 below. See also A1269a and A1334.

A1302   Dominique, Claude. "A Review of the Olivier *Hamlet* Film." *Psyché—Revue Internationale des Sciences de l'Homme et de Psychanalyse* (published in Paris under editorship of Mme Maryse Choisy-Clouzet as the *Bulletin de la Ligue d'Hygiène Mentale*), III, Nos. 23 and 24 (Sept.-Oct., 1948), 1179-82.

A1303   Dupee, F. W. "Adjusting Hamlet." *Partisan Review*, XV (1948), 1136-39.
Review of Ernest Jones's edition of *Hamlet.*
Very unsympathetic both to Jones and to historical scholarship, but in itself rather trivial.

A1304 Frye, Northrop. "The Argument of Comedy." *EIE, 1948*. New York: Columbia University Press, pp. 58-73.
Discusses Shak.'s comedies in terms of myth.

A1305 Hyman, Stanley E. "The Psychoanalytic Criticism of Literature." *Western Review*, XII (1948), 106-115.

A1306 Jones, Ernest. "The Death of Hamlet's Father." *International Journal of Psycho-Analysis*, XXIX (1948), Part III (published Aug., 1949), 174-176. Reprinted by William Phillips in *Art & Psychoanalysis*. New York: Criterion Books, 1957, pp. 146-150 (A1405 below).

A1307 K., H. "E. Jones' Hamlet: With a Psychoanalytical Study." *Punch*, 214 (Feb. 11, 1948), 128-129.

A1308 Kris, E. "Prince Hal's Conflict." *Psychoanalytic Quarterly*, XVII (1948), 487-505.
Asserts that Hal felt life-long guilt over his father's treatment of Richard II, and withdrew from the court because of it.

A1309 Lindner, Robert M. "The Equivalents of Matricide." *Psychoanalytic Quarterly*, XVII, No. 4 (1948), 453-470.
Support for Wertham's *Dark Legend*, A1272.

A1310 Lindsay, Jack. "Shakespeare and Tom Thumb." *Life and Letters*, LVIII (1948), 119-127.
Discusses the "psychic process" revealed by Shakespeare's "invention" of the small-sized Fairy.

A1311 White, David M. "Shakespeare and Psychological Warfare." *Public Opinion Quarterly* (Princeton), XII (1948), 68-72.

A1312 Ashworth, John. "Olivier, Freud, and Hamlet." *Atlantic Monthly*, May, 1949, pp. 30-33.
Uses discussion of Olivier film as occasion for attack on Freudian interpretation of *Hamlet*. See A1379.

A1313 Glicksberg, Charles I. "Literature and Freudianism." *Prairie Schooner*, XXIII (1949), 359-372.

A1314 Jones, Ernest. *Hamlet and Oedipus*. London: Victor Gollancz; New York: Norton, 1949. Pp. 166. Paperback ed., Doubleday Anchor, 1954.
Revised version of the psychoanalytical study first published in 1910.
Rev: *TLS*, Sept. 9, 1949, p. 586; by John Whale, *Spectator*, Sept. 9, 1949, p. 336; by Marshall W. Stearns, "Hamlet and Freud," *CE*, X, 265-272; by Robert Withington, "Why Put Freud into Hamlet?", ibid., X, 475-476; by E. M. Schrero, "A Misinterpretation of Freud," ibid., X, 476; by Patrick Mullahy, *NYTBR*, Aug. 6, 1950, p. 23; by O. J. Campbell, *SQ*, II (1951), 108-109; by Harry Slochower, *Complex*, III (Winter, 1951); by J. G. Weightman, "Edinburgh, Elsinore, and Chelsea," *TC*, 154 (1953), 302-310.

A1315 Moloney, James Clark, and Laurence Rochelein. "A New Interpretation of Hamlet." *International Journal of Psycho-Analysis*, XXX (1949), 92-107.

A1316 Reik, Theodor. *Fragment of a Great Confession*. New York: Farrar, Straus, & Co., 1949. *Hamlet*, pp. 269-270; *Henry IV*, p. 336.

A1317 Sharpe, Ella M. "An Unfinished Paper on *Hamlet*." *International Journal of Psycho-Analysis*, XXIX (1948), Part II (published May, 1949), 98-109.

A1318 Cancelled.

A1319 Stevenson, G. H. "Social Psychiatry and *Hamlet*." *Trans. of Royal Society of Canada* (Ottawa), XLIII, Series III (June, 1949), Section 2, pp. 143-151.

A1320 Stewart, J. I. M. *Character and Motive in Shakespeare*. London: Longmans, Green & Co., 1949. Pp. vii, 147.
A critique of discussions by Bridges, Schücking, and Stoll, of character and motive in Shak. See also A1408 below.
Rev: A6518.

A1321 Stewart, J. I. M. "Shakespeare and his World: Shakespeare's Characters." *Listener*, XLII (Aug. 25, 1949), 312-316.
Review of critical works: Dr. Johnson, Bradley, Bridges, Schücking, Stoll, T. S. Eliot, Granville-Barker, Ernest Jones (whose book he calls "deeply persuasive").

A1322 Webster, Peter Dow. "A Critical Fantasy or Fugue." *American Imago*, VI (1949), 297-309. On "Venus and Adonis."

A1323 Wormhoudt, Arthur. *The Demon Lover*. New York: Exposition Press, 1949.
Denies that Oedipus conflict can fully account either for *Hamlet* or for Shak.'s character, pp. 7-8.

A1324 Baker, Sidney J. "Shakespeare and Sex." *International Journal of Sexology*, IV (1950), 35-39.
The devices of the literary analysis of Shak.'s imagery is applied to the terms used by Shak. in dealing with sexual contacts. The author concludes that Shak. was free "from sexual inhibitions, without any asocial or psychopathic tendencies."

A1325 Bergler, Edmund. *The Writer and Psychoanalysis*. New York: Doubleday, 1950. Pp. xvii, 265.
Rev: by Frank G. Slaughter, *NYTBR*, Feb. 26, 1950, p. 20; by H. G. McCurdy, *Journal of Aesthetics*, IX, 65; by R. M. Wendlinger, *HR*, III, 303,312; by Patrick Mullahy, *NR*, June 19, 1950, pp. 19-20; by William S. Milburn, *Arizona Quarterly*, VI, 188-189; by Gorham Munson, *SRL*, Aug. 12, pp. 16-17; by Robert Gorham Davis, *Partisan Review*, XVII, 872-876.

A1326 Hoffman, Frederick J. "Psychoanalysis and Literary Criticism." *American Quarterly*, II (1950), 144-154.

A1327 Huhner, Max. *Shakespeare's Hamlet.* New York: Farrar, Straus, 1950. Pp. xi, 163. Pp.
       135-142 an extended quotation from Jones's 1910 paper.
       Rev: B7445.

A1328 Jankélévitch, S. "Le Délire Onirique dans les Drames de Shakespeare." *Psyché* (Paris), V,
       No. 42 (1950). 305-324.

A1329 Rank, Otto. *Psychology and the Soul.* Tr. by William D. Turner. Oxford Univ. Press; Univ.
       of Pennsylvania Press, 1950. Pp. viii, 195.

A1330 Schneider, Daniel E. *The Psychoanalyst and the Artist.* New York: Farrar, Straus; Toronto:
       Clarke, Irwin, 1950. Pp. xiv, 306.
       Rev: by Robert Gorham Davis, *Partisan Review,* XVII (1950), 872-876.

A1331 Schwerer, Margarethe. *Shakespeares tragische Helden im Lichte der Kretschmerschen Lehre.* DD,
       Vienna, 1950. Pp. 119. Typewritten.

A1332 Sharpe, Ella Freeman. *Collected Papers on Psycho-Analysis.* Ed. by Marjorie Brierley, pref. by
       Ernest Jones. International Psycho-Analytic Library No. 36. London: Hogarth Press, 1950.
       Contains: "From *King Lear* to *The Tempest*," pp. 214-241.
                 "The Impatience of Hamlet," pp. 203-213.
                 "An Unfinished Paper on Hamlet," pp. 242-265.
       Rev: by G. Gorer, *NstN,* XL (1950), 518-520.

A1333 Slochower, Harry. "*Hamlet*: Myth of Renaissance Sensibility." *American Imago,* VII (1950),
       197-238.

A1334 Trilling, Lionel. "Freud and Literature." *The Liberal Imagination.* New York: The Viking
       Press, 1950, pp. 34-57. Reprint of A1301. See also A1269a.
       Rev: by Philip Toynbee, *NYTBR,* Apr. 9, 1950, p. 5; by George F. Whicher, *NYHTBR,*
       Apr. 9, p. 5; by R. P. Blackmur, *KR,* XII, 663-673; by Ben Ray Redman, *SRL,* Apr. 15,
       pp. 44-45; by Sidney E. Lind, *NR,* July 3, p. 18; by R. H. Rovere, *Harper's Magazine,* May,
       p. 118; by R. W. B. Lewis, *Hudson Review,* III, 313-317; by W. P. Clark, *Western Humanities
       Review,* IV, 353-354; by Thomas W. Copeland, *YR,* XL, 167-169; by Douglas Bush, *VQR,*
       XXVI, 472-476; *Canadian Forum,* XXX, 160-161; by Harold Nicolson, *Obs.,* Mar. 25, 1951, p. 7;
       by Raymond Mortimer, *Sun. Times,* Apr. 1, p. 3; by Herbert Read, *Listener,* XLV, 671; *TLS,*
       Apr. 20, 1951, p. 240; by Clifton Fadiman, *New Yorker,* Apr. 22, pp. 115-118; by J. Vallette,
       EA, V (1952), 82-83.

A1335 Wangh, Martin. "Othello: The Tragedy of Iago." *Psychoanalytic Quarterly,* XIX (1950),
       202-212.

A1336 Wormhoudt, Arthur. "The Unconscious Bird Symbol in Literature." *American Imago,* VII
       (1950), 35-39.

A1337 Bodkin, Maud. *Studies of Type-Images in Poetry, Religion, and Philosophy.* New York: Oxford
       Univ. Press, 1951.
       Lear as child, p. 138. Also as archetype of man in his godlike kingly role.

A1338 Emde Boas, C. van. *Shakespeares Sonneten en Hun Verband met de Travesti-Double Spelen.* Am-
       sterdam: Wereldbibliotheek, 1951. Pp. 528.
       Rev: A870. See also A869.

A1339 Flatter, Richard. "Sigmund Freud on Shakespeare." *SQ,* II (1951), 368-369.

A1340 Kanzer, Mark. "The Central Theme in Shakespeare's Works." *Psychoanalytic Review,* XXXVIII
       (1951), 1-16.

A1341 McCullen, Joseph T., Jr. "Madness and Isolation of Character in Elizabethan and Early Stuart
       Drama." *SP,* XLVIII (1951), 206-218.

A1342 Pauncz, Arpad. "The Concept of Adult Libido and the Lear Complex." *American Journal of
       Psychotherapy,* V (1951).

A1343 Rashbrook, R. F. "Keats, *Oberon* and Freud." *N &Q,* 196 (1951), 34-37.

A1344 Reik, Theodor. "Shakespeare Visits a Psychoanalyst." *Complex,* VI (1951), 34-39.
       Hamlet, III.ii.135.

A1345 Reik, T. " 'Jessica, My Child'." *American Imago,* VIII (1951), 3-27. Reprinted in *The
       Secret Self,* A1356.

A1346 Feldman, Abraham B. "Othello's Obsessions." *American Imago,* IX (1952), 147-164.

A1347 Feldman, Harold. "Unconscious Envy in Brutus." *American Imago,* IX (1952), 307-355.

A1348 Hartwig, Theodor. *Hamlets Hemmungen.* Psycholog. Studie. Vienna: Cerny, 1952. Pp. 104.

A1349 Hodgart, Matthew. "The Progress of Criticism-III. Psychology and Literary Criticism."
       Listener, Sept. 11, 1952, pp. 420-421; Alan Over, ibid., Sept. 25, p. 508.

A1350 Hubler, Edward. *The Sense of Shakespeare's Sonnets.* Princeton Univ. Press, 1952. Pp. x, 170.
       Chapter II: "The Unromantic Lady," discusses Freudian criticism of Shak.
       Rev: C85.

A1351 Katz, Joseph. "Faith, Reason and Art." *American Scholar,* XXI (1952), 151-160. Comments
       by A. J. Levin, ibid., 363.
       Comments, pp. 157-158, on the Freud-Jones interpretation of Hamlet: "Most people are by
       now convinced of the Freudian aspects of Shak.'s *Hamlet.*"

A1352 Kris, Ernst. *Psychoanalytic Explorations in Art.* New York: International Universities Press,

1952. Pp. 358, 79 pl.
"Approaches to Art," pp. 13-63.
"Aesthetic Ambiguity" (with Abraham Kaplan), pp. 243-264.
"Freudianism and the Literary Mind," pp. 265-272.
"Prince Hal's Conflict," pp. 273-288.
"Psychology of Creative Processes," pp. 289-318.

A1353 Meltzer, J. "Some Psycho-Analytical Angles on Aspects of Shakespearean Drama." *Discussion* (South Africa), I, No. 6 (1952), 47-50.

A1354 Muir, Kenneth. "Some Freudian Interpretations of Shakespeare." *Proceedings of the Leeds Philosophical and Literary Society*, VII (1952), 43-52.
Contains summaries of Freud, Jones, Sharpe, Wertham, and Stewart (on Hamlet, Lear, Othello, and Macbeth). Defends Freudian approach and attacks Stoll and Schücking, pp. 49-50. Considers Freudian approach valid.

A1355 Pauncz, Arpad. "Psychopathology of Shakespeare's *King Lear*: Exemplification of the Lear Complex (A New Interpretation)." *American Imago*, IX (1952), 57-78.

A1356 Reik, Theodor. *The Secret Self*. New York: Farrar, Straus, and Young, 1952. Pp. 329.
Rev: by Sylvan Barnet (with reference to its studies of Shak.) in *SQ*, IV (1953), 351-352.

A1357 Weilgart, Wolfgang J. *Shakespeare Psychognostic: Character Evolution and Transformation*. Tokyo: Hokuseido Press; Rutland, Vt.: Tuttle, 1952. Pp. viii, 276.
Rev: by Lawrence Babb, *SQ*, VI (1955), 190.

A1358 Donnelly, Mabel Collins. "Freud and Literary Criticism." *CE*, XV (1953), 155-158.

A1359 Ehrenzweig, Anton. *The Psycho-Analysis of Artistic Vision and Hearing*. London: Routledge and Kegan Paul, 1953.

A1360 Eissler, K. R. "On Hamlet." *Samiksa*, VII (1953), 85-132, 155-202.

A1361 Feldman, A. Bronson. "The Confessions of William Shakespeare." *American Imago*, X (1953), 113-116.

A1362 Lucas, F. L. *Literature and Psychology*. London: Cassell, 1951. Pp. 340. Paperback reprint: Ann Arbor: Univ. of Michigan Press, 1957. Pp. 340.
Rev: *TLS*, Feb. 16, 1951, p. 104; *Listener*, XLV, 309; by Harold Nicolson, *Obs.*, Feb. 4, p. 7; by Desmond MacCarthy, *Sun. Times*, Jan. 28, p. 3; by F. C. Danchin, *EA*, V (1952), 87-88; by K. R. S. Iyengar, *Aryan Path*, XXIII (1952), 129-130; by O. J. Campbell, *SQ*, IV (1953), 467-468.

A1363 Reik, Theodor. *The Haunting Melody*. New York: Farrar, Straus, and Young, 1953.

A1364 Weisinger, Herbert. "Iago's Iago." *Univ. Kansas City Rev.*, XX (1953), 83-90.

A1365 Feldman, A. Bronson. "Othello in Reality." *American Imago*, XI (1954), 147-179.

A1366 Lassen, Erik. "Shakespeare som Kriminalist." *Berlingske Aften* (Copenhagen), Oct. 11, 1954.

A1367 Pauncz, Arpad. "The Lear Complex in World Literature." *American Imago*, XI (1954), 51-83.

A1368 Strong, L. A. G. "Shakespeare and the Psychologists." *Talking of Shakespeare*, ed. by John Garrett. London: Hodder & Stoughton & Max Reinhardt, 1954.

A1369 Desmonde, William H. "The Ritual Origin of Shakespeare's *Titus Andronicus*." *International Journal of Psycho-Analysis*, XXXVI (1955), 61-65.

A1370 Donnelly, John. "Incest, Ingratitude, and Insanity." *Psychoanalytic Review*, XL (1955), 149-155.

A1371 Feldman, A. Bronson, ed. "Fifty Years of the Psychoanalysis of Literature: 1900-1951." *Literature and Psychology*, V (1955), 40-42, 54-64.
Contains 26 Shak. items, all of which are entered separately in this bibliography.

A1372 Feldman, A. Bronson. "Shakespeare Worship." *Psychoanalysis*, II, i (1955), 57-72.

A1373 Feldman, A. Bronson. "Imaginary Incest." *American Imago*, XII (1955), 117-155.
Another of Dr. Feldman's Earl-of-Oxford papers.

A1374 Feldman, A. Bronson. "Shakespeare's Early Errors." *International Journal of Psycho-Analysis*, XXXVI (1955), 114-133.

A1375 Geyer, Horst. *Dichter des Wahnsinns. Eine Untersuchung über die dichterische Darstellbarkeit seelischer Ausnahmezustände*. Göttingen: Musterschmidt, 1955. Pp. 322.
Chapter 6, "Ein psychogener Dämmerzustand. Shakespeares Ophelia," pp. 73-94; 269-282.
Chapter 11, "Eifersuchtswahn. Shakespeares Leontes und Othello," pp. 178-196; 282-295.
Chapter 14, "Altersschwachsinn. Shakespeares Lear," pp. 234-256; 295-310.

A1376 Gui, Weston A. "Bottom's Dream." *American Imago*, IX (1952), 251-305.

A1377 Hannah, Barbara. "*All's Well That Ends Well*." *Studien z. analyt. Psychologie C. G. Jungs*. Zurich, 1955. Vol. II, pp. 344-363.

A1378 Krapf, E. E. "Shylock and Antonio: A Psychoanalytic Study of Shakespeare and Anti-semitism." *Psychoanalytic Review*, XLII (1955), 113-130.

A1379 Lesser, Simon O. "Freud and *Hamlet* Again." *American Imago*, XII (1955), 207-220.
An answer to John Ashworth's article, A1312.

A1380 Müller-Hegemann, D. "Über die Beziehungen der Psychopathologie zur Literatur." *Psychia., Neurol. med. Psychol.* (Leipzig), V (1953), 341-346.

A1381   Daiches, David. *Critical Approaches to Literature*. London: Longmans, 1956. Pp. ix, 404. "Shakespearean Criticism and Scholarship," pp. 336-338. "Psychoanalytic Study of the Characters in a Literary Work," pp. 348-355, discusses Hanns Sachs' "The Measure in *Measure for Measure*," A1280.
Rev: by James Michie, *London Mag.*, IV (1957), 4, 75, 77, 79; by H. Sergeant, *ConR*, 191 (1957), 252-253; by J. B. Hall, *CL*, IX, 263-264; by J. Vallette, *MdF*, 329 (1957), 334; by K. W. Gransden, *TC*, 161 (1957), 496-498; *TLS*, Jan. 11, 1957, p. 22.

A 1382   Dracoulides, N. N. "Tracé Psychoanalytique sur *Hamlet* de Shakespeare." *Psyché* (Paris), XI (1956), 129-155.

A1383   Dührssen, Annemarie. "Lebensproblem und Daseinkrise bei Hamlet und Ophelia (Life Problems and Existential Crisis of Hamlet and Ophelia)." *Zeitschrift für Psychosomatische Medizin*, II (1956), 220-235, 295-311.
Existentialist. Cf. Wylie Sypher. "*Hamlet*: The Existential Madness," *Nation*, June 21, 1946.

A1384   Feldman, A. Bronson. "The Yellow Malady: Short Studies of Five Tragedies of Jealousy." *Literature and Psychology*, VI (1956), 38-52.

A1385   Fraiberg, Louis Benjamin. *The Use of Psychoanalytic Ideas by Literary Critics*. DD, University of Michigan, 1956. Pp. 393. Mic 57-2143. *DA*, XVII (1957), 1336. Publication No. 21,177.

A1386   Fraiberg, Louis. "Freud's Writings on Art." *International Journal of Psycho-Analysis*, XXXVII (1956), 82-96. Reprinted in *Literature and Psychology*, VI (1956), 116-130, and in *Psychoanalysis and American Literary Criticism*, Detroit: Wayne State Univ. Press, 1960, pp. 1-46.

A1387   Frost, William. "Shakespeare His Own Granpaw." *CE*, XVII (1956), 219-222.

A1388   García Reinoso, Diego. "Notas Sobre la Obesidad a través del Estudio de Falstaff (Notes on Obesity through a Study of Falstaff)." *Revista de Psicoanálisis* (Buenos Aires), XIII (1956) 170-177.

A1389   Grinstein, Alexander. "The Dramatic Device: A Play Within a Play." *Journal of the American Psychoanalytic Association*, IV (1956), 49-52.

A1390   Hankins, John Erskine. "Hamlet and Oedipus Reconsidered." *ShN*, VI (1956), 11. Disapproves.

A1391   Kirschbaum, Leo. "Hamlet and Ophelia." *PQ*, XXXV (1956), 376-393.
Critique of Freud-Jones view. Argues the play is a mystery that can't be plucked out.

A1392   Morrell, Roy. "The Psychology of Tragic Pleasure." *EIC*, VI (1956), 22-37.
With reference to Freudian psychoanalysis, and to several Shak. tragedies, argues that tragedy must end disastrously and must, by a rehearsal of the harsher realities of life, jolt the psyche out of its delusive security.

A1393   Ogdon, J. A. H. *An Examination of Imagery and Libido Symbolism in Certain Literary Works*. Master's thesis, Liverpool, 1956.
Considerable work done on *Richard II* alluded to in introduction but not given *in extenso*.

A1394   Reik, Theodor. *The Search Within: The Inner Experiences of a Psychoanalyst*. Selections from the Works of T. Reik. New York: Grove Press, 1956. Pp. xi, 659.

A1395   Smith, Gordon Ross. *Good in Evil in Shakespearean Tragedy*. DD, The Pennsylvania State University, 1956. Pp. 446. Mic 57-568. *DA*, XVII (1957), 358. Publication No. 19,323.

A1396   Wormhoudt, Arthur. *Hamlet's Mouse Trap*. A Psychoanalytical Study of the Drama. New York: Philosophical Library, Inc., 1956. Pp. 221.
Rev: B7904.

A1397   Cancelled.

A1398   Fliess, Robert. *Erogeneity and Libido*. New York: International Universities Press, 1957.

A1399   Grotjahn, Martin. *Beyond Laughter*. New York: McGraw-Hill, 1957. Pp. 285.

A1400   Hofling, Charles K. "An Interpretation of Shakespeare's *Coriolanus*." *American Imago*, XIV (1957), 407-435.

A1401   Jones, Ernest. *The Life and Work of Sigmund Freud*. Vol. III, The Last Phase, 1919-1939. New York: Basic Books, Inc., 1957. Pp. xvi, 537.
Shak. criticism and theories of authorship, pp. 425-430.

A1402   Kanzer, Mark. "Contemporary Psychoanalytic Views of Aesthetics." *Journal of American Psychoanalytic Association*, V (1957), 514-523.

A1403   Lesser, Simon O. *Fiction and the Unconscious*. Boston: Beacon Press, 1957. Pp. xiii, 322.
Shak. and characters in the plays *passim*.

A1404   Lowenthal, Leo. *Literature and the Image of Man: Sociological Studies of the European Drama and Novel, 1600-1900*. Boston: Beacon Press, 1957. Pp. 242. Shakespeare, pp. 57-97.
Rev: briefly by Laura Jepsen, *English Journal*, XLVI (1957), 372; by Hazard Adams, *Amer. Scholar*, XXVI, 514; by William G. McCollom, *QJS*, XLIII, 436-437; by L. Lowenthal and W. G. McCollom, ibid., XLIV (1958), 179-181.

A1405   Phillips, William, ed. *Art and Psychoanalysis*. Criterion Books, 1957. Pp. 552.
Includes Ernest Jones's "Death of Hamlet's Father," pp. 146-150 (A1306).
Rev: by Herbert Marcuse, *Nation*, Sept. 28, 1957, pp. 200-202.

A1406   Smith, Gordon Ross. "A Note on Shakespeare's Sonnet 143." *American Imago*, XIV (1957), 33-36.

A1407   Vredenburgh, Joseph L. "The Character of the Incest Object: A Study of Alternation Between Narcissism and Object Choice." *American Imago*, XIV (1957), 45-52.

A1408   Williams, Philip. "The Birth and Death of Falstaff Reconsidered." *SQ*, VIII (1957), 359-365. Supports and develops J. I. M. Stewart's interpretation of a Freudian relationship between Hal and Falstaff as given in his *Character and Motive in Shakespeare*, A1320 above.

A1409   Zuk, Gerald H. "A Note on Richard's Anxiety Dream." *American Imago*, XIV (1957), 37-39.

A1410   Eastman, Richard M. "Drama As Psychological Argument." *CE*, XIX (1958), 327-332.

A1411   Lynd, Helen Merrell. *On Shame and the Search for Identity*. New York: Harcourt, Brace, and Co., 1958.
Speaks of Shakespeare only in very general terms.

A1412   McPeek, James A. S. "Richard and His Shadow World." *American Imago*, XV (1958), 195-212.

A1413   Reed, Robert R., Jr. "Hamlet the Pseudo-Procrastinator." *SQ*, IX (1958), 177-186.

3. RELIGION AND THE CHURCH (35,175;13,61)

a. RELIGION IN THE 16th AND 17th CENTURIES
(The following items are included here because they occurred in the sources from which this bibliography was compiled. This section should by no means be considered a comprehensive bibliography of its subject.)

A1414   Jordan, W. K. *The Development of Religious Toleration in England from the Beginning of the English Reformation to the Death of Queen Elizabeth*. London, 1932.
Rev: by E. Préclin, *RH*, 178 (1936), 104-105; by G. D., *EHR*, LIII (1938), 166-167.

A1415   Jordan, W. K. *The Development of Religious Toleration in England from the Accession of James I to the Convention of the Long Parliament (1603-1640)*. Harvard Univ. Press, 1936. Pp. 542.
Rev: by Robert Hastings Nichols, *JMH*, IX (1937), 220-221; by T. S. Gregory, *Criterion*, XVI, 326-328; by F. Brompton Harvey, *London Quar. and Holborn Rev.*, Apr., pp. 274-276; by S. L., *Church Quar. Rev.*, 124 (1937), 368-370.

A1416   Jordan, W. K. *The Development of Religious Toleration in England, 1640-1660*. Vol. III. Harvard Univ. Press, 1938. Pp. 560.
Rev: by H. J. Laski, *NstN*, NS, XVI (1938), 90; *TLS*, July 16, p. 476; *National Rev.*, 111 (1938), 549-550; by Ethyn W. Kirby, *AHR*, XLIII, 155-156; by Hugh Watt, *History*, NS, XXII, 365-366; by M. M. Baldwin, *Catholic Hist. Rev.*, XXIII, 490-492; by Ethyn W. Kirby, *AHR*, XLIV (1939), 881-882; by R. H. Bainton, *Philos. Rev.*, XLVIII, 440-442; by R. H. Nichols, *JMH*, XI, 211-212; by J. L. Connolly, *Catholic Hist. Rev.*, XXV, 78-80; by S. L., *Church Quar. Rev.*, 129 (1939), 173-174; *TLS*, Dec. 14, 1940, p. 628.

A1417   Jordan, W. K. *The Development of Religious Toleration in England*. Vol. IV: Attainment of the Theory and Accommodations in Thought and Institutions (1640-1660). Harvard Univ. Press, 1940. Pp. 499.
Rev: by J. L. Connolly, *Catholic Hist. Rev.*, XXVII (1941), 356-357; by R. Martin Pope, *London Quar. and Holborn Rev.*, Jan., pp. 110-111; by M. M. Knappen, *Church Hist.*, X, 287-288; by R. H. Nichols, *JMH*, XIII, 552-553; by R. B. Schlatter, *New England Quar.*, XIV, 745-748; by A. S. P. Woodhouse, "Background for Milton," *UTQ*, X, 500-502; by Ethyn W. Kirby, *AHR*, XLVII (1942), 327-329.

A1418   Kapp, R. *Heilige und Heiligenlegenden in England*. Vol. I, 1934.
Rev: by L. André, *RCHL*, LXVIII, NS, 101 (1934), 288; by K. Hammerle, *Archiv*, 167 (1935), 273-275; by Marie Schütt, *Lbl*, LVI, 490-493; by G. H. Gerould, *MLN*, L, 543-544; by F. M., *RG*, XXVI, 190-191; by A. Taylor, *MP*, XXXIII, 214-215; by K. Brunner, *Eng. Studn.*, LXX, 313-316; by W. Hågi, *HZ*, 153 (1936), 153-156.

A1419   Mathew, David. *Catholicism in England, 1535-1935. Portrait of a Minority, Its Culture and Tradition*. London: Longmans, 1936. Pp. 316. Enlarged and revised ed. London: Eyre and Spottiswoode, 1949. Pp. 304.
Rev: by A. L. Rowse, *Spectator*, Apr. 10, 1936, p. 672; by Shane Leslie, *Dublin Rev.*, 199 (1936), 89-104.

A1420   Zweig, Stefan. *The Right to Heresy: Castellio Against Calvin*. Tr. by Eden and Cedar Paul· London: Cassell, 1936. Pp. 277. A translation of *Castellio gegen Calvin oder ein Gewissen gegen die Gewalt*. Vienna: Reichner, 1936. Pp. 336.
Rev: by George Jackson, *MGW*, Nov. 6, 1936, p. 374; *TLS*, Nov. 7, 1936, p. 910; by Garrett Mattingly, *SRL*, Nov. 28, 1936, p. 10; by Alice Beal Parsons, *Nation* (N. Y.), 143 (1936), 488-491; by A. L. Rowse, *Spectator*, Dec. 25, p. 1131; by Bertrand L. Conway, *Catholic World*, 144 (1937), 499-500.

A1420a Harrison, A. H. W. *Arminianism*. London: Duckworth, 1937.
Rev: by P. J. Boyling, *London Quar. and Holborn Rev.*, Apr., 1938, pp. 273-274.

A1421   Coulton, George Gordon. *Inquisition and Liberty*. London: Heinemann, 1938. Pp. viii, 446.
Rev: *TLS*, March 12, 1938, p. 164.

A1422   Dodd, A. H. "The Spanish Treason, the Gunpowder Plot, and the Catholic Refugees." *EHR*, LIII (1938), 627-650.

A1423   Garrett, Christina Hallowell. *The Marian Exiles: A Study in the Origins of Elizabethan Puritanism*. Cambridge Univ. Press, 1938. Pp. x, 388.
Rev: *TLS*, June 25, 1938, p. 427; by A. L. Rowse, *NstN*, NS, XVI, 622-624; by R. N. C. H.,

Church Quar. Rev., 126 (1938), 353-355; by J. E. Neale, *EHR*, LIV (1939), 501-504; by A. H. Sweet, *JMH*, XI, 69-70; by Conyers Read, *AHR*, XLIV, 350-352; by E. F. Hawks, *Catholic Hist. Rev.*, XXV, 105; by J. W. Ashton, *PQ*, XIX (1940), 223-224.

A1424   Haller, William. *The Rise of Puritanism, or the Way to the New Jerusalem as Set Forth in Pulpit and Press from Thomas Cartwright to John Lilburne and John Milton, 1570-1643.* Columbia Univ. Press, 1938. Pp. vii, 464.
        Rev: by A. S. P. Woodhouse, *AHR*, XLV (1939), 123-125; by M. M. Knappen, *JMH*, XI, 209-211; by R. T. F., *Personalist*, XX, 418-419; by Florence Higham, *History*, NS, XXIV, 147-148; by A. E. Barker, *UTQ*, VIII, 472-477; by T. Wilkinson, *London Quar. and Holborn Rev.*, July, 1939, pp. 399-400; by Henry S. Lucas, *Catholic Hist. Rev.*, XXVI (1940), 106-107; by A. R. Denham, *MLQ*, I, 115-119; by C. Je., *EHR*, LV, 680-681; by R. B. Schlatter, *JHI*, IV (1943), 362-364; by H. J. C. Grierson, *MLR*, XXXIX (1944), 97-107.

A1425   Knappen, M. M. *Tudor Puritanism: A Chapter in the History of Idealism.* Chicago: Univ. of Chicago Press; London: Cambridge Univ. Press, 1939. Pp. xii, 555.
        Rev: *TLS*, Aug. 5, 1939, p. 470; by E. N. S. Thompson, *PQ*, XVIII, 411; by J. E. Neale, *History*, XXIV, 146-147; by H. Craig, *MLN*, LIV, 600-603; by J. H. Gleason, *New England Quar.*, XII, 558-562; by R. G. Usher, *AHR*, XLV, 121-137; by P. Hutchison, *NYTBR*, Feb. 26, 1939, p. 19; by F. L. Baumer, *YR*, XXIX, 208-211.

A1426   Watson, Y. "The Attitude of the Church Toward Drama." *Thought*, XIII (1938), 226-239.

A1427   Mary Charlotte Bonville, Sister. *The Catholic Church in the Jacobean Drama.* DD, St. Louis University, 1939. Pp. 250. *Microf. Ab.*, II (1940), 45. Publication No. 207.
        "Shakespeare . . . is omitted from this study," p. 6.

A1428   Collins, Joseph B. *Christian Mysticism in the Elizabethan Age with its Background in Mystical Methodology.* The Johns Hopkins Press, 1940. Pp. xvi, 251.
        Rev: by V. R. Stallbaumer, *Catholic Hist. Rev.*, XXVII (1941), 385-386; by Joseph McSorley, *Catholic World*, 154 (1942), 627; by Hardin Craig, *AHR*, XLVII, 325-326; by F. E. Hutchinson, *RES*, XVIII, 340-341; by Helen White, *MLN*, LVIII (1943), 312-314; by Bertha Kuhn, *MLQ*, IV, 115-116.

A1429   Wright, Louis B. "The Significance of Religious Writings in the English Renaissance." *JHI*, I (1940), 59-68.

A1430   Bainton, Roland H. "The Struggle for Religious Liberty." *Church Hist.*, X (1941), 95-124.

A1431   Bush, Douglas. "Two Roads to Truth: Science and Religion in the Early Seventeenth Century." *ELH*, VIII (1941), 81-102.

A1432   Cremeans, Charles D. *The Reception of Calvinistic Thought in England.* DD, University of Illinois, 1942.

A1433   Hutton, Edward. *Catholicism and English Literature.* London: Frederick Muller, 1942. Pp. 224.
        Rev: by Charles Williams, *Spectator*, Nov. 20, 1942, p. 486.

A1434   Ryan, C. J. "The Jacobean Oath of Allegiance and English Lay Catholics." *Catholic Hist. Rev.*, XXVIII (1942), 159-183.

A1435   Baumer, Franklin Le Van. "England, the Turk, and the Common Corps of Christendom." *AHR*, L (1944), 26-48.

A1436   Baumer, Franklin Le Van. "The Church of England and the Common Corps of Christendom." *JMH*, XVI (1944), 1-22.

A1437   Penry, John. *The Notebook of John Penry, 1593.* Ed. for the Royal Hist. Soc. from the original in the Huntington Lib., by Albert Peel. Camden 3rd S., Vol. LXVII. London: Royal Hist. Soc., 1944. Pp. 99.
        Rev: *TLS*, Oct. 21, 1944, p. 514.

A1438   Baumer, Franklin Le Van. "The Concept of Christendom in Renaissance England." *JHI*, VI (1945), 131-156.

A1439   Hudson, Winthrop S. "Democratic Freedom and Religious Faith in the Reformed Tradition." *Church History*, XV (1946), 177-194.

A1440   Hecht, David, and George L. Mosse. "Liturgical Uniformity and Absolutism in the Sixteenth Century." *Anglican Theol. Rev.*, XXIX (1947), 158-166.

A1441   Leatherbarrow, J. S. *The Lancashire Elizabethan Recusants.* Remains Historical and Literary connected with the Palatine Counties of Lancaster and Chester, Vol. 110, New Series. Manchester: Chetham Society, 1947. Pp. xi, 176.
        Rev: *MGW*, Aug. 5, 1948, p. 11; by A. G. D., *EHR*, LXIV (1949), 400-401; by M. C. Wren, *AHR*, LIV, 347-349.

A1442   Rupp, E. G. *Studies in the Making of the English Protestant Tradition (Mainly in the Reign of Henry VIII).* Cambridge Univ. Press, 1947. Pp. xvi, 220.
        Rev: by R. Cant, *Church Quar. Rev.*, 145 (1948), 261-266; by P. V. Norwood, *Anglican Theol. Rev.*, XXX, 187; *TLS*, Oct. 23, 1948, p. 602; by F. W. Buckler, *Church History*, XVII, 248-250; by N. M., *QQ*, LV, 366-367; by H. S. Darby, *London Quar. & Holborn Rev.*, 173 (1948), 173; by A. G. Dickens, *Jour. Theol. Studies*, L (1949), 106-107; by F. L. Baumer, *Jour. Religion*, XXIX, 148-149.

A1443   Shires, Henry M. "The Conflict between Queen Elizabeth and Roman Catholicism." *Church History*, XVI (1947), 221-223.

A1444 Davies, Horton. *The Worship of the English Puritans*. London: Dacre Press, 1948. Pp. xii, 304.
       Rev: *TLS*, Feb. 26, 1949, p. 141; by E. G. Rupp, *London Quar. & Holborn Rev.*, Jan.,
       pp. 81-82.

A1445 Smith, H. Maynard. *Henry VIII and the Reformation*. London and New York: Macmillan,
       1948. Pp. xv, 480.
       Rev: by David Knowles, *Spectator*, Dec. 17, 1948, pp. 817-818; *TLS*, Feb. 5, 1949, p. 92;
       by G. Smith, *Church Quar. Rev.*, 147 (1949), 208-210; by Norman Sykes, *CamJ*, II, 565-567;
       by J. J. Smithen, *Hibbert Jour.*, XLVII, 312-313; by Marshall Knappen, *Church Hist.*, XVIII, 113;
       by Garrett Mattingly, *SRL*, XXXII, 42, and *AHR*, LIV, 871-873; by P. C., *RHE*, XLIV, 369-370.

A1446 Knox, John. *John Knox's History of the Reformation in Scotland*. Ed. by William Croft Dickinson.
       2 Vols. New York, Edinburgh: Nelson, 1949. Pp. 374,498.
       Rev: by H. R. Trevor-Roper, *Spectator*, Dec. 16, 1949, p. 864; by Sir F. M. Powicke, *Hibbert
       Jour.*, XLVIII (1950), 296-298; " 'Jesus and No Quarter'!" *TLS*, May 19, 1950, pp. 301-303;
       by A. F. Scott-Pearson, *EHR*, LXV, 521-522; by W. L. Sachse, *AHR*, LV, 969; by Charles D.
       Cremeans, *JMH*, XXIII (1951), 406 (brief); by William A. Clebsch, *Hist. Mag. Prot. Episcopal
       Church*, XX, 235-236; by Henry G. J. Beck, *Theol. Studies*, XII, 421-429; by John T. McNeill,
       Theology Today, VIII (1952), 401-409 (important); by J. E. Neale, *History*, XXXVII, 164-165.

A1447 McGinn, Donald J. *The Admonition Controversy*. Rutgers Univ. Press, 1949. Pp. xii, 589.
       Rev: *N &Q*, 195 (1950), 301-308; by C. Smythe, *Church Quar. Rev.*, 150 (1950), 266-268;
       by R. H. Bainton, *RN*, III, 43-44; by J. M. Batten, *Church Hist.*, XIX, 138-139; by I. M. Calder,
       AHR, LV, 664-665; by A. Adams, *Anglican Theol. Rev.*, XXXII, 305-306; by P. M. Dawley,
       Hist. Mag. Prot. Episcopal Church, XIX, 289-290; by H. Fletcher, *JEGP*, XLIX, 255; by H. M.
       Relton, *MLR*, XLV, 372-373; by D. C. Allen, *MLN*, LXV, 576.

A1448 Morris, William Dale. *The Christian Origins of Social Revolt*. New York: Macmillan, 1949.
       Pp. 239.
       Rev: A1665.

A1449 Craig, Hardin, Jr. "Religious Disputation in Tudor England." *Rice Inst. Pamphlet*, XXXVII,
       No. 1 (1950), 21-47.

A1450 Holden, William P. *The Religious Controversy and Anti-Puritan Satire, 1572-1642*. DD, Harvard
       University, 1950.

A1451 Johansson, Bertil. *Religion and Superstition in the Plays of Ben Jonson and Thomas Middleton*.
       Essays & Stud. on Eng. Lang. & Lit., VII. Uppsala: A.-B. Lundequistska Bokhandeln, 1950.
       Pp. 339.
       Rev: by Jean Jacquot, *EA*, V (1952), 248.

A1452 Neale, J. E. *The Elizabethan Age*. The Creighton Lecture in History, 1950. London: Athlone
       Press, for University of London, 1951. Pp. 22.
       Rev: *TLS*, Oct. 12, 1951, p. 645.

A1453 McLachlan, H. J. *Socinianism in Seventeenth Century England*. Oxford Univ. Press, 1951.
       Rev: *TLS*, Apr. 27, 1951, Religious Books Sec., p. iii; *N &Q*, 196 (1951), 351-352; by
       Duncan P. Stewart, *Hibbert Jour.*, L, 95-97; by D. N., *EHR*, LXVII (1952), 600-601; by
       Winthrop S. Hudson, *Jour. Religion*, XXXII, 76; by Earl Morse Wilbur, *Jour. Ecclesias. Hist.*, III,
       118-119.

A1454 Bloomfield, Morton W. *The Seven Deadly Sins*. Michigan State College Press, 1952. Pp. xiv,
       482.
       Rev: by Mary McDonald Long, *Catholic Hist. Rev.*, XXXIX (1953), 224.

A1455 Kocher, Paul H. "The Old Cosmos: A Study in Elizabethan Science and Religion." *HLQ*,
       XV (1952), 101-121.

A1456 Kocher, Paul H. *Science and Religion in Elizabethan England*. San Marino, Calif.: The Hunting-
       ton Library, 1953. Pp. 340.
       Rev: by Charles T. Harrison, *SR*, LXII (1954), 161-162; by Francis R. Johnson, *Isis*, XLV,
       209-212; by Professor Johnson, *RES*, V, 405-407; by Hardin Craig, *JEGP*, LIII, 469-472; by
       Jackson I. Cope, *MLN*, LXIX, 423-427; by J. F. Scott, *Cath. Hist. Rev.*, XXXIX (1953/54),
       454-456; by F. R. Johnson, *The Library*, VIII, 5th Ser. (1954), 286-287; by Q. Breen, *Church
       History*, XXIV (1955), 78-79; by Charles Tyler Prouty, *SQ*, VII (1956), 110-111.

A1457 Antheunis, L. "La Législation Persécutrice des Catholiques sous le Règne d'Elizabeth Ire
       d'Angleterre." *RHE*, L (1955), 900-909.

A1458 Curran, M. *St. Thomas More's "Treatice Upon the Passion."* DD, National University, Ireland,
       1957.

A1459 Hawkins, Eliza Merideth. "Theological and Political Aspects in the Development of Religious
       Heterogeneity in England: A Study of Sixteenth and Seventeenth Century England." DD,
       University of Nebraska, 1957. *DA*, XVII (1957), 2579-80.

A1460 Loomie, A. J. *Spain and the English Catholic Exiles, 1580-1604*. DD, London, University
       College, 1957.

A1461 Thompson, Craig R. *The English Church in the Sixteenth Century*. Folger Booklets on Tudor
       and Stuart Civilization. Washington, D. C.: The Folger Shakespeare Library, 1958. Pp. 57.

                              b. RELIGION AND SHAKESPEARE

A1462 Bradley, Francis. *Apostles' Creed in Shakespeare*. MA thesis, Ottawa, 1927. Pp. 43.

A1463 Mary St. Andrew, Sister. (Gertrude Teresa Adams). *Liturgical Elements in English Drama*. MA thesis, University of Ottawa, 1930. Pp. 50.

A1464 Curry, Walter Clyde. "Sacerdotal Science in Shakespeare's *The Tempest*." *Archiv*, 168 (1935), 25-36 and 185-196.

A1465 Vollert, W. "Shakespeares Religiöse Lebensweisheit." *Die Wartburg*, XXXIV (1935), 315-320.

A1466 Cameron, K. W. "Hamlet's Fourth Soliloquy and S. Ward." *SAB*, XI (1936), 59-60.
On Irving Richard's "Meaning of Hamlet's Soliloquy." *PMLA*, XLVIII (1933), 741 ff. Parallels to Richard's interpretation from Ward.

A1467 Huhner, Max. "Shakespeare's Conception of the Clergy." *Unity*, 119 (1937), 92-94; also in *SAB*, XI (1936), 161-170.

A1468 Hunkin, J. W. "Shakespeare's Religion." *Stratford-on-Avon Herald*, May 1, 1936, p. 2.

A1469 O'Hagan, Thomas. *What Shakespeare Is Not*. Toronto: Hunter-Rose, 1936. Pp. x, 115.

A1470 Gill, F. C. "Homiletic Values in Shakespeare." *London Quar. and Holborn Rev.*, 1937, pp. 433-444.

A1471 Cancelled.

A1472 Klein, T. "Die Religiöse Wirklichkeit bei Shakespeare." *Zeitwende*, XIII (1937), 641-650.

A1473 Matthes, H. "Shakespeares Dramen, Theologisch Gesehen." *Luthertum*, NF, XLVIII (1937), 263-277.

A1474 Adkins, Mrs. Mary G. M. *Puritanism in Elizabethan Drama as Represented by Beaumont and Fletcher, Johnson, Dekker, and Shakespeare*. DD, University of Texas, 1938.

A1475 Bachmann, H. "Shakespeares religiöse Einstellung." *Schönere Zukunft*, XIII (1938), Bd. 2, 1064.

A1476 Murry, John Middleton. *Heaven—and Earth*. London: Cape, 1938. Pp. 318.
Chap. VI: Shakespeare: "Religion and the Middle Class," pp. 81-91.
Rev: A1791.

A1477 Schindler, P. "Den religiøse baggrund for Shakespeare." *Edda*, XXV (1938), 340-349.

A1478 Mary C. Bonville, Sister. *The Catholic Church in the Jacobean Drama*. DD, St. Louis University, 1939.

A1479 Burgert, Helmuth. "Das Christentum in Shakespeares Drama." *Schönere Zukunft*, XIV (1939), II, 1059-60.

A1480 Greenewald, Rev. Gerard M. *Shakespeare's Attitude Towards the Catholic Church in "King John."* DD, Catholic University of America, 1939. Pp. x, 195.
Rev: by H. Marcus, *Beiblatt*, LI (1940), 88-89; by T. W. Baldwin, *MLN*, LV, 457; by N. Zwager, *Neophil*, XXVI, 73-74.

A1481 McCarthy, Leo J. *Shakespeare's Dramatic Use of the Catholic Doctrine of Retributive Justice*. DD, Boston College, 1939.

A1482 Miller, Carol Rice. *A Study of the Anachronisms in Some Religious Concepts Expressed in the Tragedies of Shakespeare*. DD, University of Washington, 1939. Abstract in University of Washington *Abstracts of Theses*, IV (1939), 138-140.

A1483 Müller, Wolfgang. "Hamlet-Rätsel. Zur religiösen Problematik Shakespeares." *Die Furche* (Berlin), XXV (1939), 168-174.

A1484 Olivero, F. "Shakespeare in Rapporto alla Religione ed alla Morale." *Atti della Società Italiana per il Progresso delle Scienze* (Turin, Rome), XX, ii (1939), 544-546.

A1485 Eckhardt, Eduard. *Shakespeares Anschauungen über Religion und Sittlichkeit, Staat und Volk*. Weimar: Böhlaus Nachfolger, 1940. Pp. 156.
Rev: by W. Kalthoff, *GA*, VII, No. 21 (1940), 8; by A. Heinrich, *DNS*, XLVIII, 204; by W. Fischer, *Götting. Gel. Anzeigen*, 202 (1940), 545-548; by W. Keller, *SJ*, LXXVI (1940), 207-208; by Willy Casper, *ZNU*, XXXIX, 279-281; by P. Meissner, *Beiblatt*, LII (1941), 60-64; by W. Horn, *Archiv*, 180 (1941), 50-52; by W. S., *GRM*, XXIX, 74; by R. Pechel, *Dts. Rundschau*, 267 (1941), 116; by Karl Brunner, *Lbl*, LXIII (1942), 262-265; by H. H. Glunz, *DLZ*, LXIII (1942), 254-257; by A. Eichler, *Eng. Studn.*, LXXV (1943), 248-249.

A1486 Hankins, John Erskine. *The Character of Hamlet and Other Essays*. University of North Carolina Press, 1941. Pp. xii, 264. Two essays on religion, pp. 172-221.
Rev: B7664.

A1487 Law, Robert Adger. "Shakespeare in the Garden of Eden." *Univ. Texas Studies in English*, XXI (1941), 24-38.

A1488 Myrick, Kenneth O. "The Theme of Damnation in Shakespearean Tragedy." *SP*, XXXVIII (1941), 221-345.

A1489 Adkins, M. G. M. "Sixteenth Century Religious and Political Implication in *Sir John Oldcastle*." *Univ. Texas Studies in English*, 1942, pp. 86-104.

A1490 Grant, John Weldon. *The Religion of Shakespeare*. MA thesis, Dalhousie University, 1942. Pp. 208.

A1491 Battenhouse, Roy W. "*Measure for Measure* and Christian Doctrine of the Atonement." *PMLA*, LXI (1946), 1029-59.

A1492 Garde, Axel. *Hamlet. I Generationernes Spejl. Et Essay*. Copenhagen: Gyldendal, 1946. Pp. 52. Also in *Tilskueren*, L, i, 138-159.

A1493 Semper, I. J. *Hamlet Without Tears*. Dubuque, Iowa: Loras College Press, 1946. Pp. 107.
Rev: briefly, *TLS*, Jan. 11, 1947, p. 27; *TAr*, XXXI, 74-75; by Paul E. McLane, *Thought*, XXII, 344-345; by J. J. H., *Studies*, XXXVII (1948), 127-128; by M. A. Shaaber, *MLN*, LXIII, 194-197; by Mabel C. Livingston, *Catholic World*, 165 (1947), 283; by John Pledger, *MLR*, XLIII, 106.

A1494 Broszinski, Hans. "Christian Reality in *Macbeth*." *Theology*, L (1947).

A1495 Eastman, F. "The Drama Before Shakspere." *Christ in Drama*, New York, 1947, pp. 1-22.

A1495a Eastman, F. "The Influence of Christ in Shakspere's Plays." *Christ in Drama*, New York, 1947, pp. 23-39.

A1496 Flint, Robert W. "The Tragedy of Hamlet." *Union Seminary Quarterly Review*, II, iii (1947), 20-25.
Suggests much scepticism in the times and in Shak. Discusses philos. views and religions. Declares the tragedies non-Christian.

A1497 Lloyd, Roger. "The Rack of This Tough World." *QR*, 285 (1947), 530-540.

A1498 Mårtens, Ilse. *Shakespeare und die Christliche Botschaft*. Lüneburg: Heliand-Verl., 1947. Pp. 56.

A1499 Thiess, F. *Shakespeare und die Idee der Unsterblichkeit*. Dortmund: Schwalvenberg, 1947. Pp. 37.
Rev: A1053.

A1500 Yates, Frances A. "Elizabeth as Astraea." *JWCI*, No. 10, 1947, pp. 27-82.
Section titled "Shakespeare and Astraea," pp. 70-72.

A1501 Clarke, G. H. "Christ and the English Poets." *QQ*, LV (1948), 292-307.

A1502 Culdee, C. "Shakespeare and Reincarnation." *Ba*, XXXII (1948), 47-48.

A1503 Danby, John F. "*King Lear* and Christan Patience." *CamJ*, I (1948), 305-320.
Suggests that what has "often been taken for Stoicism" is "the orthodox teaching on Christian Patience" which also can be found, e.g. in Chaucer, Bacon, Hutchinson, and Coverdale.

A1504 Harrison, G. B. "Shakespeare's Religion." *Commonweal*, XLVIII (July 2, 1948), 281-284; also in *Kath. Digest* (Schaffenburg), III, No. 4 (1949), 29-33.

A1505 McGinn, Donald. "The Precise Angelo." *AMS*, pp. 129-139.

A1506 Carmody, Robert J. *An Investigation of Shakespeare's Knowledge and Use of Dogmatic Theology*. DD, University of Washington, Seattle, 1949.

A1507 Garwood, H. P. "Shakespeare's Church." *NstN*, XXXVII (1949), 182.
Discussed on pp. 206, 230, 254.

A1508 Knight, George Wilson. *Christ and Nietzsche*. London: Staples Press, 1949. Pp. 244.
Rev: *TLS*, Jan. 1, 1949, p. 13; by W. D. Williams, *MLR*, XLV (1950), 412-415.

A1509 Pope, Elizabeth Marie. "The Renaissance Background of *Measure for Measure*." *ShS*, II (1949), 66-82.
Comment by G. Wilson Knight in *Scrutiny*, XVI (1949), 326-327.

A1510 Brock, F. H. C. "Shakespeare's *Macbeth* and the Christian Tradition." *ConR*, 1950, pp. 176-181.

A1511 Leech, Clifford. "The 'Meaning' of *Measure for Measure*." *ShS*, III (1950), 66-73.
Objects to "historical" approaches. Declares the play contains "a passionate sympathy with the unfortunate and hard-pressed."

A1512 Leube, Hans. "Shakespeares Glaube." *Neuphilol. Zs.*, II (1950), 417-428.

A1513 Parker, M. H. *Shakespeare and the Idea of Justice*. B. Litt. thesis, Oxford, St. Anne's Society, 1950.

A1514 Pope, Elizabeth Marie. "Shakespeare on Hell." *SQ*, I (1950), 162-164.
See Mr. T. W. Baldwin's comment, ibid., 296.

A1515 Simpson, Lucie. "Shakespeare—The Mystic." *The Secondary Heroes of Shakespeare and Other Essays*. London: Kingswood Press, 1950, pp. 79-84.

A1516 Speaight, Robert. "La Nature et la Grâce dans l'Univers Shakespearien." *Laval Théologique et Philosophique*, VI (1950), 63-127.

A1517 Stevenson, Robert. "Shakespeare's Cardinals and Bishops." *Crozer Quar.*, XXVII (1950), 116-138.

A1518 Koenigsberger, Hannelore. *The Untuned String: Shakespeare's Concept of Chaos*. DD, Columbia University, 1951. Pp. 222. *DA*, XII (1952), 66. Publ. No. 3353.

A1519 Ralli, Augustus. *Poetry and Faith*. London: The Bodley Head, 1951. Pp. 160.
Shak.: pp. 113-130.
Rev: by N. Nicholson, *FortnR*, 169 (1951), 422-423; *TLS*, April 27, p. 263.

A1520 Roberts, Preston. "A Christian Theory of Dramatic Tragedy." *Jour. Religion*, XXXI (1951), 1-20.

A1521 Frye, Roland Mushat. "Macbeth and the Powers of Darkness." *Emory Univ. Quar.*, VIII (1952), 164-174.

A1522 Huhner, Max. *Shakespearean Studies and Other Essays.* With an Introd. by George S. Hellman. New York: Farrar Straus, 1952. Pp. 115.
"Shakespeare's Conception of the Clergy," pp. 17-29.

A1523 Elliott, G. R. "Shakespeare's Christian, Dramatic Charity." *Theology*, LVI (1953), 459-463.
See also A. T. P. Byles, "How Christian was Shakespeare?" LVII (1954), 63.

A1524 Glover, A. S. B. "Shakespeare and the Jewish Liturgy." *TLS*, May 22, 1953, p. 333.

A1525 Lee, Alberta E. *Preaching in Elizabethan and Jacobean Drama.* DD, Columbia University, 1953. Pp. 341. Mic A54-164. *DA*, XIV (1954), 112. Publ. No. 6657.

A1526 Rinehart, Keith. "The Moral Background of *King Lear*." *The Univ. of Kansas City Review*, XX (1953), 223-228.

A1527 Schneider, Reinhold. *Über Dichter und Dichtung.* Cologne, Olten: Hegner, 1953. Pp. 346. Includes Shak., pp. 133-141; "Tod und Unsterblichkeit in Shakespeares Dramen," pp. 142-156.

A1528 Semper, I. J. "The Ghost in *Hamlet*: Pagan or Christian?" *The Month*, NS, IX (1953), 222-234.
Contradicts Battenhouse, A1572.

A1529 Speaight, Robert. "Nature and Grace in *The Tempest*." *Dublin Review*, No. 459, (1953), pp. 28-51.

A1530 Swander, Homer D. *The Design of "Cymbeline."* DD, University of Michigan, 1953. Pp. 224. Mic A53-1499. *DA*, XIII (1953), 814. Publication No. 5744.

A1531 Milunas, Joseph George, S. J. *Shakespeare and the Christian View of Man.* DD, Stanford University, 1954. Pp. 378. Mic A54-749. *DA*, XIV (1954), 526-527. Publication No. 7500.

A1532 Parker, Marion Hope. *The Slave of Life: A Study of Shakespeare and the Idea of Justice.* London: Chatto & Windus; New York: Macmillan, 1955. Pp. 264.
Rev: by F. S. Boas, *ConR*, 188 (1955), 281-283; *TLS*, July 1, p. 367 (protest by author and reply by reviewer, July 8, p. 381; further comments by R. H. Hill, July 15, p. 397; M. H. D. Parker, July 22, p. 413; reply by R. H. Hill, July 29, p. 429); by J. Vallette, *MdF*, 325 (1955), 151; by Carmen Rogers, *English Journal*, XLV, 52; by Hardin Craig, *CE*, XVII, 243-244; by Philip Henderson, *Time and Tide*, XXXVI, 843; by Christopher Devlin, *Month*, NS, XIV, 372-374; *NstN*, L, 195; by H. Dinwiddy, *Tablet*, 206 (1955), 108-109; by P. E. McLane, *America*, April 21, 1956, p. 89; by Hermann Heuer, *SJ*, 92 (1956), 371-374; by L. G. Salingar, *Universities Quarterly*, X, 199-204; by L. D. Lerner, *London Mag.*, III, 83-86; by Dom Raphael Appleby, *Downside Rev.*, LXXIV, 181-183; by Michel Poirier, *EA*, IX, 254-255; by A. A., *Personalist*, XXXVII (1957), 212-214; by Virgil K. Whitaker, *SQ* VIII, 108-112; by K. Muir, *ShS*, X (1957), 135-136.

A1533 Raphael, D. Daiches. "Tragedy and Religion." *Listener*, LII (1954), 360-361.
Includes comments on *King Lear*. See also letters to the editor, ibid., pp. 403-404, and p. 529.

A1534 Rosier, James L. "The Lex Aeterna and *King Lear*." *JEGP*, LIII (1954), 574-580.

A1535 Barnet, Sylvan. "Some Limitations of a Christian Approach to Shakespeare." *ELH*, XXII (1955), 81-92.

A1536 Coleman, H. *Shakespeare and the Bible.* A Reprint. New York: Vantage, 1955.

A1537 Frye, Roland Mushat. *The Accepted Ethics and Theology of Shakespeare's Audience as Utilized by the Dramatist in Certain Representative Tragedies, with Particular Attention to Love and Marriage.* DD, Princeton University, 1952. Pp. 372. Mic A55-745. *DA*, XV (1955), 581. Publication No. 10,901.
Rev: A2563.

A1538 Frye, Roland Mushat. " 'Out, Out, Brief Candle', and the Jacobean Understanding." *N &Q*, NS, II (1955), 143-145.

A1539 Miller, Robert P. *The Double Hunt of Love, A Study of Shakespeare's "Venus and Adonis" as a Christian Mythological Narrative.* DD, Princeton University, 1955. Pp. 587. Mic A54-3471. *DA*, XIV (1954), 2338. Publication No. 9436.

A1540 Speaight, Robert. *Nature in Shakespearean Tragedy.* London: Hollis & Carter, 1955. Pp. viii, 179.
Rev: A1035.

A1541 Donno, Elizabeth Story. "Cleopatra Again." *SQ*, VII (1956), 227-233.
See also Dolora G. Cunningham, "The Characterization of Shakespeare's Cleopatra," *SQ*, VI (1954), 9-17.

A1542 Hankins, John E. "The Pains of the Afterworld: Fire, Wind, and Ice in Milton and Shakespeare." *PMLA*, LXXI (1956), 482-495.

A1543 Keller, Isaac Clayton. *Literature and Religion.* Rindge, N. H.: Richard R. Smith, 1956. Pp. 64.

A1544 Santayana, George. "The Absence of Religion in Shakespeare." *Essays in Literary Criticism.* Ed. Irving Singer. New York: Scribner's, 1956, pp. 137-148.

A1545 Siegel, Paul N. "The Damnation of Othello: An Addendum." *PMLA*, LXXI (1956), 279-280.

A1546 Thaler, Alwin. "The Gods and God in *King Lear*." *Renaissance Papers, 1955.* University of South Carolina and Duke University, 1955, pp. 32-39.

Disputes T. M. Parrott's argument in *SQ*, IV (1953), 427-432.

A1547   Battenhouse, Roy W. "Shakespearean Tragedy: A Christian Interpretation." *The Tragic Vision & The Christian Faith.* Ed. Nathan A. Scott, Jr. New York: Association Press, 1957, pp. 56-98.
Rev: briefly, *Georgia Review*, XII (1958), 12; briefly, *CE*, XIX, 282.

A1548   Speaight, Robert. "Shakespeare's Religion: The Enquiries of the Countess of Chambrun." *Tablet*, Dec. 14, 1957.

A1549   Thaler, Alwin. "Shakespeare and Our World." *Tennessee Studies in Lit.*, II (1957), 105-120.

A1550   Elton, William. *"King Lear" and the Gods: Shakespeare's Tragedy and Renaissance Religious Thought.* DD, Ohio State University, 1958.

A1551   Stevenson, Robert. *Shakespeare's Religious Frontier.* The Hague: Martinus Nijhoff, 1958. Pp. x, 97.

(1) THE ROMAN CATHOLIC THESIS

A1552   Chambrun, Clara Longworth, Comtesse de. "Shakespeare and the Elizabethan Statutes." *Dublin Review*, 198 (1936), 84-98.

A1553   Colby, E. *English Catholic Poets: Chaucer to Dryden.* Milwaukee: Bruce Publishing Co., 1936. Pp. xx, 208.
Shak. and Catholicism, pp. 97-118; clerical characters in Shak., pp. 118-136.

A1554   Messiaen, Pierre. "Shakespeare et le Catholicisme." *Bulletin Joseph Lotte*, Oct., 1937.

A1555   Chambrun, Clara Longworth, Comtesse de. *Shakespeare Rediscovered by Means of Public Records, Secret Reports and Private Correspondence Newly Set Forth as Evidence on his Life and Work.* Preface by G. B. Harrison. New York: Scribner's, 1938. Pp. xii, 323.
Rev: A509.

A1556   Cancelled.

A1557   Greenewald, Gerard M. *Shakespeare's Attitude Towards the Catholic Church in "King John."* DD, Catholic University of America, Washington, 1938. Pp. x, 195.
Rev: by T. W. Baldwin, *MLN*, LV (1940), 455; by Hans Marcus, *Beiblatt*, LI, 88-89; by T. W. Baldwin, *JEGP*, XI (1941), 292-295.

A1558   Lanoire, Maurice. "La Redécouverte de Shakespeare." *Rev. de France*, July 15, 1938, pp. 203-225.

A1559   Messiaen, Pierre. "Shakespeare et le Catholicisme: Le Roi Jean." *Bulletin Joseph Lotte*, June, 1938, pp. 402-408.

A1560   "Le 'Papisme' de Shakespeare." *Nouvelle Review*, Oct., 1938.

A1561   Lemonnier, Léon. "Du Nouveau sur Shakespeare." *NRFH*, XXX (1942), 425-435.

A1562   H., A. J., and C. L'Estrange Ewen. "John Shakespeare's Confession of Faith." *N &Q*, 184 (1943), 145.

A1563   Semper, I. J. "Shakespeare's Religion Once More." *Catholic World*, 156 (1943), 589-596.

A1564   "John Shakespeare." *N &Q*, 184 (1943), 47-48.
See replies by A. R. Bayley, ibid., p. 113, and by A. J. H., ibid., p. 145.

A1565   de Groot, John Henry. *The Shakespeares and "The Old Faith."* New York: King's Crown Press, 1946. Pp. x, 258.
Rev: A633.

A1566   Scherer, Johannes. "Shakespeares Christentum." *Stimmen der Zeit*, 140 (1947), 98-117.

A1567   Everitt, Ephraim B. "Bricks Without Straw." *SAB*, XXIII (1948), 114-118. On A1565.

A1568   Mutschmann, Heinrich, and Karl Wentersdorf. "Shakespeares katholischer Hintergrund." *Stimmen der Zeit*, 142 (1948), 462-468.

A1569   Hollis, Christopher. "Was Shakespeare a Catholic?" *Catholic World*, 170 (1949), 70.

A1570   Mutschmann, Heinrich, and Karl Wentersdorf. *Shakespeare und der Katholizismus.* Speyerer Studien, R. II, Bd. II. Speyer: Pilger Verlag, 1950. Pp. 256.
Rev: by Helmuth Reitz, *Welt und Wort*, VI (1951), 162-163; by Wolfgang Stroedel, *SJ*, 87/88 (1952), 220-221; by Thomas O. Brandt, *Monatshefte* (Madison), XLV (1953), 58-59.

A1571   Mutschmann, Heinrich, and Karl Wentersdorf. *Shakespeare and Catholicism.* New York: Sheed & Ward, 1952. Pp. xvii, 446. A translation.
Rev: by E. Edward Cain, *Catholic Hist. Rev.*, XXXIX (1953), 190-193.

A1572   Battenhouse, Roy W. "The Ghost in *Hamlet*: A Catholic 'Lynchpin'?" *SP*, XLVIII (1951), 161-192.
See also A1528.

A1573   Jacobi, Johannes. "Shakespeare—Zentrum Bochum." *Die Zeit*, VI, No. 19 (1951), 3.

A1574   Bruers, Antonio. *Shakespeare Cattolico.* Rome: G. Bardi, 1952. Pp. 76.

A1575   Tucker, William John. "Shakespeare, a Catholic?" *Catholic World*, Oct., 1952, pp. 14-19.

A1576   Schümmer, Karl. "Um Shakespeares Religion." *Hochland*, XLV (1952/53), 194-196.

A1577   Keen, Alan, and Roger Lubbock. *The Annotator: The Pursuit of an Elizabethan Reader of*

Halle's "Chronicle" Involving Some Surmises About the Early Life of William Shakespeare. London: Putnam, 1954. Pp. xiii, 216.
  Rev: A425.

A1578 Semper, I. J. "Shakespeare and his Catholicizers." *ShN*, IV (1954), 6.

A1579 Lupo, Valeria. "Shakespeare era Cattolico?" *La Fiera Letteraria*, No. 13, Mar. 27, 1955, pp. 1-2.

A1580 Schwarzstein, Leonard. "Knight, Ireland, Steevens, and the Shakespeare Testament." *N &Q*, NS, II (1955), 76-78.

A1581 Walker, L., O. P. "How Catholic Was Shakespeare?" *Dominicana*, XL (1955), 159-177.

A1582 Devlin, Christopher. *The Life of Robert Southwell: Poet and Martyr.* New York: Farrar & Straus; London: Longmans, 1956. Pp. x, 367.
  Rev: (primarily for Shak. relevance) by John Crow, *SQ*, IX (1958), 73-76.

4. THE SUPERNATURAL (36;13)

a. IN GENERAL
(Not comprehensive: contains only items in sources of this compilation.)

A1583 Hutchins, Randall. "Randall Hutchins' *Of Specters* (ca. 1593)." Tr. by Virgil B. Heltzel and Clyde Murley. *HLQ*, XI (1948), 407-429.

A1584 Zilboorg, Gregory. *The Medical Man and the Witch During the Renaissance.* Baltimore: Johns Hopkins Press, 1935. Pp. x, 215.
Contains an especially valuable study of the work of the Flemish physician Johann Weyer (1515-1588).
  Rev: *TLS*, Sept. 26, 1935, p. 588; by L. T., *AHR*, XLI (1936), 620; by George Sarton, *Isis*, XXV, 147-152; by P. T., *Life and Letters Today*, XIV, No. 3, 203-204.

A1585 Sergeant, Philip W. *Witches and Warlocks.* With an Introd. by Arthur Machen. London: Hutchinson, 1936. Pp. 290, il.
  Rev: *TLS*, Oct. 10, 1936, p. 810.

A1586 Rudd, Dorothea. "The Witches." *QR*, 269 (1937), 24-38.

A1587 Lea, Henry Charles. *Materials Toward a History of Witchcraft.* 3 Vols. Ed. by Arthur C. Howland. Univ. Penna. Press, 1939. Pp. xliv, 434; 435-1038; 1039-1548.
  Rev: by C. L'Estrange Ewen, *AHR*, XLV (1939), 96-98.

A1588 West, Robert H. *The Invisible World: A Study of Pneumatology in Elizabethan Drama.* DD, Vanderbilt University, 1939. Abstr. publ. in *Bulletin of Vanderbilt University*, XXXIX (Aug., 1939), 34-35.

A1589 West, Robert H. *The Invisible World: A Study of Pneumatology in Elizabethan Drama.* Univ. Georgia Press, 1939. Pp. xviii, 275.
  Rev: by T. W. Baldwin, *MLN*, LV (1940), 455-462; by Margaret Bushnell, *MLQ*, I, 245-248; by R. B. Sharpe, *South Atlantic Bul.*, Oct. 1940, p. 5; by Una Ellis-Fermor, *MLR*, XXXVII (1942), 496-497; by J. W. Ashton, *PQ*, XXI, 447-448.

A1590 Doran, Madeleine. "On Elizabethan 'Credulity': With Some Questions Concerning the Use of the Marvellous in Literature." *JHI*, I (1940), 151-176.
That the commonalty were less credulous than the learned in Elizabethan times, and more inductive, because less bookish, p. 166.

A1591 Williams, Charles. *Witchcraft.* London: Faber & Faber, 1941. Pp. 320.
  Rev: by C. E. West, *MGW*, May 23, 1941, p. 376; by F. M. Powicke, *Spectator*, Apr. 18, 1941, p. 428; *TLS*, Apr. 26, p. 200; by Pennethorne Hughes, *NstN*, Aug. 2, pp. 118-119; by Hilda Johnstone, *Church Quar. Rev.*, 133 (1941), 93-96; by S. R. Brett, "Witchcraft," *QR*, 179 (1942), 206-217.

A1592 Wilson, W. G. "The Mandrake Myth." *Life and Letters Today*, XXVII (1941), 197-203.

A1593 Cancelled.

A1594 Hole, Christina. *Witchcraft in England.* Illus. by Marvin Peake. London: Batsford, 1945. Pp. 167.
  Rev: *TLS*, Mar. 24, 1945, p. 142; *QR*, 283 (1945), 374; by Anne Fremantle, *NYHTBR*, July 6, 1947, p. 4; by H. E. Wedeck, *NYTBR*, July 27, p. 3.

A1595 Camden, Carroll. "Elizabethan Chiromancy." *MLN*, LXII (1947), 1-7.

A1596 Davies, R. Trevor. *Four Centuries of Witch Beliefs: With Special Reference to the Great Rebellion.* London: Methuen, 1947. Pp. xii, 222.
Emphasizes the rise and development of the witch-mania from Elizabethan times to its decline in the late seventeenth century, and suggests that the balance may have been turned against the Royalists because of their adherence to the common-sense views of James I and Charles I.
  Rev: *TLS*, May 31, 1947, p. 268; by Frances Paul, *FortnR*, 162 (1947), 156-157; by A. J. P. T., *MGW*, June 5, p. 11; by Maurice Ashley, *Spectator*, May 16, pp. 563-564; by H. N. Brailsford, *NstN*, June 14, p. 440.

A1597 Pavia, Mario N. *Magic and Witchcraft in the Literature of the Siglo de Oro, Especially in the Drama.* DD, Chicago University, 1948. Pp. 186.

A1598 Trefethen, Mrs. Florence Marion Newman. *Demonology, Magic, and Witchcraft in the English*

Drama, 1580-1642. M. Litt. thesis, Cambridge. *Cam Abs.*, 1949-50, p. 96.
"The historical picture demonstrates uniform credulity . . . . The pre-Commonwealth dramatic history of demonology . . . is . . . correlated with the stage's response to a changing political-religious situation and demonstrated to be only an indirect reflexion of contemporary evaluations of witchcraft and magic."

A1599   Buell, Llewellyn M. "Elizabethan Portents: Superstition or Doctrine?" *Essays . . . Dedicated to Lily B. Campbell,* Berkeley: Univ. of Calif. Press, 1950, pp. 27-41.

A1600   Johansson, Bertil. *Religion and Superstition in the Plays of Ben Jonson and Thomas Middleton.* Essays & Stud. on Eng. Lang. & Lit., VII. Uppsala: A.-B. Lundequistska Bokhandeln, 1950. Pp. 339.
        Rev: A1451.

A1601   Nomachi, Susumu. "English Literature and the Supernatural." *Eibungaku-kenkyu,* XXVII (1950), 46-60.

A1602   Haraszti, Zoltan. "The Impostures of the Devil." *Boston Public Lib. Quar.,* IV (1952), 185-189. Gives some account of the *De Praestigiis Daemonum,* by Johann Weyer, or Wierus (Basel 1563), which was intended as a reply to the *Malleus Maleficarum.*

A1603   West, Robert H. "Elizabethan Belief in Spirits and Witchcraft." *Studies in Shakespeare.* Ed. Matthews and Emery, pp. 65-73.

A1604   Goldman, Marcus S. "Sidney and Harington as Opponents of Superstition." *JEGP,* LIV (1955), 526-548.

A1605   Walker, D. P. *Spiritual and Demonic Magic from Ficino to Campanella.* Studies of the Warburg Institute, XXII. London: Warburg Inst., Univ. of London, 1958. Pp. vii, 264.

b. SHAKESPEARE AND THE SUPERNATURAL

A1606   Larkey, Sanford V. "Astrology and Politics in the First Years of Elizabeth's Reign." *Bulletin of the Inst. of the History of Medicine,* III (1935), 171-186.
        Cites views of Wm. Faulke, who refuted belief in the supernatural "several decades before Reginald Scot." "Here in William Faulke as early as 1563 is a Renaissance English skeptic talking about the supernatural in a fashion which can hardly be distinguished by a hair's breadth from a modern skeptic working in 1941."—G. C. Taylor, A1619.

A1607   Seaton, Ethel. *Literary Relations of England and Scandinavia in the Seventeenth Century.* Oxford: Clarendon Press, 1935. Pp. 384; pl.
        Chap. VII: "Popular Superstitions," pp. 275-296.

A1608   Heline, Theodore. *The Occult in Shakespeare: "The Merchant of Venice;" "Romeo and Juliet."* New York: New Age Press, 1936. Pp. 31.

A1609   Fryxell, Burton L. *Ghosts and Witches in Elizabethan Tragedy, 1560-1625.* DD, University of Wisconsin, 1937. Abstr. publ. in *Summaries of Doctoral Dissertations, 1936-1937,* Vol. II, Madison: Univ. of Wisconsin Press, 1938, pp. 295-297.

A1610   Rogers, L. W. "Clairvoyance in Shakespeare." *Theosophist,* LVIII (1937), 219-225.

A1611   Rogers, L. W. "Ghosts in Shakespeare." *Theosophist,* LVIII (1937), 491-494.

A1612   Rogers, L. W. "Shakespeare and Theosophy." *Theosophist,* LVIII (1937), 400-405.

A1613   Rogers, L. W. "Symbolical Dreams in Shakespeare." *Theosophist,* LVIII (1937), 21-35.

A1614   Burcham, C. "An Examination of Shakespeare's Use of the Supernatural." *Research,* Jan., 1939, pp. 14-32.

A1615   Grosauer, Gunda. *Die Frage der Realität der Geistererscheinungen in Shakespeares Dramen.* DD, Erlangen, 1939. Erlangen: K. Döres, 1939. Pp. vii, 81.

A1616   Saleski, R. E. "Supernatural Agents in Christian Imagery: Word Studies in Elizabethan Dramatists." *JEGP,* XXXVIII (1939), 431-439.

A1617   Doran, Madeleine. "That Undiscovered Country: A Problem Concerning the Use of the Supernatural in *Hamlet* and *Macbeth.*" *Renaissance Studies in Honor of Hardin Craig.* Stanford Univ. Press, 1941, pp. 221-235; also *PQ,* XX (1941), 413-427.

A1618   Stanford, W. B. "Ghosts and Apparitions in Homer, Aeschylus, and Shakespeare." *Hermathena,* LVI (1941), 84-92.

A1619   Taylor, G. C. "Two Notes on Shakespeare." *PQ,* XX (1941), 371-376.

A1620   Calhoun, Howell V. "James I and the Witch Scenes in *Macbeth.*" *SAB,* XVII (1942), 184-189.

A1621   McGlinchee, Claire. "Magic—Of an Age and for All Time." *SAB,* XVIII (1943), 72-74.

A1622   Semper, I. J. *Hamlet Without Tears.* Dubuque, Iowa: Loras College Press, 1946. Pp. 107.
        Rev: A1493.

A1623   Röling, B. V. A. *De Criminologische Betekenis van Shakespeares Macbeth.* Nijmegen: Dekker & Van de Vegt, 1947. Pp. xvi, 143.

A1624   Carrère, Félix. "Le Surnaturel dans *La Tempête.*" *LanM,* July-August, 1950, pp. 252-257.

A1625   Johnson, W. Stacy. "The Genesis of Ariel." *SQ,* II (1951), 205-210.

A1626   Arnold, Paul. "Occultisme Elizabéthain." *CS,* XXXVIII, No. 308 (1951), 88-101.

A1627   Heninger, S. K. *The Interpretation of 'Meteors' in Elizabethan and Jacobean Literature.* B. Litt. thesis, Oxford, 1952.

A1628   Chapman, G. E. *Demonology in Elizabethan Drama.* MA thesis, Sheffield University, 1953.

A1629   McPeek, James A. S. "The 'Arts Inhibited' and the Meaning of *Othello.*" *Studies in English*, I (1955), 129-147.

A1630   Hoeniger, F. D. "Prospero's Storm and Miracle." *SQ*, VII (1956), 33-38.

A1631   Maxwell, J. C. "The Ghost from the Grave: A Note on Shakespeare's Apparitions." *DUJ*, XVII (1956), 55-59.

A1632   Thompson, Marvin Orville. *Uses of Music and Reflections of Current Theories of the Psychology of Music in the Plays of Shakespeare, Jonson, and Beaumont and Fletcher.* DD, University of Minnesota, 1956. Pp. 272. Mic 56-3899. *DA*, XVI (1956), 2448. Publication No. 18,954.

A1633   West, Robert H. "Night's Black Agents in *Macbeth.*" *Renaissance Papers*, 1956, pp. 17-24.

A1634   Behrens, Ralph. "Some Observations on Rationality vs. Credulity in Shakespeare." *N &Q*, NS, IV (1957), 420-421.

A1635   Nielsen, Johannes. "Shakespeares Trolddomskraft" ("Shakespeare's Witchcraft"). *Jyllandsposten* (Aarhus, Denmark), June 29, 1957.

A1636   West, Muriel. *The Devil and John Webster: A Study of the Characters in The White Devil and The Duchess of Malfi Based on Imagery in the Plays Related to Ideas Current in the Jacobean Period Concerning Demonology and Witchcraft.* DD, University of Arkansas, 1957. Pp. 411. Mic 57-1720. *DA*, XVII (1957), 1077. Publication No. 20,607.
Shak. passim.

A1637   Cutts, John P. "Music and the Supernatural in *The Tempest*: A Study in Interpretation." *Music and Letters*, XXXIX (1958), 347-358.
See also A5319.

5. THE STATE, POLITICAL THOUGHT, AND PATRIOTISM (38,176;14,61)
a. EUROPE AS A WHOLE
A selection of items published 1936-1958. (Chronological order by period treated, then by date of publication.)
(1) GENERAL

A1638   Sabine, George H. *A History of Political Theory.* New York: Holt, 1937. Pp. xvi, 797.
Rev: by C. H. McIlwain, *AHR*, XLIII (1938), 567-569.

A1639   Gierke, Otto Friedrich von. *The Development of Political Theory.* Tr. by Bernard Freyd. London: Allen & Unwin, 1939. Pp. 364.
Includes a study of Johannes Althusius (or Althaus), 1557-1638.

A1640   Fink, Zera S. *The Classical Republicans.* An Essay in the Recovery of a Pattern of Thought in Seventeenth Century England. Northwestern University Studies in the Humanities, No. 9. Evanston: Northwestern University, 1945. Pp. xi, 225.
Reviews, i.a., the comments of Aristotle, Cicero, Polybius, Machiavelli, analyzes the constitution of Venice, and discusses James Harrington's *Oceana* (1656).
Rev: by Clarence J. Ryan, *Catholic Hist. Rev.*, XXXI (1945), 332-333; by A. S. P. Woodhouse, *UTQ*, XV, 100-101; by David Harris Willson, *South Atlantic Quar.*, XLV (1946), 119-120; by M. M., *QQ*, LIII, 106-107; by E. S., *Greece and Rome*, XV, 79; by Wm. Haller, *MLQ*, VII, 246-247; by Arthur Barker, *MLN*, LXI, 196-199; by W. C. Abbott, *Jour. Mod. Hist.*, XVIII, 71; by Hardin Craig, Jr., *AHR*, LI, 296-297; by Margaret Spahs, *Am. Pol. Sci. Rev.*, XL, 173-174; by James Hutton, *Phil. Rev.*, LVI (1947), 223-225.

A1641   Bowle, John. *Western Political Thought: An Historical Introduction from the Origins to Rousseau.* London: Cape, 1947. Pp. 464.
Rev: *TLS*, Dec. 27, 1947, pp. 669-670.

A1642   Doyle, Phyllis. *A History of Political Thought.* London: Cape, 1949. Pp. 319.

(2) MEDIEVAL

A1643   Carlyle, R. W., and A. J. Carlyle. *A History of Mediaeval Political Theory in the West.* Vol. VI: Political Theory from 1300 to 1600. London: Blackwood, 1936. Pp. 578.
Rev: by Igor Vinogradoff, *Spectator*, May 29, 1936, pp. 986-987; by Francis W. Coker, *AHR*, XLII (1937), 734-737; by F. M. Powicke, *EHR*, LIII (1938), 126-128; by Richard Scholz, *DLZ*, LIX, 28-31.

A1644   Lewis, Ewart. "Organic Tendencies in Medieval Political Thought." *Amer. Pol. Sci. Rev.*, XXXII (1938), 849-876.

A1645   Schoenstedt, F. *Der Tyrannenmord im Spätmittelalter.* DD, Leipzig. Berlin: Junker and Dünnhaupt, 1938. Pp. 124.
Rev: by Richard Scholz, *DLZ*, LX (1939), 743-746; by Hans Weirich, *Hist. Zeitschrift*, 161 (1940), 350-354.

A1646   D'Entreves, Alexander Passerin. *The Mediaeval Contribution to Political Thought.* Thomas Aquinas, Marsilius of Padua, Richard Hooker. Oxford Univ. Press, 1939. Pp. viii, 148.

Rev: by J. J. Rolbiecki, *Catholic Hist. Rev.*, xxv (1939), 228-229; by R. N. C. Hunt, *Church Quar. Rev.*, 128 (1939), 325-327.

A1647 Gilmore, Myron Piper. *Argument from Roman Law in Political Thought, 1200-1600.* Harvard Univ. Press, 1941. Pp. 148.
Rev: by Sigmund Neumann, *Amer. Pol. Sci. Rev.*, xxxv (1941), 774-775.

A1648 Carlyle, A. J. *Political Liberty: A History of the Conception in the Middle Ages and Modern Times.* Oxford Univ. Press, 1941. Pp. viii, 220.
Rev: by F. S. Marvin, *Hibbert Jour.*, xl (1941), 106-108; by Leonard Woolf, *NstN*, May 24, p. 536; by C. D. B., *Ethics*, lii (1942), 120-121; by R. M., *Amer. Pol. Sci. Rev.*, xxxvi, 151-152.

A1649 Jarrett, Bede. *Social Theories of the Middle Ages, 1200-1500.* Westminster: Newman Book Shop, 1942. Pp. ix, 280.
Rev: by G. G. Walsh, *AHR*, xlviii (1943), 548-549.

A1650 The Royal Historical Society. *Transactions of the Royal Historical Society.* 4th Ser., xxv (1943). Pp. 165.
Includes, i.a., "Manuscripts and the War" by C. T. Flower, pp. 15-33; "The Significance of the Baronial Reform Movement, 1258-1267" by R. F. Treharne, pp. 35-72; "Medieval Democracy in the Brandenburg Towns and Its Defeat in the Fifteenth Century" by F. L. Carsten, pp. 73-91; "The Study and Use of Archdeacons' Court Records: Illustrated from the Oxford Records (1566-1759)" by E. R. Brinkworth, pp. 93-119.
Rev: *TLS*, July 10, 1943, p. 335.

A1651 Koht, Halvdan. "Medieval Liberty Poems." *AHR*, xlviii (1943), 281-290.
The call for liberty in the last centuries of the Middle Ages.

A1652 De Lagarde, Georges. "La Conception Médiévale de l'Ordre en Face de l'Humanisme, de la Renaissance et de la Réforme." *Umanesimo e Scienza Politica. Atti del Congresso Internazionale di Studi Umanistici, Roma, Firenze, 1949* (A cura di Enrico Castelli; Centro internazionale di studi umanistici; Milan: Carlo Marzorati, 1951), pp. 237-245.

(3) RENAISSANCE

A1653 Gierke, Otto. *Natural Law and the Theory of Society, 1500 to 1800.* Tr. by Ernest Barker. 2 Vols. Cambridge Univ. Press, 1934.
Rev: by G. E. G. Catlin, *Pol. Sci. Quar.*, l (1935), 441-442; by John D. Lewis, *Amer. Pol. Sci. Rev.*, xxxix, 302-304; by Preserved Smith, *AHR*, xl, 550; by J. C. Walker, *History*, ns, xix, 341-342; by L. J. Younce, *Catholic Hist. Rev.*, xxi (1936), 474-476; by A. Schultze, *DLZ*, lvii, 2228-35; by Mary Glover, *EHR*, lii (1937), 326-328.

A1654 Hayes, Carlton J. H. *A Political and Cultural History of Modern Europe.* Vol. I: 1500-1830. New York: Macmillan, 1936. Pp. xviii, 863.
Rev: by Herbert F. C. Bell, *Catholic World*, 143 (1936), 497-499.

A1655 Yung Chi Hoe. *The Origin of Parliamentary Sovereignty or "Mixed" Monarchy: Calvinism and Bodinism, 16th to 17th Century, Chiefly in France and England.* London: Kegan Paul, 1936. Pp. 391.

A1656 Mesnard, Pierre. *L'Essor de la Philosophie Politique au XVIe Siècle.* Paris: Boivin, 1936. Pp. 714.
Rev: *Criterion*, xv (1936), 756-757; by G. Cirot, *BH*, xxxix (1937), 272-273; *TLS*, Feb. 27, 1937, pp. 137-138; by Jean Hértier, *Rev. des Questions Historiques*, Nov., 1937, pp. 117-118.

A1657 Kallen, G. *Nikolaus von Cues als Politischer Erzieher.* Leipzig: Meiner, 1937. Pp. 47.

A1658 McGovern, William M. *From Luther to Hitler: The History of Fascist-Nazi Political Philosophy.* Boston: Houghton Mifflin, 1941. Pp. ix, 683.
Rev: by J. D. Lewis, *Amer. Pol. Sci. Rev.*, xxxv (1941), 968-969.

A1659 Gilbert, Felix. "Political Thought of the Renaissance and Reformation: A Report on Recent Scholarship." *HLQ*, iv (1941), 443-468.

A1660 Kernodle, George R. "Renaissance Artist in the Service of the People. Political Tableaux and Street Theatres in France, Flanders, and England." *Art Bulletin*, xxv (1943), 59-64.

A1661 Williams, Arnold. "Politics and Economics in Renaissance Commentaries on Genesis." *HLQ*, vii (1944), 207-222.

A1662 Baron, Hans. "Articulation and Unity in the Italian Renaissance and in the Modern West." *Annual Report Amer. Hist. Assoc. 1942*, iii (1944), 123-138.

A1663 Jones, W. T. *Masters of Political Thought.* Vol. II: Machiavelli to Bentham. Ed. by Edward M. Sait. London: Harrap, 1947. Pp. 338.
Rev: by F. A. Lea, *Adelphi*, xxiv (1948), 175-179.

A1664 Hearnshaw, F. J. C., ed. *The Social and Political Ideas of Some Great Thinkers of the Renaissance and the Reformation. The Social and Political Ideas of Some Great Thinkers of the Sixteenth and Seventeenth Centuries.* New York: Barnes & Noble, 1949. Pp. 216; 220.

A1665 Morris, William Dale. *The Christian Origins of Social Revolt.* New York: Macmillan, 1949. Pp. 239. Concerns, i.a., Luther and the 17th Century Puritans.
Rev: by Stevie Smith, *Spectator*, May 20, 1949, pp. 694-696; by Norman MacKenzie, *NstN*, xxxvii, 306-307.

A1666   Quadri, Goffredo. *Niccolò Machiavelli e la Costruzione Politica della Coscienza Morale.* Florence: La Nuova Italia, n.d. Pp. 253.
Rev: by Ernesto Ragionieri, *Belfagor*, IV (1949), 250.

A1667   Sternfeld, Frederick W. "Metropolitan Symposium." *RN*, V (1952), 5-10, 32-34, 58-63. Abstracts of papers given at the Symposium on the Renaissance held at the New York Metropolitan Museum of Art (Feb. 8-10, 1952). Summary of Wallace K. Ferguson's "Toward the Modern State," pp. 58-63.

b. ENGLISH POLITICAL THOUGHT
(Selections, 1936-1958.)
(1) TEXTS

A1668   Dunham, William Huse, Jr., and Stanley M. Pargellis, eds. *Complaint and Reform in England 1436-1714: Fifty Writings of the Time on Politics, Religion, Society, Economics, Architecture, Science, and Education.* New York: Oxford Univ. Press, 1938. Pp. xxxv, 925; pl.
Rev: *N&Q*, 174 (1938), 414; by H. H. Coulson, *Catholic Hist. Rev.*, XXIV, 241-242; *TLS*, May 7, p. 322; *Nation* (N. Y.), 146 (1938), 161-162; by R. L. Schuyler, *AHR*, XLIV, 71-74; by C. H. Karraker, *JMH*, X, 417-418.

A1669   Orwell, G., and R. Reynolds, eds. *British Pamphleteers.* I: *From the Sixteenth Century to the French Revolution.* London: Allan Wingate, 1948. Pp. 264.
Rev: *TLS*, Dec. 11, 1948, p. 694; by J. Freeman, *Life and Letters*, LXI (1949), 262, 264; by R. M. Fox, *Dublin Mag.*, XXIV, 3, 71-72; *MGW*, Jan. 20, 1949, p. 12.

A1670   White, Frederick Randolph, ed. *Famous Utopias of the Renaissance.* New York: Farrar, Straus, 1948. Pp. xxiii, 250. Includes More's *Utopia* and selections from the work of Rabelais, Montaigne, Shakespeare, Campanella, and Bacon.

A1671   Hudson, Winthrop S. *John Ponet (1516?-1556), Advocate of Limited Monarchy.* Univ. of Chicago Press, 1942. Pp. ix, 246, 183.
Biography of John Ponet and facsimile reproduction of *A Short Treatise of Politike Power.*
Rev: by Hardin Craig, Jr., *AHR*, XLVIII (1943), 780-781; by C. F. Mullett, *Pol. Sci. Quar.*, LVIII, 151-152; by F. L. Baumer, *JMH*, XV, 238-239; by Quirinus Breen, *Jour. Religion*, XXIV (1944), 70-71.

A1672   Buchanan, George. *The Powers of the Crown in Scotland: Being a Translation, with Notes and an Introductory Essay, of George Buchanan's 'De Jure Regni apud Scotos'.* Tr. by Charles Flinn Arrowood. Univ. Texas Press, 1949. Pp. ix, 150.

A1673   Dudley, Edmund. *The Tree of Commonwealth: A Treatise Written by Edmund Dudley.* Ed. by D. M. Brodie. Cambridge Univ. Press, 1948. Pp. viii, 110.
Rev: by Michael Oakeshott, *CamJ*, II (1949), 763-764; *TLS*, Sept. 23, p. 615; by G. L. Mosse, *Speculum*, XXIV, 267-269; by D. H., *EHR*, LXIV, 268; *N&Q*, 194 (1949), 66.

A1674   Lambarde, William. *Archeion, or A Discourse Upon the High Courts of Justice in England.* Ed. Charles H. McIlwain and Paul L. Ward. Cambridge: Harvard Univ. Press, 1957. Pp. 176.
Rev: by Margaret A. Judson, *JMH*, XXX (1958), 51-52; by William Huse Dunham, Jr., *Manuscripta*, II, 110-112.

A1674a   Winny, James, ed. *The Frame of Order.* London Allen & Unwin, 1957. Pp. 224.
An outline of Elizabethan belief taken from treatises of the late 16th century. Considerable applicability to the drama.
Rev: A1168.

(2) STUDIES
(Chronological order by period treated; thereafter, chronological order by date of publication.)
(a) SEVERAL PERIODS

A1675   Chrimes, S. B. *English Constitutional Ideas in the XV Century.* Cambridge Univ. Press, 1936. Pp. xx, 415.
Rev: *N&Q*, 172 (1936), 304-305; *TLS*, Oct. 31, p. 876; see letter by Mr. Chrimes, ibid., Nov. 21, p. 980; *QR*, 268 (1937), 363-364; by S. E. Gleason, *Speculum*, XII, 397-399; by Charles Smyth, *Criterion*, XVI, 685-687; by A. F. Pollard, *History*, NS, XXII, 162-165; by H. L. Gray, *AHR*, XLII, 519-523; by K. B. McFarlane, *EHR*, LIII (1938), 707-710; by R. L. Schuyler, *Pol. Sci. Quar.*, LIII, 308.

A1676   Wedgwood, Josiah C., and Anne D. Holt. *History of Parliament. Biographies of the Members of the Commons House, 1439-1509.* I: London: H. M. Stationery Office, 1936. II: London, 1938.
Rev: "The Mother of Parliaments: English Democracy in the Making," *TLS*, Dec. 5, 1936, pp. 1001-02; see authors' reply, ibid., Dec. 19, p. 1052; by S. B. Chrimes, *NstN*, NS, XIII (1937), 20-22; by W. M. Childs, *London Mercury*, XXXV, 432-433; by Hilaire Belloc, *FortnR*, NS, 141 (1937), 241-243; by Robert Livingston Schuyler, *Pol. Sci. Quar.*, LII, 448-450; by N. S. B. Gras, *Speculum*, XII, 536-537; by Charles Mallet, *Spectator*, Jan. 1, 1937, pp. 22-23; see the authors' article "*The History of Parliament:* A Review of Reviews," *Nineteenth Century and After*, 121 (1937), 658-665; by May McKisack, *EHR*, LIII (1938), 503-506; by H. L. Gray, *AHR*, XLIII, 111-113; by Conyers Read, *JMH*, X, 411-413; *TLS*, Nov. 12, 1938, p. 719; see

correspondence between author and reviewer, ibid., Nov. 19, pp. 741-742, Nov. 26, p. 755, Dec. 3, p. 770; by E. G. Hawke, *FortnR*, NS, 145 (1939), 238-239; by May McKisack, *EHR*, LIV, 315-317; by H. L. Gray, *AHR*, XLIV, 876-878; *Spectator*, Jan. 6, p. 30; by J. A. R. Marriott, *QR*, 272 (1939), 189-205; by Conyers Read, *JMH*, XII (1940), 234-236; by Robert Livingston Schuyler, *Pol. Sci. Quar.*, LIV, 614-617.

A1677   Bond, Donald F. "English Legal Proverbs." *PMLA*, LI (1936), 921-935.
Cites "Peoples' voice is God's voice" from the 9th Century on.

A1678   Poppers, H. *Der Religiöse Ursprung des Modernen Englischen Freiheits- und Staatsideals. Die Geschichtsgestaltung des Independentismus.* Prague: Taussig & Taussig, 1936. Pp. 127.
Rev: *AHR*, XLIII (1938), 688.

A1679   Williams-Ellis, A., and F. J. Fisher. *A History of English Life: Political and Social.* Vol. III: 1485-1800. London: Methuen, 1936.

A1680   Dobrée, Bonamy. *English Revolts.* London: Herbert Joseph, 1937. Pp. 202.
Rev: *TLS*, Jan. 8, 1938, p. 19.

A1681   Keir, D. L. *The Constitutional History of Modern Britain, 1485-1937.* London: Black, 1938. Pp. 568.
Rev: by A. Barriedale Keith, *EHR*, LIV (1939), 317-319; by M. M. Knappen, *JMH*, XI, 584.

A1682   Kohn, Hans. "The Genesis and Character of English Nationalism." *JHI*, I (1940), 69-94.

A1683   Fitzsimons, Matthew A. "Politics and Men of Learning in England, 1540-1640." *Rev. Politics*, VI (1944), 452-483.

A1684   Taswell-Langmead, T. P. *English Constitutional History from the Teutonic Conquest to the Present Time.* 10th ed., revised and enlarged by T. F. T. Plucknett. London: Sweet and Maxwell, 1947. Pp. xxviii, 833.
Rev: *History*, XXXII (1947), 165.

A1685   Thompson, Faith. *Magna Carta: Its Role in the Making of the English Constitution, 1300-1629.* Univ. Minn. Press, 1948. Pp. ix, 410, il. 5.
Rev: *TLS*, June 10, 1949, p. 379; by H. W. Rice, *Catholic Hist. Rev.*, XXXV, 323-324; by E. D. Re, *NYTBR*, Jan. 9, p. 21.

A1686   MacNeill, Duncan H. *The Scottish Realm: An Approach to the Political and Constitutional History of Scotland.* Glasgow: A. and J. Donaldson, 1948. Pp. 296.
From early Roman times to 1745.

A1687   Chrimes, Stanley Bertram. *English Constitutional History.* Home Univ. Lib. Oxford Univ. Press, 1948. Pp. 201.
Rev: by C. K. Allen, *Spectator*, July 9, 1948, pp. 54-56.

A1688   Haskins, George L. *The Growth of English Representative Government.* Univ. Penna. Press, 1948. Pp. xi, 131.
Rev: by Hartley Simpson, *YR*, XXXVII (1948), 553-555; *TLS*, Jan. 1, 1949, p. 7; by G. Post, *Speculum*, XXIV, 120-125.

A1689   Brauer, Jerald C. "Puritan Mysticism and the Development of Liberalism." *Church History*, XIX (1950), 151-170.

A1690   Hurstfield, Joel. "Tudor and Stuart Experiments in Absolutism." *MGW*, June 11, 1953, p. 7.

A1691   Løkse, Olav. "Folkestyretankar i England i renessansetida." ["Thoughts about Democratic Government in England during the Renaissance."] *Edda*, LV (1955), 328-337.

A1692   Bennett, Josephine Waters. "Britain Among the Fortunate Isles." *SP*, LIII (1956), 114-140.

A1693   Hawkins, Elza Merideth. "Theological and Political Aspects in the Development of Religious Heterogeneity in England: A Study of Sixteenth and Seventeenth Century England." DD, University of Nebraska, 1957. *DA*, XVII (1957), 2579-80.

A1694   Salmon, J. H. M. *The French Religious Wars in English Politics and Political Theory.* M. Litt., Cambridge, St. John's, 1957.

(b) EARLY TUDOR

A1695   Williams, C. H. *The Making of the Tudor Despotism.* London: Nelson, 1935. Pp. vii, 280.

A1696   Read, Conyers. *The Tudors: Personalities and Politics in Sixteenth Century England.* New York: Holt, 1936. Pp. xvii, 285.
Rev: *TLS*, Oct. 10, 1936, p. 806; by A. L. Rowse, *Spectator*, Oct. 23, pp. 693-694; by E. M. H., *Social Studies*, XXVII, 503; by Wm. A. Morris, *JMH*, IX (1937), 415; by J. B. B., *History*, NS, XXI, 380-381; by W. E. C. Harrison, *QQ*, XLIII, 325-326.

A1697   Baumer, Frederick Le Van. *The Early Tudor Theory of Kingship.* Yale Univ. Press, 1940. Pp. x, 259.
"Before 1588 the cult of authority was fashionable in England. After that date it became, to a certain extent, an object of ridicule, and was at any rate cultivated by only a minority."
Rev: *TLS*, Sept. 7, 1940, p. 436; by Roland G. Usher, *JMH*, XII, 392-393; by A. B. White, *AHR*, XLVI, 118-119; by R. N. Carew Hunt, *Church Quar. Rev.*, XXXI, 150-153; by A. F. Pollard, *EHR*, LVII (1941), 310-313; by Conyers Read, *Pol. Sci. Quar.*, LVI, 309.

A1698   Zeeveld, W. G. "A Tudor Defense of Richard III." *PMLA*, LV (1940), 946-957.

A1699 Sandison, Helen E. "An Elizabethan Economist's Method of Literary Composition." *HLQ*, VI (1943), 205-211.
       Gerard de Malynes: "Malynes' concern for the poor, evidenced in various pamphlets and projects, partakes somewhat of More's resentment at the conspiracy of rich men for their own commodity."

A1700 Smelser, Marshall. "Political Philosophy of Sir Thomas More." *Studies in Honor of St. Thomas Aquinas*, St. Louis Univ. Press, 1943, pp. 12-32.

A1701 Thrupp, Sylvia. "The Problem of Conservatism in Fifteenth Century England." *Speculum*, XVIII (1943), 363-368.

A1702 White, Helen C. *Social Criticism in Popular Religious Literature of the Sixteenth Century.* New York: Macmillan, 1944. Pp. xii, 330.
       Rev: by S. B. Colby, *NYTBR*, June 18, 1944, p. 24; by Margaret Williams, *Catholic World*, 160 (1944), 185-186; by Mary L. Carlson, *Class. Weekly*, XXXVIII, 61-62; by V. M. Hamm, *Thought*, XIX, 725-727; by Mildred Campbell, *AHR*, L (1945), 316-317; by Robert Hastings Nichols, *Church History*, XIV, 75-76; by D. F. Putnam, *Lutheran Church Quar.*, XVIII, 323; by Brents Stirling, *MLQ*, VII (1946), 112-114.

A1703 Adams, Robert P. "Designs by More and Erasmus for a New Social Order." *SP*, XLII (1945), 131-145.

A1704 Zeeveld, W. Gordon. "Social Equalitarianism in a Tudor Crisis." *JHI*, VII (1946), 35-55.

A1705 Nolan, H. *The Social Doctrine of St. Thomas More.* DD, Louvain, 1944-1948.

A1706 Stone, Laurence. "State Control in Sixteenth Century England." *Economic Hist. Rev.*, XVII (1947), 103-120.

A1707 Zeeveld, William Gordon. *Foundations of Tudor Policy.* Harvard Univ. Press, 1948. Pp. vii, 291.
       Rev: by Conyers Read, *Pol. Sci. Quar.*, LXIII (1948), 622-625; *TLS*, June 17, 1949, p. 400; by F. L. Baumer, *JMH*, XXI, 239-240; by C. F. Mullett, *Church History*, XVIII, 58-59; by F. L. Baumer, *RN*, II, 46-47; by E. V. Cardinal, *Catholic Hist. Rev.*, XXXV, 240-241; by R. H. Tawney, *MGW*, Aug. 4, 1949, p. 11; by W. K. Jordon, *AHR*, LIV, 578-580; by D. Hays, *EHR*, LXIV, 519-520; by Silvio Policardi, *Erasmus*, IV, 49-51; by J. E. Neale, *History*, XXXVI, 255-256.

A1708 Shavelenko, Igor A. *English Metrical Propaganda and Other Partisan Verse: 1525-1600.* DD, University of Pennsylvania, 1952.

A1709 Smith, Lacey Baldwin. *Tudor Prelates and Politics.* Princeton Studies Hist., VIII. Princeton Univ. Press, 1953. Pp. viii, 333.
       Rev: by W. Gordon Zeeveld, *AHR*, LIX (1953), 104-105; by Philip Hughes, *Catholic Hist. Rev.*, XL (1954), 296-298; by Eric McDermott, S. J., *Theol. Studies*, XV, 143-146; by George L. Mosse, *JMH*, XXVI, 185-186.

(c) ELIZABETHAN

A1710 Campbell, Lily B. "The Use of Historical Patterns in the Reign of Elizabeth." *HLQ*, I (1937/38), 135-167.

A1711 Evans, E. "Of the Antiquity of Parliaments in England: Some Elizabethan and Early Stuart Opinions." *History*, NS, XXIII (1938), 206-221.

A1712 Brown, Louise Fargo. "Ideas of Representation from Elizabeth to Charles II." *JMH*, XI (1939), 23-40.

A1713 Jenkins, Gladys. "Ways and Means in Elizabethan Propaganda." *History*, NS, XXVI (1941), 105-114.

A1714 Praz, Mario. *Machiavelli in Inghilterra ed altri saggi.* Rome: Tumminelli, 1942.

A1715 Kuhl, E. P. "The Earl of Essex and Liberalism." *PQ*, XXIX (1945), 187-190.

A1716 Armstrong, W. A. "The Elizabethan Conception of the Tyrant." *RES*, XXII (1946), 161-181.

A1717 Davies, E. T. *The Political Ideas of Richard Hooker.* London: S. P. C. K., 1946. Pp. xii, 98.
       Rev: "Hooker in the Modern World," *TLS*, May 11, 1946, p. 217; by H. R. Trevor-Roper, *NstN*, Feb. 9, p. 109; by C. H. Williams, *Church Quar. Rev.*, 162 (1946), 262-265.

A1718 Orsini, N. "Policy or the Language of Elizabethan Machiavellianism." *JWCI*, IX (1946), 122-134.

A1719 Dirksen, Cletus F. *A Critical Analysis of Richard Hooker's Theory of the Relation of Church and State.* Notre Dame: Univ. Notre Dame Press, 1947. Pp. viii, 148.
       Rev: by C. J. Ryan, *Catholic Hist. Rev.*, XXXIV (1948), 180-181.

A1720 Neale, John Ernest. *The Elizabethan Political Scene.* The Raleigh Lecture on History. Oxford Univ. Press, 1948. Pp. 23.

A1721 Mosse, George L. "The Influence of Jean Bodin's *République* on English Political Thought." *Medievalia et Humanistica*, V (1948), 73-83.

A1722 Neale, John Ernest. *The Elizabethan House of Commons.* London: Cape, 1949. Pp. 455.
       Rev: *TLS*, Oct. 21, 1949, pp. 673-675; by Strathearn Gordon, *Spectator*, Oct. 7, pp. 470, 2; by H. J. Laski, *NstN*, XXXVIII, 518; by L. Stone, *EHR*, LXV (1950), 119-122; by C. B. Owens,

QJS, XXXVI, 415-416; by P. Laslett, *CamJ*, III, 762-763; by G. B., *SRL*, May 6, 1950, p. 51; by J. B. Conacher, *Canadian Hist. Rev.*, XXXI, 71-73; by D. H. Willson, *AHR*, LV, 885-886; by Caroline Robbins, *NYHTBR*, Sept. 17, p. 18; by J. Cournos, *NYTBR*, Feb. 19, p. 33; by Conyers Read, *JMH*, XXIII (1951), 75-77.

A1723 Shirley, F. J. *Richard Hooker and Contemporary Political Ideas*. London: S. P. C. K., 1949. Pp. vi, 274.
    Rev: *TLS*, July 1, 1949, p. 432; by C. J. Wright, *Hibbert Jour.*, XLVIII, 100-102; by J. S. Marshall, *Hist. Mag. Protestant Episcopal Church*, XVIII, 462-464; by N. Micklem, *QQ*, LVII (1950), 227; by R. W. Greaves, *Church Quar. Rev.*, 149 (1950), 236-238; by A. P. d'E., *EHR*, LXVI (1951), 149-150.

A1724 Neale, John Ernest. "The Elizabethan House of Commons." *Listener*, XLIII (1950), 145-146.

A1725 Morris, Christopher. *Political Thought in England, Tyndale to Hooker*. Home Univ. Library. Oxford Univ. Press, 1953. Pp. 220.
Valuable discussion of Shak.'s ideas of government, the ruler, and the concept of order, pp. 98-109.
    Rev: by C. V. Wedgwood, *Time and Tide*, Aug. 1, 1953, pp. 1019-20; *TLS*, Sept. 4, p. 563; by Richard Mayne, *NstN*, Nov. 7, p. 575; by Maurice Cranston, *Spectator*, Dec. 11, p. 710; *Listener*, L, 875; by H. T. Price, *SQ*, V (1954), 110-111; by Michel Poirier, *EA*, VII, 344-345; by Roy C. Macridis, *Amer. Pol. Sci. Rev.*, XLVIII, 906; by Alan Simpson, *JMH*, XXVII (1955), 308-310; by A. L. Rowse, *EHR*, LXX, 324-325.

A1726 O'Brien, Gordon Worth. *Renaissance Poetics and the Problem of Power*. Institute of Elizabethan Studies (Dir.: Ralph Graham Palmer), Publ. No. 2. Chicago: Inst. Elizabethan Studies, 1956. Pp. xxvi, 127.
    Rev: by Jackson I. Cope, *MLN*, LXXII (1957), 364-368; by Ruth Wallerstein, *JEGP*, LVI, 626-628; *ShN*, VII, 22; by M. C. Bradbrook, *RES*, IX (1958), 234 (brief); by Lillian Feder, *SCN*, XVI, 4; by Jewel Wurtzbaugh, *Books Abroad*, XXXII, 191; *VQR*, XXXIV, No. 1, xvii.

A1727 Cancelled.

A1728 Praz, Mario. " 'The Political Brain': Machiavelli and the Elizabethans." Praz: *The Flaming Heart*. New York: Doubleday, 1958, pp. 90-145.

(d) EARLY STUART

A1729 Parsons, E. J. S., ed. *Some Proclamations of Charles I*. Being Addenda to Bibliotheca Lindesiana: A Bibliography of Royal Proclamations of the Tudor and Stuart Sovereigns by Robert Steele. Suppl. to *Bodleian Quar. Record*, VIII, No. 90 (1936). Pp. 28.

A1730 Lyon, T. *The Theory of Religious Liberty in England, 1603-1639*. Cambridge Univ. Press, 1937. Pp. 242.
    Rev: by David Garnett, *NstN*, NS, XIV (1937), 1018; by J. W. G., *EHR*, LIII (1938), 542-543; *TLS*, Mar. 26, 1938, p. 196; by H. Watkin-Jones, *London Quar. and Holborn Rev.*, Apr., 1938, pp. 272-273; by R. H. M., *Church Quar. Rev.*, 126 (1938), 161; by W. K. Jordan, *AHR*, XLIV (1939), 355-356; by J. L. Connelly, *Catholic Hist. Rev.*, XXV, 80-81.

A1731 Jordan, W. K. *The Development of Religious Toleration in England, 1603-1640*. London: Allen & Unwin, 1937. Pp. 542.
    Rev: by T. S. Gregory, *Criterion*, XVI (1937), 326-328; by R. H. Murray, *ConR*, 151 (1937), 251-252; by F. B. Harvey, *London Quar. Rev.*, 162 (1937), 274-276; by H. Watt, *History*, XXII (1938), 365-366; by R. H. Bainton, *Philosophical Rev.*, XLVII, 223-226; by M. W. Baldwin, *Catholic Hist. Rev.*, XXIII, 490-492.

A1732 Bock, Hellmut. *Staat und Gesellschaft bei Francis Bacon*. Berlin: Junker und Dünnhaupt, 1937.
    Rev: by Alois Brandl, *Archiv*, 172 (1938), 250; by Rudolf Metz, *Eng. Studn.*, LXXII, 433-435; by Hans Rühl, *DLZ*, LIX, 1420-22; by D. N., *EHR*, LIV (1939), 177.

A1733 Allen, J. W. *English Political Thought, 1603-1660*. Vol. I: 1603-1644. London: Methuen, 1938. A major authority.
Comments upon Shakespeare's influence, p. 228.
    Rev: by A. L. Rowse, *Spectator*, Feb. 11, 1938, pp. 234, 236; by J. Vallette, *EA*, II, 321-322; *TLS*, Feb. 12, 1938, p. 101; by H. J. Laski, *NstN*, NS, XV, 336-338; by C. H. McIlwain, *Amer. Pol. Sci. Rev.*, XXXII, 1175-77; by Reginald Cant, *Church Quar. Rev.*, 126 (1938), 133-136; by M. M. Knappen, *AHR*, XLIV (1939), 602-604; by A. S. P. Woodhouse, *EHR*, LIV, 731-734; by A. E. Barker. "The Two-Handed Engine," *UTQ*, VIII, 472-477; by George Catlin, *Pol. Sci. Quar.*, LV (1940), 136-138.

A1734 Sisson, C. J. "King James as Poet and Political Writer." *17th Century Studies*, pp. 47-63.

A1735 Bock, H. "Francis Bacon als Staatsdenker und Wissenschaftstheoretiker." *N. Mon.*, IX (1938), 255-268.

A1736 Wormuth, Francis D. *The Royal Prerogative, 1603-1649: A Study in English Political and Constitutional Ideas*. Cornell Univ. Press, 1939. Pp. x, 124.
    Rev: by Elisabeth Hodder, *JMH*, XI (1939), 585-586; by M. M. Knappen, *AHR*, XLVI (1941), 630; by G. D., *EHR*, LVII (1942), 280-281.

A1737 Davies, Godfrey. "English Political Sermons, 1603-1640." *HLQ*, III (1939), 1-22.

A1738 Fink, Z. S. "Venice and English Political Thought in the Seventeenth Century." *MP*, XXXVIII (1940), 155-172.

A1739 Fitch, W. O. "Nazism in the Seventeenth Century." *Church Quar. Rev.*, 131 (1940), 119-133.

A1740 Tenney, Mary F. "Tacitus in the Politics of Early Stuart England." *Classical Jour.*, XXXVI (1941), 151-163.

A1741 Jordan, W. K. *Men of Substance*. Univ. of Chicago Press, 1942. Pp. 283.
Studies of the political convictions of Henry Parker and Henry Robinson, seventeenth-century men of substance.
    Rev: by W. S. Hudson, *Church History*, XI (1942), 337-338; by R. M. Krapp, *AHR*, XLVIII (1943), 553-554; by E. A. Bellar, *JMH*, XV, 143-144; by J. H. Clapham, *Economica*, X, 72-73; by R. P. Stearns, *Jour. Religion*, XXIII, 148-149; by Godfrey Davies, *EHR*, LIX (1944), 273-275; by A. S. P. Woodhouse, *Philos. Rev.*, LIII, 80-82.

A1742 Wright, Louis B. "Propaganda Against James I's 'Appeasement' of Spain." *HLQ*, VI (1943), 149-172.

A1743 Bush, Douglas. *English Literature in the Earlier Seventeenth Century, 1600-1660*. Oxford: Clarendon Press, 1945. Pp. 621.
This work, Vol. V of the *Oxford History of English Literature*, ed. by F. P. Wilson and Bonamy Dobrée, is the first of twelve volumes to appear.
Chapter on political thought, pp. 232-257.
    Rev: A8045.

A1744 Abel, Deryck. "Liberty v. Authority in Stuart England." *ConR*, 165 (1944), 47-52.
James I to Charles II. Asserts that James was authoritarian and that the English were at first astounded.

A1745 Elson, James Hinsdale. *John Hales of Eton*. New York: King's Crown Press, 1948. Pp. 199.
    Rev: by Godfrey Davies, *Church History*, XVIII (1949), 114-115; by D. N., *EHR*, LXIV, 274; by L. I. Bredvold, *AHR*, LIV, 662-663; by J. C. Brauer, *Rev. Religion*, XIV (1950), 394-396; by H. Gifford, *RES*, NS, I, 174-175.

A1746 Judson, Margaret Atwood. *The Crisis of the Constitution: An Essay in Constitutional and Political Thought in England, 1603-1645*. Rutgers Studies in History, No. 5. Rutgers Univ. Press, 1949. Pp. xi, 444.
    Rev: by P. R. L., *SRL*, May 6, 1950, pp. 50-51; by W. H. Coates, *AHR*, LV, 887-888; by G. D., *EHR*, LXVI (1951), 444; by Matthew A. Fitzsimons, *JMH*, XXIII, 276; by Bernard Norling, *Catholic Hist. Rev.*, XXXVII, 328-330.

A1747 Hinton, R. W. K. "Government and Liberty under James I." *Cambridge Hist. Jour.*, XI (1953) 48-64.

A1748 Mitchell, William M. *The Rise of the Revolutionary Party in the English House of Commons, 1603-1629*. New York: Columbia Univ. Press, 1957. Pp. 212.
    Rev: by William H. Stockdale, *RN*, XI (1958), 277-278; by Carl B. Cone, *Manuscripta*, II, 113-114; by R. W. K. Hinton, *Hist. Rev.*, I, 185-187; by D. H. Pennington, *History*, XLIII, 235-236; *TLS*, Mar. 21, 1958, p. 158.

A1749 Eusden, John Dykstra. *Puritans, Lawyers, and Politics in Early Seventeenth Century England*. Yale Studies in Religious Educ., XXIII. New Haven: Yale Univ. Press, 1958. Pp. xii, 238.

A1750 Moir, Thomas L. *The Addled Parliament of 1614*. Oxford: Clarendon Press, 1958. Pp. 212.
    Rev: by D. H. Pennington, *History Today*, VIII (1958), 287; by M. M. Reese, *Time and Tide*, June 21, p. 778; by Christopher Hill, *Spectator*, Feb. 28, p. 270; by Harold Hume, *AHR*, LXIV, 149-150; by R. W. K. Hinton, *Hist. Rev.*, I, 185-187; by Ivan Roots, *History*, XLIII, 236; *TLS*, Feb. 21, p. 99.

A1751 Tawney, R. H. *Business and Politics under James I: Lionel Cranfield as Merchant and Minister*. Cambridge: Cambridge Univ. Press, 1958. Pp. xii, 325.
    Rev: by Christopher Hill, *Spectator*, Oct. 10, 1958, p. 493; by Hugh Ross Williamson, *Time and Tide*, Oct. 18, pp. 1251-52; by Asa Briggs, *NstN*, Oct. 11, pp. 496-497; *TLS*, Dec. 26, pp. 745-746.

c. IN ENGLISH LITERATURE
(1) SPECIFIC POETS AND WORKS OTHER THAN SHAKESPEARE'S. (General studies followed by studies of specific writers and works.)

A1752 Paletta, Gerhard. *Fürstengeschick und innerstaatlicher Machtkampf im englischen Renaissance-Drama*. Breslau, 1934.
    Rev: by Eduard Eckhardt, *Beiblatt*, XLVII (1936), 50-52; by Max J. Wolff, *Eng. Studn.*, LXXI, 94-95.

A1753 Grosse, F. *Das englische Renaissance-Drama im Spiegel zeitgenössischer Staatstheorien*. Breslau, LXXII, 1935.
    Rev: by Eduard Eckhardt, *Beiblatt*, XLVII (1936), 137-140; by Hans Marcus, *DLZ*, LVII, 236-238; by Wolfgang Keller, *SJ*, LXXII (1936), 152-153; by W. Wehe, *Bausteine z. dts. Nat. Theat.*, IV (1936), 281; by H. E., *GRM*, XXVI (1938), 323.

A1754 Hobday, C. H. *Political Thought in English Drama, 1588-1625*. MA thesis, University of London, 1941.

A1755 Anderson, R. L. "Kingship in Renaissance Drama." *SP*, XLI (1944), 136-155.

A1756   Reese, Gertrude C. *Reflection of Political Thought in the Elizabethan Drama as Studied Through the Subject of Kingship.* DD, University of Texas, 1941.

A1757   Reese, Gertrude C. "The Question of the Succession in Elizabethan Drama." *TxSE*, XXII (1942), 59-85.

A1758   Ribner, Irving. *The English History Play in the Age of Shakespeare.* Princeton Univ. Press, 1957. Rev: B5137.

A1759   Jenkins, Sadie F. *The Treatment of Tyranny in Elizabethan English History Plays.* DD, University of North Carolina, 1935. Abstr. publ. in *Univ. of North Carolina Record, Research in Progress, 1934-1935,* Chapel Hill, 1935, p. 36.

A1760   Turner, Lilian F. *The Elizabethan Drama as the Newspaper of the Age: A Study of the Influence of External Controlling Factors on the Drama of the Early Seventeenth Century as a Potential Medium for Reflecting Popular Opinion on Political and Social Questions.* MA thesis, University of London, 1938.

A1761   Quinn, H. M. *The Presentation of Dissension in the State as a Moral Theme in Early Elizabethan Historical Drama.* B. Litt. thesis, Oxford, 1954.

A1762   Lowers, James K. *Elizabethan Non-Dramatic Literature Relating to the Northern Rebellion of 1569.* DD, University of California, Los Angeles, 1950.

A1763   Armstrong, W. A. "The Influence of Seneca and Machiavelli on the Elizabethan Tyrant." *RES*, XXIV (1948), 19-35.

A1764   Ribner, Irving. "Machiavelli and Sidney's *Discourse to the Queens Majestie.*" *Italica*, XXVI (1949), 117-187.

A1765   Ribner, Irving. "Machiavelli and Sidney: The *Arcadia* of 1590." *SP*, XLVII (1950), 152-172. Is not concerned with indebtedness but with ideas in the revised *Arcadia* which are similar to Machiavelli's.

A1766   Ribner, Irving. "Sidney's *Arcadia* and the Machiavelli Legend." *Italica*, XXVII (1950), 225-235.

A1767   Burton, K. M. "The Political Tragedies of Chapman and Ben Jonson." *EIC*, II (1952), 397-412.

A1768   Watson, Sara Ruth. "*Gorboduc* and the Theory of Tyrannicide." *MLR*, XXXIV (1939), 355-366. Parallels between Goodman's *How Superior Powers Oght To Be Obeyd* and *Gorboduc*.

A1769   Phillips, James E. "A Revaluation of *Horestes* (1567)." *HLQ*, XVIII (1954-55), 227-244. Believes that the playwright adapted his Senecan material to support the arguments for the deposition of Queen Mary Stuart. Reproduces statements from both aristocracy and populace on nature of royal sovereignty: "Scottish rebels and their partisans in England expounded the doctrine that while rulers are indeed responsible only to God, He for that very reason will sometimes raise up instruments to punish those of His anointed deputies who are guilty of gross immorality and misconduct," p. 231. "Nicholas Throckmorton, the English ambassador wrote at the same time to Elizabeth herself that 'It is public speech among all the people, that their queen hath no more liberty nor privilege to commit murder nor adultry, than any other private person, neither by god's laws, nor the laws of the realm'," pp. 231-232.

A1770   Adkins, M. G. M. "Sixteenth Century Religious and Political Implication in *Sir John Oldcastle.*" *TxSE*, XXII (1942), 86-104.

A1771   Adkins, Mary G. M. "A Theory About *The Life and Death of Jack Straw.*" *TxSE*, XXVIII (1949), 57-82.

A1772   Reese, G. "Political Import of *The Misfortunes of Arthur.*" *RES*, XXI (1945), 81-91.

A1773   Rossiter, A. P., ed. *Woodstock: A Moral History.* London: Chatto & Windus, 1946. Pp. 255. Contains preface (seventy-six pages), edition, and modernized text.
        Rev: *TLS*, Nov. 23, 1946, p. 578; by Bonamy Dobrée, *Spectator*, Dec. 6, p. 618; by Grace Banyard, *FortnR*, 960 (1946), 462; by J. M. Nosworthy, *Life and Letters*, LIII (1947), 56-57; by George Rylands, *NstN*, Feb. 8, pp. 118-119; by H. Jenkins, *RES*, XXIV (1948), 66-68.

A1774   Mohle, Ruth. *Studies in Spenser, Milton and the Theory of Monarchy.* Columbia Univ. Press, 1949. Pp. 144.

(2) SHAKESPEARE

A1775   Bayer, Hermann. *Shakespeares Politisches Denken.* DD, Tübingen, 1924. Pp. 108. Typewritten.

A1776   Empson, W. *Some Versions of Pastoral.* London, 1935. Pp. 298. Publ. in USA as *English Pastoral Poetry.* New York: Norton, 1938. Pp. 298.
        Shak., pp. 89-115.
        Rev: B5290.

A1777   Morrow, Donald. *Where Shakespeare Stood. His Part in the Crucial Struggles of His Day.* Milwaukee, Wisc.: Casanova Press, 1935. Pp. 13, 89. Marxist.
        Rev: by R. P. Blackmur, *NR*, 86 (1936), 52.

A1778   Bestian, Hans. "Shakespeares *Macbeth* und sein Politischer Hintergrund." *Gelbe Hefte*, XII (1935-36), 370-374.

A1779   Draper, John W. "Political Themes in Shakespeare's Later Plays." *JEGP*, XXXV (1936), 61-93.

A1780 O'Hagan, Thomas. *What Shakespeare Is Not.* Toronto: Hunter-Rose, 1936. Pp. xx, 115. "The purpose of this work is to combat the theory that William Shakespeare, in his dramas, is a propagandist, either political or religious."

A1781 Papiroff, S. "Shakespeare's Idea of Kingship as Seen in *Richard II* and *Henry IV." The Silver Falcon,* New York: Hunter College, 1936, pp. 16-20.

A1782 Pongs, H. "Shakespeare und das Politische Drama." *DuV,* xxxvii (1936), 257-281.

A1783 Rebora, Piero. *Civiltà italiana e civiltà inglese. Studi e ricerche.* Florence: Felice Le Monnier, 1936. Pp. xi, 271. "Shakespeare e il Cesarismo," pp. 3-47.

A1784 "Shakespeare's Politics." *AglGR,* I (1937), 500, 502. Review of "Shakespeare as a Political Dramatist." *Berliner Tagblatt,* Oct. 13, 1937.

A1785 Hofmüller, Rudolf. "Shakespeares *Richard III* . . . im Residenztheater. Der Epilog zu den Königsdramen. Politische Weltschau im Drama. Charakterbild eines Tyrannen." *VB,* Oct. 15, 1937.

A1786 Bachmann, H. "Wo stand Shakespeare innerlich? Die Durchdringung einer politischen Welt und eines Dichterischen Werkes." *Germania,* 1938, No. 159.

A1787 Eckloff, L. "Heroismus und Politisches Führertum bei Shakespeare." *ZNU,* xxxvii (1938), 97-112.

A1788 Schmidt, Wolfgang. "Zur Freiheitsauffassung der Engländer." *ZNU,* xxxvii (1938), 28-38. "Shakespeares Freiheitsbegriff," pp. 33-35.

A1789 Knowlton, Edgar. "Nature and Shakespeare." *PMLA,* li (1936), 719-744.

A1790 Messiaen, Pierre. "Jugements Politiques de Shakespeare." *Revue de l'Enseignement des Langues Vivantes,* lv (1938), 58-62.

A1791 Murry, John Middleton. *Heaven—and Earth.* London: Cape; Toronto: Nelson, 1938. Pp. 318. American edition titled *Heroes of Thought.* New York: Julian Messner, 1938. Chap. V: Shakespeare: "The Mystery of Order," pp. 68-80.
    Rev: by Humphrey House, *NstN,* ns, xvi (1938), 656; *TLS,* Sept. 3, p. 568.

A1792 Salter, C. H. "Poetry and Politics." *Poetry Review,* xxx (1939), 345-361.

A1793 Wilson, John Dover. "The Political Background of Shakespeare's *Richard II* and *Henry IV." SJ,* lxxv (1939), 36-51.

A1794 Winter, J. W. "Shakespeare als Politischer Dramatiker. Gespräch mit Dover Wilson." *MNN,* No. 112, April 22, 1939.

A1795 Glunz, Hans H. "Shakespeares Staat." *Rheinisch-westfäl. Ztg.,* Jan. 3, 1939.

A1796 Glunz, H. H. "Shakespeares Staat." *FuF,* xv (1939), 6-7.

A1797 Glunz, Hans H. "Shakespeares Staat." *SJ,* lxxv (1939), 59-76.

A1798 Glunz, H. H. *Shakespeares Staat.* Frankfurter wiss. Beiträge. Kulturwiss. Reihe, Bd. 3. Frankfurt am Main: Vittorio Klostermann, 1940. Pp. 182.
    Rev: by Wolfgang Keller, *SJ,* lxxvi (1940), 208-209; by Hans W. Kalthoff, *GA,* vii, No. 21 (1940), 8; by Hans Marcus, *DLZ,* lxii (1941), 210-211; by Paul Meissner, *GRM,* xxix, 73; by Willy Casper, *ZNU,* xl, 138-140; by Karl Schummer, *N. Mon.,* xii, 305-308; by Albert Eichler, *Eng. Studn.,* lxxv (1942), 364-368; by E. Eckhardt, *Lbl,* lxiii, 26-27.

A1799 Deutschbein, Max. "Die Politischen Sonette Shakespeares." *SJ,* lxxvi (1940), 161-188. See Boerner's comments, A1812.

A1800 Dietz, Heinrich. "Demagogie als Literarisches Motiv." *ZNU,* xxxix (1940), 59-70.

A1801 Eckhardt, Eduard. *Shakespeares Anschauungen über Religion und Sittlichkeit, Staat und Volk.* Weimar: Böhlaus Nachfolger, 1940. Pp. 156. Anhang: "Shakespeares Stellung zum Judentum," pp. 79-83.
    Rev: A1485.

A1802 De Selincourt, Ernest, ed. *English Poets and the National Ideal.* (Four Lectures on Shakespeare, Milton, Wordsworth, English Poetry since 1815.) Oxford: Clarendon Press, 1940. Pp. 120. Political comments in wartime; first published in 1915.

A1803 Phillips, James Emerson, Jr. *The State in Shakespeare's Greek and Roman Plays.* DD, Columbia University, 1941. Published in Columbia Univ. Studies in English and Comparative Literature, 149. New York: Columbia Univ. Press, 1940. Pp. ix, 230.
    Rev: *N &Q,* 180 (1941), 179; by Brents Stirling, *MLQ,* ii, 144-147; by G. C. Taylor, *YR,* xxx, 418-421; *BJRL,* xxvi, 27-28; by Allardyce Nicoll, *JEGP,* xl, 408-409; by Louis Teeter, *MLN,* lviii (1943), 151-152.

A1804 Baldensperger, Fernand. "Le Siège de Rouen (1591-1592) et son Importance pour l'Information de Shakespeare." *Comparative Literature Studies* (Cardiff), iii (1941), 1-8.

A1805 Fleming, Edith Alice. *Shakespeare's Recurring Ideas.* MA thesis, Alberta, 1941. Pp. 314.

A1806 Hankins, John Erskine. *The Character of Hamlet and Other Essays.* Univ. North Carolina Press, 1941. Pp. xii, 264. Politics in Hamlet, p. 95.
    Rev: B7664.

A1807 Schümmer, K. "Shakespeares Staat." *N. Mon.,* xii (1941), 305-308.

A1808 Stirling, Brents. "Anti-Democracy in Shakespeare." *MLQ,* ii (1941), 487-502.

A1809   Thaler, Alwin. *Shakespeare and Democracy.* Univ. Tennessee Press, 1941. Pp. xii, 312.
        Rev: by Alfred Harbage, *MLN*, LVII (1942), 376-378; by A. H. Carter, *Lib. Quar.*, XII,
        330-332; by G. I. Duthie, *RES*, XVIII, 346-349; by Brents Stirling, *MLQ*, III, 334-337; by
        B. T. Spencer, "Shakespeare, With and Without Tears," *SR*, L, 551-553; by Allardyce Nicoll,
        JEGP, XLI, 380-381; by C. A. Robertson, "Where Did Shakespeare Stand?" *South Atlantic
        Bul.*, VIII (Feb., 1943), 4-5.

A1810   Traversi, D. A. *"Henry V."* *Scrutiny*, IX (1941), 352-374. Also in Eric Bentley, ed., *The
        Importance of Scrutiny.* New York: Stewart, 1948, pp. 120-140.

A1811   Deutschberger, Paul. "Shakspere on Degree: A Study in Backgrounds." *SAB*, XVII (1942),
        200-207.

A1812   Boerner, Oskar. "Zur Frage der Politischen Sonette Shakespeares." *Archiv*, 180 (1942), 9-18.
        Comments upon A1799.

A1813   McCloskey, John C. "Fear of the People as a Minor Motive in Shakspere." *SAB*, XVII (1942),
        67-72.

A1814   Stirling, Brents. "The Social Significance of Elizabethan Drama." *HLQ*, VI (1942-43), 31-33.
        George Sensabaugh comments on Mr. Stirling's papers, ibid., p. 34.

A1815   Wright, Louis B. "Humanistic Education and the Democratic State." *South Atlantic Quar.*,
        XLII (1943), 142-153.
        Emphasis placed on the Renaissance.

A1816   "The Political Wisdom of the English Poets." *Nineteenth Century*, 134 (1943), 1-11.

A1817   Craig, Hardin. "Shakespeare and the Normal World." *Rice Inst. Pamphlet*, XXXI (1944), 1-49.

A1818   Dean, Leonard F. "Shakespeare's Treatment of Conventional Ideas." *SR*, LII (1944), 414-423.
        Argues that Shakespeare's plays are more than dramatic confirmations of conventional beliefs.
        Particularly attacks Spencer's *Shakespeare and the Nature of Man*, A1044.

A1819   Knight, G. Wilson. *The Olive and the Sword: A Study of England's Shakespeare.* Oxford: Univ.
        Press; London: Milford, 1944. Pp. 102.
        Rev: *TLS*, July 29, 1944, p. 369; by W. M. T. Dodds, *MLR*, XXXIX, 423-424; by René
        Pruvost, "Etudes sur Shakespeare," *R. de la Méditerranée*, IV (1947), 615-618.

A1820   Pinto, V. de S. "Shakespeare and the Dictators." *Essays by Divers Hands.* Transactions Royal
        Soc. Lit., XXI, ed. by Walter de la Mare. Oxford Univ. Press, 1945, pp. 82-102.
        "By 'holding the mirror up to Nature', Shakespeare certainly did not mean what we call
        'photographic realism'. His mirror is a magic mirror which shows us the essential quality of
        the things it reflects, 'their form and pressure.' He meant, I think, very much what Aristole
        meant when he defined dramatic poetry as an 'imitation' of Nature. The dramatic poet is to
        give us a convincing picture of what Aristotle calls 'universals', and defines as the way in which
        'a person of a certain type will on occasion speak or act, according to the law of probability
        or necessity'."

A1821   "Shakespeare's Kings." *TLS*, Jan. 6, 1945, p. 6.
        Review of B5072.

A1822   Palmer, John. *Political Characters of Shakespeare.* Macmillan, 1945. Pp. xii, 335.
        Rev: A6550a.

A1823   Ellis-Fermor, Una. *The Frontiers of Drama.* London: Methuen, 1945; New York: Oxford
        Univ. Press, 1946. Pp. vii, 154.
        Chap. III: "Shakespeare's Political Plays."
        Chap. IV: " 'Discord in the Spheres': The Universe of *Troilus and Cressida*."
        Rev: A5941.

A1824   Donatelli, O. G. *The Political Lessons in Shakespeare's English Historical Plays.* MS thesis,
        Columbia University, 1946.

A1825   Lackey, Katharine. *Shakespeare's Political Philosophy.* Master's thesis, University of North
        Carolina, 1944. Abstr. publ. in *University of North Carolina Record, Research in Progress*, Grad.
        School Series, No. 50, 1946, p. 157.

A1826   Laird, John. *Philosophical Incursions into English Literature.* Cambridge Univ. Press, 1946.
        Pp. 223. Chap. I: "Shakespeare on the Wars of England."
        Rev: by H. I'A. F., *MGW*, Jan. 23, 1947, p. 11; by Bonamy Dobrée, *Spectator*, Jan. 3, p. 17;
        N&Q, 192 (1947), 176; by V. de Sola Pinto, *RES*, XXIII, 282-283.

A1827   Muir, Kenneth. *"Timon of Athens* and the Cash-Nexus." *Modern Quar. Miscellany*, No. 1,
        1946.
        Cites Karl Marx: "Shakespeare was one of the spiritual godfathers of the *Communist Manifesto*."

A1828   Speaight, Robert. *Shakespeare and Politics.* The Wedmore Memorial Lecture, May 21, 1946.
        With a Foreword by F. S. Boas. The Royal Society of Literature, 1946. Pp. 20.
        Also in *Essays by Divers Hands: Being the Transactions of the Royal Society of Literature of the
        United Kingdom*, XXIV, NS (Oxford Univ. Press, 1947), 2-20.
        Rev: *TLS*, Oct. 26, 1946, p. 521.

A1829   Campbell, Lily B. *Shakespeare's Histories: Mirrors of Elizabethan Policy.* San Marino, Calif.:
        The Huntington Library, 1947. Pp. xiv, 346.
        Rev: by G. B. Harrison, *PQ*, XXVI (1947), 380-381; *TLS*, Apr. 26, 1947, p. 203, and June 21,

p. 311; see the letter by Miss Campbell, *TLS*, Aug. 9, 1947, p. 403, and reviewer's answer, idem; *N &Q*, 192 (1947), 241; by Conyers Read, *AHR*, LII, 725-727; by M. E. Prior, *MP*, XLV, 135-138; by William Haller, *Pol. Sci. Quar.*, LXII, 477-478; by G. Greever, *Personalist*, XXVIII, 101-102; by W. J. Grace, *Thought*, XXIII (1948), 156-157; by E. M. W. Tillyard, *RES*, XXIV, 153-155; by R. B. Heilman, *MLN*, LXIII, 275-277; by R. G., *TAr*, XXXII, 71-72; by O. J. Campbell, *YR*, XXXVII, 357-360; by M. A. Fitzsimons, *Catholic Hist. Rev.*, XXXIII, 488-489; by F. C. Dietz, *JEGP*, XLVII, 302-303; by R. S. Knox, *UTQ*, XVIII, 94-97; by W. A. Armstrong, *Library*, II, 294-295; by F. L. Baumer, *JMH*, XXI (1949), 57-58; by John E. Hankins, *MLQ*, X, 237-239.

A1830 Muir, Edwin. *The Politics of King Lear.* The Seventh W. P. Ker Memorial Lecture. Glasgow Univ. Pub. No. 72. Glasgow: Jackson, Son & Co., 1947. Pp. 24. Republished in Muir's *Essays on Literature and Society.* London: Hogarth Press, 1949. Pp. 168.
Rev: "Shakespeare's Politics," *TLS*, Dec. 4, 1948, p. 681; *TLS*, June 10, 1949, p. 382; by B. I. Evans, *MGW*, May 26, p. 12; by T. H. Jones, *Life and Letters*, LXIII, 162-164.

A1831 Thiess, F. *Shakespeare und die Idee der Unsterblichkeit.* Dortmund: Schwalvenberg, 1947. Pp. 37.
Rev: A1053.

A1832 Wilson, J. D. "Shakespeare and Humanity." *LanM*, XLI (1947), 264-270.

A1833 Eckhoff, Lorentz. *Shakespeare: Spokesman of the Third Estate.* Oslo Studies in English, No. 3. Tr. by R. I. Christophersen. Oslo, Norway: Akademisk Forlag; Oxford: Basil Blackwell, 1954. Pp. xiv, 201. English transl. of the 2nd ed. of *William Shakespeare*, which was published in Norwegian in 1948. Presented to Dr. Eckhoff on his 70th birthday by colleagues, students, and friends.
"Those who have followed my exposition will recognize that Shakespeare has expressed in play upon play his dissatisfaction with the government of the world, his dissatisfaction with the government of the state; his scepticism with regard to love; his mistrust of passion, of boundless ambition, of unruly energy; his trust in, and approval of, the completely opposite attitude; of level-headedness, of consistency, moderation, impassivity, and balance."—p. 188.
Rev: A941.

A1834 Lambin, Georges. "Shakespeare était-il Essexien?" *LanM*, XLII (1948), 14-22.

A1835 Renner, Ida. *Der Ordnungsgedanke bei Shakespeare mit besonderem Hinblick auf "King Lear."* DD, Münster, 1948. Pp. 114. Typewritten.

A1836 White, David M. "Shakespeare and Psychological Warfare." *Public Opinion Quarterly*, XII (Spring, 1948), 68-72.

A1837 Boxallová, A. M. "Shakespeare a Politika." *Slovesná Věda*, II (1949), 124-125.

A1838 Pope, Elizabeth Marie. "The Renaissance Background of *Measure for Measure*." *ShS*, II (1949), 66-82.
Comment by G. Wilson Knight, *Scrutiny*, XVI (1949), 326-327.

A1839 Hobday, C. H. "The Social Background of *King Lear*." *Modern Quarterly Miscellany*, I (1949), 37-56.

A1840 Waterston, G. Chychele. "Shakespeare and Montaigne: A Footnote to *The Tempest*." *RR*, XL (1949), 165-172.
"The passage selected by Shakespeare is one which epitomizes that part of Montaigne's philosophy which must have made the deepest impression upon Shakespeare's age: his attack upon kingship and his desire to 'execute all things by contraries', contrary, that is, to the hierarchy of the universe which was accepted at that time."—p. 167.

A1841 Mary Alphonsa Carpenter, Sister. *The Tragedy of Richard II: Its Background and Meaning.* DD, University of Illinois, 1950. Pp. 340. Mic A51-55. *Microf. Ab.*, XI (1951), 104. Publication No. 2225.

A1842 Heuer, Hermann. "Der Geist und seine Ordnung bei Shakespeare." *SJ*, 84/86 (1950), 40-63.

A1843 Cancelled.

A1844 Neale, J. E. *The Elizabethan Age.* The Creighton Lecture in History, 1950. London: Athlone Press, for University of London, 1951. Pp. 22.
Rev: A1452.

A1845 Simpson, Lucie. "Is Shakespeare Anti-Democratic?" *The Secondary Heroes of Shakespeare and Other Essays.* London: Kingswood Press, 1950, pp. 63-70.

A1846 Zaal, J. *The Concept of Kingship in Shakespeare's History Plays.* MA thesis, University of London, 1950.

A1847 Bowling, Lawrence E. "The Theme of Natural Order in *The Tempest*." *CE*, XII (1951), 203-209.

A1848 Bruers, Antonio. "La dottrina sociale di Shakespeare." *Osservatore Romano*, 91, No. 254 (1951), 3.

A1849 Campbell, Lily B. "Political Ideas in *Macbeth* IV.iii." *SQ*, II (1951), 281-286.

A1850 Fischer, Walther. "Zur Frage der Staatsauffassung in Shakespeares Königsdramen." *Shakespeare-Studien, Festschrift für Heinrich Mutschmann* (Marburg: Verlag N. G. Elwert), pp. 64-79.

A1851 Hauser, Arnold. *The Social History of Art.* 2 vols. New York: Alfred A. Knopf; London: Routledge, 1951. Pp. xxi, 500; ix, 501-1022.

A1852 Reeg, L. *Shakespeare und die Weltordnung.* Stuttgart: Schröder, 1950.

A1853 Reynolds, George F. "Comedy and the Crisis." *Western Humanities Review,* V (1951), 143-151.

A1854 Blackett, Douglas. "Shakespeare's Views on the Ethical Foundations of Society." *Studien aus dem Inst. f. natur- und geisteswiss. Anthropologie.* Berlin: Dahlem, 1952, pp. 96-107.

A1855 Dean, Leonard F. "Richard II: The State and the Image of the Theatre." *PMLA,* LXVII (1952), 211-218.

A1856 Koenigsberger, Hannelore. *The Untuned String: Shakespeare's Concept of Chaos.* DD, Columbia University, 1951. Pp. 222. *DA,* XII (1952), 66. Publication No. 3353.

A1857 Meurling, P. *Shakespeare.* Stockholm, 1952. Pp. 255.
Emphasizes the influence of political events on Shak.'s plays.
Rev: A549.

A1858 Ribner, Irving. "The Political Problem in Shakespeare's Lancastrian Tetralogy." *SP,* XLIX (1952), 171-184.

A1859 Gilbert, Allan. "Patriotism and Satire in *Henry V.*" Matthews and Emery, eds., *Studies in Shakespeare,* pp. 40-64.

A1860 Reese, Max M. *Shakespeare and the Welfare State.* London: Printed at the London School of Printing and Graphic Arts, 1953. Pp. 34.

A1861 Ribner, Irving. "Political Doctrine in *Macbeth.*" *SQ,* IV (1953), 202-205.

A1862 Uhler, John Earle. "*Julius Caesar:* A Morality of Respublica." Matthews and Emery, eds., *Studies in Shakespeare,* pp. 96-106.

A1863 Kleinstück, Johannes. "The Problem of Order in Shakespeare's Histories." *Neophil,* XXXVIII (1954), 268-277.
Challenges the view that Shak. in his Histories followed the Elizabethan concept, showing horror of rebellion and pointing to its remedies; instead Shak. implies in his own concept a criticism of that order which devotees like Henry IV, Prince John, and the Archbishop of Canterbury in *H. V* use simply as a Machiavellian instrument for gaining personal power.

A1864 Knights, Lionel Charles. *Poetry, Politics and the English Tradition.* London: Chatto and Windus, 1954. Pp. 32.

A1865 Merchant, W. M. "The Status and Person of Majesty." *SJ,* 90 (1954), 285-289.

A1866 Waith, Eugene M. "*Macbeth:* Interpretation versus Adaptation." *Shakespeare: Of an Age and for all Time.* The Yale Shakespeare Festival Lectures, pp. 103-122.

A1867 Borinski, Ludwig. " 'Soldat' und 'Politker' bei Shakespeare und seinen Zeitgenossen." *SJ,* 91 (1955), 87-120.

A1868 Jorgensen, Paul A. "Divided Command in Shakespeare." *PMLA,* LXX (1955), 750-761.

A1869 MacLure, Millar. "Shakespeare and the Lonely Dragon." *UTQ,* XXIV (1955), 109-120.

A1870 Sehrt, Ernst Theodor. *Shakespeare und die Ordnung.* Veröffentlichungen der Schleswig-Holsteinischen Universitätsgesellschaft, N.F. 12. Kiel, 1955.
Rev: by Robert Fricker, *Archiv,* 193 (1956), 60; by J. Kleinstück, *NS,* V (1956), 199.

A1871 Spira, Theodor. "Shakespeares Dichtung und die Welt der Geschichte." *SJ,* 91 (1955), 65-86.

A1872 Cancelled.

A1873 Atkinson, Brooks. "Political Shakespeare." *New York Times,* Oct. 14, 1956, Part IV, p. 2.
Shak. quotations for the presidential campaign.

A1874 Knights, Lionel Charles. "Beyond Politics: An Aspect of Shakespeare's Relation to Tradition." Paper delivered at Stratford. Abstract in *ShN,* VI (1956), 14.

A1875 Ribner, Irving. "Shakespeare and Legendary History: *Lear* and *Cymbeline.*" *SQ,* VII (1956), 47-52.

A1876 Schmitt, Carl. "Hamlet y Jacobo I de Inglaterra (Política y Literatura)." *Revista de Estudios Políticos,* LVI, No. 85 (1956), 59-91.

A1877 Braun, Erich. *Das Legitimitätsprinzip in Shakespeares Königsdramen.* DD, Cologne, 1957. Pp. 149.

A1878 Jaffa, H. V. "Limits of Politics: An Interpretation of *King Lear,* Act. I, Scene I." *American Political Science Review,* LI (1957), 405-427.

A1879 Kantorowicz, Ernest H. "Shakespeare: *King Richard II.*" *The King's Two Bodies: A Study in Medieval Political Theology.* Princeton Univ. Press, 1957, pp. 24-41.

A1880 Knights, L. C. "Shakespeare's Politics: With Some Reflections on the Nature of Tradition." *Proceedings British Academy,* XLIII (1958), 115-119. Also published separately, Oxford Univ. Press, 1958.
Prefers "living tradition" to "background of literature." Shak.'s comments on politics "spring from an insight that is spiritual, moral, and psychological rather than political in any narrow sense."
Rev: *TLS,* July 25, 1958, p. 423.

A1881 Ribner, Irving. "Political Issues in *Julius Caesar.*" *JEGP,* LVI (1957), 10-22.

A1882 Siegel, Paul N. *Shakespearean Tragedy and the Elizabethan Compromise.* New York Univ. Press, 1957. Pp. xvi, 243.

Rev: by G. B. Harrison, *SatR*, Aug. 3, 1957, p. 17; by George Freedley, *Library Journal*, 82 (1957), 1792; *ShN*, VII, 40; *SCN*, XV, 32; by Robert Shedd, *MLN*, LXXIII (1958), 211-214; by Peter G. Phialas, *SQ*, IX, 409-411; by J. R. Brown, *JEGP*, LVII, 335-337; by Bernard Harris, *MLR*, LIII, 563-564; by Reed Whittemore, *Poetry*, 92 (1958), 189-195; by R. M. Wiles, *RN*, XI, 276-277; by G. P. V. Akrigg, *QQ*, LXV, 540-541; *VQR*, XXXIV, No. 2, lxiv-lxv; *Books Abroad*, XXXII, 84; *SR*, LXVI (1958), 330-331; by Aerol Arnold, *Personalist*, XXXIX, 419-420.

A1883 Thaler, Alwin. "Shakespeare and Our World." *Tennessee Studies in Literature*, II (1957), 105-120. Shak.'s message for today on education, government, and religion.

A1884 Knight, G. Wilson. *The Sovereign Flower.* On Shakespeare as the Poet of Royalism together with Related Essays and Indexes [by Patricia M. Ball] to Earlier Volumes. London: Methuen, 1958. Pp. 324.
Rev: *TLS*, Oct. 17, 1958, p. 596; by Eric Gillett, *National and English Rev.*, Oct., 1958, p. 162; by J. I. M. Stewart, *NstN*, Sept. 28, 1958, pp. 390-391.

A1885 McDonnell, Robert Francis. *The "Aspiring Minds": A Study of Shakespearean Characters Who Aspire to Political Sovereignty, against the Background of Literary and Dramatic Tradition.* DD, University of Minnesota, 1958. Pp. 307. Mic 58-7015. *DA*, XIX (1959), 1365-66.

A1886 Markels, Julian. *The Public and Private Worlds of Shakespeare's Roman Plays.* DD, University of Minnesota, 1958. Pp. 289. Mic 58-311. *DA*, XVIII (1958), 221. Publication No. 23,940.

6. THE SOCIAL CLASSES (39,177;15,61)

a. THE SOCIAL CLASSES AND ECONOMIC CONDITIONS IN GENERAL (Selection from the sources of this bibliography.)

(1) ECONOMICS AND THE STRUCTURE OF SOCIETY (176;61)
(a) ECONOMICS

A1887 Massie, Joseph, ed. *Bibliography of the Collections of Books and Tracts on Commerce, Currency, and Poor Law (1557-1763).* Transcribed from Lansdowne MS MXLIX with hist. and bibl. Introd. by William A. Shaw. London: George Harding's Bookshop, Ltd., 1937. Pp. xlii, 173.
Rev: A13.

A1888 Beer, Max. *Early British Economics, from the XIIIth to the Middle of the XVIIIth Century.* London: Allen & Unwin, 1938. Pp. 250.
Rev: *FortnR*, 144 (1938), 119-120; *NstN*, NS, XVI, 224-225; by A. E. Monroe, *AHR*, XLIV (1939), 875-876.

A1889 Beveridge, Sir William. *Prices and Wages in England from the Twelfth to the Nineteenth Century.* Vol. I. London: Longmans, 1939. Pp. 816.
Rev: *TLS*, June 17, 1939, p. 358; by G. D. H. Cole, *NstN*, NS, XVIII, 24; by W. W. Rostow, *JMH*, XII (1940), 91-92; by Herbert Heaton, *AHR*, XLV, 622-623; by N. S. B. Gras, *Amer. Econ. Rev.*, XXX, 139-141; by Shepard B. Clough, *Pol. Sci. Quar.*, LV, 274-277.

A1890 Clark, George Norman. *The Wealth of England from 1496 to 1760.* The Home Univ. Lib. Series. Oxford Univ. Press, 1946. Pp. 199.
Rev: by N. S. B. Gras, *AHR*, LIII (1947), 155-156; by C. R. Fay, *Economic Jour.*, LVII, 350-352; by T. S. Ashton, *Economica*, XIV, 226-227; by W. H. Coates, *Jour. Econ. Hist.*, VII, 232-233; by Honor Croome, *Spectator*, Jan. 10, 1947, pp. 51-52; *NstN*, Jan. 25, 1947, p. 80.

A1891 Clapham, Sir John. *A Concise Economic History of Britain: From the Earliest Times to A.D. 1750.* Cambridge Univ. Press, 1949. Pp. xv, 324.
Rev: by T. S. Ashton, *Spectator*, Dec. 23, 1949, pp. 893-894; *TLS*, Dec. 30, p. 854.

A1892 Johnson, Edgar Augustus Jerome. *Predecessors of Adam Smith: The Growth of British Economic Thought.* New York: Prentice-Hall, 1937. Pp. xii, 426.
Rev: by G. N. C., *EHR*, LIII (1938), 342-343; by E. R. A. Seligman, *AHR*, XLIII, 375-376; by Herbert Heaton, *Jour. Mod. Hist.*, X, 261-262; by J. H. Hollander, *Amer. Econ. Rev.*, XXVIII, 329-330.

A1893 Nef, S. U. "The Progress of Technology and the Growth of Large Scale Industry in Great Britain, 1540-1640." *Econ. Hist. Rev.*, V (1936), 3-24.

A1894 Gay, Edwin F. "Economic Depression, 1603-1660." *HLQ*, V (1942), 193-198.

A1895 Bridgewater, H. "The Value of Money in Queen Elizabeth's Time." *Ba*, XXIX (1945), 66-68.

A1896 Burstein, Sona Rose. "Care of the Aged in England from Medieval Times to the End of the 16th Century." *Bul. Hist. Medicine*, XXII (1948), 738-746.

(b) THE SOCIAL CLASSES GENERALLY

A1897 Martin, Alfred von. *Sociology of the Renaissance.* London: Kegan Paul, 1944. Pp. x, 100. Tr. by Manuel Pedroso as *Sociología del Renacimiento.* Mexico: Fondo de Cultura Económica, 1946. Pp. 164. First published in Germany in 1932.
Rev: *NstN*, Feb. 10, 1945, p. 98; by Frederick E. Welfle, *Catholic Hist. Rev.*, XXXI, 197-198; by Frederic C. Church, *AHR*, LI, 108-109; by E. K. B., *ConR*, 167 (1945), 256; by C. R. Smith, *London Quar. Rev.*, Jan., pp. 91-92. Of Spanish tr.: by José A. Portuondo, *Cuadernos Americanos*, V, No. 5 (1946), 205-208; by Víctor Rico González, *Filosofía y Letras* (Mex.), XII, No. 23, 179-180.

A1898   Trevelyan, G. M. *English Social History. A Survey of Six Centuries, Chaucer to Queen Victoria.*
         New York and London: Longmans, Green & Co., 1942. Pp. 628.
                Rev: by Christopher Morley, "English History and Social Solicitude," *SRL*, XXVI, Feb. 20,
                1943, pp. 9-10; by C. R. Sanders, *South Atlantic Quar.*, XLII, 102-104; by Keith Hutchison,
                Nation (N.Y.), March 13, 1943, pp. 387-388; *TLS*, Aug. 12, 1944, pp. 389, 393; by E. L.
                Woodward, *Spectator*, Aug. 25, p. 176; by D. C. H., *Dalhousie Rev.*, XXIV, 360-361; by
                John Armitage, *FortnR*, NS, 154 (1944), 334-335; by F. J. C. Hearnshaw, *ConR*, 166 (1944),
                380-381.

A1899   Rowse, Alfred Leslie. *The England of Elizabeth: The Structure of Society.* London, Toronto:
         Macmillan, 1950; New York: Macmillan, 1951. Pp. xv, 546.
         Is concerned primarily with the structure of society; to be followed by a 2nd vol. on achieve-
         ments and culture.
                Rev: by J. B. Black, *Spectator*, Dec. 15, 1950, p. 704; *TLS*, Dec. 15, pp. 793-794; by G. M.
                Trevelyan, London *Sun. Times*, Nov. 26, p. 3; by C. V. Wedgwood, *Obs.*, Dec. 10, p. 7;
                by Maurice Ashley, *Listener*, XLIV (1950), 706; by Conyers Read, *William and Mary Quar.*,
                VIII, 458-463; by Alan Bullock, *History Today*, Feb., 1951, pp. 75-76; by J. B. Conacher,
                Canadian Hist. Rev., XXXII, 161-163; by Garrett Mattingly, *SRL*, July 28, 1951, pp. 8-9; *N &Q*,
                196 (1951), 86-87; by H. R. Trevor-Roper, *NstN*, Jan. 13, pp. 42-43; by Alfred Harbage,
                Nation (N. Y.), June 16, pp. 567-568; by Samuel C. Chew, *NYHTBR*, June 24, p. 6; by
                R. H. Tawney, *MGW*, March 15, p. 11; by Theodore Roscoe, *ConR*, 179 (1951), 253-254;
                SQ, II, 175-176; by Paul Goodman, *KR*, XIII, 714-719; by C. F. B., *Dalhousie Rev.*, XXXI, 2,
                xvii; by Thomas Caldecot Chubb, *NYTBR*, July 8, 1951, p. 4; by Jack Simmons, *National &
                Eng. Rev.*, 136 (1951), 44-45; *TC*, 149 (1951), 79; by Millar MacLure, *UTQ*, XXI, 90-93; by
                Louis B. Wright, *AHR*, LVII, 125-126; by Gladys Scott Thomson, *EHR*, LXVI, 589-592;
                Dublin Mag., XXVI, 51-52; by Hubert Dauphin, *RHE*, XLVI, 285-286; by William B. Hamil-
                ton, *South Atlantic Quar.*, LI (1952), 142-145; by J. E. Neale, *History*, XXXVII, 58-59.

A1900   Neale, J. E. *The Elizabethan Age.* The Creighton Lecture in History, 1950. London: Athlone
         Press, for University of London, 1951. Pp. 22.

A1900a   Rowse, A. L. *An Elizabethan Garland.* London: Macmillan, 1953. Pp. viii, 162.
                Rev: *TLS*, Oct. 23, 1953, p. 675; by C. V. Wedgwood, *Time and Tide*, Oct. 31, pp. 1425-26;
                by Virgil B. Heltzel, *SQ*, VI (1955), 98; by Hermann Heuer, *SJ*, 91 (1955), 315.

A1901   Notestein, Wallace. *The English People on the Eve of Colonization, 1603-1630.* New York:
         Harper; London: Hamish Hamilton, 1954. Pp. xvii, 302.
                Rev: by H. Heuer, *SJ*, 91 (1955), 314-315; by J. P. Cooper, *YR*, XLIV, 464-466.

A1902   Rowse, A. L. *The Expansion of Elizabethan England.* London: Macmillan; New York:
         St. Martins Press, 1955. Pp. 450.
                Rev: by Jack Simmons, *Time and Tide*, Oct. 8, 1955, pp. 1295-96; by Philip Magnus,
                Spectator, Oct. 28, pp. 560-561; *History Today*, V, 876-877; by Sir John Squire, *Illus. London
                News*, Oct. 29, p. 726; by Michael Howard, *NstN*, Nov. 12, pp. 632-633; by Robert L.
                Schuyler, *NYTBR*, Dec. 18, p. 6; *TLS*, Oct. 28, pp. 629, 631; by S. C. Chew, *NYHTBR*,
                Nov. 13, p. 6; by Caroline Robbins, *RN*, VIII, 217-219; by E. E. Rich, *Cambridge Hist. Jour.*,
                XII (1956), 94-97; by Robert Blackburn, *ConR*, No. 1083, Mar., pp. 188-189; by Davis Harris
                Willson, *AHR*, LXI, 627-628; by J. A. Williamson, *EHR*, LXXII, 284-286; by Hermann Heuer,
                SJ, 92 (1956), 357-358; by L. M., *Books and Bookmen*, I, No. 4, Jan., p. 30 (brief); by George
                P. Rice, Jr., *QJS*, XLII, 191-192; by J. B. Conacher, *Canadian Hist. Rev.*, XXXVII, 280-282.

A1903   Clair, Colin. *Shakespeare's England: The England of the Poets.* By C. L. R. Nicolai (pseudonym).
         London: Watford, Herts, Bruce and Gawthorn, 1957. Pp. 64.

A1904   Williamson, Hugh Ross. *The Day Shakespeare Died.* London, 1958.
         A panoramic reconstruction of English life in 1616.

A1905   Sherwin, Oscar. " 'All That Glisters Is Not Gold': A Devaluation of the Elizabethan Age."
         Amer. Jour. of Econ. and Sociology, VI (1947), 387-399, 549-560.
         Sections upon "The Land" [Enclosures], "The Rogue," and "The Plague."

i. Upper Classes

A1906   Stone, Laurence. "The Anatomy of the Elizabethan Aristocracy." *The Economic Hist. Rev.*,
         XVIII (1948), 1-53.

A1907   Finch, Mary E. *The Wealth of Five Northamptonshire Families, 1540-1640.* Publs. Northampton-
         shire Rec. Soc., XIX. Northampton: The Society, 1956. Pp. xx, 246.
                Rev: by J. P. Cooper, *Jour. Ecclesias. Hist.*, VIII (1957), 252-253; by Perez Zagorin, *Jour.
                Econ. Hist.*, XVIII (1958), 202-204; by G. W. Hoskins, *Econ. Hist. Rev.*, XI, 163-164.

A1908   Ross, Dorothy. "Class Privilege in Seventeenth Century England." *History*, XXVIII (1943),
         148-155.

ii. Middle Classes

A1909   Wright, Louis B. *Middle-class Culture in Elizabethan England.* Univ. of North Carolina Press,
         1935. Pp. xiv, 733. Reprinted, Cornell Univ. Press, 1958.
                Rev: by W. A. Neilson, *Nation* (N.Y.), 141 (1935), 25-26; *London Mercury*, XXXII, 612; by
                E. P. Cheyney, *AHR*, XLI (1936), 530-532; by M. M. Knappen, *JMH*, VIII, 101-102; by

Warner G. Rice, *JEGP*, xxxv, 427-429; *TAr*, xx, 166; by W. M. Dodd, *QR*, 266 (1936), 272-284; by W. T. Laprade, *VQR*, xII, 146-150; by E. A. Strathmann, *Library Jour.*, lI, 154; by K. Brunner, *HZ*, 154 (1936), 166-168; by D. S. Staines, *SR*, xLV (1937), 234-237; by Franz Grosse, *Beiblatt*, xLVIII, 171-176; by R. B. Werham, *History*, NS, xxII, 166-168; by Floris Delattre, *EA*, i, 246-247; by J. E. N., *EHR*, lII, 159-160; by M. St. C. Byrne, *MLN*, lIII (1938), 212-214; by E. R. Adair, *ES*, xx, 36-38; by L. C. Knights, *Scrutiny*, vI, 341-347; by C. Bowie Millican, *RES*, xvI (1940), 84-87.

A1910   Cancelled.

A1911   Laski, Harold J. *The Rise of European Liberalism.* London: Allen & Unwin, 1936. Pp. 287.
        Rev: "The Background of Liberalism: Emergence of the Middle Class," *TLS*, May 30, 1936, pp. 445-446; by J. L. Hammond, "The Liberal Past," *Spectator*, May 22, p. 939.

iii.   Lower Classes

A1912   Campbell, Mildred. *The English Yeoman Under Elizabeth and the Early Stuarts.* Yale Hist. Publs., xIV. Yale Univ. Press, 1942. Pp. xiii, 453.
        Rev: by Conyers Read, *AHR*, xLVIII (1943), 777-779; by R. E. Roberts, "English History and Social Solicitude," *SRL*, xxVI (Feb. 20, 1943), 9; by Fulmer Mood, *JMH*, xv, 318-319; "The English Yeoman," *TLS*, 1944, p. 361; by J. P. Hennessy, *NstN*, July 1, 1944, pp. 13-14; by G. E. Fussell, *Econ. Jour.*, lIV, 103-106; by W. G. Hoskins, *Econ. Hist. Rev.*, xIV, 193-196; by R. V. L., *EHR*, lX (1945), 126-127; by A. M. C. Latham, *Life and Letters*, xLVIII, 126-127.

A1913   Fussell, G. E. *The English Rural Labourer: His Home, Furniture, Clothing and Food from Tudor to Victorian Times.* London: Batchworth Press, 1949. Pp. viii, 160.

A1914   Steinbicker, C. R. *Poor-relief in the Sixteenth Century.* DD, Catholic University of America, 1937. Washington, 1937. Pp. xxxi, 272.
        Rev: by Conyers Read, *AHR*, xLIII (1938), 673.

A1915   Trehern, E. M. " 'Dear, They Durst Not' . . . Notes on an Elizabethan Commonplace." *English*, x (1954), 59-60.
        On the fear of conspirators to murder the deposed because of popular favor toward the latter. Cites five such passages.

iv.   Literary Reflections

A1916   Wheeler, Harold Peyton. *Studies in Sixteenth Century English Literature of Rustic Life.* DD, University of Illinois, 1938.

A1917   Wells, Henry W. "A Mirror of National Integration: A New Summary of Four Decades of the English Theatre [1550-1590]." *SAB*, xVIII (1943), 30-40.
        The efflorescence of drama in the eighties was due to the assimilation of earlier experiments to a democratic outlook that embraced the interests and tastes of all classes. The turning point is the organization of the Queen's men in 1583.

A1918   Saunders, J. W. "The Façade of Morality." *ELH*, xIX (1952), 81-114.
        On the impact of middle-class morality upon 16th-century poetry, with particular reference to Spenser.

A1919   Thomas, Lewis Ralph. *Jacobean Comedy Examined in the Light of Marxian Principles.* MA thesis, Dalhousie University, 1952.

A1920   Knights, L. C. *Aspects of the Economical and Social Background of Comedy in the Early 17th Century.* MS thesis, Cambridge, 1936.

A1921   Long, Dorothy R. *The Middle Class: Its Treatment in Early Seventeenth Century English Drama.* DD, University of Texas, 1941.

(2)   ECONOMIC AND SOCIAL PROTEST
(a)   GENERAL

A1922   Dunham, William Huse, Jr., and Stanley M. Pargellis, eds. *Complaint and Reform in England 1436-1714: Fifty Writings of the Time on Politics, Religion, Society, Economics, Architecture, Science, and Education.* New York: Oxford Univ. Press, 1938. Pp. xxxv, 925; pl.
        Rev: A1668.

A1923   "Thomas Dekker and the Underdog. The Compassionate Realist: From Pamphlet Prose to Lyric Beauty." *TLS*, May 31, 1941, p. 262.

A1924   Sandison, Helen E. "An Elizabethan Economist's Method of Literary Composition." *HLQ*, vI (1943), 205-211.
        Gerard de Malynes: "Malynes' concern for the poor, evidenced in various pamphlets and projects, partakes somewhat of More's resentment at the conspiracy of rich men for their own commodity."

A1925   Milligan, Burton. "Satire Concerning the Ale and Wine Trades in the Shakespearian Period and Later." *SAB*, xVIII (1943), 147-155.

A1926   White, Helen C. *Social Criticism in Popular Religious Literature of the Sixteenth Century.* New York: Macmillan, 1944. Pp. xii, 330.
        A major contribution.
        Rev: A1702.

A1927 Zeeveld, W. Gordon. "Social Equalitarianism in a Tudor Crisis." *JHI*, VII (1946), 35-55.
A1928 Mackerness, E. D. "Thomas Deloney and the Virtuous Proletariat." *CamJ*, V (1951), 34-50.
A1929 Fuz, J. K. *Welfare Economics in English Utopias.* The Hague: Martinus Nijhoff, 1952. Pp. viii, 113.
    Rev: by J. E. C. H., *EHR*, LXVII (1952), 603-605; *TLS*, Jan. 2, 1953, p. 5; by J. F. Bell, *Econ. Jour.*, LXIII, 705-706; by Paul Marcel Glaude, *Books Abroad*, XXVII, 310.
A1930 Blum, Irving D. *Avarice in English Utopias and Satires from 1551 to 1714.* DD, Rutgers University, 1953.
A1931 Elton, G. R. "An Early Tudor Poor Law." *Econ. Hist. Rev.*, VI (1953), 55-67.
    Discusses the discarded draft of the poor law which was composed in the Autumn of 1535 and which displays "vastly greater scope, ingenuity and originality" than the act of 1536.
A1932 Abernethy, Francis Edward. *Popular Literature and Social Protest, 1485-1558.* DD, Louisiana State University, 1957. Pp. 226. Mic 57-983. *DA*, XVII (1957), 619. Publication No. 17,433.

(b) FASHIONS AND THE PARVENU
See also English Ideal of a Gentleman, A4537-A4562.

A1933 Howard, Edwin J., ed. *Pleasant Quippes for Vpstart Newfangled Gentlewomen.* Oxford, Ohio: The Anchor Press, 1942. Pp. xx, 5-22.
    A page-for-page reprint of the 1595 edition of this satirical poem, sometimes attributed to Stephen Gosson.
    Rev: *TLS*, May 8, 1943, p. 228; by M. A. Shaaber, *MLQ*, IV, 508-509; by Katherine Koller, *MLN*, LIX (1944), 428-429.
A1934 Mason, John E. *Gentlefolk in the Making: Studies in the History of English Courtesy Literature and Related Topics from 1531 to 1774.* Univ. of Pennsylvania Press, 1935. Pp. xiv, 394; il.
    Rev: by C. D. A., *SRL*, July 20, 1935, pp. 19, 22; by S. A. T., *SAB*, X, 175-176; *TLS*, Sept. 19, p. 557; by Virgil B. Heltzel, *MP*, XXXIV (1936), 204-205; by M. C. Pitman, *MLR*, XXXI, 261-262; by Ruth Kelso, *JEGP*, XXXV, 285-286; by John W. Draper, *RES*, XII, 350-351; by W. L. Ustick, *MLN*, LII (1937), 593-596; by F. Grosse, *Beiblatt*, XLVIII, 134.
A1935 Kelso, Ruth. *Doctrine for the Lady of the Renaissance.* Urbana: Univ. of Illinois Press, 1956. Pp. xi, 475.
    Rev: by C. A. Meyer, *BHR*, XVIII (1956), 462-464; by W. L. Wiley, *RR*, XLVII, 301-303; *N&Q*, NS, III, 458; by Kitty W. Scoular, *ES*, XXXVIII (1957), 272-273; by Anna T. Sheedy, *Cath. Hist. Rev.*, XLII, 513-514; by Harold S. Wilson, *MP*, LV, 55-57; by K. Sneyder de Vogel, *Neophil*, XLI, 318-319; by C. V. Auburn, *BH*, LIX, 238-240 (brief); by F. Pierce, *BHS*, XXXIV, 49-50; by Ernest W. Nelson, *AHR*, LXII, 381-382; by Karl Brunner, *Anglia*, LXXV, 245-247; by M. Poirier, *EA*, X, 50-51; by Carroll Camden, *JEGP*, LVI, 126-131; by M. C. Bradbrook, *MLR*, LII, 411-412; by G. D. Willcock, *RES*, IX (1958), 186-187; by O. H. Green, *HR*, XXVI, 71-75; by Elizabeth Armstrong, *French Studies*, XII, 64-65; by Ramond Lebègue, *RLC*, XXX, 111-114; by Marc J. Bensimon, *Romance Philol.*, XI, 317-320; by E. Garin, *Giornale italiano di filologia*, X, 82-85.
A1936 Fisher, F. J. "The Development of London as a Centre of Conspicuous Consumption in the Sixteenth and Seventeenth Centuries." *Trans. Royal Hist. Soc.*, XXX (1948), 37-50.
A1937 Josephson, L. "Adeln i Renässansens Litteratur." *Edda*, XLIX (1949), 179-228.
A1938 Norris, Herbert. *Costume and Fashion.* Vol. III: The Tudor Period; Book 1: 1485-1547; Book 2: 1547-1603. Ill. by the author. London: Dent, 1938; New York: Dutton, 1939. Pp. 864.
    Rev: *TLS*, Jan. 7, 1939, p. 13.
A1939 Wilson, F. P. "The Funeral Obsequies of Sir All-in-New-Fashions." *ShS*, XI (1958), 98-99.

b. SHAKESPEARE AND SOCIO-ECONOMIC CONDITIONS (-;18)
(1) GENERAL

A1940 Knights, L. C. "Shakespeare and Profit Inflations. Notes for the Historian of Culture." *Scrutiny*, V (1936), 48-60.
A1941 Herzig, P. "Shakespeare als Klassenkämpfer." *Neue Zürcher Ztg.*, 1935, No. 2207.
A1942 Tannenbaum, Samuel A. "Shakspere an Anti-Semite?" *SAB*, XIX (1944), 47-48.
A1943 Wilson, J. D. "Shakespeare and Humanity." *LanM*, XLI (1947), 264-270.
A1944 Hahn, Herbert. "Über die Menschlichkeit bei Shakespeare." *Die Kommenden*, III, iv (1949), 6.
A1945 Danby, John F. *Shakespeare's Doctrine of Nature: A Study of "King Lear".* London: Faber and Faber, 1949. Pp. 234.
    Comment by G. Wilson Knight in *Scrutiny*, XVI (1949), 325.
    Rev: A934.
A1946 Fort, Joseph B. "Quelques Problèmes Shakespeariens: L'Homme, le Texte, la 'Sagesse Pourpre'." *LanM*, Nov., 1950, pp. 38-41.
    A critical examination of Danby's *Shakespeare's Doctrine of Nature*, A1945, among others.
A1947 Meyer, Justus. "Shakespeares Sociologie." *Vlam*, June 9, 1951.
A1948 Hoskins, Frank Lawrence, Jr. *Master-Servant Relations in Tudor and Early Stuart Literature*:

With Special Reference to the Drama of Shakespeare and his Contemporaries. DD, Columbia University, 1955. Pp. 294. Mic A55-1832. *DA*, xv (1955), 1387. Publication No. 12,440. Shak. section, pp. 63-121.

A1949   Siegel, Paul N. *Shakespearean Tragedy and the Elizabethan Compromise.* New York Univ. Press, 1957.
        Rev: A1882.

A1950   Kolmer, Herbert. *Die Entwicklung des sozialen Bewusstseins W. Shakespeares aus einer Analyse seiner Werke.* DD, Vienna, 1956. Pp. 150. Typewritten.

(2)   UPPER CLASSES (Arranged by "degree".)
See also Social Types, A6747-A6764.

A1951   Schirmer, Walter F. *Glück und Ende der Königinen Shakespeares Historien.* Arbeitsgemeinschaft für Forschung des Landes Nordrhein Westfalen, Heft 22. Cologne: Westdeutscher Verlag, 1954. Pp. 18.

A1952   Mettin, H. C. "Shakespeares Fürstenspiegel." *Die Tat*, xxviii (1937), 816-828.

A1953   Watson, Curtis B. "Shakspere's Dukes." *SAB*, xvi (1941), 33-41.

A1954   Stevenson, Robert. "Shakespeare's Cardinals and Bishops." *Crozer Quar.*, xxvii (1950), 116-138.

A1955   Mettin, Hermann Christian. "Die Bedeutung des Adels bei Shakespeare." *Deut. Adelsblatt*, lv (1937), 994-996.

A1956   Schneider, Reinhold. "Das Bild der Herrschaft in Shakespeares Drama." *SJ*, 93 (1957), 9-37. Earlier version: *Prisma* (Bochum), 1955/56, pp. 113-115.

A1957   Draper, John W. "Falstaff's Robin and Other Pages." *SP*, xxxvi (1939), 476-490.

(3)   MIDDLE CLASSES
See also Social Types, A6765-A6777.

A1958   Murry, John Middleton. *Heaven—and Earth.* London: Cape, 1938. Pp. 318.
        Chap. VI: "Shakespeare: Religion and the Middle Class," pp. 81-91.
        Rev: A1791.

A1958a Daniels, R. Balfour. "Shakspere and the Puritans." *SAB*, xiii (1938), 40-53.

A1959   Awad, Lewis Hanna Khalil. *The Theory and Practice of "Poetic Diction" in English, with Reference to the Same in Arabic and French.* M. Litt. thesis, Cambridge. Abstr. in *Cam Abs.*, 1942-43, p. 26. Shakespeare's diction represents a rising and progressive bourgeoisie.

A1960   Muir, Kenneth. "*Timon of Athens* and the Cash-Nexus." *Modern Quarterly Miscellany*, No. 1, 1946.
        Cites Karl Marx: "Shakespeare was one of the spiritual godfathers of the *Communist Manifesto.*" —*Das Kapital.*

A1961   Brunner, Karl. "Middle-Class Attitudes in Shakespeare's Histories." *ShS*, vi (1953), 36-38.

A1962   Marković, Vida. "The Social and Economic Background of Shakespeare's Characters in the *Merchant of Venice.*" *Zbornik Filozofskog Fakulteta* (Belgrade), ii (1952), 383-403.

(4)   LOWER CLASSES
See also Scenes, A6216-A6268, and
Character Types, A6594-A6818.

A1963   Wood, F. T. "Shakespeare and the Plebs." *Essays and Studies*, xviii (1933), 53-73.
        (In Ebisch and Schücking Supplement, p. 15.)
        Rev: by Ed. Eckhardt, *DLZ*, lvii (1936), 670-671.

A1964   Ringeling, Gerhard. "Shakespeare und der Landmensch." *Zeitwende*, xiv (1937-38), 739-746.

A1965   Murphy, George H. *Shakespeare and the Ordinary Man.* With a foreword by Sir Joseph Chisholm. Toronto: Ryerson Press, 1939. Pp. x, 41.

A1966   Ewen, C. L'Estrange. *Shakespeare and Seamen.* London: Author, 1939.

A1967   McCloskey, John C. "Fear of the People as a Minor Motive in Shakespeare." *SAB*, xvii (1942), 67-72.

A1968   Stirling, Brents. "Shakespeare's Mob Scenes: A Reinterpretation." *HLQ*, viii (1945), 213-240.

A1969   Watkins, W. B. C. "Shakespeare and the Populace." *SR*, liv (1946), 548-551.

A1970   Eckhoff, Lorentz. *Shakespeare: Spokesman of the Third Estate.* Oslo Studies in English, No. 3. Tr. by R. I. Christophersen. Oxford: Basil Blackwell; Oslo, Norway: Akademisk Forlag, 1954. Pp. xiv, 201.
        Rev: A941.

A1971   Shanker, Sidney. "Some Clues for *Coriolanus.*" *SAB*, xxiv (1949), 209-213.
        Clues about attitudes to the poor during the grain riots of 1607-08.

A1972   Stirling, Brents. *The Populace in Shakespeare.* Columbia University Press, 1949. Pp. 203.
        Rev: A6219.

A1973   Pervas, D. "Šekspirov stav prema narodu." *Naša reč*, Jan., 1950, pp. 50-64.

A1974   Reese, Max M. *Shakespeare and the Welfare State.* London: Printed at the London School of
        Printing and Graphic Arts, 1953. Pp. 34.

A1975   Kaieda, Susumu. "The Mob in Shakespearian Plays" (in Japanese). *Tokyo Univ. of Foreign
        Studies Journal,* Nov., 1956.

A1976   Schlösser, Anselm. "Zur Frage 'Volk und Mob' bei Shakespeare." *ZAA,* IV (1956), 148-171.

7. THE LAW (39,181;15,-)
a. GENERAL ITEMS
(Comprehensiveness limited to that of the sources of this bibliography.)

A1977   Massie, Joseph, ed. *Bibliography of the Collections of Books and Tracts on Commerce, Currency,
        and Poor Law (1557-1763).* Transcribed from Lansdowne MS MXLIX with hist. and bibl.
        Intro. by William A. Shaw. London: George Harding's Bookshop, Ltd., 1937. Pp. xlii, 173.
        Rev: A13.

A1978   Cecil, William. *Execution of Justice in England (1583).* Ed. by F. Baumer. With introduction
        and bibliographical note. New York: Scholars' Facsimiles and Reprints, 1938. Pp. xiv, 40.

A1979   Mosse, George L. "Change and Continuity in the Tudor Constitution." *Speculum,* XXII
        (1947), 18-28.

A1979a Lacy, Edgar W. "The Relation of Property and Dominion to the Law of Nature." *Speculum,*
        XXIV (1949), 407-409.
        Explains and qualifies Mr. Mosse's remark about Fortesque's conception of property, A1979.

A1980   Hastings, Margaret. *The Court of Common Pleas in Fifteenth Century England: A Study of Legal
        Administration and Procedure.* Publ. for Amer. Hist. Assoc., Cornell Univ. Press, 1947. Oxford
        Univ. Press, 1948. Pp. xviii, 302, pl. 4.
        Rev: by G. L. Haskins, *Speculum,* XXIII (1948), 701-704; by Richard A. Newhall, *AHR,*
        LIII, 800-801; by W. B. Hamilton, *South Atlantic Quar.,* XLVIII (1949), 290-291; by S. B.
        Chrimes, *EHR,* LXIV, 249-251; by G. O. Sayles, *Medium Aevum,* XVIII, 74-75.

A1981   Eusden, John Dykstra. *Puritans, Lawyers, and Politics in Early Seventeenth Century England.*
        Yale Studies in Religious Educ., XXIII. New Haven: Yale Univ. Press, 1958. Pp. xii, 238.
        Rev: by George L. Mosse, *AHR,* LXIV (1958), 150-151.

A1982   Stone, Margaret. "AYTOXEIPIA: A Sixteenth Century Lawyer on Suicide." *Bul. Hist.
        Medicine,* XIV (1943), 173-180.
        An English version of the summation made in 1592 by the French Advocate General concern-
        ing the case of William Coffin, which involved witchcraft, madness, murder, and suicide.

A1983   Ullmann, W. "The Right of Asylum in Sixteenth Century Theory and Practice." *Dublin Rev.,*
        Oct., 1944, pp. 103-110.

(1) LAW AND LANGUAGE

A1984   Bond, Donald F. "The Law and Lawyers in English Proverbs." *American Bar Association
        Journal,* XXI (1935), 724-727.

A1985   Bond, Donald F. "English Legal Proverbs." *PMLA,* LI (1936), 921-935.
        Cites "Peoples' voice is God's voice" from the 9th century on.

A1986   Woodbine, George. "The Language of English Law." *Speculum,* XVIII (1943), 395-436.

A1987   Schoeck, R. J. "Rhetoric and Law in Sixteenth Century England." *SP,* L (1953), 110-127.
        Discusses the meeting of the traditions of law and rhetoric, principally in the treatises of
        Sir Thomas Elyot, Sir Thomas Wilson, John Ferne, Abraham Fraunce, and Sir Edward Coke.

A1988   Bland, D. S. "Rhetoric and the Law Student in Sixteenth Century England." *SP,* LIV (1957),
        498-508.

b. SHAKESPEARE AND LAW
(1) GENERAL STUDIES

A1989   Chambrun, Clara Longworth, Comtesse de. "Shakespeare Under the Elizabethan Statutes."
        Dublin Rev., 198 (1937), 84-98.

A1990   Wears, T. M. "Shakespeare's Legal Acquirements." *Canadian Bar Rev.,* Jan., 1938, pp. 28-42.

A1991   Wigmore, J. H. "Shakespeare's Legal Documents." *American Bar Association Journal,*
        XXVIII (1942), 134.

A1992   Calvin, W. W. "Shakespeare and the Law." *Case and Comment,* LI (1946), 6-8.

A1993   Watts, P. R. "Shakespeare's 'Double' Purchase of New Place." *Australian Law Journal,*
        XX (1947), 330-336.

A1994   Young, George Malcolm. *Shakespeare and the Termers.* Annual Shakespeare Lecture of the
        British Academy, 1947. *Proceedings of the British Academy,* XXXIII (1947). Oxford Univ. Press,
        1948. Pp. 19.
        Rev: "The Dyer's Hand," *TLS,* March 20, 1948, p. 163; by C. J. Sisson, *MLR,* XLIII (1948),
        436-437.

A1995   Norman, C. H. "Shakespeare and the Law." *TLS,* June 30, 1950, p. 412.
        See the letters by D. Somervell, *TLS,* July 21, 1950, p. 453; by C. H. Norman, ibid., Aug. 4,

p. 485. Mr. Norman calls attention to two cases in Plowden's *Law Reports*, the arguments of which he believes to be reflected in *Hamlet*, in order to argue against the identification of "Shakespeare, the actor" and "Shakespeare, the playwright"; Mr. Somervell objects; rejoinder by Mr. Norman.

A1996   Axelrad, A. José. "Un Point de Droit Elizabéthain sur la Scène Dramatique." *Revue du Nord*, XXXVI (1954), 195-200.
On marriage contracts and precontract conjugal rights.

A1997   Frye, Roland Mushat. "Shakespeare's 'Second Best Bed' and a Contemporary Parallel." *N &Q*, NS, I (1954), 468-469.
Comment ibid., K. B. Danks, II (1955), 227.

(2) LAW IN LITERATURE

A1998   Ransom, Harry. "Some Legal Elements in Elizabethan Plays." *TxSE*, XVI (1936), 53-76.

A1999   Davis, Cushman K. *The Law in Shakespeare*. Washington, D. C.: Washington Law Book Co., 1941. Pp. 303. First published 1883.

A2000   Clarkson, Paul S., and Clyde T. Warren. *The Law of Property in Shakespeare and the Elizabethan Drama*. Johns Hopkins Press, 1942. London: Milford, 1943. Pp. xxvii, 346. Tabulation of dramatic references, pp. 302-330.
Rev: by T. W. Baldwin, *MLQ*, IV (1943), 242-243; *TLS*, May 5, p. 238; by Leslie Hotson, *JEGP*, XLII, 436-440; by Tucker Brooke, *MLN*, LVIII, 310-312; by G. B. Harrison, *RES*, XX (1944), 250; by G. E. Bentley, *MP*, XLII (1945), 193-194.

A2001   Draper, John W. "Dogberry's Due Process of Law." *JEGP*, XLII (1943), 563-576.

A2002   Youel, Donald B. *The Idea of Law in English Literary Criticism: Sixteenth and Seventeenth Centuries*. DD, State University of Iowa, 1945. Abstr. in Univ. Iowa, *Programs Announcing Candidates for Higher Degrees, 1944*. Unpaged.

A2003   Polak, Alfred Laurence. *More Legal Fictions: A Series of Cases from Shakespeare*. London: Stevens, 1946. Pp. 134.

A2004   Harding, Davis P. "Elizabethan Betrothals and *Measure for Measure*." *JEGP*, XLIX (1950), 139-158.
Distinguishes between the legal and moral status of the Elizabethan *de praesenti* nuptial contract. Asserts, however, that an Elizabethan audience would not have been morally repelled by the "bed-trick" or the inconsistency in the actions of the Duke and Isabella.

A2005   Marder, Louis. "Law in Shakespeare." *Renaissance Papers* (University of South Carolina), 1954, pp. 40-44.

A2006   Windolph, Francis Lyman. *Reflections of the Law in Literature*. Univ. of Pennsylvania Press, 1956. "Shakespeare and the Law," pp. 35-58.
Rev: by Albrecht B. Strauss, *Books Abroad*, XXXI (1957), 311-312.

8. NATURE AND SCIENCE (40;16)
a. SCIENCE IN CONTEMPORANEOUS EUROPE
(Compiled from the specified literary sources; not more comprehensive than the source. See initial items below for comprehensive listings.)
(1) BIBLIOGRAPHY

A2007   International Committee of Historical Sciences. *International Bibliography of Historical Sciences*.

I, 1926, publ. 1930	XIII, 1938, publ. 1941
II, 1927, publ. 1932	XIV, 1939, publ. 1942
III, 1928, publ. 1933	XV, 1940-46, Not publ. to date
IV, 1929, publ. 1933	XVI, 1947, publ. 1949
V, 1930, publ. 1934	XVII, 1948, publ. 1950
VI, 1931, publ. 1936	XVIII, 1949, publ. 1951
VII, 1932, publ. 1934	XIX, 1950, publ. 1952
VIII, 1933, publ. 1935	XX, 1951, publ. 1953
IX, 1934, publ. 1936	XXI, 1952, publ. 1954
X, 1935, publ. 1938	XXII, 1953, publ. 1955
XI, 1936, publ. 1938	XXIII, 1954, publ. 1956
XII, 1937, publ. 1939	XXIV, 1955, publ. 1957

XXV, 1956, publ. 1958

A2008   *Isis*. "Critical Bibliography of the History of Science and of the History of Civilization." *Isis*, successive issues. Sometimes entitled "Critical Bibliography of the History and Philosophy of Science and of the History of Civilization," and sometimes numbered, and dated, e.g., "Seventy-first Critical Bibliography of the History and Philosophy of Science and of the History of Civilization (to October 1947)."

(2) HISTORY AND PHILOSOPHY OF SCIENCE
(Reserved for general accounts extending beyond 1300-1700.)

A2009   Chalmers, Gordon Keith. "Three Terms of the Corpuscularian Philosophy." *MP*, XXXIII (1936), 243-260.

A2010   Taylor, F. Sherwood. *A Short History of Science.* London: Heinemann, 1938. Pp. xiv, 320.
        Rev: *TLS,* Jan. 21, 1939, p. 47.
A2011   Partington, J. R. "The Origins of the Atomic Theory." *Annals of Science,* IV (1939), 245-282.
A2012   Pledge, H. T. *Science Since 1500: A Short History of Mathematics, Physics, Chemistry, Biology.*
        London: H. M. Stationery Office, 1939. Pp. 357.
        Rev: *TLS,* Feb. 10, 1940, p. 69.
A2013   Wellmuth, John. *The Nature and Origins of Scientism.* The Aquinas Lecture, 1944. Milwaukee,
        1944. Pp. 60.
        Rev: by J. R. Cresswell, *Philosophical Rev.,* LV (1946), 203-204.
A2014   Collingwood, R. G. *The Idea of Nature.* Oxford: Clarendon Press, 1945. Pp. viii, 183.
        Rev: by A. E. Murphy, *Philosophical Rev.,* LV (1946), 199-202; by C. C. J. Webb, *Hibbert
        Jour.,* XLV, 83-86.
A2015   Crombie, A. C. "Discovery in Medieval Science and Its Contribution to the Scientific Revolu-
        tion." *CamJ,* I (1947), 56-66.
        Sketches the medieval background out of which grew the "so-called Scientific Revolution of
        the sixteenth and seventeenth" centuries.
A2016   Jeans, Sir James. *The Growth of Physical Science.* New York: Macmillan, 1947. Pp. x, 364.
        Rev: by A. C. C., *CamJ,* I (1947), 138; by Ernest Nagel, *NYTBR,* March 14, 1948, p. 4;
        by J. K. R., *QQ,* LV, 94-95; by P. N. Powers, *Scientific Monthly,* LXVII, 70; by W. J. Archibald,
        Dalhousie Rev., XXVIII, 198-199; by F. S. Hogg, *UTQ,* XVIII, 110-112.
A2017   Eliphas, Levi. *The History of Magic: Including a Clear and Precise Exposition of its Procedure, its
        Rites and its Mysteries.* Tr. with Preface and Notes by Arthur Edward White. New York:
        Rider, 1948. Pp. 384.
        Fourth ed. of work publ. in 1913.
A2018   Sarton, George. *The Life of Science: Essays in the History of Civilization.* Foreword by Max H.
        Fisch. Life of Science Lib. New York: Henry Schuman, 1948. Pp. vii, 197.
        Rev: by William Beebe, *NYHTBR,* Dec. 5, 1948, p. 22.
A2019   Sarton, George. *Horus: A Guide to the History of Science.* A First Guide for the Study of the
        History of Science. With Introductory Essays on Science and Tradition. Waltham, Mass.:
        Chronica Botanica Co., 1952. Pp. xvii, 316.
        Rev: by P. Diepgen, *Sudhoffs Archiv f. Gesch. der Medizin und der Naturwissenschaften,*
        XXXVII (1953), 94-95; by D. McKie, *Annals of Science,* IX, 377; by M. Clagett, *Isis,* XLIV, 91-93.
A2020   Crombie, A. C. *Augustine to Galileo: The History of Science A.D. 400-1650.* London: Falcon
        Press, 1953. Pp. 436, il.
        Rev: by A. W. Heathcote, *London Quar. and Holborn Rev.,* Apr., 1953, pp. 150-151; by
        A. R. Hall, *CamJ,* VII, 116, 118; by Sir Edmund Whittaker, *Science Progress,* XLI, 689-691;
        by Marshall Clagett, *Isis,* XLIV, 398-403 (important); by E. F. Jacob, *British Jour. Philos. Sci.,*
        IV (1954), 173-175; by I. Bernard Cohen, *JHI,* XV, 188-191; by A. L. Gabriel, *Cath. Hist.
        Rev.,* XL, 220-221; by Lynn Thorndike, *Speculum,* XXIX, 541-545; by Jean Jacquot, *Rev. d'Hist.
        des Sciences et de Leurs Applications,* VII, 86-89.
A2021   Underwood, E. Ashworth, ed. *Science, Medicine, and History.* Essays on the Evolution of
        Scientific Thought and Medical Practice, written in Honour of Charles Singer. 2 Vols.
        Oxford Univ. Press, 1954.
        The second, third and fourth books (in Vol. I) deal respectively with The Medieval World,
        The Renaissance, and the New Philosophy; the fifth book (in Vol. II), with the 17th Century.
        Includes, i.a., essays by Armando Cortesao (on natural science in the Renaissance), Agnes
        Arber (on the development of botany from the medieval herbal), F. J. Cole (on the history of
        Albrecht Dürer's Rhinoceros in zoological literature), Sir Arthur MacNalty (on Sir Thomas
        More as Student of Medicine and Public Health Reformer).
A2022   Singer, Charles, E. J. Holmyard, A. R. Hall, and T. I. Williams, eds. *A History of Technology.*
        Vol. III: *From the Renaissance to the Industrial Revolution, c. 1500-c. 1750.* Oxford: Clarendon
        Press, 1957. Pp. xxxvii, 766.
        Rev: by Harold Hartley, *Endeavour,* XVII (1958), 110; by David S. Lamdes, *Jour. Econ. Hist.,*
        XVIII, 377-379.

(3)   MEDIEVAL AND RENAISSANCE SCIENCE (1300-1700)

A2023   Thorndike, Lynn. *A History of Magic and Experimental Science.* Vols. III and IV: *Fourteenth
        and Fifteenth Centuries.* Columbia Univ. Press, 1934. Pp. xxvi, 827; xviii, 767.
        Rev: by G. Cirot, BH, XXXVIII (1936), 96-98.
A2024   Thorndike, Lynn. *A History of Magic and Experimental Science.* Vols. V and VI: *The Sixteenth
        Century.* Columbia Univ. Press, 1941. Pp. xxii, 695; xviii, 766.
        Rev: *TLS,* Nov. 1, 1941, p. 546; by D. B. Durand, "Magic and Experimental Science:
        The Achievement of Lynn Thorndike," *Isis,* XXXIII (1942), 691-712; by C. B. Boyer, *AHR,*
        XLVII, 552-555; by E. L. Tinker, "New Editions, Fine and Otherwise," *NYTBR,*
        July 25, 1943, p. 25; by F. R. Johnson, *MLQ,* V (1944), 115; by A. K. Ziegler, *Catholic Hist.
        Rev.,* XXX, 64-66.
A2025   Thorndike, Lynn. *A History of Magic and Experimental Science.* Vols. VII and VIII: *The
        Seventeenth Century.* Columbia Univ. Press, 1957. Pp. 705, 640.
A2026   Wolf, Abraham. *A History of Science, Technology, and Philosophy in the 16th and 17th Centuries.*

With the cooperation of F. Dannenmann and A. Armitage. London: Allen & Unwin, 1935. Pp. xxvii, 692; 316 il. Reissued, 1951.
  Rev: by E. A. Burt, *Nation* (N.Y.), 141 (1935), 485-487; by Michael Roberts, *Spectator*, June 7, p. 984; by G. Sarton, *Isis*, XXIV, 164-167; by Carroll Mason Sparrow, "Science Looks Backward," *VQR*, XI 634-640; *London Mercury*, XXXII, 306; *More Books*, X, 366; *Catholic World*, 143 (1936), 507-508; by G. S. Brett, *UTQ*, V, 605-611; by Bert James Loewenberg, *AHR*, XLI, 738-739; by Charles Atwood Koford, *SRL*, Aug. 1, 1936, p. 15; by F. S. Marvin, *Hibbert Jour.*, XXXIV, 315-317; by E. M. da C. A., *Science Progress*, XXXI, 193-195.

A2027   Jones, Richard Foster. *Ancients and Moderns: A Study of the Background of the Battle of the Books.* Washington Univ. Studies, NS, Lang. and Lit., VI, 1936. Pp. xi, 358.
  Rev: by Robert K. Merton, *Isis*, XXVI (1936), 171-172; by Harcourt Brown, *Annals of Science*, II (1937), 130-133; by L. B. Wright, *Philos. Rev.*, XLVIII (1939), 223-225.

A2028   Strong, Edward W. *Procedures and Metaphysics: A Study in the Philosophy of Mathematical-Physical Science in the Sixteenth and Seventeenth Centuries.* Univ. of California Press, 1936. Pp. vii, 301.
  Rev: by Francis Johnson, *Isis*, XXIX (1938), 110-113.

A2029   Wiener, P. P. "The Tradition Behind Galileo's Methodology." *Osiris*, I (1936), 733-746.

A2030   Taylor, F. Sherwood. *Galileo and the Freedom of Thought.* The Library of Science and Culture. London: C. A. Watts & Co., 1938. Pp. xvi, 212; 4 pl.
  Rev: by A. A., *Science Progress*, XXXIV (1939), 428-429.

A2031   Dow, Neal. *The Concept and Term "Nature" in Montaigne.* DD, University of Pennsylvania, 1938.

A2032   Johnson, Francis R., and Sanford V. Larkey. "Science." *MLQ*, II (1941), 363-401.
  This bibliographical essay forms part of the survey of Renaissance scholarship published under the auspices of the Committee on Renaissance Studies.

A2033   Stewart, Herbert L. "The Spirit of Renaissance Scientists." *Personalist*, XXII (1941), 285-296.

A2034   Durand, Dana B. "Tradition and Innovation in Fifteenth Century Italy. 'Il primato dell' Italia' in the Field of Science." *JHI*, IV (1943), 1-20.
  A paper delivered at the Renaissance section of American Historical Association meeting at Chicago in December, 1941, and published in *JHI* as the basis of a symposium on Italian science. See also following notes, A2034a-A2034f.

A2034a Baron, Hans. "Towards a More Positive Evaluation of the Fifteenth-Century Renaissance." *JHI*, IV (1943), 21-49.
  Critique of Professor Durand's paper on Science in Fifteenth-Century Italy.

A2034b Cassirer, Ernst. "Some Remarks on the Question of the Originality of the Renaissance." *JHI*, IV (1943), 49-56.

A2034c Johnson, Francis R. "Preparation and Innovation in the Progress of Science." *JHI*, IV (1943), 56-59.

A2034d Kristeller, Paul Oskar. "The Place of Classical Humanism in Renaissance Thought." *JHI*, IV (1943), 59-63.

A2034e Lockwood, Dean P. "It is Time to Recognize a New 'Modern Age'." *JHI*, IV (1943), 63-65.

A2034f Thorndike, Lynn. "Renaissance or Prenaissance?" *JHI*, IV (1943), 65-74.

A2035   Johnson, Francis R. "*A Newe Herball of Macer* and Banckes' *Herball*: Notes on Robert Wyer and the Printing of Cheap Handbooks of Science in the Sixteenth Century." *Bul. Hist. of Medicine*, XV (1944), 246-260.

A2036   Singer, Charles, and C. Rabin. *A Prelude to Modern Science: Being a Discussion of the History, Sources and Circumstances of the Tabulae Anatomicae Sex of Vesalius.* Wellcome Hist. Museum Pub., NS, No. 1. Cambridge Univ. Press, 1946. Pp. lxxxvi, 58, pl. 59.
  Rev: *TLS*, Aug. 30, 1947, p. 441; by J. B. de C. M. Saunders, *Isis*, XXXVIII, 109-111.

A2037   Weisinger, Herbert. "The Idea of the Renaissance and the Rise of Science." *Lychnos*, X (1946-47), 11-35.

A2038   Haraszti, Zoltán. "Dr. Sarton on Scientific Incunabula." *Isis*, XXXII (1940, publ. 1947), 52-62.

A2039   Sarton, George. *Introduction to the History of Science.* Vol. III: *Science and Learning in the Fourteenth Century.* 2 Pts. Washington, D. C.: Carnegie Inst. of Washington, 1948. Pp. 2, 155.
  Rev: by Waldemar Kaempffert, *NYTBR*, Nov. 28, 1948, p. 6.

A2040   Butterfield, Herbert. *The Origins of Modern Science, 1300-1600.* London: Bell, 1949. Pp. 227.
  Rev: by Charles Singer, *Spectator*, Sept. 16, 1949, pp. 362-364; *TLS*, Nov. 25, pp. 761-762.

A2041   Hinton, R. W. K. "The Transformation of the Universe, 1500-1700." *CamJ*, III (1950), 674-685.

A2042   Callot, Emile. *La Renaissance des Sciences de la Vie au XVIe Siècle.* Bibl. de Philosophie Contemporaine. Paris: Presses Universitaires, 1951. Pp. viii, 204.
  Rev: by François Russo, *Etudes*, Dec., 1952, pp. 433-434; by P.-M. Schuhl, *Rev. Phil. de la France et de l'Etranger*, 142 (1952), 146; by H. Bouchet, *Monde Nouveau-Paru*, LVIII, 127; by H. Erjel, *Centaurus*, II, 250-257.

A2043   Thorndike, Lynn. "Newness and Craving for Novelty in Seventeenth-Century Science and Medicine." *JHI*, XII (1951), 584-598.

A2044   Sternfeld, Frederick W. "Metropolitan Symposium." *RN*, V (1952), 5-10, 32-34, 58-63.

Abstracts of papers given at the Symposium on the Renaissance held at the New York Metropolitan Museum of Art (Feb. 8-10, 1952).
George Sarton: "The Quest for Truth: Being an Account of Scientific Progress During the Renaissance (1350-1600)," pp. 7-8.

A2045   Mason, S. F. "The Scientific Revolution and the Protestant Reformation. I: Calvin and Servetus in Relation to the Astronomy and the Theory of the Circulation of the Blood. II: Lutheranism in Relation to Iatrochemistry and the German Nature-Philosophy." *Annals of Science*, IX (1953), 64-87, 154-175.

A2046   Thorndike, Lynn. "Mediaeval Magic and Science in the Seventeenth Century." *Speculum*, XXVIII (1953), 692-704.

A2047   Hellman, C. Doris. "Science in the Renaissance: A Survey." *RN*, VIII (1955), 186-200.

A2048   Sarton, George. *The Appreciation of Ancient and Medieval Science During the Renaissance (1450-1600)*. Rosenbach Fellowship in Bibliography Series. Univ. Penna. Press, 1955. Pp. 250.
Rev: by Wallace K. Ferguson, *AHR*, LXI (1956), 429; by Philip Shorr, *RN*, IX, 110-113; by Dorothy Stimson, *Jour. Hist. Medicine and Allied Sciences*, XI, 112-113; by Charles D. O'Malley, *Speculum*, XXXI, 717-719; by Ernest Wickersheimer, *BHR*, XVIII, 329-330; by J. Malye, *Bul. de l'As. G. Budé*, No. 2, pp. 121-122; by Curtis Wilson, *Bul. Hist. Medicine*, XXX, 383-385; by Francis R. Johnson, *Isis*, XLVIII (1957), 373-375.

A2049   Sarton, George. *Six Wings: Men of Science in the Renaissance*. Patten Foundation Lectures, 1955. Bloomington: Univ. Indiana Press, 1958. Pp. xv, 318.
Rev: *Hist. Ideas Newsletter*, III (1957), 66 (brief); by Frederick M. Feiker, *Amer. Scholar*, XXVI, 380; by C. Doris Hellman, *Isis*, XLVIII, 375-377; by John Pfeiffer, *NYTBR*, Feb. 24, 1957, p. 14; by Giorgio de Santillana, *YR*, XLVII (1958), 453-458; by Trevor I. Williams, *Endeavour*, XVII, 54 (brief); by Emmanuel Poulle, *BHR*, XX, 235-236; by C. D. O'Malley, *Jour. Hist. Med. & Allied Sci.*, XIII, 109-111; by Walter Pagel, *Bul. Hist. Med.*, XXXII, 575-576.

A2050   Cancelled.
A2051   Cancelled.

b. SCIENCE IN CONTEMPORANEOUS ENGLAND (178;-)
(1) GENERAL STUDIES

A2052   Wright, Louis B. *Middle-class Culture in Elizabethan England*. Univ. of North Carolina Press, 1935. Pp. xiv, 733. Reprinted, Cornell Univ. Press, 1958.
Rev: A1909.

A2053   Larkey, Sanford V. "Scientific Glossaries in Sixteenth Century English Books." *Bul. of the Institute of Hist. of Medicine*, V (1938), 105-114.

A2054   Gunther, R. T. *Early Science in Cambridge*. Oxford: The Author, The Old Ashmolean Museum, 1937. Pp. 513, pl.
Rev: *TLS*, Feb. 6, 1937, p. 95; ibid., Dec. 25, p. 973; by M. F. Ashley Montagu, *Isis*, XXVIII (1939), 134.

A2055   Hornberger, Theodore. "Puritanism and Science. The Relationship Revealed in the Writings of John Cotton." *New England Quar.*, X (1937), 503-515.

A2056   Merton, Robert K. "Science in Seventeenth Century England." *Osiris*, IV (1938), 360-632.

A2057   Stimson, Dorothy. "Amateurs of Science in Seventeenth Century England." *Isis*, XXXI (1939), 32-47.

A2058   Stearns, Raymond Phineas. "The Scientific Spirit in England in Early Modern Times (c. 1600)." *Isis*, XXXIV (1943), 293-300.

A2058a   Johnson, Francis R. "Latin Versus English: The Sixteenth Century Debate Over Scientific Terminology." *SP*, XLI (1944), 109-135.

A2059   Dodd, A. H. "The Influence of Early Science on English Thought." *Hibbert Jour.*, XLIII (1945), 216-225.

A2060   Allen, Phyllis. "Scientific Studies in the English Universities of the Seventeenth Century." *JHI*, X (1949), 219-253.

A2061   Kocher, Paul H. "The Old Cosmos: A Study in Elizabethan Science and Religion." *HLQ*, XV (1952), 101-121.

A2062   Kocher, Paul H. *Science and Religion in Elizabethan England*. San Marino, Calif.: Huntington Library, 1953.
Rev: A1456.

A2063   Davy, Norman, ed. *British Scientific Literature in the Seventeenth Century*. London: Harrap, 1954. Pp. 125.
Rev: by Philip George, *National & Eng. Rev.*, 142 (1954), 176-177; *TLS*, Apr. 9, p. 237; *CE*, XVI, 75 (brief); by Renee Haynes, *Time and Tide*, Mar. 6, p. 312.

(2) INDIVIDUALS
(Arranged alphabetically by individuals discussed.)

A2064   Jacquot, Jean. "Humanisme et science dans l'Angleterre Elizabéthaine: L'Œuvre de Thomas Blundeville." *Rev. d'Hist. des Sciences et le Leurs Applications*, IV (1953), 189-202.

A2065 McCulloch, Samuel Clyde. "John Dee: Elizabethan Doctor of Science and Magic." *South Atlantic Quar.*, L (1951), 72-85.

A2066 Webb, Henry J. "The Mathematical and Military Works of Thomas Digges, with an Account of His Life." *MLQ*, VI (1945), 389-400.

A2067 McColley, Grant. "William Gilbert and the English Reputation of Giordano Bruno." *Annals of Science*, II (1937), 353-354.

A2068 Guthrie, Douglas. "King James the Fourth of Scotland: His Influence on Medicine and Science." *Bul. Hist. Medicine*, XXI (1947), 173-191.
Gives evidence for considering James "a worthy pioneer of science and medicine."

A2069 McColley, Grant. "The Debt of Bishop John Wilkins to the *Apologia Pro Galileo of Tomaso Campanella*." *Annals of Science*, IV (1939), 150-168.

c. SCIENCE AND LITERATURE
(Arrangement: from general to specific, then chronologically by periods.)

A2070 Dudley, Fred A., with the assistance of Norbert Fuerst, Francis R. Johnson, and Hyatt H. Waggoner. *The Relations of Literature and Science: A Selected Bibliography, 1930-1949.* Publ. for "General Topics VII" of MLA by the Dept. of English, State College of Washington. Pullman, Wash., 1949. Pp. 59.
Rev: A32.

A2071 Spielmann, Percy E. "The Effect of Scientific Thought on the Arts and Literature." *Essays by Divers Hands*, XVIII (1940), 67-88.

A2072 Bennett, H. S. "Science and Information in English Writings of the Fifteenth Century." *MLR*, XXXIX (1944), 1-8.

A2073 Bush, Douglas. "Two Roads to Truth: Science and Religion in the Early Seventeenth Century." *ELH*, VIII (1941), 81-102.

A2074 Bush, Douglas. *English Literature in the Earlier Seventeenth Century, 1600-1660.* Oxford: Clarendon Press, 1945. Pp. 621.
Chapter on Science, pp. 258-293.
Rev: A8045.

A2075 Bush, Douglas. *Science and English Poetry: An Historical Sketch, 1590-1950.* Oxford Univ. Press, 1950. Pp. vii, 166.
Rev: by B. Dobrée, *Spectator*, Dec. 8, 1950, p. 659; by J. G. Villa, *NYTBR*, Oct. 15, p. 31; *CE*, XI, 58-59; by D. A. Stauffer, *SRL*, July 29, 1950, p. 10.

A2076 Walsh, R. F. *Nature and Its Themes in English Poetry from the Beginnings up to and including James Thomson and the "Sylvan School" of Poets.* DD, Ireland, National University, 1956.

A2077 Kummer, Manfred. *Studien zum Wissenschaftlichen Denken im Drama der Shakespeare-Zeit.* DD, Hamburg, 1955. Pp. vii, 99. Typewritten.

A2078 Heninger, Simeon K., Jr. *A Study of Renaissance Meteorology in Relation to Elizabethan and Jacobean Literature.* DD, Johns Hopkins University, 1955.

A2079 Allen, Don C. *The Legend of Noah: Renaissance Rationalism in Art, Science, and Letters.* Urbana, Ill.: Ill. Studies in Lang. and Lit., XXXIII, Nos. 3-4, 1949.
Rev: A3943.

A2080 Allen, Don Cameron. "Science and Invention in Greene's Prose." *PMLA*, LIII (1938), 1007-18.

A2081 Nicolson, Marjorie Hope. *The Breaking of the Circle: Studies in the Effect of the "New Science" upon Seventeenth Century Poetry.* The Norman Wait Harris Lectures delivered at Northwestern University, July, 1949. Northwestern Univ. Press, 1950. Pp. xxii, 193.
Note by Samuel Mintz, "Galileo, Hobbes and the Circle of Perfection," *Isis*, XLIII (1952), 98-100.
Rev: by Donald A. Stauffer, *NYHTBR*, Feb. 18, 1951, p. 14; by Harcourt Brown, *Isis*, XLII, 251-252; by Joan Bennett, *RES*, III (1952), 178-180; by William Blackburn, *South Atlantic Quar.*, LI, 469-470; by H. J. C. Grierson, *MLR*, XLVII, 390-392; by R. Wallerstein, *JEGP*, LI, 101-103.

A2082 Hofsten, N. von. "Ideas of Creation and Spontaneous Generation Prior to Darwin." *Isis*, XXV (1936), 80-94.

d. SCIENCE AND SHAKESPEARE
(1) NATURE (i.e., As an abstract force or principle,
rather than as landscape, flora, or fauna.)

A2083 Jacob, Georg. *Shakespeare-Studien.* Herausgegeben nach dem Tode des Verfassers von H. Jensen. Hamburg; New York: Augustin, 1938. Pp. 37.
Essays on Nature.
Rev: B4476a.

A2084 Kerl, Wilhelm. *Fortuna und Natura in ihrem Verhältnis zum Menschen in Shakespeares Barockdramen.* DD, Marburg, 1949. Pp. 187. Typewritten.

A2085 Danby, John F. *Shakespeare's Doctrine of Nature: A Study of "King Lear."* London: Faber & Faber, 1949. Pp. 234.

Comment by G. Wilson Knight in *Scrutiny*, XVI (1949), 325.
Rev: A934.

A2086   Bush, G. D. *The Idea of Nature in Shakespeare's Four Principal Tragedies.* B. Litt, thesis, Oxford, 1952.

A2087   Baldwin, T. W. "Nature's Moulds." *SQ*, III (1952), 237-241.

(2) SPECIFIC SCIENCES
(except those for which special sections follow.)

A2088   Willard, Bradford. "The Geology of Shakespeare." *Scientific Monthly*, LXV (1947), 399-404.

A2089   King, Thomson. "The Science of Shakespeare's Time." *The Baltimore Engineer*, XXI (Feb., 1947).

A2090   Ewing, S. Blaine. "Scientists and Shakespeare." *SAB*, XXIII (1948), 5-11.
A review of A2088 and A2089.

A2091   Rubin, E. L. "Shakespeare and Radiography." *Radiography*, April, 1950, pp. 67-72.

A2092   Brotherton, Bertram. "Weather in Shakespeare's Plays." *Weather* (London), VIII (1953), 361-367.

A2093   Hoffman, Banesh. "Shakespeare the Physicist." *Scientific American*, 184 (April, 1951), 52-53.

(3) DETAILS IN PLAYS

A2094   Davenport, A. "Notes on Lyly's *Campaspe* and Shakespeare." *N &Q*, 199 (1954), 19-20.
Finds parallels in I *Henry IV*. Suggests a possible Elizabethan notion that things weighed heaviest at midnight. Draws quotations from *Measure for Measure* and *Much Ado*.

A2095   Heninger, S. K., Jr. " 'Wondrous Strange Snow': *Midsummer-Night's Dream*, V.i.66." *MLN*, LXVIII (1953), 481-483.

A2096   Camden, Carroll. "The Mind's Construction in the Face." *Renaissance Studies in Honor of Hardin Craig.* Stanford Univ. Press, 1941, pp. 208-220; also *PQ*, XX (July, 1941).
The line an allusion to the pseudo science of physiognomy.

e. ASTROLOGY AND ASTRONOMY

A2097   Parr, Johnstone. "Bibliography: Sources of the Renaissance Englishman's Knowledge of Astrology: A Bibliographical Survey and A Bibliography, 1473-1625." *Tamburlaine's Malady*, Univ. of Alabama Press, 1953, pp. 112-150.

A2098   Carmody, Francis J. *Astronomical and Astrological Sciences in Latin Translation: A Critical Bibliography.* Univ. California Press, 1956.
Rev: by S. S., *BHR*, XIX (1957), 145.

(1) ASTROLOGY, ITS NATURE AND THE EXTENT OF BELIEF

A2099   Bosanquet, E. F. "Notes on Further Addenda to English-Printed Almanacks & Prognostications to 1600." *Library*, XVIII (1937), 39-66.

A2100   Wilson, F. P. "Some English Mock-Prognostications." *Library*, XIX (1938), 6-43.
Concerned with parodies of astrological prognostications.

A2101   Dick, Hugh G. *The Doctrines of the Ptolemaic Astronomy in the Literature of the English Renaissance.* DD, Cornell University, 1938. Abstr. publ. in *Abstracts of Theses*, Ithaca: Cornell Univ. Press, 1938, pp. 17-19.
Chap. VII: "The Sceptical Attitude Towards Astrology."
Rejection of astrology by Church and early humanists began with *A Mery Prognostication* (1544) and continued with burlesque almanacs and "serious and extended refutations of the principles of the art. Moreover, periods in which numerous astrological prophecies appeared, for example, from 1580 to 1590, were also times in which attacks upon the superstition increased. In fine, the common view that the pseudo-science of astrology was universally accepted during the English Renaissance is not borne out by . . . the available evidence."

A2102   Allen, Don Cameron. *The Star-crossed Renaissance: The Quarrel about Astrology and Its Influence in England.* Durham, N. C.: Duke Univ. Press; London: Cambridge Univ. Press, 1941. Pp. 291.
Rev: by Una Ellis-Fermor, *MLR*, XXXVII (1942), 497-498; by Carroll Camden, *MLN*, LVIII (1943), 145-147; by Hardin Craig, *JEGP*, XLII, 433-436; by T. H. English, "Man and the Stars," *South Atlantic Bull.*, VIII (Feb., 1943), 1, 7; by F. R. Johnson, *Isis*, XXXIV (1944), 377-378.

A2103   Tallmadge, G. Kasten. "On the Influence of the Stars on Human Birth." *Bul. Hist. Medicine*, XIII (1943), 251-267.

A2104   Dick, Hugh G. "Students of Physic and Astrology: A Survey of Astrological Medicine in the Age of Science." *Jour. Hist. Med. & Allied Sciences*, I (1946), 300-317.
Discusses, i.a., Robert Fludd, Nicholas Fiske, John Evans, Dr. Simon Forman, John Lambe, William Lilly, Nicholas Culpeper, John Heydon.

A2105   Eisler, Robert. *The Royal Art of Astrology.* London: Michael Joseph, 1947. Pp. 296.

A history and description of basic astrological principles and beliefs.
Rev: *TLS*, June 21, 1947, p. 307.

A2106   Smith, Warren D. "The Elizabethan Rejection of Judicial Astrology and Shakespeare's Practice." *SQ*, IX (1958), 159-176.
Shak.'s practice was in accord with that of large numbers of enlightened, influential Elizabethans, who were skeptical of what we would now call astrology.

A2107   Patrides, C. A. "The Numerological Approach to Cosmic Order During the English Renaissance." *Isis*, XLIX (1958), 391-397.

A2108   Camden, Carroll. "Elizabethan Chiromancy." *MLN*, LXII (1947), 1-7.

(2) ASTRONOMY, THE DEVELOPMENT OF VALID IDEAS
(This section is not comprehensive; it is limited to the stipulated sources of this compilation. See A2007-A2008.)
(a) GENERAL STUDIES

A2109   Abbot, C. G. "Astronomy in Shakespeare's Time and in Ours." *Annual Report of . . . the Smithsonian Inst.*, 1936, pp. 108-122.

A2110   Johnson, Francis R. *Astronomical Thought in Renaissance England: A Study of the English Scientific Writings from 1500 to 1645.* Johns Hopkins Press, 1937. Pp. xi, 357.
Dr. Johnson's book concerns itself primarily with the history of science but shows so great a consciousness of literary thought that it may well be considered as a book of the most general importance in the Renaissance field. It shows accuracy, originality, and clarity of comprehension. The book is also bibliographically very valuable.
Rev: *TLS*, Jan. 1, 1938, p. 30; by H. M., *EHR*, LIII (1938), 538-539; by Frederick Barry, *AHR*, XLIII, 846-847; by Lynn Thorndike, *JMH*, X, 418-421; by S. V. Larkey, *Beiblatt*, XLIX, 340-341; by Grant McColley, *Isis*, XXVIII, 514-516; by Dorothy Stimson, *MLN*, LIII, 442-443; by C. M. Coffin, *JEGP*, XXXVIII (1939), 143-147.

A2111   McColley, Grant. "The Theory of the Diurnal Rotation of the Earth." *Isis*, XXVI (1937), 392-402.

A2112   Davidson, Martin. *The Stars and the Mind: A Study of the Impact of Astronomical Development on Human Thought.* London: Watts & Co., 1947. Pp. x, 210.

A2113   McColley, Grant. "Humanism and the History of Astronomy." *Studies and Essays in the History of Science and Learning Offered in Homage to George Sarton . . . ,* ed. M. F. Ashley Montagu, New York, pp. 323-347.

A2114   Dingle, Herbert. *The Scientific Adventure: Essays in the History and the Philosophy of Science.* New York: Philos. Library, 1953. Pp. ix, 372.
Includes, i.a., "Astronomy in the Sixteenth and Seventeenth Centuries," pp. 41-57; "Nicolaus Copernicus (1473-1543)," pp. 58-83; "The Quest of Accuracy in Astronomy: The Message of Four Centenaries," pp. 84-103; "Galileo Galilei (1564-1642)," pp. 104-112.
Rev: by I. Bernard Cohen, *AHR*, LIX (1954), 347-348.

A2115   Winny, James, ed. *The Frame of Order. An Outline of Elizabethan Belief Taken from Treatises of the Late Sixteenth Century.* London: Allen & Unwin, 1957. Pp. 224.
Rev: A1168.

(b) COPERNICUS (Texts and general studies followed by more specific studies.)

A2116   Copernicus, Nicolaus. *Révolutions des Orbes Célestes.* Trad. avec Introd. et notes par A. Koyré. Paris: Alcan, 1934. Pp. viii, 156.
Rev: by Edward Rosen, *Isis*, XXIV (1936), 439-442.

A2117   Brachvogel, A. *Nikolaus Koppernikus (1473-1543) und Aristarch von Samos (etwa 310-330 v. Chr.).* Braunsberg, 1935. Pp. 73.
Rev: by E. Zinner, *DLZ*, LVII (1936), 2018-20.

A2118   Armitage, Angus. *Copernicus: The Founder of Modern Astronomy.* London: Allen & Unwin, 1938. Pp. 183.
Rev: *TLS*, Dec. 10, 1938, p. 791; by C. Lester Johnson, *London Quar. and Holborn Rev.*, Jan. 1939, p. 124; by A. H., *Science Progress*, XXXIV, 429.

A2119   Kesten, Herman. *Copernicus and His World.* New York: Roy Publishers, 1945. Pp. ix, 408. Tr. as *Copernic et Son Temps.* Paris: Calmann-Lévy, 1951. Pp. 432.
Rev: by Waldemar Kaempffert, *SRL*, XXVIII (Mar. 17, 1945), 26; by James B. Macelwane, *Catholic Hist. Rev.*, XXXI, 368-370; by Jean Desbois, *Monde Nouveau-Paru*, VII, Nos. 51-52 (1951), 161; by Joseph Lecler, *Études*, No. 10, p. 121.

A2120   Kuhn, Thomas S. *The Copernican Revolution: Planetary Astronomy in the Development of Western Thought.* Cambridge: Harvard Univ. Press, 1957. Pp. xviii, 297.
Rev: by C. Doris Hellman, *RN*, X (1957), 217-220; by M. W. Burke-Gaffney, *Dalhousie Rev.*, XXXVII, 208-209; by A. Vibert Douglas, *QQ*, LXV (1958), 153-154; by Luise Herzberg, *Canadian Forum*, XXXVIII, 19; by Harry Woolf, *Isis*, XLIX, 366-367.

A2121   Ginzburg, Benjamin. "The Scientific Value of the Copernican Induction." *Osiris*, I (1936), 303-313.

A2122   McColley, Grant. "Nicolas Copernicus and an Infinite Universe." *Popular Astronomy*, XLIV (1937), 525-533.

A2123   McColley, Grant. "Notes on William Gilbert and the English Reputation of Giordano Bruno, and The Eighth Sphere of *De Revolutionibus*." *Annals of Science*, II (1937), 353-356.

A2124   McColley, Grant. "An Early Friend of the Copernican Theory: Gemma Frisius." *Isis*, XXVI (1937), 322-325.

A2125   McColley, Grant. "The Universe of *De Revolutionibus*." *Isis*, XXX (1939), 452-472.

A2126   McColley, Grant. "An Early Poetic Allusion to the Copernican Theory." *JHI*, III (1942), 355-357.
        In John Norden's *Vicissitudo Rerum*, 1600.

A2127   Thorndike, Lynn. "Concerning Astronomical Books Published Soon After Copernicus' *De Revolutionibus*." *Isis*, XLI (1950), 53.

(c)   OTHER INDIVIDUALS
i.   GENERAL STUDIES
(Arranged chronologically by subject.)

A2128   Gunther, R. T. "The Newly Found Astrolabe of Queen Elizabeth." *The Illustrated London News*, Oct. 24, 1936, pp. 738-739.

A2129   McCusker, Honor. "The Science of the Stars." *More Books*, XII (1937), 300-303.
        Description of several sixteenth-century books on astronomy.

A2130   Johnson, Francis R. "Astronomical Textbooks in the Sixteenth Century." *Science, Medicine and History. Essays . . . in Honour of Charles Singer*, ed. E. A. Underwood (Oxford), I (1954), 285-302.

A2131   Kocher, Paul H. "Use of the Bible in English Astronomical Treatises During the Renaissance." *HLQ*, IX (1946), 109-120.

A2132   Nicolson, Marjorie. *A World in the Moon: A Study of the Changing Attitude Toward the Moon in the Seventeenth and Eighteenth Centuries*. Smith College Studies in Modern Languages, XVII, 2. Northampton, Mass.: Smith College, 1936. Pp. vi, 72.
        Rev: by Johannes Speck, *Archiv*, 171 (1937), 247-248.

A2133   Nicolson, Marjorie. "English Almanacs and the New Astronomy." *Annals of Science*, IV (1939), 1-33.

A2134   McColley, Grant. "The Second Edition of *The Discovery of a World in the Moone*." *Annals of Science*, I (1936), 330-334.

A2135   McColley, Grant. "The Seventeenth Century Doctrine of a Plurality of Worlds." *Annals of Science*, I (1937), 385-430. See also "Saint Bonaventure, Francis Mayron, William Vorilong, and the Doctrine of a Plurality of Worlds," by Grant McColley and H. W. Millar, *Speculum*, XII, 386-389.

ii.   Individuals (Arranged chronologically by subject.)

A2136   Ionides, S. A. "Caesar's Astronomy (Astronomicum Caesareum) by Peter Apian, Ingolstadt, 1540." *Osiris*, I (1936), 356-389.

A2137   Patterson, Louise Diehl. "Recorde's *Cosmography*, 1556." *Isis*, XLII (1951), 208-218.

A2138   Naiden, James R. *The "Sphera" of George Buchanan (1506-1582): A Literary Opponent of Copernicus and Tycho Brahe*. DD, Columbia University, 1948. Revised and published without place or date. Available from Wm. H. Allen, 2031 Walnut St., Philadelphia 3, Pa. Pp. 184.

A2139   McColley, Grant. "A Facsimile of Salusbury's Translation of Didacus a Stunica's *Commentary Upon Job*." *Annals of Science*, II (1937), 179-282.
        Dr. McColley reproduces Salusbury's 1661 translation of part of the *Commentary Upon Job* (Toledo, 1584), whose author was the first to attempt a reconciliation between Scripture and the heliocentric theory.

A2140   Johnson, Francis R. "The Influence of Thomas Digges on the Progress of Modern Astronomy in Sixteenth Century England." *Osiris*, I (1936), 390-410.

A2141   Rosen, Edward. "Kepler's Defense of Tycho Against Ursus." *Popular Astronomy*, LIV (1946), 405-412.

A2142   M., M. "Astronomy in Shakespeare's England." *More Books*, XVIII (1943), 433.
        Upon *A Brief Treatise of the Use of the Globe* by R. T(anner?).

A2143   Watson, A. G. "An Identification of Some Manuscripts Owned by Dr. John Dee and Sir Simonds D'Ewes." *Library*, 5th Series, XIII (1958), 194-198.

(3)   ASTROLOGY AND ASTRONOMY IN LITERATURE
(In that order; arrangement thereafter:
chronologically by authors discussed.)

A2144   Dick, Hugh G. *The Doctrines of the Ptolemaic Astronomy in the Literature of the English Renais-*

sance. DD, Cornell University, 1938. Abstr. publ. in *Abstracts of Theses,* Ithaca: Cornell Univ. Press, 1938, pp. 17-19.
First five chapters on Ptolemaic astronomy. Chap. VI on Pt. Astr. in Engl. Lit., notably Greene's *Planetomachia* and Lyly's *The Woman in the Moone.* Breakdown illustrated in Spenser's *Mutabilitie Cantos* and Norden's *Vicissitudo Rerum.*

A2145 Parr, Johnstone. *Cosmological Fortune: Astrology in the Elizabethan and Jacobean Drama.* DD, Vanderbilt University, 1942. Abstr. publ. in *Bulletin of Vanderbilt University, Abstracts of Theses,* August 1, 1942, pp. 22-23.

A2146 Parr, Johnstone. "The Duke of Byron's Malignant *Caput* Algol." *SP,* XLIII (1946), 194-202.

A2147 Parr, Johnstone. "Sources of the Astrological Prefaces in Robert Greene's *Planetomachia.*" *SP,* XLVI (1949), 400-410.

A2148 Parr, Johnstone. *Tamburlaine's Malady.* Univ. of Alabama Press, 1953. Pp. xiv, 158.
Chap. VI: "Shakespeare's Artistic Use of Astrology," pp. 57-69.
Chap. VII: "The Late Eclipses in *King Lear,*" pp. 70-79.
Chap. VIII: "Edmund's Birth under Ursa Major," pp. 80-84.
    Rev: *N &Q,* 199 (1954), 181-182; *VQR,* xxx, xlv; by Clifford Leech, *MLR,* XLIX, 540; by Carroll Camden, *MLN,* LXIX, 512-514; by John W. Draper, *SQ,* v, 421-422; by C. D. Hellman, *Isis,* XLV, 398-399; by A. J. Axelrad, *RLC,* XXIX (1955), 402-403; by J. C. Bryce, *RES,* VI, 306-308.

A2149 Heninger, S. K. *The Interpretation of 'Meteors' in Elizabethan and Jacobean Literature.* B. Litt. thesis, Oxford, 1952.

A2150 Howard, Edwin J. "Sir Thomas Elyot on the Turning of the Earth." *PQ,* XXI (1942), 441-443.

A2151 Johnson, Francis R. "Marlowe's Astronomy and Renaissance Skepticism." *ELH,* XIII (1946), 241-254.

A2152 Shapiro, I. A., W. F. Mitchell, M. F. Ashley Montagu, P. Legouis, and C. M. Coffin. "John Donne the Astronomer." *TLS,* 1937, pp. 492 (July 3); 512 (July 10); 528 (July 17); 560 (July 31); 576 (Aug. 7); 592 (Aug. 14); 675 (Sept. 18).

A2153 Maxwell, J. C. "Donne and the 'New Philosophy'." *DUJ,* XII (1951), 61-64.
Observes (1) the lack of evidence for regarding the "new philosophy" (here, the Copernican cosmology) as "an emotionally disconcerting theory"; and (2) Donne's rhetorical utilization of the sciences, new and old.

A2154 Thompson, Marvin Orville. *Uses of Music and Reflections of Current Theories of the Psychology of Music in the Plays of Shakespeare, Jonson, and Beaumont and Fletcher.* DD, University of Minnesota, 1956. Pp. 272. Mic 56-3899. *DA,* XVI (1956), 2448. Publication No. 18,954.

(4) ASTROLOGY AND ASTRONOMY IN SHAKESPEARE
(In that order; arrangement thereafter: by date of publication.)

A2155 Larkey, Sanford V. "Shakespeare and the Prognostications." *Bul. of the Institute of the Hist. of Medicine,* III (1935), 171-186.
"Here in William Fulke as early as 1563 is a Renaissance English skeptic talking about the supernatural in a fashion which can hardly be distinguished by a hair's breadth from a modern skeptic working in 1941."—George Coffin Taylor, in B8806.

A2156 Darby, Robert H. "Astrology in Shakespeare's 'Lear'." *ES,* xx (1938), 250-257.

A2157 Draper, John W. "Shakespeare's Star-crossed Lovers." *RES,* xv (1939), 16-34.

A2158 Sondheim, Max. "Shakespeare and the Astrology of his Time." *Jour. of the Warburg Institute,* II (1938-39), 243-259.

A2159 Cambillard. "Le Songe d'une Nuit d'Été, Thème Astrologique." *EA,* III (1939), 118-126.

A2160 Parr, Johnstone. "Edmund's Nativity in *King Lear.*" *SAB,* XXI (1946), 181-185.

A2161 Smith, Warren Dale. "The Elizabethan Rejection of Judicial Astrology and Shakespeare's Practice." *SQ,* IX (1958), 159-176.
An excellent statement of what is not entirely new but has been too much ignored.

A2162 Wilson, J. Dover. "Shakespeare's Universe." *Univ. of Edin. Jour.,* XI (1942), 216-233.
Ptolemaic and Copernican influences.

A2163 Eagle, R. L. "Shakespeare's Astronomy in *Hamlet.*" *N &Q,* 189 (1945), 43.

A2164 Goodhart, L. McC. "Shakespeare and the Stars." *Popular Astronomy,* LIII (1945), 489-503.

A2165 Schrickx, W. "Solar Symbolism and Related Imagery in Shakespeare." *RBPH,* XXIX (1951), 118-128.

A2166 Walker, Roy. "The Celestial Plane in Shakespeare." *ShS,* VIII (1955), 109-117.

A2167 Cancelled.
A2168 Cancelled.
A2169 Cancelled.

f. NATURE (landscape, flora, and fauna.)
(1) GENERAL

A2170 Jacob, G. *Shakespeares Naturverbundenheit im Vergleich mit Schillers und Goethes Verhältnis zur*

Natur. Hamburg and Glückstadt: Augustin, 1937. Pp. 35.
Rev: by W. Keller, *SJ*, LXXIII (1937), 160; by A. Eichler, *Beiblatt*, XLIX (1938), 103-104; by H. W., *GRM*, XXVI, 324.

A2171 Jacob, Georg. *Shakespeare-Studien.* Nach dem Tode des Verfassers hrsg. v. H. Jensen. Glückstadt; Hamburg; New York: Augustin, 1938. Pp. 37.

A2172 Hering, Gerhard F. "Shakespeare-Studien." *DL*, XLIII (1941), 230-232, 399-400, 501-503. First is titled: "Umgebende Natur."

A2173 Wilson, W. G. "Elizabethan Natural History." *Life and Letters Today*, XXXIV (1943), 11-17.

A2174 Truhelka, Agata. "Shakespeare i priroda (Shakespeare and Nature)." *Hrvatsko kolo* (Zagreb: Matica Hrvatska), V (1952), 9-10, pp. 697-701.

A2175 Fredén, Gustaf. "En strand dår timjan blommar vild. En studie i Shakespeare-dramats bakgrund. *Orestes och försoningen*, Lund, 1955, pp. 85-108.

A2176 Stamm, Rudolf. *Shakespeare's Word-Scenery.* With Some Remarks on Stage-History and the Interpretation of His Plays. Veröffentlichungen der Handels-Hochschule St. Gallen, Reihe B, Heft 10. Zurich and St. Gallen: Polygraphischer Verlag, 1954. Pp. 34.
Rev: A5603.

A2177 Korninger, Siegfried. *Die Naturauffassung in der englischen Dichtung des 17. Jahrhunderts.* *Wiener Beiträge zur Englischen Philologie*, bd. 64. Vienna: Braumüller, 1956. Pp. 260. Only Ref. to Shak., p. 220.

(a) THE SEA

A2178 Vallese, Tarquinio. "Il mare agitato nel dramma Shakespeariano." *Annali del R. Istituto Super. Navale* (Naples), III (1938), 161-187.

A2178a Vallese, Tarquinio. "Cognizioni nautiche dello Shakespeare." *Annali del R. Istituto Super. Navale* (Naples), IV (1938), 31-60. This and A2178 republished in Vallese's *Saggi di Letteratura Inglese*, Naples: Pironti, 1949. Pp. 153.

A2179 Doherty, W. O. *Shakespeare's Sea Lore.* MS thesis, Columbia University, 1947. Pp. 145.

A2180 Atkinson, A. D. " 'Full Fathom Five'." *N&Q*, 194 (1949), 465-468, 493-495. Traces underseas imagery in many poets, especially Shak.

A2181 Pettet, E. C. "Dangerous Sea and Unvalued Jewels: Some Notes on Shakespeare's Consciousness of the Sea." *English*, X (1955), 215-220.

(2) ZOOLOGY (40;16)
(a) ANIMALS

A2182 Kirmse, Persis. *Shakespeare at the Zoo: A Book of Drawings.* London: Methuen, 1936. Pp. 55.

A2183 McPeek, James A. S. "Shakspere's Chameleons and Salamanders." *SAB*, XVI (1941), 237-242.

A2184 White, T. H. *The Book of Beasts, Being a Translation of a Latin Bestiary of the Twelfth Century.* London: Jonathan Cape, 1954. Pp. 296.
Shak.'s indebtedness to bestiary lore, pp. 11, 18, 20, 32, 36, 47, 92, 96, 121, 128, 154 (all notes). See also pp. 261-268 on Elizabethan in general.

(b) BIRDS

A2185 Friedmann, Herbert. *The Symbolic Goldfinch, Its History and Significance in European Devotional Art.* The Bollingen Series, VII. New York: Pantheon Books, 1946. Pp. xxiv, 254. In Italian art. Shak., pp. 53, 180.
Rev: by E. Faye Wilson, *Speculum*, XXIII (1948), 121-125.

A2186 Kirmse, Persis. *Shakespeare and the Birds: A Book of Drawings.* London: Methuen, 1938. Pp. 57.

A2187 *New York Times.* "Paintings of Shakespeare's Birds Exhibited." Dec. 14, 1940, p. 12.

A2188 McCormick-Goodhart, L. "Birds of Shakespeare." *Nature Magazine*, XXXIX (1946), 413-416, 444.

A2189 Stockelbach, Lavonia. *The Birds of Shakespeare.* Verona, New Jersey: The Author, 1940. Pp. 52. Also, London: Batsford, 1954. Pp. xiv, 94.
Rev: *TLS*, July 30, 1954, p. 491.

A2190 Harrison, Thomas P. "Shakespeare's Birds." *Tennessee Studies in Literature*, III (1958), 53-62.

(c) VERMIN

A2191 Harris, C. A. "The Bee in Shakespeare." *Poet Lore*, XLIII (1937), 328-338.

A2192 Twinn, Cecil Raymond. *Insect Life in the Poetry and Drama of England.* DD, Ottawa, 1942. Pp. 281.

A2193 Dodson, Sarah. "Caterpillars, Sponges, Horseleeches, in Shakspere and Holinshed." *SAB*, XIX (1944), 41-46.

(3) BOTANY (41;16)
(a) HERBALS AND THEIR INFLUENCE
ON SHAKESPEARE

A2194   Arber, Agnes. *Herbals: Their Origin and Evolution: A Chapter in the History of Botany, 1470-1670.* New ed. Cambridge Univ. Press, 1938. Pp. xxiv, 326; 25 pl.
    Rev: by Conway Zirkle, *Isis,* xxx (1939), 131-132; by H. G. F., *Connoisseur,* 103 (1939), 172.

A2195   Wilson, Winfred Graham. "Elizabethan Natural History." *Life and Letters Today,* xxxvi (1943), 11-17.

A2196   Johnson, Francis R. "*A Newe Herball of Macer* and Banckes's *Herball:* Notes on Robert Wyer and the Printing of Cheap Handbooks of Science in the Sixteenth Century." *Bul. Hist. of Medicine,* xv (1944), 246-260.

A2197   Harrison, Thomas P., Jr. "Flower Lore in Spenser and Shakespeare: Two Notes." *MLQ,* vii (1946), 175-178.

A2198   Lever, J. W. "Three Notes on Shakespeare's Plants." *RES,* iii (1952), 117-129.
    Argues Shakespeare's knowledge and use of Gerarde's *Herball* (1597) and concludes: (1) the songs at the end of *L. L. L.* were part of the revision mentioned on the t.p. of 1598 Q; (2) the herbals of Gerarde and Lyte explain the various Shakespearean descriptions of *mandrake* and *mandragora;* (3) Ophelia's words and actions with her flowers are "in keeping with her character, her good intentions, her abysmal ignorance of life."

A2199   Stevenson, Hazel Allison. "The Major Elizabethan Poets and the Doctrine of Signatures." *Fla. State Univ. Studies,* No. 5 (1952), 11-31.
    Discusses the herbal theory of signatures popularized by Giambattista della Porta, with references from English dramatic and nondramatic poets.

A2200   Wilson, W. G. "The Mandrake Myth." *Life and Letters Today,* xxvii (1941), 197-203.

(b) PLANTS IN SHAKESPEARE

A2201   Jacob, Georg. *Shakespeare-Studien.* Nach dem Tode des Verfassers hrsg. v. H. Jensen. Glückstadt; Hamburg; New York: Augustin, 1938. Pp. 37.

A2202   Cook, Phyllis. "William Shakspere, Botanist." *SAB,* xv (1940), 149-165.
    Concludes with list of plant references alphabetically by common name.

A2203   Harrison, Thomas P., Jr. "Flower Lore in Spenser and Shakespeare: Two Notes." *MLQ,* vii (1946), 175-178.

A2204   Harrison, Thomas P., Jr. "Hang Up Philosophy." *SAB,* xxii (1947), 203-209.
    Plant lore in *Romeo.*

A2205   Hammerle, Karl. "Das Laubenmotiv bei Shakespeare und Spenser." *Anglia,* lxxi (1953), Heft 3, 310-331.

A2206   Macht, David I. "Calendula or Marigold in Medical History and in Shakespeare." *Bulletin of the History of Medicine,* xxix (1955), 491-502.

A2207   Sörrensen, W. "Gärten und Blumen bei Shakespeare." *Das Gartenamt* (Frankfurt/M.), iv (1955), 211-213.

A2208   Myers, A. J. Wm. "Flowers in Shakespeare." *Dalhousie Rev.,* xxxvi (1956), 369-377.

(c) GARDENS

A2209   Carter, Annie B. *Shakespeare Gardens: Design, Plants and Flower Lore.* London and Philadelphia: Dorrance, 1936. Pp. 85.

A2210   Cancelled.

A2211   McFaddan, Liam. "Shakespearean Garden." *Catholic World,* 165 (1947), 51-55.
    At St. Elizabeth's College.

A2212   Clark, A. [Shakespeare Gardens, New Rochelle]. *Wilson Library Bulletin,* xxx (1955), 272.

A2213   Tannenbaum, Samuel A. "A Shakespeare Garden in Cleveland." *SAB,* xvii (1942), 208.

g. MEDICINE (41;16)
(Compiled only from the specified sources; not to be considered a comprehensive bibliography of medicine.)
(1) REPRINTS OF OLD TEXTS

A2214   Vesalius, Andreas. *The Epitome of Andreas Vesalius.* Tr. by L. R. Lind. Anatomical Notes by C. W. Asling. Yale Medical Lib., Hist. Lib., Publ. No. 22. New York: Macmillan, 1949. Pp. 107.
    Rev: by L. J. Warshaw, *NYTBR,* June 26, 1949, p. 12.

A2215   Laurentius, M. Andreas. *A Discourse of the Preservation of the Sight; of Melancholike Diseases; of Rheumes, and of Old Age.* Tr. by Richard Surphlet. Introd. by Sanford V. Larkey. Shakespeare Assoc. Facsimiles: No. 15. Oxford Univ. Press, 1938. Pp. 236.
    Rev: *TLS,* Sept. 24, 1938, p. 619; by C. J. Sisson, *MLR,* xxxiv (1939), 91.

A2216   Elyot, T. *The Castel of Helth* (London, 1541). New York: Scholars' Facsimiles & Reprints, 1936. Pp. xvi, 194.

A2217   Clowes, William. *Profitable and Necessarie Book of Observations. An Elizabethan Book of Surgery and Medicine.* Ed. by DeWitt T. Starnes and Chauncy D. Leake. New York: Scholars' Facsimiles, 1944.

A2218   Clowes, William. *Selected Writings of William Clowes, 1544-1604.* Ed. by F. N. L. Poynter.

London: Harvey & Blythe, 1948. Pp. 184, pl. 8.
Rev: "An Elizabethan Surgeon," *Spectator*, Aug. 19, 1949, pp. 228-229.

(2) GENERAL
(See also A3474, A3475, A3485, A3492.)
(a) HISTORIES

A2219   *Histoire Générale de la Médecine, de la Pharmacie, de l'Art Dentaire et de l'Art Vétérinaire*. Publ.
sous la direction du M. Laignel-Lavastine. Tome ii, Paris: A. Michel, 1938. Pp. 672.
Contains chapter on medicine of the Renaissance by O. Béliard.

A2220   Castiglioni, Arturo. *A History of Medicine*. Tr. and ed. by E. B. Krumbhaar. New York:
Alfred A. Knopf, 1947. Pp. xxx, 1192, lxi.
Rev: by A. H. Weiler, *NYTBR*, Jan. 4, 1948, p. 22.

A2221   Cole, F. J. *A History of Comparative Anatomy from Aristotle to the Eighteenth Century*. London:
Macmillan, 1944. Pp. viii, 524.
Rev: by W. L. Straus, Jr., *Bul. Hist. Med.*, xviii (1946), 566-568.

A2222   Heischkel, Edith. *Die Medizingeschichtschreibung von ihren Anfängen bis zum Beginn des 16.
Jahrhunderts*. Abhandlungen zur Geschichte der Med. und der Naturwiss., Heft 28. Berlin:
E. Ebering, 1938. Pp. 91.
Rev: by W. Haberling, *DLZ*, lx (1939), 754-756.

A2223   Mettler, Cecilia C. *History of Medicine*. Philadelphia: Blakiston Co., 1947. Pp. 1215; pl 16.
Rev: by Douglas Guthrie, *Bul. Hist. Med.*, xxii (1948), 337-339.

A2224   Temkin, Owsei. *The Falling Sickness. A History of Epilepsy from the Greeks to the Beginnings of
Modern Neurology*. Johns Hopkins Press, 1945. Pp. 380; il.
Rev: by M. F. Ashley Montagu, *NYTBR*, Dec. 9, 1945, p. 22.

(b) SYPHILIS

A2225   Zimmermann, E. L. "Early Collections of Syphilologic Works." *Bul. of the Inst. of the Hist.
of Medicine*, iv (1936), 582-599.

A2226   Krause, K. "Erasmus von Rotterdam über die Gefahr der Syphilis in der Ehe und über
Eugenik." *Zeitschrift für ärztl. Forthbildung*, xxxiv (1937), 152-154.

A2227   Wickersheimer, Ernest. "Sur la Syphilis au XVe et XVIe siècles." *H &R*, 1937, pp. 157-207.

A2228   Zimmermann, E. L. "An Early English Manuscript on Syphilis: A Fragmentary Translation
from the Second Edition of Gaspar Torrella's *Tractatus cum consiliis contra pudendagram seu
morbum gallicum*." *Bul. of the Inst. of Hist. of Medicine*, v (1937), 461-482.
The manuscript may be dated ca. 1500.

A2229   Munger, Robert S. "Guaiacum, the Holy Wood from the New World." *Jour. Hist. Medicine
& Allied Sciences*, iv (1949), 196-229. See the letter by Harry Keil, ibid, iv (1949), 475-477.
Surveys the controversy and literature about syphilis, principally during the 16th and 17th
centuries, as revealed by discussions of the wood thought to be its specific; emphasizes the
work of Ulrich von Hutten.
See also A2327 and A2345.

(c) MORE SPECIFIC SUBJECTS
(Arranged alphabetically by author.)

A2230   Barraud, G. *L'Humanisme et la Médecine au XVIe Siècle*. Paris: Vigot, 1942. Pp. 136.
A2230a Bloch, Joshua. "More on Early Medical Books." *Library Quar.*, xi (1941), 97-98.
See A2233.

A2231   Elton, William. "A Renaissance Forerunner of Pavlov." *Jour. Hist. Medicine & Allied
Sciences*, ii (1947), 576-577.
Refers to John Caius' *De canibus britannicis libellus* (1570), tr. 1576 by Abraham Fleming.

A2232   Jarcho, Saul. "Medicine in Sixteenth Century New Spain as Illustrated by the Writings of
Bravo, Farfan, and Vargas Machuca." *Bul. Hist. Med.*, xxxi (1957), 425-441.

A2233   Keys, Thomas E. "The Earliest Medical Books Printed with Movable Type: A Review."
Lib. Quar., x (1940), 220-230.

A2234   Marsden, W. H. "Early Books on Surgery." *British Museum Quar.*, xi (1937), 85-87.

A2235   Mayer, Claudius F. *Bio-Bibliography of XVI Century Medical Authors*. Fasc. I: *Abarbanel-
Alberti*, S. Washington: U. S. Gov't Printing Office, 1941. Pp. xi, 55.
Rev: by J. F. Ballard; *Papers Bibl. Soc. Amer.*, xxxvi (1942), 69-72; by E. Weil, *Library*,
ns, xxvi (1946), 217-218.

A2236   Neuburger, Max. "An Historical Survey of the Concept of Nature from a Medical Viewpoint." *Isis*, xxxv (1944), 16-28.
Paracelsus, Jean Fernel, Van Helmont, Sir Thomas Browne, and others.

A2237   Pagel, Walter. "Prognosis and Diagnosis: A Comparison of Ancient and Modern Medicine."
JWCI, ii (1939), 382-398.
Discusses, as necessary to the comparison, the abandonment of Greek medical ideology
during the sixteenth and seventeenth centuries.

A2238   Rucker, M. Pierce. "Leaves from a Bibliotheca Obstetrica." *Bul. Hist. Med.*, XIX (1946), 177-199.
Describes, i.a., Rosslin's *Der Swangern Frawen und Hebammen Roszgarten* (1513, 1536, 1545, 1554, 1580, 1591, 1594). English tr. *The Byrth of Mankynde* (1552-1654), the works of Jason a Pratis, and Damian Carbon's *Libro del arte de las Comadres* (1541).

A2239   Thorndike, Lynn. "Newness and Craving for Novelty in Seventeenth Century Science and Medicine." *JHI*, XII (1951), 584-598.

A2240   Waller, Erik. "Der Arzt und sein Buch." *Philobiblon*, X (1938), 305-334.
Contains cuts and descriptions of numerous 16th century books on surgery.

A2241   Wilson, Leonard Gilcrest. "Theories of Respiration in the Seventeenth Century." DD, University of Wisconsin. *DA*, XIX (1958), 1064.
"An Historical Account of Theories of Respiration in Relation to Anatomical Knowledge from the Greek through the Seventeenth Century."

A2242   Zilboorg, Gregory. *The Medical Man and the Witch During the Renaissance.* Baltimore: Johns Hopkins Press, 1935. Pp. x, 215.
Rev: A1584.

(3) IN ENGLAND
(a) BIBLIOGRAPHY

A2243   Russell, K. F. "A Check List of Medical Books Published in England Before 1600." *Bul. Hist. Med.*, XXI (1947), 922-958.

A2244   Russell, K. F. "A Bibliography of Anatomical Books Published in England Before 1800." *Bul. Hist. Med.*, XXIII (1949), 268-306.

A2245   Kurz, Myrtis T. *Health Books of Renaissance England.* DD, University of North Carolina, 1944. Abstract in *Univ. of North Carolina Record, in Research Progress,* No. 429, 1946, pp. 140-141.

(b) GENERAL

A2246   Larkey, Sanford V. "The Hippocratic Oath in Elizabethan England." *Bul. of the Inst. of the Hist. of Medicine*, IV (1936), 201-219.

A2247   Miller, J. L. "A Discussion of Burton's *Anatomy of Melancholy.*" *Annals of Medical History*, VIII (1936), 44-53.

A2248   Larkey, Sanford V. "Scientific Glossaries in Sixteenth Century English Books." *Bul. of the Inst. of the Hist. of Medicine*, V (1938), 105-114.

A2249   Silvette, Herbert. "Philemon Holland in Coventry." *Annals of Medical History*, 3rd Series, I (1938), 99-100.

A2250   Noack, Jeannette Snyder. *Social Aspects of Elizabethan Medicine: A Background for the Study of Elizabethan Literature.* DD, Stanford University, 1941. Abstract publ. in *Abstracts of Dissertations, 1940-41*, Stanford, 1941, pp. 90-94.

A2251   Smith, Golwin. "The Practice of Medicine in Tudor England." *Scientific Monthly*, L (1940), 65-72.

A2252   Allen, Phyllis. "Medical Education in 17th Century England." *Jour. Hist. Med. & Allied Sciences*, I (1946), 115-143.

A2253   Dick, Hugh G. "Students of Physic and Astrology: A Survey of Astrological Medicine in the Age of Science." *Jour. Hist. Med. & Allied Sciences*, I (1946), 300-317, 419-433.
Discusses, i.a., Robert Fludd, Nicholas Fiske, John Evans, Dr. Simon Forman, John Lambe, William Lilly, Nicholas Culpeper, John Heydon.

A2254   MacNalty, Arthur Salusbury. *The Renaissance and Its Influence on English Medicine, Surgery and Public Health. Being the Thomas Vicary Lecture for 1945.* London: Christopher Johnson, 1946. Pp. 30.
Discusses hospitals after dissolution of the monasteries.
Rev: briefly, *TLS*, Dec. 14, 1946, p. 620; by S. V. Larkey, *Jour. Hist. Med. & Allied Sciences*, IV (1949), 249-250.

A2255   Kocher, Paul H. "The Physician as Atheist in Elizabethan England." *HLQ*, X (1947), 229-249.

A2256   Kocher, Paul H. "Paracelsan Medicine in England." *Jour. Hist. Med. & Allied Sciences*, II (1947), 460-480.

A2257   Kocher, Paul H. "John Hester, Paracelsan (fl. 1576-93)." *AMS*, pp. 621-638.

A2258   Dickson, Sarah. "The 'Humours' of Samuel Rowlands." *Papers Bibl. Soc. Amer.*, XLIV (1950), 101-118.

A2259   Kocher, Paul H. "The Idea of God in Elizabethan Medicine." *JHI*, XI (1950), 3-29.

A2260   Cruttwell, Patrick. "Physiology and Psychology in Shakespeare's Age." *JHI*, XII (1951), 75-89.

A2261   Poynter, F. N. L., and W. J. Bishop. *A Seventeenth Century Doctor and His Patients: John Symcotts 1592(?)-1662.* Bedfordshire Hist. Rec. Soc., XXXI, 1951. Pp. 126.
Rev: by Walter Pagel, *Isis*, XLIII (1952), 66.

A2262 Ashworth, E. Underwood. "English Medicine and the Italian Renaissance." *Riv. di storia delle scienze mediche e naturali*, XLIII (1952), 215-222.

A2263 Clark, Sir George N. "Jacobean England, 1603-1625." *Bul. Hist. Med.*, XXXI (1957), 391-407.

A2264 Keevil, J. J. *Medicine and the Navy, 1200-1900.* Vol. I: 1200-1649. Edinburgh: E. & S. Livingstone, 1957. Pp. xii, 255.
Rev: by E. J. Holmyard, *Endeavour*, XVII (1958), 53-54.

A2265 Rossky, William. "Imagination in the English Renaissance: Psychology and Poetic." *Studies in the Renaissance* (Ren. Soc. Amer.), V (1958), 49-73.
Cites his examples from Batman, Bright, Burton, the two John Davies', Greville, Jonson, La Primaudaye, Sidney, Spenser, and others.

(c) HARINGTON

A2266 Reynolds, Reginald. *Cleanliness and Godliness, or the Further Metamorphosis.* London: Allen & Unwin, 1943. Pp. v, 7-266.
A discussion of the problems of sanitation raised by Sir John Harington.
Rev: *TLS*, July 3, 1943, p. 320.

A2267 Sigerist, Henry E. "An Elizabethan Poet's Contribution to Public Health: Sir John Harington and the Water Closet." *Bul. Hist. Medicine*, XIII (1943), 229-243; 4 pl.

(d) HARVEY

A2268 Keynes, Geoffrey. *A Bibliography of the Writings of Dr. William Harvey, 1573-1657.* 2nd ed. revised. Cambridge Univ. Press, 1953. Pp. xii, 79. (First edition appeared in 1928.)
Rev: by Thomas E. Keys, *Lib. Quar.*, XXIV (1954), 262-263.

A2269 William, Arthur. *An Analysis of the "De Generatione Animalium" of William Harvey.* Stanford Univ. Press, 1936. Pp. xx, 167.
Rev: by Chauncey D. Leake, *Isis*, XXVI (1936), 174-176.

A2270 Zurbach, K. "Vorstellungen und Lehren von der Blutbewegung vor William Harvey." *Ciba Zeitschrift*, IV (1937), 1255-59.

A2271 Bayon, H. P. "William Harvey, Physician and Biologist: His Precursors, Opponents and Successors." *Annals of Science*, III (1938), 59-118, 435-456; ibid., IV (1939), 65-106, 329-389.

A2272 Meyer, A. W. "Harvey's Appraisal of His *De Generatione*." *Bul. Hist. Medicine*, XI (1942), 264-272.

A2273 Weil, E. "William Fitzer, the Publisher of Harvey's 'De Motu Cordis', 1628." *Library*, NS, XXIV (1944), 142-164.

A2274 Arcieri, John P. *The Circulation of the Blood and Andrea Cesalpino of Arezzo.* New York: S. R. Vanni, 1945. Pp. 193.
Would prove that the powers of Harvey have been exaggerated and those of Cesalpino underestimated.
Rev: by Charles Singer, *Bul. Hist. Med.*, XIX (1946), 122-124.

A2275 Langdon-Brown, Sir Walter. *Some Chapters in Cambridge Medical History.* Cambridge Univ. Press, 1946. Pp. viii, 120. Discusses, i.a., John Caius, Gilbert, Harvey, and Bacon.
Rev: by H. H. Bashford, *Spectator*, Aug. 30, 1946, p. 222; *N &Q*, 191 (1946), 88.

A2276 Bayon, H. P. "William Harvey (1578-1657): His Application of Biological Experiment, Clinical Observation, and Comparative Anatomy to the Problems of Generation." *Jour. Hist. Med. & Allied Sciences*, II (1947), 51-98.

A2277 Keynes, Geoffrey. *The Portraiture of William Harvey.* The Thomas Vicary Lectures, 1948. London Royal College of Surgeons, 1949. Pp. 42, pl. 32.
Rev: *TLS*, Nov. 11, 1949, p. 736.

A2278 Izquierdo, J. J. "On Spanish Neglect of Harvey's 'De Motu Cordis' for Three Centuries, and How It was Finally Made Known to Spain and Spanish-speaking Countries." *Jour. Hist. Med. & Allied Sciences*, III (1948), 105-124.

A2279 Hunter, William B., Jr. "The Seventeenth Century Doctrine of Plastic Nature." *Harvard Theol. Rev.*, XLIII (1950), 197-213.
Wm. Harvey, among other 17th century figures.

A2280 Pagel, Walter. "The Circular Motion of the Blood and Giordano Bruno's Philosophy of the Circle." *Bul. Hist. Med.*, XXIV (1950), 398-399.
Suggests Bruno as a link between Cesalpino and Harvey; see also Mr. Pagel's "Harvey's Role in the History of Medicine," ibid., XXIV, 70-73 (on the Harvey-Cesalpino controversy).

A2281 Huntley, Frank Livingstone. "Sir Thomas Browne, M. D., William Harvey, and the Metaphor of the Circle." *Bul. Hist. Med.*, XXV (1951), 236-247.

A2282 Pagel, Walter. "William Harvey and the Purpose of Circulation." *Isis*, XLII (1951), 22-38.

A2283 Fleming, Donald. "William Harvey and the Pulmonary Circulation." *Isis*, XLVI (1955), 319-327.

A2284 Boenheim, Felix. "From Huang-Ti to Harvey." *Jour. Hist. Med. & Allied Sciences*, XII (1957), 181-188.

A2285   Chauvois, Louis. *William Harvey: His Life and Times, His Discoveries, His Methods.* Foreword by Sir Zachary Cope. London: Hutchinson, 1957. Pp. 271.
        Rev: by Roger Pilkington, *Time and Tide,* June 29, 1957, p. 820; by A. M., *Science Progress,* XLV, 787.

A2286   Chauvois, Louis. "On William Harvey at Padua and the Way in Which He was Stimulated to Reinvestigate the Problem of Heart and Blood Movements and on the Credit He Merits for the Discovery." *Jour. Hist. Med. & Allied Sciences,* XII (1957), 175 ff.

A2287   Cohen of Birkenhead, Lord. "The Germ of an Idea, or What Put Harvey on the Scent?" *Jour. Hist. Med. & Allied Sciences,* XII (1957), 102-105.

A2288   Cole, F. J. "Henry Power on the Circulation of the Blood." *Jour. Hist. Med. & Allied Sciences,* XII (1957), 291-324.

A2289   Cole, F. J. "Harvey's Animals." *Jour. Hist. Med. & Allied Sciences,* XII (1957), 106-113.

A2290   Laín Entralgo, Pedro. "Harvey in the History of Scientific Thought." *Jour. Hist. Med. & Allied Sciences,* XII (1957), 220-231.

A2291   Francis, W. W., ed. "On the Death of Harvey: A Premature Threnody by N. Kolaas van Assendelft." *Jour. Hist. Med. & Allied Sciences,* XII (1957), 254-255.
        Dutch text and English translation.

A2292   Franklin, Kenneth J. "On Translating Harvey." *Jour. Hist. Med. & Allied Sciences,* XII (1957), 114-119.

A2293   Gotfredsen, Edv. "The Reception of Harvey's Doctrine in Denmark." *Jour. Hist. Med. & Allied Sciences,* XII (1957), 202-208.

A2294   Guthrie, Douglas. "The Harveian Tradition in Scotland." *Jour. Hist. Med. & Allied Sciences,* XII (1957), 120-125.

A2295   Hunter, Richard A., and Ida Macalpine. "William Harvey: His Neurological and Psychiatric Observation." *Jour. Hist. Med. & Allied Sciences,* XII (1957), 126-139.

A2296   Kilgour, Frederick G. "Harvey's Use of Galen's Findings in His Discovery of the Circulation of the Blood." *Jour. Hist. Med. & Allied Sciences,* XII (1957), 232-234.

A2297   Krumbhaar, E. B. "Thoughts on Bibliographies and Harvey's Writings." *Jour. Hist. Med. & Allied Sciences,* XII (1957), 235-240.

A2298   Leibowitz, Joshua O. "William Harvey's Diploma from Padua." *Jour. Hist. Med. & Allied Sciences,* XII (1957), 264-265.

A2299   Lindroth, Sten. "Harvey, Descartes, and Young Olaus Rudbeck." *Jour. Hist. Med. & Allied Sciences,* XII (1957), 209-219.

A2300   Poynter, F. N. L. "William Harvey's Last Will and Testament." *Jour. Hist. Med. & Allied Sciences,* XII (1951), 165-166.
        See also A2322 and A2323.

(e)   THE PLAGUE

A2301   Mullett, Charles Frederic. "Some Neglected Aspects of Plague Medicine in Sixteenth Century England." *Scientific Monthly,* XLIV (1937), 325-327.

A2302   Mullett, C. F. "The Plague of 1603 in England." *Annals of Medical History,* IX (1937), 230-247.

A2303   Viets, Henry R., and James F. Ballard. "Notes on the Plague Tracts in the Boston Medical Library." *Bul. Hist. Medicine,* VIII (1940), 370-380.
        A German broadside and 28 French, German and Italian tracts on the Black Death printed in the period 1472-1501.

A2304   Hirst, L. Fabian. *The Conquest of Plague: A Study of the Evolution of Epidemiology.* Oxford: Clarendon Press, 1953. Pp. 478; figs, pl.
        Rev: by René J. Dubos, *Isis,* XLV (1954), 206-208; by Gaylord W. Anderson, *AHR,* LX (1954-55), 62.

A2305   Wright, Herbert G. "Some Sixteenth and Seventeenth Century Writers on the Plague." *Essays and Studies* (Eng. Assoc.), VI (1953), 41 ff.
        Nashe, Lodge, Dekker and others.

A2306   Mullett, Charles F. *The Bubonic Plague and England: An Essay in the History of Preventive Medicine.* Lexington, 1956.
        Rev: by George Rosen, *AHR,* LXII (1957), 382-383; by F. N. L. Poynter, *Jour. Hist. Med. & Allied Sciences,* XII, 90-92; by John O'Connor, *Catholic Hist. Rev.,* XLIII, 375-376.

(4)   IN ENGLISH RENAISSANCE LITERATURE GENERALLY

A2307   Robinson, Herbert S. "Galen in Chaucer, Shakespeare and Jonson." *Medical Life,* XXXV (1928).

A2308   Silvette, H. "The Doctor on the Stage: Medicine and Medical Men in 17th Century English Drama." *Annals of Medical History,* VIII (1936), 520 ff; IX (1937), 62-88, 174-189, 264-279, 482-507.

A2309   Willcox, Alice. "Medical References in the Dramas of John Lyly." *Annals of Medical History,* X (1938), 117-126.

A2310   Rebora, Piero. "Motivi medici nel teatro inglese del Rinascimento." *Rinascita*, III (1940).

A2311   Babb, Lawrence. "The Physiological Conception of Love in the Elizabethan and Early Stuart Drama." *PMLA*, LVI (1941), 1020-35.

A2312   Randolph, Mary C. "The Medical Concept in English Renaissance Satiric Theory: Its Possible Relationships and Implications." *SP*, XXXVIII (1941), 125-157.
        Suggests that the medical imagery of Renaissance satire may be a survival of the incantational and magical verse of the Celts and, so far as it assigns a cathartic effect to satire, seems to point forward to 18th century moral and philosophical satire.

A2313   Duffy, Philip Howlett. *The Theory and Practice of Medicine in Elizabethan England as Illustrated by Certain Dramatic Texts*. DD, Harvard University, 1942. Abstr. publ. in *Summaries of Ph.D. Theses, 1942*. Cambridge: Harvard Univ. Press, 1946, pp. 268-271.

A2314   Allen, D. C. "John Donne's Knowledge of Renaissance Medicine." *JEGP*, XLII (1943), 322-342.

A2315   Price, George R. "Medical Men in *A Faire Quarrel*." *Bul. Hist. Med.*, XXIV (1950), 38-42.

A2316   MacGowan, C. E. *The Semantics of Certain Selected Medical Terms (nerve, liver, heart, blood, bile, phlegm, fever, digestion) in Seventeenth Century English Literature, with Special Reference to Their Use in Poetry and Poetic Drama*. Master's thesis, London, University College, 1956.

(5)   IN SHAKESPEARE
(a)   SHAKESPEARE'S KNOWLEDGE

A2317   Edgar, Irving I. "Shakespeare's Medical Knowledge, with Particular Reference to his Delineation of Madness." *Annals of Medical History*, VI (1935), 150-168.

A2318   Matthews, W. "Peter Bales, Timothy Bright, and W. Shakespeare." *JEGP*, XXXIV (1935), 483-510.

A2319   Watson, E. M. "Medical Lore in Shakespeare." *Annals of Medical History*, VIII (1936), 249-265.

A2320   Pomeranz, Herman. *Medicine in the Shakespearean Plays, and Dickens' Doctors."* New York: Powell Publishing Co., 1936. Pp. 410.

A2321   Goldbloom, A. "Shakespeare and Pediatrics." *Amer. Jour. of Diseases of Children*, LI (1936), 653-665.

A2322   Edgar, I. I. "Shakespeare, Harvey, and the Circulation of the Blood." *Medical Record*, 144 (1936), 37-39.

A2323   Edgar, Irving I. "Elizabethan Conceptions of the Physiology of the Circulation." *Annals of Medical History*, VIII (1936), 359-370, 456-465.
        Demolishes the idea that Shakespeare knew of the circulation of the blood before Harvey.

A2324   Wolff, L. "Medical Concepts in Shakespeare's Works." *Hygeia*, 99 (1937), 177-204.

A2325   de Lorde, A. "La Médecine au Théâtre: Shakespeare et Brieux." *Les Nouvelles Littéraires*, Nov. 13, 1937, p. 10.

A2326   Witt, W. H. "Medical References in Shakespeare." *Jour. of the Tennessee Medical Assoc.*, III (1938), 1-10.

A2327   Vest, W. E. "William Shakespeare, Syphilographer." *West Va. Medical Jour.*, XXXIV (1938), 130-137.

A2328   White, William. "Osler on Shakespeare, Bacon and Burton." *Bul. of Hist. Medicine*, VII (1939), 392-408.

A2329   Mikulowski, W. [La Médecine chez Shakespeare.] *Archivum historii i filozofii medycyny oraz historii nauk przyrodniczych* (Poznan), XVI (c. 1939), 28-58.

A2330   Walsh, G., and R. M. Pool. "Shakespeare's Knowledge of Twins & Twinning." *Southern Medicine & Surgery*, Apr., 1940, pp. 4. Reprint.

A2331   Walsh, G., and R. M. Pool. "Antithetical Views on Twinning Found in the Bible and Shakespeare." *Southern Medicine & Surgery*, 1941, pp. 12. Reprint.

A2332   Walsh, Groesbeck, and R. M. Pool. "Laterality Dominance in Shakespeare's Plays." *Southern Medicine & Surgery*, 104 (1942), 51-58. Also separately printed.

A2333   Schmutzer, R. "Tierkrankheiten im Werke Shakespeares." *Wiener Archiv für innere Medizin*, XXXV (1943), 325.

A2334   Vest, W. E. "William Shakespeare, Therapeutist." *Southern Medical Jour.*, Aug., 1944, pp. 457-464.

A2335   Johnson, E. D. "Shakespeare's Medical Knowledge." *Ba*, XXVIII (1944), 98-102.

A2336   Ficarra, Bernard J. "Surgical References in Shakespeare." *Essays on Historical Medicine*, New York, 1948, pp. 89-93.

A2337   Brussel, James A. "Doctor William Shakespeare." *General Magazine and Historical Chronicle* (Univ. of Penna.), LI (1949), 163-166.

A2338   Fabricant, Noah D. "Shakespeare's References to the Ear, Nose and Throat." *Eye, Ear, Nose and Throat Monthly*, XXIX (1950), 496.

A2339   Simpson, R. R. "Shakespeare on the Ear, Nose and Throat." *Jour. of Laryngology and Otology*, LXIV (1950), 342-352.

A2340   Vest, Walter E. "Shakespeare's Knowledge of Chest Diseases." *Jour. of the Am. Med. Assoc.*, 144 (1950), 1232-34.

A2341   Rose, B. T. "Medycyna w dcielach Wiliama Szekspira." *Wiadomosci lekarskie* (Warsaw), 1953, No. 2, pp. 116-118.

A2342   Plichet, A., and P. Plichet. "Shakespeare et ses Connaissances en Médecine." *Presse Médicale*, LXII (1954), 1845-49.

A2343   Sreenivasan, B. R. "Shakespeare on Medicine." *Medical Jour. of Malaya*, X (June, 1956), 279-288.

A2344   Rudolf, Werner. "Shakespeare und kein Ende." *Medizinische Klinik*, LII (1957), 436-437.

(b) CHARACTERS AND PASSAGES

A2345   Woods, Andrew H. "Syphilis in Shakespeare's Tragedy of Timon of Athens." *The American Jour. of Psychiatry*, Baltimore, 1934, pp. 95-107.

A2346   Edgar, Irving I. "Medical Practice and the Physician in Elizabethan England and in Shakespeare's Dramas." *Medical Life*, XLI (1935), 331-350.

A2347   Stender, John L. "Master Doctor Caius." *Bul. Hist. Medicine*, VIII (1940), 133-138.

A2348   Sims, Ruth E. "The Green Old Age of Falstaff." *Bul. Hist. Medicine*, XIII (1943), 144-157. On Falstaff as illustrating Elizabethan concepts of old age.

A2349   Camden, Carroll. "The Suffocation of the Mother." *MLN*, LXIII (1948), 390-393. On the medical background of the well-known passage in *Lear*.

A2350   Danks, K. B. " 'Grease That's Sweaten'." *N &Q*, NS, I (1954), 334. See letter by P. W. F. Brown, ibid., p. 545.
The phrase from *Macbeth* IV. i. 65, supported by passages from *H. VIII*, V. iv. 4-7; *1 H. IV*, II. i. 65-67; and *Timon*, IV. iii. 12-13, may be indicative of Shakespeare's firsthand knowledge of public hangings. Mr. Brown notes that the belief in the magical properties of human fat was widely accepted in Shakespeare's time.

A2351   Kocher, Paul H. "Lady Macbeth and the Doctor." *SQ*, V (1954), 341-349.

A2352   Summerskill, William H. J. "Aguecheek's Disease." *Lancet*, 269 (1955), 288 ff. See also Rudolf Werner, "Shakespeare als Medizinischer Autor." *Medizin. Klinik*, L (1955), 1758.

A2353   Steadman, John M. "Falstaff's 'Facies Hippocratica': A Note on Shakespeare and Renaissance Medical Theory." *SN*, XXIX (1957), 130-135.

A2354   Wilson, J. Dover. "A Note on *Richard III*: The Bishop of Ely's Strawberries." *MLR*, LII (1957), 563-564.
Quotes and evaluates (mostly with acceptance) the letter of Dr. J. Swift Joly (*British Medical Journal*, June 15, 1956) arguing that Richard's withered arm, which he attributes to witchcraft, was really only suffering from a rash, which he intentionally produced by sending for and eating the strawberries.

A2355   Mendilow, A. A. "Falstaff's Death of a Sweat." *SQ*, IX (1958), 479-483.
Dame Quickly's account of Falstaff's death is shown to accord in detail with Renaissance (and classical) medical description of the last stages of a plague victim.

h. ALCHEMY, CHEMISTRY, AND PHARMACY (41;-)
(1) IN GENERAL

A2356   Reidy, J. *An Edition of "The Ordinal of Alchemy" by Thomas Norton.* Edited from MS. Bod. E. Mus. 63 with variants from B.M. Add. 10302, introduction, commentary, and glossary of technical terms and uses. Ph.D., London, External, 1957.

A2357   Read, John. *Prelude to Chemistry: An Outline of Alchemy. Its Literature and Relationships.* London: G. Bell, 1936. Pp. 352, il.
Shak. passim.
Rev: *TLS*, Dec. 12, 1936, p. 1028; by F. Sherwood Taylor, *Annals of Science*, II (1937), 136; by J. R. P., *Science Progress*, XXXII, 193-194; by Tenney L. Davis, *Isis*, XXVII, 528-531; by Rudolph J. Anderson, *YR*, XXVI, 626-628; by John Riordan, *SRL*, Jan. 25, 1937, p. 6; by Allan C. Topp, *Dalhousie Rev.*, XVII, 394.

A2358   Duveen, Denis. "Notes on Some Alchemical Books." *Library*, 5th Series, I (1946), 56-61.

A2359   Read, John. *The Alchemist in Life, Literature and Art.* London: Nelson, 1947. Pp. xii, 100. Nothing on Shak. but much on his times.
Rev: *TLS*, Jan. 31, 1948, p. 63.

A2360   Taylor, F. Sherwood. *The Alchemists.* London: Heinemann, 1952. Pp. x, 246.
Rev: by C. E. Vulliamy, *Spectator*, July 25, 1952, pp. 136-137; *TLS*, Aug. 29, 1952, p. 567; by J. R. F. Calder, *NstN*, Sept. 20, 1952, pp. 324-326; by C. E. M. Joad, *Time and Tide*, July 5, 1952, pp. 752-753.

A2361   Princeton University Library. "A Sixteenth Century Scroll of Alchemical Emblems." *Princeton Univ. Lib. Chronicle*, XIX (1958), 201-202.
The scroll, work of a late 16th century copyist, is similar to the scroll of George Ripley, preserved in the British Museum.

A2362   Dickson, Sarah Augusta. *Panacea or Precious Bane: Tobacco in Sixteenth Century Literature*

(Arents Tobacco Collection, Publication No. 5). New York: The New York Public Library, 1954. Pp. xiv, 230.
The only mention of Shak. is to say he said nothing about tobacco.
Rev: by James G. McManaway, *SQ*, VI (1955), 350-351; by Lawrence C. Wroth, *Papers of the Bibliographical Society of America*, XLIX, 281-284.

A2363 Singer, Charles. *The Earliest Chemical Industry: An Essay in the Historical Relations of Economics and Technology Illustrated from the Alum Trade.* Preface by Derek Spence. London: Folio Soc., 1948. Pp. xviii, 337, illus. 181.
Contains excellent sections on medieval and Renaissance periods.
Rev: by E. A. Underwood, *Spectator*, May 27, 1949, pp. 730-732.

A2364 Rehor, Charles F. *Of Many Simples: A Study of the Elizabethan Melancholic in Medicine and Literature (1586-1621).* DD, Western Reserve University, 1941.

(2) IN SHAKESPEARE

A2365 Harrison, Thomas P., Jr. "Shakespeare's 'Hebenon' Again." *MLR*, XL (1945), 310-311.

A2366 Sullivan, Frank. "Hamlet's Hebona and Mercury Poisoning." *Los Angeles Tidings*, Dec. 31, 1948, pp. 9.
Hydrargyrum, called Mercury, was administered by ear as a poison.

A2367 Macht, David I. "A Physiologic and Pharmacologic Appreciation of *Hamlet*, Act I, Scene 5, lines 59-73." *Bul. Hist. Medicine*, XXIII (1949), 186-195.

A2368 Savage, D. S. "Heraldry and Alchemy in Shakespeare's *Hamlet*." *Univ. of Kansas City Rev.*, XVII (1951), 231-240.

A2369 Savage, D. S. "An Alchemical Metaphor in *Hamlet*." *N &Q*, 197 (1952), 157-160.

A2370 Savage, D. S. "Alchemy in Shakespeare's *Hamlet*: An Essay in Creative Interpretation." *The Aryan Path*, XXXIII (1952), 366-369.

A2371 Macht, David I. "Shakespeare's Allusions to Clotting and Blood Clotting Drugs." *Jour. of the American Pharmaceutical Assoc.*, XII, No. 3 (March, 1951).

A2372 Macht, David I. "Calendula or Marigold in Medical History and in Shakespeare." *Bul. Hist. Medicine*, XXIX (1955), 491-502.

9. ART (41,177;16,62)
a. TUDOR ART IN GENERAL
(Occasional items from literary bibliographies.)

A2373 Ogden, Henry V., and Margaret S. Ogden. "A Bibliography of Seventeenth Century Writings on the Pictorial Arts in English." *Art Bulletin*, XXIX (1947), 196-201.

A2374 Panofsky, Erwin. *Studies in Iconology: Humanistic Themes in the Art of the Renaissance.* Oxford Univ. Press, 1939. Pp. xxxiii, 262.
Rev: by Leicester Bradner, *MP*, XXXVIII (1940), 103-104; by C. S. Singleton, *MLN*, LV, 478-479; by A. H. Gilbert, *Art. Bul.*, XXII, 172-174; by H. W. Johnson, ibid., XXII, 174-175.

A2375 Sitwell, Sacheverell. *British Architects and Craftsmen: A Survey of Taste, Design and Style During Three Centuries, 1600-1830.* London: B. T. Batsford, Ltd., 1946. Pp. vii, 196.
Rev: by G. P. G., *ConR*, 169 (1946), 64; by R. D. Middleton, *Hist. Mag. Protestant Episcopal Church*, XV, 251-252.

A2376 Dutton, Ralph. *The English Interior, 1500 to 1900.* London; New York: Batsford, 1949. Pp. 192.
Rev: *TLS*, April 16, 1949, p. 254; by James Lees-Milne, *Spectator*, March 18, p. 372.

A2377 Winter, C. *The British School of Miniature Portrait Painters.* Annual Lecture on Aspects of Art. Henriette Hertz Trust of the British Academy. Oxford Univ. Press, 1949. Pp. 19, pl. 10.
Rev: *TLS*, Nov. 18, 1949, p. 744.

b. SHAKESPEARE AND ART

A2378 Fairchild, Arthur H. R. *Shakespeare and the Arts of Design (Architecture, Sculpture, and Painting).* Univ. of Missouri Studies, XII, No. 1. Columbia, Mo.: Univ. of Missouri, 1937. Pp. xii, 198.
Professor Fairchild has concerned himself with the possible influence of the decorative arts on Shakespeare, and he has carried the investigation much further than it has ever been carried before. In order to achieve his purpose he has made background studies in Elizabethan architecture, sculpture, and painting, which, in turn, are not without their originality and thoroughness. It turns out that Shakespeare's allusions to the decorative arts, always casual, are extensive and widespread in his work. Professor Fairchild has worked *con amore*, and his book will be delightful to all Shakespeareans.
Rev: by G. W. Knight, *MLR*, XXXIII (1938), 68; by Alwin Thaler, *JEGP*, XXXVII, 81-84; by Robert Withington, *MLN*, LIII, 619-623; by Georges Connes, *EA*, II, 45-46; by Albert Eichler, *Beiblatt*, XLIX, 100-103.

A2379 Baughan, Denver Ewing. "Shakespeare's Probable Confusion of the Two Romanos." *JEGP*, XXXVI (1937), 35-39.

On the painter who made the statue of Hermione; and on Shak.'s taste in art (for naturalness and realism).

A2363-A2396 101

A2380 Laux, Karl August. "Shakespeare und die bildende Kunst." *Deutschland-Italien. Festschrift für W. Waetzoldt.* Berlin: Grote, 1941, pp. 209-243.

A2381 Hammerle, Karl. "The Poet's Eye (*MND* 5.1.12): Zur Auffassung Shakespeares vom Wesen des Dichters." *Ammann-Festgabe,* Innsbruck, 1953, pp. 101-107.

A2382 Merchant, W. M. "*Timon* and the Conceit of Art." *SQ*, VI (1955), 249-257.
Vindicates the dramatic function of the Poet and Painter scenes. Poetry and painting, as argued in Renaissance controversy, present appearance as a revelation of reality; and this kind of presentation becomes the business of the play.

A2383 Künstler, Ernst. "Julio Romano im Wintermärchen." *SJ*, 92 (1956), 291-298.

A2384 Eggar, Katharine. "Shakespeare as a Musician." *Musical Times,* Sept., 1958, pp. 480-481.

A2385 Giannini, V. "Shakespeare's Musical Training." *Music Journal,* XVI (1958), 8 ff.

A2386 Hoffman, Mary. "Shakespeare Knew His Music." *Music Journal,* Sept., 1958, pp. 90-92.

10. SHAKESPEARE'S ATTITUDE TOWARDS EDUCATION
(Cancelled; contents transferred to Shakespeare's Education,
Reading and Book Knowledge, IV,I,e.)

11. GEOGRAPHICAL KNOWLEDGE. SHAKESPEARE'S ALLEGED TRAVELS
AND LOST YEARS
a. RENAISSANCE TRAVEL AND GEOGRAPHY (181;-)

A2387 Cox, Edward G. *A Reference Guide to the Literature of Travel.* Vol. I: The Old World. Univ. of Washington Pubs. in Lang. and Lit., IX. Seattle: Univ. of Washington, 1935. Pp. x, 401. Vol. II: The New World. Univ. of Washington Pubs. in Lang. and Lit., x, 1938. Pp. vii, 591. Vol. III: Great Britain. Univ. of Washington Pubs. in Lang. and Lit., XII, 1949. Pp. xiii, 732.
Rev: Vol. I: by George B. Parks, *MLN*, LII (1937), 310; Vol. II: by J. I. Wyer, *Lib. Quar.*, IX (1939), 355-357; by Jane Louise Mesick, *American Lit.*, x, 522-523; by R. W. Frantz, *MP*, XXXVIII (1940), 101-103; Vol. III: by W. H. Bonner, *JEGP*, XLIX (1950), 257-260.

A2388 Burpee, Lawrence J. *The Search for the Western Sea.* The Story of the Exploration of Northwestern America. New and Revised ed., 2 Vols. Toronto: Macmillan, 1935. Pp. lxi, 304; ix, 305; il. and maps.
Rev: by D. C. Harvey, *Dalhousie Rev.*, xv (1936), 529-530; by Reginald G. Trotter, *QQ*, XLIII, 101-103.

A2389 Penrose, Boies. *Travel and Discovery in the Renaissance, 1420-1620.* Cambridge, Mass., 1952. Pp. xvi, 369.
Rev: by Thomas Caldecot Chubb, *NYTBR*, Nov. 30, 1952, p. 50; *TLS*, July 17, 1953, p. 458; by Robert Sabatino Lopez, *Speculum*, XXVIII, 412-415; by E. G. R. Taylor, *Mariner's Mirror*, XXXIX, 316-317; by Garrett Mattingly, *SatR*, Jan. 3, pp. 15, 61-62; by George B. Parks, *RN*, VI, 5-6; by Manoel Cardozo, *Catholic Hist. Rev.*, XXXIX, 200-201.

A2390 Jones, Howard M. "The Image of the New World." *Elizabethan Studies . . . in Honor of George F. Reynolds,* 1945, pp. 62-84.

A2391 Lynam, Edward, ed. *Richard Hakluyt and His Successors.* Hakluyt Soc., 2nd Series, No. CXIII. London: Bernard Quaritch, for the Soc., 1946. Pp. 192, lxviii, pl. 8.
Rev: by Honor Croome, *Spectator*, Dec. 6, 1946, p. 614; "Hakluyt Society," *TLS*, Dec. 7, p. 603; by George Sarton, *Isis*, XXXVIII (1947), 130; by A. E. Hall, *Mariner's Mirror*, XXXIII, 132; by S. T. Sheppard, *NstN*, Mar. 15, p. 178.

A2392 Wright, Louis B. *Middle-class Culture in Elizabethan England.* Univ. of North Carolina Press, 1935. Pp. xiv, 733. Republished 1958.
Rev: A1909.

A2393 Bush, Douglas. *English Literature in the Earlier Seventeenth Century, 1600-1660.* Oxford: Clarendon Press, 1945. Pp. 621. Chapters on Travel, pp. 170-180.
Rev: A8045.

A2394 Thomson, J. A. K. *Classical Influences on English Prose.* London: Allen & Unwin, 1956. Pp. xiii, 303.
Chap. XVII: "The Literature of Travel," pp. 262-277.
Rev: A4145.

A2395 Cawley, Robert Ralston. *The Voyagers and Elizabethan Drama.* Mod. Lang. Assoc. Monograph Series, VIII. Boston: Heath, 1938. Pp. xiv, 428.
Rev: by A. Walker, *RES*, xv (1939), 475-476; by J. H. Walter, *MLR*, XXXIV, 86-87; by G. B. Parks, *MP*, XXXVI, 318-319; by Una Ellis-Fermor, *MLN*, LIV, 603-604; EA, III, 330; by Alois Brandl, *DLZ*, LX, 771-772; by G. R. C., *Geog. Jour.*, 93 (1939), 369-370; by P. Meissner, *Beiblatt*, L, 110-112; by M. H. Braaksma, *ES*, XXI, 278-279; by W. G. Rice, *JEGP*, XXXIX (1940), 288-290.

A2396 Cawley, R. R. *Unpathed Waters: Studies in the Influence of the Voyagers on Elizabethan Literature.* Princeton Univ. Press; Oxford Univ. Press, 1940. Pp. viii, 285.
Rev: by G. B. Parks, *JEGP*, XL (1941), 582-584; by R. W. Frantz, *MP*, XXXIX (1942),

321-322; by Edward Godfrey Cox, *MLQ*, III, 123-125; E. G. R. Taylor, *RES*, XVII, 475-479; by J. H. Walter, *MLR*, XXXVII, 203; by Warner G. Rice, *MLN*, LVIII (1943), 322-324.

A2397 McManaway, James G. "Women and Ships." *TLS*, Feb. 20, 1937, p. 131. See letter by R. G. Howarth, *TLS*, Sept. 25, 1937, p. 695.

A2398 Couldridge, F. T. *Voyages and Travels in the Works of Some Prominent Men of Letters of the Shakespearian Age (1558-1625)*. MA thesis, University of South Africa, 1940.

A2399 Ramsaran, J. A. *The West Indies in English Literature Mainly During the Sixteenth and Seventeenth Centuries*. MA thesis, University of London, 1951.

b. SHAKESPEARE'S GEOGRAPHY (42;17)

A2400 Robertson, J. Minto. "Wanted—a Shakespeare Atlas and Gazetteer." *English*, VI (1946), 69-73.

(1) ENGLAND AND SCOTLAND

A2401 Platter, Thomas. *Thomas Platter's Travels in England, 1599*. Rendered into English from the German and with introductory matter by Clare Williams. London: Cape, 1937. Pp. 245.
Rev: *TLS*, Sept. 11, 1937, pp. 645-646; see letter by Everard W. Pepys, ibid., Sept. 18, p. 675; by P. Laver, ibid., Sept. 25, p. 695; by Clare Williams, ibid., Oct. 16, p. 759; by A. L. Rowse, *Spectator*, Sept. 24, pp. 510, 512; by W. J. Lawrence, *London Mercury*, XXXVI, 584; by A. Desmond Hawkins, *NstN*, NS, XIV, 958-960; by W. E. C. Harrison, *QQ*, XLIV, 587-588; by Pierre Janelle, *EA*, II (1938), 48-49; by A. V. Judges, *History*, NS, XXIII, 77-78.

A2402 Thorndike, Russell. *In the Steps of Shakespeare*. London: Rich and Cowan, 1948. Pp. 308. Originally publ. as *Wanderer with Shakespeare*.

A2403 Langdale, A. Barnett. "Did Shakspere Miss the Road to Warkworth? (A Note on *Henry the Fourth, Part Two*.)" *SAB*, XVII (1942), 156-159.

A2404 Pohl, Frederick, J. "Where Shakespeare Saw Mountains." *ShN*, VIII (1958), 37.

A2405 Gierow, K. R. "På spår i en mordaffar (Tracking a murder case)." *Svenska Dagbladet* (Stockholm), Mar. 18, 1955.

A2406 Fergusson, Sir James. *Shakespeare's Scotland*. Andrew Lang Lecture delivered before the University of St. Andrew's, Nov. 14, 1956. Edinburgh: Nelson, 1957. Pp. ii, 21.

(2) ITALY

A2407 Farinelli, Arturo. "La Visión de Italia en la Obra de Shakespeare." *La Nación* (Buenos Aires), July 9, 16, 1939.

A2408 Draper, John W. "Shakespeare and Florence and the Florentines." *Italica*, XXIII (1946), 287-293.

A2409 Draper, John W. "Shakespeare and the Doge of Venice." *JEGP*, XLVI (1947), 75-81.

A2410 Colafelice, Franco L. "Shakespeare in Italia." *Insegnare* (Rome), VIII, No. 11 (Nov., 1953), 25-30.

A2411 Draper, John W. "Shakespeare and the Lombard Cities." *Rivista di Letterature Moderne*, IV (1953), 54-58.

A2412 Steer, Barbara D. G. "Shakespeare and Italy." *N &Q*, 198, No. 1 (1953), 23.

A2413 Praz, Mario. "Shakespeare's Italy." *ShS*, VII (1954), 95-106. Also in *The Flaming Heart*. Essays on Crashaw, Machiavelli, and Other Studies in the Relations between Italian and English Literature from Chaucer to T. S. Eliot (Doubleday Anchor Books). Garden City: Doubleday & Company, 1958, pp. 146-167.

A2414 Cancelled.

(3) ISLAM

A2415 Chew, Samuel C. *The Crescent and the Rose: Islam and England During the Renaissance*. Oxford Univ. Press, 1937. Pp. xviii, 583.
Rev: *TLS*, Mar. 19, 1938, p. 183; by David Garnett, *NstN*, NS, XV, 370-372; by Tucker Brooke, *SRL*, Jan. 15, 1938, p. 16; by H. A. R. Gibb, *MLR*, XXXIII, 579-580; by R. T. F., *Personalist*, XIX, 411-416.

A2416 Baumer, Franklin Le Van. "The Church of England and the Common Corps of Christendom." *JMH*, XVI (1944), 1-22.

A2417 Baumer, Franklin Le Van. "England, the Turk, and the Common Corps of Christendom." *AHR*, L (1944), 26-48.

A2418 Baumer, Franklin Le Van. "The Conception of Christendom in Renaissance England." *JHI*, VI (1945), 131-156.

A2419 Lebel, R. "Le Maroc dans le Théâtre de Shakespeare." *Revue de la Méditerranée*, IV (1948), 299-308.

A2420 Burian, Orhan. "Interest of the English in Turkey as Reflected in English Literature of the Renaissance." *Oriens* (Jour. International Soc. Oriental Research), V (1952), 209-229.

A2421   Spencer, Terence. "Turks and Trojans in the Renaissance." *MLR*, XLVII (1952), 330-333.
A2422   Draper, John W. "Shakespeare and the Turk." *JEGP*, LV (1956), 523-532.

(4) ELSEWHERE

A2423   Feldman, Abraham B. "Playwrights and Pike-trailers in the Low Countries." *N &Q*, 198 (May, 1953), 184-187.
A2424   Langenfelt, Gösta. "The Geographical Position of *Dansk(e)*, *Danskin*, *Danskyn*." *Studier i Modern Språkvetenskap (Stockholm Studies in Modern Philology)*, XVII (1949), 62-70.
A2425   Künstler, Ernst. "Böhmen am Meer." *SJ*, 91 (1955), 212-216.
A2426   Parks, George B. "Shakespeare's Map for *The Comedy of Errors*." *JEGP*, XXXIX (1940), 93-97.
A2427   Spencer, Terence. "Shakespeare's Isle of Delphos." *MLR*, XLVII (1952), 199-202.
A2428   Draper, John W. "Shakespeare and Muscovy." *The Slavonic and East European Review*, XXXIII, No. 80 (1955), 217-221.
A2429   Draper, John W. "Ethiopian in Shakespeare." *Anglia*, LXXIII, No. 1 (1955), 65-70.
A2430   Lockhart, Laurence. "Shakespeare's Persia." *Journal of the Iran Soc.* (London), I (1952), 141-146.
A2431   Winsteadt, R. "The East in English Literature." *Indian Art and Letters*, XXI (1947), 1-12.
A2432   Draper, John W. "Shakespeare and India." *Littératures: Etudes de Littérature Moderne* (Annales publiées par la Faculté des Lettres de Toulouse), II (Novembre, 1953), 1-12.
A2433   Draper, John W. "*Indian* and *Indies* in Shakespeare." *N. Mitt.*, LVI (1955), 103-112.
A2434   Lesher, Clara R. *The South Sea Islanders in English Literature, 1519-1798.* DD, University of Chicago, 1938.
A2435   Nutt, Sarah M. "The Arctic Voyages of William Barents in Probable Relation to Certain of Shakespeare's Plays." *SP*, XXXIX (1942), 241-264.
A2436   Walmsley, D. M. "Shakespeare's Link with Virginia." *History Today*, VII (1957), 229-235.

(5) TRAVEL

A2437   Baughan, Denver Ewing. "Shakespeare's Attitude toward Travel." *Essays in Honor of W. C. Curry*, pp. 207-220.
A2438   Ewen, C. L'Estrange. *Shakespeare No Seaman.* London, 1938.
        Rev: *TLS*, Dec. 31, 1938, p. 831.
A2439   Knight, F. E. "How Did Shakespeare Know? An Essay to Suggest that Shakespeare was a Sailor." *The Seafarer*, No. 67 (July, 1950), pp. 60-62.

c. THE LOST YEARS
(Alphabetical by author.)

A2440   Baker, Oliver. *In Shakespeare's Warwickshire and the Unknown Years.* London, 1937. Pp. 328.
        Rev: A811.
A2441   Günther, Alfred. *Der Junge Shakespeare: Sieben Unbekannte Jahre.* Stuttgart: Deutsche Verlaganstalt, 1947; Zürich: Ex-Libris Verlag, 1949. Pp. 249.
        Rev: by J. Thielmann, *Die Lücke* (1948), Beil. Neue Lit., p. 35; by G. G., *Neues Abendland*, III (1948), 255; by H. Reitz, *Welt und Wort*, III (1948), 269-270.
A2442   Duff Cooper, Sir A. *Sergeant Shakespeare.* London: Rupert Hart-Davis; Toronto: Clarke, Irwin & Co., 1949. Pp. 100.
        Tr. into Italian by Elena Canino as *Il Sergente Shakespeare.* Naples: Ed. scientifiche ital., 1950. Pp. 97.
        Summary: "Unteroffizier Shakespeare," *Die Brücke*, No. 160 (1949), 13-14.
        Rev: by George Rylands, *Spectator*, Dec. 9, 1949, p. 824; *TLS*, Dec. 30, 1949, p. 858; by Desmond MacCarthy, *Sunday Times*, Dec. 11, p. 3; by H. Smith, *YR*, XXXIX (1950), 743-746; *Blackwood's Mag.*, 267 (1950), 191-192; by Esther C. Dunn, *SRL*, Apr. 1, 1950, p. 15; by W. P. Eaton, *NYHTBR*, May 7, p. 25; by F. D. Hoeniger, *Canadian Forum*, XXX, 71; by D. A. Stauffer, *SQ*, I, 89-90; *CE*, XI, 122; by D. Bush, *NR*, Apr. 24, p. 20; by H. Levin, *NYTBR*, Mar. 26, pp. 7, 30; by P. Williams, *South Atlantic Quar.*, XLIX, 553-554; *Elseviers Weekblad*, Feb. 4; by J. B. Fort, *LanM* XLIV (1950), 266; by E. Brennecke, *SQ*, I, 275-276; *TAr*, XXXIV, 13; by Hamilton Basso, *New Yorker*, Apr. 8, pp. 117-118; *Listener*, XLIII, 307-308; by W. van Maanen, *De Gids*, 114 (1951), 378-379.
A2443   Gray, Cecil G. "Shakespeare's Lost Years." *John o' London's Weekly*, LIX (April 28, 1950), 249-250.
A2444   Mutschmann, Heinrich. "Shakespeare's Lost Years." *Players Magazine*, July 26, 1950, p. 154 f.
A2445   Keen, Alan. "In the Quick Forge and Working-House of Thought . . . Lancashire and Shropshire and the Young Shakespeare." *BJRL*, XXXIII (Mar., 1951), 256-270. Also published separately, Manchester: Univ. Press, 1951. Pp. 15.
        Rev: *TLS*, Aug. 10, 1951, p. 498.

A2446   Lambin, G. "Sur la Trace d'un Shakespeare Inconnu: I. Shakespeare à Florence; II. Shakespeare et la Ligue." *LanM*, XLV (1951), 1-21.

A2447   Wentersdorf, Karl. "Shakespeares Erste Truppe. Ein Beitrag zur Aufklärung des Problems der sog. 'verlorenen Jahre'." *SJ*, 84/86 (1948-50), 114-130.
         Rev: by R. A. Law, *SQ*, III (1952), 86.

A2448   Isaacs, J. *Shakespeare's Earliest Years in the Theatre*. Annual Shakespeare Lecture of the British Academy, 1953. *Proceedings of the British Academy*, XXXIX. London: Cumberlege, 1955. Pp. 26.
         Rev: A604.

A2449   Everitt, E. B. *The Young Shakespeare: Studies in Documentary Evidence*. Vol. II: *Anglistica*. Copenhagen: Rosenkilde and Bagger, 1954. Pp. 188.
         Rev: *TLS*, May 7, 1954, p. 302; by Robert Adger Law, *JEGP*, LIII, 624-628; by Hermann Heuer, *SJ*, 90 (1954), 328-330; brief notice in *The Library*, 5th Series, IX, 218; by Peter P. Rohde, *Information* (Copenhagen), July 8; by T. S. Dorsch, *YWES*, XXXV, 84; by M. M. Reese, *RES*, NS, VI (1955), 310-313; by Clifford Leech, *MLN*, LXX, 206-208; *CE*, XVI, 199; by C. J. Sisson, *SQ*, VI, 455-457; by Levin L. Schücking, *Anglia*, LXXIII, 221-224; by J. R. Brown, *SN*, XXVII, 161-163; by Robert Adger Law, *TxSE*, XXXIV, 47-50; by Hermann Heuer, *Archiv*, 193 (1956), 56-57; by Harold Jenkins, *MLR*, LI, 96.

A2450   Keen, Alan, and Roger Lubbock. *The Annotator: the Pursuit of an Elizabethan Reader of Halle's "Chronicle" Involving Some Surmises About the Early Life of William Shakespeare*. London: Putnam, 1954. Pp. xiii, 216.
         Rev: A425.

A2451   Lambin, Georges. "Sur les Traces d'un Shakespeare Inconnu. Réponse à Mario Praz et à quelques Autres." *LanM*, XLVIII (1954), 505-507.

A2452   Cancelled.

A2453   Law, Robert Adger. "Guessing About the Youthful Shakespeare." *TxSE*, XXXIV (1955), 43-50.

A2454   Broadbent, C. "Shakespeare and Shakeshaft." *N&Q*, NS, III (1956), 154-157.

A2455   Neilson, Francis (Rhadamanthus, pseudonym). *Shakespeare and the Tempest*. New Hampshire: Richard R. Smith, 1956.
         Rev: B9830.

12.   SPORT

a.   GENERAL (181;-)

(Items from the sources of this bibliography only.)

A2456   Bentley, Gerald Eades, ed. *The Arte of Angling, 1577*. With an Introd. by Carl Otto v. Kienbusch, & Explanatory Notes by Henry L. Savage. Princeton: Princeton Univ. Press, 1958. Pp. 178.
         Rev: by Arthur M. Coon, *SCN*, XVI (1958), 43; by Marcus Selden Golden, *JEGP*, LVII, 136-146; by V. de S. Pinto, *N&Q*, NS, V, 551-552.
         Second facsimile ed.; the first was published in 1956.

A2457   Aylward, J. D. "Playing a Prize." *N&Q*, 196 (1951), 201-204.

A2458   Aylward, J. D. "Saviolo's Ghost." *N&Q*, 195 (1950), 226-229.
         Suggests that Saviolo's treatise on fencing was ghostwritten by John Florio.

A2459   Indorf, Hans. " 'Fair Play' und der 'Englische Sportgeist'." *Britannica*, Heft 15. Hamburg: Friederichsen u. de Gruyter & Co., 1938.
         Comments by Wolfgang Schmidt, "Ist England noch das Land des Sports?" *ZNU*, XXXIX (1940), 37.

A2460   M., M. "The Booke of Falconrie." *More Books*, XVIII (1943), 427.

b.   IN SHAKESPEARE (43;17)

A2461   Jacob, Georg. *Shakespeare-Studien*. Nach dem Tode des Verfassers hrsg. v. H. Jensen. Glückstadt; Hamburg; New York: Augustin, 1938. Pp. 37.

A2462   Schultz, John Howard. "A Glossary of Shakespeare's Hawking Language." *TxSE*, XVIII (1938), 174-205.

A2463   Fatout, Paul. "With Horn and Hound." *SAB*, XX (1945), 63-75.

A2464   Gibson, F. D. *The Use of Sport for Imagery and Incident in the Works of Shakespeare*. MA thesis, Leeds University, 1951.

A2465   Huhner, Max. *Shakespearean Studies and Other Essays*. With an Introd. by George S. Hellman. New York: Farrar Straus, 1952. Pp. 115.
         "Was Shakespeare an Angler?" pp. 42-49.
         Rev: B4476.

A2466   McCullen, Joseph T., Jr. "The Use of Parlor and Tavern Games in Elizabethan and Early Stuart Drama." *MLQ*, XIV (1953), 7-14.

13.   HERALDRY (43,180;17,-)

A2467 Tannenbaum, Samuel A. "Almost Right: Shakespeare's Coat-of-Arms." *SAB*, XI (1936), 58.

A2468 Baker, H. Kendra. "Shakespeare's 'Coat of Arms'." *Ba*, XXIV (1938/39 [?]), 77-84.

A2469 Scott-Giles, C. W. *Shakespeare's Heraldry*. London: Dent, 1950. Pp. x, 237.
       Rev: by M. St. Clare Byrne, *English*, VIII (1950), 89; *TLS*, Mar. 10, 1950, p. 154; by R. M. Smith, *SQ*, I, 183-184; by H. L. Savage, ibid., I, 286-292; by A. R. W., *History*, NS, XXXIX, 179-180.

A2470 Holmes, Martin. "A Heraldic Allusion in *Henry V*." *N &Q*, 195 (1950), 333.

A2471 Kingston, H. B. "The Martlets." *TLS*, Mar. 16, 1951, p. 165. Comment by Scott-Giles, *TLS*, Apr. 13, 1951, p. 229.

A2472 Savage, D. S. "Heraldry and Alchemy in Shakespeare's *Hamlet*." *Univ. of Kansas City Rev.*, XVII (1951), 231-240.

A2473 Walker, Saxon. "Mime and Heraldry in *Henry IV, Part I*." *English*, XI (1956), 91-96.

14. WOMEN, LOVE, MARRIAGE, THE FAMILY
a. GENERAL (179;63)
(1) REPRINTS OF OLD TEXTS

A2474 Parry, J. P., translator and ed. *"The Art of Courtly Love" by Andreas Capellanus*. New York: Columbia Univ. Press, 1941. Pp. xii, 218.

A2475 Fraser, Russell A., ed. *The Court of Venus*. Duke Univ. Press, 1955. Pp. x, 168.
       Rev: briefly by James G. McManaway, *SQ*, VIII (1957), 126.

A2476 Plat, Sir Hugh. *Delights for Ladies to Adorne Their Persons, Closets and Distillatories*. London, 1609. Facsimile reprint: Trovillion Private Press, Herrin, Illinois, 1939. With Introd. by G. E. and Kathleen R. Fussell. London: Crosby Lockwood, 1948. Pp. xci, 106.
       Rev: by Kenneth Young, *Spectator*, Apr. 22, 1949, pp. 550-552; *TLS*, Jan. 8, p. 30.

A2477 Byrne, Muriel St. Clare, ed. *The Elizabethan Home: Discovered in Two Dialogues by Claudius Hollyband and Peter Erondell*. A new and enlarged ed. of work publ. in 1925. London: Methuen, 1949. Pp. xxiii, 91.
       Rev: by Kenneth Young, *Spectator*, May 6, 1949, p. 622.

(2) THE DOMESTIC SCENE: WOMEN, CHILDREN, AND THE HOME (Arrangement by subject.)

A2478 Bradford, Gamaliel. *Elizabethan Women*. Ed. by Harold Ogden White. Boston: Houghton Mifflin, 1936. Pp. 243.
       Rev: by D. O., *SRL*, Apr. 11, 1936, p. 19; *More Books*, XI, 183; by Samuel A. Tannenbaum, *SAB*, XI, 125-126; by Katherine Brégy, *Catholic World*, 143 (1936), 761-762; *Nation* (N.Y.), 142 (1936), 558-559; by P. Hutchinson, *NYTBR*, Mar. 15, p. 6.

A2479 Galinsky, Hans. *Die Familie im Drama von Thomas Heywood*. Eine Studie zur dichterischen Entwicklung des englischen Gemeinschaftsgefühls. Sprache und Kultur d. Germ.-rom. Völker. A: Anglist. R. Bd. 22. Breslau: Priebatsch, 1936. Pp. xvii, 134.
       Rev: by W. Keller, *SJ*, LXXIII (1937), 166-167.

A2480 Kohler, Charlotte. *The Elizabethan Woman of Letters: The Extent of her Literary Activities*. DD, University of Virginia, 1936. Abstr. in Univ. of Virginia *Abstracts of Dissertations, 1936*. pp. 14-18.

A2481 Kahin, Helen A. *Controversial Literature About Women: A Survey of the Literature of this Type with Special Reference to the Writings of the English Renaissance*. DD, University of Washington, 1937. Abstr. in Univ. of Washington *Abstracts of Theses*, II (1937), 575-578.

A2482 Tipping, H. Avray. *English Homes*. Vol. II: *Mediaeval and Early Tudor, 1066-1558*. London: Country Life, 1937. Pp. 412.

A2483 "Elizabethan Decoration. Patterns in Art and Passion." *TLS*, July 3, 1937, pp. 485-486.

A2484 Pearson, Lu Emily. "Elizabethan Widows." *Stanford Studies in Language and Literature* (Stanford Univ. Press, 1941), pp. 124-142.

A2485 O'Connor, William V. *The New Woman of the Renaissance*. New York, 1942.

A2486 Stauffer, Ruth Mary. *The Relation of Women to English Literature from 1558 to 1660*. DD, Radcliffe College, 1942.

A2487 Wright, Celeste T. "Something More About Eve." *SP*, XLI (1944), 156-168.

A2488 Wright, Celeste T. "The Elizabethan Female Worthies." *SP*, XLIII (1946), 628-643.

A2489 Hole, Christina. *English Home-Life, 1500-1800*. London: Batsford, 1947. Pp. 184.
       Rev: *TLS*, Dec. 13, 1947, p. 643; *National Rev.*, 130 (1948), 436-437; *QR*, 276 (1948), 273-284.

A2490 Byrne, Muriel St. Clare. *Elizabethan Life in Town and Country*. 6th rev. ed. London: Methuen, 1950. Pp. xxiv, 302.

A2491 Camden, Carroll. *The Elizabethan Woman*. Houston, Texas: Elsevier Press; London: Cleaver-Hume; Toronto: Burns and MacEachern, 1952. Pp. 333.
       Rev: by J. E. Neale, *Sunday Times*, Dec. 7, 1952, p. 4; by Joseph Wood Krutch, *Nation*,

Sept. 6, 1952, pp. 195-196; by A. L. Rowse, *Time and Tide*, Dec. 6, pp. 1460-61; by Lillian de la Torre, *NYTBR*, Sept. 7, p. 16; by Margaret Evans, *NYHTBR*, Sept. 7, p. 5; *TLS*, Jan. 16, 1953, p. 34; by Kathleen M. Williams, *MLN*, LXVIII, 500-502; by Ruth Kelso, *JEGP*, LII, 256-258; by M. T. Jones-Davies, *EA*, VI, 357-358; by D. M. S., *English*, IX, 150 (brief); by Catherine Strateman Sims, *AHR*, LVIII, 684-685; by Gladys Scott Thomson, *EHR*, LXVIII, 472-473; by W. F. McNeir, *PQ*, XXXIII (1954), 445-447.

A2492   Putnam, Maxine. "A Glimpse into the Lives of English Women During the Renaissance." *Florida State Univ. Stud.*, V (1952), 67-78.

A2493   Hole, Christina. *The English Housewife in the Seventeenth Century*. London: Chatto & Windus, 1953. Pp. 248.
Rev: by Maurice Ashley, *Spectator*, July 10, 1953, p. 68; *TLS*, June 5, p. 362; by R. H., *Time and Tide*, June 6, p. 766 (brief); by Naomi Lewis, *NstN*, July 11, p. 54; by Catherine Ing, *National & Eng. Rev.*, 141 (1953), 117-118; by Sir John Squire, *Illus. London News*, July 11, 1953, p. 52.

A2494   Willett, C., and Phillis Cunnington. *Handbook of English Costume in the Sixteenth Century*. Ill. by Barbara Phillipson. London: Faber & Faber, 1954. Pp. 244.
Rev: A7264.

A2495   Brewer, D. S. "The Ideal of Feminine Beauty in Medieval Literature, Especially *Harley Lyrics*, Chaucer, and Some Elizabethans." *MLR*, L (1955), 257-269.

A2496   Brooks, Charles B. *The Dramatization of Attitudes Toward Women (1585-1595)*. DD, University of California, Berkeley, 1955.

A2497   Kelso, Ruth. *Doctrine for the Lady of the Renaissance*. Urbana: Univ. of Illinois Press, 1956. Pp. xi, 475.
Rev: A1935.

A2498   Pearson, Lu Emily. *Elizabethans at Home*. Stanford: Stanford Univ. Press, 1957. Pp. x, 630.
Rev: *ShN*, VII (1957), 40; by H. C. Kiefer, *Arizona Quar.*, XIV (1958), 76-77; by Helen E. Sandison, *RN*, XI, 35-37; by Lacey Baldwin Smith, *JMH*, XXX, 140; by Thomas W. Cunningham, *Catholic Hist. Rev.*, XLIV, 41-42; by J. Hurtsfield, *History*, XLIII, 232-234; in *ConR*, 1105 (1958), p. 56.

A2499   Burton, Elizabeth. *The Elizabethans at Home*. Ill. by Felix Kelly. London: Secker & Warburg; New York: Scribner's, 1958. Pp. 276. New York edition entitled *The Pageant of Elizabethan England*.
Rev: by Philip Henderson, *Time and Tide*, Oct. 11, 1958, p. 1226; *NstN*, Nov. 8, p. 651; *TLS*, Oct. 3, p. 558; by J. Vallette, *MdF*, 334 (1958), 695.

(3) LOVE: IDEALS AND PRACTICE

A2500   Stoll, Elmer Edgar. "Modesty in the Audience." *MLN*, LV (1940), 570-575.

A2501   Babb, Lawrence. "The Physiological Conception of Love in the Elizabethan and Early Stuart Drama." *PMLA*, LVI (1941), 1020-35.

A2502   Haller, William, and Malleville Haller. "The Puritan Art of Love." *HLQ*, V (1942), 235-272. Concerned with Puritan ideas of love and marriage for the three or four generations before 1643.

A2503   Morgan, Edmund S. "The Puritans and Sex." *New England Quar.*, XV (1942), 591-607.

A2504   Babb, Lawrence. "Sorrow and Love on the Elizabethan Stage." *SAB*, XVIII (1943), 137-142.

A2505   Babb, Lawrence. "Love Melancholy in the Elizabethan and Early Stuart Drama." *Bul. Hist. Medicine*, XIII (1943), 117-132.

A2506   Stevenson, David Lloyd. *The Love-Game Comedy*. Columbia Univ. Press, 1946. Pp. xii, 259.
Rev: A3530.

A2507   Pettet, E. C. "Sidney and the Cult of Romantic Love." *English*, VI (1947), 232-240.

A2508   Rowe, Kenneth Thorpe. *Romantic Love and Parental Authority in Sidney's Arcadia*. Univ. Michigan Contributions in Mod. Phil., No. 4. Univ. Michigan Press, 1947. Pp. 58.

A2509   Bruser, Fredelle. *Concepts of Chastity in Literature, Chiefly Non-dramatic, of the English Renaissance*. DD, Radcliffe College, 1948.

A2510   Smith, J. H. "The Love Duel in English Comedy Before the Restoration." *The Gay Couple in Restoration Comedy* (Cambridge), 1948, pp. 3-28.

A2511   Falk, Signi L. *The Vogue of the Courtesan Play, 1602-1610*. DD, University of Chicago, 1949.

A2512   Sylvester, William Arthur. *War and Lechery: Four Themes in the non-Shakespearean Elizabethan Theater, 1587-1603*. DD, University of Minnesota, 1951. Pp. 189. *DA*, XII (1952), 192. Publication No. 3207.

A2513   Helton, Tinsley. *The Concept of Woman's Honour in Jacobean Drama*. DD, University of Minnesota, 1953. Pp. 371. *DA*, XII (1952), 795. Publication No. 4334.
"Shak. before 1600," pp. 95-113.
"Shak. after 1600," pp. 159-175.

A2514   McDowell, Dimmes A. *Courtly Love in the Early English Renaissance: 1485-1557*. DD, Cornell University 1953.

A2515   Axelrad, A. José. "Un Point de Droit Elizabéthain sur la Scène Dramatique." *Revue du Nord*, XXXVI (1954), 195-200.

A2516 Bossard, Richard. *Die Liebe in der erzählenden Prosa Englands von Lyly bis Defoe.* DD, Zurich, 1955.

A2517 Finn, Dorothy M. *Love and Marriage in Renaissance Literature.* DD, Columbia University, 1955. Pp. 299. Mic 55-1104. *DA*, xv (1955), 2188-89. Publication No. 12,428.

A2518 Williams, Gwyn. "The Cuckoo, the Welsh Ambassador." *MLR*, li (1956), 223-225.

A2519 Ashley, Maurice. "Love and Marriage in Seventeenth Century England." *History Today*, viii (1958), 667-675.

b. SHAKESPEARE (43;17)
(1) WOMEN

A2520 Kronacher, B. "Shakespeares Bild von der Frau." *Die deutsche höhere Schule*, xxiii (Feb., 1935).

A2521 Blos, Hanna. *Die Auffassung der Frauengestalten Shakespeares in dem Werk der Mrs. Cowden Clarke.* DD, Erlangen, 1936. Pp. 131.

A2522 Kurrelmeyer, W. "Weiblichkeit (Womanhood)." *MLN*, li (1936), 443-445.

A2523 Garbe, H. "Shakespeares Mädchen und Frauen in lebenskundlicher Betrachtung." *Nordische Stimmen*, vii (1937), 378.

A2524 Günther, H. F. K. "Shakespeares Mädchen und Frauen in lebenskundlicher Betrachtung." *SJ*, lxxiii (1937), 85-108.
Short version, *Rasse*, viii (1941), 46-58.

A2525 Lemme, H. "Shakespeares Frauen und Mädchen in lebenskundlicher Betrachtung." *Nationalsozialist Monatshefte*, viii (1937), 548-550.

A2526 Trinker, Martha K de. *Las Mujeres en el "Don Quijote" de Cervantes Comparadas con las Mujeres en los Dramas de Shakespeare.* DD, Mexico, 1938. Pp. 123.

A2527 McCormick, Virginia T. "Women and Love as Shakespeare Sees Them." *Catholic World*, 150 (1939), 330-334.

A2528 Huhner, Max. "Male and Female Created He Them." *Medical Times*, Mar., 1940, p. 4. Reprinted in B4476.

A2529 Sampley, Arthur M. "A Warning-piece Against Shakespeare's Women." *SAB*, xv (1940), 34-39.

A2530 Imhoff, Ruth. "Anna Jameson, Englands 'kleine Frau von Staël'." *N. Mon.*, xii (1941), 267-276.

A2531 Auld, Ina B. *Woman in the Rennaissance: A Study of the Attitude of Shakespeare and His Contemporaries.* DD, State University of Iowa, 1939. Abstr. in Univ. of Iowa *Doctoral Dissertations: Abstracts and References, 1938*, ii (1941), 103-109.

A2532 Gordon, G. "Shakespeare's Women." *Shakespearian Comedy and Other Studies*, London, 1944, pp. 52-59.

A2533 Plank, Patricia Gertrude. *The Function of Women in Shakespeare Comedy.* MA thesis, Saskatchewan, 1944. Pp. 113.

A2534 Anna of Mary, Sister. *Les Charactères de Femmes dans les Tragédies Romaines de Corneille et de Shakespeare.* MA thesis, Laval, 1945. Pp. 115.

A2535 Muhlberger, Margarethe. *Shakespeare und Grillparzer. Mit besonderer Berücksichtigung ihrer Frauengestalten.* DD, Vienna, 1945.

A2536 "Women in Shakespeare." *Fujinbunko* (Japan), No. 6, 1947.

A2537 Gjedde, Georg. "Shakespeares Kvinder." *Mandens Blad* (Copenhagen), Feb. 13, 1947, pp. 20-22 and 32-33.

A2538 Smith, Fred M. "Shylock on the Rights of Jews and Emilia on the Rights of Women." West Virginia Univ. Bul.: *Philological Papers*, v (1947), 32-33.

A2539 Jain, S. A. *Shakespeare's Conception of Ideal Womanhood.* Madras: Madras Publishing House, 1948. Pp. 223.

A2540 Berger, Alfred von. "Das Weib auf der Bühne Shakespeares." *Erato* (Hamburg), 1948, pp. 51-57.

A2541 Bandel, Betty. *Shakespeare's Treatment of the Social Position of Women.* DD, Columbia University, 1951. Pp. 326. Mic A51-530. *Microf. Ab.*, xi (1951), 1030-32. Publication No. 2793.

A2542 Camden, Carroll. "The Elizabethan Imogen." *The Rice Institute Pamphlet*, xxxviii (1951), 1-17.

A2543 Swinnerton, Frank. "Shakespeare's Heroines." *John o' London's Weekly*, lxiii (1954), 913.

A2544 Percival, Alicia C. "The Shakespearian Woman—'Human As She Is'." English Association Lecture, April 23, 1955, as noted in *English*, x (1955), 204-205.

A2545 Taylor, William Edwards. *The Villainess in Elizabethan Drama.* DD, Vanderbilt University, 1957. Pp. 402. Mic 57-2820. *DA*, xvii (1957), 1756. Publication No. 22,025.

A2546 Brown, John Russell. *Shakespeare and his Comedies.* London: Methuen, 1957. Pp. 208.
Rev: B5210.

(2) LOVE, COURTSHIP, AND MARRIAGE
(See also the sections on relevant plays and poems and general sections on tragedy, comedy, aesthetic criticism, etc.)

A2547   Stoll, Elmer Edgar. *Shakespeare's Young Lovers.* Oxford Univ. Press, 1937. Pp. 118.
        Rev: by E. C., *SRL*, Dec. 25, 1937, p. 21; by R. S. Knox, *UTQ*, VII (1938), 249-261; by
        George Rylands, *NstN*, NS, XV, 531-532; by W. Keller, *SJ*, LXXIV, 178-180; by Kathleen
        Tillotson, *RES*, XV (1939), 98-99; by Theodore Spencer, *MLN*, LIV, 396; by Eduard Eck-
        hardt, *Eng. Studn.*, LXXIII, 273-274; by Joan Bennett, *MLR*, XXXIV, 89-90.

A2548   Davies, W. Robertson. *Shakespeare's Boy Actors.* London: Dent, 1939. Pp. 208, pl.
        Rev: A7322.

A2549   Pettigrew, Helen P. *The Elizabethan Lover in Shakespeare's Comedies.* DD, University of
        Washington, Seattle, 1939.

A2550   Horne, Herman Harrell. *Shakespeare's Philosophy of Love.* Bradenton Beach, Fla.: Harmon H.
        Horne, 1946. Pp. xviii, 205.

A2551   Wilson, Arthur H. "The Great Theme in Shakespeare." *Susquehanna Univ. Studies*, IV (1949),
        5-62.
        "Love is the greatest force in the world."

A2552   Leech, Clifford. *Shakespeare's Tragedies: And Other Studies in Seventeenth-Century Drama.*
        London: Chatto and Windus, 1950. Pp. viii, 232.
        Rev: B4967.

A2553   Watkins, W. B. C. *Shakespeare and Spenser.* Princeton Univ. Press, 1950. Pp. ix, 339.
        Rev: A8549.

A2554   Wisser, Heinz. *Shakespeares Ideen über Liebe, Frauen und Freundschaft, abgeleitet aus Zitaten und
        Aphorismen der 8 grossen Tragödien seiner dritten Schaffensperiode.* DD, Vienna, 1950. Pp. 138.
        Typewritten.

A2555   Höllinger, Helene. *Konflikte zwischen Liebe und Pflicht bei Shakespeare.* DD, Innsbruck, 1951.

A2556   Thompson, Karl F. "Shakespeare's Romantic Comedies." *PMLA*, LXVII (1952), 1079-93.

A2557   Cancelled.

A2558   *Roméo et Juliette.* Paris: Ed. mondiale, 1953. Pp. 136.
        Contains, i.a., two essays "Jeunesse de Shakespeare," by André Obey, and "Le thème de
        l'amour chez William Shakespeare," by Jean-Jacques Mayoux.

A2559   Meader, William Granville. *Courtship in Shakespeare.* DD, Columbia University, 1951.
        Pp. 269. *DA*, XII (1952), 68. Publication No. 3109. Published also in New York: King's
        Crown Press, 1954. Pp. viii, 266.
        Rev: *CE*, XVI (1955), 522; by William Dace, *Players Magazine*, XXXI, 68; *SCN*, XIII, 13; *JHI*,
        XVI, 563; by Georges A. Bonnard, *SQ*, VII (1956), 130-131; by Michel Poirier, *EA*, IX,
        156-157; by J. C. Maxwell, *RES*, VII, 439; by T. S. Dorsch, *YWES*, XXXV (1954), 86-87; by
        Joseph H. Marshburn, *Books Abroad*, Winter, 1957, p. 82.

A2560   Milunas, Joseph George, S. J. *Shakespeare and the Christian View of Man.*" DD, Stanford
        University, 1954. Pp. 378. Mic A54-749. *DA*, XIV (1954), 526-527. Publication No. 7500.

A2561   Dickey, Franklin M. *Shakespeare's Presentation of Love in "Romeo and Juliet," "Antony and
        Cleopatra," "Troilus and Cressida."* DD, University of California (Los Angeles), 1954.

A2562   Dickey, Franklin M. *Not Wisely but Too Well: Shakespeare's Love Tragedies.* San Marino, Calif.:
        The Huntington Library, 1957. Pp. ix, 205.
        Rev: by L. L. Schücking, *Anglia*, LXXV (1957), 472; by Albert Howard Carter, *SQ*, IX (1958),
        403-405; by Roy Walker, *MLR*, LIII, 424-425; by Vernon Hall, Jr., *RN*, XI, 31-33; by Irving
        Ribner, *JEGP*, LVII, 337-340; by Robert D. Horn, *CL*, X, 276-279; briefly in *ShN*, VIII, 38;
        by Hermann Heuer, *SJ*, 94 (1958), 272-275; by J. A. Bryant, *SR*, LXVI, 329-333.

A2563   Frye, Roland Mushat. *The Accepted Ethics and Theology of Shakespeare's Audience as Utilized by
        the Dramatist in Certain Representative Tragedies, with Particular Attention to Love and Marriage.*
        DD, Princeton University, 1952. Pp. 372. Mic A55-745. *DA*, XV (1955), 581. Publication
        No. 10,901.
        Rev: by Nellie Shoemaker, *ShN*, V (1955), 29.

A2564   Murry, John Middleton. "Shakespeare and Love." *John Clare and Other Studies.* London:
        Nevill, 1950, pp. 31-44.

A2565   Thompson, Marvin Orville. *Uses of Music and Reflections of Current Theories of the Psychology
        of Music in the Plays of Shakespeare, Jonson, and Beaumont and Fletcher.* DD, University of
        Minnesota, 1956. Pp. 272. Mic 56-3899. *DA*, XVI (1956), 2448. Publication No. 18,954.

A2566   Loftus, Margaret Florence. *Shakespeare's Comic Treatment of Courtship and Marriage: Back-
        ground and Technique as Illustrated in Four Comedies.* DD, University of California (Los Angeles),
        1958.

(3) THE FAMILY

A2567   Clark, Cumberland. *Shakespeare and Home Life.* London, 1935.
        Rev: by W. Keller, *SJ*, LXXIV (1938), 177-178.

A2568   Hewins, N. "Shakespeare and Children." *Drama*, XVI (1938), 111-112.

A2569   Fleming, Edith Alice. *Shakespeare's Recurring Ideas.* MA thesis, Alberta, 1941. Pp. 314.

A2570   Bielau, Gertrud. *Die Familie im Drama von William Shakespeare.* DD, Graz, 1944. Pp. 98.
        Typewritten.

A2571   Schücking, Levin L. "Die Familie bei Shakespeare." *Essays über Shakespeare, Pepys, Rossetti, Shaw und Anderes*. Wiesbaden: Dietrich, 1948, pp. 222-273.

A2572   Holbrook, Sybil C. "Husbands in Shakespeare." *SAB*, XX (1945), 173-190.

(4) SEX, SEX-NAUSEA, AND SATIRE
(See also sections on Satire and on the Sonnets.)

A2573   Murry, John Middleton. *Heaven—and Earth*. London: Cape, 1938. Pp. 318.
Chap. VII: Shakespeare, "The Cuckoo Call," pp. 92-98.
Chap. IX: Shakespeare, "The Redemption of Generation," pp. 109-117.
Rev: A1791.

A2574   Watkins, W. B. C. "Shakespeare's Banquet of Sense." *Southern Rev.*, VII (1942), 706-734.

A2575   Partridge, Eric. *Shakespeare's Bawdy*. London: Routledge & Kegan Paul, 1955. Pp. x, 226.
A revised ed. Addenda on p. 226. Previous edition, 1947.
Rev: A5408.

A2576   Pyles, Thomas. "Ophelia's 'Nothing'." *MLN*, LXIV (1949), 322-323.
Elaborates Eric Partridge.

A2577   Hanser, Richard. "Shakespeare, Sex . . . and Dr. Bowdler." *SatR*, Apr. 23, 1955, pp. 7-8, 50.

A2578   Camden, Carroll. "Iago on Women." *JEGP*, XLVIII (1949), 57-71.

A2579   Baker, Sidney J. "Shakespeare and Sex." *International Jour. of Sexology*, IV (1950), 35-39.

A2580   Mason, E. C. "Satire on Woman and Sex in Elizabethan Tragedy." *ES*, XXXI (1950), 1-10.

A2581   Henderson, Archibald, Jr. *Family of Mercutio*. DD, Columbia University, 1954. Pp. 270.
Mic A54-2044. *DA*, XIV (1954), 1395. Publication No. 8684.

A2582   Fitch, Robert Elliot. *The Decline and Fall of Sex*. New York: Harcourt Brace, 1957.
"Romeo and Juliet, or the Nurse," pp. 31-39.
"Shakespeare, Lucretius, and the Reverend T. R. Malthus," pp. 105-114.
Rev: by Philip Wylie, *SatR*, Aug. 3, 1957, p. 25; by J. Donald Adams, *NYTBR*, July 14, p. 2.

15.   MILITARY LIFE
a. IN ELIZABETHAN AND JACOBEAN TIMES (179;-)

A2583   Marriott, J. A. R. "Projects of World Peace." *QR*, 267 (1936), 153-169.
Summary of projects from the sixteenth century.

A2584   Ballis, William. *The Legal Position of War: Changes in Its Practice and Theory from Plato to Vattel*.
The Hague: Nijhoff, 1937. Pp. xii, 188.
Chapters on Renaissance and Reformation.
Rev: by Clyde Eagleton, *Amer. Pol. Sci. Rev.*, XXX (1938), 152-153.

A2585   Oman, C. "Military History of England under the Tudors." *A History of the Art of War in the Sixteenth Century*, 1937, pp. 285-389.
Rev: *National Rev.*, 109 (1937), 123-127; *TLS*, June 12, p. 438; see letter by Bertrand Roland, ibid., July 3, p. 496; by R. Ernest Dupuy, *SRL*, July 31, pp. 18-19; *QR*, 269 (1937), 177-178; by A. L. Rowse, *Spectator*, July 2, p. 23; by A. J. Grant, *History*, NS, XXIII (1938), 75-77; by Adrian Taylor, *EHR*, LIII, 301-303; by J. M. Scammell, *AHR*, XLIII, 601-603; by R. A. Newhall, *JMH*, X, 101-103.

A2586   Vagts, Alfred. *A History of Militarism: Romance and Realities of a Profession*. New York: Norton, 1937. Pp. ix, 510.
Rev: by R. C. Albion, *AHR*, XLIV (1939), 318-319.

A2587   Cruickshank, Charles G. "Dead-Pays in the Elizabethan Army." *EHR*, LIII (1938), 93-97.

A2588   Richmond, Sir Herbert W. *The Invasion of Britain: An Account of Plans, Attempts, and Counter-measures from 1586 to 1918*. London: Methuen, 1941. Pp. v, 81.
Rev: *AHR*, XLVII (1942), 163.

A2589   Webb, Henry J. "The Elizabethan Translation of Vegetius' *De Re Militari*." *MLN*, LVI (1941), 605-606.
Suggests that the translation of Vegetius' treatise, published by Sadler in 1572, might have been used to call attention to evils of mustering rogues and giving commissions to flatterers.

A2590   The Bodleian Library Record. "The Art of War, An Exhibition." *Bodleian Lib. Rec.*, II (1942), 43-50.
Includes descriptions of a number of English Renaissance books on war.

A2591   Pearce, Brian. "Elizabethan Food Policy and the Armed Forces." *Econ. Hist. Rev.*, XII (1942), 39-46.

A2592   Webb, Henry J. "English Military Books, Laws, and Proclamations Published from 1513 to 1610." *PQ*, XXIII (1944), 116-128.

A2593   Knight, G. Wilson. *The Olive and the Sword: A Study of England's Shakespeare*. Oxford Univ. Press, 1944. Pp. 112.
Rev: A1819.

A2594   Cruickshank, C. G. *Elizabeth's Army*. Oxford Univ. Press, 1946. Pp. 156.
The fifteenth volume to appear in the Oxford Historical Series. Discusses the organization

of the military expeditions which left England between 1585 and 1603.
>Rev: *TLS*, May 25, 1946, p. 250; by Samuel C. Chew, *NYHTBR*, June 9, p. 12; by T. M. Spaulding, *AHR*, LII, 170-171; by W. E. C. H., *QQ*, LIII, 511-512.

A2595   Spaulding, Thomas M. "Elizabethan Military Books." *AMS*, pp. 495-507.

A2596   Jorgensen, Paul A. "Moral Guidance and Religious Encouragement for the Elizabethan Soldier." *HLC*, XIII (1950), 241-259.
>Is concerned primarily with conduct literature for the soldier.

A2597   Webb, Henry J. "Elizabethan Soldiers: A Study in the Ideal and the Real." *Western Humanities Review*, IV (1950), 19-33, 141-154.

A2598   Webb, Henry J. "Military Newsbooks During the Age of Elizabeth." *ES*, XXXIII (1952), 241-251.

A2599   Jorgensen, Paul A. "Theoretical Views of War in Elizabethan England." *JHI*, XIII (1952), 469-481.
>"What is truly remarkable in English pro-war thinking of the latter sixteenth century is its prevailing reasonableness, especially in view of the reputedly passionate intensity of Elizabethan patriotism."

A2600   Pearce, T. M. "The Ideal of the Soldier-Scholar in the Renaissance." *Western Humanities Review*, VII (1953), 43-52.

A2601   Webb, Henry J. "Classical Histories and Elizabethan Soldiers." *N &Q*, NS, II (1955), 466-469.

A2602   Jorgensen, Paul A. "Alien Military Doctrine in Renaissance England." *MLQ*, XVII (1956), 43-49.

A2603   Clark, Sir George. *War and Society in the Seventeenth Century.* Cambridge: Cambridge Univ. Press, 1958. Pp. 157.
>Rev: by Stanford E. Lehmberg, *RN*, XI (1958), 211-213; by Michael Howard, *NstN*, Sept. 28, 1958, pp. 388-389.

b. IN SHAKESPEARE AND HIS LITERARY CONTEMPORARIES

A2604   Boas, Frederick S. "The Soldier in Elizabethan and Later English Drama." *Essays by Divers Hands: Being the Transactions of the Royal Society of Literature*, NS, XIX (1942), 121-156.
>Also in Boas's *Queen Elizabeth in Drama, and Related Studies*, London, 1950, pp. 163-189.

A2605   Webb, Henry Jameson. *Criticism of the Military Profession in Sixteenth Century Literature.* DD, State University of Iowa, 1942. Abstract in Univ. of Iowa *Doctoral Dissertations: Abstracts and References*, III (1943), 247-255.

A2606   Izard, Thomas C. *George Whetstone, Mid-Elizabethan Gentleman of Letters.* Columbia Univ. Studies in English and Comp. Lit., 158. Columbia Univ. Press, 1942. Pp. viii, 297.
>Contains chapter on Whetstone's *Honorable Reputation of a Souldier.*
>Rev: B8362.

A2607   Laird, John. "Shakespeare and the Wars of England." *Philosophy*, XVIII (1943), 140-154.
>Also in Laird's *Philosophical Incursions into English Literature*. Cambridge Univ. Press, 1946, pp. 1-20.

A2608   Webb, Henry J. "Falstaff's 'Tardy Tricks'." *MLN*, LVIII (1943), 377-379.

A2609   Bhanu, D. "Shakespeare as a War Prophet." *Indian Review*, XLIV (1944), 445-446.

A2610   Paige, Douglass D. *The Art of War in the Jacobean Drama, 1603-1625.* Master's thesis, University of North Carolina, 1944. Abstr. publ. in *Univ. of North Carolina Record, Research in Progress*, Grad. School Series, No. 50, 1946, pp. 159.

A2611   Webb, Henry J. "Falstaff's Clothes." *MLN*, LIX (1944), 162-164.

A2612   Jorgensen, Paul A. *The Elizabethan "Plain Soldier" in Shakespeare's Plays.* DD, University of California, Berkeley, 1946.

A2613   Delattre, Floris. "Shakespeare et la Guerre." *LanM*, XLI (1947), 271-297.

A2614   Pettigrew, Helen P. "*Troilus and Cressida*, Shakespeare's Indictment of War." West Virginia Univ. Bul.: *Philological Papers*, V (1947), 34-48.

A2615   Harbage, Alfred. "Shakespeare's Ideal Man." *AMS*, pp. 65-80.

A2616   Duff Cooper, Sir A. *Sergeant Shakespeare.* London, 1949.
>Rev: A2442.

A2617   Luciani, Vincent. "Raleigh's *Discourse of War* and Machiavelli's *Discorsi.*" *MP*, XLVI (1948), 122-131.

A2618   Waggoner, George R. *The School of Honor: Warfare and the Elizabethan Gentleman.* DD, University of Wisconsin, 1948. Abstr. publ. in *Summaries of Doctoral Dissertations, 1947-49*, X, Madison: Univ. of Wisconsin Press, 1950, pp. 624-626.

A2619   Jorgensen, Paul A. "Shakespeare's Coriolanus: Elizabethan Soldier." *PMLA*, LXIV (1949), 221-235.

A2620   Jorgensen, Paul A. "Military Rank in Shakespeare." *HLQ*, XIV (1950), 17-41.

A2621   Jorgensen, Paul A. "The Courtship Scene in *Henry V.*" *MLQ*, XI (1950), 180-188.

A2622   Jorgensen, Paul A. " 'My Name Is Pistol Call'd'." *SQ*, I (1950), 73-75.

A2623   Langsam, G. Geoffrey. *Martial Books and Tudor Verse.* New York: King's Crown Press, 1951. Pp. 213.
         Rev: *TLS*, Dec. 14, 1951, p. 802; by P. A. Jorgensen, *JEGP*, LI (1952), 100-101; by Henry J. Webb, *SQ*, III, 377-378; by Arthur B. Ferguson, *South Atlantic Quar.*, LI, 340-341.

A2624   Sylvester, William Arthur. *War and Lechery: Four Themes in the non-Shakespearean Elizabethan Theater, 1587-1603.* DD, University of Minnesota, 1951. Pp. 189. *DA*, XII (1952), 192. Publication No. 3207.

A2625   Webb, Henry J. "The Military Background in *Othello.*" *PQ*, XXX (1951), 40-52.

A2626   Moore, John R. "Othello, Iago, and Cassio as Soldiers." *PQ*, XXXI (1952), 189-194.

A2627   Nichols, Doris J. *The Code of Honor and Arms in Shakespeare's Plays.* DD, University of Missouri, 1953.

A2628   Greer, C. A. "The Source of Falstaff's Contamination of the Army." *N &Q*, 198 (1953), 236-237.
         Probably Shakespeare used direct observation as a principal source of information about abuses of impressment, especially since they are shown to be common at the time of the composition of *1 Henry IV* in such testimony as that in Moryson's *Itinerary*, and Sir John Smythe's protest to Burghley against them.

A2629   Jorgensen, Paul A. "Shakespeare's Use of War and Peace." *HLQ*, XVI (1953), 319-352.

A2630   Traversi, D. A. "Love and War in Shakespeare's *Troilus and Cressida.*" *Essays in Love and Violence* (translation by George Lamb of an issue of *Etudes Carmélitaines* in 1946 called *Amour et Violence*), New York: Sheed & Ward, 1954, pp. 35-49.

A2631   Waggoner, G. R. "An Elizabethan Attitude Towards Peace and War." *PQ*, XXXIII (1954), 20-33.

A2632   Borinski, Ludwig. " 'Soldat' und 'Politker' bei Shakespeare und seinen Zeitgenossen." *SJ*, 91 (1955), 87-120.

A2633   Jorgensen, Paul A. "Divided Command in Shakespeare." *PMLA*, LXX (1955), 750-761.

A2634   Wavell, Major the Earl. "Shakespeare and Soldiering." *Essays by Divers Hands: Being the Transactions of the Royal Society of Literature*, NS, XXVII (1955), 140-151.

A2635   Kaula, David Charles. *The Moral Vision of Shakespeare's "Troilus and Cressida."* DD, Indiana University, 1956. Pp. 262. Mic 56-3417. *DA*, XVI (1956), 2150. Publication No. 17,963. Two chapters on war.

A2636   Jorgensen, Paul A. *Shakespeare's Military World.* Univ. of California Press, 1956. Pp. x, 345.
         Rev: by Robert Adger Law, *JEGP*, LVI (1957), 483-484; by Michel Poirier, *EA*, XI, 54-55; by J. Max Patrick, *SCN*, XV, 15; by S. F. Johnson, *RN*, X, 42-43; by John W. Draper, *SQ*, VIII, 395-396; by William G. McCollom, *ETJ*, IX, 357-359; by C. G. Thayer, *Books Abroad*, XXXI, 83; *The Humanist* (British), Feb., 1957, p. 26; *ShN*, VII, 14; *TAr*, Apr., 1957, p. 94; by T. R. Henn, *MLR*, LIII (1958), 104-105; by Allan Gilbert, *MLN*, LXXIII, 613-614.

A2637   Maclean, Hugh N. "Fulke Greville on War." *HLQ*, XXI (1958), 95-109.

V.   TEXT: TRANSMISSION AND EMENDATION (44;18)
1.   PRINTING OF WORKS IN SHAKESPEAREAN TIMES (44;18)
a.   PRINTING IN GENERAL AND THE TRANSMISSION OF SHAKESPEARE'S TEXT (44;18)
(1)   ELIZABETHAN PRINTING IN GENERAL
(Contents limited to specified sources of this compilation.)
(a)   HISTORIES OF PRINTING

A2638   Updike, Daniel B. *Printing Types: Their History, Forms, and Use. A Study in Survivals.* 2 Vols. 2nd ed. Harvard Univ. Press, 1937. Pp. xl, 292; xix, 326.
         Rev: by Josef Benzing, *DLZ*, LX (1939), 505-506.

A2639   McMurtrie, Douglas. *The Book: The Story of Printing and Bookmaking.* New York: Covici-Friede, 1937. Pp. xxx, 676.
         Rev: by C. P. R., *SRL*, July 9, 1938, p. 21; by A. E., *Lib. Assoc. Rec.*, XL, 445-446.

A2640   Wroth, Lawrence C. *A History of the Printed Book. Being the Third Number of The Dolphin.* New York: Limited Editions Club, 1938. Pp. 522.
         Rev: by B. H. Newdigate, *London Mercury*, XXXVIII (1938), 369-370; *TLS*, July 9, 1938, p. 472; *SRL*, July 2, p. 21.

A2641   Barge, Hermann. *Geschichte der Buchdruckerkunst von ihren Anfängen bis zur Gegenwart.* Leipzig: Ph. Reclam., 1940. Pp. 520, illus. 134.

A2642   Besterman, Theodore. *Early Printed Books to the End of the Sixteenth Century.* London: Quartich, 1940. Pp. 309.
         Rev: *TLS*, Dec. 21, 1940, p. 648; by F. C. Francis, *Library*, NS, XXII (1941), 91-97.

A2643   Nash, Ray, and Stanley Morrison, eds. *An Account of Calligraphy and Printing in the Sixteenth Century from Dialogues Attributed to Christopher Plantin.* Harvard Univ. Press, 1940. Pp. viii, 38. Reprinted in *Liturgical Arts*, XVII, No. iv, Pt. ii (Aug., 1949).
         Rev: *TLS*, Mar. 30, 1940, p. 164; by H. F. Bouchery, *De Gulden Passer*, NR, XVIII (1941), 196-198.

A2644   Aldis, Harry G. *The Printed Book*. The second edition revised and brought up to date by John Carter and E. A. Crutchley. Cambridge Univ. Press, 1941. Pp. vi, 141.
        Rev: by F. C. Francis, *Library*, NS, XXI (1941), 343-345; *TLS*, Mar. 8, p. 120; by A. E., *Lib. Assoc. Rec.*, XLIII, 78; *QR*, 277 (1941), 307; by G. L. M., *Papers Bibl. Soc. Amer.*, XXXVI (1942), 77-78.

A2645   Meynell, Francis. *English Printed Books*. Britain in Pictures Series. London: William Collins Sons & Co., 1946. Pp. 48.
        Rev: *TLS*, Oct. 19, 1946, p. 508; *MGW*, Jan. 2, 1947, p. 11.

A2646   Mummendey, Richard. *Von Büchern und Bibliotheken*. Bonn: Verlag der Buchgemeinde, 1950. Pp. 348.
    Substantial portions devoted to the Renaissance book.

A2647   Goldschmidt, E. P. *The Printed Book of the Renaissance*. Cambridge Univ. Press, 1950. Pp. x, 93; ill. 32; pl. 8.
    Contains three lectures (delivered 1947) on "the significance of Type, Illustration, and Ornament in disseminating Renaissance culture."
        Rev: by J. G. McManaway, *RN*, III (1950), 21-24; by V. Scholderer, *Signature*, No. 11, 48-49; *TLS*, May 26, p. 332 (see Mr. Goldschmidt's letter, ibid., June 9, 1950, p. 357); by C. F. Bühler, *Papers Bibl. Soc. Amer.*, XLIV, 290-292; by L. S. Thompson, *Speculum*, XXV, 567-568. See A2647a.

A2647a   Pearce, T. M. "The Vernacular Tongue in English Education." *RN*, IV (1951), 11-12.
    Takes exception to the statement in A2647 that only Latin was spoken in schools before 1550. See reply by James G. McManaway, ibid., pp. 12-14; and notes by William Nelson, ibid., pp. 39-40, and Eva Matthews Sanford, ibid., pp. 70-72.

A2648   Lehmann-Haupt, Hellmut. *One Hundred Books about Bookmaking: A Guide to the Study and Appreciation of Printing*. Columbia Univ. Press, 1949. Pp. 81.
        Rev: by D. W. Davies, *Lib. Quar.*, XX (1950), 228-229.

(b) ORIGINS OF PRINTING

A2649   Butler, Pierce. *The Origin of Printing in Europe*. Univ. Chicago Press, 1940. Pp. xv, 155.
        Rev: by H. M. Lydenberg, *Lib. Quar.*, XI (1941), 222-226.

A2650   Guppy, Henry. "The Evolution of the Art of Printing. In Commemoration of the Five Hundredth Anniversary of the Invention of the Art of Typography." *BJRL*, XXIV (1941), 198-233.

A2651   Meier, Henry. "The Origin of the Printing and Roller Press." *Print Collector's Quar.*, XXVIII (1941), 9-55, 165-205, 339-379, 497-527.

A2652   McMurtrie, Douglas C. *The Invention of Printing*. Chicago: Chicago Club of Printing House Craftsmen, 1942. Pp. xxiv, 413.
        Rev: by C. P. Rollins, "The Bibliographical Mine," *SRL*, Aug. 7, 1943, p. 28.

A2653   Audin, Marius. *Somme Typographique*. I: *Les Origines*. II: *L'Atelier et le Matériel*. Lyon: Audin, 1948, 1949.
        Rev: by A. F. Johnson, *Library*, IV (1950), 282-283.

(c) INFLUENCE OF INVENTION OF PRINTING

A2654   Taylor, Archer, and Gustave O. Arlt. *Printing and Progress: Two Lectures by Archer Taylor and Gustave O. Arlt*. Univ. Calif. Press, 1941. Pp. 67.
    Contains:
    Taylor, Archer. "The Influence of Printing (1450-1650)," pp. 1-34.
    Arlt, Gustave O. "Printing and the Democratic Movement in the Western World," pp. 37-67.

A2655   Bockwitz, Hans H. *Buch und Papier: Buchkundliche und papiergeschichtliche Arbeiten Hans H. Bockwitz zum 65. Geburtstage dargebracht*. Leipsiz: Otto Harrassowitz, 1949. Pp. 164.
    Contains, i.a., a study by William H. Lange of the economic, intellectual, and cultural aspects of the spread of the printer's art in the 15th and 16th centuries; and an article by Karl Schottenloher on the booktrade in relation to the "Schwärmer" and "Wiedertäufer" of Germany.

A2656   Wroth, Lawrence C. *Typographical Heritage: Selected Essays*. Typophile Chap Books, Vol. XX. New York: The Typophiles, 1949. Pp. viii, 162.
    Contains, i.a., "Printing and the Rise of Modern Culture in the Fifteenth Century," delivered 1940, formerly prefixed to catalogue of exhibition of Pierpont Morgan Lib. celebrating 500th anniversary of invention of printing (*The Fifteenth Century Book*).
        Rev: by K. J. Holzknecht, *Papers Bibl. Soc. Amer.*, XLIV (1950), 299-300.

(d) PHYSICAL ASPECTS OF BOOK PRINTING IN GENERAL

A2657   Condit, Lester. *A Provisional Index to Roman Printing Types of the Fifteenth Century*. Univ. of Chicago Press, 1935. Pp. x, 37; pl.
        Rev: by Carl Purington Rollins, *SRL*, May 30, 1936, p. 24; by Edwin Eliott Willoughby, *Lib. Quar.*, VI, 312-313.

A2658   Johnson, A. F. "Sources of Roman and Italic Types Used by English Printers in the Sixteenth Century." *Library*, NS, XVII (1936), 70-82.

A2659 Isaac, Frank Swinton. *English Printers' Types of the Sixteenth Century.* Oxford Univ. Press, 1936. Pp. xix, 60; pl. 80.
Rev: by Carl Purington Rollins, *SRL*, May 30, 1936, p. 24; by A. E., *Lib. Assoc. Rec.*, XXXVIII, 124-125; *N &Q*, 171 (1936), 106-107; by B. H. Newdigate, *London Mercury*, XXXIII, 632-633; by D. B. Thomas, *Library*, NS, XVIII (1937), 216-218.

A2660 Reed, Talbot Baines. *A History of the Old English Letter Foundries: With Notes Historical and Bibliographical on the Rise and Progress of English Typography.* A New edition revised and enlarged by A. F. Johnson. London: Faber & Faber, 1952. Pp. xiv, 400.
Rev: by R. W. P., *Lib. Assoc. Rec.*, LIV (1952), 380; *TLS*, Sept. 5, 1952, p. 588.

A2661 Heawood, Edward. *Watermarks, Mainly of the Seventeenth and Eighteenth Centuries.* Monumenta Chartae Papyraceae Historia Illustrantia or Collection of Works and Documents Illustrating the History of Paper, Vol. I. Hilversum: Paper Publ. Soc., 1950.
Continues Briquet's *Les Filigranes* (1282-1600).
Rev: *TLS*, Nov. 3, 1950, p. 700; by Allan H. Stevenson, "A Critical Study of Heawood's Watermarks," *Papers Bibl. Soc. Amer.*, XLV (1951), 23-36 (important); by John Harthan, *Signature*, No. 12, 54-55.

A2662 Stevenson, Allan H. "Watermarks are Twins." *SB*, IV (1951), 57-91, 235.

A2663 Hind, Arthur M. *Engraving in England in the Sixteenth and Seventeenth Centuries: A Descriptive Catalogue with Introductions. Part I: The Tudor Period,* London: Cambridge Univ. Press, 1952. Pp. xxx, 335; 156 pl. *Part II: Reign of James I.* Cambridge Univ. Press, 1955. Pp. xxxii, 413; 253 pl.
Rev: by Edwin Eliott Willoughby, *Lib. Quar.*, XXIII (1953), 314-315; *TLS*, Jan. 2, p. 4; by H. A. Hammelmann, *Book Collector*, V (1956), 80, 82, 84; by R. A. Skelton, *Geographical Jour.*, 122 (1953), 100-101, *TLS*, Jan. 13, p. 16; by Carl Zigrosser, *RN*, IX, 104-105; by A. F. Johnson, *Library*, 5th Series, XI, 129-130.

A2664 Bernard, Erwin. "Maps in Early English Printed Books in the Huntington Library." *HLQ*, III (1940), 67-68.

(e) ENTRANCE AND COPYRIGHT

A2665 Meyer, Catharine. "Elizabethan Gentlemen and the Publishing Trade: A Study in Literary Conventions." *Summaries of Theses*, Radcliffe College, 1935-38, pp. 72-76.

A2666 Pollard, Graham. "The Company of Stationers Before 1557." *Library*, NS, XVIII (1937), 1-38.

A2667 Pollard, Graham. "The Early Constitution of the Stationers' Company." *Library*, NS, XVIII (1937), 235-260.

A2668 Pforzheimer, Walter L. "Copyright and Scholarship." *English Institute Annual, 1940.* Columbia Univ. Press, 1941, pp. 164-199.

A2669 Bald, R. C. "Early Copyright Litigation and Its Bibliographical Interest." *Papers Bibl. Soc. Amer.*, XXXVI (1942), 81-96.

A2670 Greg, W. W. "The Copyright of *Hero and Leander*." *Library*, NS, XXIV (1944), 165-174.

A2671 Greg, W. W. "Entrance, Licence, and Publication." *Library*, 4th Series, XXV (1944-45), 1-22.

A2672 Kirschbaum, Leo. "Entrance, Licence, and Publication." *Library*, 4th Series, XXVI (1945), 195. A letter supplying additional data relative to A2671.

A2673 Greg, W. W. "Entrance and Copyright." *Library*, 4th Series, XXVI (1946), 308-310. Answer to A2672.

A2674 Kirschbaum, Leo. "Author's Copyright in England Before 1640." *Papers Bibl. Soc. Amer.*, XL (1946), 43-80.

A2674a Jackson, William A. "Note on the Pforzheimer Catalogue." *Papers Bibl. Soc. Amer.*, XL (1946), 159.
Answer to A2674.

A2675 Dawson, Giles E. "Copyright of Plays in the Early Seventeenth Century." *EIE, 1947* (New York, 1948), pp. 169-192.

A2676 Davis, Richard Beale. "George Sandys v. William Stansby: The 1632 Edition of Ovid's *Metamorphosis*." *Library*, III (1948), 193-212.
Reproduces and discusses documents in Sandys suit (in His Majesty's Court of Exchequer) against Stansby for money Sandys believed due him in 1635; points out how the information throws light upon cost of printing and upon the Stuart book trade in general.

A2677 Thomas, Sidney. "Richard Smith: 'Foreign to the Company'." *Library*, III (1948), 186-192.
Points out that details of Smith's career elucidate the prohibition "against printing for foreigns," suggests that entries in *S.R.* cannot always be taken at face value, and raises doubts that entry always secured copyright.

A2678 Shapiro, I. A. "Publication Dates Before 1600." *TLS*, Feb. 6, 1953, p. 96.
See letter by Allardyce Nicoll and C. J. Sisson, *TLS*, Feb. 20, p. 121, on a chronological Short-Title Catalogue. Urges cooperative effort in providing information which will reduce uncertainty about the relationship entry in *S.R.* and date of publication; offers a short table of information of some three dozen books as illustrative; calls attention to the compilation of the Chronological Index under way at the Shakespeare Institute.

A2679 Greg, W. W. " 'Ad Imprimendum Solum'." *Library*, IX (1954), 242-247.

A2680 Simpson, Percy. "The Official Control of Tudor & Stuart Printing." *Studies in Elizabethan Drama*. Oxford: Clarendon Press, 1955, pp. 179-262.

A2681 Ransom, Harry. *The First Copyright Statute*. An Essay on An Act for the Encouragement of Learning, 1710. Austin: Univ. Texas Press, 1956. Pp. xiv, 145.
Examines the formulation of English theories of copyright from 1476 to 1710, and the history of their expression in the establishment of the English press, the founding of the Stationers, and the regulations of the press by Throne and Parliament.

(f) PIRACY (See also Shorthand, A2853-A2865.)

A2682 Judge, C. B. *Elizabethan Book Pirates*. Harvard Studies in English, 8. Cambridge: Harvard Univ. Press, 1934. Pp. xiv, 198.
Rev: by T. W. Baldwin, *JEGP*, XXXIV (1935), 595-597.

A2683 Gosse, Philip. "Pirates and Their Books." *Essays by Divers Hands*, XVI (1937), 21-42.

A2684 Duthie, George Ian. *Elizabethan Pirated Dramas, With Special Reference to the "Bad" Quartos of "Hamlet," "Henry V," and "Romeo and Juliet": With an Appendix on the Problem of "The Taming of a Shrew."* DD, Edinburgh, 1939.

A2685 Kirschbaum, Leo. "An Hypothesis Concerning the Origin of the Bad Quartos." *PMLA*, LX (1945), 697-715.
Memorization by reporters produced the bad quartos.

A2686 Simpson, Percy. "Literary Piracy in the Elizabethan Age." *Oxford Bibl. Soc. Publ.*, NS, I (1947; pr. 1948), 1-23.

A2687 Thomas, Sidney. "A Note on the Reporting of Elizabethan Sermons." *Library*, 5th Series, III (1949), 120-121.
New evidence on methods of Eliz. literary piracy affecting view of bad Shak. quartos.

A2688 Greg, W. W. "Was the First Edition of *Pierce Penniless* a Piracy?" *Library*, VII (1952), 122-124.
Argues against A. W. Pollard's citation of Nashe's work as example of an author's substitutions of an authorized text for a piratical edition.

A2689 Kirschbaum, L. "Texts of *Mucedorus*." *MLR*, L (1955), 1-5.
Reply by W. W. Greg, ibid., p. 322.
Argues that *Mucedorus* is a bad quarto, and that "the extant text can tell us only about the taste of the *reading* public"—and not about the author, the dramatic company, or the theatre public. Questions the stage vogue of the play. And declares the attribution of "primitive" qualities to the Eliz. stage comes from the assumption that "bad" quartos are accurate texts.

(2) THE NEW BIBLIOGRAPHY (See also Textual Criticism, A3241 ff, and sections on Folios and Quartos, A2931 ff. These sections are limited by the sources. For fuller listings, see A133-A139.)

(a) GENERAL

A2690 Hirsch, Rudolf, Lucy Clark, and Fredson Bowers. "A Selective Check List of Bibliographical Scholarship for 1949," et seq. See Nos. A133 to A139.

A2691 Bowers, Fredson, ed. *Studies in Bibliography*, I-VIII. Charlottesville, Virginia: Bibliographical Society of the Univ. of Va., 1948-56.
All Shakespearean essays entered separately.
Rev: B3830-B3840.

A2692 Haselden, R. B. *Scientific Aids for the Study of Manuscripts*. Oxford Univ. Press, for the Bibliographical Soc., 1935. Pp. x, 108; 16 pl.
Rev: "Bibliographical Notes," *TLS*, Feb. 29, 1936, p. 188; by A. E., *Lib. Assoc. Rec.*, XXXVIII, 125-126; by Samuel A. Tannenbaum, *SAB*, XI, 126-127.

A2693 Besterman, Theodore. *The Beginnings of Systematic Bibliography*. Oxford Bibliographical Series III. Oxford Univ. Press, 1935. Pp. 94, pl. 12.
Rev: by G. P. Winship, *MLN*, LII (1937), 151-152; by H. F. B. B.-S., *Oxf. Mag.*, LV (1936), 172; by C. P. Rollins, *SRL*, XIII (Nov., 1935), 20; *TLS*, Nov. 9, 1935, p. 728; cf. T. Besterman, ibid., Nov. 30, p. 820; by S. de Ricci, *MLR*, XXXI (1936), 412-413.

A2694 Newton, A. E. *Bibliography and Pseudo-Bibliography*. London: Milford, 1936. Pp. 116.
Comments of a collector.

A2695 "What is Bibliography?" *TLS*, July 18, 1942, p. 355.

A2696 Greg, W. W. "Bibliography—A Retrospect." *The Bibliographical Society, 1892-1942. Studies in Retrospect* (ed. by F. C. Francis, London: Bibl. Soc., 1945), pp. 23-31.

A2697 Thomas, H. "The Bibliographical Society's Contribution to Foreign Bibliography." *The Bibliographical Society, 1892-1942. Studies in Retrospect* (ed. by F. C. Francis, London: Bibl. Soc., 1945), pp. 159-174.

A2698 Bowers, Fredson. "Certain Basic Problems in Descriptive Bibliography." *Papers Bibl. Soc. of Amer.*, XLII (1948), 211-228.

A2699 Bowers, Fredson. *Principles of Bibliographical Description*. Princeton Univ. Press, 1949. Pp. xviii, 505.
Rev: by A. Esdaile, *English*, VIII (1950), 148; *TLS*, Sept. 29, p. 620; by C. F. Bühler, *VQR*,

XXVI, 614-617; by W. R. Parker, *Papers Bibl. Soc. Amer.*, XLIV, 216-223; by Paul S. Dunkin, *Lib. Quar.*, XXI (1951), 61-64 (important); by Lewis Leary, *South Atlantic Quar.*, L, 267-269; by R. W. Chapman, *MLN*, LXVI, 568-569.

A2700   Bühler, Curt F., James G. McManaway, and Lawrence C. Wroth. *Standards of Bibliographical Description.* Univ. of Pennsylvania Press, 1949. Pp. viii, 120.
Contains three separate papers, of which the one by J. G. McManaway discusses the bibliography of English literature from 1475 to 1700, with specific references to problems relating to the works of Shak.
Rev: *TLS*, Sept. 29, 1950, p. 620; by M. E. Kronenberg, *Het Boek*, XXX, 252-253; by W. R. Parker, *Papers Bibl. Soc. Amer.*, XLIV, 216-223; by A. T. Hazen, *Lib. Quar.*, XXI (1951), 64-66.

A2701   Bowers, Fredson. "Bibliography, Pure Bibliography, and Literary Studies." *Papers Bibl. Soc. Amer.*, XLVI (1952), 186-208.

A2702   McManaway, James G. "Bibliography." *Literature and Science* (Proceedings of the Sixth Triennial Congress, Oxford, 1954), pp. 27-35. Oxford: Basil Blackwell (for The International Federation for Modern Languages and Literatures), 1955.

A2703   Cauthen, I. B., Jr. "Recent Bibliographical Studies." *ShN*, V (1955), 4-5.
Twelve abstracts.

A2704   Willoughby, Edwin Eliott. *The Uses of Bibliography to the Students of Literature and History.* Hamden, Conn.: Shoe String Press, 1958. Pp. 105. Printed by offset from typescript.
Four lectures delivered in England in 1952, including (No. 4) a summary of *The Printing of the First Folio.*

(b) INDIVIDUAL STUDIES

A2705   Simpson, Percy. *Proof-reading in the Sixteenth, Seventeenth, and Eighteenth Centuries.* Oxford Univ. Press, 1935. Pp. 264; 16 pl.
Rev: by A. E., *Lib. Assoc. Rec.*, 4th Series, II (1935), 253; by John Hayward, *NstN*, NS, IX, 820, by A. K. McIlwraith, *Bodleian Quar. Record*, VIII, 111-112; by R. B. McK., *Library*, NS, XVI, 347-352; by H. Marcus, *Dt. Litztg.*, 3 F., VI, 1821-46; *N&Q*, 168 (1935), 376-378; by B. H. Newdigate, *London Mercury*, XXXII, 62-63; by Carl Purington Rollins, *SRL*, Dec. 28, p. 21; by John Sparrow, *Spectator*, May 10, pp. 795-796; by Geoffrey Tillotson, *History*, NS, XX, 168-169; *More Books*, XI (1936), 353; by Hazelton Spencer, *MLN*, LI, 551-552; by Margarete Rösler, *Eng. Studn.*, LXXI, 96-98; by W. W. Greg, *RES*, XIII (1937), 190-205.

A2706   Allen, Don Cameron. "Some Contemporary Accounts of Renaissance Printing Methods." *Library*, NS, XVII (1936), 167-171.

A2707   Ferguson, F. S. "Additions to Title-Page Borders, 1485-1640." *Library*, NS, XVII (1936), 264-311.

A2708   Greg, W. W. "From Manuscript to Print." *RES*, XIII (1937), 190-205.

A2709   Greg, W. W. "A Proof-sheet of 1606." *Library*, NS, XVII (1937), 454-457.

A2710   Pershing, James H. "Storage of Printed Sheets in the Seventeenth Century." *Library*, NS, XVII (1937), 468-471.

A2711   Bowers, Fredson. "Notes on Running-titles as Bibliographical Evidence." *Library*, NS, XIX (1938/39), 315-338.

A2712   Price, Hereward T. "Grammar and the Compositor in the Sixteenth and Seventeenth Centuries." *JEGP*, XXXVIII (1939), 540-548.

A2713   Hinman, Charlton. "Principles Governing the Use of Variant Spellings as Evidence of Alternate Setting by Two Compositors." *Library*, XXI (1940), 78-94.
The principles proposed are based on a study of the variant spellings of *The Sun's Darling* (1656) and *Othello* (1622).

A2714   Hummel, Ray O., Jr. "Seventeenth Century Publishing Economy." *MLN*, LIV (1941), 61-62.

A2715   Bald, R. C. "Evidence and Inference in Bibliography." *English Institute Annual, 1941*, Columbia Univ. Press, 1942, pp. 159-183.

A2716   Bond, William H. "Imposition by Half-sheets." *Library*, NS, XXII (1942), 163-167.

A2717   Bowers, Fredson. "The Headline in Early Books." *English Institute Annual, 1941*, Columbia Univ. Press, 1942, pp. 186-205.

A2718   Hinman, Charlton. "New Uses for Headlines as Bibliographical Evidence." *English Institute Annual, 1941*, Columbia Univ. Press, 1942, pp. 207-222.

A2719   Schulz, H. C. "Manuscript Printer's Copy for a Lost English Book." *Library*, NS, XXII (1942), 138-144.

A2720   Wolf, Edwin, 2nd. "Press Corrections in Sixteenth and Seventeenth Century Quartos." *Papers Bibl. Soc. Amer.*, XXXVI (1942), 187-198.

A2721   Shaaber, M. A. "The Meaning of the Imprint in Early Printed Books." *Library*, NS, XXIV (1944), 120-141.

A2722   Hinman, Charlton. "Mechanized Collation: A Preliminary Report." *Papers Bibl. Soc. Amer.*, XLI (1947), 99-106.

A2723   Bowers, Fredson. "Bibliographical Miscellanea." *Library*, 5th Series, I (1946), 131-134.

A2724   Ferguson, F. S. "English Books Before 1640." *The Bibliographical Society, 1892-1942. Studies in Retrospect* (ed. by F. C. Francis, London: Bibl. Soc., 1945), pp. 42-75.

A2725   Johnson, Francis R. "Press Corrections and Presswork in the Elizabethan Printing Shop." *Papers Bibl. Soc. Amer.*, XL (1946), 276-286.

A2726   Oliver, Leslie Mahin. "Single-page Imposition in Foxe's *Acts and Monuments*, 1570." *Library*, 5th Series, I (1946), 49-56.

A2726a Dunkin, Paul S. "Foxe's *Acts and Monuments*, 1570, and Single-page Imposition." *Library*, 5th Series, II (1947), 159-170.

A2727   Bowers, Fredson. "Notes on Standing Type in Elizabethan Printing." *Papers Bibl. Soc. Amer.*, XL (1946), 205-224.

A2728   Carter, Albert Howard. "On the Use of Details of Spelling, Punctuation, and Typography to Determine the Dependence of Editions." *SP*, XLIV (1947), 497-503.
        Cautions against placing too much dependence upon such features by examining the relationship between the printings of "The Passionate Sheepheards Song," i.e., *Love's Labour's Lost*, Q₁ (1598); *The Passionate Pilgrim*, Q₁, Q₂ (1599); and *England's Helicon* (1600).

A2729   Peery, William. "Correction at Press in the Quarto of Law-Trickes." *Library*, 5th Series, II (1947), 186-190.

A2730   Tarr, John C. "Measurement of Type." *Library*, 5th Series, I (1947), 248-249.

A2731   Bond, William H. "New Examples of Imposition by Half-sheets." *Harvard Lib. Bul.*, II (1948), 402-403.

A2732   Bowers, Fredson. "Two Notes on Running-titles as Bibliographical Evidence." *Papers Bibl. Soc. Amer.*, XLII (1948), 143-148.
        Concerns George Sandys' *Ovid's Metamorphosis* (1632) and *Christ's Passion* (1640).

A2733   Bowers, Fredson. "Elizabethan Proofing." *AMS*, pp. 571-586.

A2734   Bowers, Fredson. "Criteria for Classifying Hand-printed Books as Issues and Variant States." *Papers Bibl. Soc. Amer.*, XLI (1947), 271-292.
        See the article, *TLS*, Sept. 4, 1948, p. 504, which summarizes Mr. Bowers' points and also briefly applies them to problems confronting the bibliographer and collector of modern books.

A2734a Dunkin, Paul S. "The State of the Issue." *Papers Bibl. Soc. Amer.*, XLII (1948), 239-255.
        Considers the arguments of Mr. Bowers, A2734; rejoinder by Mr. Bowers, ibid., XLII, 341-343; answer by Mr. Dunkin, ibid., XLIII (1949), 83.

A2735   Bowers, Fredson. "Running-title Evidence for Determining Half-sheet Imposition." *Papers Bibl. Soc. Univ. Virginia*, I (1948-49), 199-202.

A2736   Bond, William H. "Casting Off Copy by Elizabethan Printers: A Theory." *Papers Bibl. Soc. Amer.*, XLII (1948), 281-291.

A2737   Bowers, Fredson. "Bibliographical Evidence from Printer's Measure." *SB*, II (1949), 153-167.

A2738   Bühler, Curt F. "A Note on a Fifteenth Century Printing Technique." *Univ. Penna. Lib. Chronicle*, XV (1949), 52-55.

A2739   Willoughby, Edwin Eliott. "A Long Use of a Setting of Type." *SB*, II (1949), 173-175.
        Concerns the use of the same setting of type from 1631 until at least 1640 for issues of an octavo ed. of John Speed's *The Genealogies Recorded in the Holy Scriptures*.

A2740   Bald, R. C. "Editorial Problems: A Preliminary Survey." *SB*, III (1950), 3-17.

A2741   Greg, W. W. "The Rationale of Copy-text." *SB*, III (1950), 19-36.

A2742   Hill, Archibald A. "Some Postulates for Distributional Study of Texts." *SB*, III (1950), 63-95.

A2743   McIlwraith, A. K. "Marginalia on Press-Corrections in Books of the Early Seventeenth Century." *Library*, 5th Series, IV (1950), 238-248.

A2744   Price, George R. "Compositors' Methods with Two Quartos Reprinted by Augustine Mathewes." *Papers Bibl. Soc. Amer.*, XLIV (1950), 269-274.

A2745   Crow, John. "Thomas Goad and *The Dolefull Euen-Song*: An Editorial Experiment." *Trans. Cambridge Bibl. Soc.*, I, iii (1951), 238-259.
        Concerned with the bibliographical problems of Goad's tract of 1623 as a means of learning from a printed text of the 17th Century about the printer's copy and "the obstacles a manuscript might have to surmount before it could become a printed text."

A2746   Jackson, William A. "Printed Wrappers of the Fifteenth to the Eighteenth Centuries." *Harvard Lib. Bul.*, VI (1952), 313-321.

A2747   Shields, Alciun. "Seventeenth Century Pamphlets." *TLS*, Feb. 22, 1952, p. 141.
        Quotes *A Beacon set on Fire, The Beacon Quenched* and *The Beacon Flameing* (all London, 1652) as evidence that 1500 was a usual number of copies of an impression of a book or pamphlet in the first half of the 17th Century. Stanley Gardner, *TLS*, Mar. 7, 1952, p. 173, offers additional evidence in support of the number; H. John McLachlan, ibid., argues that 1500 copies to an impression is probably an exaggeration.

A2748   Bowers, Fredson. "The Problem of the Variant Forme in a Facsimile Edition." *Library*, 5th Series, VII (1953), 262-272.

A2749   Hunter, G. K. "The Marking of Sententiae in Elizabethan Printed Plays, Poems, and Romances." *Library*, 5th Series, VI (1951), 171-178.

A2750   Jackson, William A. "Printed Quire and Sheet Numbers." *Harvard Lib. Bul.*, VIII (1954), 96-102, 363-364.

A2751   Povey, K. "Variant Formes in Elizabethan Printing." *Library*, 5th Series, X (1955), 41-48.

A2752   Borinski, Ludwig. "Vers und Text in den Dramenmanuskripten der Shakespeare-Zeit." *Anglia*, 85 (1957/58), 391-410.

A2753   Williams, George Walton. "Setting by Formes in Quarto Printing." *SB*, XI (1958), 39-53.

(3) SHAKESPEARE

(a) SHAKESPEARE'S INFERRED ATTITUDES TOWARD PUBLICATION

A2754   Allen, Percy. "Stage or Study?" *TLS*, Apr. 11, 1936, p. 316.
See letters by W. W. Greg, *TLS*, May 2, 1936, p. 379; by Mr. Allen, ibid., May 9, p. 400; by Levin L. Schücking, ibid., May 6, p. 420, and June 12, 1937, p. 442.
Allen argues against the traditional belief that Shakespeare considered his plays as stage plays only, and expresses a conviction that the great tragedies in uncut form were written for publication and, in particular, that Q_2 of *Hamlet* was intended not for stage presentation but "as a counterblast to, and protest against, the pirated Q_1." Greg also doubts the plays were meant only for the stage. Schücking heartily endorses notion that they were also meant for reading and subsequently cites *Spanish Tragedy* additions.

A2755   "Stage or Study." *TLS*, Oct. 7, 1944, p. 487.
The writer of the article questions whether Shak. wrote only and exclusively for the stage. Answered by H. S. Bennett, *TLS*, Oct. 14, p. 499, to the effect that plays could have been written from retirement only after 1610 and that earlier plays were for the stage and the stage only.

A2756   Chambers, Sir E. K. "William Shakespeare: An Epilogue." *RES*, XVI (1940), 385-401. Reprinted in his *Shakespearean Gleanings*, Oxford Univ. Press, 1944.
That drama is "character in action." Cites many Elizabethan sources to indicate acting was "natural" as opposed to theory it was "formal." That plays ran 2 to 2 ½ hours. Doubts the full text as we have it was given on the Globe or Blackfriars stage. Concludes that Shak. wrote for publication or to please himself.

A2757   Duthie, George Ian. (*1*) *Two Shakespeare Problems; (a) The "Bad" Quarto of "Hamlet," (b) "The Taming of a Shrew" and "The Taming of the Shrew"; (2) Shakespeare's "King Lear": A Critical Edition.* DD, Edinburgh, 1946.

A2758   Duthie, George Ian. *Elizabethan Shorthand and the First Quarto of "King Lear".* Oxford: Blackwell, 1950. Pp. iv, 82. Argues that while Q_1 of *Lear* is certainly a reported text, no system of shorthand used in 1608 could have produced so "good" a version of a stage performance.
    Rev: *TLS*, May 12, 1950, p. 290: *N &Q*, 195 (1950), 308; by J. G. McManaway, *SQ*, II (1951), 85-86; by William Matthews, *MLR*, XLVI, 263-265; by R. Flatter, *SJ*, 87/88 (1952), 233-234.

A2759   McManaway, James G. "Where Are Shakespeare's Manuscripts?" *The New Colophon*, II (1950), 357-369.

(b) ENTRANCE AND COPYRIGHT

A2760   Clarkson, Paul S., and Clyde T. Warren. "Copyhold Tenure and *Macbeth*, III, ii, 38." *MLN*, LV (1940), 483-493.

A2761   Dawson, Giles E. "The Copyright of Shakespeare's Dramatic Work." *Studies in Honor of A. H. R. Fairchild*, pp. 9-35.

A2762   Danks, K. B. "*Hamlet*: The Problem of Copyright." *N &Q*, 197 (1952), 47-48.

A2763   Danks, K. B. "A Notable Copyright Award." *N &Q*, NS, III (1956), 283.

(c) PIRACY (See also Shorthand, A2853 ff.)

A2764   Price, H. T., and W. Matthews. "Shakespeare and the Reporters." *Library*, XVII (1936), 225-230.

A2765   Pollard, A. W. *Shakespeare's Fight with the Pirates and the Problems of the Transmission of his Text.* 2nd ed. Cambridge Univ. Press, 1937. Pp. 140.

A2766   Parrott, Thomas Marc. "*Pericles*: The Play and the Novel." *SAB*, XXIII (1948), 105-113.
Discusses John Munro's letter to *TLS*, Oct. 11, 1942, suggesting Wilkins' *Painful Adventures of Pericles Prince of Tyre* follows and is based upon Shak.'s play. Agrees, suggesting novel was pushed because the King's Men refused to permit publication.

A2767   Nosworthy, J. M. "Hamlet and the Player Who Could Not Keep Counsel." *ShS*, III (1950), 74-82.
The pirate responsible for Q_1 was an actor who played, successively, Marcellus, Lucianus, and an Attendant Lord.

A2768   Savage, D. S. *Hamlet and the Pirates.* London: Eyre and Spottiswoode, 1950.
Argues that the pirate episode in *Hamlet* "is a postscript written by Shakespeare to the original

play of 1601." Further, the sea robbers stand also for copyright thieves, and the whole episode is Shak.'s veiled treatment of the circumstances surrounding the publication of the bad quarto of *Hamlet*.

Rev: *TLS*, Dec. 15, 1950, p. 796 and Jan. 5, 1951, p. 7 (see the author's letter, ibid., Dec. 22, 1950, p. 815); by J. I. M. Stewart, *NstN*, Dec. 30, 1950, p. 683; by Bernard Raymund, *Arizona Quar.*, VII, 177-178; by Eugênio Gomes, *Correio da Manhã* (Rio de Janeiro), Mar. 4, 1953.

A2769   Rubow, Paul Victor. *Hamlet og Boghandlerne*. Det Kgl. Danske Videnskabernes Selskab. Hist.-filol. Meddelelser, 32, 7. Copenhagen: Munksgaard, 1952. Pp. 13.

A2770   Danks, K. B. "Macbeth and the Word 'Strange'." *N&Q*, NS, I (1954), 425.

A2771   Craig, Hardin. "Proof and Probability in the Study of Shakespeare and His Contemporaries." *McNeese Rev.*, VII (1955), 26-38.
An address delivered at the fourth annual Renaissance Conference at Tulane University, Nov. 4, 1954. Disposes of bad Qs from stenographic or piratic origins.

(d) SHAKESPEARE AND THE NEW BIBLIOGRAPHY

A2772   Wallace, Paul Anthony Wilson. *Shakespeare and His Printers*. DD, Toronto, 1925. Pp. 203.

A2773   Wilson, F. P. "Shakespeare and the 'New Bibliography'." *The Bibliographical Society, 1892-1942. Studies in Retrospect* (ed. by F. C. Francis, London: Bibl. Soc., 1945), pp. 76-135.

A2774   Parrott, Thomas M. "Shakespeare and the New Bibliography." *Library*, 5th Series, III (1948), 63-65.
Comments upon A2773.

A2775   Bowers, Fredson. "Some Relations of Bibliography to Editorial Problems." *SB*, III (1950), 37-62.

A2776   Sampson, Antony. "The Printing of Shakespeare's Plays." *Signature*, No. 15, 1952, 40-53.

A2777   Cauthen, Irby B. "Studies in Shakespeare Bibliography." *ShN*, VI (1956), 29, 40-41.
Abstracts.

A2778   Wilson, J. Dover. "The New Way with Shakespeare's Texts: An Introduction for Lay Readers. IV: Towards the High Road." *ShS*, XI (1958), 78-88.

b. PRINTERS, PUBLISHERS, AND BOOKSELLERS (45;19)
(1) READING PUBLIC TASTE
(See also Popular Taste, A7667 ff.)

A2779   Willard, Oliver M. *The Circulation of Books in Elizabethan England*. DD, Harvard University, 1936. Abstr. publ. in *Summaries of Ph.D. Theses, 1936*, Cambridge: Harvard Univ. Press, 1938, pp. 359-362.
Copies of largest editions now less frequent than those from smaller. "I have concluded . . . that the more there are, the less there were."

A2780   Boothe, Bert E. *The Contribution of the Italian Novella to the Formation and Development of Elizabethan Prose Fiction; 1506-1582*. DD, University of Michigan, 1936.

A2780a   Schücking, L. L. "The *Spanish Tragedy* Additions: Acting and Reading Versions." *TLS*, June 12, 1937, p. 442.
Upon the change of public taste around 1600. Suggests some quarto versions were for publication only, not for acting.

A2781   Eccles, Mark. "A Survey of Elizabethan Reading." *HLQ*, V (1942), 180-182.

A2782   Akrigg, G. P. V. "Middleton: An Allusion to the Shakspere First Folio?" *SAB*, XXI (1946), 25-26.
Suggests that Middleton and Webster were happy to see their plays published in their own lifetimes.

A2783   Mish, Charles C. "Comparative Popularity of Early Fiction and Drama." *N&Q*, 197 (1952), 269-270.
Shows that the number of editions of works of fiction printed 1475-1642 (717) is almost as large as that of plays (881).

A2784   Mish, Charles C. "Best Sellers in Seventeenth-Century Fiction." *Papers Bibl. Soc. Amer.*, XLVII (1953), 356-373.

(2) THE BOOK TRADE

A2785   Morrison, Paul G. *Index of Printers, Publishers and Booksellers in A. W. Pollard and G. R. Redgrave: A Short-title Catalogue of Books . . . 1475-1640*. Bibl. Soc. of the Univ. of Va., c/o Univ. Va. Lib., 1950. Pp. 82, "Errata," "Add. & Corr."
Rev: by A. Esdaile, *English*, VIII (1950), 148; *TLS*, Oct. 13, 1950, p. 652; by Edwin Eliott Willoughby, *Lib. Quar.*, XXI (1951), 136; by Rudolf Juchhoff, *Anglia*, LXX, 214-215; by R. L. C., *Lib. Assoc. Rec.*, LIII, 99-100; by J. Gerritsen, *ES*, XXXIII (1952), 88.

A2786   Morrison, Paul G. *Index of Printers, Publishers, and Booksellers in Donald Wing's Short-title Catalogue of Books . . . 1641-1700*. Charlottesville, Univ. Virginia Press, 1955. Pp. 217.
Rev: by Edwin Eliott Willoughby, *Lib. Quar.*, XXV (1955), 261-262.

A2787 Moore, John F. *A Topographical Directory of London Printers and Booksellers, 1475-1640.* DD, Ohio State University, 1941. Abstr. in *Ohio State Univ. Abstracts of Doctors' Diss.*, No. 34 (1941), pp. 447-448.

A2788 Plant, Marjorie. *The English Book Trade: An Economic History of the Making and Selling of Books.* London: Allen & Unwin, 1939. Pp. 499; il.
Rev: by Michael Sadleir, *Spectator*, June 16, 1939, pp. 1044-45; by Frederic Littman, *Life and Letters Today*, XXI, 249-253; *TLS*, July 22, 1939, p. 444; by David Garnett, *NstN*, NS, XVIII, 250; by Austin Robinson, *Econ. Jour.*, L (1940), 310-311; by L. Hanson, *Library*, NS, XXII (1942), 249-250.

A2789 Bockwitz, H. H., ed. *Das Buchgewerbe. Eine Gesamtdarstellung des graphischen Gewerbes, in seinen wissenschaftlichen, technischen und künstlerischen Grundzügen.* Leipzig: Verlag. d. Deutch. Buchgewerbevereins, 1941. Pp. 659.

A2790 Bennett, H. S. *English Books and Readers, 1475-1557: Being a Study in the History of the Book Trade from Caxton to the Incorporation of the Stationers' Company.* Cambridge Univ. Press, 1952. Pp. xiv, 335.
Rev: by J. D. R., *Lib. Assoc. Rec.*, LIV (1952), 348; by Oliver Warner, *Time and Tide*, Nov. 29, p. 1406; *TLS*, Aug. 8, p. 524; by F. Mossé, *EA*, VI (1953), 148; by Denys Hay, *EHR*, LXVIII, 273-275; by Arthur Brown, *MLR*, XLVIII, 330-332.

A2791 Hirsch, Rudolf. *The Emergence of Printing and Publishing as a Trade, 1450-1550.* DD, University of Pennsylvania, 1955. Pp. 194. Mic 55-100. *DA*, XV (1955), 802-803. Publication No. 11,413.

A2792 Greg, W. W. *Some Aspects and Problems of London Publishing Between 1550 and 1650.* Oxford: The Clarendon Press, 1957. Pp. viii, 131.
A reprint of the Lyall Lectures given at Oxford, summer, 1955.
Rev: by Christopher Hill, *Spectator*, June 15, 1956, p. 835 (brief); *TLS*, Aug. 10, p. 480; by S. C. Roberts, *RES*, IX (1958), 343-344; by Giles E. Dawson (with a discussion of the blocking entries of James Roberts), *SQ*, IX, 563-564.

A2793 Johnson, Francis R. "Notes on English Retail Book-prices, 1550-1640." *Library*, 5th Series, V (1950), 83-112.

A2793a Bennett, H. S. "Notes on English Retail Book-prices, 1480-1560." *Library*, 5th Series, V (1951), 172-178.

A2794 Evans, G. Blakemore. "Notes on English Retail Book-prices, 1550-1640." *Library*, 5th Series, V (1951), 275-276.
Addendum to A2793.

A2795 Muir, Kenneth. "Elizabethan Remainders." *Library*, 5th Series, XIII (1958), 56-57.

A2796 Johnson, F. R. "Printers' 'Copy Books' and the Black Market in the Elizabethan Book Trade." *Library*, 5th Series, I (1946), 97-105.
See letter by F. C. Johnson, ibid., I, 244-245. Gives evidence for believing that badly printed quires, corrected proof-sheets, and "similar abnormalities" in volumes printed before 1635 may be the result of journeymen and apprentices making up more than their allowed number of "copy books." F. C. Johnson cautions against basing any conclusions on notes of "warranty," which are not as rare as F. R. Johnson seemed to imply.

A2796a Oates, J. C. T. "Booksellers' Guarantees." *Library*, 5th Series, VI (1952), 212-213.
Adds four inscriptions in books of the Cambridge University Library to the list of those noted in A2796.

A2796b Oates, J. C. T. "Booksellers' Guarantees." *Library*, 5th Series, X (1955), 125-126.
See A2796 and A2796a.

A2797 Klotz, Edith L. "A Subject Analysis of English Imprints for Every Tenth Year from 1480-1640." *HLQ*, I (1938), 417-419.

A2798 Mish, Charles C. "Black Letter as a Social Discriminant in the Seventeenth Century." *PMLA*, LXVIII (1953), 627-630.
Romances designed to suit the tastes of the middle class are set in black letter, those written to appeal to the upper class in roman type; "there is strong presumption, and one which grows stronger as the century progresses, that anything in black letter was intended for a culturally retarded audience."

A2799 Williams, Franklin B. "Scholarly Publication in Shakespeare's Day: A Leading Case." *AMS*, pp. 755-773.

A2800 Rickert, C. H. *Books and Readers, 1598-1600. A Survey and Analysis of All Books Printed in England or in English Abroad During the Last Three Years of the Sixteenth Century.* DD, Birmingham, 1955.

A2801 "Elizabethan Publishing." *TLS*, Oct. 5, 1940, p. 507.

A2802 Alden, John. "Deception Compounded: Further Problems in Seventeenth Century Irish Printing." *SB*, XI (1958), 246-249.

A2803 Kirschbaum, Leo. *Shakespeare and the Stationers.* Ohio State Univ. Press, 1955.
Rev: A7021.

A2804 Dickins, Bruce. "Stationers Made Free of the City in 1551/52 and 1552." *Trans. Cambridge Bibl. Soc.*, I, ii (1951), 130-138.

A2805   McKenzie, D. F. "Men Made Free of the Stationers' Company, 1605-1640: Some Corrections to the List in Arber's Transcript." *N &Q*, NS, V (1958), 429-430.

A2806   Munby, A. N. L. "The Gifts of Elizabethan Printers to the Library of King's College, Cambridge." *Library*, 5th Series, II (1948), 224-232.

A2807   Davies, David. "The Geographic Extent of the Dutch Book Trade in the Seventeenth Century." *Lib. Quar.*, XXII (1952), 200-207.

(3) INDIVIDUAL PRINTERS

A2808   Willoughby, Edwin Eliott. *A Printer of Shakespeare: The Books and Times of William Jaggard.* London, 1934.
   Rev: by H. S., *MLN*, L (1935), 139; *SAB*, X, 44; by Arundell Esdaile, *Lib. Quar.*, VI (1936), 99-100.

A2809   Willoughby, Edwin E. "Who Saved Shakespeare?" *Coronet*, April, 1937, pp. 179-182.
   The Jaggards and their troubles.

A2810   Willard, Oliver M. "Jaggard's Catalogue of English Books." *Stanford Studies in Language and Literature*, Stanford Univ. Press, 1941, pp. 152-172.

A2811   Shield, H. A. "Links with Shakespeare. IV." *N &Q*, 194 (1949), 536-537.
   Family of second husband of I. Jaggard's widow.

A2812   Wood, E. R. "*A Discoverie of Errours* in 'The Case of William Jaggard (1619)'." *N &Q*, NS, IV (1957), 62-63.
   A defense of Jaggard against the attack of Raphe Brooke.

A2813   Shield, H. A. "Links with Shakespeare. X." *N &Q*, 197 (1952), 387-389.
   Identifies the publisher Thomas Thorpe with a person of the same name who became Mayor of Chester in 1615.

A2814   Willoughby, Edwin Eliott. "Francis Bacon and the King's Printer." *Lib. Quar.*, XXII (1952), 285-287.
   The King's Printer is Robert Barker, mentioned as giving the Lord Chancellor £700, in Bacon's *Confession and Submission to the House of Lords*.

A2815   Lievsay, John L. "William Barley, Elizabethan Printer and Bookseller." *SB*, VIII (1956), 218-225.

A2816   Hill, T. H. "Hugh Broughton and Some Elizabethan Printers." *N &Q*, NS, IV (1957), 286-288.

A2817   Rosenberg, Eleanor. "Giacop Castelvetro: Italian Publisher in Elizabethan London and His Patrons." *HLQ*, VI (1943), 119-148.

A2818   Murgatroyd, T. "John Haviland, Printer." *N &Q*, 189 (1945), 216.
   Answer to query by Roderick L. Eagle, ibid., p. 170.

A2819   Brown, John Russel. "A Proof-sheet from Nicholas Okes' Printing-Shop." *SB*, XI (1958), 228-231.

A2820   Thomas, Sidney. "Richard Smith: 'Foreign to the Company'." *Library*, 5th Series, III (1948), 186-192.
   On the activities of a publisher who was not a member of the Stationers' Company.

A2821   Bühler, Curt F. "Robert Waldegrave and the Pirates of Dunkirk." *New Colophon*, I (1948), 377-382.
   Concerns the career of the London and Edinburgh printer.

A2822   Johnson, Francis R. "*A Newe Herball of Macer* and Banckes's *Herball*: Notes on Robert Wyer and the Printing of Cheap Handbooks of Science in the Sixteenth Century." *Bul. Hist. Medicine*, XV (1944), 246-260.

(4) PRINTING OUTSIDE LONDON

A2823   Johnson, John, and Strickland Gibson. *Print and Privilege at Oxford to the Year 1700.* Oxford Univ. Press, 1946. Pp. 212.
   Rev: by Laurence Hanson, *RES*, XXIII (1947), 364-366; *TLS*, Nov. 29, p. 617.

A2824   "A Note on Joseph Barnes, Printer to the University, 1584-1618." *Bodleian Lib. Rec.*, II (1948), 188-190.

A2825   Thompson, W. D. J. Cargill. "The Two Editions of Thomas Bilson's *True Difference Between Christian Subjection and Unchristian Rebellion*." *Trans. Cambridge Bibl. Soc.*, II (1955), 199-203.
   Discusses the part which the editions by Joseph Barnes (Oxford, 1585), and John Jackson and Edmund Bollifant (London, 1586) played in the war of the Stationers' Company against the right of the universities to have their own presses.

A2826   Gibson, S., and D. M. Rogers. "The Earl of Leicester and Printing at Oxford." *Bodleian Lib. Rec.*, II (1949), 240-245.

A2827   Goldschmidt, E. P. *The First Cambridge Press in Its European Setting.* Cambridge Univ. Press, 1955.
   Rev: by Hellmut Lehmann-Haupt, *RN*, X (1957), 30-32.

A2828   Blagden, Cyprian. "Early Cambridge Printers and the Stationers' Company." *Trans. Cambridge Bibl. Soc.*, II, iv (1958), 275-289.

A2829   Roberts, S. C. *The Evolution of Cambridge Publishing.* The Sanders Lectures, 1954. Cambridge:
        Cambridge Univ. Press, 1956. Pp. x, 67.
            Rev: George Whalley, *QQ*, LXV (1958), 361-363.
A2830   Clarke, W. J. *Early Nottingham Printers and Printing.* Nottingham: Thos. Forman & Sons,
        1942. Pp. 79.
            Rev: by G. E. Flack, *Library*, NS, XXIV (1944), 91.
A2831   Sheppard, L. A. "Printing at Deventer in the Fifteenth Century." *Library*, NS, XXIV (1944),
        101-119.
A2832   Johnson, A. F. "English Books Printed Abroad." *Library*, 5th Series, IV (1950), 273-276.
        Attempts to assign Sayle's Zurich books to correct presses or towns, revises much in *STC*.

(5) BOOKBINDING

A2833   Goldschmidt, E. P. "The Study of Early Bookbinding." *The Bibliographical Society, 1892-
        1942. Studies in Retrospect.* Ed. F. C. Francis. London: Bibl. Soc., 1945, pp. 175-187.
A2834   "Sixteenth Century Bindings." *TLS*, Nov. 24, 1950, p. 756.
        Concerns the more than 100 bindings which have survived from the library of Thomas Wotton,
        father of Sir Henry and "one of the greatest of English book collectors."
A2835   Oldham, J. Basil. *English Blind-stamped Bindings."* Cambridge Univ. Press, 1952. Pp. xi,
        72; 61 pl.
            Rev: *TLS*, Sept. 19, 1952, p. 620; by A. R. A. Hobson, *Library*, VII, 284-285; by A. T.
        Hazen, *Lib. Quar.*, XXIII (1953), 50-51.
A2836   Moss, William E. *Bindings from the Library of Robt. Dudley, Earl of Leicester, K./G., 1533-1588.
        A New Contribution to the History of English Sixteenth Century Gold-tooled Book-bindings.* Crawley,
        Sussex: Privately printed, 1940.
            Rev: *TLS*, Nov. 30, 1940, p. 608; Dec. 14, 1940, p. 636.
A2837   Hobson, G. D. *Les Reliures à la Fanfare—Le Problème de l'S Fermé.* London: Chiswick Press,
        1936. Pp. 151; 37 pl.
        A study of the kind of bookbinding popular in 1570-1620.
            Rev: by S. G., *Bodleian Quar. Rev.*, VIII (1936), 178-179; by R. B. McKerrow, *Library*,
        NS, XVII, 365-368.

(6) MISCELLANEOUS

A2838   Davies, Hugh William. *Devices of the Early Printers, 1457-1560.* Their history and develop-
        ment. With a chapter on portrait figures of printers. London: Grafton, 1935. Pp. 720.
            Rev: by A. E., *Library Assoc. Rec.*, 4th Series, II (1935), 167; *TLS*, May 16, 1935, p. 315; by
        R. B. McKerrow, *Library*, NS, XVI (1936), 466-469; by H. Stein, *Rev. des Bibliothèques*, XLI, 94.
A2839   Willard, O. M. "The Survival of English Books Printed Before 1640: A Theory and Some
        Illustrations." *Library*, XXIII (1943), 171-190.
A2840   Bennett, H. S. "Printers, Authors, and Readers, 1475-1557." *Library*, 5th Series, IV (1949),
        155-165.
        Concerns England from the printing of Caxton's first book to the foundation of the Stationers'
        Company.
A2841   Cohnen, I. "Les Libraires-Imprimeurs Français en Angleterre aux XVᵉ et XVIᵉ Siècles."
        Courrier Graphique, XV, No. 43 (1950).
A2842   Howe, Ellie, and Sidney K. Eastwood. "The Patron Saint of Printers." *N &Q*, 195 (1950),
        547-548.
        St. John, the Evangelist, but St. Luke in the very early days of printing.
A2843   Stellfeld, J. A. *Bibliographie des Editions Musicales Plantiniennes.* Brussels: Palais des Académies,
        1949. Pp. 248, pl. 20.
            Rev: *Signature*, No. 11 (1950), p. 53.
A2844   Southern, A. C. *Elizabethan Recusant Prose: 1559-1582.* Foreword by H. O. Evennett.
        London: Sands, 1950. Pp. 533.
        An historical and critical account of books by Catholic refugees publ. abroad and at secret
        presses in England, with annotated bibl.
            Rev: *TLS*, Nov. 3, 1950, p. 691; by Helen C. White, *Catholic Hist. Rev.*, XXXVII (1951),
        325-326; by A. F. Allison and D. M. Rogers, *Library*, 5th Series, VI, 49-57 (important);
        by Hubert Dauphin, *RHE*, XLVI, 287-289.
A2845   Dickins, Bruce. "John Heaz, Elizabethan Letter-founder to the Printers." *Trans. Cambridge
        Bibl. Soc.*, I, iii (1951), 287.
A2846   Miller, C. William. "A London Ornament Stock: 1598-1683." *SB*, VII (1955), 125-151.
A2847   Ferguson, W. Craig. "Some Additions to McKerrow's *Printers' and Publishers' Devices.*"
        Library, 5th Series, XIII (1958), 201-203.

c. ELIZABETHAN HANDWRITING (47;19)

A2848   Judge, Cyril Bathurst, ed. *Specimens of Sixteenth Century Handwriting Taken from Contemporary
        Public and Private Records.* Harvard Univ. Press, 1935. Pp. xvi, 24 pl.

Rev: *TLS*, May 9, 1936, p. 401; *SAB*, XI, 59; by C. J. Sisson, *MLR*, XXXI, 465-466; by W. W. Greg, *RES*, XII, 456-458; by Samuel A. Tannenbaum, *MLN*, LII (1937), 74.

A2849   Nash, Ray, and Stanley Morrison, eds. *An Account of Calligraphy and Printing in the Sixteenth Century from Dialogues Attributed to Christopher Plantin.* Harvard Univ. Press, 1940. Pp. viii, 38. Republished in *Liturgical Arts*, XVII (Aug., 1949).
Rev: A2643.

A2850   Grieve, Hilda E. P. *Some Examples of English Handwriting.* From Essex Official, Ecclesiastical, Estate and Family Archives of the Twelfth to the Seventeenth Century. With Transcripts and Translations. Chelmsford: Essex Rec. Office Publ., 1949. Pp. 30.
Rev: *TLS*, Aug. 26, 1949, p. 560; *N &Q*, 194 (1949), 351-352.

A2851   Schulz, Herbert C. "The Teaching of Handwriting in Tudor and Stuart Times." *HLQ*, VI (1943), 381-425.

A2852   Borinski, Ludwig. "Vers und Text in den Dramenmanuskripten." *Anglia*, LXXV (1957), 391-410.

d. ELIZABETHAN SHORTHAND (48;19)

A2853   Butler, E. H. *The Story of British Shorthand.* London: Pitman, 1951. Pp. 247.

A2854   Hoppe, Harry R. "The Third (1600) Edition of Bales's *Brachygraphy.*" *JEGP*, XXXVII (1938), 537-541.

A2855   Matthews, William. "English Pronunciation and Shorthand in the Early Modern Period." *Univ. Calif. Pubs. Eng.*, IX (1943), 135-214.
Rev: *N &Q*, 188 (1945), 22; by Simeon Potter, *MLR*, XL, 317-318.

A2856   Morley, Morris. "Conjectures about Sixteen Century Stenography." *N &Q*, 189 (1945), 112-114.
The systems of Edmund and John Willis, Timothy Bright, and Peter Bale.

A2857   Morley, Morris. "John Willis: Elizabethan Stenographer. The Art of Stenographie, 1602." *N &Q*, 189 (1945), 222-227.

A2858   Fryckberg, Marjorie. "Pirates in the Pews." *Hist. Mag. Prot. Episcopal Church*, XVI (1947), 260-266.
Discusses the use of shorthand to provide illegal editions of sixteenth century sermons.

A2859   Thomas, Sidney. "A Note on the Reporting of Elizabethan Sermons." *Library*, 5th Series, III (1949), 120-121.
New evidence on methods of Eliz. literary piracy affecting view of "bad" Shak. quartos.

A2860   Matthews, W. "Shakespeare and the Reporters." *Library*, NS, XV (1936), 481-498.
See letter by H. T. Price and reply by Dr. Matthews, *Library*, NS, XVII, 225-230.

A2861   Greg, W. W. "King Lear—Mislineation and Stenography." *Library*, NS, XVII (1936), 172-183.

A2862   Förster, Max. "Shakespeare and Shorthand." *PQ*, XVI (1937), 1-29.

A2863   Stössel, Oskar. *Stenographische Studien zu Shakespeares"King Lear".* DD, Munich, 1937. Pp. 80.

A2864   Duthie, G. I. *Elizabethan Shorthand and the First Quarto of "King Lear".* Oxford, 1950.
Rev: A2758.

A2865   Craig, Hardin. "Proof and Probability in the Study of Shakespeare and His Contemporaries." *McNeese Rev.*, VII (1955), 26-38.
An address delivered at the fourth annual Renaissance Conference at Tulane University, Nov. 4, 1954.

e. CENSORSHIP IN ELIZABETHAN TIMES (48;20)

A2866   Clyde, William M. *The Struggle for the Freedom of the Press from Caxton to Cromwell.* Oxford Univ. Press, 1935. Pp. 372.
Chiefly 1640-1658, but thirty or so pages on Elizabethan times.
Rev: by A. S. Collins, *RES*, XI (1935), 243-246; by Harris Fletcher, *JEGP*, XXXIV, 599-601; by W. W. Greg, *MLR*, XXX, 513-514; by Oron James Hale, *AHR*, XLI, 338-340; by M. P., *Lib. Assoc. Rec.*, 4th Series, II, 250-251; *TLS*, Feb. 14, 1935, p. 82; see letters by J. D. Muddiman, ibid., Mar. 21, p. 176; Apr. 4, p. 228; May 2, p. 288; and May 16, p. 313; by the author, ibid., Mar. 28, p. 210; Apr. 25, p. 272; by G. D., *EHR*, LI (1936), 365; by Wm. Haller, *MLN*, LI, 562-563.

A2867   Craig, Alec. *The Banned Books of England.* Foreword by E. M. Forster. London: Allen & Unwin; New York: Macmillan, 1937. Pp. 207.
Rev: *TLS*, Apr. 10, 1937, p. 268.

A2868   Callanan, James A. S. *A History of Literary Censorship in England.* DD, Boston University, 1941.

A2869   Siebert, Frederick Seaton. *Freedom of the Press in England, 1476-1776: The Rise and Decline of Government Controls.* Univ. Ill. Press, 1952. Pp. ix, 411.
Rev: by J. R. Wiggins, *AHR*, LVIII (1953), 349-350.

A2870   Griffin, William J. *Tudor Control of Press and Stage.* DD, State University of Iowa, 1940. Abstr. in Univ. of Iowa *Abstracts and References*, III (1943), 239-246.

A2871 Griffin, William J. "Notes on Early Tudor Control of the Stage." *MLN*, LVIII (1943), 50-54.
Corrects and supplements information in Chambers' *Medieval Stage* and Gildersleeve's *Government Regulation of the Elizabeth Drama*.

A2872 Clark, Eleanor Grace. *Elizabethan Fustian*. A Study in the social and political background of the drama with particular reference to Christopher Marlowe. New York: Oxford Univ. Press, 1937. Pp. 226.
Reprinted as Part I of A2872a.
Rev: by Blanche M. Kelly, *Catholic World*, 145 (1937), 374-375; by Tucker Brooke, *SAB*, XIII (1938), 256; letter by Miss Clark, *SAB*, XIV (1939), 57-59.

A2872a Clark, Eleanor Grace. *Ralegh and Marlowe*. Fordham Univ. Press, 1941. Pp. 488.
Rev: by R. A. Sille, *SRL*, Dec. 27, 1941, p. 16; by Una Ellis-Fermor, *RES*, XVIII (1942), 342-344; by Helen C. White, *Catholic World*, 156 (1942), 117-118; by E. A. Strathmann, *MLN*, LVIII (1943), 473-477.

A2873 Siebert, Fred S. "Regulation of the Press in the Seventeenth Century: Excerpts from the Records of the Court of the Stationers' Company." *Jour. Quar.*, XIII (1936), 381-393.

A2874 Greg, W. W. "Ad Imprimendum Solum." *Library*, 5th Series, IX (1954), 242-247.
Takes issue with Alfred Pollard and A. W. Reed in the interpretation of the Proclamation of Henry VIII, Nov. 16, 1538, relating to royal license and royal privilege in printing.

A2875 Greg, W. W. "Samuel Harsnett and Hayward's *Henry IV*." *Library*, 5th Series, XI (1956), 1-10.
Transcribes and interprets Harsnett's self-defence against suspicion of treason aroused by his favorable examination for licensing of John Hayward's history; notes that apparently "at the end of Elizabeth's reign ecclesiastical licensing for the press was more casual and less effective than the authorities can have intended or perhaps realized."

f. SOCIAL POSITION OF WRITERS (49;20)

A2876 Gebert, Clara. *An Anthology of Elizabethan Dedications and Prefaces*. London: Milford; Philadelphia: Univ. of Penna. Press, 1934. Pp. x, 302.
Rev: by El. Deckner, *Beiblatt*, XLVII (1936), 199-202; by H. N. Hillebrand, *MLN*, LI, 462.

A2877 Wolff, Max J. "Die Soziale Stellung der Englischen Renaissancedramatiker." *Eng. Studn.*, LXXI (1936/37), 171-190.

A2878 Meyer, Catharine. *Elizabethan Gentlemen and the Publishing Trade: A Study in Literary Conventions*. DD, Radcliffe College, 1936. Abstr. in *Summaries of Theses*, Radcliffe College, *1935-38*, pp. 72-76.

A2879 Smith, M. Ellwood. "The Lunatic, The Lover and The Poet." *SAB*, XVI (1941), 77-88.

A2880 Clements, Robert J. "The Cult of the Poet in Renaissance Emblem Literature." *PMLA*, LIX (1944), 672-685.

A2881 Clements, Robert J. "Pen and Sword in Renaissance Emblem Literature." *MLQ*, V (1944), 131-141.

A2882 Clements, Robert J. "Condemnation of the Poetic Profession in Renaissance Emblem Literature." *SP*, XLIII (1946), 213-232.

A2883 Stafford, John. "The Social Status of Renaissance Literary Critics." *TxSE*, 1945-46, pp. 72-97.

A2884 Orsini, Napoleone. "L'Arte degli autori al Tempo di Shakespeare." *Rivista Italiana del Teatro*, VII (1943), 135-151.

A2885 Danby, John Francis. "The Poets on Fortune's Hill: Literature and Society, 1580-1610." *CamJ*, II (1949), 195-211.

A2886 Pallette, Drew B. "The English Actor's Fight for Respectability." *Theatre Annual*, VII (1949), 27-34.

A2887 Saunders, J. W. "The Stigma of Print: A Note on the Social Bases of Tudor Poetry." *EIC*, I (1951), 139-164.
Concludes: "One question which it is suggested in the future be asked in any discussion of a particular Tudor poet is 'Did he write for a manuscript audience or for a printed-book audience?' The reaction to the stigma of print is a test that may perhaps deserve a place even in the critic's laboratory."

A2888 Saunders, J. W. "The Façade of Morality." *ELH*, XIX (1952), 81-114.
Two connected essays: "Ambivalence in Tudor Professional Poetry," and "Spenser's Dualism." In part an elaboration of "The Stigma of Print" by Mr. Saunders, A2887.

A2889 Goodman, Randolph G. *That Strumpet the Stage: Poems About Playgoers, Players, and Playwrights*. DD, Columbia University, 1953. Pp. 357. Mic H53-781. *DA*, XIII (1953), 450. Publication No. 5189.

A2890 Patrides, C. A. "A Note on Renaissance Plagiarism." *N &Q*, NS, III (1956), 438-439.

A2891 Durling, Robert Marlowe. *The Figure of the Poet in Renaissance Epic*. DD, Harvard University, 1958.

A2892 Heltzel, Virgil B. "The Dedication of Tudor and Stuart Plays." Brunner *Festschrift*, pp. 74-86.

2. OLDEST PRINTED TEXTS. FOLIOS AND QUARTOS (49;21)

a. BIBLIOGRAPHY OF OLDEST TEXTS IN GENERAL (49;21)
(1) SHORT TITLE CATALOGUE—POLLARD AND REDGRAVE

A2893   Pollard, A. W., G. R. Redgrave, et al. *A Short-Title Catalogue of Books Printed in England,
Scotland, and Ireland and of English Books Printed Abroad, 1475-1640.* London: Bibl. Soc.,
1946. Pp. xviii, 609.
Reproduced by photolithography from the edition of 1926.
Rev: by K. J. Holzknecht, *Papers Bibl. Soc. Amer.*, XL (1946), 314-316; by E. E. Willoughby,
Lib. Quar., XVI, 247-250, which covers Donald Wing's continuation of *STC* (1641-1700);
by J. R. Sutherland, *RES*, XXIII (1947), 275-276.

A2894   Morrison, Paul G. *Index of Printers, Publishers and Booksellers in A. W. Pollard and G. R.
Redgrave: A Short-Title Catalogue of Books Printed in England, Scotland, and Ireland and of
English Books Printed Abroad, 1475-1640.* Charlottesville: Bibl. Soc. of the Univ. of Va.,
1950. Pp. 82.
Rev: A2785.

A2895   Bishop, William Warner, ed. *A Preliminary Checklist of American Copies of Short-Title Catalog
Books.* Ann Arbor, Mich.: Univ. Mich. General Lib., 1941. Pp. v, 173.
The first fruits of an important undertaking, based upon Pollard and Redgrave's *Short-Title
Catalogue.*

A2896   Bishop, William Warner. *A Checklist of American Copies of "Short-Title Catalogue" Books.*
General Lib. Publs., No. 6. Univ. Michigan Press, 1944. Pp. xvi, 250. Second edition,
revised and expanded, 1950. Pp. xi, 203.
Rev: by Edwin Eliott Willoughby, *Lib. Quar.*, XXI (1951), 60-61.

A2897   Allison, A. F., and D. M. Rogers. *A Catalogue of Catholic Books in English Printed Abroad or
Secretly in England, 1558-1640.* Bognor Regis: Arundel Press, 1956. Pp. xiii, 89; (90-)187.
Rev: by Eugene P. Willging, *Catholic Hist. Rev.*, XLIII (1957), 370 (brief); by A. I. Doyle,
Library, XII, 127-130.

A2898   The Newberry Library. *English Books and Books Printed in England Before 1641 in the Newberry
Library.* A Supplement to the Record in the *Short-Title Catalogue.* Chicago, 1939. Pp. viii,
118.

A2899   Allison, A. F. "Early English Books at the London Oratory: A Supplement to *STC.*" *Library*,
II (1947), 95-107.

A2900   Francis, F. C. "Three Unrecorded English Books of the Sixteenth Century." *Library*, XVII
(1936), 184-199.

A2901   Seaton, Ethel. "Richard Gallis and the Witches of Windsor." *Library*, XVIII (1937), 268-278.
Info. on STC 23267. Concludes with references to influence upon *Wives.*

A2902   Pafort, Eloise. "A Group of Early Tudor School-books." *Library*, 4th Series, XXVI (1945),
227-261.
Lists a number of issues not recorded in the *STC.*

A2903   Harrison, Thomas P., Jr. "The Folger *Secret of Secrets*, 1572." *AMS*, pp. 601-620.
Describes a copy of an edition not listed in the *STC* and re-examines the importance of the
work in Elizabethan thought.

A2904   Bühler, Curt F. "Two Unrecorded Jacobean Proclamations." *Library*, III (1948), 121.
Notes two works not listed in Steele's bibliography or in the *STC.*

A2905   Hagedorn, Ralph. "Bibliotheca Thordarsoniana: The Sequel." *Papers Bibl. Soc. Amer.*,
XLIV (1950), 29-54.
Describes the Thordason collection acquired by the University of Wisconsin and lists, i.a.,
one book (*God Speede the Plough*, 4°. J. Harison, 1601), and a number of editions not listed
in *STC.*

A2906   Johnson, A. F. "English Books Printed Abroad." *Library*, IV (1950), 273-276.
Attempts to assign Sayle's Zurich books to correct presses or towns, revises much in *STC.*

A2907   Williams, George Walton. "Two Corrections of the *Short-Title Catalogue.*" *N &Q*, NS, IV
(1957), 232.
Two volumes in 1593 and 1595 are erroneously assigned to Thomas Creed in the *STC.*

A2908   Shapiro, I. A. "Publication Dates Before 1600." *TLS*, Feb. 6, 1953, p. 96.
See letter by Allardyce Nicoll and C. J. Sisson, *TLS*, Feb. 20, p. 121, on a chronological
Short-Title Catalogue.
Urges cooperative effort in providing information which will reduce uncertainty about the
relationship entry in S. R. and date of publication; offers a short table of information of some
three dozen books as illustrative; calls attention to the compilation of the Chronological
Index under way at the Shakespeare Institute.

A2909   Williams, Franklin B., Jr. "Tracking Down *STC* Authors." *TLS*, Jan. 7, 1955, p. 9.
Calls for the assistance of all scholars in the work of revising the *Short-Title Catalogue.*

A2910   University Microfilms. Catalogues of microfilms of Pollard and Redgrave STC books. Title
varies: *English Books, 1475-1640*, 1956. Pp. 96. Reels 1-162. The First Five years [1938-1942].
Partial List of Microfilms of Books Printed in England Before 1600, 1943 (4 issues); 1944 (2 issues);
1945 (3 issues); 1946; 1948; 1949.
Partial List of Microfilms of Books Printed in England Before 1640, 1950; 1951.

Partial List of Microfilms of STC Books and A Cross Index by STC Number, 1952; 1953; 1954; 1955. *English Books, 1475-1640. A Cross Index by STC Number and Partial List of Microfilms.* 1956; 1957; 1958; 1959.
English Books, 1475-1640. Consolidated Cross Index by STC Numbers, Years 1-19, 1956.

(2) SHORT TITLE CATALOGUE—DONALD WING

A2911 Wing, Donald G., ed. *A Short-Title Catalogue of Books Printed in England, Scotland, Ireland, Wales, and British America, and of English Books Printed in Other Countries, 1641-1700.* New York: Index Soc., 1945-51. 3 Vols. Pp. 590; 562; 521.
   Rev: by Carl Purington Rollins, *SatR,* Aug. 16, 1952, p. 21; by Edwin Eliott Willoughby, *Lib. Quar.,* xx, 144-145; by Karl J. Holzknecht, *Papers Bibl. Soc. Amer.,* xlvi, 400-406; *TLS,* Nov. 14, p. 752.

A2912 Morrison, Paul G. *Index of Printers, Publishers, and Booksellers in Donald Wing's Short-Title Catalogue of Books . . . 1641-1700.* Charlottesville: Univ. Virginia Press, 1955. Pp. 217.
   Rev: A2786.

A2913 Wing, Donald G. "The Making of the 'Short-Title Catalogue, 1641-1700'." *Papers of the Bibl. Soc. America,* xlv (1951), 59-69.

A2914 Wing, Donald G. "Interim Report on the Second *STC.*" *TLS,* Nov. 7, 1958, p. 648.

A2915 Fry, Mary Isabel, and Godfrey Davies. "Supplements to the *Short-Title Catalogue, 1641-1700.*" *HLQ,* xvi (1953), 393-436.
   About 250 items not in Wing.

A2916 Alden, John. *Bibliographica Hibernica: Additions and Corrections to Wing.* Charlottesville: Bibliographical Society of the University of Virginia, 1955. Pp. 39.

A2917 Hiscock, W. G. *The Christ Church Supplement to Wing's Short-Title Catalogue, 1641-1700.* Oxford: Holywell Press, 1956. Pp. 47.

(3) OTHER

A2918 *English Plays to 1700, including an Unique Shakespeare Collection.* Philadelphia and New York: The Rosenbach Company, 1940. Pp. 104.

A2919 Cancelled.

A2920 Greg, W. W. *A Bibliography of the English Printed Drama to the Restoration.* Illustrated Monographs issued by the Bibliographical Society No. XXIV (I, II, III). Printed for the Bibliographical Society at the University Press, Oxford.
   Vol. I: Stationers Records, Plays to 1616: Nos. 1-349, 1940. Pp. xxxiii, 492. Plates.
   Vol. II: Plays, 1617-1689: Nos. 350-836. Latin Plays. Lost Plays. 1951. Pp. xxxiii, 493-1008. Plates.
   Vol. III: Collections, Appendix, Reference Lists, 1957. Pp. 1009-1642. Plates.
   Rev: Vol. I: *TLS,* July 20, 1940, p. 356; by E. E. Willoughby, *Papers Bibl. Soc. Amer.,* xxxvi (1942), 166-168; Vol. II: by Karl J. Holzknecht, *Papers Bibl. Soc. Amer.,* xlv (1951), 363-365; by A. K. McIlwraith, *RES,* iv (1953), 180-182; *TLS,* Sept. 7, 1951, p. 572.

A2921 Greg, W. W. *A Bibliography of the English Printed Drama to the Restoration.* Vol. IV. Oxford University Press for the Bibliographical Society, 1959. Pp. 283.

A2922 Cancelled.

A2923 Harbage, Alfred. *Annals of English Drama, 975-1700: An Analytical Record of all plays, extant or lost, chronologically arranged and indexed by authors, titles, dramatic companies, etc.* Univ. of Pennsylvania Press, 1940. Pp. 264.
   Rev: by J. G. McManaway, *MLQ,* ii (1941), 141-143; by E. E. Willoughby, *Lib. Quar.,* xi, 236-237; by Allardyce Nicoll, *JEGP,* xl, 415-416; by H. S., *MLN,* lvi, 561; *TLS,* June 21, p. 303; by Albert Howard Carter, *MP,* xl (1942), 201-212.

A2924 Wells, Henry W. *A Chronological List of Extant Plays Produced in or about London 1581-1642.* Columbia Univ. Press, 1940. Pp. 17.
   Prepared as a supplement to Prof. Wells's *Elizabethan and Jacobean Playwrights,* A7066.

A2925 Woodward, Gertrude L., and James G. McManaway. *A Check-list of English Plays, 1641-1700.* Chicago: Newberry Lib., 1945. Pp. 155.
   Rev: by W. W. Greg, *Library,* 5th Series, i (1946), 81-85; by T. W. Baldwin, *JEGP,* xlv, 457-458; by D. F. Bond, *MLQ,* vii, 504-505; by Hugh Macdonald, *RES,* xxii, 328-329; by A. H. Carter, *Lib. Quar.,* xvi, 361-362; by Alfred Harbage, *MLN,* lxii (1947), 60-61; by K. J. Holzknecht, *Papers Bibl. Soc. Amer.,* xli, 65-67; by I. A. Shapiro, *MLR,* xliii, 112-113.

A2926 Bowers, Fredson. *A Supplement to the Woodward and McManaway Check-list of English Plays, 1641-1700.* Bibl. Soc. Univ. Va., c/o Univ. Va. Library, 1949. Pp. 22.

A2927 Bibliothèque Nationale. *Catalogues des Ouvrages de William Shakespeare Conservés au Département des Imprimés et dans les Bibliothèques de l'Arsenal, Mazarine, Sainte-Geneviève, de l'Institut et l'Université de Paris.* Paris: Imprimerie Nationale, 1948. Pp. vii, 424 columns.

b. THE FOUR FOLIOS (50;21)
(1) THE FIRST FOLIO (50;21)
(a) REPRINTS (50;21)

A2928   Shakespeare, William. *Mr. William Shakespeares Comedies, Histories, and Tragedies.* Facsimile ed. prepared by Helge Kökeritz. New Haven, 1954. Pp. xxix, 889.
     Rev: *ShN*, IV (1954), 40; by Thomas E. Cooney, *SatR*, Dec. 18, p. 12; by T. S. Dorsch, *YWES*, xxxv, 79; by Karl J. Holzknecht, *Papers Bibl. Soc. Amer.*, XLIX (1955), 190-191; by Fredson Bowers, *MP*, LIII, 50-57; by Louis Marder, *Amer. Scholar*, XXIV, 241-242 (brief); by E. D. O'Brien, *Illus. London News*, July 23, p. 164; by H. B. Charlton, *MGW*, July 14, p. 10 (brief); by J. I. M. Stewart, *NstN*, Apr. 30, p. 622; by D. F. Foxon, *Book Collector*, Autumn, 261-262; *TLS*, Oct. 14, p. 612 (letters by W. W. Greg, and R. C. Bald, Oct. 28, p. 629); by George Freedley, *Lib. Jour.*, 80 (1955), 83; by Nils Molin, *Göteborgs handels- o. sjöfartstidning*, Feb. 22; by Arthur Brown, *Library*, 5th Series, XI (1956), 57-59; by Hermann Heuer, *SJ*, 92 (1956), 393-394; by Francis R. Johnson, *SQ*, VII, 114-115; *Dublin Mag.*, Apr.-June, 32-34; by J. G. McManaway, *MLR*, LI, 588-590; by M. Poirier, *EA*, IX, 153-154.

A2929   Baldwin, T. W. "Shakespeare Facsimiles." *TLS*, May 6, 1939, p. 265.

A2930   Hinman, Charlton. "The 'Halliwell-Phillipps Facsimile' of the First Folio of Shakespeare." *SQ*, V (1954), 395-401.
    Long the most accessible reproduction, and consulted even by modern editors, this facsimile derives from enough different folios to make it a hodge-podge. It also shows tamperings.

(b) STUDIES (51;21)

A2931   Seh, L. H. "Shakespeares erste Verleger [John Heminge and Henry Condell]." *Weltkunst.*, IX, No. 49 (1935), 3.

A2932   Casson, F. F. "Notes on a Shakespearean First Folio in Padua." *MLN*, LI (1936), 417-423.

A2933   Clow, R. M. *Shakespeare's "Merry Wives of Windsor": A Study of the 1602 Quarto and the 1623 Folio Texts.* MS thesis, Stanford University, 1936. Pp. 364.

A2933a   Black, Matthew W. "Shakespeare's Seventeenth Century Editors." *Proc. Amer. Philos. Soc.*, LXXVI (1936), 707-717.
    Preliminary report of the results of an exhaustive study of the four folios made in collaboration with Matthias A. Shaaber. The evidence shows unmistakable editorial supervision in the later folios, especially in the second.

A2934   Black, Matthew W., and Matthias A. Shaaber. *Shakespeare's Seventeenth Century Editors, 1632-1685.* New York: Mod. Lang. Assoc., 1937. Pp. xi, 420.
    Rev: by Hazelton Spencer, *MLN*, LIII (1938), 450-453; by R. C. Smith, *JEGP*, XXXVII, 305-307; by F. E. Budd, *MLR*, XXXIII (1938), 460; *SAB*, XIII, 62; by Kurt Wittig, *Beiblatt*, XLIX, 150-154; by W. Keller, *SJ*, LXXIV, 186-187; by Georges Connes, *EA*, III (1939), 42; by Wolfgang Clemen, *Eng. Studn.*, LXXIII, 395-396.

A2935   R. "Actors in Shakespeare's Plays." *N &Q*, 174 (1938), 387.
    Asks names of contemporaneous actors. Cites 3 in F_1: Wilson, Cowley, and Kemp.

A2936   "Wieder eine Shakespeare-Erstausgabe entdeckt." *NS*, XLVI (1938), 519.

A2937   Smith, R. M. "Why a First Folio Shakespeare Remained in England." *RES*, XV (1939), 257-264.

A2938   Stainer, C. L. "The F_1 Text of *Hamlet*." *TLS*, Jan. 6, 1940, p. 7.

A2939   Crundell, H. W. "Actors' Parts and Elizabethan Play-Texts." *N &Q*, 180 (1941), 350-351.

A2940   Dawson, Giles E. "A Bibliographical Problem in the First Folio of Shakespeare." *Library*, NS, XXII (1941), 25-33.

A2941   Hitchcock, R. M. "Case of a Missing First Folio." *Esquire*, XVI (1941), 93, 254, 256-258, 260.

A2942   Hinman, Charlton. "A Proof Sheet in the First Folio of Shakespeare." *Library*, NS, XXIII (1942), 101-107; 3 pl.

A2943   Jaggard, W. "The Editorial Problem." *N &Q*, 184 (1943), 148.

A2944   Rosenbach, A. S. W. *A Description of the Four Folios of Shakespeare, 1623, 1632, 1663-64, 1685, in the Original Bindings, the Gift of Mr. P. A. B. Widener and Mrs. Josephine Widener Wichfeld to the Free Library of Philadelphia in Memory of their Father, Joseph E. Widener.* Philadelphia, 1945.

A2945   Kirschbaum, Leo. *The True Text of "King Lear."* Johns Hopkins Press, 1945. Pp. ix, 81.
    Rev: *TLS*, Oct. 13, 1945, p. 488; by Baldwin Maxwell, *PQ*, XXIV, 280-281; *DUJ*, XXXVIII, 32; by Madeleine Doran, *JEGP*, XLV (1946), 227-230; by Samuel Asa Small, *MLN*, LXI, 68-70; by J. M. Nosworthy, *Library*, 5th Series, I, 77-79; by W. W. Greg, *RES*, XXII, 230-234; by G. I. Duthie, *MLR*, XLI, 326-330; by R. H. Parkinson, *MLQ*, VII, 503-504; by H. B. Charlton, *MGW*, LIV, 151; by J. B. Fort, *LanM*, XLIV (1950), 415-416.

A2946   Akrigg, G. P. V. "An Allusion by Thomas Middleton to the First Folio?" *SAB*, XXI (1946), 25-26.

A2947   Greg, W. W. "The Staging of *King Lear*." *RES*, XXII (1946), 229.
    Revises his opinion to accept Mr. John Berryman's view that act and scene division in the Folio is not "original" and may be the work of the Folio editor.

A2948   Nosworthy, J. M. "The Bleeding Captain Scene in *Macbeth*." *RES*, XXII (1946), 126-130.

A2949   "Shakespeare Folio Is Sold for $50,000." [The Rosebery Folio] *New York Times*, Apr. 25, 1946, p. 12.
    From Frank J. Hogan Library.

A2950 Bald, Robert C. "Tables for the Identification and Collation of the Shakespeare Folios." *Book Handbook*, No. 2 (1947), 101-109; No. 4, 113-126.

A2951 Nosworthy, J. M. "*Macbeth* at the Globe." *Library*, II (1947), 108-118.
Discusses agreements in Forman's account of the play and in the "Argument" of Davenant's version (1674) which have the support of Shakespeare's source material and which afford clues to matter deleted from the Folio text.

A2952 Hinman, Charlton. "Why 79 First Folios?" Read before Bibl. Soc. of the Univ. of Virginia, June 6, 1947. Mimeographed.

A2953 Brooke, C. F. Tucker. "The Folio of 1623." *Essays on Shakespeare and Other Elizabethans*, Yale Univ. Press, 1948, pp. 78-92.

A2954 Flatter, Richard. *Shakespeare's Producing Hand*. London, 1948.
Rev: A5944.

A2955 Smith, Warren D. *Shakespeare's Stagecraft as Denoted by the Dialogue in the Original Printings of his Texts*. DD, University of Pennsylvania, 1948. Pp. 256. Mic A50-217. *Microf. Ab.*, x (1950), 163. Publication No. 1731.

A2956 Secord, Arthur W. "I. M. of the First Folio Shakespeare and Other Mabbe Problems." *JEGP*, XLVII (1948), 374-381.

A2957 Parsons, Howard. "The Identify of I. M. (of 'First Folio' Celebrity)." *N &Q*, 194 (1949), 38.
Suggests James Mervyn as the I. M. of laudatory poem in F_1.

A2958 Atkinson, A. D. "Notes on *Richard II*." *N &Q*, 194 (1949), 190-192, 212-214.

A2959 Williams, Philip, Jr. *The 1609 Quarto of "Troilus and Cressida" and Its Relation to the Folio Text of 1623*. DD, University of Virginia, 1949. Abstr. publ. in Univ. of Virginia *Abstracts of Dissertations*, Charlottesville: Univ. of Va., 1949, pp. 31-35.

A2960 Williams, Philip. "Shakespeare's *Troilus and Cressida*: The Relationship of Quarto and Folio." *SB*, III (1950), 131-143.

A2961 Hinman, Charlton. "Mark III: New Light on the Proof-reading for the First Folio of Shakespeare." *SB*, III (1950), 145-153.

A2962 Robinson, A. M. Lewin. "The Grey Copy of the Shakespeare First Folio." *Quarterly Bulletin of the South African Library*, V (1950), 11-16.

A2963 Greg, W. W. "The Printing of Shakespeare's *Troilus and Cressida* in the First Folio." *Papers Bibl. Soc. Amer.*, XLV (1951), 273-282.

A2964 Cauthen, Irby B., Jr. *Shakespeare's "King Lear": An Investigation of Compositor Habits in the First Folio and their Relation to the Text*. DD, University of Virginia, 1951. Abstr. publ. in Univ. of Virginia *Abstracts of Dissertations*, Charlottesville: Univ. of Va., 1951, pp. 13-18.

A2965 Walker, Alice. "Quarto 'Copy' and the 1623 Folio: *2 Henry IV*." *RES*, NS, II (1951), 217-225.

A2966 Walker, Alice. "The Textual Problem of *Hamlet*: A Reconsideration." *RES*, NS, II (1951), 328-338.

A2967 Cauthen, I. B., Jr. "Compositor Determination in the First Folio *King Lear*." *SB*, V (1952/53), 73-80.

A2968 Hasker, Richard E. "The Copy for the First Folio *Richard II*." *SB*, V (1952/53), 53-72.
Rev: by H. T. Price, *SQ*, V (1954), 119-120.

A2969 Muir, Kenneth. "Split Lines in the First Folio." *N &Q*, 197 (1952), 271-272.

A2970 Muir, Kenneth. "Folio Sophistications in *Othello*." *N &Q*, 197 (1952), 335-336.

A2971 Walker, Alice. "The 1622 Quarto and the First Folio Texts of *Othello*." *ShS*, V (1952), 16-24.

A2972 Flatter, Richard. " 'The True Originall Copies' Shakespeare's Plays—Outline of a New Conception." *Proc. Leeds Philos. and Lit. Soc.*, Lit. & Hist. Sec. VII, Pt. 1 (1952), 31-42.

A2973 Flatter, Richard. "Der Setzer der Ersten Shakespeare-Folio." *Das Antiquariat*, VIII (1952), No. 17/18; IX (1953), 5-6; XI (1955), 275-276.

A2974 Feuillerat, Albert. *The Composition of Shakespeare's Plays: Authorship, Chronology*. Yale University Press, 1953. Pp. viii, 340.
Rev: A3286.

A2975 Hinman, Charlton. "Variant Readings in the First Folio of Shakespeare." *SQ*, IV (1953), 279-288.

A2976 Hinman, Charlton. "The Proof-reading of the First Folio Text of *Romeo and Juliet*." *SB*, VI (1954), 61-70.

A2977 Shedd, Robert Gordon. *The "Measure for Measure" of Shakespeare's 1604 Audience*. DD, University of Michigan, 1953. Pp. 430. Mic A53-1478. *DA*, XIII (1953), 801. Publication No. 5730.

A2978 Williams, Philip. Two Problems in the Folio Text of *King Lear*." *SQ*, IV (1953), 451-460.

A2979 Walker, Alice. *Textual Problems of the First Folio: "Richard III," "King Lear," "Troilus & Cressida," "2 Henry IV," "Othello."* Shakespeare Problems Series VII, J. Dover Wilson, gen. ed. Cambridge Univ. Press, 1953. Pp. viii, 170.
Rev: *TLS*, July 24, 1953, p. 482; by Philip Williams, *SQ*, IV, 481-484 (important); R. A. Foakes, *English*, IX, 220-221; *N &Q*, 198 (1953), 454-455; by James G. McManaway, *Papers*

Bibl. Soc. Amer., XLVIII (1954), 105-107; by M. A. Shaaber, *MLN*, LXIX, 436-438; by Philip Williams, *South Atlantic Quar.*, LIII, 272; by G. Blakemore Evans, *JEGP*, LIII, 473-476; by J. M. Nosworthy, *Library*, 5th Series, IX, 63-65; by G. B. Harrison, *Dublin Review*, 118 (1954), 226-228; Philip Edwards, *MLR*, XLIX, 365-367; by Hermann Heuer, *SJ*, 90 (1954), 324-326; by A. Koszul, *EA*, VII, 321-322; by Joseph Warren Beach, *JEGP*, LIII, 127-130; by James G. McManaway, *ShS*, VII, 152-153; by H. T. Price, *SQ*, V, 112; by Peter Alexander, *RES*, NS, IX (1958), 188-193.

A2980 Walker, Alice. "The Folio Text of *1 Henry IV*." *SB*, VI (1954), 45-59.

A2981 Hinman, Charlton. "Variant Readings in First Folios." *ShN*, IV (1954), 41.

A2982 Parsons, Howard. *Shakespearian Emendations and Discoveries*. London: Ettrick Press, 1954. Pp. 136.
Rev: A3330.

A2983 Smith, Warren D. "The *Henry V* Choruses in the First Folio." *JEGP*, LIII (1954), 38-57. See A3005.

A2984 Cairncross, A. S. "The Quartos and the Folio Text of *King Lear*." *RES*, VI (1955), 252-258.

A2985 Danks, K. B. " 'What Heminges and Condell Really Meant'." *N&Q*, NS, II (1955), 16-19.

A2986 Greg, W. W. *The Shakespeare First Folio*. Its Bibliographical and Textual History. Oxford: Clarendon Press, 1955. Pp. 496.
Rev: by John Wain, *Spectator*, July 15, 1955, p. 101; by H. B. Charlton, *MGW*, July 14, p. 10; *QR*, 293 (1955), 424 (brief); by R. A. Foakes, *English*, X, 227-228; by David Daiches, *TC*, 158 (1955), 180-183; *N&Q*, NS, II, 412-413; *TLS*, Oct. 14, p. 612; Oct. 21, p. 621; Oct. 28, p. 639; by A. Brown, *Listener*, LIII, 1037-38; *Times Weekly Rev.*, June 16, p. 12; by Karl J. Holzknecht, *Papers Bibl. Soc. Amer.*, L (1956), 88-95; by Alice Walker, *Library*, 5th Series, XI, 56-57; by Kenneth Muir, *MLR*, LI, 97; by James G. McManaway, *ShS*, IX, 148-149; by Charlton Hinman, *SQ*, VII, 97-101; *Dublin Mag.*, XXXI, 32-34; by Burns Martin, *Dalhousie Rev.*, XXXVI, 289-291; by Hermann Heuer, *SJ*, 92 (1956), 385-390; by H. S. Wilson, *UTQ*, XXVI (1957), 271-272; by Peter Alexander, *RES*, NS, IX (1958), 69-70.

A2987 Hinman, Charlton. "Cast-off Copy for the First Folio of Shakespeare." *SQ*, VI (1955), 259-273.

A2988 Jenkins, Harold. "The Relation Between the Second Quarto and the Folio Text of *Hamlet*." *SB*, VII (1955), 69-83.

A2989 Shaaber, M. A. "The Folio Text of *2 Henry IV*." *SQ*, VI (1955), 135-144.

A2990 Walton, J. K. *The Copy for the Folio Text of "Richard III."* With a Note on the Copy for the Folio Text of *King Lear*. Monograph Series, No. 1. Auckland University College, New Zealand: The Pilgrim Press, 1955. Pp. 164.
Rev: A3301.

A2991 Akrigg, G. P. V. "The Arrangement of the Tragedies in the First Folio." *SQ*, VII (1956), 443-445.

A2992 Brock, Elizabeth. *Shakespeare's "The Merry Wives of Windsor": A History of the Text from 1623 Through 1821*. DD, University of Virginia, 1956. Pp. 623. Mic 57-1351. *DA*, XVII (1957), 847. Publication No. 20,349.

A2993 Flatter, Richard. "Some Instances of Line Division in the First Folio." *SJ*, 92 (1956), 184-196.

A2994 Greer, C. A. "An Actor-Reporter in the *Merry Wives of Windsor*." *N&Q*, NS, III (1956), 192-194.

A2995 Greer, C. A. "The Quarto-Folio Relationship in *2* and *3 Henry VI* Once Again." *N&Q*, NS, III (1956), 420-421.

A2996 Mackenzie, Barbara. "Shakespeare's First Folio." *Quar. Bul. of the South African Lib.*, X (1955/56), 57-60.

A 2997 Scott, R. I. *A Study of the First Quarto and First Folio Editions of Shakespeare's "Othello."* B. Litt., Glasgow, 1956.

A2998 Shroeder, John W. *The Jaggard Shakespeare: A Bibliographical Study of the First Folio*. DD, Yale University, 1954. Pp. 162, 29 pl. Abstr. in *ShN*, VI (1956), 11.

A2999 Shroeder, John W. *The Great Folio of 1623: Shakespeare's Plays in the Printing House*. Hamden, Conn.: The Shoe String Press, 1956. Pp. 126; 29 pl.
Rev: by W. W. G., *Book Collector*, VI (1957), 95; by I. B. Cauthen, Jr., *JEGP*, LVI, 631-633; by W. W. Greg, *Library*, XII, 130-133; by Charlton Hinman, *SQ*, VIII, 219-222; by George Walton Williams, *RN*, XI, 33-35; by R. A. Foakes, *ES*, XXXIX, 261-263.

A3000 Walker, Alice. "Some Editorial Principles (with special reference to *Henry V*)." *SB*, VIII (1956), 95-111.

A3001 Weld, John S. "Old Adam New Apparelled." *SQ*, VII (1956), 435-456.

A3002 Danks, K. B. "Is F_1 *Macbeth* a Reconstructed Text?" *N&Q*, NS, IV (1957), 516-519.

A3003 Danks, K. B. "Are There Any Memorially Reconstructed Texts in the Shakespeare First Folio?" *N&Q*, NS, IV (1957), 143-144.

A3004 Hinman, Charlton. "The Prentice Hand in the Tragedies of the Shakespeare First Folio: Compositor E." *SB*, IX (1957), 3-20.

A3005   Law, Robert Adger. "The Choruses in *Henry the Fifth.*" *TxSE*, XXXV (1956), 11-21. Disputes A2983.

A3006   "Eighth International Shakespeare Conference at Stratford." *ShN*, VII (1957), 39, 48. Contains Abstract of: Michael MacOwan, "The Value of the First Folio Text for the Speaking of the Verse."

A3007   Musgrove, S. "*King Lear* I. i. 170 ('To come betwixt our sentence/sentences and our power')." *RES*, VIII (1957), 170-172.

A3008   Nathan, Norman. "Compositor Haste in the First Folio." *SQ*, VIII (1957), 134-135.

A3009   Barton, Thomas P. "The Library's First Folio of Shakespeare." *Boston Public Lib. Quar.*, X (1958), 63-75.

A3010   Foakes, R. A. "On the First Folio Text of *Henry VIII.*" *SB*, XI (1958), 55-60.

A3011   Willoughby, Edwin Eliott. *The Uses of Bibliography to the Students of Literature and History.* Hamden, Conn.: Shoe String Press, 1958. Pp. 105. Printed by offset from typescript. Four lectures delivered in England in 1952, including (No. 4) a summary of *The Printing of the First Folio*, pp. 89-100.

(2)   THE 2nd-4th FOLIOS (52;-)
(a)   SEVERAL FOLIOS

A3012   Black, Matthew W., and Matthias A. Shaaber. *Shakespeare's Seventeenth Century Editors, 1632-1685.* New York: Mod. Lang. Assoc., 1937. Pp. xi, 420.
        Rev: A2934.

A3013   "A Shakespeare Collection." *TLS*, January 3, 1942, p. 12.

A3014   Rosenbach, A. S. W. *A Description of the Four Folios of Shakespeare, 1623, 1632, 1663-64, 1685, in the Original Bindings, the Gift of Mr. P. A. B. Widener and Mrs. Josephine Widener Wichfeld to the Free Library of Philadelphia in Memory of their Father, Joseph E. Widener.* Philadelphia, 1945.

A3015   Bald, R. C. "Tables for Identification and Collation of the Shakespeare Folios." *Book Handbook*, No. 2 (1947), pp. 100-109; No. 4, pp. 113-126.

A3016   Brock, Elizabeth. *Shakespeare's "The Merry Wives of Windsor": A History of the Text from 1623 Through 1821.* DD, University of Virginia, 1956. Pp. 623. Mic 57-1351. *DA*, XVII (1957), 847. Publication No. 20,349.

(b)   SECOND FOLIO

A3017   Dawson, Giles E. "Second Folio Variants." *TLS*, Feb. 1, 1947, p. 65.

A3018   Todd, William B. "The Issues and States of the Second Folio and Milton's Epitaph on Shakespeare." *SB*, V (1952), 81-108.
        Rev: by P. Edward, *SQ*, IV (1953), 185-186; by H. T. Price, *SQ*, V (1954), 120.

A3019   Robinson, A. M. Lewin. "The Grey Copy of the Shakespeare Second Folio [1632]." *Quar. Bul. of the South African Lib.*, VI (1952), 120-125.

A3020   Partridge, A. C. "Another Shakespeare Find in South Africa." *Rand Daily Mail*, Sept. 20, 1952.

A3021   McManaway, James G. "The Colophon of the Second Folio of Shakespeare." *Library*, 5th Series, IX (1954), 199-200.

A3022   "Blake Water-colours: Illustrations from the British Museum's Newly-acquired Second Folio." *Illustrated London News*, Dec. 25, 1954, p. 1163.

A3023   Boase, T. S. R. "An Extra-illustrated Second Folio of Shakespeare." *British Museum Quar.*, XX (1955), 4-8.
        The copy of F_2 recently purchased by the British Museum containing single well-known water colors by William Blake and drawings by other artists of ca. 1800.

(c)   THIRD FOLIO

A3024   Brooks, P. "An Alleged Pepys Third Folio." *NYTBR*, June 12, 1939, p. 20.

A3025   McManaway, James G. "Additional Prompt-Books of Shakespeare from the Smock Alley Theatre." *MLR*, XLV (1950), 64-65.

A3026   McManaway, J. G. "A Miscalculation in the Printing of the Third Folio." *Library*, IX (1954), 129-133.

(d)   FOURTH FOLIO

A3027   Dawson, Giles E. "Some Bibliographical Irregularities in the Shakespeare Fourth Folio." *SB*, IV (1951), 93-103.

A3028   Bowers, Fredson. "Robert Roberts: A Printer of Shakespeare's Fourth Folio." *SQ*, II (1951), 241-246.

A3029   R., S. "An Old London Bookshop." *N&Q*, NS, III (1956), 310-311.

(3)   THE QUARTOS (52;21)
(a)   BAD QUARTOS IN GENERAL, CHIEFLY NON-SHAKESPEAREAN

A3030 Kirschbaum, Leo. *Elizabethan and Jacobean Bad Quartos Among the Stationers.* DD, University of Michigan, 1937.

A3031 Kirschbaum, Leo. "A Census of Bad Quartos." *RES,* XIV (1938), 20-43.

A3032 Kirschbaum, Leo. "An Hypothesis Concerning the Origin of the Bad Quartos." *PMLA,* LX (1945), 697-715.

A3033 Hoppe, Harry R. "John of Bordeaux: A Bad Quarto That Never Reached Print." *Studies in Honor of A. H. R. Fairchild,* pp. 119-132.

A3034 Ashe, Dora J. *A Survey of Non-Shakespearean Bad Quartos.* DD, University of Virginia, 1953.

A3035 Ashe, Dora Jean. "The Non-Shakespearean Bad Quartos as Provincial Acting Versions." *Renaissance Papers,* 1954, pp. 57-61.

(b) SHAKESPEAREAN QUARTOS

(All studies of and facsimiles of quartos of single, individual plays are listed in Texts sections under play titles in Part B.)

A3036 Bartlett, Henrietta C. "First editions of Shakespeare's Quartos." *Library,* 4th Series, XVI (1935/36), 166-172.

A3037 Clow, R. M. "Shakespeare's *Merry Wives of Windsor:* A Study of the 1602 Quarto and the 1623 Folio Texts." MS thesis, Stanford University, 1936. Pp. 364.

A3038 Stoll, Elmer Edgar. "*Hamlet* and the *Spanish Tragedy,* Quartos I and II: A Protest." *MP,* XXXV (1937), 31-46.

A3039 Bartlett, Henrietta C. "Shakespeare Census." *TLS,* June 4, 1938, p. 386. See also "Shakespeare Quartos." *SRL,* XVI (1937), 9.

A3040 Bartlett, Henrietta C., and Alfred W. Pollard. *A Census of Shakespeare's Plays in Quarto, 1594-1709.* Yale Univ. Press, 1939. Pp. v, 165.
Rev: by G. E. Dawson, *MLN,* LV (1940), 226-227; *TLS,* Mar. 9, 1940, p. 115; by W. W. Greg, *RES,* XVI, 208-211; by J. Q. Adams, *JEGP,* XXXIX, 405-407; by B. M., *PQ,* XIX, 413-414; *N&Q,* 178 (1940), 161-162; by A. E., *Lib. Assoc. Rec.,* XLII, 132; by H. Sellers, *Library,* XX, 432-433; by Evelyn May Albright, *MP,* XVII (1941), 101-102.

A3041 Duthie, George Ian. *Elizabethan Pirated Dramas, with Special Reference to the "Bad" Quartos of "Hamlet," "Henry V" and "Romeo and Juliet": With an Appendix on the Problem of "The Taming of a Shrew."* DD, Edinburgh, 1939.

A3042 McManaway, J. G. "Shakespeare Quartos in Collotype Facsimiles." *MLN,* LV (1940), 632-634.

A3043 Hart, Alfred. *Stolne and Surreptitious Copies: A Comparative Study of Shakespeare's Bad Quartos.* Oxford Univ. Press, 1942. Pp. xi, 478.
Rev: *TLS,* May 1, 1943, p. 216; by G. I. Duthie, *RES,* XIX, 416-418; by Leo Kirschbaum, *MLN,* LIX (1944), 196-198; by Madeleine Doran, *MLR,* XXXIX, 190-193; by Eva Turner Clark, *Shakespeare Fellowship Quar.,* V, 6-8.

A3044 Sisson, Charles J. "Shakespeare Quartos as Prompt Copies." *RES,* XVIII (1942), 129-143.

A3045 Shapin, Betty. "An Experiment in Memorial Reconstruction." *MLR,* XXXIX (1944), 9-17.

A3046 Danks, K. B. "The Good and Bad Quartos." *English,* VI (1946), 154.

A3047 Duthie, George Ian. (1) *Two Shakespeare Problems; (a) The "Bad" Quarto of "Hamlet," (b) "The Taming of a Shrew" and "The Taming of the Shrew"; (2) Shakespeare's "King Lear": A Critical Edition.* DD, Edinburgh, 1946.

A3048 Bowers, Fredson. "An Examination of the Method of Proof Correction in Lear." *Library,* II (1947), 20-44.
The evidence of headlines casts doubts upon Mr. Greg's solution of the Pide Bull puzzle and hence upon some aspects of general bibliographical research.

A3049 Flatter, Richard. *Shakespeare's Producing Hand.* London, 1948.
Rev: A5944.

A3050 Smith, Warren D. *Shakespeare's Stagecraft as Denoted by the Dialogue in the Original Printings of his Texts.* DD, University of Pennsylvania, 1948. Pp. 256. Mic A50-217. *Microf. Ab.,* X (1950), 163. Publication No. 1731.

A3051 Rubinstein, William C. *Shakespearean Bad Quartos: A Critical Study.* DD, Yale University, 1950.

A3052 Flatter, Richard. " 'The True Originall Copies' of Shakespeare's Plays—Outline of a New Conception." *Proc. Leeds Philos. and Lit. Soc.,* Lit. & Hist. Sec. VII, Pt. 1 (1952), 31-42.

A3053 Feuillerat, Albert. *The Composition of Shakespeare's Plays: Authorship, Chronology.* Yale Univ. Press, 1953. Pp. viii, 340.
Rev: A3286.

A3054 Suschko, Leo J. *Können die 'schlechten' Quartos der Shakespeare-Dramen abgekürzte Provinzfassungen sein?* DD, Erlangen, 1953. Pp. 140. Typewritten.

A3055 Partridge, A. C. "Shakespeare's Orthography in *Venus and Adonis* and Some Early Quartos." *ShS,* VII (1954), 35-47.

A3056 Brown, John Russell. "The Compositors of *Hamlet* Q₂ and *The Merchant of Venice.*" *SB,* VII (1955), 17-40.

A3057   Craig, Hardin. "Proof and Probability in the Study of Shakespeare and his Contemporaries." *McNeese Rev.*, VII (1955), 26-38.

A3058   Danks, K. B. " 'What Heminges and Condell Really Meant'." *N &Q*, NS, II (1955), 16-19; III (1956), 11-13.

A3059   Kirschbaum, Leo. *Shakespeare and the Stationers*. Ohio State Univ. Press, 1955.
        Rev: A7021.

A3060   Bolton, Joseph S. G. "Worn Pages in Shakespearian Manuscripts." *SQ*, VII (1956), 177-182.

A3061   Byvanck, W. G. C. *Keur uit het ongebundelde Werk*. Zwolle Drukken en Herdrukken, 16. Zwolle: Tjeenk Willink, 1956. Pp. 247.
        Includes a long introduction to *Hamlet* and tells how English play quartos were acquired by the Royal Library.

A3062   Greer, C. A. "An Actor-Reporter in *The Merry Wives of Windsor*." *N &Q*, NS, III (1956), 192-194.

A3063   Greer, C. A. "The Quarto-Folio Relationship in *2* and *3 Henry VI* Once Again." *N &Q*, NS, III (1956), 420-421.

A3064   Linton, Marion. "The Bute Collection of English Plays." *TLS*, Dec. 21, 1956, p. 772.

A3065   Martin, Burns. "Shakespeare Quartos." *TLS*, Sept. 21, 1956, p. 553. See also Sept. 28, p. 569.

A3066   Hosley, Richard. "Quarto Copy for Q$_2$ *Romeo and Juliet*." *SB*, IX (1957), 129-141.

A3067   Sale, Roger Hiller. *The Development of Narrative Technique in the English Drama, 1585-1595*. DD, Cornell University, 1957. Pp. 253. Mic 57-4208. *DA*, XVII (1957), 2616. Publication No. 23,143.
        Appendix: "The bad quartos of *H. VI*, *Shrew*, and *John*," pp. 232-237.

(c)   SUPPLEMENT: THE PAVIER QUARTOS OF 1619
(53;21)

A3068   "Library Notes and News." *BJRL*, XXIX (1945), 22-23.

A3069   "A Treasure Restored." *TLS*, May 18, 1946, p. 235.

A3070   "Frank Hogan's Library." *TLS*, June 14, 1946, p. 288.
        The last substantial section of the late Frank Hogan's library was sold by the Parke-Bernet Galleries, New York, on April 23 and 24, 1946. It included the Rosebery copy of the First Folio, several later folios, and numerous quartos.

A3071   Hodgson and Co. *The Remarkable Story of the Shakespearian Quartos of 1619. Being a Brief Record of the Unraveling of a Puzzle in Shakespearian Bibliography and an Account of the Unlooked-for Discovery of a 'Set' of the Quartos of 1619*. London: Printed for Messrs. Hodgson & Co., 1946. Pp. 12.
        Rev: by J. M. N., *Library*, 5th Series, I (1947), 257.

A3072   Dunkin, Paul S. "Two Notes on Richard Hooker." *Papers Bibl. Soc. Amer.*, XLI (1947), 344-346.

A3073   Cancelled.

A3074   Stevenson, Allan H. "Shakespearian Dated Watermarks." *SB*, IV (1951), 159-164.
        Reports the discovery of two dated watermarks in the Jaggard-Pavier Quartos of 1619: a 1608 date in the "1600" *Sir John Oldcastle*, and a 1617 or 1619 date in the "1608" *Henry V*.

A3075   Danks, K. B. " 'What Heminges and Condell Really Meant'." *N &Q*, NS, II (1955), 16-19; III (1956), 11-13.

A3076   Danks, K. B. "The Case of William Jaggard 1619." *N &Q*, NS, III (1956), 329-330.

A3077   Wood, E. R. "A Discoverie of Errours in 'The Case of William Jaggard' 1619 (cci. 329)." *N &Q*, NS, IV (1957), 62-63. Answer to A3076.

A3078   Willoughby, Edwin Eliott. *The Uses of Bibliography to the Students of Literature and History*. Hamden, Conn.: Shoe String Press, 1958. Pp. 105. Printed by offset from typescript.
        Pavier, pp. 83-89.

3.   LATER EDITIONS WITH CRITICAL TEXT REVISION (53;22)
a.   GENERAL LITERATURE (53;22)
(1)   EIGHTEENTH CENTURY
(a)   GENERAL

A3079   Ford, H. L. *Shakespeare, 1700-1740: A Collation of the Editions and Separate Plays with Some Account of T. Johnson and R. Walker*. Oxford Univ. Press, 1935. Pp. viii, 145.
        Rev: by R. B. McKerrow, *Library*, NS, XVII (1936), 117-120; *TLS*, Feb. 1, 1936, p. 100; by W. Keller, *SJ*, LXXIV (1938), 187-188.

A3080   Dawson, Giles E. "Three Shakespeare Piracies in the Eighteenth Century." *Papers Bibl. Soc. Univ. Va.*, I (1948/49), 47-58.

A3081   Todd, William B. *Procedures for Determining the Identity and Order of Certain Eighteenth Century Editions*. DD, University of Chicago, 1950.

A3082   Brock, Elizabeth. *Shakespeare's "The Merry Wives of Windsor": A History of the Text from 1623*

Through 1821. DD, University of Virginia, 1956. Pp. 623. Mic 57-1351. *DA*, XVII (1957), 847. Publication No. 20,349.

A3083 Bronson, Bertrand H. "Printing as an Index of Taste in Eighteenth Century England. Part II." *Bul. of the New York Public Library*, LXII (1958), 443-462.

(b) ROWE

A3084 Summers, Montague. "The First Illustrated Shakespeare." *Connoisseur*, 102 (1938), 305-309.
A3085 Suling, Karl-Heinz. *Die Shakespeare-Ausgabe Nicholas Rowes (1709).* DD, Göttingen, 1939. Pp. 111. Publ. in *England. Sprache und Kultue*, II. Würzburg: Triltsch, 1939.
A3086 Clark, Donald B. *Nicholad Rowe: A Study in the Development of the Pathetic Tragedy.* DD, George Washington University, 1947.
A3087 Schwarz, Alfred. *The Literary Career of Nicholas Rowe.* DD, Harvard University, 1951.

(c) POPE

A3088 Butt, John. *Pope's Taste in Shakespeare.* Oxford Univ. Press, 1936. Pp. 22.
A3089 Wasserman, Earl R. "Elizabethan Poetry 'Improved'." *MP*, XXXVII (1940), 357-369.
A3090 Crundell, H. W. "Actors' Parts and Elizabethan Play-Texts." *N&Q*, 180 (1941), 350-351.
A3091 Hart, John A. *Alexander Pope's Edition of Shakespeare: A Critical Study.* DD, Yale University, 1943.
A3092 Goldstein, M. "Pope, Sheffield, and Shakespeare's *Julius Caesar*." *MLN*, LXXI (1956), 8-10.
A3093 Goldstein, Malcolm. *Pope and the Augustan Stage.* Stanford Univ. Press, 1958. Pp. 139.
       Rev: briefly by James Preu, *English Journal*, XLVII (1958), 590.

(d) THEOBALD

A3094 Cadwalader, John. "Theobald's Alleged Shakespeare Manuscript." *MLN*, LV (1940), 108-109.
A3095 King, H. M. *The Work of Theobald and his Predecessors on the Text of Shakespeare.* DD, University of London, 1940.

(e) WARBURTON

A3096 Dawson, Giles E. "Warburton, Hanmer, and the 1745 Edition of Shakespeare." *SB*, II (1949) 35-48.
A3097 Sherbo, Arthur. "Warburton and the 1745 Shakespeare." *JEGP*, LI (1952), 71-82.
A3098 Gilbert, V. M. "The Warburton-Edwards Controversy, (I) Mr. Toby Dismissed." *N&Q*, 199 (1954), 257-259 and 291-293.

(f) STEEVENS

A3099 Thompson, Lawrence. "The Boydell Shakespeare." *Princeton Univ. Library Chronicle*, I, No. 2 (1940), 17-24.
A3100 Horne, Colin J. "Malone and Steevens." *N&Q*, 195 (1950), 56.
A3101 Wenner, Evelyn W. *George Steevens and the Boydell Shakespeare.* DD, George Washington University, 1952.
       Abstr. publ. in Geo. Washington University Bulletin, *Summaries of Doctoral Dissertations, 1951 and 1952*, Washington, D. C., 1953, pp. 43-52.
A3102 Schwarzstein, Leonard. "Knight, Ireland, Steevens, and the Shakespeare Testament." *N&Q*, NS, II (1955), 76-78.
A3103 Barnet, Sylvan. "George Steevens, Editor." *ShN*, VII, No. 2 (1957), 2.

(g) DR. JOHNSON (See also other sections on Johnson, A7858-A7869, A8896-A8915.)

A3104 Hazen, A. T. "Johnson's Shakespeare: A Study in Cancellation." *TLS*, Dec. 24, 1938, p. 820.
A3105 Bronson, Bertrand H. *Joseph Ritson, Scholar-at-Arms.* 2 Vols. Berkeley: Univ. of Calif. Press, 1938. Pp. 819.
       Rev: by W. Keller, *SJ*, LXXV (1939), 164-166.
A3106 Hart, C. W. "Dr. Johnson's 1745 Shakespeare Proposals." *MLN*, LIII (1938), 367-368.
A3107 Eastman, Arthur M. *Johnson's Edition of Shakespeare: 1765.* DD, Yale University, 1947.
A3108 Eastman, Arthur M. "Johnson's Shakespearean Labors in 1765." *MLN*, LXIII (1948), 512-515.
A3109 Evans, G. Blakemore. "The Text of Johnson's Shakespeare (1765)." *PQ*, XXVIII (1949), 425-428.
A3110 Eastman, Arthur M. "The Texts from Which Johnson Printed his Shakespeare." *JEGP*, XLIX (1950), 182-191.
A3111 Eastman, Arthur M. "Johnson's Shakespeare and the Laity: A Textual Study." *PMLA*, LXV (1950), 1112-21.

A3112 Fleischauer, Warren L. *Dr. Johnson's Editing and Criticism of Shakespeare's Lancastrian Cycle.* DD, Western Reserve University, 1952. Abstr. publ. in Western Reserve Univ. *Bibliography of Published Research, 1950-1952,* (?1957), pp. 146-148.

A3113 Sherbo, Arthur. "Dr. Johnson on *Macbeth:* 1745 and 1765." *RES,* NS, II (1951), 40-47.

A3114 Sherbo, Arthur. "The Proof-Sheets of Dr. Johnson's Preface to Shakespeare." *BJRL,* XXXV (1952), 206-210.

A3115 Monaghan, T. J. "Johnson's Addition to His Shakespeare for the Edition of 1773." *RES,* IV (1953), 234-248.
        Rev: by A. Sherbo, *PQ,* XXXIII (1954), 283-284.

A3116 Liebert, Herman W. "Proposals for Shakespeare, 1756." *TLS,* May 6, 1955, p. 237.
        Letter correcting reviewer's statement (*TLS,* Mar. 18) that the two Rothschild copies of Johnson's *Proposals* (1756) are the only two known.

A3117 Sherbo, Arthur. *Samuel Johnson, Editor of Shakespeare.* With an Essay on *The Adventurer.* Illinois Studies in Language and Literature, XLII. Urbana: Univ. of Illinois Press, 1956. Pp. xi, 181.
        Rev: A8910.

A3118 Eastman, Arthur M. "In Defense of Dr. Johnson." *SQ,* VIII (1957), 493-500. (Takes issue with Sherbo's *Samuel Johnson,* A3117.)

A3119 Sherbo, Arthur. "Sanguine Expectations: Dr. Johnson's Shakespeare." *SQ,* IX (1958), 426-428.

A3120 Sherbo, Arthur. "Correspondence." *SQ,* IX (1958), 433.

(h) MALONE

A3121 Smith, D. N. "E. Malone." *HLQ,* III (1939), 23-36.

(i) OTHERS

A3122 Byrne, M. St. Clare. "Bell's Shakespeare." *TLS,* Jan. 31, 1948, p. 65.

A3123 Schmitz, R. Morrell. "Scottish Shakspere." *SAB,* XVI (1941), 229-236.

A3124 Rostenberg, Leona. "Nathaniel Butter and Nicholas Bourne, First 'Masters of the Staple'." *Library,* XII (1957), 23-33.

A3125 Fairchild, Arthur Henry Rolph. "A Shakespearean Who Was Hanged (William Dodd)." *Western Humanities Rev.,* VII (1953), 313-321.

A3126 Willoughby, Edwin E. "A Deadly Edition of Shakespeare." *SQ,* V (1954), 351-357.

A3127 Willoughby, Edwin E. "The Unfortunate Dr. Dodd: The Tragedy of an Incurable Optimist." *Essays by Divers Hands,* ed. by E. V. Rieu for the Royal Society of Literature, NS, XXXIX (1958), 124-143.

A3128 Crosse, Gordon. "Charles Jennenns as Editor of Shakespeare." *Library,* 4th Series, XVI (1935/36), 236-240.

A3129 Geduld, H. M. *Jacob Tonson: His Life and Work and the Enterprises of his Publishing House from 1678 to his Death in 1736* (with handlist). MA thesis, Sheffield, 1955.

(2) NINETEENTH CENTURY

A3130 Paul, Henry N. "Billy Jones' Shakespeare." *Colophon,* NS, I (1936), 461-462.

A3131 Timperly, Charles Henry. *William Bulmer and the Shakespeare Press:* A biography of William Bulmer from *A Dictionary of Printers and Printing,* London, 1839, with an introductory note on the Bulmer-Martin types by Laurence B. Siegfried. Syracuse Univ. Press, 1957. Pp. 34.

A3132 Isaac, C. G. "William Bulmer, 1757-1830: An Introductory Essay." *Library,* XIII (1958), 37-50.

A3133 "Shakespeare: Standard Emendations." *N&Q,* 179 (1941), 388, 466.
        See letters by Philomot, *N&Q,* 180 (1941), 283; by W. H. J., ibid., 304.

A3134 Coyle, William. "Trollope and the Bi-columned Shakespeare." *Nineteenth Century Fiction,* VI (1951), 33-46.

A3135 Bakeless, J. "The Most Famous Edition of Shakespeare: the Furness Variorum." *Common-weal,* XXVIII (1938), 637-638.

A3136 Brooke, C. F. T. "Report on the Furness Variorum." *Miscellanea,* I (1936), 41-42.

A3137 "W. J. Craig (1843-1906), Editor of *The Oxford Shakespeare.*" *N&Q,* 185 (1943), 137-138.

A3138 A., G. "The 'Edina' Edition of Shakespeare: Introduction." *N&Q,* 170 (1936), 9.

(3) TWENTIETH CENTURY
(General Comments upon current editions
or editions issued before 1936.)

A3139 Beaujon, P. "Some Recent Editions of Shakespeare's Works." *Signature,* Nov., 1937, pp. 17-32.

A3140 Hastings, William T. "To the Next Editor of Shakspere: Notes for his Prospectus." *Colophon,* NS, II (1937), 487-503.

A3141   Rogers, B., H. Farjeon, and G. Macy. *Some Notes Upon a Project for an Illustrated Shakespeare.* New York, 1938. Pp. 16.

A3142   Law, Robert Adger. "Mr. Kittredge and his Shakespeare." *Southwest Rev.*, XXVI (1940), 125-131.

A3143   Tannenbaum, Samuel A. "The American Shakspere" (a notice of G. L. Kittredge's edition of the plays published separately). *SAB*, XVI (1941), 127.

A3144   Sutherland, J. R. "The Dull Duty of an Editor." *RES*, XXI (1945), 202-215.

A3145   Jazayery, Mohammad Ali, and Robert Adger Law. "Three Texts of *King Lear*: Their Differences." *TxSE*, XXXII (1954), 14-24.
Differences between three standard texts: Globe, Neilson, Kittredge.

A3146   Granville-Barker, Harley. "Introduction to 'The Players Shakespeare'." *The Shakespeare Stage*, No. 2, Sept., 1953, pp. 11-22.

A3147   Sisson, Charles Jasper. "A New Edition of Shakespeare is Always a Major Venture." *The Bookseller*, Mar. 27, 1954, pp. 1016-18.

A3148   Cruttwell, Patrick. "Another Part of the Wood." *EIC*, V (1955), 382-390.

A3149   Bowers, Fredson. "Old-spelling Editions of Dramatic Texts." *Studies in Honor of T. W. Baldwin*, 1958, pp. 9-15.

b.   RECENT EDITIONS (53;22)
(1)   THE IMPORTANT SERIES   (Generally one play to a volume and usually with various editors. Review entries occur under the Individual Plays, Texts.)

A3150   *Shakespeare Quartos in Collotype Facsimile (Shakespeare Assoc. Q facsimiles).* Ed. and Introd. by Walter Wilson Greg. London: Shakespeare Assoc., and Sidgwick & Jackson.
See Text sections of plays for those issued.

A3151   *New Variorum Editions since 1935.* Philadelphia: Lippincott.
I Henry IV, ed. S. B. Hemingway, 1936.
Poems, ed. Hyder Rollins, 1938.
II Henry IV, ed. M. A. Shaaber, 1941.
The Sonnets, ed. Hyder Rollins, 1944.
Troilus and Cressida, ed. H. N. Hillebrand and T. W. Baldwin, 1953.
Richard II, ed. M. W. Black, 1955.
Rev: See entries in Individual Plays, Texts.

A3152   The Arden Edition of the Works of William Shakespeare. New and revised version. General ed. Una Ellis-Fermor. London: Methuen.
Rev: See entries for each volume under Individual Plays.

A3153   New (Cambridge) Shakespeare. Ed. for the syndics of Cambridge Univ. Press by John Dover Wilson.
Rev: See entries for each volume under Individual Plays.

A3154   The Cambridge Pocket Shakespeare. Gen. ed. John Dover Wilson. Cambridge Univ. Press.

A3155   McManaway, J. G. " 'The New Cambridge' Edition of *The Complete Plays and Poems of William Shakespeare.*" *MLN*, LVIII (1943), 483-485.

A3156   Flatter, Richard. "Modern Stage-directions in Shakspere." *SAB*, XXI (1946), 116-123.
Objects to Dover Wilson's expansion of the stage-directions of the text and his invention of new ones.

A3157   Wilson, J. Dover. "Letter to the Editor." *MP*, XLIX (1952), 274-275.
Replies to Dr. Flatter's criticisms of the editorial methods of the New Shakespeare.

A3158   New Clarendon Shakespeare. London: Oxford Univ. Press; Clarendon Press, 1938.
Julius Caesar, ed. R. E. C. Houghton, 1938. Pp. 102.
Merchant of Venice, ed. R. F. W. Fletcher, 1938. Pp. 192.
Richard II, ed. J. M. Lothian, 1938. Pp. 206.
Twelfth Night, ed. J. C. Dent, 1938. Pp. 159.
As You Like It, 1941. Pp. 190.
Macbeth, ed. Bernard Groom, 1939. Pp. 191.
The Merchant of Venice, 1938. Pp. 192.
A Midsummer Night's Dream, ed. F. C. Horwood, 1939. Pp. 192.
The Tempest, ed. J. B. Sutherland, 1939.
Hamlet, ed. George Rylands, 1947. Pp. 256.
Romeo and Juliet, ed. Ralph E. C. Houghton, 1947. Pp. 192.
Coriolanus, 1954.
Rev: See entries for each volume under Individual Plays.

A3159   Croft's Classics. New York: Appleton-Century-Crofts.
The Tragedy of Antony and Cleopatra, ed. Theodore Spencer, 1948. Pp. 115.
Much Ado about Nothing, ed. Charles T. Prouty, 1948. Pp. xi, 78.
Romeo and Juliet, ed. Harry Reno Hoppe, 1947. Pp. ix, 116.
Twelfth Night; or, What you Will, ed. Marc Eccles, 1948. Pp. vi, 87.

Julius Caesar, ed. Hereward Thimbleby Price, 1949. Pp. xiii, 78.
King Lear, ed. Robert Cecil Bald, 1949. Pp. xii, 114.
The Tragedy of King Richard II, ed. Theodore Spencer, 1949. Pp. xii, 83.
The Tragedy of Macbeth, ed. Matthias Adam Shaaber, 1949. Pp. xi, 77.

A3160   The New Eversley Shakespeare. London: Macmillan, 1935-36.
Coriolanus, ed. V. de Sola Pinto. Pp. 174.
Cymbeline, ed. Guy Boas. Pp. 192.
King Henry IV, Pt. II, ed. M. Alderton Pink. Pp. 170.
King Richard III, ed. Lionel Aldred. Pp. 212.
Love's Labour's Lost, ed. F. E. Budd. Pp. 192.
Midsummer Night's Dream, ed. Cyril Aldred with Introd. by Walter de la Mare. Pp. 166.
Much Ado about Nothing, ed. F. E. Budd. Pp. 178.
Romeo and Juliet, ed. Guy Boas. Pp. 154.
Winter's Tale, ed. Buy Boas. Pp. 160.
    Rev: *TLS*, July 25, 1936, p. 613.

A3161   Folger Library General Reader's Shakespeare. New York: Pocket Library.
King Lear, 1957.
The Tragedy of Othello, the Moor of Venice, ed. Louis Booker Wright, and Virginia L. Freund, 1957. Pp. xxxviii, 128.
The Merchant of Venice, ed. Louis Booker Wright, and Virginia L. Freund, 1957. Pp. xxxvii, 94.
Hamlet, Prince of Denmark, ed. Louis Booker Wright, and Virginia L. Freund, 1958.
Julius Caesar, ed. Louis Booker Wright, and Virginia A. LaMar, 1958. Pp. 136.
A Midsummer Night's Dream, ed. Louis Booker Wright, and Virginia A. LaMar, 1958.

A3162   The Laurel Shakespeare. New York: Dell Publishing Co.
Hamlet, with a modern commentary by Maurice Evans, 1958. Pp. 255.
Richard III, with a modern commentary by Stuart Vaughan. Text ed. by Charles Jasper Sisson, 1958. Pp. 254.
Romeo and Juliet, with a modern commentary by Wystan Hugh Auden, 1958. Pp. 223.
The Taming of the Shrew, text ed. by Charles Jasper Sisson; commentary by Margaret Webster, 1958. Pp. 191.
    Rev: *ShN*, VIII (1958), 20.

A3163   The Pelican Shakespeare. Gen. ed., Alfred Harbage. *Coriolanus*, ed. Harry Levin; *Hamlet*, ed. Willard Farnham; *Henry IV, Pt. I*, ed. M. A. Shaaber; *Henry IV, Pt. II*, ed. Allan Chester; *Henry V*, ed. Louis B. Wright, and Virginia Freund; *Macbeth*, ed. Alfred Harbage; *Measure for Measure*, ed. R. C. Bald; *Much Ado about Nothing*, ed. Josephine Bennett; *Othello*, ed. Gerald Bentley; *Richard II*, ed. Matthew Black; *The Winter's Tale*, ed. Baldwin Maxwell.
    Rev: Entries under Individual Plays, Texts.

A3164   *The Penguin Shakespeare*. Ed. by G. B. Harrison. London: Penguin Books, Ltd., 1937.
    Rev: *TLS*, Nov. 6, 1937, p. 833.

A3165   *The New Temple Shakespeare*. Ed. by M. R. Ridley. London: Dent, 1935-36.
Cymbeline. Pp. xii, 178.
King Henry VI, Pts. I, II, and III. Pp. x, 132; xii, 158; xii, 146.
King Richard II. Pp. x, 136.
Measure for Measure. Pp. xxii, 140.
Much Ado about Nothing. Pp. xii, 133.
The Tempest. Pp. xix, 121.
Winter's Tale. Pp. xiv, 157.
Venus and Adonis; The Rape of Lucrece; The Phoenix and the Turtle. Pp. xiii, 178.

A3166   The Yale Shakespeare. Revised ed. by Helge Kökeritz and Charles Tyler Prouty. New Haven: Yale Univ. Press; Oxford Univ. Press.
    Rev: Entries under Individual Plays, Texts.

(2) INDIVIDUAL EDITORS
(a) P. ALEXANDER

A3167   *William Shakespeare: The Complete Works*. Ed. with Introd. and Glossary by Peter Alexander. London: Collins, 1951. Pp. xxxii, 1376. Republished in New Classics edition, 4 Vols., 1954-58. Republished in Players Edition, 1958.
A newly revised text, with a biography, introductory material, and glossary.
    Rev: by H. B. Charlton, *MGW*, Aug. 23, 1951, p. 11; *TLS*, Sept. 28, 1951, p. 613; by Kenneth Muir, *Spectator*, July 13, pp. 69-70; by J. I. M. Stewart, *NstN*, Sept. 22, pp. 319-320; by I. Brown, *Obs.*, July 8, p. 7; *Adelphi*, XXVIII, 553-554; by Vanoriot, *EA*, V (1952), 73; *DUJ*, XLIV (1952), 73-74; *Listener*, XLVII, 32-33; answers by P. Alexander, *ibid.*, p. 150, and J. D. Wilson, *ibid.*, p. 187; by H. Heuer, *SJ*, 87/88 (1952), 254; by G. Bullough, *MLR*, XLVIII (1953), 332-333; by H. Craig, *SQ*, IV, 117; by W. Clemen, *Archiv*, 190 (1954), 237.

A3168   *The Heritage Shakespeare*. Ed. by Peter Alexander. New York: The Heritage Press, 1958. Two of three vols. have appeared: *The Comedies*, with Introd. by Tyrone Guthrie, and illustrated with 32 color drawings by Edward Ardizzone; *The Histories*, with Introd. by James G. McManaway, and with color engravings by John Farleigh.

A3169   Cancelled.

A3170   Cancelled.
A3171   Cancelled.

(b)   A. H. BULLEN

A3172   *The Works of William Shakespeare Gathered into One Volume.* Ed. Arthur Henry Bullen. Printed for the Shakespeare Head Press. Oxford Univ. Press, 1934. Pp. xii, 1264. Republished 1937; New edition Odhams Press, 1944.
    Rev: by H. S., *MLN*, LI (1936), 272; *TLS*, June 10, 1944, p. 287.

(c)   O. J. CAMPBELL

A3173   *The Living Shakespeare: Twenty-Two Plays and The Sonnets.* Ed. Oscar James Campbell. New York: Macmillan, 1949. Pp. 1239. Based on the Globe text, with extensive notes, introductions to each work, and a long general introduction (pp. 1-75).
    Rev: by E. Hubler, *CE*, XI (1950), 414-415; by R. Davril, *LanM*, XLIV, 424.

(d)   CLARK & WRIGHT

A3174   *The Complete Works of William Shakespeare.* The Cambridge edition text, as edited by William Aldis Wright, including Temple notes. Illus. by Rockwell Kent. New York: Garden City Publishing Co., 1936. Pp. xviii, 1527.
A3175   *Complete Works, Arranged in their Chronological Order.* Ed. William George Clark and William Aldis Wright. New York: Blue Ribbon Books, 1937. Pp. 1233.
A3176   *Five Great Comedies: As You Like It; A Midsummer Night's Dream; The Merchant of Venice; Twelfth Night; The Tempest.* Cambridge text as ed. by William Aldis Wright, introds. by John Masefield. New York: Pocket Books, 1941. Pp. 458.
A3176a *Five Great Tragedies.* New York: Pocket Books, 1939.
A3177   *Complete Works: With the Complete Temple Notes and a Comprehensive Glossary.* Ed. William George Clark and William Aldis Wright. New York: Grosset & Dunlop, 1947. Pp. x, 1420.
A3177a *Four Great Comedies: A Midsummer Night's Dream, As You Like It, Twelfth Night, The Tempest.* Cambridge text and glossaries. Ill. by Frederick E. Banbery. New York: Pocket Books, 1950. Pp. 383.
A3177b *Four Great Tragedies: Romeo and Juliet, Julius Caesar, Hamlet, Macbeth.* Cambridge text and glossaries. Ill. by Louis L. Glanzman. New York: Pocket Books, 1950. Pp. 477.
A3178   *Shakespeare: Comedies; Historical Plays; Poems and Sonnets; Tragedies.* Everyman's Lib., 3 Vols. London: Dent, 1953. Pp. 848, 888, 982. Reprint following Clark and Wright's *Cambridge Shakespeare.*
    Rev: by R. M., *Spectator*, May 1, 1953, p. 558.

(e)   HARDIN CRAIG

A3179   *The Complete Works of Shakespeare.* Ed. Hardin Craig. Chicago: Scott, Foresman, 1951. Pp. xi, 1338.
    Rev: by Matthew W. Black, *SQ*, II (1951), 361-363; by Peter Alexander, *MLR*, XLVII (1952), 218-219; by R. A. Law, *SQ*, III, 83; by W. Clemen, *Archiv*, 190 (1954), 237.
A3180   *Shakespeare:* A Historical and Critical Study with Annotated Texts of Twenty-one Plays. Ed. Hardin Craig. Chicago: Scott, Foresman and Co., 1931. Pp. vi, 1194. Revised ed. 1958.
    Rev: by Samuel A. Tannenbaum, *SAB*, XII (1937), 192-193.
A3181   *Introduction to Shakespeare: Eight Plays, Selected Sonnets.* Ed. Hardin Craig. New York: Scott Publications, 1952.

(f)   W. J. CRAIG

A3182   *The Complete Works of William Shakespeare.* Ed. W. J. Craig. (Oxford Shakespeare). Oxford Univ. Press, 1936. Pp. 1174. Republished 1956.
Additions include 32 illustrations of modern stage presentations.
    Rev: briefly, *Essential Books*, April, 1956, p. 32.

(g)   ALAN S. DOWNER

A3183   *Hamlet, King Lear, I Henry IV, Much Ado about Nothing, and The Tempest.* Ed. with an Introd. and notes by Alan S. Downer. New York: Rinehart, 1951. Pp. xxiii, 473.
A3184   *As You Like It, Julius Caesar, and Macbeth.* Ed. with Introd. and Notes by Alan S. Downer. New York: Rinehart, 1958. Pp. xx, 242.
A3185   *Three Plays: Othello, Twelfth Night, Romeo and Juliet.* Ed. by Alan S. Downer. New York: Rinehart, 1957. Pp. 320.
A3185a *Three Plays: Macbeth, Julius Caesar, As You Like It.* Ed. Alan S. Downer. New York: Rinehart, 1957. Pp. 320.
A3186   *Twelfth Night, Othello.* Ed. Alan S. Downer. New York: Rinehart, 1958. Pp. 186.

(h)   H. FARJEON

A3187   *Works.* Limited, numbered, signed edition by Herbert Farjeon. Folio 36 Vols. New York:

Limited Editions Club, 1939-41.
Text based on the Lee facsimile of the First Folio.
    Rev: by E. L. Tinker, *NYTBR*, Sept. 4, 1939, p. 24.

A3188   *Comedies and Tragedies.* Complete and unabridged, with notes and glossary. 4 Vols. New York: Random House, 1947.

A3189   *The Complete Works of William Shakespeare.* The Nonesuch Text established 1929 by Herbert Farjeon, with new Introd. by Ivor Brown. 4 Vols. London: Nonesuch Press; New York: Random House, 1953. Pp. liv, 1081; 1199; 1473; xvi, 249.
Text based on the Lee facsimile of the First Folio, with marginal additions from the good quartos, and complete reprintings of the bad quartos.
    Rev: *TLS*, July 3, 1953, p. 428; by John Roselli, *MGW*, July 2, p. 10; J. I. M. Stewart, *NstN*, July 25, pp. 106, 108; by John Crow, *Listener*, June 25, pp. 1063, 1065; by W. R. Davies, *Saturday Night*, July 11, pp. 16-17; by J. G. McManaway, *SQ*, v (1954), 92-93; by J. Vallette, *MdF*, 321 (1954), 727-728.

A3190   Cancelled.

(i) G. B. HARRISON

A3191   *The Penguin Shakespeare.* Ed. G. B. Harrison. London, New York, and Baltimore: Penguin Books, various dates, 1939-1956. One play to a volume.
    Rev: *TLS*, Nov. 6, 1937, p. 833.

A3192   *Shakespeare, The Complete Works.* Ed. G. B. Harrison. New York: Harcourt Brace, 1952. Pp. vi, 1666.
    Rev: by Eric Bentley, *NR*, Sept. 1, 1952, p. 23.

A3193   *The New Stratford Shakespeare.* With introd. and commentary by Tyrone Guthrie. London: Harrap.
Julius Caesar, 1954. Pp. 152.
Macbeth, 1954. Pp. 147.
The Merchant of Venice, 1954. Pp. 139.
A Midsummer-Night's Dream, 1954. Pp. 122.
Twelfth Night, 1954. Pp. 131.

A3194   *Shakespeare: Twenty-three Plays and the Sonnets.* New York: Harcourt, Brace & Co., 1948. Pp. 1090.
    Rev: by W. B. C. Watkins, *NYTBR*, Aug. 1, 1948, p. 3; by B. R. Redman, *SRL*, June 5, p. 46.

A3195   *Six Plays of Shakespeare.* New York: Harcourt, Brace & Co., 1949. Pp. 252.

A3196   *Four Plays.* New York: Harcourt, Brace, 1954. Pp. 172. *Henry V, As You Like It, King Lear, Antony and Cleopatra.*

(j) GEORGE LYMAN KITTREDGE

A3197   *The Works of Shakespeare.* Boston: Ginn and Co., 1936. Pp. 1561.
    Rev: by Tucker Brooke, *SRL*, Nov. 7, 1936, p. 12; *More Books*, xi, 453-454; by Mabel C. Livingston, *Catholic World*, 154 (1937), 634-635; by C. J. Sisson, *MLN*, lv (1940), 145-147; *TLS*, Sept. 13, 1942, p. 461; by Theodore Spencer, *NR*, 110 (1944), 57-59.

A3198   *Plays of Shakespeare.* Ed. George Lyman Kittredge. Boston: Ginn, 1939-41. Separate volumes. *As You Like It, Hamlet, I Henry IV, Julius Caesar, Macbeth, A Midsummer Night's Dream, Othello, Romeo and Juliet, The Tempest, Much Ado about Nothing, King Lear.*
    Rev: *N &Q*, 176 (1938), 395-396; by W. T. Hastings, *SRL*, Aug. 19, 1939, p. 13; by R. A. Law, *JEGP*, xxxix (1940), 578-581.

A3199   Cancelled.

A3200   *The Portable Shakespeare.* New York: Viking Press, 1944. Pp. 800. Reissued 1956.
Kittredge text of *Hamlet, Macbeth, Romeo and Juliet, Julius Caesar, Midsummer Night's Dream, As You Like It, The Tempest,* the *Sonnets* and selections from the other plays.
    Rev: by W. H. Auden, *NYTBR*, Oct. 1, 1944, pp. 7, 24.

A3201   *Sixteen Plays.* Preface by A. C. Sprague. New York: Ginn & Co., 1946. Pp. ix, 1541.
    Rev: by G. F. Reynolds, *CE*, viii (1947), 332.

(k) NEILSON & HILL

A3202   *The Complete Plays and Poems of William Shakespeare.* Boston: Houghton Mifflin Co., 1942. Pp. xxviii, 1420.
    Rev: by J. G. McManaway, *MLN*, lviii (1943), 483-485; by Theodore Spencer, *NR*, 110 (1944), 57-59.

(l) PARROTT & HUBLER

A3203   *Shakespeare: Twenty-three Plays and the Sonnets.* New York: Scribner's, 1938. Pp. viii, 1116. Revised ed. 1953.
    Rev: by G. C. Taylor, *MLN*, liv (1939), 313-314.

A3204   *Shakespeare: Six Plays and the Sonnets.* New York: Scribner's, 1956. Pp. 290.
Includes *Romeo, I Henry IV, Hamlet, Othello, As You Like It, The Tempest.*
    Rev: by I. B. Cauthen, *CE*, xviii (1956), 125-126.

(m) C. J. SISSON

A3205   *The Complete Works.* Including A Biographical and General Introd., Glossary and Index of
Characters. London: Odhams Press; New York: Harper & Bros., 1954. Pp. lii, 1376.
The Introduction includes the following: Biographical Essay, by Harold Jenkins; The Canon
and the Text, by W. M. T. Nowottny; Editors, Editions and Critics, by W. M. T. Nowottny;
The Theatre and the Actors, by Terence Spencer; Shakespeare's Language, by Hilda Hulme;
Music and Masque, by Bruce Pattison.
Rev: by David Hardman, *John O' London's Weekly,* LXIII (1954), 414; by G. Lambin, *LanM,*
XLVIII, 91-92; *TLS,* June 18, p. 394; by B. Ifor Evans, *MGW,* July 1, p. 11; by Thom Gunn,
Spectator, July 2, pp. 32-33, *QR,* 292 (1954), 405-406; by Kenneth Muir, *London Mag.,* I, 102,
105-106, 108; by T. S. Dorsch, *YWES,* XXXV, 79; by J. Vallette, *MdF,* 321 (1954), 728; by
G. Blakemore Evans, *JEGP,* LIV (1955), 127-128; by William T. Hastings, *SQ,* VI, 114-115
(see letters of Mr. Sisson and Mr. Hastings, ibid., p. 475); by M. A. Shaaber, *SQ,* VI, 340-341;
by Hermann Heuer, *SJ,* 91 (1955), 328-330; by J. Dover Wilson, *MLR,* LI (1956), 240-242;
TLS, June 8, p. 345; by A. Koszul, *EA,* IX, 345-346; by M. Lehnert, *ZAA,* IV, 248-251.

(n) MINOR EDITORS AND
ANONYMOUS TRADE EDITIONS

A3206   *The Most Popular Plays: A Midsummer-Night's Dream, Twelfth Night, The Merchant of Venice,
Julius Caesar, Macbeth, Hamlet.* Ed. Francis L. Bacon and James D. Kirkpatrick. New York:
Row, Peterson and Co., 1937. Pp. 608.

A3207   *Four Shakespearean Plays.* Ed. Helen Louise Cohen and Karl Young. 4th edition. Philadelphia:
Lippincott, 1937. Pp. 528.

A3208   Dinamov, S. S., and A. A. Smirnov, eds. *Shakespeare's Complete Works.* Vol. III. Moscow,
1937. Pp. 486.

A3209   Cancelled.

A3210   *Selected Plays of Shakespeare.* Ed. Karl J. Holzknecht, and Norman E. McClure. New York:
American Book Co., 1936. 4 Vols.
Vol. I: *Richard II, I Henry IV, Much Ado, Julius Caesar, Hamlet, Winter's Tale.* Pp. vi, 673.
Vol. II: *Comedy of Errors, Romeo and Juliet, Midsummer Night's Dream, Henry V, Lear, Antony
and Cleopatra, Tempest.* Pp. vii, 739.
Vol. III: *Richard III, As You Like It, Twelfth Night, Othello, Macbeth, Cymbeline,* 1937. Pp. 722.
Vol. IV: *King John, Merchant of Venice, Measure for Measure, Coriolanus, Henry VIII, Sonnets,*
1941.
Rev: *TLS,* Dec. 26, 1936, p. 1071.

A3211   *Six Plays.* Ed. S. Fred Johnson (Riverside Editions). Boston: Houghton Mifflin Company,
1956.

A3212   *The London Shakespeare.* Ed. John Munro. London: Eyre and Spottiswoode, 1957. New
York: Simon and Shuster, 1958. 6 Vols. Vols. I and II contain the General Introduction by
G. W. G. Wickham, The Dedicatory Poems and Addresses, and The Comedies; Vols. III and
IV, The Histories and The Poems; Vols. V and VI, The Tragedies.
Rev: briefly, *ShN,* VIII (1958), 12; *TLS,* Oct. 31, p. 620 (comment by R. W. David, Nov.
14, p. 657); by J. C. Maxwell, *Spectator,* Oct. 3, p. 451; by Harry T. Moore, *NR,* Apr. 21,
pp. 20-21; by J. A. Bryant, *SR,* LXVI, 323-324.

A3213   *The Nelson Shakespeare.* Ed. John Hampden. London: Nelson, 1937.
Rev: by A. Wills, *Life and Letters Today,* XVI, No. 8 (1937), 191-192.

A3214   *King Richard II; Julius Caesar; Twelfth Night, or What You Will; Hamlet, Prince of Denmark.*
Ed. E. E. Reynolds. (Traveller's Libr. Vol. I). London: Cape, 1937. Pp. 381.

A3215   *Under the Greenwood Tree.* Ed. Julia Louise Reynolds; ill. by Leonard Weisgard. New York:
Oxford Univ. Press, 1939.
A pretty edition of songs from the plays.

A3216   *Romeo and Juliet.* Ed. G. Sampson. Pitt Press Shakespeare. Cambridge Univ. Press; New
York: Macmillan, 1936. Pp. 238

A3217   *Mercury Shakespeare.* Ed. for reading and arranged for staging by Orson Welles and Roger
Hill. New York: Harper, 1939.
Julius Caesar. Pp. 91.
The Merchant of Venice. Pp. 92.
Twelfth Night. Pp. 96.

A3218   *Comedies and Tragedies.* London: Dent, 1936. Pp. 982.

A3219   *Complete Works.* Containing the plays and poems with special introductory matter, index of
characters and glossary of unfamiliar terms. London: Collins, 1937. Pp. 1372.

A3220   *Collection Théâtre de Shakespeare.* Paris: Presses Universitaires Françaises, 1938. *As You like
It, Julius Caesar, King Lear, Macbeth, Merchant of Venice, Midsummer Night's Dream, Othello,
Romeo and Juliet, The Tempest.*

A3221   *The Kingsway Shakespeare.* Works. London: Harrap, 1938.

A3222   *Historical Plays.* (Canterbury classics). London: Collins, 1939. Pp. 506.

A3223 *The Merchant of Venice; Twelfth Night; Julius Caesar.* New York: Harper, 1939.

A3224 *Complete Works.* With the Temple notes; containing all of Shakespeare's plays and poems, the history of his life, his will, an introd. to each play, and an index to characters. Cleveland: World Publishers, 1948. Pp. lxxxvi, 1173.

A3225 *The Best Loved Plays.* With 16 original ill. by Marion Kunzelman. Chicago: Fountain Press, 1949. Pp. xi, 480.

A3226 *The Complete Works.* London: Universal Textbooks, 1949. Pp. 1098.

A3227 *The Complete Works.* Comprising his plays and poems, also history of his life, his will and an introd. to each play, to which is added an index to the characters. London: Gawthorn, 1950. Pp. lxxxvi, 1097.

A3228 *The Complete Works.* Incl. a biography, glossary, and index of characters. London: Ward, Lock, 1950. Pp. xvi, 1599.

A3229 *Complete Dramatic and Poetic Works.* Red letter edition, with the most famous quotations printed in red. Introd., biography, and introd. to each play by F. D. Losey. Philadelphia: Winston, 1952. Pp. xvi, 1344.

A3230 *Scenes.* By J. Bouten. Revised by P. A. Jongsma. 8th edition. Zwolle: Tjeenk Willink, 1953. Pp. 108.

A3231 *The Complete Works* of William Shakespeare. With 32 ill. from modern stage productions. Oxford Univ. Press, 1955. Pp. 1178.

A3232 *Chaucer to Shakespeare.* Ed. D. K. Roberts. London: Penguin Books, 1955. Pp. 223.
    Rev: *MdF*, 323 (1955), 721-722.

(o) REPRINTS OF OUTMODED EDITIONS

A3233 *Complete Works.* New York: Van Nostrand, 1948; London: Macmillan, 1949. Pp. xxxii, 1312. (Classics club college ed.)
    Reissued Princeton, N. J.: D. Van Nostrand Co., 1956. Johnson-Steevens-Reed edition of 1803.

A3234 *Works, 3 Vols.* Comedies; Histories and Poems; Tragedies. General introduction by Algernon Charles Swinburne; introductory studies of the several plays by Edward Dowden; and a note by Theod. Watts-Dunton. With glossary. New York: Oxford Univ. Press, 1936. Pp. 527; 529; 547.

A3235 *Works.* Prefaces by Israel Gollancz, introductions by Henry Norman Hudson; with the notes of the Temple Shakespeare. New York: Grosset, 1936. Single play to a volume; entered under Plays, Texts.

(p) "ACTING" EDITIONS

A3236 *Shakespeare.* (French's Acting Edition.) Ed. George Skillan. London: French, 1937.
    Rev: *TLS*, Nov. 6, 1937, p. 833.

A3237 Bloch, Albert. "Karl Kraus' Shakespeare." *Books Abroad*, xi (1937), 21-24.
    Versions Kraus read.

A3238 *The Players' Shakespeare.* (*As You Like It, Taming of the Shrew, Midsummer Night's Dream,* condensed.) Ed. by T. P. Robinson. New York: Viking, 1941.

A3239 *Shakespeare Arranged for Modern Reading.* Ed. by Frank W. Cady and Van H. Cartmell. New York: Doubleday, 1946. Pp. ix, 1165.
    Rev: by W. B. C. Watkins, *NYTBR*, Nov. 17, 1946, p. 22; by Charles Norman, *SRL*, Apr. 19, 1947, p. 23.

A3240 *The Dramatic Experience.* Ed. by Juda Bierman, James Hart, and Stanley Johnson. New York: Prentice-Hall, 1958. Pp. 549. Includes *Twelfth Night* and *Othello,* text and notes.
    Rev: by W. J. Friederich, *QJS*, xliv (1958), 339-340.

4. TEXTUAL CRITICISM (58;23)
a. PROBLEMS OF TEXTS AND EDITING

A3241 McManaway, James G. "The Year's Contributions to Shakespearean Study. III: Textual Studies." *ShS*. Annually in each issue.

A3242 Bowers, Fredson, ed. *Studies in Bibliography,* i-xi. Charlottesville, Virginia: Bibliographical Society of the Univ. of Virginia, 1948-58. All Shakespearean essays entered separately.
    Rev: B3830-B3840.

A3243 Ford, H. L. *Shakespeare, 1700-1740: A Collation of the Editions and Separate Plays, with Some Account of T. Johnson and R. Walker.* Oxford Univ. Press, 1935. Pp. viii, 145.
    Rev: A3079.

A3244 Black, Matthew W., and Matthias A. Shaaber. *Shakespeare's Seventeenth Century Editors, 1632-1685.* New York: Mod. Lang. Assoc., 1937. Pp. xi, 420.
    Rev: A2934.

A3245 Mavrogordato, John. "Shakespeare: A Suggestion." *TLS*, Apr. 10, 1937, p. 275.
    See also R. W. Chapman, ibid., Apr. 17, 1937, p. 292; A. J. Hawkes, ibid., Apr. 24, p. 308.

A3246   Price, H. T. "Towards a Scientific Method of Textual Criticism for the Elizabethan Drama."
        JEGP, XXXVI (1937), 151-167.

A3247   Hinkle, George H. *Shakespeare's Poems of 1640*. DD, Stanford University, 1937. Abstr. publ.
        in *Abstracts of Dissertations, 1936-37*, Stanford University, 1937, pp. 41-46.

A3248   McKerrow, Ronald B. *Prolegomena for the Oxford Shakespeare*. Oxford: Clarendon Press,
        1939. Pp. 127.
        Rev: *TLS*, May 27, 1939, p. 315; by R. W. Zandvoort, *ES*, XXI, 169-171; by F. P. Wilson,
        Library, NS, XX, 234-239; by Wolfgang Keller, *SJ*, LXXV, 145-146; by Georges Connes, *EA*,
        III, 377; by John Wilcox, *SAB*, XV (1940), 59-60; by W. Kalthoff, *Beiblatt*, LI, 76-78; by
        H. E. Rollins, *MLN*, LV, 150-151; by J. B. Leishman, *RES*, XVI, 92-95; by Peter Alexander,
        MLR, XXXV, 386-387; by W. Fischer, *DLZ*, LXII, 1221-22; by W. W. Greg, *RES*, XVII, 139-
        149; by Max Priess, *Eng. Studn.*, LXXV (1942), 236-241.

A3249   Petersen J. "Grundlegen d. Shakespeare-Textes." *Die Wissenschaft von d. Dichtung*, I (1939),
        141-156.

A3250   Phelps, William L. "Notes on Shakespeare." *Proc. of Amer. Philos. Soc.*, 81 (1939), 573-579.

A3251   Phelps, William L. "More Notes on Shakespeare." *Proc. of Amer. Philos. Soc.*, 83 (1940),
        493-502.

A3252   Crundell, H. W. "Actors' Parts and Elizabethan Texts." *N &Q*, 180 (1941), 350.

A3253   Severs, J. Burke. "Quentin's Theory of Textual Criticism." *English Institute Annual, 1941*.
        Columbia Univ. Press, 1942, pp. 65-93.

A3254   Doran, Madeleine. "An Evaluation of Evidence in Shakespearian Textual Criticism." *English
        Institute Annual, 1941*. Columbia Univ. Press, 1942, pp. 95-114.

A3255   Friedman, Arthur. "Principles of Historical Annotation in Critical Editions of Modern Texts."
        English Institute Annual, 1941. Columbia Univ. Press, 1942, pp. 115-128.

A3256   Cancelled.

A3257   Greg, W. W. *The Editorial Problem in Shakespeare: A Survey of the Foundations of the Text*.
        Oxford: Clarendon Press, 1942. Pp. lv, 210. Second edition, 1951; third edition, 1954.
        Rev: *TLS*, May 1, 1943, p. 216; by G. I. Duthie, *MLR*, XXXVIII (1943), 255-257; by Paul
        Mueschke, "Three Valuable New Studies in the Drama," *NYTBR*, Aug. 1, 1943, p. 22;
        N &Q, 184 (1943), 29-30; by William Jaggard, ibid., p. 148; by John Berryman, *Nation*
        (N. Y.), Aug. 21, 1943, pp. 218-219; by Trevor James, *Life and Letters*, XXXVI, 72; by P. Maas,
        RES, XIX, 410-413; by M. A. Shaaber, *MLN*, LIX (1944), 139-141; by P. Maas, *RES*, XX,
        73-77; *TLS*, Apr. 27, 1951, p. 262; by C. J. Sisson, *MLR*, XLVII (1952), 100-101; by J. C.
        Maxwell, *RES*, III, 200; by A. Koszul, *EA*, VII (1954), 322; *TLS*, Mar. 4, 1955, p. 139;
        by Hermann Heuer, *SJ*, 92 (1956), 385.

A3258   Evans, G. B. "Shakespeare's *Julius Caesar*, a Seventeenth Century Manuscript." *JEGP*,
        XLI (1942), 401-417.

A3259   Weitenkampf, Frank. "What is a Facsimile?" *Papers Bibl. Soc. Amer.*, XXXVII (1943), 114-130.

A3260   Philbrick, N. "Act and Scene Division in First Editions of Shakespeare." *Theatre Annual*,
        1944, pp. 36-46.

A3261   "The Text of *King Henry V*." *N &Q*, 187 (1944), 200-203.
        See comment by M. H. Dodds, ibid., 302.

A3262   Kirschbaum, Leo. "Shakespeare's Hypothetical Marginal Additions." *MLN*, LXI (1946),
        44-49.

A3263   Shaaber, M. A. "Problems in the Editing of Shakespeare: Text." *EIE*, 1947, pp. 97-116.

A3264   Black, Matthew W. "Problems in the Editing of Shakespeare: Interpretation." *EIE*, 1947,
        pp. 117-136.

A3265   Brooke, C. F. Tucker. "Shakespeare and the Textus Receptus." *Essays on Shakespeare and
        Other Elizabethans*. Yale Univ. Press, 1948, pp. 103-107. Also in *The Yale Shakespeare*,
        Henry IV, Part I, Yale Univ. Press, 1947.

A3266   Harrison, G. B. "A Note on *Coriolanus*." *AMS*, pp. 239-252.

A3267   Flatter, Richard. *Shakespeare's Producing Hand*. London, 1948.
        Rev: A5944.

A3268   Smith, Warren D. *Shakespeare's Stagecraft as Denoted by the Dialogue in the Original Printings of
        his Texts*. DD, University of Pennsylvania, 1948. Pp. 256. Mic A50-217. *Microf. Ab.*, X
        (1950), 163. Publication No. 1731.

A3269   Bowers, Fredson. *Principles of Bibliographical Description*. Princeton Univ. Press, 1949. Pp.
        xviii, 505.

A3270   Dawson, Giles E. "Warburton, Hanmer, and the 1745 Edition of Shakespeare." *SB*, II
        (1949), 35-48.

A3271   Wolf, E., II. *The Textual Importance of Manuscript Commonplace Books of 1620-1660*. Bibl. Soc.
        Univ. Virginia, 1949. Mimeographed pamphlet.

A3272   Bald, R. C. "Editorial Problems: A Preliminary Survey." *SB*, III (1950), 3-17.

A3273   Bowers, Fredson. "Current Theories of Copy-Text, with an Illustration from Dryden."
        MP, XLVIII (1950), 12-20.

A3274 Bowers, Fredson. "Some Relations of Bibliography to Editorial Problems." *SB*, III (1950), 37-62.

A3275 Fort, J. B. "Quelques Problèmes Shakespeariens: L'Homme, le Texte, la 'Sagesse Pourpre'." *LanM*, XLIV (1950), 414-417.

A3276 Greg, W. W. "The Rationale of Copy-Text." *SB*, III (1950), 19-36.

A3277 Muir, Kenneth. "A Test for Shakespearian Variants." *N &Q*, 195 (1950), 513-514.

A3278 Capocci, Valentina. "Poeti et attori nel Dramma Elisabettiano." *Il Ponte* (Florence), 7th Year, No. 12 (Dec., 1951), pp. 1593-1600.

A3279 Schücking, Levin Ludwig. "Über einige Probleme der neueren und neuesten Shakespeare-Forschung (Textgestaltung u. Echtheitsfragen)." *GRM*, XXXIII (1951/52), 208-228.

A3280 Alexander, Peter. "Restoring Shakespeare: The Modern Editor's Task." *ShS*, V (1952), 1-9.

A3281 Baldini, Gabriele. "La Critica Testuale Shakespeareana e l'Aggriornamento del Gusto." *Letterature Moderne*, III (1952), 711-719.

A3282 Bowers, Fredson. "A Definitive Text of Shakespeare: Problems and Methods." Matthews and Emery, eds., *Studies in Shakespeare*, pp. 11-29.

A3283 Flatter, Richard. " 'The True Originall Copies' of Shakespeare's Plays—Outline of a New Conception." *Proc. of Leeds Philos. and Literary Soc.*, VII (1952), 31-42.

A3284 Kirschbaum, Leo. "The Authorship of *1 Henry VI*." *PMLA*, LXVII (1952), 809-822.

A3285 Nicoll, Allardyce. "Cooperation in Shakespearian Scholarship." *Proc. British Academy 1952*. Oxford Univ. Press, pp. 71-88.

A3286 Feuillerat, Albert. *The Composition of Shakespeare's Plays: Authorship, Chronology.* Yale Univ. Press, 1953. Pp. viii, 340.
    Rev: by Hallett Smith, *YR*, XLIII (1953), 121-125; by G. B. Harrison, , *SatR*, Oct. 10, p. 20; by Fredson Bowers, *MP*, LI, 132-133; *TLS*, Mar. 5, 1954, p. 154; by Philip Williams, *South Atlantic Quar.*, LIII, 270-272; by A. Koszul, *EA*, VII, 213-219; by Kenneth Muir, *RES*. V, 411-413; by M. A. Shaaber, *MLN*, LXIX, 427-430; by J. Swart, *Neophil*, XXXVIII, 221-224; by Peter Alexander, *SQ*, V, 70-77; by G. E. Bentley, *MLR*, XLIX, 496; by A. José Axelrad, *RLC*, XXVIII, 344-345; by Hermann Heuer, *SJ*, 90 (1954), 326-328; *VQR*, XXX, xvii-xviii; by J. Vallette, *LanM*, XLIX, No. 1 (1955), 90-91; by H. W. Donner, *Moderna språk*, XLIX, 112-116; by Wolfgang Clemen, *Archiv*, 191 (1955), 88-89; by Robert Adger Law, *TxSE*, XXXIV, 43-47; by L. L. Schücking, *Anglia*, LXXIII (1956), 527-532 (important).

A3287 Orsini, Napoleone. "Stato attuale della filologia shakespeariana." *Paideia* (Arona), VIII, No. 3 (May-June, 1953), 153-176.
    Important trends and achievements in Shak. textual studies are discussed.

A3288 Walker, Alice. *Textual Problems of the First Folio.* Cambridge Univ. Press, 1953. Pp. viii, 170.
    Rev: A2979.

A3289 Ashe, Dora Jean. *A Survey of Non-Shakespearean Bad Quartos.* DD, University of Virginia, 1953. Pp. 286. Mic 54-1567. *DA*, XIV (1954), 1070. Publication No. 7952.

A3290 Bowers, Fredson. "Shakespeare's Text and the Bibliographical Method." *SB*, VI (1954), 71-79.

A3291 McManaway, James G. "Bibliography." *Literature and Science* (Proceedings of the Sixth Triennial Congress, Oxford, 1954). Oxford: Basil Blackwell (for The International Federation for Modern Languages and Literatures), 1955, pp. 27-35.

A3292 Wilson, J. Dover. "On Editing Shakespeare with Special Reference to the Problems of *Richard III*." *Talking of Shakespeare*, ed. by John Garrett. London: Hodder & Stoughton & Max Reinhardt, 1954.

A3293 Wilson, J. Dover. "The New Way with Shakespeare's Texts: An Introduction for Lay Readers. I: The Foundations." *ShS*, VII (1954), 48-56.

A3294 "Report of the Advisory of the Shakespeare Group of M. L. A." *ShN*, IV (1954), 45.
    See letters by Fredson Bowers and Hardin Craig, *ShN*, V (1955), 4.

A3295 Bowers, Fredson. "McKerrow's Editorial Principles for Shakespeare Reconsidered." *SQ*, VI (1955), 309-324.
    Reconsiders, with a view to their serviceability today, the theories of *Prolegomena for the Oxford Shakespeare*, and finds them—though recoiling from "Wilsonian" extravagance—unresponsive to scientific textual scholarship.

A3296 Bowers, Fredson. *On Editing Shakespeare and the Elizabethan Dramatists.* Philadelphia: Published for the Philip H. and A. S. W. Rosenbach Foundation by the University of Pennsylvania Library, 1955. Pp. 200.
    Rev: *VQR*, XXXI, (1955) civ; by Howard W. Winger, *Lib. Quar.*, XXVI (1956), 141; by C. J. Sisson, *MLR*, LI, 242-244; by James G. McManaway, *ShS*, IX, 149-150; by W. W. Greg, *SQ*, VII, 101-104; *TLS*, Dec. 28, p. 788; by Herbert Davis, *MLN*, LXXI, 521-523; by J. C. Maxwell, *RES*, VIII (1957), 293-298; by Roy Stokes, *JEGP*, LVI, 142-144; by L. L. Schücking, *Anglia*, LXXVI (1958), 312-313.

A3297 Crow, John. "Editing and Emending." *Essays and Studies, 1955*, ed. for the English Association by D. M. Low, NS, VIII 1-20. See also *TLS*, Dec. 28, 1955, p. 639.

A3298 Craig, Hardin. "Proof and Probability in the Study of Shakespeare and His Contemporaries." *McNeese Rev.*, VII (1955), 26-38.

A3299 Walker, Alice. "Compositor Determination and Other Problems in Shakespearean Texts." *SB*, VII (1955), 3-15.

A3300 Walker, Alice. "Collateral Substantive Texts (with Special Reference to *Hamlet*)." *SB*, VII (1955), 51-67.

A3301 Walton, J. K. *The Copy for the Folio Text of "Richard III."* With a Note on the Copy for the Folio Text of *King Lear*. Monograph Series, No. 1. Auckland University College, New Zealand: The Pilgrim Press, 1955. Pp. 164.
Rev: *TLS*, Dec. 9, 1955, p. 750; by W. W. Greg, *Library*, 5th Series, XI (1956), 125-129; by I. B. Cauthen, Jr., *JEGP*, LV, 503-505; by R. Davril, *EA*, XI (1958), 51; by Hermann Heuer, *SJ*, 94 (1958), 294.

A3302 *King Henry VI, Part 2*. Ed. Andrew S. Cairncross (Arden Shakespeare). London: Methuen, 1956. Pp. liv, 197.
Introduction offers detailed study of the text, principally the problem of the copy behind Q_1 and F_1. 1590 proposed as date of play.
Rev: B5304.

A3303 Bolton, Joseph S. G. "Worn Pages in Shakespearian Manuscripts." *SQ*, VII (1956), 177-182.

A3304 Brown, Arthur. "Editorial Problems in Shakespeare: Semi-Popular Editions." *SB*, VIII (1956), 15-26.

A3305 Kaindl, Elisabeth Maria. *Shakespeares Methoden, Regiebemerkungen in den Text zu verarbeiten*. DD, Vienna, 1956. Pp. 195. Typewritten.

A3306 Leech, Clifford. "Studies in *Hamlet*, 1901-1955." *ShS*, IX (1956), 1-15.

A3307 Otsuka, Takanobu. "On the Text of Shakespeare." Special lecture at the English Literary Society. Kochi Joshi Daigu: Shikoku, Oct., 1956.

A3308 Smirnov, A. A. "Problemy tekstologii Šekspira." *Izvestia* (Moscow), XV, ii (1956), 122-123.

A3309 Walker, Alice. "Some Editorial Problems (with Special Reference to *Henry V*)." *SB*, VIII (1956), 95-112.

A3310 Williams, Philip, Jr. "New Approaches to Textual Problems in Shakespeare." *SB*, VIII (1956), 3-14.

A3311 Brock, Elizabeth. *Shakespeare's "The Merry Wives of Windsor": A History of the Text from 1623 Through 1821*. DD, University of Virginia, 1956. Pp. 623. Mic 57-1351. *DA*, XVII (1957), 847. Publication No. 20,349.

A3312 Cairncross, Andrew S. "The Quartos and Folio Text of *Richard III*." *RES*, NS, VIII (1957), 225-233.

A3313 Cairncross, Andrew S. "Coincidental Variants in *Richard III*." *Library*, XII (1957), 187-190. See A3323.

A3314 Nowottny, Winifred M. T. "The Application of Textual Theory to Hamlet's Dying Words." *MLR*, LII (1957), 161-167.

A3315 Wälterlin, Oskar. "Randglossen zur Shakespeare-Inszenierung." *SJ*, 93 (1957), 128-140.

A3316 Walker, Alice. "Principles of Annotation: Some Suggestions for Editors of Shakespeare." *SB*, IX (1957), 95-105.

A3317 "The Critics Criticized." *TLS*, Feb. 7, 1958, p. 80.

A3318 Craig, Hardin. "Criticism of Elizabethan Dramatic Texts." *Studies in Honor of T. W. Baldwin*, ed. by Don Cameron Allen, Univ. of Illinois Press, 1958, pp. 3-8.

A3319 Hulme, Hilda M. "The Spoken Language and the Dramatic Text: Some Notes on the Interpretation of Shakespeare's Language." *SQ*, IX (1958), 379-386.

A3320 Hulme, Hilda M. "Shakespeare's Text: Some Notes on Linguistic Procedure and Its Relevance to Textual Criticism." *ES*, XXXIX (1958), 49-56.

A3321 Stevenson, Allan. "Thomas Thomas Makes a Dictionary." *Library*, XIII (1958), 234-246.

A3322 Waller, Frederick O. "Printer's Copy for *The Two Noble Kinsmen*." *SB*, XI (1958), 61-81.

A3323 Walton, J. K. "Coincidental Variants in *Richard III*." *Library*, XIII (1958), 139-140. See A3313.

b. COLLECTIONS OF EMENDATIONS

A3324 Johnson, Samuel. *Notes to Shakespeare*. Vol. I: Comedies, ed. with an introd. by Arthur Sherbo (Augustan Reprint Society, Nos. 59-60). Los Angeles: William Andrews Clark Memorial Library, University of California, 1956. Pp. viii, 140.

A3325 Johnson, Samuel. *Notes to Shakespeare*. Vol. II: Histories, ed. with an introd. by Arthur Sherbo (Augustan Reprint Society, Nos. 65-66). Los Angeles: William Andrews Clark Memorial Library, University of California, 1957. Pp. 123.

A3326 Johnson, Samuel. *Notes to Shakespeare*. Vol. III: Tragedies, ed. with an introd. by Arthur Sherbo (Augustan Reprint Society, Nos. 71-73). Los Angeles: William Andrews Clark Memorial Library, University of California, 1958. Pp. 202.

A3327 Baker, Arthur E. *A Shakespeare Commentary*. Taunton: Author, Borough Librarian, 1938. Pp. 964. Reissue. New York: Ungar. Two Vols., 1957. Pp. 482, 484-964.
Entitled in 14 of the 15 parts, *A Shakespeare Dictionary*.
Parts: I, *Caesar;* II, *AYLI;* III, *Macb.;* IV, *Temp.;* V, *Ham.;* VI, *Lear;* VII, *John;* VIII, *Merch.;*

IX, *R. II;* X, *I Hry. IV;* XI, *II Hry. IV;* XII, *Hry. V;* XIII, *I Hry. VI;* XIV, *II Hry. VI;* XV, *III Hry. VI.*
Rev: briefly by L. LaMont Okey, *QJS,* XLIV (1958), 201-202; by M. E. Bradford, *SQ,* IX, 581-582; *ShN,* VIII, 21.

A3328 J., W. H. "Shakespeare: Standard Emendations." *N &Q,* 179 (1939), 388-389; Wm. Jaggard, ibid., p. 466; Philomot, ibid., 180 (1941), 283; W. H. J., ibid., p. 304.

A3329 Munro, John. "Some Matters Shakespearian." *TLS,* Sept. 13, 1947, p. 472; ibid., Sept. 27, p. 500; ibid., Oct. 11, p. 528; S. G. Thomas, ibid., Oct. 11, p. 528 (re *Wives*); J. M. Nosworthy, ibid., Sept. 27, p. 497 (re *Wives*).

A3330 Parsons, Howard. *Emendations to Three of Shakespeare's Plays.* London: Ettrick Press, 1953. Pp. viii, 128. Subsequent publication: *Shakespearian Emendations and Discoveries,* London: Ettrick Press, 1954. Pp. 136.
Emendations to passages in *AYLI, MND, Hamlet, Tempest, R &J, Macbeth, Othello.*
Rev: *N &Q,* NS, I (1954), 275-276; by Emma Gurney Salter, *ConR,* 186, No. 1064 (1954), 126; *NstN,* May 29, p. 710 (see letter by Charles E. Raven, June 5, p. 733); by I. B. Cauthen, Jr., *SQ,* V, 423-424; *TLS,* Jan. 29, p. 78; by Hermann Heuer, *SJ,* 91 (1955), 345-347.

A3331 Bateson, F. W. "Editorial Commentary." *EIC,* V (1955), 91-95.

A3332 Sisson, C. J. *New Readings in Shakespeare* (Shakespeare Problems Series). London: Cambridge Univ. Press, 1956. 2 Vols. Pp. viii, 218; vi, 300.
Play by play discussion of recent textual emendations and explanations of readings accepted in Sisson's own edition. Principally concerned with errors occurring between manuscript and printing and with corrections made possible by knowledge of Elizabethan handwriting and printing.
Rev: *QR,* 294 (1956), 271-272; by Anthony A. Stephenson, *Month,* NS, XV, 294-300; *Dublin Magazine,* XXXI, No. 2, 34-36; by Jacques Vallette, *MdF,* June, pp. 363-365; *N &Q,* NS, III, 272; by Hermann Peschmann, *English,* XI, 69; by Arthur Colby Sprague, *TN,* XI, No. 1, 31-32; by F. S. Boas, *ConR,* 190 (1956), 58; *Listener,* LV, 521, 523; by J. G. McManaway, *ShS,* X (1957), 153; by L. L. Schücking, *Anglia,* LXXIV, 371-373; by Alfred Harbage, *MLN,* LXXII, 53-55; by Hereward T. Price, *MP,* LV, 53-55; by Alice Walker, *RES,* VIII, 298-301; by Arthur Brown, *Library,* XII, 60-62; by Giles E. Dawson, *MLR,* LII, 97-100; by M. A. Shaaber, *SQ,* VIII, 104-107; by J. A. Bryant, Jr., *SR,* LXV, 152-160; by Fredson Bowers, *MLQ,* XVIII, 156-157; by Hermann Heuer, *SJ,* 94 (1958), 284.

5. LIBRARIES
a. GENERAL (Items from the sources specified only.)

A3333 Gilder, Rosamond, and George Freedley. *Theatre Collections in Libraries and Museums.* London: Stevens & Brown, 1936. Pp. 182.
Rev: by F. C. F., *Library,* NS, XVIII (1937), 119-120.

A3334 Norris, Dorothy May. *A History of Cataloguing and Cataloguing Methods, 1100-1850; With an Introductory Survey of Ancient Times.* Foreword by H. M. Cashmore. London: Grafton, 1939. Pp. x, 246.
Rev: by J. C. M. Hanson, *Lib. Quar.,* X (1940), 115-116.

A3335 Hessel, Alfred. *A History of Libraries.* Tr., with supplementary material, by Reuben Peiss. Washington 7, D. C.: Scarecrow Press, 1950. Pp. 198.
Chap. V: "The Renaissance," pp. 39ff.
Rev: by Jesse H. Shera, *Lib. Quar.,* XXI (1951), 46-48.

A3336 Friedlaender, Marc. *Growth in the Resources for Studies in Earlier English History, 1534-1625.* DD, University of Chicago, 1943.

A3337 Spargo, John W. "Book Selection for Reference Work." *The Reference Function of the Library,* ed. by Pierce Butler. Univ. Chicago Press, 1943, pp. 267-280.
Rev: by Mabel Louise Conat, *Lib. Quar.,* XIII (1943), 351.

b. MANUSCRIPTS

A3338 De Ricci, Seymour, and W. J. Wilson. *Census of Medieval and Renaissance Manuscripts in the United States and Canada.* Publ. under the Auspices of the American Council of Learned Socs. Vol. I, New York: H. W. Wilson Co., 1935. Pp. xxiii, 1098. Vol. II, New York: Wilson, 1938. Pp. xviii, 1103-2343. Vol. III, Indices, 1940.
Rev: *TLS,* July 4, 1936, p. 566; by E. C. R., *Library Assoc. Record,* XXXVIII, 639; by Charles H. Beeson, *MP,* XXXIV (1937), 425-427; by R. B. McKerrow, *Library,* NS, XVII, 479-480; *TLS,* June 18, 1938, p. 424; by Mario Roques, *Rom,* LXIV, 281; by B. S., *Library,* NS, XIX, 380-382; *BJRL,* XXII (1939), 318-320; *Personalist,* XXI (1940), 217; *TLS,* May 4, p. 223; by Lynn Thorndike, *AHR,* XLV, 857-859; by George Sarton, *Isis,* XXXIII (1942), 719-720.

A3338a Ives, Samuel A. "Corrigenda and Addenda to the Descriptions of the Plimpton Manuscripts as Recorded in the de Ricci *Census.*" *Speculum,* XVII (1942), 33-49.

A3338b Bühler, Curt F., and Robert H. Bowers. "A Medical Manuscript Presented to Charles VIII of France." *Bul. Hist. Medicine,* XI (1942), 69-86.
The Latin manuscript (Pierpont Morgan Library, MS. 509), composed between February 1492 and September 1494, does not appear in the de Ricci *Census.*

A3338c Munby, A. N. L. "Jacob Bryant's Caxtons: Some Additions to de Ricci's *Census*." *Library*
III (1948), 218-222.

A3338d Sheppard, L. A. "The Early Ownership of the British Museum Copy of Caxton's *Recuyell of
the Histories of Troy*." *Library*, III (1948), 216-218.
Carries ownership of the copy book to Thomas Sackville, Lord Buckhurst (100 years earlier
than the date noted by de Ricci).

A3339   De Ricci, Seymour. "Survey of Manuscripts in the British Isles." *Bul. of the Institute of Hist.
Research*, XV (1937), 65-68.

A3340   Adams, Joseph Quincy. "Hill's List of Early Plays in Manuscript." *Library*, NS, XX (1939),
71-99.

A3341   Cancelled.

A3342   Upton, Eleanor S. "The Location of Seventeenth Century Documents Described in the First
Nine Reports of the Historical Manuscripts Commission." *Bul. of the Institute of Hist. Research*,
XVI (1937), 73-78.

A3343   Historical Manuscripts Commission. *Report on the Manuscripts of Lord de l'Isle and Dudley
Preserved at Penshurst Place*. Vol. III. Ed. by W. A. Shaw. H. M. Stationery Office, 1936.
Pp. lxxix, 547. Vol. IV: *Sidney Papers, 1608-1611*. London: H. M. Stationery Office, 1942.
Pp. 395.
Rev: *TLS*, Dec. 12, 1936, p. 1034; by J. E. Neale, *EHR*, LIII (1938), 712-713; by Hartley
Simpson, *AHR*, XLVIII (1943), 323-325; by Wallace Notestein, *JMH*, XV, 239-240.

A3344   MacKinney, Loren C. "Manuscript Photoreproductions in Classical, Mediaeval, and Renaissance Research." *Speculum*, XXI (1946), 244-252.

A3345   Kristeller, Paul Oskar. "Latin Manuscript Books Before 1600: A Bibliography of the Printed
Catalogues of Extant Collections." *Traditio*, VI (1948), 227-317.
Rev: by M. Cappuyns, *Recherches de Théologie ancienne et médiévale*, XIX (1952), 182-183; by
Tönnes Kleberg, *Nordisk Tidskrift för Bok- och Biblioteksväsen*, XXXVII, 48.

c. SEVENTEENTH CENTURY LIBRARIES
(1) GENERAL

A3346   Kibre, Pearl. "The Intellectual Interests Reflected in Libraries of the Fourteenth and Fifteenth
Centuries." *JHI*, VII (1946), 257-297.

A3347   Irwin, Raymond. "The English Domestic Library." *Lib. Assoc. Record*, LVI (1954), 196-201.

A3348   Jayne, Sears. *Library Catalogues of the English Renaissance*. Berkeley and Los Angeles: Univ.
Calif. Press, 1956. Pp. viii, 225.
Rev: by William Le Fanu, *Book Collector*, VII (1958), 305-306; by Thelma Eaton, *JEGP*,
LVII, 100-101; by A. J. Doyle, *Library*, 5th Series, XIII, 64-66; by Denys Hay, *EHR*, LXXIII,
289-290.

A3349   Wormald, Frances, and C. E. Wright, eds. *The English Library Before 1700*. London: Athlone
Press, 1958. Pp. 273.
Rev: *TLS*, Dec. 12, 1958, p. 728.

(2) COLLEGE LIBRARIES

A3350   Liddell, J. R. "The Library of Corpus Christi College, Oxford, in the Sixteenth Century."
Library, NS, XVIII (1938), 385-416.

A3351   Oates, J. C. T., and H. L. Pink. "Three Sixteenth Century Catalogues of the University
Library." *Trans. Cambridge Bibl. Soc.*, I, iv (1952), 310-340.

A3352   Thompson, W. D. J. "Notes on King's College Library, 1500-1570, in Particular for the
Period of the Reformation." *Trans. Cambridge Bibl. Soc.*, II, i (1955), 38-54.

(3) PRIVATE LIBRARIES
(Arranged by surname of original collector.)

A3353   "John Aubrey's Books—I, II." *TLS*, Jan. 13, 20, 1950, pp. 32, 48.

A3354   Nuttall, Geoffrey. "A Transcript of Richard Baxter's Library Catalogue: A Bibliographical
Note." *Jour. Ecclesias. Hist.*, II (1951), 207-221. See also ibid., III (1952), 74-100.

A3355   Lievsay, John L., and Richard B. Davis. "A Cavalier Library—1643." *SB*, VI (1954), 141-160.
The list of books in the library of Sir Thomas Bludder, supporter of King Charles I.

A3356   Hassall, W. O. *A Catalogue of the Library of Sir Edward Coke*. Yale Univ. Press, 1950. Pp.
xxvi, 98.
Rev: by S. B. C., *EHR*, LXVI (1951), 623.

A3357   Pafford, J. H. P. "John Donne's Library." *TLS*, Sept. 2, 1949, p. 569.
See the letter by Canon A. C. Powell, ibid., Sept. 23, p. 617. Mr. Pafford and Canon Powell
add five vols. to the list of books known to have been in Donne's library.

A3357a Keynes, G. "Books from Donne's Library." *Trans. Cambridge Bibl. Soc.*, I (1949), 64-68.

A3358   Jackson, William A. "Humphrey Dyson and His Collections of Elizabethan Proclamations."
Harvard Lib. Bul., I (1947), 76-89.

A3358a   Jackson, William A. "Humphrey Dyson's Library, or Some Observations on the Survival of Books." *Papers Bibl. Soc. Amer.*, XLIII (1949), 279-287.

A3359   Oxford Architectural and Historical Society. *Oxoniensia.* Vols. XI, XII, 1946-47. Pp. 194, pl. 18. Contains an article by W. C. Costin on an inventory of more than 500 books left by John English of St. John's College (d. 1613).

A3360   Gray, W. Forbes. "A Seventeenth-Century Scottish Library." *TLS*, June 5, 1948, p. 324. Notes the appearance of religious and theological material in this library left to Haddington by the Rev. John Gray (d. 1717).

A3361   Hassall, W. O. "The Books of Sir Christopher Hatton at Holkham." *Library*, V (1950), 1-13.

A3362   Curtis, Mark H. "Library Catalogues and Tudor Oxford and Cambridge." *Studies in the Renaissance* (Ren. Soc. Amer.), V (1958), 111-120. Reproduces the inventory of books owned by Edward Higgins of Brasenose College, Oxford (d. 1588).

A3363   Doyle, A. I. "Books Belonging to R. Johnson." *N &Q*, 197 (1952), 293-294. Books collected between 1503 and 1523 by R. Johnson, whose exact identity has not been established.

A3364   M., M. "From the Library of Ben Jonson." *More Books*, XVIII (1943), 230. A folio edition of the *De Architectura* of Vitruvius (Venice, 1567).

A3365   Moss, William E. *Bindings from the Library of Robt. Dudley, Earl of Leicester, K/G, 1533-1588: A New Contribution to the History of English Sixteenth Century Gold-Tooled Bookbindings.* Crawley, Sussex: Privately printed, 1940.
Rev: A2836.

A3366   Jayne, Sears, and Francis R. Johnson. *The Lumley Library: The Catalogue of 1609.* Published by the Trustees of the British Museum, 1956. Pp. xiii, 372.
Rev: *TLS*, Dec. 14, 1956, p. 756; by R. George Thomas, *English*, XI (1957), 233-234; by I. G. Philip, *Book Collector*, VI, 186-190; by J. C. T. Oates, *Library*, XII, 63-65; by Leicester Bradner, *MLN*, LXXII (1958), 58-60.

A3367   Barratt, D. M. "The Library of John Selden and Its Later History." *Bodleian Lib. Rec.*, III (1951), 128-142, 208-213, 256-274.

A3368   Hotson, Leslie. "The Library of Elizabeth's Embezzling Teller." *SB*, II (1949), 49-61. Reprints a list of books drawn from the complete appraisal of Richard Stonley's goods in 1597.

A3369   Mitchell, R. J. "A Renaissance Library: The Collection of John Tiptoft, Earl of Worcester." *Library*, NS, XVIII (1937), 67-83.

A3370   Young, Patrick. *Catalogus Librorum Manuscriptorum Bibliothecae Wigorniensis.* Made in 1622-1623. Ed. with Introd. by Ivor Atkins and Neil R. Ker. Cambridge Univ. Press, 1944.
Rev: *TLS*, Dec. 23, 1944, p. 624; by E. Ph. Goldschmidt, *Library*, 4th Series, XXV (1944/45), 188-189.

A3371   "Sixteenth Century Bindings." *TLS*, Nov. 24, 1950, p. 756. Concerns the more than 100 bindings which have survived from the library of Thomas Wotton, father of Sir Henry and "one of the greatest of English book collectors."

d. MODERN LIBRARIES
(1) ENGLISH

A3372   Ramage, David. *A Finding-list of English Books to 1640 in Libraries in the British Isles.* Durham, England: Durham Univ., 1958. Pp. xvi, 101. Uses *STC* numbers; does not include Oxford, Cambridge, and the national Libraries.
Rev: by A. N. L. Munby, *Book Collector*, VII (1958), 199-200.

A3373   Hands, M. S. G. "The Cathedral Libraries Catalogue." *Library*, II (1947), 1-13.

A3374   Sisson, C. J. "Elizabethan Life in Public Records." *Listener*, June 21, 1951, pp. 998-999.

(a) BRITISH MUSEUM

A3375   Isaac, Frank. *An Index to the Early Printed Books in the British Museum.* Part II, Sections 2, 3. London: Quaritch, 1939. Pp. xv, 286. Continuation of Robert Proctor's *Index*, 1898-1899, 1903.
Rev: *TLS*, June 17, 1939, p. 384.

A3376   Scholderer, Victor. *Catalogue of Books Printed in the XVth Century now in the British Museum.* VIII: *France, French-speaking Switzerland.* London: British Museum, 1949. Pp. lxxxvii, 441, facs. 21, pl. 72. Continuation of series begun in 1912.
Rev: by C. F. Bühler, *Papers Bibl. Soc. Amer.*, XLIV (1950), 280-283; *TLS*, Dec. 8, 1950, p. 792.

A3377   Francis, F. C. "The Shakespeare Collection in the British Museum." *ShS*, III (1950), 43-57.

A3378   Boase, T. S. R. "An Extra-illustrated Second Folio of Shakespeare." *British Museum Quar.*, XX (1955), 4-8. The copy of F_2 recently purchased by the B. M. containing single well-known water colors by William Blake and drawings by other artists of ca. 1800.

A3378a   "Blake Water-Colours: Illustrations from the British Museum's Newly-acquired Second Folio." *Ill. London News*, 225 (Dec. 25, 1954), 1163.

A3378b   "Illustrated Second Folio Shakespeare for British Museum." *Music Jour.*, LIV (Jan., 1955), 268.

A3379   "Mechanized Collation." *TLS*, Mar. 9, 1956, p. 156.
Describes Charlton Hinman's collating machine; one is now in operation in the British Museum.

(b) BIRMINGHAM AND STRATFORD

A3380   Fox, Levi. "The Stratford Collections." *TN*, VI (1952), 60-62.

A3381   Isaac, Winifred F. E. C. *Alfred Wareing*. London: Privately printed and published, 1952. Pp. xxii, 221.
A biography of the late Librarian of Shak. Memorial Library at Stratford.

A3382   Patrick, F. J. "The Birmingham Shakespeare Memorial Library." *ShS*, VII (1954), 90-94.

A3383   Patrick, F. J. "Shakespeariana." *TLS*, Aug. 27, 1954, p. 503.
Letter asking for donations to fill gaps in the collection of the Shakespeare Memorial Library of Birmingham.

A3384   *Shakespeare's Birthplace Trust*. Library. English books published between 1500 and 1640 with *STC* references. Privately printed, Stratford-upon-Avon, Shakespeare's Birthplace Trust, 1955. Typescript 19ff.

A3385   Payne, Waveney R. N. "The Shakespeare Memorial Library, Birmingham." *Lib. Assoc. Rec.*, LX (1958), 120-123.

A3386   Robinson, Eileen. "The Shakespeare Memorial Library Stratford-upon-Avon: Items of Interest to Research Workers." *TN*, XII (1957/58), 114-116.

(c) JOHN RYLANDS

A3387   Taylor, F. "Court Rolls, Rentals, Surveys, and Analogous Documents in the John Rylands Library." *BJRL*, XXXI (1948), 345-386.

A3388   Taylor, F. "Hand-list of the Crutchley Manuscripts in the John Rylands Library," *BJRL*, XXXIII (1950), 138-187, 327-352.

A3389   Taylor, F. "Hand-list of Additions to the Collection of English Manuscripts in the John Rylands Library, 1937-1951." *BJRL*, XXXIV (1951), 191-240.

(d) CAMBRIDGE

A3390   Oates, John C. T. *A Catalogue of the Fifteenth Century Printed Books in the University Library, Cambridge*. Cambridge Univ. Press, 1954. Pp. xiv, 898; pl.
Rev: by Curt F. Bühler, *Papers Bibl. Soc. Amer.*, XLIX (1955), 82-84, and *Lib. Quar.*, XXV, 262-263; by L. A. Sheppard, *Library*, 5th Series, X, 218-222; by John F. Fulton, *Jour. Hist. Medicine and Allied Sciences*, XI (1956), 235-236.

A3391   Munby, A. N. L. "The Gifts of Elizabethan Printers to the Library of King's College, Cambridge." *Library*, II (1948), 224-232.

A3392   Adams, H. M. "The Shakespeare Collection in the Library of Trinity College, Cambridge." *ShS*, V (1952), 50-54.

A3393   Wormald, Francis, and Phyllis M. Giles. "A Handlist of the Additional Manuscripts in the Fitzwilliam Museum, Part I." *Trans. Cambridge Bibl. Soc.*, I, iii (1951), 197-207.

(e) OXFORD

A3394   Boas, F. S. "Sir Thomas Bodley and His Library." *Essays by Divers Hands: Being the Transactions of the Royal Society of Literature of the United Kingdom*, NS, XXIII (1947), 20-36.
Reprinted in Boas's *Queen Elizabeth in Drama and Related Studies*. London, 1950, pp. 122-140.

A3395   Bachrach, A. G. H. "The Foundation of the Bodleian Library and XVIIth Century Holland." *Neophil*, XXXVI (1952), 101-114.

A3396   Hanson, L. W. "The Shakespeare Collection in the Bodleian Library, Oxford." *ShS*, IV (1951), 78-96.

A3397   "The Art of War: An Exhibition." *Bodleian Lib. Rec.*, II (1942), 43-50.

A3398   Toynbee, Margaret R. "Two Letterbooks of Charles I in the Bodleian Library." *N &Q*, 193 (1948), 358-362.

A3399   Lamborn, E. A. Greening. "Notes on Some Wood MSS, in the Bodleian." *N &Q*, 193 (1948), 420-422.

A3400   Myres, J. N. L. "Two Hundred Oxford 'Worthies' See the Light Again: First Photographs of a Remarkable Bodleian Find." *Ill. London News*, 125 (1949), 814-815.

A3401   The Bodleian Library. "Notable Accessions." *Bodleian Lib. Rec.*, II (1944), 86-90, 106-110, 125-126; II (1949), 260-265; IV (1953), 52-56, 115-120, 173-176, 227-232, 279-288.

A3401a Rogers, David. "The Holkham Collection." *Bodleian Lib. Rec.*, IV (1953), 255-266.

A3402   Fordyce, C. J., and T. M. Knox. "The Library of Jesus College, Oxford, with an Appendix on the Books Bequeathed Thereto by Lord Herbert of Cherbury." *Oxford Bibl. Soc., Proceedings and Papers*, V (1937), 53-115.

A3403   Hiscock, W. G.   *A Christ Church Miscellany.* Oxford Univ. Press, 1946. Pp. 260.
        Includes material from the college records about plays performed in Christ Church before
        Elizabeth and James.

A3404   Smith, Robert M.   "Why A First Folio Shakespeare Remained in England."   *RES*, XV (1939),
        257-264.

(f) TOWN LIBRARIES

A3405   Bristol Public Libraries.   *A Catalogue of Books in the Bristol Reference Library Printed in England
        and Ireland Up to the Year 1640 and of English Books Printed Abroad During the Same Period.*
        Bristol: The Corporation, 1954.   Pp. 51.
        Rev: by J. C. T. Oates, *Library*, 5th Series, IX (1954), 278.

A3405a *Early Printed Foreign Books (1473-1700) in the Bristol Reference Library.*   Bristol: Corporation
        of Bristol, 1956.   Pp. 194.
        Rev: by W. W. G., *Book Collector*, VI (1957), 95.

A3406   William Shakespeare: *Select Catalogue of Books in Newcastle-upon-Tyne City Libraries.* Newcastle-
        upon-Tyne, 1952.
        Rev: *N &Q*, 197 (1952), 155; by Sidney Thomas, *SQ*, VI (1955), 192.

A3407   "Parochial Libraries."   *TLS*, Mar. 24, 1950, p. 192.   See the letters by G. G. Greenwood, ibid.,
        April 7, 1950, p. 215; by G. K. Scott, ibid., April 28, p. 261.
        Concerns the library in Boston parish church, Lincolnshire, which has just been catalogued
        for the first time (about 150 items printed before 1600; about 1200 from 1600 to 1700).

A3408   "An Ancient Public Library."   *TLS*, Aug. 18, 1950, p. 524.
        Describes the foundation (1588-1612) and contents of the Old Town Library at Ipswich,
        emphasizes vols. of 16th and 17th centuries.

A3409   Ewing, S. Blaine.   "A New Manuscript of Greville's 'Life of Sidney'."   *MLR*, XLIX (1954),
        424-427.
        Describes MS 295 of the Shrewsbury Public Library, discovered by Professor William Ringler.

(g) MISCELLANEOUS

A3410   *The Player's Library.   The Catalogue of the Library of the British Drama League.* With an Introd.
        by Frederick S. Boas.   London: Faber, for the British Drama League, 1950.   Subsequent
        supplements, e.g., 1951, 1954.
        Rev: *TLS*, May 5, 1950, p. 283.

A3411   Jones, Philip E., and Raymond Smith.   *A Guide to the Records in the Corporation of London
        Records Office and the Guildhall Library Muniment Room.*   London: English Universities Press,
        1951.
        Rev: by T. F. Reddaway, *Bul. Inst. Hist. Research*, XXIV (1951), 191-192.

A3412   Taylor, F., ed.   "An Early Seventeenth Century Calendar of Records Preserved in Westminster
        Palace Treasury."   *BJRL*, XXIII (1939), 228-341.

A3413   Allison, A. F.   "Early English Books at the London Oratory: A Supplement to *S. T. C.*"
        Library, II (1947), 95-107.

A3414   Jackson, William A.   "The Lamport Hall—Brittwell Court Books."   *AMS*, pp. 587-599.

A3415   Birley, Robert.   "The Storer Collection in the Eton College Library."   *Book Collector*, V (1956),
        115-126.

A3416   Linton, Marion.   "The Bute Collection of English Plays."   *TLS*, Dec. 21, 1956, p. 772.

A3417   Schenk, Wilhelm.   "An English Cathedral Library in the 17th Century."   *Church Quar. Rev.*,
        148 (1949), 72-81.
        Briefly discusses books in the Library of Exeter Cathedral and their donors.

A3418   Sprague, Arthur Colby.   "Falstaff Hackett."   *TN*, IX (1955), 61-67.
        Five promptbooks in Gabrielle Enthoven Collection.

A3419   Speaight, George.   "The M. W. Stone Collection."   *TN*, XI (1957), 62-63.

A3420   The John Rylands Library.   "Library Notes and News."   *BJRL*, XXIX (1945).
        Includes "A link with Shakespeare," pp. 22-23, announcing the exhibition of a 1619 edition
        of the *Merry Wives*, believed to have remained since its publication in Charlecote Park, the
        house of the Lucys.

A3421   Wright, W. S.   "Dulwich College Library."   *TN*, VIII (1954), 58-60.

(2) AMERICAN

A3422   Bishop, William Warner.   *A Checklist of American Copies of "Short-Title Catalogue" Books.*
        2nd Ed.   Univ. Michigan General Lib. Publs., No. 6.   Univ. Michigan Press, 1950.   Pp.
        xxi, 203.
        Rev: A2896.

A3423   "Additions and Corrections to List of Medieval and Renaissance Holdings in American
        Libraries."   *Progress of Medieval and Renaissance Studies in the United States and Canada.*   Bul.
        No. 17.   Boulder, Colo.: Univ. of Colorado, 1942.   Pp. 49.

A3424   *A Contribution to a Union Catalog of Sixteenth Century Imprints in Certain New England Libraries.* Providence: Brown Univ. Library, 1953.
A3425   VanMale, John. "Notable Materials Added to American Libraries, 1941-42." *Lib. Quar.,* XIV (1944), 132-158.
A3426   Sternfeld, Frederick W. "Library News." *RN,* II (1949), 11-12, 29-30, 49-53, 79.
        Lists recent acquisition of Renaissance items by various libraries in the United States.
A3427   Hintz, Carl W. "Notable Materials added to North American Libraries, 1943-47." *Lib. Quar.,* XIX (1949), 105-118.
A3428   "Library News." *RN,* VI (1953), 12-15, 29-30.
        Recent Renaissance acquisitions of Houghton Library of Harvard University, New York Public Library, Toledo Museum of Art, Bibliotheca Parsoniana of New Orleans.

(a) THE FOLGER LIBRARY

A3429   Adams, Joseph Quincy. *The Folger Shakespeare Memorial Library: A Report on Progress, 1931-1941.* Published for the Trustees of Amherst College, 1942. Pp. 61.
        Rev: *TLS,* Aug. 1, 1942, p. 384; by F. C. Francis, *Library,* NS, XXIII (1943), 148-150; by H. B. Charlton, "The Folger Shakespeare Memorial Library," *BJRL,* XXVII, 70-73.
A3430   *The Folger Shakespeare Library.* Published for the Trustees of Amherst College, 1954.
A3431   King, Stanley. *Recollections of The Folger Shakespeare Library.* Cornell Univ. Press, 1950. Reprinted 1959.
A3432   Willoughby, Edwin E. "The Classification of the Folger Shakespeare Library." *Library Quar.,* VII (1937), 396-400.
A3433   Dawson, Giles E. "The Resources and Policies of the Folger Shakespeare Library." *Library Quar.,* XIX (1949), 178-185.
A3434   Wright, Louis B. "The Folger Library as a Research Institution." *College and Research Libraries,* XIII (1952), 14-17.
A3435   McManaway, James G. "The Folger Shakespeare Library." *ShS,* I (1948), 57-78. See also *N&Q,* 193 (1948), 388.
A3436   Foster, Joseph T. "Folger: Biggest Little Library in the World." *National Geographic,* Sept., 1951, pp. 411-424.
A3437   "Open House." *Time,* May 9, 1955, pp. 85-86. Reply by Louis B. Wright, May 23, p. 8.
A3438   Belskie, Abram. "John Gregory's Shakespeare Bas-reliefs." *SQ,* IX (1958), 397-398.
A3439   Hergel, Frederik. "The Folger Shakespeare Library." *Bokvännen,* XII (1957), 43-45.
A3440   Sadler, M. "Grösste Shakespeare-Bücherei." *Kölnische Ztg.,* June 17, 1938.
A3441   McManaway, James G. "A Survey of the Harmsworth Collection." *Amherst Graduates Quarterly,* XVII (1938), 329-336.
A3442   McManaway, James G. "Additions to the Harmsworth Collection." *Amherst Graduates Quarterly,* XVIII (1939), 192-205.
A3443   Wright, Louis B. "The Harmsworth Collection and the Folger Library." *Book Collector,* VI (1957), 123-128.
A3444   Smith, Robert M. "The Pursuit of a First Folio." *Colophon,* NS, III (1938), 41-53.
        An account of H. C. Folger's negotiations for the acquisition of the Vincent-Jaggard copy.
A3445   "One of Shakespeare's Books?" *TLS,* May 1, 1943, p. 216.
        See also "Shakespeare in Washington," *TAr,* XXVII (1943), 248-251.
A3446   Price, Hereward T. "Shakespeare's Classical Scholarship." *RES,* IX (1958), 54-55.
        Is inclined to accept as authentic the signature *W Shakspere* on the flyleaf of the Folger copy of William Lambarde's *Archaionomia* (1564); argues that Shak.'s ownership of the book indicates his good knowledge of Latin and his wide interests.
A3447   Akrigg, G. P. V. "A Plague Bill of 1609." *N&Q,* 192 (1947), 99-100.
A3448   Harrison, Thomas P., Jr. "The Folger *Secret of Secrets,* 1572." *AMS,* pp. 601-620.
A3449   Hinman, Charlton. "Variant Readings in First Folios." *ShN,* IV (1954), 41.
A3450   E., S. Y. "A Shakespeare MS?" *N&Q,* 189 (1945), 193; Wm. Jaggard, ibid., p. 263; James G. McManaway, ibid., p. 284; Wm. Jaggard, *N&Q,* 190 (1946), 65; S. Y. E., *N&Q,* 191 (1946), 85, and *N&Q,* 192 (1947), 218.
A3451   E., S. Y. "A Shakespeare MS." *N&Q,* 193 (1948), 388; James G. McManaway, ibid., p. 525; S. Y. E., ibid., p. 547, and 194 (1949), 19.
A3452   Wright, Louis B. *Report from the Folger Library.* Washington, D. C.: The Folger Library. Irregularly issued mimeographed reports.
        Rev: of V, No. 3 (1956), *TLS,* May 4, 1956, p. 276; of VI, No. 1 (1957), *TLS,* Mar. 29, 1957, p. 200; *ShN,* VII (1957), 8.

(b) HUNTINGTON LIBRARY

A3453   Davies, Godfrey. "The Huntington Library." *ShS,* VI (1953), 53-63.
A3454   "Research at the Huntington Library." *HLQ,* VIII (1944), 1-5.

A3455   "Huntington Library Shakespeariana." *HLQ*, IX (1946), 431-432.

A3456   Bickley, Francis, ed. *Report on the Manuscripts of the Late Reginald Rawdon Hastings, Esq. of the Manor House, Ashby de la Zouch*. Vol. IV. Hist. Manuscripts Commission, No. 78. London: Stationery Office, 1947. Pp. liii, 464.
Most of the papers here described, now in the Henry E. Huntington Library, relate almost exclusively to Irish affairs in the seventeenth century.
Rev: by Godfrey Davies, *AHR*, LIII (1948), 323-325; by W. H. Coates, *JMH*, XXI (1949), 76-77; by R. H. Tawney, *Economic Hist. Rev.*, 2nd Series, I, 171-172; by F. J. R., *History*, XXXIV, 173-174.

A3457   Wright, Lyle H. *Sporting Books in the Huntington Library*. Huntington Library Lists, No. 2. San Marino, Calif.: The Huntington Library, 1937. Pp. vii, 132.
Rev: by V. B. Heltzel, *JEGP*, XXXVII (1938), 123-124.

A3458   Rollins, Hyder E. "A Small Handful of Fragrant Flowers (1575)." *Huntington Library Bul.*, No. 9 (April, 1936), pp. 27-35.
Discussion of the apparently unique copy of a sixteen-page miscellany in octavo, preserved in the Huntington Library.

A3459   Schulz, H. C. "Manuscript Printer's Copy for a Lost English Book." *Library*, NS, XXII (1942), 138-144.
The manuscript, now in the Huntington Library, is a text of the *Prick of Conscience*, formerly attributed to Richard Rolle.

A3460   Bernard, Erwin. "Maps in Early English Printed Books in the Huntington Library." *HLQ*, III (1940), 67-68.

A3461   Newdigate, B. H. "The Constant Lovers." *TLS*, Apr. 18, 1942, p. 204; Apr. 25, 1942, p. 216.
A review and reproduction in part of the contents of a commonplace book from the Huntington Library (H. M. 904), originally in the Tixall collection of manuscript poetry.

(c) OTHER PRIVATELY ENDOWED LIBRARIES

A3462   The Newberry Library. *English Books and Books Printed in England Before 1641 in the Newberry Library*. A Supplement to the Record in the Short-Title Catalogue. Chicago, 1939. Pp. viii, 118.

A3463   Heltzel, Virgil B. *A Check-List of Courtesy Books in the Newberry Library*. Chicago: Newberry Library, 1942. Pp. 161.
List of works written or published before 1775.

A3464   Thurston, Ada, and Curt F. Bühler. *Check-List of Fifteenth Century Printing in the Pierpont Morgan Library*. New York: Pierpont Morgan Library, 1939. Pp. xv, 348.
Rev: by V. S., *Library*, XXI (1940), 99-101; by E. E. Willoughby, *Lib. Quar.*, x, 298.

A3465   *The Pierpont Morgan Library: English Drama from the Mid-Sixteenth to the Later Eighteenth Century*. New York, 1946. Pp. 96.

A3466   The Carl H. Pforzheimer Library. *English Literature, 1475-1700*. 3 Vols. New York: Privately printed, 1940. Pp. xli, 1305.
Rev: by C. F. Bühler, *Library*, NS, XXIII (1943), 140-142.

A3467   Wolf, Edwin, II. "Early American Playbills." *SQ*, VII (1956), 285-286.
Describes the significance of the collection recently purchased by the Library Company of Philadelphia.

(d) PRIVATE COLLECTIONS

A3468   Brooks, Philip. "Notes on Rare Books." *NYTBR*, Apr. 18, 1937, p. 27; New York Times, Apr. 23, 1937, p. 19.

A3469   *An Exhibit of Shakespeare Books from the Collection of Mr. Sidney Fisher of Montreal*. Montreal, Canada: Halcyon Press, 1956. Pp. 38.
Rev: by Frederick Goff, *SQ*, VIII (1957), 125-126.

A3470   "Frank Hogan's Library." *TLS*, June 14, 1946, p. 288.

A3471   Hyde, Donald and Mary. "Contemporary Collectors VI. The Hyde Collection." *Book Collector*, IV (Autumn, 1955), 208-216.

A3472   The Rosenbach Company. *English Plays to 1700, Including an Unique Shakespeare Collection*. Philadelphia and New York: The Rosenbach Co., 1940. Pp. 104.

A3473   Goff, Frederick R. "The Rosenwald Library." *Book Collector*, v (1956), 28-37.

(e) UNIVERSITY LIBRARIES

A3474   Viets, Henry R., and James F. Ballard. "Notes on the Plague Tracts in the Boston Medical Library." *Bul. Hist. Medicine*, VIII (1940), 370-380.

A3475   Ballard, James F., ed. *Catalogue of Medieval and Renaissance Manuscripts and Incunabula in the (Boston Medical) Library*. Boston: Boston Med. Library, 1944. Pp. xx, 246.
Rev: by Curt F. Bühler, *Papers Bibl. Soc. Amer.*, XXXIX (1945), 325-328; by George Sarton, *Isis*, XXXV, 218-219; by E. Ashworth Underwood, *Library*, 4th Series, XXVI (1946), 215-216; by H. E. Sigerist, *Bul. Hist. Med.*, XVII, 527-528.

A3476   William Andrews Clark Memorial Library. *Report of the First Decade, 1934-44.* Berkeley and Los Angeles, 1946.

A3477   Tannenbaum, Samuel A. "Editorial Notes and Comments." *SAB*, XVII (1942), 63, 112.
"A Portrait of Anne Hathaway," p. 112, in a F₃ in Colgate University Library.

A3478   Wells, Henry W. "New Shakespeare Collection at Columbia." *ShN*, VII (1957), 27.

A3479   *The Shakespeare Folios in the Cornell University Library.* Published under the auspices of the Cornell University Library Associates. Ithaca, New York, 1954. Pp. 16.
Summarizes publishing history of the four Folios.
    Rev: *Library*, 5th Series, IX (1954), 217.

A3480   Hinman, Charlton. "Mechanized Collation at the Houghton Library." *Harvard Library Bulletin*, IX (1955), 132-134.

A3481   *The William Pyle Philips Collection in the Haverford College Library: An Introd. Essay and a Descriptive Catalogue to his Rare Books.* Haverford, 1952. Pp. viii, 133.
Shak., pp. 115-127.

A3482   Baldwin, Thomas W., and Isabella Grant. *Shakspere at Illinois. Notes on an Exhibition of the Ernest Ingold Folios and Other Shakespeareana in the University of Illinois Library.* Univ. of Illinois Press, 1951. Pp. 22.

A3483   Savage, Henry L. "The Shakespearean Library of Henry N. Paul." *Princeton Univ. Library Chronicle*, XVII (1955), 49-50.

A3484   Ferguson, J. Wilson. "The Iconography of the Kane Suetonius." *Princeton Univ. Library Chronicle*, XIX (1957), 34-45.

A3485   Burke, Margaret N. "The Miller Collection in the Library of the Richmond Academy of Medicine." *Bul. Hist. Med.*, XIX (1946), 200-225, 319-344.

A3486   Scouten, A. H. "II. Shakespeare." *Library Chronicle of the University of Texas*, I, No. 3 (Spring, 1945), 12-13.

A3487   Skinner, A. E. "Fifteenth Century Books in the University of Texas Library: An Interim Check-List." *Library Chronicle of the Univ. of Texas*, V, No. 1 (1954), 3-8.

A3488   Perry, William. "Renaissance Dictionaries in the University of Texas Library." *Library Chronicle of the Univ. Texas*, V, No. 2 (1954), 3-11.

A3489   Allen, Don Cameron. *A Short-Title Catalogue of English Books Prior to 1700 in the Library of the State College of Washington.* Research Studies of the State College of Washington, V, 1937. Supplement, pp. 109-126.

A3490   Brooks, P. "A First Folio Stolen From Williams College." *NYTBR*, Mar. 3, 1940, p. 23, 2 illus.

A3491   Hagedorn, Ralph. "Bibliotheca Thordarsoniana: The Sequel." *Papers Bibl. Soc. Amer.*, XLIV (1950), 29-54.
Describes the Thordarson collection acquired by the University of Wisc.

(f)   PUBLIC LIBRARIES

A3492   Schullian, Dorothy M., and Francis E. Somer. *A Catalogue of Incunabula and Manuscripts in the Army Medical Library.* New York: Henry Schuman, Inc., 1950. Pp. xiii, 361.
    Rev: by Janet Doe, *Papers Bibl. Soc. Amer.*, XLV (1951), 181-183.

A3493   Stark, Lewis M. "The Whitney Cookery Collection." *Bul. New York Public Library*, I (1946), 103-126.

A3494   Goldberg, M. J. "List of Hebrew Translations of Shakespeare in the Library of Congress." *Chavrutha* (Hebrew), Feb. 27, 1945, pp. 26-28.

A3495   "The Library's First Folio of Shakespeare." *Boston Public Lib. Quar.*, X (1958), 63-77.
Reprints Thomas P. Barton's account, first printed in 1860, of the Library's copy of the first folio then in his possession.

A3496   Rosenbach, A. S. W. *A Description of the Four Folios of Shakespeare, 1623, 1632, 1663-64, 1685, in the Original Bindings, the Gift of Mr. P. A. B. Widener and Mrs. Josephine Widener Wichfeld to the Free Library of Philadelphia in Memory of their Father, Joseph E. Widener.* Philadelphia, 1945.

(g)   MISCELLANEOUS

A3497   Wright, Louis B. "The Gentleman's Library in Early Virginia: The Literary Interests of the First Carters." *HLQ*, I (1937), 3-61.

A3498   Adams, Randolph G. "Who Uses a Library of Rare Books?" *English Institute Annual, 1940.* Columbia Univ. Press, 1941, pp. 144-163.

A3499   Lawler, Percy E., John Fleming, and Edwin Wolf, eds. *To Doctor R.: Essays Here Collected and Published in Honor of the Seventieth Birthday of Dr. A. S. W. Rosenbach.* Philadelphia: Privately Printed, 1946. Pp. 301.

A3500   Brooke, C. F. Tucker. "The Shakespeare Tercentenary." *Essays on Shakespeare and Other Elizabethans.* Yale Univ. Press, 1948, pp. 93-102.

A3501   Dain, Neville E. "Notes on the Editing and Collecting of Shakespeareana." *The Librarian*, Sept., 1956, pp. 149-153.

(3) CONTINENTAL
(a) FRENCH, SWISS, AND ITALIAN

A3502 Bibliothèque Nationale. *Catalogues des Ouvrages de William Shakespeare Conservés au Départment des Imprimés et dans les Bibliothèques de l'Arsenal, Mazarine, Sainte-Geneviève, de l'Institut et de l'Université de Paris.* Paris: Imprimerie Nationale, 1948. Pp. vii, 424 columns.

A3503 Ritter, François. *Catalogue des Incunables et Livres du XVIe Siècle de la Bibliothèque Municipale de Strasbourg.* Strasbourg: P. H. Heitz, 1948. Pp. xiii, 925.
       Rev: by Y. R., *RHE*, XLIV (1949), 323-324; by Charles Wittmer, *ZfSchKg*, XLV (1951), 225-226.

A3504 Schutz, A. H. "Gleanings from Parisian Private Libraries of the Early Renaissance (1494-1558)." *Rom. Phil.*, V (1951), 25-34.

A3505 The Rosenbach Company. *English Plays to 1700, Including an Unique Shakespeare Collection.* Philadelphia and New York: the Rosenbach Company, 1940. Pp. 104.

A3505a Fleming, John. "The Rosenbach-Bodmer Shakespeare Folios and Quartos." *SQ*, III (1952), 257-259.

A3505b Flatter, Richard. "Die neuen Shakespeare-Schätze in der 'Sammlung Martin Bodmer'." *Das Antiquariat*, VIII, Nos. 7/8 (Apr. 10, 1952).

A3505c Hayward, John. "The Rosenbach-Bodmer Shakespeare Collections." *Book Collector*, I (1952), 112-116.

A3505d Bonnard, Georges A. "Shakespeare in the Bibliotheca Bodmeriana." *ShS*, IX (1956), 81-85.

A3506 *Calendar of the State Papers and Manuscripts, Relating to English Affairs, Existing in the Archives and Collections of Venice and in Other Libraries of Northern Italy.* Vol. XXXVII, 1671-72. Ed. by Allen B. Hinds. London: H. M. Stationery Office, 1939. Pp. 439.
       Rev: by Clarence P. Gould, *Mississippi Valley Hist. Rev.*, XXVII (1940), 89-90.

(b) GERMANIC

A3507 Mummendey, Richard. *Von Büchern und Bibliotheken.* Bonn: Verlag der Buchgemeinde, 1950. Pp. 348.
       Substantial portions devoted to the Renaissance book.

A3508 Pflaume, Heinz. "Die Bibliothek der deutschen Shakespeare-Gesellschaft." *SJ*, 92 (1956), 532-539.

A3508a Pflaume, Heinz. "Die Bibliothek der deutschen Shakespeare-Gesellschaft 1955/56." *SJ*, 93 (1957), 289-291.

A3508b Pflaume, Heinz. "Sammelstätte des Shakespeare-Schrifttums. Die Bibliothek der deutschen Shakespeare-Gesellschaft." *Shakespeare-Tage* (Bochum), 1956, pp. 6-9.

A3509 *Katalog der Bücherei der deutschen Shakespeare-Gesellschaft in Weimar.* Weimar: Gutenberg-Dr., 1951. Pp. 357.

A3510 Hodes, Fr. "Kurzer Bericht über die Ausstellung Shakespeare im Wandel der Jahrhunderte der Bibliothek für Neuere Sprachen u. Musik in Frankfurt a. M." *Zbl. f. Bibl.*, LV (1938), 675-676.

A3511 *Katalog der Shakespeare-Ausstellung veranstaltet aus Anlass des 25 jährigen Bestehens der Österreichischen Nationalbibliothek.* Vienna: Bauer, 1947. Pp. 93.

A3512 Davidsson, Ake. *Catalogue Critique et Descriptif des Imprimés de Musique des 16e et 17e Siècles Conservés à la Bibliothèque de l'Université Royale d'Upsala.* 2 Vols. Upsala: Almqvist et Wiksells, 1951. Pp. 168, 204.
       Rev: by Charles van den Borren, *Erasmus*, IV (1951), 431-433.

A3513 "Age of Shakespeare: Exhibition at the Gemeentemuseum, the Hague." *Museums Journal*, LVII (1958), 268.

A3514 Byvanck, W. G. C. *Keur uit het Ongebundelde Werk.* Zwolle Drukken en Herdrukken, 16. Zwolle: Tjeenk Willink, 1956. Pp. 247.
       Includes a long introduction to *Hamlet* and tells how English play quartos were acquired by the Royal Library.

VI. SHAKESPEARE'S SOURCES, LITERARY INFLUENCES,
     AND CULTURAL RELATIONS (61;24)
     1. GENERAL (61;24)
        a. COLLECTED SOURCES OF SHAKESPEARE'S WORKS (61;24)

A3515 Guttman, Selma. *The Foreign Sources of Shakespeare's Works: An Annotated Bibliography of the Commentary on this Subject Between 1904 and 1940, Together with Lists of Certain Translations Available to Shakespeare.* New York: King's Crown Press, 1947. Pp. xxii, 168.
       Rev: A179.

A3516 Bullough, Geoffrey, ed. *Narrative and Dramatic Sources of Shakespeare.* Vol. I: Early Comedies, Poems, *Romeo and Juliet.* London: Routledge & Kegan Paul; New York: Columbia Univ. Press, 1957. Pp. xx, 352.

Rev: *TLS*, Nov. 20, 1957, p. 716; by Robin Skelton, *MGW*, Dec. 31, 1957, p. 2; by George Freedley, *Library Journal*, 83 (1958), 94; briefly in *SCN*, XVI, 20; by Kester Svendsen, *Books Abroad*, XXXII, 321; *NstN*, Nov. 29, 1958, pp. 772-773; by Gordon Ross Smith, *Colorado Review*, III (Winter, 1958), 9-10.

A3517   Bullough, Geoffrey, ed. *Narrative and Dramatic Sources of Shakespeare*. Vol. II: The Comedies, 1597-1603. London: Routledge & Kegan Paul; New York: Columbia Univ. Press, 1957. Pp. xiv, 543.
Rev: *TLS*, Nov. 7, 1958, p. 642.

b. REPRINTS OF VARIOUS SOURCES

A3518   Grismer, R. L., and E. Atkins. *The Book of Apollonius Translated into English Verse*. Minneapolis: Univ. of Minnesota Press, 1936. Pp. xx, 114.

A3519   O'Brien, Edward J., ed. *Elizabethan Tales*. Ed. with an Introd. London: Allen & Unwin, 1937. Pp. 317.
Rev: *TLS*, Mar. 6, 1937, p. 167; *Spectator*, Apr. 2, p. 634; by Trevor James, *Life and Letters Today*, XVI, No. 8, 153-154; by John Hayward, *NstN*, NS, XIII, 256-258; *London Mercury*, XXXVI, 533; *SRL*, Sept. 18, p. 18.

A3520   Pettie, George. *A Petite Pallace of Pettie His Pleasure*. Ed. by Herbert Hartman. Oxford Univ. Press, 1938. Pp. xxxiv, 327.
Rev: *TLS*, Jan. 28, 1939, p. 62; by C. J. Vincent, *MLN*, LIV, 316; by G. D. Willcock, *RES*, XV, 473-475; *N &Q*, 176 (1939), 71; by H. S. V. J., *JEGP*, XXXIX (1940), 440; by S. Gorley Putt, *MLR*, XXXV, 230-232; by René Pruvost, *EA*, IV, 56-57; by R. W. Zandvoort, *ES*, XXII, 148-149.

A3521   Jourdain, Silvester. *A Discovery of the Barmudas (1610)*. With Introd. by Joseph Quincy Adams. New York: Scholars' Facsimiles & Reprints, 1940. Pp. x, 24.

A3522   Novellen, Italienische. Vols. I, II, III. Tr. into German by Eduard von Bülow and others. Berlin: Lambert Schneider, 1942. Contains reprints of various novelle which directly or indirectly influenced Shakespeare: those of Fiorentino, Masuccio, da Porto, Bandello, Straparola, Giraldi, and others.

A3523   Saxo Grammaticus. *Amlethus*. M. dt. Übertr. v. Gerhart Sieveking. Hamburg: Ges. d. Bücherfreunde, 1947. Pp. 87. Latin and German texts.
Rev: by W. Horn, *Archiv*, 186 (1949), 160.

A3524   *The French Bandello. A Selection. The Original Text of Four of Belleforest's 'Histoires Tragiques' Translated by Geoffrey Fenton and William Painter Anno 1567*. Ed. with an Introd. by Frank S. Hook. *The Univ. of Missouri Studies*, XXII, No. 1. Columbia: Univ. of Missouri, 1948. Pp. 185.
Rev: by D. J. Gordon, *RES*, I (1949), 62-63.

A3525   Wilkins, George. *The Painfull Adventures of Pericles, Prince of Tyre*. Ed. by Kenneth Muir. Univ. of Liverpool Press, 1953. Pp. xv, 120.
The introduction, by Prof. Muir, examines the relationship between Wilkins' novel and Shak.'s *Pericles*.
Rev: *TLS*, Nov. 13, 1953, p. 731 (brief); *N &Q*, NS, I (1954), 182; by R. A. Foakes, *English*, X, 20-21; by J. R. Brown, *MLR*, XLIX, 540-541; by E. A. J. Honigmann, *SQ*, VI (1955), 98-100; by Philip Edwards, *RES*, VI, 85-86.

A3526   Secchi, Nicolò. *Self-Interest*. Tr. by William Reymes; ed. by Helen Andrews Kaufman. Seattle: Univ. of Washington Press, 1955. Pp. xxix, 106.
(For Secchi's influence on Shak., see Mrs. Kaufman's article in *SQ*, VI (1955), 271-280.)
Rev: by R. E. Davril, *SQ*, VI (1955), 352-353; by Marvin T. Herrick, *JEGP*, LIV, 416; by M. Poirier, *RLC*, XXIX, 409.

A3527   Holinshed, Raphael. *Holinshed's Chronicle, as Used in Shakespeare's Plays*. Ed. by Allardyce and Josephine Nicoll. (Reissue.) London: Dent, 1955. Pp. xiii, 233.

See also Variorum and Arden editions for reprints of various sources, A3151-A3152.

c. GENERAL STUDIES (62;24)
(1) LARGE-SCALE GENERAL STUDIES

A3528   Whitaker, V. K. "Shakespeare's Use of his Sources." *Renaissance Studies in Honor of Hardin Craig*, pp. 185-197; also *PQ*, XX (1941), 377-389.

A3529   Tillyard, E. M. W. *Shakespeare's History Plays*. London: Chatto & Windus, 1944. Pp. viii, 336.
Rev: B5072.

A3530   Stevenson, David Lloyd. *The Love-Game Comedy*. Columbia Univ. Press, 1946. Pp. xii, 259.
Rev: *CE*, VIII (1947), 278; by W. L. Renwick, *RES*, XXIII, 166-167; by D. J. Gordon, *MLR*, XLIII (1948), 109-111; by Helen A. Kaufman, *MLQ*, X (1949), 109-110.

A3531   Baldwin, T. W. *Shakspere's Five-Act Structure: Shakspere's Early Plays on the Background of Renaissance Theories of Five-Act Structure from 1470*. Univ. Illinois Press, 1947. Pp. xiii, 848.
Rev: A5938.

A3532   Baldwin, T. W. "Respice Finem: Respice Funem." *AMS*, pp. 141-155.
Sketches the background for *The Comedy of Errors*, IV, iv, 44-46.

A3533   Andersson, H. O. E. *The Study of Shakespeare's Sources from Langbaine to Malone*. B. Litt. thesis, Oxford, Merton, 1949.

A3534   Bradbrook, M. C. *Shakespeare and Elizabethan Poetry*: *A Study of his Earlier Work in Relation to the Poetry of the Time.* London: Chatto & Windus, 1951. Pp. viii, 279.
     Rev: by J. I. M. Stewart, *NstN*, Nov. 17, 1951, p. 571; *TLS*, Feb. 1, 1952, p. 94; by J. B. Fort, *EA*, v, 245; by L. A. Cormican, *Scrutiny*, xviii, 320-324; by Raymond Mortimer, *Sunday Times*, Jan. 6, p. 3; by J. M. Cohen, *Spectator*, Jan. 4, p. 24; by G. B. Harrison, *SatR*, June 14, pp. 28-29; by Hermann Heuer, *SJ*, 87/88 (1952), 253; by F. S. Boas, *FortnR*, 1021 (Jan.), 66-67; by G. Rylands, *ConR*, LXXIII (1951/52), 344-346; by M. A. Shaaber, *SQ*, IV (1953), 343-344; by Clifford Leech, *ShS*, VI, 155; by W. Clemen, *Archiv*, 189 (1953), 364.

A3535   Whitaker, Virgil K. *Shakespeare's Use of Learning*: *An Inquiry into the Growth of his Mind and Art.* San Marino, Calif.: Huntington Lib., 1953. Pp. ix, 366.
     Rev: by Hallett Smith, *YR*, XLIII (1953), 121-125; *TLS*, Oct. 23, p. 675; by Douglas Bush, *JEGP*, LIII (1954), 104-107; by Charles T. Harrison, *SR*, LXII, 164-165; by Matthias A. Shaaber, *MLN*, LXIX, 430-433; by Nelson Magill, *QJS*, XL, 88; by M. C. Bradbrook, *RES*, NS, V, 413-414; by H. T. Price, *SQ*, V, 110; by H. Edward Cain, *Catholic Hist. Rev.*, XL, 371; by I. A. Shapiro, *ShS*, VIII (1955), 146-147; by L. C. Knights, *SR*, LXIII, 224-230; by Giles E. Dawson, *MP*, LII, 205-206; by H. Nørgaard, *ES*, XXXVI, 117-121; by R. G. Cox, *SQ*, VIII (1957), 94-98.

A3536   Knights, L. C. "On Historical Scholarship and Interpretation of Shakespeare." *SR*, LXIII (1955), 223-240.
     See comments of Virgil K. Whitaker, "Vindicating the Historical Approach," *ShN*, V, 39; and John Lawlor, "On Historical Scholarship and the Interpretation of Shakespeare; A Reply to L. C. Knights," *SR*, LXIV (1956), 186-206.

A3537   Hankins, John Erskine. *Shakespeare's Derived Imagery.* Lawrence: Univ. of Kansas Press, 1953. Pp. 289.
     Rev: by G. B. Harrison, *SatR*, Sept. 25, 1954, p. 22; by R. C. Bald, *MP*, LI, 278-281; by William C. McAvoy, *JEGP*, LIII, 637-639; by Michel Poirier, *EA*, VII, 415; by Paul N. Siegel, *ShN*, IV, 34; *CE*, XVI, 145; by E. D. Pendry, *MLR*, L (1955), 105-106; by M. C. Bradbrook, *RES*, NS, VI, 313-314; by Madeleine Doran, *MLN*, LXX, 134-138; by Alan S. Downer, *SQ*, VI, 466-468; by J. Swart, *Neophil*, XL (1956), 236-237.

A3538   Muir, Kenneth. *Shakespeare's Sources.* I: Comedies and Tragedies. London: Methuen, 1957. Pp. ix, 267.
     Rev: by G. Wilson Knight, *TC*, 161 (1957), 590-591; *TLS*, May 17, p. 306; by F. S. Boas, *English*, XI, 189; by C. J. Sisson, *MLR*, LII, 585-586; by Hermann Heuer, *SJ*, 93 (1957), 265-266; by Helen Gardner, *London Mag.*, IV, No. 12, 73-74, 77-78; *Dublin Mag.*, July-Sept., 69-70; *N &Q*, NS, IV, 458-459; by J. Vallette, *MdF*, 330 (1957), 711-712; by Clifford Leech, *ES*, XXXIX (1958), 83-85; by Rufus Putney, *SQ*, IX, 407-409; by G. Blakemore Evans, *JEGP*, LVII, 343-344; by J. C. Maxwell, *RES*, NS, IX, 314-316; by Brita Tigerschiöld, *Göteborgs Handelstidning* (Göteborg), June 2; *ShN*, VIII, 20.

(2)   SPECIFIC INFLUENCES NOT EXCLUSIVELY NATIONAL
(a)   CONTINUING CLASSICAL-MEDIEVAL-RENAISSANCE INFLUENCES

A3539   Walker, Eirene Margaret. *The Impact of the Renaissance on the English Drama.* MA thesis, Dalhousie University, 1934. Pp. 84.

A3540   M. Rose-Isabel, Sister. *The Effect of the Renaissance on French and English Literature.* MA thesis, Montreal, 1935. Pp. 67.

A3541   Mary Ann Eva, Sister. *Shakespeare's Art.* MA thesis, Montreal, 1939. Pp. 103.
Apprenticeship and influence.

A3542   Cunningham, James Vincent. *Tragic Effect and Tragic Process in Some Plays of Shakespeare, and Their Background in the Literary and Ethical Theory of Classical Antiquity and the Middle Ages.* DD, Stanford University, 1945. Abstr. in Stanford Univ., *Abstracts of Dissertations*, 1944-45, pp. 29-34.

A3543   Chew, Samuel C. "This Strange Eventful History." *AMS*, pp. 157-182.

A3544   Sledd, James. "A Note on the Use of Renaissance Dictionaries." *MP*, XLIX (1951), 10-15.

A3545   Arnold, Aerol. "The Hector-Andromache Scene in Shakespeare's *Troilus and Cressida*." *MLQ*, XIV (1953), 335-340.

A3546   Bradner, Leicester. "From Petrarch to Shakespeare." *The Renaissance.* A Symposium. Feb. 8-10, 1952. New York: The Metropolitan Museum of Art, 1953, pp. 63-76.

A3547   Goolden, P. "Antiochus's Riddle in Gower and Shakespeare." *RES*, NS, VI (1955), 245-251.

A3548   Bradner, Leicester. "The Rise of Secular Drama in the Renaissance." *Studies in the Renaissance*, III (1956), 7-22.

(b)   LITURGICAL INFLUENCES

A3549   Cormican, L. A. "Medieval Idiom in Shakespeare: (I) Shakespeare and the Liturgy." *Scrutiny*, XVII (1950), 186-202.

A3550   Baldwin Peter, Brother, F. S. C. "*Hamlet* and *In Paradisum*." *SQ*, III (1952), 279-280; idem, *SQ*, IV, 209.
Corrects a statement in his note in *SQ*, III, 279.

A3551 Roth, Cecil. "Shakespeare and the Jewish Liturgy." *TLS*, May 15, 1953, p. 317.
       See letter by A. S. B. Glover, May 22, p. 333.
       Notes parallel between Richmond's prayer before sleep (Richard III, V.iii.112-114) and the
       traditional Jewish night prayer; observes that the Jewish liturgy in translation was available to
       Shak. Mr. Glover suggests the Office of Compline as a more probable source than the
       Jewish liturgy.

A3552 Quinlan, Maurice J. "Shakespeare and the Catholic Burial Services." *SQ*, v (1954), 303-306.

(c) MISCELLANEOUS

A3553 Muir, Kenneth, and Sean O'Loughlin. *The Voyage to Illyria*. A New Study of Shakespeare.
       London: Methuen, 1937. Pp. 242.
       Rev: A8307.

A3554 Heron-Allen, Edward. "The Sources of Shakespeare." *N &Q*, 178 (1940), 20; ibid., p. 61.

A3555 Harrison, Thomas P., Jr. "Aspects of Primitivism in Shakespeare and Spenser." *TxSE*,
       xx (1940), 39-71.

A3556 Bhattacherje, M. M. *"Courtesy" in Shakespeare*. With a Foreword by C. J. Sisson and Introd.
       by Louis Cazamian. Calcutta Univ. Press, 1940. Pp. xix, 225.
       Rev: A4560.

A3557 Wilson, Harold S. " 'Nature and Art' in *Winter's Tale* (IV.iv.86 ff.)." *SAB*, xviii (1943),
       114-120.

A3558 Tucker, William John. "Irish Aspects of Shakespeare." *Catholic World*, 156 (1943), 698-704.

A3559 Munro, James. "Some Matters Shakespearian." *TLS*, Sept. 13, 1947, p. 472; Sept. 27, p. 500;
       See the letter by S. G. Thomas, ibid., Oct. 11, 1947, p. 528.

A3560 Krzyżanowski, Juliusz. *Shakespearean Modifications. Methodical Prolegomena*. Wrocław
       (Breslau): Nakładem Wrocławskiego Towarzystwa Naukowego, 1948. Pp. 31.

A3561 Parrott, Thomas M. *Shakespearean Comedy*. New York: Oxford Univ. Press, 1949. Pp. xiv, 417.
       Rev: A8323.

A3562 Isaacs, J. "Shakespeare and his World: Sources of Shakespeare's Plays." *Listener*, XLII (1949),
       183-184, 199. Comment, ibid., by W. Bliss and P. Carr, p. 230; by J. Isaacs, p. 274; by W.
       Bliss, pp. 323-324, 405; by G. H. Moore and D. Evans, p. 363.

A3563 Heilman, Robert B., et al. "Myth in the Later Plays of Shakespeare." *EIE, 1948* (1949),
       pp. 27-119.

A3564 Lord, John Bigelow. *Certain Dramatic Devices Studied in the Comedies of Shakespeare and in Some
       of the Works of his Contemporaries and Predecessors*. DD, University of Illinois, 1951. Pp. 296.
       DA, XII (1952), 66. Publication No. 3154.

A3565 Hutton, James. "Some English Poems in Praise of Music." *English Miscellany*, ed. by
       Mario Praz (Rome: Edizioni di Storia e Letteratura), 1951, pp. 1-63.

A3566 Craig, Hardin. "Motivation in Shakespeare's Choice of Materials." *ShS*, IV (1951), 26-34.

A3567 Waith, Eugene M. *"Pericles* and Seneca the Elder." *JEGP*, L (1951), 180-182.

A3568 Krempel, Daniel Spartakus. *The Theatre in Relation to Art and to the Social Order from the
       Middle Ages to the Present*. DD, University of Illinois, 1953. Pp. 373. Mic A54-596. *DA*,
       XIV (1954), 421. Publication No. 6957. Chap. III: "Elizabethan Society and its Theatre,"
       pp. 113-141.

A3569 Soellner, Rolf H. *Anima and Affectus: Theories of the Emotions in Sixteenth Century Grammar
       Schools and Their Reflections in the Works of Shakspere*. DD, University of Illinois, 1954. Pp. 275.
       Mic A54-489. *DA*, XIV (1954), 351. Publication No. 6983.

A3570 Muir, Kenneth. "Pyramus and Thisbe: A Study in Shakespeare's Method." *SQ*, v (1954),
       141-153.

A3571 Greer, C. A. "Shakespeare a Researcher." *N &Q*, NS, II (1955), 479-480.

A3572 Born, Walter. *Shakespeares Verhältnis zu seinen Quellen in "The Comedy of Errors" und "The
       Taming of the Shrew."* DD, Hamburg, 1955. Pp. 211. Typewritten.

A3573 Løkse, Olav. "The Story and the Play." *Orbis*, XI (1956), 237-244.

A3574 Stamm, Rudolf. "Elizabethan Stage-Practice and the Transmutation of Source Material by
       the Dramatists." Abstr. in *ShN*, VII (1957), 48.

d. MEDIEVAL ELEMENTS
(1) GENERAL

A3575 Harvey, J. H. *Gothic England: A Survey of National Culture, 1300-1550*. London, New York,
       1946.
       Rev: by H. M. Colvin, *History*, xxxII (1947), 126-127; *TLS*, July 5, p. 335 (rejoinder by
       Mr. Harvey, ibid., July 19, p. 365); by K. B. McF., *MGW*, Sept. 18, p. 10; by Lionel Brett,
       Spectator, July 18, p. 86; by Abbott Martin, *NYTBR*, Jan. 11, 1948, p. 16.

A3576 Artz, Frederick B. *The Mind of the Middle Ages, A. D. 200-1500: An Historical Survey*.
       New York: Alfred A. Knopf, 1953. Pp. xiv, 552, viii.
       Rev: by Thomas C. Van Cleve, *Speculum*, xxviii (1953), 858-862.

A3577   Cancelled.

(a) DANCE OF DEATH

A3578   Stegemeier, Henri. *The Dance of Death in Folksong, with an Introduction on the History of the Dance of Death.* DD, University of Chicago. Private ed. distributed by the University of Chicago Libraries. Chicago, 1939.
Rev: by S. Thompson, *JEGP*, XLIII (1944), 365-366.

A3579   Stammler, Wolfgang. *Der Totentanz: Entstehung und Deutung.* Munich: Carl Hanser, 1948. Pp. 95, il. 28.
Second revised edition of *Die Totentänze des Mittelalters* (1922).
Rev: by H. Stegemeier, *JEGP*, XLIX (1950), 401-405; by E. Rooth, *Niederdeutsche Mitteilungen*, IV, 96.

A3580   Enklaar, D. Th. *De Dodendans, een Cultuur-Historische Studie.* Amsterdam: L. J. Veens Uitgeversmaatschappij N. V., 1950.
Rev: by J. J. Mak, *Tijdschrift voor Nederlandse Taal- en Letterkunde*, LXIX (1951), 147-157.

A3581   Clark, James M. *The Dance of Death in the Middle Ages and the Renaissance.* Glasgow Univ. Publ., 86. Glasgow: Jackson, Son & Co., 1950. Pp. xi, 131; pl. 20.
See article by the author, "The Dance of Death in Medieval Literature: Some Recent Theories of Its Origin," *MLR*, XLV, 336-345.
Rev: *TLS*, Sept. 1, 1950, p. 551; by Archer Taylor, *Speculum*, XXVI (1951), 151-152; by John C. Lapp, *QQ*, LVIII, 460-462; by Arthur Brown, *MLR*, XLVI, 78-80.

(b) POLITICAL THOUGHT

A3582   Carlyle, R. W., and A. J. Carlyle. *A History of Mediaeval Political Theory in the West.* Vol. VI: *Political Theory from 1300 to 1600.* London: Blackwood, 1936. Pp. 578.
Rev: A1643.

A3583   Lewis, Ewart. "Organic Tendencies in Medieval Political Thought." *Amer. Pol. Sci. Rev.,* XXXII (1938), 849-876.

A3584   Koht, Halvdan. "Medieval Liberty Poems." *AHR*, XLVIII (1943), 281-290.
The call for liberty in the last centuries of the Middle Ages.

A3585   Jarrett, Bede. *Social Theories of the Middle Ages, 1200-1500.* Westminster: Newman Book Shop, 1942. Pp. ix, 280.

(c) MISCELLANEOUS

A3586   Lewis, Clive S. *The Allegory of Love: A Study in Mediaeval Tradition.* Oxford: Clarendon Press, 1936. Pp. ix, 378.
Rev: *TLS*, June 6, 1936, p. 475; by William Empson, *Spectator*, Sept. 4, p. 389; *N &Q*, 172 (1936), 250-251; by Stephen Gaselee, *CR*, L, 183; by E. H. W. Meyerstein, *London Mercury*, XXXIV, 270-271; by G. L. Brook, *MLR*, XXXII (1937), 287-288; by Edgar C. Knowlton, *JEGP*, XXXVI, 124-126; by Thomas A. Kirby, *MLN*, LII, 515-518; by Kathleen Tillotson, *RES*, XIII, 477-479; by Vera S. M. Fraser, *Criterion*, XVI, 383-388; by Oliver Elton, *Medium Aevum*, VI, 34-40; by Howard R. Patch, *Speculum*, XII, 272-274; by Mona Wilson, *English*, I, 344-346; by F. Krog, *Beiblatt*, XLVIII, 333-338.

A3587   Meissner, Paul. "Mittelalterliches Lebensgefühl in der englischen Renaissance." *DVLG*, XV (1937), 433-472.

A3588   Tervarent, Guy de. *Les Enigmes de l'Art du Moyen Age.* 2 Vols. Paris: Éd. d'Art et d'Histoire, 1938 and 1941.
Rev: by Jean Adhémar, *BHR*, II (1942), 196-197.

A3589   Thorndike, Lynn. "Mediaeval Magic and Science in the Seventeenth Century." *Speculum*, XXVIII (1953), 692-704.

A3590   Sarton, George. *The Appreciation of Ancient and Medieval Learning During the Renaissance (1450-1600).* Philadelphia, 1957.
Rev: by A. C. Crombie, *Medium Aevum*, XXVII (1958), 55-56.

A3591   Wittkower, Rudolf. "Marvels of the East: A Study in the History of Monsters." *JWCI*, V (1943), 159-197.

A3592   Trachtenberg, Joshua. *The Devil and the Jew.* The Medieval Conception of the Jew and Its Relation to Modern Anti-Semitism. Yale Univ. Press, 1944. Pp. xiv, 279.
Rev: *TLS*, May 20, 1944, p. 249; by H. J. Laski, *NstN*, Feb. 5, pp. 96-97; by Gaines Post, *AHR*, XLIX, 698-699.

(2) IN ELIZABETHAN LITERATURE

A3593   Chambers, Sir E. K. *The English Folk Play.* Oxford, 1933.
Rev: A5023.

A3594   Farnham, Willard. *The Medieval Heritage of Elizabethan Tragedy.* Univ. California Press; Cambridge Univ. Press, 1936. First ed. reprinted with corrections. Oxford: Blackwell, 1957. Pp. xiv, 487.
Rev: by H. R. Patch, *Eng. Studn.*, LXXI (1937), 396-398; by W. W. Lawrence, *MLN*, LII,

435-437; by W. Keller, *SJ*, LXXIV (1938), 191-192; by G. R. Coffman, *SP*, XXXV, 505-509; by C. J. Sisson, *MLR*, XXXIV (1939), 88-89; by Cyrus Hoy, *CE*, XX (1958), 100; by Hermann Heuer, *SJ*, 94 (1958), 263.

A3595   Spencer, Theodore. *Death and Elizabethan Tragedy*. A Study of Convention and Opinion on the Elizabethan Drama. Harvard Univ. Press, 1936. Pp. xiii, 288.
Rev: A6823.

A3596   Withington, Robert. *Excursions in English Drama*. New York: Appleton-Century, 1937. Pp. xvii, 264.
Rev: by G. C. Taylor, *MLN*, LIV (1939), 314; by H. S. V. J., *JEGP*, XXXIX (1940), 163.

A3597   Coffman, George R. "Some Trends in English Literary Scholarship, with Special Reference to Mediaeval Backgrounds." *SP*, XXXV (1938), 500-514.

A3598   Kernodle, George R. "The Medieval Pageant Wagons of Louvain." *Theatre Annual*, 1943, pp. 58-62; 13 pl.

A3599   Atkins, J. W. H. *English Literary Criticism: The Medieval Phase*. Cambridge Univ. Press, 1944. Pp. ix, 211.
Rev: *TLS*, Feb. 12, 1944, p. 82; see also leading article, "An Ancient Quarrel," ibid., Feb. 12, p. 79; by E. E. Kellett, *NstN*, June 3, pp. 370-371; by H. J. Paris, *Spectator*, Mar. 17, pp. 248, 250; by J. D. R., *Canadian Forum*, XXIV, 95; by Geoffrey Tillotson, *English*, V, 57-58; by Blanche M. Kelly, *Catholic World*, 159 (1944), 566-567; by Richard McKeon, *MP*, XLII, 59-60; by J. F. Lockwood, *MLR*, XXXIX, 399-401; *N &Q*, 176 (1944), 235-236; by A. H. Gilbert, *JEGP*, XLIV (1945), 212-215; by Elizabeth J. Sweeting, *RES*, XXI, 63-64; by G. H. Gerould, *MLN*, LX, 65-67; by F. M. Powicke, *EHR*, LX, 111.

A3600   Gardiner, H. C. *Mysteries' End . . . The Last Days of the Medieval Religious Stage*. New Haven, 1946. Pp. xvi, 140.

A3601   Farnham, Willard. "The Mediaeval Comic Spirit in the English Renaissance." *AMS*, pp. 429-437.

A3602   Schirmer, Walter Franz. "The Importance of the Fifteenth Century for the Study of the English Renaissance with Special Reference to Lydgate." *English Studies Today*. Oxford Univ. Press, 1951, pp. 104-110.

A3603   Goodman, Randolph G. *That Strumpet the Stage: Poems about Playgoers, Players, and Playwrights*. DD, Columbia University, 1953. Pp. 357. Mic A53-761. *DA*, XIII (1953), 450. Publication No. 5189.

A3604   Spivack, Bernard. *Allegory of Evil*. DD, Columbia University, 1953. Revised and published as *Shakespeare and the Allegory of Evil*. New York: Columbia University Press, 1958.
Rev: A4951.

A3605   Hieatt, A. Kent. *Medieval Symbolism and the Dramatic Imagery of the English Renaissance*. DD, Columbia University, 1954. Pp. 510. Mic 55-108. *DA*, XV (1955), 817. Publication No. 11,456.

A3606   Kesler, Charlotte Ruth. *The Importance of the Comic Tradition of English Drama in the Interpretation of Marlowe's Doctor Faustus*. DD, University of Missouri, 1954. Pp. 258. Mic 55-234. *DA*, XV (1955), 1387. Publication No. 9183. Shak., pp. 153-155.

A3607   Ribner, Irving. "Morality Roots of the Tudor History Play." *Tulane Studies in English*, IV (1954), 21-43.

A3608   Brewer, D. S. "The Ideal of Feminine Beauty in Medieval Literature, Especially 'Harley Lyrics', Chaucer, and Some Elizabethans." *MLR*, L (1955), 257-269.

A3609   Craig, Hardin. *English Religious Drama of the Middle Ages*. Oxford: Clarendon Press, 1955. Pp. 432.
Rev: by R. R. Rylands, *Church Quar. Rev.*, 156 (1955), 432-434; by Arnold Williams, *Speculum*, XXXI (1956), 348-351; *TLS*, Jan. 20, p. 36; by J. S. Purvis, *Jour. Eccl. Hist.*, VII, 96-98; by Henry W. Wells, *Rev. of Religion*, XX, 186-192; by Aerol Arnold, *Personalist*, XXXVII, 415; by M. W. Bloomfield, *MP*, LIV, 129-131; by A. P. Berthet, *EA*, IX, 344-345.

A3610   Mares, F. H. *An Investigation of the Origin and Development of the Figure Called 'The Vice' in Tudor Drama*. B. Litt. thesis, Oxford, Lincoln, 1955.

A3611   Mares, Francis Hugh. "The Origin of the Figure Called 'The Vice' in Tudor Drama." *HLQ*, XXII (1958), 11-29.

A3612   Taylor, William Edwards. *The Villainess in Elizabethan Drama*. DD, Vanderbilt University, 1957. Pp. 402. Mic 57-2820. *DA*, XVII (1957), 1756. Publication No. 22,025.

(3) IN SHAKESPEARE
(a) GENERAL MEDIEVAL INFLUENCES

A3613   Curry, Walter Clyde. *Shakespeare's Philosophical Patterns*. Louisiana State Univ. Press, 1937. Pp. xii, 244.
Rev: A931.

A3614   Taylor, George C. "The Medieval Element in Shakspere." *SAB*, XII (1937), 208-216.
A critical review of Willard Farnham's *Medieval Heritage of Elizabethan Tragedy*.

A3615   Bhattacherje, M. M. "Feudal Manners in Shakespeare." *Calcutta Rev.*, LXX (1938/39), 181-194.

A3616   Hussey, Richard. "Shakespeare and Gower." *N &Q*, 180 (1941), 386.

A3617   O'Donnell, Joseph Leo. *Ethical Principles of the Christian Middle Ages in Shakespeare.* MA thesis, Western Ontario, 1941. Pp. 206.

A3618   Cox, Ernest H. "Shakespeare and Some Conventions of Old Age." *SP*, XXXIX (1942), 36-46.

A3619   Deutschberger, Paul. "Shakspere on Degree: A Study in Backgrounds." *SAB*, XVII (1942), 200-207.

A3620   Wade, James Edgar. *Medieval Rhetoric in Shakespeare.* DD, St. Louis University, 1942. Pp. 185. Mic A44-671. *Microf. Ab.*, V (1944), 72. Publication No. 613.

A3621   Yates, Frances A. "Shakespeare and the Platonic Tradition." *Univ. of Edin. Jour.*, XII (1942), 2-12.

A3622   Cunningham, James Vincent. *Tragic Effect and Tragic Process in Some Plays of Shakespeare, and Their Background in the Literary and Ethical Theory of Classical Antiquity and the Middle Ages.* DD, Stanford University, 1945. Abstr. publ. in *Abstracts of Dissertations, 1944-45*, Stanford, 1945, pp. 29-34.

A3623   Patchell, Mary F. *The Palmerin Romances in Elizabethan Prose Fiction.* Columbia Univ. Stud. in Engl. and Comp. Lit., No. 166. Pp. 157. DD, Columbia University, 1946.

A3624   Sinsheimer, Hermann. *Shylock: The History of a Character of the Myth of the Jew.* With a Foreword by John Middleton Murry. London: Gollancz, 1947. Pp. 147, pl. 16.
Rev: by H. B. C., *MGW*, July 3, 1947, p. 11; by Nevill Coghill, *Shakespeare Quarterly* (London), I (Summer, 1947), 107-109; brief mention, *TLS*, Apr. 26, p. 203.

A3625   Richard, William Kenneth. "Miracle, Mystery and Shakespeare." *Poetry and the People.* London, 1947, pp. 53-81.

A3626   Monro, M. T. "Shakespeare's Medieval Faith." *Blessed Margaret Clitherow.* New York: Longmans, Green, 1947.

A3627   Danby, John F. *Shakespeare's Doctrine of Nature: A Study of King Lear.* London: Faber and Faber, 1949. Pp. 234.
Rev: A934.

A3628   Parrott, Thomas M. *Shakespearean Comedy.* New York: Oxford University Press, 1949., Pp. xiv, 417.
Rev: A8323.

A3629   Coghill, Nevill. "The Basis of Shakespearian Comedy: A Study in Medieval Affinities." *Essays and Studies*, III (1950), 1-28.
Rev: by M. A. Shaaber, *SQ*, II (1951), 260-261; by C. J. Sisson, *MLR*, XLVI, 545.

A3630   Cormican, L. A. "Medieval Idiom in Shakespeare. I: Shakespeare and the Liturgy. II: Shakespeare and the Medieval Ethic." *Scrutiny*, XVII (1951), 186-202, 298-317.

A3631   Curtius, Ernst Robert. *Europäische Literatur und Lateinisches Mittelalter.* 2nd ed., Bern: Francke 1954. Pp. 608. Shak., pp. 335-346.

A3632   Meader, William G. *Courtship in Shakespeare.* New York: Columbia Univ. Press, 1954. Pp. 266.
Rev: A2559.

A3633   White, T. H. *The Book of Beasts, Being a Translation of a Latin Bestiary of the Twelfth Century.* London: Jonathan Cape, 1954. Pp. 296.
Shak.'s indebtedness to bestiary lore, pp. 11, 18, 20, 32, 36, 47, 92, 96, 121, 128, 154 (all notes). See also pp. 261-268 on Elizabethan in general.

A3634   Fredén, Gustaf. "En strand där timjan blommar vild. En studie i Shakespeare-dramats bakgrund.' *Orestes och försoningen*, Lund, 1955, pp. 85-108.

A3635   MacCarthy, S. "Shakespeare the Medievalist." *Irish Ecclesastical Rev.*, 84 (Sept., 1956), 193-200.

A3636   Gallagher, Ligera Cécile. *Shakespeare and the Aristotelian Ethical Tradition.* DD, Stanford University, 1956. Pp. 338. Mic 56-3017. *DA*, XVI (1956), 1898. Publication No. 17,720.

A3637   Hankins, John E. "The Pains of the Underworld: Fire, Wind, and Ice in Milton and Shakespeare." *PMLA*, LXXI (1956), 482-495.

A3638   Barroll, John L., III. *Shakespeare and Roman History.* DD, Princeton University, 1956. Pp. 675. Mic 57-996. *DA*, XVII (1957), 626. Publication No. 20,101.

(b) SPECIFIC MEDIEVAL INFLUENCES
i. Medieval Drama

A3639   McMahon, Amos Philip. *The Mediaeval Conception of Tragedy and Comedy.* DD, Harvard University, 1916.

A3640   Thaler, A. "Shakespeare, Daniel, and *Everyman*." *PQ*, XV (1936), 217-218.

A3641   Thaler, A. "Shakespeare and *Everyman*." *TLS*, July 18, 1936, p. 600.

A3642   Fredén, Gustaf. "The Tide of Verona." *Studier tillägnade Anton Blanck*, Dec. 29, 1946, pp. 54-60.

A3643   McDowell, J. H. "Conventions of Medieval Art in Shakespearean Staging." *JEGP*, XLVII (1948), 215-229.

A3644 McDowell, J. H. "Medieval Influences in Shakespearian Staging." *Players Magazine*, XXVI (1949), 52-53.

A3645 Craig, Hardin. "Morality Plays and Elizabethan Drama." *SQ*, I (1950), 64-72.

A3646 Salter, K. W. "*Lear* and the Morality Tradition." *N &Q*, NS, I (1954), 109-110.

A3647 Felver, Charles Stanley. *William Shakespeare and Robert Armin his Fool—A Working Partnership.* DD, University of Michigan, 1956. Pp. 352. Mic 56-3895. *DA*, XVI (1956), 2446. Publication No. 18,601.

ii. Bartholomaeus Anglicus (via Stephen Batman)

A3648 Draper, John W. "Jacques' 'Seven Ages' and Bartholomaeus Anglicus." *MLN*, LIV (1939), 273-276.

A3649 Gilbert, Allan H. "Jacques' 'Seven Ages' and Censorinus." *MLN*, LV (1940), 103-105.

A3650 Heninger, S. K., Jr. " 'Wondrous Strange Snow'—*Midsummer Night's Dream*, V.i.66." *MLN*, LXVIII (1953), 481-483.

iii. Chaucer

A3651 Bethurum, Dorothy. "Shakespeare's Comment on Mediaeval Romance in *Midsummer Night's Dream.*" *MLN*, LX (1945), 85-94. Suggests that either Chaucer's *Knight's Tale* or the anonymous (and lost) play *Palamon and Arcette* first inspired the main plot of *Midsummer Night's Dream.*

A3652 McNeal, Thomas H. "*Henry IV, Parts I* and *II*, and Speght's First Edition of *Geoffrey Chaucer.*" *SAB*, XXI (1946), 87-93.

A3653 Shakespeare, William. *The Tragedy of Romeo and Juliet.* Introd. by Nevill Coghill. Designs by Jean Hugo. London: Folio Soc., 1950. Pp. 131.
Introd. discusses, i.a., the influence of Chaucer on Shakespeare.
    Rev: *Adelphi*, XXVII (1950), 88.

A3654 Schlauch, Margaret. "*Troilus i Kressyda* Szekspira i Chaucera." *Kwartalnik Neofilologiczny*, I (1954), 3-19.

A3655 Bradbrook, M. C. "What Shakespeare Did to Chaucer's *Troilus and Criseyde.*" *SQ*, IX (1958), 311-319.

iv. Analogues

A3656 Wilson, James L. "Another Medieval Parallel to the Jessica and Lorenzo Story." *SAB*, XXIII (1948), 20-23.
Parallel in story of Floripas in *The Sultan of Babylon.*

A3657 Braddy, Haldeen. "Shakespeare and Three Oriental Tales." *Midwest Folklore*, I (1951), 91-92.
Early Oriental analogues to *Othello* I.ii.167-168, *Merchant of Venice* IV.i.340-342, and *Hamlet* I.ii.140.

A3658 Bowers, R. H. "A Medieval Analogue to *As You Like It*, II.vii.137-166." *SQ*, III (1952), 109-112.

v. Specific Details in Shakespeare

A3659 Cox, Ernest H. "Another Medieval Convention in Shakspere." *SAB*, XVI (1941), 249-253.
The *ubi sunt* formula in *Hamlet.*

A3660 Hatto, A. T. " 'Venus and Adonis'—and the Boar." *MLR*, XLI (1946), 353-361.

A3661 Semper, I. J. " 'Yes, by St. Patrick'." *TLS*, Aug. 3, 1946, p. 367.
Ref. to Clarence Brownfield's suggestion that Holinshed is the source of Ham.'s phrase (*TLS*, May 25, 1946). Semper suggests Voragine's *Golden Legend.*

A3662 Elton, William. "Two Shakesperian Parallels." *SAB*, XXII (1947), 115-116. In *Winter's Tale* and *Cor.*

A3663 Lascelles, Mary. " 'Glassie Essence,' *Measure for Measure*, II.ii.120." *RES*, II (1951), 140-142.
The phrase apparently refers to man's soul, figuratively or descriptively a vessel of glass, the vas vitreum et sphaericum of the thirteenth-century *Dialogus Miraculorum* of Caesarius of Heisterbach.

A3664 Brewer, D. S. "Brutus' Crime: A Footnote to *Julius Caesar.*" *RES*, NS, III (1952), 51-54.

A3665 Cunningham, J. V. " 'Essence' and *The Phoenix and Turtle.*" *ELH*, XIX (1952), 265-276.

A3666 Semper, I. J. "The Ghost in *Hamlet*: Pagan or Christian?" *The Month*, NS, IX (1953), 222-234.

A3667 Bonnard, Georges A. "Note sur les Sources de *Timon of Athens.*" *EA*, VII (1954), 59-69.
Suggests that Shakespeare, later the author of the anonymous comedy, and finally Shadwell in his version of *Timon*, used a common source now lost, in which the original story had been elaborated with details of oriental origin and had received in Italy a form unknown to classical authors; notes parallel between the tale of Ali-Nour in the *Arabian Nights* and the first part of *Timon.*

A3668 Honigmann, E. A. "Secondary Sources of *The Winter's Tale.*" *PQ*, XXXIV (1955), 27-38.

Presents evidence that Shak. owed far more than has been realized to three secondary sources: Francis Sabie's *The Fisherman's Tale*, 1595; *Amadis de Gaule*; and the Proserpine-myth.

A3669 Semper, I. J. "On the Dignity of Man." *Month*, 199 (1955), 292-301.
Hamlet's great lines on the dignity of man viewed as an ordered, phrase-by-phrase presentation of Medieval Thomistic philosophy.

A3670 Siegel, Paul N. "Adversity and the Miracle of Love in *King Lear*." *SQ*, VI (1955), 325-326.

e. SHAKESPEARE'S EDUCATION, READING, AND BOOK KNOWLEDGE (42,62;-,24)
(1) RENAISSANCE EDUCATION (178;62)

A3671 Korpikallio, Jaakko. *Yksilön ja kansalaisen kasvatus Englannissa.* I: *Kasvatuspäämäärän kehitys renessanssista nykyaikaan.* (*Die Erziehung des Individuums und des Staatsbürgers in England.* I: *Die Entwicklung des Erziehungs-Zieles von der Renaissance bis zur Gegenwart.*) DD, Helsinki, 1937. Pp. 398.

A3672 Morison, Samuel Eliot. "The Universities of the Middle Ages and the Renaissance." *Rice Institute Pamphlet*, XXIII (1937), 211-245.

A3673 Gee, John Archer. "Berthelet's Latin-English Publication of the *Apophthegmata Graeciae Sapientum* and other Sayings formerly Edited by Erasmus." *SP*, XXXV (1938), 164-177.

A3674 Warren, Leslie C. *Humanistic Doctrines of the Prince from Petrarch to Sir Thomas Elyot: A Study of the Principal Analogues and Sources of "The Boke Named the Governour."* DD, University of Chicago, 1939.

A3675 Ashton, J. W. "The Fall of Icarus." *Renaissance Studies in Honor of Hardin Craig*, 1941, pp. 153-159; also *PQ*, XX, 345-351.

A3676 Schulz, Herbert C. "The Teaching of Handwriting in Tudor and Stuart Times." *HLQ*, VI (1943), 381-425.

A3677 Wright, Louis B. "Humanistic Education and the Democratic State." *South Atlantic Quar.*, XLII (1943), 142-153.

A3678 Adamson, John William. *"The Illiterate Anglo-Saxon" and Other Essays on Education, Medieval and Modern.* Cambridge Univ. Press, 1946. Pp. 167.
Includes, i.a., "Literacy in England in the Fifteenth and Sixteenth Centuries."
Rev: "The Early English Schools," *TLS*, Mar. 29, 1947, p. 138; *DUJ*, XXXIX, 77-78; by Angela Cave, *Catholic World*, 166 (1947), 181-182.

A3679 Pafort, Eloise. "A Group of Early Tudor School-books." *Library*, XXVI (1946), 227-261.

A3680 Curtis, S. J. *History of Education in Great Britain.* With a Foreword by W. R. Niblett. London: Univ. Tutorial Press, 1948. Pp. 407.

A3681 Allen, Phyllis. "Scientific Studies in the English Universities of the Seventeenth Century." *JHI*, X (1949), 219-253.

A3682 Barrington, Michael. " 'Learning and Virtue': Free Education." *N &Q*, 194 (1949), 359.

A3683 Richards, I. A. "The Places and the Figures." *KR*, XI (1949), 17-30.
Critical comment upon Donald L. Clark's *John Milton at St. Paul's School* and Sister Miriam Joseph's *Shakespeare's Use of the Arts of Language.*

A3684 Simonini, Rinaldo Charles, Jr. *Florio's Second Frutes: A Critical Edition.* DD, University of North Carolina, 1949. Abstr. publ. in *Univ. of North Carolina Record, Research in Progress*, Jan.-Dec., 1949, Grad. School Series, No. 58, pp. 115-116.

A3685 Goldschmidt, E. P. *The Printed Book of the Renaissance.* Cambridge Univ. Press, 1950. Pp. x, 93; il. 32; pl. 8. See T. M. Pearce, "The Vernacular Tongue in English Education." *RN*, IV, 11-12. (Takes exception to the statement in A3685 that only Latin was spoken in schools before 1550.) See reply by James G. McManaway, ibid., pp. 12-14; and notes by William Nelson, ibid., pp. 39-40; and Eva Matthews Sanford, ibid., pp. 70-72.
Rev: A2647.

A3686 Hexter, J. H. "The Education of the Aristocracy in the Renaissance." *JMH*, XXII (1950), 1-20.

A3687 Simonini, R. C., Jr. "The Genesis of Modern Language Teaching." *MLJ*, XXXV (1951), 179-186. Teachers and texts of Renaissance England.

A3688 Nelson, William. "The Teaching of English in Tudor Grammar Schools." *SP*, XLIX (1952), 119-143.

A3689 Stevens, Linton C. "Humanistic Education and the Hierarchy of Values in the Renaissance." *Renaissance Papers*, Univ. of South Carolina, 1955, pp. 55-64.

A3690 MacKinnon, M. H. M. "School Books Used at Eton College about 1600." *JEGP*, LVI (1957), 429-433.

A3691 Costello, William T., S. J. *The Scholastic Curriculum at Early Seventeenth-Century Cambridge.* Cambridge, Mass.: Harvard Univ. Press, 1958. Pp. 228.
Rev: by H. C. Porter, *Canadian Forum*, XXXVIII (1958), 186-187; *SCN*, XVI, 33; *TLS*, Dec. 5, p. 709.

A3692 Sherwin, Wilma. *The Rhetorical Structure of the English Sermon in the Sixteenth Century.* DD, University of Illinois, 1958. Pp. 180. Mic 58-5495. *DA*, XIX (1958), 1072.

A3693   Thompson, Craig R. *Schools in Tudor England*. Folger Booklets on Tudor and Stuart Civilization. Washington, D. C.: The Folger Shakespeare Library, 1958. Pp. 36, pl. 12.

(a) DICTIONARIES
i. Reprints

A3694   Cotgrave, Randle. *A Dictionarie of the French and English Tongues. Compiled by Randle Cotgrave.
London, Printed by Adam Islip. Anno 1611*. Facsimile Reproduction. Univ. South Carolina
Press, 1950. Pp. viii, 984.
Rev: by B. J. Whitney, *Speculum*, XXVII (1952), 94-96.

A3695   Holyband, Claudius. *The French Littleton*. Ed. of 1609 with an Introd. by M. St. Clare Byrne.
Cambridge Univ. Press, 1953. Pp. xxxii, 220.
A reprint of the 1609 ed. of this delightful manual for teaching French to Elizabethan children.
Rev: *TLS*, Mar. 20, 1953, p. 184 (see letter by Miss St. Clare Byrne, Mar. 27, p. 205);
N &Q, 198 (1953), 318; by D. M. S., *English*, IX, 193 (brief); by W. L. Wiley, *French Rev.*,
XXVII, 153-154.

ii. Studies

A3696   Starnes, D. T. "Bilingual Dictionaries of Shakespeare's Day." *PMLA*, LII (1937), 1005-18.

A3697   Starnes, D. T. "English Dictionaries of the Seventeenth Century." *TxSE*, XVII (1937), 15-51.
See also A3699.

A3698   Austin, Warren B. "Claudius Hollyband: An Elizabethan Schoolmaster." *N &Q*, 177 (1939),
237-240, 255-258.

A3699   Noyes, Gertrude "Some Interrelations of English Dictionaries of the Seventeenth Century."
PMLA, LIV (1939), 990-1006.

A3700   Starnes, D. T. "Literary Features of Renaissance Dictionaries." *SP*, XXXVII (1940), 26-50.

A3701   Noyes, Gertrude. "The First English Dictionary, Cawdrey's *Table Alphabeticall*." *MLN*,
LVIII (1943), 600-605.

A3702   Starnes, D. T., and E. W. Talbert. "John Milton and Renaissance Dictionaries." *TxSE*,
1943, pp. 50-65.

A3703   Starnes, D. T. "The Poetic Dictionary and the Poet." *Lib. Chron. Univ. Texas*, II (1946), 75-85.
Concerns the sixteenth and seventeenth centuries.

A3704   Starnes, DeWitt T., and Gertrude E. Noyes. *The English Dictionary from Cawdrey to Johnson,
1604-1755*. Univ. North Carolina Press, 1946. Pp. x, 299, facs. 16.
Rev: by Doris B. Saunders, *UTQ*, XVI (1946), 98-101; by Douglas Bush, *AHR*, LII, 172;
by R. W., *Lib. Chron. Univ. Texas*, II, 159-163; by F. K. Mitchell, *South Atlantic Quar.*, XLVI
(1947), 297; *TLS*, Aug. 9, p. 404; by A. G. Kennedy, *MLQ*, VIII, 376-379; by E. Coyle,
Classical Weekly, XLI, 23-27.

A3705   Smalley, Vera E. *The Sources of "A Dictionarie of the French and English Tongues" by Randle
Cotgrave (London, 1611)*. The Johns Hopkins University Studies in Romance Languages and
Literatures. Extra vol., XXV. The Johns Hopkins Press, 1948. Pp. 252.
Rev: by Raphael Levy, *MLN*, LXIV (1949), 431-432; by James Sledd, *MP*, XLVII, 135-139.

A3706   Starnes, De Witt T. "Thomas Cooper's 'Thesaurus': A Chapter in Renaissance Lexicography."
TxSE, XXVIII (1949), 15-48.

A3707   DeJongh, William F. J. *Western Language Manuals of the Renaissance*. Univ. New Mexico
Publ. in Lang. and Lit., No. 1. Univ. New Mexico Press, 1949. Pp. 46.

A3708   Starnes, D. T. "An Elizabethan *Dictionarie for Yonge Beginners*." *TxSE*, XXIX (1950), 51-76.
Concerns the provenance, sources, and history (1556-1634) of John Withals' dictionary.

A3709   Starnes, D. T. "Thomas Cooper and the *Bibliotheca Eliotae*." *TxSE*, XXX (1951), 40-60.

A3710   Sledd, James. "A Note on the Use of Renaissance Dictionaries." *MP*, XLIX (1951/52), 10-15.

A3711   Simonini, R. C., Jr. "The Italian Pedagogy of Claudius Hollyband." *SP*, XLIX (1952),
144-154.

A3712   Starnes, DeWitt T. *Renaissance Dictionaries: English-Latin and Latin-English*. Univ. of Texas
Press, 1954. Pp. 427.
Rev: by G. H. Valins, *English*, X (1955), 233-234 (brief); by Louis Bakelants, *RBPH*,
XXXIII, 638-639; by G. Shepherd, *MLR*, L, 522-523; by F. Mossé, *EA*, VIII, 249; by R. W.
Chapman, *RES*, VI, 79-80.

A3713   Starnes, DeWitt T., and Ernest W. Talbert. *Classical Myth and Legend in Renaissance Diction-
aries*. A Study of Renaissance Dictionaries in their Relation to the Classical Learning of
Contemporary English Writers. Univ. of North Carolina Press, 1956. Pp. vi, 517.
Rev: A4397.

A3714   Cancelled.

(2) SHAKESPEARE'S EDUCATION: NATURE AND EVIDENCE
(a) GENERAL STUDIES

A3715   Baldwin, T. W. *William Shakspere's Petty School*. Univ. of Illinois Press, 1943.

Rev: by H. S. Bennett, *RES*, xx (1944), 312-313; by Hardin Craig, *MLN*, LIX, 136-137; *TLS*, Feb. 5, p. 67; by G. D. Willcock, *MLR*, XXXIX, 76-78; by T. M. Parrott, *JEGP*, XLIII, 115-117; *TLS*, July 1, p. 318; by W. Clemen, *Archiv*, 188 (1951), 147-149.

A3716 Baldwin, Thomas Whitfield. *William Shakspere's Small Latine and Lesse Greeke.* 2 Vols. Univ. Illinois Press, 1944. Pp. xviii, 753; vi, 772.
Rev: A4163.

A3717 Marder, Louis. *Aspects of Shakespeare's Education.* DD, Columbia University, 1950. Pp. 291. Mic A50-149. *Microf. Ab.*, x (1950), 218. Publication No. 1880.

A3718 Whitaker, Virgil K. *Shakespeare's Use of Learning.* San Marino, California, 1953.
Rev: A3535.

(a) DETAILS AND BRIEF DISCUSSIONS

A3719 Anders, Heinrich. *Shakespeares Belesenheit.* DD, Berlin, Humboldt University, 1900. Pp. 32.

A3720 Barker, E. "A Shakespeare Discovery." *Spectator*, 158 (1937), 615-616.
Troil. & Elyot's *Governor.*

A3721 Münch, R. "Shakespeares Schule. Zum 375. Geburtstag des Dichters." *Der niedersächsische Erzieher*, July, 1939, pp. 182-185.

A3722 Messiaen, Pierre. "L'Érudition de Shakespeare." *Rev. Bleue Politique et Littéraire*, LXXVII (1939), 181-185.

A3723 Baldwin, T. W. "Perseus Purloins Pegasus." *Renaissance Studies in Honor of Hardin Craig*, 1941, pp. 169-178; also *PQ*, xx, 361-370.
See also John M. Steadman, " 'Perseus upon Pegasus' and *Ovid Moralized.*" *RES*, IX (1958) 407-410.

A3724 Brown, D. "What Shakespeare Learned at School." *Bucknell University Studies*, I (1941), 1-20.

A3725 Ott, Karl. "Über Zweisprachigkeit." *N. Mon.*, XII (1941), 81-101; 121-143; 175-194.

A3726 Ray, P. C. "The Learning of Shakespeare." *Calcutta Rev.*, LXXVII (1941), 131-140.

A3727 "Shakespeare's Learning." *TLS*, May 15, 1943, p. 235.

A3728 Law, Robert Adger. "Some Books That Shakespeare Read." *Lib. Chron. Univ. Texas*, (1944/45), 14-18.

A3729 Harbage, Alfred. "Shakespeare's Ideal Man." *AMS*, pp. 65-80.

A3730 Simonini, Rinaldo Charles, Jr. *The Language Lesson Dialogue in Shakespearean Drama.* MA thesis, University of North Carolina, 1946. Abstr. publ. in *Univ. of North Carolina Record, Research in Progress*, Grad. School Series, No. 56, 1949, pp. 229.

A3731 Baldwin, T. W. "Shakspere's Aphthonian Man." *MLN*, LXV (1950), 111-112.

A3732 Boas, F. S. *Queen Elizabeth in Drama, And Related Studies.* London, 1950. "Aspects of Shakespeare's Reading," pp. 56-71.
Rev: B4458.

A3733 Wilson, F. P. "Shakespeare's Reading." *ShS*, III (1950), 14-21.

A3734 Simonini, R. C., Jr. "Language Lesson Dialogues in Shakespeare." *SQ*, II (1951), 319-329.

A3735 Wickham, Glynne. "Shakespeare's 'Small Latine and Less Greeke'." *Talking of Shakespeare.* Ed. by John Garrett. London: Hodder & Stoughton & Max Reinhardt, 1954.

A3736 Nakamura, Rikuo. "Shakespeare and Education" (in Japanese). *Shinshu Daigaku Study Report* (Uyeda), March, 1956.

A3737 Sheppard, Sir John. "Shakespeare's Small Latin." *Rice Institute Pamphlet*, XLIV (1957), 70-86.

A3738 Thaler, Alwin. "Shakespeare and Our World." *Tennessee Studies in Literature*, II (1957), 105-120.

A3739 Wilson, J. Dover. "Shakespeare's 'Small Latin'—How Much?" *ShS*, x (1957), 12-26.

A3740 Price, Hereward Thimbleby. "Shakespeare's Classical Scholarship." *RES*, IX (1958), 54-55.

f. SUPPLEMENT: THE THOUGHT AND LEARNING OF SHAKESPEARE'S TIMES (63,173;24,60)
See also earlier sections on Science, Astrology, Astronomy, Alchemy, Chemistry, etc.
(1) THE NATURE OF THE RENAISSANCE

A3741 Delattre, F. "E. Legouis et la Renaissance Anglaise." *EA*, July, 1939, pp. 240-257.

A3742 Ferguson, W. K. *The Renaissance.* New York, 1940. Pp. viii, 148.

A3743 Förster, Max. "The Psychological Basis of Literary Periods." *Studies for William A. Read. A Miscellany Presented by Some of His Colleagues and Friends.* Ed. by Nathaniel M. Caffee and Thomas A. Kirby. University, Louisiana: La. State Univ. Press, 1940, pp. 254-268.

A3744 Wilkinson, Walter W. J. "The Meaning of the Renaissance." *Thought*, XVI (1941), 444-456.

A3745 Weisinger, Herbert. *The Idea of the Renaissance from Petrarch to Hallam.* DD, University of Michigan, 1941. Pp. 555. *Microf. Ab.*, III, No. 2 (1941), 62. Publication No. 280.

A3746 Weisinger, Herbert. "Renaissance Theories of the Revival of the Fine Arts." *Italica*, XX (1943), 163-170.

A3747 Baron, Hans. "Articulation and Unity in the Italian Renaissance and in the Modern West." *Annual Report Amer. Hist. Assoc., 1942*, III (1944), 123-138.

A3748 Weisinger, Herbert. "The Self-Awareness of the Renaissance as a Criterion of the Renaissance." *Papers Michigan Acad. Sci., Arts, and Letters*, XXIX (1943), 650-657.

A3749 Akrigg, G. P. V. "The Renaissance Reconsidered." *QQ*, LII (1945), 311-319.

A3750 Weisinger, Herbert. "Who Began the Revival of Learning? The Renaissance Point of View." *Papers Michigan Acad. Sci., Arts, and Letters*, XXX (1945), 625-638.

A3751 Weisinger, Herbert. "The Renaissance Theory of the Reaction Against the Middle Ages as a Cause of the Renaissance." *Speculum*, XX (1945), 461-467.

A3752 Williams, John Rodney. "The Concept of the Renaissance: Its Development Among the Great French Historians of the Nineteenth Century." DD, Harvard University, 1942. Abstr. in Harvard Univ. *Summaries of Ph. D. Theses, 1942* (1946), pp. 320-324.

A3753 Weisinger, Herbert. "The Study of the Revival of Learning in England from Bacon to Hallam." *PQ*, XXV (1946), 221-247.

A3754 Weisinger, Herbert. "The Idea of the Renaissance and the Rise of Science." *Lychnos*, X (1946/47), 11-35.

A3755 Weisinger, Herbert. "English Attitudes Toward the Relationship Between the Renaissance and the Reformation." *Church Hist.*, XIV (1945), 167-187.

A3756 Ferguson, Wallace K. *The Renaissance in Historical Thought: Five Centuries of Interpretation.* Boston: Houghton Mifflin, 1948. Pp. xiii, 429.
       See the tr., *La Renaissance dans la Pensée Historique*, préface de V. L. Saulnier (Paris: Payot, 1950, pp. 384); and the brief article by Mr. Ferguson "The Renaissance: A Synthesis," *RN*, III (1950), 41-43.
       Rev: by W. W. J. Wilkinson, *Catholic Hist. Rev.*, XXXV (1949), 322-323; by W. F. Church, *Speculum*, XXIV, 431-433; by Garrett Mattingly, *SRL*, XXXII, 10; by J. W. Swain, *JEGP*, XLIX (1950), 252-254; by C. Trinkaus, *RN*, III, 1-4; by H. Baron, *AHR*, LV, 864-866; by H. Baron, *JHI*, XI, 493-510; by Francis R. Johnson, *MLQ*, XII (1951), 108-110; by J. H. Hexter, *JMH*, XXIII, 257-261 (of French tr. by Jacques Marty [Paris: Payot, 1950]); by V. L. Saulnier, *BHR*, XIII, 212-213; by Walter J. Ong, *Etudes*, September, 1951, pp. 272-273; by Dom Leon Robert, *RHE*, XLVI, 270-280.

A3757 Gérard, A. "Shakespeare et l'Esprit de la Renaissance." *Synthèses*, III (1948), 170-176.

A3758 Weisinger, Herbert. "Renaissance Accounts of the Revival of Learning." *SP*, XLV (1948), 105-118.

A3759 Bennett, Josephine W. "On the Causes of the Renaissance." *RN*, II (1949), 5-6.

A3760 Ferguson, Wallace K. "The Renaissance: A Synthesis." *RN*, III (1950), 41-43.

A3761 Sellery, George Clarke. *The Renaissance: Its Nature and Origins.* Univ. Wisconsin Press, 1950. Pp. xii, 296.
       Rev: by Hardin Craig, *YR*, XL (1950), 343-345; *Catholic World*, 172 (1950), 80; *ConR*, Dec., 1950, p. 382; by T. C. Chubb, *NYTBR*, Sept. 17, p. 20; by Robert Halsband, *SRL*, March 17, 1951, p. 40; by R. W., *EHR*, LXVI, 290-291; by Arthur B. Ferguson, *South Atlantic Quar.*, L, 127-129; by Charles T. Harrison, *SR*, LIX, 693-694; by Elio Gianturco, *Erasmus*, IV, 766-770; by Jewell Wurtzbaugh, *RN*, IV, 44-45 (see letter by George B. Parks, ibid., 70); by J. P. Heisler, *Dalhousie Rev.*, XXXI, No. 1, xxxii-xxxiii; by Bernard Mandel, *JMH*, XXIII, 291-292; by Walter W. J. Wilkinson, *Catholic Hist. Rev.*, XXXVII, 323-324.

A3762 Weisinger, Herbert. "The English Origins of the Sociological Interpretation of the Renaissance." *JHI*, XI (1950), 321-338.

A3763 Ferguson, Wallace K. "The Interpretation of the Renaissance: Suggestion for a Synthesis." *JHI*, XII (1951), 483-495.

A3764 Tillyard, E. M. W. *English Renaissance: Fact or Fiction?* Baltimore: Johns Hopkins Press; London: Hogarth; Toronto: Clarke, Irwin, 1952. Pp. 118.
       Rev: *TLS*, June 20, 1952, p. 405; by Michel Poirier, *EA*, V, 355; by Oliver Warner, *Time and Tide*, May 10, 1952, p. 496; *NstN*, May 24, p. 627; by B. Ifor Evans, *MGW*, May 29, p. 11; by Rosemond Tuve, *MLN*, LXVIII (1953), 421-423 (important); by J. Vallette, *MdF*, 317 (1953), 529-531.

A3765 Montano, Rocco. "Idea del Rinascimento." *Delta*, NS, No. 10 (1957), pp. 1-32; No. 13, pp. 1-35.

A3766 Schalk, Fritz. "Zur Interpretation des Humanismus und der Renaissance." *Wissenschaftliche Annalen*, VI (1957), 93-100.

(2) THOUGHT AND LEARNING
(a) REPRINTS OF TEXTS

A3767 Elyot, Sir Thomas. *Of the Knowledge Which Maketh a Wise Man.* Ed. by Edwin Johnston Howard. Oxford, Ohio: Anchor Press, 1946. Pp. xxxii, 260.
       Rev: *TLS*, Sept. 21, 1946, p. 452; by D. C. Allen, *MLN*, LXII (1947), 58-59; by John Butt,

RES, XXIII, 273-275; by J. L. Lievsay, *MLQ*, IX (1948), 245; by G. D. Willcock, *MLR*, XLIII, 103-104.

A3768 Cassirer, Ernst, Paul Oskar Kristeller, and John Herman Randall, Jr., eds. *The Renaissance Philosophy of Man*. Univ. of Chicago Press, 1948. Pp. viii, 405. Reissued 1956. Selections from the work of Petrarch, Valla, Ficino, Pico Della Mirandola, Pomponazzi, and Vives translated into English with a general introduction and with separate introductions for each.
Rev: by W. F. Church, *Speculum*, XXIV (1949), 112-113; by E. Williamson, *MLN*, LXIV, 210-211; by Quirinus Breen, *Church Hist.*, XVIII, 185-187; by A. R. Caponigri, *NYTBR*, Feb. 6, p. 21; by E. H. Wilkins, *Italica*, XXVI, 298-300; by E. W. Talley, *Thought*, XXIV, 548-549; by W. W. J. Wilkinson, *Catholic Hist. Rev.*, XXXVI (1950), 351-352; by H. Weisinger, *MLQ*, XI, 106-108; by R. Weiss, *MLR*, XLV, 401-402; by R. W. Battenhouse, *Jour. of Religion*, XXX, 74-75; by Max H. Fisch, *Philos. Rev.*, LX (1951), 109-111; by J. B. Hawkins, *PQ*, XXXVI (1957), 379.

A3768a Nugent, Elizabeth M., ed. *The Thought and Culture of the English Renaissance: An Anthology of Tudor Prose, 1481-1555.* Cambridge Univ. Press, 1956.

A3769 Winny, James, ed. *The Frame of Order*. An Outline of Elizabethan Belief Taken from Treatises of the Late Sixteenth Century. London: Allen & Unwin, 1957. Pp. 224.
Rev: by Helen Gardner, *London Mag.*, IV, No. 12 (1957), 73-74; 77-78.

A3770 Hearnshaw, F. J. C., ed. *The Social and Political Ideas of Some Great Thinkers of the Renaissance and the Reformation. The Social and Political Ideas of Some Great Thinkers of the Sixteenth and Seventeenth Centuries.* New York: Barnes & Noble, 1949. Pp. 216; 220.

(b) SCHOLASTICISM, ARISTOTELIANISM,
CHRISTIAN HUMANISM, AND PLATONISM

A3771 Nathan, Walter Ludwig. *Sir John Cheke und der englische Humanismus*. DD, Bonn, 1928. Pp. 106.

A3772 Elliott-Binnx, L. E. *England and the New Learning: A Fresh Study of the Renaissance*. London: Lutterworth Press, 1937. Pp. 110.
Rev: *TLS*, Dec. 18, 1937, pp. 905-906.

A3773 Amar, André. "Entretiens sur l'Humanisme." *Revue hebdomadaire*, July 1, 1939, pp. 44-55. Essay on the spirit of the Renaissance.

A3774 Bush, Douglas. *The Renaissance and English Humanism*. Univ. Toronto Press, 1939. Pp. 139.
Rev: by Alice Walker, *RES*, XVI (1940), 337-338; by N. J. E., *Canadian Forum*, XX, 61; by R. V. Cram, *Classical Weekly*, XXXIII, 212-213; *TLS*, Jan. 18, 1941, p. 32; by B. E. C. Davis, *MLR*, XXXVI, 256-258; by J. M. Lenhart, *Catholic Hist. Rev.*, XXVII, 124-125.

A3775 Meissner, Paul. "Renaissance und Humanismus im Rahmen der nationalenglischen Kulturidee." *SJ*, LXXII (1937), 9-30. See also supplementary article with the same title in *FuF*, XIII (1937), 231-232.

A3776 Warren, Leslie C. *Humanistic Doctrines of the Prince from Petrarch to Sir Thomas Elyot: A Study of the Principal Analogues and Sources of "The Boke Named the Governour."* DD, University of Chicago, 1938.

A3777 Lockwood, Dean P., and Roland H. Bainton. "Classical and Biblical Scholarship in the Age of the Renaissance and Reformation." *Church Hist.*, X (1941), 125-143.

A3778 Weiss, Roberto. *Humanism in England During the Fifteenth Century*. Oxford: Blackwell, 1941. Pp. xxiii, 190.
Rev: *TLS*, June 7, 1941, p. 278; by A. L. Rowse, *Spectator*, June 20, pp. 658-660; by Douglas Bush, *Speculum*, XVII (1942), 149-150; by S. Gaselee, *CR*, LVI, 47-48; by Cecilia M. Ady, *Medium Aevum*, X, 173-175; by J. W. H. Atkins, *MLR*, XXXVIII (1943), 353-354.

A3779 Wilson, Harold S. *Concepts of 'Nature' in the Rhetorical Tradition: A Chapter in the History of Classical Humanism Before Ben Jonson*. DD, Harvard University, 1939. Abstr. in Harvard Univ., *Summaries of Theses, 1939* (1942), pp. 255-257.

A3780 Guppy, Henry. "The Dawn of the Revival of Learning." *BJRL*, XXVI (1942), 206-223, 413-430.

A3781 Renaudet, Augustin. "Autour d'une Définition de l'Humanisme." *BHR*, VI (1945), 7-49.

A3782 Dupront, A. "Espace et Humanisme." *BHR*, VIII (1946), 7-104.

A3783 Hering, Jean. *Die Biblische Grundlagen des Christlichen Humanismus*. Zurich: Zwingli Verlag, 1946. Pp. 358.

A3784 Toffanin, G. *Geschichte des Humanismus*. Tr. by Dr. Lili Sartorius. Amsterdam, 1941. Pp. vii, 528.
Rev: by Marie Delcourt, *RBPH*, XXII (1943), 244-245.

A3785 Oppel, Horst. *Der englische Humanismus im Zeitalter Elisabeths*. Mainz: Kupferberg, 1947. Pp. 24.

A3786 Van Gelder, H. A. Enno, K. H. Heeroma, G. Kazemier, and M. D. E. De Leve. *Humanisme et Renaissance*. The Hague: Servire, 1948. Pp. 148.

A3787 Hermans, Francis. *Histoire Doctrinale de l'Humanisme Chrétien*. 4 Vols. Paris: Casterman, 1948. Pp. 244; 392; 544; 348.
Rev: by Parl Vuillaud, *Paru*, No. 47, Oct., 1948, pp. 57-58.

A3788 Phillips, Elias H. *Humanitas in Tudor Literature (1475-1575)*. DD, Pennsylvania University, 1949.

A3789 Trinkaus, Charles. "The Problem of Free Will in the Renaissance and the Reformation." *JHI*, x (1949), 51-62. As expressed, i.a., in Ficino, Pico, Valla, and Pomponazzi.

A3790 De Lagarde, Georges. "La Conception Médiévale de l'Ordre en Face de l'Humanisme, de la Renaissance et de la Réforme." *Umanesimo e scienza politica. Atti del Congresso Internazionale di Studi Umanistici, Roma, Firenze, 1949* (A cura di Enrico Castelli; Centro internazionale di studi umanistici; Milan: Carlo Marzorati, 1951), pp. 237-245.

A3791 Castelli, A. *Note sull'Umanesimo in Inghilterra*. Milan: Vita e Pensiero, 1950. Pp. 86.

A3792 Jayne, Sears. "Ficino and the Platonism of the English Renaissance." *CL*, IV (1952), 214-238.

A3793 Meissner, Paul. *England im Zeitalter von Humanismus, Renaissance und Reformation*. Heidelberg: F. H. Kerle, 1952. Pp. 656.
       Rev: by S. B. Liljegren, *SN*, xxv (1953), 195-196; by R. Spindler, *NS*, NS, II, 410-412; by K. Brunner, *SJ*, 90 (1954), 351-354.

A3794 Siegel, Paul N. "English Humanism and the New Tudor Aristocracy." *JHI*, xiii (1952), 450-468.

A3795 Caspari, Fritz. *Humanism and the Social Order in Tudor England*. Univ. Chicago Press, 1954. Pp. ix, 293. Includes studies on Erasmus, Sir Thomas More, Sir Thomas Elyot, Thomas Starkey, Sir Philip Sidney, and Edmund Spenser.
       Rev: by R. A. Preston, *Canadian Hist. Rev.*, xxxv (1954), 336-337; by William A. Armstrong, *YWES*, xxxv, 89; by Myron P. Gilmore, *RN*, VIII (1955), 24-27; by Quirinus Breen, *Church Hist.*, xxiv, 375-376; *TLS*, Sept. 30, p. 567; *N &Q*, NS, II, 492-495, 502-503; by Douglas Bush, *Speculum*, xxx, 96-97; by G. R. Elton, *EHR*, lxx, 483-484; by H. R. Trevor-Roper, *History Today*, VI (1956), 69-70; by D. P. Walker, *BHR*, xviii, 153.

A3796 Cassirer, Ernst. *The Plantonic Renaissance in England*. Tr. by J. P. Pettegrove. Univ. Texas Press, 1954. Pp. 216.
       Rev: by Rose Macaulay, *NstN*, May 29, 1954, p. 708.

A3797 Weiss, Roberto. "Codici Umanistici in Inghilterra." *GSLI*, 136 (1954), 386-395.

A3798 Chester, Allan G. "The 'New Learning': A Semantic Note." *Studies in the Renaissance*, Vol. II. Ed. M. A. Shaaber. New York, 1955, pp. 139-147.

A3799 Gallagher, Ligera Cécile. *Shakespeare and the Aristotelian Ethical Tradition*. DD, Stanford University, 1956. Pp. 338. Mic 56-3017. *DA*, xvi (1956), 1898. Publ. No. 17,720.

A3800 Ray, Don Eldon. *"In Whom Lay the Pattern of a Christian Hero:" Milton and the Elizabethan Tradition of Christian Learning*. DD, Rice Institute, 1957.

A3801 Renaudet, Augustin. *Humanisme et Renaissance. Dante, Pétrarque, Standonck, Erasme, Lefèvre d'Etaples, Marguerite de Navarre, Rabelais, Guichardin, Giordano Bruno*. Travaux d'Humanisme et Renaissance, No. 30. Geneva: Droz, 1958. Pp. 280.

(c) OPTIMISM AND PESSIMISM

A3802 Allen, Don Cameron. "The Degeneration of Man and Renaissance Pessimism." *SP*, xxxv (1938), 202-227.

A3803 Osenburg, Frederic C. *The Ideas of the Golden Age and the Decay of the World in the English Renaissance*. DD, University of Illinois, 1939. Abstr. in Univ. of Illinois *Abstracts of Theses*, Urbana, 1939, p. 18.

A3804 Williams, Arnold L. "A Note on Pessimism in the Renaissance." *SP*, xxxvi (1939), 243-246.

A3805 Harris, Victor I. *The Seventeenth Century Controversy Over the Decay of Nature*. DD, University of Chicago, 1945. Pp. 287.

A3806 Adams, Robert P. "Designs by More and Erasmus for a New Social Order." *SP*, xlii (1945), 131-145.

A3807 Dewey, Rebecca A. *The Idea of Progress in Elizabethan Literature*. DD, Stanford University, 1947. Abstr. publ. in *Abstracts of Dissertations, 1946-1947*, Stanford, 1947, pp. 31-36.

A3808 Harris, Victor. *All Coherence Gone*. Univ. Chicago Press, 1949. Pp. x, 255.
       Concerns the seventeenth century controversy on the decay of Nature, emphasizing Godfrey Goodman's *The Fall of Man* (1616, 1618, etc.) and George Hakewill's attacks on Goodman's position (1627-35), sketches the development of the controversy with emphasis on sixteenth century English writers of prose and verse, and discusses the basic arguments.

A3809 Strathmann, Ernest A. "The Idea of Progress: Some Elizabethan Considerations." *RN*, II (1949), 23-25.

A3810 Tuveson, Ernest L. *Millenium and Utopia: A Study in the Background of the Idea of Progress*. Univ. Calif. Press, 1949. Pp. xi, 254.
       Rev: by G. N. Conklin, *RN*, III (1950), 47-48; by G. R. Stephenson, *NYTBR*, Mar. 5, p. 18; by Clark Emery, *MLQ*, xii (1951), 501-502.

A3811 Keller, A. C. "Zilsel, the Artisans, and the Idea of Progress in the Renaissance." *JHI*, xi (1950), 235-240.
       Criticizes the theories of Edgar Zilsel by focussing attention on Rabelais, Bodin, and LeRoy.

A3812 Keller, Abraham C. "Ancients and Moderns in the Early Seventeenth Century." *MLQ*, XI (1950), 79-82.
Notes possible relationships among writers who "believed in progress" (particularly the Sieur de Pampalle, George Hakewill, Lancellotti).

A3813 Borinski, Ludwig. "Die Tragische Periode der Englischen Literatur." *NS*, NS, IV (1955), 289-307.

A3814 Bennett, Josephine Waters. "Britain Among the Fortunate Isles." *SP*, LIII (1956), 114-140.

(d) FAITH, REASON, SCEPTICISM, AND FREE THOUGHT

A3815 Lindsay, Jack. "Donne and Giordano Bruno." *TLS*, June 20, 1936, p. 523.
See letters by Richard Ince, *TLS*, June 27, 1936, p. 544; by Frances A. Yates, ibid., July 4, p. 564; by Mr. Lindsay, ibid., July 11, p. 580.

A3816 Whitaker, Virgil K. "Du Bartas' Use of Lucretius." *SP*, XXXIII (1936), 134-146.

A3817 Coffin, Charles Monroe. *John Donne and the New Philosophy*. Columbia Univ. Press, 1937. Pp. ix, 311.
Rev: *TLS*, Aug. 21, 1937, p. 604; by Mark Van Doren, *Nation* (N. Y.), 144 (1937), 442-443; by Grant McColley, *Annals of Science*, II, 475-476; by Pierre Legouis, *EA*, II (1938), 46-48; by R. F. Jones, *SR*, XLVI, 261-263; by M. F. Ashley Montagu, *Isis*, XXVIII, 473-475; by F. R. Johnson, *MLN*, LIII, 290-293; by I. A. Shapiro, *MLR*, XXXIII, 280-281; by R. T. F., *Personalist*, XIX, 315-318; by Rudolf Metz, *Eng. Studn.*, LXXIII (1939), 397-401; by F. E. Budd, *RES*, XV, 101-103.

A3818 Henderson, P., et al. "Philip Sidney and Bruno." *TLS*, Oct. 9, 1937, p. 735; Oct. 16, p. 759.

A3819 Orsini, N. *Bacon e Machiavelli*. Genoa: E. degli Orfini, 1936. Pp. 211.
Rev: by W. Keller, *SJ*, LXXIII (1937), 171; by J. G. Fucilla, *Books Abroad*, XI (1938), 488; by J. H. Whitfield, *English*, I (1939), 359-360.

A3820 Moloney, Michael F. *John Donne: The Flight from Mediaevalism*. DD, University of Illinois, 1939.

A3821 Collins, Joseph B. *Christian Mysticism in the Elizabethan Age with Its Background in Mystical Methodology*. Baltimore: Johns Hopkins Press; London: Milford, 1940. Pp. xvi, 251.

A3822 Doran, Madeleine. "On Elizabethan 'Credulity': With Some Questions Concerning the Use of the Marvelous in Literature." *JHI*, I (1940), 151-176.

A3823 Wiley, Margaret L. *Scepticism in the Writings of John Donne, Richard Baxter, Jeremy Taylor, Sir Thomas Brown, and Joseph Glanvill*. DD, Radcliffe College, 1940.

A3824 Strathmann, Ernest A. "The *History of the World* and Ralegh's Skepticism." *HLQ*, III (1940), 265-287.

A3825 Strathmann, Ernest A. "Sir Walter Ralegh on Natural Philosophy." *MLQ*, I (1940), 49-61.

A3826 Doran, Madeleine. "That Undiscovered Country: A Problem Concerning the Use of the Supernatural in *Hamlet* and *Macbeth*." *Renaissance Studies in Honor of Hardin Craig*, 1941, pp. 221-235. Also, *PQ*, XX, 413-427.

A3827 Hudson, Hoyt H. "The Transition in Poetry." *HLQ*, V (1942), 188-190.
Taking place about 1595. "Psychological and erotic realism" "rationalism, skepticism and cynicism."

A3828 Johnson, Francis R. "Marlowe's Astronomy and Renaissance Skepticism." *ELH*, XIII (1946), 241-254.

A3829 Greenwood, Thomas. "L'Éclosion du Scepticisme pendant la Renaissance et les Premiers Apologistes." *Rev. de l'Univ. d'Ottawa*, XVII (1947), 66-99.

A3830 Flint, Robert W. "The Tragedy of *Hamlet*." *Union Seminary Quarterly Rev.*, II, iii (1947), 20-25.
Suggests much scepticism in the times and in Shak. Declares the tragedies non-Christian.

A3831 Allen, D. C. "*Hamlet* and the Wages of Reason." *The Univ. of Chicago Magazine*, XLI, No. 11 (1948), 6-9, 21.

A3832 Allen, D. C. "Style and Certitude." *ELH*, XV (1948), 167-175. On the relations between philosophic certainty and style in the late sixteenth and early seventeenth centuries.

A3833 Jacquot, Charles Jean Marcel. *Etude sur la Question de l'Athéisme dans l'Angleterre Elisabéthaine*. Thèse de lettres complémentaire, Lyon, 1949.

A3834 Ribner, Irving. *Machiavelli and Sir Philip Sidney* DD, University of North Carolina, 1949. Abstr. publ. in *Univ. of North Carolina Record, Research in Progress*, Grad. School Series, No. 58, Jan.-Dec., 1949, pp. 113-115.

A3835 Ribner, Irving. "The Significance of Gentillet's *Contre-Machiavel*." *MLQ*, X (1949), 153-157.

A3836 Haydn, Hiram. *The Counter-Renaissance: A Comprehensive History of the Intellectual Cross-currents of the Renaissance and Reformation and their Impact upon the Elizabethans, with Special Reference to Shakespeare, Bacon, Donne and Marlowe*. DD, Columbia University, 1950. New York: Scribner's 1950. Pp. xvii, 705.
Shak., pp. 598-667.
Rev: by Hardin Craig, *YR*, XL (1950), 343-345; by W. K. Ferguson, *RN*, III, 64-65; by D. M. Frame, *RR*, XLI, 284, 289; by J. H. Randall, Jr., *SRL*, June 24, p. 21; by D. Bush,

NYHTBR, May 21, p. 14; by H. Kohn, *NYTBR*, Apr. 23, p. 18; *CE*, XI, 58; by Hugh I'A. Fausset, *MGW*, July 12, 1951, p. 11, by Charles T. Harrison, *SR*, LIX, 694-696; by Paul Oskar Kristeller, *JHI*, XII, 468-472; by J. H. Hexter, *JMH*, XXIII, 257-261; by W. Gordon Zeeveld, *AHR*, LVI, 330-332; by Malcolm Ross, *QQ*, LVIII, 276-279; by C. Cantimori, *Annali della Scuola Norm. Sup. di Pisa*, XX, 164-167; by A. A., *Personalist*, XXXIII (1952), 293-294; by Myron P. Gilmore, *Speculum*, XXVIII (1953), 170-174; by Yves Bonnefoy, *Annales*, VIII, 123-125.

A3837 Nicolson, Marjorie Hope. *The Breaking of the Circle: Studies in the Effect of the "New Science" upon Seventeenth Century Poetry.* The Norman Wait Harris Lectures delivered at Northwestern University, July, 1949. Northwestern Univ. Press, 1950. Pp. xxii, 193.
Rev: A2081.

A3838 Pagel, Walter. "The Circular Motion of the Blood and Giordano Bruno's Philosophy of the Circle." *Bul. Hist. Med.*, XXIV (1950), 398-399.
Suggests Bruno as a link between Cesalpino and Harvey; see also Mr. Pagel's "Harvey's Role in the History of Medicine," ibid., XXIV, 70-73 (on the Harvey-Cesalpino controversy).

A3839 Parkes, H. B. "Nature's Diverse Laws: The Double Vision of the Elizabethans." *SR*, LVIII (1950), 402-418.
Examines the conflict between traditional moral and religious attitudes and the new naturalistic attitudes, in late Eliz. and Jacobean literature, with numerous references to the plays of Shak.

A3840 Wiley, Margaret L. "John Donne and the Poetry of Scepticism." *Hibbert Jour.*, XLVIII (1950), 163-172. Is based on C. M. Coffin's *John Donne and the New Philosophy*, A3817.

A3841 Maxwell, J. C. "Donne and the 'New Philosophy'." *DUJ*, XII (1951), 61-64.
Observes (1) the lack of evidence for regarding the "new philosophy" (here, the Copernican cosmology) as "an emotionally disconcerting theory;" and (2) Donne's rhetorical utilization of the sciences, new and old.

A3842 Hoopes, Robert. "Fideism and Skepticism During the Renaissance: Three Major Witnesses." *HLQ*, XIV (1951), 319-347. The three witnesses are Luther, Calvin, and Montaigne.

A3843 Strathmann, Ernest A. *Sir Walter Ralegh: A Study in Elizabethan Skepticism.* New York: Columbia Univ. Press; London, Toronto: Oxford Univ. Press, 1951. Pp. ix, 292.
Rev: *TLS*, August 24, 1951, p. 533; by Harold S. Wilson, *SQ*, II, 358-359; by Margaret Wintringham, *Time and Tide*, Sept. 29, pp. 925-926; by George L. Mosse, *AHR*, LVII, 126-127; by Winthrop S. Hudson, *Church Hist.*, XX, 4, 88-90; by Raymond P. Stearns, *William and Mary Quar.*, IX (1952), 112-114; by Arthur B. Ferguson, *South Atlantic Quar.*, LI (1952), 164-165; by Garland Greever, *Personalist*, XXXIII, 214-215; by J. Jacquot, *EA*, V, 247-248.

A3844 Wiley, Margaret L. *The Subtle Knot: Creative Scepticism in Seventeenth Century England.* Cambridge: Harvard Univ. Press; London: Allen & Unwin, 1952. Pp. 303.
Rev: by A. L. Hilliard, *Western Humanities Rev.*, VI (1952), 389-391; by H. L. Short, *Hibbert Jour.*, LI (1953), 316, 319; *TLS*, Jan. 16, p. 36; *Adelphi*, XXIX, 261-262; by Ernest Sirluck, *MP*, LI, 68; by F. S. Boas, *English*, IX, 142-143; by Jackson I. Cope, *MLN*, LXIX (1954), 192-197.

A3845 Ornstein, Robert. *The Ethics of Jacobean Tragedy, A Study of the Influence of Renaissance Free Thought.* DD, University of Wisconsin, 1954. Abstr. publ. in *Summaries of Doctoral Dissertations, 1953-54*, Vol. XV, Madison: Univ. of Wisconsin Press, 1955, pp. 622-624.

A3846 Warhaft, Sidney. *New Worlds of Ignorance: A Survey of Counter-Humanistic Attitudes toward Learning and Knowledge in England, 1595-1670.* DD, Northwestern University, 1954. Pp. 367. Mic A54-2548. *DA*, XIV (1954), 1737. Publication No. 9284.

A3847 Carre, Meyrick H. "The New Philosophy and the Divines." *Church Quar. Rev.*, 156 (1955), 33-44.

A3848 Goldman, Marcus S. "Sidney and Harington as Opponents of Superstition." *JEGP*, LIV (1955), 526-548.

A3849 Bodtke, Richard A. *Tragedy and the Jacobean Temper: A Critical Study of John Webster.* DD, Columbia University, 1957. Pp. 454. Mic 57-2485. *DA*, XVII (1957), 1550. Publication No. 21,630. Chap. I: An Age of Skepticism, pp. 25-76.

A3850 West, Muriel. *The Devil and John Webster: A Study of the Characters in "The White Devil" and "The Duchess of Malfi" Based on Imagery in the Plays Related to Ideas Current in the Jacobean Period Concerning Demonology and Witchcraft.* DD, University of Arkansas, 1957. Pp. 411. Mic 57-1720. *DA*, XVII (1957), 1077. Publication No. 20,607. Skepticism of Webster the physician, pp. 341-342.

A3851 Smith, Warren D. "The Elizabethan Rejection of Judicial Astrology and Shakespeare's Practice." *SQ*, IX (1958), 159-176.

A3852 Whitlock, Baird W. "The Counter-Renaissance." *BHR*, XX (1958), 434-449.
Proposes a new name for the period 1520-1620.

(e) MISCELLANEOUS

A3853 Litchfield, Florence LeD. *The Treatment of the Theme of Mutability in the Literature of the English Renaissance: A Study of the Problems of Change Between 1558 and 1660.* DD, University of Minnesota, 1935. Abstr. publ. in Univ. of Minnesota *Summaries of Ph.D. Theses*, Minneapolis, 1939, pp. 164-168.

A3854 Wright, Louis B. *Middle-class Culture in Elizabethan England.* Univ. of North Caroline Press, 1935. Pp. xiv, 733. Republished 1958.
Rev: A1909.

A3855 Allen, Don Cameron. "Symbolic Color in the Literature of the English Renaissance." *PQ*, XV (1936), 81-92. See also A3876.

A3856 Bainton, Roland H. "Changing Ideas and Ideals in the Sixteenth Century." *JMH*, VIII (1936), 417-443.

A3857 Craig, Hardin. *The Enchanted Glass. The Elizabethan Mind in Literature.* Oxford Univ. Press, 1936. Pp. ix, 293.
Rev: by Mark Van Doren, *Nation* (N. Y.), 143 (1936), 108-109; by A. L. Rowse, *Spectator*, July 31, pp. 208-209; by James Southall Wilson, *VQR*, XII, 636-640; by L. C. Knights, *Criterion*, LXII, 187-188; *N &Q*, 171 (1936), 359; *TLS*, Dec. 5, p. 1017; by Tucker Brooke, *SRL*, Aug. 1, p. 13; by Albert Guérard, Jr., *NYHTBR*, Sept. 20, p. 14X; by Thomas Good, *Life and Letters*, XV, 200-201; by Percy Hutchinson, *NYTBR*, May 31, p. 2; by Georges Connes, *EA*, I (1937), 137; by Edwin E. Willoughby, *Library Quar.*, VII, 290; by George Herbert Clarke, *QQ*, XLIV, 114-115; by A. Brandl, *Archiv*, 170 (1937), 284; by George Coffin Taylor, *SR*, XLV, 234-237; by B. M., *Dalhousie Rev.*, XVII, 260; by L. L. McVay, *Catholic Hist. Rev.*, XXIII, 392; by B. E. C. Davis, *MLR*, XXXII, 90-91; by Douglas Bush, *MLN*, LII, 443-444; by Garland Greever, *Personalist*, XVIII, 323-324; by W. Keller, *SJ*, LXXIII, 167-169; by Y. Hirn, *N. Mitt.*, XXXVIII, 396-397; by R. S. Knox, *UTQ*, VII (1938), 249-261; by Eduard Eckhardt, *Beiblatt*, XLIX, 97-99; by Heinz Nicolai, *DLZ*, LIX, 1272-77; by V. B. Heltzel, *JEGP*, XXXVII, 594-597; by F. O. Matthiessen, "Towards our Understanding of Elizabethan Drama," *Southern Rev.*, Autumn, 398-428; by Giulio Vallese, *Rinascita*, II (1939), 125-126; by A. A. Prins, *Neophil*, XXV (1940), 307-308.

A3858 Funck-Brentano, Franz. *The Renaissance.* New York: Macmillan, 1936. Pp. 320.
Rev: by Wallace K. Ferguson, *JMH*, VIII (1936), 520-521; *London Mercury*, XXXIV, 188; *NstN*, NS, XI, 727; *TLS*, May 2, p. 367; *QR*, 267 (1936), 176-177; by Joseph J. Reilly, *Catholic World*, 144 (1937), 498-499; by Louis Cons, *Books Abroad*, XI, 319; by E. Anagnine, *Leonardo*, VIII, 24-27.

A3859 Hammerle, Karl. *Von Ockham zu Milton.* Innsbruck, 1936.
Rev: by Karl Brunner, *Archiv*, 171 (1937), 119; by Rudolf Metz, *Beiblatt*, XLVIII, 271-273; *LZ*, 87 (1937), 1065; by H. E., *GMR*, XXVI (1938), 324; by P., *Zeit. f. katholische Theologie*, LXII, 140-141.

A3860 Lovejoy, A. O. *The Great Chain of Being: A Study of the History of an Idea.* Harvard Univ. Press, 1936. Pp. ix, 382.
Rev: by Raphael Demos, *MLN*, LII (1937), 518-520; by H. T. Davis, *Isis*, XXVII, 111-114; by G. R. Coffman, *SP*, XXXV (1938), 502-505; by A. S. P. Woodhouse, *JEGP*, XXXVII, 109-114; by E. C. Knowlton, *South Atlantic Quar.*, XXXVII, 93-94; by Henry Ogden, *Isis*, XXVIII, 537-540.

A3861 Medicus, Fritz. "The Scientific Significance of Paracelsus." Tr. by Fritz Marti. *Bul. of the Inst. Hist. Med.*, IV (1936), 353-366.

A3862 Meissner, Paul. "Empirisches und Ideelles Zeiterleben in der englischen Renaissance." *Anglia*, LX (1936), 165-180.

A3863 Oman, Sir Charles. *The Sixteenth Century.* London: Methuen, 1936. Pp. 254.
Rev: *TLS*, July 18, 1936, p. 590; *QR*, 267, 177-178; *NstN*, NS, XI, 986-988; by G. M., *SLR*, Feb. 13, 1937, p. 23; by Garrett Mattingly, *JMH*, IX, 218-219; by A. J. G., *EHR*, LII, 541-542; *Personalist*, XVIII, 444; by J. D. M., *History*, NS, XXII, 87-88.

A3864 Shillinglaw, Arthur T. "Hobbes and Ben Jonson." *TLS*, April 18, 1936, p. 336.

A3865 Spencer, Theodore. *Death and Elizabethan Tragedy.* A Study of Convention and Opinion on the Elizabethan Drama. Harvard Univ. Press, 1936. Pp. xiii, 288.
Chap. II: The Sixteenth Century Conflict, pp. 35-65;
Chap. IV: The Eliz. Drama: Ideas, pp. 111-181;
Chap. VI: The Drama—the Renaissance Mind, pp. 221-271.
Rev: A6823.

A3866 Allen, Don Cameron. "The Relation of Drayton's 'Noah's Flood' to the Ordinary Learning of the Early Seventeenth Century." *MLN*, LII (1937), 106-111.

A3867 Arnold, Aerol. *Thomas Nashe's Criticism of the State of Learning in England.* DD, University of Chicago, 1938. Chapter III lithoprinted, the Univ. of Chicago Libraries, 1937.

A3868 Curry, Walter Clyde. *Shakespeare's Philosophical Patterns.* Louisiana State Univ. Press, 1937. Pp. xii, 244.
Rev: A931.

A3869 Koldewey, E. *Über die Willensfreiheit im älteren Englischen Drama.* DD, Berlin, 1937. Wurzburg: Triltsch, 1937. Pp. 98.
Rev: A985.

A3870 Riese, Teut. *Die Englische Psalmendichtung im sechzehnten Jahrhundert.* DD, Freiburg/Breisgau, 1937. Pp. viii, 119.

A3871 Cancelled.

A3872 Cawley, Robert Ralston. *The Voyagers and Elizabethan Drama.* Mod. Lang. Assoc. Monograph Series, VIII. Boston: Heath, 1938. Pp. xiv, 428.
Rev: A2395

A3873 Klotz, Edith L. "A Subject Analysis of English Imprints for Every Tenth Year from 1480-1640." *HLQ*, I (1938), 417-419.

A3874 Papini, Giovanni. "La Renaissance Reconciliant l'Homme avec lui-même, en Fait le Collaborateur de Dieu." *Les Nouv. Litt.*, 816 (1938), 1-2.

A3875 Pinto, Vivian De Sola. *The English Renaissance, 1510-1688; with a Chapter on Literature and Music by Bruce Pattison.* New York: McBride; London: Cresset Press, 1938. Pp. 380.
Rev: by W. F. Schirmer, *Beiblatt*, L (1939), 81-84; by Monica Redlich, *Spectator*, Aug. 4, pp. 192-193.

A3876 Portal, Frédéric. *Des Couleurs Symboliques, dans l'Antiquité, le Moyen Âge et les Temps Modernes.* Paris: Niclaus, 1938. Pp. 200. See also A3855.

A3877 Anderson, Ruth L. *The Mirror Concept and its Relation to the Drama of the Renaissance.* Northwest Missouri State Teachers College Studies, III, No. 1, 1939. Pp. 30.

A3878 Butt, John. "The Facilities for Antiquarian Study in the Seventeenth Century." *Essays and Studies by Members of the English Assoc.*, XXIV Oxford: Clarendon Press, 1939.

A3879 Campbell, L. B. "The Use of Historical Patterns in the Reign of Elizabeth." *HLQ*, I (1937), 135-167.

A3880 Chew, Samuel C. "Time and Fortune." *ELH*, VI (1939), 83-113.

A3881 Langston, A. D. Beach. *Tudor Books of Consolation.* DD, University of North Carolina, 1940. Abstr. publ. in *University of North Carolina Record, Research in Progress, 1939-1940*, Chapel Hill, 1940, pp. 82-83.

A3882 Lewalter, Ernst. *Francis Bacon, ein Leben zwischen Tat und Gedanke.* Berlin: G. Kiepenheuer, 1939. Pp. 352.
Rev: by Hans Marcus, *Archiv*, 177 (1940), 55-56; by W. Keller, *SJ*, LXXVI (1940), 215.

A3883 Nicolson, Marjorie. "The History of Literature and The History of Thought." *English Institute Annual, 1939.* New York: Columbia Univ. Press, 1940, pp. 56-89.

A3884 Rowe, Kenneth Thorpe. "Elizabethan Morality and the Folio Revisions of Sidney's *Arcadia*." *MP*, XXXVII (1939/40), 151-172.

A3885 Siebeck, Berta. *Das Bild Sir Philip Sidneys in der engl. Renaissance.* DD, Freiburg, 1939. Weimar: Böhlau, 1939. Pp. xvi, 198.
Rev: by W. Keller, *SJ*, LXXV (1939), 170-171; by Willy Casper, *ZNU*, XXXIX, 141-142; by T. W. Baldwin, *MLN*, LV, 458; by Hans Marcus, *Beiblatt*, LI, 98-99; by W. F. Schirmer, *Eng. Studn.*, LXXIV, 225-226; by O. Müller, *DNS*, L (1942), 110.

A3886 Hall, Vernon, Jr. *The Social Content of Renaissance Literary Criticism.* DD, University of Wisconsin, 1940. Abstr. publ. in Univ. of Wisconsin *Summeries of Doctoral Dissertations, 1939-40*, Madison, 1940, pp. 256-258.

A3887 Jaloux, Edmond. "L'Esprit Élizabéthain." *Le Théâtre Élizabéthain.* Paris: Les Cahiers du Sud, 1940, pp. 25-39.

A3888 Lovett, Robert Morss. "Shakespeare in Relation to His Age." *University of Puerto Rico Bul.*, Series XII, No. 2, Dec., 1941, pp. 77-89.

A3889 Ashton, J. W. "The Fall of Icarus." *Renaissance Studies in Honor of Hardin Craig*, 1941, pp. 153-159; also *PQ*, XX, 345-351.
Discussion of the English Renaissance attitude toward the spread of knowledge.

A3890 Kristeller, Paul O., and John H. Randall, Jr. "The Study of the Philosophies of the Renaissance." *JHI*, II (1941), 449-496.

A3891 Morgan, R. "Some Stoic Lines in *Hamlet* and the Problem of Interpretation." *PQ*, XX (1941), 549-558.

A3892 Mary Bonaventure Mroz, Sister. *Divine Vengeance: A Study in the Philosophical Backgrounds of the Revenge Motif as It Appears in Shakespeare's Chronicle History Plays.* DD, Catholic University of America, 1941. Pp. x, 168.
Rev: B5068.

A3893 Orsini, Napoleone. *Fulke Greville tra il mondo e Dio.* Reale Università di Milano, Facoltà di lettere e filosofia, Ser. II: Letteratura italiana e filologia moderna. Milan: Gius. Principato, 1941. Pp. 119.

A3894 Stewart, Herbert L. "Philosophy in Renaissance Art." *UTQ*, X (1941), 401-416.

A3895 Williams, Arnold. "The Two Matters: Classical and Christian in the Renaissance." *SP*, XXXVIII (1941), 158-164.

A3896 Wilson, Harold S. "Some Meanings of 'Nature' in Renaissance Literary Theory." *JHI*, II (1941), 430-448.
Discusses 35 differences of meaning.

A3897 Davies, Godfrey, ed. "The Renaissance Conference at the Huntington Library." *HLQ*, V (1942), 155-201.

Remarks by a number of scholars upon various aspects of the English Renaissance.

A3898   Dean, Leonard F. "Bodin's *Methodus* in England Before 1625." *SP*, XXXIX (1942), 160-166.

A3899   Deutschberger, Paul. "Shakspere on Degree: A Study in Backgrounds." *SAB*, XVII (1942), 200-207.

A3900   O'Connor, Mary Catharine. *The Art of Dying Well: The Development of the Ars Moriendi.* New York: Columbia Univ. Press, 1942. Pp. xiv, 258.
    Rev: by H. Caplan, *MLN*, LIX (1944), 191-193.

A3901   Parr, Johnstone. *Cosmological Fortune: Astrology in the Elizabethan and Jacobean Drama.* DD, Vanderbilt University, 1942. Abstr. publ. Bul. of Vanderbilt Univ., *Abstracts of Theses*, August 1, 1942, pp. 22-23.
    Most Eliz. dramatists had little "thorough knowledge of the science." "None of the Elizabethan playwrights appear to have been specialists in astrology."

A3902   Willey, Basil. *The Seventeenth Century Background: Studies in the Thought of the Age in Relation to Poetry and Religion.* Columbia Univ. Press, 1942. Pp. viii, 315.
    Rev: by Garrett Mattingly, *SRL*, Nov. 28, 1942, pp. 16-17; by Arthur Barker, *Philos. Rev.*, LII (1943), 413-414; *Nation* (N. Y.), Jan. 9, p. 67; by D. C. A., *MLN*, LIX (1944), 437-438.

A3903   Wilson, J. Dover. "Shakespeare's Universe." *Univ. of Edinburgh Jour.*, XI (1942), 216-233·

A3904   Yates, Frances A. "Shakespeare and the Platonic Tradition." *Univ. of Edinburgh Jour.*, XII (1942), 2-12.

A3905   Adams, Henry H. *English Domestic, or Homiletic Tragedy, 1575 to 1642; Being an Account of the Development of the Tragedy of the Common Man Showing its Great Dependence on Religious Morality, Illustrated with Striking Examples of the Interposition of Providence for the Amendment of Men's Manners.* DD, Columbia University, 1944. Columbia Univ. Studies in Engl. & Comp. Lit., 159. Columbia Univ. Press, 1944. Pp. 228.

A3906   Lindsay, Jean Stirling. *A Survey of the Town-Country and Court-Country Themes in Non-dramatic Elizabethan Literature.* DD, Cornell University, 1943.

A3907   Sullivan, Frank. "The Renaissance Ideal." *Studies in Honor of St. Thomas Aquinas* (St. Louis Univ. Press, 1943), pp. 32-43.

A3908   Tillyard, E. M. W. *The Elizabethan World Picture.* London: Chatto & Windus, 1943. Pp. 108.
    Rev: *TLS*, May 1, 1943, p. 205; by H. W. Crundell, *TLS*, July 17, p. 343; by Margaret Willy, *English*, IV, 165-166; by Sarah M. Nutt, *NYTBR*, Apr. 2, 1944, p. 18; by G. B. Harrison, *RES*, XX, 71-73; by H. J. C. Grierson, *MLR*, XXXIX, 69-73; by E. Harris Harbison, *JMH*, XVI, 252-253; by Frank Aydelotte, *AHR*, L, 112-113; by J. J. Dwyer, *Shakespeare Fellowship Quar.*, V, 28-29; by H. P. Lazarus, *Nation*, 158 (1944), 601-602; by Ludwig Edelstein, *Bul. Hist. Med.*, XVI (1944), 216-217; by D. C. Allen, *AJP*, LXVI (1945), 435-436; by Garland Greever, *Personalist*, XXVI, 108; by Hardin Craig, *CE*, VI, 236-238; by R. H. Perkinson, *Theatre*, XX, 551-552.

A3909   Wright, Louis B. "The Noble Savage of Madagascar in 1640." *JHI*, IV (1943), 112-118.

A3910   Allen, Don Cameron. "The Rehabilitation of Epicurus and His Theory of Pleasure in the Early Renaissance." *SP*, XLI (1944), 1-15.

A3911   Anderson, Ruth L. "Excessive Goodness A Tragic Fault." *SAB*, XIX (1944), 85-96.

A3912   Craig, H. "Shakespeare and the Normal World." *Rice Institute Pamphlet*, XXXI (1944), 1-49·

A3913   Dilthey, Wilhelm. *Hombre y mundo en los siglos XVI y XVII.* Versión y pról. por E. Imaz. Mexico: Fondo de Cultura Económica, 1944. Pp. 501.
    Rev: by J. D. García Bacca, *Filosofía y Letras* (Mexico), VIII, No. 15 (1944), 17-82.

A3914   Knights, L. C. "Shakespeare and the Elizabethan Climate." *Scrutiny*, XII (1944), 146-152.

A3915   Martin, Alfred von. *Sociology of the Renaissance.* London: Kegan Paul, 1944. Pp. x, 100.
    Rev: A1897.

A3916   Spitzer, Leo. "Classical and Christian Ideas of World Harmony. Part I." *Traditio*, II (1944), 409-464.
    "Classical and Christian Ideas of World Harmony: Prolegomena to an Interpretation of the Word 'Stimmung'. Part II." *Traditio*, III (1945), 307-364.

A3917   Taylor, George C. "The Elizabethan Legacy (A Glance Towards the Renaissance)." *SAB*, XIX (1944), 60-70, 99-109.

A3918   Benesch, Otto. *The Art of the Renaissance in Northern Europe: Its Relation to the Contemporary Spiritual and Intellectual Movements.* Harvard Univ. Press, 1945. Pp. xiv, 174, il. 80.
    Rev: by H. McC., *More Books*, XXI (1946), 28; by Dayton Phillips, *AHR*, LII, 111-113; by Hugo Leichtentritt, *Jour. of Aesthetics*, V, 66-69; by P. O. Kristeller, *Art. Bul.*, XXIX (1947), 60-61.

A3919   Craig, Hardin. "Renaissance Ideal: A Lecture on Shakespeare." *Univ. of North Carolina Extension Bulletin*, XXIV, No. 4 (1945), 25-38.

A3920   Gaupp, Friedrich. *Pioniere der Neuzeit in der Frührenaissance.* Bern: Verlag Paul Haupt, 1945.
    Rev: *ConR*, 168 (1945), 382; by F. W. Wasserman, *Books Abroad*, XXI (1947), 169.

A3921   Randall, Henry John. *The Creative Centuries: A Study in Historical Development.* London: Longmans, 1945. Pp. xxix, 409; maps.
    Rev: *TLS*, Apr. 21, 1945, p. 184.

A3922   Raven, Charles E. *Synthetic Philosophy in the Seventeenth Century.* The Herbert Spencer Lecture for 1945. Oxford: Blackwell, 1945. Pp. 24.
        Rev: *TLS*, Sept. 15, 1945, p. 442.

A3923   Weisinger, Herbert. "Ideas of History During the Renaissance." *JHI*, VI (1945), 415-435.

A3924   Dunn, Catherine E. *The Concept of Ingratitude in Renaissance English Moral Philosophy.* Catholic Univ. America Press, 1946. Pp. xv, 133.
        Rev: by Lilian Haddakin, *MLR*, XLII (1947), 540; by Rosemond Tuve, *MLN*, LXIII (1948), 427-428.

A3925   Garrod, H. W. *Scholarship: Its Meaning and Value.* The J. H. Gray Lectures for 1946. Cambridge Univ. Press, 1946. Pp. 79.
        Takes notice, i.a., of some of the scholars of the early Renaissance.
        Rev: *TLS*, Jan. 25, 1947, p. 53; *N &Q*, 192 (1947), 110; by T. E. Mommsen, *AHR*, LII, 765-766; by J. A. Chapman, *English*, VI, 257-258.

A3926   Halblützel, Margrit Elisabeth. *Die Bildwelt Thomas Deloneys: Ein Beitrag zur Erkenntnis von Zeitgeist und Gattungsgeschichte der Englischen Renaissance.* DD, Zurich, 1946. Siebnen: Kürzi, 1946. Pp. 109. Schweizer anglistische Arbeiten, Vol. XVI. Bern: A. Francke, 1946. Pp. 119.
        Rev: by J. S., *ES*, XXVIII (1947), 95.

A3927   Howell, A. C. "Res et Verba: Words and Things." *ELH*, XIII (1946), 131-142.

A3928   Jarratt, Louise Paschal. *A Study of Death in English Renaissance Tragedy.* Master's thesis, University of North Carolina, 1943. Abstr. publ. in *Univ. of North Carolina Record, Research in Progress*, Grad. School Series, No. 50, 1946, pp. 156-157.

A3929   Pintard, Pene. *Le Libertinage Erudit dans la Première Moitié du XVIIe Siècle.* 2 Vols. Paris: Boivin, 1943.
        Rev: by Mary Elizabeth Storer, *MLN*, LXI (1946), 481-483.

A3930   Prym-von Becherer, Gisela. *Das Weltbild der Shakespearezeit mit besonderer Berücksichtigung von Shakespeares "Hamlet".* DD, Marburg, 1946. Pp. xviii, 159. Typewritten.

A3931   Seelye, Mary-Averett. *Nature in "King Lear" as a Basis for the Unity of Action.* Master's thesis, University of North Carolina, 1944. Abstr. publ. in *Univ. of North Carolina Record, Research in Progress*, Grad. School Series, No. 50, 1946, pp. 160-161.

A3932   Stewart, H. L. "Scholastic Philosophy in Renaissance Thought." *Personalist*, XXVII (1946), 285-298.

A3933   Weise, Georg. "Der Realismus des 16. Jahrhunderts und seine geistigen Voraussetzung und Parallelen." *Die Welt als Geschichte*, VIII (1946), 133-163, 300-322.

A3934   Baker, Herschel C. *The Dignity of Man: Studies in the Persistence of an Idea.* Harvard Univ. Press, 1947. Pp. xii, 365.
        Rev: *Phil. Rev.*, LVII (1948), 201-202; by Douglas Bush, *JEGP*, XLVII, 196-198; *MGW*, Oct. 24, 1948, p. 10.

A3935   Grace, William J. "The Conception of Society in More's *Utopia*." *Thought*, XXII (1947), 283-296.

A3936   Nakanishi, Shintaro. "Shakespeare and English Literary Thought." *Bungei-Gaku* (Japan), No. 1 (1947).

A3937   De Santillana, Giorgio, ed. *The Age of Adventure: The Renaissance Philosophers.* Boston: Houghton Mifflin, 1947. Pp. 283.
        Rev: by W. Barrett, *NYTBR*, Mar. 17, 1947, p. 44.

A3938   Zavala, Silvio. "The American Utopia of the Sixteenth Century." *HLQ*, X (1947), 337-347. See also the same author's "La Utopia de América en el siglo XVI." *Rev. Nacional de Cultura* (Caracas), No. 58 (1946), 117-127.

A3939   Elson, James Hinsdale. *John Hales of Eton.* New York: King's Crown Press, 1948. Pp. 199.
        Rev: A1745.

A3940   Gérard, Albert. "Shakespeare et l'Esprit de la Renaissance." *Synthèses*, III, No. 5 (1948), 170-176.

A3941   Harrison, Thomas P., Jr. "The Folger *Secret of Secrets*, 1572." *AMS*, pp. 601-620.

A3942   Lievsay, John Leon. "Some Renaissance Views of Diogenes the Cynic." *AMS*, pp. 447-455.

A3943   Allen, Don Cameron. *The Legend of Noah: Renaissance Rationalism in Art, Science, and Letters.* Ill. Stud. in Lang. and Lit., XXXIII, Nos. 3-4. Urbana, Ill., 1949. Pp. vii, 221.
        Rev: by A. Williams, *JEGP*, XLIX (1950), 581-583; by S. Stein, *MLR*, XLV, 526-528; by F. L. Utley, *MLN*, LXVIII (1953), 240-244.

A3944   Craig, Hardin. "An Aspect of Shakespearean Study." *SAB*, XXIV (1949), 247-257.

A3945   Carre, Meyrick H. *Phases of Thought in England.* Oxford: Clarendon Press, 1949. Pp. xix, 392.
        Rev: *TLS*, Aug. 19, 1949, p. 541; by M. Ross, *QQ*, LVII (1950), 423-425; by F. H. Anderson, *Phil. Rev.*, LIX, 394-397; by P. T. Geach, *Mind*, LIX, 278-279.

A3946   Dain, A. "Mediaeval and Renaissance Latin Translations and Commentaries." *Bul. de l'Assoc. Guillaume Budé*, No. 7 (June, 1949), 103-105.

A3947   Harrison, George Bagshawe. *England in Shakespeare's Day.* 2nd ed. London: Methuen, 1949. Pp. 239.

A3948   Pope, Elizabeth Marie. "The Renaissance Background of *Measure for Measure*." *ShS*, II
        (1949), 66-82.
        Comment by G. Wilson Knight, *Scrutiny*, XVI (1949), 326-327.

A3949   Prym-von Becherer, Gisela. "Der Makrokosmos im Weltbild der Shakespearezeit." *SJ*,
        82/83 (1948), 52-87.

A3950   Wilson, John Dover. *Life in Shakespeare's England*. Harmondsworth: Penguin Books, 1949.
        Pp. 365. Reprint of Compilation of 1926.

A3951   Mary Alphonsa Carpenter, Sister. *The Tragedy of Richard II: Its Background and Meaning*.
        DD, University of Illinois, 1950. Pp. 340. Mic A51-55. *Microf. Ab.*, XI (1951), 104. Publi-
        cation No. 2225.

A3952   Hartmeyer, Käthe. *Die Sozial- und Kulturverhältnisse Englands in der elisabethanischen Zeit,
        gesehen mit den Dichtern Thomas Deloney, Thomas Dekker und Ben Jonson*. DD, Münster, 1950.

A3953   Hinton, R. W. K. "The Transformation of the Universe, 1500-1700." *CamJ*, III (1950),
        674-685.

A3954   Kendrick, T. D. *British Antiquity*. London: Methuen, 1950. Pp. 171.
        Rev: *TLS*, Oct. 6, 1950, p. 632; by E. F. Jacob, *MGW*, Sept. 14, p. 12; by C. E. Vulliamy,
        Spectator, Aug. 4, p. 151; by Jacquetta Hawkes, *NstN*, Dec. 2, p. 560.

A3955   Ritter, Gerhard. *Die Neugestaltung Europas im 16. Jahrhundert. Die kirchlichen und staatlichen
        Wandlungen im Zeitalter der Reformation und der Glaubenskämpfe*. Berlin: Verlag des Druck-
        hauses Tempelhof, 1950. Pp. 384.
        Rev: by Ernest G. Schwiebert, *Archiv f. Reformationsgesch.*, XLII (1951), 262-263; by Delio
        Cantimori, *Belfagor*, VI, 232-237.

A3956   Wilkins, Ernest H. "A General Survey of Renaissance Petrarchism." *CL*, II (1950), 327-342.

A3957   Boas, Frederick S. "The Four Cardinal Virtues: A Fragmentary Moral Interlude." *QQ*,
        LVIII (1951), 85-91.

A3958   Hauser, Arnold. *The Social History of Art*. 2 Vols. New York: Alfred A. Knopf, 1951.
        Pp. xxi, 500; ix, 501-1022.

A3959   James, D. G. *The Dream of Learning: An Essay on "The Advancement of Learning", "Hamlet",
        and "King Lear"*. Oxford: Clarendon Press, 1951. Pp. 126.
        Rev: by R. W. Zandvoort, *ES*, XXXIII (1952), 93-94; by J. B. Fort, *EA*, V, 153; by Virgil K.
        Whitaker, *SQ*, III, 371-373; *TLS*, Mar. 7, 1952, p. 174; by D. S. Savage, *Atlantic Quar.*, VIII,
        282-285; by F. Wölcken, *Archiv*, 190 (1953), 133-134; by M. C. Bradbrook, *ShS*, VI, 148-149;
        by L. C. Knights, *RES*, IV, 75-76; by Ernest Sirluck, *MLN*, LXVIII, 262-264; by Hermann
        Heuer, *SJ*, 89 (1953), 232-233; by I. A. Shapiro, *MLR*, XLVIII, 69-70.

A3960   Myres, J. N. L. "The Painted Frieze in the Picture Gallery." *Bodleian Lib. Rec.*, III (1950),
        82-91. See also by the same author "Thomas James and the Painted Frieze." *Bodleian Lib.
        Rec.*, IV (1952), 30-51.

A3961   Schirmer, Walter F. "The Importance of the Fifteenth Century for the Study of the English
        Renaissance, with Special Reference to Lydgate." *English Studies Today*. Papers read at the
        International Conference of University Professors. Held in Magdalen College, Oxford,
        August, 1950. Oxford: Univ. Press, 1951, pp. 104-110.

A3962   Shanker, Sidney. *Conservatism and Change: A Study of the Relationship Between the Elizabethan-
        Jacobean Milieu and the Works of Jonson and Chapman for the Decade, 1605-1614*. DD, New York
        University, 1951.

A3963   Bethell, S. L. *The Cultural Revolution of the Seventeenth Century*. London: Dobson, 1952. Pp. 161.
        Includes a discussion of Shak.'s debt to the thought of his age.
        Rev: by M. C. Bradbrook, *NstN*, Aug. 4, 1951, pp. 133-134; by Hugh I'A. Fausset, *MGW*,
        July 12, p. 11; *TLS*, Aug. 3, p. 483; by Raymond P. Stearns, *William and Mary Quar.*, IX,
        556-558; by Lilian Haddakin, *MLR*, XLVII (1952), 575-577; by P. Courant, *EA*, V, 254; by
        M. M. Mahood, *RES*, IV (1953), 76-78.

A3964   Browne, Robert M. "Robert Burton and the New Cosmology." *MLQ*, XIII (1952), 131-148.

A3965   Burton, K. M. "The Political Tragedies of Chapman and Ben Jonson." *EIC*, II (1952),
        397-412.

A3966   Fuz, J. K. *Welfare Economics in English Utopias*. The Hague: Martinus Nijhoff, 1952. Pp.
        viii, 113.
        Rev: A1929.

A3967   Haller, William. " 'What Needs My Shakespeare?' " *SQ*, III (1952), 1-16.
        Adaptation of a lecture given at the Folger Shakespeare Library, April 23, 1951.

A3968   Obertello, Alfredo. "Tempo elisabettiano (specie e realtà storica)." *A. C. M. E. Annali della
        Facoltà di Filosofia e Lettere dell'Università statale di Milano*, V (Aug., 1952), 163-176.

A3969   Rothe, Hans. "Die elisabethanischen Zeitalter." *Shakespeare-Tage* (Bochum), 1952, pp. 6-7.

A3970   Simonini, R. C., Jr. *Italian Scholarship in Renaissance England*. The Univ. of North Carolina
        Studies in Comparative Literature, No. 3. Chapel Hill: Univ. of North Carolina Press, 1952.
        Pp. viii, 126.
        Studies teachers of Italian in 16th and 17th century England, and concludes with a section on
        their influence on Shak. and Jonson.

Rev: by Allan Gilbert, *South Atlantic Quar.*, LII (1953), 490-491; by M. C. Bradbrook, *SQ*, IV, 93; by S. B. Liljegren, *SN*, XXVI (1954), 196-197; by Giuliano Pellegrini, *Riv. di lett. mod. e comp.*, VI (1955), 127-128; by Frances S. Yates, *CL*, VII, 281-283.

A3971   Sternfeld, Frederick W. "Metropolitan Symposium." *RN*, V (1952), 5-10, 32-34, 58-63. Abstracts of papers given at the Symposium on the Renaissance held at the New York Metropolitan Museum of Art, Feb. 8-10, 1952; Leicester Bradner, "From Petrarch to Shakespeare," pp. 32-34.

A3972   White, Frances E. *The Theological, Moral, and Political Thought of William Tyndale as Revealed in Two of his Treatises: "The Parable of the Wicked Mammon" and "The Obedience of a Christian Man."* DD, University of Colorado, 1962. Abstr. in *Univ. of Colorado Stud.*, General Ser., XXIX, No. 1 (1952), 100-103.

A3973   Zitt, Hersch L. "The Jew in the Elizabethan World-Picture." *Historia Judaica*, XIV (1952), 53-60.

A3974   Ackert, E. "Die Zeitepoche W. Shakespeares." *Befreiung* (Aarau), I (1953), 127-130.

A3975   Finney, Gretchen L. "A World of Instruments." *ELH*, XX (1953), 87-120.

A3976   Friedell, Egon. *A Cultural History of the Modern Age*, I: *The Crisis of the European Soul from the Black Death to the Thirty Years' War.* New York: Alfred A. Knopf, 1953. Pp. xxiv, 353. See the author's *Die Krisis der europäischen Seele von der Schwarzen Pest bis zum Ersten Weltkrieg.* 3 Vols. 27th ed., 1950.

A3977   Kocher, Paul H. *Science and Religion in Elizabethan England.* San Marino, Calif.: Huntington Lib., 1953. Pp. xii, 340.
     Rev: A1456.

A3978   Lee, Alberta E. *Preaching in Elizabethan and Jacobean Drama.* DD, Columbia University, 1953. Pp. 341. Mic A54-164. *DA*, XIV (1954), 112. Publication No. 6657.

A3979   Stone, Walter B. *The Prediction of Regiomontanus: A Study in the Eschatology of Elizabethan England.* DD, Harvard University, 1953.

A3980   Bliss, Frank Walker, Jr. *Studies in the Background of the Idea of Pride in Eighteenth Century Thought.* DD, University of Minnesota, 1954. Pp. 332. Mic A55-498. *DA*, XV (1955), 403. Publication No. 11,069.
     Shak., pp. 157-164.

A3981   Jacquot, Jean. "Acontius and the Progress of Tolerance in England." *BHR*, XVI (1954), 192-206.

A3982   Mazzeo, Joseph A. "Universal Analogy and the Culture of the Renaissance." *JHI*, XV (1954), 299-304.

A3983   Morris, I. *Shakespeare and Greville: Their Tragic Characters Compared. An Attempt to Re-define the Principles of Shakespearean Tragedy in the Light of Elizabethan Thought.* B. Litt. thesis, Oxford, 1954.

A3984   Soellner, Rolf H. *Anima and Affectus: Theories of the Emotions in Sixteenth Century Grammar Schools and Their Reflections in the Works of Shakspere.* DD, University of Illinois, 1954. Pp. 275. Mic A54-489. *DA*, XIV (1954), 351. Publication No. 6983.

A3985   Ferguson, Arthur B. "Renaissance Realism in the 'Commonwealth' Literature of Early Tudor England." *JHI*, XVI (1955), 287-305. Robert Crowley, Clement Armstrong, John Hales, Thomas Starkey, and others.

A3986   Gilbert, Neal Ward. *Concepts of Method in the Renaissance and their Ancient and Medieval Antecedents.* DD, Columbia University, 1956. *DA*, XVI (1956), 1261. Publication No. 16,809.

A3987   Kristeller, Paul Oskar. *Studies in Renaissance Thought and Letters.* Rome, 1956.
     Rev: *SCN*, XVI (1958), 31; by R. J. Schoeck, *Neo-Latin News*, XVI (Summer), 31.

A3988   Cancelled.

A3989   O'Brien, Gordon Worth. *Renaissance Poetics and the Problem of Power.* Institute of Elizabethan Studies, No. 2. Chicago: Inst. Elizabethan Studies, 1956. Pp. xxvi, 127.
     Rev: A1726.

A3990   Barroll, John L., III. *Shakespeare and Roman History.* DD, Princeton University, 1956. Pp. 675. Mic 57-996. *DA*, XVII (1957), 626. Publication No. 20,101.
     Caesar and *Antony* are the only two plays discussed. Comparisons are made with other Cleopatra plays.

A3991   Batard, Yvonne. "L'Idée de la Tolérance chez les Humanistes de la Renaissance." *Littérature Générale et Histoire des Idées. Actes du Premier Congrès National de Littérature Comparée.* Bordeaux, 2, 3, 4, March, 1957. Études de Littérature Etrangère et Comparée, No. 34. Paris: M. Didier, 1957.

A3992   Brandt, William Jeans. *The Continental Origins of English Renaissance Conceptions of the Nature of Man.* DD, University of California, Berkeley, 1957.

A3993   Dieckmann, Liselotte. "Renaissance Hieroglyphics." *CL*, IX (1957), 308-321.

A3994   Rosier, James Louis. *The Chain of Sin and Privation in Elizabethan Literature.* DD, Stanford University, 1957. *DA*, XVIII (1958), 583.

A3995   Siegel, Paul N. *Shakespearean Tragedy and the Elizabethan Compromise.* New York Univ.

Press, 1957.
Rev: A1882.

A3996   Surtz, Edward, S. J. *The Praise of Pleasure. Philosophy, Education, and Communism in More's*
        "Utopia." Cambridge, Mass.: Harvard Univ. Press, 1957. Pp. 246.
        Rev: by Robert P. Adams, *RN*, XI (1958), 129-133; by Allan Holaday, *JEGP*, LVII, 801-803;
        by Sears Jayne, *CE*, XX, 153; by Hugh Maclean, *Dalhousie Rev.*, XXXVIII, 243-244; *TLS*,
        Sept. 12, 1958, p. 514.

A3997   Surtz, Edward, S. J. *The Praise of Wisdom. A Commentary on the Religious and Moral Problems*
        and Backgrounds of St. Thomas More's "Utopia." Jesuit Studies, No. 6. Chicago: Loyola
        Univ. Pres, 1957. Pp. 402.
        Rev: *SCN*, XVI (1958), 48; by Allan Holaday, *JEGP*, LVII, 801-803; by Sears Jayne, *CE*, XX,
        153.

A3998   Wright, Celeste Turner. "The Queen's Husband: Some Renaissance Views." *Studies in*
        English, III (1957), 133-138.

A3999   "Shakespeare Lectures at the Oregon Festival." *ShN*, VIII (1958), 28-29.
        Includes abstract of George Vernon Blue, "Makers of the Tudor Myth."

A4000   Bowers, R. H. "Heraclitus and Democritus in Elizabethan England." *Southern Folklore Quar.*,
        XXII (1958), 139-143.

A4001   Gleason, John Bernard. *Studies in the Thought of John Colet.* DD, University of Chicago, 1958.

A4002   Koryé, Alexandre. *From the Closed World to the Infinite Universe.* Baltimore: Johns Hopkins
        Press, 1958.
        Rev: by Giorgio de Santillana, *YR*, XLVII (1958), 453-458.

A4003   Rice, Eugene F., Jr. *The Renaissance Idea of Wisdom.* Harvard Univ. Historical Monographs,
        XXXVII. Cambridge, Mass.: Harvard Univ. Press, 1958. Pp. xvi, 220.

A4004   Soellner, Rolf. "The Four Primary Passions: A Renaissance Theory Reflected in the Works
        of Shakespeare." *SP*, LV (1958), 549-567.

A4005   Williamson, Hugh Ross. *The Day Shakespeare Died.* London, 1958.

(f) GOSSIP OF THE TIMES

A4006   Matthews, William. *British Diaries: An Annotated Bibliography of British Diaries Written*
        Between 1442 and 1942. Univ. Calif. Press, 1950. Pp. xxiv, 339.
        Rev: A37.

A4007   Collins, D. C. *A Handlist of News Pamphlets, 1590-1610.* Southwest Essex Technical College,
        1944. Pp. xix, 129.
        Rev: *TLS*, Jan. 27, 1945, p. 48; by E. A., *MGW*, Feb. 23, p. 110; *History*, NS, XXIX, 213.

A4008   *Anecdotes, Traditionary, of Shakespeare, Collected in Warwickshire in the Year 1693, Now First*
        Published from the Original MS. London: T. Rodd, 1938. Pp. 20.

A4009   Harrison, G. B. *A Last Elizabethan Journal, 1599-1603.* London, 1933.
        Rev: by Margarete Rösler, *Eng. Studn.*, LXX (1936), 418-419.

A4010   Harrison, G. B. *The Elizabethan Journals: Being a Record of Those Things Most Talked of During*
        the Years 1591-1603. London: George Routledge and Sons, 1938. New York: Macmillan,
        1939. Pp. xiii, 395, 379, 364. Ann Arbor: Univ. Michigan Press, 1955. Pp. 1204.
        Rev: by C. J. Sisson, *MLR*, XXXIV (1939), 474-475; by Conyers Read, *SRL*, Jan. 27, 1940,
        pp. 18-19; by L. B. Wright, *AHR*, XLVI, 120; by L. Cazamian, *EA*, IV, 57-58.

A4011   Harrison, George B. *Jacobean Journal: Being a Record of Those Things Most Talked of During*
        Years 1603-1606. London: Routledge; New York: Macmillan, 1941. Pp. xii, 406.
        Rev: *TLS*, Feb. 8, 1941, p. 68; *DUJ*, II, 224-225; by Henry Grattan, *NYTBR*, Sept. 28, p. 3;
        by A. L. Rowse, *Spectator*, Feb. 21, pp. 208-210; by Rose Macaulay, *NstN*, Mar. 8, p. 254;
        by D. H. Willson, *AHR*, XLVII (1942), 839-840.

A4012   Harrison, G. B. *A Second Jacobean Journal: Being a Record of Those Things Most Talked of*
        During the Years 1607 to 1610. Ann Arbor: Univ. Michigan Press; London: Routledge, 1958.
        Pp. x, 278.
        Rev: *TLS*, Nov. 14, 1958, p. 654.

A4013   Akrigg, G. P. V. "England in 1609." *HLQ*, XIV (1950), 75-94.

g. WORKS ON SIXTEENTH CENTURY TRANSLATORS
OF CONTINENTAL WRITERS (63;25)
(1) REPRINTS OF OLD TRANSLATIONS (64;-)

A4014   Laurentius, M. Andreas. *A Discourse of the Preservation of the Sight; of Melancholike Diseases;*
        of Rheumes, and of Old Age. Tr. by Richard Surphlet. intro. by Sanford V. Larkey. Shakespeare
        Assoc. Facsimiles: No. 15. Oxford Univ. Press, 1938. Pp. 236.

A4015   Dickson, A., ed. *Valentine and Orson.* Tr. from the French by Henry Watson. Oxford:
        Univ. Press; London: Milford, 1937. Pp. 440.
        Rev: *TLS*, Aug. 28, 1937, p. 620.

A4016   Baptista Spagnuoli (Mantuanus). *The Eglogs.* Turned into English Verse by George Turber-
        vile. London: Henry Bynneman, 1567. Facsimile. Ed. with Introd. Essay and Biblio-

graphical Note by Douglas Bush. New York: Scholars' Facsimiles and Reprints, 1937.

A4017 Cancelled.

A4018 Trotter, Margret Guthrie, ed. "Sir John Harington's *Orlando Furioso*, Books I-V. Edited in Facsimile from the 1591 Edition." In *Abstracts of Doctoral Dissertations*, Ohio State Univ., Summer Quarter, 1943. Ohio State Univ., 1944, pp. 193-199.

A4019 Machiavelli, Niccolò. *Machiavelli's The Prince: An Elizabethan Translation*. Edited with an Introduction and Notes from a Manuscript in the Collection of Mr. Jules Furthman by Hardin Craig. Chapel Hill: Univ. of North Carolina Press; London: Milford, 1944. Pp. xli, 177.
  Rev: by Leonard Bacon, *SRL*, June 17, 1944, pp. 21, 53; by E. Baughan, *South Atlantic Bul.*, Oct. 1944, pp. 7-8; by Una Ellis-Fermor, *RES*, XXI (1945), 155-156; by A. H. Gilbert, *MLN*, LX, 418-420; by Helen C. White, *AHR*, L, 382-383; by A. J. G., *EHR*, LX, 269-270; by C. J. Sisson, *MLR*, XL, 136-137; by Paul Hyland Harris, *Italica*, XXII, 149-152; by A. M. Pellegrini, *MLQ*, VI, 105.

A4020 Tuve, Rosemond, ed. *The Zodiacke of Life by Marcellus Palingenius Translated by Barnabe Googe*. New York: Scholars' Facsimiles & Reprints, 1947.

A4021 Flenley, R. "The First English Translation of Champlain." *Canadian Hist. Rev.*, XXVIII (1947), 178-182.
  Discusses and reprints Grimston's translation in *A General Inventorie of the History of France* . . . (1607).

A4022 Hook, Frank S., ed. *The French Bandello: A Selection. The Original Text of Four of Belleforest's "Histoires Tragiques," Tr. by Geoffrey Fenton and William Painter, Anno 1567*. Univ. Missouri Studies, Vol. XXII, No. 1, 1948. Pp. 185.
  Rev: by H. W. Lawton, *Fr. Studies*, III (1949), 162-163; by W. H. Bowen, *Books Abroad*, XXIII, 156; by G. Hainsworth, *MLR*, XLIV, 442-443.

A4023 Heltzel, Virgil B., and Clyde Murley. "Randall Hutchins' *Of Specters* (ca. 1593), Translated from the Latin." *HLQ*, XI (1948), 407-429.
  Provides a translation of Hutchins' *Tractatus de spectris*, from a MS in the Huntington Library.

A4024 Crane, William G., ed. *The Castle of Love (1549?), A Translation by John Bourchier, Lord Berners, of Cárcel de Amor (1492) by Diego de San Pedro*. Gainesville, Florida: Scholars' Facsimiles & Reprints, 1950.

A4025 Kirk, Rudolph, ed. *The Moral Philosophie of the Stoicks*. Written in French by Guillaume du Vair. Englished by Thomas James. Rutgers Studies in English, No. 8. New Brunswick, New Jersey: Rutgers Univ. Press, 1951. Pp. ix, 134.
  Rev: *N &Q*, 197 (1952), 395-396.

A4026 Starnes, DeWitt T., ed. *Proverbs or Adages by Desiderius Erasmus Gathered Out of the Chiliades and Englished (1569) by Richard Taverner*. Gainesville, Florida: Scholars' Facsimiles and Reprints, 1956.

(2) ENGLISH TRANSLATORS
(a) GENERAL

A4027 Larwill, P. H. *La Théorie de la Traduction au Début de la Renaissance*. DD, Munich, 1934. Pp. 64.

A4028 Calver, Edward Thomas. *Translations into English 1523-1600: A Catalogue Raisonné with a Bibliography of Secondary Studies*. DD, University of Michigan, 1944.

A4029 Clements, Arthur Frederick. *Tudor Translations*. Oxford: Blackwell, 1929. Pp. 227.
  Rev: *TLS*, Feb. 10, 1940, p. 74; by Rose Macaulay, *NstN*, NS, XIX, 80; by Charles E. Hydes, *Illus. London News*, 106, 250; by A. L. Rowse, *Spectator*, Feb. 23, 1940, p. 258.

A4030 Orsini, Napoleone. "Elizabethan MS. Translations of Machiavelli's *Prince*." *Jour. of the Warburg Institute*, I (1937), 166-169.

A4031 Yates, F. A. "Italian Teachers in Elizabethan England." *Jour. of the Warburg Institute*, I (1937), 103-116.

A4032 Workman, Samuel K. *Fifteenth Century Translation as an Influence on English Prose*. Princeton Studies in Eng. 18. Princeton Univ. Press, 1940. Pp. 218.
  Rev: by J. I., *RES*, XVII (1941), 248-250; by K. M., *MLN*, LVII (1942), 79-80.

A4033 Hall, Marie-Louise Michaud. *Montaigne et ses Traducteurs*. DD, University of Wisconsin, 1940.

A4034 Hudson, Hoyt H. "Current English Translations of *The Praise of Folly*." *PQ*, XX (1941), 250-265. Also in Craig Festschrift, B4402.

A4035 Wright, H. G. "The Elizabethan Translations of the *Questioni d'Amore* in the *Filocolo*." *MLR*, XXXVI (1941), 289-303.

A4036 Pellegrini, Angelo M. "Giordano Bruno on Translations." *ELH*, X (1943), 193-207.

A4037 Mary Jeremy, Sister. "The English Prose Translation of *Legenda Aurea*." *MLN*, LIX (1944), 181-183.

A4038 Mary Jeremy, Sister. "Caxton and the Synfulle Wretche." *Traditio*, IV (1946), 423-428.

A4039   Pane, Remigio U. *English Translations from the Spanish, 1484-1943*. Rutgers Univ. Studies in
        Span., No. 2. Rutgers Univ. Press, 1944. Pp. vi, 218.
        Rev: *N &Q*, 187 (1944), 219-220; by Harry Bernstein, *HAHR*, xxvi, 224-225.

A4040   Gilbert, Allan H. "Nervizanus, Ariosto, Florio, Harington and Drummond." *MLN*, lxii
        (1947), 129-130.

A4041   Mosse, George L. "The Influence of Jean Bodin's *République* on English Political Thought."
        Medievalia et Humanistica, v (1948), 73-83.

A4042   Grierson, Sir Herbert J. C. *Criticism and Creation: Essays and Addresses*. London: Chatto
        and Windus, 1949. Pp. 127.
        Contains essay on verse translations.

A4043   Tucker, Joseph E. "The Earliest English Translations of Scarron's Nouvelles." *RLC*, xxiv
        (1950), 557-563.

A4044   Kristeller, P. O. "Mediaeval and Renaissance Latin Translations and Commentaries."
        Scriptorium, vi, No. 1 (1952).

A4045   Rees, D. G. "Petrarch's *Trionfo della Morte* in English." *Italian Studies*, vii (1952), 82-96.

A4046   Wright, H. G. *The First English Translation of the "Decameron" (1620)*. Essays and Studies
        Eng. Lang. & Lit., xii. Uppsala: A. B. Lundequistska Bokhandeln, 1952. Pp. 327. See also
        Herbert G. Wright, *MLR*, xxxi (1936), 500-512.
        Rev: by Douglas Bush, *MLR*, xlix (1954), 227-228; by Kathleen M. Lea, *RES*, v, 419-420;
        by Geoffrey Bullough, *SN*, xxvi, 185-187; by Alfredo Obertello, "Traduttori Inglesi del
        Decameron," *Studium* l (1954), 610-612.

A4047   Reckmann, Kurt. "Dr. Martin Luthers Kirchenlieder in den Englischen und Schottischen
        Übersetzungen des 16. Jahrhunderts: Ein Beitrag zur Anglo-deutschen Literaturbeziehung."
        Monatshefte, l (1958), 215-216.

A4048   Fellheimer, Jeannette. "The Section on Italy in the Elizabethan Translations of Giovanni
        Botero's *Relazioni Universali*." *English Miscellany*, viii (1957), 289-306.

A4049   Randall, Dale B. J. *Renaissance English Translations of Non-chivalric Spanish Fiction (with Special
        Reference to the Period from 1620 to 1657)*. DD, University of Pennsylvania, 1958. Pp. 670.
        Mic 58-1864. *DA*, xviii (1958), 2129.

(b) SPECIFIC INDIVIDUALS
i. Ashley

A4050   Ashley, Robert. *Of Honour*. Ed. with Introduction and Commentary by Virgil B. Heltzel.
        San Marino: Huntington Lib., 1947. Pp. 80.
        Rev: by D. C. A., *MLN*, lxiii (1948), 435; by A. M. C. Latham, *RES*, xxiv, 325-326;
        N &Q, 193 (1948), 220; by C. J. Sisson, *MLR*, xliii, 436.

A4051   Heltzel, Virgil B. "Robert Ashley: Elizabethan Man of Letters." *HLQ*, x (1947), 349-363.

ii. Fairfax

A4052   "Fairfax's Tasso." *TLS*, Mar. 11, 1944, p. 127.

A4053   Bell, Charles G. "Edward Fairfax, a Natural Son." *MLN*, lxii (1947), 24-27.

A4054   Bell, Charles G. "A History of Fairfax Criticism." *PLMA*, lxii (1947), 644-656.
        Charts the judgment of the Tasso translation.

A4055   Grundy, Joan. "Tasso, Fairfax, and William Browne." *RES*, iii (1952), 268-271.

A4056   Bell, Charles G. "Fairfax's Tasso." *CL*, vi (1954), 26-52.

iii. Fenton

A4057   Fellheimer, Jeannette. *Geoffrey Fenton, Elizabethan Translator*. DD, Yale University, 1941.

A4058   Fellheimer, Jeannette. "Barnabe Barnes' Use of Geoffrey Fenton's *Historie of Guicciardin*."
        MLN, lvii (1942), 358-359.

A4059   Fellheimer, Jeannette. "Notes on Geoffrey Fenton's Minor Translations." *PQ*, xxii (1943),
        343-346.

A4060   Fellheimer, Jeannette. "Geoffrey Fenton's *Historie of Guicciardin* and Holinshed's *Chronicles*
        of 1587." *MLQ*, vi (1945), 285-298.

A4061   Fellheimer, Jeannette. "Some Words in Fenton's *Certaine Tragicall Discourses*." *MLN*, lxi
        (1946), 538-540.

A4062   Fellheimer, Jeannette. "Hellowes' and Fenton's Translations of Guevara's *Epístolas Familiares*."
        SP, xliv (1947), 140-156.

A4063   Fellheimer, Jeannette. "The Episode of 'The Villain of the Danube' in Fenton's *Golden
        Epistles*." *MLQ*, xiv (1953), 331-334.

iv. John Florio

A4064   Dieckow, Fritz. *John Florios Englische Übersetzung der Essays Montaignes und Lord Bacons, Ben
        Jonsons und Robert Burtons Verhältnis zu Montaigne*. DD, Strassburg, 1902. Pp. 117.

A4065 Yates, F. A. *John Florio, an Italian in Shakespeare's England.* Cambridge Univ. Press, 1934. Pp. 364. In Ebisch & Schücking Suppl., p. 63.
Rev: by A. Brandl, *Archiv*, 168 (1935), 251.

A4066 Yates, F. A. "Florio and Love's Labor's Lost." *A Study of "Love's Labor's Lost,"* 1936, pp. 27-49.

A4067 Yates, F. A. "Italian Teachers in Elizabethan England." *Journ. of the Warburg Institute*, I (1937), 103-116.

A4068 Gillet, Louis. "Nouvelles Recherches sur Shakespeare." *RddxM*, 108, Tome 47 (1938), 443-457.
Includes review of Clara Longworth de Chambrun's *Giovanni Florio*, 1921.

A4069 Florio, John. *Florio's First Fruites.* In two parts. Ed. by Arundel del Re. Formosa, Japan: Taihoku Imperial Univ., 1936.
Rev: *TLS*, Dec. 19, 1936, p. 1053; by G. D. Willcock, *MLR*, XXXII (1937), 607-608; by Francesco Viglione, *Beiblatt*, XLVIII, 120-123; by Mario Praz, *ES*, XIX, 226-232; by F. Olivero, *GSLI*, 109, 155-157.

A4070 Ignoto. "Shakespeare and Florio." *N & Q*, 184 (1943), 283-285; Frederick Page, ibid., pp. 42-44; ibid., pp. 107-108.

A4071 Policardi, Silvio. *John Florio e le Relazioni Culturali fra l'Inghilterra e l'Italia nel XVI Secolo.* Biblioteca di saggi e di lezioni accademiche—opera No. 27. Venice: Casa Editrice F. Montuoro, 1947. Pp. 170.

A4072 Policardi, Silvio. "Montaigne e Florio." *Belfagor*, IV (1949), 716-721.

A4073 Simonini, Rinaldo Charles, Jr. *Florio's Second Frutes: A Critical Edition.* DD, University of North Carolina, 1949. Abstract publ. in *Univ of North Carolina Record, Research in Progress*, Jan.-Dec. 1949, Grad. School Series No. 58, pp. 115-116.

A4073a Simonini, R. C., Jr., ed. *Second Frutes* (1591) by John Florio. A Facsimile Reproduction with an Introd. Gainesville, Florida: Scholars' Facsimiles & Reprints, 1953.

A4074 Villa, Carlo. *Parigi Vale Bene una Messa! William Shakespeare & il Poeta Valtellinese Michelagnolo Florio.* Milan: Editrice Storica, 1951.

A4075 Aylward, J. D. "Saviolo's Ghost." *N & Q*, 195 (1951) 226-229.

A4076 Simonini, R. C., Jr. "John Florio, Scholar and Humanist." *A Tribute to George Coffin Taylor*, pp. 67-82.

A4077 del Re, Arundel. *The Place of John Florio in Renaissance English Literature (1553-1625).* DD, Tokyo. Abstract publ. in *Japan Science Review*, VI (1955), 12-15.

v. Golding
(See also section on Ovid below, A4263-A4276.)

A4078 *An Elizabethan Puritan, Arthur Golding, Translator of Ovid and Calvin.* New York: R. R. Smith, 1937. Pp. x, 276.
Rev: *Spectator*, Feb. 25, 1938, p. 336; *National Rev.*, 110 (1938), 544-545; *QR*, 271 (1938), 180; *ConR*, 154 (1938), 126; *TLS*, April 2, 1938, p. 273; by F. B. Williams, Jr., *MLN*, LIII, 394-395; by J. E. N., *EHR*, LIV (1939), 553; by F. H., *History*, NS, XXIII, 375; by H. S. V. J., *JEGP*, XXXIX (1940), 306.

A4079 Brooks, E. St. J. "A Pamphlet by A. Golding (1573)." *N & Q*, 174 (1938), 182-184.

A4080 Buell, Llewellyn M. "Arthur Golding and the Earthquake of 1580." *PQ*, XXIV (1945), 227-232.

A4081 Wortham, James. "Arthur Golding and the Translation of Prose." *HLQ*, XII (1949), 339-367.

A4081a Blythe, Ronald. "Arthur Golding." *Essex Rev.*, 1950, pp. 213-215.

vi. Harington

A4082 Rich, Townsend. *Harington's Fountain.* *TLS*, May 30, 1936, p. 460.

A4083 Rich, Townsend. *Harington & Ariosto: A Study in Elizabethan Verse Translation.* Yale Studies in English, Vol. 92. New Haven, 1940.
Rev: by B. E. C. Davis, *MLR*, XXXVI (1941), 258; by H. N. Hillebrand, *MLN*, LVI, 620-623.

A4084 Trotter, Margret Guthrie. "Harington's Sources." *TLS*, Dec. 30, 1944, p. 631.

vii. Holland

A4085 Silvette, Herbert. *A Short-Title List of the Writings of Philemon Holland of Coventry, Doctor of Physicke.* Charlottesville: Privately Printed, 1939. Pp. x, 18.

A4086 Silvette, Herbert. *Catalogues of the Works of P. Holland of Coventry.* Charlottesville, 1940. Pp. xviii plus 30, port.

A4087 Silvette, Herbert. "Philemon Holland in Coventry." *Annals of Medical History*, 3rd Series, I (1938), 99-100, 196.

A4088 Schäfer, Alfred. *Die Volkstümliche Liviusübersetzung Philemon Hollands.* DD, Leipzig, 1910. Pp. 113.

viii. Mabbe

A4089 Houck, Helen Phipps. "Mabbe's Paganization of the *Celestina*." *PMLA*, LIV (1939), 422-431.
A4090 Secord, Arthur W. "I. M. of the First Folio Shakespeare and Other Mabbe Problems." *JEGP*, XLVII (1948), 374-381.
A4091 Pierce, Frank. "James Mabbe and *La Española Inglesa*." *RLC*, XXIII (1949), 80-85.
A4092 Russell, P. E. "A Stuart Hispanist: James Mabbe." *BHS*, XXX (1953), 75-84.

ix. Painter

A4093 Kimmelman, Elaine. "*The Palace of Pleasure*." *Boston Public Libr. Quar.*, II (1950), 231-244.
A4094 Wright, Herbert G. "The Indebtedness of Painter's Translations from Boccaccio in *The Palace of Pleasure* to the French Version of Le Macon." *MLR*, XLVI (1951), 431-435.
A4095 Maxwell, J. C. "William Painter's Use of Mexía." *N &Q*, 199 (1954), 16.
A4096 Wright, H. G. "How Did Shakespeare Come to Know the *Decameron*?" *MLR*, L (1955), 45-48.
A4097 Buchert, Jean Ruth. *A Critical Study of Painter's Palace of Pleasure.* DD, Yale University, 1957.

x. Countess of Pembroke

A4098 Jackson, Paul Joseph. *An Elizabethan Translator: the Countess of Pembroke with Particular Attention to Her Discourse of Life and Death.* DD, University of Washington, Seattle, 1940. Abstract publ. in *Abstracts of Theses*, Vol. V, Seattle: Univ. of Washington, 1941, pp. 279-284.
A4099 Beauchamp, Virginia Walcott. "Sidney's Sister as Translator of Garnier." *RN*, X (1957), 8-13.

xi. Thomas Shelton

A4100 George, J. "Thomas Shelton, Translator, in 1612-14." *BHS*, XXXV (1958), 157-164.
A4101 Knowles, Edwin B. "Thomas Shelton, Translator of *Don Quixote*." *Studies in the Renaissance*, V (1958), 160-175.

xii. Others (Alphabetically by translator.)

A4102 Schlauch, Margaret. "A Sixteenth-Century English Satirical Tale about Gdańsk." *Kwartalnik Neofilologiczny*, IV (1957), 95-120.
. Reprints "A New Deceyt Doone of Latest Dauswyke in Pruyse" from the 1560 edition of *The Deceyt of Women*, and argues that the book may be a translation from the Dutch by Lawrence Andrewe, who may also be translator of *Frederick of Jennen* (1518), a source of *Cym*.
A4103 R., M. U. H. *Lady Anne Bacon's Translations.* *N &Q*, 170 (1936), 441.
A4104 Parks, George B. "William Barker, Tudor Translator." *Papers Bibliog. Soc. Amer.*, LI (1957), 126-140.
A4105 Tucker, Joseph E. "John Davies of Kidwelly (1627?-1693), Translator from the French." *Papers of the Bibliog. Soc. of Amer*, XLIV (1950), 119-152.
A4106 Wortham, James. "Sir Thomas Elyot and the Translation of Prose." *HLQ*, XI (1948), 219-240.
A4107 Henning, Richard. *George Gascoigne als Übersetzer Italienischer Dichtungen.* DD, Königsberg, 1913. Pp. vii, 112.
A4108 Gee, John Archer. *Hervet's English Translation, With its Appended Glossary of Erasmus' "De immensa dei misericordia."* *PQ*, XV (1936), 136-152.
A4109 Musgrove, S. "Some Manuscripts of Heywood's *Art of Love*." *Library*, 5th Ser., I (1946), 106-112.
A4110 Atkinson, Dorothy F. "One R. P." *MLQ*, VI (1945), 3-12.
Presents internal evidence to show that the "R. P." who englished a number of Spanish works was Robert Parke, translator of González de Mendoza's *History of China*.
A4111 Binder, James. "More's *Utopia* in English: A Note on the Translation." *MLN*, LXII (1947), 370-376.
Discusses some of Ralph Robinson's alterations.
A4112 Webb, Henry J. "The Elizabethan Translation of Vegetius' *De Re Militari*." *MLN*, LVI (1941), 605-606.
John Sadler translated and published the fourth century treatise as a means of showing the dangers of mustering rogues into military service.
A4113 Strathmann, Ernest. "The 1595 Translation of Du Bartas' *First Day*." *HLQ*, VIII (1945), 185-191.
A4114 Williams, Franklin B., Jr. "Robert Tofte." *RES*, XIII (1937), 282-296; 405-424.
A4115 M., M. "Tragical Tales." *More Books*, XVIII (1943), 343.
The first (1587) edition of George Turberville's translation.
A4116 Roe, F. C. "A Double Centenary: Sir Thomas Urquhart and His Translation of Rabelais." *Aberdeen Univ. Rev.*, XXXV (1953), 121-129.
A4117 Anderson, D. M. "Sir Thomas Wilson's Translation of Montemayor's Diana." *RES*, VII (1956), 176-181.

A4118   Russell, G. H. "Philip Woodward: Elizabethan Pamphleteer and Translator." *Library*,
        IV (1949), 14-24.

A4119   Rees, D. G. "Sir Thomas Wyatt's Translations from Petrarch." *CL*, VII (1955), 15-24.

A4120   Wright, Herbert G. "The Italian Edition of Boccaccio's *Fiammetta* Used by Bartholomew
        Young." *MLR*, XXXVIII (1943), 339-340.

2. SHAKESPEARE AND CLASSICAL LITERATURE (64;25)
a. GENERAL TREATISES (64;25)
(1) GENERAL

A4121   Brown, H. "The Classical Tradition in English Literature: a Bibliography." *Harvard Studies
        and Notes in Philology.* Cambridge, 1935, pp. 7-46.

A4122   *England und Die Antike.* Vorträge d. Bibl. Warburg, IX, 1932. Pp. xii, 304.
        Rev: by Helm Kuhn, *ZAAK*, XXX (1936), 293-294; by E. C. Batho, *MLR*, XXXI, 222-224.

A4123   Hickman, Ruby Mildred. *Ghostly Etiquette on the Classical Stage.* Iowa Studies in Classical
        Phil., VII. Cedar Rapids, Iowa: Torch Press, 1938. Pp. 226.

A4124   Toretta, L. *Studi Romani e Motivi Anti-Romani nel Rinascimento Inglese.* Rome: Istituto di
        Studi Romani, 1938.

A4125   J., W. H. "Swan Signifying Poet: 'Swan Song'." *N&Q*, 177 (1939), 311-313.
        See letter by Hibernicus, ibid., pp. 353-354.

A4126   Perry, Henry Ten Eyck. *Masters of Dramatic Comedy and Their Social Themes.* Harvard Univ.
        Press, 1940. Pp. xxi, 428.
        Rev: by Allardyce Nicoll, *JEGP*, XXXIX (1940), 399; by H. S., *MLN*, LV, 641.

A4127   Lockwood, Dean P., and Roland H. Bainton. "Classical and Biblical Scholarship in the Age
        of the Renaissance and Reformation." *Church History*, X (1941), 125-143.

A4128   Warburg and Courtauld Institutes. *England and the Mediterranean Tradition: Studies in Art,
        History and Literature.* Oxford Univ. Press, 1946. Pp. viii, 232.
        Rev: *Illus. London News*, 208 (1946), 422; by N., *MGW*, LIV, 268; by Michael Ayrton,
        Spectator, June 14, 1946, pp. 612-614; by Leicester Bradner, *MP*, XLIV, 61-62; by Lynn White,
        Jr., *AHR*, LII (1947), 502-503.

A4129   Brunner, K. *England und Die Antike.* Innsbruck: Rauch, 1947. Pp. 47.

A4130   Durnell, B. H. "The Humanistic Concept of the Latin Classics in Thomas Elyot's *Book of
        the Governour.*" MS thesis, Columbia University, 1947. Pp. 78.

A4131   Von Salis, Arnold. *Antike und Renaissance: Über Nachleben und Weiterwirken der Alten in der
        Neueren Kunst.* Erlenbach-Zürich: Eugen Rentsch, 1947. Pp. 280; pl. 64; text figs. 30.
        Rev: by Margarete Bieber, *AJP*, 80 (1949), 320-325; by Ch. Picard, *Rev. Hist.*, 201 (1949),
        290-293; by Ch. Picard, "La Renaissance et l'art Antique," *Jour. des Savants*, Jan.-June, 1948,
        pp. 33-60.

A4132   Thomson, J. A. K. *The Classical Background of English Literature.* London: Allen and Unwin,
        1948. Pp. 272.
        Rev: by J. M. D. P., *MGW*, May 13, 1948, p. 10; by Gilbert Murray, *Spectator*, March 5,
        1948, p. 290; by W. A. Armstrong, *Life and Letters*, LVIII, 249-252; by V. de Sola Pinto,
        English, VII, 139-140; H. L. T., *QQ*, LV, 516-517.

A4133   Harmon, Alice I. "*Loci Communes*" on Death and Suicide in the Literature of the English Renais-
        sance.. DD, University of Minnesota, 1949. Abstract in *Summaries of PhD Theses*, Univ. of
        Minnesota, III (1949), 121-124.

A4134   Highet, Gilbert. *The Classical Tradition: Greek and Roman Influences on Western Literature.*
        Oxford Univ. Press, 1949. Pp. xxxviii, 763.
        Rev: by H. W. Garrod, *Spectator*, Sept. 30, 1949, pp. 424, 426; by G. F. Whicher, *NYHTBR*,
        Dec. 18, 1949, p. 7; *TLS*, Jan. 6, 1950, p. 12; by F. C. G., *Anglican Theol. Rev.*, XXXII, 244:
        by F. M. Combellack, *CL*, II, 376-379; by A. C., *Dublin Mag.*, XXV, 2, 44-46; by G. Romilly,
        NstN, Feb. 11, 1950, pp. 171-172; by C. A. Robinson, Jr., *SRL*, Mar. 4, 1950, p. 21; by
        Huntington Brown, *JEGP*, L (1951), 118-121; by Isidore Silver, *RR*, XLII, 69-71; (of Span.
        sec.) E. J. Webber, *HR*, XIX, 87-88; by J. Hutton, *AJP*, LXXIII (1952), 79-87; by F. Wölc-
        ken, *Archiv*, 190 (1952), 133; by G. B. A. Fletcher, *RES*, NS, III, 85-87.

A4135   Sackton, Alexander H. "The Paradoxical Encomium in Elizabethan Drama." *TxSE*, XXVIII
        (1949), 83-104.

A4136   Herrick, Marvin T. *Comic Theory in the Sixteenth Century.* Illinois Stud. in Lang. & Lit.,
        XXXIV, Nos. 1-2. Univ. Illinois Press, 1950. Pp. viii, 248.
        Rev: A7513.

A4137   Keller, Abraham C. "Ancients and Moderns in the Early Seventeenth Century." *MLQ*, XI
        (1950), 79-82.

A4138   Zocca, Louis R. *Elizabethan Narrative Poetry.* Rutgers Univ. Press, 1950. Pp. xii, 306.
        Rev: C191.

A4138a Thomson, J. A. K. *Classical Influences on English Poetry.* London: Allen & Unwin, 1951.
        Pp. 281.

A kind of sequel to Professor Thomson's *Classical Background of English Literature*, 1948, A4132. Rev: *TLS*, Sept. 28, 1951, p. 614; by Peter Russell, *Time and Tide*, Oct. 13, 1951, pp. 986-987.

A4139 Williamson, George. *The Senecan Amble: A Study in Prose Form from Bacon to Collier*. London: Faber & Faber, 1951. Pp. 377.
Rev: *TLS*, Nov. 2, 1951, p. 694 (see letter by H. R. Trevor-Roper and reviewer's reply, ibid., Nov. 16, 1951, p. 731); by Anthony Curtis, *NstN*, Sept. 29, 1951, pp. 344-345.

A4140 Bush, Douglas. *Classical Influences in Renaissance Literature*. Martin Classical Lectures, XIII. Oberlin College, 1952. Pp. 60.
Rev: by Rudolf Gottfried, *MLN*, LXVIII (1953), 505-506; Northrop Frye, *RN*, VI, 47-48; by Hardin Craig, *JEGP*, LII, 255-256; *Personalist*, XXXVI (1954), 192 (brief); by Terence Spencer, *MLR*, XLIX, 539-540.

A4141 Bolgar, R. R. *The Classical Heritage and Its Beneficiaries*. Cambridge, 1954.
Rev: by Martin R. P. McGuire, *Cath. Hist. Rev.*, XLII (1957), 501-503; by Revilo P. Oliver, *AJP*, LXXV, 307-313; *TLS*, Dec. 31, 1954, p. 852; by Douglas Bush, *RN*, VIII (1955), 14-19; by Frederick A. Artz, *SatR*, Jan. 1, p. 58; by Darsie Gillie, *Spectator*, Jan. 7, p. 22; *NstN*, Jan. 1, p. 24.

A4142 Herrick, Marvin T. *Tragicomedy*. Urbana: The Univ. of Illinois Press, 1955. Pp. 331.
Rev: B5201.

A4143 Kristeller, Paul Oskar. *The Classics and Renaissance Thought*. Martin Classical Lectures, XV. Cambridge: Harvard Univ. Press for Oberlin College, 1955. Pp. 106.
Rev: by James Hutton, *RN*, IX (1956), 149-152; by Quirinus Breen, *Church History*, XXVI (1957), 293-294; by R. R. Bolgar, *CR*, VII, 156-158; by Edward Williamson, *RR*, XLVIII, 295-297; by Otis H. Green, *Rom. Phil.*, X, 281-284; by R. F. Harvanak, S. J., *Jour. of Religion*, XXXVII, 207-208; by A. A., *Personalist*, XXXVII, 214-215; by Charles Trinkaus, *Rev. of Religion*, XXII, 189-193; by Panos Paul Morphos, *CL*, X (1958), 77-80.

A4144 Langenfelt, Gösta. "'The Noble Savage' Until Shakespeare." *ES*, XXXVI (1955), 222-227.

A4145 Thomson, J. A. K. *Classical Influences on English Prose*. London: Allen & Unwin, 1956. Pp. xiii, 303.
Rev: *TLS*, May 18, 1956, p. 294.

A4146 Mahoney, John Leo. *Classical Form in English Oratory of the Golden Age*. DD, Harvard University, 1957.

A4147 Sarton, George. *The Appreciation of Ancient and Medieval Learning During the Renaissance (1450-1600)*. Philadelphia: Univ. of Pennsylvania Press, 1957.

A4148 Taylor, William Edwards. *The Villainess in Elizabethan Drama*. DD, Vanderbilt University, 1957. Pp. 402. Mic 57-2820. *DA*, XVII (1957), 1756. Publ. No. 22,025.
Chapters 2 and 3 on classical influences.

A4149 Summerell, Joseph Howard. *Backgrounds of Elizabethan Pastoral Drama*. DD, Columbia University, 1958. Pp. 268. Mic 58-7055. *DA*, XIX (1959), 2941.

(2) SHAKESPEARE

A4150 Cunningham, Cornelius C. *Persuasive Factors in Shakespearean Address*. DD, State University of Iowa, 1936. Abstract in Univ. of Iowa *Programs Announcing Candidates for Higher Degrees* . . . , no pagination.

A4151 Formichi, Carlo. *Roma nell'Opera di Shakespeare*. Rome: Istituto di Studi Romani, 1937. Pp. 15.

A4152 Kennedy, Milton B. *The Oration in Shakespeare*. DD, University of Virginia, 1937. Abstract publ. in *Abstracts of Dissertations, 1937*, Charlottesville: Univ. of Virginia, 1937, pp. 16-18.
Rev: by W. H. MacKellar, *SR*, L (1942), 424-426; by Alfred Harbage, *MLN*, LIX (1944), 131; by Una Ellis-Fermor, *RES*, XXI (1945), 151-152; by W. Clemen, *Archiv*, 188 (1951), 147-149.

A4153 Kranz, Walther. "Shakespeare und die Antike." *Eng. Studn.*, LXXIII (1938), 32-38.

A4154 Rüdiger, H. "Shakespeare und die Antike." *Darmstädter Tageblatt*, Nov. 27, 1938.

A4155 Hadas, Moses. "Clytemnestra in Elizabethan Dress." *Class. Weekly*, XXXII (1939), 255-256.

A4156 Messiaen, Pierre. "Shakespeare et l'Histoire Romaine." *Culture*, II (Mar., 1939), 351-357.

A4157 Staedler, E. "Die Klassischen Quellen der Antoniusrede in Shakespeares *Julius Caesar*." *N. Mon.*, X (1939), 235-245.

A4158 Harrison, Thomas P., Jr. "Aspects of Primitivism in Shakespeare and Spenser." *TxSE*, XX (1940), 39-71.

A4159 Hastings, William T. "The Ancestry of Autolycus." *SAB*, XV (1940), 253.

A4160 Hughes, Merritt Y. "A Classical vs a Social Approach to Shakespeare's Autolycus." *SAB*, XV (1940), 219-226.

A4161 Law, Robert A. "The Roman Background of *Titus Andronicus*." *SP*, XL (1943), 145-153.

A4162 Nelson, Lawrence Gerald. *Classical History in Shakespeare*. DD, University of Virginia, 1943. Abstract publ. in *Abstracts of Dissertations*, Charlottesville: Univ. of Virginia, 1943, pp. 5-8.

A4163   Baldwin, Thomas Whitfield. *William Shakspere's Small Latine and Lesse Greeke*. 2 V., Univ. Illinois Press, 1944. Pp. xviii, 753; vi, 772. Reissued, 1956.
A work of great learning and importance which seems to fix definitely the nature and extent of Shakespeare's schooling.
Rev: *TLS*, July 1, 1944, p. 318; by R. A. Law, *JEGP*, XLIV (1945), 216-220; by Tucker Brooke, *MLN*, LX, 125-127; by G. D. Willcock, *MLR*, XL, 54-56; by G. B. H., *QQ*, LII, 119-121; by W. Clemen, *Archiv*, 188 (1951), 147-149; by S. Musgrove, *Erasmus*, x (1957), 539-540.

A4164   Boas, Frederick S. *Aspects of Classical Legend and History in Shakespeare*. Proceedings of the British Academy, XXIX. London: Milford, 1944. Pp. 28.
Rev: *N &Q*, 186 (1944), 191-192.

A4165   Wolff, Emil. "Shakespeare und die Antike." *Die Antike*, xx (1944), 134-174.

A4166   Cunningham, James Vincent. *Tragic Effect and Tragic Process in Some Plays of Shakespeare, and Their Background in the Literary and Ethical Theory of Classical Antiquity and the Middle Ages*. DD, Stanford University, 1945. Abstract publ. in *Abstracts of Dissertations, 1944-45*, Stanford, 1945, pp. 29-34.

A4167   Ransom, John Crowe. "On Shakespeare's Language." *SR*, LV (1947), 181-198.

A4168   Yoder, Audrey. *Animal Analogy in Shakespeare's Character Portrayal*. New York: King's Crown Press, 1947. Pp. x, 150. DD, Columbia University, 1946.
Rev: A5728.

A4169   Boyce, Benjamin. "The Stoic *Consolatio* and Shakespeare." *PMLA*, LXIV (1949), 771-780.

A4170   Baldwin, T. W. *On the Literary Genetics of Shakspere's Poems and Sonnets*. Urbana: Univ. of Illinois Press, 1950. Pp. xi, 399.
Rev: by Virgil K. Whitaker, *SQ*, II (1951), 137-139; by W. Clemen, *Archiv*, 189 (1952/53), 224-225.

A4171   Leon, Harry J. "Classical Sources for the Garden Scene in *Richard II*." *PQ*, XXIX (1950), 65-70.

A4172   Schirmer, Walter F. "Chaucer, Shakespeare und die Antike." *Kleine Schriften*. Tübingen: Niemeyer, 1950, pp. 57-82.

A4173   Clark, Donald Lemen. "Ancient Rhetoric and English Renaissance Literature." *SQ*, II (1951), 195-204.

A4174   Hower, Charles C. "The Importance of a Knowledge of Latin for Understanding the Language of Shakespeare." *Classical Journal*, XLVI (1951), 221-227.

A4175   Sledd, James. "A Note on the Use of Renaissance Dictionaries." *MP*, XLIX (1951/52), 10-15.

A4176   Sheppard, J. T. *Music at Belmont and Other Essays and Addresses*. London: Rupert Hart-Davis, 1952. Pp. 192.

A4177   Thomson, J. A. K. *Shakespeare and the Classics*. London: Allen and Unwin, 1952. Pp. 254.
Rev: by H. B. Charlton, *MGW*, May 29, 1952, p. 10; by Anthony Curtis, *NstN*, Apr. 26, 1952, pp. 503-504; *TLS*, July 11, 1952, p. 450; by Douglas Bush, *SQ*, III 375-377; by E. M. Rynaud, *EA*, v, 357-358; by F. S. Boas, *FortnR*, 1030 (Oct., 1952), 281-282; *Listener*, XLVIII, 33; by T. P. D., *Irish Ecclesiastical Record*, LXXVIII (1952), 391-392; by J. Oliver Thomson, *MLR*, XLVIII (1953), 68-69; by Clifford Leech, *ShS*, VI (1953), 155.

A4178   Haywood, Richard M. "Shakespeare and the Old Roman" *CE*, XVI (1954-5), 98-101, 151.

A4179   McAvoy, William C. "Form in *Richard II*, II. i. 40-46." *JEGP*, LIV (1955), 355-361.
Gaunt's praise of England indebted to directions for praising a city found in Aphthonius' *Progymnasmata* and the scholia of R. Lorichius.

A4180   Simpson, Percy. *Studies in Elizabethan Drama*. Oxford: Clarendon Press, 1955. Pp. 265.
Includes "Shakespeare's Use of Latin Authors," pp. 1-63.

A4181   Svoboda, Karel. "Shakespeare a Antika." *Časopis pro Moderní Filologii* (Československá Akademie Věd), XXXVII, Nos. 2-3 (1955), 82-96.

A4182   Barroll, John L., III. *Shakespeare and Roman History*. DD, Princeton University, 1956. Pp. 675. Mic 57-996. *DA*, XVII (1957), 626. Publ. No. 20,101.
See also B5049.

A4183   Wilson J. Dover. "Shakespeare's 'Small Latin'—How Much?" *ShS*, x (1957), 12-26.
Partly a summing up of scholarship; partly an independent, experimental study based mainly on *Merch.*, V. i. 1-14, in which he is able to trace all classical allusions to native sources, notably Chaucer and Golding.

A4184   Price, Hereward T. "Shakespeare's Classical Scholarship." *RES*, NS, IX (1958), 54-55.
Accepts the contention that Shak.'s signature, in the Folger copy of W. Lambarde's *Archaionomia* (1564), is genuine, deducing that Shak.'s Latin was not "small" and that he had wide intellectual interests.

b. CONTEMPORANEOUS ENGLISH TRANSLATORS
OF THE ANCIENT CLASSICS (64;25)
(1) SEVERAL OR MANY TRANSLATORS

A4185   Witz, Edmund. *Die Englischen Ovidübersetzungen des 16. Jahrhunderts*. DD, Strassburg, 1915. Pp. viii, 59.

A4186 Clements, Arthur Frederick. *Tudor Translations*. Oxford: Blackwell, 1929. Pp. 227.
       Rev: A4029.
A4187 Lathrop, H. B. *Translations from the Classics into English from Caxton to Chapman, 1475-1620.*
       Madison, 1933.
       Rev: by René Pruvost, *RAA*, xiii (1936), 337; by T. Weevers, *ES*, xix (1937), 223-225.
A4188 Wortham, James Lemuel. *English Prose Style in Translations from the Classics, 1489-1580.* DD,
       Princeton University, 1939. No abstract available to date. Microfilm, Publ. No. 3072.
       Pp. 228.
A4189 Musgrove, S. *The Changing Values in the Critical and Literary Outlook of the Seventeenth Century,
       as Manifested in English Verse Translation from the Greek and Latin Classics.* DD, Oxford,
       Merton, 1944.
A4190 Musgrove, S. "Anonymous Translations from Seneca." *N &Q*, 187 (1944), 120-121.
A4191 Swan, Marshall W. S. "Seneca: Texts and Translations." *More Books*, xx (1945), 347-354.
       English and Spanish translations.
A4192 Webb, Henry J. "English Translations of Caesar's *Commentaries* in the Sixteenth Century."
       PQ, xxviii (1949), 490-495.
       Briefly describes the 1530 edition of John Tiptoft; the 1565 one by Arthur Golding and its
       second edition in 1590; the 1600 *Observations* by Sir Clement Edmondes and its 1604 reprint;
       indicates how the *Commentaries* had become a text on the art of war.
A4193 Weinberg, Bernard. "Translations and Commentaries of Longinus, *On the Sublime*, to 1600:
       A Bibliography." *MP*, xlvii (1951), 145-151.
       Includes in chronological list editions of the Greek text, Latin commentaries and translations,
       and vernacular translations.
A4194 Clark, S. *English Renaissance Translations from Classical Latin.* DD, Cambridge, 1951.
       Cam Abs. 1950-51, p. 88.
A4195 Weinberg, Bernard. "Translations and Commentaries of Demetrius' *On Style* to 1600; A
       Bibliography." *PQ*, xxx (1951), 353-380.
A4196 Nørgaard, Holger. "Translations of the Classics into English Before 1600." *RES*, ix (1958),
       164-172.
A4197 Benham, Allen R. "Horace and His *Ars Poetica* in English: A Bibliography." *Classical
       Weekly*, xlix (1956), 1-5.
A4198 Crossett, John Maurice, Jr. *English Translations of Homer's "Iliad."* DD, Harvard University,
       1958.

(2) SPECIFIC TRANSLATORS
(a) ADLINGTON

A4199 Adlington, William, tr. *The Golden Ass of Apuleius: Translated Out of Latin by William Ad-
       lington in the Year 1566.* With an Introduction by Louis MacNeice. Chiltern Lib., No. 1.
       London: John Lehmann, 1946. Pp. xi, 239.
       An unabridged reprint.
       Rev: by J. F. Burnet, *FortnR*, 161 (1947), 207.
A4200 Montgomerie, William. "Lucianus Nephew to the King (Hamlet III. ii. 238)." *N &Q*, ns
       iii (1956), 149-151.
A4201 Montgomerie, William. "Provincial Roses." *N &Q*, ns, iii (1956), 361.
       A further point on his previous note, A4200.

(b) CHAPMAN

A4202 Nicoll, Allardyce, ed. *Chapman's Homer: The Iliad, The Odyssey and The Lesser Homerica.*
       With Introd., Notes, Commentaries, and Glossaries. 2 vols. Bollingen Ser. xli. New York:
       Pantheon Books, 1956.
A4203 Rouse, W. H. D. "Chapman's Homer." *TLS*, Jan. 4, 1936, p. 15.
A4204 Loane, George G. "The Text of Chapman's Homer." *TLS*, Apr. 18, 1936, p. 336.
A4205 L., G. G. "Queries from Chapman's *Iliad*." *N &Q*, 169 (1936), 261-262.
A4206 L., G. G. "Queries from Chapman's *Odyssey*." *N &Q*, 169 (1936), 330-331.
A4207 Weever, T. "Coornhert's and Chapman's Odysseys, an Early and a Late Renaissance Homer."
       ES, xviii (1936), 145-152.
A4208 Loane, George G. "Chapman's Method." *TLS*, July 24, 1937, p. 544.
A4209 Loane, George G. "Chapman's Homer." *CM*, 156 (1937), 637-644.
A4210 Loane, George G. "Misprints in Chapman's Homer." *N &Q*, 173 (1937), 399-402, 453-455.
A4211 Loane, George G. "Misprints in Chapman's Homer." *N &Q*, 174 (1938), 367; 175 (1938),
       331-332.
A4212 Fay, H. C. "Chapman's Materials for His Translation of Homer." *RES*, ii (1951), 121-128.
A4213 Fay, H. C. "Poetry, Pedantry, and Life in Chapman's *Iliads*." *RES*, iv (1953), 13-25.
A4214 Fay, H. C. "Chapman's Text Corrections in His *Iliads*." *Library*, vii (1952), 275-280.

A4215 Lord, George deF. *Homeric Renaissance: "The Odyssey" of George Chapman*. New Haven, 1956.
Rev: by Robert G. Hoerber, *Books Abroad*, XXXI (1957), 309-310; by Robert K. Presson,
JEGP, LVI, 629-631; by J. I. M. Stewart, *NstN*, Jan. 26, p. 109; by Phyllis Bartlett, *RN*, X,
95-98; by Douglas Bush, *YR*, XLVI, 430-432.

A4216 Ure, Peter. "Chapman as Translator and Tragic Playwright." *Guide to Eng. Lit.*, ed. Boris
Ford, II (1956), 318-333.

(c) GOLDING

A4217 Kish, George, ed. *The Excellent and Pleasant Worke "Collectanea Rerum Memorabilium" of
Caius Julius Solinus; Translated from the Latin (1587) by Arthur Golding*. A Facsimile Reproduction with an Introd. Gainesville, Florida: Scholars' Facsimiles & Reprints, 1955.

A4218 Leonard, Edwin S. *Golding's Translation of Ovid's "Metamorphoses."* DD, University of
Missouri, 1938.

A4219 Swan, Marshall Wilbur Stephen. *A Study of Golding's Ovid*. DD, Harvard University, 1942.
Abstract publ. in *Summaries of PhD Theses, 1942*. Cambridge: Harvard Univ. Press, 1946,
pp. 287-290.

A4220 Swan, Marshall W. S. " 'Concerning Benefyting'." *More Books*, XXI (1946), 123-128.
Deals with Golding's 1578 English translation of Seneca's *De Beneficiis*.

A4221 Steiner, Grundy. "Golding's Use of the Regius-Micyllus Commentary Upon Ovid." *JEGP*,
XLIX (1950), 317-323.

(d) STANYHURST

A4222 Schmidt, Heinrich. *Richard Stanyhursts Übersetzung von Virgils Aeneide, I-IV. Ihr Verhältnis
zum Original, Stil und Wortschatz*. DD, Breslau, 1887. Pp. 44.

A4223 Grose, Nancy P. "Studies in the Life and English Works of Richard Stanyhurst (1547-1618)."
MA thesis, London, 1948.

A4224 Greig, Margaret. "An Elizabethan Joyce." *English*, IX (1953), 166-167. Richard Stanyhurst.

A4225 Hoppe, Harry R. "The Period of Richard Stanyhurst's Chaplaincy to the Archduke Albert."
Biographical Studies, Arundel, Sussex, III (1955), 115-117

(e) STUDLEY

A4226 Dowlin, C. M. "Two Shakespeare Parallels in Studley's Translation of Seneca's *Agamemnon*."
SAB, XIV (1939), 256. See also "A Correction," *SAB*, XV (1940), 128.

A4227 Muir, Kenneth. "Seneca and Shakespeare." *N &Q*, NS, III (1956), 243-244.
Finds verbal echoes in Macbeth's soliloquies from Studley's tr. of the *Agamemnon*.

(f) SURREY

A4228 Fest, Otto. *Über Surreys Virgilübersetzung*. DD, Berlin, Humboldt University, 1903. Pp.
46. Publ. in *Palaestra*, XXXIV.

A4229 Oras, Ants. "Surrey's Technique of Phonetic Echoes: A Method and Its Background."
JEGP, L (1951), 289-308.
Studies assonance, approximate rime, occasional true rime, and consonance in the tr. of the
Aeneid; examines briefly similar practices in Surrey's Italian predecessors.

A4230 Webb, H. J. "The Elizabethan Translation of Vegetius' *De re militari*." *MLN*, LVI (1941),
605-606.

(g) "W. B." (OF APPIAN)

A4231 Schanzer, Ernest, ed. *Shakespeare's Appian*. A Selection from the Tudor Translation of
Appian's *Civil Wars* (English Reprints Series). Liverpool Univ. Press, 1956. Pp. xxviii, 101.
Rev: *TLS*, Aug. 24, 1956, p. 503; by G. Blakemore Evans, *JEGP*, LVI (1957), 282-283; by
R. Davril, *EA*, X, 57; by J. Chalker, *SN*, XXIX, 104; by E. T. Sehrt, *Anglia*, LXXV, 472-473;
by Clifford P. Lyons, *SQ*, IX (1958), 72-73; by E. A. J. Honigmann, *RES*, NS, IX 187-188;
N &Q, NS, V, 133; by T. J. B. Spencer, *MLR*, LIII, 460; by H. Heuer, *SJ*, 94 (1958), 295.

A4232 Ryan, Pat M., Jr. "Appian's *Civil Wars* Yet Again as Source for Antony's Oration." *QJS*,
XLIV (1958), 72-73.
Ref to A4231.

(h) OTHERS (Alphabetically by translator)

A4233 Parks, George B. "William Barker, Tudor Translator." *Papers Bibliog. Soc. Amer.*, LI (1957),
126-140.

A4234 Lenaghan, Robert Thomas. *William Caxton's Translation of the "Subtyl Historyes and Fables of
Esope"*: *An Annotated Edition*. DD, Harvard University, 1957.

A4235 Riddlehough, Geoffrey B. "Queen Elizabeth's Translation of Boethius' *De Consolatione
Philosophiae*." *JEGP*, XLV (1946), 88-94.

A4236 Jackson, William A. "The First Separately Printed English Translation of Horace." *Harvard*

Lib. Bul., I (1947), 238-241.
Describes one of the broadsides from Helmingham Hall, the translation done by Lewis Evan and published on or shortly before July 22, 1565.

A4237   M., M. "Roman History in Elizabethan English." *More Books*, XVIII (1943), 184.
Thomas Heywood's translation of *Catelin and Jugurth* of Sallust.

A4238   M., M. "The First English Edition of Josephus." *More Books*, XVIII (1943), 229.
Thomas Lodge's translation.

A4239   Martin, L. C. "Lucan-Marlowe? Chapman." *RES*, XXIV (1948), 317-321.
Concerns the authorship of *Lucans First Book Translated . . . by Chr. Marlowe* (1600).

A4240   Thompson, C. R. *The Translations of Lucian by Erasmus and St. Thomas More*. Ithaca, New York, 1940. Pp. 52. First published *RBPH*, XVIII (1939), 855-881.
See note on circumstances of publication by Mr. Thomson in *MLR*, XXXVIII, 76.
      Rev: by Douglas Bush, *Speculum*, XVII (1941), 148-149; by J. F. Lockwood, *MLR*, XXXVII, 235; by L. R. Lind, *Class. Week.*, XXXV, 103-104; by William Nelson, *MLQ*, II, 647-648.

A4241   Law, Robert A. "The Text of 'Shakespeare's Plutarch'." *HLQ*, VI (1943), 197-203.

A4242   Brenner, Eduard J. W. *Phaers Virgilübersetzung in Ihrem Verhältnis zum Original*. DD, Würzburg, 1912. Pp. 68.
Publ. under the title *Thomas Phaer m. bes. Berücksichtigung seiner Aeneis-Übersetzung* in *Würzburger Beiträge zur Englischen Literaturgeschichte* (Heidelberg) II.

A4243   Palmer, Ralph Graham. *Seneca's "De Remediis Fortuitorum" and the Elizabethans*. Institute of Elizabethan Studies I. Chicago, 1953. Pp. 66.
Essay on Senecan influence in 16th Century, with reprint of newly edited Latin text and Whyttynton's 1547 translation on facing pages.
      Rev: A4304.

c. INFLUENCE OF INDIVIDUAL LATIN CLASSICAL AUTHORS (65;25)
(1) APULEIUS

A4244   M. Generosa, Sister. "Apuleius and *A Midsummer-Night's Dream*: Analogue or Source, Which?" *SP*, XLII (1945), 198-204.

A4245   Starnes, D. T. "Shakespeare and Apuleius." *PMLA*, LX (1945), 1021-50.

A4246   Montgomerie, William. "Lucianus, Nephew to the King (*Hamlet* III. ii. 238)." *N &Q*, NS, III (1956), 149-151, 361.

(2) BOETHIUS

A4247   Soellner, Rolf. "Shakespeare and the *Consolatio*." *N &Q*, 199, (1954), 108-109.

(3) CATULLUS

A4248   "Shakespeare and Catullus." *Ba*, XXXI (1947), 3.

A4249   McPeek, James Andrew Scarborough. *The Influence of Catullus Upon English Literature*. MA thesis, Acadia, Canada, 1928.

A4250   McPeek, James A. S. *Catullus in Strange and Distant Britain*. Harvard Studies in Comp. Lit., XV. Harvard Univ. Press, 1939. Pp. xvii, 411.
      Rev: by B. E. C. Davis, *MLR*, XXXV (1940), 235-236; by James Hutton, *MLN*, LV, 639-640.

A4251   Kan, A. H. "Plagiaat? (Hamlet en Catullus.)" *Hermeneus* (Zwolle), XX (1948), 24.

A4252   Eagle, Roderick L. "Shakespeare and Catullus." *N &Q*, NS, IV (1957), 521-522.

(4) CICERO

A4253   C., T. C. "Three Notes on Hamlet." *N &Q*, 175 (1938), 114, 158. See answer by Hibernicus, " 'The Mind's Eye'," ibid., pp. 158-159.

A4254   Jones, Robert E. "Brutus in Cicereo and Shakespeare." *Classical Journal*, XXXVIII (1943), 449-457.
Declares Cicero a better source on Brutus than Plutarch.

A4255   Ruegg, W. *Cicero und der Humanismus*. Zurich: Rhein-Verlag, 1946.
Analyzes the reasons for the admiration of Renaissance scholars for Cicero.
      Rev: *TLS*, July 13, 1946, p. 328; by H. Bouchery, *De Gulden Passer*, NR, XXIV (1947), 88-92; by Dorothy Robathan, *Classical Weekly*, XL, 63.

A4256   Venezky, Alice S. *Pageantry on the Shakespearean Stage*. New York, 1951. Pp. 242.
Cicero, p. 63 ff.
      Rev: A7238.

A4257   Kennedy, William Henry Joseph, Jr. *The Influence of Cicero in England During the Sixteenth Century*. DD, Harvard University, 1957.

(5) HORACE

A4258   Westbrook, Perry D. "Horace's Influence on Shakespeare's *Antony and Cleopatra*." *PMLA*, LXII (1947), 392-398.

A4259   Wilkinson, L. P. "Shakespeare and Horace." *TLS*, May 6, 1955, p. 237.

A4260   Maximilianus, P. "Shakespeare en Horatius." *Neophil*, XL (1956), 144.

A4261   Benham, Allen R. "Horace and His *Ars Poetica* in English: A Bibliography." *Classical Weekly*, XLIX (1956), 1-5.

A4262   Lever, J. W. "Chapman and Shakespeare." *N &Q*, NS, V (1958), 99-100.
Both Shak. and Chapman drew heavily on Horace, *Odes*, III. XXX. And Ovid, *Metam.*, XV, 871 ff.
See also A4321.

(6)   OVID

A4263   Sedgwick, W. B. "The Influence of Ovid." *19th Century*, 122 (1937), 483-494.

A4264   Parry, J. P., tr. and ed. *"The Art of Courtly Love" by Andreas Capellanus*. New York: Columbia Univ. Press, 1941. Pp. xii, 218.

A4265   Swan, Marshall Wilbur Stephen. *A Study of Golding's Ovid*. DD, Harvard University, 1942. Abstract publ. in *Summaries of PhD Theses, 1942*, Cambridge: Harvard Univ. Press, 1946, pp. 287-290.

A4266   Forrest, John. *The Elizabethan Ovid: A Study of the Ovidian Spirit in Elizabethan Poetry, 1589-1610*. DD, Edinburgh, 1945.

A4267   Boas, Frederick S. *Ovid and the Elizabethans*. A Lecture delivered at a Joint Meeting of the English Association and the London Branch of the Classical Association. London: English Association, 1947. Pp. 16.
Rev: *TLS*, Dec. 27, 1947, p. 678; *N &Q*, 193 (1948), 484.

A4268   Davenport, A. "Weever, Ovid and Shakespeare." *N &Q*, 194 (1949), 524-525.

A4269   Starnes, D. T. "Shakespeare's Sonnet 60: Analogues." *N &Q*, 194 (1949), 454.

A4270   Head, E. A. *The Ovidian Mythological Verse Romance in England During the Early Seventeenth Century*. MA thesis, University of London, 1953.

A4271   Smith, Hallett. *Elizabethan Poetry: A Study in Conventions, Meaning, and Expression*. Cambridge, Mass.: Harvard Univ. Press, 1953. Pp. xii, 355.
Rev: A8369.

A4272   Miller, Robert P. *The Double Hunt of Love, a Study of Shakespeare's "Venus and Adonis" as a Christian Mythological Narrative*. DD, Princeton University, 1955. Pp. 587. Mic A54-3471. *DA*, XIV (1954), 2338. Publ. No. 9436.

A4273   Starnes, DeWitt Talmage. "Acteon's Dogs." *Names*, III (1955), 19-25.

A4274   Wilkinson, L. P. *Ovid Recalled*. Cambridge Univ. Press, 1955. Pp. 483.

A4275   Waith, Eugene M. "The Metamorphosis of Violence in *Titus Andronicus*." *ShS*, X (1957), 39-49.

A4276   Eagle, Roderick L. "Shakespeare's Learned Ladies." *N &Q*, NS, V (1958), 197.
See also A4256 and A4262.

(7)   PLAUTUS

A4277   Draper, John W. "Falstaff and the Plautine Parasite." *Classical Journ.*, XXXIII (1938), 390-401.

A4278   Knox, Bernard. *"The Tempest* and the Ancient Comic Tradition," in *English Stage Comedy*. *EIE*, 1954, pp. 52-73. See also *VQR*, XXXI, 73-89, and comment in *CE*, XVI, 455.

A4279   Salingar, L. G. "Messaline in *Twelfth Night*." *TLS*, June 3, 1955, p. 301.

A4280   Etherton, A. R. B. *The Influence of Classical Dramatists, Particularly Plautus and Terence, on English Comedy from 1520-1556*. DD, University of London, 1956.

(8)   PLINY

A4281   Jaggard, Wm. " 'The Phoenix and the Turtle': Translation of Pliny." *N &Q*, 180 (1941), 51.

A4282   Meyerstein, E. H. W. "Othello and C. Furius Cresinus." *TLS*, Feb. 7, 1942, p. 72.

A4283   Muir, Kenneth. "Holland's Pliny and *Othello*." *N &Q*, 198 (1953), 513-514.

(9)   SENECA

A4284   Reimers, A. L. *Seneca and Elizabethan Tragedy*. MA thesis, Stellenbosch, South Africa, 1933.

A4285   Williamson, George. "Senecan Style in the Seventeenth Century." *PQ*, XV (1936), 321-351.

A4286   Beckingham, C. F. "Seneca's Fatalism and Elizabethan Tragedy." *MLR*, XXXII (1937), 434-438.

A4287   Sawler, Harold Hall. *The Influence of Seneca on Elizabethan Tragedy*. MA thesis, Dalhousie University, 1937. Pp. 112.

A4288   Dowlin, C. M. "Two Shakespeare Parallels in Studley's Translation of Seneca's *Agamemnon*." *SAB*, XIV (1939), 256. See also "A Correction," *SAB*, XV (1940), 128.

A4289   Craig, Hardin. "The Shackling of Accidents: A Study of Elizabethan Tragedy." *PQ*, XIX (1940), 1-19.

A4290 Mendell, Clarence W. *Our Seneca.* New Haven: Yale Univ. Press, 1941. Pp. viii, 285.
Rev: by H. D. Kitto, "Classical and Elizabethan Drama," *CR*, LVII (1943), 29-30.

A4291 Montgomerie, William. "English Seneca." *Life and Letters Today*, XXXVI (1943), 25-28.

A4292 Morel, W. "On Some Passages in Shakespeare's Tragedies." *AJP*, LXIV (1943), 94-97.

A4293 Heller, J. L., and R. L. Grismer. "Seneca in the Celestinesque Novel." *HR*, XII (1944), 29-48.

A4294 Wells, Henry W. "Senecan Influence on Elizabethan Tragedy: A Re-Estimation." *SAB*, XIX (1944), 71-84.

A4295 Charlton, H. B. *Senecan Tradition in Renaissance Tragedy: A Re-issue of an Essay Published in 1821.* Victoria Univ. Manchester, Publ. No. 296, English Ser. No. 24. Manchester Univ. Press, 1946. Pp. vii, ccv.

A4296 Bandel, B. *The Debt of Shakespearian Tragedy to Early English Comedy.* MS thesis, Columbia University, 1947. Pp. 130.

A4297 Reed, R. R., Jr. *Seneca and Elizabethan Tragedy.* MS thesis, Columbia University, 1947. Pp. 61.

A4298 Armstrong, W. A. "The Influence of Seneca and Machiavelli on the Elizabethan Tyrant." *RES*, XXIV (1948), 19-35.

A4299 Craig, Hardin. "Shakespeare and the History Play." *AMS*, pp. 55-64.

A4300 Johnson, Francis R. "Shakespearian Imagery and Senecan Imitation." *AMS*, pp. 33-53.

A4301 Ure, Peter. "On Some Differences Between Senecan and Elizabethan Tragedy." *DUJ*, XLI (1948), 17-23.

A4302 Muir, Kenneth. "A Borrowing from Seneca." *N &Q*, 194 (1949), 214-216.

A4303 Atherton, J. S. "Shakespeare's Latin, Two Notes." *N &Q*, 196 (1951), 337.

A4304 Palmer, Ralph G. *Seneca's "De Remediis Fortuitorum" and the Elizabethans.* An Essay on the Influence of Seneca's Ethical Thought in the Sixteenth Century, together with the Newly-edited Latin Text and English Translation of 1547 Entitled: *Lucii Annei Senecae ad Gallioneni de Remedis Fortuitorum. The Remedyes agaynst all Casuall Chances. Dialogus inter Sensum et Rationem. A Dialogue betwene Sensualyte and Reason. Lately Translated out of Latyn into Englyshe by Robert Whyttyton Poet Laureat and nowe Newely Imprynted.* Inst. of Elizabethan Stud. Pub. No. 1. Chicago, 1953. Pp. 66.
Rev: *N &Q*, NS, I (1954), 547; *RN*, VII (1954), 104; by R. Kirk, *MLN*, LXX (1955), 204-205; by R. T. Bruère, *Classical Philology*, L (1955), 61; by R. Davril, *EA*, VII (1955), 149; by L. Herrmann, *RBPH*, XXXIII (1955), 1046; *Études Classiques*, 1955, p. 215; by J. Chalker, *SN*, XXVIII (1956), 258; by J. Espiner-Scott, *RLC*, XXXII (1958), 118-120.

A4305 Tolbert, James M. "A Source of Shakespeare's *Lucrece*." *N &Q*, 198 (1953), 14-15.

A4306 Clemen, W. H. "Tradition and Originality in Shakespeare's *Richard III*." *SQ*, V (1954), 247-257.

A4307 Riley, Bryan M. *L'Influence de Sénèque sur Shakespeare.* DD, Paris, 1954. Typewritten.

A4308 Förg, Josef. *Typische Redeformen und Motive im Vorshakespeareschen Drama und ihre Vorbilder bei Seneca.* DD, Munich, 1955.

A4309 Muir, Kenneth. "Buchanan, Leslie and *Macbeth*." *N &Q*, NS, II (1955), 511-512.

A4310 Muir, Kenneth. "Seneca and Shakespeare." *N &Q*, III (1956), 243-244.

A4311 Schanzer, Ernest. "*Hercules Oetaeus* and *King John*." *N &Q*, NS, III (1956), 509-510.

A4312 Fleming, N. E. *The Influence of Seneca on Shakespeare.* MA thesis, Liverpool University, 1957.

A4313 Taylor, William Edwards. "The Villainess in Elizabethan Drama." DD, Vanderbilt University, 1957. Pp. 402. Mic 57-2820. *DA*, XVII (1957), 1756-1757.

A4314 Ornstein, Robert. "Seneca and the Political Drama of *Julius Caesar*." *JEGP*, LVII (1958), 51-56.

A4315 Soellner, Rolf. "The Madness of Hercules." *CL*, X (1958), 309-324.

(10) VIRGIL

A4316 Nosworthy, J. M. "The Narrative Sources of *The Tempest*." *RES*, XXIV (1948), 281-294.

A4317 Maxwell, J. C. "Virgilian Half-Lines in Shakespeare's 'Heroic Narrative'." *N &Q*, 198 (1953), 100.

(11) OTHERS (Alphabetically by Latin Author.)

A4318 Hamilton, Marie Padgett. "A Latin and English Passage on Dreams." *SP*, XXXIII (1936), 1-9. Claudian.

A4319 Kaiser, Leo. "Shakespeare and St. Jerome." *Classical Journal*, XII (1946), 219-220.

A4320 Blissett, William. "Lucan's Caesar and the Elizabethan Villain." *SP*, LIII (1956), 553-575.

A4321 Turner, Paul. "True Madness (A Note on *Hamlet* II. ii. 92-95)." *N &Q*, NS, IV (1957, 194-196. From Juvenal or from Horace.

A4322 Tolbert, James M. "The Argument of Shakespeare's *Lucrece*: Its Sources and Authorship." *TxSE*, XXIX (1950), 77-90.

Argues that the source is a Latin epitome of Livy, also used by Thomas Languet in *Cooper's Chronicle* (1549), doubts that Shakespeare is the author; suggests John Harrison, the publisher.

A4323   Martin, L. C. "Shakespeare, Lucretius, and the Commonplaces." *RES*, XXI (1945), 174-182.

A4324   Berry, E. G. "Hamlet and Suetonius." *The Phoenix*, II (1948), 73-81.

A4325   García, V. B. "Tácito y Shakespeare." *Universidad* (Saragossa), XXIV (1948), 38-41.

d. INFLUENCE OF THE GREEK CLASSICAL AUTHORS (67;25)
(1)   GENERAL STUDIES (67;25)

A4326   Allen, Don Cameron. "The Rehabilitation of Epicurus and His Theory of Pleasure in the Early Renaissance." *SP*, XLI (1944), 1-15.

A4327   Lever, Katherine. *Early Tudor Drama and Old Greek Comedy: A Study of Didactic and Satiric Drama.* DD, Bryn Mawr College, 1945. *Mcf. Ab.*, VI, No. 1 (1945), 77-79.

A4328   Lever, Katherine. "Greek Comedy on the Sixteenth-Century English Stage." *CamJ*, XLI (1946), 169-174.

A4329   Cancelled.

A4330   Wolff, Ernst. *Die goldene Kette: Das Nachleben des homerischen Bildes von der goldenen Kette in der englishen Literatur von Chaucer bis Wordsworth.* Hamburg: Hansischer Gildenverlag, 1947. Pp. 83.
          Rev: by J. E. Housman, *MLR*, XLIV (1949), 141-142.

A4331   Barker, Sir Ernest. *Traditions of Civility: Eight Essays.* Cambridge Univ. Press, 1948. Pp. ciii, 369.
          Includes "Greek Influences in English Life and Thought."

A4332   Warner, William. *William Warner's "Syrinx or Sevenfold History."* Ed. with Intro. and Notes by Wallace A. Bacon. Northwestern Univ. Press, 1950. Pp. lxxxv, 223.
          Long introduction upon the Greek romance.
          Rev: *N &Q*, 196 (1951), 372-373; by H. L. Tracy, *QQ*, LVIII, 447-448.

A4333   Jayne, Sears. "Ficino and the Platonism of the English Renaissance." *CL*, IV (1953), 214-238·

A4334   Spencer, Terence. *Fair Greece Sad Relic.* Literary Panhellenism from Shakespeare to Byron. London: Weidenfeld & Nicolson, 1954. Pp. 312, pl.
          Rev: *TLS*, May 14, 1954, p. 307; by E. I. Watkin, *Church Quar. Review*, 156 (1955), 223-225; by A. J. B. Wace, *RES*, VII (1956), 99-100; by Herbert G. Wright, *MLR*, LII (1957), 415-416.

(2)   SHAKESPEARE AND GREEK AUTHORS
(a)   GENERAL

A4335   Zitzmann, Irene Jane. *The Greek Influence on Shakespeare.* MA thesis, McGill University, 1930.

A4336   Hutton, James. "Analogues of Shakespeare's Sonnets 153-54; Contributions to the History of a Theme." *MP*, XXXVIII (1941), 385-403.

A4337   Yates, Frances A. "Shakespeare and the Platonic Tradition." *Univ. of Edin. Jour.*, XII (1942), 2-12.

A4338   Roussel, L. "Shakespeare's Greek." *TLS*, Feb. 2, 1946, p. 55. Further correspondence: D. Koffler, ibid., pp. 91, 115; R. L. Eagle, p. 127; John Berryman, p. 151; A. de Quincey, p. 199. Various sources for *Lear* and comments on the "anvil of my sword" passage in *Cor.*

A4339   Ellis, Oliver C. de C. *Cleopatra in the Tide of Time.* London: Williams & Norgate, 1947. Pp. xv, 287.
          Rev: B9407.

A4340   Taylor, E. M. M. "Lear's Philosopher." *SQ*, VI (1955), 364-365.

A4341   Cancelled.

A4342   Gesner, Carol. *The Greek Romance Materials in the Plays of Shakespeare.* DD, Louisiana State University, 1956. Pp. 352. Mic 56-3435. *DA*, XVI (1956), 2162. Publ. No. 17,442.

(b)   INDIVIDUAL GREEK AUTHORS (67;25)
i.   Apthonius

A4343   Johnson, Francis R. "Two Renaissance Textbooks of Rhetoric: Aphthonius' *Progymnasmata* and Rainolde's *A Booke Called the Foundacion of Rhetorike.*" *HLQ*, VI (1943), 427-444.

A4343a Baldwin, T. W. "Shakspere's Aphthonian Man." *MLN*, LXV (1950), 111-112.

A4344   McAvoy, William Charles. *Shakespeare's Use of the Laus of Apthonius.* DD, University of Illinois, 1952. Pp. 225. Mic A53-237. *DA*, XIII (1953), 97. Publ. No. 4464.

ii.   Aristotle and Plato

A4345   Anderson, Ruth L. " 'As Heart Can Think'." *SAB*, XII (1937), 246-251.
          Illustrates the survival of Aristotelian notion that the reasonable soul resides in the heart.

A4346   Klibansky, Raymond. "Plato's *Parmenides* in the Middle Ages and the Renaissance." *The Warburg Institute, Mediaeval and Renaissance Studies*, I (1943), 281-334.

A4347   Jayne, Sears R. *Platonism in English Drama of the Renaissance, 1442-1642.* DD, Yale University, 1948.

A4348   Lees, F. N. "*Coriolanus*, Aristotle, and Bacon." *RES*, NS, I (1950), 114-135.

A4349   Caldiero, Frank M. "The Source of Hamlet's 'What a Piece of Work is a Man!' " *N&Q*, 196 (1951), 421-424.

A4350   Hammerle, Karl. "The Poet's Eye (*MND* V.i.12): Zur Auffassung Shakespeares vom Wesen des Dichters." *Innsbrucker Beiträge zur Kulturwissenschaft*, (Ammann-Festgabe I. Teil), I (1954), 101-107.

A4351   Hammerle, Karl. "Shakespeares Platonische Wende." *Anglo-Americana, Festschrift für Leo Hibler-Lehmannssport, Wiener Beiträge z. engl. Philologie*, LXII (1955), 62-71.

A4352   Nitze, W. A. "*Midsummer Night's Dream*, V. i. 4-17." *MLR*, L (1955), 495-497.
        The madness of lunatics, lovers, and poets passage recalls Plato's *Phaedrus*.

A4353   Richards, I. A. *Speculative Instruments.* Univ. of Chicago Press, 1955. Pp. xii, 216.
        Eighteen essays on meaning, with the general theme of "How do we understand anything or one another?" Includes "*Troilus and Cressida* and Plato," pp. 198-213.

A4354   Suberman, Jack. *Platonism in Shakespeare.* DD, University of North Carolina, 1955.

A4355   Gallagher, Ligera Cécile. *Shakespeare and the Aristotelian Ethical Tradition.* DD, Stanford University, 1956. Pp. 338. Mic 56-3017. *DA*, XVI (1956), 1898. Publ. No. 17,720.

A4356   Steadman, John M. "The 'Fairies' Midwife': *Romeo and Juliet*, I. iv." *N&Q*, NS, III (1956), 424.

iii. Plutarch

A4357   Fleming, Rudd. *Plutarch in the English Renaissance.* DD, Cornell University, 1935.

A4358   Heuer, Hermann. "Shakespeare und Plutarch in Shakespeares Römerdramen." *ZNU*, XXXVII (1938), 65-90.

A4359   Heuer, Hermann. "Shakespeare und Plutarch. Studien zu Wertwelt und Lebensgefühl im *Coriolanus*." *Anglia*, LXII (1939), 321-346.

A4360   Law, Robert A. "The Text of 'Shakespeare's Plutarch'." *HLQ*, VI (1943), 197-203.

A4361   Barnett, George L. " 'The Glass of Fashion and the Mould of Form': *Hamlet*, III. i. 161." *N&Q*, 185 (1943), 105.

A4362   Campbell, Lily B. "Polonius: The Tyrant's Ears." *AMS*, 1948, pp. 295-313.

A4363   Law, Robert Adger. "Porcia's Curiosity: A Tale Thrice Told by Shakespeare." *TxSE*, XXVII (1948), 207-214.

A4364   Nyland, Waino S. "Pompey as the Mythical Lover of Cleopatra." *MLN*, LXIV (1949), 515-516.

A4365   Law, Robert Adger. "On Certain Proper Names in Shakespeare." *TxSE*, XXX (1951), 61-65.
        Rev: by M. Eccles, *SQ*, IV (1953), 352.

A4366   Stull, Joseph S. "Shakespeare and Plutarch's *Life of Pelopidas*." *N&Q*, 198 (1953), 512-513.

A4367   Oakeshott, Walter. "Shakespeare and Plutarch." *Talking of Shakespeare*, ed. by John Garrett. London: Hodder & Stoughton & Max Reinhardt, 1954.

A4368   Norman, Arthur M. Z. "Source Material in *Antony and Cleopatra*." *N&Q*, NS, III (1956), 59-61.

A4369   Thomas, Mary Olive. *Plutarch in "Antony and Cleopatra".* DD, Duke University, 1956.

A4370   Heuer, Hermann. "From Plutarch to Shakespeare: A Study of *Coriolanus*." *ShS*, X (1957), 50-59.

A4371   Honda, Akira. "Antonius to Antony." *Hōsei Daigaku Bungakubu Kiyō.* (Hōsei Univ. Studies in English and American Literature), No. 3, 1958, pp. 1-15.
        Shak.'s use of Plutarch's account.

iv. Theophrastus

A4372   Greenough, Chester Noyes. *A Bibliography of the Theophrastian Character in English.* Prepared for pub. by J. Milton French. Harvard Univ. Press, 1947. Pp. xii, 347.
        Rev: A36.

A4373   *A Strange Metamorphosis of Man Transformed into a Wildernesse. Deciphered into Characters.* London, 1634. Edited with an Introduction and Notes by Don Cameron Allen. Baltimore: Johns Hopkins Press; London: Oxford Univ. Press, 1949. Pp. xviii, 64.
        Rev: by J. M. French, *MLN*, LXV (1950), 566-567; bv A. K. Croston, *RES*, II (1951), 280-281.

A4374   Overbury, Sir Thomas. *The Overburian Characters.* Edited by W. J. Paylor. Oxford, 1936.
        Rev: by W. M. Clyde, *RES*, XIV (1938), 221-223; by G. Bonnard, *ES*, XXI (1939), 279-283.

A4375   Paylor, W. J. "The Editions of the 'Overburian' Characters." *Library*, XVII (1936), 340-348.

A4376   Paylor, W. J. "Thomas Dekker and the 'Overburian' Characters." *MLR*, XXXI (1936), 155-160.

A4377   Boyce, Benjamin. *The Theophrastan Character in England to 1642.* Harvard Univ. Press, 1947. Pp. ix, 324.

Rev: by D. C. A., *MLN*, LXIII (1948), 211-212; by J. M. French, *JEGP*, XLVII, 198-202; TLS, Sept. 11, p. 517; by V. B. Heltzel, *PQ*, XXVII, 285-288.

A4378 Thomson, J. A. K. *Classical Influences on English Prose.* London: Allen & Unwin, 1956. Pp. xiii, 303. Chap. XIV: "Characters," pp. 219-234.
Rev: A4145.

v. Others

A4379 Roussel, Louis. "Shakespeare's Greek." *TLS*, Feb. 2, 1946, p. 55.
See letters by Dosio Koffler, ibid., Feb. 23, 1946, p. 91, and Mar. 9, p. 115; by Roderick L. Eagle, Mar. 16, p. 127; by John Berryman, Mar. 30, p. 151; and A. de Quincey, Apr. 27, p. 199. Includes comments on Aeschylus.

A4380 Glasson, T. Francis. "Did Shakespeare Read Aeschylus?" *London Quar. & Holborn Rev.,* 173 (1948), 57-66.

A4381 Schanzer, Ernest, ed. *Shakespeare's Appian.* A Selection from the Tudor Translation of Appian's *Civil Wars* (English Reprints Series). Liverpool Univ. Press, 1956. Pp. xxviii, 101. Selections probably drawn upon for *Caesar* and *Antony.*
Rev: A4231.

A4382 Ryan, Pat M., Jr. "Appian's *Civil Wars* Yet Again as Source for Antony's Oration." *QJS*, XLIV (1958), 72-73.
Ref. to Schanzer's ed. of Tudor Appian.

A4383 Raanes, Florence E. *The Celestial Hierarchy of the Pseudo-Dionysius and its Influence Upon English Poetry of the Sixteenth and Seventeenth Centuries.* DD, New York University, 1952.

A4384 Schapira, Elisabeth. *Der Einfluss des Euripides auf die Tragödie des Cinquecento.* DD, Munich, 1935.

A4385 Scott, John A. "An Unnoticed Homeric Phrase in Shakespeare." [*Coriolanus*, IV. vi. 144.] *Classical Philology*, XXXIII (1938), 414.

A4386 Law, Robert Adger. "An Echo of Homer in *Henry the Fifth?*" *TxSE*, (1942), 105-109.

A4387 Bennett, Josephine Waters. "Characterization in Polonius' Advice to Laertes." *SQ*, IV (1953), 3-9.
See note by R. H. Bowers, pp. 362-364. Suggests source is *Ad Demonicum* of Isocrates.

A4388 Weinberg, Bernard. "Translations and Commentaries of Longinus, *On the Sublime*, to 1600: A Bibliography." *MP*, XLVII (1950), 145-151.

A4389 Bond, R. W. "Lucian and Boiardo in *Timon.*" *Studia Otiosa*, 1938, pp. 75-105.
Rev: B4459.

A4390 Wilson, Knox. *Xenophon in the English Renaissance from Elyot to Holland.* DD, New York University, 1945.

e. CLASSICAL MYTHOLOGY (68;26)
(1) MYTHOLOGY AND THE ENGLISH RENAISSANCE

A4391 Bush, Douglas. *Mythology and the Renaissance Tradition in English Poetry.* Univ. of Minnesota Press, 1932.
Rev: by H. Glunz, *Beiblatt*, XLVIII (1937), 38-45; by A. Koszul, *JEGP*, XXXVIII (1939), 311.

A4392 McCain, John Walker, Jr. "John Heywood and Classical Mythology." *N&Q*, 174 (1938), 368.

A4393 Seznec, Jean. *La Survivance des Dieux Antiques: Essai sur le Rôle de la Tradition Mythologique dans l'Humanisme et l'Art de la Renaissance.* London: Warburg Institute, 1940.

A4394 Wright, Celeste Turner. "The Amazons in Elizabethan Literature." *SP*, XXXVII (1940), 433-456.

A4395 LeComte, Edward S. *Endymion in England: The Literary History of a Greek Myth.* New York: King's Crown Press, 1944. Pp. 189.
Rev: by Douglas Bush, *JEGP*, XLIV (1945), 105-106; by D. T. Starnes, *MLN*, LX, 423-424.

A4396 Merrill, Robert V. "Eros and Anteros." *Speculum*, XIX (1944), 265-284.
Traces the career of Eros' brother from Plato's time into the Renaissance.

A4397 Starnes, De Witt T., and Ernest W. Talbert. *Classical Myth and Legend in Renaissance Dictionaries: A Study of Renaissance Dictionaries in Their Relation to the Classical Learning of Contemporary English Writers.* Univ. of North Carolina Press, 1956. Pp. vi, 517.
Rev: by A. Taylor, *RN*, IX (1956), 108-110; by D. C. Allen, *MLN*, LXXI, 598; by W. J. Ong, *Classical Bul.*, XXXII, 70; by R. T. Bruère, *Classical Phil.*, LI, 260-263; *SCN*, XIV, 10; by R. A. Fraser, *South Atlantic Quar.*, LV, 511-512; by C. R. Thompson, *SQ*, VIII (1957), 233-235; by Ralph Waterbury Condee, *CE*, XIX, 92; by M. Poirier, *EA*, X, 247-248; by D. Bush, *MP*, LIV, 200-202; by Rudolph Willard, *Lib. Chron. Univ. Texas*, VI, 24-29; by J. P. Pritchard, *Books Abroad*, XXXI, 83-84; by Herbert Weisinger, *Jour. Amer. Folklore*, LXX, 93-94; by Hardin Craig, *Manuscripta*, I, 45-47; by Louis Bakelants, *Latomus*, XVI, 369; by R. R. Bolgar, *RES*, IX (1958), 63-65.

(2) SHAKESPEARE AND MYTHOLOGY

A4398 Baldwin, T. W. "Perseus Purloins Pegasus." *PQ*, XX (1941), 361-370.

A4399 Boas, Frederick S. *Aspects of Classical Legend and History in Shakespeare.* Annual Shakespeare Lecture. *Proceedings of the British Academy,* XXIX. London: Milford, 1944. Pp. 28.
Reprinted in Boas's *Queen Elizabeth in Drama and Related Studies,* pp. 72-100.
Rev: by C. J. Sisson, *MLR,* XXXIX (1944), 205-206; *N &Q,* 184 (1944), 191-192; by George Cookson, *English,* V, 55-56.

A4400 Honigmann, E. A. "Secondary Sources of *The Winter's Tale.*" *PQ,* XXXIV (1955), 27-38.

A4401 Dodd, E. M. "Autolycus and Odysseus." *TLS,* Nov. 22, 1957, p. 705.
Corrects a *TLS* reviewer (Nov. 1) p. 656, by pointing out that Autolycus was the maternal grandfather, not the father, of Odysseus. Discusses Shak.'s knowledge of class. mythology.

3. INFLUENCE OF CONTEMPORARY CONTINENTAL LITERATURE (69;26)
See also A7486-A7538, and Literary Genesis, Sources and Analogues, in individual play sections.
a. GENERAL (69;26)
(1) IN ENGLAND

A4402 Hyma, A. "The Continental Origins of English Humanism." *HLQ,* IV (1940), 1-26.

A4403 Winsteadt, R. "The East in English Literature." *Indian Art and Letters,* XXI (1947), 1-12.

A4404 Harrison, Thomas P., Jr. "The Literary Background of Renaissance Poisons." *TxSE,* XXVII (1948) 35-67.

A4405 Herrick, Marvin T. *Comic Theory in the Sixteenth Century.* Illinois Stud. in Lang. & Lit., XXXIV, Nos. 1-2. Univ. Illinois Press, 1950. Pp. viii, 248.
Rev: A7513.

A4406 Simonini, R. C., Jr. "The Genesis of Modern Language Teaching." *MLJ,* XXXV (1951), 179-186.

A4407 Ruffmann, K. H. *Das Russlandbild im England Shakespeares.* Göttingen, 1952.
Rev: by A. L. Mersen, *Erasmus,* VIII (1953), 438-439; by M. S. Anderson, *EHR,* LXIX (1954), 149-150.

A4408 Simonini, R. C., Jr. *Italian Scholarship in Renaissance England.* The Univ. of North Carolina Studies in Comparative Literature, No. 3. Chapel Hill: Univ. of North Carolina Press, 1952. Pp. viii, 126.
Rev: A3970.

A4409 Hieatt, A. Kent. *Medieval Symbolism and the Dramatic Imagery of the English Renaissance.* DD, Columbia University, 1954. Pp. 510. Mic 55-108. *DA,* XV (1955), 817. Publ. No. 11,456.

A4410 Crump, G. M. *Some Aspects of Continental Influence on English Poetry During the First Half of the 17th Century.* MA thesis, Reading, England, 1955.

A4411 Herrick, Marvin T. "The New Drama of the Sixteenth Century." *JEGP,* LIV (1955), 555-577.

A4412 Herrick, Marvin T. *Tragicomedy.* Urbana: The Univ. of Illinois Press, 1955. Pp. 331.
Rev: B5201.

A4413 Brandt, William Jeans. *The Continental Origins of English Renaissance Conceptions of the Nature of Man.* DD, University of California, Berkeley, 1957.

A4414 Myer, William Hoogland. *The Pastoral Drama in Italy and France: 1573-1632.* DD, University of North Carolina, 1957.

A4415 Summerell, Joseph Howard. *Backgrounds of Elizabethan Pastoral Drama.* DD, Columbia University, 1958. Pp. 268. Mic 58-7055. *DA,* XIX (1959), 2941.
Classical and continental antecedents.

(2) SHAKESPEARE
(Reserved for very general treatments of continental influences and for countries not included immediately below.)

A4416 Carrère, Félix. "Shakespeare et la Méditerranée." *Annales de la Fac. des Lettres d'Aix,* XXXI (1957), 141-161.

A4417 Draper, R. P. *Shakespeare and the Pastoral.* DD, Nottingham, 1953.

A4418 Felver, Charles Stanley. *William Shakespeare and Robert Armin His Fool—a Working Partnership.* DD, University of Michigan, 1956. Pp. 352. Mic 56-3895. *DA,* XVI (1956), 2446. Publ. No. 18,601.

A4419 Gordon, Cyrus H. " 'A Daniel Come to Judgment'." *SAB,* XV (1940), 206-209. Reply by John E. Hannigan, "Which Daniel?" *ibid.,* XVI (1941), 63-64, 190-192.
Comment by R. Withington, ibid., XVI, 256.

A4420 Grégoire, Henri. "The Bulgarian Origins of *The Tempest* of Shakespeare." *SP,* XXXVII (1940), 236-256.

A4421 Hatto, A. T. " 'Venus and Adonis'—and the Boar." *MLR,* XLI (1946), 353-361.

A4422 Henderson, Archibald, Jr. *Family of Mercutio.* DD, Columbia University, 1954. Pp. 270. Mic A54-2044. *DA,* XIV (1954), 1395. Publ. No. 8684.
Baldassare Castiglione, Étienne Pasquier, Annibale Romei, and others.

A4423 Hutton, James. "Analogues of Shakespeare's Sonnets 153-154: Contributions to the History of a Theme." *MP,* XXXVIII (1941), 385-403.

A4424 Langenfelt, Gösta. " 'The Noble Savage' Until Shakespeare." *ES*, xxxvi (1955), 222-227.

A4425 Rathe, Kurt. *Un Detto Shakespeariano e la sua Fonte*. Florence: Leo S. Olschki, 1947.

A4426 S., E. B. "A Polish Source for Shakespeare." *More Books, Bull. Boston Publ. Lib.*, xv (May 1940), 192.

A4427 Zocca, Louis R. *Elizabethan Narrative Poetry*. Rutgers Univ. Press, 1950. Pp. xii, 306.
	Rev: C191.

b. INFLUENCE OF ITALIAN LITERATURE (69:26)
(1) GENERAL (69;26)
(a) IN ENGLAND

A4428 Scott, Mary Augusta. *The Elizabethan Drama, Especially in its Relations to the Italians of the Renaissance*. DD, Yale University, 1894.

A4429 Bonaschi, A. and C. *Italian Currents and Curiosities in the English Literature from Chaucer to Shakespeare*. New York: Italian Chamber of Commerce, 1937. Pp. 28.

A4430 Orsini, Napoleone. *Studi sul Rinascimento italiano in Inghilterra*. Florence, 1937.
	Machiavelli, Boccaccio, Guicciardini.
	Rev: by P. Rebora, *Leonardo*, viii (1937), 344-345; by A. H. Gilbert, *MLN*, liii (1938), 623-625; by J. Raith, *Beiblatt*, xlix, 260-263; by Henri Peyre, *EA*, ii, 417-418; by E. Allodoli, *Rinascita*, i, 3, 113-122; by Friedrich Brie, *SJ*, lxxiv, 193-195.

A4431 Wright, Herbert G., ed. *Early English Versions of the Tales of Guiscardo and Ghismonda and Titus and Gisippus from the Decameron*. Early English Text Society. Oxford Univ. Press, 1937. Pp. cxv, 256.
	Rev: *TLS*, Mar. 12, 1938, p. 174; by W. W. Greg, *MLR*, xxxiii, 425-427; by Gavin Bone, *Medium Aevum*, viii (1939), 161-164.

A4432 B., A. "An Echo of the 'Paragone' in Shakespeare." *Journal of the Warburg Institute*, ii (1939), 260-262.

A4433 Chard, Joseph E. *The Influence of the Italian Literary Renaissance on English Literature and Culture*. MA thesis, Montreal, 1939. Pp. 59.

A4434 Rebora, Piero. "Motivi Medicei nel Teatro inglese del Rinascimento." *Rinascita*, iii (1940).

A4435 Fink, Z. S. "Venice and English Political Thought in the Seventeenth Century." *MP*, xxxviii (1941), 155-172.

A4436 Bhattacherje, M. M. "Italy in Elizabethan Pamphlets." *Calcutta Review*, 83 (1942), 129-135.

A4437 Orsini, Napoleone. "La Scena Italiana in Inghilterra: Il Trattato di Serlio." *Anglica*, (1946), 100-102.

A4438 Krey, A. C. "Padua in the English Renaissance." *HLQ*, x (1947), 129-134.

A4439 Policardi, Silvio. *John Florio e le Relazioni Culturali fra l'Inghilterra e l'Italia nel XVI Secolo*. Biblioteca di saggi e di lezioni accademiche—opera No. 27. Venice: Casa Editrice F. Montuoro, 1947. Pp. 170. See also Florio, A4064-A4077.

A4440 Viglione, Francesco. *L'Italia nel Pensiero degli Scrittori Inglesi*. Milan: Fratelli Bocca, 1947. Pp. 545.
	An account of English prejudice and/or hostility to Rome and Italy, without recognition of English acknowledgment and acclaim. From Geoffrey of M. to G. B. Shaw.
	Rev: by H. Craig, *CL*, ii (1950), 286-287.

A4441 Obertello, Alfredo. *Madrigali Italiani in Inghilterra: Storia, Critica, Testi*. Milan: Bompiani, 1949. Pp. 550.
	Rev: by Elio Gianturco, *SQ*, ii (1951), 267-269; by Edward J. Dente, *Ital. Studies*, vi, 94-100; by Carlo Calcaterra, *Convivium Raccolta Nuova*, 1951, p. 783-787; by Joseph Kerman, *Jour. Amer. Musicological Soc.*, iv, 159-160.

A4442 Guicciardini, Paolo. "Le Traduzioni Inglesi della *Storia* Guicciardiniana nel XVI e XVII Secolo. Quarto Contributo alla Bibliografia Guicciardiniana." *Biblio.*, lii (1950), 227-240.

A4443 Firpo, Luigi. "Francesco Pucci in Inghilterra." *Rev. Internationale de Philosophie*, v (1951), 158-173.

A4444 Pazzini, Adalberto. "Shakespeare Lesse un Libro Anatomico Italiano?" *Osservatore Romano*, 91, No. 44 (1951), 3.

A4445 Simonini, R. C., Jr. "Italian-English Language Books of the Renaissance." *RR*, xlii (1951), 241-244.
	Lists thirteen titles of language books, 1550-1657, not noted in Mary A. Scott's *Elizabethan Translations from the Italian*, Boston, 1916.

A4446 Underwood, E. Ashworth. "English Medicine and the Italian Renaissance." *Riv. di Storia delle Scienze Mediche e Naturali*, xliii (1952), 215-222.

A4446a Byler, Arthur W. *Italian Currents in the Popular Music of England in the Sixteenth Century*. DD, University of Chicago, 1953.

A4447 Hale, J. R. *England and the Italian Renaissance*. The Growth of Interest in its History and Art. London: Faber & Faber, 1954. Pp. 216.
	Rev: *TLS*, June 18, 1954, p. 392; by Alwin Thaler, *SQ*, vi (1955), 178-179; by G. Robertson,

EHR, LXX, 325-326; by Sidney Warhaft, *QQ*, LXII (1956), 637-639; by R. Holland, *DUJ*, XLVIII, 123-124.

A4448 Kaufman, Helen. "The Influence of Italian Drama on Pre-Restoration English Comedy." *Italica*, XXXI (1954), 9-23.

A4449 Praz, Mario. "Shakespeare's Italy." *ShS*, VII (1954), 95-106.
Reprinted in *The Flaming Heart*. Essays on Crashaw, Machiavelli, and Other Studies in the Relations between Italian and English Literature from Chaucer to T. S. Eliot (Doubleday Anchor Books). Garden City: Doubleday & Company, 1958, pp. 146-167.

A4450 Sells, A. Lytton. *The Italian Influence in English Poetry from Chaucer to Southwell*. Bloomington: Indiana Univ. Press, 1955. Pp. 346.
Rev: *CL*, VII (1955), 283-285; by D. S. Carne-Ross, *Spectator*, July 22, p. 132; by R. A. Foakes, *English*, X, 227-228; by B. Evan Owen, *ConR*, 188 (1955), 355-356; by K. Foster, *Tablet*, 206 (1955), 476-477; by Hermann Heuer, *SJ*, 92 (1956), 377-378; by Stanley T. Williams, *Books Abroad*, XXX, 224; by Mario Praz, *MP*, LIII, 274-275 and *SQ*, VII, 248-250; by Joseph A. Mazzeo, *RN*, IX, 25-27; by H. H. Blanchard, *MLN*, LXXI, 515-518; *TLS*, July 6, p. 410; by J. Voisine, *RLC*, XXXI (1957), 442-444.

A4451 Weiss, Roberto. "Il Debito degli Umanisti Inglesi verso l'Italia." *Lettere Italiane*, VII (1955), 298-313.

A4452 Baldi, E. "The Secretary of the Duke of Norfolk and the First Italian Grammar in England." *Studies in English Language and Literature presented to Prof. Karl Brunner*, ed. S. Korninger. Wiener Beiträge zur Englischen Philologie, LXV. Vienna, 1957.

(b) SHAKESPEARE

A4453 Henneberger, Olive P. *Proximate Sources for the Italianate Elements in Shakespeare*. DD, University of Illinois, 1937.

A4454 Rebora, Piero. *Civiltà Italiana e Civiltà Inglese. Studi e Ricerche*. Florence: Felice Le Monnier, 1936. Pp. xi, 271.
All the essays in the collection with one exception, deal with the sixteenth and seventeenth centuries; and four are concerned directly with Shakespeare.

A4455 Bennett, Mackie Langham. "Shakespeare's *Much Ado* and Its Possible Italian Sources." *TxSE*, XVII (1937), 52-74.

A4456 Djivelegov, A. "The Influence of Italian Culture on Marlowe's and Shakespeare's Way of Thinking." *Transactions of the Lunacharsky State Institute of Theatrical Art* (USSR), 1940, pp. 143-160.

A4457 Farinelli, Arturo. "Shakespeares Italien." *SJ*, LXXV (1939), 16-35.

A4458 Borgese, G. A. "The Dishonor of Honor: Francesco Giovanni Mauro to Sir John Falstaff." *RR*, XXXII (1941), 44-55.

A4459 Boughner, Daniel C. "Sir Toby's Cockatrice." *Italica*, XX (1943), 171-172.

A4460 Rebora, Piero. "Di Alcune Fonti Italiane di Shakespeare." *Rinascita*, VI (1943), 145-165.

A4461 Vigano, Paolo. *Shakespeare, Genio Italiano*. Dimostrazioni e prove della sua Italianità; documentazioni e rivelazioni psicografiche su Guglielmo Crollalanza. Treviso: Tip. ed. Trevigiana, 1947. Pp. 30.
Demonstration and proof of his being Italian.

A4462 Ridenti, Lucio, ed. *Shakespeare degli Italiani. I testi scespiriani inspirati da fatti e figure della nostra storia e della nostra leggenda*. Turin: Società Editrice Torinese, 1950. Pp. lxxvii, 686.
Contents: A Pastore, "W. Shakespeare," pp. xiii-xxxv. B. Brunelli, "Interpreti di Shakespeare in Italia," pp. xxxix-lv. L. Gigli, "La storia romana nel teatro di Shakespeare," pp. lix-lxviii. J. Copeau, "Shakespeare ou la livraison de l'émotion humaine," pp. lxxi-lxxvii. Various translations follow. See B870.

A4463 Simpson, Lucie. "Shakespeare and Italy." *The Secondary Heroes of Shakespeare and Other Essays*. London: Kingswood Press, 1950, pp. 87-92.

A4464 Sjögren, Gunnar. *Var Othello Neger och Andra Shakespeareproblem*. Stockholm: Natur och Kultur, 1958. Pp. 196.
Contains essay, "Shakespeare och Italien."

(2) ITALIAN NOVEL AND DRAMA (70;)

A4465 Novellen, Italienische. Vols. I, II, III. Tr. into German by Eduard von Bülow and others. Berlin: Lambert Schneider, 1942.
Rev: A3522.

A4466 Boothe, Bert E. *The Contribution of the Italian Novella to the Formation and Development of Elizabethan Prose Fiction, 1506-1582*. DD, University of Michigan, 1936.

A4467 Colucci, Loris. "La Novella di Giulietta e Romeo e le sue Fonti Classiche." *Rassegna Nazionale*, Ser. IV, XXVII (1939), 426-434.

A4468 Meozzi, Antero. *La Drammatica della Rinascita Italiana in Europa* (sec. XVI-XVII). Pisa: Nistri-Lischi, 1940. Pp. 216.

A4469 Gordon, Donald James. *The "Commedia Erudita" and Elizabethan Comedy*. DD, Cambridge

University. *Cam Abs.*, 1940-41, p. 60.
3 Shak. plays discussed: *Shrew, Much, Twelf.*

A4470   Günther, Johannes von. *Italienische Shakespeare Novellen aus der Renaissance. Nach. d. Übertr. v. Adalbert Keller hrsg.* Die kleinen Bücher, 59. Heidelberg: Meister, 1947. Pp. 66.

A4471   Gilbert, Allan H. "The Duel in Italian Cinquecento Drama and its Relation to Tragicomedy." *Italica*, XXVI (1949), 7-14.

A4472   Wright, Margaret M. *Shakespeare and the Italian Novellieri.* DD, Manchester University, 1951.

A4473   Wilkins, E. H. "The Tale of Julia and Pruneo." *Harvard Libr. Bulletin*, VIII (1954), 102-107. Enlarges upon James Wardrop's description of an anonymous novella in a 15th century MS at Harvard. Wilkins shows Luigi da Porto, who gave the story its standard form, based it on Masuccio da Salerno's tale of Mariotto and Ganozza.

A4474   Taylor, William Edwards. *The Villainess in Elizabethan Drama.* DD, Vanderbilt University, 1957. Pp. 402. Mic 57-2820. *DA*, XVII (1957), 1756. Publ. No. 22,025. Chap. IV, Italian Novella, pp. 195-232.

A4475   Borinski, Ludwig. "The Origins of the Euphuistic Novel and its Significance for Shakespeare." *Studies in Honor of T. W. Baldwin*, 1958, pp. 38-52.

(3) INDIVIDUAL ITALIAN AUTHORS (71;26)
(a) BANDELLO

A4476   Cancelled.

A4477   Pruvost, René. *Matteo Bandello and Elizabethan Fiction.* Thesis, Paris, 1938. Paris: E. Champion, 1938.

A4478   Snell, Otto. "Hier Irren Shakespeare und Bandello." *Der Erbarzt. Beilage z. Dts. Ärzteblatt*, VI (1939), 71-72.
Rev: by F. Dx., "Das Unmögliche Zwillingspaar." *VB* (Mü), June 30, 1939.

A4479   Gordon, D. J. "*Much Ado About Nothing:* A Possible Source for the Hero-Claudio Plot." *SP*, XXXIX (1942), 279-290.

A4480   Griffith, T. G. *Historical Background and Fiction in the Novelle of Bandello.* B. Litt thesis, Oxford, 1951.

A4481   Griffith, T. Gwynfor. *Bandello's Fiction.* An Examination of the Novelle. Modern Language Studies. Oxford: Blackwell, 1955. Pp. 147.
Rev: by Hermann Heuer, *SJ*, 92 (1956), 378.

A4482   Hoeniger, F. D. "Two Notes on *Cymbeline.*" *SQ*, VIII (1957), 132-133.

(b) BOCCACCIO

A4483   Brunneman, Martha. *Dekamerone III, 3 im Englischen Drama.* DD, Rostock, 1910. Pp. 105.

A4484   Raith, J. *Boccaccio in der Englischen Literatur von Chaucer bis Painters "Palace of Pleasure."* Ein Beitrag zur Geschichte der Italienischen Novelle in England. Leipzig: Noske, 1936. Pp. viii, 167.
Rev: by Hans Marcus, *Beiblatt*, XLVII (1936), 295-296; by Herbert G. Wright, *MLR*, XXXII (1937), 288-289; by Karl Brunner, *Lbl*, LVIII, 164-165; by Alois Brandl *Archiv*, 171 (1937), 82-83; by R. Stamm, *ES*, XX (1938), 261-266.

A4485   Nosworthy, J. M. "The Sources of the Wager Plot in *Cymbeline.*" *N &Q*, 197 (1952), 93-96.

A4486   Wright, Herbert G. "How Did Shakespeare Come to Know the *Decameron?*" *MLR*, L (1955), 45-48.

A4487   Wright, H. G. *Boccaccio in England, from Chaucer to Tennyson.* London: Athlone Press, 1957.
Rev: by W. F. Schirmer, *Anglia*, LXXV (1957), 450-453; *TLS*, Aug. 15, 1958, p. 458; by V. de Sola Pinto, *N &Q*, NS, V, 275-276; by Gunnar Boklund, *SN*, XXX, 116-118; by R. A. Foakes, *English*, XII, 62; *SCN*, XVI, 4; by S. B. Liljegren, *RLC*, XXXIII, 589-591; by M. Praz, *MLR*, LIII, 559-561; by G. N. G. Orsini, *MP*, LVI, 61-62, and *GSLI*, 125 (1958), 434-437; by Joseph A. Mazzeo, *RR*, XLIX, 209; by E. R. Vincent, *Ital. Studies*, XIII, 100-101.

(c) BRUNO

A4488   Whitebrook, J. C. "Fynes Moryson, G. Bruno, and William Shakespeare." *N &Q*, 171 (1936), 255-260.

A4489   Yates, F. A. *A Study of "Love's Labor's Lost,"* 1936. G. Bruno, pp. 89-136.
Rev: B5645.

A4490   Limentani, Ludovico. "Giordano Bruno ad Oxford." *Civiltà Moderna*, Florence, July-October, 1937.

A4491   Yates, Frances A. "Shakespeare and the Platonic Tradition." *Univ. of Edin. Jour.*, XII (1942) 2-12.

A4492   Pellegrini, Angelo Mario. *Bruno and the Elizabethans.* DD, University of Washington, Seattle, 1942. Abstract publ. in *Abstracts of Dissertations*, VII. Seattle: Univ. of Washington, 1943, pp. 211-216.

A4493   Pellegrini, Angelo. "Giordano Bruno and Oxford." *HLQ*, v (1942), 303-316.
A4494   Pellegrini, Angelo M. "Giordano Bruno on Translations." *ELH*, x (1943), 193-207.
A4495   Pellegrini, Angelo M. "Bruno, Sidney, and Spenser." *SP*, xl (1943), 128-144.
A4496   Yates, Frances. "The Emblematic Conceit in Giordano Bruno's *De Gli Eroici Furori* and in the Elizabethan Sonnet Sequences." *JWCI*, vi (1944), 101-121.
A4497   Martin, L. C. "Shakespeare, Lucretius, and the Commonplaces." *RES*, xxi (1945), 174-182. Suggests Bruno as an intermediary between Shak. and Lucretius.
A4498   Giusso, Lorenzo. "Barocco. Bruno e Shakespeare." *Il Giornale di Sicilia*, June 1, 1948.
A4499   Garnier, Ch.-M. "Giordano Bruno en Angleterre." *LanM*, xlvi (1952), 333-335.
See also A721, A2280, A3815, A3818.

(d) DANTE

A4500   Vida, A. "Reminiscenze Dantesche in un Dramma di Shakespeare." *Rassegna Nazionale*. Ser. IV, lx (1939-41 ?), 506-512.
A4501   Friedrich, Werner P. *Dante's Fame Abroad, 1350-1850. The Influence of Dante Alighieri on the Poets and Scholars of Spain, France, England, Germany, Switzerland and the United States: A Survey of Scholarship*. Univ. North Carolina Stud. in Comp. Lit., No. 2. Rome: Ed. *Storia e Letteratura*, 31, 1950. Pp. 582.
Shak., pp. 196-197.
Rev: by H. H., *CL*, iii (1951), 272-274.

(e) FICINO

A4502   Jayne, Sears. "Ficino and the Platonism of the English Renaissance." *CL*, iv (1953), 214-238.
A4503   Hawkes, Terry. "Ficino and Shakespeare." *N&Q*, ns, v (1958), 185-186.
A4504   McAvoy, William C. "Falstaff, Erasmus, and Ficino." *Carroll Quarterly*, xi (1957), 10-14

(f) MACHIAVELLI

A4505   Beck, H. *Machiavellismus in der Renaissance*. DD, Bonn, 1935. Pp. 45.
Rev: by H. Schütt, *HZ*, 156 (1936), 634.
A4506   Hashagen, J. "Um Machiavelli." *Deutsche Rundschau*, lxiv (1938), 117-120.
A4507   Orsini, Napoleone. "Nuove Ricerche sul Machiavellismo nel Rinascimento Inglese. II. Appunti Inediti dalle 'Storie' del Machiavelli e del Guicciardini." *Rinascita*, ii (1939), 299-304.
A4508   Praz, Mario. *Machiavelli in Inghilterra ed Altri Saggi*. Rome: Tumminelli, 1942.
A4509   Ribner, Irving. "The Significance of Gentillet's *Contre-Machiavel*." *MLQ*, x (1949), 153-157. Minimizes the influence of Gentillet and argues that knowledge of Machiavelli's own writings combined with the Senecan tradition and that of the morality play to produce the Elizabethan stage 'Machiavel'.
A4510   Armstrong, W. A. "The Influence of Seneca and Machiavelli on the Elizabethan Tyrant." *RES*, xxiv (1948), 19-35.
A4511   Ribner, Irving. *Machiavelli and Sir Philip Sidney*. DD, University of North Carolina, 1949 Abstract publ. in *Univ. of North Carolina Record, Research in Progress*, Jan.-Dec. 1949, Grad. School Series No. 58, pp. 113-115.
Declares Machiavelli was widely read in Eliz. England.
A4512   Schieder, Theodor. *Shakespeare und Machiavelli*. *Archiv f. Kulturgeschichte*, xxxiii (1951), 131-173.
A4513   Wada, Yuchi. "Machiavellism and *Richard III*." *Eibungakukenkyu*, xxvii (1951), 179-191.
A4514   Walters, R. N. *Machiavelli and the Elizabethan Drama*. M. Litt thesis, Cambridge University, 1953. *Cam. Abs.*, 1952-53, p. 80.
A4515   Mosse, George L. "The Assimilation of Machiavelli in English Thought: The Casuistry of William Perkins and William Ames." *HLQ*, xvii (1954), 315-326.
A4516   Berry, R. T. *Webster's Interpretation and Treatment of Machiavelli*. MA thesis, London, External, 1956.
A4517   Gasquet, E. S. "Machiavelli's *Discourses*: A Forgotten English Translation." *N&Q*, ns, v (1958), 144-145.
A4518   Praz, Mario. " 'The Political Brain': Machiavelli and the Elizabethans," and "Shakespeare's Italy." *The Flaming Heart*. New York: Doubleday, 1958.
A4519   Wheeler, Thomas. "Bacon's Henry VII as a Machiavellian Prince." *Renaissance Papers*. A selection of papers presented at the Renaissance Meeting in the Southeastern States, Duke University, April 12-13, 1957. Ed. Allan H. Gilbert. Southeastern Renaissance Conference, 1958, pp. 111-117.
A4519a Stevens, Linton C. "Machiavelli's *Virtù* and the Voluntarism of Montaigne." *Renaissance Papers*, April 12-13, 1957. Ed. Allan H. Gilbert. Southeastern Renaissance Conference, 1958, pp. 118-124.
See also items A1764-A1766.

(g) PETRARCH

A4520   Valente, Pier Luigi. "Petrarca e Shakespeare." *Studi Petrarcheschi*, I, diretti da Carlo Calcaterra. Accademia Petrarca di Lettere, Arti e Scienze di Arezzo. Bologna: Zanichelli, 1948, pp. 195-211.

A4521   Thomson, P. "Petrarch and the Elizabethans." *English*, x (1955), 177-180.

(h) TASSO

A4522   Castelli, Alberto. *"La Gerusalemme Liberata" nell'Inghilterra di Spenser.* Milan, 1936.
             Rev: by R. W. Baldner, *JEGP*, xxxvII (1938), 122-123.

A4523   Borgese, G. A. "The Dishonor of Honor: Francesco Giovanni Mauro to Sir John Falstaff." *RR*, xxxII (1941), 44-45.
             Tasso's influ. via Daniel, p. 50.

A4524   Praz, Mario. "Tasso in Inghilterra." *Comitato per le celebrazioni di Torquato Tasso, Ferrara, 1954.* Milan: Marzorati, 1957, pp. 673-710.

(i) OTHERS (Alphabetically by Italian Author)

A4525   Jardini, Anna Maria. *The Influence of Pietro Aretino on English Literature of the Renaissance.* DD, University of Southern California, 1957. Abstract publ. in *Univ. of Southern California Abstracts of Dissertations, 1957,* 1958, pp. 91-93.

A4526   Bond, R. W. "Lucian and Boiardo in *Timon.*" *Studia Otiosa*, 1938, pp. 75-105.
             Rev: B4459.

A4527   DeJongh, William F. J. "A Borrowing from Caviceo for the Legend of Romeo and Juliet." *SAB*, xvi (1940), 118-119.

A4528   Ball, Robert Hamilton. "Cinthio's 'Epitia' and *Measure for Measure.*" *Elizabethan Studies and Other Essays in Honor of George F. Reynolds,* 1945, pp. 132-146.

A4529   Muir, Kenneth. "Shakespeare and Lewkenor." *RES*, NS, VII (1956), 182-183.
             Offers additional evidence that *Oth.* was influenced by Cardinal Gaspar Contarino's *The Commonwealth and Government of Venice,* tr. by Sir Lewes Lewkenor.

A4530   Villa, Carlo. *Parigi vale bene una messa! William Shakespeare & il Poeta Valtellinese Michelagnolo Florio.* Milan: Editrice Storica, 1951.

A4531   Perella, Nicolas James. *The Pastor Fido and Baroque Sensibility.* DD, Harvard University, 1957.

A4532   Fellheimer, Jeannette. "Geoffrey Fenton's *Historie of Guicciardin* and Holinshed's *Chronicles* of 1587." *MLQ*, vi (1945), 285-298.

A4533   Guinn, John A. *Aeneas Sylvius Piccolomini: His Relationship to 16th Century English Literature.* DD, University of Texas, 1939.

A4534   Caldiero, Frank M. "The Source of Hamlet's 'What a Piece of Work is a Man!'" *N&Q*, 196 (1951), 421-424.
             Corrects J. Dover Wilson who, following Pater, names as the source of Hamlet's discourse Pico's *Oratio de Hominis Dignitate* rather than the same writer's *Heptaplus;* suggests that Pico's source may have been Photius' Life of Pythagoras; and observes that the major influence in the Renaissance was Neo-Platonic rather than Neo-Aristotelian.

A4535   Stevenson, Hazel Allicon. "The Major Elizabethan Poets and the Doctrine of Signatures." *Florida State Univ. Studies,* v (1952), 11-31.
             Discusses the herbal theory of signatures popularized by Giambattista della Porta.

A4536   Schaar, Claes. "Shakespeare's Sonnets L-LI and Tebaldeo's Sonnet CVII." *ES*, xxxvIII (1957), 208-209.

(4) ITALIAN CONDUCT BOOKS AND THE ENGLISH
IDEAL OF A GENTLEMAN (72;27)
(a) BIBLIOGRAPHY

A4537   Noyes, Gertrude E. *Bibliography of Courtesy and Conduct Books in Seventeenth-Century England.* New Haven: Tuttle, Morehouse and Taylor, 1937. Pp. iv, lll.
             Rev: by R. Kelso, *JEGP*, xxxvII (1938), 601; by W. Ebisch, *Beiblatt*, L (1939), 12-13; by G. Murphy, *Library*, xix, 495-496; by W. L. Ustick, *MLN*, LIV, 476; by Ernest Alker, *Lbl*, LX, 386.

A4538   Heltzel, Virgil B. *A Check List of Courtesy Books in the Newberry Library.* Chicago: Newberry Lib., 1942. Pp. 161.
             List of works written or published before 1775.

(b) CASTIGLIONE

A4539   McDowell, M. M. *Shakespeare's Likeness to Castiglione as Indication of Probable Indebtedness.* DD, University of Washington, Seattle, 1936. Pp. 117.

A4540   Cancelled.

A4541   Schrinner, Walter. *Castiglione und die Englische Renaissance.* DD, Breslau, 1939. Pp. 174.

Publ. *Neue deutsche Forschungen. Abt. Englische Philologie*, XIV, 234. Berlin: Junker and Dünnhaupt, 1939. Pp. 174.
   Rev: by Wolfgang Keller, *SJ*, LXXVII (1941), 199-201.

A4542   Praz, Mario. "Shakespeare, il Castiglione e le Facezie." *Riv. Italiana del Dramma*, IV (1940), 55-76.

(c)   ENGLAND IN GENERAL

A4543   Mason, John E. *Gentlefolk in the Making*. Univ. of Pennsylvania Press, 1935.
   Rev: A1934.

A4544   Molyneux, Max. *Hero-Paideia or the Institution of a Young Noble Man by James Cleland*. Edited with Introduction and Notes. 2v. DD, Cornell University, 1938. Abstract publ. in *Abstracts of Theses*, Ithaca, Cornell Univ. Press, 1938, pp. 27-29.

A4545   Siebeck, Berta. *Das Bild Sir Philip Sidneys in der Englischen Renaissance*. DD, Freiburg/Breisgau, 1939. Pp. xii, 198.

A4546   Smith, Rhea. "The Courtesy Book Convention in the English Drama from 1535-1595." *Abstracts of Theses*, Southern Methodist University, Dallas, Texas, VIII (1941), 51-52.

A4547   Fife, Hilda Mary. *"Gli Asolani" by Pietro Bembo, a Translation with an Introduction*. DD, Cornell University, 1942. Abstract publ. in *Cornell Univ. Abstracts of Theses*, 1942, pp. 39-41.

A4548   Lievsay, John Leon. "Trends in Tudor and Stuart Courtesy Literature." *HLQ*, V (1942), 184-188.

A4549   Barker, Sir Ernest. *Traditions of Civility: Eight Essays*. Cambridge Univ. Press, 1948. Pp. viii, 369. Includes "The Education of the English Gentleman in the Sixteenth Century."

A4550   M. Loretta Langendorf, Sister. *The Attitude Toward History in English Renaissance Courtesy Literature*. DD, St. Louis, 1948. Pp. 350.

A4551   Cremeans, Charles D. *The Renaissance Gentleman in England*. Williamstown, Mass: Chapin Lib., Williams College, 1949. Pp. 31.
   Describes an exhibit, March 1949, with commentaries on the social, intellectual, and literary backgrounds of the works exhibited.

A4552   Schwalb, Harry M. "Cicero and the English Gentleman." *Classical Jour.*, XLVI (1950), 33-34, 44.

A4553   de Bruyn, J. *A Study of Seventeenth-Century Courtesy and Conduct Literature as a Revelation of the Concept of the English Gentleman*. MA thesis, University of London, 1951.

A4554   Hazlett, McCrea. *Richard Whitlock's "Zootomia": An Edition*. DD, University of Chicago, 1952. Wing, 2030.

A4555   Buys, William E. *Speech Education of the English Gentleman in Tudor Behavior Books*. DD, University of Wisconsin, 1953. Abstract publ. in Univ. of Wisconsin *Summaries of Doctoral Dissertations*, 1952-53, Madison, 1954, pp. 400-402. Abstract in *Speech Monographs*, XX (1953), 152.

A4556   Kelso, Ruth. *Doctrine for the Lady of the Renaissance*. Urbana: Univ. of Illinois Press, 1956. Pp. xi, 475.
   Rev: A1935.

A4557   Starnes, D. T. *"The Institucion of a Gentleman* (1555) and Carion's *Chronicles.*" *PQ*, XXXVI (1957), 244-252.

A4558   Potts, Abbie Findlay. *Shakespeare and "The Faerie Queene"*. Cornell Univ. Press, 1958. Pp. xii, 269.
   Rev: A4819.

(d)   SHAKESPEARE

A4559   McDowell, M. M. *Shakespeare's Likeness to Castiglione as Indication of Probable Indebtedness*. DD, University of Washington, Seattle, 1936. Pp. 117.

A4560   Bhattacherje, M. M. *"Courtesy" in Shakespeare*. With a Foreword by C. J. Sisson and Intro. by Louis Cazamian. Calcutta Univ. Press, 1940. Pp. xix, 225.
   Rev: by Hardin Criag, MLN, LIX (1944), 134-135; by B. E. C. Davis, *MLR*, XXXIX, 206.

A4561   Praz, Mario. "Shakespeare, il Castiglione e le Facezie." *Riv. Italiana del Dramma*, IV (1940), 55-76.

A4562   Draper, J. W. "Shakespeare and the *Conversazione*." *Italica*, XXIII (1946), 7-17.

c.   INFLUENCE OF FRENCH LITERATURE (72;27)
(1)   GENERAL (72;-)

A4563   Lester, J. A. *Connection Between the Drama of France and Great Britain, Particularly in the Elizabethan Period*. DD, Harvard University, 1902.

A4564   Lefranc, Abel. "Les Eléments Français de *Peines d'Amour Perdues* de Shakespeare." *RH*, 178 (1937), 411-432.

A4565   "Our Debts to France." *TLS*, Dec. 3, 1938, p. 769.

A4566   Maxwell, Ian. *French Farce and John Heywood*. Melbourne Univ. Press, 1946. Pp. 175.
   Rev: *TLS*, Aug. 3, 1946, p. 368; by Grace Frank, *MLN*, LXI, 492-493; by Una Ellis-Fermor,

English, VI, 140-141; *N &Q*, 191 (1946), 22; by J. H. Walter, *MLR*, XLII (1947), 259-260; by Jules Bernard, *JEGP*, XLVI, 102-109; by F. S. Boas, *RES*, XXIII, 157-159.

A4567   Ure, Peter. "Shakespeare's Play and the French Sources of Holinshed's and Stow's Account of *Richard II*." *N &Q*, 198 (1953), 426-429.

A4568   Aboul-Enein, A. M. *Cleopatra in French and English Drama from Yodelle to Shakespeare.* DD, Trinity College, Dublin, 1953-54.

(2)   INDIVIDUAL FRENCH AUTHORS (73;27)
(a)   BELLEFOREST

A4569   Tremolières, Dr. "La Part de Belleforest (de Samattan) dans Trois Œuvres de Shakespeare." *Bul. de la Société d'Histoire et d'Archéologie du Gers*, XXXIX (1939), 154-161, 201-207.

A4570   Law, Robert Adger. "Belleforest, Shakespeare, and Kyd." *AMS*, pp. 279-294.

(b)   FROISSART

A4571   Lehmann, John. "Shakespeare and Froissart." *TLS*, Mar. 3, 1945, p. 103.

A4572   Braddy, Haldeen. "The Flying Horse in *Henry V*." *SQ*, V (1954), 205-207.
Symbolism indebted to Berners' translation of Froissart.

A4573   Braddy, Haldeen. "Shakespeare's Puck and Froissart's Orthon." *SQ*, VII (1956), 276-280.

(c)   GARNIER

A4574   Carrère, Félix Jean. *Le Théâtre de Thomas Kyd. Contribution à l'Etude du Drame Elizabéthain.* Thèse de Lettres, Paris, 1949. Publ. Toulouse: Edouard Privat, 1951.
A parallel of Garnier's *Cornelia* with temptation scene in *Caesar* thru Kyd's tr.
Rev: A4979.

A4575   Beauchamp, Virginia Walcott. "Sidney's Sister as Translator of Garnier." *RN*, X (1957), 8-13.

A4576   McDiarmid, Matthew P. "The Influence of Robert Garnier on Some Elizabethan Tragedies." *EA*, XI (1958), 289-302.

(d)   MONTAIGNE

A4577   Allen, Percy. "Montaigne and *Twelfth Night*." *TLS*, Sept. 18, 1937, p. 675.

A4578   Dow, Neal. *The Concept and Term "Nature" in Montaigne.* DD, University of Pennsylvania, 1938.

A4579   Henderson, W. B. Drayton. "Montaigne's *Apologie of Raymond Sebond*, and *King Lear*." *SAB*, XIV (1939), 209-225. Concluded, ibid., XV (1940), 40-56.

A4580   Best, G. Percival. "Le Montaigne de Shakespeare." *Bulletin des Amis de Montaigne*, 2 sér. No. 8. Paris: Conard, March 1, 1940. Pp. 40.

A4581   Hall, Marie-Louise Michaud. *Montaigne and His Translators.* DD, University of Wisconsin, 1940. Abstract publ. in *Summaries of Doctoral Dissertations, 1939-40*, Vol. 5, Madison: Univ. of Wisconsin Press, 1940, pp. 272-274.

A4582   Harmon, Alice. "How Great was Shakespeare's Debt to Montaigne?" *PMLA*, LVII (1942), 988-1008.

A4583   M., A. "*Hamlet* Once More." *N &Q*, 184 (1943), 255, 282-283.
Matthew Arnold on Shakespeare's thinking about Montaigne.

A4584   Page, Frederick. "Shakespeare and Florio." *N &Q*, 184 (1943), 283-285. See also Frederick Page, ibid., 185 (1943), 42-44, and 107-108.

A4585   Taylor, George C. "Montaigne-Shakespeare and the Deadly Parallel." *PQ*, XXII (1943), 330-337.
Largely an attempt to refute the conclusions of Miss Alice Harmon in A4582.

A4586   Dédéyan, Charles. *Montaigne chez ses Amis Anglo-Saxons.* 2v. Paris: Boivin, 1946. Pp. 448, 118.
    Rev: by Robert Kemp, "Montaigne et ses Amis Anglais." *Nouv. Littéraires*, August 8, 1946, p. 3; by G. J.-A., *Rev. de Paris*, LIII, No. 11, 161-162; by E. V., *MGW*, LV, 58.

A4587   Deutschbein, Max. "Shakespeares *Hamlet* und Montaigne." *SJ*, 80/81 (1944/45), 70-107.

A4588   Hardy, R. G. "Michel Montaigne Among the English." *TLS*, Sept. 13, 1947, p. 465.

A4589   Faure, E. *Montaigne et ses Trois Premiers-Nés: Shakespeare, Cervantes, Pascal.* Paris: Prolibro, 1948. Pp. 230.

A4590   Maxwell, J. C. "Montaigne and *Macbeth*." *MLR*, XLIII (1948), 77-78.

A4591   Atkinson, A. D. "Additional Florio-Shakespeare Resemblances." *N &Q*, 194 (1949), 356-358.

A4592   Schmid, Eduard Eugen. "Shakespeare, Montaigne und die Schauspielerische Formel." *SJ*, 82/83 (1946/47), 103-135.

A4593   Waterston, G. Chychele. "Shakespeare and Montaigne: A Footnote to *The Tempest*." *RR*, XL (1949), 165-172.
". . . not only does the commonwealth passage resemble the words of Montaigne, but the

character [Gonzalo] who utters it exhibits two salient traits of Montaigne's character."
"Moreover the passage selected by Shakespeare is one which epitomizes that part of Montaigne's philosophy which must have made the deepest impression upon Shakespeare's age: his attack upon kingship and his desire to 'execute all things by contraries,' contrary, that is, to the hierarchy of the universe which was accepted at that time."—p. 167.

A4594   Legge, M. Dominica. "An English Allusion to Montaigne Before 1595." *RES*, NS, I (1950), 341-344.

A4595   Hodgen, Margaret T. "Montaigne and Shakespeare Again." *HLQ*, XVI (1952), 23-42.
Shows that Montaigne's description of New World savages in his essay "Of the Caniballes" was preceded by many like descriptions in Continental and English writers. Concludes, however, that Gonzalo's speech in *The Tempest* is probably specifically indebted to Montaigne.

A4596   James, D. G. *The Dream of Learning: An Essay on "The Advancement of Learning," "Hamlet" and "King Lear."* Oxford: Clarendon Press, 1951. Pp. 126.
Infl. of Montaigne, pp. 57-62.
Rev: A3959.

A4597   Janaro, Richard Paul. "Dramatic Significance in *Hamlet*." *Studies in Shakespeare*, ed. by Arthur D. Matthews and Clark M. Emery, Coral Gables: Univ. of Miami Press, 1953, pp. 107-115.

A4598   Hennings, Elsa. *"Hamlet:" Shakespeares "Faust"-Tragödie*. Bonn, 1954. Pp. 296.
Several chapters on Montaigne.
Rev: A8574.

A4599   Whitman, Robert Freeman. *The Opinion of Wisdom: Montaigne and John Webster*. DD, Harvard University, 1956.

A4600   Greene, Thomas M. "Montaigne and the Savage Infirmity." *YR*, XLVI (1957), 191-205.
For Shak. parallels, see pp. 192, 203.

A4601   Stevens, Linton C. "Machiavelli's *Virtù* and the Voluntarism of Montaigne." *Renaissance Papers*. A selection of papers presented at the Renaissance Meeting in the Southeastern States, Duke University, April 12-13, 1957. Ed. by Allan H. Gilbert. Southeastern Renaissance Conference, 1958, pp. 118-124.

(e) OTHERS

A4602   Ribner, Irving. "The Significance of Gentillet's *Contre-Machiavel*." *MLQ*, X (1949), 153-157.

A4603   Wagner, Anthony R. "Shakespeare and the Agincourt Ennoblement." *N &Q*, 195 (1950), 105.
Points out that the full story, apparently utilized by Shak., is found in Jean Juvénal de Ursins *Histoire de Charles VI* (an ed. in 1572).

d. INFLUENCE OF SPANISH AND PORTUGUESE LITERATURE (74;27)
(1) GENERAL (74;-)

A4604   Mathews, Ernst G. *Studies in Anglo-Spanish Cultural and Literary Relations, 1598-1700*. DD, Harvard University, 1938. Abstract publ. in Harvard Univ. *Summaries of Theses, 1938*, Cambridge, 1940, pp. 304-311.

A4605   Patchell, Mary. *The Palmerin Romances in Elizabethan Prose Fiction*. Columbia Univ. Studies in Eng. and Comp. Lit. No. 166. Columbia Univ. Press, 1947. Pp. xiii, 157.
Rev: by J. L. Lievsay, *MLN*, LXIII (1948), 504-506; by F. L. Utley, *MLQ*, IX, 497-498.

A4606   Housman, J. E. *Parallel Plots in English and Spanish Drama of the Early 17th Century*. DD, University of London, 1951.

A4607   Salazar Chapela, Esteban. "Clásicos Españoles en Inglaterra." *Claudernos Americanos*, XI, No. 1 (1952), 256-261.

A4608   Hogan, Floriana T. *The Spanish Comedia and the English Comedy of Intrigue With Special Reference to Aphra Behn*. DD, Boston, 1955.

A4609   Ungerer, Gustav. *Anglo-Spanish Relations in Tudor Literature*. DD, Bern, 1956. Publ. in Schweizer Anglistische Arbeiten, Band 38. Berne, 1956. Pp. 231.
Rev: by M. Poirier, *EA*, X (1957), 51-52; by R. M. Wilson, *Erasmus*, X, 228-230; by T. Riese, *Archiv*, 194 (1957), 238-239; by Edwin B. Knowles, *HR*, XXV, 305-306; by K. Muir, *BHS*, XXXV (1958), 41-43; by Carmine Rocco Linsalata, *RN*, XI, 154-156; by André Stegmann, *RLC*, XXXII, 121-122; by K. L. Selig, *BHR*, XXI, 247-248.

A4610   Funke, Otto. "Spanische Sprachbücher im Elisabethanischen England." *Brunner Festschrift*, Vienna, 1957, pp. 43-57.

A4611   Randall, Dale B. J. *Renaissance English Translations of Non-Chivalric Spanish Fiction (With Special Reference to the Period from 1620 to 1657)*. DD, University of Pennsylvania, 1958. Pp. 670. Mic 58-1864. *DA*, XVIII (1958), 2129.

(2) INDIVIDUAL SPANISH AUTHORS (74;27)
(a) CERVANTES

A4612   Knowles, Edwin B. "Cervantes y la Literatura Inglesa." *Realidad*, I, II No. 5, (1947), 268-297.

A4613   Bruton, J. G. "Cervantes en Inglaterra." *Cervantes*. Montevideo: Inst. de Estudios Superiores, 1948. Pp. 108.

A4614   Peers, E. Allison. "Cervantes in England." *BSS*, XXIV (1947), 226-238.

A4615   Wilson, Edward M. "Cervantes and English Literature of the Seventeenth Century." *BH*, L (1948), 27-52.

(b) F. DE ROJAS

A4616   Allensworth, Clairenne. *Estudio Comparativo Entre "La Celestina" y "Romeo y Julieta."* MAE thesis, Mexico, 1940. Pp. 68. Typewritten.

A4617   Russel, Mary Elanor. *Una Comparación Entre Melibea y Julieta.* MAE thesis, Mexico, 1940. Pp. 113. Typewritten.

A4618   Heller, J. L., and R. L. Grismer. "Seneca in the Celestinesque Novel." *HR*, XII (1944), 29-48.

A4619   Hillard, Ernest H. Kilgore. *Spanish Imitations of the "Celestina."* DD, University of Illinois, 1958. Pp. 479. Mic 58-4335. *DA*, XVIII (1958), 588. Publ. No. 25,229.

(c) GIL VICENTE

A4620   Livermore, Ann. "Gil Vicente and Shakespeare." *Book Handbook*, II (1951), 1-12. Idem., *Revista da Fac. de Letras* (Univ. of Lisbon), XVII (1951), No. 1.

A4621   Revah, I. S. "Edition Critique du *Romance de Don Duardos et Flérida.*" *Bul. d'Hist. du Théâtre Portugais*, III (1952), 107-139.

(d) OTHERS

A4622   Allen, Don Cameron. "Jacques' 'Seven Ages' and Pero Mexía." *MLN*, LVI (1941), 601-603.

A4623   Leech, Clifford. "Catholic and Protestant Drama." *DUJ*, XXXIII (1941), 171-187.

A4624   Alcalá, M. "Don Juan Manuel y Shakespeare: Una Influencia Imposible." *Filosofía y Letras*, Mexico, X, No. 19 (1945), 55-67.

A4625   Evans, Dorothy Atkinson. "Some Notes on Shakespeare and *The Mirror of Knighthood.*" *SAB*, XXI (1946), 161-167; XXII (1947), 62-68.

A4626   Hunter, G. L. "A Source for Shakespeare's *Lucrece.*" *N &Q*, 197 (1952), 46.

A4627   Villarejo, Oscar Milton. *Lope De Vega and the Elizabethan and Jacobean Drama.* DD, Columbia University, 1953. Pp. 418. Mic A53-1502. *DA*, XIII (1953), 816. Publ. No. 5763.

A4628   Anderson, D. M. "Sir Thomas Wilson's Translation of Montemayor's *Diana.*" *RES*, VII (1956), 176-181.

A4629   Muir, Kenneth. "A Mexican Marina." *ES*, XXXIX (1958), 74-75.

e. INFLUENCE OF GERMANIC LITERATURE (75;28)
(1) GENERAL (75;-)

A4630   Seaton, Ethel. *Literary Relations of England and Scandinavia in the Seventeenth Century.* Oxford: Clarendon Press, 1935. Pp. 384; pl.
        Rev: *TLS*, March 28, 1936, p. 262; by A Brandl, *Archiv*, 169 (1936), 135-136; by Jens Kruuse, *RLC*, XVI, 608-612; by Y. Hirn, *N. Mitt.*, XXXVII, 320-322; by J. Nordström, *Lychnos* (Uppsala and Stockholm), I, 353; by A. G. van Hamel, *Museum*, XLIII, 298-299; by H. D. Leach, *American Scandinavian Rev.*, XXIV, 180; by Eduard Eckhardt, *Beiblatt*, XLVII, 365-367; by Gunnar Ahlström, *ES*, XIX (1937), 32-35; by v. H., *Neophil*, XXIII, 74; by Oscar James Campbell, *MLN*, LII, 596-598; by Herbert G. Wright, *RES*, XIII, 106-109; by Edith C. Batho, *MLR*, XXXII, 134-135; by Otto Springer, *Lbl*, LVIII, 388-389; by K. Litzenberg, *Scandinavian Studies and Notes*, XV (1938), 29-30; by Henry Tronchon, *RG*, XXIX, 409-410.

A4631   Claus, Else. *Deutschland und die Deutschen in Englischen Reiseberichten des 16. Jahrhunderts.* DD, Würzberg, 1942. Pp. 140, 63. Typewritten.

A4632   Feldman, Abraham. *Dutch Influence in the Tudor Theatre.* DD, University of Pennsylvania, 1950.

A4633   Feldman, Abraham. "Dutch Exiles and Elizabethan Playwrights." *N &Q*, 196 (1951), 530-533.

A4634   Feldman, A. Bronson. "Dutch Humanism and the Tudor Dramatic Traditions." *N &Q*, 197 (1952), 357-360.

A4635   Diederichsen, Diedrich. *Shakespeare und das Deutsche Märchendrama.* DD, Hamburg, 1952. Pp. 332. Typewritten.

(2) INDIVIDUAL GERMANIC AUTHORS (75;28)
(a) ERASMUS

A4636   Exner, Helmut. *Der Einfluss des Erasmus auf die Englische Bildungsidee.* DD, Breslau, 1939. Pp. 159. Publ. *Neue deutsche Forschungen. Abt. Englische Philologie*, XIII, 222. Berlin: Junker and Dünnhaupt, 1939. Pp. 159.
        Rev: by Kalthoff, *GA*, VI (1940), 22; by Wolfgang Keller, *SJ*, LXXVI, 214; by Wolfgang

Mann, *Beiblatt*, LII (1941), 109-110; by Edward Roditi, *Books Abroad*, XV, 447-448; by Paul Van Tieghem, *Rev. de Synthèse*, 1940-1945, p. 155.

A4637　Matthes, Heinrich Christoph. "Francis Meres und Erasmus von Rotterdam." *Anglia*, LXIII (1939), 426-435.

A4638　Larkin, James F. *Erasmus' "De Ratione Studii": Its Relationship to Sixteenth Century English Literature*. DD, University of Illinois, 1942.

A4639　White, Olive B. "Richard Taverner's Interpretation of Erasmus in *Proverbs or Adagies*." *PMLA*, LIX (1944), 928-943.

A4640　Edgerton, William L. "Shakespeare and the 'Needle's Eye'." *N &Q*, 196 (1951), 549-550. Observes that "the postern of a small needle's eye" (*R. II*, V.v.17) is the phrasing of an explanation known to Elizabethans in Erasmus' *Paraphrases*.

A4641　Hegland, Leonard. *The "Colloquies" of Erasmus: A Study in the Humanistic Background of English Literature*. DD, University of Illinois, 1951.

A4642　Marcel, Raymond. "Les *Découvertes* D'Erasme en Angleterre." *BHR*, XIV (1952), 117-123.

A4643　Muir, Kenneth. "Shakespeare and Erasmus." *N &Q*, NS, III (1956), 424-425.

A4644　Soellner, Rolf. "The Troubled Fountain: Erasmus Formulates a Shakespearian Simile." *JEGP*, LV (1956), 70-74.

A4645　McAvoy, William C. "Falstaff, Erasmus, and Ficino." *Carroll Quar.*, XI (1957), 10-14.

(b) GNAPHAEUS

A4646　Feldman, A. Bronson. "Gnaphaeus in England." *MLN*, LXVII (1952), 325-328.

A4647　Feldman, Abraham Bronson. "Dutch Humanism and the Tudor Dramatic Tradition." *N &Q*, 197 (1952), 357-360.

A4648　Atkinson, W. E. D. *"Acolastus," by Gulielmus Gnapheus: A Study of its Dramatic Structure and Didactic Intent, and of its Relation to English Literature in the Sixteenth Century*. DD, University of Chicago, 1954.

4. INFLUENCE OF CONTEMPORANEOUS ENGLISH NONDRAMATIC LITERATURE (75;28)
a. GENERAL STUDIES OF VARIOUS SOURCES

A4649　Hart, Alfred. *Shakespeare and the Homilies, and Other Pieces of Research into the Elizabethan Drama*. Melbourne Univ. Press, 1934.
　　　　Rev: by Max. J. Wolff, *Eng. Studn.*, LXXI (1936), 107-111; by Peter Alexander, *RES*, XII, 343-344.

A4650　Collins, D. C. *The Collection and Dissemination of News During the Time of Shakespeare, with Particular Reference to the News Pamphlets, 1590-1610*. DD, University of London, 1938.

A4651　Turner, Lilian F. *The Elizabethan Drama as the Newspaper of the Age: A Study of the Influence of External Controlling Factors on the Drama of the Early Seventeenth Century as a Potential Medium for Reflecting Popular Opinion on Political and Social Questions*. MA thesis, University of London, 1938.

A4652　Herr, A. F. *The Elizabethan Sermon: A Survey & Bibliography*. DD, University of Pennsylvania, 1940.

A4653　Greg, W. W. "The Date of *King Lear* and Shakespeare's Use of Earlier Versions of the Story." *Library*, XX (1940), 377-400.

A4654　Lindsay, Jean S. *A Survey of the Town-Country and Court-Country Themes in Non-Dramatic Elizabethan Literature*. DD, Cornell University, 1943. Abstract publ. in *Cornell Univ. Abstracts of Theses*, 1943, pp. 37-40.

A4655　Wilson, John Dover. "The Origins and Development of Shakespeare's *Henry IV*." *Library*, 4th S., XXVI (1945), 2-16.

A4656　Miriam Joseph, Sister, C. S. C. *Shakespeare's Use of the Arts of Language*. Columbia Univ. Press, 1947. Pp. xii, 423.
　　　　Rev: A5570.

A4657　Nearing, Homer, Jr. "Julius Caesar and the Tower of London." *MLN*, LXIII (1948), 228-233.

A4658　Nosworthy, J. M. "The Narrative Sources of *The Tempest*." *RES*, XXIV (1948), 281-294.

A4659　Bland, D. S. "*Macbeth* and the *Battle of Otterburn*." *N &Q*, 194 (1949), 335-336.

A4660　Jorgensen, Paul A. "The Courtship Scene in *Henry V*." *MLQ*, XI (1950), 180-188.
Concerns Shak's sympathetic handling of the plain soldier and its background in Churchyard, Lyly, Riche, Dekker, Beaumont-Fletcher, etc.

A4661　Paul, Henry N. *The Royal Play of Macbeth: When, Why, and How It Was Written by Shakespeare*. New York: Macmillan, 1950. Pp. 438.
　　　　Rev: B9143.

A4662　Frye, Roland M. " 'The World's a Stage': Shakespeare and the Moralists." *N &Q*, 198 (1953), 429-430.

A4663　Muir, Kenneth. "Menenius's Fable." *N &Q*, 198 (1953), 240-242.

A4664   Shedd, Robert Gordon. *The "Measure for Measure" of Shakespeare's 1604 Audience.* DD, University of Michigan, 1953. Pp. 430. Mic A53-1478. *DA*, XIII (1953), 801. Publ. No. 5730.

A4665   Henderson, Archibald, Jr. *Family of Mercutio.* DD, Columbia University, 1954. Pp. 270. Mic A54-2044. *DA*, XIV (1954), 1395. Publ. No. 8684.
Elyot, Tilney, Whetstone, Greene, and others.

A4666   Frye, Roland Mushat. " 'Out, Out, Brief Candle', and the Jacobean Understanding." *N &Q*, NS, II (1955), 143-145.

A4667   Honigmann, E. A. "Secondary Sources of *The Winter's Tale.*" *PQ*, XXXIV (1955), 27-38.

A4668   Wilson, J. Dover. "Shakespeare's 'Small Latin'—How Much?." *ShS*, X (1957), 12-26.
Chaucer, Golding, and others.

b. CHRONICLES AND HISTORIES
(1) TUDOR PRINCIPLES

A4669   Campbell, L. B. "The Use of Historical Patterns in the Reign of Elizabeth." *HLQ*, I (1937), 135-167.

A4670   Dick, H. G. "T. Blundeville's *The True Order and Methode of Wryting and Reading Hystories.*" (1574). *HLQ*, III (1940), 149-170.

A4671   Dean, Leonard Fellows. *The Theory and Background of Tudor History Writing.* DD, University of Michigan, 1940.

A4672   Dean, L. F. *Tudor Theories of History Writing.* Univ. of Michigan, Contributions in Modern Phil., No. 1, 1947, p. 24.

A4673   Buford, Albert H. *Theory and Practice of Biography in Holinshed's Chronicles.* DD, University of North Carolina, 1947. Abstr. publ. in *Univ. of North Carolina Record, Research in Progress, 1945-1948*, Chapel Hill, 1949, pp. 182-183.

A4674   Trimble, Walter Raleigh. "Early Tudor Historiography, 1485-1548." *JHI*, XI (1950), 30-41.

A4675   Jenkins, Owen. *The Art of History in Renaissance England: A Chapter in the History of Literary Criticism.* DD, Cornell University, 1954. Pp. 293. Mic A55-174. *DA*, XV (1955), 123-124. Publ. No. 10,587.

(2) HISTORY AND LITERATURE

A4676   Messiaen, P. "Shakespeare et l'Histoire d'Angleterre." *RCC*, XXXIX (1938), 692-709.

A4677   Elson, John. "Studies in the King John Plays." *AMS*, pp. 183-197.
Foxe, Holinshed, Polydore Vergil, John Bale, and others as sources of the *Troublesome Reign.*

A4678   Meierl, Elisabeth. *Shakespeares "Richard III" und seine Quelle. Die Bedeutung der Chronik für die Entwicklung des Shakespeareschen Dramas.* DD, Munich, 1955.

A4679   Gisi, Othmar. *Historische Elemente in der Englischen Tragödie vor der Romantik.* DD, Basel, 1953. Aarau: Keller, 1953. Pp. 119.

A4680   Ribner, Irving. *The English History Play in the Age of Shakespeare.* Princeton: Princeton Univ. Press, 1957. Pp. 369.
Rev: B5137.

A4681   Shubik, I. *The Use of English History in the Drama, 1599-1642.* MA thesis, University of London, 1954.

A4682   Ware, Eunice L. *King John in Tudor Chronicle and Drama.* DD, University of Texas, 1936.

A4683   Wiley, Paul L. "Renaissance Exploitation of Cavendish's *Life of Wolsey.*" *SP*, XLIII (1946), 121-146.

(a) GEOFFREY OF MONMOUTH

A4684   Hammer, J. "Remarks on the Sources and Textual History of Geoffrey of Monmouth's *Historia.*" *Quarterly Bulletin of the British Institute of Arts and Sciences*, 1944, pp. 501-564.

A4685   Hammer, J. "Note sur l'Histoire du Roi Lear dans Geoffrey de Monmouth." *Latomus: Revue d'Etudes Latines*, 1946, pp. 299-301.

A4686   Tatlock, J. S. P. *The Legendary History of Britain: Geoffrey of Monmouth's 'Historia Regum Britanniae' and Its Early Vernacular Versions.* Univ. Calif. Press, 1950. Pp. xi, 545.

(b) T. MORE

A4687   Glunz, H. *Shakespeare und Morus.* Kölner Anglistische Arbeiten: XXXII. Bochum Langendreer: Pöppinghaus, 1938. Pp. ix, 267.
Rev: by Alois Brandl, *DLZ*, LX (1939), 18-21; by Wolfgang Schmidt, *Beiblatt*, L, 101-103; by Wolfgang Keller, *SJ*, LXXV, 153-154; by Eduard Eckhardt, *Eng. Studn.* LXXIV (1940), 125-127.

A4688   Visser, F. T. "Borrowings by Shakespeare from St. Thomas More." *Tijdschrift voor Taal en Letteren*, XXVII (1939), 232-241.

A4689   Semper, I. J. "Shakespeare and St. Thomas More." *Catholic Educational Review*, XXXIX (1941), 166-172.

(c) POLYDORE VERGIL

A4690   Fulton, John F., and Charlotte H. Peters. *Hand List of Editions of Polydore Vergil's "De Inventoribus Rerum."* Compiled . . . from a bibliography in manuscript by . . . Professor John Ferguson. With an appendix on *Anglica Historia.* Historical Library, Yale University School of Medicine, 1944. Pp. 15.

A4691   Vergil, Polydore. *The Anglica Historia of Polydore Vergil, A. D. 1485-1537.* Ed. with a tr. by Denys Hay. Camden Series, LXXIV. London: Royal Hist. Soc., 1950. Pp. xlii, 373.
        Rev: by Helen M. Cam, *Speculum,* XXVI (1951), 161-163; by G. R. E., *EHR,* LXVI, 147-148; by Charles Johnson, *Bul. Inst. Hist. Research,* XXIV, 78-79.

A4692   Hay, Denys. "The Life of Polydore Vergil of Urbino." *JWCI,* XII (1949), 132-151.
        Enlarges and corrects the account in the *DNB*; contains list of letters to and from Polydore Vergil.

A4693   Hay, Denys. *Polydore Vergil. Renaissance Historian and Man of Letters.* Oxford: Clarendon Press, 1952. Pp. xiii, 233.
        Rev: *Listener,* XLVII (1952), 971, 973; by J. D. Mackie, *History Today,* II, 719-720; *TLS,* May 23, p. 349; by G. R. Elton, *EHR,* LXVII, 573-575; by D. J. Gordon, *RN,* V, 55-56; by E. M. W. Tillyard, *RES,* IV (1953), 155-156; by R. D. Richardson, *Speculum,* XXVIII, 892-894; by R. W., *Italian Studies,* VII, 96-97.

A4694   Koebner, Richard. " 'The Imperial Crown of This Realm': Henry VIII, Constantine the Great, and Polydore Vergil." *Bul. Inst. Hist. Research,* London Univ., XXVI (1953), 29-52.

(d) HALL AND HOLINSHED

A4695   King, Lucille. *The Relations of the Henry VI Plays to the Chronicle Histories of Hall and Holinshed.* DD, University of Texas, 1936.

A4696   Mutz, Wilhelm. *Der Charakter Richards III. in der Darstellung des Chronisten Holinshed und des Dramatikers Shakespeare mit einem Beitrag zu seiner Charakterpsyche.* DD, Berlin, Humboldt-Univ., 1936. Pp. 74.

A4697   Zeeveld, W. Gordon. "The Influence of Hall on Shakespeare's English Historical Plays." *ELH,* III (1936), 317-353.
        Rev: by G. L., *Archiv,* 171 (1937), 256.

A4697a Zeeveld, W. Gordon. *The Influence of Hall on Shakespeare's English Plays; A Portion of Edward Hall; A Study of 16th Century Historiography in England.* Baltimore: Johns Hopkins Press, 1937. Pp. 44.

A4698   Brownfield, Clarence. "Holinshed and His Editors." *TLS,* Aug. 7, 1937, p. 576.

A4699   Fletcher, Baylis J., Jr. *Shakespeare's Use of Holinshed's Chronicles in "Richard III," "Richard II," "Henry IV," and "Macbeth."* DD, University of Texas, 1937.

A4700   Dodson, Sarah. "The Northumberland of Shakespeare and Holinshed." *TxSE,* 1939, pp. 74-85.

A4701   Dodson, Sarah. "Caterpillars, Sponges, Horseleeches, in Shakespere and Holinshed." *SAB,* XIX (1944), 41-46.

A4702   Fellheimer, Jeannette. "Geoffrey Fenton's *Historie of Guicciardin* and Holinshed's *Chronicles* of 1587." *MLQ,* VI (1945), 285-298.

A4703   Semper, I. J. " 'Yes, by St. Patrick'." *TLS,* Aug. 3, 1946, p. 367.

A4704   Dodson, Sarah. "Holinshed's Sources for the Prognostications About the Years 1583 and 1588." *Isis,* XXXVIII (1947), 60-62.

A4705   Hay, D. "Hall and Shakespeare." *TLS,* May 17, 1947, p. 239.

A4706   Law, Robert Adger. "Holinshed's Leir Story and Shakespeare's." *SP,* XLVII (1950), 42-50.

A4707   Law, Robert Adger. "Deviations from Holinshed in *Richard II.*" *TxSE,* XXIX (1950), 91-101.

A4708   Law, Robert Adger. "The Composition of *Macbeth* with Reference to Holinshed." *TxSE,* XXXI (1952), 35-41.

A4709   Law, Robert Adger. "Edmund Mortimer in Shakespeare and Hall." *SQ,* V (1954), 425-436.

A4710   Law, Robert Adger. "The Chronicles and the Three Parts of *Henry VI.*" *TxSE,* XXXIII (1955), 13-32.

A4711   Muir, Kenneth. "*King Lear* IV. 6." *N &Q,* NS, II (1955), 15.

c. PROSE FICTION GENERALLY

A4712   Mish, C. C. *English Prose Fiction 1600-1640; 1641-1660.* Charlottesville, Virginia: Bibl. Soc. Univ. Virginia, 1952. Pp. v, 34; iii, 21.

A4713   Pruvost, René. *Matteo Bandello and Elizabethan Fiction.* Bibl. de la Rev. de Litt. Comp., 113. Paris: Champion, 1937. Pp. 348.

A4714   Bernbaum, Ernest. "Recent Works on Prose Fiction Before 1800." *MLN,* LV (1940), 54-65.

A4715   Patchell, Mary. *The Palmerin Romances in Elizabethan Prose Fiction.* Columbia Univ. Studies in Eng. and Comp. Lit. No. 166. Columbia Univ. Press, 1947. Pp. xiii, 157.
        Rev: A4605.

A4716　O'Dell, Willis H. S. *The Vogue of Prose Fiction in Elizabethan England.* DD, Harvard University, 1949.

A4717　Hurrell, J. D. *Themes and Conventions of Elizabethan Prose Fiction* (1558-1603). DD, Birmingham University, 1955.

A4718　Borinski, Ludwig. "The Origin of the Euphuistic Novel and its Significance for Shakespeare." *Studies in Honor of T. W. Baldwin,* pp. 38-52.

d. INDIVIDUAL WRITERS
(1) BEVERLEY

A4719　Prouty, C. T. "George Whetstone, Peter Beverley, and the Sources of *Much Ado About Nothing.*" *SP,* xxxviii (1941), 211-220.

A4720　Prouty, Charles T. *The Sources of "Much Ado About Nothing:" A Critical Study, Together with the Text of Peter Beverley's "Ariodanto and Ieneura."* New Haven: Yale Univ. Press, 1950. Pp. vi, 142.
　　　　Rev: B6593.

(2) BRIGHT (See also A1069)

A4721　Elton, William. "Timothy Bright and Shakespeare's Seeds of Nature." *MLN,* lxv (1950), 196-197.

A4722　Riesenfeld, Kurt. "Timothy Bright und Shakespeare." *Sudhoffs Archiv. f. Geschichte d. Medizin u. d. Naturwiss.,* xli (1957), 244-254.

(3) BROOKE

A4723　Moore, Olin H. *The Legend of Romeo and Juliet.* Columbus: Ohio State Univ. Press, 1950. Pp. 9, 167.
　　　　Rev: B5788.

A4724　Muir, Kenneth. "Arthur Brooke and the Imagery of *Romeo and Juliet.*" *N &Q,* NS, iii (1956), 241-243.

(4) BUCHANAN

A4725　Starnes, D. T. "Shakespeare's Sonnet 60: Analogues." *N &Q,* 194 (1949), 454.

A4726　Muir, Kenneth. "Buchanan, Leslie and *Macbeth.*" *N &Q,* NS, ii (1955), 511-512.

(5) DANIEL

A4727　Thaler, A. "Shakespeare, Daniel, and *Everyman.*" *PQ,* xv (1936), 217-218.

A4728　Borgese, G. A. "The Dishonor of Honor: Francesco Giovanni Mauro to Sir John Falstaff." *RR,* xxxii (1941), 44-55.

A4729　Law, Robert Adger. "Daniel's *Rosamond* and Shakespeare." *TxSE,* xxvi (1947), 42-48.

A4730　Parr, Johnstone. "A Note on Daniel." *SAB,* xxiii (1948), 181-182.

A4731　Greer, C. A. "Did Shakespeare Use Daniel's *Civile Warres?*" *N &Q,* 196 (1951), 53-54.

A4732　Michel, Laurence, and Cecil C. Seronsy. "Shakespeare's History Plays and Daniel: An Assessment." *SP,* lii (1955), 549-577.

A4733　Bludau, Diethild. "Sonettstruktur bei Samuel Daniel." *SJ,* 94 (1958), 63-89.

A4734　Daniel, Samuel. *The Civil Wars.* Ed. with Introduction and Notes by Laurence Michel. New Haven: Yale Univ. Press, 1958. Pp. vii, 366.
　　　　Rev: by G. B. Evans, *JEGP,* lvii (1958), 808-810.

(6) DELONEY

A4735　Sievers, Richard. *Thomas Deloney. Eine Studie über Balladenliteratur der Shakespeare-Zeit. Nebst Neudruck von Deloneys Roman "Jack of Newbury."* DD, Berlin, Humboldt Univ., 1903. Pp. iv, 32.

A4736　Bache, William B. " 'The Murder of Old Cole': A Possible Source for *Macbeth.*" *SQ,* vi (1955), 358-359.

A4737　Lawlis, Merritt E. "Shakespeare, Deloney, and the Earliest Text of the Arthur Ballad." *Harvard Library Bulletin,* x (1956), 130-134.

(7) SYLVESTER'S DUBARTAS

A4738　Taylor, G. C. "Two Notes on Shakespeare." *PQ,* xx (1941), 371-376.

A4739　Ure, Peter. "Two Passages in Sylvester's Du Bartas and Their Bearing on Shakespeare's *Richard II.*" *N &Q,* 198, (1953), 374-377.

(8) J. ELIOT

A4740　Hard, F. "Notes on J. Eliot's *Ortho-epia Gallica (1593).*" *HLQ,* i (1937), 169-187.

A4741　Lever, J. W. "Shakespeare's French Fruits." *ShS,* vi (1953), 79-90.

Points out numerous parallels between Shak.'s works and John Eliot's *Ortho-epia Gallica*.
Rev: by D. M. Stuart, *English*, IX (1952/53), 230-231.

(9) T. ELYOT

A4742   Barker, E. "A Shakespeare Discovery." *Spectator*, Apr. 2, 1937, p. 615.
Troilus and Cressida and Elyot's *Governor*.

A4743   Grether, Emil. *Das Verhältnis von Shakespeares "Heinrich V" zu Sir Thomas Elyots "Governour."*
DD, Marburg, Bauer, 1938. Pp. 46.

A4744   Schlotter, Josef. *Thomas Elyots "Governour" in seinem Verhältnis zu Francesco Patrici.* DD,
Freiburg/Breisgau, 1938. Pp. 118.

A4745   Warren, Leslie C. *Humanistic Doctrines of the Prince from Petrarch to Sir Thomas Elyot.* DD,
University of Chicago, 1938.

A4746   Lassen, Willi. *Das Verhältnis des "Governour" von Thomas Elyot zur Humanistischen Literatur
über Fürstenerziehung.* DD, Hamburg, 1939.
Mummendey reported no copy could be found.

A4747   Durnell, B. H. *The Humanistic Concept of the Latin Classics in Thomas Elyot's "Book of the Governour."* MS thesis, Columbia University, 1947. Pp. 78.

A4748   Sargent, Ralph M. "Sir Thomas Elyot and the Integrity of *The Two Gentlemen of Verona*."
PMLA, LXV (1950), 1166-80.

A4749   Maxwell, J. C. "*Julius Caesar* and Elyot's *Governour*." *N&Q*, NS III (1956), 147.

(10) GASCOIGNE

A4750   Going, William T. "Gascoigne and the Term 'Sonnet Sequence'." *N&Q*, NS, I (1954),
189-191.

A4751   Sasek, Lawrence A. "Gascoigne and the Elizabethan Sonnet Sequences." *N&Q*, NS, III
(1956), 143-144.

(11) GREENE

A4752   Pruvost, René. *Robert Greene et ses Romans (1558-1592), Contribution à l'Histoire de la Renaissance en Angleterre.* Thesis, Paris, 1938. Paris: Les Belles-Lettres, 1938. Pp. 650.
Rev: by Heinz Reinhold, *Beiblatt*, LI (1940), 100-107.

A4753   Muir, Kenneth. "Greene and *Troilus and Cressida*." *N&Q*, NS, II (1955), 141-142.

(12) HARSNETT

A4754   Muir, Kenneth. "Samuel Harsnett and *King Lear*." *RES*, NS, II (1951), 11-21.

A4755   Muir, Kenneth. "Shakespeare and Harsnett." *N&Q*, 197 (1952), 555-556.

A4756   Stevenson, Robert. "Shakespeare's Interest in Harsnet's *Declaration*." *PMLA*, LXVII (1952),
898-902.

(13) LEWKENOR

A4757   Jorgensen, Paul A. "Enobarbus' Broken Heart and *The Estate of English Fugitives*." *PQ*,
XXX (1951), 387-392.

A4758   Muir, Kenneth. "Shakespeare and Lewkenor." *RES*, VII (1956), 182-183.

(14) LODGE

A4759   Seronsy, Cecil C. "The Seven Ages of Man Again." *SQ*, IV (1953), 364-365.

A4760   Fox, Charles A. O. "Thomas Lodge and Shakespeare." *N&Q*, NS, III (1956), 190.

(15) NASHE

A4761   Wilson, J. Dover (trans.). "Nashe's 'Kid in Æsop': A Danish Interpretation by V. Østerberg." *RES*, XVIII (1942), 385-394.

A4762   Lea, Kathleen, and Ethel Seaton. " 'I Saw Young Henry'." *RES*, XXI (1945), 319-322.

A4763   Shaaber, M. A. "Shylock's Name." *N&Q*, 195 (1950), 236.

A4764   Ebbs, John Dale. "A Note on Nashe and Shakespeare." *MLN*, LXVI (1951), 480-481.

A4765   Davenport, A. "Shakespeare and Nashe's 'Pierce Penilesse'." *N&Q*, 198 (1953), 371-374.

A4766   Evans, G. Blakemore. "Thomas Nashe and the 'Dram of Eale'." *N&Q*, 198 (1953), 377-378.

A4767   York, Ernest C. "Shakespeare and Nashe." *N&Q*, 198 (1953), 370-371.

A4768   Bradbrook, Frank W. "Thomas Nashe and Shakespeare." *N&Q*, NS, I (1954), 470.

A4769   Taylor, E. M. M. "Lear's Philosopher." *SQ*, VI (1955), 364-365.

(16) RICH

A4770   Hinton, Edward M. "Rych's *Anothomy of Ireland*, With an Account of the Author." *PMLA*,
LV (1940), 73-101.
Prints an unpublished text with a biographical account serving to explain it.

A4771   Bruce, Dorothy Hart. "*The Merry Wives* and Two Brethren." *SP*, XXXIX (1942), 265-278.

A4772   Webb, Henry J. "Barnabe Riche—Sixteenth Century Military Critic." *JEGP*, XLII (1943), 240-252.

A4773   Bruce, Dorothy Hart. *Barnabe Riche and His Acquaintances*. DD, Stanford University, 1944. Abstr. publ. in Stanford *Abstracts of Dissertations*, XIX, 1943-44, pp. 17-18.

A4774   Cranfill, Thomas Mabry. *Barnaby Rich's Farewell and the Drama*. DD, Harvard University, 1944. Abstr. publ. in *Summaries of PhD Theses, 1943-1945*, Cambridge: Harvard Univ. Press, 1947, pp. 466-469.
         Partial source for Shak.'s *Twelf.*, *Oth.*, *Wives*.

A4775   Welply, W. H. "Seven Anglo-Irishmen of the Tudor Time." *N &Q*, 187 (1944), 90-94.

A4776   Cranfill, T. M. "Barnaby Rich's 'Sappho' and *The Weakest Goeth to the Wall*." *TxSE*, XXV (1945-46), 142-171.

A4777   Cranfill, T. M. "Barnaby Rich: An Elizabethan Reviser at Work." *SP*, XLVI (1949), 411-418.

A4778   Cranfill, T. M. "Barnaby Rich and King James." *ELH*, XVI (1949), 65-75.

A4779   Cranfill, Thomas M. "Thomas North at Chester." *HLQ*, XIII (1949), 93-99.

A4780   Miller, Edwin H. "Repetition in Barnaby Rich." *N &Q*, 198 (1953), 511-512.

A4781   Cranfill, Thomas Mabry, and Dorothy Hart Bruce. *Barnaby Rich: A Short Biography*. Austin: Univ. of Texas Press, 1953. Pp. x, 135.
         Rev: by Edwin E. Willoughby, *SQ*, V (1954), 423; by Paul A. Jorgensen, *JEGP*, LIII, 478-479; *TLS*, Dec. 10, 1954, p. 794; by Jean Robertson, *RES*, NS, VII (1956), 105-106.

A4782   Muir, Kenneth. "The Sources of *Twelfth Night*." *N &Q*, NS, II (1955), 94.

A4783   Jorgensen, Paul A. "Barnaby Rich: Soldierly Suitor and Honest Critic of Women." *SQ*, VII (1956), 183-188.

A4784   Lievsay, John Leon. "A Word About Barnaby Rich." *JEGP*, LV (1956), 381-392.
         On the Cranfill-Bruce biography of Rich.

A4785   Wilson, F. P. "Dekker, Segar, and Some Others." *HLQ*, XVIII (1954-55), 297-300.
         Includes comments upon Riche's *The Honestie of This Age*.

A4786   Ferrara, Fernando. "Barnabe Riche, Difensore del Soldato Inglese e Autore di *A Larum for London*." *English Miscellany*, VIII (1957), 21-54.

(17) THE SCHOOL OF NIGHT

A4787   Bradbrook, M. C. *The School of Night*. A Study in the Literary Relationships of Sir Walter Ralegh. Cambridge Univ. Press, 1936. Pp. viii, 190.
         Rev: *TLS*, Oct. 31, 1936, p. 887; by H. Ross Williamson *FortnR*, NS, 140 (1936), 632-633; by T. W. Ramsey, *Poetry Review*, XXVII, 483-485; *QR*, 268 (1937), 179-180; by Thomas Good, *Life and Letters*, XVI, No. 7, 163-164; by F. S. Boas, *English*, I, 346-348; by J. Burns Martin, *Dalhousie Rev.*, XVII, 116; by George Herbert Clarke, *QQ*, XLIV, 116; by A. L. R., *Criterion*, XVI, 758-759; by F. C. Danchin, *EA*, I, 248-249; by Walter G. Friedrich, *MLN*, LII, 616-617; by W. Keller, *SJ*, LXXIII, 161-162; by Paul Meissner, *DLZ*, LIX (1938), 482-485; by F. R. Johnson, *Isis*, XXIX, 113-115; by Peter Alexander, *MLR*, XXXIII, 622.

A4788   Strathmann, Ernest A. "The Textual Evidence for 'The School of Night'." *MLN*, LVI (1941), 176-186.

A4789   Schrickx, W. "Shakespeare and the School of Night: An Estimate and Further Interpretations." *Neophil*, XXXV (1950), 35-44.
         See also *LLL*, Texts and Lit. Gen.

(18) SIDNEY

A4790   Watson, Sara Ruth. "Shakespeare's Use of the *Arcadia*. An Example in *Henry V*." *N &Q*, 175 (1938), 364-365.
         See letter by Joseph E. Morris, ibid., p. 409.

A4791   Siebeck, Berta. *Das Bild Sir Philip Sidneys in der Englischen Renaissance*. DD, Freiburg/Breisgau, 1939. Pp. xii, 198.

A4792   Pellegrini, Angelo M. "Bruno, Sidney, and Spenser." *SP*, XL (1943), 128-144.

A4793   Thaler, Alwin. *Shakespeare and Sir Philip Sidney*. Harvard Univ. Press, 1947. Pp. 100.
         Rev: by A. H. Gilbert, *Tennessee Alumnus*, XXVII (1947), 12-14; by M. Webster, *TAr*, XXXII (1948), 78-79; *TLS*, Feb. 28, 1948, p. 127; by M. T. Herrick, *JEGP*, XLVII, 193-196; by G. Bullough, *MLR*, XLIV (1949), 559-560; by F. T. Prince, *RES*, NS, I (1950), 63-64; by W. Clemen, *Archiv*, 189 (1952/53), 66.

A4794   Poirier, Michel. "Sidney's Influence Upon *A Midsummer Night's Dream*." *SP*, XLIV (1947), 483-489.

A4795   Ribner, Irving. "A Note on Sidney's *Arcadia* and *A Midsummer Night's Dream*." *SAB*, XXIII (1948), 207-208.

A4796   Pyle, Fitzroy. "*Twelfth Night, King Lear* and *Arcadia*." *MLR*, XLIII (1948), 449-455.

A4797   Armstrong, William A. "*King Lear* and Sidney's *Arcadia*." *TLS*, Oct. 24, 1949, p. 665.

A4798   D(avenport), Arnold. "Possible Echoes from Sidney's *Arcadia* in Shakespeare, Milton and Others." *N &Q*, 194 (1949), 554-555.

A4799   Disher, M. Willson. "The Trend of Shakespeare's Thought." *TLS*, Oct. 20, 27, Nov. 3, 1950, pp. 668, 684, 700.
        See the letters "The Rival Poet" by J. M. Murry, ibid., Nov. 17, 1950, p. 727; by A. S. Cairn-cross, ibid., Dec. 1, 1950, p. 767; by Lynette Feasey, ibid., Dec. 8, 1950, p. 785; by Howard Murry and Lawrence Durrell, ibid., May 1, 1951, p. 7; by C. Longworth de Chambrun, ibid., Feb. 2, 1951, p. 69.

A4800   Cancelled.

A4801   Muir, Kenneth, and John Danby. "Arcadia and *King Lear*." *N &Q*, 195 (1950), 49-51.

A4802   D., A. "Shakespeare's *Sonnets*." *N &Q*, 195 (1950), 5-6.

A4803   Zandvoort, R. W. "Fair Portia's Counterfeit." *Rivista di Letterature Moderne*, II (1951), 351-356. Also in Zandvoort's *Collected Papers, A Selection of Notes and Articles originally Published in English Studies and Other Journals*. Groningen Studies in English, V. Groningen: J. B. Walters, 1954, pp. 50-57. Also in *Atti del V Congresso Internazionale di Lingue e Letterature Moderne nei loro Rapporti con le Belle Arti*. Florence, 27-31 March 1951. Florence: Valmartina, 1955.

A4804   Ribner, Irving. "Sidney's *Arcadia* and the Structure of *King Lear*." *SN*, XXIV (1952), 63-68.

A4805   Danby, J. F. *Poets on Fortune's Hill*. London, 1952. Chapter 3 "Sidney and the Late-Shakespearian Romance," pp. 74-107.
        Rev: A8156.

A4806   Bludau, Diethild. "Sonettstruktur bei Samuel Daniel." *SJ*, 94 (1958), 63-89.
        See also A5466 and A5466a.

(19)   SPENSER

A4807   Thaler, Alwin. "Shakespeare and Spenser: The Epithalamion." *SAB*, XI (1936), 33-40.

A4808   Thaler, Alwin. "Mercutio and Spenser's Phantastes." *PQ*, XVI (1937), 405-407.

A4809   Harrison, Thomas P., Jr. "Aspects of Primitivism in Shakespeare and Spenser." *TxSE*, XX (1940), 39-71.

A4810   Thaler, Alwin. "Spenser and *Much Ado About Nothing*." *SP*, XXXVII (1940), 225-235.

A4811   Gordon, D. J. "*Much Ado About Nothing*: A Possible Source for the Hero-Claudio Plot." *SP*, XXXIX (1942), 279-290.

A4812   Potts, Abbie Findlay. "Spenserian 'Courtesy' and 'Temperance' in *Much Ado About Nothing*." *SAB*, XVII (1942), 103-111, 126-133.

A4813   Montgomerie, William. "Sporting Kid (The Solution of the 'Kidde in Æsop' Problem)." *Life and Letters*, XXXVI (1943), 18-24.

A4814   Harrison, Thomas P., Jr. "Flower Lore in Spenser and Shakespeare: Two Notes." *MLQ*, VII (1946), 175-178.

A4815   McPeek, James A. S. "The Genesis of Caliban." *PQ*, XXV (1946), 378-381.

A4816   Watkins, W. B. C. *Shakespeare and Spenser*. Princeton Univ. Press, 1950.
        Rev: A8549.

A4817   Hammerle, Karl. "Das Titanialager des Sommernachtstraumes als Nachhall des Topos vom *Locus Amoenus*." *SJ*, 90 (1954), 279-284.

A4818   Potts, Abbie Findlay. "Hamlet and Gloriana's Knights." *SQ*, VI (1955), 31-43.

A4819   Potts, Abbie Findlay. *Shakespeare and "The Faerie Queene."* Cornell Univ. Press, 1958. Pp. xii, 269.
        Rev: (None through terminal date).

A4820   Hammerle, Karl. "Ein Muttermal des Deutschen Pyramus und die Spenserechoes in *Midsummer Night's Dream*." *Festschrift z. 70. Geburtstag von Friedrich Wild*. Vienna, Stuttgart: Braumüller, 1958, pp. 52-66.

(20)   GEORGE WILKINS

A4821   Dickson, George B. "The Identity of George Wilkins." *SAB*, XIV (1939), 195-208.

A4822   Parrott, Thomas Marc. "*Pericles*: The Play and the Novel." *SAB*, XXIII (1948), 105-113. Discusses John Munro's letter in *TLS*, Oct. 11, 1942, suggesting Wilkins' *Painful Adventures of Pericles Prince of Tyre* follows and is based upon Shak.'s play. Agrees, suggesting novel was pushed because the King's Men refused to permit publication.

A4823   Muir, K. "The Problem of *Pericles*." *ES*, XXX (1949), 65-83.

A4824   Evans, Bertrand. "The Poem of Pericles." *The Image of the Work, Essays in Criticism* by B. H. Lehman and Others. Berkeley and Los Angeles: Univ. of California Press, 1955, pp. 35-56.

(21)   WILSON

A4825   Kennedy, Milton B. *The Oration in Shakespeare.* DD, University of Virginia, 1937. Abstr,
publ. in *Abstracts of Dissertations, 1937.* Charlottesville: Univ. of Virginia, 1937, pp. 16-18.

A4826   Peterson, Douglas L. "A Probable Source for Shakespeare's Sonnet CXXIX." *SQ,* V (1954),
381-384.

<h4 style="text-align:center">(22)   OTHERS   (Arranged alphabetically by surname of subject.)</h4>

A4827   Sargent, Ralph M. "The Source of *Titus Andronicus.*" *SP,* XLVI (1949), 167-183.
Discusses the prose History of *Titus Andronicus* and the ballad that represents an undated but
early English treatment of the story; compares play with *History* in an attempt to demonstrate
that the prose treatise is a version of Shakespeare's source, "if not that source itself."

A4828   James, D. G. *The Dream of Learning: An Essay on "The Advancement of Learning," "Hamlet"
and "King Lear."* Oxford: Clarendon Press, 1951. Pp. 126.
Influence of Bacon, *passim.*
Rev: A3959.

A4829   Nutt, Sarah M. "The Arctic Voyages of William Barents in Probable Relation to Certain
of Shakespeare's Plays." *SP,* XXXIX (1942), 241-264.

A4830   Frankis, P. J. "Shakespeare's *King John* and a Patriotic Slogan." *N &Q,* NS, II (1955), 424-425.
Notes the famous patriotic ending of Shak.'s *John* has its parallel in Andrew Borde's *The Fyrst
Boke of the Introduction of Knowledge* published in 1548. Though editor Honigmann (1954) has
cited other later parallels, certain aspects are common only to Borde and Shakespeare.

A4831   Kentish-Wright, U. "Shakespeare and N. Breton." *Cornhill Magazine,* 159 (1939), 815-826.

A4832   Musgrove, S. "The Nomenclature of *King Lear.*" *RES,* VII (1956), 294-298.
Sees Shak.'s indebtedness to Camden's *Remaines* (1605) in a number of details including three
Anglo-Saxon names in the subplot—Edgar, Edmund, and Oswald.

A4833   Wicks, George A. *Henry Constable: Elizabethan Courtier and Poet of the Counter-Reformation.*
DD, University of California, 1954.
According to Malone, Constable's *Shepheard's Song of Venus and Adonis,* first printed in *Eng-
land's Helicon* (1600), suggested Shak.'s *Venus and Adonis.*

A4834   Cauthen, I. B. "Shakespeare's 'Moat Defensive' (*Richard II,* II. i. 43-49)." *N &Q,* NS, III
(1956), 419-420.
Another source for this passage found in Thomas Diggs's *Arithmetical Warlike Treatise Named
Stratioticos,* first published in 1579.

A4835   Allen, Don Cameron. "Three Notes on Donne's Poetry with a Side Glance at *Othello.*" *MLN,*
LXV (1950), 102-106.

A4836   Davenport, A. "The Seed of a Shakespeare Sonnet?" *N &Q,* 182 (1942), 242-244.
Calls attention to the resemblance of a group of images in Shak.'s second sonnet to those in
Drayton's Second Eglog of *The Shepheards Garland.*

A4837   Maas, P. "Henry Finch and Shakespeare." *RES,* IV (1953), 142.
Parallel between Finch's speech in the Debate in Commons, March 21, 23, 1593, and *The Booke
of Sir Thomas More,* sc. vi in Shak.'s hand.

A4838   Muir, Kenneth. "Shakespeare and Florio." *N &Q,* 197 (1952), 493-495.
Florio's other works, not Montaigne.

A4839   Sitwell, Osbert. " 'The Sole Arabian Tree'." *TLS,* Apr. 26, 1941, pp. 199, 206.
See editorial comment, *TLS,* Apr. 26, 1941, p. 203; letters by Malcolm Letts, ibid., May 3, 1941,
p. 215; C. H. Wilkinson, ibid., May 3, 1941, pp. 215, 216; Margaret Cooper, ibid., May 24,
1941, p. 251; T. W. Baldwin, ibid., June 14, 1941, p. 287.
Suggests John Frampson's (1579) translation of Marco Polo as a possible source for *The
Phoenix and the Turtle.*

A4840   Lever, J. W. "Three Notes on Shakespeare's Plants." *RES,* III (1952), 117-129.
Argues Shak.'s knowledge and use of Gerarde's *Herball* (1597) and concludes: (1) the songs
at the end of *Love's Labour's Lost* were part of the revision mentioned on the t.p. of 1598 Q;
(2) the herbals of Gerarde and Lyte explain the various Shak. descriptions of *mandrake* and
mandragora; (3) Ophelia's words and actions with her flowers are "in keeping with her character, her good intentions, her abysmal ignorance of life."

A4841   Hunter, G. K. "A Source for Shakespeare's *Lucrece.*" *N &Q,* 197 (1952), 46.
Suggests the version of the Lucrece story in Barnaby Googe's translation of a work by Peter
Diaz, as "well worth consideration."

A4842   Lambin, G. "Une Première Ebauche d'*Hamlet* (mars 1587)." *LanM,* XLIX (May-June 1955),
229-237.
Suggests that John Gordon's "Mânes d'Henri" addressed in 1587 to James VI, upon the
execution of the Queen, directly influ. Shak.'s Hamlet in his treatment of Gertrude.

A4843   Nathan, Norman. "The Marriage of Duke Vincentio and Isabella." *SQ,* VII (1956), 43-45.
Parallel to James I's *Basilikon Doron.*

A4844   "One of Shakespeare's Books?" *TLS,* May 1, 1943, p. 216.
Signature in the Folger copy of Lambarde's *Archaionomia,* London, 1568, and circumstances of
its acquisition suggests Shak. and Lambarde were friends. Cites Lambarde's "Eirenarcha"
as known to Shak.

A4845 Whitebrook, J. C. "Fynes Moryson, G. Bruno, and William Shakespeare." *N &Q*, 171 (1936), 255-260.

A4846 Fisher, A. S. T. "The Sources of Shakespeare's Interlude of Pyramus and Thisbe: A Neglected Poem." *N &Q*, 194 (1949), 376-379, 400-402.
Treats Thomas Mouffet's *The Silkewormes, and Their Flies*, 1599.

A4847 Pruvost, René. "Le Drame Romanesque du *Marchand de Venise*." *LanM*, March-April, 1951, pp. 51-61.
A study of the "romanesque" in *Merch.* in relation to Munday's *Zelauto*.

A4848 Joseph, B. L. "Correspondence." *English*, VIII (1950), 47-48.
Writes explaining Hamlet's references to the "handsaw," i.e. *heronshaw* (cf. Joseph Hall's *Quo Vadis*), and to "French falconers"; suggests a source for his jingle on the stricken deer (Henry Petowe's *Hero and Leanders Further Fortunes*, London, 1598).

A4849 Babcock, C. Merton. "An Analogue for the Name Othello." *N &Q*, 196 (1951), 515.
John Reynolds' *God's Revenge* as Shakespeare's source for the name Othello is either a mis-interpretation of George Steevens' commentary or a deliberate falsification by Steevens himself.

A4850 Chester, Allan G. "John Soowthern's *Pandora* and *Othello* II.i.184." *MLN*, LXVI (1951), 481-482.
Notes that Steevens in his comment on the line in *Othello* is correct in claiming for Soowthern the Ronsardian application of *warrior* (*guerrière*) to his lady; that the rare term of *orgulous* occurs on Sig. C 2v; and that evidence of Shak.'s knowledge of *Pandora* is slight.

A4851 Walmsley, D. M. "Shakespeare's Link with Virginia." *History Today*, VII (1957), 299-235.
William Leveson, Sir Dudley Digges, the Virginia Company, and William Strachey's *A True Repertory of the Wrack and Redemption of Sir Thomas Gates*.

A4852 Muir, Kenneth. "Henry Swinburne and Shakespeare." *N &Q*, NS, IV (1957), 285-286.

A4853 Ure, Peter. "*Macbeth* and Warner's *Albion's England*." *N &Q*, 194 (1949), 232-233.

A4854 Rose, Norma V. *Amintae Gavdia* by Thomas Watson. DD, Yale University, 1944.

A4855 Atkinson, Dorothy F. "The Source of *Two Gentlemen of Verona*." *SP*, XLI (1944), 223-234.
The fifth tale in Henry Wotton's *Courtlie Controversie of Cupids Cautels* (1578).

5. INFLUENCE OF CONTEMPORANEOUS ENGLISH DRAMATISTS (76;28)
a. COLLABORATION AND OTHER PROBLEMS OF AUTHORSHIP (18;4,5)

A4856 Tiegs, Alexander. *Zur Zusammenarbeit Englischer Berufsdramatiker Unmittelbar vor, neben und nach Shakespeare*. Breslau, 1933.
Rev: by Max J. Wolff, *Eng. Studn*, LXX (1936), 395-397; by W. A. O., *ES*, XVIII, 236-237; by Wolfgang Keller, *SJ*, LXXII, 155-156; by J. Delcourt, *RAA*, XIII, 510-511; by H. N. Hillebrand, *MLN*, LI, 458-463.

A4857 Stalker, Archibald. *Shakespeare and Tom Nashe*. Stirling: Learmouth, 1935. Pp. 178.

A4858 Castle, Eduard. "Theobalds *Double Falsehood* und *The History of Cardenio* von Fletcher und Shakespeare." *Archiv*, 169 (1936), 182-199.

A4859 Knight, G. Wilson. "A Note on *Henry VIII*." *Criterion*, XV (1936), 228-236.

A4860 Knight, G. Wilson. "The Vision of Jupiter in *Cymbeline*." *TLS*, Nov. 21, 1936, p. 958.

A4861 Taylor, Rupert. "A Tentative Chronology of Marlowe's and Some Other Elizabethan Plays." *PMLA*, LI (1936), 643-688.

A4862 Jacob, Georg. *Shakespeare-Studien*. Herausgegeben nach dem Tode des Verfassers von H. Jensen. Hamburg; New York, 1938. Pp. vii.
Contains essay on authenticity of *Per.* and *Errors*.

A4863 Schücking, Levin L. *Die Zusätze zur "Spanish Tragedy"* [Kyd]. Berichte über die Verhand-lungen d. Sächs. Akad. d. Wiss. Philol. Kl. 90, 1938, H. 2. Leipzig: Hirtzel, 1938. Pp. 82.
Chap. 5, "The Question of Authorship," Shak., p. 55 ff.
Rev: by Rolf Kaiser, *Archiv*, 176 (1939), 92-93; by T. W. Baldwin, *MLN*, LV (1940), 459; by W. Keller, *SJ*, LXXVI, 216; by Pet. W. Biesterfeldt, *ADA*, LIX, (1940/41), 15-16; by W. Kalthoff, *NS*, XLIX (1941), 35.

A4864 Birkin, Keith Oswald. *Authorship of "Titus Andronicus."* MA thesis, Ottawa, 1939. Pp. 108.

A4865 Dickson, George B. "The Identity of George Wilkins." *SAB*, XIV (1939), 195-208.

A4866 Maxwell, Baldwin. *Studies in Beaumont, Fletcher, and Massinger*. Univ. North Carolina Press, 1939. Pp. vii, 238.
Rev: by T. A. Bisson, *SRL*, Feb. 3, 1940, p. 18; by R. A. Law, *JEGP*, XXXIX, 582-583; by A. Hart, *MLR*, XXXV, 390-391; by Evelyn May Albright, *MP*, XXXVIII (1941), 465-468; by J. G. McManaway, *MLN*, LVI, 144-145; by F. S. Boas, *RES*, XIX (1943), 80-83; by Bryher, *Life and Letters*, XXXVI, 66.

A4867 Boas, F. S. *Christopher Marlowe: A Biographical and Critical Study*. Clarendon Press, 1940. Pp. 347.
Rev: by Una Ellis-Fermor, *RES*, XVI (1940), 342-345; *TLS*, June 1, p. 268; by Peter Quen-nell, *NstN*, NS, XIX, 278; by A. L. Rowse, *Spectator*, Mar. 22, p. 419; by B. Ivor Evans, *MGW*,

Mar. 29, p. 255; by William Empson, *Life and Letters Today*, XXVI, 173-175; *N &Q*, 178 (1940), 197-198; *DUJ*, NS, I, 25-26; by E. G. S., *ConR*, Oct., pp. 475-477; by E. C. Knowlton, *South Atlantic Quar.*, XXXIX, 481; by E. K. Chambers, *English*, III, 134-135; by Paul H. Kocher, *MLQ*, I, 553-555; by T. M. Parrott, *MLN*, LVI (1941), 141-144; by Mark Eccles, *MLR*, XXXVII (1942), 83-85.

A4868   Cadwalader, John. "Theobald's Alleged Shakespeare Manuscript." *MLN*, LV (1940), 108-109.

A4869   Chevalley, Abel. "Shakespeare et les Poètes Elizabéthains." *Le Théâtre Elizabéthain*. Paris: Les Cahiers du Sud, 1940, pp. 48-55.

A4870   Haug, Ralph A. "The Authorship of *Timon of Athens*." *SAB*, XV (1940), 227-248.

A4871   Price, H. T. "Like Himself." *RES*, XVI (1940), 178-181.

A4872   Ray, P. C. "Shakespeare as a Reviser of Plays of Others." *Calcutta Review*, LXXVII (1941), 241-248.

A4873   Bentley, Gerald E. "Authenticity and Attribution in the Jacobean and Caroline Drama." *English Inst. Annual, 1942* (1943), pp. 101-118.

A4874   Reinhold, Heinz. "Die Metrische Verzahnung als Kriterium für Fragen der Chronologie und Authentizität im Drama Shakespeares und einiger Zeitgenossen und Nachfolger." 1. Teil. *Archiv*, 181 (1942), 83-96; 182 (1943), 7-24.

A4875   Greg, W. W. "Authorship Attributions in the Early Play-Lists." *Edinburgh Bibl. Soc. Trans.*, II (1946), 305-329.

A4875a   Greg, W. W. "The Date of the Earliest Play-Catalogues." *Library*, II (1947), 190-191.

A4876   Kermode, Frank. "What is Shakespeare's *Henry VIII* About?" *DUJ*, NS, IX (1948), 48-55.

A4877   Partridge, A. C. *The Problem of Henry VIII Re-opened*. Cambridge: Bowes & Bowes, 1949. Pp. 35.
     Rev: B9885.

A4878   Vančura, Zdeněk. "The Problems of the Shakespearean Canon." *Časopis pro moderní filologii*, Prague, XXXII (1949), Suppl., pp. 17-18.

A4879   Walker, Roy. *The Time is Free: A Study of Macbeth*. London: Dakers, 1949. Pp. xvii, 234.
     Rev: B9226.

A4880   Maxwell, J. C. "Peele and Shakespeare: A Stylometric Test." *JEGP*, XLIX (1950), 557-561.

A4881   Segerström, Sigurd. *Shakespeares liv och Författarskap*. Skrifter utg. av Modersmålslärarnas Förening, 38. Stockholm: Bonnier, 1950. Pp. 10.

A4882   Lyman, Dean B. "Apocryphal Plays of the University Wits." *English Studies in Honor of James Southall Wilson*, pp. 211-221.

A4883   Seiler, Grace E. *Shakespeare's Part in "Pericles."* DD, University of Missouri, 1951.

A4884   James, Wilfred P. *The Life and Work of Richard Barnfield*. DD, Northwestern University, 1952. Abstr. publ. in *Summaries of Doctoral Dissertations, 1952*, XX, Chicago & Evanston: Northwestern Univ., 1953.

A4885   Kirschbaum, Leo. "The Authorship of *1 Henry VI*." *PMLA*, LXVII (1952), 809-822.

A4886   Schücking, Levin Ludwig. "Über einige Probleme der Neueren und Neuesten Shakespeare-Forschung. (Textgestaltung und Echtheitsfragen)." *GRM*, XIII (1951-52), 208-228.

A4887   Feuillerat, Albert. *The Composition of Shakespeare's Plays: Authorship, Chronology*. Yale Univ. Press, 1953. Pp. viii, 340.
     Rev: A3286.

A4888   Oras, Ants. 'Extra Monosyllables' in *Henry VIII* and the Problem of Authorship." *JEGP*, LII (1953), 198-213.

A4889   Hoy, Cyrus. *An Examination into the Shares of Fletcher and His Collaborators in the Beaumont and Fletcher Canon: An Essay in the Use of Linguistic Criteria as a Source of Authorial Evidence*. DD, University of Virginia, 1954. Pp. 533. Mic A54-3062. *DA*, XIV (1954), 2057. Publ. No. 9648.

A4890   Kernan, Alvin. "A Comparison of the Imagery in *3 Henry VI* and *The True Tragedie of Richard Duke of York*." *SP*, LI (1954), 431-442.

A4891   Charlton, H. B., and R. D. Waller, eds. *Edward II*. London: Methuen, 1955. 2nd ed. "Reviser's Note" (pp. 212-225) discusses interrelations of this and Shak.'s early history plays. First publ. 1933.

A4892   Johnston, D. R. Lukin. "Var Shakespeare en Revisor?" *Revision og Regnskabsvaesen* (Copenhagen), XXIV (1955), 501-506. Radio talk.

A4893   Law, Robert Adger. "The Chronicles and the Three Parts of *Henry VI*." *TxSE*, XXXIII (1954 [publ. 1955]), 13-32.

A4894   Appleton, William W. *Beaumont and Fletcher*. A Critical Study. London: Allen & Unwin; Fair Lawn, N. J.: Essential Books, 1956. Pp. 131.
     Rev: *TLS*, Apr. 13, 1956, p. 218; D. M. S., *English*, XI, 77; by M. A. Shaaber, *RN*, IX, 217-219; by Kenneth Muir, *London Mag.*, Nov., pp. 89-93; by Michel Poirier, *EA*, IX, 258; by M. T. Herrick, *JEGP*, LVI (1957), 283; by Clifford Leech, *MLR*, LII, 256-257; by Samuel Schoenbaum, *MLN*, LXXII, 442-444; by Hermann Heuer, *SJ*, 94 (1958), 261; by Harold S. Wilson, *SQ*, IX, 81-82.

A4895 Beecham, Sir Thomas. *John Fletcher* (Romanes Lecture). Oxford: Clarendon Press, 1956. Pp. 23.
Rev: by Clifford Leech, *MLR*, LII (1957), 626.

A4896 Cutts, John P. "The Original Music to Middleton's *The Witch*." *SQ*, VII (1956), 203-209.

A4897 Felver, Charles Stanley. *William Shakespeare and Robert Armin His Fool—A Working Partnership*. DD, University of Michigan, 1956. Pp. 352. Mic 56-3895. *DA*, XVI (1956), 2446. Publ. No. 18,601.

A4898 Hoy, Cyrus. "The Shares of Fletcher and His Collaborators in the Beaumont and Fletcher Canon (I)." *SB*, VIII (1956), 129-146.

A4898a Hoy, Cyrus. "The Shares of Fletcher and His Collaborators in the Beaumont and Fletcher Canon (II)." *SB*, IX (1957), 143-162.

A4899 Flatter, Richard. "Who Wrote the Hecate-Scene?" *SJ*, 93 (1957), 196-210.

A4899a Cutts, John P. "Who Wrote the Hecate-Scene?" *SJ*, 94 (1958), 200-202.
Disagrees with A4899.

A4900 Law, Robert Adger. "Holinshed and *Henry the Eighth*." *TxSE*, XXXVI (1957), 3-11.

A4901 Barker, Richard Hindry. *Thomas Middleton*. New York: Columbia Univ. Press, 1958. Pp. ix, 216.

b. THE WAR OF THE THEATRES (19;5)

A4902 Sharpe, Robert Boies. *The Real War of the Theatres. Shakespeare's Fellow in Rivalry with the Admiral's Men, 1594-1603. Repertories, Devices, and Types*. Boston, 1935.
Rev: by G. Connes, *RAA*, XIII (1935/36), 153-155; by A. Brandl, *Archiv*, 168 (1936), 252; by L. L. Schücking, *Beiblatt*, XLVII, 118-127; by H. Harvey Wood, *MLR*, XXXI, 213-215; by E. K. Chambers, *RES*, XII, 344-346; by Wolfgang Keller, *SJ*, LXXII, 153-155; by Mario Praz, *ES*, XIX (1937), 226-232; by R. C. Bald, *Eng. Studn.*, LXXII, 105-107; by Oscar James Campbell, *MLN*, LII, 59-61; by T. W. Baldwin, *JEGP*, XXXVI, 272-275.

A4903 Ellis-Fermor, Una M. *The Jacobean Drama: An Interpretation*. London: Methuen, 1936. Pp. 351. Appendix I "The Theatre War."
Rev: A6005.

A4904 Harrison, G. B. *Elizabethan Plays and Players*. London: Routledge, 1940. Pp. viii, 306. Paperback ed.: Univ. of Michigan Press, 1956.
Rev: A7079.

A4905 Berringer, Ralph W. "Jonson's *Cynthia's Revels* and the War of the Theatres." *PQ*, XXII (1943), 1-22.

A4906 Halstead, W. L. "What *War of the Theatres*?" *CE*, IX (1948), 424-426.
See the comment by Robert Withington, ibid., X, 163-164.

A4907 Leishman, J. B., ed. *The Three Parnassus Plays*. London: Nicholson, 1949.
Rev: A7549.

A4908 Gray, Henry David. "The Chamberlain's Men and *The Poetaster*." *MLR*, XLII (1947), 173-179.

A4909 Simpson, Percy. "A Modern Fable of Aesop." *MLR*, XLIII (1948), 403-405.
Comments on A4908.

A4910 Gray, H. David, and Percy Simpson. "Shakespeare or Heminge? A Rejoinder and a Surrejoinder." *MLR*, XLV (1950), 148-152.
More on A4908.

A4911 Zbierski, H. *Shakespeare and the "War of the Theatres": A Reinterpretation*. Poznański Towarzystwo Przyjaciół Nauk. Wydział Filologiczno-filozoficzny. Poznan: Panstw. wydawn. naukowe, 1957. Pp. 150.
Rev: by Hermann Heuer, *SJ*, 94 (1958), 261-262.

c. GENERAL STUDIES

A4912 Ellis-Fermor, Una M. *The Jacobean Drama: An Interpretation*. London: Methuen, 1936. Pp. 351.
Rev: A6005.

A4913 Campbell, Oscar J. *Comicall Satyre and Shakespeare's "Troilus and Cressida."* San Marino, California: The Henry E. Huntington Library, 1938. Pp. ix, 246.
Rev: by René Lalou, *EA*, III (1939), 265-266; *N &Q*, 172 (1939), 305; *TLS*, July 29, p. 458; by Tucker Brooke, *MLN*, LV (1940), 71-73; by Alwin Thaler, *JEGP*, XXXIX, 282-284; by Alice Walker, *RES*, XVI, 90-92; by Wolfgang Schmidt, *Beiblatt*, LI, 13-18; by Una Ellis-Fermor, *MLR*, XXXVII (1942), 498-500; by Richard Flatter, *SJ*, 89 (1953), 200-202.

A4914 Baker, Howard. *Induction to Tragedy. A Study in the Development of Form in "Gorboduc", "The Spanish Tragedy" and "Titus Andronicus"*. Louisiana State Univ. Press, 1939. Pp. 247.
Rev: by Tucker Brooke, *MLN*, LIV (1939), 629; by B. H., *QJS*, XXV, 504; *QR*, 273 (1939), 184; by Rolf Kaiser, *Archiv*, 165 (1939), 230-233; by René Pruvost, *EA*, III, 376-377; by J. Wilcox, *SRL*, July 8, 1939, p. 18; by H. H. Glunz, *Beiblatt*, LI (1940), 182-191; by Alwin Thaler, *JEGP*, XXXIX, 399-400; by F. E. Budd, *MLR*, XXXVI, (1941), 260-262; by Austin Wright, *JA*, III, Nos. 11-12 (1944), 94-96.

A4915 Boas, F. S. *Shakespere and His Predecessors.* Seventh Impression, with a New Introductory Chapter. London: Murray, 1939. Pp. xxiii, 555. First publ. 1896.

A4916 Bing, Just. "Shakespeare's Debut." *Edda,* XL (1940), 1-30.

A4917 Hastings, W. T. "The Ancestry of Autolycus." *SAB,* XV (1940), 253.

A4918 Adams, Henry H. *English Domestic, or Homiletic Tragedy, 1575 to 1642; Being an Account of the Development of the Tragedy of the Common Man Showing its Great Dependence on Religious Morality, Illustrated with Striking Examples of the Interposition of Providence for the Amendment of Men's Manners.* DD, Columbia University, 1944. Columbia Univ. Studies in Engl. & Comp. Lit., No. 159. Columbia Univ. Press, 1944. Pp. 228.
       Rev: C282.

A4919 Bandel, B. *The Debt of Shakesperian Tragedy to Early English Comedy.* MS thesis, Columbia University, 1947. Pp. 130.

A4920 Eichhorn, Traudl. *Prosa und Vers im Vorshakespeareschen Drama. Ein Beitrag zum Form-problem des Englischen Renaissancedramas.* DD, Munich, 1949. Pp. iii, 173. Also in *SJ,* 84-86 (1951), 140-198.

A4921 Pettet, E. C. *Shakespeare and the Romance Tradition.* London: Staples, 1949.
       Rev: B5175.

A4922 Rossiter, Arthur Percival. *English Drama from Early Times to the Elizabethans. Its Background, Origins and Developments.* London: Hutchinson, 1950. Pp. 176.
       Rev: by F. S. Boas, *FortnR* (1950), 196-197; by A. Brown, *MLR,* XLV, 369-372; by D. Traversi, *Scrutiny,* XVII, 181-184; *TLS,* Feb. 10, p. 90; by R. Davril, *LanM,* XLV (1951), 266.

A4923 Munday, Mildred B. *The Influence of Shakespeare's Predecessors on His Early Blank Verse.* DD, University of Wisconsin, 1953. Abstr. publ. in *Summaries of Doctoral Dissertations, 1952-53,* Vol. 14. Madison: Univ. of Wisconsin Press, 1954, pp. 437-438. Also in *ShN,* VI (1956), 2.

A4924 Helton, Tinsley. *The Concept of Woman's Honour in Jacobean Drama.* DD, University of Minnesota, 1953. Pp. 371. *DA,* XII (1952), 795. Publ. No. 4334. "Shak. Before 1600," pp. 95-113. "Shak. After 1600," pp. 159-175.

A4925 Förg, Josef. *Typische Redeformen und Motive im Vorshakespeareschen Drama und ihre Vorbilder bei Seneca.* DD, Munich, 1955.

A4926 Rubow, Paul Victor. *Shakespeares Ungdomsstykker.* Copenhagen: Munksgaard, 1955. Pp. 33.

A4927 Schrickx, W. *Shakespeare's Contemporaries. The Background of the Harvey-Nashe Polemic and "Love's Labour's Lost."* Antwerp, 1956. Pp. vii, 291.
       Rev: A622.

d. LOST AND ANONYMOUS PLAYS

A4928 Greg, W. W. "The Date of *King Lear* and Shakespeare's Use of Earlier Versions of the Story." *Library,* XX (1940), 377-400.

A4929 Ray, P. C. "Shakespeare as a Reviser of Plays of Others." *Calcutta Review,* LXXVII (1941), 241-248.

A4930 Rossiter, A. P., ed. *Woodstock: A Moral History.* London: Chatto & Windus, 1946. Pp. 255.
       Rev: A1773.

A4931 Elton, William. "Two Shakespeare Parallels." *SAB,* XXII (1947), 115-116.

A4932 Elson, John. "Studies in the King John Plays." *AMS,* pp. 183-197.

A4933 Greer, C. A. "A Lost Play in the Case of *Richard II.*" *N &Q,* 197 (1952), 24-25.

A4934 Greer, C. A. "A Lost Play the Source of Shakespeare's *Henry IV* and *Henry V.*" *N &Q,* 199 (1954), 53-55.

A4935 Schanzer, Ernest. "A Neglected Source of *Julius Caesar.*" *N &Q,* 199 (1954), 196-197.

A4936 Greer, C. A. "Shakespeare's Use of *The Famous Victories of Henry the Fifth.*" *N &Q,* 199 (1954), 238-241.

A4937 Honigmann, E. A. J. "Shakespeare's *Lost Source-Plays.*" *MLR,* XLIX (1954), 293-307.

e. INDIVIDUAL DRAMATISTS
(1) SEVERAL

A4938 Glunz, H. *Shakespeare und Morus.* Kölner Anglistische Arbeiten, XXXII. Bochum Langen-dreer: Pöppinghaus, 1938. Pp. ix, 267.
       Rev: A4687.

A4939 McAnally, A. M. *Influence of the Masque on English Drama, 1608-10.* DD, University of Oklahoma, 1939. Abstr. publ. in *Univ. of Oklahoma Bulletin,* Jan. 1939, p. 114.

A4940 Law, Robert A. "The 'Pre-Conceived Pattern' of *A Midsummer Night's Dream.*" *TxSE* (1943), 5-14.
       Indebtedness to Lyly and Greene.

A4941 McCutchan, J. Wilson. "Similarities Between Falstaff and Gluttony in Medwall's *Nature.*" *SAB,* XXIV (1949), 214-219.

A4942   Jorgensen, Paul A. "The Courtship Scene in *Henry V*." *MLQ*, XI (1950), 180-188.
Background in Churchyard, Lyly, Riche, Dekker, Beaumont-Fletcher, etc.

A4943   Lyman, Dean B. "Apocryphal Plays of the University Wits." *English Studies in Honor of James Southall Wilson*, pp. 211-221.

A4944   Maugeri, Aldo. *Greene, Marlowe, Shakespeare: Tre Studi Biografici*. Messina: V. Ferrara, 1952. Pp. 103.

A4945   Isaacs, J. *Shakespeare's Earliest Years in the Theatre*. Annual Shakespeare Lecture of the British Academy, 1953. *Proceedings of the British Academy*, XXXIX. London: Cumberlege, 1955. Pp. 26.
Rev: A604.

A4946   Shedd, Robert Gordon. *The "Measure for Measure" of Shakespeare's 1604 Audience*. DD, University of Michigan, 1953. Pp. 430. Mic A53-1478. *DA*, XIII (1953), 801. Publ. No. 5730.

A4947   Greenfield, Thelma Nelson. "The Clothing Motif in *King Lear*." *SQ*, V (1954), 281-286.

A4948   Hunter, G. K. "*Henry IV* and the Elizabethan Two-Part Play." *RES*, V (1954), 236-248.
Finds in Chapman's *Byron*, Marlowe's *Tamburlaine*, Marston's *Antonio and Mellida*, and *Henry IV* that the form of each two-part play "depends *primarily* on a parallel presentation of incidents . . . and only secondarily on a preservation of traits of character or strands of the plot."

A4949   Felver, Charles Stanley. *William Shakespeare and Robert Armin His Fool—A Working Partnership*. DD, University of Michigan, 1956. Pp. 352. Mic 56-3895. *DA*, XVI (1956), 2446. Publ. No. 18,601.

A4950   Spivack, Bernard. "Falstaff and the Psychomachia." *SQ*, VIII (1957), 449-459.
The "warlike parts of Falstaff" were collected from the vices of two moralities, Medwall's *Nature* and John Rastell's *Four Elements*.

A4951   Spivack, Bernard. *Shakespeare and the Allegory of Evil*. Columbia Univ. Press, 1958. Pp. ix, 508.
Six chapters are devoted to an exploration of the Vice's changing roles in Tudor drama.
Rev: *TLS*, Dec. 5, 1958, p. 702; *SCN*, XVI, 40; *ShN*, VIII, 30; by Harry Levin, *RN*, XI, 279-281; by Rosalie L. Colie, *Hist. Ideas News Letter*, IV, 64-66; *NstN*, Nov. 29, 1958, pp. 772-773.

A4952   Summersgill, Travis. "Structural Parallels in *Eastward Ho* and *The Tempest*." *Bucknell Rev.*, VI, iv (1957), 24-28.

(2)   DANIEL

A4953   Schütze, Johannes. "Daniels *Cleopatra* und Shakespeare." *Eng. Studn.*, LXXI (1936), 58-72.

A4954   Leavenworth, Russell E. *Daniel's "Cleopatra": A Critical Study*. DD, University of Colorado, 1953. Abstr. publ. in *Abstracts of Theses for Higher Degrees, 1953*. Univ. of Colorado Studies, XXIX, April, 1954, pp. 26-27.

A4955   Nørgaard, Holger. "The Bleeding Captain Scene in *Macbeth* and Daniel's *Cleopatra*." *RES*, VI (1955), 395-396.

A4956   Nørgaard, Holger. "Shakespeare and Daniel's *Letter From Octavia*." *N&Q*, NS, II (1955), 56-57.

A4957   Norman, Arthur M. Z. "Daniel's *The Tragedie of Cleopatra* and *Antony and Cleopatra*." *SQ*, IX (1958), 11-18.

(3)   GREENE

A4958   McLean, A. T. *Shakespeare and Robert Greene: A Study of Seven Plays*. MS thesis, University of Texas, 1937.

A4959   McNeal, Thomas H. "Who Is Silvia?—and Other Problems in the Greene-Shakespeare Relationship." *SAB*, XIII (1938), 240-254.

A4960   Houk, Raymond A. "Shakespeare's *Shrew* and Green's *Orlando*." *PMLA*, LXII (1947), 657-671.

A4961   Walker, Roy. " 'The Upstart Crow'." *TLS*, August 10, 1951, p. 501.

A4962   Ekeblad, Inga-Stina. "*King Lear* and *Selimus*." *N&Q*, NS, IV (1957), 193-194.

(4)   JONSON

A4963   Howarth, R. G. *Shakespeare's "Tempest."* A public lecture delivered for the Australian English Assoc., Oct. 1, 1936. Sydney: Australian English Assoc., 1936. Pp. 55. Revised and abridged, 1947. Much on Jonson's influence.
Rev: B9753.

A4964   Currey, R. N. "Jonson and *The Tempest*." *N&Q*, 192 (1947), 468.

A4965   Sewell, Sallie Wimberly. *The Relation of "The Merry Wives of Windsor" to Jonson's "Every Man In His Humour."* MS thesis, University of North Carolina, 1939. Abstr. publ. in *Univ. of North Carolina Record, Research in Progress*, Grad. School Series No. 36, 1939, p. 82.

A4966   Sewell, Sallie. "The Relation Between *The Merry Wives of Windsor* and Jonson's *Every Man in His Humour*. *SAB*, XVI (1941), 175-189.

A4967 Potts, L. J. "Ben Jonson and the Seventeenth Century." *ES*, NS, II (1949), 7-24.

A4968 Honig, Edwin. "*Sejanus* and *Coriolanus*: A Study in Alienation." *MLQ*, XII (1951), 407-421.

A4969 Olive, W. J. "*Sejanus* and *Hamlet*." *A Tribute to George Coffin Taylor*, 1952, pp. 178-184.

A4970 Potts, Abbie Findlay. "*Cynthia's Revels, Poetaster*, and *Troilus and Cressida*." *SQ*, V (1954), 297-302.

A4971 Maxwell, J. C. "The Relation of *Macbeth* to *Sophonisba*." *N &Q*, NS, II (1955), 373-374.

A4972 McGlinchee, Claire. "Still Harping. . . ." *SQ*, VI (1955), 362-364.

A4973 Norman, Arthur M. Z. "Source Material in *Antony and Cleopatra*." *N &Q*, NS, III (1956), 59-61.

(5) KYD

A4974 Stoll, Elmer Edgar. "*Hamlet* and *The Spanish Tragedy*, Quartos I and II: A Protest." *MP*, XXXV (1937), 31-46.

A4975 Stoll, Elmer Edgar. "*Hamlet* and *The Spanish Tragedy* Again." *MP*, XXXVII (1939), 173-186.

A4976 Wells, William. "Thomas Kyd and the Chronicle-History." *N &Q*, 178 (1940), 218-224, 238-243.

A4977 Priess, Max. "Thomas Kyds *Spanish Tragedy* und die Zusätze in der Ausgabe von 1602." *Eng. Studn.*, LXXIV (1941), 329-341.

A4978 Law, Robert Adger. "Belleforest, Shakespeare, and Kyd." *AMS*, 1948, pp. 279-294.

A4979 Carrère, Félix. *Le Théâtre de Thomas Kyd. Contribution à l'Etude du Drame Elizabéthain*. Thèse de Lettres, Paris, 1949. Publ. Toulouse: Edouard Privat, 1951. Pp. 462.
       Rev: by Michel Poirier, *EA*, V (1952), 156-158; *Annales de l'Univ. de Paris*, XX, 502-505.

A4980 Rees, Joan. "*Julius Caesar*—An Earlier Play, and an Interpretation." *MLR*, L (1955), 135-141.

A4981 McDiarmid, Matthew P. "A Reconsidered Parallel Between Shakespeare's *King John* and Kyd's *Cornelia*." *N &Q*, NS, III (1956), 507-508.

(6) LYLY

A4982 Swart, Jr. "Lyly and Pettie." *ES*, XXIII (1941), 10-18.

A4983 Davenport, A. "Notes on Lyly's *Campaspe* and Shakespeare." *N &Q*, NS, I (1954), 19-20.

(7) MARLOWE

A4984 Mawdsley, M. Dorothy. *The Influence of Marlowe on Shakespeare*. MA thesis, British Columbia, 1927. Pp. 141.

A4985 Brown, Royden Anthony. *Influence of Christopher Marlowe on William Shakespeare*. MA thesis, Ottawa, 1935. Pp. 69.

A4986 Bakeless, John E. *Christopher Marlowe: A Biographical and Critical Study*. DD, Harvard University, 1936. Abstr. publ. in *Summaries of PhD Theses, 1936*, Cambridge: Harvard Univ. Press, 1938, pp. 302-307.

A4987 Bakeless, John. *Christopher Marlowe: The Man in His Time*. New York: Morrow, 1937. Pp. viii, 404.
       Rev: by Douglas Bush, *SRL*, Nov. 27, 1937, p. 11; *TLS*, Jan. 29, 1938, p. 72; by W. J. Lawrence, *NstN*, NS, XV, 424-426; by Richard David, *London Mercury*, XXXVIII, 464; *More Books*, XIII, 14; *Nation* (N.Y.), 146 (1938), 135; by E. R. Adair, *JMH*, X, 455; by R. T. F., *Personalist*, XIX, 97-98; by Kenneth Muir, *Spectator*, Feb. 11, p. 234; by J. C. Metcalf, *VQR*, XIV, 306-308; by Trevor James, *Life and Letters Today*, XVIII, No. 11, 173-174; by F. C. Danchin, *EA*, II, 392-393.

A4988 Henderson, Philip. *And Morning in His Eyes. A Study of Christopher Marlowe*. London: Boriswood, 1937. Pp. 352.

A4989 Bakeless, John. *The Tragicall History of Christopher Marlowe*. 2 v. Harvard Univ. Press, 1942. Pp. xvi, 376; viii, 432. Chap. XVI. "Marlowe and Shakespeare," II, 205-267.
       Rev: by Hazelton Spencer, *MLN*, LVIII (1943), 217-220; by B. M., *PQ*, XXII (1943), 189-192; by H. W. Wells, "Elizabethan Giant," *SRL*, XXVI, Feb. 6, pp. 10-11; by Leslie Hotson, *YR*, XXXII, 801-803; by George Barker, *Nation* (N.Y.) Jan. 9, p. 66; by H. McC., *More Books*, XVIII, 23; "Marlowe Mysteries: Essays in Detection," *TLS*, Feb. 12, 1944, pp. 78, 83; by F. S. Boas, *MLR*, XXXIX, 75-76; by Mark Eccles, *JEGP*, XLIV (1945), 299-301; by Una Ellis-Fermor, *RES*, XXI, 65-66.

A4990 Walley, Harold R. "Shakespeare's Debt to Marlowe in *Romeo and Juliet*." *PQ*, XXI (1942), 257-267.

A4991 Darby, Robert H. "Christopher Marlowe's Second Death." *West Virginia Univ. Bull., Philological Studies*, IV (1943-44), 81-85.

A4992 Stewart, J. I. M. "King Cambyses's Vein [1 *Henry IV*, II. iv. 423-425]." *TLS*, May 26, 1945, p. 247.

A4993 Norman, Charles. *The Muses Darling. The Life of Christopher Marlowe*. New York: Rinehart & Co., 1946. Pp. xvi, 272.
       Chap. VI. "Marlowe & Shakespeare," pp. 57-73. Chap. XVIII. "Apology to Marlowe and

Shakespeare," pp. 167-177.
   Rev: A616.

A4994   Puknat, Siegfried. "Doktor Faustus and *Love's Labour's Lost.*" *Program*, Philol. Assoc. of the Pacific Coast. Eugene, Oregon, 1950.

A4995   Liu, J. Y. "A Marlo-Shakespearian Image Cluster." *N &Q*, 196 (1951), 336-337.

A4996   Wilson, F. P. *Marlowe and the Early Shakespeare.* Clark Lectures, Trinity College, Cambridge, 1951. Oxford: Clarendon Press, 1953. Pp. 144.
   Rev: *TLS*, Apr. 17, 1953, p. 254; by Hallett Smith, *YR*, XLIII, 121-125; by H. B. Charlton, *MGW*, Apr. 16, p. 11; by J. I. M. Stewart, *NstN*, Apr. 18, pp. 460, 462; by Philip Henderson, *Spectator*, Aug. 28, p. 227; by J. Vallette, "Shakespeariana," *MdF*, 1078, (1953), 336-341; by J. Crow, *CamR*, LXXV, 138-140; by F. Wölcken, *Archiv*, 190 (1954), 238-239; by H. T. Price, *SQ*, V, 113-114; *VQR*, XXX, 17; by H. S. Wilson, *UTQ*, XXIV, 102-105; by Peter Ure, *RES*, NS, V, 71-73; by T. M. Parrott, *SQ*, V, 179-186; by E. M. W. Tillyard, *MLR*, XLIX, 223-224; by Michel Poirier, *EA*, VII, 319; by Clifford Leech, *ShS*, VII, 132; by Harold Jenkins, ibid., 142; by James G. McManaway, ibid., 147; by Walter H. Walters, *ETJ*, VII (1955), 76-77; by Robert Fricker, *ES*, XXXIX (1958), 38-39; by Hans Georg Heun, *DLZ*, LXXIX, 514-515.

A4997   Maugeri, Aldo. "*Edward II,*" "*Richard III*" e "*Richard II.*" *Note Critiche.* Messina: V. Ferrara, 1952. Pp. 63.

A4998   Maxwell, J. C. "*Hero and Leander* and *Love's Labour's Lost.*" *N &Q*, 197 (1952), 334-335.

A4999   Röhrman, H. *Marlowe and Shakespeare: A Thematic Exposition of Some of Their Plays.* Arnhem: van Loghum Slaterus, 1952. Pp. x, 109.
   Rev: A1023.

A5000   McNeal, Thomas H. "The Names 'Hero' and 'Don John' in *Much Ado.*" *N &Q*, 198 (1953), 382.

A5001   Oras, Ants. "Lyrical Instrumentation in Marlowe: A Step Towards Shakespeare." Matthews and Emery, eds., *Studies in Shakespeare*, 1953, pp. 74-87.

A5002   Charlton, H. B., and R. D. Waller, eds., *Edward II.* London: Methuen, 1955. 2nd ed.

A5003   Byller, Harald. "Shakespeare och Marlowe." *Bonniers Litterära Magasin*, XXV (1956), 138-140.

A5004   Harrison, Thomas P. "Shakespeare and Marlowe's *Dido, Queen of Carthage.*" *TxSE*, XXXV (1956), 57-63.

A5005   Hart, Jeffrey P. "Prospero and Faustus." *Boston Univ. Studies in English*, II (1956), 197-206.

A5006   Christ, Henry I. "*Macbeth* and the Faust Legend." *English Jour.*, XLVI (1957), 212-213.

A5007   Cutts, John P. "*Dido, Queen of Carthage.*" *N &Q*, NS, V (1958), 371-374.

A5008   Leech, Clifford. "The Two-Part Play: Marlowe and the Early Shakespeare." *SJ*, 94 (1958), 90-106.

(8) MIDDLETON

A5009   Sullivan, Frank. "*Macbeth*, Middleton's *Witch*, and *Macbeth* Again." *Los Angeles Tidings*, Sept. 24, 1948, p. 6.

A5010   Bradbrook, M. C. "*Lucrece* and *Othello.*" *TLS*, Oct. 27, 1950, p. 677.
   Suggests an indebtedness in *Othello*, V. ii. 177-180, to Middleton's *The Ghost of Lucrece* (ca. 1596), in turn indebted to Shak.'s poem.

(9) PORTER

A5011   Nosworthy, J. M. "*The Merry Wives of Windsor.*" *TLS*, Sept. 27, 1947, p. 497.

A5012   Nosworthy, J. M. "The Shakespearian Heroic Vaunt." *RES*, II (1951), 259-261.

A5013   Nosworthy, J. M. "The Two Angry Families of Verona." *SQ*, III (1952), 219-226.

(10) OTHERS (Arranged chronologically by dramatist.)

A5014   Wallis, Lawrence B. *Fletcher, Beaumont and Company: Entertainers to the Jacobean Gentry.* New York: Kings Crown Press, 1947. Pp. xii, 315.
   Rev: *TLS*, Sept. 6, 1947, p. 448; by John Garrett, *Spectator*, Nov. 7, 1947, pp. 600-602; by G. F. Sensabaugh, *MLQ*, IX (1948), 246-247; by M. C. Bradbrook, *MLR*, XLIII, 260-261; by C. Leech, *RES*, XXV (1949), 74-75; by B. Maxwell, *MLN*, LXIV, 206-207; by M. Eccles, *PQ*, XXIX (1950), 95-96.

A5015   Bowers, Fredson. "The Pictures in *Hamlet* III. iv: A Possible Contemporary Reference." *SQ*, III (1952), 280-281.
   Sees a possible reflection of Hamlet's "Looke heere vpon this Picture, and on this" in the last scene of Thomas Dekker's *Satiromastix*, where Tucca displays and comments upon the two pictures he has brought in.

A5016   Muir, Kenneth. "*Macbeth* and *Sophonisba.*" *TLS*, Oct. 9, 1948, p. 569. See the letters by D. S. Bland, ibid., Oct. 16, 1948, p. 583; by Kenneth Muir, ibid., Oct. 23, 1948, p. 597. Mr. Muir argues that Shak. is indebted to Marston for I. ii. 49-51 and that, consequently, "very little remains of the theory that *Macbeth* was performed before May 1606" and of Mr.

J. Dover Wilson's assumption that references to Garnet were interpolated for a Court performance; Mr. Bland doubts the value of such an inquiry; rejoinder by Mr. Muir.

A5017   Danchin, F. C. "Une Source de *Much Ado About Nothing*." *RAA*, XIII (1936), 430-431. Indicates the plot parallel between *Much Ado* and A. M.'s *A Pleasant Comedie of Two Italian Gentlemen* (1585).

A5018   Rees, Joan. "A Passage in *Henry VI*, Part 3." *N &Q*, 199, (1954), 195-196. Suggests a source for the father-son episode in *3 Henry VI*, II.v, in *Gorboduc*, V.ii.180 ff.

A5019   Ribner, Irving. "Shakespeare and Peele: The Death of Cleopatra." *N &Q*, 197 (1952), 244-246. See letters by John D. Reeves, ibid., 441-442, and Holgar Nørgaard, ibid., 442-443.

A5020   Schanzer, Ernest. "*Antony and Cleopatra* and the Countess of Pembroke's *Antonius*." *N &Q*, NS, III (1956), 152-154.

A5021   Izard, Thomas C. *George Whetstone, Mid-Elizabethan Gentleman of Letters*. DD, Columbia University, 1943. Columbia Univ. Stud. in Engl. and Comp. Lit., No. 158. Columbia Univ. Press, 1943. Pp. 297.
Meas., pp. 52-74.

6. INFLUENCE OF FOLK TALES, JESTBOOKS, EMBLEM BOOKS, ETC.
(**78;28**) (Not complete on any of these topics, but limited by defined sources. See Introduction.)
a. SEVERAL POPULAR GENRES

A5022   Putnam, Adelaide Donalda. *Folklore and Balladry in Shakespeare*. MA thesis, McGill, 1933.

A5023   Chambers, Sir E. K. *The English Folk Play*. Oxford: 1933.
Rev: by Margarete Rösler, *Eng. Studn.*, LXXI (1936), 304-306.

A5024   McNeely, Samuel Sidney, Jr. *Popular Anecdotal Literature in Sixteenth Century England*. DD, Louisiana State University, 1940. Pp. 366.

A5025   Stříbrný, Zdeněk. "Shakespeare a Lidoyé Tradice." (Shakespeare and the popular tradition), *Časopis pro Moderní filologii*, Prague, XL (1958), 65-79.

b. BALLADS (**22;7**)

A5026   Sievers, Richard. *Thomas Deloney. Eine Studie über Balladenliteratur der Shakespeare-Zeit. Nebst Neudruck von Deloneys Roman "Jack of Newbury."* DD, Berlin, Humboldt Univ., 1903. Pp. iv, 32.

A5027   Firth, Sir Charles. "Ballads and Broadsides." Firth's *Essays: Historical and Political*. Oxford: Clarendon Press, 1938, pp. 1-33. Reprinted from *Shakespeare's England*, 1916, Chap. 24.

A5028   Hodgson, N. H. "The Murder of N. Turberville: Two Elizabethan Ballads." *MLR*, XXXIII (1938), 520-527.

A5029   Lamson, Roy, Jr. *English Broadside Ballad Tunes, 1550-1770*. DD, Harvard University, 1936. Abstr. publ. in *Summaries of PhD Theses, 1936*, Cambridge: Harvard Univ. Press, 1938, pp. 336-338.

A5030   Esdaile, Arundell. *Autolycus' Pack and Other Light Wares: Being Essays, Addresses and Verses*. London: Crafton & Co., 1940. Pp. x, 221.
Rev: by F. C. F., *Library*, 4th Ser., XXI (1940), 96-97.

A5031   Cauthen, I. B., Jr. "The Twelfth Day of December: *Twelfth Night*, II. iii. 91." *SB*, II (1949), 182-185.

A5032   Fangl, Walter. *Die Einwirkung alter Balladen auf Shakespeares Dramen*. DD, Vienna, 1949. Pp. 115. Typewritten.

A5033   Brennecke, Ernest. " 'Nay, That's Not Next!' The Significance of Desdemona's 'Willow Song'." *SQ*, IV (1953), 35-38.

A5034   Halpert, Herbert. "Shakespeare, Abelard, and The Unquiet Grave." *Jour. of Amer. Folklore*, LXIX (1956), 74-75.

A5035   Lawlis, Merritt E. "Shakespeare, Deloney, and the Earliest Text of the Arthur Ballad." *Harvard Lib. Bul.*, X (1956), 130-134; pl.

A5036   "Shakespeare Verse Traced to Source." *New York Times*, Nov. 18, 1958, p. 35M.

c. EMBLEMS

A5037   Yates, Frances. "The Emblematic Conceit in Giordano Bruno's *De Gli Eroici Furori* and in the Elizabethan Sonnet Sequences." *JWCI*, VI (1944), 101-121.

A5038   Johnson, E. D. "Examples of Shakespeare's Use of Emblem Books." *Ba*, XXIX (1945), 145-146.

A5039   Johnson, E. D. "Shakespeare's Use of Emblem Books." *Ba*, XXX (1946), 65-68.

A5040   Praz, Mario. *Studies in Seventeenth-Century Imagery*. I. London, 1939. Tr. in *Studi sul Concettismo*. Florence: G. C. Sansoni, 1946. Pp. viii, 321.
Rev: *TLS*, March 11, 1939, p. 151; by Joan Bennett *NstN*, NS, XIX (1940), 648; by Jean Adhémar, *HR*, VI (1941), 404-405; by Silvio Policardi, *Anglica*, I (1946), 280-281; by Fr.

A. Pompen, O. F. M., *ES*, XXVIII, 50-52; *TLS*, Jan. 29, 1949, p. 80; by K. L. Selig, *MLN*, LXIV, 203-204; by G. S. Haight, *Eng. Studn.*, XXX, 48-50; by T. H. Jones, *MLQ*, XI (1950), 109-110; by M. Y. Hughes, *MLR*, XLV, 224-226; by Rosemary Freeman, *RES*, NS, I, 72-73.

A5041   Freeman, Rosemary. *English Emblem Books*. London: Chatto & Windus, 1948. Pp. xiv, 256.
Rev: *TLS*, Nov. 13, 1948, p. 640; by N. Braybrooke, *English*, VII (1948/49), 243; by M. Praz, *ES*, XXX (1949), 51-54; by T. H. Jones, *Life and Letters*, LXI, 172-173; by J. Hawks, *NstN*, XXXVII, 282-283; by W. Clemen, *Archiv*, 188 (1951), 143-144.

A5042   Lewis, Arthur O., Jr. *Emblem Books and English Drama: A Preliminary Survey, 1581-1600*. DD, The Pennsylvania State University, 1951.

A5043   Leisher, John F. "George Puttenham and Emblemata." *Boston Univ. Studies in English*, I (1955), 1-8.

A5044   Greene, David Mason. *Mediaeval Backgrounds of the Elizabethan Emblem-Book*. DD, University of California, Berkeley Campus, 1958.
See also A2880-A2882.

d. JESTBOOKS

A5045   "English Humour 1500 to 1800." *TLS*, May 21, 1938, p. 360.

A5046   Wilson, F. P. "The English Jestbooks of the Sixteenth and Early Seventeenth Centuries." *HLQ*, II (1939), 121-158.

A5047   Praz, Mario. "Shakespeare, il Castiglione e le Facezie." *Riv. Italiana del Dramma*, IV (1940), 55-76.

A5048   Long, Littleton. *Tudor Jest-Books: A Study in Sixteenth Century Humor*. DD, Yale University, 1949.

A5049   Mish, Charles C. "Will Summers: An Unrecorded Jestbook." *PQ*, XXXI (1952), 215-218.

A5050   Violi, Unicio J. *Shakespeare and the Lazzo*. DD, Columbia University, 1955. Pp. 282. Mic A55-1834. *DA*, XV (1955), 1391. Publ. No. 12,479.

A5051   Felver, Charles Stanley. *William Shakespeare and Robert Armin His Fool—A Working Partnership*. DD, University of Michigan, 1956. Pp. 352. Mic 56-3895. *DA*, XVI (1956), 2446. Publ. No. 18,601.

A5052   Muir, Kenneth. " 'Wits Fittes' and Shakespeare." *N & Q*, NS, V (1958), 186-187.

e. FOLKLORE (179;62)

A5053   Chandler, Frank Wadleigh. *The Literature of Roguery*. 2 vols. New York: Franklin, 1958. Pp. viii, 584.
First published in 1907. In Ebisch and Schücking, p. 78.

A5053a   Gurd, Jean Marjorie S. *The Treatment and Use of the Fairy Element in the Elizabethan and Modern Drama: A Contrast*. MA thesis, McGill, 1926.

A5054   Hohmann, B. "Bäuerliches Brauchtum in Shakespeares Dramen." *Berlin Börsenzeitung*, Sept. 15, 1938.

A5055   Hohmann, E. "Volksbrauch in Shakespeares Dramen." *Magdeburger Zeitung*, Nov. 12, 1938.

A5056   Stroup, Thomas B. "Shakespeare's Use of a Travel-Book Commonplace." *PQ*, XVII (1938), 351-358.

A5057   Spargo, John Webster. *Juridical Folklore in England Illustrated by the Cucking Stool*. Duke Univ. Press, 1944. Pp. vii, 163.
Rev: by Joseph R. Strayer, *JMH*, XVII (1945), 163-164; by Thomas Dodson, *Jour. Religion*, XXV, 156; by K. M., *MLN*, LX, 502; *Rev. Religion*, IX, 218; by J. G. Kunstmann, *Cal. Folklore Quar.*, IV, 188-192.

A5058   Adler, Alfred. "Falstaff's Holy Dying, Pagan as Well as Christian." *MLN*, LXI (1946), 72.

A5059   Crow, John. "Folklore in Elizabethan Drama." *Folklore*, LVIII (1947), 297-311.

A5060   Spence, Lewis. *The Fairy Tradition in Britain*. London: Rider & Co., 1948. Pp. 374.

A5061   Nearing, Homer, Jr. "The Legend of Julius Caesar's British Conquest." *PMLA*, LXIV (1949), 889-929. Comments on Shak. pp. 927-928.

A5062   Nearing, Homer, Jr. "Local Caesar Traditions in Britain." *Speculum*, XXIV (1949), 218-227.

A5063   Hewitt, Douglas. "The Very Pompes of the Divell—Popular and Folk Elements in Elizabethan and Jacobean Drama." *RES*, XXV (1949), 10-23.

A5064   Jackson, James L. "Shakespeare's Dog-and-Sugar Imagery and the Friendship Tradition." *SQ*, I (1950), 260-263.

A5065   Johnson, W. Stacy. "The Genesis of Ariel." *SQ*, II (1951), 205-210.

A5066   Johnson, W. Stacy. "Folklore Elements in *The Tempest*." *Midwest Folklore*, I (1951), 223-228.

A5067   Briggs, K. M. *Some Aspects of Folk-lore in Early Seventeenth Century Literature*. DD, Oxford, 1952.

A5068   Diederichsen, Diedrich. *Shakespeare und das Deutsche Märchendrama*. DD, Hamburg, 1952. Pp. 332. Typewritten.

A5069   Chapman, Raymond. "The Fair-Haired Man: An Elizabethan Superstition." *N&Q*, NS, II (1955), 332. Reply by W. H. W. Sabine, II, 547.

A5070   Cheney, David Raymond. *Animals in "A Midsummer Night's Dream."* DD, State University of Iowa, 1955. Pp. 288. Mic 55-1103. *DA*, XV (1955), 2188. Publ. No. 14,094.

A5071   Ashton, John W. "Folklore in the Literature of Elizabethan England." In "Folklore in Literature: A Symposium." *Jour. Amer. Folklore*, LXX (Jan.-Mar., 1957), 10-15.

A5072   Lüthi, Max. "Shakespeare und das Märchen." *Zeitschrift f. Volkskunde* (Stuttgart), LIII (1956/57), 141-149.

A5073   Montgomerie, William. "Folk-Play and Ritual in *Hamlet*." *Folklore*, LXVII (1956), 214-227.

A5074   Smith, S. A. *The Folk Element in Tudor Drama.* MA thesis, University of London, King's College, 1956.

A5075   Briggs, K. M. "The English Fairies." *Folklore*, LXVIII (1957), 270-287.

A5076   Campbell, J. L. "Gaelic Folk Song." *TLS*, June 27, 1958, p. 361. On the source of "Calen O Costure Me"; see also Kevin P. Neary, "Padraic Colum's Poems," *TLS*, May 23, p. 283.

A5077   Frankis, P. J. "The Testament of the Deer in Shakespeare." *N. Mitt.*, LIX (1958), 65-68.

7. INFLUENCE OF THE BIBLE (79;-)
a. ELIZABETHAN BIBLES AND BIBLICAL SCHOLARSHIP
(Selection from the specified sources only.)

A5078   Lockwood, Dean P., and Roland H. Bainton. "Classical and Biblical Scholarship in the Age of the Renaissance and Reformation." *Church History*, X (1941), 125-143.

A5079   Harrison, F. *The Bible in Britain.* New York: Nelson, 1949. Pp. vii, 200, pl. 12.

A5080   Siegel, Ben. *Elements of the Old Testament in Early Seventeenth Century English Poetry.* DD, University of Southern California, 1957.

A5081   Thompson, Craig R. *The Bible in English 1525-1611.* Folger Booklets on Tudor and Stuart Civilization. Washington, D. C.: The Folger Shakespeare Library, 1958. Pp. 37.

b. SHAKESPEARE AND THE BIBLE
(1) GENERAL

A5082   Noble, Richmond S. H. *Shakespeare's Biblical Knowledge and Use of the Book of Common Prayer, as Exemplified in the Plays of the First Folio.* London, 1935. Pp. 72, 390.
        Rev: by D. C. Macgregor, *RES*, XIII (1937), 90-91; by Paul Dottin, *Rev. de France*, XVII, i (1937), 323.

A5083   Ackermann, C. *The Bible in Shakespeare.* Columbus: Lutheran Book Concern, 1936. Pp. 124.

A5084   Weber, Carl J. "On Shakspere's Biblical Knowledge." *SAB*, XI (1936), 184.

A5085   Gill, Frederick C. "Homiletic Values in Shakespeare." *London Quar. and Holborn Rev.*, Oct. 1937, pp. 433-444.

A5086   Dodds, M. H. "*The Book of Proverbs* in Shakespeare." *N&Q*, 179 (1940), 34.

A5087   Hankins, John Erskine. *The Character of Hamlet and Other Essays.* Univ. of North Carolina Press, 1941. Pp. xii, 264.
        Contains essay on the Bible in *Hamlet*.
        Rev: B7664.

A5088   Law, Robert Adger. "Shakespeare in the Garden of Eden." *TxSE*, XXI (1941), 24-38.

A5089   Eastman, Fred. *Christ in the Drama: A Study of the Influence of Christ on the Drama of England and America.* Northwestern University. John C. Shaffer Foundation, Lectures, 1946. New York: Macmillan, 1947. Pp. x, 174.
        Rev: by Deane Edwards, *Christendom*, XII (1947), 546-547.

A5090   de Groot, John Henry. *The Shakespeares and "The Old Faith."* New York: King's Crown Press, 1946. Pp. x, 258.
        Rev: A633.

A5091   Preis, A. "Bacon, Shakespeare, and the Bible." *N&Q*, 190 (1946), 59.

A5092   "Shakespeare's Bible." *TLS*, Jan. 11, 1947, p. 23.

A5093   Baldwin, T. W., and P. Alexander. "Shakespeare's Bible." *TLS*, Jan. 18, 1947, p. 37.
        Comments upon A5092.

A5094   Pope, Elizabeth Marie. "The Renaissance Background of *Measure for Measure*." *ShS*, II (1949), 66-82.

A5095   Rashbrook, R. F. "Shakespeare and the Bible." *N&Q*, 197 (1952), 49-50.

A5096   Coleman, H. *Shakespeare and the Bible.* Reprint. New York: Vantage, 1955.
        Rev: *ShN*, VII (1957), 28.

A5097   Felver, Charles Stanley. *William Shakespeare and Robert Armin His Fool—A Working Partnership.* DD, University of Michigan, 1956. Pp. 352. Mic. 56-3895. *DA*, XVI (1956), 2446. Publ. No. 18,601.

A5098   Ross, Lawrence J. "Two Supposed 'Defects in Shakespeare's Biblical Knowledge'." *N&Q*, NS, V (1958), 462-463.

(2) SPECIFIC ECHOES

A5099 Traver, Hope. "I Will Try Confusions With Him." *SAB*, XIII (1938), 108-120.

A5100 Dodds, M. H. "*The Book of Proverbs* in Literature." *N &Q*, 174 (1940), 34.

A5101 Hankins, John E. "Lear and the Psalmist." *MLN*, LXI (1946), 88-90.

A5102 Seaton, Ethel. "*Antony and Cleopatra* and the *Book of Revelation*." *RES*, XXII (1946), 219-224.

A5103 Kōkeritz, Helge. "Five Shakespeare Notes." *RES*, XXIII (1947), 310-320.

A5104 Lindsay, Jack. "*Antony and Cleopatra* and the *Book of Revelation*." *RES*, XXIII (1947), 66. See A5102.

A5105 Abend, Murray. "Some Biblical Influences in Shakespeare's Plays." *N &Q*, 195 (1950), 554-558.

A5106 Lees, F. N. "A Biblical Connotation in *Macbeth*." *N &Q*, 195 (1950), 534.

A5107 Edgerton, W. L. "Shakespeare and the 'Needle's Eye'." *MLN*, LXVI (1951), 549-550.

A5108 Harrison, Thomas P. "A Biblical Echo in *Hamlet*." *N &Q*, 196 (1951), 235.

A5109 Heist, William W. " 'Fulness of Bread'." *SQ*, III (1952), 140-142.

A5110 Parrott, T. M. "Fulness of Bread." *SQ*, III (1952), 379-381.

A5111 Harrison, G. B. "Distressful Bread." *SQ*, IV (1953), 105.

A5112 Nathan, Norman. " 'On the Hip'." *N &Q*, 197 (1952), 74.

A5113 Kane, Robert J. "A Passage in *Pericles*." *MLN*, LXVIII (1953), 483-484.

A5114 Cauthen, I. B., Jr. "Richard II and the Image of the Betrayed Christ." *Renaissance Papers*, Univ. South Carolina, 1954, pp. 45-48.

A5115 Nathan, Norman. "Duncan, Macbeth and Jeremiah." *N &Q*, 199 (1954), 243.

A5116 Bryant, J. A., Jr. "Shakespeare's Allegory: *The Winter's Tale*." *SR*, LXIII (1955), 202-222.

A5117 Frye, Roland M. "Macbeth's 'Out, Out, Brief Candle' Speech and the Jacobean Understanding." *N &Q*, NS, II (1955), 143-154.

A5118 Jack, Jane H. "Macbeth, King James, and the Bible." *ELH*, XXII (1955), 173-193.

A5119 Macht, David I. "Biblical Allusions in Shakespeare's *The Tempest* in the Light of Hebrew Exegesis." *The Jewish Forum*, Aug. 1955, pp. 3-5.

A5120 Siegel, Paul N. "Echos of the Bible Story in *Macbeth*." *N &Q*, NS, II (1955), 142-143.

A5121 McManaway, James G. "A Probable Source of *Romeo and Juliet*, III. i. 100-101." *N &Q*, NS, III (1956), 57.

A5122 Nathan, Norman. "Pericles and Jonah." *N &Q*, NS, III (1956), 10-11.

A5123 Nathan, Norman. "Balthasar, Daniel and Portia." *N &Q*, NS, IV (1957), 334-335.

VII. THE ART OF SHAKESPEARE: LANGUAGE, VOCABULARY, PROSODY, AND STYLE (79;29)
1. LANGUAGE AND VOCABULARY (79;29)
a. GENERAL STUDIES OF THE LANGUAGE

A5124 Pendered, Mary L. "Word Magic." *Poetry Rev.*, XXVII (1936), 193-202.

A5125 Francis, J. H. *From Caxton to Carlyle: A Study in the Development of Language, Composition and Style in English Prose.* Cambridge Univ. Press, 1937. Pp. ix, 240.

A5126 Delcourt, M. J. "Some Aspects of Sir Thomas More's English." *Essays and Studies by Members of the English Association*, XXI. Oxford: Clarendon Press, 1937.

A5127 Wells, Henry W. "Ben Jonson, Patriarch of Speech Study." *SAB*, XIII (1938), 54-62.

A5128 Wyld, Henry Cecil. "Aspects of Style and Idiom in Fifteenth Century English." *Essays and Studies by Members of the English Association*, XXVI, 1940. Oxford: Clarendon Press, 1941, pp. 30-44.

A5129 Jolas, Eugène. "La Révolution du Langage Chez les Elizabéthains." *Le Théâtre Elizabéthain*. Paris: Les Cahiers du Sud, 1940, pp. 73-76.

A5130 Tillotson, Geoffrey. "Elizabethan Decoration." *Essays in Criticism and Research.* Cambridge Univ. Press, 1942, pp. 5-16.

A5131 Craigie, Sir William A. *The Critique of Pure English from Caxton to Smollett.* S. P. E. Tract No. LXV. Oxford, 1946. Pp. 60.
Rev: by Hilda Hulme, *MLR*, XLII (1947), 398; "Other Words," *TLS*, Nov. 23, 1946, p. 577.

A5132 Hulme, Hilda. "Manuscript Material for the Study of Tudor and Stuart English." *MLR*, XLI (1946), 108-112.

A5133 Q., D. "The English Language in 1573." *N &Q*, 190 (1946), 100-101; Roderick L. Eagle, ibid., p. 150.

A5134 Prior, M. *The Language of Tragedy.* Columbia Univ. Press, 1947.
Rev: by Rosemond Tuve, *JAAC*, VI (1948), 349-352; by P. F. Baum, *South Atlantic Quar.*, XLVII, 242-244; by D. A. Stauffer, *Amer. Lit.*, XX, 80-82; by F. S. Tupper, *MLN*, LXIII, 560-562.

A5135   Richards, I. A. "The Places and the Figures." *KR*, XI (1949), 16-30.

A5136   Empson, William. *The Structure of Complex Words*. London: Chatto & Windus, 1951. Pp. 449.
Rev: by C. Madge, *NstN*, XLII (1951), 232; by P. Hughes, *FortnR*, 176 (1951), 711-712; *Listener*, XLVI, 473; by J. M. Cohen, *Spectator*, No. 6430 (1951), 372; by I. Watt, *ConR*, LXXIII (1951/52), 133-134; by R. G. Davis, *Partisan Rev.*, XIX (1952), 368-371; *TLS*, June 27, 1952, p. 420; by Richard Sleight, *EIC*, II, 325-337; by R. Williams, *English*, IX, 27-28; by Cleanth Brooks, *KR*, XIV, 669-678; by James Sledd, *MP*, L, 138-141; by Hugh Kenner, *Hudson Review*, V, 137-144; by R. C. Bald, *SQ*, V (1954), 83-84.

A5137   Evans, Maurice. "Elizabethan Spoken English." *CamJ*, IV (1951), 401-414.

A5138   Pearce, T. M. "The Vernacular Tongue in English Education." *RN*, IV (1951), 11-12. See reply by James G. McManaway, ibid., pp. 12-14; and notes by William Nelson, ibid., pp. 39-40, and Eva Matthews Sanford, ibid., pp. 70-72.

A5139   Jones, Richard Foster. *The Triumph of the English Language*. A Survey of Opinions Concerning the Vernacular from the Introduction of Printing to the Restoration. Stanford Univ. Press, 1952. Pp. xii, 340.
Rev: *TLS*, Sept. 18, 1953, p. 592; by D. T. Starnes, MP, LI, 130-132; by Charles T. Harrison, *SR*, LXII (1954), 160-161; by Franklin L. Baumer, *Isis*, XLV, 304-305; by Simeon Potter, *RES*, V, 294-296.

A5140   Krook, D. *Language Consciousness in the Seventeenth Century in England*. DD, Cambridge, 1952.

b. GENERAL STUDIES OF SHAKESPEARE'S LANGUAGE

A5141   Willcock, Gladys Dodge. *Shakespeare as Critic of Language*. London: Shak. Assoc., 1934. Pp. 30.
Rev: by H. N. Hillebrand, *MLN*, LI (1935), 458-463.

A5142   Bradbrook, M. C. *Themes and Conventions of Elizabethan Tragedy*. Cambridge Univ. Press, 1935.
Rev: A6269.

A5143   Mackie, W. S. "Shakespeare's English: and How Far it Can Be Investigated with the Help of the *New English Dictionary*." *MLR*, XXXI (1936), 1-10.

A5144   Spencer, Theodore. *Death and Elizabethan Tragedy*. A Study of Convention and Opinion on the Elizabethan Drama. Harvard Univ. Press, 1936. Pp. xiii, 288. Language, pp. 66-110.
Rev: A6823.

A5145   Lievsay, J. L. "Shakespeare's 'Golden World'." *SAB*, XIII (1938), 77-81.

A5146   Scholte. "Goethe, Shakespeare en Philologie." *De Weegschaal*, V (1938), Heft 12.

A5147   Davies, W. Robertson. *Shakespeare's Boy Actors*. London: Dent, 1939. Pp. 208, pl.

A5148   Hunter, Edwin R. "Shakspere's Mouthpieces: Manner of Speech as a Mark of Personality in a Few Shakspere Characters." *SR*, XLVII (1939), 406-430.

A5149   Evans, Maurice. *The Language of the Elizabethan Drama*. DD, Cambridge. Abstr. publ. in *Cam Abs.*, 1939-40, p. 52.

A5150   Morsbach, Lorenz. *Shakespeares Dramatische Kunst und ihre Voraussetzungen. Mit e. Ausblick auf d. Hamlet-Tragödie*. Göttingen: Vanderhoek and Reprecht, 1940. Pp. 167.
Rev: by W. Keller, *SJ*, LXXVI (1940), 205-207; by Hans Marcus, *DLZ*, LXII (1941), 207-209; by Wilhelm Horn, *Archiv*, 178 (1941), 26-30; by Eduard Eckhardt, *Eng. Studn.*, LXXV (1942), 92-94.

A5151   Morozov, M. "Language and Style of Shakespeare." *History of English Realism*. Ed. I. Anisimov. Moscow, 1941, pp. 5-56.

A5152   Thomas, Sidney. *The Antic Hamlet and "Richard III."* New York: King's Crown Press, 1943. Pp. 92.

A5153   Hinman, Charlton. "'Nether' and 'Neither' in the Seventeenth Century." *MLN*, LXIII (1948), 333-335.

A5154   Smith, Roland M. "Anglo-Saxon Spinsters and Anglo-Saxon Archers." *MLN*, LXIV (1949), 312-315.
Page and a half on Shak.'s language.

A5155   Becker, Dietrich. "Shakespeares Englisch und seine Erforschbarkeit mit Hilfe des *New English Dictionary*." *SJ*, 86 (1950), 199.

A5156   Schmetz, Lotte. *Sprache und Charakter im Drama Shakespeares*. DD, Munich, 1950. Pp. 190. Typewritten.

A5157   Hower, Charles C. "The Importance of a Knowledge of Latin for Understanding the Language of Shakespeare." *Classical Jour.*, XLVI (1951), 221-227.

A5158   Otsuka, Takanobu. *The English of Shakespeare and the Bible*. Tokyo, 1951. Pp. xviii, 236, frontispiece. In Japanese.

A5159   Bradbrook, M. C. "Fifty Years of the Criticism of Shakespeare's Style." *ShS*, VII (1954), 1-11.

A5160   Kökeritz, Helge. "Shakespeare's Language." *Shakespeare: of an Age and for all Time*. The Yale Shakespeare Festival Lectures, 1954, pp. 35-51.

A5161 Willcock, Gladys D. "Shakespeare und Elizabethan English." *ShS*, VII (1954), 12-24.

A5162 Zandvoort, R. W. *Collected Papers, A Selection of Notes and Articles Originally Published in English Studies and Other Journals.* Groningen Studies in English, V. Groningen: J. B. Walters, 1954. Pp. 186. "On the Perfection of Experience," pp. 106-121.

A5163 Hulme, Hilda. "Shakespeare and the *Oxford English Dictionary:* Some Supplementary Glosses." *RES*, NS, VI (1955), 128-140.

A5164 Flatter, Richard. "Der Schleier der Schönheit. Einiges über das Problem von Prosa und Vers bei Shakespeare und Goethe." *Chronik d. Wiener Goethe-Vereins*, LIX (1955), 38-46.

A5165 Draper, John W. *The Tempo-Patterns of Shakespeare's Plays.* Angl. Forschungen, Heft 90, 1957. Heidelberg: Carl Winter, 1958. Pp. 161.
  Rev: by Kenneth Muir, *MLR*, LIII (1958), 562-563; by Michel Poirier, *EA*, XI, 161-162; by Gunnar Boklund, *SN*, XXX, 118-120; by Hermann Heuer, *SJ*, 94 (1958), 280-281; by H. Schnyder, *Archiv*, 195 (1958), 201; by Hermann Fischer, *Anglia*, LXXVI, 306-307.

A5166 Hulme, Hilda M. "On the Interpretation of Shakespeare's Text." *ES*, XXXVIII (1957), 193-200.

A5167 Prager, Leonard. *The Language of Shakespeare's Low Characters.* DD, Yale University, 1957.

c. GRAMMAR, MORPHOLOGY, ACCIDENCE (79,82;-,-)
(1) REPRINTS OF ELIZABETHAN GRAMMARS

A5168 Funke, Otto, ed. *Grammatica Anglicana von P. Gr.* 1594. Wiener Beiträge zur Englischen Philologie, LX. Vienna: Braumuller, 1938. Pp. li, 39.
  Rev: by Bogislav v. Lindheim, *Beiblatt*, XLIX (1938), 331-334; by Eilert Ekwall, *Lbl*, LX (1939), 18-19.

A5169 Lily, William. *A Shorte Introduction of Grammar* (1567). Ed. by Vincent J. Flynn. New York: Scholars' Facsimiles and Reprints, 1945. Pp. xii, 204.

(2) GENERAL STUDIES

A5170 Lehnert, M. *Die Grammatik des Englischen Sprachmeisters John Wallis (1616-1703).* Breslau: Priebatsch, 1936. Pp. 156.
  Rev: by E. Kruisinga, *Beiblatt*, XLVII (1937), 360-364; by Eilert Ekwall, *ES*, XIX, 87-90; by G. Scherer, *Archiv*, 172 (1937), 88-90; by Herbert Koziol, *DLZ*, LIX (1938), 53-55.

A5171 Breejen, Bastiaan den. *The Genitive and its of-Equivalent in the Latter Half of the Sixteenth Century.* DD, Amsterdam, 1937.

A5172 Funke, Otto. "William Bullokars *Bref Grammar for English* (1586)." *Anglia*, LXII (1938), 116-137.

A5173 Neumann, Joshua H. "Notes on Ben Jonson's English." *PMLA*, LIV (1939), 736-763.

A5174 Price, Hereward T. "Grammar and the Compositor in the Sixteenth and Seventeenth Centuries." *JEGP*, XXXVIII (1939), 540-548.

A5175 Eccles, Mark. "Francis Beaumont's *Grammar Lecture.*" *RES*, XVI (1940), 402-414.

A5176 Funke, Otto. "Ben Jonsons *English Grammar* (1640)." *Anglia*, LXIV (1940), 117-134.

A5177 Funke, O. *Die Frühzeit der Englischen Grammatik. Die Humanistisch-antike Sprachlehre und der National-Sprachliche Gedanke im Spiegel der Frühneuenglischen Grammatiker von Bullokar (1586) bis Wallis (1653). Die Grammatische Systematik und die Klassifikation der Redeteile.* Schriften der Literarischen Gesellschaft Bern, IV. Bern: Lang, 1941. Pp. 91.

A5178 Niederstenbruch, Alex. "Zur Sprachhaltung des Englischen." *N. Mon.*, XII (1941), 205-217. Shak., pp. 209-213.

A5179 Flynn, Vincent Joseph. "The Grammatical Writings of William Lily, ?1468-?1523." *Papers Bibl. Soc. Amer.*, XXXVII (1943), 85-113.

A5180 Nelson, William. "Thomas More, Grammarian and Orator." *PMLA*, LVIII (1943), 337-352.

A5181 Miles, Josephine. *Major Adjectives in English Poetry from Wyatt to Auden.* Univ. California Pubs. Eng., XII, No. 3. Univ. California Press, 1946. Pp. 305-426.
  Rev: by H. W. Wells, *Amer. Lit.*, XVIII (1946), 267-268; by Rosemary Freeman, *RES*, XXIII (1947), 81-82.

A5182 Pafort, Eloise. "A Group of Early Tudor School-Books." *Library*, 4th S., XXVI (1946), 227-261. Also Bennett, H. S. "A Check-List of Robert Whittinton's Grammars." *Library*, VII (1952), 1-14.

A5183 Bambas, Rudolph C. "Verb Forms in -*S* and -*TH* in Early Modern English Prose." *JEGP*, XLVI (1947), 183-187.

A5184 Hulbert, J. R. "On the Origin of the Grammarian's Rules for the Use of *Shall* and *Will.*" *PMLA*, LXII (1947), 1178-82.

A5185 Lee, Donald Woodward. *Functional Change in Early English.* Menasha, Wisconsin: George Banta, 1948. Pp. ix, 128.
  Rev: by H. T. Price, *JEGP*, XLVIII (1949), 151-152; by Stefán Einarsson, *MLN*, LXIV, 498-500; by P. M. Kean, *Medium Aevum*, XVIII, 78-80.

A5186 Höller, Helmut. *Wortbildung und Wortformen in den Dramen Thomas Middletons: ein Vergleich mit der Sprache Shakespeares.* DD, Graz, 1950. Pp. 155. Typewritten.

A5187 Dahl, Torsten. *An Inquiry into Aspects of the Language of Thomas Deloney.* Linguistic Studies in Some Elizabethan Writings, I. Acta Jutlandica, Aarsskrift for Aarhus Universitet, XXIII, Humanistick Series 36. Aarhus: Universitetsforlaget; Copenhagen: Ejnar Munksgaard, 1951. Pp. 215.
> Rev: by Norman E. Eliason, *MLR*, XLVII (1952), 569-570; *TLS*, Aug. 1, 1952, p. 499; by Fernand Mossé, *EA*, VIII (1955), 67.

A5188 Legouis, Pierre. "The Epistolary Past in English." *N &Q*, 198 (1953), 111-112.

A5189 Brunner, Karl. "Expanded Verbal Forms in Early Modern English." *ES*, XXXVI (1955), 218-221.

A5190 Bačelis, T. "Svjaź Vremen." *Teatr* (Moscow), XVII (1956), 84-97.

A5191 Lindheim, Bogislav von. "Zur Problematik der Grammatischen Kategorien im Englischen." *NS*, V (1956), 417-428. See also Gustav Kirchner, "Guiltless Bloodshedding," ibid., VI (1957), 83-84; Lindheim: "Eine Replik," ibid., 280-281.

(3) SHAKESPEARE'S GRAMMAR

A5192 Ritzenfeld, Emil. *Der Gebrauch des Pronomens, Artikels und Verbs bei Thomas Kyd im Vergleich zu dem Gebrauch bei Shakespeare.* DD, Kiel, 1889. Pp. 75.

A5193 Soltau, Jens. *Die Sprache im Drama.* Germanische Studien, 139. Berlin: Ebering, 1933. Pp. 126.
> Rev: by Wilhelm Emrich, *ZDP*, LXII (1937), 194-199.

A5194 Lennox-Short, A. *The Development of the Use of "Thou" and "You" to the End of the Eighteenth Century.* MA thesis, Capetown, 1934.

A5195 Archer, C. "*Thou* and *You* in the Sonnets." *TLS*, June 27, 1936, p. 544.

A5196 Bohlen, Adolf. "Von der Sprachform zum Sprachgeist." *N. Mon.*, VII (1936), 81-104.

A5197 Saint Geraldine Byrne, Sister. *Shakespeare's Use of the Pronoun of Address: Its Significance in Characterization and Motivation.* Washington, D. C.: Catholic Univ. of America, 1936. Pp. xxxvi, 189.

A5198 Shewmake, Edwin F. "Shakespeare and Southern 'You All'." *American Speech*, XIII (1938), 163-168.

A5199 Long, E. H. "The Southerners' 'You All'." *Southern Literary Messenger*, I (1939), 652-655.

A5200 Franz, W. *Die Sprache Shakespeares, in Vers und Prosa.* Shakespeare-Grammatik in 4 Auflage. Halle: Max Niemeyer, 1939. Pp. xl, 730.
> Rev: by Wolfgang Keller, *SJ*, LXXV (1939), 154-156; by Georges Connes, *EA*, IV (1940), 58; by W. Fischer, *Beiblatt*, LI, 73-75; by Hans Marcus, *Archiv*, 177 (1940), 54; by F. A. Pompen, *Museum*, XLVII, 337-339; by Willy Casper, *ZNU*, XXXIX, 278-279; by Simeon Potter, *MLR*, XXXV (1940), 129-130; by T. W. Baldwin, *MLN*, LV, 460; by H. T. Price, *JEGP*, XXXIX, 577; by S. B. Liljegren, *SN*, XIII (1940-41), 158-159; by M. Niederstenbruch-Tietze, *DDHS*, VIII (1941), 70; by Herman Heuer, *Lbl*, LXII, 201-202; by F. T. Visser, *ES*, XXV (1943), 6; by Hans Marcus, *DLZ*, LXXI (1950), 497-498.

A5201 Rudolph, O. *Die Umschreibung der einfachen Verben mit "to do" in Shakespeares "Julius Caesar."* DD, Marburg, 1939. Pp. 86.

A5202 Glunz, Hans H. "Shakespeare und die Sprache." *Blätter des Hessischen Landestheaters*, 1939-40, Heft. 4.

A5203 Herr, A. F. "An Elizabethan Usage of 'Quoth'." *N &Q*, 178 (1940), 152.

A5204 Niederstenbruch, Alex. "Nordisch-westliche Züge in Shakespeares Sprache." *DNS*, XLIX (1941), 37-50.

A5205 Gordon, G. "Shakespeare's English." *Shakespearian Comedy and Other Studies.* London, 1944, pp. 129-154.

A5206 Tenney, C. D. *Studies in the Language of Shakespeare's Characters.* DD, University of Oregon, 1946.

A5207 Visser, F. Th. "Two Remarkable Constructions in Shakespeare." *Neophil*, XXX (1946), 37-43

A5208 Beckers, Günther. *Die Kausative Kraft des Adjektivums in Shakespeares Sprachgebrauch.* DD Marburg, 1947. Pp. 94. Typewritten.

A5209 Fridén, Georg. *Studies on the Tenses of the English Verb from Chaucer to Shakespeare with Special Reference to the Late Sixteenth Century.* DD, Uppsala, 1948. Publ. in *Essays and Studies on Eng. Lang. & Lit.*, II. Ed. by S. B. Liljegren. Uppsala, 1948. Harvard Univ. Press, 1949. Pp. 222.
> Rev: by Friedrich Schubel, *SN*, XXI (1949), 300-302; by F. Mossé, *Bulletin de la Soc. ling. de Paris*, XLV, 175-176; by B. M. Charleston, *Moderna Språk*, XLIII, 216-219; by W. E. Collison, *Studia Linguistica*, IV (1950), 113-117; by S. M. Kuhn, *JEGP*, XLIX, 104-106; by S. Potter, *MLR*, XLV, 77-78; by J. Sledd, *MP*, XLVII, 208-209; by A. A. Hill, *Studies in Linguistics*, IX (1951), 98-99; by F. Mossé, *EA*, V (1952), 69-70.

A5210 Grünberg, née Fränkel, Ellen. *Die Verben mit Doppeltem Objekt und Verwandte Konstruktionen bei Shakespeare.* DD, Jena, 1948. Pp. 123. Typewritten.

A5211   Flesch, Rudolf. "Did Shakespeare Make Mistakes in English." *The Art of Readable Writing,* New York: Harper, 1949, pp. 94-105.
       Ham., V.i.315.

A5212   Partridge, A. C. *The Problem of "Henry VIII" Re-opened.* Cambridge: Bowes & Bowes, 1949. Pp. 35.
       Rev: B9885.

A5213   Abend, Murray. "Two Unique Gender Forms in the Shakespeare Sonnets." *N &Q,* 195 (1950), 325.

A5214   Becker, Dietrich. *Shakespeares Präfixbildungen. Ein Beitrag zur Erforschung der Sprachlichen Neuprägungen Shakespeares.* DD, Münster, 1950. Pp. 143. Typewritten.

A5215   Maxwell, J. C. "Peele and Shakespeare: A Stylometric Test." *JEGP,* XLIX (1950), 557-561.

A5216   Biese, Yrjo M. "Notes on the Compound Participle in the Works of Shakespeare and His Contemporaries." *Suomalaisen Tiedeakatemian Toimituksia. Annales Academiae Scientiarum Fennicae,* Helsinki, B, LXIII 2 (1950), 1-18.
       Rev: by H. M. Flasdieck, *Anglia,* LXX (1951), 327.

A5217   Schlothauer, Günter. *Der Reine Verbalstamm als Substantiv bei Shakespeare.* DD, Jena, 1951. Pp. 357. Typewritten.

A5218   Biese, Y. M. "Notes on the Use of the Ingressive Auxiliary in the Works of William Shakespeare." *N. Mitt.,* LIII (1952), 9-18.

A5219   Kiendler, Helga. *Wortformen und Wortbildung in den Dramen F. Beaumonts und J. Fletchers: Ein Vergleich mit der Sprache Shakespeares sowie Middletons und Massingers.* DD, Graz, 1952. Pp. 183. Typewritten.

A5220   Price, H. T. "Shakespeare's Parts of Speech." *Univ. of San Francisco Quarterly,* XVIII (1952), 19-28.

A5221   Kilian, Friedhelm. *Shakespeares Nominalkomposita. Ein Beitr. zur Erforschung s. Neuprägungen.* DD, Münster, 1953. Pp. 218.

A5222   Partridge, A. C. *The Accidence of Ben Jonson's Plays, Masques and Entertainments.* With an Appendix of Comparable Uses in Shakespeare. Cambridge: Bowes and Bowes, 1953. Pp. xiv, 333.
       Rev: *TLS,* July 17, 1953, p. 466; by E. G. Stanley, *MLR,* XLIX (1954), 368-369; by Hermann Heuer, *SJ,* 90 (1954), 345-347; by Hereward T. Price, *SQ,* VI (1955), 102-103; by E. J. Dobson, *RES,* NS, VI, 197-201; by Mark Eccles, *JEGP,* LIV, 283.

A5223   Stahl, Hannelore Eleonore. *Studien zum Problem der Sprachlichen Neuschöpfungen bei Shakespeare. Die Suffixbildungen.* DD, Freiburg/Br., 1953. Pp. 231. Typewritten.

A5224   Williams, Charles. "The Use of the Second Person in *Twelfth Night.*" *English,* IX (1953), 125-128.

A5225   Sonderegger, Erwin. *Die Fügung von "to be" mit dem Partizipium des Präsens bei Shakespeare im Vergleich zum Heutigen Gebrauch.* DD, Innsbruck, 1954. Pp. 162. Typewritten.

A5226   Veuhoff, Karl Friedrich. *Shakespeares Funktionsverschiebungen. Ein Beitrag zur Erforschung der Sprachlichen Neuprägungen Shakespeares.* DD, Münster, 1954. Pp. 118. Typewritten.

A5227   Harada, Shigeo. "The Progressive Tense in Shakespeare." *Kurume Daigaku Ronso,* Kurume, Japan, IV, No. 2 (1956). In Japanese.

A5228   Jud-Schmid. *Der Indefinite Agens von Chaucer bis Shakespeare.* Die Wörter und Wendungen für "man." DD, Zurich, 1956. Publ. in Schweizer anglist. Arbeiten. Bern: Francke, 1956. Pp. 128.
       Rev: by Friedrich Schubel, *DLZ,* LXXVIII (1957), 613-616; by E. Standop, *Archiv,* 194 (1957-58), 236-237; by R. Derolez, *RBPH,* XXXV, 422-425; by R. Quirk, *MLR,* LIII (1958), 458.

A5229   O'Brien, Gordon Worth. *Renaissance Poetics and the Problem of Power.* Publ. No. 2 of Institute of Elizabethan Studies, 1956. Pp. 127.
       Rev: A1726.

A5230   Berry, Francis. *Poets' Grammar.* London: Routledge and Kegan Paul, 1958. Pp. 190.
       Rev: *TLS,* May 16, 1958, p. 270; by R. Fuller, *London Mag.,* V, No. 9, 67-68.

A5231   Berry, Francis. "'Thou' and 'You' in Shakespeare's *Sonnets.*" *EIC,* VIII (1958), 138-146.
       Comment by Thomas Finkenstaedt, ibid., pp. 456-457.

A5232   Harada, Shigeo. "The Be Going To Infinitive Form in Shakespeare." *Otsuka Festschrift,* 1958, pp. 317-322.

A5233   Hulme, Hilda M. "The English Language as a Medium of Literary Expression." *EIC,* VIII (1958), 68-76.
       Comment by F. W. Bateson, ibid., 76-78. Also, W. Haas, Vivian Salmon, F. W. Bateson, "More on 'Language and Literature'," ibid., 325-326.

A5234   Hulme, Hilda M. "Shakespeare's Text: Some Notes on Linguistic Procedure and Its Relevance to Textual Criticism." *ES,* XXXIX (1958), 49-56.

A5235   Hulme, Hilda M. "The Spoken Language and the Dramatic Text: Some Notes on the Interpretation of Shakespeare's Language." *SQ,* IX (1958), 379-386.

A5236   Matsuda, Yutaka. "Shakespeare's Use of an Indirect Negative Form." Otsuka *Festschrift*, 1958, pp. 323-333.

A5237   Mitsui, Takayuki. "Relative Pronouns in Shakespeare's Colloquial English." Otsuka *Festschrift*, 1958, pp. 335-349.

d. PHONOLOGY, PRONUNCIATION, AND ORTHOGRAPHY (81;29)
(1) GENERAL

A5238   Zachrisson, R. E. *The English Pronunciation at Shakespeare's Time as Taught by William Bullokar.* Uppsala and Leipzig, 1927.
Rev: by W. van der Gaaf, *ES*, XVIII (1936), 39-43.

A5239   Askew, C. C. *The Light Thrown on Seventeenth Century Pronunciation by the Rhymes in Herrick, Lovelace, and Crashaw.* MA thesis, Cape Town, South Africa, 1934.

A5240   Davies, Constance. *English Pronunciation from the Fifteenth to the Eighteenth Century.* London, 1934.
Rev: by C. G., *Amer. Speech*, X (1935), 222; *TLS*, May 23, 1935, p. 330; by C. L. W., *RES*, XII (1936), 372-374; by J. Delcourt, *RAA*, XIII, 508.

A5241   Bloom, J. *The Rhymes of Sir John Suckling and Lord Herbert, and the Rhymes and Manuscript Spellings of Sir Walter Raleigh, as Evidence of Contemporary Pronunciation.* MA thesis, Cape Town, South Africa, 1936.

A5242   Fiedler, H. G. *A Contemporary of Shakespeare on Phonetics and on the Pronunciation of English and Latin.* Oxford Univ. Press, 1936. Pp. 21.
Rev: by Wolfgang Schmidt, *Beiblatt*, XLVIII (1937), 78-79; by Mary S. Serjeantson, *English*, I, 449-450; by C. K. Thomas, *QJS*, XXIII, 673-674; by W. Keller, *NS*, XLV, 172-173; *SJ*, LXXIII, 163; by Herbert Koziol, *Archiv*, 172 (1938), 223-225; by F. Brittain, *CR*, LII, 87; by Albert Eichler, *Lbl*, LIX, 388-389; by A. Dekker, *Neophil*, XXVII (1941/42), 75-76.

A5243   Zachrisson, R. E., and W. van der Gaaf. "The English Pronunciation at Shakespeare's Time." *ES*, XVIII (1936), 39-43.

A5244   Grosse, Eginhard. *Die Neuenglische ea-Schreibung: Ein Beitrag zur Geschichte der Englischen Orthographie.* Leipzig: Mayer and Muller, 1937. Pp. 271.
Rev: by G. Linke, *Archiv*, 173 (1938), 85-87; by Karl Brunner, *Beiblatt*, XLIX, 330-331.

A5245   Sommer, I. *Die Frühneuenglische Orthographie und Lautlehre in Lord Bacons Englischen Werken nach den Wichtigsten Drucken und Handschriften.* DD, Heidelberg, 1937. Pp. xii, 168; pl.
Rev: by Herbert Koziol, *Eng. Studn.*, LXXIII (1939), 255-257; by K. Hammerle, *Beiblatt*, L, 47-49; by Karl Brunner, *Lbl*, LX, 321-322; by Simeon Potter, *MLR*, XXXIV, 534.

A5246   Wijk, Axel. *The Orthography and Pronunciation of Henry Machyn the London Diarist.* DD, Uppsala, 1937. Pp. xi, 299.
Rev: by Herbert Koziol, *Beiblatt*, XLIX (1938), 70-73; by F. Mossé, *EA*, III (1939), 373-374; by Karl Thielke, *Eng. Studn.*, LXXIII, 254-255.

A5247   Lehnert, Martin. "Die Anfänge der Wissenschaftlichen und Praktischen Phonetik in England." *Archiv*, 173 (1939), 163-180; 174 (1940), 28-35.

A5248   Matthews, William. "Variant Pronunciations in the Seventeenth Century." *JEGP*, XXXVII (1938), 189-206.

A5249   Sheldon, Esther Keck. *Standards of English Pronunciation According to the Grammarians and Orthoepists of the Sixteenth, Seventeenth and Eighteenth Centuries.* DD, University of Wisconsin, 1938. Abstr. publ. in *Summaries of Doctoral Dissertations*, 1937-38, Vol. 3, Madison: Univ. of Wisconsin Press, 1938, pp. 304-305.

A5250   Franck, M. *Englische Schreibung und Aussprache in Zeitalter der Tudor und Stuarts.* DD, Berlin, 1939. Pp. 121.

A5251   Gill, W. W. "Pronunciation of 'Daughter'." *N &Q*, 177 (1939), 15.

A5252   Hultzén, Lee S. "Seventeenth Century Intonation." *Amer. Speech*, XIV (1939), 39-43.

A5253   Hinman, C. "Principles Governing the Use of Variant Spellings as Evidence of Alternate Setting of Two Compositors." *Library*, XXI (1940), 78-94.

A5254   Horn, W. "Der Lautwandel von sj zu š im Neuenglischen." *Beiblatt*, LI (1940), 21-24. In Shak.'s time.

A5255   Eckhardt, Eduard. "Der Übergang zur Germanischen Betonung bei den Wörtern Französischer Herkunft im Frühneuenglischen." *Eng. Studn.*, LXXV (1942/43), 287-352.

A5256   Matthews, William. "English Pronunciation and Shorthand in the Early Modern Period." *Univ. Cal. Pubs. Eng.*, IX (1943), 135-214.
Rev: A2855.

A5257   Scholl, Evelyn H. "New Light on Seventeenth Century Pronunciation from the English School of Lutenist Song Writers." *PMLA*, LIX (1944), 398-445.

A5258   Spielmann, M. H. "Sixteenth and Seventeenth Century Spelling: A Suggested Reason for its Variability." *Essays by Divers Hands.* London XXII (1947), 94-102.

A5259   Danielsson, Bror. *Studies on the Accentuation of Polysyllabic Latin, Greek, and Romance Loan-Words in English, with Special Reference to Those Ending in -able, -ate, -ator, -ible, -ic, -ical, and -ize.*

Stockholm Studies in Eng., III. Stockholm: Almqvist & Wiksell, 1948. Pp. xvi, 664, 6.
Rev: by O. R. Reuter, *N. Mitt.*, L (1949), 254-259; by F. Schubel, *SN*, XXII (1950), 214-217; by N. E. Eliason, *MLR*, XLV, 360-362.

A5260   Hinman, Charlton. " 'Nether' and 'Neither' in the Seventeenth Century." *MLN*, LXIII (1948), 333-335.

A5261   Graves, Robert. *The Common Asphodel.* Collected Essays on Poetry, 1922-49. London: Hamilton, 1949. Pp. xii, 335. Punctuation and spelling, pp. 84-85.

A5262   Kökeritz, Helge. "John Hart and Early Standard English." *Malone Anniversary Studies*, 1949, pp. 239-248.

A5263   Dobson, E. J. *English Pronunciation, 1500-1700, According to the Evidence of the English Ortho-epists.* DD, Oxford, 1951.

A5264   Haase, Gladys D. *Spenser's Orthography: An Examination of a Poet's Use of the Variant Pronunciations of Elizabethan English.* DD, Columbia University, 1952.

A5265   Svendsen, Bent. "Verdens Største Forfatter Kunde Ikke Stave." ("The Greatest Author in the World Could Not Spell." *Aalborg Amtstidende*, Aalborg, Denmark, March 2, 1954.

A5266   Danielsson, Bror. *John Hart's Works on English Orthography and Pronunciation.* Part I, Biographical and Bibliographical Introduction. Texts and Index Verborum. Stockholm: Almqvist & Wiksell, 1955. Pp. 338.
Rev: by S. B. Liljegren, *Archiv*, 193 (1956), 55-56; by Fernand Mossé, *EA*, IX, 34-38; by Harris Fletcher, *JEGP*, LV, 142-144; by Pamela Gradon, *RES*, VIII (1957), 187-189; by Randolph Quirk, *MLR*, LII, 94-95.

A5267   Kusakabe, Tokuji. "The Orthography and Pronunciation of the Diary of Richard Cocks, Cape-Merchant in the English Factory in Japan, 1615-1622." *Bull. of the Kyoto Gajugei Univ.*, Ser. A, No. 7 (1955), 1-16.

A5268   Dobson, E. J. *English Pronunciation 1500-1700.* Vol. I, *Survey of the Sources*; Vol. II, *Phonology.* Oxford: Clarendon Press, 1957. Pp. xxiii, 444; vi, [445-] 1078.
Rev: *TLS*, May 24, 1957, p. 324; by Eilert Ekwall, *RES*, IX (1958), 303-312; by Herbert Koziol, *ES*, XXXIX, 138-141; by R. P. Roberts, *SCN*, XVI, 1-2; by Randolph Quirk and W. M. Smith, *MLR*, LIII, 228-231; by Angus McIntosh, *EHR*, LXXIII, 522-523.

A5269   Palmer, Rupert Elmer, Jr. *Thomas Whythorne's Speech—A Study of English Pronunciation in the Sixteenth Century.* DD, Yale University, 1957.

A5270   Robinson, Robert. *The Phonetic Writings of Robert Robinson.* Ed. E. J. Dobson. *Early English Texts Society*, No. 238, for 1953. London: Oxford Univ. Press for the Society, 1957. Pp. xxi, 96.
Includes Robinson's *The Art of Pronunciation* and a transcription in Robinson's phonetic script of Richard Barnfield's *Lady Pecunia*, in MS Ashmole 1153, ff. 117-119, 122-138.
Rev: by Norman E. Eliason, *SQ*, IX (1958), 405-406.

A5271   London, H. Stanford. "John Hart, Orthographic Reformer and Chester Herald, 1567-74." *N &Q*, NS, V (1958), 222-224.

(2) SHAKESPEARE

A5272   Kökeritz, Helge. "Two Sets of Shakespearean Homophones." *RES*, XIX (1943), 357-365.

A5273   Kenyon, John S. "Shakespeare, Sonnet CXI, 12." *MLN*, LX (1945), 357-358.

A5274   Crow, J. " 'Anathomize': Shakespeare's Spelling." *TLS*, May 10, 1947, p. 225.

A5275   Kernodle, G. R. "Basic Problems in Reading Shakespeare." *QJS*, XXXV (1949), 36-43.

A5276   Kökeritz, Helge. "Shakespeare's Pronunciation: A Preliminary Survey." *Moderna Språk*, XLIII (1949), 149-168.

A5277   Sansom, Clive. "On the Speaking of Shakespeare." London Academy of Music and Dramatic Arts, 1949.

A5278   Schratzer, Erich. *Wortformen und Syntax in den Shirburn Ballads (1585-1616): ein Vergleich mit der Sprache Shakespeares.* DD, Graz, 1950. Pp. 125. Typewritten.

A5279   Le Page, R. B. "The Dramatic Delivery of Shakespeare's Verse." *ES*, XXXII (1951), 63-68.

A5280   Pöll, Margit. *Wortformen und Syntax in Thomas Nashs "Unfortunate Traveller": ein Vergleich mit der Sprache Shakespeares.* DD, Graz, 1951. Pp. 163. Typewritten.

A5281   Schmid, Ilse. *Wortformen und Syntax in Stephen Gossons "School of Abuse" und Sir Philip Sidneys "Apologie for Poetrie": ein Vergleich mit der Sprache Shakespeares.* DD, Graz, 1951. Pp. 143. Typewritten.

A5282   Auty, R. A. "Pronouncing Shakespearian Names." *TLS*, Sept. 19, 1952, p. 613.

A5283   Kökeritz, Helge. *Shakespeare's Pronunciation.* Yale Univ. Press, 1953. Pp. xv, 516.
Rev: by Hallett Smith, *YR*, XLIII (1953), 121-125; by Harold Whitehall, *KR*, XVI (1954), 322-328; by Philip Williams, *South Atlantic Quar.*, LIII, 273; by Hilda M. Hulme, *MLR*, XLIX, 367-368; by Norman E. Eliason, *SQ*, V, 413-415; by F. G. Cassidy, *CE*, XVI (1954-55), 198-199; by Eilert Ekwall, *Moderna Språk*, XLVIII, 104-114; by Hermann Heuer, *SJ*, 90 (1954), 343-345; by Hereward T. Price, *JEGP*, LIV (1955), 418-421; by Herbert Dean Meritt, *MP*,

LII, 275-276; by Bertil Sundby, *ES*, XXXVI, 78-83; by E. J. Dobson, *RES*, VI 404-414; by Stanley Richards and Paul Slocumb, *Players Magazine*, XXXI, 187; by M. Pagnini, *Rivista di Letterature Mod.*, NS, VI, 73; by Otto Funke, *Anglia*, LXXIV (1956), 260-265; by S. B. Liljegren, *Archiv*, 193 (1956), 56; by Fernand Mossé, *EA*, IX, 34-38.

A5284   Masson, David I. "Free Phonetic Patterns in Shakespeare's Sonnets." *Neophil*, XXXVIII (1954), 277-289.

A5285   Partridge, A. C. "Shakespeare's Orthography in *Venus and Adonis* and Some Early Quartos." *ShS*, VII (1954), 35-47.

A5286   Hebbe, Agneta. " 'Snacka' med Shakespeare." *Gaudeamus*, Stockholm, 1955, p. 8. Shak.'s pronunciation as recorded by Kökeritz.

A5287   Kökeritz, Helge. *Examples of Shakespeare's Pronunciation. A Recording.* Bridgeport, Conn.: Columbia Records, Inc. 10" LP, 1955.
         Rev: by F. G. Cassidy, *CE*, XVI (1955), 199.

A5288   Hulme, Hilda. "Three Notes on the Pronunciation and Meanings of Shakespeare's Text: *Let Him be Made an Ouerture for th' Warres* (*Coriolanus*, I.ix.46)); *And Either the Deuill, or Throwe Him Out* (*Hamlet*, III. iv. 169); *A Whole Armado of Conuicted Saile* (*King John*, III. iv. 2)." *Neophil*, XLI (1957), 275-281.

A5289   Muir, Kenneth. "The Speaking of Shakespeare." *English Speech*, IV. Year Book of the English Speaking Board. London: English Speaking Board, 1957.

A5290   Lane, Ralph H. "Shakespearean Spelling." *ShN*, VIII (1958), 28.

e. ACCIDENCE (Transferred to GRAMMAR, VII,1,c.)

f. SYNTAX (83;-)

A5291   Visser, Frederikus Theodorus. *A Syntax of the English Language of St. Thomas More.* DD, Nijmegen Rooms-Katholieke Universiteit, 1941.
         Part I, The Verb, publ. Louvain: Uystpsuyst, 1946. Pp. xxxiii, 443. *Part II, The Verb*, also Louvain: Uystpsuyst, 1952. Pp. xx, 449-752.

A5292   Partridge, A. C. *The Problem of "Henry VIII" Re-opened.* Cambridge: Bowes & Bowes, 1949. Pp. 35.
         Rev: B9885.

A5293   Schratzer, Erich. *Wortformen und Syntax in den Shirburn Ballads (1585-1616): ein Vergleich mit der Sprache Shakespeares.* DD, Graz, 1950. Pp. 125. Typewritten.

A5294   Pöll, Margit. *Wortformen und Syntax in Thomas Nashs "Unfortunate Traveller": ein Vergleich mit der Sprache Shakespeares.* DD, Graz, 1951. Pp. 163. Typewritten.

A5295   Schmid, Ilse. *Wortformen und Syntax in Stephen Gossons "School of Abuse" und Sir Philip Sidneys "Apologie for Poetrie": ein Vergleich mit der Sprache Shakespeares.* DD, Graz, 1951. Pp. 143. Typewritten.

A5296   Partridge, A. C. *Studies in the Syntax of Ben Jonson's Plays.* Cambridge: Bowes & Bowes, 1953. Pp. x, 104.
         Rev: by E. G. Stanley, *MLR*, XLIX (1954), 368-369; by Hermann Heuer, *SJ*, 90 (1954), 345-347; by E. J. Dobson, *RES*, VI, 197-201.

A5297   Lindheim, Bogislav von. "Syntaktische Funktionsverschiebung als Mittel des barocken Stils bei Shakespeare." *SJ*, 90 (1954), 229-251.

A5298   Munday, Mildred B. *The Influence of Shakespeare's Predecessors on His Early Blank Verse.* DD, University of Wisconsin, 1953. Abstr. publ. in *Summaries of Doctoral Dissertations, 1952-53*, Vol. 14, Madison: Univ. of Wisconsin Press, 1954, pp. 437-438. Also in *ShN*, VI, 2.

A5299   Davie, Donald. *Articulate Energy.* An Inquiry into the Syntax of English Poetry. London: Routledge, 1955. Pp. vii, 173. Chapter V. "Syntax as Action in Sidney, Shakespeare and Others," pp. 43-55.
         Rev: by J. J., *NstN*, L (1955), 637; by J. Holloway, *Spectator*, 6649 (1955), 776; by D. Donoghue, *TC*, 158, 588 and 590; *TLS*, Nov. 4, 1955, p. 658; *Listener*, LV (1956), 691, 693; by R. Fuller, *London Magazine*, III, ii, 77-80; by J. Vallette, *MdF*, 326 (1956), 776-777; by J. G. Ritz, *EA*, x (1957), 175-176; by E. Morgan, *RES*, VIII, 212-214; by A. D. S. Fowler, *EIC*, VIII (1958), 79-87; by M. Price, *YR*, XLVII (1957/58), 617-623.

A5300   Kirchner, Gustav. "Direct Transitivation." *ES*, XXXVI (1955), 15-23.

A5301   Dunn, T. A. *Philip Massinger.* London: Nelson, for the Univ. College of Ghana, 1958. Pp. 285.
         Much comparison with Shak. Syntax, pp. 217-218, 224 ff.
         Rev: A8855.

g. PUNCTUATION (84;29)

A5302   Ong, W. J. "Historical Backgrounds of Elizabethan and Jacobean Punctuation Theory." *PMLA*, LIX (1944), 349-360.

A5303   Kane, Robert J. "Hamlet's Apotheosis of Man—Its Punctuation." *RES*, XIV (1938), 67-68.

A5304   Alexander, Peter. *Shakespeare's Punctuation.* Annual Shakespeare Lecture of the British

Academy. London: Cumberlege, 1945. Pp. 24.
Rev: by J. D. Wilson, *RES*, XXIII (1947), 70-78 (see Mr. Alexander's answer to Mr. Wilson's review, "Shakespeare's Punctuation," *RES*, XXIII, 263-266).

A5305 Knight, G. Wilson. "Shakespeare's Angels." *TLS*, Sept. 14, 1946, p. 439.
See letters by Evan John, ibid., Oct. 19, 1946, p. 507; G. Wilson Knight, ibid., Oct. 26, 1946, p. 521.

A5306 Cancelled.

A5307 Carter, Albert Howard. "The Punctuation of Shakespeare's *Sonnets* of 1609." *AMS*, pp. 409-428.

A5308 Flatter, Richard. *Shakespeare's Producing Hand.* London, 1948.
Rev: A5944.

A5309 Smith, Warren D. *Shakespeare's Stagecraft as Denoted by the Dialogue in the Original Printings of His Texts.* DD, University of Pennsylvania, 1948. Pp. 256. Mic A50-217. *Mcf Ab*, X (1950), 163. Publ. No. 1731.

A5310 Graves, Robert. "A Study in Original Punctuation and Spelling." *The Common Asphodel*, London, 1949, pp. 84-95.

A5311 Flatter, Richard. " 'True Originall Copies' Shakespeare's Plays — Outline of a New Conception." *Proc. Leeds Philos. and Lit. Soc.*, Lit. & Hist. Sec. VII, Pt. 1 (1952), 31-42.

A5312 Hunter, G. K. "The Marking of Sententiae in Elizabethan Printed Plays, Poems, and Romances." *Library*, VI (1952), 171-188.

A5313 Maxwell, J. C. "The Punctuation of *Macbeth*, I.i.1-2." *RES*, NS, IV (1953), 356-358.

A5314 Partridge, A. C. "Shakespeare's Orthography in *Venus and Adonis* and Some Early Quartos." *ShS*, VII (1954), 35-47.

A5315 Blayney, Glenn H. "Dramatic Pointing in the *Yorkshire Tragedy*." *N &Q*, NS, IV (1957), 191-192.

h. THE VOCABULARY OF SHAKESPEARE AND HIS CONTEMPORARIES (85;29)
(1) VOCABULARY IN GENERAL (85;29)

A5316 Nottrott, Marianne. *Der Formale Gebrauch des Epithetons in Shakespeares Dramen "Othello," "King Lear," "Macbeth," und "Coriolanus."* DD, Leipzig, 1922. Pp. vi, 254. Handwritten. Publ. in *Jahrbuch der Philosophischen Fakultät Leipzig*, I (1923).

A5317 Corth, Konstantin. *Zur Würdigung von Leon Kellners Shakespeare-Wörterbuch.* DD, Rostock, 1925. Pp. v, 50. Typewritten.

A5318 Morris, C. M. J. *Shakespeare's Vocabulary in "Love's Labour's Lost"; The Effect of the Elizabethan Age and the Renascence on the Creation, Use and Interpretation of Words.* MA thesis, Capetown, 1934.

A5319 Allen, H. E. "The influence of Superstition on Vocabulary." *PMLA*, LI (1936), 904-920.

A5320 Empson, William. "The Best Policy." *Life and Letters*, XIV, No. 4 (1936), 37-45.
Discusses the forty-eight uses of the word "honesty" in *Othello*.

A5321 Hart, Alfred. "The Vocabulary of the First Quarto of *Hamlet*." *RES*, XII (1936), 18-30.

A5322 Larrabee, S. A. " 'Bydding Base' in *Two Gentlemen of Verona*, etc." *MLN*, LI (1936), 535-536.

A5323 Llewellyn, E. C. *The Influence of Low Dutch on the English Vocabulary.* Oxford Univ. Press, 1936. Pp. xii, 223.
Rev: by J. F. Bense, *ES*, XIX (1937), 165-172.

A5324 Serjeantson, Mary S. *A History of Foreign Words in English.* New York: Dutton, 1936. Pp. ix, 354.
Rev: by J. Alexander Kerns, *Class. Weekly*, XXX (1937), 214-215.

A5325 Taylor, Rupert. "*Folks* in Elizabethan English." *Amer. Speech*, XI (1936), 187-188.

A5326 Groom, Bernard. *The Formation and Use of Compound Epithets in English Poetry from 1579.* S.P.E. Tract, XLIX. Oxford: Clarendon Press, 1937. Pp. 30.
Rev: *TLS*, July 31, 1937, p. 562; *N &Q*, 173 (1937), 18.

A5327 Hammerschlag, Johannes. *Dialekteinflüsse im Frühneuenglischen Wortschatz Nachgewiesen an Caxton und Fabyan.* Bonn: Hanstein, 1937. Pp. 142.
Rev: by W. Héraucourt, *Eng. Studn.*, LXXIII (1938), 65-67; by Rudolf Hittmair, *Beiblatt*, XLIX, 327-330; by G. Linke, *Archiv*, 174 (1938), 255; by F. Mossé, *EA*, III (1939), 258-259; by W. Héraucourt, *Lbl*, XL, 387-389.

A5328 Partridge, Eric. *Slang and Unconventional English from the Fifteenth Century to the Present Day.* London: Routledge, 1937. Pp. xv, 999.
Rev: *N &Q*, 172 (1937), 305-306; by Karl Thielke, *Eng. Studn.*, LXXIII (1938), 280-283; *N &Q*, 174, (1938), 449-450.

A5329 Rubel, Veré L. *A Study of Poetic Diction in the English Renaissance* (to 1590). DD, New York University, 1938.

A5330 Clark, Eleanor G. [Concerning the Elizabethan Use of the Term 'Fustian']. *SAB*, XIV (1939), 57-59.

A5331   Vaughan, D. N. *Satire Upon Language in the Plays of Shakespeare and Ben Jonson*. MA thesis, Capetown, 1939.

A5332   Elson, John J. "Items of Elizabethan Usage." *N &Q*, 179 (1940), 314.

A5333   Wilson, Frank P. *Shakespeare and the Diction of Common Life*. The Annual Shakespeare Lecture Before the British Academy. Oxford Univ. Press, 1941. Pp. 34.
         Rev: *TLS*, Sept. 27, 1941, p. 483; by C. J. Sisson, *MLR*, XXXVII (1942), 108.

A5334   W., E. F. " 'Bugs' in Shakespeare." *American N &Q*, I (Dec. 19, 1941), 138.

A5335   M., J. G. " 'Bug' in Shakespeare and His Contemporaries." *American N &Q*, II (1942), 24-26.

A5336   Awad, Lewis Hanna Khalil. *The Theory and Practice of "Poetic Diction" in English, with Reference to the Same in Arabic and French*. M. Litt thesis, Cambridge, *Cam Abs.*, 1942-43, p. 26.

A5337   Howard, Edwin J. "Four Words in Coxe's *A Short Treatise . . . of Magicall Sciences*." *MLN*, LVII (1942), 674-675.
         Notes use of *proclivity, adhere, devastation* in Coxe's work of 1561, antedating earliest examples in the *O.E.D.*; as well as of *arologie*, a synonym of *aeromancy*.

A5338   Marquardt, Hertha. "Der Englishce Wortschatz als Spiegel Englischer Kultur." *GRM*, 1942, pp. 273-285. Shak., p. 279.

A5339   Rubel, Veré L. *Poetic Diction in the English Renaissance, from Skelton through Spenser*. New York: M.L.A. Revolving Fund Series, No. 12, 1941. Oxford Univ. Press, 1942. Pp. xiv, 312.
         Rev: by H. E. Rollins, *MLN*, LVIII (1943), 317-318; by W. L. Renwick, *RES*, XIX, 216-217; by Elizabeth Sweeting, *MLR*, XXXVIII, 354-355.

A5340   Lexicographer. "The Derivation of 'Clown'." *TLS*, Jan. 2, 1943, p. 7.

A5341   Eccles, Mark. "Shakespeare's Use of *Look How* and Similar Idioms." *JEGP*, XLII (1943), 386-400.

A5342   Hart, Alfred. "The Growth of Shakespeare's Vocabulary." *RES*, XIX (1943), 242-254.

A5343   Hart, Alfred. "Vocabularies of Shakespeare's Plays." *RES*, XIX (1943), 128-140.

A5344   Page, Frederick. "Shakespeare and Florio." *N &Q*, 184 (1943), 283-285. See also Frederick Page, ibid., 185 (1943), 42-44, and 107-108.

A5345   Wittlake, Käthe. *Die Bedeutung von Wit bei Shakespeare*. DD, Marburg, 1943. Pp. 138.

A5346   Gordon, George. *Shakespearian Comedy and Other Studies*. Ed. by Sir Edmund Chambers. Oxford Univ. Press, 1944. Pp. 168.
         Rev: B5165.

A5347   Yule, G. Udny. *The Statistical Study of Literary Vocabulary*. Cambridge Univ. Press, 1944. Pp. x, 306.
         Rev: by W. W. Greg, *MLR*, XXXIX (1944), 291-293; by Angus McIntosh, *Medium Aevum*, XVI (1946), 51-56.

A5348   Q., D. "Shakespeare, Bacon and the O. E. D." *N &Q*, 190 (1946), 37-38.
         See further notes on the same subject by D. Q., "Bacon, Nashe and Dante," *N &Q*, 190 (1946), 78; "Shakespeare, Bacon and English Proverbs," ibid., p. 146; "Shakespeare and Bacon," ibid., p. 259; see D. Q.'s article on "Bacon, Shakespeare and the Bible," ibid., p. 59, and the answer by Reviewer, "Bacon-Shakespeare Parallels," ibid., pp. 99-100. See also W. H. Welply's article, "Shakespeare, Bacon, and the 'O.E.D.'," ibid., pp. 150-151.

A5349   Beckers, Günther. *Die Kausative Kraft des Adjektivums in Shakespeares Sprachgebrauch*. DD, Marburg, 1947. P. 94.

A5350   Ransom, John Crowe. "On Shakespeare's Language." *SR*, LV (1947), 181-198.

A5351   Elton, W. " 'Sooth' in Shakespeare, Milton and Keats." *MLN*, LXIII (1948), 436.

A5352   Goepp, Philip H., II. "Verstegan's 'Most Ancient Saxon Words'." *Malone Anniversary Studies*, 1949, pp. 249-255.

A5353   Partridge, A. C. *The Problem of "Henry VIII" Re-opened*. Cambridge: Bowes & Bowes, 1949. Pp. 35.
         Rev: B9885.

A5354   Sledd, James. "A Footnote on the Inkhorn Controversy." *TxSE*, XXVIII (1949), 49-56.

A5355   Greene, D. J. " 'Sooth' in Keats, Milton, Shakespeare, and Dr. Johnson." *MLN*, LXV (1950), 514-517.

A5356   Marder, Louis. *Aspects of Shakespeare's Education*. DD, Columbia University, 1950. Pp. 291. Mic A50-149. *Mcf Ab*, x (1950), 218. Publ. No. 1880.

A5357   Bland, D. S. "Shakespeare and the 'Ordinary' Word." *ShS*, IV (1951), 49-55.

A5358   Brown, J. R. "Some Notes on the Native Elements in the Diction of *Paradise Lost*." *N &Q*, 196 (1951), 424-428.
         Contains some Shak. usages.

A5359   Sledd, James. "A Note on the Use of Renaissance Dictionaries." *MP*, XLIX (1951), 10-15.

A5360   Hotson, Leslie. *Shakespeare's Motley*. London: Rupert Hart-Davis, 1952. Pp. 133.
         Rev: A6671.

A5361   Price, Hereward T. "Shakespeare's Parts of Speech." *Univ. of San Francisco Quart.*, XVIII (1952), 19-28.

A5362 Ridley, M. R. "Missing the Meaning." *Listener*, Jan. 15, 1953, pp. 98-99, 102.

A5363 Shedd, Robert Gordon. *The "Measure for Measure" of Shakespeare's 1604 Audience.* DD, University of Michigan, 1953. Pp. 430. Mic A53-1478. *DA*, XIII (1953), 801. Publ. No. 5730.
Appendix A. "Once-words" in *Meas.*, pp. 405-410.

A5364 Flatter, Richard. "Das Schauspielerische in der Diktion Shakespeares." Vienna: Krieg, 1954. Pp. 52.

A5365 Lüdeke, H. "Shakespeare as Preserver of English Speech." *English Miscellany*, ed. by Mario Praz. Rome: Edizioni di Storia e Letteratura, V (1954), 95-106.

A5366 Maxwell, J. C. " 'At Once' in Shakespeare." *MLR*, XLIX (1954), 464-466.

A5367 Reetz, Olaf. *Die Entwicklung der Sprachkomik in den Komödien Shakespeares.* DD, Berlin, 1954. Pp. xv, 283. Typewritten.

A5368 Stahl, Hannelore. "Schöpferische Wortbildung bei Shakespeare." *SJ*, 90 (1954), 252-278.

A5369 Cronin, P. J. *Diction and Dramatic Character in Shakespearian Tragedy, with Special Attention to Characteristic Use of Imagery.* B. Litt thesis, Oxford, 1955.

A5370 Groom, Bernard. *The Diction of Poetry from Spenser to Bridges.* Univ. of Toronto Press, 1955. Pp. viii, 284.
Rev: by Burns Martin, *Dalhousie Review*, XXXVI (1957), 419-421; by V. de Sola Pinto, *N &Q*, NS, IV, 364-365; *TLS*, Jan. 25, p. 54; by Howard Sergeant, *English*, XI, 237-238; by Wilhelmina Gordon, *QQ*, LXIV, 151-152; by John Arthos, *JEGP*, LVI, 473-476; by Roy C. Moose, *English Journal*, XLVII (1958), 308; by L. Bonnerot, *EA*, XI, 266; by Edwin Morgan, *RES*, IX, 346-347; by Betty D. Evans, *Books Abroad*, XXXII, 87; by Norman Jeffares, *MLR*, LIII, 100-101.

A5371 Nicolson, Harold. "Shakespeares Lieblingswort." *Die österr. Furche*, XI, No. 30 (1955), 2.

A5372 Pafford, J. H. P. "Words Used Only Once in Shakespeare." *N &Q*, NS, V (1958), 237-238.

(2) ENGLISH DIALECTS (86;-)

A5373 Alexander, Rose. *Slang and Popular Phrases Used by Shakespeare.* Los Angeles: Author, 1936. Pp. 64.

A5374 Mawer, A., and F. M. Stenton. "The Dialect of Warwickshire." *The Place-Names of Warr*, 1936, pp. 25-27.

A5375 Hulme, Hilda M. *Dialect in Tudor Drama.* MA thesis, University of London, 1937.

A5376 Matthews, William. "The Vulgar Speech of London in the XV-XVII Centuries." *N &Q*, 172 (1937), 2-5, 21-24, 40-42, 56-60, 77-79, 92-96, 112-115, 130-133, 149-151, 167-170, 186-188, 204-206, 218-220, 241-243.
See letters by M. H. Dodds, *N &Q*, 172 (1937), 286, and E. K. Sheldon, ibid., 173 (1937), 409-410.

A5377 Matthews, William. *Cockney Past and Present: A Short History of the Dialect of London.* London: Routledge, 1938. Pp. xv, 245.
Rev: *N &Q*, 174 (1938), 286-287; by B. Ifor Evans, *MGW*, Mar. 25, p. 234; by H. K. Fisher, *Life and Letters Today*, XVIII, No. 11, 173-174; by Harry Morgan Ayres, *Amer. Speech*, XIV (1939), 127-129; by M. Schubiger, *ES*, XXI, 39-41; *YR*, XXVIII, 197-200; by Wilhelm Hard, *Archiv*, 178 (1941), 49-51.

A5378 Noyes, Gertrude. "The Development of Cant Lexicography in England, 1566-1785." *SP*, XXXVIII (1941), 462-479.

A5379 Kökeritz, Helge. "Elizabethan 'Che Vore Ye' 'I Warrant You'." *MLN*, LVII (1942), 98-103.

A5380 Marchwardt, Albert H. "An Unnoted Source of English Dialect Vocabulary." *JEGP*, XLVI (1947), 177-182.

A5381 Wagenvoorde, Hanno v. "Het Engelse Volkstoneel in Shakespeares Tijd." *Toneelschild*, II (1947), 132-133.

A5382 Kökeritz, Helge. "Shakespeare's Use of Dialect." *Transactions of the Yorkshire Dialect Society*, Part LI, IX (1951), 1-16.

A5383 Hulme, Hilda M. "A Warwickshire Word-list." *MLR*, XLVI (1951), 321-330.

A5384 Kökeritz, Helge. *Shakespeare's Pronunciation.* Yale Univ. Press, 1953. Pp. xv, 516.
Rev: A5283.

(3) PROPER NAMES (87;-)

A5385 Griffin, William J. "Names in *The Winter's Tale*." *TLS*, June 6, 1936, p. 480.
See letter by Percy Allen, *TLS*, July 18, 1936, p. 600.

A5386 Sennewaid, Charlotte. *Die Namengebung bei Dickens, eine Studie über Lautsymbolik.* Palästra, 203. Leipzig: Mayer & Müller, 1936. Pp. 121.
"Namen bei Shakespeares Nebenpersonen," pp. 14-21.

A5387 Baker, Arthur E. *A Shakespeare Commentary.* Vol. I. Taunton, England: Author, Borough Librarian, 1938. Pp. 964.
Rev: A3327.

A5388   Moore, J. R. "The Name 'Seacole'." *N &Q*, 174 (1938), 60-61.

A5389   Tannenbaum, Samuel A. "The Names in *As You Like It*." *SAB*, xv (1940), 255-256.

A5390   Brennan, J. H. "Nerissa's Name." *American N &Q*, iii (1943), 88.

A5391   C., T. C. "London Place-Names and Men of Letters." *N &Q*, 190 (1946), 12-13.

A5392   Law, Robert A. "On Certain Proper Names in Shakespeare." *TxSE*, xxx (1951), 61-65.
        Rev: *SQ*, iv (1953), 352.

A5393   Kane, Robert J. " 'Richard du Champ' in *Cymbeline*." *SQ*, iv (1953), 206-207.

A5394   Williams, Franklin B., Jr. "Renaissance Names in Masquerade." *PMLA*, lxix (1954),
        314-323.

A5395   Kellogg, Allen B. "Place Names and Epithets in Homer and Shakespeare." *Names*, iii
        (1955), 169-171.

A5396   Kellogg, A. B. "Nicknames and Noncenames in Shakespeare's Comedies." *Names*, iii
        (1955), 1-4.

A5397   Salingar, L. G. "Messaline in *Twelfth Night*." *TLS*, June 3, 1955, p. 301.

A5398   Starnes, DeWitt Talmage. "Acteon's Dogs." *Names*, iii (1955), 19-25.
        Dogs names in *Wives*, *Macb.*, probably from Golding's Ovid.

A5399   Muir, Kenneth, "Shakespeare and Erasmus." *N &Q*, ns, iii (1956), 424-425.

A5400   Musgrove, S. "The Nomenclature of *King Lear*." *RES*, vii (1956), 294-298.

A5401   Malone, Kemp. "Meaningful Fictive Names in English Literature." *Names*, v (1957), 1-13.
        Discusses meanings of names in *Twel.*: Toby Belch, Andrew Aguecheek, Feste, and Malvolio.

A5402   Nathan, Norman. "Balthasar, Daniel, and Portia." *N &Q*, ns, iv (1957), 334-335.

A5403   Knight, G. Wilson. *The Sovereign Flower*. On Shakespeare as the Poet of Royalism Together
        with Related Essays and Indexes to Earlier Volumes. London: Methuen; New York:
        Macmillan, 1958.
        Contains an examination of Shak.'s use of proper names.

(4) DICTIONARIES & GLOSSARIES (87;30)

A5404   Corth, Konstantin. *Zur Würdigung von Leon Kellners Shakespeare-Wörterbuch*. DD, Rostock,
        1925. Pp. v, 50. Typewritten.

A5405   Baker, Arthur E. *A Shakespeare Commentary*. Vol. I. Taunton, England: Author, Borough
        Librarian, 1938. Pp. 964.
        Rev: A3327.

A5406   Schultz, John Howard. "A Glossary of Shakespeare's Hawking Language." *TxSE*, xviii
        (1938), 174-205.

A5407   Michelagnoli, Alfredo. *Dizionario Shakespeariano Inglese-Italiano* (Presentazione di Carlo
        Izzo). Venice: C. Ferrari, 1947. Pp. 139.

A5408   Partridge, Eric. *Shakespeare's Bawdy: A Literary and Psychological Essay and a Comprehensive
        Glossary*. London: Routledge, 1947; New York: Dutton, 1948. Pp. 10, 225. New ed.,
        revised, 1955. Pp. x, 226.
        Rev: by R. H., *Life & Letters*, lv (1947), 264-266; by Raymond Mortimer, *NstN*, Nov.
        29, p. 434; *TLS*, Dec. 6, p. 632; by John Bryson, *Spectator*, Jan. 2, 1948, pp. 21-22; by
        Edward Hubler, *JEGP*, xlvii, 424-425; by Ivor Brown, *Obs.*, Jan. 4, p. 3; by George S.
        McCue, *American Quar.*, v (1949), 188; by Margaret Webster, *NYHTBR*, Mar. 6, 1949,
        p. 5; by E. Brennecke, *SQ*, i (1950), 276; by Richard Flatter, *SJ*, 87/88 (1952), 223-224;
        by Michel Poirier, *EA*, ix (1956), 253-254; by J. Russell Reaver, *English Journal*,
        xlv, 108; by Arthur Brown, *RES*, ns, ix (1958), 118-119.

A5409   Hulme, Hilda M. "A Warwickshire Word-list." *MLR*, xlvi (1951), 321-330.

A5410   Thomson, W. H. *Shakespeare's Characters: A Historical Dictionary*. Altrincham, Manchester:
        John Sherratt and Company, the Saint Ann's Press, 1951. Pp. 320.
        Rev: *TLS*, July 13, 1951, p. 435; by H. B. Charlton, *MGW*, June 14, p. 11 (adverse);
        TLS, July 13, p. 437; by Ivor Brown, *Obs.*, July 8, p. 7; by J. Loiseau, *EA*, v (1952), 153.

(5) CONCORDANCES (88;30)

A5411   Parker, W. M. "Shakespeare Concordances." *TLS*, May 12, 1945, p. 228.

A5412   McGlinchee, Claire. "Romance in a Reference Book." *SAB*, xxi (1946), 64-65.

(6) DICTIONARIES OF QUOTATIONS (Transferred to class of
        same title, XV, 5.)

2. SHAKESPEARE'S PROSODY (89;30)
a. GENERAL WORKS ON ENGLISH PROSODY (89;30)

A5413   Klothilde, Mother. *The Development (or Expansion) (a) of the Content and Style of Poetry, and
        (b) of the Conceptions of Poetry From Shakespeare and Sidney to Hardy and T. S. Eliot*. MA thesis,
        Saskatchewan, 1934. Pp. 129.

A5414   Bernard, Jules E., Jr. *The Prosody of the Tudor Interlude: A Survey*. DD, Yale University, 1937.

A5415 Fogarty, E. *Rhythm*. London: Allen & Unwin, 1937. Pp. 246.
A5416 De La Mare, Walter. *Poetry in Prose*. Warton Lecture, 1935. Oxford: Univ. Press; London: Milford., 1937.
Rev: by K. Brunner, *Beiblatt*, XLVIII (1937), 347.
A5417 Smart, G. K. "English Non-Dramatic Blank Verse in the Sixteenth Century." *Anglia*, LXI (1937), 370-397.
A5418 Sorensen, Frederick C. *Metre and Rhythm in English Prosody*. DD, Stanford University, 1938. Abstr. publ. in *Abstracts of Dissertations*, Stanford Univ., XIII (1937-38), 50-51. His findings applied to first two scenes of *Hamlet*.
A5419 Loane, George G. "Final S in Rhyme." *TLS*, Jan. 15, 1938, p. 44. Examples from Hall's Satires, Chapman, and others.
A5420 Anderson, J. R. "The Principle of Uniformity in English Metre." *DUJ*, XXXIII (June, 1941), 188-200; XXXIV (Dec., 1941), 33-49.
A5421 Simpson, Percy. "The Rhyming of Stressed with Unstressed Syllables in Elizabethan Verse." *MLR*, XXXVIII (1943), 127-129; P. Maas, ibid., XXXIX (1944), 179.
A5422 Scholl, Evelyn H. "English Metre Once More." *PMLA*, LXIII (1948), 293-326. Considers the problem of the basis of English metre in the light provided by the English School of Lutenist Song Writers (1597-1632).
A5423 Eliot, T. S. *Poetry and Drama*. Harvard Univ. Press, 1951. The first Theodore Spencer Memorial Lecture, given at Harvard in Nov. 1950. Considers Hamlet.
Rev: by Francis Fergusson, *NYTBR*, June 10, 1951, p. 14; by D. Paul, *Listener*, XLVI, 751-753; by F. Fergusson, *Partisan Rev.*, XVIII, 582-586; by M. Redgrave, *NstN*, XLII, 370; by F. W. Bateson, *SQ*, III (1952), 271-273; by B. Lupini, *English*, IX (1952/53), 28.
A5424 Fluchère, Henri. "The Function of Poetry in Drama." *English Studies Today*, ed. by C. L. Wren and G. Bullough, Oxford: 1951, pp. 22-34.
A5425 Smith, Hallet. *Elizabethan Poetry*. Harvard Univ. Press, 1952. Pp. viii, 355.
Rev: A8369.
A5426 Hunter, G. K. "The English Hexameter and the Elizabethan Madrigal." *PQ*, XXXII (1953), 340-342.
A5427 Kellogg, George A. "Bridges' *Milton's Prosody* and Renaissance Metrical Theory." *PMLA*, LXVIII (1953), 268-285.

b. SHAKESPEARE'S PROSODY (89;30)

A5428 König, Goswin. *Zu Shakespeares Metrik*. DD, Strassburg, 1888. Pp. 76.
A5429 David, Richard. *The Janus of Poets: Being an Essay on the Dramatic Value of Shakespeare's Poetry, Both Good and Bad*. Cambridge Univ. Press, 1935.
A5430 Franz, Wilhelm. *Shakespeares Blankvers*. Mit Nachträgen zu des Verfassers Shakespeare-Grammatik (in 3 Auflage). 2 Auflage. Tübingen: Komm.-Verlag d. Osianderschen Buchhandlung, 1935. Pp. 104.
Rev: by Karl Brunner, *Beiblatt*, XLVII (1936), 108-109.
A5431 Poisson, Rodney Peter Dominic. *The Heroic Couplet in the Plays of Shakespeare*. MA thesis, British Columbia, 1939. Pp. 123.
A5432 Skinner, B. F. "Alliteration in Shakespeare's Sonnets." *Psychological Record*, Oct. 1939. Reply by E. E. Stoll, *MLN*, LV (1939), 388-390.
A5433 Tannenbaum, Samuel A. "Shakespeare's Verse. Prepared for Students." *SAB*, XIV (1939), 60-61.
A5434 Ness, Frederic W. *The Use of Rhyme in Shakespeare's Plays*. DD, Yale University, 1940.
A5435 Ness, Frederic W. *The Use of Rhyme in Shakespeare's Plays*. New Haven: Yale Univ. Press; London: Milford, 1941. Pp. xvi, 168.
Rev: by J. W. Draper, *MLN*, LVII (1942), 379-380; by J. W. R. Purser, *MLR*, XXXVIII (1943), 50-51; by Paul Landis, *JEGP*, XLII, 587-589.
A5436 Tannenbaum, Samuel A. "Shakspere's Rimes." *SAB*, XVI (1941), 255-256.
A5437 Smith, Lewis W. "Shakespeare and the Speaking Line." *Poet Lore*, XLVIII (1942), 61-70.
A5438 Maas, P. "Shakespeare and Rime." *MLR*, XXXIX (1944), 179.
A5439 Ungaretti, G. "Appunti sull'arte Poetica di Shakespeare." *Poesia*, I (1946), 132-135.
A5440 Griffith, Hubert. "Antony, Cleopatra, and Others." *New English Review*, XIV (1947), 162-165.
A5441 "Shakespeare's Rhythms." *Bulletin* (Australia), LXIX (Aug. 1948), 2.
A5442 Flatter, Richard. *Shakespeare's Producing Hand*. London, 1948.
Rev: A5944.
A5443 Smith, Warren D. *Shakespeare's Stagecraft as Denoted by the Dialogue in the Original Printings of His Texts*. DD, University of Pennsylvania, 1948. Pp. 256. Mic A50-217. *Mcf Ab*, X (1950), 163. Publ. No. 1731.
A5444 Ing, C. M. *Metrical Theory and Practice in the Elizabethan Lyric*. DD, Oxford, Lady Margaret Hall, 1949.

A5445 Meyerstein, E. H. W. "You Might Have Rimed." *ES 1949*, English Association, NS, II (1949), 64-74.

A5446 Eliot, T. S. "Shakespeares Verskunst." *Der Monat*, XX (May, 1950), 198-207.

A5447 Pasternak, Boris. "Shakespeare's Imagery and Rythm." Tr. by Peter Meadows. *Arena*, I (1950), 33-37.

A5448 Pettet, E. C. "Shakespeare's Conception of Poetry." *Essays and Studies*, III (1950), 29-46.

A5449 Sitwell, Edith. *A Poet's Notebook*. Boston, 1950. "Notes on Shak.," pp. 104-147.
       Rev: B4970.

A5450 Cancelled.

A5451 Ing, Catherine. *Elizabethan Lyrics: A Study in the Development of English Metres and Their Relation to Poetic Effect*. London: Chatto and Windus, 1951. Pp. 252.
       Rev: *NstN*, XLIII (1952), 135; *TLS*, May 9, p. 314; by F. W. Sternfeld, *SQ*, IV (1953), 79-83; by H. Heuer, *SJ*, 89 (1953), 239-240; by M. Poirier, *EA*, VII (1954), 155-156.

A5452 Flatter, Richard. " 'The True Originall Copies' Shakespeare's Plays—Outline of a New Conception." *Proc. Leeds Philos. and Lit. Soc.*, Lit. & Hist. Sec. VII, Pt. 1 (1952), 31-42.

A5453 Guzzo, Augusto. "Prosa nei Drammi di Shakespeare." *Paragone*, Florence, III (July-Aug. 1952).

A5454 Baldini, Gabriele. "Mellifluous Shakespeare." *Engl. Miscellany*, IV (1953), 67-94.

A5455 Maxwell, J. C. "Vergilian Half-Lines in Shakespeare's 'Heroic Narrative'." *N &Q*, 198 (1953), 100.

A5456 Munday, Mildred B. *The Influence of Shakespeare's Predecessors on His Early Blank Verse*. DD, University of Wisconsin, 1953. Abstr. publ. in *Summaries of Doctoral Dissertations, 1952-53*, Vol. 14, Madison: Univ. of Wisconsin Press, 1954, pp. 437-438. Also in *ShN*, VI, 2.

A5457 Viswanathan, K. "Shakespeare's Poetics." *English Studies*, Andhra Univ. (Waltair), Nov. 1953.

A5458 Finkenstaedt, Thomas. "Zur Methodik der Versuntersuchung bei Shakespeare." *SJ*, 90 (1954), 82-107.

A5459 Halliday, F. E. *The Poetry of Shakespeare's Plays*. London: Duckworth, 1954. Pp. 196.
       Rev: *TLS*, July 2, 1954, p. 424 (see letter by F. R. Leavis, *TLS*, July 9, p. 441, and reply by reviewer *TLS*, July 16, p. 457); by Thom Gunn, *Spectator*, July 2, pp. 32-33; *Dublin Magazine*, July-Sept., pp. 60-61; by M. W., *John o' London's Weekly*, LXIII, 457; by J. Vallette, *MdF*, 321 (1954), 729-730; *Reviewer*, July 16, p. 457; by Alice Griffin, *TAr*, XXXIX (1955), 7-8; by A. C. Partridge, *SQ*, VI, 343-345; by William T. Hastings, *SQ*, VI, 111; by J. B. Fort, *EA*, X (1957), 444-445.

A5460 Hart, Walter Morris. "Shakespeare's Use of Verse and Prose." *Five Gayley Lectures, 1947-1954*, Berkeley and Los Angeles: Univ. of California Press, 1954, pp. 1-17.

A5461 Willcock, Gladys D. *Language and Poetry in Shakespeare's Early Plays*. Annual Shakespeare Lecture of the British Academy, 1954. London: Geoffrey Cumberlege, 1955. *Proceedings of the British Academy*, XL (1954), 103-117.
       Rev: A5604.

A5462 Finkenstaedt, Thomas. *Die Verskunst des Jungen Shakespeare: "Richard III," "Richard II," "King John."* DD, Munich, 1955. Pp. x, 155. Typewritten.

A5463 Simpson, Percy. *Studies in Elizabethan Drama*. Oxford: Clarendon Press, 1955.
       Chapter II, "Shakespeare's Versification: A Study of Development," pp. 64-88.
       Rev: B4492.

A5464 Granville-Barker, Harley. *On Dramatic Method*. New York: Hill and Wang, 1956.
       Chapter III, "Shakespeare's Progress," pp. 68-116.

c. PROSODY OF SHAKESPEARE'S CONTEMPORARIES (91;31)
(See also sections upon Shak.'s contemporaries e.g. A4912-A5021.)

A5465 Bakeless, John. *Christopher Marlowe: The Man in His Time*. New York: Morrow, 1937. Pp. viii, 404.
       Rev: A4987.

A5466 Poirier, Michel. *Sir Philip Sydney, Chevalier, Poète et Puritain*. Thèse de lettres. Paris, 1944.

A5466a Poirier, Michel. *Sir Philip Sydney and English Quantitative Verse*. Thèse de lettres complémentaires. Paris, 1944.

A5467 Vančura, Z. "K Metodě Renesanční Poesie." (The Method of Renaissance Poetry.) *Český Časopis Filologický*, III (1944), 12-15; ibid., III, 190-201.

A5468 Eichhorn, Traudl. *Prosa und Vers im Vorshakespeareschen Drama. Ein Beitrag zum Formproblem des Englischen Renaissancedramas*. DD, Munich, 1949. Pp. iii, 173. Typewritten. See also *SJ*, 84/86 (1950), 140-198.

A5469 Moloney, Michael F. "Donne's Metrical Practice." *PMLA*, LXV (1950), 232-239.
       Donne's metrical "revolution" was achieved by the "unrevolutionary means" utilized also, e.g., by Milton and Shakespeare.

A5470 Peltz, Catharine W. "Thomas Campion, An Elizabethan Neo-Classicist." *MLQ*, XI (1950), 3-6.

A5471 Ringler, William. "Master Drant's Rules." *PQ*, xxix (1950), 70-74.

A5472 Swallow, Alan. "The Pentameter Line in Skelton and Wyatt." *MP*, xlviii (1950), 1-11.

A5473 Oras, Ants. "Surrey's Technique of Phonetic Echoes: A Method and Its Background." *JEGP*, l (1951), 289-308.

A5474 Thompson, John. *The Iambic Line from Wyatt to Sidney.* DD, Columbia University, 1958. Pp. 260. Mic 58-4692. *DA*, xviii (1958), 1040. Publ. No. 25,156.

3. SHAKESPEARE'S LITERARY STYLE (92;31)
a. RENAISSANCE, MANNERIST, AND BAROQUE
(1) DEFINITIONS AND GENERAL DISCUSSIONS

A5475 Meissner, Paul. *Die Geistesgeschichtlichen Grundlagen des Englischen Literaturbarocks.* Munich, 1934.
Rev: by Johannes Speck, *Archiv*, 169 (1936), 100-103; by Eduard Eckhardt, *Eng. Studn.*, lxx, 402-405; by Ben. Rosenberg, *PQ*, xv, 301-306; A5479 below; by Hermann Heuer, *Lbl*, lviii (1937), 103-104.

A5476 Rosenberg, Benjamin B. *The Changing Concepts of the Literary Baroque in the Criticism of the Twentieth Century.* DD, Johns Hopkins University, 1935.

A5477 Read, Herbert Edward. "Obscurity in Poetry," and "Parallels in English Painting and Poetry." *In Defence of Shelley*, London, 1936, pp. 147-163; 225-248.

A5478 Schaller, Heinrich. *Die Welt des Barock.* Munich: Reinhardt, 1936. Pp. 77.
Rev: by B. B. Rosenberg, *MLN*, liii (1938), 225-226.

A5479 Woesler, Richard. "Über Englisches Literaturbarock." *Literaturwiss. Jahrbuch der Görresgesellschaft*, viii (1936), 139-150.

A5480 Isaacs, J. "Baroque and Rococo: A History of Two Concepts." *Bull. of the International Committee of Hist. Sciences*, ix (1937), 347-348.

A5481 Mathew, David. *The Jacobean Age.* London: Longmans, 1938. Pp. 354.
Rev: by A. L. Rowse, *Spectator*, Nov. 18, 1938; pp. 16, 18; by E. V. Cardinal, *Catholic Hist. Rev.*, xxv (1939), 203-204; by C. E. Byles, *Illustrated London News*, Feb. 25, p. 308; by H. M. Smith, *Church Quar. Rev.*, 128 (1939), 160-161; *ConR*, 155 (1939), 126; by J. Loiseau, *EA*, iii, 148-149; *National Rev.*, 152 (1939), 270; by Godfrey Davies, *EHR*, lv (1940), 313-314; by J. Isaacs, *Nineteenth Century*, 125 (1940), 722-727; by Gladys Scott Thomson, *History*, ns, xxiv, 344-346.

A5482 Hoffmann, H. *Hochrenaissance, Manierismus, Frühbarock: Die Italienische Kunst des 16. Jahrhunderts.* Zurich: Leemann, 1939. Pp. 187.

A5483 Heywood, Terence. "Some Notes on English Baroque." *Horizon*, ii (1940), 267-70.

A5484 Lewis, John Colby. *A Correlation of the Theatre with the Graphic Arts, According to the Dominant Artistic Theories of Several Times, from the Middle Ages to the Present Day.* DD, Cornell University, 1940. Abstr. publ. in *Abstracts of Theses, 1940*, Ithaca, 1941.

A5485 Steiner, Arpad. "A Mirror for Scholars of the Baroque." *JHI*, i (1940), 320-334.

A5486 Kindermann, Heinz. *Kampf um die dts. Lebensform. Reden und Aufsätze über die Dichtung im Aufbau der Nation.* Vienna: Wiener Vlg.-Ges., 1941. Pp. 461.

A5487 Wellek, René. "The Parallelism Between Literature and the Arts." *English Institute Annual 1941*, Columbia Univ. Press, 1942, pp. 29-63.

A5488 Pope-Hennessy, John. "Nicholas Hilliard and Mannerist Art Theory." *JWCI*, vi (1944), 89-100.

A5489 Daniells, Roy. "Baroque Form in English Literature." *UTQ*, xiv (1945), 393-408.

A5490 Mayor, A. Hyatt. "The Art of the Counter-Reformation." *Metropolitan Museum Art Bull.*, iv (1945), 101-105.

A5491 Daniells, Roy. "English Baroque and Deliberate Obscurity." *JAAC*, v (1946), 115-121.

A5492 Hassold, Ernest C. "The Baroque as a Basic Concept of Art." *College Art Jour.*, vi (1946), 3-28.

A5493 Wellek, René. "The Concept of Baroque in Literary Scholarship." *JAAC*, v (1946), 77-109.

A5494 Chew, Samuel C. *The Virtues Reconciled: An Iconographic Study.* Univ. Toronto Press, 1947. Pp. xi, 163; pl. 18.
Rev: by H. P. G., *QQ*, lv (1948), 224-225; by B. M., *Dalhousie Rev.*, xxviii, 191; by M. M. Ross, *UTQ*, xviii, 106-110; by W. S. Heckscher, *Art Bull.*, xxxi (1949), 65-68.

A5495 Friederich, W. P. "Late Renaissance, Baroque or Counter-Reformation?" *JEGP*, xlvi (1947), 132-143.

A5496 Mincoff, Marco. *Baroque Literature in England.* Sofia Univ. Press, 1947. Pp. 71.
Rev: by G. Kitchin, *MLR*, xliv (1949), 106-107; by C. Leech, *RES*, xxv, 74-75; by K. de Wit, *ES*, xxxiii (1952), 267-269.

A5497 Clercx, Suzanne. *Le Baroque et la Musique: Essai d'Esthétique Musicale.* Brussels: Ed. de la Librairie Encyclopédique, 1948. Pp. 235.
Rev: by Fernand Desonay, "Baroques et Baroquisme," *BHR*, xi (1949), 248-259.

A5498 Hatzfeld, Helmut. "A Clarification of the Baroque Problem in the Romance Literatures." *CL*, i (1949), 113-139.

A5499   Dédéyan, Charles. "Position Littéraire du Baroque." *L'Information Litt.*, II (1950), 127-135.

A5500   Groult, P. "Le Problème du Baroque." *Lettres Romances*, IV (1950), 241-242.

A5501   Schirmer, Walter F. *Kleine Schriften.* Tübingen: Max Niemeyer Verlag, 1950. Pp. 200.
Includes essays on "Chaucer, Shakespeare und die Antike," "Shakespeare und die Rhetorik,"
and "Über das Historiendrama in der Englischen Renaissance," and "Die Geistesgeschichtlichen Grundlagen der Englischen Barockliteratur."

A5502   Wilkinson, L. P. "The Baroque Spirit in Ancient Art and Literature." *Essays by Divers Hands*,
XXV (1950), 1-11.

A5503   Carter, William H., Jr. *Ut Pictura Poesis: A Study of the Parallel Between Painting and Poetry
from Classical Times Through the Seventeenth Century.* DD, Harvard University, 1951.

A5504   Hauser, Arnold. *The Social History of Art.* 2 vols. New York: Alfred A. Knopf, 1951.
Pp. xxi, 500; ix, 501-1022.
Calls Shak.'s language Mannerist, pp. 422-423.

A5505   Oppenheimer, Max, Jr. "Tendencies and Bias in Baroque Literary Studies." *MLJ*, XXXV
(1951), 258-262.

A5506   Friedrich, Carl Joachim. *The Age of the Baroque: 1610-1660.* Rise of Modern Europe Series,
v. New York: Harper; London: Hamish Hamilton; Toronto: Musson, 1952. Pp. xv, 367.
Rev: by Geoffrey Bruun, *NYHTBR*, Apr. 20, 1952, p. 7; by Leo Gershoy, *SatR*, Apr. 19,
pp. 51-52; by Margaret A. Judson, *JMH*, XXV (1953), 297-298; by Roland G. Visher, *AHR*,
LVIII, 348-349; by U. Scheuner, *Das Historisch-politische Buch*, I, 173-174; by P. Coles, *British
Jour. Sociology*, IV, 94.

A5507   Turnell, Martin. "Baroque Art and Poetry." *Commonweal*, May 16, 1952, pp. 146-149.

A5508   Béguin, Albert. "Du Baroque en Littérature." *Esprit*, Feb., 1954, pp. 282-288.

A5509   De Mourgues, Odette. *Metaphysical, Baroque and Précieux Poetry.* Oxford Univ. Press, 1954.
Pp. viii, 184.
Rev: by Charles S. Holmes, *SR*, LXII (1954), 705-710; by Mario Praz, *CL*, VI, 357-360; by
Michel Poirier, *EA*, VII, 415-416; by A. M. Boase, *Fr. Studies*, VIII, 265-268; by Pierre Kohler,
RLC, XXVIII, 492-496; by Philip A. Wadsworth, *RR*, XLV, 203-207; by A. J. Steele, *MLR*,
L (1955), 211-212.

A5510   Hatzfeld, Helmut. "The Baroque from the View Point of the Literary Historian." *JAAC*,
XIV (1955), 156-164.

A5511   Martin, John Rupert. "The Baroque from the Point of View of the Art Historian." *JAAC*,
XIV (1955), 164-171.

A5512   Stechow, Wolfgang. "The Baroque." *JAAC*, XIV (1955), 171-173.

A5513   Stamm, Rudolf, ed. *Die Kunstformen des Barockzeitalters.* Sammlung Dalp, Vol. 82. Berne:
Francke, 1956. Pp. 467.
Rev: by Karl Brunner, *SQ*, VIII (1957), 231-233; *JEGP*, LVI, 91-92; by E. Th. Sehrt, *SJ*, 94
(1958), 302-305.

A5514   Sypher, Wylie. *Four Stages of Renaissance Style.* New York: Doubleday Anchor Books, 1956.
Pp. 312.
Rev: by Wallace K. Ferguson, *NYTBR*, June 19, 1955, p. 3; by Klaus Berger, *RN*, VIII,
147-149; by Creighton Gilbert, *JAAC*, XIV (1956), 394-395; by Sidney Warhaft, *QQ*, LXIV
(1957), 155.

A5515   Cioranescu, Alejandro. *El Barroco. El Descubrimiento del Drama.* Universidad de La Laguna,
1957. Pp. 445.
Rev: by H. Hatzfeld, *CL*, X (1958), 179-181; by Cecilia Rizza, *Studi Francesi*, II, 98-100.

A5516   Colombier, Pierre du. "Conquêtes et Itinéraires du Baroque." *Revue de Paris*, March, 1957.

A5517   Elwert, W. T. "Le Varietà Nazionali della Poesia Barocca." *Convivium*, No. 6 (1957), 670-679;
No. 1 (1958), 27-42.

A5518   Maddison, Carol Hopkins. *Apollo and the Nine: The Renaissance-Baroque Ode in Italy, France,
and England.* DD, Johns Hopkins University, 1957.

A5519   Miller, Gustavus Hindman. *A Comparison of Late Renaissance and Early Baroque Aesthetics as
Seen Through Two Dramatic Interpretations of the Inés de Castro Story.* DD, University of
Michigan, 1957. Pp. 149. Mic 57-231. *DA*, XVII (1957), 144. Publ. No. 18,630.

A5520   Perella, Nicolas James. *The Pastor Fido and Baroque Sensibility.* DD, Harvard University, 1957.

A5521   Sayce, R. A. "The Use of the Term Baroque in French Literary History." *CL*, X (1958),
246-253.

A5522   Cancelled.

A5523   Neumann, Alfred R., David Erdman, Calvin S. Brown, et al. *Literature and the Other Arts:
A Select Bibliography, 1952-1958.* New York: New York Public Library, 1959. Pp. 39.

(2) SHAKESPEARE

A5524   Albrecht, J. "O Problému Baroknosti v Shakespearově Díle Dramatickém." *Časopis pro
Moderní Filologii*, (Prague), XXIII (1937), 33-43, 152-163, 254-260, 390-400.
The problem of baroque features in Shak.'s dramatic work. English summary.

A5525 Deutschbein, Max. *Shakespeares "Macbeth" als Drama des Barock.* Leipzig: Quelle and Meyer, 1936. Pp. 130.
Rev: LZ, 87 (1936), 359; by P. Meissner, *SJ*, LXXII, 163-166; by H. Pongs, *DuV*, XXXVII, 387; by Jos. Sprengler, *DL*, XXXVIII, 588; by Johannes Speck, *Archiv*, 171 (1937), 227-229; by Hermann Heuer, *Beiblatt*, XLVIII, 100-105; by Joh. Gg. Sprengel, *DDHS*, IV, 35-36; by A. Potthoff, *NS*, XLV, 97; by W. Keller, *ZNU*, XXXVII (1938), 330-332; by Ernst Weigelin, *DDHS*, VI (1939), 37; by P. P. Kies, *MLN*, LVI (1941), 385-387.

A5526 Cherix, Pierre. "L'Evolution de la Pensée de Shakespeare; la Thèse de Max Deutschbein." *Etudes de Lettres*, XXIII (1950), 16-27.

A5527 Boerner, O. "Shakespeare und der Barock." *German.-roman. Mscher.*, XXV (1937), 363-381.

A5528 Schücking, Levin L. *The Baroque Character of the Elizabethan Tragic Hero.* Annual Shakespeare Lecture of the British Academy. *Pro. British Academy*, XXIV. Oxford Univ. Press, 1938. Pp. 29. Also appeared as "Der Barocke Charakter des Tragischen Helden in Elisabethanischen Drama." *Essays über Shakespeare, Pepys, Rossetti, Shaw und Anderes.* Wiesbaden: Dietrich, 1948, pp. 274-312.
Rev: by Wolfgang Keller, *SJ*, LXXV (1939), 152; by T. W. Baldwin, *MLN*, LV (1940), 459-460.

A5529 Niederstenbruch, Alex. "Kunstgeschichtliche Parallelen im Neusprachlichen Unterricht." *DDHS*, VI (1939), 431-438.

A5530 Frank, J. *Shakespeare, Galilei, Rubens.* Schicksale und Epochen. Stuttgart: Franckh, 1941. Pp. 213.

A5531 Smirnov, A. *Shekspir. Renessans i Barokko (k Voprosu o Prirode i Razvitii Shekspirovskogo Gumanizma).* Vestnik Leningradskogo Universiteta, 1946, No. 1, pp. 96-112. *Shakespeare: Renaissance and Baroque (On the Question of the Nature and Development of Shakespeare's Humanism.)*

A5532 Giusso, Lorenzo. "Barocco. Bruno e Shakespeare." *Il Giornale di Sicilia*, June 1, 1948.

A5533 Kerl, Wilhelm. *Fortuna und Natura in Ihrem Verhältnis zum Menschen in Shakespeares Barockdramen.* DD, Marburg, 1949. Pp. 187. Typewritten.

A5534 Kleinschmidt von Lengefeld, W. F. "Shakespeare und die Kunstepochen des Barock und des Manierismus." *SJ*, 82/83 (1948), 88-98.

A5535 Kleinschmidt von Lengefeld, W. F. "Ist Shakespeares Stil Barock? Bemerkungen zur Sprache Shakespeares und Drydens." *Shakespeare-Studien, Festschrift für Heinrich Mutschmann*, pp. 88-106.

A5536 Pellegrini, Giuliano. *Barocco Inglese.* Messina-Florence: Casa Editrice G. D'Anna, 1953. Pp. 245. Includes "Shakespeare e gli Studi sul Barocco Inglese."
Rev: by J. L. Lievsay, *MLN*, LXX (1955), 211-213.

A5537 Lindheim, Bogislav von. "Syntaktische Funktionsverschiebung als Mittel des Barocken Stils bei Shakespeare." *SJ*, 90 (1954), 229-251.

A5538 Swanston, Hamish F. G. "The Baroque Element in *Troilus and Cressida*." *DUJ*, NS, XIX (1957), 14-123.

(3) OTHERS

A5539 Kortemme, Josef. *Das Verhältnis John Donnes zur Scholastik und zum Barock. Eine Untersuchung zu den Anfängen des Englischen Barock.* DD, Münster, 1933. Pp. 85.

A5540 Koszul, A. "Beaumont et Fletcher et le Baroque." *Le Théâtre Elizabéthain.* Paris: Les Cahiers du Sud, 1940, pp. 272-280.

A5541 Cancelled.

A5542 McCalmon, George. *A Study of Some of the Renaissance and Baroque Factors in the Theatre Style of Inigo Jones.* DD, Western Reserve University, 1946.

A5543 Bottrall, Margaret. "The Baroque Element in Milton." *English Miscellany: A Symposium of History, Literature and the Arts*, ed. by Mario Praz, Ronald Bottrall, Edwin Muir. Vol. I. Rome: Edizioni di Storia e Letteratura, 1950, pp. 31-42.

A5544 Nelson, Lowry, Jr. "Góngora and Milton: Towards a Definition of the Baroque." *CL*, VI (1954), 53-63.

A5545 Praz, Mario. *La Poesia Metafisica Inglese del Seicento: John Donne.* Rome, 1945.
Rev: by Fr. A. Pompen, O. F. M., *ES*, XXVIII (1947), 50-52.

A5546 Barish, Jonas A. "Baroque Prose in the Theater: Ben Jonson." *PMLA*, LXXIII (1958), 184-195.

b. LINGUISTIC ASPECTS

A5547 David, Richard. *The Janus of Poets: Being an Essay on the Dramatic Value of Shakespeare's Poetry, Both Good and Bad.* Cambridge Univ. Press, 1935.
Rev: A5905.

A5548 Cunningham, Cornelius C. *Persuasive Factors in Shakespearean Address.* DD, State University of Iowa, 1936. Abstr. publ. in Univ. of Iowa *Programs Announcing Candidates for Higher Degrees* . . . , no pagination.

A5549 Garrett, J. "Drama and the Poet's Tongue." *Nineteenth Century*, 119 (1936), 350-360.

A5550   Roberts, Donald R. *Shakespeare and the Rhetoric of Stylistic Ornamentation.* DD, Cornell University, 1936.

A5551   Trench, W. F. "Shakespeare's Unfinished Sentences." *TLS*, Apr. 4, 1936, p. 300.

A5552   "Elizabethan Decoration: Patterns in Art and Passion." *TLS*, July 3, 1937, pp. 485-486.

A5553   Berkelman, Robert G. "Shakespeare: Ventriloquist." *SR*, XLVI (1938), 353-364.

A5554   Draper, John W. "King James and Shakespeare's Literary Style." *Archiv*, 171 (1937), 36-48.

A5555   Franz, Wilhelm. "Zur Sprachkunst Shakespeares." *Anglia*, LXII (1938), 347-355.

A5556   Messiaen, Pierre. "Préciosité de Shakespeare." *Revue de l'Enseignement des Langues Vivantes*, LV (1938), 289-296.

A5557   Elton, Oliver. *Style in Shakespeare.* Brit. Acad. Shakespeare Lecture. Oxford Univ. Press, 1936. Pp. 29. Repr. in *Essays and Addresses.* London: Arnold, 1939. Pp. 275.
    Rev: by C. J. Sisson, *MLR*, XXXII (1937), 137; by Wolfgang Schmidt, *Beiblatt*, XLIX (1938), 113-114; by J. Dover Wilson, *MLR*, XXXV (1940), 532-533; by Gwyn Jones, *Life and Letters Today*, XXIV, 89-90; by George Cookson, *English*, III, 32-34.

A5558   Lewis, C. S. *Rehabilitations and Other Essays.* Oxford Univ. Press, 1939. Pp. viii, 197.
    Rev: by J. B. Leishman, *RES*, XVI (1940), 109-113.

A5559   Förster, Max. "The Psychological Basis of Literary Periods." *Studies for William A. Read*, pp. 254-268.

A5560   Morozov, M. M. "Shakespeare's Language and Style." *History of English Realism.* A Symposium, Moscow, 1941, pp. 5-56.

A5561   Morozov, M. M. "Shakespeare's Stylistic Peculiarities." *Literary Heritage* (USSR), IV (1941), 172-178.

A5562   Thaler, Alwin. "Shakespeare on Style, Imagination, and Poetry." *PMLA*, LIII (1938), 1019-36. Republished in Thaler's *Shakespeare and Democracy.* Univ. Tennessee Press, 1941. Pp. xii, 312.
    Rev: A1809.

A5563   Wade, James Edgar. *Medieval Rhetoric in Shakespeare.* DD, St. Louis University, 1942. Pp. 185. Mic A44-671. *Mcf Ab*, V (1944), 72. Publ. No. 613.

A5564   Willcock, Gladys D. "Shakespeare and Rhetoric." *Essays and Studies*, XXIX (1943), 50-61.

A5565   Earp, F. R. "Change of Style in Shakespeare." *The Style of Sophocles*, Cambridge, 1944, pp. 159-177.

A5566   Brooks, Cleanth. "Shakespeare as a Symbolist Poet." *YR*, XXXIV (1945), 642-665.
See Nicholas Bravo Bockmeyer's summary, "Shakespeare como poeta simbolista," *Rev. Cubana*, XIX (1945), 140-142.

A5567   Orsini, N. "La Lingua Poetica Inglese: Note Storiche." *Anglica*, I (1946), 139-148, 193-203, 241-252.

A5568   Stein, Arnold. "Donne's Obscurity and the Elizabethan Tradition." *ELH*, XIII (1946), 98-118.

A5569   Huchon, R. "Le Style de Shakespeare." *LanM*, XLI (1947), 241-263.

A5570   Miriam Joseph, Sister, C. S. C. *Shakespeare's Use of the Arts of Language.* Columbia Univ. Studies in Eng. and Comp. Lit., No. 165. Columbia Univ, Press, 1947. Pp. xii, 423.
    Rev: by Mark Van Doren, *NYHTBR*, July 4, 1948, p. 6; by M. T. Herrick, *JEGP*, XLVII, 423-424; by M. Livingston, *Catholic World*, 167 (1948), 573; by W. M. T. Nowottny, *MLR*, XLIV (1949), 560-561; by I. A. Richards, *KR*, XI, 17-30; by T. W. Baldwin, *MLN*, LXIV, 120-122; by Gladys D. Willcock, *RES*, XXV, 269-271; by F. R. Johnson, *QJS*, XXXV, 94; by Ewing S. Blaine, *SAB*, XXIV, 223-228; by W. Clemen, *Archiv*, 188 (1951), 147-149

A5571   Mackerness, E. D. "A Note on Thomas Nashe and 'Style'." *English*, VI (1947), 198-200.

A5572   Fluchère, Henri. *Shakespeare: Dramaturge Elizabéthain.* Marseille: Cahiers du Sud, 1948. Pp. 400. Tr. as *Shakespeare.* London: Longmans Green, 1953. Pp. x, 272. Style, pp. 151-185 in Engl. edition.
    Rev: A8187.

A5573   Sackton, A. H. *Rhetoric as a Dramatic Language in Ben Jonson.* Columbia Univ. Press, 1948. Contrasts with Jonson, pp. 124ff.
    Rev: by Marcia L. Anderson, *South Atlantic Quar.*, XLVIII (1949), 156; by Sr. Miriam Joseph, *JEGP*, XLVIII, 409-411; by D. C. Bryant, *QJS*, XXXV, 94-95; by R. G. Cox, *Scrutiny*, XVI, 71-74; by C. T. Harrison, *SR*, LVII, 709-714; by J. Gerritsen, *ES*, XXXI (1950), 223-224; by A. K. McIlwraith, *RES*, NS, I, 167-168; by Ernest William Talbert, *MLQ*, XII (1951), 110-111.

A5574   Chang, Hsin-Chang. *Early Elizabethan Dramatic Style with Particular Regard to the Works of George Peele.* DD, Edinburgh, 1949.

A5575   Draper, John W. "Patterns of Style in *Romeo and Juliet.*" *SN*, XXI (1949), 195-210.

A5576   Mayhall, Jane. "Shakespeare and Spenser: A Commentary on Differences." *MLQ*, X (1949), 356-363.

A5577   Partridge, A. C. *The Problem of "Henry VIII" Re-opened.* Cambridge: Bowes & Bowes, 1949. Pp. 35.
    Rev: B9885.

A5578 Schiller, Andrew. "Shakespeare's Amazing Words." *KR*, XI (1950), 43-49.
       Comment by Allan Gilbert, ibid., pp. 484-488.

A5579 Fort, J. B. "Quelques Problèmes Shakespeariens: l'Homme, le Texte, la 'Sagesse Pourpre'." *LanM*, XLIV (1950), 414-417.

A5580 De Giorgi, C. B. Elsa. *Shakespeare e L'Attore*. Milan: Tipografia Industrie Grafichi Italiane Stucchi, 1950. Pp. 26.
       A refutation of the theory expressed by Valentina Capocci in her book *Genio e Mestiere* that Shak. wrote only the verse passages in the plays, with the actors writing the prose.

A5581 Goldsmith, Ulrich K. "Words Out of a Hat? Alliteration and Assonance in Shakespeare's Sonnets." *JEGP*, XLIX (1950), 33-48.

A5582 Leech, Clifford. *Shakespeare's Tragedies: And Other Studies in Seventeenth-Century Drama.* London: Chatto and Windus, 1950. Pp. viii, 232.
       Rev: B4967.

A5583 Schirmer, Walter Franz. "Shakespeare und die Rhetorik." *Kleine Schriften.* Tübingen: Niemeyer, 1950, pp. 83-108.

A5584 Berkelman, Robert. "The Quintessence of Shakespeare." *South Atlantic Quar.*, L (1951), 233-238.
       Concludes that Shak.'s "ultimate stylistic achievements arise more from dramatization of emotion and character than from the crystallization of thought."

A5585 Burris, Quincy Guy. " 'Soft! Here Follows Prose'—*Twelfth Night* II. v. 154." *SQ*, II (1951), 233-239.
       Finds no consistency or design in Shak.'s choice of rhyme, blank verse, or prose.

A5586 Schmidt-Hidding, Wolfgang. "Shakespeares Stilkritik in den Sonetten." *Shakespeare-Studien, Festschrift für Heinrich Mutschmann*, pp. 119-126.

A5587 Wilson, F. P. *Marlowe and the Early Shakespeare.* Clark Lectures, Trinity College, Cambridge, 1951. Oxford: Clarendon Press, 1953. Pp. 144.
       Rev: A4996.

A5588 Evans, B. Ifor. *The Language of Shakespeare's Plays.* London: Methuen, 1952. Pp. 190.
       Rev: *TLS*, Mar. 21, 1952, p. 206 (see letters, *TLS*, 1952, by Mr. Evans and Dora E. Yates, Apr. 4, p. 237, by W. W. Greg, Apr. 25, p. 281; by E. P. Kuhl, May 9, p. 313); by E. G., *National & Eng. Rev.*, 138 (1952), 186-187; *NstN*, Feb. 23, pp. 225-226; by Allardyce Nicoll, *Adelphi*, XXVIII, 727-729; by H. B. Charlton, *MGW*, Feb. 21, p. 10; by G. B. Harrison, *SatR*, June 14, pp. 28-29; by Henry Popkin, *NR*, July 14, p. 23; by F. S. Boas, *FortnR*, 1024 (April), 283-284; by D. Hewlett, *Aryan Path*, XXIII, 328; M. J. C. Grierson, *ConR*, LXXIV, 220-223; by Hubert Heffner, *QJS*, XXXVIII, 476-477; by Ivor Brown, *Obs.*, Apr. 20, p. 7; *Listener*, XLVIII, 313, 315; by B. Ifor Evans, ibid., XLVIII, 387; by Peter Alexander, *John O'London's*, Mar. 28, pp. 322-323; by M. C. Bradbrook, *ShS*, VI (1953), 151; by Michel Poirier, *EA*, VI, 257-258; by D. S. Bland, *CamJ*, VI, 497-499; by Hermann Heuer, *SJ*, 89 (1953), 238-239; by James Southall Wilson, *SQ*, IV, 190-192.

A5589 Guzzo, Augusto. "Prosa nei Drammi di Shakespeare." *Paragone* (Florence), III, July,Aug., 1952.
       Supports the theory put forth by Valentina Capocci in *Genio e Mestiere* that Shak. wrote only the verse passages in the plays, with the actors supplying the prose.

A5590 Krook, D. *Language Consciousness in the Seventeenth Century in England.* DD, Cambridge, 1952.

A5591 McAvoy, William Charles. *Shakespeare's Use of the Laus of Apthonius.* DD, University of Illinois, 1952. Pp. 225. Mic A53-237. *DA*, XIII (1953), 97. Publ. No. 4464.

A5592 Ellis-Fermor, Una. "Shakespeare and the Dramatic Mode." *Neophil*, XXXVII (1953), 104-112.

A5593 Rossky, William. *The Theory of Imagination in Elizabethan Literature: Psychology, Rhetoric and Poetic.* DD, New York University, 1953.

A5594 Bradbrook, M. C. "Fifty Years of the Criticism of Shakespeare's Style." *ShS*, VII (1954), 1-11.

A5595 Burrell, Margaret D. "*Macbeth*: A Study in Paradox." *SJ*, 90 (1954), 167-190.

A5596 Cruttwell, Patrick. *The Shakespearean Moment.* London, 1954.
       Rev: B5257.

A5597 Ellis-Fermor, Una. "Some Functions of Verbal Music in Drama." *SJ*, 90 (1954), 37-48.

A5598 Foakes, R. A. "Contrasts and Connections: Some Notes on Style in Shakespeare's Comedies and Tragedies." *SJ*, 90 (1954), 69-81.

A5599 Halliday, F. E. *The Poetry of Shakespeare's Plays.* London: Duckworth, 1954. Pp. 196.
       Rev: A5459.

A5600 Hill, R. F. *Shakespeare's Use of Formal Rhetoric in His Early Plays up to 1596.* B. Litt thesis, Oxford, 1954.

A5601 Knights, Lionel Charles. *Poetry, Politics and the English Tradition.* London: Chatto and Windus, 1954. Pp. 32.

A5602 Muir, Kenneth. "Shakespeare and Rhetoric." *SJ*, 90 (1954), 49-68.

A5603 Stamm, Rudolf. *Shakespeare's Word-Scenery.* With Some Remarks on Stage-History and the Interpretation of His Plays. Veröffentlichungen der Handels-Hochschule St. Gallen, Reihe B, Heft 10. Zurich and St. Gallen: Polygraphischer Verlag, 1954. Pp. 34.
       Rev: by Arthur Colby Sprague, *TN*, VIII (1954), 96; by Hermann Heuer, *SJ*, 90 (1954),

321-322; Z., *ES*, xxxv, 191; by Ernst Th. Sehrt, *Anglia*, LXXII (1954-55), 485-488; by J. B. Fort, *EA*, VIII (1955), 68-69.

A5604 Willcock, Gladys D. "Language and Poetry in Shakespeare's Early Plays." *Proceedings of the British Academy*, XL (1954), 103-117.
Annual Shak. Lecture read April 21, 1954.
Rev: by Harold S. Wilson, *SQ*, VIII (1957), 399; by Kenneth Muir, *RES*, NS, VIII, 347.

A5605 Gerstner-Hirzel, Arthur. "Stagecraft and Poetry." *SJ*, 90 (1955), 196-211.
Abstract of A5611.

A5606 Nosworthy, J. M. "The Integrity of Shakespeare: Illustrated from *Cymbeline*." *ShS*, VIII (1955), 52-56.

A5607 Flatter, Richard. " 'Sprachmelodie,' Konsonanten, Vokale und Sonstiges Werkzeug der Sprache." Flatter: *Triumph der Gnade. Shakespeare Essays*. Vienna and Munich: Kurt Desch, 1956, pp. 61-69.

A5608 Halio, Jay Leon. *Rhetorical Ambiguity as a Stylistic Device in Shakespeare's Problem Comedies*." DD, Yale University, 1956. 2 Vols. Pp. vi, 210; iv, 244. Abstr. publ. in *ShN*, VI (1956), 39.

A5609 Tschopp, Elisabeth. *Zur Verteilung von Vers und Prosa in Shakespeare*. DD, Zurich, 1956. Schweizer Anglistische Arbeiten, 41. Bern, 1956.
Rev: by H. Schnyder, *Archiv*, 195 (1958), 207-208.

A5610 Bennett, Paul E. "The Statistical Measurement of a Stylistic Trait in *Julius Caesar* and *As You Like It*." *SQ*, VIII (1957), 33-50.

A5611 Gerstner-Hirzel, A. *The Economy of Action and Word in Shakespeare's Plays*. DD, Basel, 1955. The Coopers Monographs on English and American Language and Literature, 2. Bern: Francke, 1957. Pp. 134. For abstract, see A5605.
Rev: by Philip Edwards, *MLR*, LIII (1958), 300-301; by Michel Poirier, *EA*, XI, 248-249; by Rudolf Stamm, *Archiv*, 195 (1958), 203-204.

A5612 Schanzer, Ernest. "Atavism and Anticipation in Shakespeare's Style." *EIC*, VII (1957), 242-256.
Proposes a flexible answer to the question of how "functional" in general are passages that seem stylistically too late or early for the play in which they occur.

A5612a Hunter, G. K., E. M. W. Tillyard, and R. A. Foakes. "The Critical Forum: Atavism and Anticipation in Shakespeare's Style." EIC, VII (1957), 450-457.
Commentaries on Ernest Schanzer's article A5612.

A5613 Trimpi, William Wesley, Jr. *The Classical Plain Style and Ben Jonson's Poems*. DD, Harvard University, 1957.

A5614 Donoghue, Denis. "Shakespeare's Rhetoric." *Studies: Irish Quarterly Review*, XLVII (1958), 431-440.

A5615 Kenner, Hugh. "Words in the Dark." *Essays by Divers Hands*, NS, XXIX (1958), 113-123.
Shak.'s influ. on poetic style in England to the twentieth century.

c. IMAGERY (93;31)
See also EMBLEMS, A5037-A5044
Studies of imagery in individual plays are listed in Language sections of the plays concerned. A few book-length studies of single plays are included here because of their general importance.

A5616 Kerl, Erich. *Das Hendiadyoin bei Shakespeare*. DD, Marburg, 1922. Pp. 80. Typewritten.

A5617 Sedgewick, G. G. *Of Irony, Especially in Drama*. University of Toronto Studies, No. 10. Univ. of Toronto Press, 1935. Pp. 150.

A5618 Sedgewick, G. G. *Of Irony, Especially in Drama*. Univ. of Toronto Press, 1948. Pp. 139. Second edition. Oxford Univ. Press, 1949. Pp. ix, 127.
Rev: by A. W., *Culture*, June, 1949; by B. M., *Dalhousie Rev.*, XXIX, 226; *TLS*, May 13, p. 308; by Clifford Leech, *RES*, NS, II (1951), 175-177.

A5619 Spurgeon, Caroline F. E. *Shakespeare's Imagery and What It Tells Us*. Cambridge Univ. Press, 1935. Pp. xvi, 408. Reissued, Cambridge Univ. Press, 1952. Reissued as Beacon Paperback, BP53. Boston: Beacon Press, 1958.
Rev: *QR*, 266 (1936), 170-171; by Mabel C. Livingston, *Catholic World*, 142 (1936), 758-759; by Émile Legouis, *RAA*, XIII, 338-340; by Mario Praz, *ES*, XVIII, 177-181; by Anne Bayard Dick, *SR*, XLIV, 249-252; by Theodora Bosanquet, *English*, I, 62-66; by William T. Hastings, *SAB*, XI, 131-141; by Morton Dauwen Zabel, *MP*, XXXIV, 78-83; by U. M. Ellis-Fermor, *MLR*, XXXI, 423-426; by Kathleen Tillotson, *RES*, XII, 458-461; by Tucker Brooke, *YR*, XXV, 632-633; by Wolfgang Keller, *SJ*, LXXII, 141-142; by G. N. Shuster, *Commonweal*, XXIII, 279; by E. C. Dunn, *Atlantic Monthly*, 157 (May, 1936), "Bookshelf"; by R. P. Blackmur, *NR*, 86 (1936), 52; by Paul Dottin, "La Littérature anglaise en 1935," *Rev. de France*, XVII, i (1937), 323-324; by Wolfgang Schmidt, *Beiblatt*, XLVIII, 107-116; by Robert Adger Law, *MLN*, LII, 526-530; by R. S. Knox, *UTQ*, VII (1938), 249-261; by E. E. Stoll, *SJ*, LXXIV, 63-66; by F. E. C. H., and W. S. M., *Ba*, XXV (1941), 213-228; by R. G. Cox, "Statistical Criticism," *The Importance of Scrutiny*, New York: Stewart, 1948, pp. 166-168 (Reprinted from *Scrutiny*, 1935); by J. Vallette, "Shakespeariana," *MdF*, 1078 (June, 1953), pp. 336-341; by James G. McManaway, *SQ*, VI (1955), 355.

A5620 Isaacs, J. "Shakespeare's Imagery." *TLS*, Sept. 12, 1936, p. 729. D. Whiter and C. Spurgeon.

A5621 Cancelled.

A5622 Hornstein, Lillian H. "Analysis of Imagery: A Critique of Literary Method." *PMLA*, LVII (1942), 638-653.
Criticizes Miss Spurgeon's method of studying poetical imagery, especially her assumptions regarding the images and the poet's experiences, predilections, etc.

A5623 Muraoka, I. "Some Problems of Miss Caroline Spurgeon's Method." *Annual Reports of the Faculty of Arts and Letters of Tohoku Univ.*, II (1951).

A5624 Gildersleeve, Virginia C. "Literary Expeditions." *Many a Good Crusade*. New York: Macmillan, 1954, pp. 230-246.
Reminiscences of Caroline Spurgeon's study of imagery.

A5625 Clemen, Wolfgang. *Shakespeares Bilder. Ihre Entwicklung und ihre Funktionen im dramatischen Werk*. DD, Bonn, 1936. Pp. iv, 56. *Bonner Studien zur englischen Philologie, XXVII*.

A5626 Clemen, Wolfgang. *Shakespeares Bilder, ihre Entwicklung und ihre Funktionen im dramatischen Werk*. Bonn: Peter Hanstein, 1936. Pp. viii, 339.
Rev: *TLS*, May 2, 1936, p. 384; by A. Brandl, *Archiv*, 169 (1936), 298; by Mario Praz, *ES*, XVIII, 177-181; by Karl Brunner, *Lbl*, LVII, 390-394; *LZ*, LXXXVII, 647, 839; by Wolfgang Keller, *SJ*, LXXII, 142-143; by Georges Connes, *RAA*, XIII, 514; by Albert Eichler, *Eng. Studn.*, LXXI, 251-254; by Jos. Sprengler, *DL*, XXXVIII, 588; by H. Pongs, *Dichtung und Volkstum*, XXXVII (1936), 387-388; by W. Meineke, *NS*, XLIV, 527-528; by Alfred Ehrentreich, *DLZ*, LVIII (1937), 1224-26; by Wolfgang Schmidt, *Beiblatt*, XLVIII, 107-116; by J. B. Leishman, *RES*, XIV (1938), 213-216; by W. Keller, *ZNU*, XL (1941), 140.

A5627 Clemen, W. H. *The Development of Shakespeare's Imagery*. Cambridge: Harvard University Press; London: Methuen, 1951. Pp. xii, 236.
A revision and expansion of the author's *Shakespeares Bilder* (1936). Contains a Preface by J. Dover Wilson.
Rev: by George Rylands, *Spectator*, August 10, 1951, p. 191; by H. B. Charlton, *MGW*, Sept. 6, p. 11; *TLS*, Sept. 7, p. 566; by J. I. M. Stewart, *NstN*, Sept. 22, pp. 319-320; by Derek Stanford, *ConR*, 180 (1951), 113-116; by Milton Crane, *SRL*, Oct. 20, pp. 12-13; by Kenneth Muir, *ES*, XXXII, 264-267; by R. A. Law, *SQ*, III, 85-86; by Sir Desmond MacCarthy, *Sunday Times*, Dec. 2, 1951, p. 3; by M. C. Bradbrook, *SQ*, III (1952), 125-126; by Sister Miriam Joseph, *JEGP*, LI, 419-422; by R. G. Cox, *Scrutiny*, XVIII, 238-241; by Allardyce Nicoll, *Adelphi*, XXVII, 727-729; by W. F. Schirmer, *Anglia*, LXXI, 112-113; by Lorentz Eckhoff, *Erasmus*, V, 33-36; by Michel Poirier, *EA*, V, 74-75; by Elkins C. Wilson, *RN*, V, 56; *Listener*, XLVII, 275, 277; by M. C. Bradbrook, *ShS*, VI, 150-151; by O. J. Campbell, *MLN*, LXVIII, 50-51; by Lilian Haddakin, *MLR*, XLVIII, 202-204; by Robert B. Heilman, *MLQ*, XV (1954), 183-184; by H. Heuer, *Archiv*, 190 (1954), 233.

A5628 "The Imagery of Shakespeare: Dr. Clemen and Walter Whiter." Leading article. *TLS*, Sept. 5, 1936, pp. 701-702.

A5629 Hastings, William T. "Shakespeare's Imagery." *SAB*, XI (1936), 131-141.

A5630 Ellis-Fermor, Una. *Some Recent Research in Shakespeare's Imagery*. Oxford Univ. Press, 1937. Pp. 39.
Rev: by Wolfgang Schmidt, *Beiblatt*, XLIX (1938), 110-113; by Wolfgang Clemen, *Eng. Studn.*, LXXIII (1939), 274-275.

A5631 Muir, Kenneth, and Sean O'Loughlin. *The Voyage to Illyria*. A New Study of Shakespeare. London: Methuen, 1937. Pp. 242.
Rev: A8307.

A5632 Cancelled.

A5633 Petsch, R. "Die dramatischen Figuren bei Shakespeare, Goethe, Kleist, u. a. Dramatikern." *Archiv*, 173 (1938), 12-23.

A5634 Taylor, Warren. *Tudor Figures of Rhetoric*. DD, University of Chicago, 1938. Lithoprinted by Univ. of Chicago Libraries, 1937, p. 59.

A5635 Chew, Samuel C. "Time and Fortune." *ELH*, VI (1939), 83-113.

A5636 Evans, Maurice. *The Language of the Elizabethan Drama*. DD, Cambridge. *Cam Abs.*, 1939-40, p. 52.

A5637 Pongs, Hermann. *Das Bild in der Dichtung*. II: *Voruntersuchungen zum Symbol*. Marburg: Elwert, 1939. Pp. viii, 632.
Rev: by Horst Oppel, *DLZ*, LXI (1940), 282-288.

A5638 Skinner, B. F. "The Alliteration in Shakespeare's Sonnets: A Study in Literary Behavior." *Psychological Record*, III (1939), 186-192.
Answered by E. E. Stoll, *MLN*, LV (1939), 388-390.

A5639 Potter, George Reuben. "A Protest Against the Term Conceit." *Renaissance Studies in Honor of Hardin Craig*, pp. 282-291; also *PQ*, XX (1941), 474-483.

A5640 Tillotson, Kathleen. "Windows in Shakespeare." *RES*, XVII (1941), 332-334.

A5641 Curtius, Ernst Robert. "Schrift- und Buchmetaphorik in der Weltliteratur." *DVLG*, XX (1942), 359-411.
Shak., pp. 397-403.

A5642   Fröhlich, Armin. "Zum bildlichen Ausdruck. III: Grundsätzliches." *N. Mon.*, XIII (1942), 217-227.
Shak., pp. 219-225.

A5643   Stamm, Rudolf. "Sir William Davenant and Shakespeare's Imagery." *Eng. Studn.*, LXXV (1942), 67-73.

A5644   Stephenson, A. A. "The Significance of *Cymbeline*." *Scrutiny*, X (1942), 329-338.

A5644a Leavis, F. R. "The Criticism of Shakespeare's Late Plays: A Caveat." *Scrutiny*, X (1942), 339-345.

A5645   Selz, William Aaron. *Conventional Imagery in Religious Verse of the English Renaissance*. DD, Harvard University, Abst. in *Summaries of Theses, 1943-45*, pp. 477-480.

A5646   Price, Hereward T. "Shakespeare's Imagery." *Michigan Alumnus Quar. Rev.*, L (1944), 207-220.

A5647   Armstrong, Edward A. *Shakespeare's Imagination*. London: Lindsay Drummond, 1946. Pp. 191.
Rev: *TLS*, Sept. 21, 1946, p. 452; by J. R. Sutherland, *RES*, XXIII (1947), 278-280; by R. S. Knox, *UTQ*, XVII, 101; by Roy Walker, *Life and Letters*, LIV, 168-174; by T. P. Harrison, Jr., *MLN*, LXIII (1948), 431-432; by Mario Praz, *ES*, XXIX, 53-58; by T. W. Baldwin, *JEGP*, XLVIII (1949), 404-405.

A5648   Hatto, A. T. "*Venus and Adonis*—and the Boar." *MLR*, XLI (1946), 353-361.

A5649   Ellis-Fermor, Una. *The Frontiers of Drama*. Oxford Univ. Press, 1947.
Rev: A5941.

A5650   Hornstein, Lillian Herlands. "Imagery and Biography: They Are Of the Imagination All Compact." *CE*, VIII (1947), 248-250.

A5651   Lewis, Cecil Day. *The Poetic Image*. The Clark Lectures, Cambridge, 1946. London: J. Cape; New York: Oxford Univ. Press, 1947. Pp. 157.

A5652   Arnheim, Rudolf. "Psychological Notes on the Poetical Process." *Poets at Work*, New York: Harcourt Brace, 1948. Pp. ix, 186.
Discussions of imagery in *H. V*, pp. 154-155, and in *Romeo*, pp. 156-158.

A5653   Curtius, E. R. "Das Buch als Symbol." *Europäische Literatur und lateinisches Mittelalter*, Bern: Francke, 1948. Shak., pp. 335-346.

A5654   Heilman, Robert B. *This Great Stage: Image and Structure in "King Lear."* Louisiana State Univ. Press, 1948. See particularly William R. Keast, "Imagery and Meaning in the Interpretation of *King Lear*," *MP*, XLVII (1949/50), 45-64.
Rev: B8892.

A5655   Johnson, Francis R. "Shakespearian Imagery and Senecan Imitation." *AMS*, pp. 33-53.

A5656   Rajan, Balachandra. "Similes and Metaphors in Shakespeare." *Paradise Lost and the Seventeenth Century Reader*, London, 1947, pp. 118-121.

A5657   Severs, Kenneth. "Imagery and Drama." *DUJ*, XLI (1948), 24-33.

A5658   Thompson, Alan Reynolds. *The Dry Mock: A Study of Irony in Drama*. Univ. Calif. Press, 1948. Pp. ix, 278.
Emphasizes post-Renaissance drama except for Shakespeare.
Rev: A6868.

A5659   Abend, Murray. " 'Ingratitude' and the 'Monster' Image." *N &Q*, 194 (1949), 535-536.

A5660   Atkinson, A. D. " 'Full Fathom Five'." *N &Q*, 194 (1949), 465-468, 493-495.

A5661   Beall, Chandler B. "A Quaint Conceit from Guarini to Dryden." *MLN*, LXIV (1949), 461-468. Concerns the use of *die* with sexual signification: examples mainly from English poetry in the Renaissance.

A5662   Downer, Alan S. "The Life of Our Design." *Hudson Review*, II (1949), 242-263.

A5663   Ellis-Fermor, Una. "Shakespeare and his World: The Poet's Imagery." *Listener*, XLII (July 28, 1949), 157-158.

A5664   Flasche, Hans. "Similitudo templi. Zur Geschichte einer Metapher." *DVLG*, XXIII (1949), 81-125.
Shak., pp. 100-101.

A5665   Morozov, Mikhail M. "The Individualization of Shakespeare's Characters through Imagery." *ShS*, II (1949), 83-106.

A5666   Walker, Roy. *The Time is Free: A Study of "Macbeth"*. London: Dakers, 1949. Pp. xvii, 234.
Rev: B9226.

A5667   Abend, Murray. "Two Unique Gender Forms in the Shakespeare Sonnets." *N &Q*, 195 (1950), 325.

A5668   Goldsmith, Ulrich K. "Words Out of a Hat? Alliteration and Assonance in Shakespeare's Sonnets." *JEGP*, XLIX (1950), 33-48.

A5669   Jackson, James L. "Shakespeare's Dog-and-Sugar Imagery and the Friendship Tradition." *SQ*, I (1950), 260-263.

A5670   Pasternak, Boris. "Shakespeare's Imagery and Rhythm." Tr. by Peter Meadows. *Arena*, I (1950), 33-37.

A5671   Poethen, Wilhelm. "Shakespeares Bildersprache im Unterricht." *Leb. Fremdspr.*, II (1950), 260-266.

A5672   Wormhoudt, Arthur. "The Unconscious Bird Symbol in Literature." *American Imago*, VII (1950), 35-39.

A5673   Atkinson, A. D. " 'The Poet's Eye'." *N &Q*, 196 (1951), 121-122.
        Finds that Keats was particularly struck by the "eye-imagery" in Shak.

A5674   Cordero y Leon, Rigoberto. "Figuras de Shakespeare." *Anales de la Universidad de Cuenca*, VII (1951), 69-83.

A5675   Dorius, Raymond J. *The Coherence of Metaphor in Shakespeare's English History Plays.* DD, Harvard University, 1951.

A5676   Gibson, F. D. *The Use of Sport for Imagery and Incident in the Works of Shakespeare.* MA thesis, Leeds University, 1951.

A5677   Liu, J. Y. "A Marlo-Shakespearian Image Cluster." *N &Q*, 196 (1951), 336-337.
        Finds in *I. Tamburlaine* and in Shakespeare the use of the Association of *love* with *book* or *bookbinding*, and with *eyes*, *reading commentary* and the like; notes the possibility of study of "image clusters" as an auxiliary in determining authorship.

A5678   Schrickx, W. "Solar Symbolism and Related Imagery in Shakespeare." *RBPH*, XXIX (1951), 112-128.

A5679   Venezky, Alice S. *Pageantry on the Shakespearean Stage.* New York: Twayne Publishers, 1951. Pp. 242.
        Rev: A7238.

A5680   Aronson, Alex. "A Note on Shakespeare's Dream Imagery." *Visva-Bharati Quarterly*, XVIII (Oct., 1952), 168-182.

A5681   Charney, Maurice M. *Shakespeare's Roman Plays: A Study of the Function of Imagery in the Drama.* DD, Princeton University, 1952. Pp. 458. Mic A54-173. *DA*, XIV (1954), 118. Publication No. 6796.
        Discusses, among other things, the "presentational" image, i.e., symbolic stage events.

A5682   Foakes, R. A. *Imagery in Elizabethan and Jacobean Drama.* DD, Birmingham, 1952.

A5683   Foakes, R. A. "Suggestions for a New Approach to Shakespeare's Imagery." *ShS*, V (1952), 81-92.

A5684   Zeeveld, W. Gordon. " 'Food for Powder'—'Food for Worms'." *SQ*, III (1952), 249-253.

A5685   Evans, Maurice. "Metaphor and Symbol in the Sixteenth Century." *EIC*, III (1953), 267-284. Comment by D. S. Brewer, ibid., IV (1954), 108-111.

A5686   Finney, Gretchen L. "A World of Instruments." *ELH*, XX (1953), 87-120.
        The pervasiveness of musical imagery in English Renaissance literature.

A5687   Frye, Roland M. " 'The World's a Stage': Shakespeare and the Moralists." *N &Q*, 198 (1953), 429-430.

A5688   Gardner, W. H. "Aspects of Shakespeare's Imagery." *Month*, X (1953), 41-51.

A5689   Hankins, John Erskine. *Shakespeare's Derived Imagery.* Lawrence: Univ. of Kansas Press, 1953. Pp. 289.
        Rev: A3537.

A5690   Holloway, John. "Dramatic Irony in Shakespeare." *Northern Miscellany of Literary Criticism*, Autumn, 1953, pp. 3-16.

A5691   Jepsen, Laura. *Ethical Aspects of Tragedy.* Gainesville: Univ. of Florida Press, 1953.
        Rev: A975.

A5692   Oyama, Toshiko. *A Study of Shakespeare's Imagery.* Tokyo: Shinozaki-shorin, 1953. Pp. 190.

A5693   Wheelwright, Philip. "Philosophy of the Threshold." *SR*, LXI (1953), 56-75.

A5694   Colbrunn, Ethel B. *The Simile as a Stylistic Device in Elizabethan Narrative Poetry: An Analytical and Comparative Study.* DD, University of Florida, 1954. Pp. 315. Mic A54-3073. *DA*, XIV (1954), 2065. Publication No. 9541.

A5695   Danks, K. B. "Shakespeare and 'Peine Forte et Dure'." *N &Q*, NS, I (1954), 377-379.

A5696   Halliday, F. E. *The Poetry of Shakespeare's Plays.* London: Duckworth, 1954. Pp. 196.
        Divides Shak.'s work into five periods and considers, among other things, the use of metaphor and imagery.
        Rev: A5459.

A5697   Hieatt, A. Kent. *Medieval Symbolism and the Dramatic Imagery of the English Renaissance.* DD, Columbia University, 1954. Pp. 510. Mic 55-108. *DA*, XV (1955), 817. Publication No. 11, 456.

A5698   Hoeniger, F. J. D. *The Function of Structure and Imagery in Shakespeare's Last Plays.* DD, University of London, 1954. Abst. publ. in *ShN*, V (1955), 42.

A5699   Kernan, Alvin B. "A Comparison of the Imagery in *3 Henry VI* and *The True Tragedie of Richard Duke of York.*" *SP*, LI (1954), 431-442.

A5700   Stamm, Rudolf. *Shakespeare's Word-Scenery.* With Some Remarks on Stage-History and the Interpretation of His Plays. Veröffentlichungen der Handels-Hochschule, St. Gallen, Reihe

B, Heft 10. Zurich und St. Gallen: Polygraphischer Verlag, 1954. Pp. 34.
Rev: A5603.

A5701   Wentersdorf, K. "The Authenticity of *The Taming of the Shrew*." *SQ*, V (1954), 11-32.
Imagery indicates that the play could have had only one author, and that was Shak.
See answer, A5701a.

A5701a Prior, Moody E. "Imagery as a Test of Authorship." *SQ*, VI (1955), 381-386.
Questions, after testing them with reference to other plays and dramatists, three of the major
premises used by K. Wentersdorf (A5701), in applying imagery as a test of authorship to the
Shrew.

A5702   Willcock, Gladys D. *Language and Poetry in Shakespeare's Early Plays.* Annual Shakespeare
Lecture of the British Academy, 1954. London: Geoffrey Cumberlege, 1955. *Proceedings
of the British Academy*, XL (1954), 103-117.
Rev: A5604.

A5703   Cronin, P. J. *Diction and Dramatic Character in Shakespearian Tragedy, with Special Attention to
Characteristic Use of Imagery.* B. Litt. thesis, Oxford, Balliol, 1955.

A5704   Ong, Walter J., S. J. "Metaphor and the Twinned Vision." *SR*, LXIII (1955), 202-222.

A5705   Partridge, Eric. *Shakespeare's Bawdy.* London: Routledge & Kegan Paul, 1955. Pp. x, 226.
"A new popular revised edition." Addenda on p. 226. Previous edition, 1947.
Rev: A5408.

A5706   Provost, George Foster. *The Techniques of Characterization and Dramatic Imagery in "Richard II"
and "King Lear."* DD, Louisiana State University, 1955. Pp. 274. Mic 55-280. *DA*, XV
(1955), 1616. Publication No. 12,525.

A5707   Walker, Roy. "The Celestial Plane in Shakespeare." *ShS*, VIII (1955), 109-117.

A5708   Broadbent, C. "Shakespeare and Shakeshaft." *N &Q*, NS, III (1956), 154-157.

A5709   Burckhardt, Sigurd. "The Poet as Fool and Priest." *ELH*, XXIII (1956), 279-298.

A5710   Heilman, Robert B. *Magic in the Web: Action and Language in "Othello".* Lexington: Univ.
of Kentucky Press, 1956. Pp. 316.
Rev: B8609.

A5711   Heninger, S. K., Jr. "The Heart's Meteors, a Microcosm—Macrocosm Analogy." *SQ*, VII
(1956), 273-275.

A5712   Muraoka, Isamu. "Poetic Images in the Elizabethan Period" (Japanese). *Bunka* (Tohoku
Univ., Sendai), XX, No. 3 (1956).

A5713   Smith, Stella Tilley. *Imagery of Motion in Shakespeare's Tragedies.* DD, University of Florida
(Gainesville), 1956.

A5714   Williams, Gwyn. "The Cuckoo, the Welsh Ambassador." *MLR*, LI (1956), 223-225.

A5715   Fehrman, Carl. "The Study of Shakespeare's Imagery." *Moderna Språk* (Stockholm), LI
(1957), 7-20.

A5716   Fliess, Robert. *Erogeneity and Libido.* New York: International Universities Press, 1957.
Pp. 325. Pp. 129, 133, in particular.

A5717   Lawlor, John. "Mind and Hand: Some Reflections on the Study of Shakespeare's Imagery."
SQ, VIII (1957), 179-193.

A5718   Peacock, Ronald. *The Art of Drama.* London: Routledge, 1957. Pp. vi, 263.
Rev: by M. B. Peppard, *Monatshefte*, XLIX (1957), 378-379; by F. Shaw, *Anglia*, LXXV
(1957/58), 475-477; by R. Williams, *EIC*, VIII (1958), 290-298; by J. A. Bryant, *SR*, LXVI
(1958), 321-323.

A5719   Fricker, Robert. "Das szenische Bild bei Shakespeare." *Annales Universitatis Saraviensis:
Philosophie-Lettres*, V (1956), 227-240.

(1)   RAMUS
See also other section on Ramus, A7534-A7538.

A5720   Tuve, Rosemond. "Imagery and Logic: Ramus and Metaphysical Poetics." *JHI*, II (1941),
365-400.

A5721   Tuve, Rosemond. *Elizabethan and Metaphysical Imagery: Renaissance Poetic and Twentieth
Century Critics.* Univ. of Chicago Press, 1947. Pp. xiv, 442.
Rev: by Kenneth Young, *Spectator*, Nov. 28, 1947, pp. 686-688; by V. B. Heltzel, *PQ*,
XXVI, 382-384; by W. K. Wimsatt, Jr., *JAAC*, VI (1948), 277-279; *TLS*, Jan. 17, p. 39; by
T. H. Jones, *Life and Letters*, LVIII, 247-249; by G. R. Potter, *MLQ*, IX, 359-360; by S. G.
Putt, *English*, VII, 136-138; by Rosemary Freeman, *RES*, XXIV, 331-332; by Kenneth Burke,
Accent, VIII, 125-127; by Josephine Miles, *SR*, LVI, 312-315; by Helen C. White, *CE*, X,
53-54; *N &Q*, 193 (1948), 484; by H. M. McLuhan, *Hudson Review*, I, 270-273; by M. T.
Herrick, *MLN*, LXIV (1949), 125-127; by W. Clemen, *Archiv*, 188 (1951), 149-150; by
R. G. Cox, *Scrutiny*, XIX (1952/53), 82-89; by J. Vallette, *MdF*, 317 (1953), 346.

A5722   Nelson, Norman E. *Peter Ramus and the Confusion of Logic, Rhetoric, and Poetry.* Ann Arbor:
Univ. of Michigan Contributions in Mod. Phil., No. 2, 1947. Pp. 22.

A5723   Duhamel, Pierre Albert. "The Logic and Rhetoric of Peter Ramus." *MP*, XLIV (1946),
163-171.

A5724   Howell, Wilbur S. "Ramus and English Rhetoric: 1574-1681." *QJS*, XXXVII (1951), 299-310.

A5725   Watson, George. "Ramus, Miss Tuve, and the New Petromachia." *MP*, LV (1958), 259-262. Rejects Miss Tuve's linking of metaphysical style with Ramism (A5721), on the grounds that (1) the only poets who are clearly Ramists—Sidney, Jonson, and Milton—are not metaphysical, and (2) Ramism was understood by English Renaissance poets as a simplification (or even over-simplification) of logic and hence would scarcely appeal to the metaphysicals.

(2)   ANIMAL IMAGERY

A5726   Dayton, B. E. *Animal Similes and Metaphors in Shakespeare's Plays.* DD, University of Washington. Abstr. in Univ. of Washington *Abstracts of Theses*, II (1937), 119-122.

A5727   Laxson, A. H. *Animal Symbolism in Shakespeare.* DD, State University of Iowa, 1937.

A5728   Yoder, Audrey. *Animal Analogy in Shakespeare's Character Portrayal.* New York: King's Crown Press, 1947. Pp. x, 150. DD, Columbia University, 1946.
        Rev: by J. C. Maxwell, *MLR*, XLIII (1948), 562; by J. Hannigan, *SAB*, XXIV (1949), 132.

A5729   Cheney, David Raymond. *Animals in "A Midsummer Night's Dream."* DD, State University of Iowa, 1955. Pp. 288. Mic 55-1103. *DA*, XV (1955), 2188. Publication No. 14,094.

(3)   COLOR IMAGERY

A5730   Allen, Don Cameron. "Symbolic Color in the Literature of the English Renaissance." *PQ*, XV (1936), 81-92.

A5731   Portal, Frédéric. *Des Couleurs Symboliques, dans l'Antiquité, le Moyen Âge et les Temps Modernes.* Paris: Niclaus, 1938. Pp. 200.

A5732   Seard, S. "The Use of Color in Literature." *Proceedings of the American Philosophical Society*, XX (1946), 163-249. Shak., pp. 191, 225-226.

d.   SHAKESPEARE'S PROSE AND EUPHUISM (94;32)
(1)   SHAKESPEARE'S PROSE (94;32)

A5733   Harrison, John Robert. *An Investigation of the Use of Prose in the Elizabethan Verse Drama, 1566-1595.* MA thesis, University of Toronto, 1937. Pp. 122.

A5734   Wells, Henry W. "The Continuity of Shaksperian Prose." *SAB*, XV (1940), 175-183.

A5735   Zandvoort, R. W. "Brutus's Forum Speech in *Julius Caesar.*" *RES*, XVI (1940), 62-66.

A5736   Buell, Llewellyn M. "A Prose Period in Shakespeare's Career?" *MLN*, LVI (1941), 118-122.

A5737   Crane, Milton. *The Prose of Shakespeare.* DD, Harvard University, 1942. Abstr. publ. in *Summaries of Ph.D. Theses, 1942*, Cambridge: Harvard Univ. Press, 1946, pp. 265-268.

A5738   Crane, Milton. *Shakespeare's Prose.* Chicago: Univ. of Chicago Press, 1951. Pp. 219.
        Rev: by Alfred Harbage, *SRL*, June 16, 1951, pp. 25, 59; by H. B. Charlton, *MGW*, Sept. 6, p. 11; by Frederick S. Boas, *FortnR*, NS, 1017 (Sept.), 636; by Esther Cloudman Dunn, *NYTBR*, Dec. 2, 1951, p. 20; by Rosemond Tuve, *JAAC*, X, 181-183; by K. Young, *Spectator*, 6440 (1951), 749; by A. P. Rossiter, *CamR*, LXXIII (1951/52), 488, 490; by G. Blakemore Evans, *SQ*, III (1952), 57-59; by A. P. Rossiter, *English*, IX, 68-69; *Adelphi*, XXVIII, 721; *NYHTBR*, Sept. 21, p. 20; by Hermann Heuer, *SJ*, 87/88 (1952), 262-263; by Michel Poirier, *EA*, V, 154-155; *Listener*, XLVII, 275; by R. A. Law, *SQ*, III, 83-84; by W. Clemen, *Archiv*, 189 (1953), 364-365.

A5739   Reed, Henry. "Towards The Cocktail Party. II." *Listener*, XLV (1951), 803-804.

A5740   Williamson, George. *The Senecan Amble: A Study in Prose Form from Bacon to Collier.* London: Faber & Faber, 1951. Pp. 377.
        Shak., pp. 118-120, 148, 331.
        Rev: A4139.

A5741   Guzzo, Augusto. "Prosa nei Drammi di Shakespeare." *Letterature Moderne*, III (1952), 476-482.

A5742   Hart, Walter Morris. "Shakespeare's Use of Verse and Prose." *Five Gayley Lectures, 1947-1954*, Berkeley and Los Angeles: Univ. of Calif. Press, 1954, pp. 1-17.

A5743   Borinski, Ludwig. "Shakespeare's Comic Prose." *ShS*, VIII (1955), 57-68.

(2)   EUPHUISM AND ELIZABETHAN PROSE (95;32)

A5744   Knights, Lionel Charles. *Aspects of the Economic and Social Background of Comedy in the Early Seventeenth Century.* DD, Cambridge, 1936. *Cam Abs.*, 1935-36, p. 63.
        Appendix C: "Elizabethan Prose."

A5745   Ringler, William. "The Immediate Source of Euphuism." *PMLA*, LIII (1938), 678-686.

A5746   Tillotson, Geoffrey. "The Prose of Lyly's Comedies." *Essays in Criticism and Research*, Cambridge Univ. Press, 1947, pp. 17-30.

A5747   Allen, D. C. "Style and Certitude." *ELH*, XV (1948), 167-175.

A5748   Borinski, Ludwig. *Englischer Geist in der Geschichte Seiner Prosa.* Freiburg i. B.: Herder, 1951. Pp. 253. "Die vorklassische Prosa," pp. 1-18; "Der Aufsteig zur klassischen Prosa (1580-

1660)," pp. 19-34.
    Rev: by A. J. Farmer, *Erasmus*, v (1952), 174-176.

A5749   Fisch, Harold. "The Puritan and the Reform of Prose-Style." *ELH*, xix (1952), 229-248.

A5750   Hebel, J. William, Hoyt H. Hudson, Francis R. Johnson, and A. Wigfall Green, eds. *Prose of the English Renaissance: Selected from Early Editions and Manuscripts*. New York: Appleton-Century-Crofts, 1952. Pp. xii, 882.

A5751   Thomson, J. A. K. *Classical Influences on English Prose*. London: Allen & Unwin, 1956. Pp. xiii, 303.
No extended discussion of Shak.
    Rev: A4145.

e. PROVERBS, MAXIMS, RIDDLES, PUNS, ETC. (96;32)
(1) PROVERBS AND MAXIMS (96;32)
(a) RECORDED FORMS
i. Collections (96;32)

A5752   Champion, Selwyn. *Racial Proverbs: A Selection of the World's Proverbs Arranged Linguistically*. London: Routledge; New York: Macmillan, 1938. Pp. cxxix, 767.
    Rev: by D. B. Porter, *Jour. of Negro Hist.*, xxiv (1939), 106-109.

A5753   Smith, William George, comp. *The Oxford Dictionary of English Proverbs*. Oxford: Clarendon Press; London: Milford, 1935. Pp. 672. 2nd ed. Revised by Sir Paul Harvey. Oxford: Clarendon Press, 1948. Pp. xxxii, 740.
Includes material from the sixteenth and seventeenth century collections of Prof. F. P. Wilson.
    Rev: by R. Huchon, *MLR*, xxxii (1937), 286-287; by B. J. Whiting, *MLN*, lii, 433-434; by E. Thommen, *ES*, xx (1938), 234-236; by H. W. B., *American Speech*, xiv (1939), 51-52; *Dublin Mag.*, xxiv, No. 3 (1949), 73-74; by J. R. Newman, *NR*, 120 (1949), 19-22.

A5754   Tilley, Morris Palmer. *A Dictionary of the Proverbs in England in the Sixteenth and Seventeenth Centuries*. Ann Arbor: Univ. of Michigan Press, 1950. Pp. xiii, 854.
    Rev: by Charles Philip Wagner, *MLJ*, xxxv (1951), 580-581; by James Sledd, *MP*, xlix, 62-63; by Richard Jente, *JEGP*, li (1952), 252-255; by H. S. Wilson, *UTQ*, xxi, 205-207; by Hermann M. Flasdieck, *Anglia*, lxx, 327-335; by Hilda Hulme, *MLR*, xlvii, 384-790; by John Crow, *SQ*, iii, 261-267; by F. P. Wilson, *RES*, ns, iii, 190-198; by H. Heuer, *SJ*, 91 (1955), 312-313.

A5755   Whiting, B. J. "Proverbs and Proverbial Sayings from Scottish Writings Before 1600. Part I. A-L." *Mediaeval Studies*, xi (1949), 123-205. "Part II. M-Y," ibid., xiii (1951), 87-164.

A5756   Heywood, John. *John Heywood's Works and Miscellaneous Short Poems*. Ed., with an Introd. and notes by Burton A. Milligan. Illinois Studies in Lang. & Lit., xli. Urbana: Univ. Illinois Press, 1956. Pp. xi, 297.
Contains Heywood's "Dialogue conteinying the number in effect of all the proverbs in the englishe tongue, . . ."

A5757   Starnes, DeWitt T., ed. and introd. *Proverbs or Adages by Desiderius Erasmus Gathered out of the Chiliades and Englished (1569) by Richard Taverner*. Gainesville, Fla.: Scholars' Facsimiles and Reprints, 1956.

ii. Uncollected Examples

A5758   Bond, Donald F. "English Legal Proverbs." *PMLA*, li (1936), 921-935.

A5759   Taylor, Archer. "The Proverb 'The Black Ox Has Not Trod on His Foot' in Renaissance Literature." *Renaissance Studies In Honor of Hardin Craig*, pp. 74-86; also *PQ*, xx (1941), 266-278.

A5760   Steiner, Arpad. "The Vernacular Proverb in Mediaeval Latin Prose." *AJP*, lxv (1944), 37-68. Appendix, pp. 67-68, contains 22 "Vernacular Proverbs in the Epistolae Obscurorum Virorum."

A5760a Oldfather, W. A. "Brief Notes on 'The Vernacular Proverb in Mediaeval Latin Prose'." *AJP*, lxvi (1945), 310-312.

A5761   Smith, Roland M. "Three Obscure English Proverbs." *MLN*, lxv (1950), 441-447.

A5762   Hotson, Leslie. "What Wood Is the Ship Made of?" *TLS*, Nov. 8, 1957, p. 673.
The stock answer to this saw, current in Shak.'s time was a sick "O—O—Oak!"

(b) STUDIES (96;33)
i. English Proverbs in General

A5763   Bond, Donald F. "The Law and Lawyers in English Proverbs. *American Bar Association Journal*, xxi (1935), 724-727.

A5764   Whiting, Bartlett Jere. *Proverbs in the Earlier English Drama, with Illustrations from Contemporary French Plays*. Harvard Studies in Comp. Lit., xiv. Harvard Univ. Press, 1938. Pp. xx, 505.
    Rev: *N&Q*, 175 (1938), 369-370; by A. T., *MP*, xxxvi, 102-103; by M. P. Tilley, *MLN*, liv (1939), 295-299; by Angus McIntosh, *RES*, xvi (1940), 81-83.

A5765   Robertson, Jean. "Nicholas Breton's Collections of Proverbs." *HLQ*, vii (1944), 307-315.

A5766   White, Olive B. "Richard Taverner's Interpretation of Erasmus in *Proverbs or Adagies.*"
        PMLA, LIX (1944), 928-943.
A5767   Jente, Richard. "The Untilled Field of Proverbs." *SP*, XLII (1945), 490-497.
A5768   Wilson, F. P. "English Proverbs and Dictionaries of Proverbs." *Library*, 4th Series, XXVI
        (1945), 51-70.
A5769   Wilson, F. P. "English Proverbs." *Bodleian Lib. Rec.*, II (1948), 219-221.
A5770   Bland, D. S. "Proverbs as Passwords." *N &Q*, 194 (1949), 469.
A5771   Hunter, G. K. "The Marking of Sententiae in Elizabethan Printed Plays, Poems and Ro-
        mances." *Library*, 5th Series, VI (1951), 171-188.
A5772   McNeir, Waldo F. "A Proverb of Green's Emended." *N &Q*, 197 (1952), 117.

ii.   In Shakespeare

A5773   Whiting, B. J. " 'Old Maids Lead Apes in Hell'." *Eng. Studn.*, LXX (1936), 337-351.
A5774   Anderson, Ruth L. " 'As Heart Can Think'." *SAB*, XII (1937), 246-251.
A5775   Lever, Katherine. "Proverbs and *Sententiae* in the Plays of Shakespeare." *SAB*, XIII (1938),
        173-183, 224-239.
A5776   Dowlin, C. M. "Two Shakespeare Parallels in Studley's Translation of Seneca's *Agamemnon.*"
        SAB, XIV (1939), 256.
        See also "A Correction," *SAB*, XV (1940), 128.
A5777   Preis, A. "Shakespeare, Bacon, and English Proverbs." *N &Q*, 190 (1946), 146.
A5778   Taylor, Archer. "Shakespeare's Wellerisms." *Southern Folklore Quarterly*, XV (1951), 170.
A5779   Thaler, Alwin. " 'In My Mind's Eye, Horatio'." *SQ*, VII (1956), 351-354.
A5780   Weinstock, Horst. *Die dramatische Funktion elisabethanischer Sprichwörter und Sentenzen bei
        Shakespeare* (einschliesslich der Sprichwortanspielungen). DD, Munich, 1956. Pp. 171.
A5781   M. Clarita Felhoelter, Sister, O. S. U. *Proverbialism in "Coriolanus".* DD, Catholic University
        of America, 1956. Abstracted by Jack R. Brown, *ShN*, VII (1957), 12.
A5782   Purcell, J. M. "*Commedy of Errors*, II. ii. 57." *N &Q*, NS, V (1958), 180.
A5783   Purcell, J. M. "*Antony and Cleopatra*, I. i. 42-43." *N &Q*, NS, V (1958), 187-188.
        See Constance I. Smith, "A Further Note . . . ," p. 371.
A5784   Purcell, J. M. "*Twelfth Night*, II. ii. 27-28." *N &Q*, NS, V (1958), 375-376.

(2)   RIDDLES (97;-)

A5785   Goolden, P. "Antiochus's Riddle in Gower and Shakespeare." *RES*, NS, VI (1955), 245-251.

(3)   POSIES (Omitted) (97;33)

(4)   PUNS (98;-)

A5786   Pollard, A. F. "A Shakespearean Pun?" *TLS*, Apr. 3, 1937, p. 256.
A5787   Horn, Wilhelm. "Zu Shakespeares Wortspielen." *Archiv*, 178 (1940), 119-121.
A5788   King, Arthur H. "Some Notes on Ambiguity in *Henry IV, Part 1.*" *SN*, XIV (1942), 161-183.
A5789   Siler, Henry D. "A French Pun in *Love's Labour's Lost.*" *MLN*, LX (1945), 124-125.
A5790   Altick, Richard D. " 'Conveyers' and Fortune's Buckets in *Richard II.*" *MLN*, LXI (1946),
        179-180.
A5790a Nearing, Homer, Jr. "A Three-Way Pun in *Richard II.*" *MLN*, LXII (1947), 31-33.
        Comments on A5790.
A5791   Kökeritz, Helge. "Touchstone in Arden. *As You Like It*, II. iv. 16." *MLQ*, VII (1946), 61-63.
A5792   Kökeritz, Helge. "Five Shakespeare Notes." *RES*, XXIII (1947), 310-320.
        A pun in *Timon*.
A5793   Baldwin, T. W. "Respice Finem: Respice Funem." *AMS*, pp. 141-155.
A5794   Herbert, T. Walter. "Shakespeare's Word-Play on 'Tombe'." *MLN*, LXIV (1949), 235-241.
A5795   Kökeritz, Helge. "Shakespeare som skämtare." *Ord och Bild* (Stockholm)), LVIII (1949),
        444-448.
A5796   Maxwell, J. C. " 'Rope-Tricks'." *N &Q*, 194 (1949), 556.
A5797   Kökeritz, Helge. "Punning Names in Shakespeare." *MLN*, LXV (1950), 240-243.
A5798   Kökeritz, Helge. "Thief and Stealer: A Sample of Shakespeare's Punning Technique."
        English and Germanic Studies, III (1950), 57-60.
A5799   Louthan, Doniphan. "The 'Tome-Tomb' Pun in Renaissance England." *PQ*, XXIX (1950),
        375-380.
A5800   Muir, Kenneth. "The Uncomic Pun." *CamJ*, III (1950), 472-485.
A5801   Mahood, M. M. "The Fatal Cleopatra: Shakespeare and the Pun." *EIC*, I (1951), 193-207.
A5802   Main, W. W. "Shakespeare's 'Fear No More the Heat o' th' Sun'. *Cymbeline*, IV. ii."
        Expl., IX (1951), 36.

A5803 O'Hanlon, Redmond L. "Shakespeare's Puns." *ShN*, Mar.-Apr., 1952, p. 15.

A5804 Rowse, A. L. "*Haud Credo*: A Shakespearian Pun." *TLS*, July 18, 1952, p. 469.

A5805 Bluestone, Max. "An Anti-Jewish Pun in *A Midsummer Night's Dream*, III. i. 97." *N&Q*, 198 (1953), 325-329.

A5806 Kökeritz, Helge. *Shakespeare's Pronunciation*. Yale Univ. Press, 1953. Pp. xv, 516.
A detailed study. Concludes that Shak.'s pronunciation was probably much closer to modern pronunciation than popularly supposed. Most striking differences in pronunciation of certain individual words.
Rev: A5283.

A5807 Spevack, Marvin. *The Dramatic Function of Shakespeare's Puns*. DD, Harvard University, 1953. Abstr. in *ShN*, VI (1956), 11.

A5808 Jorgensen, Paul. "*Much Ado About Nothing*." *SQ*, V (1954), 287-295.

A5809 O'Hanlon, R. L. "Shakespeare and the Hard of Hearing." *Volta Review*, LVI (May, 1954), 214-216.

A5810 Mustanoja, Tauno F. "Middle English 'With an O and an I' with a Note on Two Shakespearean 'O-I' Puns." *N. Mitt.*, LVI (1955), 161-173.

A5811 Partridge, Eric. *Shakespeare's Bawdy*. London: Routledge & Kegan Paul. First ed., 1947; second ed., 1955. Pp. x, 226. Addenda on p. 226.
Rev: A5408.

A5812 Brown, James. "Eight Types of Puns." *PMLA*, LXXI (1956), 14-26.

A5813 Burckhardt, Sigurd. "The Poet as Fool and Priest." *ELH*, XXIII (1956), 279-298.

A5814 McKenzie, James J. "Edgar's 'Persian Attire'." *N&Q*, NS, III (1956), 98-99.

A5815 Mahood, M. M. *Shakespeare's Word Play*. London: Methuen, 1957. Pp. 192.
Rev: *TLS*, June 14, 1957, p. 360; by John Wain, *Dublin Review*, July, pp. 89-91; by C. V. Wedgewood, *Time and Tide*, Aug. 31, pp. 1081-82; *Dublin Magazine*, XXXII (Oct.-Dec.), 76; by R. A. Foakes, *English*, XI, 232; by Helen Gardner, *London Mag.*, IV, No. 12, 73-74, 77-78; by John Wain, *TC*, 162 (1957), 89-91; by J. Vallette, *MdF*, 330 (1957), 713-714; *N&Q*, NS, IV, 458-459; *Dublin Magazine*, (July-Sept.), pp. 69-70; by Ernest Schanzer, *EIC*, VIII (1958), 199-207; by Edward Hubler, *SQ*, IX, 192-193; by G. K. Hunter, *MLR*, LIII, 426-427; by Hermann Heuer, *SJ*, 94 (1958), 281-283; by S. F. Johnson, *MP*, LVI, 62-64; by Roy Walker, *Aryan Path*, XXIX, 514-515; by John McEwen, *Month*, XIX, 249-250; by Michel Poirier, *EA*, XI, 349-350; *ShN*, VIII, 38.

A5816 Parish, John E. "Another Pun on 'Will'." *N&Q*, NS, IV (1957), 147-148.

A5817 Barnet, Sylvan. "Coleridge on Puns: A Note To His Shakespeare Criticism." *JEGP*, LVI (1957), 602-609.

A5818 Barnet, Sylvan. "Coleridge's Marginalia in Stockdale's Shakespeare of 1784." *Harvard Lib. Bul.*, XII (1958), 210-219.

VIII. THE ART OF SHAKESPEARE: HIS DRAMATIC ART (98;33)
1. SHAKESPEARE'S CREATIVE FACULTIES (98;33)

A5819 Rank, Otto. *Art and Artist*, tr. by Charles F. Atkinson. New York: Knopf, 1932. Pp. xxvii, 431, xii.
Ill-informed about Shak.

A5820 Sisson, C. J. *The Mythical Sorrows of Shakespeare*. Annual Shakespeare Lecture. London, 1934. Pp. 28.
In Ebisch and Schücking Supplement, p. 33.
Rev: by M. Praz, *ES*, XVIII (1936), 177-181; by B. Maxwell, *MLN*, LI (1936), 202-203.

A5821 Nussberger, Max. *Die künstlerische Phantasie in der Formgebung der Dichtkunst, Malerei und Musik*. Munich: F. Bruckmann, 1935. Pp. xi, 464.
Rev: by Rob. Petsch, *DLZ*, LVIII (1937), 701-710.

A5822 Kittredge, George L. "The Man Shakespeare." *SAB*, XI (1936), 171-174.

A5823 Schick, J. "Drei Genies und ein Talent, oder Bacons Stellung unter den Grossen seiner Zeit." *SJ*, LXXII (1936), 42-78.
The three geniuses are Shakespeare, Galileo, and Kepler. Bacon is merely talented.

A5824 Caudwell, Christopher (pseudonym for Sprigg, Christopher St. John). *Illusion and Reality: A Study of the Sources of Poetry*. London: Macmillan, 1937. Pp. 336.
Rev: by Lucien Wolff, *EA*, I (1937), 546-549; by J. Middleton Murry, *Criterion*, XVII (1938), 373-377; by H. A. Mason, *Scrutiny*, VI (1938), 429-433.

A5825 Higgins, G. M. P. "Imagination: Shakespeare and Wordsworth." *Discovery*, XVIII (1937), 119.

A5826 James, D. G. *Scepticism and Poetry*. London: Allen & Unwin, 1937. Pp 276.
Rev: *TLS*, Mar. 20, 1937, p. 200.

A5827 Murry, John Middleton. *Heaven—and Earth*. London: Cape, 1938. Pp. 318.
Chap. VIII, "Shakespeare: Imagination & the Machine", pp. 99-108.
Rev: A1791.

A5828 Shaftel, O. H. "Universality as a Canon of Criticism." *Summaries of Theses* (Harvard University), 1938, pp. 347-350.

A5829 Baker, Courtland D. *The Continuity of the Literary Tradition of the Inspired Poet.* DD, Johns Hopkins University, 1939.

A5830 Knight, G. Wilson. *The Burning Oracle.* Oxford Univ. Press, 1939. Pp. 299.
Contains an essay, "The Shakespearian Integrity."
Rev: "The Dynamics of Poetry," *TLS*, Sept. 2, 1939, p. 514; by A. C., *SRL*, Sept. 16, 1939, p. 20; by H. I'A. Fausset, *MGW*, Sept. 8, 1939, p. 194; by R. O. C. Winkler, *Scrutiny*, VIII (1940), 233-236; by Wilfred Gibson, *English*, III, 35-36; by B. E. C. Davis, *MLR*, XXXV, 268-269; by Kathleen Tillotson, *RES*, XVII (1941), 245-246; by Paul Meissner, *DLZ*, LXII, 448-450.

A5831 Lalou, René. "Universalité de Shakespeare." *Europe*, L (1939), 33-40. "Sur l'universalité de Shakespeare." *Revue théâtrale*, No. 26 (1954), pp. 9-12.

A5832 Rokotov, T. "Shakespeare: A Contemporary of Eternity." *International Literature* (USSR), June, 1939, pp. 38-46.

A5833 Lovett, Robert Morse. *Shakespeare's Permanence: An Address Delivered at the Univ. of Puerto Rico on the Occasion of the Anniversary of Shakespeare's Birth.* Univ. of Puerto Rico, 1940. Pp. 15.

A5834 Ridley, M. R. *On Reading Shakespeare.* Annual Shakespeare Lecture of the British Academy, 1940. London: Milford, 1940. Pp. 31.
Rev: A8346.

A5835 Slade, Frederick E. "On Reading Shakespeare." *Poetry R*, XXXI (1940), 347-349.

A5836 Wilson, Arthur Herman. "Universal Appeal of Shakespeare." *Susquehanna Univ. Studies*, I (1940), No. 5, 204-208.

A5837 Spencer, Benjamin T. "This Elizabethan Shakespeare." *SR*, XLIX (1941), 536-552.
A review of recent books by Messrs. Stoll, Van Doren, and Draper and Miss Dunn, protesting against interpretations which reconstruct "the Elizabethan mind," assume that it is a constant, and thus make "the rigid and commonplace mentality" of Shakespeare's contemporaries the measure of his plays.

A5838 Craig, Hardin. "Shakespeare's Development as a Dramatist in the Light of his Experience." *SP*, XXXIX (1942), 226-238.

A5839 Von Oppell, Baron. "Beauty in Shakespeare and in Kant." *Hibbert Journal*, XL (1942), 166-173.

A5840 Kahler, Erich. *Man the Measure: A New Approach to History.* New York: Pantheon Books, 1943. Pp. 700.
Shak., pp. 500ff.
Rev: by J. H. Nichols, *Jour. Religion*, XXIV (1944), 133-134.

A5841 McGlinchee, Claire. "Magic—of an Age and for all Time." *SAB*, XVIII (1943), 72-74.

A5842 Mizener, Arthur. "Some Notes on the Nature of English Poetry." *SR*, LI (1943), 27-51.

A5843 Pinto, V. de S. "Shakespeare and the Dictators." *Essays by Divers Hands: Transactions of the Royal Society of Literature.* Oxford Univ. Press, 1944. Pp. xviii, 124.

A5844 Bishop, Roger J. *The Doctrine of Poetic Inspiration in English Renaissance and 17th Century Literature, and Its Background.* MA thesis, Toronto, 1944. Pp. 162.

A5845 Dean, Leonard F. "Shakespeare's Treatment of Conventional Ideas." *SR*, LII (1944), 414-423.
Argues that Shakespeare's plays are more than dramatic confirmations of conventional beliefs.

A5846 Granville-Barker, H. *The Use of the Drama.* Princeton Univ. Press, 1945. Pp. vi, 92.
"The Exemplary Case of Shakespeare," pp. 80-83.

A5847 Armstrong, Edward A. *Shakespeare's Imagination.* London: Lindsay Drummond, 1946. Pp. 191.
Rev: A5647.

A5848 Mincoff, Marco. "Geniyat na Shakespeare" [Shakespeare's Genius]. *Izkustvo*, II (1946), 3, 172-176.

A5849 Wolff, Emil. *Gedanken über das Shakespeare-Problem.* Hamburg: Hoffman u. Campe-Verlag, 1946. Pp. 51.
Rev: by K. Wentersdorf, *SJ*, 82/83 (1946-47), 209-211.

A5850 King, Thomson. "Shakespeare, the Master Builder." *The Aryan Path*, XVIII (1947), 387-391.

A5851 Strodthoff, Emil. "Shakespeare, vox humana." *Neues Europa*, II (1947), x, 8-13.

A5852 Vivante, Leone. "Shakespeare." In *La poesia inglese ed il suo contributo alla conoscenza dello spirito*. Florence: Vallecchi, 1947. Pp. 7-96.
Rev: by V. de Sola Pinto, *Erasmus*, II (1948-49), 223-225.

A5853 Wilson, J. D. "Shakespeare and Humanity." *LanM*, XLI (1947), 264-270.

A5854 Craig, Hardin. "Shakespeare's Bad Poetry." *ShS*, I (1948), 51-56.

A5855 Ellis-Fermor, Una. *Shakespeare the Dramatist.* Annual Shakespeare Lecture of the British Academy, 1948. London: Oxford Univ. Press, 1948. Also in *Proceedings of the British Academy*, XXXIV.

Rev: *TLS*, Feb. 12, 1949, p. 107; by J. R. Sutherland, *MLR*, XLIV, 438-439; by J. H. Pafford, *RES*, I (1950), 163-166.

A5856 Felheim, Marvin. "Landmarks of Criticism: 'Shakespeare the Dramatist', Una Ellis-Fermor." *ShN*, VIII (1958), 36.

A5857 Lawrence, Sir H. S., and T. M. Aitken. *The Inspiration of Shakespeare*. Oxford: Privately printed at the University Press, 1948. Pp. 20.

A5858 Schiller, A. "Shakespeare's Amazing Words." *KR*, XI (1948), 43-49.

A5859 Walker, James. "A Personal Approach to Shakespeare." *English*, VII (1948-49), 220-222.

A5860 Van Brakell Buys, W. R. *De Magiër van Stratford. Shakespeares Karakter-tekenning*. Naarden: In den Toren, 1949.

A5861 Mayhall, Jane. "Shakespeare and Spenser: A Commentary on Differences." *MLQ*, X (1949), 356-363.

A5862 Partridge, A. C. *The Problem of Henry VIII Re-opened*. Cambridge: Bowes & Bowes, 1949. Pp. 35.
      Rev: B9885.

A5863 Potts, L. J. "Ben Jonson and the Seventeenth Century." *Essays and Studies*, NS, II (1949), 7-24.

A5864 Brown, Ivor. "Vom Wunder und Geheimnis Shakespeares." *Neue Schweizer Rundschau*, XVIII (1950), 473-479.

A5865 Lewisohn, Ludwig. *The Magic Word. Studies in the Nature of Poetry*. New York: Farrar, Straus, 1950. Pp. xv, 151.
      Chap. III, "Shakespeare", pp. 67-108.

A5866 Pettet, E. C. "Shakespeare's Conception of Poetry." *Essays and Studies*, NS, III (1950), 29-46.
      Rev: by M. A. Shaaber, *SQ*, II (1951), 260-261; by C. J. Sisson, *MLR*, XLVI, 545.

A5867 Ray, Sibnarayan. "A Note on Shakespeare." *Mysindia* (Bangalore), July 9, 1950, pp. 17-18.

A5868 Frings, Josef Kardinal. "Die Grösse Shakespeares." *Rhein Merkur*, VI (1951), xxii, 8.

A5869 James, D. G. *The Dream of Learning: An Essay on "The Advancement of Learning", "Hamlet", and "King Lear"*. Oxford: Clarendon Press, 1951. Pp. 126.
      Rev: A3959.

A5870 Law, Robert A. "On Certain Proper Names in Shakespeare." *TxSE*, XXX (1951), 61-65.
      Rev: *SQ*, IV (1953), 352.

A5871 Rylands, George. "Shakespeare's Poetic Energy." *Proceedings British Academy*, XXXVII (1951), 99-120. Annual Shakespeare Lecture, 1951.
      Rev: in *TLS*, Sept. 4, 1953, p. 565; by H. Heuer, *SJ*, 90 (1954), 349-350.

A5872 Wilde, Hans-Oskar. "Wort und dramatische Existenz." *Shakespeare-Studien*, Festschrift für Heinrich Mutschmann, pp. 194-206.

A5873 Reynolds, George F. "Of Imagination all Compact." *Colorado Quarterly*, I (1952), 44-57.

A5874 Barker, George. "William Shakespeare and the Horse with Wings." *Partisan Review*, XX (1953), 410-420.

A5875 Bing, Just. "Shakespeare-karakterer." *Edda*, LIII (1953), 324-330.

A5876 Capocci, Valentina. "Shakespeare e la tradizione." *Lo spettatore italiano*, VI (1953), 311-315.

A5877 Rossky, William. *The Theory of Imagination in Elizabethan Literature: Psychology, Rhetoric and Poetic*. DD, New York University, 1953.

A5878 Dickinson, Patric. "Shakespeare Considered as a Poet," *Talking of Shakespeare*, ed. by John Garrett. London: Hodder & Stoughton & Max Reinhardt, 1954.

A5879 Dilthey, Wilhelm. "Shakespeare und seine Zeitgenossen," *Die grosse Phantasiedichtung*. Göttingen, 1954, pp. 53-108.
      Rev: by H. Oppel, *NS*, III (1954), 478-479.

A5880 Frings, Josef Kardinal. "Ansprache beim Festakt der Shakespeare-Gesellschaft." *SJ*, 90 (1954), 9-10. Excerpt as "Shakespeares Masse," *Rhein Merkur*, IX (1954), xviii, 9.

A5881 Hunter, Edwin R. *Shakespeare and Common Sense*. Boston: Christopher Publ. House, 1954. Pp. 312.
      Chap. XIII: "Some Observations On the Processes of the Creative Mind."
      Rev: A971.

A5882 Twiss, John. "Shakespeare's 'Preying Monsters'." *N &Q*, NS, I (1954), 334-335.

A5883 Watkin, Edward Ingram. *Poets and Mystics*. London: Sheed & Ward, 1954. Pp. ix, 318.
      Chap. II: " 'He Wanted Art'," pp. 21-37.
      Rev: *TLS*, Mar. 5, 1954, p. 157; by Robert Ellrodt, *EA*, VII (1954), 418-419.

A5884 Johnston, D. R. Lukin. "Var Shakespeare en Revisor?" *Revision og Regnskabsvaesen* (Copenhagen), XXIV (1955), 501-506. Radio Talk.

A5885 Pettet, E. C. "Dangerous Sea and Unvalued Jewels: Some Notes on Shakespeare's Consciousness of the Sea." *English*, X (1955), 215-220.

A5886 Speaight, Robert. *Nature in Shakespearean Tragedy*. London: Hollis and Carter, 1955. Pp. viii, 179.
      Rev: A1035.

A5887   Vinaver, Stanislav. "Šekspir u punom blesku i zamahu." *Književnost* (Belgrade), XXI (1955), 213-217; 306-313.

A5888   Bodmer, Martin. "Zum Thema Shakespeare." In *Variationen zum Thema Weltliteratur.* Frankfurt a. M.: Suhrkamp, 1956, pp. 208-211.

A5889   Burckhardt, Sigurd. "The Poet as Fool and Priest." *ELH*, XXIII (1956), 279-298.

A5890   Ingersoll, Robert G. "On Shakespeare." *Wisdom*, July, 1956, p. 3.

A5891   Miyauchi, Bunshichi. "Quintessence of Poetic Drama in Shakespeare" (in Japanese). *Studies in English Literature and Language* (Hiroshima), II, No. 2.

A5892   Nemerov, Howard. "The Marriage of Theseus and Hippolyta." *KR*, XVIII (1956), 633-641.

A5893   Rossmann, Hermann. "Shakespeare, eine Welt und ihr Schöpfer." *Prisma* (Bochum), 1956-57, No. 7, pp. 82-84. Also in *Shakespeare-Tage* 1957, pp. 1-3.

A5894   Stroedel, Wolfgang. "Shakespeares Entwicklung von 'Romeo und Julia' zu 'Macbeth'." *ZAA*, IV ii, (1956), 137-148.

A5895   Eastman, Arthur M. "Shakespeare's Negative Capability." *Papers of the Michigan Academy of Science, Arts, and Letters*, XLII (1957), 339-347.

A5896   Flatter, Richard. "Triumphierende Tragödie oder Shakespeares wahre Grösse." *Chronik des Wiener Goethevereins*, LXI (1957), 1-9. Also in *Triumph der Gnade: Shakespeare Essays.* Vienna/Munich: Kurt Desch, 1956, pp. 158-174.

A5897   Musgrove, S. *Shakespeare and Jonson.* The Macmillan Brown Lectures. Auckland Univ. College Bull. No. 51, English Series No. 9, Auckland, 1957. Pp. 55.
         Rev: A623.

A5898   Samarin, R. "On the Problem of Realism in West European Literature of the Renaissance Period." *Voprosi Literaturi* (Moscow), August, 1957, pp. 40-62.

A5899   Wilson, John Dover. "The Shakespeare Paradox. Universal Stage of the Man from Stratford." *Times* (London), September 2, 1957, pp. 9-10.

A5900   Kennedy, A. L. "The Two Greatest Englishmen: Shakespeare and Churchill?" *Quarterly Review*, April, 1958, pp. 123-137.

A5901   Rossky, William. "Imagination in the English Renaissance: Psychology and Poetic." *Studies in the Renaissance*, V (1958), 49-73.

2. SHAKESPEARE'S DRAMATIC TECHNIQUE (99;33)
a. GENERAL TREATISES ON DRAMATIC TECHNIQUE (99;33)
(1) TECHNIQUE OF THE DRAMA IN GENERAL (99;33)
(Omitted by nature of the sources of this bibliography)
(2) SHAKESPEARE'S TECHNIQUE IN GENERAL (99;34)

A5902   Ludwig, Wilhelm. *Der Schluss der Shakespeareschen Lustspiele.* DD, Münster, 1925. Pp. 103.

A5903   Schäfer, Walter. *Beiträge zur vergleichenden Dramaturgie der alten und neuren, insbes. Shake-speareschen Dramatik.* DD, Tübingen, 1926. Pp. 75. Typewritten.

A5904   Stoll, E. E. *Art and Artifice in Shakespeare.* Cambridge Univ. Press, 1933.
         Rev: A8390.

A5905   David, Richard. *The Janus of Poets: Being an Essay on the Dramatic Value of Shakespeare's Poetry, Both Good and Bad.* Cambridge Univ. Press, 1935.
         Rev: by E. Olson, *MP*, XXXIII (1935/6), 221-222; G. Connes, *RAA*, XIII, 150; by Wolfgang Keller, *SJ*, LXXII, 140-141; by Geoffrey Tillotson, *RES*, XIII (1937), 354-356; by Robert Adger Law, *MLN*, LII, 526-530; by J. H. Walter, *MLR*, XXXII, 660-661.

A5906   Squire, Sir John. *Shakespeare as a Dramatist.* London, 1935.
         In Ebisch & Schücking Supplement, p. 34.
         Rev: by Floris Delattre, *RAA*, XIII (1935/6), 513.

A5907   Allen, Percy. "Stage or Study?" *TLS*, Apr. 11, 1936, p. 316.
         See letters by W. W. Greg in *TLS*, May 2, 1936, p. 379; by Mr. Allen, ibid., May 9, 1936, p. 400; by Levin L. Schücking, ibid., May 6, 1936, p. 420.
         Argues against the traditional belief that Shakespeare considered his plays as stage plays only, and expresses a conviction that the great tragedies in uncut form were written for publication.

A5907a   "Stage or Study?" *TLS*, Oct. 7, 1944, p. 487. Answered by H. S. Bennett, *TLS*, Oct. 14, 1944, p. 499.

A5908   Brandl, A. "Zur Szenenführung bei Shakespeare." In Brandl, *Forschungen und Charakteristiken* (Berlin), 1936, pp. 147-160.

A5909   Cunningham, Cornelius C. "Persuasive Factors in Shakespearean Address." [Univ. of Iowa] *Programs Announcing Candidates for Higher Degrees . . .* , no pagination. (Abstract.) DD, State University of Iowa, 1936.

A5910   Deaton, M. "Some Scenes Shakespeare Left Out." *SAB*, XI (1936), 52-56.

A5911   Knickerbocker, William S. "The Pragmatic Shakespeare." *SR*, XLIV (1936), 482-500.

A5912   Lawrence, W. J. "Something New About Shakespeare." *London Mercury*, XXXIV (1936), 224-228.

A5913 Nosworthy, J. M., and W. F. Trench. "Shakespeare's Unfinished Sentences." *TLS*, April 4, 1936, p. 300; April 25, 1936, p. 356.

A5914 Walker, Albert L. "Conventions in Shakespeare's Dramatic Poetry." [Univ. of Iowa] *Programs Announcing Candidates for Higher Degrees.* (Abstract.) DD, State University of Iowa, 1936.

A5915 Wilson, Arthur H. "The Principle of Rest in the Shakespearean Plays." *Susquehanna Univ. Studies*, I (1936), 63-69.

A5916 Fallon, G. "Naturalism & Revolt in the Theatre." *Irish Monthly*, LXV (1937), 542-547.

A5917 Lawrence, W. J. *Speeding Up Shakespeare.* Studies of the Bygone Theatre and Drama. London: Argonaut Press, 1937. Pp. 220.
Rev: A7402.

A5918 Campbell, O. J. *Comicall Satyre and Shakespeare's "Troilus and Cressida."* San Marino, Cal., 1938.
Rev: A4913.

A5919 Gardner, Helen L. "Lawful Espials." *MLR*, XXXIII (1938), 345-355.

A5920 Charlton, H. B. *Romeo and Juliet as an Experimental Tragedy.* London: Milford, 1939. Pp. 45.
Rev: by C. J. Sisson, *MLR*, XXXV (1940), 268; by Georges Connes, *EA*, IV (1940), 59; by H. N. Hillebrand, *MLN*, LVI (1941), 620-623.

A5921 Poisson, Rodney Peter Dominic. *The Heroic Couplet in the Plays of Shakespeare.* MA thesis, British Columbia, 1939. Pp. 123.

A5922 Zeissig, Gottfried. "*Sprecherziehung und Dramenbehandlung.*" *ZDK*, LIII (1939), 413-420.

A5923 Granville-Barker, H. "Progrès du Drame Shakespearien." *Le Théâtre Élizabéthain.* Paris: Les Cahiers du Sud, 1940, pp. 44-47.

A5924 Stoll, Elmer Edgar. *Shakespeare and other Masters.* Harvard Univ. Press, 1940. Pp. xv, 430.
Rev: A8394.

A5925 Tannenbaum, Samuel A. "The Names in *As You Like It.*" *SAB*, XV (1940), 255-256.

A5926 Kreider, Paul V. *Repetition in Shakespeare's Plays.* Princeton Univ. Press, 1941. Pp. ix, 306.
Rev: by Fredson Bowers, *MLN*, LVII (1942), 469-470; by F. W. Chandler, *SR*, L, 130-133; by Hardin Craig, *MLQ*, II, 648-650; by Alwin Thaler, *JEGP*, XLII, 126-129.

A5927 Craig, Hardin. "Shakespeare's Development as a Dramatist in the Light of his Experience." *SP*, XXXIX (1942), 226-238.

A5928 Peach, Earle Sanford. *A Critical Study of the Openings of Shakespeare's Plays.* MA thesis, Acadia (Canada), 1942.

A5929 Campbell, Oscar James. *Shakespeare's Satire.* Oxford Univ. Press, 1943. Pp. 227.
Rev: B5164.

A5930 Small, Samuel A. "Shakspere's Stage Business." *SAB*, XVIII (1943), 66-71.

A5931 Rostosky, F. "Vers und Prosa auf dem Theater." *Dt. Dramaturgie*, II (1943), 82-87.

A5932 Cady, Frank W. "Motivation of the Inciting Force in Shakespeare's Tragedies." *Elizabethan Studies and Other Essays in Honor of George F. Reynolds*, pp. 166-171.

A5933 Gaubert, Hélène. *Shakespeare's Theory of the Drama and its Relation to Contemporary Stagecraft.* DD, Montreal, 1944.

A5933a Gaubert, H. A. *La Dramaturgie de Shakespeare.* Montreal: L. Parizeau, 1945. Pp. 250.

A5934 McCollom, William G. "Formalism and Illusion in Shakespearian Drama, 1595-1598." *QJS*, XXXI (1945), 446-453.

A5935 Sewell, Arthur. "Place and Time in Shakespeare's Plays." *SP*, XLII (1945), 205-224.

A5936 Stewart, J. I. M. " 'Julius Caesar' and 'Macbeth.' Two Notes on Shakespearean Technique." *MLR*, XL (1945), 166-173.

A5937 McCloskey, John C. "The Plot Device of False Report." *SAB*, XXI (1946), 147-158.

A5938 Baldwin, T. W. *Shakspere's Five-Act Structure: Shakspere's Early Plays on the Background of Renaissance Theories of Five-Act Structure from 1470.* Univ. Illinois Press, 1947. Pp. xiii, 848.
Rev: "This Figure," *TLS*, April 26, 1947, pp. 189-190; by Clifford Leech, *MLR*, XLII (1947), 502-503; by H. S. Wilson, *MLN*, LXIII (1948), 494-496; by J. M. Nosworthy, *RES*, XXV (1949), 359-361.

A5939 Clemen, W. "Shakespeares erste Dramen." *Geistige Welt*, I (Jan., 1947), 7-16.
Rev: by W. Azzalino, *SJ*, 82/83 (1948), 220-221.

A5940 Craig, M. R. *The Technique of the Chronicle Play.* MS thesis, Columbia University, 1947. Pp. 79.

A5941 Ellis-Fermor, Una. *The Frontiers of Drama.* London: Methuen & Co., 1945. Pp. viii, 154.
Rev: by Harley Granville-Barker, *RES*, XXII (1946), 144-147; by Paul Dombey, *NstN*, Jan. 5, 1946, pp. 13-14; by Elizabeth Sweeting, *MLR*, XLI, 324-326; by Alwyn Andrew, *Life & Letters*, XLVIII, 130-140; by Alan Downer, *KR*, IX (1947), 148-151; by Paul H. Kocher, *MLN*, LXIV (1949), 127-128; by J. H. Pafford, *RES*, NS, I (1950), 166.

A5942 Nakano, Yoshio. "Shakespeare's Psychological Techniques." *Rising Generation* (Japan), 93 (1947), No. 1.

A5943 Ellis-Fermor, Una. *Shakespeare the Dramatist*. London, 1948.
       Rev: A5855.

A5944 Flatter, Richard. *Shakespeare's Producing Hand: A Study of His Marks of Expression to be Found in the First Folio*. London: Heinemann, 1948. Pp. 184.
       Rev: by H. B. C., *MGW*, June 24, 1948, p. 10; *TLS*, Oct. 9, 1948, p. 570; by Margaret Webster, *NYHTBR*, Nov. 21, 1948, p. 20; by Giles E. Dawson, *SAB*, XXIV (1949), 229-236; by R. A. Law, *Southwest Review*, XXXIV, 100-101; by F. Bowers, *MP*, XLVIII (1950), 64-68; by P. Alexander, *RES*, NS, I, 66-70; by C. Hinman, *MLN*, LXV, 558-560; by Hallett Smith, *YR*, XXXIX, 743-746; by Hermann Heuer, *SJ*, 84/86 (1951), 257-258.

A5945 Fluchère, Henri. *Shakespeare: Dramaturge Élizabéthain*. Marseille: Cahiers du Sud, 1948. Pp. 400. *Shakespeare*. London: Longmans, Green, 1953. Pp. x, 272. (A translation by Guy Hamilton. Forword by T. S. Eliot.)
       Rev: A8187, A8188.

A5946 Maurer, Friedrich. *Theatereinsichten. Von Shakespeare bis Max Reinhardt*. Berlin: Cornelsen, 1948. Pp. 99.

A5947 Price, Hereward T. "Mirror Scenes in Shakespeare." *AMS*, pp. 101-113.

A5948 Smith W. "The Shakespearean Apostrophe." *SAB*, XXIII (1948), 195-200.

A5949 Smith, Warren D. *Shakespeare's Stagecraft as Denoted by the Dialogue in the Original Printings of his Texts*. DD, University of Pennsylvania, 1948. Pp. 256. Mic A50-217. *Microf. Ab.*, X. (1950), 163. Publ. No. 1731.

A5950 Wiles, Roy McKeen. 'In My Mind's Eye, Horatio'." *UTQ*, XVIII (1948), 57-67.

A5951 Möller, Kr. Langdal. "Shakespeare Som Praktisk Teatermand." *Nationaltidende* (Copenhagen), 81, May 4, 1949.

A5952 Reynolds, G. F. "Shakespeare and his World: Staging Elizabethan Plays." *Listener*, XLII, Aug. 11, 1949, pp. 223-224.

A5953 Smith, Warren. "The Third Type of Aside in Shakespeare." *MLN*, LXIV (1949), 510-513.

A5954 Stirling, Brents. *The Populace in Shakespeare*. Columbia Univ. Press, 1949. Pp. 203.
       Rev: A6219.

A5955 Smith, Warren. "New Light on Stage Directions in Shakespeare." *SP*, XLVII (1950), 173-181

A5956 Thaler, Alwin. "Delayed Exposition in Shakespeare." *SQ*, I (1950), 140-145.

A5957 Yeaton, Robert Kniss. *The Dramatic Techniques of William Shakespeare and Their Importance to the Modern Realistic Theatre*. DD, Innsbruck, 1950.

A5958 Brock, James Wilson. "A Study of the Use of Sound Effects in Elizabethan Drama." *Summaries of Doctoral Diss . . . Northwestern Univ.*, XVIII (1951), 99-103.

A5959 Frye, Northrop. "A Conspectus of Dramatic Genres." *KR*, XIII (1951), 543-562.

A5960 Price, Hereward T. *Construction in Shakespeare*. The Univ. of Michigan Contributions in Mod. Philol., No. 17 (May, 1951), Univ. Michigan Press, 1951. Pp. 42.
       Rev: A6063.

A5961 Salter, F. M. "Shakespeare's Use of Silence." *TRSC*, XLV, Ser. III, June 1951 (pub. 1952), Sect. Two, pp. 59-81.

A5962 Venezky, Alice S. *Pageantry on the Shakespearean Stage*. New York: Twayne Publishers, 1951· Pp. 242.
       Rev: A7238.

A5963 Weil, Nordon, P. *Shakespeare's Dramatic Technique in the Opening Scenes of his Tragedies*. MA thesis, Birmingham, 1951.

A5964 Clemen, Wolfgang H. *Wandlung des Botenberichts bei Shakespeare*. Sitzungsberichte der Bayerischen Akademie der Wissenschaften, Philosophisch-historische Klasse, 4 (1952). Munich, 1952. Pp. 46.
       Rev: by Hereward T. Price in *SQ*, V (1954), 186; by J. C. Maxwell in *RES*, NS, V, 217; by Ernst Th. Sehrt, *Anglia*, LXXII (1954-5), 485-488.

A5965 Ebrahim, C. "The Drama and Society." *Discussion* (South Africa), I, vi (1952), 21-30.

A5966 Flatter, Richard. " 'True Original Copies' Shakespeare's Plays—Outline of a New Conception." *Proc. Leeds Philos. and Lit. Soc.*, Lit. & Hist. Sec. VII, Pt. 1 (1952), 31-42.

A5967 Lord, John B. "Certain Dramatic Devices Studied in the Comedies of Shakespeare and in Some of the Works of his Contemporaries and Predecessors." DD, University of Illinois, 1952. *DA*, XII (1952), 66-67.

A5968 Smith, Warren D. "Stage Settings in Shakespeare's Dialogue." *MP*, L (1952), 32-35.

A5969 Thomson, J. A. K. *Shakespeare and the Classics*. London: Allen and Unwin, 1952. Pp. 254.
       Rev: A4177.

A5970 Adams, Robert M. "Trompe-L'Oeil in Shakespeare and Keats." *SR*, LXI (1953), 238-255.

A5971 Desai, Chintamani N. *Shakespearean Comedy*. (With a Discussion on Comedy, the Comic, and the Sources of Shakespearean Comic Laughter.) Indore City, M. B., India: The Author, 1953. Pp. 204.
       Rev: B5187.

A5972 Smith, Warren D. "The Elizabethan Stage and Shakespeare's Entrance Announcements." *SQ*, IV (1953), 405-410.

A5973 Smith, Warren D. "Stage Business in Shakespeare's Dialogue." *SQ*, IV (1953), 311-316.

A5974 Coghill, Nevill. "Shakespeare as a Dramatist," in *Talking of Shakespeare*, ed. by John Garrett. London: Hodder & Stoughton & Max Reinhardt, 1954.

A5975 Schlüter, Kurt. "Die Erzählung der Vorgeschichte in Shakespeares Dramen." *SJ*, 90 (1954), 108-123.

A5976 Schopf, Alfred. "Leitmotivische Thematik in Shakespeares Dramen." *SJ*, 90 (1954), 124-166.

A5977 Watkin, Edward Ingram. *Poets and Mystics*. London: Sheed & Ward, 1954. Pp. ix, 318.
Rev: A5883.

A5978 Aldus, Paul J. "Analogical Probability in Shakespeare's Plays." *SQ*, VI (1955), 397-414. See also L. J. Mills & P. J. Aldus, *SQ*, VII (1956), 133-134.

A5979 Arnold, Aerol. "The Recapitulation Dream in *Richard III* and *Macbeth*." *SQ*, VI (1955), 51-62.

A5980 Gerstner-Hirzel, Arthur. "Stagecraft and Poetry." *SJ*, 90 (1955), 196-211.

A5981 Laqueur, Richard. *Shakespeares Dramatische Konzeption*. Tübingen: Max Niemeyer Verlag, 1955. Pp. viii, 356.
Rev: by Clifford Leech, *SQ*, VIII (1957), 115-117; by E. A. J. Honigmann, *RES*, NS, VIII, 301-302; by Hermann Heuer, *SJ*, 93 (1957), 266-268; by Hans Schnyder, *Archiv*, 193 (1957), 330; by Anselm Schlösser, *DLZ*, LXXVIII, 897-899; by K. Muir, *ShS*, X, 138.

A5982 Pearce, Josephine Anna. *The Manipulations of Time in Shakespeare's English History Plays*. DD, University of Missouri, 1955. Pp. 236. Mic 55-1110. *DA*, XV (1955), 2192. Publ. No. 14,618.

A5983 Beckerman, Bernard. *The Production of Shakespeare's Plays at the Globe Playhouse, 1599-1609*. DD, Columbia University, 1956. Pp. 468. Mic 56-2257. *DA*, XVI (1956), 1440. Publ. No. 17,039.

A5984 Granville-Barker, Harley. *On Dramatic Method*. New York: Hill and Wang, 1956. Chap. III: "Shakespeare's Progress," pp. 68-116.

A5985 Heuser, Georg. *Die aktlose Dramaturgie William Shakespeares*. Eine Untersuchung über das Problem der Akteinteilung und angeblichen Aktstruktur der Shakespeareschen Dramen. DD, Marburg, 1956. Marburg: Erich Mauersberger, 1956. Pp. x, 430.

A5986 Kaindl, Elizabeth Maria. *Shakespeares Methoden, Regiebemerkungen in den Text zu verarbeiten*. DD, Vienna, 1956.

A5987 Stroedel, Wolfgang. "Shakespeares Entwicklung von 'Romeo und Julia' zu 'Macbeth'." *ZAA*, IV ii, (1956), 137-148.

A5988 Draper, John W. *The Tempo-Patterns of Shakespeare's Plays*. Angl. Forschungen, Heft 90, 1957. Pp. 180.
Rev: A5165.

A5989 Gerstner-Hirzel, A. *The Economy of Action and Word in Shakespeare's Plays*. DD, Basel, 1957. The Coopers Monographs on English and American Language and Literature, 2. Bern: Francke, 1957. Pp. 134. For abstract see A5605.
Rev: A5611.

A5990 Hegenbarth, Josef. *Zeichnungen zu fünf Shakespeare-Dramen*. Berlin: Rütten & Loening, 1957. Pp. 305.

A5991 Leech, Clifford. "Shakespeare's Use of a Five-Act Structure." *NS*, Heft 6 (1957), 249-263.

A5992 Main, William W. "Dramaturgical Norms in the Elizabethan Repertory." *SP*, LIV (1957), 128-148.

A5993 Peacock, Ronald. *The Art of Drama*. London: Routledge, 1957. Pp. vi, 263.
Rev: A5718.

A5994 Sale, Roger Hiller. "The Development of Narrative Technique in the English Drama, 1585-1595." DD, Cornell University, 1957. *DA*, XVII (1957), 2616.

A5995 Suk Kee Yoh. "The Convention of Place in Shakespeare." *English Language & Literature* (Eng. Lit. Soc. of Korea), No. 4 (1957), 279-294.

A5996 Wilson, H. S. *On the Design of Shakespearean Tragedy*. Univ. of Toronto Press, 1957. Pp. 256.
Rev: A6073.

A5997 Bonjour, Adrien. *Résonances Shakespeariennes* (Leçon inaugurale). Neuchâtel: Secrétariat de l'Université, 1958. Pp. 24.

A5998 Chujo, Kazuo. "The Development of Structural Devices in Shakespeare's Tragicomedies." *Otsuka Festschrift*, 301-316.

A5999 Levý, Jiří. "Divadelní prostor a čas v dramatech Williama Shakespeara a Bena Jonsona." (Dramatic space and time in the plays of Shakespeare and Jonson), in *F. Wollmanovi k sedmdesátinám* (Collection of articles in tribute to Professor Wollman's 70th birthday). Prague: Státní pedagogické nakladatelství, 1958, pp. 648-656.

A6000 Salingar, L. G. "The Design of *Twelfth Night*." *SQ*, IX (1958), 117-139.

A6001 Schlüter, Kurt. *Shakespeares dramatische Erzählkunst* (Schriftenreihe der deutschen Shakespeare-Gesellschaft, N. F. Bd. 7). Heidelberg: Quelle and Meyer, 1958. Pp. 159.

(3) TECHNIQUE OF SHAKESPEARE'S CONTEMPORARIES
(101;34)

A6002 Tomlinson, Warren Everett. *Herodes-Charakter im Englischen Drama.* DD, Berlin. Leipzig, 1933. Pp. x, 46.
Rev: by K. Arns, *Beiblatt,* XLVII (1936), 18-20; by Karl Hammerle, *Archiv,* 169 (1936), 95-96; by H. Lüdeke, *ES,* XXI (1939), vi.

A6003 Bradbrook, M. C. *Themes and Conventions of Elizabethan Tragedy.*
In Ebisch and Schücking *Supplement,* pp. 3, 34.
Rev: A6269.

A6004 Biesterfeldt, Peter Wilhelm. *Die dramatische Technik Thomas Kyds: Studien zur inneren Struktur und szenischen Form des Elisabethanischen Dramas.* Halle: Niemeyer, 1936. Pp. 115.
Rev: by Hans Marcus, *Archiv,* 170 (1937), 283; by H. Nicolai, *Beiblatt,* XLVIII, 123-124; by Robert Petsch, *Eng. Studn.,* LXXI, 398-402; by W. Keller, *SJ,* LXXIII, 165-166; by P. Meissner, *DLZ,* LVIII, 1787-790; by R. Stamm, *ES,* XX (1938), 170-172; by Eduard Eckhardt, *Lbl,* LIX, 168-169.

A6005 Ellis-Fermor, Una M. *The Jacobean Drama: An Interpretation.* London: Methuen, 1936. Pp. 351. 2nd ed., rev. London: Methuen, 1947. 3rd ed., rev. London: Methuen, 1953. 4th ed., rev. London: Methuen, 1958.
Rev: "Machiavelli and the Jacobean Drama from Despair to Serenity," *TLS,* Feb. 29, 1936, p. 179; by Frank Chapman, *Criterion,* XV, 739-742; by Mario Praz, *ES,* XVIII, 177-181; by Bonamy Dobrée, *Spectator,* Mar. 20, 1936, pp. 530, 532; by E. K. Chambers, *English,* I, 159-161; *London Mercury,* XXXIII, 670-671; by C. J. Sisson, *MLR,* XXXI, 568-569; by K. John, *NstN,* NS, XI, 399-400; by Hugh Ross Williamson, *FortnR,* NS, 139 (1936), 505-506; by Wolfgang Keller, *SJ,* LXXII, 150-151; by J. Hayward, *Obs.,* March 1, 1936; by Trevor James, *Life and Letters Today,* XV (1937), No. 6, 213-214; by G. Tillotson, *RES,* XIV (1938), 94-97; by E. E. Stoll, "Recent Elizabethan Criticism," *ELH,* VI (1939), 39-52; by W. Clemen, *Eng. Studn.,* LXXIII (1938/39), 274-275; by Szenczi, *Archivum Philologicum,* LXII, Hefte 10-12.

A6006 Lawson, J. H. *Theory and Technique of Playwriting.* New York: G. P. Putnam's Sons, 1936. Pp. xvi, 316.

A6007 Stoll, E. E. "Tartuffe and the 'optique du théâtre'." *RAA,* Feb., 1936, pp. 193-213.

A6008 Legouis, E., and L. Cazamian. "A Propos d'une Critique de E. E. Stoll." *RAA,* Feb., 1936, pp. 214-218.

A6009 Petersen, Julius. "Das Motiv in der Dichtung." *DuV,* XXXVIII (1937), 44.

A6010 Spencer, Theodore. *Death and Elizabethan Tragedy.* A Study of Convention and Opinion on the Elizabethan Drama. Harvard Univ. Press, 1936. Pp. xiii, 288.
Rev: A6823.

A6011 Iwatsuki, Tachiwo. "On the Changing Literary Modes in the Development of Renaissance Tragedy." *Studies in English Literature* (Japan), XVIII (1938), 486-505.

A6012 Anderson, Ruth L. "The Mirror Concept and Its Relation to the Drama of the Renaissance." *Northwest Missouri State Teachers College Studies,* III (1939), No. 1, 1-30.

A6013 Stoll, Elmer Edgar. "Recent Elizabethan Criticism." *ELH,* VI (1939), 39-57.
Chiefly on A6003 and A6005.

A6014 Craig, Hardin. "The Shackling of Accidents: A Study of Elizabethan Tragedy." *PQ,* XIX (1940), 1-19.

A6015 Empson, William. "La Double Intrigue et l'Ironie Dans le Drame Élizabéthain." In *Le Théâtre Élizabéthain.* Paris: Les Cahiers du Sud, 1940. Pp. 56-60.

A6016 Outram, A. E. *Some Conventions of Elizabethan Drama.* DD, Oxford, 1939. *Ox Abs* 1940, pp. 97-102.

A6017 Kluckhohn, Paul. "Die Arten des Dramas." *DVLG,* XIX (1941), 241.

A6018 Durfee, Joseph. *A Study of Expectation and Surprise in Tragedy, Especially Elizabethan and Jacobean.* DD, University of Colorado, 1951. Abstract in *Univ. of Colorado Studies,* XXVI (1941), No. 4, 75-77.

A6019 Bouvier, Arthur Paul. *Studies in the Development of Dramatic Conventions in 16th Century England.* DD, University of Minnesota, 1944.

A6020 McCollom, William Gilman. *Illusion and Formalism in Elizabethan Tragedy.* DD, Cornell University, 1944. Abstract in Cornell Univ. *Abstracts of Theses,* 1944, 17-20.

A6021 Sprague, Arthur C. "Off-stage Sounds." *UTQ,* XV (1945), 70-75.

A6022 Lever, Katherine. *Early Tudor Drama and Old Greek Comedy: A Study of Didactic and Satiric Drama.* DD, Bryn Mawr College, 1945. Abstract in *Microfilm Abstracts,* VI (1945), No. 1, 77-79.

A6023 Mincoff, Marco. "Verbal Repetition in Elizabethan Tragedy." *Annuaire de l'Univ. Sv. Climent Ochridski* (Sofia), XLI (1945), 128.
Rev: by L. Ceijp, *Časopis pro mod. filol.,* XXXIII (1950), Suppl., 44.

A6024 Ryan, Harold F. *Heroic Play Elements in Earlier English Drama.* DD, St. Louis University, 1944. *Microfilm Abstracts,* VI (1946), Pt. 2, 27-28. Publication No. 766.

A6025 Sawyer, P. S. *A Comparative Study of the Exposition in Elizabethan Drama and Modern Drama.* MS thesis, Columbia University, 1946. Pp. 80.

A6026 Straumann, Heinrich. "Zur Auffassung vom Wesen der Tragödie in der englischen Literatur vor Shakespeare." *Eumusia. Festgabe für E. Howald.* Zürich, 1947, pp. 140-153.

A6027 Thompson, Alan Reynolds. *The Dry Mock: A Study of Irony in Drama.* Univ. Cal. Press, 1948. Pp. ix, 278.
Rev: A6868.

A6028 Ure, Peter. "On Some Differences between Senecan and Elizabethan Tragedy." *DUJ*, x (1948), 17-23.

A6029 Cancelled.

A6030 Prior, Moody E. "Poetic Drama: An Analysis and a Suggestion." *EIE, 1949*, Columbia Univ. Press, 1950, pp. 3-32.

A6031 Hyde, Mary Crapo. *Playwriting for Elizabethans.* Columbia Univ. Press. Pp. ix, 258.
Rev: A6061.

A6032 Eber, Brigitte. *Die Apostrophe als Selbstäusserungsform in der englischen Tragödie des 16. Jahrhunderts.* DD, Munich, 1950. Pp. 125. Typewritten.

A6033 Hewitt, Ray S. *Foreshadowing in Elizabethan Tragedy.* DD, University of California, Berkeley, 1951.

A6034 Linn, John G. *The Court Masque and Elizabethan Dramatic Structure, 1558-1604.* DD, Cornell University, 1951.

A6035 Popkin, Henry. *Dramatic Theory of the Elizabethan and Jacobean Playwrights.* DD, Harvard University, 1951.

A6036 Dietrich, Margret. *Europäische Dramaturgie. Der Wandel ihres Menschenbildes von der Antike bis zur Goethezeit.* Wien-Meisenheim: A. Saxl, 1952. Pp. 404.
Rev: P. M. Wild, *Universitas*, VIII (1953), 305-306; G. Konrad, *Welt und Wort*, VIII (1953), 65.

A6037 Dugan, John T. *The First Principles of Dramatic Composition: A Comparative Study of Selected Theories of Dramaturgy.* DD, University of Minnesota, 1952.

A6038 Doran, Madeleine. *Endeavors of Art: A Study of Form in Elizabethan Drama.* Madison: Univ. of Wisconsin Press, 1953. Pp. xv, 482.
Rev: A7827.

A6039 Bradbrook, M. C. *The Growth and Structure of Elizabethan Comedy.* London: Chatto and Windus, 1955. Pp. ix, 246.
Rev: B5197.

A6040 Clemen, Wolfgang. *Die Tragödie vor Shakespeare.* Schriftenreihe der Deutschen Shakespeare-Gesellschaft, 5. Heidelberg: Quelle and Meyer, 1955. Pp. 270.
Rev: by E. A. J. Honigmann, *MLR*, LI (1956), 583-584; briefly by Muriel C. Bradbrook, *SQ*, VII, 434-435; by Ernst Th. Sehrt, *SJ*, 92 (1956), 435-438; by Ernest Schanzer, *RES*,NS, VII, 304-305; by J. Kleinstück, *NS*, V, 359-360; by Robert Fricker, *Archiv*, 193 (1957), 327-328; by Clifford Leech, *MLN*, LXXII, 317-320; by Hans Georg Heun, *DLZ*, LXXVIII, 1087-88; by Rudolf Stamm, *Anglia*, LXXV, 453-458; by Richard Gerber, *ES*, XXXIX, 81-83.

A6041 Samarin, R. "On the Problem of Realism in West European Literature of the Renaissance Period." *Voprosi Literaturi* (Moscow), Aug., 1957, pp. 40-62.

A6042 James, William. "The Judgement Denouement of Renaissance Comedy." *DA*, XVII (1957), 621.

A6043 Lombardo, Agostino. *Il Dramma Pre-Shakespeariano: Studi sul Teatro Inglese dal Medioevo al Rinascimento.* ("Collana di varia critica," Vol. XIV, ed. by Neri Pozza). Venice, 1957. Pp. viii, 224.
Rev: by Theodore Silverstein, *MP*, LV (1958), 202-203; by Hardin Craig, *MLN*, LXXIII, 612-613; by F. Kermode, *RES*, IX, 450.

A6044 Sale, Roger Hiller. *The Development of Narrative Technique in the English Drama, 1585-1595.* DD, Cornell University, 1957. Pp. 253. Mic 57-4208. *DA*, XVII (1957), 2616. Publication No. 23,143.

A6045 Mann, Otto. *Poetik der Tragödie.* Bern: Francke, 1958. Pp. 344.

A6046 Holt, Albert Hamilton. *The Nature of the Dramatic Illusion and Its Violations in Jonson's Comedies—His Precedents in Theory and Practice.* DD, Vanderbilt University, 1958. Pp. 401. Mic 58-1545. *DA*, XVIII (1958), 1786. [No publication no.]

A6047 Schirmer, W. F. "Shakespeares klassizistische Gegenspieler." *Anglia*, LXXVI (1958), 90-116.

A6048 Weimann, Robert. *Drama und Wirklichkeit in der Shakespearezeit.* Ein Beitrag zur Entwicklungsgeschichte des elisabethanischen Theaters. Halle (Saale): Max Niemeyer Verlag, 1958. Pp. 334.

b. VARIOUS ASPECTS OF SHAKESPEARE'S DRAMATIC TECHNIQUE (102;35)

(1) DEPENDENCE OF THE DRAMATIC FORM ON EXTERNAL INFLUENCES (102;35)

(a) ON THEATRICAL CONDITIONS (102;35)
     (Transferred to General Treatises on dramatic technique)
(b) ON PUBLIC TASTE (102;35)
     (Transferred to Theatre Public, X,3)
(c) CUSTOMS OF THE PRINTING AND PUBLISHING
     TRADES (103;-)
     (Transferred to Printing, V,1.)
(d) POLITICAL PROPAGANDA AND THE DRAMA
     (103;-)
     (Transferred to Politics, IV,5.)
(2) PLAY CONSTRUCTION OF SHAKESPEARE AND THE
     ELIZABETHAN DRAMATISTS; CONVENTIONS; INDUC-
     TIONS (103;-)

A6049 Walker, Albert L. *Conventions in Shakespeare's Dramatic Poetry.* DD, State University of Iowa, 1936.

A6050 Jacobi, Walter. *Form und Struktur der Shakespeareschen Komödien: Eine Vorstudie zum Problem des Dramatischen bei Shakespeare.* DD, Berlin, Humboldt U., 1937. Pp. 134. Berlin: Triltsch & Huther, 1937.
  Rev: by J. B. Leishman, *RES,* xv (1939), 371-372; by W. Keller, *SJ,* LXXVI (1940), 213-214; by Elise Deckner, *Beiblatt,* LII (1941), 58-60.

A6051 Armbrister, Victor S. *The Origins and Functions of Subplots in Elizabethan Drama.* Summary, Joint University Libraries, Nashville, Tennessee. DD, Vanderbilt University, 1938.

A6052 Raysor, Thomas M. "Intervals of Time and Their Effect upon Dramatic Values in Shakespeare's Tragedies." *JEGP,* XXXVII (1938), 21-47.

A6053 Olmsted, Sterling P. *The Development of the "Induction" in the English Drama, 1582-1642.* DD, Yale University, 1940.

A6054 Patterson, Berta M. "Stock Plot Devices in Elizabethan Drama." *Abstracts of Theses, S. Methodist Univ.,* No. 7 (1940), p. 47.

A6055 Durfee, Joseph. *A Study of Expectation and Surprise in Tragedy, Especially Elizabethan and Jacobean.* DD, University of Colorado, 1941. Abstr. publ. in U. of Colorado "Abstracts of Theses for Higher Degrees," in *University of Colorado Studies,* XXVI (Nov. 1941), 75-77.

A6056 Mincoff, Marco. "Plot Construction in Shakespeare." *Godišnik na Sofiiskiya Universitet, Itoriko-filologičeski Fakultet,* (Annuaire de l'Université de Sofia, Faculté Historico-philologique), XXXVII (1941), 1-51.

A6057 Adams, Joseph Quincy. "The Author-Plot of an Early Seventeenth Century Play." *Library,* 4th S., XXVI (1945), 17-27.

A6058 Sewell, Arthur. "Place and Time in Shakespeare's Plays." *SP,* XLII (1945), 205-224.

A6059 Schücking, Levin L. *Shakespeare und der Tragödienstil seiner Zeit.* Bern: A Francke, 1947. Pp. 184.
  Rev: by Scheurweghs in *Leuvense Bijdragen,* XXXVIII (1948), 70; by G. Kirchner, *DLZ,* LXX (1949), 12-17; by O. E. Schoen-René, *MLN,* LXIV, 124-125; by G. Blakemore Evans, *JEGP,* XLVIII, 291-292; by J. B. Leishman, *RES,* XXV, 357-359; E. A. Taylor, *MLQ,* X, 531-532; by H. Lüdeke, *ES,* XXX, 309-312; by A. Koszul, *LanM,* V, 189-190; by J. P. Pritchard, *Books Abroad,* XXIII, 72-73; by J. M. S. Tompkins *MLR,* XLVI (1951), 87-89; by W. Kleinschmidt von Lengefeld, *SJ,* 84/86 (1951), 242-245.

A6060 Schücking, Levin L. "Das Problem der Überlänge Shakespearescher Dramen," in *Essays über Shakespeare, Pepys, Rossetti, Shaw und Anderes.* Wiesbaden: Dietrich, 1948, pp. 313-330. Also in *FuF,* XX (1944), 29-31.

A6061 Hyde, Mary C. *Playwriting for Elizabethans, 1600-1605.* Studies in Eng. and Comp. Lit., No. 167, Columbia Univ. Press, 1949. Pp. ix, 258. (DD, Columbia University.)
  Rev: by Harry Levin, *NYTBR,* Aug. 7, 1949; by T. W. Baldwin, *JEGP,* XLVIII, 439-440; by Marcia L. Anderson, *South Atlantic Quar.,* XLVIII, 622-623; by L. M. Parrott, Jr., *TAr,* XXXIII (Aug., 1949), 107-108; by R. B. Sharpe, *MLR,* XLV (1950), 377-379; *CE,* XI, 470; by M. C. Bradbrook, *RES,* III (1952), 89; by Baldwin Maxwell, *MLN,* LXVIII (1953), 53-55; by Albert H. Carter, *MLQ,* XIV, 220-221; by H. Heuer, *SJ,* 89 (1953), 214.

A6062 Mincoff, Marco. "The Structural Pattern of Shakespeare's Tragedies." *ShS,* III (1950), 58-65.

A6063 Price, H. T. *Construction in Shakespeare.* The University of Michigan Contributions in Modern Philology, Number 17, (May, 1951), Univ. of Michigan Press, 1951. Pp. 42.
  Rev: by Una Ellis-Fermor, *SQ,* III (1952), 55-57; by R. A. Law, ibid., p. 87; by A. P. Rossiter, *English,* IX, 68-69; by Philip Edwards, *MLR,* XLVII, 272 [brief]; by Hermann Heuer, *SJ,* 87/88 (1952), 263; by H. B. Charlton, *MLN,* LXVIII (1953), 52-53; by H. C. Matthes, *Archiv,* 189 (1952/53), 228-229; by L. Bonnerot, *EA,* VII (1954), 115.

A6064 Williams, George C. "Shakespeare's Basic Plot Situation." *SQ,* II (1951), 313-317.

A6065 Goodman, Randolph G. *That Strumpet the Stage: Poems about Playgoers, Players, and Playwrights.* DD, Columbia University, 1953. Pp. 357. Mic A53-761. *DA,* XIII (1953), 450. Publication No. 5189.

A6066   Greenfield, Thelma N. *The Use of the Induction in Elizabethan Drama.* DD, University of Wisconsin, 1952. Abstract publ. in *Summaries of Doctoral Dissertations, 1951-1952,* Vol. 13. Madison: University of Wisconsin Press, 1953, pp. 378-380.

A6067   Cancelled.

A6068   Hoeniger, F. J. D. *The Function of Structure and Imagery in Shakespeare's Last Plays.* DD, University of London, 1954.

A6069   Voitl, Herbert. *Neubildungswert und Stilistik der Komposita bei Shakespeare.* DD, Freiburg i. Br., 1954. Typewritten.

A6070   Gaul, E. M. *Zur Struktur der Tragödien Shakespeares.* DD, Cologne, 1955. Pp. 149.

A6071   Main, William W. "Dramaturgical Norms in the Elizabethan Repertory." *SP,* LIV (1957), 128-148.

A6072   Summersgill, Travis. "Structural Parallels in *Eastward Ho* and *The Tempest.*" *Bucknell Review,* VI, iv, (1957), 24-28.

A6073   Wilson, H. S. *On the Design of Shakespearean Tragedy.* Univ. of Toronto Press, 1957. Pp. 256.
Rev: by G. B. Harrison, *SatR,* Aug. 3, 1957, p. 17; C. L. Bennet, *Dalhousie Rev.,* XXXVII, 213; by Philip Edwards, *MLR,* LIII (1958), 427-428; by William G. McCollom, *QJS,* XLIV, 88-89; by G. P. V. Akrigg, *QQ,* LXV, 146-148; by Clifford Leech, *SQ,* IX, 565-566; by Irving Ribner, *JEGP,* LVII, 127-130; by R. A. Foakes, *MLN,* LXXIII, 294-297; Alfred Harbage, *UTQ,* XXVII, 461-463; F. D. Hoeniger, *Canadian Forum,* XXXVIII, 112-113; *ShN,* VIII, 20.

A6074   Hoffmann, Friedrich. "Die typischen Situationen im Elisabethanischen Drama und ihr Pattern." *SJ,* 94 (1958), 107-120.

A6075   Leech, Clifford. "The Two-Part Play. Marlowe and the Early Shakespeare." *SJ,* 94 (1958), 90-106.

A6076   Levin, Richard Lewis. *The Punitive Plot in Elizabethan Drama.* DD, University of Chicago, 1958.

(3)   ACT AND SCENE DIVISION (104;35)

A6077   Kirschbaum, Leo. "The Sequence of Scenes in *Hamlet.*" *MLN,* LV (1940), 382-387.

A6078   Klaiber, Joachim. *Die Aktform im Drama und auf dem Theater.* Ein Beitrag zur dts. Theatergeschichte des 19. Jh. [Sh. passim.] Berlin: Elsner, 1936. Pp. viii, 291.

A6079   Philbrick, Norman. "Act and Scene Division in the First Editions of Shakespeare." *Theatre Annual for 1944,* pp. 36-46.

A6080   Jewkes, Wilfred Thomas. *Act Division in Elizabethan Plays, 1583-1616.* DD, University of Wisconsin, 1956. Pp. 387. Mic 57-1713. *DA,* XVII (1957), 1073. Publication No. 18,410. Subsequently revised and published as *Act Division in Elizabethan and Jacobean Plays,* Hamden, Conn.: Shoe String Press; London: Paterson, 1959. Pp. 374.

(4)   SCENE TECHNIQUE (105;35)

A6081   Deaton, Mary. "Something Shakespeare Left Out." *SAB,* XI (1936), 52-56.

A6082   Brandl, Alois. "Zur Szenenführung bei Shakespeare." (First published in *Sitz.-Ber. Preuss. Akad. d. Wiss.* 1906.) In Brandl, *Forschungen,* pp. 147-160.

A6083   Fiedler, Leslie A. "The Defense of the Illusion and the Creation of Myth." *EIE, 1948.* New York: Columbia Univ. Press, 1949, pp. 74-94.

A6084   Holt, Albert Hamilton. *A Study of the Extra-Dramatic Scenes in Shakespeare.* Master's thesis, University of North Carolina, 1947. Abstr. publ. in *University of North Carolina Record, Research in Progress,* Grad. School Series, No. 56, 1949. Pp. 212.

A6085   Stamm, Rudolf. *Shakespeare's Word Scenery with Some Remarks on Stage-History and the Interpretation of his Plays.* Zurich, St. Gallen: Polygr. Verl., 1954. Pp. 34.
Rev: A5603.

(5)   DEPICTION OF MILIEU AND INTERPRETATION OF NATURE (103;35)
(Transferred to Nature IV, 8, f.)

(6)   USE OF MUSIC, SONGS, ACROBATICS AND DANCES (106;36)
(a)   COLLECTIONS OF SONGS

A6086   *England's Helicon,* 1600, 1614. Vol. 1: Text. Pp. xiv, 228. Vol. 2: Introd., notes and indexes. Pp. viii, 242. Ed. by Hyder Edw. Rollins. Cambridge, Mass.: Harvard University Press, 1935.
Rev: by R. Hittmair, *DLZ,* LVIII (1937), 1855-57.

A6087   Black, Matthew W., ed. *Elizabethan and Seventeenth-Century Lyrics.* London: Lippincott, 1938. Pp. xi, 624.
Rev: by D. F., *SRL,* Jan. 14, 1939, p. 22; by Joan Bennett, *MLR,* XXXIV, 636-637; by R. D. H., *MLN,* LV (1940), 239; by H. S. V. J., *JEGP,* XXXIX, 310-311; by John Butt, *RES,* XVI, 115.

A6088   Whimster, Donald Cameron, ed. *A Century of Lyrics, 1550-1650*. London: Arnold, 1938. Pp. 127.

A6089   Boas, Frederick S., ed. *Songs and Lyrics from the English Playbooks*. London: Cresset Press, 1945. Pp. xviii, 258.

A6090   Stevens, Denis, ed. *The Mulliner Book*. Musica Britannica, V. I. Pub. for the Royal Musical Assoc. London: Stainer & Bell, 1951. Pp. xvi, 97.
Rev: by Manfred F. Bukofzer, *RN*, iv (1951), 43-44.

A6091   Auden, W. H., Chester Kallman, and Noah Greenberg. *An Elizabethan Song Book*. London: Faber & Faber, 1955. Pp. xxix, 243.
Rev: by Ralph Lawrence, *English*, xi (1957), 232-233; by Naomi Lewis, *Statesman*, Aug. 3, p. 150; *TLS*, July 12, 1957, p. 424.

A6092   Crum, M. C. "A Seventeenth-Century Collection of Music Belonging to Thomas Hammond, A Suffolk Landowner." *Bodleian Lib. Rec.*, vi (1958), 373-386.

(b) EUROPEAN MUSIC OF THE RENAISSANCE
(Items listed in the specified sources only)

A6093   Stellfeld, J. A. *Bibliographie des Editions Musicales Plantiniennes*. Brussels: Palais des Académies, 1949. Pp. 248, pl. 20.
Rev: A2843.

A6094   Schnapper, Edith B., ed. *The British Union-Catalogue of Early Music Printed before the Year 1801*. 2 vols. London: Butterworth, 1958. Pp. 583, 593.
Rev: A31.

A6095   Besseler, Heinrich. *Musik des Mittelalters und der Renaissance*. (Handbuch der Musikwissenschaft. Bd. 11). Wildpark-Potsdam: Athenaion, 1931-1935. Pp. 338.
Rev: by Hermann Halbig, *DLZ*, lvii (1936), 1104-10; by Isabel Pope, *Speculum*, xiii (1938), 240-241.

A6096   Parry, C. Hubert H. *The Oxford History of Music*. Vol. III: *The Music of the Seventeenth Century*. 2 ed. Revised, with intro. by E. J. Dent. Oxford Univ. Press, 1938. Pp. xi, 486.
Rev: *National Rev.*, 110 (1939), 824-830; by C. T. Harrison, *VQR*, xv, 157-160.

A6097   Prunieres, Henry. *A New History of Music: The Middle Ages to Mozart*. New York: The Macmillan Co., 1943. Pp. xv, 413.
Rev: by Ralph Bates, *Nation* (N. Y.), Feb. 27, 1943, p. 320; *TLS*, Jan. 1, 1944, p. 9.

A6098   Mellers, W. H. "Voice and Dance in the Sixteenth and Seventeenth Centuries." *Scrutiny*, xii (1944), 119-135, 204-222.

A6099   Smith, Carleton Sprague, and William Dinneen. "Recent Work on Music in the Renaissance." *MP*, xlii (1944), 41-58.

A6100   Bukofzer, Manfred F. *Music in the Baroque Era: From Monteverdi to Bach*. New York: W. W. Norton & Co., 1947. London: Dent, 1948. Pp. xv, 489.
Rev: by Martin Cooper, *Spectator*, Sept. 17, 1948, p. 378.

A6101   Finney, Gretchen L. "Ecstacy and Music in Seventeenth-Century England." *JHI*, viii (1947), 153-186.

A6101a Finney, Gretchen L. " 'Organical Musick' and Ecstacy." *JHI*, viii (1947), 273-292.

A6102   Clercx, Suzanne. *Le Baroque et la Musique: Essia d'Esthétique Musicale*. Brussels. Ed. de la Librairie Encyclopédique, 1948. Pp. 235.
Rev: A5497.

A6103   Manifold, J. "Theatre Music in the Sixteenth and Seventeenth Centuries." *Music and Letters*, xxix (1948), 366-397.

A6104   Ulrich, Homer. *Chamber Music: The Growth and Practice of an Intimate Art*. Columbia Univ. Press, 1948. Pp. xvi, 430.
Devotes nearly half of the book to the sixteenth and seventeenth centuries.
Rev: *TLS*, Aug. 26, 1949, p. 548.

A6105   Bedbrook, Gerald Stares. *Keyboard Music from the Middle Ages to the Beginnings of the Baroque*. London, New York: Macmillan, 1949. Pp. xvi, 170, pl. 15, music exx. 140.
Rev: by Dorothy Swainson, *Spectator*, Oct. 7, 1949, p. 475; by J. F. R., *MGW*, Oct. 6, 1949, p. 13; *TLS*, Dec. 9, 1949, p. 811.

A6106   Walker, D. P. *Der Musikalische Humanismus im 16. und frühen 17. Jahrhundert*. Kassel: Bärenreiter, 1949. Pp. 76.

A6107   Bukofzer, Manfred F. *Studies in Medieval and Renaissance Music*. New York: Norton, 1950. Pp. 324.
Rev: by Gustave Reese, *SRL*, Mar. 31, 1951, p. 33; by Carter Harmon, *NYTBR*, Oct. 21, 1951, p. 28; by William Kimmel, *JAAC*, ix, 341; *TLS*, March 7, 1952, p. 177; by Willi Apel, *Speculum*, xxvii, 207-208.

A6108   Milner, R. "Music and Poetry in the Sixteenth Century." *EA*, ix (1956), 28-33. Rev. art. devoted to *Musique et Poésie au XVIe Siècle*, Paris, 1954.

A6109   Harman, Alec. *Medieval and Early Renaissance Music*. London: Rockliff, 1958. Pp. 268.
        Rev: *TLS*, Oct. 10, 1958, p. 580.

i. Tudor and Stuart Music

A6110   Bontoux, Germaine. *La Chanson en Angleterre au temps d'Élisabeth*. Oxford Univ. Press, 1936.
        Pp. 699, pl. 11.
        Rev: by Émile Legouis, *EA*, I (1937), 248.

A6111   Lamson, Roy, Jr. *Some Elizabethan Tunes*. *MLR*, XXXII (1937), 584-585.

A6112   Porter, I. *Aspects of the Early English Opera—Libretto*. DD, Leeds, 1938. Abstr. publ. in
        Univ. of Leeds *Publications and Abstracts of Theses, 1837/38*, p. 18.
        Traces the song tradition from Elizabethan times.

A6113   Boyd, Morrison Comegys. *Elizabethan Music and Musical Criticism*. Philadelphia: Univ.
        of Pennsylvania Press; Oxford Univ. Press, 1940. Pp. xi, 363.
        Rev: by M. B. B., *SRL*, Mar. 9, 1940, p. 21; by W. G. Hill, *JEGP*, XXXIX, 585-588; *TLS*,
        Nov. 16, 1940, p. 583; by Leicester Bradner, *MLN*, LVI (1941), 242.

A6114   Saugnet, Henri. "La Musique Élisabéthaine." In *Le Théâtre Élizabéthain*. Paris: Les Cahiers
        du Sud, 1940, pp. 133-134.

A6115   Evans, Willa McClung. *Henry Lawes, Musician and Friend of Poets*. New York: Mod. Lang.
        Assoc., 1941. Pp. xvi, 250.
        Rev: by J. T. Wisely, *RES*, XIX (1943), 86-88; by H. E. Rollins, *MLN*, LVIII, 317-318; by
        John Butt, *MLR*, XXXVIII, 51-52; by E. N. S. Thompson, *PQ*, XXII, 284-285.

A6116   Simpson, Claude M. "Tudor Popular Music: Its Social Significance." *HLQ*, V (1942),
        176-179; comments by Clair C. Olson, ibid., pp. 182-183.

A6117   Miller, Hugh Milton. *English Plainsong Compositions for Keyboard in the Sixteenth Century*.
        DD, Harvard University, 1943. Abstr. in *Summaries of Theses*, 1937-45, pp. 530-532.

A6118   Meyer, Ernst Hermann. *English Chamber Music: The History of a Great Art from the Middle
        Ages to Purcell*. New York: Universal Distributors Co.; London: Lawrence & Wishart,
        1946. Pp. xiv, 318.
        Rev: *TLS*, Jan. 25, 1947, p. 53.

A6119   Delattre, Floris, and Camille Chemin. *Les Chansons Élizabéthaines*. Bibl. des Langues Modernes,
        Vol. II. Paris: Marcel Didier, 1948. Pp. 459.
        Rev: by L. W. Wilson, *Mod. Languages*, XXIX (1948), 118; by Desmond MacCarthy in
        Sun. Times, June 6, 1948, p. 3; by Cecily Mackworth, *Paru*, Jan., 1949, pp. 77-78; by D. C.
        A., *MLN*, LXIV, 287; by O. E. Schoen-René, *JEGP*, XLVIII, 292-293; by F. Kermode, *RES*,
        XXV, 356-357; by R. Derolez, *RBPH*, XXVIII (1950), 210-215; by J. Loiseau, *LanM*, XLIV,
        119-120; by G. A. Bonnard, *ES*, XXXIII (1952), 72-76.

A6120   Scholl, Evelyn H. "English Metre Once More." *PMLA*, LXIII (1948), 293-326.
        Considers the problem of the basis of English metre in the light provided by the English
        School of Lutenist Song Writers (1597-1632).

A6121   Tegnell, John C., Jr. *Elizabethan Musical Prosody: A Study of the Style of the English Madrigal
        and Ayre*. DD, Northwestern University, 1948. Pp. 224. Abstract publ. in *Summaries of
        Doctoral Dissertations*, XVI. Chicago & Evanston: Northwestern U., 1949, pp. 36-39.

A6122   Einstein, Alfred. *The Italian Madrigal*. Tr. by Alexander H. Krappe, Roger H. Sessions, and
        Oliver Strunk, 3 vols. Princeton Univ. Press, 1949. Pp. xvi, 887 (I, II); xxx, 333; pl. 24.
        Rev: by Otto Kinkeldey, *RN*, II (1949), 25-28; by Howard Taubman, *NYTBR*, April 3,
        1949, p. 16; by P. H. Lang, *NYHTBR*, May 29, 1949, p. 7; by Leo Schrade, *YR*, XXXIX,
        378-380; by Kathleen Hoover, *SRL*, XXXII, 21; by P. H. Lang, *Musical Quarterly*, XXXV,
        437-447.

A6123   Fellowes, Edmund Horace. *The English Madrigal Composers*. 2nd ed. Oxford Univ. Press,
        1949. Pp. 364. First publ. in 1921; some corrections and revisions.

A6124   Obertello, Alfredo. *Madrigali Italiani in Inghilterra*. Milan: Bompiani, 1949. Pp. 560.
        Rev: A4441.

A6125   Woodfill, Walter L. "Education of Professional Musicians in Elizabethan England." *Medie-
        valia et Humanistica*, VI (1950), 101-108.
        See A6107 and A6141.

A6126   Kerman, Joseph W. *The Elizabethan Madrigal: A Comparative Study*. DD, Princeton Uni-
        versity, 1950.

A6127   Bright, Robert H. *The Early Tudor Part-song from Newarke to Cornyshe*. DD, University of
        Southern California, 1952.

A6128   Mackerness, E. D. *The English Musical Sensibility: Studies in Representative Literary Discussions
        and Periodical Criticism from Thomas Morley (1557-1603?) to W. J. Turner (1899-1946)*. DD,
        Manchester, 1952.

A6129   Byler, Arthur W. *Italian Currents in the Popular Music of England in the Sixteenth Century*. DD,
        University of Chicago, 1953.

A6130   Milner, R. H. "The Study of Elizabethan Music." *EA*, VI (1953), 214-226.

A6131 Woodfill, Walter L. *Musicians in English Society from Elizabeth to Charles I.* Princeton Univ. Press, 1953. Pp. xv, 372; pl. 8.

A6132 Mason, Dorothy E. *Music in Elizabethan England* (Folger Booklets on Tudor and Stuart Civilization). Washington, D. C.: The Folger Shakespeare Library, 1958. Pp. 38.

A6133 Stevens, John. "The Elizabethan Madrigal." In *Essays and Studies, 1958.* Collected for the English Association by Basil Willey. London: Murray, 1958. Pp. 17-37.

ii. Music and English Renaissance Literature

A6134 Lamson, Roy, Jr. *English Broadside Ballad Tunes, 1550-1770.* DD, Harvard University, 1936. Abstract publ. in *Summaries of Ph.D. Theses, 1936.* Cambridge: Harvard Univ. Press, 1938, pp. 336-338.

A6135 Policardi, S. *Lyrical Poetry in Renaissance England.* Milan: Montuoro, 1943. Pp. 192.

A6136 Ottieri, Ottiero. "Lirica nel dramma inglese." *Anglica,* I (1946), 154-159.

A6137 Eldredge, Frances. *Criteria for Lyric in the Later English Renaissance.* DD, University of Chicago, 1948. Pp. 331.

A6138 Pattison, B. *Music and Poetry of the English Renaissance.* London: Methuen, 1948. Pp. ix, 220.
Rev: *TLS,* May 8, 1948, p. 256; by E. J. Dent, *MLR,* XLIII (1948), 526-527; by R. Davril, *LanM,* XLII, 469; by Frank Kermode, *RES,* xxv (1949), 265-269; *Scrutiny,* xv, 331.

A6139 Sabol, Andrew J. *Music for the English Drama from the Beginnings to 1642.* DD, Brown University, 1948. Pp. 271.

A6140 Hart, E. F. *The Relationship between English Poetry and Music in the Seventeenth Century.* MA thesis, London (King's), 1949.

A6141 Carpenter, Nan C. "Musicians in Early University Drama." *N & Q,* 195 (1950), 470-472.

A6142 Bowden, William R. *The English Dramatic Lyric, 1603-42: A Study in Stuart Dramatic Technique.* Yale Univ. Stud. Eng., 118. Yale Univ. Press, 1951. Pp. xii, 219.
Rev: *TLS,* Oct. 31, 1952, p. 710; by Albert Howard Carter, *SQ,* IV (1953), 348-350.

A6143 Ingram, R. W. *Dramatic Use of Music in English Drama, 1603-1642.* DD, London University, 1955.

(c) MUSIC AND SONGS IN SHAKESPEARE
i. General Dramatic Function of Music in Shakespeare

A6144 Lambertson, Chester Lee. *Shakespeare's Use of Music as a Dramatic Device.* MA thesis, Alberta, 1941. Pp. 263.

A6144a Wood, Warren Welles. *A Comparison between Shakespeare and His Contemporaries in Their Use of Music and Sound Effects.* DD, Northwestern University, 1944. Abstract publ. in *Summaries of Doctoral Dissertations, 1944,* XII. Chicago and Evanston: Northwestern U., 1945, pp. 33-38.

A6145 Vogel, R. R. *An Evaluation of the Love Songs in Shakespeare's Dramatic Works.* MS thesis, Columbia University, 1948. Pp. 66.

A6146 Sterling, Alfred M. *Shakespeare's Dramatic Use of Music.* DD, Harvard University, 1949.

A6147 Long, John H. *Shakespeare's Use of Music: A Study of the Music and its Performance in the Original Performances of Seven Comedies.* DD, University of Florida, 1951.
See number A6151.

A6148 McCullen, Joseph T., Jr. "The Functions of Songs Aroused by Madness in Elizabethan Drama." *A Tribute to George Coffin Taylor* (Univ. North Carolina Press, 1952), pp. 185-196.

A6149 Sternfeld, Frederick W. "*Troilus and Cressida:* Music for the Play." *EIE, 1952.* New York: Columbia Univ. Press, 1954, pp. 107-137.

A6150 Schomburg, Wolfgang. *Das Lyrische in Shakespeares Dramen.* DD, Kiel, 1953. Typewritten.

A6151 Long, John H. *Shakespeare's Use of Music: A Study of the Music and Its Performance in the Original Production of Seven Comedies.* Gainesville: Univ. of Florida Press, 1955. Pp. xv, 213.
Rev: by Edwin S. Lindsey, *South Atlantic Bul.,* XXI, No. 2 (1955), 12; by D. W. Stevens, *Music and Letters,* XXXVI, 398-399; *SCN,* XIII, 30-31; by Peter J. Seng, *JEGP,* LV (1956), 309-311; *CE,* XVIII, 176; *ShN,* VI, 42; by Frederick W. Sternfeld, *RES,* VIII (1957), 64-66; Denis Arnold, *MLR,* LII, 416-417; by Cécile de Banke, *SQ,* VIII, 107-108; by R. A. Foakes, *ShS,* X, 150; by Bruce Pattison, *ES,* XXXIX (1958), 91-92.

A6152 Seng, Peter J. *The Dramatic Function of the Songs in Shakespeare's Plays: A Variorum Edition.* DD, Harvard University, 1955. 2 vols. Pp. 696. Abstracted by Jack R. Brown in *ShN,* VII (1957), 31.

A6153 Sternfeld, Frederick W. "The Dramatic and Allegorical Function of Music in Shakespeare's Tragedies." *Annales Musicologiques,* III (1955), 265-282.

A6154 Manifold, John Streeter. *The Music in English Drama.* From Shakespeare to Purcell. London: Rockliff, 1956. Pp. ix, 208.
Shak: pp. 2-103, 171-182.
Rev: *TLS,* Aug. 17, 1956, p. 488; briefly by Julian Hall in *English,* XI, 106; by Ivor Brown, *Time and Tide,* July 7, 1956, p. 822; by R. W. Ingram, *Music and Letters,* XXXVII, 375-376; by Hermann Heuer, *SJ,* 94 (1958), 297-299.

A6155   Thompson, Marvin Orville. *Uses of Music and Reflections of Current Theories of the Psychology of Music in the Plays of Shakespeare, Jonson, and Beaumont and Fletcher.* DD, University of Minnesota, 1956. Pp. 272. Mic A56-3899. *DA*, XVI (1956), 2448. Publication No. 18,954.

A6156   Auden, W. H. "Music in Shakespeare." *Encounter*, IX (1957), 31-44.

A6156a   Seng, Peter J. "Music in Shakespeare." *Encounter*, X (1958), 67-68. On A6156.

A6157   Wey, James J. *Musical Allusion and Song as Part of the Structure of Meaning of Shakespeare's Plays.* An Abstract of a Dissertation. Washington, D. C.: Catholic University of America Press, 1957. Pp. 17.

A6158   Cutts, John P. "Music and the Super-natural in *The Tempest*: A Study in Interpretation." *Music & Letters*, XXXIX (1958), 347-358.

A6159   Doss, E. Sue Harrison. *The Unity of Play and Song in Shakespeare.* DD, University of Arkansas, 1958. Pp. 223. Mic A58-1488. *DA*, XVIII (1958), 1786.

A6160   Nosworthy, J. M. "Music and Its Function in the Romances of Shakespeare." *ShS*, XI (1958), 60-69.

A6161   Sternfeld, Frederick W. "Le Symbolisme Musical dans Quelques Pièces de Shakespeare Présentées à la Cour d'Angleterre." *Fêtes de la Renaissance* (B4438a), pp. 319-333.

ii.   Morley and Shakespeare

A6162   Morley, Thomas. *Plaine and Easie Introduction to Practicall Musicke.* Introd. by Edmund H. Fellowes. Shakespeare Assoc. Facsimiles No. 14. Oxford Univ. Press, 1937. Pp. 218.
         Rev: *TLS*, Aug. 14, 1937, p. 588; *N & Q*, 174 (1938), 269; by Bruce Pattison, *MLR*, XXXIV (1939), 294.

A6162a   Morley, Thomas. *A Plain and Easy Introduction to Practical Music.* Ed. by R. Alec Harman. With a foreword by Thurston Dart. London: Dent, 1952. Pp. xxx, 326.
         Rev: *TLS*, Aug. 8, 1952, p. 512; *N & Q*, 197 (1952), 550; *DUJ*, XVI (1952), 35-36; by J. Jacquot, *EA*, VI (1953), 335-357.

A6163   Uhler, John Earle. *Morley's Canzonets for Two Voices.* Louisiana State Univ. Press, 1954. Pp. 17, Sigs. [A2]-D4.
         Includes facsimile reproductions of both cantus book and tenor book.
         Rev: by John H. Long, *SCN*, XIII (1955), 14; by Charles W. Hughes, *RN*, VIII, 116.

A6163a   Uhler, John Earle. *Morley's Canzonets for Three Voices.* Louisiana State Univ. Studies, Humanities Series, 7, ed. Waldo McNeir. Baton Rouge: Louisiana State Univ. Press, 1957. Pp. 49, (plus 118 unpaged).
         Reproduces the German ed. of 1624.
         Rev: *Georgia Rev.*, XII (1958), 229.

A6164   Brennecke, Ernest, Jr. "Shakespeare's Musical Collaboration with Morley." *PMLA*, LIV (1939), 139-149. See also "A Reply and a Symposiun" by Robert Moore, ibid., 149-152, and "Postscript" by author, ibid., 152.

A6165   Deutsch, Otto Erich. "The Editions of Morley's *Introduction*." *Library*, XXIII (1942), 127-129.

A6166   Fellowes, Edmund H. " 'It Was a Lover and his Lass': Some Fresh Points of Criticism." *MLR*, XLI (1946), 202-206.

A6167   Gordon, P. "The Morley-Shakespeare Myth." *Music and Letters*, XXVIII (1947), 121-125.

A6168   Mackerness, E. D. "Morley's Musical Sensibility." *CamJ*, II (1949), 301-308.

A6169   Reymes-King, John. *An Aesthetic and Musical Analysis of the Madrigals of Thomas Morley, with Special Reference to Relations between Text and Music and Some Comparison with the Madrigals of John Wibye, John Bennet, and the "Triumphs of Oriana."* DD, Toronto, 1950.

A6170   Long, John H. "Shakespeare and Thomas Morley." *MLN*, LXV (1950), 17-22.
         Comment by Louis Marder, *MLN*, LXV, 501-503; by John R. Moore, ibid., pp. 504-505.

A6171   Beck, Sydney. "The Case of 'O Mistresses mine'." *RN*, IV (1953), 19-23.
         See comments by John H. Long, *RN*, VII, 15-16; by Vincent Duckles, ibid., 98-100.

iii.   Settings of Specific Songs

A6172   Adams, J. Q. "A New Song by Robert Jones." *MLQ*, I (1940), 45-48.

A6173   Castelnuovo-Tedesco, Mario. "Shakespeare and Music." *SAB*, XV (1940), 166-174.

A6174   Thewlis, G. A. "An Unpublished Contemporary Setting of 'Hark, hark'!" *Music and Letters*, XXII (1941), 32-35.

A6175   McEvans, Willa. *Shakespeare's 'Harke, Harke, Ye Larke'.* *PMLA*, LX (1945), 95-101.

A6176   Brennecke, Ernest. " 'What Shall He Have that Killed the Deer?' A Note on Shakespeare's Lyric and Its Music." *Musical Times*, 93 (1952), 347-351.

A6177   Cutts, J. P. "Robert Johnson: King's Musician in His Majesty's Public Entertainment." *Music and Letters*, XXXVI (1955), 110-125.

A6178   Cutts, John P. "The Original Music of a Song in *2 Henry IV*." *SQ*, VII (1956), 385-392.

A6179   Cutts, John P. "The Original Music to Middleton's *The Witch*." *SQ*, VII (1956), 203-209.

A6180   Cutts, John P. "An Unpublished Contemporary Setting of a Shakespeare Song." *ShS*, IX (1956), 86-89.

A6181   Stevens, Denis. *The Five Songs in Shakespeare's "As You Like It,"* adapted and arranged from sources contemporary with the play. London: Hinrichson, 1957.
Rev: *Music and Letters*, XXXVIII (1957), 300-301.

A6182   Osborn, James J. "Benedick's Song in 'Much Ado'." *The Times* (London), Nov. 17, 1958, p. 11.

A6183   Seng, Peter J. "The Earliest Known Music for Desdemona's 'Willow Song'." *SQ*, IX (1958), 419-420.

A6184   Seng, Peter J. "An Early Tune for the Fool's Song in *King Lear*." *SQ*, IX (1958), 583-585.

A6185   Seng, Peter J. "The Riddle Song in 'Merchant of Venice'." *N &Q*, NS, V (1958), 191-193.

A6186   Sternfeld, Frederick W. "Lasso's Music for Shakespeare's 'Samingo'." *SQ*, IX (1958), 105-115.

iv.   Production Problems, etc.

A6187   M. "Shakespeare und die Musik." *Stuttg. Neues Tagbl.*, 1936, Nr. 276.

A6188   Ghisi, Federico. "Shakespeare e le sue Relazioni con la Musica." *Studi Inglesi*, April, 1939.

A6189   Mantey, K. G. *Shakespeare-Volkslieder*. Lieder aus Shakespeares Dramatischen Werken. Leipzig: H. H. Kreisel Verlag, 1939. Pp. 80.

A6190   Prick van Wely, M. "Muziek bij Shakespeare." *Gemeenschap.*, 1939, pp. 650-654.

A6191   Sollertinsky, I. I. "Shakespeare and the World Music." *Shakespeare—A Symposium*. Leningrad, Moscow: The State Scientific Institute of Music and the Theatre, 1939, pp. 97-130.

A6192   Davis, Reginald. *Shakespeare's Contribution to Music*. MA thesis, Ottawa, 1943. Pp. 99.

A6193   Gombosi, Otto. "Some Musical Aspects of the English Court Masque." *Journal of the American Musicological Society*, I (1948), 3-19.

A6194   Marder, Louis. *Aspects of Shakespeare's Education*. DD, Columbia University, 1950. Pp. 291. Mic A50-149. *Microf. Ab.*, X (1950), 218. Publication No. 1880.

A6195   Purdom, C. B. *Producing Shakespeare*. London: Pitman, 1950. Pp. xii, 220.
Rev: B1729.

A6196   Hutton, James. "Some English Poems in Praise of Music." *English Miscellany*, ed. by Mario Praz. Rome: Edizioni di Storia e Letteratura, 1951, pp. 1-63.

A6197   Baldini, Gabriele. "Mellifluous Shakespeare." *English Miscellany*, IV (1953), 67-94.

A6198   Banke, Cécile de. *Shakespearean Stage Production: Then & Now*. New York: McGraw-Hill, 1953. Pp. xviii, 342.
Rev: A7409.

A6199   Long, John H. "Music for the Replica Staging of Shakespeare." Matthews and Emery, eds., *Studies in Shakespeare*, 1953, pp. 88-95.
See B4448.

A6200   Kahan, Gerald. *A Shakespeare Production Handbook for Nonprofessionals*. DD, University of Wisconsin, 1954. Abstr. publ. in Univ. of Wisconsin *Summaries of Doctoral Dissertations, 1953-54*, Madison, 1955, pp. 576-578.
Chap. VI, "Music," discusses Eliz. music.

A6201   Pleijel, Bengt. "Shakespeare och musikerna" ("Shakespeare and the musicians"). *Teatern* (Norrköping), XXIII (1956), 13-16.

A6202   Cutts, J. P. *Music for Shakespeare's Company, The King's Men*. DD, Birmingham, 1957.

A6203   Cutts, John P. "Music for Shakespeare." *ShN*, VII (1957), 28.

A6204   Fortner, Wolfgang. "Festival of Music and Musicians from South Africa." *Musical Opinion*, 80 (1957), 265.

A6205   Eggar, Katharine. "Shakespeare as Musician." *Musical Times* (1958), pp. 480-481.

A6206   Giannini, V. "Shakespeare's Musical Training." *Music Journal*, XVI (1958), 8 ff.

A6207   Hollander, John. "Musica Mundana and Twelfth Night." *EIE, 1956*. Columbia Univ. Press, 1958, pp. 55-82.

(d)   DANCES AND ACROBATICS

A6208   Sullivan, Norah (E. M.) Cleaver. *The Purpose and Development of the Dance in the English Drama from 1590-1642*. MA thesis, McGill, 1931.

A6209   Dolmetsch, Mabel. *Dances of England and France from 1450 to 1600: With their Music and Authentic Manner of Performance*. London: Routledge and Kegan Paul, 1949. Pp. xii, 163.
Rev: *TLS*, Feb. 17, 1950, p. 100.

A6210   Richey, Dorothy. *The Dance in the Drama of the Elizabethan Public Theatre: A Production Problem*. DD, Northwestern University, 1951. Abstr. publ. in Northwestern Univ. *Summaries of Doctoral Dissertations*, 1951, XIX, Chicago and Evanston: Northwestern Univ., 1952, pp. 169-174.

A6211 Prange, Gerda. "Shakespeares Ausserungen über die Tänze seiner Zeit." *SJ*, 89 (1953), 132-161.

A6212 Violi, Unicio J. *Shakespeare and the Lazzo*. DD, Columbia University, 1955. Pp. 282. Mic A55-1834. *DA*, xv (1955), 1391. Publication No. 12,479.

A6213 Sorell, Walter. "Shakespeare and the Dance." *SQ*, viii (1957), 367-384. (Earlier condensation: *Dance Magazine*, Aug., 1955, p. 24 ff.)

A6214 Mitchell, Lee. "Shakespeare's Legerdemain." *Speech Monographs*, xvi (1949), 144-161.

A6215 Schneideman, Robert Ivan. *Elizabethan Legerdemain, and Its Employment in the Drama, 1576-1642*. DD, Northwestern University, 1956. Pp. 274. *DA*, xvi (1956), 2558.

(7) TYPICAL SCENES—MOBS, GHOSTS, MADNESS, ETC. (107;36)
(a) MOBS

A6216 McCloskey, John C. "Fear of the People as a Minor Motive in Shakspere." *SAB*, xvii (1942), 67-72.

A6217 Stirling, Brents. "Shakespeare's Mob Scenes: A Reinterpretation." *HLQ*, viii (1945), 213-240.

A6218 Watkins, W. B. C. "Shakespeare and the Populace." *SR*, liv (1946), 548-551.

A6219 Stirling, Brents. *The Populace in Shakespeare*. Columbia Univ. Press, 1949. Pp. 203.
　　Rev: by Harry Levin, *NYTBR*, Aug. 7, 1949; by Justus Meyer, *Elseviers Weekblad* (Amsterdam), Apr. 8, 1950; *TLS*, Feb. 10, 1950, p. 94; by H. E. Cain, *Catholic Hist. Rev.*, xxxv, 500-501; by D. Bush, *NR*, Apr. 24, 1950, p. 22; by Marcia L. Anderson, *South Atlantic Quar.*, xlix, 417-418; by Sidney Thomas, *MLN*, lxvi (1951), 114-115; by E. C. Pettet, *RES*, ii, 378-379; by John Arthos, *MLQ*, xii, 499-501; by W. Clemen, *Archiv*, 189 (1952/53), 65; by H. Heuer, *SJ*, 89 (1953), 229-230.

A6220 Kaieda, Susumu. "The Mob in Shakespearian Plays" (in Japanese). *Tokyo Univ. of Foreign Studies Journal*, Nov., 1956.

(b) GHOSTS AND OTHER SUPER-NATURAL REPRESENTATIONS

A6221 Small, Samuel A. "Shakespeare's Ghosts." *SAB*, xi (1936), 118-119.

A6222 Rogers, L. W. "Ghosts in Shakespeare." *Theosophist*, lviii (1937), 491-494.

A6223 Fryxell, Burton L. *Ghosts and Witches in Elizabethan Tragedy, 1560-1625*. DD, University of Wisconsin, 1937. Abstr. publ. in Univ. of Wisconsin *Summaries of Doctoral Dissertations*, ii (1938), 295-297.

A6224 Gronauer, G. *Die Frage der Realität der Geistererscheinungen in Shakespeares Dramen*. DD, Erlangen, 1939. Erlangen: K. Döres, 1939. Pp. vii, 81.

A6225 West, Robert H. *The Invisible World: A Study of Pneumatology in Elizabethan Drama*. DD, Vanderbilt University, 1939. Abstr. publ. in *Bulletin of Vanderbilt University*, xxxix (Aug., 1939), 34-35.

A6226 West, Robert H. *The Invisible World: A Study of Pneumatology in Elizabethan Drama*. Univ. Georgia Press, 1939. Pp. xviii, 275.
　　Rev: A1589.

A6227 C., T. C. "Ghosts on Stage and in Cinema." *N &Q*, 178 (1940), 444-445; M. H. Dodds, ibid., 179 (1940), 104-105; H. G. L. K., ibid., 138-139.

A6228 Doran, Madelaine. "On Elizabethan 'Credulity': With some questions concerning the Use of the Marvellous in Literature." *JHI*, i (1940), 151-176.
　　That the Commonalty were less credulous than the learned in Elizabethan times, and more inductive, because less bookish.

A6229 Doran, Madeleine. "That Undiscovered Country. A Problem concerning the use of the Supernatural in *Hamlet* and *Macbeth*." *Renaissance Studies in Honor of Hardin Craig*, Stanford Univ. Press, 1941, pp. 221-235; also *PQ*, xx, 413-427.
　　"There is no Elizabethan state of mind; there are many Elizabethan states of mind."

A6230 Hankins, John Erskine. *The Character of Hamlet and Other Essays*. Univ. of North Carolina Press, 1941. Pp. xii, 264. "On Ghosts," p. 131.
　　Rev: B7664.

A6231 Stanford, W. B. "Ghosts and Apparitions in Homer, Aeschylus, and Shakespeare." *Hermathena*, lvi (1941), 84-92.

A6232 Semper, I. J. "The Ghost in Hamlet." *Catholic World*, 162 (1946), 510-517.

A6233 Jones, D. E. *The Ghost in the Drama*. MS thesis, Columbia University, 1948.

A6234 Herbert, T. Walter. "Shakespeare Announces a Ghost." *SQ*, i (1950), 247-254.

A6235 Chapman, G. E. *Demonology in Elizabethan Drama*. MA thesis, Sheffield University, 1953.

A6236 Semper, I. J. "The Ghost in *Hamlet*: Pagan or Christian?" *The Month*, ns, ix (1953), 222-234.
　　Avers it's Christian.

A6237   West, Robert H. "Elizabethan Belief in Spirits and Witchcraft." Matthews and Emery, eds. *Studies in Shakespeare*, pp. 65-73.
        Asserts the strength of the Elizabethan belief in demons, but also cites Harsnett, Scot, and other doubters.

A6238   Christian, Margarette. "Shakespeare's Ghosts." *Ashland Studies in Shakespeare, 1955*, pp. 42-77.

A6239   Maxwell, James Coutts. "The Ghost from the Grave: A Note on Shakespeare's Apparitions." *DUJ*, XLVIII (1956), 55-59.

A6240   Craig, Edward Gordon. *On the Art of Theatre*. 5th impr. with new ill. London: Heinemann, 1957. Pp. xxiii, 294. "The Ghosts in the Tragedies of Shakespeare," pp. 264-280.
        Rev: A8133.

A6241   Dahinten, Gisela. *Die Geisterszene in der Tragödie vor Shakespeare. Zur Seneca-Nachfolge im englischen und lateinischen Drama des Elisabethanismus* (*Palaestra*, Band 225). Göttingen: Vandenhoeck & Ruprecht, 1958. Pp. 193.

(c) MAD SCENES

A6242   Adnès, André. *Shakespeare et la Folie*. Étude Médicopsychologique. Paris: Librairie Maloine, 1936. Pp. 315.
        Rev: A1237.

A6243   Smith, M. Ellwood. "The Lunatic, The Lover and The Poet." *SAB*, XVI (1941), 77-88.

A6244   McCullen, Joseph T., Jr. *The Functions or Uses of Madness in Elizabethan Drama Between 1590 and 1638*. DD, University of North Carolina, 1948. Abstr. publ. in *Univ. of North Carolina Record, Research in Progress, 1945-1948*, Grad. School Ser., No. 56, 1949, pp. 193-194.

A6245   McCullen, Joseph T., Jr. "Madness and the Isolation of Characters in Elizabethan and Early Stuart Drama." *SP*, XLVIII (1951), 206-218.

A6246   McCullen, J. T., Jr. "The Functions of Songs Aroused by Madness in Elizabethan Drama." *A Tribute to George Coffin Taylor*, ed. by Arnold Williams, Univ. of North Carolina Press, 1952.

(d) PRISONS

A6247   Dobb, C. *Life and Conditions in London Prisons, 1553-1643, with Special Reference to Contemporary Literature*. B. Litt thesis, Oxford, 1953.

A6248   Pendry, E. D. *Elizabethan Prisons and Prison Scenes*. DD, Birmingham, 1955.

(e) GAMES AND SPORTS

A6249   Brewster, Paul G. "Games and Sports in Sixteenth and Seventeenth Century English Literature." *Western Folklore*, VI (1947), 143-156.

A6250   Solem, Delmar E. *Indoor Game Scenes in the Elizabethan Drama and the Problem of Their Staging*. DD, Northwestern University, 1953. Abstr. publ. in Northwestern Univ. *Summaries of Doctoral Dissertations*, 1952, XX. Chicago and Evanston, 1953, pp. 163-167. Also in *Speech Monographs*, XX (1953), 142-143.

A6251   McCullen, Joseph T., Jr. "The Use of Parlor and Tavern Games in Elizabethan and Early Stuart Drama." *MLQ*, XIV (1953), 7-14.

(f) INTERNAL DRAMATIC REPRESENTATIONS
See also Numbers B7878-B7906 on the Mousetrap in *Hamlet*.

A6252   Gaw, A. "The Impromptu Masque in Shakespeare with Special Reference to *Romeo and Juliet*." *SAB*, XI (1936), 149-160.

A6253   Eastmond, M. *Formative Influences Upon Elizabethan Dumbshow*. MS thesis, Columbia University, 1947. Pp. 84.

A6254   Lüthi, M. "Theater im Theater bei Shakespeare." *Volkshochschule* (Zürich), XVII (1948), Heft 5.

A6255   Fiedler, Leslie A. "The Defense of the Illusion and the Creation of Myth." *EIE, 1948*. New York: Columbia Univ. Press, 1949, pp. 74-94.

A6256   Flatter, Richard. "The Dumb-Show in 'Macbeth'." *TLS*, March 23, 1951, p. 181.
        See letters by Peter Ure, *TLS*, April 6, 1951, p. 216; C. B. Purdom, ibid., April 20, 1951, p. 245.

A6257   Venezky, Alice S. *Pageantry on the Shakespearean Stage*. New York: Twayne Publishers, 1951. Pp. 242.
        Dumb Shows, pp. 111 ff.
        Rev: A7238.

A6258   Hunter, E. K. *Shakespeare and Common Sense*. Boston: Christopher, 1954. Pp. 312.
        Chapter on Plays Within Plays.
        Rev: A971.

A6259   Sunesen, Bent. "Marlowe and the Dumb Show." *ES*, XXXV (1954), 241-253.

A6260   Gerhardt, Mia I. "Het Toneelstuk in Het Toneelstuk." *LT* (1955), pp. 258-275.

A6261   Schmidtbonn, Wilhelm. *Das festliche Haus.* Cologne, 1955. "Die Fahrt in den Sommernachts-traum," pp. 122-124.

A6262   Voigt, Joachim. *Das Spiel im Spiel.* Versuch einer Formbestimmung an Beispielen aus dem deutschen, englischen und spanischen Drama. DD, Göttingen, 1955. Pp. 179. Typewritten.

A6263   Grinstein, Alexander. "The Dramatic Device: A Play within a Play." *Journal of the American Psycho-Analytic Association,* IV (1956), 49-52.

A6264   Nelson, Robert J. *Play Within a Play: The Dramatist's Conception of His Art, Shakespeare to Anouilh* (Yale Romanic Studies, 2nd Series, Vol. V). Yale Univ. Press, 1958. Pp. xiii, 182.

(g)   MISCELLANEOUS

A6265   Kennedy, Milton Boone. "The Oration in Shakespeare." *Abstracts of Dissertations,* Univ. of Virginia, 1937, pp. 16-18.

A6266   Hoffmann, Friedrich. "Die Typischen Situationen im Elisabethanischen Drama und ihr Pattern." *SJ,* 94 (1958), 107-120.

A6267   Sutton, Vivian Ryan. *Inns and Taverns and English Literature, 1558-1642.* DD, Bryn Mawr College, 1942. Pp. 223. Mic A44-3353. *Microf. Ab.,* VI (1945), 80. Publication No. 669.

A6268   Upton, K. S. *Nocturnal Devices and Occasions in Elizabethan and Jacobean Drama, 1584-1610.* Master thesis, Wales, 1956.

(8)   DEFINITE MOTIFS—FRIENDSHIP, SUICIDE, DREAMS, ETC. (109;-)
(a)   GROUPS OF MOTIFS

A6269   Bradbrook, M. C. *Themes and Conventions of Elizabethan Tragedy.* Cambridge Univ. Press, 1935. In Ebisch and Schücking *Supplement,* pp. 3, 34.
        Rev: by Richard David, *NstN,* NS, IX (1935), 290-292; by Esther Cloudman Dunn, *SRL,* May 4, 1935, p. 22; by Gorley Putt, *MP,* XXXIII, 203-206; *N &Q,* 168 (1935), 215; *SAB,* X, 114; by G. B. Harrison, *MLR,* XXXI (1936), 78; by W. Kalthoff, *Beiblatt,* XLVII (1936), 144-147; by U. M. Ellis-Fermor, *RES,* XIII (1937), 94-96; by W. H. Durham, *MLN,* LIII (1938), 211-212; by E. E. Stoll, "Recent Elizabethan Criticism," *ELH,* VI (1939), 52-57.
        2nd edition, Cambridge Univ. Press, 1952. Pp. viii, 275.
        Rev: by M. Poirier, *EA,* VI (1953), 358-359; by J. Vallette, *MdF,* 318 (1953), p. 548.

A6270   Messiaen, Pierre. "Thèmes Moraux et Sentimentaux dans Shakespeare." *Rev. Universitaire,* Dec., 1936, pp. 420-427.

A6271   Petersen, Julius. "Das Motiv in der Dichtung." *DuV,* XXXVIII (1937), 44-65.

A6272   Gorrell, Robert Mark. *The Popular Drama in England, 1600-1642.* DD, Cornell University, 1940. Abstract publ. in *Abstracts of Theses, 1939,* Ithaca: Cornell Univ. Press, 1940, pp. 35-37.

A6273   Outram, A. E. *Some Conventions of Elizabethan Drama.* DD, Oxford, 1939. *OxAbs,* 1940, pp. 97-102.

A6274   Fleming, Edith Alice. *Shakespeare's Recurring Ideas.* MA thesis, Alberta, 1941. Pp. 314.

A6275   Cox, Ernest H. "Shakespeare and Some Conventions of Old Age." *SP,* XXXIX (1942), 36-46.

A6276   Bouvier, Arthur Paul. *Studies in the Development of Dramatic Conventions in 16th Century England.* DD, University of Minnesota, 1944.

A6277   McClure, Charles R. *Devices in English Plays of 1600-1607, with Particular Reference to "Hamlet".* DD, Indiana University, 1947.

A6278   Schneider, R. *Macht und Gewissen in Shakespeares Tragödie.* Berlin: Suhrkamp, 1947.

A6279   Hubler, Edward. "Three Shakespearean Myths: Mutability, Plenitude, and Reputation." *EIE, 1948.* New York: Columbia Univ. Press, 1949, pp. 95-119.

A6280   Hyde, Mary Crapo. *Playwriting for Elizabethans.* Columbia Univ. Press, 1949. Pp. ix, 258.
        Rev: A6061.

A6281   Utter, Robert P., Jr. "In Defense of Hamlet." *CE,* XII (1950), 138-144.
        Discusses 5 medieval themes with which Shak. concerned himself: (1) usurpation, (2) dueling, feuding and brawling, (3) overzealous honor, (4) war over trifles, and (5) hasty revenge.

A6282   Lord, John Bigelow. *Certain Dramatic Devices Studied in the Comedies of Shakespeare and in Some of the Works of His Contemporaries and Predecessors.* DD, University of Illinois, 1951. Pp. 296. *DA,* XII (1952), 66. Publication No. 3154.
        Reform, the Vow and the Law, Love Tokens, the Bribe and Reward, Misdelivery, Betrayal, Substitute, the Man Behind the Arras, Disguise.

A6283   Melián Lafinur, Luis. "El *humour,* la fantasía, la pasión, el crimen y la virtud en Shakespeare." *Rev. Nacional* (Montevideo), Tomo LV, Año XV, No. 163 (July 1952), 128-145.
        From the author's book *Las mujeres en Shakespeare,* Montevideo [?], 1884.

A6284   Lee, Alberta E. *Preaching in Elizabethan and Jacobean Drama.* DD, Columbia University, 1953. Pp. 341. Mic A54-164. *DA,* XIV (1954), 112. Publication No. 6657.
        Discusses 4 homiletic themes: gluttony and drunkenness, excess of apparel, usury, brawling.

A6285   McAvoy, William Charles. *Shakespeare's Use of the Laus of Apthonius.* DD, University of Illinois, 1952. Pp. 225. Mic A53-237. *DA,* XIII (1953), 97. Publication No. 4464.

A6286 Provost, George Foster. *The Techniques of Characterization and Dramatic Imagery in "Richard II" and "King Lear".* DD, Louisiana State University, 1955. Pp. 274. Mic 55-280. *DA*, xv (1955), 1616. Publication No. 12,525.

A6287 Jacquot, Jean. "Le Théâtre du Monde de Shakespeare à Calderón." *RLC*, xxxi (1957), 341-372.

A6288 Tillyard, Eustace M. W. "Reality and Fantasy in Elizabethan Literature." *Sprache und Literatur*, pp. 69-81.
See B4447a.

(b) MOTIFS INSEPARABLE FROM ETHICAL CONSIDERATIONS
i. Friendship

A6289 Burre, H. *Das Freundschaftsmotiv und seine Abwandlung in den Dramen Shakespeares.* DD, Marburg, 1938. Marburg: Bauer, 1938. Pp. viii, 56.

A6290 Mills, Laurens J. *One Soul in Bodies Twain: Friendship in Tudor Literature and Stuart Drama.* Bloomington, Ind.: Principia Press, Inc., 1937. Pp. vii, 470.
Rev: by Robert Withington, *MLN*, LIII (1938), 619-623.

A6291 Jackson, James L. "Shakespeare's Dog-and-Sugar Imagery and the Friendship Tradition." *SQ*, I (1950), 260-263.

A6292 Wisser, Heinz. *Shakespeares Ideen über Liebe, Frauen und Freundschaft, abgeleitet aus Zitaten und Aphorismen der 8 grossen Tragödien seiner dritten Schaffensperiode.* DD, Vienna, 1950. Pp. 138. Typewritten.

A6293 Piloto, A. E. *The Theme of Friendship in Elizabethan Literature.* MLitt thesis, Cambridge, Jesus, 1955.

A6294 Potts, Abbie Findlay. *Shakespeare and "The Faerie Queene."* Cornell University Press, 1958. Pp. xii, 269.
Chapter on Friendship and Chastity.

ii. Deception and Intrigue

A6295 Evans, Viola M. *Self-deception in the Plays of Six Comic Dramatists.* DD, University of California, 1935.
Chapter IV: "Shakespeare," pp. 63-81.

A6296 Messiaen, Pierre. "L'Intrigue et l'Action dans les Comédies de Shakespeare." *Rev. Universitaire*, June, 1937, pp. 25-35.

A6297 McCloskey, John C. "The Plot Device of False Report." *SAB*, xxi (1946), 147-158.

A6298 Curry, Rev. John Vincent. *Deception in Elizabethan Comedy: An Analytical Study.* DD, Columbia University, 1951. Pp. 229. Mic A51-541. *Microf. Ab.*, xi (1951), 840. Publication No. 2804. Chicago: Loyola Univ. Press, 1955. Pp. viii, 197.
Rev: *N &Q*, NS, II (1955), 504; Robert Withington, *CE*, xvii (1956), 244; by Arthur Colby Sprague, *MLN*, LXXI, 216-218; by Marvin T. Herrick, *JEGP*, LV, 311-313; by M. C. Bradbrook, *MLR*, LI, 623; by C. G. Thayer, *Books Abroad*, xxx, 441; by Erwin W. Geissman, *Thought*, xxxII (1957), 145-146; by Moody E. Prior, *MP*, LIV, 275-276; by R. Davril, *EA*, x, 52; by Ray L. Heffner, Jr., *SQ*, VIII, 117-119.

A6299 Bradbrook, M. C. "Shakespeare and the Use of Disguise in Elizabethan Drama." *EIC*, II (1952), 159-168.

A6300 Bradbrook, M. C. *The Growth and Structure of Elizabethan Comedy.* London: Chatto and Windus, 1955. Pp. ix, 246.
Shak. Disguise, pp. 86-93.
Rev: B5197.

A6301 Unger, Leonard. "Deception and Self-Deception in Shakespeare's *Henry IV*." *The Man in the Name: Essays on the Experience of Poetry.* Univ. of Minnesota Press, 1956. Pp. xii, 249. Deception and self-deception, pp. 3-17.
Rev: by Elisabeth Schneider, *Expl.*, June, 1957, R5; by David Laird, *QJS*, XLIII, 441; by John J. McLaughlin, *Thought*, xxxII, 452-454; by Grover Smith, Jr., *South Atlantic Quar.*, LVI, 527-529; by A. Norman Jeffares, *MLR*, LIII (1958), 233-234; by J. Loiseau, *EA*, xi, 273-274.

iii. Guilt, Pride and Various Sins

A6302 Draper, J. W. "Flattery, A Shakespearian Tragic Theme." *PQ*, xvii (1938), 240-250.

A6303 Hoche, A. C. "Geisteskranke bei Shakespeare." *Kölner Ztg.*, 1939, Nos. 407, 408.

A6304 Dietz, H. "Demagogie als literar. Motiv." *ZNU*, xxxix (1940), 59-70.

A6305 Jones, Carol Whitt. *Reason versus Passion in Shakespeare's Comedies.* Master's thesis, University of North Carolina, 1941. Abstr. publ. in *U. of North Carolina Record, Research in Progress*, Grad. School Series, No. 40, 1941, p. 74.

A6306 Hamilton, Robert. "Shakespeare: The Nemesis of Pride." *Nineteenth Century*, 143 (1948), 335-340. German trl: "Die Nemesis des Hochmutes bei Shakespeare." *Die Brücke*, 1948, No. 86, pp. 8-10.

A6307   D., A. " 'Henry IV' Part Two and the Homily against Drunkenness." *N &Q*, 195 (1950), 160-162.

A6308   Pöhl, Margarete. *Die Geisteskrankheiten in Shakespeares Dramen.* DD, Vienna, 1951. Pp. 174. Typewritten.

A6309   Bliss, Frank Walker, Jr. *Studies in the Background of the Idea of Pride in Eighteenth Century Thought.* DD, University of Minnesota, 1954. Pp. 332. Mic A55-498. *DA*, xv (1955), 403. Publication No. 11,069.
        Shakespeare, pp. 157-164.

A6310   Cunningham, Dolora E. G. *The Doctrine of Repentance as a Formal Principle in Some Elizabethan Plays.* DD, Stanford University, 1954. Pp. 259. Mic A54-746. *DA*, xiv (1954), 524-525.

A6311   Cunningham, Dolora. "Repentance and the Art of Living Well." *Ashland Studies in Shakespeare*, ed. Margery Bailey, ii (1956). Stanford, Calif.: Shakespeare Festival Institute, 1956.

A6312   Daiches, David. "Guilt and Justice in Shakespeare." *Literary Essays*, London: Oliver and Boyd, 1956. Pp. vii, 225.
        Objects to a synthetic "Elizabethan point of view."

A6313   Rosier, James Louis. *The Chain of Sin and Privation in Elizabethan Literature.* DD, Stanford University, 1958. Pp. 240. Mic 58-4326. *DA*, xviii (1958), 583. Publication No. 25,387.

iv. Curses and Oaths

A6314   Echols, Clara Dale. *The Curse in Shakespeare's Plays.* Master's thesis, University of North Carolina, 1942. Abstr. publ. in *Univ. of North Carolina Record, Research in Progress*, Grad. School Series, No. 42, 1942, p. 79.

A6315   Walpole, V. " 'And Cassio High in Oath' (*Othello*, II. iii. 227)." *MLR*, xl (1945), 47-48.

A6316   Rice, James G. *Shakespeare's Curse: Relation to Elizabethan Curse Tradition and to Drama.* DD, University of North Carolina, 1947. Abstr. publ. in *Univ. of North Carolina Record, Research in Progress*, Grad. School Series, No. 56, 1949, pp. 197-198.

A6317   Akrigg, G. P. V. "The Name of God and *The Duchess of Malfi.*" *N &Q*, 195 (1950), 231-233.

v. Honor

A6318   Cramer, Ilse. *Der Ehrbegriff bei Shakespeare.* DD, Marburg, 1925. Pp. 53. Typewritten.

A6319   Bryson, F. R. *The Point of Honor in Sixteenth-Century Italy: An Aspect of the Life of the Gentleman.* Chicago: Univ. of Chicago Libraries, 1935. Pp. v, 129.

A6320   Whidden, Reginald W. *Chivalry in pre-Shakespearean Drama.* DD, Yale University, 1937.

A6321   Borgese, G. A. "The Dishonor of Honor: Francesco Giovanni Mauro to Sir John Falstaff." *RR*, xxxii (1941), 44-55.

A6322   Cooper, F. R. *The Theme of Honour as Present in the English Drama, 1485-1642, with Special Reference to the Dramatic Use of the Duel.* MA thesis, University of London, 1946.

A6323   Ashley, Robert. *Of Honour.* Ed. with Introduction and Commentary by Virgil B. Heltzel. San Marino: Huntington Lib., 1947. Pp. 80.

A6324   Heltzel, Virgil B. "Robert Ashley: Elizabethan Man of Letters." *HLQ*, x (1947), 349-363.

A6325   Josephson, L. "Adeln i Renässansens Litteratur." *Edda*, xlix (1949), 179-228.

A6326   Waggoner, George R. *The School of Honor Warfare and the Elizabethan Gentleman.* DD, University of Wisconsin, 1948. Abstr. publ. in *Summaries of Doctoral Dissertations, 1947-1949*, Vol. 10, Madison: Univ. of Wisconsin Press, 1950, pp. 624-626.

A6327   Haydn, Hiram. *The Counter-Renaissance.* New York, 1950. Theme of Honor, pp. 598-618.
        Rev: A3836.

A6328   Waith, Eugene M. "Manhood and Valor in Two Shakespearean Tragedies." *ELH*, xvii (1950), 262-272.

A6329   Watson, Curtis B. *Shakespeare and the Renaissance Concept of Honour.* DD, Harvard University, 1950.

A6330   Höllinger, Helene. *Konflikte zwischen Liebe und Pflicht bei Shakespeare.* DD, Innsbruck, 1951. Pp. 187. Typewritten.

A6331   Harris, William Oliver. *Honour and Ambition in Shakespeare, with Special Reference to Julius Caesar.* MA thesis, University of North Carolina, 1952. Abstr. publ. in *Univ. of North Carolina Record, Research in Progress, 1952*, Grad. School Series, No. 64, 1953, pp. 114-115.

A6332   Nichols, Doris J. *The Code of Honor and Arms in Shakespeare's Plays.* DD, University of Missouri, 1953.

A6333   Wilson, Edward M. "Family Honour in the Plays of Shakespeare's Predecessors and Contemporaries." *Essays and Studies* (Eng. Assoc.), vi (1953), 19-40.

A6334   Schopf, Alfred. "Leitmotivische Thematik in Shakespeares Dramen." *SJ*, 90 (1954), 124-166.

A6335   Gallagher, Ligera Cécile. *Shakespeare and the Aristotelian Ethical Tradition.* DD, Stanford University, 1956. Pp. 338. Mic 56-3017. *DA*, xvi (1956), 1898. Publication No. 17,720.
        Chap. VI, "Aristotelian Treatment of Honor."

A6336   Jackson, B. A. W. *The Concept of Honour in Elizabethan and Early Stuart Times.* DD, Oxford, Lincoln, 1956.

A6337   Barber, C. L. *The Idea of Honour in the English Drama, 1591-1700.* Gothenburg Studies in Eng., VI, ed. Frank Behre. Gothenburg: Elanders Boktryckeri Aktiebolag; distr. Stockholm: Almquist & Wiksell, 1957. Pp. 364.
        Rev: by H. W. Donner, *SN*, xxx (1958), 120-124; by George I. Jones, *Archiv*, 195 (1958), 199; by John Harold Wilson, *SQ*, IX, 576-577; by Hans Andersson in *Moderna språk*, LII, 301-304.

vi. Dueling

A6338   Bowers, Fredson. "Henry Howard Earl of Northampton and Duelling in England." *Eng. Studn.*, LXXI (1937), 350-355.
        Evidence is cited to show Howard's vigorous opposition to duelling.

A6339   Bowers, Fredson. "Middleton's *Fair Quarrel* and the Duelling Code." *JEGP*, XXXVI (1937), 40-65.

A6340   Bryson, F. R. *The 16th Century Italian Duel: A Study in Renaissance Social History.* Univ. of Chicago Press, 1938. Pp. xxviii, 248.

A6341   Craig, Horace S. "Duelling Scenes and Terms in Shakespeare's Plays." *Univ. Cal. Pubs. in Eng.*, IX (1940), 1-28.
        Rev: by Samuel A. Tannenbaum, *SAB*, XVI (1941), 60.

A6342   Jackson, James L. "The Fencing Actor-Lines in Shakespere's Plays." *MLN*, LVII (1942), 615-621.

A6343   Gilbert, Allan H. "The Duel in Italian Cinquecento Drama and its Relation to Tragicomedy." *Italica*, XXVI (1949), 7-14.

A6344   Aylward, J. D. "Saviolo's Ghost." *N &Q*, 195 (1950), 226-229.

A6345   Grossman, Harvey. "Kunskap i fäktning väsentlig för god Shakespearetolkning." *Göteborgstidningen* (Gothenburg), Aug. 30, 1956.

vii. Justice

A6346   Rude, Jack Leland. *Poetic Justice: A Study of the Problem of Human Conduct in Tragedy from Aeschylus to Shakespeare.* DD, Harvard University, 1934.

A6347   Lacy, E. W. "Justice in Shakespeare." (Abst. of Thesis). *Bulletin of Vanderbilt Univ.*, XXXVII (1937), 42.

A6348   Vries, Theun de. "Recht en gezag bij Shakespeare." I, II, III: *Criterium*, I (1940), 217-226, 280-288, 338-343.

A6349   Mary Bonaventure Mroz, Sister. *Divine Vengeance: A Study in the Philosophical Backgrounds of the Revenge Motif as It Appears in Shakespeare's Chronicle History Plays.* DD, Catholic University of America, 1941. Catholic Univ. Amer. Press, 1941. Pp. x, 168.
        Rev: B5068.

A6350   Hart, Thomas Alonzo, Jr. *The Development and Decline of the Doctrine of Poetic Justice, from Plato to Johnson.* DD, University of Michigan, 1942.

A6351   Gardner, Helen. "Milton's 'Satan' and the Theme of Damnation in Elizabethan Tragedy." *Essays and Studies*, I (1948), 46-66.

A6352   Hafele, Melanie. *Gnade und Recht bei Shakespeare, Besonders Untersucht an "Mass für Mass," dem "Kaufmann von Venedig" und "Sturm."* DD, Innsbruck, 1949. Pp. 129. Typewritten.

A6353   Pace, Caroline J. *The Anatomy of Justice in Shakespeare's Plays.* DD, University of North Carolina, 1949. Abstr. publ. in *Univ. of North Carolina Record, Research in Progress*, Grad. School Series, No. 58, 1950, pp. 111-112.

A6354   Rogers, Carmen. "Heavenly Justice in the Tragedies of Shakespeare." Matthews and Emery, eds., *Studies in Shakespeare*, pp. 116-128.

A6355   Daiches, David. "Guilt and Justice in Shakespeare." *Literary Essays*, London, 1956, pp. 1-25.

A6356   Mullen, Richard D. *Reward and Punishment in English Comedy, 1599-1613.* DD, University of Chicago, 1956.

A6357   Wood, Glena Decker. *Retributive Justice: A Study of the Theme of Elizabethan Revenge Tragedy.* DD, University of Kentucky, 1958.

viii. Mercy, Forgiveness, and Grace

A6358   Reimer, Christian Josef. *Der Begriff der Gnade in Shakespeares "Measure for Measure."* DD, Marburg, 1937. Pp. xi, 110.

A6359   Hafele, Melanie. *Gnade und Recht bei Shakespeare, Besonders Untersucht an "Mass für Mass," dem "Kaufmann von Venedig" und "Sturm."* DD, Innsbruck, 1949. Pp. 129. Typewritten.

A6360   Sehrt, Ernst Theodor. "Der Gedanke der Vergebung bei Shakespeare." *Die Sammlung*, (Göttingen), Mar., April and May, 1949, pp. 145, 213, 275.

A6361   Sehrt, Ernst Theodor. *Vergebung und Gnade bei Shakespeare.* Stuttgart: K. F. Koehler Verlag, 1952. Pp. 260.

Rev: by Karl Brunner, *Anglia*, LXXI (1952), 113-115; by J. C. Maxwell, *RES*, IV (1953), 281-282; by Hermann Heuer, *SJ*, 89 (1953), 227-229; by W. Clemen, *Archiv*, 189 (1953), 366; by W. Stroedel, *Mittag*, June 11, 1953; by H. Oppel, *NS*, II, 148-149; by F. H. Link, *SJ*, 90 (1954), 355-360; by A. Koszul, *EA*, VII (1954), 320-321; by Clifford Leech, *ShS*, VII, 132; by John Leon Lievsay, *SQ*, V, 327-330; by M. Lüthi, *GRM*, XXXV, 75-76; by Oscar James Campbell, *MLN*, LXX (1955), 366-369; by Robert Fricker, *ES*, XXXVII (1956), 217-220.

A6362 Elliott, George Roy. *Dramatic Providence in "Macbeth": A Study of Shakespeare's Tragic Theme of Humanity and Grace.* Princeton Univ. Press, 1958. Pp. xvi, 234.
Rev: B9274.

ix. Poisons

A6363 Bowers, Fredson. "The Audience and the Poisoners of Elizabethan Tragedy." *JEGP*, XXXVI (1937), 491-504.

A6364 Harrison, Thomas P., Jr. "The Literary Background of Renaissance Poisons." *TxSE*, XXVII (1948), 35-67.

x. Revenge and Violence

A6365 Simpson, Percy. *The Theme of Revenge in Elizabethan Tragedy.* Annual Shakespeare Lecture of the British Academy, 1935. Oxford Univ. Press, 1935. Pp. 38. Reprinted in Simpson's *Studies in Elizabethan Drama.* Oxford: Clarendon Press, 1955, pp. 138-178.
Rev: by Mario Praz, *ES*, XVIII (1936), 177-181; by L. L. Schücking, *Beiblatt*, XLVII, 75; by Robert Adger Law, *MLN*, LII (1937), 526-530.

A6366 Polfliet, Marie-Louise. *The Elizabethan Tragedy of Revenge for Murder.* Thèse présentée pour l'obtention du grade de Licencié en Philos. et Lettres, 1939/40, Univ. de Gent.

A6367 Bowers, Fredson. *Elizabethan Revenge Tragedy, 1587-1642.* Princeton Univ. Press, 1940. Pp. viii, 288.
Rev: B4941.

A6368 Mitchell, Lee. *Elizabethan Scenes of Violence and the Problem of Their Staging.* DD, Northwestern University, 1941. Abstr. publ. in *Summaries of Doctoral Dissertations*, IX (1941), Chicago and Evanston: Northwestern Univ. Press, 1942, pp. 69-73.

A6369 Kirschbaum, Leo. "Shakespeare's Stage Blood and Its Significance." *PMLA*, LXIV (1949), 517-529.

A6370 Carrère, Félix Jean. *Le Théâtre de Thomas Kyd. Contribution à l'Etude du Drame Elizabéthain.* Thèse de Lettres, Paris, 1949. Publ. Toulouse: Edouard Privat, 1951. Pp. 462.
Rev: A4979.

A6371 Wadsworth, Frank Whittemore. *The White Devil, an Historical and Critical Study.* DD, Princeton University, 1951. Pp. 416. Mic A55-1111. *DA*, XV (1955), 832. Publication No. 11,051.

A6372 Brennan, E. M. *The Theme of Revenge in Elizabethan Life and Drama, 1580-1605.* Master's thesis, Queens University, Belfast, 1956.

xi. Death, Murder, and Suicide

A6373 Thompson, W. Meredith. *Der Tod in der Englischen Lyrik des siebzehnten Jahrhunderts.* Breslau: Priebatsch, 1935. Pp. 97.
Rev: by A. Brandl in *Archiv*, 169 (1936), 137; by S. B. Liljegren, *Lbl*, LVII, 249-250; by H. Marcus, *DLZ*, LVII, 1397-99; by Wolfgang Keller, *SJ*, LXXII (1936), 159.

A6374 Spencer, Theodore. *Death and Elizabethan Tragedy: A Study of Convention and Opinion on the Elizabethan Drama.* Harvard Univ. Press, 1936. Pp. xiii, 288.
Rev: A6823.

A6375 Harmon, Alice I. *"Loci Communes* on Death and Suicide in the Literature of the English Renaissance." DD, University of Minnesota, 1940. *Summaries of Ph.D. Theses, Univ. of Minnesota*, III, pp. 121-124.

A6376 Reik, Theodore. "The Way of All Flesh." *From Thirty Years with Freud.* trans. Richard Winston. New York: Farrar and Rinehart, Inc., 1940, pp. 197-212.
Discusses death in *Hamlet* and *Tempest*.

A6377 Hankins, John Erskine. *The Character of Hamlet and Other Essays.* Univ. North Carolina Press, 1941. Pp. xii, 264. Suicide in Shak., p. 222.
Rev: B7664.

A6378 O'Connor, Mary Catharine. *The Art of Dying Well: The Development of the Ars Moriendi.* New York: Columbia Univ. Press, 1942. Pp. xiv, 258.
Rev: A3900.

A6379 Jarratt, Louise Paschal. *A Study of Death in English Renaissance Tragedy.* Master's thesis, University of North Carolina, 1943. Abstr. publ. in *University of North Carolina Record, Research in Progress*, Grad. School Series, No. 50, 1946, pp. 156-157.

A6380 Engel, Werner. *Veränderlichkeit, Vergänglichkeit, Tod in Shakespeares Sonetten.* DD, Marburg, 1949. Pp. 107. Typewritten.

A6381 Frye, Roland Mushat. *The Accepted Ethics and Theology of Shakespeare's Audience as Utilized by*

the Dramatist in Certain Representative Tragedies, with Particular Attention to Love and Marriage.
DD, Princeton University, 1952. Pp. 372. Mic A55-745. *DA*, xv (1955), 581. Publication
No. 10,901.
Rev: A2563.

A6382   McCullen, Joseph T., Jr. "Brother Hate and Fratricide in Shakespeare." *SQ*, III (1952),
335-340.

A6383   Schneider, Reinhold. *Über Dichter und Dichtung.* Cologne, Olten: Hegner, 1953. Pp. 346.
"Tod und Unsterblichkeit in Shakespeares Drama," pp. 142-156.

A6384   Wickert, Maria. "Das Schattenmotiv bei Shakespeare." *Anglia*, LXXI, iii (1953), 274-310.

xii.   Satire and Complaint

A6385   Campbell, Oscar J. *Comicall Satyre and Shakespeare's "Troilus and Cressida".* San Marino:
Huntington Library, 1938. Pp. ix, 246.
Rev: A4913.

A6386   McCullen, Joseph Thomas, Jr. *The Use of Madness in Shakespearean Tragedy for Characterization
and for Protection in Satire.* Master's thesis, University of North Carolina, 1939. Abstr. publ.
in *Univ. of North Carolina Record, Research in Progress*, Grad. School Series, No. 36, 1939, p. 81.

A6387   Vaughan, D. N. *Satire upon Language in the Plays of Shakespeare and Ben Jonson.* MA thesis,
Cape Town, 1939.

A6388   Worcester, David. *The Art of Satire.* Harvard Univ. Press, 1940. Pp. x, 191.
Rev: by L. I. Bredvold, *JEGP*, XL (1941), 434-435.

A6389   Milligan, B. "Sixteenth and Seventeenth Century Satire Against Grain Engrossers." *SP*,
XXXVII (1940), 585-597.

A6390   Randolph, Mary C. "The Medical Concept in English Renaissance Satiric Theory: Its
Possible Relationships and Implications." *SP*, XXXVIII (1941), 125-157.

A6391   Campbell, Oscar James. *Shakespeare's Satire.* Oxford Univ. Press, 1943. Pp. 227.
Rev: B5164.

A6392   Frye, Northrop. "The Nature of Satire." *UTQ*, XIV (1945), 75-89.

A6393   Johnson, E., ed. "Satiric Overtones in Shakespeare." *A Treasury of Satire.* New York:
Simon and Schuster, 1945, pp. 155-174.

A6394   Milligan, Burton A. "Some Sixteenth and Seventeenth Century Satire Against Money
Lenders." *SAB*, XXII (1947), 36-46, 84-93.

A6395   Cazamian, Louis. *The Development of English Humor.* Duke Univ. Press, 1952. Pp. viii, 421.
Rev: B5186.

A6396   Goldsmith, Robert Hillis. *Wise Men in Motley: The Fool in Elizabethan Drama.* DD, Columbia
University, 1952. Pp. 226. *DA*, XII (1952), 618. Publication No. 4186.

A6397   Waith, Eugene M. *The Pattern of Tragicomedy in Beaumont and Fletcher.* Yale Studies Eng.,
120. Yale Univ. Press, 1952. Pp. xiv, 212.
"Satyr and Shepherd in Shakespeare," pp. 80-83.
Rev: A6894.

A6398   Brockett, Oscar Gross. *Satire in English Drama, 1590-1603.* DD, Stanford University, 1953.
Pp. 314. Mic A53-1467. *DA*, XIII (1953), 793. Publication No. 5784.
(Shakespeare excluded.)

A6399   Holden, William P. *Anti-Puritan Satire, 1572-1642.* New Haven: Yale Univ. Press, 1954.
Pp. 165.
Section on Shak: *Twelf.* and *Meas.*, pp. 123-128.
Rev: A7128.

A6400   Bogard, Travis. *The Tragic Satire of John Webster.* Berkeley and Los Angeles: Univ. Cal.
Press, 1955. Pp. xii, 158.
Rev: by R. A. Foakes, *English*, X (1955), 227-228; by John Leon Lievsay, *SQ*, VI, 472-473;
by C. G. Thayer, *Books Abroad*, XXX (1956), 220-221; *TLS*, Feb. 17, 1956, p. 102; Michel
Poirier, *EA*, IX, 157-158; by J. A. Bryant, Jr., *SR*, LXIV, 508-520.

A6401   Peter, John. *Complaint and Satire in Early English Literature.* Oxford: Clarendon Press, 1956.
Pp. 323.
Rev: by D. W. Robertson, Jr., *Speculum*, XXXII (1957), 600-603; *TLS*, Jan. 11, 1957, p. 24;
by James Kinsley and S. W. Dawson, *RES*, IX (1958), 60-63; Leicester Bradner, *MLN*,
LXXIII, 57-58; by N. J. Endicott, *UTQ*, XXVII, 463-464; Sears Jayne, *MP*, LV, 200-202; by
Brice Harris, *SQ*, IX, 577-578.

A6402   Stempel, Daniel. "The Transmigration of the Crocodile." *SQ*, VII (1956), 59-72.

A6403   Diekmann, Gisela. *Die Klage im Drama Shakespeares.* DD, Göttingen, 1957. Pp. 208.

xiii.   Usury

A6404   Wright, C. T. "The Usurer's Sin in Elizabethan Literature." *SP*, XXXV (1938), 178-194.

A6405   Taeusch, Carl F. "The Concept of 'Usury'. The History of an Idea." *JHI*, III (1942), 291-318.

A6406   Pettet, E. C. "*The Merchant of Venice* and the Problem of Usury." *Essays and Studies by Members of English Association*, XXXI (1945), 19-33.

A6407   Nelson, Benjamin N. "The Usurer and the Merchant Prince: Italian Business Men and the Ecclesiastical Law of Restitution, 1100-1550." *Jour. Econ. Hist.*, VII (1947), 104-122.

A6407a Nelson, B. N. *The Idea of Usury*. Princeton Univ. Press, 1949. Pp. xxi, 258.
        Rev: by T. P. McLaughlin, *Catholic Hist. Rev.*, XXXVI (1950), 223-224; by J. A. Cabaniss, *Church Hist.*, XIX, 135-136; by S. E. Stumpf, *Jour. of Rel.*, XXX, 284; by Robert Sabantino Lopez, *Speculum*, XXVI (1951), 401-404; by Garrett Mattingly, *JMH*, XXIII, 73.

A6408   Ramp, Ernst. *Das Zinsproblem: Eine Historische Untersuchung*. Zurich: Zwingli-Verlag, 1949. Pp. 122.
        Surveys in detail the problem of usury and interest in Luther, Calvin, and Zwingli; considers later development in Protestantism.
        Rev: by C. C. R., *Anglican Theol. Rev.*, XXXII (1950), 85; by J. H. S. Burleigh, *Evangelical Quar.*, XXII, 73-74.

A6409   Wagner, Russell H. "Thomas Wilson's Speech against Usury." *QJS*, XXXVIII (1952), 13-22.
See also listings under *Merchant of Venice*, and A6807.

xiv.   Miscellaneous

A6410   Turolla, E. "Fede e speranza in Omero, Dante, Shakespeare." *Nuova Riv. Storica*, XX (1936), 82-87.

A6411   Bhattacherje, M. M. *Courtesy in Shakespeare*. With a Foreword by C. J. Sisson and Introduction by Louis Cazamian. Calcutta Univ. Press, 1940. Pp. xix, 225.
        Rev: A4560.

A6412   Russev, Russi. "Tema na Sinovnost u Shakespeare." *Annuaire de l'Université de Sofia, Faculté Historicophilologique*, XXXVI (1940), 1-7.

A6413   Lindsay, Jean S. "A Survey of the Town-Country and Court-Country Themes in Non-Dramatic Elizabethan Literature." *Cornell Univ. Abstracts of Theses*, 1943, pp. 37-40.

A6414   Maurois, André. "Shakespeare und die Bedrohung." *Universitas*, II (1947), 1135-36.

A6415   Bruser, Fredelle. *Concepts of Chastity in Literature, Chiefly Non-dramatic, of the English Renaissance*. DD, Radcliff College, 1948.

A6416   Powell, Arnold F. *Pathos in English Tragedy through Shakespeare*. DD, Vanderbilt University, 1948. Abstr. publ. in *Bulletin of Vanderbilt Univ., Abstracts of Theses*, Dec. 1, 1948, pp. 10-11. Reprinted: *Bull. of Birmingham Southern Coll.*, XLII, No. 4. *The Melting Mood, a Study of the Function of Pathos in English Tragedy through Shakespeare*. Nashville, 1949.

A6417   Appel, Louis D. *The Concept of Fame in Tudor and Stuart Literature*. DD, Northwestern University, 1949. Abstr. publ. in *Summaries of Doctoral Dissertations*, 1949, Vol. 17, Chicago and Evanston: Northwestern Univ. Press, 1950, pp. 9-13.

A6418   Wilson, Arthur H. "The Great Theme in Shakespeare." *Susquehanna Univ. Studies*, IV (1949), 5-62. (Love.)

A6419   Trienens, Roger. *The Green-eyed Monster: A Study of Sexual Jealousy in the Literature of the English Renaissance*. DD, Northwestern University, 1951. Abstr. publ. in *Summaries of Doctoral Dissertations*, 1951, Vol. 19, Chicago and Evanston: Northwestern Univ. Press, 1952, pp. 45-49.

A6420   Hoskins, Frank L. "Misalliance: A Significant Theme in Tudor and Stuart Drama." In *Renaissance Papers 1956*, ed. Hennig Cohen and J. Woodrow Hassell, Jr., Columbia, S. C., 1956, pp. 72-81.

A6421   Hoffmann, Gerhard. *Das Gebet im ernsten englischen Drama von der älteren Moralität bis zu William Shakespeare*. DD, Göttingen, 1957. Pp. 236. Typewritten. Abstr. by Jack R. Brown in *ShN*, VII (1957), 12.

A6422   Levitsky, Ruth Mickelson Jones. *Shakespeare's Treatment of the Virtue of Patience.*. DD, University of Missouri, 1957. Pp. 237. Mic 59-1929. *DA*, XIX (1959), 2940. Publication No. 24,367.

(c)   DEVICES AND ETHICALLY NEUTRAL PHENOMENA
i.   Fortune

A6423   Chew, Samuel C. "Time and Fortune." *ELH*, VI (1939), 83-113.

A6424   Hammerle, Karl. "Das Fortunamotiv von Chaucer bis Bacon." *Anglia*, LXV (1941), 87-100.

A6425   Chapman, R. *Fortune in Elizabethan Drama: An Attempt to Discover, Chiefly from Plays Written between 1570 and 1620, the Conception of that Period Concerning the Person and Activities of the Goddess Fortuna*. MA thesis, University of London, 1947.

A6426   Wertsching, P. *Fate in Elizabethan Drama*. DD, Columbia University, 1948. Pp. 218.

A6427   Kerl, Wilhelm. *Fortuna und Natura in ihrem Verhältnis zum Menschen in Shakespeares Barock-dramen*. DD, Marburg, 1949. Pp. 187. Typewritten.

A6428   Chapman, Raymond. "Fortune and Mutability in Elizabethan Literature." *CamJ*, V (1952), 374-382.

ii.   Time

A6429 Wilson, H. M. " 'Time and the Hour' in Literature." *ConR*, 154 (1938), 617-624.

A6430 Litchfield, Florence L. *The Treatment of the Theme of Mutability in the Literature of the English Renaissance: A Study of the Problem of Change between 1558 and 1660.* DD, Minnesota, 1939. Abstr. in *Summaries of Ph.D. Theses, Univ. of Minn.*, I (1939), 164-168.

A6431 Azzalino, W. "The Time und Time bei Shakespeare." *N. Mon.*, X (1939), 96-109.

A6432 Chew, Samuel C. "Time and Fortune." *ELH*, VI (1939), 83-113.

A6433 Spender, Stephen. "Time, Violence and Macbeth." *Penguin New Writing*, III (1940-41), 115-20.

A6434 Spencer, Benjamin T. "*2 Henry IV* and the Theme of Time." *UTQ*, XIII (1944), 394-399.

A6435 Newman, Franklin B. *The Concept of Time in Elizabethan Poetry.* DD, Harvard University, 1947.

A6436 Craig, Hardin. "Shakespeare and the Here and Now." *PMLA*, LXVII (1952), 87-94.
       Shak.'s concept and use of time closer to modern relativistic ideas than to the physical science of the last three centuries.

A6437 Witte, W. "Time in *Wallenstein* and *Macbeth*." *Aberdeen Univ. Review*, XXXIV (1952), 217-224.

A6438 Otten, Kurt. *Die zeit in Gehalt und Gestalt der frühen Dramen Shakespeares.* DD, Tübingen, 1954. Pp. 184. Typewritten.

A6439 Pearce, Josephine Anna. *The Manipulations of Time in Shakespeare's English History Plays.* DD, University of Missouri, 1955. Pp. 236. Mic 55-1110. *DA*, XV (1955), 2192. Publication No. 14,618.

A6440 Bush, Douglas. *Themes and Variations in English Poetry of the Renaissance.* Two Lectures: "God and Nature" and "Time and Man." Under the auspices of the Francis Bacon Foundation, Inc. Claremont, Cal.: The Claremont Graduate School, 1957. Pp. 45.

A6441 Driver, Tom Faw. *The Sense of History in Greek and Shakespearean Dramatic Form.* DD, Columbia University, 1957. Pp. 397. Mic 57-2807. *DA*, XVII (1957), 1748. Publication No. 21,781.
       Frequently concerned with kinds of time.

A6442 Levý, Jiří. "Divadelní prostor a čas v dramatech Williama Shakespeara a Bena Jonsona." (Dramatic space and time in the plays of Shakespeare and Jonson) in *F. Wollmanovi k sedmdesátinám.* (Collection of articles in tribute to Professor Wollman's 70th birthday). Prague: Státní pedagogické nakladatelství, 1958, pp. 648-656.

iii. Sleep and Dreams

A6443 Sartorius, Ella. *Der Traum und das Drama.* Munich: Max Hueber, 1936. Pp. 79.
       Rev: by Kurt May, *Lbl*, LXIII (1942), 183-184.

A6444 Camden, Carroll, Jr. "Shakespeare on Sleep and Dreams." *Rice Institute Pamphlet*, XXIII (1936), 106-133.

A6445 Rogers, L. W. "Symbolical Dreams in Shakespeare." *Theosophist*, LVIII (1937), 21-25.

A6446 Stewart, Bain Tate. *The Renaissance Interpretation of Dreams and Their Use in Elizabethan Drama.* DD, Northwestern University, 1942. Abstr. publ. in *Summaries of Doctoral Dissertations*, 1942, Vol. 10, Northwestern Univ., 1943, pp. 33-36.

A6447 Hatto, A. T. " 'Venus and Adonis'—and the Boar." *MLR*, XLI (1946), 353-361.

A6448 Jankélévitch, S. "Le Délire Onirique dans les Drames de Shakespeare." *Psyché* (Paris), V, No. 42 (1950), 305-324.

A6449 Venezky, Alice S. *Pageantry on the Shakespearean Stage.* New York: Twayne Publishers, 1951. Pp. 242.
       Rev: A7238.

A6450 Aronson, Alex. "A Note on Shakespeare's Dream Imagery." *Visva-Bharati Quarterly*, XVIII (Oct. 1952), 168-182.

A6451 Stewart, Bain T. "The Misunderstood Dreams in the Plays of Shakespeare and his Contemporaries." *Essays in Honor of W. C. Curry*, pp. 197-206.

A6452 Arnold, Aerol. "The Recapitulation Dream in *Richard III* and *Macbeth*." *SQ*, VI (1955), 51-62.

A6453 Chandler, Simon B. "Shakespeare and Sleep." *Bul. Hist. Medicine*, XXIX (1955), 255-260.

A6454 Clemen, Wolfgang. *Clarences Traum und Ermordung (Shakespeare: Richard III. 1.4).* Sitzungsberichte der Bayerischen Akademie der Wissenschaften, Philosophisch-historische Klasse, 5 (1955). Munich: Verlag der Bayerischen Akademie der Wissenschaften, 1955. Pp. 46.
       Rev: by Aerold Arnold in *SQ*, VIII (1957), 117; by E. A. J. Honigmann, *RES*, VIII, 347.

A6455 Hindenberg, Gisela. *Der Traum im Drama Shakespeares.* DD, Göttingen, 1956. Pp. iii, 179. Typewritten.

iv. Letters

A6456 Guinn, John A. "The Letter Device in the First Act of *The Two Gentlemen of Verona*." *TxSE*, XX (1940), 72-81.

A6457 Robertson, Jean. *The Art of Letter Writing. An Essay on the Handbooks Published in England during the Sixteenth and Seventeenth Centuries.* Univ. Press of Liverpool, 1942. Pp. 80.

A6458   Moroney, Katharine Elizabeth. *The Letter as a Dramatic Device in Shakespeare's Plays.* DD, Oklahoma University, 1956. Pp. 155. Mic 56-2263. *DA*, XVI (1956), 1443. Publication No. 16,979. Abstracted by Jack R. Brown, *ShN*, VII (1957), 31.

A6459   Hawkes, Terry. "Ficino and Shakespeare." *N &Q*, NS, V (1958), 185-186.

v. Animals

A6460   Fatout, Paul. "Roan Barbary." *SAB*, XV (1940), 67-74.

A6461   Cheney, David Raymond. *Animals in "A Midsummer Night's Dream."* DD, State University of Iowa, 1955. Pp. 288. Mic 55-1103. *DA*, XV (1955), 2188. Publication No. 14,094.

vi. Miscellaneous

A6462   Hübner, Walter. *Der Vergleich bei Shakespeare.* DD, Berlin, Humboldt Univ., 1908. Pp. 149.

A6463   " 'Senex'." "Swooning in Literature." *N &Q*, 171 (1936), 58-60.

A6464   Daube, David. *Shakespeare on Aliens Learning English.* Cambridge: Heffer, 1942. Pp. 20.

A6465   Pace, Caroline Jennings. *The Interest in Learning in Shakespeare's Plays.* Master's thesis, University of North Carolina, 1942. Abstr. publ. in *Univ. of North Carolina Record, Research in Progress*, Grad. School Series, No. 42, 1942, p. 81.

A6466   Smalt, A. "Le Rôle du Hasard dans les Tragédies de Shakespeare." *LT*, X (1944), 50-59.

A6467   Pipes, G. A. "Numismatics of Shakespeare." *Numismatist*, LVIII (1945), 1185-88.

A6468   Bauer, Robert V. *The Use of Humours in Comedy by Ben Jonson and his Contemporaries.* DD, University of Illinois, 1948.

A6469   Morton, Lena. *The Influence of the Sea Upon English Poetry from the Anglo-Saxon Period to the Victorian Period.* DD, Western Reserve University, 1947. Abstr. publ. in Western Reserve Univ. *Bibliography of Published Research, 1946-1947,* 1949, pp. 28-30.

A6470   Simonini, Rinaldo Charles, Jr. *The Language Lesson Dialogue in Shakespearean Drama.* Master's thesis, University of North Carolina, 1946. Abstr. publ. in *Univ. of North Carolina Record, Research in Progress*, Grad. School Series, No. 56, 1949, pp. 229. "Language Lesson Dialogues in Shakespeare." *SQ*, II (1951), 319-329.

A6471   Clemen, W. H. *Wandlung des Botenberichts bei Shakespeare.* Sitzungsberichte der Bayerischen Akademie der Wissenschaften, Philosophisch-historische Klasse, 4 (1952). Munich, 1952. Pp. 46.
        Rev: A5964.

A6472   Huhner, Max *Shakespearean Studies and Other Essays.* With an Introduction by George S. Hellman. New York: Farrar Straus, 1952. Pp. 115.
        Chap. V, "Was Shakespeare an Angler?" pp. 42-49; VI, "A New Aspect of Shakespeare's Depiction of Shamming," pp. 50-65.
        Rev: B4476.

A6473   Schilling, K. *Shakespeare: Die Idee des Menschseins in seinen Werken.* Munich/Basel: Ernst Reinhardt, 1953. Pp. 294.
        Rev: by Karl Brunner, *SJ*, 89 (1953), 197-200; by S. F. Johnson, *JAAC*, XII (1954), 527-528; by Hereward T. Price, *SQ*, VI (1955), 188-189; by C. A. Weber, *DLZ*, LXXVII (1956), 30-31; by H. Straumann, *Anglia*, LXXV (1957/58), 464-466.

A6474   Baughan, Denver E. "Shakespeare's Attitude Toward Travel." *Essays in Honor of Walter Clyde Curry,* Vanderbilt Univ. Press, 1954.

A6475   Blayney, Glenn H. "Wardship in English Drama (1600-1650)." *SP*, LIII (1956), 470-484.

(d) LITERARY MOTIFS
i. Anachronism

A6476   Braun, Hans. *Hier irrt Goethe—unter anderen. Eine Lese von Anachronismen von Homer bis auf unsere Zeit.* Munich: Heimeran, 1937. Pp. 121.
        "Kåsi kosåi billai und Shakespeare," pp. 49-60; "Hamlet im Frack," pp. 95-99.
        Rev: by F. Märker, *DL*, XL (1937/38), 125.

A6477   Muir, Kenneth. "The Dramatic Function of Anachronism." *Proceedings of the Leeds Philosophical and Literary Society* (Literary and Historical Section), VI (1951), 529-533.

ii. Burlesque

A6478   Olive, William J. *Burlesque in Elizabethan Drama.* DD, University of North Carolina, 1937. Abstr. publ. in *Univ. of North Carolina Record, Research in Progress, 1936-1937,* Chapel Hill, 1937, pp. 53-54.

A6479   Lailey, Constance. *The Use of Paradox and Burlesque in Shakespeare.* MA thesis, Toronto, 1940. Pp. 122.

A6480   Aldus, Paul J. *The Use of Physical Comic Means in English Drama from 1420 to 1603.* DD, University of Chicago, 1951.

iii. Miscellaneous

A6481   Stallmann, H. *Malapropismen im Englischen Drama von den Anfängen bis 1800.* DD, Berlin, 1938. Pp. 113. Bottrop i. W.: Wilh. Postberg, 1938.
Rev: by Wolfgang Keller, *SJ,* LXXV (1939), 157-158.

A6482   Seard, S. "The Use of Color in Literature." *Proceedings of the American Philosophical Society,* XX (1946), 163-249. *Shak.:* pp. 191, 225-226.

A6483   Sackton, Alexander H. "The Paradoxical Encomium in Elizabethan Drama." *TxSE,* XXVIII (1949), 83-104.

A6484   Simpson, Lucie. "Shakespeare's Farewells." *The Secondary Heroes of Shakespeare and Other Essays.* London: Kingswood Press, 1950, pp. 111-116.

A6485   Ritter, Federica de. "El Gran Teatro del Mundo." *Rev. Nacional de Cultura* (Caracas), XIV, No. 95 (Nov.-Dec. 1952), 133-153.

A6486   Tison, John L., Jr. *The Dramatic Consolatio in Shakespeare.* DD, University of North Carolina, 1953. Abstr. publ. in *Univ. of North Carolina Record, Research in Progress, 1953,* Grad. School Series, No. 66, 1954, pp. 103-104.

(9) MONOLOGUE, DIALOGUE, AND CHORUS (109;36)
(a) MONOLOGUE (109;36)

A6487   Kilian, E. "Der Shakespeare Monolog u. s. Spielweise." *Dramaturgische Blätter,* Munich, 1905, pp. 63-91.

A6488   Heller, R. *Der Monolog in Shakespeares Tragödien.* DD, Vienna, 1923.

A6489   Hinterwaldner, A. *Der Monolog in Shakespeares Königsdramen.* DD, Vienna, 1932.

A6490   Vollmann, Elisabeth. *Ursprung und Entwicklung des Monologs bis zu seiner Entfaltung bei Shakespeare.* Bonn, 1934.
Rev: by G. Connes, *RAA,* XII (1934/35), 537-538; by Albert Eichler, *Beiblatt,* XLVII (1936), 109-113; by Karl Brunner, *Lbl,* LVII, 390-394; by Eduard Eckhardt, *Eng. Studn.,* LXXI, 106-107; by J. B. Leishman, *MLR,* XXXI, 466-467; by Harold Hillebrand, *MLN,* LI, 458-463; by K. Arns, *NS,* XLIV, 213-218; by H. Pongs, *DuV,* XXXVII, 388-389; by T. W. Baldwin, *JEGP,* XXXV, 150-151; by D. de Vries, *Neophil,* XXII (1937), 218-219; by H. Lüdeke, *ES,* XXI (1939), Heft 6.

A6491   Kennedy, Milton B. *The Oration in Shakespeare.* DD, University of Virginia, 1937. Abstr. publ. in *Abstracts of Dissertations,* 1937, Charlottesville: Univ. of Virginia, 1937, pp. 16-18.

A6492   Kennedy, Milton B. *The Oration in Shakespeare.* Univ. North Carolina Press, 1942. Pp. 270.
Rev: A4152.

A6493   Günther-Konsalik, Heinz. "Der Monolog . . . unmodern?" *Dts. Dramaturgie,* II (1943), 88-89.

A6494   Joseph, B. L. *Monologue, Soliloquy and Aside in the Pre-Restoration Drama.* DD, Oxford, Magdalen, 1946.

A6495   Smith, Warren. "The Shakespearean Apostrophe." *SAB,* XXIII (1948), 195-200.

A6496   Smith, Warren. "Artful Brevity in Shakespeare's Monologs." *SAB,* XXIV (1949), 275-279.

A6497   Eber, Brigitte. *Die Apostrophe als Selbstäusserungsform in der Englischen Tragödie des 16. Jahrhunderts.* DD, Munich, 1950. Pp. 125. Typewritten.

A6498   Cancelled.

A6499   Langbaum, Robert. *The Poetry of Experience: The Dramatic Monologue in Modern Literary Tradition.* New York: Random House, 1957. Pp. 246.
Rev: A6512.

A6500   Shackford, Martha Hale. "Stichomythia, Chorus, Soliloquy: *Antigone, Julius Caesar, Hamlet, Macbeth.*" *Shakespeare, Sophocles: Dramatic Modes.* Natick, Mass., 1957.
Rev: B4489.

(b) DIALOGUE (110;36)

A6501   Smith, Warren D. *Shakespeare's Stagecraft as Denoted by the Dialogue in the Original Printings of his Texts.* DD, University of Pennsylvania, 1948. Pp. 256. Mic A50-217. *Microf. Ab.,* X (1950), 163. Publication No. 1731.

A6502   Sutherland, James, ed. *The Oxford Book of English Talk.* Oxford Univ. Press, 1953.
Includes comments on Shak.'s use of dialogue.
Rev: *SCN,* XII (1954), 10; by Robert Graves, *Hudson Review,* VII, 155-166.

A6503   Gruner, Helene. *Studien zum Dialog im vorshakespeareschen Drama.* DD, Munich, 1955. Shak. passim.

(c) CHORUS (110;36)

A6504   Petsch, Robert. "Der Chor im Drama." *Helicon,* III (1941), 1-8.
Shak. passim.

A6505   See A6500.

(10) PROLOGUE AND EPILOGUE (110;36)

A6506   Hirte, Helmut. *Entwicklung des Prologs und Epilogs in frühneuenglischen Dramen.* DD, Giessen, 1928. Pp. 21.

A6507   Leech, Clifford. "Shakespeare's Prologues and Epilogues." *Studies in Honor of T. W. Baldwin*, pp. 150-164.

(11)   ACTION AND CHARACTER (110;36)

A6508   Schmid, Eduard Eugen. "Shakespeare, Montaigne und die schauspielerische Formel." *SJ*, 82/83 (1948), 103-135.

A6509   Regnoli, Piero. "Shakespeare e l'azione visiva." *Osservatore Romano*, 91 (1951), No. 295, p. 3.

A6510   Schlüter, Kurt. *Shakespeares dramatische Erzählkunst. Eine Untersuchung über den Wandel von Funktion und Gestalt der Erzählung in Shakespeares Dramen.* DD, Munich, 1954. Pp. 169. Typewritten.

A6511   Langbaum, Robert. "Character Versus Action in Shakespeare." *SQ*, VIII (1957), 57-69.

A6512   Langbaum, Robert. *The Poetry of Experience: The Dramatic Monologue in Modern Literary Tradition.* New York: Random House, 1957. Pp. 246.
Chap. V, "Character versus Action in Shakespeare," pp. 160-181.
Rev: *TLS*, Aug. 2, 1957, p. 472.

A6513   Lombard, Edwin Henderson. *Plot, Character, and Action: A Study of Dramatic Theory and Practice.* DD, Cornell University, 1940. Abstr. publ. in Cornell University, *Abstracts of Theses*, 1940, Ithaca, 1941, pp. 37-39.

(12)   ART OF CHARACTER DEPICTION (111;37)
(a)   PROBLEMS OF CHARACTER IN GENERAL (111;37)
i.   Nature of Shakespeare's Character Depiction

A6514   Schücking, Levin Ludw. *Die Charakterprobleme bei Shakespeare.* Leipzig: Koehler & Amelang, 1941. Pp. 302. Reprint of 3rd edition. *Character Problems in Shakespeare's Plays: A Guide to Better Understanding of the Dramatist.* New York: P. Smith, 1948. Pp. 269. Reprint of W. H. Peters 1922 edition.
Rev: by L. M. Parrott, Jr., *TAr*, XXXIII (Aug. 1949) 107-108.

A6515   Keller, Wolfgang. "Shakespeare und die Deutsche Jugend." *NS*, XLV (1937), 259-278.
In this article Professor Keller disagrees with ideas expressed by Professor L. L. Schücking in *Die Charakterprobleme bei Shakespeare* (3rd ed. 1932); see "Entgegnung" by Professor Schücking in *NS*, XLV, 413, with "Nachschrift" by Professor Keller. See also O. Urbach, "Shakespeare und die dt. Jugend," *Berliner Börsenztg.*, 1937, Nr. 413.

A6516   Bethell, S. L. *Shakespeare and the Popular Dramatic Tradition.* With an Intro. by T. S. Eliot. London: King & Staples, 1944. Pp. 160.
Rev: A7690.

A6517   Ellis-Fermor, U. *Shakespeare the Dramatist.* Proceedings of the British Academy, Annual Shakespeare Lecture, 1948. "We . . . remain convinced that though only a slender arc of each personality enters the frame of the play, the circle is complete beyond it, living full and whole in the poet's imagination."
Rev: A5855.

A6518   Stewart, J. I. M. *Character and Motive in Shakespeare.* London: Longmans, Green & Co., 1949. Pp. vii, 147.
Rev: *TLS*, May 6, 1949, p. 298; by Milton Crane, *NYTBR*, Nov. 20, 1949; by G. W. Stonier, *NstN*, XXXVII, 563-564; by Edward J. West, *SQ*, I (1950), 84-88; by J. F. Danby, *CamJ*, III, 314-315; by Joseph B. Fort, *LanM*, XLV (1951), 405; by G. Baldini, *Belfagor*, VI, 616; by A. Norman Jeffares, *ES*, XXXIV (1953), 85-86.

A6519   Stoll, Elmer E. "A Freudian Detective's Shakespeare." *MP*, XLVIII (1950), 122-132.
Inspired by Mr. Stewart's study, A6518.

A6520   Duthie, G. I. *Shakespeare.* London: Hutchinson's University Library, 1951. Pp. 206.
Rev: A8162.

A6521   Ellis-Fermor, Una. "The Nature of Character in Drama, with Special Reference to Tragedy." *English Studies Today.* Papers read at the International Conference of University Professors. Held in Magdalen College, Oxford, August, 1950. Oxford Univ. Press, 1951, pp. 11-21.

A6522   Sewell, Arthur. *Character and Society in Shakespeare.* Oxford: Clarendon Press, 1951. Pp. 149.
Rev: *TLS*, Dec. 14, 1951, p. 802; by M. C. Bradbrook, *CamR*, LXXIII (1951/52), 442, 444; by G. B. Harrison, *SatR*, June 14, 1952, pp. 28-29; by L. C. Knights, *MLR*, XLVII, 573-574; by Pierre Chamaillard, *EA*, v, 246; by Harry Levin, *SQ*, III, 370-371; *Listener*, XLVII, 395; by M. C. Bradbrook, *ShS*, VI (1953), 149-150; by John F. Danby, *RES*, IV, 282-283; by Hermann Heuer, *SJ*, 89 (1953), 230-232; by H. Craig, *SQ*, IV, 116; by H. Reinhold, *Archiv*, 189 (1953), 367; by S. Thomas, *MLN*, LXXI (1956), 218-220.

A6523   Muir, Kenneth. "Some Freudian Interpretations of Shakespeare." *Proc. Leeds Philos. and Lit. Soc.*, Lit. & Hist., VII, Pt. 1 (1952), 43-52.
Contains summaries of Freud, Jones, Sharpe, Wertham, and Stewart (on *Ham.*, *Lear*, *Oth.*, & *Mach.*). Defends Freudian approach and attacks Stoll and Schücking, pp. 49-50.

A6524   Bradbrook, M. C. *Shakespeare and Elizabethan Poetry: A Study of his Earlier Work in Relation to the Poetry of the Time.* London: Chatto and Windus, 1951. Pp. viii, 279.
Rev: A3534.

A6525   Doran, Madeleine. *Endeavors of Art: A Study of Form in Elizabethan Drama.* Madison: Univ.
of Wisconsin Press, 1953. Pp. xv, 482.
Rev: A7827.

A6526   Stirling, Brents. *Unity in Shakespearian Tragedy: The Interplay of Theme and Character.* New
York: Columbia Univ. Press, 1956. Pp. 212.
Rev: B5018.

ii.   The Humours

A6527   Draper, John W. *The Humors and Shakespeare's Characters.* Duke Univ. Press, 1945. Pp. vii,
126.
Rev: *TLS*, Sept. 29, 1945, p. 464; by Carroll Camden, *JEGP*, XLV (1946), 230-232; by Una
Ellis-Fermor, *RES*, XXII, 234-235; by Ludwig Edelstein, *Bul. Hist. Med.*, XIX, 349-351; by
A. A. Prins, *ES*, XXVII, 180-182; by Lawrence Babb, *MLN*, LXII (1947), 56-57; by J. L.
Lievsay, *MLQ*, VIII, 125-126; by Dudley Wynn, *New Mexico Quarterly Review*, XVII, 117; by
Mario Praz, *ES*, XXIX (1948), 53 ff.

A6528   Snuggs, Henry L. "The Comic Humours: A New Interpretation." *PMLA*, LXII (1947),
114-122.

A6529   Bauer, Robert V. *The Use of Humours in Comedy by Ben Jonson and his Contemporaries.* DD,
University of Illinois, 1948.

iii.   Characterization through Language

A6530   Saint Geraldine Byrne, Sister. *Shakespeare's Use of the Pronoun of Address: Its Significance in
Characterization and Motivation.* Washington, D. C.: Catholic Univ. of America, 1936.
Pp. xxxvi, 189.

A6531   Berkelman, Robert G. "Shakespeare: Ventriloquist." *SR*, XLVI (1938), 353-364.

A6532   Hunter, Edwin R. "Shakespeare's Mouthpieces: Manner of Speech as a Mark of Personality
in a Few Shakespeare Characters." *SR*, XLVII (1939), 406-430. Reprinted in *Shakespeare and
Common Sense.* Boston: Christopher, 1954.
Rev: A971.

A6533   Tenney, Charles Dewey. "Studies in the Language of Shakespeare's Characters." *Graduate
Theses*, 1932-1942, Oregon State System of Higher Education, pp. 45-49.

A6534   Yoder, Audrey. *Animal Analogy in Shakespeare's Character Portrayal.* New York: King's
Crown Press, 1947. Pp. x, 150. DD, Columbia University, 1946.
Rev: A5728.

A6535   Morozov, Mikhail M. "The Individualization of Shakespeare's Characters through Imagery."
ShS, II (1949), 83-106.

A6536   Schmetz, Lotte. *Sprache und Charakter im Drama Shakespeares.* DD, Munich, 1950. Pp. 190.
Typewritten.

A6537   Schmetz, Lotte. "Die Charakterisierung der Personen durch die Sprache in *Macbeth.*" *SJ*
84/86 (1950), 96-113.

A6537a Cheney, David Raymond. *Animals in "A Midsummer Night's Dream."* DD, State University
of Iowa, 1955. Pp. 288. Mic 55-1103. *DA*, XV (1955), 2188. Publication No. 14,094.

A6538   Cronin, P. J. *Diction and Dramatic Character in Shakespearian Tragedy, with Special Attention
to Characteristic Use of Imagery.* B. Litt thesis, Oxford, 1955.

A6539   Ehrl, Charlotte. *Sprachstil und Charakter bei Shakespeare.* Schriftenreihe der Deutschen
Shakespeare-Gesellschaft, N. F. Bd VI. Heidelberg: Quelle & Meyer, 1957. Pp. 192.
Rev: by Hermann Heuer, *SJ*, 94 (1958), 279-280.

A6540   Joseph, Bertram L. "Verse and Character: the Elizabethan Solution and the Modern Actor."
Abstract in "Eighth International Shakespeare Conference at Stratford," *ShN*, VII (1957), 39, 48.

iv.   Contrast

A6541   Fricker, Robert. *Kontrast und Polarität in den Charakterbildern Shakespeares.* Swiss studies in
English, XXII. Bern: A. Francke, 1951. Pp. 275.
Rev: by T. W. Baldwin, *SQ*, III (1952), 129-131; by Heinz Reinhold, *Anglia*, LXXI, 115-116;
by A. G. van Kranendonk, *ES*, XXXIII, 166-168; by Hermann Heuer, *SJ*, 87/88 (1952),
263-265; by A. Koszul, *EA*, VI (1953), 354-355; by W. Clemen, *Archiv*, 189 (1953),
365-366; by E. T. Sehrt, *Gött. Gel. Anz.*, 208 (1954), 179-184; by W. Schrickx, *RBPH*, XXXV
(1957/58), 425-429.

A6542   Hanawalt, Lloyd A. *Character Foils in Shakespeare's Comedies and Histories.* DD, The Pennsylvania State University, 1957. Pp. 483. Mic 57-2130. *DA*, XVII (1957), 1328. Publication
No. 20,958.

v.   Comic Characters

A6543   Kreider, Paul V. *Elizabethan Comic Character Conventions as Revealed in the Comedies of George
Chapman.* Univ. of Michigan Press, 1935. Pp. xi, 206.
Rev: *TLS*, Feb. 29, 1936, pp. 185-186; by L. C., *RAA*, XIII, 515; by Alwin Thaler, *JEGP*,

XXXVI (1937), 126-128; by Hazelton Spencer, *MLN*, LII, 437-442; by J. H. Walter, *MLR*, XXXII, 489; by Eduard Meissner, *Lbl*, LVIII, 102-103; by A. Brandl, *Archiv*, 170 (1937), 283-284; by H. Nicolai, *Beiblatt*, XLVIII, 125-126.

A6544 Palmer, John. *Comic Characters of Shakespeare.* New York: Macmillan, 1946. Pp. 135.
Rev: "Berowne as Shakespeare," *TLS*, Nov. 16, 1946, p. 562; by W. R. Calvert, *Illus. London News*, 209 (1946), 664; by Bonamy Dobrée, *Spectator*, Oct. 11, 1946, p. 368; by R. Flatter, *Shakespeare Quarterly* (London), I (Summer, 1947), 109-112; by Claire McGlinchee, *NYTBR*, May 18, 1947, p. 14; by R. G., *TAr*, XXXI, 72; by O. J. Campbell, *YR*, XXXVI (1947), 555-557; *Dalhousie Rev.*, XXVII, 117-118; by R. S. Knox, *UTQ*, XVII, 99; by Roy Walker, *Life & Letters*, LIV, 168-174; by A. V. Cookman, *Britain Today*, 129 (1947), 41; by C. Leech, *Erasmus*, I (1947), 425-426; by Hermann Heuer, *SJ*, 84/86 (1951), 254-256.

A6545 Desai, Chintamani N. *Shakespearean Comedy.* (With a Discussion on Comedy, the Comic, and the Sources of Shakespearean Comic Laughter.) Indore City, M. B., India: The Author, 1953. Pp. 204.
Rev: B5187.

A6546 Lawton, Robert O., Jr. *Stock Comic Characters in Shakespeare; A Study of their Relation to the Plot.* DD, Duke University, 1953. Abstract in *ShN*, VI (1956), 22.

A6547 Frye, Northrop. "Characterization in Shakespearian Comedy." *SQ*, IV (1953), 271-277.

A6548 Holland, R. A. *Comedy and Character in Shakespeare in Relation to Shakespearean Criticism Since 1903.* DD, London, Queen Mary College, 1957.

A6549 Hussain, A. M. M. A. *Development of Comic Characters in the Plays of Shakespeare.* MA thesis, Bristol, 1957.

vi. Political Characters

A6550 Eckloff, L. "Heroismus und politisches Führertum bei Shakespeare." *ZNU*, XXXVII (1938), 97-112.

A6550a Palmer, John. *Political Characters of Shakespeare.* London: Macmillan, 1945. Pp. xii, 335.
Rev: "Shakespeare in Politics: A Democratic Study," *TLS*, June 2, 1945, p. 258; by Bonamy Dobrée, *Spectator*, June 29, 1945, p. 597; by J. D. Wilson, *Britain Today*, July, 1945, pp. 38-39; by R. S. Knox, *UTQ*, XVII (1947), 97-99; by O. J. Campbell, *YR*, XXXVI, 555-557; by Hermann Heuer, *SJ*, 84/86 (1951), 254-256.

A6551 Ramin, Reinbold. *Die Gestalt des Politiker und Statesman in Shakespeares Historien und Tragödien bis zum Abschluss der Hamlet-Periode.* DD, Marburg, 1945. Pp. iv, 129. Typewritten.

A6552 Borinski, Ludwig. " 'Soldat' und 'Politiker' bei Shakespeare und seinen Zeitgenossen." *SJ*, 91 (1955), 87-120.

A6553 McDonnell, Robert F. *The "Aspiring Minds": A Study of Shakespearean Characters Who Aspire to Political Sovereignty Against the Background of Literary and Dramatic Tradition.* DD, University of Minnesota, 1958. Pp. 307. Mic 58-7015. *DA*, XIX (1959), pp. 1365-66.

vii. Miscellaneous
(Arranged alphabetically by author.)

A6554 Peregrinus. "The Age of Shakespeare's Characters." *N &Q*, 177 (1939), 83; H. Kendra Baker, *ibid.*, 123; M. H. Dodds, *ibid.*, 197.

A6555 Anderson, Ruth L. "Excessive Goodness A Tragic Fault." *SAB*, XIX (1944), 85-96.

A6556 Baldwin, T. W. "Shakspere's Aphthonian Man." *MLN*, LXV (1950), 111-112.

A6557 Berhens, Ralph. "Some Observations on Rationality vs. Credulity in Shakespeare." *N &Q*, NS, IV (1957), 420-421.

A6558 Bowden, William R. "The Human Shakespeare and *Troilus and Cressida.*" *SQ*, VIII (1957), 167-177.

A6559 Boyce, Benjamin. *The Theophrastan Character in England to 1642.* Harvard Univ. Press, 1947. Pp. ix, 324.
Shak's approaches to character, pp. 113-115, 155-157.
Rev: A4377.

A6560 Van Brakell Buys, W. R. *De Magiër van Stratford: Shakespeares Karakter-tekening.* Naarden: In den Toren, 1949. Pp. 67.
Rev: by C. de Groot in *Nieuwe Eeuw*, Nov. 19, 1949.

A6561 Campbell, Oscar James. *Shakespeare's Satire.* Oxford Univ. Press, 1943. Pp. 227.
Rev: B5164.

A6562 Carré, Henri. "C'est Shakespeare qui a, le premier, réhabilité Jeanne d'Arc dans l'opinion anglaise." *Figaro Litt.*, May 7, 1949, p. 3.

A6563 Cunningham, Edward. *Vehicle Characters in Shakespeare's Plays.* MA thesis, Ottawa, 1936. Pp. 85.

A6564 Draper, John W. "Characterization in Shakespeare's Plays." *West Virginia University Bulletin*, Philological Papers, Series 58, No. 11-12 (1958), pp. 1-15.

A6565 Druhman, Rev. Alvin W. *An Analysis of Four of the Level-of-Life Characters in Shakespeare's*

Tragedies. DD, St. John's University, Brooklyn, 1952. Abstr. publ. in *Abstracts of Dissertations, 1951-1952*, Brooklyn: St. John's Univ., 1952, pp. 14-15.

A6566 Edwards, Eleanor. *The Evolution of the Tragic Flaw with Special Reference to Shakespeare's Chronicle History Plays*. MA thesis, University of North Carolina, 1939. Abstr. publ. in *Univ. of North Carolina Record, Research in Progress*, Grad. School Series, No. 36, 1939, pp. 78-79.

A6566a Ellis-Fermor, Una. "Shakespeare and the Dramatic Mode." *Neophil*, XXXVII (1953), 104-112.

A6567 Fergusson, Francis. *The Human Image in Dramatic Literature*. New York: Doubleday & Company, 1957. Pp. xx, 217.
Shak., pp. 115-157.

A6568 Gates, William Bryan. "The Reality of Shakespeare's 'Supers'." *SAB*, XX (1945), 160-172.

A6569 Grosse, Franz. "Persönlichkeit und Gemeinschaft bei Shakespeare." *NS*, XLVIII (1940), 205-208.

A6570 Günther-Konsalik, Heinz. "Der Gegenspieler im Drama." *Dts. Dramaturgie*, II (1943), 172-175.

A6571 Haas, Rudolf. *Die Gestaltung der dramatischen Person in den grossen Tragödien Shakespeares*. DD, Tübingen, 1953. Pp. v, 242. Typewritten.

A6572 Harbage, Alfred. "Shakespeare's Ideal Man." *AMS*, pp. 65-80.

A6573 Harrison, G. B. *Elizabethan Plays and Players*. London: Routledge, 1940. Pp. viii, 306. Paperback ed.: Univ. of Michigan Press, 1956. Pp. viii, 306.
Rev: A7079.

A6574 Herbert, T. Walter. "Diversive Estimates of Polonius' Character: An Example of a Dramatic Technique." *Renaissance Papers*, 1957, pp. 82-86.

A6575 Kerl, Wilhelm. *Fortuna und Natura in ihrem Verhältnis zum Menschen in Shakespeares Barockdramen*. DD, Marburg, 1949. Pp. ix, 187. Typewritten.

A6576 Langsam, G. Geoffrey. *Martial Books and Tudor Verse*. New York: King's Crown Press, 1951. Pp. 213.
Rev: A2623.

A6577 Lindsay, J. "Shakespeare & Tom Thumb." *Life & Letters*, LVIII (1948), 119-127.

A6578 Lord, John Bigelow. *Certain Dramatic Devices Studied in the Comedies of Shakespeare and in Some of the Works of His Contemporaries and Predecessors*. DD, University of Illinois, 1951. Pp. 296. *DA*, XII (1952), 66. Publication No. 3154.

A6579 Lovett, David. *Shakespeare's Characters in Eighteenth Century Criticism*. DD, Johns Hopkins University, 1935.

A6580 McCutchan, John W. *Personified Abstractions as Characters in Elizabethan Drama*. DD, University of Virginia, 1949. Abstract in *Univ. of Virginia Abstracts of Diss.*, 1949, pp. 11-14.

A6581 Matheson, Belle Seddon. *The Invented Personages of Shakespeare's Plays*. Univ. of Pennsylvania Press, 1932.
Rev: by Eduard Eckhardt, *Eng. Studn.*, LXX (1936), 401-402; by H. N. Hillebrand, *MLN*, LI (1936), 462.

A6582 Mettin, H. C. "Die Bedeutung des Adels bei Shakespeare." *Deut. Adelsblatt*, LV (1939), 994-996.

A6583 Nikolajev, V. N. "On Certain Peculiarities in the Development of Shakespearean Characters." *Transactions of the Pedagogical Institute in Gorki* (USSR), VIII (1940), 121-134.

A6584 Ryan, Rev. Harold Francis, S. J. *Heroic Play Elements in Earlier English Drama*. DD, St. Louis University, 1944. Pp. 366. Mic A45-5307. *Microf. Ab.*, VI (1945), 27. Publication No. 766.

A6585 Schlumberger, Jean. "Sur les Personnages de Shakespeare." In *Le Théâtre Élizabéthain*. Paris: Les Cahiers du Sud, 1940, pp. 40-43.

A6586 Smith, M. Ellwood. "The Lunatic, The Lover and The Poet." *SAB*, XVI (1941), 77-88.

A6587 Soellner, Rolf H. *Anima and Affectus: Theories of the Emotions in Sixteenth Century Grammar Schools and Their Reflections in the Works of Shakespere*. DD, University of Illinois, 1954. Pp. 275. Mic A54-489. *DA*, XIV (1954), 351. Publication No. 6983.

A6588 Waith, Eugene M. *The Pattern of Tragicomedy in Beaumont and Fletcher*. Yale Studies Eng., 120. Yale Univ. Press, 1952. Pp. xiv, 212. "Satyr and Shepherd in Shakespeare," pp. 80-83.
Rev: A6894.

A6589 Watkins, W. B. C. *Shakespeare and Spenser*. Princeton Univ. Press, 1950. Pp. ix, 339.
Rev: B8549.

A6590 Weilgart, Wolfgang J. *Shakespeare Psychognostic: Character Evolution and Transformation*. Tokyo: 1952.
Rev: by Lawrence Babb, *SQ*, VI (1955), 190.

A6591 Wilson, M. G. *An Interpretation of Shakespeare's Character Additions*. Thesis, Univ. of New Zealand, 1952.

A6592 Yamoto, Sadamiki. "Personalities in Shakespeare's Plays." *Eibungaku-kenkyu*, XXVI (1950).

A6593 Yozovsky, Y. *The Character and the Epoch: On Shakespeare Themes*. Moscow, 1947. Pp. 190.

(b) PARTICULAR PROBLEMS OF CHARACTER (111;37)
(Transferred to Problems of Character in General)
(c) INDIVIDUAL CHARACTERS (112;37)
(Omitted; studies of individual characters are listed under
the play they appear in.)
(d) CHARACTER TYPES (112;37)
    i. Artisan and Professional Types (112;37)
        aa. Soldiers, Braggarts and Roaring Boys

A6594 Boughner, Daniel C. "Pistol and the Roaring Boys." *SAB*, xi (1936), 226-237.

A6595 Withington, R. "Braggart, Devil and 'Vice': A Note on the Development of Comic Figures in the Early English Drama." *Speculum*, xi (1936), 124-129.

A6596 Bowden, Nancy Jane. *The Dramatic Tradition of the Miles Gloriosus*. MA thesis, Acadia (Canada), 1938.

A6597 Boughner, Daniel C. *The Braggart Soldier in Elizabethan Drama, 1580-1616*. DD, Princeton University, 1939.

A6598 Boughner, Daniel C. "Don Armado and the *Commedia dell'Arte*." *SP*, xxxvii (1940), 201-224.

A6599 Milligan, Burton. "The Roaring Boy in Tudor and Stuart Literature." *SAB*, xv (1940), 184-190.

A6600 Webb, Henry Jameson. *Criticism of the Military Profession in Sixteenth Century Literature*. DD, State University of Iowa, 1942.

A6601 Boughner, Daniel C. "Sir Toby's Cockatrice." *Italica*, xx (1943), 171-172.

A6602 Dangel, Anneliese. *Fähnrich Pistol und die Anfänge des Begriffes Rant*. DD, Leipzig, 1944. Pp. 118. Typewritten.

A6603 Jorgensen, Paul A. *The Elizabethan "Plain Soldier" in Shakespeare's Plays*. DD, University of California, Berkeley, 1946.

A6604 Peery, William. "The Roaring Boy Again." *SAB*, xxiii (1948), 12-15, 78-86. Criticizes A6599.

A6605 Gilbert, Allan H. "The Duel in Italian Cinquecento Drama and Its Relation to Tragicomedy." *Italica*, xxvi (1949), 7-14.

A6606 Boas, F. S. *Queen Elizabeth in Drama, and Related Studies*. London, 1950. "The Soldier in Elizabethan Drama," pp. 163-189.
       Rev: B4458.

A6607 Cordasco, Francesco. *Don Adriano de Armado of Love's Labour's Lost*. Bologna, 1950. Pp. 6.

A6608 Boughner, Daniel C. *The Braggart in Renaissance Comedy: A Study in Comparative Drama from Aristophanes to Shakespeare*. Minneapolis: Univ. of Minnesota Press, 1954. Pp. vii, 328.
       Rev: by Joseph G. Fucilla, *RN*, vii (1954), 101-102; by William Armstrong, *YWES*, xxxv (1954), 77; by W. P. F[riederich], *CL*, vii (1955), 88-89; by Virgil B. Heltzel, *SQ*, vi, 342-343; by L. Bradner, *MLN*, lxx, 205-206; by Norman B. Spector, *Italica*, xxxii, 193-194; by Marvin T. Herrick, *JEGP*, lv (1956), 144-145; by J. E. Gillet, *HR*, xxiv, 151-153; by K. L. Selig, *RBPH*, xxxv (1957), 834-835; by Maria Rosa Lida de Malkiel, *Romance Philol.*, xi, 268-291.

A6609 Bradner, L. "The First Cambridge Production of *Miles Gloriosus*." *MLN*, lxx (1955), 400-403.
See also discussions of the military, A2583-A2637, and of character in the Falstaff plays.

bb. Pillars of Society

A6610 Liebe, Karl. *Der Arzt im Elisabethanischen Drama*. DD, Halle, 1907. Pp. 50.

A6611 Silvette, Herbert. "The Doctor on the Stage." *Annals of Medical History*, ns, ix (1937), 62-88, 174-188, 264-279, 371-394, 482-507.

A6612 Sleeth, C. R. "Shakespeare's Counsellors of State." *RAA*, xiii (1936), 97-113.

A6613 Evans, H. A. *The Scholar on the London Stage, 1580-1620*. MA thesis, Birmingham, 1954.

A6614 Mirtschuk, Johanna. *Die Gestalt des guten Fürstenberaters im ernsten elisabethanischen Drama*. DD, Munich, 1956.

ii. Female Characters (113;37)

A6615 Passmann, Hans. *Der Typus der Kurtisane im Elisabethanischen Drama*. DD, Münster, 1926. Pp. vii, 75.

A6616 Blos, Hanna. *Die Auffassung der Frauengestalten Shakespeares in dem Werk der Mrs. Cowden Clarke, "The Girlhood of Shakespeares Heroines."* DD, Erlangen, 1936. Pp. 131.

A6617 Günther, Hans F. K. "Shakespeares Mädchen und Frauen." *SJ*, lxxiii (1937), 85-108.

A6618 Lemme, H. "Shakespeares Frauen und Mädchen in lebenskundlicher Betrachtung." *Nationalsozialist Mhe.*, viii (1937), 548-550.

A6619 Vallese, Tarquinio. *Donne Shakespeariane*. Rome: Albrighi Segati, 1937. Pp. 72.

A6620 Trinker, Martha K de. *Las Mujeres en el "Don Quijote" de Cervantes, Comparadas con las Mujeres en los Dramas de Shakespeare*. DD, Mexico, 1938. Pp. 123.

A6621   Davies, W. Robertson. *Shakespeare's Boy Actors*. London: Dent, 1939. Pp. 208.
         Rev: A7322.

A6622   Sampley, Arthur M. "A Warning-Piece Against Shakespeare's Women." *SAB*, xv (1940), 34-39.

A6623   Melián Lafinur, Luis. *Las Mujeres de Shakespeare. Con un Prólogo de Alvaro Melián Lafinur*. Montevideo: Claudio García, 1942.

A6624   Gordon, George. *Shakespearian Comedy and Other Studies*. Ed. by Sir Edmund Chambers. Oxford Univ. Press, 1944. Pp. 168.
         Rev: B5165.

A6625   Falk, Signi L. *The Vogue of the Courtesan Play, 1602-1610*. DD, University of Chicago, 1949.

A6626   Bandel, Betty. *Shakespeare's Treatment of the Social Position of Women*. DD, Columbia University, 1951. Pp. 326. Mic A51-530. *Microf. Ab.*, xi (1951), 1030. Publication No. 2793.

A6627   Camden, Carroll. "The Elizabethan Imogen." *The Rice Institute Pamphlet*, xxxviii (No. 1, April, 1951), 1-17.

A6628   Boyd, Catharine B. "The Isolation of Antigone and Lady Macbeth." *Classical Journal*, xLVII (1952), 174-177, 203.

A6629   Helton, Tinsley. *The Concept of Woman's Honour in Jacobean Drama*. DD, University of Minnesota, 1953. Pp. 371. *DA*, xii (1952), 795. Publication No. 4334.
"Shak. Before 1600," pp. 95-113; "Shak. After 1600," pp. 159-175.

A6630   Wadsworth, Frank Whittemore. *The White Devil, an Historical and Critical Study*. DD, Princeton University, 1951. Pp. 416. Mic A55-1111. *DA*, xv (1955), 832. Publication No. 11,051.
Shak. plays discussed: *Antony, Hamlet, Lear, Richard III, Macbeth, Othello, Romeo, Titus*.

A6631   Taylor, William Edwards. "The Villainess in Elizabethan Drama." DD, Vanderbilt University, 1957. *DA*, xvii (1957), 1756-57.

A6632   Eagle, Roderick L. "Shakespeare's Learned Ladies." *N&Q*, NS, v (1958), 197.

iii.   Ghosts (114;38)
(Transferred to Scenes, VIII, 2, b, (7), (b).)
iv.   Children and Old Men (114;38)

A6633   Davies, W. Robertson. *Shakespeare's Boy Actors*. London: Dent, 1939. Pp. 208.
         Rev: A7322.

A6634   Krjijanovsky, S. "The Children in Shakespeare's Plays." *Literature for Children* (USSR), vi (1940), 13-15.

A6635   Miles, L. Wardlaw. "Shakespeare's Old Men." *ELH*, vii (1940), 286-299.

A6636   Draper, John W. "Shakespeare's Attitude Toward Old Age." *Journal Gerontology*, i (1946), 118-126.

A6637   Raynor, Henry. "The Little Victims." *FortnR*, August, 1953, pp. 104-114.

A6638   Whitehouse, J. Howard. *The Boys of Shakespeare*. Birmingham: Cornish Brothers, 1953. Pp. 30.
         Rev: *TLS*, Mar. 27, 1953, p. 211; by H. T. Price, *SQ*, v (1954), 113.

v.   The Melancholy Type (114;38)

A6639   Knights, Lionel Charles. *Aspects of the Economic and Social Background of Comedy in the Early Seventeenth Century*. Thesis, Cambridge. *Cam Abs.*, 1935/36, p. 63.
Appendix B: "Seventeenth Century Melancholy."

A6640   Draper, John W. "The Melancholy Duke Orsino." *Bul. Inst. Hist. Medicine*, vi (1938), 1020-29.

A6641   Cole, John W. "Romeo and Rosaline." *Neophil*, xxiv (1939), 285-288.

A6642   Babb, Lawrence. "Melancholy and the Elizabethan Man of Letters." *HLQ*, iv (1941), 247-261.

A6643   Rehor, Charles F. *Of Many Simples: A Study of the Elizabethan Melancholic in Medicine and Literature (1586-1621)*. DD, Western Reserve University, 1941.

A6644   Thomas, Sidney. "The Elizabethan Idea of Melancholy." *MLN*, lvi (1941), 261-263.

A6645   Floyd, John Paul. *The Convention of Melancholy in the Plays of Marston and Shakespeare*. DD, Harvard University, 1942. Abstr. publ. in *Summaries of Ph.D. Theses, 1942*, Cambridge: Harvard Univ. Press, 1946, pp. 271-272.

A6646   Uhler, J. E. "Shakespeare's Melancholy." *Studies for William A. Read*. (B4418)

A6647   Babb, Lawrence. "Melancholic Villainy in the Elizabethan Drama." *Papers Michigan Acad. Sci. Arts, and Letters*, xxix (1943), 527-535.

A6648   Babb, Lawrence. "Love Melancholy in the Elizabethan and Early Stuart Drama." *Bul. Hist. Medicine*, xiii (1943), 117-132.

A6649   Babb, Lawrence. "Hamlet, Melancholy, and the Devil." *MLN*, lix (1944), 120-122.

A6650   Draper, John W. *The Humors and Shakespeare's Characters.* Duke Univ. Press, 1945. Pp. vii, 126.
        Rev: A6527.

A6651   Siegel, Paul Noah. *Studies in Elizabethan Melancholy.* DD, Harvard University, 1941. Abstr. publ. in *Summaries of Ph.D. Theses, 1941,* Cambridge: Harvard Univ. Press, 1945, pp. 341-344.

A6652   Ritze, F. H. *Shakespeare's Men of Melancholy and His Malcontents.* MS thesis, Columbia University, 1947. Pp. 98.

A6653   Babb, Lawrence. *The Elizabethan Malady: A Study of Melancholia in English Literature from 1580 to 1642.* East Lansing: Michigan State College Press, 1951. Pp. xi, 206.
        Rev: *TLS,* Jan. 11, 1952, p. 22; by Alexander M. Saunders, *Books Abroad,* XXVI, 396; by John W. Draper, *MLR,* XLVII, 571-572; by Murray W. Bundy, *SQ,* III, 275-278; by Hermann Heuer, *SJ,* 87/88, (1952), 252-253; by Paul H. Kocher, *Bul. Hist. Medicine,* XXVI, 390-392; by R. Davril, *EA,* V, 250-251; by Carmen Rogers, *ShN,* II, 38; by R. A. Law, *SQ,* III, 84; by William Van O'Connor, *Journal of Esthetics,* XI, 177-178; *Dalhousie Review,* XXXI, 13-15; by Clifford Leech, *ShS,* VI (1953), 154-155; by Paul V. Kreider, *MLN,* LXVIII, 250-252; by C. T. Harrison, *SR,* LXII (1954), 160-166.

A6654   Rogers, Carmen. "English Renaissance Melancholy: A Prologue of Men and Moods." *Fla. State Univ. Studies,* V (1952), 45-66.

vi.   Fools, Clowns, and the Devil (115;38)

A6655   Withington, R. "Braggart, Devil and 'Vice': A Note on the Development of Comic Figures in the Early English Drama." *Speculum,* XI (1936), 124-129.

A6656   Schell, J. S. "Shakespeare's Gulls." *SAB,* XV (1940), 23-33.

A6657   Draper, John W. "Et in Illyria Feste." *SAB,* XVI (1941), 220-228, and XVII (1942), 25-32.

A6658   Vassilieva, T. N. "The Character of the Buffoon in Shakespeare." *Transactions of the Hertzen State Pedagogical Institute in Leningrad,* XLI (1941), 129-172.

A6659   Campbell, Oscar James. *Shakespeare's Satire.* Oxford Univ. Press, 1943. Pp. 227.
        Rev: B5164.

A6660   Babb, Lawrence. "Hamlet, Melancholy, and the Devil." *MLN,* LIX (1944), 120-122.

A6661   Gordon, George. *Shakespearian Comedy and Other Studies.* Ed. by Sir Edmund Chambers. Oxford Univ. Press, 1944. Pp. 168.
        Rev: B5165.

A6662   Nakahashi, Kazuo. *Destiny of the Fool.* Tokyo: Chuokoronsha, 1948.

A6663   Sitwell, Edith. "On the Clowns and Fools of Shakespeare." *Life & Letters,* LVII (1948), 102-109.

A6664   Sitwell, Edith. *A Notebook on William Shakespeare.* New York, London: Macmillan, 1948. Pp. xii, 233.
        Rev: A8365.

A6665   Empson, William. "The Fool in Lear." *SR,* LVII (1949), 177-214.

A6666   Vallese, Tarquinio. *Saggi di Letteratura Inglese.* Naples: Pironti, 1948. Pp. 153. "X. Folle Shakespeariane."

A6667   Orwell, George. "Lear, Tolstoy, and the Fool." *Shooting an Elephant and Other Essays.* New York, 1950, pp. 32-52.

A6668   Curry, Rev. John Vincent. *Deception in Elizabethan Comedy: An Analytical Study.* DD, Columbia University, 1951. Pp. 229. Mic A51-541. *Microf. Ab.,* XI (1951), 840. Publication No. 2804.
        Rev: A6298.

A6669   Cazamian, Louis. *The Development of English Humor.* Duke Univ. Press, 1952. Pp. viii, 421.
        Rev: B5186.

A6670   Goldsmith, Robert Hillis. *Wise Men in Motley: The Fool in Elizabethan Drama.* DD, Columbia University, 1952. Pp. 226. *DA,* XII (1952), 618. Publication No. 4186.

A6671   Hotson, Leslie. *Shakespeare's Motley.* London: Rupert Hart-Davis, 1952. Pp. 133.
        Rev: *TLS,* July 25, 1952, p. 482 (comment by Oliver Lodge and R. F. Rattray, Aug. 1, p. 501; by Louise S. Boas, Sept. 12, p. 597); *SatR,* Aug. 2, 1952, p. 12; by Theodore Hoffman, *NR,* Sept. 1, 1952, p. 23; *NstN,* XLIII (1952), 782; by Ivor Brown, *Obs.,* June 29, 1952, p. 7; by Joseph Carroll, *TAr,* Nov., 1952, pp. 10-11; *NYHTB,* Nov. 23, 1952, p. 24; by P. H., *Spectator,* May 8, 1953, p. 584; by Hermann Heuer, *SJ,* 89 (1953), 212-213; by Kenneth Muir, *RES,* IV, 378; by John Crow, *SQ,* IV, 344-346; by M. St. Clare Byrne, *TN,* IX (1955), 83-84.

A6671a Hotson, Leslie. "False Faces on Shakespeare's Stage." *TLS,* May 16, 1952, p. 336. Comment, ibid., by Howard Schless, June 6, p. 377; Oliver Lodge and R. F. Rattray, August 1, p. 501.

A6672   Di Stefano, Carlo. "Il Buffone nel Teatro Elisabettiano e Shakespeariano." *Teatro Scenario* (Milan), Feb. 1, 1952, pp. 48-49.

A6673   Auerbach, Erich. *Mimesis: The Representation of Reality in Western Literature,* tr. by Willard R. Trask. Princeton Univ. Press, 1953.

Study of Fools and Madmen, pp. 347-349.
Rev: A6859a.

A6674   Goldsmith, Robert Hillis. "Touchstone: Critic in Motley." *PMLA*, LXVIII (1953), 884-895.

A6675   Boughner, D. C. "Vice, Braggart, and Falstaff." *Anglia*, LXXII (1954), 35-61.

A6676   Goldsmith, Robert H. *Wise Fools in Shakespeare*. Michigan State Univ. Press, 1955. Pp. xi, 123.
Rev: by Glenn H. Blayney, *SQ*, VIII (1957), 119-120; by Edwin B. Benjamin, *CE*, XVIII,
291; by R. A. Foakes, *English*, XII (1958), 105-106.

A6677   Violi, Unicio J. *Shakespeare and the Lazzo*. DD, Columbia University, 1955. Pp. 282. Mic
A55-1834. *DA*, XV (1955), 1391. Publication No. 12,479.

A6678   Felver, Charles Stanley. *William Shakespeare and Robert Armin his Fool—A Working Partnership*.
DD, University of Michigan, 1956. Pp. 352. Mic 56-3895. *DA*, XVI (1956), 2446. Publica-
tion No. 18,601.
Appendix III discusses Hotson's *Shakespeare's Motley*, A6671.

A6679   Felver, Charles S. "Robert Armin, Shakespeare's Source for Touchstone." *SQ*, VII (1956),
135-137.

A6680   Bekker, Hugo. *The Lucifer Motif in the German and Dutch Drama of the Sixteenth and Seventeenth Centuries*. DD, University of Michigan, 1958. Pp. 248. Mic 58-7680. *DA*, XIX (1958),
1364.
Nothing explicit on Shak.

vii.   National Types (115;38)
aa.   General

A6681   Clark, E. G. "Racial Antagonisms in Shakespeare—and His Contemporaries." *Opportunity*,
XIV (1936), 138-140.

A6682   Withington, Robert. "Shakespeare and Race Prejudice." *Elizabethan Studies in Honor of
George F. Reynolds*, 1945, pp. 172-184.

A6683   Faggett, Harry L. *Attitudes Toward Foreigners Reflected in Elizabethan Drama*. DD, Boston
University, 1948.

bb.   Irish, Welsh, and Scotch

A6684   Bartley, J. O. *Teague, Shenkin and Sawney*. Cork Univ. Press, 1954.
Rev: by Denis Donoghue in *Studies*, LXIV (1955), 255.

A6685   Dugan, G. C. *The Stage Irishman*. New York: Longmans, Green, 1937. Pp. 322.
Rev: *TLS*, Apr. 3, 1937, p. 251.

A6686   Bartley, J. O. "The Development of a Stock Character: I. The Stage Irishman to 1800."
MLR, XXXVII (1942), 438-447.

A6687   Bartley, J. O. "The Development of a Stock Character: II. The Stage Scotsman; III. The
Stage Welshman (to 1800)." *MLR*, XXXVIII (1943), 279-288.

A6688   Wilson, W. G. "Welshmen in Elizabethan London." *Life and Letters Today*, XLI (1944),
177-186.

A6689   Scott, Florence R. "Teg—the Stage Irishman." *MLR*, XLII (1947), 314-320.

cc.   Jewish

A6690   Coleman, Edward D. "The Jew in English Drama: An Annotated Bibliography." *Bul.
New York Public Lib.*, XLII (1938), 827-850; 919-932.

A6691   Coleman, E. D. "The Jew in English Drama: An Annotated Bibliography." Pts. III and IV.
Bul. New York Public Lib., XLIII (1939), 45-52; 374-378.

A6692   Coleman, E. D. "The Jew in English Drama: An Annotated Bibliography." Pts. VI, VII,
VIII, IX, X, XI, XII, XIII. *Bul. New York Pub. Lib.*, XLIV (1940), 361-372; 429-444; 495-504;
543-558; 620-634; 675-698; 777-788; 843-866.

A6693   Sisson, C. J. "A Jewish Colony in Shakespeare's London." *Essays and Studies by Members of
the English Association* (Oxford), 1938, pp. 38-51.

A6694   Marcus, Jacob Rader. *The Jew in the Medieval World: A Source Book, 315-1791*. Cincinnati:
Union of Amer. Hebrew Congregations, 1938. Pp. xxiv, 504.
Rev: by S. W. Baron, *AHR*, XLIV (1939), 421-422; by Dorothy Mackay Quinn, *South
Atlantic Quar.*, XXXVIII, 238-239; *Medium Aevum*, VIII, 82-83; by T. P. Oakley, *Catholic
Hist. Rev.*, XXVI (1941), 255-256.

A6695   Cancelled.

A6696   Hobman, B. L. "The Jew in Gentile Fiction." *ConR*, 157 (1940), 97-103.

A6697   Roth, Cecil. *A History of the Jews in England*. Oxford: Clarendon Press, 1942. Pp. xii, 306.
Rev: *N&Q*, 182 (1942), 210; *TLS*, Mar. 14, 1942, p. 128; by I. C., *MGW*, Mar. 27, 1942,
p. 198; by James Parkes, *Econ. Hist. Rev.*, XII, 98-99.

A6698   Roth, C. "Expulsion of Jews from England in 1610." *N&Q*, 185 (1943), 82-83.

A6699   Trachtenberg, Joshua. *The Devil and the Jew*. The Medieval Conception of the Jew and Its

Relation to Modern Anti-Semitism. Yale Univ. Press, 1944. Pp. xiv, 279.
Rev: A3592.

A6700 Zitt, Hersch L. "The Jew in the Elizabethan World-Picture." *Historia Judaica*, XIV (1952), 53-60.

A6701 Charlton, H. B. "Shakespeare's Jew." *BJRL*, XXII (1938), 34-68. Reprinted in Charlton's *Shakespearian Comedy*, B5155.
Rev: by E. E. Stoll, *SJ*, LXXIV (1938), 53-55.

A6702 Modder, M. F. *The Jew in the Literature of England to the End of the 19th Century.* Philadelphia: Jewish Publication Society of America, 1939. Pp. xvi, 436.

A6703 Stoll, Elmer Edgar. "Shakespeare's Jew." *UTQ*, VIII (1939), 139-154.

A6704 Tannenbaum, Samuel A. "Shakspere an Anti-Semite?" *SAB*, XIX (1944), 47-48.

A6705 Smith, Fred M. "Shylock on the Rights of Jews and Emilia on the Rights of Women." *West Virginia Univ. Bul., Philological Papers*, V (1947), 32-33.

A6706 Nathan, Norman. "Three Notes on *The Merchant of Venice.*" *SAB*, XXIII (1948), 152-173.

A6707 Lelyveld, Toby Bookholtz. *Shylock on the Stage: Significant Changes in the Interpretation of Shakespeare's Jew.* DD, Columbia University, 1951. Pp. 196. Mic A51-284. *Microf. Ab.,* XI (1951), 772. Publication No. 2541.

A6708 Shackford, J. B. "Bond of Kindness: Shylock's Humanity." *Univ. of Kansas City Rev.,* XXI (1954), 85-91.

A6709 Krapf, E. E. "A Psychoanalytic Study of Shakespeare and Antisemitism." *Psychoanalytic Rev.,* XLII (1955), 113-130.

A6710 Macht, David I. "Biblical Allusions in Shakespeare's *The Tempest* in the Light of Hebrew Exegesis." *The Jewish Forum*, Aug., 1955, pp. 3-5.

A6711 Warhaft, Sidney. "Anti-Semitism in *The Merchant of Venice.*" *Manitoba Arts Rev.,* X (1956), 3-15.

A6712 Gross, Harvey. "From Barabas to Bloom: Notes on the Figure of the Jew." *Western Humanities Review*, XI (1957), 149-156.

A6713 "Shakespeare Lectures at the Oregon Festival." *ShN*, VIII, 28-29. Abstracts of the Gresham Lecture: Arthur Kreisman, "The Jews of Marlowe and Shakespeare."

dd. Continental

A6714 Keller, Wolfgang. "Die Franzosen in Shakespeares Dramen." *SJ*, LXXVI (1940), 34-56.

A6715 Keller, W. "Shakespeare und die Gascogner." *Weltliteratur*, XV (1940), 124-125.

A6716 Feldman, Abraham. "Netherlanders on the Early London Stage." *N &Q*, 196 (1951), 333-335.

A6717 Feldman, A. Bronson. "The Flemings in Shakespeare's Theatre." *N &Q*, 197 (1952), 265-269.

A6718 Peery, William. "Spanish Figs and Conjectural Thistles." *Neophil*, XXXVI (1952), 50-53.

ee. Non-European

A6719 Hunekuhl-Keller, Klåre. *Die Neger- und Indianerromantik in der englischen Literatur von der Renaissance bis zum Ende des 18. Jahrhunderts.* DD, Münster, 1932. Pp. iv, 107, 7. Typewritten.

A6720 Troesch, Mrs. Helen de Rusha. *The Negro in English Dramatic Literature and on the Stage and a Bibliography of Plays with Negro Characters.* DD, Western Reserve University, 1940.

A6721 Poag, T. E. *The Negro in Drama and the Theatre.* DD, Cornell University, 1944. Abstract in *Cornell University Abstracts of Theses* (Ithaca), 1944, pp. 23-25.

viii. Social Types (116;38)
aa. Heroes

A6722 Lewis, [Percy] Wyndham. *The Lion and the Fox: The Role of the Hero in the Plays of Shakespeare.* New edition. London: Methuen, 1955. Pp. 326.
Originally published in 1927.

A6723 Campbell, Lily B. *Shakespeare's Tragic Heroes.* A Reprint. New York: Barnes & Noble, 1955. Pp. xii, 296. First published 1930.
Rev: B5002.

A6724 Schneider, Hermann. *Germanische Heldensage.* II. 1. Abt. Nord, germ. Heldensage; 2. Abt. Englische Heldensage. Festländische Heldensage in . . . engl. Überlieferung. Berlin and Leipzig: de Gruyter, 1933/34. Pp. 326; 181.
Rev: by F. Panzer, *DLZ*, LVII (1936), 200-202; by W. Golther, *Lbl*, LVII (1936), 171-172.

A6725 Bodkin, Maud. *Archetypal Patterns in Poetry.* Oxford Univ. Press, 1934. Pp. xiv, 340.
Rev: A8096.

A6726 Raglan, Lord. *The Hero: A Study in Tradition, Myth, and Drama.* London: Watts, 1936. Republished 1949. Pp. x, 310.

A6727 Wilson, Arthur H. "At the Elbow of the Shakespearean Protagonist." *Susquehanna Univ. Studies*, I (1936), 38-40.

A6728 Eckloff, L. "Heroismus und politisches Führertum bei Shakespeare." *ZNU*, XXXVII (1938), 97-112.

A6729 Schücking, Levin L. *The Baroque Character of the Elizabethan Tragic Hero*. Annual Shakespeare Lecture of the British Academy. Oxford Univ. Press, 1938. Pp. 29. Also in *Proceedings of British Academy*, XXIV, 85-111.
Rev: A5528.

A6730 Magill, Thomas Nelson. *Character in the Drama*. DD, Cornell University, 1941. Abstr. publ. in *Cornell University Abstracts of Theses, 1941*, Ithaca, 1942, pp. 45-47.

A6731 Woesler R. "Der Mensch und seine Grösse bei Shakespeare." *NS*, XLVIII (1941), 181-187.

A6732 Sachs, Hanns. "What Would Have Happened if . . . ?" *The Creative Unconscious*, Cambridge (Mass.): Sci-Art, 1942, pp. 339-340.
2nd edition 1951.

A6733 Stoll, Elmer E. "Heroes and Villains: Shakespeare, Middleton, Byron, Dickens." *RES*, XVIII (1942), 257-269.

A6734 Spencer, Theodore. "The Isolation of the Shakespearean Hero." *SR*, LII (1944), 313-331.

A6735 Pitcher, Seymour. "Aristotle's Good and Just Heroes." *PQ*, XXIV (1945), 1-11.
See letter by Mr. Pitcher, ibid., XXIV, 190-191.

A6736 Schücking, Levin L. "Der barocke Charakter des tragischen Helden in Elisabethanischen Drama." *Essays über Shakespeare, Pepys, Rossetti, Shaw und Anderes*. Wiesbaden: Dietrich, 1948, pp. 274-312.
English version: A6729.

A6737 Draper, John W. "The Heroes of Shakespeare's Tragedies." *West Virginia Univ. Bul., Philol. Papers*, VI (1949), 12-21.

A6738 Schwerer (née Krumbholz), Margarethe. *Shakespeares tragische Helden im Lichte der Kretschmerschen Lehre*. DD, Vienna, 1950. Pp. 119. Typewritten.

A6739 Simpson, Lucie. "The Secondary Heroes of the Plays." *The Secondary Heroes of Shakespeare and Other Essays*. London: Kingswood Press, 1950, pp. 11-24.

A6740 Cruttwell, Patrick. "The War's and Fortune's Son." *EIC*, II (1952), 24-37.

A6741 Eppler, Erhard. *Der Aufbegehrende und der Verzweifelnde als Heldenfigur der elisabethanischen Tragödie*. DD, Tübingen, 1952. Pp. xiv, 145. Typewritten.

A6742 Brown, Huntington. "Enter the Shakespearean Tragic Hero." *EIC*, III (1953), 285-302.
Rev: by H. T. Price, *SQ*, V (1954), 127-128.

A6743 Gaither, Mary Elizabeth. *Ancient and Modern Concepts of the Tragic Hero*. DD, Indiana University, 1953. Pp. 151. Mic A53-905. *DA*, XIII (1953), 547. Publication No. 5313.
Chap. III: "The Tragic Heroes of Shakespeare and Racine," pp. 54-84.

A6744 Wollmann, Alfred. *Die Personenführung in Shakespeares Historien*. DD, Munich, 1955. Pp. 152. Typewritten.

A6745 "Shakespeare Lectures at the Oregon Festival." *ShN*, VIII (1958), 28-29. Abstract of Margery Bailey, "Shakespeare's Doubled Heroes."

A6746 Coles, Blanche. *Shakespeare's Four Giants: Hamlet, Macbeth, Othello, Lear*. Rindge, New Hampshire: Richard R. Smith, 1957. Pp. 126.
Rev: *ShN*, VII (1957), 22; by Hereward T. Price, *SQ*, IX (1958), 417.

bb. Kings and Courtiers

A6747 Papiroff, S. "Shakespeare's Idea of Kingship as Seen in *Richard II* and *Henry IV*." *The Silver Falcon*. New York: Hunter College, 1936, pp. 16-20.

A6748 Peregrinus. "Early English Kings in Drama and Fiction." *N&Q*, 179 (1940), 280; A. R. Bayley, ibid., 341; G. Catalini, ibid., 353; M. H. Dodds and P. J. Fynmore, ibid., 463.

A6749 Draper, John W. "Falstaff's Robin and Other Pages." *SP*, XXXVI (1939), 476-490.

A6750 Reese, Gertrude C. *Reflection of Political Thought in the Elizabethan Drama as Studied through the Subject of Kingship*. DD, University of Texas, 1941.

A6751 Anderson, Ruth L. "Kingship in Renaissance Drama." *SP*, XLI (1944), 136-155.

A6752 Lawton, H. W. "The Confidant in and Before French Classical Tragedy." *MLR*, XXXVIII (1943), 18-31.

A6753 Fermaud, Jacques A. "The Confidant in Literature and Life." *MLR*, XLI (1946), 419-422.
Maintains that the previous treatment of the subject by Mr. H. W. Lawton does not give sufficient attention, in particular, to Renaissance tragedy; that instead of being a device invented by seventeenth-century French dramatists, the confidant is the offspring of a long literary tradition and a lively human one.

A6754 "Shakespeare's Kings." *TLS*, Jan. 6, 1945, p. 6.

A6755 Rosenmayr, Maria. *Könige bei Grillparzer und Shakespeare*. DD, Vienna, 1946.

A6756 Knoll, Robert E. *Fortinbras and his Character Type in Elizabethan Drama*. DD, University of Minnesota, 1950.

A6757 Merchant, W. M. "The Status and Person of Majesty." *SJ*, 90 (1954), 285-289.

A6758 Schirmer, Walter F. *Glück und Ende der Königinen Shakespeares Historien.* (Arbeitsgemeinschaft für Forschung des Landes Nordrhein Westfalen, Heft 22). Cologne: Westdeutscher Verlag, 1954. Pp. 18.

A6759 Schoff, Francis G. "Horatio: A Shakespearian Confidant." *SQ*, VII (1956), 53-57.

A6760 Brustein, Robert Sanford. *Italianate Court Satire and the Plays of John Marston.* DD, Columbia University, 1957. Pp. 346. Mic 57-2139. *DA*, XVII (1957), 1334. Publication No. 20,574.

A6761 Schneider, Reinhold. "Das Bild der Herrschaft in Shakespeares Drama." *SJ*, 93 (1957), 9-37.

A6762 Hoskins, Frank L. "Shakespeare and the Prodigious Page Tradition." *Renaissance Papers,* 1957, pp. 106-110. Abstr: *ShN*, VII (1957), 12.

cc. Clergy

A6763 Colby, E. *English Catholic Poets: Chaucer to Dryden.* Milwaukee: Bruce Publishing Co., 1936. Pp. xx, 208. Clerical characters in Shak., pp. 118-136.

A6764 Stevenson, Robert. "Shakespeare's Cardinals and Bishops." *Crozer Quar.*, XXVII (1950), 116-138.

dd. Commoners

A6765 Maitland, J. A. B. *An Introduction to the Study of Lower-class Characters in Shakespeare's Comedies.* MA thesis, Toronto, 1925. Pp. 68.

A6766 Ringeling, Gerhard. "Shakespeare und der Landmensch." *Zeitwende*, XIV (1937/38), 739-746.

A6767 Shirley, John W. *The Parasite, the Glutton, and the Hungry Knave in English Drama to 1625.* DD, State University of Iowa, 1938.

A6768 Ewen, C. L'E. *Shakespeare and Seamen.* London: The Author, 1939.

A6769 McCloskey, John C. "Fear of the People as a Minor Motive in Shakspere." *SAB*, XVI[I] (1942), 67-72.

A6770 Milligan, Burton A. "Some Sixteenth and Seventeenth Century Satire against Money Lenders." *SAB*, XXII (1947), 36-46, 84-93.

A6771 Hoskins, Frank L., Jr. *Master-Servant Relations in Shakespeare with Some Reference to the Same Relations in the Drama of the Elizabethan and Stuart Periods.* Master's thesis, University of North Carolina, 1947. Abstr. publ. in *University of North Carolina Record, Research in Progress,* Grad. School Series, No. 56, 1949, pp. 213-214.

A6772 Pervas, D. "Šekspirov stav prema narodu." *Naša reč,* Jan., 1950, pp. 50-64.

A6773 Hoskins, Frank Lawrence, Jr. *Master-Servant Relations in Tudor and Early Stuart Literature: With Special Reference to the Drama of Shakespeare and his Contemporaries.* DD, Columbia University, 1955. Pp. 294. Mic A55-1832. *DA*, XV (1955), 1387. Publication No. 12,440.

A6774 Kaieda, Susumu. "The Mob in Shakespearian Plays" (in Japanese). *Tokyo Univ. of Foreign Studies Journal,* Nov., 1956.

A6775 Schlösser, Anselm. "Zur Frage 'Volk und Mob' bei Shakespeare." *ZAA*, IV (1956), 148-172.

A6776 Prager, Leonard. *The Language of Shakespeare's Low Characters.* DD, Yale University, 1957.

A6777 Lüthi, Max. "Zur Rolle des Volks bei Shakespeare." *Anglia,* LXXVI (1958), 74-89.

ix. Criminal Types (116;39)

A6778 Brock, J. H. *Iago and Some Shakespearean Villains.* Cambridge: W. Heffer and Sons, 1937. Pp. viii, 48.
Rev: A1245.

A6779 Goll, J. A. "Criminal Types in Shakespeare." *Journal of Criminal Law and Criminology* (Chicago), XXIX (1939), 492-516, 645-667.

A6780 Milligan, Burton A. *Rogue Types and Roguery in Tudor and Stuart Literature.* DD, Northwestern University, 1939. Abstr. publ. in *Summaries of Doctoral Dissertations, 1939,* Vol. 7, Chicago and Evanston: Northwestern Univ., 1939, pp. 14-18.

A6781 Kreider, P. V. *Repetition in Shakespeare's Plays.* Princeton Univ. Press, 1941.
Rev: A5926.

A6782 Howell, James. *The Rogue in English Comedy to 1642.* DD, University of North Carolina, 1942. Abstr. publ. in *Univ. of North Carolina Record, Research in Progress, 1941-42,* Chapel Hill, 1942, pp. 75-76.

A6783 Stoll, Elmer E. "Heroes and Villains: Shakespeare, Middleton, Byron, Dickens." *RES*, XVIII (1942), 257-269.

A6784 Röling, B. V. A. *De Criminologische Betekenis van Shakespeares Macbeth.* Nijmegen: Dekker & Van de Vegt, 1947. Pp. xvi, 143.

A6785 Kelly, Mary Louise. *Villains in Shakespeare's Comedies.* Master's thesis, University of North Carolina, 1948. Abstr. publ. in *Univ. of North Carolina Record, Research in Progress,* Grad. School Series, No. 56, 1949, pp. 215.

A6786 Hooker, Ward. "Shakespeare's Apprenticeship in the Portrayal of Villainy." *Bucknell Univ. Stud.,* II (1950), 80-89.

A6787 Curry, Rev. John Vincent. *Deception in Elizabethan Comedy: An Analytical Study.* DD, Columbia University, 1951. Pp. 229. Mic A51-541. *Microf. Ab.*, XI (1951), 840. Publication No. 2804.
Rev: A6298.

A6788 Ribner, Irving. "The Significance of Gentillet's *Contre-Machiavel.*" *MLQ*, X (1949), 153-157.

A6789 Wadsworth, Frank Whittemore. *The White Devil: An Historical and Critical Study.* DD, Princeton University, 1951. Pp. 416. Mic A55-1111. *DA*, XV (1955), 832. Publication No. 11,051.
Shakespearean plays discussed: *Ant., Ham., Lear, R. III, Macb., Oth., Romeo, Titus.*

A6790 Stroedel, Wolfgang. "Die Gestalt des Usurpators in Shakespeares Dramen." *SJ*, 87/88 (1952), 102-115.

A6791 Walters, R. N. *Machiavelli and the Elizabethan Drama.* M Litt thesis, Cambridge, 1953. *Cam Abs.*, 1952-1953, p. 80.

A6792 Lassen, Erik. "Shakespeare som Kriminalist." *Berlingske Aften* (Copenhagen), Oct. 11, 1954.

A6793 Barnet, Sylvan. "Coleridge on Shakespeare's Villains." *SQ*, VII (1956), 9-21.

A6794 Blissett, William. "Lucan's Caesar and the Elizabethan Villain." *SP*, LIII (1956), 553-575.

A6795 Bennett, G. A. *A Study of the English Stage Villain, 1588-1900.* MA thesis, Wales, 1957.

A6796 Coe, Charles Norton. *Shakespeare's Villains.* New York: Bookman Associates—Twayne Publishers, 1957. Pp. xii, 76.
Rev: by John P. Cutts, *SQ*, IX (1958), 417-418.

A6797 Smith, Calvin Clifton. *Milton's Satan and the Elizabethan Stage Villain.* DD, Duke University, 1957.

A6798 Taylor, William Edwards. *The Villainess in Elizabethan Drama.* DD, Vanderbilt University, 1957. Pp. 402. Mic 57-2820. *DA*, XVII (1957), 1756. Publication No. 22,025.

A6799 Cancelled.

A6800 Spivack, Bernard. *Allegory of Evil.* DD, Columbia University, 1953. Revised and published as *Shakespeare and the Allegory of Evil*, New York: Columbia Univ. Press, 1958.
Rev: A4951.

x. Various Types (117;39)

A6801 Stoll, Elmer Edgar. *Shakespeare's Young Lovers.* Oxford Univ. Press, 1937. Pp. 118.
Rev: A2547.

A6802 Draper, John W. "Bastardy in Shakespeare's Plays." *SJ*, LXXIV (1938), 123-136.

A6803 Pettigrew, Helen P. *The Elizabethan Lover in Shakespeare's Comedies.* DD, University of Washington, Seattle, 1939.

A6804 Camille, Georgette. "Des Travestis." *Le Théâtre Élizabéthain.* Paris: Les Cahiers du Sud, 1940, pp. 77-91.
Boy actors playing girls masquerading as boys.

A6805 Chassé, Charles. "Les Personnages de la Pègre dans le Théâtre Élizabéthain." *Le Théâtre Élizabéthain.* Paris: Les Cahiers du Sud, 1940, pp. 298-310.

A6806 Hastings, William T. "The Ancestry of Autolycus." *SAB*, XV (1940), 253.

A6807 Outram, A. E. *Some Conventions of Elizabethan Drama.* DD, Oxford, 1939. *Ox Abs*, 1940, pp. 97-102.
Part I: Usurer and Usury.

A6808 Robertson, J. Minto. "The Middle of Humanity as Shakespeare Saw it." *Hibbert Jour.*, XXXIX (1941), 143-155.

A6809 Smith, M. Ellwood. "The Lunatic, The Lover and The Poet." *SAB*, XVI (1941), 77-88.

A6810 Forrest, Louise T. *The Elizabethan Malcontent and his Significance in the Drama, 1596-1616.* DD, Yale University, 1943.

A6811 Holbrook, Sybil C. "Husbands in Shakespeare." *SAB*, XX (1945), 173-190.

A6812 Spencer, Theodore. "The Elizabethan Malcontent." *AMS*, pp. 523-535.

A6813 Hyde, Mary Crapo. *Playwriting for Elizabethans.* Columbia University Press, 1949. Pp. ix, 258.
Rev: A6061.

A6814 Stoll, Elmer E. "Iago Not a 'Malcontent'." *JEGP*, LI (1952), 163-167.
Opposes the views advanced by Theodore Spencer in "The Elizabethan Malcontent," A6812.

A6815 Guillén, Claudio. *The Anatomies of Roguery: A Comparative Study in the Origins and the Nature of Picaresque Literature.* DD, Harvard, 1953.

A6816 Henderson, Archibald, Jr. *Family of Mercutio.* DD, Columbia University, 1954. Pp. 270. Mic A54-2044. *DA*, XIV (1954), 1395. Publication No. 8684.
"Mockers in Shakespeare," pp. 172-261. Upon scoffers at love and antifeminists.

A6817 Meader, William G. *Courtship in Shakespeare.* New York: Columbia Univ. Press, 1954. Pp. 266.
Rev: A2559.

A6818 Goldsmith, Robert Hillis. "The Wild Man on the English Stage." *MLR*, LIII (1958), 481-491.

3. THE TRAGIC AND THE COMIC; IRONY (117;39)

A6819 Linkenbach, Baldur. *Das Prinzip des Tragischen.* Munich: Einhorn Verlag, 1934. Pp. 110.

A6820 Hanekom, J. R. *Tragic Conception in Elizabethan Drama.* MA thesis, Stellenbosch, South Africa, 1936.

A6821 Perkinson, Richard H. *Aspects of English Realistic Comedy in the Seventeenth Century.* DD, Johns Hopkins University, 1936.

A6822 Spencer, Theodore. *The Treatment of Death in Elizabethan Drama: A Study in the History of Convention and Opinion.* DD, Harvard University, 1928.

A6823 Spencer, Theodore. *Death and Elizabethan Tragedy: A Study of Convention and Opinion on the Elizabethan Drama.* Harvard Univ. Press, 1936. Pp. xiii, 288.
Rev: *TLS*, July 18, 1936, p. 595; *N &Q*, 171 (1936), 198; by L. C. Knights, *Criterion*, LXII, 157-162; by Leicester Bradner, *SRL*, Dec. 12, 1936, p. 18; by J. H. Walter, *MLR*, XXXII (1937), 294-295; by Hazelton Spencer, *MLN*, LII, 437-442; by Thomas Good, *Life and Letters Today*, XV, No. 6, 212; by J. Burns Martin, *Dalhousie Rev.*, XVI, 534; by Kathleen Tillotson, *RES*, XIV (1938), 346-348; by G. R. Coffman, *SP*, XXXV, 507-509; by W. Keller, *SJ*, LXXIV (1938), 192-193.

A6824 Stoll, E. E. "The Tragic Fallacy, So-called." *UTQ*, V (1936), 457-481.

A6825 Srinivasan, P. R. "Melpomene or the Muse of Tragedy." *Twentieth Century* (Allahabad), III (1937), 347-357, 424-432, 550-559.

A6826 "English Humour, 1500 to 1800." *TLS*, May 21, 1938, p. 360.

A6827 de Casseres, B. "Shakespeare: Nihiliste Tragique." *L'en Dehors*, March, 1938.

A6828 Dobrée, B. "Shakespeare and the Comic Idea." *Spectator*, Feb. 25, 1938, p. 318.

A6829 Feibleman, James. "The Meaning of Comedy." *Jour. of Philos.*, XXXV (1938), 421-432.

A6830 Flügel, Heinz. "Die Tragödie und der Mythos." *DL*, XL (1938), 582-586.

A6831 Lawrence, C. E. "English Humor." *QR*, 270 (1938), 132-145.

A6832 Schmidt, Wolfgang. "Shakespeares Leben und der Sinn der Tragödien." *NS*, XLVI (1938), 339-353.

A6833 Sellmair, Joseph. "Katharsis oder der Sinn der Tragödie." *ZDG*, I (1938), 269-279.

A6834 Anderson, Maxwell. *The Essence of Tragedy.* Washington: Anderson House, 1939. Pp. 53. Also published as an essay in Anderson's *Off Broadway: Essays About the Theater*, New York: William Sloane, 1947, pp. 55-66.
Rev: by E. C. Knowlton, *South Atlantic Quar.*, XXXVIII (1939), 473.

A6835 Casson, T. E. "Tragedy and the Infinite." *Poetry Review*, XXX (July, 1939), 265-275; (Sept., 1939), 363-370.

A6836 Charlton, H. B. *Romeo and Juliet as an Experimental Tragedy.* London: Milford, 1939. Pp. 45.
Rev: A5920.

A6837 Feibleman, James. *In Praise of Comedy: A Study in Theory and Practice.* London: Allen and Unwin; New York: Macmillan, 1939. Pp. 284.
Rev: *TLS*, Aug. 26, 1939, p. 506; by E. S. Robinson, *KR*, II (1940), 493-496; by T. M. G., *Jour. of Philos.*, XXXVII, 249.

A6838 Fleming, Rudd. "Of Contrast between Tragedy and Comedy." *Jour. of Philos.*, XXXVI (1939), 543-553.

A6839 Mueller, W. "Komödie und Tragödie." *Neue Rundschau*, Nov., 1939, pp. 398-400.

A6840 O'Connor, William Van. "When Elizabethans Laughed." *SAB*, XIV (1939), 243-247.

A6841 Ellis-Fermor, Una. "Tragedy." *English*, III (1940), 84-86.

A6842 Empson, William. "Le Double Intrigue et l'Ironie dans le Drame Élizabéthain." *Le Théâtre Élizabéthain*. Paris: Les Cahiers du Sud, 1940, pp. 56-60.

A6843 Hollowell, Annabelle. *Shakespeare's Use of Comic Materials in Tragedy: A Survey of Criticism.* MA thesis, University of North Carolina, 1940. Abstr. publ. in *Univ. of North Carolina Record, Research in Progress*, Grad. School Series, No. 38, 1940, p. 89.

A6844 Woesler, R. "Der Mensch und seine Grösse bei Shakespeare." *NS*, XLVIII (1940), 165-181.

A6845 O'Connor, W. V. "The Rebirth of Tragedy." *SAB*, XVI (1941), 67-76.

A6846 Büchler, Franz. *Über das Tragische.* Strassburg: Hünenburg-Verlag, 1942. Pp. 45.

A6847 Charlton, H. B. "Hamlet." *BJRL*, XXVI (1942), 265-286.

A6848 Grace, William J. "Cosmic Sense in Shakespearean Tragedy." *SR*, L (1942), 433-444.

A6849 Mayer-Exner, Karl. "Schicksal und Tragik." *Dts. Dramaturgie*, II (1943), 27-29.

A6850 O'Connor, William Van. *Climates of Tragedy.* Louisiana State Univ. Press, 1943. Pp. vii, 115.
Rev: by C. D. Thorpe, *CE*, VI (1944), 122-123.

A6851 Rommell, Otto. "Komik und Lustspieltheorie." *DVLG*, XXI (1943), 252-286.

A6852 Schneider, Hans Ernst. "Das Problem des Tragischen. Zu einigen Neuerscheinungen." *DW*, XVIII (1943), 69-74.

A6853 Fairchild, Arthur H. R. *Shakespeare and the Tragic Theme.* Univ. Missouri Studies, XIX, No. 2.
Univ. Missouri Press, 1944. Pp. 145.
Rev: by D. T. Starnes, *MLQ*, VI (1945), 496-497; by J. H. Walter, *MLR*, XL, 220-221; by
Samuel Asa Small, *MLN*, LXI (1946), 562-565; by G. Bullough, *RES*, XXIII (1947), 163-164;
by W. Clemen, *Archiv*, 188 (1951), 143.

A6854 Meissner, Paul. "Gestaltung und Deutung des Tragischen bei Shakespeare." *SJ*, 80/81
(1946), 12-30.

A6855 Spencer, T. "The Isolation of the Shakespearian Hero." *SR*, LII (1944), 313-331.

A6856 App, Austin J. "Aristotle's Tragic Murder and Shakespeare." *Classical Bul.*, XXII (1945), 5-7.

A6857 Cunningham, James Vincent. *Tragic Effect and Tragic Process in Some Plays of Shakespeare, and
their Background in the Literary and Ethical Theory of Classical Antiquity and the Middle Ages.*
DD, Stanford University, 1945. Abstr. publ. in *Abstracts of Dissertations, 1944-45*, Stanford,
1945, pp. 29-34.

A6858 Weber, Carl J. "Tragedy and the Good Life." *Dalhousie Rev.*, XXV (1945), 225-233.

A6859 Auerbach, Erich. "Der müde Prinz." *Mimesis*, Bern: A. Francke Verlag, 1946, pp. 298-319.

A6859a Auerbach, Erich. *Mimesis: The Representation of Reality in Western Literature*, tr. by Willard R.
Trask. Princeton Univ. Press, 1953. Pp. 563.
"The Weary Prince," pp. 312-333, discusses mixture of comic and tragic in Shakespeare.
Rev: by P. F. Baum, *South Atlantic Quar.*, LIII (1954), 429-430; by Rosemond Tuve, *YR*,
XLIII, 619-622; by Arnold Isenberg, *JAAC*, XII, 526-527; by W. H. D., *Personalist*, XXXVI
(1955), 90-91; by Harry Bergholz, *MLJ*, XXXIX, 109.

A6860 Deutschbein, Max. *Die kosmischen Mächte bei Shakespeare.* Dortmund: Schwalvenberg, 1947.
Pp. 45.
Rev: by H. Oppel, *Literatur der Gegenwart*, I (1948), 41-43.

A6861 Leech, Clifford. "The Implications of Tragedy." *English*, VI (1946/47), 177-182.

A6862 Quadri, Goffredo. *Guglielmo Shakespeare e la Maturità della Coscienza Tragica.* Florence:
La nuova Italia, 1947. Pp. 110.
Rev: A1016.

A6863 Farnham, Willard. "The Mediaeval Comic Spirit in the English Renaissance." *AMS*, pp.
429-437.

A6864 Hamilton, R. "Shakespeare: The Nemesis of Pride." *Nineteenth Century*, 143 (1948), 335-
340. Tr: "Die Nemesis des Hochmutes bei Shakespeare." *Die Brücke*, No. 86 (1948), pp.
8-10.

A6865 Orna, Norah E. *The Relation between Theory and Practice in Elizabethan and Jacobean Comedy,
1570-1616.* MA thesis, London, 1948.

A6866 Powell, Arnold F. *Pathos in English Tragedy through Shakespeare.* DD, Vanderbilt University,
1948. Abstr. publ. in *Bulletin of Vanderbilt Univ., Abstracts of Theses*, Dec. 1, 1948, pp. 10-11.

A6867 Sitwell, Edith. *A Notebook on William Shakespeare.* London: Macmillan, 1948. Pp. xii, 233.
Rev: A8365.

A6868 Thompson, Alan Reynolds. *The Dry Mock: A Study of Irony in Drama.* Univ. Cal. Press,
1948. Pp. ix, 278.
Rev: *TLS*, Oct. 14, 1949, p. 662; by H. Jenkins, *MLR*, XLV (1950), 255-256; by Dorothy
F. Mercer, *JAAC*, VIII, 201-202.

A6869 Parrott, Thomas M. *Shakespearean Comedy.* New York: Oxford Univ. Press, 1949. Pp.
xiv, 417.
Rev: A8323.

A6870 Pastore, Annibale. "La Rivelazione Tragica di William Shakespeare." *Il Dramma*, LXXV/
LXXVI (Jan. 1, 1949), 101-106.

A6871 Sedgewick, G. G. *Of Irony, Especially in Drama.* Univ. of Toronto Studies, No. 10. Univ.
of Toronto Press, 1935. Pp. 150. Republ. 1949.
Rev: A5618.

A6872 Sypher, Wylie. "Nietzsche and Socrates in Messina." *Partisan Rev.*, XVI (1949), 702-713.

A6873 Yoshida, Kenichi. "Shakespeare's Tragedy and Comedy." *Bungei*, May, 1949.

A6874 Bing, Just. "Veien til Hamlet." *Edda* (Oslo), L (1950), 39-55.

A6875 Brock, F. H. Cecil. "Oedipus, Macbeth and the Christian Tradition." *ConR*, 177 (Mar., 1950),
176-181.

A6876 Cunningham, J. V. " 'Tragedy' in Shakespeare." *ELH*, XVII (1950), 36-46.

A6877 Dyson, H. V. D. "The Emergence of Shakespeare's Tragedy." Annual Shakespeare Lecture
of the British Academy, 1950. *Proceedings of the British Academy*, XXXVI (1953), 69-93.
Rev: B4987.

A6878 Farnham, Willard. *Shakespeare's Tragic Frontier: The World of His Final Tragedies.* Univ. of
California Press, 1950.
Rev: A8183.

A6879 Leech, Clifford. *Shakespeare's Tragedies: And Other Studies in Seventeenth-Century Drama.*
London: Chatto and Windus, 1950. Pp. viii, 232.
Rev: B4967.

A6880   Sen Gupta, S. C. *Shakespearian Comedy*. Calcutta: Oxford University Press, 1950. Pp. ix, 287.
        Rev: B5178.

A6881   Tave, S. M. *Comic Theory and Criticism from Steele to Hazlitt*. DD, Oxford, Oriel, 1950.

A6882   Aldus, Paul J. *The Use of Physical Comic Means in English Drama from 1420 to 1603*. DD,
        University of Chicago, 1951.

A6883   Cunningham, J. V. *Woe or Wonder*. Denver, 1951.
        Rev: B4972.

A6884   Koenigsberger, Hannelore. *The Untuned String: Shakespeare's Concept of Chaos*. DD, Columbia
        University, 1951. Pp. 222. *DA*, XII (1952), 66. Publication No. 3353.

A6885   Roberts, Preston. "A Christian Theory of Dramatic Tragedy." *Journal of Religion*, XXXI
        (1951), 1-20.

A6886   Carrère, Félix. "La Conception Shakespearienne du Tragique et le Drame d'Othello." *Litté-
        ratures. Annales publ. par la Faculté des Lettres de Toulouse*, I (1952), 77-85.

A6887   Cazamian, Louis. *The Development of English Humor*. Duke University Press, 1952. Pp. viii,
        421.
        Rev: B5186.

A6888   Frye, Northrop. "Comic Myth in Shakespeare." *TRSC*, 3rd Ser., XLVI, Sect. 2 (June, 1952),
        47-58.

A6889   Kronenberger, Louis. *The Thread of Laughter: Chapters on English Stage Comedy from Jonson
        to Maugham*. New York: Knopf; Toronto: McClelland, 1952. Pp. x, 297, vi.
        Rev: Edmund Wilson, *NYHTBR*, Nov. 2, 1952, p. 6; by Joseph Carroll, *TAr*, Nov. 1,
        pp. 9-10; by Howard Mumford Jones, *SatR*, Oct. 18, p. 24; by J. W. Krutch, *NYTBR*,
        Sept. 28, p. 26; by Francis Fergusson, *YR*, XLII, 289-290.

A6890   McCulley, Cecil Michael. *A Study of Dramatic Comedy*. DD, Columbia University, 1952.
        Pp. 348. *DA*, XII (1952), 614. Publication No. 4214.

A6891   Margeson, John M. R. *Dramatic Irony in Jacobean Tragedy*. DD, University of Toronto, 1952.

A6892   Müller, Joachim. "Das Tragische und die tragische Situation in Shapespeares Dramen."
        Wiss. Zs. d. Friedr.-Schiller-Univ. Jena. Gesellschafts- u. sprachwiss. Reihe II, 2 (1952/53),
        73-100.

A6893   Rebora, P. "I toni comici nelle tragedie di Shakespeare." *Rivista di Studi Teatrali* (Milan), I
        (1952), 116-131.

A6894   Waith, Eugene M. *The Pattern of Tragicomedy in Beaumont and Fletcher*. Yale Studies Eng.,
        120. Yale Univ. Press, 1952. Pp. xiv, 212.
        Rev: John Russell Brown, *MLN*, LXVIII (1953), 495-497; Marvin T. Herrick, *JEGP*, LII,
        580-582; Peter Ure, *RES*, V (1954), 73-74; Harold Jenkins, *ShS*, VII, 142; Baldwin Maxwell,
        MLR, XLIX, 498-499; M. Poirier, *EA*, VIII (1955), 261-262.

A6895   Desai, Chintamani N. *Shakespearean Comedy*. (With a Discussion on Comedy, the Comic,
        and the Sources of Shakespearean Comic Laughter.) Indore City, M. B., India: The Author,
        1953. Pp. 204.
        Rev: B5187.

A6896   Ornstein, Robert. *The Ethics of Jacobean Tragedy, a Study of the Influence of Renaissance Free
        Thought*. DD, University of Wisconsin, 1954. Abstr. publ. in *Summaries of Doctoral Disserta-
        tions, 1953/54*, Vol. 15, Madison: Univ. of Wisconsin Press, 1955, pp. 622-624.

A6897   Weisinger, Herbert. *Tragedy and the Paradox of the Fortunate Fall*. Michigan State Univ.
        Press, 1953. Pp. 300.
        Rev: S. G. F. Brandon, *Hibbert Jour.*, LI (1953), 407-410; *TLS*, Aug. 14, p. 522; Philip
        Mairet, *Time and Tide*, June 27, p. 858; Henry Popkin, *NR*, Sept. 28, p. 20; David Daiches,
        MGW, May 28, p. 19; Anthony Curtis, *NstN*, May 30, pp. 651-652; J. A. Bryant, "Out-
        flying Tragedy," *SR*, LXII (1954), 319-328.

A6898   Gindin, James J. *Renaissance and Modern Theories of Irony: Their Application to Donne's "Songs
        and Sonnets."* DD, Cornell University, 1954. Pp. 192. Mic A54-3076. *DA*, XIV (1954),
        2066-67. Publication No. 9750.

A6899   Holloway, John. "Dramatic Irony in Shakespeare." *Northern Miscellany of Literary Criticism*,
        I (1953), 3-16.

A6900   Lehman, Benjamin Harrison. "Comedy and Laughter." *Five Gayley Lectures, 1947-1954*.
        Berkeley and Los Angeles: Univ. of Cal. Press, 1955, pp. 81-101.

A6901   Morris, I. *Shakespeare and Greville: Their Tragic Characters Compared. An Attempt to Re-
        define the Principles of Shakespearean Tragedy in the Light of Elizabethan Thought*. B Litt thesis,
        Oxford, 1954.

A6902   Müller, Joachim. *Das Tragische in Shakespeares Dramen*. Rudolstadt: Greifenverlag, 1954.
        Pp. 97.
        Rev: by H. Schnyder, *Archiv*, 193 (1957), 331-332; by W. Schrickx, *RBPH*, XXXIV (1956),
        926.

A6903   Abrams, Sherwin Frederic. *The Tragic Impulse*. DD, University of Wisconsin, 1955. Pp. 325.
        Mic 55-1788. *DA*, XV (1955), 2596. Publication No. 14,754.

A6904 Braun, Felix. "Shakespeare und der arme Mann (Ulrich Braeker)." Braun: *Die Eisblume*, Salzburg, 1955, pp. 78-84.

A6905 Kesler, Charlotte Ruth. *The Importance of the Comic Tradition of English Drama in the Interpretation of Marlowe's Doctor Faustus*. DD, University of Missouri, 1954. Pp. 258. Mic 55-234. *DA*, xv (1955), 1387. Publication No. 9183.

A6906 Lynch, William F. "Theology and the Imagination III. The Problem of Comedy." *Thought*, xxx, No. 116 (1955), 18-36.

A6907 Muschg, Walter. *Tragische Literaturgeschichte*. Zweite, umgearbeitete und erweiterte Auflage. Bern: Francke Verlag, 1953. Pp. 747.
   Rev: A8035.

A6908 Schadewaldt, Wolfgang. "Von der Wirkung des Trauerspiels." *Shakespeare-Tage, 1955* (Bochum), pp. 5-8.

A6909 Bush, Geoffrey. *Shakespeare and the Natural Condition*. Harvard Univ. Press, 1956. Pp. 140.
   Rev: A921.

A6910 Flatter, Richard. "Triumphierende Tragödie, oder: Shakespeares wahre Grösse." Flatter: *Triumph der Gnade. Shakespeare Essays*. Vienna/Munich: Kurt Desch, 1956, pp. 158-174.

A6911 Forster, A. Haire. *Wit, Humor and the Comic in Shakespeare and Elsewhere*. New York: William Frederick Press, 1956.
   Rev: J. R. Brown, *SQ*, ix (1958), 415-416.

A6912 Henn, T. R. *The Harvest of Tragedy*. London: Methuen, 1956. Pp. xv, 304.
   Rev: *Dublin Magazine*, xxxi, No. 4 (1956), 60-62; by John Heath-Stubbs, *Time and Tide*, Sept. 22, pp. 1127-28; *TLS*, Dec. 14, pp. 741-742; *MdF*, Dec., p. 736; *MGW*, Oct. 25, p. 10; by Geoffrey Brereton, *NstN*, Oct. 13, p. 458; by J. B. Thomas, *Books of the Month*, Oct. 16; by G. W. Horner, *ConR*, 190 (1956), 377-378; by J. Holloway, *Spectator*, Sept. 21, 389-390; by J. M. Murry, *London Magazine*, iv (March, 1957), 61-63; by H. Popkin, *SR*, lxv (1957), 304-309.

A6913 Morrell, Roy. "The Psychology of Tragic Pleasure." *EIC*, vi (1956), 22-37.

A6914 Muller, Herbert J. *The Spirit of Tragedy*. New York: Knopf, 1956. Pp. ix, 335.
   Rev: by Marvin Lowenthal, *NYHTBR*, Nov. 11, 1956, p. 10; by R. J. Kaufmann, *Nation*, Apr. 27, 1957, pp. 367-370; by Jay Leyda, *NR*, May 6, pp. 18-19; by Howard Mumford Jones, *SatR*, June 8, pp. 21, 36; by Gariff B. Wilson, *QJS*, xliii, 205-206; by Henry Popkin, *SR*, lxv, 304-309; by W. T. Stace, *VQR*, xxxiii, 287-292; by Helen D. Lockwood, *The Humanist*, xvii, 248-249.

A6915 Murphy, H. H. "Reflections on the Tragedies of Shakespeare." *Dalhousie Rev.*, xxxvi (1956), 266-274.

A6916 Myers, Henry Alonzo. *Tragedy: A View of Life*. Cornell Univ. Press, 1956. Pp. 218.
   Rev: by Hermann Heuer, *SJ*, 93 (1957), 255; by J. B. Fort, *EA*, x, 459; by B. R. McElderry, *Personalist*, xxxvii, 427-428; by Willard Farnham, *SQ*, ix (1958), 59-61.

A6917 Schwartz, Elias. "Detachment and Tragic Effect." *CE*, xviii, (1956/57), 153-156.

A6918 Zumwalt, Eugene Ellsworth. *Divine and Diabolic Irony: The Growth of a Tudor Dramatic Sense*. DD, University of California (Berkeley), 1956.

A6919 Knox, Norman D. *The Word "Irony" and Its Context, 1500-1755*. DD, Duke University, 1957.

A6920 Malekin, Peter. "Tragedy and Comedy: A Western View." *Aryan Path*, xxviii (1957), 100-104.

A6921 Oppel, Horst. "Shakespeare und das Leid." *SJ*, 93 (1957), 38-81.

A6922 De Berry, Frances C. *All the World's a Stage for Shakespeare Comedies*. A Modern Interpretation of the Bard's Humor by a Shakespeare Winner on "The $64,000 Question." New York: Exposition Press, 1958. Pp. 130.

A6923 Birrell, T. A. "The Shakespearian Mixture: Recent Approaches to Shakespeare's Handling of the Comic and Tragic Kinds." *Museum*, lxiii (1958), 97-111.

A6924 Bonjour, Adrien. *Résonances Shakespeariennes* (Leçon inaugurale). Neuchâtel: Secrétariat de l'Université, 1958. Pp. 24.

A6925 Krieger, Murray. "Tragedy and the Tragic Vision." *KR*, xx (1958), 281-299.

A6926 "Shakespeare Lectures at the Oregon Festival." *ShN*, viii (1958), 28-29. Abstracts of James Sandoe, William Nye, and Nagle Jackson, "Conversation on Comedy."

A6927 Tillyard, E. M. W. *The Nature of Comedy and Shakespeare*. English Association Presidential Address. Oxford: Oxford University Press, 1958. Pp. 15.
   Rev: *N&Q*, ns, v (1958), 504-505.

4. SYMBOLISM: ALLUSIONS TO PLACES AND TO CONTEMPORARY PERSONS AND EVENTS (118;40)

A6928 Akrigg, G. P. V. "Shakespeare's Living Sources: An Exercise in Literary Detection." *QQ*, lxv (1958), 239-250.

A6929 Anderson, Viola Hadlock. "Othello and Peregrina, 'Richer Than All His Tribe'." *MLN*, lxiv (1949), 415-417.

A6930   Angell, P. K. "Light on the Dark Lady: A Study of Some Elizabethan Libels." *PMLA*, LII (1937), 652-674.

A6931   Angell, Pauline K., and T. W. Baldwin. " 'Light on the Dark Lady'." *PMLA*, LV (1940), 598-602.
        See A6930.

A6932   Ashe, Geoffrey. " 'Several Worthies'." *N &Q*, 195 (1950), 492-493.

A6933   Aylward, J. D. "Saviolo's Ghost." *N &Q*, 195 (1950), 226-229.

A6934   Barnard, E. A. B. "Shakespeare and Shylock." *TLS*, May 12, 1950, p. 293.

A6935   Bastian, F. "George Vargis, Constable." *N &Q*, NS, IV (1957), 11.

A6936   Baughan, Denver Ewing. "A Compliment to Sidney in *Hamlet*." *N &Q*, 177 (1939), 133-136.

A6937   Blair, Frederick G. "Shakespeare's Bear 'Sackerson'." *N &Q*, 198 (1953), 514-515.

A6938   Bowers, R. H. "Polonius: Another Postscript." *SQ*, IV (1953), 362-363.

A6939   Brennecke, Ernest. "Shakespeare's 'Singing Man of Windsor'." *PMLA*, LXVI (1951), 1188-92.

A6940   Brennecke, Ernest. "A Singing Man of Windsor." *Music and Letters*, XXXIII (1952), 33-40.

A6941   Bromberg, Murray. "Shylock and Philip Henslowe." *N &Q*, 194 (1949), 422-423.

A6942   Cheney, David Raymond. *Animals in "A Midsummer Night's Dream."* DD, State University of Iowa, 1955. Pp. 288. Mic 55-1103. *DA*, XV (1955), 2188. Publication No. 14,094.

A6943   LeComte, Edward S. "The Ending of *Hamlet* as a Farewell to Essex." *ELH*, XVII (1950), 87-114.

A6944   LeComte, Edward S. "Shakspere, Guilpin, and Essex." *SAB*, XXIII (1948), 17-19.

A6945   Crundell, H. W. "Shakespeare and Clement Swallow." *N &Q*, 189 (1945), 271-272.

A6946   Crundell, H. W. "*All's Well That Ends Well*: The Episode of the King's Ring." *N &Q*, 170 (1941), 26-27.

A6947   Dobbs, Leonard. *Shakespeare Revealed.* Ed. with Intro. Memoir by Hugh Kingsmill. London: Skeffington & Son, 1951. Pp. 222.
        Rev: A513.

A6948   Draper, John W. "*As You Like It* and 'Belted Will' Howard." *RES*, XII (1936), 440-444.

A6949   Draper, John W. "Historic Local Colour in *Macbeth*." *RBPH*, XVII (1938), 43-52.

A6950   Draper, John W. "*Macbeth* as a Compliment to James I." *Eng. Studn.*, LXXII (1938), 207-220.

A6951   Elton, William. "Shakespeare's Portrait of Ajax in *Troilus and Cressida*." *PMLA*, LXIII (1948), 744-748.

A6952   Gray, H. David, and Percy Simpson. "Shakespeare or Heminge? A Rejoinder and a Surrejoinder." *MLR*, XLV (1950), 148-152. See A4908.

A6953   Harrison, G. B. *Shakespeare at Work: 1592-1603.* 1933. Republished, Ann Arbor Paperbacks, Univ. of Michigan Press, 1958. Pp. 325.
        Rev: by W. Keller, *SJ*, LXXIII (1937), 156; *ShN*, VIII (1958), 12.

A6954   Hoepfner, Theodore C. "Hamlet and the Polonian Ambassador." *N &Q*, 198 (1953), 426.

A6955   Kane, Robert J. " 'Richard du Champ' in *Cymbeline*." *SQ*, IV (1953), 206.

A6956   Keen, Alan. "*Love's Labour's Lost* in Lancashire." *TLS*, Sept. 21, 1956, p. 553.

A6957   Keen, Alan. "Shakespeare and the Chester Players." *TLS*, Mar. 30, 1956, p. 195.

A6958   Keen, Alan. "Shakespeare's Northern Apprenticeship." *TLS*, Nov. 18, 1955, p. 689.

A6959   Kuhl, E. P. "Hamlet's Mousetrap." *TLS*, July 8, 1949, p. 445.
        See the letter by W. W. Greg, *TLS*, July 22, 1949, p. 473.

A6960   Kuhl, E. P. "Hercules in Spenser and Shakespeare." *TLS*, Dec. 31, 1954, p. 860.

A6961   L., G. G. "Chapman and Holofernes." *N &Q*, 172 (1937), 7; M. H. Dodds, ibid, 286-287.

A6962   Lambin, G. "Sur la Trace d'un Shakespeare Inconnu: III. Il Signor Prospero." *LanM*, Nov., 1951, pp. 1-23.

A6963   Lambin, Georges. "Sur la trace d'un Shakespeare Inconnu: V. W. Shakespeare à Paris." *LanM*, Nov./Dec., 1953, pp. 28-48.

A6964   Loomis, Edward Alleyn. "Master of the *Tiger*." *SQ*, VII (1956), 457.

A6965   Marañón, Gregorio. *Antonio Pérez*, tr. by Charles David Ley. London: Hollis and Carter, 1954. Pp. xiv, 382.
        Rev: by Salvador de Madariaga, "The Original of Armado," *MGW*, May 6, 1954, p. 10.

A6966   Montgomery, Roy F. "A Fair House Built on Another Man's Ground." *SQ*, V (1954), 207-208.

A6967   Moore, John Robert. "*Much Ado About Nothing*: Seacole." *N &Q*, 174 (1938), 60-61.

A6968   Morris, Joseph E. "*Twelfth Night*: 'The Lady of the Strachy'." *N &Q*, 175 (1938), 347-348.
        See letter by H. Kendra Baker, *N &Q*, 175 (1938), 411.

A6969   Muir, Kenneth. "The Dramatic Function of Anachronism." *Proceedings of the Leeds Philosophical and Literary Society* (Literary and Historical Section), VI (1951), 529-533.

A6970 Nathan, Norman. "Is Shylock Philip Henslowe?" *N &Q*, 193 (1948), 163-165.

A6971 Nathan, Norman. *"Julius Caesar* and *The Shoemaker's Holiday."* *MLR*, XLVIII (1953), 178-179.

A6972 Newdigate, B. H. " 'The Phoenix and the Turtle': Was Lady Bedford the Phoenix?" *TLS*, Oct. 24, 1936, p. 862. See letters by Mr. Newdigate, *TLS*, Nov. 28, 1936, p. 996; by W. B. Kempling, ibid., Dec. 5, 1936, p. 1016; by R. W. Short and B. H. Newdigate, "Was Lady Bedford the Phoenix?" *TLS*, Feb. 13, 1937, p. 111; *TLS*, Feb. 20, p. 131.

A6973 Oppel, Horst. "Gabriel Harvey." *SJ*, 82/83 (1949), 34-51.

A6974 Perkinson, Richard H. "A Tutor from Rheims." *N &Q*, 174 (1938), 168-169.

A6975 Phillips, Gerald William. *Lord Burghley in Shakespeare: Falstaff, Sly and Others.* London: Thorton Butterworth, 1936. Pp. 285.
       Rev: *TLS*, Jan., 1937, p. 13.

A6976 Savage, D. S. *Hamlet and the Pirates.* London: Eyre and Spottiswoode, 1950.
       Rev: A2768.

A6977 Schmitt, Carl. "Hamlet y Jacobo I de Inglaterra (Política y Literatura)." *Revista de Estudios Políticos* (Madrid), 85 (1956), 59-91.
       Rev: *TLS*, July 27, 1956, p. 453.

A6978 Shanker, S. "Shakespeare Pays Some Compliments." *MLN*, LXIII (1948), 540-541.

A6979 Shedd, Robert Gordon. *The "Measure for Measure" of Shakespeare's 1604 Audience.* DD, University of Michigan, 1953. Pp. 430. Mic A53-1478. *DA*, XIII (1953), 801. Publication No. 5730.

A6980 Siegel, Paul N. "Shylock and the Puritan Usurers." Matthews and Emery, eds., *Studies in Shakespeare*, 1953, pp. 129-138.

A6981 Simonini, R. C., Jr. "The Pedant and Church in *Twelfth Night*, III. ii. 80." *MLN*, LXIV (1949), 513-515.

A6982 Smith, Warren D. "The *Henry V* Choruses in the First Folio." *JEGP*, LIII (1954), 38-57.

A6983 Southern A. C. "The Elephant Inn." *TLS*, June 12, 1953, p. 381.

A6984 Strathmann, Ernest A. "The Textual Evidence for 'The School of Night'." *MLN*, LVI (1941), 176-186.

A6985 Thaler, Alwin. *Shakespeare and Democracy.* Univ. Tennessee Press, 1941. Pp. xii, 312. Chap. VI, "The Original Malvolio?"
       Rev: A1809.

A6986 Venezky, Alice S. *Pageantry on the Shakespearean Stage.* New York: Twayne Publishers, 1951. Pp. 242.
       Rev: A7238.

A6987 Walbridge, Earle F. "Drames à Clef: A List of Plays with Characters Based on Real People." *Bul. New York Public Lib.*, LX (1956), 156-174.

A6988 Williams, Gwyn. "Correspondence." *RES*, XXI (1945), 147.
       Speculates that Hamlet is Essex.

A6989 Young, G. M. "Master Holofernes." *TLS*, July 3, 1937, p. 496.

IX. SHAKESPEARE'S STAGE AND THE PRODUCTION OF HIS PLAYS (119;41)
    1. THE THEATRE (119;41)
        a. HISTORY OF THE ELIZABETHAN THEATRE (119;41)
            (1) SOURCES (119;-)
                (a) THE REVELS AT COURT (119;-)

A6990 Boas, F. S. *Queen Elizabeth, the Revels Office and Edmund Tilney.* Annual Elizabeth Howland Lecture delivered on Nov. 17, 1937. Oxford Univ. Press, 1938. Pp. 27. Republ. in F. S. Boas, *Queen Elizabeth in Drama and Related Studies.* London, 1950, pp. 35-55.
       Rev: by V. de S. Pinto, *English*, II (1938), 183-184; by E. K. C., *EHR*, LIV (1939), 176-177; see also Number B4458.

A6991 Adams, Joseph Quincy. "The Office-Book, 1622-1642, of Sir Henry Herbert, Master of the Revels." *To Doctor R.: Essays Here Collected and Published in Honor of the Seventieth Birthday of Dr. A. S. W. Rosenbach.* Philadelphia: Privately printed, 1946, pp. 1-9.

A6992 Benger, F. B. *A Calendar of References to Sir Thomas Benger (Master of the Revels and Masques to Queen Elizabeth, 1560-1572).* Privately printed, 1946. Pp. 23.

A6993 Tilney-Bassett, J. G. "Edmund Tilney's *The Flower of Friendshippe."* *Library*, 4th Series XXVI (1946), 175-181.

A6994 Wilson, John Dover, and R. W. Hunt. "The Authenticity of Simon Forman's 'Bocke of Plaies'." *RES*, XXIII (1947), 193-200.

A6995 Edinborough, Arnold. "The Early Tudor Revels Office." *SQ*, II (1951), 19-25.

A6996 Race, Sydney. "John Payne Collier and His Fabrications." *N &Q*, Feb. 2, 1952, pp. 54-56.

A6997 Schoeck, R. J. "Christmas Revels at the Inns of Court: 'A Sudden Order Against Plays' in 1520." *N & Q*, 197 (1952), 226-229.

A6998 Challen, W. H. "Sir George Buck, Kt., Master of the Revels." *N &Q*, NS, IV (1957), 290-292, 324-327.

A6999 Hunter, G. K. "Sir Edmund Chambers and *Perseus and Andromeda* (1572)." *N &Q*, NS, IV (1957), 418.

(b) PHILIP HENSLOWE (119;-)

A7000 Ewen, C. L'Estrange. "Philip Henslowe." *N &Q*, 171 (1936), 61.

A7001 Greg, W. W. "A Fragment From Henslowe's Diary." *Library*, NS, XIX (1938), 180-184.

A7002 Adams, Joseph Quincy. "Another Fragment From Henslowe's Diary." *Library*, NS, XX (1939), 154-181.

A7003 Nathan, Norman. "Is Shylock Philip Henslowe?" *N &Q*, 193 (1948), 163-165.

A7004 Bromberg, Murray. "Shylock and Philip Henslowe." *N &Q*, 194 (1949), 422-423.

A7005 Bromberg, Murray. "The Reputation of Philip Henslowe." *SQ*, I (1950), 135-139.

A7006 Patterson, Remington. "Shakespearian Connexions." *TLS*, Dec. 23, 1955, p. 777.

A7007 Malone Society. *Collections*, Vol. IV. *MSR*, Oxford University Press, 1956. Pp. 75. Includes, i.a.: W. W. Greg, "Fragments from Henslowe's Diary," pp. 27-32, pl.

A7008 Patterson, Remington Perrigo. *Philip Henslowe and the Rose Theatre*. DD, Yale University, 1957.

A7009 Briley, John. "Edward Alleyn and Henslowe's Will." *SQ*, IX (1958), 321-330.

(c) MASTER OF ROLLS (120;-)
(Transferred to Sources, Other, IX,1,a,(1), (h).)
(d) THE LORD CHAMBERLAIN'S ACCOUNTS (120;-)
(Transferred to Sources, Other, IX,1,a,(1), (h).)
(e) THE PRIVY COUNCIL (120;-) (Same)
(f) THE MALONE SOCIETY COLLECTIONS (120;-)

A7010 Robertson, Jean, and D. J. Gordon, eds. *A Calendar of Dramatic Records in the Books of the Livery Companies of London, 1485-1640*. Malone Society, Vol. III. London: Malone Soc., 1954. Pp. xlix, 204.
Rev: *TLS*, May 13, 1955, p. 260; by J. R. Brown, *MLR*, LI (1956), 307 [brief].

A7010a The Malone Society. *The First Fifty Years: 1906-1956*. Collections, IV. London: Malone Society, 1956. Pp. 75.

(g) THE STATIONERS' COMPANY (120;-)

A7011 Greg, W. W. *A Bibliography of the English Printed Drama to the Restoration*. Illustrated Monographs issued by the Bibliographical Society No. XXIV (I, II, III). Printed for the Bibliographical Society at the University Press, Oxford.
Vol. I: Stationers Records, Plays to 1616: Nos. 1-349. 1940. Pp. xxxiii, 492. Plates.
Vol II: Plays, 1617-1689: Nos. 350-836. Latin Plays. Lost Plays. 1951. Pp. xxxiii, 493-1008. Plates.
Vol III: Collections, Appendix, Reference Lists. 1957. Pp. 1009-1642. Plates.
Vol IV: Oxford University Press for the Bibliographical Society. 1959. Pp. 283.
Rev: A2920.

A7012 Jackson, William A., ed. *The Records of Court of the Stationers' Company, 1602-1640*. London: The Bibliographical Society, 1957. Pp. xxiv, 556.
Rev: *TLS*, May 3, 1957, p. 280; by James G. McManaway, *Papers of the Bibliographical Society of America*, LII (1958), 65-67; by Cyrian Blagden, *Book Collector*, VII, 81-82; by Norma H. Russell, *EHR*, LXXIII, 491-492.

A7013 Siebert, Fred S. "Regulation of the Press in the Seventeenth Century: Excerpts from the Records of the Court of the Stationers' Company." *Journalism Quar.*, XIII (1936), 381-393.

A7014 Kirschbaum, Leo. *Elizabethan and Jacobean Bad Quartos Among the Stationers*. DD, University of Michigan, 1937.

A7015 Kirschbaum, Leo. "The Elizabethan Licenser of 'Copy' and His Fee." *RES*, XIII (1937), 453-455.

A7016 Pollard, Graham. "The Company of Stationers Before 1557." *Library*, NS, XVIII (1937), 1-38.

A7017 Pollard, Graham. "The Early Constitution of the Stationers' Company." *Library*, NS, XVIII (1937), 235-260.

A7018 Greg, W. W. "Entrance, Licence, and Publication." *Library*, 4th Series, XXV (1944/45), 1-22.

A7019 Thomas, Sidney. "Richard Smith: 'Foreign to the Company'." *Library*, III (1948), 186-192.

A7020 Hodgson, Sidney. *The Worshipful Company of Stationers and Newspaper Makers*. Notes in its Origin and History. London: Stationers' Hall, 1953. Pp. 16.
Rev: *TLS*, Oct. 9, 1953, p. 646.

A7021 Kirschbaum, Leo. *Shakespeare and the Stationers*. Ohio State Univ. Grad. School Monographs, Contributions in Langs. and Lit. No. 15 (Fifth in Eng. Series). Columbus: Ohio State Univ. Press, 1955. Pp. x, 421.
Rev: by Hyder E. Rollins, *JEGP*, LV (1956), 147-149; by Cyprian Blagden, *Library*, 5th Series, XI, 54-56; by R. E. Hill, *MLR*, LI, 97-98; by Karl Brunner, *SJ*, 92 (1956), 427-431; by Arthur Brown, *SQ*, VII, 426-429; by G. F. Dawson, *MP*, LIV, 58-61; by S. F. Johnson, *RN*, X (1957), 43-44.

A7022 Race, Sydney. "John Payne Collier and the Stationers' Registers." *N &Q*, NS, II (1955), 492-495; *ibid.*, III (1956), 120-122.

A7023 Blagden, Cyprian. "The English Stock of the Stationers' Company. An Account of Its Origins." *Library*, 5th Series, X (1955), 163-185.

A7024 Greg, W. W. "The English Stock of the Stationers' Company." *Library*, 5th Series, XI (1956), 53.

A7025 Greg, W. W. "Richard Robinson and the Stationers' Register." *MLR*, L (1955), 407-413.

A7026 Greg, W. W. *Some Aspects and Problems of London Publishing Between 1550 and 1650.* Oxford: Clarendon Press, 1956.
       Rev: A2792.

A7027 Jackson, W. A. "Variant Entry Fees of the Stationers' Company." *Papers of the Bibliographical Society of America*, LI (1957), 103-110.

A7028 Blagden, Cyprian. "The Accounts of the Wardens of the Stationers' Company." *SB*, IX (1957), 69-93.

A7029 Blagden, Cyprian. "The English Stock of the Stationers' Company in the Time of the Stuarts." *Library*, 5th Series, XII (1957), 167-186.

A7030 Blagden, Cyprian. "Early Cambridge Printers and the Stationers' Company." *Trans. Cambridge Bibliog. Soc.*, II, iv, (1958), 275-289.

A7031 McKenzie, D. F. "Men Made Free of the Stationers' Company, 1605-1640. Some Corrections to the List in Arber's 'Transcript'." *N &Q*, NS, V (1958), 429-430.

(h) SOURCES, OTHER
i. Simon Forman's *Bocke of Plaies*

A7032 Meyerstein, E. H. W. "The Death of S. Forman." *N &Q*, 190 (1946), 258.

A7033 Nosworthy, J. M. "*Macbeth* at the Globe." *Library*, II (1947), 108-118.

A7034 Wilson, J. Dover, and R. W. Hunt. "The Authenticity of Simon Forman's *Bocke of Plaies*." *RES*, XXIII (1947), 193-208.

A7035 Bullard, J. E., and W. M. Fox. "*The Winter's Tale*." *TLS*, Mar. 14, 1952, p. 189; C. B. Purdom, *ibid.*, Mar. 21, p. 205; Richard Flatter, *ibid.*, Apr. 4, p. 237; E. P. Kuhl, *ibid.*, May 9, p. 313.

A7036 Race, Sydney. "Simon Forman's 'Bocke of Plaies': MS Ashmole 208." *N &Q*, 197 (1952), 116-117.

A7037 Amneus, Daniel A. *A Textual Study of Macbeth.* DD, University of Southern California, 1953. Discusses Forman.

A7038 Race, Sydney. "Simon Forman's 'Bocke of Plaies' Examined." *N &Q*, NS, V (1958), 9-14.

A7039 Race, Sydney. "J. O. Halliwell and Simon Forman." *N &Q*, NS, V (1958), 315-320.

ii. Keeling Journal

A7040 Race, Sydney. "J. P. Collier's Fabrications." *N &Q*, 195 (1950), 345-346.
       Comment by William Foster, *N &Q*, Sept. 16, 1950, pp. 414-415
       Reply by Race, ibid., Oct. 28, pp. 480-481.

A7041 Evans, G. Blakemore. "The Authenticity of Keeling's Journal Entries on *Hamlet* and *Richard II*." *N &Q*, 196 (1951), 313-315.
       See comment by Sidney Race, *ibid.*, pp. 513-515.

A7042 Evans, G. Blakemore. "The Authenticity of the Keeling Journal Entries Reasserted." *N &Q*, 197 (1952), 127-128. See letters referring to Mr. Sidney Race's charge of forgery by Mr. J. C. Maxwell, *TLS*, Feb. 22, 1952, p. 141, and by F. S. Boas, *TLS*, Mar. 7, 1952, p. 173; and Mr. Race's restatement of the case, *N &Q*, 197 (1952), 181-182.

iii. Manningham's Diary

A7043 Hotson, Leslie. "Manningham's 'Mid . . .'." *TLS*, Sept. 9, 1949, p. 585.

A7044 Race, Sydney. "Collier's History of English Dramatic Poetry." *N &Q*, 195 (1950), 33-35; "Manningham's Diary." *N &Q*, 195 (1950), 218.

A7045 Race, Sydney. "John Payne Collier and His Fabrications." *N &Q*, 195 (1950), 501-502.

A7046 Race, Sydney. "Manningham's Diary: The Case for Re-examination." *N &Q*, 199 (1954), 380-383.

iv. Other

A7047 Platter, Thomas. *Thomas Platter's Travels in England, 1599.* Tr. and intro. by Clare Williams. London: Cape, 1937. Pp. 245.
       Rev: A2401.

A7048 Schanzer, Ernest. "Thomas Platter's Observations on the Elizabethan Stage." *N &Q*, NS, III (1956), 465-467.

A7049 Bentley, Gerald Eades. "The Diary of a Caroline Theatergoer." *MP*, XXXV (1937), 61-72.

A7049a Ralph, Philip L. "References to the Drama in the Mildmay Diary." *MLN*, LV (1940), 589-591.

A7050   Hiscock, W. G. *A Christ Church Miscellany*. Oxford Univ. Press, 1946. Pp. 260.
        Includes, i.a., material from the college records about plays performed in Christ Church before
        Elizabeth and James.
             Rev: *TLS*, Nov. 2, 1946, p. 534.

A7051   McManaway, James G. "A New Shakespeare Document." *SQ*, II (1951), 119-122.
        Reproduces the Lord Chamberlain's warrant for payment to the King's Men for their per-
        formance of twenty-one plays before the King and Queen in 1630-31 (Folger MS. 2068.7),
        and the schedule of the plays (Folger MS. 2068.8); indicates, i.a., that the *Oldcastle* listed as
        being acted Jan. 6, 1631, was not the play by Drayton and others but *1 Henry IV*.

A7052   Semper, I. J. "The Jacobean Theater Through the Eyes of Catholic Clerics." *SQ*, III (1952),
        45-51.

A7053   Semper, I. J. "Jacobean Playhouses and Catholic Clerics." *The Month*, July, 1953, pp. 28-39.

A7054   Prouty, Charles T. "An Early Elizabethan Playhouse." *ShS*, VI (1953), 64-74.

A7055   Danks, K. B. "What Heminges and Condell Really Meant." *N &Q*, NS, III (1956), 11-13.
        Continued from *N &Q*, NS, II, 16-19.

A7056   Dodds, Madeleine Hope. "The First Night of *Twelfth Night*." *N &Q*, NS, III (1956), 57-59.

A7057   Feil, J. P. "Dramatic References from the Scudamore Papers." *ShS*, XI (1958), 107-116.

(2) GENERAL TREATISES (120;41)
(a) GENERAL STUDIES
This class reserved for general secondary accounts.

A7058   Tighe, E. J. *Rise and Fall of British Drama*. MA thesis, Ottawa, 1929. Pp. 87.

A7059   Lawrence, W. J. *Those Nut-cracking Elizabethans*. London, 1935.
             Rev: J. B. Harrison, *RES*, XII (1936), 468-469.

A7060   Hiebel, Friedrich. "England und die Entwicklung des Dramas." *Das Goetheanum*, XV (1936),
        379-380.

A7061   Nicoll, Allardyce. *The English Theatre: A Short History*. London: Nelson, 1936. Pp. 163.
             Rev: *TLS*, Oct. 10, 1936, p. 808; by I. Brown, *Obs.*, Oct. 18, 1936; by W. Browne, *EngR*,
             LXIV (1937), 136; by B. Dobrée, *Criterion*, XVI, 546; by A. V. Cookman, *London Mercury*,
             XXXV, 433; by R. P. C., *Dublin Mag.*, Apr., p. 84; by R. Gilder, *TAr*, XXI, 79-80; by J. Spens,
             RES, XIV (1938), 218-221.

A7062   Mantzius, K. *A History of Theatrical Art*. New York, 1937, 6 vols. Vol III: "The Shake-
        spearean Period in England."

A7063   Nicoll, Allardyce. *The Development of the Theatre*. 2nd ed. New York: Harcourt, Brace and
        Co., 1937. Pp. 309. 3rd ed, 1948. (First ed. was in 1927.)
             Rev: Tom Squire, *TAr*, XXI (1937), 823; by Richard Lockridge, *SRL*, Oct. 30, p. 18; by
             B. R. Redman, *SRL*, June 5, 1948, p. 46.

A7064   Vito, Maria S. de. *L'Origine del Dramma Liturgico*. Milan: Soc. An. Ed. Dante Alighieri,
        1938. Pp. 181.
             Rev: Karl Young, *MLN*, LIV (1939), 299-301.

A7065   Peach, L. du Garde. *A Dramatic History of England, 900-1901*. London: London Univ.
        Press, 1939. Pp. 367.

A7066   Wells, Henry W. *Elizabethan and Jacobean Playwrights*. New York: Columbia Univ. Press;
        Oxford: Univ. Press, 1939. Pp. xiv, 327.
        See also A2924.
             Rev: T. M. Pearce, *New Mexico Quarterly*, X (1940), 116-117; J. G. E. Hopkins, *Common-
             weal*, Jan. 12, XXXI, 269-270; T. W. Baldwin, *MLN*, LV, 455-462; A. Thaler, *JEGP*, XL
             (1941), 150-151.

A7067   Gorrell, Robert M. "The Popular Drama in England, 1600-1642." *Cornell Univ. Abstracts
        of Theses, 1939*, Cornell Univ. Press, 1940, pp. 35-37.

A7068   Detmold, George Ernst. "The Origins of Drama." *Cornell Univ. Abstracts of Theses, 1943*,
        Cornell Univ. Press, 1944, pp. 23-25.

A7069   Brook, D. *The Romance of the English Theatre*. London, 1945. Pp. 208.

A7070   Bachler, Karl, and Paul Zimmermann. *Das Englische Drama von den Anfängen bis zur Gegen-
        wart*. Gelsenkirchen-Buer: Post, 1947. Pp. 63.
        Shak., pp. 1-19.

A7071   Evans, B. Ifor. *A Short History of English Drama*. Harmondsworth: Penguin Books, 1948·
        Pp. 172.
        Shak., pp. 51-69.

A7072   Cancelled.

A7073   Rossiter, Arthur P. *English Drama from Early Times to the Elizabethans: Its Background, Origins,
        and Developments*. London: Hutchinson; Toronto: Ryerson, 1950. Pp. 176.
             Rev: A4922.

A7074   Stamm, Rudolf. *Geschichte des Englischen Theaters*. Bern: A. Franke, 1951. Pp. 484.
        "Die Shakespearezeit" covered on pp. 55-116.
             Rev: K. Ude, *Welt und Wort*, VI (1951), 205; M. B. Evans, *JEGP*, LI (1952), 99-100; Karl

Brunner, *SQ*, III, 132-133; *TLS*, Jan. 25, 1952, p. 75; H. Oppel, *DLZ*, LXXIII, 245-250; H. Reinhold, *GRM*, XXXIII, 237-239; H. Heuer, *SJ*, 87/88 (1952), 251-252; A. M. C. Kahn, *TN*, VI, 23; H. C. Matthes, *Archiv*, 189 (1952/1953), 230; I. Simon, *RBPH*, XXXI (1953), 121-123; H. H. Borcherdt, *Anglia*, LXXI, 367-371, E. Poulenard, *EA*, VII (1954), 439-440.

A7075 Baldini, Gabriele. "A proposito di due recenti studi sul teatro di Shakespeare." *Nuova Antologia*, 88 (April, 1953), 490-500.

A7076 Nagler, A. M. *Sources of Theatrical History.* New York: Theatre Annual, 1952. Pp. xxiii, 611.
Rev: Hubert Heffner, *SQ*, IV (1953), 187-189.

A7077 Krempel, Daniel Spartakus. *The Theatre in Relation to Art and to the Social Order from the Middle Ages to the Present.* DD, University of Illinois, 1953. Pp. 373. Mic A54-596. *DA*, XIV (1954), 421. Publication No. 6957.

A7078 Bradner, Leicester. "The Rise of Secular Drama in the Renaissance." *Studies in the Renaissance* (Renaissance Soc. Amer.), III (1956), 7-22.

A7079 Harrison, G. B. *Elizabethan Plays and Players.* London: Routledge, 1940. Pp. viii, 306. Paperback ed.: Univ. of Michigan Press, 1956. Pp. viii, 306.
Rev: *TLS*, May 18, 1940, p. 239; *ibid.*, Dec. 7, 1940, p. xxii; E. E. Kellett, *NstN*, NS, XX, 144-145; C. E. Byles, *Illus. London News*, Sept. 7, 1940, p. 318; Trevor James, *Life and Letters Today*, XXVI, 84-85.

A7080 Bridges-Adams, W. *The Irresistible Theatre.* Vol. I: From the Conquest to the Commonwealth. London: Secker and Warburg, 1957. Pp. xiv, 446. Illustrated.
Rev: *TLS*, July 5, 1957, p. 412; Ivor Brown, *Obs.*, June 23; Richard Findlater, *TC*, 162 (1957), 275-276; Gerald Meath, *The Tablet*, Aug. 10, pp. 113-114; Jan Bussel, *Drama* (Autumn, 1957), pp. 40-41; briefly by John Cournos, *The Key Reporter*, Oct., p. 4; Douglas Hewitt, *MGW*, July 23, p. 4; T. C. Worsley, *NstN*, Aug. 3, p. 151; *Booklist*, LIV, 69; Alfred Harbage, *NYTBR*, Sept. 15, p. 4; Barnard Hewitt, *ETJ*, X (1958), 76-77; Pat M. Ryan, Jr., *QJS*, XLIV, 89-90; *Players Mag.*, XXXIV, 126; briefly in *ShN*, VIII, 38; James G. McManaway, *SQ*, IX, 574; E. M. Browne, *TN*, XII, 73-74.

A7081 Weimann, Robert. *Drama und Wirklichkeit in der Shakespearezeit.* Ein Beitrag zur Entwicklungsgeschichte des elisabethanischen Theaters. Halle: Max Niemeyer, 1958. Pp. 334.

A7082 Wright, Louis B. *Shakespeare's Theatre and the Dramatic Tradition.* Folger Booklets on Tudor and Stuart Civilization. Washington, D. C.: The Folger Shakespeare Library, 1958. Pp. 36.

(b) MORE SPECIFIC STUDIES

A7083 Chambers, Sir E. K. *Sir Henry Lee: An Elizabethan Portrait.* Oxford: Clarendon Press; London: Milford, 1936. Pp. viii, 328.
Rev: Hans Ruhl, *DLZ*, LX (1939), 342-343.

A7084 Granville-Barker, H. "The Canadian Theatre." *QQ*, XLIII (1936), 256-267.

A7085 Sisson, Charles Jasper. *Lost Plays of Shakespeare's Age.* Cambridge Univ. Press; New York: Macmillan, 1936. Pp. 231.
Rev: W. Keller, *SJ*, LXXII (1936), 151-152; L. C. Knights, *Criterion*, XVI (1937), 187-188; W. Fischer, *DLZ*, LVIII, 775-788; H. Spencer, *MLN*, LII, 437-441; G. C. Moore Smith, *MLR*, XXXII, 94-95; Georges Connes, *RAA*, XIII, 435; A. Walker, *RES*, XIII, 229-232.

A7086 White, B. *Index to "Elizabethan Stage" and "Shakespeare, Study of Facts" by Sir E. K. Chambers.* 1934. Pp. 463.
Rev: H. Spencer, *MLN*, LI (1936), 272.

A7087 Withington, R. "Braggart, Devil and 'Vice': A Note on the Development of Comic Figures in the Early English Drama." *Speculum*, XI (1936), 124-129.

A7088 Cancelled.

A7089 McCabe, W. M. "Notes on St. Omers College Theatre." *PQ*, XVII (1938), 225-239.

A7090 Marshall, Mary Hatch. "Dramatic Tradition Established by the Liturgical Plays." *PMLA*, LVI (1941), 962-991.

A7091 Kearney, James J. "The Suppression of the Mystery Plays: Culmination of Social, Literary and Religious Forces in the Sixteenth Century." Fordham University, *Dissertations Accepted for Higher Degrees in the Grad. School of Arts and Sciences*, 1942, pp. 59-62.

A7092 Sisson, C. J. "Notes on Early Stuart Stage History." *MLR*, XXXVII (1942), 25-36.

A7093 Wells, Henry W. "A Mirror of National Integration: A New Summary of Four Decades of the English Theatre [1550-1590]." *SAB*, XVIII (1943), 30-40.

A7094 Knepler, Heinrich Wilhelm. *The Playgoer's Fare, 1603-1613.* MA thesis, Queen's (Canada), 1946. Pp. 142.

A7095 Nosworthy, J. M. "*Macbeth* at the Globe." *Library*, II (1947), 108-118.

A7096 Johnson, Samuel F. *Early Elizabethan Tragedies of the Inns of the Court.* DD, Harvard University, 1948.

A7097 Stratman, Carl J. *Dramatic Performances at Oxford and Cambridge, 1603-1642.* DD, University of Illinois, 1948.

A7098 Purdom, C. B. *Producing Shakespeare.* London: Pitman, 1950. Pp. xii, 220.
Rev: B1729.

A7099   Goodman, Randolph G. *That Strumpet the Stage: Poems About Playgoers, Players, and Playwrights.* DD, Columbia University, 1953. Pp. 357. Mic A53-761. *DA*, XIII (1953), 450. Publication No. 5189.

A7100   Reese, M. M. *Shakespeare: His World and His Work.* New York: St. Martin's Press, 1953. Pp. xiii, 589.
     Rev: A871.

A7101   Allen, James S. *Changes in the Structure and Characterization of the English Moral Play after 1516.* DD, Vanderbilt University, 1954. Pp. 274. Mic A54-2056. *DA*, XIV (1954), 1404. Publication No. 9215.

A7102   Jenkins, Harold. "The Year's Contributions to Shakespearian Study. 2. Shakespeare's Life, Times, and Stage." *ShS*, VII (1954), 138-146.

A7103   McCabe, J. C. *A Study of the Blackfriars Theatre, 1608-1642.* DD, Birmingham, 1954.

A7104   Markward, W. B. *A Study of the Phoenix Theatre in Drury Lane, 1617-1638.* DD, Birmingham, 1954.

A7105   Borinski, Ludwig. "Die Tragische Periode der Englischen Literatur." *NS*, NF, IV (1955), 289-307.

A7106   Stevenson, Allan. "The Case of the Decapitated Cast or *The Night-walker* at Smock Alley." *SQ*, VI (1955), 275-296.

A7107   Norberg, Lars. "Shakespearetidens Teater." *Borås Tidning*, XXIX (1955), 10.

A7108   Speight, George. *The History of the English Puppet Theatre.* New York: John de Graff, 1956. Pp. 350.
     Rev: B1318.

A7109   Weimann, Robert. "Zur Enstehungsgeschichte des elisabethanischen Dramas." *ZAA*, IV (1956), 200-242.

A7110   Williams, S. H. *The Lord Mayor's Shows from Peele to Settle: A Study of Literary Content, Organisation, and Methods of Production.* DD, London, Queen Mary College, 1957.

A7111   Pokorný, Jaroslav. *Shakespeareova doba a divadlo* (Shakespeare's Time and Theatre). Prague: Orbis, 1958. Pp. 172.

(3) PURITAN ATTACK UPON THE STAGE (122;-)

A7112   Howard, Edwin J., ed. *Pleasant Quippes for Vpstart Newfangled Gentlewomen.* Oxford, Ohio, 1942.
     Rev: A1933.

A7113   Ringler, William. "Another Collier Forgery." *TLS*, Oct. 29, 1938, p. 693.

A7114   Adkins, Mrs. Mary G. M. *Puritanism in Elizabethan Drama as Represented by Beaumont and Fletcher, Jonson, Dekker, and Shakespeare.* DD, University of Texas, 1938.

A7115   Haller, William. *The Rise of Puritanism: The Way to the New Jerusalem as Set Forth in Pulpit and Press from Thomas Cartwright to John Lilburne and John Milton, 1570-1643.* New York: Columbia Univ. Press, 1938. Pp. 472.

A7116   Allen, Don Cameron. "Melbancke and Gosson." *MLN*, LIV (1939), 111-114.

A7117   Ringler, William. "The Source of Lodge's *Reply to Gosson*." *RES*, XV (1939), 164-171.

A7118   Ringler, William A. *Stephen Gosson: A Biographical and Critical Study.* (Princeton Studies in English, Vol. 25.) Princeton: Princeton Univ. Press; London: Milford, 1942. Pp. v, 151.
     Rev: J. F. Larkin, *JEGP*, XLII (1943), 431-432; M. A. Shaaber, *MLQ*, IV, 508-509; J. Robertson, *MLR*, XXXIX (1944), 189-190; K. Koller, *MLN*, LIX, 427-429; F. S. Boas, *RES*, XX (1944), 311-312.

A7119   Ringler, William. "The First Phase of the Elizabethan Attack on the Stage, 1558-1579." *HLQ*, V (1942), 391-418.

A7120   Davis, Joe Lee. "Comedy in Caroline Theatrical Apologetics." *PMLA*, LVIII (1943), 353-371.

A7121   Adkins, Mary Grace Muse. "The Genesis of Dramatic Satire Against the Puritan, as Illustrated in *A Knack to Know a Knave*." *RES*, XXII (1946), 81-95.

A7122   McIlwraith, A. K. "Stephen Gosson." *TLS*, Sept. 20, 1947, p. 479.

A7123   Feasey, Lynette. "A Note on William Rankins." *N &Q*, 195 (1950), 20. See also George, J. "A Note on William Rankins." *N &Q*, 194 (1949), 420-421.

A7124   Holden, William P. *The Religious Controversy and Anti-Puritan Satire, 1572-1642.* DD, Harvard University, 1950.

A7125   Sandberg, Edwin T. "*Anti-Puritan Satire in Selected Seventeenth-Century Plays.*" DD, Indiana University, 1952.

A7126   Goodman, Randolph G. *That Strumpet the Stage: Poems about Playgoers, Players, and Playwrights.* DD, Columbia University, 1953. Pp. 357. Mic A53-761. *DA*, XIII (1953), 450. Publication No. 5189.

A7127   Meadley, T. D. "Attack on the Theatre (*circa* 1580-1680)." *London Quar. & Holborn Rev.*, Jan., 1953, pp. 36-41.

A7128   Holden, William P. *Anti-Puritan Satire, 1572-1642.* New Haven: Yale Univ. Press, 1954.
         Pp. 165.
             Rev: Burton A. Milligan, *JEGP*, LIV (1955), 281-283; Roger Sharrock, *MLR*, LII (1957),
         137; J. E. Neale, *EHR*, LXXII, 171.

A7129   Trace, Arthur S., Jr. *The Continuity of Opposition to the Theater in England from Gosson to Collier.*
         DD, Stanford University, 1954.

A7130   Zitner, S. P. "Gosson, Ovid, and the Elizabethan Audience." *SQ*, IX (1958), 206-208.

b. THE COURT AND THE STAGE (122;-)

A7131   Sisson, C. J. "King James as Poet and Political Writer." *17th Century Studies*, 1938, pp. 47-63.

A7132   Turner, Lilian F. *The Elizabethan Drama as the Newspaper of the Age: A Study of the Influence
         of External Controlling Factors on the Drama of the Early Seventeenth Century as a Potential Medium
         for Reflecting Popular Opinion on Political and Social Questions.* MA thesis, University of London,
         1938.

A7133   Griffin, William J. *Tudor Control of Press and Stage.* DD, State University of Iowa, 1940.
         Abstract in *Programs Announcing Candidates for Higher Degrees*, Univ. of Iowa, 1939, No.
         378, pp. 239-246.

A7134   Stunz, Arthur N. *The Contemporary Setting of Macbeth.* DD, State University of Iowa, 1940.

A7135   Griffin, William J. "Notes on Early Tudor Control of the Stage." *MLN*, LVIII (1943), 50-54.

A7136   Heuer, Hermann. "Shakespeares Verhältnis zu König Jakob I." *Anglia*, LXVI (1943), 223-237.

A7137   McDowell, John H. "Tudor Court Staging: A Study in Perspective." *JEGP*, XLIV (1945),
         194-207.

A7138   Yates, Frances A. "Elizabeth as Astraea." *JWCI*, X (1947), 27-82.

A7139   Boas, F. S. *Queen Elizabeth in Drama and Related Studies.* London, 1950.
             Rev: B4458.

A7140   Paul, Henry N. *The Royal Play of Macbeth: When, Why, and How It Was Written by Shake-
         speare.* New York: Macmillan, 1950. Pp. 438.
             Rev: B9143.

A7141   Linn, John G. *The Court Masque and Elizabethan Dramatic Structure, 1558-1604.* DD, Cornell
         University, 1951.

A7142   Walton, Charles E. *The Impact of the Court Masque and the Blackfriars Theatre upon the Staging
         of Elizabethan-Jacobean Drama.* DD, University of Missouri, 1953. Pp. 198. Mic A54-200.
         DA, XIV (1954), 136-137. Publication No. 6100.

A7143   Wilson, F. P. "Court Payments for Plays 1610-1611, 1612-1613, 1616-1617." *Bodleian
         Lib. Rec.*, V, No. 4 (Oct., 1955), 217-221.

A7144   Brustein, Robert Sanford. *Italianate Court Satire and the Plays of John Marston.* DD, Columbia
         University, 1957. Pp. 346. Mic 57-2139. *DA*, XVII (1957), 1334. Publication No. 20,574.

c. PUBLIC AND PRIVATE THEATRES (123;41)
(1) PLAN AND SITUATION (123;41)
(a) ELIZABETHAN THEATRES IN GENERAL

A7145   Jouvet, L. "The Elizabethan Theatre: A Reconstruction." *TAr*, XX (1936), 222-223.

A7146   Gilder, Rosamond. "The World in the Mirror of the Theatre." *TAr*, XXI (1937), 595-671.
         The entire August 1937 issue of Theatre Arts Monthly is devoted to a sketch of the history
         of the drama, with seventy illustrations, chiefly from the medieval and renaissance periods.

A7147   Baty, Gaston. "La Scène Élizabéthaine." *Le Théâtre Élizabéthain.* Paris: Les Cahiers du
         Sud, 1940, pp. 127-132.

A7148   Chambers, Sir E. K. *Shakespearean Gleanings.* Oxford Univ. Press, 1944.
         Chap. IX: "The Stage of the Globe."
             Rev: B4466.

A7149   Brereton, J. Le Gay. "The Elizabethan Playhouse." *Writings on Elizabethan Drama*, Mel-
         bourne Univ. Press, 1948, pp. 81-88.

A7150   Shapiro, I. A. "The Bankside Theatres: Early Engravings." *ShS*, I (1948), 25-37.

A7151   Bennett, H. S. "Shakespeare's Stage and Audience." *Neophil*, XXXIII (1949), 40-51.

A7152   Hotson, Leslie. "The Projected Amphitheatre." *ShS*, II (1949), 24-35.

A7153   Hodges, C. Walter. "Unworthy Scaffolds: A Theory for the Reconstruction of Elizabethan
         Playhouses." *ShS*, III (1950), 83-94.

A7154   Bald, R. C. "The Entrance to the Elizabethan Theatre." *SQ*, III (1952), 17-20.

A7155   Feldman, Abraham Bronson. "Dutch Theatrical Architecture in Elizabethan London."
         N&Q, 197 (1952), 444-446.

A7156   Freeman, Sidney L. *The Forms of Non-proscenium Theatre: Their History and Theories.* DD,
         Cornell University, 1952.

A7157   Nagler, A. M. *Sources of Theatrical History.* New York: Theatre Annual, 1952. Pp. xxiii, 611.
        Rev: A7076.

A7158   Hotson, Leslie. "Shakespeare's Arena." *SR*, LXV (1953), 347-361.
        See also A7159-7160.

A7159   Hotson, Leslie. "Shakespeare's Arena-Stage at Court." *RN*, VI (1954), 17-18.

A7160   Harbage, Alfred. "Shakespeare's Inner Stage." *RN*, VI (1954), 18-19.

A7161   Hodges, C. Walter. "Some Comments upon Dr. Leslie Hotson's 'Shakespeare's Arena'."
        The Shakespeare Stage, No. 3, Dec., 1953, pp. 26-29.

A7162   Hodges, C. Walter. "New Light on the Old Playhouses: Notes on Some Researches by
        Richard Southern and Leslie Hotson." *The Shakespeare Stage*, June, 1954, pp. 41-44.

A7163   Hotson, Leslie. "The Elizabethan Stage." *TLS*, Jan. 7, 1955, p. 9.
        See also A7164.

A7164   Empson, William. "The Elizabethan Stage." *Literary Guide*, LXX, No. 3 (1955), 12-14.

A7165   Golden, Joseph. *The Position and Character of Theater-in-the-Round in the United States.* DD,
        University of Illinois, 1954. Pp. 160. Mic A55-235. *DA*, XV (1955), 166. Publication
        No. 10,482.

A7166   Joseph, Bertram. "The Elizabethan Stage and Acting." *The Age of Shakespeare*, ed. Boris
        Ford. Aylesbury and London: Pelican Books, 1955, pp. 147-161.

A7167   "Eighth International Shakespeare Conference at Stratford." *ShN*, VII (1957), 39, 48. Con-
        tains abstract of: C. Walter Hodges, "The Elizabethan Stage and the Lantern of Taste";
        Richard Southern, "Some Considerations on Reconstructing an Elizabethan Playhouse";
        Richard Hosley, "The Curtained Space for Discovery in Shakespeare's Globe."

A7168   Armstrong, William A. " 'Canopy' in Elizabethan Theatrical Terminology." *N &Q*, NS,
        IV (1957), 433-434.

A7169   Hosley, Richard. "The Gallery over the Stage in the Public Playhouse of Shakespeare's
        Time." *SQ*, VIII (1957), 16-31.

A7170   Hosley, Richard. "Shakespeare's Use of a Gallery over the Stage." *ShS*, X (1957), 77-89.

A7171   Hotson, Leslie. " 'This Wooden O': Shakespeare's Curtain Theatre Identified." *Times*
        (London), Mar. 26, 1954, pp. 7, 14.
        Rev: H. Leclerc, *RHT*, VII (1955), 86.

A7172   Shuttleworth, Bertram. "W. J. Lawrence: A Handlist." *TN*, VIII (1954), 52-54. Part I.
        See also B3988-B3990.

A7173   Wilson, F. P. "The Elizabethan Theatre." *Neophil*, XXXIX (1955), 40-58.
        Rev: H. Oppel, *NS*, IV (1955), 517.

A7174   Wright, Louis Booker. *Shakespeare's Theatre and the Dramatic Tradition.* Folger Booklets
        on Tudor and Stuart Civilization, 3. Washington: Folger Shakespeare Library, 1958. Pp. 36.

A7175   Hosley, Richard. "An Elizabethan Tiring-House Façade." *SQ*, IX (1958), 588.

A7176   Nagler, A. M. *Shakespeare's Stage*, tr. by Ralph Manheim. Yale Univ. Shakespeare Supple-
        ments. Yale Univ. Press, 1958. Pp. ix, 117.

i. Specific Theatres

aa. Theatre and Globe

A7177   Adams, John C. *The Structure of the Globe Playhouse Stage.* DD, Cornell University, 1935.

A7178   "The Globe Theatre Plan." *TLS*, Dec. 3, 1938, p. 761.

A7179   Adams, John Cranford. *The Globe Playhouse: Its Design and Equipment.* Harvard Univ. Press,
        1942. Pp. xiii, 420.
        Rev: *Nation* (N.Y.), Sept 5, 1942, p. 198; by S. A. T., *SAB*, XVII, 160; John Corbin, *NYTBR*,
        Sept. 27, 1942, p. 34; Rosamond Gilder, *TAr*, XXVI, 730; John Dolman, *QJS*, XXVIII, 484-
        485; S. C. Chew, *NYHTBR*, Aug. 2, p. 14; B. R. Lewis, "Shakespeare's 'Globe'," *TLS*,
        Mar. 6, 1943, p. 120; G. F. Reynolds, *JEGP*, XLII, 122-126; John Wilcox, *PQ*, XXII, 95-96;
        A. D., *MGW*, July 16, 1943, p. 36; J. H. Marshburn, *Books Abroad*, XVII, 278; G. E. Bentley,
        MP, XL, 359-361; F. R. Johnson, *MLN*, LIX (1944), 198-200; Harley Granville-Barker,
        MLR, XXXIX, 296-299; H. S. Bennett, *RES*, XX (1944), 313-315; H. Lüdeke, *ES*, XXVII
        (1947), 45-48.

A7180   Cancelled.

A7181   Hodges, C. Walter. "The Globe Playhouse: Some Notes on a New Reconstruction." *TN*,
        I (1947), 108-111.
        Comments upon A7179.

A7182   Barker, Rennie. "The Structure of the First Globe Theatre." *SAB*, XXIV (1949), 106-111.

A7183   Shapiro, I. A. "An Original Drawing of the Globe Theatre." *ShS*, II (1949), 21-23.

A7184   Fronius, Hans. *Zeichnungen um Shakespeare.* Vienna-Linz: Gurlitt Verlag, 1950.
        Eight lithographs on Shak. and the Globe Theatre.

A7185   Lüdeke, H. "Shakespeares Globus-Theater nach den neuesten Ergebnissen der Forschung."
        SJ, 84/86 (1948-50), 131-139.

A7186 Adams, John Cranford. " 'That Virtuous Fabrick'." *SQ*, II (1951), 3-11.
See letter by Richard Flatter, ibid., 171; and Irwin Smith's "Notes on the Construction of the Globe Model," ibid., 13-18.

A7187 Hayward, W. C. *The Globe Theatre, 1599-1608.* DD, Birmingham, 1951.

A7188 Reynolds, George F. "Was There a 'Tarras' in Shakespeare's Globe?" *ShS*, IV (1951), 97-100.

A7189 Smith, Irwin. "Notes on the Construction of the Globe Model." *SQ*, II (1951), 13-18.

A7190 Saunders, F. R. "Capacity of the Second Globe Theatre." *TLS*, Nov. 14, 1952, p. 743.

A7191 Smith, Irwin. "Theatre into Globe." *SQ*, III (1952), 113-120.

A7192 Hodges, C. Walter. *The Globe Restored: A Study of the Elizabethan Theatre.* London: Ernest Benn, 1953. Pp. 199.
Rev: *TLS*, Nov. 13, 1953, p. 720; by A. Nicoll, *Drama*, NS, XXXI, 37-38; William Scawen, *Adelphi*, XXX, 86-88; Bertram Joseph, *Spectator*, Nov. 20, 1953, p. 616; *NstN*, Nov. 14, pp. 510-511; M. St. Clare Byrne, *English*, X (1954), 19-20; Paul Jordan-Smith, *Los Angeles Times*, Nov. 14, 1954, Part IV, p. 6; G. B. Harrison, *SatR*, Sept. 25, 1954, p. 32; G. R. Kernodle, *ETJ*, VI, 271-272; J. Vallette, *MdF*, 321, (1954), 732-733; H. Leclerc, *RHT*, VI, 316-321; H. T. Price, *SQ*, V, 112-113; Alfred Harbage, *YR*, XLIV (1955), 443-446; George F. Reynolds, *SQ*, VI, 96-97; *ShN*, V, 7; *CE*, XVI, 199-200; Rudolf Stamm, *SJ*, 91 (1955), 356-365; I. A. Shapiro, *ShS*, VIII, 151-152.

A7193 Swinney, D. H. "The Globe Playhouse of Hofstra College." *ETJ*, V (March, 1953), 1-11.

A7194 "Shakespeare's Theater: The Globe Playhouse." An educational film.
Rev: *Quarterly of Film, Radio, and Television*, VIII (1954), 322-355.

A7195 Montgomery, Roy F. "A Fair House Built on Another Man's Ground." *SQ*, V (1954), 207-208.

A7196 Saunders, J. W. "Vaulting the Rails." *ShS*, VII (1954), 69-81.

A7197 Hodges, C. Walter. *Will Shakespeare and the Globe Theater.* New York: Random House, 1955. Pp. 182.

A7198 Müller-Bellinghausen, Anton. *Die Wortkulisse bei Shakespeare.* DD, Freiburg im Breisgau, 1955. Pp. 327. Typewritten. Part published in *SJ*, 91 (1955), 182-195.

A7199 Beckerman, Bernard. *The Production of Shakespeare's Plays at the Globe Playhouse, 1599-1609.* DD, Columbia University, 1956. Pp. 468. Mic 56-2257. *DA*, XVI (1956), 1440. Publication No. 17,039.

A7200 Smith, Irwin. " 'Gates' on Shakespeare Stage." *SQ*, VII (1956), 159-176.

A7201 Smith, Irwin. *Shakespeare's Globe Playhouse.* A modern reconstruction in text and scale drawings, based upon the reconstruction of the Globe by John Cranford Adams, with an Introduction by James G. McManaway. New York: Charles Scribner's Sons, 1956. Pp. xxiii, 240.
Rev: Alice Griffin, *TAr*, April, 1957, p. 62; J. D. Clay, *QJS*, XLIII, 101; *VQR*, XXXIII, xlv; G. B. Harrison, *SatR*, Aug. 3, pp. 17, 28; *ShN*, VII, 40; Joseph W. Young, *ETJ*, IX, 263; H. C. Kiefer, *Arizona Quar.*, XIII, 375-376; Charles H. Shattuck, *JEGP*, LVI, 624-626; J. A. Bryant, Jr., *SR*, LXV, 152-160; John Russell Brown, *MLN*, LXXIII (1958), 364-367; C. Walter Hodges, *SQ*, IX, 194-197.

bb. Swan

A7202 Barrell, Charles Wisner. "Documentary Notes on the Swan Theatre." *Shakespeare Fellowship Quar.*, V (1944), 8-9.

A7203 Nicoll, Allardyce. "A Note on the Swan Theatre Drawing." *ShS*, I (1948), 23-24.

A7204 Triebel, L. A. "Sixteenth-Century Stagecraft in European Drama: A Survey." *MLQ*, XI (1950), 7-16.

A7205 Chapman, Raymond. " 'Twelfth Night' and the Swan Theatre." *N &Q*, 196 (1951), 468-470.

A7206 Hodges, C. Walter. "De Witt Again." *TN*, V (1951), 32-34.

A7207 Southern, Richard, and C. Walter Hodges. "Colour in the Elizabethan Theatre." *TN*, VI (1952), 57-60.

A7208 Holmes, Martin. "A New Theory about the Swan Drawing." *TN*, X (1956), 80-83.

cc. Blackfriars

A7209 Isaacs, J. *Production and Stage-Management at the Blackfriars Theatre.* Oxford Univ. Press, 1933.
Rev: Robert Adger Law, *MLN*, LII (1937), 526-530.

A7210 Bentley, G. E. "Shakespeare and the Blackfriars Theatre." *ShS*, I (1948), 38-56.

A7211 *The Site of the Office of the Times, 1276-1956.* London: Privately printed, 1956.

dd. Court Performances

A7212 Feldman, Abraham. "Hans Ewouts, Artist of the Tudor Court Theatre." *N &Q*, 195 (1950), 257-258.

A7213 Bordinat, Philip. "A New Site for the Salisbury Court Theatre." *N &Q*, NS, III (1956), 51-52.

ee. The Continent

A7214 Skopnik, Günter. "Niederländische Bühnenformen des 16. Jahrhunderts." *DuV*, XXXIX (1938), 411-426.

A7215 Pascal, R. "The Stage of the 'Englische Komödianten': Three Problems." *MLR*, XXXV (1940), 367-376.

A7216 Nagler, A. M. "Sixteenth-Century Continental Stages." *SQ*, V (1954), 359-370.

A7217 Bernheimer, Richard. "Another Globe Theatre." *SQ*, IX (1958), 19-29.

A7218 Bradbrook, M. C. "An 'Ecce Homo' of the Sixteenth Century and the Pageant and Street Theatres of the Low Countries." *SQ*, IX (1958), 424-426.

(2) STAGING AND STAGE MACHINERY (125;42)
(a) STAGING IN GENERAL

A7219 Bradbrook, M. C. *Themes and Conventions of Elizabethan Tragedy.* Cambridge Univ. Press, 1935.
Rev: A6269.

A7220 Ellis-Fermor, Una M. *The Jacobean Drama: An Interpretation.* London: Methuen, 1936. Pp. 351.
Chap. XIV: "The Jacobean Stage."
Rev: A6005.

A7221 Perrigard, Elma E. *The Development of Properties in Drama on the English Speaking Stage.* MA thesis, McGill, 1936.

A7222 Kernodle, George R. *Perspective in the Renaissance Theatre. The Pictorial Sources and the Development of Scenic Forms.* DD, Yale University, 1937.

A7223 Nicoll, Allardyce. *Stuart Masques and the Renaissance Stage.* London: Harrap, 1937. Pp. 224, 197 il.
Rev: "Stuart Court Masques. 'A Noble and Lovely Scene'," *TLS*, Nov. 20, 1937, pp. 877-879; by W. J. Lawrence, *NstN*, NS, XV (1938), 138-140; by John Hayward, *London Mercury*, XXXVII, 344-345; by Rosemond Gilder, *TAr*, XXII, 388-389; by P. Meissner, *Eng. Studn.*, LXXIII (1939), 275-279; by Floris Delattre, *EA*, III, 42-43.

A7224 Fulford, G. L. *The History and the Development of Scenery, Costumes and Lighting of the English Stage from Mediaeval Times to the Year 1700.* MA thesis, McGill, 1940.

A7225 Reynolds, George Fullmer. *The Staging of Elizabethan Plays at the Red Bull Theater, 1605-1625.* Mod. Lang. Assoc. America, Gen. Ser., IX. Oxford Univ. Press, 1940. Pp. 203.
Rev: *TLS*, May 18, 1940, p. 239; ibid., Dec. 7, 1940, p. xxii; by Hazelton Spencer, *MLN*, LV, 540-541; by C. J. Sisson, *RES*, XVII (1941), 102-104; by R. A. Law, *JEGP*, XL, 151-152; by G. E. Bentley, *MP*, XXXIX, 213-215; by George R. Kernodle, *QJS*, XXVII (1942), 332-333; by G. E. Bentley, *MLN*, LVI, 213-215.

A7226 Reynolds, George F. "Some Problems of Elizabethan Staging." *Univ. of Colorado Studies*, XXVI, No. 4 (1941), 3-19.

A7227 Mitchell, Lee. *Elizabethan Scenes of Violence and the Problem of Their Staging.* DD, Northwestern University, 1941. Abstr. publ. in *Summaries of Doctoral Dissertations*, IX (1941), Chicago and Evanston: Northwestern Univ., 1942, pp. 69-73.

A7228 Kernodle, George R. "Renaissance Artist in the Service of the People. Political Tableaux and Street Theatres in France, Flanders, and England." *Art Bulletin*, XXV (1943), 59-64.

A7229 Kernodle, George R. *From Art to Theatre: Form and Convention in the Renaissance.* Univ. Chicago Press, 1944. Pp. 255.
Rev: by Paul McPharlin, *NYTBR*, Oct. 15, 1944, p. 9; by H. C. Lancaster, *MLN*, LIX, 572-573; by Harold Whitehall, *KR*, VII, 357; by B. Hewitt, *QJS*, XXXI, 248-249; by George F. Védier, *MP*, XLII, 249-251; by G. F. Reynolds, *JEGP*, XLIII, 299-301; by Paul Zucker, *Journal of Aesthetics*, IV, 194-195; by A. C., *Connoisseur*, 115 (1945), 63-64; by H. W. Janson, *Art Bulletin*, XXVII, 212-213.

A7230 McDowell, John H. "Tudor Court Staging: A Study in Perspective." *JEGP*, XLIV (1945), 194-207.
Finds little evidence that the staging of plays at Court employed perspective scenery before the time of Inigo Jones, and suggests that this failure to employ Serlian principles may be attributed to English indifference to scientific thought.

A7231 Sprague, A. C. "Off-stage Sounds." *UTQ*, XV (1945), 70-75.

A7232 McDowell, John H. "Some Pictorial Aspects of Early Mountebank Stages." *PMLA*, LXI (1946), 84-96.

A7233 Orsini, Napoleone. "La scena italiana in Inghilterra: il trattato di Serlio." *Anglica*, I (1946), 100-102.

A7234 Nicoll, A. "Studies in the Elizabethan Stage Since 1900." *ShS*, I (1948), 1-16.

A7235 Reynolds, George F. "Staging Elizabethan Plays." *SAB*, XXIV (1949), 258-263.

A7236 Brock, James W. *A Study of the Use of Sound Effects in Elizabethan Drama.* DD, Northwestern

University, 1950. Abstr. publ. in Northwestern Univ. *Summaries of Doctoral Dissertations,* XVIII (1950), Chicago and Evanston: Northwestern Univ., 1951, pp. 99-103.

A7237 Triebel, L. A. "Sixteenth-Century Stagecraft in European Drama: A Survey." *MLQ,* XI (1950), 7-16.

A7238 Venezky, Alice S. *Pageantry on the Shakespearean Stage.* New York: Twayne Publishers, 1951. Pp. 242.
Rev: by Robert Withington, *JEGP,* L (1951), 548-549; by Ernest A. Strathmann, *SQ,* II, 363-364; *SRL,* Sept. 29, 1951, pp. 30, 34; by H. Christian Kiefer, *Ariz. Quar.,* VIII, 171-173; by R. A. Law, *SQ,* III (1952), 84; by W. Clemen, *Archiv,* 189 (1953), 367.

A7239 Richey, Dorothy. *The Dance in the Drama of the Elizabethan Public Theatre: A Production Problem.* DD, Northwestern University, 1951. Abstr. publ. in Northwestern Univ. *Summaries of Doctoral Dissertations,* XIX (1951), Chicago and Evanston: Northwestern Univ., 1952, pp. 169-174.

A7240 Altman, George, Ralph Freud, Kenneth MacGowan, William Melnitz. *Theater Pictorial.* Berkeley and Los Angeles: Univ. of California Press, 1953.

A7241 Rothwell, William F., Jr. *Methods of Production in the English Theatre from 1550-1598.* DD, Yale University, 1953.

A7242 Solem, Delmar E. *Indoor Game Scenes in the Elizabethan Drama and the Problem of Their Staging.* DD, Northwestern University 1952. Abstr. publ. in Northwestern Univ. *Summaries of Doctoral Dissertations,* XX (1952), Chicago and Evanston: Northwestern Univ., 1953, pp. 163-167, and in *Speech Monographs,* XX (1953), 142-143.

A7243 Walton, Charles E. *The Impact of the Court Masque and the Blackfriars Theatre Upon the Staging of Elizabethan-Jacobean Drama.* DD, University of Missouri, 1953. Pp. 198. Mic A54-200. *DA,* XIV (1954), 136-137. Publication No. 6100.

A7244 "Producing Shakespeare: The Stage in Two Elizabethan Ages." *Times* (London), March 5, 1954, p. 9.

A7245 Biggins, D. B. O. *The Continuity in English Stage and Dramatic Tradition Between the Restoration and the Earlier Seventeenth Century.* MA thesis, Southampton, 1954.

A7246 Rosenberg, Marvin. "Public Night Performances in Shakespeare's Time." *TN,* VIII (1954), 44-45.

A7247 Joseph, Bertram L. "The Elizabethan Stage and the Art of Elizabethan Drama." *SJ,* 91 (1955), 145-160.

A7248 Wilson, F. P. "The Elizabethan Theatre." *Neophil,* XXXIX (1955), 40-58.

A7249 Schneideman, Robert Ivan. *Elizabethan Legerdemain and Its Employment in the Drama, 1576-1642.* DD, Northwestern University, 1956. Pp. 274. Mic 56-5385. *DA,* XVI (1956), 2558. Publication No. 19,596.

A7250 Stamm, Rudolf. "Elizabethan Stage-practice and the Transmutation of Source Material by the Dramatists." *ShN,* VII (1957), 48.

A7251 Quinn, Seabury Grandin, Jr. *Ideological Spectacle: Theories of Staging Methods.* DD, Yale University, 1958.

(b) SCENERY

A7252 MacGachen, Freda Kathleen. *The History and Development of Scenery on the English Stage from Mediaeval Times to the Year 1700.* MA thesis, McGill, 1931.

A7253 Nicoll, Allardyce. "Scenery Between Shakespeare and Dryden." *TLS,* Aug. 15, 1936, p. 658.

A7254 Mitchell, Lee. "The Advent of Scenic Design in England." *QJS,* XXIII (1937), 189-197.

A7255 Southern, Richard. "He Also, Was a Scene-Painter. (Wm. Lyzarde 1572)." *Life and Letters Today,* XXIII (1939), 294-300.

A7256 Southern, Richard. "The 'Houses' of the Westminster Play." *TN,* III (1949), 46-52.

A7257 Southern, Richard. *Changeable Scenery: Its Origin and Development in the British Theatre.* London: Faber & Faber, 1952. Pp. 411.
Rev: *TLS,* June 20, 1952, p. 403; by E. Carrick, *RES,* V (1954), 217-218.

(c) COSTUME
i. English

A7258 Calthrop, Dion Clayton. *English Costume from William I to George IV, 1066-1830.* With 61 colour plates by author, 91 illustr. London: Black, 1937. Pp. 463.

A7259 Bradfield, Nancy M. *Historical Costumes of England, 1066-1936.* London: Harrap, 1938. Pp. 155.

A7260 Norris, H. *Costume and Fashion.* III: The Tudor Period, London: Dent, 1938. 1485-1603. Illustrated.

A7261 Laver, James. *Early Tudor, 1485-1558.* Costume of the Western World Series. London: Harrap, 1951. Pp. 24, pl.
Rev: *TLS,* May 11, 1951, p. 288; by Sidney J. Maiden, *National & Eng. Rev.,* 136 (1951), 376.

A7262 Reynolds, Graham. *Elizabethan and Jacobean, 1558-1625.* Costume of the Western World

Series. London: Harrap, 1951. Pp. 23, pl.
Rev: *TLS*, May 11, 1951, p. 288; by Sidney J. Maiden, *National & Eng. Rev.*, 136 (1951), 376.

A7263   Yarwood, Doreen. *English Costume: From the Second Century B.C. to 1950*. London: Batsford, 1952. Pp. xiv, 290.
Rev: by Margaret Lane, *NstN*, Aug. 30, 1952, pp. 243-244.

A7264   Willett, C., and Phillis Cunnington. *Handbook of English Costume in the Sixteenth Century*. Ill. by Barbara Phillipson. London: Faber & Faber, 1954. Pp. 244.
Rev: *TLS*, May 28, 1954, p. 340 (see letter by David Piper and reviewer's reply, June 11, p. 377); *TLS*, April 29, 1955, p. 205; *NstN*, April 16, p. 553.

ii.   Continental

A7265   Brooke, Iris. *Western European Costume, and Its Relation to the Theatre*. Vol. I: Thirteenth to Seventeenth Century. London: Harrap, 1939. Pp. 151.
Rev: *TLS*, June 10, 1939, p. 346; by Lucy Barton, *QJS*, xxv (1939), 682-683.

A7266   Reade, Brian. *The Dominance of Spain, 1550-1660*. Costume of the Western World. London: Harrap, 1951. Pp. 27, pl.
Rev: *TLS*, Oct. 12, 1951, p. 640.

A7267   Blum, André. *Early Burbon, 1590-1643*. Costume of the Western World. London: Harrap, 1951. Pp. 28, pl.
Rev: *TLS*, Oct. 12, 1951, p. 640.

iii.   On the Stage

A7268   Linthicum, M. Channing. *Costume in the Drama of Shakespeare and his Contemporaries*. Oxford: Clarendon Press, 1936. Pp. xii, 307; pl.
Rev: *TLS*, June 20, 1936, p. 516; *N &Q*, 171 (1936), 89-90; by T. B., *SRL*, Sept. 5, 1936, p. 22; *London Mercury*, xxxiv, 379; by Wolfgang Keller, *SJ*, LXXII, 157-158; by Trevor James, *Life and Letters Today*, xv, No. 6 (1937), 213-214; by G. S. T., *History*, NS, XXII, 88; by G. B. Harrison, *MLR*, XXXII, 456-457; M. Q., *EHR*, LII, 739-740; by R. C. Bald, *RES*, XIV (1938), 91-93.

A7269   Merchant, W. M. "Classical Costumes in Shakespearian Productions." *ShS*, x (1957), 71-76.

A7270   Russell, Douglas A. "Shakespearean Costume: Contemporary or Fancy Dress." *ETJ*, x (1958), 105-112.

(d)   SHAKESPEAREAN DETAILS IN GENERAL

A7271   Liebscher, Frida Margot. *Wie ersetzt Shakespeare seinem Publikum Theaterzettel, Bühnendekorationen und künstliche Beleuchtung? Nachgewiesen am Hamlet, zugleich ein Beitrag zur Kenntnis des altenglischen Theaters*. DD, Leipzig, 1920. Pp. 89. Handwritten. Excerpt in *Jahrbuch der Philosophischen Fakultät Leipzig*, 1921.

A7272   Adams, John C. "Shakespeare's Stage: New Facts and Figures." *TAr*, xx (1936), 812-818.

A7273   Gaw, Allison. "The Impromptu Mask in Shakspere." (With especial reference to the stagery of *Romeo and Juliet*, I, iv-v.) *SAB*, XI (1936), 149-160.

A7274   Moody, Dorothy B. *Shakespeare's Stage Directions*. DD, Yale University, 1938.

A7275   Hart, Alfred. "Did Shakespeare Produce His Own Plays?" *MLR*, XXXVI (1941), 173-183.

A7276   Jackson, Joan S. *An Analysis of Some Elizabethan and Some Twentieth Century Methods of Producing Shakespeare's "Hamlet."* MA thesis, McGill, 1943.

A7277   Burrell, J. "Réflexions sur la mise en scène des tragédies de Shakespeare." *La Revue Théâtrale*, 1947, pp. 169-170.

A7278   Gorelik, M. "Shakespeare, Liberator." *New Theatres for Old*. New York: S. French, 1940; London: D. Dobson, 1947, pp. 100-105.

A7279   Mitchell, Lee. "Shakespeare's Sound Effects." *Speech Monographs*, XIV (1947), 127-138.

A7280   Mitchell, Lee. "Shakespeare's Lighting Effects." *Speech Monographs*, xv (1948), 72-84.

A7281   McDowell, John H. "Conventions of Medieval Art in Shakespearian Staging." *JEGP*, XLVII (1948), 215-229.

A7282   Smith, Warren D. *Shakespeare's Stagecraft as Denoted by the Dialogue in the Original Printings of his Text*. DD, University of Pennsylvania, 1948. *Microf. Ab.*, x (1950), 163. Publication No. 1731.

A7283   Kernodle, G. R. "Basic Problems in Reading Shakespeare." *QJS*, xxxv (1949), 36-43.

A7284   McDowell, J. H. "Medieval Influences in Shakespearian Staging." *Players Magazine*, xxvi (1949), 52-53.

A7285   Mitchell, Lee. "Shakespeare's Legerdemain." *Speech Monographs*, xvi (1949), 144-161.

A7286   Purdom, C. B. *Producing Shakespeare*. London: Pitman, 1950. Pp. xii, 220.
Rev: B1729.

A7287 Watkins, Ronald. *On Producing Shakespeare*. London: Michael Joseph, 1950; New York: Norton, 1951. Pp. 335.
Rev: by Desmond MacCarthy, *Sun Times*, Dec. 17, 1950, p. 3; *TLS*, Jan. 12, 1951, p. 22; by Peter Brook, *NstN*, April 28, 1951, p. 482; by Michael MacOwan, *Spectator*, Feb. 2, 1951, pp. 156, 158; by J. Banyard, *FortnR*, 169 (1951), 212; by Henry Popkin, *SatR*, LX (1952), 327-336; by Margaret Webster, *SQ*, III, 63-68; by Rudolf Stamm, *SJ*, 87/88 (1952), 216-217; by Richard Flatter, ibid., 236-238.

A7288 Budde, Fritz. "Shakespeare und die Frage der Raumbühne." *Shakespeare-Studien, Festschrift für Heinrich Mutschmann*, pp. 21-47.

A7289 Smith, Warren D. "Evidence of Scaffolding on Shakespeare's Stage." *RES*, II (1951), 22-29.

A7290 Crouch, Jack H. *Some Shakespearean Stage Conventions Developed from a Study of the Architectural Antecedents of the Elizabethan Public-outdoor Playhouse and a Staging Study of "Romeo and Juliet" and "Anthony [sic] and Cleopatra."* DD, Cornell University, 1952.

A7291 Smith, Warren D. "Stage Settings in Shakespeare's Dialogue." *MP*, L (1952), 32-35.

A7291a "Shakespeare on the Stage, 1928: A Players' Shakespeare." *TLS*, Aug. 28, 1953, pp. xxxii-xxxv.

A7292 Banke, Cécile de. *Shakespearean Stage Production: Then & Now*. New York: McGraw-Hill, 1953. Pp. xviii, 342.
Rev: A7409.

A7293 Smith, Warren D. "Stage Business in Shakespeare's Dialogue." *SQ*, IV (1953), 311-316.

A7294 Smith, Warren D. "The Elizabethan Stage and Shakespeare's Entrance Announcements." *SQ*, IV (1953), 405-410.

A7295 Harbage, Alfred. *Theatre for Shakespeare*. (The Alexander Lectures for 1954-55). Toronto: Univ. of Toronto Press, 1955. Pp. xii, 118.
Rev: B1748.

A7296 Beckerman, Bernard. *The Production of Shakespeare's Plays at the Globe Playhouse, 1599-1609*. DD, Columbia University, 1956. Pp. 468. Mic 56-2257. *DA*, XVI (1956), 1440. Publication No. 17,039.

A7297 Merchant, W. M. "Visual Elements in Shakespeare Studies." *SJ*, 92 (1956), 280-290.

A7298 Wälterlin, Oskar. "Randglossen zur Shakespeare-Inszenierung." *SJ*, 93 (1957), 128-140.

(e) SPECIFIC SHAKESPEAREAN DETAILS

A7299 Adams, John C. "The Staging of *Romeo and Juliet*." *TLS*, Feb. 15, 1936, p. 139.
See W. J. Lawrence, "The Original Staging of *Romeo and Juliet*, Act III, Scene V", *TLS*, Sept. 19, 1935, p. 580. Letters by Percy Allen, ibid., p. 612; by George Sampson, ibid., p. 722; by Harley Granville-Barker and by George Sampson, *TLS*, Feb. 22, 1936, p. 163; by W. J. Lawrence, ibid., Feb. 29, 1936, p. 184; letters by Mr. Adams, ibid., May 23, 1936, p. 440; by Mr. Granville-Barker and by Mr. Lawrence, ibid., May 30, p. 460.

A7300 Adams, John C. "*Romeo and Juliet*: As Played on Shakespeare's Stage." *TAr*, xx (1936), 896-904.

A7301 Crundell, H. W. "*The Taming of the Shrew* on the XVII. Century Stage." *N &Q*, 173 (1937), 207.

A7302 Adams, John C. "The Staging of *The Tempest*, III, iii." *RES*, XIV (1938), 404-419.

A7303 Greg, W. W. "The Staging of *King Lear*." *RES*, XVI (1940), 300-303.

A7304 Levin, Harry. "Falstaff Uncolted." *MLN*, LXI (1946), 305-310.

A7305 Adams, John C. "The Original Staging of *King Lear*." *AMS*, pp. 315-335.

A7306 Reynolds, George F. "*Troilus and Cressida* on the Elizabethan Stage." *AMS*, pp. 229-238.

A7307 Wilson, J. Dover. "*Titus Andronicus* on the Stage in 1595." *ShS*, I (1948), 17-22.

A7308 Flatter, Richard. "The Dumb-Show in *Macbeth*." *TLS*, March 23, 1951, p. 181.
See letters by Peter Ure, ibid., April 6, 1951, p. 216; by C. B. Purdom, ibid., April 20, 1951, p. 245.

A7309 Kirschbaum, Leo. "Shakespeare's Stage Blood and Its Significance." *PMLA*, LXIV (1949), 517-529.

A7310 Stroup, Joseph Bradley. *The Problems of Staging in the Second Quarto of "Romeo and Juliet."* Master's thesis, University of North Carolina, 1951. Abstr. publ. in *Univ. of North Carolina Record, Research in Progress*, Grad. School Series, No. 62, 1951, pp. 128-129.

A7311 Hotson, Leslie. "False Faces on Shakespeare's Stage." *TLS*, May 16, 1952, p. 336.

A7312 Hosley, Richard. "The Use of the Upper Stage in *Romeo and Juliet*." *SQ*, V (1954), 371-379.

A7313 Byrne, M. St. Clare. "*Twelfth Night* 'In the Round'." *TN*, IX (1955), 46-52.

A7314 Fusillo, Robert James. "Tents on Bosworth Field." *SQ*, VI (1955), 193-194.

A7315 Hosley, Richard. "More about 'Tents' on Bosworth Field." *SQ*, VII (1956), 458-459.

A7316 Saunders, J. W. "The Elizabethan Theatre." *TLS*, Nov. 11, 1955, p. 680.
An objection to Hotson's *First Night of Twelfth Night* as to staging.

A7317   Adams, John C. "Shakespeare's Use of the Upper Stage in *Romeo and Juliet*, III, v." *SQ*, VII (1956), 145-152.

A7318   McNeir, Waldo F. "The Closing of the Capulet Tomb." *SN*, XXVIII (1956), 3-8.

A7319   Reynolds, George F. "*Hamlet* at the Globe." *ShS*, IX (1956), 49-53.

2. THE ACTORS AND THEIR ART (127;42)
a. CHILD-ACTORS (127;-)

A7320   Brown, Ivor. "The Boy-Player." *TAr*, XX (1936), 385-391.

A7321   Boas, Guy. "The Influence of the Boy-Actor on Shakespeare's Plays." *ConR*, 152 (1937), 69-77.

A7322   Davies, W. Robertson. *Shakespeare's Boy Actors*. London: Dent, 1939; New York: William Sollach, 1941. Pp. 208, pl.
  Rev: *N&Q*, 176 (1939), 215-216; *QR*, 272 (1939), 370; *TLS*, Feb. 4, 1939, p. 74; by R. S. Knox, *UTQ*, IX, 115-116.

A7323   Brawner, James Paul, ed. *The Wars of Cyrus: An Early Classical Narrative Drama of the Child Actors*. Univ. Illinois Press, 1942. Pp. 163.
  Rev: by Madeleine Doran, *JEGP*, XLII (1943), 424-429; by Tucker Brooke, *MLQ*, V (1944), 120-122; by Alfred Harbage, *MLN*, LIX, 130; by F. S. Boas, *TLS*, Mar. 31, 1945, p. 156; see letter by W. W. Greg, ibid., Apr. 14, 1945, p. 175.

A7324   Schücking, Levin L. "Die Kindertruppenstelle in *Hamlet*." *Archiv*, 179 (1941), 8-14.

A7325   Goodman, Randolph G. *That Strumpet the Stage: Poems about Playgoers, Players, and Playwrights*. DD, Columbia University, 1953. Pp. 357. Mic A53-761. *DA*, XIII (1953), 450. Publication No. 5189.

A7326   Walton, Charles E. *The Impact of the Court Masque and the Blackfriars upon the Staging of Elizabethan-Jacobean Drama*. DD, University of Missouri, 1953. Pp. 198. Mic A54-200. *DA*, XIV (1954), 136-137. Publication No. 6100.

b. DRAMATIC COMPANIES (128;42)

A7327   Sharpe, Robert Boies. *The Real War of the Theatres. Shakespeare's Fellow in Rivalry with the Admiral's Men, 1594-1603. Repertories, Devices, and Types*. Boston, 1935.
  Rev: A4902.

A7328   Sisson, C. J. "Mr. and Mrs. Browne of the Boar's Head." *Life and Letters Today*, XV, No. 6 (1937), 99-107.

A7329   Eliot, S. A., Jr. "The Lord Chamberlain's Company as Portrayed in *Every Man Out of His Humour*." *Essays Contributed in Honor of President William Allan Neilson*. 1939.

A7330   Castle, Eduard. "Shakespeare und seine Truppe." *SJ*, LXXVI (1940), 57-111.

A7331   Harbage, Alfred. *Annals of English Drama, 975-1700: An Analytical Record of all Plays, Extant or Lost, Chronologically Arranged and Indexed by Authors, Titles, Dramatic Companies, etc.* Univ. of Penna. Press, 1940. Pp. 264.
Dramatic companies listed.
  Rev: A2923.

A7332   Harrison, G. B. *Elizabethan Plays and Players*. London: Routledge, 1940. Pp. viii, 306. Paperback ed.: Univ. of Michigan Press, 1956. Pp. viii, 306.
  Rev: A7079.

A7333   Wilson, Winifred Graham. "Skinners' Pageants." *Life and Letters Today*, XXVII (1940), 10-16.

A7334   Cancelled.

A7335   Brawner, James Paul, ed. *The Wars of Cyrus: An Early Classical Narrative Drama of the Child Actors*. Univ. of Illinois Press, 1942. Pp. 163.
  Rev: A7323.

A7336   Sisson, Charles J. "Notes on Early Stuart Stage History." *MLR*, XXXVII (1942), 25-36.

A7337   Chambrun, Clara Longworth de. "La compagnie de Shakespeare." *Revue Théâtrale*, 1946, pp. 176-186.

A7338   Greenslade, S. L. "The Elizabethan Theatre." *TLS*, Apr. 25, 1952, p. 281.
One of a bundle of Chapter Vouchers, Durham Cathedral, 1590-1591, signed by Tobie Matthew, reads: "November 1590/5 To the Earle of Essex his players xxˢ/Auguste To her Maties playes liiiˢ iiijᵈ."

A7339   Rosenberg, Eleanor. *Maecenas in England: The Earl of Leicester as Patron of Literature and Propaganda, 1559-1588*. DD, Columbia University, 1953. Publ. as *Leicester, Patron of Letters*, New York: Columbia Univ. Press, 1955. Pp. xx, 395.

A7340   Sisson, Charles J. "The Red Bull Company and the Importunate Widow." *ShS*, VII (1954), 57-68.

A7341   Lane, Robert Philips. *A Study of the Repertory of Queen Elizabeth's Company*. DD, University of North Carolina, 1956.

A7342   Kerr, S. Parnell. "The Constable Kept an Account." *N&Q*, NS, IV (1957), 167-170.

c. ENGLISH PLAYERS ON THE CONTINENT (129;42)
(1) COLLECTIONS OF THEIR PLAYS AND GENERAL TREATISES
(129;42)

A7343 McCabe, William H. "Notes on the St. Omers College Theatre." *PQ*, XVII (1938), 225-239.

(2) SPECIAL ESSAYS ON VISITS TO VARIOUS CITIES AND
COUNTRIES (130;43)
(a) ENGLAND

A7344 Crundell, H. W. "Visits of Dramatic Companies to Bristol, 1587-1600." *N &Q*, 171 (1936), 24.

A7345 Gray, M. M. "Queen Elizabeth's Players." *TLS*, Jan. 14, 1939, p. 25.

A7346 Thaler, Alwin. *Shakespeare and Democracy*. Univ. Tennessee Press, 1941. Pp. xii, 312. Chap. VIII: "Travelling Players in Shak.'s England."
Rev: A1809.

A7347 Stratman, Carl J. *Dramatic Performances at Oxford and Cambridge, 1603-1642*. DD, University of Illinois, 1948.

A7348 Ashe, Dora Jean. "The Non-Shakespearean Bad Quartos as Provincial Acting Versions." *Renaissance Papers* (Univ. of South Carolina, 1954), pp. 57-61.

A7349 Rosenfeld, Sybil. "Dramatic Companies in the Provinces in the Sixteenth and Early Seventeenth Centuries." *TN*, VIII (1954), 55-58.

(b) GERMANY

A7350 Baesecke, Anna. *Das Schauspiel der englischen Komödianten in Deutschland*. Halle, 1935.
Rev: *LZ*, 86 (1935), 608; by Harry Kurz, *Books Abroad*, X (1936), 75-76; *SAB*, XI, 58; by Franz Grosse, *Beiblatt*, XLVII, 114-116; by P. Meissner, *ES*, XVIII, 269; by Wolfgang Keller, *SJ*, LXXII, 160-161; by Walch, *Museum*, XLIII, No. 9; by J. H. Walter, *MLR*, XXXII (1937), 138; by Robert Adger Law, *MLN*, LII, 526-530; by Maurice Denis, *RG*, XXVIII, 207; by W. Keller, *ZNU*, XXXVI, 50-51; by N. C. Brooks, *JEGP*, XXXVII (1938), 592-593; by Günter Skopnik, *DLZ*, LIX, 15-19.

A7351 Hartleb, H. *Landgraf Moritz der Gelehrte von Hessen-Kassel als Förderer der englischen Komödianten und Erbauer des ersten deutschen Theaters*. DD, Munich, 1936. Published as *Deutschlands erster Theaterbau. Eine Geschichte des Theaterlebens und der englischen Komödianten unter Landgraf Moritz*. Berlin: de Gruyter, 1936. Pp. vii, 162.

A7352 Fredén, Nils Gustaf Tsin Mei. *Friedrich Menius und das Repertoire der englischen Komödianten in Deutschland*. DD, Uppsala, 1939. Published by Palmers, Stockholm, 1939. Pp. 527. "Englische Comedien und Tragedien" of 1620 was probably put together by Menius.
Rev: by L. M. Price, *GR*, XVII (1942), 153-155. See also A7354.

A7353 Pascal, R. "The Stage of the 'Englische Komödianten': Three Problems." *MLR*, XXXV (1940), 367-376.

A7354 "Elizabethan Plays in Germany." *TLS*, Apr. 26, 1941, p. 208; May 3, 1941, p. 220. See A7352.

A7355 Möhring, Hans. "Als Shakespeare zu uns kam. Shakespeare-Aufführungen englischer Komödianten in Deutschland." *Theater d. Zeit*, VIII (1953), Heft 12, 6-12.

A7356 Bernheimer, Richard. "Another Globe Theatre." *SQ*, IX (1958), 19-29.

A7357 Brett-Evans, D. "Der 'Sommernachtstraum' in Deutschland 1600-1650." *ZDP*, LXXVII (1958), 371-383.

A7358 Freudenstein, Reinhold. *Der bestrafte Brudermord. Shakespeares "Hamlet" auf der Wanderbühne des 17. Jhd*. (Britannica et Americana, Bd. 3). Hamburg, 1958. Pp. 130.

(c) LOW COUNTRIES

A7359 Bald, R. C. "Leicester's Men in the Low Countries." *RES*, XIX (1943), 395-397.

A7360 Hoppe, Harry R. "English Actors at Ghent in the Seventeenth Century." *RES*, XXV (1949), 305-321.

A7361 Hoppe, Harry R. "George Jolly at Bruges, 1648." *RES*, NS, V (1954), 265-268.

A7362 Hoppe, Harry R. "English Acting Companies at the Court of Brussels in the Seventeenth Century." *RES*, NS, VI (1955), 26-33.

(d) ELSEWHERE

A7363 Chambrun, Clara Longworth, Comtesse de. "Shakespeare Across the Channel." *AMS*, pp. 97-100.

A7364 Clark, William Smith. *The Early Irish Stage*. Oxford: Clarendon Press, 1955. Pp. 225.
Rev: B1362.

d. INDIVIDUAL ACTORS (130;43)
(1) GENERAL

A7365   Lawrence, W. J. *Speeding Up Shakespeare*. Studies of the Bygone Theatre and Drama. London: Argonaut Press, 1937. Pp. 220.
        Rev: A7402.

A7366   R. "Actors in Shakespeare's Plays." *N &Q*, 174 (1938), 387.

A7367   Evans, Allan. "Actors in the Account Rolls of Battle Abbey." *HLQ*, VI (1942), 103-105.

A7368   Jackson, James L. "The Fencing Actor-Lines in Shakespeare's Plays." *MLN*, LVII (1942), 615-621.

A7369   Darlington, William Aubrey. *The Actor and his Audience*. London: Phoenix House, 1949. Pp. 188.
        Rev: *TLS*, June 24, 1949, p. 412; by G. Vallet, *RHT*, II (1950), 91-92.

A7370   Brook, Donald. *A Pageant of English Actors*. New York: Macmillan; London: Rockliff, 1950. Pp. viii, 9-286, pl. 15.

A7371   Hoston, Leslie. *Shakespeare's Motley*. London: Rupert Hart-Davis, 1952. Pp. 133.
        Rev: A6671.

A7372   Nagler, A. M. *Sources of Theatrical History*. New York: Theatre Annual, 1952. Pp. xxiii, 611.
        Rev: A7076.

(2)   INDIVIDUALS
(a)   ALLEYN

A7373   Hosking, G. L. *The Life and Times of Edward Alleyn*. Actor, Master of the King's Bears, Founder of the College of God's Gift at Dulwich. With a Brief Account of the Foundation up to its Remodelling in 1857 and a Note on the Picture Gallery. With a Foreword by Lord Gorell. London: Cape, 1952. Pp. 285.
        Rev: *TLS*, May 2, 1952, p. 292; reply by G. L. Hosking, ibid., May 16, 1952, p. 329; by Ivor Brown, *Obs.*, Apr. 20, 1952, p. 7; *RHT*, IV, 275; by John Bryson, *Spectator*, May 9, 1952, pp. 622, 624; by E. D. O'Brien, *Illus. London News*, May 3, 1952, p. 770; by Clifford Leech, *ShS*, VI (1953), 160-161; by J. B. Fort, *EA*, VI, 258; by Arnold Edinborough, *SQ*, IV, 83-84.

A7374   Armstrong, William A. "Shakespeare and the Acting of Edward Alleyn." *ShS*, VII (1954), 82-89.

See also A7397, A7398.

(b)   ARMIN

A7375   Dudley, O. H. T. "John in the Hospital." *TLS*, June 17, 1949, p. 397.

A7376   Felver, Charles Stanley. *William Shakespeare and Robert Armin his Fool: A Working Partnership*. DD, University of Michigan, 1956. Pp. 352. Mic 56-3895. *DA*, XVI (1956), 2446. Publication No. 18,601.

A7377   Felver, Charles S. "Robert Armin, Shakespeare's Source for Touchstone." *SQ*, VII (1956), 135-137.

(c)   TARLTON

A7378   "English Humour 1500 to 1800." *TLS*, May 21, 1938, p. 360.

A7379   Campbell, Lily B. "Richard Tarlton and the Earthquake of 1580." *HLQ*, IV (1941), 293-301.

A7380   Bryant, Joseph Allen, Jr. "Shakespeare's Falstaff and the Mantle of Dick Tarlton." *SP*, LI (1954), 149-162.

(d)   OTHERS

A7381   Seh, L. H. "Shakespeares erste Verleger." *Weltkunst*, IX, No. 49 (1935), 31.

A7382   Nosworthy, J. M. "A Note on John Heminge." *Library*, 5th Series, III (1949), 287-288.

A7383   Gray, Cecil G. "The Sixteenth-Century Burbages of Stratford on Avon." *N &Q*, 196 (1951), 490.

A7384   Shield, H. A. "Links with Shakespeare." *N &Q*, 196 (1951), 250-252.

e.   ANIMALS AS ACTORS ON THE ELIZABETHAN STAGE (131;-)
     (Transferred to Motifs, Animals, VIII,2,b,(8),(c), v. above)

f.   INTERNAL ORGANIZATION OF THE ELIZABETHAN THEATRE
     (Relations of Actors, Managers & Audiences) (131;-)

A7385   Gorrell, Robert Mark. *The Popular Drama in England, 1600-1642*. DD, Cornell University, 1940. Abstr. publ. in *Abstracts of Theses, 1939*, Ithaca: Cornell Univ. Press, 1940, pp. 35-37.

A7386   Harbage, Alfred. *Shakespeare's Audience*. Columbia Univ. Press, 1941. Pp. viii, 201.
        A major work on the subject. It quite demolishes the nineteenth-century conception of the late Tudor theatre audience and consequently the basis for much of that so-called realist criticism which assumed that primitive dramatic techniques and popular intellectual stereotypes were the necessary and inevitable fare of an ignorant audience.
        Rev: by David Mathew, *Spectator*, May 15, 1942, p. 467; by J. W. Krutch, (N.Y.) *Nation*, Feb. 21, 1942, pp. 233-234; by G. F. Reynolds, *MLQ*, III, 332-334; by J. J. Knights, *Cana-*

dian Forum, XXI, 380; by B. T. Spencer, "Shakespeare, With and Without Tears," *SR*, L, 550-551; by B. R. Lewis, "Shakespeare's Audience as Viewed by Doctor Harbage," *SAB*, XVII, 150-155; by Allardyce Nicoll, *JEGP*, XLI, 381-382; by H. S. Bennett, *RES*, XVIII, 496-498; by T. W. Baldwin, *MLN*, LVIII (1943), 481-483.

A7387   Akrigg, G. P. V. "Middleton: An Allusion to the Shakspere First Folio?" *SAB*, XXI (1946), 25-26.

A7388   Gerold, A. W. "The Organization of Representative Acting Companies Since Elizabethan Times." MS thesis, Columbia University, 1948. Pp. 78.

A7389   Parrott, Thomas Marc. "*Pericles:* The Play and the Novel." *SAB*, XXIII (1948), 105-113. Suggests the novel was published because the King's Men refused to permit publication of the play.

A7390   Purdom, C. B. *Producing Shakespeare.* London: Pitman, 1950. Pp. xii, 220.
Rev: B1729.

A7391   Bromberg, Murray. "Theatrical Wagers: A Sidelight on the Elizabethan Drama." *N &Q*, 196 (1951), 533-535.

A7392   Capocci, Valentina. "Poeti e attori nel dramma elisabettiano." *Il Ponte*, VII (1951), 1593-600.

A7393   Hayward, W. C. *The Globe Theatre, 1599-1608.* DD, Birmingham, 1951.

A7394   Goodman, Randolph G. *That Strumpet the Stage: Poems about Playgoers, Players, and Playwrights.* DD, Columbia University, 1953. Pp. 357. Mic A53-761. *DA*, XIII (1953), 450. Publication No. 5189.

A7395   McCabe, J. C. *A Study of the Blackfriars Theatre, 1608-1642.* DD, Birmingham, 1954.

A7396   Markward, W. B. *A Study of the Phoenix Theatre in Drury Lane, 1617-1638.* DD, Birmingham, 1954.

A7397   Briley, John. "Of Stake and Stage." *ShS*, VIII (1955), 106-108.
Prints and comments upon two documents attesting Edward Alleyn's services in his royally sponsored office in charge of bear-baiting at the Bear Garden, where this sport alternated with stage plays.

A7398   Briley, John. "Edward Alleyn and Henslowe's Will." *SQ*, IX (1958), 321-330.

A7399   Eccles, Mark. "Martin Peerson and the Blackfriars." *ShS*, XI (1958), 100-106.

g. THE ART OF THE ACTOR IN THE TIME OF SHAKESPEARE (132;43)
(1) GENERAL (132;43)

A7400   Bradbrook, M. C. *Themes and Conventions of Elizabethan Tragedy.* Cambridge Univ. Press, 1935.
Rev: A6269.

A7401   Lewes, G. H. "Shakespeare: Actor and Critic." *Theatre Workshop*, Oct., 1936, pp. 41-50. (Repr. from *On Actors and the Art of Acting.*)

A7402   Lawrence, W. J. *Speeding Up Shakespeare.* Studies of the Bygone Theatre and Drama. London: Argonaut Press, 1937. Pp. 220.
Rev: *TLS*, Dec. 25, 1937, p. 977; by George Rylands, *NstN*, NS XV (1938), 174-176; by Bonamy Dobrée, *London Mercury*, XXXVII, 4478; by Kenneth Muir, *Spectator*, Feb. 4, 1938, pp. 191-192.

A7403   Huang, John. *A Short History of Shakespearean Production.* M. Litt. thesis, Cambridge, 1937. *Cam Abs.*, 1937-1938, pp. 84.

A7404   Davies, W. Robertson. *Shakespeare's Boy Actors.* London: Dent, 1939. Pp. 208, pl.
Rev: A7322.

A7405   McNeir, Waldo F. "Gayton on Elizabethan Acting." *PMLA*, LVI (1941), 579-583.

A7406   Purdom, C. B. *Producing Shakespeare.* London: Pitman, 1950. Pp. xii, 220.
Rev: B1729.

A7407   Downer, Alan S. "The Tudor Actor: A Taste of his Quality." *TN*, V (1951), 76-81.

A7408   Nagler, A. M. *Sources of Theatrical History.* New York: Theatre Annual, 1952. Pp. xxiii, 611.
Rev: A7076.

A7409   Banke, Cécile de. *Shakespearean Stage Production: Then and Now.* New York: McGraw-Hill, 1953. Pp. xviii, 342.
Rev: by Stewart Cowan, *Canadian Forum*, XXXIII (1953), 91-92; by Walter Prichard Eaton, *NYHTBR*, Feb. 8, p. 13; by Hubert Heffner, *SQ*, IV, 477-479; by Ivor Brown, *Obs.*, May 30, 1954, p. 8; by David Hardman, *John o'London's Weekly*, LXIII (1954), 414; *TLS*, Apr. 16, p. 244 (see letter by Stanley Gardner, ibid., May 14, p. 319, and reviewer's reply, May 21, p. 335); by Harold Jenkins, *ShS*, VII, 144; *QR*, 292 (1954), 410; by G. W. Horner, *FortnR*, NS, 1050 (1954), 426-427.

A7410   Goodman, Randolph G. *That Strumpet the Stage: Poems about Playgoers, Players, and Playwrights.* DD, Columbia University, 1953. Pp. 357. Mic A53-761. *DA*, XIII (1953), 450. Publication No. 5189.

A7411   Mead, Robert S. *A Study of Factors Influencing the Development of Acting Technique in England,*

1576-1642, with Applications to the Problems of Educational Theatre. DD, Northwestern University, 1952. Abstr. publ. in Northwestern Univ. *Summaries of Doctoral Dissertations,* xx (1952), Chicago and Evanston, 1953, pp. 149-151.

A7412 Rothwell, William F., Jr. *Methods of Production in the English Theatre from 1550-1598.* DD, Yale University, 1953.

A7413 Hunter, E. R. *Shakespeare and Common Sense.* Boston: Christopher, 1954. Pp. 312.
Rev: A971.

A7414 Ellis, Brobury Pearce. *Creative Relationships Between Dramatist, Actor, and Audience in the Acted Play.* DD, Cornell University, 1954. Pp. 203. Mic A55-233. *DA,* xv (1955), 164. Publication No. 10,578.

A7415 Beckerman, Bernard. *The Production of Shakespeare's Plays at the Globe Playhouse, 1599-1609.* DD, Columbia University, 1956. Pp. 468. Mic 56-2257. *DA,* xvi (1956), 1440. Publication No. 17,039.

A7416 Bolton, Janet. *A Historical Study of English Theories and Precepts of Vocal and Gestural Expressiveness from Stephen Hawes to John Bulwer: 1509-1644.* DD, University of Southern California, 1958.

A7417 Nagler, A. M. *Shakespeare's Stage,* tr. by Ralph Manheim (Yale Univ. Shakespeare Supplements). Yale Univ. Press, 1958. Pp. ix, 117.

A7418 Weiner, Albert Byron. *Acting on the Medieval Religious Stage.* DD, Yale University, 1958.

(2) THE FORMALISTIC-NATURALISTIC CONTROVERSY

A7419 Harbage, Alfred. "Elizabethan Acting." *PMLA,* LIV (1939), 685-708.

A7420 Chambers, Sir E. K. "William Shakespeare: An Epilogue." *RES,* xvi (1940), 385-401. Republished in *Shakespearean Gleanings.* Oxford Univ. Press, 1944.
Rev: B4466.

A7421 McCollom, William Gilman. *Illusion and Formalism in Elizabethan Tragedy.* DD, Cornell University, 1945. Abstr. publ. in *Abstracts of Theses, 1944,* Ithaca: Cornell Univ. Press, 1945, pp. 17-20.

A7422 Bowers, Robert H. "Gesticulation in Elizabethan Acting." *Southern Folklore Quar.,* xii (1948), 267-277.

A7423 Bachrach, A. G. H. "The Great Chain of Acting." *Neophil,* xxxiii (1949), 160-172.

A7424 Bethell, S. L. "Shakespeare's Actors." *RES,* NS, I (1950), 193-205.
After a critical consideration of various points made by Baldwin, Harbage, and others, concludes that "acting, like the drama itself, was in a mixture of styles."

A7425 Joseph, Bertram L. "How the Elizabethans Acted Shakespeare." *Listener,* XLIII (1950), 17-18.

A7426 Joseph, B. L. *Elizabethan Acting.* London: Oxford University Press, 1951. Pp. x, 157.
Rev: *TLS,* May 4, 1951, p. 274; by Alfred Harbage, *SQ,* II, 360-361; *DUJ,* xII, 119; by A. F., *Time and Tide,* May 19, 1951, p. 477; by F. S. Boas, *English,* VIII, 254-255; by M. E. Prior, *SRL,* Sept. 29, 1951, p. 30; by R. Southern, *TN,* v, 94; by Sir Desmond MacCarthy, *Sunday Times,* Mar. 11, 1951, p. 3; by G. Baldini, *Belfagor,* VII (1952), 366; by Frank Kermode, *RES,* NS, IV (1953), 70-73; by Rudolf Stamm, *SJ,* 87/88 (1953), 213; by J. Gerritsen, *ES,* xxxv (1954), 222-224.

A7427 Brown, John Russell. "On the Acting of Shakespeare's Plays." *QJS,* xxxix (1953), 474-484.
Argues that "formalism on the stage was fast dying out in Shakespeare's age, and that a new naturalism was a kindling spirit in his theatre."

A7428 Miles, Bernard. "Elizabethan Acting." *TLS,* Apr. 2, 1954, p. 217.
Passage in a bill now in the Public Record Office addressed to Cardinal Wolsey and supporting B. Joseph's theory that "Elizabethan Acting was founded entirely on the art of rhetoric." This piece of evidence, however, is dated 1528.

A7429 Rosenberg, Marvin. "Elizabethan Actors: Men or Marionettes?" *PMLA,* LXIX (1954), 915-927.
A plea, in opposition to "formalists" like Bradbrook and Joseph, for Elizabethan actors as individual artists, sharing with the dramatist the problems of interpretation.

A7430 Brockett, Lenyth Spenker. *Theories of Style in Stage Production.* DD, Stanford University, 1954. Pp. 315. Mic A54-2724. *DA,* xiv (1954), 1841. Publication No. 9481.

A7431 Foakes, R. A. "The Player's Passion: Some Notes on Elizabethan Psychology and Acting." *Essays and Studies,* VII (1954), 62-77.
A warning for critics who make excessive use of the approach to Shak. through Elizabethan psychology. Elizabethan acting was thought at the time to be lifelike.

A7432 Joseph, Bertram. "The Elizabethan Stage and the Art of Elizabethan Drama." *SJ,* 91 (1955), 145-160.
Citing examples from John Bulwer's *Chironomia,* Joseph suggests that Elizabethans understood the "action of the orator and the stage-player as being substantially the same," at once natural and theatrical, with the style suited to the words.

A7433 Joseph, Bertram. "The Elizabethan Stage and Acting." *The Age of Shakespeare,* ed. Boris Ford. Aylesbury and London: Pelican Books, 1955, pp. 147-161.

A7434   Harbage, Alfred. *Theatre for Shakespeare*. (The Alexander Lectures for 1954-55.) Toronto:
        Univ. of Toronto Press, 1955. Pp. xii, 118.
        Rev: B1748.

A7435   Klein, David. "Elizabethan Acting." *PMLA*, LXXI (1956), 280-282.
        See Also A7429.
        Considerable further evidence is offered that Elizabethan acting was natural.

A7436   Goldstein, Leonard. "On the Transition from Formal to Naturalistic Acting in the Elizabethan
        and Post-Elizabethan Theatre." *Bul. N. Y. Public Lib.*, LXII (1958), 330-349.

(3) SPECIFIC ASPECTS OF ELIZABETHAN ACTING
(a) DELIVERY

A7437   Sansom, Clive. "On the Speaking of Shakespeare." London Academy of Music and Dramatic
        Arts, 1949.

A7438   Annan, N. G. "The Marlowe Society Tradition." *CamJ*, III (1950), 592-612.

A7439   Le Page, R. B. "The Dramatic Delivery of Shakespeare's Verse." *ES*, XXXII (1951), 63-68.
        Argues against Draper's tempo work.

A7440   Loper, Robert Bruce. "Shakespeare 'All of a Breath'." *QJS*, XXXIX (1953), 193-196.

A7441   Rylands, George. "The Poet and the Player." *ShS*, VII (1954), 25-34.

A7442   Mattingly, Alethea S. "The Playing Time and Manner of Delivery of Shakespeare's Plays in
        the Elizabethan Theatre." *Speech Monographs*, XXI (1955), 29-38.

A7443   Müller-Bellinghausen, Anton. "Die Wortkulisse bei Shakespeare." *SJ*, 91 (1955), 182-195.

A7444   Draper, John W. *The Tempo-Patterns of Shakespeare's Plays*. Angl. Forschungen, Heft 90,
        1957. Pp. 180.
        Rev: A5165.

(b) TEXTUAL EVIDENCES

A7445   Spencer, Hazelton. "A Note on Cutting and Slashing." *MLR*, XXXI (1936), 393-395.

A7446   Crundell, H. W. "Actors' Parts and Elizabethan Texts." *N &Q*, 180 (1941), 350-351.

A7447   Sturman, Berta S. *Renaissance Prompt Copies: A Looking Glasse for London and England*. DD,
        University of Chicago, 1948. Pp. 95.

A7448   Ashe, Dora Jean. "The Non-Shakespearean Bad Quartos as Provincial Acting Versions."
        Renaissance Papers (Univ. South Carolina), 1954, pp. 57-61.

A7449   Flatter, Richard. "Some Instances of Line-Division in the First Folio." *SJ*, 92 (1956), 184-196.

A7450   Muir, Kenneth. "An Unfinished Prompt-Book." *SQ*, IX (1958), 420-422.

(c) MISCELLANEOUS

A7451   Engelen, Julia. *Die Schauspieler-Ökonomie in Shakespeares Dramen*. DD, Munster, 1926. Publ.
        in *SJ*, LXII (1926), 36-97.

A7452   Brandl, A. "Shakespeare-Möglichkeiten." Brandl, *Forschungen und Charakteristiken* (B4460),
        pp. 177-182.

A7453   Lawrence, W. J. "Something New About Shakespeare." *London Mercury*, XXXIV (1936),
        224-228.

A7454   Babb, Lawrence. "Sorrow and Love on the Elizabethan Stage." *SAB*, XVIII (1943), 137-142.

A7455   Sprague, Arthur Colby. *Shakespeare and the Actors. The Stage Business in His Plays (1660-1905)*.
        Harvard Univ. Press, 1944. Pp. xxvi, 440; il.
        Rev: by Edward Wagenknecht, *NYTBR*, July 16, 1944, p. 19; by J. W. Krutch, *Nation*,
        Aug. 16, 1944, pp. 216-217; by C. F. Tucker Brooke, *YR*, XXXIV, 169-171; by A. B. William-
        son, *QJS*, XXXI (1945), 249-250; by M. D., *Dublin Mag.*, XX, 57-59; by H. K. Fisher, *Life
        and Letters*, XLVI, 64-66; by Allardyce Nicoll, *UTQ*, XIV, 217-218; by E. Bradlee Watson,
        JEGP, XLIV, 220-222; by Bernard Jenkin, *RES*, XXI, 152-153; by Harley Granville-Barker,
        MLN, LX, 127-131; by H. S. Bennett, *NstN*, Apr. 21, 1945, pp. 260-261; by La Tourette
        Stockwell, *CE*, VI, 415; by F. S. Boas, *MLR*, XLI (1946), 72-73; *N &Q*, 192 (1947), 418; by
        L. L. Schücking, *Neues Europa*, III, Issue 6 (1948), 57-58; by Rudolf Stamm, *SJ*, 87/88 (1952),
        213.

A7456   Jordan, John E. "The Reporter of *Henry VI, Part 2*." *PMLA*, LXIV (1949), 1089-113.

A7457   Sprague, Arthur Colby. *The Stage Business in Shakespeare's Plays: A Postscript*. London: Society
        for Theatre Research Pamphlet Series, No. 3, 1953. Pp. 35.
        Rev: *TLS*, July 30, 1954, p. 491; by T. S. Dorsch, *YWES*, XXV, 102; by C. J. Sisson, *MLR*,
        L (1955), 364; by W. M. Merchant, *SQ*, VI, 179-180; by Glynne Wickham, *RES*, NS, VII
        (1956), 106.

A7458   Bromberg, Murray. "Theatrical Wagers: A Sidelight on the Elizabethan Drama." *N &Q*,
        196 (1951), 533-535.

A7459   Gerstner-Hirzel, Arthur. "Stagecraft and Poetry." *SJ*, 91 (1955), 196-211. Abstract of
        A7463.

A7460   Krabbe, Henning. *Bernard Shaw on Shakespeare and English Shakespearean Acting.* Publs. of
        Univ. Aarhus, XXVII, Supp. B. Aarhus, Denmark: Univ. Press, 1955.
            Rev: St. Vincent Troubridge, *SQ*, VIII (1957), 101-104.
A7461   Wilson, F. P. "The Elizabethan Theatre." *Neophil*, XXXIX (1955), 40-58.
            Rev: by H. Oppel, *NS*, IV (1955), 517.
A7462   Felver, Charles Stanley. *William Shakespeare and Robert Armin his Fool: A Working Partnership.*
        DD, University of Michigan, 1956. Pp. 352. Mic 56-3895. *DA*, XVI (1956), 2446. Publica-
        tion No. 18,601.
A7463   Gerstner-Hirzel, A. *The Economy of Action and Word in Shakespeare's Plays.* DD, Basel, 1955.
        For abstract, see A7459.
            Rev: A5611.
A7464   Schneideman, Robert Ivan. *Elizabethan Legerdemain and Its Employment in the Drama, 1576-
        1642.* DD, Northwestern University, 1956.
A7465   Smith, Irwin. "Ariel as Ceres." *SQ*, IX (1958), 430-432.

                        (4) "ACT TIME"; ACT AND SCENE DIVISIONS;
                             INTERVALS AND HOW FILLED (133;-)
                             (Transferred to Act and Scene Division VIII,2,b,(3).)
                        (5) COMMEDIA DELL'ARTE (133;43)
                             (a) THE ITALIAN IMPROVISED COMEDY (133;-)

A7466   Lea, K. M. *Italian Popular Comedy: A Study in the Commedia dell'arte 1560-1620 with Special
        Reference to the English Stage.* Oxford Univ. Press, 2 vols., 1934. Pp. 714.
        Ebisch & Schücking *Supplement*, p. 44.
            Rev: by Rob. Stumpfl, *DLZ*, LVII (1936), 1568-1570; by P. Meissner, *Beiblatt*, XLVIII
            (1937), 116-120.
A7467   Nicoll, Allardyce. *The Development of the Theatre.* New edition. New York: Harcourt Brace,
        1937. Pp. 309. Commedia dell'arte, pp. 105-115.
            Rev: A7063.
A7468   Boughner, Daniel C. "Don Armado and the *Commedia dell'arte*." *SP*, XXXVII (1940), 201-224.
A7469   McDowell, J. H. "Some Pictorial Aspects of Early *Commedia dell'arte* Acting." *SP*, XXXIX
        (1942), 47-64.
A7470   McDowell, John H. "Some Pictorial Aspects of Early Mountebank Stages." *PMLA*, LXI
        (1946), 84-96.
A7471   Cancelled.
A7472   Salerno, Henry Frank. *The Elizabethan Drama and the Commedia dell'arte.* DD, University of
        Illinois, 1956. Pp. 209. Mic 56-3021. *DA*, XVI (1956), 1901. Publication No. 18,195.
        Chap. III: "Traces of *Commedia dell'arte* in Shakespeare's plays."

                        (b) SHAKESPEARE AND THE IMPROVISED COMEDY
                             (134;-)

A7473   Capocci, Valentina. "Il dramma Shakespeariano e la commedia dell'arte." *Quaderni della
        Critica* (August, 1945), pp. 65-79.
A7474   Gentry, R. J. W. "Shakespeare and the Italian Comedy." *Ba*, XXXI (1947), 42-47.
A7475   Moore, John Robert. "Pantaloon as Shylock." *Boston Public Library Quarterly*, I (1949), 33-42.
A7476   Capocci, Valentina. *Genio e mestiere: Shakespeare e la Commedia dell'arte.* Bari: Laterza & figli,
        1950. Pp. 129.
            Rev: by Elio Gianturco, *Symposium*, V (1951), 368-372; by Gabriele Baldini, *NA*, April,
            1953, pp. 490, 500.
A7477   De Giorgi, C. B. Elsa. *Shakespeare e L'Attore.* Florence: Electa, 1950. Pp. 26.
A7478   Boughner, Daniel C. *The Braggart in Renaissance Comedy: A Study in Comparative Drama from
        Aristophanes to Shakespeare.* Minneapolis: Univ. of Minnesota Press, 1954. Pp. vii, 328.
            Rev: A6608.
A7479   Violi, Unicio J. *Shakespeare and the Lazzo.* DD, Columbia University, 1955. Pp. 282. Mic
        A55-1834. *DA*, XV (1955), 1391. Publication No. 12,479. Abstracted by Jack R. Brown,
        ShN, VII (1957), 4.
A7480   Hoeniger, F. D. "Two Notes on Cymbeline." *SQ*, VIII (1957), 132-133.
A7481   Kaufman, Helen Andrews. "*Trappolin Supposed a Prince* and *Measure for Measure*." *MLQ*,
        XVIII (1957), 113-124.

                        (6) DRAMATIC PLOTS (STAGE ABRIDGEMENTS) (134;44)
                             (Transferred to Art of the Actor, IX,2,g.
                             Specific Aspects (3), Miscellaneous (c).)
                        (7) THE DOUBLING OF ROLES AND NUMBER OF ACTORS
                             (134;-)
                             (Transferred along with preceding class)

X.   LITERARY TASTE IN SHAKESPEARE'S TIME (135;-)
     1.   RENAISSANCE LITERARY THEORY IN GENERAL
          a.   SOURCES

A7482   Smith, James Harry, and Edd W. Parks. *The Great Critics: An Anthology of Literary Criticism.*
        Rev. and enlarged ed.   New York: Norton, 1939.   Pp. 786.

A7483   Taille, J. de la. *De l'art de la tragédie.* Ed. by F. West. Editions de l'Université de Manchester,
        1939.   Pp. 39.
              Rev: by B. Weinberg, *MP*, xxxviii (1940), 216-217.

A7484   Gilbert, Allan H., ed. *Literary Criticism: Plato to Dryden.* Cincinnati: American Book Co.,
        1940.   Pp. 704.
              Rev: by C. P. Lyons, *South Atlantic Bulletin*, Oct., 1940, p. 11; by F. B. R. Godolphin,
              Classical Philology, xxxvi (1941), 315-316; by George Boas, *MLN*, lvi, 560; by A. S. P.
              Woodhouse, *UTQ*, xi (1942), 241-243.

A7485   Lawton, H. W., ed. *Handbook of French Renaissance Dramatic Theory.* Manchester: Univ.
        Press, 1950.   Pp. 150.
        Introduction and Reprints.

          b.   STUDIES
               See also Influence of Continental Literature, General, A4402-A4427, and
               subsequent sections.

A7486   Crane, William G. *Wit and Rhetoric in the Renaissance.* Columbia Univ. Press, 1937. Pp. viii,
        285.
              Rev: by Kathleen Tillotson, *RES*, xiv (1938), 466-467; by H. H. Hudson, *MLN*, liv
              (1939), 147-148; by G. D. Willcock, *MLR*, xxxiv, 84-85; by Clarence D. Thorpe, *JEGP*,
              xxxviii, 466-468; by René Pruvost, *EA*, iii (1939), 144-146; by Friedrich Brie, *Eng. Studn.*,
              lxxiii, 289-291.

A7487   Baldwin, Charles Sears. *Renaissance Literary Theory and Practice. Classicism in the Rhetoric and
        Poetic of Italy, France, and England, 1400-1600.* Ed. by Donald L. Clark. Columbia Univ.
        Press, 1939.   Pp. xiv, 251.
              Rev: by T. M. Pearce, *New Mexico Quarterly*, x (1940), 47-48; by Alice Walker, *RES*, xvi,
              336-337; by R. V. Merrill, *Library Quar.*, x, 301-302; by G. M., *Books Abroad*, xiv, 321; by
              F. M. Padelford, *MLQ*, ii (1941), 123-124; by A. H. Gilbert, *MLN*, lvi, 149-150; by J. W. H.
              Atkins, *MLR*, xxxvi, 522-524; by Louis Cons, *RR*, xxxii, 83-85; by C. D. Thorpe, *JEGP*,
              xl, 401-403.

A7488   Ashton, J. W. "Peter Martyr on the Function and Character of Literature." *PQ*, xviii (1939),
        311-314.

A7489   Ernst, Earle. *Cycles in the Development of the Dramatic Arts.* DD, Cornell University, 1940.
        Abstr. publ. in Cornell University *Abstracts of Theses*, 1940, Ithaca, 1941.

A7490   Hall, Vernon, Jr. *The Social Content of Renaissance Literary Criticism.* DD, University of
        Wisconsin, 1940. Abstr. publ. in Univ. of Wisconsin *Summaries of Doctoral Dissertations*,
        V (1940), 256-258.

A7491   Hite, John B. E. "Renaissance Criticism." *Abstracts of Theses, Bulletin of Tulane University*,
        1940, pp. 43-44.

A7492   Kuiper, G. *Orbis Artium en Renaissance. I. Cornelius Valerius en Sebastianus Foxius Morzillus
        als bronnen van Coornhert.* DD, Vrije Univ., Amsterdam. Harderwijk: Drukkerij Flevo,
        1941.   Pp. xx, 381.
        A study of manuals of dialectics, grammar, physics, ethics, rhetoric, etc., by Cornelius Valeria-
        nus and his pupil Foxius Morzillus with a consideration of their influence on contemporary
        authors—particularly on Coornhert's *Wellevenskunste* and Thomas Wilson's *Rule of Reason*
        (1551).
              Rev: by Z., *ES*, xxiii (1941), 158-159; by Z. Zyderveld, *Tijdschrift voor Ned. Taal- en
              Letterkunde*, lxiv, afl. 1-2, 77-80; by H. F. Bouchery, *De Gulden Passer*, nr, xx, 328-331; by
              E. Rombauts, *Leuvensche Bijdragen*, xxxiv (1942), nos. 1-2, Bijblad, 31-33.

A7493   Randolph, Mary C. "The Medical Concept in English Renaissance Satiric Theory: Its
        Possible Relationships and Implications." *SP*, xxviii (1941), 125-157.

A7494   Dean, Leonard F. "Bodin's *Methodus* in England Before 1625." *SP*, xxxix (1942), 160-166.

A7495   Johnson, Francis R. "Two Renaissance Textbooks of Rhetoric: Aphthonius' 'Progymnas-
        mata' and Rainolde's 'A Booke called the Foundacion of Rhetorike'." *HLQ*, vi (1943),
        427-444.

A7496   Wilson, Harold S. "Some Meanings of 'Nature' in Renaissance Literary Theory." *JHI*, ii
        (1941), 430-448.
        Identifies 35 differences of meaning.

A7497   Weinberg, Bernard. "The Poetic Theories of Minturno." *Studies in Honor of Frederick W.
        Shipley* (Washington Univ. Press, 1942), pp. 101-129.

A7498   Campbell, Lily B. "The Conflict Between History and Literature." *HLQ*, vi (1942/43), 31.
        George Sensabaugh comments upon Miss Campbell's papers, p. 34.

A7499   Giovannini, G. "Agnolo Segni and a Renaissance Definition of Poetry." *MLQ*, VI (1945), 167-173.

A7500   Hall, Vernon, Jr. *Renaissance Literary Criticism: A Study of Its Social Content.* Columbia Univ. Press, 1945. Pp. viii, 264.
         Rev: by Robert J. Clements, *NYTBR*, Oct. 21, 1945, p. 14; by L. Hughes, *Thought*, XXI (1946), 163-165; *TLS*, Mar. 9, 1946, p. 116; by F. Michael Krouse, *MLN*, LXI, 135-136; by Hardin Craig, *AHR*, LI, 493-495; by J. W. H. Atkins, *MLR*, XLI, 429-430; by Elizabeth Sweeting, *RES*, XXIII (1947), 68-69.

A7501   Taylor, Archer. *Renaissance Guides to Books: An Inventory and Some Conclusions.* Univ. Calif. Press, 1945. Pp. 130.
         Rev: by A. T. Hazen, *Library Quar.*, XVI (1946), 250-252; by Felix Gilbert, *AHR*, LI, 740; by D. Bush, *JEGP*, XLV, 456-457; by R. Offor, *MLR*, XLI, 428-429; by F. R. Johnson, *MLQ*, VIII (1947), 124-125; by F. P. Wilson, *RES*, XXIII, 276-277; by K. J. Holzknecht, *Papers Bibl. Soc. Amer.*, XLI, 71-72.

A7502   Carapetyan, Armen. "The Concept of *Imitazione della natura* in the Sixteenth Century." *Jour. of Renaissance and Baroque Music*, I (1946), 47-67.

A7503   Herrick, Marvin T. *The Fusion of Horatian and Aristotelian Literary Criticism, 1531-1555.* Univ. Illinois Studies in Lang. and Lit., XXXII, No. 1. Univ. Illinois Press, 1946. Pp. vii, 117.
         Rev: by F. S. Boas, *English*, VI (1947), 313-314; by Allan H. Gilbert and Henry Snuggs, *JEGP*, XLVI, 233-247; by J. W. H. Atkins, *RES*, XXIV (1948), 152-153; by V. Hall, Jr., *MLN*, LXIII, 209-211; by H. T. Swedenberg, Jr., *MLQ*, IX, 355-357; by H. L. Tracey, *Classical Philology*, XLIII, 280; by A. M. Clark, *CR*, LXII, 30-31; by G. D. Willcock, *MLR*, XLIII, 525-526; by H. F. Bonchery, *RBPH*, XXVII (1949), 175-179.

A7504   Stafford, J. "The Social Status of Renaissance Literary Critics." *Studies in English, 1945-1946,* University of Texas, pp. 72-97.

A7505   Baldwin, T. W. *Shakspere's Five-Act Structure: Shakspere's Early Plays on the Background of Renaissance Theories of Five-Act Structure from 1470.* Univ. Illinois Press, 1947. Pp. xiii, 848.
         Rev: A5938.

A7506   Herrick, Marvin T. "Some Neglected Sources of Admiratio." *MLN*, LXII (1947), 222-226.

A7507   Roditi, Edouard. "The Genesis of Neoclassical Tragedy." *South Atlantic Quar.*, XLVI (1947), 93-108.

A7508   Hall, Vernon, Jr. "Scaliger's Defense of Poetry." *PMLA*, LXIII (1948), 1125-30.

A7509   Robbins, Edwin W. *Theories of Characterization in Commentaries on Terence Before 1600.* DD, University of Illinois, 1948. Pp. 377.

A7510   Allen, Don C. *The Legend of Noah: Renaissance Rationalism in Art, Science, and Letters.* Urbana: Ill. Studies in Lang. and Lit., XXXIII, Nos. 3-4, 1949.
         Rev: A3943.

A7511   Herrick, Marvin T. "The Theory of the Laughable in the Sixteenth Century." *QJS*, XXXV (1949), 1-16.

A7512   Baroway, Israel. "The Accentual Theory of Hebrew Prosody: A Further Study in Renaissance Interpretation of Biblical Form." *ELH*, XVII (1950), 115-135.

A7513   Herrick, Marvin T. *Comic Theory in the Sixteenth Century.* Illinois Studies in Lang. and Lit., XXXIV, Nos. 1-2. Urbana: Univ. of Illinois Press, 1950. Pp. viii, 248.
         Rev: by H. Carrington Lancaster, *MLN*, LXVI (1951), 428; by Douglas Bush, *JEGP*, L, 265-266; by Bernard Weinberg, *MP*, XLVIII, 271-273; by L. Bakelants, *RBPH*, XXX (1952), 202-205; by G. D. Willcock, *RES*, NS, IV (1953), 73-74.

A7514   Keller, Abraham C. "Ancients and Moderns in the Early Seventeenth Century." *MLQ*, XI (1950), 79-82.

A7515   Wilkins, Ernest H. "A General Survey of Renaissance Petrarchism." *CL*, II (1950), 327-342.

A7516   Carter, William H., Jr. *Ut pictura poesis: A Study of the Parallel Between Painting and Poetry from Classical Times through the Seventeenth Century.* DD, Harvard University, 1951.

A7517   Kristeller, Paul O. "The Modern System of the Arts: A Study in the History of Aesthetics." *JHI*, XII (1951), 495-527. The Renaissance, pp. 510-521.

A7518   Lawton, Harold W. "L'heatontimorumenos de Térence, J.-C. Scaliger, et les unités dramatiques." *Mélanges Chamard*, 1951, pp. 205-209.

A7519   Robbins, Edwin W. *Dramatic Characterization in the Printed Commentaries on Terence, 1473-1600.* Illinois Stud. in Lang. and Lit., XXXV, No. 4. Univ. Illinois Press, 1951. Pp. ix, 122.
         Rev: by Peter Ure, *RES*, NS, IV (1953), 229; by Terence Spencer, *MLR*, XLVIII, 458-459; by Harry Caplan, *JEGP*, LII, 110-112.

A7520   Kermode, Frank, ed. *English Pastoral Poetry: From the Beginnings to Marvell.* Life, Literature and Thought Library, London: Harrap, 1952. Pp. 256.
         Chapters on Renaissance Pastoral theory and form and nearly 200 pages of texts. Excerpt from *Winter's T.*

A7521   Gaither, Mary E. *Ancient and Modern Concepts of the Tragic Hero.* DD, Indiana University, 1953. Pp. 151. Mic A53-905. *DA*, XIII (1953), 547. Publication No. 5313.

A7522 Givoannini, G. "Historical Realism and the Tragic Emotions in Renaissance Criticism." *PQ*, XXXII (1953), 304-320.

A7523 Kellogg, George A. "Bridges' *Milton's Prosody* and Renaissance Metrical Theory." *PMLA*, LXVIII (1953), 268-285.

A7524 Dollarhide, Louis E. *Shakespeare's "Richard III" and Renaissance Rhetoric.* DD, University of North Carolina, 1954.

A7525 Gindin, James J. *Renaissance and Modern Theories of Irony: Their Application to Donne's "Songs and Sonnets."* DD, Cornell University, 1954. Pp. 192. Mic A54-3076. *DA*, XIV (1954), 2066-67. Publication No. 9750.

A7526 O'Brien, G. W. *Renaissance Poetics and the Problem of Power.* Chicago, 1956.
Rev: A1726.

A7527 Fucilla, Joseph G. "A Rhetorical Pattern in Renaissance and Baroque Poetry." *Studies in the Renaissance*, III (1957), 23-48.

A7528 Janssen, Anna Mae. *The Guilds of Rhetoric in the Low Countries During the Fifteenth and Sixteenth Centuries.* DD, Northwestern University, 1957. Pp. 208. Mic 57-4970. *DA*, XVII (1957), 3122. Publication No. 23,517.

A7529 Soens, Adolph L., Jr. *Criticism of Formal Satire in the Renaissance.* DD, Princeton University, 1957.

A7530 Armstrong, W. A. "*Damon and Pithias* and Renaissance Theories of Tragedy." *ES*, XXXIX (1958), 200-207.

A7531 Holt, Albert Hamilton. "The Nature of the Dramatic Illusion and Its Violations in Jonson's Comedies: His Precedents in Theory and Practice." DD, Vanderbilt University. *DA*, XVIII (1958), 1786-87.

A7532 Ukas, Michael William. *The Theory and Practice of Italian Tragicomedy During the Sixteenth Century.* DD, University of Toronto, 1958.

A7533 Bryant, Donald, ed. *The Rhetorical Idiom. Essays . . . Presented to Herbert August Wichelns.* Ithaca: Cornell Univ. Press, 1958. Pp. viii, 334.
Includes, *i.a.*, Wilbur Samuel Howell, "Renaissance Rhetoric and Modern Rhetoric: A Study in Change," pp. 53-70; Karl R. Wallace, "Rhetoric, Politics, and Education of the Ready Man," pp. 71-95; Frederick G. Marcham, "Oliver Cromwell, Orator," pp. 179-200; Marvin T. Herrick, "The Revolt in Tragicomedy Against the Grand Style," pp. 271-280; Donald C. Bryant, " 'A Peece of a Logician': The Critical Essayist as Rhetorician," pp. 293-314 (Sidney, Dryden and others); James Hutton, "Rhetorical Doctrine and Some Poems of Ronsard," pp. 315-334.

(1) SUPPLEMENT: RAMUS
See also section on Ramus in Imagery, A5720-A5725.

A7534 French, J. Milton. "Milton, Ramus, and Edward Phillips." *MP*, XLVII (1949), 82-87.

A7535 Moltmann, Jürgen. "Zur Bedeutung des Petrus Ramus für Philosophie und Theologie im Calvinismus." *Zeitschrift für Kirchengeschichte*, 1957, Heft iii-iv.

A7536 Ong, Walter J., S. J. *Ramus, Method, and the Decay of Dialogue.* Harvard Univ. Press, 1958. Pp. 408.

A7537 Ong, Walter J., S. J. *Ramus and Talon Inventory.* Harvard Univ. Press, 1958. Pp. 558.
Rev: by Thomas R. Hartmann, *SCN*, XVII (1959), 32-33; by Pierre Mesnard, *BHR*, XXI, No. 2 (April, 1959), 568-576.

A7538 Hooykaas, R. *Humanisme, Science et Réforme: Pierre de la Ramée (1515-1572).* Leiden: E. J. Brill, 1958. Pp. xii, 133.

2. ENGLISH RENAISSANCE LITERARY THEORY (135;-)
a. SOURCES (135;-)

A7539 Ebisch, Walther, and L. L. Schücking. "Bibliographie zur Gesch. d. literar. Geschmacks in England." *Anglia*, LXIII (1939), 1-64.

A7540 Smith, G. G., ed. *Elizabethan Critical Essays.* (With an introduction.) 2 Vols. Oxford Univ. Press, 1937.

A7541 Smith, James Harry, and Edd W. Parks. *The Great Critics: An Anthology of Literary Criticism.* Rev. and enlarged ed. New York: Norton, 1939. Pp. 786.

A7542 Gilbert, Allan H., ed. *Literary Criticism: Plato to Dryden.* Cincinnati: American Book Co., 1940. Pp. 704.
Rev: A7484.

A7543 Ward, A. C., ed. *Specimens of English Dramatic Criticism, Seventeenth-Twentieth Centuries.* Oxford, 1945. Pp. 356.
Rev: A7730.

A7544 Meres, Francis. *Francis Meres' Treatise "Poetrie."* A critical edition by Don Cameron Allen. Univ. of Illinois Press, 1933.
Rev: by H. B. Lathrop, *MLN*, L (1935), 198-200; by C. R. Baskervill, *MP*, XXXIII, 195-197;

by A. Koszul, *RCHL*, 68e an., 393-394; by G. C. Moore Smith, *MLR*, xxx, 361-363; by Norman E. Nelson, *JEGP*, xxxiv, 285-286; by R. B. McK., *RES*, xiv (1938), 88-91; by H. C. Matthes, *Beiblatt*, L (1939), 72-79.

A7545   Meres, Francis. *Palladis Tamia*. With Preface by Don Cameron Allen. Scholars' Facsimiles and Reprints. New York, 1939.
Rev: by S. A. T., *SAB*, xiv (1939), 128; *TLS*, Apr. 28, 1939, p. 239.

A7546   Hoskins, John. *Directions for Speech and Style*. Ed. with introduction and notes by Hoyt H. Hudson. Princeton Univ. Press, 1935.
See letter by Bernard M. Wagner, *TLS*, Oct. 3, 1936, p. 791, which calls attention to the existence of a second MS copy of the *Directions*, preserved in the Bodleian Library.
Rev: *TLS*, June 27, 1936, p. 539; by Karl Brunner, *Beiblatt*, xLVII, 264-265; *N &Q*, 171 (1936), 305; by J. Delcourt, *RAA*, xiii, 511; by A. Dekker, *Neophil*, xxii (1937), 217-218; by R. W. Zandvoort, *ES*, xix, 177-178; by G. D. Willcock, *MLR*, xxxii, 291-293; by Don Cameron Allen, *MLN*, LII, 444-445; by Norman E. Nelson, *JEGP*, xxxvi, 608-609; by G. Tillotson, *RES*, xiv (1938), 97-99.

A7547   Puttenham, George. *The Arte of English Poesie*. Ed. by Gladys Doidge Willcock and Alice Walker. Cambridge Univ. Press, 1936. Pp. cx, 359.
Rev: *TLS*, Feb. 29, 1936, p. 179; by Geoffrey Tillotson, *Criterion*, xv, 716-718; by A. Koszul, *RAA*, xiii, 433; *Spectator*, Mar. 20, 1936, p. 544; *N &Q*, 171 (1936), 180; *London Mercury*, xxxiii, 670; by Don Cameron Allen, *MLN*, LII (1937), 444-445; by Geoffrey Bullough, *MLR*, xxxii, 605-607; by George Williamson, *MP*, xxxv, 197-198; by H. F. B. B.-S., *Oxford Mag.*, LVI (Oct. 14, 1937), 33; by H. J. Byrom, *RES*, xiv (1938), 81-86.

A7548   Rainolde, R. *The Foundacion of Rhetorike . . . 1563*. Ed. by F. R. Johnson. New York: Scholars' Facsimiles & Reprints, 1945. Pp. xxiv, facs (124).

A7549   Leishman, J. B., ed. *The Three Parnassus Plays*. London: Nicholson, 1949.
Rev: by Giles Romilly, *NstN*, xxxviii (1949), 586, 588; *TLS*, Jan. 27, 1950, p. 59; by Harold Jenkins, *RES*, NS, ii (1951), 165-166; by M. W. Stephens, *CamJ*, iv, 438-443.

A7550   Peacham, Henry. *The Garden of Eloquence, 1593*. A Facsimile Reprod. with an Introd. by William S. Crane. Gainsville, Fla.: Scholars' Facsimiles & Reprints, 1954. Pp. 280.

A7551   Jonson, Ben. *Ben Jonson's Timber or Discoveries*. Ed. by Ralph S. Walker. Syracuse: Syracuse Univ. Press, 1955.
Rev: J. C. Bryce, *Aberdeen Univ. Rev.*, xxxvi (1955), 189-190.

b. STUDIES
See also entries under VI, 4, b, (1), Tudor Principles, A4669-A4675.
(1) GENERAL (137;-)

A7552   Bateson, F. W. *English Poetry and the English Language: An Experiment in Literary History*. New York and London: Oxford Univ. Press, 1934. Pp. vii, 129.
Rev: by M. E. Prior, *MP*, xxxiii (1936), 87-91; by Owen Barfield, *MLN*, LI, 407-408; by B. Fehr, *Lbl*, LVII, 31-34; by K. Arns, *Eng. Studn.*, LXXI, 281-282.

A7553   White, Harold Ogden. *Plagiarism and Imitation During the English Renaissance: A Study in Critical Distinctions*. Harvard Studies in Eng., XII. Harvard Univ. Press, 1935. Pp. x, 209.
Rev: by E. W. N., *Dalhousie Rev.*, xv (1935), 130-131; *TLS*, April 11, 1935, p. 246; by Don Cameron Allen, *JEGP*, xxxiv, 597-599; by Douglas Bush, *MLN*, LI (1936), 198-199; by Geoffrey Bullough, *MLR*, xxxi, 211-213; by Austin Warren, *SR*, xLIV, 244-246; by Alice Walker, *RES*, xiii (1937), 88-90.

A7554   Woesler, Richard. *Die ständische Schichtung des Schriftstellertums in der englischen Renaissance*. DD, Berlin, Humboldt Univ., 1936. Pp. x, 92.
Rev: by A. Brandl, *Archiv*, 171 (1937), 120; by W. Keller, *SJ*, LXXIII (1937), 169-170; by Walter Schrinner, *Beiblatt*, xLIX (1938), 13-16.

A7555   Cancelled.

A7556   Bottrall, Margaret. "George Chapman's Defense of Difficulty in Poetry." *Criterion*, xvi (1937), 638-654.

A7557   Mason, V. *An Historical and Critical Background for the Study of English Romantic Tragedy*. DD, University of Washington, 1937. Abstr. in Univ. of Washington, *Abstracts of Theses*, ii (1937), 123-125.

A7558   Iwatsuki, Tachiwo. "On the Changing Literary Modes in the Development of Renaissance Tragedy." *Studies in Eng. Lit.* (Eng. Lit. Soc. Japan), xviii (1938), 486-505.

A7559   Kreuzer, J. R. "Some Earlier Examples of the Rhetorical Device in *Ralph Roister Doister*." *RES*, xiv (1938), 321-323.

A7560   Wilson, Harold S. *Concepts of 'Nature' in the Rhetorical Tradition: A Chapter in the History of Classical Humanism Before Ben Jonson*. DD, Harvard University, 1939. Abstr. publ. in Harvard University *Summaries of Theses*, 1939, Cambridge, 1942, pp. 255-257.

A7561   Giovannini, G. *The Theory of Tragedy as History in Renaissance and Neo-Classical Criticism*. DD, University of Michigan, 1940.

A7562   Hall, Vernon, Jr. *The Social Content of Renaissance Literary Criticism*. DD, University of Wisconsin, 1940. Abstr. publ. in Univ. of Wisconsin *Summaries of Doctoral Dissertations, 1939-40*, Madison, 1940, pp. 256-258. Published version, A7500.

A7563   Rushton, Urban Joseph Peters. *The Development of Historical Criticism in England, 1532-1700.*
        DD, Princeton University, 1940. Pp. 307. *DA*, XII (1952), 308. (No abstract published.)
        Publication No. 3037.
        Chapter II: "The Elizabethan Critics," pp. 31-80.

A7564   Sweeting, E. J. *Studies in Early Tudor Criticism.* Oxford: Blackwell, 1940. Pp. xvi, 176.
        Rev: *Life and Letters Today*, XXVI (1940), 284; *TLS*, Aug. 31, 1940, p. 424; by F. M.
        Padelford, *MLQ*, II (1941), 124-126; by J. W. H. Atkins, *MLR*, XXXVI, 522-524.

A7565   Berringer, Ralph W. "The Reaction in the Poetry of 1595-1620 Against Elizabethan Con-
        ventionalism." DD, University of California, 1941. Abstr. in Univ. of California, *Programme
        of Final Examination*, Jan. 24, 1941.

A7566   Macclean, Norman F. *The Theory of Lyric Poetry in England from the Renaissance to Coleridge.*
        DD, University of Chicago, 1941. Pp. 193.

A7567   McCulley, Cecil Michael. "Dramatic Criticism in the English Renaissance." DD, Southern
        Methodist University, 1941. Abstr. in Southern Methodist Univ., *Abstracts of Theses*, Dallas,
        Texas, VIII (1941), 45-46.

A7568   Potter, George Reuben. "A Protest Against the Term *Conceit.*' *Renaissance Studies in Honor
        of Hardin Craig* (Stanford Univ. Press, 1941), pp. 282-291; also *PQ*, XX (1941), 474-482.

A7569   Randolph, Mary Claire. "The Medical Concept in English Renaissance Satiric Theory: Its
        Possible Relationships and Implications." *SP*, XXXVIII (1941), 125-157.

A7570   Wetzel, Günther. *Die literarische Kritik in England von Sidney bis Dryden.* DD, Kiel, 1941.
        Pp. 168. Typewritten.

A7571   Wilson, Harold S. "Some Meanings of 'Nature' in Renaissance Literary Theory." *JHI*, II
        (1941), 430-448.

A7572   Dean, Leonard F. "Bodin's 'Methodus' in England Before 1625." *SP*, XXXIX (1942), 160-166.

A7573   Hudson, Hoyt H. "The Transition in Poetry." *HLQ*, V (1942), 188-190.
        Taking place about 1595. "Psychological and erotic realism"; "rationalism, skepticism and
        cynicism."

A7574   Jones, Richard F. "The Moral Sense of Simplicity." *Studies in Honor of Frederick W. Shipley*
        (Washington Univ. Press, 1942), pp. 265-287.

A7575   Swallow, Alan. "Principles of Poetic Composition from Skelton to Sidney." *Univ. Bulletin
        Louisiana State Univ.*, NS, XXXIV (1942), 21-23. Abstr. of dissertation.

A7576   Johnson, Francis R. "Two Renaissance Textbooks of Rhetoric: Aphthonius' *Progymnasmata*
        and Rainolde's *A Booke called the Foundacion of Rhetorike.*" *HLQ*, VI (1943), 427-444.

A7577   Jones, Juanita. *The Theory of Comic Drama in England Before 1625.* DD, State University of
        Iowa, 1943. Abstr. in Univ. of Iowa *Doctoral Diss.: Abstracts and References*, VI (1953), 426-427.

A7578   Orsini, Napoleone. "L'arte degli autori al tempo di Shakespeare." *Riv. Italiana del Teatro,*
        VII (1943), 135-151.

A7579   Renfer, Katharina. *A Contribution to the Study of Style in Elizabethan Classical Drama.* DD,
        Neuchâtel, 1943. Berne: Grunau, 1943. Pp. 109.

A7580   Atkins, J. W. H. *English Literary Criticism: The Medieval Phase.* Cambridge Univ. Press, 1944
        Pp. ix, 211.
        Rev: A3599.

A7581   Bishop, Roger J. *The Doctrine of Poetic Inspiration in English Renaissance and Seventeenth Century
        Literature, and Its Background.* MA thesis, Toronto, 1944. Pp. 162.

A7582   Musgrove, S. *The Changing Values in the Critical and Literary Outlook of the Seventeenth Century,
        as Manifested in English Verse Translation from the Greek and Latin Classics.* DD, Oxford,
        Merton, 1944.

A7583   Orsini, N. "La coscienza della lingua nel Rinascimento: Shakespeare." *Anglica*, I (1946),
        200-203.

A7584   Stafford, John. "The Social Status of Renaissance Literary Critics." *Univ. Texas Studies in
        Eng., 1945/46*, pp. 72-97.

A7585   Atkins, J. W. H. *English Literary Criticism: The Renascence.* London: Methuen, 1947. Pp.
        xi, 371.
        Rev: by F. G. Mackarill, *Life and Letters*, LVII (1948), 268-272; *TLS*, Feb. 14, 1948, p. 91;
        by H. B. C., *MGW*, Jan. 1, 1948, p. 11; by A. P. Rossiter, *CamJ*, I, 385-388; by D. C. Allen,
        MLN, LXIII, 508; by E. H. W. Meyerstein, *English*, VII, 138-139; by Malcolm Ross, *Canadian
        Forum*, XXVIII, 21; by *NstN*, June 19, 1948, p. 509; by F. R. Johnson, *QJS*, XXXIV, 515-516; by
        Desmond MacCarthy, *Sun. Times*, Mar. 21, 1948, p. 3; by G. D. Willcock, *RES*, XXV (1949),
        70-71; by M. T. Herrick, *JEGP*, XLVIII, 286-289; by H. S. Wilson, *UTQ*, XVIII, 402-405;
        by K. Dockhorn, *Archiv*, 188 (1951), 140-142.

A7586   McClennen, Joshua. *On the Meaning and Function of Allegory in the English Renaissance.* Univ.
        Michigan Contributions in Mod. Phil., No. 6, Univ. Michigan Press, 1947. Pp. 38.

A7587   Eldredge, Frances. *Criteria for Lyric in the Later English Renaissance.* DD, University of Chicago,
        1948. Pp. 331.

A7588   Orna, Norah E. *The Relation Between Theory and Practice in Elizabethan and Jacobean Comedy,
        1570-1616.* MA thesis, University of London, 1948.

A7589   Brooks, Harold F. "The 'Imitation' in English Poetry, Especially in Formal Satire, Before the Age of Pope." *RES*, xxv (1949), 124-140.

A7590   Wallerstein, Ruth C. "Rhetoric in the English Renaissance: Two Elegies." *EIE, 1948.* New York: Columbia Univ. Press; London: Oxford Univ. Press, 1949, pp. 153-178.

A7591   Baine, Rodney M. "The First Anthologies of English Literary Criticism, Warton C. Haselwood." *SB*, III (1950), 262-265.

A7592   Bredvold, Louis I. "The Rise of English Classicism: A Study in Methodology." *CL*, II (1950), 253-268.

A7593   Thaler, Alwin. "Literary Criticism in *A Mirror for Magistrates*." *JEGP*, xLIX (1950), 1-13.

A7594   Wallerstein, Ruth. *Studies in Seventeenth Century Poetic.* Madison: Univ. of Wisconsin Press, 1950. Pp. x, 421.
        Rev: *N &Q*, 195 (1950), 528; by M. Mincoff, *ES*, xxxII, 38-39; by Harriet Zinnes, *Poetry*, 80 (1950), 163-165; by Louis L. Martz, *YR*, xL, 562-565; *UTQ*, xxI, 97-99; by Allan Gilbert, *South Atlantic Quarterly*, LI, 177-179; *TLS*, Sept. 15, 1950, p. 582; by K. Koller, *MLN*, LXVII, 567-569; by L. C. Martin, *MLR*, xLVI, 486-487.

A7595   West, Bill Covode. *Anti-Petrarchism: A Study of the Reaction Against the Courtly Tradition in English Love-Poetry from Wyatt to Donne.* DD, Northwestern University, 1950. Abstr. in Northwestern Univ. *Summaries of Doctoral Dissertations*, xVIII (1950), 35-37.

A7596   Allison, Alexander W. "Poetry and Rhetoric: In Defense of Elizabethan Criticism." *English Studies in Honor of James Southall Wilson*, ed. by Fredson Bowers, Charlottesville, 1951, pp. 203-210.

A7597   Clark, Donald Lemen. "Ancient Rhetoric and English Renaissance Literature." *SQ*, II (1951), 195-204.

A7598   Dundas, Oenone J. *The Concept of Wit in English Literary Criticism, 1579-1650.* MA thesis, University of London, 1951.

A7599   Popkin, Henry. *Dramatic Theory of the Elizabethan and Jacobean Playwrights.* DD, Harvard University, 1951.

A7600   Bethell, S. L. *The Cultural Revolution of the Seventeenth Century.* London: Dobson, 1952. Pp. 161. Chapter IV: "The Two Universes in Literary Theory and Practice," pp. 69-114. (Shak., p. 73-86).
        Rev: A3963.

A7601   Clark, Donald L. "The Rise and Fall of Progymnasmata in Sixteenth and Seventeenth Century Grammar Schools." *Speech Monographs*, xIX (1952), 259-263.

A7602   Evans, Maurice. "Metaphor and Symbol in the Sixteenth Century." *EIC*, III (1953), 267-284.

A7603   Condon, Helen M. *The Ethical Element in Literary Criticism of the English Renaissance.* DD, Stanford University, 1954.

A7604   Davie, Donald. "Sixteenth-Century Poetry and the Common Reader. The Case of Thomas Sackville." *EIC*, IV (1954), 117-127.
        Rev: by J. B. Broadbent, "Sixteenth-Century Poetry and the Common Reader," *EIC*, IV (1954), 421-426. Davie answers, ibid., pp. 426-428; F. W. Bateson comments, ibid., pp. 428-430.

A7605   Doran, Madeleine. *Endeavors of Art: A Study of Form in Elizabethan Drama.* Univ. Wisconsin Press, 1954. Pp. xv, 482.
        Rev: A7827.

A7606   Bradbrook, M. C. *The Growth and Structure of Elizabethan Comedy.* London: Chatto and Windus, 1955. Pp. ix, 246.
        Rev: B5197.

A7607   Benham, Allen R. "Horace and His *Ars Poetica* in English: A Bibliography." *Classical Weekly*, xLIX (1956), 1-5.

A7608   Howell, Wilbur Samuel. *Logic and Rhetoric in England, 1500-1700.* Princeton Univ. Press, 1956.
        Rev: by Donald C. Bryant, *QJS*, xLII (1956), 304-306; by W. J. Ong, S. J., *RN*, IX, 206-211; by William T. Costello, S. J., *New Scholasticism*, xxxI (1957), 287-288; by Francis R. Johnson, *MP*, LIV, 273-275; by Harris Fletcher, *JEGP*, LVI, 266-268; by Marvin T. Herrick, *SQ*, VIII, 551-552; by Porter G. Perrin, *MLQ*, xVIII, 339-340; by Rosemond Tuve, *MLN*, LXXIII (1958), 206-211; by H. L. S., *Personalist*, xxxIX, 283.

A7609   Gilbert, Allan H., ed. *Renaissance Papers.* A selection of papers presented at the Renaissance Meeting in the Southeastern States, Duke University, April 12-13, 1957.
        Contains: A. G. D. Wiles, "James Johnstown and the *Arcadian Style*," pp. 72-81; Philip J. Traci, "The Literary Qualities of Puttenham's *Arte of English Poesie*," pp. 87-93.

A7610   Hale, Hilda Louise Hanson. *Conventions and Characteristics in the English Funeral Elegy of the Earlier Seventeenth Century.* DD, University of Missouri, 1957.

A7611   Shafter, Edward Merl, Jr. *A Study of Rhetorical Invention in Selected English Rhetorics, 1550-1600.* DD, University of Michigan, 1957. Pp. 243. Mic 57-2274. *DA*, xVII (1957), 1415. Publication No. 21,360.

A7612 McMahon, Fred R., Jr. *A History of the Concepts of Style in English Public Address: 1600-1700.* DD, University of Southern California, 1958.

A7613 Sherwin, Wilma. *The Rhetorical Structure of the English Sermon in the Sixteenth Century.* DD, University of Illinois, 1958. Pp. 180. Mic 58-5495. *DA*, XIX (1958), 1072.

A7614 Staton, Walter F., Jr. ""The Characters of Style in Elizabethan Prose." *JEGP*, LVII (1958), 197-207.

(a) HARVEY, NASHE, AND THE PARNASSUS PLAYS

A7615 Sackton, Alexander H. "Thomas Nashe as an Elizabethan Critic." Univ. of Texas, *Studies in English*, 1947, pp. 18-25.

A7616 Latham, Agnes M. C. "Satire on Literary Themes and Modes in Nashe's 'Unfortunate Traveller'." *ES*, NS, I (1948), 85-100.

A7617 Schrickx, W. "The Portraiture of Gabriel Harvey in the Parnassus Plays and John Marston." *Neophil*, XXXVI (1952), 225-234.

A7618 Summersgill, Travis L. "Harvey, Nashe, and the Three Parnassus Plays." *PQ*, XXXI (1952), 94-95.

A7619 Tate, Gary Lee. *Gabriel Harvey: Catalyst in the English Literary Renaissance.* DD, University of New Mexico, 1958.

(b) LAW

A7620 Youel, Donald B. *The Idea of Law in English Literary Criticism: 16th and 17th Centuries.* DD, State University of Iowa, 1945. Abstr. in Univ. of Iowa *Programs Announcing Candidates for Higher Degrees*, 1944.

A7621 Schoeck, R. J. "Rhetoric and Law in Sixteenth-Century England." *SP*, L (1953), 110-127.

A7622 Bland, D. S. "Rhetoric and the Law Student in Sixteenth-Century England." *SP*, LIV (1957), 498-508.

(2) SPECIFIC AUTHORS (136;-)
(a) BACON

A7623 Wallace, Karl R. *Francis Bacon on Communication and Rhetoric, or: The Art of Applying Reason to Imagination for the Better Moving of the Will.* Univ. North Carolina Press, 1943. Pp. 277.
Rev: by J. E. Baker, *PQ*, XXII (1943), 287-288.

A7624 McNamee, Maurice B., S. J. "Literary Decorum in Francis Bacon." *St. Louis Univ. Studies*, Ser. A, I (1950), 1-52.

(b) DONNE

A7625 Stein, Arnold. "Donne's Harshness and Elizabethan Tradition." *SP*, XLI (1944), 390-409.

A7626 Stein, Arnold. "John Donne's Obscurity and the Elizabethan Tradition." *ELH*, XIII (1946), 98-118.

(c) GREVILLE

A7627 Edwards, D. C. "Fulke Greville on Tragedy." *TLS*, June 8, 1940, p. 279.

A7628 Morris, I. *Shakespeare and Greville: Their Tragic Characters Compared. An Attempt to Re-define the Principles of Shakespearean Tragedy in the Light of Elizabethan Thought.* B. Litt. thesis, Oxford, 1954.

(d) JONSON

A7629 Shillinglaw, A. T. "New Light on *Discoveries*." *Eng. Studn.*, LXXI (1937), 356-359.

A7630 Neumann, Joshua H. "Notes on Ben Jonson's English." *PMLA*, LIV (1939), 736-763.

A7631 Baum, Helena Watts. *The Satiric and the Didactic in Ben Jonson's Comedies.* Univ. North Carolina Press, 1947. Pp. x, 192.
Rev: by G. B. Johnston, *South Atlantic Bul.*, XIV (1948), 13-14; by G. B. Evans, *JEGP*, XLVII, 306-308; by F. R. Johnson, *MLN*, LXIV (1949), 213; by A. Davenport, *MLR*, XLIV, 402-403.

A7632 Snuggs, Henry L. "The Source of Jonson's Definition of Comedy." *MLN*, LXV (1950), 543-544.

A7633 Walker, Ralph S. "Literary Criticism in Jonson's Conversations with Drummond." *English*, VIII (1950/1951), 222-227.

A7634 Bryant, Joseph Allen, Jr. "The Significance of Ben Jonson's First Requirement for Tragedy: 'Truth of Argument'." *SP*, XLIX (1952), 195-213.

A7635 Walker, Ralph S. "Ben Jonson's *Discoveries*: A New Analysis." (The Eng. Assoc.) *Essays and Studies*, V (1952), 32-51.

A7636 Withington, Eleanor. "Nicholas Briot and Jonson's Commendation of Joseph Rutter." *N & Q*, 198 (1953), 152-153.

A7637 McGinnis, Paul J. "Ben Jonson's *Discoveries*." *N &Q*, NS, IV (1957), 162-163.

(e) MERES

A7638   Matthes, H. Ch. "Zur ersten eingehenderen Lobpreisung Shakespeares." *SJ*, LXXV (1939), 116-126.

A7639   Matthes, Heinrich Christoph. "Francis Meres und Erasmus von Rotterdam." *Anglia*, LXIII (1939), 426-435.

A7640   Matthes, Heinrich Christoph. "Zum Quellenproblem der *Palladis Tamia*." *Anglia*, LXV (1941), 104-152.
        Rev: Germ Mann, *Archiv*, 180 (1941), 54.

A7641   Va Unger, Emma. "A Note on Three Copies of Meres's *Palladis Tamia*, 1598." *To Doctor R.: Essays Here Collected and Published in Honor of the Seventieth Birthday of Dr. A. S. W. Rosenbach.* Philadelphia: Privately printed, 1946, pp. 215-217.

(f) PUTTENHAM

A7642   Madden, Wilhelm Heinrich. *Die Sprache in George Puttenhams "The Arte of English Poesie."* DD, Tübingen, 1893.

A7643   Eagle, R. L. "Authorship of *The Arte of English Poesie* (1589)." *Ba*, XXVII (1943), 38-41.

A7644   Graham, N. H. "The Puttenham Family." *N &Q*, 199, No. 3 (Mar., 1954), 100-101. See also K. B. Danks, "Shakespeare Connexions." *N &Q*, 199 (1954), 362.

A7645   Graham, N. H. "The Puttenham Family." (Part II). *N &Q*, NS, IV (1957), 424-431.

A7646   Korn, A. L. "Puttenham and the Oriental Pattern-Poem." *CL*, VI (1954), 289-303.

A7647   Leisher, John F. "George Puttenham and Emblemata." *Boston University Studies in English*, I (1955), 1-18.

A7648   Eagle, R. L. " 'The Arte of English Poesie' (1589)." *N &Q*, NS, III (1956), 188-190. See also N. H. Graham, ibid., 362 and M. H. Dodds, ibid., 317.

(g) SHAKESPEARE

A7649   Roberts, Donald R. *Shakespeare and the Rhetoric of Stylistic Ornamentation.* DD, Cornell University, 1936.

A7650   Price, Hereward T. "Shakespeare as a Critic." *Renaissance Studies in Honor of Hardin Craig.* Stanford Univ. Press, 1941, pp. 198-207. Also *PQ*, XX (1941), 390-399.

A7651   Laltoo, Ralph Clarence. *Shakespeare as a Literary Critic.* MA thesis, Dalhousie University, 1942. Pp. 395.

A7652   Miriam Joseph, Sister, C. S. C. *Shakespeare's Use of the Arts of Language.* Columbia Univ. Studies in Eng. and Comp. Lit., No. 165. Columbia Univ. Press, 1947. Pp. xii, 423.
        Rev: A5570.

A7653   Chwalewik, Witwold. "Hamlet Jako Krytyk Teatru." *Polska Akademia Umiejętności*, LI (1950), 580-583.

A7654   Schirmer, Walter Franz. *Kleine Schriften.* Tübingen: Niemeyer, 1950. Pp. 200. "Shakespeare und die Rhetorik," pp. 83-108.

A7655   Thaler, Alwin. *Shakespeare and Sir Philip Sidney. The Influence of "The Defense of Poesy".* Harvard University Press, 1947.
        Rev: A4793.

(h) SIDNEY

A7656   Bronowski, J. *The Poet's Defence.* Cambridge Univ. Press, 1939. Pp. viii, 258.
        Rev: *N &Q*, 176 (1939), 359-360; by V. de S. Pinto, *English*, II, 317-318; by J. B. Leishman, *RES*, XVI (1940), 369-372; by Louis Bonnerot, *EA*, IV, 72-73.

A7657   Samuel, Irene. "The Influence of Plato on Sir Philip Sidney's 'Defense of Poesy'." *MLQ*, I (1940), 383-391.

A7658   Dowlin, Cornell March. "Sidney's Two Definitions of Poetry." *MLQ*, III (1942), 573-581.

A7659   Duhamel, P. Albert. "Sidney's *Arcadia* and Elizabethan Rhetoric." *SP*, XLV (1948), 134-150.

A7660   Duhamel, Pierre Albert. *Sir Philip Sidney and the Traditions of Rhetoric.* DD, University of Wisconsin, 1945. Abstr. publ. in Univ. of Wisconsin *Summaries of Doctoral Dissertations, 1943-1947*, Madison, 1949, pp. 483, 484.

(i) WILSON

A7661   Engelhardt, George J. "The Relation of Sherry's *Treatise of Schemes and Tropes* to Wilson's *Arte of Rhetorique*." *PMLA*, LXII (1947), 76-82.

A7662   Wagner, Russell H. "Thomas Wilson's Speech Against Usury." *QJS*, XXXVIII (1952), 13-22.

A7663   Kuiper, G. "Thomas Wilson's *Rule of Reason* (1551) en het Continentale Humanisme." *De Nieuwe Taalgids*, Bijzondere Afl., XLVI (1953), 58-63.

(j) OTHERS

A7664   Pace, George B. "Sir Thomas Elyot Against Poetry." *MLN*, LVI (1941), 597-599.

A7665 Willson, David Harris. "James I and His Literary Assistants." *HLQ*, VIII (1944), 35-57.

A7666 Ellrodt, R. "Sir John Harington and Leone Ebreo." *MLN*, LXV (1950), 109-110. See letter by P. W. Long, ibid., p. 292.

3. POPULAR TASTE AND THE ELIZABETHAN THEATRE AUDIENCE (102,138; 35,44)

A7667 Sprague, Arthur Colby. *Shakespeare and the Audience.* Harvard Univ. Press, 1935. Pp. xiii, 327.
Rev: by Alwin Thaler, *JEGP*, XXXV (1936), 605-606; *MGW*, Jan. 31, 1936, p. 94; by Burns Martin, *Dalhousie Rev.*, XVI, 267; by James Southall Wilson, *VQR*, XII, 636-640; by Hoyt H. Hudson, *QJS*, XXII, 131-133; by Wolfgang Keller, *SJ*, LXXII, 139-140; by G. B. Harrison, *MLR*, XXXII (1937), 296-297; by Geoffrey Tillotson, *RES*, XIII, 354-356; by Tucker Brooke, *YR*, XXVI, 176-177; by T. W. Baldwin, *MLN*, LII, 530-532; by J. Vallette, *RH*, 178 (1937), 633-634.

A7668 Knickerbocker, William S. "The Pragmatic Shakespeare." *SR*, XLIV (1936), 482-500.

A7669 Knights, Lionel Charles. *Aspects of the Economic and Social Background of Comedy in the Early Seventeenth Century.* Thesis, Cambridge, 1935. *Cam Abs.*, 1935-36, p. 63.

A7670 Allen, Percy. "Stage or Study?" *TLS*, April 11, 1936, p. 316.
See letters by W. W. Greg, *TLS*, May 2, 1936, p. 379; by Mr. Allen, ibid., May 9, 1936, p. 400; by Levin L. Schücking, ibid., May 6, 1936, p. 420.
Allen argues against the traditional belief that Shakespeare considered his plays as stage plays only; and expresses a conviction that the great tragedies in uncut form were written for publication and, in particular, that Q2 of Hamlet was intended not for stage presentation but "as a counterblast to, and protest against, the pirated Q1." Greg and Schücking concur.

A7670a "Stage or Study?" *TLS*, Oct. 7, 1944, p. 487. Answered by H. S. Bennett, *TLS*, Oct. 14, p. 499.
The writer of the article questions whether Shak. wrote only and exclusively for the stage. See also A7689.

A7671 "Elizabethan Decoration: Patterns in Art and Passion." *TLS*, July 3, 1937, pp. 485-486.

A7672 Bowers, Fredson. "The Audience and the Poisoners of Elizabethan Tragedy." *JEGP*, XXXVI (1937), 491-504.

A7673 Olive, William J. *Burlesque in Elizabethan Drama.* DD, University of North Carolina, 1937. Abstr. publ. in *Univ. of North Carolina Record, Research in Progress, 1936-1937*, Chapel Hill, 1937, pp. 53-54.
Chapter IV: "Burlesque of Shakespeare by his Contemporaries."

A7674 Simpson, Percy. "King Charles the First as a Dramatic Critic." *Bodleian Quar. Record*, VIII (1937), 257-262. See note by Mr. Simpson, ibid., 320.

A7675 Draper, John W. *The Hamlet of Shakespeare's Audience.* Duke Univ. Press, 1938. Pp. xi, 254.
Rev: B7539.

A7676 Mitchell, Charles B. *The English Sonnet in the 17th Century, Especially after Milton.* DD, Harvard University, 1939. Abstr. publ. in Harvard University *Summaries of Theses, 1939*, Cambridge, 1942, pp. 239-243.

A7677 Doran, Madelaine. "On Elizabethan 'Credulity': With Some Questions Concerning the Use of the Marvellous in Literature." *JHI*, I (1940), 151-176.
That the commonalty were less credulous than the learned in Elizabethan times.

A7678 Evans, Maurice. *The Language of the Elizabethan Drama.* DD, Cambridge, 1939. *Cam Abs.*, 1939-40, p. 52.

A7679 Stoll, Elmer Edgar. "Modesty in the Audience." *MLN*, LV (1940), 570-575.

A7680 Harbage, Alfred. *Shakespeare's Audience.* Columbia Univ. Press, 1941. Pp. viii, 201.
A major work on the subject. It quite demolishes the nineteenth-century conception of the late Tudor theatre audience and consequently the basis for much of that so-called realist criticism which assumed that primitive dramatic techniques and popular intellectual stereotypes were the necessary and inevitable fare of an ignorant audience.
Rev: A7386.

A7681 Hotson, Leslie. " 'Not of an Age': Shakespeare." *SR*, XLIX (1941), 193-210.
From an address delivered at the Folger Library, April 23, 1940. Reprinted in *Shakespeare's Sonnets Dated, and Other Essays.*
Rev: C21.

A7682 Leech, Clifford. "The Caroline Audience." *MLR*, XXXVI (1941), 304-319.

A7683 Reynolds, George F. "Aims of a Popular Elizabethan Dramatist." *Renaissance Studies in Honor of Hardin Craig*, pp. 148-152. Also in *PQ*, XX (1941), 340-344.

A7684 Spencer, Benjamin T. "This Elizabethan Shakespeare." *SR*, XLIX (1941), 536-552.
A review of recent books by Messrs. Stoll, Van Doren, and Draper and Miss Dunn, protesting against interpretations which reconstruct "the Elizabethan mind," assume that it is a constant, and thus make "the rigid and commonplace mentality" of Shakespeare's contemporaries the measure of his plays.

A7685   Willard, Oliver M. "Jaggard's *Catalogue of English Books*." *Stanford Studies in Language and Literature*. Stanford Univ. Press, 1941, pp. 152-172.

A7686   Hudson, Hoyt H. "The Transition in Poetry." *HLQ*, V (1942), 188-190.

A7687   McLeod, A. *The Nature of the Relations Between the Theatre Audience, the Drama and the Mise-en-scène*. Cornell University *Abstracts of Theses*, Ithaca, 1943, pp. 65-68.

A7688   Wells, Henry W. "A Mirror of National Integration: A New Summary of Four Decades of the English Theatre, 1550-1590." *SAB*, XVIII (1943), 30-40.

A7689   Bennett, H. S. *Shakespeare's Audience*. Annual Shakespeare Lecture of the British Academy. Oxford Univ. Press; London: Milford, 1944. Pp. 16.
        See also A7670a.
        Rev: briefly by C. J. Sisson, *MLR*, XL (1945), 78.

A7690   Bethell, S. L. *Shakespeare and the Popular Dramatic Tradition*. With an Intro. by T. S. Eliot. London: King & Staples, 1944. Pp. 160.
        Rev: *TLS*, July 8, 1944, p. 333; by H. B. Charlton, *NstN*, July 22, 1944, p. 60; by Trevor James, *Life and Letters*, XLII, 181-182; by A. I. Doyle, *Scrutiny*, XII, 236-238; by J. C. Ransom, *KR*, VII (1945), 515-520; by Bonamy Dobrée, *Spectator*, Aug. 31, 1945, p. 200; by J. W. R. Purser, *MLR*, XL, 221-222; by W.B.C. Watkins, *SR*, LIV (1946), 548-551; by Garland Greever, *Personalist*, XXVII, 331-332; by G. E. Bentley, *MLN*, LXII (1947), 53-55; by Richard Flatter, *SQ* (Vienna), No. I (1947), 112-115; by Dudley Wynn, *New Mexico Quar. Rev.*, XVII, 270-271; by R. Pruvost, "Études sur Shakespeare," *R. de la Méditerranée*, IV (1947), 615-618; *Dalhousie Rev.*, XXX (1950), 430-431; by R. Flatter, *SJ*, 88 (1952), 243-244.

A7691   Schücking, L. L. *The Sociology of Literary Taste*. London: Kegan Paul, 1944. Pp. 78.
        Rev: by H. I'A. F., *MGW*, July 28, 1944, p. 48; by F. R. Leavis, *Scrutiny*, XIII (1945), 74-79.

A7692   Wade, James Edgar. *Medieval Rhetoric in Shakespeare*. DD, St. Louis University, 1942. Pp. 185. Mic A44-671. *Microf. Ab.*, V (1944), 72. Publication No. 613.
        Chapter II: "Rhetoric and the Elizabethan Audience," pp. 31-38.

A7693   Stewart, J. I. M. "The Blinding of Gloster." *RES*, XXI (1945), 264-270.

A7694   Knepler, Heinrich Wilhelm. *The Playgoer's Fare, 1603-1613*. MA thesis, Queen's (Canada), 1946. Pp. 142.
        Part II: Assessment of audience preferences at that time.

A7695   Gates, William B. "Did Shakespeare Anticipate Comments from his Audience?" *QJS*, XXXIII (1947), 348-354.

A7696   Harbage, Alfred. *As They Liked It*. New York, 1947.
        Rev: A959.

A7697   Bentley, Gerald Eades. "Shakespeare and the Blackfriars Theatre." *ShS*, I (1948), 38-50.

A7698   Bennett, H. S. "Shakespeare's Stage and Audience." *Neophil*, XXXIII (1949), 40-51.

A7699   Isaacs, J. "Shakespeare and his World: The Elizabethan Audience." *Listener*, XLII (Sept. 1, 1949), 353-355.
        See also: P. Bedford, ibid., 451; J. Isaacs, ibid., 496; P. Bedford, ibid., 538; A. Harbage, ibid., 724-725; J. Isaacs, ibid., 771.

A7700   Draper, John W. *The "Twelfth Night" of Shakespeare's Audience*. Stanford Univ. Press, 1950. Pp. xiii, 280.
        Rev: B7044.

A7701   Purdom, C. B. *Producing Shakespeare*. London: Pitman, 1950. Pp. xii, 220.
        Rev: B1729.

A7702   Stoll, E. E. " 'Multi-Consciousness' in the Theatre." *PQ*, XXIX (1950), 1-14.

A7703   Cohen, Hennig. "Shakespeare's *Merchant of Venice* II, vii, 78-99." *SQ*, II (1951), 79.

A7704   Gardner, S. *The Relationship Between Poet and Audience from 1603 to 1660*. B. Litt. thesis, Oxford, 1951.

A7705   Prior, Moody E. "The Elizabethan Audience and the Plays of Shakespeare." *MP*, XLIX (1951), 101-123.
        ". . . A general defect of the criticism which refers the plays to the audience is a failure to understand the limitations of the method. It has been applied to questions which it cannot properly answer, and it has been used as though it could provide final judgments on the art and meaning of the plays of Shakespeare."
        Attacks "the monotonous error of taking the measure of Shakespeare by the limitations and prejudices of his most conventional customers."

A7706   Draper, John W. *The "Othello" of Shakespeare's Audience*. Paris, 1952.
        Rev: B8579.

A7707   Frye, Roland Mushat. *The Accepted Ethics and Theology of Shakespeare's Audience as Utilized by the Dramatist in Certain Representative Tragedies, with Particular Attention to Love and Marriage*. DD, Princeton University, 1952. Pp. 372. Mic A55-745. *DA*, XV (1955), 581. Publication No. 10,901.
        Rev: A2563.

A7708 Harbage, Alfred. *Shakespeare and the Rival Traditions.* New York: Macmillan, 1952. Pp. xviii, 393.
Rev: by James G. McManaway, *NYTBR*, Nov. 16, 1952, p. 6; by Joseph Wood Krutch, *NYHTBR*, Dec. 7, 1952, p. 7; by Marchette Chute, *Nation*, Dec. 6, p. 528; by G. B. Harrison, *SatR*, Oct. 10, 1953, p. 19; by Garland Greever, *Personalist*, xxxiv, 429-430; by Charles Tyler Prouty, *RN*, vi, 49-51; by Sandford Salyer, *Books Abroad*, xxvii, 432; by Charles T. Harrison, *SR*, lxii (1954), 165-166; by Philip Williams, *South Atlantic Quar.*, liii, 273-274; by Harold Jenkins, *ShS*, vii, 141; by R. C. Bald, *MP*, li, 278-281; *VQR*, xxix (1954), xxxii; by John Gassner, *TAr*, xxxviii (1954), 12-13; Daniel Boone Dodson, *Thomas Middleton's City Comedies*, DD, Columbia University, 1954, pp. 253, Mic A54-3074 (Discussion of Harbage's *Shak. & the Rival Traditions*, pp. 137-141); by Clifford Leech, *MLN*, lxx (1955), 292-295.

A7709 Mish, Charles C. "Comparative Popularity of Early Fiction and Drama." *N & Q*, 197 (1952), 269-270.

A7710 Nagler, A. M. *Sources of Theatrical History.* New York: Theatre Annual, 1952. Pp. xxiii, 611.
Rev: A7076.

A7711 Bhattacherje, M. M. *Elizabethan Stage and Audience and Shakespeare's Plays.* Pilani: The Arts College, 1953. Pp. 13.

A7712 Goodman, Randolph G. *That Strumpet the Stage: Poems about Playgoers, Players, and Playwrights.* DD, Columbia University, 1953. Pp. 357. Mic A53-761. *DA*, xiii (1953), 450. Publication No. 5189.

A7713 Shedd, Robert Gordon. *The "Measure for Measure" of Shakespeare's 1604 Audience.* DD, University of Michigan, 1953. Pp. 430. Mic A53-1478. *DA*, xiii (1953), 801. Publication No. 5730.

A7714 West, Robert H. "Elizabethan Belief in Spirits and Witchcraft." Matthews and Emery, eds. *Studies in Shakespeare*, pp. 65-73.

A7715 Ellis, Brobury Pearce. *Creative Relationships Between Dramatist, Actor, and Audience in the Acted Play.* DD, Cornell University, 1954. Pp. 203. Mic A55-233. *DA*, xv (1955), 164. Publication No. 10,578.

A7716 Gardner, Stanley. "Shakespeare's Audiences." *TLS*, May 14, 1954, p. 319.
Takes issue with *TLS* reviewer who regarded Shak.'s audiences as illiterate, and submits evidence to the contrary. Reply in *TLS*, May 21, p. 335.

A7717 Harding, Davis P. "Shakespeare the Elizabethan." *Shakespeare: Of an Age and For all Time.* The Yale Shakespeare Festival Lectures, pp. 13-32.
The economic and educational level of Shak.'s audience is described to prove that Shak. wrote to please a heterogeneous group of people, about whom generalized assumptions are dangerous.

A7718 Rowse, A. L. "Elizabethan Drama and Society: An Historian's View." *Talking of Shakespeare*, ed. by John Garrett. London: Hodder & Stoughton & Max Reinhardt, 1954.

A7719 Wilson, Frank Percy. "The Elizabethan Theatre." *Neophil*, xxxix (1955), 40-58.
Rev: by H. Oppel, *NS*, iv (1955), 517.

A7720 Hodges, Cyril Walter. "The Elizabethan Stage and the Lantern of Taste." Summary in *ShN*, vii (1957), 39.

A7721 Braun, Margarete. "Das Drama vor Shakespeare und seine Beziehungen zum Publikum." *SJ*, 94 (1958), 191-199.

A7722 Nagler, A. M. *Shakespeare's Stage.* Tr. from the German by Ralph Mannheim. New Haven, Conn.: Yale Univ. Press, 1958. Pp. ix, 117.

A7723 Zitner, S. P. "Gosson, Ovid, and the Elizabethan Audience." *SQ*, ix (1958), 206-208.

XI. AESTHETIC CRITICISM OF SHAKESPEARE (139; 44)
    1. AESTHETIC CRITICISM FROM THE SEVENTEENTH
        TO THE TWENTIETH CENTURIES
        a. REPRINTS

A7724 Ebisch, Walther, and Levin Ludwig Schücking. "Bibliographie zur Geschichte des literarischen Geschmacks in England." *Anglia*, lxiii (1939), 1-64.

A7725 Baker, Blanch Merritt. *Theatre and Allied Arts. A Guide to Books Dealing with the History, Criticism, and Technic of the Drama and Theatre.* New York: Wilson, 1952. Pp. xiii, 536. Shakespeare, pp. 57-70.

A7726 Agate, James. *The English Dramatic Critics. An Anthology, 1660-1932.* New ed. London: Barker, 1936. Pp. xiii, 370.
Republ. Paperback ed., New York: Hill & Wang; London: Calder, 1958. Pp. xiii, 370.
Rev: D. Nichols, *ETJ*, x (1958), 365-366.

A7727 Smith, James Harry, and Edd W. Parks. *The Great Critics: an Anthology of Literary Criticism.* Rev. & enlarged ed. New York: Norton, 1939. Pp. 786.
Includes Scaliger, Du Bellay, Ronsard, Sidney, Daniel, Jonson, Boileau, and others up to the present.

A7728 Gilbert, Allan H., ed. *Literary Criticism: Plato to Dryden.* Cincinnati: American Book Co., 1940. Pp. 704.
Rev: A7484

A7729 Allen, G. W., and H. H. Clark, eds. *Literary Criticism: Pope to Croce.* New York: American Book Co., 1942. Pp. xii, 660.

A7730 Ward, A. C., ed. *Specimens of English Dramatic Criticism, XVII-XX Centuries.* Oxford: Univ. Press, 1946. Pp. x, 355.
Rev: in *TAr*, XXXI (1947), 75-76.

A7731 Wagner, Bernard M. *The Appreciation of Shakespeare: A Collection of Criticism—Philosophic, Literary, and Esthetic—by Great Writers and Scholar-Critics of the Eighteenth, Nineteenth, and Twentieth Centuries.* Georgetown Univ. Press, 1949. Pp. xiii, 481, 40.
Rev: by D. C. Allen, *MLN*, LXV (1950), 576; *Catholic World*, 172 (1950), 160; by H. Levin, *NYTBR*, Mar. 26, 1950, pp. 7, 30; *N & Q*, 195, (1950), 132; by H. T. Price, *JEGP*, L (1951), 137; by Clifford P. Lyons, *SQ*, IV (1953), 355.

A7732 Williamson, C. C. H., ed. *Readings on the Character of Hamlet, 1661-1947.* London: Allen and Unwin, 1950. Pp. xiv, 783.
Rev: B7730.

A7733 Sehrt, Ernst Th., ed. and tr. *Shakespeare. Englische Essays zum Verständnis seiner Werke* (Göttinger Anglist., Bd. 249). Stuttgart: Alfred Kröner, 1958. Pp. 304.
Selections from Pope, Johnson, Hazlitt, Coleridge, de Quincey, Pater, Bradley, Bridges, Chambers, Eliot, Spurgeon, Granville-Barker, Murry, and Tillyard.
Rev: by Hermann Heuer, *SJ*, 94 (1958), 267-268; by L. L. Schücking, *GRM*, XXXIX, 312-313; by H. Oppel, *NS*, VII, 349-350.

A7734 Ralli, Augustus. *History of Shakespearean Criticism.* 2 vols. (Reissue). New York: Humanities Pr., 1958.

b. STUDIES

A7735 Baxter, F. C. *Criticism and Appreciation of the Elizabethan Drama: Dryden to Swinburne.* DD, Cambridge University, 1933.

A7736 Littlewood, S. R. *Dramatic Criticism.* Foreword by Sir Barry Jackson. London: Pitman, 1938. Pp. viii, 324. Chapter VIII "Shakespeare in Criticism," pp. 144-170.
Rev: Karl Arns, *Beiblatt*, LI (1940), 225-227.

A7737 Lombard, Edwin Henderson. *Plot, Character, and Action: A Study of Dramatic Theory and Practice.* DD, Cornell University, 1940. Abstr. publ. in Cornell University *Abstracts of Theses, 1940*, Ithaca, 1941, pp. 37-39.

A7738 Macclean, Norman F. *The Theory of Lyric Poetry in England from the Renaissance to Coleridge* DD, University of Chicago, 1941. Pp. 193.

A7739 "Which Shakespeare?" *TLS*, Jan. 6, 1945, p. 7.
Discusses varying interpretations of Shakespeare in different centuries.

A7740 Wickert, Maria. *Shakespeare-Interpretationen.* DD, Cologne, 1947. Pp. 106. Typewritten.

A7741 Nakanishi, Nobutaro. *Studies in Shakespeare Criticism* (Shakespeare Studies Series). DD, Kyoto University. Tokyo: Sogen-sha, 1949. Pp. viii, 268 (in Japanese).
Abstract in *Japan Science Review*, II (1951), 137-138.

A7742 McKean, A. K. F. *Ethical Judgments in the Criticism of Irving Babbitt, Paul Elmer More, and Yvor Winters.* DD, University of Michigan, 1950. Pp. 246. Mic A50-39. *Micr. Abstr.* X, No. 1 (1950), 85. Publ. No. 1518.
Begins in the Renaissance, with Gosson and Sidney.

A7743 Carlisle, Carol J. *Contributions of the English Actors to Shakespearean Criticism to 1902.* DD, University of North Carolina, 1951. Abstr. publ. in *Univ. of North Carolina Record, Research in Progress*, Jan.-Dec. 1951, Grad. School Series No. 62, 1952, pp. 110-111.

A7744 Cancelled.

A7745 Schirmer, Walter F. *Alte und Neue Wege der Shakespeare-Kritik.* Schriften der Universität Bonn, Heft. 9. Bonn: Hanstein Verlag, 1953. Pp. 33.
Rev: by F. W. Schulze, *ZAA*, III (1955), 189-190.

A7746 Sisson, Charles J. *Shakespeare.* British Council Series Writers and Their Work, No. 58. London: Longmans, 1955. Pp. 50.
Surveys Shak. scholarship and criticism since 17th century. Includes *A Select Shakespeare Bibliography* by J. R. Brown, pp. 33-50.
Rev: A159.

A7747 Wellek, René. *A History of Modern Criticism, 1750-1950.* Yale Univ. Press, 1955.
Vol. 1, The later 18th century. Vol. 2. The romantic age. To be completed in 4 volumes.
Rev: *Listener*, LIV (1955), 755, 757; by J. Wain, *Spectator*, No. 6644 (1955), pp. 559-560; *TLS*, Feb. 10, 1956, pp. 77-78; by C. T. Harrison, *SR*, LXIV, 520-524; by E. R. Wasserman, *PQ*, XXXV, 274-275; by N. Arvin, *Partisan Rev.*, XXIII, 124-127; by G. Bullough, *English*, XI, 26-27; by W. Silz, *GR*, XXXI, 307-309; by L. Cazamian, *EA*, X (1957), 226-230; by G. Watson, *EIC*, VII, 81-84; by A. Gillies, *MLN*, LXXII, 202-204.

A7748 Halliday, F. E. *The Cult of Shakespeare.* London: Duckworth, 1957. Pp. xiii, 218, with 16 pp. of plates.

Rev: *MGW*, Jan. 16, 1958, p. 11; *TLS*, Jan. 10, p. 16; by J. Vallette, *MdF*, 332 (1958), 521; by W. Bridges-Adams, *Drama* (Summer, 1958) pp. 39, 41; *Players Magazine*, XXXIV, 126; by Gösta Langenfelt, *Sundsvalls Tidning* (Sundsvall), July 3, 1958.

A7749   Morris, Harry Caesar. *Nineteenth and Twentieth Century Criticism of Shakespeare's Problem Comedies.* DD, University of Minnesota, 1957. Pp. 553. Mic 57-2479. *DA*, XVII (1957), 1546. Publ. No. 21,252.

A7750   Wimsatt, William K., and Cleanth Brooks. *Literary Criticism: A Short History.* New York: Knopf, 1957. Pp. 795.
Rev: by Charles I. Glicksberg, *Arizona Quar.*, XIV (1958), 172-177; by Douglas Knight, *Christian Scholar*, XLI, 167-169; by Harry Levin, *MLN*, LXXIII, 155-160 (see author's comment and reviewer's reply, pp. 557-560); by Nathan A. Scott, Jr., *New Scholasticism*, XXXII, 402-407; by F. W. Bateson, *Spectator*, Mar. 28, 1958, pp. 402-403; by Robert Marsh, *MP*, LV, 263-265.

c. HISTORIES OF THE CRITICISM OF SPECIFIC PLAYS OR CHARACTERS

A7751   Wales, J. G. "A Suggestion for a (Chronological) History of Shakespearean Criticism by Plays." *Transactions of the Wisconsin Acad. of Sciences, Arts, and Letters*, XXX (1937), 313-316.

A7752   Bracy, William. *Jacques: A Study in Shakespearean Criticism.* MA thesis, University of North Carolina, 1939. Abstr. publ. in *Univ. of North Carolina Record, Research in Progress*, Grad. School Series No. 36, 1939, pp. 76-77.

A7753   Conklin, Paul S. *A History of Hamlet Criticism: Part I 1601-1800.* DD, University of Minnesota, 1938. Abstract publ. in *Summaries of PhD Theses*, University of Minnesota, 1939, pp. 151-154.

A7754   Gore, Arabella. *The History of the Interpretation of Shylock in English and American Literary Criticism, 1796 to 1935.* MA thesis, University of North Carolina, 1939. Abstract publ. in *University of North Carolina Record, Research in Progress*, Grad. School Series No. 36, 1939, p. 79.

A7755   MacDowell, David Archibald. *The History of the Interpretation of Lady Macbeth in English and American Literary Criticism, 1747-1939.* MA thesis, University of North Carolina, 1939. Abstract publ. in *University of North Carolina Record, Research in Progress*, Grad. School Series No. 36, 1939, p. 81.

A7756   Pritchett, Frances G. *The History of the Interpretation of Cordelia in English and American Literary Criticism, 1710 to 1940.* MA thesis, University of North Carolina, 1944. Abstract publ. in *University of North Carolina Record, Research in Progress*, Grad. School Series No. 50, 1946, pp. 159-160.

A7757   Dukes, William J. *Shakespeare Criticism and Richard II.* MA thesis, University of North Carolina, 1943. Abstract publ. in *University of North Carolina Record, Research in Progress*, Grad. School Series No. 50, 1946, p. 151.

A7758   Thomas, Mary Olive. *A Study of the Criticism of Iago.* MA thesis, University of North Carolina, 1944. Abstract publ. in *University of North Carolina Record, Research in Progress*, Grad. School Series No. 50, 1946, p. 163.

A7759   Edmunds, Winifred Egan. *The History of the Criticism of the Character of Richard III.* MA thesis, University of North Carolina, 1945. Abstract publ. in *University of North Carolina Record, Research in Progress*, Grad. School Series No. 50, 1946, p. 152.

A7760   Nicholson, Catherine. *The History of the Criticism of the Character of Othello.* MA thesis, University of North Carolina, 1945. Abstract publ. in *University of North Carolina Record, Research in Progress*, Grad. School Series No. 50, 1946, p. 159.

A7761   Schartle, Patty McFarland. *Aristocratic Coriolanus: A Study in Shakespearean Criticism.* MA thesis, University of North Carolina, 1946. Abstract publ. in *University of North Carolina Record, Research in Progress*, Grad. School Series No. 56, 1949, p. 228.

A7762   Conklin, Paul S. *A History of Hamlet Criticism, 1601-1821.* New York: King's Crown Press, 1947. Pp. viii, 176.
Reprinted, New York, 1957.
Rev: Brief mention *TLS*, Feb. 28, 1948, p. 127; by T. M. Pearce, *New Mexico Quar.*, XVIII, 241-242; by D. C. A., *MLN*, LXIII, 434; by J. W. Draper, *South Atlantic Quar.*, XLVII, 431-432; by R. S. Knox, *UTQ*, XVIII, 97-99; by J. B. Fort, *LanM*, XLII, 295-296; by J. I. M. Stewart, *RES*, XXV (1949), 168-169; by R. M. Smith, *SAB*, XXIV, 13-15; by Fernand Baldensperger, *RLC*, XXIV (1950), 127-128; by Claude M. Newlin, *MLQ*, XI, 108-109; by G. I. Duthie, *MLR*, XLV, 531-533; by Thomas Hogan, *Spectator*, Aug. 23, 1957, pp. 253-254; by C. V. Wedgwood, *Time & Tide*, Aug. 31, p. 1082; briefly by Giles Dawson, *SQ*, IX (1958), 418.

A7763   Ribner, Irving. *King Lear: A Study in Shakespearean Character Criticism.* MA thesis, University of North Carolina, 1947. Abstract publ. in *University of North Carolina Record, Research in Progress*, Grad. School Series No. 56, 1949, pp. 227-228.

A7764   Cochran, Ruth Maidee. *Prospero: A Study in Shakespeare Character Criticism.* MA thesis, University of North Carolina, 1948. Abstract publ. in *University of North Carolina Record, Research in Progress*, Grad. School Series No. 56, 1949, p. 204.

A7765   Glover, Allison. *A Survey of Shakespeare's Cleopatra.* MA thesis, University of North Carolina, 1948. Abstract publ. in *University of North Carolina Record, Research in Progress*, Grad. School Series No. 56, 1949, p. 207.

A7766   Negueloua, Lillian Mary. *The Literary Reputation of Shakespeare's Cressida.* MA thesis, University of North Carolina, 1948. Abstract publ. in *University of North Carolina Record, Research in Progress*, Grad. School Series No. 56, 1949, pp. 224-225.

A7767   Springer, R. *A History of Falstaff Criticiam.* DD, Columbia University, 1948. Pp. 94.

A7768   Shoemaker, Lisle N. *The Whole History of Hamlet.* DD, Western Reserve University, 1950. Abstract publ. in Western Reserve Univ. *Bibliography of Published Research, 1948-1950*, pp. 140-142.

A7769   Poindexter, James E. *Criticism of Falstaff to 1860.* DD, University of North Carolina, 1950. Abstract publ. in *University of North Carolina Record, Research in Progress*, Jan.-Dec., 1949, Grad. School Series No. 58, pp. 112-113.

A7770   Lief, Leonard. *The Fortunes of King Lear: 1605-1838.* DD, Syracuse University, 1953. Pp. 291. Abstracted in *ShN*, VI (1956), 22.

2. SEVENTEENTH AND EIGHTEENTH CENTURY CRITICISM (139; 44)
a. REPRINTS (139; 44)

A7771   Adams, Henry Hitch and Baxter Hathaway, eds. *Dramatic Essays of the Neoclassic Age.* New York: Columbia Univ. Press; London, Toronto: Oxford Univ. Press, 1950. Pp. xix, 412.
         Rev: by Monroe K. Spears, *SA*, LX (1952), 336-347; by Allan H. Gilbert, *South Atlantic Quarterly*, L, 283-284; by Marvin T. Herrick, *QJS*, XXXVII, 102-103; by H. C. Lancaster, *MLN*, LXVI, 197-198; *TLS*, Jan. 19, 1951, p. 34; by J. W. R. Purser, *MLR*, XLVI, 487-488; by Pierre Legouis, *EA*, V, 161.

A7772   Wells, Staring B. *A Comparison Between the Two Stages.* DD, Princeton University, 1935. Revised version published by Princeton Univ. Press, 1942. Pp. xxi, 206.
         A reprint of Gildon's book of 1702, with copious notes. Shak. passim.

A7773   Thorpe, Clarence D., ed. Anonymous [attributed to Thomas Hammer]. *Some Remarks on the Tragedy of Hamlet, Prince of Denmark, Written by Mr. William Shakespeare* (1736). Ann Arbor, 1947. Augustan Reprint Soc., Ser. III, No. 3.

A7774   Herder, Johann Gottfried. *Shakespeare.* Sel., trad. y pról. de Juan C. Probst. Antología alemana. Ser. 1, fasc. 39. Buenos Aires: Univ., Fac. de fil., 1949. Pp. 56.
         In German and Spanish.

A7775   Johnson, Samuel. *Notes to Shakespeare. Vol. I, Comedies.* Ed., with an introduction by Arthur Sherbo. Augustan Reprint Society, nos. 59-60. Los Angeles: William Andrews Clark Memorial Library, Univ. of California, 1956. Pp. viii, 140.

A7776   Johnson, Samuel. *Notes to Shakespeare. Vol. II, Histories.* Ed. with an introduction by Arthur Sherbo. Augustan Reprint Society, nos. 65-66. Los Angeles: William Andrews Clark Memorial Library, Univ. of California, 1957. Pp. 123.

A7777   Johnson, Samuel. *Notes to Shakespeare. Vol. III, Tragedies.* Ed., with an introduction by Arthur Sherbo. Augustan Reprint Society, nos. 71-73. Los Angeles: William Andrews Clark Memorial Library, Univ. of California, 1958. Pp. 202.

A7778   Johnson, Samuel. *Preface to Shakespeare, with Proposals for Printing the Dramatic Works of William Shakespeare.* Oxford Univ. Press, 1957. Pp. iv, 63.

A7779   Monaghan, T. J. "Johnson's Addition to His *Shakespeare* for the Edition of 1773." *RES*, NS, IV (1953), 234-248.
         Rev: by A. Sherbo, *PQ*, XXXIII (1954), 283-284.

A7780   McCall, John Joseph. *Gerard Langbaine's "An Account of the English Dramatick Poets" 1691.* Edited with an introduction and notes. DD, The Florida State University, 1957.

A7781   Rowe, Nicholas. *Some Account of the Life of Mr. William Shakespeare* (1709). With an introduction by Samuel H. Monk. Augustan Reprint Soc. Extra Ser. 1. Los Angeles: Augustan Reprint Soc., 1948. Pp. 11, XI.

A7782   Zimansky, Curt A. "A Manuscript Poem to Thomas Rymer." *PQ*, XXX (1951), 217-220.

A7783   Zimansky, Curt A., ed. *The Critical Works of Thomas Rymer.* Yale Univ. Press, 1956.
         Rev: *TLS*, June 7, 1957, p. 350; briefly in *VQR*, XXXIII, xliv; by G. L. Anderson, *SCN*, XV, 1-2; briefly in *SNL*, VII, 28; by George Sherburn, *PQ*, XXXVI, 402-403; by M. H. Abrams, *MP*, LV (1958), 206-208; by H. T. Swedenberg, Jr., *MLN*, LXXIII, 439-442; by Benjamin Boyce, *SQ*, IX, 200-201; by Clifford Leech, *ES*, XXXIX, 85-87; by A. Mavrocordato, *EA*, XI, 255-256; by J. Kinsley, *RES*, NS, IX, 325-327.

A7784   Theobald, Lewis. *Preface to the Works of Shakespeare.* (1734). With an introduction by Hugh G. Dick. Augustan Reprint Soc. Publ. Nr. 20, Extra Ser. 2. Los Angeles: Augustan Reprint Soc., 1949. Pp. 6, lxviii.
         Rev: P. Legouis, *LanM*, XLIV (1950), 424-425.

A7785   Lewis, W. S., ed. *Notes by H. Walpole on Several Characters of Shakespeare.* Farmington, 1940. Pp. viii, 22.

b. STUDIES (140; 44)
(1) GENERAL

A7786   Eich, Louis M. *Alterations of Shakespeare, 1660-1710; and an Investigation of the Critical and Dramatic Principles and Theatrical Conventions which Prompted these Revisions.* DD, University of Michigan, 1923. Pp. 211. Mic A48-50. *Mic Ab*, VIII (1948), 90. Publication No. 920.

A7787 Mirabent y Vilaplana, Francisco. *La Estética inglesa del Siglo XVIII.* DD, Madrid, 1923-1926. Pp. 271.

A7788 Lovett, David. *Shakespeare's Characters in Eighteenth Century Criticism.* DD, Johns Hopkins University, 1935.

A7789 Noyes, Robert Gale. *Ben Jonson on the English Stage, 1660-1774.* Harvard Studies in English, 17. Harvard Univ. Press, 1935. Pp. xii, 351.
Rev: by Allardyce Nicoll, *JEGP*, xxxv (1936), 434-435; by H. P. Gundy, *MP*, xxxiv, 99-100; by Burns Martin, *Dalhousie Rev.*, xvi, 267; *TLS*, March 14, 1936, p. 219; by F. C. Danchin, *RAA*, xiii, 435; by F. E. Budd, *MLR*, xxxii (1937), 297-298; by Hazelton Spencer, *MLN*, lii, 437-442; by W. Kalthoff, *Beiblatt*, xlviii, 140-141; by Frederick T. Wood, *Eng. Studn.*, lxxi, 407-408.

A7790 Lovett, David. "Shakespeare as a Poet of Realism in the Eighteenth Century." *ELH*, II, (1935/6), 267-289.

A7791 Pennink, R. *Nederland en Shakespeare.* The Hague, 1936.
Rev: A9739.

A7792 White, Irving Hamilton. *Studies in English Dramatic Criticism, 1750-1800.* DD, Harvard University, 1936. Abstract publ. in *Summaries of PhD Theses, 1936.* Cambridge: Harvard Univ. Press, 1938, pp. 356-359.

A7793 Allen, B. Sprague. *Tides in English Taste (1619-1800): A Background for the Study of Literature.* Harvard Univ. Press, 1937.
Rev: by A. S. P. Woodhouse, *UTQ*, viii (1939), 461-467; by L. Cazamian, *EA*, iii, 46-47.

A7794 Wasserman, Earl Reeves. "The Scholarly Origin of the Elizabethan Revival." *ELH*, iv (1937), 213-243.

A7795 Draper, J. W. "The Theory of the Comic in the 18th Century." *JEGP*, xxxvii (1938), 207-223.

A7796 Smyth, Miriam. *The Ethical Conception of Literature in English Literary Theory.* DD, University of Kansas, 1938.

A7797 Williams, Robert D. "Antiquarian Interest in Elizabethan Drama before Lamb." *PMLA*, liii (1938), 434-444.

A7798 Wassermann, Earl R. "Henry Headley and the Elizabethan Revival." *SP*, xxxvi (1939), 491-502.

A7799 Giovannini, G. *The Theory of Tragedy as History in Renaissance & Neo-Classical Criticism.* DD, University of Michigan, 1940.

A7800 Hathaway, Baxter Levering. *The Function of Tragedy in Neo-Classic Criticism.* DD, University of Michigan, 1940.

A7801 Tieze, Wilhelm. "Die Leidenschaften reinigen. . . Zur Kritik des Ästhetischen seit Lessing." *DL*, xliv (1941/42), 53ff.

A7802 Wellek, René. *The Rise of English Literary History.* Univ. North Carolina Press, 1941. Pp. 273.
Rev: by E. R. Wasserman, *JEGP*, xli (1942), 115-118.

A7803 Wetzel, Gunther. *Die Literarische Kritik in England von Sidney bis Dryden.* DD, Kiel, 1941. Pp. 168. Typewritten.

A7804 Appelberg, Bertel. *Teorierna om det Komiska Under 1600-och 1700 talet.* [Die Theorien des Komischen im 17 und 18 Jahrhundert.] DD, Helsinki, 1944. Pp. 292.

A7805 Musgrove, S. *The Changing Values in the Critical and Literary Outlook of the Seventeenth Century, as Manifested in English Verse Translation from the Greek and Latin Classics.* DD, Oxford, Merton, 1944.

A7806 Kallick, Martin. *The Association of Ideas and Critical Theory in 18th Century England: A History of a Psychological Method in English Criticism.* DD, Johns Hopkins University, 1945.

A7807 Weisinger, H. "The 17th-Century Reputation of the Elizabethans." *MLQ*, vi (1945), 13-20.

A7808 Youel, Donald B. *The Idea of Law in English Literary Criticism: 16th and 17th Centuries.* DD, State University of Iowa, 1945. Abstr. in Univ. of Iowa *Programs Announcing Candidates for Higher Degrees, 1944.*

A7809 Jörgensen, Bodil. "Aesthetic Criticism in England from 1675 to 1725. Some Problems." *Orbis*, ii (1946), 43-66.

A7810 Knights, L. C. *Explorations: Essays in Criticism, Mainly on the Literature of the Seventeenth Century.* London, 1946.
Rev: A8269.

A7811 Van Tieghem, Paul. "Shakespeare devant la critique continentale au XVIIIe siècle." *Essais et Etudes Universitaires*, 1945-46, Nr. 1.

A7812 Dodson, D. B. *German Shakespeare Critics in the 18th Century.* DD, Columbia University, 1947. Pp. 104.

A7813 Snuggs, Henry L. "The Comic Humours: A New Interpretation." *PMLA*, lxii (1947), 114-122.

A7814 Stahl, Ernst Leopold. *Shakespeare und das deutsche Theater.* Stuttgart: Kohlhammer, 1947. Pp. viii, 768. Includes 48 pp. of illustrations.
Rev: A9465.

A7815   Fluchère, Henri. "Shakespeare in France: 1900-1948." *ShS*, II (1949), 115-124.

A7816   Bailey, Helen Phelps. *Hamlet in France from Voltaire to Laforgue, 1733-1886.* DD, Columbia University, 1950. Pp. 405. Mic A50-92. *Mcf Ab*, x (1950), 114. Publication No. 1632.

A7817   Leech, Clifford. *Shakespeare's Tragedies: and Other Studies in Seventeenth-Century Drama.* London: Chatto and Windus, 1950. Pp. viii, 232.
    Rev: B4967.

A7818   Atkins, J. W. H. *English Literary Criticism: 17th and 18th Centuries.* London: Methuen; Toronto: British Book Service, 1951; New York: Barnes and Noble, 1952. Pp. xi, 383.
    Rev: by G. S. Fraser, *NstN*, XLII (1951), 468; by B. Dobrée, *Spectator*, No. 6436 (1951), pp. 580-581; *TLS*, Nov. 9, 1951, p. 710; by Desmond MacCarthy, *Sunday Times*, Dec. 2, 1951, p. 3; by E. M. W. Tillyard, *CR*, LXXIII, 370; by O. Brunet, *EA*, v (1952), 272-273; by D. A. Stauffer, *Erasmus*, v, 428-430; by M. T. Herrick, *JEGP*, LI, 429-430; by G. Bullough, *English*, IX, 26-27; by W. K. Wimsatt, *JAAC*, XI (1953), 421-422; by J. R. Sutherland, *RES*, NS, IV, 184-185; by R. S. Crane, *UTQ*, XXII, 376-391; by T. A. Birrell, *ES*, XXXV (1954), 25-27.

A7819   Chute, Marchette. "The Bubble, Reputation." *VQR*, XXV (1949), 575-584.

A7820   Kiendler, Grete. *Konvertierte Formen in den Dramen Otways und Lees: ein Vergleich mit der Sprache Shakespeares.* DD, Graz, 1951. Pp. 202. Typewritten.

A7821   Wilcox, Angeline T. *The "True Critic" in England in the Eighteenth Century.* DD, Northwestern University, 1951. Abstract publ. in Northwestern University *Summaries of Doctoral Dissertations*, XIX (1951), Chicago & Evanston: Northwestern University, 1952, pp. 55-59.

A7822   Wiley, Margaret Lee. "A Supplement to the Bibliography of 'Shakespeare Idolatry'." *SB*, IV (1951), 164-166.

A7823   Cooney, Madeleine Sophie. "The Beauties-and-Faults Criticism in the Neo-Classical Period of English Literature." *Stanford Univ. Abstracts of Dissertations, 1952,* pp. 214-216.

A7824   Freimarck, Vincent. "The Bible and Neo-classical Views of Style." *JEGP*, LI (1952), 507-526.

A7825   Hanzo, Thomas Andrew. "English Latitudinarian Thought and the Literary Criticism of the Restoration." *Stanford Univ. Abstracts of Dissertations, 1952,* pp. 223-225.

A7826   Tave, Stuart M. "Corbyn Morris: Falstaff, Humor, and Comic Theory in the Eighteenth Century." *MP*, L (1952), 102-115.

A7827   Doran, Madeleine. *Endeavors of Art: A Study of Form in Elizabethan Drama.* Madison: Univ. of Wisconsin Press, 1953. Pp. xv, 482.
    Rev: *TLS*, Mar. 5, 1954, p. 152; *N &Q*, NS, I, 183-184; by Marvin T. Herrick, *JEGP*, LIII, 472-473; by Una Ellis-Fermor, *SQ*, v, 411-412; by Hermann Heuer, *SJ*, 90 (1954), 347-349; by Arthur Brown, *YWES*, XXXV, 104; by Levin L. Schücking, *Anglia*, LXXIII (1955), 219-221; by H. D. Gray, *RN*, VIII, 116-117; by William T. Hastings, *SQ*, VI, 109-110; by M. C. Bradbrook, *MLR*, L, 68-70; by E. T. Sehrt, *MLN*, LXX, 524-527; by M. Poirier, *EA*, VIII, 152-153; *CE*, XVI, 466; by B. L. Joseph, *RES*, NS, VII (1956), 73-74; by R. Fricker, *Archiv*, 193 (1957), 328-329.

A7828   Bliss, Frank Walker, Jr. *Studies in the Background of the Idea of Pride in Eighteenth Century Thought.* DD, University of Minnesota, 1954. Pp. 332. Mic A55-498. *DA*, XV (1955), 403. Publication No. 11,069.

A7829   Sellers, William H. *Literary Controversies Among Restoration Dramatists, 1660-1685.* DD, Ohio State University, 1954.

A7830   Fiehler, Rudolph. "How Oldcastle Became Falstaff." *MLQ*, XVI (1955), 16-28.

A7831   Howell, Elmo H. *The Role of the Critic in the Restoration and Early Eighteenth Century.* DD, University of Florida, Gainesville, 1955.

A7832   Branam, George C. *Eighteenth-Century Adaptations of Shakespearean Tragedy.* University of California Publications. English Studies: 14. Univ. of California Press, 1956. Pp. viii, 220.
    Rev: B144.

A7833   Hazard, Benjamin Munroe. *The Theory of Comedy in the Restoration and Early Eighteenth Century.* DD, Northwestern University, 1958. Pp. 195. Mic 58-4322. *DA*, XVIII (1958), 581. Publication No. 24,905.

(2)   SPECIFIC AUTHORS (See Various English Authors, XIII, 2, b, for Addison, Dryden, Walpole, etc.)
(a)   COLLIER

A7834   Ressler, Kathleen. *Jeremy Collier.* DD, University of Cincinnati, 1935.

A7835   Anthony, R. *The Jeremy Collier Stage Controversy, 1698-1726.* Milwaukee: Marquette Univ. Press, 1937. Pp. xvi, 328.
    Rev: by E. N. Hooker, *MLN*, LIV (1939), 386-389.

(b)   DENNIS

A7836   Wilkins, Arthur N. *An Essay on John Dennis's Theory and Practice of the Art of Tragedy Together with the Text of his Tragedy of "Appius and Virginia."* DD, Washington University, St. Louis, 1953.

A7837 Hardy, Gene B. *John Dennis as Comic Dramatist.* DD, University of Illinois, 1955. Pp. 193. Mic 55-1107. *DA*, xv (1955), 2190-91. Publication No. 13,489.

A7838 Wilkins, A. N. "John Dennis and Poetic Justice." *N &Q*, NS, IV (1957), 421-424.

A7839 Wilkins, A. N. "John Dennis on Love as a 'Tragical Passion'." *N &Q*, v (1958), 396-398, 417-419.

(c) DRYDEN

A7840 Weselmann, Christian Adolph Franz. *Dryden als Kritiker.* DD, Göttingen, 1893. Pp. 54.

A7841 Treadaway, Brother Thomas J. *The Critical Opinions of John Dryden.* DD, St. Louis University, 1938.

A7842 Huntley, Frank Livingstone. *The Unity of John Dryden's Dramatic Criticism, 1664-1681.* DD, University of Chicago, 1943. Pp. 264.

A7843 Margaret Joseph Burke, Sister, S. S. J. *Dryden and Eliot—a Study in Literary Criticism.* DD, Niagara University, 1945.

A7844 Ribner, Irving. "Dryden's Shakesperian Criticism and the Neo-Classical Paradox." *SAB*, XXI (1946), 168-171.

A7845 Gohn, Ernest S. *Seventeenth-Century Theories of the Passions and the Plays of John Dryden.* DD, Johns Hopkins University, 1948.

A7846 Aden, John Michael. *The Question of Influence in Dryden's Use of the Major French Critics.* DD, University of North Carolina, 1950. Abstract publ. in *University of North Carolina Record, Research in Progress*, Jan.-Dec. 1950, Grad. School Series No. 60, 1951, pp. 121-122.

A7847 Tillyard, E. M. W. "A Note on Dryden's Criticism." *Richard Foster Jones Studies*, 1951, pp. 330-338.

A7848 Moore, Frank H. *Dryden's Theory and Practice of Comedy.* DD, University of North Carolina, 1953. Abstract publ. in *University of North Carolina Record, Research in Progress*, Jan.-Dec. 1953, Grad. School Series No. 66, 1954, pp. 96-99.

A7849 Edward O. Carm. Ramagosa, Sister. *A Compendium of the Opinions of John Dryden.* DD, Tulane University, 1958.

A7850 Mary Franzita Kane, Sister. *John Dryden's Doctrine of "Wit" as "Propriety": A Study of the Terms and Relations Involved in the Definition of 1677.* DD, University of Notre Dame, 1958. Pp. 418. Mic 58-7098. *DA*, xix (1959), 1741.

(d) GARRICK

A7851 Stone, George Winchester, Jr. *Garrick's Treatment of Shakespeare's Plays, and His Influence Upon the Changed Attitude of Shakespearean Criticism During the Eighteenth Century.* DD, Harvard University, 1940. Abstract publ. in *Summaries of PhD Theses, 1940.* Cambridge: Harvard Univ. Press, 1942, pp. 368-372.

A7852 Bodtke, R. A. "Garrick's Revisions of Shakespeare: a Mirror for 18th Century Tastes." DD, Columbia University, 1947. Pp. 94.

A7853 Stone, George Winchester, Jr. "David Garrick's Significance in the History of Shakespearean Criticism." *PMLA*, LXV (1950), 183-197.

(e) GENTLEMAN

A7854 Highfill, Philip Henry, Jr. *Francis Gentleman, Critic: A Biographical Study of the Author of "The Dramatic Censor."* MA thesis, University of North Carolina, 1948. Abstract publ. in *University of North Carolina Record, Research in Progress*, Grad. School Series No. 56, 1949, p. 211.

A7855 Highfill, Philip Henry, Jr. *A Study of Francis Gentleman's "The Dramatic Censor," (1770).* DD, University of North Carolina, 1950. Abstract publ. in *University of North Carolina Record, Research in Progress*, Jan.-Dec. 1950, Grad. School Series No. 60, 1951, pp. 127-129.

(f) HILL

A7856 Sutherland, William Owen Sheppard. *A Study of the Prompter (1734-1736).* DD, University of North Carolina, 1950. Abstract publ. in *University of North Carolina Record, Research in Progress*, Jan.-Dec. 1950, Grad. School Series, No. 60, 1951, pp. 135-136.

A7857 Sutherland, W. O. S. "Polonius, Hamlet, and Lear in Aaron Hill's Prompter." *SP*, XLIX (1952), 605-618.

(g) JOHNSON

A7858 Christiani, Sigyn. *Samuel Johnson als Kritiker. Im Lichte von Pseudoklassizismus und Romantik.* DD, Munich, 1931. Pp. 120. Publ. *Beiträge zur englischen Philologie*, XVIII, (Halle/Saale).

A7859 Lam, George L. *Johnson's "Lives of the Poets": Their Origin, Text, and History, with Remarks on Sources and Comment on His "Life of Cowley."* DD, Cornell University, 1938.

A7860 Hesketh-Williams, P. K. *The Earlier Literary Criticism of Samuel Johnson.* B. Litt. Thesis, Oxford, St. Hugh's, 1940.

A7861   Leavis, F. R. "S. Johnson as Critic." *Scrutiny*, XII (1944), 187-204.

A7862   Wieder, Robert. *Le Docteur Johnson Critique Littéraire (1709-1784).* Thèse de lettres, Paris, 1944.

A7863   Keast, William R. *The Foundations of Samuel Johnson's Literary Criticism.* DD, University of Chicago, 1948. Pp. 156.

A7864   Carroll, Richard A. *Johnson's "Lives of the Poets" and Currents of English Criticism, 1750-1779.* DD, University of Michigan, 1950. Pp. 420. Mic A50-421. *Micro Abstr.* X, No. 4 (1950), 208. Publication No. 1952.

A7865   Fleischauer, Warren L. *Dr. Johnson's Editing and Criticism of Shakespeare's Lancastrian Cycle.* DD, Western Reserve University, 1952. Abstract publ. in Western Reserve University *Bibliography of Published Research, 1950-1952,* (?1957), pp. 146-148.

A7866   Lubbers-van der Brugge, Catharina Johanna Maria. *Johnson and Baretti. Some Aspects of Eighteenth-Century Literary Life in England and Italy.* DD, Groningen, 1951. Publ. as Groningen studies in English #2.

A7867   Sherbo, Arthur. "Dr. Johnson on *Macbeth:* 1745 and 1765." *RES,* NS, II (1951), 40-47.

A7868   Hagstrum, Jean Howard. *Samuel Johnson's Literary Criticism.* Univ. of Minnesota Press, 1952. Oxford Univ. Press, 1953. Pp. 212.
        Rev: by E. Morgan, *CamJ,* VII (1953), 124-126; *DUJ,* XLV, 121-122; by I. Jack, *PQ,* XXXII, 275-276; by C. Tracy, *QQ,* LX, 121-122; by D. C. Bryant, *QJS,* XXXIX, 236; by W. H. Irving, *South Atlantic Quar.,* LII, 473-475; *TLS,* March 20, 1953, p. 188; by G. Sherburn, *SR,* LXII (1954), 344-345; by D. J. Greene, *RES,* NS, V, 200-203; by W. K. Wimsatt, *MLN,* LXIX, 128-130.

A7869   Keast, William R. "*The Theoretical Foundations of Johnson's Criticism.*" In: *Critics and Criticism, Ancient and Modern.* Univ. of Chicago Press, 1952, pp. 389-407.
        Rev: by J. H. Hagstrum, *PQ,* XXXII (1953), 276-278.

(h) MORGANN

A7870   Gordon, George Stuart. *The Lives of Authors.* London: Chatto & Windus; Toronto: Clarke, Irwin, 1950. Pp. 216.
        Rev: *TLS,* June 9, 1950, p. 355; by R. G. Cox, *MGW,* May 11, 1950, p. 11.

A7871   Tave, Stuart Malcolm. "Notes on the Influence of Morgann's Essay on Falstaff." *RES,* NS, III (1952), 371-375.

A7872   Felheim, Marvin. "Landmarks of Criticism: *Essay on the Dramatic Character of Sir John Falstaff.*" *ShN,* VI (1956), 15.

(i) RICHARDSON

A7873   Boulton, M. *A Study of William Richardson with Special Reference to His Shakespearian Criticism.* B. Litt Thesis, Oxford, Somerville, 1948.

A7874   Cordasco, Francesco. "William Richardson's Essays on Shakespeare (1784): A Bibliographical Note on the First Edition." *N&Q,* 196 (1951), 148.
        See letter by Howard Parsons, ibid., 196 (1951), 174.

A7875   Felheim, Marvin. "Landmarks of Criticism: 'On the Faults of Shakespeare', William Richardson." *ShN,* VII (1957), 45.

(j) RYMER

A7876   Zimansky, Curt A. *Critical and Dramatic Works of Thomas Rymer.* DD, Princeton University, 1937.

A7877   Walcott, Fred. "John Dryden's Answer to Thomas Rymer's *The Tragedies of the Last Age.*" *PQ,* XV (1936), 194-214.

A7878   Dollard, Frank D. *French Influence on Thomas Rymer's Dramatic Criticism.* DD, University of California, Berkeley, 1953.

(k) WHITER

A7879   "The Imagery of Shakespeare. Dr. Clemen and Walter Whiter." *TLS,* Sept. 5, 1936, pp. 701-702.

A7880   Isaacs, J. "Shakespeare's Imagery." *TLS,* Sept. 12, 1936, p. 729.

A7881   Smith, Rev. Paul F., S. J. *Whiter's "A Specimen of a Commentary on Shakespeare."* DD, St. Louis University, 1946.

A7882   Cleobury, A. W. *The Shakespearian Criticism of Walter Whiter.* B. Litt. thesis, Oxford, 1951.

A7883   Hardy, Barbara. "Walter Whiter and Shakespeare." *N&Q,* 198 (1953), 50-54.

(l) OTHER INDIVIDUALS
(Arranged alphabetically by author discussed.)

A7884   M. Ambrosia Jackiewicz, Sister. *Edmund Burke's Opinions on Literature.* DD, Fordham University, 1953.

A7885 Thorpe, Clarence DeW. *The Aesthetic Theory of Thomas Hobbes, with Special Reference to His Contribution to the Psychological Approach in English Literary Criticism.* Univ. of Michigan Press, 1940. Pp. ix, 339.

A7886 Russell, Percy, ed. *Report and Transactions of the Devonshire Association for the Advancement of Science, Literature and Art.* Vol. 98. Lynton, 1956. Pp. 304.
Includes assessment, by E. D. Mackerness, of the qualities of the Rev. Richard Hole (1746-1803) as a Shak. critic.
Rev: *TLS*, July 5, 1957, p. 418.

A7887 Montague, Edwine. *Bishop Hurd as Critic.* DD, Yale University, 1939.

A7888 Watkin-Jones, A. "Langbaine's Account of the English Dramatick Poets (1691)." *Essays and Studies.* Vol. XXI. Collected by Herbert Read. Oxford: Clar. Press; London: Milford, 1936, pp. 75-85.

A7889 Small, Miriam Rossiter. *Charlotte Ramsay Lennox, an 18th Century Lady of Letters.* Yale studies in English. Vol. 85. New Haven: Yale Univ. Press, 1935. Pp. 268.

A7890 Tuveson, Ernest. "Locke and the 'Dissolution of the Ego'." *MP*, LII (1955), 159-174.

A7891 Parsons, H. "A. Pope's Essay on Criticism and the Present Day." *Poetry Review*, XXXV (1944), 137-145.

A7892 Mandel, Elias Wolf. *Christopher Smart: Scholar of the Lord. A Study of His Poetic Theory and its Eighteenth-century Background.* DD, University of Toronto, 1957.

A7893 Brown, Ernest A. *A Study of the Materials on the History of the Drama in Warton's "History of English Poetry."* DD, University of North Carolina, 1953. Abstract publ. in *University of North Carolina Record, Research in Progress*, Jan.-Dec. 1952, Grad. School Series No. 64, 1953, pp. 104-106.

A7894 Cancelled.

3. NINETEENTH CENTURY CRITICISM (141; 45)
a. REPRINTS (141; 45)

A7895 Coleridge, Samuel Taylor. "Marginalia on Shakespeare," in *Miscellaneous Criticism*, ed. by Thomas M. Raysor. Cambridge: Harvard Univ. Press; London: Constable, 1936. Pp. xvi, 468.

A7896 Brinkley, Roberta Florence, ed. *Coleridge on the Seventeenth Century.* Introd. by Louis I. Bredvold. Durham, North Carolina: Duke Univ. Press, 1956. Pp. xxxviii, 704.
Rev: by John M. Raines, *Books Abroad*, XXX (1956), 89; by Lucyle Werkmeister, *Personalist*, XXXVII, 314-315; by Roland Mushat Frye, *South Atlantic Bul.*, XXII, (May 1), 14-15; by George Whalley, *UTQ*, XXV, 259-262; by G. Blakemore Evans, *JEGP*, LV, 337-338; by M. H. Abrams, *MLN*, LXXII (1957), 56-60; by H. M. Margoliouth, *RES*, NS, VIII, 101-102.

A7897 Holmes, Charles Shively, Edwin Fussel, and Ray Frazer, eds. *Major Critics.* New York: Knopf, 1957.
Includes "Shakespeare's Judgement Equal to his Genius," "Shakespeare as a Poet Generally," and "Character of Hamlet," from *Coleridge's Shakespearian Criticism;* Dr. Johnson's "Preface to Shakespeare."

A7898 Hazlitt, William. *Hazlitt on Theatre*, ed. by William Archer and Robert Lowe, with an Introduction by William Archer (Dramabooks). First American ed. New York: Hill and Wang, 1957. Pp. 256.

A7899 Hazlitt, William. *The Round Table* and *Characters of Shakespeare's Plays.* New Everyman ed. London: Dent, 1957.

A7900 Charlton, H. B. *Senecan Tradition in Renaissance Tragedy: A Re-issue of an Essay Published in 1821.* Victoria Univ. Manchester, Publ. No. 296; English Ser., No. 24. Manchester Univ. Press, 1946. Pp. vii, 205.

A7901 Hunt, Leigh. *Dramatic Criticism, 1808-1831.* Ed. by Lawrence Huston Houtchens and Carolyn Washburn Houtchens. New York: Columbia University Press, 1949. Oxford Univ. Press, 1950. Pp. xiii, 347.
Rev: *TAr*, XXXIV (1950), 7; *TLS*, Oct. 20, p. 660; *Spectator*, No. 6387 (1950), 590; by E. Schneider, *PQ*, XXX (1951), 115.

A7902 Melián Lafinur, Luis. "El *humour*, la fantasía, la pasión, el crimen y la virtud en Shakespeare." *Rev. Nacional* (Montevideo), LV, Año XV, No. 163 (July, 1952), 128-145.

A7903 Taine, Hippolyte. *Šekspir i njegovi savremenici.* Serbian tr. by Nikola Trajković. Belgrade: Novo pokolenje, 1953. Pp. 350.

b. STUDIES (146; 46)
See also sections on Shakespeare's Significance for Various English, American, French, German, etc., Authors, A8953-B130.
(1) SURVEYS OF HISTORICAL CRITICISM
Articles and theses devoted to this topic. *Not exhaustive;* see also listings in 20th Century criticism, A8012-A8446. Pro and con comments upon this topic are numberless and may appear anywhere.

A7904 Miller, George Morey. *The Historical Point of View in Elizabethan Criticism.* DD, Heidelberg, 1912. Pp. 67.

A7905   Rushton, Urban Joseph Peters. *The Development of Historical Criticism in England 1532-1700.* DD, Princeton University, 1940. Pp. 307. *DA*, XII (1952), 308. No abstract published. Publication No. 3037.

A7906   Guérard, Albert. "The Growth of the Historical Spirit." *Stanford Studies in Lang. and Lit.*, ed. by Hardin Craig. Stanford University, California, 1941, pp. 1-10.

A7907   McCluskey, Donald. *The Rise of Historical Criticism of Shakespeare.* DD, Yale University, 1941.

A7908   Popper, Karl. "The Poverty of Historicism." *Economica*, NS, XI (1944), 86-103; 119-137; ibid., XII (1945), 69-89.

A7909   Orsini, Napoleone. "La pregiudiziale storicista nella critica di Shakespeare." *Anglica*, I (1946), 89-95.

A7910   Pearce, Roy Harvey. " 'Pure' Criticism and the History of Ideas." *JAAC*, VII (1948), 122-132.

A7911   Peery, Thomas A. "Emerson, the Historical Frame, and Shakespeare." *MLQ*, IX (1948), 440-447.

A7912   Robertson, D. W., Jr. "Historical Criticism." *EIE*, (1950), 3-31.

A7913   Babcock, R. W. "Historical Criticism of Shakespeare." *MLQ*, XIII (1952), 6-20.

A7914   Rathbun, John Wilbert. *The Development of Historical Literary Criticism in America, 1800-1860.* DD, University of Wisconsin, 1957.

A7915   Knights, L. C. "On Historical Scholarship and the Interpretation of Shakespeare." *SR*, LXIII (1955), 223-240.
        Answered by Whitaker in *ShN*, V (1955), 39.

A7916   Lawlor, John. "On Historical Scholarship and the Interpretation of Shakespeare: A Reply to L. C. Knights." *SR*, LXIV (1956), 186-206.

(2) NINETEENTH CENTURY CRITICISM IN GENERAL

A7917   Pennink, R. *Nederland en Shakespeare.* The Hague, 1936.
        Rev: A9739.

A7918   Colum, M. M. *From These Roots: The Ideas That Have Made Modern Literature.* New York, 1937. Pp. viii, 386.

A7919   Smyth, Miriam. *The Ethical Conception of Literature in English Literary Theory.* DD, University of Kansas, 1938.

A7920   Stolle, E. *Die Zeitgenossen und unmittelbaren Nachfolger Shakespeares in der englischen Kritik des neunzehnten Jahrhunderts.* DD, Hamburg, 1938. Pp. 230.

A7921   Stemmler, Walter. *Der Renaissancebegriff in der Shakespeare-Kritik.* DD, Hamburg, 1942. Pp. 277. Typewritten.

A7922   Peyre, Henri. *Writers and Their Critics.* Ithaca: Cornell Univ. Press, 1944. Pp. xii, 340.

A7923   McCollom, William Gilman. *Illusion and Formalism in Elizabethan Tragedy.* DD, Cornell University, 1945. Abstract publ. in *Abstracts of Theses, 1944*, Ithaca: Cornell Univ. Press, 1945, pp. 17-20.

A7924   Zanco, Aurelio. *Shakespeare in Russia e altri saggi.* Turin: Gheroni, 1945. Pp. 200.
        Rev: A9787.

A7925   Millward, James Bert. *The Restoration of Shakespeare's Personality.* MA thesis, Bishop's University (Canada), 1946. Pp. 87.

A7926   Jorgensen, Paul A. "Accidental Judgements, Casual Slaughters, and Purposes Mistook: Critical Reaction to Shakespeare's *Henry the Fifth*." *SAB*, XXII (1947), 51-61.

A7927   Ribner, Irving. "Lear's Madness in the Nineteenth Century." *SAB*, XXII (1947), 117-129.

A7928   Stahl, Ernst Leopold. *Shakespeare und das deutsche Theater.* Stuttgart: Kohlhammer, 1947. Pp. viii, 768.
        Rev: A9465.

A7929   Fluchère, Henri. "Shakespeare in France: 1900-1948." *ShS*, II (1949), 115-124.

A7930   Halliday, F. E. *Shakespeare and His Critics.* London: Gerald Duckworth & Co., 1949. Pp. 522.
        Rev: A8596.

A7931   Mercer, D. F. *Trends in Modern Criticism, 1800-1940.* B. Litt. Thesis, Oxford: St. Anne's Society, 1949.

A7932   Bailey, Helen Phelps. *Hamlet in France from Voltaire to Laforgue, 1733-1886.* DD, Columbia University, 1950. Pp. 405. Mic A50-92. *Mcf Ab*, X (1950), 114. Publication No. 1632.

A7933   Carlisle, Carol Jones. "The Nineteenth-Century Actors *Versus* the Closet Critics of Shakespeare." *SP*, LI (1954), 599-615.

A7934   Aldus, Paul J. "Analogical Probability in Shakespeare's Plays." *SQ*, VI (1955), 397-414. See also L. J. Mills and P. J. Aldus, ibid., VII (1956), 133-134.

A7935   Morris, Harry Caesar. *Nineteenth and Twentieth Century Criticism of Shakespeare's Problem Comedies.* DD, University of Minnesota, 1957. Abstract in *DA*, XVII (1957), 1546-47.

(3) ROMANTIC CRITICISM

A7936 O'Neill, Ada Gertrude. *English Literary Criticism of the Early 19th Century, 1798-1830.* MA thesis, Manitoba, 1931. Pp. 100.

A7937 Sisson, C. J. *The Mythical Sorrows of Shakespeare.* Oxford Univ. Press, 1934.
   Rev: by Baldwin Maxwell, *MLN*, LI (1936), 202-203; *London Mercury*, XXXIV, 92; by Mario Praz, *ES*, XVIII, 177-181; *N &Q*, 171 (1936), 53-54.

A7938 Knox, I. *The Aesthetic Theories of Kant, Hegel, and Schopenhauer.* New York: Columbia Univ. Press, 1936. Pp. xii, 220.

A7939 Davies, John Roberts. *The English Romantic Criticism of Shakespeare.* MA thesis, Dalhousie University, 1937. Pp. 182.

A7940 Mary M. O'Donnell, Sister. *The Genesis of Two Fallacies in Romantic Shakespearean Criticism.* DD, University of St. Louis, 1938.

A7941 Sanderlin, George. "The Repute of Shakespeare's Sonnets in the Early Nineteenth Century." *MLN*, LIV (1939), 462-466.

A7942 Shen, Yao. *Some Chapters on Shakespearean Criticism: Coleridge, Hazlitt and Stoll.* DD, University of Michigan, 1944. Pp. 306. Mic A47-33. *Mcf Ab*, VII (1947), 91. Publication No. 825.

A7943 Weisinger, Herbert. "English Treatment of the Classical-Romantic Problem." *MLQ*, VII (1946), 477-488.

A7944 Grober, Lydia. *Die Shakespeare-Kritik, in der englischen Romantik: Samuel Taylor Coleridge, Charles Lamb und William Hazlitt.* DD, Kiel, 1948. Pp. xvi, 286. Typewritten.
   See also "Shakespeare in der Kritik der englischen Romantik." *Neuphilol. Zeitschr.*, II (1950), 263-267.

A7945 Tave, S. M. *Comic Theory and Criticism from Steele to Hazlitt.* DD, Oxford, Oriel, 1950.

A7946 Barnet, Sylvan S. *Studies in Romantic Theory of Tragedy.* DD, Harvard University, 1954.

A7947 Russell, Bertrand. *Nightmares of Eminent Persons.* New York: Simon and Schuster, 1955. Includes "Mr. Bowdler's Nightmare" (pp. 11-16) and "The Psychoanalyst's Nightmare" (pp. 17-28), the latter concerning Romeo, Hamlet, Othello, Lear, Macbeth, and Antony. Repr. from *Courier*, XXII (Apr. 1954), 81-87.

A7948 Felheim, Marvin. "Landmarks of Criticism: *On the Tragedies of Shakespeare* by Charles Lamb, and *On the Knocking at the Gate in Macbeth* by Thomas De Quincey." *ShN*, VI (1956), 37.

A7949 Tomkins, A. R. *The Elizabethan Revival: A Study of the Contribution of Elizabethan Drama to the Romantic Movement.* DD, Cambridge, King's, 1957.

(4) LATER NINETEENTH CENTURY CRITICISM

A7950 'Rhedecynian.' "Shakespeare, Handel, and Gervinus." *N &Q*, 171 (1936), 327-328.

A7951 Schröter, Werner. "Grundsätzliches zur Deutung von Meisterwerken fremdsprachlicher Literatur." *NS*, XLVI (1938), 199-207.

A7952 Westfall, Alfred Van Rensselaer. *American Shakespearean Criticism, 1607-1865.* New York: H. W. Wilson, 1939. Pp. xii, 305.
   Rev: by H. R. Steeves, *Amer. Lit.*, XI (1939), 321-323; by Giles Dawson, *Lib. Quar.*, X (1940), 146-148; by Esther Cloudman Dunn, *SRL*, XXI (No. 12), 18.

A7953 Falk, Robert Paul. *Representative American Criticism of Shakespeare, 1830-1885.* DD, University of Wisconsin, 1940. Abstract publ. in *Summaries of Doctoral Dissertations, 1939-40*, Madison: Univ. of Wisconsin Press, 1940, pp. 258-260.

A7954 Quinlan, Maurice J. *Victorian Prelude.* A History of English Manners, 1700-1830. Number 155 of the Columbia University Studies in English and Comparative Literature. New York: Columbia Univ. Press, 1941. Pp. 301.
   "The Expurgators of Shakespeare," pp. 240-250. On Bowdler, Pitman, Hannah More and others.

A7955 Taylor, Warren. "The Uses of Shakespeare." *CE*, II (1941), 476-485.

A7956 Holzer, Gustav. *Kuno Fischers irrige Erklärung der Poetik Bacons.* Karlsruhe i. B.: Gutsch, 1942. Pp. 43.
   See also: Scholte: "Gregors Shakespeare herdrukt," *De Weegschaal*, IX (1943), H. 4.

A7957 Nye, Russel B. "George Bancroft's View of Shakspere." *SAB*, XVIII (1943), 109-113.

A7958 Pedigo, Frances. *Literary Criticism in the "Christian Examiner," 1824-1839.* MA thesis, University of North Carolina, 1946. Abstract publ. in *University of North Carolina Record, Research in Progress*, Grad. School Series No. 56, 1949, p. 226.

A7959 Henriques, Alf. "Shakespeare and Denmark: 1900-1949." *ShS*, III (1950), 107-115.

A7960 Link, Franz. *Die Begriffe des "Poet" und des "Writer" in ihrer Stellung im Ganzen der Lebensauffassung Ralph Waldo Emersons auf Grund einer Interpretation der Essays "Shakespeare or the Poet" und "Goethe or the Writer."* DD, Frankfurt am Main, 1950. Pp. 168. Typewritten.

A7961 Rubow, Paul V. *En Studie Bog (A Book of Studies).* Copenhagen: Gyldendal, 1950. Pp. 161.

A7962 South, R. J. *Changes in the Interpretation of Shakespeare in the Second Half of the 19th Century: the Treatment of the Plays by the Theatres and Dramatic Critics.* DD, University of London, 1952.

(5) SPECIFIC AUTHORS
(a) COLERIDGE

A7963   Coburn, Kathleen H. *Philosophical Tendencies in the Writings of S. T. Coleridge.* MA thesis, Toronto, 1930. Pp. 67.

A7964   Leavis, F. R. "S. T. Coleridge in Criticism." *Scrutiny,* IX (1940), 57-69.

A7965   Benziger, James George. *The Background of Coleridge's Doctrine of Organic Form.* DD, Princeton University, 1941.

A7966   Creed, Howard H. *Coleridge as Critic.* DD, Vanderbilt University, 1943.

A7967   Thorpe, C. D. "S. T. Coleridge as Aesthetician and Critic." *JHI,* V (1944), 387-414.

A7968   Stein, R. *Scientific Terminology and Analogy in Coleridge's Poetic Theory and Practice.* B. Litt. thesis, Oxford, Lady Margaret Hall, 1946.

A7969   Suppan, Adolph A. *Coleridge: the Shaping Mind.* DD, University of Wisconsin, 1947.

A7970   Willey, Basil. *Coleridge on Imagination and Fancy.* Warton Lecture on English Poetry, 1946. Oxford: Univ. Press; London: Cumberlege, 1947. Pp. 15.
        Rev: *TLS,* Nov. 9, 1946, p. 555; *N &Q,* 192 (1946), 21-22.

A7971   Waters, Leonard A. *Coleridge and Eliot: A Comparative Study of Their Theories of Poetic Composition.* DD, University of Michigan, 1948. Pp. 390. Mic A48-180. *Mic Abstr.* VIII (1948), 112. Publication No. 1081.

A7972   Hardy, Barbara C. *Coleridge's Theory of Communication.* MA thesis, London, University College, 1949.

A7973   Read, Herbert. "Coleridge as Critic." *Lectures in Criticism.* The Johns Hopkins University. Bollingen Series XVI. New York: Pantheon, 1949, pp. 73-116.

A7974   Whalley, A. G. C. *Samuel Taylor Coleridge: Library Cormorant. The History of His Use of Books; With a Consideration of Purpose and Pattern in His Reading, and an Account of the Books he Owned, Annotated and Borrowed.* DD, Univ. of London, 1950.

A7975   Benziger, James. "Organic Unity: Leibniz to Coleridge." *PMLA,* LXVI (1951), 24-48.

A7976   Millar, Kenneth. *The Inward Eye: A Revaluation of Coleridge's Psychological Criticism.* DD, University of Michigan, 1952. Pp. 458. *DA,* XII (1952), 190. Publication No. 3533.

A7977   Brennan, Maynard J. *Organic Unity: The Principle and its Application in the Criticism of Coleridge.* DD, University of Michigan, 1953. Pp. 254. Mic A53-1466. *DA,* XIII (1953), 792-793. Publication No. 5642.

A7978   Monroe, Dougald M., Jr. *Coleridge's Theories of Dreams, Hallucinations, and Related Phenomena in Relation to His Critical Theories.* DD, Northwestern University, 1953. Pp. 222. Mic A53-2032. *DA,* XIII (1953), 1186-87. Publication No. 6226.

A7979   Baker, James V. *The Subterranean Fountain: The Role of the Unconscious in Coleridge's Theory of Imagination.* DD, University of Michigan, 1954. Pp. 418. Mic A54-965. *DA,* XIV (1954), 670-671. Publication No. 7600.

A7980   Colmer, J. A. *Coleridge as a Critic of Political and Social Problems in His Prose Writings, 1795-1832.* DD, London, University College of Khartoum, 1955.

A7981   Beer, J. B. *The Development of Coleridge's Mind and Art Up to 1800.* DD, Cambridge, St. John's, 1956.

A7982   Yarlott, G. *Coleridge's Theory of the Whole Man and its Relation to His Ode on Dejection."* DD, Nottingham, 1956.

A7983   Haven, Richard. *Vision and Intellect: The Role of Mystical Experience in the Work of Samuel Taylor Coleridge.* DD, Princeton University, 1958.

(b) DE QUINCEY

A7984   Jordan, John E. *De Quincey's Criticism of English Literature.* DD, Johns Hopkins University, 1947. Pp. 506.

A7985   Jordan, John Emory. *Thomas de Quincey, Literary Critic. His Method and Achievement.* Univ. of California Publications. Engl. Studies. 4. Berkeley: Univ. of California Press, 1952; Cambridge Univ. Press, 1953. Pp. ix, 301.
        Rev: G. Carnall, *RES,* NS, V (1954), 424-426.

A7986   Bilsland, John Winstanley. *De Quincey's Theory of Literature of Power.* DD, University of Toronto, 1958.

(c) DOWDEN

A7987   "Edward Dowden: Shakespearean Critic." *TLS,* May 1, 1943, p. 214.

A7988   Hoeniger, F. D. "Dowden Marginalia on Shakespeare." *SQ,* VIII (1957), 129-132.

(d) MRS. JAMESON

A7989   Imhoff, Ruth. "Anna Jameson, Englands 'kleine Frau von Staël'." *N. Mon.,* XII (1941), 267-276.

A7990   Swinnerton, Frank. "Shakespeare's Heroines." *John o' London's Weekly,* LXIII (1954), 913.

(e) HAZLITT

A7991 Wilcox, Stewart C. *The Development of William Hazlitt with Particular Reference to the Familiar Essay.* DD, Johns Hopkins University, 1938.

A7992 Wulling, Emerson G. *William Hazlitt as a Literary Critic.* DD, University of Minnesota, 1939.

A7993 Lewis, I. *The Critical Writings of William Hazlitt.* MA thesis, Wales, 1952.

A7994 Slater, D. *Hazlitt as a Dramatic Critic.* MA thesis, Manchester, 1952.

A7995 Wilkerson, Leon C. *The Eighteenth Century Background of Hazlitt's Criticism.* DD, Vanderbilt University, 1954.

A7996 Klingopulos, G. D. "Hazlitt as Critic." *EIC,* VI (1956), 386-403.

(f) NORTH

A7997 Struve, Hugo. *John Wilson (Christopher North) als Kritiker.* DD, Berlin, Humboldt Univ., 1921. Pp. 67.

A7998 Swann, Elsie. *The Life of Christopher North.* DD, Leeds, 1933. Abstract publ. in University of Leeds *Publications and Abstracts of Theses, 1932-33,* p. 19.

A7998a Strout, Alan Lang. "John Wilson (Christopher North) as a Shakespeare Critic. A Study of Shakespeare in the English Romantic Movement." *SJ,* LXXII (1936), 93-123.

(g) PATER

A7999 Meaney, John W. *A Study in the Critical Method of Walter Pater.* DD, University of Texas, 1951.

A8000 Allison, J. M. *Walter Pater and the Function of Criticism.* MA thesis, London, Royal Holloway College, 1955.

(h) WINTER

A8001 McGaw, Charles J. *An Analysis of the Theatrical Criticism of William Winter.* DD, University of Michigan, 1940.

A8002 Ludwig, Richard M. *The Career of William Winter, American Drama Critic: 1836-1917.* DD, Harvard University, 1950.

A8003 Rubenstein, Gilbert M. *The Shakespearean Criticism of William Winter: An Analysis.* DD, University of Indiana, 1951.

(i) OTHERS

A8004 Lyon, B. R. *William Archer and the English Theatre.* MA thesis, London, Queen Mary College, 1955.

A8005 Capon, Reginald L. *Gamaliel Bradford as Literary Critic, with Particular Reference to Elizabethan Drama.* DD, Boston University, 1955.

A8006 Blos, Hanna. *Die Auffassung der Frauengestalten Shakespeares in dem Werk der Mrs. Cowden Clarke "The Girlhood of Shakespeare's Heroines."* DD, Erlangen, 1936. Pp. 131.

A8007 Stafford, John. "Henry Norman Hudson and the Whig Use of Shakespeare." *PMLA,* LXVI (1951), 649-661.

A8008 Carlisle, Carol Jones. "William Macready as a Shakespearean Critic." *Renaissance Papers,* 1954, pp. 31-39.

A8009 White, William. "Osler on Shakespeare, Bacon and Burton with a Reprint of His Creators, Transmuters, and Transmitters as Illustrated by Shakespeare, Bacon, and Burton." *Bul. Hist. Medicine,* VII (1939), 392-408.

A8010 Saintsbury, G. *Shakespeare.* Cambridge Univ. Press, 1934. Pp. 131.
   Rev: by L. C. Knights, *Criterion,* XIV (1934-35), 533-534.

A8011 Falk, Robert P. "Critical Tendencies in Richard Grant White's Shakespeare Commentary." *Amer. Lit.,* XX (1948), 144-154.

4. TWENTIETH CENTURY CRITICISM
   a. HISTORIES OF LITERATURE
   (1) LITERARY HISTORIES OF ENGLAND AND THE WORLD

A8012 Ghosh, J. C., and E. G. Withycombe. *Annals of English Literature, 1475 to 1925; the Principal Publications of Each Year.* Oxford: Clarendon Press, 1935. Pp. vi, 339.
   Rev: *TLS,* Feb. 1, 1936, p. 97; also (Leading article), June 6, p. 465; *N &Q,* 170 (1936), 414; by W. Fischer, *Beiblatt,* 47 (1936), 215; by J. E. Baker, *JEGP,* XXXVI (1937), 136-138; by W. W. Miller, *MLR,* XXXII, 490-491; briefly by R. D. H., *MLN,* LII, 153-154; by G. Becker, *DLZ,* LVIII, 701; by A. Brandl, *Archiv,* 171 (1937), 226; by Cl.-E. Engel, *RLC,* XIX (1939), 359-360.

A8013 Osgood, C. G. *The Voice of England: A History of English Literature.* New York and London, 1935. Pp. xiii, 627.
   Rev: by R. O. Rivera, *South Atlantic Quar.,* XXXV (1936), 348; by B. M. K., *Catholic World,*

142 (1936), 755-756; by O. Elton, *MLR*, XXXII (1937), 107-108; by K. Arns, *Beiblatt*, XLVIII, 237-242.

A8014 Kelly, B. M. *The Wells of English.* New York: Harper & Bros., 1936. Pp. xx, 402. Shak., pp. 97-103.

A8015 Praz, Mario. *Storia della Letteratura Inglese.* Florence: Sansoni, 1937. Pp. 411.
Rev: *TLS*, July 3, 1937, p. 494; by A. Zanco, *Rivista italiana del dramma*, Sept. 15, 1937; by O. Williams, *Criterion*, XVII, 186-187; by H. J. C. Grierson, *ES*, XX (1938), 124-126; by R. D. Waller, *MLR*, XXXIII, 88-89; by W. Hübner, *N. Mon.*, IX, 235-236.

A8016 Schirmer, Walter F. *Geschichte der Englischen Literatur von den Anfängen bis zur Gegenwart.* Halle: Niemeyer, 1937. Pp. vii, 679.
Rev: by H. S. V. Jones, *JEGP*, XXXVI (1937), 617-618; by A. Heinrich, *NS*, XLV, 427-428; by H. Lüdeke, *ES*, XX (1938), 219-223; by Max Wildi, *DLZ*, LIX, 702-708; by Friedrich Brie, *Eng. Studn.*, LXXII, 283-286; by H. W. Häusermann, *RES*, XIV, 492-493; by W. Keller, *SJ*, LXXIV, 186-190; by K. Arns, *ZNU*, XXXVII, 266-267; *RLC*, XVIII, 559-565; by A. Heinrich, *NS*, XLVI (1939), 82-87; by W. E. Süskind, *DL*, XL, 758; by W. Hübner, *N. Mon.*, IX, 234-235; by W. Keller, *ZNU*, XXXVII, 265-266; by H. G. Fiedler, *English*, II, 247-249; by K. M., *MLN*, LIV, 626-627; by F. Wild, *Archiv*, 175 (1939), 108-111; by K. Brunner, *Lbl*, LX, 179-181; by W. Fischer, *Beiblatt*, LI (1940), 49-54; by S. B. Liljegren, *SN*, XIII, 154-158; by A. Macdonald, *MLR*, XXXV, 128; by W. D. Robson-Scott, *RES*, XXV (1949), 183-184.

A8017 Ford, F. M. *The March of Literature.* New York: Dial Press, 1938. Pp. 878. London: Allen and Unwin, 1939.
Rev: *TLS*, Dec. 9, 1939, p. 716.

A8018 Guérard, A. *Preface to World Literature.* New York, 1940. Pp. 536.

A8019 Sampson, George. *The Concise History of English Literature.* Cambridge Univ. Press, 1941. Pp. xiv, 1094.
Rev: *N &Q*, 181 (1941), 83-84; *Spectator*, Sept. 19, p. 292; *TLS*, Aug. 16, p. 398; by H. B. C., *MGW*, Sept. 5, p. 156; by B. G. Brooks, *Nineteenth Century*, 130 (1941), 300-301; by Trevor James, *Life and Letters*, XXX, 236-240; by Raymond Mortimer, *NstN*, July 26, 90; by A. J. W., *Lib. Assoc. Rec.*, XLIII, 175-176; by R. E. Roberts, *SRL*, Oct. 11, pp. 6-7; by G. P. G., *ConR*, 160 (1941), 268-269; by H. C. Minchin, *FortnR*, NS, No. 897 (1941), 308-309; by L. Trilling, *Nation* (New York), 153 (1941), 546; by Blanche M. Kelly, *Catholic World*, 154 (1942), 625; by Edith J. Morley, *RES*, XVIII, 375-378; by L. B. Wright, *MLQ*, III, 493; by Edith C. Batho, *MLR*, XXXVII, 491-493; by Boris Ford, *Scrutiny*, X, 200-205; by W. W. Greg, *MLR*, XXXVIII (1943), 249-250; by Robert Shafer, *MLN*, LIX (1944), 350-354.

A8020 Van Tieghem, Paul. *Histoire Littéraire de l'Europe et de l'Amérique de la Renaissance à nos Jours.* Paris: A. Colin, 1941. Pp. vi, 422.
Rev: by R. Lebègue, *BHR*, II (1942), 202-203; by Albert Dauzat, *Le Français Moderne*, X, 234-235; *Rev. Universitaire*, LI, 27.

A8021 Shipley, Joseph T., ed. *A Dictionary of World Literature: Criticism, Forms, Technique.* New York: Philosophical Lib., 1943. Pp. xv, 633.
Rev: by M. F. Ashley Montagu, *Isis*, XXXV (1944), 87; by R. T. House, *Books Abroad*, XVIII, 152-153; by J. W. Ashton, *Jour. Amer. Folklore*, LVII, 146; by R. Wellek, *PQ*, XXIII, 186-189; (note on Mr. Wellek's review by W. A. Oldfather, ibid., XXIII, 378-379); by J. E. Tobin, *Thought*, XIX, 150-151.

A8022 Evans, B. Ifor. *English Literature.* London: Longmans, 1944. Pp. 42.
Rev: "Form in Literature," *TLS*, Mar. 25, 1944, p. 147.

A8023 Grierson, Herbert J. C., and J. C. Smith. *A Critical History of English Poetry.* London: Chatto & Windus, 1944. Pp. 527.
Rev: by Gwyn Jones, *Life and Letters Today*, XLIII (1944), 170, 172, 174; *TLS*, Dec. 2, p. 582; also editorial comment, ibid., p. 583; by Raymond Mortimer, *NstN*, Nov. 11, pp. 324-325; by Sheila Shannon, *Spectator*, Nov. 24, pp. 484, 486; by B. Ifor Evans, *MGW*, Feb. 23, 1945, p. 107; by Hermann Peschmann, *English* V, 124-126; by Babette Deutsch, *NYHTBR*, Dec. 1, 1946, p. 46; by Leonard Bacon, *SRL*, Dec. 7, p. 70; by F. A. Pottle, *YR*, XXXVI (1947), 731-734; by D. C. A., *MLN*, LXII, 360; by Earl Daniels, *CE*, VIII, 443-444.

A8024 Funke, Otto. *Epochen der Neueren Englischen Literatur. Eine Überschau von der Renaissance zum Beginn des 20. Jahrhunderts.* I. Teil, *16. und 17. Jahrhundert.* Bern: A Francke Verlag, 1945. Pp. iv, 192.
Rev: *Universitas*, II (1947), 1356; by G. Scheurweghs, *Erasmus*, II (1948/49), 96-97.

A8025 Zanco, Aurelio. *Storia della Letteratura Inglese.* 1. Delle Origini alla Restaurazione, 650-1660. Turin: Chiantore, 1946. Pp. xi, 610.

A8026 Baugh, Albert C., ed. *A Literary History of England.* New York: Appleton-Century-Crofts, 1948. Pp. xii, 1673.
The Renaissance is treated by the late C. F. Tucker Brooke.
Rev: by De Lancey Ferguson, *NYHTBR*, May 2, 1948, p. 11; by Charles Duffy, *NYTBR*, May 23, p. 25; *TLS*, March 26, 1949, p. 202; by J. J. Parry, *JEGP*, XLVIII, 147-149; by René Wellek, *MP*, XLVII, 39-45; by E. A. Cross, *CE*, X, 293; by J. Slattery, *Thought*, XXIV, 143-145; by R. A. Law, *MLN*, LXV (1950), 560-563; by V. de S. Pinto, *RES*, NS, I, 399-402; by Norman Callan, *MLR*, XLV, 84-85.

A8027 Suzuki, Sachio. *Main Currents in English Literature.* Aoyama-shoin, 1949.

A8028 Vallese, Tarquinio. *Saggi di Letteratura Inglese.* Naples: Pironti, 1949. Pp. 157.

A8029 Craig, Hardin, ed. *A History of English Literature.* Oxford Univ. Press, 1950. Pp. xiii, 697. Written by George K. Anderson, Hardin Craig (Renaissance), Louis I. Bredvold, and Joseph Warren Beach.
  Rev: by D. A. Stauffer, *CE,* xii (1950), 298-299.

A8030 Pellegrini, Giuliano. *Appunti di Letteratura Inglese,* 1949-50. Dalle lezioni. A cura di Bernardini Brunero e Iris Evangelisti. Pisa: Libr. goliardica, 1950. Pp. 187.

A8031 Ségur, Nicolas. *Histoire de la Littérature Européenne.* II: *Moyen Age et Renaissance.* Paris: Athinger, 1950. Pp. 348.
  Rev: by Pierre Courtines, *Books Abroad,* xxv (1951), 356; by Jean Roudaut, *Monde Nouveau-Paru,* Nos. 51-52, vii, 117-118.

A8032 Spemann, Adolf. *Vergleichende Zeittafel der Weltliteratur vom Mittelalter bis zur Neuzeit, 1150-1939.* Stuttgart: Engelhorn, 1951. Pp. 161.

A8033 Williams, Thomas George. *English Literature: A Critical Survey.* New York, London: Pitman, 1951. Pp. vii, 316.
  Rev: *TLS,* Aug. 17, 1951, p. 518; by Cazes, *EA,* v, 186.

A8034 Joseph, Bertram L. "Shakespeare." *Cassell's Encyclopaedia of World Literature.* Vol. II. London, 1953, pp. 1472-1475.

A8035 Muschg, Walter. *Tragische Literaturgeschichte.* 2nd ed. Bern: Francke, 1953. Pp. 747. Shak., pp. 41-46.
  Rev: by W. D. Williams, *Erasmus,* vi (1953), 790-795; by H. Uhlig, *Monat,* lxviii (1954), 189-191; by A. Oras, *JEGP,* liv (1955), 135-139; by F. M. Wasserman, *Monatshefte,* xlvii, 257-258.

A8036 Lüdeke, Henry. "Renaissance: Shakespeare." Lüdeke's *Die engl. Literatur.* Dalp-Taschenbücher, 307. Bern, 1954, pp. 26-37.

A8037 Pongs, Hermann. "Shakespeare." Pongs' *Das kleine Lexikon d. Weltliteratur.* Stuttgart, 1954, pp. 1242-48.

A8038 Baugh, Albert C. *History of the English Language.* 2nd ed. New York: Appleton-Century-Crofts, 1957. Pp. 550. Chapter VIII: The Renaissance, 1500-1650.

A8039 Legouis, Émile, and Louis Cazamian. *A History of English Literature.* New York: Macmillan, 1957. Pp. 1427.
  A thorough revision, with a new expanded bibliography.
  Rev: by Henry Pettit, *Western Humanities Review,* xi (1957), 196-197; briefly, *Arizona Quar.,* xiii, 282.

A8039a Delattre, Floris. "Émile Legouis et la Renaissance Anglaise." *EA,* ii (1938), 240-257.

A8040 Stamm, Rudolph. *Englische Literatur. Wissenschaftliche Forschungsberichte.* Geisteswissenschaftliche Reihe, Bd. II. Bern: Francke, 1957. Pp. 422.
  Shak., pp. 90-133.
  Rev: by Hermann Heuer, *SJ,* 94 (1958), 257-258.

(2) ENGLISH PERIOD HISTORIES

A8041 Dunn, Esther Cloudman. *The Literature of Shakespeare's England.* New York: Scribner's, 1936. Pp. viii, 336.
  Rev: by T. M. Parrott, *SRL,* Jan. 23, 1937, p. 17; by Alexander M. Witherspoon, *YR,* xxvii, 202-204.

A8042 Meissner, Paul. *Englische Literaturgeschichte.* II: *Von der Renaissance bis zur Aufklärung.* Berlin: de Gruyter, 1937. Pp. 139.
  Rev: by Hans Marcus, *DLZ,* lix (1938), 195-196; by Karl Brunner, *Eng. Studn.,* lxxiii, 87-88; by W. Keller, *SJ,* lxxiv, 190-191; by Alois Brandl, *Archiv,* 175 (1939), 116-117; by G. Kirchner, *Lbl,* lx, 388-391; by W. Keller, *ZNU,* xxxviii, 57-58; by H. W. Häusermann, *Beiblatt,* li (1940), 272-277; by H. S. V. J., *JEGP,* xxxix, 163-164.

A8043 Mathew, David. *The Jacobean Age.* London: Longmans, 1938. Pp. 354.
  Rev: A5481.

A8044 Pinto, Vivian de Sola. *The English Renaissance, 1510-1688.* With a chapter on Literature and Music by Bruce Pattison. Introductions to English Literature, ed. by Bonamy Dobrée: II. London: Cresset Press, 1938. Pp. 381.
  Rev: by J. B. Fort, *EA,* ii (1938), 391-392; *TLS,* May 28, p. 368; by W. F. Schirmer, *Beiblatt,* l (1939), 81-84; by Monica Redlich, *Spectator,* Aug. 4, pp. 192-193.

A8045 Bush, Douglas. *English Literature in the Earlier Seventeenth Century, 1600-1660.* Oxford: Clarendon Press, 1945. Pp. 621.
  Perhaps the best history in this period.
  Rev: by Geoffrey Tillotson, *English,* vi (1946), 28-30; *DUJ,* ns, vii, 66-67; by J. H. P. P., *Library,* 5th Series, i, 79-81; by C. J. Sisson, *MLR,* xli, 432-433; by H. B. Charlton, *MGW,* liv, 49; by H. J. C. Grierson, *Spectator,* Jan. 18, p. 68; by J. F. Macdonald, *Canadian Forum,* xxvi, 187; by B. M., *Dalhousie Rev.,* xxvi, 387-388; by C. R. T., *QQ,* liii, 397-399; *ES,* xxvii,

62; by L. C. Martin, *RES*, XXIII (1947), 167-169; by M. E. Prior, *MP*, XLV, 139-142; by Louis L. Martz, *YR*, XXXVI, 568-570; by Harris Fletcher, *JEGP*, XLVI, 315; by Rafael Koskimies, *Erasmus*, I, 288-290; by Arthur Barker, *UTQ*, XVI, 206-210; by S. C. Chew, *NYHTBR*, Mar. 30, 1947, p. 6; by Merritt Y. Hughes, *MLN*, LXIII (1948), 190-194; by A. Guidi, *Belfagor*, III, 383-384; by R. Kirk, *MLQ*, IX, 108-109.

A8046   Chambers, Sir Edmund K. *English Literature at the Close of the Middle Ages*. Oxford History of English Literature. Ed. F. P. Wilson and Bonamy Dobrée, Vol. II, Part 2. Oxford Univ. Press, 1946.
Rev: *TLS*, March 16, 1946, p. 127; *DUJ*, NS, VII, 66-67; by J. R. Hulbert, *MP*, XLIV (1947), 195-196; by J. M. N., *Library*, 5th Series, I, 255-257; by A. C. Baugh, *JEGP*, XLVI, 304-307; by J. A. W. Bennett, *RES*, XXIII, 271-273; by Laura H. Loomis, *MLQ*, VIII, 496-498; by S. C. Chew, *NYHTBR*, Mar. 30, 1947, p. 6.

A8047   Lattanzio, Michele. *History of English Literature, XVI and XVII Centuries*. Bari: Filli D'Ecclesia di Giovanni, 1949. Pp. 178.

A8048   Teesing, H. P. H. *Das Problem der Perioden in der Literaturgeschichte*. Groningen: J. B. Wolters, 1949. Pp. 146.
Rev: by J. E. Housman, *MLR*, XLV (1950), 237.

A8049   Schück, Henrik. *Allmän Litteraturhistoria*. 2nd ed. III, 3: *Renåssansen*. Stockholm: Hugo Gebers Forlag, 1950. Pp. 676.

A8050   Wedgwood, C. V. *Seventeenth Century English Literature*. Oxford Univ. Press, 1950. Pp. 186.
Rev: *TLS*, Oct. 6, 1950, p. 626; by H. B. Charlton, *MGW*, Nov. 2, p. 11; by B. Dobrée, *Spectator*, Oct. 6, p. 372; by W. Allen, *NstN*, Oct. 28, p. 390.

A8051   Lewis, C. S. *English Literature in the Sixteenth Century Excluding Drama*. Oxford History of English Literature, III. Oxford: Clarendon Press, 1954. Pp. vii, 696.
Rev: *TLS*, Sept. 17, 1954, p. 592; by Helen Gardner, *NstN*, Oct. 30, p. 546; by John Wain, *Spectator*, Oct. 1, pp. 403-405; *Listener*, LII, 773; by William A. Armstrong, *YWES*, XXXV, 66-68; by Donald Davie, *EIC*, V (1955), 159-164; by Leicester Bradner, *RN*, VIII, 19-22; *CE*, XVI, 466; by H. S. Wilson, *UTQ*, XXIV, 429-433; by Hermann Peschmann, *English*, X, 144-145; by Hermann Heuer, *SJ*, 91 (1955), 319-322; by J. C. Maxwell, *DUJ*, XVI (June), 133-137; *VQR*, XXXI (Spring), 44; *ShN*, V, 14; by Elizabeth Sewell, *Thought*, XXX, 454-455; by Barbara Cooper, *London Mag.*, II, No. 7 (1955), 86-91; by Wolfgang Clemen, *Archiv*, 192 (1955), 202-203; by H. B. Charlton, *MGW*, Feb. 10, p. 11; by Yvor Winters, *Hudson Rev.*, VIII, 281-287; by F. S. Boas, *ConR*, 187 (1955), 345-347; by Jacques Vallette, *MdF*, Jan., pp. 145-149; by M. MacLure, *Canadian Forum*, July, p. 94; by C. T. Harrison, *SR*, LXIII, 153-161; by James Roy King, *QQ*, LXIII (1956), 151-153; by G. D. Willcock, *RES*, NS, VII, 195-197; by Michel Poirier, *EA*, IX, 131-135; by R. W. Zandvoort, *ES*, XXXVII, 271-274; by J. Chalker, *Studia Neophil.*, XXVIII, 56-59.

A8052   Ward, A. C. *Illustrated History of English Literature*. Vol. I: *Chaucer to Shakespeare*. London: Longmans, 1954. Pp. xv, 244.
Rev: *TLS*, May 14, 1954, p. 311; *Listener*, LI, 269.

A8053   Schubel, F. *Englische Literaturgeschichte*. II: *Von der Renaissance bis zur Aufklärung*. Berlin: Walter de Gruyter, 1956. Pp. 160.
Rev: briefly by Hans Marcus, *Archiv*, 193 (1957), 332.

A8054   Morris, Helen. *Elizabethan Literature*. Home Univ. Library. Oxford Univ. Press, 1958. Pp. ix, 239.
Rev: briefly, *ShN*, VIII (1958), 30; by Philip Henderson, *Time and Tide*, Oct. 11, pp. 1225-26; by R. A. Foakes, *English*, XII, 105-106, *N &Q*, NS, V, 489; by J. Fuzier, *LanM*, LII, 401.

(3) THEATRE HISTORIES OTHER THAN EXCLUSIVELY ELIZABETHAN-STUART

A8055   Borcherdt, H. H. *Das Europäische Theater im Mittelalter und in der Renaissance*. Leipzig, 1935.
Rev: *LZ*, 86 (1935), 511-512; by H. K., *ZDK*, L (1936), 299; by M. Bl. Evans, *GR*, XI, 56-57; by Günter Skopnik, *DLZ*, LVIII (1937), 449-452; by J. W. Kurtz, *MP*, XXXIV, 427-428; by P. Abrahams, *Medium Aevum*, VII (1938), 72-73; by H. Wehe, *Hochschule und Ausland*, XIV (1939?), Heft 5; by N. N., *Hochland*, XXXV (1940), 12.

A8056   Drew, Elizabeth. *Discovering Drama*. London: Cape, 1937. Pp. 252.

A8057   Nicoll, A. *The Development of the Theatre: A Study of Theatrical Art from the Beginning to the Present Day*. New York: Harcourt, Brace & Co., 1937. Pp. 310.

A8058   D'Amico, Silvio. *Storia del Teatro Drammatico*. Vol. I. Milan, Rome: Rizzoli e C., 1939.
Rev: by D. Mondrone, S. J., *La Civiltà Cattolica*, 90, iii (1939), 257-265.

A8059   Mokulsky, S. *The History of the Theatre in Europe*. Vol. II. Moscow, Leningrad: Iskusstvo, 1939. Pp. 512.

A8060   Gassner, John. *Masters of the Drama*. New York: Random House, 1940. Pp. xvii, 804.
Excerpt, "William Shakespeare Playwright of Infinite Scope." *Wisdom*, July, 1956, pp. 7-11.
Rev: by Edwin Duerr, *QJS*, XXVI (1940), 680-681.

A8061   Freedley, G., and I. A. Reeves. *A History of the Theatre*. New York, 1941. Pp. xvi, 688.

A8062   Pfeiffer, Arthur. *Ursprung und Gestalt des Dramas.* Studien zu einer Phänomenologie der Dichtkunst und Morphologie des Dramas. Berlin: Junker & Dünnhaupt, 1943. Pp. 395. Shak. *passim.*
  Rev: by F. Baser, *Deutsche Dramaturgie,* II (1943), 118.

A8063   Weber, Alfred. *Das Tragische und die Geschichte.* Hamburg: H. Goverts, 1943. Pp. 446.
  Rev: by Heinrich Jacobi, *EL,* III (1944), 14-17.

A8064   Gregor, Joseph. *Weltgeschichte des Theaters.* I: *Von den Ursprüngen bis zum Ausgang des Barocktheaters.* Munich, 1944. Pp. 481.

A8065   Bridie, James. *The British Drama.* British Way Pamphlets, No. 12. Glasgow: Craig & Wilson, 1946. Pp. 40.
  Rev: *TLS,* Mar. 2, 1946, p. 103.

A8066   Cleaver, James. *The Theatre Through the Ages.* London: George G. Harrap & Co., 1946. Pp. 146.
  Rev: *TLS,* Nov. 23, 1946, p. 575.

A8067   Nicoll, Allardyce. *World Drama from Aeschylus to Anouilh.* New York: Harcourt, Brace, 1950. Pp. 1000. Section on Shak., pp. 257-277.
  Rev: by L. Eyrignoux, *LanM,* XLIV (1950), 446; by C. Morgenstern, *Spectator,* No. 6352, pp. 394; by J. Gassner, *TAr,* XXXIV (July, 1950), 2, 4, 6-7.

A8068   Kindermann, Heinz. *Meister der Komödie.* Von Aristophanes bis G. B. Shaw. Vienna, Munich: Donau-Verlag, 1952. Pp. 297. Shak. and Jonson, pp. 121-148.
  Rev: by H. Heuer, *SJ,* 89 (1953), 217-218; by H. Moenkemeyer, *MLN,* LXIX (1954), 60-61.

A8069   Nagler, A. M. *Sources of Theatrical History.* New York: Theatre Annual, 1952. Pp. xxiii, 611.
  Rev: A7076.

A8070   Kerr, Alfred. "Shakespeare." Kerr's *Die Welt im Drama.* Cologne, Berlin, 1954, pp. 363-373.

A8071   Hartnoll, Phyllis, ed. *The Oxford Companion to the Theatre.* New York: Oxford Univ. Press, 1951. Pp. 888. Second ed. Oxford Univ. Press, 1957. Pp. 984. Illustrated.
  Rev: by Russell Rhodes, *SRL,* Sept. 29, 1951, p. 30; *N &Q,* 196 (1951), 417-418; by Henry Popkin, *SR,* LX, 329-336; *Listener,* XLVI, 152; by Sir Desmond MacCarthy, *Sunday Times,* July 29, p. 3; *TLS,* July 13, p. 435; by Louis Bonnerot, *EA,* V, 89; by S. Deas, *Erasmus,* V (1952), 766-768; by T. C. Worsley, *NstN,* XLII, 161-162; by J. Gielgud, *Spectator,* No. 6417, p. 828; by Rudolf Stamm, *SJ,* 87/88 (1952), 219-220; *TLS,* Dec. 13, 1957, p. 758; by William A. Armstrong, *TN,* XII (1958), 98-100; *Drama,* Spring, p. 43; *Players Mag.,* XXXIV, 125.

b. OTHER AESTHETIC CRITICISM OF SHAKESPEARE (144-6;46)
Articles which are chiefly discussions of some one other author's work are entered after the listings of that author. E.g., see Croce, Granville-Barker, Stoll.

A8072   "Nieuwe Shakespeare-Studien." [Bradley, Wilson Knight, F. R. Leavis und L. C. Knights]. *De Stem,* 1937, pp. 641-644.

A8073   Abrams, M. H. "Belief and Suspension of Disbelief." *Literature and Belief, EIE,* 1957 (1958), pp. 1-30.

A8074   Alexander, Peter. *Shakespeare's Life and Art.* London: Nisbet, 1938. Pp. vi, 248. See "Many Shakespeares." *TLS,* Feb. 25, 1939, p. 121.
  Rev: A505.

A8075   Alexander, Peter. *Hamlet: Father and Son.* The Lord Northcliffe Lectures, University College, London, 1953. Oxford: Oxford Univ. Press, 1954. Pp. 196. Discusses major considerations of Shak. criticism.
  Rev: B7759.

A8076   Arnoux, Alexandre. "À la Recontre de Shakespeare." *Rev. de Paris,* February (1953), pp. 102-115.

A8077   Aynard, Joseph. "Exotisme et Humanisme dans la Poésie Élizabéthaine." *Le Théâtre Élizabéthain.* Paris: Les Cahiers du Sud, 1940, pp. 61-65.

A8078   Babb, Lawrence. "On the Nature of Elizabethan Psychological Literature." *AMS,* pp. 509-522.
  Points out that there is no agreement about such fundamental matters as the classification of the passions, or the number of spirits in the body: that the Elizabethan dramatists apply psychological concepts only intermittently to their characters; and, one might add, that the newer psychological interpretation may often be imposed upon an older stage character type, with little regard for consistency.

A8079   Babcock, Robert W. "A Note on Modern Sceptical Criticism of Shakespeare." *N &Q,* 193 (1948), 491-494.
  Distinguishes between sceptical and historical criticism and declares the former may exist without the latter. The former simply denies the plausibility of the characters, the latter explains them by source, tradition, etc.

A8080   Babcock, R. W. "Historical Criticism of Shakespeare." *MLQ,* XIII (1952), 6-20.

A8081 Bachrach, A. G. H. *Naar Het Hem Leek. Een Inleiding tot Shakespeare in Vijf Brieven.* The Hague: Bert Bakker/Daamen; Antwerp: De Sikkel, 1957. Pp. 272.
Rev: A366.

A8082 Bailey, Helen P. *"Hamlet" in France from Voltaire to Laforgue (1733-1886).* DD, Columbia University, 1950. Pp. 405. Mic A50-92. *Microf. Ab.,* x, ii (1950), 114. Publication No. 1632.

A8083 Baldini, Gabriele. "La Critica Testuale Shakespeariana e l'Aggiornamento del Gusto." *Letterature Moderne,* III (Dec., 1952), 711-719.

A8084 Baldwin, T. W. "Review of Some Recent Books on Shakespeare." *MLN,* LV (1940), 455-462.

A8085 Baldwin, T. W. "On Atomizing Shakespeare." *SJ,* 91 (1955), 136-144.

A8086 Bateson, F. W. "The Function of Criticism at the Present Time." *EIC,* III (1953), 1-27.
Discusses, as one among a number of examples of "critical irresponsibility," Empson's analysis of Sonnet 73. Comment by W. Empson, reply by F. W. Bateson, further comment by W. Empson, *EIC,* III, 357-363.

A8087 Beck, Martha Ryan. *An Estimate of Brander Matthews as Teacher, Writer, and Critic in the Field of Drama.* DD, University of Washington, 1939. Abstr. in Univ. of Washington *Abstracts of Theses,* IV (1939), 106-108.

A8088 Bender, Jack Earl. *The Theatre of Brander Matthews.* DD, University of Michigan, 1954. Pp. 476. Mic A54-1627. *DA,* XIV (1954), 1112. Publication No. 8270.

A8089 Bentley, Eric. "Maiming the Bard." *NR,* Sept. 22, 1952, p. 27.

A8090 Bentley, Eric. "Doing Shakespeare Wrong." *Perspectives,* No. 3, Spring, 1953, pp. 97-109.

A8091 Berenson, Bernard. "Noterelle su Shakespeare (Pagine di diario)." *Letteratura,* VIII (May-June, 1946), 13-16.

A8092 Berger, Ludwig. *Wir Sind vom Gleichen Stoff, aus dem Träume Sind.* Tübingen: Wunderlich, 1953. Pp. 403. Shak., pp. 83-101.

A8093 Bertocci, Angelo Philip. *Charles Du Bos and English Literature: A Critic and his Orientation.* New York: King's Crown Press; Oxford Univ. Press, 1949. Pp. viii, 285.

A8094 Bethell, S. L. *Essays on Literary Criticism and the English Tradition.* London: Dennis Dobson, 1948. Pp. 99.

A8095 Bliss, William. *The Real Shakespeare: A Counterblast to Commentators.* London: Sidgewick & Jackson, 1947. Pp. x, 311.
Rev: *TLS,* July 12, 1947, p. 352; by W. R. Calvert, *Illus. London News,* Sept. 6, p. 278; by H. B. C., *MGW,* Aug. 7, p. 10; by Goronwy Rees, *Spectator,* Mar. 21, pp. 307-308; by Arthur Sewell, *NstN,* Oct. 25, p. 336. See rejoinder by Mr. Bliss and reply by reviewer, *TLS,* July 26, 1947, p. 379; ibid., Aug. 9, p. 403; by J. Vallette, *La Nef,* December; by A. Koszul, *LanM,* XLIII (1949), 334; by E. Brennecke, *SQ,* I (1950), 279; by Harry Levin, *NYTBR,* Mar. 26, p. 7; by Hamilton Basso, *New Yorker,* Apr. 8, 1950, p. 113.

A8096 Bodkin, Maud. *Archetypal Patterns in Poetry.* Oxford Univ. Press, 1934. Pp. xiv, 340.
Chiefly concerned with Virgil, Dante, Shakespeare, and Milton.
Hamlet & Oedipus considered, pp. 11-13; Othello, pp. 217-224; Hamlet & Lear, pp. 280-285; Psych. Crit. & Dr. Conventions," pp. 332-334.
Rev: by G. D. Willcock, *MLR,* XXXI (1936), 91-92; *Cornhill Mag.,* 153 (1936), 253-254.

A8097 Bohannan, Laura. " 'Miching Mallecho, that means Witchcraft'." *London Magazine,* I (1954), 51-60.
How a woman anthropologist told the Hamlet story to a group of African natives.

A8098 Borinski, Ludwig. "Die Tragische Periode der Englischen Literatur." *NS,* IV (1955), 289-307.

A8099 Bradbrook, M. C. *Shakespeare and Elizabethan Poetry: A Study of his Earlier Work in Relation to the Poetry of the Time.* London: Chatto and Windus, 1951. Pp. viii, 279.
Rev: A3534.

A8100 Bradley, A. C. *Shakespearean Tragedy. Hamlet, Othello, King Lear, Macbeth.* New York: Noonday, 1956. Pp. 448. Also London: Macmillan, 1957. Pp. xv, 432.
Reprints.

A8101 "Shakespeare and A. C. Bradley." *N &Q,* 185 (1943), 25.

A8102 Campbell, Lily B. "Bradley Revisited: Forty Years After." *SP,* XLIV (1947), 174-194.

A8103 Siegel, Paul N. "In Defense of Bradley." *CE,* IX (1948), 250-256.

A8104 Campbell, Lily B. "Concerning Bradley's *Shakespearean Tragedy.*" *HLQ,* XIII (1949), 1-18.
See also J. Gassner, *TAr,* XXXIII, viii (1949), 5, 108-109.

A8105 "A. C. Bradley." *TLS,* March 30, 1951, p. 197.

A8106 Joseph, Bertram. "The Problem of Bradley." *Use of Engl.,* Feb. 5, 1953, pp. 87-91.

A8107 Emslie, Macdonald. "Burning Bradley." *ShN,* IV (1954), 30.

A8108 Bush, Douglas. "Seventeenth Century Poets and the Twentieth Century." *Annual Bulletin of the Modern Humanities Research Association,* pp. 16-28.
The 1955 presidential address. Mentions Bradley but has nothing else on Shak.

A8109 Cancelled.

A8110 Brandl, Alois. "Von der Unwahrheit und Wahrheit Shakespeares." *Blätter d. Dts. Theaters,* II, Reihe No. 22, p. 337 ff. Also in Brandl's *Forschungen,* pp. 175-176.

A8111 Braun, Hanns. "Shakespeare als Nothelfer der Kritik." *SJ*, 93 (1957), 82-88.

A8112 Brennecke, Ernest. "All Kinds of Shakespeares—Factual, Fantastical, Fictional." *SQ*, I (1950), 272-280.

A8113 Brooke, C. F. Tucker. "Shakespeare Apart." *Essays on Shakespeare and Other Elizabethans*, Yale Univ. Press, 1948, pp. 16-31.

A8114 Brooke, Stopford A. *On Ten Plays of Shakespeare*. Cheap edition. London: Constable, 1937. Pp. 311. Reprint.

A8115 Brooks, Cleanth. "Literary History vs. Criticism." *KR*, II (1940), 403-412.

A8116 Brooks, Cleanth. *The Well Wrought Urn: Studies in the Structure of Poetry*. New York: Reynal & Hitchcock, 1947. Pp. xi, 270.
Rev: by D. A. Stauffer, *MLN*, LXII (1947), 427-429; by Dudley Fitts, *KR*, IX, 612-616; by A. Mizener, "The Desires of the Mind," *SR*, LV, 460-469; by W. Empson, "Thy Darling in an Urn," ibid., LV, 690-697; by Theodore Maynard, *Catholic World*, 165 (1947), 570; by R. P. Blackmur, *NYTBR*, June 8, 1947, p. 6; by G. F. Whicher, *NYHTBR*, April 20, p. 2; by H. W. Wells, *SRL*, April 12, p. 50; by J. W. R. Purser, *MLR*, XLII, 541-542; by Josephine Miles, *JAAC*, VI, 185-186; by R. S. Crane, "Cleanth Brooks; or the Bankruptcy of Critical Monism," *MP*, XLV (1948), 226-245; by Norman Callan, *RES*, XXIV, 347-349; by A. Mizener, *Poetry*, LXXI, 318-324; *TLS*, Jan. 13, 1950, p. 26.

A8117 Brooks, Cleanth. "A Note on the Limits of 'History' and the Limits of 'Criticism'." *SR*, LXI (1953), 129-135.

A8118 Brooks, Cleanth. "Implications of an Organic Theory of Poetry." *Literature and Belief, EIE*, 1957 (1958), pp. 53-79.

A8119 Burke, Kenneth. *The Philosophy of Literary Form: Studies in Symbolic Action.*. Louisiana State Univ. Press, 1941. Pp. xvii, 546. Paperback edition, N. Y. Vintage Books, 1957.

A8120 Burke, Kenneth. *Counter-Statement*. Univ. of Chicago Press, 2nd edition, 1953. Paperback edition, 1957.

A8121 Burke, Kenneth. *A Rhetoric of Motives*. New York: Prentice-Hall, 1952. Pp. 340.

A8122 Burke, Kenneth. *A Grammar of Motives*. New York: Prentice-Hall, 1952. Pp. 530.

A8123 Bush, Geoffrey. *Shakespeare and the Natural Condition*. Harvard Univ. Press, 1956. Pp. 140.
Rev: A921.

A8124 Campbell, O. J. "Shakespeare and the 'New' Critics." *AMS*, 1948, pp. 81-96.

A8125 Carrère, Félix. "L'Imagination dans le Théâtre de Shakespeare." *LanM*, March-April, 1950, pp. 100-113.

A8126 Centeno, Augusto, ed. *The Intent of the Artist*. Princeton Univ. Press, 1941. Pp. 162.

A8127 Chambers, Sir E. K. *Shakespearean Gleanings*. Oxford Univ. Press, 1944.
Reprint of a number of his well-known essays.

A8128 Chambers, E. K. *Shakespeare: A Survey*. Fifth reprinting. New York: Macmillan, 1955. Pp. x, 325. Also New York: Hill and Wang, 1958. Pp. 336. Dramabooks reprint, paperback.
Noticed by James G. McManaway, *SQ*, VI (1955), 473.

A8129 Chambers, R. W. *The Jacobean Shakespeare and "Measure for Measure."* Annual Shakespeare Lecture of the British Academy, 1937. Oxford Univ. Press, 1938. Pp. 60.
Rev: by Wolfgang Schmidt, *Beiblatt*, XLIX (1938), 108-110; by O. Elton, *MLR*, XXXIII, 428-429; by W. Keller, *SJ*, LXXIV, 180-182; *N &Q*, 176 (1939), 449-450; by T. W. Baldwin, *MLN*, LV (1940), 460.

A8130 Chapman, J. A. "*King Lear*." *Nineteenth Century*, 142 (1947), 95-100.

A8131 Clemen, Wolfgang. "Zur Methodik der Shakespeare-Interpretation." *Sprache und Literatur Englands und Amerikas* (Tübingen), II (1956), 83-102.

A8132 Clurman, Harold. *Lies Like Truth*. New York: Macmillan, 1958. Pp. 300.
Rev: by John Gassner, *Nation*, Oct. 11, 1958, pp. 215-216; by Babette Brimberg, *TAr*, Sept., pp. 8, 74-75.

A8133 Craig, Edward Gordon. *On the Art of Theatre*. Fifth impr. with new ill. London: Heinemann, 1957. Pp. xxiii, 294.
Rev: by T. C. Worsley, *NstN*, LIII (1957), 311-312; by J. Stephens, *TN*, XI, 142-143; by G. W. Knight, *TC*, 162 (1957), 92-93; *TLS*, Feb. 22, p. 113; by G. R. Kernodle, *ETJ*, IX, 256-257; by O. G. Brockett, *Players Mag.*, XXXIV (1958), 143; by P. Nordmann, *EA*, XI, 362-363.

A8134 Craig, Hardin. *The Enchanted Glass: The Elizabethan Mind in Literature*. Oxford Univ. Press, 1936. Pp. ix, 293.
Rev: A3857.

A8135 Craig, Hardin. *Shakespeare and the Normal World*. Rice Institute Pamphlet, XXXI, No. 1, Houston, Texas, 1944. Pp. vi, 49.
Rev: A929.

A8136 Craig, Hardin. *An Interpretation of Shakespeare*. New York: Dryden Press, 1948. Pp. 400.
Rev: by W. B. C. Watkins, *NYTBR*, Aug. 1, 1948, p. 3; by C. R. Florey, *South Atlantic Bul.*, XIV, No. 2 (1948), 10-11; by W. T. Hastings, *SAB*, XXIII, 201-203; by George R. Potter, *CE*, X (1949), 231; *TLS*, Aug. 5, p. 508; by Una Ellis-Fermor, *RES*, NS, I (1950), 259-260.

A8137 Craig, Hardin. "An Aspect of Shakespearean Study." *SAB*, XXIV (1949), 247-257.

A8138 Craig, Hardin. "Trend of Shakespeare Scholarship." *ShS*, II (1949), 107-114.
Recommends all fields of knowledge be brought to bear on interpretation. Deplores specialization.

A8139 Crane, R. S., ed. *Critics and Criticism, Ancient and Modern.* Univ. of Chicago Press, 1952.
Rev: by Northrop Frye, *SQ*, V (1954), 78-80.

A8140 Crane, R. S. *The Languages of Criticism and the Structure of Poetry.* Toronto Univ. Press, 1953.
Pp. xxi, 214.

A8141 Croce, Benedetto. *Saggi Filosofici. VIII: La Poesia. Introduzione alla Critica e Storia della Poesia e della Letteratura.* Bari: Laterza, 1936. Pp. 352.

A8142 Croce, Benedetto. *Shakespeare.* Ed. by Napoleone Orsini. Biblioteca di Cultura Moderna. Bari: Laterza, 1948. Pp. xxx, 213.

A8143 Croce, Benedetto. *Ariosto, Shakespeare e Corneille.* 4th revised edition. Bari: Laterza, 1950. Pp. viii, 280.

A8144 Croce, Benedetto. *Conversazioni Critiche. Serie V.* Bari: Laterza, 1939. *Serie III, IV.* 2nd rev. ed. Bari: Scritti di Storia Letteraria e Politica, Laterza, 1951. Pp. 397.
The last chapter of *Serie III*, "Letterature Straniere," includes a discussion of Croce's attitude to Shak. philology. Other comments on Shak. throughout.

A8145 Lawrie, J. G. *The Basic Principles of the Esthetic of Benedetto Croce, with Reference to English Literature.* MA thesis, Univ. of South Africa, 1921.

A8146 Meldrum, M. S. *Croce and the Einfühlung Theory on the Relation of Feeling to the Work of Art.* B. Litt. thesis, Oxford, Somerville, 1941.

A8147 Praz, Mario. "Literary History." *CL*, II (1950), 97-106.

A8148 Orsini, Napoleone. "Croce e la Critica Shakespeariana." *Rivista di Letterature Moderne* (Florence), IV, ii (April-June, 1953), 145-154.

A8149 Crow, John. "Deadly Sins of Criticism, or, Seven Ways to Get Shakespeare Wrong." *SQ*, IX (1958), 301-306. See Harold S. Wilson, "Commentary," *SQ*, IX (1958), 307-310.
Remarks on the three MLA papers printed in *SQ*.

A8150 Cruttwell, Patrick. "Another Part of the Wood." *EIC*, V (1955), 382-390.
Objects to the old historical criticism on the grounds it neglects other considerations.

A8151 Cunningham, J. V. "Logic and Lyric." *MP*, LI (1953), 33-41.

A8152 Daiches, David. *A Study of Literature.* Ithaca: Cornell Univ. Press, 1948. Pp. ix, 240.

A8153 Daiches, David. "Guilt and Justice in Shakespeare." *Literary Essays.* London: Oliver and Boyd, 1956, pp. vii, 225.
Opening remarks deal with "historical" criticism. "We distort the meaning of Shakespeare's plays sadly if we lay them on the Procrustean bed of a synthetic 'Elizabethan point of view'." p. 1.

A8154 Daiches, David. *Critical Approaches to Literature.* London: Longmans, 1956. Pp. ix, 404.
"Shakespearean Criticism & Scholarship," pp. 336-338.
Rev: A1381.

A8155 Danby, John F. *Shakespeare's Doctrine of Nature: A Study of "King Lear".* London: Faber and Faber, 1949. Pp. 234.
Rev: A934.

A8156 Danby, John F. *Poets on Fortune's Hill: Studies in Sidney, Shakespeare, Beaumont and Fletcher.* London: Faber and Faber, 1952. Pp. 212.
Rev: *TLS*, Nov. 14, 1952, p. 744; by R. A. Foakes, *English*, IX (1952/53), 141-142; by J. I. M. Stewart, *NstN*, XLIV, 324; by M. Poirier, *EA*, VI (1953), 58-59; by F. T. Prince, *RES*, NS, IV, 374-376; by J. C. F. Littlewood, *Scrutiny*, XIX, 154-160; by Clifford Leech, *ShS*, VII (1954), 135 [brief]; by Harold Jenkins, ibid., 141 [brief].

A8157 Dean, Leonard F. "Shakespeare's Treatment of Conventional Ideas." *SR*, LII (1944), 414-423.
Argues that Shakespeare's plays are more than dramatic confirmations of conventional beliefs.

A8158 Delius, Rudolf von. *Shakespeare: Eine Neudeutung seines Geistes.* Reinbek bei Hamburg: Parus, 1947. Pp. 160.
Rev: by H. Oppel, *Lit. d. Gegenw.*, 1948, i, pp. 41-43; by G. G., *Neues Abendland*, III (1948), 255.

A8159 Dilthey, Wilhelm. *Die Grosse Phantasiedichtung und Andere Studien zur Vergleichenden Literaturgeschichte.* Göttingen: Vanderhoek und Ruprecht, 1954. Pp. 324. Shak., pp. 53-108.

A8160 Dobrée, Bonamy. "On (Not) Enjoying Shakespeare." *Essays and Studies*, NS, IX (1956), 39-55.

A8161 Doyle, A. I. "Approach to Shakespeare." *Scrutiny*, XII (1944), 236-238.

A8162 Duthie, G. I. *Shakespeare.* London: Hutchinson's University Library, 1951. Pp. 206.
First Chapter offers objections to the critical principles of certain so-called historical critics.
Rev: *TLS*, Aug. 31, 1951, p. 550; by Frederick S. Boas, *FortnR*, NS, 1017 (1951), 634-635; by J. I. M. Stewart, *NstN*, Sept. 22, pp. 319-320; *Adelphi*, XXVII, 361-362; *N &Q*, 196 (1951), 549-550; *DUJ*, NS, XIII, 32; by K. Young, *Spectator*, 6440 (1951), 749; by A. P. Rossiter,

English, IX (1952), 68-69; briefly by R. W. Zandvoort, *ES*, XXXII, 283; *Dalhousie Rev.*, XXXII, 31; by G. A. Dudok, *LT*, p. 302; *Listener*, XLVII, 32-33; by Hereward T. Price, *SQ*, IV (1953), 194-196; by E. E. Stoll, ibid., 434-436; by Desmond W. Cole, *QQ*, LX, No. 3 (1953), 447-448.

A8163   Dutt, T. K. *Critical Studies of English Poets*. Allahabad, 1956.
Shak., pp. 41-47.

A8164   Earley, Clarence Luther Steven. *English Dramatic Criticism, 1920-1930*. Richmond, Virginia: William Byrd Press, 1952. DD, University of Geneva.

A8165   Edgerton, F. "Indirect Suggestion in Poetry: A Hindu Theory of Literary Aesthetics." *Proc. of Amer. Philos. Soc.*, LXXVI (1936), 687-706.
Shak. *passim*.

A8166   Eliot, T. S. *Elizabethan Essays*, 1934.
Rev: by W. Keller, *SJ*, LXXII (1936), 156-157; by Paul de Réal, *RUnBrux*, XLII (1936/37), 270-281; by Szenczi, *Archivum Philologicum*, LXII (1940?), Heft 10-12.

A8167   Eliot, T. S. "Was ist ein Klassiker?" Tr. by W. E. Süskind. *Antike und Abendland*, III (1948), 8-25.

A8168   Eliot, T. S. "Shakespeares Verskunst." *Der Monat*, No. 20 (May, 1950), 198-207.

A8169   Eliot, T. S. *Poetry and Drama*. Cambridge: Harvard Univ. Press, 1951. Pp. 44.
Rev: A5423.

A8170   Eliot, T. S. *On Poetry and Poets*. New York: Farrar, Straus and Cudahy, 1957. Pp. xii, 308.
Rev: by Richard Rees, *TC*, 162 (1957), 499-500.

A8171   Eliot, T. S. *Ausgewählte Essays, 1917-1947*. Ausgew. u. eingel. v. Hans Hennecke. Berlin, Frankfort a. M.: Suhrkamp, 1950. Pp. 510.

A8172   Margaret Joseph Burke, Sister, S. S. J. *Dryden and Eliot: A Study in Literary Criticism*. DD, Niagara University, 1945.

A8173   M. Cleophas Costello, Sister. *Between Fixity and Flux: A Study of the Concept of Poetry in the Criticism of T. S. Eliot*. DD, Catholic University of America, 1947.

A8174   Waters, Leonard A. *Coleridge and Eliot: A Comparative Study of their Theories of Poetic Composition*. DD, University of Michigan, 1948. Pp. 390. Mic A48-180. *Microf. Ab.*, VIII ii, (1948), 112. Publication No. 1081.

A8175   Orsini, Napoleone. "T. S. Eliot e la Teoria delle Convenzioni Drammatiche." *Letterature Moderne*, IV (1953), 621-635.

A8176   Thompson, Marion C. *The Dramatic Criticism of Thomas Stearns Eliot*. DD, Cornell University, 1953.

A8177   Wellek, René. "The Criticism of T. S. Eliot." *SR*, LXIV (1956), 398-443.

A8178   Williamson, Mervyn Wilton. *A Survey of T. S. Eliot's Literary Criticism: 1917-1956*. DD, The University of Texas, 1958. Pp. 594. Mic 58-1676. *DA*, XVIII (1958), 2131.
See also other Eliot entries A7690, A9267, and A9276-A9283.

A8179   Empson, William, and George Garrett. *Shakespeare Survey*. London: Brendin, 1937. Pp. 63.
Rev: B4454.

A8180   Endo, Shingo. "Shakespeare's World." *Higeki-Kigeki*, VI (1949).

A8181   Evans, B. Ifor. *Tradition and Romanticism: Studies in English Poetry from Chaucer to W. B. Yeats*. London: Methuen, 1940. Pp. x, 213.
Chap. III: Chaucer to Shakespeare, pp. 23-43.
Rev: by R. G. Cox, *Scrutiny*, VIII (1940), 441-443; by Michael Roberts, *Spectator*, Feb. 16, p. 222; by V. de S. Pinto, *English*, III, 36-37; by Gwyn Jones, *Life and Letters*, XXIV, 326-328; by E. G. S., *ConR*, Aug., 1940, pp. 232-233; *TLS*, Feb. 3, p. 58; by B. E. C. Davis, *RES*, XVII (1941), 210-211.

A8182   Farinelli, A. *Shakespeare, Kant, Goethe. Drei Reden*. Berlin: Junker und Dünnhaupt, 1942. Pp. 94.
Rev: by P. Leibrecht, *DNL*, XLIII (1942), 215; *Theolog. Littrztg.*, LXVIII (1943), Heft 11/12.

A8183   Farnham, Willard. *Shakespeare's Tragic Frontier: The World of His Final Tragedies*. Berkeley and Los Angeles: Univ. of California Press, 1950. Pp. 289.
Rev: by H. Smith, *YR*, XXXIX (1950), 743-746; by R. A. Law, *JEGP*, XLIX, 583-584; by T. M. Parrott, *SQ*, I, 281-285; by Mabel Livingston, *Catholic World*, 172 (1950), 78-79; by Douglas Bush, *NR*, Apr. 24, p. 22; by B. I. Evans, *MGW*, June 29, p. 12; by R. Walker, *English*, VIII, 144-145; by Robert Halsband, *SRL*, July 8, p. 16; by Henry Popkin, *TAr*, June, p. 4; *TLS*, July 14, p. 442; by Robert Roth ("Another World of Shakespeare"), *MP*, XLIX (1951), 42-61; by Howard Nemerov, *SR*, LIX, 161-167; by H. S. Wilson, *UTQ*, XXI, 83-88; by Peter Alexander, *MLR*, XLVI, 89-90; by O. J. Campbell, *SQ*, II, 107-108; by M. E. Prior, *MLN*, LXVII (1952), 569-571; by F. T. Prince, *RES*, NS, III, 283-285.

A8184   Felheim, Marvin. "Landmarks of Criticism: Lascelles Abercrombie, 'A Plea for the Liberty on Interpreting', *Proceedings of the British Academy 1930*." *ShN*, VI (1956), 24.

A8185   Felheim, Marvin. "Landmarks of Criticism: 'Shakespeare and the Language of Poetry', Otto Jespersen." *ShN*, VII (1957), 5.

A8186   Florenne, Yves. "Le Théâtre Élizabéthain." *Table Ronde*, No. 37, 1951, pp. 151-154.

A8187   Fluchère, Henri. *Shakespeare: Dramaturge Élizabéthain.* Marseille: Cahiers du Sud, 1948. Pp. 400.
        Rev: *Figaro Littéraire*, April 10, 1948, p. 5; by Robert Kemp, *Nouv. Littéraires*, June 10, p. 2; by René Laporte, *Les Lettres Françaises*, July 1, p. 3; by Robert Delince, *Gazette des Lettres*, August 7, p. 5; by Una Ellis-Fermor, *MLR*, XLIV (1949), 401-402; *TLS*, Jan. 22, p. 58; by Mary H. Marshall, *Symposium*, IV (1950), 193-199.

A8187a Ruyssen, Yvonne. "Shakespeare et la Critique Française." *Europe*, Sept., 1950, pp. 34-41. Chiefly on A8187.

A8188   Fluchère, Henri. *Shakespeare.* New York, London: Longmans, Green, 1953. Pp. x, 272. Republ. New York: Hill & Wang, 1956. Pp. 254.
        A translation by Guy Hamilton of A8187. Foreword by T. S. Eliot.
        Rev: *TLS*, July 3, 1953, p. 428; by R. A. Foakes, *English*, IX, 220-221; by John Wain, *TC*, 154 (1953), 141-145; by R. G. Cox, *Scrutiny*, XIX, 331-333; *Listener*, L, 112; by F. S. Boas, *FortnR*, 1038 (1953), 426-428; by Richard Murphy, *Spectator*, May 15, pp. 648-650; by H. Smith, *YR*, XLIII, 121-125; by G. B. Harrison, *SatR*, Oct. 10, pp. 19-20; *NstN*, May 16, p. 591 [brief]; by Ivor Brown, *Obs.*, May 10, p. 10; by H. T. Price, *SQ*, V (1954), 109; by Milton Crane, ibid., pp. 186-188; by Michel Poirier, *EA*, VII, 115-116; by Clifford Leech, *ShS*, VII, 129 [brief]; *SatR*, Aug. 3, 1957, p. 28; briefly, *ShN*, VII, 28; by David S. Hawes, *Players Mag.*, Nov., pp. 44-45.

A8189   Fluchère, Henri. "Shakespeare in France: 1900-1948." *ShS*, II (1949), 115-124.

A8190   Fluchère, Henri. "The Function of Poetry in Drama." *English Studies Today.* Papers read at the International Conference of University Professors. Magdalen College, Oxford, August, 1950. Oxford Univ. Press, 1951, pp. 22-34.

A8190a Foerster, Norman. "Literary Scholarship and Criticism." *English Journal*, College ed., XXV (1936), 224-232.

A8191   Foerster, Norman, John C. McGalliard, René Wellek, Austin Warren, and Wilbur L. Schramm. *Literary Scholarship: Its Aims and Methods.* Univ. North Carolina Press, 1941. Pp. ix, 269.
        Rev: by Douglas Bush, *JEGP*, XLI (1942), 248-249; by E. K. Brown, "Humane Scholarship in the Humanities," *UTQ*, XI, 217-225; by Harcourt Brown, *MLQ*, III, 469-471; by Emery Neff, "Calliope," *SR*, L, 214-220; by Lane Cooper, *MLN*, LVIII (1943), 215-217; by Elizabeth Sweeting, *MLR*, XXXVIII, 59-60.

A8192   Forrest, Louis C. Turner. "A Caveat for Critics Against Invoking Elizabethan Psychology." *PMLA*, LXI (1946), 651-672.

A8193   Fraiberg, Louis Benjamin. *The Use of Psychoanalytic Ideas by Literary Critics.* DD, University of Michigan, 1956. Pp. 393. Mic 57-2143. *DA*, XVII (1957), 1336. Publication No. 21,177.

A8194   Frank, Tenney. "Changing Conception of Literary and Philological Research." *JHI*, III (1942), 401-414.

A8195   Gardner, Helen. *The Limits of Literary Criticism.* Reflections on the Interpretation of Poetry and Scripture. Riddell Memorial Lectures. Oxford Univ. Press, for the Univ. of Durham, 1956. Pp. 63.
        Expresses respectful skepticism toward approaches of critics who, rejecting Bradley's concern with plot and character, seek "meaning through the study of patterns of imagery" and those who are obsessed with "the climate of ideas," especially with the medieval thought-patterns behind complex characterizations.
        Rev: *TLS*, Dec. 28, 1956, p. 781; by Clifford Leech, *DUJ*, L (1957), 42-43; by W. W. Robson, *EIC*, VII, 303-317; by Basil Willey, *RES*, NS, IX (1958), 106-109; by Pierre Legouis, *EA*, XI, 178-179.

A8196   Gearhart, Sally Miller. *Aristotle and Modern Theorists on the Elements of Tragedy.* DD, University of Illinois, 1957. Pp. 189. Mic 57-685. *DA*, XVII (1957), 429. Publication No. 19, 822.

A8197   Gilbert, Allan. "Shakespeare's Amazing Words." *KR*, XI (1949), 484-488.

A8198   Glunz, Hans H. "Der Elisabethanische Weg zu Shakespeare." *SJ*, LXXVIII/LXXIX (1943), 29-72.

A8199   Goddard, Harold C. *The Meaning of Shakespeare.* The University of Chicago Press, 1951. Pp. xii, 691.
        Rev: by R. M. Smith, *SQ*, II (1951), 353-358; by O. J. Campbell, *SRL*, July 14, p. 22; *TLS*, Nov. 2, p. 694; *Nation* (N. Y.), July 14, p. 37 (brief); by Frederick S. Boas, *FortnR*, NS, 1017 (Sept., 1951), 635-636; by Sandford Salyer, *Books Abroad*, XXV, 282 (brief); by Milton Crane, *NYTBR*, July 8, pp. 4, 15; by F. C. G., *Anglican Theol. Rev.*, XXXIII, 264; by Charles A. McLaughlin, *MP*, XLIX (1952), 207-213; by W. Clemen, *Archiv*, 189 (1952/53), 227; by H. Heuer, *SJ*, 87/88 (1952), 257; by R. A. Law, *SQ*, III, 85; by Joseph Remenyi, *Jahrbuch für Amerikastudien*, X, 285; by David L. Patrick, *American Quarterly*, VIII, 89-91; by George R. Kernodle, *QJS*, XXXVIII, 85-86; by H. Trowbridge, *CL*, V (1953), 168-169; by M. C. Bradbrook, *ShS*, VI, 147-148.

A8200   Gowda, H. H. Anniah. "The Twentieth Century Critics of Shakespeare." *The Literary Criterion* (India), I (1952).

A8201   Granville-Barker, Harley. *Prefaces to Shakespeare.* 2 Vols. Princeton Univ. Press, 1946, 1947. Pp. viii, 543; viii, 449.
        First American edition of the well-known series. Vol. I contains the discussion of *Hamlet*,

Lear, The Merchant of Venice, Antony and Cleopatra, Cymbeline; Vol. II: the discussions of *Othello, Coriolanus, Romeo and Juliet, Julius Caesar, Love's Labour's Lost.* For the English editions and their reviews, see the individual plays concerned.

Rev: by Hardin Craig, *JEGP*, XLVI (1947), 312-315; by A. S. Downer, *SR*, LV, 627-645; by S. C. Chew, *NYHTBR*, July 6, p. 6; by Margaret Webster, *NYTBR*, Jan. 26, p. 4 (Vol. I); by Eric Bentley, ibid., July 20, p. 4 (Vol. II); by J. W. Draper, *South Atlantic Quar.*, XLVI, 409-412; *TAr*, XXXI, 70; by Arthur Mizener, *Nation*, 164 (1947), 549-550; by Robert Adger Law, *Southwest Review*, XXXII, 213-214; by Allardyce Nicoll, *RES*, XXIII, 69-70; by Robert Adger Law, *Southwest Review*, XXXII, 427-428; by John Gielgud, *TAr*, XXXI, 58-59; by P. E. McLane, *Thought*, XXII, 342-343; by M. A. Shaaber, *MLN*, LXIII (1948), 194-197; by J. W. Draper, *South Atlantic Quar.*, XLVII, 118-119; by O. J. Campbell, *YR*, XXXVII, 357-360 (Vol. II); by H. T. Price, *MLQ*, IX, 357-359 (Vol. I); by Hardin Craig, *JEGP*, XLVII, 303-304; by G. F. Reynolds, *CE*, IX, 457-458; by P. E. McLane, *Thought*, XXIII, 155-156; by G. G., *Personalist*, XXIX, 214-215; by G. Rylands, *NstN*, XXXV (1948), 157; by R. M. Smith, *SAB*, XXIV (1949), 291-293; *TLS*, Aug. 28, 1953, pp. xxxiv-xxxv.

A8202 Granville-Barker, Harley. *Prefaces to Shakespeare. Third Series: Hamlet.* London, 1936.
Rev: B7354.

A8203 Granville-Barker, Harley. *Prefaces to Shakespeare. Fourth Series: Othello.* London, 1947.
Rev: B8555.

A8204 Granville-Barker, Harley. *Prefaces to Shakespeare. Fifth Series: Coriolanus.* London, 1948.
Rev: B9553.

A8204a Granville-Barker, Harley. *Prefaces to Shakespeare.* Reissued in 2 Vols. London: Batsford, 1958.

A8205 "H. Granville-Barker's *On Poetry in Drama.*" *TLS*, Aug. 7, 1937, pp. 565-566.

A8206 Downer, Alan S. "Harley Granville-Baker." *SR*, LV (1947), 627-645.

A8207 Cancelled.

A8208 Vallette, J. "Granville-Barker and Shakespeare." *MdF*, 305 (1949), 535-537.

A8209 Rutledge, F. P. *Harley Granville-Barker and the English Theatre.* MA thesis, National University of Ireland, 1951.

A8210 Salenius, Elmer W. *Harley Granville-Barker and the Modern English Theatre.* DD, Boston, 1951.

A8211 Britton, L. J. *The Achievement of Harley Granville-Barker (1877-1946).* MA thesis, Wales, 1955.

A8212 Glick, Claris. *An Analysis of Granville-Barker's Criticism of Shakespeare.* DD, University of Texas, 1956. Abstr. by Jack R. Brown, "Dissertation Digest," *ShN*, VII (1957), 19.

A8213 Purdom, C. B. *Harley Granville-Barker: Man of the Theatre, Dramatist and Scholar.* Harvard Univ. Press, 1956. Pp. xiv, 322.
Rev: B1803.

A8214 Thomas, N. K. *A Study of Harley Granville-Barker as Producer and Dramatist.* MA thesis, Bristol, 1956.

A8215 Gray, Henry David. "Some Methods of Approach to the Study of *Hamlet.*" *SP*, XLV (1948), 203-215.
"No man can really know a past age with sufficient fullness and accuracy to say what that age was capable of thinking and of producing," p. 207.

A8216 Grierson, H. J. C. "Criticism and Creation: Their Interactions." *Essays and Studies by Members of the English Association*, XXIX (1943), Oxford: Clarendon Press, 1944, pp. 7-29.

A8217 Griffiths, G. S. "*Antony and Cleopatra.*" *Essays and Studies by Members of the English Association*, XXXI (1945). Oxford: Clarendon Press, 1946, pp. 34-67.

A8218 Guidi, Augusto. "L'Ultimo Shakespeare." Published serially in Nos. 31-45. *Idea* (Rome), IX (1957).

A8218a Guidi, Augusto. *L'Ultimo Shakespeare.* Padua: Liviana editrice, 1958. Pp. 129.

A8219 Gutteling, J. F. C. "Modern Hamlet-Criticism." *Neophil*, XXV (1941), 276-285.
Reviews Jones (pp. 278-279) and finds him plausible. Examines Stoll and finds him wanting. Notices C. M. Lewis' *Genesis of Hamlet* (1907), A. J. A. Waldock's *Hamlet: A Study in Critical Method* (which he calls fine), Dover Wilson, and J. Draper.

A8220 Halliday, F. E. *Shakespeare and His Critics.* London: Gerald Duckworth & Co., 1949. Pp. 522.
Rev: A8596.

A8221 Harbage, Alfred. "Materials for the Study of English Renaissance Drama." *MLN*, LIX (1944), 128-133.

A8222 Harbage, Alfred. *As They Liked It.* New York, 1947. Pp. xvi, 238.
See Chapter II, pp. 21-39, for considered objections to the historical approaches of Stoll, Schücking, Lily Campbell, and others.
Rev: A959.

A8223 Hastings, William T. "The Hardboiled Shakspere." *SAB*, XVII (1942), 114-125.

A8224 Hastings, William T. "The New Critics of Shakespeare: An Analysis of the Technical Analysis of Shakespeare." *SQ*, I (1950), 165-176.
Comments upon essays by R. B. Heilman, Northrop Frye, Leslie Fiedler, Edward Hubler, G. Wilson Knight, D. A. Traversi, and T. S. Eliot.

A8225 Häusermann, Hans Walter. *Studien zur Englischen Literaturkritik 1910-30*. Kölner Anglistische Arbeiten, Bd. 34. Bochum-Langendreer: Pöppinghaus, 1938. Pp. vi, 244.

A8226 Hauser, Arnold. *The Social History of Art*. 2 vols. New York: Alfred A Knopf, 1951. Pp. xxi, 500, ix, 501-1022.
Vol. I, pp. 401-423, contains an extended discussion of Shak.'s works in terms of his society. Finds in him a sense of social responsibility, and sees his drama as springing from "the basic experience of political realism."

A8227 Hawdon, F. E. *A Survey of English Shakespearean Criticism, 1907-1939*. MA thesis, University of London, 1948.

A8228 Hegenbarth, Josef. *Zeichnungen zu fünf Shakespeare-Dramen*. Berlin: Rütten & Loening, 1957. Pp. 305.

A8229 Henriques, Alf. "Shakespeare and Denmark: 1900-1949." *ShS*, III (1950), 107-115.

A8230 Hergešić, Ivo. *Shakespeare, Molière, Goethe. Književno-kazališne Studije*. Zagreb: Zora, 1957. Pp. 300.

A8231 Hicks, Granville. "Assumptions in Literature." *English Journal*, xxv (1936), 709-717.

A8232 Holland, R. A. *Comedy and Character in Shakespeare in Relation to Shakespearean Criticism Since 1903*. DD, London, Queen Mary College, 1957.

A8233 Hoskawa, Senjiro. "Shakespeare Scholarship and Aesthetic Criticism." *The Rising Generation*, 98 (1952), 7-10.

A8234 Hotson, Leslie. "Literary Serendipity." *ELH*, ix (1942), 79-94.

A8235 Hotson, Leslie. " 'Not of an Age': Shakespeare." *SR*, xLIX (1941), 193-210. Republ. in *Shakespeare's Sonnets Dated, and Other Essays*. London: Rupert Hart-Davis; Toronto: Clarke, Irwin & Co., 1949.
Inspiration for the war effort drawn from Shak., support for historical criticism, and its suggestion that on the basis of vocabulary-intelligence correlations, an Eliz. audience was more intelligent than a modern.

A8236 Hubler, Edward. "The Sunken Aesthete." *EIE, 1950*. New York: Columbia Univ. Press, 1951, pp. 32-56.

A8237 Hughes, Merritt Y. "A Meditation on Literary Blasphemy." *JAAC*, xIV (1955), 106-115. On Ernest Boyd's *Literary Blasphemies*, (1927), and F. R. Leavis' *The Common Pursuit*, (A8276).

A8238 Hunter, Kermit H. *Dramatic Unity in Shakespeare: A Critical and Historical Study (1880-1950)*. DD, University of North Carolina, 1955.

A8239 Hurst, H. Norman. *Four Elements in Literature*. London: Longmans, 1936. Pp. xx, 192.

A8240 Hyman, Stanley Edgar. "The Critical Achievement of Caroline Spurgeon." *KR*, x (1948), 92-108.
I. a., discusses sympathetically "extensions and modifications" of her work in the writing of G. Wilson Knight, Edward A. Armstrong, Kenneth Burke, Theodore Spencer, Cleanth Brooks.

A8241 Jacquot, Jean. "Connaissance du Théâtre Anglais." *EA*, vII (1954), 389-394.

A8242 Jaffé, Gerhard. "Shaws Oppfatning av Dramatisk Diktkunst Sammenlignet med Shakespeares." *Edda* (Oslo), L (1950), 56-92.
Rejects Shaw's criticism of Shak., and supports the findings of German critics (Walzel, M. Klein) who have applied the methods of Wölfflin to an analysis of Shak.'s art.

A8243 James, D. G. *The Dream of Learning: An Essay on "The Advancement of Learning", "Hamlet" and "King Lear"*. Oxford: Clarendon Press, 1951. Pp. 126.
Objections to medievalism and historicism in Shak. studies, pp. 33-36.
Rev: A3959.

A8244 John, E. "Shakespeare's Angels." *TLS*, Oct. 19, 1946, p. 507.

A8245 Johnson, S. F. "The Regeneration of Hamlet: A Reply to E. M. W. Tillyard with a Counter-proposal." *SQ*, III (1952), 187-207.
Also discusses "marked reaction" to Stoll in last 20 years.

A8246 Jorgensen, Paul A. "Accidental Judgements, Casual Slaughters, and Purposes Mistook: Critical Reaction to Shakespeare's *Henry the Fifth*." *SAB*, xxII (1947), 51-61.
Upon criticism of Hazlitt, Palmer, G. B. Shaw, Dowden, John Masefield, Moulton, Bradley, Kittredge.

A8247 Joseph, B. L. *Elizabethan Acting*. London: Oxford Univ. Press, 1951. Pp. x, 157.
Chap. VI: "The Grounds of Criticisms in Elizabethan Drama," pp. 113-140.
Rev: A7426.

A8248 Jouvet, Louis. "A L'Instar de Cuvier." *Le Théâtre Élizabéthain*. Paris: Les Cahiers du Sud, 1940, pp. 119-120.
That we must understand a play in the theatre of its time, but can never entirely do so.

A8249 Keast, W. R. "Imagery and Meaning in the Interpretation of *King Lear*." *MP*, xLVII (1949), 45-64.
An important review article criticizing the basic assumptions and the method of "New Critics," with particular reference to Mr. Heilman's study.

A8250   Keast, William R. "The New Criticism and *King Lear*." In *Critics and Criticism, Ancient and Modern*. Chicago, 1952, pp. 108-137.
        Rev: *TLS*, Feb. 6, 1953, p. 90; by N. Frye, *SQ*, v (1954), 80.

A8251   Keudel, R. "Kritik an Shakespeare." *Thuringische Landesztg.*, 1936, No. 112.

A8252   Kirschbaum, Leo. "The Authorship of *1 Henry VI*." *PMLA*, LXVII (1952), 809-822.

A8253   Kirschbaum, L. "Texts of *Mucedorus*." *MLR*, L (1955), 1-5.
        Reply by W. W. Greg, ibid., p. 322. Argues that *Mucedorus* is a bad quarto, and that "the extant text can tell us only about the taste of the *reading* public"—and not about the author, the dramatic company, or the theatre public. Questions the stage vogue of the play. And declares the attribution of "primitive" qualities to the Eliz. stage comes from the assumption that "bad" quartos are accurate texts.

A8254   Kitto, H. D. F. *Form and Meaning in Drama: A Study of Six Greek Plays and of "Hamlet"*. London: Methuen, 1956. Pp. 541.
        Main thesis: *Hamlet* and other great tragedies should be judged not by their period but by the author himself. The critic should presume some dramatists great enough to be "in complete command of their own art and (with) very good reasons for shaping the play as they did."
        Rev: B7506.

A8255   Klein, David. "Elizabethan Acting." *PMLA*, LXXI (1956), 280-282.
        Comment on Marvin Rosenberg's article, A8348. Considerable further evidence is offered that Elizabethan acting was natural.

A8256   Klein, Karl. *Der Dichterbegriff in der Modernen Englischen Literaturkritik*. DD, Cologne, 1953. Pp. 289.

A8257   Knight, G. Wilson. *The Wheel of Fire: Essays in Interpretation of Shakespeare's Sombre Tragedies*. Oxford Univ. Press, 1930. Fourth ed., with Three New Essays. London: Methuen & Co.; New York: Oxford Univ. Press, 1949. Pp. 363. Fifth revised ed., Introduction by T. S. Eliot. New York: Meridian Books, 1957. Pp. xx, 343.
        Rev: by Georges Connes, *EA*, II (1938), 45; by R. Walker, *English*, VIII (1950), 144; by F. Berry, *Erasmus*, III (1950), 748-750; by A. Laffay, *LanM*, XLIV (1950), 121; by A. G. van Kranendonk, *Neophil*, XXXVII (1953), 254.

A8258   Knight, G. Wilson. *The Imperial Theme*. Further Interpretation of Shakespeare's Tragedies Including the Roman Plays. Oxford Univ. Press, 1939. Pp. 376. Third ed. London: Methuen, 1951. Pp. xiii, 367. Third ed. reprinted with minor corrections. London: Methuen, 1955. Pp. xv, 367.
        Rev: *TLS*, July 1, 1939, p. 395; by Hardin Craig, *SQ*, III (1952), 267-271; by K. Muir, *ES*, XXXIII, 94.

A8259   Knight, G. Wilson. *The Burning Oracle*. Oxford Univ. Press, 1939.
        Contains an essay, "The Shakespearian Integrity."
        Rev: A5830.

A8260   Knight, G. Wilson. *The Shakespearian Tempest*. Oxford Univ. Press, 1940. Pp. x, 332. Originally published 1932. Third ed., London: Methuen, 1953.
        Rev: by J. R. S., *RES*, XVII (1941), 377-378; *TLS*, July 3, 1953, p. 428 (see letter by Mr. Knight, July 10, p. 445); by H. B. Charlton, *MGW*, Sept. 24, pp. 10, 11; by R. G. Cox, *Scrutiny*, XIX, 333-336; by Michel Poirier, *EA*, VII (1954), 323-324.

A8261   Knight, G. Wilson. *The Olive and the Sword*. A Study of England's Shakespeare. Oxford Univ. Press, 1944. Pp. 112.
        Rev: A1819.

A8262   Knight, G. Wilson. *The Crown of Life: Essays in Interpretation of Shakespeare's Final Plays*. Oxford Univ. Press, 1947.
        Rev: B5241.

A8262a Knight, G. Wilson. *The Mutual Flame: An Interpretation of Shakespeare's Sonnets*. London: Methuen, 1955. Pp. xi, 233.
        Rev: C93.
        See also A1508, A1884, A9841, and B1718.

A8263   Knight, G. Wilson. "The New Interpretation." *EIC*, III (1953), 382-395. See also A. E. Rodway, G. Salgado, G. W. Knight and F. W. Bateson, "The School of Knight." *EIC*, IV (1954), 212-224.

A8264   Purdom, C. B. "Shakespeare and Mr. Wilson Knight." *The Listener*, Dec. 23, 1954, p. 1120.

A8265   Felheim, Marvin. "Landmarks of Criticism: Critical Theories of G. Wilson Knight." *ShN*, VIII (1958), 6, 13.

A8266   Felheim, Marvin. "Landmarks of Criticism: 'On the Principles of Shakespeare Interpretation,' Chapter I of *The Wheel of Fire, 1930*." *ShN*, VIII (1958), 13.

A8267   Jones, John. "Shakespeare and Mr. Wilson Knight." *Listener*, LII (1954), 1011-12.

A8268   Knights, L. C. "On the Social Background of Metaphysical Poetry." *Scrutiny*, XIII (1945), 37-52.

A8269   Knights, Lionel Charles. *Explorations: Essays in Criticism, Mainly on the Literature of the Seventeenth Century.* London: Chatto & Windus, 1946. Pp. xii, 198.
Rev: *TLS*, July 20, 1946, p. 341; by H. I'A. F., *MGW*, LV, 46; by Anthony Powell, *Spectator*, Aug. 30, pp. 220-221; by Joan Bennett, *NstN*, Aug. 24, p. 137; by Eric Bentley, *KR*, VIII, 672-674; by B. M., *Dalhousie Rev.*, XXVII (1947), 121; by S. G. Putt, *ES*, XXVIII, 81-82; *English*, VI, 216-217; by F. O. Matthiessen, *NYTBR*, June 15, p. 4; by John Farrelly, *NR*, Oct. 13, pp. 27-28; by Theodore Spencer, *SRL*, Aug. 16, p. 14; by Rafael Koskimies, *Erasmus*, I, 288-290; by G. H. C., *QQ*, LV (1948), 361-362; by Mark Schorer, *SR*, LVI, 179-184.

A8270   Knights, L. C. *Some Shakespearean Themes.* London: Chatto and Windus, 1959.

A8271   Felheim, Marvin. "Landmarks of Criticism: 'How Many Children Had Lady Macbeth?', L. C. Knights." *ShN*, VII (1957), 37.

A8272   Knox, R. S. "Shakespeare: A Diversity of Doctrine." *UTQ*, VII (1938), 249-261.

A8273   Kulisheck, Clarence L. "The Critics' Shakespeare." *ShN*, V (1955), 38.

A8274   Kyd, Thomas [pseud.]. "Cosmic Card Game." *American Scholar*, XX (1951), 325-333.
Parodies the methods of the "new critics" through an analysis of *Antony.*

A8275   Landauer, Gustav. *Shakespeare Dargestellt in Vorträgen.* Potsdam: Rütten and Loening, 1948. 2 Vols. Pp. 362, 386. Reprint of 1920 work.

A8275a Leavis, F. R. "Diabolic Intellect and the Noble Hero." *Scrutiny*, VI (1937), 259-283. Republished in A8276.

A8276   Leavis, F. R. *The Common Pursuit.* New York: George W. Stewart; London: Chatto and Windus; Toronto: Clarke, Irwin, 1952. Pp. viii, 307.
Rev: by Dudley Fitts, *NR*, April 21, 1952, pp. 18-19; by R. W. B. Lewis, *HR*, V, 308-311; by Edwin Muir, *Obs.*, Jan. 20, p. 7; *Listener*, XLVII, 191; by Raymond Mortimer, *Sunday Times*, Feb. 3, p. 3; *TLS*, Feb. 29, p. 156; by J. M. Cohen, *Spectator*, No. 6448 (1952), p. 118; by G. S. Fraser, *NstN*, XLIII, 130; by F. Fergusson, *Partisan Rev.*, XX (1953), 232-235; by M. C. Bradbrook, *ShS*, VI, 153; by Henri Fluchère, *EA*, VI, 73-75; by Derek Stanford, *ConR*, 183 (1953), 161.

A8277   Leavis, F. R. "Shakespeare's Craft of Verse." *TLS*, July 9, 1954, p. 441. See also July 2, p. 424; July 16, p. 457.

A8278   Hughes, Merritt Y. "A Meditation on Literary Blasphemy." *JAAC*, XIV (1955), 106-115. F. R. Leavis and others.

A8279   Brannigan, P. *The Literary Criticism of F. R. Leavis.* MA thesis, Manchester, 1956.

A8280   Lebègue, Raymond. "Le Théâtre de Démesure et d'Horreur en Europe Occidentale aux XVIᵉ et XVIIᵉ Siècles." *Forschungsprobleme der Vergleichenden Literaturgeschichte*, 1951, pp. 35-36.

A8281   Leech, Clifford. "The 'Meaning' of *Measure for Measure.*" *ShS*, III (1950), 66-73.
Objects to "historical" approaches. Declares the play contains "a passionate sympathy with the unfortunate hard-pressed."

A8282   Lewis, C. S. "Hamlet, the Prince or the Poem?" *Proceedings of the British Academy*, XXVIII (1942).
Rev: B7673.

A8283   Lewis, Percy Wyndham. *The Lion and the Fox: The Role of the Hero in the Plays of Shakespeare.* New edition. London: Methuen, 1955. Pp. 326. Originally published in 1927.

A8284   Lewisohn, Ludwig. *The Magic Word. Studies in the Nature of Poetry.* New York: Farrar, Straus, 1950. Pp. xv, 151.
Chap. III, Shak., pp. 67-108.

A8285   Lovejoy, A. O. "The Meaning of Romanticism for the Historian of Ideas." *JHI*, II (1941), 257-278.

A8286   Lüthi, Max. *Shakespeares Dramen.* Berlin: Walter De Gruyter & Co., 1957. Pp. 447.
Rev: by Hermann Heuer, *SJ*, 93 (1957), 258-260; by Heinrich Meyer, *Books Abroad*, XXXI, 394-395; by K. Schneider, *Archiv*, 194 (1957), 334-335; by Heinrich Straumann, *Anglia*, LXXV, 458-466; by Ernest Schanzer, *MLR*, LIII (1958), 425-426; by E. A. J. Honigmann, *RES*, NS, IX, 432-434; by Virgil B. Heltzel, *SQ*, IX, 575-576; by Christof Wegelin, *CL*, X, 375; by L. L. Schücking, *GRM*, XXXIX, 97-99; by A. Schlösser, *ZAA*, VI, 70-72.

A8287   Lyons, Clifford P. " 'It Appears so by the Story': Notes on Narrative-Thematic Emphasis in Shakespeare." *SQ*, IX (1958), 287-294. See also Wilson, H. S. "Commentary." *SQ*, IX, 307-310.
Commentary on papers read at the MLA meeting in Sept., 1957, by Clifford P. Lyons, Edward Hubler, and John Crow.

A8288   McCollom, William Gilman. *Illusion and Formalism in Elizabethan Tragedy.* DD, Cornell University, 1945. Abstract publ. in *Abstracts of Theses, 1944*, Ithaca: Cornell Univ. Press, 1945, pp. 17-20.

A8289   McKeon, Richard. "The Philosophic Bases of Art and Criticism." *MP*, XLI (1944), 65-87, 129-171.

A8290   MacLaurin, Jean C. *An Examination of Some Oppositions in the Shakespeare Criticism of A. C. Bradley, E. E. Stoll, and J. Dover Wilson.* MA thesis, Toronto, 1940. Pp. 218.

A8291 McMullen, Frank. "Producing Shakespeare." *Shakespeare: of an Age and for all Time*. The Yale Shakespeare Festival Lectures, 1954, pp. 55-57.

A8292 Marks, Emerson. "The Achieve of, The Mastery." *JAAC*, XVI (1957), 103-111.

A8293 Marder, Louis. "Stage vs. Study." *ShN*, VIII (1958), 10, 18.

A8294 Martin, M. S. *The Redirection of Critical Interest in Shakespeare's Last Plays, 1930-1948*. Thesis, University of New Zealand, 1949.

A8295 Masefield, John. *William Shakespeare*. London: Butterworth, 1938. Pp. 256. Subsequent ed., London: Heinemann, 1954. Pp. vii, 184. Revised ed. of book first published in 1911.
Rev: *TLS*, Dec. 24, 1954, p. 834; by T. S. Dorsch, *YWES*, XXXV, 85; by A. S. T., *Spectator*, No. 6601 (1954), p. 836; by G. Lambin, *LanM*, XLIX (1955), 271; by Kenneth Muir, *London Mag.*, II, No. 6, 104-106, 108; by Robert Halsband, *SatR*, Feb. 26, p. 26; by William T. Hastings, *SQ*, VI, 111-112; by Hermann Heuer, *SJ*, 91 (1955), 324-325; by Sir Ralph Richardson, *Adelphi*, XXXI, No. 3, pp. 291-292; by M. Poirier, *EA*, VII, 153-154; by Oscar James Campbell, *SQ*, VII (1956), 108-110.

A8296 Matthes, H. "Shakespeares Dramen, Theologisch Gesehen." *Luthertum*, NS, XLVIII (1937), 263-277.

A8297 Matthiessen, F. O. "Towards Our Understanding of Elizabethan Drama." *Southern Rev.*, Autumn 1938, pp. 398-428.

A8298 Maxwell, J. C. "Simple or Complex? Some Problems in the Interpretation of Shakespeare." *DUJ*, XLVI (1954), 112-113.
Strictures upon over-simplifying character and then looking askance at resulting inconsistencies.

A8299 Menon, C. Narayan. *Shakespeare Criticism: An Essay in Synthesis*. London: Humphrey Milford, Oxford Univ. Press, 1938. Pp. 276.
Rev: by Y. D. Bhare, *Journal of the Univ. of Bombay*, NS, VII (Sept., 1938), 196-198; by L. L. Schücking, *Beiblatt*, L (1939), 80; *RLC*, XIX, 672; by S. Rice, *Asiatic Review*, XXXV, 123-129; *Baconiana*, XXIV, 43-46; by A. W. Pirkhofer, *Eng. Studn.*, LXXIII, 393-395; by T. W. Baldwin, *MLN*, LV (1940), 455-462.

A8300 Mercer, D. F. *Trends in Modern Criticism, 1800-1940*. B. Litt. thesis, Oxford, St. Anne's Society, 1949.

A8301 Merchant, W. M. "Visual Elements in Shakespeare Studies." *SJ*, 92 (1956), 280-290.

A8302 Mizener, Arthur. "The Scrutiny Group." *KR*, X (1948), 355-360.

A8303 Möller, Kr. Langdal. "Shakespeare Som Praktisk Teatermand." *Nationaltidende* (Copenhagen), LXXXI (1949).

A8304 Morozov, M. M. *A Commentary on Shakespeare's Plays*. Moscow, Leningrad: Vserossiiskoe Teatralnoe Obshchestvo, 1941. Pp. 104.

A8305 Morrison, T. " 'The Fault Dear Brutus': Poetic Example and Poetic Doctrine Today." *Pacific Spectator*, I (1947), 235-250.

A8306 Müller-Schwefe, Gerhard. "Wandlungen des Shakespeare-Bildes im 20. Jahrhundert." *NS*, X (1954), 433-445.

A8307 Muir, Kenneth, and Sean O'Loughlin. *The Voyage to Illyria*. A New Study of Shakespeare. London: Methuen, 1937. Pp. 242.
Rev: *TLS*, Aug. 21, 1937, p. 605; by Ronald Lewin, *NstN*, NS XIV, 496-498; *QR*, 269 (1937), 368-369; by W. J. Lawrence, *Spectator*, Aug. 20, p. 322; by Hugh Kingsmill, *FortnR*, NS, 142 (1937), 754-755; by Bernard Blackstone, *Criterion*, XVII (1938), 355-357; by Clara Longworth, Comtesse de Chambrun, *EA*, II, 159; by Wolfgang Schmidt, *Beiblatt*, XLIX, 108-110; by G. Tillotson, *MLR*, XXXIII, 317-318; by Max Priess, *Eng. Studn.*, LXXIII, 95-99; by W. Keller, *SJ*, LXXIV, 174-176; by Kathleen Tillotson, *RES*, XV (1939), 217-218; by B. T. Spencer, *SR*, XLVII, 119-129.

A8308 Muir, Kenneth. "The Future of Shakespeare." *Penguin New Writing*, XXVIII (1946/47), 101-121.

A8309 Muir, Kenneth. "Some Freudian Interpretations of Shakespeare." *Proceedings of the Leeds Philosophical and Literary Society*, VII (1952), 43-52.
Contains summaries of Freud, Jones, Sharpe, Wertham, and Stewart (on *Hamlet, Lear, Othello*, and *Macbeth*). Defends some Freudian approaches and attacks Stoll and Schücking, pp. 49-50.

A8310 Muir, Kenneth. "Changing Interpretations of Shakespeare." *The Age of Shakespeare*, ed. Boris Ford, pp. 282-301.

A8311 Murry, John Middleton. *Shakespeare*. London: Jonathan Cape, 1936. Pp. 448. Repr. 1955. Tr. by R. Krauschaar, *NR*, XLVIII (1937), 604-620.
Rev: *TLS*, Feb. 8, 1936, pp. 101-102; *Cornhill Mag.*, 153 (1936), 378-379; by T. S. Eliot, *Criterion*, XV, 708-710; *More Books*, 234-235; by Herbert Read, *Spectator*, Feb. 21, pp. 312, 314; by J. Dover Wilson, *MGW*, Apr. 17, p. 314; *QR*, 266 (1936), 258-259; by Christopher Martin, *Catholic World*, 143 (1936), 631; by James Southall Wilson, *VQR*, XII, 636-640; by Edwin Muir, *London Mercury*, XXXIII, 540-541; by G. W. Stonier, *NstN*, NS, XI, 192-193; by Stephan Potter, *FortnR*, NS, 139 (1936), 373-374; by Hugh Kingsmill, *Nineteenth Century*, 120 (1936), 112-117; by Mark Van Doren, *Nation* (N.Y.), 142 (1936), 520-522; by

Wolfgang Keller, *SJ*, LXXII, 137-138; by B. de Selincourt, *Obs.*, Feb. 9; by R. G. Cox, *Scrutiny*, V, 105-107; *Bull. Boston Pub. Lib.*, XI, 234-235; by H. E. Stearns, *Scribner's*, July, p. 4; by P. M. Jack, *NYTBR*, April 19, p. 2; by A. G. van Kranendonk, *De Groene Amsterdammer*, March 28; by R. Van Gelder, *New York Times*, April 16, p. 23; *New York Sun*, April 18; *Adelphi*, XII, 104-111; by Paul de Réal, *RUnBrux*, XLII (1936/37), 270-281; by H. T. P., *English Jour.*, XXVI (1937), 378; by Tucker Brooke, *YR*, XXVI, 176-177; by George Herbert Clarke, *QQ*, XLIV, 114-115; by Paul Dottin, *Rev. de France*, XVII, iii, 706-707; by R. S. Knox, *UTQ*, VII (1938), 249-261; *TLS*, May 13, 1955, p. 258; by Hermann Heuer, *SJ*, 92 (1956), 364-365.

A8312   Murray, John Middleton. *Shakespeare*. Tr. into Italian by Francesco Lo Bue. Turin: G. Einaudi, 1953. Pp. 441.

A8313   Cancelled.

A8314   Heath, William W. "The Literary Criticism of John Middleton Murry." *PMLA*, LXX (1955), 47-57.

A8315   Nakano, Yoshio, et al. *Studies in Shakespeare*. Shingetsu-sha, 1949.

A8316   Neri, Ferdinando. "Alla Ricerca di Shakespeare" and "I Sonnetti." *Saggi di Letteratura Italiana Francese e Inglese*. Naples: Loffredo, 1936, pp. 245-250, 251-256.

A8317   Nicoll, Allardyce. "Co-operation in Shakespearian Scholarship." *Proc. British Academy 1952*, Oxford Univ. Press, pp. 71-88.
The Shakespeare Lecture, read April 23, 1952.

A8318   O'Connor, Frank [pseud.] *The Road to Stratford: A Critical Study of Shakespeare*. London: Methuen, 1948. Pp. 156.
Rev: *TLS*, Feb. 12, 1949, p. 107.

A8319   Orsini, Napoleone. "Shakespeare, il Romanticismo e la Filologia." *Leonardo*, X (1939), 337-343.

A8320   Orsini, Napoleone. "La Critica Shakespeariana." *Anglica*, I (1946), 5-17.

A8321   Orsini, Napoleone. "Caratteri Estetici del Drama Elisabettiano." *Anglica*, II (1948), 1-19.

A8322   Orsini, Napoleone. "Stato Attuale della Filologia Shakespeariana." *Paideia*, VIII (1953), 153-176.

A8323   Parrott, Thomas M. *Shakespearean Comedy*. New York: Oxford Univ. Press, 1949. Pp. xiv, 417.
Rev: by Mary C. Hyde, *SAB*, XXIV (1949), 294-297; by Harry Levin, *NYTBR*, Aug. 7, p. 5; by S. C. Chew, *NYHTBR*, Sept. 18, p. 13; by L. M. Parrott, Jr., *TAr*, XXXIII, 107-108; by A. Laffay, *LanM*, XLIV (1950), 422-423; by Kenneth Muir, *MLR*, XLV, 529-531; by H. V. Routh, *English*, VIII, 87-88; *TLS*, March 10, p. 154; by D. Bush, *NR*, Apr. 24, p. 22; by Una Ellis-Fermor, *RES*, NS, II, 269-271; by John E. Hankins, *MLQ*, XIII (1952), 214-215; by H. Oppel, *NS*, I, 403-404; by F. L. Schoell, *EA*, VI (1953), 28-34.

A8324   Pearson, Hesketh, and Malcolm Muggeridge. *About Kingsmill*. London: Methuen, 1951. Pp. 185.
Rev: *TLS*, Sept. 21, 1951, p. 594.

A8325   Pearson, Norman Holmes. "Literary Forms and Types, Or a Defense of Polonius." *English Institute Annual, 1940*. Columbia Univ. Press, 1941, pp. 61-72.

A8326   Perger, Arnulf. *Die Wandlung der Dramatischen Auffassung*. Berlin: O. Elsner, 1936. Pp. 136.

A8327   Pinto, V. de Sola. "Shakespeare and the Dictators." *Essays by Divers Hands*, NS, XXI (1944), 82-102.
The dramatic poet is to give us a convincing picture of what Aristotle calls "universals," and defines as the way in which "a person of a certain type will on occasion speak or act, according to the law of probability or necessity."

A8328   Petsch, Robert. *Deutshes Literaturwissenschaft. Aufsätze zur Begründung der Methode*. Berlin: Ebering, 1940. Pp. 274.

A8329   Peyre, Henri. *Writers and Their Critics*. Ithaca: Cornell Univ. Press, 1944. Pp. xii, 340.

A8330   Pisharoti, K. R. "Aesthetic Pleasure in Drama." *Calcutta Rev.*, LVIII (1936), 297-301.

A8331   Pogson, Beryl. *In the East My Pleasure Lies: An Esoteric Interpretation of Some Plays of Shakespeare*. London: Stuart and Richards, 1950. Pp. 120.
Rev: by J. Duncan Spaeth, *SQ*, III (1952), 61-63.

A8332   Policardi, Silvio. *Lyrical Poetry in Renaissance England*. Milan: F. Montuoro, 1943.

A8333   Pollock, Thomas Clark. *The Nature of Literature. Its Relation to Science, Language and Human Experience*. Princeton Univ. Press, 1942. Pp. xxiv, 218.
Shak. pp. 111-112.
Rev: by J. C. Bryce, *MLR*, XXXIX (1944), 64-65; by E. C. Pettet, *English*, V, 58-59; by E. F. Carritt, *Mind*, LIII, 184-185.

A8334   Pottle, Frederick A. *The Idiom of Poetry*. Cornell Univ. Press, 1941. Pp. xi, 139.
Rev: by S. K. Winther, *MLQ*, IV (1943), 123; by J. C. Ransom, *MLN*, LVIII, 321; by R. K. Root, *JEGP*, XLII, 278-279.

A8335 Praz, Mario. *Cronache Letterarie Anglo-Sassoni*. Rome: Edizioni di Storia e Letteratura, 1951. 2 vols. Pp. 297, 295.
Rev: by Augusto Guidi, *Notiziario della Scuola*, Oct. 15-30, 1951, pp. 10-12

A8336 Price, Hereward T. "Shakespeare as a Critic." *Renaissance Studies In Honor of Hardin Craig*, pp. 198-207; also *PQ*, xx (1941), 390-399.

A8337 Prior, Moody, E. "The Elizabethan Audience and the Plays of Shakespeare." *MP*, XLIX (1951), 101-123.
Attacks "the monotonous error of taking the measure of Shak. by the limitations and prejudices of his most conventional customers."

A8338 Provost, George Foster. *The Techniques of Characterization and Dramatic Imagery in "Richard II" and "King Lear."* DD, Louisiana State University, 1955. Pp. 274. Mic 55-280. *DA*, xv (1955), 1616. Publ. No. 12,525.

A8339 Quiller-Couch, Sir A. *Shakespeare's Workmanship*. Cambridge Univ. Press, New York: Macmillan, 1931. Pp. 323.
Rev: by G. Baldini, *Belfagor*, III (1948), 628.

A8340 Ransom, John Crowe. *The New Criticism*. Norfolk, Conn., 1941. Pp. xiv, 340.

A8341 Remenyi, J. "Sincerity in Literature." *Personalist*, XXVI (1945), 375-386.

A8342 Reyher, Paul. *Essai sur les Idées dans l' Œuvre de Shakespeare*. Bibliothèque des Langues Modernes. Vol. I. Paris: Didier, 1947. Pp. xxix, 662.
Rev: A1021.

A8343 Richards, Ivor Armstrong. "*Troilus and Cressida* and Plato." *Speculative Instruments*. London, 1955, pp. 198-213.
Rev: by W. Empson, *NstN*, L (1955), 799-800; by J. Wain, *Spectator*, No. 6644 (1955), p. 559; *TLS*, October 21, p. 621; by R. Fuller, *London Magazine*, Feb. 3, 1956, pp. 77-80.

A8344 Bradby, Anne, ed. (Anne Ridler) *Shakespeare Criticism, 1919-1935*. World's Classics. Oxford Univ. Press, 1936. Pp. xiv, 388.
Rev: by Rosamond Gilder, *TAr*, XXI (1937), 330-331; by Joseph Wood Krutch, "Interpreting Shakespeare," *Nation* (N. Y.), 144 (1937), 270-271; by L. C. K., *Criterion*, XVI, 576-577; by W. Fischer, *Beiblatt*, XLVIII, 107; by W. Keller, *SJ*, LXXIII, 160-161; by A. Brandl, *Archiv*, 173 (1938), 232-234; *TLS*, Oct. 26, 1946, p. 521.

A8345 Ridley, M. R. *William Shakespeare: A Commentary*. The New Temple Shakespeare. London: Dent, 1936. Pp. vii, 195. Republished, London: Dent, 1957. Pp. vi, 227.
Rev: by J. Middleton Murry, *Criterion*, LXII (1936), 125-128; by F. C. Danchin, *EA*, I (1937), 186; *TLS*, Oct. 16, p. 752; by Hugh Kingsmill, *FortnR*, NS, 142 (1937), 754-755; *National Rev.*, 110 (1938), 135; by Trevor James, *Life and Letters Today*, XVIII, No. 11, 174-175; *QR*, 170 (1938), 183-184; by B. T. Spencer, *SR*, XLVII (1939), 119-129; *TLS*, May 17, 1957, p. 306; by Richard Findlater, *Drama* (Summer, 1957), pp. 37, 39; by Frank Granville-Barker, *Plays and Players*, Sept. 1957, p. 17; by H. Heuer, *SJ*, 94 (1958), 263-264.

A8346 Ridley, M. R. *On Reading Shakespeare*. Annual Shakespeare Lecture of the British Academy, 1940. London: Milford, 1940. Pp. 31.
Rev: by Alice Walker, *RES*, XVII (1941), 250.

A8347 Rohrmoser, Günter. *Kritische Erörterungen zu Gundolfs Shakespeare-Bild unter den Kategorien der Geschichte und der Person*. DD, Münster, 1955. Pp. iii, 222. Typewritten.

A8348 Rosenberg, Marvin. "Elizabethan Actors: Men or Marionettes?" *PMLA*, LXIX (1954), 915-927.
A plea, in opposition to "formalists" like Bradbrook and Joseph, for Elizabethan actors as individual artists, sharing with the dramatist the problems of interpretation. See also A8255.

A8349 Rottsolk, James E. *Criticism of the Drama in the Twenties*. DD, University of Chicago, 1951.

A8350 Rubow, Paul V. *Shakespeare i Nutidsbelysning*. Copenhagen: Munksgaard, 1948. Pp. 86.
Rev: by P. Krüger, *Orbis*, VII (1949), 308-310.

A8351 Rudin, Seymour. *George Jean Nathan: A Study of His Criticism*. DD, Cornell University, 1953.

A8352 Rylands, George. "Shakespeare's Poetic Energy." *Proceedings of the British Academy*, XXXVII (1951), 99-119.
Comment in *TLS*, Sept. 4, 1953, p. 565.

A8353 Saito, Takeshi. *A Study of Shakespeare*. Kenkyusha, 1949. See B49.

A8354 Sanders, Charles Richard. "Lytton Strachey as a Critic of Elizabethan Drama." *PQ*, xxx (1951), 1-21.

A8355 Schlumberger, Jean. *Essais et Dialogues*. Paris: Gallimard, 1937.
Contains an essay on Shak.

A8356 Schmitt, Saladin. "Shakespeare, Drama und Bühne." *SJ*, 89 (1953), 18-34.

A8357 Schnier, Jacques. "The Function and Origin of Form." *JAAC*, XVI (1957), 66-75.

A8358 Schoff, Francis G. *Aspects of Shakespearean Criticism, 1914-1950: A Commentary Centered on British and American Criticism of Hamlet*. DD, University of Minnesota, 1952. Pp. 504. Mic A53-430. *DA*, XIII (1953), 230. Publ. No. 4877.

A8359   Schomerus, Hans. *Shakespeare.* Stuttgart: Kreuz Verlag, 1958. Pp. 59.

A8360   Schrey, K., and K. Arns. "Kurz- oder Ganzausgabe von Shakespeare-Dramen." *N. Mon.,* VII (1936), 319-320.

A8361   Shaw, G. Bernard. *Shaw on Theatre.* Ed. by E. J. West. New York: Hill and Wang, 1958. Pp. xi, 306.
        Rev: *ShN,* VIII (1958), 38.

A8362   Shoemaker, Francis. *Aesthetic Experience and the Humanities.* Columbia Univ. Press, 1943. Pp. xviii, 339.
        Includes a somewhat detailed critique of *Hamlet* as an illustration of method in "teaching" literature.
        Rev: by M. T. Herrick, *JEGP,* XLIII (1944), 258-260.

A8363   Simon, Irène. "Les Progrès de la Critique Shakespearienne au XXᵉ Siècle." *Revue des Langues Vivantes,* XVI (1950), 303-329.

A8364   Sisson, C. J. "Elizabethan Life in Public Records." *The Listener,* June 21, 1951, pp. 998-999.

A8365   Sitwell, Edith. *A Notebook on William Shakespeare.* New York, London: Macmillan, 1948. Pp. xii, 233.
        Rev: by H. B. Charlton, *MGW,* Dec. 2, 1948, p. 11; *TLS,* Nov. 20, p. 654; *DUJ,* X, 37-38; by Margaret Willy, *English,* VII (1949), 185-186; *Dublin Mag.,* XXIV, 1, 49-50; by R. S. Knox, *UTQ,* XIX, 98-99; by Helen Thomas, *Adelphi,* XXV, 147; by P. Danchin, *LanM,* V, 66-67; by J. H. P. Pafford, *RES,* NS, I (1950), 166; by L. Eckhoff, *ES,* XXXII (1951), 37-38; by Richard Flatter, *SJ,* 87/88 (1952), 225-226.

A8366   Sklare, Arnold Beryl. *Arthur Symons, Critique et Poète.* DD, Paris, 1949.

A8367   Smirnov, A. A. *Shakespeare: A Marxist Interpretation.* Tr. by Sonia Volochova and others. New York: Critics' Group, 1936. Pp. 93.
        Rev: by M. Howard, *New Masses,* XX (Sept. 15, 1936), 22-24; by P. M. Jack, *NYTBR,* Aug. 16, p. 4; by B. D. N. Grebanier, *New Theatre,* Sept., p. 10.

A8367a Smirnov, A. A. *Tvorchestvo Shekspira.* Das Werk Shakespeares Zsgest. u. bearb. v. E. Tungler. Neue russ. Bibliothek. 37. Berlin: Volk u. Wissen, 1952. Pp. 72. German tr. of Smirnov's study.

A8368   Smith, Gordon Ross. *Good in Evil in Shakespearean Tragedy.* DD, The Pennsylvania State University, 1956. Pp. 446. Mic 57-568. *DA,* XVII (1957), 358. Publ. No. 19,323.

A8369   Smith, Hallett. *Elizabethan Poetry: A Study in Conventions, Meaning, and Expression.* Harvard Univ. Press, 1953. Pp. xii, 355.
        Rev: *TLS,* June 5, 1953, p. 366; by John Buxton, *Time and Tide,* June 27, p. 859; by Henry Popkin, *NR,* Jan. 5, p. 28; by H. S. Wilson, *UTQ,* XXIII, 96-98; by Leicester Bradner, *MLN,* LXVIII, 425-429; by W. H. D., *Personalist,* XXXIV, 430-431; by R. A. Foakes, *SQ,* IV, 350-351; by Herschel Baker, *JEGP,* LII, 401-403; *NstN,* XLVI, 83; by M. Poirier, *EA,* VII (1954), 116-117; by B. E. C. Davis, *RES,* NS, V, 285-287; by Herbert Goldstone, *MLQ,* XV, 275-276; by Geoffrey Bullough, *MLR,* LI (1956), 92-93.

A8370   Smith, Logan Pearsall. *On Reading Shakespeare.* London, 1933.
        Rev: by H. de Groot, *ES,* XVIII (1936), 37-39).

A8371   Smith, M. Ellwood. "The Lunatic, The Lover and The Poet." *SAB,* XVI (1941), 77-88.

A8372   Smith, Robert M. "An Agnostic Life of Shakespeare." *SAB,* XV (1940), 75-87.
        Discussion of various recent studies, including objections to interpreting Shak. in terms of "historical" criticism.

A8373   Smith, Robert M. "Current Fashions in *Hamlet* Criticism." *SAB,* XXIV (1949), 13-21.

A8374   Spalding, Kenneth J. *The Philosophy of Shakespeare.* New York, 1953.
        Rev: A1034.

A8375   Speaight, Robert. *Nature in Shakespearean Tragedy.* London: Hollis and Carter, 1955. Pp. viii, 179.
        Rev: A1035.

A8376   Spencer, Benjamin T. "This Elizabethan Shakespeare." *SR,* XLIX (1941), 536-552.
        A review of recent books by Messrs. Stoll, Van Doren, and Draper and Miss Dunn, protesting against interpretations which reconstruct "the Elizabethan mind," assume that it is a constant, and thus make "the rigid and commonplace mentality" of Shakespeare's contemporaries the measure of his plays.

A8377   Spencer, Hazelton. *The Art and Life of William Shakespeare.* New York: Harcourt, Brace, 1940. Pp. xx, 495.
        Rev: A522.

A8378   Squire, Sir John. *Shakespeare as a Dramatist.* London, 1935.
        Rev: by Floris Delattre, *RAA,* XIII (1936), 513.

A8379   Stalker, Archibald. *Shakespeare and Tom Nashe.* Stirling: Learmonth, 1935. Pp. 178.

A8380   Stallman, Robert Wooster, ed. *Critiques and Essays in Criticiam, 1920-1948.* Foreword by Cleanth Brooks. New York: Ronald Press, 1949. Pp. xxii, 571.
        Essays on specific plays by Shak. entered separately.

A8381 Stamm, Rudolf. *Shakespeare's Word Scenery.* With Some Remarks on Stage-History and the Interpretation of His Plays. Zurich and St. Gallen: Polygraph. Verlag, 1954. Pp. 34.
Rev: A5603.

A8382 Stauffer, Donald A. *Shakespeare's World of Images: The Development of His Moral Ideas.* New York: W. W. Norton, 1949. Pp. 393.
Rev: A1046.

A8383 Steiner, Rudolf. *Drama und Dichtung im Bewusstseins-Umschwung der Neuzeit: Shakespeare Goethe und Schiller.* Ed. Robert Friedenthal. Dornach: R. Steiner Nachlassverwaltung, 1956.

A8384 Stammler, Walter. *Der Renaissancebegriff in der Shakespeare-Kritik.* DD, Hamburg, 1942. Pp. 277. Typewritten.

A8385 Stewart, J. I. M. *"Julius Caesar* and *Macbeth.* Two Notes on Shakespearean Technique." *MLR,* XL (1945), 166-173.

A8386 Stewart, J. I. M. *Character and Motive in Shakespeare.* London: Longmans, Green & Co., 1949. Pp. vii, 147.
A critique of discussions by Bridges, Schücking and Stoll, of character and motive in Shak.
Rev: A6518.

A8387 Stewart, J. I. M. "Shakespeare and His World: Shakespeare's Characters." *Listener,* XLII (Aug. 25, 1949), 312-316.
Review of critical works: Dr. Johnson, Bradley, Bridges, Schücking, Stoll, T. S. Eliot, Granville-Barker, Ernest Jones (whose book he calls "deeply persuasive").

A8388 Still, Colin. *The Timeless Theme: A Critical Theory Formulated and Applied.* London: I. Nicholson & Watson, 1936. Pp. x, 244.
Part II: "An Interpretation of Shakespeare's *Tempest,* pp. 127-244.

A8389 Stoessl, O. "Über einige Dramen von Shakespeare: *Der Kaufmann von Venedig. König Richard II. Macbeth. Antonius und Kleopatra. Troilus und Kressida. Viel Lärm um Nichts.* Shakespeares Problem in *Hamlet. Mass für Mass. Der Sturm.*" In *Geist und Gestalt* (Vienna), III (1935), 260-312.

A8390 Stoll, E. E. *Art and Artifice in Shakespeare.* Cambridge Univ. Press, 1933. Republ. New York: Barnes and Noble, 1955. Pp. xvi, 178.
Rev: by Floris Delattre, *RAA,* XII (1934/35), 219-221; by Harold N. Hillebrand, *JEGP,* XXXIV (1935), 442-444; by Johannes Speck, *Archiv,* 169 (1936), 135; by Eduard Eckhardt, *Eng. Studn.,* LXX, 397-400; by Paul de Réal, *RUnBrux,* XLII, 270-281; by L. C. Knights, *Scrutiny,* 1934. Reprinted in *The Importance of Scrutiny,* New York: Stewart, 1948, pp. 163-166; by James G. McManaway, *SQ,* VI (1955), 474.

A8391 Stoll, E. E. "The Dramatic Texture in Shakespeare." *Criterion,* XIV (1934/35), 586-607.

A8392 Stoll, E. E. "Tartuffe and the *Optique du Théâtre.*" *RAA,* XIII (1936), 193-214.
See the joint reply by Émile Legouis and L. Cazamian, *À Propos d'une Critique de Mr. Edgar Stoll,* ibid., pp. 214-218.

A8393 Stoll, Elmer Edgar. "Jacques, and the Antiquaries." *MLN,* LIV (1939), 79-85.

A8394 Stoll, Elmer Edgar. *Shakespeare and Other Masters.* Harvard Univ. Press, 1940. Pp. xv, 430.
Rev: by J. Corbin, *NYTBR,* Dec. 8, 1940, p. 34; by Wolfgang Keller, *SJ,* LXXVII (1941), 197-198; by Douglas Bush, *UTQ,* X, 241-245; by E. C. Knowlton, *South Atlantic Quar.,* XL, 186-188; by G. C. Taylor, *YR,* XXX, 418-421; by Allardyce Nicoll, *JEGP,* XL, 290-292; by R. A. Law, *MLQ,* II, 510-512; by H. S. Bennett, *RES,* XVIII (1942), 344-345; by B. T. Spencer, "This Elizabethan Shakespeare," *SR,* XLIX, 545-548; by Baldwin Maxwell, *MLN,* LVIII (1943), 147-149; by B. E. C. Davis, *MLR,* XXXVIII, 48-50; by Rufus Putney, *PQ,* XXII, 83-84.

A8395 Stoll, Elmer Edgar. "Poetry and the Passions: An Aftermath." *PMLA,* LV (1940), 979-992.

A8395a Stoll, Elmer Edgar. "Poetry and the Passions Again." *JEGP,* XL (1941), 509-525.

A8396 Stoll, Elmer E. "Heroes and Villains: Shakespeare, Middleton, Byron, Dickens." *RES,* XVIII (1942), 257-269.
On Mark Van Doren's *Shakespeare,* which he calls "present-day highbrow criticism;" expresses doubts that Van Doren is "thinking."

A8397 Stoll, Elmer Edgar. *From Shakespeare to Joyce: Authors and Critics. Literature and Life.* New York: Doubleday Doran, 1944. Pp. 442.
Rev: by Mark Schorer, *NYTBR,* Feb. 6, 1944, p. 7; by G. W. Stonier, *NstN,* June 10, pp. 390-391; by J. T. S., *American Bookman,* I, 127; by Louis Kronenberger, *Nation,* Feb. 19, pp. 229-231; by R. Ellis Roberts, *SRL,* March, pp. 9-10; by S. C. Chew, *NYHTBR,* April 30, Sec. 6, p. 8; *TLS,* March 18, 1944, p. 138; by Roy Daniells, *UTQ,* XIV (1945), 214-216; by J. R. Sutherland, *RES,* XXI, 153-155; by E. C. Pettet, *English,* V, 212-213.

A8398 Stoll, Elmer Edgar. "Mainly Controversy: Hamlet, Othello." *PQ,* XXIV (1945), 289-316.
Answers to Professor Lawrence in his "Hamlet's Sea-Voyage," *PMLA,* LIX (1944), 45-70, and to Rufus Putney in his review of Shakespeare and Other Masters, *PQ,* XXII (1943), 83-84.

A8399 Stoll, Elmer Edgar. "Symbolism in Shakespeare." *MLR,* XLII (1947), 9-23.
A criticism of the "new criticism."

A8400 Stoll, Elmer Edgar. " 'Multi-Consciousness' in the Theatre." *PQ,* XXIX (1950), 1-14.
Inspired by Mr. Harbage's *As They Liked It,* and Mr. Bethell's *Shakespeare and the Popular*

Dramatic Tradition; objects to a basic assumption in those works and in that of the "Imaginatives (Messrs. G. W. Knight, L. C. Knights, F. R. Leavis, and others)."

A8401   Stoll, Elmer E. "A Freudian Detective's Shakespeare." *MP*, XLVIII (1950), 122-132.
Inspired by Mr. Stewart's study A8386.

A8402   Stoll, E. E. "Intentions and Instinct." *MLQ*, XIV (1953), 375-412.
An attack on G. W. Knight, Bonamy Dobrée, Lionel Trilling, E. Jones, etc.
The following items out of alphabetical order are chiefly concerned with Professor Stoll's criticism. They by no means exhaust the published objections to his work. Other relevant sections should be consulted and also annotations of other items elsewhere in this section.

A8403   Teeter, Louis. "Scholarship and the Art of Criticism." *ELH*, V (1938), 173-194.

A8404   Sampley, Arthur M. "Hamlet Among the Mechanists." *SAB*, XVII (1942), 134-149.

A8405   Putney, Rufus. " 'What Praise to Give?' Jonson vs. Stoll." *PQ*, XXIII (1944), 307-319.

A8406   Shen, Yao. *Some Chapters on Shakespearean Criticism: Coleridge, Hazlitt and Stoll.* DD, University of Michigan, 1944. Pp. 306. Mic A47-33. *Mcf Ab*, VII (1947), 91. Publ. No. 825.

A8407   Stirling, Brents. "Psychology in *Othello.*" *SAB*, XIX (1944), 135-144.

A8408   Pitcher, Seymour. "Aristotle's Good and Just Heroes." *PQ*, XXIV (1945), 1-11.
See letter by Mr. Pitcher, ibid., pp. 190-191.

A8409   Babcock, R. W. "Mr. Stoll Revisited Twenty Years After." *PQ*, XXVII (1948), 289-313.

A8410   Rosenberg, Marvin. "A Sceptical Look at Sceptical Criticism." *PQ*, XXXIII (1954), 66-77.
Questions whether E. E. Stoll, despite his professed concern with theatrical conventions, really understands the resources of the theater.

A8411   Morgan, George Alan. *Illustrations of the Critical Principles of E. E. Stoll.* DD, Iowa State University, 1957. Pp. 224. Mic 57-4807. *DA*, XVII (1957), 3020. Publ. No. 23,772.
See also A8236.

A8412   Swinnerton, Frank. "Shakespeare's Heroines." *John o'London's Weekly*, LXIII (1954), 913.

A8413   Taylor, Warren. "The Uses of Shakespeare." *CE*, II (1941), 476-485.

A8414   Thompson, Stith. "The Use and Abuse of Books. Literary Scholarship During the Past Century." *American Scholar*, IX (Winter, 1939-40), 85-96.

A8415   Tillyard, E. M. W. *Shakespeare's Last Plays.* London: Chatto & Windus, 1938. Pp. 85.
Rev: B5233.

A8416   Tillyard, E. M. W., and C. S. Lewis. *The Personal Heresy, A Controversy.* Oxford Univ. Press, 1939. Pp. vii, 150.
Rev: *N &Q*, 176 (1939), 394-395; by D. F., *SRL*, Aug. 19, p. 20; by Ruth Z. Temple, *SR*, XLVII, 596-599; by T. Merton, *NYTBR*, July 9, p. 16; by F. W. Bateson, *RES*, XVI (1940), 487-489; by G. Tillotson, *MLR*, XXXV, 250-251; by G. Boas, *MLN*, LV, 233-234.

A8417   Tillyard, E. M. W. "Is a New History of Criticism Possible?" *CamJ*, II (1949), 543-551.
See the comment "Splendid Fossils," *TLS*, June 17, 1949, p. 397.

A8418   Tillyard, E. M. W. *Shakespeare's Problem Plays.* Toronto, 1949; London, 1950.
Rev: B5222.

A8419   Tillyard, Eustace M. W. "Reality and Fantasy in Elizabethan Literature." In *Sprache und Literatur*, pp. 69-81.
Rev: B4447a.

A8420   Traversi, D. A. *An Approach to Shakespeare.* London: Sands, Paladin Press, 1938. Pp. 152.
Second edition, revised and enlarged, New York: Doubleday, 1956. Pp. 304.
Rev: by R. G. Cox, *Scrutiny*, VII (1939), 459-461; *SCN*, XIV (1956), 4-5; *English Journal*, XLV, 234; *TLS*, Sept. 13, 1957, p. 551; *N &Q*, NS, V (1958), 134-135; by Hermann Heuer, *SJ*, 94, (1958), 264-265; *The Month*, XIX, 190.

A8421   Traversi, Derek A. *Visión de Shakespeare.* Tr. Concha Vásquez. Barcelona: Janes, 1948. Pp. 159.

A8421a   Traversi, Derek. *Shakespeare.* Tr. por Concepción Vásquez de Castro. Barcelona: Labor, 1951. Pp. 275.

A8422   Trilling, Lionel. "The Sense of the Past." In *The Liberal Imagination*, New York, 1949.
Paperback ed.: New York: Doubleday Anchor, 1957.
Contains a discussion of Prof. E. E. Stoll's criticism. "Professor Stoll seems to go on the assumption that Shakespeare's audiences were conscious of convention; they were aware of it, but certainly not conscious of it; what they were conscious of was life, into which they made an instantaneous translation of all that took place on the stage."

A8423   Van Doren, Mark. "Literature and Propaganda." *VQR*, XIV (1938), 203-208.

A8424   Van Doren, Mark. *Shakespeare.* New York: Holt, 1939. Pp. viii, 344. Repr. New York: Doubleday, 1953.
Rev: by W. T. Hastings, *SRL*, Oct. 7, 1939, p. 7; by W. H. Auden, *Nation* (N. Y.), 149 (1939), 444-445; by M. M. Colum, *Forum*, 102 (1939), 161-162; by P. M. Jack, *NYTBR*, Nov. 12, p. 2; by Leland Schubert, *QJS*, XXVI (1940), 118-119; by T. W. Baldwin, *MLN*, LV, 460-461; by M. C. L., *Catholic World*, 150 (1940), 504-505; *South Atlantic Quar.*, XXXIX,

246-247; by Philip Timberlake, *KR*, II, 112-116; by H. N., *Standard*, XXVII, 21; by A. Guérard, *VQR*, XVI, 150-156; by Bonamy Dobrée, *Spectator*, Mar. 21, 1941, pp. 318, 320; *QR*, 276 (1941), 310; *TLS*, Apr. 5, p. ii; by George Cookson, *English*, III, 226-227; by E. Bowen, *NstN*, Apr. 19, pp. 413-414; by M. P., *Adelphi*, XVII, 296-298; by G. C. Taylor, *YR*, XXX, 418-421; by B. T. Spencer, *SR*, XLIX, 550-553; by Richard Flatter, *SJ*, 84/86 (1950), 240-242; by Nelson Magill, *QJS*, XL (1955), 88; *ShN*, VIII (1958), 3.

A8425   Van Doren, Mark. "The Secret of Shakespeare's Power." *Catholic World*, 150 (1939), 225-226. A quotation from A8424.

A8426   Vinaver, Stanislav. "Šekspir u punom Blesku i Zamahu." *Književnost* (Belgrade), X (1955), 105-113.

A8427   Waldock, A. J. A. *Sophocles the Dramatist*. Cambridge Univ. Press, 1951. Pp. x, 228. First chapter: "The Historical Method and Its Limitations."
Rev: by R. Mayhead, *Scrutiny*, XVIII (1951), 233-238; by William T. Hastings, *SQ*, III (1952), 135-136; *Listener*, XLVII, 353.

A8428   Webb, Kaye, ed. *An Experience of Critics*, by Christopher Fry, and *The Approach to Dramatic Criticism*, by W. A. Darlington and Others. With a Prologue by Alec Guinness. London: Perpetua, 1952.
Rev: *TLS*, Oct. 24, 1952, p. 690; by Ivor Brown, *Obs.*, Oct. 19, p. 8.

A8429   Weber, Carl August. "Die Neuere Entwicklung der Literaturwissenschaft in der Anglistik." In *Sprache u. Literatur*, pp. 99-123, B4447a.

A8430   Webster, Margaret. *Shakespeare Without Tears*. New York: McGraw-Hill, 1942. Pp. xii, 319. Revised ed., New York: World Publishing Co., 1955.
Rev: by Rosamond Gilder, *TAr*, XXVI (1942), 282; by John Corbin, *NYTBR*, Feb. 1, p. 8; by Barnard Hewitt, *QJS*, XXVIII, 487-488; by Mabel C. Livingston, *Catholic World*, 155 (1942), 369-370; by H. McC., *More Books*, XVII, 161; by B. T. Spencer, *SR*, L, 553-556; *English Journal*, XLIV (1955), 549; *ShN*, VI (1956), 28; by St. Vincent Troubridge, *SQ*, VII, 268-270; *SatR*, Aug. 3, 1957, p. 28; by R. A. Foakes, *English*, XI, 232.

A8431   Webster, Margaret. "Interpretation of Shakespeare Today." *Wisdom*, July, 1956, pp. 23-27. Excerpted from A8430.

A8432   Webster, Margaret. *Shakespeare Today*. Intro. by M. R. Ridley. London: Dent, 1956. Pp. 319.
Rev: by Helen Gardner, *London Mag.*, IV, no. 12 (1957), 73-74, 77-78; by Hermann Heuer, *SJ*, 93 (1957), 274; by Philip Hope-Wallace, *Time and Tide*, June 1, p. 692; by R. A. Foakes, *English*, XI, 232; by J. B. Fort, *EA*, X, 447-448; *TLS*, May 17, p. 306; *Theatre World*, April, p. 53; by Frank Granville-Barker, *Plays and Players*, Sept., p. 17; by J. Vallette, *MdF*, 330 (1957), 714; by M. St. Clare Byrne, *TN*, XII, 72-73.

A8433   Weisinger, Herbert. "The Study of Shakespearian Tragedy since Bradley." *SQ*, VI (1955), 387-396.
Objections to certain modern tendencies undermining Bradley: emphasis on text instead of idea; studies of imagery; use of Elizabethan psychology; highlighting of native medieval elements; semantic revolt against generic terms; and the claim that tragedy cannot be created.

A8434   Wellek, René. "The Nature and Scope of Literary History." *HLQ*, VI (1942-43), 35-39, with comments by William H. Dunham, Jr., pp. 39-40, D. H. Wills, pp. 40-41, Merritt Y. Hughes, pp. 41-42, Louis B. Wright, pp. 42-43, and C. H. Collins Baker, p. 43.

A8435   Wellek, René, and Austin Warren. *Theory of Literature*. London: Cape; New York: Harcourt, Brace, 1949. Pp. x, 403.
Rev: by W. K. Wimsatt, Jr., *YR*, XXXIX (1949), 180-182; by H. H., *CL*, I, 277-281; by Alwyn Berland, *Western Rev.*, XIV, 74-76; by D. A. Stauffer, *NYTBR*, Jan. 30, p. 14; by G. F. Whicher, *NYHTBR*, March 27, p. 14; by William Troy, *Hudson Rev.*, II, 619-621; by Newton Arvin, *Partisan Rev.*, XVI, 318-321; *Accent*, IX, 172-175; by A. Mizener, *Furioso*, IV (Summer), 84-88; by H. Levin, *GR*, XXIV, 303-306; by Howard Mumford Jones, *SRL*, Apr. 30, p. 12; by I. Howe, *Nation*, 169 (1949), 64-65; by Richard Harter Fogel, *CE*, XI, 52-53; by M. Geismar, *NR*, Apr. 11, pp. 22-23; by W. M. Frohock, *Rom*, XL, 306-310; by Carl Grabo, *Chicago Jewish Forum*, VIII, 99-106; by S. M. Pitcher, *PQ*, XXVIII, 520-523; by T. Spencer, *MLR*, XLIV, 555-557; by Isabel C. Hungerland, *JAAC*, VIII (1950), 196-198; *TLS*, Feb. 24, p. 119; by H. S. Wilson, *UTQ*, XIX, 194-197; by H. S. Benjamin, *Antioch Rev.*, X, 147-150; by E. Vivas, *KR*, XII, 161-165; by J. D. Jump, *MGW*, Jan. 5, p. 12; by Harriet Zinnes, *Poetry*, LXXV, 303-306; by Kemp Malone, *Language*, XXVI, 311-313; by Alexander C. Kern, *MLQ*, XII (1951), 360-361; by Rudolf Sühnel, *Anglia*, LXX, 210-213.

A8436   Wheelwright, Philip, Cleanth Brooks, I. A. Richards, and Wallace Stevens. *The Language of Poetry*. Ed. with a Preface by Allen Tate. Princeton Univ. Press, 1942. Pp. viii, 125.
Rev: by D. A. Stauffer, *KR*, IV (1942), 411-415; by Marvin T. Herrick, *JEGP*, XLII (1943), 293-294; by Delmore Schwartz, *MLN*, LVIII, 647-648.

A8437   Wickert, Maria. *Shakespeare-Interpretationen*. DD, Cologne, 1947. Pp. 160. Typewritten.

A8438   Williams, Philip. "The Birth and Death of Falstaff Reconsidered." *SQ*, VIII (1957), 359-365.

A8439   Williams, Raymond. "Criticism into Drama 1888-1950." *EIC*, I (1951), 120-138.

A8440   Wilson, F. P. *Elizabethan and Jacobean*. Oxford Univ. Press, 1945. Pp. 144. Toronto Univ. Alexander lectures in English, 1943. Shak., pp. 109-130.

Rev: *TLS*, Nov. 10, 1945, p. 539; ibid., Jan. 12, 1946, p. 16; by C. J. Sisson, *MLR*, XLI, 208; by Una Ellis-Fermor, *English*, VI, 34-35; by S. E. C., *NYHTBR*, May 12, p. 25; by H. B. Charlton, *MGW*, LIV, 154; *DUJ*, VII, 65-66; by F. R. Johnson, *MLN*, LXII (1947), 208-210; by Douglas Bush, *UTQ*, XVI, 199-202; by Hardin Craig, *MLQ*, VIII, 124-125; by Theodore Spencer, *RES*, XXIII, 79-80; by Sergio Baldi, *Rivista di Letterature Moderne*, I (1950), 156-157; by Hermann Heuer, *SJ*, 84/86 (1951), 250-251.

A8441 Wilson, John Dover. "New Ideas and Discoveries about Shakespeare." *VQR*, XXIII (1947), 537-542.

A8442 Wimsatt, W. K., Jr., and M. C. Beardsley. "The Intentional Fallacy." *SR*, LIV (1946), 468-488. A criticism of the author's intention as the measure of a poem.

A8443 Wimsatt, W. K., Jr. "The Structure of the 'Concrete Universal' in Literature." *PMLA*, LXII (1947), 262-280.

A8444 Yamato, Motoo. *Appreciation of English Literature.* Tokyo: Kenkyusha, 1949.

A8445 Zandvoort, R. W. "*King Lear:* The Scholars and Critics." *Mededelingen der Koninklijke Nederlandse Academie van Wetenschappen, afd. Letterkunde.* Amsterdam: N. V. Noord-Hollandsche Uitgevers Maatschappij, *NR*, XIX, No. 7 (1956), 229-244.

A8446 Zukofsky, Louis. *A Test of Poetry.* London: Routledge & Kegan Paul, 1952.
Rev: *TLS*, Oct. 24, 1952, p. 691.

XII. COMPARISONS WITH OTHER WRITERS
1. WITH AUTHORS OF VARIOUS NATIONALITIES

A8447 Rank, Otto. *Art and Artist.* Tr. by Charles F. Atkinson. New York: Knopf, 1932. Pp. xxvii, 431, xii.
Shak. compared to Michelangelo, pp. 55-58. To Homer, 381.

A8448 Kassner, R. "Über Shakespeare." *Corona*, VI (1936), 256-283, 408-423.

A8449 Stoll, Elmer Edgar. *Shakespeare and Other Masters.* Harvard Univ. Press, 1940. Pp. xv, 430.
Rev: A8394.

A8450 Williams, E. E. *Tragedy of Destiny, Oedipus Tyrannus, Macbeth, Athalie.* Cambridge, Mass.: Eds. XVII siècle, 1940. Pp. 35.
Rev: B9208.

A8451 Ellis-Fermor, Una. *Shakespeare the Dramatist.* British Acad. Annual Shakespeare Lecture. Oxford Univ. Press, 1948. Pp. 16.
A multitude of comparison with various famous poets.
Rev: A5855.

A8452 Sitwell, Edith. *A Notebook on William Shakespeare.* New York, London: Macmillan, 1948. Pp. xii, 233.
Rev: A8365.

A8453 Ellis-Fermor, Una. "Die Spätwerke grosser Dramatiker." *Deutsche Vierteljahrsschrift*, XXIV (1950), 423-439. With Aeschylus, Sophocles, Euripides, and Ibsen.

A8454 Boas, F. S. "Joan of Arc in Shakespeare, Schiller, and Shaw." *SQ*, II (1951), 35-45.

A8455 Kilga, Johanna F. *Joan of Arc bei Shakespeare, Schiller und Shaw.* DD, Vienna, 1951. Pp. 87. Typewritten.

A8456 Bruers, Antonio. "Dante—Shakespeare—Hugo." *Osservatore Romano* 92 (1952), No. 279, 3.

A8457 Custodio, Alvaro. "Poesía y Realismo Dramáticos." *Excelsior*, Mexico City, Oct. 6, 1957, p. 3. Comparison between Spanish realistic poetry, the Greek classics, and Shak.

2. CLASSICAL LITERATURE
a. GENERAL

A8458 Crutchfield, H. M. *Elizabethan and Athenian Tragic Drama Compared and Contrasted.* MA thesis, University of South Africa, 1922.

A8459 Stanford, W. B. "Ghosts and Apparitions in Homer, Aeschylus, and Shakespeare." *Hermathene*, LVI (1941), 84-92.

A8460 Jones, Robert E. "Brutus in Cicero and Shakespeare." *Classical Journal*, XXXVIII (1943), 449-457.

A8461 Martin, L. C. "Shakespeare, Lucretius, and the Commonplaces." *RES*, XXI (1945), 174-182. "There are, to put it bluntly, signs of too great a readiness to remain content with the easier discipline of noting the correspondences between Shakespeare, for example, and those numerous writers who said the same sort of thing before him." (p. 175.)
Suggests Bruno as the intermediary between Shak. and Lucretius.

A8462 Ure, Peter. "On Some Differences Between Senecan and Elizabethan Tragedy." *DUJ*, X (1948), 17-23.

A8463 Grosjean, Jean. "D'où vient Shakespeare?" *NRF*, No. 28, Jan. 3, 1955, pp. 697-701.

A8464 Kellogg, Allen B. "Place Names and Epithets in Homer and Shakespeare." *Names*, III (1955), 169-171.

b. GREEK DRAMA

A8465 Lever, Katherine. *Early Tudor Drama and Old Greek Comedy: a Study of Didactic and Satiric Plays.* DD, Bryn Mawr College, 1943.

A8466 Pfeiffer, Arthur. "Griechisches und Deutsches Drama." *DW*, XVIII (1943), 86-91.

A8467 Jepsen, Laura P. *Ethos in Classical and Shakespearean Tragedy.* DD, State University of Iowa, 1946. Abstract publ. by State Univ. of Iowa in *Doctoral Dissertations: Abstracts and References (1942 Through 1948)*, Vol. VI, 418-425. Publ. as *Ethical Aspects of Tragedy.* Gainesville: Univ. of Florida Press, 1953.
Rev: A975.

A8468 Glasson, T. Francis. "Did Shakespeare Read Aeschylus?" *London Quar. & Holborn Rev.*, 173 (1948), 57-66.

A8469 Maxwell, J. C. "Creon and Angelo: A Parallel Study." *Greece & Rome*, XVII (1949), 32-36.

A8470 Brock, F. H. Cecil. "*Oedipus, Macbeth* and the Christian Tradition." *ConR*, Mar., 1950, pp. 176-181.

A8471 Boyd, Catharine B. "The Isolation of Antigone and Lady Macbeth." *Classical Journal*, XLVII (1952), 174-177, 203.

A8472 Auden, Wystan Hugh. "The Dyer's Hand." *Listener*, LIII (1955), 1063-66.
Compares *Oedipus Rex* with *Macbeth.*

A8473 Kitto, H. D. F. *Form and Meaning in Drama: A Study of Six Greek Plays and of "Hamlet".* London: Methuen, 1956. Pp. 541.
Rev: B7506.

A8474 Driver, Tom Faw. *The Sense of History in Greek and Shakespearean Dramatic Form.* DD, Columbia University, 1957. Pp. 397. Mic 57-2807. *DA*, XVII (1957), 1748. Publication No. 21,781.

A8475 Knoll, Robert E. "Drama of Fulfillment and Drama of Choice: A Note on Greek and Elizabethan Drama." *Western Humanities Review*, XI (1957), 371-376.

A8476 Flanagan, Sarah Patricia. "A Reinterpretation of *King Lear*." *DA*, XVIII (1958), 581.

3. ITALIAN LITERATURE
a. INDIVIDUALS
(1) DANTE

A8477 Muir, Kenneth. "Shakespeare and Dante." *N &Q*, 194 (1949), 333.

A8478 Thompson, W. Lawrence. "*Hamlet* and Dante's Paradiso." *N &Q*, Apr. 28, 1951, pp. 181-182.

A8479 Cetrangolo, Giuseppe. *L'universo dantesco e la terra di Shakespeare.* Incontro con F. Lucas critico e prosatore inglese. Rome: Opere nuove, 1953. Pp. 47.

A8480 Dwyer, J. J. "Did Shakespeare Read Dante?" *Tablet*, 206 (July 9, 1955), 33-34.

A8481 Harrison, Charles T. "The Poet as Witness." *SR*, LXIII (1955), 539-550.
Comparison of Shak. with Dante.

A8482 Rebora, Piero. "Espressioni sulla vita in Dante e in Shakespeare." *Studi Urbinati*, (Urbino), XXIX (1955), 23-35.

(2) OTHERS

A8483 Kernan, Joseph. "Verdi's *Otello*, or Shakespeare Explained." *Hudson Review*, VI (1953), 266-267.

A8484 Blanco, Julio Enrico. "Las Pruebas del Alter Ego en D'Annunzio y en Shakespeare." *Ideas y Valores*, Bogotá, No. 6, 1952.

4. FRENCH LITERATURE
a. GENERAL

A8485 MacKerracher, Christina Jean. *Similarites in Shakespeare's Sonnets and the French Poetry of the 16th Century.* MA thesis, Western Ontario, 1928. Pp. 77.

b. INDIVIDUALS
(1) MOLIÈRE

A8486 Stoll, E. E. "Molière and Shakespeare." *RR*, XXXV (1944), 1-18.

A8487 Schevill, James. "Towards a Rhythm of Comic Action." *Western Speech*, XX (1956), 5-14.
Concerns Falstaff and Tartuffe.

A8488 Brittin, Norman A. "*Coriolanus, Alceste,* and Dramatic Genres." *PMLA*, LXXI (1956), 799-807.

(2) RACINE

A8489 Soderman, Hilda Marjorie. *Racine's Women and Lady Macbeth.* MA thesis, Alberta, 1935. Pp. 93.

A8490   Ternois, René. *Stendhal, Racine et Shakespeare.* Collection Classique Larousse. Paris: Larousse, 1936.
Rev: *RUnBrux*, XLII (1936), 14-15.

A8491   Schlumberger, Jean. "Sur Les Personnages de Shakespeare." *Le Théâtre Élizabéthain.* Paris: Les Cahiers du Sud, 1940, pp. 40-43.
Comparisons with Racine.

A8492   Mary Carmel, Sister. *"Macbeth" et "Britannicus."* MA thesis, Laval, 1942. Pp. 104.

A8493   Arnold, Paul. "Racine et Shakespeare." *Cahiers du Nord*, 1950, pp. 263-269.

A8494   Stendhal. *Rasin i Shekspir.* Tr. by Milan Predić into Serbo-Croatian. Belgrade: Novo pokolenje, 1953. Pp. 180.

A8495   Wain, Marianne. "Racine Revisited." *Mandrake*, II (Autumn & Winter, 1955-56), 427-432. A rev. of Eugène Vinavers' *Racine and Poetic Tragedy* (tr. P. M. Jones), with a comparison of *Ham.* and *Phèdre.*

(3) OTHERS

A8496   Neri, Ferdinando. *Poesia nel tempo.* Turin: Francesco de Silva, 1948. "Corneille e Shakespeare," pp. 51-55.

A8497   Hugo, Howard E. "The Madman of the Heath and the Madwoman of Chaillot." *Chrysalis* (Boston), V (1952), 3-4, 3-11.

A8498   Fowlie, Wallace. "Swann and Hamlet: A Note on the Contemporary Hero." *Partisan Review*, IX (1942), 195-202.

A8499   Gus, M. "Racine and Shakespeare. On Stendhal's Pamphlet 'Of a Heroic Art and of Our Classics'." *Theatre* (USA), VI (1940), 26-37.

A8500   Legouis, Émile. *"La Terre* de Zola et le *Roi Lear."* *RLC*, XXVII (1953), 417-427.
See also B7672.

5. SPANISH LITERATURE
a. GENERAL

A8501   Leech, Clifford. "Catholic and Protestant Drama." *DUJ*, XXXIII (1941), 171-187.
Primarily concerned with a comparison of the plays of Lope and Calderón and those of Elizabethan and Jacobean playwrights.

A8502   Housman, J. E. *Parallel Plots in English and Spanish Drama of the Early 17th Century.* DD, University of London, 1951.

A8503   Crocker, Lester G. *"Hamlet, Don Quijote, La vida es sueño:* The Quest for Values." *PMLA*, LXIX (1954), 278-313.

b. INDIVIDUALS
(1) DE ROJAS

A8504   Allensworth, Clairenne. *Estudio comparativo entre "La Celestina" y "Romeo y Julieta."* MAE thesis, Mexico, 1940. Pp. 68. Typewritten.

A8505   Russel, Mary Eleanor. *Una comparación entre Melibea y Julieta.* MAE thesis, Mexico, 1940. Pp. 113. Typewritten.

A8506   Quijano Terán, Margarita. *"La Celestina" y "Otelo": Estudio de Literatura Dramática Comparada.* Mexico: Univ. Nacional Autónoma de México, 1957.

(2) LOPE

A8507   Pujals, Esteban. "Shakespeare y Lope de Vega." *Revista de Literatura*, I (1952), 25-45.

A8508   Villarejo, Oscar M. *Lope de Vega and the Elizabethan and Jacobean Drama.* DD, Columbia University, 1953. Pp. 418. Mic A53-1502. *DA*, XIII (1953), 816. Publication No. 5763.

A8509   Heald, William F. *A Comparison of the Plot Patterns in the Plays of Shakespeare and Lope de Vega.* DD, University of North Carolina, 1954.

(3) CALDERÓN

A8510   Werekshagen, Carl. "Calderón und Shakespeare." *Blätter des Hessischen Landestheaters,* 1939/40, Heft. 14.

A8511   Parker, A. A. *"Henry VIII* in Shakespeare and Calderón. An Appreciation of *La Cisma de Ingalaterra."* *MLR*, XLIII (1948), 327-352.

A8512   Irving, Thomas B. "Hamlet y Segismundo ante la Vida." *Universidad de San Carlos* (Guatemala), No. 19 (1950), pp. 7-18.

(4) CERVANTES

A8513   Trinker, Martha K. de. *Las Mujeres en el "Don Quijote" de Cervantes, Comparadas con las Mujeres en los Dramas de Shakespeare.* DD, Mexico, 1938. Pp. 123.

A8514   Wyneken, H. "Falstaff und *Don Quichotte."* *MNN*, 1939, No. 113.

A8515   Rusch, Heinz. "Schöpfer der Weltliteratur. Zum 325. Todestag von Shakespeare und Cervantes." *Westfälische Landesztg.*, Rote Erde, No. 110, 1941.

A8516   Weller, Earl F. *Una Comparación de la Filosofía de Shakespeare con la de Cervantes.* MAE thesis, Mexico, 1942. Pp. 117. Typewritten.

A8517   González Ruiz, Nicolás. *Dos Genios Contemporáneos: Cervantes, Shakespeare.* Barcelona: Imp. Clarasó, 1945. Pp. 160.

A8518   Madariaga, Salvador de. "Hamlet and Don Quixote." *Shakespeare Quarterly,* (London), I (Summer, 1947), 22-25.

A8519   Starkie, W. "Cervantes et Shakespeare." *Revista nacional de educación* (Madrid), VII (1947), No. 7.

A8520   Madariaga, Salvador de. *On Hamlet.* London, 1948.

A8521   Ardura, E. "Shakespeare and Cervantes." *Américas,* VII (Nov. 1955), 14-18.

6. ENGLISH LITERATURE
a. GENERAL

A8522   Gurd, Jean Marjorie S. *The Treatment and Use of the Fairy Element in the Elizabethan and Modern Drama: A Contrast.* MA thesis, McGill, 1926.

A8523   Ryan, Rev. Harold Francis, S. J. *Heroic Play Elements in Earlier English Drama.* DD, St. Louis University, 1944. Pp. 366. Mic A45-5307. *Mcf Ab,* VI (1945), 27. Publication No. 766. "Shak. and the Restoration Heroic Play," pp. 249-311.

A8524   Wood, Warren Welles. *A Comparison Between Shakespeare and His Contemporaries in Their Use of Music and Sound Effects.* DD, Northwestern University, 1944. Abstract publ. in *Summaries of Doctoral Dissertations, 1944,* XII (1945), Chicago & Evanston: Northwestern Univ., pp. 33-38.

A8525   Schücking, Levin L. *Shakespeare und der Tragödienstil seiner Zeit.* Bern: A. Francke, 1947. Pp. 182.
          Rev: A6059.

A8526   Poirier, Michel. "Le 'Double Temps' dans *Othello.*" *EA,* V (1952), 107-116.
          On Shakespeare's skillful use of double time in the play. Comparison with Marlowe and Ford.

A8527   Colbrunn, Ethel B. *The Simile as a Stylistic Device in Elizabethan Narrative Poetry: An Analytical and Comparative Study.* DD, University of Florida, 1954. Pp. 315. Mic A54-3073. *DA,* XIV (1954), 2065. Publication No. 9541.
          Numerous comparisons with contemporaries.

A8528   Lacy, Margaret Swanson. *The Jacobean Problem Play: A Study of Shakespeare's "Measure For Measure" and "Troilus and Cressida" in Relation to Selected Plays of Chapman, Dekker, and Marston.* DD, University of Wisconsin, 1956. Pp. 216. Mic. 56-3019. *DA,* XVI (1956), 1899. Publication No. 18,418.

b. INDIVIDUALS
(1) BACON

A8529   James, D. G. *The Dream of Learning: An Essay on "The Advancement of Learning", "Hamlet" and "King Lear."* Oxford: Clarendon Press, 1951. Pp. 126.

A8530   Eagle, R. L. "Bacon and Shakespeare on Companionship in Misfortune." *N&Q,* NS, II (1955), 472-473.

(2) BEAUMONT & FLETCHER

A8531   Wallis, Lawrence B. *Fletcher, Beaumont and Company: Entertainers to the Jacobean Gentry.* New York: Kings Crown Press, 1947. Pp. xii, 315.
          Comparisons of B & F with Shak. *passim.*
          Rev: A5014.

A8532   Wilson, Harold S. "Philaster and Cymbeline." *EIE,* 1951, pp. 146-167.

(3) CHAUCER

A8533   Chute, Marchette. "Chaucer and Shakespeare." *CE,* XII (1950), 15-19.

A8534   Schlauch, Margaret. "Troilus i Kressyda Szekspira i Chaucera-Język Metaforyczny w świetle Przemian Spolecznych." *Kwartalnik Neofilologiczny,* I (1954), 3-19.
          Contrasts the two versions, stressing Shak's mercantile metaphors, in the light of social and economic change.

(4) JONSON

A8535   Bentley, Gerald Eades. *Shakespeare and Jonson. Their Reputations in the Seventeenth Century Compared.* 2 vols. Univ. Chicago Press, 1945. Pp. vi, 148; 307.
          Rev: A8732.

A8536   Sackton, A. H. *Rhetoric as a Dramatic Language in Ben Jonson.* Columbia Univ. Press, 1948.
          Rev: A5573.

A8537   Bentley, Gerald Eades. *The Swan of Avon and the Bricklayer of Westminster.* Inaugural Lecture in Princeton University, March 15, 1946. Princeton Univ. Press, 1948. Pp. 18.

A8538   Frye, Northrop. "Comic Myth in Shakespeare." *Transactions of the Royal Soc. of Canada,* Ser. 3, XLVI, Sect. 2 (1952), 47-58.
          Jonson & Shak. compared.

A8539 Honig, Edwin. *"Sejanus* and *Coriolanus*: A Study in Alienation." *MLQ*, XII (1952), 407-421.

A8540 Bacon, Wallace A. "The Magnetic Field: The Structure of Jonson's Comedies." *HLQ*, XIX (1956), 121-153.
For comparisons with Shak. see particularly pp. 122, 125-128.

A8541 Levý, Jiří. "Ben Jonson a William Shakespeare, dva typy dramatu." *Ben Jonson: Alchymista*. Prague: *Orbis* (1956), pp. 33-51.

A8542 Levý, Jiří. "Divadelní prostor a čas v dramatech Williama Shakespeara a Bena Jonsona." (Dramatic space and time in the plays of Shak. and Jonson), in *F. Wollmanovi k sedmdesátinám* (Collection of articles in tribute to Professor Wollman's 70th birthday). Prague: Státní pedagogické nakladatelství, 1958, pp. 648-656.

(5) MILTON

A8543 Kellett, E. E. "*Macbeth* and Satan." *London Quar. and Holborn Rev.*, July 1939, pp. 289-299.

A8544 Lewis, C. S. *Rehabilitations and Other Essays*. Oxford Univ. Press, 1939. Pp. viii, 197.
Contains a comparison with Milton.
Rev: A5558.

A8545 Hankins, John Erskine. "The Pains of the Afterworld: Fire, Wind, and Ice in Milton and Shakespeare." *PMLA*, LXXI (1956), 482-495.

(6) SPENSER

A8546 Harrison, Thomas P., Jr. "Aspects of Primitivism in Shakespeare and Spenser." *TxSE*, XX (1940), 39-71.

A8547 Mayhall, Jane. "Shakespeare and Spenser: A Commentary on Differences." *MLQ*, X (1949), 356-363.

A8548 Watkins, W. B. C. "The Kingdom of Our Language." *Hudson Review*, II (1949), 343-376.
Compares poetic styles of Spenser and Shak.

A8549 Watkins, W. B. C. *Shakespeare and Spenser*. Princeton Univ. Press, 1950. Pp. ix, 339.
Eight loosely connected essays, exploring various aspects of the art of Shak. and Spenser.
Rev: by Samuel C. Chew, *NYHTBR*, Oct. 1, 1950; by A. H. R. Fairchild, *SQ*, II (1951), 133-134; by Charles T. Harrison, *SR*, LIX, 696-697; by Louis L. Martz, *YR*, XL, 562-565; by O. J. Campbell, *SQ*, II, 108; by Roland M. Smith, *JEGP*, LI (1952), 250-253; by Hermann Heuer, *SJ*, 87/88 (1952), 253-254; by W. Clemen, *Archiv*, 189 (1952/53), 230-231; by D. J. Gordon, *RES*, NS, IV (1953), 90-91; by R. B. Heilman, *MLN*, LXVIII, 46-49; by Brents Stirling, *MLQ*, XV (1954), 75-76.

A8550 Potts, Abbie Findlay. "*Hamlet* and Gloriana's Knights." *SQ*, VI (1955), 31-43.

(7) SWIFT

A8551 Watkins, W. B. "Absent Thee From Felicity." *Southern Review*, V (1939), 346-365.

A8552 Clarkson, Paul S. "Swift and Shakespeare." *N &Q*, 193 (1948), 151; Harold Williams, ibid., pp. 194-195.

A8553 Cancelled.

(8) OTHERS

A8554 Sensabaugh, G. F. "John Ford and Elizabethan Tragedy." *Renaissance Studies in Honor of Hardin Craig*, 1941, pp. 250-261; also *PQ*, XX, 442-453.

A8555 Morris, I. *Shakespeare and Greville: Their Tragic Characters Compared. An Attempt to Re-Define the Principles of Shakespearean Tragedy in the Light of Elizabethan Thought*. B. Litt thesis, Oxford, 1954.

A8556 Wilson, F. P. *Marlowe and the Early Shakespeare*. Clark Lectures, Trinity College, Cambridge, 1951. Oxford: Clarendon Press, 1953. Pp. 144.
Rev: A4996.

A8557 Smith, J. C. "Scott and Shakespeare." *Essays and Studies by Members of the English Association*, XXIV (1939), 114-131.

A8558 Henderson, Archibald. *George Bernard Shaw: Man of the Century*. New York: Appleton-Century-Crofts, 1956. Pp. xxxii, 969.
"Contrasts: Shaw and Shakespeare," pp. 703-716.

A8559 Watson, Sara Ruth. "Shelley and Shakespeare: An Addendum—A Comparison of *Othello* and *The Cenci*." *PMLA*, LV (1940), 611-614.

A8560 Sorg, J. L. *Synge and Shakespeare: a Comparison of Approaches to Tragi-Comedy*. B. Litt thesis, Trinity College, Dublin, 1954.

A8561 Bogard, Travis Miller. *A Preface to Websterian Tragedy: A Critical Study of "The White Devil" and "The Duchess of Malfi."* DD, Princeton University, 1947. Pp. 348. Mic A55-511. *DA*, XV (1955), 411. Publication No. 10,849.
Shak. passim.

A8562 Higgins, G. M. P. "Imagination: Shakespeare and Wordsworth." *Discovery*, XVIII (1937), 119.

7. GERMANIC LITERATURE
a. INDIVIDUALS
(1) GOETHE AND SCHILLER

A8563 Jacob, Georg. *Shakespeares Naturverbundenheit im Vergleich mit Schillers und Goethes Verhältnis zur Natur*. Hamburg and Glückstadt: Augustin, 1937. Pp. 35.
Rev: A2170.

A8564 Petsch, R. "Die dramatischen Figuren bei Shakespeare, Goethe, Kleist, u. a. Dramatikern." *Archiv*, 173 (1938), 12-23.

A8565 Hollander, L. M. "Erlkönig and Sommernachtstraum." *Monatshefte*, XXXVI (1944), 145-146.

A8566 Hartlaub, Gustav Friedrich. *Prospero und Faust. Ein Beitr. z. Problem d. Schwarzen u. Weissen Magie*. Shakespeare-Schriften, 3. Dortmund: Schwalvenberg, 1948. Pp. 32.
Rev: by H. Reitz, *Welt und Wort*, III (1948), 311.

A8567 Kirchner, Gustav. "Goethe und Shakespeare als typische Vertreter grosser Dichtung (m. bes. Berücks. ihres Bildergebrauchs)." *Dem Tüchtigen ist diese Welt nicht stumm. Jenaer Goethe-Festschrift*, 1949, pp. 166-183.

A8568 Schröder, Rudolf Alexander. "Goethe und Shakespeare." *SJ*, 84/86 (1948/50), 17-39.

A8569 Flatter, Richard. "The Veil of Beauty. Some Aspects of Verse and Prose in Shakespeare and Goethe." *JEGP*, L (1951), 437-450.

A8570 Kaufmann, Walter. "Goethe versus Shakespeare. Some Changes in Dramatic Sensibility." *Partisan Review*, XIX (Dec. 1952), 621-634.

A8571 Uhler, John Earle. "Goethe and Shakespeare." *Goethe after Two Centuries*, Louisiana State Univ. Press (1952), pp. 97-102.

A8572 Witte, W. "Time in *Wallenstein* and *Macbeth*." *Aberdeen Univ. Review*, XXXIV (1952), 217-224.

A8573 Flatter, Richard. "Der Schleier der Schönheit." Flatter: *Triumph der Gnade. Shakespeare Essays*. Vienna and Munich: Kurt Desch, 1956, pp. 10-26.

A8574 Hennings, Elsa. *"Hamlet." Shakespeares "Faust"-Tragödie*. Bonn: H. Bouvier, 1954. Pp. 296.
Rev: by L. Bergel, *Books Abroad*, XXX (1956), 308; by J. Gerritsen, *SQ*, VII, 437-438.

A8575 Steiner, Rudolf. *Drama und Dichtung im Bewusstseins-Umschwung der Neuzeit: Shakespeare, Goethe und Schiller*. Ed. Robert Friedenthal. Dornach: R. Steiner Nachlassverwaltung, 1956.

(2) IBSEN

A8576 Williams, Raymond. *Drama in Performance*. Man and Society Series, ed. by Lady Simon of Wythenshawe and others. London: Frederick Muller, 1954. Pp. viii, 9-128.
Chap. 4 compares duel scene of *Hamlet* with goblet scene of Ibsen's *Feast at Solhoug*.

A8577 Ellis-Fermor, Una. "Ibsen and Shakespeare as Dramatic Artists." *Edda A*, 43, Bd. 56 (1956), 364-379.

(3) KIERKEGAARD

A8578 Granchi, Danilo. "I Due Danesi." *L'Ultima* (Florence), IV (July 1949), 32-36.
A comparison between Hamlet's melancholy and Kierkegaard's.

A8579 Rougemont, Denis de. "Kierkegaard and *Hamlet:* Two Danish Princes." *The Anchor Rev.*, I (1955), 109-127.

(4) OTHERS

A8580 Sampson, George. "Bach and Shakespeare." *Seven Essays*. Cambridge Univ. Press, 1947, pp. 112-136. See also "Johann Sebastian Bach und W. Shakespeare." *Universitas*, IX (1954), 127-133.

A8581 Von Oppell, Baron. "Beauty in Shakespeare and in Kant." *Hibbert Journal*, XL (1942), 166-173.

A8582 Polak, A. Laurence. *"The Tempest* and *The Magic Flute*." *English*, IX (1952), 2-7.

A8583 Sypher, Wylie. "Nietzsche and Socrates in Messina." *Partisan Rev.* XVI (1949), 702-713.

8. MISCELLANEOUS

A8584 Eastman, M. "By the Eternal." *The Stage* (April 1937), 51-52.
Shakespeare and S. Anderson compared.

A8585 Kobayashi, Hideo. "Hamlet and Roskolnikof." *Shincho* (Tokyo), LII (1956), No. 8.

A8586 Webster, Peter Dow. "A Critical Fantasy or Fugue." *American Imago*, VI (Dec., 1949), 297-309.
Compares *V & A* to Kafka's "Country Doctor."

A8587 Mansinha, Mayadhar. *Shakespeare and Kalidas*. DD, Durham, 1939. Abstract publ. in Univ. of Durham *Abstracts of Theses for Doctorates*, 1938-39, p. 3.

A8588   Goto, Takeshi. "*Moby Dick* and Shakespeare." *Kyushu Daigakue English Literary Proceedings*, Fukuoka, Aug. 1956, (in Japanese).

A8589   Siegel, Paul N. "Willy Loman and King Lear." *CE*, XVII (1956), 341-345.

A8590   Baum, Bernard. "*Tempest* and *Hairy Ape:* The Literary Incarnation of Mythos." *MLQ*, XIV (1953), 258-273.

9. SUPPLEMENT: SHORT INTRODUCTIONS TO THE STUDY OF SHAKESPEARE (146;47)
a. THE MORE IMPORTANT HANDBOOKS AND INTRODUCTIONS
(1) IN ENGLISH

A8591   Alexander, Peter. *A Shakespeare Primer.* London: James Nisbet, 1951.
Rev: *TLS*, Mar. 7, 1952, p. 174; by T. M. Parrott, *SQ*, III, 367-370; by Clifford Leech, *ShS*, VI (1953), 158; by Hermann Heuer, *SJ*, 89 (1953), 220-222.

A8592   Boas, F. S. *An Introduction to the Reading of Shakespeare.* London, 1927.
Rev: by H. de Groot, *ES*, XVIII (1936), 29-31.

A8593   Clarke, D. Waldo. "W. Shakespeare Drawings by D. M. Rossolymos." London: Longmans, 1950. Pp. 86.

A8594   Ford, Boris, ed. *The Age of Shakespeare.* A Guide to English Literature, Vol. II. Aylesbury and London: Pelican Books, 1955. Pp. 479.

A8595   Granville-Barker, Harley, and G. B. Harrison, eds. *A Companion to Shakespeare Studies.* Cambridge Univ. Press, 1934.
Rev: by H. de Groot, *ES* XVIII (1936), 32-36; by Eduard Eckhardt, *Eng. Studn.*, LXXI, 100-106; by Hoyt H. Hudson, *QJS*, XXII, 131-133; by Louis Gillet, "Nouvelles recherches sur Shakespeare," *RddxM*, 108 (1938), 443-457.

A8596   Halliday, F. E. *Shakespeare and His Critics.* London: Gerald Duckworth & Co., 1949. Pp. 522.
Rev: *TLS*, Dec. 16, 1949, p. 827; by John Garrett, *Spectator*, Nov. 25, 1949, p. 750; *Blackwoods Mag.*, 266 (1949), 479-480; by G. W. Stonier, *NstN*, XXXVIII, 618, 620; letter by Paul Vaughan, *Spectator*, Dec. 9, 1949, pp. 815-816; by Rudolf Stamm, *SJ*, 87/88 (1952), 213; by Marie Schutt, *Anglia*, LXXI, 116-117; by W. Clemen, *Archiv*, 189 (1952/53), 227-228; by Robert Halsband, *SatR*, April 25, 1953, p. 23; by G. B. Harrison, *SQ*, V (1954), 334-335; by J. Vallette, *MdF*, 334 (1958), 318-319.

A8597   Halliday, F. E. *A Shakespeare Companion, 1550-1950.* London: Duckworth, 1952. Pp. 742.
Rev: *TLS*, June 6, 1952, p. 376; by Joyce Emerson, *Sun. Times*, Apr. 20, 1952, p. 3; by Ivor Brown, *Obs.*, Apr. 20, 1952, p. 7; *Listener*, XLVII, 761; *Adelphi*, XXVIII, 645; *SatR*, Aug. 2, 1952, p. 12; by H. B. Charlton, *MGW*, May 29, 1952, p. 10; by J. G. McManaway, *SQ*, IV (1953), 357-359; by Clifford Leech, *ShS*, VI, 157; John M. Raines, *Books Abroad*, XXVII, 87.

A8598   Harrison, G. B. *Introducing Shakespeare.* London: Penguin Books, 1939. Pp. 184. Tr. into Danish by Jørgen Sinding as *En Introduktion til Shakespeare*, Copenhagen: Wangel, Prisme-Bogerne, 1955. Pp. 130. Tr. into Serbo-Croatian by Blanka Pečnik as *Uvod u Shakespearea*. Zagreb: Mladost, 1954. Pp. 213.
Rev: *TLS*, Apr. 8, 1939, p. 204; by R. W. Zandvoort, *ES*, XXI, 144; by Clara Longworth de Chambrun, *EA*, III (1939), 378-379; *Ba*, XXIV, 158-161; by P. E. McLane, *Thought*, XXII (1947), 721-722.

A8599   Holzknecht, Karl J. *The Backgrounds of Shakespeare's Plays.* New York: American Book Company, 1950. Pp. x, 482.
Rev: by E. Brennecke, *SQ*, I (1950), 273; by R. A. Law, *JEGP*, XLIX, 584-585; by Arleigh B. Williamson, *QJS*, XXXVI, 423-424; by R. Flatter, *SJ*, 87/88 (1952), 238-239.

A8600   Macintosh, Joan. *An Introduction to Shakespeare.* London: Macmillan, 1957. Pp. 144.

A8601   Nicoll, Allardyce. *The Elizabethans.* Cambridge Univ. Press, 1958. Pp. viii, 174.
Rev: by James G. McManaway, *SQ*, VIII (1957), 397; by Eugene K. Bristow, *ETJ*, IX, 260-261; by Hermann Heuer, *SJ*, 93 (1957), 252; *Dublin Mag.*, April-June, p. 47; by Margaret Willy, *English*, XI, 189-191; *N &Q*, NS, IV, 271-272; by Arthur B. Ferguson, *South Atlantic Quar.*, LVI, 406; A. H. Dodd, *History Today*, VII, 411; by A. V. C., *Time & Tide*, Mar. 30, p. 397; by Wallace A. Bacon, *QJS*, XLIII, 308; by G. B. Harrison, *SatR*, Oct. 12, pp. 57-58; by A. W. Stockwell, *AUMLA*, No. 7, Nov., pp. 56-57; by J. Vallette, *MdF*, 330, (1957), 158-159; *N &Q*, NS, IV, 271-272; *ShN*, VII, 14; by M. T. Jones Davies, *EA*, XI (1958), 345-346; by J. W. Draper, *MLR*, LIII, 622; by Helen E. Sandison, *RN*, XI, 35-37; by Joel Hurstfield, *History*, XLIII, 139-141; by F. N. L. Poynter, *Jour. of Hist. of Med. & Allied Science*, XIII, 110-111; by Aerol Arnold, *Personalist*, XXXIX, 193.

A8602   Nicoll, Allardyce. *Shakespeare.* Home Study Books. London: Methuen, 1952. Pp. 181.
Rev: *The Listener*, Nov. 6, 1952, p. 779; ibid. by A. P. Rossiter, Nov. 13, pp. 811-813; reply by reviewer, Nov. 27, p. 895; further comment by Rossiter, Dec. 4, p. 935; *TLS*, Dec. 26, 1952, p. 854; by A. Koszul, *EA*, VI (1953), 150-151; by G. B. Harrison, *SatR*, Oct. 10, p. 20; by Hermann Heuer, *SJ*, 89 (1953), 222-223; by Charles Tyler Prouty, *YR*, XLIII (1954), 471-473; by Clifford Leech, *ShS*, VII, 132; Matthew W. Black, *SQ*, V, 417-418; *N &Q*, 199 (1954), 457.

A8603   Parrott, Thomas Marc. *William Shakespeare: A Handbook.* Oxford Univ. Press, 1934.
        Revised Edition. New York: Charles Scribner's Sons, 1953. Pp. xiv, 266.
          Rev: by H. S., *MLN*, LI (1936), 414; by H. de Groot, *ES*, XVIII, 31-32; by Geoffrey
          Tillotson, *RES*, NS, VIII (1957), 354-356.

A8604   Pollard, Alfred William, and John Dover Wilson. *The Great Tudors.* 2d ed. London, 1956,
        pp. 285-296.

A8605   Reese, M. M. *Shakespeare: His World and His Work.* New York: St. Martin's Press, 1953.
        Pp. xiii, 589.
          Rev: A871.

A8606   Ridley, M. R. *William Shakespeare: A Commentary.* The New Temple Shakespeare. London,
        1936.
          Rev: A8345.

A8607   Sanders, Gerald DeWitt. *Shakespeare Primer.* New York: Rinehart, 1950. Pp. 224.

A8608   Sisson, C. J. *Shakespeare.* Writers and Their Work, No. 58. London: Longmans, 1955.
        Pp. 50.
          Rev: A159.

A8609   Williams, Frayne. *Mr. Shakespeare of the Globe.* New York: Dutton, 1941. Pp. v, 396.
          Rev: by Rosamond Gilder, *TAr*, XXV (1941), 851-852; by V. Nabokov, *NR*, 104 (1941),
          702; by John Corbin, *NYTBR*, June 29, 1941, p. 10.

A8610   Wilson, J. Dover. *The Essential Shakespeare.* Cambridge Univ. Press, 1932.
          Rev: by H. de Groot, *ES*, XVIII (1936), 36-37; by B. G. Theobald, *Ba*, XXIII (1938), 107-114;
          by A. Maurois, *La Victoire*, 1945, p. 7.

A8610a Wilson, John Dover. "Der wesentliche Shakespeare." *Die Brücke*, XLII (1947), 10-11.

A8611   Wilson, John Dover. *Shakespeare der Mensch (The Essential Shakespeare).* Tr. into German by
        Franziska Meister. Hamburg: M. von Schröder, 1953. Pp. 168.
          Rev: by Wolfgang Grothe, *Deutsche Rundschau*, Nov. 1954, p. 1207.

A8612   Wilson, Richard. *The Approach to Shakespeare.* Nelson Classics. London: Nelson, 1938.
        Pp. 256.

(2)   IN OTHER LANGUAGES

A8613   Delius, R. von. *Shakespeare: Eine Neudeutung seines Geistes.* Reinbek bei Hamburg: Parus,
        1947. Pp. 160.

A8614   Formichi, Carlo. *Guglielmo Shakespeare.* Milan: Bietti, 1939. Pp. 79.

A8615   Fuhara, Yoshiaki. *Shakespeare Nyumon.* (*Introduction to Shakespeare.*) Tokyo: Kenkyusha,
        1955. Pp. 248.

A8616   Huch, R. *William Shakespeare. Eine Studie.* Hamburg: Hanseatische Verlagsanstalt, 1941.
        Pp. 92.
          Rev: by Christian Tränkner, *DNL*, XLIII (1942), 215; by Joachim Müller, *ZDK*, LVII
          (1943), 39.

A8617   Hübner, Walter. *Die Stimmen der Meister. Eine Einf. in Meisterwerke engl. Dichtens u. Denkens.*
        Berlin: de Gruyter, 1950. Pp. xii, 536.
          Rev: by R. Münch, *Neuphilologische Zeitschrift*, III (1951), 180-185; by G. Kirchner, *DLZ*,
          LXXIV (1953), 16-22; by W. Schmidt-Hidding, *Anglia*, LXXI (1953), 348-349.

A8618   Kinoshita, Junji. *Watashi-tachi no Shakespeare.* Tokyo: Chikuma, 1953. Pp. 210.

A8619   Kramskoi, Miguel. *Shakespeare.* Barcelona: G. P., 1957. Pp. 96.

A8620   Maugeri, Aldo. *Greene, Marlowe, Shakespeare: Tre Studi Biografici.* Messina: V. Ferrara,
        1952. Pp. 103.

A8621   Rüegg, August. *Shakespeare: Eine Einführung in seine Dramen.* Bern: A. Francke, 1951.
        Pp. 303.
          Rev: by Hermann Heuer, *SJ*, 87/88 (1952), 255-256; by E. Honigmann, *MLR*, XLVII, 423;
          by H. Reitz, *Welt und Wort*, VII, 28; by L. Eckhoff, *Erasmus*, VI (Spring, 1953), 358-362.

A8622   Saito, Takeshi. *Shakespeare: A Survey of His Life and Works.* Tokyo: Kenkyusha, 1949.
        Pp. xviii, 568 (in Japanese).

A8623   Sanvic, Romain [Robert de Smet]. *Le Théâtre Élizabéthain.* Brussels: Office de Publicité,
        S. A., 1955.
          Rev: *TLS*, Sept. 30, 1955, p. 568; by F. S. Boas, *ConR*, 188 (1955), 281-283; by J. Vallette,
          MdF, 325 (1955), 722; by Hermann Heuer, *SJ*, 92 (1956), 361; by Michel Poirier, *EA*, IX,
          151-152; by Paul Blanchart, *RHT*, VII, 362-363.

A8624   *Shakespeare. Ein Lesebuch für unsere Zeit.* Weimar: Thür. Volksverlag, 1953. Pp. vii, 507.

A8625   Vallese, Tarquinio. *Donne Shakespeariane.* Rome: Albrighi, Segati and Co., 1937. Pp. 72.

A8625a Vallese, Tarquinio. *Shakespeare.* Corso Ufficiale di Letteratura Inglese. Naples, 1940. Pp.
        224.
          Rev: by W. Keller, *SJ*, LXXVII (1941), 196-197.

b. CASUAL ESSAYS, INTRODUCTORY EXCERPTS, POPULAR AND JUVENILE WORKS, ETC.

A8626 Brasch, Alfred. "Das neue Shakespeare-Bild." *Industriekurier*, v, No. 166 (1952), 4.

A8627 Braun, Hanns. *Vor den Kulissen*. Munich: Heimeran, 1938. Pp. 179.

A8628 Chute, Marchette. *An Introduction to Shakespeare*. New York: E. P. Dutton, 1951. Pp. 123.

A8629 Chute, Marchette. *Shakespeare and His Stage*. Pathfinder Library. Univ. of London Press, 1953. Pp. 128.
       For children.
       Rev: by Johannes Nielsen, *Berlingske Aften*, Copenhagen, June 18, 1954; by Hermann Heuer, *SJ*, 91 (1955), 322; by Michel Poirier in *EA*, VIII, 260.

A8630 Christen, Marcel. *Petite Promenade dans le Grand Jardin de Shakespeare*. Ill. par André Christen. Niort, Deux Sèvres: Impr. A. Chiron, 1939. Pp. 82.

A8631 Clair, Colin. *Shakespeare's England: The England of the Poets* by C. L. R. Nicolai (pseudonym). London: Watford, Herts, Bruce and Gawthorn, 1957. Pp. 64.

A8632 Drinkwater, John. *Shakespeare*. Great Lives Series. New York: Macmillan, 1956. Pp. 122. Illustrated.
       Rev: by Hudson Rogers, *English Journal*, XLV (1956), 569.

A8633 Fleming, J. R. "Shakespeare's World." *The Highway of Reading*, 1936, pp. 61-65.

A8634 Hardman, D. R. *What About Shakespeare?* London: Nelson, 1939. Pp. 174. Tr. into Italian by Maria Gallone as *Shakespeare*. Milan: Garzanti, 1955. Pp. 184.

A8635 Harrison, David. *Tudor England*. 2 Vols. London: Cassell, 1953. Pp. xv, 172; xiii, 204.
       Rev: by H. L. Short, *Time and Tide*, Sept. 26, 1953, p. 1254.

A8636 Hodges, C. Walter. *Shakespeare and the Players*. New York: Coward-McCann, 1949. Pp. 100.
       Rev: by F. C. Danchin, *LanM*, v (1949), 191; by Louis S. Bechtel, *NYHTBR*, April 24, p. 9; *TLS*, Jan. 29, 1949, p. 79; by M. T. Jones-Davies, *EA*, VII (1954), 114-115.

A8637 Isaac, Winifred F. E. C. *Alfred Wareing*. London: Privately printed and published, 1952. Pp. xxii, 221.
       A biography of the late Librarian of the Shak. Memorial Library at Stratford, which includes as an appendix an unfinished brief introductory work on Shak. by Wareing, called *Enter Shakespeare*, pp. 178-220.

A8638 Knickerbocker, William S. "Shakespeare." *Twentieth-Century English*, ed. by W. S. Knickerbocker, pp. 432-452. New York: Philosophical Library, 1946. Pp. xv, 460.

A8639 Malcolmson, D. "Shakespeare." *Ten Heroes: A Book on the Making of Literature*, 1941, pp. 237-239.

A8640 Marx Milton. *The Enjoyment of Drama*. New York: F. S. Crofts & Co., 1940. Pp. ix, 242.

A8641 Metcalf, John C. *Know Your Shakespeare*. Boston: D. C. Heath & Co., 1949. Pp. viii, 245.

A8642 Meyer, Justus. *De Schoonheid van Shakespeare*. Utrecht: W. de Haan, I (1948), 338; II (1949), 267; III (1949), 290.
       Appreciative introductions to the plays, intended for the general reader.
       Rev: *Elseviers Weekblad*, Oct. 1, 1949; *Streven*, Jan. 3, 1949, p. 215; *Vrij Nederland*, March 1, 1950; *De Gids*, 113 (1950), 311-312; by B. Stroman, *Critisch Bulletin*, XVIII (1951), 405-412.

A8643 Morris, Christopher. *The Tudors*. London: Batsford, 1955.
       Rev: *TLS*, Dec. 23, 1955, p. 779; by Richard Mayne, *NstN*, Jan. 14, 1956, p. 50; by J. B. Conacher, *Canadian Hist. Rev.*, XXXVII, 280-282.

A8644 Ouchi, Shuko. *Shakespeare and His Age*. Japan: Kenkyusha, 1947. Pp. 88.

A8645 Paris, Jean. *Shakespeare par lui-même*. Paris: Ed. du Seuil 1954. Pp. 191.
       Rev: by Marguerite Fernagu, *Rev. d'Esthétique*, VIII (1955), 225-228.

A8646 Penzoldt, Ernst. "Freude an Shakespeare. Entdeckungen eines liebenden Lesers." Penzoldt's *Die Liebende und andere Prosa aus dem Nachlass*. Frankf./M: Suhrkamp, 1958, pp. 292-325.

A8647 Powys, John Cowper. *The Pleasures of Literature*. London: Cassell; New York: Simon and Schuster, 1938. Pp. vi, 670.
       Rev: by Karl Arns, *Eng. Studn.*, LXXV (1942), 112-113.

A8648 *Shakespeare, the Swan of Avon*. Scenes from his life and the Elizabethan stage, ed. by Martin S. Allwood and Michael Taylor. Swedish translations by Carl August Hagberg. Stockholm: Halmstad, 1957. Pp. 220.
       English and Swedish text.
       Rev: by Carl Ernolv, *Moderna språk*, LII (1958), 328-329.

A8649 *Shakespearean Manuel*. Vest Pocket Library Series. New York: Ottenheimer, 1955.

A8650 Shipley, Joseph T. *Guide to Great Plays*. Washington: Public Affairs Press, 1956. Pp. xii, 867.
       Eighty pages devoted to *Shak.*
       Rev: by Calvin D. Linton, *SQ*, VIII (1957), 241-242.

A8651 Taylor, George C. "William Shakespeare, Thinker." *Univ. of North Carolina Extension Bulletin*, XXVI (March, 1946), 39-52.

XIII. SHAKESPEARE'S INFLUENCE THROUGH THE CENTURIES (148;48)
1. LITERARY ALLUSIONS TO SHAKESPEARE (148;48)

A8652 Crosse, Gordon. *A Shakespeare Allusion*. *TLS*, July 11, 1936, p. 580.

A8653   Howarth, R. G. "Allusions in Byron's Letters." *N &Q*, 171 (1936), 401-403.

A8654   McCutcheon, Roger P. "A Shakespeare Allusion." *TLS*, March 14, 1936, p. 224.

A8655   Mitchell, P. B. "Falstaff in the 'Mercurius Aulicus'." *MLN*, LI (1936), 241.

A8656   Mitchell, P. B. "Shakespeare Allusion." *TLS*, Feb. 1, 1936, p. 96.
         See letter by Roger P. McCutcheon, *TLS*, Mar. 14, 1936, p. 224.
         Points out a Shakespeare allusion in *Mercurius Britannicus*, No. 49 (August 26-Sept. 2, 1644).

A8657   Price, H. T. "Allusions to Shakspere." *SAB*, XI (1936), 250.
         Lists several 17th Century references to *Macbeth*, *Lear*, and *Henry VIII*.

A8658   Babcock, R. W. "An Early Eighteenth Century Note on Falstaff." *PQ*, XVI (1937), 84-85.

A8659   Crundell, H. W. "Marston's 'Drusus'." *TLS*, Oct. 30, 1937, p. 803.

A8660   Yamagiwa, Joseph K. "A Shakespeare Allusion." *MLN*, LII (1937), 201-202; and "An
         Allusion to Shakespeare by Morley, 1694." *MLN*, LII (1937), 201-202.

A8661   Sloane, William. "Four Early Shakspere Allusions." *SAB*, XIII (1938), 123-124.
         Robt. Roche 1599, Wm. Martyn 1612.

A8662   Schultz, Howard. "An Early *Hamlet* Allusion." *SAB*, XVI (1941), 50-51.

A8663   Sisson, Charles J. "Shakespeare Quartos as Prompt-Copies. With Some Account of Chol-
         meley's Players and a New Shakespearean Allusion." *RES*, XVIII (1942), 129-143.

A8664   Crundell, H. W. "*Love's Labour's Lost:* A New Shakespeare Allusion." *N &Q*, 183 (1942),
         44-45.
         An allusion to Berowne's speech at the end of Act IV appears in the "Jane Shore" of Drayton's
         Heroicall Epistles.

A8665   Bentley, Gerald Eades. *Shakespeare and Jonson. Their Reputations in the Seventeenth Century
         Compared.* 2 vols. Univ. Chicago Press, 1945. Pp. vi, 148; 307.
              Rev: A8732.

A8666   Aubin, Robert A. "Black as the Moor of Venice." *TLS*, July 13, 1946, p. 331.

A8667   Chambers, Sir Edmund K. *Sources for a Biography of Shakespeare.* Oxford: Clarendon Press,
         1946. Pp. 80.
              Rev: A395.

A8668   Dunkin, Paul S. "A Shakespeare Allusion." *N &Q*, 190 (1946), 15.
         In Nathaniel Lee.

A8669   Nearing, Homer, Jr. " 'Yorke in Choller' and Other Unrecorded Allusions to *Richard II.*"
         N &Q, 191 (1946), 46-47.
         Allusions in George Daniel's *Trinarchodia* (MS, 1649) and John Trussell's continuation of
         Samuel Daniel's history (1636).

A8670   Austin, Warren B. "An Early Shakespeare Allusion." *N &Q*, 192 (1947), 275.
         Robert Roche refers to *Lucrece* in *Eustathia, or the Constancie of Susanna*, Oxford: Barnes, 1599.

A8671   Sparrow, John. "Some Later Editions of Sir John Davies's *Nosce Teipsum*." *Library*, 5th
         Series, I (1947), 136-42.
         Lists an unnoticed Shakespeare allusion of 1697.

A8672   Young, G. M. " 'Pretty and Pathetical'." *TLS*, April 26, 1947, p. 197.
         Chapman's *A Humorous Day's Mirth*, I. i. 29.

A8673   Akrigg, G. P. V. "The Curious Marginalia of Charles, Second Lord Stanhope." *AMS*, 1948,
         pp. 785-801.
         References to Shak. p. 800.

A8674   Boas, F. S. "Edward Howard's Lyrics and Essays." *ConR*, 174 (1948), 107-111.

A8675   Westfall, Alfred. "A New American Shakespeare Allusion." *MLN*, LXIII (1948), 401-403.
         Discusses the 1730 allusion that apparently came through Dryden from Charles Hart, the
         actor and grandnephew of Shakespeare.

A8676   Evans, G. Blakemore. "Two Early Shakespeare Allusions: *Hamlet*, V; *Twelfth Night*, I, i."
         N &Q, 194 (1949), 275-276.

A8677   Keast, W. R. "Some Seventeenth-Century Allusions to Shakespeare and Jonson." *N & Q*,
         194 (1949), pp. 468-469.
         Three previously unrecorded allusions, 1 in Wm. Sampson, 2 in Thomas Killigrew.

A8678   Olive, W. J. "Davenant and Davenport." *N &Q*, 194 (1949), 320.
         Corrects error in *Shakespeare Allusion Book*.

A8679   Fox, Charles O. "Shakespearean Allusion." *N &Q*, 196 (1951), 535.
         Possible echo of *R. II* in a 1616 poem.

A8680   Fox, Charles O. "Shakespearean Allusion." *N &Q*, 196 (1951), 412.
         Finds a resemblance between a poem printed in Overbury's *Wife* and Shak.'s Sonnet 66.

A8681   Fox, Charles O. "Shakespearean Allusion." *N &Q*, 196 (1951), 535.
         Finds an allusion to John of Gaunt's speech (*R. II*, II. i) in Thomas Scott's "Monarchia" in
         Philomythie (1616).

A8682   Jones, H. W. "A New Allusion in Gray's Elegy?" *N &Q*, 196 (1951), 184-185; ibid.,
         J. C. Maxwell, p. 262.

A8683   Peery, William. "Shakhisbeard at Finnegan's Wake." *TxSE*, xxx (1951), 243-257.

A8684   Abend, Murray. "More Allusions to Shakespeare in Beaumont and Fletcher." *N&Q*, 198 (1953), 191-192.

A8685   Bowers, R. H. "A New Shakespeare Allusion." *SQ*, IV (1953), 362.
        Misquotation of Shak. for comic effect in a ms. farce of the late 17th century, *The Merry Loungers*.

A8686   Fox, Charles O. "Early Echoes of Shakespeare's 'Sonnets,' and 'The Passionate Pilgrim'." *N&Q*, 198 (1953), 370.
        John Guillim's *A Display of Heraldrie* (1610).

A8687   Howarth, R. G. "An Unnoted Allusion to Shakespeare." *N&Q*, 198 (1953), 101.
        Notes three recollections of *Hamlet*, in "The Christian Duell," of Humphrey Sydenham's *Sermons Upon Solemne Occasions* (1637).

A8688   Rees, Joan. "An Elizabethan Eyewitness of *Antony and Cleopatra*?" *ShS*, VI (1953), 91-93.
        Suggests that a passage in the 1607 version of Daniel's *Cleopatra* is a reminiscence of an actual performance of Shak.'s play.

A8689   Fox, Charles O. "A Shakespeare Parallel." *N&Q*, NS, I (1954), 111.
        Finds Parallel to *R. II* in Niccols' *Sir Thomas Overburies Vision* (1616).

A8690   Thayer, C. G. "Ben Jonson, Markham, and Shakespeare." *N&Q*, 199 (1954), 469-470.

A8691   Austin, Warren B. "A Supposed Contemporary Allusion to Shakespeare as Plagiarist." *SQ*, VI (1955), 373-380.
        Sonnet IX of *Greenes Funerals* attacks Harvey's stealing from Greene and therefore may not be used to support the view that the famous *Groatsworth of Wit* passage charges Shakespeare with plagiarism.

A8692   Bennett, P. E. "An Apparent Allusion to *Titus Andronicus*." *N&Q*, NS, II (1955), 422-424.

A8693   Biswanger, Raymond A., Jr. "More Seventeenth Century Allusions to Shakespeare." *N&Q*, NS, II (1955), 301-302.
        In Thomas D'Urfey.

A8694   Blayney, Glenn H. "Arden of Feversham—an Early Reference." *N&Q*, II (1955), 336.

A8695   Sirluck, Ernest. "Shakespeare and Jonson Among the Pamphleteers of the First Civil War: Some Unreported Seventeenth-Century Allusions." *MP*, LIII (1955), 88-99.

A8696   Fox, Charles O. *Notes on William Shakespeare and Robert Tofte*. Swansea: Privately published, 1956. Pp. 15.
        Rev: *ShN*, VI (1956), 42; *TLS*, May 10, 1957, p. 294.

A8697   Frank, Joseph. "An Early Newspaper Allusion to Shakespeare." *SQ*, VII (1956), 456.

A8698   Maxwell, J. C. "An Uncollected Shakespeare Allusion." *N&Q*, NS, III (1956), 236.
        Allusion to Bottom (II. 127, 186, 316) discovered in a letter of Edward Norgate in 1639.

A8699   Harrison, G. B. "A New Shakespeare Allusion." *SQ*, VIII (1957), 127.
        Letter of William Cecil, 2nd Earl of Salisbury, dated Jan. 29, 1627/28, alluding to *I H. IV*, III.i.96.

A8700   Forker, Charles R. "*A Midsummer Night's Dream* and Chapman's Homer: An Unnoted Shakespeare Allusion." *N&Q*, NS, V (1958), 524.

2. SHAKESPEARE'S INFLUENCE IN ENGLAND (148;48)
a. GENERAL (148;48)
(1) VARIOUS PERIODS

A8701   Abercrombie, L. "Most Precious Possession of the English-Speaking Peoples." *Stratford-on-Avon Herald*, Apr. 24, 1936, p. 10.

A8702   Meighen, Arthur. *The Greatest Englishman of History. An Address*. Foreword by Sir Robert Falconer. Toronto: Oxford Univ. Press, 1936. Pp. 39.

A8703   Adams, H. P. "Shakespeare: For An Age or For All Time?" *Stratford Herald*, Mar. 26, 1937.

A8704   "Poetry and Freedom." *TLS*, Jan. 21, 1939, p. 41. Shak. in *Lear, Timon*, & sonnets.

A8705   "This Bardolatry Business." *TLS*, Apr. 8, 1939, p. 203.

A8706   Brown, Ivor, and George Fearon. *Amazing Monument: A Short History of the Shakespeare Industry*. London: Heinemann, 1939. Pp. xii, 332.
        Published in America under title *This Shakespeare Industry*.
        Rev: *TLS*, Apr. 1, 1939, p. 185; by J. T. W., *SRL* Sept. 9, 1939, p. 20; by B. Ifor Evans, *MGW*, Apr. 14, 1939, p. 294; *Spectator*, Apr. 28, 1939, p. 732; by R. Gilder, *TAr*, XXIII (1939), 73-74; by K. Woods, *NYTBR*, Jan. 7, 1939, p. 4; by A. W. Porterfield, *N. Y. Evening Sun*, Sept. 16, 1939, p. 25.

A8707   Cancelled.

A8708   Jorgensen, Paul A. "Accidental Judgements, Casual Slaughters, and Purposes Mistook: Critical Reaction to Shakespeare's *Henry the Fifth*." *SAB*, XXII (1947), 51-61.

A8709   Nakanishi, Shintaro. "Shakespeare and English Literary Thought." *Bungei-Gaku* (Japan), 1947, No. 1.

A8710   Wallis, Lawrence B. *Fletcher, Beaumont and Company*: *Entertainers to the Jacobean Gentry*. New York: Kings Crown Press, 1947. Pp. xii, 315.
Includes comments upon Shak.'s reputation in various centuries.
Rev: A5014.

A8711   Tave, S. M. *Comic Theory and Criticism from Steel to Hazlitt*. DD, Oxford, Oriel, 1950.

A8712   Schröder, Rudolf Alexander. "Shakespeare als Dichter des Abendlandes." *Theater-Almanach*, II (1947), 220-233. Also in *Gesammelte Werke*, Berlin, 1952, pp. 218-230, and in Schröder's *Fülle des Daseins. Eine Auslese aus dem Werk*. Ausgew. v. Siegfried Unseld. Berlin: Suhrkamp 1958, pp. 437-457.

A8713   Straumann, Heinrich. "Shakespeare in England." *Hesperia* (Zurich), III (Oct. 1952), 173-190.

A8714   With, Mogens K., ed. *Om Shakespeare. Engelski og tyske Udtalelser 1660-1825*. Udvalgt og oversat. Hasselbalchs Kultur-Bibliotek, 112. Copenhagen: Hasselbalch, 1952. Pp. 64.

A8715   Borinski, Ludwig. "Die Funktion der Literatur in der englischen Gesellschaft." *NS*, III (1954), 221-239.

A8716   Lüdeke, H. "Shakespeare as Preserver of English Speech." *English Miscellany* (Rome), V (1954), 95-106.

A8717   Feldman, A. Bronson. "Shakespeare Worship." *Psychoanalysis*, II (1955), 57-72.

A8718   Sparks, W. H. M. "The Immortal Memory of William Shakespeare," *The Central [Birmingham] Literary Magazine*, XXXVIII, iv (1955).

A8719   Groom, Bernard. *The Diction of Poetry from Spenser to Bridges*. Univ. of Toronto Press, 1955. Pp. viii, 284. Chapter II (pp. 26-47) devoted to Shak.
Rev: A5370.

A8720   *Shakespeare im britischen Theater*. Eine vom British Council Zusammengestellte Ausstellung (Katalog). Vienna: Theater in d. Josefsstadt, 1958. Pp. 16.

A8721   Kenner, Hugh. "Words in the Dark." *Essays by Divers Hands*, NS, XXIX (1958), 113-123.
Shak.'s influ. on poetic style in England.

(2)   17TH CENTURY

A8722   Harbage, Alfred. *Cavalier Drama: An Historical and Critical Supplement to the Study of the Elizabethan and Restoration Stage*. New York: Mod. Lang. Assoc. of Amer.; London: Oxford Univ. Press, 1936. Pp. ix, 302.
Rev: by Rosamond Gilder, *TAr*, XXI (1937), 493-494; in *QQ*, XLIV, 275; by Allardyce Nicoll, *JEGP*, XXXVI, 586-588; *Catholic World*, 145 (1937), 250; *N & Q*, 173 (1937), 413-414; by Pierre Legouis, *EA*, II (1938), 300-301; by Alois Brandl, *Archiv*., 172 (1938), 250; *TLS*, Jan. 8, 1938, p. 25; by D. M. Walmsley, *RES*, XIV, 352-355; by A. K. McIlwraith, *MLR*, XXXIII, 435-436; by Rudolf Kirk, *PQ*, XVII, 92-94; by Rudolf Stamm, *Eng. Studn.*, LXXIII, 99-103; by Eduard Eckhardt, *Lbl*, LX (1939), 113-115; by Fletcher Henderson, *MLN*, LIV, 209-210; by Walther Ebisch, *Beiblatt*, L, 13-14.

A8723   Smith, Dane Farnsworth. *Plays About the Theatre in England from 1671 to 1737*. London and New York: Oxford Univ. Press, 1936. Pp. xxii, 287.

A8724   Knights, L. C. *Drama and Society in the Age of Jonson*. London: Chatto & Windus, 1937. Pp. xii, 347.
Rev: by John Hayward, *Spectator*, Apr. 30, 1937, p. 828; *TLS*, June 5, 1937, pp. 417-418; by W. J. Lawrence, *London Mercury*, XXXVI, 196-198; by Lambert Ennis, *MP*, XXXV, 199-200; by J. E. Neale, *MGW*, May 21, 1937, p. 422; by Theodore Spencer, *Criterion*, XVII (1938), 345-348; by Pierre Legouis, *EA*, II, 397-398; of 2 ed. by F. S. Boas, *FortnR*, 169 (1951), 421-422.

A8725   McGinn, Donald Joseph. *Shakespeare's Influence on the Drama of His Age*. Studies in English: I. Rutgers Univ. Press, 1938. Pp. 254.
Rev: *QR*, 271 (1938), 371-372; by F. T. Bowers, *MLN*, LIV (1939), 214-215; *TLS*, Dec. 10, p. 791; by A. J. A. Waldock, *MLR*, XXXIV, 294-295; by Alice Walker, *RES*, XV, 351-353; by John W. Draper, *JEGP*, XXXVIII, 618-618; by Floris Delattre, *EA*, III (1939), 267-268; by L. L. Schücking, *Beiblatt*, LIII (1942), 59-61.

A8726   Harbage, Alfred. "Elizabethan-Restoration Palimpsest." *MLR*, XXXV (1940), 287-319.

A8727   Spassky, Y. "Tragedy in the 17th and 18th Centuries." *The Theater* (USSR), V (1941), 89-105.

A8728   Bentley, Gerald Eades. "John Cotgrave's *English Treasury of Wit and Language* and the Elizabethan Drama." *SP*, XL (1943), 186-203.

A8729   Herring, Robert. "The Whale Has a Wide Mouth or Harlequin Faustus. (A survey of Some Lesser-known Late Elizabethan Plays With Deductions Therefrom.)" *Life and Letters Today*, XXXVI (1943), 44-65.
Frequent reference to Shakespearean influences.

A8730   Nearing, Homer, Jr. *English Historical Poetry, 1599-1641*. DD, University of Pennsylvania, 1944.
Occasional references to Shakespeare's influence on epics and historical ballads.

A8731   Ryan, Rev. Harold Francis, S. J. *Heroic Play Elements in Earlier English Drama*. DD, St. Louis

University, 1944. Pp. 366. Mic A45-5307. *Mcf Ab.*, VI (1945), 27. Publ. No. 766. Chap. VI "Shak. & the Restoration Heroic Play," pp. 249-311.

A8732   Bentley, Gerald Eades. *Shakespeare and Jonson. Their Reputations in the Seventeenth Century Compared.* 2 vols. Univ. Chicago Press, 1945. Pp. vi, 148; 307.
    Rev: *TLS*, Apr. 28, 1945, p. 200; *N &Q*, 188 (1945), 241-242; by Alfred Harbage, *MLN*, LX, 414-417; by Baldwin Maxwell, *PQ*, XXIV, 91-93; by Pierce Butler, *Lib. Quar.*, XV, 268-269; by Percy Simpson, *RES*, XXI, 334-336; *TAr*, XXIX, 254-255; by C. J. Sisson, *MLR*, XLI (1946), 73-74; by T. W. Baldwin, *JEGP*, XLV, 232-234; by F. P. Wilson, *Library*, XXVI, 199-202; by W. W. Greg, "Shakespeare and Jonson," *RES*, XXII (1946), 58; by R. S. Knox, *UTQ*, XVII (1947), 100-101.

A8733   Evans, G. Blakemore. "A Seventeenth-Century Reader of Shakespeare." *RES*, XXI (1945), 271-279.

A8734   Weisinger, Herbert. "The Seventeenth-Century Reputation of the Elizabethans." *MLQ*, VI (1945), 13-20.

A8735   Boas, Frederick Samuel. *An Introduction to Stuart Drama.* Oxford Univ. Press, 1946. Pp. viii, 443.
    Rev: by G. Tillotson, *English*, VI (1946/47), 88-89; by G. F. Sensabaugh, *MLQ*, VIII (1947), 500; by J. H. Walter, *MLR*, XLII, 132-133; by U. Ellis-Fermor, *RES*, XXIII, 169-170.

A8736   Bogorad, Samuel Nathaniel. *The English History Play in Restoration Drama.* DD, Northwestern University, 1946. Abstract publ. in *Summaries of Doctoral Dissertations*, XIV (1946), Chicago and Evanston: Northwestern Univ., 1947, pp. 5-10.

A8737   Brooke, C. F. Tucker. "Willobie's *Avisa*," in *Essays on Shakespeare and Other Elizabethans.* Yale Univ. Press, 1948, pp. 167-178. Also in *Essays in Honor of Albert Feuillerat.* Yale Romanic Studies, XXII. Yale Univ. Press, 1943.
Only passing reference to Shak.

A8738   Chute, Marchette. "The Bubble, Reputation." *VQR*, XXV (1949), 575-584.
A brief popular survey of the history of Shak.'s reputation to the end of the 17th century.

A8739   Taylor, Aline Mackenzie. *Next to Shakespeare. Otway's "Venice Preserv'd" and "The Orphan", and Their History on the London Stage.* Duke Univ. Press, 1950. Pp. viii, 328.
    Rev: by St. V. Troubridge, *English*, VIII (1950/51), 255-256; *N &Q*, 196 (1951), 175-176; by C. Leech, *RES*, NS, IV (1953), 179-180; by H. Popkin, *TAr*, XXXV, v (1951), 6-7; *TLS*, March 23, 1951, 178.

A8740   Sirluck, Ernest. "Shakespeare and Jonson Among the Pamphleteers of the First Civil War: Some Unreported Seventeenth-Century Allusions." *MP*, LIII (1955), 88-99.

A8741   Shield, H. A. "Links with Shakespeare, XIV." *N &Q*, NS, III (1956), 421-423.

A8742   Brocker, Harriet Durkee. *The Influence of "Othello" in Jacobean and Caroline Drama.* DD, University of Minnesota, 1957. Pp. 349. Mic 57-3223. *DA*, XVII (1957), 2006. Publ. No. 22,444.

(3) 18TH CENTURY

A8743   Ford, H. L. *Shakespeare, 1700-1740.* Oxford Univ. Press, 1935.
    Rev: A3079.

A8744   Lovett, David. *Shakespeare's Characters in Eighteenth Century Criticism.* DD, Johns Hopkins University, 1935.

A8745   Spriggs, Charles O. "*Hamlet* on the Eighteenth Century Stage." *QJS*, XXII (1936), 78-85.

A8746   Wasserman, Earl Reeves. "The Scholarly Origin of the Elizabethan Revival." *ELH*, IV (1937), 213-243.

A8747   Pratt, John M. *The Influence of Shakespeare on English Tragedy, 1700-1750.* DD, Harvard University, 1938. Abstract publ. in *Summaries of Ph.D. Theses, 1938*, Cambridge: Harvard Univ. Press, 1940, pp. 320-325.

A8748   Stone, George Winchester, Jr. *Garrick's Treatment of Shakespeare's Plays, and His Influence Upon the Changed Attitude of Shakespearean Criticism During the Eighteenth Century.* DD, Harvard University, 1940. Abstract publ. in *Summaries of Ph.D. Theses, 1940*, Cambridge: Harvard Univ. Press, 1942, pp. 368-372.

A8749   Wasserman, Earl R. *Elizabethan Poetry in the Eighteenth Century.* Univ. Illinois Studies in Lang. and Lit., XXXII, Nos. 2-3. Univ. of Illinois Press, 1947. Pp. 291.
    Rev: by E. N. Hooker, *JEGP*, XLVII (1948), 310-311; by B. H. Bronson, *MLN*, LXIII, 496-500; by W. H. Irving, *South Atlantic Quar.*, XLVII, 432-433; by C. J. Horne, *RES*, XXV (1949), 367-369; by Hoyt Trowbridge, *MLQ*, X, 536-538; by John Butt, *ES*, XXX, 57-58.

A8750   Margaret J. Purcell, Sister. *English History Plays of the Early Eighteenth Century.* DD, University of Missouri, 1950. Pp. 246. Mic A49-235. *Mcf. Ab.*, IX, iii (1949), 142. Publ. No. 1478.

A8751   Stone, George Winchester, Jr. "Shakespeare in the Periodicals, 1700-1740." *SQ*, II (1951), 221-231. Part I.

A8752   Sherbo, Arthur. "George III, Franklin, and Dr. Johnson." *N &Q*, 197 (1952), 37-38.
Franklin and Dr. Johnson characterized by George III in two quotations from Shak.

A8753   Stone, George Winchester, Jr. "Shakespeare in the Periodicals, 1700-1740." *SQ*, III (1952), 313-328. Part II.

A8753a Noyes, Robert G. "Shakespeare in the Eighteenth-Century Novel." *ELH*, XI (1944), 213-236.

A8754   Noyes, Robert Gale. *The Thespian Mirror: Shakespeare in the Eighteenth-Century Novel.* Brown Univ. Studies, xv. Providence, 1953. Pp. v, 200.
Rev: by G. B. Harrison, *SatR*, Oct. 10, 1953, p. 38; by George Winchester Stone, Jr., *SQ*, v (1954), 191-192; by Bernard Harris, *MLR*, xlix, 392-393; by A. H. Scouten, *MLN*, lxix, 524-525; by J. M. S. Tompkins, *RES*, ns, v, 83-84; by Clifford Leech, *ShS*, vii, 137.

A8755   Willoughby, Edwin Eliott. "A Deadly Edition of Shakespeare." *SQ*, v (1954), 351-357.

A8756   Avery, Emmett L. "The Shakespeare Ladies Club." *SQ*, vii (1956), 153-158.

A8757   Wills, Geoffrey. "Shakespeare in Porcelain." *Apollo*, lxv (1957), 150.

(4) 19TH CENTURY

A8758   Ross, Malcolm Mackenzie. *Shakespeare and Romantic Tragedy: A Study of the Fate of the Shakespearean Influence on Romantic Currents in English Tragedy from Dryden to Keats, with Special Reference to the Decline of Poetic Drama.* MA thesis, Toronto, 1934. Pp. 111.

A8759   Sanderlin, George. "The Repute of Shakespeare's Sonnets in the Early Nineteenth Century." *MLN*, liv (1939), 462-466.

A8760   Hudson, Arthur Palmer. "Romantic Apologiae for Hamlet's Treatment of Ophelia." *ELH*, ix (1942), 59-70.

A8761   Gorelik, M. "Shakespeare, Liberator." *New Theatres for Old.* New York: S. French, 1940; London: D. Dobson, 1947, pp. 100-105.
Brief discussion of Eliz. stage practice and Shak.'s impact on Romantic Theater.

A8762   Ribner, Irving. "Lear's Madness in the Nineteenth Century." *SAB*, xxii (1947), 117-129. Coleridge, Lamb, Hazlitt, Hallam.

A8763   Wheat, Cathleen Hayhurst. *Tudor Poetry and Drama Reprinted in England Between 1800 and 1835: A Bibliography with Introduction and Notes.* DD, University of California, Los Angeles, 1945.

A8764   Taupin, René. "Le Mythe de Hamlet à l'Epoque Romantique." *French Rev.*, xxvii (1953), 15-21.

A8765   Jones, Margaret (Mrs.) "Shakespeare's Bust as a Trade-Mark." *Country Life*, October 13, 1955, p. 801.

A8766   Orsini, Napoleone. "Critica e Filologia Shakespeariana nell'Epoca Romantica." *Rivista di Letterature Moderne e Comparate* (Florence), ix, i (1956), 5-16.

A8767   Browne, Ray B. "Shakespeare in the Nineteenth Century Songsters." *SQ*, viii (1957), 207-218.

A8768   Tomkins, A. R. *The Elizabethan Revival: A Study of the Contribution of Elizabethan Drama to the Romantic Movement.* DD, Cambridge, King's, 1957.

(5) 20TH CENTURY

A8769   Sears, William P., Jr. "A London Shrine for Shakespeare." *Eng. Jour.*, xxvi (1937), 822-826.

A8770   Dietz, Carl. "Ein Englisches Nationaltheater?" *DL*, xl (1938), 597-599.

A8771   Mackail, John William. *Studies in Humanism.* London: Longmans, 1938. Pp. ix, 271.
Rev: by George Cookson, *English*, ii (1938), 112-114; by F. R. Earp, *CR*, lii, 169-170.

A8772   Brown, Ivor. "The Shakespeare Industry." *Harper's Mag.*, 179 (June, 1939), 97-104.

A8773   Castle, Eduard. "Shakespeare-Feier vor 75 Jahren." *SJ*, lxxv (1939), 52-58.

A8774   Tomkinson, G. "Shakespeare in Newfoundland." *Dalhousie Rev*, xx (1940), 60-70.

A8775   Hayes, K. "Shakespeare Didn't Gilt the Lily." (Shakespeare Misquoted.) *Irish Digest*, xx (Nov. 1944), 44-45.

A8776   Edwards, Hayden. "Shakespeare-Heute in England." *Welt und Wort*, ii (1947), 135-137.

A8777   Hilterman, G. B. J. "Shakespeare-Cultuur in Engeland." *Elseviers Weekblad*, v, Jan. 4, 1947.

A8778   Collier, R. "They Made a Salesman Out of Shakespeare." *Saturday Evening Post* (May 1, 1955), pp. 32-33.

A8779   Priestley, John Boynton. "The Case Against Shakespeare." *Theatre, 1954-1955.* London: Reinhardt, 1955, pp. 111-114.
Rev: B2086.

A8780   Fyvel, T. R. "Der Shakespeare-Kult." *Der Monat*, viii, Heft 86 (Nov., 1955), 74-77.

A8781   Masefield, John. "Festival Theater." *Atlantic*, (Jan., 1955), pp. 60-64.
Reply by Christine Stewart in March, p. 25. A rather popular appeal which assumes non-Shak. Eliz. plays are never produced. Proposes a new festival theater.

A8782   McGeachy, J. B. "Debate on Shakespeare Has Everything." *Financial Post* (Canada), Aug. 3, 1957, p. 7.

A8783   Stříbrný, Zdeněk. "O Shakespearovském Bádání v Anglii." *Věstník Čsl. Akademie Věd* (Bulletin of the Czechoslovak Academy of Sciences, Prague), lxvii (1958), 636-638.
Report on a visit to the Shakespeare Institute at Stratford-on-Avon.

b. SHAKESPEARE'S SIGNIFICANCE FOR VARIOUS
ENGLISH AUTHORS (148;48)
See also sections on 17th, 18th, 19th and 20th century criticism, A7735-A8446, for the more general discussions of critical principles.

(1) CONTEMPORANEOUS TO 1660
(a) BEAUMONT AND FLETCHER

A8784   McKeithan, Daniel M. *A Study of the Debt to Shakespeare in the Beaumont-and-Fletcher Plays.*
DD, University of Texas, 1935. Austin: Texas Book Store, 1938. Pp. vii, 233.
Rev: by Mark Van Doren, *Nation* (N. Y.) 146 (1938), 728; by Robert Withington, *MLN*,
LIII, 619-623; by T. W. Baldwin, *JEGP*, XXXIX (1940), 407-408.

A8785   McKeithan, D. M. "Shakespearian Echoes in the Florimel Plot of Fletcher and Rowley's
The Maid in the Mill." *PQ*, XVII (1938), 396-398.

A8786   Wallis, Lawrence B. *Fletcher, Beaumont and Company: Entertainers to the Jacobean Gentry.*
New York: Kings Crown Press, 1947. Pp. xii, 315.
Influences of Shakespeare on Beaumont and Fletcher *passim.*
Rev: A5014.

A8787   Maxwell, Baldwin. " 'Twenty Good Nights.' *The Knight of the Burning Pestle* and Middleton's
Family of Love." *MLN*, LXIII (1948), 233-237.
Suggests Middleton's play was being ridiculed, not Romeo.

A8788   Olive, W. J. " 'Twenty Good Nights'—*The Knight of the Burning Pestle, The Family of Love,*
and *Romeo and Juliet.*" *SP*, XLVII (1950), 182-189.
Opposes Mr. Maxwell (A8787), argues, *i.a.*, that Beaumont here and elsewhere burlesques
Shakespeare, that Middleton's play imitates Shakespeare's *R & J.*

A8789   Abend, Murray. "Shakespeare's Influences in Beaumont and Fletcher." *N &Q*, 197 (1952),
272-274, 360-363.
Traces Shakespeare's influences in many passages of plays by Beaumont and Fletcher. Finds
the influence of *Hamlet* particularly heavy.

A8790   Wilson, Harold S. "*Philaster* and *Cymbeline.*" *EIE, 1951* (1952), 146-166.
Rev: by W. H. Clemen, *SQ*, V (1954), 190.

(b) CHAPMAN

A8791   Bartlett, Phyllis. "Ovids 'Banquet of Sense'?" *N &Q*, 197 (1952), 46-47.
No evidence that there is any such work by Ovid, but the theme of Chapman's poem, Ovid's
Banquet of Sense, may have been suggested by Shakespeare's *Venus and Adonis.*

A8792   Lever, J. W. "Chapman and Shakespeare." *N &Q*, NS, V (1958), 99-100.
Shakespeare's sonnet LV (Not marble nor the gilded monuments Of princes) influenced
Chapman's prefatory verses to Prince Henry in his *Homer.*

(c) CHESTER

A8793   Bonnard, G. "Shakespeare's Contribution to R. Chester's *Love's Martyr.* 'The Phoenix and
the Turtle'." *ES*, XIX (1937), 66-69.

A8794   Green, Charles H. *The Sources of "Love's Martyr," by Robert Chester.* DD, University of
Texas, 1952.

(d) DANIEL

A8795   Daniel, Samuel. *The Civil Wars.* Ed. with Introduction and Notes by Laurence Michel.
Yale Univ. Press, 1958. Pp. vii, 366.
Introduction contains (pp. 7-28) "*The Civil Wars* and Shakespeare," an evaluation of the
indebtedness of Daniel and Shak. to each other. The two poets shared the same view of
English history. Shak., shortly after *The Civil Wars'* first publication, drew upon it for *Richard
II* and *Henry IV.* Daniel, while indifferent to Shak.'s plays until 1604, was influenced by
them in his important revisions and continuation of the poem in 1609.
Rev: A4734.

A8796   Schanzer, Ernest. "Daniel's Revision of His 'Cleopatra'." *RES*, NS, VIII (1957), 375-381.
Shak.'s influence upon the revision.

(e) DAVENPORT

A8797   Olive, W. J. "Davenport's Debt to Shakespeare in *The City-Night-Cap.*" *JEGP*, XLIX (1950),
333-344.

A8798   Olive W. J. "Shakespeare Parody in Davenport's *A New Tricke to Cheat the Divell.*" *MLN*,
LXVI (1951), 478-480.

(f) DEKKER

A8799   Seronsy, Cecil C. "Dekker and Falstaff." *SQ*, IV (1953), 365-366.

A8800   Manheim, L. M. "The King in Dekker's *The Shoemaker's Holiday.*" *N &Q*, NS IV (1957),
432-433.
The King in *The Shoemaker's Holiday* was influenced by Shakespeare's characterizations of
Henry V.

(g) FIELD

A8801   Field, Nathan. *The Plays of Nathan Field*. Ed. by William Peery. Univ. Texas Press, 1950. Pp. xiii, 346. Pp. 28-29 discuss Field's indebtedness to Shak. Parallels cited in the notes.
  Rev: *TLS*, April 7, 1950, p. 218; by R. Halsband, *SRL*, May 6, 1950, pp. 56-57; by R. Moody, *QJS*, XXXVI, 425; by R. A. Law, *Library Chronicle, Univ. Texas*, IV, 47-48; *N &Q*, 196 (1951), 21-22; by T. M. Parrott, *JEGP*, L, 268-269; by R. Florence Brinkley, *South Atlantic Quar.*, L, 149-150; by A. K. McIlwraith, *RES*, NS, III (1952), 75-77; *TLS*, Aug. 22, 1952, p. 547; by Harold Jenkins, *MLR*, XLVI (1951), 484-486; by Joh. Gerritsen, *ES*, XXXIV (1953), 86-89; by R. Davril, *EA*, VI, 156-157; by Irving Ribner, *MLQ*, XIV, 311-312.

A8802   Perry, William. "Shakespeare and Nathan Field." *Neophil*, XXXIV (1950), 238-245.

(h) FORD

A8803   Ewing, S. Blaine. *Burtonian Melancholy in the Plays of John Ford*. Princeton Univ. Press, 1940. Pp. x, 132.
  Influence of Shak. on Ford passim.
  Rev: A1100.

A8804   Sensabaugh, G. F. "John Ford and Elizabethan Tragedy." In *Renaissance Studies in Honor of Hardin Craig*. Stanford Univ. Press, 1941, pp. 250-261; also *PQ*, XX, 442-453.

A8805   Davril, Robert. *Le Drame de John Ford*. Bibliothèque des Langues Modernes, 5. Paris: Librairie Marcel Didier, 1954. Pp. 554.
  Rev: by Peter Ure, *RES*, VI (1955), 201-202; by Una Ellis-Fermor, *EA*, VIII, 70-71; by C. G. Thayer, *Books Abroad*, XXX (1956), 180; by Mario Praz, *ES*, XXXVII, 24-29; by Arthur Brown, *YWES*, XXXV (1954), 106.

A8806   Oliver, H. J. *The Problem of John Ford*. Melbourne, Univ. Press; New York: Cambridge Univ. Press, 1955. Pp. vi, 146.
  Shak.'s influence on Ford passim.
  Rev: *N & Q*, NS, III (1956), 230; by William W. Appleton, *RN*, IX, 95-97; by E. M. Waith, *MP*, LIV, 134-136; by S. F. Johnson, *MLN*, LXXI, 599-602; by R. Davril, *EA*, X (1957), 56-57; by A. L. McLeod, *Books Abroad*, XXXI, 82-83; by R. Davril, *SQ*, IX (1958), 80-81.

A8807   Leech, Clifford. *John Ford and the Drama of His Time*. London: Chatto & Windus, 1957. Pp. 144.
  Rev: by R. Davril, *SQ*, IX (1958), 413-414; by *N &Q*, NS, V, 184; by A. L. McLeod, *Books Abroad*, XXXII, 323-324.

A8808   Davril, R. "Shakespeare and Ford." *SJ*, 94 (1958), 121-131.

(i) HEYWOOD

A8809   Halstead, W. L. "New Source Influence on *The Shoemaker's Holiday*." *MLN*, LVI (1941), 127-129.
  Suggests that the impressment scene may have been influenced by the similar scene in *The Famous Victories*.

A8810   Adams, Joseph Quincy, ed. *Oenone and Paris by T. H.* Washington, D. C.: Folger Lib., 1943. Pp. xlv, 46.
  Probably by Thomas Heywood ". . . earliest known imitation of Shak."
  Rev: by Marie L. Edel, *JEGP*, XLIII (1944), 110-112; by W. W. Greg, *Library*, NS, XXIV, 88-89; by R. H. Perkinson, *MLQ*, VI (1945), 101-102.

A8811   Holaday, Allan Gibson. *Thomas Heywood's "The Rape of Lucrece."* DD, George Washington University, 1943.
  Rev: by James G. McManaway, *JEGP*, L (1951), 266-268; by Philip Edwards, *MLR*, XLVI (1951), 483-484; by Arthur Melville Clark, *RES*, III (1952), 285-289; by M. A. Shaaber, *MLN*, LXVII, 564-567.

A8811a Heywood, Thomas. *Thomas Heywood's "The Rape of Lucrece."* Ed. by Allan Holaday. Illinois Studies in Lang. & Lit., XXXIV, No. 3. Univ. Illinois Press, 1950. Pp. ix, 185.
  Rev: C219.

A8812   Powell, Woodrow W. *A Critical Edition of Thomas Heywood's "A Challenge for Beauty," with Introduction and Notes*. DD, Duke University, 1958. Pp. 345. Mic 58-2832. *DA*, XIX (1958), 525-526.
  Includes parallels between the main plot of *A Challenge for Beauty* and *Cymbeline*.

(j) JONSON

A8813   Withington, Eleanor M. *Studies in the Commendation of Poetry: Ben Jonson to Edmund Waller*. DD, Radcliffe College, 1947.

A8814   Potts, L. J. "Ben Jonson and the Seventeenth Century." *Essays and Studies*, NS, II (1949), 7-24.

A8815   Wilson, J. Dover. "Ben Jonson and *Julius Caesar*." *ShS*, II (1949), 36-43.

A8816   Wronker, Stanley S. "Pope and Ben Jonson." *N &Q*, 196 (1951), 495-496.
  Sees a "more than superficial" parallelism between Pope's description of man in *Essay on Man*, II, 18, and Jonson's characterization of Shakespeare.

A8817   Bennett, Alvin L. *The Renaissance Personal Elegy and the Rhetorical Tradition*. DD, University of Texas, 1952.

A8818   McNeal, Thomas H. *"Every Man Out of His Humour* and Shakespeare's Sonnets." *N &Q,* 197 (1952), 376.

A8819   Musgrove, Sydney. *Shakespeare and Jonson.* The Macmillan Brown Lectures. Auckland: Univ. College Bulletin. No. 51, Engl. ser. No. 9. Auckland: Univ. Coll., 1957. Pp. 56. Rev: A623.

(k)   MIDDLETON

A8820   Middleton, Thomas. *The Ghost of Lucrece.* Ed. by Joseph Quincy Adams. New York: Scribner's 1937. Pp. xxxiii, 43.
Reproduced in facsimile from the unique copy in the Folger Shakespeare Library.
Rev: C218.

A8821   Middleton, Thomas. *The Witch.* Ed. by Walter Wilson Greg and Frank Percy Wilson. London: Malone Soc. 1948 (1950). Pp. xv, 94, 4 facs.
See articles by Baldwin Maxwell and W. J. Olive on "Twenty Good Nights" in Beaumont Section, A8787.

A8822   Lane, Ralph H. *Thomas Middleton's "A Mad World, My Masters."* DD, George Washington University, 1946. Echoes of 9 Shak. plays.

A8823   Olive, W. J. "Imitation of Shakespeare in Middleton's *The Family of Love.*" *PQ,* XXIX (1950), 75-78.

A8824   Schoenbaum, Samuel. *Middleton's Tragedies: A Critical Study.* DD, Columbia University, 1953.

A8825   Schoenbaum, Samuel. *Middleton's Tragedies: A Critical Study.* Columbia Univ. Press, 1955. Pp. xix, 275.
Rev: by Robert V. Bauer, *CE,* XVII (1956), 321; by J. I. M. S., *NstN,* Jan. 21, p. 81 [brief]; by J. A. Bryant, Jr., *SR,* LXIV, 508-520; by C. G. Thayer, *Books Abroad,* XXX, 223-224 [brief]; *TLS,* Feb. 17, p. 102; by Mark Eccles, *JEGP,* LV, 316-318; by Una Ellis-Fermor, *MLR,* LI, 421-422; by Gerald J. Eberle in *SQ,* VIII (1957), 121-123; by Harold Jenkins, *MLN,* LXXII, 214-217; by Clifford Leech, *RES,* VIII, 193-194; by A. José Axelrad, *EA,* X, 254-256.

(l)   MILTON

A8826   Loane, G. G. "Shakespeare, Milton, and Pope." *TLS,* Jan. 23, 1937, p. 60.

A8827   Wilson, J. Dover. "Shakespeare, Milton, and Congreve." *TLS,* Jan. 16, 1937, p. 44.

A8828   McColley, Grant. *"Macbeth* and *Paradise Lost."* *SAB,* XIII (1938), 146-150.

A8829   Murry, John Middleton. "Lear Without Cordelia." *Adelphi,* XIV (1938), 289-292, 350-353

A8830   Spencer, Theodore. "Shakespeare and Milton." *MLN,* LIII (1938), 366-367.
See letter by W. P. Parker, ibid., 556.

A8831   Kellett, E. E. "Macbeth and Satan." *London Quar. and Holborn Rev,* July, 1939, pp. 289-299.

A8832   C., T. C. "Milton: Marble for Thinking." *N &Q,* 184 (1943), 314.
See comment by Richard Hussey and reply by editor, ibid., 381.

A8833   Schaus, Hermann. "The Relationship of *Comus* to *Leander* and *Venus and Adonis.*" Univ. of Texas, *Studies in Eng.,* 1945-1946, 129-141.

A8834   Seaton, Ethel. *"Comus* and Shakespeare." In *Essays and Studies by Members of the English Association,* XXXI (1945), 68-80.
Traces in the masque Milton's memory of Shak.'s plays, particularly *A Midsummer Night's Dream, The Tempest,* and, most frequently, *Romeo and Juliet.*

A8835   Elton, W. " 'Sooth' in Shakespeare, Milton and Keats." *MLN,* LXIII (1948), 436.

A8836   Gardner, Helen. "Milton's 'Satan' and the Theme of Damnation in Elizabethan Tragedy." *Essays and Studies,* NS, I (1948), 46-66.

A8837   Adams, Henry Hitch. "The Development of the Flower Passage in *Lycidas.*" *MLN,* LXV (1950), 468-472.

A8838   Greene, D. J. " 'Sooth' in Keats, Milton, Shakespeare, and Dr. Johnson." *MLN,* LXV (1950), 514-517.

A8839   Leishman, James Blair. *"L'Allegro* and *Il Penseroso* in Their Relation to Seventeenth-Century Poetry." *Essays and Studies,* NS, IV (1951), 1-36.

A8840   Thompson, W. Lawrence. "The Source of the Flower Passage in *Lycidas.*" *N &Q,* 197 (1952), 97-99.
The source not in *The Winter's Tale* but in Jonson's *Pan's Anniversary.*

A8841   Thaler, Alwin. "Shakespeare and Milton Once More." *SAMLA Studies in Milton* (Essays in John Milton and his Works). Ed. by J. Max Patrick. Gainesville: Univ. of Florida Press, 1953, pp. 80-99.

A8842   Smith, Calvin Clifton. *Milton's Satan and the Elizabethan Stage Villain.* DD, Duke University, 1957.

(m)   OTHERS
(Alphabetically by authors influenced)

A8843   Fiehler, Rudolph. " 'I Serve the Good Duke of Norfolk'." *MLQ*, X (1949), 364-366.
Both influ. on *Merry Devil* (1604) and genesis of Falstaff.

A8844   Friedman, Lee M. " '*A Jewes Prophesy*' and Caleb Shilock." *More Books*, XXII (1947), 43-51.

A8845   Schwartzstein, Leonard. "The Test of *The Double Falsehood*." *N &Q*, NS, I (1954), 471-472.
Indicates passages in *The Double Falsehood* paralleling lines in *Hamlet*, *Romeo & Juliet*, *Lucrece*,
as evidence of Shakespearean imitation by the anonymous author.

A8846   Thaler, Alwin. *Shakespeare and Democracy*. Univ. Tennessee Press, 1941. Pp. xii, 312.
Chap. X. Sir Thomas Browne.
Rev: A1809.

A8847   Currie, H. Macl. "Notes on Sir Thomas Browne's *Christian Morals*." *N &Q*, NS, V (1958), 143.
One note observes that III, vii, 268 (Everyman ed.) echoes *Lear* II, ii, 134.

A8848   Gottlieb, Hans J. *Robert Burton's Knowledge of English Poetry*. DD, New York University, 1937.

A8849   Biggs, Alan J. "Carew and Shakespeare." *N &Q*, NS, III (1956), 225.
The influence of Shakespeare's Sonnet 116 upon Carew's poem to his mistress in absence,
bearing the subtitle "A Ship."

A8850   Cartwright, William. *The Plays and Poems of William Cartwright*. Ed. with Introduction and
Notes by G. Blakemore Evans. Univ. Wisconsin Press, 1951. Pp. xiii, 861.
Rev: by S. M., *SRL*, June 16, 1951, p. 61; *N &Q*, 196, 285-286; by Alfred Harbage, *JEGP*,
L, 423-425; *TLS*, Dec. 28, 1951, p. 832; by Esther Cloudman Dunn, *NYTBR*, June 10, 1951,
p. 14; by F. P. W., *Library*, VI, 128-129; by Fredson Bowers, *MP*, L (1952), 60-64; by V.
de S. Pinto, *MLR*, XLVII, 222-223; by Peter Ure, *RES*, NS, III, 392-397.

A8851   Thomas, Sidney. "The Earthquake in *Romeo and Juliet*." *MLN*, LXIV (1949), 417-419.
Calls attention to Covell's *Polimanteia* (1595), wherein the author refers to an earthquake of
1584 and elsewhere praises Shakespeare. Comments by Sarah Dodson, "Notes on the Earthquake in *Romeo and Juliet*." *MLN*, LXV (1950), 144.

A8852   O'Donnell, Norbert F. *The Tragedy of Orestes by Thomas Goffe: A Critical Edition*. DD, Ohio
State University, 1950. Abstract in *Ohio State Univ. Abstr. of Doct. Diss.* LXIII (1952), 289-293.

A8853   Carter, Burnham, Jr. [Article suggesting Greville may have satirized Navarre in his *Treatise of
Humane Learning*.] *Ashland Studies in Shakespeare*, ed. by Margery Bailey II, Stanford, Calif:
Shakespeare Festival Institute, 1956.

A8854   O'Donnell, Norbert F. "Shakespeare, Marston, and the University: The Sources of Thomas
Goffe's *Orestes*." *SP*, L (1953), 476-484.
Finds that *Hamlet* is one of the sources of Goffe's play.

A8855   Dunn, T. A. *Philip Massinger*. London: Nelson, for the Univ. College of Ghana, 1957.
Pp. 285.
Much comparison with Shakespeare with particular attention to Massinger's debasement
of Shakespeare.
Rev: *TLS*, Aug. 1, 1958, p. 436; by R. A. Foakes, *English*, XII, 20-21; *NstN*, Jan. 18, p. 79;
by Michel Poirier, *EA*, XI, 351; by Geraint Lloyd Evans, "*The Unnatural Combat*." *N &Q*,
NS, V, 96.

A8856   Mary Ransom Burke, Sister, S.C.N. "*The Tragedy of Cleopatra, Queen of Aegypt*," *by Thomas
May: Edited with an Introduction*. DD, Fordham University, 1943. Pp. 102.

A8857   Strube, Hans. *S. Centlivres Lustspiel "The Stolen Heiress" und sein Verhältnis zu "The Heir" von
Thomas May*. With Appendix: "May und Shakespeare." DD, Halle, 1900. Pp. 51.

A8858   Cross, Gustav. "More's *Historie of Kyng Rycharde the Thirde* and *Lust's Dominion*." *N &Q*,
NS, IV (1957), 198-199.

A8859   Ebbs, John Dale. "A Note on Nashe and Shakespeare." *MLN*, LXVI (1951), 480-481.

A8860   Randolph, Thomas. *The Fary Knight or Oberon the Second*. Ed. by F. T. Bowers. Univ.
North Carolina Press, 1942. Pp. ix, 87.
Rev: *TLS*, Aug. 8, 1942, p. 395; by C. L. Day, *JEGP*, XLII (1943), 432-433; by J. B. Leish-
man, *RES*, XX (1944), 321-322; by Alfred Harbage, *MLN*, LIX, 130-131.

A8861   Wallerstein, Ruth. "Suckling's Imitation of Shakespeare." *RES*, XIX (1943), 290-295.

A8862   Fox, Charles O. *Notes on William Shakespeare and Robert Tofte*. Swansea: Privately published,
1956. Pp. 15. 2nd ed., corrected and enlarged, 1957. Pp. 60.
Tofte's allusions to Shakespeare: a preliminary assessment.
Rev: A8696.

A8863   Weever, John. *Faunus and Melliflora (1600)*. Ed. by Arnold Davenport. Liverpool Reprints,
No. 2. Liverpool Univ. Press, 1949. Pp. viii, 85.
Rev: by W. A. Armstrong, *Library*, 5th Series, IV (1950), 148-150; *N &Q*, 194 (1949), 351;
by A. M. C. Latham, *RES*, NS, II (1951), 81-83. See also D(avenport), "Weever, Ovid and
Shakespeare." *N &Q*, 194 (1949), 524-525.

A8864   Parrott, Thomas Marc. "*Pericles*: The Play and the Novel." *SAB*, XXIII (1948), 105-113.
Discusses John Munro's Letter in *TLS*, Oct. 11, 1942, suggesting Wilkins' *Painful Adventures
of Pericles Prince of Tyre* follows and is based upon Shakespeare's play. Agrees, suggesting novel
was pushed because the King's Men refused to permit publication of the play.

(2) RESTORATION AND EIGHTEENTH CENTURY
(a) ADDISON

A8865   Kabelmann, Karl. *Joseph Addisons literarische Kritik im Spectator.* DD, Rostock, 1899. Pp. 73.

A8866   Saude, Emil. *Die Grundlagen der literarischen Kritik bei Joseph Addison.* DD, Berlin, Humboldt Univ., 1906. Pp. vii, 67.

A8867   Zagel, Hans. *Shakespeare in England um 1700 im Spiegel der moralischen Wochenschriften Richard Steeles und Joseph Addisons.* DD, Erlangen, 1922. Pp. 54. Typewritten.

A8868   Marcus, Mitchell. *Joseph Addison as Literary Critic.* DD, Stanford University, 1951. Abstracts published in *Abstracts of Dissertations*, Stanford University, XXVI (1950-51), 135-137.

A8869   Schreinert, Kurt. "Der '*Spectateur*' und sein Shakespeare-Bild 1714-26. Zugleich ein Beitrag zur Kontinentalen Frühgeschichte der moralischen Wochenschriften." *Shakespeare-Studien, Festschrift für Heinrich Mutschmann*, pp. 127-160.

(b) BLAKE

A8870   Meyerstein, E. H. " '*A True Maid*' and 'The Sick Rose'." *TLS*, June 22, 1946, p. 295.

A8871   "Blake Water-Colours: Illustrations from the British Museum's Newly-acquired Second Folio." *Illustrated London News*, 225 (Dec. 25, 1954), 1163.

A8872   Boase, T. S. R. "An Extra-Illustrated Second Folio of Shakespeare." *British Museum Quar.*, XX (1955), 4-8.

(c) THE CIBBERS

A8873   Avery, Emmett L. "Cibber, *King John*, and the Students of the Law." *MLN*, LIII (1938), 272-275.

A8874   Thexton, B. *Colley Cibber, Dramatist.* MA thesis, Leeds, 1955.

A8875   Peterson, W. M. *Colley Cibber as a Comic Dramatist.* B. Litt thesis, Oxford, Wadham, 1955.

A8876   Scouten, A. H. "Theophilus Cibber's *The Humorists*." *N &Q*, NS, II (1955), 114-115.

(d) DAVENANT

A8877   Laig, Friedrich. *Englische und französische Elemente in Sir William Davenants Dramatischer Kunst.* DD, Münster, 1934. Pp. vi, 133.

A8878   Harbage, Alfred. *Sir William Davenant.* Univ. of Pennsylvania Press, 1935.
Rev: by Geoffrey Tillotson, *RES*, XII (1936), 471-473; by V. de Sola Pinto, *MLR*, XXXI, 216-217; by Paul Meissner, *Beiblatt*, XLVII, 148-150; by R. W. Babcock, *SR*, XLV (1937), 248-250.

A8879   Nethercot, Arthur Hobart. *Sir William Davenant, Poet Laureate and Playwright-Manager.* Chicago Univ. Press, 1938. Pp. 495.
Numerous references to Shakespeare.
Rev: by Haz. Spencer, *MLN*, LIV (1939), 606-607; by A. K. McIlwraith, *RES*, XV, No. 59; by W. Keller, *SJ*, LXXV (1939), 168-169; *Eng. Studn.*, LXXV (1943), 249-250.

A8880   Stamm, R. "Sir William Davenant and Shakespeare's Imagery." *Eng. Studn.*, LXXIV (1942), Heft 3, 4.

A8881   Spencer, Christopher. *The Problems of Davenant's Text of Shakespeare's 'Macbeth' Together with a Typed Facsimile of the Yale Manuscript.* DD, Yale University, 1955.

(e) DRYDEN
See also *Various Adapters, Dryden*, B150-B154.

A8882   Allen, N. B. "The Sources of J. Dryden's Comedies." Ann Arbor: Univ. of Michigan Press, 1935. Pp. xviii, 298.

A8883   Eidson, John Olin. *Dryden's Criticism of Shakespeare.* SP, XXXIII (1936), 273-281.

A8884   Walcott, F. G. "J. Dryden's Answer to T. Rymer's 'The Tragedies of the Last Age'." *PQ*, XV (1936), 194-214.

A8885   Ribner, I. "Dryden's Shakespearean Criticism and the Neo-Classical Paradox." *SAB*, XXI (1946), 168-171.

A8886   Russell, Trusten W. *Voltaire, Dryden & Heroic Tragedy.* DD, Columbia, 1946. New York: Columbia Univ. Press, 1946. Pp. 178.

A8887   Wallerstein, Ruth. "Dryden and the Analysis of Shakespeare's Techniques." *RES*, XIX (1943), 165-185. Deals with *All For Love*.

A8888   Sherwood, John C. "Dryden and the Rules: The Preface to *Troilus and Cressida*." *CL*, II (1950), 78-83.
Discusses Dryden's criticism of Shakespeare in the Preface to his adaptation of *Troilus and Cressida*. Finds that Dryden applies standards of French neo-classical critics to Shakespeare "not only to expose his faults but to emphasize his virtues."

A8889   Bevan, Allan R. *Dryden as a Dramatic Artist.* DD, Toronto, 1953.

A8890   Aden, John M. "Shakespeare in Dryden's First Published Poem?" *N &Q*, NS, II (1955), 22-23.
        Echoes of *Hamlet* in Dryden's "Upon the Death of the Lord Hastings."

A8891   Freedman, Morris. *"All for Love"* and *"Samson Agonistes."* *N &Q*, NS, III (1956), 514-517.
        Miltonic influence in Dryden's adaptation.

A8892   Ramsey, Paul, Jr. *The Image of Nature in John Dryden.* DD, University of Minnesota, 1957.

A8893   Maurer, Wallace. "From Renaissance to Neo-Classic." *N &Q*, NS, V (1958), 287.
        Ulysses's lines on degree as rewritten by Dryden in his *Troilus and Cressida* "swing the emphasis
        from the very present wide universal world of Shakespeare to the narrowed . . . plane of
        inspection and clean-clicking logic of Dryden."

(f) GOLDSMITH

A8894   Kirsch, A. C. *A Study of the Essays of Oliver Goldsmith.* B. Litt. thesis, Oxford, St. John's, 1955.

A8895   Golden, Morris. "Goldsmith and *The Universal Museum and Complete Magazine.*" *N &Q*,
        IV (1957), 339-348. Passages on *Hamlet*, p. 347.

(g) JOHNSON

See also section on Johnson in Editions, Eighteenth Century, A3104-A3120, and Seventeenth and
Eighteenth Century Critical Treatises, Johnson, A7858-A7869.

A8896   Johnson, Samuel. *Preface to Shakespeare, with Proposals for Printing the Dramatic Works of
        William Shakespeare.* Oxford Univ. Press, 1957. Pp. iv, 63. See also 3 volumes of *Notes
        to Shakespeare*, Augustan Reprint Society, nos. 59-60, 65-66, 71-73, A7775-A7777.

A8897   Wohlers, Heinz. *Der persönliche Gehalt in den Shakespeare-Noten Samuel Johnsons.* DD, Ham-
        burg, 1934. Pp. 92.

A8898   Watkins, W. B. C. *Johnson and English Poetry Before 1660.* Princeton Univ. Press, 1936.
        Pp. 120.
            Rev: *N &Q*, 170 (1936), 233-234; by R. Stamm, *ES*, XVIII, 87-88; by P. Meissner, *Beiblatt*,
        XLVII, 333-334; *TLS*, Aug. 22, p. 682; by Doris B. Saunders, *MP*, XXXIV (1937), 326-329;
        by Clarissa Rinaker, *JEGP*, XXXVI, 282; by G. Tillotson, *MLR*, XXXII, 489-490.

A8899   Sato, Kiyoshi. "Samuel Johnson on Milton and Shakespeare." *Studies in English Literature
        by the English Lit. Soc. of Japan*, XIX (1939), 339-350.

A8900   Loane, George. "Time, Johnson, and Shakespeare." *N &Q*, 184 (1943), 184.

A8901   Krutch, J. W. *Samuel Johnson.* New York: Holt, 1944. Pp. xvi, 600.
        Shakespeare, pp. 265-336.

A8902   O'Brien, M. E. *Samuel Johnson as a Reviewer.* B. Litt. thesis, Oxford, St. Hilda's, 1946.

A8903   Eastman, Arthur M. *Johnson's Edition of Shakespeare: 1765.* DD, Yale University, 1947.

A8904   Greene, D. J. " 'Sooth' in Keats, Milton, Shakespeare, and Dr. Johnson." *MLN*, LXV (1950),
        514-517.

A8905   Hagstrum, Jean Howard. *Samuel Johnson's Literary Criticism.* Univ. of Minnesota Press,
        1952; Oxford Univ. Press, 1953. Pp. 212.

A8906   Monaghan, T. J. "Johnson's Addition to His 'Shakespeare' for the Edition of 1773." *RES*,
        NS, IV (1953), 234-248.
            Rev: by A. Sherbo, *PQ*, XXXIII (1954), 283-284.

A8907   Sherbo, Arthur. "The Proof Sheets of Dr. Johnson's Preface." *BJRL*, XXXV (1953), 206-210.

A8908   Sherbo, Arthur. "Dr. Johnson's *Dictionary* and Warburton's *Shakespeare.*" *PQ*, XXXIII (1954),
        94-96.
        In his *Dictionary* Johnson often cited from the notes as well as from the text of Warburton's
        Shakespeare.

A8909   Tucker, Susie I. "Johnson and Lady Macbeth." *N &Q*, NS, IV (1957), 210-211.
        Lady Macbeth's invocation to Night is used by Johnson to illustrate the 18th century offensive
        or undignified connotations of "blanket," "dark," "dun," "knife," "pall," and "peep."

A8910   Sherbo, Arthur. *Samuel Johnson, Editor of Shakespeare.* With an Essay on *The Adventurer.*
        Illinois Studies in Language and Literature, XLII. Univ. of Illinois Press, 1956. Pp. xi, 181.
        First complete examination of Johnson's commentary on Shakespeare.
            Rev: *Essential Books*, June, 1956, p. 37; by A. M. Eastman, *SQ*, VIII (1957), 548-549; in
        N &Q, NS, IV, 88-89; *ShN*, VII, 14; by M. R. Ridley, *RES*, NS, IX (1958), 91-93; by W. K.
        Wimsatt, Jr., *MLN*, LXXIII, 214-217; by Georges Bonnard, *Erasmus*, XI, 43-46.

A8911   Eastman, Arthur M. "In Defense of Dr. Johnson." *SQ*, VIII (1957), 493-500.
        Takes issue with Sherbo's *Samuel Johnson, Editor of Shakespeare*, A8910.

A8912   Sherbo, Arthur. "Correspondence." *SQ*, IX (1958), 433.
        A brief vindication, against the strictures of Arthur Eastman, of his position that Dr. Johnson
        borrowed widely, and without full acknowledgment, from other critics in his edition of Shak.

A8913   Maxwell, J. C. "*Othello* and Johnson's *Irene.*" *N &Q*, NS, IV (1957), 148.

A8914   Emley, Edward. *Dr. Johnson and the Writers of Tudor England.* DD, New York University,
        1958.

A8915   Sherbo, Arthur. "Sanguine Expectations: Dr. Johnson's Shakespeare." *SQ*, IX (1958), 426-428.

(h) OTWAY

A8916   Taylor, Aline Mackenzie. *Next to Shakespeare: Otway's "Venice Preserv'd" and "The Orphan," and Their History on the London Stage.* Durham, North Carolina: Duke Univ. Press, 1950. Pp. viii, 328.
          Rev: A8739.
A8917   Kiendler, Grete. *Konvertierte Formen in den Dramen Otways und Lees: ein Vergleich mit der Sprache Shakespeares.* DD, Graz, 1951. Pp. 202. Typewritten.
A8918   Batzer, Hazel Margaret. *Heroic and Sentimental Elements in Thomas Otway's Tragedies.* DD, University of Michigan, 1957. Pp. 378. Mic 57-218. *DA*, XVII (1957), 136. Publ. No. 19,679.
          Discusses influ. of Shak.

(i) PEPYS

A8919   Pendleton, L. "Samuel Pepys as Dramatic Critic." *South Atlantic Quar.*, XXXV (1936), 411-419.
A8920   Spencer, Hazelton. "Mr. Pepys is Not Amused." *ELH*, VII (1940), 163-176.
A8921   Emslie, Macdonald. "Pepys' Shakespeare Song." *SQ*, VI (1955), 159-170.

(j) POPE

A8922   Butt, J. *Pope's Taste in Shakespeare.* New York: Oxford Univ. Press, 1936. Pp. 21.
A8923   Loane, G. G. "Shakespeare, Milton, and Pope." *TLS*, Jan. 23, 1937, p. 60.
A8924   Maxwell, J. C. "Sporus and Patroclus." *RES*, XXIV (1948), 141.
          Influ. of *Troilus* V. i. 34ff. upon Pope.
A8925   Wronker, Stanley S. "Pope and Ben Johnson." *N &Q*, 196 (1951), 495-496.
A8926   Bawcutt, N. W. "More Echoes in Pope's Poetry." *N &Q*, NS, V (1958), 220-221.
          Cites *Shakespeare.*
A8927   Goldstein, Malcolm. *Pope and the Augustan Stage.* Stanford Univ. Press, 1958. Pp. 139.
          Rev: A3093.

(k) SHADWELL

A8928   Iacuzzi, Alfred. "The Naive Theme in *The Tempest* as a Link Between Thomas Shadwell and Ramón de la Cruz." *MLN*, LII (1937), 252-256.
A8929   Milton, William M. "*Tempest* in a Teapot." *ELH*, XIV (1947), 207-218.

(l) SMOLLETT

A8930   Kahrl, George Morrow. "The Influence of Shakespeare on Smollet." *Parrott Festschrift*, pp. 399-420.
A8931   Heilman, Robert B. "Falstaff and Smollett's Mickelwhimmen." *RES*, XXII (1946), 226-228.

(m) SWIFT

A8932   Clarkson, Paul S. "Swift and Shakespeare." *N &Q*, 193 (1947), 151; Harold Williams, ibid., pp. 194-195.
A8933   C., A. "Swift and Shakespeare." *American N &Q*, VII (1948), 155-156.
A8934   Peake, C. H. *Jonathan Swift as a Critic of Literature and Language.* MA thesis, London, University College, 1955.

(n) WALPOLE

A8935   Kilby, Clyde S. *Horace Walpole as Literary Critic.* DD, New York University, 1939.
A8936   Kilby, Clyde S. "Horace Walpole on Shakespeare." *SP*, XXXVIII (1941), 480-493.

(o) OTHERS
          (Arranged alphabetically by the surnames of the authors influenced.)
See A9601 (Akenside).

A8937   Blair, Thomas Marshall Howe, ed. *The Unhappy Favorite, or the Earl of Essex.* Columbia Univ. Press, 1939. Pp. xii, 144.
          Shak.'s influ. on Banks, pp. 9, 12, 16.
          Rev: by Arthur E. DuBois, *SR*, XLVIII (1940), 424-427.
A8938   Miller, C. William. "A Source Note on Boyle's *The General.*" *MLQ*, VIII (1947), 146-150.
          Points out, i.a., the possible influence of *Romeo and Juliet* upon *Parthenissa*, as well as upon *The General.*
A8939   Greany, Helen J. "Some Interesting Parallels." *N &Q*, NS, V (1958), 252-253.
          One such parallel is that between Churchill's *The Prophecy of Famine* (1763), 93-108, and *Lear* I. ii. 1-22.

A8940 Wilson, J. D. "Shakespeare, Milton, and Congreve." *TLS*, Jan. 16, 1937, p. 44.

A8941 Hering, Gerhard F. "Crabbe und Shakespeare." *SJ*, LXXVII (1941), 93-115.

A8942 Moore, John Robert. "*The Tempest* and *Robinson Crusoe*." *RES*, XXI (1945), 52-56.
Suggests some incidents in *Robinson Crusoe* are derived from *The Tempest*.

A8943 Crundell, H. W. *Two Notes on "The Merry Wives of Windsor."* *N &Q*, 173 (1937), 112-113.
The notes relate to the stage history of the play in the seventeenth century and indicate parallels in Etherege's *Love in a Tub*.

A8944 Loomis, Ralph A. *George Farquhar as Dramatic Theorist.* DD, Northwestern University, 1957.
Pp. 327. Mic 57-564. *DA*, XVII (1957), 355. Publ. No. 19,013.

A8945 Fukuhara, Rintaro. "Shakespeare and Thomas Gray." *The Rising Generation*, 98 (1952), 149-150.

A8946 Brunius, Jan Axel Teodor (Teddy). *David Hume on Criticism.* DD, Uppsala, 1952. *Figura*, Studies ed. by the Institute of Art History, University of Uppsala. Stockholm: Almquist and Wiksell, 1952. Pp. 137.
Shak. passim, esp. pp. 103-104 and 106-107.

A8947 Horsley, Phyllis M. "George Keate and the Voltaire Shakespeare Controversy." *Comparative Literature Studies*, XVI (1945), 5-7.

A8948 Kiendler, Grete. *Konvertierte Forman in den Dramen Otways und Lees: ein Vergleich mit der Sprache Shakespeares.* DD, Graz, 1951. Pp. 202. Typewritten.

A8949 Kermode, Frank. "Two Notes on Marvell." *N &Q*, 197 (1952), 136-138.

A8950 Cordasco, Francesco. "William Richardson's *Essays on Shakespeare* (1784): A Bibliographical Note on the First Edition." *N &Q*, 196 (1951), 148.
Comment by Howard Parsons, *N &Q*, 196 (1951), p. 174.

A8951 Boswell, James. *London Journal, 1762-1763.* New York: McGraw-Hill, 1950. Pp. xxix, 370·
Reports "a most ingenious dissertation on the character of Hamlet" by Thomas Sheridan, in conversation with Boswell and others, April 6, 1763, pp. 234-235. Probably the first recorded statement in detail of the theory of Hamlet as an irresolute intellectual, shrinking from an unwelcome task. Also contains remarks by Sheridan on *2 Henry IV* (pp. 135-136), criticizing Garrick's performance, and references to Garrick's playing of *Henry IV* and *Lear* (pp. 134, 256).

A8952 Croce, Benedetto. "Un viaggiatore in Italia nel settecento, apostolo dello Shakespeare (Martin Sherlock)." Croce: *Variatà di storia letteraria e civile.* 2 ed. Ser. 1, Bari, 1949, pp. 135-144. (First edition: 1935).
See also section on Rowe under Later Editions, Eighteenth Century, Rowe, A3084-A3087.

(3) ROMANTIC PERIOD
(a) SEVERAL AUTHORS

A8953 Weisinger, Herbert. "English Treatment of the Classical-Romantic Problem." *MLQ*, VII (1946), 477-488. Coleridge, Hazlitt, Scott & De Quincey.

A8953a Grober, Lydia. *Die Shakespeare-Kritik in der englischen Romantik: Samuel Taylor Coleridge, Charles Lamb und William Hazlitt.* DD, Kiel, 1948. Pp. xvi, 286. Typewritten.

(b) BYRON

A8954 Howarth, R. G. "Allusions in Byron's Letters." *N &Q*, 171 (1936), 401-403.

A8954a Taborski, B. *Lord Byron and the Theatre.* MA thesis, Bristol, 1953.

(c) S. T. COLERIDGE

A8955 Milne, W. S. *Coleridge as Shakespeare Critic.* MA thesis, Toronto, 1927. Pp. 67.

A8956 Schnöker, Otto. *Shakespeares Einfluss auf S. T. Coleridge.* DD, Vienna, 1938.

A8957 Morgan, Roberta. "The Philosophic Basis of Coleridge's *Hamlet* Criticism." *ELH*, VI (1939), 256-270.

A8958 Merz, née Foerster, Lavinia. *Der Romantiker Samuel Coleridge in den grundlegenden Ideen seiner Shakespeare-Kritik.* DD, Hamburg, 1949. Pp. 230. Typewritten.

A8959 Hardy, Barbara. "Keats, Coleridge and Negative Capability." *N &Q*, 197 (1952), 299-300.

A8960 Nethery, Wallace. "Coleridge's Use of 'Judgment' in Shakespearean Criticism." *Personalist*, XXXIII (1952), 411-415.

A8961 Badawi, M. M. *Coleridge's Shakespearean Criticism.* DD, University of London, 1954.

A8962 Schanzer, Ernest. "Shakespeare, Lowes, and 'The Ancient Mariner'." *N &Q*, NS, II (1955), 260-261.
Suggests as more likely sources for two passages in the *Ancient Mariner*, lines from *Caesar* and *Tempest*.

A8963 Barnet, Sylvan. "Coleridge on Shakespeare's Villains." *SQ*, VII (1956), 9-20.

A8964 Barnet, Sylvan. "Coleridge on Puns: A Note on his Shakespeare Criticism." *JEGP*, LVI (1957), 602-609.

A8965 Snipes, Wilson Currin. *An Analysis of the Critical Principles in Coleridge's Shakespearean Criticism With Some Attention to Their Background and Development.* DD, Vanderbilt University, 1957. Pp. 229. Mic 57-4182. *DA*, XVII (1957), 2601. Publication No. 22,024.

A8966   Barnet, Sylvan. "Coleridge's Marginalia in Stockdale's Shakespeare of 1784." *Harvard Library Bulletin*, XII (1958), 210-219.
Reprint of Coleridge's comments in a copy of *Stockdale's Edition of Shakespeare*.

A8967   Hardy, Barbara. " 'I Have a Smack of Hamlet': Coleridge and Shakespeare's Characters." *EIC*, VIII (1958), 238-255.

(d) HAZLITT

A8968   Bennion, Lynn B. *William Hazlitt's Shakespearean Criticism*. DD, Johns Hopkins University, 1947.

A8969   Wilcox, Stewart C. "Stylistic Echoes in Hazlitt." *N &Q*, 197 (1952), 211-212.
See also D. S. Bland, "More Hazlitt Allusions," ibid., p. 319.

A8970   Miller, Edmund G. *The Intellectual Development of the Young William Hazlitt*. DD, Columbia University, 1955.

A8971   Albrecht, W. P. "Hazlitt's Preference for Tragedy." *PMLA*, LXXI (1956), 1042-51.
Frequent reference to *Characters of Shakespeare's Plays*.

A8972   Barnet, Sylvan, and W. P. Albrecht. "More on Hazlitt's Preference for Tragedy." *PMLA*, LXXIII (1958), 443-445.

(e) HUNT

A8973   Moebus, Otto. *Leigh Hunts Kritik der Entwicklung der englischen Literatur bis zum Ende des 18. Jahrhunderts*. DD, Strassburg, 1917. Pp. xii, 180.

A8974   Stout, George D. "Leigh Hunt's Shakespeare: a 'Romantic' Concept." *Washington Univ. Studies*, NS, *Lang. and Lit.*, No. 20, 1951, pp. 14-33.

A8975   Fleece, Jeffrey. "Leigh Hunt's Shakespearean Criticism." *Essays in Honor of W. C. Curry*, (1955), pp. 181-195.

(f) JOHN KEATS

A8976   Murry, John Middleton. *Keats and Shakespeareare*. Oxford Univ. Press, 1935. Pp. 260.

A8977   Stroup, T. B. "*Cymbeline* II, ii and 'The Eve of St. Agnes'." *ES*, XVII (1935), 144-145.

A8978   Brooks, Philip. "Notes on Rare Books." *NYTBR*, Apr. 18, 1937, p. 27. *New York Times*, Apr. 23, 1937, p. 19.
What Shak. meant to Keats.

A8979   Viebrock, Helmut. "Die Anschauungen von John Keats über Dichter und Dichtung nach seinen Briefen." *Essays und Gedichten*. Habilitationsschrift, Marburg, 1943. Pp. 110.

A8980   B., K. J. "Keats and the Elizabethans." *N &Q*, 185 (1943), 110.

A8981   Dudley, O. H. T. "Keats, Shakespeare, and *Cymbeline*." *TLS*, May 4, 1946, p. 211.

A8982   Young, C. B. "St. Agnes' Eve and *Cymbeline*." *TLS*, Apr. 6, 1946, p. 163.

A8983   Maxwell, J. C. "*Troilus and Cressida*." *TLS*, Aug. 2, 1947, p. 391.

A8984   Muir, Kenneth. "Shakespeare and Keats." *TLS*, July 5, 1947, p. 337.

A8985   Elton, William. " 'Sooth' in Shakespeare, Milton and Keats." *MLN*, LXIII (1948), 436.

A8986   Rashbrook, R. F. " 'This Living Hand'. A Note on Keats and Shakespeare." *N &Q*, 192 (1947), 24-25.

A8987   Rashbrook, R. F. "Keats and Others." *N &Q*, 192 (1947), 161-164.

A8988   Rashbrook, R. F. "Keats's 'La Belle Dame sans Merci'." *N &Q*, 194 (1949), 210.

A8989   Rashbrook, R. F. "Keats's 'Ode to a Nightingale'." *N &Q*, 194 (1949), 14-16.

A8990   Rashbrook, R. F. "Keats and *Hamlet*." *N &Q*, 195 (1950), 253-254.

A8991   Greene, D. J. " 'Sooth' in Keats, Milton, Shakespeare, and Dr. Johnson." *MLN*, LXV (1950), 514-517.

A8992   Atkinson, A. D. " 'The Poet's Eye'." *N &Q*, 196 (1951), 121-122.

A8993   Rashbrook, R. F. "Keats, *Oberon* and Freud." *N &Q*, 196 (1951), 34-37.

A8994   Atkinson, A. D. "Keats and Compound-Epithets." *N &Q*, 197 (1952), 186-189.

A8995   Hardy, Barbara. "Keats, Coleridge and Negative Capability." *N &Q*, 197 (1952), 299-300.

A8996   Maxwell, J. C. "Keats as a Guide to Shakespeare." *N &Q*, 197 (1952), 126.

A8997   Sperry, Stuart M. "Madeline and Ophelia: A Source for 'The Eve of St. Agnes'." *N &Q*, NS, IV (1957), 29.

A8998   Eastman, Arthur M. "Shakespeare's Negative Capability." *Papers of the Michigan Academy of Science, Arts, and Letters*, XLII (1957), 339-347.

(g) LAMB

A8999   Chappel, Mary Haru. *Charles Lamb as a Literary Critic*. MA thesis, Toronto, 1927, Pp. 77.

A9000   Boas, F. S. "Charles Lamb and the Elizabethan Dramatists." *Essays and Studies by Members of the English Association*. XXIX (1943), 62-81. Republ. in *Queen Elizabeth in Drama, and Related Studies*. London, 1950, pp. 141-162.

A9001   Bald, R. C. "Charles Lamb and the Elizabethans." *Studies in Honor of A. H. R. Fairchild*, pp. 167-174.

A9002   McGlinchee, Claire. "Romance in a Reference Book." *SAB*, xxi (1946), 64-65.
        The Lambs are mentioned.

A9003   Barnet, Sylvan. "Charles Lamb and the Tragic Malvolio." *PQ*, xxxiii (1954), 178-188.

A9004   Barnet, Sylvan. "Charles Lamb's Contribution to the Theory of Dramatic Illusion." *PMLA*,
        lxix (1954), 1150-59.
        A clarification of Lamb's theory of actor's "distance," particularly in reference to *Oth.*, *Lear*,
        and *Macb.* (pp. 1154, 1156-59).

(h) SCOTT

A9005   Sweeney, John Meredith. *The Relationship Between Scott and Shakespeare.* MA thesis, Alberta,
        1938. Pp. 25.

A9006   Gordon, Robert K. "Shakespeare and Some Scenes in the Waverley Novels." *QQ*, xlv
        (1938), 478-85.

A9007   Smith, J. C. "Scott and Shakespeare." *Essays and Studies by Members of the English Association.*
        xxiv, Oxford: Clarendon Press, 1939, pp. 114-131.

A9008   Gordon, R. K. "Shakespeare's *Henry IV* and the Waverley Novels." *MLR*, xxxviii (1943),
        304-316.

A9009   Gordon, R. K. "Scott and Shakespeare's Tragedies." *TRSC*, Section 11, xxxix (1945),
        111-117.

A9010   Parker, W. M. "Scott's Knowledge of Shakespeare." *QR*, 290 (1952), 341-354.

A9011   Skelton, L. M. *The Influence of Shakespeare's Plays on the Waverley Novels.* B. Litt thesis,
        Oxford, 1953.

A9012   Tillyard, E. M. W. "Scott's Linguistic Vagaries." *EA*, xi (1958), 112-118.
        The archaized language of Scott's novels has a "riotous eclecticism" which reflects many
        earlier authors, including Shak.

(i) SHELLEY

A9013   Leavis, F. R. *Revaluation. Tradition and Development in English Poetry.* London: Chatto &
        Windus; Toronto: Macmillan, 1936. Pp. 285.
        "Shelley and *Othello*," pp. 235-238.
            Rev: *TLS*, Oct. 17, 1936, p. 833; by Stephen Spender, *Criterion*, xvi (1937), 350-353; by
            Herbert Davis, *UTQ*, vi, 282-290; by Karl Arns, *Eng. Studn*, lxxii, 122-124.

A9014   Clark, David L. "Shelley and Shakespeare." *PMLA*, liv (1939), 261-287.

A9015   Watson, Sara Ruth. "Shelley and Shakespeare: An Addendum—A Comparison of *Othello*
        and *The Cenci*." *PMLA*, lv (1940), 611-614.

A9016   Jones, Frederick L. "Shelley and Shakespeare: A Supplement." *PMLA*, lix (1944), 586-589.
        Supplement to A9014.

A9017   Prior, M. *The Language of Tragedy.* Columbia Univ. Press, 1947. Influence on Shelley,
        pp. 226-227.
            Rev: A5134.

A9018   Langston, Beach. "Shelley's Use of Shakespeare." *HLQ*, xii (1949), 163-190.

A9019   Taylor, E. M. M. "Shelley and Sheakespeare." *EIC*, ii (1953), 367-368.
        Finds Shak.'s lines often misused and muddled by Shelley, as in *Prometheus Unbound*, II, ii.

(j) WORDSWORTH

A9020   Maxwell, J. C. "Wordsworth and Prospero." *N &Q*, 194 (1949), 477.

A9021   Smith, Charles J. "The Effect of Shakespeare's Influence on Wordsworth's 'The Borderers'."
        SP, l (1953), 625-639.

A9022   Noyes, Russell. "Wordsworth's 'Ode: Intimations of Immortality' and *Hamlet*" *N &Q*,
        ns, iii (1956), 115-116.

(k) OTHERS

A9023   Jordan, John E. "De Quincey's Dramaturgic Criticism." *ELH*, xviii (1951), 32-49.

A9024   Cancelled.

A9025   Cancelled.

(4) VICTORIAN PERIOD
(a) ARNOLD

A9026   M., A. "M. Arnold on *Much Ado*." *N &Q*, 184 (1943), 340-341.

A9027   Hussey, Richard. "Arnold on Shakespeare." *N &Q*, 182 (1942), 221.
        See letters by Wm. Jaggard and by W. H. J., ibid., 276, and by Mr. Hussey, ibid., 348.

A9028   M., A. "*Hamlet* Once More." *N &Q*, 184 (1943), 255, 282-283.
        Asserts Arnold believed Shak. much infl. by Montaigne, from the evidence in Feis's *Shake-
        speare and Montaigne*.

A9029   Philbrick, F. A. "On M. Arnold's Sonnet on Shakespeare." *Expl.* (Dec. 1946), item 24.

(b) THE BRONTËS

A9030   Drew, Arnold P. "Emily Brontë and *Hamlet*." *N &Q*, 199 (1954), 81-82.
Finds a pattern in *Hamlet* IV.i for a scene in Chapter 12 of *Wuthering Heights*. Cathy's mad speech shows resemblances to Ophelia's.

A9031   Girdler, Lew. "*Wuthering Heights* and Shakespeare." *HLQ*, XIX (1956), 385-392.

(c) BROWNING

A9032   Browning, Rob. "Caliban upon Setebos. Der Naturhafte Gottesbegriff des Inselbewohners." Deutsch von Cécile Gräfin Keyserling. *Corona*, V (1934/5), 590-599.

A9033   Heuer, H. "H. Hovelaque's *Browning's English in 'Sordello'*." *Beiblatt*, XLVII (1936), 79-83. Discusses Shak's. infl. on Browning.

A9034   Carr, Geraldine Wildon. "Shakespeare, Browning and the Self." *Personalist*, XXIX (1948), 391-395.

(d) CARLYLE

A9035   Shine, H. "T. Carlyle's Views on the Relation Between Poetry and History up to Early 1832." *SP*, XXXIII (1936), 487-506.

A9036   Felheim, Marvin. "Landmarks of Criticism: 'The Hero as Poet', Thomas Carlyle." *ShN*, VII (1957), 20.

(e) DICKENS

A9037   Sennewaid, Charlotte. "Die Namengebung bei Dickens, eine Studie über Lautsymbolik." *Palästra*, 203, Leipzig: Mayer and Müller, 1936. Pp. 121. "Namen bei Shakespeares Nebenpersonen," pp. 14-21.

A9038   McNulty, J. H. "*Bleak House* and *Macbeth*." *Dickensian*, XL (1944), 188-91.

A9039   Vandiver, Edward P., Jr. "Dickens' Knowledge of Shakspere." *SAB*, XXI (1946), 124-128.

A9040   Staples, L. C. "Dickens and Macready's *Lear*." *Dickensian*, XLIV (1948), 78-80.

(f) HARDY

A9041   Von der Muhll. *Shakespeare and Hardy: A Study of Some Similarities Between the Two Authors.* MA thesis, Toronto, 1931. Pp. 132.

A9042   Griesbach, Ilse. *Das tragische Weltgefühl als Gestaltungsprinzip in Thomas Hardys Wessexromanen unter Hineinbeziehung Shakespeares in seiner "Lear"- und "Macbeth"-Periode.* DD, Marburg, 1934. Pp. iv, 79.

A9043   Chakravarty, Amiya. *The Dynasts and the Post-War Age in Poetry* [Hamlet and Napoleon]. Oxford Univ. Press, 1938.
      Rev: *TLS*, Dec. 31, 1938, p. 827.

A9044   Vandiver, E. P., Jr. "Hardy and Shakspere Again." *SAB*, XIII (1938), 87-95.

A9045   Weber, C. J. "T. Hardy's Debt to Shakespeare." *Hardy of Wessex*. New York: Columbia Univ. Press, 1940, pp. 246-57.

A9046   Gwynn, Frederick L. "*Hamlet* and Hardy." *SQ*, IV (1953), 207-208.

A9047   Hammerle, Karl. "Transpositionen aus Shakespeares *King Lear* in Thomas Hardys *Return of the Native*." *Studies . . . Presented to Karl Brunner* (B4400). *Wiener Beiträge zur Englischen Philologie* (Wien-Stuttgart), LXV (1957), 58-74.

(g) SWINBURNE

A9048   Probst, Elfride. *Der Einfluss Shakespeares auf die Stuart-Trilogie Swinburnes.* Munich, 1934.
      Rev: by Wolfgang Keller, *SJ*, LXXII (1936), 160.

A9049   Spivey, Gaynell Callaway. "Swinburne's Use of Elizabethan Drama." *SP*, XLI (1944), 250-263. In the writing of his own plays. Much on Shak.

A9050   Walker, Roy. "Swinburne, Tolstoy, and *King Lear*." *English*, VII (1949), 282-284.
Swinburne praised *Lear* for its spiritual democracy and its socialism. Furness's excerpts are inadequate because it was inaccessible to him.

(h) TENNYSON

A9051   Thislethwaite, George. *Über die Sprache in Tennysons "Idylls of the King" in ihrem Verhältnis zur "Bibel" und zu Shakespeare.* DD, Halle, 1896. Pp. 53.

A9052   Brandon, L. A. *Shakespeare's Influence on Tennyson.* MS thesis, Univ. of Tenn. Libr., 1936. Pp. 114.

A9053   Mooney, E. A., Jr. "Tennyson's Earliest Shakspere Parallels." *SAB*, XV (1940), 118-124. Specific Shakespearian parallels in *The Devil and the Lady* are indicated.

A9054   Harrison, Thomas P., Jr. "Tennyson's *Maud* and Shakspere." *SAB*, XVII (1942), 80-85.

A9055   Bush, Douglas. "Tennyson's *Ulysses* and *Hamlet*." *MLR*, XXXVIII (1943), 38.

(i) OTHERS

A9056   Vandiver, E. P., Jr. "W. S. Gilbert and Shakspere." *SAB*, XIII (1938), 139-145.

A9057 Haber, Tom Burnes. "What Fools These Mortals Be! Housman's Poetry and the Lyrics of Shakespeare." *MLQ*, VI (1945), 449-58.

A9058 Patrick, Arthur W. *Lionel Johnson (1867-1902), poète et critique.* DD, Paris, 1938. Paris: L. Rodstein, 1939.

A9059 Roesen, Bobbyann. "*Love's Labour's Lost.*" *SQ*, IV (1953), 411-426.
Pater's essay on *L.L.L.* in *Appreciations.*

A9060 Sklare, Arnold Beryl. *Arthur Symons, critique et poète.* DD, Paris, 1949.

A9061 Vandiver, Edward P., Jr. "Thackeray and Shakespeare." *Furman Studies*, XXXIV (1951), 30-45.

A9062 Coyle, William. "Trollope and the Bi-columned Shakespeare." *Nineteenth-Century Fiction*, VI (June, 1951), 33-46.

A9063 Wilde, Oscar. *The Portrait of Mr. W. H.* The Greatly Enlarged Version Prepared by the Author after the Appearance of the Story in 1889, but not Published; ed. with an Introduction by Vyvyan Holland. London: Methuen 1958. Pp. iii-xv, 90.
Rev: *TLS*, Nov. 21, 1958, p. 668; *ibid.*, by H. Montgomery Hyde, December 5, p. 705.

(5) TWENTIETH CENTURY
(a) COMMENTS OF LITERARY FIGURES
i. Auden

A9064 Auden, W. H. "The Sea and the Mirror." In *For the Time Being.* New York: Random House, 1944.

A9065 Auden, W. H. "The Dyer's Hand: Poetry and the Poetic Process." *The Anchor Review*, no. 2 (1957), 255-301.
Earlier version: "The Dyer's Hand." *Listener*, LIII (1955), 1063-1066.
Sections on *Oth.* & *Macb.*

A9066 Auden, Wystan Hugh, and Chester Kallman: *An Elizabethan Song Book. Lute Songs, Madrigals and Rounds.* Music ed. by Noah Greenberg. London: Faber, 1957. Pp. xv, 240. Shak., pp. 204-207.
Rev: A6091.

A9067 Auden, W. H. "Music in Shakespeare. Its Dramatic Use in His Plays." *Encounter*, Dec., 1957, pp. 31-44. Ibid., Peter J. Seng, January 10, 1958, pp. 67-88.

ii. Masefield

A9068 Masefield, John. *William Shakespeare.* Leipzig: Rohmkopf, 1938. Pp. 32.
A selection from Masefield's articles on Shak.'s plays.

A9069 Masefield, John. *A "Macbeth" Production.* London: Heinemann, 1945, pp. 64; New York, 1946. Also in *Thanks Before Going*, A9070. Cf. "The Poet in the Theatre." *TLS*, Apr. 14, 1945, p. 175.
Rev: by H. K. Fisher, *Life and Letters*, XLVI (1945), 66-68; by Margaret Webster, *NYHTBR*, Feb. 24, 1946, p. 6; by G. H. C., *QQ*, LIII, 126.

A9070 Masefield, John. *Thanks Before Going* . . . Includes "A *Macbeth* Production" and various papers. London: Heinemann, 1947. Pp. vi, 215.
The American edition of *Thanks Before Going* does not include "A *Macbeth* Production."

A9071 Masefield, John. *William Shakespeare.* London: Heineman, 1954. Pp. vii, 184.
Rev: A8295.

iii. Sitwell

A9072 Sitwell, Edith. "A Note on *Measure for Measure.*" *Nineteenth Century*, 140 (1946), 131-135.

A9073 Sitwell, Edith. "On the Clowns and Fools of Shakespeare." *Life and Letters*, LVII (1948), 102-109.

A9074 Sitwell, Edith. *A Notebook on William Shakespeare.* New York, London: Macmillan, 1948. Pp. xii, 233.
Rev: A8365.

A9075 Sitwell, Edith. "*King Lear.*" *Atlantic Monthly* (May, 1950), pp. 57-62.

A9076 Sitwell, Edith. "*Macbeth.*" *Atlantic Monthly* (April, 1950), pp. 43-48.

A9077 Sitwell, Edith. *A Poet's Notebook.* Boston, 1950. "Notes on Shak.," pp. 104-147.
Rev: B4970.

iv. Spender

A9078 Spender, Stephen. "Time, Violence and Macbeth." *Penguin New Writing*, III (1940/41), 115-120.

A9079 Spender, Stephen. "Pages from a Journal." *SR*, LXIII (1955), 614-630.
See also B3537.

v. Others

A9080 Baldwin, Stanley. "Shakespeare." In *On England.* New York: Stokes, 1936, pp. 119-122.
An address to a boy's school.

A9081   Barrie, James M. "The Truth About William Shakespeare." *The Greenwood Hat*. New York, 1938, pp. 109-116.

A9082   Belloc, Hilaire. *Elizabethan Commentary*. London: Cassell, 1942. Pp. 202.
Shak. pp. 21, 52-53. Otherwise, on Elizabeth I.
        Rev: by C. V. Wedgwood, *Spectator*, Apr. 3, 1942, p. 334; *TLS*, Apr. 4, 1942, p. 178.

A9083   Bowen, Elizabeth. "*King Lear* at Cambridge." *NstN*, XV (1938), 478.

A9084   De la Mare, Walter. "The Dream." In *Pleasures and Speculations*. London, 1940, pp. 270-305.
The plot, sources, structure, etc.

A9085   Drinkwater, John. *English Poetry: An Unfinished History*. Preface by St. John Ervine. London: Methuen, 1938. Pp. 227.
Shak.'s *Venus*, pp. 92-94. *Sonnet* 30, p. 137.
        Rev: *TLS*, Sept. 3, 1938, p. 565.

A9086   Duncan, Ronald. "How *The Rape of Lucrece* Became an Opera." *Shakespeare Quarterly* (London), I (Summer, 1947), 95-100.
How Shak.'s poem influenced him in composing his libretto.

A9087   Forster, E. M. *Two Cheers for Democracy*. London: Arnold, 1951. Pp. 371.
Includes essays on *Caesar* (pp. 162-166), and the Stratford Jubilee of 1769 (pp. 166-169), the first originally written in 1942, the second in 1932.
In Harcourt Brace, New York edition (n.d.) *Julius Caesar* essay, pp. 154-158; Stratford essay, pp. 158-161.
        Rev: by P. H. Newby, *Listener*, XLVI (1951), 749; by R. Cazes, *EA*, V (1952), 266-267.

A9088   Fry, Christopher. "Letters to an Actor Playing Hamlet." *ShS*, V (1952), 58-61.

A9089   Orwell, George. "Lear, Tolstoy, and the Fool." *Shooting an Elephant and Other Essays*. New York, 1950, pp. 32-52. Also in *Polemic*, March, 1947, No. 7, pp. 2-17.

A9090   Orwell, George. *The Orwell Reader*. New York: Harcourt Brace, 1956. Pp. 456.
Includes an essay "Lear, Tolstoy, and the Fool," pp. 300-315.

A9091   Russell, Bertrand. *Nightmares of Eminent Persons*. New York: Simon and Schuster, 1955.
Includes "Mr. Bowdler's Nightmare" (pp. 11-16) and "The Psychoanalyst's Nightmare" (pp. 17-28), the latter concerning Romeo, Hamlet, Othello, Lear, Macbeth, and Anthony (repr. from *Courier*, XXII [Apr. 1954], 81-87).

A9092   Waugh, Evelyn. "Titus with a Grain of Salt." *Spectator*, 194 (Sep. 2, 1956), 300-301.

A9093   Wilson, Colin. "The Outsider." *TLS*, Dec. 21, 1956, p. 765.
In response to a skeptical commentary (*TLS*, Dec. 14, p. 749), clarifies and defends his opinion that Shak. was a second-rate mind.

A9094   Wodehouse, P. G. "William Shakespeare and Me." *NYTBR*, Aug. 26, 1956, pp. 3, 28-29.

(b)   STUDIES OF THE ATTITUDES OF AUTHORS
TOWARD SHAKESPEARE
i. Conrad

A9095   Sherbo, Arthur. "Conrad's *Victory* and *Hamlet*." *N&Q*, 198 (1953), 492-493.

A9096   Bache, William B. "*Othello* and Conrad's *Chance*." *N&Q*, NS, III (1956), 478-479.

ii. Joyce

A9097   Morse, B. J. "Mr. Joyce and Shakespeare." *Eng. Studn.*, LXV (1930), 367-381.

A9098   Leavis, F. R. "Joyce and 'The Revolution of the Word'." *Scrutiny*, II (Sept. 1933), 193-201.
Compares Joyce's innovations in language unfavorably with Shakespeare's.

A9099   Budgen, Frank. *James Joyce and the Making of "Ulysses"*. London: Grayson, 1934, pp. 107-120.
Dedalus on *Hamlet*.

A9100   Cantwell, Robert, and J. H. Friend. "Joyce and the Elizabethans." *NR*, 88 (Sept. 9, 1936), 131-132.

A9101   Vander Vat, D. G. "Paternity in *Ulysses*." *ES*, XIX (August, 1937), 145-158.

A9102   Baake, Josef. *Das Riesenscherzbuch Ulysses*. Bonner Studien zur engl. Philologie, 32. Bonn: Peter Hanstein, 1937. Pp. iii, 101. Earlier form: Bonn dissertation entitled: *Sinn und Zweck der Reproduktionstechnik im Ulysses von James Joyce*. Hagen, 1937.
        Rev: by W. Héraucourt, *Beiblatt*, XLIX (1938), 373-375; by Wolfgang Schmidt, *NS*, XLVI, 383-384; Karl Arns, *ZNU*, XXXVII, 333; by W. Héraucourt, *Lbl*, LXI (1940), 29-31.

A9103   Stoll, Elmer Edgar. *From Shakespeare to Joyce*. Garden City: Doubleday, Doran, 1944, pp. 350-388.

A9104   Rogers, Howard Emerson. "Irish Myth and the Plot of *Ulysses*." *ELH*, XV (1948), 306-327.
Dedalus on *Hamlet*.

A9105   Damon, S. Foster. "The Odyssey in Dublin," in Seon Givens, ed., *James Joyce: Two Decades of Criticism*. New York: Vanguard Press, 1948, pp. 203-242. [From *Hound and Horn*, 1929.]
Says the psychology of the father-son relationship in *Ulysses* is derived from *Hamlet*.

A9106   Heine, Arthur. "Shakespeare in James Joyce." *SAB*, XXIV (1949), 56-70.
A collection of "quotations, adaptations, and echoes" from Shakespeare in *Ulysses*.

A9107   Duncan, Edward. "Unsubstantial Father: A Study of the *Hamlet* Symbolism in Joyce's *Ulysses.*" *UTQ*, XIX (1950), 126-140.

A9108   Edwards, Calvin R. "The Hamlet Motif in Joyce's *Ulysses.*" *Western Review*, XV (Autumn, 1950), 5-13.

A9109   Mayhew, George. "Joyce on Shakespeare." *Southwestern Journal*, V (Summer, 1950), 109-126.

A9110   Perry, William. "Shakhisbeard at Finnegans Wake." *TxSE*, XXX (1951), 243-257.
Reviews fifty-five passages in Joyce's novel with "close Shakespearean associations."

A9111   Peery, William. "The Sources of Joyce's Shakespeare Criticism." *ShN*, I (1951), 23.

A9112   Gilbert, Stuart. *James Joyce's "Ulysses".* New York: Knopf, second ed., 1952, pp. 208-222.
Dedalus on *Hamlet.*

A9113   Kenner, Hugh. "Joyce's *Ulysses*: Homer and Hamlet." *EIC*, II (1952), 85-104.

A9114   Perry, William. "The Hamlet of Stephen Dedalus." *TxSE*, XXXI (1952), 109-119.

A9115   Hodgart, M. J. C. "Shakespeare and *Finnegan's Wake.*" *CamJ*, VI (1953), 735-752.

A9116   Schutte, William M. *James Joyce's Use of Shakespeare in "Ulysses".* DD, Yale University, 1954.
Summary in *ShN*, VI (1956), 30.

A9117   Edwards, Philips. "*Ulysses* and the Legends." *EIC*, V (1955), 118-128.

A9118   Holmes, Lawrence Richard. "Joyce's 'Ecce Puer'." *Expl.*, XIII, no. 12, 1955.
Echoes of *Lear* and *Temp.* cited.

A9119   Jones, William Powell. *James Joyce and the Common Reader.* Norman: Univ. of Oklahoma Press, 1955, pp. 76-78.
Dedalus on *Hamlet.*

A9120   Beebe, Maurice. "James Joyce: Barnacle Goose and Lapwing." *PMLA*, LXXI (1956), 302-320.
Includes examination (pp. 317-318) of the theory of *Hamlet* which Stephen Dedalus advances in *Ulysses.*

A9121   Kenner, Hugh. *Dublin's Joyce.* Bloomington: Indiana Univ. Press, 1956, pp. 251-253.
Dedalus on *Hamlet.*

A9122   Magalaner, Marvin, and Richard M. Kain. *Joyce: The Man, the Work, the Reputation.* New York: New York Univ. Press, 1956, pp. 159-161.
Dedalus on *Hamlet.*

A9123   Sternfeld, Frederick W. "Poetry and Music—Joyce's *Ulysses*," in Northrop Frye, ed., *Sound and Poetry*: EIE, 1956. New York: Columbia Univ. Press, 1957, pp. 16-54.
Dedalus on *Hamlet.*

A9124   Goldberg, S. L. "Art and Freedom: The Aesthetic of *Ulysses.*" *ELH*, XXIV (1957), 44-64.
Discussion centers upon Stephen Dedalus' theory of *Hamlet* put forward in the library chapter of *Ulysses.*

A9125   Noon, William T., S.J. *Joyce and Aquinas.* New Haven: Yale Univ. Press, 1957, pp. 105-125.
Dedalus on *Hamlet.*

A9126   Schutte, William M. *Joyce and Shakespeare. A Study in the Meaning of "Ulysses".* Yale Univ. Press, 1957. Pp. xiv, 197.
Rev: by Mary M. Colum, *SatR*, June 15, 1957, pp. 32-33; briefly *ShN*, VII, 28; by Herbert Cahoon, *Library Journal*, 82 (1957), 1771; by Herbert Howarth, *CL*, IX, 252-254; by Marvin Magalaner, *JAAC*, XVI (1958), 412-413; by J. I. M. Stewart, *MLR*, LIII, 579-580; by Joseph L. Blotner, *CE*, XX, 154; by C. G. Thayer, *Books Abroad*, XXXII, 84.

A9127   Russell, H. K. "The Incarnation in *Ulysses.*" *Modern Fiction Studies*, IV (Spring, 1958), 53-61.
Dedalus on *Hamlet.*

iii. G. B. Shaw

A9128   Timmler, M. *Die Anschauungen B. Shaws über d. Aufgabe d. Theaters.* Breslau, 1937. Pp. xiv, 94.

A9129   "G. B. Shaw's *Cymbeline.*" *Time*, XXX (Nov. 29, 1937), 33.

A9130   "A Scene from G. B. Shaw's Version of *Cymbeline.*" *TAr*, XXII (1938), 112.

A9131   Chesterton, G. K. "Shaw and Shakespeare." *Deut. Allgem. Ztg.*, 1938, p. 225.

A9132   Keunen, J. "Het shakespeareaansche pessimisme en de verklaring ervan door B. Shaw." *Dietsche Warande* (1939), pp. 837-848.

A9133   Breitburg, S. "The Bernard Shaw-Tolstoy Controversy about Shakespeare." *Literary Heritage*, XXXVII (1940), 617-632.

A9134   West, E. J. "G. B. S., Music, and Shakespearean Blank Verse." *Elizabethan Studies and Other Essays In Honor of George F. Reynolds*, pp. 344-356.

A9135   Shaw, Bernard. "*Cymbeline* Refinished. A Variation on Shakespeare's Ending." *Geneva, Cymbeline Refinished and Good King Charles.* London: Constable, 1946, pp. 133-150. Also in *London Mercury*, XXXVII (1938), 373-389.

A9136   Ellis, Oliver C. de C. *Cleopatre in the Tide of Time.* London: Williams & Norgate, 1947. Pp. xv, 287.
Rev: B9407.

A9137   Shaw, G. B. "Sullivan, Shakespeare, and Shaw." *The Atlantic*, 181 (March, 1948), 56-58.

A9138   West, E. J. "G. B. S. on Shakespearean Production." *SP*, XLV (1948), 216-235.

A9139   Worsley, Thomas C. "G. B. S. and *Cymbeline*." *NstN*, XXXVIII (July 2, 1949), 11.

A9140   Ellis, Havelock. *From Marlowe to Shaw: Studies, 1876-1936, in English*. Edited with a Fore-word by John Gawsworth. With a Prefatory Letter from Thomas Hardy. London: Williams and Norgate, 1950, pp. 320.
         Rev: *TLS*, Jan. 5, 1951, p. 8; by Sylvere Monod, *EA*, v, (1952), 81.

A9141   Shaw, Bernard. "Shakes versus Shav. A Puppet Play." *Buoyant Billions, Farfetched Fables and Shakes versus Shav*. London, 1950, pp. 133-143. First publ. in *Arts Council Bulletin*. Sept. 1949.

A9142   West, E. J. "Shaw, Shakespeare, and *Cymbeline*." *Theatre Annual*, VIII (1950), 7-24.

A9143   Wilshire, Lewis. "Shaw's Last Play (*Shakes versus Shav*)." *English*, VIII (1950/51), 193-195.

A9144   Boas, Frederick S. "Joan of Arc in Shakespeare, Schiller, and Shaw." *SQ*, II (1951), 35-45.

A9145   Gassner, John. "Shaw as Drama Critic." *TAr* (May, 1951), 26-29, 91-95.

A9146   Kilga, Johanna F. *Joan of Arc Bei Shakespeare, Schiller und Shaw*. DD, Vienna, 1951. Pp. 87. Typewritten.

A9147   Reed, Henry. "Towards the Cocktail Party. II." *Listener*, XLV (1951), 803-804.
         Shak.'s influence on Shaw and the mixture of prose and verse in Shak.

A9148   Elliott, Robert C. "Shaw's Captain Bluntschli: A Latter-Day Falstaff," *MLN*, LXVII (1952), 461-464.

A9149   Smith, J. P. "Superman Versus Man: Bernard Shaw on Shakespeare." *YR*, XLII (1952), 67-82.

A9150   Henderson, Archibald. "Shaw and Shakespeare." *Shaw Bulletin*, VI (Sept. 1954), 1-6.

A9151   Rylands, George. "The Poet and the Player." *ShS*, VII (1954), 25-34.
         Repeated references to G. B. Shaw.

A9152   Barnet, Sylvan. "Bernard Shaw on Tragedy." *PMLA*, LXXI (1956), 888-899.
         Devoted in large part to Shak.

A9153   Henderson, Archibald. *George Bernard Shaw: Man of the Century*. New York: Appleton-Century-Crofts, 1956. Pp. xxxii, 969.
         Three chapters deal with Shakespeare.

A9154   Krabbe, Henning. "Bernard Shaw on Shakespeare and English Shakespearean Acting." *Acta Jutlandicâ*, XXVII, Supplementum B. Humanities Series 41. Aarhus: Universitets-forlaget, 1955. Pp. 66.
         Rev: A7460.

A9155   Collins, P. A. W. "Shaw on Shakespeare." *SQ*, VIII (1957), 1-13.

A9156   Silverman, Albert H. "Bernard Shaw's Shakespeare Criticism." *PMLA*, LXXII (1957), 722-736.

A9157   Fiske, Irving. "My Correspondence with GBS." *Shavian*, no. II, 1958, pp. 12-15.
         On the author's modern English version of *Ham*.

A9158   Shaw, G. Bernard. *Shaw on Theatre*. Ed. by E. J. West. New York: Hill and Wang, 1958. Pp. xi, 306.
         Rev: A8361.

A9159   Stamm, Rudolf. "Shaw und Shakespeare." *SJ*, 94 (1958), 9-28.

A9160   Stamm, Rudolf. "George Bernard Shaw and Shakespeare's *Cymbeline*." *Studies in Honor of T. W. Baldwin*, ed. by Don Cameron Allen, 1958, pp. 254-266.

iv. Others

A9161   Rutledge, F. P. *Harley Granville-Barker and the English Theatre*. MA thesis, National University of Ireland, 1951.
         See also listings in 20th Century Criticism, XI, 4.

A9162   Britton, L. J. *The Achievement of Harley Granville-Barker* (1877-1946). MA thesis, Wales, 1955.

A9163   Greene, Graham. "The Theatre." *Britain Today*, (Jan., 1945), 29-30.
         Shak.'s appeal in wartime Britain.

A9164   Wilson, Robert H. "*Brave New World* as Shakespeare Criticism." *SAB*, XXI (1946), 99-107.

A9165   Carter, Thomas H. " 'An Universal Prey': A Footnote to *The Lion and the Fox*." *Shenandoah*, IX, ii (1958), 25-34.

A9166   Vandiver, E. P., Jr. "Stevenson and Shakspere." *SAB*, XIV (1939), 232-238.

A9167   Sanders, Charles Richard. "Lytton Strachey as a Critic of Elizabethan Drama." *PQ*, XXX (1951), 1-21.

A9168   Sorg, J. L. *Synge and Shakespeare: a Comparison of Approaches to Tragi-Comedy*. B. Litt thesis, Trinity College, Dublin, 1954.

A9169   King, S. K. "Eliot, Yeats and Shakespeare." *Theoria* (Pietermartitzburg) 1953, pp. 113-119.

3. SHAKESPEARE'S INFLUENCE OUTSIDE ENGLAND
a. AMERICA (150;49)
(1) GENERAL SURVEYS

A9170   Felheim, Marvin. "Landmarks of Criticism: 'Shakespeare in America', Ashley Thorndike."
        ShN, VII (1957), 10.
        Thorndike's *Annual Shak. Lect.* of Brit. Acad., 1927.

A9171   Paul, H. N. "Shakespeare in Philadelphia." *Proc. Amer. Philosophical Soc.*, LXXVI (1937),
        719-729.

A9172   Alden, Barbara. *The History and Interpretation of Shakespeare's "Othello" on the American Stage.*
        DD, University of Chicago, 1942.

A9173   Morozov, M. "From the History of the American Shakespeareology." *International Litera-*
        ture (USSR), 1942, pp. 3-5, 192-196.

A9174   Schröder, Rudolf Alexander. "Shakespeare als Dichter des Abendlandes." *Theater-Alman-*
        ach, II (1947), 220-233.
        Also in *Gesammelte Werke*, Berlin, 1952, pp. 218-230, and in *Fülle des Daseins, Eine Auslese aus*
        dem Werk, Berlin: Suhrkamp, 1958.

A9175   Nakanishi, Shintaro. *Studies in Shakespeare Criticism.* Shakespeare Studies Series. Tokyo:
        Sogen-sha, 1949. Pp. viii, 268 (in Japanese).

A9176   Bab, Julius. "Shakespeare in Amerika." *SJ*, 82/83 (1949), 164-174.

A9177   Monson, Leland Hans. *Shakespeare in Utah (1847-1900).* DD, University of Utah, 1956.
        Pp. 322. Mic 57-1354. *DA*, XVII (1957), 848. Publication No. 17,574.

A9178   Willson, Lawrence. "Shakespeare and the Genteel Tradition in America." *New Mexico*
        Quarterly, XXVI (1956), 14-30.

(2) PERIODS

(a) UP TO 1880

i. General

A9179   Westfall, Alfred Van Rensselaer. *American Shakespearean Criticism, 1607-1865.* New York:
        H. W. Wilson, 1939. Pp. xii, 305.
        Rev: A7952.

A9180   Dunn, Esther C. *Shakespeare in America.* New York: Macmillan, 1939. Pp. xiv, 310.
        Rev: by Otis Skinner, *SRL*, Oct. 28, 1939, p. 12; by W. T. Hastings, "E. Dunn's *Shake-*
        speare in America," *Providence Sunday Journal*, Dec. 10, 1939; by G. F. Whicher, *NYHTBR*,
        Nov. 19, 1939, p. 16; by Samuel A. Tannenbaum, "Shakespeare in Miscaloosa." *SAB*,
        XV (1940), 127; by Tucker Brooke, *Amer. Lit.*, XII (1940), 130-133; by Rosamond Gilder,
        TAr, XXIV, 73-74; by Joseph S. Schick, *AHR*, XLVI, 221; by B. T. Spencer, "This Elizabethan
        Shakespeare," *SR*, XLIX (1942), 548-550.

A9181   Quinn, A. H. *A History of American Drama . . . to the Civil War.* New York, 1943. Pp.
        xviii, 530.

A9182   Shiffler, Harrold C. *The Opposition of the Presbyterian Church in the United States of America to*
        the Theatre in America, 1750-1871. DD, University of Iowa, 1953. Pp. 511. Mic A53-2209.
        DA, XIII (1953), 1305-1306. Publication No. 4990.

ii. The Colonies

A9183   Freedley, George. "An Early Performance of *Romeo and Juliet* in New York." *Bull. of the*
        New York Public Library, XL (1936), 494.

A9184   Shurter, Robert L. "Shakespearean Performances in Pre-Revolutionary America." *South*
        Atlantic Quar., XXXVI (1937), 53-58.

A9185   Willoughby, Edwin Eliott. "The Reading of Shakespeare in Colonial America." *Papers*
        Bibl. Soc. of Amer., XXXI (1938), 45-56.

A9186   Rosenbach, A. S. W. "The First Theatrical Company in America." *Proc. of the American*
        Antiquarian Society, XLVII (1938), 3-13; XLVIII (1939), 300-310.

A9187   Schmitz, R. Morrell. "Scottish Shakspere." *SAB*, XVI (1941), 229-236.
        On Hugh Blair and his Shakespearean criticism.

A9188   Turner, Vivian. "Our Colonial Theatre." *QJS*, XXVII (1941), 559-573.

A9189   Gale, Cedric. *Shakespeare on the American Stage in the Eighteenth Century.* DD, New York
        University, 1945.

A9190   Walsh, Charles R. *Shakespeare on the Colonial Stage.* DD, Fordham University, 1948. Pp. 276.
        Abstract publ. in *Dissertations . . . Fordham Univ.*, XV (1948), 64-68.

A9191   Bailey, James H. "Shakespeare and the Founders of Virginia." *Virginia Cavalcade*, I (1951), 9.

A9192   Wolf, Edwin, 2nd. "Early American Playbills." *SQ*, VII (1956), 285-286.

A9193   Walmsley, D. M. "Shakespeare's Link with Virginia." *History Today*, VII (April, 1957), 229.

iii. The Nineteenth Century

A9194   Brooks, V. W. *The Flowering of New England.* New York: Doubleday, 1936. Pp. xxi, 550.

A9195   Pierce, Ella J. *Appreciation of the Elizabethans During the New England Renaissance (1830-1880).*
        DD, Cornell University, 1936.

A9196   Hoole, William Stanley. "Two Famous Theatres of the Old South." *South Atlantic Quar.*, XXXVI (1937), 273-277.

A9197   Kimball, LeRoy E. "Miss Bacon Advances Learning." *Colophon*, NS, II (1937), 338-354.
An account of the American anti-Shakespearean, Delia Bacon.

A9198   Mangan, Nora Aileene. *Augustin Daly as a Producer of Shakespearian Drama*. DD, University of Washington. Abstract in *Univ. of Washington Abstracts of Theses*, IV (1939), 133-138.
See A9208.

A9199   Falk, Robert Paul. *Representative American Criticism of Shakespeare, 1830-1885*. DD, University of Wisconsin, 1940. Abstract publ. in *Summaries of Doctoral Dissertations, 1939-40*, Madison: Univ. of Wisconsin Press, 1940, pp. 258-260.

A9200   Durilin, S. "Ira Aldridge." *SAB*, XVII (1942), 33-39.
An account of the American Negro actor who played Shakespeare in Russia, 1858-1867. See also A9838.

A9201   Swan, Marshall W. S. "Shakespeare's 'Poems': The First Three Boston Editions." *Papers Bibl. Soc. Amer.*, XXXVI (1942), 27-36.

A9202   Gates, W. B. "Performances of Shakespeare in Ante-Bellum Mississippi." *Journal of Miss. History*, V (1943), 28-37.

A9203   Hoole, W. Stanley. "Shakespeare on the Ante-Bellum Charleston Stage." *SAB*, XXI (1946), 37-45.

A9204   Felheim, Marvin L. *The Career of Augustin Daly*. DD, Harvard University, 1948.
See A9208.

A9205   Stafford, John. "Henry Norman Hudson and the Whig Use of Shakespeare." *PMLA*, LXVI (1951), 649-661.

A9206   Young, G. M. "'To the Manor Born'." *TLS*, Nov. 7, 1952, p. 725.
Comment by Evan John, ibid., Nov. 21, p. 761.
Quotes a passage which suggests that this reading of the phrase in *Hamlet* was current in America in 1865.

A9207   Pedigo, Frances. *Critical Opinions of Poetry, Drama, and Fiction, in "The Christian Examiner," 1824-1869*. DD, North Carolina, 1953. Abstr. publ. in *Univ. of North Carolina Record, Research in Progress*, Jan.-Dec. 1953, Grad. School Series No. 66, 1954, pp. 99-100.
Abstract mentions no Shak.

A9208   Felheim, Marvin. *The Theatre of Augustin Daly*. Harvard Univ. Press, 1956. Pp. 329.
Shak., pp. 219-284.
See A9198 and A9204.
    Rev: *ShN*, VI (1956), 42; *TAr*, XL (Oct.), 66-68, 90-91; by St. Vincent Troubridge, *TN*, XI (1957), 144-145; by Pat M. Ryan, Jr., *QJS*, XLII, 334-335; by Alan S. Downer, *SQ*, VIII, 546-547.

A9209   Roppolo, Joseph Patrick, "*Hamlet* in New Orleans." *Tulane Studies in English*, VI (1956), 71-86.
    Rev: by Ewald Standof, *Anglia*, LXXV (1957), 252-254.

A9210   Browne, Ray B. "Shakespeare in the Nineteenth-Century Songsters." *SQ*, VIII (1957), 207-218.

A9211   Halpert, Herbert. "Shakespeare, Abelard, and The Unquiet Grave." *Journal of American Folklore*, LXIX (1956), 74-75.

A9212   Rathbun, John Wilbert. *The Development of Historical Literary Criticism in America, 1800-1860*. DD, University of Wisconsin, 1957.

A9213   Roppolo, Joseph Patrick. "American Premieres of Two Shakespearean Plays in New Orleans." *Tulane Studies in English*, VII (1957), 125-132.

(b)   AFTER 1880
(See also section on Gardens, A2209-A2213.)

A9214   Brown, I. "The Shakespeare Industry." *Harper's Magazine*, 179 (1939), 97-104.

A9215   Peyre, Henri. *Writers and Their Critics*. Ithaca: Cornell Univ. Press, 1944. Pp. xii, 340.
Particularly cites failings of conservative scholarship.

A9216   Clow, Ruth M. *A Study of the Rated Eminence of Authors of the Several Periods of English Literature*. DD, Stanford University, 1946. Abstract publ. in *Abstracts of Dissertations*, Stanford University, XXI (1945-46), 136-140.

A9217   Schwarz, D. "The Present and Future of Shakespeare." *New York Times Magazine*, May 12, 1946, pp. 22-23.

A9218   Schwartz, Frederick. *The Attitude of the Working Class Toward Literature and Art*. DD, University of Iowa, 1949. Pp. 119.

A9219   Harbage, Alfred. "The Shakespeare Boom?" *Atlantic*, Oct., 1956, pp. 80-84.

A9220   Rothe, Hans. "Shakespeare in USA." *Prisma* (Bochum), 1955/56, pp. 115-116.
Also in *Shakespeare-Tage, 1956*, Bochum, pp. 14-18.

A9221   Hastings, William T. "Shakespeare in Providence." *SQ*, VIII (1957), 335-351.

(3)   SHAKESPEARE'S SIGNIFICANCE FOR
VARIOUS AMERICAN AUTHORS

(a) NINETEENTH CENTURY AUTHORS
i. General

A9222   Dunn, Esther C. *Shakespeare in America.* New York: Macmillan, 1939. Pp. xiv, 310.
        Influ. on colonial and later writers; specifically Emerson, Thoreau, Alcott, Whitman, Lincoln,
        Hawthorne.
        Rev: A9180.

A9223   Vandiver, Edward P., Jr. "Longfellow, Lanier, Boker and *King Lear.*" *SAB*, XIX (1944),
        132-134.

ii. Individuals
aa. Cooper

A9224   Vandiver, Edward P., Jr. "James Fenimore Cooper and Shakspere." *SAB*, XV (1940), 110-117.

A9225   Gates, W. B. "Cooper's Indebtedness to Shakespeare." *PMLA*, LXVII (1952), 716-731.

A9226   Vandiver, Edward P., Jr. "Cooper's *The Prairie* and Shakespeare." *PMLA*, LXIX (1954),
        1302-04.

bb. Emerson

A9227   Falk, Robert P. "Emerson and Shakespeare." *PMLA*, LVI (1941), 532-543.

A9228   Peery, Thomas A. "Emerson, the Historical Frame, and Shakespeare." *MLQ*, IX (1948),
        440-447.

A9229   Link, Franz. *Die Begriffe des "Poet" und des "Writer" in ihrer Stellung im Ganzen der Lebensauf-
        fassung Ralph Waldo Emersons auf Grund einer Interpretation der Essays "Shakespeare or the Poet"
        und "Goethe or the Writer."* DD, Frankfurt am Main, 1950. Pp. 168. Typewritten.

A9230   Anderson, John Quincy. *Emerson's Concept of the Poet.* DD, University of North Carolina,
        1952. Abstract publ. in *Univ. of North Carolina Record, Research in Progress,* Jan.-Dec., 1952,
        Grad. School Series No. 64, 1953, pp. 103-104.

A9231   Felheim, Marvin. "Landmarks of Criticism: 'Shakespeare; or, the Poet', Ralph Waldo
        Emerson." *ShN*, VII (1957), 20.

cc. Hawthorne

A9232   Davidson, F. "Hawthorne's Hive of Honey." *MLN*, LXI (1946), 14-21.

A9233   Abel, D. "Immortality vs. Mortality in *Septimus Felton*: Some Possible Sources." *American
        Literature*, XXVII (1956), 569-570.

dd. Melville

A9234   Olson, Charles. "Lear and Moby Dick." *Twice a Year*, I (1938), 165-189.

A9235   Olson, Charles. *Call Me Ishmael.* New York: Reynal & Hitchcock, 1947. Pp. 120.
        Part II is "Source: Shakespeare," pp. 35-73.

A9236   Lash, Kenneth. "Captain Ahab and King Lear." *New Mexico Quarterly Review*, XIX (1949),
        438-445.

A9237   Olson, Charles. "Melville et Shakespeare ou la découverte de *Moby Dick.*" *Temps Modernes*,
        VII (1951), 647-676.

A9238   Vogelback, A. L. "Shakespeare and Melville's *Benito Cereno.*" *MLN*, LXVII (1952), 113-116.

A9239   Yaggy, Elinor. "Shakespeare and Melville's *Pierre.*" *Boston Public Lib. Quar.*, VI (1954), 43-51.

A9240   Goto, Takeshi. "*Moby Dick* and Shakespeare." *Kyushu Daigakue English Literary Proceedings*
        (Fukuoka), Aug., 1956. (In Japanese.)
        Compares Melville's work with *Lear.*

A9241   Stewart, George R. "The Two Moby-Dicks." *Amer. Literature*, XXXV (1954), 417-418.

A9241a Stone, Edward. "*Moby Dick* and Shakespeare: A Remonstrance." *SQ*, VII (1956), 445-448.

A9242   Vogel, Dan. "The Dramatic Chapters in *Moby Dick.*" *Nineteenth Century Fiction*, XIII (1958),
        239-247.

ee. Poe

A9243   Olybrius. "The Character of Hamlet." *N &Q*, 189 (1945), 130. [See *N &Q*, 188 (1945), 125.]
        Comments upon Poe's opinions of Hamlet.

A9244   Hunter, W. B., Jr. "Poe's 'The Sleeper' & *Macbeth.*" *American Literature*, XX (1948), 55-57.

ff. Simms

A9245   Holman, Clarence Hugh. "Simms and the British Dramatists." *PMLA*, LXV (1950), 346-359.

A9246   Vandiver, Edward P., Jr. "Simms's Border Romances and Shakespeare." *SQ*, V (1954),
        129-139.

gg. Thoreau

A9247   Whaling, Anne. *Studies in Thoreau's Reading of English Poetry and Prose, 1340-1660.* DD, Yale
        University, 1946.

A9248   Craig, George D. *Literary Criticism in the Works of Henry David Thoreau.* DD, University of
        Utah, before 1952.

hh. Whitman

A9249   Thaler, Alwin. *Shakespeare and Democracy*. Univ. Tennessee Press, 1941. Pp. xii, 312.
        Chap. II. "Shakespeare and Walt Whitman."
            Rev: A1809.
A9250   Falk, Robert P. "Shakspere's Place in Walt Whitman's America." *SAB*, XVII (1942), 86-96.
A9251   Allen, Gray. *Walt Whitman Handbook*. Chicago: Packard & Co., 1946. Pp. xviii, 560.
        Shak. passim.
A9252   Stovall, Floyd. "Whitman's Knowledge of Shakespeare." *SP*, XLIX (1952), 643-669.
A9253   Stovall, Floyd. "Whitman, Shakespeare, and the Baconians." *PQ*, XXXI (1952), 27-38.
A9254   Stovall, Floyd. "Whitman, Shakespeare, and Democracy." *JEGP*, LI (1952), 457-472.

ii.   Others

A9255   Nye, Russel B. "George Bancroft's View of Shakspere." *SAB*, XVIII (1943), 109-113.
A9256   Davidson, F. "A Note on Emily Dickinson's Use of Shakespeare." *New England Quarterly*,
        XVIII (1945), 407-408.
A9257   Cancelled.
A9258   Reichart, Walter A. "Impromptu by Washington Irving." *N &Q*, 198 (1953), 531.
A9259   Stafford, William T. "James Examines Shakespeare: Notes on the Nature of Genius."
        PMLA, LXXIII (1958), 123-128.
A9260   Berkelman, Robert. "Lincoln's Interest in Shakespeare." *SQ*, II (1951), 303-312.
A9261   McElderry, B. R., Jr. "J. R. Lowell and *Richard III*—a Bibliographical Error." *N &Q*, NS,
        V (1958), 179-180.
A9262   Smith, M. Elwood. "Note on 'Shakespeare in America'." *SAB*, XVII (1942), 61-62.

(b)   TWENTIETH CENTURY AUTHORS
i.   Comments of Literary Figures

A9263   Auslander, Joseph. "Shakespeare to Our Time." *New York Times Magazine*, Apr. 24, 1955,
        p. 40.
A9264   Chapman, John Jay. *The Selected Writings of John Jay Chapman*. Ed. with an introduction by
        Jacques Barzun. New York: Farrar, Strauss and Cudahy, 1957. Pp. 294.
        Includes four Shak. criticisms: "Each Play a World," pp. 261-268; "Troilus & Cressida,"
        pp. 268-276; "The Melancholy Plays," pp. 277-284; "Shakespeare's Influence," pp. 284-289.
            Rev: by William Hudson Rogers, *English Journal*, XLVI (1957), 589; by Melvin H. Bernstein,
        Nation, Nov. 9, 1957, p. 328.
A9265   D(oolitle), H(ilda). *By Avon River*. New York: Macmillan, 1949. Pp. 98.
        A collection of poems about Shak.
            Rev: by M. W., *Canadian Forum*, Nov., 1949.
A9266   D(oolittle), H(ilda). *Avon*. Tr. by Johannes Urzidil. Berlin: Suhrkamp, 1955. Pp. 135.
            Rev: by H. Hennecke, *Krit. Blätter* (Gütersloh), II (1955/56), Heft 4, pp. 2-3.
A9267   Eliot, T. S. "Hamlet and His Problems." *Critiques and Essays in Criticism, 1920-1948*. New
        York: Ronald Press, 1949, pp. 384-388.
        See also Eliot entries A7690, A8166-A8178 above, and A9276-A9283 below.
A9268   Hughes, Langston. *Shakespeare in Harlem*. New York: A. A. Knopf, 1942.
A9269   Miller, Henry, and Michael Fraenkel. *Hamlet: A Philosophical Correspondence*. New York
        and Paris: Carrefour, 1939. Pp. 330.
        A book on contemporary philosophy, listed here because of its title. The book shows an
        incredibly mistaken conception of Shakespeare's hero.
            Rev: by Winifred Smith, *Books Abroad*, XIV (1940), 440-441; by Paul Rosenfeld, *Nation*
        (N. Y.), 153 (1941), 146.
A9270   Santayana, George. "Hamlet." *Obiter Scripta*, ed. Buchler and Schwartz, New York: Charles
        Scribner's Sons, 1936, pp. 41-67.
A9271   Santayana, George. "Hamlet." *Essays in Literary Criticism*, ed. Irving Singer, New York:
        Charles Scribner's Sons, 1956, pp. 120-136.
        "Tragic Philosophy" (on Macb.), pp. 266-277.
A9272   Young, Stark. "To Madame Frijsh." *NR*, 89 (1936), 146.
        On the prayer scene and Hamlet's irresolution as portrayed by Leslie Howard and John
        Gielgud.

ii.   Studies of the Attitudes of Authors
aa.   Maxwell Anderson

A9273   Sampley, A. M. "Maxwell Anderson's Poetic Tragedies." *CE*, V (1944), 412-417.
A9274   Petty, J. M. *A Study of "Winterset" Especially in the Light of "Hamlet"*. MS thesis, Columbia
        University, 1948. Pp. 46.
A9275   Adler, Jacob. "Shakespeare in *Winterset*." *ETJ*, Oct. 1954, pp. 241-248.

bb.   T. S. Eliot

A9276   Fussell, Paul.   "A Note on 'The Hollow Men'."   *MLN*, LXV (1950), 254-255.

A9277   Roby, Robert C.   *T. S. Eliot and the Elizabethan and Jacobean Dramatists.*   DD, Northwestern University, 1950.   Abstract publ. in *Summaries of Doctoral Dissertations*, 1949, Vol. 17, Chicago and Evanston: Northwestern Univ., 1950, pp. 42-46.

A9278   Melchiori, Giorgio.   "Echoes in *The Waste Land.*"   *ES*, XXXII (1951), 1-11.
Particularly of *Cymbeline*.

A9279   King, S. K.   "Eliot, Yeats and Shakespeare."   *Theoria* (Pietermaritzburg), 1953, pp. 113-119.

A9279a   Thompson, Marion C.   *The Dramatic Criticism of Thomas Stearns Eliot.*   DD, Cornell University, 1953.

A9280   Stevenson, David L.   "An Objective Correlative for T. S. Eliot's *Hamlet.*"   *JAAC*, XIII (1954), 69-79.

A9281   Eliot, T. S.   "Gordon Craig's Socratic Dialogues."   *Drama* (Spring, 1955), pp. 16-21.

A9282   Blum, Margaret Morton.   "The *Fool* in 'The Love Song of J. Alfred Prufrock'."   *MLN*, LXXII (1957), 424-426.
Eliot meant not Polonius, nor a generalized fool, but Yorick.

A9283   Major, John M.   "Eliot's 'Gerontion' and *As You Like It.*"   *MLN*, LXXIII (1958), 28-31.
See also A7690, A8166-A8178, and A9267.

cc.   Others

A9284   Prior, M.   *The Language of Tragedy.*   Columbia Univ. Press, 1947.
Discusses Shakespearean influence on Sherwood Anderson, pp. 318-325.
Rev: A5134.

A9285   Collins, Carvel.   "The Interior Monologues of *The Sound and the Fury.*"   *EIE*, 1952, pp. 29-56.
Faulkner influenced by *Macbeth*.

A9285a   Ryan, Marjorie.   "The Shakespearean Symbolism in *The Sound and the Fury.*"   *Faulkner Studies*, II, (Autumn, 1953), 40-44.

A9286   Newdick, Robert S.   "Some Notes on Robert Frost and Shakspere."   *SAB*, XII (1937), 187-189.

A9287   Gates, William Bran.   "O. Henry and Shakspere."   *SAB*, XIX (1944), 20-25.

A9288   Myers, Henry Alonzo.   *Tragedy: A View of Life.*   Ithaca: Cornell Univ. Press, 1956.   Pp. viii, 210.
Contains a comparison of *Macbeth* and *The Iceman Cometh*.
Rev: A6916.

A9289   Frye, Roland M.   "Macbeth and the Powers of Darkness."   *Emory Univ. Quarterly*, VIII (1953), 164-174.
On religion in Shakespeare, with objections to comments of Santayana in his essay "Religion in Shakespeare."

b.   THE CONTINENT IN GENERAL (150;49)
See also Surveys for Shakespeare's influence in various countries, A339-A381.

A9290   Praz, M.   "La fortuna del dramma elisabettiano."   *Studi e svaghi inglesi.*   Florence: Sansoni, 1937.   Pp. vii, 348.

A9291   Castle, Eduard.   "Shakespeare-Feier vor 75 Jahren."   *SJ*, LXXV (1939), 52-58.

A9292   Houg, Ragnar.   *Shakespeare. Diktiner "for alle tider" i lys av vår tids kjensle og viten.*   Bergen (Norway), 1945.

A9293   Van Tieghem, Paul.   "Shakespeare devant la critique continentale au XVIIIᵉ siècle."   *Essais et Études Universitaires.*   1945/46, No. 1.

A9293a   Van Tieghem, Paul.   "Adaptations scéniques de Shakespeare sur le continent."   *Rivista di letterature moderne*, I (1946), 22-38.

A9294   Schröder, Rudolf Alexander.   "Shakespeare als Dichter des Abendlandes."   *Theater-Almanach*, II (1947), 220-233.   Also in *Gesammelte Werke*, Berlin, 1952, pp. 218-230, and in *Fülle des Daseins. Eine Auslese aus dem Werk.*   Berlin: Suhrkamp, 1958.

A9295   Van Tieghem, Paul.   *Le Préromantisme: Études d'histoire littéraire européenne (La Découverte de Shakespeare sur le continent).*   Paris: Sfelt, 1947.   Pp. xi, 412.
Rev: by L. G., *Paru*, July, 1948, pp. 56-57; by A. Koszul, *LanM*, V (1949), 64; by H. C. Lancaster, *MLN*, LXIV, 201-202; by L. M. Price, *CL*, I, 88-90; by F. Baldensperger, *RLC*, XXIII, 137-144.

A9296   Stahl, Ernst L.   "Shakespeare heute in Europa."   *Die Quelle*, II (1948), Heft 4, pp. 11-18.

A9297   Abreu, Bricio de.   "Shakespeare em todo o mundo."   *Comoedia* (Rio de Janeiro), 1950, p. 100.

A9298   Bonnard, Georges A.   "Suggestions Towards an Edition of Shakespeare for French, German and Other Continental Readers."   *ShS*, V (1952), 10-15.

A9299   Calgari, Guido.   "Fortuna di Shakespeare in Italia e in Francia."   *Hesperia* (Zurich), III (Oct. 1953), 191-199.

A9300 Taupin, René. "Le Mythe de Hamlet à l'Epoque Romantique." *French Rev*, XXVII (1953), 15-21.

A9301 "World's Most Translated Authors." *Unesco Courier*, Feb., 1957, pp. 8-10.

c.   THE LATIN COUNTRIES (150;49)
(1)   FRANCE (150;49)
(a)   GENERAL STUDIES (150;-)

A9302 Krüger, Paul. *Fransk litteraer Kritik indtil 1830. Ideer og Metoder.* DD, Copenhagen, 1936. Pp. viii, 304.

A9303 Lebègue, Raymond. "La Tragédie 'shakespearienne' en France au temps de Shakespeare." *RCC*, XXXVIII (1937), 385-404, 621-628, 683-695.

A9304 Radulescu, I. Horia. "Les Intermédiaires français de Shakespeare en Roumanie." *RLC*, XVIII (1938), 252-271.

A9305 "Shakespeare in France." *TLS*, Oct. 21, 1939, p. 609.

A9306 Marye, Edouard. "Shakespeare et Nous." *Les Nouvelles Littéraires*, Feb. 25, 1939, p. 5.

A9307 Vaudoyer, J. J. "Shakespeare et les *Peintres* Français." *Beaux-Arts*, 327 (Apr. 7, 1939), 1, 4.

A9308 Brulé, André. "Du Théâtre Élizabéthain en France." *Le Théâtre Elizabéthain.* Paris: Les Cahiers du Sud, 1940, pp. 314-321.

A9309 Fluchère, Henri. "Shakespeare en France." *Le Théâtre Elizabéthain.* Paris: Les Cahiers du Sud, 1940, pp. 7-22.

A9310 Rose, Francis. "Les Poètes Elizabéthains et Nous." *Le Théâtre Elizabéthain.* Paris: Les Cahiers du Sud, 1940, pp. 311-313.

A9311 Marie de Bon Secours, Sister. *L'Influence de Shakespeare sur le Théâtre Romantique Français.* MA thesis, Montreal, 1940. Pp. 78.

A9312 Keller, W. "Shakespeares Eindringen in Frankreich und die deutsche Shakespeare-Begeisterung." *EWD*, II (1942), 2-3.

A9313 Travers, Seymour. *Catalogue of 19th Century French Theatrical Parodies; a Compilation of the Parodies Between 1789 and 1914 of Which Any Record Was Found.* DD, Columbia University, 1942. Publ: New York: King's Crown Press, 1942. Pp. 130. Shak. pp. 96-97.

A9314 Whitridge, Arnold. "Shakspere and Delacroix." *SAB*, XVII (1942), 167-183.

A9315 Monaco, Marion. *Shakespeare on the French Stage in the Eighteenth Century.* DD, Bryn Mawr College, 1943. Pp. 235. Mic A43-2178. *Mcf Ab*, V (1943), 18. Publication No. 581.

A9316 Mary Magdalen Murphy, Sister. *Essai sur l'Influence de Shakespeare en France jusqu'à l'Epoque Romantique.* MA thesis, McGill University, 1943.

A9317 Rudwin, Maximilien. "Shakspere en France." *SAB*, XX (1945), 110-117.

A9318 Barrault, Jean-Louis. "Shakespeare et les Français." *RddxM*, Dec. 15, 1948, pp. 650-659.

A9319 Chambrun, Clara Longworth de. "Shakespeare en France." *Hommes et Mondes*, V (1948), 261-278.

A9320 Chambrun, Clara Longworth de. "Shakespeare Across the Channel." *AMS*, pp. 97-100. See A9319.

A9321 Lancaster, H. Carrington. "The Alleged First Foreign Estimate of Shakespeare." *MLN*, LXIII (1948), 509-512.
       The so-called Clémont estimate (1675-84) derives from a *Dissertation* of 1717.

A9322 Fluchère, Henri. "Shakespeare in France: 1900-1948." *ShS*, II (1949), 115-124.

A9323 Bailey, Helen P. *Hamlet in France from Voltaire to Laforgue (1733-1886).* DD, Columbia University, 1950. Pp. 405. Mic A50-92. *Mic Ab*, X (1950), 114. Publication No. 1632.

A9324 Barrault, Jean-Louis. "Shakespeare et Nous." *RHT*, II (1950), 131-136.

A9325 Ruyssen, Yvonne. "Shakespeare et la Critique Française." *Europe*, Sept., 1950, pp. 34-41.

A9326 De Smet, Robert. "*Othello* in Paris and Brussels." *ShS*, III (1950), 98-106.

A9327 Vigo Fazio, Lorenzo. "Come Parigi Apprezzò Shakespeare." *Francia coi poeti.* Catania: Arione, 1952, pp. 41-52.

A9328 Benchettrit, Paul. *A History of "Hamlet" in France.* DD, Birmingham, 1953.

A9329 Keys, A. C. "Shakespeare in France. An Early Stage Adaptation." *Jour. Australian Univ. Mod. Lang. Assoc.*, Aug., 1953.

A9330 Taupin, René. "The Myth of Hamlet in France in Mallarmé's Generation." *MLQ*, XIV (1953), 432-447.

A9331 Barrault, Jean-Louis. "Actualité de Shakespeare." *Revue théâtrale*, No. 26, 1954, pp. 5-8.

A9332 Dasté, Jean. "Lettre sur nos Spectacles Shakespeare (Comédie de St.-Etienne). *Revue théâtrale*, No. 26, 1954, pp. 28-30.

A9333 Eisner, Doris. "*Richard II* und das Théâtre National Populaire." *Shakespeare-Tage* (Bochum), 1954, pp. 20-24.

A9334 Lamont, Rosette. *The Hamlet Myth in French Symbolism.* DD, Yale University, 1954.

A9335 Saint-Denis, Michel. "Shakespeare en France et en Angleterre." *Revue théâtrale*, No. 26, 1954, pp. 13-18.

A9336 Platt, P. *Le roi Lear en France*. MA thesis, Edinburgh, 1955.

A9337 Benchettrit, Paul. "*Hamlet* at the Comédie Française: 1769-1896." *ShS*, IX (1956), 59-68.

A9338 England, Martha Winburn. "Garrick's Stratford Jubilee: Reactions in France and Germany." *ShS*, IX (1956), 90-100.
       In contrast with English cynicism to the jubilee, French reaction was enthusiastic and German reaction was a precursor of *Sturm und Drang*.

A9339 *L'Encyclopédie du Théâtre Contemporain*, Vol. I, 1850-1914. Paris: Plaisir de France, 1957. Pp. 208. (Vol. II, 1914-1950.)
       Includes notes and commentary on Shak. adaptations and translations produced in France.
          Rev: by Stanley Richards, *Players Magazine*, XXXIV (1958), 126, 141.

A9340 Cannaday, Robert Wythe, Jr. *French Opinion of Shakespeare from the Beginnings Through Voltaire, 1604-1778*. DD, University of Virginia, 1957. Pp. 401. Mic 57-4190. *DA*, XVII (1957), 2605. Publication No. 22,886.

A9341 Keys, A. C. "Shakespeare en France: *La Mégère Apprivoisée* en 1767." *RLC*, XXXI (1957), 426-428.

A9342 Junge, E. "La France et Shakespeare." *Bulletin culturel du British Council* (Paris), May, 1958.

(b) INFLUENCE ON INDIVIDUAL FRENCH WRITERS
     (150;49)
     i. Ducis

A9343 Vanderhoof, Mary B. *Hamlet: A Tragedy Adapted from Shakespeare (1770) by Jean François Ducis. A Critical Edition. Proceedings Amer. Philos. Soc.*, 97, No. 1 (1953), 88-142.
          Rev: by H. Carrington Lancaster, *SQ*, IV, (1953), 470-471; by Willard B. Pope, "Ducis' *Hamlet*." *SQ*, V (1954), 209-211.

A9344 De Beaumont, V. *The Shakespearean Tragedies of Ducis*. MA thesis, University of California, 1904.

A9345 Downs, B. W. "Ducis's Two *Hamlets*." *MLR*, XXXI (1936), 206-208.
       Versions of 1770 and 1803.

A9346 Pennink, R. "Ducis." *Nederland en Shakespeare*, 1936, pp. 261-269.

A9347 Shackleton, Robert. "Shakespeare in French Translation." *Modern Languages*, XXIII (1941), 15-21.

A9348 Nicholson, G. R. *Shakespeare for the Age of Reason—A Study of J. F. Ducis*. MA thesis, University of London, 1951.

A9349 Pope, Willard B. "Ducis's *Hamlet*." *SQ*, V (1954), 209-211.

A9350 Lombard, Charles M. "Ducis' *Hamlet* and Musset's *Lorenzaccio*." *N &Q*, V (1958), 72-75.

ii. Hugo

A9351 Hugo, Victor. *W. Shakespeare*. Introd., trad. y notas de José López y López. Madrid: Aguilar, 1950. Pp. 547.

A9352 Daubray, Cécile. "Sur le *Shakespeare* de Victor Hugo." *Rev. de France*, 17e an., II (1937), 268-300.

A9353 Vandérem, F. "Chronique: les livres négligés. Victor Hugo: William Shakespeare." *Bulletin du bibliophile et du bibliothécaire*, XVII (1938), 1-5.

A9354 Grant, E. M. *The Career of V. Hugo*. Cambridge, 1945. Shak., pp. 268-271.

A9355 Moore, Olin H. "Victor Hugo as a Humorist Before 1840." *PMLA*, LXV (1950), 133-153.

A9356 Levaillant, M. "Quand Shakespeare à Jersey parle à Victor Hugo." *RLC*, XXVI (1952), 296-312.

A9357 Patterson, H. Temple. "Shakespeare and the Imagery of Victor Hugo." *Studies in Romance Philology and French Literature Presented to John Orr*. Manchester Univ. Press, 1953, pp. 198-217.

A9358 Barrère, Jean-Bertrand. "Victor Hugo et la Grande-Bretagne." *RLC*, XXVIII (1954), 137-167.

iii. Musset

A9359 Silver, Edith. *L'Influence de Shakespeare sur le Théâtre d'Alfred de Musset*. MA thesis, McGill, 1924.

A9360 Morgan, M. *The Influence of Shakespeare on Alfred de Musset*. MA thesis, Univ. of Witwatersrand, South Africa, 1926.

A9361 Chillemi, Guglielmo. "Lorenzaccio, Amleto romantico." *Teatro Scenario*, (Milan), NS, V, No. 12 (June 16-30, 1953), 44-45.

iv. Stendhal

A9362 Gus, M. "Racine and Shakespeare. On Stendhal's Pamphlet 'Of a Heroic Art and of Our Classics'." *Theatre* (USA), VI (1940), 26-37.

A9363   Cordiè, Carlo. "Inedite Postille di Stendhal a Shakespeare." *Letterature Moderne* (Milan), III (March-April 1952), 129-157.

A9364   Stendhal. *"Rasin i Shekspir."* (Serbo-Croatian translation by Milan Predić.) Belgrade: Novo pokolenje, 1953. Pp. 180.

v.   Voltaire

A9365   Maurois, André. *Voltaire*. Paris, 1935. Pp. 144. English version, trans. by Hamish Miles, 1932.

A9366   Naves, Raymond. *Le Goût de Voltaire*. DD, Paris, 1938. Paris: Garnier frères. Pp. 566.

A9367   Adams, Percy G. "How Much Shakespeare Did Voltaire Know?" *SAB*, XVI (1941), 126.

A9368   Havens, George R. "Voltaire and English Critics of Shakespeare." New York: Franco-American Pamphlets, Second Ser., No. 16, 1944. Also in *Amer. Soc. Legion of Honor Magazine*, XV (1944), 176-186.

A9369   Horsley, Phyllis M. "George Keate and the Voltaire-Shakespeare Controversy." *Comp. Lit. Studies*, XVI (1945), 5-8.

A9370   Russell, Trusten W. *Voltaire, Dryden & Heroic Tragedy*. DD, Columbia University, 1946. New York: Columbia Univ. Press, 1946. Pp. 178.

A9371   Mönch, Walter. "Voltaire und Shakespeare: Eine Begegnung zweier Geistesmächte." In Mönch's *Das Gastmahl*, Hamburg, 1947, pp. 172-233.

A9372   Fenger, Henning. "Voltaire et le Théâtre Anglais." *Orbis*, VII (1949), 161-287.

A9373   Price, Lawrence M. "Shakespeare as Pictured by Voltaire, Goethe, and Oeser." *GR*, XXV (1950), 83-84.

A9374   Lubbers-van der Brugge, Catharine Johanna Maria. *Johnson and Baretti. Some Aspects of Eighteenth-Century Literary Life in England and Italy*. DD, Gröningen, 1951. Chap. VII. "A Discussion of the *Discours sur Shakespeare et sur Monsieur de Voltaire* with More of Baretti's Miscellaneous Borrowings from Johnson."

A9375   Guicharnaud, Jacques. "Voltaire and Shakespeare." *American Society Legion of Honor Magazine*, XXVII (1956), 159-169.

vi.   Others

A9376   Evrard, Claude. "Apollinaire et Shakespeare." *Revue des Sciences Humaines*, 84 (1956),461-465.

A9377   Smith, Stephen Réginald-Birt. *Essai sur l'Influence de l'Angleterre sur l'Œuvre de Balzac*. DD, Besançon, 1950. London: Williams, Lea & Co., 1953.

A9378   Baym, Max I. "Baudelaire and Shakspere." *SAB*, XV (1940), 131-148.

A9379   Spencer, Bessie. *The Influence of Shakespeare on the Life and Work of Hector Berlioz*. DD, Leeds, 1936. Abstr. publ. in Univ. of Leeds *Publications and Abstracts of Theses, 1935/36*, p. 20.

A9380   Lebois, A. "Elémir Bourges et les Elizabéthains." *RLC*, XXII (1948), 237-254.

A9381   Book, Ernest Truett. *Les Influences Anglaises dans l'Œuvre de Chateaubriand jusqu'en 1802*. DD, Paris, 1950.

A9382   Berton, Jean-Claude. *Shakespeare et Claudel. Le Temps et l'Espace au Théâtre*. Geneva: La Palatine; Paris: Plon, 1958. Pp. 224.

A9383   Forsberg, Roberta J. *Madame de Staël: The English Period*. DD, University of Southern California, 1950.

A9384   Heitner, Robert R. *Lessing, Diderot, and the Bourgeois Drama*. DD, Harvard University, 1949. Shakespeare's influence in liberating Lessing and Diderot from classical drama.

A9385   Bertocci, Angelo Philip. *Charles Du Bos and English Literature. A Critic and His Orientation*. New York: King's Crown Press; Oxford Univ. Press, 1949. Pp. viii, 285.

A9386   Cassagnau, M. "Théophile Gautier et Shakspere." *RLC*, XXIV (1950), 577.

A9387   Hottot, A. L. F. H. *André Gide as Translator From English and Interpreter of Great Britain*. B. Litt. thesis, Oxford, 1951.

A9388   Ewen, Frederic. "Criticism of English Literature in Grimm's Correspondance Littéraire." *SP*, XXXIII (1936), 397-404.

A9389   Maurois, André. *Profiles of Great Men*. Translated from the French by Helen Temple Patterson. London: Tower Bridge Publications, 1955. Pp. 148.
Includes study of Shak. as one of Maurois' masters.
          Rev: *TLS*, Feb. 11, 1955, p. 94.

A9390   Cellier, L. "Sur un Vers des Chimères. Nerval et Shakespeare." *CS*, (Paris), No. 311, 1952, pp. 146-153.

A9391   Boyle, James-Louis. *Marcel Proust et les Ecrivains Anglais*. Thèse, Univ. of Paris, 1953.

A9392   Klein, David. "Shakespeare in France." *N &Q*, NS, IV (1957), 336.

A9393   Lehmann, A. G. "Sainte-Beuve Critique de la Littérature Anglaise." *RLC*, XXVIII (1954), 417-439.

A9394 Taine, Hippolyte. *Shakespeare i njegovi savremenici.* Tr. into Serbo-Croat. Belgrade: 1953. Pp. 349.

A9395 Legouis, Emile. "*La Terre* de Zola et le *Roi Lear.*" *RLC*, XXVII (1953), 417-427.

A9396 Iacuzzi, Alfred. "The Naive Theme in *The Tempest* as a Link Between Thomas Shadwell and Ramón de la Cruz." *MLN*, LII (1937), 252-256.
Influence of French version of Dryden-Shadwell version of *Temp.* in Spain.

(2) SPAIN AND PORTUGAL (151;49)

A9397 Coe, Ada M. *Catálogo Bibliográfico y Crítico de las Comedias Anunciadas en Los Periódicos de Madrid Desde 1661 Hasta 1819.* Johns Hopkins Studies in Romance Literatures and Languages. Extra Vol. 9. Baltimore: Johns Hopkins Press, 1935. Pp. xii, 270. Includes Shak.

A9398 Par. A. *Shakespeare en la Literatura Española.* Madrid, 1935.
Rev: by S. R., *Bol. de Biblioteca Menéndez y Pelayo,* XVII (1936), 188-190; by H. Thomas, *MLR*, XXXI, 594-595; by E. M. W., *Criterion*, XV, 361-362; by T. Heinermann, *SJ*, LXXIII (1937), 177-178; by Richard Ruppert y Ujaravi, *Beiblatt*, XLIX (1938), 119-122.

A9399 Par. A. *Representaciones Shakespearianas en España. I: Epoca galoclásica. Epoca romántica.* Pp. 268. *II: Epoca realista y tiempos modernos.* Pp. 220. San Felíu de Guixols: O. Viader, 1936.

A9400 Esquerra, Ramón. *Shakespeare a Catalunya.* Barcelona: Generalitat de Catalunya, Publicacions de la Institució del Teatre, 1937. Pp. 194.
Rev: by H. Thomas, *MLR*, XXXIV (1939), 459-460.

A9401 Iacuzzi, Alfred. "The Naive Theme in *The Tempest* as a Link Between Thomas Shadwell and Ramón de la Cruz." *MLN*, LII (1937), 252-256.

A9402 Herder, Johann Gottfried. *Shakespeare* [Spanish and German.] Sel., trad. y pról. de Juan C. Probst. Antología alemana. Ser. 1, fasc. 39. Buenos Aires: Univ., Fac. de fil., 1949. Pp. 56.

A9403 Figueiredo, Fidelino de. *Shakespeare e Garrett.* Universidade de São Paulo, 1950. Pp. 50.
Almeida Garrett was leader of the Romantic movement in Portugal.
Rev: by Gerald M. Moser, *Books Abroad*, XXV (1951), 294.

A9404 Thomas, Sir Henry. *Shakespeare in Spain.* London: G. Cumberlege, 1950. Pp. 24.
Rev: *TLS*, July 21, 1950, p. 446; by C. J. Sisson, *MLR*, XLV, 423.

A9405 FitzGerald, Thomas A. "Shakespeare in Spain and Spanish America." *MLJ*, XXXV (1951), 589-594.

A9406 Ley, Charles David. *Shakespeare para los Españoles.* Madrid: Revista de Occidente, 1951.
Rev: *TLS*, Dec. 28, 1951, p. 839; by J. L. Cano, *Insula*, VI, No. 68 (Aug. 15, 1951), p. 4; by G. G. de la S., *Clavileño*, II, No. 11 (Sept.-Oct., 1951), 73.

A9407 Gomes, Eugênio. "O Drama de Leonor de Mendonça." *Correio da Manhã,* Rio de Janeiro, Oct. 23, 1954.
The influence of *Othello* on the play *Leonor de Mendonça* by Gonçalves Dias.

A9408 Shoemaker, William H. "Galdós' *La de los tristes destinos* and Its Shakespearean Connections." *MLN*, LXXI (1956), 114-119.

(3) ITALY (151; 49)
(a) GENERAL

A9409 "Shakespeare e l'Italia." *Bibliografia fascista,* VIII (1933), 805-868.
See also A189a.

A9410 Rebora, Piero. *Civiltà Italiana e Civiltà Inglese. Studi e ricerche.* Florence: Felice Le Monnier, 1936. Pp. xi, 271.
Rev: by Louis Bonnerot, *EA*, I (1937), 328-329; by C. Pellizzi, *Leonardo*, VIII, 102-103.

A9411 Orsini, N. "Gli Studi inglesi in Italia nel 1935." *Leonardo,* VIII (1937), 289-290.

A9412 Praz, Mario. "Come Shakespeare è letto in Italia." *Rivista Italiana del Dramma,* II (1938), 4.

A9413 Buck, August. "Gedanken zur Entwicklung des Italienischen Schrifttums um die Wende des 18. Jahrhunderts." *GRM*, XXX (1942), 285-293.

A9414 Praz, Mario. *Richerche Anglo-Italiane.* Rome: Edizioni di Storia e Letteratura, 1944.
Reprints studies published at various times between 1922 and 1938, including "Come Shakespeare è letto in Italia," pp. 169-196.
Rev: by Anna Maria Crinò, *Anglica*, II (1948), 50-52.

A9415 Corsi, Mario. "Interpreti di Shakespeare in Italia." *Il Dramma,* No. 75/76, Jan. 1, 1949, 108-121.

A9416 Rebora, Piero. "Compresione e Fortuna di Shakespeare in Italia." *CL*, I (1949), 210-224.

A9417 Ridenti, Lucio, ed. *Shakespeare degli Italiani. I testi scespiriani inspirati da fatti e figure della nostra storia e della nostra leggenda.* Turin: Società Editrice Torinese, 1950. Pp. lxxvii, 686.
Contents: A. Pastore, "W. Shakespeare," pp. xiii-xxxv. B. Brunelli, "Interpreti di Shakespeare in Italia," pp. xxxix-lv. L. Gigli, "La storia romana nel teatro di Shakespeare," pp. lix-lxviii. J. Copeau, "Shakespeare ou la livraison de l'émotion humaine," pp. lxxi-lxxvii.
For the ten plays translated, see B870.

A9418 Orsini, N. "Shakespeare in Italy." *CL*, III (1951), 178-180.

A9419 Baldini, Gabriele. "Riletture Shakespeariane." *Nuova Antologia*, July, 1954, pp. 353-368.

A9420 Guerrieri, Gerardo. "Saper, Sachespar, Shakespeare ovvero l'interpretazione di Shakespeare in Italia dal Settecento al Novecento." *Cinquant' anni di Teatro in Italia*. Rome: Marzorati, 1954, pp. 69-86.

A9421 Pellegrini, Giuliano. "The Roman Plays of Shakespeare in Italy." *Italica*, XXXIV (1957), 228-233.

(b) INDIVIDUALS

A9422 Lubbers-van der Brugge, Catharina Johanna Maria. *Johnson and Baretti. Some Aspects of Eighteenth-Century Literary Life in England and Italy.* DD, Gröningen, 1951. Publ. as Gröningen studies in English No. 2.
Chap. VII. "A Discussion of the *Discours sur Shakespeare et sur Monsieur de Voltaire* with More of Baretti's Miscellaneous Borrowings from Johnson."

A9423 Wolff, Max J. "Antonio Conti in seinem Verhältnis zu Shakespeare." *JEGP*, XXXVII (1938), 555-558.

A9424 Lombardo, Agostino. "De Sanctis e Shakespeare." *English Miscellany*, Rome, VII (1956), 91-146.

A9425 Ortolani, G. "Goldoni e Shakespeare. Appunti e Note." *Riv. italiana del dramma*, IV (1940), 280-301.

A9426 Guidi, Augusto. "Manzoni and Shakespeare." *N &Q*, Mar. 19, 1949, p. 126.

A9427 Guidi, Augusto. "*Henry VIII e I Promessi Sposi.* Sulla interpretazione di un sostantivo in *Julius Caesar*." *Letterature Moderne*, May-June, 1954. pp. 314-315.
The first of these two notes deals with reminiscences of Shakespeare in Manzoni's *I Promessi Sposi;* the second with the interpretation of the word *Creature* in Shakespeare's *Julius Caesar*.

A9428 Zanco, Aurelio. *Shakespeare in Russia e Altri Saggi.* Turin: Gheroni, 1945. Pp. 200.
"Ernesto Rossi interprete e critico shakespeariano," pp. 123-141.
Rev: A9787.

A9429 Ungaretti, Giuseppe. "Appunti sull'arte poetica di Shakespeare." *Poesia*, I Jan., 1945, pp. 132, 135.

A9430 Fleischer, Hernest. "I Contemporanei e la Rinascenza Verdiana. Melodramma Shakespeariano." *La Fiera Letteraria* (Rome), V (Apr. 22, 1950), 4.

D. GERMANY AND THE GERMANIC COUNTRIES (152;50)
(1) GERMANY (152;50)
(a) GENERAL TREATISES (152;50)
i. Various Periods

A9431 Beam, Jacob. *Die Ersten Deutschen Übersetzungen Englischer Lustspiele im Achtzehnten Jahrhundert.* DD, Jena, 1904. Pp. iv, 91.

A9432 Drews, Wolfgang. "*König Lear*" auf der Deutschen Bühne bis zur Gegenwart. Berlin, 1932.
Rev: by Wolfgang Keller, *SJ*, LXXII (1936), 161-162; by Hans Heinrich Borcherdt, *ZDP*, LXI (1937), 451-452; see other reviews listed in Ebisch and Schücking Supplement, p. 87.

A9433 Lucas, Wilfrid Irvine, M. A. *Die Epischen Dichtungen Shakespeares in Deutschland.* DD, Heidelberg, 1934. Philippsburg: J. Kruse und Söhne, [1936]. Pp. 113.

A9434 Price, Mary Bell, and Lawrence Marsden Price. *The Publication of English Literature in Germany in the Eighteenth Century.* Univ. of California Publ. in Modern Philology. Vol. 17, Berkeley: Univ. of California Press, 1934. Pp. viii, 228.
Rev: by A. R. Hohlfeld, *JEGP*, XXXIV (1935), 451-457; by Rob. D. Horn, *MLN*, LI (1936), 122-126; by Kurt Schrey, *ZDB*, XII, 411-412; by Eb. Semrau, *ZDP*, LXII (1937), 199-201.

A9435 Kahn, Ludwig W. *Shakespeares Sonnette in Deutschland: Versuch einer Literarischen Typologie.* Bern, Leipzig, 1935. Pp. 122.
Rev: by A. Brandl, *Archiv*, 168 (1935), 291; by J. Decroos, *ES*, XVII, 185-186; by W. Keller, *SJ*, LXXI, 122-123; by J. Shawcross, *MLR*, XXXI (1936), 253-254; by B. von Wiese, *GRM*, XXIV, 156; by E. Kast, *ZAAK*, XXX, 341-343; by W. Kayser, *ADA*, LV, 54-56; by J. E. Eilenberg, *GR*, XI, 58-59; by Henri Tronchon, *RG*, XXVIII (1937), 306-307; by Robert Adger Law, *MLN*, LII, 526-530; by H. Papajewski, *GA*, IV (1937).

A9436 Ulshöfer, Robert. *Die Theorie des Dramas in der dts. Romantik.* Neue dts. Forschungen 29. Abt. Neuere dts. Literaturgesch., Bd. 1. Berlin: Junker und Dünnhaupt, 1935. Pp. 183.
Shak., Schlegel, and Tieck.

A9437 Brandl, A. "Shakespeare and Germany." Third Annual British Academy Lecture. Republ. in Brandl's *Forschungen und Charakteristiken*, Berlin, 1936, pp. 161-172.

A9438 Hartleb, H. *Deutschlands erster Theaterbau. Eine Geschichte des Theaterlebens und der englischen Komödianten unter Landgraf Moritz dem Gelehrten von Hessen-Kassel.* Berlin: de Gruyter, 1936. Pp. 162.

A9439 Kelly, J. A. *German Visitors to English Theatres in the Eighteenth Century.* Princeton Univ. Press, 1936. Pp. viii, 178.
Rev: by Walter Graham, *JEGP*, XXXVI (1937), 614-615; by G. J. Ten Hoor, *MP*, XXXV, 205-208; by A. Brandl, *Archiv*, 171 (1937), 120-121; by Aug. Closs, *DuV*, XXXIX (1938), 258;

by Curtis C. D. Vail, *GR*, XIII, 68-69; by John A. Walz, *MLN*, LIII (1938), 70; by v. Kranendonk, *Neophil*, XXVII (1941/42), Heft 2.

A9440 Knox, I. *The Aesthetic Theories of Kant, Hegel, and Schopenhauer.* New York: Columbia Univ. Press, 1936. Pp. xii, 220.

A9441 Brüggemann, F., ed. *Die Aufnahme Shakespeares auf der Bühne der Aufklärung in den Sechziger und Siebziger Jahren.* Leipzig, 1937.
Rev: by L. M., *RG*, XXIX (1938), 211-212; by Marian P. Whitney, *Books Abroad*, XIII (1939), 224-225.

A9442 Pascal, R. *Shakespeare in Germany, 1740-1815.* Cambridge Univ. Press, 1937.
Rev: *TLS*, Oct. 9, 1937, p. 730; by J. Corbin, *NYTBR*, Dec. 5, p. 34; by A. R., *Criterion*, XVII (1938), 378; by L. M. Price, *GR*, XIII, 220-222; by W. Kalthoff, *Beiblatt*, XLIX, 117-118; by Albert Eichler, *Eng. Studn.*, LXXII, 410-411; by J. G. Kunstmann, *MP*, XXXVI, 83-85; by J. W. Eaton, *Monatshefte*, XXX, 337-338; by W. Keller, *SJ*, LXXIV, 188-189; by Léon Polak, *ES*, XX, 266-267; by G. Kitchin, *MLR*, XXXIV (1939), 297; by J. B. Leishman, *RES*, XVI (1940), 242-243; by P. P. Kies, *MLN*, LVI (1941), 385; by W. Fischer, *DLZ*, LXII, 929-931.

A9443 Ritter, E. *Die Dramaturgie der Zyklenaufführungen von Shakespeares Königsdramen in Deutschland.* Emsdetten: Lechte, 1937. Pp. 52.
Rev: *LZ*, 88 (1937), 1087.

A9444 Durian, Hans. *Jocza Savits und die Münchener Shakespeare-Bühne. Ein Beitrag zur Geschichte der Regie um die Jahrhundertwende.* DD, Munich, 1937. Emsdetten: Lechte, 1938. Pp. 132.

A9445 Frehn, Paul. *Der Einfluss der Englischen Literatur auf Deutschlands Musiker und Musik im 19. Jahrhundert.* Düsseldorf: G. H. Nolte, 1938. Pp. 196.
Shak., pp. 36-105 and Appendices 1-3.

A9446 Kluckhohn, Paul. "Die Dramatiker der Deutschen Romantik als Shakespeare-Jünger." *SJ*, LXXIV (1938), 31-49.

A9447 Stahl, Ernst Leopold. "Englische Dramatiker auf der dts. Bühne." *Dts. Kultur im Leben der Völker*, XIII (1938), 38-44.

A9448 Würtenberg, Gustav. *Shakespeare in Deutschland.* Beilefeld: Velhagen und Klasing, 1939. Pp. xiv, 145. Reprinted 1951. Pp. xxii, 140.
Rev: by W. Fischer, *Beiblatt*, LII (1941), 65.

A9449 Petsch, Robert. *Dts. Literaturwissenschaft. Aufsätze zur Begründung der Methode.* Germanische Studien, 222. Berlin: Ebering, 1940. Pp. 274.

A9450 Platz, H. "Houston Stewart Chamberlain, Bayreuth und Shakespeare." *N. Mon.*, XI (1940), 210-224.

A9451 Wiem, Irene. *Das Englische Schrifttum in Deutschland von 1518 bis 1600.* DD, Berlin, Humboldt-Univ., 1940. Pp. 150. Publ. Palaestra, 219. Leipzig: Akadem. Verlagsges. Becker u. Erler, 1940. Pp. 150.
Rev: by Marie Schütt, *DLZ*, LXII (1941), 644-646; by L. M. Price, *MLN*, LVII (1942), 161.

A9452 "Elizabethan Plays in Germany." *TLS*, April 26, 1941, p. 208.

A9453 Kies, P. P. "Shakespeare in Germany." *MLN*, LVI (1941), 385-388.

A9454 Pfitzner, Hans. "Shakespeare-Dämmerung?" *SJ*, LXXVII/LXXVIII (1941), 74-92. Republ. in Pfitzner's *Reden, Schriften, Briefe.* Berlin, 1955, pp. 69-85.

A9455 Buck, August. "Gedanken zur Entwicklung des Italienischen Schrifttums um die Wende des 18. Jh." *GRM*, XXX (1942), 285-293.

A9456 Schellenberg, Ernst Ludwig. *Das Buch der Deutschen Romantik.* 2nd ed. Bamberg: Buchner, 1943. Pp. 356.
Shak., pp. 202-236 passim.

A9457 Kreysler, Friedrich. "Deutsche Shakespeare-Ausgaben seit 1945." *MDtShG*, I (1949), 5.

A9458 Reiff, P. *Die Ästhetik der Deutschen Frühromantik.* Urbana: Univ. of Illinois Press, 1946. Pp. 306.

A9459 Schoen-René, Otto Eugene. *Shakespeare's Sonnets in Germany, 1787-1939.* DD, Harvard University, 1942. Abstr. publ. in *Summaries of PhD Theses, 1942.* Cambridge: Harvard Univ. Press, 1946, pp. 284-287.

A9460 Weber, Alfred. *Abschied von der Bisherigen Geschichte.* Hamburg: Claassen & Goverts, 1946. Shak., pp. 44-61.

A9461 Dodson, D. B. *German Shakespeare Critics in the Eighteenth Century.* MS thesis, Columbia University, 1947. Pp. 104.

A9462 Gundolf, Friedrich. *Shakespeare und der Deutsche Geist.* Godesberg: Küpper vorm. Bondi, 1947. Pp. x, 320.
Rev: by H. Eyl, *Lit. d. Gegenw.*, I (1948), 41.

A9463 Mårtens, Ilse. "Shakespeare Heute." *Pädagog. Rundschau*, I (1947), 89-93.

A9464 Sinden, Margaret J. *English Drama in Germany in the Later Enlightenment.* DD, Toronto, 1947.

A9465 Stahl, Ernst Leopold. *Shakespeare und das Deutsche Theater.* Stuttgart: Kohlhammer, 1947. Pp. viii, 768. 48 pp. of illustrations.
Rev: by G. Ross, *Die Lücke*, 1948, Beil. Neue Lit., p. 35; by Ernst Martin, *SJ*, 84/86 (1951), 237-240.

A9466 Cancelled.

A9467 Böchmann, Paul. "Der Dramatische Perspektivismus in der Deutschen Shakespearedeutung des 18. Jahrhunderts." *Vom Geist der Dichtung*, Hamburg, 1949, pp. 65-119.

A9468 Dorn, Ernst. "Shakespeare bei Deutschen Kriegsgefangenen in Frankreich." *SJ*, 82/83 (1949), 195-198.

A9469 Magon, Leopold. "Deutschland, Shakespeare und der Norden." *SJ*, 82/83 (1949), 136-153.

A9470 "Deutsche Veröffentlichungen über Shakespeare seit 1945." *MDtShG*, II (1950), 3-5.

A9471 Brandt, Thomas O. "Die Eindeutschung Shakespeares." *Monatshefte*, XLII (1950), 33-36.

A9472 Bruford, Walter Horace. *Theatre, Drama and Audience in Goethe's Germany*. London: Routledge, 1950. Pp. xii, 338.
Rev: *German Life and Letters*, NS, IV (1950/51), 221; *Listener*, XLV (1951), 32-33; by A. Gillies, *MLR*, XLVII (1952), 93.

A9473 Schmidt-Jhms, M. "Shakespeare's Influence on German Drama." *Theoria* (a journal of studies of the Arts faculty, Univ. of Natal), 1950. Pp. 14.

A9474 Goerres, Karlheinz. *Hamlet im Spiegel der Deutschen Dichtung und Literatur, Insbesondere der Romantik*. DD, Freiburg, 1951. Pp. 269. Typewritten.

A9475 Lüthi, Hans Jürg. *Das Deutsche Hamletbild seit Goethe*. Sprache und Dichtung, LXXIV. Bern: Verlag Paul Haupt, 1951. Pp. 192.
Rev: by G. Bianquis, *Erasmus*, V (1952), 179-180; by H. Heuer, *SJ*, 87/88 (1952), 260-261; by H. Reitz, *Welt und Wort*, VII, 28; by G. Blakemore Evans, *JEGP*, LII (1953), 265-266; by T. O. Brandt, *Monatshefte*, XLV, 155-157.

A9476 Sternfeld, Frederick W. "The Musical and Rhythmical Sources of Poetry." *EIE*, 1951, pp. 126-145.

A9477 Diederichsen, Diedrich. *Shakespeare und das Deutsche Märchendrama*. DD, Hamburg, 1952. Pp. 332. Typewritten.

A9478 Glaser, Hermann. *Hamlet in der Deutschen Literatur*. DD, Erlangen, 1952. Pp. v, 189. Typewritten.

A9479 Gregor, Joseph. "Was Ist Uns Hamlet?" *SJ*, 87/88 (1952), 9-25.

A9480 Rodger, G. B. B. *The Presentation of the Artist-Hero in Nineteenth Century German Drama*. DD, Glasgow, 1952.

A9481 Staiger, Emil. "Shakespeare in Deutschland." *Hesperia* (Zurich), III (Oct., 1952), 183-190.

A9482 Drews, Wolfgang. *Die Grossen Zauberer*. Vienna, Munich, 1953. Pp. 362.
Rev: B1281.

A9483 Price, Lawrence Marsden. *English Literature in Germany*. Univ. of California Publications in Modern Philology, XXXVII. Berkeley: Univ. of California Press, 1953. Pp. viii, 548.
Rev: by G. Waterhouse, *CL*, VI (1954), 82-84; by A. Gillies, *GQ*, XXVII, 69-71; by Th. C. van Stockrun, *ES*, XXXV, 132-134; by R. L. Wilkie, *MLQ*, XV, 86-87; by H. A. Pochmann, *Monatshefte*, XLVI, 236-237; by H. Sparnaay, *Neophil*, XXXVIII, 235-236; by C. B. Woods, *PQ*, XXXIII, 309-310; by H. Heuer, *Archiv*, 192 (1955), 73-74; by L. L. Schücking, *GRM*, XXXVI, 179-182; by W. Paulsen, *JEGP*, LIV, 140-141; by H. Schneider, *MLN*, LXX, 144-147; by K. W. Maurer, *MLR*, L, 76.

A9484 Schmitt, Saladin. *Shakespeare, Drama und Bühne*. Beiträge z. Duisburger Theatergeschichte, 1. Duisburg, 1953. Pp. 33.

A9485 Schwamborn, Heinrich. "Die Shakespeare-Lektüre. Ihre Bedeutung und ihre Möglichkeiten." *NS*, II (1953), 494-501.

A9486 Fehrle-Burger, L. "Der Geist Shakespeares in der Kurpfälzischen Theatertradition." *Baden* (Karlsruhe), VI (1954), Heft 2, pp. 15-19.

A9487 Oppel, Horst. "Der Einfluss der Englischen Literatur auf die Deutsche." *Deutsche Philologie im Aufriss*. Ed. Wolfgang Stammler. Bd. III. Berlin: Schmidt, 1954, pp. 47-144.
Rev: by W. F. Schirmer, *Anglia*, LXXII (1954), 510-511; by J. T. Krumpelmann, *Archiv*, 192 (1955), 73; by L. Polak, *ES*, XXXVI, 129-131; by A. Gillies, *MLR*, L (1955), 354-355; by L. M. Price, *NS*, IV, 189-190; by M. Lehnert, *ZAA*, III, 92-96; by L. Borinski, *Euphorion*, XLIX, 379-380; by G. Rodger, *RES*, VI, 438.

A9488 Scott, A. P. *The Evaluation of Shakespeare in Germany from Johann Elias Schlegel to the Schlegel Brothers*. B. Litt thesis, Oxford, 1955.

A9489 "Library Notes." *Newberry Library Bulletin*, III (1955), 254-255.

A9490 Dietrich, Gerhard. "Zur Geschichte der Englischen Philologie an der Martin-Luther-Universität Halle-Wittenberg." *Wiss. Zs. d. Martin-Luther-Univ. Halle-Wittenberg. Gesellsch. u. Sprachwiss. Reihe.*, V (1955/56), 1041-56.

A9491 Klingemann, Robert. "Wie Steht die Heutige Jugend zu Shakespeare?" *Prisma* (Bochum), 1955/56, pp. 117-120.

A9492 Leuca, George. "Wieland and the Introduction of Shakespeare into Germany." *GQ*, XXVIII (1955), 247-255.

A9493 Worsley, Thomas Cuthbert. "A German Troilus." *NstN*, L (1955), 572-573.

A9494 England, Martha Winburn. "Garrick's Stratford Jubilee: Reactions in France and Germany." *ShS*, IX (1956), 90-100.

A9495 Orsini, Napoleone. "Critica e Filologia Shakespeariana nell'Epoca Romantica." *Rivista di Letterature Mod. e Comp.*, IX (1956), 5-16.

A9496 Schaller, Rudolf. "Shakespeare für die Deutsche Bühne." *Neue dt. Literatur* (Berlin), IV, No. 6 (1956), 120-127.

A9497 Steiner, Rudolf. *Drama und Dichtung im Bewusstseins-Umschwung der Neuzeit.* Dornach: Rudolf Steiner Nachlassverwaltung, 1956.
Essay I, "Shak., Goethe, und Schiller," pp. 9-24.

A9498 Zacharias, Gerhard P. "Macbeth in Uns." *Das neue Forum* (Darmstadt), V (1955/56), 113-114.

A9499 Kraft, Werner. "Das Opfer: Gedanken über Shakespeare." *Eckart*, XXVI (1957), 295-303.

A9500 Linder, Hans R. "Shakespeare als Test. Notizen zum Heutigen Theater." *SJ*, 93 (1957), 89-97.

A9501 McNamee, Lawrence Francis. *"Julius Caesar" on the German Stage in the Nineteenth Century.* DD, University of Pittsburgh, 1957. Pp. 324. Mic 57-1716. *DA*, XVII (1957), 1074. Publ. No. 21,009.

A9502 Brett-Evans, D. *"Der Sommernachtstraum* in Deutschland 1600-1650." *ZDP*, LXXVII (1958), 371-383.

ii. 1933-1945
See also various items in Political Thought, A1775-A1886, and Rothe, B334-B343.

A9503 Gerlach, Kurt. *Drama und Nation. Beitrag zur Wegbereitung des Nationalsozialistischen Dramas.* Breslau: F. Hirt, 1934. Pp. 87.

A9504 Deubel, Werner. *Der Deutsche Weg zur Tragödie.* Dresden: Jess, 1935. Pp. 80.
Rev: by Mart. Kiessig, *DNL*, XXXVII (1936), 44.

A9505 Meyer-Erlach, Wolf. *Shakespeare. Die Verkörperung Nordischer Schöpferkraft.* Munich: J. F. Lehmans, 1935. Pp. 65.

A9506 Steffen, Albert. *Dramaturgische Beiträge zu den Schönen Wissenschaften.* Dornach: Verlag der Schönen Wissenschaften, 1935.
Shak., pp. 70-78.

A9507 "Shakespeare und das Deutsche Volkstheater." *Thüringer Gauztg.*, 1936, No. 96, and *LNN*, 1936, No. 117, p. 50.
On A9511.

A9508 "Shakespeare under Hitler." *Living Age*, 350 (1936), 166.

A9509 "Shakespeare, William, der Dramatiker der Politischen Totalität." *Bücherkunde der Reichsstelle zur Förderung des Deutschen Schrifttums*, III (1936), 125-126.

A9510 Braumüller, W. "William Shakespeare. Der Dramatiker der Politischen Totalität." *Berliner Börsenztg.*, No. 95 (1936).

A9510a Harlander, Otto. "Französisch und Englisch im Dienste der Rassen-politischen Erziehung." *NS*, XLIV (1936), 45-67.

A9511 Kindermann, Heinz. *Shakespeare und das Deutsche Volkstheater.* *SJ*, LXXII (1936), 9-41.

A9512 Klitscher, H. "Des Menschen Wille und sein Schicksal. Ein Beitrag zu der Frage: Was Bedeutet Shakespeare für die Deutsche Jugend?" *Englische Kultur in Sprachwissenschaftlicher Deutung. Festschrift für Max Deutschbein.* Leipzig: Quelle & Meyer, 1936, pp. 85-100.

A9513 Reich, B. "Fascist Interpretation of Shakespeare." Tr. S. D. Kogan. *International Literature*, 1936, pp. 90-99.

A9514 Schulz, B. "Der Shakespeare d. 20. Jahrhunderts." *ZDB*, May 1936.

A9515 Tannenbaum, Samuel A. "All to the Rescue." *SAB*, XI (1936), 186-187.

A9516 Trotha, Th. von. "William Shakespeare zu seinem 320. Todestag." *VB* (B), No. 114 (1936), 5.

A9517 Wanderscheck, Hermann. "Shakespeare und die Junge Generation." *Ostdts. Monatshefte*, XVII (1936/37), 125-126.

A9518 "Shakespeares Zweite Heimat: Göttingen. Zum 200. Jährigen Jubiläum." *Die Woche*, No. 24 (1937).

A9519 Baser, Friedrich. "Heidelberger Shakespeare-Erinnerungen. Zur Eröffnung der Reichsfestspiele am 20. Juli." *VB*, July 20, 1937.

A9520 K., G. "Die Völkische Sendung Shakespeares." *VB*, April 26, 1937.

A9521 Lemme, H. "Shakespeares Frauen und Mädchen in Lebenskundlicher Betrachtung." *Nationalsozialist Monatshefte*, VIII (1937), 548-550.

A9522 Plessow, G. *Um Shakespeares Nordentum.* Aachen: Mayersche Buchhandlung, 1937. Pp. 43.
Rev: by Hm., *Archiv.*, 174 (1938), 260-261; by P. M., *GRM*, XXVI, 324; by Hermann Heuer, *Beiblatt*, LI (1939), 85-87; by E. Weigelin, *DDHS*, VI, 37; by W. Keller, *SJ*, LXXV, Heft 1, 151-152.

A9523 Urbach, O. "Shakespeare und die Deutsche Jugend." *Berl. Börsenztg.*, No. 413 (1937).

A9524   Voss, K. "Shakespeare und der Deutsche Geist." *Hannoverscher Kurier*, Nos. 269, 270 (1937).

A9525   Wieber, H. "Shakespeare der Jugend." *Germania* (Berlin), March 20, 1937.

A9526   "Die Brücke." *DL*, XLI (1938/39), 65-66.

A9527   Eckloff, L. "Heroismus und Politisches Führertum bei Shakespeare." *ZNU*, XXXVII (1938), 97-112.

A9528   Keller, Wolfgang. "Shakespeare und die Deutsche Jugend." *NS*, XLV (1938), 259-278.

A9529   Kindermann, Heinz. "Begegnungen des Deutschen und Englischen Geisteslebens." *Wille und Macht*, VI (1938), Heft 6, 34-38.

A9530   Kroepelin, H. "Shakespeare-Fragen heute und Morgen." *Rhein.-Westfäl. Ztg.* (Essen), Oct. 22, 1938.

A9531   Kroepelin, Hermann. "Die Shakespeare-Texte." *Berliner Tagblatt*, No. 298 (1938).

A9532   Kroepelin, H. "Shakespeare und der Deutsche Leser." *Deutsche Allgemeine Zeitung*, No. 229 (May 14, 1939).

A9533   Pick, F. W. "Shakespeare and the German Stage." *AglGR*, II (1938), 34-35.

A9534   Schröter, Werner. "Grundsätzliches zur Deutung von Meisterwerken Fremdsprachlicher Literatur." *DNS*, XLVI (1938), 199-207.

A9535   Wagner, Joseph. "Was ist uns Shakespeare?" *SJ*, LXXIV (1938), 13-19.

A9536   Wirtz, René. "Das Werk Shakespeares im dts. Geistesleben." *Blätter des Hessischen Landestheaters*, 1938/39, Heft 4.

A9537   Woesler, R. "Das Germanische Menschenbild Shakespeares." *Kölnische Volksztg.*, Sept. 18, 1938.

A9538   "Shakespeare sur les Scènes de Berlin." *Dts.-Französische Monatshefte*, VI (1939), 418.

A9539   Shakespeare, William. "Von der Ordnung der Welt." [Excerpts] Ausgewählt von Herm. Christian Mettin. Deutsche Reihe 87. Jena: Diederichs, 1939. Pp. 63.

A9540   "Hamlet im Wandel der Zeit. Zur Heutigen Erstaufführung von Hamlet auf der Freilichtbühne Augsburg." *Neue Augsburger Ztg.*, No. 170, July 25, 1939.

A9541   "Wie sieht Unsere Zeit Shakespeare?" *Freiheitskampf* (Dresden), April 23, 1939.

A9542   Dietz, Heinrich. "Nordischer Mythus in der Englischen Literatur." *N. Mon.*, X (1939), 305-319.

A9543   Goetz, Wolfgang. "Salut für Shakespeare zum 375. Geburtstag." *Berliner Lokal-Anzeiger*, No. 97 (1939).

A9544   Huch, Rud. "*Hamlet* und Wir." *MDG*, XLI (1939), 100-103.

A9545   Knudsen, Hans. "Shakespeare auf der Deutschen Bühne." *GA*, May 5, 1939, pp. 9-10.

A9546   Koch. "Shakespeare und wir Deutschen." *Dts. Pfarrerblatt* (Essen), XLIII (1939), 469f.

A9547   Kosch, Wilhelm. *Das dts. Theater und Drama im 19. und 20. Jahrhundert.* Würzburg: Wächter-Vlg., 1939. Pp. 165.

A9547a Krieger, H. *England und der Judenfrage.* Frankfurt, 1939. Pp. 116.

A9548   Krug, Werner G. "Schacher um Shakespeare?" *Berliner Lokal-Anzeiger*, No. 188 (1939).

A9549   Schmidt, W. "Shakespeare im Leben und in der Wissenschaft des Neuen Deutschlands." *ZNU*, XXXVIII (1939), 174-177.

A9549a Schrey, Kurt. "Nationalpolitische Erziehung als Ziel der Gedichtbehandlung im Engl. Unterricht." *ZNU*, XXXVIII (1939), 201-208. Shak. p. 204.

A9550   Schümmer, K. "Shakespeare: Nordischer Mythus und Christliche Metaphysik." *Hochland*, XXXVI (1939), 191-205.

A9551   Vorwahl, H. "Shakespeares Weltanschauung: Nordisch oder Christlich?" *Protestantenblatt*, LXXII (1939), 418.

A9552   Wittko, Paul. "Shakespeare in Deutschland. Zu seinem 375. Geburtstag." *Königsberger Tageblatt*, No. 112, 1939.

A9553   Zickel-von Jan, R. "William Shakespeare und Wir." *Danziger Neueste Nachrichten*, March 18, 19, 1939.

A9554   Zickel-von Jan, R. "Shakespeare und Wir." *Schlesische Ztg.*, April 22, 1939 and *Der Dts. Schriftsteller*, IV (1939), 78.

A9555   "Shakespeare 1940." *Wille und Macht* (Berlin), VIII (1940), Heft 3, p. 1.

A9556   "Whose is Shakespeare?" *TLS*, May 4, 1940, p. 219.

A9557   St-g. "Franzosenfreundlich und Staatsgefährlich. Shakespeare auf den Englischen Bühnen Verboten." *VB(Mü)*, No. 322, Nov. 17, 1940.

A9558   Bethge, Friedrich. "Das Drama der Zukunft." *MNN*, No. 354 (Dec. 19, 1940).

A9559   Burte, H. "Der Englische und der Deutsche Tag." *Wille und Macht* (Berlin), VIII (1940), Heft. 3, 3-9.

A9560   Dichter. "Deutsche, über Shakespeare." *Wille und Macht* (Berlin), VIII (1940), No. 3, 9-14.

A9561   Dringenberg, Willibert. "Shakespeare contra Chamberlain." *VB*(Mü), No. 114, April 4, 1940.

A9562   Eckhardt, Eduard. *Shakespeares Anschauungen über Religion und Sittlichkeit, Staat und Volk.* Weimar: Böhlaus Nachfolger, 1940. Pp. 156.
Anhang: "Shakespeares Stellung zum Judentum," pp. 79-83.
Rev: A1485.

A9563   Eckhardt, F. O. "Sollen wir Shakespeare Feiern?" *Neues Wiener Tagblatt*, April 26, 1940.

A9564   Franke, Hans. "Die Tragödie aus dem Willen des Geistes. Zu Langenbecks Schrift, 'Wiedergeburt des Dramas'." *Weltlit.*, 1940, Heft 9.

A9565   Franke, Hans. "Die Wiedergeburt des Dramas aus dem Geist der Zeit. (Eine Erörterung an Hand der Ideen von C. Langenbeck und E. Bacmeister)." *Geist der Zeit*, XVIII (1940), 504-507.

A9566   Frenzel, Herbert A. "Ist Shakespeare ein Problem?" *Wille und Macht* (Berlin), VIII (1940), Heft 3, 2-3.

A9567   Gerlach, K. "Das dts. Drama zwischen Antike und Shakespeare." *Der Türmer*, XLIII (1940/41), No. 1, 1-6.

A9568   Keller, W. "Deutschlands Arbeit an Shakespeare." *DWD*, XXI (1940), 4-5.

A9569   Kölli, Josef Georg. "Die Notwendige Wiedergeburt der Tragödie." *MDG*, II (1940), 280-282. On Langenbeck's *Wiedergeburt des Dramas*.

A9570   Langenbeck, Curt. "Wiedergeburt des Dramas aus dem Geist der Zeit." *Das Innere Reich*, VI (1939/40), 923-957.

A9570a Langenbeck, Curt. *Wiedergeburt des Dramas aus dem Geist der Zeit.* Munich: Langen and Müller, 1940. Pp. 54.
Rev: by Hans Knudsen, *DNL*, XLI (1940), 215-216; by Heinz Hügel, *Eckart* (Monatsschrift), XVI, 178; by R. Fink, *ZDG*, III (1940/41), 149; by A. von Blumenthal, *Beiblatt*, LII (1941), 56-58; by Teesing, *De Weegschaal*, VII (1941?), Heft 9; by Emil Kast, *Lbl*, LXIII (1942), 140.

A9571   Langenbeck, Curt. "Christentum und Tragödie. Eine Antwort." *MNN*, No. 55/56, Feb. 24/25, 1940.

A9572   Langenbeck, Curt. "Shakespeare ein Problem für Unsere Zeit." *MNN*, No. 62/63, March 2/3, 1940.

A9573   Wehner, Jos. Magn. "Der Dichter und der Hades. Zu Curt Langenbecks Rede über die Wiedergeburt des Dramas." *MNN*, No. 47, Feb. 16, 1940.

A9574   Wehner, Jos. Magn. "Curt Langenbeck und Shakespeare. Bekenntnis gegen Bekenntnis." *MNN*, No. 49, Feb. 18, 1940.

A9575   Wehner, Jos. Magn. "Die Wiedergeburt des Dramas. Der Weg zur Weltgültigen dts. Form." *MNN*, No. 52, Feb. 21, 1940.

A9576   Wehner, Jos. Magn. "Der Streit um den Hades. Schlusswort zu einer Zeitgemässen Auseinandersetzung." *MNN*, No. 66, March 6, 1940.

A9577   Wehner, Jos. Magn. "Götter, Sowohl-als-auch-Leute und Shakespeare; Schicksal u. Religion —Der Gott der Tragödie—Versöhnung der Gegensätze." *MNN*, No. 69/70, March 9/10, 1940.

A9578   Cancelled.

A9579   Saekel, Herbert. "Tragisches Lebensgefühl. Um das Drama der Zukunft." *DL*, XLII (1939/40), 360-363.

A9580   Platz, H. "H. S. Chamberlain, Bayreuth u. Shakespeare." *N. Mon.*, XI (1940), 210-224.

A9581   Sauter, H. "William Shakespeare Heute?" *Der Buchhändler im Neuen Reich*, V (1940), 53-56.

A9582   Siemonsen, Hans. *Die dts. Dichtung im Unterricht.* Vol. 2: *Die Dramatische Dichtung.* Leipzig: Brandstetter, 1940. Pp. 335.
Shak. chapter.

A9583   Bacmeister, Ernst. *Der dts. Typus der Tragödie. Dramaturgisches Fundament.* Berlin: Langen/ Müller, 1941. Pp. 122.
Rev: by Joachim Müller, *ZDWDU*, 1943, pp. 185-186.

A9584   Bethge, Friedrich. Das Deutsche Theater—Eine Quelle für Kraft durch Freude [Shak. passim]. *DNL*, XLII (1941), 281-283.

A9585   Frenzel, E. "Shakespeare in Deutschen Zahlen." *Wille und Macht* (Berlin), VIII (1940), Heft 3, 22-23.

A9586   Kindermann, Heinz. *Kampf um die dts. Lebensform. Reden u. Aufsätze über die Dichtung im Aufbau der Nation.* Vienna: Wiener Vlg.-Ges., 1941. Pp. 461.
Shak. passim.

A9587   Resch, Hans. "Zum Kampf um die neue Tragödie." *Zs. f. dts. Kulturphilosophie*, VII (1941), 63-73.
On A9570a.

A9588   Rostosky, Friedrich. "Eine neue Tragödie." *MDG*, XLIII (1941), 390-392.
On A9570a.

A9589 Schulz, Helmut. "Warum Spielen wir Shakespeare?" *Die Bühne*, VII (1941), 102-104.

A9590 Schulze-Maizier, Friedr. "Deutschland und Shakespeare." *Wir und die Welt*, III (1941), 48-53.

A9591 Busch, Ernst. *Die Idee des Tragischen in der dts. Klassik*. Halle: Niemeyer, 1942. Pp. 165.
       Rev: by H. Oehler, *DLZ*, LXIV (1943), 382-390.

A9592 Keller, Wolfgang. "Shakespeares Eindringen in Frankreich und die dts. Shakespeare-Begeisterung." *EWD*, II (1942), Heft 9, 2-3.

A9593 Niederstenbruch, Alex. "Einige Gedanken zur Rassischen Betrachtung von Shakespeares *Hamlet*." *ZNU*, XLI (1942), 31-33.

A9594 Buchheld, Kurt. "Die Fortsetzung der Tragödie. Eine neue Sicht aus der Wandlung des Schicksals in Unserer Zeit." *DW*, XVIII (1943), 38-43.

A9595 Gregor, Joseph. *Das Theater des Volkes in der Ostmark*. Vienna: Dts. Vlg. für Jugend u. Volk, 1943. Pp. 287.

A9596 Kindermann, Heinz. *Theater und Nation*. Reclams Universalbibliothek. No. 7563. Leipzig: Reclams, 1943. Pp. 64.

A9597 Kindermann, Heinz. "Die Europäische Sendung des Deutschen Theaters." *EL*, III (1944), Heft 3, 2-6.

(b) SHAKESPEARE'S SIGNIFICANCE FOR VARIOUS GERMAN AUTHORS (153; 50)
i. Several Authors

A9598 Jacob, Georg. *Shakespeares Naturverbundenheit im Vergleich mit Schillers und Goethes Verhältnis zur Natur*. Hamburg and Glückstadt: Augustin, 1937. Pp. 35.
       Rev: A2170.

A9599 Borden, C. "J. E. Schlegel als Vorläufer Lessings." DD, University of California, 1937.

A9600 Gjødesen, Rigmor. "Forholdet Kleist, Goethe, Shakespeare." *Edda* (Oslo), L (1950), 1-38.

A9601 Price, Lawrence Marsden. "Herder and Gerstenberg or Akenside." *MLN*, LXV (1950), 175-178.

A9602 *Meisterwerke Deutscher Literaturkritik*. Ed. by Hans Mayer. Vol. 1. *Aufklärung, Klassik, Romantik*. Berlin: Ruetten & Loening, 1954. Pp. 966.
       Partial contents: Johann Elias Schlegel: "Vergleichung Shakespeares u. Andreas Gryphs," pp. 63-98; Ulrich Bräker: "Etwas über W. Shakespeares Schauspiele," pp. 359-370; Johann Wolfgang Goethe: "Zum Shakespeares Tag," pp. 371-375, "Shakespeare und kein Ende," pp. 408-422.

A9603 Fechter, Paul. *Das Europäische Drama. Geist und Kultur im Spiegel des Theaters*. Vol. 1. *Vom Barock zum Naturalismus*. Mannheim: Bibliogr. Inst., 1956. Pp. 511.
       Chap. VI, "Die Entdeckung Shakespeares," pp. 90-97. Discusses German translations. Also Wieland, Schlegel, and Herder.

A9604 Lehmann, Jakob, and Hermann Glaser. *Shakespeares "Hamlet." Ein Arbeitsheft zur Lektüre*. Bamberg, Wiesbaden: Bayer. Verl.-Anst., 1956. Pp. 51.
       A general discussion of the play followed by excerpts from famous German critics—Goethe, Schlegel Grillparzer, Tieck, Heine, Nietzsche, Jaspers, etc.

A9605 Wiese, Benno von. *Deutsche Dramaturgie vom Barock bis zur Klassik*. Tübingen: Niemeyer, 1956. Pp. vii, 144. Herder & Goethe.

A9606 Purdie, Edna. "Hamann, Herder and *Hamlet*: Shakespeare's Penetration into Germany." *German Life and Letters*, April 1957, pp. 198-209.

ii. Blankenburg

A9607 Beasley, Shubael T. *Christian Friedrich von Blankenburg's (1744-1796) Relation to the English Language and Literature*. DD, Cornell University, 1949.

A9608 Schioler, Margarethe C. "Blankenburg's Advocacy of Shakespeare." *Monatshefte*, XLII (1950), 161-165.

iii. Brecht

A9609 Brecht, Bertolt. "On Shakespeare's Play *Hamlet*." *Adam and Encore*, No. 254 (1956), p. 9.
       Poem.

A9610 Brecht, Bertolt. *Hamlet*. Tr. by Helmut W. Bonheim. *CE*, XIX (1957), 82.
       Poem.

A9611 Zéraffa, Michel. "Shakespeare, Brecht und die Gesichte." *Geist und Zeit*, IV (1957), 37-38.

iv. George

A9612 Farrell, Ralph. *Stefan Georges Beziehungen zur Englischen Dichtung*. DD, Berlin, 1937. Berlin: Ebering, 1937. Pp. 239.
       Rev: by Henri Tronchon, *RG*, XXX (1939), 297-299.

A9613 Hoffmann, Friedrich. "Stefan Georges Übertragung der Shakespeare-Sonette." *SJ*, 92 (1956), 146-156.

v. Goethe

A9614 Petsch, Robert. "Die Grundlagen der Dramatischen Dichtung Goethes." *DVLG*, xv (1937) 362-384.

A9615 Sengle, Friedrich. "Goethe und das Drama." *ZDK*, LI (1937), 593-605.

A9616 Sengle, Friedrich. *Goethes Verhältnis zum Drama. Die Theoretischen Bemerkungen im zusammenhang mit seinem Dramatischen Schaffen.* Neue Deutsche Forschungen, 116. Abt. Neuere dts. Literaturgesch. Bd. 9. Berlin: Junker and Dünnhaupt, 1937. Pp. 131.
　　Rev: by F. Stuckert, *ADA*, LVI (1937), 48-52; by G. Fricke, *ZDK*, LI, 588-589.

A9617 Friese, H. "Zu Goethes Hamletklärung." *ZNU*, XXXVII (1938), 173-179.

A9618 *Goethes Rede zum Shåkespears Tag. Wiedergabe der Handschrift. Mit einem Geleitwort von Ernst Beutler.* Schriften der Goethe-Gesellschaft, Bd. 50. Weimar: Goethe-Gesellschaft; Leipzig: Haag-Drugulin, 1938. Pp. 18, fasc. 4.
　　Rev: by Wolfgang Keller, *SJ*, LXXV (1939), 163-164; by W. A. Reichart, *Books Abroad*, XIII, 478; by L. M. Price, *GR*, xv (1940), 64-65; by Berta Siebeck, *Lbl*, LXII (1941), 307-308.

A9619 Roos, Carl. "Goethe og Shakespeare." *Tilskueren* (Copenhagen), I (1939), 97-108.

A9620 Zucker, A. E. "The Courtiers in *Hamlet* and *The Wild Duck.*" *MLN*, LIV (1939), 196-198. Shak., Goethe, Ibsen.

A9621 Schöffler, Herbert. "Shakespeare und der Junge Goethe." *SJ*, LXXVI (1940), 11-33. Reprinted in *Deutscher Geist im 18. Jahrhundert.* Göttingen: Vandenhoeck and Ruprecht, 1956, pp. 97-113.

A9622 Barthel, Ernst. *Goethe, das Sinnbild dts. Kultur.* 2nd ed. Kolmar (Alsace): Alsatia Verlag, 1941. Pp. 364. First ed., 1929.

A9623 Kindermann, Heinz. *Kampf um die dts. Lebensform. Reden und Aufsätze über die Dichtung im Aufbau der Nation.* Vienna: Wiener Vlg.-Ges., 1941. Pp. 461. "Persönlichkeit und Gemeinschaft in Goethes Dichterischem Werk," pp. 87-127.

A9624 Verschaeve, C. *Goethe en Shakespeare.* Brugge: Zeemeeuw, 1941. Pp. 55.

A9625 *Herder-Goethe. Von Deutscher Art und Kunst. Einige Fliegende Blätter.* Nebst Goethes Aufsatz Zum S.-Tag. Hrsg. mit einem Nachwort von Heinz Kindermann. Leipzig: Reclam, 1942. Pp. 165.
　　Rev: by J. G. Sprengel, *DDHS*, x (1943), 95-96.

A9626 Spring, P. "Shakespeare and Goethe." *The Spirit of Literature* (Winter Park, Florida), 1945, pp. 96-118.

A9627 Kane, Robert J. "Tolstoy, Goethe, and *King Lear.*" *SAB*, XXI (1946), 159-160.

A9628 Kudo, Yoshimi. "Goethe and Shakespeare." *Ningen* (Japan), No. 7 (1947).

A9629 Lambda, Beta. "Hamlet Miscellany." *Shakespeare Quarterly* (London), I (Summer, 1947), 50-75.
　　Goethe as producer of *Hamlet* and his conception of Hamlet's character.

A9630 Kruhm, August. "Goethe und Shakespeares Hamlet." *Dramaturg. Blätter*, June 2, 1948, pp. 263-266.

A9631 Schirmer, Walter Franz. "Shakespeare und der Junge Goethe." *Publications of the Engl. Goethe Society*, NS, XVIII (1948), 26-42.

A9632 Kamps, H. "Englisches Leben und Englische Literatur in Goethes Urteil." *Neuphilol. Zs.*, I (1949), Heft 5, 25-37.

A9633 Oppel, Horst. *Das Shakespeare-Bild Goethes.* Mainz: Kirchheim, 1949. Pp. 118.
　　Rev: by H. Heuer, *SJ*, 87/88 (1952), 257-258; by L. Leibrich, *Etude Germaniques*, VII, 207; by Werner P. Friederich, *CL*, VII (1955), 93-94.

A9634 Schröder, Rudolf A. *Goethe und Shakespeare.* Shakespeare-Schriften No. 4. Bochum: Schürmann und Klagges, 1949. Pp. 28. Also in *SJ*, 84/86 (1950), 17-39 and Schröder's *Gesammelte Werke*, Berlin, 1952, pp. 420-451. See *MDtShG*, II (1950), 8.

A9635 Vermeil, Edmond. "Goethe and the West." Tr. by W. E. Delp. *MLR*, XLIV (1949), 504-513.

A9636 Wolff, Emil. "Goethe und Shakespeare. Zwei Formen der Universität." *Zeit*, IV (1949), No. 34, 4.
　　Comment by Paul Gerhard Manzke, *Neuphilologische Zeitschrift*, I (1949), 75-77.

A9637 Link, Franz Heinrich. *Die Begriffe des "Poet" und des "Writer" in ihrer Stellung im Ganzen der Lebensauffassung Ralph Waldo Emersons auf Grund einer Interpretation der Essays "Shakespeare or the Poet" und "Goethe or the Writer."* DD, Frankfurt, 1950. Pp. 168. Typewritten.

A9638 Price, Lawrence M. "Shakespeare as Pictured by Voltaire, Goethe, and Oeser." *GR*, XXV (1950), 83-84.

A9639 Abend, Murray. "A Shakespearean Image in *Faust* II." *N &Q*, 196 (1951), 249-250.

A9640 Jantz, Harold. "Goethe and an Elizabethan Poem." *MLQ*, XII (1951), 451-461.

A9641 Kaufmann, Walter. "Goethe Versus Shakespeare: Some Changes in Dramatic Sensibility." *Partisan Rev*, XIX (1952), 621-634.

A9642 Cancelled.

A9643   Willoughby, L. A. "Goethe Looks at the English." *MLR*, L (1955), 464-484.
A9644   Blummenthal, Marie Luise. "Zur Erinnerung an Goethes Enkelkinder." *Sammlung*, XI (1956), 234-242.
A9645   Tykesson, Elisabeth. "Shakespeare-analysen i Goethes *Wilhelm Meister*." *En Goethebok till Algot Werin*. Lund, 1958, pp. 59-75.

vi. Grabbe

A9646   Bergmann, A. "Einleitung in die 'Shakespearo-Manie'." C. D. Grabbes. *Jb. d. Grabbe-Ges.*, I (1939), 25-29.
A9646a Grabbe, Christian Dietrich. "Über die Shakspearo-Manie." *Jahrbuch der Grabbe-Ges.*, I (1939).
A9647   Busch, Ernst. "Geschichte und Tragik in Grabbes Drama." *DuV*, XLI (1941), 440-459.
A9648   Martini, Fritz. "Chr. D. Grabbes Niederdeutsches Drama. I." *GRM*, XXX (1942), 87-106.
A9649   Hering, Gerhard F. "Grabbe und Shakespeare." *SJ*, LXXVII (1941), 93-115.

vii. Grillparzer

A9650   Grillparzer, Franz. *Sämtliche Werke*. I. Abt. Bd. 8/9: Dramat. Pläne und Bruchstücke seit 1816. Vienna: Schroll, 1936.
        Contains his tr. from *Shrew*, pp. 22-25.
A9651   Salinger, H. "Shakespeare's Tyranny over Grillparzer." *Monatshefte* (Madison), XXXI (1939), 222-229.
A9652   Görlich. "Grillparzer und Shakespeare. Versuch einer Deutung." *SJ*, LXXVIII/LXXIX (1943), 73-80.
A9653   Mühlberger, Margarethe. *Shakespeare und Grillparzer. Mit Besonderer Berücksichtigung ihrer Frauengestalten*. DD, Vienna, 1945.
A9654   Rosenmayr, Maria. *Könige bei Grillparzer und Shakespeare*. DD, Vienna, 1946.

viii. Gryphius

A9655   Keppler, Ernst. *Gryphius und Shakespeare*. DD, Tübingen, 1921. Pp. 123. Typewritten.
A9656   Kappler, Helmut. *Der Barocke Geschichtsbegriff bei Andreas Gryphius*. Frankfurt a. M.: Diesterweg, 1936. Pp. 76.
A9657   Wentzlaff-Eggebert, F. W. *Dichtung und Sprache des Jungen Gryphius*. Berlin: de Gruyter, 1936. Pp. 121.
A9658   Brett-Evans, D. *Andreas Gryphius and the Elizabethan Drama*. MA thesis, Wales, 1951.

ix. Hauptmann

A9659   Hauptmann, Gerhart. *Hamlet in Wittenberg*. Schauspiel. Berlin: Fischer, 1935. Pp. 189.
        Rev: by Marian P. Whitney, *Books Abroad*, X (1936), 421-422; *DL*, XXXVIII (1935/36), 153-154; *RG*, XXVII (1936), 277-278.
A9659a Trask, C. "Berlin Sees Hauptmann's *Hamlet in Wittenberg*." *New York Times*, Nov. 15, 1936, p. 2x.
A9659b Hering, Gerhard F. "Gerhard Hauptmanns Jüngstes Schauspiel *Hamlet in Wittenberg*." *Westermanns Monatshefte*, 159 (1935/36), 587-588.
A9659c Stirk, S. D. "A Note on Gerhart Hauptmann's *Hamlet in Wittenberg*." *MLR*, XXXII (1937), 595-597.
        Influence of Gutzkow's play of the same title.
A9659d Prahl, A. J. "Bemerkungen zu Gerhart Hauptmanns *Hamlet in Wittenberg*." *Monatshefte* (Madison), XXIX (1937), 153-157.
A9660   Hauptmann, Gerhart. *Im Wirbel der Berufung*. Berlin: Fischer, 1936. Pp. 281.
        Rev: by Hermann Barnstorff, *Books Abroad*, X (1936), 422; by A. Brandl, *Archiv*, 170 (1936), 278-279.
A9661   "G. Hauptmann and the Hamlet theme." *TLS*, Aug. 15, 1936, p. 660.
A9662   Gillet, Louis. "Un *Hamlet* de Gerhard Hauptmann," *RddxM*, Pér. VIII, t. 32 (1936), 207-220.
A9663   Stirk, S. D. "G. Hauptmann and *Hamlet*." *German Life and Letters*, I (1937), Heft 3.
A9664   Voigt, Felix A. "Gerhart Hauptmann und England: die Bedeutung Shakespeares für sein Schaffen." *GRM*, XXV (1937), 321-329.
A9665   Wahr, F. B. *The Hauptmann "Hamlet."* *PQ*, XVI (1937), 124-138.
A9666   Busse, A. "The Case of Hauptmann's *Hamlet*." *Monatshefte*, XXX (1938), 162-170.
A9667   Voigt, F. A., and W. A. Reichart. *Hauptmann und Shakespeare, mit einem Aufsatz und Dramatischen Szenen von G. Hauptmann*. Breslau: Maruschke and Berendt, 1938. Pp. viii, 154.
        Rev: by A. Brandl, *Archiv*, 174 (1938), 210-211; by Hermann Barnstorff, *Monatshefte*, XXX, 464-465.
A9668   Ruppel, K. H. "Die neue Theaterspielzeit in Berlin." *DL*, XLI (1938/39), 170.
A9669   Voigt, Felix A. "Gerhart Hauptmann und Shakespeare." *SJ*, LXXVIII/LXXIX (1943), 6-28.
A9670   Voigt, F. A., and W. A. Reichart. *Hauptmann und Shakespeare, mit einem Aufsatz und Drama-*

tischen Szenen von G. Hauptmann. Breslau, 1938. Second ed., *Hauptmann und Shakespeare: Ein Beitrag zur Geschichte des Fortlebens Shakespeares in Deutschland.* Goslar: Deutsche Volksbücherei, 1947. Pp. 153.

Rev: by C. F. W. Behl, *DL*, XLI (1938/39), 375-376; by H. Steinhauer, *MLN*, LIV (1939), 545-546; by Walther Preusler, *Beiblatt*, L, 119-21; by Winifred Smith, *Books Abroad*, XIII, 356; by F. Piquet, *RG*, XXX, 273-275; by H. H. Borcherdt, *DLZ*, LXI (1940), 1050-53; by W. Baumgart, *ZDP*, LXV, 223-224; by W. J. Mueller, *JEGP*, XL (1941), 164-165; by J. Albrecht, *Die Lücke*, 1948, p. 28; by G. Haug, *Welt und Wort*, III, 26-27.

A9671 Galambos, Wilhelm. *Gerhart Hauptmanns Interesse für Shakespeares "Hamlet."* DD, Vienna, 1948. Pp. 120. Typewritten.

x. Hebbel

A9672 Graham, Paul G. "Hebbel's Study of *King Lear.*" William Allan Neilson *Festschrift*, 1939. Pp. vii, 269.

A9673 Rau, Fritz. "Hebbels Shakespeare-Bild." *Wirkendes Wort*, II (1951/52), 228-231.

xi. Hegel

A9674 Wolff, Emil. "Hegel und Shakespeare." *Vom Geist der Dichtung: Gedächtnisschrift für Robert Petsch.* Hamburg, 1949.

A9675 Fornacca, Daisy C. *Hegel, Hegeliani e la Letteratura Italiana; Variazioni su Temi di Hegel, con Appendice su Hegel e Shakespeare.* DD, Columbia University, 1952. Florence: Soc. Edit. Univ., 1952. Pp. 238.

A9676 Steels, Theodore M. *Hegel's Influence on Shakespearean Criticism.* DD, Columbia University, 1953.

xii. Herder

A9677 Herder, Johann Gottfried. *Shakespeare* (Spanish and German) Sel., trad. y pról. de Juan C. Probst. Antología alemana. Ser. 1, fasc. 39. Buenos Aires: Univ., Fac. de fil., 1949. Pp. 56.

A9678 Isaacsen, Hertha. *Der Junge Herder und Shakespeare.* Berlin: Emil Ebering, 1930. Pp. 103. Rev: by E. P., *MLR*, XXXI (1936), 129.

A9679 Gillies, A. "Herder's Essay on Shakespeare: 'Das Herz der Untersuchung'." *MLR*, XXXII (1937), 262-280.

A9680 William-Wilmont, N. N. "Herder on Shakespeare." *International Literature* (USSR), 1939, pp. 3-4, 284-289.

A9681 Thost. H. *Nachlass-Studien zu Herder. 1: Herder als Shakespeare-Dolmetsch.* Leipzig: Poeschel und Trepte, 1940. Pp. 33. Rev: by W. Keller, *SJ*, LXXVI (1940), 217.

A9682 Schuetze, M. "J. G. Herder." *Monatshefte*, XXXVI (1944), 257-287.

A9683 Blättner, Fritz. "Das Shakespearebild Herders." *Vom Geist der Dichtung* (Hamburg), 1949, pp. 49-64.

A9684 Dobbek, Wilhelm. "Herder und Shakespeare." *SJ*, 91 (1955), 25-51.

xiii. Kleist

A9685 Fries, Carl. "Shakespeare bei Kleist." *Archiv*, 168 (1936), 232-235.

A9686 Sembdner, Helmut. *Die Berliner Abendblätter Heinrich von Kleists, ihre Quellen und ihre Redaktion.* Mit 1 Faks. und 9 Abb. auf 7 Taf. Schriften der Kleist-Ges. Bd. 19. Berlin: Weidmann, 1939. Pp. 16, 402.

A9687 Busch, Ernst. "Das Wesen des Tragischen in Kleists Drama." *GRM*, XXVIII (1940), 280-289.

A9688 Krumpelmann, John T. "Shakespeare's Falstaff Dramas and Kleist's *Zerbrochener Krug.*" *MLQ*, XII (1951), 462-472.

A9689 Krumpelmann, John T. "Kleist's *Krug* and Shakespeare's *Measure for Measure.*" *GR*, XXVI (1951), 13-21.

xiv. Lessing

A9690 Vail, Curtis C. D. *Lessing's Relation to the English Language and Literature.* DD, Columbia University, 1937. Publ. in Columbia Univ. Germanic Studies, NS, No. 3, 1936. Pp. vi, 220. Rev: by L. M. Price, *GR*, XII (1937), 132-133; by G. J. Ten Hoor, *MP*, XXXV, 205-208; by W. Kalthoff, *Beiblatt*, XLIX (1938), 19; by Hans G. Heun, *DLZ*, LIX, 740-742; by Paul P. Kies, *PQ*, XVII, 414-416; by O. W. Long, *JEGP*, XXXVIII (1939), 134-136; by Edna Purdie, *MLR*, XXXIV, 461-463.

A9691 Cancelled.

A9692 Tieze, Wilhelm. "Die Leidenschaften Reinigen . . . Zur Kritik des Ästhetischen seit Lessing." *DL*, XLIV (1941-42), 53ff.

A9693 Heitner, Robert R. *Lessing, Diderot, and the Bourgeois Drama.* DD, Harvard University, 1949.

A9694 Krumpelmann, John T. "Lessing's *Faust Fragment* and *Romeo and Juliet.*" *MLN*, LXIV (1949), 395-397.

A9695   Brinton, Clarence Crane, ed. *Portable Age of Reason Reader*. New York: Viking, 1956.
        Includes "On Shakespeare, Voltaire, and Others," by G. E. Lessing, pp. 526-533.

A9696   Friebert, Stuart A. "A Note on Lessing's Early Attitude toward Shakespeare." *GQ*, XXXI
        (1958), 178-182.

xv. Ludwig

A9697   Richter, F. *Otto Ludwigs Trauerspielplan "Tiberius Gracchus" und sein Zusammenhang mit den
        "Shakespeare-Studien."* Breslau: Priebatsch, 1935. Pp. vii, 89.
        Rev: by Kurt Vogtherr, *DLZ*, LVI (1935), 1786-90; by J. Speck, *Archiv*, 169 (1936), 131;
        by W. Baumgart, *ZDP*, LXII (1937), 86.

A9698   Kracke, Arthur. "Und die Dramatischen Studien?" *Otto Ludwig-Jahrbuch*, XI (1939), 71-82;
        XII (1940), 39-50.

A9699   Alfes, Leonhard. *Otto Ludwigs Shakespeare-Studien und ihre Beziehungen zur Romantisch-idealist-
        ischen Shakespeare-Krktik*. DD, Bonn, 1942. Pp. 285, 18. Typewritten.

A9700   Schwarz, Alfred. "Otto Ludwig's Shakespearean Criticism." *Perspectives of Criticism*, ed. by
        Harry Levin. Harvard Univ. Press, 1950, pp. 85-101.

xvi. Marx

A9701   Jackson, T. A. "K. Marx and Shakespeare." *International Literature*, Feb. 1936, pp. 75-97.

A9702   Kreft, Dr. Bratko. "Marx in Shakespeare." (Marx and Shakespeare) *Gledališni List* (Ljubl-
        jana), I (1946), 10.

xvii. Schiller

A9703   Schwendt, Friedrich. *Schillers Shakespeare-Bearbeitungen*. DD, Tübingen, 1901.
        Mummendey reported no copy could be found.

A9704   Valentin, Erich. "Schiller, Shakespeare und Verdi. Eine Stilgeschichtliche Betrachtung."
        VB(Mü), Dec. 4, 1937. Also in *Dts. Volksbildung*, XIII (1938/39), 22-24.

A9705   Kilga, Johanna F. *Joan of Arc Bei Shakespeare, Schiller und Shaw*. DD, Vienna, 1951. Pp. 87.
        Typewritten.

A9706   Brugger, Ilse. *El Porter de Shakespeare y el Pförtner de Schiller*. Estudios Germánicos, 11.
        Buenos Aires, 1955.

xviii. Schlegel

A9707   Eichner, Hans. "Friedrich Schlegel's Theory of Romantic Poetry." *PMLA*, LXXI (1956),
        1018-41.

A9708   Schirmer, Walter F. *Kleine Schriften*. Tübingen: Max Niemeyer Verlag, 1950.
        Several essays on Schlegel.

xix. The Tiecks

A9709   Stricker, Käthe. "Dorothea Tieck und ihr Schaffen für Shakespeare." *SJ*, LXXII (1936), 79-92.

A9710   Gillies, A. "Ludwig Tieck's English Studies at the University of Göttingen, 1792-1794."
        JEGP, XXXVI (1937), 206-223.

A9711   Immerwahr, Raymond M. *Ludwig Tieck's Contribution in Theory and Practice to the German
        Romanticists' Conception of Comedy*. DD, University of California, 1941.

A9712   Speck, Hans. "Sitzungsberichte der Berliner Ges. für das Studium der neueren Sprachen;
        Sitzung vom 28. 2. 39." *Archiv*, 179 (1941), 130-132.
        On L. Tieck as critic and historian of English literature.

xx. Other Individual Authors

A9713   Becker, G. "Johann Jakob Bodmers 'Sasper'." *SJ*, LXXIII (1937), 139-141.

A9714   Zierow, U. "John Brinckman und Shakespeare." *SJ*, LXXIII (1937), 132-133.

A9715   Knight, A. H. J. "Duke Heinrich Julius of Brunswick's *Comedy of Vincentius Ladislaus*."
        MLR, XXXIV (1939), 50-61.

A9716   Landauer, Gustav. *Shakespeare Dargestellt in Vorträgen*. Hrsg. v. Martin Buber. Potsdam:
        Rütten & Loening, 1948.

A9717   Majut, Rudolf. "Some Literary Affiliations of Georg Büchner with England." *MLR*, L
        (1955), 30-32.

A9718   Holzer, Gustav. *Kuno Fischers irrige Erklärung der Poetik Bacons*. Karlsruhe i. B.: Gutsch,
        1942. Pp. 43. See also *De Weegschaal*, IX (1943), Heft 4.

A9719   Jones, Ernest. *The Life and Work of Sigmund Freud*. Vol. III, The Last Phase, 1919-1939.
        New York: Basic Books, Inc., 1957. Pp. xvi, 537.
        Shak. criticism and theories of authorship, pp. 425-430.

A9720   Guthke, Karl S. "Johann Heinrich Füssli und Shakespeare." *N. Mitt.*, LVIII (1957), 206-215.
        Rev: by H. Oppel, *NS*, VII (1958), 290.

A9721 Grappin, Pierre. "Gerstenberg, Critique d'Homère et de Shakespeare." *Etudes Germaniques*, April and June, 1951, pp. 81-92.

A9722 Rohrmoser, Günter. *Kritische Erörterungen zu Gundolfs Shakespeare-Bild unter den Kategorien der Geschichte und der Person.* DD, Münster, 1955. Pp. iii, 222. Typewritten.

A9723 Wadepuhl, Walter. "Heine and Shakespeare." *SAB*, XXI (1946), 51-59.

A9724 Kayser, Rudolf. "Georg Herweghs Shakespeare-Auffassung." *GQ*, XX (1947), 231-238.

A9725 Spee, Hubert. *Franz Herwig als Dichter und Kritiker.* Dts. Quellen und Studien, Bd. 16. Graz: Wächter-Vlg., 1938.
Shak.'s influence, pp. 210-211.

A9726 Zucker, A. E. "Ibsen, Hettner, *Coriolanus, Brand.*" *MLN*, LI (1936), 99-106.

A9727 Nock, Francis J. "E. T. A. Hoffmann and Shakespeare." *JEGP*, LIII (1954), 369-382.
Rev: by H. Oppel, *NS*, IV (1955), 94.

A9728 Proske, Max. *Hugo von Hofmannsthal und sein Verhältnis zu Shakespeare Begegnung und Erkenntnis.* DD, Munich, 1956.

A9729 Lanz, Max. *Klinger und Shakespeare.* DD, Zürich, 1941. Zurich: E. Lang., 1941. Pp. 95.

A9730 Fischer, Walther. *Des Darmstädter Schriftstellers Joh. Heinr. Künzel (1810-1872) Beziehungen zu England—mit ungedruckten (oder wenig bekannten) Briefen von Carlyle, Dickens . . . u.a.* Giessener Beiträge zur dts. Philologie, 67. Giessen: v. Münchow, 1939. Pp. 80.

A9731 Maurer, K. W. "Tonio Kröger und Hamlet." *MLR*, XLIII (1948), 520.

A9732 Rehder, H. "Novalis and Shakespeare." *PMLA*, LXIII (1948), 604-624.

A9733 Wood, Frank. "Rilke's 'Der Geist Ariel', An Interpretation." *GR*, XXXII (1957), 35-44.

A9734 Kendzia, Maria Luise. "Friedrich Ludwig Schröder und Shakespeare." *Theater d. Zeit*, X (1955), No. 12, pp. 23-27.

A9735 Kurrelmeyer, W. "Weiblichkeit—Womanshood." *MLN*, LI (1936), 443-445.
On a reference in Wieland's *Agathon* to Shak.'s use of the word "womanhood."

(2) THE REMAINING GERMANIC COUNTRIES (155; 52)
(a) GENERAL

A9736 Molin, Nils Rikard. *Shakespeare och Sverige intill 1800-talets mitt. En Översikt av hans Inflytande.* DD, Gothenburg, 1931. Pp. iv, 308.

A9737 Seaton, Ethel. *Literary Relations of England and Scandinavia in the Seventeenth Century.* Oxford: Clarendon Press; London: Milford, 1935. Pp. 384.
Rev: A4630.

A9738 Leeloux, G. *"Othello" in Holland. A Contribution to the Study of Shakespeare in Holland.* Thèse, Liège, 1936-37.

A9739 Pennink, Renetta. *Nederland en Shakespeare. Achttiende Eeuw en Vroege Romantiek.* DD, Utrecht Rijksuniversiteit, 1936. The Hague: Nijhoff, 1936. Pp. viii, 304.
Rev: by J. Decroos, *SJ*, LXXII (1936), 168-169; *TLS*, April 10, 1937, p. 271; by C. A. Zaalberg, *ES*, XIX, 233-234; by Brian W. Downs, *MLR*, XXXII, 610-612; by Adr. Jac. Barnouw, *GR*, XII, 141-142; by B. H. Erné, *De Nieuwe Taalgids*, XXXII (1938), 40-42; by Gerhard Buck, *Lbl*, LX (1939), 383-384.

A9740 Tennant, P. "*Romeo och Julia* i Norrköping, 1776." *Samlaren* (Uppsala, Skrifter udg. af Svensk. Litt. Selskapet), XVII (1936), 215.

A9741 Funke, Otto. *Die Schweiz und die Englische Literatur. Ein Vortrag.* Bern: A. Francke, 1937. Pp. 57.

A9742 Büsser, Max. *Die Römerdramen in der Theatergeschichte der Deutschen Schweiz (1500-1800).* DD, Freiburg (Schweiz). Luzern: Theaterkultur Vlg., 1938. Pp. x, 169.

A9743 Schweinshaupt, G. *Shakespeares Dramtik in Ihrer Gehaltlichen und Formalen Umwandlung auf dem Österreichischen Theater des 18. Jhdts.* DD, Königsberg, 1938. Pp. 120.

A9744 Einarsson, Stefán. *Shakespeare á Íslandi.* Sérprent úr Tímaritinu 1937 og 1938. Winnipeg: The Viking Press, 1939.

A9745 Einarsson, Stefán. "Shakespeare in Iceland: An Historical Survey." *ELH*, VII (1940), 272-285.

A9746 Henriques, Alf. *Shakespeare og Danmark Indtil 1840.* DD, Copenhagen, 1941. Copenhagen: Munksgaard, 1941. Pp. 292.
Rev: by Frederick Schyberg, *Politiken*, Feb. 6, 1941, pp. 9-10; by Hakon Stangerup, *Nationaltidende*, Feb. 6, pp. 7-8; by Jens Kruuse, *Aarhus Amtstidende*, Feb. 7, p. 8; by Leopold Magon, *SJ*, 82/83 (1946/47), 211-213.

A9747 Engel, C. E. "Shakespeare in Switzerland in the Eighteenth Century." *Comparative Literature Studies*, XVII/XVIII (1945), 2-8.

A9748 Wilson, Charles. *Holland and Britain.* Nations and Britain Ser. London: William Collins Sons & Co., 1946. Pp. 126.
Rev: *Illus. London News*, 208 (1946), 142.

A9749 Magon, Leopold. "Deutschland, Shakespeare und der Norden." *SJ*, 82/83 (1948), 136-153.

A9750   Henriques, Alf. "Shakespeare and Denmark: 1900-1949." *ShS*, III (1950), 107-115.
A9751   Decroos, J. "Deutschlands Einfluss auf die Shakespeare-Pflege im Niederländischen Sprach-
         gebiet." *SJ*, 87/88 (1952), 116-157.
A9752   Downs, Brian W. "Anglo-Norwegian Literary Relations 1867-1900." *MLR*, XLVII (1952),
         449-494.
         Shak., pp. 455-457.
A9753   Eisner, Dora. "Sieben Jahre Shakespeare in Österreich (1945-1951)." *SJ*, 87/88 (1952),
         180-197.
A9754   Thorén, Birger. "Aktuellt for lärarna i moderna språk." *Aktuellt från Skolöverstyrelsen*, VIII
         (1955), 177-180.
A9755   Matsson, Ragnar. "Hamlet i Uppsala." *Studiekamraten*, XXXVIII (1956), 54-57.
A9756   Brown, Ivor. "Shakespeare og Danmark." *Berlingske Tidende* (Copenhagen), May 21, 1957.

                              (b) INDIVIDUALS
                                   i. Ibsen

A9757   Zucker, A. E. "Ibsen—Hettner—*Coriolanus—Brand*." *MLN*, LI (1936), 99-106.
A9758   Zucker, A. E. "The Courtiers in *Hamlet* and *The Wild Duck*." *MLN*, LIV (1939), 196-198.
A9759   Koht, Halvdan. "Shakespeare and Ibsen." *JEGP*, XLIV (1945), 79-86.
A9760   Arestad, Sverre. "Ibsen and Shakespeare: A Study in Influence." *SS*, XIX (1946), 89-104.
A9761   Simonsen, Peter. "*Hamlet og Vildanden*." *Edda*, L (1950), 281-288.

                                   ii. Kierkegaard

A9762   Oppel, Horst. "Shakespeare und Kierkegaard. Ein Beitrag zur Geschichte der *Hamlet*-
         Deutung." *SJ*, LXXVI (1940), 112-136.
A9763   Rougemont, Denis de. "Kierkegaard et *Hamlet*." *Preuves*, No. 24, 1953. German version,
         "Kierkegaard und Hamlet." *Der Monat*, LVI (1953), 115-124.
A9764   Boehlich, Walter. "Noch Einmal Kierkegaard und Hamlet: Sören, Prinz von Dänemark."
         Der Monat, LXVI (1954), 628-634. Comment by Helmut Uhlig, "Hamlet in Wittenberg,
         Kierkegaard in Berlin"; by P. Orlowski, "Kierkegaard und Hamlet über sich Selbst," ibid.,
         LXVIII (1954), 208-209.
A9765   Madariaga, Salvador de. "Noch Einmal Kierkegaard und Hamlet: War Hamlet Melan-
         cholisch?" *Der Monat*, LXVI (1954), 625-628.

                                   iii. Strindberg

A9766   Börge, Vagn. "Strindberg und Shakespeare." *SJ*, LXXIII (1937), 142-149.
A9767   Anderson, H. *Strindberg, Master Olof and Shakespeare*. Essays and Studies on English Language
         and Literature. Uppsala, 1952. Pp. 63.
         Rev: by Alrik Gustafson, *N. Mitt.*, LVI (1955), 74-76.

                                   iv. Others

A9768   Bull, Francis. "The Influence of Shakespeare on Wergeland, Ibsen and Björnson." Tr. from
         the Norwegian by E. M. Huggard, *Norseman*, XV (1957), 89-95.
A9769   House, Roy Temple. "Shakespeare and a Poor Swiss Peasant." *Books Abroad*, IX (1935),
         375-377.
         Ulrich Bräker, gifted Swiss peasant pauper of the later eighteenth century. See also A6904.
A9769a   Bräker, Ulrich. *Etwas über William Shakespeares Schauspiele. Von einem armen Ungelehrten
         Weltbürger, der das Glück genoss, ihn zu Lesen*. Basel: B. Schwabe & Co., 1942. Pp. viii, 156.
A9770   Küry, Hans. *Simon Grynaeus von Basel, 1725-1799, der Erste Deutsche Übersetzer von Shakespeares
         "Romeo und Julia."* Zurich, Leipzig: Niehans, 1935. Pp. 83.
A9771   Konow, Sten. "Holberg og Shakespeare." *Edda*, XLVI (1946), 69-71.
A9772   Rubow, Paul V. "Johannes Vilhelm Jensens Hamlet eller den Flaaede Marsyas." *Epistler*,
         Copenhagen: Levin and Munksgaard, 1938, pp. 21-35.
         Rev: by Frederick Schyberg, *Politiken*, May 6, 1938, pp. 17-19.
A9773   Gielen, Jos. J. "Kees Meekel en Shakespeare." (De Invloed van Shakespeare op Meekel).
         Nieuwe Taalgids, XXX (1936), 341-350.
A9774   Gielen, Jos. J. "Vondel en Shakespeare." *De Gids*, 1937, pp. 162-176.

                         e. THE SLAVONIC COUNTRIES (155; 52)
                              (1) RUSSIA (155; 52)
                                   (a) GENERAL
                                        i. Surveys from Outside Russia

A9775   Haughton, N. *Moscow Rehearsals: Methods of Production in the Soviet Theatre*. New York,
         London, 1936. Pp. xx, 292.
         Rev: *TLS*, Sept. 10, 1938, p. 584.

A9776   Simmons, Ernest J. *English Literature and Culture in Russia (1553-1840).* Harvard Univ. Press, 1935. Pp. 357.
Chap. VIII. "The Early History of Shakspere in Russia," pp. 204-236. Includes a bibliog. on the subject at the end of the chapter.
Rev: by Georg Sacke, *DLZ*, LVIII (1937), 487-488.

A9777   Gourfinkel, Nina. *Shakespeare chez les Soviets. DF*, 268 (1936), 319-330.

A9777a Zanco, Aurelio. *Shakespeare in Russia.* Annali della R. Scuola Normale Superiore di Pisa. Lettere, Storia, Filosofia. Ser. II, Vol. 7, fasc. 2/3. Bologna: N. Zanichelli, 1938.
See A9787.

A9778   "Soviet Shakespeare." *TLS*, April 29, 1939, p. 249.

A9779   Gury, J. "Shakespeare in the USSR." *American Quarterly of the Soviet Union*, II (July, 1939), 45-59.

A9780   Bryner, Cyril. "Shakespeare Among the Slavs." *ELH*, VIII (1941), 107-118.

A9781   Tannenbaum, Samuel A. "Shakspere in Russia." *SAB*, XVI (1941), 127-128.

A9782   Salingar, L. G. "The Soviet Public and Shakespeare." *Anglo-Soviet Journal*, III (1942), 228-234.

A9783   Blum, E. "Shakespeare in the USSR." *The Worker*, Dec. 26, 1943, p. 7.

A9784   Zagorsky, Mikhail. "Shakespeare in Russia." *TLS*, Aug. 12, 1944, p. 396.

A9785   "Shakespeare in Armenia." *American Review on the Soviet Union*, VI (1945), 59-60.

A9786   Blum, Eugene. "Shakspere in the USSR." *SAB*, XX (1945), 99-102.

A9787   Zanco, Aurelio. *Shakespeare in Russia e Altri Saggi.* Turin: Gheroni, 1945. Pp. 200.
"Shakespeare in Russia," pp. 5-39.
Rev: by Sergio Baldi, *Anglica*, I (1946), 169-171; by Giuliano Pellegrini, *Rivista di Letterature Moderne*, II (1947), 328-329; by Carlo Cordiè, *La Rassegna d'Italia*, III (1948), 987-989.

A9788   "Bardolatry Abroad." *TLS*, April 13, 1946, p. 175.
Comments on Moscow conference of scholars.

A9789   Kreft, Dr. Bratko. "Shakespeare v Z S S R" (Shakespeare in the USSR). *Gledališni List* (Ljubljana), I (1946), 10.

A9790   Canterbury, Dean of. "Shakespeare in Russia." *Shakespeare Quarterly* (London), I (Summer, 1947), 76-81.

A9791   Wolff, Tatiana A. *The Russian Romantics and English Literature.* MA thesis, University of London, 1947.

A9792   Gibian, George J. *Shakespeare in Russia.* DD, Harvard University, 1951.

A9793   Luther, Arthur. "Shakespeare in Russland." *SJ*, 84/86 (1950), 214-228.

A9794   Gibian, George. "Shakespeare in Soviet Russia." *Russian Review*, XI (1952), 24-34.

A9795   Krehayn, Joachim. "Die Englische Literatur in der Sowjetunion." *ZAA*, I (1953), 170-185. Shak., pp. 175-178.

A9796   Lehrman, Edgar Harold. *Soviet Shakespeare Appreciation (1917-1952).* DD, Columbia University, 1954. Pp. 465. Mic A54-2072. *DA*, XIV (1954), 1413.
Bibliography of 100 pages totals over a thousand items.

A9797   "Shakespeare's Roman Plays: And Other Subjects." *ShN*, V (1955), 41.

A9798   Ilyin, Eugene. "Two Centuries of Russian Shakespeare." *Plays and Players*, Dec., 1957, pp. 10-11.

A9799   "Eighth International Shakespeare Conference at Stratford." *ShN*, VII (1957), 39, 48.
Contains abstr. of Samuel Marshak, "Shakespeare in the USSR."

A9800   Alexander, Edward. "Shakespeare's Plays in Armenia." *SQ*, IX (1958), 387-394.

ii.   Surveys from Inside Russia

A9801   Reich, B. "Fascist Interpretation of Shakespeare." Tr. S. D. Kogan. *International Literature* (USSR), 1936, pp. 90-99.

A9802   Dinamov, S. "Shakespeare on the Soviet Stage." *Soviet Land*, VI (1937), 4-5, 16, 30.

A9803   Morozov, M. "Shakespeare en U.R.S.S." *Europe*, L (1939), 676-678.

A9804   Nels, S. "Shakespeare and the Soviet Theatre." *October* (USSR), IV (1941), 186-203.

A9805   Nels, S. "Shakespeare and European Culture." *The Theater* (USSR), IV (1941), 3-15.

A9806   Spassky, Y. "Tragedy in the Seventeenth and Eighteenth Centuries." *The Theater* (USSR), V (1941), 89-105.

A9807   Zabludovsky, M. "New Books on Shakespeare (in England and America)." *International Literature* (USSR), V (1941), 190-197.

A9808   Morozov, M. "Shakespeare Studies in the Soviet Union." *Indian Review*, XLIV (1943), 117.

A9809   Morozov, M. "Soviet Shakespeare Studies." *International Literature* (USSR), XI (1944), 67-68.

A9810   Morozov, M. M. "Shakespeare on the Stages of Erevan, Tbilisi, Baku." *SAB*, XX (1945), 105-109.

A9811   Anikst, Alexandre. "Shakespeare in Russia." *Soviet Literature*, April 1946, pp. 60-65.

A9812   *Shekspirovskii Sbornik*, 1947. Redkollegiia. G. N. Boiadzhiev, M. B. Zagorskii, M. M. Morozov. Moscow: Vserossiiskoe Treatral'noe Obschestvo, 1948. Pp. 296.
Contains M. B. Zagorskii, "Shekspir v Rossii," and E. Subbotina, "Sovetskaia Shekspiriana," among others.

A9813   Borovoi. L. "Na Shekspirovskie temy (0 10-i Shekspirovskoi Konferentsii i o Rabotakh Sovetskikh Shekspirovedov.)" *Teatr*, XI (1948), 40-46.
[L. Borovoi. "On Shakespearean Themes (On the Tenth Shakespeare Conference and on the Work of Soviet Shakespeare Specialists.)"]

A9814   Morozov, Mikhail M. "The Study of Shakespeare in the Soviet Union." *Amer. Rev. of the Soviet Union*, VIII (March 1947), 3-15.

A9815   Morozov, Mikhail M. *Shakespeare on the Soviet Stage*. Tr. David Magarshack. London: Soviet News Publ., 1947. Pp. 71.
Rev: by M. St. Clare Byrne, *English*, VI (1947), 317-318; by Una Ellis-Fermor, *MLR*, XLIII, 258-259; *TLS*, April 26, p. 202.

A9816   Nikolsky, D. "Shakespearean Plays in Soviet Russia." *Soviet Literature*, 1948, pp. 62-64.

A9817   Morozov, Mikhail M. *Szekspir*. Warsaw: Czytelnik, 1950. Pp. 222.
Rev: by Z. Hierowski, *Swiat i życie*, No. 8 (1952), 2.

A9818   Sapir, Mikhail. "The Ever-Living Hamlet." *News* (Moscow), No. 8 (1956), 17-20.

A9819   Morozov, Mikhail Mikhailovich. "*Hamlet* in Sowjetischer Beleuchtung." *Theater u. Zeit* (Wuppertal), IV (1956/57), 188-190.

(b) INDIVIDUAL AUTHORS
i. Chekhov

A9820   Wilson, Arthur H. "The Influence of *Hamlet* upon Chekhov's *The Sea Gull*." *Susquehanna Univ. Stud.*, IV (1952), 309-316.

A9821   Winner, T. G. "Chekhov's *Seagull* and Shakespeare's *Hamlet*: A Study of a Dramatic Device." *American Slavic and East European Review*, XV (1956), 103-111.

A9822   Stroud, T. A. "*Hamlet* and *The Seagull*." *SQ*, IX (1958), 367-372.

ii. Pasternak

(For Pasternak's comments upon translation into Russian, see B990-B998.)

A9823   Pasternak, Boris. "Shakespeare's Imagery and Rhythm." Tr. by Peter Meadows. *Arena*, I (1950), 33-37.

A9824   Pasternak, Boris. "*Hamlet*." The Poems of Yurii Zhivago." (From the novel *Dr. Zhivago*). Tr. Bernard Guilbert Guerney. New York: Pantheon Books, 1958, p. 523.

A9825   Pasternak, Boris. "*Hamlet*." *Poesie*. Introduzione, Traduzione e Note di Angelo Maria Ripellino. Florence: Einaudi, 1958.
Poem.

A9826   William-Wilmont, N. N. "Boris Pasternak's Translation of *Hamlet*." *International Literature* (USSR), (1939), 7-8, 284-285.

A9827   Morozov, M. M. "Boris Pasternak's Translation of *Othello*." *SAB*, XX (1945), 103-104.

A9828   Frank, Victor S. "A Russian *Hamlet*: Boris Pasternak's Novel." *Dublin Review*, Autumn, 1958, pp. 212-220.

iii. Pushkin

A9829   Pushkin, A. S. "Notes on Shylock, Angelo and Falstaff." *SAB*, XVI (1941), 120-121.
Four paragraphs translated by Albert Siegel from a collected edition of Pushkin's works.

A9830   Simmons, Ernest J. "La Littérature Anglaise et Pouchkine." *RLC*, XVII (1937), 79-107.

A9831   Spasskii, J. A. "Pushkin & Shakespeare." *Bull. de l'Académie des Sciences de l'URSS*, Nos. 2 & 3, (1937), 413-430.

A9832   Bobrova, M. N. "On the Influence of Shakespeare in Pushkin's Tragedy of *Boris Godunov*." *Literature in School* (USSR), II (1940), 69-80.

A9833   Gifford, H. "Shakespearean Elements in *Boris Godunov*." *The Slavonic and East European Rev.*, XXVI (1947), 152-160.

A9834   Lavrin, Janko. "Pushkin and Shakespeare." *Pushkin and Russian Literature*, New York, 1948, pp. 140-160.

A9835   Gibian, George. "Pushkin's Parody on *The Rape of Lucrece*." *SQ*, I (1950), 264-266.

A9836   Gibian, George. "*Measure for Measure* and Pushkin's *Angelo*." *PMLA*, LXVI (1951), 426-431.

A9837   Wolff, Tatiana A. "Shakespeare's Influence on Pushkin's Dramatic Work." *ShS*, V (1952), 93-105.

iv. Shevchenko

A9838   Finkel, M. "T. Shevchenko and Ira Aldridge." *International Literature* (USSR), March, 1939, pp. 92-93.

A9839   Bojko, Jurij. "Taras Shevchenko and West European Literature." *Slavonic and East European Review*, XXXIV (1955), 77-98.
Shevchenko's passion for Shak., pp. 94-96.

v. Tolstoi

A9840 Tolstoy, L. "Shakespeare and the Drama." *Recollections & Essays*, Vol. 21 of *Tolstoy Centenary Edition*, 1937.

A9841 Knight, G. Wilson. *Shakespeare and Tolstoy*. Oxford Univ. Press, 1934.
Rev: by Albert Eichler, *Beiblatt*, XLVII (1936), 113-114.

A9842 Wassenberg, R. *Tolstois Angriff auf Shakespeare: Ein Beitrag zur Charakterisierung Östlichen und Westlichen Schöpfertums*. DD, Bonn, 1935. Pp. 44.

A9843 Breitburg, S. "Tolstoy Reading *Hamlet* and Assisting at its Performance." *International Literature* (USSR), 1939, pp. 11-12, 233-250.

A9844 Turel, A. "Tolstoi und Shakespeare." Bachofen-Freud: *Emanzipation d. Mannes vom Reich d. Mütter*. Bern: H. Huber, 1939, pp. 24-26.

A9845 Breitburg, S. "The Bernard Shaw-Tolstoy Controversy About Shakespeare." *Literary Heritage* (USSR), XXXVII (1940), 617-632.

A9846 Kane, Robert J. "Tolstoy, Goethe, and *King Lear*." *SAB*, XXI (1946), 159-160.

A9847 Bischoff, D. "Shakespeare und Tolstoi." *Die Sammlung*, II (1948), 134-143.

A9848 Walker, Roy. "Swinburne, Tolstoy, and *King Lear*." *English*, VII (1949), 282-284.
Tolstoi ill-informed.

A9849 Orwell, George. "Lear, Tolstoy, and the Fool." *Polemic*, No. 7 (March 1947), 2-17. Reprinted in *Shooting an Elephant and Other Essays*. New York, 1950, pp. 32-52. Reprinted in *The Orwell Reader*. New York: Harcourt-Brace, 1956, pp. 300-315.

A9850 Orwell, George. "Tolstoj e Shakespeare." *Inventario*, III (Spring, 1950), 21-34.

A9851 Simpson, Lucie. "Tolstoy and Shakespeare." *The Secondary Heroes of Shakespeare and Other Essays*. London: Kingswood Press, 1950, pp. 53-60.

A9852 Gibian, George. *Tolstoi and Shakespeare*. The Hague: Mouton, 1957. Pp. 47. Paperback.
Demonstrates the novelist's lifelong hostility to the plays, based "in part on Tolstoi's adherence to the literary criteria and tastes of the French eighteenth-century neo-classicists and in part on Tolstoi's personal religious and puritanical fanaticism."
Rev: *TLS*, Oct. 18, 1957, p. 630; by Earl H. Rovit, *Books Abroad*, XXXII (1958), 188.

A9853 Stříbrný, Zdeněk. "Několik Poznámek ke Králi Learovi." ("Some Remarks on *King Lear*"). *Divadlo* (Prague), VIII (1957), 915-920.
A polemic on Tolstoi's condemnation of *Lear*.

vi. Turgenev

A9854 Turgenev, I. "A Speech about Shakespeare." *International Literature*, June, 1939, pp. 47-49.

A9855 Toergeniev (Turgenev), Ivan. *Hamlet en Don Quichote*. Uit het Russ. vert. en Ingel. door Aleida G. Schot. Amsterdam: Meulenhoff, 1947. Pp. 48.

vii. Others

A9856 Muir, Kenneth. "The Jealousy of Iago." *English Miscellany*. Ed. Mario Praz (Rome: Edizioni di Storia e Letteratura), II (1952), 65-83.
Opening pages on Dostoevski, Pushkin, and Ostuzhev.

A9857 Fridlender, G. M. "Belinskii i Šekspir." *Belinskii. Stat'i i Materialy* (Leningrad), 1949, pp. 147-173.

A9858 Kassner, R. "Über Shakespeare." *Corona*, VI (1936), 256-283, 408-423.
Dostoievski and Shak.

A9859 Mandin, L. "Gorki et Shakespeare." *MdF*, 269 (1936), 436-437.

A9860 Lang, D. M. "Sumarkov's *Hamlet*: A Misjudged Russian Tragedy of the Eighteenth Century." *MLR*, XLIII (1948), 67-72.

(c) MISCELLANEOUS

A9861 "A Shakespeare Conference in USSR." *SAB*, XI (1936), 123-124.

A9862 Holdaway, N. A. "Shakespeare and the Moscow Trial." *Adelphi*, XIII (1936), 115-116.

A9863 Jackson, T. A. "K. Marx and Shakespeare." *International Literature*, Feb., 1936, pp. 75-97.

A9864 Lukas, G. "The Intellectual Physiognomy of Literary Characters." Tr. L. E. Mins. *International Literature*, 1936, pp. 55-83.

A9865 Lunacharski, A. "F. Bacon in Shakespearean Surroundings." Tr. S. D. Kogan. *International Literature*, Jan., 1936, pp. 85-99.

A9866 Smirnov, A. A. *Shakespeare: A Marxist Interpretation*. Tr. by Sonia Volochova and others. New York: Critics' Group, 1936. Pp. 93.
Rev: A8367.

A9867 Smirnov, A. A. *Tvorchestvo Shekspira*. Neue russ. Bibliothek, 37. Berlin: Volk u. Wissen, 1952. Pp. 72.

A9868 Morozov, M., ed. "Shakespeare." Bulletin No. 1. Moscow: Iskusstvo, 1939. Pp. 92.

A9869 Morozov, M. "Shakespeare's *Hamlet*." *The Young Guard* (USSR), 1939, pp. 5-6, 251-253.

A9870 Odartchenko, P. V. *William Shakespeare. Material Collected for the Anniversary*. Kursk: Kurskoje, 1939. Pp. 24.

A9871   Rokotov, T. "The Great Brotherly Soul." *International Literature* (USSR), 1939, pp. 3-4, 262-270.

A9872   Rokotov, T. "Shakespeare: A Contemporary of Eternity." *International Literature*, June, 1939, pp. 38-46.

A9873   Sollertinsky, I. I. "Shakespeare and the World Music." *Shakespeare. A Symposium.* Leningrad, Moscow: The State Scientific Institute of Music and the Theatre, 1939, pp. 97-130.

A9874   Spassky, Y. "Shakespeare Without End." *Theatre* (USSR), IV (1939), 13-32.

A9875   Verchovsky, N. P., K. N. Derjavin, S. E. Radlov, et al. *Shakespeare. A Symposium.* Leningrad, Moscow: Iskusstvo, 1939. Pp. 184.

A9876   William-Wilmont, N. N. "Herder on Shakespeare." *International Literature* (USSR), 1939, pp. 3-4, 284-289.

A9877   Morozov, M. "Notes on *Hamlet.*" *Theatre* (USSR), IV (1940), 45-52.

A9878   Morozov, M. M. "How We Study Shakespeare." *Sovietland*, IX (1940), 34.

A9879   Nikolajev, V. N. "On Certain Peculiarities in the Development of Shakespearean Characters." *Transactions of the Pedagogical Institute in Gorki* (USSR), VIII (1940), 121-134.

A9880   Morozov, M. "Language and Style of Shakespeare." *History of English Realism.* Ed. I. Anisimov, 1941.

A9881   Morozov, M. M. *A Commentary on Shakespeare's Plays.* Moscow, Leningrad: Vserossiiskoe Teatral'noe Obschestvo, 1941. Pp. 104.

A9882   Scopin, G. A. *William Shakespeare. A Short Bibliography.* For the 325th Anniversary of his Death. The Fundamental Library of the Tatar Autonomous Soviet Socialist Republic at the Kazan State Univ., 1941. Pp. 30.

A9883   Morozov, M. "From the History of the American Shakespeareology." *International Literature* (USSR), 1942, pp. 3-5, 192-196.

A9884   "Russians' Love of Shakespeare." *The Times* (London), May 15, 1943, pp. 3, 5.

A9885   Morozov, M. M. "Humanism in Shakespeare's Works." *SAB*, XVIII (1943), 51-61.

A9886   Kemenov, V. "Shakespeare on the Occasion of the 330th Anniversary of His Death." *VOKS-Bulletin* (Moscow), No. 5-6, 1946.

A9887   Morozov, M. *Shakespeare (1564-1616).* With Illustration and 1 Portrait. Lives of Remarkable People [series]. Moscow: Molodaia Gvardiia, 1947. Pp. 280.
         Rev: A569.

A9888   Yozovsky, Y. *The Character and The Epoch: On Shakespeare Themes.* Moscow, 1947. Pp. 190.

A9889   Samarin, P. M. "Novyi Sbornik o Shekspire." *Sovietskaia Kniga*, I (1949), 109-111.

A9890   Drahomanov, M. "*Taming of the Shrew* in the Folklore of the Ukraine." *Annals of the Ukrainian Academy of Arts and Sciences in the US*, II (1952), 214-218.

A9891   Anikst, A. "Literatura k Teme Shekspira." *Literatura v Schkole*, No. 6 (1953), 80-82.

A9891a   Anikst, Alexander. "*Hamlet*, Tragedy of William Shakespeare." *Literatura v Schkole*, No. 2 (1954), 14-29.

A9891b   Anikst, Alexander. "A Valuable Heritage. On the 390th Anniversary of William Shakespeare's Birth." *Smena*, No. 10 (1954), 22.

A9891c   Kirsanova, T. "In the Native Land of Shakespeare. On the Occasion of the 390th Anniversary of His Birth." *Voknug Sveta*, No. 4 (1954), 20-23.

A9892   Plekhanov, Georgii Valentinovič. *Kunst und Literatur.* Tr. Joseph Harhammer. Berlin: Dietz, 1955. Pp. xxxviii, 1034.

A9893   Simonov, G. "*Gamlet.*" *Ogonek* (Moscow), XXXIII (Sept. 1955), 20-21.

A9894   "I Interviewed Hamlet." Intercepted over radio by Sergei Datlin, *News* (Moscow), No. 1 (1955), 17.

A9895   Bačelis, T. "Svjaź Vremen." *Teatr* (Moscow), XVII (1956), 84-97.

A9896   Smirnov, A. A. "Problemy Tekstologii Šekspira." *Izvestia.* Akademii Nauk SSR. Otdelenie Literatury i Jazyka (Moscow), Feb. 15, 1956, pp. 122-132.

A9897   *Sonety Shekspira.* Desiat Sonetov Shekspira. Moscow, 1957. Pp. 37.
         Muscial settings for Shak.'s sonnets.

A9898   Kostetzky, Eaghor G. "Grŭndungsbericht." *SJ*, 94 (1958), 315.
         On the Ukrainian Shak. Assocation.

(d) PRODUCTIONS
i. General

A9899   Lidin, V. "An Amateur Performance of *Hamlet.*" *International Literature*, March, 1938, pp. 57-60.

A9900   Mokulsky, S. *The History of the Theatre in Europe.* Vol. II. Moscow, Leningrad: Iskusstvo, 1939. Pp. 512.

A9901   Radlov, S. "Producing Shakespeare." *International Literature*, June, 1939, pp. 49-58.

A9902   Banu, T., A. Lakhuti, and E. Chemodurov. *Dekada Tadzhikskovo Iskusstva: "Otello."* Moscow, 1941. Pp. 18.

A9903 Kozintsev, G. "*King Lear.*" *The Theater* (USSR), IV (1941), 16-32.
A9904 Papazyan, V. "He Played Othello 2000 Times." *Sovietland*, April 1941, pp. 6-7, 37.
A9905 Reich, B. "*Macbeth.*" *The Theater* (USSR), I (1941), 74-85.
A9906 Schwartz-Bostunitsch, Gregor. "Shakespeare im Moskauer Künstlertheater." *SJ*, LXXVII (1941), 138-150.
A9907 Durilin, S. "Ira Aldridge." *SAB*, XVII (1942), 33-39.
A9908 Macleod, J. "Shakespeare in the New Soviet Theatre." *Anglo-Soviet Journal*, III (Jan., 1942), 17-24.
A9909 Macleod, J. "Shakespeare on the Soviet Stage." *The New Soviet Theatre* (London), 1943, pp. 208-218.
A9910 Arbat, Y. "Khidoyatov Plays *Hamlet* and *Othello* in Uzbek." *International Literature*, XI (1944), 73-75.
A9911 Freidkina, L. "*König Lear* im Moskauer Staatlichen Jüdischen Theater." *Theater der Zeit*, IV (1946), 25-26.
A9912 Luther, Arthur. "Moskaus erster *Hamlet.*" *SJ*, 82/83 (1948), 175-185.
A9913 Johnston, Robert A. *The Moscow Art Theatre in America.* DD, Northwestern University, 1951. Abstr. publ. in Northwestern Univ. *Summaries of Doctoral Dissertations, 1951*, Vol. 19, Chicago and Evanston, 1952, pp. 145-150.
A9914 Shchepkina-Kupernik, Tat'iana L'vovna. "My Work on Shakespeare." *News* (Moscow), No. 5 (1952), 17-19.
A9915 "New Shakespearean Productions." *News* (Moscow), May 1, 1954, pp. 24-25.
       A symposium by three Russian producers, one actor, and one actress, giving views on their productions of *Hamlet, Macbeth, Twelfth Night,* and *Romeo and Juliet.*
A9916 "Russian Dressing." *TAr*, XXXVIII (Sept. 1954), 15.
A9917 "*Hamlet* in Moscow." *Time*, Dec. 12, 1955, p. 67.
       Russians respond enthusiastically to *Ham.* as played by Paul Scofield in English.
A9918 "Theater." *News* (Moscow), No. 19 (Oct. 1, 1955), 31.
A9919 Anikst, Alexander. "Two Hamlets." *News* (Moscow), May 10, 1955, pp. 24-26.
A9920 Alpers, B. "Russkij Gamlet." *Teatr* (Moscow), XVI, viii (1955), 65-80.
A9921 Anikst, Alexander. "Byt' ili ne byt' u nas Gamletu." *Teatr* (Moscow), March 16, 1955, pp. 62-81.
A9922 Gogoleva, Elena. "My Conception of Lady Macbeth." *News* (Moscow), No. 19 (Oct. 1, 1955), 29.
A9923 Ochlopkov, N. "Iz Režisserskoj Eksplikacii Gamleta." *Teatr* (Moscow), XVI, i (1955), 60-73.
A9924 Turovskaja, M. "Ešče o *Gamlete.*" *Teatr* (Moscow), Sept. 16, 1955, pp. 54-62.
A9925 Velekhova, N. "*Hamlet* at the Mayakovsky Theatre." *VOKS-Bulletin* (Moscow), VI, 95 (1955), 43-48.
A9926 Anikst, Alexander. "*Macbeth* at the Moscow Maly." *News* (Moscow), No. 5 (1956), 28-29.
A9927 Anikst, Alexander. "Sein oder Nichtsein Unseres *Hamlet.*" *Sowjetwissenschaft. Kunst und Literatur* (Berlin), IV (1956), 41-60.
A9928 Juzovskij, Ju. "*Gamlet* i Drugie." *Teatr* (Moscow), Feb. 17, 1956, pp. 140-157.
A9929 Rudnitsky, Konstantin. "Shakespeare and Shaw in Moscow." *Plays and Players*, Sept. 1956, p. 13.
A9930 "Shakespeare's Plays on Soviet Stages." *USSR*, No. 13 (1957), 56.
A9931 Levin, M. "U Každogo 'Svoj' Šekspir." *Teatr* (Moscow), Aug. 18, 1957, pp. 67-78.
A9932 Rylsky, Maxim. "Cultural Progress of the Ukrainian People." *USSR*, No. 8 (1957), 11-13.
A9933 Yura, Gnat. "Theatre in the Ukraine." *USSR*, No. 8 (1957), 44-47.
A9934 Zingerman, B. "Šekspir." *Teatr* (Moscow), Oct. 18, 1957, pp. 104-107.
A9935 Mitchell, John D. and Miriam. "The Theatre in Russia." *Today's Speech*, April 1958.
A9936 Rudnitsky, Konstantin. "Moscow's Mammoth Festival." *Plays and Players*, Sept. 1958, pp. 16-17.

ii. Stanislavski

A9937 Stanislavski, K. S. *Rejisserkii Plan "Othello."* Leningrad: State Publishing House, 1944. Pp. 392.
A9938 *Stanislavski (Constantin) Produces "Othello."* Tr. from the Russian by Helen Nowak. London: Bles, 1948. Pp. 244.
       Rev: by P. Fleming, *Spectator*, 180 (1948), 740, 742; *TLS*, June 19, p. 340; by Harold Hobson, *Sun Times*, June 20, p. 3; by R. Flatter, *SJ*, 87/88 (1952), 247-248.
A9939 Cancelled.
A9940 "*Othello.*" Trad. de F. Victor Hugo, Entièrement Ref. par Christine et René Lalou. Mise en Scène . . . de Constantin Stanislavski. Trad. du russe par Nina Gourfinkel. Coll. Mises en Scènes. Paris: Ed. du Seuil, 1948. Pp. 352.

A9941 Stanislavski, Constantin. *Building a Character*. Tr. Elizabeth Reynolds Hapgood: Intro. by Joshua Logan. New York: Theatre Arts; Toronto: Ambassador, 1949. Pp. xx, 292.
　　　Rev: by George R. Kernodle, *QJS*, xxxv (1949), 553-554; by Lewis Funke, *NYTBR*, Jan. 1, 1950, p. 13.

A9942 Ilyin, Eugene K. "Gordon Craig's Mission to Moscow." *TAr*, May 1954, pp. 78-79, 88-90.

A9943 Afanasieva, Olga, and Alexander Vasiliev. "Behind the Scenes at the Moscow Theatre." *USSR*, No. 9 (1957), 48-53.
　　　Stanislavsky influenced production of *W.T.* in Moscow.

A9944 Hetler, Louis. *The Influence of the Stanislavsky Theories of Acting on the Teaching of Acting in the United States*. DD, University of Denver, 1957.

A9945 Ilyin, Eugene. "How Stanislavsky and Gordon Craig Produced *Hamlet*." *Plays and Players*, March 1957, pp. 6-7, 21.
　　　Story of the Stanislavsky and Craig production of *Ham*. at the Moscow Art Theatre in 1908. Includes a conversation transcribed by L. A. Soolergitsky, between Craig and Stanislavsky.

A9946 Marowitz, Charles. "Stanislavsky and Shakespeare." *Encore*, IV, iv, No. 13 (1958), 26-30.

iii. Films

A9947 Lvov-Anokhin, B. "The Film-Ballet *Romeo and Juliet*." *VOKS-Bulletin* (Moscow), v, 94 (1955), 48-50.

A9948 Michaut, Pierre. "La Danse: *Roméo et Juliette*, Film-Ballet Soviétique." *La Revue de Paris*, June, 1956, pp. 168-169.

A9949 Prouse, Derek. "*Othello*." *Sight and Sound*, Summer, 1956, pp. 29-30.
　　　Sergei Yutkevitch's Russian film.

A9950 Sibirtsev, Gennadi. "Her Debut is a Promise." *USSR*, Sept., 1956, pp. 42-43.

A9951 Weightman, J. G. "Many Othellos." *TC*, Aug., 1956, pp. 166-169.

A9952 Robleto, Hernán. "*Otelo* ha Vuelto." *El Universal* (Mexico City), April 1, 1957, p. 3.

A9953 Rozental, Gennadi. "Sergei Yutkevitch, Film Director, Writer, Artist." *USSR*, No. 10 (1957), 50-53.

A9954 Sibirtsev, Gennadi. "How a Film Star is Made: Alla Larionova." *USSR*, No. 4 (1956), 54-56.
　　　Notes Russian film of *Twel*.

iv. The English Visit

A9955 "The Tennent Company in Moscow." *News* (Moscow), No. 1 (1956), 28-29.

A9956 Tynan, Kenneth. "Curtain Time in Moscow." *Harper's Magazine*, March, 1956, pp. 61-65.

A9957 Zavadsky, Yuri. "English Produce *Hamlet* in Moscow." *VOKS-Bulletin* (Moscow), I, 96 (1956), 33-34.

(2) POLAND (156;-)

A9958 Bryner, Cyril. "Shakespeare Among the Slavs." *ELH*, VIII (1941), 107-118.

A9959 Hahn, Wiktor. [Shakespeare's Influence on Polish Drama.] *Teatr Miesoceznik* (Poland), Nos. 1-2 (1945).

A9960 Hahn, Wiktor. [*Hamlet* at Lwow in 1797.] *Teatr Miesoceznik* (Poland), Nos. 4-5 (1945).

A9961 Rulikowski, M. [Shakespeare na Scenach Polskich.] *Teatr Miesoceznik* (Poland), Nos. 4-5 (1945).
　　　Shak.'s fortunes on the Polish stage.

A9962 Byrne, Clare. "Szekspir w Naszych Czasach." *Glos Anglii* (Cracow), No. 47 (1947), 9.
　　　"Shak. in Our Times."

A9963 Borowy, Wacław. "Jak Słuchać *Otella*." *Łódź Teatr*, No. 8 (1948), 2-11.
　　　How to listen to *Othello*.

A9964 Kudlinski, Tadeusz. *Dziedzietwo Zemstypolpowiesc* (*The Heritage of Revenge: A Semi-Novel*). Wrocław-Warsaw: Ksiaznica-Atlas, 1948. Pp. 342.
　　　In a semi-novelistic manner the author traces the evolution of the Hamlet Saga up to Shak. and sketches the story of Hamlet production on the Polish stage.

A9965 Melcer, Wanda. "Szekspir na Półmisku." *Odrodzenie* (Warsaw), No. 28 (1948), 7.

A9966 Berwińska, Krystyna. "Ardeński Las." *Teatr* (Warsaw), Nos. 11/12 (June 1951), 55-63.

A9967 "William Shakespeare und G. B. Shaw in Polen." *Kulturprobleme d. Neuen Polen* (Berlin), No. 4 (April, 1952), 3-6.

A9968 Borowy, Wacław. "Przekłady Shakespeare a Teatr." *Teatr*, No. 1-2 (1948), 19-25.

A9968a Borowy, Wacław. "Przekłady Shakespeare a i Teatr." *Studia i Rozprawy*, II, 33-16. Wrocław: Zakł. Narod. im. Ossolińskich, 1952. Pp. 382.

A9969 Helsztyński, Stanislaw. "Przekłady Szekspirowskie w Polsce Wczoraj i Dzis." *Pamietnik Teatralny*, Feb. 1954.
　　　Shak. translation in Poland Yesterday and Today.

A9970 Grzegorczyk, P. "*Hamlet* w Nowym Spojrzeniu." *Twórczość* (Warsaw), June 12, 1956, pp. 172-175.

A9971 Raszewski, Zbigniew. "Against Some Part of Poland." *Drama*, Spring, 1956, pp. 24-28. The influence of Shak. on the Polish Theatre.

(3) CZECHOSLOVAKIA

A9972 Albrecht, J. "Vodákův Shakespeare." *Jindřich Vodák, Poeta k Jeho Sedmdesátinám*. Prague, 1937, pp. 274-280.

A9973 Bryner, Cyril. "Shakespeare Among the Slavs." *ELH*, VIII (1941), 107-118.

A9974 Mráz, Andreas. *Die Literatur der Slowaken*. Berlin: Volk und Reich-Vlg., 1943. Pp. 202.

A9975 Kodicek, J. "Shakespeare on the Czech Stage." *Central European Observer*, XXI (1944), 247-248.

A9976 Selver, Paul. "Czech Shakespeare Studies." *TLS*, Aug. 25, 1945, p. 408.
Notes that F. Chudoba's *Kniha o Shakespearovi*, [*A Book about Shak.*], edited by Professor Chudoba's son was published in Prague, 1941-43, by Jan Laichter, in two volumes.

A9977 Babler, O. F. "Shakespeare's *Macbeth* in Czech Literature." *N &Q*, 193 (1948), 268.

A9978 Strnad, Miroslav. "Několik Poznámek o Shakespearovi v Čechách." *Slovesná Věda*, II (1949), 119-124.
["Some Remarks Concerning Shakespeare in Bohemia."]

A9979 Bejblik, A. "Dvě Poznámky k Shakespeareovi v Čechách." *Listy Filologické* (Prague), XV (1951), No. 5-6.

A9980 Simko, Ján. "Shakespeare in Slovakia." *ShS*, IV (1951), 109-116.

A9981 Babler, O. F. "Shakespeare's *Tempest* in Czech." *N &Q*, NS, II (1955), 15-16.

A9982 Pokorný, Jaroslav. *Shakespeare in Czechoslovakia*. Prague: Československá Akademie Věd Kabinet pro Moderní Filologii, 1955.
Rev: by O. Vočadlo, *The Slavonic Review*, XXXV (1956), 272-274; by Milton Crane, *SQ*, VII (1956), 119.

A9983 Vočadlo, Otakar. "Shakespeare and Bohemia." *ShS*, IX (1956), 101-110.

A9984 Boor, Ján. "Poznámky k Našej Shakespearovskej Drmaturgii." *Slovenské Divadlo* (Bratislava), VI (1958), 68-70.

A9985 Jeřábek, Dušan. "Hálek a Shakespeare." *F. Wollmanovi k Sedmdesátinám* (Collection of articles in tribute to Professor Wollman's 70th birthday). Prague: Státní Pedagogické Nakladatelství, 1958, pp. 603-616.

A9986 Stříbrný, Zedněk. "První Shakespearovský Festival v Olomouci." *Časopis pro Moderní Filologii* (Prague), XL (1958), 234-235.

(4) OTHER SLAVONIC REGIONS

A9987 Radulescu, I. Horia. "Les Intermédiares Français de Shakespeare en Roumanie." *RLC*, XVIII (1938), 252-271.

A9988 Bryner, Cyril. "Shakespeare Among the Slavs." *ELH*, VIII (1941), 107-118.

A9989 Dedinac, M. "Povodom Šekspirovog Otela na Beogradskoj Pozornici." *Književnost* (Belgrade), II (1947), pp. 478-486.

A9990 Filipović, Rudolf. *Shakespeare i Hrvati u 19. Stoljeću* [Shakespeare and Croats in the 19th Century]. Zagreb, 1948. Pp. 16. Also in Slovene translation, "Shakespeare in Hrvati v 19. Stoletju." *Slavistični Revija* (Ljubljana), II, Nos. 3-4 (1949), 306-317.
This is one chapter in the doctoral thesis, *Echoes of English Literature in 19th Century Croatia* (MS), Univ. of Zagreb, 1948.

A9991 Hergešić, Ivo. "Shakespeare u Hrvatskoj." (Shakespeare in Croatia). *Hrvatsko Kolo* (Zagreb), II, Nos. 2-3 (1949), 505-528.

A9992 Klajn, Hugo. "Savremeni Problemi u Hamletu." *Književnost* (Belgrade), IV (1949), 210-237.

A9993 Matković, Marijan. "Shakespeare i Današnjica." *Izvor*, II (1949), 509-516. Also in his *Dramaturški Eseji* (Zagreb), 1949, pp. 23-35.

A9994 Moravec, Dušan. "Shakespeare pri Slovencih" (Shakespeare in Slovenia). *Slavistična Revija* (Ljubljana), II, Nos. 1-2, 3-4 (1949), 51-74, 250-291.

A9995 Moutaftchiev, I. "Shakespeare and Bulgaria." *TLS*, Nov. 18, 1949, p. 751.
Comment by Peter Alexander and Norman Davis, *TLS*, Dec. 16, 1949, p. 825.

A9996 Grün, Herbert. "*Kralj Lear*. Meditacije pred Premiero." *Mladinska Revija* (Ljubljana), V (1950), 220-224.

A9997 Hergešić, I. "Shakespeare u Hrvata Nekoć i Danas." *Narodna Knjiga*, III (July 1950), 43-45.

A9998 Koš, Erih. "Šekspir: Kako vam Drago." *Književnost* (Belgrade), V (1950), 381-383.

A9999 Pervas, D. "Šekspirov stav prema narodu." *Naša Reč*, Jan. 1950, pp. 50-64.

A10000 Dolar, Jaro. "O Shakespearu in Njegovi Ejubezenski Tragediji." *Gledališni List* (Maribor), June 6, 1951, pp. 27-29.

B1 Petančić, M. "*Hamlet* (Kraljević Danski). William Shakespeare." [Program] Osijek: Narodno Kazalište, 1951. Pp. 15.

B2   Popović, Vladeta. "Shakespeare Among the South Slavs, Especially in Post-War Yugoslavia."
      Zbornik Filozofskog Fakulteta (Belgrade), II (1952), 281-291.

B3   Javarek, V. *English Influence on the Works of Dositej Obradović—Its Extent and Importance.* DD,
      London, 1954.
      See Noyes tr. of Obradović's Autobiography, Vol. 39 of *Univ. of California Publ. in Modern
      Philology.*

B4   Klajn, Hugo. "Shakespeare in Yugoslavia." *Review of International Affairs* (Belgrade), V
      (June 1, 1954), 17-18.

B5   Klajn, Hugo. "Shakespeare in Yugoslavia." *SQ,* V (1954), 41-45.

B6   Checkley, C. S. *Rumanian Interpretations of "Hamlet."* MA thesis, Birmingham, 1956.

f. HUNGARY (156; 52)

B7   Hevesi, Sándor. "A Huszadik Század Shakespeare-je." *Budapesti Szemle,* Band 242, Heft 706
      (1936), 287-303.
      Shak. in the 20th century.

B8   Anon. "English and American Drama in the Hungarian National Theatre." *Theater d. Welt,*
      I (1937), 520-525.

B9   Sebestyén, Ch. "Cult of Shakespeare in Hungary." *The Hungarian Quarterly* (Budapest),
      III (1937), 154-163.

B10   Yoland, A. "The Cult of Shakespeare in Hungary." *The Hungarian Quarterly* (Budapest), V
      (1938), 285-296.

B11   Császár, Elemér. *Deutsche Elemente in der Ungarischen Dichtung des 18. Jahrhunderts.* Südost-
      europäische Arbeiten des Dts. Auslandwissenschaftl. Instituts [Berlin] und des Südost-
      instituts München. No. 31. Munich: Schick, 1942. Pp. 71.
      Shak. translations, p. 64, and Shak. passim.

B12   Mikes, George. *Shakespeare and Myself.* London: Wingate, 1952. Pp. 121. Tr. into
      German by Luise Wasserthal-Zuccari as *Shakespeare und Mikes.* Hamburg: Zsolnay, 1953.
      Pp. 161.
        Rev: by C. E. Vulliamy, *Spectator,* 6484 (1952), 438-439; *TLS,* Sept. 19, p. 615.

B13   Mark, Thomas Raymond. *Shakespeare in Hungary: A History of the Translation, Presentation,
      and Reception of Shakespeare's Dramas in Hungary, 1785-1878.* DD, Columbia University, 1955.
      Pp. 354. Mic 56-1174. *DA,* XVI (1956), 751. Publ. No. 16,287. Abstracted by Jack R.
      Brown, *ShN,* VII (1957), 31.

g. JAPAN

This section is chiefly listings of Japanese items in the sources of this bibliography. Most of
those not specifically on Shakespeare's influence in Japan were either of too general and re-
capitulative or of too uncertain content to warrant listing elsewhere. Japanese items of
obvious relevance to other classes have been listed appropriately.

B14   *Studies in English Literature.* A Quarterly Review Compiled and Issued by the English Literary
      Society of Japan, Tokyo Imperial Univ. 35 volumes through 1958.
      Many essays on Shak.

B15   Saisho, F. "An Oriental Appreciation of Shakespeare's Personality." *Cultural Nippon,* IV
      (1936), 91-93.

B16   Iwatsuki, Tachiwo. "On the Changing Literary Modes in the Development of Renaissance
      Tragedy." *Studies in English Literature,* XVIII (1938), 486-505.

B17   Oktski, Kenji. "Analytische Würdigung von Shakespeares *Hamlet." Tokyo Zeitschrift für
      Psychoanalyse,* 1938.

B18   Thaler, A. "Shakespeare in Japan." *SAB,* XIV (1939), 192.
      On Yuzo Tsubouchi's tr. of Shak.

B19   Toyoda, Minoru. *Shakespeare in Japan: An Historical Survey.* Tokyo: The Iwanami Shoten,
      1940. Pp. xi, 139 (in English).
      An outline history of Shak. studies in Japan, from the origins up to the date of publication.
      "Direct Translation," pp. 32-50; "Stories and Adaptations of Shak.'s plays," pp. 61-74;
      "Shak. on the Stage," pp. 107-120; "A Japanese Shak. Bibliog.," pp. 121-139.

B20   Tannenbaum, Samuel A. "Shakspere and Japan." *SAB,* XVI (1941), 59-60.

B21   Toyoda, Minoru. *Shakespeare in Japan: An Historical Survey.* S. Pasadena, California: P. D. &
      Jone Perkins, 1941. Pp. 150.

B22   Saito, Takeshi. "Studies of English Literature in Japan, 1936-1940." *Studies in Eng. Lit.*
      (Eng. Lit. Soc. Japan), XX (1941), 565-584.

B23   "Women in Shakespeare." *Fujinbunko* (Japan), No. 6 (1947).

B24   Abe, Tomoji. "*Hamlet.*" *World Literature* (Japan), No. 1 (1947).

B25   Kudo, Yoshimi. "Goethe and Shakespeare." *Ningen* (Japan), No. 7 (1947).

B26   Saito, Takeshi. *A Shakespeare Survey.* Tokyo: Shingetsu-sha, 1946. Pp. 148 (in Japanese).

B27   Fukuhara, Rintaro. *"Romeo and Juliet."* *Rising Generation* (Japan), 93, No. 3, (1947).

B28   Hijikata, Yoshi. *"The Taming of the Shrew."* *Teatoro* (Japan), No. 79 (1947).

B29   Ishida, Kenji. "Shakespeare's Historical Plays." *Rising Generation* (Japan), 93, No. 3 (1947).

B30   Nakahaski, Kazuo. "The Spirit of Shakespeare's Comedies." *Rising Generation* (Japan), 93, No. 3 (1947).

B31   Nakanishi, Shintaro. "Shakespeare and English Literary Thought." *Bungei-Gaku* (Japan), No. 1 (1947).

B32   Nakano, Yoshio. "Shakespeare: A Man of Renaissance." *Kaizo* (Japan), No. 2 (1947).

B33   Nakano, Yoshio. "Shakespeare's Psychological Techniques." *Rising Generation* (Japan), 93, No. 1 (1947).

B34   Ouchi, Shuko. *Shakespeare and His Age.* Japan: Kenkyusha, 1947. Pp. 88.

B35   Tachibana, Tadae. *A Study of Shakespeare.* Japan: Sakuraishoten, 1947. Pp. 226 (in Japanese).

B36   "Chikamatsu and Shakespeare." *Kaishaku to Kansho,* Feb. 1948.

B37   Nakahashi, Kazuo. *Destiny of the Fool.* Tokyo: Chuokoronsha, 1948.

B38   Yamoto, Sadamiki. *The Literature in the Elizabethan Age.* Tokyo: Akitaya, 1948.

B39   Endo, Shingo. "Shakespeare's World." *Higeki-Kigeki,* VI (1949).

B40   Honda, Akira. *A Study of Shakespeare.* Kobundo, 1949.

B41   Hondo, Masao. "A Study of *Hamlet.*" *The Literature* (Japan), No. 1 (1949).

B42   Mikami, Isao. "Shakespearean Comedy." *Eibungakushicho,* XXII, No. 1 (1949).

B43   Myoga, Sachiya. "Shakespeare and Chikamatsu." *Eibungakushicho,* XXII (1949), 2.

B44   Nakanishi, Shintaro. *Studies in Shakespeare Criticism* (Shakespeare Studies Series). Tokyo: Sogen-sha, 1949. Pp. viii, 268 (in Japanese).

B45   Nakano, Yoshio. "Ophelia's Death." *World News* (Japan), Nov. 1949.

B46   Nakano, Yoshio, ed. *Studies of Shakespeare.* Tokyo: Shingetsu-sha, 1949. Pp. 322 (in Japanese).

B47   Cancelled.

B48   Otsuka, Takanobu. *A Study of Shakespeare's Handwriting* (Shakespeare Studies Series). Tokyo: Sogen-sha, 1949. Pp. 138, 22 (in Japanese). Republ. Tokyo: Shinozaki Shorin, 1952. Pp. 167, 17 plates.

B49   Saito, Takeshi. *Shakespeare: A Survey of His Life and Works.* Tokyo: Kenkyusha, 1949. Pp. xviii, 568 (in Japanese).
       Standard Shak. handbook in Japan.

B50   Cancelled.

B51   Shimada, Kinji. *English Literature in Japan.* *Albion* (Japan), I (1949).

B52   Suzuki, Sachio. *Main Currents in English Literature.* Aoyama-shoin, 1949.

B53   Yamato, Motoo. *Appreciation of English Literature.* Tokyo: Kenkyusha, 1949.

B54   Yamoto, Teikan. "Personalities in Shakespeare's Plays." *Eibungakukenkyu,* XXVI, No. 1 (1949).

B55   Yoshida, Kenichi. *English Literature.* Yukei-sha, 1949.

B56   Yoshida, Kenichi. *Modern English Literature.* *Albion* (Japan), I (1949).

B57   Yoshida, Kenichi. "Shakespeare's Tragedy and Comedy." *Bungei,* May 1949.

B58   Nakanishi, Shintaro. *An Introduction to "Hamlet."* Tokyo: Kenkyusha, 1950. Pp. 226.

B59   Nomachi, Susumu. "English Literature and the Supernatural." *Eibungakukenkyu,* XXVII (1950), 46-60.

B60   The Theatre Arts Society of Japan, ed. *Studies in Shakespeare,* with a list of the performances of Shakespeare's plays in Japan (*Journal of Theatre Arts,* II, No. 1). Tokyo: Chuokoron-sha (in Japanese).

B61   Nakanishi, Shintaro. "The Opening Scene of *Hamlet.*" *The Rising Generation,* 97 (1951), 149-151.

B62   Otsuka, Takanobu. *English of Shakespeare and the Bible.* Tokyo: Kenkyusha. Pp. xvii, 234 (in Japanese).

B63   Wada, Yuchi. "Machiavellism and *Richard III.*" *Eibungakukenkyu,* XXVII (1951), 179-191.

B64   Fukuhara, Rintaro. "Shakespeare and Thomas Gray." *The Rising Generation,* 98 (1952), 149-150.

B65   Hoskawa, Senjiro. "Shakespeare Scholarship and Aesthetic Criticism." *The Rising Generation,* 98 (1952), 7-10.

B66   Kinoshita, Junji. *Watashi-tachi no Shakespeare.* Tokyo: Chikuma, 1953. Pp. 210.
       Introduction for young readers by a representative playwright of Japan.

B67   Oyama, Toshiko. *A Study of Shakespeare's Imagery.* Tokyo: Shinozaki-shorin, 1953. Pp. 190.

B68   Kaneda, Tamayo. " 'Patience' in *King Lear.*" *Essays and Studies in British and American Literature.* Tokyo Woman's Christian College, II, i (Summer, 1954), 1-26 (in English).

B69   Kashiwakura, Shunzo. *Shakespeare and His Environs.* Tokyo: Kenkyusha, 1954. Pp. 250.

B70   Saito, Kinuko. "A Note on *The Tempest*—The Utopian Notion in Shakespeare." *Essays and Studies in British and American Literature*, Tokyo Woman's Christian College, I, i (Spring, 1954), 35-43 (in English).

B71   Higashi, Tosiko. "On *Macbeth*." *Essays and Studies in British and American Literature*, Tokyo Woman's Christian College, III, i (Autumn, 1955), 1-26 (in English).

B72   Honda, Akira. "How to Handle Fools in Shakespeare." *The Rising Generation* (Tokyo), 101, No. 4 (1955) (in Japanese).

B73   Kashiwakura, Shunzo. "Shakespeare." *Literature* (Sapporo), Nov. 1955 (in Japanese).

B74   Fukuhara, Rintaro. *Ars Longa*. Tokyo: Tarumizu Shobo, 1956. Pp. 214.

B75   Fuhara, Yoshiaki. *Shakespeare Nyumon (Introduction to Shakespeare.)* Tokyo: Kenkyusha, 1955. Pp. 248.

B76   Goto, Takeshi. "Moby Dick and Shakespeare." *Kyushu Daigakue English Literary Proceedings* (Fukuoka), Aug., 1956 (in Japanese).

B77   Harada, Shigeo. "The Progressive Tense in Shakespeare." *Kurume Daigaku Ronso* (Kurume, Japan), IV, No. 2 (1956) (in Japanese).

B78   Hiraoka, Tomokazu. "From *Rosalynde* to *As You Like It*." *Toyama Daigaku Bungaku Kiyo* (Toyama, Japan), March 1956 (in Japanese).

B79   Hondo, Masao. "The Essence and Environments of Shakespeare Plays." *Bunka* (Tohoku Univ., Sendai), XX, No. 3 (1956) (in Japanese).

B80   Kaieda, Susumu. "The Mob in Shakespearian Plays." *Tokyo Univ. of Foreign Studies Journal*, Nov. 1956 (in Japanese).

B81   Kobayashi, Hideo. "*Hamlet* and Roskolnikof." *Shincho* (Tokyo), LII, No. 8 (1956), (in Japanese).

B82   Matsumoto, Kan. "An Essay on *King Lear*." *Studies in English Literature and Language* (Hiroshima), III No. 2 (1956), (in Japanese).

B83   Miyauchi, Bunshichi. "Quintessence of Poetic Drama in Shakespeare." *Studies in English Literature and Language* (Hiroshima), II, No. 2 (1956), (in Japanese).

B84   Muraoka, Isamu. "Poetic Images in the Elizabethan Period." *Bunka* (Tohoku Univ., Sendai), XX, No. 3 (1956), (in Japanese).

B85   Muraoka, Isamu. "*Troilus and Cressida* of Shakespeare." *Studies in English Literature* (Tokyo), XXXII, No. 2 (1956), (in Japanese).

B86   Nakamura, Rikuo. "Shakespeare and Education." *Shinshu Daigaku Study Report* (Uyeda), March, 1956, (in Japanese).

B87   Nishida, Kunio. "On the Imagery of *Othello*." *Kanazawa English Studies* (Kanazawa Univ.), Jan., 1956, (in Japanese).

B88   Okubo, Junichiro. "Robert Greene and Shakespeare." *Kanazawa English Studies* (Kanazawa Univ.), Jan., 1956, (in Japanese).

B89   Oyama, Toshikazu. *Saikinno Shakespeare Kenkyuho* (A Bibliographical Approach to Recent Shakespearean Studies). Tokyo: Shinozaki Shorin, 1956. Pp. iv, 242, ix.

B90   Ozu, Jiro. "Restoration and Modernization of Shakespeare." *The Rising Generation* (Tokyo), 102, No. 6 (1956) (in Japanese).

B91   Tazawa, Keito. "On the Imagery in *Othello*." *Kyoto Joshidai English Studies* (Kyoto), May, 1956 (in Japanese).

B92   Yamanouchi, Ryuji. "Shakespeare and *The Fairy Way of Writing*." *Meiji Daigaku English Studies*, II (Aug. 1956) (in Japanese).

B93   Yamoto, Teikan. "Ben Jonson in His *Discoveries*." *Bunka* (Tohoku Univ., Sendai), XX, No. 3, (1956).

B94   Yano, Banri. "On Some Scenes in *Henry V*." *Studies in English Literature* (Tokyo), XXXII, No. 2 (1956) (in Japanese).

B95   Yoshida, Ken-ichi. "On *Hamlet*." *Bungei* (Tokyo), XII, No. 6 (1956) (in Japanese).

B96   Yoshida, Ken-ichi. *Shakespeare*. Tokyo: Tarumizu Shobo, 1956. Pp. 254.

B97   Kimura, Keiko. "A Study of *King Lear*." *Essays and Studies in British and American Literature*, Tokyo Woman's Christian College, V, i (Summer, 1957), 1-28.

h. INDIA

Listings of Indian items as well as of discussions of Shak.'s influence in India: Same reservations as with Japanese items above.

B98   Pisharoti, K. R. "Aesthetic Pleasure in Drama." *Calcutta Rev.*, LVIII (1936), 297-301.

B99   Shahani, R. G. "Kalidasa and Shakespeare." *Aryan Path*, VII (1936), 456-459.

B100   Tyabji, F. B. "The Value of Shakespeare to Modern India." *Aryan Path*, VII (1936), 231-235.

B101   Sinha, A. B. N. "Tulsidas and Shakespeare." *Hindustan Rev.*, LXIX (Feb., 1937), 560-564.

B102   Menon, C. Narayana. *Shakespeare Criticism: An Essay In Synthesis*. Oxford Univ. Press, 1938. Pp. 276.

Rev: *TLS*, Oct. 1, 1938, p. 629; *N &Q*, 175 (1938), 215-216; by J. W. Crowfoot, *English*, II, 186-187; by J. Crofts, *MLR*, XXXIV (1939), 636; by Georges Connes, *EA*, III, 103; by L. L. Schücking, *Beiblatt*, L, 80; by R. S. Knox, *UTQ*, IX, 113-115; by A. W. Pirkhofer, *Eng. Studn.*, LXXIII, 393-395; by T. W. Baldwin, *MLN*, LV (1940), 460.

B103   Mansinha, Mayadhar. *Shakespeare and Kalidas*. DD, Durham, 1939. Abstr. publ. in Univ. of Durham *Abstracts of Theses for Doctorates, 1938-39*, p. 3.

B104   Bhave, Y. D. "Shakespeare Criticism Through Indian Eyes." *Journal of Univ. of Bombay*, VII (1939), 196-198.

B105   Bhattacherje, M. M. "Feudal Manners in Shakespeare." *Calcutta Review*, LXX (1938/39), 181-194.

B106   Bhattacherje, M. M. "Evolution of Hamlet's Personality." *Calcutta Review*, LXX (1939), 288-299.

B107   Mansinha, M. "At the Birthplace of Shakespeare." *The Modern Review* (Calcutta), LXIV (1938), 677.

B108   Bhattacherje, M. M. "Italy in Elizabethan Pamphlets." *Calcutta Review*, LXXIII (1942), 129-135.

B109   Bhanu, D. "Shakespeare as a War Prophet." *Indian Review*, XLIV (1944), 445-456.

B110   Gupta, A. "Studies of English Through Indian Eyes." *Hindustan Review*, LXXIX (1946), 101-106.

B111   King, T. "Shakespeare, The Master-Builder." *The Aryan Path*, XVIII (1947), 387-391.

B112   Winsteadt, R. "The East in English Literature." *Indian Art and Letters*, XXI (1947), 1-12.

B113   Sethna, K. D. *Shakespeare and "Things to Come."* Bombay: Sri Aurobindo Circle, 1948, pp. 96-112.

B114   Ray, Sibnarayan. "A Note on Shakespeare." *Mysindia* (Bangalore), July 9, 1950, pp. 17-18.

B115   Wasi, Muriel. "Shakespeare in Delhi." *Mysindia* (Bangalore), Nov. 26, 1950, pp. 19-20.

B116   Marshall, Norman. "Shakespeare in India." *Theatre Newsletter*, April 28, 1951, p. 3.

B117   Krishnaswami, P. R. *Four Lectures on Shakespeare*. Madras, 1955.
        Rev: *The Hindu* (Madras), Oct. 23, 1955.

B118   Omkarananda, Swami. *Shakespeare on Sivananda*. Rishakesh: Divine Life Society, Yoga Vedanta Forest Univ., n.d., (1955?). Pp. 66.
        Rev: by K. C. Varadachari, *The Hindu* (Madras), March 27, 1955.

B119   *The Tempest*. Ed. V. H. Kulkarni. With complete paraphrase printed opposite to the text. Bombay: Booksellers' Publ. Co., 1955. Pp. 278.

B120   *Othello*. Introd., paraphrase, word meaning and notes by Shiv Kumar. Delhi, India: Chand, 1956.

B121   Prema, S. "Producing Shakespeare in India." *SQ*, IX (1958), 395-396.
See also B7455.

i. CHINA

B122   Atkinson, Brooks. "*Hamlet* at the Kuo T'ai Theatre in Chungking, Is Not Yet Quite Ready for Broadway." *New York Times*, Dec. 18, 1942, pp. 1, 38.

B123   Chang Chen-Hsien. *Shakespeare in China*. MA thesis, Birmingham, 1951.

B124   Chang Chen-Hsien. "Shakespeare in China." *ShS*, VI (1953), 112-116.

B125   "Shakespeare in China." *Illustrated London News*, Oct. 13, 1956, p. 615.

j. TURKEY

B126   Dengi. *Shakispeare Kimdi?* [Who Was Shakespeare?] (In Turkish New Script) London: Luzac, 1939. Pp. 31.

B127   Burian, Orhan. "Shakespeare in Turkey." *SQ*, II (1951), 127-128.

B128   Burian, Orhan, and Perihan Cambel. "Theatre in Turkey." *Players Magazine*, May, 1952.

k. Other Countries (not included above)

B129   Parry, John. *A Guide to Shakespeare for Malayan Students*. London: Harrap, 1956. Pp. 72.

B130   "Shakespeare Lectures at the Oregon Festival." *ShN*, VIII (1958), 28-29.
        Includes abstr. of paper by Myna Brunton Hughes, "Shak. in South America."

4. ALTERATIONS AND ADAPTATIONS (156;53)
a. GENERAL TREATISES (GROUP STUDIES) (156;53)

B131   Eich, Louis M. *Alterations of Shakespeare, 1660-1710: and an Investigation of the Critical and Dramatic Principles and Theatrical Conventions which Prompted these Revisions*. DD, University of Michigan, 1923. Pp. 211. Mic A 48-50. *Mcf Ab*, VIII (1948), 90. Publ. No. 920.

B132   L., L. "Imitations of Shakespeare." *N &Q*, 173 (1937), 334.
        See letters by William Jaggard, *N &Q*, 173 (1937), 370-373, and Frederic Connett White, ibid., p. 373.

B133   Huang, John. *A Short History of Shakespearean Production.* M. Litt thesis, Cambridge. *Cam Abs.*, 1937-38, p. 84.

B134   Toyoda, Minoru. *Shakespeare in Japan: An Historical Survey.* Tokyo: The Iwanami Shoten, 1940. Pp. xi, 139 (in English).
        "Stories and Adaptations of Shak.'s Plays," pp. 61-74.

B135   Foster, George Harding. *British History on the London Stage, 1660-1760.* DD, University of North Carolina, 1941. Abstr. publ. in *Univ. of North Carolina Record, Research in Progress, 1940-41.* Chapel Hill, 1941, pp. 65-67.
        Abstr. does not mention Shak.

B136   Monaco, Marion. *Shakespeare on the French Stage in the Eighteenth Century.* DD, Bryn Mawr College, 1943. Pp. 235. Mic A43-2178. *Mcf Ab.*, v (1943), 18. Publ. No. 581.

B137   Bogorad, Samuel Nathaniel. *The English History Play in Restoration Drama.* DD, Northwestern University, 1946. Abstr. Publ. in *Summaries of Doctoral Dissertations, 1946*, xiv. Chicago and Evanston: Northwestern Univ., 1947, pp. 5-10.

B138   Dunkel, W. D. "An Error in *Shakespeare Improved* Corrected." *CEA Critic*, x (1948), 1-3.
        In *Shakespeare Improved* by Hazelton Spencer, Harvard Univ. Press, 1927.

B139   Margaret J. Purcell, Sister. *English History Plays of the Early Eighteenth Century.* DD, University of Missouri, 1950. Pp. 246. Mic A49-235. *Mic Ab*, ix:3 (1949), 142. Publ. No. 1478.

B140   Ashin, Mark. *Restoration Adaptations of Jacobean and Caroline Comedy.* DD, University of Chicago, 1951.

B141   Hook, Lucyle. "Shakespeare Improv'd, or A Case for the Affirmative." *SQ*, iv (1953), 289-299.

B142   Branam, George C. *Eighteenth-Century Adaptations of Shakespearean Tragedy.* DD, University of California, Berkeley, 1954.

B143   Stone, M. W. "Shakespeare and the Juvenile Drama." *TN*, viii (1954), 65-66.
        A list of the juvenile dramas adapted from Shakespeare, with their publishers and dates.

B144   Branam, George C. *Eighteenth-Century Adaptations of Shakespearean Tragedy.* DD, University of California, Berkeley, 1954. Univ. of California Publications. English Studies: 14. Univ. of California Press, 1956. Pp. viii, 220.
        Rev: *ShN*, vi (1956), 39; by George W. Stone, Jr., *MLN*, lxxii (1957), 451-452; by Arthur H. Scouten, *SQ*, viii, 547-548; by John Loftis, *PQ*, xxxvi, 319-320; by A. Parreaux, *LanM*, li, 610-611; by Marvin Rosenberg, *JEGP*, lvii (1958), 130-133.

B145   Kaplan, Milton. "Retarding Shakespeare." *Harper's Magazine*, Jan., 1956, pp. 37-38.

b.   VARIOUS ADAPTERS OF SHAKESPEARE (157;53)
        Both discussions of individual adapters
        and their published adaptations.
        (1) STUDIES OF INDIVIDUAL ADAPTATIONS
              IN ENGLISH
              (a) RESTORATION

B146   Milton, William M. "*Tempest* in a Teapot." *ELH*, xiv (1947), 207-218.

B147   Spencer, Christopher. *The Problems of Davenant's Text of Shakespeare's "Macbeth" Together with a Typed Facsimile of the Yale Manuscript.* DD, Yale University, 1955.

B148   *Theatre Miscellany. Six Pieces Connected with the Seventeenth-Century Stage.* Oxford, 1953.
        Contains "Songs and Masques in The Tempest [c. 1674]. Ed. J. G. McManaway.
        Rev: by Harold Jenkins, *RES*, ns, vi (1955), 86-88.

B149   Haywood, Charles. "The Songs and Masque in the *New Tempest:* An Incident in the Battle of the Two Theatres, 1674." *HLQ*, xix (1955), 39-56.
        Support for B148.

i. Dryden

B150   Leavis, F. R. "*Antony and Cleopatra* and *All For Love.* A Critical Exercise." *Scrutiny*, v (1936), 158-169.

B151   Hooker, Helene M. "Dryden's and Shadwell's *Tempest.*" *HLQ*, vi (1943), 224-228.

B152   Wallerstein, Ruth. "Dryden and the Analysis of Shakespeare's Techniques." *RES*, xix (1943), 165-185.

B153   Lill, James V. *Dryden's Adaptation from Milton, Shakespeare and Chaucer.* DD, University of Minnesota, 1954. Pp. 284. Mic A54-1780. *DA*, xiv (1954), 1214. Publ. No. 8462. Abstr. in *ShN*, iv (1954), 51.

B154   Freedman, Morris. "*All for Love* and *Samson Agonistes.*" *N &Q*, ns, iii (1956), 514-517.

ii. Otway

B155   Eich, Louis. "A Previous Adaptation of *Romeo and Juliet.*" *QJS*, xxiii (1937), 589-594.

B156   Mackenzie, Aline Freeman-Fayers. *Otway and the History of His Plays on the London Stage: A Study of Taste.* DD, Bryn Mawr College, 1943.

B157   Kiendler, Grete. *Konvertierte Formen in den Dramen Otways und Lees: ein Vergleich mit der Sprache Shakespeares.* DD, Graz, 1951. Pp. 202. Typewritten.

B158   Spring, Joseph E. *Two Restoration Adaptations of Shakespeare's Plays "Sauny the Scot;" or, the "Taming of the Shrew" by John Lacy and "The History and Fall of Caius Marius," Thomas Otway's Appropriation of "Romeo and Juliet."* DD, University of Denver, 1953. Abstr. publ. in *Speech Monographs,* xx (1953), 180.

(b) EIGHTEENTH CENTURY

B159   Lehner, Francis C. *The Literary Views of Colley Cibber.* DD, University of Wisconsin, 1955. Abstr. Publ. in Univ. of Wisconsin *Summaries of Doctoral Dissertations,* 1954-55, Madison, 1956, pp. 544-545.

B160   Takeuchi, Hideo. *"King Richard the Third and Colley Cibber."* *Yokahoma Kokudai Proceedings in Humanities* (Tokyo), Jan., 1956 (in Japanese).

B161   Scouten, A. H. "Theophilus Cibber's *The Humourists.*" *N &Q,* NS, II (1955), 114-115.

B162   Stone, G. W., Jr. *"Midsummer Night's Dream* in the Hands of Garrick and Colman." *PMLA,* LIV (1939), 467-482.

B163   Bodtke, R. A. *Garrick's Revisions of Shakespeare: A Mirror for Eighteenth Century Tastes.* MS thesis, Columbia University, 1947. Pp. 94.

B164   Goldstein, Malcolm. "Pope, Shefield, and Shakespeare's *Julius Caesar.*" *MLN,* LXXI (1956), 8-10.

(c) NINETEENTH AND TWENTIETH CENTURIES
i. General
(For Shaw see A9128-A9160)

B165   Thompson, William F. *Edwin Booth's Acting Versions of "Richard III," "Julius Caesar," and the "Merchant of Venice."* DD, University of Nebraska, 1937.

B166   Nathan, Norman. "Three Notes on *The Merchant of Venice.*" *SAB,* XXIII (1948), 152-173.

B167-171 Cancelled..

B172   *"Julius Caesar."* *A Basic English Expansion by A. P. Rossiter.* Cambridge: The Basic English Publishing Co., 1942. Pp. 330.
        Rev: *DUJ,* III (1942), 187-188.

B173   Hastings, William T. "Basic Shakespeare Too?" *Books at Brown,* XVIII (1957), 35-59.

ii. Bowdler

B174   Jha, A. "The Bowdler and His *Shakespeare.*" *Calcutta Rev.,* LXII (1937), 148-152.

B175   Quinlan, Maurice J. *Victorian Prelude.* A History of English Manners, 1700-1830. Number 155 of the Columbia Univ. Studies in English and Comparative Literature. New York: Columbia Univ. Press, 1941. Pp. 301. "The Expurgators of Shakespeare," pp. 240-250. On Bowdler, Pitman, Hannah More and others.

B176   Hanser, Richard. "Shakespeare, sex . . . and Dr. Bowdler." *SatR,* April 23, 1955, pp. 7-8, 50.

B177   Russell, Bertrand. "Mr. Bowdler's Nightmare." *Nightmares of Eminent Persons.* New York: Simon & Schuster, 1955, pp. 11-16.

B178   Rosenberg, Marvin. "Reputation, Oft Lost Without Deserving. . . ." *SQ,* IX (1958), 499-506. A defense of the practicality and artistic integrity of Thomas Bowdler, especially in view of the mutilated "refinements" of Shak. that held the stage at the time.

B179   Yonge, Stanley. "Two Thomas Bowdlers, Editors of Shakespeare." *N &Q,* NS, V (1958), 383-384.

(2) IN NON-ENGLISH COUNTRIES
(For Ducis, see A9343-A9350.)

B180   Van Tieghem, Paul. "Adaptations Scéniques de Shakespeare sur le Continent." *Rivista di Letterature Moderne,* I (1946), 22-38.

B181   Lang, D. M. "Sumarkov's *Hamlet*: A Misjudged Russian Tragedy of the Eighteenth Century." *MLR,* XLIII (1948), 67-72.

B182   Keys, A. C. "Shakespeare in France. An Early Stage Adaptation." *Jour. Australian Univ. Mod. Lang. Assoc.,* Aug., 1953.

B183   Dufour, Emile H. "World Information: Chile." *World Theatre,* IV, No. 3, (1955), 62-64.

(3) EDITIONS OF ADAPTATIONS
(a) IN ENGLISH
i. Several Plays

B184   Nathan, G. J. *The Avon Flows.* New York: Random House, 1937. Pp. 290.

Adaptations of *Romeo*, *Oth.*, and *Shrew*.
  Rev: by P. M. Jack, *NYTBR*, Feb. 14, 1937, p. 4.

B185   Welles, O., and R. Hill, eds. *The Mercury Shakespeare*. New York, 1939.
       Adaptations of *Merch*, *Caesar*, and *Twelf*.

B186   Windross, Ronald, adapter. *Three Comedies. The Stories of These Abridged and Simplified*. Tales
       from England, 2nd degree. 3. Paris, Brussels: Didier, 1950. Pp. 80. *Dream*, *Temp*, *AYL*.

B186a Windross, Ronald, adapter. *Three Mediterranean Plays*. Abridged and simplified. Tales
       from England, 2nd degree. 4. Paris, Brussels: Didier, 1952. Pp. 80. *Romeo*, *Merch.*, *Twelf.*

B187   Taylor, Henry S. *A Shorter Shakespeare*. Arranged by Henry S. Taylor. London: Ginn.
       As You Like It, 1956. Pp. viii, 96. *King Henry V*, 1956. Pp. viii, 88. *The Merchant of Venice*,
       1956. Pp. viii, 72. *Julius Caesar*, 1956. Pp. viii, 103. *Henry IV, Part 1*, 1956. Pp. ix, 86.
       Macbeth, 1956. Pp. ix, 102. *A Midsummer Night's Dream*, 1956. Pp. ix, 86. *Twelfth Night*,
       or What You Will, 1956. Pp. viii, 108. *Hamlet*, 1957. Pp. viii, 143. *The Tempest*, 1957. Pp.
       viii, 88. *Richard II*, 1958. Pp. viii, 96. *The Taming of the Shrew*, 1958. Pp. viii, 104.
       Rev: B4195, B4198, B4205, B4207.

B188   *Shakespeare for Young Actors: 40-minute Versions of A Midsummer Night's Dream, The Merchant
       of Venice, The Taming of the Shrew, As You Like It, Julius Caesar, and The Tempest*. For secondary
       school study and production. Ed. with introduction and comments by Eleanor Patmore
       Young. New York: Exposition Press, 1958. Pp. 248.
       Rev: by Hudson Rogers, *English Journal*, XLVII (1958), 308-309.

B189   *Radio Plays from Shakespeare*. Ten Plays Adapted for Royalty-Free Performance by Lewy
       Olfson. Boston: Plays Incorporated, 1958. Pp. 193.
       Version of *Macb.* previously publ. in *Plays*, April, 1955, pp. 87-95. Of *AYL* and *Ham.*,
       Plays, 1958.
       Rev: by T. C. Kelly, *Library Journal*, 83 (1958), 2076.

                              ii.   Single Plays
                                    (Arranged by play in chronological
                                    order of their composition)

B190   *The Comedy of Errors*. Adapted by Klaus Fuss. Braunsche Schulbücherei, Series 3, No. 10.
       Karlsruhe: Braun, 1953. Pp. 83.

B191   *The Taming of the Shrew*. Adapted for the Blackfriars of Alabama by L. Raines. Alabama
       Univ., 1942. Pp. 25.

B192   *A Midsummer Night's Dream*. Arranged by L. Green. London: Nelson, 1937. Pp. 55.

B193   *Romeo and Juliet*. Ed. and Abr. by Donald G. Kobler. New York: Henry Holt, 1956. Pp. 90.

B194   *The Merchant of Venice*. Adapted by Hubert Hüsges. Schöninghs Englische Lesebogen.
       Paderborn: Schöningh, 1954. Pp. 103.

B195   "Beatrice and Benedick." An Adaptation of *Much*, as edited by M. Mantle. *Plays*, XIV
       (May, 1955), 13-18.

B196   *Julius Caesar*. Telescoped from Shakespeare's play by Alicia C. Percival. London: Nelson,
       1938. Pp. 111.

B197   *Julius Caesar*. Adapted by Jack A. Wapon and Leroy S. Layton. New York: Globe Book Co.,
       1952. Pp. xii, 99.

B198   *Julius Caesar in Modern English*. Adapted from Shakespeare's Play by Elsie M. Katterjohn.
       Chicago: Scott, Foresman, 1957. Pp. 120.
       Rev: (from an invited letter by Miss Katterjohn), "Shakespeare for the Retarded," *ShN*,
       VII (1957), 45.

B199   *As You Like It. Das Spiel von Celia und Rosalinde im Ardennerwald. Aus Shakespeares Lustspiel
       "Wie es euch Gefällt."* Arranged for amateurs by Eva Ultsch. Kassel, Basel: Barenreiter-
       Verlag, 1953. Pp. 60.

B200   *Maurice Evans' G. I. Production of "Hamlet": Acting Edition with a Preface; Designer's Sketches
       by Frederick Stover*. New York: Doubleday, 1947. Pp. 7, 187.
       Rev: B3023.

B201   *Hamlet*. As Arranged for the Stage of the Globe Theatre at the San Diego Exposition (Globe
       Theatre Version), ed. Thomas Wood Stevens. New York: Samuel French, 1952. Pp. 88.

B202   *The Portable "Hamlet."* Adapted for the Modern Reader by George Haimsohn. Ill. New
       York: Coward-McCann, 1951.

B203   Freund, Philip. *Prince Hamlet*. New York: Bookman Associates, 1953. Pp. 70.
       Rev: B4066.

B204   *Othello*. With Introd., Paraphrase, Word Meaning and Notes by Shiv Kumar. Delhi, India:
       Chand, 1956.

B205   *The Tragedy of King Lear*. Adapted and Annotated by J. Verwey. Purmerend: Muusses,
       1952. Pp. 117.
       Rev: by L. E. de Vries, *LT*, 1952, pp. 416-417.

B206   *Macbeth*. Classics Illustrated, No. 4. New York: Gilberton and Company, 1957.
       Adapted, pictorial version for children.

B207   *Macbeth*. Telescoped by J. P. Walker. London: Nelson, 1937. Pp. 106.

B208   *Macbeth*. Translated into a more modern speech and clarified by Frank P. Zeidler. Milwaukee: Milwaukee Publishers, 1957. Pp. 83.

B208a *Macbeth*. Adapted by Elsie Katterjohn and Esther W. Currie. Chicago: Scott, Foresman, 1957.

(b) IN OTHER LANGUAGES

B209   *Richard III*. Adaptation de Charles Antonetti. *Éducation et Théâtre* (Paris), Nos. 42-43 (1957).

B210   *Le Songe d'une Nuit d'Été*. Adaptation pour la Jeunesse par Charles Vildrac. Petite Bibliothèque Théâtrale. Paris: Éditions Sociales Internationales, 1937.

B211   *La Tempête. Le Songe d'une Nuit d'Été*. Adapt. de Claude Lussier. Montréal: Éd. Fides, 1948. Pp. 61.

B212   *Songe d'une Nuit d'Été*. Adaptation de Paul Arnold. *Revue Théâtrale*, No. 26 (1954), 31-84.

B213   *Roméo et Juliette*. Adapt. par Jean Sarment. Paris: Nagel, 1948. Pp. 248.

B214   Quéval, J. "*Les Amants de Vérone* (d'Après un Scénario de Jacques Prévert, Transposé de *Roméo et Juliette*)." *MdF*, 306 (1949), 314-317.

B215   *Henry IV*. Adapt. de Maurice Clavel. Paris: Nagel, 1950. Pp. 196.

B216   *Le Chevalier à la Lune, ou Sir John Falstaff*. Comédie en cinq actes restituée en sa forme originale et précédée d'un argument par Fernand Crommelynck. Brussels: Éditions des Artistes, 1954. Pp. 245.

B217   *Macbeth*. Adapt. du Drame de Shakespeare par Rose Laurence Gignoux. Paris: Larousse, 1950. Pp. 142.

B218   *Le Prodigue de Londres*. Comédie en 5 actes. Adapt. par Henri Ghéon selon la version d'Ernest Kamnitzer. Paris: Impr. Artistique, 1947. Pp. xiii, 206.

B219   *Connaissance de Shakespeare*. Cahiers de la Compagnie Madeleine Renaud—J.-L. Barrault, No. 16. Paris: Julliard, 1956. Pp. 128.

B220   *Hamlet, Prince of Denmark*. In leicht gekürzter Form hrsg. u. m. Anm. u. e. Einl. vers. v. Stephan Hartmann. Vienna: Österr. Bundesverl., 1951. Pp. 111.

B221   *Historias*. Adaptación de María Luz Morales Godoy. 7 ed. Barcelona: Araluce, 1955.

B222   *Más Historias*. Adaptación de Jeanie Lang. 5 ed. Las obras maestras al alcance de los niños. Barcelona: Araluce, 1956. Pp. 115.

c. COLLECTIONS OF EXCERPTS

B223   *The Shakespeare Anthology: Poems, Poetical Passages, Lyrics*. London: Nonesuch Press; New York: Random House, 1935. Pp. vii, 525.
       Rev: *TLS*, Dec. 14, 1935, p. 850; by B. de Selincourt, *Obs.*, Jan. 26, 1936.

B224   Colborne-Smith, H. *Gatherings from Shakespeare*. London: S. Nott, 1936. Pp. 207.

B225   Shakespeare, William. *A Shakespeare Anthology*. By W. Dodd. Mermaid Poets. London: Collins, 1936.

B226   Shakespeare, William. *Reif sein ist Alles*. Ein Brevier. Zusammengestellt u. eingel. von Oskar Jancke. Munich: R. Piper, 1940. Pp. 278. Republ. 1941, 1946.
       Rev: by W. Keller, *SJ*, LXXVII (1941), 193-194; by J. Sprengler, *DL*, XLIV (1941/42), 255.

B227   Knight, G. Wilson. *This Sceptred Isle*. Oxford: Blackwell, 1940. Pp. 35.
       Rev: *TLS*, Nov. 30, 1940, p. 607; *TLS*, Jan. 4, 1941, p. 7.

B228   Reynolds, A. L., ed. *Under the Greenwood Tree*. Oxford Univ. Press, ills. by L. Weisgard, 1940.

B229   *Fifteen Poets*. Oxford: Clarendon Press, 1941. Pp. xiv, 503.
       Rev: *TLS*, Feb. 8, 1941, p. 67; by J. B. Leishman, *RES*, XVII, 206-209; *NstN*, Feb. 22, p. 196.

B230   Shakespeare, William. *Scenes*. By J. Bouten. 6th ed. Selections from the Classics, No. 2. Zwolle: W. E. J. Tjeenk, 1941. Pp. vi, 111.

B231   Cosulich, G. "Did Shakespeare Say That?" *Timely Quotations*. New York, 1944. Pp. xiv, 300.

B232   Shakespeare, William. *Pensamientos de Shakespeare*. Selección y notas de Antonio C. Gavaldá. Barcelona: Eds. Símbolo, 1944. Pp. 74.

B233   *Lend Me Your Ears*. An Anthology of Shakespearean Quotations. Comp. by Reyner Barton. Rev. and Enl. ed. London: Jarrolds, 1947. Pp. 320.

B234   Fordham, H., ed. *Hey Nonny Yes: Passions and Conceits from Shakespeare*. London: Saturn Press, 1947.

B235   *Shekspirovskii Sbornik*, 1947. Redkollegiia. G. N. Boiadzhiev, M. B. Zagorskii, M. M. Morozov. Moscow: Vserossiiskoe Teatral'noe Obschestvo, 1948. Pp. 296.

B236   Taylor, George Coffin. *Essays of Shakespeare: An Arrangement*. New York: G. P. Putnam's Sons, 1947. Pp. xv, 144.
       Rev: by A. Thaler, *South Atlantic Bul.*, XIII No. 4, (1948), 1; by A. H. Buford, *NYTBR*, April 4, p. 4; by R. M. Smith, "Shakspere, the Montaigne of England," *SAB*, XXIII, 155-162; by LeGette Blythe, *SRL*, XXXI, 28, 32; by D. C. Allen, *MLN*, LXIV (1949), 144.

B237   Wilson, Leslie. *Six Portraits from Shakespeare.* Arr. with Commentary Notes and Questions. London: Murray, 1947. Pp. 168.

B238   *Lebensweisheit. Geflügelte Worte.* Dt. u. engl. Unt. Zugrundelegung d. Schlegel-Tieckschen Übers. zsgest. durch Doroth. Gerke. Ulm: Aegie-Verl., 1948. Pp. 48.

B239   *Shakespeare.* Hrsg. v. Alfred Günther. Stuttgart: Mayer, 1948. Pp. 143.

B240   Kingston, W., ed. *Shakespeare Companion: A Selective Anthology.* London: Saturn Press, 1948. Pp. vii, 236.
        Rev: *TLS*, Mar. 13, 1948, p. 154.

B241   Stanley, Arthur, ed. *The Bedside Shakespeare: An Anthology.* London: Gollancz, 1948. Pp. 287.

B242   *Scenes from "Macbeth".* Ed. by Josef Raith. Munich: Hueber, 1949. Pp. 35.
        Rev: by H. Mannhart, *Leb. Fremdspr.*, I (1949), 352.

B243   *Scenes from "Romeo and Juliet" and "King Henry the Fourth", Part I, Sonnets.* Ed. by Josef Raith. Munich: Hueber, 1949. Pp. 31.

B244   *Shakespeare-Klenodium.* Sammanst. av Nils Molin. Lund: Gleerup, 1949. Pp. 244.

B245   Pearson, Hesketh. *A Life of Shakespeare.* London: Carroll & Nicholson, 1949. Pp. 240. A revised edition. Includes anthology of Shak.'s poetry.
        Rev: A519.

B246   *Meet W. Shakespeare.* By Hubert Phillips and P. Falconer. New ed. Watford, Herts.: Cornleaf Press, 1950. Pp. vi, 106.

B247   Smith, Logan Pearsall, ed. *The Golden Shakespeare.* London: Constable, 1950. Pp. xii, 700.
        Rev: *TLS*, Feb. 3, 1950, p. 74; by Desmond MacCarthy, *Sun Times*, Feb. 19, p. 3; by G. Rylands, *Spectator*, 6349 (1950), 282.

B248   *The Ages of Man.* Arranged by George Rylands. London: Heinemann, 1939, 1941. New ed., 1951. Pp. xviii, 358.
        Rev: *TLS*, Dec. 2, 1939, p. 701; by B. E. Sears, *The Adelphi*, XVI (1940), 169-172; by H. Nicolson, *Spectator*, 6407 (1951), 488; comment by F. R. Dale, ibid., 6408, pp. 524, 526.

B249   *A Shakespeare Tapestry.* Compiled by Andrew Scotland. Ill. by Eric Fraser. London: Nisbet, 1951. Pp. vii, 200.

B250   *Worte über die Musik.* Aus seinen Werken ausgelesen u. ges. v. Kurt Sydow. Wolfenbüttel: Möseler, 1951. Pp. 31.
        Shak.'s comments on music.

B251   *Gedanken sind frei.* Ein Brevier der Lebensweisheit. Hrsg. v. Adolf Spemann. Stuttgart: Engelhorn-Verl., 1952. Pp. 90.

B252   Filho, Samuel McDowell. *Pequena Sequência Shakespereana.* [A Short Shakespearean Sequence] Rio de Janeiro: Oficinas Graficas Yornal do Brasil, 1952.

B253   Sen, N. B. *Thoughts of Shakespeare, Being a Treasury of Over 3,000 Valuable Thoughts Collected from the Complete Poetic and Dramatic Works of the Immortal Poet and Classified Under 240 Subjects.* Third Rev. Ed. Lahore: New Book Society, n.d. [1950].

B254   *King Lear.* A Selection of the Chief Scenes. Ed. by Alfred Bernhard. Huebers Fremdsprachliche Texte, No. 50. Munich: Hueber, 1954. Pp. 36.

B255   *A Shakespeare Anthology.* Selections from the Comedies, Histories, Tragedies, Songs, and Sonnets. Ed. by G. F. Maine (Fontana Series). London: Collins, 1954. Pp. 160.

B256   *Shakespeare par lui-même.* Textes choisis par Jean Paris. Paris: Éd. du Seuil, 1954. Pp. 190.
        Rev: by R. Saurel, *Cahiers de la Compagnie M. Renaud—J. -L. Barrault*, IX (1954); by J. Vallette, *MdF*, 322 (1954), 546.

B256a   *William Shakespeare in Selbstzeugnissen und Bilddokumenten.* Aus d. Franz. übertragen v. Oswalt v. Nostiz, bearb. v. Paul Raabe. Rowohlts Monographien 2. Hamburg, 1958. Pp. 169. German ed. of B256.

B257   *Shakespearean Manual of Quotations, Characters, Scenes and Plays.* Vest-Pocket Library. Baltimore: Ottenheimer Publishers, 1955. Pp. 224.
        Rev: *ShN*, VII (1957), 40.

B258   "From the Wisdom of William Shakespeare." *Wisdom*, July 1956, pp. 34-35.

B259   *Pensamientos.* Sel. y notas de Antonio C. Gavaldá. Literatos y pensadores, No. 2. 2nd ed. Barcelona: Sintes, 1956. Pp. 69.

B260   Carr, John, ed. *What Shakespeare Says: A Christian Anthology.* Dublin: Clonmore and Reynolds, 1956. London: Burns Oates, 1956. Pp. 60.
        Excerpts arranged by subjects for the consolation of the godly.
        Rev: *TLS*, Oct. 19, 1956, p. 622.

B261   Gilbert, M. "Bard at the Polls." *New York Times Magazine*, Oct. 14, 1956, p. 22.

5. TRANSLATIONS OF SHAKESPEARE (158;53)
a. GERMAN TRANSLATIONS (158;53)
(1) GENERAL WORKS DEALING WITH TRANSLATORS AND TRANSLATIONS (158;53)

(a) PRINCIPLES OF TRANSLATION

B262   Heun, Hans Georg. "Probleme der Shakespeare-Übersetzungen. Eine Bibliographie." *SJ*,
92 (1956), 450-463.

B263   Hochgesang, Michael. *Wandlungen des Dichtstils, Aufgezeigt an Deutschen "Macbeth"-Übertra-
gungen.* DD, Munich, 1925. Pp. ii, 162. Typewritten.

B264   Kahn, Ludwig W. *Shakespeares Sonnette in Deutschland: Versuch einer Literarischen Typologie.*
Bern and Leipzig, 1935.
Rev: A9435.

B265   Schulz, B. "Der Shakespeare des 20. Jahrhunderts? Eine Wegweisung zu Deutscher
Sprachkunst." *ZDB*, XII (1936), 253-267.

B266   Kramp, Willy. "Über das Hören des Worts." *Das Innere Reich*, III (1936/37), 1505-1522.

B267   Kriebaum, Rudolf. *Übersetzungsversuche aus Shakespeare vor Wieland.* DD, Vienna, 1938.

B268   Winter, J. W. "Probleme der Shakespeare-Übersetzung." *Berl. Börsenztg.*, June 30, 1938.

B269   Cancelled.

B270   Jones, Oscar Frederick. *The Treatment of Shakespearian Obscenity by Eighteenth Century German
Translators.* DD, Stanford University, 1940. Abstr. in *Abstracts of Dissertation, Stanford Univ.*,
XV (1940), 77-81.

B271   Ruths, Heiner. "Probleme der Shakespeare-Übersetzung. Von Wieland über Schlegel-Tieck
zu Rud. Alex. Schröder." *VB*(Mü), No. 320, Nov. 16, 1940.

B272   Schröder, Rudolf Alexander. "Zur Frage einer neuen Shakespeare-Übersetzung," (1941).
Gesammelte Werke. Berlin: Suhrkamp, Bd. 1, 1952, pp. 231-237. Also in *Shakespeare-Tage*,
1954 (Bochum), pp. 13-19.

B273   Schoen-René, Otto Eugene. *Shakespeare's Sonnets in Germany, 1787-1939.* DD, Harvard
University, 1942. Abstr. publ. in *Summaries of Ph.D. Theses, 1942*, Cambridge: Harvard Univ.
Press, 1946, pp. 284-287.

B274   Schramm, E. "Zum Problem der Modernen Shakespeare-Übersetzung." *Hamburger akad.
Rundschau*, II (1947/48), 355-361.

B275   Schwarz, Hedwig. "Meine Bemühung um Shakespeare." *SJ*, 82/83 (1948), 199-202.

B276   Kratky, Herbert. *Übersetzungsideal und seine Verwirklichung, Dargetan an Übersetzungen von
Shakespeares "Hamlet."* DD, Vienna, 1949. Pp. 120. Typewritten.

B277   Purdie, Edna. "Some Problems of Translation in the Eighteenth Century in Germany." *ES*,
XXX (1949), 191-205.

B278   Schücking, Levin L. "Shakespeares Stil als Übersetzungsproblem." *SJ*, 84/86 (1950), 69-74.

B279   Kirchner, Gustav. "Direct Transitivation." *ES*, XXXVI (1955), 15-23.
Syntax as discussed by Schücking in B278.

B280   Fechter, Paul. "Die Entdeckung Shakespeares." *Das Europäische Drama. Geist u. Kultur im
Spiegel des Theaters.* Mannheim: Bibliogr. Inst., Bd 1. *Vom Barock zum Naturalismus*, 1956,
pp. 90-97.

B281   Hilty, Hans Rudolf. "Zur Behandlung der Eigennamen in Shakespeare-Übersetzungen."
SJ, 92 (1956), 255-267.

B282   Hübner, Hans. *Sonette in Deutscher Sprache und Italienischer Versform.* Dresden: Dresdener
Verlagsgesellschaft, 1949. Pp. 154. Rostock: C. Hinstorff, 1956. Pp. 196.

B283   Kachler, K. G. "Weshalb immer noch die Shakespeare-Übertragungen der Romantiker vor-
zuziehen sind." *SJ*, 92 (1956), 90-95.

B284   Korninger, Siegfried. "Shakespeare und seine Deutschen Übersetzer." *SJ*, 92 (1956), 19-44.

B285   Schwartz, Hedwig. "Arbeit für Shakespeare durch Shakespeare-Bearbeitungen." *SJ*, 92
(1956), 175-183.

B286   Heun, Hans Georg. *Shakespeare in Deutschen Übersetzungen.* Berlin, 1957. Pp. 74.
Rev: by Hermann Heuer, *SJ*, 94 (1958), 299; by H. Schnyder, *Archiv*, 195 (1958), 208.

B287   Koziol, Herbert. "Shakespeares Komposita in Deutschen Übersetzungen." *NS*, 1957,
pp. 457-463.

B288   McNamee, Lawrence Francis. *"Julius Caesar" on the German Stage in the Nineteenth Century.*
DD, University of Pittsburgh, 1957. Pp. 324. Mic 57-1716. *DA*, XVII (1957), 1074. Publ.
No. 21,009.

B289   "World's Most Translated Authors." *Unesco Courier*, Feb. 1957, pp. 8-10.

(b) INDIVIDUAL TRANSLATORS
i. Several

B290   Brües, Otto. "Shakespeare-Übersetzungen." *Köln. Ztg.*, Nos. 191/192 (1937).

B291   Fleischhauer, H. "Ist Schlegel-Tieck Klassisch? Eine neue Shakespeare-Übersetzung
[by W. Josten]." *Dresd. Anz.*, Aug. 5, 1937.

B292   "Der erste Hamlet-Monolog. I. Akt, 2. Auftritt. Orig. u. Übers. v. J. J. Eschenburg, A. W. Schlegel, W. Josten u. R. Flatter." *Shakespeare-Tage*, 1952 (Bochum), pp. 12-15.

B293   Buck, Eva. "Vier Zeilen von Shakespeare in Berühmten Französischen und Deutschen Übersetzungen." *Archiv*, 190 (1954), 21-31.

B294   Candidus, Irmentraud, and Erika Roller. "Der Sommernachtstraum in Deutscher Übersetzung von Wieland bis Flatter." *SJ*, 92 (1956), 128-145.

B295   Falkenberg, Hans-Geert. "Zur Bühnen- und Übersetzungsgeschichte von *Antonious und Cleopatra*." *Blätter d. Dt. Theaters in Göttingen*, 1956, Heft 89.

B296   Lüdeke, Harry. "Gundolf, Flatter, und Shakespeares *Macbeth*." *SJ*, 92 (1956), 110-127.

B297   Purdie, Edna. "Observations on Some Eighteenth-Century German Versions of the Witches Scenes in *Macbeth*." *SJ*, 92 (1956), 96-109.

B298   Stricker, Käthe. "Deutsche Shakespeare-Übersetzungen im Letzten Jahrhundert (etwa 1860-1950)." *SJ*, 92 (1956), 45-89.

ii.   von Baudissin

B299   Kroepelin, H. "Die Shakespeare-Texte." *Berliner Tageblatt*, No. 298 (1938).
Other articles by this writer: "Für einen Shakespeare: Übersetzer: Wolf Graf Baudissin zum 150. Geburtstag." *VB*(B), No. 40 (1939); "Shakespeare, der Freilichtspiel Dichter," *Dt. Allgem. Ztg.*, No. 345; "Shakespeare und der Deutsche Leser," ibid., No. 229.

B300   Kroepelin, H. "Was Könnte man Wolf Baudissin Schenken? Zu Seinem 150. Geburtstag." *MNN*, Jan. 30, 1939, p. 4.

B301   Hofmüller, Rudolf. "Diplomat und Sprachmeister. Zum 150. Geburtstag des Shakespeare Übersetzers Wolf Graf von Baudissin." *VB*(Mü), Jan. 30, 1939, p. 5.

iii.   Flatter

B302   Flatter, Richard. "Auf den Spuren von Shakespeares Wortregie." *SJ*, 84/86 (1951), 93-96.

B303   *Richard Flatter. Seine Bedeutung als Shakespeare-Übersetzer*. Bad Bocklet: Krieg, 1952. Pp. 22.

B304   Flatter, Richard. " 'Sein oder Nichtsein': Bemerkungen zu Einigen Hamlet-Worten." *Neue Zürcher Zeitung* (Zurich), Dec. 7, 1952.
A criticism of Schlegel's translation of Hamlet's soliloquy.

B305   Flatter, Richard. "Das Schauspielerische in der Diktion Shakespeares." In *Shakespeare-Schriften*. Ed. by Richard Flatter, Heft 1, Vienna, 1954. Pp. 53.

B306   Flatter, Richard. "Bühnensprachliche und andere Eigenheiten der Diktion Shakespeares: Anmerkungen eines Shakespeare Übersetzers." *Anglo-Americana*. Ed. by Karl Brunner. Vienna, 1955, pp. 42-52.

B307   Flatter, Richard. "Lässt sich Shakespeare Übersetzen?" In Flatter's *Triumph der Gnade. Shakespeare Essays*. Vienna, Munich: Kurt Desch, 1956, pp. 46-60.

B308   Flatter, Richard. " 'Sprachmelodei'. Konsonanten, Vokale und Sonstiges Werkzeug der Sprache." In Flatter's *Triumph der Gnade. Shakespeare Essays*. Vienna, Munich: Kurt Desch, 1956, pp. 61-69.

B309   Flatter, Richard. "Schlegel und 'Schlegel-Tieck'." In Flatter's *Triumph der Gnade. Shakespeare Essays*. Vienna, Munich: Kurt Desch, 1956, pp. 70-83.

B310   Flatter, Richard. "Zum Problem der Shakespeare-Übersetzung. Versuch einer Antwort auf einige von Anselm Schlösser aufgeworfene Fragen." *ZAA*, IV (1956), 473-483.

B311   Flatter, Richard. "Shakespeare-Übersetzung und Weltanschauung." *Theater und Zeit*, 1956/57, pp. 109-111.

B312   Flatter, Richard, and Irmentraud Candidus. "Eine Berichtigung und eine Antwort." *SJ*, 93 (1957), 214-215.

B313   Stamm, Rudolf. "*Hamlet* in Richard Flatter's Translation." *ES*, XXXVI (1955), 228-238, 299-308.

B314   Sehrt, Ernst Theodor, Karen Kramp, and Wolfgang Stroedel. "Einzelbesprechungen." *SJ*, 91 (1955), 348-355.
Flatter's tr. of *Oth.*, *Macb.*, *Dream*, *H.IV*, *Shrew*, *Meas.*, *Romeo*, *Lear*, pp. 353-355.

B315   Brack, J. Paul. "Shakespeare-Deutsch für unser Jahrhundert." *Nationalzeitung* (Basel), Dec. 11, 1955.

iv.   George

B316   Norwood, Eugene. "Stefan George's Translation of Shakespeare's Sonnets." *Monatshefte* (Madison), XLIV (1952), 217-224.

B317   Hoffmann, Friedrich. "Stefan Georges Übertragung der Shakespeare-Sonette." *SJ*, 92 (1956), 146-156.

B318   "Zwei gegen Stefan George Shakespeares *Sonnets* und *Les Fleurs du Mal* von Baudelaire neu Übersetzt." *Die Weltwoche* (Zurich), XXV (May 31, 1958).

v. Gryphius

B319 Keppler, Ernst. *Gryphius und Shakespeare.* DD, Tübingen, 1921. Pp. 123. Typewritten.
B320 Brett-Evans, D. *Andreas Gryphius and the Elizabethan Drama.* MA thesis, Wales, 1951.

vi. Josten

B321 Josten, Walter. "Schwierigkeiten der Shakespeare-Übersetzung." *N.Mon.*, XII (1941), 300-305, and *ZNU*, XL (1941), 274-279.
B322 Josten, Walter. "Schwierigkeiten der Shakespeare-Übersetzung." *Archiv*, 180 (1941/42), 114-117, and *Geist der Zeit*, XX (1942), 48-51, Heft 1.
B323 Josten, Walter. "Schwierigkeiten der Shakespeare-Übersetzung." *SJ*, 82/83 (1948), 202-206.
B324 Josten, Walter. "Schwierigkeiten der Shakespeare-Übersetzung." *SJ*, 92 (1956), 168-174. See also *Die Zeit*, X (1955), No. 9, p. 4.
B325 Josten, Walter. "Schwierigkeiten der Shakespeare-Übersetzung." *Shakespeare-Tage 1957* (Bochum), pp. 3-8.
B326 Lassaulx, C. von. "Neue Versuche zu Shakespeare-Übertragungen." *Köln. Ztg.*, 1936, No. 179/180, p. 9; No. 185/186, p. 9.
B327 Ackermann, E. *Shakespeare-Deutsch: Eine Einführung in das Übersetzungswerk von W. Josten.* Hamburg: Hartung, 1937. Pp. 77.
    Rev: *GA*, V (1938), 6; by Joh. Speck, *Archiv*, 175 (1939), 224-227; by W. Fischer, *Beiblatt*, LII (1941), 66-67.
B328 Lützeler, H. "Eine Bemerkenswerte Shakespeare-Übersetzung." *Köln. Volksztg. Lit. Beilage.*, 1937, No. 146.
B329 Pechel, Rudolf. "Eine neue Shakespeare-Übersetzung." *Dts. Rundschau*, 253 (1937), 156.
B330 Bleckmann, Henry. "Eine neue *Lear*-Übersetzung." *VB*, Dec. 1, 1938.
B331 Ehrentreich, A. "Ein Deutscher Shakespeare von Walter Josten." *N. Mon.*, IX (1938), 224-233.
B332 Cancelled.
B333 Schwarz, Hedwig, and Walter Josten. "Neue Shakespeare-Übersetzungen in Selbstanzeigen." *SJ*, 82/83 (1949), 199-206.

vii. Rothe

B334 Rothe, Hans. *Der Kampf um Shakespeare.* Ein Bericht. Leipzig: Paul List Verlag, 1936. Pp. 106. Second revised ed. Baden-Baden, 1956. Pp. 96.
Extended controversy: see comments by R. Bach, "Shakespeare in neuer Übertragung," *Frankfurter Ztg.*, Nos. 652-653 (1935), *Lbl*, No. 51; by W. Braumüller, "*Der Kampf um Shakespeare.* Eine Entgegnung auf H. Rothes Bericht," *Bausteine zum dt. Nationaltheater*, IV, 51-62; by Bütow, "Ein 'moderner' Shakespeare," *Frankfurter Ztg.*, Nos. 662-663, *Lbl*, No. 52; by H. Glunz, "Shakespeare in der Deutschen Gegenwart," *Kölnische Ztg.*, Nos. 124-125 (1936), p. 17; by H. Jhering, "Braucht das Theater den Banalisierten Shakespeare?" *Berliner Tagebl.*, No. 17; by K. Künkler, "Hans Rothe und das Theater," *Bausteine zum dt. Nationaltheater*, IV, 43-47; by W. Kurz, "Verbrechen an Shakespeare," ibid., pp. 33-42; by L. L. Schücking, "Die Frage der Rotheschen Shakespeare-Übersetzung," *Kölnische Ztg.*, No. 147, 154; by R. Zickel-von Jan, "Wir Brauchen Shakespeare!" *Bausteine zum dt. Nationaltheater*, IV, 37-51; by W. Fischer, "Zu Rothes Shakespeare-Übersetzung," *Beiblatt*, XLVII, 97-102; "Rothe oder Shakespeare?" *Germania*, No. 49; by G. Steinböhmer, "Shakespeare und kein Ende," *Münchener Neueste Nachrichten*, No. 39; "Ein Theater-Urteil zu Rothes Shakespeare-Übersetzung," *Die Bühne*, II, 2-3; by J. M. Wehner, "Der Shakespeare des 20. Jahrunderts," *Westfälische Landesztg.* Rote Erde, No. 55 and *Münchener Neueste Nachrichten*, No. 36; by R. Bach, "Kampf um Shakespeare," *Der Bücherwurm*, XXI, 132-135; by W., "Shakespeare, Carew und Rothe," *Wille und Macht*, IV, 21-23; by Wolfgang Keller, *SJ*, LXXII, 162-163; by H. C. Mettin, "Shakespeare oder Rothe," *Die Tat*, XXVII, 669-677; by C. von Lassaulx, "Neue Versuche zu Shakespeare-Übersetzung," *Köln. Ztg.*, Nos. 179, 180; by Wolfgang Keller, "Zum Streit um Rothes Shakespeare," *Wille u. Macht*, IV, 14-15; "Die Entscheidung gegen Rothe," *DL*, XXXVIII, 452-453; "Stimmen aus Theaterpraxis und Presse [zum Fall Rothe]," *Bausteine zum dt. Nationaltheater*, IV, 63-67; by H. G., "Rothe—oder Schlegel?" *VB* (Norddts. Ed.), 1936, No. 77; by Wolfgang Keller, "Zum Kampf um Shakespeare," *Westfälische Landesztg.*, Rote Erde, Dortmund, Feb. 23; by Wolfgang Keller, "Der Kampf um Shakespeare," *Münsterischer Anzeiger*, May 21; by Marg. Kurlbaum-Siebert, "Der Kampf um Shakespeare und—Hans Rothe," *Das Deutsche Wort*, XII, 312-317; by Gustav Steinböhmer, "Zum Streit um Rothes Shakespeare," *Wille und Macht*, IV, 11-14; by Hermann Wanderscheck, "Kampf um Shakespeare Gegen die Textverfälschungen des Übersetzers Rothe," *Lpz. Tagesztg.*, No. 18; by Joseph Magnus Wehner, "Zum Streit um Rothes Shakespeare," *Wille und Macht*, IV, 15 and in *DL*, XXXVIII, 324; of 2nd edition: by H. Heuer, *SJ*, 93 (1957), 279-280.

B335   Rothe, H. "Shakespeare in German." Tr. by C. P. Magill. *German Life & Letters*, I (1937), 255-269.
B335a   Schneider, Karl. *Der wahre Kampf um Shakespeare.* Würzburg: Triltsch, 1937. Pp. 44.
        Rev: by W. Fischer, *Beiblatt*, XLIX (1938), 123.
B336   Rilla, P. "Kampf um die Shakespeare-Übersetzung." *Dramaturg. Blätter*, I (1947), v, 1-11.
B337   Heerwagen, Fritz. "Shakespeare und der Humanismus. Nachdenkliches zu den Bochumer Shakespeare-Tagen." *Theater d. Zeit*, v, vi (1950), 18-19.
B337a   Fries, Martin. "Enthumanisierter Shakespeare?" *Theater d. Zeit*, v, viii (1950), 25.
B337b   Heerwagen, Fritz. "Hans Rothes Shakespearesche Stimmqualität." *Theater d. Zeit*, v, x (1950), 5-8.
B338   Wittlinger, Karl. *Hans Rothes neuer Shakespeare.* DD, Frankfurt/Main, 1950. Pp. 353.
B339   Rothe, Hans. "Choreographie und Shakespeare-Inszenierung." *Das neue Forum* (Berlin), 1951, 72-73.
B340   Rothe, Hans. "Translating Shakespeare." *International Theatre*, Spring, 1951, pp. 19-20.
B341   Wittlinger, Karl. "Hans Rothe und die Shakespeare-Forschung." *SJ*, 87/88 (1952), 158-173.
B342   McNamee, Lawrence Francis. "Translating Principles of Hans Rothe and *Henry V.*" *ShN*, VIII (1958), 10.
B343   Stamm, Rudolf. "Shakespeare und Hans Rothe." *Der Bund* (Bern), Dec. 1, 1958.
        Virulent attack on Rothe's Shak. translations, successful only because their mediocrity and simplifications bring Shak. down to the level of the most stupid spectator.

viii. Schaller

B344   Schaller, Rudolf. "Meine Nachdichtung der Lustigen Weiber von Windsor." *Theater d. Zeit*, VII, xviii (1952), 5-7.
B345   Schaller, Rudolf. "Eine neue *Macbeth*-Übertragung. Der Übersetzer über seine Arbeit." *Theater d. Zeit*, VII, vii (1952), 25-29.
B346   Schaller, Rudolf. "Schiller als Dramatischer Übersetzer." *Theater d. Zeit*, x, vi (1955), 4-6.
B347   Schaller, Rudolf. "Gedanken zur Übertragung Shakespeares in unsere Sprache." *SJ*, 92 (1956), 157-167.
B348   Schaller, Rudolf. "Shakespeare für die Deutsche Bühne." *Neue Deutsche Literatur* (Berlin), IV (1956), No. 6, pp. 120-127.
B349   Schaller, Rudolf. "Shakespeare in Deutscher Sprache, Einige Probleme bei der Arbeit des Übersetzers." *Theater der Zeit*, x, xi (1955), 30-37. See also Gerhard Wahnrau, ibid., pp. 38-41.
B350   Magon, Leopold. "Zu Rudolf Schallers *Macbeth*-Übersetzung." *Neue Zeit*, May 30-31, 1952.
B351   Schlösser, Anselm. "Besser als Baudissin (Betrachtungen zu Rudolf Schallers Übersetzung des *King Lear*)." *ZAA*, IV, ii (1956), 172-191.

ix. Schlegel-Tieck

B352   Zeydel, E. H. *L. Tieck and England; A Study . . .* 1931.
        Rev: by H. Lüdeke, *DLZ*, LIX (1938), 433-446.
B353   Zeydel, E. H. *Ludwig Tieck, the German Romanticist: A Critical Study.* Princeton Univ. Press, 1935. Pp. xvi, 406.
        Rev: by J. Sp., *Archiv*, 170 (1936), 276; by H. W. Hewett-Thayer, *GR*, II, 278-280; by Minder, *RLC*, XVI; by W. E. Suskind, *DL*, XXXIX (1936/37), 694-695; by J. H. Scholte, *Neophil*, XXII, 152; by Marianne Thalmann, *MLN*, LII (1937), 295-296; by A. Gillies, *MLR*, XXXII, 129-131; by J. Rouge, *RG*, XXVIII, 201-202; by H. Lüdeke, *DLZ*, LIX (1938), 433-446; by Aug. Closs, *DuV*, XXXIX, 254-255; by Herm. J. Weigand, *JEGP*, XXXVII, 100-107; by Jos. Körner, *Lbl*, LIX, 153-160; by Y. Hirn, *N. Mitt.*, XLI (1940), 188-191.
B354   Hewett-Thayer, Harvey W. "Tieck and the Elizabethan Drama: His Marginalia." *JEGP*, XXXIV (1935), 377-407.
B355   Minder, Rob. "Un Poète Romantique Allemand: Ludwig Tieck (1773-1853)." Paris: Les Belles-Lettres, 1936. Pp. 508.
        Rev: by H. Lüdeke, *DLZ*, LIX (1938), 433-446; by Jos. Körner, *Lbl*, LIX, 153-160.
B356   Petroczi, Stefan. *Künstlertypen bei Tieck.* Specimina dissertationum Fac. Philos. Reg. Hungar. Universitatis Elis. Quinqueecclesiensis. 94. Rt. Pécs, 1936.
        Rev: by Emil Kast, *Lbl*, LIX (1938), 17.
B357   Zeydel, E. H. "Ludwig Tieck as a Translator of English." *PMLA*, LI (1936), 221-242.
        Rev: by Joh. Speck, *Archiv*, 171 (1937), 254.
B358   v. Langermann. "Wie Entstand die Grosse Schlegel-Tiecksche Shakespeare-Übersetzung." *Magdeburger Ztg.*, Jan. 25, 1937.
B359   Winter, J. W. "Dorothea Tiecks *Macbeth*-Übersetzung." DD, Berlin: Elsner, 1938. Pp. 113.
        Rev: by E. Mühlbach, *LZ*, 90 (1939), 358; by H. Kügler, *Zeitschrift d. Vereins f. Geschichte Berlins*, LVI, 89; by Karl Brunner, *Beiblatt*, LII (1941), 67-70; by Bertha Siebeck, *Lbl*, LXII, 306-307; by Max Priess, *Eng. Studn.*, LXXV (1942), 357-360.

B360   Lazenby, Marion Chandler. *The Influence of Wieland and Eschenburg on Schlegel's Shakespeare Translation.* DD, Johns Hopkins University, 1941.

B361   Speck, Hans. [On Ludwig Tieck as Critic and Historian of English Literature.] *Archiv*, 179 (1941), 130-132.

B362   Neale, T. "Dorothea Tiecks *Macbeth*-Übersetzung." *Beiblatt*, LII (1942), 67-70.

B363   Brentano, Bernard von. "*August Wilhelm Schlegel. Geschichte eines romantischen Geistes.* Stuttgart: Cotta, 1949. Pp. 296.
        Rev: by F. Braig, *Stimmen d. Zeit*, 146 (1949/50), 476-477; by H. P. H. Teesing, *Museum*, LVI (1951), 184-185.

B364   Schirmer, Walter Franz. "August Wilhelm Schlegel und England." *SJ*, LXXV (1939), 77-107. Republ. in Schirmer's *Kleine Schriften*. Tübingen: Niemeyer, 1950, pp. 152-200.

B365   Richter, Werner. *August Wilhelm Schlegel. Wanderer Zwischen Weltpoesie und Altdeutscher Dichtung.* Rektoratsrede. Bonn: Bouvier, 1954. Pp. 27.

B366   Wohlfarth, Paul. "Zwei Übersetzungsfehler bei Schlegel-Tieck." *SJ*, 92 (1957), 211-213.

x. Miscellaneous

B367   Beam, Jacob. *Die Ersten Deutschen Übersetzungen Englischer Lustspiele im Achtzehnten Jahrhundert.* DD, Jena, 1904. Pp. iv, 91.

B368   Gaiser, Konrad. *Die Übersetzungen Ludwig Seegers aus Shakespeare.* DD, Tübingen, 1911. Pp. 158.

B369   Küry, Hans. *Simon Grynaeus von Basel, 1725-1799, der erste Deutsche Übersetzer von Shakespeares "Romeo und Julia."* Zürich, 1935.
        Rev: by W. Milch, *DL*, XXXVIII (1935/36), 50; by Al. Brandl, *Archiv*, 169 (1936), 286; by Hans Lutz, *Lbl*, LIX (1938), 12; by Günther Scherer, *DLZ*, LIX, 708-709.

B370   Keudel, R. "Kritik an Shakespeare." *Allgem. Thüringische Landeszig Deutschland*, No. 112, 1936.

B371   Bloch, Albert. "Karl Kraus' Shakespeare." *Books Abroad*, XI (1937), 21-24.

B372   Kraft, Werner. *Karl Kraus, Beiträge zum Verständnis Seines Werkes.* Salzburg: Müller, 1956. Pp. 366.

B373   Bergmann, Alfred. "Probe einer Vergessenen *Lear*-Übersetzung." *SJ*, LXXIV (1938), 123-132. The reference is to a translation by A. von Sieten (1814).

B374   Thiel, R. *Otto Gildemeister als Übersetzer Englischer Dichtungen.* DD, Breslau, 1938. Reichenbach (Eulengebirge): Ernst Töbing, 1938. Pp. 90. Shak., pp. 36-42.
        Rev: by A. Brandl, *Archiv*, 176 (1939), 119; by A. Closs, *Beiblatt*, L, 122-124.

B375   Uhde-Bernays, H. "Einige Fehler alter Shakespeare-Übersetzungen." *Werke und Tage. Festschr. f. Rud. Alex. Schröder z. 60. Geburtstag am 26. Jan. 1938.* Berlin: Eckart Vlg., 1938, pp. 145-147.

B376   Schorf, Wilhelm. "Dingelstedts Plan einer neuen Shakespeare-Übersetzung." *SJ*, LXXVI (1940), 137-160.

B377   Sehrt, E. Th. "Der Entromanisierte *Sommernachtstraum*: Zu Rudolf Alexander Schröders Neuübertragung." *GRM*, XXIX (1941), Heft 7/9.

B378   "Bardolatry Abroad." *TLS*, April 13, 1946, p. 175. Some comments on German translation.

B379   Borcherdt, Hans Heinrich. "Schillers Bühnenbearbeitungen Shakespearescher Werke." *SJ*, 91 (1955), 52-64.

B380   Meyen, Fritz. *Johann Joachim Eschenburg, 1743-1820.* Braunschweig, 1957. Pp. 130. On translating Shak., pp. 35-49.
        Rev: by K. J. Höltgen, *Anglia*, LXXVI (1958), 313-314.

(2) THE MOST IMPORTANT GERMAN TRANSLATIONS (158;53)
(a) SCHLEGEL-TIECK
i. Collected Works

B381   *Dramatische Werke.* Übers. von Aug. Wilh. von Schlegel und Ludwig Tieck. Berlin: Lambert Schneider, 1939. 3 vols. Pp. 1032, 960, 973.
        Rev: by F. Brie, *Beiblatt*, LI (1940), 90-91; by Will Vesper, *DNL*, XLI, 66; by W. Keller, *SJ*, LXXVI, 203-204; by G. Lüdtke, *GA*, VII, No. 23, p. 3; by E. T. Sehrt, *Eng. Studn.*, LXXVI (1944), 124-128.

B382   *Dramatische Werke.* Übers. von August Wilhelm v. Schlegel und Ludwig Tieck. Hrsg. und revid. von Hans Matter. Bd. 1-10. Basel: Birkhäuser, 1943.

B383   *Dramatische Werke.* Baden-Vienna: Buchgemeinschaft der Klassiker Verlagsgesellschaft m.b.H. 9 vols., 1949-1950. A reprint after the "Ausgabe letzter Hand" of 1839-40, with introductions to single plays by E. Zellwecker, biographical introduction by Karl Brunner.

B384　*Werke.* Ed. by I. E. Walter. Salzburg: Verlag 'Das Bergland-Buch,' 1952. 2 vols. Pp. 1136, 1051.
Reprint of the Schlegel-Tieck translation of the plays, of the Ferdinand Freiligrath translation of *Venus and Adonis,* of the Frederick Bodenstedt translation of the Sonnets, with introduction by the editor.

B385　Cancelled.

B386　*Sämtliche Werke.* Übers. v. August Wilhelm v. Schlegel u. Ludwig Tieck. 4 vols. Heidelberg: Schneider, 1953.
Poems tr. by Friedrich Bodenstedt, Ferdinand Freiligrath and others.

B387　*Werke.* In dt. Sprache durch August Wilhelm Schlegel u. Ludwig Tieck. (Hrsg.) Karl Balser, Reinhard Buchwald u. Karl Franz Reinking. Standard-Klassiker-Ausg. in 10 Bdn. Hamburg: Standard-Verl., 1953.

B388　*Dramatische Werke.* Übers. v. August Wilhelm v. Schlegel u. Ludwig Tieck. Frankfurt a.M.: Büchergilde Gutenberg, 1953. 3 vols. Pp. 1032, 960, 973.

B389　*Werke.* Engl. u. deutsch. Hrsg. v. Levin Ludwig Schücking. Übers. d. Dramen von Aug. Wilh. Schlegel u. Ludwig Tieck. Bd 1-6. Berlin and Darmstadt: Tempel-Verl., 1956.

B390　*Dramatische Werke.* Übers. v. August Wilhelm v. Schlegel u. Ludwig Tieck. Hrsg. u. rev. v. Hans Matter. 10 vols. Basel: Birkhäuser, 1950-54.

ii. Selected Plays

B391　*Tragödien.* Übers. v. A. W. Schlegel u. L. Tieck. Vienna: Ullstein, 1946. Pp. 349.
Romeo u. Julia, Othello, Hamlet.

B392　*Dramen.* In d. Übers. v. A. W. Schlegel. Düsseldorf: Bastion-Verl., 1947. 1. *Hamlet, Der Sturm, Romeo u. Julia.* Pp. 269. 2. *Julius Caesar, Kaufmann v. Venedig, Sommernachtstraum, Was ihr wollt.* Pp. 277.

B393　*Dramen.* Engl. u. dt. Dt. v. A. W. Schlegel. Mit e. Nachw. v. Emil Greeff. Bearb. u. hrsg. v. Hubert Tigges. Wuppertal: Marées-Verl., 1948. Pp. 244.

B394　*Dramatische Werke, Liebes- u. Heldentragödien.* Engl. u. dt. Übers. v. Schlegel-Tieck. Rev. v. Friedr. Schwiecker. Bd. 1-3. Hamburg: Eckardt & Messtorff, 1948. 1. *Othello, Romeo u. Julia.* Pp. 187. 2. *Antonius u. Kleopatra, Coriolanus.* Pp. 209. 3. *Julius Caesar, Hamlet.* Pp. 190.

B395　*Lustspiele. Die lust. Weiber v. Windsor. Mass für Mass. Viel Lärmen um Nichts. Ein Sommernachtstraum. Wie es euch gefällt. Der Widersp. Zähmung. Ende gut, alles gut. Was ihr Wollt.* Nach d. Übers. v. Schlegel-Tieck neu bearb. v. Karl u. Renate Lerbs. M. e. Einf. v. Bernh. Sengfelder. Wiesentheid, Munich: Droemer, 1948. Pp. 283.

B396　*Komödien.* Translated by Ludwig Tieck. Vienna: Ullstein, 1949.

B397　*Ausgewählte Werke.* (Schlegel-Tiecksche Übersetzung.) Eingel. u. hrsg. v. Oskar Rühle. 4 Teile in 2 Bdn. Stuttgart: Kohlhammer, 1956.
1. Einführung. *Sonette, Romeo u. Julia, Hamlet, Othello, Macbeth, König Lear.* Pp. 574.
2. *Richard III, Richard II, Mass für Mass, Julius Caesar, Coriolanus, Antonius u. Cleopatra.* Pp. 598.
3. *Der Widerspenstigen Zähmung, Die lustigen Weiber von Windsor, Wie es euch gefällt, Was ihr wollt, Sommernachtstraum, Der Kaufmann von Venedig, Sturm.* Pp. 576.
4. *Troilus u. Cressida, Ende gut, alles gut, Liebes Leid u. Lust, Komödie der Irrungen, Cymbeline, Wintermärchen, Viel Lärmen um Nichts.* Pp. 660.

iii. Comedies

B398　*Ein Sommernachtstraum.* Reclams Universalbibliothek, 73. Leipzig: Reclam, 1941. Pp. 64. Republ. 1948.

B399　*Ein Sommernachtstraum* (Engl. u. dt.) M. Schattenbildern v. Paul Konewka. Dt. v. A. W. Schlegel. Wuppertal: Marées-Verl., 1947. Pp. 132.

B400　*Ein Sommernachtstraum.* Übers. v. A. W. Schlegel. M. Anm. u. Nachw. v. Christian Jenssen. Hamburg: Laatzen, 1947. Pp. 76.

B401　*Ein Sommernachtstraum.* Tr. by A. W. Schlegel. Lindau: Apollo Verlag, 1947. Pp. 64. Offenburg: Lehrmittel Verlag, 1947. Pp. 88.

B402　*Ein Sommernachtstraum.* Dt. v. A. W. v. Schlegel. Berlin, Bielefeld: Cornelsen, 1949. Pp. 110.

B403　*Ein Sommernachtstraum.* Tr. A. W. Schlegel. Stuttgart: Reclam, 1950. Pp. 64.

B404　*Ein Sommernachtstraum.* Tr. A. W. Schlegel. Basel: Birkhäuser, 1952. Pp. 75.

B405　*Ein Sommernachtstraum.* Dt. Übertr. v. August Wilhelm v. Schlegel. M. 5 farb. Lithogr. v. Jack v. Reppert-Bismarck. Bern: Scherz, 1956. Pp. 134.

B406　*Der Kaufmann von Venedig.* Übers. von Aug. Wilh. von Schlegel. Mit Federzeichnungen von Frz. Stassen. Berlin: L. Schroeter, 1934.

B407　*Der Kaufmann von Venedig.* Übers. von August Wilhelm Schlegel. Bielefeld, Leipzig: Velhagen & Klasing, 1943. Pp. vi, 91.

B408　*Der Kaufman von Venedig.* Dt. v. A. W. Schlegel. Braunschweig: Westermann, 1949. Pp. 99.

B409　*Der Kaufmann von Venedig.* Übers. v. August Wilhelm von Schlegel. Stuttgart: Reclam, 1951. Pp. 83.

B410 *Der Kaufmann von Venedig.* Tr. A. W. Schlegel. Editiones Helveticae, Abt. Deutsche Texte, 22. Basel: Birkhäuser, 1952. Pp. 89.

B411 *Wie es euch gefällt.* Tr. A. W. Schlegel. Lindau: Apollo Verlag, 1948. Pp. 95.

B412 *Wie es euch gefällt.* Dt. v. A. W. v. Schlegel. Berlin, Bielefeld: Cornelsen, 1949. Pp. 142.

B413 *Wie es euch gefällt.* Übers. v. August Wilhelm von Schlegel. Stuttgart: Reclam, 1952. Pp. 87.

B414 *Twelfth Night, or What You Will. Was Ihr Wollt.* Engl. u. dt. Dt. v. A. W. Schlegel. Oberursel: Kompass-Verl., 1947. Pp. 231.

B415 *Was Ihr Wollt.* Übers. v. A. W. Schlegel. Leipzig: Reclam, 1948. Pp. 79.

B416 *Was Ihr Wollt.* Dt. v. A. W. Schlegel. Berlin, Bielefeld: Cornelsen, 1949. Pp. 104.

B417 *Der Sturm.* Übers. v. August Wilhelm v. Schlegel. Stuttgart: Reclam, 1951. Pp. 79.

B418 *Der Sturm.* Übers. v. August Wilhelm v. Schlegel. Leipzig: Reclam, 1956. Pp. 68.

B419 *Der Sturm.* Ein Zauberlustspiel von W. Sh. Dt. Übers. v. August Wilhelm v. Schlegel. Klavierauszug m. Singstimmen von Frank Martin. Reproduktion d. Originalmanuskriptes. Vienna, Zurich, London: Universal Ed., 1956. Pp. iv, 472.

iv. Histories

B420 *König Richard der Dritte.* Übers. v. August Wilhelm v. Schlegel. Stuttgart: Reclam, 1954. Pp. 110.

B421 *Richard III.* Dt. v. A. W. Schlegel. Kuno Fischer: "Shakespeares Charakterentwicklung Richards III." Oberursel: Kompass-Verl., 1948. Pp. 215.

B422 *König Richard III.* Engl. u. dt. In d. Übers. v. August Wilhelm v. Schlegel u. Ludwig Tieck hrsg. v. Levin Ludwig Schücking. M. e. Essay "Zum Verständnis d. Werkes," u. e. Bibliographie v. Wolfgang Clemen. Hamburg: Rowohlt, 1958. Pp. 228.

B423 *König Richard der Zweite.* Übers. v. A. W. Schlegel. Leipzig: Reclam, 1947. Pp. 85.

B424 *König Heinrich der Vierte.* Übers. v. A. W. Schlegel. Leipzig: Reclam, 1947.

B425 *King Henry the Fourth. König Heinrich der Vierte.* (engl. u. dt.) Übertr. v. A. W. v. Schlegel. Einf. v. Reinhold Schneider. Freiburg: Herder, 1949. Pp. 289.

B426 *König Heinrich der Vierte.* Übers. v. August Wilhelm v. Schlegel. Reclams Universalbibl., No. 81/82. Stuttgart: Reclam, 1956. Pp. 204.

v. Tragedies

B427 *Romeo und Julia* (Engl. u. dt.) Dt. v. A. W. Schlegel. Oberursel: Kompass-Verl., 1947. Pp. 221.

B428 *Romeo und Julia.* Engl. u. dt. Nach d. Übers. v. A. W. Schlegel. Textrev., Einl. u. Anm. v. Karl Brunner. Linz: Österreichischer Verlag für Belletristik und Wissenschaft, 1947. Pp. 288.

B429 *Romeo und Julia.* Übertr. v. Schlegel-Tieck in d. Bearb. d. Dt. Shakespeare-Ges. durch W. Oechelhäuser. Dortmund: Schwalvenberg, 1947. Pp. 79.

B430 *Romeo und Julia.* Übers. v. A. W. Schlegel. Berlin: Dressler, 1947. Pp. 80.

B431 *Romeo und Julia.* Übers. v. A. W. Schlegel. M. Anm. v. Christian Jenssen u. e. Nachw. v. Wilh. Etzrodt. Hamburg: Laatzen, 1948. Pp. 118.

B432 *Romeo und Julia.* Leipzig: Reclam, 1948. Pp. 88. Republ. Stuttgart, 1950. Leipzig, 1953.

B433 *Romeo und Julia.* Englisch und deutsch i. d. Übersetzung v. Schlegel u. Tieck. Hrsg. v. L. L. Schücking. Mit einem Essay "Zum Verständnis des Werkes" u. einer Bibliographie v. Wolfgang Clemen. Hamburg: Rowohlt, 1957. Pp. 203.

B434 *Julius Cäsar.* Übers. v. A. W. Schlegel. Berlin: Dressler, 1947. Pp. 72.

B435 *Julius Cäsar.* Nach d. Übers. v. A. W. Schlegel. Hrsg. v. Karl Heinz Dworczak. Vienna: Hölder-Pichler-Tempsky, 1948. Pp. 136.

B436 *Julius Cäsar.* Übers. v. A. W. Schlegel. Leipzig: Reclam, 1948. Pp. 80. Stuttgart, 1950.

B437 *Julius Cäsar.* Nach d. Übers. v. A. W. Schlegel. M. e. Vorw. v. Gottfried Ippisch. Vienna: Humboldt-Verl., 1947. Pp. 93.

B438 *Julius Cäsar.* Tr. A. W. Schlegel. Editiones Helveticae, Abt. Deutsche Texte, 19. Basel: Birkhäuser, 1952. Pp. 89.

B439 *Hamlet, Prinz von Dänemark.* Trauerspiel in 5 Aufzügen. Übers. von Aug. Wilh. von Schlegel. Leipzig: Reclam, 1943. Pp. 115.

B440 *Hamlet.* Englischer Text mit deutscher Übersetzung nach August Wilhelm Schlegel. Textrevision, Einleitung und Anmerkungen von Karl Brunner. Linz: Österreichischer Verlag für Belletristik und Wissenschaft, 1946. Pp. 315.

B441 *Hamlet, Prinz von Dänemark.* Übers. v. A. W. Schlegel. Vienna: Humboldt-Verl., 1946. Pp. 135. Republ. 1947.

B442 *Hamlet.* Übertr. v. Schlegel-Tieck in der Bearb. d. Dt. Shakespeare-Ges. durch Wilhelm Oechelhäuser. Dortmund: Schwalvenberg, 1947. Pp. 98.

B443 *Hamlet.* Dt. v. A. W. Schlegel. M. Abhandl. v. Kuno Fischer. Oberursel: Kompass-Verl., 1947. Pp. 344.

B444   *Hamlet.* Übers. v. A. W. Schlegel. Rendsburg: Wilkens, 1947. Pp. 128.

B445   *Hamlet.* Übers. v. A. W. Schlegel. Berlin: Dressler, 1947. Pp. 103.

B446   *Hamlet.* Übers. v. A. W. Schlegel. Leipzig: Reclam, 1947. Pp. 115.

B447   *Hamlet, Prinz von Dänemark.* Übers. v. A. W. Schlegel. Linz: Oberösterr. Landesverl., 1948.
        Pp. xxix, 162.

B448   *Hamlet.* Übers. v. A. W. Schlegel. Mit Anm. u. Nachw. v. Christian Jenssen. Hamburg:
        Laatzen, 1948. Pp. 134.

B449   *Hamlet.* Tr. A. W. Schlegel. Stuttgart: Reclam, 1950. Pp. 115.

B450   *Hamlet.* Tr. A. W. Schlegel. Editiones Helveticae, Abteilung Deutsche Texte, 14. Basel:
        Birkhäuser, 1952. Pp. 135.

B451   *Hamlet.* English und deutsch i. d. Übersetzung von Schlegel u. Tieck. Hrsg. v. L. L. Schücking.
        Mit einem Essay "Zum Verständnis der Werkes" und einer Bibliographie v. Wolfgang Clemen.
        Hamburg: Rowohlt, 1957. Pp. 248.

B452   *King Lear.* Engl. u. dt. Dt. v. L. Tieck. M. e. Nachw. v. M. Maeterlinck. Wuppertal:
        Marées-Verl., 1947. Pp. 195.

B453   *König Lear.* Dt. v. L. Tieck. Wuppertal: Marées-Verl., 1946. Pp. 98.

B454   *König Lear.* Übertr. v. A. W. Schlegel. L. Tieck in d. Bearb. d. Dt. Shakespeare-Ges. durch
        Wilhelm Oechelhäuser. Dortmund: Schwalvenberg, 1947. Pp. 90.

B455   *King Lear.* Tr. A. W. Schlegel. Stuttgart: Reclam, 1950.

B456   *Macbeth.* Englisch und Deutsch i.d. Übersetzung von Schlegel u. Tieck. Hrsg. v. L. L.
        Schücking. Mit einem Essay "Am Verständnis des Werkes" u. einer Bibliographie v. W. F.
        Schirmer. Hamburg: Rowohlt, 1958. Pp. 172.

B457   *Macbeth.* Übers. v. August Wilhelm Schlegel u. Ludwig Tieck. Berlin: Volk u. Wissen, 1958.
        Pp. 88.

(b) DOROTHEA TIECK

B458   *Coriolanus.* Trauerspiel in 5 Aufz. Deutsch von Dorothea Tieck. Leipzig: Reclam, 1941.
        Pp. 107.

B458a   *Coriolanus.* Übers. v. Dorothea Tieck. Berlin: Dressler, 1948. Pp. 96.

B459   *Das Wintermärchen.* Dt. v. Dorothea Tieck. Stuttgart: Reclam, 1957. Pp. 103.

B460   *Macbeth.* Trauerspiel in 5 Aufz. Deutsch von Dorothea Tieck. Leipzig: Reclam, 1938.
        Pp. 73. Republ. 1947, 1953.

B461   *Macbeth.* Tr. Dorothea Tieck, redaction of L. Tieck. Editiones Helveticae, Abt. Deutsche
        Texte, 21. Basel: Birkhäuser, 1952. Pp. 85.

B462   *Macbeth.* Übers. v. Dorothea Tieck. Iserlohn: Silva-Verl., 1947. Pp. 103.

B463   *Macbeth.* Übers. v. Dorothea Tieck. Berlin: Dressler, 1947. Pp. 66.

B464   *Macbeth.* In d. Übers. v. Dorothea Tieck. Bochum-Wattenscheid: Turm-Verl., 1947. Pp. 90.

B465   *Macbeth.* Übertr. auf Grund d. Dorothea Tieckschen. Übers. v. Fr. Theod. Vischer. Karls-
        ruhe: Braun, 1949. Pp. xi, 71.

(c) VON BAUDISSIN

B466   *Viel Lärmen um Nichts.* Dt. v. W. H. Graf Baudissin. Bühnenbearb. v. L. Barnay u. C. F.
        Wittmann. Leipzig: Reclam, 1948. Pp. 80.

B467   *Die Lustigen Weiber von Windsor.* Lustspiel in 5 Aufzügen. Dts. von Wolf Heinrich Graf
        Baudissin. Leipzig: Reclam, 1940. Pp. 86. Republ. 1949.

B468   *König Lear.* Übers. v. W. H. Graf Baudissin unt. d. Red. v. L. Tieck. Textgest. u. Erl. v.
        Hans Matter. Basel: Birkhäuser, 1948. Pp. 119. Republ. Vienna: Österr. Bundesverl.,
        1949. Pp. 168. Stuttgart: Reclam, 1950. Pp. 104. Leipzig: Reclam, 1953. Pp. 72.

B469   *Mass für Mass.* Dt. v. W. H. Graf Baudissin. Leipzig: Reclam, 1948. Pp. 96.

B470   *Der Widerspenstigen Zähmung.* Lustsp. in 5 Aufz. Deutsch von Wolf Heinrich Graf Baudissin.
        Leipzig: Reclam, 1938. Pp. 80. Republ. Berlin: Dressler, 1947. Pp. 70. Stuttgart: Reclam,
        1952. Pp. 86.

B471   *Othello, der Moor von Venedig.* Trauerspiel in 5 Aufzügen. Dts. von Wolf Heinrich Graf
        Baudissin. Leipzig: Reclam, 1941. Pp. 96. Republ. Berlin: Dressler, 1948. Pp. 91.
        Linz: Österreichischer Verlag für Belletristik und Wissenschaft, 1947. Pp. 279. Vienna:
        Humboldt-Verl., 1948. Pp. 108. Stuttgart: Reclam, 1950. Pp. 103. Leipzig: Reclam, 1953.
        Pp. 100.

B472   *Shakespeares Zeitgenossen.* 2 Bde. 1: Komödien. 2: Tragödien. Berlin: Lambert Schneider,
        1941. Pp. 889, 807. Republ. Heidelberg: Schneider, 1956. Contains *Der Londoner verlorene
        Sohn.* Übers. v. Wolf Graf v. Baudissin, I, 95-115, and *König Eduard der Dritte.* Übers. v. Wolf
        Graf v. Baudissin, II, 235-303.
            Rev: by Hans Bütow, *Frankf. Ztg.*, Lit. Beil. 75 (1942), No. 10, p. 4; by F. Brie, *Beiblatt,*
        LIV (1943), 58-60.

(d) FLATTER

B473   *Werke neu Übersetzt*, von Richard Flatter.   Vienna, Leipzig u. Zürich: Herb. Reichner, 1938.
        Bd. 1: *Macbeth—Romeo u. Julia.—Hamlet*, 1938.   Pp. 474.

B474   *Shakespeare neu Übersetzt*, von Richard Flatter.   Vienna, Munich: Walter Krieg, 1952.   Vol. I:
        Oth, Macb, Dream, H. IV.
        Rev: by E. A. J. Honigmann, *MLR*, XLIX (1954), 66-67; by Ludwig Kahn, *SQ*, v, 198-201.

B475   *Shakespeare neu Übersetzt*, von Richard Flatter.   Vienna, Munich: Walter Krieg, 1954.   Vol.
        II, III, IV, V.
        Vol. II: *Shrew, Meas, Romeo, Lear*.
        Vol. III: *Ham, Caes, Temp, Errors*.
        Vol. IV: *Merch, Troil, Winter's Tale, AYL*.
        Vol. V: *R. II, Twelf, Much, R. III*.
        Rev: (*Hamlet*) by Rudolf Stamm, *ES*, XXVI (1955), 228-238; 289-299; by Wolfgang Stroedel,
        SJ, 91 (1955), 353-355; by Ludwig W. Kahn, *SQ*, VII (1956), 124-125.

B476   *Shakespeare neu Übersetzt*, von Richard Flatter.   Vienna, Munich: Walter Krieg, 1955.   Vol. VI:
        Ant, Wives, TGV, All's Well.
        Rev: by Hereward T. Price, *JEGP*, LV (1956), 305-309; by Hermann Heuer, *SJ*, 92 (1956),
        407-422.

B477   Cancelled.

B478   *Shakespeares Sonette*, Übersetzt von Richard Flatter.   Vienna, Munich, Basel: Kurt Desch,
        1957.   Pp. 173.
        Rev: by Hermann Heuer, *SJ*, 93 (1957), 277-279.

(e) HENNECKE

B479   Jonson, Ben.   "Ode auf William Shakespeare."   Übertrag. u. eingel. v. H. Hennecke. *Europä-
        ische Rev*, XIII (1937), 735-739.

B480   Hennecke, H.   *Englische Gedichte von Shakespeare bis W. B. Yeats*.   Einführungen, Urtexte und
        Übertragungen.   Berlin: Kiepenheuer, 1938.   Pp. 160.

B481   "Sonnet 146."   Tr. by Hans Hennecke in his *Gedichte von Shakespeare bis Ezra Pound*.   Wies-
        baden, 1955, pp. 56-57.   English and German.

(f) JOSTEN

B482   *König Richard III, Hamlet, Macbeth*.   Deutsch aus dem Urtext von Walter Josten.   Hamburg:
        Paul Hartung Verl., 1937.   Pp. 163; 171; 109.
        Rev: by W. Keller, *SJ*, LXXIII (1937), 154-155; by Marg. Kurlbaum-Siebert, *Das dt. Wort*,
        XIII, 179; by W. Schmiele, *Frankf. Ztg.*, Nov. 28; by Johannes Speck, *Archiv*, 175 (1939),
        224-227.

B483   *Hamlet, Prinz von Dänemark*.   Dt. Übers. nebst sachl. u. sprachl. Erl. v. Walter Josten.   Bonn:
        Röhrscheidt, 1950.   Pp. 215.

(g) KELLER

B484   *Macbeth*.   Hrsg. von Wolfg. Keller.   Der Ausgabe liegt die Tiecksche Übersetzung zugrunde
        nach der Revision des Schlegel-Tieckschen Textes von Wolfgang Keller.   Cologne: Schaff-
        stein, 1940.   Pp. 88.
        Rev: by W. Keller, *SJ*, LXXVII (1941), 194.

B485   *Der Kaufmann von Venedig*.   Hrsg. v. W. Keller.   Cologne: Schaffstein, 1940.   Pp. 88.
        Rev: by W. Keller, *SJ*, LXXVII (1940), 205.

(h) ROTHE

B486   *Shakespeare.   In neuer Übersetzung von Hans Rothe*.   3 Bde.   I: *Lustspiele;* II: *Komödien;* III:
        Jugendwerke.   Leipzig: Paul List Verlag, 1927, 1934, 1935.   Pp. xxxvi, 439; xxiv, 511; 480.
        Rev: (of Bde. I, II, III) by W. Fischer, *Beiblatt*, XLVII (1936), 97-102.   But see B334-B343.

B487   *Shakespeare-Trostbüchlein für viele Lagen des Lebens*.   Zusammengestellt von Hans Rothe.
        Leipzig: Paul List Verlag, 1937.   Pp. 63.   Republ. 1940, 1947.

B488   *Der Elisabethanische Shakespeare*.   Übers. v. Hans Rothe.   Baden-Baden u. Genf: Holle,
        1956/58.   9 vols.

B489   Cancelled.

(i) SCHALLER

B490   *König Lear*.   Nach d. Urtexten Übertr. v. Rudolf Schaller.   Als Unverkäufl. Bühnen-Ms. gedr.
        Berlin: Henschel, 1950.   Pp. 139.

B491   *Macbeth*.   Aus d. Urtext Übertr. v. Rudolf Schaller.   Unverkäufl. Bühnen-Ms.   Berlin:
        Henschel, 1951.   Pp. 88.

B492   *Die Lustigen Weiber von Windsor*.   Dt. Nachdichtung u. Bühnenfassung in 12 Szenen v. Rudolf
        Schaller.   Unverkäufl. Bühnen-Ms.   Berlin: Henschel, 1952.   Pp. 93.

B493   *Hamlet Prinz von Dänemark.* Übertragung v. Rudolf Schaller. Berlin: Henschel, 1957.
        Pp. 164.
        Rev: by Hermann Heuer, *SJ*, 94 (1958), 299-301.

(j) SCHRÖDER

B494   *Was ihr Wollt.* Komödie in 5 Akten. Dts. von Rud. Alex. Schröder. Leipzig: Der junge
        Bühnenvertrieb, 1941. Pp. 128.

B495   *Wie es Euch Gefällt.* Lustspiel in 5 Aufz. Deutsch von Rudolf Alexander Schröder. Urverkäufl.
        [Bühnen-] Manuskript. Leipzig: R. Steyer, 1939. Pp. 86. Typewritten.

B496   *Ein Sommernachtstraum.* Komödie in 5 Akten. Dts. von Rud. Alex. Schröder. Leipzig:
        Der junge Bühnenvertrieb, 1941. Pp. 65. Two scenes published earlier in *Corona*, x (1940/41),
        292-308.

B497   *Troilus und Cressida.* Tr. by Rudolf A. Schröder. Hamburg: Maximilian-Gesellschaft, 1949.
        Pp. 194. Two scenes (I.iii. and II.i.), publ. in *SJ*, 84/86 (1948-50), 75-92.

B498   *Romeo und Julia.* Tr. by Rudolf A. Schröder. Berlin: Suhrkamp, 1949.

B499   *Sturm.* Deutsch von R. A. Schröder. Bibliothek Suhrkamp, Bd. 46. Berlin u. Frankfurt:
        Suhrkamp, 1958. Pp. 141. Act V publ. in *SJ*, 89 (1953), 5-17, and in Schröder's *Fülle des
        Daseins. Eine Auslese aus dem Werk.* Berlin: Suhrkamp, 1958.

B500   "Sonette." Übers. von Rudolf Alexander Schröder. [Son. 1, 4, 5], *Corona*, VI (1936), 253-255.

B500a   *Sonette.* Tr. into German by Rudolf A. Schröder. Stuttgart: *Merkur*, No. 5 (1949).
        Sonnets 1-6, 15, 18, 22, 31.

B500b   *Sonette* 1-6, 15, 18, 22, 25, 29, 31, 116. Übertr. v. Rudolf Alexander Schröder. In Schröder's
        Gesammelte Werke. Bd 1, 1952, pp. 547-553. Republ. in his *Fülle des Daseins. Eine Auslese
        aus dem Werk.* Berlin: Suhrkamp, 1958.

(k) SCHWARTZ

B501   *Macbeth.* Trauerspiel in 5 Aufzügen. Dts. von H. Schwarz. [Unverkäufliches Bühnen-Ms.]
        Leipzig: Der junge Bühnenvertrieb, 1941. Pp. 77.

B502   *Mass für Mass.* Tragikomödie in 5 Aufzügen. Dts. von H. Schwarz. [Unverkäufliches
        Bühnen-Ms.] Leipzig: Der junge Bühnenvertrieb, 1941. Pp. 96.

B503   *Der Sturm.* Übers. u. Bearb. v. Hedwig Schwarz. Als Ms. gedr. Hamburg: Chronos-Verl.,
        1955. Pp. 159.

B504   *Ende gut, alles gut.* Ubers. u. Bearb. v. Hedwig Schwarz. Als Ms. gedr. Hamburg: Chronos-
        Verl., 1955. Pp. 166.

(1) ZEYNEK

B505   *Shakespeare in neuer Übertragung*, von Theodor von Zeynek. Munich, Salzburg: Stifterbibliothek
        (Klassiker der Bühne). Vol. 16/16½, *Hamlet*, 1952, pp. 164. Vol. 24, *Ein Sommernachtstraum*,
        1953, pp. 96. Vol. 45, *Julius Caesar*, 1953, pp. 116. Vol. 48, *Romeo und Julia*, 1954, pp. 150.
        Rev: by I. Meidinger-Geise, *Welt u. Wort*, VIII (1953), 238; by Hermann Heuer, *SJ*, 92
        (1956), 407-422.

B506   *Macbeth.* In dt. Sprache Übertr. v. Theodor v. Zeynek. Stifterbibliothek, 132. Munich,
        Salzburg: Stifterbibl., 1955. Pp. 119.

B507   *Der Kaufmann von Venedig.* In dt. Sprache Übertr. v. Theodor v. Zeynek. Stifterbibliothek,
        Bd. 117. Salzburg: Stifterbibl., 1956. Pp. 120.

B508   *König Lear.* In dt. Sprache Übertr. v. Theodor v. Zeynek. Stifterbibliothek, Bd. 133/133½.
        Salzburg: Stifterbibl., 1956. Pp. 174.
        Rev: by Hermann Heuer, *SJ*, 93 (1957), 279.

B509   *Perikles.* In dt. Sprache Übertr. v. Theodor v. Zeynek. Stifterbibliothek, 134/135. Salzburg:
        Stifterbibl., 1958. Pp. 131.

(m) MISCELLANEOUS

B510   *Complete Works.* 4 vols. *Poetical Works.* Tr. by Friedrich Bodenstedt, Ferdinand Freiligrath
        and others. Heidelberg: L. Schneider, 1953. Pp. 479.

B511   *Poetische Werke.* Übers. v. Friedrich Bodenstedt, Ferdinand Freiligrath (u.a.). Frankfort:
        M. Büchergilde Gutenberg, 1957. Pp. 479.

B512   *Das Leben des Timon von Athen.* Übers. u. Bearb. v. Ludwig Berger. Als Ms. gedr. Berlin,
        Munich: Weiss, 1955. Pp. 49.

B513   *Sonett* 18, 21, 29, 50, 54, 64, 66, 71, 76, 90, 94, 104, 116, 129, 130, 132, 146. Übertr. v. Karl
        Theodor Busch. Busch's *Sonette der Völker*. Heidelberg, 1954. Pp. 221-229.

B514   *Antonius und Cleopatra.* Dts. von Rochus Gliese. Unverkäufliches [Bühnen-] Ms. Leipzig:
        Der Junge Bühnenvertrieb. Leipzig: Ralf Steyer, 1943. Pp. 161. Typewritten.

B515   *Sonette* (Engl. u. dt.) Dt. v. Walther Freund. Bern: Scherz, 1948. Pp. 219. Selection republ.
        1950. Pp. 77.

B516   *Der Liebesbrief. Die Szenen um Malvolio aus der Komodie "Was ihr wollt."* Nach d. Erfahrungen
        e. Einstudierung f. dramatische Zirkel eingerichtet u. mit Regiehinweisen vers. v. Peter Fischer.
        Leipzig: Hofmeister, 1955. Pp. 84.

B517   *Sonette.* In dt. Sprache u. Ital. Versform v. Hans Hübner. Dresdner Verlagsgesellschaft, 1949.
        Pp. 154. Republ. Rostock: Hinstorff, 1953, 1956. Pp. 196.

B518   *Sonnette.* Übers. von Ilse Krämer. Basel: B. Schwabe & Co., 1945. Pp. iv, 168.

B519   *Shakespeares Sonette.* Nachdichtung von Karl Kraus. Vienna, Leipzig: Verlag "Die Fackel,"
        1933. Pp. 81.
            Rev: by Albert Bloch, *Books Abroad*, XI (1937), 22-24.

B520   *Dramen für Hörer und Leser.* Bearb., Teilweise Sprachlich Erneuert von K. Kraus. Bd. II.
        Vienna: Lanyi, 1935. Pp. 336.

B521   *Shakespeare-Volkslieder.* Lieder aus Shakespeares Dramatischen Werken Übersetzt u. Eingeleitet
        v. Karl Georg Mantey. Leipzig: H. H. Kreisel Verlag, 1939. Pp. 80.
            Rev: by Wolfgang Keller, *SJ*, LXXV (1939), 149-150.

B522   *Hamlet, Prince of Denmark.* Eine Auswahl mit Übersetzungen und Sprachvergleichendem
        Kommentar von Wilh. Poethen. Heidelberg: Winter, 1940. Pp. viii, 65.
            Rev: by W. Héraucourt, *Lbl*, LXIII (1942), 312-313; by W. Hübner, *N. Mon.*, XIII, 39.

B523   *Sonette.* Engl. u. dt. In d. Übertr. v. Gottlob Regis. Hamburg: v. Schröder, 1945. Pp. 163.
        Republ. 1958. Pp. 322.

B524   *Macbeth.* Bearb. v. Friedrich von Schiller. In Schiller's *Werke.* Nationalausg., Bd. 13.
        Weimar: Böhlau, 1949, pp. 73-162; 306-315; 362-405.
            Rev: by W. Stroedel, *SJ*, 91 (1955), 368.

B525   *Der Kaufmann von Venedig.* Tr. by K. Schümmer. Paderborn: Schöningh, 1941. Pp. 80.

B526   *Phönix und Taube.* Tr. by Heinrich Straumann. Zurich: Artemis-Verlag, 1953.

B527   Brüggemann, F., ed. *Die Aufnahme Shakespeares auf der Bühne der Aufklärung in den Sechziger
        und Siebziger Jahren.* Leipzig, 1937.
        Contains Wieland's prose transl. of *Lear* (1760's).
            Rev: A9441.

B528   *Sonnette.* Englisch und Deutsch. Neue Übertragung von Gustav Wolff. Munich: Reinhardt,
        1938. Pp. 163.

(n) TRANSLATOR NOT IDENTIFIED IN SOURCES
(Arranged alphabetically by publisher)
i. Lindau: Apollo-Verlag

B529   *Romeo und Julia.* Vienna, Innsbr., Lindau: Apollo-Verl., 1947. Pp. 93.

B530   *Ein Sommernachtstraum.* Vienna, Innsbr., Lindau: Apollo-Verl., 1947. Pp. 64.

B531   *Wie es euch gefällt.* Lindau: Apollo-Verl., 1948. Pp. 95.

B532   *König Richard III.* Vienna, Innsbr., Lindau: Apollo-Verl., 1948. Pp. 110.

B533   *Julius Cäsar.* Lindau: Apollo-Verl., 1948. Pp. 64.

ii. Dieterich

B534   *Hamlet.* Englisch und Deutsch. Mit Einleitung und Anmerkungen Hrsg. von L[evin]
        L[udwig] Schücking. Leipzig: Dieterich, 1941. Pp. lxxxiii, 414. Republ., 1943.
            Rev: by W. Keller, *SJ*, LXXVII (1941), 192-193; by Hans Bütow, *Frankf. Ztg.*, Lit. Beil. 75
            (1942), No. 10, p. 4.

B535   "Sonnel 29, 66, 116, 147 [Engl. u. dt.]." In Levin Ludwig Schücking's *Englische Gedichte aus
        sieben Jahrhunderten.* Sammlung Dieterich, 109. Bremen, 1956, pp. 58-65.

iii. Berlin: Dressler

B536   *Dramen.* Berlin: Dressler, Vol. I, *Ham, Macb, Lear, Cor, Caes, Ant, Romeo, Oth*, 1948. Vol. II,
        Errors, Shrew, Dream, Wives, Merch, Twelf, AYL, Meas, 1949.

B537   *Ein Sommernachtstraum.* Berlin: Dressler, 1947. Pp. 56.

iv. Hamburg: Internat. Klassiker

B538   *Hamlet.* Illustrierte Klassiker, No. 4. Hamburg: Verl. Internat. Klassiker, 1956.

B539   *Macbeth.* Illustrierte Klassiker, No. 22. Hamburg: Verl. Internat. Klassiker, 1956.

B540   *Romeo und Julia.* Illustrierte Klassiker, 34. Hamburg: Verl. Internat. Klassiker, 1957.

B541   *Ein Sommernachtstraum.* Illustrierte Klassiker, 64. Hamburg: Bildschriftenverl., 1958.

v. Other Publishers

B542   *Sämtliche Werke.* Hrsg. v. Anselm Schlösser. In 3 Bdn. Berlin: Aufbau-Verl., 1956. 1.
        Historien. Pp. 913. 2. Komödien. Pp. 1276. 3. Tragödien. Poetische Werke. Pp. 1055.

B543   *Gesammelte Werke* in 6 Bänden. Eingel. v. Reinhold Schneider. Hrsg. v. Hans Jürgen Meinerts.

Gütersloh: Bertelsmann, 1958. 1. Einleitung. Sonette. Komödien. Pp. 573. 2. Komödien.
Pp. 573. 5. Tragödien. Pp. 518.
Rev: by W. Westecker, *Christ und Welt*, July 3, 1958, p. 16.

B544 *König Richard III.* Bearb. v. Emil Steiger. Anm. Karlsruhe: Braun, 1951. Pp. xix, 121, 55.

B545 *Der Sturm.* M. e. Einf. v. Adolf v. Grolman. Hamburg: Ellermann, 1948. Pp. 92.

B546 *Englische Dichtung des 16. Jahrhunderts. Eine Anthologie.* Ed. by Wolfgang Clemen. Munich-
Pasing: Filser, 1948. Pp. 167.
Shak., pp. 98-109.

B547 *Komödien.* Einl. v. Helmut Viebrock. Fischer-Bücherei, Bd. 148. Frankfort: M. Fischer,
1957. Pp. 224.

B548 *Shakespeare, Dramen* (Goldmanns Gelbe Taschenbücher, Bd. 397, Bd. 400-402, Bd. 407-408).
3 Bände. Munich: Wilhelm Goldmann, 1956, 1957.
I.   Schicksals- und Königsdramen. (*Romeo, Ham, Oth*).
II.   Komödien. (*Shrew, Dream, AYL, Twelf, Wives, All's Well*).
III. Schicksals- und Königsdramen. (*Caesar, Lear, Macb, R. II, H. IV, R. III*).

B549 *Romeo und Julia.* M. e. Vorw. v. Gottfried Ippisch. Vienna: Humboldt-Verl., 1947. Pp. 118.

B550 *Shakespeare's Works* (English and German). Ed. by L. L. Schücking. Munich: Knaur;
Vienna: Österr. Buchgemeinschaft, 1955.
Vol. 1. Dramen. Romanzen. Pp. 1318.
Vol. 2. Tragödien. Komödien. Pp. 1341.

B551 *Ausgewählte Werke.* Hrsg. u. eingel. v. Oskar Rühle. Stuttgart: Kohlhammer, 1950. 3 Vols.
Pp. 574, 598, 576.
Vol. I: *Sonnets, Rom, Ham, Oth, Macb, Lear.*
Vol. II: *R. III, R. II, Meas, Caesar, Cor, Ant.*
Vol. III: *Shrew, Wives, Twelf, AYL, Dream, Merch, Temp.*

B552 *Ein Sommernachtstraum.* Offenburg, Mainz: Lehrmittelverl., 1947. Pp. xvi, 88.

B553 *Sonette.* Cologne: Pick, 1947. Pp. 54.

B554 *Geleitspruch aus Hamlet.* Polonius, Oberkämmerer d. Königs v. Dänemark, an seinen nach
Frankreich ausreisenden Sohn Laertes. Einblattdr., 2 farb., z. Jahreshauptvers. 1951 d. Ges.
d. Bibliophilen, Wuppertal. Krefeld: Scherpe, 1951.

B555 *Ein Sommernachtstraum: Eine Kömodie mit Fünf Farbigen.* Lithographien von Jack von Reppert-
Bismarck. Bern: Alfred Scherz Verlag, 1956. Pp. 134.

B556 *Ein Lesebuch für unsere Zeit.* Ed. by Walther Victor. Weimar: Thüringer Volksverlag, 1953.
Pp. 509.

B557 *Komödien.* Vienna: Ullstein.
Vol. I: *Shrew, Dream, Merch, Wives*, 1946. Pp. 351.
Vol. II: *All's Well, AYL, Twelf*, 1947. Pp. 292.
Vol. III: *Troil, Cym, Winter's Tale*, 1947. Pp. 349.

B558 *König Lear.* Braunschweig: Westermann, 1949. Pp. 126.

B559 *Dramen in Einzelbänden.* Engl. u. dt. Hrsg. u. eingel. v. Paul Wiegler. Berlin: Transmare-
Verl. *Hamlet, Prinz von Dänemark*, 1947. Pp. 408. *Romeo und Julia*, 1948. Pp. 324. *Wie es
euch gefällt*, 1948. Pp. 288.

b. TRANSLATIONS INTO OTHER GERMANIC LANGUAGES (162;54)
(1) DUTCH

B560 Pennink, R. *Nederland en Shakespeare.* The Hague, 1936.
Rev: A9739.

(a) BRABANDER

B561 *Leer om Leer.* Bewerking door Gerard den Brabander. Amsterdam: von Oorschot, 1950.
Pp. 128. Republ. 1952.
Rev: by J. Meyer, *Elseviers Weekblad*, Oct. 7, 1950; by H. de Vries, *Critisch Bulletin*, xviii
(1951), 401-405; by W. van Maanen, *De Gids*, 114, i (1951), 379-381.

B562 *Een Midzomernachtdroom.* Bew. door Gerard den Brabander. Amsterdam: van Kampen,
1952. Pp. 94.

(b) BUNING

B563 *Het Spel der Vergissingen.* [*Comedy of Errors.*] Vert. door J. W. F. Werumeus Buning. *Gids*, IV
(1939), 151-168, 249-285. Republ. Amsterdam: Querido, 1940. Pp. 56.

B564 *Een Midzomernachtsdroom.* Vert. door J. W. F. Werumeus Buning. Toneelfonds Maestro,
196. Amsterdam: Strengholt, 1957. Pp. 64.

B565 *Een Winteravondsprookje.* Vert. door J. W. F. Werumeus Buning. Toneelfonds Maestro, 197.
Amsterdam: Strengholt, 1958. Pp. 88.

(c) BURGERSDIJK

B566   *Een Midzomernacht-droom.* Vert. door L. A. J. Burgersdijk. Film-editië. Med ill. . . . en een voorwoord van Max Reinhardt. Leiden: A. W. Sijthoff, 1936. Pp. viii, 70.

B567   *De Complete Werken van William Shakespeare.* In de Vertaling van L. A. J. Burgersdijk. Bewerkt en van een inleidung voorzien door F. de Baker en G. A. Dudok. 3 v. Leiden, A. W. Sijthoff, 1941, 1944, 1945. Pp. 679, 722, 783.
Rev: by R. W. Zandvoort, *ES,* xxiii (1941), Heft 6.

B568   *Toneelspelen.* In de Vert. van Leendert A. J. Burgersdijk. Bew. door Frans de Backer en G. A. Dudok. Leiden: Sijthoff; Antwerpen: Nederl. Boekh. 1952.
1. *De Koopman van Venetië.* Pp. 95.
2. *Een Midzomernachtdroom.* Pp. 84.
3. *Drie-Koningenavond of wat gij wilt.* Pp. 102.
4. *Hamlet.* Pp. 173.
5. *Romeo en Julia.* Pp. 109.
6. *Othello.* Pp. 122.
7. *Macbeth.* Pp. 96.
8. *Koning Lear.* Pp. 138.
9. *Julius Caesar.* Pp. 104.
10. *Een Winteravondsprookje.* Pp. 115.
11. *Elk wat Wils.* Pp. 96.

B569   *De Toneelspelen. Romeo en Julia. Een Midzomernachtsdroom. Julius Caesar. Hamlet.* In de Vertaling van Leendert A. J. Burgersdijk. Bew. door C. Buddingh. Utrecht: Bruna, 1955. Pp. 325.

B570   *Koning Richard de Derde. De Vrolijke Vrouwtjes van Windsor. De Storm.* In de Vertaling van Leendert A. J. Burgersdijk. Bew. door Frans de Backer en G. A. Dudok. Utrecht: Spectrum, 1955. Pp. 264.

B571   *De Toneelspelen. De Koopman van Venetië. Driekoningenavond. Othello. Macbeth.* In de Vert. van Leendert Alexander Johannes Burgersdijk. Bew door C. Buddingh. Utrecht: Bruna, 1957.

B572   *Maat voor Maat.* In de Vertaling van Leendert A. J. Burgersdijk. Bew. door Frans de Backer en G. A. Dudok. Antwerpen: Nederl. Boekh.; Leiden: Sijthoff, 1954.

B573   *De Getemde Feeks.* In de Vert. v. Leendert A. J. Burgersdijk. Bew. door Frans de Backer en G. A. Dudok. Leiden: Sijthoff, 1956. Pp. 49.

B574   *Veel Leven om Niets.* In de Vert. van Leendert Alexander Johannes Burgersdijk. Bew. door Frans de Backer en Gerard Anton Dudok. Leiden: Sijthoff, 1957. Pp. 51.

(d) COURTEAUX

B575   *Hendrik IV.* Ingel. en vert. door Wim Courteaux. Antwerpen: Nederl. Boekh.; Amsterdam: Wereldbibl., 1956. Pp. xviii, 213.

B576   *De Feeks Wordt Getemd.* Ingel. en vert. door Wim Courteaux. Klassieke galerij, 121. Amsterdam: Wereldbibl., 1957. Pp. xii, 90.

B577   *Julius Caesar.* Ingel. en vert. door Wim Courteaux. Amsterdam: Wereldbibl., 1958. Pp. xii, 88.

B578   *Hamlet.* Ingel. en vert. door Wim Courteaux. Antwerpen: De Nederl. Boekh., 1958. Pp. xlviii, 144.

B579   *De Storm.* Ingel. en vert. door Wim Courteaux. Amsterdam: Wereldbibl., 1958. Pp. xviii, 75.

(e) DEELEN

B580   *Hamlet.* Vert. door Martin Deelen. Illustrated Classics. Beroemde Boeken in Woord en Beeld. 4. Amsterdam: van Ditmar, 1956. Pp. 48.
Rev: by Noud van den Eerenbeemt, *Nieuwe Eeuw,* March 24, 1956.

B581   *Een Midzomernachtdroom.* Vert. door Martin Deelen. Illustrated Classics. Beroemde Boeken in Woord en Beeld. 64. Bussum: Classics Nederland, 1958. Pp. 48.

B582   *Romeo en Julia.* Vert. door Martin Deelen. Illustrated Classics. Beroemde Boeken in Woord en Beeld. 34. Bussum: Classics Nederland, 1957. Pp. 48.

(f) FLEERACKERS

B583   *Macbeth.* Vert. door E. Fleerackers, S. J. Antwerpen: Standaard Boekhandel, 1939. Pp. 103. Republ. 1947. Pp. 100.

B584   *Julius Caesar.* Vert. door E. Fleerackers, S. J. Antwerpen: Standaard Boekhandel, 1938. Pp. 108. Republ. 1951. Pp. 95.

(g) MESSELAAR

B585   "Bruidslied uit Romeo en Julia." Vert. door Gerard Messelaar. *Kunst en Kunstleven*, Aug.
        1949, p. 48.

B586   "Sonnet 8. Sonnet 98." Vert. door Gerard Messelaar. *Kunst en Kunstleven*, Jan. 1949, p. 14.

(h) VAN SUCHTELEN

B587   *Een Midzomernachtsdroom.* Tr. into Dutch by Nico van Suchtelen. Amsterdam: Wereldbibl.,
        1949. Pp. 82.
            Rev: by Justus Meyer, *Elseviers Weekblad*, April 16, 1949.

B588   *Het Treurspel van Hamlet, Prins van Denemarken.* Uit het Engels vert. door Nico van Suchtelen.
        Amsterdam: Wereldbibl., 1947. Pp. 152. Republ. 1952.

B589   *Macbeth.* Uit het Engels vert. door Nico van Suchtelen. Amsterdam: Wereldbibl., 1950.
        Pp. 93.
            Rev: by H. de Vries, *Vrij Nederland*, Nov. 11, 1950.

(i) VOETEN

B590   *De Koopman van Venetië.* Tr. into Dutch by Bert Voeten. Amsterdam-Antwerpen: Wereldbibl.,
        1951. Pp. 108.
            Rev: by H. de Vries, *Critisch Bulletin*, XVIII (1951), 401-405.

B591   *De Vrolijke Vrouwtjes van Windsor.* Vert. door Bert Voeten. Amsterdam: Wereldbibl., 1952.
        Pp. 127. Republ. 1958.
            Rev: by P. H. Breitenstein, *LT*, 1952, p. 303.

B592   *Hamlet, Prins van Denemarken.* In de Vert. van Bert Voeten. Amsterdam: De Bezige Bij,
        1958. Pp. 207.

B593   "Sonnet 18, 71, 132." Vert. door Bert Voeten, Hans Berghuis, H. W. J. M. Keuls. *Ad
        Interim*, v (1948), 227-229.

(j) OTHERS

B594   *The Merchant of Venice.* M. verkl. aantek. voor school en huis door K. ten Bruggencate. 21.
        dr., nagezijn door C. D. ten Bruggencate. Groningen: Wolters, 1956. Pp. 103.

B595   "Sonnet XVII en LXV." Vert. door Jan Campert. *Groot Nederland*, 1941, ii, 91-92.

B596   "Vier Sonnetten (XXIX, LXI, LXVI, LXXI)." Vert. door Jan Campert. *Groot Nederland*,
        1942, i, 142-143.

B597   *De Storm.* Losbandig Bewerkt door Charivarius. 3 de druck. Haarlem: Tjeenk Willink &
        Zoon, 1936. Pp. 43.

B598   *Hamlet.* Engelsch en Nederlandsch, Tegenover Elkaar door J. Decroos. Kortrijk: Verlag
        Steenlandt, n.d. (1936).
            Rev: by M. van Der Kerckhove, *SJ*, LXXII (1936), 167-168; by H. de Groot, *ES*, xx (1938),
        225-226.

B599   "Sonnetten." Vert. door H. W. J. M. Keuls, *Criterium*, 1941, ii, 309-310.

B600   "Sonnet 129." Vert. door H. W. J. M. Keuls. *Gids*, 113 (1950), 97.

B601   *Richard III.* Treurspel. Vert. door A. Roland Holst. 2 de druck. Maastricht: A. A. M. Stols,
        1937. Pp. 174. Republ. Amsterdam: Wereldbibl., 1951. Pp. 134. Republ. 1955. Pp. 157.

B602   *Fragmenten uit Een Midzomernachtdroom.* Vert. en vew. door J. H. Hoornweg. Assen: Van
        Gorcum & Comp., 1937. Pp. 43.

B603   "Sonnet LXXII." Vert. door H. Kron, *Nieuwe Gids*, 1941, i, p. 175.

B604   *Storm.* Een spel van Tooverij. Vert. door M. Nijhoff. 2 de druck. Maastricht: A. A. M.
        Stols, 1937. Pp. 109. Republ. Amsterdam: Querido, 1952. Pp. 80. Amsterdam: van
        Oorschot, 1954.

B605   *De Klucht der Vergissingen.* Tr. into Dutch, ed. by P. H. Schröder. Assen: Van Gorcums
        Niew Dilettantentoneel No. 1, 1951. Pp. 1-44.

B606   "Drie Sonnetten" [27, 76, 121]. Vert. door Jan Spierdijk. *Gids*, 120, ii (1957), 163-165.

(2) FRISIAN

B607   Foppema, Yge. "Shakespeare in het Fries." *Vry Nederland* (Amsterdam), Aug. 12, 1950.
        On translating Shak. into Frisian.

B608   "Untearing fan Lucretia." Fragment ("Lucretia foar it Skilderij") in het Fries vert. en ingel.
        d. D. Kalma. *Tsjerne*, III (1948), 367-374.

B609   *In Midsummernachtdream.* Tr. into Frisian by D. Kalma. Drachten: Laverman, 1949. Pp. 96.

B610   *Shakespeares Wurk yn Fryske, Diel I, Komeedzjes.* Tr. by D. Kalma. Ljouwert: Fryske Shake-
        speare Stifting, 1956. Pp. 235. Komeedzes. *In Komeedzje fol Forsinnen. Leafde's lêst net
        leanne. De twa eallju fan Verona.* (*Errors, LLL, TGV.*)
        Tr. by Dourve Kalma (1896-1953), this is Vol. II of the projected three-volume translation
        into Frisian of the complete works of Shak.
            Rev: by B. Folkertsma, *Heitelân*, 1956, pp. 188-189; by K. Dykstra, *LT*, 1957, pp. 93-96,
        and in *Tsjerne*, XI, 326-329; by Bernard J. Fridsma, Sr., *Books Abroad*, XXXI, 323.

(3) AFRIKAANS

B611   Van Heyningen, Christina. "Afrikaans Translations of Shakespeare." *Vista* (publication of the Council of Cultural Societies, Univ. of the Witwatersrand), 1950. Pp. 9.
A critical discussion of Afrikaans translations of Shak., particularly those by Professor Coertze of *Macbeth* and *Hamlet*.

B611a   Malherbe, E. F. "Iets oor die Vertaling van *The Merchant of Venice*" ["Something about the translation of *The Merchant of Venice*"], *Huisgenoot*, Nov. 9, 1951, p. 13.
The author comments on his own recent translation of the play into Afrikaans.

B612   *Macbeth*. Vert. deur L. I. Coertze. Tekeninge Nerine Desmond. Kapstad: Stewart, 1948. Pp. 120.

B613   *Die Koopman van Venesië*. Vert. deur D. F. Malherbe. Johannesburg: Afrik. Pers, 1949. Pp. v, 90.

(4) DANISH
(a) TRANSLATION PROBLEMS

B614   Børge, V. "Oversaettelsesproblemet og Shakespeare paa Dansk." *Danske Studier*, 1932, pp. 57-68.

B615   Jensen, Johannes. "Rebuserne i Hamlet." *Politiken*, Feb. 18, 1937, pp. 11-12.

B616   Henriques, Alf. "Shakespeare and Denmark: 1900-1949." *ShS*, III (1950), 107-115.

B617   Beyer, Edvard. *Problemer Omkring Oversettelser av Shakespeares Dramatikk*. With English Summary. Historiskantikvarisk Rekke, No. 3. Bergen: A. S. John Briegs Boktrykkeri, 1956. Pp. 64.
Rev: B626.

B618   Rubow, Paul V. "Om Shakespere Oversaettelser—Endnu Engang." *Berlingske Aften* (Copenhagen), No. 12, 1958.

(b) TRANSLATIONS

B619   *Hamlet*. Tr. by Johannes V. Jensen. Copenhagen: Gyldendal, 1937. Pp. 202.
Rev: by Gay W. Allen, *EA*, I (1937), 445; by G. W. Allen, *Books Abroad*, XI (1938), 502.

B620   *Hamlet, Prins af Denmark*. Tr. by Valdemar Østerberg. Copenhagen: Schultz, 1954. Pp. 210.

B621   *Dramatiske Vaerker*, Ed. by Kr. Langdal Möller; tr. into Danish by V. Østerberg. Copenhagen: Schultz, 1958. Pp. 507.

B622   *Skuespil*. Tr. by Edvard Lembcke. Copenhagen: Reitzel, 1953. Pp. 128.

B623   *A Midsummer Night's Dream*. *En Sommernattsdrøm* (Excerpts). Tr. by André Bjerke. *Ordet* (Oslo), VI, No. 4 (1955), 181-188.

B624   *Henrik IV*. Tr. by Niels Möller. Ed. by Alf. Henriques. Copenhagen: Gyldendal, 1958. Pp. 167.

(5) NORWEGIAN
(a) TRANSLATION PROBLEMS

B625   Dale, Johannes A. "Henrik Rytters Omsetjingar." *Syn og Segn* (Oslo), LV, No. 4 (1949), 161-174.

B626   Beyer, Edvard. *Problemer Omkring Oversettelser av Shakespeares Dramatikk*. With English Summary. Historiskantikvarisk Rekke, No. 3. Bergen: A. S. John Briegs Boktrykkeri, 1956. Pp. 64.
Emphasizes Norwegian translation—hitherto neglected—but makes comparison with the most important Danish and Swedish versions.

B627   Eckhoff, Lorentz. "Shakespeare in Norwegian Translations." *SJ*, 92 (1956), 244-254.

(b) TRANSLATIONS

B628   *Dramatiske Verker i Norsk Oversettelse*. Hefte 28, 29, 30. Oslo: Aschehoug & Co., 1936. Hefte 31-43, Aschehoug, 1942.

B629   Cancelled.

B630   *Dramatiske Verker*. I Norsk Oversettelse ved Carl Burchardt, . . . Innledninger og Oplysninger til Teksten ved A. Trampe Bødtker. Oslo: Aschehoug, 1942.
8.: *Troll Kan Temmes*. Oversatt av Gunnar Larsen. Pp. 130
Othello. Oversatt av Gunnar Larsen. Pp. 158.
Macbeth. Oversatt av Aasmund Sveen. Pp. 116.

B631   *Leken i Skogen [As You Like It]*. På Norske Vers av Herman Wildenvey. Tegninger av Gunnar Bratlie. Oslo: E. G. Mortensen, 1942. Pp. 206.

B632   *Fra En Sommernattsdrøm*. Ved André Bjerke. *Ordet* (Oslo), VI, No. 4 (1955), 181-188.

B632a   *En Sommernattsdrøm*. Tr. into Norwegian by André Bjerke. Oslo: H. Aschehoug & Co., 1958. Pp. i, 130.

B633 *Hamlet* (Selections). Tr. into Norwegian by André Bjerke. *Ordet* (Oslo), IX, Nos. 5, 6, 8, 9 (1958).
Includes Acts I-II (with omissions) and parts of Act III.

(6) SWEDISH
(a) TRANSLATION PROBLEMS

B634 Donner, H. W. *Svenska Översättningar av Shakespeares Macbeth.* I: *Schillers Inflytande på Geijers Översättnung. Acta Academiae Aboensis, Humaniora* (Åbo), XX, No. 1 (1950). Pp. vii, 148.
Rev: by Esbjörn Blohmé, *ES*, XXXIII (1952), 266-267; by J. M. Nosworthy, *RES*, III, 298.

B635 Donner, H. W. "Kunna Tankar oversättas?" *Skrifter utg. av Föreningen för Filosofi och Specialvetenskap* (Uppsala), III (1955), 44-58.
Mostly instances from Shak. on the subject: Can thoughts be translated?

B636 Beyer, Edvard. *Problemer Omkring Oversettelser av Shakespeares Dramatikk.* With English Summary. Historiskantikvarisk Rekke, No. 3. Bergen: A. S. John Briegs Boktrykkeri, 1956. Pp. 64.
Rev: B626.

B637 Molin, Nils. "Shakespeare Translated into Swedish." *SJ*, 92 (1956), 232-243.

(b) TRANSLATIONS

B638 *Macbeth.* Övers. av Sigvard Arbman. Illustrerad av Yngve Kernell. Stockholm: Sällskapet Bokvännerna, 1954. Pp. 128.

B639 *En Midsommarnatts Dröm* . . . By Svensk Översattning av Allan Bergstrand. Stockholm: Bröderne Lagerströms Forlag, 1946.

B640 *Macbeth.* Övers. av Hagberg. Med inledn. Förklaringar och Studieuppgifter utg. av Josua Mjöberg. Skrifter utg. av Modersmålslärarnas Förening, 69. Lund: Gleerup, 1948. Pp. 95.

B641 *Hamlet.* Övers. av K. A. Hagberg i ny Bearbetning Jämte Anmärkningar och Kommentarer av Nils Molin. Stockholm: Tiden, 1954. Pp. 195.

B642 *Hamlet.* Övers. av Per Hallström. Skoluppl. m. Inledning av Sigurd Segerström. Skrifter utg. av Modersmålslärarnas Förening, 40. Stockholm: Bonnier, 1948. Pp. 146.

B643 *Köpmannen i Venedig.* Övers. av Per Hallström. Skoluppl. med Inledn. av Sigurd Segerström. Skrifter utg. av Modersmålslärarnas Förening, 39. Stockholm: Bonnier, 1949. Pp. 88.

B644 *Sonetter.* Tolkning av Eva von Koch. Göteborg, 1951. Pp. 46.

B645 *Hamlet, Prins av Danmark.* Tr. by Sven Rosén. Stockholm: Bokförlaget Fornted och Nutid, 1952. Pp. 330.
Rev: by H. Gillqvist in *Moderna Språk*, XLVIII (1954), 341-348.

B646 Tigerschiöld, Brita. "Dödsperspektivet i en grupp Shakespearesonetter." *Ord och Bild*, No. 9 (1954), pp. 553-561.

B647 *Så Tuktas en Argbigga.* Bearb. f. Amatörteatern av Torsten Friedlander. Göteborg: Elander, 1950. Pp. 80.

B648 *Coriolan,* gez. Hannsferdinand Döbler. Rec. av Carl-Henning Wijkmark. *Sydsvenska Dagbladet Snällposten*, XV (1958), 1.

c. TRANSLATIONS INTO ROMANCE LANGUAGES (162;54)
(1) FRENCH (162;54)
(a) TRANSLATION PROBLEMS AND TRANSLATORS

B649 Downs, B. W. *Ducis's Two "Hamlets." MLR*, XXXI (1936), 206-208.
Versions of 1770 and 1803. See also A9343-A9350.

B650 Lemaire, M. *Some French Translations of Shakespeare's "Macbeth".* (Thèse Pour le Degré de) Licence, Liège, 1936/7.

B651 Radulescu, I. Horia. "Les Intermédiaires Français de Shakespeare en Roumanie." *RLC*, XVIII (1938), 252-271.

B651a Montaigne, André. *"Arden de Feversham,* adapté par H.-R. Lenormand." *Le Mois*, Oct. 1939, pp. 226-228.

B652 Underwood, V. P. "Verlaine et Coppé, Traducteurs de Shakespeare." *Nouvelles Littéraires*, Jan. 14, 1939, p. 1.

B653 Shackleton, Robert. "Shakespeare in French Translation." *Mod. Languages*, XXIII (1941), 15-21.
Discusses the eighteenth century translations of La Place, Le Tourneur, and Ducis.

B654 Beresford-Howe, Constance. *The French Translations of "Hamlet".* DD, Brown University, 1950.

B655 Fluchère, Henri. "Shakespeare in France: 1900-1948." *ShS*, II (1949), 115-124.

B656 Buck, Eva. "Vier Zeilen von Shakespeare in Berühmten Französischen und Deutschen Übersetzungen." *Archiv*, 190, Nos. 1-2 (October, 1953), 21-32.

B657   Davril, R. "Shakespeare in French Garb." *SJ*, 92 (1956), 197-206.
        In the controversy over the best method of translation, Gide has demonstrated the right course
        to follow: the translator must combine the virtues of the scholar and the artist.

B658   Haldimann-Roman, Eva. *Stilkritische Untersuchungen an Le Tourneurs Übersetzungen der Shake-
        speareschen Lustspiele.* DD, Zurich, 1956. Publ. in *Zürcher Beiträge zur Vergleichenden Litera-
        turgesch.*, 7. Zurich: Juris-Verlag, 1956.

B659   Keys, A. C. "Shakespeare en Français." *RLC*, xxx (1956), 98-102.
        Critical evaluation of Louis Direy's translation of *Sonn.* in 1891 in New Zealand.

B660   Koszul, A. "L'Éternel Problème de la Traduction: À Propos d'une Nouvelle Version des
        Sonnets de Shakespeare." *EA*, ix (1956), 1-9.
        See also B660a and response by Pierre Leyris in *EA*, ix, 10-13.
        The version is that of P. J. Jouve.

B660a   Loiseau, J. "L'Éternel Problème de la Traduction: À Propos d'une Nouvelle Édition avec
        Traduction de Shakespeare." *EA*, ix (1956), 10-13.
        See response by Pierre Leyris, ibid., pp. 225-228.

B661   Gide, André. "Shakespeare en Francés." *Sur*, Buenos Aires, Nov. 1938, pp. 7-16.

B662   D'Estournelles, Paul. "Hamlet in French." Tr. by André Gide. *TAr*, xxix (1945), 665-666.

B663   Levin, Harry. "Meditation on a Battlement." *NR*, 112 (1945), 559-560.

B664   Brunot, Henriette. "*Hamlet* de Shakespeare, Traduction d'André Gide." *Psyché*, i (1946),
        229-232.

B665   Milwitsky, W. "A. Gide's 'Hamlet'." *Symposium*, i (1947), 147-151.

B666   Roddiman, P. "Gide's *Hamlet*." *Partisan Review*, xvi (1949), 213-220.

B667   Hottot, A. L. E. H. *André Gide as Translator from English and Interpreter of Great Britain.*
        B. Litt. thesis, Oxford, 1951.

B668   Brown, John Mason. "Etre ou ne pas Etre." *SatR*, xxxv, No. 52 (1952), pp. 24-25.
        On Gide's translation.

B669   Brock-Sulzer, Elisabeth. "André Gide als Übersetzer Shakespeares." *SJ*, 92 (1956), 207-219.

(b) TRANSLATIONS

B670   *Œuvres Complètes* (English and French). Publ. Sous la Direction de Pierre Leyris et Henri Evans
        Dans une Trad. Nouv. Accompagnée d'Études, Préf., Notices, Notes et Glossaires. Paris:
        Formes et Reflects, 1954. *1. Henry VI.* Trad. de Georges Garampon, Henri Thomas et
        Armand Guilbert. *Richard III.* Trad. de Pierre Leyris. *La Comédie des Méprises.* Trad. de
        Francis Ledoux, 1954. Pp. xviii, xciv, 1402.
            Rev: Yves Florenne, *Le Monde*, Aug. 18, 1955; J. Loiseau, ibid., Aug. 28; Yves Florenne,
            ibid., Sept. 6; Robert Escarpit, ibid., Sept. 20; Pierre Leyris and J. Loiseau, ibid., Sept. 24:
            J. Loiseau, *EA*, ix (1956), 10-13.

B670a   *Œuvres Complètes.* Publ. sous la Direction de Pierre Leyris et Henri Evans dans une Traduction
        Nouvelle, Accompagnée d'Études, Préfaces, Notices, Notes et Glossaires. Quatre Tomes.
        Texte Anglais et Traduction Française en Regard. Paris: Formes et Reflects, 1957. Pp. 1488.
        La critique Shakespearienne par Marjorie Thompson. *Henry V*, préface et notice par R. G.
        Cox, traduction de Sylvère Monod. *Jules César*, préface par Ernest Schanzer, notice par
        F. N. Lees, traduction d'Yves Bonnefoy. *Comme Il Vous Plaira*, préface et notes par F. N. Lees,
        traduction d'Antoine Tavera. *La Nuit des Rois*, préface par Leo Salingar, notice par F. N. Lees
        traduction de Pierre Leyris. *Hamlet*, préface par Karl Jaspers, notice par R. G. Cox, traduction
        d'Yves Bonnefoy.

i. Individual Translators
aa. Carrère

B671   *Arden de Feversham.* Étude Critique. Trad. et Notes par Félix Carrère. [Coll. Bilingue Anglaise.
        Paris: Aubier, 1950. Pp. 253.
            Rev: by J. B. Fort, *LanM*, xlv (1951), 266-267.

B672   *La Nuit des Rois.* Introd. Trad. et Préf. par Félix Carrère et Camille Chemin. Coll. Bilingue.
        Paris: Éd. Montaigne, 1956.

bb. Castelain

B673   *La Mégère Apprivoisée.* Trad. de Maurice Castelain. Paris, 1934.
            Rev: by E. Buyssens, *Rev. Belge*, xiv, 1383-84.

B674   *Macbeth.* Tr. par Maurice Castelain. Coll. Bilingue des Classiques Étrangers. Paris: Aubier,
        1937. Pp. xlii, 162.
            Rev: by F. C. Danchin, *EA*, i (1937), 357; by Paul Dottin, *Eng. Studn.*, lxxii, 104-105.

B675   *Vénus et Adonis*, Suivi du *Pèlerin Passionné.* Collection Shakespeare. Tr. With an Introduction
        by Maurice Castelain. Paris: Belles-Lettres, 1939. Pp. xvi, 161.

B676   *Othello.* Traduit, avec une Introd., par Maurice Castelain. Coll. Bilingue des Classiques
        Étrangers. Paris: Aubier, 1942. Pp. 293.

B677   *Le Songe d'une Nuit d'Été.* Collection Bilingue des Classiques Étrangers. Paris: Aubier, 1943.
        Pp. 231.
B678   *Conte d'Hiver.* Trad. et Préf. de Maurice Castelain. Coll. Bilingue des Classiques Étrangers.
        Paris: Éd. Montaigne, 1947. Pp. 275.
B679   *Hamlet.* Trad. et Préf. de Maurice Castelain. Coll. Bilingue des Classiques Étrangers. Paris:
        Éd. Montaigne, 1947. Pp. 335.

cc.   Derocquigny

B680   *La Tragédie de Hamlet.* Trad. par Jules Derocquigny, ornée de 16 lithographies par Dela-
        croix. Le Livre et l'Estampe, No. 5. Paris: Horizons de France, 1942. Pp. 159.
B681   *La Tragédie de Macbeth.* Trad. de Jules Derocquigny. Paris: Les Belles-Lettres, 1951.
        Pp. 186.
B682   *La Tragédie de Coriolan.* Traduction de Jules Derocquigny. Paris: Les-Belles Lettres, 1957.
        Pp. xvi, 290.

dd.   Gide

B683   Gide, André. Tr. *Arden de Feversham.* *Le Théâtre Élizabéthain.* Paris: Les Cahiers du Sud,
        1940, pp. 137-151.
B684   *Hamlet.* Éd. Bilingue. Trad. Nouvelle d'André Gide. Éd. by Jacques Schiffrin. Paris:
        Gallimard; New York: Pantheon Books, 1945. Pp. 286.
        Rev: by Harry Levin, "Meditation on a Battlement." *NR*, 112 (1945), 559-560; by Fernand
        Baldensperger, *Books Abroad*, XIX, 272; by Paul d'Estournelles, *TAr*, XXIX, 665-666; by
        Joseph Wood Krutch, *Nation* (N.Y.), Apr. 21, 1945, p. 456; by William Milvitsky, *Sym-
        posium*, I (1947), 147-151.
B684a   *Hamlet.* Tr. by André Gide. Paris: Gallimard, 1946. Pp. 239.
        Rev: *TLS*, June 14, 1947, p. 297.
B685   "Selection From Gide's Translation." *Theatre Today*, April, 1947, p. 11.
B686   *Antoine et Cléopâtre.* Trad. par André Gide. Paris: Gallimard, 1948. Pp. 181.

ee.   F.-Victor Hugo

B687   *Œuvres.* Trad. de François-Victor Hugo. Entièrement revue et annotée par Christine et
        René Lalou. Bibliothèque Classique de Cluny. Paris: Éd. de Cluny, 1938.
        Le Conte d'Hiver—La Tempête. Reissued, 1942.
        *Macbeth—Othello. Jules César—Antoine et Cléopâtre. Le Songe d'une Nuit d'Été—Le Mar-
        chand de Venise. Hamlet—Roméo et Juliette.* Revised, 1949.
        Rev: by G. Connes, *LanM*, XLIV (1950), 266.
B688   *Peines d'Amour Perdues. Comme il Vous Plaira.* Trad. de François-Victor Hugo. Entièrement
        rev. et ann. par Christine et René Lalou. Bibliothéque de Cluny. No. 43. Paris: Éd. de
        Cluny, 1941. Pp. xvi, 239. Reissued, 1943.
B689   *Le Marchand de Venise.* Trad. de François-Victor Hugo. Paris: Simon, 1947. Pp. 287.
B690   *Othello.* Trad. de F.-Victor Hugo. Entièrement rev. par Christine et René Lalou. Mise en
        scène . . . de Constantin Stanislavski. Trad. du russe par Nina Gourfinkel. Coll. Mises en
        scènes. Paris: Éd. du Seuil, 1948. Pp. 352.
B691   *Le Songe d'une Nuit d'Été.* Trad. de François-Victor Hugo. Ill. de 12 aquarelles en couleurs
        d'Edouard Chimot. Paris: Guillot, 1949. Pp. 119.
B692   *Le Marchand de Venise. Tout est Bien qui Finit Bien. Beaucoup de Bruit pour Rien. Œuvres
        Complètes.* Trad. par François-Victor Hugo.
        Petite Bibliothèque Littéraire. Paris: Lemerre, 1950. Vol. VII. Pp. 456.
B693   *Hamlet. Mesure pour Mesure. Œuvres Complètes.* Trad. par François-Victor Hugo. Petite
        Bibliothèque Littéraire. Paris: Lemerre, 1951. Vol. X. Pp. 365.
B694   *Œuvres Complètes.* Trad. de François-Victor Hugo. Ill. de Maurice Leroy. Vol. XV. Paris:
        Éd. Arc-en-ciel, 1950-51.
B695   *La Sauvage Apprivoisée.* Trad. de François-Victor Hugo. Lithos Orig. de Paul Aïzpiri. Paris:
        Les Francs-Bibliophiles, 1957. Pp. 149.

ff.   Jouve

B696   *La Tragédie de Roméo et Juliette.* Traduite par Pierre Jean Jouve et G. Pitoëff. Paris: Éditions
        de la *NRF*, 1938.
        Rev: by Pierre Leyris, *NRF*, L (1938), 144.
B697   *Tombeau d'Amour, Deux sonnets de Shakespeare.* [Sonn. 20 and 31.] Tr. par Pierre Jean Jouve.
        Paris: *GLM*, [1938].
        Rev: by Pierre Leyris, *NRF*, L (1938), 144.
B698   "Scènes de *Macbeth*." Tr. by Pierre Jean Jouve. *MdF*, June, 1956, pp. 228-262.
B699   Jouve, Pierre Jean. "Sonnets de Shakespeare." *MdF*, 324 (1955), 5-16.

B700   *Sonnets.* Version Française par Pierre Jean Jouve. Paris: Sagittaire, 1955. Pp. 188.
       Rev: by J. Vallette, *MdF*, 324 (1955), 724; by A. Koszul, *EA*, IX (1956), 1-9.

B701   *Sonnets.* Version Française par Pierre Jean Jouve. Paris: Club Français du Livre, 1956. Pp.
       xviii, 318.

B702   Jouve, Pierre Jean. "Sur Les Sonnets de W. S." *La Revue de Paris*, LXII (1955), 112-119.
       Commented on by M. P. in *La Revue de Paris*, LXII (Oct.), 173.

gg.   Koszul (See also Sauvage below.)

B703   *Un Songe d'une Nuit d'Été.* Tr. by A. Koszul. Antwerp; Paris: Belles-Lettres, 1938. Pp.
       xxiv, 175.
       Rev: by F. C. Danchin, *EA*, III (1939), 191-192.

B704   *La Comédie des Erreurs.* Translated into French by André Koszul. Paris: Collection Shake-
       speare, Les Belles-Lettres, 1949. Pp. xxxiii, 164.
       Rev: by Irène Simon, *ES*, XXXII (1951), 48.

B705   *La Tragédie de Roméo et Juliette.* Trad. de A. Koszul. Coll. Shakespeare. Soc. des Belles-
       Lettres, 1950. Pp. xxiii, 241.

hh.   Matthey

B706   *La Tempête.* Texte Français de Pierre-Louis Matthey. Éd. du Cheval Ailé. Genève: C.
       Bourquin, 1944. Pp. iv, 177.

B707   *Roméo et Juliette.* Texte de Pierre-Louis Matthey. Coll. du Bouquet, 32. Lausanne: Mermod,
       1947. Pp. iv, 271.

ii.   Mayoux

B708   *Comme Il Vous Plaira.* Trad., Introd., Notes et Bibliographie par Jean-Jacques Mayoux. Coll.
       Bilingue. Paris: Éd. Montaigne, 1956. Pp. 264.
       Rev: by J. Vallette, *MdF*, 328 (1956), 320-321.

B709   *La Tempête.* Traduction et Préface de J. J. Mayoux. Collection Bilingue des Classiques
       Étrangers. Paris: Aubier, 1943. Pp. 200.

jj.   Messiaen

B710   *Les Comédies.* Traduction Nouvelle par Pierre Messiaen. Paris, Bruges: Désclée de Brouwer,
       1939. Pp. xi, 1478.
       Rev: *TLS*, Oct. 21, 1939, p. 614; by Ch. Bastide, *Rev. Universitaire*, L (1941), 359-361; by
       Winifred Smith, *Books Abroad*, XIV, 407-408; by Louis Mandin, *MdF*, March 1, 1940, pp.
       713-719.

B711   *Tragédies.* Nouvelle Traduction Française avec Remarques et Notes par Pierre Messiaen.
       Paris, Bruges: Désclée de Brouwer, 1941. Pp. 1556.
       Rev: by Mario Meunier, *Journal des Débats*, Apr. 18, 1942, p. 19.

B712   *William Shakespeare.* I: *Les Comédies.* Pp. 1479. II: *Les Tragédies.* Pp. 1557. III: *Les
       Drames Historiques et les Poèmes Lyriques.* Pp. 1533. Nouvelle Trad. Française avec Remarques
       et Notes par Pierre Messiaen. Bruges, Paris: Désclée de Brouwer, 1949.
       Rev: by H. Carrington Lancaster, *SQ*, III (1952), 59-60.

kk.   Piachaud

B713   *Le Songe d'une Nuit d'Été.* Traduction Libre et Rythmée de René-Louis Piachaud. Lausanne:
       A. Gonin, 1944. Pp. 149.

B714   *Le Songe d'une Nuit d'Été.* Tr. and adapted by René-Louis Piachaud. Beaux textes, textes
       rares, textes inédits, 9. Vésenaz-Genève: Cailler, 1947. Reissued 1949.

B715   *Le Marchand de Venise.* Comédie Trad. et Adapt. par René-Louis Piachaud. Vésenaz-Genève:
       Cailler, 1946. Pp. 131.

B716   *La Tragédie d'Othello, le More de Venise.* Trad. et Adapt. par René-Louis Piachaud. Beaux
       textes, textes rares, textes inédits, 6. Vésenaz-Genève: Cailler, 1946. Pp. 157. Reissued
       1949.

B717   *La Tragédie de Coriolan.* Trad. Librement et Adaptée à la Scène Française par René-Louis
       Piachaud. Beaux textes, textes rares, textes inédits, 11. Vésenaz-Genève: Cailler, 1947. Pp.
       147. Reissued 1949.

B718   *La Farce des Joyeuses Commères.* Tr. by René-Louis Piachaud. Beaux textes, textes rares, textes
       inédits, No. 21. Geneva: Pierre Cailler, 1949. Pp. 134.

B719   *Le Roi Lear.* Tr. and adapted by René-Louis Piachaud, with a study of Piachaud as dramatic
       critic by Hilaire Theurillat. Beaux textes, textes rares, textes inédits, No. 23. Geneva: Pierre
       Cailler, 1949. Pp. 144.

ll.   Sauvage

B720   *Les Joyeuses Commères de Windsor.* Tr. de Félix Sauvage. Paris: Les Belles-Lettres, 1935.
       Pp. xxxiii, 230.

Rev: by Maurice Castelain, *EA*, I (1937), 173-174.

B721   *Le Roi Henri IV, Première Partie.* Texte, traduction, introduction et notes par F. Sauvage et A. Koszul. Coll. Shakespeare. Paris: Belles-Letters, 1955. Pp. xx, 218.
Rev: by J. B. Fort, *EA*, IX (1956), 48-49; by J. Vallette, *LanM*, L (1956), 555; by H. Heuer, *SJ*, 92 (1956), 362-363.

mm. Others.

B722   *Le Théâtre Complet de Shakespeare.* Avantpropos par André Gide. Traductions de J. Copeau et S. Bing. Ed. Fleg, A. Gide, F.-V. Hugo, P. J. Jouve et G. Pitoëff, P. Leyris et E. Holland, Maeterlinck, E. Morand et M. Schwob, G. De Pourtalès, J. Superveille. 2 Vols. Bibliothèque de la Pléiade. Paris: Nouvelle Revue Fr., 1938. Pp. 2700.
Rev: by J. Prévost in *NRF*, LIII (1939), 492-493.

B723   *Trois Comédies. Comme il Vous Plaira. Un Conte d'Hiver. La Nuit des Rois.* Trad. et adaptation de Jean Anouilh et Claude Vincent. Paris: La Table Ronde, 1952. Pp. ii, 357.

B724   *La Mégère Apprivoisée.* Adaptée par J. Audiberti, dans une adaptation théâtrale. Paris: Gallimard, 1957.

B725   *Les Sonnets de Shakespeare Traduits en Vers Français et Accompagnés d'un Commentaire Continu.* Par Fernand Baldensperger. Berkeley: Univ. California Press, 1943. Pp. xx, 370.
Rev: by S. A. T., *SAB*, XVIII (1943), 144; by Rosamund Thomson, *Books Abroad*, XVIII (1944), 251-252; by Dudley Fitts, "Shakespeare Rearranged," *SR*, LIII (1945), 153-158.

B726   *La Tragédie de Jules César.* Texte Français de Georges Beaume. *Paris Théâtre*, No. 112 (1956), pp. 20-57.
Includes photographs of the production at the Baalbeck Festival.

B726a *Douze Sonnets.* Texte Anglais. Trad. et présentation par Maurice Blanchard. Paris: G. L. M., 1947. Pp. 34.

B727   *Jules César.* Trad. par Gabriel Boissy. Paris: Grasset, 1937. Pp. 160.
Rev: by F. C. Danchin, *EA*, II (1938), 195-196.

B728   "Scènes de *Jules César* de Shakespeare." Tr. by Yves Bonnefoy, *MdF*, 329 (1957), 193-208. Scenes in French from the version of *Caesar* to appear in *Œuvres Complètes de Shakespeare* of the Club Français du Livre.

B729   *Arden de Faversham, Drame en 5 Actes.* Trad. de l'Anglais par Laurette Brunius et Loleh Bellon. Répertoire pour un théâtre populaire, 9. Paris: l'Arche, 1957. Pp. 77.

B730   *Tout Est Bien Qui Fini Bien.* Trad. de C. Cambillard. Coll. Shakespeare. Paris: Belles-Lettres, 1952. Pp. xxv, 232.
Rev: by J. B. Fort, *EA*, VII (1954), 326-327; by Irène Simon, *ES*, XXXIV (1953), 40-41; by G. Lambin, *LanM*, XLVII (1953), 74.

B731   *Les Comédies.* Trad. par Suzanne Bing et Jacques Copeau. Ill. de Berthold Mahn Vol. 1-7. Paris: Union Latine d'Éditions, 1952.
Rev: by M. Rat, *Éducation Nationale*, X, No. 11 (1954), 12-13.

B732   *Le Marchand de Venise.* Traduit, avec une introduction par F. C. Danchin. Collection Bilingue des Classiques Anglais. Paris: Aubier, 1938. Pp. liii, 187, xxiii.
Rev: by C. Bastide, *EA*, III (1939), 409-410.

B733   *Richard III.* Tr. by J. Delcourt. Coll. Shakespeare. Paris: Belles-Lettres, 1957. Pp. 274.

B734   *Hamlet: A Tragedy Adapted from Shakespeare (1770) by Jean François Ducis.* Ed. by Mary B. Vanderhoof. *Proceedings of the American Philosophical Society*, 97, No. 1 (1953), 88-142.
Rev: A9343.

B735   *XXV Sonnets.* Traduction Nouvelle par Monsieur Mélot Du Dy. Brussels: Éditions du Cercle d'Art, 1943. Pp. 60.

B736   *Roméo et Juliette.* Adaptation nouv. en vers par Edgard Gamard. Paris: Éd. de l'Odéon, 1952.

B737   *Macbeth.* Trad. Nouv. par Madeleine Gérard-Bultot et Albert Gérard. Coll. nouv. des classiques, 104. Brussels: Éd. Labor, 1949. Pp. 64.

B738   *Measure for Measure.* Edition avec introduction, traduction et notes par Michel Grivelet. Thèse complémentaire, Paris, 1956. Typewritten. Published Éditions Montaigne, Collection Bilingue. Paris: Aubier, 1957. Pp. 288.

B739   *Roméo et Juliette. Hamlet.* Traduction et présentation de Christine et René Lalou. Bibliothèque Cluny. Paris: A Colin, 1958. Pp. xvi, 286.
Rev: by M. Antier, *LanM*, LII (1958), 403.

B740   *Antoine et Cléopâtre.* Trad. de J. Lambin. Collection Shakespeare. Paris: Belles-Lettres, 1957. Pp. 312.

B741   *Henri V.* Préf. et trad. de M. J. Lavelle. Coll. Bilingue des Classiques Étrangers. Paris: Aubier, 1947. Pp. 294.

B742   *Le Conte d'Hiver.* Tr. d'Émile Legouis. Coll. Shakespeare. Paris: Les Belles-Lettres, 1936. Pp. xxvi, 249.
Rev: *TLS*, Aug. 8, 1936, p. 648; by Floris Delattre, *EA*, I (1937), 174-176.

B743   Cancelled.

B744   *Pièces Féeriques.* Trad., notice et notes de Sylvère Monod. Préf. de Jean Sarment. Les Grands
        Maîtres. Paris: Bordas, 1949. Pp. xvi, 831.

B745   *La Tragique Histoire d'Hamlet.* Trad. par Eugène Morand et Marcel Schwob. Ill. en couleurs
        par Phillippe Jullian, gravées sur bois par Théo Schmied. Paris: Blaizot, 1952. Pp. 145.

B746   *Le Marchand de Venise d'après William Shakespeare.* Raconté par Jean Muray. Ill. de Jean
        Reschofsky. Idéal Bibliothèque, 124. Paris: Hachette, 1957. Pp. 186.

B747   *Le Songe d'une Nuit d'Été.* Texte français de G. Neveux. Paris: Gallimard, 1945.

B747a   *Othello.* Texte français de Georges Neveux. Suppl. Théâtral et Littéraire, 55. France Illustra-
        tion, 1950. Pp. 32.

B748   *Richard III.* Pièce en 4 Actes. Tr. by André Obey. Théâtre de l'Atelier. Paris: Ramlot,
        1933. Pp. 159.

B749   *Hamlet.* Trad. et préface de Marcel Pagnol. Paris: Nagel, 1947. Pp. 302.

B750   *Connaissance de Shakespeare. Cahiers de la Compagnie Madeleine Renaud-J. L. Barrault,* No. 16.
        Paris: Julliard, 1956. Pp. 128.
        Présentation et traduction par J. Paris.

B751   Phelps, John. "French Translation of a Passage in *Love's Labour's Lost.*" *SAB,* XXII (1947), 94.

B752   Pollet, Maurice. *La Tragédie de "Roméo et Juliette" de William Shakespeare.* Édition critique
        avec traduction [sans le texte anglais] par Maurice Pollet. DD, Paris, 1955. Typewritten.

B753   *Hamlet,* III, iii. Trad. par C. Pons. *CS,* LXVIII (1947), 435-455.

B754   *Les Sonnets de Shakespeare.* Essai d'interprétation poétique française et introduction par André
        Prudhommeau. Porrentruy: Aux Portes de France, 1945. Pp. iv, 113.

B755   *Un Conte d'Hiver.* Adaptation de Claude André Puget. Suppl. Théâtral et Littéraire, 78.
        France Illustration, 1951. Pp. 32.

B756   *Jules César.* Adaptation de Jean-Francis Reille. Paris: L'Arche, 1957. Pp. 79.

B757   Rose, M. Félix. *Les Grands Lyriques Anglais.* Paris: Didier, 1940. Pp. 441.
        Rev: *ConR,* Oct. 1940, p. 480; by A. Will, *Life and Letters Today,* XXVI, 77-78.

B758   *Théâtre Choisi.* Traduction et notices par G. Roth. 5 vols. Paris: Larousse, 1938.

B759   Rousselot, Jean. "Shakespeare Poète ou le Théâtre Intérieur." *Cahiers de la Compagnie
        Madeleine Renaud-Jean Louis Barrault,* Paris, No. 17, 1957, pp. 115-124.
        Sone sonnets translated.

B760   *Sonnets.* Tr. by G. d'Uccle. Paris: Charlot, 1945.

B761   *Mesure pour Mesure.* Adaptation par B. Vigny. Marseille: R. Laffont, 1945.

B762   *Comme Il Vous Plaira.* Trad. et introd. de Lucien Wolf. Texte et traduction. Collection
        Shakespeare. Paris: Les Belles-Lettres, 1935. Pp. xx, 197.

                                nn. Translator not indicated in source.

B763   *Antoine et Cléopâtre.* Paris: Aubier, 1942.

B764   *Le Roi Lear.* Paris: Aubier, 1942.

B765   *Le Songe d'une Nuit d'Été.* Paris: Aubier, 1943.

B766   *Jules César.* Paris: Aubier, 1945. Pp. 256.

B767   *Timon d'Athènes.* Paris: Belles-Lettres, 1944.

B768   *Le Viol de Lucrèce.* Paris: Belles-Lettres, 1944.

B769   *La Tragique Histoire d'Hamlet.* Illustrated in water colors by Philippe Jullian, improved on
        wood in color by Théo Schmied, printed in two colors. Limited ed., 190 copies. Paris:
        Librairie Auguste Blaizot, 1952.

B770   *Tragédies.* Préf. d'André Maurois. Notes de Jacques Gouelou. Les Grands Maîtres. Paris:
        Bordas, 1950. Pp. 368.

B771   *Le Roi Lear.* Paris: Le Fleuve étincelant, 1947. Pp. 212.

B772   *Les CLIV Sonnets.* Paris: Librairie Le François, 1945. Pp. 176.

B773   *Hamlet.* Trad. Française. Brussels: Éd. du Frêne, 1949. Pp. 143.

B774   *Le Songe d'une Nuit d'Été.* Ill. de 12 gouaches en couleur de Brunelleschi. Paris: Guillot, 1947.

B775   *La Tempête.* Avec introd. et notes par G. Guibillon. Les Classiques pour Tous, 391. Paris:
        Hatier, 1948. Pp. 64.

B776   *L'Œuvre de Shakespeare.* 1 Vol. Paris: Ley, 1950. Pp. 1344.

B777   *Romeo and Juliet.* Tr. into French. Paris: Éditions de la Bibliothèque Mondiale, 1953. Pp. 136.
        With texts of Jean Davy, "Shakespeare Vu par un Acteur du XX Siècle"; A. Obey, "Jeunesse
        de Shakespeare"; J. J. Mayoux, "Le Thème de l'Amour chez William Shakespeare."

B778   *Roméo et Juliette. Le Songe d'une Nuit d'Été.* Geneva: Éd. Au Grand Passage, 1944. Pp. iv, 171.

B779   *La Sauvage Apprivoisée (Shrew).* Lithographies originales de Paul Aïzpiri. Les Francs-Biblio-
        philes, 1957. Pp. 149.

                              (2) SPANISH (163;54)

(a) TRANSLATIONS

B780 Esquerra, Ramón. *Shakespeare a Catalunya*. Barcelona: 1937.
      Rev: by H. Thomas, *MLR*, xxxiv (1939), 459-460.

B781 Ley, Charles David. *Shakespeare para los Españoles*. Madrid: Revista de Occidente, 1951.
      Rev: A9406.

B782 Madariaga, Salvador de. "On Translating *Hamlet*." *ShS*, vi (1953), 106-111.

(b) INDIVIDUAL TRANSLATORS
i. Astrana Marín

B783 *Obras Completas*. Estudio preliminar, traducción y notas por Luis Astrana Marín. Primera
      versión íntegra del inglés. Unica edición completa en lengua castellana. Madrid: Edit.
      M. Aguilar, 1943. Pp. cliii, 1742. Reissued 1949, 1951.

B784 Cancelled.

B785 *Obras Completas de William Shakespeare. I Macbeth, Trabajos de Amor Perdidos, Mucho Ruido
      Para Nada*, ed. by Luis Astrana Marín. Edición Bilingüe Ilustrada. Madrid: Ediciones de
      la Universidad de Puerto Rico, 1955.

B786 *La Tragedia de Ricardo III*. Colección Universal, No. 467-468. Traducción por Luis Astrana
      Marín. Madrid: Espasa-Calpe, 1941. Pp. 196.

B787 *Tito Andrónico*. Trad. por Luis Astrana Marín. Madrid: Espasa-Calpe, 1943. Pp. 175.

B788 *La Doma de la Bravía*. Colección Universal, No. 1074-1075. Trad. por Luis Astrana Marín.
      Madrid: Espasa-Calpe, 1941.

B789 *Trabajos de Amor Perdidos*. Col. Más Allá, 19. Trad. por Luis Astrana Marín. Madrid:
      Afrodisio Aguado, 1950. Pp. 184.

B790 *La Tragedia de Romeo y Julieta*. Colección Universal, 378-380. Traducción por Luis Astrana
      Marín. Madrid: Espasa-Calpe, 1941. Pp. 233.

B791 *El Mercader de Venecia*. Collección Universal, 432-433. Traducción por Luis Astrana Marín.
      Madrid: Espasa-Calpe, 1940. Pp. 178.

B792 *La Vida del Rey Enrique V*. Trad. de Luis Astrana Marín. Madrid: Espasa-Calpe, 1943.
      Pp. 211.

B793 *Hamlet, Príncipe de Dinamarca. La Tragedia de Macbeth*. Traducción, introducción y notas
      de Luis Astrana Marín. Col. Crisol, 61. Madrid: Edit. M. Aguilar, 1944. Pp. 481.

B794 *Hamlet, Príncipe de Dinamarca*. Nueva trad. especial para la ed. presente por Luis Astrana
      Marín. Col. Clásicos y maestros. Madrid: Afrodisio Aguado, 1957. Pp. 276.

B795 *A Buen Fin no Hay Mal Principio*. Trad. por Luis Astrana Marín. Colección Universal, 1009-
      1010. Madrid: Espasa-Calpe, 1940. Pp. 200.

B796 *Otelo. La Tragedia de Romeo y Julieta*. Trad. de L. Astrana Marín. Buenos Aires: Espasa-
      Calpe, 1939. Pp. 248.

B797 *Sonetos*. Prólogo, traducción y notas de Luis Astrana Marín. Madrid: Afrodisio Aguado,
      1944. Pp. xxxix, 372.

ii. Ballester Escalas

B798 *Julio César*. Pról., texto y trad. por Rafael Ballester Escalas. Barcelona: Flors, 1950. Pp. 123.

B799 *Coriolano*. Pról., texto y trad. por Rafael Ballester Escalas. Barcelona: Flors, 1950. Pp. 134.

iii. Clark

B800 *Tragedias. Romeo y Julieta. Hamlet. Otelo. Rey Lear*. Clásicos Jackson, 10. Estudio pre-
      liminar por Antonio Pagés Larraya. Trad. de Jaime Clark y Jacinto Benavente. Barcelona:
      Exito, 1951. Pp. lviii, 452.

B801 *Comedias. El Mercader de Venecia. Como Gustéis. Noche de Reyes. La Tempestad*. Clásicos
      Jackson, 9. Estudio preliminar por Ezequiel Martínez Estrada. Trad. de Jaime Clark, rev.
      Barcelona: Exito, 1951. Pp. xlvi, 368.

iv. González Ruiz

B802 *Romeo y Julieta, y la Tragedia de Macbeth*. En la versión escénica de Nicolás González Ruiz.
      Col. Mediterráneo, Clásicos Universales. Madrid: Edit. Mediterráneo, 1944. Pp. 255.

B803 *Romeo y Julieta*. Versión escénica de Nicolás González Ruiz. Col. Capitel, II. Madrid: Edit.
      Alhambra, 1945. Pp. 121.

v. Méndez Herrera

B804 *Cuento de Invierno. La Tempestad*. Col. Crisol, 396. Trad., pról. y notas de José Méndez
      Herrera. Madrid: Aguilar, 1957. Pp. 439.

B805 *Hamlet, Príncipe de Dinamarca. Macbeth*. Trad., prólogo y notas por José Méndez Herrera
      Col. Crisol, No. 61. 4th ed. Madrid: Aguilar, 1956. Pp. 499.

vi. Pemán

B806   *Hamlet.* Versión libre, en verso, de José María Pemán. Madrid: Escelicer, 1949. Pp. 152.

B807   *Julio César.* Col. Teatro, 125. Versión libre, en verso, de José María Pemán. Madrid: Alfil, 1955. Pp. 164.

vii. Vedia y Mitre

B808   "Sonetos de Shakespeare." Tr. by M. Vedia y Mitre. *Nosotros,* II, No. 12 (1937), 248-256; also separately, Buenos Aires: Kraft, 1955.

B809   *Venus y Adonis: Traducción poética directa del inglés, precedida de una introducción y seguida de notas críticas y autocríticas por el académico.* Tr. by Marino de Vedia y Mitre. Buenos Aires: Academia Argentina de Letras, 1946.
        Rev: *TLS,* Sept. 27, 1947, p. 495.

viii. Others

B810   *Julio César.* Versión de Ramón Alva. Enciclopedia Pulga, 110. Barcelona: Pulga, 1954. Pp. 224.

B811   *Historias.* Según adaptación de Julia F. Castañón. Madrid: Bureba, 1952. Pp. 120.

B812   *Troilo y Crésida.* Trad. de Luis Cernuda. Madrid: Insula, 1953. Pp. 218.

B813   *El Hámlet de Shakespeare: Edición Bilingüe.* Tr. with Introd. Essay by Salvador de Madariaga. Buenos Aires: Edit. Sudamericana, 1950. Pp. 620.
        Rev: *TLS,* June 23, 1950, p. 386; by José Izquierdo, *Revista nacional de cultura* (Caracas), XIII (1950), 90-93.

B814   *El Rey Lear.* Adapt. de Fernando Palacios Vera. Enciclopedia Pulga., No. 350. Barcelona: Pulga, 1957. Pp. 224.

B815   *El Sueño de una Noche de Verano.* Narrado por Ángel Puigmiquel. Ilustraciones de Emilio Freixas. Barcelona: Edit. Enrique Meseguer, 1943. Pp. 97.

B816   *Hamlet, Príncipe de Dinamarca.* Versión castellana de F. Rodríguez Moya. Medellín: Ed. Granamétrica, 1955. Pp. 214.

B817   *Coriolá. Juli César. Antoni i Cleopatra.* Trad. de Josep María de Sagarra. Barcelona: Alpha 1958. Pp. 352.

B818   *Sonnet 71.* Tr. by Eduardo San Martín, *SQ,* IV (1953), 486.

B819   *Vida y Muerte de Ricardo III.* Versión de Bernardo Vásquez. Enciclopedia Pulga, 310. Barcelona: Pulga, 1956. Pp. 224.

ix. Translator not indicated in source

B820   *Romeo y Julieta.* Col. Desirée. Madrid: Gráf. Canales, 1956. Pp. 80.

B821   *Julio César.* Novelas y cuentos. Una obra dramática completa. Madrid: Ed. Dédalo, 1942.

B822   *Otelo, el Moro de Venecia.* Novelas y cuentos. Madrid: Diana, 1953. Pp. 61.

B823   *Las Alegres Comadres de Windsor.* Novelas y cuentos. Madrid: Diana, 1954. Pp. 38.

B824   *La Tempestad y La Doma de la Bravía.* Colección Austral, 116. Buenos Aires: Espasa-Calpe Argentina, 1940. Pp. 220.

B825   *Hamlet, Principe de Dinamarca.* Col. Austral, 27. Il. ed. Madrid: Espasa-Calpe, 1956. Pp. 146.

B826   *Las Comedias de Shakespeare.* Contiene *Los Dos Hidalgos de Verona, La Comedia de las Equivocaciones, Penas Por Amor Perdidas, La Doma de la Tarasca.* Madrid: Ediciones Ibéricas, 1958.

(3) PORTUGESE (163;54)
(a) TRANSLATION PROBLEMS AND TRANSLATORS

B827   Gomes, Eugênio. "Uma Tradução de *Henrique IV.*" *Correio da Manhã,* Rio de Janeiro, Feb. 4, 1951.
        Critical article on a translation of *Henry IV* by Carlos Alberto Nunes.

B828   Gomes, Eugênio. "Sonetos de Shakespeare." *Correio da Manhã,* Rio de Janeiro, March 10, 1953.
        Critical article on trans. of the sonnets into Portuguese by Eugênio Péricles da Silva Ramos.

B829   Gomes, Eugênio. "Um Pássaro de Shakespeare." (A Bird in Shakespeare). *Correio da Manhã,* Rio de Janeiro, April 29, 1951.
        Commentary on Artur de Sales's translation of the word *martlet* (*Macbeth*).

B830   Gomes, Eugênio. "Traduções de *Hamlet.*" *Correio da Manhã,* Rio de Janeiro, July 23, 1950; and in *Prata de Casa,* Rio de Janeiro, ed. Noite, 1952, p. 157.
        Commentaries on some translations of *Hamlet* into Portuguese.

B831   Carpeaux, Otto Maria. "Shakespeare e Nos Outros" (Shakespeare and We). *Diario Carioca,* Rio de Janeiro, Oct. 10, 1954.
        Critical article on Onestaldo Pennafort's translation of *Romeo and Juliet.*

(b) INDIVIDUAL TRANSLATORS
i. Braga

B832   *O Rei Henrique VI*. Trad. por Henrique Braga. Vol. 1-3. Porto: Lello & Irmão, 1955.

B833   *O Rei Ricardo III*. Trad. por Henrique Braga. Porto: Lello & Irmão, 1955. Pp. 240.

B834   *A Comédia dos Equívocas*. Traduzida directamente do original inglês por Henrique Braga.
        Porto: Lello & Irmão, 1955. Pp. 182.

B835   *Tito Andronico*. Trad. por Henrique Braga. Porto: Lello & Irmão, 1955. Pp. 159.

B836   *Amansia de uma Fúria*. Tradução directa da edição de Collins por Henrique Braga. Porto:
        Lello & Irmão, 1955. Pp. 224.

B837   *O Rei João*. Traduzida directamente de edição da Collins por Henrique Braga. Porto: Lello &
        Irmão, 1955. Pp. 196.

B838   *O Rei Henrique V*. Tradução directa do inglês por Henrique Braga. Porto: Lello & Irmão,
        1955. Pp. 210, 1.

B839   *Como lhe Aprouver* [*A.Y.L.*] Trad. por Henrique Braga. Porto: Lello & Irmão, 1955. Pp. 190.

B840   *Tróilo e Créssida*. Trad. por Henrique Braga. Porto: Lello & Irmão, 1955. Pp. 244.

B841   *Medida por Medida*. Trad. por Henrique Braga. Porto: Lello & Irmão, 1955. Pp. 201.

B842   *Cymbeline*. Traduzido da edição Collins por Henrique Braga. Porto: Lello & Irmão, 1955.
        Pp. 239.

B843   *Conto de Inverno* [*W.T.*] Trad. por Henrique Braga. Porto: Lello & Irmão, 1955. Pp. 196.

B844   *O Rei Henrique VIII*. Tradução da edição Cassell por Henrique Braga. Porto: Lello & Irmão,
        1955. Pp. 185, 1.

ii. Bragança

B845   *Ricardo III*. Tr. by Luis de Bragança. Porto: Lello & Irmão, 1956.

B846   *O Mercador de Veneza*. Tr. by Luis de Bragança. Porto: Lello & Irmão, 1956.

B847   *Hamlet*. Tr. by Luis de Bragança. Porto: Lello & Irmão, 1956.

B848   *Otello, o Mouro de Veneza*. Tr. by Luis de Bragança. Porto: Lello & Irmão, 1956.

iii. Pennafort

B849   *Otelo, o Mouro de Veneza*. Trad. de Onestaldo Pennafort. Obras imortals, 5. Rio de Janeiro:
        Civilização Brasileira, 1956. Pp. 191.

B850   *Romeu e Julieta*. Tradução integral, em prosa e verso, por Onestaldo de Pennafort. Rio de
        Janiero: Edição do Ministerio da Educação e Saude, 1940. Pp. 277.
        Rev: by Samuel Putnam, *Books Abroad*, xv (1941), 233.

iv. Silva Ramos

B851   *Macbeth*. Tr. by Eugênio Péricles da Silva Ramos. Rio de Janeiro: José Olympo, 1955.
        Pp. 280.

B852   *A Tragédia de Hamlet, Príncipe da Dinamarca*. Tr. by Eugênio Péricles da Silva Ramos. Rio de
        Janeiro: José Olympo, 1956. Pp. 181.

B853   *Sonetos*. Trad. por Eugênio da Silva Ramos. S. Paolo: Saraiva, 1953. Pp. 165.

v. Others

B854   *Romeu e Julieta*. Trad. por Maria José Martins. Lisbon: Publ. Europa-América, 1955. Pp. 191.

B855   *Obras Completas de Shakespeare*. Tr. by Carlos Alberto Nunes. 15 Vols. São Paulo: Edicões
        Melhoramentos, 1954.
        Rev: by Fred P. Ellison, *SQ*, VIII (1957), 388-391.

B856   *Macbeth*. Tr. by António Pedro. Porto: Círculo de Cultura Teatral, 1956.

B857   *A Comédia dos Equívocos*. Ed. by Henrique Pongetti and Willy Keller. Rio de Janeiro:
        Departmento de Imprensa Nacional, 1955.

(4) ITALIAN (-;55)
(a) TRANSLATION PROBLEMS AND TRANSLATORS

B858   Crinò, Anna Maria. "Le Traduzioni Shakespeariane di Giustina Renier Michiel." *Gior.
        Storico*, 108 (1937), 242-249.

B858a   Michelagnoli, Alfredo. *Dizionario Shakespeariano Inglese-Italiano*. Venice: Ferrari, 1947.
        Pp. 139.

B859   Rebora, Piero. "Shakespeare Tradotto in Italiano." *Leonardo*, XVI (1947), 334-337.

B860   De Robertis, Domenico. "Ungaretti Traduttore di Shakespeare." *Leonardo*, XVI (June-Aug.,
        1947), 194-202.

B861   Galletti, Alfredo. "Shakespeare e i Suoi Nuovi Traduttori." *NA*, 83 (1948), 376-389.

B862   Crinò, Anna Maria. "In Margine alle Traduzioni Shakespeariane." *GSLI*, 126 (1949), 330-331.

B863   Baldini, Gabriele. "Come Vien Tradotto Shakespeare." *Belfagor* (Florence), v, No. 1 (Jan. 31, 1950), 102-108.
       A review of Salvatore Quasimodo's translation of *Romeo* (Milan, Verona, 1949).

B864   Crinò, Anna Maria. *Le Traduzioni di Shakespeare in Italia nel settecento.* Letture di Pensiero e d'Arte, No. 9. Rome: Ed. di Storia e Lett., 1950. Pp. 117.
       Rev: by Elio Gianturco, *MLN*, LXVI (1951), 212-213, *SQ*, II, 84-85, and *Symposium*, v, 368-372; by F. Schalk, *Anglia*, LXX, 218-219; by Augusto Guidi, *La Fiera Letteraria*, Feb. 11, p. 5, and *Notiziario della Scuola*, Oct. 15-30, pp. 10-13; by Terence Spencer, *MLR*, XLVII (1952), 101; by Ch. Dédéyan, *RLC*, XXVII, 103-104.

B865   Vigoni, Carlo. "Quasimodo Prepara Amleto." *La Fiera Letteraria* (Rome), VII (June 15, 1952), 1-2.

B866   Gamberini, S. "Del Tradurre Shakespeare." *Rivista di Studi Teatrali*, VI (Apr.-June, 1953), 160-166.

B867   Praz, Mario. "Shakespeare Translations in Italy." *SJ*, 92 (1956), 220-231.
       A critical survey of Italian translators up to the present day.

B868   Guidi, Augusto. "Una Traduzione Italiana dei Sonetti di Shakespeare." *Lettere Italiane*, X, No. 3 (July-Sept., 1958), 363-366.
       On a translation of *Sonn.* into Italian by Luigi De Marchi.

(b) TRANSLATIONS
i. Several Hands

B869   *Teatro.* Tr. by Fedele Bajocchi, Aldo Camerino, Emilio Cecchi, Cino Chiarini, Guido Ferrando, G. S. Gargano, Eugenio Montale, Mario Praz, Salvatore Rosati, Aurelio Zanco. Sotto la direzione di Mario Praz. 3 vols. Florence: Sansoni, 1943-47. Vol. I, pp. xvi, 1112. Vol. II, pp. 1294. Vol. III, pp. 1167.
       Rev: of Vol. III, by A. Castelli, *Humanitas*, IV (1948), 219.

B870   *Shakespeare Degli Italiani: I Testi Scespiriani Inspirati da Fatti e Figure Della Nostra Storia e della Nostra Leggenda.* I Capolavori, No. 5. Turin: Società Editrice Torinese, 1950. Pp. lxxvii, 686.
       Includes: *I Due Gentiluomini di Verona*, versione italiana di G. Caimi, pp. 3-51. *Romeo e Giulietta*, versione italiana di L. Milani, pp. 55-114. *Il Mercante di Venezia*, versione italiana di M. A. Andreoni, pp. 117-179. *La Bisbetica Domata*, versione italiana di S. Policardi, pp. 183-240. *Molto Rumore per Nulla*, versione italiana di C. A. Menetoo, pp. 243-299. *Giulio Cesare*, versione italiana di N. Neri, pp. 303-352. *Otello, il Moro di Venezia*, versione italiana di L. Gigli, pp. 355-423. *Antonio e Cleopatra*, versione italiana di E. A. Gambino, pp. 427-556. *Coriolano*, versione italiana di L. Aimerito, pp. 559-631. *La Tempesta*, versione italiana di Gigi Cane, pp. 635-684.

ii. Individuals
aa. Baldini

B871   *Re Enrico VI 1. 2. 3.* Tr. by Gabriele Baldini. Biblioteca Universale Rizzoli, 931-934. Milan: A. Rizzoli, 1955. Pp. 342.

B872   *Storie Inglesi: La Tragedia di Re Riccardo III.* Tr. di Gabriele Baldini. Biblioteca Universale Rizzoli, 1006-1007. Milan: Rizzoli, 1956. Pp. 152. Rome: A. Signorelli (Tip. Castaldi), 1957. Pp. 278.

B873   *La Tragedia di Re Riccardo II.* Tr. di Gabriele Baldini. Biblioteca Universale Rizzoli, 591. Milan: Rizzoli, 1953. Pp. 103. Naples: R. Pironti & Son, 1954. Pp. 275. Bilingual edition.

B874   *King John.* Tr. with an introduction by Gabriele Baldini. Milan: Rizzoli, 1952. Pp. 103.

B875   *La Storia di Re Enrico IV.* Tr. by Gabriele Baldini. Biblioteca Universale Rizzoli, 750-752. Milan: Edizioni Rizzoli & Co., 1954. Pp. 233.

B876   *Re Enrico IV, Prima Parte.* Tr. with texts printed side by side, by Gabriele Baldini. Rome: Angelo Signorelli, 1956. Pp. 221.

B877   *La Vita di Re Enrico Quinto.* Testo riveduto, introduzione e commenti di Gabriele Baldini. Biblioteca Sansoniana Straniera, 96-97. Versione italiana a fronte di F. Bajocchi. Florence: G. C. Sansoni, 1950. Pp. lxii, 373.

B878   *La Cronica di Re Enrico V.* Tr. by Gabriele Baldini. Biblioteca Universale Rizzoli, 843-844. Milan: Edizioni Rizzoli & Co., 1955. Pp. 123.

B879   *Venus and Adonis.* Testo criticamente riveduto e commentato, saggio di una interpretazione e versione italiana a fronte di Gabriele Baldini. Parma: Guanda, 1952. Pp. xx, 199.

bb. Chiarini

B880   *Romeo e Giulietta.* Tr. by Cino Chiarini. Collezione Sansoniana Straniera, No. 4. Florence: Sansoni, 1954. Pp. xxxviii, 243.
       Bilingual edition, revised text, with introduction and notes. A reprint.

B881   *Macbeth.* Tr. by Cino Chiarini. Biblioteca Sansoniana Teatrale, 10. Florence: Sansoni,
        1950. Pp. 86. A reprint.

cc. Dèttore

B882   *La Bisbetica Domata (Shrew).* Tr. di Ugo Dèttore. Biblioteca Universale Rizzoli, No. 1115.
        Milan: Rizzoli, 1957. Pp. 91.
B883   *King Lear.* Tr. by Ugo Dèttore. Milan: Rizzoli, 1951. Pp. 139.
B884   *Macbeth.* Tr. by Ugo Dèttore. Biblioteca Universale Rizzoli, 351. Milan: Rizzoli, 1951.
        Pp. 83.
B885   *La Tempesta.* Tr. by Ugo Dèttore. Biblioteca Universale Rizzoli, No. 1280. Milan: Biblio-
        teca Universale Rizzoli, 1958. Pp. 77.

dd. Errante

B886   *La Tragedia di Romeo e Giulietta.* Tr. di Vincenzo Errante. Florence: Sansoni, 1947. Pp.
        xi, 193.
B887   *Il Sogno di una Notte d'Estate.* Tr. di Vincenzo Errante. Le opere di Vincenzo Errante. Florence:
        Sansoni, 1948. Pp. xxiii, 124.
B888   *Il Mercante di Venezia.* Tr. di Vincenzo Errante. Florence: Sansoni, 1948. Pp. xv, 160.
B889   *La Tragedia di Giulio Cesare.* Tr. di Vincenzo Errante. Florence: Sansoni, 1946. Pp. xiii, 142.
B890   *La Tragedia di Amleto, Principe di Danimarca.* Tr. e introduzione di Vincenzo Errante. Florence:
        Sansoni, 1946. Pp. xvii, 256.
B891   *La Tragedia di Otello.* Tr. di Vincenzo Errante. Florence: Sansoni, 1946. Pp. xii, 181.
B891a   *La Tragedia di Re Lear.* Tr. di Vincenzo Errante. Florence: Sansoni, 1946. Pp. vii, 198.
B892   *La Tragedia di Macbeth.* Tr. di Vincenzo Errante. Florence: Sansoni, 1946. Pp. xviii, 134.
B893   *La Tempesta.* Tr. di Vincenzo Errante. Florence: Sansoni, 1947. Pp. 143.

ee. Hochkofler

B894   *Sogno di una Notte di Mezza Estate.* Tr. letteraria di Mary de Hochkofler. L'Ulivo, 14. Florence:
        Salani, 1950. Pp. 106.
B895   *Hamlet.* Tr. by Mary de Hochkofler, with an introduction by Enrico Bianche. L'Ulivo, 3.
        Florence: Salani, 1950. Pp. 193.
B896   *Othello.* Tr. by Mary de Hochkofler. Florence: Salani, 1951. Pp. 128.

ff. Lodovici

B897   *Riccardo III.* Tr. di Cesare Vico Lodovici. Piccola Biblioteca Scientifico-Letteraria, 73. Turin:
        Einaudi, 1956. Pp. 196.
B898   *The Taming of the Shrew.* Tr. by Cesare Vico Lodovici. Piccola Biblioteca Scientifico-Letteraria,
        28. Turin: G. Einaudi, 1950. Pp. 160.
B899   *Romeo and Juliet.* Tr. by Cesare Vico Lodovici. Piccola Biblioteca Scientifico-Letteraria, 15.
        Turin: G. Einaudi, 1950. Pp. 169.
B900   *Riccardo II.* Tr. by Cesare Vico Lodovici. Teatro. Dir. da L. Ridenti, 31. Turin: 1948.
        Pp. 100. Republished in Piccola Biblioteca Scientifico-Letteraria, 67. Turin: G. Einaudi,
        1955. Pp. 197.
B901   *Il Mercante di Venezia.* Tr. by Cesare Vico Lodovici. Piccola Biblioteca Scientifico-Letteraria,
        68. Turin: G. Einaudi, 1955. Pp. 193.
B902   *Henry IV Part I.* Tr. by Cesare Vico Lodovici. Piccola Biblioteca Scientifico-Letteraria, 45.
        Turin: G. Einaudi, 1952. Pp. 160.
B903   *Molto Rumore per Nulla (Much).* Tr. by Cesare Vico Lodovici. Piccola Biblioteca Scientifico-
        Letteraria, 83. Turin: G. Einaudi, 1958. Pp. 145.
B904   *Julius Caesar.* Tr. by Cesare Vico Lodovici. Piccola Biblioteca Scientifico-Letteraria, 17.
        Turin: G. Einaudi, 1950. Pp. 138.
B905   *As You Like It.* Tr. by Cesare Vico Lodovici. Piccola Biblioteca Scientifico-Letteraria. Turin:
        G. Einaudi, 1952. Pp. 144.
B906   *La Dodicesima Notte.* Tr. by Cesare Vico Lodovici. Piccola Biblioteca Scientifico-Letteraria,
        60. Turin: G. Einaudi, 1954. Pp. 146.
B907   *Amleto.* Tr. di Cesare Vico Lodovici. Piccola Biblioteca Scientifico-Letteraria, 75. Turin:
        G. Einaudi, 1956. Pp. 208.
B908   *Le Allegre Comari di Windsor.* Tr. by Cesare Vico Lodovici. Piccola Biblioteca Scientifico-
        Letteraria, 79. Turin: G. Einaudi, 1957. Pp. 162.
B909   *Troilus and Cressida.* Tr. by Cesare Vico Lodovici. Piccola Biblioteca Scientifico-Letteraria, 27.
        Turin: G. Einaudi, 1950. Pp. 169.
B910   *Misura per Misura.* Tr. by Cesare Vico Lodovici. Piccola Biblioteca Scientifico-Letteraria, 80.
        Turin: G. Einaudi, 1957. Pp. 148.

B911   *Otello*. Tr. di Cesare Vico Lodovici. Piccola Biblioteca Scientifico-Letteraria, 56. Turin:
       G. Einaudi, 1953. Pp. 183.

B912   *Re Lear*. Tr. di Cesare Vico Lodovici. Piccola Biblioteca Scientifico-Letteraria, 76. Turin:
       G. Einaudi, 1956. Pp. 188.

B913   *Macbeth*. Tr. by Cesare Vico Lodovici. Piccola Biblioteca Scientifico-Letteraria. Turin:
       G. Einaudi, 1951. Pp. 131.
       Rev: by Achille Fiocco, *La Fiera Letteraria*, VI, No. 44 (Nov. 18, 1951).

B914   *Timone d'Atene (Tim.)*. Tr. by Cesare Vico Lodovici. Piccola Biblioteca Scientifico-Letteraria,
       84. Turin: G. Einaudi, 1958. Pp. 135.

B915   *Antony and Cleopatra*. Tr. by Cesare Vico Lodovici. Piccola Biblioteca Scientifico-Letteraria.
       Turin: G. Einaudi, 1952. Pp. 160.

B916   *Coriolano*. Tr. by Cesare Vico Lodovici. Piccola Biblioteca Scientifico-Letteraria. Turin:
       G. Einaudi, 1953. Pp. 192.

B917   *Cimbelino (Cym.)*. Tr. by Cesare Vico Lodovici. Piccola Biblioteca Scientifico-Letteraria, 85.
       Turin: G. Einaudi, 1958. Pp. 182.

B918   *Racconto d'Inverno*. Tr. di Cesare Vico Lodovici. Piccola Biblioteca Scientifico-Letteraria, 53.
       Turin: Einaudi, 1953. Pp. 160.

B919   *La Tempesta*. Tr. by Cesare Vico Lodovici. Piccola Biblioteca Scientifico-Letteraria. Turin:
       G. Einaudi, 1953. Pp. 126.

gg. Montale

B920   *Hamlet*. Tr. by Eugenio Montale. Milan: Cederna, 1949. Pp. 211.

B921   *Sonetti*. Tr. Eugenio Montale. Milan: Quaderno di Traduzioni, 1948.

hh. Obertello

B922   *La Tragedia di Giulio Cesare*. Tr. by Alfredo Obertello. Biblioteca Moderna Mondadori,
       Nuova Serie, 368. Milan, Verona: Mondadori, 1953. Pp. 182.
       Rev: *EA*, VIII (1955), 184.

B923   *Misura per Misura (Meas.)*. Tr. by Alfredo Obertello. Biblioteca Moderna Mandadori diretta
       da A. Mondadori, 503. Milan: A. Mandadori, 1958. Pp. 179.

B924   *La Tragedia di Coriolano*. Tr. by Alfredo Obertello. Biblioteca Moderna Mondadori diretta
       da A. Mondadori, 516. Milan: A. Mondadori, 1958. Pp. 194.

ii. Ojetti

B925   *Romeo e Giulietta*. Tr. di Paola Ojetti. Biblioteca Universale Rizzoli, 76. Milan: Rizzoli,
       1949. Pp. 96.

B926   *A Midsummer Night's Dream*. Tr. by Paola Ojetti. Biblioteca Universale Rizzoli, 195. Milan:
       Rizzoli, 1950. Pp. 86.

B927   *Il Mercante di Venezia*. Tr. di Paola Ojetti. Biblioteca Universale Rizzoli, 134. Milan:
       Rizzoli, 1950. Pp. 92.

B928   *Come vi Garba*. Tr. di Paola Ojetti. Biblioteca Universale Rizzoli, 166. Milan: Rizzoli,
       1950. Pp. 91.

B929   *Otello*. Tr. di Paola Ojetti. Milan: Rizzoli, 1949. Pp. 93.

jj. Piccoli

B930   *Otello*. Versione di Raff. Piccoli. Testo riveduto, introduz. di Guido Ferrando. Florence:
       Sansoni, 1934.

B931   *Amleto*. Tr. by Raff. Piccoli. Collezione Sansoniana Straniera, 63. Florence: Sansoni, 1955.
       Pp. xxxii, 316.
       Bilingual edition, revised text, with introduction and notes. A reprint.

kk. Quasimodo

B932   *Romeo e Giulietta*. Tr. di Salvatore Quasimodo. Milan, Verona: Mondadori, 1949. Pp. 297.
       Rev: by Guglielmo Petroni, *La Fiera Letteraria*, 1949, p. 3; by G. Baldini, *Belfagor*
       (Florence), V (1950), 102-108.

B933   *Macbeth*. Tr. by Salvatore Quasimodo. Turin: G. Einaudi, 1952. Pp. 96.

B934   *Richard III*. Tr. by Salvatore Quasimodo. Milan, Verona: A. Mondadori, 1952. Pp. 149.

B935   *La Tempesta*. Tr. by Salvatore Quasimodo. Introd. by Luigi Berti. Universale Einaudi, 23.
       Turin: G. Einaudi, 1956. Pp. xiv, 108.

ll. Rebora

B936   *I Sonetti*. Versione col testo a fronte, introd. e note a cura di P. Rebora. Biblioteca Sansoniana
       Straniera. Florence: Sansoni, 1941. Pp. xliii, 197.
       Rev: by Benvenuto Cellini, *ICS*, XXV (1942), 74-75; by Mario Praz, *ES*, XXIX (1948), 53-58.

B937   *I Sonetti.* Translation, introduction and notes by Piero Rebora. Biblioteca Sansoniana
        Straniera, 82. Florence: Sansoni, 1953. Pp. 197.
        Revised text and Italian translation printed side by side.

B938   *Canti Lirici.* Tr. da Piero Rebora. Florence: Cya, 1947. Pp. 46.

mm. Rusconi

B939   *Tragedie Scelte: Macbeth, Re Lear, Romeo e Giulietta, Otello, Amleto.* Tr. di Carlo Rusconi,
        riveduta. Sancasciano Pesa: Soc. Ed. Toscana, 1936. Pp. xv, 499. I Classici Azzurri, 25.
        Rome: Ed. Cremonese, 1955. Pp. xii, 499.

B940   *Commedie Scelte: La Tempesta, Il Mercante di Venezia, Molto Strepito per Nulla, La Bisbetica
        Domata, Le Allegre Donne di Windsor.* Tr. di Carlo Rusconi. Con introd. e note di Ferdinando
        Carlesi. I Classici Azzurri, 11. Rome: Ed. Cremonese, 1955. Pp. xvi, 396.

B941   *Teatro.* Tr. di Carlo Rusconi. Rome: Astra, 1956.
        1. *Amleto, Macbeth, Otello, Romeo e Giulietta.* Pp. 356.
        2. *Re Lear, La Bisbetica Domata, Le Allegre Comari di Windsor, Il Sogno di una Notte di Mezza
        Estate.* Pp. 300.

nn. Others

B942   *La Bisbetica Domata. Le Allegre Comari di Windsor.* A cura e trad. di Maria Antonietta Andreoni.
        I Grandi Scrittori Stranieri, 132. Turin: Utet, 1948. Pp. 243.

B943   *Il Sogno di una Notte di Mezza Estate.* Nuova Traduzione di Diego Angeli. Milan: Treves,
        1936. Pp. ix, 175.

B944   *Enrico V.* Tr. di Fedele Bajocchi. Biblioteca Sansoniana Teatrale, 6. Florence: Sansoni,
        1950. Pp. 103. The same translation also issued in a revised text, with introduction and
        commentary by Gabriele Baldini. Pp. lxii, 375.

B945   *Sonnets.* Tr. by Gustavo Barbensi. Florence: L. S. Olschki, 1952. Pp. iv, 51.

B946   *Giulietta e Romeo.* Libera versione in vernacolo veronese de la Romeo e Giulietta de Memo
        Sespir di Giuseppe Barni (Bepo Spela). Quaderni di "Vita veronese," 13-15. Verona:
        Ghidini e Fiorini, 1949. Pp. 39.

B947   *Ricardo III.* Tr. e adattamento . . . a cura di Odoardo Campa. Teatro. Dir. da L. Ridenti, 22.
        Turin: Set, 1946. Pp. 101.

B948   *Coriolano.* Versione con testo a fronte, introd. e note a cura di Guido Ferrando. Biblioteca
        Sansoniana Straniera, 53. Florence: Sansoni, 1946. Pp. xxxix, 271. Bilingual edition.

B949   *The Tempest.* Tr. by G. S. Gargano. Biblioteca Sansoniana Straniera, 71. Florence: Sansoni,
        1952. Pp. 222.

B950   *Giulio Cesare, Antonio e Cleopatra, Romeo e Giulietta.* A cura di Augusto Grosso Guidetti.
        I Grandi Scrittori Stranieri, 108. Turin: Utet, 1949. Pp. 412.

B951   *Giulietta e Romeo.* Tr. e adattamento di Luigi Lazzarini. Milan: Aurora, 1936. Pp. 223.
        Milan: Tipografia Editrice Lucchi, 1955. Pp. 223.

B952   *Giulio Cesare.* Tr. di Emidio Martini. Prefazione di Benedetto Croce. Turin: G. B. Paravia
        e C., 1942. Pp. 126.

B953   Cancelled.

B954   *I Colloqui di Giulietta e Romeo Nella Tragedia di Guglielmo Shakespeare.* Ed. and tr. by Luigi
        Motterle. Bari: Società Editrice Tipografica, 1953. Pp. 52.

B955   *Opere Complete.* Tradotte da Alessandro Muccioli. Nos. 23, 38. Florence: La Nuova Italia.
        Giulio Cesare. 2a ed., 1936. Pp. 176. La *Tempesta.* 1936. Pp. 159.

B956   *Coriolano.* Intro., versione e com. a cura di Emilio Nazaro. Palermo: Priulla, 1937. Pp.
        xxxii, 144.

B957   *Il Mercante di Venezia. Tutto è Bene quel che Finisce Bene.* Tr. with an introd. and notes by
        Nicoletta Neri. Grandi Scrittori Stranieri. Collana di Traduzioni diretta da G. V. Amoretti,
        169. Turin: Utet, 1954. Pp. 279.

B958   *Liriche.* Intro. e com. a cura di Napoleone Orsini. Messina: G. Principato, 1937. Pp. 88.

B959   *Hamlet.* Tr. by Corrado Pavolini. Milan: Rizzoli, 1951. Pp. 125.

B960   *Sonnets.* Tr. by Francesco Politi. Turin: Chiantore, 1952. Pp. 124. Bilingual edition.

B961   *Giulio Cesare.* Tr. by Aldo Ricci. Collezione Sansoniana Straniera, 1. Florence: Sansoni,
        1949. Pp. xlvii, 216.
        Bilingual edition, revised text, with introd. and notes. A reprint.

B962   *Sonetti.* Introd., tr. e note di Alberto Rossi. Nuova Collana di Poeti Trad. con Testo a fronte,
        1. Turin: G. Einaudi, 1952. Pp. 375.
        Bilingual edition. Republished Turin, 1956; Milan: Mondadori, 1957.
            Rev: *TLS*, Mar. 19, 1954, p. 186; by Terence Spencer, *MLR*, xlix (1954), 541-542; by
            Hermann Heuer, *SJ*, 91 (1955), 326-327.

B963   Cancelled.

B964   *Amleto.* Tr. by Luigi Squarzina. With an Introd. by Silvio D'Amico and directions for the stage by Vittorio Gassman and Luigi Squarzina. Bologna-Rocca San Casciano: Tipografia Licineo Cappelli, 1953. Pp. 293.

B965   *Coriolano.* Tr. by Alessandro De Stefani. Universale Economica, 254. Serie Teatro, 2. Milan: G. Feltrinelli, 1958. Pp. 235.

B966   *Otello, il Moro di Venezia; Re Lear; Macbeth.* Introd. e tr. a cura di Laura Toretta. I Grandi Scrittori Stranieri, 130. Turin: Utet, 1948. Pp. 359.

B967   *XXII Sonetti.* Scelti e tradotti da Giuseppe Ungaretti. Rome: Ed. Documento, 1944. Pp. 55. Bilingual edition.

B968   *XL Sonetti di Shakespeare.* Tr. di Giuseppe Ungaretti. Vita d'un Uomo, IV. Milan: Mondadori, 1946. Pp. 127.
       Rev: by Renato Poggioli, *Books Abroad*, XXI (1947), 100-101.

B969   *Antonio e Cleopatra.* Revised text, introd., and tr. by Aurelio Zanco. Biblioteca Sansoniana Straniera, 70. Florence: Sansoni, 1954. Pp. xlii, 251.

oo. Translator not identified in Source

B970   *Sogno di una Notte di Mezza Estate.* Cinema-Biblioteca, 43. Milan: Bietti, 1936. Pp. 221. Versione romanzata.

B971   *Re Enrico IV.* Piccola Biblioteca Scientifico-Letteraria. Turin: Einaudi, 1958. Pp. 176.

B972   *Amleto.* Biblioteca Moderna Mondadori. Milan: Mondadori, 1958. Pp. 240.

B973   *La Tragedia di Re Riccardo III.* Biblioteca Universale. Milan: Rizzoli, 1958. Pp. 152.

B974   *Romeo e Giulietta.* Biblioteca Universale. Milan: Rizzoli, 1958. Pp. 96.

B975   *Sogno d'una Notte d'Estate.* Biblioteca Universale. Milan: Rizzoli, 1958. Pp. 88.

B976   *Il Mercante di Venezia.* Biblioteca Universale Rizzoli. Milan: Rizzoli, 1958. Pp. 96.

B977   *Come vi Garba.* Biblioteca Universale Rizzoli. Milan: Rizzoli, 1958. Pp. 96.

B978   *Amleto.* Biblioteca Universale Rizzoli. Milan: Rizzoli, 1958. Pp. 128.

B979   *Re Lear.* Biblioteca Universale. Milan: Rizzoli, 1958. Pp. 144.

B980   *Una Tragedia Nella Contea di York.* Florence: Sansoni, 1952. Pp. 90. Bilingual edition.

B981   *La Tragedia di Amleto, Principe di Danimarca.* Versione italiana conforme all'originale inglese e presentazione di Alessandro De Stefani. Teatro, Vol. 13. Turin: Set, 1945. Pp. 159. Il Dramma, Suppl. NS 4. Turin: Set, 1949. Pp. 100.

(5) RUMANIAN

B982   *Opere.* 3 vols. Bucharest: Ed. de Stat Pentru Lit. si Arta.
       1. *Regele Joan. Comedia Erorilor. Romeo si Julieta.* Tr. by Mihnea Gheorghiu, 1955. Pp. 419.
       2. *Richard II. Negutatorul din Venetia. Juliu Cezar.* Tr. by Mihnea Gheorghiu, 1955. Pp. 395.
       3. *Cei doi Tineri. Zadarnicele Chinuri ale Dragostei. Visul Unei Nopti de Vara. Mult Zgomot Pentru Nimic.* Tr. by Mihnea Gheorghiu, Ion Frunzetti, and others, 1956. Pp. 340.
       First Rumanian collected edition.
       Rev: by Agerpres, *Inf.-Bull.*, VI, No. 3 (1955), 9-10 (vols. 1 and 2); by Fritz Behr, *SJ*, 92 (1956), 424-426 (vols. 1 and 2).

B983   *Romeo si Julieta.* St. O. Iosif. Bucharest: Ed. Tineretului, 1956. Pp. 182.

B984   *Hamlet, Princ al Denemarčei.* Andrej Lupan. Kisinev: Škoala Sovetike, 1956. Pp. 208.

B985   *Hamlet, Princ al Denemarčei, Tragedie.* In romineste de Petru Dumitriv. Bucharest: Editura de Stat Pentru Literatura si Arta, 1955. Pp. 231.

d. SLAVONIC TRANSLATIONS (163; -)
(1) RUSSIAN
(a) TRANSLATION PROBLEMS AND TRANSLATORS

B986   Kojevnkov, V. "The New Translations of *Hamlet* and the Problems of Translation." *Literary Critic* (USSR), 1939, pp. 10-11, 252-266.

B987   Morozov, M. " 'Read Him, Therefore, and Again and Again . . .'." *Theatre* (USSR), VIII (1940), 121-130.

B988   Morozov, Mikhail M. *Shakespeare on the Soviet Stage.* Tr. by David Magarshack. London: Soviet News Publ., 1947. Pp. 71.

B989   Gibian, George. "Shakespeare in Soviet Russia." *Russian Review*, XI (1952), 24-34.

i. Pasternak

B990   Pasternak, B. "Some Remarks by a Translator of Shakespeare." *Soviet Literature*, Sept., 1946, pp. 51-57.

B991   Pasternak, Boris. "Comment J'Ai Traduit Shakespeare en Russe." *Lettres Françaises*, No. 647 (1956).

B992   Pasternak, Boris. "Notes on the Translation of Shakespeare's Tragedies." *Literaturnaya Moskva* (Moscow), 1956.

B993　Pasternak, Boris. "On Translating Shakespeare." *The New Leader*, Oct. 13, 1958, pp. 18-25.

B994　Pasternak, Boris. "Translating Shakespeare." *TC*, 164, No. 979 (1958), 213-228. Tr. by Manya Harari.

B995　William-Wilmont, N. N. "Boris Pasternak's Translation of *Hamlet*." *International Literature* (USSR), 1939, pp. 7-8, 284-285.

B996　Morozov, M. M. "Boris Pasternak's Translation of *Othello*." Ed. by Eugene Blum. *SAB*, xx (1945), 103-104.

B997　Pollak, Seweryn. "Otello po Rosyjsku w Przekladzie Borysa Pasternaka." *Łódź Teatr*, No. 8 (1948), 38-41.

B998　Bruskov, N. "The Tragedies of William Shakespeare. Translated by Boris Pasternak." *News* (Moscow), No. 4 (1952), 21-22.

(b) TRANSLATIONS
i. Pasternak

B999　*Hamlet*. Tr. by Boris Pasternak. Moskva: Gihl, 1941. Pp. 171. Reprinted, Moskva: Detgiz, 1947. Pp. 320. Reprinted, Moskva, Leningrad: Iskusstvo, 1951. Pp. 242. Reprinted, Moskva: Detgiz, 1956. Pp. 188.
　　　Rev: by Alexander Kaun, *Books Abroad*, xvi (1942), 450.

B1000　*Otello, Venetsianskii Mavr*. Tr. by Boris Pasternak. Moscow: State Publishing House of Belles-Lettres, 1944. Pp. 140. Reprinted, Moskva, Leningrad: Iskusstvo, 1951. Pp. 227.

B1001　*Genrich IV*. Perev. B. Pasternaka. Moskva: Detgiz, 1949. Pp. 256.

B1002　*Romeo i Džuletta*. Perev. B. Pasternaka. Moskva, Leningrad: Iskusstvo, 1951. Pp. 182.

B1003　*Vil'jam Šekspir v perev. B. Pasternaka*. Obšč. red. perev. M. M. Morozova. Moskva: Iskusstvo, 1950.
　　　1. *Romeo i Džul'etta; Korol' Genrich Cetvertyi; Gamlet, Princ Datskij*. Pp. 606.
　　　2. *Otello; Korol' Lir; Antonij i Kleopatra*. Pp. 518.

ii. Others

B1004　Dinamov, S. S., and A. A. Smirnov, eds. *Shakespeare's Complete Works*. Vol. III. Moscow, 1937. Pp. 486.

B1005　*Twelfth Night*. Tr. by A. I. Kronberg and A. A. Smirnov. Moscow, 1937. Pp. 150.

B1006　*Hamlet*. Tr. by A. Radlovaya. Moscow, 1937. Pp. 254.

B1007　*Merry Wives of Windsor*. Tr. by T. L. Shchepkina-Kupernik. Moscow, 1937. Pp. 135. Directing comments by N. M. Gorchakov.

B1008　*Othello*. Tr. by A. L. Sokolovski. Moscow, 1937. Pp. 256.

B1009　*Taming of the Shrew*. Tr. by M. A. Kusmin, adapted to the stage with notes. A. Popov and P. Urbanovich, eds. Moscow, 1940. Pp. 168.

B1010　*Othello*. With literal translation and commentary by M. M. Morozov. Published in USSR, 1946.

B1011　*Sonety*. Perev. S. Maršaka. Moskva: Sovetskij Pisatel', 1948. Pp. 198. Reissued, 1952.

B1012　*Tragičeskaja Istorija o Gamlete, Princ Datskom*. Voronezh: Oblastnoe Izd., 1949. Pp. 124.

B1013　*Korol Lir*. Moskva: Goslitizdat, 1949. Pp. 164.

B1014　*Korol Genrich IV*. Moskva: Goslitizdat, 1949. Pp. 280.

B1015　*Izbrannye Proizvedeniia*. Vorr. Ebda u. d. T.: Smirnov, A.: Predislovie k Knige. Moskva: Goslitizdat, 1950. Pp. 1328.

B1016　*Vindzorski Nasmešnicy*. Prevoschodnaja i prijatnaja komedija o sere Džone Falstafe i vindzorskich nasmešnicach. Per. S. Maršaka i M. Morozova. Moskva: Iskusstvo, 1951. Pp. 115.

B1017　*Ukroščenie Stroptivoj*. Per. A. I. Kuroševoj pod red. A. A. Smirnova. Moskva, Leningrad: Iskusstvo, 1952. Pp. 179.

B1018　*Korol Lir*. Per. T. L. Ščepkinoj-Kupernik pod red. A. A. Smirnovoj. Moskva, Leningrad: Iskusstvo, 1952. Pp. 231.

B1019　*Isbrannye Proizvedenija*. Perev. S. Maršaka, B. Pasternaka, T. Ščepkinoj-Kupernik. Moskva: Goslitizdat, 1953. Pp. 548.

B1020　*Dvenadcataja Noč*. Moskva: Izd. Inostr. Lit., 1954. Pp. 93.

B1021　Morozov, Mikhail Mikhailovich. *Izbrannye Stati i Perevody*. Moskva: Goslitizdat, 1954. Pp. 594.

(c) OTHER LANGUAGES OF THE USSR

B1022　*Komedija Ošibok* (Ukrain). Kiev: Mistectvo, 1954. Pp. 116.

B1023　*Romeo and Juliet*. Ins Ukrainische übersetzt und eingeleitet von Eaghor G. Kostetzky. Munich, 1957. Pp. 100.

B1023a　*Shakespeares Sonette*. Erste vollständige ukrainische Übersetzung mit Kommentar und Anmerkungen von Eaghor G. Kostetsky. Munich, 1958. Pp. 254.

B1024 *Tragedies.* Vol. I: *Othello, Antony and Cleopatra, Richard III, Julius Caesar.* Tr. by I Machabeli. Tiflis, 1938. Pp. 510.

B1025 *Veselye Vindzorskie Kumuški.* Georgian tr. by V. Čelidze. Tiflis: Helovneba, 1956. Pp. 119.

B1026 Alexander, Edward. "Shakespeare's Plays in Armenia." *SQ,* IX (1958), 387-394.

B1027 *Izbrannye Proizvedenija.* Armenian tr. by Khačik Daštenc. Erevan: Ajpetrat, 1955. Pp. 472.

B1028 *Sonetlăr.* Azerbaidjánian tr. by Tălăt Äjubov. Baku: Azernešr, 1955. Pp. 159.

B1029 *Otello. Romeo Belăn Džuleta.* Tatar tr. by Gabdulla Šamukov. Kazan: Tatknigoizdat, 1956. Pp. 336.

B1030 *Otello. Venecianskij Mavr.* Yakuts tr. by G. Vasilev. Jakutsk: Jakutknigoizdat, 1956. Pp. 149.

(2) POLISH
(a) TRANSLATION PROBLEMS

B1031 Chwalewik, Witold. "Z Poetyki Przekladów Szekspira." *Twórczość,* VII (1952), 120-217.

(b) INDIVIDUAL TRANSLATORS
i. Berwinska

B1032 *Wesołe Kumoszki z Windsoru.* Tr. by Krystyna Berwinska. Warsaw: Pánstwowy Instytut Wydawniczy, 1954.

B1033 *Otello.* Tr. by Krystyna Berwinska. Warsaw: Pánstwowy Instytut Wydawniczy, 1956. Pp. 222.

ii. Brandstaettera

B1034 *Król Ryszard III.* Tr. by Romana Brandstaettera. Warsaw: Pánstwowy Instytut Wydawniczy, 1952.

B1035 *Kupiec Wenecki.* Tr. by Romana Brandstaettera. Warsaw: Pánstwowy Instytut Wydawniczy, 1953, 1954.

B1036 *Hamlet Królewicz Dunski.* Tr. by Romana Brandstaettera. Warsaw: Pánstwowy Instytut Wydawniczy, 1952, 1953. Pp. 227.

iii. Iwaszkewicz

B1037 Iwaszkewicz, J. [Tr. into Polish of a scene from *Hamlet.*] *Teatr Miesoceznik,* Nos. 4-5, 1946.

B1038 *Romeo i Julia., Hamlet.* Tr. by Jaroslaw Iwaszkewicz. Warsaw: Pánstwowy Instytut Wydawniczy, 1954. Pp. 324.

iv. Paszkowski

B1039 *Makbet.* Tr. by J. Paszkowski. Ed. by A. Gorski. Krakow: Anczyc, 1949. Pp. 126.

B1040 *Makbet.* Tr. by J. Paszkowski. Ed. by A. Tretiak, 4th ed. rev. by J. Krzyżanowski. Wrocław: Biblioteka Narodowa, 1949. Pp. 139.

B1041 *Hamlet.* Tr. by J. Paszkowski. Biblioteczka Universytetow Ludowych. Warsaw: Gebethnera i Wolffa, 1951. Pp. 178.

v. Paszkowskiego

B1042 *Hamlet.* Przeklad Jozefa Paszkowskiego. Wyd. 3, nakl. 3. Warsaw: Nakl. Geberthnera i Wolffa, 1951. Pp. 178.

B1043 *Makbet.* Tr. by Jozefa Paszkowskiego. Warsaw: Ossolineum, 1956.

vi. Siwicka

B1044 *Makbet.* Przeklad, wstep i objašnienia Zofii Siwicka. Biblioteka Pisarzy polskich i obcych, 51. Warsaw: Ksiazka i Wiedza, 1950. Pp. 122.

B1045 *Othello, King Lear, Macbeth.* Tr. by Z. Siwicka. Warsaw: Ksiazka i Wiedza, 1951. Pp. 532.

B1046 *Juliusz Cezar.* Ed. by Zofia Siwicka. Warsaw: Pánstwowy Instytut Wydawniczy, 1953.

B1047 *Koriolan.* Tr. by Zofia Siwicka. Warsaw: Pánstwowy Instytut Wydawniczy, 1955. Pp. 222.

B1048 *Burza (The Tempest).* Tr. by Zofia Siwicka. Warsaw: Pánstwowy Instytut Wydawniczy, 1956. Pp. 135.

B1049 *Romeo i Julia.* Tr. by Zofia Siwicka. Warsaw: Pánstwowy Instytut Wydawniczy, 1956. Pp. 182.

B1050 *Król Lir.* Tr. by Zofia Siwicka. Warsaw: Pánstwowy Instytut Wydawniczy, 1956. Pp. 202.

vii. Tarnawski

B1051 *Hamlet.* Ed. by Stanislaw Helsztynski and tr. by Wladyslaw Tarnawski. Biblioteka Narodowa, No. 20, Series II. Breslau: Ossolinski, 1955. Pp. c, 260. Reprint.
       Rev: by Witwold Chwalewik, *Komitet Neofilologiczny,* III (1956), 269-271.

B1052 *Król Ryszard Drugi.* Tr. by Wladyslaw Tarnawski. Warsaw: Pánstwowy Instytut Wydawniczy, 1956. Pp. 174.

viii. Others

B1053 *A Midsummer Night's Dream.* Tr. by S. E. Koźmian. Biblioteka Accydziel Poezji i Prozy, 101.
Krakow: Wydawnictwo M. Kot, 1950. Pp. 100.

B1054 *Macbeth.* Tr. by J. Kasprowicz. Biblioteczka Universytetow Ludowych, 172. Warsaw:
Gebethnera i Wolffa, 1950. Pp. 132.

B1055 Morozov, Mikhail Mikhailovič. "Poskromienie Zlośnicy: Komedia Szekspira." Tr.
Aleksander Balinski. *Pamietnik Teatralny* (Warsaw), IV (1952), 118-136.

B1056 *Tymon Aténczyk.* Ed. by Czesław Jastrzebiec-Kosłowski. Warsaw: Pánstwowy Instytut
Wydawniczy, 1954.

B1057 *Sen Nocy Letniej. Król Henryk IV. Burza.* Tr. by Konstanty Ildefons Galczynski. Warsaw:
Pánstwowy Instytut Wydawniczy, 1954. Pp. 252.

B1058 *Wieczór Trzech Króli, Albo, co Chcecie (Twel.).* Tr. by Stanislaw Dygat. Warsaw: Pánstwowy
Instytut Wydawniczy, 1955. Pp. 179.

B1059 *Pięć Dramatów. Dream, Romeo, Wives, Ham.,* and *Mach.* Tr. by Stanislaw Koźmian, Józef
Paszkowski, and Leon Ulrich. Warsaw: Pánstwowy Instytut Wydawniczy, 1956. Pp. 437.

(3) SERBO-CROATIAN
(a) TRANSLATION PROBLEMS AND TRANSLATORS

B1060 Batušić, Slavko. "Naši Prijevodi *Otela*" (Our translations of *Othello*). *Kazališni List* (Zagreb),
II, No. 34 (1947), 3-5.
Four translations of the play in Croatia: 1875, 1885, 1910, 1919.

B1061 Popović, Vladeta. "Shakespeare in Post-War Yugoslavia." *ShS*, IV (1951), 117-122.
Translations and performances.

B1062 Potokar, Tone. "Shakespeare v Hrvaščini." *Naša Sodobnost* (Ljubljana), I, Nos. 2-3 (1953),
274-276.

B1063 Klajn, Hugo. "Shakespeare in Yugoslavia." *SQ*, V (1954), 41-45.

B1063a Klajn, Hugo. "Shakespeare in Yugoslavia." *Review of International Affairs* (Belgrade), V
(June 1, 1954), 17-18.

B1064 Čulić, Ćiro. "Shakespearova *Mjera za Mjeru* u Izvedbi Splitskoz Narodnog Kazališta."
Mogućnosti (Split), VII (July, 1955), 555-558.
About *Meas.* and its translation into Croatian.

B1065 "Shakespeare's Works Among the Yugoslavs." *Aryan Path*, XXVIII (1957), 72-76.

(b) INDIVIDUAL TRANSLATORS
i. Antelinović

B1066 "Susret Venere s Veprom" (from *Venus and Adonis*). Tr. by Danko Antelinović. *Republika*
(Zagreb), VI, Nos. 8-9 (1950), 534-535.

B1066a *Venera i Adonis.* Tr. with notes by Danko Antelinović. Zagreb: Zora, 1950. Pp. 70.

B1067 *Soneti.* Tr. with notes by Danko Antelinović. Mala Biblioteka, 106. Zagreb: Zora, 1951.
Pp. 200.

B1068 *Poezija.* Tr. Danko Antelinović. Kol Svjetski Klasici. Zagreb: Zora, 1958. Pp. 280.

ii. Bogdanović

B1069 *Koriolan.* Tr. by Dr. Milan Bogdanović. Zagreb: Hrvatski Izdavalački Zavod, 1943. Pp. 198.

B1070 *San Ivanjske Noći (A Midsummer Night's Dream).* Tr. by Dr. Milan Bogdanović. Revised,
introd., and notes by Prof. Josip Torbarina. *Sabrana Djela W. Shakespearea* (Compl. Works),
ed. by Prof. Josip Torbarina. Zagreb: Matica Hrvatska, 1947. Pp. 151.

B1071 *Mletacki Trgovac (The Merchant of Venice).* Tr. by Dr. Milan Bogdanović. Revised, introd.,
and notes by Prof. Josip Torbarina. *Sabrana Djela W. Shakespearea* (Compl. Works), ed. by
Prof. Josip Torbarina. Zagreb: Matica Hrvatska, 1947. Pp. 172.

B1072 *Hamlet Kraljević Danski.* Tr. by Dr. Milan Bogdanović. Revised, introd. and notes by Prof.
Josip Torbarina. *Sabrana Djela W. Shakespearea* (Compl. Works), ed. by Prof. Josip Torbarina.
Zagreb: Matica Hrvatska, 1950. Pp. 252. Second edition, 1956.

B1073 *Romeo i Julija.* Tr., introd., and notes by Dr. Milan Bogdanović. Second ed. Zagreb: Matica
Hrvatska, 1950. Pp. 180.

B1074 *Otelo.* Tr., with notes, by Dr. Milan Bogdanović. Second ed. Zagreb: Matica Hrvatska,
1950. Pp. 193.

B1075 *Kralj Lear.* Tr. with notes by Dr. Milan Bogdanović. Second ed. Zagreb: Matica Hrvatska,
1950. Pp. 199.

B1076 *Rikard III.* Tr., introd., and notes by Dr. Milan Bogdanović. Second ed. Zagreb: Matica
Hrvatska, 1951. Pp. 282.

B1077   *Julije Cezar*. Tr. with notes by Dr. Milan Bogdanović. Second ed. Zagreb: Matica Hrvatska, 1951. Pp. 159.

B1078   *Na Tri Kralja ili Kako Hoćete* (*Twelfth Night; or, What You Will*). Tr., introd., and notes by Dr. Milan Bogdanović. Second ed. Zagreb: Matica Hrvatska, 1951. Pp. 171.

B1079   *Oluja* (*The Tempest*). Tr., introd., and notes by Dr. Milan Bogdanović. Second ed. Zagreb: Matica Hrvatska, 1951. Pp. 152.

B1080   *Mnogo Vike ni za Šta* (*Much Ado About Nothing*). Tr., introd., and notes by Dr. Milan Bogdanović. Second ed. Zagreb: Matica Hrvatska, 1952. Pp. 154.

B1081   *Ukrocena Goropadnica* (*The Taming of the Shrew*). Tr., introd., and notes by Dr. Milan Bogdanović. Second ed. Zagreb: Matica Hrvatska, 1952. Pp. 172.
See also B1094.

iii. Nedić and Živojinović

B1082   *Kako Vam Drago* (*As You Like It*). Tr. by B. Nedić and V. Živojinović. Introd. by B. Nedić. Belgrade: Prosveta, 1949. Pp. 208. Printed in Cyrillic.

B1083   *Julije Cezar*. Tr. by B. Nedić and V. Živojinović. Introd. by B. Nedić. Belgrade: Prosveta, 1949. Pp. 288. Printed in Cyrillic.

B1084   *Zimska Bajka* (*The Winter's Tale*). Tr. by B. Nedić and V. Živojinović. Introd. and Notes by B. Nedić. Belgrade: Prosveta, 1951. Pp. 251. Printed in Cyrillic.

B1085   *Tragedija Romea i Djulijete*. Tr. by B. Nedić and V. Živojinović. Introd. and notes by B. Nedić. Belgrade: Prosveta, 1951. Pp. 260. Printed in Cyrillic.

B1086   *Antonije i Kleopatra*. Tr. by B. Nedić and V. Živojinović. Introd. by Nedić. Belgrade: Prosveta, 1953. Pp. xiii, 308. Printed in Cyrillic.

iv. Simić and Pandurović

B1087   *Hamlet, Danski Kraljević*. Tr. by Sima Pandurović. Sarajevo: Sojetlost, 1951. Pp. 135. Printed in Cyrillic.

B1088   *Kralj Henri Cetvrti. Dio I i II* (*I and II Henry IV*). Tr. with notes by Živojin Simić and Sima Pandurović. Belgrade: Novo Pokolenje, 1952. Pp. 333. Printed in Cyrillic.

B1089   *Život i Smrt Kralja Džona* (*King John*). Tr. with notes by Živojin Simić and Sima Pandurović. Belgrade: Novo Pokolenje, 1952. Pp. 114.

B1090   *Kralj Ričard Drugi* (*Richard II*). Tr. by Živojin Simić and Sima Pandurović. Belgrade, 1953. Pp. 163. Printed in Cyrillic.

B1091   *Kralj Lir. Makbet*. Tr. by Živojin Simić and Sima Pandurović. Belgrade: Nolit, 1955. Pp. 304.

B1092   *Hamlet, Danski Kraljević*. Tr. by Živojin Simić and Sima Pandurović. Cetinje: Narodna Knjiga, 1955. Pp. 270.

B1093   *Celokupna Dela* (Complete Works). Vol. I: *Tragedije*. Tr. by Živojin Simić and Sima Pandurović. Cetinje: Narodna Knjiga, 1957. Pp. 1572.
This first volume comprises 13 plays: *Titus, Romeo, Caesar, Ham., Troi., Oth., Lear, Macb., Antony, Cor., Tim., Per., Cym.* Appendix of 101 pages consisting of: 1. Life of William Shakespeare; 2. Shakespeare's Tragedies; 3. Bibliography (this being incomplete because it covers only Servian translations, omitting all the Croatian and Slovenian).

v. Torbarina

B1094   *Sabrana Djela W. Shakespearea* (Compl. Works). Ed. by Prof. Josip Torbarina, with introd. and notes. Zagreb: Matica Hrvatska, 1948.
Vesele Žene Wendsorske (*Wives*). Tr. by Milan Bogdanović, 1948. Pp. 177.

B1095   *Mjer za Mjeru* (*Meas.*). Tr. by Josip Torbarina. Zagreb: Matica Hrvatska, 1957. Pp. 200.

vi. Others

B1096   *Studija o Hamletu*. Tr. by Bjelinski. Belgrade, 1953. Pp. 156.

B1097   *Kako Vam Drago* (*As You Like It*). Tr. by Branko Gavela. *Teatar* (Zagreb), III (1957), 17-48.

B1098   *Vesele Windsorke* (*Wives*). Tr. by Hebert Grün. Maribor: Založba "Obzorja," 1955. Pp. 141.

B1099   *Kako Wam se Svita* (*As You Like It*). Tr. with notes by Slavko Ježić. Zagreb: Matica Hrvatska, 1951. Pp. 149.

B1100   "Soneti (Sonnets 1, 2, 3)." Tr. by Dorte Kostić. *Mladost* (Belgrade), II, No. 6 (1946), 65-66.

(4) SLOVENE
(a) TRANSLATION PROBLEMS AND TRANSLATORS

B1101   Mráz, Andreas. *Die Literatur der Slowaken*. Berlin: Volk und Reich-Verlag, 1943. Pp. 202. Shak. passim.

B1102   Moravec, Dušan. "Shakespeare pri Slovencih" (Shakespeare in Slovenia). *Slavistična Revija* (Ljubljana), II, Nos. 1-2, 3-4 (1949), pp. 51-74, 250-291.

B1103 "Shakespeare's Works Among the Yugoslavs." *Aryan Path*, XXVIII (1957), 72-76.

B1104 G., H. "William Shakespeare." *Mladinska Revija* (Ljubljana), I, No. 4 (1946), 140-141.
Discusses a projected edition of the complete works of Shak., translated into Slovene, to be published by the State Publishing house of Slovenia.

(b) INDIVIDUAL TRANSLATORS
i. Bor

B1105 *Richard III* (three excerpts). Tr. into Slovenian by Matej Bor. *Novi Svet*, VI, No. 12 (1951), 1057-69.

B1106 *Richard III*. Tr. by Matej Bor. Ljubljana: Slovenska Matica, 1955. Pp. 242.

B1107 *Henrik IV*. (I in II. dél). Tr. by M. Bor. Ljubljana: Slovenska Matica, 1957. Pp. 293, iii. Commentary and Notes by Bratko Kreft.

ii. Menart

B1108 "Iz Shakespeareovih Sonetov" (Sonnets 42, 66). Tr. into Slovene by Janez Menart. *Gledališni List* (Kranj), II (1951), 4-5.

B1109 "Iz Shakespeareovih Sonetov" (Sonnets 2, 17, 32, 66, 130, 144). Tr. by Janez Menart. *Mladinska Revija*, V, Nos. 4-5 (1949), 220-224.

B1110 "Iz Sonetov" (from the *Sonnets*). Tr. by Janez Menart. *Obzornik*, VII, No. 4 (1952), 210-212.

B1111 "Iz Sonetov" (from the *Sonnets*). Tr. by Janez Menart. *Novi Svet*, VII, No. 11 (1952), 990-993.

iii. Zupančič
(See also B1119.)

B1112 *Koriolan* (*Coriolanus*). Tr. into Slovene by Oton Zupančič. Introd. and Notes by Dr. Francè Koblar. Ljubljana: Slovenska Matica, 1946. Pp. 168.

B1113 *Izbrano Delo* (Selected Works, 3rd revised edition). Tr. into Slovene, with Notes, by Oton Zupančič. Ljubljana: Državna Založba Slovenije. Vol. I, 1947, pp. 243. Vol. II, 1948, pp. 271.
Vol. I includes *Sen kresne noči* (*A Midsummer Night's Dream*), *Komedija Zmesnjav* (*The Comedy of Errors*), *Romeo in Julija*.
Vol. II includes *Beneski Trgovec* (*The Merchant of Venice*), *Kar Hočete* (*Twelfth Night*), *Julij Cezar* (notes by Dr. Francè Koblar).

B1114 *Kakor Vam Drago* (*As You Like It*). Tr. by Oton Zupančič. Introd. and Notes by Francè Koblar. Ljubljana, 1954. Pp. 160.

B1115 *Hamlet*. Tr. by Oton Zupančič. Ljubljana: Mladinska Knjiga, 1956. Pp. 196.

iv. Others

B1116 "Sonet 42." Tr. into Slovene by Dr. Alojz Gradnik. *Mladinska Revija*, V, No. 4-5 (1949), 180.

B1117 "*King John*" (excerpt). Tr. into Slovenian by Branko Rudolf. *Večer*, VIII (1952), 238.

B1118 "*Henrik IV (I. del). III. Dejanje*" (*I Henry IV*, Act III). Tr. into Slovenian. *Naša Sodobnost* (Ljubljana), IV, No. 2 (1954), 306-317.

B1119 Lamb, Charles, and Mary Lamb. *Pripovedke iz Shakespearea*. Tr. by Anton Cernigoj and Oton Zupančič. Ljubljana: Mladinska Knjiga, 1952. Pp. 310.

(5) CZECH
(a) TRANSLATION PROBLEMS AND TRANSLATORS

B1120 Fencl, A. "Prvni České Překlady ze Shakespeara." *Časopis pro Moderní Filologii*, XXIV (1938), 161-168.

B1121 Vodička, T. "K Novému Překladu Shakespearova Caesara." *Listy pro Umění a Kritiku* (Prague), IV (1935), 274-282.

B1122 Albrecht, J. "Vodákův Shakespeare." *Jindřich Vodák, Poeta k Jeho Sedmdesátinám* (Prague), 1937, pp. 274-280.

B1123 Albrecht, J. "Saudkův Nový Shakespeare v Perspektivě Vývojové." *Lumír*, LXIV (1938), 397-401.

B1124 Babler, O. F. "Shakespeare's *King Lear* in Czech." *N &Q*, 196 (1951), 55-56.
Names as translators Prokop Frantisek Sedivy, Josef Kajetán Tyl, Ladislav Celakovsky, Josef V. Sládek, Bohumil Stepánek, and himself.

B1125 Babler, O. F. "Shakespeare's *Midsummer Night's Dream* in Czech and Slovakian." *N &Q*, NS, IV (1957), 151-153.

B1126 Bejblík, Alois. "K. Vrchlického Překladu Shakespearových Sonetů" (On Vrchlický's Translation of Shakespeare's *Sonnets*). *Časopis pro Moderní Filologii* (Prague), XXXVIII, Nos. 2-3 (1956), 157-166.

(b) INDIVIDUAL TRANSLATORS
i. Saudek and Stříbrný

B1127   *Othello.* Tr. by E. A. Saudek. Prague: Orbis, 1953. Pp. 235.

B1128   *Večer Tříkrálovy Nebo Cokoli Chcete.* Tr. by E. A. Saudek. Prague: Orbis, 1954. Pp. 196.

B1129   *Romeo a Julie.* Tr. by Erik Adolf Saudek. Prague: Orbis, 1955. Pp. 199.

B1130   *Benatský Kupec (Merch.).* Tr. by Erik Adolf Saudek. Prague: Orbis, 1955. Pp. 189.

B1131   *Král Lear.* Tr. by E. A. Saudek. Introd. and Commentary by Zdeněk Stříbrný. Prague: Státní Nakladatelství Krásné Literatury, 1958. Pp. 199.

B1132   *William Shakespeare—Spisy I* (Selected Works, I). Ed. and Tr. by Erik A. Saudek and Zdeněk Stříbrný. Prague: Naše Vojsko, 1956. Pp. 601.
This first volume comprises six comedies: *Shrew, Dream, Merch., A.Y.L., Twel.,* and *Wives* in new Czech tr. Each play has a preface and commentary (150 pp. of annotations in all). This volume is introduced by a general article on Shak. and his times by Jaroslav Pokorný. Illustrations by John Gilbert.

B1133   *W. Shakespeare—Tragedie I.* Tr. by Erik A. Saudek and ed. by Zdeněk Stříbrný. (*Works,* No. 4). Prague: Státní Nakladatelství Krásné Literatury, 1958. Pp. 701. *Romeo, Caesar, Ham., Oth., Macb.,* with prefaces and commentaries.

ii. Others

B1134   *Mnoho Povyky pro Nic.* Tr. by Frank Tetauer. Prague: Orbis, 1953. Pp. 130.

B1135   *Sonety.* Tr. by Ján Vladislav. 2. vyd. Prague: SNKLHU, 1955. Pp. 179.

B1136   *Sonety.* Tr. by Jaroslav Vrchlický. Red. Karel Jansky. Prague: Čs. Spis, 1954. Pp. 166.

B1137   *Kupec z Venedyku nebo Láska a Přátelství. Makbet, Vůdce Skotského Wogska. Rokokové Povídky ze Shakespeara.* Prague: Čs. Divadelni a lit. Jednatelstvi, 1954. Pp. 144.

(6) SLOVAKIAN

B1138   Kramoris, I. J. "Shakespeare in Slovakia." *Books Abroad,* XXIII (1949), 34.

B1139   Simko, Ján. "Shakespeare in Slovakia." *ShS,* IV (1951), 109-116.
A historical survey, and a discussion of two modern productions: *A.Y.L.* and *Shrew.*

B1140   Babler, O. F. "Shakespeare's *Midsummer Night's Dream* in Czech and Slovakian." *N &Q,* NS, IV (1957), 151-153.
Surveys the translations of *Dream* by Frantisek Doucha, Josef V. Sládek, Bohumil Stepánek, Erik A. Saudek, and Jirí Valja into Czech, and that of Pavel Országh Hviezdoslav into Slovakian.

B1141   Bejblík, Alois. "Hviezdoslavův Překlad Hamleta" (Hviezdoslav's translation of *Hamlet*). *Slovenská Literatura* (Bratislava), IV (1957).

B1142   Ormis, Ján V. "Ďalšie Údaje o Michalovi Bosom, Našom Prvom Prekladatelóvi Shakespeara." *Slovenské Divadlo* (Bratislava), VI (1958), 431-434.
New findings about the first Slovak translator of Shak., Michal Bosý—pseudonym: Bohuslav Křižák (d. 1847).

B1143   Ormis, Ján V. "Do Tretice Michal Bosý." *Slovenské Divadlo* (Bratislava), VI (1958), 549-550.

(7) MACEDONIAN

B1144   *Kako Što Miluvate (As You Like It).* Tr. into Macedonian by V. Iljoski and I. Milčin. Skopje: Državno Knjigoizd. na Makedonija, 1949. Pp. 226. Printed in Cyrillic.

B1145   *Starinska Pesna. Ljubovno Priznarie* (Two passages from *Twelfth Night*). Tr. by Blaže Koneski. *Kulturen Život* (Skopje), III, No. 5 (1951), 1-2.

B1146   *Otelo.* Tr. by Blaže Koneski. Skopje: "Kočo Racìn," 1953. Pp. 256. Printed in Cyrillic.

(8) BULGARIAN
(a) OGNJANOV-RIZOR

B1147   *Ukrotjavane na Opurničavata.* Tr. by Ljubomir Ognjanov-Rizor. Sofia: Durž. Izd. Nar. Prosveta, 1947. Pp. 122.

B1148   *Komedija ot Greški.* Tr. by Ljubomir Ognjanov-Rizor. Sofia: Durž. Izd. Nar. Prosveta, 1948. Pp. 102.

B1149   *Dvamata Veronci.* Tr. by Ljubomir Ognjanov-Rizor. Sofia: Durž. Izd. Nar. Prosveta, 1948. Pp. 90.

B1150   *Burja.* Tr. by Ljubomir Ognjanov-Rizor. Sofia: Durž. Izd. Nar. Prosveta, 1948. Pp. 103.

B1151   *Zimna Prikazka.* Tr. by Ljubomir Ognjanov-Rizor. Sofia: Durž. Izd. Nar. Prosveta, 1948. Pp. 133.

B1152   *Romeo i Džuleta.* Tr. by Ljubomir Ognjanov-Rizor. Sofia: Nar. Kultura, 1951. Pp. 156. 2nd ed. Sofia: Nar. Kultura, 1955. Pp. 184.

B1153   *Otelo.* Tr. by Ljubomir Ognjanov-Rizor. Sofia: Nar. Kultura, 1952. Pp. 186. 2nd ed. Sofia: Nar. Kultura, 1955. Pp. 216.

B1154   *Makbet.* Tr. by Ljubomir Ognjanov-Rizor. Sofia: Nar. Kultura, 1954. Pp. 158.
B1155   *Hamlet.* Tr. by Ljubomir Ognjanov-Rizor. Sofia: Nar. Kultura, 1955. Pp. 230.

(b) OTHERS

B1156   *Chamlet.* Tr. by K. Kiulavkov. Kiev, 1936. Pp. 134.
B1157   *Chamlet Princ Datski.* Tr. by Geo Milev. 3. Sofia: Chemus, 1947. Pp. 256.
B1158   *Soneti.* Tr. by Vladimir Svintila. Sofia: Balg Pisatel, 1956. Pp. 172.
B1159   *Chamlet Datski Princ.* Tr. by G. Zečev. Bibl. Svetovni Pisateli, 13. Sofia: Nar. Peč., 1949.
        Pp. 136.

e. OTHER INDO-EUROPEAN
(1) GREEK AND LATIN
(a) PROBLEMS AND TRANSLATIONS

B1160   "Shakespeare in Greek and Latin." *N &Q,* 175 (1938), 389-390, 409, 464. Letters by Deme-
        trius Caclamanos, C. Kessary, William Jaggard, Paul Morgan, L. Graham H. Horton-Smith.
        A list of Shak.'s works tr. into classical or modern Greek, pp. 389-390, 409, 464. A few in
        Latin, pp. 390 and 409.
B1161   Fisher, H. K. "*Hamlet.*" *Life and Letters,* XXII (1939), 268-271.

(b) INDIVIDUAL TRANSLATORS
i. Greek
aa. Carthaios

B1162   *Ioulios Kaissaras.* Tr. by Cl. Carthaios. Athens: Icaros, 1953. Pp. 147.
B1163   *I Eftyhmes Kyratses tou Windsor (Wives).* Tr. by Cleandros Carthaios. Athens: Icaros, 1955.
        Pp. 132.
B1164   *I Striglia pou Eghine Arnaki (Shrew).* Tr. by Cleandros Carthaios. Athens: Icaros, 1955.
        Pp. 152.

bb. Rotas

B1165   *Troilos kai Krusida.* Tr. by B. Rotas. Athens: Icaros, 1952.
B1166   *Hamlet, to Vassilopoulo tis Danias.* Tr. by B. Rotas. Athens: Icaros, 1953. Pp. 163.
B1167   *Metro Idhio Metro.* Tr. by Basil Rotas. Athens: Icaros, 1956. Pp. 96.

cc. Others

B1168   *Romaios kai Ioulieta.* Tr. by P. Arghyros. Athens: Daremas, 1955. Pp. 158.
B1169   *O Emberos tis Venetias* (Merch.). Tr. by Alexander Pallas. Athens: Icaros, 1955. Pp. 101.

ii. Latin

B1170   Abel, D. H. "De Caesare Panegyricus Marci Antoni." *Classical Journal,* LIII (1958), 262.
B1171   Sidebothan, H. "Latin Translation of *Sonnet 18.*" *London Mercury,* XXXV (1937), 454.

(2) ALBANIAN

B1172   *Hamleti, Princ i Danemarkes.* Tr. by Fran S. Noli. Priština: Mustafa Bakija, 1952. Pp. xii,
        182.
B1173   *Jul Qešari (Julius Caesar).* Tr. into Albanian by Fran S. Noli. Priština, 1953. Pp. 140.

(3) GAELIC

B1174   *Coriolanus le Shakespeare.* An t-ollamh Liam O'Briaian do Chuir gaedhilg Baile Átha Cliath,
        Oifig an t Soláthain, [1945]. Pp. 161. "An Chéad Chló, 1945."

(4) INDIAN
(including non-Indo-European Languages of southern India)
(a) PROBLEMS AND TRANSLATIONS

B1175   Shah, C. R. "Shakespeare's Plays in Indian Languages." *The Aryan Path* (Bombay), XXVI
        (1955), 483-488, 541-544.

(b) INDIVIDUAL TRANSLATORS

B1176   *Vikar Vilasita Athava Shakespeare Krita Hamlet Natachen Bhasantar.* Tr. into Marathi by
        Gopal Ganesh Agarkar. 4. ed. Poona: Venus Psakashan, 1954. Pp. lxii, 147.
B1177   *Hamlet.* Tr. into Kannada by Y. N. Shanmukiah. Publisher unknown.
        Rev: by V. S., *Deccan Herald,* Supplement (Bangalore), Feb. 6, 1955.
B1178   *Othello.* Tr. into Malayalam by M. R. Nair. Kozhikode, Travancore-Cochin State: Mat-
        rubhumi Printing and Publishing Co., No. 14, 1952.

B1179   *Julius Caesar*. Tr. into Tamil. Madras: Kalai Manram, 1954. Pp. 128.
B1180   *Hamlet*. Tr. into Tamil by G. Manisekharan. Madras: Kalai Manram, 1955. Pp. 158.
B1181   *Hamlet* [film in Hindustani language, produced by K. Sahu].
        Rev: B3461.

(5) ESPERANTO

B1182   *Trojlo kaj Kresida*. Tr. by Stephen A. Andrew. Rickmansworth, Herts: Esperanto Publ.,
        1952. Pp. 94.

f. NON-INDO-EUROPEAN
(1) HEBREW

B1183   Goldberg, M. J. "List of Hebrew Translations of Shakespeare in the Library of Congress."
        Chavrutha, Feb. 27, 1945, pp. 26-28.
B1184   *Ha-Melekh Richard ha-Shelishi*. Tr. into Hebrew by Rafael Eliaz. Merhavya: Sifriyat Poalim,
        1955. Pp. 200.
B1185   *King Lear*. Tr. into Hebrew by Abraham Shlonsky. Merhavya, 1954-1955. Pp. 171.

(2) YIDDISH

B1186   *Die Soneten*. Tr. by A. Asen. New York: Bellemir Press, 1944. Pp. 176.
B1187   *Sonnets*. Tr. into Yiddish by B. Lapin. New York: Bloch, 1954. Pp. 96.
        Parallel text edition.

(3) HUNGARIAN
(a) PROBLEMS AND TRANSLATIONS

B1188   Mark, Thomas R. "The First Hungarian Translation of Shakespeare." *SQ*, IX (1958), 471-478.
        An account of the great national, linguistic, and theatrical significance of Francis Kazinczy's
        prose translation of *Ham*. (1790).
B1189   Lutter, Tibor. "The New Hungarian Edition of Shakespeare's Plays and the Hungarian
        Tradition." *ZAA*, IV, Heft 2 (1956), 191-200.
        On B1191.

(b) TRANSLATORS

B1190   *Összes Drámái Művei*. (Works) 4 Vols. Budapest: Franklin-Tarsulat Kiadasa, 1948.
B1191   *Shakespeare Összes Drámái*. Uj Magyar Könyvkiadó. Budapest, 1955. Four vols.
        Rev: by Tibor Lutter, "The New Hungarian Edition of Shak.'s Plays and the Hungarian
        Tradition," *ZAA*, IV:2 (1956), 191-200; by M. Benedek, *Irodalmi Ujság* (Budapest), Jan. 14,
        1956, p. 5.
B1192   *The Tempest* (*Kétnyelvű Klasszikusok*). With a Hungarian version by Mihály Babits. Budapest:
        Corvina, 1957. Pp. 207.
        Rev: by Nati Krivatsy, *SQ*, IX (1958), 416.
B1193   *Lear Király*. Tr. by Milán Füst. Budapest: Uj Magyar Kiadó, 1955. Pp. 189.
B1194   *The Sonnets of Shakespeare—Shakespeare Szonettjei*. Bilingual ed. Tr. by Pál Justus. Budapest:
        Corvina Publishing Co., 1956. Pp. 344.
        Rev: by Andor Klay, *SQ*, IX (1958), 189-192.
B1195   *Romeo és Julia*. Tr. by Dezső Mészöly. Budapest: Magyar Kiadó, 1956. Pp. 132.
B1196   *Ahogy Tetszik*. Tr. by Lőrinc Szabó. Budapest: Művelt Nép Könyvkiadó, 1954. Pp. 111.
B1197   *Szonettjei*. Tr. by Lőrinc Szabó. Budapest: Ifjusági Kiadó, 1956. Pp. 176.
B1198   *Richárd III*. Tr. by István Vas. Budapest: Magyar Kiadó, 1956. Pp. 162.
B1199   *Hamlet dán Királyfi; Szentivánéji álom: Lear Király*. Tr. by János Arany and Mihály Vörös-
        marty. Budapest: Magyar Kiadó, 1956. Pp. 385.

(4) FINNISH

B1200   *Kootut Draamat*. Tr. by Paavo Cajander. Helsinki: Söderström. 1. *Hamlet. Romeo ja Julia.
        Venetsian Kauppias. Kuningas Lear*, 1953. Pp. 505.
B1201   *Suuret Draamat*. Suomentanut Yrjö Jylhä. Helsinki: Otava. 1. *Romeo ja Julia. Kesäyön
        Unelma. Macbeth*, 1955. Pp. 387. 2. *Hamlet. Othello*, 1955. Pp. 319. 3. *Kuningas Lear.
        Venetsian Kauppias*, 1957. Pp. 274.
B1202   Cancelled.

(5) TURKISH
(a) PROBLEMS AND TRANSLATIONS

B1203   Burian, Orhan. "Tercümeci Gözüyle *Hamlet*." ("*Hamlet* from the Viewpoint of Translators").
        Devlet Tiyatrosu (Ankara), I, No. 5 (Oct. 1950), 3-6.

(b) TRANSLATORS
i. Burian

B1204 *Othello.* Tr. by Orhan Burian. Ankara: Maarif Matbaasi, 1943. Pp. 166.

B1205 *Beğendiğiniz Gibi (As You Like It).* Tr. by Orhan Burian. Ankara: Maarif Matbaasi, 1943. Pp. 134.

B1206 *Atinali Timon (Timon of Athens).* Tr. by Orhan Burian. Ankara: Maarif Matbaasi, 1944. Pp. 121.

B1207 *Hamlet.* Tr. by Orhan Burian. Ankara: Maarif Matbaasi, 1944. Pp. 179.

B1208 *Macbeth.* Tr. by Orhan Burian. Ankara: Millî Eğitim Basimevi, 1946. Pp. 102.

ii. Derin

B1209 *Firtina (The Tempest).* Tr. by Haldun Derin. Ankara: Maarif Matbaasi, 1944. Pp. 103.

B1210 *Windsor'un Sen Kadinlari (The Merry Wives of Windsor).* Tr. by Haldun Derin. Istanbul: Millî Eğitim Basimevi, 1945. Pp. 131.

iii. Givda

B1211 *Yanlisliklar Komediasi (The Comedy of Errors).* Tr. by Avni Givda. Ankara: Maarif Matbaasi, 1943. Pp. 94.

B1212 *Veronali Iki Centilmen (Two Gentlemen of Verona).* Tr. by Avni Givda. Ankara: Maarif Matbaasi, 1944. Pp. 106.

B1213 *Onikinci Gece (Twelfth Night).* Tr. by Avni Givda. Istanbul: Millî Eğitim Basimevi, 1946. Pp. 125.

iv. Sevin

B1214 *Julius Caesar.* Tr. by Nureddin Sevin. Istanbul: Maarif Matbaasi, 1942. Pp. 252.

B1215 *Venedik Taciri (The Merchant of Venice).* Tr. by Nureddin Sevin. Ankara: Maarif Matbaasi, 1943. Pp. xiv, 305.

B1216 *Bir Yaz Dönümü Gecesi Rüyasi (A Midsummer Night's Dream).* Tr. by Nureddin Sevin. Ankara: Maarif Matbaasi, 1944. Pp. 96.

B1217 *Hircin Kiz (The Taming of the Shrew).* Tr. by Nureddin Sevin. Istanbul: Millî Eğitim Basimevi, 1946. Pp. 127.

v. Others

B1218 *Henry VIII.* Tr. by Belkis Boyar. Istanbul: Millî Eğitim Basimevi, 1947. Pp. 136.

B1219 *Kuru Gürültü (Much Ado About Nothing).* Tr. by Hâmit Dereli. Ankara: Maarif Matbaasi, 1944. Pp. 136.

B1220 *Bir Yaz Gecesi Rüyasi.* (Dream). Tr. by Asena Dora. Istanbul: Necmettin Salman Kitap Yayma Odasi, 1956.

B1221 *Antonius ile Kleopatra (Antony and Cleopatra).* Tr. by Saffet Korkut. Ankara: Maarif Matbaasi, 1944. Pp. xvi, 161.

B1222 *Romeo and Juliet.* Tr. by Yusuf Mardin. Istanbul: Ibrahim Horoz Basimevi, 1945. Pp. 168.

B1223 *Richard III.* Tr. by Berna Moran. Istanbul: Millî Eğitim Basimevi, 1947. Pp. 172.

(6) INDONESIAN

B1224 *Hamlet di Indonesia.* Tr. by Trisno Sumardjo. Djakarta: Pembagunan, 1948.
  Rev: by Sitor Situmorang, *Indonesië* (The Hague), IV (1950/51), 565-568.

B1225 *Manasuka (As You Like It).* Djakarta: Balai Pustaka, 1952. Pp. 144.

B1226 *Impian Ditengah Musim (Dream).* Tr. by Trisno Sumardjo. Djakarta: Balai Pustaka, 1954. Pp. 116.

B1227 Cancelled.

B1228 *Macbeth.* Tr. by Trisno Sumardjo. Djakarta: Pembagunan, 1952. Pp. 128.

B1229 *Praha (Tempest).* Tr. by Trisno Sumardjo. Djakarta: Balai Pustaka, 1952. Pp. 132.

(7) JAPANESE
(a) PROBLEMS AND TRANSLATIONS

B1230 Thaler, Alwin. "Shakspere in Japan." *SAB*, XIV (1939), 192.
  Concerning Yuzo Tsubouchi's translation of Shak.

B1231 Toyoda, Minoru. *Shakespeare in Japan: An Historical Survey.* Tokyo: The Iwanami Shoten, 1940. Pp. xi, 139 (in English).
  "Direct Translation," pp. 32-50.

B1232 Ozu, Jiro. "Hamlet no Honyaku" (Japanese Versions of *Hamlet*). *Bungaku* (Tokyo), XXIV, No. 5 (1956), 569-578.

(b) TRANSLATORS
i. Fukuda

B1233 *Zenshû.* Tr. by Tsuneari Fukuda. Tokyo: Kawade Shobô. 1. *Hamlet*, 1955. Pp. 179.
4. *Macbeth*, 1955. Pp. 141. 5. *Jajauma Narashi* (*Shrew*), 1955. Pp. 164.

B1234 *Richard Sansei* (*Richard III*). Tr. by Tsuneari Fukuda. Tokyo: Kawade Shobô, 1956. Pp. 218.
Vol. IX of the Complete Works in Japanese, using the New Shakespeare and Arden texts.
Awarded Kishida drama prize for 1956.

ii. Mikami

B1235 *Hamlet.* Tr. by Isao Mikami. Tokyo: Kawade Shobô, 1953. Pp. 268.
B1236 *Romeo and Juliet.* Tr. by Isao Mikami. Tokyo: Kawade Shobô, 1954. Pp. 198.
B1237 *Manatsu no yo no Yume* (*Dream*). Tr. by Isao Mikami. Tokyo: Kawade Shobô, 1954. Pp. 150.

iii. Sawamura

B1238 *As You Like It.* Tr. and annotated by T. Sawamura. Tokyo: Kenkyusha, [1950?]. Pp. front.,
iv, 236. English and Japanese parallel texts.

B1239 *Hamlet.* Tr. and annotated by T. Sawamura. Tokyo: Kenkyusha, [1950?]. Pp. front., iv, 354.
English and Japanese parallel texts.

B1240 *Julius Caesar.* Tr. and annotated by T. Sawamura. Tokyo: Kenkyusha, [1950?]. Pp. front.,
ii, 225. English and Japanese parallel texts.

B1241 *Macbeth.* Tr. and annotated by T. Sawamura. Tokyo: Kenkyusha, [1950?]. Pp. front.,
ii, 217. English and Japanese parallel texts.

B1242 *The Merchant of Venice.* Tr. and annotated by T. Sawamura. Tokyo: Kenkyusha, [1950?].
Pp. front., iv, 232. English and Japanese parallel texts.

B1243 *Romeo and Juliet.* Tr. and annotated by T. Sawamura. Tokyo: Kenkyusha, [1950?]. Pp.
front., iv, ii, 274. English and Japanese parallel texts.

B1244 *The Tempest.* Tr. and annotated by T. Sawamura. Tokyo: Kenkyusha, [1950?]. Pp. front.,
vi, 178. English and Japanese parallel texts.

iv. Others

B1245 *Richard Sansei* (*Richard III*). Tr. by R. Fukuhara and S. Oyama. Tokyo: Kadogawa, 1956.
Pp. 234.

B1246 *Shakespeare in Japanese* (*Ham., Romeo, Oth., Macb.*). Tr. by Yoshio Nakano, Isao Mikami, and
Junji Kinoshita. Tokyo: Kawade Shobô, 1955. Pp. 364.
Vol. I of *Representative World Literature.*

B1247 *Hamlet. Manatsu no yo no Yume* (*Dream*). *Romeo to Juliet. Julius Caesar.* Tr. by Yoshio
Nakano; Isao Mikami. Tokyo: Kawade Shobô, 1953. Pp. 397.

B1248 *King Lear.* Annotated and tr. by Takeshi Saito. Tokyo: Kaibunsha, 1955. Pp. 452.

B1249 *Collected Works.* Tr. by Shôyô Tsubouchi. Tokyo: Sôgen-sha, 1952. Pp. vi, 1347.

B1250 *Shakespeare Shishu* (Shakespeare's Poems). Tr. by Kenichi Yoshida. Tokyo: Ikeda Shoten,
1956. Pp. 118.

(8) CHINESE

B1251 McCracken, Alan. "Bard in the East." ['All the world's a stage' re-translated from Chinese
ideographs.] NYTBR, Aug. 12, 1945, p. 23.

B1252 Chang Chen-Hsien. "Shakespeare in China." *ShS*, VI (1953), 112-116.
On the difficulties of translating Shak. into Chinese.

(9) MISCELLANEOUS ORIENTAL AND AFRICAN

B1253 *Romêwo-nnâ Žulyêt.* Tr. into Aethiopian by Kabbada Mikâ'êl. 2nd ed. Addis Ababa:
Artistic Press, 1955. Pp. 101.

B1254 *Othello.* Tr. into Malay by M. R. Nair. Calicut: Matribhumi Co., 1951. Pp. xiv, 152.

B1255 *Romeo and Juliet.* Tr. into Persian by G. Saman. London: Luzac, 1939. Pp. 291.

XIV. SHAKESPEARE AND THE MODERN STAGE (163;55)

1. STAGE HISTORY IN GENERAL

B1256 Shuttleworth, Bertram. "W. J. Lawrence: A Handlist." Part I. *TN*, VIII (1954), 52-54.
See B3988-B3990.

B1257   Gilder, Rosamond, and George Freedley. *Theatre Collections in Libraries and Museums*. London: Stevens & Brown, 1936. Pp. 182.
        Rev: A3333.

B1258   Ernst, Earle. *Cycles in the Development of the Dramatic Arts*. DD, Cornell University, 1940. Abstr. publ. in Cornell Univ. *Abstracts of Theses, 1940*, Ithaca, 1941.

B1259   Djivelegov, A. K., and G. B. Boyardjiev. *The History of the European Theatre from Its Origins to 1789*. Moscow, Lenigrad: Iskusstvo, 1941. Pp. 616.

B1260   Vardac, Alexander Nicholas. *From Garrick to Griffith: Transition from Stage to Screen*. DD, Yale University, 1942.

B1261   Vardac, Alexander Nicholas. *Stage to Screen: Theatrical Method from Garrick to Griffith*. Cambridge, Mass.: Harvard Univ. Press; London: Oxford Univ. Press, 1949. Pp. xxvi, 283.
        Rev: by Bosley Crowther, *NYTBR*, Nov. 20, 1949, p. 44.

B1262   Brook, D. *The Romance of the English Theatre*. London, 1945. Pp. 208.

B1263   Gerold, A. W. *The Organization of Representative Acting Companies Since Elizabethan Times*. DD, Columbia University, 1948. Pp. 78.

B1264   Nagler, A. M. *Sources of Theatrical History*. New York: Theatre Annual, 1952. Pp. xxiii, 611.
        Rev: A7076.

B1265   Altman, George, Ralph Freud, Kenneth MacGowan, William Melnitz. *Theater Pictorial*. Berkeley and Los Angeles: Univ. of California Press, 1953.

B1266   Mander, Raymond, and Joe Mitchenson. *The Artist and the Theatre*. The Story of the Paintings collected and presented to the National Theatre of W. Somerset Maugham. With an Introd. by W. Somerset Maugham. London: Heineman, 1955. Pp. xxii, 280.
        Collection of theatrical pictures, identified as to play and player.
        Rev: *TLS*, May 6, 1955, p. 232.

a. SURVEYS OF PRODUCTIONS AND PRINCIPLES (167;56)
(1) GENERAL

B1267   Lawrence, W. J. *Speeding Up Shakespeare*. Studies of the Bygone Theatre and Drama. London: Argonaut Press, 1937. Pp. 220.
        Rev: A7402.

B1268   Huang, John. *A Short History of Shakespearean Production*. M. Litt. thesis, Cambridge. *Cam Abs. 1937-38*, p. 84.

B1269   Ormsbee, H. *Backstage with Actors. From the Time of Shakespeare to the Present Day*. New York: T. Y. Crowell Co., 1938. Pp. 344.

B1270   Ball, Robert Hamilton. *The Amazing Career of Sir Giles Overreach*. Princeton Univ. Press, 1939. Pp. ix, 467.
        Rev: *TAr*, XXIII (1939), 681; *AHR*, XLV, 681; by D. M. Walmsley, *RES*, XVI, 216-219.

B1271   Downer, Alan S. "Mr. Dangle's Defense: Acting and Stage History." *EIE, 1946*. Columbia Univ. Press, 1947, pp. 159-190.

B1272   Purdom, C. B. *Producing Shakespeare*. London: Pitman, 1950. Pp. xii, 220.
        Rev: B1729.

B1273   Marshall, Norman. *The Producer and the Play*. London: Macdonald, 1957. Pp. 304.
        Rev: B1751.

B1274   Edwards, Charlene Frances. *The Tradition for Breeches in the Three Centuries that Professional Actresses Have Played Male Roles on the English-Speaking Stage*. DD, University of Denver, 1957.

B1275   Mander, Raymond, and Joe Mitchenson. *A Picture History of the British Theatre*. London: Hulton Press, 1957. Pp. 160.
        Rev: *TLS*, Nov. 8, 1957, p. 679; *Theatre World*, Dec., p. 49; *ShN*, VIII (1958), 3; *N &Q*, NS, V, 129-130; by Stanley Richards, *Players Magazine*, XXXIV, 114; by Robertson Davies, *Saturday Night* (Canada), Jan. 8, pp. 22-24; by Phyllis Hartnoll, *TN*, XII, 75-76.

(2) ACTORS

B1276   Arthur, G. *From Phelps to Gielgud*. London, 1936. Pp. 256.

B1277   Cole, Toby, and Helen Krich Chinoy, eds. *Actors on Acting: The Theories, Techniques, and Practices of the Great Actors of All Times as Told in Their Own Words*. Edited with Introd. and Biographical Notes. New York: Crown, 1949; London: Pitman; Toronto: Ambassador, 1952. Pp. xiv, 596.
        Rev: by H. Darkes Albright, *QJS*, XXXVI, 266.

B1278   Darlington, William Aubrey. *The Actor and His Audience*. London: Phoenix House, 1949. Pp. 188.
        Rev: A7369.

B1279   Brook, Donald. *A Pageant of English Actors*. New York: Macmillan; London: Rockliff, 1950. Pp. viii, 9-286, pl. 15.
        Fifteen biographies from Burbage to Olivier.

B1280   Carlisle, Carol J. *Contributions of the English Actors to Shakespearean Criticism to 1902*. DD,

University of North Carolina, 1951. Abstr. publ. in *Univ. of North Carolina Record, Research in Progress, Jan.-Dec., 1951.* Grad. School Series, No. 62, 1952, pp. 110-111.

B1281 Drews, Wolfgang. *Die Grossen Zauberer.* Bildnisse Deutscher Schauspieler aus 2 Jahrhunderten. Vienna, Munich: Donau-Verlag, 1953. Pp. 360.
Rev: by Wolfgang Stroedel, *SJ,* 91 (1955), 366-367.

B1282 Sprague, Arthur Colby. *Shakespearian Players and Performances.* Cambridge: Harvard Univ. Press, 1953; London: Black, 1954. Pp. viii, 222.
Rev: by Marchette Chute, *NYTBR,* May 24, 1953, p. 6; by G. B. Harrison, *SatR,* Oct. 10, pp. 20, 38; by Sybil Rosenfeld, *SQ,* IV, 469-470; *Nation,* May 9, p. 400; by E. J. West, *QJS,* XXXIX, 372; *TLS,* March 19, 1954, p. 180; *VQR,* No. 30, pp. xvi-xvii; by H. C. Kiefer, *Arizona Quarterly,* IX, 366-368; by George Devine, *TN,* VIII, 22; by J. Vallette, *MdF,* 321 (1954), 730-731; by A. R. B., *Dalhousie Rev.,* XXXIII (1953/54), No. 3, xxxii-iii; by C. G. Thayer, *Books Abroad,* XXVIII, 227; by M. Poirier, *EA,* VIII (1955), 68; by J. S. Baxter, *QQ,* LXII, 274-276; by Frederick T. Wood, *ES,* XXXVIII (1957), 78-79.

B1283 Rylands, George. "The Poet and the Player." *ShS,* VII (1954), 25-34.

B1284 Findlater, Richard. *Six Great Actors.* London: Hamish Hamilton, 1956. Illustrated with portraits. Garrick, Kemble, Kean, Macready, Irving, and Forbes-Robertson.

B1285 Lewes, George Henry. *On Actors and the Art of Acting.* New York: Grove, 1957. Pp. 237. (Paper.)
Rev: by Nadine Miles, *ETJ,* X (1958), 82-84; by Donald FitzJohn, *Drama,* Summer, 1958, pp. 44-45.

(3) PRODUCTIONS OF PARTICULAR PLAYS OR CHARACTERS
(a) HAMLET

B1286 Gilder, Rosamund. "Hamlet." *TAr,* XX (1936), 975-982.

B1287 Lambda, Beta. "Hamlet Miscellany." *Shakespeare Quarterly,* I (Summer, 1947), 50-75.

B1288 Shoemaker, Lisle N. *The Whole History of Hamlet.* DD, Western Reserve University, 1950. Abstr. publ. in Western Reserve Univ. *Bibliography of Published Research, 1948-50,* (?1953), pp. 140-142.

B1289 Horn-Monval, Madeleine. "Quelques Interprètes de Hamlet." *RHT,* II (1950), 137-150.

B1290 "The First Woman 'Hamlet'." *N&Q,* 197 (1952), 193-194.
Further comment by R., ibid., p. 393; by R. Mander and J. Mitchenson, ibid., p. 459; by A. Sparke and T. O. Mabbott, ibid., 198 (1953), 89.

B1291 Aylward, J. D. "Woman 'Hamlets'." *N&Q,* 199 (1954), 179.

B1292 Babler, O. F. "Women 'Hamlets'." *N&Q,* 199, (1954), 86.

B1293 Mander, R., and J. Mitchenson. *Hamlet Through the Ages: A Pictorial Record from 1709.* London: Rockliff, 1952; New York: Macmillan, 1953. Pp. xvi, 156, pl. 257. Second ed., London: Rockliff, 1955; New York: Macmillan, 1957. Pp. xvii, 158, pl. 255. Arranged by Act and Scene.
Rev: *TLS,* Nov. 14, 1952, p. 751; by R. M. Moudouès, *RHT,* IV, 392-393; by L. Irving, *Spectator,* No. 6491 (1952), 694-695; by A. C. Sprague, *TN,* VII (1952/53), 34-35; by M. St. C. Byrne, *English,* IX (1953), 184; *N&Q,* 198 (1953), 92; *NstN,* XLV, 74-75; by Brooks Atkinson, *NYTBR,* Feb. 8, 1953, p. 7; by Robert Hamilton Ball, *SQ,* V (1954), 335-336; by Hermann Heuer, *SJ,* 90 (1954), 322-323; by Jørgen Budtz-Jørgensen, *Nationaltidende* (Copenhagen), June 12, 1954.

(b) SHYLOCK

B1294 Smallwood, O. *The Stage-History of "Merchant of Venice."* DD, University of Oklahoma, 1939. Abstr. publ. in *Univ. of Oklahoma Bulletin,* Jan. 1939. Pp. 117.

B1295 "Shylocks of Bygone Days." *Shakespeare Quarterly* (London), I (Summer, 1947), 18-21.
Notes on performances from 1618 or earlier to 1894. Burbage, Macklin, Fleck, Iffland, Kean, Devrient, Döring, Irving, Mitterwurzer and Reicher in the role.

B1296 Lelyveld, Toby Bookholtz. *Shylock on the Stage: Significant Changes in the Interpretation of Shakespeare's Jew.* DD, Columbia University, 1951. Pp. 196. Mic A51-284. *Mcf Ab,* XI (1951), 772-774. Publ. No. 2541.

B1297 MacCarthy, Desmond. "Shylocks Past and Present." In MacCarthy's *Humanities.* London: Macgibbon & Kee, 1953, pp. 49-53.

(c) OTHERS

B1298 Derrick, Leland Eugene. *The Stage History of "King Lear."* DD, University of Texas, 1940.

B1299 Troubridge, St. Vincent. "Helena in *All's Well That Ends Well.*" *N&Q,* 181 (1941), 109-110; A. R. Bayley and Wm. Jaggard, ibid., p. 122.

b. PROMPT BOOKS

B1300 Clark, William S. "Restoration Prompt Notes and Stage Practices." *MLN,* LI (1936), 226-230.

B1301   Casson, F. F. "Notes on a Shakespearean First Folio in Padua." *MLN*, LI (1936), 417-423.

B1302   McManaway, J. G. "The Two Earliest Prompt Books of *Hamlet*." *Papers of the Bibliographical Society of America*, XLIII (1949), 288-320.
Describes two prompt books (annotated copies of Q1676 and Q1683) prepared and used by John Ward c. 1740.

B1303   McManaway, James G. "Additional Prompt-Books of Shakespeare from the Smock Alley Theatre." *MLR*, XLV (1950), 64-65.

B1304   Sprague, Arthur Colby. "Falstaff Hackett." *TN*, IX (1955), 61-67.
Hackett's heavily annotated prompt books throw new light on his interpretation of Falstaff.

B1305   Beck, Martha Ryan. *A Comparative Study of Prompt Copies of "Hamlet" used by Garrick, Booth, and Irving*. DD, University of Michigan, 1956. Pp. 729. Mic 57-2269. *DA*, XVII (1957), 1412. Publ. No. 21,144.

B1306   Cancelled.

B1307   Carson, William B. "*As You Like It* and the Stars: Nineteenth Century Prompt Books." *QJS*, XLIII (1957), 117-127.

c. COSTUME

B1308   Linthicum, M. Channing. *Costume in the Drama of Shakespeare and His Contemporaries*. Oxford: Clarendon Press, 1936. Pp. xii, 307; pl.
Rev: A7268.

B1309   Perrigard, Elma E. *The Development of Properties in Drama on the English-Speaking Stage*. MA thesis, McGill, 1936.

B1310   Kelly, Francis Michael. *Shakespearian Costume for Stage and Screen*. London: Black, 1938. Pp. x, 132.
Rev: *TLS*, March 26, 1938, p. 209.

B1311   Sprague, Arthur Colby. *Shakespeare and the Actors. The Stage Business in His Plays (1660-1905)*. Harvard Univ. Press, 1944. Pp. xxvi, 440; il.
Rev: A7455.

B1312   Sprague, Arthur Colby. *The Stage Business in Shakespeare's Plays: A Postscript*. London: Society for Theatre Research Pamphlet Series, No. 3, 1953. Pp. 35.
Rev: A7457.

B1313   Hotson, Leslie. *Shakespeare's Motley*. London: Rupert Hart-Davis, 1952. Pp. 133.
Rev: A6671.

B1314   Watters, Don Albert. *The Pictorial in English Theatrical Staging, 1773-1833*. DD, Ohio State University, 1954. Pp. 388. Mic 55-204. *DA*, XV (1955), 1278. Publ. No. 12,252.

B1315   Russell, D. A. "Hamlet Costumes from Garrick to Gielgud." *ShS*, IX (1956), 54-58.

B1316   Mander, Raymond, and Joe Mitchenson. "Hamlet Costumes: A Correction." *ShS*, XI (1958), 123-124.

B1317   Merchant, W. M. "Classical Costumes in Shakespearian Productions." *ShS*, X (1957), 71-76.

2. SHAKESPEARE AND THE STAGE, 1660-1880.
a. ENGLAND
(1) SEVERAL PERIODS

B1318   Speaight, George. *The History of the English Puppet Theatre*. New York: John de Graff, 1956. Pp. 350.
Rev: by James G. McManaway, *SQ*, VIII (1957), 243-244.

B1319   Foster, George Harding. *British History on the London Stage, 1660-1760*. DD, University of North Carolina, 1941. Abstr. publ. in *Univ. of North Carolina Record, Research in Progress, 1940-41*, Chapel Hill, 1941, pp. 65-67.

B1320   Smith, Dane Farnsworth. *Plays About the Theatre in England from 1671 to 1737*. London and New York: Oxford Univ. Press, 1936. Pp. xxii, 287.

B1321   Rosenfeld, Sybil. "The Players in Cambridge, 1662-1800." *Studies in English Theatre History in Memory of Gabrielle Enthoven*. Ed. M. St. Clare Byrne. London: Society for Theatre Research, 1952, pp. 24-37.

B1322   Rulfs, Donald J. "Reception of the Elizabethan Playwrights on the London Stage." *SP*, XLVI (1949), 54-69.

B1323   Stockwell, La Tourette. *The Dublin Theatre, 1637-1820*. DD, Radcliffe College, 1936.

B1324   Stockwell, La Tourette. *Dublin Theatres and Theatre Customs (1637-1820)*. Kingston, Tennessee: Kingston Press, 1938. Pp. xvii, 406.

B1325   Troubridge, Sir St. Vincent. "Theatre Riots in London [and elsewhere]." *Studies in English Theatre History in Memory of Gabrielle Enthoven*. Ed. M. St. Clare Byrne. London: Society for Theatre Research, 1952, pp. 84-97.

B1326   Trewin, J. C. *The Night Has Been Unruly*. London: Hale, 1957. Pp. 288.
Famous stories from the by-ways of theatre history, from Garrick's 1769 Shakespeare Jubilee to Olivier's 1955 *Titus*.

Rev: by George Speaight, *Drama*, Summer, 1957, pp. 42-43; by Frank Granville-Barker, *Plays and Players*, Sept., p. 17; by Guy Boas, *English*, XI, 237; *TLS*, May 10, p. 284.

B1327   Kemp, T. C. "Acting Shakespeare: Modern Tendencies in Playing and Production with Special Reference to Some Recent Productions." *ShS*, VII (1954), 121-127.

B1328   Stamm, Rudolf. *Shakespeare's Word-Scenery*. With Some Remarks on Stage-History and the Interpretation of His Plays. Veröffentlichungen der Handels-Hochschule St. Gallen, Reihe B, Heft 10. Zurich and St. Gallen: Polygraphischer Verlag, 1954. Pp. 34.
Rev: A5603.

(2)   RESTORATION

B1329   Avery, E. L. "A Tentative Calendar of Theatrical Performances, 1660-1700." *Research Studies of the State College of Washington*, XIII (1945), 225-283.

(a)   THEATERS AND AUDIENCES

B1330   Wells, Staring B. *A Comparison Between the Two Stages*. DD, Princeton University, 1935. Revised version publ. by Princeton Univ. Press, 1942. Pp. xxi, 206.
A reprint of Gildon's book of 1702, with copious notes. "The 2 Stages" means King's and Duke's playhouses.

B1331   Scanlan, Elizabeth G. *Tennis-Court Theatres and the Duke's Playhouse, 1661-1671*. DD, Columbia University, 1952.

B1332   Williams, S. H. *The Lord Mayor's Shows from Peele to Settle: A Study of Literary Content, Organization, and Methods of Production*. DD, London, Queen Mary College, 1957.

B1333   Thomas, Carl A. *The Restoration Theater Audience—A Critical and Historical Evaluation of the London Playgoers of the Late Seventeenth Century, 1660-1700*. DD, University of Southern California, 1952.

B1334   Zitner, Sheldon P. *The English Theatre Audience, 1660-1700*. DD, Duke University, 1955.

B1335   Howell, Elmo H. *The Role of the Critic in the Restoration and Early Eighteenth Century*. DD, University of Florida, Gainesville, 1955.

(b)   STAGING

B1336   Langhans, Edward A. *Staging Practices in the Restoration Theatres, 1660-1682*. DD, Yale University, 1955.

B1337   Nicoll, A. "Scenery Between Shakespeare and Dryden." *TLS*, 1936, p. 658.

B1338   Falls, Gregory Alexander. *An Analytical and Historical Investigation of the Staging of Restoration Comedy as Related to Modern Revivals*. DD, Northwestern University, 1953. Pp. 273. Mic A54-591. *DA*, XIV (1954), 417. Publ. No. 7029.

B1339   Martin, Lee Jackson. *Action Within the Scene on the English Restoration Stage*. DD, Stanford University, 1956. Pp. 249. Mic 56-3129. *DA*, XVI (1956), 1964. Publ. No. 17,729.

B1340   MacGachen, Freda Kathleen. *The History and Development of Scenery on the English Stage from Mediaeval Times to the Year 1700*. MA thesis, McGill, 1931.

B1341   Fulford, G. L. *The History and the Development of Scenery, Costumes and Lighting of the English Stage from Mediaeval Times to the Year 1700*. MA thesis, McGill, 1940.

B1342   Biggins, D. B. O. *The Continuity in English Stage and Dramatic Tradition Between the Restoration and the Earlier Seventeenth Century*. MA thesis, University of Southampton, 1953-54.

(c)   ACTORS AND ACTRESSES

B1343   Johannes, Irmgard. "Des Königs Schauspieler. Rings um Drury Lane." *Athena*, I, No. 10 (1947), 52-57.

B1344   Van Lennep, William. "Richard the Third." *TLS*, April 30, 1938, p. 296. See also Montague Summers, ibid., May 7, p. 316; also W. Van Lennep, ibid., June 18, p. 418.

B1345   Seely, Frederick Franklin. *Thomas Betterton, Dramatist*. DD, State University of Iowa, 1942

B1346   Armstrong, William A. "The Acting of Thomas Betterton." *English*, X (1954), 55-57.

B1347   Van Lennep, William. "Henry Harris, Actor, Friend of Pepys." *Studies in English Theatre History in Memory of Gabrielle Enthoven*. Ed. M. St. Clare Byrne. London: Society for Theatre. Research, 1952, pp. 9-23.

B1348   Wilson, John Harold. *All the King's Ladies—Actresses of the Restoration*. Univ. of Chicago Press, 1958. Pp. ix, 206.

(d)   VERSIONS PRODUCED

B1349   Eich, Louis M. *Alterations of Shakespeare, 1660-1710: And an Investigation of the Critical and Dramatic Principles and Theatrical Conventions Which Prompted These Revisions*. DD, University of Michigan, 1923. Pp. 211. Mic A48-50. *Mcf Ab*, VIII (1948), 90. Publ. No. 920.

B1350   Frohberg, Georg. *Das Fortleben des Elisabethanischen Dramas im Zeitalter der Restauration*. DD, Münster, 1925. Pp. 152. Typewritten.

B1351   Heil, Liselotte. *Die Darstellung der Englischen Tragödie zur Zeit Bettertons (1660-1710)*. Theater, Bühnenform, Inszenierungs- und Schauspielerstil. DD, Berlin, Humboldt Univ., 1936. Pp. vi, 131. Düsseldorf: Nolte, 1936. Pp. vi, 131.
        Rev: by H. Nicolai, *Beiblatt*, XLIX (1938), 73-75.

B1352   Bogorad, Samuel Nathaniel. *The English History Play in Restoration Drama*. DD, Northwestern University, 1946. Abstr. publ. in *Summaries of Doctoral Dissertations, 1946*, XIV. Chicago and Evanston: Northwestern Univ., 1947, pp. 5-10.

B1353   Ashin, Mark. *Restoration Adaptations of Jacobean and Caroline Comedy*. DD, University of Chicago, 1951.

B1354   Mitra, D. *Adaptations of the Plays of Molière for the English Stage, 1660-1700*. MA thesis, London, Bedford College, 1957.

B1355   McManaway, J. G. "Songs and Masques in *The Tempest*" [c. 1674]. *Theatre Miscellany. Six Pieces Connected with the Seventeenth-Century Stage*. Oxford, 1953.
        Rev: by Harold Jenkins, *RES*, NS, VI (1955), 86-88.

B1356   Haywood, Charles. "The Songs and Masque in the *New Tempest*: An Incident in the Battle of the Two Theatres, 1674." *HLQ*, XIX (1955), 39-56.
        Reports the discovery, in the Huntington Library, of this second English libretto, supporting the hypothesis of James G. McManaway, B1355.

B1357   Crundell, H. W. "*The Taming of the Shrew* on the Seventeenth-Century Stage." *N &Q*, 173 (1937), 207.

(e)   IRELAND (including the 18th century)

B1358   Bald, R. C. "Shakespeare on the Stage in Restoration Dublin." *PMLA*, LVI (1941), 369-378.

B1358a Spencer, Hazelton. "Shakespearean Cuts in Restoration Dublin." *PMLA*, LVII (1942), 575-576.

B1359   McManaway, J. G. "A Shakespeare Manuscript." *N &Q*, 189 (1945), 284; ibid., 193 (1948), 525.

B1360   Stevenson, A. H. "James Shirley and the Actors at the First Irish Theater." *MP*, XL (1942), 147-160.

B1361   Van Lennep, William. "The Smock Alley Players of Dublin." *ELH*, XIII (1946), 219-220.

B1362   Clark, William Smith. *The Early Irish Stage*. Oxford: Clarendon Press, 1955. Pp. 225.
        Rev: by A. J. L., *Dublin Mag.*, X, No. 2 (1955), 33-34; by F. S. Boas, *English*, X, 228-229.

B1363   Clark, William Smith. "The Siddons' in Dublin." *TN*, IX (July-Sept., 1955), 103-111.

B1364   Avery, Emmett L. "The Dublin Stage, 1736-1737." *N &Q*, II (1955), 61-65.

(f)   MISCELLANEOUS

B1365   Lawrence, W. J. *Old Theatre Days and Ways*. London: Harrap, 1935. Pp. 256; pl.
        Rev: *TLS*, Jan. 11, 1936, p. 27; by L. C. Knights, *London Mercury*, XXXIII (1936), 441-442.

B1366   Knights, L. C. *Drama and Society in the Age of Jonson*. London: Chatto & Windus, 1937. Pp. xii, 347.
        Rev: A8724.

B1367   Crundell, H. W. "Two Notes on *The Merry Wives*." *N &Q*, 173 (1937), 112-113.

B1368   Harbage, Alfred. *Sir William Davenant*. Univ. of Pennsylvania Press, 1935.
        Rev: A8878.

B1369   Nethercot, Arthur Hobart. *Sir William Davenant, Poet Laureate and Playwright-Manager*. Univ. of Chicago Press, 1938. Pp. 495.
        Rev: A8879.

B1370   Russell, Trusten W. *Voltaire, Dryden and Heroic Tragedy*. DD, Columbia University, 1946. New York: Columbia Univ. Press, 1946. Pp. 178.

B1371   Freedman, Morris. "*All for Love* and *Samson Agonistes*." *N &Q*, III (1956), 514-517.

B1372   Iacuzzi, Alfred. *The Naive Theme in "The Tempest"* as a Link Between Thomas Shadwell and Ramón de la Cruz. *MLN*, LII (1937), 252-256.

B1373   Mackenzie, Aline Freeman-Fayers. *Otway and the History of His Plays on the London Stage: A Study of Taste*. DD, Bryn Mawr, 1943.

B1374   Van Lennep, William. "Some Early English Playbills." *Harvard Library Bulletin*, VIII (1954), 235-241.

(3)   EIGHTEENTH CENTURY
(a)   PERFORMANCES (167;56)
i.   Lists of Performances

B1375   Hogan, C. B. "Shakespeare Performances." *TLS*, Oct. 13, 1945, p. 487.

B1376   Scouten, A. H., and Leo Hughes. "A Calendar of Performances of *1 Henry IV* and *2 Henry IV* during the First Half of the Eighteenth Century." *JEGP*, XLIII (1944), 23-41; XLIV (1945), 89-90.

B1377   Avery, Emmett L., and A. H. Scouten. "A Tentative Calendar of Daily Theatrical Performances in London 1700-1701 to 1704-1705." *PMLA*, LXIII (1948), 114-180.

B1378   Byrne, Muriel St. Clare. *A History of Shakespearian Production in England.* Part I: *1700-1800. Scenes and Characters in the Eighteenth Century, Made in Collaboration with the Arts Council of Great Britain.* London: Common Ground, Ltd., Sydney Place, S. W. 7, 1948.
Rev: by S. R. Littlewood, *English*, VII (1948/1949), 144-145; *TLS*, Jan. 24, 1948, p. 56.

B1379   Hogan, Charles Beecher. *Shakespeare in the Theatre 1701-1800.* Vol. I. *A Record of Performances in London 1701-1750.* Oxford: Clarendon Press, 1952. Pp. 517. Vol. II: *A Record of Performances in London 1751-1800.* Oxford: Clarendon Press, 1956. Pp. 720.
Rev: of Vol. I: by R. M. Moudouès, *RHT*, IV (1952), 392; by Ronald Watkins, *Time and Tide*, Aug. 23, p. 966; *TLS*, Sept. 26, p. 627; *Listener*, XLVIII, 779; by St. V. Troubridge, *TN*, VII (1952/53), 21-22; by J. Loftis, *PQ*, XXXII (1953), 245-246; by Hermann Heuer, *SJ*, 89 (1953), 216; by M. St. Clare Bryne, *RES*, IV, 379-380; by Allardyce Nicoll, *SQ*, IV, 189-190; of Vol. II: *Essential Books*, June 1956, p. 33; by Allardyce Nicoll, *TN*, XII (1957), 36-37; *ShN*, VII, 46; *TLS*, July 26, p. 458; by Hermann Heuer, *SJ*, 94 (1958), 296-297; by George Winchester Stone, Jr., *SQ*, IX, 402-403; *Players Magazine*, XXXIV, 125-126.

ii. Accounts of Performances

B1380   Kelly, J. A. *German Visitors to English Theatres in the Eighteenth Century.* Princeton Univ. Press, 1936. Pp. viii, 178.
Rev: A9439.

B1381   Ruppel, K. H. "*Hamlet*. [Von Garrick bis Gründgens]. Wandlungen einer Bühnengestalt." *Koralle* (Berlin), NS, IV (1936), 259.

B1382   Hampden, John. "Without the Prince of Denmark." *TLS*, May 27, 1939, p. 313.
See letter by Frederick Harker, *TLS*, May 27, 1939, p. 327.

B1383   Lowery, Margaret R. "Performances of Shaksperian Plays at Covent Garden and Drury Lane Theaters." *SAB*, XVI (1941), 102-103.

B1384   Scouten, Arthur H. "Shakespeare's Plays in the Theatrical Repertory when Garrick Came to London." *TxSE*, XXIV (1944), 257-268.

B1385   Wood, Frederick T. "Theatrical Performances at Bath in the Eighteenth Century, 1-7." *N &Q*, 192 (1947), 477-478; 486-490; 539-541; 552-558; 193 (1948), 38-40; 92-93; 253-255.

B1386   Lynch, James J. *Drama in the Theater During the Mid-Eighteenth Century, 1737-1777.* DD, University of California, Berkeley, 1948.
Chapter I, Section IV, "Shakespeare Dramas on the Stage," pp. 70-142.

B1387   Mann, Isabel Roome. "The First Recorded Production of a Shakespearean Play in Stratford-upon-Avon." *SAB*, XXIV (1949), 203-208.
Othello in 1746.

B1388   Rulfs, Donald J. "Reception of the Elizabethan Playwrights on the London Stage 1776-1833." *SP*, XLVI (1949), 54-69.

B1389   Speaight, George. "Eighteenth Century Performances of *Macbeth*." *TN*, V (1950/51), 72.

B1390   Yoklavich, J. "Hamlet in Shammy Shoes." *SQ*, III (1952), 209-218.

B1391   Lynch, James J. *Box, Pit and Gallery: Stage Society in Johnson's London.* Berkeley and Los Angeles: Univ. of California Press, 1953. Pp. ix, 362.
Rev: *TLS*, Feb. 19, 1954, p. 115; by Herman Schumlin, *TAr*, XXXVIII, No. 10; by John Randolph, *Chicago Sunday Tribune*, Jan. 3, p. 2; *N &Q*, 199, 457-458; *Books of the Month*, LXIX, No. 3, 7; by C. B. Woods, *PQ*, XXXIII, 250-251; by John Loftis, *MP*, LIII (1955), 66-67; by Emmett L. Avery, *MLN*, LXX, 62-64; by Charles Munro Gretchell, *Players Magazine*, Oct., pp. 23-24; by C. Price, *N.Mitt.*, LVII (1956), 160-161.

B1392   Heaton, J. P. *Shakespeare's Characters on the Stage, 1700-1840.* MA thesis, Sheffield, 1954.

B1393   Rosenberg, Marvin. "The 'Refinement' of *Othello* in the Eighteenth Century British Theatre." *SP*, LI (1954), 75-94.

B1394   Sawyer, Paul Simon. *John Rich Versus Drury Lane, 1714-1761: A Study in Theatrical Rivalry.* DD, Columbia University, 1954. Pp. 305. Mic A54-2731. *DA*, XIV (1954), 1846. Publ. No. 8824.
Chap. V: "The Managers and Shakespeare," pp. 181-192.

B1395   Scouten, A. H. "Theophilus Cibber's *The Humorists*." *N &Q*, II (1955), 114-115.

B1396   Ashley, Leonard R. N. *The Theatre-Royal in Drury Lane, 1711-1716, Under Colley Cibber, Barton Booth, and Robert Wilks.* DD, Princeton University, 1956. Pp. 553. Mic 57-994. *DA*, XVII (1957), 625. Publ. No. 20,099.

B1397   Branam, George C. *Eighteenth-Century Adaptations of Shakespearean Tragedy.* Univ. of California Publications. English Studies, 14. Berkeley: Univ. of California Press, 1956. Pp. viii, 220.
Rev: B144.

B1398   McKenzie, Jack. "Shakespeare in Scotland Before 1760." *TN*, XI, No. 1 (1956), 24-26.

B1399   Scouten, Arthur H. "The Increase in Popularity of Shakespeare's Plays in the Eighteenth Century: A *Caveat* for Interpreters of Stage History." *SQ*, VII (1956), 189-202.

B1400 Schulz, Max F. *"King Lear:* A Box-Office Maverick Among Shakespearian Tragedies on the London Stage, 1700-1 to 1749-50." *Tulane Studies in English,* VII (1957), 83-90.

(b) STAGING

B1401 Linton, Calvin Darlington. *Shakespeare Staging in London from Irving to Gielgud.* DD, Johns Hopkins University, 1940.

B1402 Thomas, Russell B. *Spectacle in the Theaters of London from 1767 to 1802.* DD, University of Chicago, 1942.

B1403 Byrne, M. St. Clare. "The Stage Costuming of *Macbeth* in the Eighteenth Century." *Studies in English Theatre History in Memory of Gabrielle Enthoven.* Ed. by M. St. Clare Byrne. London: Society for Theatre Research, 1952, pp. 52-64.

B1404 Miesle, Frank L. *The Staging of Pantomime Entertainments on the London Stage: 1715-1808.* DD, Ohio State University, 1955.

B1405 Böwe, Kurt. "Ekhof—Schröder—Iffland. Die Entwicklung des Schauspielerischen Realismus im 18. Jahrhundert." *Theater d. Zeit,* Jan. 11, 1956, pp. 13-19.

B1406 Burnim, Kalman A. "Some Notes on Aaron Hill and Stage Scenery." *TN,* XII (1957/58), 29-33.
Notes Hill's 1723 production of *H. V,* and adaptation from Shak.

(c) STYLES OF ACTING

B1407 Bahn, Eugene H. *Theories of Acting in Eighteenth Century England, 1750-1800.* DD, University of Wisconsin, 1935.

B1408 Downer, Alan S. "Nature to Advantage Dressed: Eighteenth Century Acting." *PMLA,* LVIII (1943), 1002-1037.

B1409 Cook, A. M. "Eighteenth Century Acting Styles." *Phylon,* V (1944), 219-224.

B1410 Adams, William Wall. *Relationships Between the Principles of Acting and Rhetorical Delivery in Eighteenth-Century England.* DD, University of Illinois, 1954. Pp. 146. Mic A54-3215. *DA,* XIV (1954), 2152. Publ. No. 9023.

B1411 Barrow, Bernard Elliott. *Low Comedy Acting Style on the London Stage, 1730-1780.* DD, Yale University, 1957.

(d) ACTORS (167;56)

B1412 Cooke, Anne M. *An Analysis of the Acting Styles of Garrick, Siddons, and Edmund Kean in Relation to the Dominant Trends in Art and Literature of the Eighteenth Century.* DD, Yale University, 1944.

i. David Garrick

B1413 Stein, Elizabeth P. *David Garrick, Dramatist.* New York: The Modern Language Assoc. of America, 1938. Pp. xx, 315.
Rev: by Samuel A. Tannenbaum, *SAB,* XIII (1938), 126-127; by A. Nicoll, *JEGP,* XXXVIII (1939), 462; by D. MacMillan, *MLN,* LIV, 210-213; by B. V. Crawford, *PQ,* XVIII, 93-94.

B1414 Barton, Margaret. *Garrick.* London: Faber, 1948. Pp. 324.
Rev: *TLS,* June 12, 1948, p. 330; by L. M. Parrott, *TAr,* XXXIII, No. 4 (1949), 6-7; by Richard Flatter, *SJ,* 89 (1953), 204-207.

B1415 Stewart, Anna Bird. *Enter David Garrick.* Philadelphia: Lippincott, 1951. Pp. ix, 278. Reissued 1952.

B1416 Burnim, Kalman Aaron. *David Garrick: Director.* DD, Yale University, 1958.

B1417 Oman, Carola. *David Garrick.* London: Hodder & Stoughton, 1958. Pp. 448. With 8 pp. gravure illustrations.
Contains much new material and some unpublished letters.
Rev: by J. Coleman, *Spectator* 6804 (1958), 708.

B1418 Highfill, Philip, Jr. "Biography in Brief: David Garrick, Actor-Manager." *ShN,* VII (1957), 11.

aa. Garrick Letters

B1419 Burnim, Kalman A. "The Significance of Garrick's Letters to Hayman." *SQ,* IX (1958), 149-152.

B1420 Stone, George Winchester, Jr., ed. *The Journal of David Garrick, Describing His Visit to France and Italy in 1763.* M.L.A. Revolving Fund Series, X. New York: Modern Language Association, 1939. Pp. xvi, 73. Oxford: Oxford Univ. Press, 1939.
Rev: by R. Weiss, *MLR,* XXXV (1940), 542-543; *TLS,* May 18, p. 239; by D. MacMillan, *MLN,* LV, 560.

B1421 Pedicord, H. W. "Mr. & Mrs. Garrick: Some Unpublished Correspondence." *PMLA,* LX (1945), 775-783.

B1422   Greene, Godfrey. "Notes on an Unpublished Garrick Letter and on Messink." *TN*, VIII (1953), 4-6.
On the subject of costumes for *Macbeth* in 1778.

bb.   Garrick and Shakespeare's Works

B1423   Stone, George Winchester, Jr. *Garrick's Treatment of Shakespeare's Plays, and His Influence upon the Changed Attitude of Shakespearean Criticism During the Eighteenth Century*. DD, Harvard University, 1940. Abstr. publ. in *Summaries of Ph.D. Theses, 1940*, Cambridge: Harvard Univ. Press, 1942, pp. 368-372.

B1424   Bodtke, R. A. *Garrick's Revisions of Shakespeare: A Mirror for Eighteenth Century Tastes*. MS Thesis, Columbia University, 1947. Pp. 94.

B1425   Stone, George Winchester, Jr. "Garrick's Presentation of *Antony and Cleopatra*." *RES*, XIII (1937), 20-38.

B1426   Cancelled.

B1427   Stone, George Winchester, Jr. "Garrick, and an Unknown Operatic Version of *Love's Labour's Lost*." *RES*, XV (1939), 323-328.

B1428   Stone, George W., Jr. "*A Midsummer Night's Dream* in the Hands of Garrick and Colman." *PMLA*, LIV (1939), 467-482.

B1429   Stone, George Winchester, Jr. "Garrick's Handling of *Macbeth*." *SP*, XXXVIII (1941), 609-628.

B1430   Stone, George Winchester, Jr. "Garrick's Production of *King Lear*: A Study in the Temper of the Eighteenth-Century Mind." *SP*, XLV (1948), 89-103.

B1431   Stone, George Winchester, Jr. "The God of his Idolatry: Garrick's Theory of Acting and Dramatic Composition with Especial Reference to Shakespeare." *AMS*, pp. 115-128.

B1432   Stone, George Winchester, Jr. "David Garrick's Significance in the History of Shakespearian Criticism." *PMLA*, LXV (1950), 183-197.

B1433   Boswell, James. *London Journal, 1762-1763*. Ed. by Frederick A. Pottle. New York: Mc-Graw-Hill, 1950. Pp. xxix, 370.
Contains remarks by Sheridan on *2 Henry IV* (pp. 135-136), criticizing Garrick's performance, and references to Garrick's playing of *Henry IV* and *Lear* (pp. 134, 256).

B1434   Stone, George Winchester, Jr. "Shakespeare's *Tempest* at Drury Lane During Garrick's Management." *SQ*, VII (1956), 1-7.

cc.   The Stratford Jubilee

B1435   Fox, Levi. *The Borough Town of Stratford-on-Avon*. Corporation of Stratford-upon-Avon, 1953. Pp. 168.
Rev: A801.

B1436   England, Martha W. *The Stratford Jubilee of 1769*. DD, Radcliffe College, 1953.

B1437   England, Martha Winburn. "Garrick's Stratford Jubilee: Reactions in France and Germany." *ShS*, IX (1956), 90-100.

B1438   Dunn, Lady. "The First Stratford-upon-Avon Festival." *Shakespeare Quarterly* (London), I (Summer, 1947), 82-88.

B1439   Mann, Isabel R. "The Garrick Jubilee at Stratford-upon-Avon." *SQ*, I (1950), 129-134.

B1440   Forster, E. M. *Two Cheers for Democracy*. London: Arnold, 1951. Pp. 371.
Includes essay on the Stratford Jubilee of 1769 (pp. 166-169), written in 1932.
Rev: A9087.

dd.   Garrick's Audiences

B1441   Pedicord, Harry W. *Garrick's Audiences*. DD, University of Pennsylvania, 1949.

B1442   Pedicord, Harry William. *The Theatrical Public in the Time of Garrick*. New York: King's Crown Press, 1954. Pp. 267.
Noticed by Charles Beecher Hogan, *SQ*, VI (1955), 353-354.

B1443   Motter, T. H. V. "Garrick and the Private Theatres." *ELH*, XI (1944), 63-75.

ee.   Miscellaneous

B1444   Martin, W. B. *David Garrick's Attitude Toward and Influence Upon Eighteenth-Century Sentimental Comedy*. DD, Edinburgh, 1954.

B1445   Holmes, Martin. "Portrait of a Celebrity." *TN*, XI, No. 2 (1957), 53-55.

B1446   Manvell, Brian. "Kemble Statuette." *TN*, XI (1957), 108; reply to B1445.

B1447   Mander, Raymond, and Joe Mitchenson. "Further Notes on the Porcelain Statuette of Richard III." *TN*, XI (1957), 128-130.
More on B1445-B1446.

B1448   Bergmann, Frederick L. *A Study of Garrick's Alterations of Non-Shakespearean Plays*. DD, George Washington University, 1954.

ii. John Philip Kemble

B1449   Child, Harold. *The Shakespearian Productions of John Philip Kemble.* Shakespeare Assoc.
        Lecture. Oxford Univ. Press, 1936. Pp. 22.
          Rev: by C. J. Sisson, *MLR*, XXXII (1937), 137-138; by Heinz Nicolai, *Beiblatt*, XLIX (1938),
          122.

B1450   Baker, Herschel C. *John Philip Kemble.* DD, Harvard University, 1939.

B1451   Baker, Herschel. *John Philip Kemble. The Actor in His Theatre.* Harvard Univ. Press, 1942.
        Pp. viii, 414.
          Rev: *TLS*, Jan. 16, 1943, p. 32; by H. N. Hillebrand, *JEGP*, XLII, 291-293; by Hazelton
          Spencer, *MLN*, LVIII, 75-77.

B1452   Matthews, Harold. "Ineffable Kemble." *Theatre World*, Mar. 1957, pp. 44-45, 51-52.

iii. Charles Macklin

B1453   Donoghue, D. *Charles Macklin: Actor, Dramatist, Producer.* MA thesis, National Univ. of
        Ireland, 1953.

B1454   Donoghue, D. "Macklin's Shylock and Macbeth." *Studies* (Dublin), XLIII (1954), 421-430.

B1455   Highfill, Philip, Jr. "Biography in Brief: Charles Macklin." *ShN*, VII (1957), 21.

iv. Mrs. Siddons

B1456   Ffrench, Yvonne. *Mrs. Siddons, Tragic Actress.* London: Cobden-Sanderson, 1936. Rev. ed.,
        London: Vershoyle, 1954. Pp. xvi, 356.
          Rev: *TLS*, Nov. 19, 1954, p. 732; by J. C. Trewin, *Books of the Month*, Jan., 1955, p. 28.

B1457   Macqueen-Pope, W. "Queen of the Tragic Theatre." [Sarah Siddons]. *The Listener*, July 14,
        1955, pp. 68-69.
        See also B1363.

vi. Others

B1458   Hodgson, Norma. "Sarah Baker, 1736/37-1816, 'Governess-General of the Kentish Drama'."
        Studies in English Theatre History in Memory of Gabrielle Enthoven. Ed. M. St. Clare Byrne.
        London: Society for Theatre Research, 1952, pp. 65-83.

B1459   Highfill, Philip Henry, Jr. "Susannah Cibber." *ShN*, VII (1957), 30.

B1460   Miles, Bernard. "The Missing Diary of a Great Actor (George Frederick Cooke)." *Listener*,
        XLIV (1950), 601-603.

B1461   Stone, George Winchester, Jr. "The Authorship of *A Letter to Miss Nossiter* (London, 1753)."
        SQ, III (1952), 69-70.
        Comment by Charles Beecher Hogan (identification of Miss Nossiter) ibid., pp. 284-285.

B1462   Gore-Browne, Robert. *Gay Was the Pit: The Life and Times of Anne Oldfield, Actress 1683-1730·*
        London: Max Reinhardt, 1957. Pp. 192.

(e)   DRAMATIC CRITICISM

B1463   White, Irving Hamilton. *Studies in English Dramatic Criticism, 1750-1800.* DD, Harvard
        University, 1936. Abstr. publ. in *Summaries of Ph.D. Theses, 1936.* Harvard Univ. Press,
        1938, pp. 356-359.

B1464   Highfill, Philip Henry, Jr. *Francis Gentleman, Critic: A Biographical Study of the Author of
        "The Dramatic Censor."* Master's thesis, University of North Carolina, 1948. Abstr. publ.
        in *Univ. of North Carolina Record, Research in Progress*, Grad, School Series No. 56, 1949, p. 211.

B1465   Highfill, Philip Henry, Jr. *A Study of Francis Gentleman's "The Dramatic Censor,"* (1770).
        DD, University of North Carolina, 1950. Abstr. publ. in *Univ. of North Carolina Record,
        Research in Progress*, Jan.-Dec. 1950, Grad. School Series, No. 60, 1951, pp. 127-129.

B1466   Sutherland, William Owen Sheppard. *A Study of the "Prompter" (1734-1736).* DD, University
        of North Carolina, 1950. Abstr. publ. in *Univ. of North Carolina Record, Research in Progress*,
        Jan.-Dec. 1950, Grad. School Series, No. 60, 1951, pp. 135-136.

B1467   Harper, Richard D. *The Rhetorical Theory of Thomas Sheridan.* DD, University of Wisconsin,
        1952. Abstr. publ. in Univ. of Wisconsin *Summaries of Doctoral Dissertations, 1951-52*, Madison,
        1953, pp. 362-363.

B1468   Noyes, Robert Gale. *The Thespian Mirror: Shakespeare in the Eighteenth-Century Novel.*
        Providence: Brown Univ. Studies, Vol. XV, 1953. Pp. v, 200.
          Rev: A8754.

B1469   Lehner, Francis C. *The Literary Views of Colley Cibber.* DD, University of Wisconsin, 1955.
        Abstr. publ. in Univ. of Wisconsin *Summaries of Doctoral Dissertations, 1954-55*, Madison,
        1956, pp. 544-545.

(f)   THE ATTACK ON THE STAGE

B1470   Wood, F. T. "The Attack on the Stage in the Eighteenth Century: A Bibliography." *N &Q*,
        173 (1937), 218-222.

B1471   Wilson, Willard. *The Life of the British Actor in the Eighteenth Century.* DD, University of Southern California, 1939.

B1472   Pallette, Drew B. "The English Actor's Fight for Respectability." *Theatre Annual*, VII (1949), 27-34.

B1473   Trace, Arthur S., Jr. *The Continuity of Opposition to the Theater in England from Gosson to Collier.* DD, Stanford University, 1954.

B1474   Scouten, Arthur H. "The S.P.C.K. and the Stage." *TN*, XI, No. 2 (1956/57), 58-62.

(g) MISCELLANEOUS

B1475   Webb, B. L. *Theatrical Autobiography in the Eighteenth Century.* MA thesis, Wales, 1952.

B1476   Merchant, William Moelwyn. "John Runciman's Lear in the Storm." *JWCI*, XVII (1954), 385-387.

(4) THE YEARS 1800 TO 1880
(a) PRODUCTIONS

B1477   Klaiber, Joachim. *Die Aktform im Drama und auf dem Theater. Ein Beitrag zur dts. Theatergeschichte des 19. Jh.* [Sh. passim.] Theater und Drama, 6. Berlin: Elsner, 1936. Pp. viii, 291.

B1478   Sper, Felix. *Periodical Criticism of the Drama in London, 1800-1825.* DD, New York University, 1936.
        Shak. productions in London which were reviewed in periodicals, pp. 74-81.

B1479   Spriggs, C. O. "*Hamlet* on the Nineteenth-Century Stage." *QJS*, XXII (1936), 78-85.

B1480   Stahl, E. L. "Shakespeare-Gestaltung auf dem Englischen Theater im 19. Jahrhundert." *SJ*, LXXIV (1938), 82-100.

B1481   Batchelor, Grace E. *The Acting Tradition in England Between 1800 and 1830, with Special Reference to Shakespeare's Plays.* DD, University of London, 1939.

B1482   Linton, C. D. *Shakespearean Staging in London from Irving to Gielgud.* DD, Johns Hopkins University, 1940.

B1483   West, Edward J. *Histrionic Methods and Acting Traditions on the London Stage, 1870-1890.* DD, Yale University, 1940. The Colorado Publication, Nos. 39-62 (April, 1940).

B1484   Allen, Shirley Seifried. "A Successful People's Theatre in London." *TAr*, XXVIII (1944), 598-604.
        Samuel Phelps at Sadler's Wells.

B1485   Downer, A. S. "Players and Painted Stage: [Nineteenth-Century Acting.]" *PMLA*, LXI (1946), 522-576.

B1486   Nathan, George Jean. "*Richard III.*" *American Mercury*, LXVIII (1949), 681-682.
        Casual comments on opinions of productions before 1880.

B1487   Hudson, Lynton. *The English Stage, 1850-1950.* London: Harrap, 1951.
        Rev: *TLS*, Feb. 23, 1951, p. 119.

B1488   Slater, D. *Hazlitt as a Dramatic Critic.* MA thesis, Manchester, 1952.

B1489   South, R. J. *Changes in the Interpretation of Shakespeare in the Second Half of the Nineteenth Century: The Treatment of the Plays by the Theatres and Dramatic Critics.* DD, University of London, 1952.

B1490   Hanson, Frank B. *London Theatre Audiences of the Nineteenth Century.* DD, Yale University, 1953.

B1491   Price, C. J. L. *The History of the English Theatre in Wales, 1844-1941.* DD, Wales, 1953.

B1492   Allen, Shirley Seifried. *Samuel Phelps and His Management of the Sadler's Wells Theatre.* DD, Bryn Mawr, 1949. Pp. 208. Mic A54-588. *DA*, XIV (1954), 415. Publ. No. 7151.
        Chap. III "The Middle Years—Shakespearean Drama," pp. 65-102.
        Appendix: Chart of Shakespearean performances, p. 178.

B1493   Carlisle, Carol Jones. "The Nineteenth-Century Actors *versus* the Closet Critics of Shakespeare." *SP*, LI (1954), 599-615.

B1494   Rowell, George. *The Victorian Theatre.* Oxford Univ. Press, 1956. Pp. 327.
        Rev: by St. Vincent Troubridge, *TN*, XI (1957), 63-64; by Martin T. Cobin, *QJS*, XLIII, 207; by Sybil Rosenfeld, *MLR*, LII, 595; by J. H. McDowell, *QJS*, XLIII, 206; by A. J. Farmer, *EA*, XI (1958), 167.

(b) ACTORS AND ACTRESSES
i. Several

B1495   Stahl, E. L. "Shakespeare-Gestaltung auf dem Englischen Theater im 19. Jahrhundert." *SJ*, LXXIV (1938), 82-100.

B1496   "Early Shakespearean Actors." *Wisdom*, July 1956, pp. 20-21.

B1497   Dent, Alan. "Playgoing over Here and over There." *Theatre in Review*. Ed. by Frederick Lumley. Edinburgh: Paterson, 1956, pp. 74-79. On Macready, Terry, Kean, Booth and Irving.

B1498   Trewin, J. C. "The Victorian Theatre." *Drama*, Spring, 1957, pp. 26-29.
         Victorian actors and actresses of Shak.

B1499   Brown, Eluned. "A Note on Crabb Robinson's Reactions to J. P. Kemble and Edmund Kean."
         TN, XIII (1958), 14-18.

ii.   Henry Irving

B1500   Craig, G. "H. Irving." *London Mercury*, XXXVII (1938), 400-405.

B1501   Craig, G. "H. Irving." Tr. by W. Meyer. *Theater d. Welt*, II (1938), 69-76.

B1502   Craig, G. "H. Irving." *TAr*, XXII (1938), 30-40.

B1503   Walbrook, H. M. "H. Irving." *FortnR*, 143 (1938), 202-211.

B1504   Williams, Harcourt. "*Harry Irving as Romeo.*" *Theatre Today*, Winter, 1946.

B1505   Forsythe, D. V. *Sir Henry Irving and His Art of Acting.* MS thesis, Columbia University,
         1947. Pp. 76.

B1506   Irving, Laurence. *Henry Irving. The Actor and His World.* London: Faber, 1951; New York:
         Macmillan, 1952. Pp. 734.
             Rev: *Listener*, XLVI (1951), 1031; answer by L. Irving, ibid., XLVII (1952), 105; by Philip
         Carr, ibid., p. 150; by St. Vincent Troubridge, *English*, IX (1952/53), 23-24; by Marvin
         Felheim, *SQ*, IV (1953), 347-348.

B1507   Carr, Philip. "Henry Irving as Hamlet." *Listener*, XLV (1951), 1034.

B1508   Craig, Gordon. "Henry Irving's Way." *Listener*, XLVI (1951), 133-134.

B1509   Shuttleworth, Bertram. "Irving's Macbeth." *TN*, V (Jan.-Mar., 1951), 28-31.

B1510   West, E. J. "Irving in Shakespeare: Interpretation or Creation?" *SQ*, VI (1955), 415-422.

B1511   Pollock, John. *Curtain Up.* London: Peter Davies, 1958. Pp. 200.
             Rev: *TLS*, Nov. 7, 1958, p. 647.

iii.   Charles Kean

B1512   Hardwick, John Michael Drinkrow. *Emigrant in Motley.* The Journey of Charles and Ellen
         Kean in Quest of a Theatrical Fortune in Australia and America, as told in their hitherto
         unpublished letters. London: Rockcliff, 1954. Pp. xx, 260.
             Rev: *TLS*, Dec. 24, 1954, p. 832.

B1513   Threlkeld, Budge. *A Study of the Management of Charles Kean at the Princess's Theatre: 1850-
         1859.* DD, Ohio State University, 1956. Pp. 315. Mic 56-294. *DA*, XVI (1956), 182.
         Publ. No. 14,501.

B1514   Wilson, Mardis Glen, Jr. *Charles Kean: A Study in Nineteenth Century Production of Shake-
         spearean Tragedy (Volumes I and II).* DD, Ohio State University, 1957. *DA*, XVIII, No. 4
         (1958), 1535. Abstr. also in *Speech Monographs*, XXV, 134.

B1515   Wilson, M. Glen, Jr. "The Box Set in Charles Kean's Productions of Shakespearean Tragedy."
         The Ohio State Univ. Theatre Collection Bulletin, V (1958), 7-26.

iv.   Edmund Kean

B1516   Playfair, Giles. *Kean. The Life and Paradox of the Great Actor.* London: G. Bles, 1939.
         Pp. x, 346; Reinhart & Evans, 1950. Pp. xv, 339.
             Rev: by M. Slater, *NstN*, XL (1950), 155-156; by S. Rosenfeld, *TN*, V (1950/51), 40-41.

B1517   Dent, Alan. *Preludes and Studies.* With Intro. Letter by Sir Max Beerbohm. London:
         Macmillan, 1942. Pp. xiii, 251.
         Contains essay on Kean.
             Rev: by A. S. W., *MGW*, July 10, 1942, p. 24.

B1518   Berstl, Julius. *The Sun's Bright Child: The Imaginary Memoirs of Edmund Kean.* London:
         Hammond, 1946. Pp. 192.

B1519   Disher, Maurice Willson. *Mad Genius. A Biography of Edmund Kean.* London: Hutchinson,
         1950. Pp. 192.
             Rev: by G. Banyard, *FortnR*, 169 (1951), 139.

B1520   Strasberg, Lee. *Past Performances.* *TAr*, XXXIV (May, 1950), 39-42.
         Kean as Shylock.

B1521   Dunkel, Wilbur D. "Kean's Portrayal of Cardinal Wolsey." *TN*, VI (1952), 80-82.

B1522   Bernad, Miguel A. "Othello Comes to Town: Orson Welles and Edmund Kean." *Philippine
         Studies*, IV (1956), 3-14.

B1523   Stamm, Rudolf. "Edmund Kean." *Shakespeare-Tage 1957* (Bochum), pp. 10-16.

v.   W. C. Macready

B1524   Shattuck, Charles H. *The Dramatic Collaborations of William Charles Macready.* DD, University
         of Illinois, 1939.

B1525   Downer, Alan S. "Macready's Production of *Macbeth.*" *QJS*, XXXIII (1947), 172-181.

B1526   Staples, L. C. "Dickens and Macready's Lear." *The Dickensian*, XLIV (1948), 78-80.

B1527   Carlisle, Carol Jones. "William Macready as a Shakespearean Critic." *Renaissance Papers* (Univ. of South Carolina, 1954), pp. 31-39.

B1528   Trewin, J. C. *Mr. Macready. A Nineteenth-Century Tragedian and His Theatre.* London: Harrap, 1955. Pp. 267.
        Illustrated from the Raymond Mander and Joe Mitchenson Theatre Collection.
        Rev: *TLS*, Sept. 9, 1955, p. 524; by R. Findlater, *Books of the Month*, LXX, No. 9, 8-10; *Listener*, LIV, 387-389; by M. Slater, *NstN*, L, 636-637; by J. Wain, *Spectator*, 6637 (1955), 339-340; by W. J. Igoe, *Tablet*, 206 (1955), 633; by Peter Forster, *Drama* (Winter) pp. 29-31; by Charles H. Shattuck, *TN*, x (1956), 57-58; by Guy Boas, *English*, XI (1956/57), 22-23.

vi. Others

B1529   Barnet, Sylvan. "Charles Lamb and the Tragic Malvolio." *PQ*, XXXIII (1954), 177-188.

B1530   Gill, W. W. "Shakespeare in Modern Dress." *N&Q*, 175 (1938), 186-187; A. H. Cooper-Pritchard, ibid., pp. 265-266.

B1531   Armstrong M. *F. Kemble, a Passionate Victorian.* New York, 1938. Pp. viii, 388.

B1532   Highfill, Philip Henry, Jr. "Biography in Brief: Frances Anne Kemble." *ShN*, VIII (1958), 34.

B1533   Grice, F. "Roger Kemble's Company at Worcester." *TN*, IX, No. 3 (1955), 73-75.

B1534   Shaw, Dennis. "Esther Leach, 'The Mrs. Siddons of Bengal'." *ETJ*, x (1958), 304-310.

B1535   Curry, Wade Chester. *Steele MacKaye: Producer and Director.* DD, University of Illinois, 1958. Pp. 247. Mic 58-1691. *DA*, XVIII (1958), 1896-1897.

B1536   Johnson, Albert E. "Greatest of Juliets." *TAr*, Aug. 1957, pp. 63-64, 95-96.
        The life of Lilian Adelaide Nielson.

B1537   Shaw, G. Bernard. "Sullivan, Shakespeare and Shaw." *Atlantic Monthly*, 181 (March, 1948), 56-58.

B1538   Elsna, Hebe. *The Sweet Lost Years: A Novel.* London: Hale, 1955. Pp. 192.
        Based upon the early life of Ellen Terry.

B1539   Holmes, Martin. "A Regency Cleopatra." *TN*, VIII (1954), 46-47.

b. AMERICA
(1) GENERAL

B1540   Dunn, Esther C. *Shakespeare in America.* New York: Macmillan, 1939. Pp. xiv, 310.
        Rev: A9180.

B1541   Quinn, A. H. *A History of American Drama . . . to the Civil War.* New York, 1943. Pp. xviii, 530.

B1542   Smoot, James S. *Platform Theater: Theatrical Elements of the Lyceum-Chautauqua.* DD, University of Michigan, 1954. Pp. 323. Mic A54-1062. *DA*, XIV (1954), 736. Publ. No. 7732.

B1543   *Annals of the New York Stage.* New York: Columbia Univ. Press.

Vol. I	(to 1798),	1927.	IX	(1870-1875),	1937.
II	(1798-1821),	1927.	X	(1875-1879),	1938.
III	(1821-1834),	1928.	XI	(1879-1882),	1939.
IV	(1834-1843),	1928.	XII	(1882-1885),	1940.
V	(1843-1850),	1931.	XIII	(1885-1888),	1942.
VI	(1850-1857),	1931.	XIV	(1888-1891),	1945.
VII	(1857-1865),	1931.	XV	(1891-1894),	1949.
VIII	(1865-1870),	1936.			

B1544   Stine, Richard D. *The Philadelphia Theater, 1682-1829: The Growth of a Cultural Institution.* DD, University of Pennsylvania, 1952.

(a) STAGING

B1545   Hamar, Clifford E. "Scenery in the Early American Stage." *Theatre Annual*, VII (1949), 84-103.

B1546   Richardson, Genevieve. *Costuming on the American Stage—1751-1901: A Study of the Major Developments in Wardrobe Practice and Costume Style.* DD, University of Illinois, 1953. Pp. 286. Mic A53-2208. *DA*, XIII (1953), 1305. Publ. No. 6003.

B1547   Green, John H. *The Development of Stage Rigging in the United States (1766-1893).* DD, University of Denver, 1955.

B1548   Held, McDonald Watkins. *A History of Stage Lighting in the United States in the Nineteenth Century.* DD, Northwestern University, 1955. Pp. 311. Mic 55-685. *DA*, xv (1955), 1930. Publ. No. 13,091.

(b) MISCELLANEOUS

B1549   Mauser, Ruth B. *The Influence of the American Actress on the Development of the American Theatre from 1835 to 1935.* DD, New York University, 1938.

B1550 Wilson, Garff Bell. *American Styles and Theories of Acting from Edwin Forrest to David Belasco.* DD, Cornell University, 1940. Abstr. publ. in Cornell Univ. *Abstracts of Theses, 1940,* Ithaca, 1941.

B1551 Alden, Barbara. *The History and Interpretation of Shakespeare's "Othello" on the American Stage.* DD, University of Chicago, 1942.

B1552 Lovell, John, Jr. "Shakespeare's American Play." *TAr,* XXVIII (1944), 363-370. *Othello* in America.

B1553 Belcher, Fannin S., Jr. *The Place of the Negro in the Evolution of the American Theatre, 1767-1940.* DD, Yale University, 1946.

(2) COLONIAL

B1554 Freedley, George. "An Early Performance of *Romeo and Juliet* in New York." *Bull. of the New York Public Library,* XL (1936). Pp. xi, 494.

B1555 Shurter, Robert L. "Shakespearean Performances in Pre-Revolutionary America." *South Atlantic Quarterly,* XXXVI (1937), 53-58.

B1556 Rosenbach, A. S. W. "The First Theatrical Company in America." *Proc. Amer. Antiq. Soc.,* XLVII (1938), 3-13; XLVIII (1939), 300-310.

B1557 Turner, Vivian. "Our Colonial Theatre." *QJS,* XXVII (1941), 559-573.

B1558 Michael, Mary Ruth. *A History of the Professional Theatre in Boston from the Beginning to 1816.* DD, Radcliffe College, 1942.

B1559 Gale, Cedric. *Shakespeare on the American Stage in the Eighteenth Century.* DD, New York University, 1945. Publ. in abridged form, New York, 1948.

B1560 Kendall, J. S. " 'The American Siddons': M. A. Duff." *Louisiana Historical Quarterly,* XXVIII (1945), 922-940.

B1561 Walsh, Charles R. *Shakespeare on the Colonial Stage.* DD, Fordham University, 1948. Abstr. publ. in *Dissertations Accepted for Higher Degrees,* Fordham Univ., XV (1948), 64-68.

B1562 Cohen, Hennig. "Shakespeare in Charleston on the Eve of the Revolution." *SQ,* IV (1953), 327-330.

B1563 Wolf, Edwin, 2nd. "Early American Playbills." *SQ,* VII (1956), 285-286.

(3) THE YEARS 1800-1880

B1564 Parrott, Frederick J. *The Mid-Nineteenth Century American Theatre, 1840-1860; A Survey of Theatre Production, Comment, and Opinion.* DD, Cornell University, 1948.

B1565 Woodbury, Lael Jay. *Styles of Acting in Serious Drama on the Nineteenth Century American Stage.* DD, University of Illinois, 1954. Pp. 231. Mic A55-242. *DA,* XV (1955), 171. Publ. No. 10,566.

B1566 Muldrow, Blanche. *The American Theatre as Seen by British Travellers 1790-1860.* DD, University of Wisconsin, 1954. Abstr. publ. in Univ. of Wisconsin *Summaries of Doctoral Dissertations, 1953-54,* Madison, 1955, pp. 584-586.

(a) ACTORS
i. Studies of Groups

B1567 Alden, Barbara. *Differences in the Conception of Othello's Character as Seen in the Performances of Three Important Nineteenth-Century Actors on the American Stage—Edwin Forrest, Edwin Booth, Tommaso Salvini.* DD, University of Chicago, 1950.

B1568 Ford, George D. *These Were Actors. A Story of the Chapmans and the Drakes.* New York: Library Publishers, 1955.
Rev: by Richard L. Coe, *SQ,* VII (1956), 435-436.

ii. Individuals
aa. Ira Aldridge

B1569 Finkel, M. "T. Shevchenko and Ira Aldridge." *International Literature,* March 1939, pp. 92-93.

B1570 Durilin, S. "Ira Aldridge." *SAB,* XVII (1942), 33-39.

B1571 Marshall, Herbert, and Mildred Stock. *Ira Aldridge.* New York: Macmillan, 1958. 33 illustrations.

bb. Edwin Booth

B1572 Thompson, William F. *Edwin Booth's Acting Versions of "Richard III," "Julius Caesar," and "The Merchant of Venice."* DD, University of Nebraska, 1937.

B1573 Skinner, O. *The Last Tragedian.* New York, 1939. Pp. xii, 214.

B1574 Frenz, Horst. "Edwin Booth in Polyglot Shakespeare Performances." *GR,* XVIII (1943), 280-285.

B1575   Sprague, Arthur Colby. "Edwin Booth's Iago: A Study of a Great Shakespearean Actor."
        Theatre Annual, 1947 (1948), 7-17.

B1576   Bundy, Murray W. "A Record of Edwin Booth's *Hamlet.*" *SQ*, II (1951), 99-102.

B1577   Ruggles, Eleanor. *Prince of Players: Edwin Booth.* London: Davies; New York: Norton,
        1953. Pp. 401.
        Rev: by M. Redgrave, *NstN*, XLVI (1953), 384; by William Van Lennep, *SQ*, VI (1955), 473.

B1578   Gallegly, J. S. "Edwin Booth in Galveston and Houston." *The Rice Institute Pamphlet*, XLIV
        (1958), 52-64.

cc. Augustin Daly

B1579   Mangan, Nora Aileene. *Augustin Daly as a Producer of Shakespearian Drama.* DD, University
        of Washington, 1939. Abstr. in *Univ. of Washington Abstracts of Theses*, IV (1939), 133-138.

B1580   Felheim, Marvin L. *The Career of Augustin Daly.* DD, Harvard University, 1948.

B1581   Felheim, Marvin. *The Theatre of Augustin Daly.* Harvard Univ. Press, 1956. Pp. 329.
        Rev: A9208.

dd. Others

B1582   Highfill, Philip Henry, Jr. "Junius Brutus Booth." *ShN*, VIII (1958), 23.

B1583   Swander, Homer. "Biographies in Brief: John Wilkes Booth." *ShN*, VI (1956), 15.

B1584   Hawes, David Stewart. *John Brougham as American Playwright and Man of the Theatre.* DD,
        Stanford University, 1954. Pp. 686. Mic A54-1479. *DA*, XIV (1954), 1006. Publ. No. 7494.

B1585   Puknat, Elizabeth M. "Romeo Was a Lady: Charlotte Cushman's London Triumph."
        Theatre Annual, IX (1951), 59-69.
        Rev: by P. Hartnoll, *TN*, VI (1951/52), 45.

B1586   Stolp, Dorothy E. *Mrs. John Drew, American Actress-Manager, 1820-1897.* DD, Louisiana
        State University, 1953.

B1587   Rosenberg, Marvin. "Othello to the Life." *TAr*, XLII (June 1958), 58-61.

B1588   Draper, Walter Headen. *George L. Fox, Comedian, in Pantomime and Travesty.* DD, University
        of Illinois, 1958. Pp. 183. Mic 58-4496. *DA*, XVIII (1958), 693. Publ. No. 25,210.

B1589   Overmyer, Grace. *America's First Hamlet.* New York: New York Univ. Press, 1957. Pp. 439.
        Rev: *VQR*, XXXIII (1957), 77; *TAr*, April, p. 63; by Basil Francis, *TN*, XII (1957/58), 35;
        by Pat M. Ryan, Jr., *QJS*, XLIV (1958), 191.

B1590   Skinner, Maud and Otis. *One Man in His Time: H. Watkins.* Univ. of Pennsylvania Press,
        1938. Pp. xviii, 258.

(b) REGIONAL THEATRE STUDIES
i. The East

B1591   Blymyer, Louise A. *Journalistic Dramatic Criticism: A Survey of Theatre Reviews in New York,
        1857-1927.* DD, Louisiana State University, 1939.

B1592   Lewis, Stanley T. *The New York Theatre: Its Background and Architectural Development,
        1750-1853.* DD, Ohio State University, 1954.

B1593   Shank, Theodore Junior. *The Bowery Theatre, 1826-1836.* DD, Stanford University, 1956.
        Pp. 645. Mic 56-3132. *DA*, XVI (1956), 1965. Publ. No. 17,740.

B1594   Borgers, Edward W. *A History of Dramatic Production in Princeton, New Jersey.* DD, New York
        University, 1950.

B1595   Coder, William D. *A History of the Philadelphia Theatre, 1856-1878.* DD, University of
        Pennsylvania, 1936.

B1596   Paul, Henry N. "Shakespeare in Philadelphia." *Proc. Amer. Philos. Soc.*, LXXVI (1936),
        719-729.

B1597   Sprague, Arthur Colby. "The First American Performance of *Richard II.*" *SAB*, XIX (1944),
        110-116.
        At Chestnut St. Theatre, Philadelphia, Jan. 22, 1819.

B1598   McKenzie, Ruth H. *Organization, Production, and Management at the Chestnut Street Theatre,
        Philadelphia, from 1791 to 1820.* DD, Stanford University, 1952. Abstr. publ. in *Abstracts
        of Dissertations*, Stanford Univ., XXVII (1951-52), 397-400.

ii. The Middle West

B1599   McDavitt, Elaine E. *A History of the Theatre in Detroit, Michigan, from Its Beginnings to 1862.*
        DD, University of Michigan, 1947. Pp. 556.

B1600   Behringer, Clara M. *A History of the Theatre in Ann Arbor, Michigan, from Its Beginnings to
        1904.* DD, University of Michigan, 1951. Pp. 604. Mic A51-123. *Micr. Abstr.* XI, No. 2
        (1951), 464. Publ. No. 2379.

B1601   Gaiser, Gerhard W. *The History of the Cleveland Theatre from the Beginning to 1854.* DD, State University of Iowa, 1954. Pp. 722. Mic A54-294. *DA*, xiv (1954), 204-205. Publ. No. 6509.

B1602   Dix, William S., Jr. *The Theater in Cleveland, Ohio, 1854-1875.* DD, University of Chicago, 1946. Pp. 496.

B1603   Stolzenbach, Norma Frizzelle. *The History of the Theatre in Toledo, Ohio, from Its Beginnings Until 1893.* DD, University of Michigan, 1954. Pp. 342. Mic A54-1873. *DA*, xiv (1954), 1276. Publ. No. 8418.

B1604   Dunlap, James F. *Queen City Stages: Professional Dramatic Activity in Cincinnati, 1837-1861.* DD, Ohio State University, 1954.

B1605   Langworthy, Helen. *The Theatre in the Frontier Cities of Lexington, Kentucky, and Cincinnati, Ohio, 1797-1835.* DD, State University of Iowa, 1952. Pp. 347. Mic. 4079. *DA*, xii (1952), 636. Publ. No. 4079.

B1606   Crum, Mabel Tyree. *The History of the Lexington Theatre from the Beginning to 1860.* DD, University of Kentucky, 1956.

B1607   Ludwig, Jay Ferris. *McVicker's Theatre, 1857-1896.* DD, University of Illinois, 1958. Pp. 148. Mic 58-5448. *DA*, xix (1958), 1140.

B1608   Woods, Donald Z. *A History of the Theater in Minneapolis, Minnesota, from the Beginning to 1883.* DD, University of Minnesota, 1951.

B1609   Herbstruth, Grant M. *Benedict Debar and the Grand Opera House in St. Louis, Missouri, from 1855-1879.* DD, State University of Iowa, 1954. Pp. 1097. Mic 55-122. *DA*, xv (1955), 898. Publ. No. 9580.

B1610   Johnson, Theodore Clark. *A History of the First Olympic Theatre of St. Louis, Missouri, from 1866-1879.* DD, State University of Iowa, 1958. Pp. 354. Mic 58-2970. *DA*, xix (1958), 599.

B1611   Schick, Joseph S. *Cultural Beginnings and the Rise of the Theater, German and American, in Eastern Iowa (Davenport), 1836-1863.* DD, University of Chicago, 1938.

B1612   Semper, I. J. "Shakespeare in Pioneer Dubuque." *SQ*, iv (1953), 105-106.

iii. The West

B1613   Nichols, Dean G. *Pioneer Theatres of Denver, Colorado.* DD, University of Michigan, 1938.

B1614   Hansen, Harold I. *A History and Influence of the Mormon Theatre from 1839-1869.* DD, State University of Iowa, 1948. Pp. 205.

B1615   Monson, Leland Hans. *Shakespeare in Utah (1847-1900).* DD, University of Utah, 1956. Pp. 322. Mic 57-1354. *DA*, xvii (1957), 848. Publ. No. 17,574.

B1616   Berelson, B., and H. F. Grant. "The Pioneer Theatre in Washington." *Pacific Northwest Quart.*, xxviii (1937), 115-136.

B1617   Fenton, Frank L. *The San Francisco Theatre, 1849-1859.* DD, Stanford University, 1942.

B1618   Gagey, Edmond McAdoo. *The San Francisco Stage: A History.* Based on Annals Compiled by the Research Department of the San Francisco Federal Theatre. New York: Columbia Univ. Press; London, Toronto: Oxford Univ. Press, 1950. Pp. xv, 264.
         Rev: by G. R. MacMinn, *American Literature*, xxiii (1951), 156-158; by Harold L. Hayes, *QJS*, xxxvii, 101-102; by Campton Bell, *Western Folklore*, x, 93-94.

B1619   Hume, Charles Vernard. *The Sacramento Theatre, 1849-1885.* DD, Stanford University, 1955. Pp. 504. Mic A55-1529. *DA*, xv (1955), 1141. Publ. No. 12,268.

iv. The South

B1620   Fife, Iline. *The Theatre During the Confederacy.* DD, Louisiana State University, 1949. Abstr. publ. in Louisiana State Univ., *Univ. Bulletin*, xlii (March 1950), 29-31.

B1621   Shockley, Martin S. *A History of the Theatre in Richmond, Virginia.* DD, University of North Carolina, 1939.

B1622   Shockley, Martin Staples. "Shakspere's Plays in the Richmond Theatre, 1819-1838." *SAB*, xv (1940), 88-94.

B1623   Hadley, Richard H. *The Theatre in Lynchburg, Virginia, from Its Beginnings in 1822 to the Outbreak of the Civil War.* DD, University of Michigan, 1947. Pp. 292.

B1624   Hoole, William Stanley. "Two Famous Theatres of the Old South." *South Atlantic Quarterly*, xxxvi (1937), 273-277.

B1625   Hoole, W. Stanley. "Shakspere on the Antebellum Charleston Stage." *SAB*, xxi (1946), 37-45.

B1626   Hill, West T. *A Study of the Macauley's Theatre in Louisville, Kentucky, 1873-1880.* DD, State University of Iowa, 1954. Pp. 489. Mic A54-1560. *DA*, xiv (1954), 1065. Publ. No. 7565.

B1627   Bristow, Eugene Kerr. *"Look Out for Saturday Night": A Social History of Professional Variety Theater in Memphis, Tennessee, 1859-1880.* DD, State University of Iowa, 1956. Pp. 241. Mic 56-3125. *DA*, xvi (1956), 1961. Publ. No. 18,522.

B1628 Faulkner, Seldon. *The New Memphis Theater of Memphis, Tennessee, from 1859 to 1880.* DD, State University of Iowa, 1957. Pp. 314. Mic 57-3361. *DA*, XVII (1957), 2085. Publ. No. 22,079.

B1629 Ritter, Charles Clifford. *The Theatre in Memphis, Tennessee from Its Beginning to 1859 (Parts One-Five).* DD, State University of Iowa, 1956. Pp. 405. Mic 56-3565. *DA*, XVI (1956), 2240. Publ. No. 17,484.

B1630 Gates, W. B. "Performances of Shakespeare in Ante-bellum Mississippi." *Journal of Miss. History*, V (1943), 28-37.

B1631 Smither, Nelle Kroger. *A History of the English Theatre at New Orleans, 1806-1842.* DD, University of Pennsylvania, 1942. Publ. in *Louisiana Historical Quarterly*, VIII (1945), 85-276, 361-572.

B1632 Roppolo, Joseph P. *A History of the English Language Theatre in New Orleans, 1845-1861.* DD, Tulane University, 1950.

B1633 Roppolo, Joseph Patrick. "*Hamlet* in New Orleans." *Tulane Studies in English*, VI (1956), 71-86.

B1634 Cancelled.

B1635 Roppolo, Joseph Patrick. "American Premières of Two Shakespearian Plays in New Orleans." *Tulane Studies in English*, VII (1957), 125-132.
       Two Gentlemen performed Dec. 28, 1831; *A & C*, March 8, 1838.

B1636 Yocum, Jack H. *A History of Theatre in Houston, 1836-1954.* DD, University of Wisconsin, 1955. Abstr. publ. in Univ. of Wisconsin *Summaries of Doctoral Dissertations, 1954-55*, Madison, 1956, pp. 522-523.

c. ELSEWHERE
(1) GERMANY

B1637 Drews, Wolfgang. "*König Lear*" *auf der Deutschen Bühne bis zur Gegenwart.* Berlin, 1932.
       Rev: A9432.

B1638 Brüggemann, Fritz, ed. *Die Aufnahme Shakespeares auf der Bühne der Aufklärung in den Sech-ziger und Siebziger Jahren.* Deutsche Literatur. Reihe Aufklärung. Bd. 11. Leipzig: Reclam, 1937. Pp. 306.
       Rev: A9441.

B1639 Durian, Hans. *Jocza Savits und die Münchener Shakespeare-Bühne. Ein Beitrag zur Geschichte der Regie um die Jahrhundertwende.* DD, Munich, 1937. Emsdetten: Lechte, 1938. Pp. 132.

B1640 Schweinshaupt, Georg. *Shakespeares Dramatik in ihrer Gehaltlichen und Formalen Umwandlung auf dem Österreichischen Theater des 18. Jahrhunderts.* DD, Königsberg, 1938. Pp. 120.

B1641 Schumacher, Erich. *Shakespeares "Macbeth" auf der dts. Bühne.* DD, Cologne, 1938. Emsdetten: Lechte, 1938. Pp. 295.

B1642 Kosch, Wilhelm. *Das dts. Theater und Drama im 19. und 20. Jahrhundert.* Wurzburg: Wächter-Vlg., 1939. Pp. 165.

B1643 Stahl, Ernst Leopold. *Die Klassische Zeit des Mannheimer Theaters.* Part 1: Das Europäische Mannheim: die Wege zum dts. Nationaltheater. Mannheim: Hakenkreuzbanner-Vlg., 1940. Pp. 300.
       Rev: by W. Keller, *SJ*, LXXVI (1940), 218-219.

B1644 "Ernst Possart and Jacob Adler as Shylock." *TAr*, XXVIII (1944), 469, 475.

B1645 Lambda, Beta. "Correspondence." *Shakespeare Quarterly* (London), I (Summer, 1947), 93-94.
       Karl Immerman, director of theater in Düsseldorf from 1832 to 1837, anticipated staging of dumb show suggested by Dover Wilson, Granville-Barker, and Simpson.

B1646 Sinden, Margaret J. *English Drama in Germany in the Later Enlightenment.* DD, Toronto, 1947.

B1647 Stahl, Ernst Leopold. *Shakespeare und das Deutsche Theater.* Stuttgart: Kohlhammer, 1947. Pp. viii, 768.
       Rev: A9465.

B1648 Röhler, W. "Shakespeare auf dem Kindertheater." *SJ*, 82/83 (1949), 186-189.

B1649 Bab, Julius. *Kränze dem Mimen. 30 Porträts Grosser Menschendarsteller.* Emsdetten: Lechte, 1954. Pp. 368.

B1650 Kendzia, Maria Luise. "Friedrich Ludwig Schröder und Shakespeare." *Theater d. Zeit*, X, No. 12 (October, 1955), 23-27.

B1651 Falkenberg, Hans-Geert. "Zur Bühnen- und Übersetzungsgeschichte von *Antonius und Cleopatra.*" *Blätter d. Dt. Theaters in Göttingen*, Heft 89, 1956.

B1652 Purdie, Edna. "Observations on Some Eighteenth-Century German Versions of the Witches' Scenes in *Macbeth.*" *SJ*, 92 (1956), 96-109.

B1653 McNamee, Lawrence Francis. "*Julius Caesar*" *on the German Stage in the Nineteenth Century.* DD, University of Pittsburgh, 1957. Pp. 324. Mic 57-1716. *DA*, XVII (1957), 1074. Publ. No. 21, 009.

(2) OTHER GERMANIC COUNTRIES

B1654   Tennant, P. "*Romeo och Julia* in Norrköping 1776." *Samlaren, Skrifter udg. af Svensk. Litt. Selskapet* (Uppsala), XVII (1936), 215.

B1655   Bergman, Gösta M. *Regi och Spelstil Under Gustaf Lagerbjelkes tid vid Kungl. Teatern; Studier Kring Några av hans Insceneringar.* Stockholm: P. A. Norstedt, 1946. Pp. 420.

B1656   Avén, Göran. "Hamlet på Kungl. Teatern 1819." *Skrifter utg. av Föreningen Drottningholms-teaterns Vänner*, No. 12 (1957), pp. 161-185.

B1657   Henriques, Alf. *Shakespeare og Danmark Indtil 1840.* Copenhagen: Einar Munksgaard, 1941. Pp. 291.
        Rev: A9746.

B1658   Pennink, R. *Nederland en Shakespeare.* The Hague, 1936.
        Rev: A9739.

(3) FRANCE
For Ducis, see A9343-A9350.

B1659   Shackleton, Robert. "Shakespeare in French Translation." *Mod. Languages*, XXIII (1941), 15-21.

B1660   Monaco, Marion. *Shakespeare on the French Stage in the Eighteenth Century.* DD, Bryn Mawr College, 1939. Pp. 235. Mic A43-2178. *Mcf Ab*, V (1943), 18. Publ. No. 581.

B1661   "Travels in France. A Vignette of Talma." *TAr*, XVIII (1944), 310-314.
        (1824 picture of Talma as Hamlet.)

B1662   De Smet, Robert. "*Othello* in Paris and Brussels." *ShS*, III (1950), 98-106.
        From eighteenth century on.

B1663   Eddison, Robert. "Souvenirs du Théâtre Anglais à Paris, 1827." *TN*, September 1955, pp. 99-103.

B1664   Lelièvre, Renée. "Les Représentations Italiennes de Shakespeare à Paris (1855-1878)." RHT, VII (1955), 326-329.

B1665   Benchettrit, Paul. "Hamlet at the Comédie Française 1769-1896." *ShS*, IX (1956), 59-68.

B1666   *L'Encyclopédie du Théâtre Contemporain.* Vol. I. Paris: Plaisir de France, 1957. Pp. 208.
        Rev: A9339.

B1667   Keys, A. C. "Shakespeare en France: *La Mégère Apprivoisée* en 1767." *RLC*, XXXI (1957), 426-428.

B1668   Lombard, Charles M. "Ducis' 'Hamlet' and Musset's 'Lorenzaccio'." *N &Q*, NS, V (1958), 72-75.

(4) SPAIN

B1669   Par, A. *Representaciones Shakespearianas en España.* San Felíu de Guixols: Imp. O. Viader, 1936.
        Vol. 1: Epoca Galoclásica. Epoca Romántica. Pp. 268.
        Vol. 2: Epoca Realista y Tiempos Modernos. Pp. 220.

B1670   Thomas, Sir Henry. *Shakespeare in Spain.* London: G. Cumberlege, 1950. Pp. 24.
        Annual Shak. lecture of the British Academy for 1949.
        Rev: A9404.

(5) SLAVONIC COUNTRIES

B1671   Luther, Arthur. "Moskaus Erster *Hamlet*." *SJ*, 82/83 (1948), 175-185.

B1672   Lang, D. M. "Sumarkov's *Hamlet*: A Misjudged Russian Tragedy of the Eighteenth Century." *MLR*, XLIII (1948), 67-72.

B1673   Dabrowski, Stanislaw. "Otello na Scenie Lódzkiej w XIX. w." *Lódź Teatr*, No. 8 (1948), 14-22.

B1674   Hahn, Wiktor. [*Hamlet* at Lwow in 1797]. *Teatr Miesoceznik* (Poland), Nos. 4-5 (1945).

B1675   Klajn, Hugo. "Shakespeare in Yugoslavia." *SQ*, V (1954), 41-45.

B1676   Mark, Thomas Raymond. *Shakespeare in Hungary: A History of the Translation, Presentation, and Reception of Shakespeare's Dramas in Hungary, 1785-1878.* DD, Columbia University, 1955. Pp. 354. Mic 56-1174. *DA*, XVI (1956), 751. Publ. No. 16,287.

2. THE LEGITIMATE STAGE SINCE 1880

See entries under individual plays, text sections, for editions of the plays edited by Tyrone Guthrie and G. B. Harrison (New Stratford Shakespeare) London: Harrap which abandon the Rowe stage directions and offer new ones designed for modern theatrical performance.
For Russian performances and dramaturgical principles see Russia, A9899-A9954.

a. SURVEYS OF TRENDS
  (1) REFERENCE WORKS

B1677   Gilder, Rosamond, and George Freedley. *Theatre Collections in Libraries and Museums*. London: Stevens & Brown, 1936. Pp. 182.
         Rev: A3333.

B1678   Shuttleworth, Bertram. "W. J. Lawrence: A Handlist." Part I. *TN*, VIII (1954), 52-54. See B3988-B3990.

B1679   Hartnoll, Phyllis. *The Oxford Companion to the Theatre*. Second ed. Oxford Univ. Press, 1957. Pp. 984. Illustrated.

B1680   Baker, Blanch Merritt. *Theatre and Allied Arts. A Guide to Books Dealing with the History, Criticism, and Technic of the Drama and Theatre*. New York: Wilson, 1952. Pp. xiii, 536.

B1681   Johnson, S. F. "Shakespearean Acting and Production." *ShN*, Jan.-Feb., 1952, p. 5.

(2) GENERAL SURVEYS

B1682   Ruppel, K. H. "Hamlet. [From Garrick to Gründgens]. Wandlungen einer Bühnengestalt." *Koralle* (Berlin), NS, IV (1936), 259.

B1683   Ernst, Earle. *Cycles in the Development of the Dramatic Arts*. DD, Cornell University, 1940. Abstr. publ. in Cornell Univ. *Abstracts of Theses, 1940*, Ithaca, 1941.

B1684   Linton, Calvin D. "Some Recent Trends in Shakespearean Staging." *ELH*, VII (1940), 300-324.

B1685   Vardac, Alexander Nicholas. *From Garrick to Griffith: Transition from Stage to Screen*. DD, Yale University, 1942. See B1687.

B1686   Downer, Alan S. "Mr. Dangle's Defense: Acting and Stage History." *EIE*, 1946, Columbia Univ. Press, 1947, pp. 159-190.

B1687   Vardac, Alexander Nicholas. *Stage to Screen: Theatrical Method from Garrick to Griffith*. Cambridge, Mass.: Harvard Univ. Press; London: Oxford Univ. Press, 1949. Pp. xxvi, 283.
         Rev: B1261.

B1688   Cole, Toby, and Helen Krich Chinoy, eds. *Actors on Acting: The Theories, Techniques, and Practices of the Great Actors of All Times as Told in Their Own Words*. Edited with Introductions and Biographical Notes. New York: Crown, 1949; London: Pitman; Toronto: Ambassador, 1952. Pp. xiv, 596.
         Rev: B1277.

B1689   South, R. J. *Changes in the Interpretation of Shakespeare in the Second Half of the Nineteenth Century: The Treatment of the Plays by the Theatres and Dramatic Critics*. DD, University of London, 1951.

B1690   Kerr, W. "Shakespeare and Shopping Baskets." *Commonweal*, LXIII (1956), 282-284.

(a) ENGLAND

B1691   Allen, A. B. *Drama Through the Centuries and Play Production To-day*. London: Allman & Son, 1936. Pp. 102.

B1692   Allen, J. "Conventions in the Modern Theater." *Life and Letters Today*, XVI (Mar. 1937), 138-141.

B1693   Huang, John. *A Short History of Shakespearean Production*. M. Litt thesis, Cambridge. *Cam Abs. 1937-38*, p. 84.

B1694   Stahl, E. L. *Shakespeare-Gestaltung auf dem Englischen Theater im 19. Jahrhundert*. *SJ*, LXXIV (1938), 82-100.

B1695   Linton, C. D. *Shakespearean Staging in London from Irving to Gielgud*. DD, Johns Hopkins University, 1940.

B1696   West, Edward J. *Histrionic Methods and Acting Traditions on the London Stage, 1870-1890*. DD, Yale University, 1940. *The Colorado Publication* 39-62, April, 1940.

B1697   Brook, D. *The Romance of the English Theatre*. London, 1945. Pp. 208.

B1698   Marshall, Norman. *The Other Theatre*. London: Lehmann, 1947. Pp. 240.
         Rev: *TLS*, July 5, 1947, p. 339; July 19, p. 369.

B1699   Farjeon, Herbert. *The Shakespearian Scene: Dramatic Criticisms*. London: Hutchinson, 1949. Pp. 194.
         Rev: *TLS*, June 17, 1949, p. 399; by M. St. Clare Byrne, *English*, VII, 289-290; by G. Baldini, *Belfagor*, July, 1952, pp. 125-126.

B1700   Williamson, Audrey. *Theatre of Two Decades*. New York: Macmillan, 1951. Pp. 372.

B1701   Earley, Clarence Luther Steven. *English Dramatic Criticism, 1920-1930*. DD, University of Geneva. Richmond, Va., U.S.A.: William Byrd Press, 1952. Pp. 190.

B1702   Crosse, Gordon. *Shakespearean Play-going, 1890-1952; Illustrated from the Raymond Mander and Joe Mitchenson Theatre Collection*. London: Mowbray, 1953. Pp. 164. Plates.
         Rev: by Eugênio Gomes ("Um Espectador de Shakespeare"), *Correio da Manhã* (Rio de Janeiro), Nov. 20, 1954; by Rudolf Stamm, *SJ*, 91 (1955), 356-365.

B1703 Emerson, Elizabeth. *English Dramatic Critics of the Nineties and the Acting of the "New Theatre."* DD, Bryn Mawr College, 1953.

B1704 Kemp, T. C. "Acting Shakespeare: Modern Tendencies in Playing and Production with Special Reference to Some Recent Productions." *ShS*, VII (1954), 121-127.

B1705 Leclerc, Hélène. "Scénographie et Architecture Théâtrale en Angleterre (Exposition à Londres, Juillet, 1955)." *RHT*, VIII (1956), 24-39.

B1706 Coghill, Nevill. "University Contributions to Shakespeare Production in England." *SJ*, 93 (1957), 175-185.

B1707 Walker, Roy. "Short of Shakespeare." *Listener*, May 2, 1957, pp. 728-729.

B1708 *Shakespeare im Britischen Theater. Eine vom British Council Zusammengestellte Ausstellung (Katalog).* Vienna: Theater in d. Josefsstadt, 1958. Pp. 16.

(b) AMERICA

B1709 Manser, Ruth B. *The Influence of the American Actress on the Development of the American Theatre from 1835 to 1935.* DD, New York University, 1938.

B1710 Wilson, Garff Bell. *American Styles and Theories of Acting from Edwin Forrest to David Belasco.* DD, Cornell University, 1940. Abstr. publ. in Cornell Univ. *Abstracts of Theses, 1940,* Ithaca, 1941.

B1711 Belcher, Fannin S., Jr. *The Place of the Negro in the Evolution of the American Theatre, 1767-1940.* DD, Yale University, 1946.

B1712 Schoell, Edwin R. *A Quantitative Analysis of the Contributions of the Community Theatre to the Development of the Drama.* DD, University of Denver, 1952.

B1713 West, L. Edna. *Contemporary Broadway Criticism.* DD, University of Wisconsin, 1952. Abstr. publ. in Univ. of Wisconsin *Summaries of Doctoral Dissertations, 1951/52,* Madison, 1953, pp. 404-405.

B1714 Downer, Alan S. "Shakespeare in the Contemporary American Theater." *SJ*, 93 (1957), 154-169.

B1715 Cox, Charles Wright. *The Evolution of the Stage Director in America.* DD, Northwestern University, 1958. Pp. 466. Mic 58-4764. *DA*, XVIII (1958), 1144. Publ. No. 24,900.

b. DRAMATURGIC PRINCIPLES OF SHAKESPEAREAN PRODUCTION (163;55)
(1) MAJOR DISCUSSIONS

B1716 Buzzini, Bertram G. "If Shakespeare Knew." *San Francisco Quart.*, II (1935), 21-24.

B1717 Brandl, A. "Eine neue Art, Shakespeare zu Spielen." Brandl, *Forschungen und Charakteristiken,* No. 184 (Berlin, 1936), 138-146. [Reprinted from *Deutsche Rundschau,* 123 (1905), 122 ff.]

B1718 Knight, G. Wilson. *Principles of Shakespearian Production.* London: Faber and Faber; New York: Macmillan, 1936. Pp. 246. Harmondsworth: Penguin Books, 1949. Pp. 224.
Rev: *TLS*, May 2, 1936, p. 373; by W. J. Lawrence, *Spectator*, May 8, p. 848; by E. Martin Browne, *Criterion*, LXII, 143-146; by Frederick Laws, *NstN*, NS, XI, 897-898; *London Mercury*, XXXIV, 378; by T. R. Barnes, *Scrutiny*, V, 328-329; by Rosamond Gilder, *TAr*, XXI (1937), 330-331; by Mark Van Doren, *Nation* (N. Y.), 144 (1937), 188-189; by Everett M. Schreck, *QJS*, XXIII, 504-505; by William Empson, *Life and Letters Today*, XV, No. 5, 202; by H. Voaden, *Canadian Forum*, XVI, No. 191, 34.

B1719 Centeno, Augusto, ed. *The Intent of the Artist.* Princeton Univ. Press, 1941. Pp. 162.

B1720 Gassner, J. *Producing the Play.* New York, 1941. Pp. xxx, 744. Shak., pp. 450-460.

B1721 Mitchell, Lee. "The Effect of Modern Stage Conventions on Shakespeare." *TAr*, XXVI (1942), 447-451.

B1722 McLeod, A. *The Nature of the Relations Between the Theatre Audience, the Drama and the Mise-en-scène.* Abstr. in Cornell Univ. *Abstracts of Theses* (Ithaca), 1943, pp. 65-68.

B1723 Brook, P. "Style in Shakespearean Production." *Orpheus* (London), 1948, pp. 139-146.

B1724 MacLiammóir, M. "Three Shakespearean Productions: A Conversation." *ShS*, I (1948), 89-97.

B1725 Kutscher, Arthur. *Grundriss der Theaterwissenschaft.* Munich: Desch, 1949. Pp. 495.

B1726 Reynolds, G. F. "Shakespeare and His World: Staging Elizabethan Plays." *Listener*, XLII (Aug. 11, 1949), 223-224.

B1727 Bellman, Willard F. *An Approach to an Aesthetics of the Visual Production of the Drama.* DD, Northwestern University, 1950. Abstr. publ. by Northwestern Univ. in *Summaries of Doctoral Dissertations*, XVII (1950), Chicago and Evanston, pp. 86-89.

B1728 Byrne, Muriel St. Clare. "A Stratford Production: *Henry VIII.*" *ShS*, III (1950), 120-129.

B1729 Purdom, Charles Benjamin. *Producing Shakespeare.* London: Pitman, 1950; New York: British Book Centre, 1951. Pp. xii, 220.
Rev: *TLS*, Jan. 12, 1951, p. 22; by Michael MacOwan, *Spectator*, Feb. 2, pp. 156, 158; by

John Gielgud, *SQ*, II, 255-256; by P. van Tieghem, *RHT*, III, 429-430; by A. Koszul, *EA*, V, 1952; by Henry Popkin, *SR*, LX (1952), 329-336.

B1730 Reynolds, George F. "What a Theatre for Shakespeare Should Be." *SQ*, I (1950), 12-17.

B1730a Watkins, Ronald. *On Producing Shakespeare.* London, 1950; New York, 1951.
Rev: A7287.

B1731 Yeaton, Robert Kniss. *The Dramatic Techniques of William Shakespeare and Their Importance to the Modern Realistic Theatre.* DD, Innsbruck, 1950. Pp. 171. Typewritten.

B1732 Purdom, Charles B. *Drama Festivals and Their Adjudication: A Handbook for Producers, Actors, Festival Organizers, and Adjudicators.* London, New York: Dent, 1951. Pp. xii, 138.

B1733 Walker, Roy. "Suiting the Action to the Word." *Theatre Newsletter*, Oct. 13, 1951, pp. 4-5. Comment by W. A. Armstrong and Nugent Monck, ibid., Nov. 24, p. 6.

B1733a "Shakespeare on the Stage: 1928. A Players' Shakespeare." *TLS*, Aug. 28, 1953, pp. xxxii-xxxv.

B1734 Banke, Cécile de. *Shakespearean Stage Production: Then and Now.* New York: McGraw-Hill, 1953. Pp. xviii, 342.
Part I.   Staging, pp. 3-89.
Part II.   Actors and Acting, pp. 91-138.
Part III.   Costume, pp. 139-213.
Part IV.   Music and Dancing, pp. 215-326.
Rev: A7409.

B1735 Maloff, Saul. *The Theory and Practice of the New Theatre Movement.* DD, State University of Iowa, 1953. Pp. 391. Mic. *DA*, XII (1952), 620. Publ. No. 4086.

B1736 Taylor, Mildred A. K. *The New Stagecraft; Its Relation to Easel Painting.* DD, Stanford University, 1953. Pp. 216. Mic A53-1408. *DA*, XIII (1953), 753. Publ. No. 5817.

B1737 Brockett, Lenyth Spenker. *Theories of Style in Stage Production.* DD, Stanford University, 1954. Pp. 315. Mic A54-2724. *DA*, XIV (1954), 1841. Publ. No. 9481.
Shak. is not specifically treated, but much that is relevant in current controversies is present.

B1738 Hunt, Hugh. *The Director in the Theatre.* London: Routledge and Kegan Paul, 1954. Pp. ix, 111.
Includes a lecture on modern Shak. production and holds the balance between sham archaism and overembellishment.
Rev: *TLS*, Nov. 19, 1954, p. 742; by T. C. Worsley, *NstN*, XLVIII, 692.

B1739 Hunt, Hugh. *Old Vic Prefaces: Shakespeare and the Producer.* London: Routledge and Kegan Paul, 1954. Pp. xii, 194.
A collection of the author's talks to the actors in those plays he produced at the Old Vic from 1949 to 1953, with afterthoughts on the productions themselves.
Rev: *TLS*, March 5, 1954, p. 148; by John T. Boorman, *Tablet*, 203 (1954), pp. 546-547; by T. C. Worsley, *NstN*, XLVII, 322-324; *Books of the Month*, May, p. 7; by A. Thaler, *SQ*, VII (1956), 122-124.

B1740 MacCarthy, Desmond. "*Midsummer Night's Dream.* The Production of Poetic Drama." In MacCarthy's *Theatre*, London, 1954, pp. 47-56.

B1741 McMullen, Frank. "Producing Shakespeare." *Shakespeare: Of an Age and for all Time.* The Yale Shakespeare Festival Lectures, 1954, pp. 55-57.

B1742 Williams, Raymond. *Drama in Performance.* Man and Society Series, ed. by Lady Simon of Wythenshawe and others. London: Frederick Muller, 1954. Pp. viii, 9-128.

B1743 Woodbury, Lael Jay. *Styles of Acting in Serious Drama on the Nineteenth Century American Stage.* DD, University of Illinois, 1954. Pp. 231. Mic A55-242. *DA*, XV (1955), 171. Publ. No. 10,566.

B1744 Harbage, Alfred. "The Role of the Shakespearean Producer." *SJ*, 91 (1955), 161-173.

B1745 Macgowan, Kenneth, and William Melnitz. *The Living Stage.* New York, 1955.
Rev: by Pat M. Ryan, Jr., *QJS*, XLIII (1957), 89-90; *ShN*, VII, 46.

B1746 Razum, Hannes. "Probleme der Shakespeare-Regie." *SJ*, 91 (1955), 225-232.

B1747 Gassner, John. *Form and Idea in Modern Theatre.* New York: Dryden Press, 1956. Pp. 290.
Rev: *Players Magazine*, April 1957, p. 164; by Roy Walker, *Drama*, Spring, p. 35.

B1748 Harbage, Alfred. *Theatre for Shakespeare.* The Alexander Lectures 1954/55. Toronto: Univ. of Toronto Press, 1955; Oxford Univ. Press, 1956. Pp. x, 118.
Rev: by Donald Harron, *Canadian Forum*, XXXVI (1956), 21; *Essential Books*, Feb., p. 21; by John Gassner, *TAr*, Sept., p. 9; *ShN*, VI, 28; by R. A. Foakes, *ShS*, X (1957), 148; by Charles H. Shattuck, *JEGP*, LVI, 138-142; by C. J. Sisson, *MLR*, LII, 100-101; by Sybil Rosenfeld, *SQ*, VIII, 237-239; by Arthur Colby Sprague, *TN*, XI, 64-65; by G. B. Harrison, *SatR*, Aug. 3, p. 28; by Louis Marder, *CE*, XIX, 41-42; by Hermann Heuer, *SJ*, 93 (1957), 274-276.

B1749 Schuberth, Ottmar. *Das Bühnenbild. Geschichte, Gestalt, Technik.* Munich: Callwey, 1956.

B1750 Strickland, Francis Cowles. *The Technique of Acting.* New York: McGraw-Hill, 1956. Pp. 306.

B1751 Marshall, Norman. *The Producer and the Play.* London: Macdonald, 1957. Pp. 304.

Rev: by Michael MacOwan, *Drama*, Summer, 1957, pp. 41-42; by Frank Granville-Barker, *Plays and Players*, April, p. 22; by T. C. Worsley, *NstN*, LIII, 311-312; by N. Macdermott, *TN*, XI, 144-145; *TLS*, August 3, p. 148.

B1752 Monck, Nugent. "Producing Elizabethan Plays for a Modern Audience." *ShN*, VII (1957), 39. Abstr. of paper delivered at the Shak. Institute.

B1752a "Eighth International Conference at Stratford." *ShN*, VIII (1958), 4.
Includes abstracts of Joan Miller, Maurice Daniels, Toby Robertson, and Patrick Wymark, "Actors' Forum"; Richard David, "Actors and Scholars: A View of Shak. in the Modern Theatre."

B1753 Melchinger, Siegfried. "Shakespeare und das Moderne Welttheater." *SJ*, 93 (1957), 98-113.

B1754 Braun, Margarete. "Das Drama vor Shakespeare und Seine Beziehungen zum Publikum." *SJ*, 94 (1958), 191-199.

B1755 Cochran, James Preston. *The Development of the Professional Stage Director: A Critical-Historical Examination of Representative Professional Directors on the New York Stage, 1896-1916.* DD, State University of Iowa, 1958. Pp. 494. Mic 58-1606. *DA*, XVIII (1958), 2255.

B1756 Hodek, Břetislav. "Einige Theoretische Betrachtungen über Shakespeare-Regie." *SJ*, 94 (1958), 42-50.

(2) PRODUCTION PRINCIPLES OF PROMINENT DIRECTORS AND ACTORS
(a) GEORGE PIERCE BAKER

B1757 Kinne, Wisner P. *George Pierce Baker: Scholar, Teacher, Dramatist.* DD, Harvard University, 1952.

B1758 Kinne, Wisner Payne. *George Pierce Baker and the American Theatre.* Harvard Univ. Press, 1954. Pp. xvi, 348.
Points out the influence of Baker's Lowell Institute Lectures delivered in 1905 (published as *The Development of Shakespeare as a Dramatist*).
Rev: by Walter Pritchard Eaton, *SQ*, VI (1955), 171-172; by Norreys Jephson O'Connor, *Arizona Quarterly*, XI, 277-281; by E. J. West, *ETJ*, VII, 352-354.

(b) JEAN-LOUIS BARRAULT

B1759 Barrault, Jean-Louis. *À Propos de Shakespeare et du Théâtre.* Paris: La Parade, 1949. Pp. 112.
B1760 Barrault, Jean-Louis. "Shakespeare et Nous." *RHT*, II (1950).

(c) NORMAN BEL GEDDES

B1761 Houghton, Norris. "The Designer Sets the Stage." *TAr*, XX (1936), 776-783.
B1762 Geddes, Norman Bel. "A Design for *King Lear*." *TAr*, XXV (1941), 126.

(d) ERIC BENTLEY

B1763 Bentley, Eric. "Maiming the Bard". *NR*, Sept. 22, 1952, p. 27.
B1764 Bentley, Eric. "The Modern Shakespeare." *NR*, April 28, 1952, pp. 22-23; May 5, pp. 22-23; May 12, pp. 29-30; May 26, pp. 22-23.
B1765 Bentley, Eric. "Doing Shakespeare Wrong." *Perspectives USA*, III (1953), 93-109. German Version: "Die Sünde Wider Shakespeare." Tr. by Walter Hasenclever. *Perspektiven*, III, 86-98. French Version: "Shakespeare Trompeur et Trompé." *Profils*, III (1953).
B1766 Bentley, Eric. *In Search of Theater.* New York: Knopf, 1953. Pp. xxii, 411, viii.
Includes: "Doing Shakespeare Wrong," pp. 113-133; "An Actor as Thinker," [Barrault], pp. 394-403.
B1767 Bentley, Eric. *The Dramatic Event.* New York, 1954.
Rev: by Roy Walker, *Drama*, Spring, 1957, p. 35.

(e) E. GORDON CRAIG

B1768 Werry, Wilfred Watson. *The Theories of Gordon Craig and Their Relation to the Contemporary Theatre.* MA thesis, McGill, 1932.
B1769 Craig, Gordon. "H. Irving." *London Mercury*, XXXVII (1938), 400-405. Tr. by W. Meyer, *Theater d. Welt*, II (1938), 69-76. *TAr*, XX (1939), 30-40.
B1770 Craig, G. "Propos sur Hamlet." *Arts et Lettres*, 1946, pp. 210-217.
B1771 Maśliński, Jósef. [Discussion of Gordon Craig's Ideas of Shakespearean Production.] *Teatr Miesoceznik*, Nos. 4-5 (1946).
B1772 Barshay, Bernard. "Gordon Craig's Theories of Acting." *Theatre Annual*, 1947, pp. 55-63.
B1773 Gregor, Joseph. "Edward Gordon Craig's Hamlet." *Phaidros* (Vienna), 1947, pp. 153-175.
B1774 Craig, Gordon. "Henry Irving's Way." *Listener*, XLVI (1951), 133-134.
B1775 Craig, Gordon. "Reminiscences of Myself and Ellen Terry." *Listener*, XLVI (1951), 97-98.

B1776 Ilyin, Eugene K. "Gordon Craig's Mission to Moscow." *TAr*, May 1954, pp. 78-79, 88-90. Transcription of conversation between the designer and Stanislavski, preceding their production of *Hamlet*. Concerns mainly I.iii.

B1777 Brook, Peter. "The Influence of Gordon Craig in Theory and Practice." *Drama*, Summer, 1955, pp. 32-36.

B1778 Eliot, T. S. "Gordon Craig's Socratic Dialogues." *Drama*, Spring, 1955, pp. 16-21.

B1779 Williams, Dallas S. *Edward Gordon Craig's Theory of the Theatre as Seen Through "The Mask."* DD, Louisiana State University, 1955. Pp. 266. Mic A55-1930. *DA*, xv (1955, 1463. Publ. No. 12,535.

B1780 Fletcher, Ifan Kyrle. "A Checklist of Books and Periodicals Written and Designed and Edited by Edward Gordon Craig." *TN*, x, No. 1 (1956), 50-51.

B1781 Craig, Edward Gordon. *On the Art of Theatre*. 5th impr. with new ill. London: Heinemann, 1957. Pp. xxiii, 294. "The Ghosts in the Tragedies of Shak.," pp. 264-280; "Shak.'s Plays," pp. 281-285. First publ. 1911. Rev: A8133.

B1782 Craig, Gordon. *Index to the Story of My Days; Some Memoirs, 1872-1907*. New York: Viking; London: Hulton Press, 1957. Pp. 308. Rev: by W. W. Appleton, *SatR*, Nov. 9, 1957, p. 41; *Booklist*, LIV, 37; by Harold Hobson, *Christian Science Monitor*, Oct. 17, p. 11; *Kirkus*, XXV, 578; by Norman Sharpnel, *MGW*, Oct. 4, p. 9; by John Piper, *NstN*, Oct. 5, p. 436; by Brooks Atkinson, *New York Times*, Oct. 13, p. 3; *TLS*, Oct. 25, p. 642; by John Wesley Swanson, *ETJ*, x (1958), 175-176; by Ifan Kyrle Fletcher, *TN*, XII, 74-75; by Louise Townsend, *American Scholar*, XXVII, 252-254; by Robertson Davies, *Saturday Night*, Jan. 8, pp. 22-24.

B1783 Ilyin, Eugene. "How Stanislavsky and Gordon Craig Produced *Hamlet*." *Plays and Players*, March 1957, pp. 6-7, 21.

B1784 Miller, Charles James. *An Analytical and Descriptive Study of the Contributions of Edward Gordon Craig to Modern Theater Art*. DD, University of Southern Calif., 1957.

B1785 Craig, Gordon. "The First Time I Played Hamlet." *The Listener*, Jan. 3, 1957, p. 19.

B1786 Valogne, Catherine. *Gordon Craig* ("Metteurs en Scène"). Paris, 1957. Pp. 64. Illustrated.

B1787 Moudouès, Rose-Marie. "Jacques Rouché et Edward Gordon Craig." *RHT*, x (1958), 313-319.

B1788 Shaw, G. Bernard. *Shaw on Theatre*. Ed. by E. J. West. New York: Hill and Wang, 1958. Pp. xi, 306. Includes essay on Gordon Craig. Rev: A8361.

(f) JOHN GIELGUD

B1789 Gielgud, John. "In the Margin." *TAr*, XXI (1937), 798-802.

B1790 Gilder, Rosamond. *John Gielgud's "Hamlet."* Oxford Univ. Press, 1937. Pp. 234. Rev: B3219.

B1791 Gielgud, John. "Tradition, Style and the Theatre Today." *ShS*, IV (1951), 101-108.

B1792 Gielgud, John. "Speak the Speech, I Pray You." *TAr*, April 1951, pp. 49-51.

(g) HARLEY GRANVILLE-BARKER

B1793 Granville-Barker, Harley. *Study of Drama*. Cambridge Univ. Press, 1934.

B1794 Granville-Barker, Harley. "The Casting of *Hamlet*." *London Mercury*, XXXV (Nov., 1936), 10-17.

B1795 Granville-Barker, Harley. "The Canadian Theatre." *QQ*, XLIII (1936), 256-356.

B1796 Granville-Barker, Harley. *The Use of the Drama*. Princeton Univ. Press, 1945. Pp. vi, 92. "The Exemplary Case of Shak.," pp. 80-83.

B1797 Granville-Barker, Harley. *Prefaces to Shakespeare*. 2 vols. Princeton Univ. Press, 1946, 1947. Pp. viii, 543; viii, 449. Rev: A8201.

B1798 B., G. "H. Granville-Barker." *English*, VI (1946), 110.

B1799 Rutledge, F. P. *Harley Granville-Barker and the English Theatre*. MA thesis, National Univ. of Ireland, 1951.

B1800 Bridges-Adams, W. "The Lost Leader." *The Listener*, July 30, 1953, pp. 173-175.

B1801 Britton, L. J. *The Achievement of Harley Granville-Barker (1877-1946)*. MA thesis, Wales, 1955.

B1802 Iijima, Kohei. "Granville-Barker and His Representation of Shakespearean Plays." *Waseda Appreciation and Studies in English Literature* (Tokyo), Feb. 1956. In Japanese.

B1803 Purdom, Charles Benjamin. *Harley Granville-Barker: Man of the Theatre, Dramatist and Scholar*. London: Rockliff; Cambridge: Harvard Univ. Press, 1956. Pp. xiv, 322. See also A8214. Rev: *Listener*, LIV (1955), 859; reply by C. B. Purdom, ibid., p. 943; by J. D. Wilson, ibid.,

p. 1007; *TLS*, Dec. 2, p. 716; by T. C. Worsley, *NstN*, L, 765-766; by G. Fay, *TC*, 159 (1956), 86, 88; by J. Hall, *English*, XI (1956/57); by Alec Clunes, *TN*, x (1956), 126-128; by Pat M. Ryan, Jr., *ETJ*, VIII, 336-337; by R. A. Foakes, *ShS*, x (1957), 148-149; by E. J. West, *QJS*, XLIII, 84-85; by G. B. Harrison, *SQ*, VIII, 229-231; by Hermann Heuer, *SJ*, 93 (1957), 276.

(h) GUSTAV GRÜNDGENS

B1804   Geisenheyner, M. "Gründgens Inszeniert: *Was Ihr Wollt*. Berliner Schauspielhaus." *Fr. Ztg.*, June 13, 1937.

B1805   Gründgens, Gustaf. "Shakespeare und der Schauspieler." *Wille und Macht* (Berlin), VIII, Heft 3 (1940), 9-10.

B1806   Gründgens, Gustaf. *Wirklichkeit des Theaters*. Frankfurt: Suhrkamp-Verlag, 1954. Pp. 213.
         Rev: by Wolfgang Stroedel, *SJ*, 91 (1955), 367.

B1807   Fechter, Paul. "Deutsche Shakespeare-Darsteller. 1. Gründgens als Hamlet. 2. Heinrich Georges Falstaff." *SJ*, LXXVII (1941), 123-137.

B1808   Hamlet, Wenn. "König Geworden wåre . . . Gustav Gründgens als Richard II in Wien." *MNN*, No. 160 (June 9, 1939), p. 6.

(i) ROBERT EDMOND JONES

B1809   Jones, Robert Edmond. "A Design for *Macbeth*." *TAr*, XXV (1941), 123.

B1810   Jones, Robert Edmond. "Light and Shadow." *TAr*, XXV (1941), 131-139.

B1811   Magon, Jero. "Farewell to a Great Designer." *Players Magazine*, XXXI (1955), 130.

B1812   Pendleton, Ralph, ed. *The Theatre of Robert Edmond Jones*. Middletown, Conn.: Wesleyan Univ. Press, 1957. Pp. xiii, 196. 51 plates.
         Seven tributary essays on the first American scenic designer to attain world recognition.
         Rev: (with emphasis on Jones's Shak. work) by Sir St. Vincent Troubridge, *SQ*, IX (1958), 566-568.

(j) BRANDER MATTHEWS

B1813   Matthews, Brander, ed. *Papers on Acting* (Dramabook 11). New York: Hill and Wang, 1958. Pp. 356. Paperback.

B1814   Bender, Jack Earl. *The Theatre of Brander Matthews*. DD, University of Michigan, 1954. Pp. 476. Mic A54-1627. *DA*, XIV (1954), 1112. Publ. No. 8270.

(k) STEELE MACKAYE

B1815   Curry, Wade Chester. *Steele MacKaye: Producer and Director*. DD, University of Illinois, 1958. Pp. 247. Mic 58-1691. *DA*, XVIII (1958), 1896-1897.

(l) WILLIAM POEL

B1816   Cancelled.

B1817   Bottomley, Gordon. "A Note on Poetry and the Stage." *Life and Letters Today*, XLI (1944), 21-31.

B1818   Sprague, Arthur Colby. "Shakespeare and William Poel." *UTQ*, XVII (1947), 29-37.

B1819   Littlewood, Samuel Robinson. "William Poel." *Dictionary of National Biography, 1931-1940* (London), 1949, pp. 708-709.

B1820   "William Poel." *TLS*, July 11, 1952, p. 453, J. F. Horrabin, ibid., July 18, p. 469.

B1821   Casson, Sir Lewis. "William Poel and the Modern Theatre." *Listener*, XLVII (1952), 56-58.

B1822   Speaight, Robert. "On the Elizabethan Experiments of William Poel." *Theatre*, VI (1952), 3.

B1823   Loper, Robert Bruce. "Shakespeare 'All of a Breath'." *QJS*, XXXIX (1953), 193-196.
         Discusses Poel's theory of the proper reading of Shak.'s dramatic poetry.

B1824   Speaight, Robert. "William Poel, Innovator and Restorer." *ShN*, IV (1954), 17.

B1825   Speaight, Robert. *William Poel and the Elizabethan Revival*. London: Heinemann, 1954. Pp. 302.
         Rev: *TLS*, Sept. 3, 1954, p. 551; by Gerard Fay, *Spectator*, Aug. 20, p. 235; by Barbara May, *Tablet*, 204, (1954), pp. 252-253; by Patrick Monkhouse, *MGW*, Aug. 17, p. 2; by T. C. Worsley, *NstN*, XLVIII, 268-269; reply by Robert Speaight, ibid., p. 296; by H. Ross Williamson, *The Month*, 118 (1954), 371-372; by R. Findlater, *TC*, 156 (1954), 559-570; by J. Vallette, *MdF*, 322 (1954), 712; *Books of the Month*, LXIX, No. 10, p. 6; by J. Hall, *English*, x, 150-151; by E. Evans, *TN*, IX (1954/55), 2; by R. M. Moudouès, *RHT*, VII (1955), 213-214; by Robertson Davies, *Saturday Night*, June 11; by Sir Barry Jackson, *SQ*, VI, 89-90; by Pat M. Ryan, Jr., *QJS*, XLI, 429-430; by Rudolf Stamm, *SJ*, 91 (1955), 356-365; *VQR*, XXXI, civ-cv; by J. F. Arnott, *RES*, VII (1956), 97-98; by L. Bonnerot, *EA*, IX, 151.

B1826   Poel, William. *William Poel's Prompt-Book of Fratricide Punished*. Ed. J. Isaacs. London: The Society for Theatre Research, 1956. Pp. xx, 35.
         Rev: *TLS*, July 12, 1957, p. 431; by D. Bernet, *RHT*, IX, 198-199; by Hubert C. Heffner, *SQ*, IX (1958), 63-66.

B1827   Speaight, Robert. "The Pioneers." *SJ*, 93 (1957), 170-174.

(m) MICHAEL REDGRAVE

B1828   Redgrave, Michael. *The Actor's Ways and Means.* London: Heinemann, 1953. Pp. 90.
B1829   Redgrave, Michael. "Shakespeare and the Actors." *Talking of Shakespeare.* Ed. by John Garrett. London: Hodder & Stoughton & Max Reinhardt, 1954.
B1830   Redgrave, Michael. *Mask or Face. Reflections in an Actor's Mirror.* London: Heinemann, 1958. Pp. 188. Includes "Shakespeare and the Actors."
        Rev: by J. Vallette, *MdF*, 334 (1958), 696; *TLS*, July 11, p. 395; by Norman Marshall, *London Magazine*, Oct., pp. 62-67; by John Gassner, *The Nation*, Oct. 11, pp. 215-216; by John Barton, *Spectator*, June 20, p. 813.

(n) MAX REINHARDT

B1831   Stucki, Lorenz. *Max Reinhardts Shakespeare-Inszenierungen.* DD, Vienna, 1948, Pp. 212. Typewritten.
B1832   Maurer, Driedrich. *Theatereinsichten. Von Shakespeare bis Max Reinhardt.* Berlin: Cornelsen, 1948. Pp. 99.

(o) CONSTANTIN STANISLAVSKI
See Russia, A9937-A9946.
(p) MARGARET WEBSTER

B1833   Wyatt, Euphemia Van Rensselaer. "Shakespeare, Evans, and Webster, Inc." *Catholic World*, 150 (1940), 466-467.
B1834   Webster, Margaret. "Producing Mr. Shakespeare." *TAr*, XXVI (1942), 43-48.
B1835   Webster, Margaret. "On Cutting Shakespeare—and Other Matters." *Theatre Annual*, 1946, 29-36.
B1836   Esterow, M. "Shakespeare Takes the Bus." *New York Times*, Sept. 26, 1948, Sec. II, p. 3.
B1837   Clark, Blake. "Shakespeare on the Gymnasium Circuit." *Reader's Digest*, LIV (March, 1949), 95-98.
B1838   Webster, Margaret. "Why Shakespeare Goes Right On." *New York Times Magazine*, Aug. 12, 1951, p. 10.
B1839   Engel, Lehman. *Music for the Classical Tragedy.* Foreword by Margaret Webster. New York: Harold Flammer, Inc., 1953. Pp. 96. Music, Illus.
        Rev: by Charles Haywood, *SQ*, V (1954), 332-334; by Russell Graves, *ETJ*, VII (1955), 269-270.
B1840   Webster, Margaret. *Shakespeare Today.* Introd. by M. R. Ridley. London: Dent, 1956.
B1841   Webster, Margaret. "Interpretation of Shakespeare Today." *Wisdom*, July 1956, pp. 23-35.

(q) ORSON WELLES

B1842   Welles, Orson. "Shakespeare et la Tradition." *Nouvelles Littéraires*, XXI, No. 1288 (1952), 1, 8.
B1843   Welles, Orson. "Shakespeare und Shakespeares Bühne." *Das Neue Forum* (Darmstadt), V (1955/56), 118-120.

(3) ACTORS AND SCHOLARS

B1844   Güttinger, Fritz. "Shakespeare-Forschung und das Theater." *N. Zürch. Ztg.*, Nos. 386, 394, 1937.
B1845   Stamm, Rudolf. "Die Moderne Shakespeareforschung und das Lebende Theater in England." *Neue Schweizer Rundschau*, Neue Folge, XXII (1954), 112-122. Thalwil: Schweizer Gesellschaft für Theaterkultur, 1954.
B1846   David, Richard. "Actors and Scholars: A View of Shakespeare in the Modern Theatre." Abstr. in *ShN*, VIII (1958), 4.

(4) PROBLEMS IN NON-ENGLISH-SPEAKING COUNTRIES

B1847   Marshall, Norman. "Shakespeare Abroad." *Talking of Shakespeare.* Ed. by John Garrett. London: Hodder & Stoughton & Max Reinhardt, 1954.
B1848   Ritter, E. *Die Dramaturgie der Zyklenaufführungen von Shakespeares Königsdramen in Deutschland.* Emsdetten: Lechte, 1937. Pp. 52.
B1849   Kroepelin, Hermann. "Probleme der Deutschen Shakespeare-Regie." *Berliner Tagblatt*, No. 370, 1938.
B1850   Stahl, Ernst Leopold. *Shakespeare und das Deutsche Theater.* Stuttgart: Kohlhammer, 1947. Pp. viii, 768.
        Rev: A9465.
B1851   Raeck, Kurt. "Shakespeare in the German Open-Air Theatre." *ShS*, III (1950), 95-97.
B1852   Schaller, Rudolf. "Shakespeare für die Deutsche Bühne." *Neue dt. Literatur* (Berlin), IV, No. 6 (1956), 120-127.

B1853   Berkowski, N. "Wie Spielt man Shakespeare in Alma-Ata ?" *Theater der Zeit*, II (Aug., 1946), 14-17.

B1854   Prema, S. "Producing Shakespeare in India." *SQ*, IX (1958), 395-396.

(5) ADVICE FOR AMATEURS

B1855   Watkins, Ronald. "Producing Shakespeare in an Elizabethan Setting." *CE*, XI (1949), 159-160.

B1856   Mead, Robert S. *A Study of Factors Influencing the Development of Acting Technique in England, 1576-1642, with Applications to the Problems of Educational Theatre.* DD, Northwestern University, 1952. Abstr. publ. in Northwestern Univ. *Summaries of Doctoral Dissertations, 1952,* Chicago & Evanston, XX (1953), 149-151.

B1857   Kahan, Gerald. *A Shakespeare Production Handbook for Non-Professionals.* DD, University of Wisconsin, 1954. Abstr. publ. in Univ. of Wisconsin *Summaries of Doctoral Dissertations, 1953-54,* Madison, 1955, pp. 576-578.

B1858   Boas, Guy. *Shakespeare and the Young Actor.* London, 1955.
        Rev: B4240.

B1859   Jurgensen, Kai. "Producing on a Shoestring." *Players Magazine*, XXXIV (1958), 76-77.

B1860   Vilhauer, William. "Why Not Do a Classic?" *Players Magazine*, XXXIV, 103-104.

(6) MISCELLANEOUS WORKS BEARING ON DRAMATURGICAL PRINCIPLES

B1861   Brown, John Mason. "The Will to Make Believe." *TAr*, XX (1936), 892-895.

B1862   Church, S. H. "Ben Greet and Shakespeare." *Carnegie Magazine*, X (1936), 92-93.

B1863   Heaton, Elizabeth. "Remarks on the Production of Shakespeare." *London Mercury*, XXXIII (1936), 398-402.

B1864   Lewes, G. H. "Shakespeare: Actor and Critic." *Theatre Workshop* (Oct., 1936), 41-50. Repr. from *On Actors and the Art of Acting.*

B1865   Grebanier, B. D. N. "Advice to the Players." *Theatre* (Jan., 1937), 55-59.

B1866   Ormsbee, H. *Backstage with Actors. From the Time of Shakespeare to the Present Day.* New York: T. Y. Crowell Co., 1938. Pp. 344.

B1867   Payne, B. I. "The Central Figure: Shakespeare." *Carnegie Magazine*, XIII (1939), 122-123.

B1868   Stoll, Elmer Edgar. "Modesty in the Audience." *MLN*, LV (1940), 570-575.

B1869   Wehner, Josef Magnus. "Shakespeare im Zirkus ? Eine Drastische Erwiderung auf Einen Drastischen Einfall." [Verwandlung der Bühne in die Manege eines Zirkus für die Auff. von T. of Shakespeare in Braunschweig]. *MNN*, Jan. 16, 1940, p. 3.

B1870   Selden, S. *The Stage in Action.* New York: Crofts, 1941. Pp. xviii, 324.

B1871   Tillotson, Geoffrey. "Two Productions of Elizabethan Plays." *Essays in Criticism and Research.* Cambridge Univ. Press, 1942, pp. 49-52.

B1872   MacOwan, Michael. "Problems of Producing Shakespeare." *Listener*, XL (Aug. 19, 1948), 265-266. German translation: "Inszenierungsprobleme bei Shakespeare-Aufführungen." *Die Brücke*, No. 96 (1948), 8-9.

B1873   West, E. J. "G. B. S. on Shakespearean Production." *SP*, XLV (1948), 216-235.

B1874   Boas, Guy. "Lytton Strachey, Dramatic Critic." *English*, VIII (1950/51), 8-14.

B1875   Ludwig, Richard M. *The Career of William Winter, American Drama Critic: 1836-1917.* DD, Harvard University, 1950.

B1876   Rubenstein, Gilbert M. *The Shakespearean Criticism of William Winter: An Analysis.* DD, University of Indiana, 1951.

B1877   Carr, Philip. "A Dramatic Critic's Creed." *Listener*, XLVI (1951), 422-423.

B1878   Houseman, John. "On Directing Shakespeare." *TAr*, XXXV, No. 4 (1951), 52-54.

B1879   Stamm, Rudolf. *Shakespeare's Word-Scenery.* With Some Remarks on Stage-History and the Interpretation of His Plays. Veröffentlichungen der Handels-Hochschule St. Gallen, Reihe B, Heft 10. Zurich and St. Gallen: Polygraphischer Verlag, 1954. Pp. 34.
        Rev: A5603.

B1880   Nagler, A. M. *Sources of Theatrical History.* New York: Theatre Annual, 1952. Pp. xxiii, 611.
        Rev: A7076.

B1881   Wilson, J. Dover, and T. C. Worsley. *Shakespeare's Histories at Stratford, 1951.* Photographs by Angus McBean. London: Reinhardt, 1952. Pp. x, 96.
        Rev: B2444.

B1882   "Producing Shakespeare; the Stage in Two Elizabethan Ages." *Times* (London), March 5, 1954, p. 9.

B1883   Bailey, Margery. "Shakespeare in Action." *CE*, XV (1954), 307-315; *English Journal*, XLIII (1954), 111-118.

B1884   Gabbard, Earnest Glendon. *An Experimental Study of Comedy.* DD, State University of Iowa,

1954. Pp. 383. Mic A54-3628. *DA*, XIV (1954), 2437. Publ. No. 10,212.
Audience interest in *Shrew*, *Caesar*, *AYL*, *Romeo*, *Twelf.*, *Errors* measured on machines.

B1885   Stevens, Martin. "Shakespeare into Puppets." *Puppetry Journal*, May/June, 1954.

B1886   Findlater, Richard. "Acting the Works." *TC*, Aug., 1955, pp. 130-139.

B1887   Hellberg, Martin. "Warum heute Shakespeare?" In his *Bühne und Film*. Berlin: Henschel, 1955. Pp. 197.

B1888   Honda, Akira. "How to Handle Fools in Shakespeare." *The Rising Generation* (Tokyo), 101, No. 4 (1955). In Japanese.

B1889   Masefield, John. "Festival Theater." *Atlantic*, Jan., 1955, pp. 60-64.
Reply by Christine Stewart in March, p. 25.

B1890   Russell, Douglas A. "Uses of Felt at the Shakespeare Memorial Theatre." *ETJ*, VII (1955), 202-205.

B1891   Fukuhara, Rintaro. *Ars Longa*. Tokyo: Tarumizu Shobo, 1956. Pp. 214.

B1892   Houseman, John. "Shakespeare and the American Actor." *TAr*, July, 1956, pp. 31-32, 90-91.

B1893   *Theatre in Review*. Ed. by Frederick Lumley. Edinburgh: Paterson, 1956. Pp. 218.
Shakespearian Production, pp. 61-79.

B1894   Seale, D. "Shakespeare and the Repertory Stage." *TAr*, Sept. 1956, pp. 20-21.

B1895   "Rest, Perturbed Spirit." *ShN*, VII (1957), 26.

B1896   Krutch, Joseph Wood. "On Reading Plays." *TAr*, Nov. 1957, pp. 33-34.

B1897   Kirschbaum, Leo. "Banquo and Edgar: Character or Function." *EIC*, VII (1957), 1-21.
Comments by C. Gillie and F. W. Bateson, ibid., pp. 322-325; by A. S. Knowland, ibid., pp. 325-330; by Peter Ure, ibid., pp. 457-459.

B1898   Ustinov, Peter. "Wanted: New Perspective for Playwrights." *TAr*, Oct. 1957, pp. 21-22, 93.

B1899   Cor, Etta. "Es Fällt Kein Shakespeare vom Himmel." *Theater d. Zeit*, XIII (1958), No. 6, 20-24.

B1900   Marder, Louis. "Orthodoxies in Staging." *ShN*, VIII (1958), 34.

B1901   Marder, Louis. "Stage vs. Study." *ShN*, VIII (1958), 10, 18.

B1902   Withey, J. A. "Action in Life and in Drama." *ETJ*, X (1958), 233-236.

(7) DIVERS ASPECTS OF PRODUCTION
(a) SPEAKING

B1903   Kernodle, George R. "Basic Problems in Reading Shakespeare." *QJS*, XXXV (1949), 36-43.

B1904   Sansom, Clive. "On the Speaking of Shakespeare." London Academy of Music and Dramatic Arts, 1949.

B1905   Annan, N. G. "The Marlowe Society Tradition." *CamJ*, III (1950), 592-612.

B1906   Le Page, R. B. "The Dramatic Delivery of Shakespeare's Verse." *ES*, XXXII (1951), 63-68.

B1907   Rylands, George. "The Poet and the Player." *ShS*, VII (1954), 25-34.

B1908   Joseph, Bertram L. "The Elizabethan Stage and the Art of Elizabethan Drama." *SJ*, 91 (1955), 145-160.

B1909   Joseph, Bertram L. "A Style for Shakespeare." *ETJ*, VII (1955), 212-216.

B1910   Rehner, Herbert Adrian. "Choral Speaking in the Theatre." *Players Magazine*, XXXI (1955), 160-161.

B1911   Watkins, Ronald. "The Actor's Task in Interpreting Shakespeare." *SJ*, 91 (1955), 174-181; *Drama*, NS, XXXIX, 32-36; *The Use of English*, IX (1957), 104-109.

B1912   Boas, Guy. "Shakespearian Tempo." *English*, XI (1957), 169.

B1913   Draper, John W. *The Tempo-Patterns of Shakespeare's Plays*. Angl. Forschungen. Heft 90, 1957. Pp. 180.
Rev: A5165.

B1914   Joseph, Bertram Leon. "Verse and Character: The Elizabethan Solution and the Modern Actor." Abstract, *ShN*, VII (1957), 39.

B1915   MacOwan, Michael. "The Value of the First Folio Text for the Speaking of the Verse." Abstract, *ShN*, VII (1957), 48.

B1916   Muir, Kenneth. "The Speaking of Shakespeare." *English Speech*, Vol. IV. 1957 Year Book of the English Speaking Board. London: English Speaking Board, 1958.

B1917   Sansom, Clive. "Correspondence." *Drama*, Summer, 1957, p. 36.

(b) COSTUME
i. Historical Costume (180;63)

B1918   Brooke, Iris. *A History of English Costume*. London: Methuen, 1937. Pp. 238.

B1919   Calthrop, Dion Clayton. *English Costume from William I to George IV, 1066-1830*. With 61 colour playes by author, 91 illustr. London: Black, 1937. Pp. 463.

B1920   Bradfield, Nancy M. *Historical Costumes of England, 1066-1936*. London: Harrap, 1938. Pp. 155.

B1921   Norris, Herbert. *Costume and Fashion.* Vol. III: *The Tudor Period.* Book 1: 1485-1547; Book 2: 1547-1603. Ill. by the author. London: Dent, 1938; New York: Dutton, 1939. Pp. 864.

B1922   Laver, James. *Early Tudor, 1485-1558.* Costume of the Western World Series. London: Harrap, 1951. Pp. 24, pl.
        Rev: A7261.

B1923   Reade, Brian. *The Dominance of Spain, 1550-1660.* Costume of the Western World Series. London: Harrap, 1951. Pp. 27, pl.
        Rev: A7266.

B1924   Reynolds, Graham. *Elizabethan and Jacobean, 1558-1625.* Costume of the Western World Series. London: Harrap, 1951. Pp. 23, pl.
        Rev: A7262.

B1924a Blum, André. *Early Burbon, 1590-1643.* Costume of the Western World Series. London: Harrap, 1951. Pp. 28, pl.
        Rev: A7267.

B1925   Yarwood, Doreen. *English Costume: From the Second Century B.C. to 1950.* London: Batsford, 1952. Pp. xiv, 290.
        Rev: A7263.

B1926   Willett, C., and Phillis Cunnington. *Handbook of English Costume in the Sixteenth Century.* Ill. by Barbara Phillipson. London: Faber & Faber, 1954. Pp. 244.
        Rev: A7264.

B1927   LaMar, Virginia A. *English Dress in the Age of Shakespeare.* Folger Booklets on Tudor and Stuart Civilization, No. 6. Washington, D. C.: The Folger Shakespeare Library, 1958. Pp. 42.

ii.   Stage Costume

B1928   Freeman, Bernice. "The Costumes of *Love's Labour's Lost, Twelfth Night,* and *The Tempest.*" *SAB,* XI (1936), 93-106.

B1929   Linthicum, M. Channing. *Costume in the Drama of Shakespeare and His Contemporaries.* Oxford: Claredon Press, 1936. Pp. xii, 307; pl.
        Rev: A7268.

B1930   Gilder, Rosamond. *John Gielgud's "Hamlet."* Oxford Univ. Press, 1937. Pp. 234.
        By J. Gielgud: "The Hamlet Tradition: Notes on Costume Scenery, and Stage Business," pp. 109-171.
        Rev: B3219.

B1931   Green, J. M. C. *Period Costumes and Settings for the Small Stage.* London, 1937. Pp. 168.

B1932   Miran, P. "Incorrect Costumes in Evans's *Richard II.*" *Commonweal,* XXVI (1937), 50.

B1933   "Costume Designs for *Winter's Tale.*" *TAr,* XXII (1938), 502.

B1934   Gill, W. W. "Shakespeare in Modern Dress." *N &Q,* 175 (1938), 186-187; A. H. Cooper-Pritchard, ibid., pp. 265-266.

B1935   Kelly, Francis Michael. *Shakespearian Costume for Stage and Screen.* London: Black; Boston: W. H. Baker, 1938. Pp. x, 132.
        Rev: B1310.

B1936   D'Amico, S. "Amleto in Abiti Moderni." *NA,* 402 (1939), 235-237.

B1937   Boas, G. "Shakespeare in Modern Dress." *Blackwood's Magazine,* 245 (1939), 167-173.

B1938   Brooke, Iris. *Western European Costume, and Its Relation to the Theatre.* Vol. I: Thirteenth to Seventeenth Century. London: Harrap, 1939. Pp. 151.
        Rev: A7265.

B1939   Bohet, V. "Shakespeare in Modern Dress." *LT,* IX (1943), 99-107.

B1940   J., W. H. "Shakespeare in Modern Dress." *N &Q,* 184 (1943), 329-331; comment by E. G., ibid., p. 374; by M. H. Dodds, ibid., 185, (1943), 323-324; by St. Vincent Troubridge, ibid., pp. 381-382.

B1941   Jackson, Sir Barry. "The Apparel Oft Proclaims . . . " *TAr,* XXX (1946), 734-737.

B1942   Cancelled.

B1943   Ffolkes, David. "The Glass of Fashion." *TAr,* April, 1951, 54-55.

B1944   Johnson, S. F. "Shakespeare Without Ear—the Protest of a Professor." *TAr,* Oct., 1951, pp. 38-39.

B1945   Marshall, Norman. "Shakespeare in India." *Theatre Newsletter,* April 28, 1951, p. 3.

B1946   Altman, George, Ralph Freud, Kenneth MacGowan, William Melnitz. *Theater Pictorial.* Berkeley and Los Angeles: Univ. of California Press, 1953.

B1947   Banke, Cécile de. *Shakespearean Stage Production: Then and Now.* New York: McGraw-Hill, 1953. Pp. xviii, 342.
        Rev: A7409.

B1948   Richardson, Genevieve. *Costuming on the American Stage—1751-1901: A Study of the Major Developments in Wardrobe Practice and Costume Style.* DD, University of Illinois, 1953. Pp. 286. Mic A53-2208. *DA,* XIII (1953), 1305. Publ. No. 6003.

B1949 "Russian Dressing." *TAr*, xxxviii (Sept. 1954), 15.

B1950 Kahan, Gerald. *A Shakespeare Production Handbook for Non-Professionals.* DD, University of Wisconsin, 1954. Abstr. publ. in Univ. of Wisconsin *Summaries of Doctoral Dissertations, 1953-54,* Madison, 1955, pp. 576-578.

B1951 *King Lear.* Intro. by Donald Wolfit, with Designs in Colour by Noguchi. London: Folio Society, 1956. Pp. 128.
Illustrations are reproductions of designs for sets and costumes.

B1952 Chavez, Edmund. "Heraldry." *Players Magazine,* xxxiii (1956), 40-41.
Hints for Shak. costuming.

B1953 Russell, D. A. "Hamlet Costumes from Garrick to Gielgud." *ShS*, ix (1956), 54-58.

B1954 Mander, Raymond, and Joe Mitchenson. "Hamlet Costumes: A Correction." *ShS*, xi (1958), 123-124.
Corrects B1953.

B1955 Merchant, W. M. "Classical Costumes in Shakespearian Productions." *ShS*, x (1957), 71-76.

B1956 Russell, Douglas A. "Shakespearean Costume: Contemporary or Fancy Dress." *ETJ*, x (1958), 105-112.

(c) STAGING
i. General

B1957 Myers, A. Michael. "British and American Staging of Shakespeare." *SAB*, xii (1937), 180-186.

B1958 Mitchell, Lee. *Elizabethan Scenes of Violence and the Problem of Their Staging.* DD, Northwestern University, 1941. Abstr. publ. in *Summaries of Doctoral Dissertations,* ix (1941), Chicago & Evanston: Northwestern Univ., 1942, pp. 69-73.

B1959 Coghill, Nevill. "The Governing Idea. Essays in Stage-Interpretation of Shakespeare." *Shakespeare Quarterly* (London), i (1947), 9-17.

B1960 Byrne, M. St. Clare. "Shakespeare and His World: Modern Production and Theatrical Tradition." *Listener*, xlii (Sept. 8, 1949), 393-395.

B1961 Payne, B. Iden. "This Is the Forest of Arden." *TAr* (June 1949), 51-53.

B1962 Reynolds, George F. "Staging Elizabethan Plays." *SAB*, xxiv (1949), 258-263.

B1963 Reynolds, George F. "Was There a 'Tarras' in Shakespeare's Globe?" *ShS*, iv (1951), 97-100.

B1964 Richey, Dorothy. "The Dance in *Henry VIII:* A Production Problem." *Bulletin of Furman University,* xxxv (1952), No. 3, 1-11.

B1965 Long, John H. "Music for the Replica Staging of Shakespeare." In Matthews and Emery's *Studies in Shakespeare,* 1953, pp. 88-95.

B1966 Hoak, Eugene Q. *Some Basic Specific Problems of Staging the Play in the College and University Theatre.* DD, Ohio State University, 1954.

B1967 Downer, Alan S. "A Comparison of Two Stagings: Stratford-upon-Avon and London." *SQ*, vi (1955), 429-433.

B1968 Green, John H. *The Development of Stage Rigging in the United States (1766-1893).* DD, University of Denver, 1955.

B1969 "A.E.T.A. Welcomes Shakespeare Stagers!" *Educational Theatre News,* October, 1956, p. 1.

B1970 Hewes, Henry. "Broadway Postscript: A Workingman's Guide to Shaw and Shakespeare." *SatR*, July 21, 1956, p. 30.

B1971 Barnes, T. R. "Cutting Shakespeare." *Journal of Education* (London), xxxix (1957), 395-396.

B1972 Herrey, Hermann. "Shakespeare-Interpretation auf der Bühne." *SJ*, 93 (1957), 114-127.

B1973 Hewes, Henry. "How To Use Shakespeare." *SatR*, July 13, 1957, pp. 10-13.
Twenty-one directors' opinions concerning Shak. texts, criticism, productions, types of stage, and paraphrase. (An adaptation of this article is to be found in *ShN,* vii, 30.)

B1974 Brown, Ivor. "What Kind of Stage?" *Drama,* Spring, 1958, pp. 21-22.

B1975 Hosley, Richard. "An Elizabethan Tiring-House Façade." *SQ*, ix (1958), 588.

B1976 Quinn, Seabury Grandin, Jr. *Ideological Spectacle: Theories of Staging Methods.* DD, Yale University, 1958.

B1977 Sjöberg, Alf and Vilgot Sjöman. "Plats för Stumt Spel!" *Vi* (Stockholm: Nordisk Rotogravyr), xlv, No. 45 (1958).

ii. Central Staging

B1978 Jones, Margo. "Doing What Comes Naturally." *TAr*, June, 1949, pp. 55-56.

B1979 Jones, Margo. "Shakespeare in the Round." *World Theatre,* iii (1953), 29-32.

B1980 Kloten, Edgar L. "Space for Shakespeare." *ShN*, iii (1953), 36.

B1981 Golden, Joseph. *The Position and Character of Theater-in-the-Round in the United States.* DD, University of Illinois, 1954. Pp. 160. Mic A55-235. *DA*, xv, (1955), 166. Publ. No. 10,482.
Chap. IV summarizes historical platform stages, including Elizabethan, pp. 122-125.

B1982   Purdom, C. B. "The Principles of Open Staging." *ShN*, IV (1954), 27. Abstracted from his
        article in *The Shakespeare Stage* entitled "A Note on the Use of the Open or Shakespeare Stage."

B1983   Boyle, Walden P. *Central and Flexible Staging. A New Theatre in the Making.* Univ. of
        California Press, 1956.
        Rev: by Kathleen Snuggs, *Books Abroad*, Winter 1957, p. 86; by Rev. Gilbert V. Hartke,
        O.P., *SQ*, IX (1958), 414-415.

iii. Scenery

B1984   Oenslager, Donald. *Scenery Then and Now.* New York: W. W. Norton, 1936. Pp. 265.
        Rev: by R. L. Duffus, *NYTBR*, Jan. 17, 1937, p. 7.

B1985   Whorf, Richard. "Scene and Costume Designs for *Macbeth*." *TAr*, XXV (1941), 197-198.

B1986   Burrell, J. "Réflexions sur la Mise en Scène des Tragédies de Shakespeare." *La Revue Théâtrale*,
        1947, pp. 169-170.

B1987   McDowell, John H. "Shakespeare and Modern Design." *JEGP*, XLVI (1947), 337-347.

B1988   Seyfarth, H. "Zu Modernen Shakespeare-Inszenierungen." *Hamburger akad. Rundschau*, II
        (1947/48), 361-363.

B1989   Gurzki, H. "Szenische Meditationen über Shakespeare." *Die Lücke*, Nos. 3/4 (1948), 32.

B1990   Simonson, Lee. *The Art of Scenic Design. A Pictorial Analysis of Stage Setting and Its Relation
        to Theatrical Production.* New York: Harper's; Toronto: Musson, 1950. Pp. 174.
        Rev: by Saul Colin, *NYTBR*, April 23, 1950, p. 25; by Lee Mitchell, *QJS*, XXXVI, 421-422.

B1991   Cole, Wendell G. *Scenery on the New York Stage, 1900-1920.* DD, Stanford University, 1952.
        Abstr. publ. in *Abstracts of Dissertations*, Stanford Univ., XXVII (1951-52), 382-385.

B1992   Thornton, Helen G. *Thesaurus of Terms Relating to Scenery.* DD, University of Denver, 1952.

B1993   Douty, John T. *Scenic Styles in the Modern American Theatre.* DD, University of Denver, 1953.

B1994   Rosenfeld, Sybil. "Scene Designs of William Capon." *TN*, x (1955/56), 118-122.

B1995   Hainaux, R., and Yves-Bonnat. *Stage Design Throughout the World Since 1935.* Texts and illus.
        collected by the national centres of the International Theatre Institute. New York: Theatre
        Arts Books, 1956. Pp. 219.
        Rev: B2034.

B1996   Valogne, C. "Décors pour Jouer Shakespeare." *Art et Décoration*, No. 62 (1957), pp. 40-41 ff.

B1997   Pope, Curtis L. *A Study of the Integration of Scenic Design and Directing in the Execution of Scenery
        for Three Productions.* DD, State University of Iowa, 1958.

B1998   Thompson, James Robert. *Twentieth Century Scene Design: Its History and Stylistic Origins.* DD,
        University of Minnesota, 1958.

iv. Lighting

B1999   Held, McDonald Watkins. *A History of Stage Lighting in the United States in the Nineteenth
        Century.* DD, Northwestern University, 1955. Pp. 311. Mic 55-685. *DA*, XV (1955), 1930.
        Publ. No. 13,091.

B2000   Mitchell, Lee. "Shakespeare's Lighting Effects." *Speech Monographs*, XV (1948), 72-84.

B2001   Walker, John A. *The Functions of Stage Lighting in the Changing Concepts of Stage Design.* DD,
        Cornell University, 1952.

v. Miscellaneous

B2002   Mitchell, Lee. "Shakespeare's Sound Effects." *Speech Monographs*, XIV (1947), 127-138.

B2003   Mitchell, Lee. "Shakespeare's Legerdemain." *Speech Monographs*, XVI (1949), 144-161.

B2003a Schneideman, Robert Ivan. *Elizabethan Legerdemain, and Its Employment in the Drama, 1576-
        1642.* DD, Northwestern University, 1956. Pp. 274. *DA*, XVI (1956), 2558.

B2004   Richey, Dorothy. *The Dance in the Drama of the Elizabethan Public Theatre: A Production
        Problem.* DD, Northwestern University, 1951. Abstr. publ. in Northwestern Univ. *Summaries
        of Doctoral Dissertations, 1951*, Vol. 19, Chicago and Evanston: Northwestern Univ., 1952,
        pp. 169-174.

B2005   Engel, Lehman. *Music for the Classical Tragedy.* New York: Flammer, 1953. Pp. 96.
        Rev: B1839.

B2006   Sprague, Arthur Colby. *Shakespearian Players and Performances.* Harvard Univ. Press, 1953.
        Pp. viii, 222.
        Rev: B1282.

B2007   Helpmann, Robert. "Formula for Midsummer Magic; Choreographer Principal of the Old
        Vic Production." *TAr*, XXXVIII (1954), 76-77.

B2008   Manifold, John Streeter. *The Music in English Drama.* From Shakespeare to Purcell. London:
        Rockliff, 1956. Pp. ix, 208.
        Rev: A6154.

B2009   Moulton, Robert Darrell. *Choreography in Musical Comedy and Revue on the New York Stage
        from 1925 Through 1950.* DD, University of Minnesota, 1958.

(d) PROBLEMS OF SPECIFIC PLAYS
i. Comedies

B2010   Jackson, Sir Barry. "Producing the Comedies." *ShS*, VIII (1955), 74-80.

B2011   Sisson, Charles Jasper. "*The Taming of the Shrew*." *Drama* (London), XXXVIII (Autumn, 1955), 25-27.

B2012   Vitaly, Georges. "Notes de Travail à Propos de *La Mégère Apprivoisée*." *Revue Théâtrale*, No. 26 (1954), 19-27.

B2013   Watkins, Ronald. *Moonlight at the Globe*. An Essay in Shakespeare Production based on performance of *A Midsummer Night's Dream* at Harrow School. Foreword by R. W. Moore. Drawings by Maurice Percival. London: Michael Joseph, 1946; Hollywood: Transatlantic Arts, 1949. Pp. 136.
Rev: *TLS*, Dec. 14, 1946, p. 616.

B2014   Lelyveld, Toby B. *Shylock on the Stage. Significant Changes in the Interpretation of Shakespeare's Jew*. DD, Columbia University, 1951. *Microfilm Abstracts* XI (1951), 772-774.

B2015   Worsley, Thomas Cuthbert. "A German Troilus." *NstN*, L (1955), 572-573.

B2016   Gross, Edgar. "Meine Inszenierung von Shakespeares *Sturm*." *Die Bühne*, II (1936), 10-12.

ii. Histories

B2017   Villar, J. "La Tragédie du Roi Richard II (Tableau du Matériel Scénique)." *La Revue Théâtrale*, VII (1948), 12-15.

B2018   Jackson, Sir Barry. "On Producing *Henry VI*." *ShS*, VI (1953), 49-52.

B2019   Sandoe, James. "*King Henry the Sixth. Part II:* Notes During Production." *Theatre Annual*, XIII (1955), 32-48.

iii. Tragedies

B2020   McDowell, John H. "Analyzing *Julius Caesar* for Modern Production." *QJS*, XXXI (1945), 303-314.

B2021   Sjögren, G. "Den Kallsinnige Hamlet" ("The Dispassionate Hamlet"). *Dagens Nyheter*, Aug. 27, 1951.

B2022   Trewin, J. C. "Who's There?" *Illustrated London News*, Dec. 17, 1955, p. 1070.

B2023   Tykesson, Elisabeth. "Shakespeare-analysen i Goethes *Wilhelm Meister*." *En Goethebok till Algot Werin*. Lund, 1958, pp. 59-75.

B2024   *Othello*. London: Folio Society, 1955. Pp. 128.
Contains color plates by Tanya Moiseiwitsch and an introduction, by Orson Welles, dealing with the problems of this play from the point of view of actor and producer.

B2025   Strozzi, Tito. "Redatelj o Svojoj Scenskoj Postavi *Otela*" [The Producer on his Production of *Othello*], *Kazališni List* (Zagreb), II, No. 35 (1947), pp. 1-3.

B2026   *King Lear*. Intro. by Donald Wolfit, with Designs in Colour by Noguchi. London: Folio Society, 1956. Pp. 128.
Intro. discusses the play on today's stage.

B2027   Derrick, Leland Eugene. *The Stage History of "King Lear."* DD, University of Texas, 1940.

B2028   Williams, David. "On Producing *King Lear*." *SQ*, II (1951), 247-252.

B2029   Masefield, John. *A "Macbeth" Production*. London: Heineman, 1945; New York: Macmillan, 1946. Pp. 64.
Rev: A9069.

B2030   Jenkin, Bernard. "*Antony and Cleopatra:* Some Suggestions on the Monument Scenes." *RES*, XXI (1945), 1-14.

B2031   Hilpert, Heinz. "*Antonius und Cleopatra*—Heute." *Blätter d. Dt. Theaters in Göttingen*. Hefte 89, 1956.

B2032   Falkenberg, Hans-Geert. "Zur Bühnen- und Übersetzungsgeschichte von *Antonius und Cleopatra*." *Blätter d. Dt. Theaters in Göttingen*. Hefte 89, 1956.

B2033   Ruppel, K. H. "*Antonius und Cleopatra*. Werkgestalt und Bühnenerscheinung." *SJ*, 93 (1957), 186-195.

c. SURVEYS OF PERFORMANCES IN A
SPECIFIC PERIOD
(1) SEVERAL COUNTRIES TOGETHER (167;56)

B2034   *Stage Design Throughout the World Since 1935*. Texts and Illustrations Collected by the National Centres of the International Theatre Institute Chosen and Presented by René Hainaux and Yves-Bonnat. With a Sketch to Serve as a Foreword by Jean Cocteau. Preface by Kenneth Rae. London: Harrap, 1957. Pp. 219. Illustrated.
Rev: *TLS*, May 17, 1957, p. 300; by L. L. Zimmerman, *Players Magazine*, XXXIV (1958), 142-143.

B2035   Hobson, Harold. *International Theatre Annual*. London: John Calder. No. 1, 1956; No. 2, 1957; No. 3, 1958.
        Rev: *TLS*, Nov. 15, 1957, p. 695.

B2036   "International News," *ShS*, I (1948), 112-117; II (1949), 126-129; III (1950), 116-119. "International Notes," *ShS*, IV (1951), 123-128; V (1952), 111-118; VI (1953), 117-125; VII (1954), 107-117; VIII (1955), 118-122; IX (1956), 111-118; X (1957), 115-122; XI (1958), 117-122.

B2037   Heine, Arthur. "The Actors Are Come Hither, My Lord." *SQ*, I (1950), 196-199.

B2038   Venezky, Alice. "Current Shakespearian Productions in England and France." *SQ*, II (1951), 335-342.

B2039   "Current Theater Notes." *SQ*, II (1951), 343-351; Hyde, Mary C., ed. "Current Theater Notes." *SQ*, IV (1953), 61-75; ibid., V (1954), 51-69; ibid., VI (1955), 67-88; Griffin, Alice, ed. "Current Theater Notes." *SQ*, VII (1956), 79-96; ibid., VIII (1957), 71-89; ibid., IX (1958), 39-58.

B2040   Stahl, Ernst L. "Shakespeare Heute in Europa." *Die Quelle*, II, No. 4 (1948), 11-18.

B2041   Smith, Robert M. "Productions of *Hamlet*, 1930 to the Present." *SAB*, XXIV (1949), 71-72.

B2042   Stahl, Ernst Leopold. "Shakespeare in Europa nach dem zweiten Weltkrieg." *SJ*, 82/83 (1948), 154-163.

B2043   Samachson, Dorothy, and Joseph Samachson. *The Dramatic Story of the Theatre*. New York, 1955.
        Rev: by Jan Bussel, *Drama*, Autumn, 1957, pp. 39-40.

B2044   "Around the World in Eleven Plays." *TAr*, March, 1958, pp. 54-56.
        Cym. by National Theatre of Greece in Athens, *Ham.* in Brazil by Sergio Cardoso, and Verdi's *Otelo* at the State Opera House, Ankara, Turkey.

(a) ENGLAND AND AMERICA
i.   General

B2045   Meyers, A. Michael. "British and American Staging of Shakespeare." *SAB*, XII (1937), 180-186.

B2046   Boyd, Alice K. *The Interchange of Plays Between London and New York, 1910-1939; a Study in Relative Audience Response*. DD, Columbia University, 1948. New York: King's Crown Press, 1948. Pp. 125.
        Survey does not include revivals.

B2047   Gerold, A. W. *The Organization of Representative Acting Companies Since Elizabethan Times*. MS thesis, Columbia University, 1948. Pp. 78.

B2048   Peck, Seymour. "Boom in Shakespeare." *New York Times Magazine*, March 25, 1956, pp. 28-29.

B2049   Barbour, Thomas. "Revivals and Revisions: Theatre Chronicle." *Hudson Review*, X (1957), 261-269.

B2050   Bryant, J. A., Jr. "Drama: Reinterpretations and Revivals." *SR*, LXVI (1958), 318-333.

B2051   Barrett, Mary Ellen, and Marvin Barrett. "Theatre: Shakespeare in the Summer." *Good Housekeeping*, July, 1957, p. 60.

B2052   "Grand Season for Shakespeare: The Poet's Comic Plays Are Summer Hits." *Life*, Aug. 26, 1957, pp. 124-128.

ii.   Some Specific Plays

B2053   Spriggs, C. O. "*Hamlet* on the Nineteenth Century Stage." *QJS*, XXII (1936), 78-85.

B2054   Detrick, L. E. "The Stage-History of *King Lear*." MS Dissertation, University of Texas, 1938.

B2055   Nelson, Esther A. "32 Lady Macbeths." *Emerson Quarterly*, XIX (1939), 11-16.

B2056   Smallwood, O. "The Stage-History of *The Merchant of Venice*." DD, University of Oklahoma, 1939. Abstr. in *Univ. of Oklahoma Bulletin*, January 1939, p. 117.

B2057   Heine, Arthur, and Laurie Schwab Strauss. "Productions of *The Merchant of Venice*." *SAB*, XXIII (1948), 183-187.

B2058   Flatter, Richard. "Shylock in Bygone Days." *Shakespeare Quarterly* (London), I (1947), 18-21.

B2059   Lelyveld, Toby Bookholtz. *Shylock on the Stage: Significant Changes in the Interpretation of Shakespeare's Jew*. DD, Columbia University, 1951. Pp. 196. Mic A51-284. *Mcf Ab*, XI (1951), 772. Publ. No. 2541.

(2) ENGLAND

B2060   Gielgud, John. *Early Stages*. London: Macmillan, 1939. Pp. xii, 322.
        Nothing before 1880.

B2061   Linton, Calvin Darlington. *Shakespeare Staging in London from Irving to Gielgud*. DD, Johns Hopkins University, 1940.

B2062   Agate, James. *Brief Chronicles, a Survey of the Plays of Shakespeare and the Elizabethans in Actual Performance*. London: J. Cape, 1943. Pp. 311.
        Rev: *TLS*, August 28, 1943, p. 416.

B2063 Byrne, M. St. Clare. "Fifty Years of Shakespearian Production: 1898-1948." *ShS*, II (1949), 1-20.

B2064 Farjeon, Herbert. *The Shakespearean Scene: Dramatic Criticisms.* London and New York: Hutchinson & Co., 1949. Pp. 195.
Rev: B1699.

B2065 Reiss, Hans. "Notizen über Shakespeare in Dublin." *SJ*, 82/83 (1949), 190-192.

B2066 Rylands, George, and Una Ellis-Fermor. "London Productions." *ShS*, I (1948), 103-106.

B2067 Rylands, George. "From Strolling Player to Oxford Accent." *Listener*, XLII (Sept. 15, 1949), 439-441.

B2068 Klajn, Hugo. "Šekspir u Današnjoj Engleskoj" [Shakespeare in Present-day England]. *Književne Novine* (Belgrade), III (1950), 36.

B2069 Worsley, T. C. "Von Shakespeare zu Fry. Ein Londoner Theaterbrief." *Der Monat*, II (1949/50), 208-211.

B2070 Hawkins, William. "Festive Island '51." *TAr*, Sept., 1951, pp. 28-29, 92.

B2071 Hudson, Lynton. *The English Stage, 1850-1950.* London: Harrap, 1951.
Rev: B1487.

B2072 Trewin, John Courtenay. "The Shakespearean Stage." *National and English Review*, 1951, pp. 357-360.

B2073 Stephens, Frances (compiler). *Theatre World Annual* (London). A Pictorial Review of West End Productions.
No. 1: 1949-50, London, 1950.
No. 2: 1950-51, London, 1951.
No. 3: 1951-52, London, 1952.
No. 4: 1952-53, London, 1953.
No. 5: 1953-54, London, 1954.
No. 6: 1954-55, London, 1955.
Rev: *TLS*, Dec. 7, 1956, p. 739; by Jack Clay, *QJS*, XLIII (1957), 317; *TLS*, Feb. 21, 1958, p. 107; *Drama*, Spring, p. 44; *TLS*, Nov. 7, p. 647.

B2074 "Shakespeare Productions in the United Kingdom, 1950." (Shakespeare Memorial Library.) *ShS*, V (1952), 119-120; ibid., for 1951, VI (1953), 126-128; ibid., for 1952, VII (1954), 118-120; ibid., for 1953, VIII (1955), 123-126; ibid., for 1954, IX (1956), 119-121; ibid., for 1955, X (1957), 123-125; ibid., for 1956, XI (1958), 125-127.

B2075 White, William. "Shakespeare in London, 1953." *ShN*, III (April, 1953), 12.

B2075a "Shakespeare on the Stage: 1928." *TLS*, Special Autumn No., August 28, 1953, pp. xxxii-xxxiv.

B2076 Price, C. J. L. *The History of the English Theatre in Wales, 1844-1951.* DD, Wales, 1953.

B2077 Rylands, George. "Festival Shakespeare in the West End." *ShS*, VI (1953), 140-146.

B2078 Kemp, T. C. "Acting Shakespeare: Modern Tendencies in Playing and Production with Special Reference to Some Recent Productions." *ShS*, VII (1954), 121-127.

B2079 Speaight, Robert. *William Poel and the Elizabethan Revival.* London, 1954.
Rev: B1825.

B2080 David, Richard. "Plays Pleasant and Plays Unpleasant." *ShS*, VIII (1955), 132-138.

B2081 Purdom, C. B. *Harley Granville-Barker: Man of the Theatre, Dramatist and Scholar.* London: Rockliff, 1955. Pp. xiv, 322.
Rev: B1803.

B2082 Spender, Stephen. "Pages from a Journal." *SR*, LXIII (1955), 614-630.

B2083 Wong, Helene Har Lin. *The Late Victorian Theatre: As Reflected in "The Theatre," 1878-1897.* DD, Louisiana State University, 1955. Pp. 226. Mic 55-1385. *DA*, XV (1955), 2347. Publ. No. 14,082.

B2084 "Monument Without a Tomb." *TAr*, April, 1956, p. 33.

B2085 Browne, E. Martin. "English Hamlets of the Twentieth Century." *ShS*, IX (1956), 16-23.

B2086 Brown, Ivor. *Theatre, 1954-55.* London: Max Reinhardt, 1955. Pp. vii, 200.
Rev: *TLS*, Dec. 23, 1955, p. 775; by T. C. Worsley, *NstN*, L, 793; by N. March Hunnings, *TN*, X (1956), 96.

B2087 Brown, Ivor. *Theatre, 1955-56.* With Contributions by William Douglas Home, Sir Ralph Richardson, Thomas Quinn Curtis, and Henry Sherek. London: Max Reinhardt, 1956.
Rev: by D. M. S., *English*, XI (1957), 161; by Stanley Richards, *Players Magazine*, Nov., pp. 46-47.

B2088 Robertson, Roderick. "University Theatre at Oxford." *ETJ*, VIII (1956), 194-206.

B2089 Rowell, George. *The Victorian Theatre.* Oxford Univ. Press, 1956. Pp. 327.
Rev: B1494.

B2090 Bloom, Ursula. *The Elegant Edwardian.* London: Hutchinson, 1957. Pp. 224.

B2091 Williamson, Audrey. *Contemporary Theatre, 1953-1956.* New York: Macmillan, 1956. Pp. xi, 195; 46 plates.
Summary of the major productions in the British Theatre. Includes category "Shakespeare."

Rev: by John Clay, *QJS*, XLII (1957), 317.

B2092   Thespis. "School Shakespeare Productions." *English* (London), XI (1956/57), 187-188.

B2093   Mander, Raymond, and Joe Mitchenson. *A Picture History of the British Theatre.* London: Hulton Press, 1957. Pp. 160. Illustrated.
        Rev: B1275.

B2094   Trewin, J. C. *The Night Has Been Unruly.* London: Hale, 1957. Pp. 288.
        Rev: B1326.

B2095   Cookman, A. V. "Shakespeare's Contemporaries on the Modern English Stage." *SJ*, 94 (1958), 29-41.

B2096   Muraoka, Akira. "Shakespeare in Stageland, 1816-1856." Otsuka *Festschrift*, 1958, pp. 351-367.

B2097   Walker, Roy. "Unto Caesar: A Review of Recent Productions." *ShS*, XI (1958), 128-135.

(3)   AMERICA
(a)   GENERAL SURVEYS

B2098   Blum, Daniel. *Theatre World, Season 1944-45*, Vol. I. New York: Greenberg. For 1945-46, Vol. II; for 1946-47, Vol. III; for 1947-48, Vol. IV; for 1948-49, Vol. V; for 1949-50, Vol. VI; for 1950-51, Vol. VII; for 1951-52, Vol. VIII; for 1952-53, Vol. IX; for 1953-54, Vol. X. for 1954-55, Vol XI; for 1955-56, Vol. XII; for 1956-57, Vol. XIII; for 1957-58, Vol. XIV. Listings of productions and performances, opening and closing dates, casts, and biographies of actors and actresses.
        Rev: by Wayne Bowman, *Players Magazine*, XXXIV (1958), 92.

B2099   Lovell, John, Jr. "Shakespeare's American Play." *TAr*, XXVIII (1944), 363-370.
        Othello in America.

B2100   Mulligan, L. "Shakespeare et l'Entente Cordiale." *Aujourd'hui*, Nov. 1946, pp. 12-14. (Translation from *Canadian Review of Music and Art*, V, No. 1 [Feb., 1946], 17-18.)

B2101   Mangan, Nora Aileen. *Augustin Daly as a Producer of Shakespearian Drama.* DD, University of Washington, 1939. Abstr. in *Univ. of Washington Abstracts of Theses*, IV (1939), 133-138.

B2101a Felheim, Marvin L. *The Career of Augustin Daly.* DD, Harvard University, 1948.

B2101b Felheim, Marvin. *The Theatre of Augustin Daly.* Harvard Univ. Press, 1956. Pp. 329.
        Rev: A9208.

B2102   Bab, Julius. "Shakespeare in Amerika." *SJ*, 82/83 (1949), 164-174.

B2103   Webster, Margaret. "Why Shakespeare Goes Right On." *New York Times Magazine*, Aug. 12, 1951, p. 10.

B2104   Venezky, Alice. "Shakespeare U.S.A." *TAr*, April, 1951, pp. 51-52.

B2104a Griffin, Alice Venezky. "Shakespeare Festivals in America." *TAr*, April, 1956, pp. 62-63. Annotated and anticipatory survey of the rapidly expanding Shak. Festival idea.

B2104b Griffin, Alice Venezky. "Theatre USA." *TAr*, April, 1954, pp. 88-93; April, 1955, pp. 81-85; April, 1957, pp. 59-61; Aug., 1957, pp. 71-83, 87; Sept., 1957, pp. 57-59, 95-96; July, 1958, pp. 52-55; Aug., 1958, pp. 58-71.

B2105   Bailey, Margery. "The Shakespeare Stage and American Theatre." *Colorado Quarterly*, I (Spring, 1953), 355-367.

B2106   Zimmerman, Leland L. *The Federal Theater: An Evaluation and Comparison with Foreign National Theaters.* DD, University of Wisconsin, 1955. Abstr. publ. in Univ. of Wisconsin *Summaries of Doctoral Dissertations, 1954-55*, Madison, 1956, pp. 524-525.

B2107   Davis, Frances D. "An Itinerant Playgoer." *ShN*, V (1955), 37.

B2108   Moore, Mavor. "A Theatre for Canada." *UTQ*, XXVI (1956), 1-16.

B2109   Beaulne, Guy. "World Reviews: Canada." *World Theatre*, V (1956), 244.

B2110   "Shakespeare in a Straw Hat." *Economist*, Aug. 24, 1957, pp. 617, 619.

B2111   Gordon, George Newton. *Theatrical Movements in the "Theatre Arts" Magazine from 1916 to 1948: A Description and Analysis.* DD, New York University, 1957. Pp. 379. Mic. 57-2610. *DA*, XVII (1957), 1622. Publ. No. 21,701.

B2112   McManaway, James G. "Shakespearian Productions in America in 1955-56." *SJ*, 93 (1957), 145-153.

(b)   SCHOOLS

B2113   Manders, V. E. C. "Shakespeare at St. Bernard's." *SQ*, II (1951), 123-126.

B2114   Griffin, Alice. "Bard on the Boards." *TAr*, April, 1956, pp. 63-64.

B2115   Hatlen, Theodore. "College and University Productions, 1955-1956." *ETJ*, IX (1957), 134-137.

(c)   NEW YORK

B2116   Odell, George C. D. *Annals of the New York Stage.* New York: Columbia Univ. Press, 1927-1949.
        See B1543 for volumes and years.

B2117   Crowther, Bosley. "Long Runs of Hamlet and Other Shakespeare Plays." *New York Times*, Jan. 10, 1937, p. X3.

B2118   Eaton, Walter P. "Shakespeare—with a Difference." *Atlantic Monthly*, 159 (1937), 474-477.

B2119   Mersand, Joseph. "Speech in the New Plays. The Poetic Dramas of Shakespeare and Maxwell Anderson Dominate the New York Stage." *Correct English*, xxxvii (1937), 68-69; 117-118.

B2120   Blymyer, Louise A. *Journalistic Dramatic Criticism: A Survey of Theatre Reviews in New York, 1857-1927.* DD, Louisiana State University, 1939.

B2121   Downer, Alan S. "The Dark Lady of Schubert Alley." *SR*, LIV (1946), 119-138.

B2122   Atkinson, Brooks. "*Richard II* and *Hamlet.*" *Broadway Scrapbook*, New York, 1947, pp. 160-163.

B2123   Weitenkampf, Frank. *Manhattan Kaleidoscope.* New York: Charles Scribner's Sons, 1947. Pp. 290.

B2124   Young, Stark. *Immortal Shadows. A Book of Dramatic Criticism.* New York: Scribner's, 1948. Pp. 290. Reprinted: New York: Hill and Wang; London: Calder, 1958. Pp. 270.

B2125   Boardman, Abigail Casey. *A Study of Revivals of Plays in the New York City (Broadway) Theatres from 1925 to 1940.* DD, University of Wisconsin, 1944. Abstr. publ. in *Summaries of Doctoral Dissertations, Univ. of Wisconsin, 1943-47*, Madison, 1949, pp. 453-454.

B2126   White, Natalie E. *Shakespeare on the New York Stage, 1891-1941.* DD, Yale University, 1946.

B2127   Jennings, John Henry. *A History of the New Theatre, New York 1909-1911.* DD, Stanford University, 1953. Pp. 281. Mic A53-490. *DA*, xiii (1953), 270. Publ. No. 4672.

B2128   Sprague, Arthur Colby. "Shakespeare on the New York Stage, 1953-1954." *SQ*, v (1954), 311-315. For 1954-55, vi (1955), 423-427; for 1955-56, vii (1956), 393-398.

B2129   Griffin, Alice. "Shakespeare in New York City, 1956-1957." *SQ*, viii (1957), 515-519.

B2130   Griffin, Alice. "The Shakespeare Season in New York." *SQ*, ix (1958), 531-534.

(d) REGIONAL HISTORIES

B2131   Reardon, William Robert. *Banned in Boston: A Study of Theatrical Censorship in Boston from 1630-1950.* DD, Stanford University, 1953. Pp. 253. Mic A53-996. *DA*, xiii (1953), 609. Publ. No. 5386.
        Merch. in 1937; *Ham.* in 1948. From 1630 to 1900, 7 plays were banned. From 1901 to 1950, 67 were banned, including Shak., *Tartuffe, Streetcar, Iceman Cometh, Waiting for Lefty, Tobacco Road, Juno and the Paycock, American Tragedy, What Price Glory, Desire under the Elms,* and *Birth of a Nation.*

B2132   Hastings, William T. "Shakespeare in Providence." *SQ*, viii (1957), 335-351.

B2133   Borgers, Edward W. *A History of Dramatic Production in Princeton, New Jersey.* DD, New York University, 1950.

B2134   Paul, H. N. "Shakespeare in Philadelphia." *Proc. of Amer. Philosoph. Soc.*, LXXVI (1936), 719-730.

B2135   Wentz, John Calely. *The Hedgerow Theatre: An Historical Study.* DD, University of Pennsylvania, 1954. Pp. 273. Mic A54-1301. *DA*, xiv (1954), 887. Publ. No. 7820.

B2136   Shockley, Martin S. *A History of the Theatre in Richmond, Virginia.* DD, University of North Carolina, 1939.

B2137   Arnold, John Coleman. *A History of the Lexington Theater from 1887 to 1900.* DD, University of Kentucky, 1956.

B2138   Maiden, Lewis Smith. *A Chronicle of the Theater in Nashville, Tennessee, 1876-1900.* DD, Vanderbilt University, 1955. Pp. 818. Mic 55-1140. *DA*, xv (1955), 2210-2211. Publ. No. 13,755.

B2139   Bradford, Clinton W. *The Non-Professional Theater in Louisiana.* DD, Louisiana State University, 1952.

B2140   Yocum, Jack H. *A History of Theatre in Houston, 1836-1954.* DD, University of Wisconsin, 1955. Abstr. publ. in Univ. of Wisconsin *Summaries of Doctoral Dissertations, 1954-55*, Madison, 1956, pp. 522-523.

B2141   Stolzenbach, Norma Frizzelle. *The History of the Theatre in Toledo, Ohio, from Its Beginnings Until 1893.* DD, University of Michigan, 1954. Pp. 342. Mic A54-1873. *DA*, xiv (1954), 1276. Publ. No. 8418.

B2142   Behringer, Clara M. *A History of the Theatre in Ann Arbor, Michigan, from Its Beginnings to 1904.* DD, University of Michigan, 1951. Pp. 604. Mic A51-123. *Micr Abstr*, xi, No. 2 (1951), 464. Publ. No. 2379.

B2143   Speaight, Robert. "The *Dream* in South Bend: Shakespeare in the Middle West." *Tablet*, April 27, 1957, pp. 393-394.

B2144   Jones, Charles A. *An Evaluation of the Educational Significance of the Children's Theatre of Evanston.* DD, Northwestern University, 1954. Pp. 130. Mic A54-595. *DA*, xiv (1954), 420-421. Publ. No. 7043.

B2145   Dukore, Bernard Frank. *Maurice Browne and the Chicago Little Theatre.* DD, University of Illinois, 1958. Pp. 156. Mic 58-4497. *DA*, xviii (1958), 693. Publ. No. 25,211.

B2146   Donahoe, Ned. *Theatres in Central Illinois—1850-1900.* DD, University of Illinois, 1953. Pp. 92. Mic A53-2201. *DA*, XIII (1953), 1300. Publ. No. 5954.

B2147   Rietz, Louise J. *History of the Theatre of Kansas City, Missouri, from the Beginnings Until 1900.* DD, State University of Iowa, 1940.

B2148   Thompson, Isabel C. *Amateur Theatricals in St. Louis, Missouri, 1875-1890.* DD, State University of Iowa, 1954. Pp. 611. Mic 55-123. *DA*, XV (1955), 899. Publ. No. 9595.

B2149   Hammack, James Alan. *Pope's Theatre and St. Louis Theatrical History: 1879-1895.* DD, State University of Iowa, 1954. Pp. 482. Mic 55-10. *DA*, XV (1955), 167. Publ. No. 9576.

B2150   Warfield, Jack W. *A History and Evaluation of the Wisconsin Players of Milwaukee, Wisconsin.* DD, University of Utah, 1953.

B2151   Herget, Patsy Joan. *A History and Evaluation of the Children's Theatre of Cedar Rapids.* DD, State University of Iowa, 1958.

B2152   Rothfuss, Hermann E. *The German Theater in Minnesota.* DD, University of Michigan, 1949.

B2153   Grossman, Audley Mitchell, Jr. *The Professional Legitimate Theater in Minneapolis from 1890 to 1910.* (Volumes I and II). DD, University of Minnesota, 1958. Pp. 787. Mic 58-484. *DA*, XVIII (1958), 330. Publ. No. 23,934.

B2154   Davidson, Levette J. "Shakespeare in the Rockies." *SQ*, IV (1953), 39-49.

B2155   Bell, William Campton. *A History of the Denver Theater During the Post-Pioneer Period (1881-1901).* DD, Northwestern University, 1942.

B2156   Winters, Earle William. *History of the Denver Theatre, 1901-1911, with Appended Material, 1901-1915.* DD, University of Denver, 1958.

B2157   Monson, Leland Hans. *Shakespeare in Utah (1847-1900).* DD, University of Utah, 1956. Pp. 322. Mic 57-1354. *DA*, XVII (1957), 848. Publ. No. 17,574.

B2158   Miller, William C. *An Historical Study of Theatrical Entertainment in Virginia City, Nevada.* DD, University of Southern California, 1947.

B2159   Gagey, Edmond McAdoo. *The San Francisco Stage: A History.* Based on Annals Compiled by the Research Department of the San Francisco Federal Theatre. New York: Columbia Univ. Press; London, Toronto: Oxford Univ. Press, 1950. Pp. xv, 264.
    Rev: B1618.

B2160   Earnest, Sue W. *An Historical Study of the Growth of the Theatre in Southern California.* DD, University of Southern California, 1947.

(4)   THE CONTINENT
(a)   FRANCE

B2161   Fluchère, Henri. "Shakespeare in France: 1900-1948." *ShS*, II (1949), 115-124.

B2162   De Smet, Robert. "*Othello* in Paris and Brussels." *ShS*, III (1950), 98-106.

B2163   Dasté, Jean. *Lettre sur Nos Spectacles Shakespeare (Comédie de St.-Etienne).* Revue Théâtrale, No. 26 (1954), 28-30.

B2164   "English Plays in Paris." *TLS*, May 27, 1955, p. xv.

B2165   *L'Encyclopédie du Théâtre Contemporain.* Vol. I. Paris: Plaisir de France, 1957. Pp. 208. Vol. II, 1914-1950.
    Rev: A9339.

(b)   GERMANY
i.   General Surveys

B2166   Mettin, H. Ch. "William Shakespeare auf dem Theater der Gegenwart." *Deutsches Adelsblatt*, LIV (1936), 294.

B2167   Stroedel, W. *Shakespeare-Pflege auf der dt. Bühne vom Ende des Weltkrieges bis z. Gegenwart.* DD, Erlangen. Weimar: Böhlau, 1938. Pp. 97.
    Rev: by Wolfgang Keller, *SJ*, LXXV (1939), 171-172; by J. Albrecht, *Časopis pro Moderní Filologii*, XXV, 365-368; by Hans Knudsen, *GA*, VI, Heft 9, p. 10; by Walter Jacobi, *Beiblatt*, LI (1940), 91-93; by J. B. Leishmann, *MLR*, XXXV, 85-88; by W. F. Schirmer, *Archiv*, 178 (1941), 145-146; by Berta Siebeck, *Lbl*, LXII, Sp. 13; by E. Th. Sehrt, *Eng. Studn.*, LXXVI (1944), 128-130.

B2168   Kosch, Wilhelm. *Das dts. Theater und Drama im 19. und 20. Jahrhundert.* Wurzburg: Wächter-Vlg., 1939. Pp. 165.

B2169   Mühlbach, Egon. "Theaterschau. Statistischer Überblick über die Aufführungen Shakespearescher Werke auf den Deutschen und Einigen Auslandsdeutschen Bühnen im Jahre 1936, Nebst Rundfunkbericht." *SJ*, LXXIII (1937), 224-228. For 1937, LXXIV (1938), 251-256; for 1938, LXXV (1939), 193-198; for 1939, LXXVI (1940), 254-259; for 1940, LXXVII (1941), 234-237; for 1941 and 1942, LXXX/LXXXI (1946).

B2170   Papsdorf, Werner. "Shakespeare auf der dts. Bühne 1938/40. Eine Übersicht." *SJ*, LXXVI (1940), 242-254.

B2171   Papsdorf, W., E. L. Stahl, and C. Niessen. "Shakespeare auf der Deutschen Bühne 1940-42." *SJ*, LXXVIII/LXXIX (1943).

B2172 Stahl, E. L. "Shakespeare im Aufführungsjahr 1943/44." *SJ*, 80/81 (1946).

B2173 Stroedel, Wolfgang. "Theaterschau 1947-1950." *SJ*, 84/86 (1951), 229-236. For subsequent years: 87/88 (1952), 174-180; 89 (1953), 173-177; 90 (1954), 290-294; 91 (1955), 217-224; 92 (1956), 299-304; 93 (1957), 216-222.

ii. Regional Studies

B2174 Trask, C. "Shakespeare on the Berlin Stage in 1936." *New York Times*, June 28, 1936, Sect. 2, p. x.

B2175 Ruppel, Karl H. *Berliner Schauspiel. Dramaturgische Betrachtungen 1936 bis 1942.* Berlin: Paul Neff, 1943. Pp. 350.
Rev: by Heinrich Jacobi, *EL*, III (1944), 20-21.

B2176 Hohenemser, Herbert. "Die Ersten Nachkriegs-Shakespeare-Aufführungen in Berlin." *SJ*, 82/83 (1949), 194-195.

B2177 Knudsen, Hans. "Shakespeare auf Berliner Bühnen 1945-1955." *SJ*, 91 (1955), 251-259.

B2178 Faltus, Hermann. *Vorhang Auf. Theater in Bremen.* Bremen: Verlag B. C. Heye, 1954. Pp. 119.
Rev: by Wolfgang Stroedel, *SJ*, 91 (1955), 367.

B2179 Stahl, Ernst Leopold. *Die Klassische Zeit des Mannheimer Theaters.* Part 1: Das Europäische Mannheim: Die Wege zum Dts. Nationaltheater. Mannheim: Hakenkreuzbanner-Vlg., 1940. Pp. 300. [Shakespeare passim.]
Rev: B1643.

B2180 Schön, Gerhard. "Vorwärts zu Shakespeare . . . auf Gewundenen Wegen an Rhein und Ruhr." *SJ*, 91 (1955), 233-237.

B2180a Dörnemann, Kurt. "Shakespeare an Ruhr und Rhein." *SJ*, 91 (1955), 238-250.

B2181 Braun, Hanns. "Shakespeare auf Süd-deutschen Bühnen nach dem Kriege." *SJ*, 91 (1955), 260-267.

B2182 Durian, Hans. *Jocza Savits und die Münchener Shakespeare-Bühne. Ein Beitrag zur Geschichte der Regie um die Jahrhundertwende.* DD, Münich, 1937. Emsdetten: Lechte, 1938. Pp. 132.

B2183 Hollmann, Reimar. "Niedersachsen umwirbt Shakespeare." *SJ*, 92 (1956), 316-326.

B2184 Drews, Wolfgang. *"König Lear" auf der Deutschen Bühne bis zur Gegenwart.* Berlin, 1932. Pp. 123.
Rev: A9432.

iii. More Specific Surveys

B2185 Schumacher, Erich. *Shakespeares "Macbeth" auf der dts. Bühne.* DD, Cologne, 1938. Emsdetten: Lechte, 1938. Pp. 295.

B2186 Keller, W. "Shakespeare-Pflege in Deutschland." *Berliner Börsenztg.*, No. 507 (October 26, 1940).

B2187 Sievert, Ludwig. *Lebendiges Theater. Drei Jahrzehnte Deutscher Theaterkunst.* Text von Ernst Leopold Stahl. Mit einem Vorwort von Joseph Gregor. Munich: Bruckmann, 1944. Pp. 69.

B2188 Bentley, Eric. "German Stagecraft Today." *KR*, XI (1949), 630-648.

B2189 Nagel, Hanna. *Impressionen um Shakespeare Nach 3 Aufführungen von Shakespeare-Komödien: "Komödie d. Irrungen," "Was ihr Wollt," "Wie es euch Gefällt."* Hrsg. u. eingel. v. Ernst Leopold Stahl. Dobel, Württ.: Dobel-Verl., 1949. Pp. 16, 28 plates.

B2190 "Shakespeare-Notizen." *MDtShG*, I (1949), 11-12; II (1950), 10-12; III (1950), 11-12.

B2191 Schmitt, Saladin. *Shakespeare, Drama und Bühne.* Beiträge z. Duisburger Theatergeschichte, 1. Duisburg, 1953. Pp. 33.

B2192 McNamee, Lawrence Francis. *"Julius Caesar" on the German Stage in the Nineteenth Century.* DD, University of Pittsburgh, 1957. Pp. 324. Mic 57-1716. *DA*, XVII (1957), 1074. Publ. No. 21,009.

(c) OTHER GERMANIC COUNTRIES

B2193 Eisner, Doris. "Sieben Jahre Shakespeare in Österreich (1945-1951)." *SJ*, 87/88 (1952), 180-197.

B2194 Kunz, Harald. "Wiener Shakespeare-Aufführungen 1952/54." *SJ*, 91 (1955), 268-277.

B2195 Schoop, Günther. "Shakespeare auf den Schweizer Bühnen 1953/54 bis 1954/55." *SJ*, 92 (1956), 305-313.

B2196 Benz-Burger, Lydia. "Shakespeare auf den Schweizer Bühnen." *SJ*, 94 (1958), 248-252.

B2197 Downer, Alan S. "The *Hamlet* Year." *SQ*, V (1954), 155-165.

B2198 Henriques, Alf. "Shakespeare and Denmark: 1900-1949." *ShS*, III (1950), 107-115.

B2199 Groothoff, Otto. "Minnenas Trettondagsaftnar" [*Twelfth Nights* remembered]. *Sydsvenska Dagbladet* (Malmö), Jan. 9, 1955.

(d) REMAINING CONTINENTAL COUNTRIES
For Russian productions, see Section on Russia,
A9899-A9954.

B2200 Par, A. *Representaciones Shakespearianas en España.*
Vol. 1: *Epoca Galoclásica. Época Romántica.* Pp. 268. Vol. 2: *Epoca Realista y Tiempos Modernos.* Pp. 220. San Felíu de Guixols: Imp. O. Viader, 1936.

B2201 De Smet, Robert. "*Othello* in Paris and Brussels." *ShS*, III (1950), 98-106.
From 18th century on.

B2202 de Gruyter, D., and Wayne Hayward. "Shakespeare on the Flemish Stage of Belgium, 1876-1951." *ShS*, V (1952), 106-110.

B2203 Mráz, Andreas. *Die Literatur der Slowaken.* Berlin: Volk und Reich-Vlg., 1943. Pp. 202.

B2204 Moravec, Dušan. "Shakespeare pri Slovencih" [Shakespeare in Slovenia]. *Slavistična Revija* (Ljubljana), II, Nos. 1-2, 3-4 (1949), 51-74, 250-291.

B2205 Moravec, Dušan. "Shakespeare pri Slovencih: Othello." *Gledališni List* (Celje), I (1955), 1-7.

B2206 Popović, Vladeta. "Shakespeare in Post-War Yugoslavia." *ShS*, IV (1951), 117-122.

B2207 Klajn, Hugo. "Shakespeare in Yugoslavia." *Review of International Affairs* (Belgrade), V (June 1, 1954), 17-18.

B2208 Anon. "English and American Drama in the Hungarian National Theatre." *Theater d. Welt,* I (1937), 520-525.

(5) ELSEWHERE

B2209 Toyoda, Minoru. *Shakespeare in Japan: An Historical Survey.* Tokyo: The Iwanami Shoten, 1940. Pp. xi, 139. (In English.)

B2210 The Theatre Arts Society of Japan. *Studies in Shakespeare.* With a list of the performances of Shakespeare's plays in Japan (*Journal of Theatre Arts*, II, No. I). Tokyo: Chuokoron-sha. (In Japanese.)
A series of essays by various hands; a chronological list of performances of Shak.'s plays in Japan, 1885-1951; bibliography of books, articles, and criticisms of Shak. published in Japan during the years 1930-1951.

B2211 Marshall, Norman. "Shakespeare in India." *Theatre Newsletter,* April 28, 1951, p. 3.

d. MAJOR SHAKESPEAREAN FESTIVALS AND REPERTORY THEATRES
(1) REPORTS ON TWO OR MORE REPERTORY THEATRES

B2212 The John Rylands Library. "Library Notes and News." *BJRL*, XXIX (1946).
Includes "England's National Theatre," pp. 246-247, announcing the merging of the Shak. Memorial National Theatre Committee and the Old Vic to make a new joint council for a national theatre.

B2213 David, Richard. "Shakespeare's Comedies and the Modern Stage." *ShS*, IV (1951), 129-138.

B2214 Purdom, Charles B. *Drama Festivals and Their Adjudication: A Handbook for Producers, Actors, Festival Organizers, and Adjudicators.* London, New York: Dent, 1951. Pp. xii, 138.

B2215 Walker, Roy. "Three Tempests." *Theatre Newsletter,* Sept. 29, 1951, pp. 3-4.

B2216 Worsley, Thomas Cuthbert. "Sophocles and Shakespeare." *Britain Today,* No. 182 (1951), 36-39.

B2217 Griffin, John and Alice. "Shakespeare's Stratfords." *TAr*, XXXVIII, No. 6 (June 1954), 76-77, 91.

B2218 "Boom in the Bard." *Economist,* 117 (Oct. 1, 1955), 16-17.

B2219 "Summer Circuit." *Newsweek,* August 15, 1955, pp. 88-89.

B2220 "Les Trois Stratford." 1. "Stratford, Connecticut (USA)" by Lawrence Langner. 2. "Stratford, Ontario (Canada)" by Cecil Clarke. 3. "Laurence Olivier à Stratford (GB)" by John Courtenay Trewin. *Théâtre dans le Monde* (World Theatre), V, No. 1 (1955).

B2221 David, Richard. "Plays Pleasant and Plays Unpleasant." *ShS*, VIII (1955), 132-138.

B2222 Davis, Francis D. "An Itinerant Playgoer." *ShN*, V (1955), 37.

B2223 Fellows, Hugh Price. *The Resident British Repertory Theatres in the Twentieth Century.* DD, New York University, 1955. Pp. 262. Mic 55-684. *DA*, XV (1955), 1930. Publ. No. 13,605. Part I: 1902-1919; Part II: 1919-1939; Part III: 1939-1952.

B2224 Griffin, Alice. "Shakespeare, U.S.A." *TAr*, XXXIX (April, 1955), 81-85.

B2225 Trewin, J. C. "United Kingdom." *World Theatre*, IV, No. 3 (1955), 78-80.
The Stratford Memorial's *Twelfth Night* and the Old Vic's *H. IV, Part I and II.*

B2226 "*Othello* at Stratford . . . and at the Old Vic." *Plays and Players,* July, 1956, pp. 8-9.

B2227 Brown, John Russell. "Shakespeare Festivals in Britain, 1956." *SQ*, VII (1956), 407-410.

B2228 Byrne, M. St. Clare. "Two *Titus* Productions." *TN*, X (1956), 44-48.

B2229 David, Richard. "The Tragic Curve." *ShS*, IX (1956), 122-131.

B2230 Griffin, Alice. "Summer Shakespeare." *TAr*, July, 1956, pp. 60-61.

B2231 Hewes, Henry. "Broadway Postscript: Groundling's Theatre." *SatR*, Aug. 25, 1956, p. 25.

B2232 Hewes, Henry. "United States: Shakespeare Festivals." *World Theatre*, v (1956), 84.

B2233 *Theatre in Review*. Ed. by Frederick Lumley. Edinburgh: Paterson, 1956. Pp. 218.
T. C. Worsley, "Stratford and Shakespearian Production," pp. 61-68. John Moody, "The Bristol Old Vic," pp. 69-73.

B2234 Quayle, A. "Three Stratfords, One Goal." *TAr*, May, 1956, pp. 30-32.

B2235 Trewin, J. C. "World Reviews: United Kingdom." *World Theatre*, v (1956), 260.

B2236 Byrne, M. St. Clare. "The Shakespeare Season at The Old Vic, 1956-57, and Stratford-upon-Avon, 1957." *SQ*, VIII (1957), 461-492, with 4 pages of illustrations.

B2237 David, Richard. "Drams of Eale." *ShS*, x (1957), 126-134.

B2238 Griffin, Alice. "The Stratford Story." *TAr*, Sept. 1957, pp. 68-73.

B2239 Richards, Stanley. "On and Off Broadway. Commercial Theatre." *Players Magazine*, Oct., 1957, pp. 11-15.
Much at Stratford, Conn.; *Ham.* and *Twel.* at Stratford, Ontario.

B2239a Worsley, T. C. "Two Shakespearean Companies." *London Calling*, April, 1957, pp. 13, 16.
Stratford and the Old Vic, origins and aims.

B2240 Wyatt, E. V. "Theatre." *Catholic World*, Oct. 1957, pp. 66-68.
Much at Stratford, Conn., and *T.G.V.* by the New York Summer Shak. Festival.

B2241 "Summer's Approach Heralds Shakespeare." *TAr*, April, 1958, p. 59.
Antioch (Ohio), San Diego (California), and other Shak. festivals.

B2242 Byrne, M. St. Clare. "The Shakespeare Season at The Old Vic, 1957-58, and Stratford-upon-Avon, 1958." *SQ*, IX (1958), 507-530.

B2243 Driver, T. F. "Autumn Report on Summer Theatre." *Christian Century*, LXXV (1958), 1239-1240.
Resumé of the summer's Shak. festivals.

B2244 Griffin, Alice. "Theatre, U.S.A.: Shakespeare, U.S.A." *TAr*, April, 1958, pp. 60-63.
Ashland, San Diego, Antioch, and Stratford, Ontario, Shak. festivals.

B2245 Hewes, Henry. "Broadway Postscript: Bringing up Fathers." *SatR*, Aug. 16, 1958, p. 26.
W. T. at Stratford, Connecticut, and at Stratford, Ontario.

B2246 Hewes, Henry. "Broadway Postscript: Will O' the West." *SatR*, Aug. 23, 1958, p. 28.

B2247 McBean, Angus. "Photographs of Productions of Shakespeare." *Plays and Players*, 1958.
Old Vic and Stratford-on-Avon.

B2248 McBean, Angus. "Photographs of Productions of Shakespeare." *Theatre World*, 1958.
Old Vic and Stratford-on-Avon.

B2249 Peck, S. "Three Stratfords of William Shakespeare." *New York Times Magazine*, July 13, 1958, pp. 24-25.
Stratford-upon-Avon; Stratford, Ontario; and Stratford, Connecticut.

(2) IN THE UNITED KINGDOM
(a) THE OLD VIC
i. General

B2250 Williamson, Audrey. *Old Vic Drama*. A Twelve Years' Study of Plays and Players. London: Rockliff, 1948; New York: Macmillan, 1949. Pp. xviii, 228.

B2251 Williamson, Audrey. *Old Vic Drama No. 2 (1947-1957)*. London: Rockliff, 1957. Pp. xii, 224.
Rev: *Theatre World*, Oct., 1957, p. 49; *TLS*, Oct. 25, p. 647; by T. C. Worsley, *NstN*, LIV, 424-426; by M. St. Clare Byrne, *English*, XII (1958), 67; by Stanley Richards, *Players Magazine*, XXXIV, 114.

B2252 Hunt, Hugh. *Old Vic Prefaces: Shakespeare and the Producer*. London: Routledge and Kegan Paul, 1954. Pp. xii, 194.
Rev: B1739.

B2253 Wood, Roger, and Mary Clarke. *Shakespeare at the Old Vic*. Foreword by Michael Benthall. London: A. & C. Black, 1954. (Published in U.S. in 1955.)
A record of the six plays of the 1953-54 season of the Old Vic, with illustrations.
Rev: *TLS*, March 4, 1955, p. 139; *ShN*, v, 22; by H. Heuer, *SJ*, 91 (1955), 322-323.

B2254 Wood, Roger, and Mary Clarke. *Shakespeare at the Old Vic*, Vol. II (1954-1955 Season). With a Foreword by Alfred Francis. London: A. & C. Black, 1956. Pp. xiv, 38. 137 photographs.
Rev: by Hermann Heuer, *SJ*, 91 (1955), 322-323; *TLS*, April 20, 1956, p. 243; by Jacques Vallette, *MdF*, June, p. 365; by W. Hudson Rogers, *English Journal*, XLV, 438.

B2254a Wood, Roger, and Mary Clarke. *Shakespeare at the Old Vic*, (1955-1956). London: Hamish Hamilton, for the Old Vic Trust, 1956. Pp. 102. Illustrated.
Rev: *TLS*, Dec. 21, 1956, p. 771; by Donald FitzJohn, *Drama*, Spring, 1957, pp. 38-39; by

Frank Granville-Barker, *Plays and Players*, June, p. 24; by W. Hudson Rogers, *English Journal*, XLVI, 523; by Hermann Heuer, *SJ*, 93 (1957), 276-277; by J. Vallette, *MdF*, 330 (1957), 159-160.

B2255   Clarke, Mary. *Shakespeare at the Old Vic*. With photographs by Angus McBean, Hanston Rogers, and Pamela Chandler. [1956-1957.] London: Hamish Hamilton, for the Old Vic Trust, 1957. Pp. 115.
Rev: *TLS*, Dec. 20, 1957, p. 779; by J. Vallette, *MdF*, 332 (1958), 521.

B2255a   Clarke, Mary. *Shakespeare at the Old Vic*, [1957-1958]. London: Hamish Hamilton, for the Old Vic Trust, 1958. Pp. 102. Illustrated.
Rev: *TLS*, Dec. 19, 1958, p. 743; by Stanley Richards, *Players Magazine*, XXXIV, 126.

ii.   Performances

B2256   Dukes, A. "*Hamlet* at the Old Vic." *TAr*, XXI (1937), 189-193.

B2257   Guthrie, Tyrone. "*Hamlet* at Elsinore." *London Mercury*, XXXVI (1937), 246-249. Also by Ivor Brown, *TAr*, XXI (1937), 873-880.

B2258   Mortimer, Raymond. "Passion's Slave." *NstN*, XIII (1937), 82-83.

B2259   Bridie, J. "Mr. Olivier's Iago." *NstN*, XV (1938), 405.

B2260   MacCarthy, Desmond. "A Great Unpopular Play." *NstN*, XV (1938), 829-830.

B2261   Mortimer, R. "*Othello* at the Old Vic." *NstN*, XV (1938), 287.

B2262   Stahl, Ernest Leopold. "Lilian Baylis. Das Old Vic Theatre in London." *SJ*, LXXV (1939), 108-115.

B2263   Darlington, W. A. "London's New Hamlet." *New York Times*, March 19, 1944, p. 1 of Sec. 2.

B2264   Dukes, Ashley. "A New Hamlet." *TAr*, XXVIII (1944), 338-342.

B2265   MacCarthy, D. "*Richard III* and the Old Vic Repertory." *NstN*, XXVIII (1944), 201-202.

B2266   "*King Lear* at the Old Vic." *Theatre World*, XLII (1946), 13-20.

B2267   Clurman, H. "Shakespeare and Company." *Tomorrow*, V (August, 1946), 61-62.

B2268   "The Old Vic *Henry IV* in New York." L. Nichols, *New York Times*, May 7, 1946, p. 25; May 8, p. 33; May 12, Sec. 2, p. X; V. Rice, *New York Post*; May 7, 8, 1946; B. Hudson, *New York World-Telegram*, May 8, p. 33; W. Morehouse, *New York Sun*, May 7, 8; R. Galland, *New York Journal-American*, May 7, 8; R. Coleman, *Daily Mirror*, May 8; J. Chapman, *New York Daily News*, May 8.

B2269   Nolan, J. Bennett. "Shakespeare Crosses The Rhine." *SAB*, XXI (1946), 76-79.

B2270   Wyatt, E. "The Old Vic's *Henry IV* in New York." *Catholic World*, 163 (1946), 263-264.

B2271   "The Old Vic Theatre Company in *The Taming of the Shrew*." *Theatre World*, XLIII (Dec., 1947), 13-20.

B2272   Fisher, H. K. "*Richard II*." *Life and Letters*, LIV, (1947), 63-70.

B2273   "The Old Vic Theatre Company. *Coriolanus*." *Theatre World*, May, 1948, pp. 21-27.

B2274   "The Old Vic Theater Company in *King Richard II*." *Theatre World*, Feb., 1948, pp. 21-24.

B2275   Eric. "*Twelfth Night*, Old Vic Production." *Punch*, 215 (1948), 318.

B2276   Vickers, J. *The Old Vic in Photographs*. London: Saturn Press, 1948. Pp. 96.

B2277   Williams, W. E. "*Hamlet* at Elsinore." *Listener*, XLIII (June 15, 1950), 1029-1030.

B2278   Worsley, T. C. "The New Old Vic." *NstN*, XL (1950), 498, 500.

B2279   Walker, James. "Shakespeare Again in the Waterloo Road." *English*, VIII (1951), 190-192.

B2280   David, Richard. "Shakespeare in the Waterloo Road." *ShS*, V (1952), 121-128.

B2281   Walker, Roy. "Theatre Royal." *TC*, 153 (1953), 463-470.

B2282   Worsley, Thomas Cuthbert. "Fuss, Flutter and Frizz." *NstN*, XLV (1953), 63-64.

B2283   "The Old Vic Company in *Julius Caesar*." *Theatre World*, Oct., 1954, pp. 17-23.

B2284   Helpmann, Robert. "Formula for Midsummer Magic; Choreographer Principal of the Old Vic Production." *TAr*, XXXVIII (1954), 76-77.

B2285   Worsley, Thomas Cuthbert. "Sound and Fury." *NstN*, XLVIII (1954), 358.

B2286   "As You Like It, *The Old Vic Company*." *Theatre World*, May, 1955, pp. 15-20.

B2287   "*King Henry IV*, Part I and Part II." *Theatre World*, July, 1955, pp. 34-35.

B2288   "*The Taming of the Shrew* at the Old Vic." *Theatre World*, Feb., 1955, pp. 12-13.

B2289   Hope-Wallace, Philip. "The Edinburgh Spirit." *Time and Tide*, XXXVI (1955), 1131.

B2290   Hope-Wallace, Philip. "Shakespeare Galore." *Time and Tide*, XXXVI (1955), 592, 594.

B2291   Hope-Wallace, Philip. "*The Winter's Tale*." *Time and Tide*, XXXVI (1955), 1464.

B2292   Jacquot, Jean. "The Old Vic: *Love's Labour's Lost*." *EA*, VII (1954), 443.

B2293   Trewin, J. C. [Old Vic's *Twelfth Night* and *Henry IV*, Parts One and Two]. *World Theatre*, IV, No. 3 (1955), 77-81.

B2294   Worsley, Thomas Cuthbert. "*As You Like It*." *NstN*, XLIX (1955), 354.

B2295   Worsley, Thomas Cuthbert. "*King Richard*." *NstN*, XLIX (1955), 138.

B2296 Worsley, Thomas Cuthbert. "The Two Henrys." *NstN*, XLIX (1955), 646.

B2297 "America Gets British Feast of Shakespeare." *Life*, Nov. 26, 1956, pp. 136-142.

B2298 "*King Henry V*." *Theatre World*, Feb., 1956, pp. 23-26. [Photographs of Old Vic production.]

B2299 "Old Plays in Manhattan." *Time*, Nov. 5, 1956, pp. 75-76; Nov. 12, pp. 71-72.

B2300 "*Othello* at the Old Vic." *Theatre World*, June, 1956, pp. 34-35. Photographs.

B2301 " 'Old Vic' Comes to Town." *Newsweek*, Nov. 5, 1956, p. 79. Includes: *Richard II* and *Romeo and Juliet*.

B2302 "*Romeo and Juliet*." *Catholic World*, Dec., 1956, p. 228.

B2303 "*Timon of Athens* at the Old Vic." *Plays and Players*, Nov., 1956, pp. 18-19. Photographs.

B2304 "*Timon of Athens*, Old Vic Company In." *Theatre World*, Nov., 1956, pp. 24-25. Photographs.

B2305 "*Troilus and Cressida* at the Old Vic." *Theatre World*, June, 1956, pp. 30-33. Photographs.

B2306 "*Troilus and Cressida* in Edwardian Dress." *Plays and Players*, May, 1956, pp. 10-11. Photographs.

B2307 Brahms, Caryl. "Son of Lear, Caryl Brahms Reviews *Timon of Athens* at the Old Vic." *Plays and Players*, Oct., 1956, p. 9.

B2308 Driver, T. F. "London Banquet." *Christian Century*, Dec. 19, 1956, pp. 1481-82. Evaluation of production of *Macb.* and *R. II*.

B2309 Gibbs, W. "Theatre: Old Vic Company Production." *New Yorker*, Nov. 10, 1956, pp. 71-73.
Performances of *Macb.*, *R. II*, *Romeo*.

B2310 Hayes, Richard. "Stage: Old Vic Production." *Commonweal*, Dec. 7, 1956, pp. 255-256. Performance of *Macb.*, *R. II*, and *Romeo*.

B2311 Hewes, Henry. "Broadway Postscript: England's Traveling Shakespeare Museum." *SatR*, Nov. 10, 1956, p. 24.
Performances of *R. II* and *Romeo*.

B2312 Hope-Wallace, Philip. "*Cymbeline*." *Time and Tide*, Sept. 22, 1956, p. 1123.

B2313 Hope-Wallace, Philip. "*Much Ado about Nothing*." *Time and Tide*, Oct. 27, 1956, p. 1300.

B2314 Hope-Wallace, Philip. "*Timon of Athens*." *Time and Tide*, Sept. 15, 1956, p. 1092.

B2315 Inglis, B. "Kiss Me Cressida." *Spectator*, April 13, 1956, p. 490.

B2316 Lewis, T. "Theatre: Old Vic Production." *America*, Dec. 1, 1956, p. 283.
Performance of *Macb.* and *R. II*.

B2317 Melchinger, Siegfried. "Das Blut an *Hamlets* Arm." *Melchinger Modernes Welttheater* (Bremen), 1956, pp. 45-56.

B2318 Trewin, J. C. "Michael Benthall's *Cymbeline*." *Illustrated London News*, Sept. 29, 1956, p. 522.

B2319 Weightman, J. G. "Many Othellos." *TC*, August, 1956, pp. 166-169.

B2320 Worsley, T. C. [Mr. Tyrone Guthrie's Trick Production of *Troilus*]. *NstN*, April 14, 1956, p. 370.

B2321 "*Antony and Cleopatra*." *Theatre World*, April, 1957, pp. 13-17.
Photographs of the Old Vic production.

B2322 "*Antony and Cleopatra* at the Old Vic." *Plays and Players*, May, 1957, p. 12.

B2323 "*Cymbeline* at the Old Vic." *Plays and Players*, Dec., 1956, p. 12.

B2324 "*Hamlet* at the Old Vic." *Plays and Players*, Dec., 1957, pp. 18-19.

B2325 "*Hamlet* at the Old Vic." *Theatre World*, Nov., 1957, pp. 21-24.

B2326 "*King Henry VI*, Parts 1, 2, and 3 at the Old Vic." *Theatre World*, Dec., 1957, pp. 30-34.

B2327 "*The Merchant of Venice*." *Plays and Players*, Feb., 1957, pp. 18-19.

B2328 "*The Merchant of Venice*." *Theatre World*, Feb., 1957, pp. 26-31.

B2329 "*Much Ado About Nothing*." *Theatre World*, Jan., 1957, pp. 48-49.

B2330 "*Much Ado About Nothing* at the Old Vic." *Plays and Players*, Jan., 1957, p. 12.

B2331 "Old Play in Manhattan." *Time*, Jan. 7, 1957, p. 40. Tyrone Guthrie's *Troilus and Cressida*.

B2332 "The Old Vic Company." *TAr*, Jan., 1957, pp. 17-18.
Reviews the Old Vic presentations of *R. II*, *Romeo*, and *Macb.* at the Winter Garden in autumn, 1956.

B2333 "*Richard III* at the Old Vic." *Theatre World*, Aug., 1957, pp. 19-21.
Photographs of Robert Helpmann's production.

B2334 "*Titus Andronicus* and *The Comedy of Errors*." *Theatre World*, July, 1957, pp. 34-35.

B2335 "*Troilus and Cressida*." *Time*, Jan. 7, 1957, p. 40.

B2336 "*The Two Gentlemen of Verona*." *Theatre World*, March, 1957, pp. 32-35.

B2337 "*Two Gentlemen of Verona* at the Old Vic." *Plays and Players*, March, 1957, p. 14.

B2338 Barnes, T. R. "Cold Vic." *Journal of Education* (London), XXXIX, 260 ff.
The Merch. and *Antony* at the Old Vic.

B2339   Brahms, Caryl. "Stove Pipe and Crinoline." *Plays and Players*, March, 1957, p. 15.
         Old Vic production of *T. G. V.*

B2340   Coton, A. V. "Without the Prince." *Spectator*, Sept. 27, 1957, p. 399.
         John Neville in Old Vic *Ham.*

B2341   Gibbs, Wolcott. "Of War and Lechery." *New Yorker*, Jan. 5, 1957, pp. 50 ff.
         Reviews the Old Vic production of *Troil.* in Edwardian costume at the Winter Garden.

B2342   Granville-Barker, Frank. "*Antony and Cleopatra.*" *Plays and Players*, April, 1957, pp. 13, 15.

B2343   Hartley, Anthony. "Without the Prince." *Spectator*, Sept. 27, 1957, p. 399.
         Old Vic *Ham.*

B2344   Hope-Wallace, Philip. "Theatre." *Time and Tide*, Oct. 26, 1957, pp. 1333.
         Old Vic production of *H. VI;* three parts on two evenings.

B2345   Hope-Wallace, Philip. "*Two Gentlemen of Verona.*" *Time and Tide*, Feb. 2, 1957, p. 127.

B2346   Lambert, J. W. "Plays in Performance." *Drama*, Summer, 1957, pp. 18-24.
         Old Vic production of *T. G. V.*

B2347   M., H. G. "*The Tragedy of Titus Andronicus* and *The Comedy of Errors.*" *Theatre World*, June,
         1957, pp. 7-8. The Walter Hudd productions.

B2348   M., L. "*King Richard III.*" *Theatre World*, July, 1957, p. 4.
         Douglas Seale's Old Vic production.

B2349   M., L. "*Measure for Measure.*" *Theatre World*, Dec., 1957, p. 10.

B2350   M., L. "Old Vic *King Henry VI,* Parts 1, 2 and 3." *Theatre World*, Nov., 1957, pp. 10, 38.
         Douglas Seale's production.

B2351   Marriott, Raymond. "*Richard III.*" *Plays and Players*, July, 1957, pp. 11, 13.
         Robert Helpmann in the Old Vic production.

B2352   Phillips, Eric. "Memories of the Old Vic." *The Listener*, Feb. 14, 1957, pp. 263-264.

B2353   Richards, Stanley. "On and Off Broadway. Commercial Theatre." *Players Magazine*,
         Feb., 1957, p. 110.
         Old Vic's New York productions of *Macb.*, *Romeo*, and *R. II.*

B2354   Richards, Stanley. "On and Off Broadway. Commercial Theatre." *Players Magazine*,
         April, 1957, p. 158.
         Old Vic's New York production of *Troi.*

B2355   Roberts, Peter. "*The Merchant of Venice.*" *Plays and Players*, Feb., 1957, p. 13.

B2356   Roberts, Peter. "New Plays: *Henry VI,* Parts 1, 2 and 3." *Plays and Players*, Dec., 1957, p. 15.

B2357   Roberts, Peter. "New Plays." *Plays and Players*, June, 1957, p. 13.
         Old Vic productions of *Titus* and *Errors.*

B2358   Stephens, Frances. "*The Merchant of Venice.*" *Theatre World*, Jan., 1957, p. 15.

B2359   Stephens, Frances. "Old Vic *Hamlet.*" *Theatre World*, Nov., 1957, p. 8.
         Michael Benthall's production.

B2360   Stephens, Frances. "*The Two Gentlemen of Verona.*" *Theatre World*, March, 1957, p. 9.

B2361   Trewin, J. C. "Happy Returns." *Illustrated London News*, May 4, 1957, p. 742.
         Walter Hudd's productions of *Titus* and *Errors* at the Old Vic.

B2362   Trewin, J. C. "[Robert Helpmann's production of *Antony*]." *Illustrated London News*, March
         16, 1957, p. 438.

B2363   Trewin, J. C. "Tragical-comical-historical; *Two Gentlemen of Verona*—at the Old Vic."
         Illustrated London News, Feb. 2, 1957, pp. 198-199.

B2364   Trewin, J. C. "United Kingdom." *World Theatre*, VI (1957), 78-80.
         Robert Helpmann's *Merch.* at the Old Vic.

B2365   Watt, David. "The Apple Orchard." *Spectator*, Nov. 29, 1957, p. 747.
         Old Vic *Meas.*

B2366   Watt, David. "Great Surgery." *Spectator*, Oct. 25, 1957, p. 548.
         Old Vic production of *H. VI.*

B2367   Cancelled.

B2368   Wyatt, E. V. "Theatre: Old Vic Production." *Catholic World*, Jan., 1957, p. 303.
         Performances of *Macb.* and *R. II.*

B2369   Wyatt, E. V. "Theatre." *Catholic World*, Feb., 1957, pp. 387-388.
         Review of the Old Vic *Troi.* production.

B2370   Wyatt, E. V. "Theatre." *Catholic World*, Nov., 1957, pp. 146-149.
         Summary of the Old Vic's New York season.

B2371   "*Henry VIII* at the Old Vic." *Tablet*, May 24, 1958, p. 487.

B2372   "Old Vic Over Here." *Newsweek*, Sept. 29, 1958, pp. 92-93. American tour of the Old Vic
         Company.

B2373   Brahms, Caryl. "It's all Happening." *Plays and Players*, July, 1958, p. 9.
         Michael Benthall's *H. VIII* at the Old Vic.

B2374 Brien, Alan. "Mr. Lear's Tragedy." *Spectator*, Feb. 28, 1958, p. 263.
Douglas Seale's *Lear* at the Old Vic.
B2375 Brien, Alan. "Theatre." *Spectator*, Oct. 17, 1958, pp. 513-514.
Caesar at the Old Vic.
B2376 Cancelled.
B2377 Clurman, Harold. "Theatre." *Nation*, Dec. 27, 1958, p. 501.
Twel. by Old Vic.
B2378 Hope-Wallace, Philip. "Theatre: *Julius Caesar*." *Time and Tide*, Oct. 18, 1958, p. 1248.
Douglas Seale's Old Vic production.
B2379 Hope-Wallace, Philip. "Theatre." *Time and Tide*, March 1, 1958, pp. 258-259.
Douglas Seale's Old Vic production of *Lear*.
B2380 Littlefield, Joan. "Old Vic Holds Appeal for Shakespeare Troopers." *El Universal* (Mexico City), May 2, 1958, English Section, p. 18.
B2381 Perlström, Åke. "*Henry VIII* på Old Vic." *Göteborgs-Posten* (Göteborg), Aug. 27, 1958.
B2382 Roberts, Peter. "*King Lear*." *Plays and Players*, April, 1958, p. 25.
Douglas Seale's Old Vic production.
B2383 Roberts, Peter. "*Midsummer Night's Dream*." *Plays and Players*, Feb., 1958, p. 15.
B2384 Roberts, Peter. "*Twelfth Night*." *Plays and Players*, May, 1958, p. 17.
Michael Benthall's Old Vic production.
B2385 Trewin, John Courtenay. "Hamlet à l'Old Vic." *Bulletin Culturel du British Council* (Paris) May, 1958.
B2386 Tynan, K. "Theatre: Old Vic at the Broadway Theatre." *New Yorker*, Dec. 27, 1958, pp. 52f.
Reviews *Ham.*, *Twel.*
B2387 Worsley, Thomas Cuthbert. "The Old Vic *Lear*." *NstN*, LV (1958), 266-268.

iii. Recordings
See Old Vic section under Recordings, B3538-B3541.
(b) THE MERMAID THEATRE, LONDON

B2388 Hodges, C. Walter. "London's New Elizabethan Theatre: Making a Mermaid." *Theatre Newsletter*, Nov. 24, 1951, pp. 4-5.
B2389 Miles, Bernard, and Josephine Wilson. "Three Festivals at the Mermaid Theatre." *SQ*, v (1954), 307-310.
B2390 Grayman, Dennis. "Mermaid on the Thames." *TAr*, Mar., 1957, pp. 74-75.

(c) THE BRISTOL OLD VIC

B2391 Eric. "*Hamlet* Performances." *Punch*, 215 (July 28, 1948), 88.
B2392 P., H. L. "*Othello*." *Theatre World*, Jan., 1957, p. 22.
B2393 P., H. L. "*A Midsummer Night's Dream*." *Theatre World*, July, 1957, pp. 6, 8.
B2394 Williamson, Audrey, and Charles Landstone. *The Bristol Old Vic: The First Ten Years*. London: J. Garnet Miller, 1957.
Rev: briefly, *Theatre World*, Dec., 1957, p. 49.
B2395 Brahms, Caryl. "Hamlet 1958." *Plays and Players*, Sept., 1958, pp. 9-10.
Discussion of Bristol Old Vic's production of "The Hamlet of Stepney Green."

(d) THE MEMORIAL THEATRE,
STRATFORD-UPON-AVON

B2396 Brown, Ivor. "The British and their Bard." *TAr*, xx (1936), 503-508.
B2397 Payne, B. I. "Shakespeare at his Birthplace." *Carnegie Mag.*, x (May, 1936), 35-39.
B2398 Fearon, G. "The Shakespeare Festival, 1937." *Theatre World*, XXVII (1937), 267-282.
B2399 Myers, A. Michael. "British and American Staging of Shakespeare." *SAB*, XII (1937), 180-186.
B2400 Ervine, St. J. "The Acting in the Stratford Memorial Theatre." *Obs.*, Aug. 21, 1938.
(Letters in defence in subsequent issues.)
B2401 Huebner, F. M. "Mijmeringen in Shakespeares Geboortestad." *Haagsch Maandblad*, I (1938), 394-406.
B2402 Eelssema, W. J. "Stratford upon Avon." *Op de Hoogte*, 1939, pp. 158-159.
B2403 Charteris, S. "The Shakespeare Festival in Stratford." *English-Speaking World*, XXIII (1941), 139-140.
B2404 *Stratford-upon-Avon Scene*. (Monthly). Published in Stratford. Vols. 1-3 (Nos. 1-30) Sept., 1946-Oct., 1950.
B2405 Jackson, Sir Barry. "Fifty Years of Stratford-on-Avon." *Drama*, Summer, 1946.
B2406 Westerham, P. "The Shakespeare Festival at his Birthplace." *Hindustan Review*, 80 (Aug., 1946), 92-94.

B2407　"Shakespeare Festival at Stratford." *Theatre World*, XLIII (Sept., 1947), 19-23.

B2408　Brown, I. "*Romeo and Juliet* at Stratford." *Britain Today*, June, 1947, pp. 33-34.

B2409　McBean, Angus. *Shakespeare Memorial Theatre, 1948-1950: A Photographic Record*. London:·
　　　　Reinhardt and Evans, 1951. Pp. 18 and photographs.
　　　　Rev: by F. Curtis Canfield, *SQ*, III (1952), 138.

B2410　McBean, Angus. *Shakespeare Memorial Theatre, 1951-1953: A Photographic Record*. With a
　　　　critical analysis by Ivor Brown. London: Reinhardt, 1953. Pp. 104.
　　　　Rev: *TLS*, Jan. 29, 1954, p. 79; by Hermann Heuer, *SJ*, 90 (1954), 323; by R. S., *The Hindu*
　　　　(Madras), weekly edition, Jan. 17, p. 11; *Times of India* (Bombay), Feb. 27, p. 8; briefly by
　　　　A. J. Axelrad, *EA*, IX (1956), 47.

B2411　McBean, Angus, and Ivor Brown. *Shakespeare Memorical Theatre, 1954-1956*. London:
　　　　Max Reinhardt, 1956. Pp. 109.
　　　　Rev: briefly, *TLS*, Dec. 21, 1956, p. 771; by Stanley Richards, *Players Magazine*, Dec., 1957,
　　　　p. 64; briefly by Hermann Heuer, *SJ*, 93 (1957), 276.

B2412　B., D. H. "*Winter's Tale*, Stratford Production." *Punch*, 214 (1948), 522-523.

B2413　Bennett, Henry Stanley, and George Rylands. "Stratford Productions Reviewed." *ShS*, I
　　　　(1948), 107-111.

B2414　Boas, Guy. "Shakespeare at Stratford, 1949." *English*, VII (1948/49), 260-261.

B2415　Brown, I. "The Stratford Season." *Britain Today*, June, 1948, pp. 28-31.

B2416　Darlington, W. A. "Stratford Hamlets." *New York Times*, May 9, 1948, Sec. II, p. 2.

B2417　Ellis, Ruth. *The Shakespeare Memorial Theatre*. London: Winchester Publications, 1948.
　　　　Pp. xiii, 162.
　　　　Rev: briefly, *TLS*, Oct. 2, 1948, p. 566; by M. St. Clare Byrne, *English*, VII, 195; by H.
　　　　Kerst, *LanM*, XLIII (1949), 78; *QR*, 287 (1949), 127-128.

B2418　Eric. "Stratford Theatre's *Hamlet*." *Punch*, 214 (1948), 390.

B2419　Eric. "*Taming of the Shrew*, Stratford Production." *Punch*, 214 (1948), 434.

B2420　Eric. "*Troilus and Cressida*, Stratford Production." *Punch*, 215 (July 14, 1948), 41.

B2421　Eric. "*Othello*, Stratford Production." *Punch*, 215 (Aug. 11, 1948), 132-133.

B2422　Mann, I. R. *The Production of Shakespeare's Plays at Stratford-upon-Avon*. MS thesis, Columbia
　　　　University, 1948. Pp. 137.

B2423　Martin, L., and S. Martin. "Shakespeare-on-Avon." *Forum*, 109 (1948), 147-150. Reprinted
　　　　in *Reader's Digest*, LII (1948), 65-68.

B2424　Matthews, H. G. "The Stratford Season to Date." *Theatre World*, 1948, pp. 29-30, 40.

B2425　Fleming, Peter. "Stratford, 1949." *Spectator*, 6304 (1949), 539.

B2426　Herring, Robert. "*Much Ado about Nothing* (at Stratford)." *Life and Letters*, LXI (1949), 163-165.

B2427　Herring, R. "*Henry VIII* and *Cymbeline* at Stratford." *Life and Letters*, LXII (1949), 215-220.

B2428　Vallese, Tarquinio. *Saggi di Letteratura Inglese*. Naples: Pironti, 1949. Pp. 153.
　　　　XII: "A Second *Tempest* at Stratford."

B2429　Worsley, Thomas C. "G. B. S. and *Cymbeline*." *NstN*, XXXVIII (July 2, 1949), 11.

B2430　Byrne, Muriel St. Clare. "A Stratford Production: *Henry VIII*." *ShS*, III (1950), 120-129.

B2431　Klajn, Hugo. "Tumačenje teksta i delovanje na sceni." (The Interpretation of the Text
　　　　and the Production on the Stage). *Književne Novine* (Belgrade), III (1950), 31, 32.

B2432　Smith, Robert M. "Interpretations of *Measure for Measure*." *SQ*, I (1950), 208-218.

B2433　Worsley, T. C. "*Measure for Measure*." *NstN*, XXXIX (1950), 368.

B2434　Worsley, T. C. "A Great *Lear*." *NstN*, XL (1950), 121-122.

B2435　Boas, Guy. "Stratford Again." *English*, VIII (1950/51), 111-112.

B2436　Boas, Guy. "Stratford in Festival Year." *English*, VIII (1951), 269-271.

B2437　Chambrun, Clara Longworth de. "Stratford Revisté." *Opera*, Oct. 31-Nov. 6, 1951, p. 3;
　　　　Nov. 7-13, p. 3; Nov. 14-20, p. 3.

B2438　Kreft, Dr. Bratko. "Shakespeare v današnji Angliji (Shakespeare in Present-Day England)."
　　　　Ljudska Prafica (Ljubljana), IX (1951), 29.

B2439　Lyons, Sylvia. "Ticket to Shakespeare." *TAr*, July, 1951, pp. 61, 91-92.

B2440　Venezky, Alice. "The 1950 Season at Stratford-upon-Avon: A Memorable Achievement
　　　　in Stage History." *SQ*, II (1951), 73-77.

B2441　Walker, Roy. "Shakespearean History." *Theatre Newsletter*, April 28, 1951, pp. 4-5.

B2442　Walker, Roy. "The Old and the Young King." *Theatre Newsletter*, Aug. 25, 1951, pp. 3-4.

B2443　Walker, Roy. "Soliloquy on Stratford." *Theatre Newsletter*, Oct. 27, 1951, pp. 4-5.

B2444　Wilson, J. Dover, and T. C. Worsley. *Shakespeare's Histories at Stratford, 1951*. Photographs
　　　　by Angus McBean. London: Reinhardt, 1952. Pp. x, 96.
　　　　Rev: by Eric Bentley, *NR*, Sept. 22, 1952, p. 27; by Joseph Carroll, *TAr*, Nov., pp. 10-11;
　　　　by R. Lalou, *EA*, V, 356-357; briefly, *TLS*, July 25, p. 490; by J. Bryson, *NstN*, XLIV, 80;
　　　　by R. M. Moudoùes, *RHT*, IV, 402-403; by H. Heuer, *SJ*, 89 (1953), 215-216; by A. C.
　　　　Sprague, *SQ*, IV, 360-361.

B2445   Worsley, Thomas Cuthbert. "Stratford." *NstN*, XLI (1951), 365.

B2446   Worsley, Thomas Cuthbert. "Late Shakespeare." *NstN*, XLII (1951), 10, 12.

B2447   Worsley, Thomas Cuthbert. "The Stratford Histories." *NstN*, XLII (1951), 489-490.

B2448   Anon. "The Season at Stratford." *English*, IX (1952), 93-96.

B2449   Chambrun, Clara Longworth de. "Shakespeare et Ben Jonson à Stratford." *La Table Ronde*, No. 58, 1952, pp. 165-168.

B2450   Enright, D. J. "Substitutes for Shakespeare Reflections on the Stratford Season, 1952." *The Month*, VIII (1952), 232-235.

B2451   Leech, Clifford. "Stratford, 1952." *SQ*, III (1952), 353-357.

B2452   Worsley, Thomas Cuthbert. "*As You Like It*." *NstN*, XLIII (1952), 552.

B2453   Worsley, Thomas Cuthbert. "Lesser than *Macbeth*." *NstN*, XLIII (1952), 728.

B2454   Chambrun, Clara Longworth de. "La Saison Théâtrale à Stratford." *Table Ronde*, No. 67, 1953, pp. 161-164.

B2455   David, Richard. "Shakespeare's History Plays—Epic or Drama?" *ShS*, VI (1953), 129-139.

B2456   Kemp, T. C., and J. C. Trewin. *The Stratford Festival: A History of the Shakespeare Memorial Theatre*. Birmingham: Cornish Brothers, 1953. Pp. 295.
        Rev: by P. Hartnoll, *TN*, VII (1953), 95; *TLS*, March 27, p. 206; by Arthur Colby Sprague, *SQ*, V (1954), 420-421; by Hermann Heuer, *SJ*, 90 (1954), 323-324; by Joseph H. Marshburn, *Books Abroad*, XXIX, No. 1 (1955), 104.

B2457   Leech, Clifford. "Stratford, 1953." *SQ*, IV (1953), 461-466.

B2458   Monsey, Derek. "Surprises at Stratford." *Spectator*, 6534 (1953), 294.

B2459   Quayle, Anthony. "Il Teatro Shakespeariano di Stratford-on-Avon." *Idea* (Rome), Mar. 27, 1953, p. 5.

B2460   Worsley, Thomas Cuthbert. "The Stratford *Lear*." *NstN*, XLVI (1953), 100-101.

B2461   Worsley, Thomas Cuthbert. "From Belmont to Forres." *NstN*, XLV (1953), 367.

B2462   Worsley, Thomas Cuthbert. "*Love for Love*." *NstN*, XLV (1953), 545-546.

B2463   "Olivier as Titus." *New York Times Magazine*, Sept. 4, 1954, p. 20.

B2464   Axelrad, A. J., Madeleine Axelrad, and J. Jacquot. "Le Festival, 1953, à Stratford." *EA*, VI (1953), 377-379.

B2465   David, Richard. "Stratford, 1954." *SQ*, V (1954), 385-394.

B2466   Monnier, Adrienne. "The Stratford Company in Paris: A French View." *London Magazine*, I, No. 5 (June, 1954), 74-76.

B2467   Reynolds, W. Vaughan. "Stratford, 1954." *Drama*, Autumn, 1954, pp. 24-28.

B2468   Worsley, Thomas Cuthbert. "*Twelfth Night*." *NstN*, XLVII (1954), 65-66.

B2469   Worsley, T. C. "Stratford." *NstN*, XLVII (1954), 400-402.

B2470   Worsley, Thomas Cuthbert. "Stratford." *NstN*, XLVIII (1954), 182.

B2471   "Gielgud's Fourth *King Lear*; the Stratford Company in London." *Illustrated London News*, July 30, 1955, p. 201.

B2472   "Shakespeare by the Oliviers." *New York Times Magazine*, July 10, 1955, p. 16.

B2473   "*The Merry Wives of Windsor* at the Memorial Theatre, Stratford-upon-Avon." *Theatre World*, Sept., 1955, pp. 30-32.

B2474   "Bigger than Life." *Time*, June 27, 1955, p. 48.
        Review of production of *Macb*.

B2475   Appia, C., and H. Appia. "Stratford-on-Avon, 1955." *EA*, VIII (1955), 376-378.

B2476   Brown, Ivor. "By the Avon—1955." *Drama*, No. 38, 1955, pp. 33-37.

B2477   Downer, Alan S. "A Comparison of Two Stagings: Stratford-upon-Avon and London." *SQ*, VI (1955), 429-433.

B2478   Findlater, Richard. "Shakespearean Atrocities." *TC*, Oct., 1955, pp. 364-372.

B2479   Cancelled.

B2480   Hewes, Henry. "This Other Stratford." *SatR*, Sept. 24, 1955, pp. 24-26.

B2481   Hope-Wallace, Philip. "Stratford-on-Avon." *Time and Tide*, XXXVI (1955), 133.

B2482   Hope-Wallace, Philip. [*Merry Wives of Windsor*: Review]. *Time and Tide*, XXXVI (1955), 968.

B2483   Hope-Wallace, Philip. "Stratford-on-Avon, *Titus Andronicus*." *Time and Tide*, XXXVI (1955), 1074.

B2484   Jacquot, Jean. "Stratford-upon-Avon, 1954." *EA* VII (1954), 441-442.

B2485   Kalamer, Joseph. "Geschäft mit William Shakespeare." *Berner Tagblatt*, No. 57, Feb. 27, 1955.

B2486   Matthews, Harold. "The First Three Plays" [of the Stratford Festival]. *Theatre World*, July, 1955, pp. 16-25.

B2487   Matthews, Harold. "Horror-Tragic." *Theatre World*, Sept., 1955, pp. 33-36.

B2488   Painter-Downes, M. "Letter from London: Two Companies at Stratford-on-Avon." *New Yorker*, Aug. 13, 1955, pp. 56-57.

B2489   "Controversial Noguchi Sets for *Lear.*" *Art News* LIV (Dec., 1955), 42-43.

B2490   "A Weird Kind of *Lear.*" *Life*, Aug. 8, 1955, pp. 64, 67, 68.

B2491   Priestley, John Boynton. "Thoughts in the Wilderness. Candles Burning Low." *NstN*, L (1955), 155-156. See Correspondence, pp. 187-188 and 217.

B2492   Worsley, T. C. "[Sir John Gielgud's] *King Lear.*" *NstN*, L (1955), 160.

B2493   *King Lear.* Introd. by Donald Wolfit, with Designs in Colour by Noguchi. London: Folio Society, 1956. Pp. 128.

B2494   Pritchett, V. S. "Looking at Life; the Immortal Memory." *NstN*, April 30, 1955, pp. 604-606.

B2495   Strix. "Meditations at *Macbeth.*" *Spectator*, June 24, 1955, p. 798.

B2496   Waugh, Evelyn. "Titus with a Grain of Salt." *Spectator*, 6636 (1955), 300-301.

B2497   Worsley, Thomas Cuthbert. "The Dark and the Dreadful." *NstN*, XLIX (1955), 839-840.

B2498   Worsley, Thomas Cuthbert. "The Stratford Opening." *NstN*, XLIX (1955), 575-576.

B2499   Worsley, Thomas Cuthbert. "Grand Guignol." *NstN*, L (1955), 240.

B2500   "Rewards of Trekking to Avon." *Broadside* (Theatre Library Assoc.), XVII, No. 1 (1956), 1-2.

B2501   "*Measure for Measure* at Stratford-upon-Avon: Photographs with a review by Anthony Merryn." *Plays and Players*, Oct., 1956, pp. 8, 14-15.

B2502   "Stratford Season, 1956." *Theatre World*, July, 1956, pp. 7-13.

B2503   "*Love's Labour's Lost.*" *Theatre World*, Oct., 1956, pp. 24-25.

B2504   "*Measure for Measure.*" *Theatre World*, Oct., 1956, pp. 26-27.

B2505   Hensel, Georg. "Elisabethanisches in England. Reise zu Hamlet in Stratford-upon-Avon, 1956." *Wuppertaler Bühnen. Programmblätter f. d. Spielzeit 1957/58*, Heft 2.

B2506   Hope-Wallace, Philip. "*Love's Labour's Lost.*" *Time and Tide*, July 14, 1956, p. 846.

B2507   Hope-Wallace, Philip. "*Measure for Measure.*" *Time and Tide*, Aug. 25, 1956, p. 1021.

B2508   Hume, George. "The Shakespeare Memorial Theatre: Its Constitution and Administration." Abstr. in *ShN*, VI (1956), 43.

B2509   Lamb, Warren. "Modern Art and the Actor." *Drama*, Winter, 1956, pp. 36-38.

B2510   Maurois, André. "Retour de Stratford." *Nouvelles Littéraires*, No. 1456, July 28, 1955, p. 1.

B2511   Ray, C. "Birthday Party." *Spectator*, April 27, 1956, p. 572.

B2512   Strix. "Prince of Limbo." *Spectator*, April 20, 1956, pp. 524 ff.

B2513   Strix. "Iago and Others." *Spectator*, June 8, 1956, p. 789.

B2514   Trewin, J. C. "Swans of Stratford." *Illustrated London News*, Jan. 21, 1956, p. 106.

B2515   Trewin, J. C. "Olivier at Stratford-upon-Avon (Great Britain)." *World Theatre*, V (1956), 51-60.

B2516   Trewin, J. C. "In Old Vienna." *Illustrated London News*, Aug. 25, 1956, p. 314.

B2517   Wilson, David. "An Exhibition at Stratford-on-Avon." *Listener*, LV (1956), 673.

B2518   "Stratford-upon-Avon." *Drama*, Autumn, 1957, pp. 26-27.

B2519   "Le Festival Shakespeare de Stratford-sur-Avon: L'enfant d'un Amour Jaloux." *Paris Théâtre*, No. 120, 1957, pp. 14-17.

B2520   "Angleterre—*Titus Andronicus.*" *Paris Théâtre*, No. 124, 1957, pp. 10-12.

B2521   "New Faces for Stratford." *Plays and Players*, Feb., 1957, p. 7.

B2522   "*As You Like It* at Stratford-on-Avon." *Plays and Players*, May, 1957, pp. 20-21.

B2523   "*Julius Caesar* at Stratford-on-Avon." *Plays and Players*, July, 1957, p. 7.

B2524   "*King John* at Stratford-on-Avon." *Plays and Players*, July, 1957, p. 10.

B2525   "*Titus* Goes to Europe . . . ." *Plays and Players*, Aug., 1957, pp. 8-9, 33.

B2526   "*The Tempest* at Stratford-on-Avon." *Plays and Players*, Oct., 1957, pp. 18-19.

B2527   "Stratford Festival: *King John.*" *Times* (London), April 16, 1957, p. 3.

B2528   "Stratford-upon-Avon, 1957 Season." *Theatre World*, Feb., 1957, p. 49.

B2529   "Nineteen-Fifty-Seven Stratford Season." *Theatre World*, June, 1957, pp. 25-30.

B2530   "*Julius Caesar.*" *Theatre World*, July, 1957, pp. 17-19.

B2531   "*Titus Andronicus.*" *Theatre World*, Aug., 1957, pp. 27-29.

B2532   "*Cymbeline.*" *Theatre World*, Aug., 1957, pp. 30-32.

B2533   "*The Tempest.*" *Theatre World*, Oct., 1957, pp. 12-16.

B2534   "*The Tempest* at Drury Lane." *Theatre World*, Dec., 1957, p. 9.

B2535   B., G. "La Galerie." *Paris Théâtre*, No. 123, 1957, p. 2.

B2536   Brahms, Caryl. "Money's Worth." *Plays and Players*, Sept., 1957, p. 9.

B2537   Byrne, M. St. Clare. "*The Tempest* at Stratford-on-Avon." *TN*, XII (1957), 25-29.

B2538   Clurman, Harold. "Theatre." *Nation*, July 6, 1957, p. 18.

B2539   Granville-Barker, Frank. "*As You Like It.*" *Plays and Players*, May, 1957, p. 13.

B2540   Granville-Barker, Frank. "*Julius Caesar.*" *Plays and Players*, July, 1957, p. 11.

B2541 Gregory, Kenneth. "Stratford, 1957." *Tatler*, March, 1957, pp. 588-590.

B2542 Hope-Wallace, Philip. "Theatre. Stratford—at Home and Abroad." *Time and Tide*, July 13, 1957, pp. 878-879.

B2543 Hope-Wallace, Philip. "Theatre. *The Tempest:* at Stratford." *Time and Tide*, Aug., 1957, p. 1050.

B2544 Kaufman, Wolfe. "Broadway Postscript: International Theatre Festival." *SatR*, Aug. 3, 1957, p. 21.

B2545 Knowland, A. S. "Critical Forum: Shakespeare in the Theatre." *EIC*, VII (1957), 325-330.

B2546 Lemarchand, Jacques. "Alfieri et Shakespeare au Théâtre des Nations." *NRF*, x (1957), 123-127.

B2547 Leonhardt, Rudolf Walter. "Stratford—mehr Touristen als Einwohner." In Leonhardt's *77 mal England*. Munich: Piper, 1957, pp. 107-111.

B2548 Linde, Ebbe. "Vivien Leigh och Laurence Olivier ger nytt liv åt *Titus Andronicus.*" *Dagens Nyheter* (Stockholm), June 2, 1957.

B2549 Loper, R. B. *"Macbeth" Productions at the Shakespeare Memorial Theatre, 1900-1938.* DD, Birmingham, 1957.

B2550 Matthews, Harold. *"As You Like It, King John,* and *Julius Caesar."* *Theatre World*, July, 1957, pp. 15, 19.

B2551 Matthews, Harold. *"Cymbeline."* *Theatre World*, Aug., 1957, pp. 30-32.

B2552 Matthews, Harold. *"The Tempest."* *Theatre World*, Oct., 1957, pp. 12-16.

B2553 Maulnier, Thierry. "Le Théâtre des Nations." *La Revue de Paris*, Aug., 1957, pp. 152-155.

B2554 Muir, Kenneth. "Stratford, 1956." *EIC*, VII (1957), 113-118.

B2555 Quijano, Margarita. "El Festival de Shakespeare en Stratford." *Revista de la Universidad de Mexico* (Mexico City), Jan., 1957, pp. 19-21.

B2556 Speaight, Robert. "Politics at Stratford." *NstN*, LIII (1957), 734-735.

B2557 Strix. "The Tiber and the Avon." *Spectator*, 6728 (1957), 746-747.

B2558 Trewin, J. C. "Love in the Forest." *Illustrated London News*, April 13, 1957, p. 600.

B2559 Trewin, J. C. "Mainly Roman." *Illustrated London News*, June 8, 1957, p. 956.

B2560 Trewin, J. C. "That Play Again." *Illustrated London News*, July 13, 1957, p. 80.

B2561 Trewin, J. C. "Strange Matters." *Illustrated London News*, July 20, 1957, p. 122.

B2562 Trewin, J. C. "Far-Off Seas." *Illustrated London News*, Aug. 24, 1957, p. 316.

B2563 Watts, Richard, Jr. "Busman's Holiday in Britain." *TAr*, Nov., 1957, pp. 24-27, 91.

B2564 Walker, Roy. "The Season at Stratford-on-Avon." *TAr*, May, 1957, pp. 69-71.

B2565 Worsley, Thomas Cuthbert. "Shakespeare's Oratorio." *NstN*, LIV (1957), 222.

B2566 "Bankside Players." *Drama*, Summer, 1958, p. 15.

B2567 Brahms, Caryl. "Juliet and Romeo." *Plays and Players*, May, 1958, p. 12.

B2568 Brahms, Caryl. "Not in the Folio." *Plays and Players*, Aug., 1958, p. 12.

B2569 Brien, Alan. "Theatre." *Spectator*, April 18, 1958, p. 483.

B2570 Brien, Alan. "Theatre." *Spectator*, May 2, 1958, p. 558.

B2571 Brien, Alan. "Theatre." *Spectator*, June 13, 1958, p. 768.

B2572 Brien, Alan. "Theatre." *Spectator*, July 18, 1958, p. 85-86.

B2573 Brien, Alan. "Theatre." *Spectator*, Sept. 5, 1958, pp. 305-306.

B2574 Brook, Peter. *"Titus Andronicus."* *World Theatre*, VII (1958), 27-29.

B2575 Ekeblad, Inga-Stina. *"Romeo och Julia."* *Göteborgs Handelstidning* (Göteborg), April 21, 1958.

B2576 Granville-Barker, Frank. *"Julius Caesar."* *Plays and Players*, July, 1958, p. 11.

B2577 Hewes, Henry. "Broadway Postscript: Directors at Work." *SatR*, Sept. 20, 1958, p. 31.

B2578 Matthews, Harold. "Ninety-Ninth Season at Stratford-upon-Avon." *Theatre World*, July, 1958, pp. 16-19.

B2579 Matthews, Harold. "Much Ado About Apparel." *Theatre World*, Oct., 1958, pp. 27-30.

B2580 Pritchett, Victor Sawdon. "A Stratford Charade." *NstN*, LVI (1958), 276.

B2581 Roberts, Peter. *"Hamlet."* *Plays and Players*, July, 1958, p. 14.

B2582 Speaight, Robert. "The Stratford Festival, I: Comedy; II: Tragedy." *Tablet*, Sept. 13, 1958, p. 20.

B2583 Trewin, J. C. "A Time for Festival." *Drama*, Summer, 1958, pp. 29-31.

B2584 Trewin, J. C. "El Festival de Stratford-on-Avon." *El Universal* (Mexico City), May 11, 1958, Section 4, p. 4.

B2585 Trewin, J. C. "Gielgud as Prospero." *Illustrated London News*, Dec. 21, 1957, p. 1096.

B2586 Veelo, G. van. *"Pericles* in Stratford. Het Shakespeare Festival te Stratford-on-Avon 1958." *LT*, 196 (1958), 506-512.

B2587 Wain, John. "Bring Your Own Blankets." *TC*, 164 (1958), 269-272.

B2588 Worsley, Thomas Cuthbert. "*Pericles.*" *NstN*, LVI (1958), 80, 82.

(e) EDINBURGH FESTIVAL

B2589 Weightman, J. G. "Edinburgh, Elsinore and Chelsea." *TC*, 154 (1953), 302-310.
B2590 Scott-Moncrieff, George. "At the Edinburgh Festival." *Tablet*, 206 (Sept. 3, 1955), 227.

(f) MISCELLANEOUS

B2591 B., G. "Shakespeare and Glyndebourne." *English*, II (1938), 72-74.
B2592 Turner, W. J. "*Macbeth* at Glyndebourne." *NstN*, xv (1938), 911-912.
B2593 Worsley, Thomas Cuthbert. "Amateur Shakespeare." *NstN*, XLIV (1952), 208-209.
B2594 Jackson, Sir Barry. "Producing the Comedies." *ShS*, VIII (1955), 74-80.
B2595 Macqueen-Pope, W. "Shakespeare at the Lane." *Plays and Players*, Dec., 1957, p. 7.
B2596 Green, William. "Shakespearean Alterations—Manchester Style." *ShN*, VIII (1958), 18.
B2597 Trewin, J. C. "El Nuevo Shakespeare." *El Universal* (Mexico City), May 4, 1958, Section 4, p. 4.

(3) IN AUSTRALIA AND CANADA
(a) AUSTRALIAN ELIZABETHAN THEATRE TRUST

B2598 Tildesley, E. M. "The Australian Elizabethan Theatre Trust." *Australian Quarterly*, XXVII (March, 1955), 53-60.
B2599 Hunnings, Neville March. "Elizabethans from Down Under." *Plays and Players*, April, 1957, p. 5.
B2600 Birch, Marguerite I. "Drama in Sydney." *Australian Quarterly*, XXIX (1957), 123-127.

(b) STRATFORD, ONTARIO

B2601 Guthrie, Tyrone, W. Robertson Davies, and Grant Macdonald. *Renown at Stratford*. Toronto: Clarke, Irwin, 1953. Pp. viii, 127.
 Rev: *Dalhousie Review*, XXXIII (1953), xxxvii; *UTQ*, XXIII, 289-290; *QQ*, LX, 577-578; *ShN*, v (1955), 14; by M. Bailey, *SQ*, VII (1956), 125-127; briefly by Wendell Cole, *ETJ*, VIII (1956), 73.
B2602 Guthrie, Tyrone, Robertson Davies, and Grant Macdonald. *Twice Have the Trumpets Sounded. A Record of the Stratford Shakespearean Festival in Canada, 1954*. Toronto: Clarke, Irwin, 1954. Pp. xiv, 193, 51 il.
 Rev: by R. S. Knox, *UTQ*, XXIV (1955), 305-306; *ShN*, v, 14; *TLS*, Jan. 6, 1956, p. 5; letter by Sidney Fisher, *TLS*, Feb. 10, 1956, p. 85, protesting *TLS* reviewer's reference to the "prairie public" at Stratford festival (*TLS*, Jan. 6) and accompanying reply by reviewer; by Wendell Cole, *ETJ*, VIII (1956), 73-74.
B2603 Davies, Robertson, with Tyrone Guthrie, Tanya Moiseiwitsch, and Boyd Neel. *Thrice the Brinded Cat Hath Mew'd*. Toronto: Clarke, Irwin, 1955. Pp. xii, 178. Illus.
 Rev: by R. S. Knox, *UTQ*, XXV (1956), 341-342; by B. Iden Payne, *SQ*, VIII (1957), 123-124.
B2604 *Reference Data on the Stratford Shakespearean Festival, 1956*. Fourth Annual Season of Drama, June 18-August 18, Second Annual Season of Music, July 7-August 11. Stratford: Ontario Shakespearean Festival Foundation, 1956. Pp. 10.
B2605 *Merchant of Venice* and *Julius Caesar*, being the text from *The Oxford Shakespeare* of the plays to be performed at the Stratford Shakespearean Festival of 1955, with synopses of the plays and a note on *Oedipus Rex*. Toronto, 1955.
B2606 *Background Data of the Stratford Shakespearean Festival Foundation of Canada*. Stratford: Ontario Shakespearean Festival Foundation, 1958. Pp. 23.
B2607 Brady, L. "Three Miracles in Stratford, Ontario." *Rotarian*, 85 (Nov., 1954), 24-26.
B2608 Clarke, Cecil. "An Open Stage at Stratford-on-Avon, Ontario." *TN*, VIII (1954), 40-44.
B2609 Edinborough, Arnold. "A New Stratford Festival." *SQ*, v (1954), 47-50.
B2610 Griffin, Alice. "Season at Stratford: The Second Annual Canadian Festival." *TAr*, XXXVIII (Sept., 1954), 24-25.
B2611 Guthrie, Tyrone. "Shakespeare Finds a New Stratford." *TAr*, XXXVII, No. 9 (Sept., 1953), 76-77.
B2612 Hewes, H. "Triple en Tente, Stratford, Ontario." *SatR*, XXXVII (July 31, 1954), 33-34.
B2613 Plunkett, P. M. "Stratford Letter; Canada." *America*, 91 (Sept. 18, 1954), 591-592.
B2614 "Stratford Festival." *Canadian Geographical Journal*, L (April, 1955), ix-xi.
B2615 "Lower Prices, Enlarge Stage for Stratford's Third Season." *Financial Post*, Feb. 26, 1955, p. 8.
B2616 Borth, Christy. "Will Shakespeare Comes to Canada." *The Montrealer*, Sept., 1955 (Condensed in *The Reader's Digest*, Sept., 1955, pp. 137-140).

B2617 Brown, Beatrice M. "Stratford Ontario Shakespeare Festival." *Players Magazine*, Oct., 1955, pp. 4-5.

B2618 Burgess, Mary Ellen. "A Growing Theatre." *Players Magazine*, XXXI (1955), 81.

B2619 Davies, W. R. "Stratford: Firm and Permanent Growth." *Saturday Night* (Canada), July 23, 1955, pp. 7-8.

B2620 Edinborough, Arnold. "Shakespeare Confirmed: At Canadian Stratford." *SQ*, VI (1955), 435-440.

B2621 Griffin, Alice. "Shakespeare and Sophocles at Stratford, Ontario." *TAr*, XXXIX (Sept., 1955), 30-31.

B2622 Guthrie, Tyrone. "Shakespeare at Stratford, Ontario." *ShS*, VIII (1955), 127-131.

B2623 Hewes, Henry. "Broadway Postscript: Astringency in Ontario." *SatR*, June 4, 1955, p. 26.

B2624 Hewes, Henry. "Broadway Postscript: The Bard in Canada." *SatR*, July 23, 1955, pp. 21-22.

B2625 Johnstone, M. W. "Boyd Neel and the Canadian Stratford Festival." *Etudes*, LXXIII (June, 1955), 20 ff.

B2626 Kerr, Walter F. "Three Classics Are Revitalized." *New York Herald Tribune*, June 10, 1955, Section 4, pp. 1-2.

B2627 McVicar, Leonard H. "From Little Acorns: Stratford's Shakespearian Festival." *Recreation*, XLVIII (1955), 110-111.

B2628 Moon, B. "Why Guthrie Outdraws Shakespeare." *Maclean's Magazine* (Canada), Aug. 6, 1955, pp. 18-19, 50-52.

B2629 Osman, M. "Other Adventures at Stratford." *Food for Thought*, XV (May-June, 1955), 27-30.

B2630 "New World Stratford." *American Magazine*, Aug., 1956, pp. 46-47.

B2631 "Stratford Theatre, Stratford, Ontario." *Canadian Journal*, XXXIII (1956), 176-177. See also *Journal of Royal Architectural Institute of Canada*, XXX (1956), 176-177.

B2632 "Le Bon Stratford." *Time*, July 16, 1956, pp. 30, 32.

B2633 Clarke, Cecil. "Stratford, Ontario (Canada)." *World Theatre*, V (1956), 42-50.

B2634 Davies, Robertson. "Stratford's Critical Season Opens." *Saturday Night* (Canada), July 7, 1956, pp. 7-8.

B2635 Davies, Robertson. "Stratford Revisited: Amazing Festival." *Saturday Night* (Canada), Sept. 1, 1956, pp. 14-15.

B2636 Edinborough, Arnold. "Consolidation in Stratford, Ontario." *SQ*, VII (1956), 403-406.

B2637 Guthrie, Tyrone. "Shakespeare Comes to Stratford." *New York Times Magazine*, June 10, 1956, pp. 26-27 ff.

B2638 Hyams, Barry. "The Town Shakespeare Built." *Coronet*, Aug., 1956, pp. 39-42.

B2639 MacDougall, A. J. "Quebec Letter." *America*, Dec. 29, 1956, p. 374.

B2640 Walker, Roy. "This Other Avon." *Drama*, Winter, 1956, pp. 26-29.

B2641 Weightman, J. G. "Edinburgh Diary." *TC*, Oct., 1956, pp. 344-345.

B2642 "Shakespeare Theatre Opened in Stratford." *Architectural Record*, Sept., 1957, p. 42.

B2643 "Stratford Festival Theatre, Rounthwaite and Fairfield, Architects." *Canadian Journal*, XXXIV (1957), 267-274.

B2644 "From Stratford, Ontario." *English-Speaking World*, Sept., 1957, pp. 29-32.

B2645 "Stratford Now Getting Ready for New Season in New Home." *Financial Post* (Canada), Jan. 26, 1957, p. 12.

B2646 "Langham to Head Stratford Festival." *Financial Post* (Canada), Sept. 7, 1957, p. 32.

B2647 "Canada's Shakespeare Capitol." *TAr*, July, 1957, p. 78.

B2648 Allen, R. T. "How a Tean-Ager's Dream Came True at Stratford." *Maclean's Magazine*, Oct. 12, 1957, pp. 28-29, 75-79.

B2649 Davies, Robertson. "Stratford, 1957: Magnificent, Masterful." *Saturday Night* (Canada), July 20, 1957, pp. 8-9, 35.

B2650 Edinborough, Arnold. "Canada's Permanent Elizabethan Theatre." *SQ*, VIII (1957), 511-514.

B2651 Fairfield, R. "New Theatre at Stratford." *Food for Thought* (Canada), XVII (1957), 173-174.

B2652 Grey, Earle. "Shakespeare Festival, Toronto, Canada." *ShS*, X (1957), 111-114.

B2653 Hewes, Henry. "Broadway Postscript: Master Hamlet and Saint Viola." *SatR*, July 20, 1957, p. 26.

B2654 Krehm, W. "Stratford Gleanings." *Canadian Music Journal*, Autumn, 1957, pp. 37-39.

B2655 Logan, Edgar. "Night with the Bard." *Senior Scholastic*, LXX (1957), 12T-13T.

B2656 Matson, Lowell. "The Stratford Adventure." *ETJ*, IX (1957), 51.

B2657 Mellors, Peter. "Stratford, Ontario, Season." *Theatre World*, Aug., 1957, pp. 16-18.

B2657a Moore, J. M. "Snobs at Stratford." *Canadian Commentator*, Sept., 1957, pp. 7-8.

B2658 Patterson, T. "Stratford and Education." *Food for Thought* (Canada), XVII (1957), 169-173.

B2659   Phillips, A. "What Shakespeare's Doing to Stratford." *Maclean's Magazine*, June 22, 1957, pp. 28-29, 71 ff.
B2660   Sangster, Dorothy. "Designing Woman of Stratford." *Maclean's Magazine*, July 20, 1957, pp. 16-19, 54-56 ff.
B2661   Wilson, Martin. "*Hamlet* at Stratford." *Canadian Forum*, Sept., 1957, pp. 130-131.
B2662   "Drama, Music and Mime for You at Stratford." *Financial Post* (Canada), July 19, 1958, p. 12.
B2663   "Stratford Group Will Visit Russia." *Financial Post* (Canada), Sept. 13, 1958, p. 32.
B2664   "Audiences Bigger Than Ever, Stratford Bonds a Hit Too." *Financial Post* (Canada), Oct. 4, 1958, p. 4.
B2665   Barkway, M. "Stratford Magic is Still Strong." *Financial Post* (Canada), July 19, 1958, p. 14.
B2666   Clurman, Harold. "Theatre." *Nation*, July 5, 1958, pp. 19-20.
B2667   Davies, Robertson. "The Stratford Season: A Great Poetic Theatre." *Saturday Night* (Canada), July 19, 1958, pp. 14-15, 36-37.
B2668   Edinborough, Arnold. "A Lively Season at Canada's Stratford." *SQ*, IX (1958), 535-538.
B2669   Garner, Hugh. "What Shakespeare Did to Stratford." *Saturday Night* (Canada), Aug. 16, 1958, pp. 12-13, 42-43.
B2670   Hayes, R. "Report from Stratford." *Commonweal*, Sept. 19, 1958, pp. 617-619.
B2671   Hewes, Henry. "Broadway Postscript: Plummer's Summer." *SatR*, July 12, 1958, pp. 28-29.
B2672   Plunkett, P. M. "Shakespeare in Ontario." *America*, Oct. 11, 1958, pp. 44-45.
B2673   Richards, Stanley. "On and Off Broadway." *Players Magazine*, Oct., 1958, pp. 19-20.
B2674   Stratford, P. "I Like My Meat Cut in Wedges." *Canadian Forum*, XXXVIII (1958), 107-108.
B2675   Stratford, P. "Antigonus and the Bear." *Canadian Forum*, XXXVIII (1958), 136-137.
B2676   Weales, Gerald. "The Bard in Ontario." *The Reporter*, Sept. 4, 1958, pp. 42-43.
B2677   Whittaker, Herbert. *The Stratford Festival, 1953-1957.* Toronto: Clarke, Irwin; London: Harrap, 1958. Pp. 104.
B2678   Wyatt, E. V. R. "Theatre." *Catholic World*, June, 1958, pp. 225-226.
B2679   Wyatt, E. V. R. "Theatre." *Catholic World*, Nov., 1958, pp. 156-158.

(4)   IN THE UNITED STATES OF AMERICA
(a)   THE BRATTLE PLAYERS

B2680   Miller, E. H. "Shakespeare in the Grand Style." *SQ*, I (1950), 243-246.
B2681   Miller, Edwin H. "Shakespeare at the Brattle Theatre." *SQ*, IV (1953), 59-60.
B2682   "*Othello*." *TAr*, XXXIX (Nov., 1955), 67.
B2683   Bentley, E. "*Othello* on Film and on the Stage." *NR*, Oct. 3, 1955, pp. 21-22.
B2684   Hayes, Richard. "The Bostonians." *Commonweal*, Oct. 14, 1955, p. 40.
B2685   Richards, Stanley. "On and Off Broadway." *Players Magazine*, XXXI (1955), 38.
B2686   Wyatt, E. V. R. "Brattle Shakespeare Players." *Catholic World*, 182 (Nov., 1955), 141-142.

(b)   STRATFORD, CONNECTICUT

B2687   Langner, Lawrence. "An American Shakespeare Festival." *TAr*, April, 1951, pp. 56, 93-94.
B2687a Hardwicke, Sir Cedric. "An American Home for Shakespeare." *TAr*, XXXVIII (Jan., 1954), 67.
B2688   "News and Ideas." *CE*, XVII (1955), 57.
B2689   Barrett, A. "Shakespeare at Stratford, U.S.A." *America*, 93 (1955), 512-514.
B2690   Clurman, H. "Theater." *Nation*, Aug., 6, 1955, pp. 122-124.
        Reply by L. Kirstern, Aug. 20, p. 164; rejoinder, Aug. 27, pp. 182-183.
B2691   Gassner, John. "Broadway in Review." *ETJ*, VII (1955), 219-220.
B2692   Gorell, Lord. "W. S. to Stratford, Conn." *QR*, No. 606, Oct., 1955, p. 547.
B2693   Griffin, Alice. "Summer Shakespeare." *TAr*, XXXIX (July, 1955), 27-29.
B2694   Griffin, Alice. "The American Shakespeare Festival." *SQ*, VI (1955), 441-446.
B2695   Hayes, Richard. "Denis Carey's Production [of *Julius Caesar*]." *Commonweal*, Aug. 26, 1955, pp. 516-518.
B2696   Hewes, Henry. "Broadway Postscript: Mr. Carey's Summer Chickens." *SatR*, July 9, 1955, p. 22.
B2697   Hewes, Henry. "Shakespeare via the N. Y., N. H. & H." *SatR*, Aug. 13, 1955, p. 20.
B2698   Kerr, Walter F. "Stratford-on-the-Housatonic." *New York Herald Tribune*, July 17, 1955, Section 4, p. 1.
B2699   Richards, Stanley. "Stratford, Connecticut." *Players Magazine*, XXXI (1955), 9.
B2700   Wyatt, E. V. R. "American Shakespeare Festival Production." *Catholic World*, 181 (1955), 469-470.

B2701   *The Stratford News.* American Shakespeare Festival Edition, 1956 Season. July 5, 1956. Pp. 1A-8A.
B2702   "Stratford-on-the-Housatonic: Connecticut Shakespeareans Shine in a Mirthfull *Measure for Measure.*" *Life,* Sept. 10, 1956, pp. 161-164.
B2703   Gassner, John. "Broadway in Review." *ETJ,* VIII (1956), 217-220.
B2704   Hayes, Richard. "Passion and Society; American Shakespeare Festival Theatre Production." *Commonweal,* Aug., 1956, pp. 540-542.
B2705   Hewes, Henry. "Broadway Postscript: Houseman on the Housatonic." *SatR,* July 14, 1956, p. 22.
B2706   Hosley, Richard. "The Second Season at Stratford, Connecticut." *SQ,* VII (1956), 399-402.
B2707   Langner, Lawrence. "Stratford, Connecticut (U.S.A.)." *World Theatre,* V (1956), 37-41.
B2708   Wyatt, E. V. R. "Theater." *Catholic World,* Sept., 1956, pp. 467-468.
B2709   "*The Taming of the Shrew.*" *TAr,* April, 1957, p. 23.
B2710   "*Measure for Measure.*" *Newsweek,* Feb. 4, 1957, p. 78.
B2711   "*Measure for Measure.*" *TAr,* April, 1957, p. 22.
B2712   Clurman, Harold. "Theatre." *Nation,* Aug. 3, 1957, pp. 58-59.
B2713   Colin, Saul. "Plays and Players in New York." *Plays and Players,* Sept., 1957, pp. 16-17.
B2714   Garland, H. B. "El teatro de verano de los Estados Unidos en 1957." *El Universal* (Mexico City), Oct. 6, 1957, pp. 6, 11.
B2715   Gibbs, Wolcott. "*Measure for Measure.*" *New Yorker,* Feb. 2, 1957, pp. 72-73.
B2716   Hewes, Henry. "Broadway Postscript: *Othello*—Take Three." *SatR,* June 29, 1957, p. 23.
B2717   Hewes, Henry. "Broadway Postscript: Shylock Achieved." *SatR,* July 27, 1957, p. 22.
B2718   Hewes, Henry. "Broadway Postscript: Much Ado on the Range." *SatR,* Aug. 24, 1957, p. 24.
B2719   Houseman, John. "America's Stratford: Progress and Growing Pains." *TAr,* July, 1957, pp. 76-77.
B2720   McGlinchee, Claire. "Stratford, Connecticut, Shakespeare Festival, 1957." *SQ,* VIII (1957), 507-510.
B2721   Peck, Seymour. "Much Ado About Shakespeare." *New York Times Magazine,* June 30, 1957, pp. 14-15.
B2722   Savery, Ranald. "Echoes from Broadway." *Theatre World,* Sept., 1957, pp. 22-23.
B2723   "Shakespeareans of Stratford." *TAr,* July, 1958, pp. 60-61.
B2724   Gassner, John. "Broadway in Review." *ETJ,* X (1958), 240-249.
B2725   Hewes, Henry. "Broadway Postscript: Reform It Altogether." *SatR,* July 5, 1958, p. 22.
B2726   McGlinchee, Claire. "Stratford, Connecticut, Shakespeare Festival, 1958." *SQ,* IX (1958), 539-542.

(c)   NEW YORK: THEATRE WORKSHOP, SHAKE-
       SPEARWRIGHTS, PUBLIC PARK PERFORMANCES,
       N. Y. SHAKESPEARE FESTIVAL CO.

B2727   "East Side Bard: Shakespearean Theatre Workshop, New York City." *New York Times Magazine,* Aug. 12, 1956, p. 43.
B2728   Hewes, Henry. "Broadway Postscript: No Great Shakes." *SatR,* Jan. 28, 1956, p. 18.
B2729   Hewes, Henry. "Broadway Postscript: Shakespearean Theatre Workshop, and Shakespeare-wrights." *SatR,* Mar. 17, 1956, p. 26.
B2730   Hayes, Richard. "The Climate of Illyria." *Commonweal,* Feb. 22, 1957, p. 538.
B2731   Clurman, Harold. "Theatre." *Nation,* Aug. 31, 1957, pp. 98-99.
B2732   Flagler, J. M. "Onward and Upward with the Arts." *New Yorker,* Aug. 31, 1957, pp. 56-70.
B2733   Lewis, Theophilus. "Theatre." *America,* Nov. 16, 1957, pp. 225-226.
B2734   M., H. G. "*Macbeth.*" *Theatre World,* Oct., 1957, p. 9.
B2735   Watt, David. "The Relapse." *Spectator,* Sept. 13, 1957, p. 342.
B2736   Wyatt, E. V. R. "Theatre." *Catholic World,* Feb., 1958, pp. 383-384.
B2737   Wyatt, E. V. R. "Theatre." *Catholic World,* Sept., 1958, p. 460.
B2738   Wyatt, E. V. R. "Theatre." *Catholic World,* Oct., 1958, pp. 68-69.

(d)   HOFSTRA

B2739   Dickinson, Hugh. "Shakespeare at Hofstra." *SQ,* I (1950), 193-196.
B2740   Venezky, Alice. "Shakespeare Festival at Hofstra College." *SQ,* II (1951), 253.
B2741   Fidone, W. "Three Tiers for the Bard." *Scholastic,* Nov. 29, 1956, p. 4T.
B2742   Griffin, Alice. "New Trends in American Theater." *Perspectives USA,* XIV (1956), 130-146.

(e) PHILADELPHIA SHAKESPEARE FESTIVAL PLAYERS

B2743   "Alas, Poor William! Philadelphia Ban." *Reporter*, Sept. 8, 1955, p. 4.

(f) ANTIOCH

B2744   "A Scene from *Macbeth* at Antioch College." *TAr*, XXI (1937), 535.

B2745   Marder, Louis. "History Cycle at Antioch College." *SQ*, IV (1953), 57-58.

B2746   Hutslar, Donald A. *The Creative Photographer as Exemplified in The Shakespearean Theatre at Antioch College.* MA thesis, Ohio University (Athens, Ohio), 1955. Pp. 232. Abstr. in *ShN*, V (1955), 36.

B2747   Ranney, Omar. "Antioch Shakespeare Festival." *SQ*, VI (1955), 453-454.

B2748   "The Play's the Thing, But a Push from Business Helps." *Business Week*, July 7, 1956, pp. 32-34.

B2749   Hewes, Henry. "Broadway Postscript: Bard Finds a Home In Ohio." *SatR*, Sept. 1, 1956, p. 24.

B2750   Jerome, Judson. "Shakespeare at Antioch." *SQ*, VII (1956), 411-414.

B2751   Pollak, B. "Shakespeare's Children; Antioch College Area Theater's Shakespeare Festival." *McCalls*, July, 1956, p. 6.

B2752   Radcliffe, E. B. "Ohio's Boom for the Bard." *TAr*, June, 1956, pp. 65-67.

B2753   Shedd, Robert G. "Shakespeare at Antioch, 1957: Past Record and Present Achievement." *SQ*, VIII (1957), 521-525.

(g) OREGON

B2754   Newberger, R. "Shakespeare Makes Good in Oregon." *New York Times*, Aug. 15, 1948, Section 2, p. X[1].

B2755   Sandoe, James. "The Oregon Shakespeare Festival." *SQ*, I (1950), 5-11.

B2756   Wiley, Margaret Lee. "Oregon Shakespeare Festival, 1951." *ShN*, I (1951), 13.

B2757   Bowmer, Angus L. "Renaissance Staging at Ashland." *ShN*, II (Nov., 1952), 37.

B2758   Robinson, Horace W. "Shakespeare, Ashland, Oregon." *SQ*, VI (1955), 447-451.

B2759   Wadsworth, Frank W. "Shakespeare in Action." *CE*, XVI (1955), 486-492; 524.

B2760   Chavez, Edmund. "Heraldry." *Players Magazine*, XXXIII (1956), 40-41.

B2761   Horn, Robert D. "The Oregon Shakespeare Festival." *SQ*, VII (1956), 415-418.

B2762   Griffin, Alice. "Theatre, U.S.A." *TAr*, July, 1957, pp. 70-72, 93.

B2763   Guth, Hans P. "Shakespeare unter den Sternen Oregons." *NS*, NS, VI (1957), Heft 9, pp. 439-441.

B2764   Horn, Robert D. "Shakespeare at Ashland, Oregon, 1957." *SQ*, VIII (1957), 527-530.

B2765   Cancelled.

B2766   "Shakespeare Lectures at the Oregon Festival." *ShN*, VIII (1958), 28-29.

B2767   Johnson, Gloria E. "Shakespeare at Ashland, Oregon, 1958." *SQ*, IX (1958), 543-547.

(h) SAN DIEGO

B2768   Feldman, Donna Rose. *An Historical Study of Thomas Wood Stevens' Globe Theatre Company, 1934-1937.* DD, State University of Iowa, 1953. Pp. 396. Mic A53-1643. *DA*, XIII (1953), 909. Publication No. 5467.

B2769   McMullen, Frank. "Community Theatre: A Wooden 'O' Among the Palms." *Players Magazine*, XXXI (1955), 152.

B2770   Payne, B. Iden. "Shakespeare Woman Actor." *San Diego Magazine*, August, 1955, pp. 62-73, and cover.

B2771   Sellman, Priscilla M. "The Old Globe's Sixth Season in San Diego." *SQ*, VII (1956), 419-422.

B2772   Johnson, Charles Frederick. "San Diego National Shakespeare Festival." *SQ*, VIII (1957), 531-534.

(i) MISCELLANEOUS

B2773   Johnston, Robert A. *The Moscow Art Theatre in America.* DD, Northwestern University, 1951. Abstr. publ. in Northwestern Univ. *Summaries of Doctoral Dissertations, 1951*, XIX, Chicago & Evanston, 1952, pp. 145-150.

B2774   Porterfield, Robert. "Trouping Shakespeare." *TAr*, April, 1951, pp. 55, 90-92.

B2775   "From Ham to Hamlet." *TAr*, XXXII (Oct., 1948), 56-57.

B2776   English, T. H. "Prologue to Shakespeare's *The Comedy of Errors*." *Emory Univ. Quarterly*, X (1954), 275-276.

B2777   Phares, Ross. "Shakespeare at Centenary College." *SQ*, V (1954), 409.

B2778   Prouty, Charles Tyler. "The Yale Shakespeare Festival." *Shakespeare: Of an Age and for all Time.* The Yale Shakespeare Festival Lectures, 1954, pp. 3-10.

B2779   *"Titus Andronicus* at the Stoll Theatre." *Plays and Players*, Aug., 1957, pp. 18-19.
B2780   Caghen, Shirley. "Twelve Years of Globe Productions." *Players Magazine*, XXXIV (1958), 154-155.
B2781   Cutts, Anson B. "The Phoenix Shakespeare Festival." *SQ*, IX (1958), 549-553.
B2782   Perkin, Robert L. "Shakespeare in The Rockies: A Happy Beginning." *SQ*, IX (1958), 555-559.
B2783   Small, Tom. "Why Shakespeare?" *Colorado Quar.*, VII (1958), 23-31.

(5)   IN FRANCE

B2784   Salomé, René. "Shakespeare: *Othello* à l'Odéon." *Etudes*, July, 1938, pp. 225-230.
B2785   Touchard, Pierre-Aimé. "Le Théâtre: Shakespeare à la Scène." *Esprit*, XIII (May, 1945), 879-883.
        Lear and *Antony* at the Théâtre Sarah Bernhardt.
B2786   Maulnier, Thierry. "Giraudoux, Molière, Shakespeare." *Revue de Paris*, LIX, No. 12 (1952), 143-147.
        Romeo at La Comédie Française.
B2787   Lemarchand, Jacques. "Coriolan à la Comédie Française." *NRF*, V, No. 49 (1957), 128-132.
B2788   Duvignaud, Jean. "Molière et Shakespeare." *NRF*, I, 2, X (Oct., 1953), 714-717.
        Performances at Avignon.
B2789   Mauduit, J. "Cinna, Macbeth, Le Prince de Hombourg: Le T. N. P. à Rouen et en Avignon." *Etudes*, 283 (Oct., 1954), 70-79.
B2790   Gandon, Yves. "Les Festivals d'Art Dramatique." *Biblio*, XXIII (Aug.-Sept., 1955), 27.
        Notices the performances at Nîmes of *Caesar* and *Cor*.
B2791   Mauduit, Jean. "Hermantier et la Création de *Jules César* de Shakespeare au Festival de Nîmes." *Etudes*, 267 (1950), 90-95.

(6)   IN GERMANY
(a)   BOCHUM

B2792   Deetjen, Werner. "Die Shakespeare-Pflege in Bochum." *LNN*, Oct. 5, 1937.
B2793   Gerlach, R. "Shakespeares Römerdramen, Bochum." *Darmstädter Tagebl.*, Oct. 19, 1937.
B2794   Keller, Wolfgang. *"Titus Andronicus*. Ein Vortrag bei der Bochumer Shakespeare-Woche gehalten im Oktober 1937." *SJ*, LXXIV (1938), 137-162.
B2795   Klein, Paul G. A. "Kreis der Römerdramen. Nach der 2. Deutschen Shakespeare-Woche in Bochum." *MNN*, Oct. 18, 1937.
B2796   Klein, Paul G. A. "Shakespeare auf der deutschen Bühne. Ausstellung auf der 2. Deutschen Shakespeare-Woche in Bochum." *MNN*, Oct. 15, 1937.
B2797   Sprüngli, Th. A. "Zyklische Aufführung von Shakespeares Römerdramen in Bochum." *LNN*, Oct. 19, 1937.
B2798   Stahl, E. L. "Der deutsche Bühnenweg der Römerdramen. Zur ersten zyklischen Aufführung, Bochum." *Berl. Börsenztg.*, Sept. 12, 1937.
B2799   Thomas, W. "Die Zweite Deutsche Shakespeare-Woche in Bochum." *Die Bühne*, XVIII (1938), 459-460.
B2800   Witthaus, W. "Heroisches Theater. Römerdramen in Bochum." *Köln. Zeitung*, Oct. 17, 1937.
B2801   Geldmacher, Willi. "Ein Vierteljahrhundert Shakespeare-Pflege in Bochum." *Shakespeare-Tage*, No. 2801, 1952, p. 1.
B2802   Ruppel, Karl Heinrich. "Shakespeares *Sommernachtstraum* gesehen und gehört von Carl Orff." *Prisma* (Bochum), 1953/54, pp. 73-76. See also *Shakespeare-Tage*, No. 3779, 1954, pp. 9-12.
B2803   Brinkmann, Karl. "Shakespeare am alten Bochumer Theater." *Shakespeare-Tage*, 1955, pp. 17-19. See also *Prisma* (Bochum), 1954/55, pp. 130-132.
B2804   Lufft, Peter. "Viel Lärm um nichts." *Prisma* (Bochum), No. 7, 1956/57, pp. 73-75. Also in *Shakespeare-Tage*, 1957, pp. 8-10.

(b)   ELSEWHERE

B2805   Brandl, Alois. "Shakespeare-Moglichkeiten [originally Broschüre zur Eröffnung des grossen Schauspielhaus, Berlin, 1921]." Reprinted in Brandl's *Forschungen*, B4460.
B2806   *Plays, Römerberg Festival*. Schiller: *Fiesco;* Hauptmann: *Florian Geyer;* Shakespeare: *King Henry IV;* Goethe: *Faust*. 1. Teil. Synopsis of the plays. Frankfurt on Main: Hauserpresse, 1937. Pp. 42.
B2807   Kobbe, Friedrich-Carl. "Reichsfestspiele Heidelberg." *DL*, XL (1937/38), 749-750.
B2808   "Shakespeare und die Griechen. Die künstlerischen Prinzipien des Bayerischen Staatsschauspiels." *MNN*, July 24, 1939, p. 5.

B2809 Ruppel, K. H. "Shakespeare-Pflege im Stuttgarter Staatstheater." *SJ*, 92 (1956), 313-316.

B2810 Rosen, Waldemar. "Der *Sommernachtstraum* mit Purcell-Musik. Uraufführung in der Leipziger Oper." *Allg. Musikzeitung*, LXIV (1937), 151.

B2811 Weigend, Friedrich. "Variationen über das Thema Shakespeare. Bemerkungen zu einer Woche im Staatstheater Dresden." *Theater d. Zeit*, Nov. 5, 1950, pp. 25-26.

B2812 Mettin, Herm. Christ. "*König Richard III* im Staatlichen Schauspielhaus zu Berlin." *Dts. Adelsblatt*, LX (1937), 371-372.

B2813 Fechter, Paul. "Zweimal Shakespeare." *Dts. Rundschau*, 267 (1941), 159-161. Berlin Staatstheater.

B2814 Hope-Wallace, Philip. "Berlin Festival." *Time and Tide*, XXXVI (1955), 1284.

(7) IN SWITZERLAND

B2815 Dürrenmatt, Friedrich. " 2 X Shakespeare." *Die Weltwoche* (Zurich), June 13, 1951.

B2816 Brock, Erich. "Shakespeare in Zürich." *Neue Schweizer Rundschau*, XX (1952), 239-244.

B2817 Brock-Sulzer, Elizabeth. "Shakespeare-Pflege am Schauspielhaus Zürich." *SJ*, 89 (1953), 162-172.

B2818 Brock, Erich. "Gedanken zu den Züricher Shakespeare-Festspielen." *Neue Schweizer Rundschau*, NF, XXI (1953), 175-179.

B2819 Trachsler, Reinhard. "German Switzerland." *World Theater*, IV, No. 3 (1955), 75.

(8) ELSEWHERE

B2820 Thun-Hohenstein, P. Graf. "Shakespeare und Shaw im Wiener Burgtheater." *Österr. Rundschau*, III (1937), 34-36.

B2821 Kindermann, Heinz. *Das Burgtheater* [Vienna]. *Erbe und Sendung eines Nationaltheaters.* Leipzig: Adolf Luser, 1939. Pp. 252.

B2822 Richter, Traute. "Wiener Festwochen, 1957." *Theater d. Zeit*, Sept. 12, 1957, pp. 31, 34-37.

B2823 Linde, E. "Köpmannen I Venedig at the Malmö Stadseater." *Bonniers Litterära Magasin*, Feb., 1948, pp. 152-153.

B2824 Clissold, Stephen. "In Quest of Hamlet." *Time and Tide*, XXXVI (1955), 74.
On seeing *Ham.* performed at festivals in Denmark and Yugoslavia.

B2825 Stříbrný, Zedněk. "První Shakespearovský festival v Olomouci." *Časopis pro Moderní Filologii* (Prague), XL (1958), 234-235.

B2826 Glass, Dudley. "Shakespeare in a Roman Temple." *Theatre World*, Dec., 1956, pp. 36-37. Baalbek Festival.

e. SPECIFIC INDIVIDUAL PERFORMANCES
(1) SEVERAL PRODUCTIONS OF TWO OR MORE TYPES
(a) COMEDIES

B2827 Bodeen, DeWitt. "Shakespeare's Greco-Roman Plays at the Pasadena Community Play-house." *SAB*, XII (1937), 49-53.

B2828 "*Richard III* and *Twelfth Night* on the West Coast." *TAr*, XXII (1938), 480-481.

B2829 Fuller, Rosalinde. "A Shakespeare Tour in Wartime." *TAr*, XXIV (1940), 179-181.

B2830 Linneballe, Poul. "Immermans Shakespeareiseenesettelser." *Edda*, XLIII (1943), 125-138.

B2831 Lewis, Lorna. "Shakespeare in Scandinavia, 1949." *Life and Letters*, Oct. 1949, pp. 92-100.

B2832 Moutaftchiev, I. "Shakespeare and Bulgaria." *TLS*, Nov. 18, 1949, p. 751.
Gives details concerning recent and projected Shak. editions and productions in Bulgaria. Comment by Peter Alexander and Norman Davis, *TLS*, Dec. 16, 1949, p. 825.

B2833 Wasi, Muriel. "Shakespeare in Delhi." *Mysindia*, (Bangalore), Nov. 26, 1950, pp. 19-20.

B2834 D'Amico, Silvio. "Theatre in the Open-Air." *World Theatre*, III, No. 4 (1954), 23-34.

B2835 Fallois, Bernard de. "Shakespeare à Paris." *La Revue de Paris*, March, 1955, pp. 91-96.

B2836 McCarthy, Mary T. *Sights and Spectacles, 1937-1956.* New York: Farrar, Strauss, 1956.

B2837 Matthews, Harold. "*Hamlet, The Merchant*, and *Othello*." *Theatre World*, July, 1956, pp. 14-15.

B2838 Čavojskv, Ladislav. "Shakespeare Pochopený Tradične a Jeho Nové Javiskové Vyjadrenie." *Slovenské Divadlo* (Bratislava), VI (1958), 35-56.
Analyzes traditional and new elements in Slovak performances of *Wives* (at Prešov), *A. Y. L.* (at Košice), and *Romeo* (in Bratislava); with illustrations.

B2839 Ruppel, K. H. "Berliner Theaterbericht, darin über Die Neuinszenierung von Shakespeares *Wie es Euch Gefällt* und die Eröffnungsvorstellung von Shakespeares *Sommernachtstraum*." *DL*, XLIII (1940-41), 77.

B2840 Simko, Ján. "Shakespeare in Slovakia." *ShS*, IV (1951), 109-116.

B2841 Barbour, Thomas. "Theatre Chronicle." *Hudson Rev*, VI (1953), 278-286.

i. Comedy of Errors

B2842 Gstettner, Hans. "*Komödie der Irrungen.* Neuinszeniert im Residenztheater, Munich." *VB* (Mü), No. 57, Feb. 26, 1940.

B2843 Sheets, Roberta Dinwiddie. "*Comedy of Errors.*" *Dramatics*, Nov. 1957, pp. 14-15.

ii. Taming of the Shrew

B2844 Atkinson, Brooks. "*Taming of the Shrew*, Done by A. Lunt, et al." *TAr*, xx (1936), 462.

B2845 Riedy, P. "Über eine Heutige Inszenierung der *Widerspenstigen Zähmung.*" *Freiburger Theaterblätter*, 1936-37. Pp. 48.

B2846 "H. Burger's Setting for *Taming of the Shrew.*" *TAr*, xxiii (1939), 266.

B2847 "Wir Wollen Shakespeare und Keinen Boogie-Woogie!" *MDtShG*, iii (1950), 10-11.

B2848 Brix, Hans. "Trold kan Taemmes." (*The Taming of the Shrew*). *Berlingske Aften* (Copenhagen), April 3, 1954.

B2849 Sweeney, Donald. "*Taming of the Shrew.*" *Dramatics*, Nov., 1957, p. 15.

B2850 Thespis. "Theatre Notes: *The Taming of the Shrew* (Regent's Park)." *English*, xii (1958), 105.

iii. Midsummer Night's Dream

B2851 Frank, Heinz. "*Ein Sommernachtstraum.* Hans Schweikarts Neuinszenierung im Münchener Residenztheater." *VB*, July 9, 1936.

B2852 "Eine Inszenierung von *Ein Sommernachtstraum.*" *Theater d. Welt*, I (1937), 181-185.

B2853 Delpy, E. and J. Goetz. "Festliche Barockkomödie. Neue Bühnengestaltung von Shakespeares. *Sommernachtstraum* in Leipzig." *LNN*, Feb. 18, 1937.

B2854 Frank, Heinz. "Ein *Sommernachtstraum.* Falckenbergs Neuinszenierung in den Münchener Kammerspielen." *VB* (Mü), No. 325, Nov. 20, 1940.

B2855 Wehner, Josef Magnus. "Der *Sommernachtstraum* auf Barock. Zu Falckenbergs Neuinszenierung in den Kammerspielen [Munich]." *MNN*, No. 325, Nov. 20, 1940.

B2856 "A Scene from *Midsummer Night's Dream.*" *TAr*, xxv (1941), 27.

B2857 Gelinas, P. "Le *Songe* a l'Ermitage (en Canada)." *Le Jour.*, Aug. 18, 1945.

B2858 Koht, Halvdan. "Det Norske Teatret, Vinterbolken 1948-49." *Syn og Segn* (Oslo), LV, ii (1949), 49-61.

B2859 Litten, Heinz W. "Noch einmal *Sommernachstraum.*" *Heute u. Morgen* (Schwerin), 1954, pp. 33-38.

B2860 Pocock, J. G. A. "Producer's Dream." *Landfall* [New Zealand], viii (Sept. 1954), 206-209.

B2861 Coleman, E. "Bard and O'Neill, with Trimmings." *TAr* (Oct. 1956), 76-77.

B2862 Whiting, Frank. "Shakespeare to GI's in Europe." *Players Magazine*, xxxiv (1958), 106.

iv. Merchant of Venice

B2863 Karutz, Richard. "Shylock in Africa." *Das Goetheanum*, xv (1936), 237-238.

B2864 G., J. "*Merchant of Venice*, 1939, in Brooklyn." *New York Times*, Jan. 10, 1939, p. 16.

B2865 "M. Schwartz as Shylock in the New Play." *TAr* (Dec., 1947), 66-67.

B2866 "*Merchant of Venice.*" *New York Theatre Critics' Reviews*, viii (1947), 450-451.

B2867 Bernstein, L. "Shylock Re-interpreted." [By A. Ibn-Zahav.] *New York Times*, Sept. 28, 1947, Section 2, p. X 3.

B2868 Barnett, John E. "*The Merchant of Venice* at the University of Kansas City." *SQ*, I (1950), 269-271.

B2869 Rudolf, Branko. "Shakespeareov Beneški Trgovec v Mariborskem Gledališču." *Nova Obzorja* (Maribor), 1953.

B2870 Hayes, Richard. "*Merchant of Venice.*" *Commonweal*, May 13, 1955, 149-150.

B2871 Wyatt, E. V. R. "*Merchant of Venice.*" *Catholic World*, 181 (May 1955), 149.

v. Much Ado About Nothing

B2872 Ruppel, K. H. "Vom Römerberg zur Hohensalzburg." *DL*, xlii (1939-40), 11.
With comments upon production of *Much* in the Freilichtheater, Salzburg.

B2873 Stahl, Heinrich. "*Viel Lärm um Nichts.* Shakespeares Lustspiel in Salzburg." *VB* (Mü), No. 217, Oct. 5, 1941.

B2874 Wehner, Josef Magnus. "Shakespeare-Komödie in Salzburg: *Viel Lärm um Nichts* in der Felsenreitschule." *MNN*, Oct. 6, 1938.

B2875 Bunuševac, Radmila. "Šekspir na Sceni Narodnog Pozorišta." [Shakespeare on the Stage of the National Theater.] *Politika*, vii (1951), 4.

B2876 Čolić, Milutin. "Mnogo Buke ni oko Čega." (*Much Ado about Nothing*) October 20, viii (1951), 9.

vi. *As You Like It*

B2877   "A Scene from *As You Like It.*" *TAr*, XXI (1937), 535.

B2878   "*As You Like It.*" *New York Theatre Critics' Reviews*, VIII (1947), 451-452.

B2879   Brown, John Mason. "That Forest of Arden." *SRL*, XXXIII (March 18, 1950), 24-26.

B2880   Hyde, Mary C. "Katharine Hepburn's *As You Like It.*" *SQ*, I (1950), 55-56.

B2881   Nedić, Borivoje. "*Kako vam Drago.*" [*As You Like It*] *Književne Novine* (Belgrade), III (1950), 9.

B2882   Popović, Dušan. "*Kako vam Drago* u Beogradskom Dramskom Pozorištu." [*As You Like It* in the Belgrade Dramatic Theatre]. *Borba*, III (1950), 5.

B2883   Kruuse, Jens. "Som Man Behager." [*As You Like It*] *Jyllandsposten* (Aarhus, Denmark), Oct. 29, 1954.

B2884   Bremer, Klaus. "*Wie es Euch Gefällt* 1956." *Das Neue Forum* (Darmstadt), V (1955-56), 267-272.

vii. *Twelfth Night*

B2885   Frank, H. "*Was ihr Wollt.* Neuinszenierung im Residenztheater [Munich]." *VB*, June 26, 1936.

B2886   Wehner, Josef Magnus. "*Was ihr Wollt.* Neu Einstudiert im Residenztheater [Munich]." *MNN*, June 26, 1936.

B2887   "Favorski's Setting for *Twelfth Night* in Moscow." *TLS*, Sept. 10, 1938, p. 577.

B2888   Frank, Heinz. "Shakespeare: *Was ihr Wollt.* Albert Fischels Neuinszenierung im Residenz-theater." Munich, *VB* (Mü), No. 33, Feb. 2, 1941.

B2889   Wehner, Jos. Magnus. "Shakespeares *Was ihr Wollt.* Neuinszeniert im Residenztheater [Munich]." *MNN*, No. 33, Feb. 2, 1941.

B2890   Dukes, Ashley. "*Twelfth Night* in London." *TAr*, XXIII (1939), 99-100.

B2891   Tannenbaum, Samuel A. "*Twelfth Night* (?)." *SAB*, XV (1940), 254-255.

B2892   Helen Hayes and Maurice Evans in *Twelfth Night*. B. Atkinson, *New York Times*, Nov. 20, 1940, p. 26; R. Lockridge, *New York Sun*, Nov. 20, 1940, p. 8; J. M. Brown, *New York Evening Post*, Nov. 20, 1940, p. 6; E. Jordan, *America*, Dec. 7, 1940, p. 250.

B2893   Gilder, Rosamund. "Fiddling While Rome Burns." *TAr*, XXV (Jan. 1941), 6-12.

B2894   "Three Ills to *Twelfth Night.*" *TAr*, XXIV (1940), 846-898.

B2895   "*Twelfth Night* at Webster Groves High School." *TAr*, XXIV (1940), 218.

B2896   The Chekhov Players in *Twelfth Night* in New York. Brooks Atkinson, *New York Times*, Dec. 3, 1941, p. 32; J. M. Brown, *New York World-Telegram*, Dec. 3, 1941, p. 26; R. Lockridge, *New York Sun*, Dec. 3, 1941, p. 36; R. Watts, Jr., *New York Herald-Tribune*, Dec. 3, 1941, p. 24.

B2897   Brown, John Mason. "What You Will?" *SRL*, XXXII (Oct. 29, 1949), 30-31.

B2898   M., Z. "Na Tri Kralja ili Kako Hócete u Hrvatskom Narodnom Kazalištu." [*Twelfth Night* in the Croatian National Theatre]. *Naprijed*, X (1951), 12.

B2899   Šaula, Dorte. "Jedna Neshakespearska Predstava." [An Un-Shakespearian Performance]. *Studentski List* (Zagreb), VII (1951), 20.

B2900   Engberg, Harald. "Helligtrekongers Aften." (*Twelfth Night*). *Politiken* (Copenhagen), June 25, 1954.

B2901   Kjaergaard, Helge. "Shakespeare er Evig og Viola er Yndig." [Shakespeare is eternal and Viola is Graceful]. *Aalborg Stiftstidende* (Copenhagen), June 18, 1954.

B2902   Marsh, Ngaio. "A Note on a Production of *Twelfth Night.*" *ShS*, VIII (1955), 69-73.

B2903   Nielsen, Frederik. "Shakespeare i Nörregade." *Social Demokraten* (Copenhagen), 22/156, 1957.

viii. *Merry Wives of Windsor*

B2904   Atkinson, Brooks. "*Merry Wives of Windsor* Produced in New York." *N. Y. Times*, Apr. 15, 1938, p. 32.

ix. *Troilus and Cressida*

B2905   Hughes, Elinor. "*Troilus and Cressida* at Harvard." *TAr*, XXXIII (Iune 1949), 56.

B2906   Mackenzie, C. [Mr. Glen Byam Shaw's Production of *Troilus and Cressida*.] *Spectator*, 193 (Sept. 3, 1954), 284.

B2907   Worsley, Thomas Cuthbert. "A German Troilus." *NstN*, L (1955), 572-573.

B2908   "At the Old Vic: A Ruritanian Revival of *Troilus and Cressida.*" *Illustrated London News*, April 14, 1956, p. 319.

B2909   Driver, Tom Faw. "An Eyeful." *Christian Century*, Feb. 6, 1957, p. 175.

x. *All's Well that Ends Well*

B2910   Smith, Lisa Gordon. "*All's Well That Ends Well.*" *Plays and Players*, Sept., 1957, p. 10.

xi.   *Measure for Measure*

B2911   "A Scene from *Measure for Measure*." *TAr*, xxII (1938), 456.
B2912   Reimer. "Shakespeares Tragikomödie, *Mass für Mass*." *Freiburger Theaterblätter* (Städt. Bühnen Freiburg i. Br.) 1941-42, p. 7.
B2913   Clurman, Harold. "Theatre." *Nation*, Feb. 16, 1957, p. 146.

xii.   *Cymbeline*

B2914   "A Scene from G. B. Shaw's Version of *Cymbeline*." *TAr*, xxII (1938), 112.
B2915   "*Cymbeline* at the Old Vic." *Theatre World*, Nov., 1957, pp. 26-27.

xiii.   *Winter's Tale*

B2916   Hamilton, C. "*Winter's Tale* and the 'Stars'." *N. Y. Times*, Jan. 13, 1946, Sec. 2, p. X[1].
B2917   *The Winter's Tale* at the Court. W. Morehouse, *New York Sun*, Jan. 16, 1946, p. 27; L. Kronenberger, *PM*, Jan. 16, 1946, p. 16; L. Nichols, *New York Times*, Jan. 16, 1946, p. 18; B. Rascoe, *New York World-Telegram*, Jan. 16, 1946, p. 20; R. Gilder, *TAr*, xxx (1946), 139-140.
B2918   Nathan, G. J. "*The Winter's Tale*." *The Theatre Book of the Year, 1945-46*. New York, 1946, pp. 276-279.
B2919   Venezky, Alice. "*The Winter's Tale:* French and English Productions." *SN*, I (1951), 14.
B2920   Afanasieva, Olga, and Alexander Vasiliev. "Behind the Scenes at the Moscow Theatre." *USSR*, No. 9, 1957, pp. 48-53. Stanislavski influenced production of *Winter's Tale* in Moscow.

xiv.   *Tempest*

B2921   Delpy, E. "Bühnen-Zauberer Shakespeares Abschied. Erstaufführung der Romanze *Der Sturm* in Leipzig." *LNN*, Nov. 15, 1937.
B2922   Mettin, Hermann Christian. "*Sturm* im Dts. Theater, Berlin." *Dts. Adelsblatt*, LVI (1938), 375.
B2923   Hastings, W. T. *Brown University Presents Sock and Buskin in "The Tempest" with "Revels' End."* Dialogue in 3 Scenes. Sept. 1942. Pp. 12.
B2924   Campbell, Oscar. "Miss Webster and *The Tempest*." *Amer. Scholar*, XIV (1946), 271-281.
B2925   The Webster Production of *The Tempest* in New York. L. Nichols, *New York Times*, Jan. 26, 1945, p. 17; B. Roscoe *New York World-Telegram*, Jan. 26, 1945, p. 14; J. Chapman, *Daily News*, Jan. 26, 1945, p. 37; O. L. Guernsey, Jr., *New York Herald-Tribune*, Jan. 26, 1945, p. 12; W. Morehouse, *New York Sun*, Jan. 26, 1945, p. 24; R. Garland, *Journal-American*, Jan. 26, 1945, p. 8; R. Coleman, *Daily Mirror*, Jan. 26, 1945, p. 20; L. Kronenberger, *PM*, Jan. 26, 1945, p. 20; E. V. R. Wyatt, *Catholic World*, 160 (1945), 548-549; G. J. Nathan, *Theatre Book of the Year*, 1945, pp. 254-258; *American Mercury*, LX (1945), 588-591.
B2926   Webster, M. "*The Tempest*." *New York Times*, Jan. 28, 1945, Sec. 2, p. X-10.
B2927   "Four Illustrations of M. Webster's Production of *The Tempest*." *New York Times Magazine*, Jan. 21, 1945, pp. 24, 25.
B2928   Webster, M. "Illustrations of *The Tempest*." *Life*, XVIII (Feb. 12, 1945), 74-76.
B2929   Brown, John Mason. "Miss Webster's Isle." *SRL*, XXVIII (Feb. 10, 1945), 22-23, 29.
B2930   Gilder, Rosamond. "Review of *The Tempest*, Directed by Margaret Webster." *TAr*, xxIX (Mar., 1945), 136-137.
B2931   Isaacs, Hermine Rich. "This Insubstantial Pageant. *The Tempest* in the Making." *TAr*, xxIX (1945), 89-93.
B2932   Adams, J. Donald. "Speaking of Books." *NYTBR*, Mar. 18, 1945, p. 2.
B2933   Gasper, Raymond Dominic. *A Study of the Group Theatre and Its Contributions to Theatrical Production in America*." DD, Ohio State University, 1956. Pp. 404. Mic 56-941. *DA*, xvI (1956), 597. Publ. No. 15,834.
B2934   Hopkinson, Tom. "Mood of the Month—II." *London Magazine*, v, iii (1958), 36-41. *Temp.* at Drury Lane.

xv.   *Pericles*

B2935   Millenkovich-Morold, Max. "Perikles, Fürst von Tyrus. Eine Neuheit des Wiener Burgtheaters. Ein gutes Theaterstück, Wahrscheinlich von Shakespeare." *VB*, Nov. 19, 1937.
B2936   Rieger, E. "*Pericles* im Burgtheater [Vienna]." *Neue Freie Presse*, Oct. 17, 1937.

(b)   HISTORIES

B2937   George, Louise Wright. "Shakespeare in La Ceiba." *SQ*, III (1952), 359-363. Discusses productions of *3 H. VI* and *R. III* in Spanish Honduras.

i.   *Richard III*

B2938   Frank, Heinz. "Shakespeare, *König Richard III*. Hans Schweikarts Neuinszenierung im Residenztheater [Munich]." *VB*, Oct. 18, 1937.

B2939 Geisenheyner, M. "*Richard III* im Staatlichen Schauspielhaus Berlin." *Fr. Ztg.*, March 4, 1937.

B2940 Hofmüller, Rudolf. "Shakespeares *Richard III* . . . im Residenztheater. Der Epilog zu den Königsdramen. Politische Weltschau im Drama. Charakterbild eines Tyrannen." *VB*, Oct. 15, 1937, p. 37.

B2941 Ruppel, K. H. "*Richard III* im Staatlichen Schauspielhaus Berlin." *Köln. Ztg.*, March 8, 1937.

B2942 G. Couloris's *Richard III* in New York. J. Anderson, *New York Journal-American*, March 27, 1943, p. 6; W. Morehouse, *New York Sun*, March 27, 1943, p. 4; W. Waldorf, *New York Post*, March 27, 1943, p. 8; B. Rascoe, *New York World-Telegram*, March 27, 1943.

B2943 Wyatt, E. V. R. "GI Version of *Richard III* Produced at Fordham University." *Catholic World*, 163 (1946), 553-554.

ii. *Richard II*

B2944 "The Almanac of Poor *Richard II*." *New York Times*, Jan. 31, 1937, Sec. 2, p. 3.

B2945 *Richard II* Produced in New York. B. Atkinson, *New York Times*, Feb. 6, 1937, p. 14; D. Gilbert, *New York World-Telegram*, Feb. 6, 1937, p. 6a; R. Lockridge, *The Sun* (New York), Feb. 7, 1937, p. 10; J. Anderson, *New York Journal*, Feb. 7, 1937; G. W. Gabriel, *New York American*, Feb. 7, 1937; *Literary Digest*, 123 (Feb. 20, 1937), 23; B. Atkinson, *New York Times*, Feb. 14, 1937, Sec. 2, p. 1; B. Crowther, ibid., p. 3; E. V. R. Wyatt, *Catholic World*, 144 (1937), 726-728.

B2946 M. Evans's *Richard II* in New York. B. Atkinson, *New York Times*, Sept. 26, 1937, Sec. 2, p. X [1]; E. V. R. Wyatt, *Catholic World*, 146 (Nov. 1937), 214-215.

B2947 "M. Evans as *Richard II*." *The Stage*, 1937, p. 50. *TAr*, xxi (1937), 187.

B2948 Miran, P. "Incorrect Costumes in Evan's *Richard II*." *Commonweal*, xxvi (1937), 50.

B2949 "Four Scenes from Evans's *Richard II*." *TAr*, xxi (1937), 354.

B2950 Isaacs, E. J. R. "Evans in *Richard II*." *TAr*, xxi (1937), 255-260, 333.

B2951 Reviews of *Richard II*. G. Vernon, *Commonweal*, xxv (Feb. 19, 1937), 472; G. Vernon, *Commonweal*, xxvi (June 25, 1937), 246; *Commonweal* (Oct. 1, 1937), 523; E. C. Sherburne. *Christian Science Monitor*, April 7, 1937, p. 4.

B2952 Brahan, T. "Bob Jones, Jr., Produces *Richard II* in Cleveland." *Chattanooga Times*, June 2, 1938.

B2953 "Shakespeare Einstweilen." *MDtShG*, iii (1950), 8.

B2954 Simiot, Bernard. "Shakespeare et Molière chez les Papes." *Hommes et Mondes*, Aug. 21, 1953, pp. 290-296.

B2955 Worsley, Thomas Cuthbert. "Mr. Gielgud's Colts." *NstN*, xlv (1953), 11.

B2956 *King Richard II*. Introduction by Sir John Gielgud. Designs in colour by Loudun Sainthill. London: Folio Society, 1958. Pp. 116.
Eight plates in full color reproduce the designs for the costumes and set of the 1952 Gielgud production.

iii. *Henry IV*

B2957 Brahan, T. "Bob Jones College presents *Henry IV*." *Chattanooga Times*, Feb. 27, 1938.

B2958 "M. Evans as Falstaff." *TAr*, xxii (1938), 104.

B2959 Rogers, C. "Unit Set for *I Henry IV*." *TAr*, xxii (1938), 534.

B2960 Anon. "M. Evans Presents *Henry IV*." New York: W. Kolmans, 1939.

B2961 M. Evans's Production of *I Henry IV*. B. Atkinson, *New York Times*, Jan. 31, 1939, p. 17; R. Lockridge, *New York Sun*, Jan. 31, 1939, p. 12; R. Watts, Jr., *New York Herald-Tribune*, Jan. 31, 1939, p. 12; S. B. Whipple, *New York World-Telegram*, Jan. 31, 1939, p. 8; W. Waldorf, *New York Post*, Jan. 31, 1939, p. 6; R. Gilder, *TAr*, xxiii (1939), 240.

B2962 Krutch, Joseph Wood. "Virtue in That Falstaff." *Nation*, 148 (1939), 184-185.

B2963 Fechter, Paul. "Deutsche Shakespeare-Darsteller. 2.: Henrich Georges Falstaff." *SJ*, lxxvii (1941), 123-137.

B2964 Potter, S. "*2 Henry IV*." *NstN*, xxx (1945), 244.

B2965 Cancelled.

B2966 Heaven, Sidney. "*Henry IV, Part 2*." *Plays and Players*, June, 1958, p. 15.

iv. *Henry V*

B2967 Wainwright, David. "Princes to Act." *Spectator*, No. 6421 (July 20, 1951), 90.

B2968 Hewes, Henry. "Broadway Postscript: Approval of Seale." *SatR*, July 28, 1956, p. 22.

B2969 Ridler, Anne. "Drama at Oxford." *Drama*, Autumn, 1957, p. 51.

v. *Henry VIII*

B2970 Wyatt, E. V. R. "*Henry VIII* Produced in New York." *Catholic World*, 164 (1946), 259-260.

B2971   Bab, Julius. *"Heinrich VIII* in New York." *SJ*, 82/83 (1949), 192-193.

(c) TRAGEDIES
i. *Titus Andronicus*

B2972   Walker, Roy. "Grand Guignol—By Shakespeare." *Theatre Newsletter*, Nov. 24, 1951, pp. 3-4. Comment by Ken Tynan, Dec. 8, 1951, p. 19.

B2973   Birch, Marguerite I. "Drama in Sydney." *Australian Quarterly*, xxx (1958), 123-125.

B2974   Heer, Friedrich. "Shakespeare-Uraufführung in Wien." *Die Furche, Freie Kulturpolitische Wochenschrift* (Vienna), xiii, No. 25 (1957), 14-15.

ii. *Romeo and Juliet*

B2975   Bernstein, A. "A Setting for *Romeo and Juliet.*" *TAr*, xxi (1937), 124.

B2976   Delpech, J. "Quand Pitoëff Joue Roméo et Met en Scène Shakespeare." *Les Nouvelles Littéraires*, June 5, 1937, p. 10.

B2977   Frank, Heinz. "Shakespeares *Romeo und Julia.* Reichsfestspiele in Heidelberg." *VB*, Aug. 23, 1937.

B2978   Dolar, Jaro. "O Shakespearu in Njegovi Ejubezenski Tragediji." [Shakespeare and His Love Tragedy]. *Gledališni List* (Maribor), vi, No. 4 (1951), 27-29.

B2979   Kreft, Bratko. "Shakespeareva Visoka Pesem." *Gledališni List—Drama* (Ljubljana), x (1953-54), 197-203.

B2980   "Shakespeare in China." *Illustrated London News*, Oct. 13, 1956, p. 615. *Romeo* performed in Peking. Photographs.

B2981   Driver, T. F. "Britons Abroad." *Christian Century*, Nov. 14, 1956, pp. 1328-29.

B2982   Thespis. "Theatre Notes." *English*, xi (1956), 57-58. Evaluation of Sloane School's production of *Romeo.*

iii. *Julius Caesar*

B2983   *Julius Caesar* in New York. B. Atkinson, *New York Times*, Nov. 12, 1937, p. 26; Nov. 28, 1937, Section 2, p. X[1]; R. Lockridge, *New York Sun*, Nov. 12, 1937, p. 28; *Time*, xxx (Nov. 22, 1937), p. 43.

B2984   Clark, Eleanor. "Shakespeare Resartus." *SAB*, xiii (1938), 73-76.

B2985   *Julius Caesar* in New York. S. Young, *NR*, 93 (Dec. 1, 1937), 101-102; A. MacLeish, *Nation*, 145 (Dec. 4, 1937), 617; G. Vernon, *Commonweal*, xxvii (Dec. 3, 1937), 160; E. Taggard, *Scholastic*, xxxi (Dec. 11, 1937), 6-7; J. W. Krutch, *Nation*, 145 (Nov. 27, 1937), 594-595.

B2986   "Two Scenes from the Modernised *Julius Caesar.*" *TAr*, xxii (1938), 18.

B2987   Cazamian, M. L. "La Représentation de *Jules César* à l'Atelier." *EA*, i (1937), 182-183.

B2988   Lièvre, Pierre. "*Jules César* de Shakespeare au Théâtre de l'Atelier." *MdF*, 274 (1937), 581-584

B2989   Geoghegan, H. "Reviewing *Julius Caesar.*" *Carnegie Magazine*, xiii (1939), 57-59.

B2990   Ruppel, Karl H. "Berliner Theater [Production of *Julius Caesar* by Jürgen Fehling in Berliner Staatlichen Schauspielhaus]." *DL*, xliii (1940-41), 556.

B2991   Bacon, Wallace A. "*Julius Caesar* at the Folger Shakespeare Library." *SAB*, xxiv (1949), 112-116.

B2992   "Shakespeare in Munich." *Newsweek*, xlv (May 23, 1955), 106.

B2993   Jacquot, Jean. "*Jules César* au Palais de Chaillot." *EA*, x (1957), 90-91.

B2994   Wyatt, E. V. R. "Theatre." *Catholic World*, Jan. 1958, p. 306.

iv. *Hamlet*
aa. Leslie Howard

B2995   Chaney, S. "Designs and Costumes for *Hamlet.*" *TAr*, xx (1936), 900, 905.

B2996   L. Howard as Hamlet. E. F. M., *New York Times*, Oct. 25, 1936, Section 2, p. X[1]; J. W. Krutch, *Nation*, 143 (1936), 612.

B2997   L. Howard's Production of *Hamlet* in New York. See New York newspapers of Nov. 11, 1936.

B2998   Brown, J. M. "Gielgud's and Howard's *Hamlet* Compared." *New York Post*, Nov. 14, 1936, p. 16.

B2999   Young, Stark. "To Madame Frijsh." *NR*, 89 (1936), 146.

bb. John Gielgud

B3000   Krutch, J. W. "With *Hamlet* Left Out?" *Nation*, 163 (1936), 500-501.

B3001   J. Gielgud as Hamlet. B. Atkinson, *New York Times*, Oct. 9, 1936, p. 30; R. Lockridge, *New York Sun*, Oct. 9, 1936, p. 38; J. M. Brown, *New York Post*, Oct. 9, 1936; D. Gilbert, *New York World-Telegram*, Oct. 9, 1936, p. 34; B. Atkinson, *New York Times*, Oct. 18, 1936, Sec. 2, p. X[1]; E. J. R. Isaacs, *TAr*, xx (1936), 841-843; J. D. William, *New York Times*, Nov. 1, 1936, X-3; C. Morley, *SRL*, xiv (1936), 13-14.

B3002 Cancelled.
B3003 "L. Gish and A. Byron in *Hamlet*." *TAr*, xx (1936), 839.
B3004 "Costume Design for J. Gielgud as Hamlet." *TAr*, xx (1936), 769.
B3005 Gilder, Rosamond. *John Gielgud's "Hamlet"*. Oxford University Press, 1937. Pp. 234.
       By R. Gilder: "John Gielgud's Hamlet," pp. 1-20; "Hamlet in Performance: A Scene-by-
       Scene Description," pp. 21-107; by J. Gielgud: "The Hamlet Tradition: Notes on Costume,
       Scenery, and Stage Business," pp. 109-171.
          Rev: B3219.
B3006 MacCarthy, Desmond. "End of the Lyceum." *NstN*, xviii (1939), 47-48.
B3007 Gilder, Rosamond. "*Hamlet* Revisited." *TAr*, xxiii (1939), 709-711.
B3008 Heiseler, Bernt von. "Shakespeare-Abende in London. Aus e. Tagebuch Herbst 1937."
       Neues Europa, ii, Heft 23 (1947), 33-37.

cc.   Maurice Evans

B3009 Evans' Uncut *Hamlet*. B. Atkinson, *New York Times*, Oct. 13, 1938, p. 28; Oct. 30, 1938,
       Section 2, p. X [1]; J. M. Brown, *New York Post*, Oct. 13, 1938, p. 15; R. Lockridge, *New York
       Sun*, Oct. 13, 1938, p. 30; S. R. Whipple, *New York World-Telegram*, Oct. 13, 1938, p. 29;
       G. Vernon, *Commonweal*, xxix (Oct. 28, 1938), 20-21; J. W. Krutch, *Nation*, 147 (Oct. 29,
       1938), 461-462; S. Young, *NR*, 96 (Nov. 2, 1938), 261-262.
B3010 Anon. "The Uncut *Hamlet*." *SRL*, xix (Nov. 26, 1938), 8.
B3011 Dayton, W. "M. Evans's *Hamlet*." *New York Times*, Nov. 27, 1938, Section 2, p. 2 X.
B3012 "Sketches for M. Evan's Hamlet." *TAr*, xxii (1938), 711.
B3013 Young, Stark. "The Whole Tragical Historie. *Hamlet*, St. James' Theatre." *NR*, 96 (Nov. 2,
       1938), 361-362.
B3014 Atkinson, B. "M. Evans's Return to New York in *Hamlet*." *New York Times*, Dec. 5, 1939,
       p. 35.
B3015 Atkinson, B. "M. Evans and the Full-Length *Hamlet*." *Broadway Scrapbook*, New York, 1947,
       pp. 98-102.
B3016 M. Evans' GI Production of *Hamlet*. L. Kronenberger, *PM*, Dec. 14, 1945, p. 16; J. Chapman,
       Daily News, Dec. 14, 1945, p. 47; W. Waldorf, *New York Post*, Dec. 14, 1945, p. 32; W.
       Morehouse, *New York Sun*, Dec. 14, 1945, p. 20; W. Gibbs, *The New Yorker*, Dec. 22, 1945,
       pp. 36, 38-39; J. T. Shipley, *New Leader*, Dec. 29, 1945; R. Gilder, *TAr*, xxx (1946), 75-77;
       E. Van Renssalaer, *Catholic World*, 162 (1946), 453-454; G. J. Nathan, "M. Todd's GI Version
       of *Hamlet*." *The Theatre Book of the Year*, 1945-46, New York (1946), pp. 221-224.
B3017 Ammerman, George. "Shakespeare as the GI's Do It." *New York Times Magazine*, Jan. 28,
       1945, p. 22.
B3018 Evans, M. "Alas, No Poor Yorick." *New York Times*, Dec. 9, 1945, Sec. II, Part 2, pp. 5 and 6.
B3019 Brown, John Mason. "Yankee Doodle *Hamlet*." *SRL*, xxviii (Dec. 22, 1945), 22-24.
B3020-B3022 Cancelled.
B3023 Shakespeare, William. *Maurice Evans' GI Production of "Hamlet": Acting Edition with a
       Preface; Designer's Sketches by Frederick Stover*. New York: Doubleday, 1947. Pp. 7, 187.
          Rev: by W. P. Eaton, *NYHTBR*, March 23, 1947, p. 29.

dd.   At Elsinore

B3024 Brown, Ivor. "The Very Spot." *TAr*, xxi (1937), 873-880.
B3025 Guthrie, Tyrone. "*Hamlet* at Elsinore." *London Mercury*, xxxvi (1937), 246-249.
B3026 Merrild, E. "*Hamlet* at Kronborg." *Amer. Scandinavian Rev.*, xxv (1937), 351-353.
B3027 Kragh Jacobsen, Svend. "To Play or Not to Play. At Spille eller ikke Spille." *Berlingske
       Tidende* (Copenhagen), June 17, 1954.
       Review of the yearly production of *Hamlet* at the castle of Kronborg, Elsinore.
B3028 Linneballe, Poul. "Shakespeare, Hamlet og Kronborg." *Social-Demokraten* (Copenhagen),
       June 23, 1954.

ee.   The Tennent Company

B3029 Worsley, Thomas Cuthbert. "Alas, Poor Hamlet." *NstN*, l (1955), 828.
B3030 "*Hamlet, Prince of Denmark*." *Theatre World*, Jan. 1957, pp. 23-25.
B3031 "The Tennent Company in Moscow." *News* (Moscow), No. 1, 1956, pp. 28-29.
B3032 Tynan, Kenneth. "Curtain Time in Moscow." *Harper's Magazine*, Mar., 1956, pp. 61-65.
B3033 Zavadsky, Yuro. "English Produce *Hamlet* in Moscow." *VOKS-Bulletin* (Moscow), i,
       No. 96, (1956), 33-34.

ff.   Others

B3034 Schroth, R. "Der Neue Dresdner *Hamlet*." *Dresd. Nachr.*, May 23, 1937.

B3035   Fleischhauer, H. *"Hamlet* im Schauspielhaus Dresden." *Dresd. Anz.*, May 28, 1937.

B3036   Fisher, H. K. *"Hamlet". Life and Letters*, XXII (1939), 268-271.

B3037   Wehner, Josef Magnus. "Lothar Műthels *Hamlet*-Inszenierung. Der 2. Tag der Reichstheaterfestwoche in Wien." *MNN*, XV (June 16, 1938).

B3038   Payne, B. Iden. "The Central Figure: Shakespeare." *TAr*, XXIII (1939), 496-506.

B3039   Fechter, Paul. "Deutsche Shakespeare-Darsteller. 1: Gründgens als Hamlet. 2: Heinrich Georges Falstaff." *SJ*, LXXVII (1941), 123-137.

B3040   Atkinson, Brooks. *"Hamlet* at the Kuo T'ai Theatre in Chungking, Is Not Yet Quite Ready for Broadway." *New York Times*, Dec. 18, 1942, pp. 1 and 38. Adapted by Liang Shih Chiu.

B3041   Fisher, H. K. "Dance of Death: An Approach to Robert Helpmann's *Hamlet." Life and Letters Today*, XXXVI (1943), 29-34.

B3042   MacCarthy, Desmond. "The Latest *Hamlet." NstN*, Feb. 19, 1944, p. 123; *NstN*, Mar. 11, 1944, p. 174; and Hazel B. Pollard, ibid., Mar. 18, 1944, p. 190.

B3043   MacCarthy, Desmond. *"Hamlet* at the Haymarket." *NstN*, XXVIII (1944), 267-268.

B3044   "Hamlet." *New York Theatre Critics' Reviews*, VIII (1947), 447-448.

B3045   Wendt, Herbert. *"Faust* und *Hamlet* in Alaska." *Das Goldene Tor*, V (1950), 427-432.

B3046   Walker, Roy. "The Prince in Darkness." *Theatre Newsletter*, July 7, 1951, p. 5.
        A discussion of the Alec Guinness *Hamlet*. See also the same writer's "Judgment?—A Hit," *Theatre Newsletter*, June 9, p. 8, which analyses the reception of the production, and "Who Should 'Scape Whipping," ibid., June 9, p. 3, which collects press criticisms of the production. Also, comments by Phyllis Hartnoll, et al., ibid., June 23, p. 3.

B3047   Kastropil, Stjepan. "Shakespeare na Lovrijencu." *Književni Jadran* (Split), I, ix (1952), 6.

B3048   *"Hamlet." As Arranged for the Stage of the Globe Theatre at the San Diego Exposition (Globe Theatre Version)*. Ed. by Thomas Wood Stevens. New York: Samuel French, 1952. Pp. 88.

B3049   Gassman, Vittorio. "Il Pubblico Dell' Amleto." *Teatro Scenario* (Milan), NS, V, No. 1 (Jan. 1-15, 1953), 12.

B3050   Pandolfi, Vito. "Shakespeare: Amleto." *Il Dramma* (Turin), XXIX, No. 170-172, Jan. 1, 1953, pp. 119-124.

B3051   Weightman, J. G. "Edinburgh, Elsinore and Chelsea." *TC*, 154 (1953), 302-310.

B3052   MacCarthy, Desmond. *Theatre*. London: MacGibbon & Kee, 1954. Pp. vi, 191.
        A collection of critical essays, including some on revivals of Shak.'s plays.
          Rev: B7838.

B3053   Anikst, Alexander. "Two Hamlets." *News* (Moscow), V (May 10, 1955), 24-26.

B3054   Clarke, Sylvester F. "Shakespeareana." *Players Magazine*, Oct. 1955, pp. 6-7.

B3055   "Four-Faced Hamlet: Baylor University." *Life*, June 11, 1956, pp. 97-98.

B3056   Dawson, Giles E. "The Catholic University *Hamlet." SQ*, VII (1956), 241-242.

B3057   *La Mise en Scène des Œuvres du Passé*. Ed. by Jean Jacquot and André Veinstein. Illus. Paris: Centre de la Recherche Scientifique, 1957.
        Includes a paper by Gabriel Monnet describing his production of *Hamlet* in the open air at Annecy.

B3058   Leventhal, A. J. "Dramatic Commentary." *Dublin Magazine*, Jan.-Mar., 1958, pp. 32-34.
        Cyril Cusack's production of *Hamlet* at Dublin's Gaiety Theatre.

v. *Othello*
aa. Paul Robeson

B3059   "A Scene from Robeson's *Othello." TAr*, XXVI (1942), 648.

B3059a "Scenes from Robeson's *Othello." Life*, Aug. 31, 1942, pp. 82-85.

B3059b *P. Robeson as "Othello."* (Souvenir) New York: A Greenstone, 1943. Pp. 20.

B3060   Jones, R. E. "Two Designs for *Othello." TAr*, XXVII (1943), 368-369.

B3061   Robeson's *Othello*. L. Nichols, *New York Times*, Oct. 20, 1943, p. 18; B. Rascoe, *New York World-Telegram*, Oct. 20, 1943, p. 24; W. Morehouse, *New York Sun*, Oct. 20, 1943, p. 30; L. Kronenberger, *PM*, Oct. 20, 1943, p. 22; L. Nichols, *New York Times*, Oct. 24, 1943, Sec. 2, p. X [1]; R. Gilder, *TAr*, XXVII (1943), 699-703.

B3062   "Paul Robeson in *Othello." TAr*, XXVIII (1944), 323.

B3063   Robeson, P., et al. *Othello*. 3 Albums. Columbia Master Works, MM 554.

B3064   Robeson, Paul. "Some Reflections on *Othello* and the Nature of Our Time." *Amer. Scholar*, XIV (1945), 392-393.

bb. Others

B3065   Huston's New York *Othello*. J. B. Brown, *New York Post*, Jan. 7, 1937, p. 18; B. Mantle, *Daily News*, Jan. 8, 1937, p. 53; R. Lockridge, *New York Sun*, Jan. 7, 1937, p. 18; D. Gilbert, *New York World-Telegram*, Jan. 7, 1937, p. 18; B. Atkinson, *New York Times*, Jan. 7, 1937, p. 16; S. Young, *New Republic*, 89 (1937), 385; E. J. R. Isaacs, *TAr*, XXI (1937), 178-182;

G. Vernon, *Commonweal*, xxv (1937), 360; E. V. R. Wyatt, *Catholic World*, 144 (1937), 601; J. W. Krutch, *Nation*, 144 (1937), 79.

B3066-B3067 Cancelled.

B3068 "*Othello* at the Odéon." *Revue de Paris*, July 15, 1938, pp. 460-464.

B3069 Houville, Gerard d'. "*Othello* à l'Odéon." *RddxM*, 108, viii (1938), 909-911.

B3070 Geoghegan, H. "Reviewing *Othello* and *Ralph Roister Doister*." *Carnegie Magazine*, xii (1938), 24-26.

B3071 Wehner, Josef Magnus. "Zwischen Lehrstück und Schaustück. *Othello* im Prinzregenten-theater." *MNN*, No. 86, March 26, 1940.

B3072 Fisher, H. K. "*Othello* at the Piccadilly." *Life and Letters*, liv (1947), 63-70.

B3073 Aleksieev, Konstantin S. *Stanislavski Produces "Othello."* Trans. from the Russian by Helen Nowak. London: Bles, 1938. Pp. 244.
Rev: A9938.

B3074 Batušić, Slavko. "Interpreti *Otela* u Dosadasnjih Pedeset Izvedaba na Zagrebačkoj Pozornici." [Actors who acted Othello in the fifty performances of the play on the Zagreb stage.] *Kaza-lišni List* (Zagreb), ii, No. 35 (1947), 4-6.

B3075 Dedinac, Milan. "Povodom Šekspirovog *Otela* na Beogradskoj Pozornici." [Shakespeare's *Othello* on the Belgrade stage.] *Naša Književnost* (Belgrade), ii (1947), 478-486.

B3076 Cancelled.

B3077 Bauër, Gérard. "De Shakespeare à Stéve Passeur." *Revue de Paris*, lv (Nov. 1948), 162-164. Lausanne troupe at the Théâtre Marigny.

B3078 Ray, Sibnarayan. "A Note on Shakespeare." *Mysindia* (Bangalore), July 9, 1950, pp. 17-18. A performance of *Othello* in Calcutta, April 30, 1950.

B3079 Worsley, Thomas Cuthbert. "The Orson Welles *Othello*." *NstN*, xlii (1951), 460.

B3080 Eylau, Hans Ulrich. "*Othello* 1953." *Theater d. Zeit*, viii, x (1953), 20-24.

B3081 "Pollux." "*Othello*." Review of productions. *Times of India* (Bombay), May 8, 1955, p. 10.

B3082 Alden, Barbara. "Edwin Forrest's *Othello*." *Theatre Annual*, xiv (1956), 7-18.

B3083 Bernad, Miguel A. "*Othello* Comes to Town: Orson Welles and Edmund Kean." *Philippine Stud.*, iv (1956), 3-14.

B3084 M., H. G. *Othello*. *Theatre World*, Oct., 1957, pp. 8-9. Amateur production by the Touchstone Theatre Company.

B3085 Newton, Robert G. "*Othello* in Madras." *The British Drama League* (issued as an insert in *Drama*, Spring, 1958), p. 7.

vi. *King Lear*

B3086 Stifter, Adalbert. "*König Lear* auf dem Burgtheater in Wien (aus dem Nachsommer)." *Das Wort in der Zeit*, iii (1935-36), 748-752.

B3087 Bowen, Elizabeth. "*King Lear* at Cambridge." *NstN*, xv (1939), 478.

B3088 Tannenbaum, Samuel A. "Editorial Notes and Comments." *SAB*, xiv (1939). "The Classic Players and *King Lear*," pp. 127-128.

B3089 Atkinson, J. B. [*King Lear* Produced by the New School for Social Research.] *New York Times*, Dec. 16, 1940, p. 27; R. Watts, Jr., *New York Herald-Tribune*, Dec. 16, 1940, p. 14.

B3090 Gilder, R. "Piscator's *King Lear*." *TAr*, xxv (1941), 96-97.

B3091 Heythum, A. "Scenic Designs for *King Lear*." *TAr*, xxv (1941), 172.

B3092 Tannenbaum, Samuel A. "A Unique *King Lear*." *SAB*, xvi (1941), 62-63.

B3093 Fisher, H. K. "*Antony and Cleopatra* at the Piccadilly." *Life and Letters*, lii (1947), 148-152. Reflections and recollections of several performances of Lear, Olivier, Guinness, Tearle, and others.

B3094 "*King Lear*." *New York Theatre Critics' Reviews*, viii (1947), 453-454.

B3095 Brown, John Mason. "Old Man with a Walking Stick." *Seeing More Things*, New York: Whittlesey House, 1948, pp. 249-254.

B3096 Landstone, Charles. "Four Lears." *ShS*, i (1948), 98-102.

B3097 Heider, Wolf. "Broadway Conquers Shakespeare." *International Theatre*, Spring, 1951, pp. 23-29.

B3098 Houseman, John. "On Directing Shakespeare." *TAr*, (April 1951), 52-53. Deals particularly with the Calhern *King Lear*.

B3099 Hewes, Henry. "Broadway Postscript: No Great Shakes." *SatR*, Jan. 28, 1956, p. 18.

B3100 Calendoli, Giovanni. "Re Lear non è un Gigante, ma Uomo fra Uomini." *La Fiera Let-teraria* (Rome), ix No. 7 (Feb. 1, 1956), 7. Considerations on the performance of *Lear* by Renzo Ricci in Rome.

B3101 Hayes, Richard. "Citizen Welles." *Commonweal*, Mar. 2, 1956, p. 568.

B3102 "*King Lear*: New York City Center Theatre Company Production." *TAr* (March 20, 1956), 20.

B3103   Bentley, E. R. "The Other Orson Welles." *NR*, April 30, 1956, pp. 29-30.

B3104   Heidicke, Manfred. "Shakespeare aus Distanz. *König Lear* am Deutschen Theater Berlin." *Theater d. Zeit*, XII, vii (1957), 47-48.

B3105   Vrchlická, Eva. "O Představení Krále Leara." *Divadlo* (Prague), VII (1958), 479-480. Lear as acted by Jaroslav Průcha in Prague.

vii.   *Macbeth*
aa.   Maurice Evans

B3106   The Evans-Anderson Production of *Macbeth*. Brooks Atkinson, *New York Times*, Nov. 12, 1941, p. 30; J. M. Brown, *New York World-Telegram*, Nov. 12, 1941, p. 30; R. Lockridge, *New York Sun*, Nov. 12, 1941, p. 28; W. Waldorf, *New York Post*, Nov. 12, 1941, p. 16; J. Anderson, *New York American*, Nov. 23, 1941.

B3107   Gilder, R. "Evans' *Macbeth*." *TAr*, XXVI (1942), 80-81.

bb.   Michael Redgrave

B3108   Redgrave, Michael. "A Medieval *Macbeth* Made for Moderns." *New York Times*, March 28, 1948, Section 2, pp. X [1], X 3.

B3109   The *Macbeth* Production. R. Garland, *New York Journal-American*, April 1, 1948, p. 14; R. Watts, Jr., *New York Post*, April 1, 1948, p. 33; W. Hawkins, *New York World-Telegram*, April 1, 1948, p. 22; B. Atkinson, *New York Times*, April 1, 1948, p. 30; R. Coleman, *Daily Mirror*, April 1, 1948, p. 28; W. Morehouse, *New York Sun*, April 1, 1948, p. 22; H. Barnes, *New York Herald-Tribune*, April 1, 1948, p. 18; L. Kronenberger, *PM*, April 2, 1948, p. 15.

B3110   Gibbs, W. "*Macbeth*." *New Yorker*, XXIV (April 10, 1948), 48 ff.

B3111   Atkinson, Brooks. "Murderer of a King." *New York Times*, April 11, 1948, Section 2, p. X [1].

B3112   "*Macbeth*." *Time*, LI (April 12, 1948), 76.

B3113   Brown, John Mason. "When the Hurly-Burly's Done." *SRL*, XXXI (April 17, 1948), 42-46.

B3114   Clurman, H. "Trouble with Shakespeare: *Macbeth*." *NR*, 118 (April 19, 1948), 30-33.

B3115   Krutch, J. W. "*Macbeth*." *Nation*, 166 (1948), 421-422.

B3116   Nathan, G. J. "*Macbeth* at the National Theatre." *The Theatre Book of the Year*, New York, 1947, 1948, pp. 334-340.

B3117   Phelan, K. "*Macbeth*." *Commonweal*, XLVIII (1948), 653.

B3118   Wyatt, E. V. R. "*Macbeth* Production." *Catholic World*, 167 (1948), 168-169.

B3119   Gilder, Rosamond. "Shakespeare in New York: 1947-1948." *ShS*, II (1949), 130-131.

cc.   Others

B3120   Harlem *Macbeth*. B. Crowther, *New York Times*, Apr. 5, 1936, Section 2, pp. X [1]-2 X; B. Atkinson, *New York Times*, Apr. 15, 1936, p. 25; R. Garland, *New York World-Telegram*, Apr. 15, 1936, p. 28; G. W. Gabriel, *New York American*, Apr. 26, 1936, p. M-7; E. V. R. Wyatt, *Catholic World*, 143 (1936), 336-338.

B3121   Cancelled.

B3122   Brychczynski, R. "*Macbeth* Produced by the Shakespearean Society of Hunter College." *The Silver Falcon*, Dec. 1936, pp. 25-28.

B3123   "*Macbeth* at Sloane School." *English*, I (1937), 431-432.

B3124   du Gard, M. M. "*Macbeth* in Paris." *Les Nouvelles Littéraires*, July 3, 1937, p. 8.

B3125   "Design for *Macbeth*." *TAr*, XXII (1938), 533.

B3126   "Two Scenes from the Negro Production of *Macbeth*." *London Studio*, XVI (1938), 140.

B3127   Dukes, Ashley. "The Gielgud *Macbeth*." *TAr*, XXVI (1942), 615-619.

B3128   Runnquist, A. "*Macbeth* at Göteborgs Stadsteater." *Bonniers Litterära Magasin*, April, 1948, p. 307.

B3129   Purdom, C. B. "The Crosby Hall *Macbeth*." London: Dent, for the Shakespeare Stage Society, 1951.

B3130   Dawson, Giles E. "The Catholic University *Macbeth*." *SQ*, III (1952), 255-256.

B3131   Calendoli, Giovanni. "Il Macbeth di Orazio Costa." *Teatro Scenario* (Milan), NS, V, No. 4 (Feb. 16-28, 1953), 12. Discusses a production of the play in the Teatro delle Arti, Rome.

B3132   Worsley, Thomas Cuthbert. "From Belmont to Forres." *NstN*, XLV (1953), 367.

B3133   Gribble, Dorothy Rose. "Our Hope's 'Bove Wisdom, Grace, and Fear. An Account of a Tour of *Macbeth*." *SQ*, V (1954), 403-407.

B3134   Hughes, W. R. "*Macbeth* Goes African." *Senior Scholastic*, No. 65 (Sept. 22, 1954), 43.

B3135   Lefranc, Pierre. "Première de *Macbeth* en Avignon." *EA*, VII (1954), 443-444.

B3136   Moller, Antoine. "Shakespeare paa Bermuda." *Berlingske Tidende* (Copenhagen), March 8, 1954.

B3137   Gandon, Yves. "*Macbeth:* A Production Review." *Biblio.*, XXIII (March, 1955), 31.
A "flawless" performance at the Théâtre National Populaire with Jean Vilar as Macbeth.

B3138   Hagberg, Knut. "Förälskad Macbeth." [Macbeth in Love]. *Samtid och Framtid* (Stockholm), 1955, p. 230.
On the performance of *Macbeth* at Dramatiska teatern in Stockholm.

B3139   Jacquot, Jean. "*Macbeth* au Palais de Chaillot." *EA*, VIII (1955), 89-90.

B3140   Cancelled.

B3141   Marcel, Gabriel. "*Macbeth* (au T. N. P.)." *Nouvelles Littéraires*, V (Jan. 27, 1955), 10.

B3141a Rerat, A. "*Macbeth* au T. N. P." *LanM*, XLIX (1955), 189-190.

B3142   "A Japanese *Macbeth*: Kurasawa's 'Throne of Blood'." *Sight and Sound*, Spring 1957, pp. 196-197.

B3143   Brahms, Caryl. "Taking the Mickey out of *Macbeth*." *Plays and Players*, Oct., 1957, p. 13. *Macbeth* at Theatre Workshop, London.

viii.   *Antony and Cleopatra*
aa.   Katharine Cornell

B3144   Wyatt, E. V. R. "*Antony and Cleopatra* in New York." *Catholic World*, 166 (1947), 357-358.

B3145   Beyer, William. "State of the Theatre." *School and Society*, LXVII (Jan. 31, 1948), 85-86.

B3146   Gassner, J. "*Antony and Cleopatra*." *Forum*, 109 (1948), 88-89.

B3147   Nathan, G. J. "*Antony and Cleopatra* at the Martin Beck Theatre." *The Theatre Book of the Year*, New York, 1947-48, pp. 158-162.

B3148   Gilder, Rosamond. "Shakespeare in New York: 1947-1948." *ShS*, II (1949), 130-131.
Reviews Katharine Cornell's *Antony and Cleopatra* and Michael Redgrave's *Macbeth*.

bb.   The Oliviers

B3149   Brown, John Mason. "A Queen's Story." *SatR*, XXXV, ii (1952), 24-27.

B3150   Venezky, Alice. "Shakespeare Conquers Broadway: The Olivier *Antony and Cleopatra*." *SQ*, III (1952), 121-124.

B3151   Shakespeare, William. "The Tragedy of *Antony and Cleopatra*." With an Introd. by Sir Laurence Olivier. Design for Costumes and Scenery by Audrey Cruddas and Roger Furse. London: Folio Society, 1952. Pp. 134.
Rev: by H. Heuer, *SJ*, 89 (1953), 219-220.

B3152   Shakespeare, William. *Antony and Cleopatra*. With *Caesar and Cleopatra* by George Bernard Shaw. With Photographs from the Productions Starring Laurence Olivier and Vivien Leigh. New York: Dodd, Mead, 1952.

cc.   Others

B3153   *Antony and Cleopatra* in New York. B. Atkinson, *New York Times*, Nov. 11, 1937, p. 30; S. Young, *NR*, 93 (Nov. 24, 1937), 75.

B3154   Fisher, H. K. "*Antony and Cleopatra* at the Piccadilly." *Life and Letters*, LII (1947), 148-152.

B3155   Maulnier, Thierry. "De Shakespeare à Jean Genest." *La Revue de Paris*, Feb. 1954, pp. 138-141.
On a performance of *Antony and Cleopatra* in Paris by the Memorial Theatre Company.

B3156   Eisner, Doris. "*Antonius und Cleopatra* am Wiener Burgtheater." *Shakespeare-Tage* (Bochum), 1956, pp. 19-20.

ix.   *Coriolanus*

B3157   Mettin, Hermann Christian. "Shakespeares *Coriolan*." [Production in the Berliner Staatstheater.] *Dts. Adelsblatt*, LV (1937), 512-513.

B3158   Ruppel, K. H. "*Coriolan* im Dts. Theater, Berlin." *Köln. Ztg.*, March 31, 1937.

B3159   Walker, D. "*Coriolanus* in Roslyn." *New York Times*, Oct. 17, 1937, p. 2x.

B3160   N., L. "*Coriolanus* Revived in New York." *New York Times*, Feb. 2, 1938, p. 14.

B3161   "*Coriolanus* Produced by the University of Hawaii Theatre Guild." *TAr*, XXIII (1939), 911.

B3162   Chabrier, Victor. "Coriolan aux Nuits de Bendor." *CS*, No. 337 (October 1956), n.p. (B$_1$ recto).

(d)   UNCLASSIFIED

B3163   Bütow, H. "Ein Moderner Shakespeare." *Frankf. Ztg.*, 1935, No. 662/663, *Lbl*, No. 52.

B3164   McDougald, J. F. "The Federal Government and the Negro Theatre in Harlem." *Opportunity*, XIV (1936), 135-137.

B3165   Koszul, A. "Deux Représentations Shakespeariennes à Strasbourg." *Bulletin de la Faculté des Lettres*, XVI (1939-40), 46.

B3166   Platz, H. "Houston Stewart Chamberlain, Bayreuth und Shakespeare." *N. Mon.*, XI (1940), 210-224.

B3167   "The Bard at Karamu." *Ebony*, III (Oct., 1948), 36-38.

B3168   Dörnemann, Kurt. "Shakespeare in Westfalen." *Westfalenspiegel*, I (April, 1952), 24-25.

B3169   Alwi, Syed. "Amateur Dramatics in Malaya." *News Bulletin*, Institute of International Education, December, 1954.

B3170   Baeckström, Tord. "Shakespeare med och utan Fernissa." [Shakespeare Varnished and Unvarnished]. *Göteborgs Handelstidning* (Göteborg), July 14, 1958.

B3171   Branner, Per-Axel. "Londonteater: Shakespeare och Tjechov Bjuder på Overraskningar." [Shakespeare and Chekhov have surprises in store for us.] *Dagens Nyheter* (Stockholm), June 20, 1958.

B3172   Dawson, J. "Szekspir at Nowa Huta." *Drama*, Winter, 1958, pp. 35-37.

B3173   Trewin, J. C. "Under a Dancing Star." *Illustrated London News*, Aug. 23, 1958, p. 318.

f.   INDIVIDUAL ACTORS (165;55)
(1) DISCUSSION OF TWO OR MORE PERFORMERS

B3174   Authur, G. *From Phelps to Gielgud.* London, 1936. Pp. 256.
H. Irving, pp. 75-86; Ellen Terry, pp. 98-105.

B3175   Gilder, Rosamond. "Hamlets." *TAr*, XX (1936), 975-982.

B3176   Bloch, Albert. "Karl Kraus' Shakespeare." *Books Abroad*, XL (1937), 21-24.
Review of second volume and of his one-man productions. These four volumes are the versions he read.

B3177   Ormsbee, H. *Backstage with Actors. From the Time of Shakespeare to the Present Day.* New York: T. Y. Crowell Co., 1938. Pp. 344.

B3178   Dent, Alan. *Preludes and Studies.* London: Macmillan, 1942. Pp. xiii, 251.
Includes, i.a., notes on performances of Shakespeare.
Rev: B1517.

B3179   Fechter, Paul. "Deutsche Shakespeare-Darsteller." *SJ*, LXXVIII/LXXIX (1943), 81-89.

B3180   "Ernst Possart and Jacob Adler as Shylock." *TAr*, XXVIII (1944), 469 and 475.

B3181   "A Century of Cleopatras." *TAr*, Dec., 1947, pp. 23-26.

B3182   "Shylocks of Bygone Days." *Shakespeare Quarterly* (London), I (Summer, 1947), 18-21.
Notes on performances from 1618 or earlier to 1894. Burbage, Macklin, Fleck, Iffland, Kean, Devrient, Döring, Irving, Mitterwurzer and Reicher in the role.

B3183   Darlington, William Aubrey. *The Actor and His Audience.* London: Phoenix House, 1949. Pp. 188.
Actors from Burbage through Irving to Shaw.
Rev: A7369.

B3184   Pallette, Drew B. "The English Actor's Fight for Respectability." *Theatre Annual*, VII (1949), 27-34.

B3185   Brook, Donald. *A Pageant of English Actors.* New York: Macmillan; London: Rockliff, 1950. Pp. viii, 9-286, pl 15.
Fifteen biographies from Burbage to Olivier. Popular and undocumented.

B3186   Horn-Monval, Madeleine. "Quelques Interprètes de *Hamlet.*" *RHT*, II (1950), 137-150.

B3187   Carlisle, Carol J. *Contributions of the English Actors to Shakespearean Criticism to 1902.* DD, University of North Carolina, 1951. Abstr. publ. in *Univ. of North Carolina Record, Research in Progress*, Jan.-Dec., 1951, Grad. School Series, No. 62, 1952, pp. 110-111.

B3188   Drews, Wolfgang. *Die Grossen Zauberer.* Bildnisse Deutscher Schauspieler aus 2 Jahrhunderten. Vienna, Munich: Donau Verlag, 1953. Pp. 360.
Rev: B1281.

B3189   MacCarthy, Desmond. "Shylocks Past and Present." *Humanities*, London: Macgibbon & Kee, 1953, pp. 49-53.

B3190   Bab, Julius. *Kränze dem Mimen. 30 Porträts Grosser Menschendarsteller.* Emsdetten: Lechte, 1954. Pp. 368.

B3191   Babler, O. F. "Women 'Hamlets'." *N &Q*, 199 (1954), 86.
Ref. to article in *SJ*, 1900; Siddons, Vestvali, Bernhardt, Sandrock.

B3192   Ford, George D. *These were Actors: The Story of the Chapmans and the Drakes.* New York: Libr. Publ., 1955. Pp. 314.
Rev: B1568.

B3193   Haviland, Frank. "Great Shakespearians of Fifty Years Ago." *Illustrated London News*, Nov. 9, 1956, p. 24.
Drawings from life by Frank Haviland of noted Shak. actors of the early 20th century.

B3194   McCarthy, Mary T. *Sights and Spectacles, 1937-1956.* New York: Farrar, Strauss, 1956.

Includes "Elizabethan Revivals," pp. 13-20; "Little Gate" (on *Love's Labor's Lost*), pp. 146-150.
    Rev: B2836.

B3195   Beaton, Cecil. "Princes of Players." *TAr*, Dec., 1957, pp. 32-33, 95-96.
    Biographical notes on Alec Guinness, Sir John Gielgud, Paul Scofield, and Sir Laurence Olivier.

B3196   Wood, Margaret. "Merely Players." *New Plays Quarterly*, Jan., 1957, p. 5.

B3197   Matthews, Brander, ed. *Papers on Acting* (Dramabooks D 11). New York: Hill and Wang, 1958. Pp. 356. Paperback.
    Includes essays on the art and technique of acting by Kemble and Booth.

B3198   Oppenheimer, George, ed. *The Passionate Playgoer: A Personal Scrapbook*. New York: Viking, 1958. Pp. xiv, 623.
    Includes reprints of "Disney and the Dane" by John Mason Brown, "The Barrymore Hamlet" by Percy Howard, Thurber's "The Macbeth Murder Mystery," "Welles on Wheels" by Oppenheimer, and Heywood Broun's "An Epitaph for Shylock."

(2) ACTORS
(a) JEAN-LOUIS BARRAULT

B3199   Brunot, Henriette. "*Hamlet* de Shakespeare, Traduction d'André Gide." *Psyché*, I (1946), 229-232.

B3200   Barrault, Jean-Louis. "*Hamlet*, le Message de Shakespeare." *Conferencia*, V (Nov. 15, 1947).

B3201   Cunard, N. "Jean-Louis Barrault as Hamlet." *Theatre Today*, Apr., 1947, pp. 9-11.

B3202   Barrault, Jean-Louis. "Shakespeare et les Français." *RddxM*, V (Dec. 15, 1948), 650-659.

B3203   Cocteau, Jean. "Jean-Louis Barrault als Hamlet." *Dionysos*, II, No. 7 (1948), 4.

B3204   Hussey, D. "*Hamlet* in French (Gide's version at Edinburgh)." *New York Times*, Sept. 11, 1948, p. 13.

B3205   Barrault, Jean-Louis. "Shakespeare et Nous." *RHT*, II (1950), 131-136.

B3206   Bentley, Eric. "The Actor as Thinker: Jean-Louis Barrault." *TAr*, XXXIV, No. 4 (1950), 31-34. Also in Bentley's *In Search of Theater*. New York: Knopf, 1953, pp. 394-403.

B3207   March, Louis V. "Jean-Louis Barrault's *Hamlet*." *QJS*, XXXVI (1950), 360-364.

B3208   Griffin, Alice Venezky. "Jean-Louis Barrault Acts *Hamlet*." *SQ*, IV (1953), 163-164.

B3209   Barrault, Jean-Louis. "Actualité de Shakespeare." *Revue Théâtrale*, No. 26, 1954, pp. 5-8.

B3210   Saint-Denis, Michel. "Shakespeare en France et en Angleterre." *Revue Théâtrale*, No. 26, 1954, pp. 13-18.
    Includes comments on Barrault's performance of Gide's *Hamlet*.

(b) JOHN BARRYMORE

B3211   Fowler, G. *Good Night, Sweet Prince: The Life and Times of John Barrymore*. New York: Viking Press, 1943. Pp. 468.

B3212   Fallon, Gabriel. "One Man's *Hamlet* [John Barrymore]." *Irish Monthly*, LXXVI (1948), 228-233.

(c) ALEC CLUNES

B3213   "Alec Clunes in *Hamlet*." *TAr*, XXX (Mar., 1946), 171.

B3214   "Playing a Character Part." *Plays and Players*, July, 1958, p. 7.

B3215   Trewin, J. C. *Alec Clunes*. Theatre World Monograph, No. 12. London: Rockliff, 1958. Pp. 134. Illustrated.
    Rev: *TLS*, Nov. 7, 1958, p. 647.

(d) MAURICE EVANS

B3216   Wyatt, Euphemia Van Rensselaer. "Shakespeare, Evans, and Webster, Inc." *Catholic World*, 150 (1940), 466-467.

B3217   Frye, Roland Mushat. "Maurice Evans and *Richard II*." *ShN*, IV (1954), 40.

B3218   Zolotow, Maurice. "The Foxy Dreamer of Broadway." *Saturday Evening Post*, Oct. 22, 1955, pp. 36-37, 127-128, 130.

(e) JOHN GIELGUD

B3219   Gilder, Rosamond. *John Gielgud's "Hamlet"*. Oxford Univ. Press, 1937. Pp. 234.
    Rev: by B. H., *QJS*, XXIV (1938), 158; by Walt Crane, *TAr*, XXII, 988-989; by R. Flatter, *SJ*, 87/88 (1952), 249-251.

B3220   Gielgud, J. *Early Stages*. London: Macmillan, 1939. Pp. xii, 322.
    Nothing before 1880.

B3221   Gielgud, John. "Before Macbeth." *TAr*, XXVI (1942), 113-117.

B3222   Fordham, Hallam. *John Gielgud. An Actor's Biography in Pictures. With a Personal Narrative by John Gielgud*. London: Lehmann, 1952. Pp. 128.
    Rev: by M. St. C. Byrne, *English*, IX (1952-1953), 184-185; *NstN*, XLV (1953), 74-75.

B3223 *Julius Caesar and the Life of William Shakespeare.* Introd. by John Gielgud. London: Gawthorn, 1958. Pp. 224.

B3224 Gielgud, Sir John. "Où va le théâtre anglais?" *Revue Théâtrale*, No. 28, 1954, pp. 15-19.

B3225 Johns, Eric. "Gielgud on Tour." *Theatre World*, Sept., 1955, pp. 24-29.

B3226 Stephens, Frances. "Edinburgh Festival 1957." *Theatre World*, Oct., 1957, pp. 26-27, 30-32. Gielgud's Shak. recital.

B3227 Watt, David. "Contemporary Arts. Plays at Edinburgh." *Spectator*, Aug., 1957, p. 277. Sir John Gielgud's Shak. recital at Edinburgh.

B3228 Friedman, Arthur. "John Gielgud, Shakespearean Actor." *ShN*, VIII (1958), 26. A survey of his roles and a brief appraisal.

B3229 Hewes, Henry. "Broadway Postscript: The Great Gielgud." *SatR*, Dec. 27, 1958, p. 20.

B3230 Trewin, J. C. "Sir John Gielgud." *Bulletin Culturel* (British Council, Paris), Nov., 1957.

(f) ALEXANDER GOLLING

B3231 Gstettner, Hans. "Shakespeares *Othello.* Zu Alexander Gollings Neuinszenierung im Prinzregenten-Theater [Munich]." *VB(Mü)*, March 26, 1940, No. 86.

B3232 Hübscher, Arthur. "Aufgaben der Shakespeare-Regie. Zu einem Gespräch mit Alexander Golling: Das *Othello*-Problem." *MNN*, April 28, 1940, No. 119.

(g) ALEC GUINNESS

B3233 Guinness, Alec. "My Idea of Hamlet." *Spectator*, No. 6419, 1951, pp. 8.

B3234 Tynan, Kenneth. *Alec Guinness.* London: Rockliff, 1953. Pp. 108.
       Rev: *TLS*, Nov. 20, 1953, p. 741.

(h) ROBERT HELPMANN

B3235 "Whispers from the Wings." *Theatre World*, Feb., 1957, pp. 25, 52. Robert Helpmann's interpretations of Shylock and Richard III.

B3236 Walker, Katherine Sorley. *Robert Helpmann.* Theatre World Monograph, No. 9. London: Rockliff, 1957. Pp. 126. Illustrated.
       Rev: *Theatre World*, Dec., 1957, p. 49; *TLS*, Dec. 27, p. 791; *Drama*, Spring, 1958, p. 43

(i) JOSEF KAINZ

B3237 Richter, H. "Kainz." *Theater d. Welt*, II (1938), 76-80.

B3238 Wiegler, Paul. *Josef Kainz. Ein Genius in seinen Verwandlungen.* Berlin: Dts. Verlag, 1941. Pp. 139.

B3239 "Josef Kainz as Hamlet." *TAr*, XXVIII (1944), 468.

(j) JOHN NEVILLE

B3240 "John Neville's Scrapbook." *Plays and Players*, Sept. 8, 1957, p. 8.

B3241 "Whispers from the Wings." *Theatre World*, Oct., 1957, pp. 33-34. Tribute to John Neville's interpretations of Shakespearean roles.

(k) LAURENCE OLIVIER

B3242 Bridie, J. "Mr. Olivier's Iago." *NstN*, XV (1938), 405.

B3243 Barker, Felix. *The Oliviers: A Biography.* London: Hamish Hamilton, 1953. Pp. 313.
       Rev: by A. Marshall, *NstN*, XLVI (1953), 108-109; by T. Holme, *Spectator*, No. 6522, 1953, pp. 840, 842; *TLS*, Oct. 23, 1953, p. 679.

B3244 Amery, Jean. "Im Schatten Shakespeares Laurence Olivier und Vivien Leigh." Amery's *Karrieren und Köpfe.* Zürich, 1955, pp. 241-245.

B3245 Peck, S. "Sir Laurence Again Widens His Range." *New York Times Mag.*, Feb. 26, 1956, pp. 28-29.
       Chiefly *Richard III*, with pictures and remarks on other films and stage productions by Olivier.

B3246 Webster, Margaret. "Interpretation of Shakespeare Today." *Wisdom*, July, 1956, pp. 23-35. With a section of pictures from the Olivier films, *Hamlet, Henry V, Richard III.*

B3247 "Knightly Entertainer." *Plays and Players*, May, 1957, p. 5. Olivier's contributions to Shakespearean acting, both on stage and in his films.

(l) MICHAEL REDGRAVE

B3248 Redgrave, Michael. "A Medieval *Macbeth* Made for Moderns." *The New York Times*, Mar. 28, 1948, Section 2, pp. X [1], X 3.

B3249 Redgrave, Michael. *The Actor's Ways and Means.* London: Heinemann, 1953. Pp. 90.

B3250 Findlater, Richard. *Michael Redgrave: Actor.* Introd. by Harold Clurman. London: Heinemann, 1956. Pp. xiii, 170. Illustrated.
       Rev: *TLS*, Oct. 19, 1956, p. 612; by J. B. Thomas, *Books of the Month*, LXXI, No. 11 (1956),

19; by P. W., *NstN*, LII, 497; *TC*, Apr., 1957, pp. 399-401; *TN*, XI, 141; by Fred J. Hinler, *Players Magazine*, Dec., 1957, p. 64; *Saturday Night* (Canada), Jan. 8, 1958, p. 25.

A3251 Granville-Barker, Frank. "Redgrave Reflects." *Plays and Players*, July, 1958, pp. 5.

B3252 Redgrave, Michael. *Mask or Face*. London: Heinemann, 1958. Pp. 188.
Lectures, articles, and notes by Redgrave.
Rev: B1830.

(m) PAUL SCOFIELD

B3253 "*Hamlet* in Moscow." *Time*, Dec. 12, 1955, p. 67.
Russians respond enthusiastically to *Hamlet*, as played by Paul Scofield in English.

B3254 Trewin, John Courtenay. *Paul Scofield*. An Illustrated Study of His Work, with a List of His Appearances on Stage and Screen. Theatre World Monograph, No. 6. London: Rockliff, 1956. Pp. 101.
Rev: *TLS*, Oct. 19, 1956, p. 612; by J. B. Thomas, *Books of the Month*, LXXI, No. 11 (1956), 14.

(n) BEERBOHM TREE

B3255 Booth, J. B. "Tree's *Hamlet*." *TLS*, Nov. 30, 1946, p. 591.
See replies by Max Beerbohm and by Hesketh Pearson, *TLS*, Dec. 7, 1946, p. 603.
Chiefly on the source of the remark, "Funny without being vulgar" applied to Tree's performance.

B3256 Ball, Robert Hamilton. "The Shakespeare Film as Record: Sir Herbert Beerbohm Tree." *SQ*, III (1952), 227-236.
Traces the history of Tree's acting of Shakespearian roles in films.

B3257 Carr, Philip. "A Great Actor-Manager. On Herbert Beerbohm Tree." *Listener*, L (1953), 1050-51.

B3258 Pearson, Hesketh. *Beerbohm Tree: His Life and Laughter*. London: Methuen, 1956. Pp. xiv, 250. Illustrated.
Rev: *TLS*, Nov. 23, 1956, p. 692; by C. A. Lejeune, *Time and Tide*, Dec. 1, pp. 1490-91; by T. C. Worsley, *NstN*, LII, 595-596; by H. Pearson, ibid., p. 626; by Walter Prichard Eaton, *NYHTBR*, Feb. 10, 1957, p. 3; by William W. Appleton, *SatR*, April 6, p. 16; by St. Vincent Troubridge, *TN*, XI, 104-106; *VQR*, XXXIII, lxxix; by J. Vallette, *MdF*, 329 (1957), 332; by A. J. Farmer, *EA*, XI (1958), 359-360.

B3259 Paulus, Gretchen. "Beerbohm Tree and 'The New Drama'." *UTQ*, XXVII (1957), 103-115.

(o) ORSON WELLES

B3260 Welles, Orson. "Shakespeare et la Tradition." *Nouvelles Littéraires*, XXXI, No. 1288 (1952), 1, 8.

B3261 Bentley, E. R. "The Other Orson Welles." *NR*, April 30, 1956, pp. 29-30.
Welles's *Lear* production at City Center, New York.

B3262 Bernad, Miguel A. "Othello Comes to Town: Orson Welles and Edmund Kean." *Philippine Studies*, IV (1956), 3-14.

B3263 Noble, Peter. *The Fabulous Orson Welles*. London: Hutchinson, 1956. Pp. 276.
Rev: *TLS*, Nov. 23, 1956, p. 702; *QR*, April, 1957, pp. 238-239.

B3264 Welles, Orson. "Shakespeare und Shakespeares Bühne." *Das neue Forum* (Darmstadt), V (1955/56), 118-120.

(p) DONALD WOLFIT

B3265 Wolfit, Donald. *First Interval: The Autobiography of Donald Wolfit*. London: Odhams, 1954. Pp. 256.
Rev: by Peter Forster, *Drama*, Winter, 1955, pp. 29-31.

B3266 Granville-Barker, Frank. "Lone Wolfit." *Plays and Players*, Mar., 1957, p. 13.
Wolfit has made a great contribution to the Shakespearean stage through his acting and managing.

B3267 Marriott, R. B. "Sir Donald Wolfit." *Theatre World*, Aug., 1957, pp. 33, 41.

(q) OTHERS (Arranged alphabetically by surname of actor.)

B3268 Wanderscheck, Hermann. "Shakespeare auf der Lachbühne [des Berliner Volkskomikers Erich Carow]." *LNN*, 1936, No. 126.

B3269 Martin, P. "Hamlet Isn't Hungry Any More." *Saturday Evening Post*, Apr. 22, 1944, pp. 11, 92.
John Carradine.

B3270 Davy, Jean. "Shakespeare Vu par un Acteur du XXe Siècle." William Shakespeare's *Roméo et Juliette*. Bibliothèque Mondiale, No. 15. Paris: Ed. Mondiale, 1953. Pp. 136.

B3271 "Personality of the Month." *Plays and Players*, Sept., 1957, p. 3.
Tribute to Robert Harris in the roles of King John, Cymbeline, and Jaques.

B3272   Jouvet, Louis. "The Elizabethan Theatre." *TAr*, XX (1936), 222-223.

B3273   Krauss, Werner. "Das Schauspiel meines Lebens." Stuttgart: Goverts, 1958. Pp. 258.

B3274   "At Home with Hamlet: Starring Burgess Meredith." *Newsweek*, May 21, 1956, pp. 106.

B3275   Johns, Eric. "Keith Michell and the Australian Theatre." *Theatre World*, May, 1957, pp. 10-11.
Tribute to the Australian actor, noted for Shak. interpretations.

B3276   "Mounet-Sully as Hamlet." *TAr*, XXI (1937), 732.

B3277   Moss, Arnold. "We are Such Stuff . . . ." *TAr*, XXIX (1945), 407-408.

B3278   Nicholson, Joseph. "Diario Londinese degli Olivier italiani: Renzo Ricci e Eva Magni."
Il Dramma (Turin), XXIX, No. 186 (Aug. 1, 1953), 54-56.
About Ricci's visit to Stratford.

B3279   Granville-Barker, Frank. "No Fun for Falstaff." *Plays and Players*, Oct., 1956, pp. 5.
Ralph Richardson in Shak.

B3280   Williamson, Audrey. *Paul Rogers*. London: Rockliff, 1956. Pp. 125.

B3281   Valk, Diana. *Shylock for a Summer*. London: Cassell, 1958. Pp. 134.
    Rev: *TLS*, July 11, 1958, p. 395.
A memorial volume by Mrs. Valk about her late husband, the Shak. actor Frederick Valk.

B3282   Findlater, Richard. *Emlyn Williams: An Illustrated Study of His Work, with a List of His Appearances on Stage and Screen*. Theatre World Monographs, No. 8. London: Rockliff, 1957.
Pp. 112.

B3283   Papazyan, V. "He Played Othello 2000 Times." *Sovietland*, April, 1941, pp. 6-7 and 37.

(3)   ACTRESSES
(a)   SARAH BERNHARDT

B3284   Régis, E. "Le Personnage d'Hamlet et Son Interprétation par Mme Sarah Bernhardt." *Revue Philomatique de Bordeaux et du Sud-Ouest*, II (1899), 469-480. Republ. in *Revue de Psychologie Clinique et Thérapeutique* (Paris), III (1899), 336-344. See also *Le Gaulois*, Paris, Dec. 17, 1899.

B3285   Shudofsky, M. Maurice. "Sarah Bernhardt on *Hamlet*." *CE*, III (1941), 293-295.
She was condemned because she played him as energetic and active.

B3286   Turner, B. *Sarah Bernhardt dans les Grandes Tragédies de Shakespeare*. MA thesis, Birmingham, 1954.

(b)   ELLEN TERRY

B3287   Craig, Gordon. "Reminiscences of Myself and Ellen Terry." *Listener*, XLVI (1951), 97-98.

B3288   Elsna, Hebe. *The Sweet Lost Years: A Novel*. London: Hale, 1955. Pp. 192.
Based upon the early life of Ellen Terry.

(c)   OTHERS

B3289   Seymour, May Davenport. "Viola Allen." *SAB*, XXIII (1948), 99-104.

B3290   Anderson, Marian. *A Few More Memories*. London: Hutchinson, 1936.

B3291   Keown, Eric. *Peggy Ashcroft. An Illustrated Study of Her Work, with a List of Her Appearances on Stage and Screen*. Theatre World Monographs, No. 3. London: Rockliff, 1955. Pp. 102.

B3292   Belmont, Eleanor Robson. *The Fabric of Memory*. New York: Farrar, Straus & Cudahy, 1957.
Pp. 311.
Reminiscences of the crusading actress, one of whose roles was Juliet.
    Rev: by Helen Beal Woodward, *SatR*, Nov. 23, 1957, p. 36.

B3293   Spadaro, Ottavio. "Giulietta di Charlot." *Teatro Scenario* (Milan), NS, V, No. 3 (Feb. 1-15, 1953), 12.
On Claire Bloom's acting of Juliet.

B3294   Cornell, K., and R. W. Sedgwick. *I Wanted to Be an Actress*. (An autobiography). New York: Random House, 1939. Pp. 362.

B3295   Stolp, Dorothy E. *Mrs. John Drew, American Actress-Manager, 1820-1897*. DD, Louisiana State University, 1953.

B3296   Trewin, J. C. *Edith Evans: An Illustrated Study of Dame Edith Evans' Work*. London: Rockliff, 1954. Pp. 116.
Gives a list of her appearances on stage and screen. Illustrated from the Raymond Mander and Joe Mitchenson Theatre Collection.

B3297   Gogoleva, Elena. "My Conception of Lady Macbeth." *News* (Moscow), No. 19, Oct. 1, 1955, pp. 29.
Production of *Macbeth* at the Maly Theatre.

B3298   Purdom, C. B. *Harley Granville-Barker: Man of the Theatre, Dramatist and Scholar*. Harvard Univ. Press, 1956. Pp. xiv, 322.
The first biography of Barker, including much of his correspondence and Purdom's personal recollections. For other entries see B1793-B1803.
    Rev: B1803.

B3299   Parker, J. "Helen Maud Holt: A Memoir." *The Stage*, Aug. 12, 1937.

B3300   Ross, Mary Lowrey. "Siobhan McKenna: Galway, Broadway and Stratford." *Saturday Night* (Canada), July 20, 1957, pp. 16-17, 36.
Miss McKenna's interpretation of Viola in *Twelfth Night*, and other Shak. roles.

B3301   "Julia Marlowe." *SQ*, II (1951), 129.
A brief survey of the career of the noted Shak. actress.

B3302   Mitchell, Yvonne. "Playing in *Lear*." *Spectator*, Dec. 4, 1953, pp. 664-665.
Actress who played Cordelia describes her reactions to the role after her performance at Stratford (England) theater.

B3303   Audiat, Pierre. "De Cléopâtre à Pauline Roland." *La Revue de Paris*, Sept., 1956, pp. 150-158.

B3304   Trewin, J. C. *Sybil Thorndike*. Theatre World Monograph, No. 4. London: Rockliff, 1956. Pp. 123. Illustrated.
Includes discussion of her period as actress at the Old Vic (1914-1918).
Rev: *TLS*, Feb. 3, 1956, p. 64.

3. MECHANICAL MEDIA
a. FILM
(1) GENERAL DRAMATURGIC LITERATURE

B3305   Crawford, Mary M., and Leroy Phillips. "Shakespeare as We Like Him." *English Journal*, XXVI (1937), 811-816.

B3306   Kelly, F. M. *Shakespearian Costume for Stage and Screen*. London: Black, 1938.
Rev: B1310.

B3307   Vardac, Alexander Nicholas. *From Garrick to Griffith: Transition from Stage to Screen*. DD, Yale University, 1942.

B3308   Ball, Robert H. "If We Shadows Have Offended." *Pacific Spectator*, I (1947), 97-104.
On film productions of Shakespeare's plays.

B3309   D., M. B. "Films: A Dialogue, Almost True to Life, between A Film-critic and The Editor." *Shakespeare Quarterly* (London), I (Summer, 1947), 116-118.
Generalizations and a discussion of Olivier's *Henry V*.

B3310   "Family Movie Guide: Should Children See the Tragedies of William Shakespeare?" *Parents Magazine*, XXIII (Sept., 1948), 13.

B3311   Bourgeois, J. "Le Sujet et l'Expression au Cinéma à Propos d'*Hamlet* et de *Macbeth*." *La Revue du Cinéma*, III (1948), 57-62.

B3312   Vardac, Alexander Nicholas. *Stage to Screen: Theatrical Method from Garrick to Griffith*. Cambridge, Mass.: Harvard Univ. Press; London: Oxford Univ. Press, 1948. Pp. xxvi, 283.
Rev: B1261.

B3313   Cardim, Luiz. *Os Problemas do Hamlet e as Suas Dificuldades Cénicas*. Lisbon, 1949. Pp. 125.
Olivier's and film difficulties.

B3314   Steinlechner, Helga. *Die filmischen Elemente in den Dramen Shakespeares*. Beitr. z. modernen Filmdramaturgie. DD, Vienna, 1951. Pp. 261. Typewritten.

B3315   Barbetti, Emilio. "Shakespeare Teatro e Cinema." *Teatro Scenario* (Milan), May 1, 1952, pp. 42-43.

B3316   Chiarini, Luigi. "Spettacolo e Film." *Belfagor*, VII (1952), 129-143.

B3317   Manvell, Roger. "Shakespeare as a Scriptwriter: Suitability of Shakespeare's Plays for Film or Television." *World Rev.*, May, 1952, pp. 56-59.

B3318   Ball, Robert H. "Shakespeare in One Reel." *Quarterly of Film, Radio, and Television*, VIII (1953), 139-149.
Surveys the early period of Shakespeare films.

B3319   Gowda, H. H. Anniah. "Shakespeare on the Screen." *The Literary Criterion* (India), II (1953).

B3320   Dehn, Paul. "The Filming of Shakespeare." *Talking of Shakespeare*. Ed. by John Garrett. London: Hodder & Stoughton & Max Reinhardt, 1954. Also in Dehn's *For Love and Money*. London: Max Reinhardt, 1956; New York: Vanguard Press, 1957. Pp. 135.
Rev: B3771.

B3321   Alpert, Hollis. "Movies Are Better than the Stage." *SatR*, July 23, 1955, pp. 5-6, 31.
Though interpretation of Shak. movies will always be subject to dispute, the over-all contribution of movie-versions to the popular appreciation of Shak. is greater than that of stage productions.

B3322   Haas, Willy. "Shakespeare und Shakespeare-Verfilmung." *SJ*, 91 (1955), 278-286.
Despite the excellence of certain Shak. films, generally too much of Shak.'s language is sacrificed for the sake of battle scenes and ceremonies. The film is not a proper medium for the interpretation of Shak.

B3323   Hellberg, Martin. "Warum heute Shakespeare?" Hellburg's *Bühne und Film*. Berlin: Henschel, 1955, pp. 197 ff.

B3324   Barnes, T. R. "Random Thoughts on Shakespeare in the Cinema." *Use of English*, Autumn, 1956, pp. 7-11.

B3325   Bensley, Gordon E. "Use of Shakespeare Films at Phillips Academy." *Audio-Visual Guide*, XXII, viii (1956), 35.

B3326   Fukuhara, Rintaro. *Ars Longa*. Tokyo: Tarumizu Shobo, 1956. Pp. 214.
         Essays on Shak., kabuki and noh plays. In making Shak. films, we should prepare scenarios different in construction from the plays.

B3327   Brinkmann, Karl. "Filmbericht." *SJ*, 94 (1958), 223-227.

B3328   Lewin, William, and Alexander Frazier. *Standards of Photoplay Appreciation*. Summit, New Jersey: Educational and Recreational Guides, Inc., 1957. Pp. 160.
         Final section presents a guide for the class discussion of a film version of *Caesar*.
         Rev: by Franklin Fearing, *Quarterly of Film, Radio, and Television*, XI (1957), 424-425.

B3329   Redi, Riccardo, e Roberto Chiti. "Shakespeare e il Cinema. Contributo a una Bibliografia." *Bianco e Nero* (Rome), XVIII, i (1957), 80-91.

B3330   Triscoli, Claudio. "Voci Italiane per Shakespeare Sullo Schermo." *Bianco e Nero* (Rome), XVIII, i (1957), 56-60.

B3331   Brinkmann, Karl. "Filmbericht." *SJ*, 94 (1958), 252-255.

B3332   Chenoweth, Stuart Curran. *A Study of the Adaptation of Acting Technique from Stage to Film, Radio, and Television Media in the United States, 1900-1951*. DD, Northwestern University, 1958. Pp. 393. Mic 58-4763. *DA*, XVIII (1958), 1143. Publication No. 24,896.

B3333   Jackson, Peter. "Shakespeare: Stage v. Screen." *Plays and Players*, Dec., 1958, pp. 8-9.
         Surveys Shak. on the screen in recent years.

B3334   Rider, Richard Lee. *A Comparative Analysis of Directing Television and Film Drama*. DD, University of Illinois, 1958. Pp. 192. Mic 58-1730. *DA*, XVIII (1958), 1900. (No publ. no.)

B3335   Thorp, Margaret Farrand. "Shakespeare and the Movies." *SQ*, IX (1958), 357-366.

(2) PERFORMANCES
(a) SEVERAL FILMS

B3336   Herring, Robert. "Shakespeare on the Screen." *Life and Letters Today*, XVI, No. 7 (1937), 125-130.

B3337   Thurmann, Irmgard. "Shakespeare im Film." *SJ*, LXXVI (1940), 189-198.

B3338   Smith, Garland Garvey. "Shakespeare on the Screen." *Emory Univ. Quarterly*, III (June, 1947), 88-95.

B3339   Dreimal *Hamlet* (im Film): "Laurence Olivier: Passt die Gebärde dem Wort, das Wort der Gebärde an. Claude Mauriac: Welch ein Meisterwerk . . . Robert Herring: O Hamlet, welch ein Abfall." *Der Monat*, I (1948/49), H. 2, 96-101.

B3340   Matković, Marijan. "Shakespeare i današnjica [Shakespeare and Our Times]." *Dramaturški eseji* (Zagreb), 1949, pp. 23-35.

B3341   Saint-Pierre, Michel de. "Shakespeare à l'Ecran." *Etudes*, 260 (1949), 239-245.

B3342   Lalou, R. "Shakespeare et le Cinéma." *EA*, V (1952), 309-318.

B3343   Bingham, R. "Movies: The Shakespeare Boom [*Othello*]." *Reporter*, XIII (Nov. 17, 1955), 34-37. Abstr. in *ShN*, VI (1956), 2.

B3344   Starr, Cecile. "Ideas on Film: The Film's Cousin—the Book." *SatR*, April 9, 1955, pp. 35-36.

B3345   Webster, Margaret. "Interpretation of Shakespeare Today." *Wisdom*, July, 1956, pp. 23-35.
         With a section of pictures from the Olivier films.

B3346   Weightman, J. G. "Many Othellos." *TC*, 160 (1956), 166-169.

B3347   Hazard, Patrick D., ed. "The Public Arts." *English Journal*, XLVII (1958), 41-43.
         Survey of recent drama recordings, television productions and films.

(b) PARTICULAR FILMS
i. Castellani's *Romeo and Juliet*

B3348   "Tragedy in Verona: New Film Version of *Romeo and Juliet*." *Life*, Dec. 6, 1954, pp. 133-134.
         Color pictures from recent production in Italy.

B3349   Charensol, G. "Roméo et Juliette (Film)." *Nouvelles Littéraires*, No. 1422, Dec. 2, 1954, p. 10.

B3350   Knight, Arthur. "Three Problems in Film Adaptation." *SatR*, Dec. 18, 1954, pp. 26-28.
         Includes a review of Castellani's filming of *Romeo and Juliet*.

B3351   Lewin, William. "Guide to the Technicolor Screen Version of *Romeo and Juliet*." *Audio-Visual Guide*, XXI (Dec., 1954), 19-28.
         Reviews the Castellani production with excerpts from *Juliet's* diary while she was rehearsing her role.

B3352   Walker, Roy. "In Fair Verona." *TC*, 156 (1954), 464-471.

B3353   "*Romeo and Juliet*." *Reporter*, Feb. 24, 1955, pp. 47-48.

B3354   Fayard, Jean. "L'Affaire Roméo." *Revue de Paris*, Jan., 1955, pp. 165-166.

B3355   Jorgensen, Paul A. "Castellani's *Romeo and Juliet*: Intention and Response." *Quarterly of*

Film, Radio, and Television, X (1955), 1-10.
An analysis of critical reaction to the film, and a defense of the film in terms of Castellani's intentions.

ii.   The Howard-Shearer *Romeo and Juliet*

B3356   *Romeo and Juliet.* New York: Random House, 1936. Pp. 13-290.
With the text of the play is given the screen script and articles on Shakespeare in moving pictures.

B3357   Nugent, F. S. "The *Romeo and Juliet* Film." *New York Times*, Aug. 21, 1936. (See also other New York newspapers of same date).
R. Stebbins, *New Theatre*, Sept. 21-22, 1936; E. V. R. Wyatt, *Catholic World*, 144 (1936), 85-88; O. Ferguson, *NR*, 88 (Sept. 2, 1936), 104; *Time*, XXVIII (Aug. 24), 30-32; *Scholastic*, XXIX (Sept. 19), 17; *Library Jour.*, LXI, 589-590.

B3358   Aveline, Claude. "Lettre de Londres." *Revue Bleue: Politique et Littéraire*, LXXIV (1936), 785-787.

iii.   The Gielgud-Brando-Mason *Julius Caesar*

B3359   *Julius Caesar and the Life of William Shakespeare.* Introd. by John Gielgud. London: Gawthorn, 1953. Pp. 224.
Published as a supplement to the M.G.M. film version. The Life of Shakespeare is anonymous.

B3360   Griffin, Alice Venezky. "Shakespeare Through the Camera's Eye: *Julius Caesar* in Motion Pictures; *Hamlet* and *Othello* on Television." *SQ*, IV (1953), 331-336; *SQ*, VI (1955), 63-66; *SQ*, VII (1956), 235-240.

B3361   Houseman, John. "*Julius Caesar*: Mr. Mankiewicz' Shooting Script." *Quarterly of Film, Radio, and Television*, VIII (1953), 109-124.

B3362   Houseman, John. "This Our Lofty Stage." *TAr*, XXXVII, No. 5 (May, 1953), 26-28.

B3363   Houseman, John. "Filming *Julius Caesar.*" *Sight and Sound*, July-Sept., 1953, pp. 24-27.

B3364   Pasinetti, P. M. "*Julius Caesar*: The Role of the Technical Adviser." *Quarterly of Film, Radio and Television*, VIII (1953), 131-138.
On the problem of historical accuracy in the filming of the play.

B3365   Phillips, James E. "*Julius Caesar*: Shakespeare as a Screen Writer." *Quarterly of Film, Radio, and Television*, VIII (1953), 125-130.

B3366   Walker, Roy. "Look Upon Caesar." *TC*, 154 (1953), 469-474.

B3367   Bernad, M. A. "*Julius Caesar* in Hollywood." *Philippine Studies*, II (1954), 286-290.

iv.   Olivier's *Henry V*

B3368   Lejeune, C. A. [*Henry V* in Technicolor in London.] *New York Times*, Dec. 31, 1944, Section 2, p. X 3.

B3369   B., G. "The Film of *Henry V.*" *English* V (1945), 107-108.

B3370   Manvell, R. "*Henry V* on the Films." *Britain Today*, Mar., 1945, pp. 25-26.

B3371   The Olivier Film of *Henry V. Time*, XLVII (Apr. 8, 1946), 56-59. E. Creelman, *New York Sun*, June 18, 1946, p. 29; B. Crowther, *New York Times*, June 18, 1946, p. 30; C. Ager, *PM*, June 18, 1946, p. 18.

B3372   Phillips, James E. "Adapted from a Play by Shakespeare." *Hollywood Quarterly*, II (Oct., 1946), 82-90.

B3373   Wyatt, E. V. R. "The Film of *Henry V.*" *Catholic World*, 163 (1946), 457-458.

B3374   Pandolfi, Vito. "*L'Enrico V* di Laurence Olivier." *La Rassegna d'Italia*, III (Aug., 1948), 887-891.

v.   Olivier's *Hamlet* (See also sections on
Psychology, A1171-A1413, and on Hamlet,
B7777-B7851).

B3375   "*Hamlet* & Olivier." *TAr*, XXXII (1948), 30-31.
B3376   "*Hamlet.*" *Look Magazine*, XII (1948), 84-87.
B3377   "Citizen Dane." *Harper's Magazine*, 197 (Sept., 1948), 116-117.
B3378   "*Hamlet* im Film." *Dionysos*, II, No. 14 (1948), 2-5.
B3379   "*Hamlet*: The Play and the Screenplay." *Hollywood Quarterly*, III (1948), 293-300.
B3380   "Olivier as *Hamlet.*" *Good Housekeeping*, 127 (Sept., 1948), 117.
B3381   "Scenes from the Olivier Production of *Hamlet.*" *Life*, XXIV (1948), 117-127.
B3382   "Sir Laurence Olivier's Movie of *Hamlet.*" *Time*, LI (May 17, 1948), 100; D. Cook, *New York Herald-Tribune*, May 9, 1948, Sec. 5, pp. 1-2.
B3383   Reviews of Olivier's *Hamlet.* By C. L. Ager, *New York Star*, Sept. 30, 1948, pp. 17-18; by

A. Winsten, *New York Post*, Sept. 30, 1948, pp. 42; by E. Creelman, *New York Sun*, Sept. 30, 1948, pp. 27-28; by R. Pelswick, *The New York Journal-American*, Sept. 30, 1948, p. 18; by A. Cook, *New York World-Telegram*, Sept. 30, 1948, p. 24; by B. Crowther, *New York Times*, Sept. 30, 1948, p. 32; by K. Cameron, *Daily News*, Sept. 30, 1948, p. 74.

B3384   Bayley, J. "*Hamlet* as a Film." *The National Review*, 131 (1948), 603-606.

B3385   Birin, J. "Sir Laurence Olivier's Film Representation of *Hamlet*." *Ba*, XXXII (1948), 166-168.

B3386   Cardim, Luiz. "É o Hamlet representável? A propósito do Hamlet-filme de Sir Laurence Olivier." *Seara Nova* (Lisbon), Nos. 1110-14, 1948.

B3387   Clurman, H. "Laurence Olivier's *Hamlet*." *Tomorrow*, Sept., 1948, pp. 47-48.

B3388   Cross, Brenda. *The Film Hamlet: A Record of Its Production*. London: Saturn Press, 1948. Pp. 76; 50 il.

B3389   Dent, Alan. *Hamlet, the Film and the Play*. London: World Film Publ., 1948.
Contains, i.a., complete text of *Hamlet* with excisions in square brackets and stage directions replaced by studio directions.
Rev: by G. F., *MGW*, Sept. 9, 1948, p. 11; by William Whitebait, *NstN*, Oct. 2, p. 287.

B3390   Dominique, Claude. [A Review of the Olivier *Hamlet* Film.] *Psyché—Revue Internationale des Sciences de l'Homme et de Psychanalyse* (publ. in Paris under editorship of Mme Maryse Choisy-Clouzer as the *Bulletin de la Ligue d'Hygiène Mentale*), III, Nos. 23-24 (Sept.-Oct., 1948), 1179-82.

B3391   Fallon, G. "The Film Called *Hamlet*." *Irish Monthly*, LXXVI (1948), 495-501.

B3392   Cancelled.

B3393   Fowler, R. A. "Notes sur Hamlet." *Revue du Cinéma*, III (1948), 58-66.

B3394   Herring, R. "*Hamlet*, Sir Laurence Olivier's Picture." *Life and Letters*, LVII (1948), 183-192.

B3395   Hopkins, Arthur. "*Hamlet* and Olivier." *TAr*, XXXII (1948), 30-31.

B3396   Lejeune, C. A. "The Bard Competes with the Body." *New York Times Magazine*, Dec. 12, 1948, p. 24.
On Olivier's film versions, chiefly *Hamlet*.

B3397   M., R. "The Olivier *Hamlet*." *Punch*, 214 (1948), 446.

B3398   "Olivier Explains His Cinematic Approach to *Hamlet*." *New York Times*, Sept. 19, 1948, Section 2, p. X 5.

B3399   "*Hamlet*." *Time*, LI (June 29, 1948), 54-62.

B3400   Powell, D. "*Hamlet* on the Screen." *Britain Today*, July, 1948, pp. 18-21.

B3401   *Mitteilungen der Deutschen Shakespeare-Gesellschaft*, I, August, 1949, Bochum, Germany. Pp. 12.
"Zur Diskussion um Oliviers *Hamlet*-Film," pp. 6-7.

B3402   Ashworth, John. "Olivier, Freud, and *Hamlet*." *Atlantic Monthly*, May, 1949, pp. 30-33.
See B3417.

B3403   Barbarow, George. "*Hamlet* Through a Telescope." *Hudson Review*, II (1949), 98-117.

B3404   Boas, Guy. "*Hamlet* (Film)." *English*, VII (1948/49), 55.

B3405   Cardim, Luiz. *Os Problemas do Hamlet e as Suas Dificuldades Cénicas*. Lisbon, 1949. Pp. 125.
Olivier's and film difficulties.

B3406   Carpeaux, Otto Maria. "Hamlet Diferente." *Letras e Artes* (Rio de Janeiro), July 24, 1949.

B3407   McManaway, J. G. "The Laurence Olivier *Hamlet*." *SAB*, XXIV (1949), 3-11.

B3408   Manvell, Roger. "The Film of *Hamlet*." *Penguin Film Rev.*, VIII (1949), 16-24.

B3409   Moscon, Giorgio. "L'Amleto di Laurence Olivier." *Belfagor* (Messina-Florence), IV (July, 1949), 473-479.
Critical essay on Laurence Olivier's *Hamlet* as an independent work of art.

B3410   Tyler, Parker. "*Hamlet* and Documentary." *KR*, XI (1949), 527-532.
Comment by M. D. Heckscher, *KR*, XI (1949), 673-674.

B3411   "Zur Diskussion um Oliviers *Hamlet*-Film." *MDtShG*, II (1950), 6-7.

B3412   Babcock, R. W. "George Lyman Kittredge, Olivier, and the Historical *Hamlet*." *CE*, XI (1950), 256-265.
Olivier's acting in the film seen as in the tradition of an "active" *Hamlet*, as taught by Kittredge.

B3413   Klitscher, Hermann. "Über Sir Lawrence Olivier's *Hamlet*-Film." *Shakespeare-Studien*, *Festschrift für Heinrich Mutschmann* (Marburg: N. G. Elwert), 1951, pp. 107-114.

B3414   Flatter, Richard. "*Hamlet* als Film." *SJ*, 87/88 (1952), 58-60.

B3415   Alexander, Peter. *Hamlet: Father and Son*. The Lord Northcliffe Lectures, University College, London, 1953. Oxford: Oxford Univ. Press, 1955. Pp. 196.
Rev: B7759.

B3416   *The Tragedy of Hamlet, Prince of Denmark*. London: Folio Society, 1954. Pp. 134.
Follows the *New Temple Shakespeare* text of M. R. Ridley.
Illustrated with nine designs made by Roger Furse for the J. Arthur Rank *Hamlet*.
Notices in *TLS*, Sept. 3, 1954, p. 562.

B3417   Lesser, Simon O. "Freud and *Hamlet* Again." *American Imago*, XII (1955), 207-220.
An answer to Ashworth's article, B3402.

vi.   Olivier's *Richard III*

B3418   "Filming of *Richard III*." *Illustrated London News*, 225 (Dec. 4, 1954), 1019.
B3419   Graham, Virginia. "*Richard III* (Film)." *Spectator*, 6651 (1955), 841.
B3420   Whitebait, William. "Olivier's *Richard*." *NstN*, L (1955), 830-831.
B3421   "The Dark History of a Wicked King." *Life*, Feb. 20, 1956, pp. 80-88.
        Photographic essay on Olivier's *Richard III*, including a survey of actress Claire Bloom's career.
B3422   "At Home and Abroad with *Richard III*." *TAr*, March, 1957, pp. 22-24.
        Photographs of selected scenes and the cast roster of Olivier's film.
B3423   "*Richard III*." *English*, Spring, 1956, p. 19.
B3424   Brinkmann, Karl. "Laurence Olivier's Film *Richard III*." *SJ*, 92 (1956), 440-442.
B3425   Brown, Ivor. *Theatre, 1955-56*. London: Reinhardt, 1956.
        Reviews of various performances including *Richard III*.
B3426   Bryant, A. "*Richard III*." *Illustrated London News*, April 14, 1956, pp. 290.
B3427   Dent A. "*Richard III:* A Disclaimer." *Illustrated London News*, Jan. 7, 1956, pp. 30.
        On Olivier's *Richard III*.
B3428   Griffin, Alice. "Shakespeare Through the Camera's Eye: III." *SQ*, VII (1956), 235-240.
B3429   Hatch, Robert. "Films," [*Richard III*]. *The Nation*, Mar. 10, 1956, pp. 206-207.
B3430   Knight, Arthur, Henry Hewes, and Gilbert Seldes. "Sir Laurence and the Bard." *SatR*,
        March 10, 1956, pp. 26-28.
B3431   Kozelka, Paul. "A Guide to the Screen Version of Shakespeare's *Richard III*." *Audio-Visual
        Guide*, XXII, No. 8 (1956), 51-57.
B3432   Phillips, James E. "*Richard III:* Two Views. I. Some Glories and Some Discontents."
        Quarterly of Film, Radio, and Television, X (1956), 399-407.
        The Olivier film, admirable for certain adaptations to modern audiences, has nevertheless
        received much of its critical praise for the least praiseworthy features.
B3433   Ross, Mary Lowrey. "Exercise in Diablerie." *Saturday Night* (Canada), Mar. 17, 1956, p. 20.
B3434   Schoen, Harry. "*Richard III:* Two Views. II. A Magnificent Fiasco?" *Quarterly of Film,
        Radio, and Television*, X (1956), 407-415. Tr. by Erik Wahlgren from *Bonniers Litterära Magasin*.
B3435   Thespis. "Films." *English*, XI (1956/57), 19-20.
B3436   Walker, Roy. "Bottled Spider." *TC*, Jan., 1956, pp. 58-68.
B3437   *Richard III*. Sound-Track Recording (Olivier-Film). London: RCA Victor, 1957. LM
        6126, 3 discs.
             Rev: by Franklin Behrens, "*Richard III* on Record," *ShN*, VIII (1958), 23.
B3438   Baldini, Gabriele. "Osservazioni sul *Riccardo III* di Shakespeare e di Olivier." *Bianco e Nero*
        (Rome), XVIII, i (1957).
B3439   Diether, Jack. "*Richard III:* The Preservation of a Film." *Quarterly of Film, Radio, and
        Television*, XI (1957), 280-293.
B3440   Šimko, Ján. "A Few Notes Concerning the Film Version of *Richard III*." *ZAA*, VI (1958),
        297-299.

vii.   Reinhardt's *Midsummer Night's Dream*

B3441   Pléville, M. B. "Shakespeare à l'Ecran." *La Revue Hebd.*, XXXIV, No. 52 (Dec. 28, 1935),
        493-497.
B3442   Verkade, Ed. "De verfilming van *Midzomernachtsdroom*." *De groene Amsterdammer*, Jan. 22,
        1936.
B3443   *Een Midzomernacht-droom*. Vert. door L. A. J. Burgersdijk. Film-editiě. Med ill. . . . en een
        voorwoord van Max Reinhardt. Leiden: A. W. Sijthoff, 1936. Pp. vii, 70.

viii.   Youtkevich's *Othello*

B3444   Prouse, Derek. "*Othello*." *Sight and Sound*, Summer, 1956, pp. 29-30.
        Sergei Youtkevich's Russian film.
B3445   Dent, A. "*Othello*, Russian Film." *Illustrated London News*, July 13, 1957, pp. 82.
B3446   Robleto, Hernán. "Otelo ha Vuelto." *El Universal* (Mexico City), April, 1957, pp. 3.
        On the Russian film of *Othello;* the whole situation is found to be old-fashioned.
B3447   Rozental, Gennadi. "Sergei Yutkevitch, Film Director, Writer, Artist." *USSR*, No. 10,
        1957, pp. 50-53.
B3448   Sibirtsev, Gennadi. "Her Debut is a Promise." *USSR*, Sept., 1956, pp. 42-43.
        Notes the appearance of Ivira Skobtevas in the Russian film of *Othello*.

ix.   Welles's *Othello*

B3449   MacLiammóir, Micheál. *Put Money in thy Purse, a Diary of the Film of "Othello."* London:
        Methuen, 1952. Pp. viii, 258.

Rev: by R. Lalou, *EA*, v (1952), 358-359; by C. Ray, *Spectator*, 6483 (1952), 404, 406; by R. H. Ball, *SQ*, iv (1953), 479-481.

B3450   Bentley, E. "*Othello* on Film and on the Stage. *NR*, Oct. 3, 1955, pp. 21-22.

B3451   Goldstein, R. M. "*Othello*." *High Points*, xxxvii (Oct., 1955), 46-50.

B3452   Kozelka, Paul. "A Guide to the Screen Version of Shakespeare's *Othello*." *Audio-Visual Guide*, xxii (Oct., 1955), 31-40.

B3453   Whitebait, W. "Big Brother." *NstN*, li (Mar. 10, 1956), 210, 212.
Reviews Orson Welles's *Othello*.

x.   Welles's *Macbeth*

B3454   Smeets, Marcel. "*Macbeth*. Une Adaptation Cinématographique d'Orson Welles." *Revue des Langues Vivantes*, xvii (1951), 58 ff.

B3455   Wilson, Richard. "*Macbeth* on Film." *TAr*, June, 1949, pp. 53-55.

xi.   Film Ballet

B3456   "The Moor's Pavane." Walter Strate Productions.
A modern ballet production, filmed in technicolor, and accompanied with passages from Shakespeare and seventeenth-century music. Four dancers only, representing Othello, Iago, Desdemona, and Emilia.

B3457   Lvov-Anokhin, B. "The Film-Ballet *Romeo and Juliet*." *VOKS-Bulletin* (Moscow), No. 5 (94) 1955, pp. 48-50.

B3458   Michaut, Pierre. "La Danse: *Roméo et Juliette*, Film-Ballet Soviétique." *La Revue de Paris*, June, 1956, pp. 168-169.
Review of the Prokofiev ballet.

xii.   Other Productions

B3459   "A. Nielsen as *Hamlet* in a German Film." *TAr*, xxi (1937), 197.

B3460   Quéval, J. "Les Amants de Vérone (d'Après un Scénario de Jacques Prévert, Transposé de *Roméo et Juliette*)." *MdF*, 306 (1949), 314-317.

B3461   *Hamlet* [film in Hindustani language, produced by K. Sahu].
Rev: *The Statesman* (Delhi & Calcutta), Jan. 15, 1955, p. 3; *Times of India* (Bombay), Jan. 2, 1955, p. 3.

B3462   "*Macbeth*." *National Parent-Teacher*, May, 1955, p. 40.
Film version of the Maurice Evans TV show.

B3463   Majdalany, Fred. "*Joe Macbeth*." *Time and Tide*, Oct. 29, 1955, pp. 1402-03.
Ken Hughes's attempt at creating a Chicago atmosphere and character is judged irrelevantly long.

B3464   Sibirtsev, Gennadi. "How a Film Star is Made: Alla Larionova." *USSR*, No. 4, 1956, pp. 54-56.
Notes Russian film of *Twelfth Night*.

B3465   Whitebait, William. "*Macbeth* as Stag-Beetle." *NstN*, lv (1958), 603.
Review of a Japanese movie version of *Macbeth* called *The Throne of Blood*.

xiii.   Educational Films

B3466   Jordan, William E., and Mildred R. "*Shakespeare's Theater: The Globe Playhouse*—An Educational Film. I. The Shooting Script." *Quarterly of Film, Radio, and Television*, viii (1954), 322-332.

B3467   Williamson, May Gordon. "*Shakespeare's Theater: The Globe Playhouse*—An Educational Film. II. The Film in the Classroom." *Quarterly of Film, Radio, and Television*, viii (1954), 333-339.

B3468   Adams, John Cranford. "*Shakespeare's Theater: The Globe Playhouse*—An Educational Film. III. The Film and Scholarship." *Quarterly of Film, Radio, and Television*, viii (1954), 340-349.

B3469   Jordan, William E., and Mildred R. "*Shakespeare's Theater: The Globe Playhouse*—An Educational Film. IV. Post-production Notes on the Film." *Quarterly of Film, Radio, and Television*, viii (1954), 350-355.
Comments by the directors and producers.

B3470   Krutch, Joseph Wood, educational director. "*Midsummer Night's Dream:* An Introduction to the Play."
[Film]. Coronet. 16 mm sound. 1 ¼ reels, 15 minutes.
Rev: by Richard E. Scott, *English Journal*, xliv (1955), 184.

B3471   "The Life of Shakespeare on Film." *Wisdom*, July, 1956, pp. 12-13.
Shots from the Film *Master Will Shakespeare*.

B3472   *Shakespeare's Stratford*. Color filmstrip, 73 frames, with 33⅓ RPM record. Narration by Frank Titus. Literary Backgrounds, 44 Turney Road, Fairfield, Connecticut.

B3473   Dunnington, Stephen. " 'Shakespeare's Stratford'." *English Journal*, xlvi (1957), 595.
Discussion of B3472.

b. TELEVISION
(1) PRINCIPLES

B3474   Manvell, Roger. "Shakespeare as a Scriptwriter: Suitability of Shakespeare's Plays for Film or Television." *World Rev.*, May, 1952, pp. 56-59.

B3475   Miner, Worthington. "Shakespeare for the Millions." *TAr*, June, 1951, pp. 58, 94.
Discusses problems connected with a television production of *Cor.* Suggests that John Webster was part author of the play. See protest of S. F. Johnson, "Shakespeare Without Ear—the Protest of a Professor." *TAr*, Oct., 1951, pp. 38-39.

B3476   Chenoweth, Stuart Curran. *A Study of the Adaptation of Acting Technique from Stage to Film, Radio, and Television Media in the United States, 1900-1951.* DD, Northwestern University, 1958. Pp. 393. Mic 58-4763. *DA*, XVIII (1958), 1143. Publication No. 24,896.

B3477   Rider, Richard Lee. *A Comparative Analysis of Directing Television and Film Drama.* DD, University of Illinois, 1958. Pp. 192. Mic 58-1730. *DA*, XVIII (1958), 1900.

(2) PRODUCTIONS
(a) MAURICE EVANS

B3478   Schreiber, Flora Rheta. "Television's *Hamlet.*" *Quarterly of Film, Radio, and Television*, VIII (1953), 150-156.

B3479   "Video Rushes in Where Angels Fear." *Life*, Feb. 8, 1954, pp. 53-54.
Short illustrated article on Maurice Evans's television production of *Richard II.*

B3480   Frye, Roland Mushat. "Shakespeare on TV: Maurice Evans and *Richard II.*" *ShN*, IV (1954), 40.

B3481   Howard, Leon. "Shakespeare for the Family." *Quarterly of Film, Radio, and Television*, VIII (1954), 356-366.
Reactions to the television performance of Maurice Evans's *Richard II.*

B3482   Merrill, J. F. "TV's Mr. Shakespeare: Maurice Evans." *Scholastic*, LXV (Nov., 1955), 6.

B3483   Shayon, Robert Louis. "TV's Withered Dames." *SatR*, Dec. 18, 1954, pp. 28-29.
On the Maurice Evans production, and the problem of witches on TV.

B3484   "*Macbeth.*" *National Parent-Teacher*, May, 1956, p. 40.
Film version of the Maurice Evans TV show.

B3485   Jones, Claude E. "The Imperial Theme—*Macbeth* on Television." *Quarterly of Film, Radio, and Television*, IX (1955), 292-298.
Analyzes the reasons for the success of the Hall of Fame production.

B3486   Tovatt, Anthony L., and Arno Jewett, eds. "[Kinescope Recordings of *Macb.* and *R. II*]." *English Journal*, XLIV (1955), 482.

B3487   Zolotow, Maurice. "The Foxy Dreamer of Broadway." *Saturday Evening Post*, Oct. 22, 1955, pp. 36-37, 127-128, 130.

B3488   Jorgensen, Paul A. "*The Taming of the Shrew:* Entertainment for Television." *Quarterly of Film, Radio, and Television*, X (1956), 391-398.

B3489   Hazard, Patrick D., ed. "The Public Arts." *English Journal*, XLVII (1958), 41-43.

(b) OTHERS

B3490   Coe, Fred. "Televising Shakespeare." *TAr*, XXXVI (April, 1952), 96.
Television production of *Caesar* and *Oth.*

B3491   Lemaire, Marcel. "Shakespeare à Broadway." *Revue des Langues Vivantes*, XVII (1951), 255-258.

B3492   Griffin, Alice Venezky. "Shakespeare Through the Camera's Eye—*Julius Caesar* in Motion Pictures; *Hamlet* and *Othello* on Television." *SQ*, IV (1953), 331-336.

B3493   Schnack, Sebastian. *Television bei Shakespeare: Eine aktuelle Zusammenstellung.* London, Zurich, Vienna: René Marti, New Press Agency, 1953. Pp. 4. Typewritten.

B3494   Rosenberg, Marvin. "Shakespeare on TV: An Optimistic Survey." *The Quarterly of Film, Radio, and Television*, IX (1954), 166-174.
Reviews productions of *Hamlet*, *Othello*, *Lear*, and *Richard II.*

B3495   Wadsworth, Frank. "'Sound and Fury'—*King Lear* on Television." *Quarterly of Film, Radio, and Television*, VIII (1954), 254-258.
Discusses the Peter Brook-Orson Welles television production.

B3496   "Russia's TV Viewers See 'Romeo, Juliet'." *Los Angeles Times*, Nov. 22, 1955, Pt. I, p. 20.
The first Soviet TV presentation of a full-length English play in English—Shak.'s *Romeo and Juliet*, produced by Peter Brook.

B3497   "Shakespeare on TV." *Ave Maria*, 82 (Aug. 27, 1955), 6.

B3498   Barry, Michael. "Shakespeare on Television." *BBC Quarterly*, IX, No. 3 (1955), 143-149.

B3499   Griffin, Alice. "Shakespeare Through the Camera's Eye, 1953-1954." *SQ*, VI (1955), 63-66; *SQ*, VII (1956), 235-240.
Lear, *Richard II*, and *Macbeth* on TV.

B3500   Hope-Wallace, Philip. "In the Basket." *Listener*, Oct. 6, 1955, p. 569.

Informal commentary on BBC's TV performance of the remarkably entertaining *Wives*, followed up by a broadcast of *The Dark Lady of the Sonnets*.
See Hope-Wallace's similar notice in *Time and Tide*, XXXVI (1955), 968.

B3501   Slater, Montagu. "Shakespeherian Rag." *NstN*, L (1955), 269-270.
On a TV *Romeo* in England.

B3502   Driberg, Tom. "A Break for Shakespeare." *NstN*, LI (1956), 210.
Ham. on TV in England.

B3503   Hainfield, Harold. "The Bard of Avon Makes Good on TV." *Audio-Visual Guide*, XXII (1956), 35 ff.

B3504   De Berry, Frances C. *All the World's A Stage for Shakespeare's Comedies: A Modern Interpretation of the Bard's Humor by a Shakespeare Winner on "The $64,000 Question."* New York Exposition Press, 1958. Pp. 130.

B3505   Cowburn, John. "Shakespeare and Chekhov." *Spectator*, Jan. 10, 1958, p. 49.
Henry V on BBC's World Theatre television series.

B3506   Hainfield, H. "Studying Shakespeare from Television." *School Activities*, Nov., 1958, pp. 86-87.

B3507   Kunstler, Ernst. "TV Shakespeare in West Germany." *ShN*, VIII (1958), 27.

c. RADIO

B3508   "Shakespeare on the Air." *American Library Association Bulletin*, XXXI (1938), 398.

B3509   Heppenstall, Rayner, and Michael Innes. *Three Tales of Hamlet*. London: Gollancz, 1950. Three broadcast plays on the *Hamlet* story.
Rev: B4069.

B3510   Stout, A. K. "Shakespeare on the Air in Australia." *Quarterly of Film, Radio, and Television*, VIII (1954), 269-272.

B3511   "Summer Mirth as Winter Comes." *New Zealand Listener*, XXX (June 4, 1954), 6-7.
Review of New Zealand Players' production of *Dream*.

B3512   "Alas, Poor William! Philadelphia Ban." *Reporter*, Sept. 8, 1955, p. 4.
Vicissitudes of Philadelphia Shak. Festival Players.

B3513   "*Macbeth* [adaptation for Radio Production]." Ed. by L. Olfson. *Plays*, XIV (April, 1955), 87-95.

B3514   Howarth, R. G. *Shakespeare by Air*. Sydney: Angus and Robertson, 1957. Pp. 64.
Rev: by A. L. McLeod, *QJS*, XLIV (1958), 204; *N &Q*, V (1958), 454.

B3515   *Shakespeare Tonight*. Engelsk språkserie i radio våren 1958. Scener ur dramer av William Shakespeare utvalda och komm. av Lorna Downman. Stockholm: Sveriges Radio, 1958. Pp. 248.

B3516   Chenoweth, Stuart Curran. *A Study of the Adaptation of Acting Technique from Stage to Film, Radio, and Television Media in the United States, 1900-1951*. DD, Northwestern University, 1958. Pp. 393. Mic 58-4763. *DA*, XVIII (1958), 1143. Publication No. 24,896.

B3517   Olfson, Lewy, ed. *Radio Plays from Shakespeare: Ten Plays Adapted for Royalty-Free Performance*. Boston: Plays, Inc., 1958. Pp. 193.
Rev: B189.

d. RECORDINGS
(1) BIBLIOGRAPHIES AND SURVEYS

B3518   Moore, Harry Thornton. "Shakespeare on Records." *TAr*, XXIV (June, 1940), 450-454.
Discussion of records available.

B3519   Banke, Cécile de. *Shakespearean Stage Production: Then & Now*. New York: McGraw-Hill, 1953. Pp. xviii, 342.
Recordings of Music and Songs, pp. 319-326.
Rev: A7409.

B3520   Lazar, B. "How to Sound Out Your Shakespeare." *Senior Scholastic*, Mar. 1, 1956, pp. 7T-8T.
Concludes with a list of recordings.

B3521   Browne, E. M. "Shakespeare Recorded." *Drama*, Summer, 1958, pp. 36-37.
Survey of recent Shak. recordings.

B3522   Hazard, Patrick D., ed. "The Public Arts." *English Journal*, XLVII (1958), 41-43.
Includes discussion of the RCA Victor recording of *Romeo*.

B3523   Wain, John. "Equity and Amateurs." *TC*, 164 (1958), 350-354. See also John Kimber, ibid., pp. 591-592.
Notes on recent phonograph recordings of the plays.

B3524   Whicher, Stephen E. "Current Long-Playing Records of Literature in English." *CE*, XIX (1957), 111-121.
Shak., pp. 119-120.

B3525   Woolf, L. "Shakespeare on Records." *NstN*, Aug. 2, 1958, p. 153.
Notes on phonograph recordings of the plays.

(2) DISCUSSIONS

B3526 Weingarten, S. "Use of Phonographs in Teaching Shakespeare." *CE*, I (1939), 45-61.

B3527 Ginsberg, W. "How Helpful are Shakespeare Recordings?" *English Journal*, XXIX (1940), 289-300.

B3528 Davies, Derek J. "Getting Shakespeare Taped." *Use of English*, Spring, 1956, pp. 184-188.

B3529 W., M. "Recording Shakespeare." *English*, XII (1958), 103-104.

(3) PERFORMANCES
(a) MARLOWE SOCIETY

B3530 *Othello* (Argo Record Co., London, 4 LPs). Marlowe Society of Cambridge, 1958.
Rev: by E. Martin Browne, *Drama*, Summer, 1958, pp. 36-37; by Leonard Woolf, *NstN*, Aug. 2, p. 143; by Stephen Spender, *Encounter*, Oct., pp. 83-84.

B3531 *As You Like It* (Argo Record Co., London, 3 LPs). Marlowe Society of Cambridge, 1958.
Rev: by E. Martin Browne, *Drama*, Summer, 1958, pp. 36-37; by Leonard Woolf, *NstN*, Aug. 2, p. 143; by Stephen Spender, *Encounter*, Oct., pp. 83-84.

B3532 *Troilus and Cressida* (Argo Record Co., London, 4 LPs). Marlowe Society of Cambridge, 1958.
Rev: by E. Martin Browne, *Drama*, Summer, 1958, pp. 36-37; by Leonard Woolf, *NstN*, Aug. 2, p. 143; by Stephen Spender, *Encounter*, Oct., pp. 83-84.

B3533 *Richard II* (Argo Record Co., London, LP recording). Marlowe Society of Cambridge, 1958.

B3534 *Julius Caesar* (Argo Record Co., London, LP recording). Marlowe Society of Cambridge, 1958.

B3535 *Coriolanus* (Argo Record Co., London, LP recording). Marlowe Society of Cambridge, 1958.

B3536 "Listeners' Shakespeare." *TLS*, April 11, 1958, p. 195.
LP recordings of *Oth.*, *A.Y.L.*, and *Troi.* by the Marlowe Society of Cambridge Univ. (Issued by the Argo Record Co.).

B3537 Spender, Stephen. "Speaking of Shakespeare." *Encounter*, Oct., 1958.
Review of the Shak. plays recorded by the Marlowe Society, Argo Record Co.

(b) OLD VIC

B3538 *Romeo and Juliet.* Recorded by the Old Vic Company. Juliet: Claire Bloom. Romeo: Alan Badel. London: His Master's Voice; New York: Radio Corp. of America, 1953. 3 LPs.
Rev: by J. G. McManaway, *SQ*, V (1954), 202-203; *ETJ*, IX (1957), 51.

B3539 *Macbeth.* Recorded by the Old Vic Company. Macbeth: Alec Guinness. Lady Macbeth: Pamela Brown. London: His Master's Voice; New York: Radio Corp. of America, 1954. 2 LPs.
Rev: by James G. McManaway, *SQ*, V (1954), 202-203.

B3540 *A Midsummer Night's Dream.* Recorded by the Old Vic Company. New York: Radio Corporation of America, 1954. 3 LPs.
Rev: by Irving Kolodin, "The 'Dream' Book," *SatR*, Sept. 25, 1954, p. 50; by James G. McManaway, *SQ*, VI (1955), 351-352.

B3541 *Hamlet* (RCA Victor, 2 LPs). Old Vic Company recording with Sir John Gielgud, 1957.
Rev: by Henry Hewes, *SatR*, Nov. 23, 1957, p. 33; *Time*, Dec. 9, pp. 114, 116; by Roy Plomley, *Theatre World*, Dec., p. 47.

(c) MISCELLANEOUS

B3542 Wonnberger, Carl. "The Mercury *Macbeth.*" *English Journal*, XXX (1941), 860-861.
On the Orson Welles-Roger Hill edition designed to accompany the recording. Publ. by Harper.

B3543 Robeson, P., et al. "*Othello.*" 3 albums, Columbia Master Works.
Rev: by M. A. Schubert, "The Columbia Recording of *Othello*," *New York Times*, Jan. 14, 1945, Section 2, p. X 5.

B3544 "*An Evening with William Shakespeare with an All Star Cast.*" Direction and narration by Margaret Webster. 2 LPs. New York: Theatre Masterworks, 1953.
Rev: by Fredson Bowers, *SQ*, V (1954), 330-331.

B3545 "*Sixteen Sonnets of William Shakespeare.*" 1 LP. Read by David Allen. New York: Poetry Records, 1954.
Music in the Elizabethan style composed by Curtis Biever and played on the harp by Margaret Ross.
Rev: by Alice Griffin, *SQ*, V (1954), 422.

B3546 *A Collection of Thirty-two Madrigals Dedicated to Queen Elizabeth.* Randolph Singers, Westminster, WAL 212, 1954. A recording.
Rev: by Dorothy E. Mason, *SQ*, V (1954), 85.

B3547 "*Poetry Series.*" (Readings from William Shakespeare and Rudyard Kipling by John A. Nist). Ypsilanti, Michigan: Idiom Recording Company. Division of Field Services. Michigan State Normal College, 1955. LPs.
Includes some of the sonnets and songs.
Rev: by John T. Muri, *English Journal*, XLIV (1955), 439.

B3548   Kökeritz, Helge. *Examples of Shakespeare's Pronunciation: A Recording.* Bridgeport, Conn.: Columbia Records, Inc., 1955. 10″ LP.
    Rev: by F. G. Cassidy, *CE*, XVI (1955), 199.

B3549   Kozelka, Paul. "New Shakespearean Recordings." *Audio-Visual Guide*, XX (Feb., 1954), 12-14.
    Reviews 3 current Shak. records: *Romeo and Juliet*, with the Old Vic Company (RCA Victor, LP); *John Barrymore Reads Shakespeare*, with scenes from *Hamlet, Twelfth Night, Richard III, Macbeth* (Dauntless Internat'l, LP); *Golden Age of the Theatre*, with Edwin Booth as Othello and Ellen Terry as Portia (Dauntless Internat'l, LP).

B3550   Kozelka, Paul. "Evaluation of Two Shakespearean Records." *Audio-Visual Guide*, XXII (Oct., 1955), 16-17.
    Reviews some recorded scenes from Castellani's *Romeo* film production on a CBS 12″, 33⅓ record, and Maurice Evans in scenes from *Hamlet* and *Richard II* (CBS, 12″, 33⅓).

B3551   "Extracts from Shakespeare." Sonnet 71. Mercy (from *M. of V.*). The seven ages of man (from *AYLI*). The funeral oration of Marc Antony (from *Jul. Caes.*). Speakers: Christopher Hassall and Jill Balcon. Paris: Disque Pléiade, 1955.

B3552   "Famous Dialogues." *AYLI* III, 2; *R. & J.* I, 5 and III, 5; *M. of V.* V, 1. Speakers: Robert Speaight and Heather Black. Paris: Disque Pléiade, 1956.

B3553   "*Hamlet* and *Henry V.*" Sir Laurence Olivier and the Philharmonica Orchestra with music by Sir William Walton. London: His Master's Voice, 1956. Extracts.

B3554   "Twenty Sonnets and Scenes from *As You Like It.*" Speaker: Dame Edith Evans. Columbia LP, 1956.

B3555   *The Merchant of Venice.* Recording with Michael Redgrave as Shylock. Caedmon, 2 LPs.
    Rev: *Time*, Dec. 9, 1957, p. 116.

B3556   "Hamlet Goes on Record." *Plays and Players*, Nov., 1957, p. 13.
    Review of H.M.V.'s complete recording.

B3557   Slocumb, Paul. "Players on Record." *Players Magazine*, Jan., 1957, p. 83.
    Westminster long-play record *Scenes from Shakespeare* by Paul Rogers.

B3558   *Shakespeare Read by Allan Whitley.* Readings from English literature, 1. London: BBC Disques, 1958.
See also B3437.

XV. OTHER ASPECTS OF SHAKESPEARE'S INFLUENCE THROUGH THE CENTURIES
1. ILLUSTRATIONS TO SHAKESPEARE'S WORKS (168;56)
a. GENERAL

B3559   Woodward, John. "Shakespeare and English Painting." *Listener*, XLIII (June 15, 1950), 1017-18, 1030.

B3560   Weitenkampf, F. "American Illustrators of Shakespeare." *New York Public Library Bulletin*, Feb., 1956, pp. 70-72.

B3561   Merchant, William Moelwyn. *Shakespeare and the Artist: Artist, Illustrator and Designer as Interpreters of the Text.* Oxford Univ. Press, 1959. Pp. xxx, 254.

b. BY PERIOD
(1) SEVENTEENTH AND EIGHTEENTH CENTURIES

B3562   Summers, Montague. "The First Illustrated Shakespeare." *Connoisseur*, 102 (1938), 305-309.
    The Shakespeare is the Rowe edition of 1709.

B3563   Chambers, Sir E. K. *Shakespearean Gleanings.* Oxford Univ. Press, 1944.
    V: "The First Illustration to Shakespeare."
    Rev: B4466.

B3564   Boase, Thomas Sherrer Ross. "Illustrations of Shakespeare's Plays in the Seventeenth and Eighteenth Centuries." *JWCI*, X (1947), 83-108.

B3565   Byrne, M. St. Clare. "Bell's Shakespeare." *TLS*, Jan. 31, 1948, p. 65.
    Discussion as to what year in the 1770's.

B3566   Hammelmann, H. A. "Eighteenth Century Illustrators: Francis Hayman, R. A." *The Book Collector*, II (1953), 116-132.

B3567   "Blake Water-Colours: Illustrations from the British Museum's Newly-acquired Second Folio." *Illustrated London News*, 225 (Dec. 25, 1954), 1163.

B3568   Merchant, William M. "A Poussin *Coriolanus* in Rowe's 1709 Shakespeare." *BJRL*, XXXVII (1954), 13-16.
    A report of an unusual engraving in a copy of Rowe's Shak. acquired by the Library.

B3569   Merchant, W. M. "John Runciman's *Lear in the Storm.*" *JWCI*, XVII (1954), 385-387.

B3570   Boase, Thomas Sherrer Ross. "An Extra-Illustrated Second Folio of Shakespeare." *British Museum Quarterly*, XX (1955), 4-8.
    The copy of F_2 recently purchased by the B. M. containing single well-known water colors by William Blake and drawings by other artists of *ca.* 1800.

B3571   "Falstaff and the Prince." *Country Life*, April 26, 1956, p. 856.
        A scene from *Henry IV*, by or after Francis Hayman, reproduced.

B3572   Hammelmann, H. A. "Shakespeare Illustration: The Earliest Known Originals Designed
        and Drawn by Gravelot." *Connoisseur*, 141 (1958), 144-149.
        Reproductions and text on Gravelot's illustrations.

B3573   Burnim, Kalman A. "The Significance of Garrick's Letters to Hayman." *SQ*, IX (1958),
        149-152.
        Two holograph letters (in the Folger Library) by Garrick to Francis Hayman.

B3574   Merchant, W. M. "Francis Hayman's Illustrations of Shakespeare." *SQ*, IX (1958), 141-147.
        Discussion of illustrations for the Thomas Hanmer Shak. (1744), some of which follow
        designs suggested by Garrick. Eight full-page plates.

(2) NINETEENTH CENTURY

B3575   *La Tragédie de Hamlet*. Tr. par Jules Derocquigny, ornée de 16 lithographies par Delacroix.
        Le Livre et l'Estampe, No. 5. Paris: Horizons de France, 1942. Pp. 159.

B3576   Cazamian, L., and A. Koszul. "Une Curiosité Littéraire." *EA*, VII (Oct., 1954), 353-361.
        Some account of Daniel O'Sullivan (1800-1866) and his connection with *Les Femmes de
        Shakespeare* (Paris, 1860).

B3577   "Scenes from Shakespeare's Plays As Seen Through the Painter's Eye." *Wisdom*, July, 1956,
        pp. 14-19.
        Paintings of various scenes, each accompanied by a brief quotation.

(3) TWENTIETH CENTURY
See also sections on individual plays,
modern editions.

B3578   Tilney, F. C., designer. "Shakespeare Playing Cards (52)." London, 1937.
        (With a note on the designs by F. C. T.)

B3579   Tannenbaum, Samuel A. "Shakespeare Illustrated." *SAB*, XIII (1938), 192.
        On Edward A. Wilson's illustrations, now available in prints.

B3580   Limited Editions Club [Shakespeare]: *Works*. Limited, numbered, signed edition by Herbert
        Farjeon. New York: Limited Ed. Club, 1939-41. Illustrations.
        Includes the following illustrators: Enric-Cristobal Ricart, Sylvain Sauvage, John Austen,
        C. Pal Molnar, Yngve Berg, Edy Legrand, Barnett Freedman, Edw. Bawden, Vera Willoughby,
        Graham Sutherland, Carlotta Petrina, Jean Charlot, Eric Gill, Frans Masereel, Boardman
        Robinson, Mariette Lydis, Gordon Craig, Steiner-Prog, René ben Sussan, Gordon Ross, Arthur
        Rackham, Fritz Kredel, Rob. Gibbings, Agnes Miller Parker, N. Fyodorovitch Lapshin,
        D. Galanis, Francesco Carnevali, Pierre Brissaud, Albert Rutherston.

B3581   Daudet, Léon. *Le Voyage de Shakespeare. Bois Gravés Originaux de Léon Masson.* 2 Vols.
        Paris: Les Editions de la Nouvelle France, 1943.

B3582   Lamb, Charles and Mary. *Tales from Shakespeare.* (Ils. by E. Blaisdell). New York: T. Y.
        Crowell Co., 1943. Pp. 360.

B3583   *Macbeth.* New York: Doubleday, Doran, 1946. Pp. 25. Twelve plates by Salvador Dali.
        Rev: *Time*, Dec. 9, 1946, pp. 112, 114; by W. Gibbs, *NYTBR*, Dec. 15, p. 6.

B3584   Criswell, Cloyd M. "A Note on Mr. F. Roberts Johnson's Line Drawings for *Hamlet*."
        SAB, XXIV (1949), 54-55.

B3585   *Hamlet . . . in Block Prints* by Dorothy N. Stewart. Santa Fe, New Mexico, 1949. Pp. 34.

B3586   *As You Like It.* London: Folio Society, 1954. Pp. 95.
        Contains an introduction by Peter Brook and eight designs of "décor and costumes" by
        Salvador Dali.
        Rev: B6887.

B3587   Lamb, Charles and Mary. *Tales from Shakespeare, from the Collection by Charles and Mary
        Lamb, with Illustrations by Geoffrey Whittam.* Stories Old and New. London: Blackie, 1955.
        Pp. 2, 157.

B3588   Lamb, Charles and Mary. *More Tales from Shakespeare.* Simplified by G. Horsley, illustrated
        by Geoffrey Whittam. Simplified English Series. London: Longmans Green, 1956. Pp. 112.

B3589   *King Lear.* Introd. by Donald Wolfit, with Designs in Colour by Noguchi. London: Folio
        Society, 1956. Pp. 128.
        Illustrations are reproductions of the designs for the sets and costumes of the recent European
        tour of the Shak. Memorial Theatre Company.

B3590   Lamb, Charles and Mary. *Favorite Tales from Shakespeare.* Ed. for modern readers by Morris
        Schreiber. New York: Grosset & Dunlap, 1956. Pp. 104. Illustrated by Donald Lynch.
        London: Publicity Products, 1957. Pp. [61].

B3591   Lamb, Charles and Mary. *Tales from Shakespeare.* Illustrated by Arthur Rackham. London:
        Dent, 1957.
        Rev: *TLS* (Children's Books Section), Nov. 15, 1957, xii-xiii.

B3592   *Macbeth.* Ill. de 20 eaux-fortes originales gravées par Marcel Gromaire.   Paris: Ed. Verve, 1958.

B3593   Lamb, Charles and Mary.   *Tales from Shakespeare.*   Color Plates by A. E. Jackson.   Sunshine Series.   London: Ward, Lock, 1958.   Pp. 129.

2.   MUSICAL SETTINGS OF SHAKESPEARE WORKS, SONGS, ETC. (169;57)
a.   GENERAL STUDIES (169;57)
(1)   SETTINGS AND ACCOMPANIMENTS

B3594   Rhedecynian.   "Shakespeare, Handel and Gervinus."   *N &Q,* 171 (1936), 327-328.
Notes on A. G. Gervinus' "Parallele" between Shakespeare and Handel (1868).

B3595   Castelnuovo-Tedesco, Mario.   "Shakespeare and Music."   *SAB,* xv (1940), 166-174.
Music in his plays and subsequent settings.

B3596   Davis, Reginald.   *Shakespeare's Contribution to Music.*   MA thesis, Ottawa, 1943.   Pp. 99.
Contemporaneous music and instruments, Shak.'s songs, stage directions, musical allusions, terminology.   Orchestral masterpieces that have been written to Shak. themes.

B3597   Gui, Vittorio.   "La *Tempesta* a Boboli (considerazioni musicali)."   *Il Ponte,* iv (1948), 684-698.

B3598   Brennecke, Ernest.   " 'What Shall He Have that Killed the Deer?'   A Note on Shakespeare's Lyric and Its Music."   *Musical Times,* 93 (1952), 347-351.
Prints score of a 1652 version of the music and discusses the lyric and its proper form.

B3599   Engel, Lehman.   *Music for the Classical Tragedy.*   New York: Flammer, 1953.   Pp. 96.
Rev: B1839.

B3600   Long, John H.   "Music for the Replica Staging of Shakespeare."   Ed. Matthews and Emery   *Studies in Shakespeare,* 1953, pp. 88-95.

B3601   Moore, Robert E.   "Music for Shakespearian Performance."   *TLS,* Aug. 21, 1953, p. 535.
Requests information as to the existence or whereabouts of music written to accompany Shak. performances in London during the Restoration and 18th century.

B3602   Cohen, S. J.   "*A Midsummer Night's Dream:* Shakespeare's Magical Creation Has Lured Many Composers to Attempt Musical Settings."   *Musical America,* LXXIV (Sept., 1954), 5, 18.

B3603   Sternfeld, Frederick W.   "*Troilus and Cressida:* Music for the Play."   *EIE, 1952* (1954), 107-137.
Rev: by J. H. Long, *SQ,* vi (1955), 189-190.

B3604   Walker, G. G.   "Shakespeare and Music."   *Etude,* LXXIII (Sept., 1955), 54.

B3605   *Sonety Shekspira.*   Desiat Sonetov Shekspira.   Moscow, 1957.   Pp. 37.
Musical settings for Shak.'s sonnets.

B3606   Chambers, H. A., ed.   *A Shakespeare Song Book.*   Three centuries of music settings for Shakespeare's Plays.   (With score.)   London: Brandford Press, 1956.   Pp. 62 and 24.
Rev: *Musical Opinion,* 80 (1957), 599.

(2)   OPERATIC VERSIONS (-;57)

B3607   Seymour, John L.   *Drama and Libretto: A Study of Four Libretto Adaptations of Two of Shakespeare's Plays.*   DD, University of California, 1940.

B3608   Gregor, Joseph.   *Kulturgeschichte der Oper.*   Ihre Verbindung mit dem Leben, den Werken des Geistes und der Politik.   Vienna: Gallus Verlag, 1941.   Pp. 426.

B3609   Duncan, Ronald.   "How *The Rape of Lucrece* Became an Opera."   *Shakespeare Quarterly* (London), i (Summer, 1947), 95-100.
How Shak.'s poem influenced him in composing his libretto.   With animal versi ons upon modifications of Shak. in operatic productions.

B3610   Rebora, Piero.   "Comprensione e Fortuna di Shakespeare in Italia."   *CL,* i (1949), 210-224.
Includes opera.

B3611   Parkhurst, Charles Edward.   *A Comparative Analysis of Selected European Opera Libretto Adaptations of the Romeo and Juliet Legend.*   DD, Northwestern University, 1953.   Pp. 549.   Mic A53-2207.   *DA,* xiii (1953), 1304.   Publication No. 6232.   Those of Sanseverino (1773), Gotter (1776), Ségur (1793), Foppa (1796), Romani (1825 & 1830), Marcello (1865), Barbier (1867), D'Ivry (1878), Barkworth (1916), Rossato (1922).

B3612   Koegler, Horst.   "Drei Variationen über ein Thema von Shakespeare.   Ein Beitr. z. Operndramaturgie."   *Schweizerische Musikztg.,* 94, No. 3 (1954), 95-99.

B3613   Cutts, John P.   "The Original Music to Middleton's *The Witch.*"   *SQ,* vii (1956), 203-209.
The availability in 1673 of Middleton's *Witch* songs may have been due to original music manuscripts handed down by the King's Men Musicians.

B3614   Dace, William.   "A Survey of Opera in Modern Translation, with Short Production Notes."   *ETJ,* viii (1956), 229-245.
Includes account of such Shak. adaptations as *Romeo and Juliet* by Boris Blacher, *Romeo and Juliet* by Charles Gounod, *Romeo and Juliet* by Franz Von Suppé, *The Taming of the Shrew* by Hermann Goetz, *The Merry Wives of Windsor* by Otto Nicolai, *Falstaff* [from *Wives*] by Giuseppe Verdi, *Macbeth* by Verdi, and *Otello* by Verdi.

b. INDIVIDUAL COMPOSERS (169;-)
(1) ELIZABETHAN AND CAROLINE

B3615 Evans, W. McC. "Lawes' Version of Shakespeare's Sonnet, CXVI." *PMLA*, LI (1936), 120-122.

B3616 Evans, W. McC. *Henry Lawes, Musician and Friend of Poets*. New York: Modern Language Association of America, 1940. Pp. xvi, 250.

B3617 Beck, Sydney. "The Case of 'O Mistresse Mine'." *RN*, VI (1954), 19-23.
The most likely setting is Thomas Morley's in *Consort Lessons*, and also William Byrd's *Fitzwilliam Virginal Book*.

B3617a Long, John H. "The Case of 'O Mistresse Mine'." *RN*, VII (1954), 15-16.
Examines the evidence put forward in B3617.

B3617b Duckles, Vincent. "New Light on 'O Mistresse Mine'." *RN*, VII (1955), 98-100.
Refers to B3617a.

B3618 Stevens, Denis. *The Five Songs in Shakespeare's "As You Like It"*. Adapted and arranged from sources contemporary with the play. London: Hinrichson, 1957.
Rev: A6181.

B3619 Cutts, John P. "Two Hitherto Unpublished Settings of Sonnets from *The Passionate Pilgrime*." *SQ*, IX (1958), 588-594.
The settings, reproduced here, occur side by side in a Bodleian MS. of John Wilson's songs, dating *c*. 1614. Both deal with Adonis.

(2) RESTORATION

B3620 Rosen, Waldemar. "*Der Sommernachtstraum* mit Purcell-Musik." Uraufführung in der Leipziger Oper. *Allg. Musikzeitung*, LXIV (1937), 151.

B3621 Westrup, J. A. *Purcell*. London: Dent, 1937.
Rev: *TLS*, Apr. 3, 1937, p. 251.

B3622 Sands, Mollie. "The Bicentenary of Arne's Songs in *As You Like It*." *N &Q*, 174 (1940), 416-417.

B3623 Dunkin, Paul S. "Issues of *The Fairy Queen*, 1692: An Operatic Adaptation of *Midsummer Night's Dream*." *Library*, Series 4, XXVI (1946), 297-304.

B3624 Ward, Charles E. "*The Tempest*: A Restoration Opera Problem." *ELH*, XIII (1946), 119-130.

B3625 Milton, William M. "*Tempest* in a Teapot." *ELH*, XIV (1947), 207-218.
On whether Shadwell wrote an opera on the *Tempest*.

B3626 McManaway, James G., ed. "Songs and Masques in *The Tempest* [*c*. 1674]." *Theatre Miscellany*, No. 14. Oxford: Basil Blackwell for the Luttrell Society, 1953, pp. 69-96.
Rev: by Harold Jenkins, *RES*, NS, VI (1955), 86-88.

B3627 Haywood, Charles. "The Songs and Masques in the *New Tempest*: An Incident in the Battle of the Two Theaters, 1674." *HLQ*, XIX (1955), 39-56.
Reports the discovery, in the Huntington Library, of this second English libretto, supporting the hypothesis of James G. McManaway. Further light is shed on the ensuing conflict between the Duke's and the King's players.
Rev: B3626.

B3628 Emslie, Macdonald. "Pepys' Shakespeare Song." *SQ*, VI (1955), 159-170.
Prints Cesare Morelli's musical setting—from Pepys' library—for 'To be, or not to be'."
Shows Pepys' interest in dramatic recitative and the age's use of blank verse for recitative, and offers a possible clue to Betterton's delivery.

(3) EIGHTEENTH CENTURY

B3629 Stone, George Winchester. "Garrick, and An Unknown Operatic Version of *Love's Labour's Lost*." *RES*, XV (1939), 323-328.

B3630 Cancelled.

B3631 Einstein, Alfred. "Mozart und Shakespeares *Tempest*." *Monatshefte f. dt. Unterricht*, XXXVI (1944), 43-48.

B3632 Frings, Joseph Kardinal. "Shakespeare und Mozart. Kriterien eines Vergleichs." *Rhein. Merkur*, VII, No. 18 (1952), 8.

(4) NINETEENTH CENTURY
(a) BERLIOZ

B3633 Spencer, Bessie. *The Influence of Shakespeare on the Life and Work of Hector Berlioz*. DD, Leeds, 1936. Abstr. publ. in University of Leeds *Publications and Abstracts of Theses*, 1935/36, p. 20.
Shak. the chief influence. All B's work revealing Shak. influence dealt with from musical and literary viewpoints.

B3634 Zeijen, M. H. Jac. "Goethe, Shakespeare et Virgile dans l' Œuvre de Berlioz." *LT*, 144 (1948), 55-63; 145 (1948), 116-121.

B3635 Barzun, Jacques. "Berlioz and the Bard." *SRL*, XXXIII (April 29, 1950), 45-46, 61.

(b) VERDI

B3636 Bundi, Gian. "Verdi und Shakespeare." *Der Bund* (Bern), 1936, Lit. Beil. Nos. 39-41.

B3637 Toye, F. "New Verdi Correspondence." *Music and Letters*, XVII (1936), 368-370.
Discussing *Falstaff* and *Othello*.

B3638 Brümmer, Eugen. "Verdi und Shakespeare." *Allgem. Musikztg.*, LXIV (1937), 129-131.

B3639 Valentin, Erich. "Schiller, Shakespeare und Verdi. Eine Stilgeschichtliche Betrachtung."
VB, IV, No. 12 (1937). Also in *Dts. Volksbildung*, XIII (1938/39), 22-24.

B3640 White, E. W. "Verdi and Shakespeare." *Life and Letters*, XVIII (1938), 120-123.

B3641 Hussey, D. "Verdi and Shakespeare." *Spectator*, 162 (1939), 997.

B3642 Farinelli, Arturo. "Verdi e Shakespeare." *Nuova antologia*, 410 (1940), 214-229.

B3643 O'Neal, Cothburn Madison. *A Study of the Verdi-Boito Operatic Versions of Shakespeare's Plays.*
DD, University of Texas, 1940.

B3644 Sear, H. G. "Operatic Morality." *Music and Letters*, XXI (1940), 60-74.
Sundry comments upon Verdi's *Otello* and Rossini's *Otello*.

B3645 Downes, O. "Verdi's *Falstaff* Sung in New York." *New York Times*, Jan. 15, 1943, p. 11.

B3646 Beiswanger, G. " 'From Eleven to Two'. Verdi's *Falstaff* in English." *TAr*, XXVIII (1944),
289-295.

B3647 Kames, Johanna. *Die Verdi-Opern nach Shakespeare-Dramen.* DD, Vienna, 1948. Pp. 158.
Typewritten.

B3648 Huschke, Konrad. "Verdi und Shakespeare." *Theater d. Zeit*, V, V (1950), 34.

B3649 Ruppel, Karl H. "Verdi und Shakespeare." *Das Musikleben* (Mainz), IV (1951), 35-38.

B3650 Shawe-Taylor, Desmond. "Verdi and Shakespeare." *NstN*, XLIV (1952), 39.

B3651 Kernan, Joseph. "Verdi's *Otello*, or Shakespeare Explained." *Hudson Review*, VI (1953),
266-277.

B3652 Holl, Karl. "Zu Verdis Othello." *Shakespeare-Tage* (Bochum), No. 3779, 1954, pp. 25-30.

B3653 Nolan, Edward F. "Verdi's *Macbeth*." *Renaissance Papers* (Univ. of South Carolina, 1954),
pp. 49-56.

B3654 Dean, Winton. "Verdi and Shakespeare." *Opera* (London), 1955, pp. 480-484.

B3655 Hope-Wallace, Philip. "*Otello*." *Time and Tide*, XXXVI (1955), 1371.
Covent Garden turns to Verdi's *Otello* and likes it.

B3656 "Dark Mystery: *Othello*." *Musical America*, Aug., 1956, p. 17.
Whether Othello was originally really a Moor or only a dark Venetian so nicknamed. Relative
to acting in Verdi's *Othello*.

B3657 Ruppel, K. H. "Verdi und Shakespeare." *Schweizerische Musikztg.*, 95 (1955), 137-141.
Also in *SJ*, 92 (1956), 7-18.

B3658 Kerman, Joseph. *Opera as Drama.* New York: Alfred A. Knopf, 1956. Pp. iv, 269.
Includes a discussion of Verdi's *Otello*.
Rev: by Nan Cooke Carpenter, *CL*, X (1958), 90-91; by Janet Leeper, *Drama*, Autumn,
p. 41; *Music and Letters*, XXXIX, 289-291; by Mosco Gardner, *Time and Tide*, Aug. 16, 1958,
p. 1000.

B3659 Larson, Lena. "Glyndebourne 1957." *Theatre World*, Sept., 1957, pp. 53-54.
Carl Ebert's production of Verdi's *Falstaff*.

B3660 Schueller, Herbert M. "*Othello* Transformed: Verdi's Interpretation of Shakespeare." *Studies
in Honor of John Wilcox*, pp. 129-156.

(c) OTHERS

B3661 Gilman, L. "Notes on R. Strauss's Tone Poem 'Macbeth'." New York *Stadium Concerts R.*,
August 1, 1937, pp. 9-13.

B3662 Tchaikowsky, P. I. "Incidental Music to *Hamlet*." Victor Record No. 13760 (London Phil-
harmonic Orchestra). Overture, Op. 67b.

B3663 Schubert-Liszt. "Hark, Hark, the Lark!" *Etude*, LXIII (1945), 629-630.
Music only.

B3664 Capell, Richard. "Schubert and Shakespeare." *Shakespeare Quarterly* (London), I (Summer,
1947), 101-106.

(5) TWENTIETH CENTURY
(a) SUTERMEISTER

B3665 Gerigk, Herbert. "*Romeo und Julia* als Oper." *Die Musik*, XXXII (1939/40), 279-280.
In Dresden.

B3666 Sutermeister, Heinrich. *Romeo und Julia. Oper in 2 Akten.* Mainz: Schott, 1940. Pp. 32.

B3667 Sénéchaud, Marcel. "Sutermeister and (his opera) *Romeo and Juliet*." *Opera* (London), 1953,
pp. 153-156.

(b) ZILLIG

B3668 Zillig, Winfried. *Troilus und Cressida*. Oper nach William Shakespeare. Wiesbaden: Brucknerverlag, 1950. Pp. 40.

B3669 Beckmann, Heinz. "Cressida aus Bayreuth." Düsseldorfer Uraufführung einer Shakespeare-Oper. *Rhein. Merkur*, VI, No. 7 (1951), 8.

B3670 Schab, Günter. "Winfried Zillig: *Troilus and Cressida*." *Das Musikleben*, IV (1951), 83.

B3670a Schab, Günter. "Zillig's *Troilus und Cressida* in Düsseldorf. Eine Chor-Oper nach Shakespeare." *Melos*, XVIII (1951), 113-114.

(c) OTHERS

B3671 Bertram, Ernst. *Prosperos Heimkehr. Eine Gedenkmusik z. Wiederkehr von William Shakespeares Todestag.* Donauwörth: Cassianeum, 1951. Pp. 115.

B3672 Blacher, Boris. *Romeo und Julia.* Kammeroper frei nach Shakespeare. Vienna: Universal-Ed., 1950. Pp. 24.

B3673 Cohen, A. "E. Bloch's *Macbeth*." *Music and Letters*, XIX (1938), 143-148.

B3674 Smidt, Kristian. "A Norwegian Operatic *Cymbeline*." *SQ*, III (1952), 284.
A new work composed by Arne Eggen.

B3675 Atkinson, Brooks. " 'Swinging' Shakespeare's *Dream:* With Benny Goodman, Louis Armstrong and Maxine Sullivan." *New York Times*, Nov. 30, 1939, p. 24. (See other New York papers of same date).
With Negro jitterbugs. Scene is New Orleans.

B3676 Gilman, L. "Notes on Prelude to Shakespeare's *Tempest* by A. Honegger." *New York Stadium Concerts R.*, August 1, 1937, pp. 7-8.

B3677 "Arthur Küsterers Oper *Was ihr wollt*." *MDtShG*, II (1950), 8-9.

B3678 Saather, F. "*Tempest* by F. Martin." *Music Quarterly*, XLII (1956), 533-535.
Discussion of Martin's opera, *The Tempest*.

B3679 Johnson, H. "H. Menges' Music for *Henry IV*." *New York Post*, May 6, 1946, p. 26.

B3680 Woerner, Karl H. "Orff und Shakespeare." *Musica*, VII (1953), 21-22.

B3681 Szyfman, Arnold. "Poland." *World Theater*, IV, No. 3 (1955), 73-74.
Prokofiev's opera, *Romeo and Juliet*, in Warsaw.

B3682 Wyatt, E. V. "*Errors* as a Musical Comedy." *Catholic World*, 148 (1939), 474-478.
Rodgers & Hart's musical version of *Errors* called *The Boys from Syracuse*.

B3683 Shawe-Taylor, Desmond. "The Arts and Entertainment." *NstN*, Feb. 23, 1957, pp. 232-233.
Sir William Walton's opera, *Troilus and Cressida*.

B3684 Babler, O. F. "Shakespeare's *Tempest* as an Opera." *N &Q*, 196 (1951), 30-31.
Quotes a letter by Hugo Wolf, in which he discusses his intentions of writing an opera based on Shak.'s play.

B3685 Kiessig, Martin. "*Was ihr wollt*. Eine neue Bühnenmusik zu Shakespeares klassischer Komödie." *VB*, Oct. 11, 1938.

B3686 Papenroth, Kurt. "Die *Komödie der Irrungen* als Oper. Eine Uraufführung in Beuthen." *MNN*, No. 83, March 24, 1941.

B3687 Hausswald, Günter. "Oper nach Shakespeares *Sturm*." *MNN*, No. 307, Nov. 11, 1942.

B3688 "*Romeo and Juliet*, Done in Gang Style. *West Side Story* is a Fine Dancing Show." *Life*, Sept. 16, 1957, pp. 103-108.
Musical, dealing with juvenile delinquency, borrows from *Romeo*.

B3689 "The Show's the Thing." *Newsweek*, Oct. 7, 1957, pp. 102-105.
Review of *West Side Story*.

B3690 "New Musical in Manhattan: *West Side Story*." *Time*, Oct. 7, 1957, pp. 48-49.

B3691 Gassner, John. "Broadway in Review." *ETJ*, IX (1958), 311-320.
West Side Story.

B3692 Rice, Charles D. "Juliet Lights Up Broadway." *This Week*, Dec. 1, 1957, pp. 20-22.
Carol Lawrence, star of *West Side Story*.

B3693 "*West Side Story*." *TAr*, Dec., 1957, pp. 17-18.

B3694 Wyatt, E. V. "Theatre." *Catholic World*, Dec., 1957, pp. 224-225.
West Side Story.

c. SHAKESPEARE AND THE BALLET (169;-)

B3695 Tudor, A. *Romeo and Juliet* (Ballet in one act). F. Delius, Composer. New York, 1943.

B3696 Martin, J. "The Dance *Romeo and Juliet*, by A. Tudor." *New York Times*, Apr. 18, 1943, Section 2, p. X,5.

B3697 Lvov-Anokhin, B. "The Film-Ballet *Romeo and Juliet*." *VOKS-Bulletin* (Moscow), No. 5, 94, (1955), 48-50.

B3698   Michaut, Pierre. "La Danse: *Roméo et Juliette*, Film-Ballet Soviétique." *La Revue de Paris*, June, 1956, pp. 168-169.
Review of the Prokofiev ballet.

B3699   Hall, Fernau. "Lifar's 'Romeo' in Paris." *SatR*, Feb. 25, 1956, p. 56.
Serge Lifar's production of Prokofiev ballet *Romeo and Juliet* at the Paris Opera.

B3700   Hope-Wallace, Philip. "The Moscow Ballet." *Time and Tide*, Oct. 13, 1956, p. 1213.
The Russian Bolshoi ballet *Romeo and Juliet* at Covent Garden.

3. PROSE VERSIONS OF SHAKESPEARE'S PLAYS (169;57)
a. CHARLES AND MARY LAMB
(1) EDITIONS IN ENGLISH

B3701   Birss, J. H. "C. Lamb's Revision of the *Tales*." *American Notes and Queries*, II (1942), 83-84.

B3702   Lamb, Charles and Mary. *Tales from Shakespeare*. Illustrations by E. Blaisdell. New York: T. Crowell Company, 1943. Pp. 360.

B3703   Lamb, Charles and Mary. *Tales from Shakespeare*. Hrsg. v. Fr. Behrens. Paderborn: Schöningh, 1947. Pp. 79.

B3704   Lamb, Charles and Mary. *Tales from Shakespeare*. New edition. London: Ward, Lock, 1949. Pp. 256.

B3705   Lamb, Charles and Mary. *Tales from Shakespeare*. Bearb. v. Fritz Kochendörffer. Karlsruhe: Braun, 1949. Pp. xi, 87.

B3706   Lamb, Charles and Mary. *Tales from Shakespeare*. New York: Macmillan, 1950. Pp. ix, 418.

B3707   Lamb, Charles. *Tales from Shakespeare: The Tempest, Macbeth*. Notes by P. Ferand and H. Sascuteanu; preface by J. Assénat. Paris: Sascot, 1954. Pp. 48.
Rev: by H. Kerst, *LanM*, XLIX, No. 1 (1955), 91-92.

B3708   Lamb, Charles and Mary. *Tales from Shakespeare*. Illustrations by Geoffrey Whittam. London: Blackie, 1955. Pp. 157.

B3709   Lamb, Charles and Mary. *Tales from Shakespeare*. London: Collins, 1955. Pp. 256.

B3710   Lamb, Charles and Mary. *More Tales from Shakespeare*. Simplified by G. Horsley. Illustrated by Geoffrey Whittam (Simplified English Series). London: Longmans Green, 1956. Pp. 112.

B3711   Lamb, Charles and Mary. *Favorite Tales from Shakespeare*. Ed. for modern readers by Morris Schreiber. New York: Grosset & Dunlap, 1956. Pp. 104. Illustrated by Donald Lynch. London: Publicity Products, 1957. Pp. [61].

B3712   Lamb, Charles and Mary. *Tales from Shakespeare*. London: Dent, 1957. Pp. 320.
Rev: B3591.

B3713   Lamb, Charles and Mary. *Tales from Shakespeare*. Col. plates by A. E. Jackson. London: Ward, Lock, 1958. Pp. 129.

B3714   Foxon, David. "The Chapbook Editions of the Lambs' *Tales from Shakespeare*." *The Book Collector*, Spring, 1957, pp. 41-53.

(2) TRANSLATIONS

B3715   Lamb, Charles and Mary. *Shakespeare Nacherzählt*. Tr. and introduction by Ursula Gaertner. Warendorf, West. Verlag J. Schnellsche Buchhandlung (C. Leopold), 1948. 3 Vols. Pp. 118.

B3716   Lamb, Charles and Mary. *Shakespeare-Erzählungen*. Tr. by Ernst Sander. Complete Edition with Walter Pater's Essay on Charles Lamb. Hamburg: Toth, 1949. Pp. 357.
Rev: by H. Reitz, *Welt und Wort*, IV (1949), 427.

B3717   Lamb, Charles and Mary. *Wie es Euch Gefällt und Andere Erzählungen nach Schauspielen von William Shakespeare*. Tr. by Alice Sieben. Freiburg: Herder, 1951. Pp. 172.

B3718   Lamb, Charles and Mary. *Shakespeare-Gestalten*. Tr. by Gisela Reichel. Leipzig: Wunderlich, 1956. Pp. 113.

B3719   Lamb, Charles and Mary. *Shakespeare Genfortalt*. Tr. by Johanne Kastor Hansen. Copenhagen: Henningsen, 1953. Pp. 228.

B3720   Lamb, Charles and Mary. *Shakespeares Sagor*. Tr. into Swedish by Carl Ernolv. Uppsala: Lindblad, 1947-48.

B3721   Lamb, Charles and Mary. *Vertellingen naar Shakespeare*. Tr. by A. Govaers. Louvain: Davidsfonds, 1954. Pp. 336.

B3722   Lamb, Charles and Mary. *Le Songe d'une Nuit d'Eté*. Tr. by Raymond Las Vergnas. Paris: Bias, 1954. Pp. 24.

B3723   Lamb, Charles and Mary. *Favole e racconti*. Tr. by Giulia Celenza. Milan: Corticelli, 1956. Pp. 134.

B3724   Lamb, Charles and Mary. *Cuentos de Shakespeare*. *Primera serie*. Tr. by J. Torres. Barcelona: Jano, 1956. Pp. 202.

B3725   Lamb, Charles and Mary. *Contos de Shakespeare*. Tr. by Octavia Mendes Cajado. São Paulo: Saraiva, 1954.

B3726 Lamb, Charles and Mary. *Povestiri Dupa Piesele lui Shakespeare.* (Ruman.) Tr. by Eugen B. Marian. Bucharest: Ed. Tineretului, 1956. Pp. 287.

B3727 Lamb, Charles and Mary. *Pripovedke iz Shakespeare.* Tr. into Slovene by Anton Cernigoj and Oton Zupančič. Ljubljana: Mladinska Knjiga, 1952. Pp. 310.

B3728 Lamb, Charles and Mary. *Šekspir vo prikazni.* Tr. into Macedonian by Vasil Kunoski. Slopje: Koco Racin, 1954. Pp. 207.

B3729 Lamb, Charles and Mary. *Shakespearemesék.* Tr. into Hungarian by István Vas. Budapest: Ifjusági Kiadó, 1955. Pp. 283.

B3730 Lamb, Charles and Mary. *Tregime prej Shekspirit.* Përkthyen Hilmi Agani e Mehdi Bardhi. Priština: Milladin Popoviq, 1957. Pp. 382.

B3731 Lamb, Charles and Mary. *Tales from Shakespeare.* Tr. into Japanese by Y. Nogomi. Tokyo, 1950. Pp. viii, 452. Tokyo: Iwanami, 1956. Pp. 170.

b. OTHERS
(1) GENERAL

B3732 Harrison, G. B. *New Tales from Shakespeare.* Illustr. by C. Walter Hodges. London: Nelson, 1938. Pp. 208.
       Rev: *TLS*, Dec. 10, 1938, pp. 785, 789.

B3733 Harrison, G. B. *More New Tales from Shakespeare.* London: Nelson, 1939. Pp. 220.
       A paraphrase, in the manner of Lamb's *Tales.*
       Rev: *English*, III (1940), 95-96.

B3734 Toyoda, Minoru. *Shakespeare in Japan: An Historical Survey.* Tokyo: The Iwanami Shoten, 1940. Pp. xi, 139 (in English).
       "Stories and Adaptations of Shak.'s Plays," pp. 61-74.

B3735 Gilbert, Mark. *The Short Story Shakespeare.* The story in prose with dialogue from the play. London: Earl, 1947. *Julius Caesar* and *Macbeth.*

B3736 Chute, Marchette. *Stories from Shakespeare.* New York: World Publishing Co., 1956. Pp. 351. Summaries of each play.
       Rev: *Chicago Sunday Tribune*, Aug. 26, 1956, p. 4; *Kirkus*, June 15, p. 407; *New York Times*, Aug. 26, p. 28; *English Journal*, XLV (1956), 502; by Esther Walls Pappy, *SatR*, Nov. 17, p. 67; *ShN*, VI, 42.

B3737 Joubert, J. H. S. *Verhale uit Shakespeare.* Johannesburg: Afrikaanse pers-boekhandel, 1957. Pp. 165.
       Paraphrases and tales from Shak.'s plays.

(2) SYNOPSES

B3738 Watt, H. A., Karl Julius Holzknecht, and R. Ross. *Outlines of Shakespeare's Plays.* New York: Barnes & Noble, 1938. Pp. viii, 244. Also Cambridge: Heffer, 1948. Pp. viii, 219.

B3738a Watt, Homer A. *Outlines of Shakespeare's Plays.* Revised edition. New York: Barnes & Noble, 1957. Pp. 212.

B3739 Deutsch, Babette. *The Reader's Shakespeare* (16 stories). New York: Julian Messner, 1946. Pp. 510.
       Rev: by A. S. Morris, *NYTBR*, Dec. 15, 1946, p. 6.

B3740 Drury, F. K. W. *Drury's Guide to Best Plays.* Washington: Scarecrow Press, 1954. Pp. 367. Gives synopses of over 1200 of the world's best plays from Sophocles to Tennessee Williams.
       Rev: *TLS*, Apr. 23, 1954, p. 270.

B3741 Gregor, Joseph. *Der Schauspielführer.* Stuttgart: Hiersemann, 1955.
       Summaries of 30 of Shak.'s plays, pp. 146-208.
       Rev: by M. Gravier, *RHT*, VII (1955), 358-360.

(3) SINGLE PLAYS

B3742 *The Student's Shakespeare. Tales and Scenes of Shakespeare's Plays.* Ed. by Max Draber. Leipzig: Teubner, 1936. Pp. 63.
       5. *Hamlet.*

B3743 Young, F. B. "*Hamlet* Told as a Short Story." *Scholastic*, XXVIII (Apr., 1936), 4-6.

B3744 *The Student's Shakespeare. Tales and Scenes of Shakespeare's Plays.* Ed. by Max Draber. Leipzig: Teubner, 1938. Pp. 34.
       1. *Caesar.*

B3745 Dierick, D. *Pericles. Naverteld naar William Shakespeare.* Hasselt: Maris, 1949. Pp. 32. "Retold after Shak."

B3746 Seidelin, Anna Sophie. *Hamlet. En genfortaelling.* Copenhagen: Wivel, 1950. Pp. 127.

B3747 *Julius Caesar. A Complete Paraphrase.* Ed. by Lyddon Roberts. London: Normal Press, 1950. Pp. 61.

B3748 *Henry V. Paraphrase.* Ed. by Isabel Young. London: Normal Press, 1950. Pp. 80.

B3749 *The Merchant of Venice: A Summary and Appreciation.* London: Clematis Publ., 1953. Pp. 39.

B3750   *Romeo and Juliet: A Summary and Appreciation.* London: Clematis Publ., 1953. Pp. 40.

B3751   *Le Marchand de Venise.* Raconté par Jean Muray. Illustrations by Jean Reschofsky. Idéal-Bibliothèque, 124. Paris: Hachette, 1957. Pp. 186.

(4) CHILDREN'S VERSIONS

B3752   Bocholt, H. van. *De Mooiste Vertelsels van Shakespeare.* Oudenaarde: Sanderus, 1949. Pp. 135.

B3753   Branson, Laura. *The Living Shakespeare* [Told in prose]. London: Newnes.
   1. *A Midsummer Night's Dream; Henry V; The Merchant of Venice,* 1951.
   2. *Julius Caesar; Twelfth Night; Macbeth,* 1951.
   3. *The Tempest; Richard II; As You Like It,* 1951.
   4. *Much Ado About Nothing, Henry IV,* Pt. 1; *Hamlet,* 1951.
   5. *Henry IV,* Pt. 2; *Richard III; Henry VIII,* 1953.

B3754   Brown, John Mason. "Knock, Knock, Knock!" *SRL,* XXXIII (July 29, 1950), 22-24; ibid., Sept. 2, 1956, pp. 26.
   Review of the comic book version of *Macbeth* (unfavorable).

B3755   Dodd, E. F. *Three Shakespeare Comedies* [retold]. London: Macmillan, 1954. Pp. 56.

B3756   Dodd, E. F. *Six Tales from Shakespeare* (Macmillan's Stories to Remember in Simple English). London: Macmillan, 1954. Pp. 97.
   Rev: *The Hindu* (Madras), weekly edition, Jan. 10, 1954, p. 11.

B3757   Dodd, E. F. *Three Shakespearian Tragedies Told by E. F. Dodd.* (Stories to Remember Series). London: Macmillan, 1956. Pp. 142.

B3758   Lang, Jenny. *Stories from Shakespeare. Told to Beginners.* Ed. by Heinz Thieme. Paderborn: Schöningh, 1938. Pp. 93.

B3759   Martin, Constance M., ed. *Stories from Shakespeare.* Riverside Readers. London: Philip and Tacey, 1955. Pp. 48.

B3760   Murray, Geoffrey. *Let's Discover Shakespeare.* London: Hamish Hamilton, 1957. Pp. [9], 278. Illustrated.
   Prose version of 8 plays.
   Rev: *TLS* (Children's Books Section), Nov. 15, 1957, pp. xii-xiii.

B3761   Nesbit, E. *The Children's Shakespeare.* Ill. by Rolf Klep. New York: Random House, 1938. Pp. 126.

B3762   Palmer, Harold E. *Four Stories from Shakespeare.* Adapted and rewritten within the thousand word vocabulary. Ill. by T. H. Robinson. London: Harrap, 1937. Pp. 110.

B3763   Rapaport, N. *Sippurey Shakespeare li-vney ha-neurim (Shakespeare's Tales for Younger People).* Jerusalem: Ahiassaf, 1955. Pp. 150.

B3764   Specking, Inez. *Shakespeare for Children.* New York: Vantage Press, 1955. Pp. 95.
   13 plays: *Twelf., AYL, Much, Dream, Errors, Shrew, Winter's Tale, Temp., Romeo, Ham., Lear, Oth., Macb.*

B3765   Wyatt, Horace Graham. *Stories from Shakespeare.* Stories Told and Retold Series. 2nd edition. London: Oxford Univ. Press, 1957. Pp. viii, 111.

4. TRAVESTIES OF SHAKESPEARE'S PLAYS (170;58)

B3766   Olive, W. J. "Shakespeare Parody in Davenport's *A New Tricke to Cheat the Divell.*" *MLN,* LXVI (1951), 480.
   A possible paraphrase of Falstaff's catechism on honor.

B3767   Olive, W. J. "Twenty Good Nights—*The Knight of the Burning Pestle, The Family of Love,* and *Romeo and Juliet.*" *SP,* XLVII (1950), 182-189.
   Restates the case for the burlesquing of *Romeo and Juliet* and other of Shak.'s works in *The Knight of the Burning Pestle.*

B3768   Hawes, David Stewart. *John Broughman as American Playwright and Man of the Theatre.* DD, Stanford University, 1954. Pp. 686. Mic A54-1479. *DA,* XIV (1954), 1006. Publ. No. 7494.
   Much Ado About A Merchant of Venice and other travesties.

B3769   Travers, Seymour. *Catalogue of Nineteenth Century French Theatrical Parodies; A Compilation of the Parodies Between 1789 and 1914 of Which any Record was Found.* DD, Columbia University, 1942. New York: King's Crown Press, 1942. Pp. 130.
   Shak. pp. 96-97.

B3770   "The Bachelor's Soliloquy." (Parody of Hamlet) *Encore,* VII (1945), 281.

B3771   Dehn, Paul. *For Love and Money.* London: Max Reinhardt, 1956. Pp. viii, 135. Amer. Ed. New York: Vanguard Press, 1957. Pp. 135.
   Includes a pantechnicon historical play called "Hambeline, the Moor of Tyre, or Much Ado About What You Will." In American edition called "Potted Swan."
   Rev: *TLS,* Oct. 19, 1956, p. 612.

B3772   "Smothered Teen-Age Bride." *Punch,* Nov. 26, 1956.

B3773   Armour, Richard. *Twisted Tales from Shakespeare.* New York: McGraw-Hill, 1957. Pp. 152.
   Best-known plays presented in a new light, "the old light having blown a fuse, together with

introductions, questions, appendices, and other critical apparatus intended to contribute to a clearer misunderstanding of the subject." Drawings by Campbell Grant.
Rev: by Paul Jordan-Smith, *Los Angeles Times*, Oct. 6, 1957, Part V, p. 7; *ShN*, VIII (1958), 12.

B3774 Draper, Walter Headen. *George L. Fox, Comedian, in Pantomime and Travesty.* DD, University of Illinois, 1958. Pp. 183. Mic. 58-4496. *DA*, XVIII (1958), 693. Publ. No. 25,210.

B3775 "Shakespeare Up-to-Date: The Balcony Scene from *Romeo and Juliet* Act II Scene II." *Mad*, May, 1958, p. 17.
Gives "Old Version" and "Mad Version."

5. DICTIONARIES OF QUOTATIONS (89,170;-,58)

B3776 Stevenson, Burton, ed. *The Home Book of Shakespeare Quotations.* (With concordance and glossary of unique words and phrases.) New York: C. Scribner's Sons, 1937. Pp. 2093.
Rev: by Isaac Goldberg, *SRL*, Nov. 27, 1937, p. 18; *NYTBR*, Jan. 23, 1938, p. 21; *TLS*, May 28, p. 373.

B3777 Stevenson, Burton. *The Standard Book of Shakespeare Quotations.* New York: Funk & Wagnalls, 1953. London: Mayflower Pub. Co., 1954. Pp. 766.
An abridgement of B3776.
Rev: *TLS*, May 21, 1954, p. 335; by George Freedley, *Library Journal*, LXXVIII, 2040; *Subscription Books Bulletin*, XXV, 31; by F. Wolcken, *SJ*, 90 (1954), 354.

B3778 Browning, D. C., ed. *Everyman's Dictionary of Shakespeare Quotations.* London: Dent, 1953. Pp. 576.
Rev: by J. D. Scott, *Spectator*, Dec. 25, 1953, p. 765; by G. Lambin, *LanM*, XLVIII, 435; *TLS*, Nov. 6, 1953, p. 709; by J. Vallette, *MdF*, 320 (1954), 159; by G. B. Harrison, *SatR*, Sept. 25, p. 32; *NstN*, XLVII, 49; *The Indian Review* (Madras), LVI (1955), 30.

B3779 Ichikawa, Sanki, Masami Nishikawa, and Mamoru Shimizu, eds. *The Kenkyusha Dictionary of English Quotations with Examples of their Use by Modern Authors.* Tokyo: Kenkyusha, 1953. Part II, pp. 401-618, deals with Shak.

B3780 *The Oxford Dictionary of Quotations.* Second ed. Oxford Univ. Press, 1953. Pp. xix, 1003. Shak., pp. 423-488.
Rev: by J. Crow, *Listener*, L (1953), 967; by J. D. Scott, *Spectator*, 6548 (1953), 765; *TLS*, Nov. 6, p. 709.

B3781 *Vest Pocket Shakespearean Manual of Quotations, Characters, Scenes, and Plays.* Baltimore: I. & M. Ottenheimer, 1956. Pp. 224.

B3782 Bartlett, John. *Familiar Quotations.* 13th ed. London: Macmillan, 1957. Pp. xxxiv, 1613. Shak., pp. 124-212.

6. SHAKESPEAREAN AND/OR PROFESSIONAL SOCIETIES AND THEIR PUBLICATIONS (170;58)
(Unless otherwise noted, periodicals listed here were still appearing regularly at the time this compilation went to press.)
a. ENGLAND
(1) STRATFORD ORGANIZATIONS

B3783 For listings of *Shakespeare Survey*, Volumes 1-9, and reviews thereof, see entries A205-A215.
B3784 Fox, Levi. "The Stratford Collections." *TN*, VI (1952), 60-62.
(1) Shak. Mem. Libr. attached to Theatre.
(2) Shak. Birthplace Trust Library.

(a) STRATFORD CONFERENCE

B3785 "Reports of Many 'Brilliant Lectures' in Stratford" by A. L. Rowse, W. A. Darlington, J. Isaacs, G. B. Harrison, J. Dale, A. Nicoll, H. C. A. Gaunt, etc. *The Stratford-upon-Avon Herald*, Sept. 9, 1938, pp. 9, 10.

B3786 Boas, Frederick S. "Shakespeare Conference at Stratford-on-Avon: Centenary of the Purchase of the Birthplace." *QQ*, LIV (1948), 421-428.

B3787 Lüdeke, Henry. "Die Fünfte Shakespeare-Konferenz in Stratford." *SJ*, 87/88 (1952), 73-74.

B3788 Benchettrit, Paul. "Sixth Annual Shakespeare Conference." *EA*, VI (1953), 379.

B3789 S[inko], G[rzegorz]. "VII Miedzynarodowa Konferencja Szekspirowska w Stratfordzie." *Kwartalnik Neofilologiczny* (Warsaw), III (1956), 181-184.

B3790 "Eighth International Shakespeare Conference at Stratford." *ShN*, VII (1957), 39, 48. *ShN*, VIII (1958), 4. Abstracts of papers.

B3791 Davril, Robert. "Eighth International Shakespeare Conference." *EA*, X (1957), 470-471.

B3792 Gross, Ronald. "Summer Lectures at the Shakespeare Institute." *ShN*, V (1955), 35. Abstracts of 24 lectures given in 6 series of 4 each.

B3793 Carrère, Félix. "L'International Shakespeare Conference" [Stratford-on-Avon]. *EA*, VIII (1955), 375-376.

B3794   Heuer, Hermann. "Internationale Shakespeare-Konferenz in Stratford 1955." *SJ*, 92 (1956), 447-449.
B3795   Kraft, James. "Tenth Annual Shakespeare Institute." Summer 1956. *ShN*, VI (1956), 33.
B3796   "Summer School Lectures at Stratford." *ShN*, VI (1956), 43.

(2) ENGLISH ASSOCIATION
(a) YWES
(Entered with Reviews under *Surveys* A279-A302.)
(b) ESSAYS AND STUDIES

B3797   Old Series. Vol. xx-xxxi, 1935 (publ. 1936) to 1945 (publ. 1946) inclusive. For reviews, see annual entries in *SP*.
B3798   Essays and Studies. New Series. Vols. I-XI, 1948 (publ. 1949) to 1958, inclusive. For reviews, see annual entries in *SP* and *SQ*.

(3) OTHER SOCIETIES

B3799   British Academy. Annual Shakespeare Lectures. Oxford Univ. Press. One each year, published separately and also in the Academy *Proceedings*. Those for 1936-1958 are entered separately in their appropriate classes.
B3800   Cancelled.
B3801   Avery, Emmett L. "The Shakespeare Ladies Club." *SQ*, VII (1956), 153-158.
Reviews the effective influence of "Shakespeare's Ladies" of 1737 and after, in the revivals of Shakespearian plays, all in 18th-century England.
B3802   The Bibliographical Society. *The Bibliographical Society, 1892-1942. Studies in Retrospect*. Ed. by F. C. Francis. London: Bibliographical Society, 1945. Pp. 215.
Essays entered separately.
Rev: *TLS*, March 23, 1946, p. 144.
B3803   Henderson, Archibald. *George Bernard Shaw: Man of the Century*. New York: Appleton-Century-Crofts, 1956. Pp. xxxii, 969.
"Shelley and Shakespeare Societies," pp. 147-160.
B3804   *Essays by Divers Hands. Being the Transactions of the Royal Society of Literature of the United Kingdom*. London: Milford. New Series, Vols. XV-XXIX, 1935-1958. For reviews, see annual entries in *SP*.
B3805   Bateson, F. W. "Organs of Critical Opinion. I. *The Review of English Studies*." *EIC*, VI (1956), 190-201.

b. AMERICA
(1) SHAKESPEARE ASSOCIATION OF AMERICA

B3806   *Shakespeare Association Bulletin*. Vols. XI-XXIV, 1936-1949 inclusive. Succeeded by B3807.
B3807   *Shakespeare Quarterly*. Vols. I-IX, 1950-58 inclusive.
B3808   "Shakespeareana." *The Aryan Path*, Sept. 1950.
Comments on the Shakespeare Assoc. of America and the *SQ*.

(2) RENAISSANCE SOCIETY OF AMERICA

B3809   *Studies in the Renaissance*. With Foreword by John Herman Randall, Jr. Publs. Renaissance Soc. Amer., Vol. I. Univ. Texas Press, 1954. Vol. II. New York: Renaissance Soc. Amer., 1955. Vol. III, 1956. Vol. IV, 1957. Vol. V, 1958.
Entries for the several articles appear in the appropriate sections.

(3) SOUTHEASTERN RENAISSANCE CONFERENCE

B3810   *Renaissance Papers. A Selection of Papers Presented at the Renaissance Meeting in the Southeastern States, Duke University, April 23-24, 1954*. Columbia, South Carolina: Univ. of South Carolina Press, 1954. Pp. 92.
Entries for papers appear in appropriate sections.
Rev: *N &Q*, NS, II (1955), 90-91; by Edward P. Vandiver, Jr., *SQ*, VI (1955), 180-181.
B3811   *Renaissance Papers. A Selection of Papers Presented at the Renaissance Meeting in the Southeastern States, University of North Carolina, April 22-23, 1955*. Edited by Hennig Cohen and Allan H. Gilbert. Columbia, South Carolina: Univ. of South Carolina Press; Durham, North Carolina: Duke Univ. Press, 1955.
Rev: by Glenn H. Blayney, *SQ*, IX (1958), 76-77.
B3812   *Renaissance Papers, 1956. A Selection of Papers Presented at the Renaissance Meeting in the Southeastern States, University of South Carolina, April 20-21, 1956*. Ed. Hennig Cohen and J. Woodrow Hassell, Jr. Columbia, South Carolina: Southeastern Renaissance Conference, 1956. Pp. 112.
Rev: *RN*, X (1957), 105-106.
B3813   *Renaissance Papers. A Selection of Papers Presented at the Renaissance Meeting in the Southeastern States, Duke University, April 12-13, 1957*. Ed. Allan H. Gilbert. Southeastern Renaissance Conference, 1957. Pp. 124.

Rev: by Glenn H. Blayney, *SQ*, IX (1958), 76-77.

B3814   Phialas, Peter G. "Renaissance Conference." *South Atlantic Bulletin*, XXIV (1958), 9-11. Includes notices of the reading of papers on Sex and Pessimism in *King Lear* by Robert J. West, on Tybalt's Exit in *Romeo and Juliet* by George W. Williams, on Parting and Justice in *Romeo and Juliet* by H. Edward Cain, at the 15th annual Renaissance Conference.

(4) ENGLISH INSTITUTE

B3815   *English Institute Annual, 1939.* New York: Columbia Univ. Press, 1940. Pp. xvi, 164. Relevant essays in this and subsequent issues have been listed in the appropriate classes. Rev: *N &Q*, 180 (1941), 179-180.

B3816   *English Institute Annual, 1940.* New York: Columbia Univ. Press, 1941. Pp. xii, 228. Rev: *N &Q*, 181 (1941), 280.

B3817   *English Institute Annual, 1941.* New York: Columbia Univ. Press, 1942. Pp. xi, 248. Rev: by W. W. Greg, *RES*, XIX (1943), 320-323; by J. D. Bowley, *MLR*, XXXVIII, 359-362.

B3818   *English Institute Annual, 1942.* New York: Columbia Univ. Press, 1943. Pp. xi, 207. Rev: by J. H. P. Pafford, *Library*, 4th S., XXV (1944-45), 191-192.

B3819   *English Institute Essays, 1946: The Critical Significance of Biographical Evidence; The Methods of Literary Studies.* Ed. James L. Clifford, et al. New York: Columbia Univ. Press, 1947. Pp. x, 222. Rev: by P. F. Baum, *South Atlantic Quar.*, XLVII (1948), 430; by D. M. Davin, *RES*, XXIV, 281-282; by W. K. Wimsatt, Jr., *JAAC*, VII, 264-266.

B3820   *English Institute Essays, 1947.* Ed. James L. Clifford, et al. New York: Columbia Univ. Press, 1948. Rev: *N &Q*, 194 (1949), 131-132; by P. F. Baum, *South Atlantic Quarterly*, XLVIII, 321-322; by J. C. Maxwell, *RES*, NS, I (1950), 278-279; by R. Flatter, *SJ*, 87/88 (1952), 235.

B3821   *English Institute Essays, 1948.* Ed. D. A. Robertson, Jr. New York: Columbia Univ. Press, 1949. Pp. 219. Rev: by Robert Halsband, *SRL*, July 8, 1950, p. 17; by Marcia Lee Anderson, *South Atlantic Quarterly*, XLIX, 555-556; by Carl H. Grabo, *New Mexico Quarterly*, XX, 225-232; by Frank Kermode, *RES*, NS, II (1951), 95-97; by Winifred M. T. Nowottny, *MLR*, XLVI, 469-470.

B3822   *English Institute Essays, 1949.* Ed. Alan S. Downer. New York: Columbia Univ. Press, 1950. Pp. x, 186. Rev: by John Caffrey, *Poetry*, LXXVII (1950), 49-51; by Lilian Haddakin, *MLR*, XLVII, 380-381; by Edwin R. Clapp, *Western Humanities Review*, VI, 193-195; by George R. Coffman, *Speculum*, XXVII, 371-375; *TLS*, Feb. 1, 1952, p. 98.

B3823   *English Institute Essays, 1950.* Ed. Alan S. Downer. New York: Columbia Univ. Press, 1951. Pp. 236.

B3824   *English Institute Essays, 1951.* Ed. Alan S. Downer. New York: Columbia Univ. Press, 1952. Rev: *TLS*, Dec. 26, 1952, p. 858; by Wolfgang H. Clemen, *SQ*, V (1954), 188-190.

B3825   *English Institute Essays, 1952.* Ed. Alan S. Downer. New York: Columbia Univ. Press, 1953. Rev: by John H. Long, *SQ*, VI (1955), 189-190.

B3826   *English Institute Essays, 1953.* On Ezra Pound.

B3827   *English Stage Comedy: English Institute Essays, 1954.* Ed. W. K. Wimsatt. New York: Columbia Univ. Press, 1955. Pp. x, 182. Rev: *TLS*, Nov. 4, 1955, p. 652; by John H. Long, *SQ*, VI, 189-190; by Marvin T. Herrick, *JEGP*, LV (1956), 313-314; by Bonamy Dobrée, *SQ*, VII, 423-426; by John V. Curry, S. J., *Thought*, XXI, 455-457; by Norman Philbrick, *QJS*, XLII, 424-427; by Harold Jenkins, *MLR*, LII (1957), 588-590; by J. Voisine, *EA*, X, 459-460; *ShN*, VII, 46; by J. F. Arnott, *RES*, NS, IX (1958), 75-76.

B3828   *English Institute Essays, 1955.* On the novel.

B3829   *Sound and Poetry: English Institute Essays, 1956.* Ed. Northrop Frye. New York: Columbia Univ. Press, 1957. Rev: *Music and Letters*, XXXIX (1958), 282-283.

(5) BIBLIOGRAPHICAL SOCIETY OF THE UNIVERSITY OF VIRGINIA
All *SB* essays having to do with Shakespeare have been listed in their appropriate classes.

B3830   *Papers of the Bibliographical Society of the University of Virginia.* Vol. I. Ed. Fredson Bowers. Charlottesville, Virginia: Bibliographical Society of the Univ. of Virginia, 1948. Rev: by W. W. Greg, *MLR*, XLV (1950), 76; by R. C. Bald, *MLQ*, XII (1951), 370-371.

B3831   *Studies in Bibliography*, II. Ed. Fredson Bowers. Charlottesville, Virginia: Bibliographical Society of the Univ. of Virginia, 1949. Rev: by W. H. Bond, *SQ*, I (1950), 95-96; by W. W. Greg, *MLR*, XLV, 524; by F. C. Francis, *The Library*, Fifth Ser., VI (1951), 62-64; by A. T. Hazen, *MLN*, LXVIII, 68-69.

B3832   *Studies in Bibliography: Papers of the Bibliographical Society of the University of Virginia. Vol. III* (1950-1951). Ed. Fredson Bowers. Charlottesville, Virginia: Bibliographical Society of the

Univ. of Virginia, 1950. Pp. 306.
Rev: by Lawrence S. Thompson, *South Atlantic Bulletin*, xiv, No. 4 (1951), 9-10; by
W. H. Bond, *Papers of the Bibliographical Society of America*, xlv, 170-172; by Warner G. Rice,
Library Quar., xxi, 300-301; by R. L. C., *Library Association Records*, liii, 100; by G. Blakemore Evans, *JEGP*, l, 421-423; by John Crow, *SQ*, ii, 81-84; by W. W. Greg, *MLR*, xlvi,
468-469; by F. C. Francis, *The Library*, Fifth Ser., vi, 61-64; by Joh. Gerritsen, *ES*, xxxiii
(1952), 134-136.

B3833 *Studies in Bibliography*, iv. Ed. Fredson Bowers. Charlottesville, Virginia: Bibliographical
Society of the Univ. of Virginia, 1951. Pp. xiii, 237.
Rev: *TLS*, May 4, 1951, p. 274; by Franklin B. Williams, Jr., *SQ*, iii (1952), 127-129; by
A. T. Hazen, *Papers of the Bibl. Soc. of Amer.*, xlvi, 169-171; by A. J. W., *Lib. Assoc. Rec.*, liv,
184; by Herbert Davis, *RES*, iv (1953), 397-399; by W. W. Greg, *MLR*, xlviii, 59-60.

B3834 *Studies in Bibliography*, v. Ed. Fredson Bowers. Charlottesville, Virginia: Bibliographical
Society of the Univ. of Virginia, 1952. Pp. xii, 238.
Rev: by Philip Edwards, *SQ*, iv (1953), 185-187; by Howard W. Winger, *Lib. Quar.*, xxiii,
313-314; *TLS*, Apr. 17, p. 260; by Karl J. Holzknecht, *Papers Bibl. Soc. of Amer.*, xlvii,
192-194; by Lawrence S. Thompson, *South Atlantic Bul.*, xviii, 4, 12; by James Kinsley,
RES, ns, v, 102-104; by Arthur Brown, *MLR*, xlix (1954), 219-220.

B3835 *Studies in Bibliography*, vi. Ed. Fredson Bowers. Charlottesville, Virginia: Bibliographical
Society of the Univ. of Virginia, 1953. Pp. 288.
Rev: *TLS*, Apr. 16, 1954, p. 256; by Philip Edwards, *SQ*, vi (1955), 100-101; by William T.
Hastings, *SQ*, vi, 121; by Karl Brunner, *SJ*, 92 (1956), 431-433.

B3836 *Studies in Bibliography: Papers of the Bibliographical Society of the University of Virginia*, 1955.
Pp. 540.
Rev: *ShN*, v (1955), 13; *TLS*, June 3, p. 308; by Karl J. Holzknecht, *Papers of the Bibl.
Soc. of America*, xlix, 190-195; by Lawrence S. Thompson, *South Atlantic Bul.*, xx, No. 4,
15-16; by Herbert Davis, *RES*, ns, viii (1957), 215-217.

B3837 *Studies in Bibliography*, viii. Ed. Fredson Bowers. Charlottesville, Virginia: Bibliographical
Society of the Univ. of Virginia, 1956. Pp. 275.
Rev: *TLS*, May 11, 1956, p. 288; *SCN*, xiv, 12; by Louis F. Peck, *CE*, xvii, 420; by I. B.
Cauthen, Jr., *ShN*, vi, 40-41; by P. G., *Book Collector*, v, 189; by Lawrence S. Thompson,
South Atlantic Bul., xxi, 4 (1956), 13-14; by Hugh G. Dick, *SQ*, viii (1957), 98-101; by
A. N. L. Munby, *MLR*, lii, 250-251; by Herbert Davis, *RES*, ns, viii, 454-456.

B3838 *Studies in Bibliography*, ix. Ed. Fredson Bowers. Charlottesville, Virginia: Bibliographical
Society of the Univ. of Virginia, 1957. Pp. 273.
Rev: *TLS*, May 3, 1957, p. 280; *ShN*, vii, 15; by Leo Kirschbaum, *SQ*, viii, 544-546; by
D. G. Neill, *Book Collector*, vi, 297-298; by C. William Miller, *JEGP*, lvii (1958), 106-108;
by J. C. T. Oates, *The Library*, xiii, 70-71; by A. N. L. Munby, *MLR*, liii, 232-233; by
L. F. Peck, *CE*, xix, 232-233; by Arthur Brown, *RES*, ns, ix, 340-341.

B3839 *SB*. x. Extra volume of reprinted bibliographies.
See A138.

B3840 *Studies in Bibliography*, xi. Ed. Fredson Bowers. Charlottesville, Virginia: Bibliographical
Society of the Univ. of Virginia, 1958. Pp. 297.
Rev: *TLS*, June 13, 1958, p. 336; by Lawrence S. Thompson, *South Atlantic Bul.*, xxiii,
4 (Mar.), 10-11; *SCN*, xvi, 45; by D. G. Neill, *Book Collector*, vii, 427-428.

(6) HUNTINGTON LIBRARY

B3841 "The Renaissance Conference at the Huntington Library." *HLQ*, iv (1941), 133-189.
B3842 "The Renaissance Conference at the Huntington Library." *HLQ*, v (1942), 155-201.
Relevant essays are entered in appropriate classes.
B3843 "Conference at the Huntington Library: English Renaissance." *HLQ*, vi (1942), 29-43.
Relevant essays are entered in appropriate classes.

(7) TENNESSEE PHILOLOGICAL ASSOCIATION

B3844 *Tennessee Studies in Literature, I.* Papers Selected from the Program of the Fifty-First Annual
Meeting of The Tennessee Philological Association, Feb. 24-25, 1956. Ed. Alwin Thaler
and Richard Beale Davis. Knoxville, Tennessee: Philol. Assoc. & Univ. Tennessee, 1956.
Pp. 82.
Entries for papers of special interest to students of the Renaissance appear in appropriate
classes.

B3845 *Tennessee Studies in Literature, II.* Ed. A. Thaler and R. B. Davis. Knoxville, 1957.
Rev: by Alfred G. Engstrom, *South Atlantic Bul.*, xxiv, 2 (Nov., 1958), 17-19.
B3846 *Tennessee Studies in Literature, III.* Ed. A. Thaler and R. B. Davis. Knoxville, 1958.

(8) OTHERS

B3847 Paul, Henry N. "Shakespeare in Philadelphia." *Proc. Amer. Philos. Soc.*, lxxvi (1936),
719-729.

B3848   *The Shakespeare Club of Oklahoma City.* Oklahoma City, 1936-37. Pp. 24.

B3849   Tannenbaum, Samuel A. "A Shakespeare Celebration." *SAB*, xv (1940), 125.

B3850   Savage, Henry L. "The Shakspere Society of Philadelphia." *SQ*, III (1952), 341-352.
See also Sections on Shakespeare's Influence.

c. GERMANY
(1) DIE DEUTSCHE SHAKESPEARE-GESELLSCHAFT
(a) GENERAL

B3851   Deetjen, Werner. "Die Deutsche Shakespeare-Gesellschaft (1864-1939)." *FuF*, xv (1939), 232-233.

B3852   Wendel, R. "75 Jahre Dts. Shakespeare-Gesellschaft. Die Geschichte der Gründung." *LNN*, April 13, 1939.

B3853   Witt, B. "75 Jahre Dts. Shakespeare-Gesellschaft." *Ostdtse. Monatshefte*, xx (1939/40), 120.

B3854   Stroedel, Wolfgang. "Aus dem Leben der Dt. Shakespeare-Gesellschaft 1948-1950." *SJ*, 84/86 (1950), 13-14.

B3855   Stroedel, Wolfgang. "Aus dem Leben der Dt. Shakespeare-Gesellschaft 1950-1952." *SJ*, 87/88 (1952), 270-272.

B3856   Vielhaber, Gerde. "Zwischen Bochum und Weimar: Zur Bochumer Hauptversammlung der Dt. Shakespeare-Gesellschaft." *Industriekurier*, v (1952), No. 68, p. 5; No. 77, p. 5.

B3857   Stroedel, Wolfgang. "Die Dt. Shakespeare-Gesellschaft 1952 bis 1953." *SJ*, 89 (1953), 245-246.

B3858   Davril, R. "Vingtième Anniversaire de la Dt. Shakespeare-Gesellschaft." *EA*, VII (1954), 346-347.

B3859   Frings, Josef Kardinal. "Ansprache beim Festakt der Shakespeare-Gesellschaft." *SJ*, 90 (1954), 9-10.
See also "Shakespeares Masse." *Rhein. Merkur*, IX (1954), No. 18, p. 9.

B3860   Stroedel, Wolfgang. "90th Anniversary Celebration of the Deutsche Shakespeare-Gesellschaft." *SQ*, v (1954), 317-322.

B3861   Stroedel, Wolfgang. "Aus dem Leben der Dt. Shakespeare-Gesellschaft im 90. Jahr ihres Bestehens." *SJ*, 90 (1954), 363-366.

B3862   Stroedel, Wolfgang. "90-Jahr-Feier der Dt. Shakespeare-Gesellschaft Tagungen in Bochum und Weimar April u. Juni 1954." *SJ*, 90 (1954), 367-369.

B3863   Stroedel, Wolfgang. "Die Deutsche Shakespeare-Gesellschaft 1954." *SJ*, 91 (1955), 370-371.

B3864   Behr, Fritz. "Die Dt. Shakespeare-Gesellschaft (April 1954-April 1955)." *ZAA*, III (1955), 315-319.

B3865   Cancelled.

B3866   Stroedel, Wolfgang. "Die Dt. Shakespeare-Gesellschaft 1955." *SJ*, 92 (1956), 444-447.

B3867   Pflaume, Heinz. "Die Bibliothek der Dt. Shakespeare-Gesellschaft." *SJ*, 92 (1956), 532-539.

B3868   Diekamp, Leo. "Die Deutsche Shakespeare-Gesellschaft, im Berichtsjahr 1956/57." *SJ*, 93 (1957), 285-289.

B3869   Diekamp, Leo. "Die Deutsche Shakespeare-Gesellschaft im Geschäftsjahr 1957/58." *SJ*, 94 (1958), 313-315.

(b) BOCHUM

B3870   Thomas, W. "Die Zweite Deutsche Shakespeare-Woche in Bochum." *Die Bühne*, XVIII (1937), 459-460.

B3871   Arns, K. "Zweite Deutsche Shakespeare-Woche." (Oct. 9-15). *ZNU*, XXXVI (1938), 386-388.

B3872   Braumüller, W. "Shakespeare und kein Ende?" *Bücherkunde*, IV (1937), 587-601.

B3873   Kobbe, Friedrich-Carl. "Shakespeare und kein Ende. Zweite Deutsche Shakespeare-Woche in Bochum." *DL*, XL (1937/38), 168-170; also in *Dresd. Anz.*, October 19, 1937.

B3874   Mettin, Hermann Christian. "Die Shakespeare-Woche in Bochum." *Die Tat.*, XXIX (1937-38), Bd. 2, pp. 547-553.

B3875   Zimmermann, K. "Zweite Deutsche Shakespeare-Woche." *Frankf. Ztg.*, Oct. 17, 1937.

B3876   Förster, Max. "Die Zweite Deutsche Shakespeare-Woche in Bochum, 9-15, Okt. 1937." *SJ*, LXXIV (1938), 9-10.

B3877   Schlösser, Rainer. "Der Deutsche Shakespeare. Ein Beitrag zur Bochumer Shakespeare-Woche." *SJ*, LXXIV (1938), 20-30.

B3877a Schlösser, Rainer. "Der 'deutsche' Shakespeare." *Wille und Macht* (Berlin), VIII (1940), Heft 3, p. 22.

B3878   Schmitt, Saladin. "Die 77. Hauptversammlung der Dt. Shakespeare-Gesellschaft zu Bochum am 24/25 Juli 1946." *SJ*, 80/81 (1946), 1-11.

B3879   "Bochumer Shakespeare-Tage 1947." *SJ*, 82/83 (1948), 1-6.

B3880   Frings, Joseph Kardinal. "Ansprache an die Teilnehmer der Shakespeare-Tage 1947 in Bochum." *SJ*, 82/83 (1948), 7-8.

B3881   "Jahreshauptversammlung in Bochum." *MDtShG*, I (1949), 2-4; II (1950), 1-2.

B3882   Kirchner, Gustav. "Jahreshauptversammlung der Dt. Shakespeare-Gesellschaft in Bochum." *Neuphilol. Zs.*, II (1950), 305-306.

B3883   Frings, Joseph Kardinal. "Ansprache anlässlich der Shakespeare-Tagung in Bochum am 22/24 April 1950." *SJ*, 84/86 (1950), 15-16.

B3884   "Shakespeare-Tage 1950 in Bochum." *MDtShG*, III (1950), 1-6.

B3885   Kirchner, Gustav. "Jahreshauptversammlung der Dt. Shakespeare-Gesellschaft in Bochum, 21-23 April 1951." *Neuphilol. Zs.*, III (1951), 361. For 21-23 April 1952, ibid., IV (1952), 402-404.

B3886   Hoffmann, Paul. "Von Eschenburg zu Eschenburg." *Shakespeare-Tage*, 1952 (Bochum), pp. 16-18.

B3887   Schmidt-Hidding, Wolfgang. "Bochumer Shakespeare-Tage, 1952." *NS*, NS, I (1952), 273-274.

B3888   Dörnemann, Kurt. "Moderner Shakespeare: Deutsch und Französisch. Shakespeare-Tage 1954 in Bochum." *Westfalenspiegel*, 1954, Heft 6, p. 46.

B3889   Oppel, Horst. "Bochumer Shakespeare-Tage, 1954." *NS*, III (1954), 345-348.

B3890   Itschert, Hans. "Bochumer Shakespeare-Tage, 1955." *NS*, IV (1955), 307-310.

B3890a Fabian, Bernhard. "Bochumer Shakespeare-Tage, 1956." *NS*, V (1956), 401-404.

B3891   Schaller, Rudolf. "Shakespeare-Tagung in Bochum." *Theater d. Zeit*, XI (1956), 12-16.

B3892   Itschert, Hans. "Bochumer Shakespeare-Tage." *NS*, VI (1957), 363-365.

(c) WEIMAR

B3893   Deetjen, Werner. "Die 72. Hauptversammlung der Deutschen Shakespeare-Gesellschaft zu Weimar am 22-23 April 1936." *SJ*, LXXII (1936), 1-8.

B3894   Deetjen, Werner. "Die 73. Hauptversammlung der Deutschen Shakespeare-Gesellschaft zu Weimar am 22-23 April 1937. Jahresbericht der Dts. Shakespeare-Gesellschaft." *SJ*, LXXIII (1937), 1-8.

B3895   Deetjen, Werner. "Die 74. Hauptversammlung der Deutschen Shakespeare-Gesellschaft zu Weimar am 22-23 April 1938." *SJ*, LXXIV (1938), 1-8.

B3896   Deetjen, Werner. "Zur Geschichte der Dts. Shakespeare-Gesellschaft. Ansprache bei der Festversammlung [der Dts. Shakespeare-Gesellschaft] im Weimarer Nationaltheater am 23 April 1939." *SJ*, LXXV (1939), 1-15.

B3897   Deetjen, Werner. "Die 75. Hauptversammlung der Dts. Shakespeare-Gesellschaft zu Weimar am 22-23 April 1939. Jahresbericht der Präsidenten." *SJ*, LXXV (1939), xi-xv.

B3898   "Homage to Shakespeare. The Annual Congress of the Shakespeare Society at Weimar [1939]." *AglGR*, III (1939), 186.

B3899   Keller, W. "Die 76. Hauptversammlung der Dts. Shakespeare-Gesellschaft zu Weimar am 22-23 April 1940. Ansprache und Jahresbericht." *SJ*, LXXVI (1940), 1-10.

B3900   "Bardolatry Abroad." *TLS*, April 13, 1946, p. 175.

B3901   *Katalog der Bücherei der Dt. Shakespeare-Gesellschaft in Weimar*. Weimar: Gutenberg, 1951. Pp. 357.

B3902   "Hauptversammlung, 76., der Dts. Shakespeare-Gesellschaft am 23 April 1940 in Weimar." *NS*, XLVIII (1940), 73-74.

(d) PUBLICATIONS OF DIE DEUTSCHE SHAKESPEARE-GESELLSCHAFT
i. Shakespeare-Jahrbuch

B3903   *SJ*, LXIX (1933); LXX (1934).
        Rev: by H. N. Hillebrand, *MLN*, LI (1936), 459-460.

B3904   *SJ*, LXXI (1935).
        Rev: by W. Wehe, *Bausteine z. dts. Nat.-Theat.*, IV (1936), 283; by K. Arns, *NS*, XLIV, 234; by J. Speck, *Archiv*, 171 (1937), 83-85; by R. A. Law, *MLN*, LII, 527; by G. C. Moore Smith, *MLR*, XXXII, 93-94; by W. Ebisch, *Beiblatt*, L (1939), 108-111; by Heinz Nicolai, *DLZ*, LX (1939), 520-521.

B3905   *SJ*, LXXII (1936).
        Rev: by B. Engelhardt, *NS*, XLV (1937), 336-337; by G. C. Moore Smith, *MLR*, XXXII, 609-610; by J. Speck, *Archiv*, 172 (1937), 84-86; by Léon Mis, *RG*, XXVIII, 218-219; *LZ*, 88 (1937), 213; by W. Schmidt, *ZNU*, XXXVII (1938), 131-133; by H. Heuer, *Lbl*, LIX, 389-390; by W. Ebisch, *Beiblatt*, L, 108-110; by F. A. Pompen, *Museum*, XLVII (1940), Heft 3.

B3906   *SJ*, LXXIII (1937).
        Rev: by W. Schmidt, *ZNU*, XXXVII (1938), 131-133; by N.-dt, *GA*, V, No. 17, p. 9; by J. Sprengler, *DL*, XL, 567; by H. Nicolai, *DLZ*, LX, 520-521; by A. Eichler, *Eng. Studn.*, LXXIII, 271-273;

by W. Ebisch, *Beiblatt*, L, 107-110; by P. A. B. van Dam, *Museum*, XLV, Heft 11/12; by G. Connes, *EA*, II, 396; by Léon Mis, *RG*, XXIX, 215; by C. J. Sisson, *MLR*, XXXIII, 427-428; by L. Kalpers, *NS*, XLVII (1939), 343-345; by J. Speck, *Archiv*, 178 (1940), 144-145.

B3907   *SJ*, LXXIV (1938).
     Rev: by Walther Ebisch, *Beiblatt*, L (1939), 108-110; by A. Heinrich, *NS*, XLVII, 345-346; by N-dt, *GA*, VI, Heft 9, p. 10; by Léon Mis, *GR*, XXX, 316; *RLC*, XIX, 315; by J. B. Leishman, *MLR*, XXXV (1940), 85-88; by J. Speck, *Archiv*, 178 (1940), 143-144; by F. A. Pompen, *Museum*, XLVII, Heft. 3.

B3908   *SJ*, LXXV (1939).
     Rev: by A. Heinrich, *NS*, XLVIII (1940), 224-225; by F. R. Schröder, *GRM*, XXVIII, 233; *N. Mon.*, XI, 279-280; by Eva Nienholdt, *GA*, VIII (1941), Heft 1, p. 8; by Walter Ebisch, *Beiblatt*, LIII (1942), 68-73.

B3909   *SJ*, LXXVI (1940).
     Rev: by L. Cremer, *DL*, XLIII (1940/41), 567; by A. Heinrich, *NS*, XLIX (1941), 161-162; by R. W. Zandvoort, *ES*, XXIII, Heft 6; by W. Kalthoff, *GA*, VIII, Heft 21, pp. 5-6; by A. Pompen, *Museum*, XLIX (1942), 33-34; by A. Eichler, *Eng. Studn.*, LXXV (1943), 229-232.

B3910   *SJ*, LXXVII (1941).
     Rev: by E. Goetschmann-Ravestrat, *Deutsche Dramaturgie*, I (1942), 264; by A. Heinrich, *NS*, L, 198-199; by A. Eichler, *Eng. Studn.*, LXXV (1942/43), 354-357; by R. W. Zandvoort, *ES*, XXV (1943), 111-113; by Joachim Müller, *ZDK*, LVII, 39.

B3911   *SJ*, LXXVIII/LXXIX (1943).
     Single volume.

B3912   *SJ*, 80/81 (1944-45).
     Single volume.

B3913   *SJ*, 82/83 (1946-47). Publ. 1948.
     Single volume.

B3914   *SJ*, 84/86 (1948-50). Publ. 1950.
     Rev: by Hardin Craig, *MLR*, XLVIII (1953), 67-68.

B3915   *SJ*, 87/88 (1951-52). Publ. 1952.
     Single volume.

B3916   *SJ*, 89 (1953).
     Rev: by H. T. Price, *SQ*, V (1954), 116-119; by Karl Brunner, ibid., pp. 419-420.

B3917   *SJ*, 90 (1954).
     Rev: by C. J. Sisson, *MLR*, L (1955), 525-526; by Ludwig W. Kahn, *SQ*, VII (1956), 118-120; by A. Koszul, *EA*, IX, 154-156.

B3918   *SJ*, 91 (1955).
     Rev: by C. J. Sisson, *MLR*, L (1955), 525-526; by W. G. Marigold, *SQ*, VIII (1957), 398-399.

B3919   *SJ*, 92 (1956).
     Rev: by H. Edward Cain, *SQ*, VIII (1957), 541-544; by T. J. B. Spencer, *MLR*, LII, 454-455; by Hereward T. Price, *SQ*, VIII, 541-542; *ShN*, VII, 33.

B3920   *SJ*, 93 (1957).
B3921   *SJ*, 94 (1958).

ii. Others

B3922   *Festschrift zur Deutschen Shakespeare-Woche, Bochum.* Hrsg. v. d. Stadt Bochum in Zus.-Arbeit m. d. Dts. Shakespeare-Gesellschaft. Text- und Bildgestaltung von Walter Thomas. Leipzig: Beck, 1937. Pp. 31.

B3923   *Mitteilungen der Deutschen Shakespeare-Gesellschaft*, I, Bochum, Germany, 1949. Pp. 12.

B3924   *Schriftenreihe der Dt. Shakespeare-Gesellschaft.* NS, V. Heidelberg: Quelle & Meyer, 1955.

B3925   *Schriftenreihe der Dt. Shakespeare-Gesellschaft.* NS, VII. Heidelberg: Quelle & Meyer, 1958.

B3926   *Shakespeare-Tage 1952.* Blätter d. Städt. Bühne Bochum. Hrsg. v. d. Dt. Shakespeare-Gesellschaft u. d. Bühne d. Stadt Bochum. Bochum, 1952. Pp. 18.

B3927   *Shakespeare-Tage 1954.* Schauspielhaus Bochum. Bochum, 1954. Pp. 32.

B3928   *Shakespeare-Tage 1955-1956.* Hrsg. v. d. Dt. Shakespeare-Gesellschaft u. dem Schauspielhaus Bochum. Bochum, 1955-56. Pp. 24.

B3929   *Shakespeare-Tage 1957.* Hrsg. v. d. Dt. Shakespeare-Gesellschaft u. dem Schauspielhaus Bochum. Bochum, 1957. Pp. 20.

(2) OTHERS

B3930   Kindermann, H., ed. *Von deutscher Art und Kunst.* Einige fliegende Blätter. Nebst dem Aufsatz Goethes 'Zum Shakespeare-Tag'. Leipzig: Reclam, 1942. Pp. 164.

B3931   Mandelartz, Carl. "Duisburger Shakespeare-Tage (1952)," *SJ*, 89 (1953), 247-248.

B3932   Klie, Barbara. "Shakespeare am Bodensee. Eine Tagung im Internat. Institut auf der Insel Mainau." *Christ und Welt*, June 22, 1953, p. 6.

B3933 Westecker, Wilhelm. "Die schöpferische Initiative. Beobachtungen und Gedanken bei Kulturtagungen." *Christ und Welt*, May 13, 1954, p. 7.

B3934 Pflaume, Heinz. "Meissener Shakespeare-Tage." *SJ*, 92 (1956), 447.

d. ELSEWHERE

B3935 *Studies in English Literature.* A Quarterly Review Compiled and Issued by the English Literary Society of Japan, Tokyo Imperial Univ. 35 volumes through 1958. Many essays on Shak.

7. TRIBUTES TO INDIVIDUAL SCHOLARS AND BIBLIOGRAPHIES OF THEIR WORKS
a. BRANDL

B3936 Keller, Wolfgang. "Alois Brandl Noch ein Wort der Erinnerung." *SJ*, LXXVI (1940), 199-202.

B3937 Keller, W. "In Memoriam Alois Brandl." *Eng. Studn.*, LXXIV (1940), 145-155.

b. DEUTSCHBEIN

B3938 Azzalino, Walther. "Max Deutschbein zum Gedächtnis." *Leb. Fremdspr.*, I (1949), 289-291.

B3939 Heuer, Hermann. "Max Deutschbein zum Gedächtnis." *SJ*, 84/86 (1950), 7-10.

c. FÖRSTER

B3940 Clemen, Wolfgang. "Nekrolog. Max Förster." *SJ*, 91 (1955), 369.

B3941 Huscher, Herbert. "Max Förster." *Anglia*, LXXIII (1955), 1-5.

B3942 Willard, Rudolph. "Max Förster. 8 March 1869-10 November 1954." *RES*, VI (1955), 273-279.

B3943 Göhler, Theodor. "Das Spätwerk Max Försters. Eine Bibliographie." *Anglia*, LXXIV (1956), 416-426.

d. GOLLANCZ

B3944 Boas, Frederick S. "Homage to Shakespeare." *Shakespeare Quarterly* (London), I (Summer, 1947), 6-8. Reminis. of Gallancz' *Book of Homage to Shakespeare*.

B3945 Highfill, Philip, Jr. "Sir Israel Gollancz." *ShN*, VIII (1958), 11. Brief biography.

e. GRANVILLE-BARKER

B3946 "H. Granville-Barker." *English*, VI (1946), 110.

B3947 Whitworth, Geoffrey. *Harley Granville-Barker, 1877-1946.* London: Sidgwick & Jackson, 1949. Pp. 15.
Rev: *TLS*, Feb. 12, 1949, p. 107.

B3948 Farmer, A. J. "Harley Granville-Barker (1877-1946)." *EA*, X (1957), 304-309.

f. KOSZUL

B3949 Kablé, M. "André Koszul (1878-1956)." *LanM*, L (1956), 374-375.

B3950 Lalou, René. "Souvenirs d'André Koszul." *EA*, X (1957), 16-17.

B3951 Pruvost, René. "La Carrière et l'Œuvre d'André Koszul." *EA*, X (1957), 5-15.

g. McKERROW

B3952 Francis, F. C. "A List of the Writings of Ronald Brunlees McKerrow." *Library*, NS, XXI (1941), 229-263.

B3953 Greg, W. W. *Ronald Brunlees McKerrow, 1872-1940.* From the *Proceedings of the British Academy*, XXVI. London: Humphrey Milford, 1941. Pp. 30.
Rev: *TLS*, Aug. 30, 1941, p. 419; by C. J. Sisson, *MLR*, XXXVII (1942), 107; by F. C. Francis, *Library*, NS, XXII, 257-258.

h. POLLARD

B3954 Francis, F. C. "A. W. Pollard, 1859-1944." *Library*, 4th Series, XXV (1944-45), 82-86.

B3955 "Alfred William Pollard." *TLS*, March 18, 1944, p. 140. See also letters by Miss M. St. Clare Byrne and Mr. Victor Scholderer, *TLS*, Apr. 1, 1944, p. 167.

i. SCHÜCKING

B3956 Hecht, Ilse. "L. L. Schücking—75 Jahre." *Anglia*, LXXI (1953), 257-258.

B3957 Schücking, Levin Ludwig. "Memorabilia." *Anglia*, LXXVI (1958), 1-26.

B3958 Clemen, Wolfgang. "Gedanken zu Levin L. Schückings Lebenswerk." *Anglia*, LXXVI (1958), 27-40.

B3959   Ehrl, B. "Bibliographie der Veröffentlichungen von Levin L. Schücking (ohne Besprechungen)." *Anglia*, LXXVI (1958), 217-226.
B3960   Ehrl, Lotte, ed. "Bibliographie der Shakespeare-Publikationen 1938-1958 von Levin L. Schücking." *SJ*, 94 (1958), 362-363.

j. STAHL

B3961   "Zum Tode Dr. Ernst Leopold Stahls." *MDtShG*, I (1949), 4.
B3962   Stroedel, Wolfgang. "Ernst Leopold Stahl." *SJ*, 84/86 (1950), 11-12.

k. TANNENBAUM

B3963   Smith, Robert Metcalf. "Dr. Samuel A. Tannenbaum." *SAB*, XXII (1947), 147-148.
B3964   Tannenbaum, Dorothy R. "Bibliography of Works by Samuel A. Tannenbaum." *SAB*, XXIII (1948), 87-94.

l. WOLFF

B3965   Schütt, Marie. "Nachruf—Emil Wolff." *Anglia*, LXX (1951), 337-338.
B3966   Heuer, Hermann. "Zum Tode von Emil Wolff." *SJ*, 87/88 (1952), 268-269.

m. OTHERS

B3967   Smith, John Hazel. "A Bibliography of the Scholarly Writings of Thomas Whitfield Baldwin." *Studies in Honor of T. W. Baldwin*, 1958, pp. 267-276.
B3968   Brock-Sulzer, Elisabeth. "Albert Bassermann." *SJ*, 89 (1953), 242-243.
B3969   Hofmüller, Rudolf. "Diplomat und Sprachmeister. Zum 150. Geburtstag des Shakespeare. Übersetzers Wolf Graf von Baudissin." *VB(Mü)*, Jan. 30, 1939, p. 5.
B3970   Mackail, J. W. *Andrew Cecil Bradley, 1851-1935*. Oxford: Univ. Press; London: Milford, 1936. Pp. 10.
B3971   Leslie, Sir Shane. "Henry Bradshaw, Prince of Bibliographers." *To Doctor R: Essays Here Collected and Published in Honor of the Seventieth Birthday of Dr. A. S. W. Rosenbach*. Philadelphia: Privately printed, 1946, pp. 124-135.
B3972   Sehrt, Ernst Theodor. "Friedrich Brie." *SJ*, 84/86 (1950), 64-66.
B3973   Thomas, Walther. "In Memoriam Horst Caspar." *SJ*, 89 (1953), 243-244.
B3974   Sisson, C. J. *Raymond Wilton Chambers, 1874-1942*. From the *Proceedings of the British Academy*, XXX. London: Cumberlege, 1946. Pp. 19.
          Rev: *TLS*, Jan. 26, 1946, p. 47; by William W. Lawrence, *MLR*, XLI, 423-424.
B3975   Wilson, F. P., and J. D. Wilson. "Sir Edmund Kerchever Chambers, 1866-1954." *Proceedings of the British Academy*, XLII (1957), 267-285.
B3976   B(aldensperger), Fernand. "La Comtesse de Chambrun." *RLC*, XXVIII (1954), 366-367.
B3977   Koszul, André, et Jean Simon. "Nécrologie: Fernand Danchin (1866-1953)." *EA*, VII (1954), 151.
B3978   Keller, W. "Werner Deetjen, 3 April 1877-21 May 1939." *SJ*, LXXV (1939), 139-141.
B3979   Förster, Max. "Curt Dewischeit 1874-1941." *SJ*, LXXVII (1941), 190-191.
B3980   Koziol, Herbert. "Albert Eichler. Nekrolog." *SJ*, 90 (1954), 361-362.
B3981   Chassé, Ch., et Henri Peyre. "Albert Feuillerat." *EA*, VI (1953), 85-88.
B3982   Highfill, Philip H., Jr. "Horace Howard Furness." *ShN*, VII (1957), 44.
B3983   White, Beatrice. "Frederick James Furnivall." *Essays and Studies*, NS, V (1952), 64-76.
B3984   Francis, F. C. "A List of Dr. Greg's Writings." *Library*, 4th Series, XXVI (1945), 72-97.
B3985   Highfill, Philip, Jr. "Biography in Brief: James Orchard Halliwell-Phillipps." *ShN*, VII (1957), 38.
B3986   Kapp, R. "Wolfgang Keller. Zu seinem 70. Geburtstag am 14 Feb., 1943." *Eng. Studn.*, LXXV (1942/43), 145-158.
B3987   Thorpe, James, ed. *A Bibliography of the Writings of George Lyman Kittredge*. With Intro. by Hyder Edward Rollins. Harvard Univ. Press, 1948. Pp. xiv, 125.
B3988   Shuttleworth, Bertram. "W. J. Lawrence: A Handlist." Part I, *TN*, VIII (1954), 52-54; Part II, *TN*, IX (1954/55), 15-19; Part III, ibid., pp. 34-38; Part IV, ibid., pp. 67-73; Part V, ibid., pp. 97-98; Part VI, *TN*, X (1956), 52-55; Part VII, ibid., pp. 69-73; Part VIII, ibid., pp. 114-117; Part IX, *TN*, XI, (1957), 26-30.
          Bibliog. of his writings on Elizabethan theater and subseq. stage history.
B3989   Shuttleworth, Bertram. "W. J. Lawrence: A Handlist, X-XIII." Part X, *TN*, XI (1957), 50-53; Part XI, ibid., pp. 78-81; Part XII, ibid., pp. 130-134; Part XIII, *TN*, XII (1957/58), 21-24.
B3990   Shuttleworth, Bertram. "W. J. Lawrence: A Handlist, XIV." *TN*, XII (1957/58), 65-67, 157-164.

B3991   Bailey, Cyril. *John William Mackail, O. M., 1859-1945.* *Proceedings of the British Academy,* XXXI (1946). London: Cumberlege, 1947. Pp. 12.
        Rev: *TLS*, Feb. 15, 1947, p. 95.

B3992   "Professor Mikhail Morozov." *News* (Moscow), 1952, No. 10, p. 14.

B3993   Fischer, Walther. "Nekrolog. Heinrich Mutschmann (1885-1955)." *SJ*, 93 (1957), 282-284.

B3994   Koziol, Herbert. "Helene Richter." *SJ*, 87/88 (1952), 267-268.

B3995   Seng, Peter J. "An Epitaph for Hyder E. Rollins." *ShN*, VIII (1958), 27.

B3996   Malone, Kemp. "Else von Schaubert, Septuagenarian." *MLN*, LXXI (1956), 513-514.

B3997   Heuer, Hermann. "Nachruf auf Saladin Schmitt. March 14, 1951, Präsident der Dt. Shakespeare-Gesellschaft 1943 bis 1951." *SJ*, 87/88 (1952), 5-8.

B3998   Donner, Henry Wolfgang. "Henrik Schück som Shakespeare-Forskare." *Finsk Tidskrift* (Åbo), 143 (1948), 113-131.

B3999   *A List of the Published Writings of Percy Simpson.* Oxford: Clarendon Press, 1950. Pp. 29.
        Rev: by G. Tillotson, *RES*, NS, II (1951), 299.

B4000   Blanchart, Paul. "In Memoriam Robert de Smet." *RHT*, VII (1955), 341-434.

B4001   "Robert Metcalf Smith, 1886-1952." *SQ*, III (1952), 139.

B4002   Keller, W. "W. F. Trench (1873-1939)." *SJ*, LXXV (1939), 141.

B4003   Isaac, Winifred F. E. C. *Alfred Wareing.* London: Privately printed and published, 1952. Pp. xxii, 221.
        A biography of the late librarian of the Shak. Memorial Library at Stratford.

8. LITERATURE PRODUCED UNDER SHAKESPEARE'S INFLUENCE
a. SHAKESPEARE AS A HERO IN LITERATURE (172;59)
(1) DRAMA (172;59)
(a) PLAYS

B4004   Arlett, V. I. *Unwillingly to School.* Sussex, 1938(?). Pp. 16.
        A One-act Play.

B4005   Asherman, Otto. *Shakespeare: A Comedy in One Act.* New York: French, 1956. Pp. 29.
        Based upon a German farce on "Goethe."

B4006   Atkinson, Henry. *Shakespeare in Lypiatt.* New York: Empire Subscription Booksellers; London, 1946. Pp. 80.
        Three acts, verse.

B4007   Carlton, G. *The Wooing of Anne Hathaway.* London: The Mitre Press, 1938. Pp. 124.
        A play in 3 acts.

B4008   Closson, Herman. "Shakespeare ou la Comédie de l'Aventure." Brussels: Edit. Universitaires, 1945. Pp. 128.

B4009   Constantin-Weyer, Maurice, and Clara Longworth de Chambrun. *Le Grand Will.* Drame historique en 3 actes. Paris: Editions de la Nouvelle France, 1945. Pp. 244.

B4010   Dane, Clemence. *Will Shakespeare: An Invention in Four Acts.* London: W. Heinemann, 1957. Dane is pseud. for Winifred Ashton. First publ. 1927.

B4011   Delpy, E. "Spiel um Shakespeare Wolfgang Goetz: Kuckuckseier." Erstaufführung in Leipzig. *LNN*, Jan. 16, 1938.

B4012   Dyne, Nicholas. "Master Will: A Comedy in One Act." *The New Plays Quarterly*, No. 38, 1957, p. 16ff.

B4013   Gruner, E. Hamilton. *With Golden Quill.* Stratford-on-Avon: Shakespeare Press, 1936. Pp. xii, 212. In three Acts.
        With a Tudor Cameo (as Preamble) by William Jaggard.
        Rev: *TLS*, Jan. 23, 1937, p. 62.

B4014   Haigh, Veronica. *To Dream Again.* A Romantic Play in three Acts. London: English Theatre Guild, 1946. Pp. 104.

B4015   Hone, John. *Hey, Will! Will!* A Play in One Act. London: Samuel French, 1948. Pp. 31.

B4016   Johnson, Samuel W. *The Courtship of Anne Hathaway.* A dramatic poem. New York: Exposition Press, 1952.
        Includes over 30 excerpts from the works.

B4017   King, Thomson. "*The Taming of the Shrew.*" *SAB*, XVII (1942), 73-79.
        Contains a skit including Shak.

B4018   Kipphardt, Heibar. *Shakespeare Dringend Gesucht.* A satirical comedy in three acts. Berlin: Henschel, 1954. Pp. 116.

B4019   Kriesi, Hans. *Die Heimkehr des Propheten.* [*Historisches Lustspiel; Shakespeare oder eine Shakespeare-Figur bildet den Stoff des Dramas*]. Elgg (Kanton Zürich): Volks-Verlag, 1935. Pp. 84.

B4020   Lennon, T. *The Truth About Ann.* A three-act play. New York: J. Day Company, 1942. Pp. xii, 132.

B4021   Rossmann, Hermann. *Titanen. 3 Einakter. Shakespeares Tod. König Thoas. Dante u. Beatrice.* Munich: Desch, 1955. Pp. 98.

B4022   Seiler, C. "Mistress Shakespeare: A Tragi-comedy in One Act." *Poet Lore*, XLIII (1936), 119-134.

B4023   Silliman, Sherwood. *The Laurel Bough*. Drama in three acts. New York: Privately printed, 1956.
That Marlowe wrote the plays.

B4024   Sladen-Smith, Frank. *Sweet Master William: A Play*. London: French, 1953. Pp. iv, 32.

B4025   Williams, Charles. *A Myth of Shakespeare*. Oxford Univ. Press, 1936. Pp. 146.

B4026   Williams, Emlyn. *Spring 1600: A Comedy in Three Acts*. Heinemann, 1946. Pp. 99.

(b) CRITIQUES

B4027   Boyd, Alice K. *The Interchange of Plays between London and New York, 1910-1939: A Study in Relative Audience Response*. DD, Columbia University, 1948. New York: King's Crown Press, 1948. Pp. 125.
Lists a play called "Will Shakespeare," unsuccessful in both London (1921) and New York (1923). Survey does not include revivals.

B4028   Kalthoff, Eva. *Das Literaturdrama. Berühmte Dichter als Dramenhelden*. Mit besonderer Berücksichtigung des 19. Jahrhunderts. DD, Munich, 1941. Kettwig/Ruhr: Flothmann, 1941. Pp. 78.

B4029   Nichols, J. W. *A Study of William Shakespeare as Character in the English Drama*. MA thesis, Birmingham, 1952.

B4030   Rodger, G. B. B. *The Presentation of the Artist-Hero in Nineteenth Century German Drama*. DD, Glasgow, 1952.

(2) NOVELS (172;59)

B4031   Arnoux, Alexandre. "A la Rencontre de Shakespeare." *Rev. de Paris*, Feb., 1953, pp. 102-115.
An imaginary meeting with Shak.

B4032   Brahms, Caryl, and S. J. Simon (pseud. for Doris Caroline Abrahams and S. J. Skidelsky). *No Bed for Bacon; or, Shakespeare Sows an Oat*. London: Joseph, 1941; New York: Crowell, 1950. Pp. 241.
Rev: A506.

B4033   Brophy, John. *Gentleman of Stratford*. London: Collins, 1939; New York: Harper, 1940. Pp. 384. Trl. by Margareta Angström as *Hans Namn var Shakespeare*. Stockholm: Bokförlaget Natur och Kultur, 1946.
Rev: *TLS*, Aug. 26, 1939, p. 505.

B4034   Bullett, Gerald. *The Alderman's Son*. London: Michael Joseph, 1954. Pp. 223.
A fictional study of the life of Shak.
Rev: *TLS*, Jan. 15, 1954, p. 37; by Johannes Nielsen, *Berlingske Aften* (Copenhagen), June 18, 1954; by Karen Kramp, *SJ*, 91 (1955), 352-353.

B4035   Chambrun, Clara Longworth de. *My Shakespeare, Rise!* Stratford-on-Avon: Shakespeare Press, 1935. Pp. 379; il. Chicago: Lippincott, 1936. Pp. 366. Also published as *Mon Grand Ami Shakespeare*, 1935; *Mein grosser Kollege Shakespeare*, translated by Viktor Polzer, Vienna: Zsolnoy, 1936; Berlin: P. Zsolnoy, 1936. *Mi gran amigo Shakespeare*, translated by Alejandro A. Rosa, Buenos Aires: Edit. Coepla, 1941.
Rev: by Louis Mandin, *MdF*, 257 (1935), 421-424; by L. C., *RAA*, XIII (1935/36), 513-514; *TLS*, Feb. 14, 1935, p. 88; *TLS*, March 28, 1936, p. 270; *London Mercury*, XXXIII, 559; by Louis Gillet, *RddxM*, 108 (1938), 443-457; by C. F. W. Behl, *DL*, XXXIX (1936/37), 752-753.

B4036   Cheever, J. "Homage to Shakespeare." *Story*, XI (1937), 73-81.
A short story.

B4037   Downton, Wm. *William Shakespeare, Gentleman*. Philadelphia: College Offset Press, 1948. Pp. vi, 123.

B4038   Evans, John Roland. *The Boyhood of Shakespeare*. Hutchinson's Books for Young People. London, 1947. Pp. 256.

B4039   Haemmerling, K. *Der Mann, der Shakespeare Hiess*. Berlin: Deutscher Verlag, 1938. Pp. 445. Berlin: Verlag des Druckhauses Tempelhof, 1949. Pp. 449.
Rev: by A. Ehr, *Archiv*, 174 (1938), 261-262; by C. F. W. Behl, *DL*, XL (1938), 622-623; by H. Fischer, *Stimmen der Zeit*, LXVIII (1938), 421; by Rud. Huch, *Deutsches Volkstum*, XX, 421-423; by W. Schwerdtfeger, *Badische Presse*, April 23, 1939, and *Darmstädter Tagblatt*, April 22, 1939; by Gabriele Reuter, *NYTBR*, Oct. 8, 1939, p. 8.

B4040   Hering, Ernst. *Sterne über England. Ein Roman um Shakespeare*. Leipzig: Wilh. Goldmann, 1938. Pp. 235.
Rev: by Fritz Wölcken, *DNL*, XXXIX (1938), 627.

B4041   Heugten, J. van. "Erna Grautoff en haar. Herrscher über Traum und Leben (een Shakespeare-Bacon Roman)." *Boekenshouw*, XXXIV (1940/41), 261-266.

B4042   Holland, Ruth. *One Crown with a Sun*. London: Jonathan Cape, 1952. Pp. 286. Tr. by Abeth de Beughem as *La Vie Passionnée de William Shakespeare*. Paris: Intercontinental

du Livre, 1956.
A novel about Shakespeare.
Rev: by Marchette Chute, *SQ*, v (1954), 90.

B4043 Holm, Hans. *Der Schwan von Avon*. Vienna: Amandus, 1948. Pp. 264.

B4044 Payne, Pierre Stephen Robert. *Roaring Boys*. New York: Doubleday, 1955; publ. as *The Royal Players*, London: Hale, 1956. Pp. 316. Tr. by Schlaich as *Aufruhr der Komödianten. Ein Shakespeare-Roman*. Munich: Desch, 1956. Pp. 395.
Novel about Shak. and his players between the years 1603, when Elizabeth I died, and December, 1607, when Shak.'s brother Edmond was buried.
Rev: *Booklist*, Sept. 15, 1955, p. 34; by F. E. Faverty, *Chicago Sunday Tribune*, Sept. 18, p. 11; *Kirkus*, XXIII, 441; by Caroline Tunstall, *NYHTBR*, Sept. 4, p. 5; by Frances Winwar, *NYTBR*, Sept. 4, p. 6; *San Francisco Chronicle*, Sept. 25, p. 21; *TLS*, Dec. 28, 1956, p. 777.

B4045 Cancelled.

B4046 Schendel, Arthur van. *Shakespeare*. Amsterdam: Meulenhoff, 1953. Pp. 231.
Biographical novel; 3rd edition, with 2nd edition of his *Verlaine*.

b. OTHER LITERATURE PROVOKED BY SHAKESPEARE (172;-)
(1) DRAMA
(a) HAUPTMANN

B4047 Hauptmann, Gerhart. *Hamlet in Wittenberg*. Schauspiel. Berlin: Fischer, 1935. Pp. 189.
Rev: A9659.

B4048 "Gerhart Hauptmann and the Hamlet Theme." *TLS*, Aug. 15, 1936, p. 660.

B4049 Voigt, Felix A. "Gerhart Hauptmann und England [die Bedeutung Shakespeares für sein Schaffen]." *GRM*, xxv (1937), 321-329.

B4050 Voigt, F. A., and W. A. Reichart. *Hauptmann und Shakespeare, mit einem Aufsatz und Dramatischen Szenen von G. Hauptmann*. Breslau: Maruscheke and Berendt, 1938. Pp. viii, 154.
Rev: A9667.

B4051 Voigt, F. A. "Gerhart Hauptmann und Shakespeare." *SJ*, LXXVIII/LXXIX (1943), 6-28.

B4052 Voigt, Felix A., and W. A. Reichart. *Hauptmann und Shakespeare: Ein Beitrag zur Geschichte des Fortlebens Shakespeares in Deutschland*. 2 rev. ed. Goslar: Deutsche Volksbücherei, 1947. Pp. 153.
Rev: A9670.

B4053 Galambos, Wilhelm. *Gerhart Hauptmanns Interesse für Shakespeares Hamlet*. DD, Vienna, 1948. Pp. 120. Typewritten.

(b) SHAW

B4054 Shaw, Bernard. "Cymbeline Refinished: A Variation on Shakespeare's Ending." Shaw's *Geneva, Cymbeline Refinished and Good King Charles*. London: Constable, 1946, pp. 133-150. Also in *London Mercury*, XXXVII (1938), 373-389.

B4055 Shaw, Bernard. "Shakes versus Shav. A Puppet Play." Shaw's *Buoyant Billions, Farfetched Fables*, and *Shakes versus Shav*. London: 1950; New York: Dodd Mead, 1951. First publ. in *Arts Council Bulletin*, Sept., 1949.

(c) OTHERS

B4056 *Connaissance de Shakespeare*. Cahiers de la Compagnie Madeleine Renaud—J.-L. Barrault. No. 16. Paris: Julliard, 1956. Pp. 128.
Adaptations in translation.

B4057 Abelson, A. "The Missing Scene in *Merchant of Venice* and in Ibn Zahav's Play." *The Jewish Forum*, XXX (Nov., 1947), 269, 273.

B4058 Abelson, A. "Transcending Shakespeare." *The Jewish Forum*, XXXI (Aug., 1948), 167-172. Scenes supplied for *Merch*.

B4059 Babcock, R. W. "William Shakespeare Speaks on V-E Day." *SRL*, XXVIII (June 2, 1945), 26. Mosaic of Quotations in a short dramatic dialogue on V-E Day.

B4060 Bessborough, Earl of. *Triptych, Three Plays: Like Stars Appearing, The Moon is Night*, and *Darker the Sky*, a trilogy of historical and religious plays of Plantagenet England which fills the gap in the sequence of chronicle plays between Shak.'s *John* and Marlowe's *Edward II*. New York: Theatre Arts Books; London: Heinemann, 1958.

B4061 Boldt, Harald. "Hamlet als Frau." In der Königslegende, ein Schauspiel von Just Scheu, in Kiel uraufgeführt. *MNN*, No. 9, Jan. 9, 1941.

B4062 Brien, Alan. "Theatre." *Spectator*, Aug. 1, 1958, p. 165.
Production of "The *Hamlet* of Stepney Green."

B4063 Chase, Stanley P., and George H. Quinby. "A Prologue for *The Winter's Tale*, Acts IV and V." *SAB*, xx (1945), 134-139.

B4064 Crommelynck, Fernand, ed. *Le Chevalier à la Lune, ou Sir John Falstaff*. Brussels: Editions des Artistes, 1954. Pp. 245.

B4065 Dukes, Ashley. *Return to Danes Hill*. London: Samuel French, 1958. Pp. 86.
A play using the *Hamlet* story in a modern setting.
Rev: *TLS*, June 20, 1958, p. 350.

B4066 Freund, Philip. *Prince Hamlet*. New York: Bookman Associates, 1953. Pp. 70.
Rev: by Milton Crane, *SQ*, VI (1955), 352; by Karen Kramp, *SJ*, 91 (1955), 350-352.

B4067 George, C. *When Shakespeare's Ladies Meet*. New York: Dramatists Play Service, 1942.
A one-act comedy.

B4068 H., F. E. C. "Shakespeare and the Crisis: A Masque." *Ba*, XXIII (1938), 180-187.
The Speakers are: Hitler, Chamberlain, Cooper, Chorus, Powers. The dialogue consists of quotations from Shak.

B4069 Heppenstall, Rayner, and Michael Innes. *Three Tales of Hamlet*. London: Gollancz, 1950.
Three broadcast plays on the *Hamlet* story. "Michael Innes" is the pen name of J. I. M. Stewart.
Rev: *TLS*, May 5, 1950, p. 278; by G. W. Stonier, *NstN*, XXXIX (1950), 610; *ShS*, IX (1956), 13; *NYTBR*, Sept. 15, 1957, p. 33.

B4070 MacKaye, Percy. *The Mystery of Hamlet, King of Denmark or What We Will*. New York: Bond Wheelwright, 1950. Pp. xvii, 69, 710. Trade edition, 1951. Pp. 675.
A "tetralogy with prelude and postlude." A series of plays dealing with King Hamlet and the Danish court before the period at which Shak.'s play begins.
Rev: by H. W. Wells, *SAB*, XXIV (1949), 85-90; by A. McCleery, *TAr*, XXXIII (June, 1949), 40-41; by F. E. Hill, *NYTBR*, Dec. 31, 1950, p. 4; by R. M. Hesse and W. R. Mackenzie, *QJS*, XXXVII (1950), 509; by Henry W. Wells, *SRL*, Jan. 27, 1951, p. 12; by I. A. Salomon, *ShN*, I (1951), 24.

B4071 Morris, Thomas B. *Ophelia*. A Play for Women in One Act. London: Samuel French, 1948. Pp. 35.

B4072 Renan, Ernest. *Caliban. Suite de la Tempête*. Ed. by Colin Smith. Manchester University French Classics Series. Manchester Univ. Press, 1954. Pp. 111.
Rev: by H. W. Wardman, *French Studies*, IX, No. 1 (1955), 83-84.

B4073 Saddey, Hans. *Selbst Shakespeare Hat Nicht Immer Recht*. Kassel/Basel: Bärenreiter-verlag, 1949. Pp. 60.
Shak. not a char.

B4074 San Martin, Eduardo. *La Novia de Hamlet*, Comedia en Tres Actos. Mexico City: Publicaciones del Grupo Literario "Bohemia Poblana," 1955. Pp. 98.

B4075 Schwarz, Hans. *Caesar. Eine Tragödie*. Berlin: Hans von Hugo Verlag, 1941. Pp. 122.
Rev: by Hans Joachim Schlamp, *EL*, III (1944), 40.

B4076 Weege, Robert. *Hamlet, Prinz von Dänemark*. Eine Tragödie. (Als MS. gedruckt.) Belgrade, 1943.

B4077 Willey, N. L. "Oehlenschläger's *Amleth*." *SS*, XVII (1942), 1-19.

(2) VERSE

B4078 Auslander, Joseph. "Shakespeare to Our Time." *New York Times Magazine*, April 24, 1955, p. 40. With portrait.

B4079 Bailey, R. E. *Dark Eyes and Will Shakespeare*. Milwaukee: Hampel, 1944.

B4080 Baskin, J. F. "Melancholy Jaques Interviews Jan Masefield." *SAB*, XXI (1946), 60-63.

B4081 Binding, R. G. "Wesen u. Wert d. Reims im Gedicht." *DL*, XXXIX (1936), 5-9.

B4082 Blackburn, Thomas. "Othello's Dream." *NstN*, Mar. 9, 1957, p. 312.

B4083 Brecht, Bertolt. "On Shakespeare's Play *Hamlet*." *Adam and Encore*, No. 254, 1956, p. 9.

B4084 Brecht, Bertolt. "*Hamlet*." Tr. by Helmut W. Bonheim. *CE*, XIX (1957), 82.

B4085 Brown, J. M. "Star-crossed." *SRL*, XIV (May 23, 1936), 10.

B4086 Carter, F. A. *More Haywire Shakespeare*. London: French, 1953.
Verse accounts of six plays: *Dream, Antony, Richard III, Macbeth, Othello*, and *Tempest*.

B4087 Cauley, C. "Laurence Olivier's *Richard III*." *Life and Letters*, LIV (1947), 42.
Poem upon a Glasgow performance.

B4088 Cremers, Paul Joseph. "Shakespeare." *SJ*, LXXVII (1941), 1.

B4089 Cumming, Isobel. "Shakespeare's Birthday, Stratford-upon-Avon." *English*, XI (1957), 166.

B4090 Doolittle, Hilda. *By Avon River*. New York: Macmillan, 1949. Pp. 98. *Avon*. Tr. by Johannes Urzidil. Berlin: Suhrkamp, 1955. Pp. 135.
A collection of poems about Shak.
Rev: A9265 and A9266.

B4091 Cancelled.

B4092 Fatout, Paul. "April 23, 1564-1937." *SAB*, XII (1937), 117.

B4093 Foster, Margaret. "To Shakespeare Triumphant (On the opening of the Walsingham tomb at Chislehurst)." *English*, XI (1956), 121.

B4094 Guiterman, A. "Soliloquy on *Hamlet*." *SAB*, XV (1940), 94.

B4095   Hanson, K. O. "Falstaff and The Chinese Poet." *Circle*, Nos. 7 and 8, 1946, pp. 38-40.

B4096   Hausman, J. J. "I Wonder if Will." *The Athenaeum* (Cincinnati, Ohio), XIV (1938), 48.

B4097   Herring, R. "Epitaph on Mercutio." *Life and Letters Today*, XXXVI (Jan., 1943), 28.

B4098   Herring, R. "A Praying Love-song: Hamlet to Ophelia." *Life and Letters Today*, XXXVI (1943), 35.

B4099   Herring, Robt. "Two Sonnets (Suggested by Shakespeare's *Othello*): Day's Demon and Dark Knight." *Life and Letters Today*, XXXVI (1943), 10.

B4100   Hughes, Langston. *Shakespeare in Harlem*. New York: Knopf, 1941.

B4101   Huhner, L. "William Shakespeare." *SAB*, XXII (1947), 35.

B4102   Humphries, R. "Maxim." *NYTBR*, Dec. 21, 1947, p. 2.
         Reprinted from *Forbid Thy Ravens*.

B4103   Hunter, Edwin R. "A Man from Stratford Entertains Ben Jonson, in Stratford, August 7, 1623, for Mistress Anne Shakespeare's Funeral." *SQ*, II (1951), 91-97.

B4104   Hyman, Harold M. "Hamlet's Soliloquy and American Loyalty." *American Assoc. Univ. Professors' Bulletin*, XLIV (1958), 736-739.

B4105   Johnson, A. E. "Yorick on *Hamlet*." *SR*, XLIX (1941), 476-478.

B4106   Johnson, Samuel W. *The Courtship of Anne Hathaway*. A dramatic poem. With excerpts from the plays and sonnets of Shak. in modern English. New York: Exposition Press, 1952. Pp. 95.

B4107   Lancaster, R. D. "*Richard II*." *TLS*, Oct. 28, 1955, p. 632.

B4108   Landrem, A. W. "Yon Pomegranate Tree." *SAB*, XII (1937), 167. Republished with efforts at improvement, *SAB*, XV (1940), 66.

B4109   Lanyon, C. L. "Shakespeare Answers the Scholars." *Poetry Review*, XXX (1939), 125.

B4110   Lea, F. A. "To Rosencrantz and Guildenstern." *Adelphi*, XIV (1938), 307.

B4111   Mabbott, M. C. "Shakespeare." *English Jour.*, XXV (1936), 233.

B4112   Moser, A. "On Reading Shakespeare." *Washington Post*, June 3, 1945.

B4113   Nemerov, Howard. "Orphic Scenario—for a Movie of *Hamlet*." *Quarterly Review of Literature*, IX (1957), 32-34.

B4114   O'Connor, J. F. "Oft Had I Dreamt." *The Athenaeum* (Cincinnati, Ohio), XIV (1938), 47.

B4115   Paulun, Dirks. "*Hamlet*, 1939." *MDG*, XLI (1939), Bd. 1, 134.

B4116   Provost, Foster. "On Shakespeare's Sonnet 116." *CE*, XVII (1956), 366.
         Parody inspired by the new astronomy of the twentieth century.

B4117   Quirk, C. J. "At Shakespeare's Grave." *Catholic World*, 165 (1947), 202.

B4118   Romig, E. D. "And Then Stratford." *SAB*, XXII (1947), 142.

B4119   'Sagittarius'. "Shakesperian Miscellany." *NstN*, XVII (1939), 319-320.

B4120   Saul, G. B. "Reflections on *Hamlet*." *CE*, VI (1945), 403.

B4121   Schlösser, Rainer. "Shakespeare 1939." *Wille und Macht* (Berlin), VIII (1940), Heft 3, p. 10.

B4122   Sleeper, B. R. "Questions to Gertrude." *SR*, L (1942), 77.

B4123   Sofaer, A. "A Shakespearean Actor's Lament." *New York Times*, April 18, 1937, Sec. XI, 2.

B4124   Tasker, Reuben. *A Presentation of Shakespeare* (Third Sketch). London: Privately printed by the author, 1958. Pp. 16.

B4125   Tiller, Terence. "The Fool in *Lear*." *Reading a Medal. And Other Poems*. London: Hogarth Press, 1957, pp. 51.

B4126   Van Doren, M. "To Shakespeare." *New Poems*. New York, 1948, p. 48.

B4127   Walsh, T. "A Wreath for Shakespeare." *SAB*, XII (1937), 68.

B4128   Weller, G. "Poets Cornered: Shakespeare." *Chambers' Journal*, April, 1945, p. 192.

B4129   Withington, R. " 'And Curst Be He'." *SAB*, XVIII (1943), 48.

(3)   VARIOUS FORMS OF PROSE
(a)   NOVELS

B4130   Alverdes, Paul. "Georg Brittings *Hamlet*-Roman, 1932." *Dank und Dienst. Reden und Aufsätze*. Munich: A. Langen/G. Müller, 1939, pp. 208-215.

B4131   Appleby, John. *The Stuffed Swan*. London: Hodder and Stoughton, 1956. Pp. 191.
         A novel, with Queen Elizabeth as the author of Shak.'s plays.
         Rev: *Sunday Times*, London, Nov. 4, 1956.

B4132   Baird, David. *The Thane of Cawdor: A Detective Study of Macbeth*. Oxford: Univ. Press; London: Milford, 1936; New York: Oxford Univ. Press, 1937. Pp. xii, 105.
         Rev: *TLS*, Aug. 14, 1937, p. 588; *SRL*, XVI (July 31, 1937), 19; by J. Corbin, *NYTBR*, Dec. 5, p. 34; *N&Q*, 173 (1937), 143-144.

B4133   "*Hamlet*, Królewicz Dúnski." *Teatr* (Warsaw), VI, Nos. 11/12 (1951), 14-23. Tr. of Branstaetter's novel.

Rev: by P. Grzegorczych, *Twórczość*, x (1952), 159-164; by Z. Kubiak, *Tygodnik Powszechny*, No. 26, 1952, pp. 8-9.

B4134   Bourjaily, Vance. *The Violated*. New York: Dial Press, 1958.
A novel, the second part of which is concentrated on a production of *Ham*.
Rev: by Granville Hicks, *SatR*, Aug. 23, 1958, p. 13.

B4135   Bryher (pseud. Annie Winifred Ellerman). *The Player's Boy: A Novel*. London: Collins, 1957.
Acting companies in Southwark in the time of James I.

B4136   Cabell, B. *Hamlet Had An Uncle*. New York: Farrar & Rinehart, 1940. Pp. xxiv, 272.
Rev: by L. Eshleman, *NYTBR*, Jan. 28, 1940, p. 7.

B4137   Dale, Celia. *The Wooden O: A Novel*. London: Cape, 1953. Pp. 255.

B4138   Hauptmann, Gerhart. *Im Wirbel der Berufung*. Berlin: Fischer, 1936. Pp. 281.
Rev: A9660.

B4139   Voigt, Felix A., and Walter A. Reichart. *Hauptmann und Shakespeare: Ein Beitrag zur Geschichte des Fortlebens Shakespeares in Deutschland*. 2 rev. ed. Goslar: Deutsche Volksbücherei, 1947. Pp. 153.
Rev: A9670.

B4140   Ibn-Zaham, A. *Jessica, My Daughter*. New York: Crown Publishers, 1948.

B4141   Innes, Michael (pseud. for John Innes Mackintosh Stewart). *Hamlet, Revenge!* (Red badge books). New York: Dodd, Mead; London: Gollancz, 1937. Pp. 344.
A murder mystery. Comments upon the staging of *Hamlet*.

B4142   Lanham, Edwin. *Another Ophelia*. London: Heinemann, 1938. Pp. 271.

B4143   Long, Amelia Reynolds. *The Shakespearean Murders*. New York: Phoenix Press, 1939. Pp. 255.

B4144   O'Neal, Cothburn. *The Dark Lady*. New York: Crown Press, 1954. Pp. 313.
Rev: *Time*, Sept. 27, 1954, p. 106; *SatR*, Jan. 8, pp. 12, 34; by Milton Crane, *SQ*, VI (1955), 355; by Harold C. Bohn, *ShN*, V (1955), 30.

B4145   Pargeter, Edith. *This Rough Magic: A Novel*. London: Heinemann, 1953. Pp. 5, 329.

B4146   Wenz-Hartmann, Gisela. *Amleth. Ein Kampf um Ehre, Recht und Heimaterde. Roman*. Leipzig: Quelle & Meyer, 1936. Pp. 271.
Rev: *Nordische Stimmen*, VII (1937), 126-127.

B4147   Ehrentreich, Alfred. "Bemerkungen zu einem Deutschen Hamletroman." *N. Mon.*, IX (1939), 481-483.
On B4146.

B4148   Wilson, Marion L. *The Tragedy of Hamlet Told by Horatio*. Enschede, Holland, 1956.
Rev: *ShN*, VII (1957), 22.

(b) STORIES

B4149   Foley, M. " 'One with Shakespeare'." *Story*, XVIII (1941), 9-14.

B4150   Goudge, E. "The Dark Lady." *Good Housekeeping*, November, 1938, pp. 28-31, 305-312.

B4151   Heppenstall, Rayner, and Michael Innes (John Innes Mackintosh Stewart). *Three Tales of Hamlet*. London: Gollancz, 1950. Pp. 192. Heppenstall: "Foll's Saga." Innes: "The Hawk and the Handsaw: Mysterious Affair at Elsinore."
Rev: B4069.

B4152   Ross, L. Q. "Mr. Kaplan and Shakespeare." *New Yorker*, XIII (1937), 22-24.

B4153   Thurber, James. "The Macbeth Murder Mystery." *My World—and Welcome To It*. New York: Harcourt, Brace, 1942, pp. 33-39.

B4154   Wells, C. "The Shakespeare Title-page Mystery." *The Dolphin*, No. 4, 1941, pp. 158-165.

B4155   Wylie, I. A. R. "You Never Can Tell." *NYHTBR*, April 16, 1939, p. 3.

(c) OTHERS

B4156   "Brush Up on Your Shakespeare." *Grail*, May, 1957, pp. 29-31.

B4157   "If Our Drama is Unoriginal, So Was Most of Shakespeare." *Saturday Evening Post*, Feb. 16, 1957, p. 10.
A facetious defense of literary pilfering. Cites Shak.'s use of Holinshed, etc.

B4158   "Laft Night's Firft Night." *Punch*, 215 (Aug. 11, 1948), 138.

B4159   "Mein Name ist Shakespeare." *Die Auslese aus Zeitschr. des In- u. Auslandes*, XI (1937), 22-24.

B4160   Arnoux, Alexandre. "A la Recontre de Shakespeare." *Revue de Paris*, LX (Feb., 1953), 102-115.

B4161   Bancroft, Edith M. "The Salvage of Shakespeare." *English*, I, No. 5 (1937), 424-426.
Really a jibe at modernist poetry.

B4162   Brown, Ivor. *Dark Ladies*. London: Collins, 1956. Pp. 320. Includes essays on Shak.'s *Dark Lady* and on *Cleopatra*.
Rev: *NstN*, Mar. 23, 1957, p. 390; *Scotsman*, Mar. 7; *TLS*, Dec. 4, p. 223.

B4163   Cantor, Arthur. "Shakespeare at Sardi's." *TAr*, XXXII (Oct., 1948), 34-36.

B4164 Dobrée, Bonamy. "On (Not) Enjoying Shakespeare: An Unbuttoned Conversation in a Study." *Essays and Studies* (Eng. Assoc.), IX (1956), 39-55.

B4165 Doolittle, Hilda. *By Avon River.* New York: Macmillan, 1949. Pp. 98. *Avon.* Translated by Johannes Urzidil. Berlin: Suhrkamp, 1955. Pp. 135.
Rev: A9265 and A9266.

B4166 Drew, E. "Alas, Poor Hamlet!" *Living Age*, 355 (1938), 150-152.
A compilation of student remarks from examination papers.

B4167 Durrell, Lawrence. *Prospero's Cell: A Guide to the Landscape and Manners of the Island of Corcyra.* London: Faber and Faber, 1945.
Rev: *TLS*, Oct. 27, 1945, p. 512.

B4168 Dunwald, W. "Gespräch mit Shakespeare." *Rhein.-Westfälishe Ztg.* (Essen), Dec. 15, 1940.

B4169 Förster, Max. "Shakespeare oder die heutige englische Briefmarke." *GRM*, XXXV (1954), 152-153.

B4170 Garçon, Maurice, ed. *Plaidoyers Chimériques.* Paris: Fayard, 1954.
Selections from Shak.'s famous declaimers or legal defendants, as the "romantique Antony" and "le More de Venise." Attempts to place the defendant before his literary jury with all the facts of the case, the passions and motivations analyzed.
Rev: by Armand Rio, *Biblio*, XXIII, iv (1955), 16.

B4171 Kaplan, Milton. "Retarding Shakespeare." *Harper's Magazine*, Jan., 1956, pp. 37-38.

B4172 Kirmse, Persis. *Shakespeare and the Birds: A Book of Drawings.* London: Methuen, 1938. Pp. 57.

B4173 Kirmse, Persis. *Shakespeare at the Zoo: A Book of Drawings.* London: Methuen, 1936. Pp. 55.

B4174 Klein, Knud. "Hamlet's Castle Houses Marine Mementoes." *American-Scandinavian Rev.*, XXV (1937), 122-129.

B4175 Leaf, M. "*Romeo and Juliet.*" *American Magazine*, 128 (December, 1939), 127.

B4176 Lewis, Wyndham. "War Shakespeare ein John Bull?" Wyndham Lewis's *Der mysteriöse John Bull. Ein Tugendspiegel des Engländers.* Aus dem Engl. übers. von Hans Rudolf Rieder. Essen: Essener Vlg. Anstalt, 1939, pp. 129-136.

B4177 Loizeaux, M. D. "Talking Shop; Shakespeare and the Automobile Age." *Wilson Library Bulletin*, XXXII (1957), 149.

B4178 Miller, Henry, and Michael Fraenkel. *Hamlet: A Philosophical Correspondence.* Vol. I. Paris Carrefour, 1939. Pp. 330. New York: Carrefour (342 E. 19th St.), 1943. Pp. 392.
Rev: A9269.

B4179 Oppenheimer, George, ed. *The Passionate Playgoer. A Personal Scrapbook.* New York: Viking, 1958. Pp. xiv, 623.
Includes reprints of "Disney and the Dane" by John Mason Brown, "The Barrymore Hamlet" by Percy Howard, Thurber's "The Macbeth Murder Mystery," "Welles on Wheels" by Oppenheimer, and Heywood Broun's "An Epitaph for Shylock."

B4180 Ornstein, J. A. "Th' Art a Knowing Cookie, Will." *High Points*, XXXVII (Nov., 1955), 65-69.

B4181 Oyhanarte, Horacio B. *En el Taller de Shakespeare.* Prólogo de Antonio Herrero. Buenos Aires: Guillermo Kraft, 1944. Pp. xxvi, 202.

B4182 Patrick, J. Max. "Cleopatra's Infinite Variety: A Fantasy." *Newberry Library Bulletin*, IV (1956), 110-113.
An imaginary conversation.

B4183 Russell, Bertrand. *Nightmares of Eminent Persons.* New York: Simon and Schuster, 1955.
Includes "Mr. Bowdler's Nightmare," "The Psychoanalyst's Nightmare." The latter, concerning Romeo, Hamlet, Othello, Lear, Macbeth, and Antony, repr. from *Courier*, XXII (Apr., 1954), 81-87.

B4184 Twiss, John. "Shakespeare's 'Preying Monsters': A discussion." *N &Q*, 199, (1954), 334-335.

B4185 Winterich, John T., et al. "Your Literary I. Q." *SatR*, Oct. 22, 1955, p. 17; Nov. 5, 1955, p. 40; Dec. 31, p. 6; Aug. 25, 1956, p. 10; July 12, 1958, p. 15; Aug. 2, p. 27; Sept. 20, p. 34; Nov. 22, p. 40.

9. SHAKESPEARE IN THE SCHOOLS AND UNIVERSITIES (173;60)
a. DESIGNED FOR CHILDREN
(1) EDITIONS OF SHAKESPEARE

B4186 Stone, M. W. "Shakespeare and the Juvenile Drama." *TN*, VIII (1954), 65-66.
A list of the juvenile dramas adapted from Shakespeare, with their publishers and dates.
See also Adaptations, Items B189, B190, B206, and others.

(a) SEVERAL PLAYS

B4187 *Shakespeare's Julius Caesar, A Midsummer Night's Dream, Romeo and Juliet.* Modern version ed. by Charles W. Cooper (Classics for Enjoyment). River Forest, Illinois: Laidlaw Brothers, 1958. Pp. vii, 335.
Simplified, abridged teaching versions. See B4204.

B4188   Specking, Inez. *Shakespeare for Children.* New York: Vantage Press, 1955. Pp. 95.
         Thirteen plays.

(b) SINGLE PLAYS

B4189   *The Comedy of Errors.* Bearb. v. Klaus Fuss. Karlsruhe: Braun, 1953. Pp. 83.

B4190   *Romeo and Juliet.* Ed. by G. N. Pocock for schools. The King's Treasures of Lit. London:
         Dent, 1937. Pp. 141.

B4191   *A Midsummer Night's Dream.* Arranged by Henry S. Taylor. The Shorter Shakespeare Series.
         London: Ginn, 1956. Pp. ix, 186.

B4192   *The Merchant of Venice.* Met verklarende aantekeningen voor school en huis door K. ten
         Bruggencate. 15 dr., nagezien door C. D. ten Bruggencate. Groningen: J. B. Wolters, 1939.
         Pp. 103. Also reprinted 1942, 1947, 1950, 1952.

B4193   *The Merchant of Venice.* Med innleiing og merknader til skolebruk eller sjølstudium ved Chr.
         Collin. 7th edition. Oslo: Aschehoug, 1939. Pp. 127. 9th edition, 1950. Pp. 162. 10th
         edition, 1954. Pp. lxxxviii, 162.

B4194   *The Merchant of Venice.* Ed. by Jacob Alsted and V. Østergaard. Engelske Forfattere for
         Gymnasiet. Copenhagen: Gyldendal, 1955. Pp. 148.
         Annotated edition for the Gymnasium.

B4195   *The Merchant of Venice.* Arranged by Henry S. Taylor. The Shorter Shakespeare Series.
         London: Ginn, 1956. Pp. viii, 72.
             Rev: *TLS*, Mar. 23, 1956, p. 186.

B4196   *Henry IV, Pt. 1.* Ved O. J. Madsen. Engelske Tekster for Gymnasiet, 2. Copenhagen:
         Gad, 1950. Pp. 164.

B4197   *Henry IV, Part I.* Arranged by Henry S. Taylor. The Shorter Shakespeare Series. London:
         Ginn, 1956. Pp. ix, 86.

B4198   *King Henry V.* Arranged by Henry S. Taylor. The Shorter Shakespeare Series. London:
         Ginn, 1956. Pp. viii, 88.
             Rev: *TLS*, Mar. 23, 1956, p. 186.

B4199   *Julius Caesar.* Universal-Jugendbibliothek, No. 304. Leipzig: Giegler, 1938. Pp. 134.

B4200   *Oxford Shakespeare for Schools.* New York: Oxford Univ. Press, 1938. *Julius Caesar,* ed. by
         Ralph E. C. Houghton.

B4201   *Julius Caesar.* Met verklarende aantekeningen voor school en huis door K. ten Bruggencate.
         Groningen: J. B. Wolters, 1939. Pp. vii, 109. 13th edition, 1942. Pp. 108. 16th edition,
         1947. Pp. 108.

B4202   *Julius Caesar.* Kölner Hefte f. d. akadem. Unterricht. Engl. Texte, 4. Cologne: Pick, 1947.
         Pp. 61.

B4203   *Julius Caesar:* A Tragedy. Ed. Helmut Singer. Munich: Bayer. Schulbuch-Verl., 1950.
         Pp. viii, 133.

B4204   *Julius Caesar.* Modern rev. version, ed. by Charles W. Cooper. Whittier, California: Whittier
         College, 1950. Pp. viii, 87.
         An "experimental edition." No footnotes, but a substitution of modern words for those
         needing annotation. ("A soothsayer bids you beware the fifteenth day of March.")

B4204a   *Julius Caesar.* Ed. by Jes Skovgaard. Engelsk Laesning for Gymnasiet. Copenhagen:
         Hirschsprung, 1955. Pp. 92, 64.

B4205   *Julius Caesar.* Arranged by Henry S. Taylor. The Shorter Shakespeare Series. London: Ginn,
         1956. Pp. viii, 103.
             Rev: *TLS*, Mar. 23, 1956, p. 186.

B4206   *Julius Caesar.* Ed. by Fritz Krog. Frankfurt a. M.: Hirschgraben-Verl., 1955. Pp. 141.

B4207   *As You Like It.* Arranged by Henry S. Taylor. The Shorter Shakespeare Series. London:
         Ginn, 1956. Pp. viii, 96.
         Intended for play readings at school, with stage directions and other guides to interpretation.
             Rev: *TLS*, Mar. 23, 1956, p. 186.

B4208   *Twelfth Night, or What You Will.* Arranged by Henry S. Taylor. The Shorter Shakespeare
         Series. London: Ginn, 1956. Pp. viii, 108.

B4209   *Hamlet.* Illustrerede Klassikere IV. Copenhagen, 1956. Pp. 48.
         Illustrated edition for children.

B4210   *Macbeth.* Ed. for School Use by Anna P. Butler and M. A. Feehan. Chicago: Loyola Univ.
         Press, 1935. Pp. 184.

B4211   Wonnberger, Carl. "The Mercury *Macbeth*." *English Journal,* xxx (1941), 860-861.
         On the Orson Welles-Roger Hill edition, designed to accompany the recording. Publ.
         by Harper.

B4212   *Macbeth.* Ed. with an Introd. by J. H. Schutt. A New English Library. Groningen: Wolters,
         1951. Pp. 116. Also published 1953, 1956.
         An edition for Dutch schools.
             Rev: by R. W. Zandvoort, *ES*, xxxii (1951), 262-264; by A. Bogaerts, *LT*, 1951, p. 188.

B4213   *Student's Macbeth.* Ed. by Lambert Greenawalt and Simon Hochberger. New York: Globe Book Co., 1954. Pp. 185.
        Parallel text-and-explanation of the play. School edition.
        Rev: *ShN*, IV (1954), 23.

B4214   *Macbeth.* Arranged by Henry S. Taylor. The Shorter Shakespeare Series. London: Ginn, 1956. Pp. ix, 102.

B4215   *Antony and Cleopatra.* Ed. by Nora Ratcliffe. Edinburgh: Nelson, 1948. Pp. 186.

B4216   *The Tempest.* Ed. by S. C. Boorman. The London English Literature Series. London: Univ. of London Press, 1957. Pp. 153.
        Intended for students preparing for the Ordinary level of the General Certificate in English; full introduction and notes.
        Rev: *TLS*, Oct. 11, 1957, p. 615.

(c) CONDENSATIONS

B4217   *Shakespeare for Young Actors: 40-minute Versions of A Midsummer Night's Dream, The Merchant of Venice, The Taming of the Shrew, As You Like It, Julius Caesar, and the Tempest.* For secondary school study and production. Ed. with introd. and comments by Eleanor Patmore Young. New York: Exposition Press, 1958. Pp. 284.
        Rev: B188.

B4218   "Antony and Cleopatra: Condensed Version." *Senior Scholastic*, LII (Apr. 19, 1948), 15-18.

(2) INTRODUCTIONS

B4219   Wilson, John Dover. *Through Elizabethan Eyes.* Cambridge: Univ. Press, 1939. Pp. 108.
        An abridgement of *Life in Shakespeare's England*, published in 1911. For junior readers.
        Rev: *TLS*, Sept. 30, 1939, p. 567.

B4220   Hodges, C. Walter. *Shakespeare and the Players.* With a Foreword by Allardyce Nicoll. London: Ernest Benn, 1948. Pp. 101.
        Rev: A8636.

B4221   Metcalf, John C. *Know Your Shakespeare.* Boston: D. C. Heath & Co., 1949. Pp. viii, 245.
        For schools.

B4222   Norman, Charles. *The Playmaker of Avon.* Philadelphia: David McKay & Co., 1949. Pp. 155.
        A biography for school children.

B4223   Godwin, Edward F., and S. A. *The Greenwood Tree: A Portrait of William Shakespeare.* New York: Dutton, 1950. Pp. 178.
        A biography for children.

B4224   Halliday, F. E. *The Enjoyment of Shakespeare.* London: Duckworth, 1952. Pp. 116.
        Intended for secondary schools. Very suitably written.
        Rev: by G. B. Harrison, *SQ*, V (1954), 334-335; by Roy W. Battenhouse, *SQ*, VI (1955), 469-470.

B4225   Chute, Marchette. *Shakespeare and his Stage.* Reissue. London: Univ. of London Press, 1953. Pp. 128.
        Rev: A8629.

B4226   Dodd, E. F. *Three Shakespeare Comedies.* Told by E. F. Dodd. Macmillan's Stories to Remember in Simple English. London: Macmillan, 1954. Pp. 56.
        AYL, Dream, Much.

B4227   Dodd, E. F. *Six Tales from Shakespeare.* Macmillan's Stories to Remember in Simple English. London: Macmillan, 1954. Pp. 97.
        Rev: B3756

B4228   Rapaport, N. *Sippurey Shakespeare li-vney ha-neurim.* Jerusalem: Ahiassaf, 1955. Pp. 150.
        Shakespeare's Tales for Younger People.

B4229   White, A. T. *Will Shakespeare and the Globe Theater.* New York: Random House, 1955.
        A biography for children about 10.
        Rev: *Chicago Sunday Tribune*, Nov. 13, 1955, p. 38; *Kirkus*, XXIII (Aug. 15, 1955), 604; *Library Journal*, LXXX (Nov. 15), 2648; *NYHTBR*, Oct. 30, 1955, p. 8.

B4230   Parker, Anthony. *Great Men of Warwickshire.* Bodley Head, 1956.
        Includes a life of Shak. Intended for juveniles.

B4231   Unstead, Robert John. *People in History.* New York: Macmillan, 1957.
        The lives of influential historical figures, aimed at the juvenile level. Includes a life of Shak., pp. 269-280.

B4232   Allen, John. *Great Moments in the Theatre.* Illustrated by Joanna Riley. London: Phoenix House, 1958.
        For young readers. Gives accounts of the building of the Globe Theatre and of Shak. at the two Stratfords in the New World.
        Rev: *TLS*, Nov. 21, 1958, Children's Book Section, p. xxxii.

B4233   Brown, Ivor. *William Shakespeare.* Nelson's Picture Biographies. London: Nelson, 1958.
        For young readers.

B4234 Burton, H. M. *Shakespeare and his Plays*. Illustrated by Richard G. Robinson. London: Methuen, 1958. Pp. 68.
General introduction for children, with reproductions of MS pages and Stratford buildings.
Rev: *TLS*, (Children's Books), Apr. 11, 1958, p. xxxi; by Hudson Rogers, *English Journal*, XLVII (1958), 308.

B4235 Colijn, I. *An Introduction to Shakespeare: For Secondary Schools*. Zutphen: Thieme, 1958. Pp. 52.

B4236 Duthie, Eric, ed. *Children's Book of Famous Lives*. London: Odhams, 1958. Pp. 415.
Includes "William Shakespeare: The Glory of English Literature" by J. Bayley, pp. 359-367.

B4237 Weber, J. Sherwood, Arthur Waldhorn, Jules Wein, and Arthur Zeiger. *Study Guide to Great Books*. New York: Holt, 1958. Pp. 320.
Includes *Ham.* and *Lear.*

(3) PRODUCTIONS

B4238 Röhler, W. "Shakespeare auf dem Kindertheater." *SJ*, 82/83 (1948), 186-189.

B4239 Manders, V. E. C. "Shakespeare at St. Bernard's." *SQ*, II (1951), 123-126.
Thirty-four years of Shak. productions at St. Bernard's School for Boys in New York City.

B4240 Boas, Guy. *Shakespeare and the Young Actor: A Guide to Production*. London: Rockliff, 1955. Pp. xi, 126.
An account of what the author—headmaster of Sloane School, Chelsea—has learned in almost 25 years of producing Shak. with a schoolboy cast. Special attention to 12 plays.
Rev: *RN*, XIII (1955), 126; *TLS*, March 4, p. 128; by Julian Hall, *English*, x, 190; by J. C. Trewin, *Books of the Month*, LXX (May), 9-10; by J. Vallette, *MdF*, 324 (1955), 534-535; by K. Wittlinger, *SJ*, 92 (1956), 439; by A. J. Axelrad, *EA*, IX, 157.

B4241 Lewis, George L. *A Stage Crew Handbook for Children's Theatre Directors*. DD, University of Denver, 1955.

B4242 Walker, G. G. "Shakespeare and Music." *Etude*, LXXIII (Sept., 1955), 54.
Lists musical settings of later times.

B4243 "A.E.T.A. Welcomes Shakespeare Stagers!" *Educational Theatre News*, Oct., 1956, p. 1.
"Staging Shak. in the Educational Theatre," announced as theme at regional meeting of American Educational Theatre Association.

B4244 Kildahl, Erling E. "Directing Shakespeare's Plays." *Speech Teacher*, v (1956), 296-304.
Offers practical advice on the director's attitude and on selecting, cutting, directing, and acting the play. Primarily for college and high school groups.

B4245 Kapteyn, James. "Producing Shakespeare in School." *Senior Scholastic*, Nov. 22, 1958, p. 11-T.
Suggestions for editing, casting, making props in secondary school Shak. productions.

B4246 McCaslin, Nellie. *A History of Children's Theatre in the United States*. DD, New York University, 1957. Pp. 417. Mic 57-3771. *DA*, XVII (1957), 2332. Publication No. 22,730.

B4247 Wattron, Frank Joseph, Jr. *A Descriptive Study of the Most Popular High School Plays in the United States Produced by Members of the National Thespian Society: 1938-1954*. DD, University of Southern California, 1957.

B4248 Thespis. "School Shakespeare Productions." *English*, XI (1956/57), 187-188.

B4249 Davis, Jed Horace, Jr. *The Art of Scenic Design and Staging for Children's Theater*. DD, University of Minnesota, 1958. Mic 58-3523. *DA*, XIX (1958), 906.

B4250 Jurgensen, Kai. "Producing on a Shoestring." *Players Magazine*, XXXIV (1958), 76-77.
Suggestions for school, amateur, and other low-budget groups in producing such plays as *Mach.*, *Pierre Pathelin*, and *Hedda Gabler.*

B4251 Vilhauer, William. "Why Not Do a Classic?" *Players Magazine*, XXXIV (1958), 103-104.
Suggestions for producing Shak. and Greek drama in secondary schools. Recommends *Shrew*, *AYL*, *Dream.*

b. TEACHING
(1) MATERIALS

B4252 *Stoffe und Gestalten. 100 Fragen und Antworten*. Vienna: Frisch Verlag, 1937. Pp. 8.

B4253 Weltzien, Erich. "Grundsätzliches zur Frage der neusprachlichen Lesestoffe." *N. Mon.*, VII (1936), 177-191.

B4253a Arns, K., and K. Schrey. "Kurz- oder Ganzausgabe von Shakespeare-Dramen?" *N. Mon.*, VII (1936), 319-320.
Answer to Weltzien, B4253.

B4254 McCaul, R. L. "A Worksheet for a Shakespearian Drama." *Education*, LVIII (1938), 325-329.

B4255 Butler, E. H. "Shakespeare Through the Imaginative Writers." *English Journal*, XXX (1941), 749-753.
A 3-page bibliog. of comments by famous writers upon Shak. suitable for schools. E. g., Noyes, Lewisohn, Goldsmith, Irving, Inez Haynes Irwin, Percy MacKaye.

B4256   Humphrey, Cavada. "Shakespeare in Quarto." *Equity*, xxx (July, 1945), 6.
        Abbreviated versions for reading in schools.

B4257   Kapitan, Hans. *Glimpses of Shakespeare*. Englische Lesehefte. Horn: Berger, 1951.

B4258   Magill, Lewis Malcolm, and Nelson Allen Ault. *Synopses of Shakespeare's Complete Plays*. Ames,
        Iowa: Littlefield, 1952. Pp. viii, 192.

B4259   May, Ferdinand. *Probenarbeit an Szenen aus Shakespeares "Mass für Mass"*. Bühnenbilder u.
        Figurinen v. Paul Pilowski. Halle: Mitteldt. Verl., 1953. Pp. 56.

B4260   Jordan, William E., Mildred R. Jordan, May Gordon, John Crawford Adams. "Shakespeare's
        Theater: The Globe Playhouse. An Educational Film." *Quar. of Film, Radio, and Television*,
        VIII (1954), 322-355.
        See also section on Educational Films, B3466-B3473.

B4261   Hudson, Arthur K., comp. *Shakespeare and the Classroom*. London: Heinemann, 1954.
        Pp. xii, 116.
        Compiled for the Society for Teachers of English. Makes suggestions for new teaching
        approaches.
        Rev: *TLS*, April 9, 1954, p. 238.

B4262   May, Ferdinand. *Probernarbeit an Szenen aus Shakespeares "Der Widerspenstigen Zähmung."*
        Leipzig: Hofmeister, 1955. Pp. 83.

B4263   Ornstein, J. A. "Th' Art a Knowing Cookie, Will." *High Points*, xxxvii (Nov., 1956), 65-69.
        Thirty-eight quotations applied to pedagogical situations.

B4264   Starr, Cecile. "Ideas on Film: The Film's Cousin—the Book." *SatR*, April 9, 1955, pp. 35-36.
        Includes brief reviews of several Shak. films, especially those available for classroom use.

B4265   Hodgins, Frank, and Audrey. "Teaching Guide for *Richard III*." *English Journal*, xLV (1956),
        138-140, 144.
        Richard as arch-dissembler can provide valuable educational and moral insights.

B4266   Illsley, William Allen. *A Shakespeare Manual for Schools*. Cambridge: Univ. Press, 1957.
        Pp. 96. Also published as *A Shakespeare Manual for Malayan Schools*.
        Rev: *ShN*, VIII (1958), 12; by Jacques Vallette, *LanM*, LII, 198-199; by Hudson Rogers,
        English Journal, xLVII (1958), 308.

B4267   Kiley, Frederick S. "Teaching Guide for *Twelfth Night*." *English Journal*, xLVI (1957), 582-585.
        Advance review of William Nichols' TV adaptation, starring Maurice Evans. Includes "Topics
        for Discussion."

B4268   *Notes. Including Scene-by-Scene Synopsis—Character Sketches, Selected Examination Questions and
        Answers*. Lincoln, Nebraska: Cliff's Notes and Outlines, 1958. Individual volumes available
        for the following plays: *Ham., 1 H. IV, Macb., Caesar, H. V, Oth., Dream, Lear, Temp., R. III,
        Merch., AYL, Twel., Antony, Romeo, R. II*.

B4269   Dean, Leonard F. "*Macbeth* and Modern Criticiam." *English Journal*, xLVII (1958), 57, 67.
        Macb., long considered in the class of "high school books," has been helped by the recent
        rediscovery that the play's apparent simplicity is full of absorbing problems. Includes a
        selected reading list.

B4270   Flatter, Richard. *Macbeth*. Frankfurt am Main: M. Diesterweg, 1958. Pp. 75.
        Commentary on the play, with a survey of the principal theories underlining the main ideas.

B4271   Schulze, Fritz Willy. *Shakespeare: Seine Bühne, sein Schaffen, sein Hamlet*. Berlin: Volk und
        Wissen, 1957. Pp. 89.

(2) PRINCIPLES
(a) GENERAL

B4272   Carroll, S. W. "Teaching Shakespeare in the Schools." *Conference of Educational Associations*
        (24th Annual Report), 1936, pp. 61-67.

B4273   Cancelled.

B4274   Hayden, Howard. *The Immortal Memory: A New Approach to the Teaching of Shakespeare*.
        London: Dent, 1936. Pp. 96.

B4275   Klein, M. "Shakespeares Dramatisches Formgesetz in seiner Bedeutung für die Schule. Ein
        neuer Weg zu *Macbeth* und *Hamlet*." *N. Mon.*, VI (1936), 487-498.

B4276   Crawford, Mary M., and Leroy Phillips. "Shakespeare as We Like Him." *English Journal*,
        xxvi (1937), 811-816.
        Contains suggestions for staging in a classroom.

B4277   Malm, M. H. "Interpreting *Merchant of Venice* to Youth." *English Journal*, xxvi (1937),
        317-319.

B4278   Phillips, A. L. "Shakespeare Not Closet Drama." *School & Society*, xLVI (1937), 689-691.

B4279   Pierce, Margery M. " 'Julius Caesar' and the Movies." *English Journal*, xxvi (1937), 322-324.

B4280   Taylor, Richard V. *Shakespeare for Senior Schools*. London: Macmillan, 1937. Pp. 237.

B4281   Phillips, A. L. "Letting Shakespeare Live Again." *Education*, LVIII (1938), 321-324.

B4282   Alexander, A. G. "English Stones." *Peabody Journal of Education*, XVII (1939), 35-41.

B4283   Dunn, Esther C. *Shakespeare in America.* New York: Macmillan, 1939. Pp. xiv, 310.
         In Schools, pp. 219-248.
             Rev: A9180.

B4284   Morgan, Charles. "To the Young—*Macbeth.* Philosophical Note on an Audience of Children
         at the Theatre." *New York Times,* June 4, 1939, Sec. IX, p. 2.

B4285   Müller, J. "Shakespeare im Deutschunterricht." *ZDK,* LIII (1939), 497-517.

B4286   Tannenbaum, Samuel A. "Shakespeare's Verse." *SAB,* XIV (1939), 60-61.

B4287   Tyson, I. "Shakespeare—When?" *SAB,* XV (1940), 57-59.

B4288   Poley, Irwin C. "Keeping Out of Hamlet's Way: Some Notes on the Teaching of Drama."
         English Journal, XXX (1941), 538-549.

B4289   Lyttle, Clyde F. "Teaching the Shaksperian Drama." *SAB,* XVIII (1943), 62-65.

B4290   Shoemaker, Francis. *Aesthetic Experience and the Humanities.* Columbia Univ. Press, 1943.
         Pp. xviii, 339.
         Includes a somewhat detailed critique of *Hamlet* as an illustration of method in "teaching"
         literature.
             Rev: A8362.

B4291   Ladd, William. "*Macbeth*—As a Reading Production." *English Journal,* XXXIII (1944),
         374-377.

B4292   Peat, R. C. *Presenting Shakespeare.* London: Harrap, 1947. Pp. 248.

B4293   Royster, S. "Shakespeare for the Superior." *English Journal,* XXXVI (1947), 34-38.

B4294   "Family Movie Guide: Should Children See the Tragedies of William Shakespeare?" *Parents
         Magazine,* XXIII (Sept., 1948), 13.

B4295   Donald, L. "Shakespeare in the Schoolroom." *Aberdeen University Review,* XXXII (1948),
         272-275.

B4296   Cancelled.

B4297   Cancelled.

B4298   Richards, I. A. "*Troilus and Cressida* and Plato." *Hudson Rev.,* I (1948), 362-376.

B4299   Kernodle, George R. "Basic Problems in Reading Shakespeare." *QJS,* XXXV (1949), 36-43.

B4300   Makey, H. O. "In the Literature Class: Study of the Opening Parts of *Macbeth.*" *English
         Journal,* XXXIX (1950), 360-366.

B4301   Poethen, Wilhelm. "Shakespeares Bildersprache im Unterricht." *Leb. Fremdspr.,* II (1950),
         260-266.

B4302   Salingar, L. G. "Shakespeare in School." *Use of English,* I, No. 2 (1950), 64-71.

B4303   Shapiro, Alan. "Should the *Merchant of Venice* Offend Jewish Students?" *English Journal,*
         XLI (1952), 432-433.

B4304   Walsh, William: "Shakespeare in the Class-Room: An Approach." *Jour. of Education,* 84,
         No. 990 (1952), 16-18.

B4305   Anikst, A. "Literatura k teme Shekspira." *Literatura v Schkole,* No. 6, 1953, pp. 80-82.

B4305a   Anikst, Alexander. "*Hamlet,* Tragedy of William Shakespeare." *Literatura v Schkole,* No. 2,
         1954, pp. 14-29.

B4306   Emslie, Macdonald. "Burning Bradley." *ShN,* IV (1954), 30.
         Bradley and the teaching of Shak.

B4307   Garrett, John. "Introduction." *Talking of Shakespeare.* London: Hodder & Stoughton
         & Max Reinhardt, 1954.
         Thoughts on the teaching of Shak.

B4308   Gribble, Dorothy Rose. "Our Hope's Love, Wisdom, Grace, and Fear: An Account of a
         Tour of *Macbeth.*" *SQ,* V (1954), 403-407.
         Techniques and adventures of the Plantagenet Productions' barnstorming tour through
         English Schools.

B4309   Jacobs, Elizabeth R. "Shakespeare Without Fears." *CE,* XV (1954), 347-348.

B4310   Söderwall, Margreta. "Shakespeare i engelska och svenska skolor." *Aktuellt från Skolö-
         verstyrelsen* (Stockholm), Aug. 8, 1954, pp. 180-186.

B4311   "Shakespearean Switch." *Newsweek,* Aug. 29, 1955, p. 52. Also in *New York Times Maga-
         zine,* Aug. 28, 1955, p. 47.
         Profs. Maynard Mack and Charles Prouty inaugurate a new summer-session Shak. course,
         designed especially for teachers, at Yale.

B4312   "Shakespeare's Roman Plays: And Other Subjects." *ShN,* V (1955), 41.

B4313   Poley, Irvin C. "Drama in the Classroom." *English Journal,* XLIV (1955), 148-151.

B4314   Thorén, Birger. "Aktuellt for Lårarna i moderna språk." *Aktuellt från Skolöverstyrelsen,*
         VIII (1955), 177-180.
         Shak. in Swedish schools.

B4315   Clark, A. "Shakespeare Gardens, New Rochelle." *Wilson Library Bulletin,* XXX (1955), 272.
         See also section on Gardens under Botany, A2209-A2213.

B4316 Davies, Derek J. "Getting Shakespeare Taped." *Use of English*, Spring, 1956, pp. 184-188. Use of a tape recorder in reading Shak.

B4317 Höppner, Joachim. "Zur Interpretation von Dramen im Englischunterricht der Oberstufe." *NS*, v (1956), 30-34.

B4318 Monson, Leland Hans. *Shakespeare in Utah (1847-1900)*. DD, University of Utah, 1956. Pp. 322. Mic 57-1354. *DA*, xvii (1957), 848. Publication No. 17,574. Chap. X on Shak. in schools and colleges.

B4319 Parry, John. *A Guide to Shakespeare for Malayan Students*. London: Harrap, 1956. Pp. 72.

B4320 Potter, Rachel. "Shakespeare in School." *Praxis d. neusprachl. Unterrichts* (Dortmund), iv (1957), 77-79.

B4321 Arndt, Reinhold. "Shakespeare-Lektüre in der Schule. Rückblick u. Neubesinnung." *Praxis d. neusprachl. Unterrichts* (Dortmund), v (1958), 35-42.

B4322 Walker, R. F. "Making the Most of Shakespeare." *Catholic Educator*, xxviii (1958), 539-541.

(b) ELEMENTARY AND SECONDARY

B4323 "Shakespearepreis für englische Literatur." *Hochschule u. Ausland*, xiii (1935), 65-66.

B4324 *"Merchant of Venice* Not Studied in the New York Public Schools." *New York Evening Sun*, Apr. 2, 1936.

B4325 Borgwardt, P. "Shakespeare und seine Behandlung im heutigen Klassenunterricht." *NS*, xliv (1936), 197-212.

B4326 Bridge, G. F. "Shakespeare in Schools." *Jour. of Education* (London), lxviii (1936), 525-528.

B4327 Morris, F. J. A. *"Macbeth." School* (Toronto), xxv (1936), 25-31.

B4328 Tannenbaum, Samuel A. "Exit Shakespeare." *SAB*, xii (1937), 191.

B4329 Welles, O., and R. Hill. "On the Teaching of Shakespeare and Other Great Literature." *English Journal*, June, 1938.

B4330 "Shakespeare in Primary Schools." *London Times*, Educational Supplement, June 10, 1939.

B4331 Gauger, R. *"Julius Caesar* als Lesestoff in Klasse 7." *Aus Unterricht u. Forschung*, 1939, pp. 74-83.

B4332 Henke, Wilh. "Shakespeares *Macbeth* in Klasse 7. Ein Unterrichtsbeispiel." *DDHS*, vi (1939), 25-27.

B4333 Ginsberg, W. "How Helpful are Shakespeare Recordings?" *English Journal*, xxix (1940), 289-300.

B4334 Hübner, Walter. *Die englische Dichtung in der Schule. Grundzüge einer Interpretationslehre.* Leipzig: Quelle & Meyer, 1940. Pp. viii, 224.

B4335 Keller, I. C. "Shakespeare for Pleasure." *SAB*, xv (1940), 249-253.

B4336 Sauer, E. H. "New Methods in Teaching." *Ohio Schools*, xviii (1940), 162-163.

B4337 Wehner, Jos. Magn. "Shakespeare und das Elementare." *Berliner Börsenzeitung*, No. 115, 1940.

B4338 Fleege, Urban H. "Streamlining Shakespeare." *English Journal*, xxx (1941), 408-411.

B4339 Henry, George H. "Escaping *As You Like It.*" *English Journal*, xxx (1941), 443-449.

B4339a Schultz, P. *Shakespeares "Julius Caesar" im englischen Unterricht*. Berlin: Matthiesen, 1941. Pp. 48. Rev: by E. Guntsch, *DDHS*, ix (1942), 277.

B4340 Hughes, R. G. "Shakespeare in the McGuffey Readers. An Analysis of the 4th, 5th, and 6th McGuffey Readers." *University of Pittsburgh Bulletin*, Jan. 20, 1944.

B4341 Palmer, D. E. "A Good Deed in a Naughty World." *English Journal*, xxxv (1946), 370-375.

B4342 Gray, C. E. "Listening to *Julius Caesar.*" *English Journal*, xxxvi (1947), 152-153.

B4343 Loveall, J. "Shakespeare is for Adults." *English Journal*, xxxvi (1947), 363-366.

B4344 Wood, Stanley. *The New Teaching of Shakespeare in Schools*. London: Gill, 1948. Pp. 57.

B4345 Saalbach, R. C. *"Macbeth* in Review." *English Journal*, xxxix (1950), 574-577.

B4346 Graham, Virginia. "Unwillingly to School." *Spectator*, 6402, March 9, 1951, p. 306; ibid., 6403, p. 344; 6404, p. 384.

B4347 Arnold, Elizabeth McDaniels. "No More Hurly-Burly." *English Journal*, xli (1952), 37-38.

B4348 Barnes, T. R. "Producing Shakespeare in School." *Use of English* (London), iii (March, 1952), 151-156.

B4349 Gallman, Mary N. *"Macbeth* Lives Again." *English Journal*, xli (1952), 370-371.

B4350 Finch, Hardy R. "Unbury the Bard." *Senior Scholastic*, lxiv (Apr. 7, 1954), 36-T, 37-T, 42-T.

B4351 Royster, S. "More About Shakespeare." *Education*, lxxv (Nov., 1954), 193-194.

B4352 Wåhlander, Britt. "Shakespeare i Umeå." *Tidning for Sveriges läroverk*, liv (1954), 424-425.

B4353 Goldstein, R. M. *"Othello." High Points*, xxxvii (Oct., 1955), 46-50.

B4354 Kahdy, N. "Eighth Grade Shakespeare." *High School Journal*, XXXVIII (Oct., 1954), 7-8.
A Progressive project.

B4355 Martin, Martha Wing. "Shakespeare in Today's Classroom." *English Journal*, XLIV (1955), 228-229. Also in *ShN*, V (1955), 18.
On the basis of a survey of 166 high schools it was discovered that only 14 Shak. plays were studied, and that 4 plays were the focus of 128 schools: *Caesar* (49 schools), *Macb.* (38), *Merch.* (22), and *Ham.* (19). The compiler noted the gradual increase in emphasis of Shak. in the upper grades of the secondary level.

B4356 Zink, P. M. "*Hamlet*, Caviare to the Generals." *English Journal*, XLIV (1955), 37-38.

B4357 "School Shakespeare." *Drama*, XLII (Fall, 1956), 58.

B4358 Bensley, Gordon E. "Use of Shakespeare Films at Phillips Academy." *Audio-Visual Guide*, XXII, No. 8 (1956), 35.

B4359 Fidone, William. "An Above-average Class Studies *Hamlet*." *English Journal*, XLV (1956), 470-476.
A high school English teacher describes the variety and depth of responses attainable through studying the play from many and deliberately provocative points of view.

B4360 Lazar, B. "How to Sound Out Your Shakespeare." *Senior Scholastic*, Mar. 1, 1956, pp. 7-T-8-T.
Concludes with a list of recordings.

B4361 Richeson, Emily. "Shakespeare for Fun." *Dramatics*, XXVII (April, 1956).
The "immortal slapstick" *Errors* provides the solution for cast-conscious and humor-conscious students.

B4362 Schäfer, Walter. "*Der Sturm* von Shakespeare. Ein Lebenshilfe im Deutschunterricht der höheren Schule." *Wirkendes Wort* (Düsseldorf), VI (1955/56), 173-179.

B4363 "How Well Do You Know *Macbeth*." *English Journal*, XLVI (1957), 354.
"Special Test" designed for teachers by a high school class.

B4364 "Shakespeare at School." *New York Times Magazine*, Mar. 31, 1957, p. 63.
The sponsorship by Theatre in Education, Inc., of a program of Shak. production in 16 Connecticut high schools.

B4365 Edwards, Rev. Mark. "Shakespeare in High School with an Assist from A-V." *Catholic Educator*, XXVII (April, 1958), 546-549.

B4366 Howarth, R. G. *Shakespeare by Air*. Sydney: Angus and Robertson, 1957. Pp. 64.
Rev: B3514

B4367 Rehfeldt, W. "Die Shakespeare-Lektüre im Englischunterricht der Oberschulen." *Fremdsprachenunterricht* (Berlin), I (1957), 83-88.

B4368 Atthill, Robin. "Set Books: XII: *Henry IV, Part II*." *The Use of English*, IX (1958), 253-258.

B4369 Hainfeld, H. "Studying Shakespeare from Television." *School Activities*, Nov., 1958, pp. 86-87.

B4370 Reynolds, William J. "When Thou Doest *Macbeth*, Do It Quickly!" *English Journal*, XLVII (1958), 90-91.

B4371 Ryerson, Edward. "*Julius Caesar* Once Again." *English Journal*, XLVII (1958), 1-7.

B4372 Thomas, Cleveland A. "Focus for Teaching *Hamlet*." *English Journal*, XLVII (1958), 8-14, 40.

B4373 Wells, Mary Alice. "Appreciation Follows Understanding." *NEA Journal*, Nov., 1958, p. 545.

B4374 Walter, J. H. "Shakespeare in Schools." *ShS*, X (1957), 107-110.
Answers objections of critics who contend that Shak. should not be taught in the (British) grammar school. Proposes means of improving the instruction.

(c) COLLEGES AND UNIVERSITIES
Most college productions are entered among festival, repertory or other productions, B2212-B3173.

B4375 Weingarten, S. "Use of Phonographic Recordings in Teaching Shakespeare." *CE*, I (Oct., 1939), 45-61.

B4376 Weninger, L. F. "Time Spent on *Julius Caesar*." *Carnegie Magazine*, XIII (1939), 86-90.

B4377 Jackson, Elizabeth. "The Kittredge Way." *CE*, IV (1943), 483-487.

B4378 Ellis-Fermor, Una. *The Study of Shakespeare*. London: Methuen, 1948. Pp. 16.
An inaugural lecture delivered in Oct., 1947, at Bedford College, Univ. of London.
Rev: by J. R. Sutherland, *MLR*, XLIV (1949), 438-439.

B4379 Mueller, William R. "The Class of '50 Reads *Othello*." *CE*, X (1948), 92-97.

B4380 Borgers, Edward W. *A History of Dramatic Production in Princeton, New Jersey*. DD, New York University, 1950.

B4381 Berkelman, Robert. "Teaching *Henry V*." *CE*, XIII (Nov., 1951), 94-99.

B4382 Kulkarni, N. M. *Hamlet*. Allahabad: Students' Friends, 1951.
Text and full length study in English.

B4383 Goldstone, Richard H. "Experiments with Audio-Visual Aids: I. In Teaching Shakespeare." *CE*, XIII (1952), 319-322.

B4384 Bergmann, Fredrick L. "Shakespeare in Indiana: A Report on the 'Shakespeare Meeting' of the Indiana College English Association." *SQ*, IV (1953), 337-341.

B4385 Kinne, Wisner Payne. *George Pierce Baker and the American Theatre.* Harvard Univ. Press, 1954. Pp. xvi, 348.
  Points out the influence of Baker's Lowell Institute lectures delivered in 1905 (published as *The Development of Shakespeare as a Dramatist*).
  Rev: B1758.

B4386 Swinney, D. H. "The Globe Playhouse of Hofstra College. I. Notes on Reconstruction; II. Notes on Direction." *ETJ*, March, 1953, pp. 1-11.

B4387 Warner, Alan. *Shakespeare in the Tropics: An Inaugural Address as First Professor of English, Makarere College, the University of East Africa, Kampala, Uganda, Delivered on May 10th, 1954.* London: Oxford Univ. Press, 1954. Pp. 28.
  Rev: by C. J. Sisson, *MLR*, L (1955), 567.

B4388 DeMarco, Norman. "Dance in the Basic Arts Program." *Players Magazine*, XXXII (1955), 7.
  Univ. of Arkansas' academic experiments: dance sequences for *Wives, Romeo*.

B4389 Clark, John Lewis. *Dramatic Activity in the Colleges and Universities of the United States Prior to 1905.* DD, Stanford University, 1956. Pp. 222. Mic 56-287. *DA*, XVI (1956), 178. Publication No. 15,361.
  Chap. VI: "Shakespeare in American Colleges: From Declamation to Drama," pp. 111-153.

B4390 Downs, Harold, ed. *The Fourth Anthology.* Foreword by Sir Laurence Olivier. Preface by Edric Cundell. Selections by Ambrose Marriott and Daniel Roberts. London: Herbert Jenkins, 1956. Pp. 272.
  Includes extracts from Shak. for speech and drama depts.
  Rev: *TLS*, Jan. 27, 1956, p. 58.

B4391 Griffin, Alice. "Bard on the Boards." *TAr*, April, 1956, pp. 63-64.
  Shak. in the collegiate forums; notably the presentation of *Macb.* by Gallaudet College in sign language for the deaf, while a reader on the side recited from the text.

B4392 Robertson, Roderick. "University Theatre at Oxford." *ETJ*, VIII (1956), 194-206.
  Discusses the university's policy toward dramatic activities of the Oxford Univ. Dramatic Society and the newer Experimental Theatre Club; surveys recent Shak. fare.

B4393 Coghill, Nevill. "University Contributions to Shakespeare Production in England." *SJ*, 93 (1957), 175-185.

B4394 Hatlen, Theodore. "College and University Productions, 1955-1956." *ETJ*, IX (1957), 134-137.
  Numerous college and university productions of Shak., with a chart showing the frequency of production of each play.

B4395 Reinert, Otto. "A Survey of Drama Anthologies." *CE*, XIX (1957), 134-140.
  Includes a chart showing the frequency of appearance of a selected list of plays.

10. COLLECTIONS OF ESSAYS
a. FESTSCHRIFTEN
(Arranged alphabetically by the surname of the person honored.)

B4396 *Joseph Quincy Adams: Memorial Studies.* Ed. by James G. McManaway, Giles E. Dawson, Edwin E. Willoughby. Washington, D. C.: The Folger Shakespeare Library, 1948. Pp. x, 808.
  Rev: by John Crow, *Library*, III (1948), 230-231; by Thomas Lask, *NYTBR*, April 10, 1949, p. 17; by R. A. Law, *JEGP*, XLVIII (1949), 397-399; by K. J. Holzknecht, *Papers Bibl. Soc. Amer.*, XLIII, 229-233; by Milton Crane, *Library Quar.*, XIX, 217-218; by Peter Alexander, *MLR*, XLIV, 262-264; by W. T. Hasting, *SAB*, XXIV, 237-238; by L. F. Dean, *MLQ*, XI (1950), 362-363; by J. I. M. Stewart, *RES*, NS, I, 260-262.

B4397 *Studies in Honor of Thomas Whitfield Baldwin.* Ed. by Don Cameron Allen. Urbana: Univ. of Illinois Press, 1958. Pp. 276.

B4398 *Buch und Papier: Buchkundliche und Papiergeschichtliche Arbeiten Hans H. Bockwitz zum 65. Geburtstage dargebracht.* Leipzig: Otto Harrassowitz, 1949. Pp. 164.
  Rev: by H. M. Lydenberg, *Papers Bibl. Soc. Amer.*, XLIV (1950), 289-290.

B4399 *Essays and Studies in Honor of Carleton Brown.* New York Univ. Press, 1940. Pp. xiii, 336.
  Rev: by H. S. V. J., *JEGP*, XL (1941), 397-399.

B4400 *Studies in English Language and Literature.* Presented to Karl Brunner on the Occasion of his Seventieth Birthday. Ed. S. Korninger. *Wiener Beiträge zur Englischen Philologie*, LXV. Vienna, Stuttgart: Wilhelm Braumüller, 1957. Pp. 290.
  Rev: by R. W. Zandvoort, *ES*, XXXVIII (1957), 215-216; *N &Q*, NS, IV, 505-506; by T. Riese, *Archiv*, 195 (1958), 60-61.

B4401 *Mélanges d'Histoire du Théâtre du Moyen Age et de la Renaissance Offerts à Gustave Cohen par ses Collègues, ses Elèves et ses Amis.* Paris: Nizet, 1950. Pp. 294.
  Rev: by Mario Roques, *Romania*, LXXII (1951), 247-249.

B4402 *Renaissance Studies in Honor of Hardin Craig.* Ed. by Baldwin Maxwell, W. D. Briggs, Francis R. Johnson, E. N. S. Thompson. Stanford Univ. Press, 1941. Pp. viii, 339. Reprinted from *PQ*, xx, iii (1941).
Rev: by E. A. Strathmann, *MLQ*, IV (1943), 119-120; by Leo Kirschbaum, *MLN*, LVIII, 477-481.

B4403 *Essays in Honor of Walter Clyde Curry.* With Foreword by Hardin Craig. Vanderbilt Studies in the Humanities, II. Nashville: Vanderbilt Univ. Press, 1955. Pp. 298.
Rev: by P. F. Baum, *South Atlantic Quar.*, LV (1956), 130; by Paul N. Siegel, *SQ*, VII, 438-439.

B4403a *Tribute to Walter de La Mare on his 75th Birthday.* London: Faber, 1948.

B4404 *Studies in Speech and Drama in Honor of Alexander M. Drummond.* Cornell Univ. Press, 1944. Pp. viii, 472.

B4405 *Studies in English Theatre History in Memory of Gabrielle Enthoven.* Ed. Muriel St. Clare Byrne. London, 1952. Pp. viii, 133.
Rev: by E. L. Avery, *SQ*, V (1954), 82-83.

B4406 *Essays in Honor of A. Howry Espenshade.* Contributed by His Colleagues in The Pennsylvania State College and Presented to Him in Celebration of His Thirty-ninth Year of Distinguished Service, 1898-1937. New York: Thomas Nelson and Sons, 1937. Pp. viii, 263.

B4407 *Studies in Honor of A. H. R. Fairchild.* Ed. by Charles T. Prouty. Univ. Missouri Studies, Vol. 21, No. 1. Univ. Missouri Press, 1946. Pp. 191.
Rev: *TLS*, Sept. 14, 1946, p. 440; by Hermann Peschmann, *English*, VI, 144; by M. W. Bundy, *MLN*, LXII (1947), 278-280; by Alfred Harbage, *MLQ*, VIII, 381-382; by W. A. Armstrong, *RES*, XXIII, 374-375.

B4408 *Festschrift für Alexander Rudolf Hohlfeld.* Monatshefte für dts. Unterricht, Univ. of Wisconsin. Vol. 30, Nr. 3/4. Madison, Wisconsin, 1938.
Rev: *DLZ*, LX (1939), 16.

B4409 *Anglo-Americana: Festschrift für Leo von Hibler.* Ed. Karl Brunner. *Wiener Beiträge zur Engl. Philologie*, LXII (1954).

B4410 *If By Your Art: Testament to Percival Hunt.* Ed. Agnes Lynch Starrett. Pittsburgh: Univ. of Pittsburgh Press, 1948. Pp. xiv, 293.

B4411 *The Seventeenth Century: Studies in the History of English Thought and Literature from Bacon to Pope by Richard Foster Jones and Others Writing in His Honor.* Stanford: Stanford Univ. Press; London: Oxford Univ. Press, 1951. Pp. viii, 392.
Rev: by Raymond P. Stearns, *William and Mary Quarterly*, IX (1952), 251-253; *TLS*, Feb. 22, p. 143; by Bonamy Dobrée, *Spectator*, Apr. 4, pp. 446-447; by SatR, Mar. 29, p. 32; by Richard A. Condon, *Personalist*, XXXIV (1953), 78-79; by Philip Edwards, *MLR*, XLVIII, 204-205.

B4412 *Philologica: The Malone Anniversary Studies.* In Honor of Kemp Malone. Baltimore: Johns Hopkins Press, 1949. Ed. by Thomas A. Kirby and Henry Bosley Woolf.
Rev: by D. C. Fowler, *JEGP*, L (1951), 257-258; by Garland A. Smith, *Emory Univ. Quarterly* VI, 191-192; by R. J. Menner, *Language*, XXVII, 103-105; by H. M. Smyser, *Speculum*, XXVI, 719-724; by Karl Brunner, *ES*, XXXIII, 163-166; by E. V. K. Dobbie, *MLN*, LXVII, 555-560.

B4413 *Shakespeare-Studien. Festschrift für Heinrich Mutschmann.* Zum 65. Geburtstag überreicht von den Herausgebern W. Fischer u. K. Wentersdorf. Marburg: Elwert Verlag, 1951. Pp. 208.
Rev: by Lawrence Babb, *SQ*, III (1952), 136-137; by Robert Fricker, *Anglia*, LXXII (1954-55), 482-485.

B4414 *Essays Contributed in Honor of President William Allan Nielson.* Smith Coll. Stud. in Mod. Langs., XXI (Oct. 1939-July 1940), Northampton, Mass., 1939. Pp. vii, 269.
Rev: by Hans Marcus, *Beiblatt*, LI (1940), 196-197.

B4415 *Studies in English Grammar and Linguistics: A Miscellany in Honour of Takanobu Otsuka.* Ed. by Araki, Kazuo, and others. Tokyo: Kenkyusha, 1958.

B4416 *Essays in Dramatic Literature. The Parrott Presentation Volume.* Princeton Univ. Press, 1935.
Rev: by W. Fischer, *Beiblatt*, XLVII (1936), 154-156; *SAB*, XI, 45; by Paul Meissner, *DLZ*, LVII, 579-583; by Leicester Bradner, *JEGP*, XXXV, 287-289; by Eduard Eckhardt, *Eng. Studn.*, LXXI, 248-251; by Hazelton Spencer, *MLN*, LII (1937), 61-63.

B4417 *Studies in French Language and Mediaeval Literature Presented to Mildred K. Pope.* Manchester: Univ. Press, 1939. Pp. 429.

B4418 *Studies for William A. Read. A Miscellany Presented by Some of His Colleagues and Friends.* Eds. Nathaniel M. Caffee and Thomas A. Kirby. Louisiana State Univ. Press, 1940.

B4419 *Elizabethan Studies and Other Essays: In Honor of George F. Reynolds.* Univ. Colorado Studies Series B. Studies in the Humanities, II, No. 4. Univ. Colorado Press, 1945. Pp. x, 390.
Rev: by Leo Kirschbaum, *PQ*, xxv (1946), 93-96; by J. E. Hankins, *MLN*, LXI, 478-481 *TLS*, Jan. 12, p. 23; by Walter MacKellar, *Philosophical Rev.*, LVI (1947), 225-227.

B4420 *To Doctor R.: Essays Here Collected and Published in Honor of the Seventieth Birthday of Dr. A. S. W. Rosenbach.* Eds. Percy E. Lawler, John Fleming, and Edwin Wolf. Philadelphia: Privately Printed, 1946. Pp. 301.

B4421 *Studies and Essays in the History of Science and Learning: Offered in Homage to George Sarton on the Occasion of His Sixtieth Birthday, 31 August 1944.* Ed. M. F. Ashley Montagu. New York: Henry Schuman, 1947. Pp. xiv, 594.
    Rev: *TLS*, Aug. 30, 1947, p. 441; by George Sarton, *Isis*, XXXVIII, 127-128; by I. E. Drabkin, *Jour. Hist. Med. and Allied Sciences*, II, 390-395.

B4422 *Studies in Honor of Frederick W. Shipley by His Colleagues.* Studies, Lang. and Lit., NS, No. 14. Washington Univ. Press, 1942. Pp. xi, 314.

B4423 *Science, Medicine, and History.* Essays on the Evolution of Scientific Thought and Medical Practice, written in Honour of Charles Singer. Ed. E. Ashworth Underwood. 2 Vols. Oxford Univ. Press, 1954.
    Rev: *TLS*, May 7, 1954, pp. 289-290.

B4424 *A Tribute to George Coffin Taylor, Studies and Essays, Chiefly Elizabethan, by His Students and Friends.* Ed. Arnold Williams. Univ. North Carolina Press, 1952. Pp. xv, 213.
    Rev: by John Leon Lievsay, *SQ*, IV (1953), 94-97; by Robert Adger Law, *JEGP*, LII, 258-260; by Clifford Leech, *MLR*, XLIX (1954), 112; by Selby Hansen, *South Atlantic Bull.*, XX (May, 1954), 13-14.

B4425 *Studies in Honor of John Wilcox, by Members of the English Department, Wayne State University.* Eds. A. Dayle Wallace, and Woodburn O. Ross. Detroit: Wayne State Univ. Press, 1958.

B4426 *The Rhetorical Idiom.* Essays in Rhetoric, Oratory, Language and Drama. Presented to Herbert August Wichelns. With a Reprinting of His "Literary Criticism of Oratory" (1925). Ed. Donald Bryant. Ithaca: Cornell Univ. Press, 1958. Pp. viii, 334.
    Rev: by Loren Reid, *QJS*, XLIV (1958), 313-317; *SCN*, XVI, 2.

B4427 *Festschrift zum 70. Geburtstag von Friedrich Wild.* Vienna, Stuttgart: Braumüller, 1958.

B4428 *English Studies in Honor of James Southall Wilson.* Ed. Fredson Bowers. Univ. Virginia Studies, Vol. 4. Univ. Virginia, 1951. Pp. 298.
    Rev: by Brents Stirling, *SQ*, III (1952), 133-134.

B4429 *F. Wollmanovi k Sedmdesátinám.* Articles Collected in Tribute to Professor Wollman's Seventieth Birthday. Prague: Státní Pedagogické Nakladatelství, 1958.

B4430 *Essays Honoring Lawrence C. Wroth.* Portland, Maine: Anthoensen Press, 1951. Pp. xxi, 515.
    Rev: by Thomas R. Adams, *Papers Bibl. Soc. Amer.*, XLVI (1952), 78-82; *TLS*, Mar. 21, p. 212.

b. ANTHOLOGIES
(Arranged alphabetically by title.)

B4431 Ford, Boris, ed. *The Age of Shakespeare.* A Guide to English Literature, Vol. II. Aylesburg and London: Pelican Books, 1955. Pp. 479.
    Rev: by Gordon R. Smith, *CE*, XVII (1955), 124; *English Journal*, XLIV, 436; *TLS*, May 13, p. 248; by E. C. Pettet, *English*, X, 189; *The Statesman* (Delhi and Calcutta), May 8, p. 15; by John Wain, *Spectator*, 6624 (1955), 754; by L. D. Lerner, *London Mag.*, II, Nos. 8, 86, 89, 91-2; by David Daiches, *MGW*, June 16, p. 12; *TLS*, May 13, p. 248; by Giles E. Dawson, *SQ*, VII (1956), 431-433; by Leif Lander, *Sydsvenska Dagbladet* (Malmö), July 3; by Hermann Heuer, *SJ*, 92 (1956), 358-359; by Michel Poirier, *EA*, IX, 43-44; by John Jones, *NstN*, June 9, p. 563.

B4432 *Ashland Studies in Shakespeare, 1954.* Privately published by the Division of Education and the Board of Directors of the Oregon Shakespeare Festival. Ashland, 1954.
    Rev: *ShN*, V (1955), 7.

B4433 *Ashland Studies in Shakespeare.* A book of articles, prints, and suggestions for projects: designed to accompany classwork in the Field Course established by the English Department of Stanford University in collaboration with the Oregon Shakespeare Festival of 1955. Ashland, Oregon, 1955. Folios v, 79; ix; vi. Mimeographed.
    Rev: by J. M. Yoklavich, *SQ*, VIII (1957), 243.

B4434 Crane, R. S., ed. *Critics and Criticism, Ancient and Modern.* Univ. of Chicago Press, 1952.
    Rev: by Marvin T. Herrick, *JEGP*, LI (1952), 610-611; by Northrop Frye, *SQ*, V (1954), 78-80.

B4435 Stallman, Robert Wooster, ed. *Critiques and Essays in Criticism, 1920-1948.* Foreword by Cleanth Brooks. New York: Ronald Press, 1949. Pp. xxii, 571.
    Rev: by G. L. Joughin, *NYTBR*, May 1, 1949, p. 25; see also Douglas Bush, "The New Criticism: Some Old Fashioned Queries." *PMLA*, LXIV, Suppl., Pt. 2, 13-21.

B4436 Praz, Mario, ed. *English Miscellany.* Rome. Nos. 1, 1950; 2, 1951; 3, 1952; 4, 1953; 5, 1954; 6, 1955; 7, 1956.

B4437 Wrenn, C. L., and G. Bullough. *English Studies Today.* Papers read at the International Conference of University Professors. Held in Magdalen College, Oxford, August 1950. Oxford Univ. Press, 1951.
    Rev: by Herbert G. Wright, *MLR*, XLVII (1952), 563-565.

B4438 Tillotson, Geoffrey. *Essays in Criticism and Research.* Cambridge Univ. Press, 1942. Pp. xxvii, 214.
    Rev: *N &Q*, 182 (1942), 154; by William Montgomerie, *Life and Letters Today*, XXXIII, 66, 68; *QR*, 279 (1942), 119-120; by Margaret Meagher, *Catholic World*, 155 (1942), 503-504;

by V. de Sola Pinto, *English*, IV, 59-60; by Louis Kronenberger, *Nation* (New York), Aug. 22, pp. 157-158; by R. G. Cox, *Scrutiny*, X, 395-396; by René Wellek, *MP*, XLI (1944), 261-263; by J. M. S. Tompkins, *RES*, XX, 91-93.

B4438a   Jacquot, Jean, ed. *Les Fêtes de la Renaissance.* Etudes réunies et présentées par Jean Jacquot. Paris: Editions du Centre National de la Recherche Scientifique, 1956. Pp. 492.
Rev: by Allardyce Nicoll, *SQ*, IX (1958), 399-400.

B4439   Bronson, Bertrand H., ed. *Five Studies in Literature.* Berkeley, California: Univ. of California Press; London: Cambridge Univ. Press, 1940.
Rev: by M. Galway, *MLR*, XXXVI (1941), 148-149.

B4440   Bentley, Eric, ed. *The Importance of Scrutiny.* New York: George W. Stewart, 1949. Pp. xxvi, 444.

B4441   Wain, John, ed. *Interpretations.* London: Routledge, 1956.
Rev: by Derek Stanford, *The Month*, NS, XVI (1956), 310-311; *TLS*, Jan. 6, 1956, p. 6.

B4442   Stamm, Rudolf, ed. *Die Kunstformen des Barockzeitalters.* Munich, Berne, 1956.
Rev: A5513.

B4443   Owen, Lewis J., Austere E. Claeyssens, William M. Schutte, and William F. Keirce. *Lectures on Four of Shakespeare's History Plays.* Carnegie Ser. in English, No. 1. Pittsburgh: Carnegie Press, 1953. Pp. 69.
Rev: by Robert Adger Law, *SQ*, V (1954), 331-332; by Kenneth Muir, *MLN*, LXIX, 435.

B4444   Jacquot, Jean, and André Veinstein, eds. *La Mise en Scène des Œuvres du Passé.* Illus. Paris: Centre National de la Recherche Scientifique, 1957.
Rev: by Thomas C. C. Milne, *TN*, XII (1958), 104-105.

B4445   Levin, Harry, ed. *Perspectives of Criticism.* Harvard Studies in Comparative Literature, 20. Cambridge: Harvard Univ. Press; London: Cumberlege, 1950. Pp. xviii, 248.
Rev: by G. Louis Joughin, *NYTBR*, Aug. 20, 1950, p. 15; by George F. Whicher, *NYHTBR*, Sept. 24, p. 20; by Bertram Jessup, *Jahrbuch fur Amerikastudien*, X, 85-86; by David Daiches, *NR*, Aug. 14, p. 19; by W. K. Wimsatt, Jr., *CL*, III, 368-372; by John K. Mathison, *Western Humanities Rev.*, VI, 384-385; by Thomas W. Copeland, *YR*, XL, 167-169; by Douglas Bush, *VQR*, XXVI, 472-476; *TLS*, Sept. 15, p. 582.

B4446   *The Renaissance: A Symposium.* New York: Metropolitan Museum of Art, 1954. Pp. 93. Abstracts publ. in *RN*, V (1952), 5-10, 32-34, 58-63.

B4447   Jones, Richard Foster, and others. *The Seventeenth Century.* See B4411.

B4447a   Weber, Carl August, ed. *Sprache und Literatur Englands und Amerikas: Lehrgangsvorträge der Akademie Comburg*, II. Tübingen: M. Niemeyer, 1956.

B4448   Matthews, Arthur D., and Clark M. Emery, eds. *Studies in Shakespeare.* Univ. Miami Publs. Eng. and Amer. Lit., I. Univ. Miami Press, 1953. Pp. 152.
Rev: by H. T. Price, *SQ*, V (1954), 120-121; by Francis R. Johnson, ibid., pp. 195-198.

B4449   Bronson, B. H., J. R. Caldwell, W. H. Durham, B. H. Lehman, Gordon McKenzie, and J. F. Ross, eds. *Studies in the Comic.* Univ. of California Publications in English, Vol. 8, No. 2. Berkeley: Univ. of California Press, 1941. Pp. iv, 155-298.
Essay on *Measure for Measure.*

B4450   Verchovsky, N. P., K. N. Derjavin, S. E. Radlov, et al. *Shakespeare. A Symposium.* Leningrad, Moscow: Iskusstvo, 1939. Pp. 184.

B4451   Carnegie Institute of Technology, Department of English. *Shakespeare: Lectures on Five Plays.* Carnegie Series in English, No. 4. Pittsburgh: Carnegie Press, 1958. Pp. 83.

B4452   Dean, Leonard F., ed. *Shakespeare: Modern Essays in Criticism.* New York: Oxford Univ. Press, 1957. Pp. viii, 426.
Rev: *VQR*, XXXIII (1957), lxxxviii; by Wallace A. Bacon, *QJS*, XLIII, 310-311; *ShN*, VII, 22; by William Frost, *CE*, XIX, 88-89; by Milton Crane, *SQ*, IX (1958), 188-189; by Reed Whittemore, *Poetry*, 92 (1958), 189-195; by J. A. Bryant, *SR*, LXVI, 326.

B4453   Prouty, Charles Tyler, ed. *Shakespeare: Of an Age and for all Time.* The Yale Shakespeare Festival Lectures. Hamden, Connecticut: Shoe String Press, 1954. Pp. 147.
Rev: by E. J. West, *QJS*, XLI (1955), 87; by William T. Hastings, *SQ*, VI, 113-114; by R. W. Zandvoort, *SQ*, VII (1956), 439-440.

B4454   Empson, William, and George Garrett. *Shakespeare Survey.* London: Brendin, 1937. Pp. 63. A single issue, not to be confused with the Cambridge series.
Rev: by G. W. Stonier, *NstN*, NS, XV (1938), 180.

B4455   Garrett, John, ed. *Talking of Shakespeare.* London: Hodder & Stoughton with Max Reinhardt, 1954. Pp. 264.
Rev: *TLS*, Sept. 3, 1954, p. 551; by David Hardman, *John o'London's Weekly*, LXIII, 811; by Anthony Thwaite, *Spectator*, July 30, p. 152; *NstN*, XLVIII, 243; by G. W. Horner, *FortnR*, NS, 1054 (1954), 283-284; *The Statesman* (Delhi and Calcutta), Oct. 17, p. 4; *Times of India* (Bombay), Nov. 21, p. 6; by Hermann Heuer, *SJ*, 91 (1955), 323-324; by Robertson Davies, *Saturday Night*, June 11; *English Journal*, XLIV, 549; *TAr*, Dec., p. 10; by William T. Hastings, *SQ*, VI, 112-113; by Franklin Fearing, *Quarterly of Film, Radio, and Television*, X (1956), 321; by John H. McDowell, *ETJ*, VIII, 79-80; by George F. Reynolds, *SQ*, VII, 433-434; by R. Davril, *EA*, IX, 46; by F. D. Hoeniger, *Canadian Forum*, June, p. 70; *ShN*, VII (1957), 40.

c. COLLECTIONS OF SINGLE AUTHORS
(Arranged alphabetically.)

B4456   Adams, Robert M. *Strains of Discord: Studies in Literary Openness*. Ithaca, New York: Cornell Univ. Press, 1958.

B4457   Barker, Sir Ernest. *Traditions of Civility: Eight Essays*. Cambridge Univ. Press, 1948. Pp. viii, 369.
Rev: by M. P. A., *MGW*, April 15, 1948, p. 10; by F. M. Powicke, *Spectator*, April 2, p. 410.

B4458   Boas, F. S. *Queen Elizabeth in Drama, And Related Studies*. London; New York, 1950. Pp. 212.
Rev: *TLS*, June 2, 1950, p. 339; by Emma G. Salter, *ConR*, July, p. 61; by R. G. Cox, *MGW*, June 8, p. 12; by A. C. Partridge, *CR*, LXXII, 82; by J. B. Fort, *LanM*, XLV (1951), 405; by A. C. Kettle, *MLR*, XLVI, 137; by Kenneth Muir, *RES*, NS, II, 380-381; by A. H. R. Fairchild, *SQ*, III (1952), 131-132.

B4459   Bond, R. W. *Studia Otiosa: Some Attempts in Criticiam*. London: Constable and Company, 1938. Pp. x, 228.
Rev: *Spectator*, June 17, 1938, p. 1121; by G. M. Young, *English*, II, 177-178; by V. de S. Pinto, *RES*, XV (1939), 89-91; by F. S. Boas, *MLR*, XXXIV, 98-99; by Benjamin Gilbert Brooks, *Nineteenth Century*, 126 (1940), 743-745.

B4460   Brandl, Alois. *Forschungen und Charakteristiken, zum 80. Geburtstag*. Berlin & Leipzig, 1936·
Rev: by Karl Brunner, *Lbl*, LVIII (1937), 324-326; by W. Keller, *SJ*, LXXIII, 159-160; by Hans Marcus, *DLZ*, LVIII, 1585-90; by R. Salewsky, *NS*, XLV, 171-172; by Albert Eichler, *Beiblatt*, XLIX (1938), 65-66; by Angus Macdonald, *MLR*, XXXIV (1939), 127-128.

B4461   Brereton, J. Le Gay. *Writings on Elizabethan Drama*. Collected by R. G. Howarth. Melbourne Univ. Press, 1948. Pp. 115.
Rev: *TLS*, May 12, 1950, p. 290; *N &Q*, 195 (1950), 263; by R. Davril, *LanM*, XLIV, 424; by Sidney Thomas, *MLN*, LXVI (1951), 113; by Paul H. Kocher, *MLQ*, XII, 231-232; by Kenneth Muir, *RES*, II, 380-381.

B4462   Brooke, C. F. T. *Essays on Shakespeare and Other Elizabethans*. Yale Univ. Press, 1948.
Rev: by D. C. A., *MLN*, LXIII (1948), 435; by R. A. Law, *Southwest Rev.*, XXXIII, 316-319; by Alfred Harbage, *NYTBR*, June 27, p. 17; by O. J. Campbell, *YR*, XXXVII, 752-755; by Robert Grinnell, *SR*, LVI, 721-724; by Milton Crane, *SRL*, June 19, p. 18; by Ernest Brennecke Jr., "Professor C. F. Tucker Brooke. The Scholar as Artist." *SAB*, XXIII, 144-150; by J. Gassner, *TAr*, XXXII, 92-94; by R. Davril, *LanM*, XLIII (1949), 65-66; *TLS*, April 9, p. 234; by Garland Greever, *Personalist*, XXX, 428-429; by H. B. Charlton, *MGW*, April 4, p. 10; by G. Bullough, *MLR*, XLV (1950), 277-278; by William A. Armstrong, *RES*, NS, II (1951), 76-78.

B4463   Cazamian, Louis. *Essais en Deux Langues*. Paris: Didier, 1938.
Rev: by V. Bohet, *ES*, XXI (1939), 133-138; by Henri Peyre, *EA*, III, 155-158; *TLS*, June 3, p. iii.

B4464   Cecil, Lord David. *The Fine Art of Reading and Other Literary Studies*. London, 1957.
Rev: *TLS*, Sept. 13, 1957, p. 546; by Carlos Baker, *SatR*, Sept. 28, pp. 22-23, 36; by Harold C. Gardiner, *America*, June 29, p. 368; by C. V. Wedgewood, *Time and Tide*, Aug. 3, pp. 968-969; *English Journal*, XLVI, 525; by P. Quennell, *Spectator*, 6736 (1957), 167-168; (with emphasis on Shak. essay) by James G. McManaway, *SQ*, IX (1958), 572-573.

B4465   Cecil, Lord David. *Poets and Story Tellers: A Book of Critical Essays*. New York: Macmillan; London, Constable, 1949. Pp. 201.
Rev: *TLS*, Feb. 19, 1949, p. 124; by M. J. C. Hodgart, *CamJ*, III, 124, 126; by H. Peschmann, *English*, VII, 296-297; by Carlos Miller, *NYTBR*, Mar. 13, p. 6; by George F. Whicher, *NYHTBR*, Mar. 13, p. 3; by Howard Mumford Jones, *SRL*, Apr. 16, p. 26; *American Mercury*, LXIX, 247; by D. A. Stauffer, *NR*, May 16, pp. 17-18; by J. Kraft, *Nation*, 168, 367-368; by W. H. Irving, *South Atlantic Quar.*, XLVIII, 624.

B4466   Chambers, Sir E. K. *Shakespearean Gleanings*. Oxford Univ. Press, 1944.
Rev: by H. S. Bennett, *NstN*, Sept. 30, 1944, p. 225; *TLS*, Oct. 7, p. 486; see also editorial comment, ibid., Oct. 7, p. 487; by Una Ellis-Fermor, *English*, V (1945), 123-124; by J. B. Leishman, *RES*, XXI, 148-151; by G. J., *Life and Letters*, XLIV, 52-54.

B4467   Craig, Hardin. *The Written Word and Other Essays*. Chapel Hill, North Carolina: Univ. of North Carolina Press, 1953. Pp. 90.
Rev: by Robert Adger Law, *SQ*, V (1954), 86; *ShN*, V (1955), 7.

B4468   Flatter, Richard. *Triumph der Gnade. Shakespeare Essays*. Vienna, Munich: Kurt Desch, 1956. Pp. 174.
Rev: by A. Schlösser, *ZAA*, V (1957), 105-108; by H. Lüdeke, *Anglia*, LXXV, 113-116; by William W. Lawrence, *SQ*, VIII, 540-541; by Hermann Heuer, *SJ*, 93 (1957), 260-262.

B4469   Gide, André, Edmond Jaloux, and others. *Le Théâtre Elizabéthain*. Essais et Traductions. Paris: J. Corti, 1941. Pp. 334.

B4470   Gordon, George. *Shakespearian Comedy and Other Studies*. Ed. Sir Edmund Chambers. Oxford Univ. Press, 1944. Pp. 168.
Rev: B5165.

B4471   Graves, Robert. *The Common Asphodel: Collected Essays on Poetry, 1922-1949*. London:

Hamish Hamilton, 1949. Pp. xii, 335.
Rev: *TLS*, Sept. 30, 1949, p. 632; by Barbara Cooper, *Spectator*, Sept. 23, p. 398; by H. I'A. F., *MGW*, Nov. 10, p. 11. See the letter by J. M. N. Hearn, *TLS*, Oct. 14, p. 665; the reviewer's answer with a letter by Mr. Graves, ibid., Nov. 4, p. 715; and a rejoinder by the reviewer, ibid., Nov. 11, p. 733.

B4472 Grierson, Sir Herbert J. C. *Criticism and Creation: Essays and Addresses.* London: Chatto and Windus, 1949. Pp. 127.
Rev: *TLS*, Feb. 17, 1950, p. 106; by Janet A. Smith, *NstN*, Feb. 18, pp. 196, 198; by M. H. M. MacKinnon, *Canadian Forum*, xxx, 214.

B4473 Hankins, J. E. *The Character of Hamlet and Other Essays.* Chapel Hill: Univ. of North Carolina Press and Oxford Univ. Press, 1941. Pp. ix, 269.
Rev: B7664.

B4474 Hart, Alfred. *Shakespeare and the Homilies, and Other Pieces of Research into Elizabethan Drama.* Melbourne Univ. Press, 1934.
Rev: A4649.

B4475 Hotson, Leslie. *Shakespeare's Sonnets Dated, and Other Essays.* London: Rupert Hart-Davis; Toronto: Clarke, Irwin & Co., 1949. Pp. 244.
Rev: C21.

B4476 Huhner, Max. *Shakespearean Studies and Other Essays.* With an Introd. by George S. Hellman. New York: Farrar Straus, 1952. Pp. 115.
Rev: by G. B. Harrison, *SatR*, Oct. 10, 1953, p. 38; by J. Duncan Spaeth, *SQ*, IV, 353-355.

B4476a Jacob, George. *Shakespeare-Studien.* Herausgegeben nach dem Tode des Verfassers von H. Jensen. Hamburg; New York: Augustin, 1938. Pp. 37.
Rev: by E. Weigelin, *Beiblatt*, L (1939), 101; by John Speck, *Archiv*, 175 (1939), 249; by Karl Brunner, *Lbl*, LX, 479; by W. Keller, *SJ*, LXXV, 153; by Joseph Sprengler, *DL*, XLI, 759-760.

B4477 Lawrence, W. J. *Those Nut-Cracking Elizabethans.* London, 1935.
Rev: by G. B. Harrison, *RES*, XII (1936), 468-469.

B4478 Leech, Clifford. *Shakespeare's Tragedies and Other Studies in Seventeenth Century Drama.* New York: Oxford Univ. Press; London: Chatto and Windus; Toronto: Clarke, Irwin & Company, 1950. Pp. 239.
Rev: B4967.

B4479 Morozov, Mikhail Mikhailovich. *Izbrannye Stati i Perevody.* Moscow: Goslitizdat, 1954. Pp. 594.
Rev: by Y. Kondratyev, *VOKS-Bulletin*, No. 4, 93 (1955), 84-85.

B4480 Murry, John Middleton. *John Clare and Other Studies.* London: Nevill, 1950. Pp. 252.

B4481 Parr, Johnstone. *Tamburlaine's Malady and Other Essays on Astrology in Elizabethan Drama.* Univ. Alabama Press, 1953. Pp. xiv, 158.
Rev: *N &Q*, NS I (1954), 181-182; by Carroll Camden, *MLN*, LXIX, 512-514; by John W. Draper, *SQ*, V, 421-422; by C. Doris Hellman, *Isis*, XLV, 398-399; by Clifford Leech, *MLR*, XLIX, 540; by W. L. Halstead, *South Atlantic Bul.*, xx, No. 4 (1955), 13; by J. C. Bryce, *RES*, VI, 306-308.

B4481a Rubow, Paul V. *Shakespeare og hans Samtidige.* Copenhagen: Gyldendal, 1948, Pp. 155.
Rev: C74.

B4482 Santayana, George. *Essays in Literary Criticism.* Introduction by Irving Singer. New York: Charles Scribner's Sons, 1956.

B4483 Samarin, P. M. "Novyi Sbornik o Shekspire." *Sovietskaia Kniga*, I (1949), 109-111.

B4484 Schelling, Felix Emmanuel. *Shakespeare Biography and Other Papers Chiefly Elizabethan.* Philadelphia: University of Pennsylvania Press, 1937. Pp. 143.
Rev: *TAr*, XXI (1937), 494; by J. Corbin, *NYTBR*, Dec. 5, p. 34; by A. Brandl, *DLZ*, LVIII, 1544-47; by R. Withington, *MLN*, LIII (1938), 621-623; by E. E. Willoughby, *Library Quar.*, VIII, 434-435; by George Rylands, *NstN*, NS, XV, 174-176.

B4485 Schirmer, Walter Franz. *Kleine Schriften.* Tübingen: Niemeyer, 1950. Pp. 200.
Rev: by F. Rau, *Neuphilologische Zeitschrift*, IV (1952), 143-144.

B4486 Schröder, Rudolf Alexander. *Gesammelte Werke.* Berlin: Suhrkamp. Band 1, 1952; Band 2, 1954.

B4487 Schücking, Levin Ludwig. *Essays über Shakespeare, Pepys, Rossetti, Shaw und Anderes.* Wiesbaden: Dietrich, 1948. Pp. 489.

B4488 Sehrt, Ernst Th. *Shakespeare. Englische Essays zum Verständnis seiner Werke.* Stuttgart: Alfred Kröner-Verlag, 1958. Pp. 304.
Rev: A7733.

B4489 Shackford, Martha Hale. *Shakespeare, Sophocles: Dramatic Modes.* Natick, Massachusetts: The Surburban Press, 1957. Pp. 37.
Rev: *ShN*, VII (1957), 33; by A. H. R. Fairchild, *SQ*, IX (1958), 415.

B4490 Sheppard, J. T. *Music at Belmont and Other Essays and Addresses.* London: Rupert Hart-Davis, 1951. Pp. 192.

Rev: by H. W. Garrod, *Spectator*, 6442 (1951), 825-826; *Listener*, XLVII (1952), 523; *TLS*. April 18, p. 266.

B4491 Simpson, Lucie. *The Secondary Heroes of Shakespeare and Other Essays.* London: Kingswood Press, 1950. Pp. 151.
Rev: *TLS*, Jan. 26, 1951, p. 58.

B4492 Simpson, Percy. *Studies in Elizabethan Drama.* Oxford: Oxford Univ. Press, 1955. Pp. 265.
Rev: by E. C. Pettet, *English*, X (1955) 189; by J. I. M. Stewart, *NstN*, Apr. 16, p. 552; *N &Q*, NS, II, 368; *TLS*, April 29, p. 202; ibid., Feb. 18, p. 106 (notice); ibid., May 6, p. 237; by J. Crow, *Listener*, LIII, 543, 545; by Michel Poirier, *EA*, IX (1956), 45-46; by Ludwig Borinski, *SJ*, 92 (1956), 433-435; by Sidney Thomas, *SQ*, VII, 127-129; by J. A. K. Thomson, *RES*, VII, 423-427; by M. A. Shaaber, *MP*, LIV, 56-57.

B4493 Thaler, Alwin. *Shakespeare and Democracy.* Univ. of Tennessee Press, 1941. Pp. xii, 312.
Rev: A1809.

B4494 Weber, Carl August, ed. *Sprache und Literatur Englands und Amerikas: Lehrgangsvorträge der Akademie Comburg, II.* Tübingen: M. Niemeyer, 1956.

B4495 Zandvoort, R. W. *Collected Papers, A Selection of Notes and Articles Originally Published in English Studies and Other Journals.* Groningen Studies in English, v. Groningen: J. B. Wolters, 1954. Pp. 186.
Rev: by F. Mossé, *EA*, VIII (1955), 337; by G. Storms, *LT*, pp. 611-612; by G. Pellegrini, *Rivista di Letterature Mod.*, VI, 72; by H. Heuer, *Archiv*, 193 (1956), 61; by J. M. Ure, *RES*, VII, 217; by H. B. Woolf, *MLN*, LXXII (1957), 49; by F. G. Cassidy, *JEGP*, LVII (1958), 104-106; by Claes Schaar, *SN*, XXX, 113-115.

XVI. CIVILIZATION IN SHAKESPEARE'S ENGLAND
This section is omitted; items from the sources that might have been included here have been entered in classes of similar content elsewhere.

XVII. THE SHAKESPEARE-BACON CONTROVERSY AND SIMILAR THEORIES (182;64)
1. BACON (182;64)
a. ITEMS OF SOME CONSEQUENCE

B4496 Abeck, Friedrich. *Die Shakespeare-Bacon-Frage.* DD, Tübingen, 1890. Mummendey reported no copy could be found.

B4497 Oelschläger, C. *Shakespeare-Bacon-Denkmale.* Würzburg: Triltsch, 1940. Pp. 84. 10 pl.

B4498 Glendening, L. "A Bibliographical Account of the Bacon-Shakespeare Controversy." *Colophon*, Sept. 1939, pp. 25-40.

B4499 Rubow, Paul V. "De Vanvittiges Skarpsindighed (the acumen of maniacs), i.e. Critical Remarks on the Baconian Theory." *Scrap Book*, 1939, pp. 142-151.

B4500 Winter, J. W. "Shakespeare War Nicht Bacon! Das Shakespeare-Rätsel Gelöst?" *VB(B)*, July 22, 1939.

B4501 Campbell, Oscar James. "Shakespeare Himself." *Harper's*, July, 1940, pp. 172-185.

B4502 *The Logan Clendening Collection of Books About the Bacon-Shakespeare Controversy.* Los Angeles: Zeitlin & Verbrugge, 1943. Pp. 32.

B4503 Galland, J. S. *An Historical and Analytical Bibliography of the Literature of Cryptology.* Evanston: Northwestern Univ., 1945. Pp. x, 209.

B4504 Churchill, R. C. "The Baconian Heresy: A Post Mortem." *Nineteenth Century*, 140 (1946), 260-268.

B4505 Galland, Joseph S. *Digesta Anti-Shakespeareana.* DD, University of Wisconsin, 1914. Pp. 1667. Mic. A48-384. *Mcf Ab*, IX (1949), 199. Publ. No. 1175.
Not a doctoral dissertation in its present form. Intro. dated Dec. 1948, and signed by Galland's son-in-law, Burton A. Milligan. An annotated bibliography.

B4506 Hubler, Edward. *The Sense of Shakespeare's Sonnets.* Princeton Univ. Press, 1952.
Appendix, pp. 136-151, dismisses Bacon, Oxford, Dyer, Derby.
Rev: C85.

B4507 Budd, L. J. "Baconians: Madness Through Method." *South Atlantic Quarterly*, LIV (1955), 359-368.

B4508 Stephen, Sir Leslie. *Men, Books, and Mountains.* Introd. by S. O. A. Ullman. Univ. of Minnesota Press, 1956.
Includes "Did Shakespeare Write Bacon," pp. 74-80.

B4509 Wallace, Irving. *The Square Pegs.* New York: Knopf, 1957. Pp. 328.
Delia Bacon, one of nine studies of curious Americans.
Rev: *Time*, July 29, 1958, pp. 83-84; by Louis B. Wright, *NYTBR*, July 21, p. 3; *TLS*, March 14, p. 141.

B4510 Wikland, Erik. " 'Baconiana' och Shakespeare-kritik." *Edda*, LVII (1957), 148-160.

b. REMAINDER

B4511 *Ba.* London: Bacon Society, 1947, Vol. 31.

B4512 "Timon and Francis Bacon." *Ba*, XXIII (1938), 34.

B4513 "Shakespeare and Bacon." *Ba*, XXIII (1938), 38-40.

B4514 "The Whys and Wherefores of Shakespeare's Plays." *Ba*, XXIII (1938), 45-49.

B4515 "Shakespeare's Real Life Story." *Ba*, XXIII (April, 1938), 81-84.

B4516 Anonymous. "Francis Bacon Wrote the 'Shakespeare' Plays." *Ba*, XXIII, (July, 1938), 143, 179-180.

B4517 "The Cryptographer's Corner." *Ba*, XXIV (1939), 37-39.

B4518 "Shakespeare and Bacon's Essay 'Of Love'." *Ba*, XXIV (1939), 70-76.

B4519 "Shakespeare in Verona and Poitiers." *Ba*, XXIV (1939), 151-154.

B4520 "Bacon and Freemasonry." *Ba*, XXIV (1939), 165-166.

B4521 "The Shorter Poems of Shakespeare." *Ba*, XXV (1941), 179-182.

B4522 "Duthie's Bad Quarto of *Hamlet*." *Ba*, XXV (1941), 193-199.

B4523 "Bacon-Shakespeare & *Proverbs XXIX*." *Ba*, XXVI (1942), 17-31.

B4524 "Shakespeare's Will a Forgery." *Ba*, XXVI (1942), 212-213, 217.

B4525 "Source of a Passage in *Timon* IV, iii." *Ba*, XXVII (1943), 51.

B4526 "W. A. Raleigh and the Baconians." *N &Q*, 185 (1943), 104-105.

B4527 "Did 'Shakespeare' Die in 1616?" *Ba*, XXVIII (1944), 62-65.

B4528 "Donnelly's Cryptogram Cipher Re-examined." *Ba*, XXVIII (1944), 128-136.

B4529 "Donnelly's Cryptogram Re-examined." *Ba*, XXIX (1945), 8-15.

B4530 "Another Mask of F. Bacon." *Ba*, XXIX (1945), 25-28.

B4531 "A Cipher in Psalm 46." *Ba*, XXIX (1945), 88-89.

B4532 "Honorificabilitudinitatibus." *Ba*, XXIX (1945), 125-126.

B4533 " 'Honorificabilitudinitatibus'." *Ba*, XXX (1946), 37.

B4534 "An Alleged 1st Quarto of *Hamlet*." *Ba*, XXX (1946), 42.

B4535 "Another Bacon-Oxford Debate." *Ba*, XXX (1946), 119-120.

B4536 "Bacon-Shakespeare Coincidences." *Ba*, XXX (1946), 135.

B4537 "The 'Kay' Cipher." *Ba*, XXX (1946), 136-137.

B4538 Johnson, E. D. "Honorificabilitudinitatibus." *Ba*, XXX (1946), 188-189.

B4539 "Francis Bacon on Friendship." *N &Q*, 190 (1946), 67.

B4540 Q., D. "Francis Bacon, T. Nashe and Dante." *N &Q*, 190 (1946), 78.

B4541 "Bacon-Shakespeare Parallels." *N &Q*, 190 (1946), 99-100.

B4542 Q., D. "Shakespeare and Francis Bacon." *N &Q*, 190 (1946), 259.

B4543 "Shakespeare and Catullus." *Ba*, XXXI (1947), 3.

B4544 "Shakespeare's Italian Tour." *Ba*, XXXI (1947), 126-128.

B4545 Arther, J. "Baconian Studies." *Theosophist*, LX (Aug., 1939), 429-440; (Sept., 1939), 524-536.

B4546 Arther, J. "Francis Bacon on Dreams." *Ba*, XXX (1946), 168-170, 181.

B4547 Arther, J. "Bacon's Number Cipher in *Love's Labour's Lost*." *Ba*, XXXI (1947), 31-38.

B4548 Arther, J. "The Royal Birth Theme." *Ba*, XXXII (1948), 128-135, 185-191, 208.

B4549 B., H. "A Debate on the Oxfordian Claim vs the Baconian." *Ba*, XXX (1946), 75-78.

B4550 Baker, H. K. "Bacon's Vindication." *Ba*, XXIII (1938), 57-66.

B4551 Baker, H. K. "Moderation in Moderation." *Ba*, XXIII (1938), 173-178.

B4552 Baker, H. K. "The Scholarship Bogy." *Ba*, XXV (1941), 183-188.

B4553 Baker, H. K. "Facts that Fit." *Ba*, XXVI (July, 1942), 151-157; (Oct., 1942), 204-209.

B4553a Baker, H. K. "Facts that Fit." *Ba*, XXVII (1943) 19-27.

B4553b Baker, H. K. "Facts that Fit." *Ba*, XXVII (1943) 77-86.

B4554 Barker, R. "Shakespeare's 'Ignorance'." *Ba*, XXIII (1938), 35-37.

B4555 Barker, R. "An Elizabethan Theatre." *Ba*, XXIII (1938), 87-89.

B4556 Bayley, V. "The Birth of the Name 'Shakespeare'." *Ba*, XXVIII (1944), 16-18.

B4557 Beaumont, C. "The Importance of the 'Word Cypher'." *Ba*, XXVIII (1944), 39-47.

B4558 Beaumont, C. "Donnelly's Cryptogram Cypher Re-examined." *Ba*, XXVIII (1944), 88-98.

B4559 Beaumont, C. "Francis Bacon's Cipher Signatures." *Ba*, XXX (1946), 13-17.

B4560 Beaumont, C. "The Importance of Bacon's Cipher." *Ba*, XXX (1946), 57-62.

B4561 Bénézet, L. P. "The Frauds and Stealths of Injurious Impostors." *Shak. Fellowship Quarterly*, V (1944), 2-6.

B4562 Bénézet, L. "The Stratford Defendant Compromised by His Advocates." *Shak. Fellowship Quarterly*, V (1944), 44-46; VI (1945), 13-15, 27-29, 40-45.

B4563 Bennett, R. J. A. "Bacon and the Rosicrucians." *Ba*, XXIII (1938), 67-74.

B4564 Bennett, R. J. A. "Bacon's Translation of the Psalms." *Ba*, XXVII (1943), 35-37.

B4565 Biddulph, L. "Francis Bacon and the Theatre." *Ba*, XXVII (1943), 131-134.

B4566 Biddulph, L. "Francis Bacon in Emblem." *Ba*, XXX (1946), 112-118.

B4567 Biddulph, L. "The Curious Prophecies of Paracelsus & Francis Bacon." *Ba*, XXXII (1948), 27-30, 142-148.

B4568 Birin, J. C. "The Phoenix Symbol in 'Shakespeare'." *Ba*, XXXII (1948), 209-210.

B4569 Blomberg, Adelheid Maria Freiin von. *Bacon-Shakespeare? Der Wahrheit die Ehre! Ein Beitrag zur Bacon-Shakespeare-Frage.* Karlsruhe i. B.: Gutsch, 1942. Pp. 111.

B4570 Bonac-Melvrau, F. *Défense de Will—La véritable Identité de William Shakespeare.* Paris: Librairie d'Art Ancien et Moderne, 1951. Vol. I, pp. 151; Vol. II, pp. 16.
       Rev: by G. Dumeige, *Etudes*, 273 (1952), 419.

B4571 Bond, H. "An Oxfordian on the Bacon Cyphers." *Ba*, XXXI (1947), 152-158.

B4572 Boyle, D. J., et al. "The Mystery of Honorificabilitudinatibus." *Ba*, XXXII (1948), 51-52.

B4573 Brahms, Caryl, and S. J. Simon (Pseud. for Doris Caroline Abrahams and S. J. Skidelsky). *No Bed for Bacon; or, Shakespeare Sows an Oat.* London: Joseph, 1941; New York: Crowell, 1950. Pp. 241.
       Rev: A506.

B4574 Brain, W. R. "Bacon's and Shakespeare's Eyes." *Ba*, XXIX (1945), 103-104.

B4575 Bridgewater, H. "Was Francis Bacon the Editor of the Bible?" *Ba*, XXI (1938), 11-20.

B4576 Bridgewater, H. "The Missing Historical Plays (*Edward I* and *Edward IV*) of Shakespeare." *Ba*, XXI (1938), 21-36.

B4577 Bridgewater, H. "A Plea for Moderation." *Ba*, XXIII (1938), 125-129.

B4578 Bridgewater, H. " 'Shakespeare' and Italy." *Ba*, XXIII (1938), 157-166.

B4579 Bridgewater, H., and R. J. A. Bennett. "Bacon's Royal Birth." *Ba*, XXIV (1939), 162-163.

B4580 Bridgewater, H. S. "Bacon or Shakespeare Does it Matter?" *Ba*, XXVI (Jan., 1942), 1-10.

B4581 Bridgewater, H. "Proxime Accessit!" *Ba*, XXVII (1943), 42-45.

B4582 Bridgewater, H. "Pshaw!" *Ba*, XXX (1946), 35-36.

B4583 Bridgewater, H. "Documentary Evidence of F. Bacon's Authorship of the Immortal Plays." *Ba*, XXXII (1948), 86-92.

B4584 Bennett, R. J. A. "The Sympathy and Antipathy of Things." *Ba*, XXIX (1945), 32-34.

B4585 Bennett, R. J. A. "Hermetic and Masonic Indications in Shakespeare's Plays." *Ba*, XXIX (1945), 54-57.

B4586 Calthorpe, F. A. G. "A Fair Vestal Throned by the West." *Ba*, XXVI (1942), 171-172.

B4587 Cartier, Général. "Quelques Précisions au Sujet de l'Acteur William Shakespeare." *MdF*, April, 1939, pp. 92-109.

B4588 Cartier, Général. "Le Système Cryptographique de Bacon." *MdF*, May 1, 1939, pp. 687-693.

B4589 Cornwall, Arthur Bradford. *Francis the First.* Unacknowledged King of Great Britain and Ireland known to the world as Sir Francis Bacon, Man of Mystery and Cipher. Birmingham: Cornish Brothers, 1936. Pp. 375.
       Rev: *TLS*, June 20, 1936, p. 525; by David Garnett, *NstN*, NS, XI, 229.

B4590 Crundell, H. W. "Bacon and *Troilus and Cressida*." *N&Q*, 187 (1944), 106-107; ibid., 186 (1944), 226.

B4590a Eagle, Roderick L. "Bacon and *Troilus and Cressida*." *N&Q*, 186 (1944), 275-276.

B4591 Crundell, H. W. "The First Baconian." *N&Q*, 187 (1944), 277.

B4592 Eagle, Roderick K. "The First Baconian." *N&Q*, 188 (1945), 63.

B4593 Eagle, Roderick L. " 'Discourse of Reason'; 'Fort of Reason' [*Hamlet*, I, ii, 150; I, iv, 28]." *N&Q*, 189 (1945), 257.

B4594 Cunningham, W. McC. *The Tragedy of F. Bacon, Prince of England.* Los Angeles, 1940. Pp. 96.

B4595 D., T. "The Enigma of Francis Bacon." *Ba*, XXXII (1948), 138-141.

B4596 Dodd, Alfred. *Shakespeare, Creator of Freemasonry.* London: Rider, 1937. Pp. 284.

B4597 Dodd, A. *The Secret Shakespeare.* London, 1942. *Ba*, XXVI (April, 1942), 104-106.

B4598 Dodd, A. "Will Shakespeare of Stratford." *Ba*, XXVIII (1944), 25-29.

B4599 Dodd, A. *The Immortal Master.* London: Rider, 1944.

B4599a S., M. "Dodd's Book on the *Sonnets*." *Ba*, XXVIII (1944), 160.

B4600 Dodd, A. "Francis Bacon's Diary: Shakespeare's Sonnets." *Ba*, XXX (July, 1946), pp. 93-98; (Oct.) 159-164; XXXI (1947), 23-29.

B4601 Dodd, Alfred. *Francis Bacon's Personal Life Story.* Vol. 1. *The Age of Elizabeth.* London: Rider, 1949. Pp. 384.
       Rev: by A. R. Hall, *CamJ*, II (1949), 766-767; by E. R. Ryman, *CamR*, LXXII (1950/51), 238, 240; by Comyns Beaufort and E. R. Ryman, *CamR*, LXXII, 354, 356.

B4602 Eagle, R. L. "William Shakespeare and the 'Essay of Love'." *Ba*, XXIV (1938/39), 70-76.

B4603 Eagle, R. L. "Sir Thomas More." *Ba*, XXIV (1939), 164-165.

B4604 Eagle, R. L. "The Padua First Folio." *Ba*, XXV (1941), 207-208.

B4605 Eagle, R. L. "Should Shakespeare Be Exhumed?" *Ba*, XXVI (1942), 49-52.

B4606 Eagle, R. L. "Could Bacon Have Found Time?" *Ba*, XXVI (1942), 83-87.

B4607 Eagle, R. L. "Only An Actor Could Have Written the Plays." *Ba*, XXVI (1942), 88-92.

B4608 Eagle, R. L. "Could Bacon Have Committed the 'Errors' in the Plays?" *Ba*, XXVI (1942), 109-113.

B4609 Eagle, R. L. "Ben Jonson and Shakespeare." *Ba*, XXVII (1943), 28-34.

B4610 Eagle, Roderick. *Shakespeare. New Views for Old.* London: Rider, 1943. Pp. 110.

B4611 Eagle, R. L. "John Marston, Shakespeare, and Francis Bacon." *Ba*, XXVII (1943), 129-130.

B4612 Eagle, R. L. "Another Shakespeare Signature!" *Ba*, XXVII (1943), 143-144.

B4613 Eagle, R. L. "The Seventh (!) Signature." *Ba*, XXVII (1943), 167-171.

B4614 Eagle, R. L. "W. A. Raleigh and the Baconians." *N &Q*, 185 (1943), 175.

B4615 Eagle, R. L. "Bacon, Spenser, and Shakespeare." *Ba*, XXVIII (1944), 36-38.

B4616 Eagle, R. L. "Shakespeare as a Gardener." *Ba*, XXVIII (1944), 103-107.

B4617 Eagle, R. L. "Forgers and Forgeries." *Ba*, XXVIII (1944), 108-117.

B4618 Eagle, R. L. "The Lawyer Speaks." *Ba*, XXVIII (1944), 142-145.

B4619 Eagle, R. L. "Elizabethan Audiences and Players." *Ba*, XXIX (1945), 16-22.

B4620 Eagle, R. L. "The Date of 'Shakespeare's' Sonnets." *Ba*, XXIX (1945), 39-40.

B4621 Eagle, R. L. "The Use of the Pseudonym." *Ba*, XXIX (1945), 68-71.

B4622 Eagle, R. L. "The Arcadia (1593), Spenser (1611) Title Page," *Ba*, XXIX (1945), 97-100.

B4623 Eagle, R. L. "Is the 'Kay' Cipher a Delusion?" *Ba*, XXX (1946), 52-54, 129-132.

B4624 Eagle, R. L. "Dates of Publication of Bacon-Shakespeare Works." *Ba*, XXX (1946), 132-134.

B4625 Eagle, R. L. "The Date of the Sonnets." *Ba*, XXXI (1947), 99-105.

B4626 Eagle, R. L. "Was 'Lucus' William Shakespeare?" *Ba*, XXXII (1948), 161-163.

B4627 Ellis, Walter W. *The Shakespeare Myth.* London: Bacon Soc., 1946. Pp. 30.

B4628 Ewen, C. L.'E. "Bacon's Bonds." *Ba*, XXIII (1938), 27-33.

B4629 Feely, Joseph Martin. *Shakespeare's Maze Further Deciphered.* Rochester, New York: Burns Press, 1938. Pp. 249.

B4630 Feely, Joseph Martin. *The Cypher in The Sonnets, the Dedication Key.* Rochester, New York: Author, 1940. Pp. 68.

B4631 Feely, Joseph M. *A Cypher Idyll Anent the Little Western Flower; Deciphered from a Midsommer Nights Dreame.* Rochester, New York: Privately Printed, 1942. Pp. 82.

B4632 Fischer, Walther. "Die Shakespeare-Bacon-Frage in Ihrer Geschichtlichen Entwicklung." *Nachrichten d. Giessener Hochschulgemeinschaft*, XVI (1946/47), 5-35.

B4633 Franco, J. "Visible Evidence for Francis Bacon." *Ba*, XXX (1946), 110-112.

B4634 Franco, J. "A Baconian Discovery." *Ba*, XXXI (1947), 22.

B4635 Franco, Johan Henri Gustave. *Bacon-Shakespeare Identities Revealed by Their Handwritings.* New York: Moore, 1947. Pp. 30.

B4636 Gallagher, D. J. "That Long Word." *Ba*, XXVIII (1944), 159.

B4637 Gentry, R. J. W. "Shakespeare and the Italian Comedy." *Ba*, XXXI (1947), 42-47.

B4638 Gentry, R. J. W. "Frances Bacon as Historian." *Ba*, XXXII (1948), 149-155.

B4639 Ghyka, Matila. "Le Cas Bacon-Shakespeare." *La France Libre*, No. 56, June 15, 1945, pp. 102-106.

B4640 Gibson, J. "Shakespeare and Bacon." *Ba*, XXIII (1938), 38ff.

B4641 Greenwood, Sir George. *The Shakespeare Problem Restated.* Condensed by E. Greenwood. Foreword by Lord Ponsonby. London: Athenaeum Press, 1937. Pp. viii, 171.

B4642 Grute, Harry. *Shakespeare with Bacon: An Examination of the English History Plays Commonly Attributed to Shakespeare.* Newton: Montgomeryshire Printing Co., 1954. Pp. 88.

B4643 Gundry, W. G. C. *Francis Bacon: A Map of Days, A Guide to His Homes and Haunts.* London: Bacon Soc., 1946. Pp. 50.
       Rev: *N &Q*, 191 (1946), 264.

B4644 Gundry, W. G. C. "A House Divided Against Itself." *Ba*, XXX (1946), 7-12.

B4645 Gundry, W. G. C. "Manes Verulamiani." *Ba*, XXX (1946), 48-51.

B4646 Gundry, W. G. C. "Was Shakespeare Educated?" *Ba*, XXXI (1947), 13-21.

B4646a Gundry, W. G. C. "Was Shakespeare Educated?" *Ba*, XXX (1946), 151-157.

B4647 Gundry, W. G. C. "A New Shakesperian Commentator." *Ba*, XXXI (1947), 143-151.

B4648 Habgood, F. E. C. "Seventeenth-Century Studies." *Ba*, XXIII (1938), 75-80.

B4649 Habgood, F. E. C. "Bacon's Two Lives." *Ba*, XXIV (1939), 129-143.

B4650 Habgood, F. E. C. " 'Shakspere' Not 'Shakespeare'." *Ba*, xxv (1941), 112-132.

B4651 Hadman, A. "It Doesn't Matter Who Wrote the Plays." *Ba*, xxviii (1944), 56-61.

B4652 Hare, Peter. "Neues zur Shakespeare-Bacon-Theorie." *Engl. Rundschau* (Cologne), ii, No. 9 (1952), 110-111.

B4653 Heron-Allen, Edward. "Shakespeare or Bacon." *N &Q*, 179 (1940), 26; H. G. L. K., R. L. Eagle and Wm. Jaggard, ibid., 68-69; G. W. Wright, ibid., 125.

B4654 Holbrook, S. "I. Donnelly." *NYTBR*, July 30, 1944, pp. 7, 16.

B4655 Holzer, Gustav. *Die Apotheose Bacon-Shakespeare*. Eine Studie. Karlsruhe i. Breisgau: Gutsch, 1942. Pp. 31.

B4656 Housden, K. M. "Somebody Says Bacon." *Ba*, xxix (1945), 90-96.

B4657 Huch, R. "Bacon-Shakespeare." *Deutsches Volkstum*, xx, 10 (1938), 715.

B4658 Hunt, R. "The Reality, Idealism, Humor and Sensitivity of Bacon in Shakespeare." *Ba*, xxvii (1943), 125-128.

B4659 Johnson, E. D. *Francis Bacon's Cypher Signatures*. Birmingham, 1942. Pp. 22.

B4660 Johnson, E. D. "The Testimony of Mrs. Judith (!) Hall." *Ba*, xxvi (1942), 158-160.

B4661 Johnson, E. D. "Shakespeare's Medical Knowledge." *Ba*, xxviii (1944), 98-102.

B4662 Johnson, E. D. "Authorship of *Don Quixote*." *Ba*, xxviii (1944), 155-156.

B4663 Johnson, E. D. "Francis Bacon's Cypher Signatures." *Ba*, xxix (1945), 29-30.

B4664 Johnson, E. D. "The Figure 2." *Ba*, xxix (1945), 104-106.

B4665 Johnson, E. D. "Examples of Shakespeare's Use of Emblem Books." *Ba*, xxix (1945), 145-146.

B4666 Johnson, E. D. "Baconian Cipher in *The Tempest*." *Ba*, xxix (1945), 147-150.

B4667 Johnson, E. D. "Malvolio's Cryptic M.O.A.I." *Ba*, xxx (1946), 26-28.

B4668 Johnson, E. D. "A Cipher in *Tempest*." *Ba*, xxx (1946), 63-65.

B4669 Johnson, E. D. "Shakespeare's Use of Emblem Books." *Ba*, xxx (1946), 65-68.

B4670 Johnson, E. D. "Francis Bacon, the Elizabethan Cuckoo." *Ba*, xxx (1946), 103-109.

B4671 Johnson, E. D. "The Futility of Oxfordian Claims." *Ba*, xxx (1946), 124-125.

B4672 Johnson, E. D. "Timon of Athens." *Ba*, xxx (1946), 158.

B4673 Johnson, E. D. "A Cipher in *Henry IV*." *Ba*, xxx (1946), 191.

B4674 Johnson, E. D. *Bacon-Shakespeare Coincidences*. London: The Bacon Society, 1946.

B4675 Johnson, E. D. "Where are the Shakespeare Manuscripts?" *Ba*, xxxi (1947), 104-110.

B4676 Johnson, Edward D. *Francis Bacon and Shakespeare: Similarity of Thought*. London: Lapworth, 1950. Pp. 32.

B4677 Kavanagh, M. "The Weird Sisters of Macbeth." *Ba*, xxxii (1948), 72-74.

B4678 Kimball, L. E. "Miss Bacon Advances Learning." *Colophon*, No. 2 (1937), 338-354.

B4679 Lefranc, Abel. "La Question Shakespearienne au XVIIIe Siècle." *Rev. Bleue Politique et Littéraire*, Feb. 1938, pp. 44-50.

B4680 Leftwich, H. S. "Shakespeare, Bacon and Popular Fallacies." *N &Q*, 187 (1944), 39-40.

B4681 Leith, A. A. "Shakespeare, Bacon and Gervinus." *Ba*, xxiv (1939), 32-36.

B4682 Leith, A. A. "A Conceit Somewhat Ridiculous." *Ba*, xxvi (1942), 73-77.

B4683 Leith, A. A. "Allusions and Allegories." *Ba*, xxviii (1944), 18-21.

B4684 Lemaître, Jacques. "Bacon et Shakespeare: Nouvelles Découvertes Cryptographiques." *MdF*, 293 (July 1, 1939), 206-212; Remarks by Général Cartier, ibid., p. 206.

B4685 Lloyd, J. E. "Shakespeare's Legends." *Ba*, xxix (1945), 151-154.

B4686 Mantey, Karl Georg. "Shakespeare oder Francis Bacon." *Berl. Börsenztg.*, No. 131, 1937.

B4687 Mataraly, P. V. "The Hidden Cipher in the Porter's Soliloquy in *Macbeth*." *Ba*, xxxii (1948), 226-228.

B4688 Maurice, Martin. *William Shakespeare*. Paris: Gallimard, 1953. Pp. 476. Translated into Italian by Luciana Lombardo Frezza (Collezione Sidra). Milan: Rizzoli, 1955. Pp. 359. An examination of the so-called "Shakespeare Problem."
Rev: by René Lalou, *Hommes et Mondes* (Paris), xxiii (Jan., 1954), 271-273; by G. Lambin, *LanM*, xlviii (1954), 85-86; by Paul Arnold, *Cahiers du Sud*, xxxix-xl, Nos. 323-328, 304-306; by J. B. Fort, *EA*, vii, 414-415; by J. J. Mayoux, *Lettres Nouvelles*, No. 24; by G. Lambin, *LanM*, xlviii, 273-275; by Y. Florenne, *Le Monde*, x, No. 3; by A. Guibert, *Monde Nouveau. Paru*, x, No. 78 (1954) 80-81; by A. Prudhommeaux, *Preuves*, No. 38; by Y. Florenne, *Table Ronde*, 86 (1955), 133-134; by Vladimiro Cajoli, *Idea* (Rome), viii, No. 1 (Jan. 1, 1956), 2-4.

B4689 Melsome, W. S. "Bacon-Shakespeare Anatomy." *Ba*, xxiv (1938/39), 57-69, 175-190; xxv (1941), 133-144, 166-175, 229-241.

B4690 Melsome, W. S. "Bacon, Shakespeare, and T. Nashe." *Ba*, xxvi (April, 1942), 53-66; (July, 1942), 122-137.

B4690a Melsome, W. S. "Bacon, Shakespeare, and Nashe." *Ba*, xxviii (1944), 9-15.

B4691   Melsome, W. S.   "Constant and Inconstant Love."   *Ba*, XXVI (1942), 196-203.

B4692   Melsome, W. S.   "Bacon, Shakespeare, and *Proverbs XXV*."   *Ba*, XXVII (1943), 6-18.

B4693   Melsome, W. S.   "Bacon, Shakespeare, and War."   *Ba*, XXVII (1943), 60-68.

B4694   Melsome, W. S.   "Bacon, Shakespeare, and Our Philologists."   *Ba*, XXVII (1943), 114-124.

B4695   Melsome, W. S.   " 'Also' Ran."   *Ba*, XXVII (1943), 135-136.

B4696   Melsome, W. S.   "Bacon, the Bible, and More's Famous Speech."   *Ba*, XXVII (1943), 153-166.

B4697   Melsome, William Stanley.   *Bacon-Shakespeare Anatomy*.   London: G. Lapworth & Co., 1945. Pp. xv, 250. New York: Stuyvesant Press, 1948. Pp. 247.
        Rev: *TLS*, Nov. 17, 1945, p. 551; by W. G. C. Gundry, *Ba*, XXX (1946), 29-32; by D. Q. (various references to the *Anatomy*), *N &Q*, 190 (1946), 37-38, 59, 78, 99-100, 146, 259.

B4698   Millar, J. S. L.   *The Man in the Shakespeare Mask*.   Edinburgh, 1942. Pp. 16.

B4699   Millar, J. S. L.   "Some Shakespeare Doubts."   *Ba*, XXVIII (1944), 48-55.

B4700   Millar, J. S. L.   "The Bacon-Shakespeare Mind as Exhibited in Burton's *Anatomy*."   *Ba*, XXVIII (1944), 137-141.

B4701   Moore, William.   *Shakespeare*.   Birmingham: Cornish Bros., 1934. Pp. x, 324.
        Rev: by Eduard Eckhardt, *Eng. Studn.*, LXXI (1936/37), 255-256.

B4702   Murchison, K.   "Who Wrote the 'Shakespeare' Plays?"   *Ba*, XXVI (1942), 138-144.

B4703   Page, Frederick.   "Jonson and Shakespeare."   *N &Q*, 184 (1943), 79.
        Questions the authority for identifications by Baconians.

B4704   Pares, Martin.   *Will o' the Wisp*.   London: c/o Royal Agricultural Benevolent Institution, Vincent House, Vincent Square, London, S. W. I, 1958. Pp. 13.
        Reprinted from *Ariel*, the Winchester College magazine.

B4705   Pigott, P.   "The Baconian Mysteries."   *Rosicrucian Digest*, XXII (1944), 96-98, 108.

B4706   Pogson, B. C.   "The Esoteric Meaning of *Twelfth Night*."   *Ba*, XXXII (1948), 65-71.

B4707   Pogson, B. C.   "The Estoric Significance of *Cymbeline*."   *Ba*, XXXII (1948), 192-198.

B4708   Porohovshikov, P. S.   "Fingerprints in Shakespeare."   *Ba*, XXX (1946), 179-181.

B4709   Pratt, Fletcher.   *Secret and Urgent: The Story of Codes and Ciphers*.   Indianapolis: Bobbs-Merrill, 1939. Pp. 282.
        Rev: by H. H. Peckham, *AHR*, XLV (1940), 606-607; by B. G. Theobald, *Ba*, XXV (April 1940), 43-47.

B4710   Prescott, K. H.   "Word and Bi-literal Cyphers."   *Ba*, XXIII (1938), 167-172.

B4711   Prescott, K. H.   "Dark Ladies and Lovely Boys."   *Ba*, XXIX (1945), 35-36.

B4712   Prescott, Kate H.   *Reminiscences of a Baconian*.   New York: Haven Press, 1949. Pp. 124.

B4713   Rose, E. G.   "A Biblical Reference to Francis Bacon."   *Ba*, XXVIII (1944), 146-149.

B4714   S., H.   "Shakespeare's Coat of Arms."   *Ba*, XXIII (1938), 42-44.

B4715   Samuels, Philips.   *Five Lectures on 'Shakespeare.'*   Boston: Samuels-Bacon Publishing Co., 1937. 1943. Pp. 64.

B4716   Schick, Joseph.   "Drei Genies und ein Talent, oder Bacons Stellung unter den Grossen seiner Zeit."   *SJ*, LXXII (1936), 42-78.

B4717   Seligo, Irene.   "Wer Schrieb Shakespeare?"   *Frankfurter Zeitung*, 1938. Nos. 525-526.

B4718   Sennett, M.   "The Wisdom of Shakespeare."   *Ba*, XXVI (1942), 187-195.

B4719   Sennett, M.   "This Concordant One."   *Ba*, XXX (1946), 126-128.

B4720   Sennett, Mabel.   *His Erring Pilgrimage; A New Interpretation of "As You Like It."*   London: Bacon Society, 1949. Pp. 108.

B4721   Seymour, H.   "Bacon's Cryptic Signatures in the Works of 'Shakespeare'."   *Ba*, XXI (1938), 8-10.

B4722   Spain, Margaret M.   *Who Wrote Shakespeare's Sonnets?*   Baltimore: Metropolitan Press, 1945. Pp. 36.

B4723   Stovall, Floyd.   "Whitman, Shakespeare, and the Baconians."   *PQ*, XXXI (1952), 27-38.
        Whitman did not accept Baconians, although doubting Shak.

B4724   Sydenham.   "The First Baconian."   *Ba*, XXVII (1943), 1-5.

B4725   Theobald, B. G.   "The Bacon-Shakespeare Mottoes."   *Ba*, XXV (1941), 145-148.

B4726   Turner, R. G.   "*Hamlet* and Francis Bacon."   *Ba*, XXX (1946), 187.

B4727   Walker, N. W. G.   "Was Shakespeare a Seaman?"   *Ba*, XXIV (1939), 124-128.

B4728   Walters, P.   "F. Bacon and Gray's Inn."   *Ba*, XXVIII (1944), 150-154.

B4729   Walters, P.   "Date of 'Shakespeare's' *Sonnets*."   *Ba*, XXIX (1945), 72-73.

B4730   Walters, P.   "Truth Brought to Light."   *Ba*, XXIII (1938), 115-121.

B4731   Walters, P.   "Joseph Hall Satirizes the Shakespeare Family."   *Ba*, XXIV (1939), 144-150.

B4732   Weagant, James R.   *ORMTS (Francis Bacon Prints)*.   Los Angeles, 1955. Pp. 80.

B4733   Wehner, Carl.   "Aus Shakespeare soll Bacon Werden."   *Kölnische Volksztg.*, No. 319, 1938.

B4734   Woodward, Frank Lee.   *Francis Bacon and the Cipher Story*.   Chicago: Aries Press, 1947.

B4735   Woodward, S. "Reply to R. L. Eagle." *Ba*, xxx (1946), 55-56.

B4736   Wright, G. W. "Shakespeare of Bacon." *N &Q*, 179 (1940), 125.

2. WILLIAM STANLEY, EARL OF DERBY (185;-)

B4737   Longworth de Chambrun, C. "Shakespeare est bien Shakespeare." *Hommes et Mondes*, May, 1951, pp. 709-725.
        Opposes Abel Lefranc's view that Shakespeare's plays were written by William Stanley.

B4738   Evans, A. J. *Shakespeare's Magic Circle*. London: Barker, 1956. Pp. 160.
        Rev: *TLS*, July 6, 1956, p. 410 (commentary, pointing out a farcical anticipation of Evans' thesis, by Roger Lancelyn Green, *TLS*, July 13, p. 423); by J. Hall, *English*, xi, 105-106; by J. I. M. Stewart, *NstN*, li, 493; by J. Vallette, *MdF*, 327 (1956), 526-528; by Robert Adger Law, *SQ*, ix (1958), 78-80.

B4739   Goldsmid, M. "Niet Shakespeare maar William Stanley." *Gulden Winckel* (Holland), Jan., 1941, pp. 12-14.

B4740   Guth, Paul. "La Bataille de Shakespeare." *Figaro Littéraire*, vi No. 248 (1951), 1, 4.

B4741   Halévy, H. D. [A. Lefranc's Solution of the Shakespeare Mystery.] *Les Nouvelles Littéraires*, Jan. 17, 1946, p. 5.

B4742   Lambin, G. *Sur la Trace d'un Shakespeare Inconnu. I. Shakespeare à Florence. II. Shakespeare et la Ligue. III. Il Signor Prospero. IV. Shakespeare à Milan. V. Shakespeare à Paris. LanM*, xlv (1951), 217-237, 345-367; xlvi (1952), 245-257; *LanM*, xlvi-xlviii (1952-54), passim.

B4743   Lefranc, Abel. "Les Eléments Français de *Peines d'Amour Perdues* de Shakespeare." *RH*, 178 (1937), 411-432.

B4744   Lefranc, Abel. "La Question Shakespearienne au XVIIIe Siècle." *Rev. Bleue Politique et Littéraire*, lxvi (Feb. 1938), 44-50.

B4745   Lefranc, A. "Het Shakespeare Vraagstuck in de 18de Euuw." *Wetenschappelijke Bladen*, iii (1938), 93-108.

B4746   Lefranc, Abel. "Sous le Masque de Shakespeare." *Les Nouvelles Littéraires*, Nov. 1, 1945, p. 1.

B4747   Lefranc, Abel. *A la Découverte de Shakespeare*. I. Paris: A. Michel, 1945. Pp. 600. Vol. II, B4749.
        Rev: by Jacques Vallette, *Lettres Françaises*, Feb. 22, 1946, p. 4; by Emile Henriot, *Le Monde*, Jan. 10, p. 3; *TLS*, Sept. 21, p. 452; by T. Pyles, *Books Abroad*, xxi (1947), 59-60; by Roddier, *RLC*, xxii (1948), 594; by M. Rat, *Education Nationale*, No. 10, 1951, pp. 8-9; by C. Roy, *Europe*, March, pp. 120-125; by A. Rousseaux, *Figaro Littéraire*, vi, No. 246, 2; by G. Connes, *LanM*, xlvi, 198-199; by R. Kemp, *Les Nouvelles Littéraires*, 1219; by O. J. Campbell, *SQ*, ii, 104.

B4748   Lambin, G. "Shakespeare Etait-il Essexien?" *LanM*, xlii (1948), fasc. A, A14-A22.

B4749   Lefranc, Abel. *A La Découverte de Shakespeare*. ii. Paris: Albin Michel, 1950. Pp. 560. Vol. I, B4747.
        Rev: by T. Pyles, *Books Abroad*, xxi (1947), 59-60; by André Rousseaux, *Figaro Littéraire*, Jan. 6, 1951, p. 2; by Claude Delmas, *Gazette des Lettres*, Feb. 15, pp. 121, 123; by Claude Roy, *Europe*, March, pp. 120-125; by Lienhard Bergel, *Books Abroad*, xxv, 335.

B4750   Lefranc, Abel. "Il n'y a Plus de Question Shakespearienne." *Beaux-Arts*, Dec. 29, 1950.

B4751   Lefranc, Abel. *William Stanley VIe Comte de Derby: Auteur des Œuvres Shakespeariennes*. Paris: A. L'Univers Latine D'Editions, 1951. Pp. 24.

B4752   Lucas, Richard Macdonald. *Shakespeare's Vital Secret*. (*Known to his Queen*). Keighley: Wadsworth, 1937. London: Rydal Press, 1938. Pp. 328.
        Rev: *TLS*, June 18, 1938, p. 422; see letter by author, ibid., July 9, 1938, p. 470; *Spectator*, Feb. 25, p. 336; by Beatrice White, *National Rev.*, 110 (1938), 401-404; see letters by Mr. Lucas and Miss White, ibid., 110, 532-533; by G. Eldon Manisty, ibid., 110, 680-681.

B4753   Mandin, Louis. "Les Nouvelles Révélations sur *Hamlet* et Marie Stuart." *MdF*, 270 (1936), 652-658. Discussion of Lefranc's *Derby* views.

B4754   Morhardt, Mathias. "A la Rencontre de William Shakespeare." *MdF*, 269 (1936), 336-358; 276 (1937), 75-96.

B4754a Morhardt, Mathias. *A la Recontre de William Shakespeare*. Préface de Abel Lefranc. Paris: Ed. Egard Malfère, 1938. Pp. 148.
        Rev: by Clara Longworth, Comtesse de Chambrun, *EA*, ii (1938), 298-299; by Marian P. Whitney, *Books Abroad*, xii (1939), 188.

B4755   Morsier, E. de. "La Clef de l'Enigme Shakespeare." *L'Opinion* (Paris), xxviii, No. 10 (1935), 9.

B4756   Schoell, F. L. "Deux Etudes Récentes sur Shakespeare." *EA*, vi (1953), 28-34.
        Discusses T. M. Parrott's *Shakespearean Comedy*, and Abel Lefranc's *A la Découverte de Shakespeare*.

B4757   Titherley, Arthur Walsh. *Shakespeare's Sonnets as from the Pen of William Stanley, Sixth Earl of Derby*. London and Liverpool: Philip, 1939.

B4758   Titherley, A. W. *Shakespeare's Identity. William Stanley, 6th Earl of Derby*. Winchester: Warren & Son Ltd., 1952. Pp. 338.
        Rev: *NstN*, xliv (1952), 115; by G. Lambin, *LanM*, xlvii (1953), 72-74; by P. J. Henniker-

Heaton, *Christian Science Monitor*, March 5, p. 13; by G. B. Harrison, *SatR*, Oct. 10, p. 38; by George C. Taylor, *SQ*, v (1954), 192-195.

B4759 Titherley, A. W. *Shakespeare's Earliest Poems in Approximately Chronological Order*. Winchester: Warren, 1953.
Sequel to B4758.

3. EDWARD DE VERE, EARL OF OXFORD (186;65)

B4760 Bénézet, L. P., E. T. Clark, and C. W. Barrell. *The Shakespeare Fellowship Quarterly*, v, No. 1 (1944), 1-16; No. 2, 17-32; No. 4, 49-68; vi (1945), 49-64; vii (Jan., 1946), 1-16; vii (July), 33-48.

B4761 *Shakespeare Fellowship Newsletter*. Edited at 17 E. 48th St., New York 17, New York. Vols. III-IV, 1941-43; v, 1944; VI-VII, 1945-46; VIII-IX, 1947-48.

B4762 S. "De Vere, Earl of Oxford, Author of Shakespeare's Plays." *N &Q*, 177 (1939), 368.

B4763 "The Authorship of *Othello*." *Shakespeare Fellowship Quarterly*, v (1944), 46-48.

B4764 "Documentary Notes on the Swan Theatre." *Shakespeare Fellowship Quarterly*, v (1944), 8-9.

B4765 "Another Bacon-Oxford Debate." *Ba*, xxx (1946), 119-120.

B4766 "Who Wrote What And How?" *High Points*, xxxvii (Oct., 1955), 72-73.

B4767 Allen, P. "Names in *The Winter's Tale*." *TLS*, July 18, 1936, p. 600.

B4768 Allen, Percy. *Talks with Elizabethans: Revealing the Mystery of 'William Shakespeare'*. London: Rider, 1948. Pp. 216. New York: Universal Distrib., 1948. Pp. 216.
Rev: by Ivor Brown, *Oxford Bibliographical Society*, Jan. 4, 1948, p. 3; *TLS*, Feb. 14, p. 100; *TLS*, Feb. 28, p. 127; by Trevor James, *Life and Letters*, LIX, 72-74.

B4769 Fodor, N. " 'Spirit Revelation' About Shakespeare's Identity." *Jour. of Amer. Soc. for Psychical Research*, xxx (1936), 232.
Abstr. fr. *Ali del Pensiero*.

B4770 Hansen, Norman Hall. "Manden, der har talt med Shakespeare." *Fortids Veje* (Copenhagen), vii (1949), 271-283.

B4771 Amphlett, Hilda. *Who Was Shakespeare*: A New Enquiry with an Introduction by Christmas Humphreys. London: Heinemann, 1955. Pp. xx, 218. Rindge, New Hampshire: Richard R. Smith, 1957.
Rev: *TLS*, July 1, 1955, pp. 370-371; by R. A. Foakes, *English*, x, 227-228; by J. I. M. Stewart, *NstN*, Aug. 27, p. 250.

B4772 B., H. "A Debate on the Oxfordian Claim VS the Baconian." *Ba*, xxx (1946), 75-78.

B4773 Barrell, Charles Wisner. "Elizabethan Mystery Man." *SRL*, xvi (May 1, 1937), 11-15.
Reply by E. E. Stoll, *SRL*, May 8, 1937, pp. 12-17; rejoinder C. W. Barrell, *SRL*, May 22, p. 9; by Carolyn Wells, *SRL*, June 5, p. 9.

B4773a Barrell, C. W. *Elizabethan Mystery Man*. New York: A. Gauthier, 17 E. 48th Street, 1940.

B4774 Barrell, Charles W. "Identifying Shakespeare." *Scientific Amer.*, 162 (1939), 4-8, 43-45.

B4775 Barrell, Charles Wisner. "Matinee at the Swan: A Topical Interlude in Oxford-Shakespeare Research." *Shakespeare Fellowship Quarterly*, v (1944), 10-15.

B4776 Barrell, Charles Wisner. "Newly Discovered Oxford-Shakespeare Pictorial Evidence." *Shakespeare Fellowship Quarterly*, v (1944), 24-27.

B4777 Barrell, C. W. "Oxford as Supervising Patron of Shakespeare's Theatrical Company." *Shakespeare Fellowship Quarterly*, v (1944), 33-40.

B4778 Barrell, Charles Wisner. " 'The Sole Author of Renowned Victorie': Gabriel Harvey Testifies in the Oxford Shakespeare Case." *Shakespeare Fellowship Quarterly*, vi (1945), 11-12.

B4779 Barrell, Charles Wisner. "Earliest Authenticated 'Shakespeare' Transcript Found with Oxford's Personal Poems." *Shakespeare Fellowship Quarterly*, vi (1945), 22-26.

B4780 Barrell, Charles Wisner. "Rare Military Volume Sponsored by Lord Oxford Issued by 'Shakespeare's' First Publisher." *Shakespeare Fellowship Quarterly*, vi (1945), 30-32.

B4781 Barrell, Charles Wisner. "The Wayward Water-Bearer Who Wrote 'Shakespeare's' Sonnet 109." *Shakespeare Fellowship Quarterly*, vi (1945), 37-39.

B4782 Barrell, Charles Wisner. " 'Creature of Their Own Creating': An Answer to the Present Day School of Shakespearean Biography." *Shakespeare Fellowship Quarterly*, vi (1945), 59-60.

B4783 Barrell, C. W. "Proof that Shakespeare's Thought and Imagery Dominate Oxford's Own Statement of Creative Principles." *Shakespeare Fellowship Quarterly*, vii (1946), 61-69.

B4784 Barrell, C. W. "Exploding the Ancient Play-Cobbler Fallacy." *Shakespeare Fellowship Quarterly*, vii (1946), 3-7.

B4785 Barrell, C. W. "A Literary Pirate's Attempt to Publish *The Winter's Tale* in 1594." *Shakespeare Fellowship Quarterly*, vii (1946), 20-31.

B4786 Barrell, C. W. "The Earl of Oxford Publishes *Cardanus Comfort*." *Shakespeare Fellowship Quarterly*, vii (1946), 35-42.

B4787 Barrell, C. W. "Verifying the Secret History of Shakespeare's Sonnets." *Tomorrow*, Feb., 1946, pp. 49-55; March, pp. 54-60.

B4788 Beaumont, C. "The Oxfordians' Freakish Claims." *Ba*, XXXI (1947), 87-95.

B4789 Bénézet, Louis, P. *Shakspere, Shakespeare and De Vere.* Manchester, New Hampshire, 1938.

B4790 Bénézet, Louis P. "The Frauds and Stealths of Injurious Imposters." *Shakespeare Fellowship Quarterly*, V (1944), 2-6.

B4791 Bénézet, Louis P. "The Stratford Defendant Compromised by His Own Advocates." *Shakespeare Fellowship Quarterly*, V (1944), 44-46; VI (1945), 13-15, 27-29, 40-45.

B4792 Bénézet, L. P. "Another Stratfordian (G. Saintsbury) Aids the Oxford Case." *Shakespeare Fellowship Quarterly*, VII (1946), 17-19.

B4793 Bénézet, L. P. "The Date of *Henry VIII*." *Shakespeare Fellowship Quarterly*, VII (1946), 43-44.

B4794 Bénézet, Louis P. *The Six Loves of Shakespeare.* New York: Pageant, 1958. Pp. 126.
       Rev: by Hudson Rogers, *English Journal*, XLVII (1958), 527-528.

B4795 Bowen, Gwynneth. *Shakespeare's Farewell.* Inglethorpe Buxton, Derbyshire: Bowen, 1951. Pp. 20.

B4795a Bowers, Fredson Thayer. "Gascoigne and the Oxford Cipher." *MLN*, LII (1937), 183-186. Disposes of Edward de Vere's supposed connection with *A Hundredth Sundrie Flowres.*

B4796 Campbell, Oscar James. "Shakespeare Himself." *Harper's Magazine*, July, 1940, pp. 172-185.

B4797 Clark, E. T. *The Satirical Comedy, "Love's Labour's Lost."* New York, 1933. Pp. 188.

B4798 Clark, Eva Turner. *The Man Who Was Shakespeare.* New York: Richard R. Smith, 1937. Pp. vii, 319.
       Rev: by Tucker Brooke, *JEGP*, XXXVII (1938), 311-312; by Rob. Withington, *MLN*, LIII, 619-623; by B. T. Spencer, *SR*, XLVII (1939), 294-305.

B4799 Clark, E. T. "Shakespeare Read Greek." *Shakespeare Fellowship News Letter*, I (1940), 9-10.

B4800 Clark, E. T. "The Neapolitan Prince." *Shakespeare Fellowship News Letter*, I (1940), 12.

B4801 Clark, Eva Turner. "Some Character Names in Shakespeare's Plays." *Shakespeare Fellowship Quarterly*, V (1944), 30-32; ibid., V, 41-43; ibid., V, 66-68.

B4802 Clark, Eva Turner. "Lord Oxford's Shakespearean Travels on the European Continent." *Shakespeare Fellowship Quarterly*, VI (1945), 3-10.

B4803 Clark, Eva Turner. "Lord Oxford's Letters Echoed in Shakespeare's Plays: An Early Letter Examined. Part One." *Shakespeare Fellowship Quarterly*, VI (1945), 51-53; ibid., VII (1946), 10-11.

B4804 Clark, E. T. "Shakespeare's Strange Silence When James I Succeeded Elizabeth." *Shakespeare Fellowship Quarterly*, VII (1946), 55-60.

B4805 Douglas, Montagu W. *Lord Oxford Was 'Shakespeare'.* London, 1934.
       Rev: by Henry D. Davray, *MdF*, 270 (1936), 424-425.

B4806 Douglas, Montagu William. *Lord Oxford and the Shakespeare Group.* Woodville Hotel, Ealing: The author, 1952. Pp. 168. Oxford: Alden, 1952. Pp. 168.
       A summary of evidences presented by J. T. Looney, Canon G. H. Rendall, Prof. Gilbert Slater. Third edition. Previously *Lord Oxford as Shak.* (1st ed., 1931) and *Lord Oxford was Shak.* (2nd ed., 1934).

B4807 Dwyer, J. J. "The Poet Earl of Oxford and Grays Inn." *Shakespeare Fellowship Quarterly*, VIII (1947), 21-25.

B4808 Ellis, W. "Edward de Vere." *Ba*, XXX (1946), 124-125.

B4809 Feldman, A. Bronson. "The Confessions of William Shakespeare." *American Imago*, XII (1955), 113-116.

B4810 Feldman, A. Bronson. "Othello in Reality." *American Imago*, XI (1954), 147-179.

B4811 Feldman, A. Bronson. "Imaginary Incest." *American Imago*, XII (1955), 117-155.

B4812 Flatter, Richard. "Sigmund Freud on Shakespeare." *SQ*, II (1951), 368-369.
       Prints two letters from Freud, one on *Lear*, and the other on the *Sonnets.*

B4813 Hoepfner, T. C., et al. "The Shakespearean Confusion." *SRL*, XXXI, No. 6 (1948), 21-22.

B4814 Johnson, E. D. "The Futility of Oxfordian Claims." *Ba*, XXX (1946), 124-125.

B4815 Kent, William, and Others. *Edward De Vere, the Seventeenth Earl of Oxford, the Real Shakespeare.* London: The Shakespeare Fellowship, 1947. Pp. 30. Enlarged 2nd edition, 1956. Pp. 32. Paperback.
       Rev: *TLS*, Sept. 27, 1947, p. 498; Sept. 27, 1957, p. 582.

B4816 Kittle, William. *Edward de Vere, Seventeenth Earl of Oxford, and Shakespeare.* Baltimore: Monumental Press, 1943. Pp. xiv, 209.

B4817 Lederer, Moritz. "Wer War Shakespeare?" *Neue Literar. Welt*, III, No. 10 (1952), 9.

B4818 Looney, John Thomas. "Discoverer of the True Shakespeare Passes." *Shakespeare Fellowship Quarterly*, V (1944), 17-23.

B4819 Looney, J. Thomas. *'Shakespeare' Identified in Edward de Vere, Seventeenth Earl of Oxford.* New York: Duell, Sloan & Pearce. Toronto: Collins, 1949. Pp. xxi, 476.
       A new edition with some revision, introduction by William McFee and "Afterwords" by C. W. Barrell.

Rev: by Douglas Bush, *NR*, April 24, 1950, p. 20; by Hamilton Basso, *New Yorker*, April 8, pp. 118-119.

B4820 Moerkerken, P. H. van. *Achter het Mombakkes*. Amsterdam: G. A. van Oorschot, 1950. Pp. 154.
Largely based on J. T. Looney, *Shakespeare Identified*, 1920.
Rev: by R. Blijstra, *Critisch Bulletin*, XVIII (1951), 8 ff; by W. van Maanen, *De Gids*, 114 (Jan.), 376-378; by Harry Hoppe, *SQ*, IV (1953), 355-357.

B4821 Ogburn, Dorothy. "The Wounded Name of Truth." *Shakespeare Fellowship Quarterly*, VI (1945), 61-62.

B4822 Ogburn, Dorothy, and Charlton Ogburn. *The Renaissance Man of England*. Fifth ed. New York: Ogburn, 1949. Pp. 37. New York: Coward McMann, 1954.

B4823 Ogburn, Charlton. *Der Wahre Shakespeare*. Stuttgart: Ernst Klett Verlag, 1950. Pp. 45. Zurich: Origo Verlag, 1950. Pp. 46.
A German translation by John Richard Mez.
Rev: by M. Lederer, *Dt. Ztg. u. Wirtschafts-Ztg.*, V, No. 76 (1950), 16; by Klaus Colberg, *Die neue Schau*, XI, 157; by Karl Brunner, *SJ*, 87/88 (1952), 211-213.

B4824 Ogburn, Dorothy, and Charlton Ogburn. *This Star of England: William Shake-speare Man of the Renaissance*. New York: Coward-McCann, 1952. Pp. xxiii, 1297. London: Vision Press, 1953.
Rev: by R. H. West, *Georgia Rev.*, VII (1953), 228-231; by Joseph Wood Krutch, *NYHTBR*, Jan. 11, p. 13; by Kenneth Muir, *Spectator*, June 12, p. 768; by Oscar James Campbell, *NYTBR*, Feb. 8, pp. 7, 32 (excerpts of letters to editor, March 1, p. 23); by G. E. Dawson, *SQ*, IV, 165-170; by G. B. Harrison, *SatR*, Oct. 10, p. 38; *VQR*, XXIX, xxxii-xxxiii; *NstN*, XLVII (1954), 266-267; by David Hardman, *John o' London's Weekly*, LXIII, p. 194.

B4825 Phillips, Gerald William. *Shakespears Sonnets: Addressed to Members of the Shakespeare Fellowship*. Cambridge: Privately Printed, 1954. Pp. 23.

B4826 Rendall, Gerard H. *Ben Jonson and the First Folio Edition of Shakespeare's Plays*. Colchester: Benham, 1939. Pp. 24.
Rev: *TLS*, Oct. 28, 1939, p. 631.

B4827 Le Riche, Kathleen. "Shakespeare in Essex." *Essex Rev.*, LVI (1952), 187-191.

B4828 Roscoe, Burton. "The Battle Still Rages Over Who Was Shakespeare." *Shakespeare Fellowship Quarterly*, VI (Oct., 1945), 57-59.

B4829 Stoll, E. E. "The Detective Spirit in Criticism." *SRL*, XVI, No. 2 (May 8, 1937), 12, 14, 16-17. Answered by C. W. Barrell, XVI, No. 4 (May 22, 1937), 9; by Carolyn Wells, XVI, No. 6 (June 5, 1937), 9, 16.
A reply to C. W. Barrell's "Elizabethan Mystery Man," B4773, and an attack upon criticism as a process of mystery seeking.

4. ROGER MANNERS, EARL OF RUTLAND (-;66)

B4830 Schneider, K. *Neues Zeugnis für Rutland-Shakespeare*. Berlin: Rembrandt-Verlag, 1932, 1942.
Rev: by W. Fischer, *Beiblatt*, XLIX (1938), 123.

B4831 Schneider, Karl. *Der Wahre Kampf um Shakespeare. Ein Kampf gegen Irrtum und Irreführung in der Shakespeare-Frage*. Würzburg: Triltsch, 1937. Pp. 44.

B4832 Porohovshikov, Pierre S. *Shakespeare Unmasked*. New York: Savoy Book Publisher, 1940. London: Arco, 1955. Pp. 304.

B4833 "Now Shakespeare's a Sour Quartet." *Amer. Weekly*, Sept. 24, 1944, p. 10.

B4834 Porohovshikov, P. S. "Fingerprints in Shakespeare." *Ba*, XXX (1946), 179-181.

B4835 Bridgewater, H. "The Rutland Theory and Prof. Porohovshikov." *Ba*, XXXI (1947), 214-216.

B4836 Sykes, Claud Walter. *Alias William Shakespeare?* With a Foreword by Arthur Bryant. London: Francis Aldor, 1947. Pp. 221. See *NYHT*, July 25, 1947, p. 15.
Rev: by W. R. Calvert, *Illus. London News*, Sept. 6, 1947, p. 278; *NstN*, Dec. 6, 1947, p. 457-458; by R. L. Eagle, *Ba*, XXXI, 220-224.

B4837 Eagle, R. L. "C. W. Sykes and the Rutland Theory." *Ba*, XXXI (1947), 220-224.

B4838 John, Lisle Cecil. "Roger Manners, Elizabethan Courtier." *HLQ*, XII (1948), 57-84.

B4839 Sykes, Claud Walter. "The Shakespeare Mystery." *The London Mystery Magazine*, I (1949), 19-24.

5. CHRISTOPHER MARLOWE

B4840 Stalker, Archibald. *Shakespeare, Marlowe and Nashe*. Stirling: Learmonth & Son, 1936.
Rev: *TLS*, Jan. 2, 1937, p. 13.

B4841 Poteete, Robert. "Literary Sleuth." *Senior Scholastic*, LXIV (1954), 6.

B4842 Hoffman, Calvin. *The Murder of the Man Who Was 'Shakespeare'*. New York: Messner; London: Parrish, 1955. Pp. 256.
Rev: by G. B. Harrison, *SatR*, July 9, 1955, p. 16; by Alfred Harbage, *NYTBR*, June 12, pp. 1, 10-11 (comments by several correspondents, July 10, pp. 12-13, and letter by Mr. Hoffman, Aug. 28, p. 20); *Spiegel*, IX, No. 26 (1955), 36-39; ibid., No. 28, p. 5; No. 29, p. 5;

No. 31, p. 4; *Time*, June 13, p. 108ff; *Kirkus*, XXIII, 296; by F. E. Flaverty, *Chicago Sunday Tribune*, June 26, p. 3; by E. F. Walbridge, *Library Journal*, 80 (1955), 1211; by Joseph Henry Jackson, San Francisco *Chronicle*, June 3, p. 17; by Ray Irwin, *QJS*, XLI, 316-318; by Gunnar Sjögren, *Dagens Nyheter* (Stockholm), Aug. 17; *CE*, XVII, 64; by Padraic Fallon, *Dublin Magazine*, XXXI No. 2 (1956), 36-37; by R. A. Foakes, *SQ*, VII, 270-272; by R. Bingham, *Reporter*, April 5, p. 46; by Hermann Heuer, *SJ*, 92 (1956), 399-407; by E. D. O'Brien, *Illus. London News*, Feb. 11, p. 216; by J. I. M. Stewart, *NstN*, Feb. 11, p. 160; by Gerard Fay, *Spectator*, Jan. 27, p. 127; *TLS*, Jan. 27, p. 47 (letter by Mr. Hoffman and reviewer's reply, Feb. 17, p. 108; further comment by "Another of Your Reviewers," April 27, p. 253); by G. W. Knight, *TC*, 159 (1956), 398-400; by Norman Sharpnel, *MGW*, Feb. 9, p. 10; by Ken Gay, *Books and Bookmen*, I, No. 6 (Feb.), p. 26; by N. C. Clegg-Bruinwold Riedel, *Groene Amsterdammer*, March 17; by R. Elvin, *Les Nouvelles Littéraires*, Feb. 9, p. 5.

B4843   Heilbroner, Robert L.   "The Murder of the Man Who Was William Shakespeare." *Esquire*, Dec., 1954, pp. 115-122.

B4844   Heilbroner, Robert.   "The Shakespeare Murder Mystery."   Ill. by Gustav Rehberger. *Coronet*, July, 1955, pp. 83-102.

B4845   "Walsingham Tomb at Chislehurst."   *Ill. London News*, Jan. 14, 1956, p. 69.

B4846   "Was Will Will."   *Life*, Jan. 16, 1956, pp. 63-64.

B4847   Heilbroner, Robert L.   "The Murder of the Man Who Was Shakespeare."   *Plays and Players*, May, 1956, pp. 12-15.

B4848   "Empty Theory."   *Time*, May 14, 1956, p. 37.

B4849   "Antiquarian's Labor's Lost."   *Life*, May 14, 1956, p. 42.

B4850   Frost, William.   "Shakespeare His Own Granpaw."   *CE*, XVII (1956), 219-222.

B4851   Fuhara, Yoshiaki.   "Shakespeare-Marlowe Theory."   (in Japanese). *The Rising Generation* (Tokyo), 102, No. 5 (1956).

B4852   Gyller, Harald.   "Shakespeare och Marlowe."   *Bonniers Litterära Magasin* (Stockholm), XXV (1956), 138-140.

B4853   Roe, Frank Gilbert.   "The Marlowe Fiasco: Shakespeare Is as Shakespeare Does." *QQ*, LXIV (1957), 89-100.

6. ANNE WHATELY

B4854   Ross, William.   *The Story of Anne Whately and William Shaxpere*.   London: Holmes, 1940. Pp. 231.

B4855   Hutcheson, W. J. F.   "Hall and Shakespeare."   *TLS*, May 24, 1947, p. 253.

B4856   Hutcheson, W. J. Fraser.   *Shakespeare's Other Anne*.   Glasgow, 1950; Toronto, 1950.   Pp. 128, 13.
        Rev: *TLS*, Sept. 15, 1950, p. 582; by Hyder E. Rollins, *SQ*, II (1951), 256-257.

7. FLORIO, QUEEN ELIZABETH, EDWARD DYER, ETC.

B4857   Brooks, Alden.   *Will Shakspere: Factotum and Agent*.   London: Round Table Press, 1937. Pp. 374.

B4858   Ewen, C. L'Estrange.   *Shakespeare No Poet? The Story of an Unpublished Volume*.   London: The Author, 103 Gower St., 1938.   Pp. 6.
        Rev: *N &Q*, 174 (1938), 450.

B4859   Lefranc, Abel.   "La Question Shakespearienne au XVIIIᵉ Siècle."   *Rev. Bleue Politique et Littéraire*, Feb., 1938, pp. 44-50.

B4860   Healy, T. F.   "Shakespeare Was An Irishman."   *Amer. Mercury*, LI (1940), 24-32.

B4861   Brooks, Alden.   *Will Shakespeare and the Dyer's Hand*.   New York: Charles Scribner's Sons, 1943.   Pp. xx, 704.
        Rev: by Theodore Spencer, *Nation* (New York), Feb. 27, 1943, pp. 315-316; by John Corbin, "A New Candidate for Shakespeare's Honors," *NYTBR*, Feb. 7, p. 18; by H. McC., *More Books*, XVIII, 184.

B4862   Ballester Escalas, Rafael.   *El Historiador William Shakespeare (Ensayo Sobre el Espíritu del Siglo XVI)*.   Tarragona: Edit. R. Ballester, 1945.   Pp. 476.

B4863   Vigano, Paolo.   *Shakespeare Genio Italiano. Dimostrazioni e Prove Della sua Italianità; Documentazioni e Rivelazioni Psicografiche su Guglielmo Crollalanza*.   Treviso: Tip. ed. Trevigiana, 1947.   Pp. 30.

B4864   Norman, C. H.   "Shakespeare and the Law."   *TLS*, June 30, 1950, p. 412.
        Comment by Donald Somervell, ibid., July 21, 1950, p. 453; reply by C. H. Norman, Aug. 4, p. 485.

B4865   Proper, Ida Sedgwick.   *Our Elusive Willy. A Slice of Concealed Elizabethan History*.   Monhegan, Me.: The Author, 1953.   Pp. xxiii, 641.

B4866   "A Hamlet Enigma at Elsinore."   *Life*, Aug. 9, 1954, pp. 81-92.

B4867   Georgi, Friderico Erich Gerwien.   *William Shakespeare alias Mercutio Florio*.   Bremen: Privately Printed, 1954.   Pp. 54.

B4868   Paladino, Santi.   *Un Italiano Autore Delle Opere di Shakespeare*.   Milan: Gastaldi, 1954.   Pp. 136.

Maintains Florio's authorship of Shak.'s works. For a similar claim made earlier, see Paladino's *Shakespeare Sarebbe il Pseudonimo di un Poeta Italiano*. Reggio Calabria: Casa Editrice Borga, 1929.

B4869   Arnold, Paul. *Esotérisme de Shakespeare*. Paris: Mercure de France, 1955. Pp. 272. Tr. by Marie Mankiewicz as *Esoterik im Werke Shakespeares*. Berlin: Karl H. Henssel, 1957.
Rev: by G. Lambin, *LanM*, L (1956), 169; *MdF*, May, p. 135; by Louis Cambon, *Contacts Litt. et Sociaux*, No. 60, p. 7; by Jean Jacquot, *EA*, IX, 256-258; by Glenn H. Blayney, *SQ*, VIII (1957), 239-240; by Yanette Deletang-Tardif, *CS*, No. 342, pp. 322-323; by R. A. Foakes, *ShS*, X, 143; by Jan W. Simons, *SJ*, 94 (1958), 309-312; by C. G. Thayer, *Books Abroad*, XXXII, 139.

B4870   Jensen, Thit. "Var Shakespeare en Kvinde (Elizabeth I)?" ("Was Shak. a Woman?"). *Politiken* (Copenhagen), June 10, 1955.

B4871   Sweet, George. *Shake-Speare: The Mystery*. With a Foreword by Earl Stanley Gardner. Malibu, California: Privately Printed, 1956. Pp. 125.
Rev: *TAr*, April, 1957, p. 63.

8. OPPOSITION TO THE ANTI-STRATFORDIANS

B4872   Palmer, Charles S. "A Possible Approach to the Shakespeare Question." *Johns Hopkins Alumni Magazine*, XXV (1937), 349-364.

B4873   Campbell, Lily B. "A Note for Baconians." *MLN*, LIII (1938), 21-23.

B4874   "Shakespeare ist Shakespeare. Ein Beitrag zur Shakespeare-Forschung." *VB(Mü)*, June 2, 1939, p. 9.

B4875   Longworth de Chambrun, Clara. "Une Comédie de Méprises sur Shakespeare." *Revue Hebdomadaire*, XLVIII, No. 4 (1939), 483-495.

B4876   Clendenning, Logan. "A Bibliographic Account of the Bacon-Shakespeare Controversy." *Colophon*, New Graphic Ser., No. 3 (1939). Pp. 8.

B4877   Dengi. *Shakispeare Kimdi?* (*Who was Shakespeare?*) In Turkish, new script. London: Luzac, 1939. Pp. 31.

B4878   Ernst, Paul. "Über die Shakespeare-Frage. Aus Briefen an Theodor Eichhoff." *Jahrbuch der Paul Ernst-Gesellschaft*, 1939, pp. 154-162.

B4879   Knickerbocker, William S. "Designs on Mr. Upton: A Rumination on Sciolism and its Engagements with William Shakespeare." *SR*, XLVII (1939), 106-118.

B4880   "Fünfzehn Männer sollen Shakespeare sein." *Kieler Neueste Nachrichten*, Jan. 4, 1939.

B4881   Campbell, Oscar James. "Shakespeare Himself." *Harper's*, July 1940, pp. 172-185.

B4882   Holstein, Mark. "The Shakespere-Bacon-Oxford-Whoozis Mixup." *SAB*, XVI (1941), 195-214.

B4883   Page, Frederick. "Jonson and Shakespeare." *N&Q*, 184 (1943), 79.

B4884   Ackermann, A. S. E. "Sir W. A. Raleigh and the Baconians." *N&Q*, 186 (1944), 27.
See letters by C. L'Estrange Ewen and R. L. Eagle, *N&Q*, 186 (1944), 75; the reply to Mr. Eagle by Ackermann and further comments by J. D. R. and W. W. G., ibid., 186 (1944), 121-122; also note by H. S. Leftwich, ibid., 187 (1945), 39-40.

B4885   Chambers, Sir E. K. *Shakespearean Gleanings*. London: Oxford Univ. Press, 1944.

B4886   Petit-Dutaillis, Charles. *Le Roi Jean et Shakespeare*. Paris: Gallimard, 1945.
Conclusion, pp. 153-160, contains objections to anti-Stratfordians.

B4887   Picard, R. "Qui était Shakespeare?" *Artifices et Mystifications Littéraires*. Montreal, 1945, pp. 41-42.

B4888   Churchill, R. C. "The Baconian Heresy: A Post-Mortem." *Nineteenth Century*, 140 (1946), 260-268.

B4889   McManaway, James G. "Shakespeare and the Heretics." In *To Dr. R.: Essays Here Collected and Published in Honor of Dr. A. S. W. Rosenbach*. Philadelphia, 1946, pp. 136-153.

B4890   Q., D. "Shakespeare, Bacon and the *O. E. D.*" *N&Q*, 190 (1946), 37-38.
See further notes on the same subject by D. Q., "Bacon, Nashe and Dante," 190 (1946), 78; "Shakespeare, Bacon and English Proverbs," 190 (1946), 146; "Shakespeare and Bacon," 190 (1946), 259. See D. Q.'s article on "Bacon, Shakespeare and the Bible," *N&Q*, 190 (1946), 59, and the answer by Reviewer, "Bacon-Shakespeare Parallels," *N&Q*, 190 (1946), 99-100. See also W. H. Welply's article, "Shakespeare, Bacon, and the 'O.E.D.' " *N&Q*, 190 (1946), 150-151.

B4891   Westfall, Alfred. "It Started with a Bullfight." *Studies in Honor of A. H. R. Fairchild*, pp. 47-65.

B4892   Wolff, Emil. *Gedanken über das Shakespeare-Problem*. Hamburg: Hoffmann, 1946. Pp. 51.
Rev: by L. Schulz, *Hamb. Akadem. Rundschau*, I (1946-47), 535-536; by K. Wentersdorf, *SJ*, 82-83 (1948), 209-211.

B4893   Dávila, Carlos. "Los Nueve Shakespeares." *Rev. de América*, XI, No. 31 (1947), 132-134.

B4894   Evans, Bergen. "Good Friend for Jesvs Sake Forebeare: Was Shakespeare Really Shakespeare?" *SRL*, May 7, 1949, pp. 7-8, 39-40.

B4895   Gasser, M. "Twist om's Keizer's Baard: Indentiteit van Shakespeare." *Elseviers Weekblad*, March 26, 1949.

B4896   Dawson, Giles E. "Who Wrote Shakespeare?" *Listener*, XLIV (Aug. 10, 1950), 195-196.

B4897   Chambrun, Clara Longworth de. "Shakespeare est bien Shakespeare." *Hommes et Mondes*, May 1951, pp. 709-725.

B4898   Duff Cooper, Sir Alfred. "Et si Shakespeare Etait . . . Shakespeare." *Le Figaro Littéraire*, August 11, 1951, pp. 1, 5.

B4899   Gyller, Harald. *Shakespeare eller icke Shakespeare det år Fragan*. Stockholm: Sållskapet Bokvännerna, 1951.

B4900   Hoffman, Banesh. "Shakespeare the Physicist." *Scientific American*, 184 (April 1951), 52-53.

B4901   Ashe, Geoffrey. "Shakespeare Versus Private Judgment." *Catholic World*, April, 1952, pp. 47-52.

B4902   Lebesque, Morvan. "Shakespeare s'Appelait Shakespeare." *Théâtre Populaire*, III (1953), 26-41.

B4903   Gulick, Sidney L., Jr. "Was 'Shakespeare' a Woman?" *CE*, XV (1954), 445-449.

B4904   Gyller, H. "Dimmor Kring Shakespeare." [Mists around Shak.] *Bonniers Litteråra Magasin* (Stockholm), XXIII (1954), 378-382.

B4905   Melchior, I. "Treasure Hunt Anyone?" *American Mercury*, LXXVIII (May, 1954), 111-114.

B4906   "Was Shakespeare a Playwright or an Alias?" *Saturday Evening Post*, Aug. 20, 1955, p. 10ff.

B4907   "Who Wrote What? And How? *High Points*, XXXVII (Oct. 1955), 72-73.

B4908   Andersen-Rosendal, Jørgen. "Var Geniet Shakespeare i Virkelig-heden 7 Andre?" ["Was the Genius Actually 7 Other Persons?"]. *Dagens Nyheder* (Copenhagen), 90 (1955), 13-18.

B4909   Atkinson, Brooks. "Who Wrote the Plays of Shakespeare." *New York Times*, Oct. 7, 1956, Section 2, p. X[1].

B4910   Stephen, Sir Leslie. *Men, Books, and Mountains*. Intro. by S. O. A. Ullman. Univ. of Minnesota Press, 1956.
        Includes "Did Shakespeare Write Bacon?" pp. 74-80.

B4911   Thaler, Alwin. "The Man Who Wrote Shakespeare." *Tennessee Studies in Literature* (Univ. of Tennessee Studies in the Humanities, No. 1), 1956, pp. 1-10.

B4912   Friedman, William F. and Elizebeth S. *The Shakespearean Ciphers Examined*. Cambridge Univ. Press, 1957. Pp. xvii, 303.
        Rev: by Bernard Levin, *Spectator*, Oct. 4, 1957, pp. 444-445; by David Kahn, *NYTBR*, Oct. 6, pp. 3, 41; *Time*, Oct. 14, pp. 50-52; *TLS*, Oct. 18, p. 626 (see notes by M. Pares, Nov. 8, p. 673 and authors, Dec. 13, p. 757); by Paul Pickrel, *Harper's Mag.*, Nov., pp. 94-95; by Elizabeth Cummings, *Time and Tide*, Nov. 9, p. 1405; *MGW*, Dec. 19, p. 11; by J. I. M. Stewart, *NstN*, LIV, 467; by Jacques Barzun, *The Griffin*, April, 1958, pp. 4-9; *N &Q*, NS, V, 133-134; *QR*, Jan., pp. 118-119; by J. C. T. Oates, *The Library*, XIII, 75-76; by Brigadier John H. Tiltman, *SQ*, IX, 187-188; by R. A. Foakes, *English*, XII, 21; by Erik Frykman, *Dagens Nyheter* (Stockholm), Feb. 3; by Yves Gylden, *Svenska Dagbladet* (Stockholm), Feb. 5; by Burton A. Milligan, *JEGP*, LVII, 805-806; by Gilbert Roe, *QQ*, (Canada), LXV, 348-351; *VQR*, XXXIV, No. 2, lxix; *The Month*, XIX, 292; by J. H., *Book Collector*, VII, 94; *Dublin Mag.*, March, pp. 52-54; by S. K. Heninger, *The South Atlantic Quar.*, LVII, 516; by G. Lambin, *LanM*, LII, 106; by J. Vallette, *MdF*, 332 (1958), 130; *ShN*, VIII, 20.

B4913   Pares, Martin. " 'The Shakespearean Ciphers Examined'." *TLS*, Nov. 8, 1957, p. 673. Reply by the Friedmans, ibid., Dec. 13, 1957, p. 757.

B4914   Churchill, R. C. *Shakespeare and His Betters*. Foreword by Ivor Brown. London: Max Reinhardt, 1958. Pp. 255.
        Rev: *TLS*, May 2, 1958, p. 242; by W. Bridges-Adams, *Drama*, Summer, pp. 39, 41; by A. W. Titherly, *The Humanist* (London), Aug., p. 26; by Gordon Craig, *Time and Tide*, July 5, pp. 828-829; by Eric Gillett, *National and English Rev.*, June, p. 254; by J. I. M. Stewart, *NstN*, May 31, p. 706; by J. Vallette, *MdF*, 334 (1958), 144-146.

B4915   Wadsworth, Frank W. *The Poacher from Stratford*. A Partial Account of the Controversy Over the Authorship of Shakespeare's Plays. Univ. of California Press, 1958. Pp. 174.
        Rev: by Alfred Harbage, *NYTBR*, Oct. 19, 1958, p. 32.

B. THE WORKS OF SHAKESPEARE EXAMINED INDIVIDUALLY

I. CHRONOLOGY OF THE DRAMAS (187;67)
(See also Text and Literary Genesis sections of Plays, below, and C21.)

B4916   Cairncross, A. S. *The Problem of Hamlet. A Solution.* London: Macmillan, 1936. Pp. xix, 205. Rev: by H. B. Charlton, "A New Shakespearean Theory," *MGW*, Aug. 28, 1936, p. 174; by C. M. Bowra, *Spectator*, Aug. 28, pp. 353-354; by M. E. N., *CM*, 154 (1936), 381; *QR*, 267 (1936), 371; *London Mercury*, XXXIV, 471; *TLS*, Dec. 19, p. 1053; by J. S., *Oxford Mag.*, LV, 232-233; by Georges Connes, *EA*, I (1937), 96; by William Empson, *Life and Letters Today*, XV, No. 6 (1937), 210-211; by J. Burns Martin, *Dalhousie Rev.*, XVII, 126; by Max Priess, *Eng. Studn.*, LXXI, 402-407; by W. Keller, *SJ*, LXXIV (1938), 182-184.

B4917   Kies, Paul P. "On the Dating of *Othello* and *Lear*." *Research Studies of the State College of Washington*, III, No. 2 (1936), 72-73.

B4918   Law, Robert Adger. "On the Dating of Shakspere's Plays." *SAB*, XI (1936), 46-51.

B4919   Taylor, Rupert. "A Tentative Chronology of Marlowe's and Some Other Elizabethan Plays." *PMLA*, LI (1936), 643-688.

B4920   Kirschbaum, Leo. "The Date of *Hamlet*." *SP*, XXXIV (1937), 168-175.

B4921   Houghton, Ralph E. C. "Shakespearian Comedy." *TLS*, May 4, 1940, p. 219. Objects to H. B. Charlton's chronology of the comedies in B5155.

B4922   Reinhold, Heinz. "Die Metrische Verzahnung als Kriterium für Fragen der Chronologie und Authentizität im Drama Shakespeares und Einiger seiner Zeitgenossen und Nachfolger, I. II." *Archiv*, 181 (1942), 83-96; 182 (1943), 7-24.

B4923   Baldwin, T. W. *Shakspere's Five-Act Structure: Shakspere's Early Plays on the Background of Renaissance Theories of Five-Act Structure from 1470.* Univ. Illinois Press, 1947. Pp. xiii, 848. Rev: A5938.

B4924   Sullivan, Frank. "*Macbeth*, Middleton's *Witch*, and *Macbeth* Again." *Los Angeles Tidings*, Sept. 24, 1948, p. 6.

B4925   McManaway, James G. "Recent Studies in Shakespeare's Chronology." *ShS*, III (1950), 23-33.

B4926   Honigmann, E. A. J. *Studies in the Chronology of Shakespeare's Plays.* B. Litt. thesis, Oxford, 1951.

B4927   Wentersdorf, Karl. "Shakespearean Chronology and the Metrical Tests." *Shakespeare-Studien, Festschrift für Heinrich Mutschmann.* Marburg: Verlag N. G. Elwert, 1951, pp. 161-193.

B4928   Feuillerat, Albert. *The Composition of Shakespeare's Plays: Authorship, Chronology.* Yale Univ. Press, 1953. Pp. viii, 340. Rev: A3286.

B4929   Wilson, F. P. *Marlowe and the Early Shakespeare.* Clark Lectures, Trinity College, Cambridge, 1951. Oxford: Clarendon Press, 1953. Pp. 144. Rev: A4996.

B4930   Shapiro, I. A. "The Significance of a Date." *ShS*, VIII (1955), 100-105.

B4931   Akrigg, G. P. V. "The Arrangement of the Tragedies in the First Folio." *SQ*, VII (1956), 443-445.

B4932   Honigmann, E. A. J. "The Date of *Hamlet*." *ShS*, IX (1956), 24-34.

B4933   Thomas, Sidney. "The Date of *The Comedy of Errors*." *SQ*, VII (1956), 376-384.

B4934   Rosenberg, Marvin. "On the Dating of *Othello*." *ES*, XXXIX (1958), 72-74.

B4935   Shapiro, I. A. "*Richard II* or *Richard III* or . . . ?" *SQ*, IX (1958), 204-206.

II. THE INDIVIDUAL DRAMAS (189;67)
1. INTRODUCTION: GENERAL TREATISES DEALING WITH THE VARIOUS TYPES
a. TRAGEDIES (189;67)

B4936   Powers, M. F. *Shakespeare's Tragedies and the Signs of Doom.* DD, University of Washington, 1937. Abstr. in Univ. of Washington *Abstracts of Theses*, VIII (1937), 135-136.

B4937   Raysor, Thomas M.   "Intervals of Time and Their Effect upon Dramatic Values in Shake-
        speare's Tragedies."   *JEGP*, XXXVII (1938), 21-47.

B4938   Schmidt, Wolfgang.   "Shakespeares Leben und der Sinn der Tragödien."   *NS*, XLVI, No. 9
        (1938), 339-353.

B4939   Traversi, D. A.   *An Approach to Shakespeare*.   London: Sands, Paladin Press, 1938.   Pp. 152.
        Second Edition, revised and enlarged, New York: Doubleday, 1956.   Pp. 304.
        Rev: A8420.

B4940   Sellmair, Jos.   *Der Mensch in der Tragik*.   Krailling vor München: E. Wewel, 1939.   Pp. 302.
        Shak., pp. 188-207.

B4941   Bowers, F. T.   *Elizabethan Revenge Tragedy, 1587-1642*.   Princeton Univ. Press, 1940.   Pp.
        viii, 288.
        Rev: by Hazelton Spencer, *MLN*, LV (1940), 536-540; by Leland Schubert, *QJS*, XXVI,
        464; by Willard Farnham, *MLQ*, I, 420-421; by M. C. Bradbrook, *RES*, XVII (1941), 214-215;
        by Una Ellis-Fermor, *MLR*, XXXVI, 258-260; by E. C. Knowlton, *South Atlantic Quar.*, XL,
        298-300; by J. J. Elson, *Lib. Quar.*, XI, 237-239; by T. W. Baldwin, *JEGP*, XL, 285-290;
        by R. S. K., *UTQ*, XI (1942), 245-246.

B4942   Craig, Hardin.   "The Shackling of Accidents: A Study of Elizabethan Tragedy."   *PQ*, XIX
        (1940), 1-19.

B4943   Myrick, Kenneth O.   "The Theme of Damnation in Shakespearean Tragedy."   *SP*, XXXVIII
        (1941), 221-345.

B4944   Spencer, Theodore.   *Shakespeare and the Nature of Man*.   Lowell Lectures, 1942.   New York:
        Macmillan, 1942.   Pp. xiii, 233.
        Rev: A1044.

B4945   Watkins, W. B. C.   "The Two Techniques in *King Lear*."   *RES*, XVIII (1942), 1-26.
        The two techniques: psychological realism and symbolical stylization.   Comments on most
        of the tragedies.

B4946   Fairchild, Arthur H. R.   *Shakespeare and the Tragic Theme*.   Univ. Missouri Studies, XIX, No. 2.
        Univ. Missouri Press, 1944.   Pp. 145.
        Rev: A6853.

B4947   Ryan, Rev. Harold Francis, S. J.   *Heroic Play Elements in Earlier English Drama*.   DD, St. Louis
        University, 1944.   Pp. 362.

B4948   Spencer, Theodore.   "The Isolation of the Shakespearean Hero."   *SR*, LII (1944), 313-331.

B4949   Cady, Frank W.   "Motivation of the Inciting Force in Shakespeare's Tragedies."   *Elizabethan
        Studies and Other Essays: In Honor of George F. Reynolds*, pp. 166-171.

B4950   Ramin, Reinbold.   *Die Gestalt des Politician und Statesman in Shakespeares Historien und Tragödien
        bis zum Abschluss der Hamlet-Periode*.   DD, Marburg, 1945.   Pp. iv, 129.   Typewritten.

B4951   Ellis-Fermor, Una.   *The Frontiers of Drama*.   London: Methuen, 1945; New York: Oxford
        Univ. Press, 1946.   Pp. vii, 154.
        Rev: A5941.

B4952   Meissner, Paul.   "Gestaltung und Deutung des Tragischen bei Shakespeare."   *SJ*, 80/81
        (1946), 12-30.

B4953   Prior, Moody Erasmus.   *The Language of Tragedy*.   New York: Columbia Univ. Press;
        Oxford Univ. Press, 1947.   Pp. viii, 411.
        Rev: by F. S. Tupper, *MLN*, LXIII (1948), 560-562; by P. Ure, *RES*, XXV (1949), 88-89.

B4954   Reyher, Paul.   *Essai sur les Idées dans l'Œuvre de Shakespeare*.   Bibliothèque des Langues Mo-
        dernes, I.   Paris: Didier, 1947.   Pp. xxix, 662.
        Rev: A1021.

B4955   Schneider, R.   *Macht und Gewissen in Shakespeares Tragödie*.   Berlin: Suhrkamp, 1947.   Pp. 46.
        Comment by Inge v. Wangenheim, "Shakespeares Geschichtliche Wirklichkeit," *Dramaturg.
        Blätter*, I, No. 5 (1947), 11-16.

B4956   Charlton, H. B.   *Shakespearian Tragedy*.   Cambridge Univ. Press, 1948.   Pp. ix, 246.
        Rev: by George Rylands, *MGW*, Nov. 25, 1948, p. 10; *TLS*, Dec. 11, p. 698; by T. M.
        Parrott, *JEGP*, XLVIII (1949), 393-397; *DUJ*, X, 76-77; by E. H. W. Meyerstein, *English*, VII,
        236-238; *Dublin Mag.*, XXIV, 2, 45-47; by A. E., *QQ*, LVI, 451-452; by S. C. Chew, *NYHTBR*,
        March 6, p. 18; by J. M. S. Tompkins, *MLR*, XLIV, 400-401; by R. S. Knox, *UTQ*, XIX,
        95-97; *N &Q*, 194 (1949), 87; by Albert Laffay, *LanM*, V, 63; by G. B. Harrison, *Common-
        weal*, XLIX, 523-524; by B. D. Greenslade, *TLS*, Jan. 15, p. 41; by J. H. P. Pafford, *RES*,
        NS, I (1950), 163-166; by M. E. Prior, *MLN*, LXV, 560-562; by A. Koszul, *ES*, XXXIII (1952),
        221-222; by Richard Flatter, *SJ*, 87/88 (1952), 246-247; by H. Heuer, *SJ*, 89 (1953), 224-227.

B4957   Gardner, Helen.   "Milton's 'Satan' and the Theme of Damnation in Elizabethan Tragedy."
        Essays and Studies, NS, I (1948), 46-66.

B4958   Hamilton, R.   "Shakespeare: the Nemesis of Pride."   *Nineteenth Century*, 143 (1948), 335-340.
        German tr.: "Die Nemesis des Hochmutes bei Shakespeare."   *Die Brücke*, 1948, No. 86,
        pp. 8-10.

B4959   González Ruiz, N.   "Dos Ensayos Sobre las Tragedias de Shakespeare."   *Arbor* (Madrid),
        X (1948), 39-56.

B4960   Sitwell, Edith. *A Notebook on William Shakespeare.* New York, London: Macmillan, 1948. Pp. xii, 233.
        Rev: A8365.

B4961   Wiles, Roy McKeen. " 'In My Mind's Eye, Horatio'." *UTQ*, xviii (1948), 57-67.

B4962   Draper, John W. "The Heroes of Shakespeare's Tragedies." *West Virginia Univ. Bulletin: Philological Papers*, vi (1949), 12-21.

B4963   De Chickera, E. B. *Revenge Tragedy from Kyd to Webster: Its Basis in the Society of the Age.* B. Litt. thesis, Oxford, Brasenose, 1950.

B4964   Connolly, Thomas F. "Shakespeare and the Double Man." *SQ*, i (1950), 30-35.

B4965   Cunningham, J. V. " 'Tragedy' in Shakespeare." *ELH*, xvii (1950), 36-46.

B4966   Farnham, Willard. *Shakespeare's Tragic Frontier: The World of His Final Tragedies.* Univ. of California Press, 1950.
        Rev: A8183.

B4967   Leech, Clifford. *Shakespeare's Tragedies: And Other Studies in Seventeenth-Century Drama.* London: Chatto and Windus, 1950. Pp. viii, 232.
        Rev: by F. S. Boas, *FortnR*, Dec., 1950, pp. 419-420; *TLS*, Nov. 17, p. 724; by H. B. Charlton, *MGW*, Dec. 21, p. 11; *DUJ*, xii, 30-31; by Philip Edwards, *MLR*, xlvi, 482-483; by A. C. Partridge, *ConR*, lxxii (1950-51), 509; by Willard Farnham, *SQ*, ii (1951), 131-132; by Charles T. Harrison, *SR*, lix, 697-698; by D. M. S., *English*, viii, 211-212; by Maria Wickert, *Anglia*, lxix, 378-383; by R. W. Zandvoort, *ES*, xxxiii, 76-77; by W. Clemen, *Archiv*, 189 (1951), 61; by J. B. Fort, *EA*, v (1952), 246-247; by Richard Flatter, *SJ*, 89 (1953), 202-204.

B4968   Mincoff, Marco. "The Structural Pattern of Shakespeare's Tragedies." *ShS*, iii (1950), 58-65.

B4969   Reeg, Ludwig. *Shakespeare und die Weltordnung.* Stuttgart: Schröder, 1950. Pp. 151.

B4970   Sitwell, Edith. *A Poet's Notebook.* London: Macmillan 1943. Pp. xi, 153. Boston: Little, Brown, 1950. Pp. xviii, 276.
        Rev: by Charles Prouty, *SQ*, ii (1951), 261-263, with special reference to its sections on Shak. by John Ciardi, *SRL*, July 14, p. 21.

B4971   Wisser, Heinz. *Shakespeares Ideen über Liebe, Frauen und Freundschaft, Abgeleitet aus Zitaten und Aphorismen der 8 Grossen Tragödien seiner dritten Schaffensperiode.* DD, Vienna, 1950. Pp. 138. Typewritten.

B4972   Cunningham, James Vincent. *Woe or Wonder: The Emotional Effect of Shakespearean Tragedy.* Univ. of Denver Press, 1951. Pp. 136.
        Rev: by Arnold Stein, *KR*, xiv (1952), 513-520; by Marvin T. Herrick, *SQ*, iii, 373-374.

B4973   Duthie, G. I. *Shakespeare.* London: Hutchinson's Univ. Library, 1951. Pp. 206.
        Rev: A8162.

B4974   Harrison, G. B. *Shakespeare's Tragedies.* London: Routledge and Kegan Paul, 1951. Pp. 277.
        Rev: *NstN*, xli (1951), 511; *Spectator*, No. 6437, p. 616; by A. P. Rossiter, *English*, ix (1952), 68-69; by James G. McManaway, *NYTBR*, July 13, p. 12; by Michel Poirier, *EA*, v, 153-154; *TLS*, Jan. 11, p. 26; by R. Mayhead, *Scrutiny*, xviii, 236-238; *Eng. Jour.*, xli, 511; by M. C. Bradbrook, *ShS*, vi (1953), 152; by Hermann Heuer, *SJ*, 89 (1953), 224-227; by George F. Reynolds, *SQ*, iv, 102-103; by Robert Halsband, *SatR*, Jan. 10, p. 41.

B4975   James, D. G. *The Dream of Learning: An Essay on "The Advancement of Learning," "Hamlet" and "King Lear."* Oxford: Clarendon Press, 1951. Pp. 126.
        Rev: A3959.

B4976   Koenigsberger, Hannelore. *The Untuned String—Shakespeare's Concept of Chaos.* DD, Columbia University, 1951. Pp. 222. *DA*, xii (1952), 66. Publ. No. 3353.

B4977   Cancelled.

B4978   Weil-Nordon, P. *Shakespeare's Dramatic Technique in the Opening Scenes of His Tragedies.* MA thesis, Birmingham, 1951.

B4979   Bush, G. D. *The Idea of Nature in Shakespeare's Four Principal Tragedies.* B. Litt. thesis, Oxford, 1952.

B4980   Cazamian, Louis. *The Development of English Humor.* Duke Univ. Press, 1952. Pp. viii, 421.
        Rev: B5186.

B4981   Eppler, Erhard. *Der Aufbegehrende und der Verzweifelnde als Heldenfigur der Elisabethanischen Tragödie.* DD, Tübingen, 1952. Pp. xiv, 145. Typewritten.

B4982   Kaufmann, Walter. "Goethe versus Shakespeare: Some Changes in Dramatic Sensibility." *Partisan Rev.*, xix (1952), 621-634.

B4983   McAvoy, William Charles. *Shakespeare's Use of the Laus of Apthonius.* DD, University of Illinois, 1952. Pp. 225. Mic A53-237. *DA*, xiii (1953), 97. Publ. No. 4464.

B4984   Schopf, Alfred. *Leitmotivische Thematik in Shakespeares Historien (mit einem Ausblick auf die Tragödien).* DD, Munich, 1952. Pp. 147. Typewritten.

B4985   Brown, Huntington. "Enter the Shakespearean Tragic Hero." *EIC*, iii (1953), 285-302.
        Rev: A6742.

B4986   Doran, Madeleine *Endeavors of Art: A Study of Form in Elizabethan Drama.* Madison:

Univ. of Wisconsin Press, 1953. Pp. xv, 482.
Rev: A7827.

B4987   Dyson, H. V. D. *The Emergence of Shakespeare's Tragedy*. Annual Shakespeare Lecture of the British Academy, 1950. Oxford Univ. Press, 1953.
Rev: by Clifford Leech, *ShS*, VII (1954), 129.

B4988   Gaither, Mary E. *Ancient and Modern Concepts of the Tragic Hero*. DD, Indiana University, 1953. Pp. 151. Mic A53-905. *DA*, XIII (1953), 547. Publ. No. 5313.

B4989   Gisi, Othmar. *Historische Elemente in der Englischen Tragödie vor der Romantik*. DD, Basel, 1953. Aarau: Keller, 1953. Pp. 119.

B4990   Haas, Rudolf. *Die Gestaltung der Dramatischen Person in den grossen Tragödien Shakespeares*. DD, Tübingen, 1953. Pp. v, 242. Typewritten.

B4991   Jepsen, Laura. *Ethos in Classical and Shakespearian Tragedies*. DD, State University of Iowa, 1953. Abstract published in *Abstracts and References* (Iowa), VI (1953), 418-425.

B4992   Jepsen, Laura. *Ethical Aspects of Tragedy*. Gainesville: Univ. of Florida Press, 1953. Pp. ix, 130.
Rev: A975.

B4993   Rogers, Carmen. "Heavenly Justice in the Tragedies of Shakespeare." *Studies in Shakespeare*, ed. by Matthews and Emery, 1953, pp. 116-128.

B4994   Speaight, Robert. *Nature in Shakespearean Tragedy*. London: Hollis and Carter, 1955. Pp. viii, 179.
Rev: A1035.

B4995   Ballester Escalas, Rafael. *El Historiador William Shakespeare. Ensayo sobre el Espíritu del Siglo XVI*. Second ed. Barcelona: Mateu, 1954. Pp. 476.

B4996   Flatter, Richard. "Shakespeares Triumphierende Tragödien." *Theater u. Zeit* (Wuppertal), I (1953-54), 67-68.

B4997   Oppel, Horst. *Shakespeares Tragödien und Romanzen: Kontinuität oder Umbruch?* Abhandlungen der Akademie der Wissenschaften u. der Literatur, Kl. der Lit., Jahrgang 1954, No. 2. Mainz: 1954. Pp. 46.
Rev: by Wolfgang Clemen, *Archiv*, 192 (1955), 203; by Hermann Heuer, *SJ*, 91 (1955), 525; *N&Q*, NS, II, 182-183; by H. Viebrock, "Neue Wege der Shakespeare-Forschung," *NS*, IV, 128-131; by L. Borinski, *Euphorion*, XLIX, 377-378; by J. L. Lievsay, *SQ*, VII (1956), 440; by Heinrich Straumann, *Anglia*, LXXV (1957), 466-468; by E. A. J. Honigmann, *RES*, NS, VIII, 107.

B4998   Parker, Marion Hope. *The Slave of life*. London: Chatto and Windus, 1954.
Rev: A1532.

B4999   Sabbadini, Ada. *Umanità e favola nell' arte di Shakespeare. Amleto, Macbeth, Otello, Re Lear* (Saggi di varia umanità. Collezione diretta da F. Flora. No. 8). Pisa: Nistri Lischi, 1954. Pp. 180.
Rev: by Gabriele Baldini, "Riletture Shakespeariane," *Nuova Antologia*, July 1954, pp. 353-368; by G. C. Ferretti, *Belfagor*, IX, 375-376; by M. Praz, *ShS*, VIII (1955), 120.

B5000   Barnet, Sylvan. "Some Limitations of a Christian Approach to Shakespeare." *ELH*, XXII (1955), 81-92.

B5001   Bogard, Travis. "Shakespeare's Second Richard." *PMLA*, LXX (1955), 192-209.

B5002   Campbell, Lily B. *Shakespeare's Tragic Heroes*. A Reprint. New York: Barnes & Noble, 1955. Pp. xii, 296.
Rev: by James G. McManaway, *SQ*, VI (1955), 474.

B5003   Cronin, P. J. *Diction and Dramatic Character in Shakespearian Tragedy, with Special Attention to Characteristic Use of Imagery*. B. Litt. thesis, Oxford, 1955.

B5004   Gaul, Erhard Manfred. *Zur Struktur der Tragödien Shakespeares*. DD, Cologne, 1955. Pp. 149. Typewritten.

B5005   Knights, L. C. "*King Lear* and the Great Tragedies." *The Age of Shakespeare*, ed. Boris Ford. Aylesbury and London: Pelican Books, 1955, pp. 228-256.

B5006   Laqueur, Richard. *Shakespeares Dramatische Konzeption*. Tübingen: Max Niemeyer, 1955. Pp. 356.
Rev: A5981.

B5007   Maxwell, J. C. "The Presuppositions of Tragedy." *EIC*, V (1955), 175-178.
On B4967. Reply by Clifford Leech, ibid., V, 178-181.

B5008   Maxwell, J. C. "Shakespeare: The Middle Plays." *The Age of Shakespeare*. Ed. Boris Ford. Aylesbury and London: Pelican Books, 1955, pp. 201-227.

B5009   Ribner, Irving. "*Othello* and the Pattern of Shakespearean Tragedy." *Tulane Studies in Eng.*, V (1955), 69-82.

B5010   Yamaguchi, Yusuke. *Evil in the Tragedy*. An Inquiry into Shakespeare. Tokyo: For the Author, 1955. Pp. ii, 42.
A translation into English of Chapter II of the author's *Evil and Literature*. Treats of *Ham.*, *Oth.*, *Macb.* and *Lear*.

B5011   Hapgood, Robert Derry. *A Rebirth of Tragedy: Ritual as Matrix and Element in Shakespeare's Early Tragedies.* DD, University of California (Berkeley), 1956.

B5012   Knight, G. Wilson. *The Wheel of Fire: Essays in Interpretation of Shakespeare's Sombre Tragedies.* Oxford Univ. Press, 1930. Fourth ed., with Three New Essays. London: Methuen; New York: Oxford Univ. Press, 1949. Pp. 363.

B5013   Muller, Herbert J. *The Spirit of Tragedy.* New York: Knopf, 1956. Pp. ix, 335.
        Rev: A6914.

B5014   Schweitzer, A. R. "Mathematics and Literary Composition, I, II, and III." Abstracts, numbered 368t, 369t, and 370t, in *Bulletin of the American Mathematical Society,* Vol. 62, No. 3 (May, 1956), 262.
        II treats *Lear, Hamlet, Oth., Macb.,* and *Merch.,* and finds ingratitude, indecision, jealousy, ambition, and inhumanity in them, respectively.

B5015   Smith, Gordon Ross. *Good in Evil in Shakespearean Tragedy.* DD, The Pennsylvania State University, 1956. Pp. 446. Mic 57-568. *DA,* XVII (1957), 358. Publ. No. 19,323. Abstracted by Jack R. Brown, *ShN,* VIII (1958), 36.

B5016   Smith, Stella Tilley. *Imagery of Motion in Shakespeare's Tragedies.* DD, University of Florida (Gainesville), 1956.

B5017   Sternfeld, Frederick W. "The Dramatic and Allegorical Function of Music in Shakespeare's Tragedies." *Annales Musicologiques,* III (1955), 265-282.

B5018   Stirling, Brents. *Unity in Shakespearian Tragedy: The Interplay of Theme and Character.* Columbia Univ. Press, 1956. Pp. viii, 212.
        Rev: *Essential Books,* June, 1956, p. 37; by George Freedley, *Library Jour.,* Aug., p. 1811; by Marvin Sargent, *San Francisco Chronicle,* June 24, p. 23; by Edward Hubler, *MLQ,* XVII, 366-367; *SCN,* XIV, No. 3, 2; by Arthur L. Housman, *ETJ,* VIII, 337-338; by S. F. Johnson, *RN,* X (1957), 41-42; *ShN,* VII, 4; by Robert Adger Law, *JEGP,* LVI, 274-275; by R. A. Foakes, *English,* XI, 150; by H. C. Kiefer, *Arizona Quarterly,* XIII, 266-267; by Dorothy Hewlett, *Aryan Path,* XXVIII, 126; by Kenneth Muir, *SQ,* VIII, 222-223; *Hist. Ideas News Letter,* III, No. 2, 19; by M. E. Prior, *MP,* LV (1957-58), 127-129; by L. C. Knights, *RES,* NS, IX (1958), 195-196.

B5019   Wilson, Harold S. *On the Design of Shakespearian Tragedy.* Toronto Univ. Press; Oxford Univ. Press, 1956. Pp. 208.

B5020   Battenhouse, Roy. "Shakespearean Tragedy." *The Tragic Vision and the Christian Faith,* ed. by Nathan A. Scott. New York: The Association Press, 1957.

B5021   McCollom, William G. *Tragedy.* New York: Macmillan, 1957. Pp. ix, 254.
        Rev: by Edward Partridge, *QJS,* XLIV (1958), 87-88; by Richard B. Sewall, *CE,* XIX, 57; by Herbert Blau, *ETJ,* X, 86-87; by Lawrence Michel, *Thought,* XXXIII, 289-291.

B5022   Scott, Nathan A., ed. *The Tragic Vision and the Christian Faith.* New York: The Association Press, 1957.
        Rev: *Georgia Review,* XII (1958), 12; *CE,* XIX, 282.

B5023   Siegel, Paul N. *Shakespearean Tragedy and the Elizabethan Compromise.* New York Univ. Press, 1957.
        Rev: A1882.

B5024   Weisinger, Herbert. "The Myth and Ritual Approach to Shakespearean Tragedy." *The Centennial Review of Arts and Science,* I (1957), 142-166.

B5025   Dunkel, W. D. "The Meek Shall Inherit the Earth: A Study in Shakespearean Tragedy." *Theology Today,* XV (1958), 359-365.

B5026   Hill, R. F. "Shakespeare's Early Tragic Mode." *SQ,* IX (1958), 455-469.

B5027   Johnson, Samuel. *Johnson's Notes to Shakespeare.* Ed. with an Intro. by Arthur Sherbo. Augustan Reprint Society, Nos. 71-73. Vol. III, Tragedies. Los Angeles: William Andrews Clark Memorial Library, Univ. of California, 1958. Pp. 202.

B5028   Potts, Abbie Findlay. *Shakespeare and "The Faerie Queene."* Cornell Univ. Press, 1958. Pp. xii, 269.
        Rev: A4819.

B5029   Rosen, William. *Four Shakespearean Tragedies: A Study in Point of View.* DD, Harvard University, 1958.

b. Roman Plays (180; 67)

B5030   Formichi, Carlo. *Roma nell'opera di Shakespeare.* Roma nell'opera del genio, v. Rome: Istituto di Studi Romani, 1937. Pp. 15.

B5031   Stahl, E. L. "Shakespeares Römerdramen." *Germania* (Berlin), XII, No. 9 (1937).

B5032   "Humanismus in Shakespeares Römerdramen." *Germania* (Berlin), XVI No. 6 (1938).

B5033   Heuer, Hermann. "Lebensgefühl und Wertwelt in Shakespeares Römerdramen." *ZNU,* XXXVII (1938), 65-90.

B5034   Heuer, Hermann. "Shakespeare und Plutarch in Shakespeares Römerdramen." *ZNU,* XXXVII (1938), 65-90.

B5035   Toretta, L. *Studi Romani e Motivi Anti-Romani nel Rinascimento Inglese.* Rome: Istituto di Studi Romani, 1938.

B5036   Messiaen, Pierre. "Shakespeare et l'Histoire Romaine." *Culture,* II No. 6 (1939), 351-357.

B5037   Morton, Louise Minor. *Shakespeare's Attitude toward History.* MA thesis, University of North Carolina, 1941. Abstr. publ. in *Univ. of North Carolina Record, Research in Progress,* Grad. School Series No. 40, 1941, pp. 75.

B5038   Nelson, Lawrence Gerald. *Classical History in Shakespeare.* DD, University of Virginia, 1943. Abstr. publ. in *Abstracts of Dissertations,* Charlottesville: Univ. of Virginia, 1943.

B5039   Anna of Mary, Sister. *Les Charactères de Femmes dans les Tragédies Romaines de Corneille et de Shakespeare.* MA thesis, Laval, 1945. Pp. 115.

B5040   Tachibana, Tadae. *A Survey of Shakespeare: His Roman Plays.* Tokyo: Sakuraishoten, 1947; 2nd ed., 1948. Pp. 212 (in Japanese).

B5041   Walker, Roy. "The Northern Star: An Essay on the Roman Plays." *SQ,* II (1951), 287-293.

B5042   Charney, Maurice M. *Shakespeare's Roman Plays: A Study of the Function of Imagery in the Drama.* DD, Princeton University, 1952. Pp. 458. Mic A54-173. *DA,* XIV (1954), 118. Publ. No. 6796.

B5043   "Shakespeare's Roman Plays: and Other Subjects." *ShN,* V (1955), 41; VI (1956), 4, 14, 20.

B5044   Spira, Theodor. "Shakespeares Dichtung und die Welt der Geschichte." *SJ,* 91 (1955), 65-86.

B5045   Coghill, Nevill. "The Tragic Fact in the Roman Plays." *ShN,* VI (1956), 20. Abstracts of works on Roman Plays.

B5046   Baldwin, N. G. *A Critical Study of the Criticism of Shakespeare's Roman Plays.* MA thesis, Manchester, 1957.

B5047   Maxwell, James Coutts. "Shakespeare's Roman Plays: 1900-1956." *ShS,* X (1957), 1-11.

B5048   Spencer, T. J. B. "Shakespeare and the Elizabethan Romans." *ShS,* X (1957), 27-38.

B5049   Barroll, J. Leeds. "Shakespeare and Roman History." *MLR,* LIII (1958), 327-343. See also A4182.

B5050   Markels, Julian. *The Public and Private Worlds of Shakespeare's Roman Plays.* DD, University of Minnesota, 1958. Pp. 289. Mic 58-311. *DA,* XVIII (1958), 221. Publ. No. 23,940.

c. HISTORICAL PLAYS (189;67)

B5051   Hinterwaldner, A. *Der Monolog in Shakespeares Königsdramen.* DD, Vienna, 1932.

B5052   Jenkins, Sadie F. *The Treatment of Tyranny in Elizabethan English History Plays.* DD, University of North Carolina, 1935. Abstr. publ. in *Univ. of North Carolina Record, Research in Progress, 1934-35,* Chapel Hill, 1935, p. 36.

B5053   Lindsay, Philip. *Kings of Merry England from Eadward the Confessor (1042-1066) to Richard the Third.* London: Nicholson, 1936. Pp. 617.

B5054   Greer, Clayton A. *Relationships in the Plays of the York-Lancaster Tetralogy.* DD, University of Texas, 1937.

B5055   Petsch, R. "Shakespeares König Heinrich IV. und das Geschichtsdrama in England." *SJ,* LXXIII (1937), 109-130.

B5056   Glunz, H. *Shakespeare und Morus.* Kölner Anglistische Arbeiten, XXXII. Bochum Langendreer: Pöppinghaus, 1938. Pp. ix, 267.
         Rev: A4687.

B5057   Greer, Clayton Alvis. "The Place of *I Henry VI* in the York-Lancaster Tetralogy." *PMLA,* LIII (1938), 687-701.

B5058   Messiaen, Pierre. "Les Drames Historiques de Shakespeare." *RCC,* XXXIX (1938), (1st Series), pp. 692-709; (2nd Series), pp. 137-156, 454-465, 626-639.

B5059   Messiaen, P. "Shakespeare et l'Historie d'Angleterre." *RCC,* XXXIX (1938), 692-709.

B5060   Edwards, Eleanor. *The Evolution of the Tragic Flaw, with Special Reference to Shakespeare's Chronicle History Plays.* MA thesis, University of North Carolina, 1939. Abstr. publ. in *Univ. of North Carolina Record, Research in Progress,* Grad. School Series No. 36, 1939, pp. 78-79.

B5061   Messiaen, Pierre. "Drames Historiques de Shakespeare: Style Oratoire, Style Lyrique, Style Dramatique." *Rev. Universitaire,* XLVIII (1939), 23.

B5062   Terrell, Elizabeth. *Shakespeare's Treatment of the House of York.* DD, University of Washington, 1939. Abstr. publ. in *Univ. of Washington Abstracts of Theses,* IV (1939), 145-146.

B5063   Wells, Henry W. *Elizabethan and Jacobean Playwrights.* Columbia Univ. Press, 1939. Pp. xiv, 327.
         Rev: by T. W. Baldwin, *MLN,* LV (1940), 461-462; by Alwin Thaler, *JEGP,* XL (1941), 150-151.

B5064   Ashton, J. W. *Types of English Drama.* New York: Macmillan, 1940. Pp. xii, 750.

B5065   Morton, Louise Minor. *Shakespeare's Attitude toward History.* MA thesis, University of North Carolina, 1941. Abstr. publ. in *Univ. of North Carolina Record, Research in Progress,* Grad. School Series No. 40, 1941, p. 75.

B5066   Schirmer, Walter F. "Über das Historiendrama in der Engl. Renaissance." *Archiv*, 179 (1941), 1-7. Also in Schirmer's *Kleine Schriften*. Tübingen: Max Niemeyer Verlag, 1950, pp. 109-118.

B5067   Schlamp, Hans Joachim. "Shakespeares Königsdramen." *Eckart* (Berlin-Steglitz: Eckart Verlag), XVII (1941), 25.

B5068   Mary Bonaventure Mroz, Sister, O. S. F. *Divine Vengeance: A Study in the Philosophical Backgrounds of the Revenge Motif as it Appears in Shakespeare's Chronicle History Plays.* DD, Catholic University of America, 1941. Washington, D. C.: Catholic University of America Press, 1941. Pp. x, 168.
        Rev: by Fredson Bowers, *MLN*, LVII (1942), 472; by Una Ellis-Fermor, *MLR*, XXXVII, 376-378.

B5069   Reese, Gertrude C. "The Question of the Succession in Elizabethan Drama." *TxSE*, XXII (1942), 59-85.

B5070   Wiese, Benno von. "Geschichte und Drama." *DVLG*, XX (1942), 412-434.

B5071   Knight, G. Wilson. *The Olive and the Sword. A Study of England's Shakespeare.* Oxford: Univ. Press; London: Milford, 1944. Pp. 102.
        Rev: A1819.

B5072   Tillyard, E. M. W. *Shakespeare's History Plays.* London: Chatto & Windus, 1944. Pp. viii, 336.
        Rev: "Shakespeare's Kings. A Philosophy of Our History. From Chronicle to Drama," *TLS*, Jan. 6, 1945, p. 6; see also editorial comment, ibid., p. 7; by John Lehmann, ibid., Mar. 3, p. 103; by K. H. Bell, ibid., Mar. 24, p. 139; by H. B. C., *MGW*, Mar. 16, p. 150; by H. B. Charlton, *NstN*, Feb. 17, p. 112; by Geoffrey Tillotson, *English*, V, 160; by A. M. C. Latham, *Life and Letters*, XLVI, 124-128; by J. Hampden, *Britain Today*, June, pp. 40-41; by Samuel C. Chew, "Shakespeare, Thinker," *NYHTBR*, Mar. 10, 1946, p. 28; by E. W. Talbert, *South Atlantic Quarterly*, XL, 523-525; by Mabel C. Livingston, *Catholic World*, 164 (1946), 279-280; by R. W. Babcock, *PQ*, XXV, 284-287; by Leo Hughes, *Thought*, XXI, 552-553; by J. C. McCloskey, *CE*, VIII (1947), 213; by F. L. Baumer, *JMH*, XIX, 335-336; by Virgil K. Whitaker, *MLQ*, IX (1948), 498-500; by Hermann Heuer, *SJ*, 84/86 (1951), 252-253; *ShN*, VII (1957), 26. See B5109.

B5073   Ballester Escalas, Rafael. *El Historiador William Shakespeare (Ensayo sobre el Espíritu del Siglo XVI).* Tarragona: Ed. R. Ballester, 1945. Pp. 476, il.

B5074   Cancelled.

B5075   Nearing, Homer, Jr. *English Historical Poetry, 1599-1641.* Univ. of Pennsylvania Press, 1945. Pp. 222.
        Rev: *TLS*, Aug. 31, 1946, p. 416.

B5076   Ramin, Reinbold. *Die Gestalt des Politician und Statesman in Shakespeares Historien und Tragödien bis zum Abschluss der Hamlet-Periode.* DD, Marburg, 1945. Pp. iv, 129. Typewritten.

B5077   Donatelli, O. G. *The Political Lessons in Shakespeare's English Historical Plays.* MS thesis, Columbia University, 1946. Pp. 164.

B5078   Campbell, Lily B. *Shakespeare's 'Histories': Mirrors of Elizabethan Policy.* San Marino, California: The Huntington Library, 1947. Pp. xiv, 346.
        Rev: A1820.

B5079   Craig, M. R. *The Technique of the Chronicle Play.* MS thesis, Columbia University, 1947. Pp. 79.

B5080   Ellis-Fermor, Una. *The Frontiers of Drama.* Oxford Univ. Press, 1947.
        Rev: A5941.

B5081   Greever, G. "Shakespeare's History Plays." *Personalist*, XXVIII (1947), 101-102.

B5082   Holzknecht, Karl J. "An Outline of Shakespeare's English History Plays." *SAB*, XXII (1947), 193-202.

B5083   Ishida, Kenji. "Shakespeare's Historical Plays." *Rising Generation* (Japan), 93, No. 3 (1947).

B5084   Reyher, Paul. *Essai sur les Idées dans l'Œuvre de Shakespeare.* Bibliothèque des Langues Modernes, I. Paris: Didier, 1947. Pp. xxix, 662.
        Rev: A1021.

B5085   Craig, Hardin. "Shakespeare and the History Play." *AMS*, pp. 55-64.

B5086   Sitwell, Edith. *A Notebook on William Shakespeare.* New York, London: Macmillan, 1948. Pp. xii, 233.
        Rev: A8365.

B5087   Chapman, Raymond. "The Wheel of Fortune in Shakespeare's Historical Plays." *RES*, NS, I (1950), 1-7.

B5088   Geyl, Pieter. *Tochten en Toernooien.* Utrecht: Oosthoek, 1950. Pp. 272. Includes "Shakespeare als Geschiedschrijver," pp. 1-92.
        Rev: by G. Stuiveling, "To Be or Not To Be," *Het Boek van Nu*, IV, No. 4 (1951); by A. Donker, "En Tocht Naar Stratford," *Critisch Bulletin*, XVIII, 412-416.

B5089   Reeg, L. *Shakespeare und die Weltordnung.* Stuttgart: Schröder, 1950.

B5090   Scott-Giles, C. W. *Shakespeare's Heraldry.* London: J. M. Dent and Sons, 1950. Pp. x, 237.
        Rev: A2469.

B5091 Dorius, Raymond J. *The Coherence of Metaphor in Shakespeare's English History Plays.* DD, Harvard University, 1951.

B5092 Duthie, G. I. *Shakespeare.* London: Hutchinson's Univ. Library, 1951. Pp. 206.
Rev: A8162.

B5093 Fischer, Walther. "Zur Frage der Staatsauffassung in Shakespeares Königsdramen." *Shakespeare-Studien, Festschrift für Heinrich Mutschmann,* pp. 64-79.

B5094 Langsam, G. Geoffrey. *Martial Books and Tudor Verse.* New York: King's Crown Press, 1951. Pp. 213.
Rev: A2623.

B5095 Wilson, J. Dover, and T. C. Worsley. *Shakespeare's Histories at Stratford, 1951.* London: Max Reinhardt, 1952. Pp. x, 96.
Rev: B2444.

B5096 Wilson, F. P. *Marlowe and the Early Shakespeare.* Clark Lectures, Trinity College, Cambridge, 1951. Oxford: Clarendon Press, 1953. Pp. 144.
Rev: A4996.

B5097 Baldini, Gabriele. "Introduzione alle Storie Inglesi di Shakespeare." *NA* (Rome), October 1952, pp. 161-177.

B5098 Bethell, S. L. "The Comic Element in Shakespeare's Histories: A Paper Read at the Shakespeare Conference at Stratford-upon-Avon, 1951." *Anglia,* LXXI (1952), 82-101.

B5099 Charlton, H. B. *Shakespearian Tragedy.* Cambridge Univ. Press, 1948.
Rev: B4956.

B5100 McAvoy, William Charles. *Shakespeare's Use of the Laus of Apthonius.* DD, University of Illinois, 1952. Pp. 225. Mic A53-237. *DA,* XIII (1953), 97. Publ. No. 4464.

B5101 Ribner, Irving. "The Political Problem in Shakespeare's Lancastrian Tetralogy." *SP,* XLIX (1952), 171-184.

A5102 Schopf, Alfred. *Leitmotivische Thematik in Shakespeares Historien (mit einem Ausblick auf die Tragödien).* DD, Munich, 1952. Pp. 147. Typewritten.

A5103 *Lectures on Four of Shakespeare's History Plays.* Carnegie Ser. Eng., I. Pittsburgh: Carnegie Press, 1953. Pp. 69.
Lewis J. Owen, "*Richard II,*" pp. 3-18; Austere E. Claeyssens, "*Henry IV, Part One,*" pp. 19-34; William M. Shutte, "*Henry IV, Part Two,*" pp. 35-52; William F. Keirce, "*Henry V,*" pp. 53-69.

B5104 Brunner, Karl. "Middle-Class Attitudes in Shakespeare's Histories." *ShS,* VI (1953), 36-38.

B5105 Clemen, Wolfgang H. "Anticipation and Foreboding in Shakespeare's Early Histories." *ShS,* VI (1953), 25-35.

B5106 Doran, Madeleine. *Endeavors of Art: A Study of Form in Elizabethan Drama.* Madison: Univ. of Wisconsin Press, 1954. Pp. xv, 482.
Rev: A7827.

B5107 Gisi, Othmar. *Historische Elemente in der Englischen Tragödie vor der Romantik.* DD, Basel, 1953. Aarau: Keller, 1953. Pp. 119.

B5108 Jenkins, Harold. "Shakespeare's History Plays: 1900-1951." *ShS,* VI (1953), 1-15.

B5109 Law, Robert Adger. "Links Between Shakespeare's History Plays." *SP,* L (1953), 168-188. Includes comments upon B5072.

B5110 Tillyard, E. M. W. "Shakespeare's Historical Cycle: Organism or Compilation?" *SP,* LI (1954), 34-39.
Comments upon B5109.

B5111 Law, R. A. "Shakespeare's Historical Cycle: Rejoinder." *SP,* LI (1954), 40-41.
Answer to B5110.

B5112 Pearce, Josephine A. "Constituent Elements in Shakespeare's English History Plays." Matthews and Emery, eds., *Studies in Shakespeare,* 1953, pp. 145-152.

B5113 Brockbank, J. P. *Shakespeare's Historical Myth: A Study of Shakespeare's Adaptations of his Sources in Making the Plays of "Henry VI" and "Richard III."* DD, Cambridge, 1934. *Cam Abs.* 1953-54, p. 97.

B5114 Kleinstück, Johannes. "The Problem of Order in Shakespeare's Histories." *Neophil,* XXXVIII (1954), 268-277.
Challenges the view that Shak. in his Histories followed the Elizabethan concept, showing horror of rebellion and pointing to its remedies; instead Shak. implies in his own concept a criticism of that order which devotees like Henry IV, Prince John, and the Archbishop of Canterbury in *H. V* use simply as a Machiavellian instrument for gaining personal power. Order, Shak. shows, may be dangerous for man.

B5115 Merchant, W. M. "The Status and Person of Majesty." *SJ,* 90 (1954), 285-289.

B5116 Ribner, Irving. "Morality Roots of the Tudor History Play." *Tulane Studies in English,* IV (1954), 21-43.

B5117 Ribner, Irving. "The Tudor History Play: An Essay in Definition." *PMLA,* LXIX (1954), 591-609.

B5118   Richardson, Arleigh D., III. "The Early Historical Plays." *Shakespeare: of an Age and for all Time*, The Yale Shakespeare Festival Lectures, 1954, pp. 81-100.

B5119   Rossiter, A. P. "Ambivalence: The Dialectic of the Histories." *Talking of Shakespeare*, ed. by John Garrett. London: Hodder & Stoughton & Max Reinhardt, 1954.

B5120   Schirmer, Walter F. *Glück und Ende der Königinen Shakespeares Historien.* Arbeitsgemeinschaft für Forschung des Landes Nordrhein Westfalen, XXII. Cologne: Westdeutscher Verlag, 1954. Pp. 18.
       Rev: by Hermann Heuer, *SJ*, 90 (1954), 341-342; by L. Borinski, *Euphorion*, XLIX (1955), 376-377; by Max Lüthi, *DLZ*, LXXVII (1956), 668-672.

B5121   Shubik, I. *The Use of English History in the Drama, 1599-1642.* MA thesis, Univ. of London, 1954.

B5122   Michel, Laurence, and Cecil C. Seronsy. "Shakespeare's History Plays and Daniel: An Assessment." *SP*, LII (1955), 549-577.

B5123   Pearce, Josephine Anna. *The Manipulations of Time in Shakespeare's English History Plays.* DD, University of Missouri, 1955. Pp. 236. Mic 55-1110. *DA*, XV (1955), 2192. Publ. No. 14,618.

B5124   Ribner, Irving. "Marlowe's *Edward II* and the Tudor History Play." *ELH*, XXII (1955), 243-253.

B5125   Schmid, Bernhard. *Form und Gestalt der Grossen Rede in Shakespeares Historien.* DD, Munich, 1955. Pp. 166. Typewritten.

B5126   Spira, Theodor. "Shakespeares Dichtung und die Welt der Geschichte." *SJ*, 91 (1955), 65-86.

B5127   Traversi, Derek A. "Shakespeare: The Young Dramatist." *The Age of Shakespeare*, ed. Boris Ford, pp. 179-200.

B5128   Wollmann, Alfred. *Die Personenführung in Shakespeares Historien.* DD, Munich, 1955. Pp. 152. Typewritten.

B5129   Edwards, Philip. "The Early Plays of Shakespeare." Summer Lecture at Stratford, abstracted in *ShN*, VI (1956), 41.

B5130   Kaieda, Susumu. "Analysis of Shakespeare's Historical Plays." (In Japanese). *Iwasaki Kyoju Kanreki Kimen Eigo Eibungaku Ronshu* (Essays and Studies in Celebration of Professor Iwasaki's 60th Anniversary). Tokyo, 1955.

B5131   Kreft, Bratko. "Shakespearove Historije." *Glasnik Matice Slovenske* (Ljubljana), L (1955), 97-101.

B5131a Scholz, Wilhelm von. *Das Drama: Wesen, Werden Darstellung der Dramatischen Kunst.* Tübingen: Niemeyer, 1956. Pp. viii, 256.
       "Das Fünfkönigsdrama und seine Uraufführung," pp. 197-226.

B5132   Tyler, Parker. "Phaethon: The Metaphysical Tension Between the Ego and the Universe in English Poetry." *Accent*, XVI (Winter, 1956), 29-44.

B5133   Braun, Erich. *Das Legitimitätsprinzip in Shakespeares Königsdramen.* DD, Cologne, 1957. Pp. xii, 149. Typewritten.

B5134   Johnson, Samuel. *Notes to Shakespeare.* Vol. II. Histories, ed. with an Intro. by Arthur Sherbo. Augustan Reprint Society, Nos. 65-66. Los Angeles: William Andrews Clark Memorial Library, Univ. of California, 1957. Pp. 123.

B5135   Lalou, René. "Du roi Jean à Henry VIII." *Cahiers de la Compagnie Madeleine Renaud-Jean Louis Barrault*, No. 21 (1957), 13-17.

B5136   Leech, Clifford. *John Ford and the Drama of His Time.* London: Chatto & Windus, 1957. Pp. 144.

B5137   Ribner, Irving. *The English History Play in the Age of Shakespeare.* Princeton Univ. Press, 1957. Pp. xii, 354.
       Rev: by Wallace A. Bacon, *QJS*, XLIII (1957), 309; *ShN*, VII, 28; by W. Hudson Rogers, *English Jour.*, XLVI, 523; by Arthur B. Ferguson, *South Atlantic Quarterly*, LVII (1958), 146-148; by Robert C. Roby, *CE*, XIX, 59-60; by Kenneth Muir, *MLR*, LIII, 561-562; by Robert B. Miller, *SCN*, XVI, 3; by Albert J. Schmidt, *JMH*, XXX, 50-51; by J. A. Bryant, *SR*, LXVI, 326-329.

B5138   Sale, Roger Hiller. *The Development of Narrative Technique in the English Drama, 1585-1595.* DD, Cornell University, 1957. Pp. 253. Mic 57-4208. *DA*, XVII (1957), 2616. Publ. No. 23,143.

B5139   Markels, Julian. *The Public and Private Worlds of Shakespeare's Roman Plays.* DD, University of Minnesota, 1958. Pp. 289. Mic 58-311. *DA*, XVIII (1958), 221. Publ. No. 23,940.

B5140   Stroedel, Wolfgang. "Historische Tragödie." *Prisma* (Bochum), 1958-59, pp. 9-11.

B5141   Traversi, Derek. *Shakespeare: From Richard II to Henry V.* Stanford Univ. Press, 1957. London: Hollis and Carter, 1958. Pp. 198.
       Rev: San Francisco *Chronicle*, Nov. 24, 1957, p. 15; by George Freedley, *Library Jour.*, 83 (1958), 94; *TLS*, July 18, p. 410; by B. Iden Payne, *ETJ*, X, 85-86; by Irving Ribner, *JEGP*,

LVII, 341-342; by Michel Poirier, *EA*, XI, 160-161; by Reed Whittemore, *Poetry*, 92 (1958), 189-195; by H. C. Kiefer, *Arizona Quarterly*, XIV, 367-368; by Jacques Vallette, *MdF*, Sept., 141-146; by M. M. Reese, *Time and Tide*, July 19, pp. 891-892; *Georgia Review*, XII, 112; by Frank Kermode, *Spectator*, June 27, p. 845; by Hermann Heuer, *SJ*, 94 (1958), 264-265; by Robert Adger Law, *Southwest Rev.*, XLVIII, 178-179; by T. Smalley, *Month*, NS, XX, 373-374; by Karl Miller, *MGW*, Aug. 7, p. 11; by Eric Gillett, *National and English Rev.*, August, 75-76; by J. Fuzier, *LanM*, LII, 402; *N &Q*, NS, V, 134-135; by J. Raymond, *NstN*, LVI, 117-118; *ShN*, VIII, 21.

d. COMEDIES (190;67)

B5142   Ludwig, Wilhelm. *Der Schluss der Shakespeareschen Lustspiele.* DD, Münster, 1925. Pp. 103.

B5143   Maitland, J. A. B. *An Introduction to the Study of Lower-class Characters in Shakespeare's Comedies.* MA thesis, Toronto, 1925. Pp. 68.

B5144   Lawrence, W. W. *Shakespeare's Problem Comedies.* New York, 1931. Pp. xi, 259.
    Rev: by A. G. van Kranendonk, *ES*, XVIII (1936), 81-83.

B5145   Kreider, Paul V. *Elizabethan Comic Character Conventions as Revealed in the Comedies of George Chapman.* Univ. of Michigan Press, 1935. Pp. xi, 206.
    Much, i.a., on Shak.
    Rev: A6543.

B5146   Messiaen, Pierre. "Première Comédie de Shakespeare." *Revue Polit. et Littér.* (*Rev. Bleue.*), LXXIV (1936), 382-385.

B5147   Messiaen, Pierre. "Les Premières Comédies de Shakespeare." *France-Grande-Bretagne*, May, 1937, pp. 136-143.

B5148   Charlton, H. B. "Shakespeare's Comedies: The Consummation." *BJRL*, XXI (1937), 323-351.

B5149   Jacobi, Walter. *Form und Struktur der Shakespeareschen Komödien: Eine Vorstudie zum Problem des Dramatischen bei Shakespeare.* DD, Berlin, 1937. Berlin: Triltsch & Huther, 1937. Pp. 134.
    Rev: A6050.

B5150   Messiaen, P. "L'Intrigue et l'Action dans les Comédies de Shakespeare." *Rev. Universitaire*, June, 1937, pp. 25-35.

B5151   Messiaen, Pierre. "Les Comédies de Shakespeare." *RCC*, XXXVIII (1937), 244-251, 421-429.

B5152   Stillwell, Gardiner. *The Source Approach to Shakespearean Comedy.* MA thesis, Toronto, 1937. Pp. 153.

B5153   Campbell, Oscar J. *Comicall Satyre and Shakespeare's "Troilus and Cressida."* San Marino, Calif.: The Henry E. Huntington Library, 1938. Pp. ix, 246.
    Rev: A4913.

B5154   Charlton, H. B. "*A Midsummer Night's Dream.*" *BJRL*, XXII (1938), 46-66.
    Rev: B6048.

B5155   Charlton, Henry Buckley. *Shakespearian Comedy.* London: Methuen, 1938. Pp. 303.
    Rev: *TLS*, Feb. 26, 1938, p. 136, and March 26, p. 216; by George Rylands, *NstN*, NS, XV, 531-532; by E. H. W. Meyerstein, *London Mercury*, XXXVIII, 83; by C. J. Sisson, *MLR*, XXXIII, 580-581; by Bonamy Dobrée, *Spectator*, Feb. 25, 1938, p. 318; by the Archbishop of York, *MGW*, Mar. 4, p. 174; by J. Crofts, *English*, II, 114-116; by Edwin H. Zeydel, *MLJ*, XXIII, 231; by W. Keller, *SJ*, LXXIV, 176-177; by E. E. Stoll, *SJ*, LXXIV, 50-63; by Wolfgang Schmidt, *Beiblatt*, L (1939), 104-106; by V. Bonet, *ES*, XXI (1939), 20-23; by R. S. Knox, *UTQ*, IX, 107-111; by Georges Connes, *EA*, III, 38-39; by R. E. C. Houghton, *TLS*, May 4, 1940, p. 219.

B5156   Glunz, H. *Shakespeare und Morus.* Kölner Anglistische Arbeiten, XXXII. Bochum Langendreer: Pöppinghaus, 1938. Pp. ix, 267.
    Chap. VIII: "Die Lustspiele," pp. 232-263, discusses many comedies.
    Rev: A4687.

B5157   Messiaen, Pierre. "Les Comédies de Shakespeare." *Culture* (Canada), II, i (Oct., 1938), 39-54.

B5158   Feibleman, J. *In Praise of Comedy: A Study in Theory and Practice.* New York: Macmillan, 1939. Pp. 284.
    Rev: A6837.

B5159   Pettigrew, Helen P. *The Elizabethan Lover in Shakespeare's Comedies.* DD, University of Washington, Seattle, 1939.

B5160   Weidlé, Wladimir. "Les Comédies de Shakespeare." *Les Nouvelles Littéraires*, Nov. 11, 1939, p. 1.

B5161   Wells, Henry W. *Elizabethan and Jacobean Playwrights.* Columbia Univ. Press, 1939. Pp. xiv, 327.
    Rev: B5063.

B5162   Gordon, Donald James. *The "Commedia Erudita" and Elizabethan Comedy.* DD, Cambridge. *Cam Abs.*, 1940-41, pp. 60.
    Three Shak. plays discussed: *Shrew, Much, Twelf.*

B5163   Jones, Carol Whitt. *Reason versus Passion in Shakespeare's Comedies.* MA thesis, University of

North Carolina, 1941. Abstr. publ. in *Univ. of North Carolina Record, Research in Progress*, Grad. School Series, No. 40, 1941, p. 74.

B5164   Campbell, Oscar James. *Shakespeare's Satire*. New York: Oxford Univ. Press; London: Milford, 1943. Pp. xii, 227.
Rev: by John Corbin, *SRL*, xxvi (June 19, 1943), 34; by Paul Mueschke, *NYTBR*, Aug. 1, p. 22; by Samuel A. Tannenbaum, *SAB*, xviii, 95-96; by James Southall Wilson, *VQR*, xix, 476-480; by Josephine Bennett, *SAB*, xviii, 168-174; by Hardin Craig, *MLN*, lix (1944), 133-137; by George Coffin Taylor, *MLQ*, v, 373-375; by Hoyt H. Hudson, *JEGP*, xliii, 118-120; by Bertram Jessup, *JAAC*, iii, Nos. 11-12 (1944), 93-94; by F. Meres, *Time and Tide*, xxv, 75-76; by Helen C. White, *CE*, vi (1945), 416-417.

B5165   Gordon, George. *Shakespearian Comedy and Other Studies*. Ed. by Sir Edmund Chambers. Oxford Univ. Press, 1944. Pp. 168.
Rev: *TLS*, June 24, 1944, p. 308; by H. B. Charlton, *NstN*, July 22, p. 60; by H. B. Charlton, *MGW*, July 28, p. 47; by Margaret Willy, *English*, v, 91-92; *N &Q*, 187 (1944), 43-44; by C. J. Sisson, *MLR*, xxxix, 405-406; by A. R. Cripps, *TLS*, July 1, 1944, p. 319; by H. Furst, *TLS*, July 15, p. 343, and July 29, p. 367; by F. K. Mitchell, *SAQ*, xliv (1945), 236; by T. M. Parrott, *JEGP*, xliv, 304-307; *DUJ*, xxxvii, 70-71; by M. A. Shaaber, *MLN*, lx, 417-418; by Margaret Webster, *SRL*, June 9, pp. 18-19; by W. H. Irving, *South Atlantic Quarterly*, xliv, 236; *QR*, 283 (1945), 249-251; by Joseph Wood Krutch, *Nation*, Jan. 13, p. 50; by Angelo M. Pellegrini, *MLQ*, vii (1946), 358-359.

B5166   Plank, Patricia Gertrude. *The Function of Women in Shakespeare Comedy*. MA thesis, Saskatchewan, 1944. Pp. 113.

B5167   Palmer, John. *Comic Characters of Shakespeare*. New York: Macmillan, 1946. Pp. 135.
Rev: A6544.

B5168   Nakahaski, Kazuo. "The Spirit of Shakespeare's Comedies." *Rising Generation* (Japan), 93, No. 3 (1947).

B5169   Reyher, Paul. *Essai Sur les Idées dans l'Œuvre de Shakespeare*. Bibliothèque des Langues Modernes, Vol. i. Paris: Didier, 1947. Pp. xxix, 662.
Ideas, their sources, their nature, relationships, developments, etc. Divided into sections on Comedies, Histories, Tragedies, and Last Plays.
Rev: A1021.

B5170   Frye, Northrop. "The Argument of Comedy." *EIE*, 1948. New York: Columbia Univ. Press, 1949, pp. 58-73.

B5171   Sitwell, Edith. *A Notebook on William Shakespeare*. London: Macmillan, 1948. Pp. xii, 233.
Rev: A8365.

B5172   Kelly, Mary Louise. *Villains in Shakespeare's Comedies*. MA thesis, North Carolina, 1948. Abstr. publ. in *University of North Caroline Record, Research in Progress*, Grad. School Series, No. 56, 1949, p. 215.

B5173   Mikami, Isao. "Shakespearean Comedy." *Eibungaku-shicho*, xxii, No. 1 (1949).

B5174   Parrott, Thomas M. *Shakespearean Comedy*. New York: Oxford Univ. Press, 1949. Pp. xiv, 417.
Rev: A8323.

B5175   Pettet, E. C. *Shakespeare and the Romance Tradition*. London: Staples Press, 1949. Pp. 208.
Chapters on the Romantic Comedies, the Dark Comedies, and the Romances.
Rev: *TLS*, April 28, 1950, p. 258; by M. MacLure, *Canadian Forum*, xxx, 164; by Kenneth Muir, *MLR*, xlv, 529-531; by Diwan Chand Sharma, *The Aryan Path*, Oct., 1950; *Dalhousie Rev.*, xxx, 430-431; by Hallett Smith, *SQ*, iii (1952), 60-61; by F. N. Lees, *RES*, ns, iii, 173-174; by W. Clemen, *Archiv*, 189 (1952/53), 62.

B5176   Coghill, Nevill. "The Basis of Shakespearian Comedy." *Essays and Studies*, ns, iii (1950), 1-28.
Rev: by M. A. Shaaber, *SQ*, ii (1951), 260-261.

B5177   Emde Boas, Conrad van. "The Connection Between Shakespeare's Sonnets and his 'Travesti-Double' Plays." *International Jour. of Sexology*, Nov., 1950.

B5177a Emde Boas, C. van. *Shakespeare's Sonnetten en Hun Verband met de Travesti-Double Spelen. Een Medesch-Psychologische Studie*. Amsterdam, 1951. Pp. 520.
Rev: A870.

B5178   Sen Gupta, Subodh Chandra. *Shakespearian Comedy*. Calcutta: Oxford University Press, 1950. Pp. ix, 287. New York: Oxford Univ. Press, 1952.
Rev: by J. B. Fort, *EA*, v (1952), 154; by L. Kirschbaum, *MLN*, lxviii (1953), 510-511; by Thomas Marc Parrott, *SQ*, iv, 100-102.

B5179   Barber, C. L. "The Saturnalian Pattern In Shakespeare's Comedy." *SR*, lix (1951), 593-611.

B5180   Curry, Rev. John Vincent. *Deception in Elizabethan Comedy: An Analytical Study*. DD, Columbia University, 1951. Pp. 229. Mic A51-541. *Microf. Ab.*, xi (1951), 840. Publication No. 2804.
Rev: A6298.

B5181   David, Richard. "Shakespeare's Comedies and the Modern Stage." *ShS*, iv (1951), 129-138.

B5182   Duthie, G. I. *Shakespeare*. London: Hutchinson's University Library, 1951. Pp. 206.
Rev: A8162.

B5183   Kreiger, Murray. *"Measure for Measure* and Elizabethan Comedy." *PMLA*, LXVI (1951), 775-784.

B5184   Lord, John Bigelow. *Certain Dramatic Devices Studied in the Comedies of Shakespeare and in Some of the Works of His Contemporaries and Predecessors.* DD, University of Illinois, 1951. Pp. 296. *DA*, XII (1952), 66. Publication No. 3154.
Part II treats each Shak. comedy in a separate chapter.

B5185   Reynolds, George F. "Comedy and the Crisis." *Western Humanities Rev.*, V (1951), 143-151.

B5186   Cazamian, Louis. *The Development of English Humor.* Duke Univ. Press, 1952. Pp. viii, 421. Cambridge Univ. Press, 1953.
Includes a long section on Shak.'s humor, divided into numerous parts.
Rev: by J. J. Mayoux, *Critique*, No. 67, 1952; by Stuart M. Tave, *MP*, L (1952/53), 206-208; by B. Evans, *SatR*, XXXV, No. 31 (1952), 10; by A. J. Farmer, *Erasmus*, VI (1953), 521-523; by J. Jones, *JEGP*, LII, 108-110; by C. E. Gauss, *JAAC*, XI, 423; by H. Jenkins, *MLN*, LXVIII, 492-495; by R. Escarpit, *RLC*, XXVII, 221-225; by K. J. Holzknecht, *SQ*, IV, 97-99; by Emil Pons, *EA*, VII (1954), 80-88; by V. de S. Pinto, *RES*, V, 434-436. For review of earlier French edition see R. Pruvost, "Études sur Shakespeare," *Revue de la Méditerranée*, IV (1947), 615-618.

B5187   Desai, Chintamani N. *Shakespearean Comedy.* (With a Discussion on Comedy, the Comic, and the Sources of Shakespearean Comic Laughter.) Indore City, M. B., India: The Author, 1952. Pp. 204.
Rev: *TLS*, July 10, 1953, p. 450; by Aerol Arnold, *SQ*, VI (1955), 101-102.

B5188   McAvoy, William Charles. *Shakespeare's Use of the Laus of Apthonius.* DD, University of Illinois, 1952. Pp. 225. Mic A53-237. *DA*, XIII (1953), 97. Publication No. 4464.

B5189   McCulley, Cecil Michael. *A Study of Dramatic Comedy.* DD, Columbia University, 1952. Pp. 348. *DA*, XII (1952), 614. Publication No. 4214.
Special attention to works of Shak. and other Elizabethans.

B5190   Thomas, Lewis Ralph. *Jacobean Comedy Examined in the Light of Marxian Principles.* MA thesis, Dalhousie, 1952.

B5191   Thompson, Karl F. "Shakespeare's Romantic Comedies." *PMLA*, LXVII (1952), 1079-93.

B5192   Doran, Madeleine. *Endeavors of Art: A Study of Form in Elizabethan Drama.* Madison: Univ. of Wisconsin Press, 1953. Pp. xv, 482.
Rev: A7827.

B5193   Frye, Northrop. "Characterization in Shakespearian Comedy." *SQ*, IV (1953), 271-277.

B5194   Klajn, Hugo. "Shakespearove komedije (Shakespeare's Comedies)." *Mogućnosti* (Split), X (1954).

B5195   Reetz, Olaf. *Die Entwicklung der Sprachkomik in den Komödien Shakespeares.* DD, Berlin, 1954. Pp. xv, 283. Typewritten.

B5196   Beltz, Wilhelm. "Das Böse in Shakespeares Komödien." *Shakespeare-Tage* (Bochum), 1955, pp. 1-4.

B5197   Bradbrook, M. C. *The Growth and Structure of Elizabethan Comedy.* London: Chatto and Windus, 1955. Pp. ix, 246.
Rev: by J. I. M. Stewart, *NstN*, Nov. 12, 1955, p. 636; by J. M. Cohen, *Spectator*, Nov. 4, p. 600; *TLS*, Dec. 9, p. 744 (letter by M. T. Jones-Davies, Dec. 16, p. 761); by J. Vallette, *MdF*, 325 (Dec., 1955), 721; *Listener*, LIV, 809; comment by W. Empson, *Listener*, LIV (Nov. 10), 899; by R. Speaight, *Tablet*, 206 (1955), 396; by M. Poirier, *EA*, IX (1956), 152-153; by K. Muir, *EIC*, VI (1956), 338-343; by L. D. Lerner, *London Magazine*, III, 83-86; by H. Heuer, *SJ*, 92 (1956), 366-367; by Milton Crane, *SQ*, VII, 436-437; by Patrick Cruttwell, *TC*, 159 (1956), 214-220; by Laura Jepsen, *English Jour.*, XLV, 438; *Essential Books*, June, p. 34; by Gorley Putt, *Time and Tide*, Jan. 28, pp. 112-113; by K. Muir, *ShS*, X (1957), 137; by J. A. Bryant, *SR*, LXV, 153-155; by W. Sharp, *ETJ*, IX, 261-262; by H. S. Wilson, *QQ*, LXIV, 295-297; by J. V. Curry, *Thought*, XXXII, 291-293; by John V. Curry, S.J., *MLQ*, XIX (1958), 75-76.

B5198   Brown, John Russell. "The Interpretation of Shakespeare's Comedies." *ShS*, VIII (1955), 1-13.

B5199   Crane, Milton. *"Twelfth Night* and Shakespearian Comedy." *SQ*, VI (1955), 1-8.

B5200   Goldsmith, Robert H. *Wise Fools in Shakespeare.* Michigan State Univ. Press, 1955. Pp. xi, 123.
Rev: A6676.

B5201   Herrick, Marvin T. *Tragicomedy: Its Origin and Development in Italy, France, and England.* Univ. of Illinois Press, 1955. Pp. vii, 331.
Besides discussing Shak., deals with classical and Renaissance backgrounds.
Rev: by Albert E. Johnson, *QJS*, XLI (1955), 427-428; by Frank Kermode, *MLR*, LI (1956), 93-94; by Vernon Hall, Jr., *MLN*, LXXI, 214-215; by Eugene M. Waith, *JEGP*, LV, 140-142; by G. P. V. Akrigg, *SQ*, VII, 263-265; by Allardyce Nicoll, *RES*, NS, VII, 427-429; by R. C. D. Perman, *French Studies*, X, 167-169; by Madeleine Doran, *MP*, LV (1957), 124-127; by E. B. O. Borgerhoff, *RR*, XLVIII, 46-51.

B5202   Long, John H. *Shakespeare's Use of Music: A Study of the Music and Its Performance in the*

Original Production of Seven Comedies. Gainesville: Univ. of Florida Press, 1955. Pp. xv, 213.
Rev: A6151.

B5203 Maxwell, J. C. "Shakespeare: The Middle Plays." *The Age of Shakespeare*, ed. Boris Ford, Pelican Books, 1955, pp. 201-227.

B5204 Traversi, Derek A. "Shakespeare: The Young Dramatist." *The Age of Shakespeare*, ed. Boris Ford, Pelican Books, 1955, pp. 179-200.

B5205 Culp, James William. *The Judgment Denouement of English Renaissance Comedy from 1553-1625.* DD, Vanderbilt University, 1956. Pp. 381. Mic 57-968. *DA*, XVII (1957), 621. Publication No. 20,031.

B5206 Edwards, Philip. "The Early Plays of Shakespeare." *ShN*, VI (1956), 41.
Abstract of Summer Lecture at Stratford.

B5207 Heine, Heinrich. "Im Zaubergarten der Shakespeareschen Komödie." *Das neue Forum* (Darmstadt), V (1955/56), 244-247.

B5208 Johnson, Samuel. *Notes to Shakespeare.* Vol. I: Comedies. Ed. with an introd. by Arthur Sherbo. Augustan Reprint Society, Nos. 59-60. Los Angeles: William Andrews Clark Memorial Library, Univ. of California, 1956. Pp. viii, 140.

B5209 Mullen, Richard D. *Reward and Punishment in English Comedy, 1599-1613.* DD, University of Chicago, 1956.

B5210 Brown, John Russell. *Shakespeare and his Comedies.* London: Methuen, 1957. Pp. 208.
Rev: by J. Vallette, *MdF*, 331 (1957), 696; *TLS*, Oct. 11, p. 610; by R. A. Foakes, *English*, XII (1958), 20; by Frank Kermode, *EIC*, VIII, 298-303; *ShN*, VIII, 30; by Hermann Heuer, *SJ*, 94 (1958), 276-278; by Michel Poirier, *EA*, XI, 350; *Dublin Magazine*, March, pp. 52-54.

B5211 Cecil, David. "Shakespearean Comedy." *The Fine Art of Reading and Other Literary Studies.* 1957.
Rev: B4464.

B5212 Holland, R. A. *Comedy and Character in Shakespeare in Relation to Shakespearean Criticism Since 1903.* DD, London, Queen Mary College, 1957.

B5213 Kindermann, Heinz. "Shakespeares Komödien." *Prisma* (Bochum), No. 7, 1956/57, pp. 75-78.

B5214 Chujo, Kazuo. "The Development of Structural Devices in Shakespeare's Tragicomedies." *Otsuka Festschrift*, 1958, pp. 301-316.

B5215 Potts, Abbie Findlay. *Shakespeare and "The Faerie Queen."* Cornell Univ. Press; Oxford Univ. Press, 1958. Pp. xii, 269.
Rev: A4819.

B5216 Tillyard, E. M. W. *The Nature of Comedy and Shakespeare.* English Association Presidential Addresses. London: English Association, 1958. Pp. 13.
Rev: A6927.

(1) PROBLEM PLAYS

B5217 Lawrence, W. W. *Shakespeare's Problem Comedies.* New York, 1931.
Rev: by A. G. van Kranendonk, *ES*, XVIII (1936), 81-83.

B5218 Sisson, C. J. *The Mythical Sorrows of Shakespeare.* Oxford Univ. Press, 1934.
Several pages on *Meas. & Troil.*
Rev: A7937.

B5219 Charlton, H. B. "Shakespeare's 'Dark Comedies'." *BJRL*, XXI (1937), 78-128.

B5220 Traversi, D. A. *An Approach to Shakespeare.* London: Sands, Paladin Press, 1938. Pp. 152. Second ed. revised and enlarged, New York: Doubleday, 1956. Pp. 304.
Rev: A8420.

B5221 Campbell, Oscar James. *Shakespeare's Satire.* Oxford Univ. Press, 1943. Pp. 227.
Rev: B5164.

B5222 Tillyard, E. M. W. *Shakespeare's Problem Plays.* Alexander Lectures. Toronto: Univ. Toronto Press, 1949; London: Chatto & Windus, 1950. Pp. vii, 168.
A critical rejection of the theory that *Hamlet, Troilus and Cressida, All's Well That Ends Well,* and *Measure for Measure* spring from a morbid state of mind induced by personal problems. They are normal studies of difficult moral problems.
Rev: by C. L. Bennet, *Dalhousie Rev.*, XXIX (1949), 217; by A. C. Sprague, *NYTBR*, May 1, p. 25; by R. P. W., *Culture*, June; by W. G. Stobie, *Winnipeg Free Press*, May 7; by Robert Halsband, *SRL*, May 14, pp. 20-21; by R. Davril, *LanM*, XLIV (1950), 423; by J. I. M. Stewart, *NstN*, XXXIX, 277; by H. Heuer, *SJ*, 84/86 (1950), 253-254; by J. M. Cohen, *Spectator*, No. 6351, p. 344; *TLS*, March 10, p. 154; by G. W. Knight, *TLS*, April 21, p. 245; by D. Traversi, *Scrutiny*, XVII, 181-184; by K. R. Srinivasa Lyengar, *The Aryan Path*, Oct.; by R. W. Zandvoort, *ES*, XXXIII (1952), 32.

B5223 James, D. G. *The Dream of Learning: An Essay on "The Advancement of Learning," "Hamlet" and "King Lear."* Oxford: Clarendon Press, 1951. Pp. 126.
Rev: A3959.

B5224	Whitaker, Virgil K. "Philosophy and Romance in Shakespeare's 'Problem' Comedies." *The Seventeenth Century. Studies in the History of English Thought and Literature from Bacon to Pope by Richard Foster Jones and Others Writing in His Honor*, pp. 339-354.

B5225	Johnson, S. F. "The Regeneration of Hamlet: A Reply to E. M. W. Tillyard with a Counter-proposal." *SQ*, III (1952), 187-207.
		Discusses "marked reaction" to Stoll in last 20 years and then Tillyard's *Shakespeare's Problem Plays*, B5222.

B5226	Ornstein, Robert. *The Ethics of Jacobean Tragedy, A Study of the Influence of Renaissance Free Thought.* DD, University of Wisconsin, 1954. Abstr. publ. in *Summaries of Doctoral Dissertations, 1953-54*, Vol. 15, Madison: Univ. of Wisconsin Press, 1955, pp. 622-624.

B5227	Halio, Jay Leon. *Rhetorical Ambiguity as a Stylistic Device in Shakespeare's Problem Comedies.* DD, Yale University, 1956. Abstract by Jack R. Brown, *ShN*, VI (1956), 39.

B5228	Morris, Harry Caesar. *Nineteenth and Twentieth Century Criticism of Shakespeare's Problem Comedies.* DD, University of Minnesota, 1957. Pp. 553. Mic 57-2479. *DA*, XVII (1957), 1546. Publication No. 21,252.
		Two chapters on each of the three plays, *All's Well*, *Meas.*, and *Troil.*

B5229	Chapman, John Jay. *The Selected Writings of John Jay Chapman.* Ed. with an introd. by Jacques Barzun. New York: Farrar, Strauss and Cudahy, 1957. Pp. 294.
		Includes four Shak. criticisms.
		Rev: A9264.

(2) LAST PLAYS (-;68)

B5230	Ellis-Fermor, Una M. *The Jacobean Drama: An Interpretation.* London: Methuen, 1936. Pp. 351.
		Rev: A6005.

B5231	Sargeaunt, G. M. "The Last Phase of Shakespeare's Work." *The Classical Spirit*, 1936, pp. 253-272.

B5232	James, D. G. *Scepticism and Poetry.* London: Allen & Unwin, 1937. Pp. 276.
		Declares Shak. went on creating mythology in his Last Plays that is independent of Christianity.
		Rev: *TLS*, Mar. 20, 1937, p. 200; by William Empson, *Criterion*, XVI, 705-707.

B5233	Tillyard, E. M. W. *Shakespeare's Last Plays.* London: Chatto & Windus, 1938. Pp. 85.
		Rev: by Desmond Hawkins, *Spectator*, Apr. 15, 1938, p. 682; by Beatrice White, *National Rev.*, 110 (1938), 401-404; by Bonamy Dobrée, *Criterion*, XVII, 741-743; by D. A. Traversi, *Scrutiny*, VI, 446-449; *TLS*, Jan. 22, p. 57; by G. W. Stonier, *NstN*, NS, XV, 180; by Michael Roberts, *London Mercury*, XXXVIII, 91-92; *TLS*, March 26, p. 216; by R. Huchon, *EA*, III (1939), 39-42; by R. S. Knox, *UTQ*, IX, 111-113.

B5234	Traversi, D. A. *An Approach to Shakespeare.* London: Sands, Paladin Press, 1938. Pp. 152. Second ed. revised and enlarged, New York: Doubleday, 1956. Pp. 304.
		Rev: A8420.

B5235	Bacon, Wallace Alger. *Shakespeare's Dramatic Romances.* DD, University of Michigan, 1940.

B5236	Harrison, Thomas P., Jr. "Aspects of Primitivism in Shakespeare and Spenser." *TxSE*, XX (1940), 39-71.
		Chiefly comparison, with some evidence of influence.

B5237	Leavis, F. R. "The Criticism of Shakespeare's Late Plays: A Caveat." *Scrutiny*, X (1942), 339-345.

B5238	Sachs, Hanns. "The Unconscious in Shakespeare's *Tempest*, Analytical Considerations." *The Creative Unconscious.* Cambridge, Mass.: Sci-Art, 1942, pp. 289-323. Second ed., 1951.

B5239	Spencer, Theodore. "Appearance and Reality in Shakespeare's Last Plays." *MP*, XXXIX (1942), 265-274.

B5240	Spencer, Theodore. *Shakespeare and the Nature of Man.* Lowell Lectures, 1942. New York: Macmillan, 1942. Pp. xiii, 283.
		Special chapter on Last Plays.
		Rev: A1044.

B5241	Knight, G. Wilson. *The Crown of Life: Interpretation of Shakespeare's Final Plays.* Oxford Univ. Press, 1947. Pp. viii, 9-336. Second ed. London: Methuen, 1948.
		Rev: by Roy Walker, *Life and Letters*, LIV (1947), 165-168; *DUJ*, XXXIX, 120-121; *TLS*, April 26, p. 203, and Oct. 25, p. 552; by G. M. Hort, *English*, VI, 314-315; by H. B. Charlton, *MGW*, May 29, p. 11; by H. J. Oliver, *MLR*, XLII, 503-505; by R. G. Cox, *Scrutiny*, XIV, 317-320; by Eric Bentley, *NYTBR*, Sept. 7, p. 34; *The Wind and the Rain*, IV, 120-123; by M. Webster, *TAr*, XXXII (1948), 78-79; by F. T. Prince, *RES*, XXIV, 251-252; by S. E. Hyman, *SR*, LVI, 328-332; by F. Delattre, *LanM*, XLIII (1949), 323-324; by B. C. West, *MLN*, LXIV, 137-138; by R. Fricker, *ES*, XXXI (1950), 105-107.

B5242	Reyher, Paul. *Essai sur les Idées dans l'Œuvre de Shakespeare.* Bibliothèque des Langues Modernes, I. Paris: Didier, 1947. Pp. xxix, 662.
		Sections on Last Plays.
		Rev: A1021.

B5243 Heilman, Robert B., et al. "Myth in the Later Plays of Shakespeare." *EIE, 1948* (Columbia Univ. Press, 1949), pp. 27-119.

B5244 Cancelled.

B5245 Martin, M. S. *The Redirection of Critical Interest in Shakespeare's Last Plays, 1930-1948.* Thesis, University of New Zealand, 1949.

B5246 Oppel, Horst. *Der Späte Shakespeare.* Hamburg: Heinrich Ellermann, 1949. Pp. 43.
Rev: by H. Heuer, *SJ*, 87 (1949), 258.

B5247 Pettet, E. C. *Shakespeare and the Romance Tradition.* London: Staples, 1949.
Chapter on the Romances.
Rev: B5175.

B5248 Ellis-Fermor, Una. "Die Spåtwerke grosser Dramatiker." *DVLG*, XXIV (1950), 423-439.

B5249 Megan, Robert N. E. *Shakespeare's Last Plays: An Inquiry into the Artistic Form of "Pericles," "Cymbeline," "The Winter's Tale," and "The Tempest."* DD, University of Chicago, 1950.

B5250 Wincor, Richard. "Shakespeare's Festival Plays." *SQ*, I (1950), 219-240.

B5251 Duthie, G. I. *Shakespeare.* London: Hutchinson's University Library. Pp. 206.
Rev: A8162.

B5252 Bonjour, Adrien. "The Final Scene of *The Winter's Tale.*" *ES*, XXXIII (1952), 193-208.
Much incidental discussion of recent criticisms of the Last Plays.

B5253 Danby, J. F. *Poets on Fortune's Hill.* London, 1952.
Rev: A8156.

B5254 Dobrée, Bonamy. "The Tempest." *Essays and Studies*, V (1952), 13-25.

B5255 Leavis, F. R. *The Common Pursuit.* New York: George W. Stewart, 1952. Pp. 307.
Collects previously published critical essays, including one on the Late Plays.

B5256 Bland, D. S. "The Heroine and the Sea: An Aspect of Shakespeare's Last Plays." *EIC*, III (1953), 39-44.

B5257 Cruttwell, Patrick. *The Shakespearean Moment.* London: Chatto & Windus, 1953. Pp. 256. New York: Columbia Univ. Press, 1955.
Rev: *TLS*, April 30, 1954, p. 282; by Herman Heuer, *SJ*, 90 (1954), 319-320; by J. C. Ghosh, *ConR*, 186, No. 1064 (1954), 126-127; *MGW*, Mar. 11, p. 10; *NstN*, Apr. 3, p. 447; by John Buxton, *Time and Tide*, July 17, p. 971; by F. S. Boas, *FortnR*, NS, 1051 (1954), 66-68; by D. Hoeninger, *Canadian Forum*, Aug., pp. 118-119; by James Michie, *London Mag.*, I, 94, 97-98, 100; by J. Vallette, *MdF*, 320 (1954), 726-727; by Roy Walker, *The Aryan Path*, XXV, 178-179; by Alfred Harbage, *MLN*, LXX (1955), 529-530; by Bruce Dearing, *CE*, XVII, 60-61; by Kathleen Nott, *Partisan Review*, XXII, 556-560; by Michel Poirier, *EA*, VIII, 67-68; by William Blackburn, *South Atlantic Quar.*, LIV, 562-564; by John Thompson, *Hudson Review*, VIII, 466-468; by Maynard Mack, *YR*, XLV, 267-273; *VQR*, XXXI, cii-civ; by William T. Hastings, *SQ*, VI, 110-111; by A. A., *Personalist*, XXXVII (1956), 310-312; by Hans Galinsky, *SQ*, VII, 265-266; by Edward Hubler, *JEGP*, LV, 314-316; by J. H. Marshburn, *Books Abroad*, XXX, 332-333.

B5258 **King, S. K.** "Eliot, Yeats and Shakespeare." *Theoria*, University of Natal, 1953, pp. 113-119.

B5259 Swander, Homer D. *The Design of "Cymbeline."* DD, University of Michigan, 1953. Pp. 224. Mic A53-1499. *DA*, XIII (1953), 814. Publication No. 5744.

B5260 Hoeniger, F. J. D. *The Function of Structure and Imagery in Shakespeare's Last Plays.* DD, Univ. of London, 1954. Abstr. in *ShN*, V (1955), 42.

B5261 Parker, Marion Hope. *The Slave of Life.* London: Chatto and Windus, 1954.
Sees a profound Christian faith at work in Shak.'s plays.
Rev: A1532.

B5262 Traversi, Derek. *Shakespeare: The Last Phase.* London: Hollis & Carter, 1954. Pp. vii, 272.
Rev: *NstN*, XLVIII (Dec. 11, 1954), 800; by H. B. Charlton, *MGW*, Dec. 9, p. 10; by J. Vallette, *MdF*, 322 (1954), 713; by P. Connolly, *Eccl. Record*, 83 (1954), 237-239; *TLS*, Mar. 18, 1955, p. 162; *Wisconsin Library Bulletin*, May, p. 11; *English Journal*, XLIV, 366; by George Freedley, *Library Journal*, LIII, 1606; by John Burrell, *TAr*, July, p. 8; by Ralph W. Condee, *CE*, XVII, 63; by Denis Donoghue, *Studies*, XLIV, 383-384; by I. J. Semper, *Month*, NS, XIV, 58-59; by John Thompson, *Hudson Review*, VIII, 463-466; by Maynard Mack, *YR*, XLV, 267-273; by William T. Hastings, *SQ*, VI, 127-128; by Alfred Harbage, *SQ*, VII (1956), 116-118; by J. A. Bryant, Jr., *SR*, LXIV, 517-520; by Hermann Heuer, *SJ*, 92 (1956), 367-369.

B5263 Bradbrook, M. C. *The Growth and Structure of Elizabethan Comedy.* London: Chatto and Windus, 1955. Pp. ix, 246. Last Plays, pp. 196-206.
Rev: B5197.

B5264 Fischer, Walther. "Shakespeares späte Romanzen." *SJ*, 91 (1955), 7-24.

B5265 Oppel, Horst. *Shakespeares Tragödien und Romanzen: Kontinuität oder Umbruch?* Mainz: Akademie der Wissenschaften und der Literatur, 1954. Pp. 46.
Rev: B4997.

B5266 Traversi, Derek A. "The Last Plays of Shakespeare." *The Age of Shakespeare*, ed. Boris Ford, pp. 257-281.
B5267 Guidi, Augusto. "In Margine a uno Studio dei Drammi Romanzeschi di Shakespeare." *Letteratura*, IV, No. 24 (1956), 3-10.
B5268 *Pericles, Prince of Tyre*. Ed. J. C. Maxwell. The New Shakespeare. Cambridge: Cambridge Univ. Press, 1956. Pp. xli, 211.
       Introd. contains discussion of the relationship between *Per*. and the Last Plays.
       Rev: B9904.
B5269 Guidi, Augusto. "L'Ultimo Shakespeare." *Idea*, IX, No. 31 (1958), 1, 4; No. 32, 4; No. 33, 4; No. 34, 4; No. 35, 3-4; No. 36, 4; No. 37, 4; No. 38, 4; No. 39, 4; No. 40, 4; No. 41, 4; No. 42, 4; No. 43, 4.
       On Shak.'s Last Plays.
B5270 Leech, Clifford. "The Structure of the Last Plays." *ShS*, XI (1958), 19-30.
B5271 Potts, Abbie Findlay. *Shakespeare and "The Faerie Queen."* Ithaca: Cornell Univ. Press, 1958. Pp. 264.
       Chapter on Last Plays.
       Rev: A4819.

e. DOMESTIC DRAMA (191;-)

B5272 Taylor, Edward Pyres. *Elizabethan Domestic Tragedies*. DD, University of Chicago, 1925.
B5273 Bachenheimer, M. S. *The Domestic Drama in the Time of Shakespeare*. MA thesis, University of Pittsburgh, 1933.
B5274 Wheeler, Harold P. *Studies in 16th Century English Literature of Rustic Life*. DD, University of Illinois, 1939.
B5275 Ashton, J. W. *Types of English Drama*. New York: Macmillan, 1940. Pp. xii, 750.
B5276 Adams, Henry H. *English Domestic, or Homiletic Tragedy, 1575 to 1642; Being an Account of the Development of the Tragedy of the Common Man Showing its Great Dependence on Religious Morality, Illustrated with Striking Examples of the Interposition of Providence for the Amendment of Men's Manners*. DD, Columbia University, 1944. Col. U. Studies in Engl. & Comp. Lit., No. 159. Columbia Univ. Press, 1943. Pp. 228.
       Rev: C282.
B5277 Lee, Alberta E. *Preaching in Elizabethan and Jacobean Drama*. DD, Columbia University, 1953. Pp. 341. Mic A54-164. *DA*, XIV (1954), 112. Publication No. 6657.
B5278 Austin, L. J. *Sixteenth and Seventeenth Century English Domestic Tragedy*. MA thesis, Nottingham, 1954.
B5279 Grivelet, Michel. *Thomas Heywood et le Drame Domestique Elizabéthain*. DD, Paris, 1956. Typewritten.

f. THE MASQUE (191;-)

B5280 Nicoll, Allardyce. *Stuart Masques and the Renaissance Stage*. London: Harrap, 1937. Pp. 224; 197 il. New York: Harcourt, 1938. Pp. 223.
       Rev: A7223.
B5281 McAnally, A. M. *Influence of the Masque on English Drama, 1608-1610*. DD, University of Oklahoma, 1939. Abstract in *University of Oklahoma Bulletin*, Jan., 1939, pp. 114.
B5282 Gombosi, Otto. "Some Musical Aspects of the English Court Masque." *Journal of the American Musicological Society*, I (Fall, 1948), 3-19.
B5283 Venezky, Alice S. *Pageantry on the Shakespearean Stage*. New York: Twayne Publishers, 1951. Pp. 242.
       Rev: A7238.
B5284 Long, John H. "Another Masque for *The Merry Wives of Windsor*." *SQ*, III (1952), 39-43.
B5285 Lees-Milne, James. *The Age of Inigo Jones*. London: Batsford, 1953. Pp. 242; il.
       Rev: by J. D. K. Lloyd, *Time and Tide*, Nov. 28, 1953, pp. 1557-58; by Clough Williams-Ellis, *Spectator*, Nov. 20, p. 599; *TLS*, Nov. 27, p. 756; by F. W. Wentworth-Shields, *FortnR*, 1044 (1953), 426-427; by John Summerson, *NstN*, Jan. 30, 1954, pp. 134-136.
B5286 Walton, Charles E. *The Impact of the Court Masque and the Blackfriars Upon the Staging of Elizabethan-Jacobean Drama*. DD, University of Missouri, 1953. Pp. 198. Mic A54-200. *DA*, XIV (1954), 136. Publication No. 6100.
B5287 Laird, David. *The Inserted Masque in Elizabethan and Jacobean Drama*. DD, University of Wisconsin, 1955. Pp. 196. Mic 55-1667. *DA*, XV (1955), 2527. Publication No. 14,714.
B5288 Palme, Per. *Triumph of Peace*. Stockholm: Almquist & Wiksell, 1956. Pp. 327.
       Rev: *TLS*, Dec. 21, 1956, p. 766.
B5289 Nicoll, Allardyce. "Shakespeare and the Court Masque." *SJ*, 94 (1958), 51-62.

g. PASTORAL PLAYS (191;-)

B5290 Empson, W. *Some Versions of Pastoral*. London, 1935. Pp. 298. Publ. in USA as *English*

Pastoral Poetry. New York: Norton, 1938. Pp. 298.
Shak., pp. 39-42, 89-115.
Rev: by Ben Belitt, *VQR*, XIV (1938), 602-606.

B5291 Wheeler, Harold P. *Studies in 16th Century English Literature of Rustic Life.* DD, University of Illinois, 1939.

B5292 Kirk, Florence Ada. *"The Faithful Shepherdess" by John Fletcher: A Critical Edition.* DD, Northwestern University, 1944. Abstr. publ. in *Summaries of Dissertations, 1944,* XII, Evanston: Northwestern Univ., 1945, pp. 16-19.
Sources discussed. Comparisons to Guarini and Tasso and *Dream.*

B5293 Gerhardt, Mia I. *La Pastorale: Essai d'Analyse Littéraire.* Assen: Van Gorcum, 1950. Pp. 317.
Rev: by A. Lytton Sells, *Fr. Studies,* V (1951), 161-163; by Alexandre Micha, *BHR,* XIII, 117-120; by C. Serrurier, *Neophil,* XXXV, 171-172.

B5294 Kermode, Frank, ed. *English Pastoral Poetry. From the Beginnings to Marvell.* Life, Literature and Thought Lib. London: Harrap, 1952. Pp. 256.
Chapters on Renaissance Pastoral theory and form and nearly 200 pages of texts.

B5295 Draper, R. P. *Shakespeare and the Pastoral.* DD, Nottingham, 1953.

B5296 Smith, Hallett. *Elizabethan Poetry: A Study in Conventions, Meaning, and Expression.* Harvard Univ. Press, 1953. Pp. xii, 355.
Rev: A8369.

B5297 Truesdale, Calvin William. *English Pastoral Verse from Spenser to Marvell: A Critical Revaluation.* DD, University of Washington, 1956. Pp. 342. Mic 57-1737. *DA,* XVII (1957), 1087. Publication No. 20,402.

B5298 Poggioli, Renato. "The Oaten Flute." *Harvard Library Bulletin,* XI (1957), 147-184.

B5299 Draper, R. P. "Shakespeare's Pastoral Comedy." *EA,* XI (1958), 1-17.

B5300 Summerell, Joseph Howard. *Backgrounds of Elizabethan Pastoral Drama.* DD, Columbia University, 1958. Pp. 268. Mic 58-7055. *DA,* XIX (1959), 2941.

2. THE PLAYS INDIVIDUALLY
HENRY VI (PARTS I-III) (196:70)
(1) THE TEXT
(a) OLD TEXTS

B5301 *The True Tragedy of Richard, Duke of York (Henry the Sixth, Part 3), 1595.* Ed. by Sir Walter Greg. Shakespeare Quarto Facsimiles, No. 11. Oxford: Clarendon Press, 1958. Pp. viii, 80.

(b) MODERN EDITIONS

B5302 *Henry VI.* Ed. with Introduction and notes by M. R. Ridley. New York: Dutton, 1936.

B5303 *Henry VI, Parts I, II, and III.* Ed. by J. Dover Wilson (The New Shakespeare). London and New York: Cambridge Univ. Press, 1952. Pp. lvi, 222; liv, 221; xlvi, 225.
Rev: *TLS,* Aug. 8, 1952, p. 513; by Ben Ray Redman, *SatR,* July 19, p. 30; *N &Q,* 197 (1952), 549-550; by Andrew S. Cairncross, *RES,* IV (1953), 157-160; by Hermann Heuer, *SJ,* 89 (1953), 218-219; by G. Blakemore Evans, *SQ,* IV, 84-92; by H. Craig, *SQ,* IV, 117; by A. Koszul, *EA,* VII (1954), 324; by Harold Jenkins, *ShS,* VII, 138-140; by James G. McManaway, ibid., pp. 147-148; by Robert Fricker, *ES,* XXXVII (1956), 18-24.

B5304 *King Henry VI, Part 2.* Ed. by Andrew S. Cairncross. Arden Shakespeare. London: Methuen, 1956. Pp. liv, 197. Introduction offers detailed study of the text, principally the problem of the copy behind Q_1 and F_1. 1590 proposed as date of play.
Rev: *Dublin Mag.,* July-Sept., 1957, pp. 69-70; *N &Q,* NS, IV, 227-228; by Pat M. Ryan, Jr., *QJS,* XLIII, 311-312; *TLS,* Mar. 8, p. 151; *SCN,* XV, 24; by J. Vallette, *MdF,* 330 (1957), 710-711; by George Walton Williams, *MLR,* LIII (1958), 236-237; by G. Blakemore Evans, *SQ,* IX, 61-63; by Hermann Heuer, *SJ,* 94 (1958), 288-291; by J. P. Brockbank, *RES,* NS, IX, 431-432; by R. A. Foakes, *DUJ,* XIX, 89-90; by J. G. McManaway, *ShS,* XI, 150-151; by J. A. Bryant, *SR,* LXVI, 325.

(c) EMENDATIONS

B5305 Yates, Frances A. "Elizabeth as Astraea." *JWCI,* X (1947), 27-82.

B5306 Koszul, A. "Some Notes on Shakespeare's Text." *ES,* XXXI (1950), 215-217.
1 Henry VI, I. v. 29.

B5307 Duncan-Jones, E. E. " 'Forlorn' in *Cymbeline* and *1 Henry VI.*" *N &Q,* NS, IV (1957), 64.

B5308 Hudson, Arthur Palmer. "To Shake Hands with Death." *MLN,* LIII (1938), 510-513.

2. LITERARY GENESIS AND ANALOGUES

B5309 Denny, C. F. *Discrimination of the Sources of "1 Henry VI" an Indication of Revision.* MS thesis, Stanford University, 1936. Pp. 120.

B5310 King, Lucille. *The Relations of the Henry VI plays to the Chronicle Histories of Hall and Holinshed.* DD, University of Texas, 1936.

B5311 King, Lucille. "Text Sources of the Folio and Quarto *Henry VI*." *PMLA*, LI (1936), 702-718.

B5312 Taylor, Rupert. "A Tentative Chronology of Marlowe's and Some Other Elizabethan Plays." *PMLA*, LI (1936), 643-688.

B5313 Denny, Charles F. "The Sources of *I Henry VI* as an Indication of Revision." *PQ*, XVI (1937), 225-248.

B5314 Knickerbocker, William S. "Shakespearean Alarum." *SR*, XLV (1937), 91-105. Answer by A. Gaw, ibid., pp. 106-107.

B5315 Knickerbocker, William S. "Shakespearean Excursion. Who Wrote *2 and 3 Henry VI?*" *SR*, XLV (1937), 328-342.

B5316 McKerrow, R. B. "A Note on the Bad Quartos of *2 and 3 Henry VI* and the Folio Text." *RES*, XIII (1937), 64-72.

B5317 Williams, C. "Joan of Arc." *Stories of Great Names*, London, 1937, pp. 87-111.

B5318 Greer, Clayton Alvis. "The Place of *I Henry VI* in the York-Lancaster Tetralogy." *PMLA*, LIII (1938), 687-701.

B5319 Boas, F. S. *Christopher Marlowe: A Biographical and Critical Study*. Clarendon Press, 1940. Pp. 347. Discusses, i.a., *2 and 3 Henry VI*.
     Rev: A4867.

B5320 Peterson, Earl H. *Early English Chronicle and Biographical Antecedents of 1 Henry VI*. DD, University of Illinois, 1940.

B5321 Smith, Marion B. *Marlowe's Imagery and the Marlowe Canon*. Univ. of Pennsylvania Press, 1940. Pp. vii, 213.
     Chapter on *Henry VI*.
     Rev: by Una Ellis-Fermor, *MLR*, XL (1945), 136.

B5322 McChristy, Cleo G. *A Comparative Textual Study of "The True Tragedie," "The Whole Contention," and the First Folio Edition of Shakespeare's "Henry VI, Part III."* DD, University of Texas, 1941.

B5323 Greer, C. A. "Revision and Adaptation in *1 Henry VI*." *TxSE*, 1942, pp. 110-120.

B5324 Thomas, Sidney. *The Antic Hamlet and Richard III*. New York: King's Crown Press, 1943. Pp. 92.
     Contains a note on *2 Henry VI* and its relation to the *Contention*.

B5325 Munro, John. "Some Matters Shakespearian." *TLS*, Oct. 11, 1947, p. 528.

B5326 Rubow, Paul V. *Shakespeare og hans Samtidige*. Copenhagen: Gyldendal, 1948. Pp. 155. Essay on *Henry VI*.
     Rev: C74.

B5327 Atkinson, A. D. "Notes on *Richard II*." *N &Q*, 194 (1949), 190-192, 212-214.
     I: "*Richard II* and the Revision of *2 Henry VI*, III, i."

B5328 Carrère, Félix Jean. *Le Théâtre de Thomas Kyd. Contribution à l'Etude du Drame Elizabéthain*. Thèse de lettres, Paris, 1949. Toulouse: Edouard Privat, Editeur, 14, Rue des Arts, 1951.
     Rev: A4979.

B5329 M. Clotilde Douglas, Sister. *King Henry the Sixth in Document, Chronicle and Drama*. DD, St. John's University, 1949. Pp. 174. Abstr. publ. in *Abstracts of Dissertations, 1949-1950*, Brooklyn: St. John's Univ., 1950, pp. 12-14. Authorship and sources discussed.

B5330 Greer, C. A. "More About the Revision Date of *I Henry VI*." *N &Q*, 195 (1950), 112.

B5331 Kirschbaum, Leo. "The Authorship of *I Henry VI*." *PMLA*, LXVII (1952), 809-822.

B5332 Feuillerat, Albert. *The Composition of Shakespeare's Plays: Authorship, Chronology*. Yale Univ. Press, 1953. Pp. vii, 340.
     Rev: A3286.

B5333 Richardson, Arleigh D., III. *An Edition of the First Part of the Contention Betwixt the Two Famous Houses of Yorke and Lancaster*. DD, Yale University, 1953.

B5334 Walters, R. N. *Machiavelli and the Elizabethan Drama*. M. Litt. thesis, Cambridge, 1953. *Cam Abs.*, 1952-53, p. 80.

B5335 Brockbank, J. P. *Shakespeare's Historical Myth: A Study of Shakespeare's Adaptations of His Sources in Making the Plays of "Henry VI" and "Richard III."* DD, Cambridge, 1954. *Cam Abs.*, 1953-54, p. 97.

B5336 Kernan, Alvin B. "A Comparison of the Imagery in *3 Henry VI* and *The True Tragedie of Richard, Duke of York*." *SP*, LI (1954), 431-442.

B5337 Law, Robert Adger. "Edmund Mortimer in Shakespeare and Hall." *SQ*, V (1954), 425-436.

B5338 Prouty, Charles T. *The Contention and Shakespeare's 2 Henry VI: A Comparative Study*. New Haven: Yale Univ. Press; Oxford Univ. Press, 1954. Pp. ix, 157.
     Rev: by G. B. Harrison, *SatR*, Sept. 25, 1954, p. 22; by G. Blakemore Evans, *JEGP*, LIII, 628-637; *U. S. Quarterly Book Review*, X, 333; by C. G. Thayer, *Books Abroad*, XXIX (1955), 349; by William T. Hastings, *SQ*, VI, 119-121; by H. T. Price, *MLN*, LXX, 527-529; by John Crow, *SQ*, VII (1956), 420-431; by Hermann Heuer, *SJ*, 92 (1956), 391-393; by G. I. Duthie, *MP*, LIII, 200-204; by James G. McManaway, *ShS*, IX, 153-154; by G. Lambin, *LanM*, XLIX, 463; by J. P. Brockbank, *RES*, NS, VIII (1957), 60-63.

B5339 Rees, Joan. "A Passage in *Henry VI, Part 3.*" *N &Q*, NS, I (1954), 195-196.

B5340 Charlton, H. B., and R. D. Waller, eds. *Edward II.* 2nd ed. London: Methuen, 1955. First publ. 1933.
"Reviser's Note," pp. 212-225, discusses interrelations of this and Shak.'s early history plays.

B5341 Law, Robert Adger. "The Chronicles and the Three Parts of *Henry VI.*" *TxSE*, XXXIII (1955), 13-32.

B5342 Brooking, Jack Thomas. *The Influence of the Trial Notes on Five Major Joan of Arc Plays.* DD, Western Reserve University, 1956. Abstr. publ. in *Bibliography of Publication . . . and Abstracts of Dissertations . . . of Western Reserve University*, July 1, 1954 to June 30, 1956, Cleveland: Western Reserve, n.d., pp. 125-128.
All five are 20th century plays, but some previous notice is taken of *I Henry VI.*

B5343 Greer, C. A. "The Quarto-Folio Relationship in *2 and 3 Henry VI* Once Again." *N &Q*, NS, III (1956), 420-421.

B5344 Greer, Clayton A. "More About the Actor-Reporter in *The Contention* and *True Tragedy.*" *N &Q*, NS, IV (1957), 52-53.

B5345 McManaway, James G. "*The Contention* and *2 Henry VI.*" *Brunner Festschrift.* *Wiener Beiträge zur Englischen Philologie*, LXV (1957), 143-155.

B5346 Kendall, Paul Murray. *Warwick the Kingmaker.* New York: Norton, 1957. Pp. 408. London: Allen and Unwin, 1958. Pp. 365.
Rev: by Garrett Mattingly, *SatR*, Nov. 23, 1957, p. 43; *TLS*, April 18, 1958, p. 206; by A. R. Myers, *History Today*, VIII, 64; *VQR*, XXXIV, No. 2, lx; by Gerald Hamilton, *Spectator*, Jan. 10, p. 52.

B5347 Cancelled.

B5348 McNeal, Thomas H. "Margaret of Anjou: Romantic Princess and Troubled Queen." *SQ*, IX (1958), 1-10.

B5349 McNeal, Thomas H. "Shakespeare's Cruel Queens." *HLQ*, XXII (1958), 41-50.

B5350 Salls, H. H. "Joan of Arc in English and American Literature." *South Atlantic Quar.*, XXXV (1936), 167-184.

B5351 Messiaen, P. "La Trilogie de *Henry VI.*" *RCC*, XXXIX (1938), 137-156.

B5352 Blair, Seabury M. *Shakespeare's Use of the Jack Cade Scenes in "2 Henry VI."* DD, University of Washington, 1939. Abstr. in *Abstracts of Theses*, IV (1939), 111-112.

B5353 Ruddy, J. *Typical Dramatic Treatment of Joan of Arc.* MS thesis, Columbia University, 1947. Pp. 85.

B5354 Aramus, Rudolf. "Shakespeare und die Jungfrau von Orleans." *Die Kommenden*, IV, No. 7 (1950), 5.

B5355 Cairncross, A. S. "An 'Inconsistency' in *3 Henry VI.*" *MLR*, L (1955), 492-494.
Completes the explanation, begun by Tucker Brooke, of the puzzling role of Montague.

B5356 Gerevini, S. "Shakespeare 'Corvo Rifatto'." *Letterature Moderne*, VII, No. 2 (1957).

B5357 Leech, Clifford. "The Two-Part Play. Marlowe and the Early Shakespeare." *SJ*, 94 (1958), 90-106.

(3) USE OF LANGUAGE
(4) GENERAL CRITICISM OF THE PLAY
(5) CHARACTERIZATION

B5358 Swayne, Mattie. "Shakespeare's King Henry VI as a Pacifist." *CE*, III (1941), 143-149.
Merits of pacifism and dangers when in heads of state. Henry VI as an obtuse idealist.

B5359 Carré, Henri. "C'Est Shakespeare Qui a, le Premier, Réhabilité Jeanne d'Arc dans l'Opinion Anglaise." *Figaro Litt.*, May 7, 1949, p. 3.

B5360 Friedland, Elias. *Shakespeare's Jack Cade.* MA thesis, University of North Carolina, 1949. Abstr. publ. in *Univ. of North Carolina Record, Research in Progress*, Jan.-Dec., 1949, Grad. School Series, No. 58, pp. 118-119.

B5361 M. J. Frances Hoey, Sister. *Shakespeare and Two Women: A Study of Eleanor of Aquitaine anp Margaret of Anjou.* DD, St. John's University, 1950. Abstr. publ. in *Abstracts of Dissertations, 1949-1950*, Brooklyn: St. John's Univ., 1950, pp. 14-16.
Characters of the real women according to their representations in the plays.

B5362 Itschert, Hans. *Die Warwick-Figur in Shakespeares "König Heinrich VI."* *Zum Gestaltproblem von Shakespeares früher Historientrilogie.* DD, Mainz, 1950. Pp. 152. Typewritten.

B5363 Kilga, Johanna F. *Joan of Arc bei Shakespeare, Schiller und Shaw.* DD, Vienna, 1951. Pp. 87. Typewritten.

B5364 Boas, F. S. "Joan of Arc in Shakespeare, Schiller, and Shaw." *SQ*, II (1951), 35-45.

(6) MISCELLANEOUS ITEMS

B5365 Cairncross, A. S. *The Problem of Hamlet: A Solution.* London: Macmillan, 1936. Pp. xix, 205. Rev: B4916.

B5366 Jordan, John E. "The Reporter of *Henry VI, Part 2.*" *PMLA*, LXIV (1949), 1089-113.

B5367 Atkinson, A. D. "Notes on *Richard II.*" *N &Q*, 194 (1949), 190-192; 212-214.
Connections between *Richard II* and *2 Henry VI*.

B5368 Cazamian, Louis. *The Development of English Humor.* Duke Univ. Press, 1952. Pp. viii, 421.
Rev: B5186.

B5369 Jackson, Sir Barry. "On Producing *Henry VI.*" *ShS*, VI (1953), 49-52.

B5370 Draper, John William. "The Turk in *Henry VI, Part I.*" *West Virginia University Bulletin, Philological Studies*, X (1956), 37-39.

(7) SUBSEQUENT HISTORY OF THE PLAY
(Other than productions after 1660)

KING RICHARD III (198;71)
(1) THE TEXT
(a) OLD TEXTS

B5371 Kerr, Ada B. "*The History of King Richard III*": A Critical Study. MA thesis, Toronto, 1934
Pp. 97.

B5372 Patrick, David L. *Textual History of Shakespeare's "Richard III."* DD, Stanford University, 1935. Abstr. publ. in *Abstracts of Dissertations*, Stanford Univ., X (1934-35), 43-45.

B5373 Greg, W. W. "*Richard III*—Q₅ (1612)." *Library*, NS, XVII (1936), 88-97.
Concludes that sheets A, B, and D of Q_5 were printed from Q_4; sheets C and E—M from Q_3.

B5374 Patrick, David L. *The Textual History of "Richard III."* Stanford Univ. Press, 1936. Pp. 153.
Rev: by Samuel A. Tannenbaum, *SAB*, XII (1937), 192; by O. J. Campbell, *MLN*, LIII (1938), 391-394; by H. T. Price, *JEGP*, XXXVII (1938), 428-431; by Alice Walker, *RES*, XIV, 468-469; by Alois Brandl, *Archiv*, 172 (1938), 249; by W. W. Greg, *Library*, NS, XIX, 118-120.

B5375 Griffin, William J. "An Omission in the Folio Text of *Richard III.*" *RES*, XIII (1937), 329-332.
Explains the omission of the "clock passage."

B5375a Spencer, Hazelton. "The Clock Passage in *Richard III.*" *RES*, XIV (1938), 205.

B5376 Feuillerat, Albert. *The Composition of Shakespeare's Plays: Authorship, Chronology.* Yale Univ. Press, 1953. Pp. viii, 340.
Rev: A3286.

B5377 Wilson, J. Dover. "On Editing Shakespeare with Special Reference to the Problems of *Richard III.*" *Talking of Shakespeare*, ed. by John Garrett. London: Hodder & Stoughton & Max Reinhardt, 1954.

B5378 Walton, J. K. *The Copy for the Folio Text of "Richard III."* With a Note on the Copy for the Folio Text of *King Lear.* Monograph Series, No. 1. Auckland University College, New Zealand: The Pilgrim Press, 1955. Pp. 164.
Rev: A3301.

B5379 Cairncross, Andrew S. "The Quartos and the Folio Text of *Richard III.*" *RES*, VIII (1957), 225-233.

B5380 Oyama, Toshikazu. "The Folio Copy of *Richard III.*" *Otsuka Festschrift*, 1958, pp. 369-378.

B5381 Walton, J. K. "Coincidental Variants in *Richard III.*" *Library*, 5th Series, XIII (1958), 139-140.

(b) MODERN EDITIONS

B5382 *Richard III.* Ed. by L. Aldred. London: Macmillan, 1936. Pp. 216.

B5383 *The Tragedy of King Richard III.* Ed. by Kurt Schrey. Paderborn: Schöningh, 1946. Pp. 48.

B5384 *The Tragedy of Richard the Third.* Ed. G. B. Harrison. London: Penguin Books, 1953. Pp. 159.

B5385 *Richard III.* Acting edition. London: S. French, 1953. Pp. 116.

B5386 *Richard III.* Ed. by J. Dover Wilson. (The New Shakespeare.) Cambridge Univ. Press, 1954.
Rev: *TLS*, Jan. 29, 1954, p. 79; *N &Q*, NS, I, 275; by T. S. Dorsch, *YWES*, XXXV, 81; by Wolfgang Clemen, *Archiv*, 192 (1955), 203-204; by I. B. Cauthen, Jr., *SQ*, VI, 174-176; *ShN*, V, 42; by Hermann Heuer, *SJ*, 92 (1956), 394-395.

B5387 *Richard III.* Ed. by Francis Fergusson and Charles Jasper Sisson (Laurel Shakespeare). With a Modern Commentary by Stuart Vaughan. New York: Dell Publishing Co., 1958. Pp. 254.

(c) EMENDATIONS

B5388 Praz, Mario. "*King Richard III*, I, iii, 241." *TLS*, Nov. 11, 1939, p. 655.
See letter by H. H. C., *TLS*, Nov. 18, 1939, p. 675.

B5389 Maas, P. "Two Passages in *Richard III.*" *RES*, XVIII (1942), 315-317.

B5390 Cunningham, J. V. " 'Tragedy' in Shakespeare." *ELH*, XVII (1950), 36-46. [III. v. 8.]

B5391 Parsons, Howard. "*Richard III.*" *N &Q*, NS, II (1955), 175-176; 288-289.
Readings of I.i. 9; I.i. 14; and of I.ii. 75, 117; I.iii. 289, respectively.

B5392 Thompson, Marjorie. "The Clarence Scenes in *Richard III.* A Query concerning the New

Cambridge Edition." *MLR*, LI (1956), 221-223.
Questions whether the Clarence passages (I.i), at least those derived from the *Mirror*, were an afterthought.

B5393 Cairncross, Andrew S. "Coincidental Variants in *Richard III*." *Library*, XII (1957), 187-190.

(2) LITERARY GENESIS AND ANALOGUES

B5394 Mancini, Dominic. *The Ursurpation of "Richard the Third." Dominicus Mancinus ad Angelum Catonem de Occupatione Regni Anglie per Riccardum Tercium Libellus.* Now first Printed and Translated with an Intro. by C. A. J. Armstrong. New York: Oxford Univ. Press, 1936. Pp. xv, 172.
Rev: *TLS*, July 18, 1936, p. 588; by A. B. White, *AHR*, XLII (1937), 737-738.

B5395 Spargo, J. W. "Clarence in the Malmsey-Butt." *MLN*, LI (1936), 166-173.

B5396 Taylor, Rupert. "A Tentative Chronology of Marlowe's and Some Other Elizabethan Plays." *PMLA*, LI (1936), 643-688.

B5397 Thaler, Alwin. "Shakspere, Daniel, and Everyman." *PQ*, XV (1936), 217-218.

B5398 Fletcher, B. J. *Shakespeare's Use of Holinshed's Chronicles in "Richard III," "Richard II," "Henry IV," and "Macbeth."* DD, University of Texas, 1937.

B5399 Glunz, H. *Shakespeare und Morus.* Kölner Anglistische Arbeiten, XXXII. Bochum Langen-dreer: Pöppinghaus, 1938. Pp. ix, 267.
Thomas More's *Historia Richardi Tertii* and Shak.'s *Richard III*.
Rev: A4687.

B5400 Smith, Marion B. *Marlowe's Imagery and the Marlowe Canon.* University of Pennsylvania Press, 1940. Pp. vii, 213. Chapter upon *Richard III*.
Rev: B5321.

B5401 Zeeveld, W. Gordon. "A Tudor Defense of *Richard III*." *PMLA*, LV (1940), 946-957.
Authorship of *The History of Richard III*, commonly attributed to Sir Thomas More.

B5402 Semper, I. J. "Shakespeare and St. Thomas More." *Catholic Educational Review*, XXXIX (1941), 166-172.

B5403 Thaler, Alwin. *Shakespeare and Democracy.* Univ. Tennessee Press, 1941. Pp. xii, 312. Chapter XIII contains a note on *Richard III*.
Rev: A1809.

B5404 Dean, Leonard F. "Literary Problems in More's *Richard III*." *PMLA*, LVIII (1943), 22-41.

B5405 Nearing, Homer. "Julius Caesar and the Tower of London." *MLN*, LXIII (1948), 228-233.

B5406 Carrère, Félix Jean. *Le Théâtre de Thomas Kyd. Contribution à l'Etude du Drame Elizabéthain.* Thèse de Lettres, Paris, 1949. Publ. Toulouse: Edouard Privat, Editeur, 14, Rue des Arts, 1951.
Rev: A4979.

B5407 Maugeri, Aldo. *"Edward II," "Richard III" and "Richard II," Note Critiche.* Messina: V. Ferrara, 1952. Pp. 63.

B5408 Wilson, J. Dover. "Shakespeare's *Richard III* and *The True Tragedy of Richard the Third*, 1594." *SQ*, III (1952), 299-306.
The True Tragedy is not a bad quarto of *Richard III*; rather, Shakespeare borrowed from it or from the play it "misrepresents."

B5409 Roth, Cecil. "Shakespeare and the Jewish Liturgy." *TLS*, May 15, 1953, p. 317.
Points out "a parallel to the Jewish liturgy in Richmond's prayer before sleep," *R. III*, V.iii. 112-114.

B5410 Glover, A. S. B. "Shakespeare and the Jewish Liturgy." *TLS*, May 22, 1953, p. 333.

B5411 Walters, R. N. *Machiavelli and the Elizabethan Drama.* M. Litt. thesis, Cambridge, 1953. *Cam Abs.*, 1952-53, p. 80.

B5412 Brockbank, J. P. *Shakespeare's Historical Myth: A Study of Shakespeare's Adaptations of His Sources in Making the Plays of "Henry VI" and "Richard III."* DD, Cambridge, 1954. *Cam Abs.*, 1953-54, p. 97.

B5413 *Richard III.* Ed. by J. Dover Wilson (The New Shakespeare). Cambridge Univ. Press, 1954. Pp. lxiii, 280.
Has an introduction concerning the sources of the play.
Rev: B5386.

B5414 Hallam, George W. "A Note on the O.E.D." *N &Q*, NS, II (1955), 97.

B5415 Kendall, Paul Murray. *Richard the Third.* London: Allen and Unwin, 1955. Pp. 514. New York: Norton, 1956. Pp. 602. Tr. by Arthur Seiffhart and Hermann Rinn. Munich: Callwey, 1957. Pp. 487.
Rev: by D. W., *Tablet*, 206 (1955), 551-552; by C. E. Carrington, *Time and Tide*, XXXVI, 1533-34; *TLS*, Dec. 30, p. 787; by H. R. Trevor-Roper, *NstN*, LI (1956), 18; *Listener*, LV, 67; by B. Miller, *TC*, 159 (1956), 210; by B. H. Carroll, Jr., *English Jour.*, XLV, 569; by Roger B. Dooley, *Catholic World*, Nov., pp. 153-154; by James G. McManaway, *NYTBR*, Aug. 26, p. 3; by Orville Prescott, *New York Times*, Aug. 24; by Garrett Mattingly, *NYHTBR*, Aug. 26, p. 1; by Geoffrey Bruun, *SatR*, Sept. 8, pp. 44-45;

by G. P. Cuttino, *VQR*, XXXII, 622-625; by Hermann Heuer, *SJ*, 93 (1957), 264-265; by Arthur B. Ferguson, *South Atlantic Quarterly*, LVI, 385-387.

B5416   Meierl, Elisabeth. *Shakespeare's "Richard III" und Seine Quelle. Die Bedeutung der Chronik für die Entwicklung des Shakespeareschen Dramas.* DD, Munich, 1955.

B5417   Mary Faith Schuster, Sister, O. S. B. "Philosophy of Life and Prose Style in Thomas More's *Richard III* and Francis Bacon's *Henry VII.*" *PMLA*, LXX (1955), 474-487.

B5418   Cross, Gustav. "More's *Historie of Kyng Rycharde the Third* and *Lust's Dominion.*" *N &Q*, NS, IV (1957), 198-199.
         Notes the indebtedness of *Lust's Dominion* to *Titus.*

B5419   Lordi, Robert Joseph. *Thomas Legge's "Richardus Tertius": A Critical Edition with a Translation.* DD, University of Illinois, 1958. Pp. 767. Mic 58-1719. *DA*, XVIII (1958), 1787.

B5420   Shapiro, I. A. "*Richard II* or *Richard III* or . . .?" *SQ*, IX (1958), 204-206.

B5421   Wilson, J. Dover. "The Composition of the Clarence Scenes in *Richard III.*" *MLR*, LIII (1958), 211-214.
         See Marjorie Thompson's note, *MLR*, LI, 221-223, B5392.

(3) USE OF LANGUAGE

B5422   Dollarhide, Louis E. *Shakespeare's "Richard III" and Renaissance Rhetoric.* DD, Univ. of North Carolina, 1954.

B5423   Finkenstaedt, Thomas. *Die Verskunst des Jungen Shakespeare: "Richard III," "Richard II," "King John."* DD, Munich, 1955. Pp. x, 155. Typewritten.

(4) GENERAL CRITICISM OF THE PLAY

B5424   Valentiner, T. "Shakespeares *Richard III*, Englische Politik im Spiegel Englischer Dichtung." *Der dts. Erzieher.* Beil. Mitteilungsblatt des NSLB., Gauwaltg. Weser-Ems, 1940, pp. 57-59.

B5425   Small, Samuel A. "Shakspere's Stage Business." *SAB*, XVIII (1943), 66-71.

B5426   Law, Robert Adger. "*Richard the Third*: A Study in Shakespeare's Composition." *PMLA*, LX (1945), 689-696.

B5427   Palmer, John. *Political Characters of Shakespeare.* London: Macmillan, 1945. Pp. xii, 335.
         Rev: A6550a.

B5428   Smith, Fred Manning. "The Relation of *Macbeth* to *Richard the Third.*" *PMLA*, LX (1945), 1003-20.

B5429   Draper, John W. "Patterns of Tempo in *Richard III.*" *N. Mitt.*, L (1949), 1-12.

B5430   Williams, Philip. "*Richard the Third*: The Battle Orations." *Eng. Studies in Honor of James Southall Wilson*, Univ. of Virginia, 1951, pp. 125-130.

B5431   Clemen, Wolfgang H. "Tradition and Originality in Shakespeare's *Richard III.*" *SQ*, V (1954), 247-257.

B5432   Arnold, Aerol. "The Recapitulation Dream in *Richard III* and *Macbeth.*" *SQ*, VI (1955), 51-62.

B5433   Clemen, Wolfgang. *Clarences Traum und Ermordung.* Munich, 1955. Pp. 46.
         Rev: A6454.

B5434   Nathan, Norman. "The Marriage of Richard and Anne." *N &Q*, NS, II (1955), 55-56.

B5435   Rubow, Paul V. *Shakespeares Ungdomsstykker.* The Royal Danish Scientifical Society: Historical-Philosophical Informations, Vol. XXXIV, No. 5. Copenhagen: Munksgaard, 1955. Pp. 34.

B5436   Baldini, Gabriele. "Osservazioni sul Riccardo III di Shakespeare e di Olivier." *Bianco e Nero* (Rome), XVIII (1957), No. 1.

B5437   Castello, Guilio Cesare. "La Tradizione Interpretativa di Riccardo III." *Bianco e Nero* (Rome), XVIII (1957), No. 1.

B5438   Clemen, Wolfgang. *Kommentar zu Shakespeares "Richard III."* Interpretation eines Dramas. Göttingen: Vandenhoech & Ruprecht, 1957. Pp. 356.
         Rev: by H. Oppel, *NS*, VI (1957), 491-492; by L. L. Schücking, *Neue Zürcher Ztg.*, Sept. 11; by Rudolf Stamm, *Archiv*, 195 (1958), 200-201; by Rolf Soellner, *JEGP*, LVII, 545-547; by Max Lüthi, *Anglia*, LXXVI, 307-312; by Hermann Heuer, *SJ*, 94 (1958), 268-272; by A. Schlösser, *DLZ*, LXXIX, 318-320; by A. Rousseau, *LanM*, LII, 271-272; by A. Rousseau, *RLC*, XXXII, 591-593.

B5439   Gerevini, Silvano. *Il testo del "Riccardo III" di Shakespeare.* Saggio Critico. Pavia: E. Cortina, 1957. Pp. 102.

B5440   Rosier, James Louis. *The Chain of Sin and Privation in Elizabethan Literature.* DD, Stanford University, 1958. Pp. 240. Mic 58-4326. *DA*, XVIII (1958), 583. Publ. No. 25,387.
         Chapter VI on Shak.

(5) CHARACTERIZATION

B5441   Rank, O. "Shakespeares Vaterkomplex." *Das Inzest-Motiv in Dichtung und Sage*, Leipzig, 1912, pp. 204-233.

B5442   Freud, S. "Einige Charaktertypen aus der Psychoanalyt. Arbeit." *Imago*, IV (1916), 317, and *Sammlg. kl. Schr. Z. Neur.*, IV Folge, p. 521.

B5443 Freud, S. "Some Character-Types Met with in Psycho-Analytic Work." Trans. by E. Colburn Mayne, *Collected Papers*, IV, 318-344. Also in the Standard Edition of the Complete Psychological Works, ed. James Strachey and others, Vol. XIV (1957), 309-333. *R. III*, pp. 314-315.

B5444 Adler, Charles A. "Richard III—His Significance as a Study in Criminal Life-Style." *International Journal of Individual Psychology*, II (1936), 55-60.

B5445 Mutz, W. *Der Charakter Richards III. in der Darstellung des Chronisten Holinshed und des Dramatikers Shakespeare, mit einem Beitrag zu seiner Charakterpsyche.* DD, Berlin, 1936. Pp. 74.
Rev: by A. Brandl, *Archiv*, 171 (1937), 260.

B5446 Hofmüller, Rudolf. "Shakespeares *Richard III.* im Residenztheater. Der Epilog zu den Königsdramen. Politische Weltschau im Drama. Charakterbild eines Tyrannen." *VB* (Mü), Oct. 15, 1937.

B5447 Goll, A. "Richard III as the Criminal Type." J. Moritzen, tr. *Journal of Criminal Law and Criminology*, XXX (1939), 22-35.

B5448 Cancelled.

B5449 Thomas, Sidney. *The Antic Hamlet and Richard III.* New York: King's Crown Press, 1943. Pp. 92.

B5450 Edmunds, Winifred Egan. "The History of the Criticism of the Character of Richard III." MA thesis, University of North Carolina, 1945. Abstr. publ. in *Univ. of North Carolina Record, Research in Progress*, Grad. School Series No. 50, 1946. Pp. 152.

B5451 Armstrong, W. A. "The Elizabethan Conception of the Tyrant." *RES*, XXII (1946), 161-181.

B5452 Balchin, Nigel. "The Villain as Tyrant: Richard III." Balchin's *The Anatomy of Villainy.* London, 1950, pp. 34-51.

B5453 M. J. Frances Hoey, Sister. *Shakespeare and Two Women: A Study of Eleanor of Aquitaine and Margaret of Anjou.* DD, St. John's University, 1950. Abstr. publ. in *Abstracts of Dissertations, 1949-1950*, Brooklyn: St. John's Univ., 1950, pp. 14-16.

B5454 Wada, Yuchi. "Machiavellism and Richard III." *Eibungakukenkyu*, XXVII (1951), 179-191.

B5455 Clemen, Wolfgang. "Clarences Traum und Ermordung." (*Richard III*, I.iv) *Sitzungsberichte d. Bayer. Akadmie d. Wissenschaften.* Munich, 1955. Pp. 46.

B5456 Smith, Gordon Ross. *Good in Evil in Shakespearean Tragedy.* DD, The Pennsylvania State University, 1956. Pp. 446. Mic 57-568. *DA*, XVII (1957), 358. Publ. No. 19,323.

B5457 Coe, Charles Norton. *Shakespeare's Villains.* New York, 1957.
Rev: A6796.

B5458 Wilson, J. D. "A Note on *Richard III*: The Bishop of Ely's Strawberries." *MLR*, LII (1957), 563-564.
Favorable comment on Dr. J. Swift Joly's theory (*British Med. Jour.*, June 15, 1956) that Richard ate the strawberries to produce a rash on his arm which would be accepted as witchcraft.

B5459 Zuk, Gerald H. "A Note on Richard's Anxiety Dreams." *American Imago*, XIV (1957), 37-39.

(6) MISCELLANEOUS ITEMS

B5460 Sachs, Hanns. "Aesthetics and Psychology of the Artist." *International Journal of Psycho-Analysis*, II (1921), 98-100.

B5461 Schücking, Levin L. *Über Einige Nachbesserungen bei Shakespeare.* Leipzig: Hirzel, 1943. Pp. 66.

B5462 Shanker, S. "Shakespeare Pays Some Compliments." *MLN*, LXIII (1948), 540-541.

B5463 Filipič, Lojze. "Drama o Zločincu." *Naši Razgledi* (Maribor), I, No. 6 (1952), 17-18.

B5464 Fusillo, Robert James. "Tents on Bosworth Field." *SQ*, VI (1955), 193-194.

B5464a Hosley, Richard. "More About 'Tents' on Bosworth Field." *SQ*, VII (1956), 458-459. On B5464.

B5465 Driver, Tom Faw. *The Sense of History in Greek and Shakespearean Dramatic Form.* DD, Columbia University, 1957. Pp. 397. Mic 57-2807. *DA*, XVII (1957), 1748. Publ. No. 21,781.

(7) SUBSEQUENT HISTORY OF THE PLAY
(Other than productions after 1660)

B5466 Van Lennep, William. "*Richard the Third.*" *TLS*, April 30, 1938, p. 296.
See letter by Montague Summers, *TLS*, May 7, 1938, p. 316; by William Van Lennep, ibid., June 18, p. 418. (Dating of a Restoration performance.)

B5467 McElderry, B. R., Jr. "J. R. Lowell and *Richard III*—A Bibliographical Error." *N &Q*, NS, V (1958), 179-180.
Although *Richard the Third and the Primrose Criticism* is attributed to Lowell in two major bibliographical sources, it is really an anonymous reply to Lowell's views on *Richard III*.

THE COMEDY OF ERRORS (194;69)
(1) THE TEXT
(a) Modern Editions

B5468   *Comedy of Errors.* Ed. by L. Raines. University of Alabama, 1941. Pp. 22. Acting version, printed as prose; typed and mimeographed.

B5469   *The Comedy of Errors.* Ed. by G. B. Harrison. London: Penguin Books, 1955. Pp. 96.
      Rev: *TLS*, Feb. 3, 1956, p. 75.

B5470   *The Comedy of Errors.* Ed. by Felicina Rota. Scrittori Inglesi, Collezione Diretta da G. Baldini. Rome: A Signorelli (Tip. A. Castaldi), 1956. Pp. 84.

(b) EMENDATIONS

B5471   Cunningham, J. V. " 'Tragedy' in Shakespeare." *ELH*, XVII (1950), 36-46.
      I.i.64.

B5472   Koszul, A. "Some Notes on Shakespeare's Text." *ES*, XXXI (1950), 215-217.
      III.i.65 ("weren't" for *went*).

B5473   Maxwell, J. C. "*Comedy of Errors* III.i.64-65." *ES*, XXXII (1951), 30.
      Argues against B5472.

B5474   Parsons, Howard. *Emendations to Three of Shakespeare's Plays.* London: Ettrick Press, 1953. Pp. 21.
      Rev: by I. B. Cauthen, *SQ*, V (1954), 423-424.

B5475   Weld, John S. "Old Adam New Apparelled." *SQ*, VII (1956), 453-456.
      IV.iii.13.

B5476   Main, C. F. "Benlowes, Brome, and the Bejewelled Nose." *N &Q*, NS, IV (1957), 232-233.
      II.ii.136-141.

B5477   Hulme, Hilda M. "On the Meaning of *Copy* (*Comedy of Errors*, V.i.62)." *Neophil*, Jan. 1958, pp. 73-74.

B5478   Purcell, J. M. "*Comedy of Errors*, II.ii.57." *N &Q*, NS, V (1958), 180.

(2) LITERARY GENESIS AND ANALOGUES

B5479   Parks, George B. "Shakespeare's Map for *The Comedy of Errors*." *JEGP*, XXXIX (1940), 93-97.

B5480   Baldwin, T. W. *Shakspere's Five-Act Structure: Shakspere's Early Plays on the Background of the Renaissance Theories of Five-Act Structure from 1470.* Univ. Illinois Press, 1947. Pp. xiii, 848.
      Rev: A5938.

B5481   Baldwin, T. W. "Respice Finem: Respice Funen." *AMS*, pp. 141-155.
      IV.iv.44-46.

B5482   Born, Walter. *Shakespeares Verhältnis zu Seinen Quellen in "The Comedy of Errors" und "The Taming of the Shrew."* DD, Hamburg, 1955. Pp. 211. Typewritten.

B5483   Thomas, Sidney. "The Date of *The Comedy of Errors*." *SQ*, VII (1956), 377-384.

(3) USE OF LANGUAGE

B5484   Heninger, S. K., Jr. "The Hearts Meteors, A Microcosm:Macrocosm Analogy." *SQ*, VII (1956), 273-275.

(4) GENERAL CRITICISM OF THE PLAY

B5485   Bellessort, A. "*La Comédie des Erreurs*." *Le Plaisir du Théâtre.* Paris: Perrin, 1939, pp. 83-87.

B5486   Bond, R. W. "The Framework of *Errors*." *Studia Otiosa* (1938), pp. 43-50.

B5487   Koszul, A. "Argentoratensia Britannica: *La Comédie des Erreurs* de Shakespeare." *Bulletin de la Fac. des Lettres* (Strasbourg), XIII (1938?), 181-185.

B5488   Melo, Rodrigo. "Actualidade de uma Peça de Shakespeare." *Atlântico* (Lisbon), III (1949), No. 2, 84-88.

B5489   Elliott, G. R. "Weirdness in *The Comedy of Errors*." *UTQ*, IX (1939), 95-106.

(5) CHARACTERIZATION

B5490   Fergusson, Francis. "*The Comedy of Errors* and *Much Ado About Nothing*." *SR*, LXII (1954), 24-37.

B5491   Fergusson, Francis. *The Human Image in Dramatic Literature.* Doubleday Anchor Books. New York: Doubleday & Company, 1957. Pp. xx, 217.
      Part II. Shakespeare, pp. 115-157, includes "Two Comedies" (*Errors* and *Much*).

B5492   Jacobsen, Eric. "Amphytrio or Jack Juggler." *TLS*, Jan. 4, 1957, p. 9.

(6) MISCELLANEOUS ITEMS

B5493   Walsh, Groesbeck, and Robert M. Pool. *Shakespeare's Knowledge of Twins and Twinning.* Fairfield, Alabama, 1940. Reprinted from *Southern Medicine and Surgery.*

B5494   Feldman, A. Bronson. "Shakespeare's Early Errors." *International Journal of Psycho-Analysis*, XXXVI (1955), 114-133.
      Farfetched.

(7) SUBSEQUENT HISTORY OF THE PLAY
(Other than productions after 1660)

TITUS ANDRONICUS (191;68)
(1) THE TEXT
(a) OLD TEXTS

B5495   *Titus Andronicus.* The First Quarto, 1594. Reproduced in facsimile from the unique copy in the Folger Shakespeare Library. With an Intro. by Joseph Quincy Adams. For the Trustees of Amherst College. New York: Scribner's, 1937. Pp. 41, 78.
　　Rev: *TLS*, May 8, 1937, p. 360; by T. Baird, *Amherst Graduates' Quar.*, XXVI, 401-402; by C. J. Sisson, *MLR*, XXXII, 660; by H. Spencer, *MLN*, LIII (1938), 314-315; by R. B. McKerrow, *RES*, XIV, 86-88.

B5496   Price, Hereward T. "The First Quarto of *Titus Andronicus*." *EIE* (1947). New York: Columbia Univ. Press, 1948, pp. 137-168.
　　The spellings of Q indicate that the copy was in Shak.'s handwriting.
　　Rev: *N &Q*, 194 (1949), 131.

B5497   Cantrell, Paul L. and George Walton Williams. "Roberts' Compositors in *Titus Andronicus* Q₂." *SB*, VIII (1956), 27-38.

B5498   Parrott, Thomas Marc. "Further Observations on *Titus Andronicus*." *SQ*, I (1950), 22-29.
　　Concerns the well-known drawing and Mr. J. Dover Wilson's ed. of *T. A.*

i. Dating

B5499   Munro, John. "*Titus Andronicus*." *TLS*, June 10, 1949, p. 385.
　　See the letters by Mr. J. Dover Wilson, *TLS*, June 24, 1949, p. 413; by Mr. Munro, and by Mr. A. G. Perrett, *TLS*, July 1, p. 429.

B5500   Ebbs, John Dale. "A Note on Nashe and Shakespeare." *MLN*, LXVI (1951), 480-481.

B5501   York, Ernest C. "Shakespeare and Nashe." *N &Q*, 198 (1953), 370-371.

B5502   Brubaker, Edward S. "A Note on *Titus Andronicus*, IV.ii.32-36." *SQ*, III (1952), 140.

B5503   Feuillerat, Albert. *The Composition of Shakespeare's Plays: Authorship, Chronology.* Yale Univ. Press, 1953. Pp. viii, 340.
　　Rev: A3286.

B5504   Greg, W. W. "Alteration in Act I of *Titus Andronicus*." *MLR*, XLVIII (1953), 439-440.

B5505   Bennett, Paul E. "An Apparent Allusion to *Titus Andronicus*." *N &Q*, NS, II (1955), 422-424.

B5505a Bennett, Paul E. "The Word 'Goths' in *A Knack to Know a Knave*." *N &Q*, NS, II (1955), 462-463.

B5506   Danks, K. B. " 'Ne' and 'Bad'." *N &Q*, NS, III (1956), 89. [Answer to B5505.]

(b) MODERN EDITIONS

B5507   *Titus Andronicus.* Ed. by J. Dover Wilson. The New Shakespeare. Cambridge Univ. Press, 1948. Pp. lxxii, 173, pl. 1.
　　Rev: by E. C. Pettet, *English*, VII (1949), 238-239; *N &Q*, 194 (1949), 154; by T. M. Parrott, *SAB*, XXIV, 117-123; by G. Lambin, *LanM*, XLIII, 190-191; by A. Koszul, *ES*, XXXI (1950), 182-183; by C. Hinman, *MLN*, LXV, 501; by R. C. Bald, *MLR*, XLV, 240-241 (answered by J. D. Wilson, *MLR*, XLVI [1951], 250); by J. G. McManaway, *ShS*, III (1950), 143-147; by J. C. Maxwell, *RES*, II (1951), 73-76.

B5508   *Titus Andronicus.* Ed. J. C. Maxwell. Arden Ed. London, 1953.
　　Rev: *TLS*, Oct. 30, 1953, p. 699; by Hermann Heuer, *SJ*, 90 (1954), 330-332; *Dublin Mag.*, XXX (Jan.-Mar.), 54; by W. W. Greg, *MLR*, XLIX, 360-364; *SatR*, Jan. 30, p. 23; by John Crow, *Listener*, LII, 975-977; by A. Koszul, *EA*, VII, 325-326; by Clifford Leech, *DUJ*, XV, 77-78; by F. S. Boas, *FortnR*, 1047 (1954), 211-212; by J. Vallette, *MdF*, 321 (1954), 147-148; by H. T. Price, *SQ*, V, 114; by Alice Walker, *RES*, NS, VI (1955), 80-82; by Patrick Cruttwell, *EIC*, V, 386-388.

B5509   *Titus Andronicus.* Ed. by G. B. Harrison. Harmondsworth: Penguin Books, 1958. Pp. 123.
　　Rev: *TLS*, Feb. 21, 1958, p. 107.

(c) EMENDATIONS

B5510   Worrall, W. "On a Passage in *Titus Andronicus*." *TLS*, Dec. 7, 1935, p. 838. II. iii. 124-126.

(2) LITERARY GENESIS AND ANALOGUES

B5511   Birkin, Keith Oswald. *Authorship of "Titus Andronicus."* MA thesis, Ottawa, 1939. Pp. 108.

B5512   Smith, Marion B. *Marlowe's Imagery and the Marlowe Canon.* University of Pennsylvania Press, 1940. Pp. vii, 213.
　　Rev: B5321.

B5513   Law, Robert A. "The Roman Background of *Titus Andronicus*." *SP*, XL (1943), 145-153.

B5514   Price, H. T.   "The Authorship of *Titus Andronicus*." *JEGP*, XLII (1943), 55-81.

B5515   Carrère, Félix Jean.   *Le Théâtre de Thomas Kyd. Contribution à l'Etude du Drame Elizabéthain*. Thèse de Lettres, Paris, 1949. Publ. Toulouse: Edouard Privat, Editeur, 14, Rue des Arts, 1951. Rev: A4979.

B5516   Sargent, Ralph M.   "The Source of *Titus Andronicus*." *SP*, XLVI (1949), 167-183.

B5517   Maxwell, J. C.   "Peele and Shakespeare: A Stylometric Test." *JEGP*, XLIX (1950), 557-561.

B5518   Wilson, J. Dover.   "*Titus and Vespasian* and Professor Alexander." *MLR*, XLVI (1951), 250.

B5519   Desmonde, William H.   "The Ritual Origin of Shakespeare's *Titus Andronicus*." *International Journal of Psycho-Analysis*, XXXVI (1955), 61-65.

B5520   Ratliff, John D.   *The Kydian Revenge Play*. DD, Stanford University, 1955. Pp. 465. Mic A54-3472. *DA*, XIV (1954), 2338. Publ. No. 10,386.

B5521   Hill, R. F.   "The Composition of *Titus Andronicus*." *ShS*, X (1957), 60-70.

(3) USE OF LANGUAGE

B5522   Price, Hereward T.   "The Language of *Titus Andronicus*." *Papers of the Michigan Academy of Science, Arts, and Letters*, XXI (1936), 501-507.

(4) GENERAL CRITICISM OF THE PLAY

B5523   Baker, Howard W., Jr.   *From "Gorboduc" to "Titus Andronicus": A Study in the Development of Tragic Form*. DD, University of California, 1938.

B5524   Keller, Wolfgang.   "*Titus Andronicus*. Ein Vortrag bei der Bochumer Shakespeare-Woche Gehalten im Oktober, 1937." *SJ*, LXXIV (1938), 137-162.

B5525   Baker, Howard.   *Introduction to Tragedy. A Study in the Development of Form in "Gorboduc." "The Spanish Tragedy" and "Titus Andronicus*." Louisiana State Univ. Press, 1939. Pp. 247. Rev: A4914.

B5526   Hastings, William T.   "The Hardboiled Shakspere." *SAB*, XVII (1942), 114-125.

B5527   Yates, Frances A.   "Elizabeth as Astraea." *JWCI*, X (1947), 27-82.
Section titled "Shakespeare and Astraea," pp. 70-72. Chiefly discussion of Astraea in *Titus*.

B5528   Jepsen, Laura.   "A Footnote on 'Hands' in Shakespeare's *Titus Andronicus*." *Florida State Univ. Studies: Studies in English and American Literature*, No. 19 (1955), p. 7.

B5529   "Shakespeare's Roman Plays: and Other Subjects." *ShN*, VI (1956), 4, 14, 20.

B5530   Waith, Eugene Mersereau.   "The Metamorphosis of Violence in *Titus Andronicus*." *ShS*, X (1957), 39-49. Abstr. in *ShN*, VIII (1958), 14.

B5531   McManaway, James G.   "Writing in Sand in *Titus Andronicus* IV.i." *RES*, NS, IX (1958), 172-173.

B5532   Rosier, James Louis.   *The Chain of Sin and Privation in Elizabethan Literature*. DD, Stanford University, 1958. Pp. 240. Mic 58-4326. *DA*, XVIII (1958), 583. Publ. No. 25,387.

(5) CHARACTERIZATION

B5533   Brock, J. H. E.   *Iago and Some Shakespearean Villains*. Cambridge: W. Heffer & Sons, 1937. Pp. viii, 48. Rev: A1245.

B5534   Cohen, Hennig.   "Shakespeare's *Merchant of Venice* II.vii.78-79." *SQ*, II (1951), 78-79. Portia identifies the Prince of Morocco with the Devil because of his color.

B5535   Coe, Charles Norton.   *Shakespeare's Villains*. New York, 1957. Rev: A6796.

B5536   Harris, Bernard.   "A Portrait of a Moor." *ShS*, XI (1958), 89-97.

(6) MISCELLANEOUS ITEMS

B5537   Schücking, Levin L.   *Über Einige Nachbesserungen bei Shakespeare*. Leipzig: Hirzel, 1943. Pp. 66. Rev: by S. B. Liljegren, *SN*, XVI (1943/44), 154-156.

B5538   Wilson, J. Dover.   "*Titus Andronicus* on the Stage in 1595." *ShS*, I (1948), 17-22.

(7) SUBSEQUENT HISTORY OF THE PLAY
(Other than productions after 1660)

B5539   Keller, Wolfgang.   "*Titus Andronicus*. Ein Vortrag bei der Bochumer Shakespeare-Woche Gehalten im Oktober 1937." *SJ*, LXXIV (1938), 137-162.

B5540   Nørgaard, Holger.   "Stage-Coach or 'Stage-Coach'?" *ES*, XXXVI (1955), 24-25.

THE TAMING OF THE SHREW (208;73)
(1) THE TEXT
(a) MODERN EDITIONS

B5541   *The Taming of the Shrew*. Ed. by Henry Norman Hudson and Others. **Cameo Classics**. New York: Grosset, 1936. Pp. 165.

B5542   *The Taming of the Shrew.* Ed. by G. B. Harrison. London: Penguin Books, 1951. Pp. 127.

B5543   *The Taming of the Shrew.* Ed. T. G. Bergin. Yale Shakespeare. New Haven, 1954. Pp. viii, 125.
        Rev: *CE*, XVI (1955), 258; by C. J. Sisson, *MLR*, L, 196-197; by Helen Andrews Kaufman, *SQ*, VI, 349-350; by Hermann Heuer, *SJ*, 91 (1955), 342-343.

B5544   *The Taming of the Shrew* (French's Acting Edition). London: French, 1958. Pp. x, 79.

B5545   *The Taming of the Shrew.* With Introduction and Notes by E. Ratto Corneli. Rome: Signorelli, 1957. Pp. 108.

B5546   *The Taming of the Shrew.* Ed. by Francis Fergusson and Charles Jasper Sisson (Laurel Shakespeare), With a Modern Commentary by Margaret Webster. New York: Dell Publishing Co., 1958. Pp. 190.

(b) EMENDATIONS

B5547   Whiting, B. J. " 'Old Maids Lead Apes in Hell'." *Eng. Studn.*, LXX (1936), 337-351.

B5548   Maxwell, J. C. " 'Rope-Tricks'." *N &Q*, 194 (1949), 556.

B5549   I., J. L. " 'Sessa'." *N &Q*, 197 (1952), 393.
        Comment by P. W. F. Brown, ibid., p. 437; by T. C. Hoepfner, ibid., p. 502.

B5550   Hulme, Hilda M. "Three Notes on the Interpretation of Shakespeare's Text." *Neophil*, XLII (1958), 212-215.

B5551   Tillyard, E. M. W. "Petruchio: Ribald or Pious?" *TLS*, Aug. 8, 1958, p. 447. See also defense of a ribald pun on *repaire* ("re-pair") by C. Broadbent, Aug. 15, p. 459, and insistence on ribald meaning of *weare* ("wear out") by Thomas R. Mark, Oct. 31, p. 625.

(2) LITERARY GENESIS AND ANALOGUES

B5552   Bowers, Fredson Thayer. "Dekker and Jonson." *TLS*, Sept. 12, 1936, p. 729.

B5553   Perkinson, Richard H. "A Tutor from Rheims." *N &Q*, 174 (1938), 168-169.

B5554   Duthie, George Ian. *Elizabethan Pirated Dramas, with Special Reference to the "Bad" Quartos of "Hamlet," "Henry V," and "Romeo and Juliet": With an Appendix on the Problem of "The Taming of a Shrew."* DD, Edinburgh, 1939.

B5555   Brenton, Mrs. Esther Spears. *"The Taming of the Shrew": Its Relations to "The Taming of a Shrew" and to "Supposes" with Special Reference to Sequence and Authorship.* DD, University of Texas, 1940.

B5556   Houk, Raymond A. "The Integrity of Shakespeare's *The Taming of the Shrew*." *JEGP*, XXXIX (1940), 222-229.

B5557   Smith, Marion B. *Marlowe's Imagery and the Marlowe Canon.* Univ. of Pennsylvania Press, 1940. Pp. vii, 213. Chapters upon *A Shrew* and various other plays.
        Rev: B5321.

B5558   Gray, Henry David. *"The Taming of a Shrew."* *Renaissance Studies in Honor of Hardin Craig*, 1941, pp. 133-141; also *PQ*, XX (1941), 325-333.

B5559   Taylor, George Coffin. "Two Notes on Shakespeare." *Renaissance Studies in Honor of Hardin Craig*, 1941, pp. 179-184; also *PQ*, XX (1941), 371-376. "Shakespeare and the Prognostications *King Lear*, I, ii, 111-145" and "The Strange Case of Du Bartas in *The Taming of a Shrew*" are the titles of the notes.

B5560   Houk, Raymond A. "Strata in *The Taming of the Shrew*." *SP*, XXXIX (1942), 291-302.

B5561   Houk, Raymond A. "The Evolution of *The Taming of the Shrew*." *PMLA*, LVII (1942), 1009-38.

B5562   King, Thomson. *"The Taming of the Shrew."* *SAB*, XVII (1942), 73-79.

B5563   Duthie, G. I. *"The Taming of a Shrew* and *The Taming of the Shrew."* *RES*, XIX (1943), 337-356.

B5564   Alcalá, M. "Don Juan Manuel y Shakespeare: una Influencia Imposible." *Filosofía y Letras*, X (1945), 55-67.

B5565   Craig, Hardin. "The Shrew and A Shrew: Possible Settlement of an Old Debate." *Elizabethan Studies and Other Essays: In Honor of George F. Reynolds.* Univ. Colo. Studies, Series B. Studies in the Humanities. Vol. 2, No. 4. Univ. Colorado Press, 1945, pp. 150-154.

B5566   Parrott, T. M. *"The Taming of a Shrew*—A New Study of an Old Play." *Elizabethan Studies and Other Essays: In Honor of George F. Reynolds.* Univ. Colorado Studies, Series B. Studies in the Humanities. Vol. 2, No. 4. Univ. Colorado Press, 1945, pp. 155-165.

B5567   Duthie, George Ian. *(1) Two Shakespeare Problems: (a) The "Bad" Quarto of "Hamlet," (b) "The Taming of a Shrew" and "The Taming of the Shrew"; (2) Shakespeare's "King Lear": A Critical Edition.* DD, Edinburgh, 1946.

B5568   Houk, Raymond A. *"Doctor Faustus* and *A Shrew."* *PMLA*, LXII (1947), 950-957.

B5569   Houk, Raymond A. "Shakespeare's *Shrew* and Green's *Orlando*." *PMLA*, LXII (1947), 657-671.

B5570   Carrère, Félix Jean. *Le Théâtre de Thomas Kyd. Contribution à l'Etude du Drame Elizabéthain.* Thèse de Lettres, Paris, 1949. Publ. Toulouse: Edouard Privat, Editeur, 14, Rue des Arts, 1951.
        Rev: A4979.

B5571   Thomas, Sidney. "A Note on *The Taming of the Shrew*." *MLN*, LXIV (1949), 94-96.

B5572   Mish, Charles C. "The Waking Mans Dreame." *TLS*, Dec. 28, 1951, p. 837.
"The Waking Mans Dreame" in Shak. Soc. *Papers* II (1845) is a transcription of the 1639 ed. of *Admirable Events*, an English version of the French of J. P. Camus, rather than a fragment of a lost ed. of stories by Richard Edwards, which Thomas Warton indicated as a possible source for the Induction of *The Shrew*.

B5573   Drahomanov, M. "*Taming of the Shrew* in the Folklore of the Ukraine." *Annals of the Ukrainian Academy of Arts and Sciences in the United States*, II (1952), 214-218.

B5574   Spencer, Terence. "Three Shakespearian Notes." *MLR*, XLIX (1954), 46-51.
Christopher Sly's "old John Naps of Greece" (*Shrew, Ind.* 2. 91-94) suggests a Greek veteran's polysyllabic name truncated by his English cronies.

B5575   Born, Walter. *Shakespeares Verhältnis zu Seinen Quellen in "The Comedy of Errors" und "The Taming of the Shrew*." DD, Hamburg, 1955. Pp. 211. Typewritten.

B5576   Danks, K. B. "*A Shrew* and *The Shrew*." *N &Q*, NS, II (1955), 331-332.

B5577   Soellner, Rolf. "The Troubled Fountain: Erasmus Formulates a Shakespearean Simile." *JEGP*, LV (1956), 70-74. *Shrew*, v. ii. 142-145.

B5578   Rubow, Paul V. *Trold Kan Taemmes*. The Royal Danish Scientifical Society: Historical-Philosophical Informations, Vol. XXXVII, No. 1. Copenhagen: Munksgaard, 1957. Pp. 41. Illustrated.
Commentary.

B5579   Shroeder, John W. "*The Taming of a Shrew* and *The Taming of the Shrew*: A Case Reopened." *JEGP*, LVII (1958), 424-443.

(3) USE OF LANGUAGE

B5580   Wentersdorf, K. "The Authenticity of *The Taming of the Shrew*." *SQ*, V (1954), 11-32.
Finds parallel images in Shakespearean portion and the alleged collaborator's part; finds also Shakespearean images (many of them paralleled elsewhere in Shak.); also throughout the play dramatic word pictures or running images which are peculiarly Shak. Argues against "unauthentic" division and for wholly Shakespearean authorship.

B5581   Prior, Moody E. "Imagery as a Test of Authorship." *SQ*, VI (1955), 381-386. On B5580.

(4) GENERAL CRITICISM OF THE PLAY

B5582   Karthaus, Werner. "Über die Vertonung von Shakespeares *Taming of the Shrew* durch Hermann Götz." *Die Bühne*, III (1937), 282-285.

B5583   Pander, Oscar von. " 'In Paaren Schreiten Sie'. Neueinstudierung von H. Goetz' *Der Widerspenstigen Zähmung*." *MNN*, Feb. 11, 1938.

B5584   Stahl, Heinr. "Ein Meisterwerk Wird Neu Entdeckt. *Der Widerspenstigen Zähmung* in der Bearbeitung von Hermann Goetz." *VB*, Feb. 11, 1938.

B5585   Hijikata, Yoshi. "*The Taming of the Shrew*." *Teatoro* (Japan), No. 79, 1947.

B5586   Greenfield, Thelma Nelson. "The Transformation of Christopher Sly." *PQ*, XXXIII (1954), 34-42.

B5587   Flatter, Richard. "Randnotizen zur Zähmung der Widerspenstigen." *Shakespeare-Tage*, 1955, pp. 14-16.

B5588   Sisson, Charles J. "*Taming of the Shrew*." *Drama*, XXXVII (Autumn, 1955), 25-27.

B5589   Bradbrook, M. C. "Dramatic Role as Social Image; A Study of *The Taming of the Shrew*." *SJ*, 94 (1958), 132-150.

(5) CHARACTERIZATION

B5590   Draper, John W. "Kate the Curst." *Journal of Nervous and Mental Diseases*, 89 (1939), 757-764.

B5591   Houk, Raymond A. "Shakespeare's Heroic Shrew." *SAB*, XVIII (1943), 121-132, 175-186. Answer to B5590.

B5592   Dürrenmatt, Friedrich. "*Der Widerspenstigen Zähmung*." *Die Weltwoche* (Zurich), Feb. 8, 1952.

(6) MISCELLANEOUS ITEMS

B5593   Phillips, Gerald William. *Lord Burghley in Shakespeare. Falstaff, Sly and Others*. London: Thornton Butterworth, 1936. Pp. 285.
Rev: *TLS*, Jan. 2, 1937, p. 13.

B5594   Perkinson, Richard H. "A Tutor from Rheims." *N &Q*, 174, (1938), 168-169.

B5595   Vitaly, Georges. "Notes de Travail à Propos de La Mégère Apprivoisée." *Revue Théâtrale*, No. 26 (1954), 19-27.

(7) SUBSEQUENT HISTORY OF THE PLAY
(Other than productions after 1660)

B5596   Crundell, H. W. "*The Taming of the Shrew* on the XVII Century Stage." *N &Q*, 173 (1937), 207.

THE TWO GENTLEMEN OF VERONA (195;69)
(1) THE TEXT
(a) MODERN EDITIONS

B5597 Tannenbaum, Samuel A. "The New Cambridge Shakspere and *The Two Gentlemen of Verona.*" *SAB*, XIII (1938), 151-172, 208-283. New York: The Tenny Press, 1939. Pp. 68.

B5598 Lewis, C. S. "Text Corruptions." *TLS*, March 3, 1950, p. 137. See the letter by J. Dover Wilson, ibid., March 10, 1950, p. 153.

B5599 *The Two Gentlemen of Verona.* Ed. by G. B. Harrison. London: Penguin Books, 1956. Pp. 107. Rev: *TLS*, Oct. 19, 1956, p. 623.

(b) EMENDATIONS

B5600 Sisson, Charles J., and Arthur Brown. " 'The Great Danseker': Literary Significance of a Chancery Suit." *MLR*, XLVI (1951), 339-348.
See James G. McManaway, "Additional Notes on 'The Great Danseker'," ibid., XLVII, 202-203.

(2) LITERARY GENESIS AND ANALOGUES

B5601 Parks, George B. "The Development of *Two Gentlemen of Verona.*" *Huntington Lib. Bull.*, No. 11 (April, 1937), 1-11.

B5602 Allen, Mozelle Scaff. "Brooke's *Romeus and Juliet* as a Source for the Valentine-Sylvia Plot in *The Two Gentlemen of Verona.*" *TxSE*, XVIII (1938), 25-46.

B5603 Guinn, John A. "The Letter Device in the First Act of *The Two Gentlemen of Verona.*" *TxSE*, XX (1940), 72-81.

B5604 Craig, Hardin. "Shakespeare's Development as a Dramatist in the Light of His Experience." *SP*, XXXIX (1942), 226-238.

B5605 Atkinson, Dorothy F. "The Source of *Two Gentlemen of Verona.*" *SP*, XLI (1944), 223-234.

B5606 Munro, John. "Some Matters Shakespearian." *TLS*, Sept. 13, 1947, p. 472. See also W. R. Dunstan, "It Is?" *TLS*, Nov. 1, 1947, p. 563.

B5607 Sargent, Ralph M. "Sir Thomas Elyot and the Integrity of *The Two Gentlemen of Verona.*" *PMLA*, LXV (1950), 1166-1180.

(3) USE OF LANGUAGE
(4) GENERAL CRITICISM OF THE PLAY

B5608 Messiaen, P. "La Première Comédie de Shakespeare." *Revue Politique et Littéraire*, LXXIV (1936), 382-385.

B5609 Perry, Thomas A. *"The Two Gentlemen of Verona": An Historical Study.* DD, State University of Iowa, 1944. Abstr. publ. by State University of Iowa in *Doctoral Dissertations: Abstracts and References (1942 through 1948)*, VI (1953), 445-446.

B5610 Fredén, Gustaf. "The Tide of Verona." *Studier Tillägnade Anton Blanck*, Dec. 29, 1946, pp. 54-60.

B5611 Baldwin, T. W. *Shakspere's Five-Act Structure: Shakspere's Early Plays on the Background of Renaissance Theories of Five-Act Structure from 1470.* University Illinois Press, 1947. Pp. xiii, 848. Rev: A5938.

B5612 Perry, Thomas A. "Proteus, Wry-Transformed Traveller." *SQ*, V (1954), 33-40.

(5) CHARACTERIZATION
(6) MISCELLANEOUS ITEMS
(7) SUBSEQUENT HISTORY OF THE PLAY
(Other than productions after 1660)

LOVE'S LABOUR'S LOST (193;68)
(1) THE TEXT
(a) OLD TEXTS

B5613 Kirschbaum, Leo. "Is *The Spanish Tragedy* a Leading Case? Did a Bad Quarto of *Love's Labour's Lost* Ever Exist?" *JEGP*, XXXVII (1938), 501-512.

B5614 *Love's Labour's Lost* (1598). Ed. by Sir Walter Greg. Shakespeare Quarto Facsimiles, No. 10, Oxford: Clarendon Press, 1957. Pp. 84.
Reproduced from the copy in the British Museum (C.34, 1.14: Heber-Daniel).
Rev: *TLS*, Oct. 25, 1957, p. 647; *ShN*, VII, 46; by Fredson Bowers, *MLR*, LIII (1958), 235-236; *N &Q*, NS, V, 135; by Hermann Heuer, *SJ*, 94 (1958), 294-295; by J. H. P. Pafford *RES*, IX, 451.

(b) MODERN EDITIONS

B5615 *Love's Labour's Lost.* Ed. by A. E. Morgan and W. Sherard Vines. Warwick Shakespeare. London: Blackie, 1936. Pp. 171.

B5616   *Love's Labour's Lost.* Ed. by F. E. Budd, With Introduction and Notes. London: Macmillan, 1936. Pp. 192.

B5617   *Love's Labour's Lost.* Ed. by Richard David. The Arden Ed. based on the Ed. of H. C. Hart. London: Methuen, 1951. Pp. lii, 196.
      Rev: *TLS,* Jan. 25, 1952, p. 79; *Adelphi,* XXVIII, 646-647; by Alice Walker, *RES,* III, 380-386; by A. Koszul, *EA,* V, 242-243; *Listener,* XLVII, 151; by F. W. Bateson, *EIC,* III (1953), 124; by T. M. Parrott, *JEGP,* LII, 404-409; by A. P. Rossiter, *CR,* LXXIV, 194; by S. Thomas, *SQ,* V (1954), 80-81; by Patrick Cruttwell, *EIC,* V (1955), 382-390.

B5618   *Love's Labour's Lost.* Ed. G. B. Harrison. London: Penguin Books, 1953. Pp. 128.

(c) EMENDATIONS

B5619   Dunstan, W. R. " 'Perttaunt'." [*Love's Labour's Lost,* V. ii. 67.] *TLS,* Oct. 3, 1936, p. 791. See letters by Henry Cuningham in *TLS,* Oct. 10, 1936, p. 815; by W. R. Dunstan, ibid., Oct. 17, 1936, p. 839, and Oct. 31, 1936, p. 887; by J. Dover Wilson, ibid., Oct. 24, p. 863 and Nov. 7, p. 908. Would read *forteunelike* for *perttauntlike.*

B5620   Tilley, M. P. " ' 'Twill be Thine Another Day'." [*Love's Labour's Lost,* IV. i. 109.] *MLN,* LII (1937), 394-397.

B5621   Rise, A. P. *"Tempered with Sighs."* [*Love's Labour's Lost,* IV. iii.] *TLS,* Oct. 1, 1938, p. 627.

B5622   Young, G. M. *"Love's Labour's Lost."* [II. i. 221-222.] *TLS,* April 16, 1938, p. 264. See letters by A. H. T. Clarke and W. A. Jones, *TLS,* April 23, 1938, p. 280; J. Dover Wilson, ibid., May 7, 1938, p. 316.

B5623   Wells, Staring B. *"Love's Labour's Lost,* IV. iii. 285-362.*"* *MLN,* LV (1940), 102-103.

B5624   Strathmann, E. A. "Textual Evidence for 'The School of Night'." *MLN,* LVI (1941), 176-186.

B5625   Stewart, J. I. M. *"Love's Labour's Lost* [II. i. 64-68].*"* *TLS,* Oct. 23, 1943, p. 511. See reply by W. R. Dunstan, *TLS,* Oct. 30, 1943, p. 523.

B5626   R., V. "Cuckoo-Flowers and Lady-Smocks." *N &Q,* 184 (1943), 305-306.

B5627   Siler, Henry D. "A French Pun in *Love's Labour's Lost.*" *MLN,* LX (1945), 124-125.

B5628   Simpson, Percy. " 'Pertuant-Like' [*Love's Labour's Lost,* V. ii. 67].*"* *TLS,* Feb. 24, 1945, p. 91.

B5629   Munro, John. "Some Matters Shakespearian." *TLS,* Sept. 13, 1947, p. 472.

B5630   Brereton, J. Le Gay. "Nathaniel's Accident, and Other Notes on *Love's Labour's Lost.*" *Writings on Elizabethan Drama.* Melbourne Univ. Press, 1948, pp. 89-91.

B5631   Danks, K. B. *Love's Labour's Lost.* *N &Q,* 193 (1948), 545. [Whether title is Loves or Love's, Labour, Labours or Labour's, Lost.]

B5632   Nearing, Homer, Jr. "Caesar's Sword (*Faerie Queene* II.x.49; *Love's Labour's Lost* V.ii.615).*"* *MLN,* LXIII (1948), 403-405.

B5633   Babcock, Weston. "Fools, Fowls, and Perttaunt-Like in *Love's Labour's Lost.*" *SQ,* II (1951), 211-219.

B5634   Fussell, E. S. " ' "Veal," Quoth the Dutchman' [*Love's Labour's Lost,* V.ii.247].*"* *N &Q,* 196 (1951), 136-137.

B5635   Rowse, A. L. "Haud Credo: A Shakespearian Pun." *TLS,* July 18, 1952, p. 469.

B5636   Parsons, Howard. *Emendations to Three of Shakespeare's Plays:* *"Merry Wives of Windsor,"* *"Love's Labour's Lost,"* *"Comedy of Errors."* London: Ettrick Press, 1953. Pp. 21.
      Rev: by I. B. Cauthen, *SQ,* V (1954), 423-424.

B5637   Ringler, William. "The Hobby Horse is Forgot." *SQ,* IV (1953), 485.

B5638   Fraser, Russell A. "The Dancing Horse of *Love's Labour's Lost.*" *SQ,* V (1954), 98-99.

B5639   Allen, E. G. "Cruxes in *Love's Labour's Lost.*" *N &Q,* NS, II (1955), 287. Suggests a new emendation of IV.iii.177: "With men of like inconstancy."

B5640   Shapiro, I. A. "Cruxes in *Love's Labour's Lost.*" *N &Q,* NS, II (1955), 287-288.

B5641   Austin, Warren B. "Concerning a Woodcut." *SQ,* VIII (1957), 245.

B5642   Pafford, J. H. P. "Schoole of Night." *N &Q,* NS, IV (1957), 143.

B5643   Blissett, William. " 'Strange Without Heresy' [*Love's Labour's Lost,* V.i.1-6].*"* *ES,* XXXVIII (1957), 209-211.
    Notes that "strange without heresy" possibly may be a punning allusion to the 5th Earl of Derby, Ferdinando Stanley, Lord Strange, but hesitates to accept it as part of the satire on the School of Night, which some have found in *Love's Labour's Lost.*

(2) LITERARY GENESIS AND ANALOGUES

B5644   Bradbrook, M. C. *The School of Night.* Study in the Literary Relationships of Sir Walter Ralegh. Cambridge Univ. Press, 1936. Pp. viii, 190.
    Love's Labour's Lost, pp. 153-168.
      Rev: A4787.

B5645   Yates, Frances A. *A Study of "Loves Labour's Lost."* Shakespeare Problems, V. Cambridge Univ. Press, 1936. Pp. viii, 224.
      Rev: *London Mercury,* XXXIV (1936), 286; *TLS,* May 16, 1936, p. 407; *N &Q,* 170 (1936),

341-342; see letter by M. H. Dodds, ibid., pp. 434-435; by Miss Yates, ibid., 171, p. 31; by Frederick Laws, *NstN*, NS, XI, 897-898; *Nation* (N. Y.), 142 (1936), 785; by Wolfgang Keller, *SJ*, LXXII, 143-144; by R. Galland, *RAA*, XIII, 515; by K. M. L., *Oxf. Mag.*, LV, 266-267; by William Empson, *Life and Letters Today*, XV, No. 5 (1937), 202-204; by George Herbert Clarke, *QQ*, XLIV, 115; by Alois Brandl, *DLZ*, LVIII, 666-668; by J. Crofts, *English*, I, 443-444; by Hazelton Spencer, *MLN*, LII, 437-442; by Enid Welsford, *MLR*, XXXIII (1938), 67-68.

B5646 Lefranc, Abel. "Les Eléments Francais de *Peines d'Amour Perdues* de Shakespeare." *RH*, 178 (1937), 411-432.

B5647 Boughner, Daniel C. "Don Armado and the *Commedia dell'Arte*." *SP*, XXXVII (1940), 201-224.

B5648 Phelps, John. "The Source of *Love's Labour's Lost*." *SAB*, XVII (1942), 97-102.

B5649 Pellegrini, Angelo M. "Bruno, Sidney, and Spenser." *SP*, XL (1943), 128-144. See B5645.

B5650 See B5632.

B5651 Ashe, Geoffrey. " 'Several Worthies'." *N &Q*, 195 (1950), 492-493.

B5652 Schrickx, W. "Shakespeare and the School of Night: An Estimate and Further Interpretations." *Neophil*, XXXIV (1950), 35-44.

B5653 Lever, J. W. "Three Notes on Shakespeare's Plants." *RES*, III (1952), 117-129.
Concludes the songs at the end of *Love's Labour's Lost* were part of the revision mentioned on the t.p. of 1598 Q.

B5654 Maxwell, J. C. "*Hero and Leander* and *Love's Labour's Lost*." *N &Q*, 197 (1952), 334-335.

B5655 Muir, Kenneth. "Shakespeare and Florio." *N &Q*, 197 (1952), 493-495.

B5656 Hammerle, Karl. "The Poet's Eye (*Midsummer Night's Dream*, V.i.12): Zur Auffassung Shakespeares vom Wesen des Dichters." *Innsbrucker Beiträge zur Kulturwissenschaft*, I (1954) (Amman-Festgabe, I Teil), 101-107.
Love's Labour's Lost, V.i. 758-761, and IV.ii. 70-76.

B5657 Puknat, Siegfried. "*Doktor Faustus*" and "*Love's Labour's Lost*." *Program*, Philol. Assoc. of the Pacific Coast, Eugene, Oregon, 1950.

B5658 Shield, H. A. "Links with Shakespeare—XIII." *N &Q*, NS, II (1955), 513-514.

B5659 Ungerer, Gustav. *Anglo-Spanish Relations in Tudor Literature*. DD, Bern, 1956. Publ. in Schweizer. Anglist. Arbeiten, Bern, 1956. Madrid: Artes Gráficas Clavileño, 1956. Pp. 231. Part III. "Shakespeare and Spain."
Rev: A4609.

B5660 Keen, Alan. "*Love's Labour's Lost* in Lancashire." *TLS*, Sept. 21, 1956, p. 553.

B5661 Schrickx, W. *Shakespeare's Early Contemporaries. The Background of the Harvey-Nashe Polemic and "Love's Labour's Lost*." Antwerp: Nederlandsche Boekhandel, 1956.
Rev: A622.

B5662 Baldwin, Thomas Whitfield. *Shakspere's Love's Labor's Won: New Evidence from the Account Books of an Elizabethan Bookseller*. Carbondale: Southern Illinois Univ. Press, 1957. Pp. viii, 42.
Rev: B8323.

(3) USE OF LANGUAGE

B5663 Morris, C. M. J. *Shakespeare's Vocabulary in "Love's Labour Lost": The Effect of the Elizabethan Age and the Renascence on the Creation, Use and Interpretation of Words*. MA thesis, Capetown, 1934.

B5664 Dayton, B. E. *Animal Similes and Metaphors in Shakespeare's Plays*. DD, University of Washington, 1937. Abstr. publ. in Univ. of Washington *Abstracts of Theses*, II (1937), 119-122.

B5665 Miller, William E. "Fustian Answer to a Tuftaffeta Speech." *N &Q*, NS, V (1958), 188-189.

(4) GENERAL CRITICISM OF THE PLAY

B5666 Cancelled.

B5667 Messiaen, Pierre. "*Peines d'Amour Perdues*." *Revue Universitaire*, April, 1936, pp. 328-335.

B5668 Charlton, H. B. "Shakespeare's Comedies: the Consummation." *BJRL*, XXI (1937), 323-351.

B5669 Bone, F. M. H. *Love's Labour's Lost*. *TLS*, Feb. 10, 1945, p. 67.

B5670 Baldwin, T. W. *Shakspere's Five-Act Structure: Shakspere's Early Plays on the Background of Renaissance Theories of Five-Act Structure from 1470*. Univ. of Illinois Press, 1947. Pp. xiii, 848.
Rev: A5938.

B5671 Bronson, Bertrand H. "Daisies Pied and Icicles." *MLN*, LXIII (1948), 35-38.

B5672 Draper, John W. "Tempo in *Love's Labour's Lost*." *ES*, XXIX (1948), 129-137.

B5673 West, E. J. "On the Essential Theatricality of *Love's Labour's Lost*." *CE*, IX (1948), 427-429.

B5674 Brereton, J. Le Gay. *Writings on Elizabethan Drama*, Collected by R. G. Howarth. Melbourne Univ. Press, 1949. Pp. 115.
Includes essay on *Love's Labour's Lost*.

B5675   Granville-Barker, Harley. *Prefaces to Shakespeare*. 2 Vols. Princeton Univ. Press, 1946, 1947. *Love's Labour's Lost* in 2nd vol.
        Rev: A8201.

B5676   Roesen, Bobbyann. "*Love's Labour's Lost*." *SQ*, IV (1953), 411-426.

B5677   Greenfield, Stanley B. "Moth's *L'Envoy* and the Courtiers in *Love's Labour's Lost*." *RES*, V (1954), 167-168.

B5678   Lloyd, Roger. "Love and Charity and Shakespeare." *MGW*, Feb. 16, 1956, p. 6.

B5679   Heninger, S. K., Jr. "Chapman's 'Hymnus in Noctem, 376-377,' and Shakespeare's *Love's Labour's Lost*, IV.iii.346-347." *Expl.*, XVI (1958), No. 8.

(5) CHARACTERIZATION

B5680   Horn, W. "Armado-Armada bei Shakespeare." *Archiv*, 177 (1940), 98.

B5681   Palmer, John. *Comic Characters of Shakespeare*. New York: Macmillan, 1946. Pp. 135.
        Rev: A6550a.

B5682   Cordasco, Francesco. *Don Adriano de Armado of "Love's Labour's Lost"*. Bologna, 1950. Pp. 6.

B5683   Nelson, William. "The Teaching of English in Tudor Grammar Schools." *SP*, XLIX (1952), 119-143.
        Sees Holofernes, in *Love's Labour's Lost* as typifying, though in an exaggerated way, the method of Tudor schoolmasters.

B5684   Henderson, Archibald, Jr. *Family of Mercutio*. DD, Columbia University, 1954. Pp. 270. Mic A54-2044. *DA*, XIV (1954), 1395. Publ. No. 8684. Berowne, p. 195.

(6) MISCELLANEOUS ITEMS

B5685   Freeman, Bernice. "The Costumes of *Love's Labour's Lost*, *Twelfth Night*, and *The Tempest*." *SAB*, XI (1936), 93-106.

B5686   L., G. G. "Chapman and Holofernes." *N&Q*, 172 (1937), 7. See letter by M. H. Dodds in *N&Q*, ibid., pp. 286-287.

B5687   Young, G. M. "Master Holofernes." *TLS*, July 3, 1937, p. 496.

B5688   Kishimoto, G. S. "On the End of *Love's Labour's Lost*." *Studies in Eng. Lit.* (Eng. Lit. Soc. Japan), XVIII (1938), 506-512.

B5689   Strathmann, E. A. "Textual Evidence for 'The School of Night'." *MLN*, LVI (1941), 176-186.

B5690   Copeau, Jacques. " 'Vain Labeur d'Amour,' ou les Débuts de Shakespeare." *Le Figaro*, Aug. 18, 1942.

B5691   Schücking, Levin L. *Über einige Nachbesserungen bei Shakespeare*. Berichte über die Verhandlungen d. Sächs. Akad. d. Wiss. Phil. Kl. Bd. 95, H. 1. Leipzig: Hirzel, 1943. Pp. 66.

B5692   West, E. J. "On a Purely Playful Hypothesis Concerning the Composition of *A Midsummer Night's Dream*." *CE*, IX (1948), 247-249.

B5693   Oppel, Horst. "Gabriel Harvey." *SJ*, 82/83 (1949), 34-51.

B5694   Ashe, Geoffrey. " 'Several Worthies'." *N&Q*, 195 (1950), 492-493.

B5695   Marañón, Gregorio. *Antonio Pérez, Spanish Traitor*. Tr. by Charles D. Ley. London: Hollis and Carter, 1954; New York: Roy Pubs., 1955. Pp. xiv, 382.
        Rev: by Salvador de Madariaga, "The Original of Armado," *MGW*, May 6, 1954, p. 10.

B5696   Cunningham, Delora. "Repentance and the Art of Living Well. The Tudor Interpretation of Penance, and Its Relation to Dramatic Form in Comedy. With analyses of *Love's Labour's Lost* and *All's Well That Ends Well* in Illustration." *Ashland Studies in Shakespeare*, 1955, pp. 4-18. Mimeographed.

B5697   Carter, Burnham, Jr. Article suggesting Greville may have satirized Navarre in his *Treatise of Humane Learning*. *Ashland Studies in Shakespeare*. Ed. Margery Bailey, II (1956). Stanford, California: Shakespeare Festival Institute.

B5698   Stratton, Lowell D. Article on the Nine Worthies Theme in *Love's Labour's Lost*. *Ashland Studies in Shakespeare*. Ed. Margery Bailey, II (1956). Stanford, California: Shakespeare Festival Institute.

(7) SUBSEQUENT HISTORY OF THE PLAY
(Other than productions after 1660)

ROMEO AND JULIET (202;72)
(1) THE TEXT

B5699   Tannenbaum, Samuel A., and D. R. *Shakespeare's "Romeo and Juliet" (a Concise Bibliography)*. Elizabethan Bibliographies, No. 41. New York, 1950. Pp. 133.

(a) OLD TEXTS

B5700   *Romeo and Juliet: Second Quarto, 1599*. Shakespeare Quarto Facsimiles, No. 6. London: The Shakespeare Assoc. & Sidgwick & Jackson, 1949. Pp. 100.

William Drummond of Hawthornden's copy (Edinburgh Univ. Lib.), with a prefatory note by W. W. Greg.
Rev: *TLS*, June 9, 1950, p. 352; by J. G. McManaway, *SQ*, II (1951), 84.

B5701   Klingbeil, Wilhelm. *Der Poetische Wert der beiden ersten Quartos von Shakespeares "Romeo and Juliet" und die Art ihrer Entstehung.* DD, Königsberg, 1907. Pp. 127.

B5702   Camp, G. C. "The Printing of *Romeo and Juliet.*" *TLS*, June 27, 1936, p. 544.
See letter by R. B. McKerrow, *TLS*, July 4, 1936, p. 564.

B5703   Hoppe, Harry R. "The First Quarto Version of *Romeo and Juliet*, II. vi. and IV. v. 43 ff." *RES*, XIV (1938), 271-284.

B5704   Hoppe, Harry R. "An Approximate Printing Date for the First Quarto of *Romeo and Juliet.*" *Library*, NS, XVIII (1938), 447-455.
The printing of Q_1, begun by Danter and completed by another printer, may be dated between Feb. 9 and Mar. 17, 1596-97.

B5705   Duthie, George Ian. *Elizabethan Pirated Dramas, with Special Reference to the "Bad" Quartos of "Hamlet," "Henry V," and "Romeo and Juliet": With an Appendix on the Problem of "The Taming of a Shrew."* DD, Edinburgh, 1939.

B5706   Twiss, Walter H. *1597 "Romeo and Juliet" as a Pirated Bad Quarto.* DD, University of Washington, 1939. Abstr. in Univ. of Washington *Abstracts of Theses*, IV (1939), 148-152.

B5707   Hoppe, Harry Reno. *The First Quarto of "Romeo and Juliet": A Bibliographical and Textual Study.* DD, Cornell University, 1942. Abstr. publ. in *Abstracts of Theses, 1942*, Ithaca: Cornell Univ. Press, 1943, pp. 23-26.

B5708   Hoppe, Harry R. "Borrowings from *Romeo and Juliet* in the 'Bad' Quarto of *The Merry Wives of Windsor.*" *RES*, XX (1944), 156-158.

B5709   Hoppe, Harry R. *The Bad Quarto of "Romeo and Juliet": A Bibliographical and Textual Study.* Cornell Studies in English, XXXVI. Cornell Univ. Press, 1948. Pp. ix, 230.
Rev: *TLS*, Mar. 5, 1949, p. 159; by Madeleine Doran, *JEGP*, XLIX (1950), 113-114; by Charlton Hinman, *MLN*, LXV, 66-68; by W. W. Greg, *RES*, NS, I, 64-66; by G. I. Duthie, *MLR*, XLV, 375-377; by R. Flatter, *SJ*, 88 (1952), 232-233.

B5710   Thomas, Sidney. "The Bibliographical Links Between the First Two Quartos of *Romeo and Juliet.*" *RES*, XXV (1949), 110-114.

B5711   Thomas, Sidney. "Henry Chettle and the First Quarto of *Romeo and Juliet.*" *RES*, NS, I (1950), 8-16.

B5712   Duthie, G. I. "The Text of Shakespeare's *Romeo and Juliet.*" *SB*, IV (1951), 3-29.

B5713   Eardley-Wilmot, H. " 'Write me a Prologue'." *English*, VIII (1951), 272-274.
The sonnets spoken by Chorus at the beginning of the first and second acts of *Romeo* not written by Shak.

B5714   Maxwell, J. C. "Juliet's Days, Hours, and Minutes." *RES*, NS, II (1951), 262.

B5715   Stroup, Joseph Bradley. *The Problems of Staging in the Second Quarto of "Romeo and Juliet."* MA thesis, North Carolina, 1951. Abstr. publ. in *Univ. of North Carolina Record, Research in Progress*, Grad. School Series, No. 62, 1951, pp. 128-129.

B5716   Hosley, Richard. "A Stage Direction in *Romeo and Juliet.*" *TLS*, June 13, 1952, p. 391.

B5717   Feuillerat, Albert. *The Composition of Shakespeare's Plays: Authorship, Chronology.* Yale Univ. Press, 1953. Pp. viii, 340.
Rev: A3286.

B5718   Hosley, Richard. "The Corrupting Influence of the Bad Quarto on the Received Text of *Romeo and Juliet.*" *SQ*, IV (1953), 11-33.

B5719   Leech, Clifford. "Notes on Dr. Richard Hosley's Suggestions Concerning the Received Text of *Romeo and Juliet.*" *SQ*, V (1954), 94-95.

B5720   Hosley, Richard. "The 'Good Night, Good Night' Sequence in *Romeo and Juliet.*" *SQ*, V (1954), 96-98.
Reply to B5719.

B5721   Hinman, Charlton. "The Proof-Reading of the First Folio Text of *Romeo and Juliet.*" *SB*, VI (1954), 61-70.

B5722   Culliford, S. G. "*Romeo and Juliet*, II.i.38." *N &Q*, NS, II (1955), 475.

B5723   Wilson, John Dover. "The New Way with Shakespeare's Texts: II. Recent Work on the Text of *Romeo and Juliet.*" *ShS*, VIII (1955), 81-99.

B5724   Cantrell, Paul L., and George Walton Williams. "The Printing of the Second Quarto of *Romeo and Juliet* (1599)." *SB*, IX (1957), 107-128.

B5725   Hosley, Richard. "Quarto Copy for Q_2 *Romeo and Juliet.*" *SB*, IX (1957), 129-141.

B5726   Williams, George Walton. *The Good Quarto of "Romeo and Juliet".: A Bibliographical Study.* DD, University of Virginia, 1957. Pp. 500. Mic 57-4183. *DA*, XVII (1957), 2601. Publication No. 22,913. Abstracted by Jack R. Brown, *ShN*, VII (1957), 19.

(b) MODERN EDITIONS

B5727   *Romeo and Juliet.* Ed. by Henry Norman Hudson and others. Cameo classics. New York: Grosset, 1936. Pp. 228.

B5728 *Romeo and Juliet*. Designs by O. Messel. Limited ed. London: Batsford; New York: Scribner's, 1936. Pp. 96.

B5729 *Romeo and Juliet*. Ed. by J. E. Crofts. London: Blackie, 1936. Pp. 171. (With *L.L.L.*)

B5730 *Romeo and Juliet*. Ed. by George Sampson. Cambridge Univ. Press, 1936. Pp. x, 238.
   Rev: *N &Q*, 170 (1936), 162.

B5731 *Romeo and Juliet*. Ed. by S. and E. G. Wood. London: Gill., 1936. Pp. 212.

B5732 *Romeo and Juliet*. Ed. by A. J. J. Ratcliff. Sixpenny Shakespeares. London: Nelson, 1937. Pp. 211.

B5733 *Romeo and Juliet*. Ed. with introd. and notes by G. L. Kittredge. Boston: Ginn and Co., 1941. Pp. xii, 234.

B5734 *The Tragedy of Romeo and Juliet*. Ed. by H. R. Hoppe. Crofts Classics. New York: Crofts, 1947. Pp. ix, 116.

B5735 *Romeo and Juliet*. Ed. by Ralph E. C. Houghton. The New Clarendon Shakespeare. Oxford: Clarendon Press, 1947. Pp. 6, 192.
   Rev: *QJS*, xxxiv (1948), 108.

B5736 *Romeo and Juliet*. Cornelsen-Fremdsprachenreihe, lxv. Berlin: Cornelsen, 1948. Pp. 138.

B5737 *The Tragedy of Romeo and Juliet*. Introd. by Nevill Coghill. Designs by Jean Hugo. The Folio Society, x. London: Cassell; New York: Duschnes, 1950. Pp. 131.
   Rev: *Adelphi*, xxvii (1950), 88; by A. Koszul, *EA*, vi (1953), 355.

B5738 *Romeo and Juliet and Cyrano de Bergerac by Edmond Rostand* (tr. by Howard Thayer Kingsbury). Ed. by Thomas Doyle and M. David Hoffman. Noble's Comparative Classics. New York: Noble, 1937, 1952, 1955. Pp. 483.

B5739 *La Tragédie de "Roméo et Juliette" de William Shakespeare*. Edition critique avec traduction [sans le texte anglais] par Maurice Pollet. DD, Paris, 1955. Typewritten.

B5740 *Romeo and Juliet*. Ed. by John Dover Wilson and George Ian Duthie. The New Shakespeare. Cambridge Univ. Press, 1955. Pp. liii, 249.
   Rev: by R. A. Foakes, *English*, x (1955), 227; by J. Vallette, *MdF*, 325 (1955), 147; *TLS*, Aug. 19, p. 475; by J. R. Brown, *MLR*, li (1956), 95-96; by Richard Hosley, *SQ*, vii, 256-261; by Hermann Heuer, *SJ*, 92 (1956), 395-396; by R. A. Foakes, *DUJ*, xlviii, 38-39; by J. Jacquot, *RHT*, ix (1957), 195-196.

B5741 *The Tragedy of Romeo and Juliet*. Ed. by Richard Hosley. Yale Shakespeare. Yale Univ. Press, 1954. Pp. 174. Revised ed. (paperback).
   Rev: *CE*, xvi (1955), 258; by Sidney Thomas, *SQ*, vi, 345-348; by F. E. Bowman, *South Atlantic Quarterly*, liv, 431-433; by James G. McManaway, *ShS*, ix (1956), 150-151; briefly in *SatR*, Aug. 3, 1957, 28.

B5742 *Romeo and Juliet*. Ed. by Francis Fergusson and Charles Jasper Sisson. Laurel Shakespeare. With a Modern Commentary by W. H. Auden. New York: Dell Publishing Co., 1958. Pp. 223.

(c) EMENDATIONS

B5743 Cuningham, Henry. "*Romeo and Juliet*, I. ii. 14, 15." *TLS*, May 23, 1936, p. 440.
   See letter by Walter Worral, *TLS* June 20, 1936, p. 523.

B5744 Cancelled.

B5745 Hoppe, Harry R. "Runaways' Eyes in *Romeo and Juliet*, III.ii.6." *N &Q*, 173 (1937), 171-172.

B5746 Kapstein, I. J. "Runaways' Eyes Again." *SAB*, xii (1937), 77-84.

B5747 Thompson, D. W. " 'Full of his Roperipe' and 'Roperipe Terms' [*Romeo and Juliet*, II.iv.154]." *MLN*, liii (1938), 268-272.

B5748 Allen, N. B. "*Romeo and Juliet* Further Restored." *MLN*, liv (1939), 85-92.

B5749 Gill, W. W. " 'Skains-Mate'." *N &Q*, 179 (1940), 27.

B5750 Cain, H. Edward. "An Emendation in *Romeo and Juliet* [III.i.69]." *SAB*, xvii (1942), 57-60.

B5751 Ignoto. "Rosaline: Rosalind." *N &Q*, 183 (1942), 163.

B5752 Houghton, Ralph E. C. "*Romeo and Juliet*, II. vi. 16-17." *TLS*, April 3, 1943, p. 163.
   See reply by R. C. Goffin and also by John Palmer, *TLS*, April 17, 1943, p. 187; by R. W. Cruttwell, *TLS*, April 24, p. 199; by D. S. Robertson, *TLS*, May 1, p. 211.

B5753 A., K. "Shakespeare's *Romeo and Juliet*, II.i." *Expl.*, ii (1944), No. 8, Q 36.

B5754 Dean, Leonard F. "Shakespeare's *Romeo and Juliet*, II.i.34-35." *Expl.*, iii (1945), 44.
   Answer to B5753; see also B5755.

B5755 Kirby, John P., and Louis G. Lock. "Shakespeare's *Romeo and Juliet*, II.i.34-35." *Expl.*, iii (1945), 44.

B5756 Hotson, Leslie. "In Defence of Mercutio." *Spectator*, Aug. 8, 1947, pp. 168-169.

B5757 Cohen, Hennig. "Shakespeare's *Romeo and Juliet*, V.iii.112-115." *Expl.*, viii (1949), 24.

B5758 Draper, John W. "The Date of *Romeo and Juliet*." *RES*, xxv (1949), 55-57.
   Considers that the "astronomy" in the play indicates 1596.

B5759   Thomas, Sidney. "The Earthquake in *Romeo and Juliet.*" *MLN*, LXIV (1949), 417-419.
        Comments by Sarah Dodson, "Notes on the Earthquake in *Romeo and Juliet*," *MLN*, LXV
        (1950), 144.
        Possible reference in play to 1584 earthquake.

B5760   Williams, Philip, Jr. "*Romeo and Juliet:* Littera Canina." *N &Q*, 195 (1950), 181-182.
        II.iv.200-204.

B5761   Sledd, James. "A Note on the Use of Renaissance Dictionaries." *MP*, XLIX (1951-52), 10-15.

B5762   Draper, John W. "The Objective Genitive and 'Run-Awayes Eyes'." *JEGP*, LI (1952),
        580-583.

B5763   McNeir, Waldo F. "Shakespeare, *Romeo and Juliet*, III.i.40-44." *Expl.*, XI (1953), 48.

B5764   Boyce, Benjamin. "Pope's Yews in Shakespeare's Graveyard." *N &Q*, NS, I (1954), 287.

B5765   Mustanoja, Tauno F. "Shakespeare's 'Runaways Eyes' and 'Children's Eyes'." *N. Mitt.*,
        LVI, Nos. 7-8 (1955), 250-258. Comment by Leo Spitzer, ibid., LVII (1956), pp. 257-260.

B5766   Cairncross, Andrew S. "*The Tempest*, III.i.15, and *Romeo and Juliet*, I.i.121-128." *SQ*, VII
        (1956), 448-450.

B5767   Spitzer, Leo. " 'Runaways Eyes' and 'Children's Eyes' Again." *N. Mitt.*, LVII (1956), 257-260.

B5768   Keil, Harry. "Scabies and the Queen Mab Passage in *Romeo and Juliet.*" *JHI*, XVIII (1957),
        394-410.

(2) LITERARY GENESIS AND ANALOGUES

B5769   Brandl, A. "Shakespeares Quellen zu *Romeo und Julia.*" Brandl's *Forschungen und Charakteris-
        tiken.* Berlin, 1936, pp. 183-185. First printed in 1922.

B5770   Hamilton, Marie Padgett. "A Latin and English Passage on Dreams." *SP*, XXXIII (1936), 1-9.
        A dream in Claudian and its passage through Engl. Lit. *Romeo and Juliet*, I.iv.70-88, is brought
        into the comparison.

B5771   Thaler, Alwin. "Shakspere, Daniel, and *Everyman.*" *PQ*, XV (1936), 217-218.

B5772   Kohler, E. "A. Riddin's Edition of *Novella di Giulietta e Romeo.*" *B. de la Faculté des Lettres
        de Strasbourg*, XV (1937), 277-278.

B5773   Mason, V. *An Historical and Critical Background for the Study of English Romantic Tragedy.*
        DD, University of Washington, 1937. Abstr. in *Abstracts of Theses* (Univ. of Washington),
        II (1937), 123-125.

B5774   Moore, Olin H. "Bandello and 'Clizia'." *MLN*, LII (1937), 38-44.

B5775   Moore, Olin H. "Shakespeare's Deviations from *Romeus and Iuliet.*" *PMLA*, LII (1937), 68-74.

B5776   Thaler, Alwin. "Mercutio and Spenser's *Phantastes.*" *PQ*, XVI (1937), 405-407.

B5777   Charlton, H. B. "France as Chaperone of *Romeo and Juliet.*" *Studies in French Language and
        Mediaeval Literature Presented to M. K. Pope.* Manchester: University Press, 1939, pp. 43-59.

B5778   Colucci, Loris. "La Novella di Giulietta e Romeo e le sue Fonti Classiche." *Rassegna Na-
        zionale*, Ser. IV, XXVII (1939), 426-434.

B5779   Moore, Olin H. "Da Porto's Deviations from Masuccio." *PMLA*, LV (1940), 934-945.

B5780   Campbell, Lily B. "Richard Tarlton and the Earthquake of 1580." *HLQ*, IV (1941), 293-301.

B5781   DeJongh, William F. J. "A Borrowing from Caviceo for the Legend of *Romeo and Juliet.*"
        SAB, XVI (1941), 118-119.
        Traces the source of Lady Capulet's explanation of Juliet's weeping (Act III, sc. v) through
        "Clizia" to the *Libro del Peregrino* of Jacopo di Antonio Caviceo (1443-1511).

B5782   Walley, Harold R. "Shakespeare's Debt to Marlowe in *Romeo and Juliet.*" *PQ*, XXI (1942),
        257-267.

B5783   Allen, Ned B. "Shakespeare and Arthur Brooke." *Delaware Notes*, 17th Series, 1944, pp.
        91-110.

B5784   Brooke, Tucker. "Shakespeare's Dove-House." *MLN*, LIX (1944), 160-161. Also in *Essays
        on Shakespeare and Other Elizabethans* (Yale Univ. Press, 1948), pp. 37-38.

B5785   Brooke, C. F. Tucker. "Shakespeare Remembers his Youth in Stratford." *Essays on Shake-
        speare and Other Elizabethans* (Yale Univ. Press, 1948), pp. 32-36. Also in *Essays and Studies in
        Honor of Carleton Brown*, New York Univ. Press, 1940.

B5786   Draper, John W. "The Date of *Romeo and Juliet.*" *RES*, XXV (1949), 55-57.
        Dates play July, 1596, by interpretation of its astronomical references.

B5787   Baldwin, T. W. "Shakspere's Aphthonian Man." *MLN*, LXV (1950), 111-112.

B5788   Moore, Olin H. *The Legend of Romeo and Juliet.* Columbus: Ohio State Univ. Press, 1950.
        Pp. 9, 167.
        Rev: by J. D. M. Ford, *Speculum*, XXVI (1951), 731-732; by Napoleone Orsini, *Symposium*,
        VI, 401-402; by G. I. Duthie, *SQ*, III (1952), 54-55; by C. T. Prouty, *MLN*, LXVIII (1953),
        274; by R. Weiss, *MLR*, XLIX (1954), 495-496.

B5789   Nosworthy, J. M. "The Two Angry Families of Verona." *SQ*, III (1952), 219-226.

B5790   Soellner, Rolf. "Shakespeare and the 'Consolatio'." *N &O*, NS, I (1954), 108-109.

B5791 Wilkins, E. H. "The Tale of Julia and Pruneo." *Harvard Library Bulletin*, VIII (1954), 102-107.
Enlarges upon James Wardrap's description (*HLB*, 1953) of an anonymous novella in a 15th
century MS at Harvard. Wilkins shows Luigi da Porto, who gave the story its standard form,
based it on Masuccio da Salerno's tale of Mariotto & Ganozza.

B5792 Dwyer, J. J. "Did Shakespeare Read Dante?" *Tablet*, 206 (July 9, 1955), 33-34.

B5793 Herzberg, Max J. "Sources and Stage History of *Romeo and Juliet*." *Audio-Visual Guide*, XXI
(Dec., 1955), 21-27.

B5794 Schanzer, Ernest. "*Midsummer Night's Dream* and *Romeo and Juliet*." *N &Q*, NS, II (1955),
13-14.

B5795 Lenotti, Tullio. *Giulietta e Romeo nella Storia, nella Leggenda e nell' Arte.* Collection Le Guide,
No. 27. Verona: Edizioni Vita Veronese, Tipografia Ghidini e Fiorini, 1955. Pp. 64. Tr.
by Silvana Redomi into English. Illustrated by Ameglio Trivella. Verona: Ed. di Vita
Veronese, 1957. Pp. 83.

B5796 McManaway, James G. "A Probable Source of *Romeo and Juliet*, III.i.100-101." *N &Q*, NS,
III (1956), 57.

B5797 Muir, Kenneth. "Arthur Brooke and the Imagery of *Romeo and Juliet*." *N &Q*, NS, III (1956),
241-243.

B5798 Steadman, John M. "The Fairies' Midwife: *Romeo and Juliet*, I.iv." *N &Q*, NS, III (1956), 424.

(3) USE OF LANGUAGE

B5799 Herr, A. F. "An Elizabethan Usage of 'Quoth'." *N &Q*, 178 (1940), 152.

B5800 Arnheim, Rudolf. "Psychological Notes on the Poetical Process." *Poets at Work*. New York:
Harcourt Brace, 1948. Pp. ix, 186.
Discussions of imagery in *Romeo*, pp. 156-158.

B5801 Draper, John W. "Patterns of Style in *Romeo and Juliet*." *SN*, XXI (1949), 195-210.

B5802 Pettet, E. C. "The Imagery of *Romeo and Juliet*." *English*, VIII (1950), 121-126.

B5803 Walker, Roy. "Shakespeare's Star Imagery." *English*, VIII (1951), 217-218.
Refers to B5802.

B5804 Williams, Philip. "The Rosemary Theme in *Romeo and Juliet*." *MLN*, LXVIII (1953), 400-403.

B5805 Mahood, M. *Shakespeare's Word Play.*. London: Methuen, 1956. Chapter on *Romeo*.

(4) GENERAL CRITICISM OF THE PLAY

B5806 Cancelled.

B5807 Adams, John C. "The Staging of *Romeo and Juliet*." *TLS*, Feb. 15, 1936, p. 139.
See letters by Harley Granville-Barker and George Sampson, *TLS*, Feb. 22, 1936, p. 163; by
W. J. Lawrence, ibid., Feb. 29, p. 184; letters by Mr. Adams, ibid., May 23, p. 440; by Mr.
Granville-Barker and Mr. Lawrence, ibid., May 30, p. 460.

B5808 Adams, John C. "*Romeo and Juliet*: As Played on Shakespeare's Stage." *TAr*, XX (1936),
896-904.

B5809 Gaw, Allison. "The Impromptu Mask in Shakspere, with Special Reference to the Stagery of
Romeo and Juliet, I.iv-v." *SAB*, XI (1936), 149-160.

B5810 Charlton, H. B. "*Romeo and Juliet*" as an Experimental Tragedy. London: Milford, 1939.
Pp. 45.
Rev: A5920.

B5811 Draper, John W. "Shakespeare's Star-Crossed Lovers." *RES*, XV (1939), 16-34.

B5812 Merkelbach, H. M. "*Romeo en Julia*." *Op de Hoogte*, 1939, pp. 64-66.

B5813 Reboux, Paul. *Roméo et Juliette, Amants de Vérone.* Paris: Fayard, 1939.

B5814 Hering, Gerhard F. "Shakespeare-Studien." *DL*, XLIII (1941), 230-232, 399-400, 501-503.

B5815 Mizener, Arthur. "Some Notes on the Nature of English Poetry." *SR*, LI (1943), 27-51.
Romeo, pp. 29-30.

B5816 Law, Robert Adgar. "*Richard the Third*: A Study in Shakespeare's Composition." *PMLA*,
LX (1945), 689-696.
Shows comparable structural points with *Romeo*.

B5817 Cain, H. E. "A Technique of Motivation in *Romeo and Juliet*." *SAB*, XXI (1946), 186-190.

B5818 Baldwin, T. W. *Shakspere's Five-Act Structure: Shakspere's Early Plays on the Background of
Renaissance Theories of Five-Act Structure from 1470.* Univ. Illinois Press, 1947. Pp. xiii, 848.
Rev: A5938.

B5819 Cain, H. Edward. "*Romeo and Juliet*: A Reinterpretation." *SAB*, XXII (1947), 163-192.

B5820 Draper, John W. "Contrast of Tempo in the Balcony Scene." *SAB*, XXII (1947), 130-135.

B5821 Fukuhara, Rintaro. "*Romeo and Juliet*." *Rising Generation* (Japan), 93 (1947), No. 3.

B5822 Granville-Barker, Harley. *Prefaces to Shakespeare.* 2 Vols. Princeton Univ. Press, 1946, 1947.
Rev: A8201.

B5823 Harrison, Thomas P., Jr. " 'Hang-up' Philosophy." *SAB*, XXII (1947), 203-209.

B5824   Smith, Robert Metcalf. "Three Interpretations of *Romeo and Juliet*." *SAB*, XXIII (1948), 60-77.

B5825   Bowling, Lawrence Edward. "The Thematic Framework of *Romeo and Juliet*." *PMLA*, LXIV (1949), 208-220.

B5826   Chapman, Raymond. "Double Time in *Romeo and Juliet*." *MLR*, XLIV (1949), 372-374.

B5827   Marion, Denis. "Les Amants de Vérone." *France Illustration*, v, No. 1 (1949), 281.

B5828   Evans, Bertrand. "The Brevity of Friar Laurence." *PMLA*, LXV (1950), 841-865.

B5829   Bonnard, Georges A. "*Romeo and Juliet:* A Possible Significance." *RES*, NS, II (1951), 319-327.

B5830   Dolar, Jaro. "O Shakespearu in Njegovi Ejubezenski Tragediji." *Gledališni List* (Maribor), VI, vi (1951), 27-29.

B5831   Eardley-Wilmot, H. " 'Write Me a Prologue'." *English* VIII (1951), 272-274.
        Regards the sonnet prologues of *Romeo and Juliet* as inferior verse, and Quince's introductory speech in *Midsummer Night's Dream* as Shakespeare's method of making clear his dislike of the prologue because of its inherent absurdity and clumsiness.

B5832   Condee, Ralph W. "The Apothecary's Holiday." *SQ*, III (1952), 282.

B5833   Frye, Roland Mushat. *The Accepted Ethics and Theology of Shakespeare's Audience as Utilized by the Dramatist in Certain Representative Tragedies, with Particular Attention to Love and Marriage.* DD, Princeton University, 1952. Pp. 372. Mic A55-745. *DA*, XV (1955), 581. Publication No. 10,901.
        Rev: A2563.

B5834   Waldock, A. J. A. *Sophocles the Dramatist.* Cambridge Univ. Press, 1951. Pp. x, 228.
        Comments on *Romeo and Juliet*.
        Rev: A8427.

B5835   Matthews, G. M. "Sex and the Sonnet." *EIC*, II (1952), 119-137.

B5836   Hosley, Richard. "Juliet's Entrance." *TLS*, May 22, 1953, p. 333.
        Suggests that Juliet should enter directly after line 9 in II.ii. of *Romeo and Juliet*.

B5837   Lewis, Allan. "Shakespeare y el Renacimiento: *Romeo y Julieta*." *Cuadernos Americanos* (Mexico), LXXII (1953), 235-258.

B5838   Link, Frederick M. "*Romeo and Juliet:* Character and Tragedy." *Studies in English* (Boston), I (1955), 9-19.

B5839   Durrant, G. H. "What's in a Name? A Discussion of *Romeo and Juliet*." *Theoria*, VIII (1956), 23-36.

B5840   McNeir, Waldo F. "The Closing of the Capulet Tomb." *SN*, XXVIII (1956), 3-8.

B5841   Myers, Henry Alonzo. *Tragedy: A View of Life.* Cornell Univ. Press, 1956. Pp. 218.
        Rev: A6916.

B5842   Dickey, Franklin M. *Not Wisely But Too Well: Shakespeare's Love Tragedies.* San Marino Calif.: The Huntington Library, 1957. Pp. ix, 205.
        Rev: A2562.

B5843   Falkenberg, Hans-Geert. "Shakespeares Trauerspiel *Romeo und Juliet*." *Blätter d. deutschen Theaters in Göttingen*, No. 106, 1956/57, pp. 118-120.

B5844   Fitch, Robert Elliot. *The Decline and Fall of Sex.* New York: Harcourt Brace, 1957.
        "*Romeo & Juliet*, or the Nurse," pp. 31-39.

B5845   Phialas, Peter G. "Renaissance Conference." *South Atlantic Bulletin*, XXIV (1958), 9-11.
        Includes notices of the reading of papers on Tybalt's Exit in *Romeo and Juliet* by George W. Williams (B5846), and on Parting and Justice in *Romeo and Juliet* by H. Edward Cain.

B5846   Williams, George Walton. "Tybalt's Exit in *Romeo and Juliet*." *ShN*, VIII (1958), 18. Abstract.

(5) CHARACTERIZATION

B5847   Baker, H. Kendra. "Friar Laurence." *N &Q*, 175 (1938), 367-368.

B5848   Cole, John W. "Romeo and Rosaline." *Neophil*, XXIV (1939), 285-288.

B5849   Reik, Theodor. *A Psychologist Looks at Love.* New York: Farrar & Rinehart, 1944.
        Contains comments on Romeo. See also B5856.

B5850   Cain, H. E. "A Technique of Motivation in *Romeo and Juliet*." *SAB*, XXI (1946), 186-190.

B5851   Guido, Angelina. "The Humor of Juliet's Nurse." *Bul. Hist. Med.*, XVII (1946), 297-303.

B5852   Woestijne, Karel van de. *Romeo oder der Liebhaber der Liebe. Verdt. v. Heinz Graef.* Munich: Alber, 1946. Pp. 60.
        Rev: by W. Barzel, *Stimmen d. Zt.*, 142 (1948), 156-157.

B5853   Hotson, Leslie. *Shakespeare's Sonnets Dated, and Other Essays.* London: Rupert Hart-Davis; Toronto: Clarke, Irwin & Co., 1949. Pp. 244.
        Contains essay on Mercutio.
        Rev: C21.

B5854   Dickey, Franklin M. *Shakespeare's Presentation of Love in "Romeo and Juliet," "Antony and Cleopatra," "Troilus and Cressida."* DD, University of California at Los Angeles, 1954.

B5855 Henderson, Archibald, Jr. *Family of Mercutio.* DD, Columbia University, 1954. Pp. 270. Mic A54-2044. *DA*, XIV (1954), 1395. Publication No. 8684.

B5856 Vredenburgh, Joseph L. "The Character of the Incest Object: A Study of Alternation Between Narcissism and Object Choice." *American Imago*, XIV (1957), 45-52.

(6) MISCELLANEOUS ITEMS

B5857 Heline, T. *"Romeo and Juliette."* *The Occult in Shakespeare.* New York: New Age Press, 1936.

B5858 Allensworth, Clairenne. *Estudio Comparativo entre "La Celestina" y "Romeo y Julieta."* MAE thesis, Mexico, 1940. Pp. 68. Typewritten.

B5859 Russel, Mary Eleanor. *Una Comparación entre Melibea y Julieta.* MAE thesis, Mexico, 1940. Pp. 113. Typewritten.

B5860 Remenyi, Joseph. "Cleverness in Literature." *Personalist*, XXV (1944), 405-418. *Romeo* mentioned, p. 418.

B5861 Dimitri, P. "Eternal Lovers: A Picture Story." *Coronet* (Chicago), XXIX (Nov., 1950), 45-52. Seven gaudy pictures and a jejune summary of the play.

B5862 Huber, K. "Über Shakespeare und die Naturgeschichte der Blindschleiche." *Vox Romanica*, XIV (1954/55), 155-159.

B5863 Durrant, G. H. "What's in a Name? A Discussion of *Romeo and Juliet.*" *Theoria*, VIII (1956), 23-36.

B5864 Stroedel, Wolfgang. "Shakespeares Entwicklung von *Romeo und Julia* zu *Macbeth.*" *ZAA*, IV (1946), Heft 2, 137-148.

(7) SUBSEQUENT HISTORY OF THE PLAY
(other than productions after 1660)
(a) ADAPTATIONS & TRANSLATIONS

B5865 Küry, Hans. *Simon Grynaeus von Basel, 1725-1799, der erste deutsche Übersetzer von Shakespeares "Romeo und Julia."* Zurich, Leipzig: Niehans, 1935. Pp. 83.

B5866 Maxwell, Baldwin. " 'Twenty Good Nights': *The Knight of the Burning Pestle* and Middleton's *Family of Love.*" *MLN*, LXIII (1948), 233-237.

B5867 Parkhurst, Charles Edward. *A Comparative Analysis of Selected European Opera Libretto Adaptations of the Romeo and Juliet Legend.* DD, Northwestern University, 1953. Pp. 549. Mic A53-2207. *DA*, XIII (1953), 1304. Publication No. 6232.

B5868 Falkenberg, Hans-Geert. "Zur Entstehungs- und Bühnengeschichte von Shakespeares *Romeo und Julia.*" *Blätter d. deutschen Theaters in Göttingen*, 1956/57, Heft 106, pp. 126-127.

(b) ROMEO & JULIET ON THE STAGE

B5869 Hosley, Richard. "The Use of the Upper Stage in *Romeo and Juliet.*" *SQ*, V (1954), 371-379.

B5870 Adams, John Cranford. "Shakespeare's Use of the Upper Stage in *Romeo and Juliet*, III.v." *SQ*, VII (1956), 145-152. Disagrees with B5869.

KING RICHARD II (201;71)
(1) THE TEXT
(a) THE OLD TEXTS

B5871 Greer, C. A. "The Date of *Richard II.*" *N &Q*, 195 (1950), 402-404.

B5872 Greer, C. A. "The Deposition Scene of *Richard II.*" *N &Q*, 197 (1952), 492-493.

B5873 Hasker, Richard E. "The Copy for the First Folio *Richard II.*" *SB*, V (1952), 53-72.

B5874 Feuillerat, Albert. *The Composition of Shakespeare's Plays: Authorship, Chronology.* Yale Univ. Press, 1953. Pp. viii, 340. Rev: A3286.

B5875 Greer, C. A. "More About the Deposition Scene of *Richard II.*" *N &Q*, 198 (1953), 49-50.

B5876 Danks, K. B. *"King Richard II, The Deposition Scene in Q₄."* *N &Q*, NS, II (1955), 473-474.

(b) MODERN EDITIONS

B5877 *Richard II.* Ed. by J. M. Lothian. New Clarendon Shakespeare. London: Oxford Univ. Press; Clarendon Press, 1938. Pp. 206.

B5878 *Richard II.* London, New York: Macmillan, 1939.

B5879 *King Richard II.* Ed. by J. Dover Wilson. Cambridge Univ. Press, 1939. Pp. xcii, 250. Rev: *TLS*, July 1, 1939, p. 392; *N &Q*, 176 (1939), 232-234; by Wolfgang Keller, *SJ*, LXXV, 143-145; by F. E. C. H., "J. D. Wilson's Edition of *Richard II*," *Ba*, XXIV, 217-221; by A. K. McIlwraith, *MLR*, XXXV (1940), 388-389.

B5880 *The Tragedy of King Richard the Second.* Ed. by George Lyman Kittredge. Boston: Ginn & Co., 1941. Pp. ix, 217.

B5881 *The Tragedy of King Richard II.* Velhagen & Klasings Sammlung neusprachl. Ausg. u. Lesebogen. Engl. Authors, Bd. 8. Bielefeld and Leipzig: Velhagen & Klasing., 1943. Pp. viii, 101, 31.

B5882   *Richard II.* Ed. by Theodore Spencer. Crofts Classics. New York: Appleton-Century-
         Crofts, 1949. Pp. xii, 83.
B5883   *Richard II.* Ed. by Sri P. A. Subrahmanya Ayyar. Madras: Kaviraja Publishers, 1949.
B5884   *The Tragedy of King Richard the Second.* Ed. by M. K. Shanmugan. Theagaraya Publication.
         Madras: Washermanpet, 1953. Pp. 450.
B5885   *"Richard II" and "Elizabeth the Queen"* [by Maxwell Anderson]. Ed. by Frank A. Ferguson.
         Canadian Classics. Toronto: Clarke, Irwin, & Co., 1954. Pp. xxxii, 301.
B5886   *The Tragedy of King Richard II.* Testo, versione ital. in prosa a fronte, note e appendici a cura
         di Gabriele Baldini. Naples: Pironti, 1954. Pp. 235.
B5887   *A New Variorum Edition of Shakespeare, The Life and Death of King Richard II.* Ed. by Matthew
         W. Black. Philadelphia and London: J. B. Lippincott Company, 1955. Pp. xxxii, 655.
             Rev: by Alice Walker, *SQ,* VII (1956), 243-246; by Robert A. Law, *Southwest Rev.,* XLI,
         299-300; by Kenneth Muir, *MLR,* LII (1957), 96-97; by Peter Ure, *RES,* NS, VIII, 290-293;
         by S. F. Johnson, *JEGP,* LVI, 476-483; *ShN,* VII, 14; by T. W. Baldwin, *MLN,* LXXII, 374-382;
         by Hermann Heuer, *SJ,* 93 (1957), 269; by J. G. McManaway, *ShS,* X, 151.
B5888   *King Richard II.* Ed. by K. P. Karunakara Menon. Madras: Viswanathan, n.d.
B5889   *King Richard II.* Ed. by S. C. Sen Gupta. Calcutta: A. Mukherjee and Co., Ltd., n.d.
B5890   *King Richard II.* Ed. by Peter Ure. Arden Shakespeare. London: Methuen, 1956. Pp.
         lxxxiii, 207.
             Rev: *TLS,* Sept. 7, 1956, p. 530; *Dublin Magazine,* XXXI, No. 4 (1956), 62; *N &Q,* NS, III,
         549-550; *MdF,* Dec., p. 736; by J. B. Thomas, *Books of the Month,* Oct., 1956, p. 16; *SCN,*
         XV (1957), 14-15; by Donald FitzJohn, *Drama,* Spring, pp. 38-49; by Pat M. Ryan, Jr.,
         QJS, XLIII, 311-312; by R. A. Foakes, *DUJ,* XLIX, 85-86; by Matthew W. Black, *SQ,* IX (1958),
         67-70; by Alice Walker, *RES,* NS, IX, 193-195; by Winifred M. T. Nowottny, *MLR,* LIII,
         101-104; by Hermann Heuer, *SJ,* 94 (1958), 292-293; by G. A. Bonnard, *Erasmus,* XI, 43-46.
B5891   *The Tragedy of King Richard the Second.* Ed. by Matthew W. Black. Pelican Shakespeare.
         Baltimore: Penguin Books, 1957. Pp. 131.
             Rev: by Wallace A. Bacon, *QJS,* XLIII (1957), 308-309; by Wilbur Dunkel, *SQ,* IX (1958),
         416.
B5892   *King Richard II.* Introd. by Sir John Gielgud. Designs in colour by Loudun Sainthill. London:
         Folio Society, 1958. Pp. 116.
         Eight plates in full color reproduce the designs for the costumes and set of the 1952 Gielgud
         production.
B5893   *The Tragedy of King Richard the Second.* Ed. by R. T. Petersson. Yale Shakespeare. Yale
         Univ. Press, 1957. Pp. viii, 164.

(c) EMENDATIONS

B5894   Sisson, C. J. *A Textual Study of Richard II.* DD, Stanford University, 1935. Abstr. in *Abstracts
         of Dissertations* (Stanford University), X (1936), 55-58.
B5895   Altick, Richard D. " 'Conveyers' and Fortune's Buckets in *Richard II.*" *MLN,* LXI (1946),
         179-180.
B5896   Black, Matthew W. "Problems in the Editing of Shakespeare: Interpretation." *EIE, 1947.*
         Columbia Univ. Press, 1948, pp. 117-136.
B5897   Nearing, Homer, Jr. "A Three-Way Pun in *Richard II.*" *MLN,* LXII (1947), 31-33.
B5898   Atkinson, A. D. "Notes on *Richard II.*" *N &Q,* 194 (1949), 190-192, 212-214.
B5899   Edgerton, W. L. "Shakespeare and the 'Needle's Eye'." *MLN,* LXVI (1951), 549-550.
B5900   Maxwell, J. C. "Blackstone on *Richard II.*" *SQ,* IX (1958), 595.

(2) LITERARY GENESIS AND ANALOGUES
(a) REPRINTS OF POSSIBLE SOURCES

B5901   Rossiter, A. P., ed. *Woodstock: A Moral History.* London: Chatto & Windus, 1946. Pp. 255.
         Contains long introd.: 2 Sections on Politics, Plays, and the State. 2 Sections on Literary
         Relations to *Richard II* and *2 Henry VI.*
             Rev: A1773.
B5902   Daniel, Samuel. *The Civil Wars.* Ed. with Introd. and Notes by Laurence Michel. Yale
         Univ. Press, 1958. Pp. vii, 366.
         Introduction contains (pp. 7-28) "The *Civil Wars* and Shakespeare," an evaluation of the
         indebtedness of Daniel and Shak. to each other.
             Rev: A4734.

(b) STUDIES

B5903   Kublitz, Georg. *Shakespeares "Richard II" und seine Vorstufen in der Englischen Dichtung.* DD,
         Königsberg, 1918. Pp. 82. Typewritten.
B5904   Fryxell, Burton L. *Ghosts and Witches in Elizabethan Tragedy, 1560-1625.* DD, University of
         Wisconsin, 1937. Abstr. publ. in *Summaries of Doctoral Dissertations, 1936-37,* Vol. II, Madison:
         Univ. of Wisconsin Press, 1938, pp. 295-297.

B5905 Fletcher, B. J. *Shakespeare's Use of Holinshed's Chronicles in "Richard III," "Richard II," "Henry IV," and "Macbeth."* DD, University of Texas, 1937.

B5906 Lapsley, G. *"Richard II's 'Last Parliament'."* EHR, LIII (1938), 53-78.

B5907 Dodson, Sarah Clara. "The Northumberland of Shakespeare and Holinshed." TxSE, XIX (1939), 74-85.

B5908 Tillotson, Kathleen. "Drayton and *Richard II*: 1597-1600." RES, XV (1939), 172-179.

B5909 Wilkinson, B. "The Deposition of *Richard II* and Accession of *Henry IV*." EHR, LIV (1939), 215-239.

B5910 Wilson, John Dover. "The Political Background of Shakespeare's *Richard II* and *Henry IV*." SJ, LXXV (1939), 36-51.

B5911 Rossiter, A. P. "Prolegomenon to the Anonymous Woodstock (alias *1 Richard II*)." DUJ, XXXVII (1945), 42-51.

B5912 Black, Matthew W. "The Sources of Shakespeare's *Richard II*." AMS, pp. 199-216.

B5913 Brereton, J. LeGay. "Shakespeare's *Richard the Second*," (pp. 21-40), and "Some Notes on *Richard II*," (pp. 98-109), in his *Writings on Elizabethan Drama*. Melbourne Univ. Press, 1948. Both on relations with *Woodstock*.

B5914 Nearing, Homer, Jr. *"Julius Caesar* and the Tower of London." MLN, LXIII (1948), 228-233.

B5915 Muir, Kenneth. "A Borrowing from Seneca." N&Q, 194 (1949), 214-216.

B5916 Law, Robert A. "Deviations from Holinshed in *Richard II*." TxSE, XXIX (1950), 91-101.

B5917 Leon, Harry J. "Classical Sources for the Garden Scene in *Richard II*." PQ, XXIX (1950), 65-70.

B5918 Greer, C. A. "Did Shakespeare Use Daniel's *Civile Warres?*" N&Q, 196 (1951), 53-54.

B5919 Walker, Roy. " 'The Upstart Crow'." TLS, August 10, 1951, p. 501.
See C. A. C. Davis, ibid., August 17, 1951, p. 517.

B5920 Greer, C. A. "The Play Performed at the Globe on 7 February, 1601." N&Q, 197 (1952), 270-271.

B5921 Greer, C. A. "A Lost Play in the Case of *Richard II?*" N&Q, 197 (1952), 24-25.

B5922 Leishman, James Blair. "The Garden of the World." TLS, Nov. 7, 1952, p. 732. Comment by A. S. T. Fisher, ibid., Nov. 28, 1952, p. 777. Further comment by A. Davenport and J. B. Trapp, ibid., Dec. 5, 1952, p. 797.

B5923 Maugeri, Aldo. *"Edward II," "Richard III," and "Richard II"*: *Note Critiche*. Messina: V. Ferrara, 1952. Pp. 63.

B5924 Ashe, Dora Jean. *A Survey of Non-Shakespearean Bad Quartos*. DD, University of Virginia, 1953. Pp. 286. Mic 54-1567. DA, XIV (1954), 1070. Publication No. 7952.

B5925 Kirchner, Gustav. "Das Historische und Dichterische Bild *Richards II*." ZAA (Berlin), I (1953), 131-170.

B5926 Ure, Peter. "Shakespeare's Play and the French Sources of Holinshed's and Stow's Account of *Richard II*." N&Q, 198 (1953), 436-439.

B5927 Ure, Peter. "Two Passages in Sylvester's Du Bartas and Their Bearing on Shakespeare's *Richard II*." N&Q, 198 (1953), 374-377.

B5928 Galbraith, V. H. "Richard II in Fact and Fiction." Listener, LI (1954), 691-692.

B5929 McAvoy, William C. "Form in *Richard II*, II.i.40-46." JEGP, LIV (1955), 355-361.

B5930 Bennett, Josephine Waters. "Britain Among the Fortunate Isles." SP, LIII (1956), 114-140. II.i.39-57.

B5931 Cauthen, I. B., Jr. "Shakespeare's 'Moat Defensive' (*Richard II*, II.i.43-49)." N&Q, NS, III (1956), 419-420.

B5932 Shapiro, I. A. *"Richard II* or *Richard III*, or . . . ?" SQ, IX (1958), 204-206.

(3) USE OF LANGUAGE

B5933 Doran, Madeleine. "Imagery in *Richard II* and in *Henry IV*." MLR, XXXVII (1942), 113-122.

B5934 Adkins, M. G. M. "A Variant of a Familiar Elizabethan Image." N&Q, 192 (1947), 69-70.

B5935 Altick, Richard D. "Symphonic Imagery in *Richard II*." PMLA, LXII (1947), 339-365.

B5936 Jorgensen, Paul A. "Vertical Patterns in *Richard II*." SAB, XXIII (1948), 119-134.

B5937 Kliger, Samuel. "The Sun Imagery in *Richard II*." SP, XLV (1948), 196-202.

B5938 Downer, Alan S. "The Life of our Design." Hudson Review, II (1949), 242-263.

B5939 Platt, Doris H. *The Imagery in Richard II*. DD, University of Wisconsin, 1948. Abstr. publ. in *Summaries of Doctoral Dissertations*, 1947-49, Vol. X, Madison: Univ. of Wisconsin Press, 1950, pp. 621-622.

B5940 Provost, George F., Jr. *The Techniques of Characterization and Dramatic Imagery in "Richard II" and "King Lear."* DD, Louisiana State University, 1955. Pp. 274. Mic 55-280. DA, XV (1955), 1615-16. Publication No. 12,525.

B5941 Finkenstaedt, Thomas. *Die Verskunst des jungen Shakespeare: "Richard III," "Richard II," "King John."* DD, Munich, 1955. Pp. x, 155. Typewritten.

B5942 Mahood, M. M. *Shakespeare's Word Play*. London: Methuen, 1956. Chapter on *Richard II*.

B5943 Suzman, Arthur. "Imagery and Symbolism in *Richard II*." *SQ*, VII (1956), 355-370.

B5944 Greenberg, Robert A. "Shakespeare's *Richard II*, IV.i.244-250." *Expl.*, Feb. 29, 1957.

(4) GENERAL CRITICISM OF THE PLAY

B5945 Papiroff, S. "Shakespeare's Idea of Kingship as Seen in *Richard II* and *Henry IV*." *The Silver Falcon*. New York: Hunter College, 1936, pp. 16-20.

B5946 Baym, M. I. "Recurrent Poetic Theme." *SAB*, XII (1937), 155-158.

B5947 Campbell, L. B. "The Use of Historical Patterns in the Reign of Elizabeth." *HLQ*, I (1937), 135-167.

B5948 Koszul, A. "Shakespeare, *Richard II*. Agrégation et Licence d'Anglais." *Bulletin de la Fac. des Lettres* (Strasbourg), XVI (1939-40), 113-117.

B5949 Palmer, John. *Political Characters of Shakespeare*. Macmillan, 1945. Pp. xii, 335.
       Rev: A6550a.

B5950 Atkinson, A. D. "Notes on *Richard II*." *N &Q*, 194 (1949), 190-192, 212-214.

B5951 Draper, John W. "The Tempo of Richard II's Speech." *SN*, XX (1948), 88-94.

B5952 Heer, Friedrich. "Tragödie des Königs. Shakespeares *König Richard II*." *Die österr. Furche*, VI, No. 13 (1950), 7.

B5953 Mary Alphonsa Carpenter, Sister. *"The Tragedy of Richard II"*: *Its Background and Meaning*. DD, University of Illinois, 1950. Pp. 340. Mic A51-55. *DA*, XI (1951), 104. Publication No. 2225.

B5954 Jensen, Harro. *"Richard II* als Drama der Wende." *Shakespeare-Studien, Festschrift für Heinrich Mutschmann*, pp. 80-87.

B5955 Dean, Leonard F. *"Richard II*: The State and the Image of the Theater." *PMLA*, LXVII (1952), 211-218.

B5956 Guerrini, Vittoria. "La Gravità e la Grazia nel *Riccardo II*." *Il Mattino dell'Italia Centrale* (Florence), Aug. 8, 1952, p. 3.

B5957 Kirchner, G. "Das historische und dichterische Bild *Richards II*." *Wissenschaftliche Zeitschrift der Friedrich-Schiller-Universität* (Jena), I (1951-2), Heft 2, 31-46. Republ. in *ZAA*, I (1953), 131-170.

B5958 Cancelled.

B5959 Owen, Lewis J. *"Richard II*." *Lectures on Four of Shakespeare's History Plays*. Carnegie Series in English, No. 1 (1953), pp. 3-18.

B5960 Barthes, Roland. "La Fin de *Richard II*." *Lettres Nouvelles*, No. 13 (1954).

B5961 Cauthen, I. B., Jr. *"Richard II* and the Image of the Betrayed Christ." *Renaissance Papers*, 1954, pp. 45-48.

B5962 Goodman, Paul. *The Structure of Literature*. Univ. of Chicago Press, 1954. Pp. vii, 282.
       Rev: *TLS*, Oct. 22, 1954, p. 674; by R. Greacen, *English*, X (1954/55), 232; by A. E. Rodway, *EIC*, V (1955), 55-63; by H. Levin, *MLN*, LXX, 124-126; by H. D. Aiken, "Inductive Criticism," *KR*, XVII, 304-311.

B5963 Rebora, P. *"Riccardo II* non Trova Riposte alle proprie domande." *Biennale di Venezia*, No. 15 (1954).

B5964 Freund, John Richard. *Dualism in "Richard II"*: *A Study in Thematic Structure*. DD, Indiana University, 1955. Pp. 249. Mic A55-1843. *DA*, XV (1955), 1397. Publication No. 12,827.

B5965 Rubow, Paul V. *Shakespeares Ungdomsstykker*. The Royal Danish Scientifical Society: Historical-Philosophical Informations, Vol. XXXIV, No. 5. Copenhagen: Munksgaard, 1955. Pp. 34.

B5966 Ure, Peter. "The Looking-Glass of *Richard II*." *PQ*, XXXIV (1955), 219-224.

B5967 Tyler, Parker. "Phaethon: The Metaphysical Tension Between the Ego and the Universe in English Poetry." *Accent*, XVI (Winter, 1956), 29-44.

B5968 Bryant, J. A., Jr. "The Linked Analogies of *Richard II*." *SR*, LXV (1957), 420-433.

B5969 Kantorowicz, Ernest H. "Shakespeare: *King Richard II*." *The King's Two Bodies: A Study in Medieval Political Theology*. Princeton, N. J.: Princeton Univ. Press, 1957, pp. 24-41.

B5970 Thompson, Karl F. "Richard II, Martyr." *SQ*, VIII (1957), 159-166.

(5) CHARACTERIZATION

B5971 Taylor, M. P. "A Father Pleads for the Death of his Son." *International Jour. of Psycho-Analysis*, VIII (1927), 53-55.

B5972 Dodson, Sarah Clara. "The Northumberland of Shakespeare and Holinshed." *TxSE*, XIX (1939), 74-85.

B5973 Craig, Hardin. "Shakespeare's Development as a Dramatist in the Light of his Experience." *SP*, XXXIX (1942), 226-238.

B5974 Draper, John W. "The Character of Richard II." *PQ*, XXI (1942), 228-236.

B5975 Dukes, William J. *Shakespeare Criticism and "Richard II."* MA thesis, University of North

Carolina, 1943. Abstr. publ. in *University of North Carolina Record, Research in Progress*, Grad. School Series, No. 50, 1946, p. 151.

B5976   Ribner, I. "Bolingbroke, a True Machiavellian." *MLQ*, IX (1948), 117-184.

B5977   Bonnard, Georges A. "The Actor in *Richard II*." *SJ*, 87/88 (1952), 87-101.

B5978   Stirling, Brents. "Bolingbroke's 'Decision'." *SQ*, III (1952), 27-34.

B5979   Bogard, Travis. "Shakespeare's Second Richard." *PMLA*, LXX (1955), 192-204.
        Rev: by H. Oppel, *NS*, IV (1955), 518-519.

B5980   Provost, George Foster. *The Techniques of Characterization and Dramatic Imagery in "Richard II" and "King Lear."* DD, Louisiana State University, 1955. Pp. 274. Mic 55-280. *DA*, XV (1955), 1616. Publication No. 12,525.

B5981   Smith, Gordon Ross. *Good in Evil in Shakespearean Tragedy.* DD, The Pennsylvania State University, 1956. Pp. 446. Mic 57-568. *DA*, XVII (1957), 358. Publication No. 19,323.

B5982   Kleinstück, Johannes. "The Character of Henry Bolingbroke." *Neophil*, XLI (1957), 51-56.

B5983   McPeek, James A. S. "Richard and his Shadow World." *American Imago*, XV (1958), 195-212.

(6)   MISCELLANEOUS ITEMS

B5984   "Elisabeth et la Tragédie du *Roi Richard II*." *MdF*, 269 (1936), 665-668.

B5985   Norton, C. E. "Rawdon Brown and the Gravestone of 'Banished Norfolk'." (Autograph MS), B. J. Beyer's catalogue of *Choice Books and MSS. from the 14th to the 20th Century*, New York, 1936, pp. 64.
        (MS was of 1889. Consisted of 12 pages offered at $60.)

B5986   Koszul, A. "*Richard II*: Notes Bibliographiques and Plan d'Etude." *B. de la Faculté des Lettres de Strasbourg*, XVI (1938), 113-117.

B5987   Lambin, G. "Shakespeare était-il Essexien?" *LanM*, XLII (1948), 14-22.

B5988   Nearing, Homer, Jr. "*Julius Caesar* and the Tower of London." *MLN*, LXIII (1948), 228-233.

B5989   Villar, J. "*La Tragédie du Roi Richard II* (Tableau du Matériel Scénique)." *La Revue Théâtrale*, VII (1948), 12-15.

B5990   Hunter, E. K. *Shakespeare and Common Sense.* Boston: Christopher, 1954. Pp. 312.
        Chap. II: "Shakspere's Intentions Regarding King Richard II."
        Rev: A971.

B5991   Gallagher, Ligera Cécile. *Shakespeare and the Aristotelian Ethical Tradition.* DD, Stanford University, 1956. Pp. 338. Mic 56-3017. *DA*, XVI (1956), 1898. Publication No. 17,720. Chapter on *Richard II*.

B5992   Ogdon, J. A. H. *An Examination of Imagery and Libido Symbolism in Certain Literary Works.* Master's thesis, Liverpool, 1956.
        Considerable work done on *Richard II* alluded to in introduction but not given *in extenso*.

(7)   SUBSEQUENT HISTORY OF THE PLAY
(other than productions after 1660)

B5993   Greer, C. A. "The Play Performed at the Globe on 7 February, 1601." *N &Q*, 198 (1953), 270-271.

B5994   O'Connell, Richard L. "A Stage History of *Richard II*." *Listener*, LI (1954), 225.

A MIDSUMMER NIGHT'S DREAM (206;73)
(1)   THE TEXT
(a)   OLD TEXTS

B5995   Spencer, H. "A Note on Cutting and Slashing." *MLR*, XXXI (1936), 393-395.

B5996   Draper, John W. "The Date of *A Midsommer Nights Dreame*." *MLN*, LIII (1938), 266-268.

(b)   MODERN EDITIONS

B5997   *A Midsummer Night's Dream.* Ed. by F. C. Horwood. New Clarendon Shakespeare. London, New York: Oxford Univ. Press, 1939. Pp. 192.

B5998   *A Midsummer Night's Dream.* Ed. by George Lyman Kittredge. Boston: Ginn, 1939. Pp. xiv, 160.
        Rev: by Robert Adger Law, *JEGP*, XXXIX (1940), 578-581.

B5999   *A Midsummer Night's Dream.* Ed. by F. W. Robinson. Melbourne: Milford, 1940.
        Rev: by Nowell Smith, *English*, III (1940), 147-148.

B6000   *A Midsummer Night's Dream. A Comedy in 5 Acts.* Met verklarende aantekeningen door Willem van Doorn. Groningen: J. B. Wolters, 1942. Pp. 100. Republ. 1948, 1950, 1958.

B6001   *A Midsummer Night's Dream.* Ed. by Mario Hazon. Milan: Garzanti, 1947. Pp. 58.

B6002   *A Midsummer Night's Dream.* Ed. by Sri P. A. Subrahmanya Ayyar. Madras: Kaviraja, 1948.

B6003   *A Midsummer Night's Dream.* Ed. by Tyrone Guthrie and G. B. Harrison. New Stratford Shakespeare. London: Harrap, 1954. Pp. 122.

B6004   *A Midsummer Night's Dream.* Ed. by Fritz Krog. Neusprachliche Textausgaben, English Series, No. 2. Frankfurt-am-Main: Hirschgraben, 1949, 1954. Pp. 135.

B6005   *A Midsummer Night's Dream.* Cape Town: Maskew Miller, 1957. Pp. 161.

B6006   *A Midsummer Night's Dream.* With a New Introduction by Sir Ralph Richardson. Designs in Colour by Oliver Messel. London: Folio Society, 1957. Pp. 88.

B6007   *A Midsummer Night's Dream.* Ed. by Ian Stuart. New Simplified Shakespeare. Birmingham, Alabama: Vulcan Press, 1956. Pp. 159. Paperback and cloth.

B6008   *A Midsummer Night's Dream.* Ed. by Louis B. Wright and Virginia A. LaMar. Folger Library General Reader's Shakespeare. New York: Pocket Books, 1958. Pp. xxxv, 81.

(c) EMENDATIONS

B6009   Allen, N. B. "An Insertion in *A Midsummer Night's Dream.*" [V.i.4-16]. *SAB,* XIII (1938), 121-122.

B6010   Kôkeritz, Helge. "Shakespeare's *Night-Rule* [*A Midsummer Night's Dream,* III.ii.5]." *Language,* XVIII (1942), 40-44.

B6011   Troubridge, St. V., et al. "The Nine-Men's-Morris." *N &Q,* 188 (1945), 40-41.

B6012   Munro, John. "Some Matters Shakespearian." *TLS,* Sept. 27, 1947, p. 500.

B6013   Thomas, Sidney. "The Bad Weather in *A Midsummer Night's Dream.*" *MLN,* LXIV (1949), 319-322.

B6014   Sledd, James. "A Note on the Use of Renaissance Dictionaries." *MP,* XLIX (1951/52), 10-15. Comments on passage in *Dream.*

B6015   Bluestone, Max. "An Anti-Jewish Pun in *A Midsummer Night's Dream,* III.i.97." *N &Q,* 198 (1953), 325-329.

B6016   Heninger, S. K., Jr. " 'Wondrous Strange Snow'—*Midsummer Night's Dream,* V.i.66." *MLN,* LXVIII (1953), 481-483.

B6017   Strix. "Those Choughs." *Spectator,* 6545 (1953), 655-656. Comment by Henry Willink, 6546 (1953), 697; by A. P. Rossiter, 6547 (1953), 726-727.

B6018   Hulme, Hilda. "Three Notes: . . . *Dream,* II.i.54 . . . ." *JEGP,* LVII (1958), 721-725.

(2) LITERARY GENESIS AND ANALOGUES

B6019   Kroepelin, H. "Das Niedersächsische im *Sommernachtstraum.*" *Dts. Allgem. Ztg.,* Sept. 25, 1940.

B6020   McNeal, Thomas H. "Studies in the Green-Shakspere Relationship." *SAB,* XV (1940), 210-218.
Passage in *Dream* aimed at a poem only hypothetically Greene's.

B6021   Chambers, Sir E. K. "The Occasion of *A Midsummer Night's Dream.*" In his *Shakespearean Gleanings,* Oxford Univ. Press, 1944.

B6022   Bethurum, Dorothy. "Shakespeare's Comment on Mediaeval Romance in *Midsummer Night's Dream.*" *MLN,* LX (1945), 85-94.
Suggests that either Chaucer's *Knight's Tale* or the anonymous (and lost) play *Palamon and Arcette* first inspired the main plot of *Midsummer Night's Dream.*

B6023   M. Generosa, Sister. "Apuleius and *A Midsummer Night's Dream:* Analogue or Source, Which?" *SP,* XLII (1945), 198-204.

B6024   Poirier, Michel. "Sidney's Influence upon *A Midsummer Night's Dream.*" *SP,* XLIV (1947), 483-489.

B6025   Ribner, Irving. "A Note on Sidney's *Arcadia* and *A Midsummer Night's Dream.*" *SAB,* XXIII (1948), 207-208. See B6024.

B6026   Lindsay, Jack. "Shakespeare and Tom Thumb." *Life and Letters,* LVIII (1948), 119-127.

B6027   West, E. J. "On a Purely Playful Hypothesis Concerning the Composition of *A Midsummer Night's Dream.*" *CE,* IX (1948), 247-249.

B6028   Davenport, A. "Weever, Ovid and Shakespeare." *N &Q,* 194 (1949), 524-525.

B6029   Fisher, A. S. T. "The Sources of Shakespeare's Interlude of Pyramus and Thisbe: A Neglected Poem." *N &Q,* 194 (1949), 376-379, 400-402.
Treats Thomas Mouffet's *The Silkewormes, and their Flies,* 1599.

B6030   Atherton, J. S. "Shakespeare's Latin, Two Notes." *N &Q,* 196 (1951), 337.

B6031   Rashbrook, R. F. "Shakespeare and the Bible." *N &Q,* 197 (1952), 49-50.

B6032   Hammerle, Karl. "Shakespeares Platonische Wende." *Anglo-Americana, Festschrift für Leo Hibler-Lehmannssport, Wiener Beiträge z. engl. Philologie,* LXII (1955), 62-71.

B6033   Hammerle, Karl. "The Poet's Eye (*MND,* V.i.12): Zur Auffassung Shakespeares vom Wesen des Dichters." *Innsbrucker Beiträge zur Kulturwissenschaft,* I (1954), 101-107.

B6034   Hammerle, Karl. "Das Titanialager des Sommernachtstraumes als Nachhall des Topos vom *Locus Amoenus.*" *SJ,* 90 (1954), 279-284.

B6035   Muir, Kenneth. "Pyramus and Thisbe: A Study in Shakespeare's Method." *SQ,* V (1954), 141-153.

B6036   Muir, Kenneth. "Shakespeare as Parodist." *N &Q,* NS, I (1954), 467-468.

B6037   Spencer, Terence. "Three Shakespearian Notes." *MLR*, XLIX (1954), 46-51.
        That *Demetrius* is a vile name (*MND*, II.ii. 106-107) may have originated in the Life of Deme-
        trius Poliorcetes in North's Plutarch.

B6038   Cheney, David Raymond. *Animals in "A Midsummer Night's Dream."* DD, State University of
        Iowa, 1955. Pp. 288. Mic 55-1103. *DA*, XV (1955), 2188. Publication No. 14,094.

B6039   Nitze, William A. *"A Midsummer Night's Dream*, V.i.4-17." *MLR*, L (1955), 495-497.

B6040   Schanzer, Ernest. *"Midsummer Night's Dream* and *Romeo and Juliet."* N &Q, NS, II (1955),
        13-14.

B6041   Simpson, Percy. *Studies in Elizabethan Drama.* Oxford: Clarendon Press, 1955. Pp. 265.
        Chap. III: "The 'Headless Bear' in Shakespeare and Burton," pp. 89-94.

B6042   Braddy, Haldeen. "Shakespeare's Puck and Froissart's Orthon." *SQ*, VII (1956), 276-280.

B6043   Briggs, K. M. "The English Fairies." *Folklore*, LXVIII (1957), 270-287.

B6044   Hammerle, Karl. "Ein Muttermal des deutschen Pyramus und die Spenserechos in *Mid-
        summer Night's Dream." Festschrift z. 70. Geburtstag von Friedrich Wild.* Vienna, Stuttgart:
        Braumüller, 1958, pp. 52-66.

(3) USE OF LANGUAGE

B6045   Jones, Ernest. "The Madonna's Conception Through the Ear." *Selected Essays in Applied
        Psycho-Analysis.* International Psycho-Analytical Library, No. 5. London: International
        Psycho-Analytical Press, 1923, pp. 261-359.
        Dream, II.i.128-132.

B6046   MacCarthy, Desmond. *Theatre.* London: MacGibbon & Kee. Pp. vi, 191.
        A collection of critical essays, including some on Shak.
        Rev: B7838.

(4)   GENERAL CRITICISM OF THE PLAY

B6047   Dayton, B. E. *Animal Similes and Metaphors in Shakespeare's* Plays. DD, University of
        Washington, 1937. Abstr. in Univ. of Washington, *Abstracts of Theses*, II (1937), 119-122.

B6048   Charlton, H. B. *"A Midsummer Night's Dream." BJRL*, XXII (1938), 46-66.
        Rev: by E. E. Stoll, *SJ*, LXXIV (1938), 50-53.

B6049   Kreuzer, J. R. "Some Earlier Examples of the Rhetorical Device in *Ralph Roister Doister."
        RES*, XIV (1938), 321-323.

B6050   De la Mare, Walter. "The *Dream." Pleasures and Speculations*, London, 1940, pp. 270-305.
        Also printed in the "Scholar's Library Edition" of *A Midsummer Night's Dream.*

B6051   Miller, Donald C. "Titania and the Changeling." *ES*, XXII (1940), 66-70.

B6052   Göpfert, Herbert Georg. "Über Rudolf Alexander Schröders Verdeutschung von Shake-
        speares *Sommernachtstraum." DNL*, XLII (1941), 258-261.

B6053   Schröder, Rudolf Alexander. "Ein Wort zu Shakespeares *Sommernachtstraum." Hamburg-
        ishches Jahrbuch für Theater und Musik*, 1941. Hamburg: Broschek & Co., 1941, pp. 45-57.
        Tr. by Paul Th. Hoffmann, also published in his *Gesammelte Werke*, II (1952), 237-248.

B6054   Sternberger, Dolf. " 'Puck'. Zum deutschen *Sommernachtstraum." Frankf. Ztg.*, 1941,
        Nos. 8/9.

B6055   Ellison, Florence R. "Fairy Folk in *A Midsummer Night's Dream." Jour. of the S. W. Essex
        Technical Coll.*, I (1942), 99-101.

B6056   Law, Robert A. "The 'Pre-Conceived Pattern' of *A Midsummer Night's Dream." TxSE*,
        XXIII (1943), 5-14.

B6057   Maas, P. "Shakespeare and Rime." *MLR*, XXXIX (1944), 179.

B6058   Schröder, Rudolf Alexander. "Das Menschenbild in Shakespeares *Sommernachtstraum."
        Zeitwende*, XVIII (1946/47), 86-97, 172-183. Also in his *Gesammelte Werke*, II (1952), 248-280.

B6059   Sobotta, Gerhard. "Dr. Stahls letztes Werk." *MDtShG*, I (1949), 8.

B6060   Parsons, Howard. "Letter on Shakespeare." *Forum Stories and Poems*, I, No. 2 (1950).

B6061   Schomerus, Hans. "Der Kobold und die Güte Gottes." *Zeitwende*, XXII (1950/51), 177-178.

B6062   Eardley-Wilmot, H. " 'Write Me a Prologue'." *English*, VIII (1951), 272-274.

B6063   Schanzer, Ernest. "The Central Theme of *A Midsummer Night's Dream." UTQ*, XX (1951),
        233-238.

B6064   Hammerle, Karl. "Das Laubenmotiv bei Shakespeare und Spenser und die Frage: Wer
        waren Bottom und die Little Western Flower?" *Anglia*, LXXI (1953), 310-330.

B6065   Klingmüller, Götz. *Pyramus und Thisbe oder Die Premiere um acht. Ein Stück Shakespeare und
        ein Stück Schmierentheater zusammengefügt.* Kassel: Bärenreiter, 1953. Pp. 54.

B6066   Litten, Heinz W. "Shakespeare als Beleuchtungsmeister." *Heute und Morgen* (Schwerin),
        1953, pp. 671-675.

B6067   Vierig, H. "Der Mensch ist ein Esel . . . Betrachtungen über Shakespeare und seine Zeit an
        Hand einer Szene aus dem *Sommernachtstraum." Gestaltung und Gestalten* (Dresden), IX (1954),
        75-81.

B6068   Schanzer, Ernest. *"A Midsummer Night's Dream* and *Romeo and Juliet."* N &Q, NS, II (1955), 13-14.

B6069   Schanzer, Ernest. "The Moon and the Fairies in *A Midsummer Night's Dream."* UTQ, XXIV (1955), 234-246.

B6070   Schmidtbonn, Wilhelm. "Die Fahrt in den *Sommernachtstraum."* *Das festliche Haus*, Cologne, 1955, pp. 122-124.

B6071   Bonnard, Georges A. "Shakespeare's Purpose in *Midsummer Night's Dream."* SJ, 92 (1956), 268-279.

B6072   Dillingham, William B. "Bottom: the Third Ingredient." *Emory University Quarterly*, XII (1956), 230-237.

B6073   Lüthi, Max. "Shakespeare und das Märchen." *Zeitschr. f. Volkskunde*, LIII (1956/57), 141-149.

B6074   Myers, Henry Alonzo. *Tragedy: A View of Life.* Cornell Univ. Press, 1956. Pp. 218.
        Rev: A6916.

B6075   Nemerov, Howard. "The Marriage of Theseus and Hippolyta." *Kenyon Review*, XVIII (1956), 633-641.

B6076   Chesterton, G. K. *G. K. Chesterton: An Anthology.* With an Introduction by Wyndham Lewis. The World's Classics. Oxford Univ. Press, 1957. Pp. 235.
        Contains a 12-page critical discussion of *Dream.*
        Rev: N &Q, NS, IV (1957), 321; by John Raymond, NstN, March 23, 1957, pp. 384-385; *Saturday Night* (Canada), July 6, p. 24.

B6077   Fisher, Peter F. "The Argument of *A Midsummer Night's Dream."* SQ, VIII (1957), 307-310.

B6078   Luserke, Martin. *Pan—Apollon—Prospero. "Ein Mittsommernachtstraum," "Die Winterssage" und "Der Sturm." Zur Dramaturgie von Shakespeare-Spielen.* Hamburg: Christians, 1957. Pp. 224.

B6079   Olson, Paul A. *"A Midsummer Night's Dream* and the Meaning of Court Marriage." ELH, XXIV (1957), 95-119.

B6080   Popović, D. "Vil'em Šekspir: San letnje noći." *Letopis matice srpske* (Novi Sad), 379 (1957), 626-630.

(5) CHARACTERIZATION

B6081   Legouis, Emile. "La Psychologie dans *Le Songe d'une Nuit d'Eté."* EA, III (1939), 113-117.

B6082   Hollander, L. M. "Erlkönig und *Sommernachtstraum."* *Monatshefte*, XXXVI (1944), 145-146.

B6083   Palmer, John. *Comic Characters of Shakespeare.* New York: Macmillan, 1946. Pp. 135.
        Rev: A6544.

B6084   Straumann, Heinrich. "Shakespeare und der Verblendete Mensch." *Neue Zürcher Zeitung* (Zurich), No. 1638, June 19, 1955.

B6085   Bastian, F. "George Vargis, Constable." N &Q, NS, IV (1957), 11.
        Comment by Geoffrey W. Jaggard, pp. 179.

(6) MISCELLANEOUS ITEMS

B6086   Cambillard. *"Le Songe d'une Nuit d'Eté*, Thème Astrologique." EA, III (1939), 118-126.

B6087   Lee, Harry B. "A Theory Concerning Free Creation in the Inventive Arts." *Psychiatry*, III (1940), 292.

B6088   Falckenberg, Otto. "Der neue *Sommernachtstraum*. Gedanken zum Problem der Inszenierung." MNN, No. 75, 1941.

B6088a Falckenberg, Otto. "Zur Frage der Inszenierung des *Sommernachtstraums."* SJ, LXXVII (1941), 116-122.

B6089   Harrison, Thomas P., Jr. "Flower Lore in Spenser and Shakespeare: Two Notes." MLQ, VII (1946), 175-178.

B6090   Wilson, J. D. "Variations on the Theme of *Midsummer Night's Dream." Tribute to Walter de la Mare on his 75th Birthday*, London, 1948, pp. 25-43.

B6091   Hammerle, Karl. "The Poet's Eye: Zur Auffassung Shakespeares vom Wesen des Dichters." *Ammann-Festgabe* (Innsbruck), I (1953), 101-107.

B6092   Siegel, Paul N. *"A Midsummer Night's Dream* and the Wedding Guests." SQ, IV (1953), 139-144.

B6093   MacCarthy, Desmond. *"Midsummer Night's Dream:* The Production of Poetic Drama." *MacCarthy's Theatre.* London, 1954, pp. 47-56.

B6094   Gui, Weston A. "Bottom's Dream." *American Imago*, IX (1952), 251-305.

B6095   Grinstein, Alexander. "The Dramatic Device: A Play Within a Play." *Jour. of the American Psycho-Analytic Association*, IV (1956), 49-52.
        The dream within a dream is compared to the play within a play as it occurs in *Hamlet*, in *A Midsummer Night's Dream*, and in one of Shaw's plays.

B6096   Brodersen, Chr. N. "Omkring 'En Skaersommernatsdröm'." *Vendsyssel Tidende* (Hiörring, Denmark), Dec. 12, 1957.

B6097 Gestetner, J. M. *Shakespeare's "Midsummer Night's Dream."* New Issue. London: Pitman, 1958. Pp. 32.
Commentary and questionaire.

(7) SUBSEQUENT HISTORY OF THE PLAY
(other than productions after 1660)

KING JOHN (211;74)
(1) THE TEXT
(a) OLD TEXTS

B6098 Taylor, Rupert. "A Tentative Chronology of Marlowe's and Some Other Elizabethan Plays." *PMLA*, LI (1936), 643-688.

B6099 Price, George R. "Compositors' Methods with Two Quartos Reprinted by Augustine Mathewes." *Papers Bibl. Soc. Amer.*, XLIV (1950), 269-274.

B6100 Law, Robert Adger. "On the Date of *King John.*" *SP*, LIV (1957), 119-127.

(b) MODERN EDITIONS

B6101 *King John.* Ed. by John Dover Wilson. Cambridge Univ. Press, 1936. New York: Macmillan Company, 1936. Pp. lxxxiv, 208.
Rev: *TLS*, Jan. 16, 1937, p. 40; *N &Q*, 172 (1937), 71-72; by G. B. Harrison, *MLR*, XXXII, 455-456; by L. L. Schücking, *Beiblatt*, XLVIII, 97-99; by Trevor James, *Life and Letters Today*, XVI, No. 8, 150-151; by L. C. K., *Criterion*, XVI, 757-758; by F. C. Danchin, *EA*, I, 252; by Rosamond Gilder, *TAr*, XXI, 330-331; by Mark Van Doren, *Nation* (N.Y.), 144 (1937), 517; by W. Keller, *SJ*, LXXIII, 151-152.

B6102 *King John.* Ed. by N. V. Meeres. Scholar's Libr. London: Macmillan, 1937. Pp. 178.

B6103 *King John.* Ed. by E. A. J. Honigmann. Arden Ed. London: Methuen, 1954. Pp. xxv, 176.
Rev: by John Crow, *Listener*, LII (1954), 975-977; by T. S. Dorsch, *YWES*, XXXV, 80; *English*, X (1955), 157; by J. Vallette, *MdF*, 323 (1955), 151-152; *TLS*, Feb. 4, p. 78; *Dublin Magazine*, XXXI, No. 1, 66-67; by Irving Ribner, *ShN*, V, 14; by Christopher Devlin, *Month*, XIV (Aug.), 110; by Franklin B. Williams, Jr., *SQ*, VI, 339-340; by Kenneth Muir, *London Mag.*, II, No. 6, 104-106, 108; by C. G. Thayer, *Books Abroad*, XXIX, 471; by William T. Hastings, *SQ*, VI, 117-118; by Hermann Heuer, *SJ*, 91 (1955), 330-333; *Adelphi*, XXXI, No. 2, 207-208; by Clifford Leech, *MLR*, LI (1956), 94-95; by Pat M. Ryan, Jr., *QJS*, XLII, 84-86; by Alice Walker, *RES*, NS, VII, 421-423; by T. M. Parrott, *JEGP*, LV, 297-305; by R. Davril, *EA*, XI (1958), 51-52.

B6104 *The Life and Death of King John.* Ed. by G. B. Harrison. Penguin Shakespeare. Harmondsworth: Penguin Books, 1958. Pp. 126.
Rev: *TLS*, Jan. 17, 1958, p. 35; by J. Vallette, *MdF*, 331 (1957), 693.

(c) EMENDATIONS

B6105 Graves, R. " 'To Paint the Lily', etc." *TLS*, July 10, 1943, pp. 331-332.

B6106 Nearing, Homer, Jr. "A Note on *King John*, V.vii.112-114." *N &Q*, 192 (1947), 256-257.

B6107 Maxwell, J. C. "Notes on *King John.*" "*King John*—Textual Notes." *N &Q*, 195 (1950), 75-76, 473-474.
Proposes emendations for II.i.143-144; II.i.584; III.i.196; V.vii.15-17; III.iv.1-3; II.iv.44; III.iv.170-172; IV.ii.30-31; IV.iii.123-129.

B6108 Baldini, Gabriele. "Shakespeariana. Nota a *King John*, III.iv.110." *Rivista di Letterature Moderne* (Milan), II, No. 5 (Sept.-Oct., 1951), 555-560.

B6109 Schanzer, Ernest. "*King John*, V.ii.103-104." *N &Q*, NS, II (1955), 474-475.

B6110 Hulme, Hilda. "Three Notes on the Pronunciation and Meanings of Shakespeare's Text . . . . A Whole Armado of Conuicted Saile (*King John*, III.iv.2)." *Neophil*, XLI (1957), 275-281.

(2) LITERARY GENESIS AND ANALOGUES

B6111 Barke, Herbert. *Bale's "Kynge Johan" und sein Verhältnis zur zeitgenössischen Geschichtschreibung.* DD, Berlin. Würzburg: Triltsch., 1937. Pp. x, 145.
Rev: by Alois Brandl, *Archiv*, 171 (1937), 260; by Maria Schutt, *Beiblatt*, XLIX (1938), 143-145.

B6112 Smith, Marion B. *Marlowe's Imagery and the Marlowe Canon.* Univ. of Penna. Press, 1940. Pp. vii, 213.
Rev: B5321.

B6113 Elson, John. "Studies in the King John Plays." *AMS*, pp. 183-197.

B6114 Frankis, P. J. "Shakespeare's *King John* and a Patriotic Slogan." *N &Q*, NS, II (1955), 424-425.

B6115 McDiarmid, Matthew P. "A Reconsidered Parallel Between Shakespeare's *King John* and Kyd's *Cornelia.*" *N &Q*, NS, III (1956), 507-508.

B6116 Schanzer, Ernest. "*Hercules Oetaeus* and *King John.*" *N &Q*, NS, III (1956), 509-510.

B6117   McDiarmid, Matthew P. "Concerning *The Troublesome Reign of King John*." *N &Q*, NS, IV (1957), 435-438.

B6118   Warren, W. L. "What Was Wrong with King John?" *History Today*, VII (1957), 806-812.

(3) USE OF LANGUAGE

B6119   Pettet, E. C. "Hot Irons and Fever: A Note on Some of the Imagery of *King John*." *EIC*, IV (1954), 128-144.

B6120   Finkenstaedt, Thomas. *Die Verskunst des jungen Shakespeare: "Richard III," "Richard II," "King John."* DD, Munich, 1955. Pp. 155. Typewritten.

(4) GENERAL CRITICISM OF THE PLAY

B6121   Ash, Margaret S. *An Historical Study of King John.* DD, State University of Iowa, 1936.

B6122   Greenewald, Rev. Gerard M. *Shakespeare's Attitude Towards the Catholic Church in "King John."* DD, Catholic University of America, 1939. Pp. x, 195.

B6123   Bonjour, Adrien. "Le Problème du Héros et la Structure du *Roi Jean* de Shakespeare." *Etudes de Lettres* (Lausanne), XXIII (1950), 3-15.

B6124   Bonjour, Adrien. "The Road to Swindstead Abbey: A Study of the Sense and Structure of *King John*." *ELH*, XVIII (1951), 253-274.

B6125   Schanzer, Ernest. "A Plot-Chain in *Antony and Cleopatra*." *N &Q*, 199 (1954), 379-380. Comparison with *John*, III. i. 331ff.

B6126   Tyler, Parker. "Phaethon: The Metaphysical Tension Between the Ego and the Universe in English Poetry." *Accent*, XVI (Winter, 1956), 29-44.

(5) CHARACTERIZATION

B6127   Ware, Eunice L. *King John in Tudor Chronicle and Drama.* DD, University of Texas, 1936.

B6128   Spiegelberger, W. "Shakespeares Caesarbild." *Neuphilol. Mschr.*, X (1939), 177-189.

B6129   Petit-Dutaillis, Charles. "Un Héros shakespearien: Le Bâtard de Falconbridge." *Académie des Inscriptions et Belles-Lettres, Comptes rendus des séances de l'année 1943*, 1945, pp. 519-531.

B6130   M. J. Frances Hoey, Sister. *Shakespeare and Two Women: A Study of Eleanor of Aquitaine and Margaret of Anjou.* DD, St. John's University, 1950. Abstr. publ. in *Abstracts of Dissertations, 1949-1950*, Brooklyn: St. John's Univ., 1950, pp. 14-16.

B6131   Salter, F. M. "Shakespeare's *King John*." *Transactions of the Royal Society of Canada* (Ottawa), XLIII, Series III (June, 1949), Section 2, pp. 115-136.

B6132   Henderson, Archibald, Jr. *Family of Mercutio.* DD, Columbia University, 1954. Pp. 270. Mic A54-2044. *DA*, XIV (1954), 1395. Publication No. 8684.

(6) MISCELLANEOUS ITEMS

B6133   Ash, Margaret S. *An Historical Study of "King John."* DD, State University of Iowa, 1936. Abstr. in State Univ. of Iowa *Programs Announcing Candidates for Higher Degrees . . .* , no pagination.

B6134   Messiaen, Pierre. "Shakespeare et le Catholicisme: Le Roi Jean." *Bulletin Joseph Lotte*, June, 1938, pp. 402-408.

B6135   Ash, D. F. "Anglo-French Relations in *King John*." *EA*, III (1939), 349-358.

B6136   Cancelled.

B6137   Hayes, K. "Shakespeare Didn't Gilt the Lily." *Irish Digest*, XX (Nov., 1944), 44-45.

B6138   Petit-Dutaillis, Charles. *Le Roi Jean et Shakespeare.* Paris: Gallimard, 1945.

B6139   White, D. M. "Shakespeare and Psychological Warfare." *The Public Opinion Quarterly*, XII (1948), 68-72.

(7) SUBSEQUENT HISTORY OF THE PLAY
(other than productions after 1660)

THE MERCHANT OF VENICE (211;74)

B6140   Tannenbaum, Samuel A. *Shakespeare's "The Merchant of Venice": A Concise Bibliography.* New York: Author, 1941. Pp. 150.

(1) THE TEXT

(a) OLD TEXTS

B6141   *The Merchant of Venice*, 1600 (Hayes Quarto). Shakespeare Quarto Facsimiles. London: Sidgwick & Jackson, 1939.
        Rev: *TLS*, Dec. 2, 1939, p. 707; by B. M., *PQ*, XIX (1940), 413-414; by H. Sellers, *MLR*, XXXV, 235; by James G. McManaway, *MLN*, LV, 632-634.

(b) MODERN EDITIONS

B6142   *The Merchant of Venice.* Ed. by G. Skillan. London, 1934.
        Rev: by Elise Deckner, *Beiblatt*, XLVII (1936), 106-107.

B6143   *The Merchant of Venice.* Texte anglais. Notes et notice par G. Guibillon. Les Classiques
        pour tous, 498. Paris: Hatier, 1934. Pp. 75.

B6144   *The Merchant of Venice.* Ed. by Henry Norman Hudson and others. Cameo Classics. New
        York: Grosset, 1936. Pp. 197.

B6145   *Merchant of Venice.* Interlinear ed. prepared by George Coffin Taylor and Reed Smith. Boston:
        Ginn, 1936. Pp. xxxvi, 164.
        Rev: by Samuel A. Tannenbaum, *SAB*, XI (1936), 252.

B6146   *The Merchant of Venice.* Ed. by Herzberg. New York: Holt, 1937. Pp. 300.

B6147   *The Merchant of Venice.* Bearb. von Alfred Mohrbutter. Kurze Lesestoffe, 109. Kiel:
        Lipsius and Tischer, 1937. Pp. iv, 57.
        Rev: by Bruno Engelhardt, *DNS*, XLV (1937), 419-420; by O. Glöde, *Eng. Studn.*, LXXII
        (1937/38), 157; by Paul Scholz-Wülfing, *ZNU*, XXXVII (1938), 195.

B6148   *Merchant of Venice.* Ed. by R. F. W. Fletcher. New Clarendon Shakespeare. London:
        Oxford Univ. Press, 1938. Pp. 192.

B6149   *Merchant of Venice.* Bearb. von G. Ost. Berlin: Langenscheidt, 1938. Pp. 83.
        Rev: by K. Arns, *Archiv*, 173 (1938), 239.

B6150   *Merchant of Venice.* Ed. for reading and arranged for staging by Orson Welles and Roger
        Hill. Mercury Shakespeare. New York: Harper, 1939. Pp. 92.

B6151   *Merchant of Venice.* Ed. by Max Draber. Leipzig: Quelle & Meyer, 1940. Pp. 68, 18.
        Rev: by Erich Thiele, *ZNU*, XXXIX (1940), 136.

B6152   *Merchant of Venice.* Ed. by H. W. Simon. New York: Simon & Schuster, 1940. Pp.
        lxvi, 146.

B6153   *The Merchant of Venice.* Ed. by George L. Kittredge. Boston: Ginn, 1945. Pp. x, 164.
        Rev: by R. M. Smith, *JEGP*, XLV (1946), 121.

B6154   *The Merchant of Venice.* Ed. and arr. by Joan and Robert Allan. London: Evans, 1947.
        Pp. 72.

B6155   *The Merchant of Venice.* With introd. and glossary by L. J. Guittart and P. J. Rijneke. 4th
        edition. Amsterdam: Meulenhoff, 1950. Pp. xii, 90, 32. 5th edition. Zwolle: Tjeenk
        Willink, 1957. Pp. xii, 116.

B6156   *The Merchant of Venice.* Ed. by R. Hünnerkopf. Heidelberg: Meister, 1953. Pp. 93.

B6157   *The Merchant of Venice.* Ed. by Tyrone Guthrie and G. B. Harrison. New Stratford Shake-
        speare. London: Harrap, 1954. Pp. 139.
        Rev: by Hermann Heuer, *SJ*, 91 (1955), 343-344.

B6158   *The Merchant of Venice.* Ed. by Hubert Hüsges. Text u. Anm. Paderborn: Schöningh,
        1954. Pp. 103, 29.

B6159   *The Merchant of Venice.* Ed. by J. R. Brown. Arden Shakespeare. London: Methuen,
        1955. Pp. lviii, 174.
        Rev: *TLS*, July 15, 1955, p. 402; by J. Vallette, *MdF*, 325 (1955), 151; *Dublin Magazine*,
        XXX (Oct.-Dec.), 46-47; *English Journal*, XLIV, 549; by Pat M. Ryan, Jr., *QJS*, XLII (1956),
        84-86; by Harold Jenkins, *MLR*, LI, 584-587; by Hereward T. Price, *JEGP*, LV, 640-645;
        by Hermann Heuer, *SJ*, 92 (1956), 397-399; by H. Edward Cain, *SQ*, VII, 120-121; by Alice
        Walker, *RES*, NS, VII (1956), 191-193; by J. Jacquot, *RHT*, IX, 197-198; by J. G. McMan-
        away, *ShS*, X, 151-152.

B6160   *The Merchant of Venice.* A Comedy. Ed. with Notes and glossary by Fr. Lange. Berlin:
        Velhagen & Klasing, 1955. Pp. 103, 47, 39.

B6161   *The Merchant of Venice.* Ed. by K. P. Karunakara Menon. Madras: Viswanathan, n.d.

B6162   *The Merchant of Venice* and *Julius Caesar.* Being the text from the Oxford Shakespeare of the
        plays to be performed at the Stratford Shakespearean festival of 1955. With synopses of the
        plays and a note on Oedipus Rex. 2 Vols. in one. Toronto: Oxford Univ. Press, 1955.

B6163   *The Merchant of Venice.* Ed. by Louis B. Wright and Virginia L. Freund. New York: Pocket
        Books, 1957. Pp. xxxvii, 94.
        Rev: *ShN*, VIII (1958), 3; by J. A. Bryant, *SR*, LXVI, 325.

B6164   *The Merchant of Venice.* Ed. by Francis Fergusson and Charles Jasper Sisson. With a Modern
        Commentary by Morris Carnovsky. New York: Dell Publishing Co., 1958. Pp. 188.

(c) EMENDATIONS

B6165   Rank, Otto. "Ein Beispiel von poetischer Verwertung des Versprechens." *Zentralblatt für
        Psychoanalyse*, I (1911), 109-110. Reappears in Brill's translation of Freud's *Psychopathology of Every-
        day Life*, Chapter V, "Mistakes in Speech." Example is from *Merchant of Venice*, III.ii.4-18.

B6166   Stroup, Thomas B. "A Charm from North Carolina and *The Merchant of Venice*, II.vii.75."
        Jour. Amer. Folk-Lore, XLIX (1936), 266.

B6167   Boughner, D. C. " 'Red Wine and Rennish'." *SAB*, XIV (1939), 46-50.
        Merch., III.i.35-37.

B6168   Withington, Robert. "A Second Daniel." *SAB*, XVI (1941), 123-124.

B6168a Withington, R. "A Last Word on 'Judge' Daniel." *SAB*, XVI (1941), 256.

B6169   Hibernicus. "The 'Muddy Vesture of Decay'." *N &Q*, 182 (1942), 275.

B6170   Pitcher, Seymour M. "Two Notes on Shakespeare." *PQ*, XXI (1942), 239-240.
        The first is "Lancelot's Blessing [*Merchant of Venice*, II.ii]."

B6171   Brooke, T. "An Emendation of IV.i.50-51." *MLN*, LVIII (1943), 427-428.

B6172   Wood, Frederick T. "Shylock's 'Fawning Publican'." *N &Q*, 189 (1945), 252-253.

B6173   Flatter, Richard. "The Wooing of Nerissa." *TLS*, Dec. 9, 1949, p. 809.
        III.ii.198 ff.
        Comment by J. L. Nevinson, *TLS*, Dec. 30, 1949, p. 857.

B6174   Gray, H. D. "The Wooing of Nerissa." *TLS*, Feb. 3, 1950, p. 73.
        See the letters by J. Dover Wilson, ibid., Feb. 17, 1950, p. 105; by R. Flatter, ibid., March 17,
        p. 169.

B6175   Brown, John Russell. "The Compositors of *Hamlet* Q$_2$ and *The Merchant of Venice*." *SB*,
        VII (1955), 17-40.

B6176   Galloway, David. " 'Alcides and His Rage': A Note on *The Merchant of Venice*." *N &Q*,
        NS, III (1956), 330-331.

B6177   Williams, Gwyn. "The Cuckoo, the Welsh Ambassador." *MLR*, LI (1956), 223-224.

B6178   Hulme, Hilda. "Wit, Rage, Mean: Three Notes on *The Merchant of Venice*." *Neophil*, XLI
        (1957), 46-50.

B6179   Kenyon, John S. "Shakespeare's Pronunciation of Stephano: *The Merchant of Venice*, V.i.28,
        51." *PQ*, XXXVII (1958), 504-506.

(2) LITERARY GENESIS AND ANALOGUES

B6180   Freud, S. "The Theme of the Three Caskets." *Collected Papers*, International Psycho-Analytic
        Library. London: Hogarth Press, 1950, IV, pp. 244-256. Reprinted in Standard Edition,
        Vol. 12, 1958, pp. 289-301.
        First publ. 1913 in *Imago*.

B6181   Ackermann, C. "Scriptural Allusions in *Merchant of Venice*." *The Bible in Shakespeare*, 1936,
        pp. 48-58.

B6182   Kranz, W. "Shakespeare und die Antike." *Eng. Studn.*, LXXIII (1938), 32-33.

B6183   McNeal, Thomas H. "Who Is Silvia?—and Other Problems in the Greene-Shakespeare
        Relationship." *SAB*, XIII (1938), 240-254.

B6184   Staerk, Willy. "Stoffgeschichtliches." *Anglia*, LXII (1938), 356-361.
        Contains a summary of "eine ägyptische Variante zum Shylock-Motiv."

B6185   Traver, Hope. "I Will Try Confusions with Him." *SAB*, XIII (1938), 108-120.

B6186   Gordon, Cyrus H. " 'A Daniel Come to Judgment'." *SAB*, XV (1940), 206-209.
        Jewish sources, see B6189-90.

B6187   Reznikoff, C. "A Story for a Dramatist." *Menorah J.*, XXVIII (1940), 269-279.

B6188   Clarkson, M. P. S. "Nerissa's Ring and Rabelais." *American Notes and Queries*, I (1941),
        69, 126.

B6189   Hannigan, John E. "Which Daniel?" *SAB*, XVI (1941), 63-64.
        A reply to B6186. Continued as B6190.

B6190   Hannigan, John E. "Portia, Daniel, Susanna." *SAB*, XVI (1941), 190-192.
        Comment by R. Withington, ibid., XVI, 256.
        More on B6186 and B6189.

B6191   Thayer, Tiffany. "Nerissa's Ring." *American Notes & Queries*, II (1942), 87.

B6192   Nelson, B. N., and J. Starr. "The Legend of the Divine Surety and the Jewish Moneylender."
        Annuaire de l'Institute de Philol. et d'Histoire Orientales et Slaves, 1939/44, VII (1944), 289-338.

B6193   Kaiser, Leo. "Shakespeare and St. Jerome." *Classical Jour.*, XLI (1946), 219-220.

B6194   Friedman, Lee Max. " 'A Jewes Prophesy' and Caleb Shilock." *More Books*, XXII (1947),
        43-51.

B6195   Parr, Johnstone. "A Note on Daniel." *SAB*, XXIII (1948), 181-182.

B6196   Wilson, James L. "Another Medieval Parallel to the Jessica and Lorenzo Story." *SAB*,
        XXIII (1948), 20-23.
        Parallel in story of Floripas in *The Sultan of Babylon*.

B6197   Moore, John Robert. "Pantaloon as Shylock." *Boston Public Library Quar.*, I (1949), 33-42.

B6198   Braddy, Haldeen. "Shakespeare and Three Oriental Tales." *Midwest Folklore*, I (1951), 91-92.

B6199   Hutton, James. "Some English Poems in Praise of Music." *English Miscellany*, ed. by
        Mario Praz. Rome: Edizioni di Storia e Letteratura, 1951, pp. 1-63.
        Parallels to Lorenzo's speech, V.i.55-88, on music.

B6200   Pruvost, René. "Le Drame Romanesque du *Marchand de Venise*." *LanM*, March-April,
        1951, pp. 51-61.

A study of the "romanesque" in *Merch.* in relation to Munday's *Zelauto*.

B6201 Nathan, Norman. " 'On the Hip'." *N &Q*, 197 (1952), 74.

B6202 Zandvoort, R. W. "Fair Portia's Counterfeit." *Rivista di Letterature Moderne*, II (1951), 351-356. Also in his *Collected Papers, A Selection of Notes and Articles Originally Published in English Studies and Other Journals*. Groningen Studies in English, v. Groningen: J. B. Wolters, 1954, pp. 50-57. Also in *Atti del V Congresso Internazionale di Lingue e Letterature Moderne nei loro Rapporti con le Belle Arti*. Firenze, 27-31 marzo 1951. Florence: Valmartina, 1955.

B6203 Lüders, Eva. "Ein Zigeunershylock. Die Hauptpersonen des *Merchant of Venice* im Lichte eines neuentdecktes ungarischen Romani-Mårchens." *Arv. Journal of Scandinavian Folklore* (Uppsala), XII (1956), 1-25.
Mainly on the pound-of-flesh story, in a recently discovered Hungarian Romani tale.

B6204 Maximilianus, P. "Shakespeare en Horatius." *Neophil*, XL (1956), 144.
Notes parallel between *Merch.*, IV.i.363 ff. and Horace's *Satires*, II.ii.989.

B6205 Nathan, Norman. "Balthasar, Daniel and Portia." *N &Q*, NS, IV (1957), 334-335.

B6206 Wilson, J. Dover. "Shakespeare's 'Small Latin'—How Much?" *ShS*, X (1957), 12-26.
Partly a summing up of scholarship; partly an independent, experimental study based mainly on *Merch.*, V.i.1-14, in which he is able to trace all classical allusions to native sources, notably Chaucer and Golding.

(3) USE OF LANGUAGE

B6207 Sheppard, J. T. *Music at Belmont and Other Essays and Addresses*. London: Rupert Hart-Davis, 1952. Pp. 192.
The essay on *Merch.* is classical influences and the musical quality of the verse.

(4) GENERAL CRITICISM OF THE PLAY

B6208 Koszul, A. "Argentoratensia Britannica: *The Merchant of Venice*." *Bulletin de la Faculté des Lettres* (Strasbourg), XIII (1937), 227-234.

B6209 Teeter, Louis. "Scholarship and the Art of Criticism." *ELH*, V (1938), 173-194.
E. E. Stoll vs. Brander Matthews chiefly upon *Merch.*

B6210 Best, Ann Marie. *The Dispute of Justice and Mercy with Special Reference to "The Merchant of Venice."* DD, University of Washington, 1939. Abstr. in Univ. of Washington *Abstracts of Theses*, IV (1939), 109-110.

B6211 Guardini, R. "Über Shakespeares *Kaufmann von Venedig*." *Die Rothenfelser Schildgenossen*, XIX (1940), 150-155.

B6212 Schümmer, Karl. *Shakespeare, Der Kaufmann von Venedig*. Wege zu Dichtern und ihren Werken, Heft 4. Paderborn: Schöningh, 1941. Pp. 80.

B6213 Jacob, Cary F. "Reality and *The Merchant of Venice*." *QJS*, XXVIII (1942), 307-315.

B6214 Plowman, Max. *The Right to Live*. Introd. by J. Middleton Murry. London: Dakers, 1942. "Money and *The Merchant*," pp. 177-182.

B6215 Brennan, J. H. "Nerissa's Name." *American Notes and Queries*, III (1943), 88.

B6216 Withington, R. "Shakespeare and Race Prejudice." *Elizabethan Studies and Other Essays in Honor of George F. Reynolds*, pp. 172-184.

B6217 West, E. J. "The Use of Contrast in *The Merchant of Venice*." *SAB*, XXI (1946), 172-176.

B6218 Coghill, Nevill. "The Governing Idea. Essays in Stage-Interpretation of Shakespeare. I. *The Merchant of Venice*." *Shakespeare Quarterly* (London), I (Summer, 1947), 9-17.

B6219 Draper, J. W. "Shakespeare and the Doge of Venice." *JEGP*, XLVI (1947), 75-81.

B6220 Granville-Barker, Harley. *Prefaces to Shakespeare*. 2 Vols. Princeton Univ. Press, 1946, 1947.
Rev: A8201.

B6221 Nelson, Benjamin N. "The Usurer and the Merchant Prince: Italian Business Men and the Ecclesiastical Law of Restitution, 1100-1550." *Jour. of Econ. Hist.*, VII (1947), 104-122.

B6222 Pettet, E. C. "*Timon of Athens:* The Disruption of Feudal Monarchy." *RES*, XXIII (1947), 321-336.
Timon, "a . . . tract for the times" against rising capitalism. Many comparisons with *Merch.*

B6223 Law, R. A. "Porcia's Curiosity: A Tale Thrice Told by Shakespeare." *TxSE*, XXVII (1948), 207-214.

B6224 Flatter, Richard. "The Wooing of Nerissa." *TLS*, Dec. 9, 1949, p. 809; comment by J. L. Nevinson, Dec. 30, 1949, p. 857; by H. D. Gray, Feb. 3, 1950, p. 73; by J. D. Wilson, Feb. 17, 1950, p. 105; by R. Flatter, March 3, 1950, p. 169.

B6225 Graves, Robert. "The Humorous Element." *The Common Asphodel*, London, 1949, pp. 149-167.
Rev: B4471.

B6226 Hafele, Melanie. *Gnade und Recht bei Shakespeare, Besonders Untersucht an "Mass für Mass," dem "Kaufmann von Venedig" und "Sturm."* DD, Innsbruck, 1949. Pp. 129. Typewritten.

B6227 Cassagnau, M. "Glanes à Travers Trois Littératures." *RLC*, XXIV (1950), 575-579.

B6228 Hennings, Elsa. *"Der Kaufmann von Venedig* als Komödie." *Vierteljahrszeitschrift für Literaturwissenschaft und Geistesgeschichte* (Halle), xxiv (1950), 83-100.

B6229 Meyer, Justus. "Shakespeare en zijn *Merchant of Venice.*" *Elseviers Weekblad*, Feb. 10, 1951.

B6230 Huhner, Max. *Shakespearean Studies and Other Essays.* With an Introd. by George S. Hellman. New York: Farrar Straus, 1952. Pp. 115. *Merch.*, pp. 71-91.

B6231 Graham, Cary B. "Standards of Value in *The Merchant of Venice.*" *SQ*, iv (1953), 145-151.

B6232 Danks, K. B. "The Case of Antonio's Melancholy." *N &Q*, NS, i (1954), 111.

B6233 Guardini, Romano. "Über Shakespeares *Kaufmann von Venedig.*" *Dank und Erkenntnis. Paul Fechter zum 75. Geburtstag.* Gütersloh, 1955, pp. 30-37. Also in *Neue dt. Hefte* (Gütersloh), ii (1955/56), 419-425.

B6234 Neergaard, Eric S. "Portias Justitsmord." ["Portia's Judicial Murder"]. *Kristeligt Dagblad* (Copenhagen), June 15, 1955.

B6235 Rubow, Paul V. *Shakespeares Ungdomsstykker.* The Royal Danish Scientifical Society: Historical-Philosophical Information, Vol. xxxiv, No. 5. Copenhagen: Munksgaard, 1955. Pp. 34.

B6236 Reik, Theodor. *The Search Within. The Inner Experiences of a Psychoanalyst.* Selections from the Works of T. Reik. New York: Grove Press, 1956. Pp. xi, 659. *Merch.*, pp. 356-371.

B6237 Warhaft, Sidney. "Anti-Semitism in *The Merchant of Venice.*" *Manitoba Arts Review*, x (1956), 3-15.

B6238 Windolph, Francis Lyman. *Reflections of the Law in Literature.* Philadelphia: Univ. of Pennsylvania Press; Oxford Univ. Press, 1956. Pp. 83.

B6239 Carrington, Norman T. *Shakespeare: The Merchant of Venice.* Rev. ed. Notes on Chosen English Texts. London: Brodie, 1958. Pp. 80.

(5) CHARACTERIZATION

B6240 Ross, T. A. "A Note on *The Merchant of Venice.*" *British Journal of Medical Psychology*, xiv (1934), 303-311.

B6241 Pettigrew, Helen P. "Bassanio, the Elizabethan Lover." *PQ*, xvi (1937), 296-306.

B6242 Kienscherf, Otto. "Lanzelot Gobbos Gewissen." *SJ*, lxxv (1939), 133-135.

B6243 Lord Normand. "Portia's Judgment." *Univ. of Edinburgh Jour.*, x (1939), 43-45.

B6244 Ariail, J. M. "In Defense of Bassanio." *SAB*, xvi (1941), 25-28.

B6245 Bethge, Friedrich. "Zu Lanzelot Gobbos Gewissen." *SJ*, lxxvii (1941), 189.

B6246 Lewis, C. S. *Hamlet: The Prince or the Poem?* London: Milford, 1942. Pp. 18. Contains comments on *Merch.*
       Rev: B7673.

B6247 Palmer, John. *Comic Characters of Shakespeare.* New York: Macmillan, 1946. Pp. 135.
       Rev: A6544.

B6248 Biering, Andreas, and Christian Wroldsen. *Et Resumé med Personkarakteristikk av William Shakespeares skuespill The Merchant of Venice.* Tvedestrand, 1947. Pp. 12.

B6249 Trilling, Lionel. "Freud and Literature." *The Liberal Imagination*, New York: The Viking Press, 1950, pp. 34-57.
       Rev: A1334.

B6250 Cohen, Hennig. "Shakespeare's *Merchant of Venice*, II.vii.78-79." *SQ*, ii (1951), 79.

B6251 Reik, T. " 'Jessica, My Child'!" *American Imago*, viii (Mar., 1951), 3-27. Reprinted in B6252.

B6252 Reik, Theodor. *The Secret Self.* New York: Farrar, Straus, and Young, 1952. Pp. 329.
       Rev: A1356.

B6253 Jensen, William. "Den usandsynlige Antonio [The improbable Antonio]." *Kristeligt Dagblad* (Copenhagen), April 6, 1954.

B6254 Coe, Charles Norton. *Shakespeare's Villains.* New York, 1957.
       Rev: A6796.

B6255 Dillingham, William B. "Antonio and Black Bile." *N &Q*, NS, iv (1957), 419.

B6256 Harris, Bernard. "A Portrait of a Moor." *ShS*, xi (1958), 89-97.

(a) SHYLOCK

B6257 Coriat, Isidore H. "Anal-Erotic Character Traits in Shylock." *International Journal of Psycho-Analysis*, ii (Sept., 1921), 354-360.

B6258 Grewe, W. "Shylock oder die Parodie der Rechtssicherheit." *Dt. Volkstum*, xviii (1936), 77-79.

B6259 Karutz, Richard. "Shylock in Africa." *Das Goetheanum*, xv (1936), 237-238.

B6260 Martin, Burns. "Shakespeare's Shylock." *Dalhousie Rev.*, xvii (1937), 333-338.

B6261 Weigelin, E. "Die gerichtliche Entscheidung in Shakespeares *Kaufmann von Venedig.*" *NS*, xlv (1937), 204-208.

B6262 Fijn van Draat, P. "*De Koopman van Venetië:* een pleidooi voor den Jood Shylock." *Haagsch Maandblad,* I (1938), 164-173.

B6263 Fijn van Draat, P. "Shylock: A Plea for the Jew." *Neophil,* XXIII (1938), 199-202.

B6264 Flasdieck, H. M. "Jüdisches im und zum *Merchant of Venice.*" *N. Mon.,* IX (1938), 148-160; ibid., IX (1938), 182-189.

B6265 "Der Kaufmann Konnte nur ein Jude Sein! Eine Höchst Interessante Schlussfolgerung Shakespeares." *VB(B),* No. 327, 1938.

B6266 Marcus, Jacob Rader. "The Jew in the Medieval World: A Source Book, 315-1791." *Union of American Hebrew Congregations* (Cincinnati), XXIV (1938), 504.

B6267 Wright, Celeste Turner. "The Usurer's Sin in Elizabethan Literature." *SP,* XXXV (1938), 178-194.

B6268 Beretz, M. "Shylock." *Mass und Wert,* II (1939), 504-516.

B6269 Charlton, H. B. "Shakespeare's Jew." *The Disseminator,* I (Mar., 1939), 13-14. (Abstract from *BJRL,* Jan., 1934).

B6270 Gore, Arabella. *The History of the Interpretation of Shylock in English and American Literary Criticism, 1796 to 1935.* Master's thesis, University of North Carolina, 1939. Abstr. publ. in *Univ. of North Carolina Record, Research in Progress,* Grad. School Series, No. 36, 1939, p. 79.

B6271 Hannigan, John E. "Shylock and Portia." *SAB,* XIV (1939), 169-175.

B6272 Cancelled.

B6273 Stoll, E. E. "Shakespeare's Jew." *UTQ,* VIII (1939), 139-154.

B6274 Borberg, Sv. "Den komiske Shylock." *Tilskueren* (Copenhagen), LI, No. 1, 245-270.

B6275 Draper, John W. "The Psychology of Shylock." *Bul. History Medicine,* VIII (1940), 643-650.

B6276 Hobman, B. L. "The Jew in Gentile Fiction." *ConR,* 157 (1940), 97-103.

B6277 Schwartz-Bostunitsch, G. "Shylock und Wir." *Weltkampf* (Munich), XVII (1940), 5-17.

B6278 Pushkin, A. S. "Notes on Shylock, Angelo and Falstaff." Tr. by Albert Siegel. *SAB,* XVI (1941), 120-121.

B6279 Tannenbaum, Samuel A. "Shakespeare an Anti-Semite?" *SAB,* XIX (1944), 47-48.

B6280 Draper, John W. "The Tempo of Shylock's Speech." *JEGP,* XLIV (1945), 281-285.

B6281 Murry, John Middleton. "The Significance of Shylock." *Adelphi,* XXII (1945), 1-5.

B6282 Withington, Robert. "Shakespeare and Race Prejudice." *Elizabethan Studies and Other Essays In Honor of George F. Reynolds,* 1945, pp. 172-183.

B6283 Pettet, E. C. "*The Merchant of Venice* and the Problem of Usury." *Essays and Studies by Members of English Association,* XXXI (1946), 19-33.

B6284 "Shylock and His Daughter." *The Jewish Forum,* XXX (Oct., 1947), 245, 264.

B6285 "Shylocks of Bygone Days." *Shakespeare Quarterly* (London), I (Summer, 1947), 18-21.

B6286 Abelson, A. "Shakspere's Shylock Challenged Anew." *The Jewish Forum,* XXX (Oct., 1947), 259-260.

B6287 Flatter, Richard. "Shylock, ein Spiegel der Zeiten." *Neue Zürcher Ztg.,* No. 1062, June 2, 1947.

B6288 Milligan, Burton A. "Some Sixteenth and Seventeenth Century Satire Against Money Lenders." *SAB,* XXII (1947), 36-46, 84-93.

B6289 Sinsheimer, Hermann. *Shylock: The History of a Character of the Myth of the Jew.* With a Foreword by John Middleton Murry. London: Gollancz, 1947. Pp. 147, pl. 16.
       Rev: A3624.

B6290 Smith, Fred Manning. "Shylock on the Rights of Jews and Emilia on the Rights of Women." *West Virginia Univ. Bul.: Philological Papers,* V (1947), 32-33.

B6291 Wilkins, Leah Wood. "Shylock's Pound of Flesh and Laban's Sheep." *MLN,* LXII (1947), 28-30.
       Meaning of lines I.iii.72-81 for understanding Shylock's mind.

B6292 Bishop, David H. "Shylock's Humour." *SAB,* XXIII (1948), 174-179.

B6293 Moore, J. R. "Shakespeare Gibe in Shylock Denied." *New York Times,* Jan. 1, 1948, p. 21.

B6294 Nathan, Norman. "Three Notes on *The Merchant of Venice.*" *SAB,* XXIII (1948), 152-173.

B6295 Sloan, Jacob. "Moneylender of Venice; in Shylock a Different Play Struggles to Be Born." *Commentary,* V (1948), 248-253.

B6296 Bromberg, Murray. "Shylock and Philip Henslowe." *N &Q,* 194 (1949), 422-423.

B6297 Moore, John Robert. "Pantaloon as Shylock." *Boston Public Library Quar.,* I (1949), 33-42.

B6298 Barnard, E. A. B. "Shakespeare and Shylock." *TLS,* May 12, 1950, p. 293.

B6299 Lelyveld, Toby Bookholtz. *Shylock on the Stage: Significant Changes in the Interpretation of Shakespeare's Jew.* DD, Columbia University, 1951. Pp. 196. Mic A51-284. *Microf. Ab.,* XI (1951), 772. Publication No. 2541.

B6300 Nathan, Norman. "Shylock, Jacob, and God's Judgment." *SQ,* I (1950), 255-259.
       Comment by J. W. Lever, *SQ,* III (1952), 383-386; and Norman Nathan, ibid., 386-388.

B6301   Shaaber, M. A. "Shylock's Name." *N &Q*, 196 (1951), 236.

B6302   Wasi, Muriel. "Shakespeare in Delhi." *Mysindia* (Bangalore), Nov. 26, 1950, pp. 19-20.

B6303   Cancelled.

B6304   Cancelled.

B6305   Siegel, Paul N. "Shylock and the Puritan Usurers." Matthews and Emery's *Studies in Shakespeare*, pp. 129-138.

B6306   Engle, Anita. "Was Shylock a Jew?" *Jewish Forum*, Autumn, 1954.
Rev: *CE*, XVI (1955), 319.

B6307   Shackford, J. B. "Bond of Kindness: Shylock's Humanity." *Univ. of Kansas City Rev.*, XXI (1954), 85-91.

B6308   Krapf, E. E. "Shylock and Antonio. A Psychoanalytic Study of Shakespeare and Antisemitism." *The Psychoanalytic Review*, XLII (1955), 113-130.

B6309   Nixon, Ingeborg. "Den Ubarmhjertige Jøde" ["The Merciless Jew"]. *Berlingske-Aften* (Copenhagen), Feb. 7, 1955.

B6310   Welner, Pinches. "Shylock Set med en Jødes Øjne" ["Shylock Seen with the Eyes of a Jew"]. *Socialdemokraten* (Copenhagen), Feb. 22, 1955.

B6311   Flatter, Richard. "Antonio, der *Kaufmann von Venedig*. Ist Shylock eine komische Figur?" In his *Triumph der Gnade: Shakespeare Essays*. Vienna, Munich: Kurt Desch, 1956, pp. 119-124.

B6312   Kaiser, Joachim. "Das Dilemma mit Shylock." *Hessische Hefte* (Kassel), VI (1956), 434.

B6313   Bradbrook, F. W. "Shylock and *King Lear*." *N &Q*, NS, IV (1957), 142-143.

B6314   Gross, Harvey. "From Barabas to Bloom: Notes on the Figure of the Jew." *Western Humanities Review*, XI (1957), 149-156.

B6315   Carnovsky, Morris. "Mirror of Shylock." *Tulane Drama Review*, III (1958), 35-45.

(6)   MISCELLANEOUS ITEMS

B6316   Digeon, A. "Le Jeu de l'Amour et de l'Amitié dans *Le Marchand de Venise*." *RAA*, XIII (1936), 219-231.

B6317   Heline, T. "*Merchant of Venice*." *The Occult in Shakespeare*. New York: New Age Press, 1936, p. 32.

B6318   Sisson, C. J. "A Jewish Colony in Shakespeare's London." *Essays and Studies by Members of the English Association*, Oxford, 1938, pp. 38-51.

B6319   Abelson, A. "The Missing Scene in *Merchant of Venice* and in Ibn Zahav's Play." *The Jewish Forum*, XXX (1947), 269, 273.

B6320   Draper, John W. "Shakespeare and the Doge of Venice." *JEGP*, XLVI (1947), 75-81.

B6321   Abelson, A. "Transcending Shakespeare." *The Jewish Forum*, XXXI (Aug., 1948), 167-172

B6322   Nathan, Norman. "Is Shylock Philip Henslowe?" *N &Q*, 192 (1947), 163-165.

B6323   Rank, Otto. *Psychology and the Soul*. Tr. by William D. Turner, 1950. *Merch.*, pp. 59-60.

B6324   Arnold, Paul. "Occultisme Elizabéthain." *Cahiers du Sud* (Paris), No. 308, 1951. Also in *France-Asie* (Saigon), VI (1951/52), 63.

B6325   Marković, Vida. "The Social and Economic Background of Shakespeare's Characters in *The Merchant of Venice*." *Zbornik Filozofskog Fakulteta* (Belgrade), II (1952), 383-403.

B6326   Krapf, E. E. "A Psychoanalytic Study of Shakespeare and Antisemitism." *Psychoanalytic Review*, XLII (1955), 113-130.

B6327   Danks, K. B. "A Notable Copyright Award." *N &Q*, NS, III (1956), 283.

B6328   Gallagher, Ligera Cécile. *Shakespeare and the Aristotelian Ethical Tradition*. DD, Stanford University, 1956. Pp. 338. Mic 56-3017. *DA*, XVI (1956), 1898. Publication No. 17,720. Chap. VII: "The Aristotelian Norm & 'Liberality' in *Merch.*," pp. 230-262.

B6329   Noordermeer, P. T. "Aantekeningen op Versjes in *De Koopman van Venetië*." *LT*, 1956, pp. 453-456.

B6330   Schweitzer, A. R. "Mathematics and Literary Composition, I, II, and III." Abstracts numbered 368T, 369T, & 370T, in *Bulletin of the American Mathematical Society*, LXII, No. 3 (May, 1956), 262.
Finds inhumanity in *Merch.*

B6331   Seng, Peter J. "The Riddle Song in *Merchant of Venice*." *N &Q*, NS, V (1958), 191-193.

(7)   SUBSEQUENT HISTORY OF THE PLAY
(other than productions after 1660)

B6332   Smallwood, O. "The Stage-History of *Merchant of Venice*." DD, University of Oklahoma, 1939. Abstr. in *University of Oklahoma Bulletin*, Jan., 1939, pp. 117.

B6333   Barnett, John E. "*The Merchant of Venice* at the University of Kansas City." *SQ*, I (1950), 269-271.

        See also note by R. M. Smith, *SQ*, I (1950), 293-295.

B6334   Cassagnau, M. "Théophile Gautier et Shakespeare." *RLC*, XXIV (1950), 577.

B6335   Reardon, William Robert. *Banned in Boston: A Study of Theatrical Censorship in Boston from 1630 to 1950.* DD, Stanford University, 1953. Pp. 253. Mic A53-996. *DA*, XIII (1953), 609. Publication No. 5386.
        Merch. in 1937.

B6336   "Alas, Poor William! Philadelphia Ban." *Reporter*, Sept. 8, 1955, p. 4.
        On the banning of *Merch.* in one part of Phila., but not another, and broadcasting in consequence.

B6337   Docens, P. T. *"Merchant of Venice* Revised to Date." *Catholic Educator*, XXVII (1957), 573-575.

B6338   Fram, Leon. "On Banning Shylock." *Nation*, Nov. 9, 1957, p. 311.
        Letter protesting the presentation of *Merch.* by the American Shak. Festival at Stratford, Conn. Argues that the play should be suppressed because of its anti-Semitism.

B6339   Clurman, Harold. "On Banning Shylock." *Nation*, Nov. 9, 1957, p. 311.
        Reply to B6338.

KING HENRY IV (Parts I and II) (214;75)

(1) THE TEXT

(a) OLD TEXTS

B6340   E., S. Y. "A Shakespeare MS?" *N &Q*, 189 (1945), 193; Wm. Jaggard, ibid., p. 263; James G. McManaway, ibid., p. 284; Wm. Jaggard, 190 (1946), 65; S. Y. E., *N &Q*, 193 (1948), 388; James G. McManaway, ibid., p. 525; S. Y. E., ibid., p. 547; and 194 (1949), 19.

B6341   McManaway, James G. "The Cancel in the Quarto of *2 Henry IV.*" *Studies in Honor of A. H. R. Fairchild* (Univ. Missouri Studies, Vol. 21, No. 1. Univ. Missouri Press, 1946), pp. 67-80.

B6342   Jordan, John E. "The Reporter of *Henry VI, Part 2.*" *PMLA*, LXIV (1949), 1089-113.

B6343   Walker, Alice. "The Cancelled Lines in *2 Henry IV*, IV.i.93, 95." *Library*, Fifth Series, VI (1951), 115-116.

B6344   Walker, Alice. "Quarto 'Copy' and the 1623 Folio: *2 Henry IV.*" *RES*, II (1951), 217-225.

B6345   Draper, John W. "The Date of *Henry IV.*" *Neophil*, XXXVIII (1954), 41-44.

B6346   Walker, Alice. "The Folio Text of *I Henry IV.*" *SB*, VI (1954), 45-59.

B6347   Shaaber, M. A. "The Folio of *2 Henry IV.*" *SQ*, VI (1955), 135-144.

B6348   Evans, G. Blakemore. "The 'Dering MS' of Shakespeare's *Henry IV* and Sir Edward Dering." *JEGP*, LIV (1955), 498-503. Reprinted in *Univ. of Illinois Studies by Members of the English Dept. in Memory of John Jay Parry*, 1957.

B6349   Craig, Hardin. "The Dering Version of Shakespeare's *Henry IV.*" *PQ*, XXXV (1956), 218-219.

(b) MODERN EDITIONS

B6350   *Henry IV, Parts 1 and 2.* Ed. by M. Alderton Pink. London: Macmillan, 1949. 2 Vols. Pp. vii, 166; vii, 168.

i. I Henry IV

B6351   *Henry the Fourth, Part I.* A New Variorum Edition of Shakespeare. Ed. by Samuel Burdett Hemingway. Philadelphia: Lippincott, 1936. Pp. xi, 554.
        The editor reprints the text of Q_1 (1598).
        Rev: *TLS*, Mar. 27, 1937, p. 236; by Alois Brandl, *Archiv*, 171 (1937), 261; by S. A. T., *SAB*, XII, 63-64; by W. W. L., *SRL*, July 3, p. 20; by Rosamond Gilder, *TAr*, XXI, 330-331; by W. Keller, *SJ*, LXXIII, 150-151; by George Coffin Taylor, *SAB*, XII, 159-167; by S. C. Chew, *NYHTBR*, Mar. 28, 2x; *SP*, XXXIV, 309-310; by R. B. McKerrow, *MLN*, LIII (1938), 207-211; by H. T. Price, *JEGP*, XXXVII, 307-311; by A. M. Clark, *MLR*, XXXIII, 64-67; by F. Delattre, *RUnBrux*, XLIV, 92-93.

B6352   McManaway, James G. "Supplements to the New Variorum Shakespeare." *SQ*, VI (1955), 247-248.

B6353   *Supplement to Henry IV, Part I: A New Variorum Edition of Shakespeare.* Ed. by G. Blakemore Evans. *SQ*, VII, No. 3 (1956). Pp. iv, 121.
        Supplements S. B. Hemingway's 1936 Variorum Edition. It appeared concurrently as the regular Summer number of *SQ* and in book form to range with volumes of the New Variorum.
        Rev: by John Crow, *SQ*, VIII (1957), 91-94; *ShN*, VII, 14; by Kenneth Muir, *MLR*, LIII (1958), 140-141; by J. B. Fort, *EA*, XI, 52-53; by E. A. J. Honigmann, *RES*, NS, IX, 451; by Hereward T. Price, *JEGP*, LVII, 806-807.

B6354   *The First Part of King Henry the Fourth.* Ed. by George L. Kittredge. Boston: Ginn & Co., 1940. Pp. xiv, 210.

B6355   *The First Part of the History of Henry IV.* Ed. by R. C. Bald. Crofts Classics. New York: Crofts, 1946. Pp. vi, 86.

B6356   *The First Part of the History of Henry IV*. Ed. by J. Dover Wilson. The New Shakespeare. Cambridge Univ. Press, 1946. Pp. xlviii, 210.
       Rev: by Janet Spens, *TLS*, Aug. 24, 1946, p. 403; *Spectator*, Aug. 30, p. 226; by E. C. Pettet, *English*, VI, 142; *N &Q*, 191 (1946), 176; by K. B. Danks, *TLS*, Oct. 26, p. 521; by W. M. T. Dodds, *MLR*, XLII (1947), 371-382; by R. W. Babcock, *SAB*, XXII, 69-80; by J. B. Leishman, *RES*, XXIII, 164-166; by F. C. Danchin, *LanM*, XLI, 169-170.

B6357   *Henry IV, Pt. 1*. Ed. by Bertram Newman. New Clarendon Shakespeare. Oxford: Clarendon Press, 1952. Pp. 192.

B6358   *Henry IV, Pt. I*. Ed. by J. J. Hogan. Malone Shakespeare Series. Dublin: Browne and Nolan, 1953. Pp. 176.

B6359   *The First Part of King Henry the Fourth*. Ed. by Tucker Brooke, and Samuel B. Hemingway. Yale Shakespeare. Yale Univ. Press, 1957. Pp. 169.
       Rev: *SatR*, Aug. 3, 1957, p. 28.

B6360   *The First Part of King Henry the Fourth*. Ed. by M. A. Shaaber. Pelican Shakespeare. Baltimore, 1957. Pp. 139.
       Rev: by Wallace A. Bacon, *QJS*, XLIII (1957), 308-309; by Wilbur Dunkel, *SQ*, IX (1958), 416.

ii. II Henry IV

B6361   *King Henry IV, Part 2*. Ed. by A. J. F. Collins, and Harold Osborne. Matriculation Shakespeare. London: Univ. Tut. Press, 1936. Pp. 140.

B6362   *The Second Part of Henry the Fourth*. Ed. by Matthias A. Shaaber. The New Variorum Edition. Philadelphia: Lippincott, 1941. Pp. xx, 715.
       Rev: *TLS*, Nov. 22, 1941, p. 583; by Samuel A. Tannenbaum, *SAB*, XVI, 60; by W. A. Nielson, *SRL*, May 24, p. 6; by H. T. Price, *JEGP*, XLI (1942), 97-99; by Madeleine Doran, *MLN*, LVII, 373-376.

B6363   *The Second Part of the History of Henry IV*. Ed. by W. R. Rutland. New Clarendon Shakespeare. Oxford Univ. Press, 1946. Pp. viii, 192.

B6364   *The Second Part of the History of Henry IV*. Ed. by J. Dover Wilson. The New Shakespeare. Cambridge Univ. Press, 1946. Pp. 232.
       Rev: *TLS*, Aug. 24, 1946, p. 402; *Spectator*, Aug. 30, p. 226; by E. C. Pettet, *English*, VI, 142; *N &Q*, 191 (1946), 176; by W. M. T. Dodds, *MLR*, XLII (1947), 371-382; by R. W. Babcock, *SAB*, XXII, 69-80; by J. B. Leishman, *RES*, XXIII, 164-166.

B6365   *King Henry IV, Part 2*. Produced, ed. and ill. by George Skillan. London: French, 1950. Pp. xvi, 93.

B6366   *The Second Part of King Henry the Fourth*. Ed. by Allan Chester. Pelican Shakespeare. Baltimore: Penguin Books, 1957. Pp. 147.
       Rev: by Wallace A. Bacon, *QJS*, XLIII (1957), 308-309; by Wilbur Dunkel, *SQ*, IX (1958), 416.

(c) EMENDATIONS
i. I Henry IV

B6367   Crundell, H. W. "On Three Passages of Shakespeare." *N &Q*, 172 (1937), 331-332.

B6368   Shaaber, M. A. "A Note on *1 Henry IV*." *SAB*, XIII (1938), 96-98.

B6369   Crundell, H. W. "The Text of *1 Henry IV*." *N &Q*, 177 (1939), 347-349.

B6370   Douglas-Osborn, E. H. " 'Danke as a Dog'." *TLS*, Feb. 25, 1939, p. 122.

B6371   Shaaber, Matthias A. "A Textual Dilemma in *1 Henry IV*, V.i.1-3." *MLN*, LIV (1939), 276-278.

B6372   King, Arthur H. "Some Notes on Ambiguity in *1 Henry IV*." *SN*, XIV (1941/42), 161-183.

B6373   Haight, Gordon S. "Saint Nicholas's Clerks [*I Henry IV*, II.i]." *TLS*, Sept. 16, 1944, p. 451.

B6374   Flatter, Richard. "Mad, Made, and Maid [*1 Henry IV*, II.iv.547 ff]." *TLS*, Oct. 6, 1945, p. 475.

B6375   Ogilvy, Jack D. A. "The Forced Gait of a Shuffling Nag." *Elizabethan Studies and Other Essays In Honor of George F. Reynolds*, 1945, pp. 147-149.

B6376   Lea, K. M. " 'Never Call A True Piece of Gold a Counterfeit': What Falstaff Means." *RES*, XXIV (1948), 236-240.

B6377   LeComte, Edward S. " 'Thieves of the Day's Beauty'." *MLN*, LXIII (1948), 256-257. Interprets *1 Henry IV*, I.ii.25.

B6378   Marder, Louis. "Shakespeare's 'Lincolnshire Bagpipe'." *N &Q*, 195 (1950), 383-385.

B6379   Cross, James E. "On the Meaning of 'A-Blakeberyed'." *RES*, NS, II (1951), 372-374.

B6380   Pearce, T. M. "Marlowe's *The Jew of Malta*, IV.vi.7-10." *Expl.*, IX (April, 1951).

B6381   Adams, Henry H. "Two Notes on *I Henry IV*." *SQ*, III (1952), 282-283.

B6382   McNeir, Waldo F. "Shakespeare, *Henry IV, Part I*, II.i.76-85." *Expl.*, X (1952), 37.

B6383   Pearce, T. M. "Shakespeare's 'Mother Reference', *1 Henry IV*, (II.iv.265 f)." *N &Q*, 197 (1952), 25-26.

B6384 Adams, Henry Hitch. "Falstaff's Instinct." *SQ*, v (1954), 208-209.
B6385 Evans, G. Blakemore. "Laying a Shakespearian Ghost: *I Henry IV*, II.iv.225." *SQ*, v (1954), 427.
B6386 Steele, Oliver L., Jr. "Shakespeare's *I Henry IV*, II.iii.64." *Expl.*, xiv (1956), No. 59.
B6387 Camden, Carroll. "Three Notes on Shakespeare." *MLN*, lxxii (1957), 251-253.
B6388 Main, C. F. "Benlowes, Brome, and the Bejewelled Nose." *N &Q*, ns, iv (1957), 232-233.

ii. II Henry IV

B6389 McCain, H. E. "A Note on *The Second Part of King Henry IV*." *SAB*, xiv (1939), 51-54.
B6390 Tilley, M. P., and J. K. Y. "Two Notes on Shakspere. I: Malvolio's Yellow Stockings and Cross-Garters; II: To Repent in Sack [*2 Henry IV*, I.ii.222]." *SAB*, xii (1937), 54-56.
B6391 Allen, D. "Gilded Twopences." *British Numismatic Journal*, xxiii (1939), 156.
B6392 Alspach, Russell K. "A Note on *2 Henry IV*, V.ii.112-117." *SAB*, xv (1940), 191-192.
B6393 Brinkley, Roberta Florence. "Doll Tearsheet." *TLS*, Sept. 21, 1946, p. 451.
       See letters by Audrey Jennings, ibid., Oct. 5, 1946, p. 479; by A. de Quincey, ibid., Oct. 12, p. 493.
B6394 Maxwell, J. C. "*2 Henry IV*, II.iv.91 ff." *MLR*, xlii (1947), 485.
B6395 Maxwell, J. C. "*2 Henry IV*, Epilogue 30." *N &Q*, 195 (1950), 314.
B6396 Siegel, Paul N. "Shakespeare's *King Henry IV, Part II*." *Expl.*, ix, No. 2 (Nov., 1950), item 9. Calls attention to a certain similarity between Falstaff's and the King's words about the Prince (IV.iii.126-132; IV.iv.54-56).
B6397 Baldini, Gabriele. "Mrs. Quickly, Doll Tearsheet e il Prof. Dover Wilson." *La Nuova Antologia* (Rome), March, 1952, pp. 296-306.
B6398 Fox, C. Overbury. "The 'Haunch' of Winter." *N &Q*, ns, i (1954), 21.
B6399 Sledd, James. "A Note on the Use of Renaissance Dictionaries." *MP*, xlix (1951/52), 10-15.
B6400 Carrington, Norman Thomas. *Shakespeare: "King Henry IV, Part 2."* London: Brodie, 1955. Pp. 72.
B6401 Long, J. H. "Sneak's Noyse Heard Again?" *Musical Quarterly*, xliv (1958), 76-81.
B6402 Phialas, Peter G. "Coleville of the Dale." *SQ*, ix (1958), 86-88.

(2) LITERARY GENESIS AND ANALOGUES
(a) GENERAL

B6403 Daniel, Samuel. *The Civil Wars*. Ed. with Introduction and Notes by Laurence Michel. Yale Univ. Press, 1958. Pp. vii, 366.
       Rev: A4734.
B6404 Starnes, D. T. "More About the Prince Hal Legend." *PQ*, xv (1936), 358-366.
B6405 Somerset, R., Lord Raglan. *The Hero: A Study in Tradition, Myth, and Drama*. London: Watts, 1936. Republished 1949. Pp. x, 310.
B6406 Fletcher, B. J. *Shakespeare's Use of Holinshed's Chronicles in "Richard III," "Richard II," "Henry IV," and "Macbeth."* DD, University of Texas, 1937.
B6407 Greer, Clayton Alvis. "The Place of *1 Henry VI* in the York-Lancaster Tetralogy." *PMLA*, liii (1938), 687-701.
B6408 Dodson, Sarah Clara. "The Northumberland of Shakespeare and Holinshed." *TxSE*, xix (1939). 74-85.
B6409 Wilson, John Dover. "The Political Background of Shakespeare's *Richard II* and *Henry IV*." A lecture delivered before the German Shakespearean Society, at Weimar. *SJ*, lxxv (1939), 36-51.
B6410 Baldwin, T. W. "Perseus Purloins Pegasus." *PQ*, xx (1941), 361-370.
B6411 Pearce, Josephine A. "An Earlier Talbot Epitaph." *MLN*, lix (1944), 327-329.
B6412 Crundell, H. W. "Shakespeare and Clement Swallow." *N &Q*, 189 (1945), 271-272.
B6413 Lea, Kathleen, and Ethel Seaton. " 'I Saw Young Henry'." *RES*, xxi (1945), 319-322.
B6414 Wilson, John Dover. "The Origins and Development of Shakespeare's *Henry IV*." *Library*, 4th Series, xxvi (1945), 2-16.
B6415 Byrne, M. St. Clare. "Like Images." *TLS*, June 1, 1946, p. 259.
B6416 Greer, C. A. "A Lost Play the Source of *Henry IV* and *Henry V*." *N &Q*, ns, i (1954), 53-55.
B6417 Greer, C. A. "Shakespeare's Use of *The Famous Victories of Henry the Fifth*." *N &Q*, ns, i (1954), 238-241.
B6418 Law, Robert Adger. "Edmund Mortimer in Shakespeare and Hall." *SQ*, v (1954), 425-427.

(b) FALSTAFF

B6419 Draper, John W. "Falstaff and the Plautine Parasite." *Classical Jour.*, xxxiii (1938), 390-401.

B6420   Borgese, G. A. "The Dishonor of Honor: Francesco Giovanni Mauro to Sir John Falstaff." *RR*, XXXII (1941), 44-55.

B6421   Boughner, Daniel C. "Traditional Elements in Falstaff." *JEGP*, XLIII (1944), 417-428.

B6422   Stewart, J. I. M. "King Cambyses's Vein [*1 H. IV*, II. iv. 423-425]." *TLS*, May 26, 1945, p. 247.

B6423   Oliver, Leslie Mahon. "Sir John Oldcastle: Legend or Literature?" *Library*, 5th Series, (1947), 179-183.

B6424   Fiehler, Rudolph. " 'I Serve the Good Duke of Norfolk'." *MLQ*, x (1949), 364-366.

B6425   McCutchan, J. Wilson. "Similarities Between Falstaff and Gluttony in Medwall's *Nature*." *SAB*, XXIV (1949), 214-219.

B6426   Fiehler, Rudolph. *Sir John Oldcastle, the Original of Falstaff*. DD, University of Texas, 1950.

B6427   D., A. "*Henry IV Part Two* and the Homily Against Drunkenness." *N &Q*, 195 (1950), 160-162.

B6428   Murry, John Middleton. *John Clare and Other Studies*. London: Nevill, 1950. Pp. 252. Includes "The Creation of Falstaff," pp. 181-207.

B6429   Feldman, Abraham. " 'King Cambises' Vein'." *N &Q*, 196 (1951), 98-100.

B6430   Davenport, A. "Notes on Lyly's *Campaspe* and Shakespeare." *N &Q*, NS, I (1954), 19-20.

B6431   Boughner, D. C. "Vice, Braggart, and Falstaff." *Anglia*, LXXII (1954), 35-61.

B6432   Bryant, Joseph Allen, Jr. "Shakespeare's Falstaff and the Mantle of Dick Tarlton." *SP*, LI (1954), 149-162.

B6433   Herbert, T. Walter. "The Naming of Falstaff." *Emory Univ. Quar.*, x (1954), 1-11.

B6434   Fiehler, Rudolph. "How Oldcastle Became Falstaff." *MLQ*, XVI (1955), 16-28.

B6435   McAvoy, William C. "Falstaff, Erasmus, and Ficino." *Carroll Quarterly*, XI (1957), 10-14.

B6436   Spivack, Bernard. "Falstaff and the Psychomachia." *SQ*, VIII (1957), 449-459.

(3) USE OF LANGUAGE

B6437   Dayton, B. E. *Animal Similes and Metaphors in Shakespeare's Plays*. DD, University of Washington, 1937. Abstr. in *Abstracts of Theses* (Univ. of Washington), II (1937), 119-122.

B6438   Doran, Madeleine. "Imagery in *Richard II* and in *Henry IV*." *MLR*, XXXVII (1942), 113-122.

B6439   King, Arthur H. "Some Notes on Ambiguity in *Henry IV, Part 1*." *SN*, XIV (1942), 161-183.

B6440   Barnett, Alan W. "Falstaff's Girth: Compass of Imagery." *Univ. of Kansas City Review*, XIX (1952), 51-56.

(4) GENERAL CRITICISM OF THE PLAY
(a) GENERAL

B6441   Empson, William. *Some Versions of Pastoral*. London, 1935. Pp. 298. *Henry IV*, pp. 103-109.

B6442   Brandl, A. "Von der Unwahrheit und der Wahrheit Shakespeares." Brandl's *Forschungen und Charakteristiken* (Berlin), 1936, pp. 175-176.

B6443   Papiroff, S. "Shakespeare's Idea of Kingship as seen in *Richard II* and *Henry IV*." *The Silver Falcon*, New York: Hunter College, 1936, pp. 16-20.

B6444   Charlton, H. B. *Shakespearian Comedy*. London: Methuen, 1938. Pp. 303. Chapter on Falstaff. Rev: B5155.

B6445   Charlton, H. B. "Shakespeare's 'Dark Comedies'." *BJRL*, XXI (1937), 78-128.

B6446   Traversi, D. A. *An Approach to Shakespeare*. London: Sands, Paladin Press, 1938. Pp. 152. Second edition, revised and enlarged. New York: Doubleday, 1956. Pp. 304. Rev: A8420.

B6447   Divine, Hugh W. *A Study of Some of the Problems in the Falstaff Plays*. DD, Louisiana State University, 1942. Abstr. in Louisiana State Univ. *Abstracts of Theses*, 1942, p. 51.

B6448   Spencer, Benjamin T. "*2 Henry IV* and The Theme of Time." *UTQ*, XIII (1944), 394-399.

B6449   Salter, F. M. "The Play Within the Play of *First Henry IV*." *Trans. Royal Soc. of Canada*, Third Series, Section II, XL (1946), 209-223.

B6450   Connor, Saymour V. "The Role of Douglas in *Henry IV, Part One*." *TxSE*, XXVII (1948), 215-221.

B6451   McLuhan, Herbert Marshall. "*Henry IV*, A Mirror for Magistrates." *UTQ*, XVII (1948), 152-160

B6452   Shaaber, M. A. "The Unity of *Henry IV*." *AMS*, pp. 217-227.

B6453   Traversi, D. A. "*Henry IV—Part I*." *Scrutiny*, XV (1948), 24-35.

B6454   Traversi, D. A. "*Henry IV—Part II*." *Scrutiny*, XV (1948), 117-127.

B6455   Bogorad, Samuel N. "*1 King Henry the Fourth*, II.iv.315 ff." *SQ*, I (1950), 76-77. Comment by Thomas D. Bowman, ibid., p. 295.

B6456 Cain, H. Edward. "Further Light on the Relation of *1* and *2 Henry IV*." *SQ*, III (1952), 21-38.

B6457 Zeeveld, W. Gordon. " 'Food for Powder'—'Food for Worms'." *SQ*, III (1952), 249-253.

B6458 Claeyssens, Austere E. "*Henry IV, Part 1*." *Lectures on Four of Shakespeare's History Plays*. Carnegie Series in English No. 1. 1953, pp. 19-34.

B6459 Leech, Clifford. "The Unity of *2 Henry IV*." *ShS*, VI (1953), 16-24.

B6460 Schutte, William M. "*Henry IV, Part 2*." *Lectures on Four of Shakespeare's History Plays*. Carnegie Series in English No. 1. 1953, pp. 35-42.

B6461 Barber, C. L. "From Ritual to Comedy: An Examination of *Henry IV*." *English Stage Comedy*. *English Institute Essays*, 1954, pp. 22-51.

B6462 Goodman, Paul. *The Structure of Literature*. Univ. of Chicago Press, 1954. Pp. vii, 282.
Rev: B5962.

B6463 Hunter, G. K. "*Henry IV* and the Elizabethan Two-Part Play." *RES*, NS, V (1954), 236-248.
Rev: by H. Oppel, *NS*, IV (1955), 94.

B6464 Aldus, Paul J. "Analogical Probability in Shakespeare's Plays." *SQ*, VI (1955), 397-414.
See also L. J. Mills and P. J. Aldus, *SQ*, VII (1956), 133-134.

B6465 Carrington, Norman Thomas. *Shakespeare: King Henry IV, Part 2*." Notes on chosen English texts series. London: Brodie, 1955. Pp. 72.

B6466 Jenkins, Harold. *The Structural Problem in Shakespeare's "Henry the Fourth."* An Inaugural Lecture Delivered at Westfield College, University of London, on May 19, 1955. London: Methuen, 1956. Pp. 28.
Rev: briefly in *TLS*, Nov. 9, 1956, p. 671; by Donald FitzJohn, *Drama*, 1957, pp. 38-39; by R. Davril, *EA*, X, 52-53; by H. Edward Cain, *SQ*, VIII, 542-544.

B6467 Tyler, Parker. "Phaethon: The Metaphysical Tension Between the Ego and the Universe in English Poetry." *Accent*, XVI (Winter, 1956), 29-44.

B6468 Walker, Saxon. "Mime and Heraldry in *Henry IV, Part I*." *English*, XI (1956), 91-96.

B6469 Langbaum, Robert. *The Poetry of Experience: The Dramatic Monologue in Modern Literary Tradition*. New York: Random House, 1957. Pp. 246.
Chap. V: "Character versus Action in Shakespeare," pp. 160-181. (*Henry IV*, pp. 169-179.)
Rev: A6512.

B6470 Knights, L. C. *Some Shakespearean Themes*. London: Chatto & Windus, 1959.
Chapter on *Henry IV*.

B6471 Rothe, Hans. "Shakespeares König Heinrich der Vierte in neuer Fassung." *Prisma* (Bochum), 1958/59, pp. 1-4.

(b) FALSTAFF

B6472 Alexander, Franz. "A Note on Falstaff." *Psychoanalytic Quarterly*, II (1933), 592-606.
Discussed by Lionel Trilling, "Freud and Literature," *Horizon*, XVI (1947), 182-200. See also A1269a and B6541.

B6473 Cancelled.

B6474 Waldock, A. J. A. "The Men in Buckram." *RES*, XXIII (1947), 16-23.

B6475 Reik, Theodor. *Fragment of a Great Confession*. New York: Farrar, Straus, 1949.
Henry IV, p. 336.

B6476 Reuter, Gerhard. "Falstaffs Funktion." *Prisma* (Bochum), 1958/59, pp. 4-8.

(5) CHARACTERIZATION
(a) FALSTAFF

B6477 Alexander, Franz. "A Note on Falstaff." *Psychoanalytic Quarterly*, II (1933), 592-606.
See B6472.

B6478 Charlton, H. B. *Falstaff*. Manchester Univ. Press, 1935. Pp. 46. Reprint of article in *BJRL*, XIX (1935), 46-89.
Rev: by L. Cazamian, *RAA*, XIII (1936), 340-341; by E. E. Stoll, *SJ*, LXXIV (1938), 55-63.

B6479 Stewart, G. R. "Three and Fifty Upon Poor Old Jack." *PQ*, XIV (1935), 274-275.

B6480 Somerset, R., Lord Raglan. "Falstaff." *Illus. London News*, 188 (1936), 630.

B6481 Babcock, R. W. "An Early Eighteenth Century Note on Falstaff." *PQ*, XVI (1937), 84-85.

B6482 Cazamian, Louis. *Essais en Deux Langues*. Contains "The Humour of Falstaff."
See B4463.

B6483 Clark, E. G. "Falstaff & Cobham." *A Christmas Book for the Dept. of English*, New York: Hunter College, 1937, pp. 49-59.

B6484 Bond, R. W. "Falstaff as *vox populi*." *Studia Otiosa*, 1938, pp. 51-68.

B6485 Cancelled.

B6486 Shirley, John W. "Falstaff, An Elizabethan Glutton." *PQ*, XVII (1938), 271-287.

B6487 Messiaen, Pierre. "Les Drames Historiques de Shakespeare: Falstaff." *RCC*, 1st Series, XL (1939), 84-96, 280-288.

B6488   Small, Samuel A. "The Reflective Element in Falstaff." *SAB*, XIV (1939), 108-121, 131-143.

B6489   Wyneken, H. "Falstaff und Don Quichotte." *MNN*, No. 113 (1939).

B6490   Jacobi, Walter. "Falstaff. Eine psychologisch-ästhetische Studie." *SJ*, LXXVII (1941), 2-48.

B6491   Martin, Burns. "Falstaff." *Dalhousie Rev.*, XIX (1940), 439-448.

B6492   Pushkin, A. S. "Notes on Shylock, Angelo and Falstaff." Tr. by Albert Siegel. *SAB*, XVI (1941), 120-121.

B6493   Small, Samuel A. "Hotspur and Falstaff." *SAB*, XVI (1941), 243-248.

B6494   Rebora, Piero. "Falstaff." *Riv. Italiana del Teatro*, VI (1942), 228-240.

B6495   Sims, Ruth E. "The Green Old Age of Falstaff." *Bul. Hist. of Medicine*, XIII (1943), 144-157.

B6496   Webb, Henry J. "Falstaff's 'Tardy Tricks'." *MLN*, LVIII (1943), 377-379.

B6497   Wilson, J. Dover. *The Fortunes of Falstaff*. Cambridge Univ. Press, 1943. Pp. viii, 144.
        Rev: *N &Q*, 185 (1943), 298-300; *TLS*, Oct. 30, 1943, p. 525; by R. W. Babcock, *PQ*, XXIII (1944), 189-192; by Mark Schorer, *NYTBR*, May 7, p. 4; *QR*, 282 (1944), 116-117; by G. C. Taylor, *Quar. Rev. Lit.*, I, 242-244; by Joyce Brown, *ConR*, 166 (1944), 64; by R. W. Babcock, *SAB*, XIX, 116-131, 172-185; by G. Stewart Griffiths, "Professor Dover Wilson's Falstaff," *English*, V, 51-53; by Theodore Spencer, *SRL*, June 17, pp. 36-37; by Peter Alexander, *MLR*, XXXIX, 408-409; by S. C. Chew, *NYHTBR*, May 14, Sec. 6, p. 3; by J. B. Leishman, *RES*, XX, 315-316; by J. C. S., *Univ. of Edinburgh Jour.*, XIII, 54-55; by Oscar James Campbell, *Nation*, 158 (1944), 738-739; by Harry Levin, *NR*, 110 (1944), 632-634; by Grover Cronin, Jr., *Thought*, XIX, 727-729.

B6497a Wilson, Edmund. "J. Dover Wilson on Falstaff." Wilson's *Classics and Commercials*, London, 1951, pp. 161-167.

B6497b Empson, William. "Falstaff and Mr. Dover Wilson." *KR*, XV (1953), 213-262.
        Argues against Wilson's theory that Shakespeare originally intended to introduce Falstaff as a comic figure at Agincourt. Falstaff and Prince Hal complex dramatic figures, not embodiments of the Medieval Vice and the Ideal King.
        Rev: by H. T. Price, *SQ*, V (1954), 128.

B6498   Webb, Henry J. "Falstaff's Clothes." *MLN*, LIX (1944), 162-164.

B6499   Cancelled.

B6500   Draper, John. "Falstaff, 'A Fool and Jester'." *MLQ*, VII (1946), 453-462.

B6501   Levin, Harry. "Falstaff Uncolted." *MLN*, LXI (1946), 305-310.
        Much on the increase of demand for realism and the breakdown of conventions.

B6502   Farnham, Willard. "The Mediaeval Comic Spirit in the English Renaissance." *AMS*, pp. 429-437.

B6503   Kris, E. "Prince Hal's Conflict." *Psychoanalytic Quarterly*, XVII (1948), 487-505. Reprinted in *Psychoanalytic Explorations in Art*. New York: International Universities Press, 1952. Pp. 358, 79 pl.

B6504   Springer, R. *A History of Falstaff Criticism*. DD, Columbia University, 1948. Pp. 94.

B6505   Traversi, D. A. "*Henry IV—Part I*." *Scrutiny*, XV (1948), 24-35. Part II, pp. 117-127.

B6506   Viswanathan, K. "Falstaff and the Sonnets." *Triveni* (Madras), XX (1949), 569-573.

B6507   Gordon, George Stuart. *The Lives of Authors*. London: Chatto & Windus; Clarke, Irwin & Co., 1950. Pp. 219.
        Includes "Morgan on Falstaff."
        Rev: *TLS*, June 9, 1950, p. 355; by R. G. Cox, *MGW*, May 11, p. 11.

B6508   Poindexter, James E. *Criticism of Falstaff to 1860*. DD, University of North Carolina, 1950. Abstr. publ. in *Univ. of North Carolina Record, Research in Progress*, Jan.-Dec., 1949, Grad. School Series, No. 58, pp. 112-113.

B6509   Sen Gupta, S. C. *Shakespearian Comedy*. Calcutta: Oxford University Press, 1950. Pp. ix, 287. Falstaff, pp. 250-275.
        Rev: B5178.

B6510   Hunter, William B., Jr. "Falstaff." *South Atlantic Quarterly*, L (1951), 86-95.

B6511   Nock, Samuel A. "The Metamorphosis of Sir John Falstaff." *Shakespeare-Studien, Festschrift für Heinrich Mutschmann*, pp. 115-118.

B6512   Stefano, C. "Sir John Falstaff." *Palcoscenico* (Milan), I (1951), No. 28.

B6513   Adams, Henry H. "Two Notes on *I Henry IV*." *SQ*, III (1952), 282-283.

B6514   Hemingway, Samuel B. "On Behalf of that Falstaff." *SQ*, III (1952), 307-311.

B6515   Lombardi, Olga. "Falstaff di Lodovice." *La Fiera Letteraria* (Rome), VII (May 25, 1952), 2.

B6516   Baldini, Gabriele. "Il Vino Vecchio di Sir John Falstaff." *Paragone*, IV (1953), 48-55.

B6517   Greer, C. A. "The Source of Falstaff's Contamination of the Army." *N &Q*, 198 (1953), 236-237.

B6518   Reik, Theodor. *The Haunting Melody*. New York: Farrar, Straus, and Young, 1953. Falstaff, pp. 137-145.

B6519   Sprague, Arthur Colby. "Gadshill Revisited." *SQ*, IV (1953), 125-137.

B6520   Greer, C. A. "Falstaff's Diminution of Wit." *N &Q*, NS, I (1954), 468.

B6521   Stoll, Elmer Edgar. "A Falstaff for the 'Bright'." *MP*, LI (1954), 145-159.

B6522   Bennett, Henry Stanley. "Sir John Fastolf." In his *Six Medieval Men and Women*. Cambridge Univ. Press, 1955, pp. 30-68.

B6523   Greer, C. A. "Falstaff A Coward?" *N &Q*, NS, II (1955), 176-177.

B6524   Flatter, Richard. "Der jugendliche Falstaff." In his *Triumph der Gnade. Shakespeare Essays.* Vienna, Munich: Kurt Desch, 1956, pp. 133-136.

B6525   García Reinoso, Diego. "Notas Sobre la Obesidad a través del Estudio de Falstaff [Notes on Obesity Through a Study of Falstaff]." *Revista de Psicoanálisis* (Buenos Aires), XIII (1956), 170-177.

B6526   Schevill, James. "Towards a Rhythm of Comic Action." *Western Speech*, XX (1956), 5-14.

B6527   Baldini, Gabriele. "Ruzanta e Falstaff." *Studi in onore di Pietro Silva.* Ed. by the Facoltà di Magistero of Rome. Florence: F. Le Monnier (Tip. Ariani), 1957, pp. 9-15.

B6528   Spivack, Bernard. "Falstaff and the Psychomachia." *SQ*, VIII (1957), 449-459.

B6529   Williams, Philip. "The Birth and Death of Falstaff Reconsidered." *SQ*, VIII (1957), 359-365.

(b) OTHERS

B6530   Boughner, Daniel C. "Pistol and the Roaring Boys." *SAB*, XI (1936), 226-237.

B6531   Draper, John W. "Robert Shallow Esq., J. P." *N. Mitt.*, XXXVIII (1937), 257-269.

B6532   Dangel, Anneliese. *Fähnrich Pistol und die Anfänge des Begriffes Rant.* DD, Leipzig, 1944. Pp. 118. Typewritten.

B6533   Dean, L. F. "Shakespeare's Treatment of Conventional Ideas." *SR*, LII (1944), 414-423.

B6534   Jennings, A. "Doll Tearsheet." *TLS*, Oct. 5, 1946, p. 479.

B6535   Quincey, A. de. "Doll Tearsheet." *TLS*, Oct. 12, 1946, p. 493.

B6536   Hotson, Leslie. "Ancient Pistol." *YR*, XXXVIII (1948), 51-66. Reprinted in *Shakespeare's Sonnets Dated, and Other Essays*, C21.

B6537   Ribner, Irving. "Bolingbroke, A True Machiavellian." *MLQ*, IX (1948), 177-184.

B6538   Draper, Charles L. [*sic*] "Falstaff's Bardolph." *Neophil*, XXXIII (1949), 222-226.

B6539   Hotson, Leslie. "Earl of Essex and Falstaff." *Shakespeare's Sonnets Dated, and Other Essays.* London: Rupert Hart-Davis; Toronto: Clarke, Irwin & Co., 1949, pp. 244.
         Rev: C21.

B6540   Cancelled.

B6541   Trilling, Lionel. "Freud and Literature." *The Liberal Imagination*, New York: The Viking Press, 1950, pp. 34-57.
         Rev: A1334.

B6542   Baldini, Gabriele. "Lord Bardolph e Sir John Umfreuile nell' *Henry IV* di Shakespeare." *Belfagor*, VII (1952), 573-581.

B6543   Greer, C. A. "Shakespeare and Prince Hal." *N &Q*, 198 (1953), 424-426.

B6544   Geehern, Richard J. *Fifteenth and Early Sixteenth Century Interpretations of the Character and Career of King Henry IV.* DD, University of North Carolina, 1954. Abstr. publ. in *Univ. of North Carolina Record, Research in Progress*, Jan.-Dec., 1953, Grad. School Series, No. 66, 1954, pp. 94-95.

B6545   Unger, Leonard. "Deception and Self-deception in Shakespeare's *Henry IV*." *The Man in the Name: Essays on the Experience of Poetry*, Minneapolis Univ. Press and Oxford Univ. Press, 1956, pp. 3-17.
         Rev: A6301.

B6546   Bastian, F. "George Vargis, Constable." *N &Q*, NS IV (1957), 11. See also Geoffrey W. Jaggard, ibid., p. 179.

B6547   Kleinstück, Johannes. "The Character of Henry Bolingbroke." *Neophil*, XLI (1957), 51-56.

(6) MISCELLANEOUS ITEMS

B6548   Cancelled.

B6549   Hart, Alfred. *Shakespeare and the Homilies, and Other Pieces of Research into the Elizabethan Drama.* Melbourne Univ. Press, 1934.
         2 Henry IV: "Was the Second Part . . . Censored?"
         Rev: A4649.

B6550   Oman, C. "Military History of England Under the Tudors." *A History of the Art of War in the 16th Century*, 1937, pp. 285-389.
         Rev: A2585.

B6551   Petsch, R. "Shakespeares *König Heinrich IV*, und das Geschichtsdrama in England." *SJ*, LXXIII (1937), 109-130.

B6552   Phillips, Gerald William. *Lord Burghley in Shakespeare. Falstaff, Sly and Others.* London: Thornton Butterworth, 1936. Pp. 285.
         Rev: *TLS*, Jan., 1937, p. 13.

B6553 Langdale, A. Barnett. "Did Shakespeare Miss the Road to Warkworth? (A Note on *Henry the Fourth, Part Two*)." *SAB*, XVII (1942), 156-159.

B6554 Adler, Alfred. "Falstaff's Holy Dying, Pagan as Well as Christian." *MLN*, LXI (1946), 72.

B6555 Boas, Guy. "Shakespeare and England, 1402 and 1939." *Blackwoods*, 259 (1946), 277-285.

B6556 Heath-Stubbs, John. "The Mythology of Falstaff." *Occult Observer* (London), I (1949), 21-30.

B6557 Brennecke, Ernest. "Shakespeare's 'Singing Man of Windsor'." *PMLA*, LXVI (1951), 1188-92.

B6558 Brennecke, Ernest, Jr. "A Singing Man of Windsor." *Music and Letters*, XXXIII (1952), 33-40.

B6559 Hunter, E. K. *Shakespeare and Common Sense.* Boston: Christopher, 1954. Pp. 312.
Chap. III: "Falstaff's Heir."
Rev: A971.

B6560 Waggoner, G. R. "An Elizabethan Attitude Toward Peace and War." *PQ*, XXXIII (1954), 20-33.

B6561 Cutts, John P. "The Original Music of a Song in *2 Henry IV*." *SQ*, VII (1956), 385-392.

B6562 Pabst, Walter. *Venus und die Missverstandene Dido. Literarische Ursprünge des Sibyllen und des Venusberges.* Cram: de Gruyter & Co., 1955. Pp. 154. (Hamburger Romanistische Studien, Reihe A, Vol. XL).
Review includes mention of *Henry IV* in connection with the legendary demonization of the ancient gods; see Wolfgang Leppmann, *Comparative Literature*, VIII, 249-251.

B6563 Lewis, P. S. "Sir John Fastolf's Lawsuit over Titchwell 1448-1455." *Hist. Jour.*, I (1958), 1-20.

B6564 Sternfeld, Frederick W. "Lasso's Music for Shakespeare's 'Samingo'." *SQ*, IX (1958), 105-116.

(7) SUBSEQUENT HISTORY OF THE PLAY
(other than productions after 1660)

B6565 Babcock, R. W. "An Early 18th-Century Note on Falstaff." *PQ*, XVI (1937), 84-85.

B6566 Sandison, Helen E. "The Ninth Earl of Northumberland Quotes his Ancestor Hotspur." *RES*, XII (1936), 71-75.

B6567 Boswell, James. *London Journal, 1762-1763.* Ed. by Frederick A. Pottle. New York: McGraw-Hill, 1950. Pp. xxix, 370.
Contains remarks by Sheridan on *2 Henry IV* (pp. 135-136), criticizing Garrick's Performance, and references to Garrick's playing of *Henry IV*.

B6568 McManaway, James G. "A New Shakespeare Document." *SQ*, II (1951), 119-122.

B6569 Sprague, Arthur Colby. "Falstaff Hackett." *TN*, IX (1955), 61-67.

B6570 "Falstaff and the Prince." *Country Life*, April 26, 1956, p. 856.

MUCH ADO ABOUT NOTHING (221;78)
(1) THE TEXT
(a) MODERN EDITIONS

B6571 *Much Ado about Nothing.* Ed. with introd. and notes by F. E. Budd. London: Macmillan, 1936. Pp. 181.

B6572 *Much Ado about Nothing.* Ed. by G. L. Kittredge. With introd. and notes. Boston: Ginn & Co., 1941. Pp. xiv, 166.

B6573 *Much Ado about Nothing.* Ed. by Charles T. Prouty. Crofts Classics. New York: Crofts, 1948. Pp. xi, 78.

B6574 *Much Ado about Nothing.* Ed. by P. Wayne. New Clarendon Shakespeare. Oxford: Clarendon Press, 1954. Pp. 192.

B6575 *Much Ado about Nothing.* French's Acting Edition. London: French, 1958. Pp. x, 88.

B6576 *Much Ado about Nothing.* Ed. by Josephine Waters Bennett. Pelican Shakespeare. Baltimore: Penguin Books, 1958. Pp. 126.

(b) EMENDATIONS

B6577 Thaler, Alwin. *Shakespeare and Democracy.* Univ. of Tennessee Press, 1941. Pp. xii, 312.
Chap. XIII: "Three Notes: *Much Ado, Rich. III, As You Like It.*"
Rev: A1809.

B6578 Dean, Leonard F. "Shakespeare's *Much Ado About Nothing*, IV.i.291." *Expl.*, II (1943/44), 51.

B6579 Brereton, J. Le Gay. "*Much Ado About Nothing*, IV.i.145-160." *Writings on Elizabethan Drama*, Melbourne Univ. Press, 1948, pp. 96-98.

B6580 Prouty, Charles Tyler. "A Lost Piece of Stage Business in *Much Ado About Nothing*." *MLN*, LXV (1950), 207-208.

B6581 Taylor, A. P. "The Sick Tune." *MLN*, LXV (1950), 345-347. Concerns *Much Ado*, III. iv.41: gives the words for the ditty called "The Sick Tune."

B6582 Hulme, Hilda M. "Three Notes on the Interpretation of Shakespeare's Text." *Neophil*, XLII (1958), 212-215. II.iii.45.

(2) LITERARY GENESIS AND ANALOGUES

B6583 Danchin, F. C. "Une Source de *Much Ado About Nothing.*" *RAA*, XIII (1936), 430-431. Indicates the plot parallel between *Much Ado* and A.M.'s *A Pleasant Comedie of Two Gentlemen* (1585).

B6584 Bennett, Mackie Langham. "Shakespeare's *Much Ado* and its Possible Italian Sources." *TxSE*, XVII (1937), 52-74.

B6585 Moore, John Robert. "*Much Ado About Nothing:* Seacole." *N&Q*, 174 (1938), 60-61. See also D. A. H. Moses, ibid., p. 106; J. W. Fawcett, ibid., p. 195.

B6586 Thaler, Alwin. "Spenser and *Much Ado About Nothing.*" *SP*, XXXVII (1940), 225-235. Re-published in Thaler's *Shakespeare and Democracy*, Univ. of Tenn. Press, 1941.

B6587 Prouty, C. T. "George Whetstone, Peter Beverly, and the Sources of *Much Ado About Nothing.*" *SP*, XXXVIII (1941), 211-220.

B6588 Gordon, D. J. "*Much Ado About Nothing:* A Possible Source for the Hero-Claudio Plot." *SP*, XXXIX (1942), 279-290.

B6589 Potts, Abbie Findlay. "Spenserian 'Courtesy' and 'Temperance' in *Much Ado About Nothing.*" *SAB*, XVII (1942), 103-111, 126-133.

B6590 Evans, Dorothy Atkinson. "Some Notes on Shakespeare and *The Mirror of Knighthood.*" *SAB*, XXI (1946), 161-167; XXII, 62-68.

B6591 Parrott, T. M. "Two Late Dramatic Versions of the Slandered Bride Theme." *AMS*, pp. 537-551.

B6592 Boyce, Benjamin. "The Stoic *Consolatio* and Shakespeare." *PMLA*, LXIV (1949), 771-780.

B6593 Prouty, Charles T. *The Sources of "Much Ado About Nothing": A Critical Study, Together with the Text of Peter Beverley's "Ariodanto and Ieneura."* New Haven: Yale Univ. Press, 1950. Pp. vi, 142.
    Rev: by H. B. Charlton, *MGW*, Sept. 6, 1951, p. 11; by Robert Adger Law, *JEGP*, L, 420-421; by Allardyce Nicoll, *SQ*, II, 135-136; *TLS*, Sept. 14, 1951, p. 582; by A. P. Rossiter, *English*, IX (1952), 68-69; by Kenneth Muir, *MLR*, XLVII, 219-220; by R. Flatter, *SJ*, 87/88 (1952), 241-242; by M. C. Bradbrook, *ShS*, VI (1953), 154; by Frank Kermode, *RES*, IV, 160-161.

B6594 McNeal, Thomas H. "The Names Hero and Don John in *Much Ado.*" *N&Q*, 198 (1953), 382.

B6595 Bastian, F. "George Vargis, Constable." *N&Q*, NS, IV (1957), 11.

B6596 "Shakespeare Verse Traced to Source." *New York Times*, Nov. 18, 1958, p. 35M.

B6597 McNeal, Thomas H. "Shakespeare's Cruel Queens." *HLQ*, XXII (1958), 41-50.

(3) USE OF LANGUAGE

B6598 Gallaher, L. M. *Shakespeare's Imagery in "Much Ado."* Thesis, University of Texas, 1937.
B6599 Jorgensen, Paul A. "*Much Ado About Nothing.*" *SQ*, V (1954), 287-295.

(4) GENERAL CRITICISM OF THE PLAY

B6600 Messiaen, Pierre. "*Beaucoup de Bruit pour Rien.*" *LanM*, XXXIV (1936), 361-367.
B6601 Draper, John W. "Dogberry's Due Process of Law." *JEGP*, XLII (1943), 563-576.
B6602 M., A. "M. Arnold on *Much Ado.*" *N&Q*, 184 (1943), 340-341.
B6603 Draper, John W. "Benedick and Beatrice." *JEGP*, XLI (1942), 140-149.
B6604 Smith, James. "*Much Ado About Nothing.*" *Scrutiny*, XIII (1946), 342-357.
B6605 Sell, A. L. "Englishmen in Padua, from Chaucer to Shelley." *DUJ*, XL (1947), 1-7.
B6606 West, E. J. "Much Ado about an Unpleasant Play." *SAB*, XXII (1947), 30-34.
B6607 Gulick, Sidney L., Jr. "More Ado about *Much Ado.*" *SAB*, XXIII (1948), 55-58.
B6608 Cancelled.
B6609 Sypher, Wylie. "Nietzsche and Socrates in Messina." *Partisan Rev.*, XVI (1949), 702-713.
B6610 Prouty, Charles T. *The Sources of "Much Ado About Nothing": A Critical Study, Together with the Text of Peter Beverley's "Ariodanto and Ieneura."* New Haven: Yale Univ. Press, 1950. Pp. vi, 142.
    Defends the unity of the play and the significance of the main plot.
    Rev: B6593.

B6611 Neill, Kirby. "More Ado about Claudio: An Acquittal for the Slandered Groom." *SQ*, III (1952), 91-107.

B6612 Craik, T. W. "*Much Ado about Nothing.*" *Scrutiny*, XIX (1953), 297-316.

B6613 Fergusson, Francis. "*Comedy of Errors* and *Much Ado about Nothing.*" *SR*, LXII (1954), 24-37.

B6614 Snuggs, Henry L. "The Act-Division of *Much Ado About Nothing.*" *Renaissance Papers* (Univ. of S. C.), 1955, pp. 65-74.

B6615 Lacy, Margaret Swanson. *The Jacobean Problem Play: A Study of Shakespeare's "Measure for*

Measure" and "Troilus and Cressida" in Relation to Selected Plays of Chapman, Dekker, and Marston. DD, University of Wisconsin, 1956. Pp. 216. Mic 56-3019. *DA*, XVI (1956), 1899. Publication No. 18,418.

B6616 Fergusson, Francis. *The Human Image in Dramatic Literature.* Doubleday Anchor Books. New York: Doubleday & Co., 1957. Pp. xx, 217.
Part II: Shakespeare, pp. 115-157, includes comments upon *Much.*

B6617 Hockey, Dorothy C. "Notes Notes, Forsooth . . . ." *SQ,* VIII (1957), 353-358.

B6618 Hawkes, Terry. "The Old and the New in *Much Ado about Nothing.*" *N &Q,* NS, V (1958), 524-525.

B6619 Sochatoff, A. Fred. "*Much Ado about Nothing.*" *Shakespeare: Lectures on Five Plays,* Carnegie Institute of Technology, Dept. of English, 1958, pp. 3-17.

(5) CHARACTERIZATION

B6620 Brock, J. H. E. *Iago and Some Shakespearean Villains.* Cambridge: W. Heffer & Sons, 1937. Pp. viii, 48.
Rev: A1245.

B6621 Lewis, C. S. *Hamlet: The Prince or the Poem?* London: Milford, 1942. Pp. 18.
Comments on *Much* also.
Rev: B7673.

B6622 Palmer, John. *Comic Characters of Shakespeare.* New York: Macmillan, 1946. Pp. 135.
Rev: A6544.

B6623 Henderson, Archibald, Jr. *Family of Mercutio.* DD, Columbia University, 1954. Pp. 270. Mic A54-2044. *DA,* XIV (1954), 1395. Publication No. 8684.
Chapter on *Much,* pp. 207-224.

(6) MISCELLANEOUS ITEMS

B6624 Carter, G. E. L. "A Shakespearean Holograph." *Library Assoc. Record,* XXXVIII (1936), 424-426. Unimportant, in spite of its title; sees a possible allusion in *Much Ado* (IV.i.166-172: "Call me a fool . . . biting error") to a copy of the second edition of Florio's *Worlde of Wordes* containing a manuscript guarantee by the bookseller William Aspley.

B6625 Antokolskoi, P. (French text), and T. Khrenikov (Music). *Five Songs (with Music) for "Much Ado About Nothing."* Moscow, 1939. Pp. 20.

B6626 Osborn, James M. "Benedick's Song in *Much Ado.*" *The Times* (London), Nov. 17, 1958, p. 11.

(7) SUBSEQUENT HISTORY OF THE PLAY
(other than productions after 1660)

B6627 Knight, A. H. J. "Duke Heinrich Julius of Brunswick's *Comedy of Vincentius Ladislaus.*" *MLR,* XXXIV (1939), 50-61.

KING HENRY V (216;76)
See also various sections of *Henry IV* for items touching all three plays.

(1) THE TEXT
(a) THE OLD TEXTS

B6628 *Henry the Fifth,* 1600. Shakespeare Quarto Facsimiles, No. 9. With Introd. by W. W. Greg. Oxford: Clarendon Press, 1956. Pp. viii, 52.
Rev: *MdF,* Oct., 1957, p. 319; *ShN,* VII, 46; by Fredson Bowers, *MLR,* LIII (1958), 235-236; *N &Q,* NS, V, 135; by Don Henry, *Players Magazine,* Oct., p. 10; by J. H. P. Pafford, *RES,* NS, IX, 451; by Cyrus Hoy, *SQ,* IX, 579-580.

B6629 Krauer, Werner. *Die Entstehung der ersten Quarto von Shakespeares "Heinrich V."* DD, Leipzig, 1924. Pp. 35. Publ. *Zeitschrift d. Deutsche Vereins für Buchwesen und Schrifttum,* 1923.

B6630 Duthie, George Ian. *Elizabethan Pirated Dramas, with Special Reference to the 'Bad' Quartos of "Hamlet," "Henry V," and "Romeo and Juliet": with an Appendix on the Problem of "The Taming of a Shrew."* DD, Edinburgh, 1939.

B6631 Cole, Percival R. "The Text of *King Henry V.*" *N &Q,* 187 (1944), 200-203; M. H. Dodds, ibid., p. 302.

B6632 Cairncross, Andrew S. "Quarto Copy for Folio *Henry V.*" *SB,* VIII (1956), 67-93.
F was set up from corrected copy from Q_1—Q_3, with Q_3 serving as the main copy.

(b) MODERN EDITIONS

B6633 Wells, William S. *The Famous Victories of Henry the Fifth: A Critical Edition.* DD, Stanford University, 1935. Abstr. publ. in *Abstracts of Dissertations,* Stanford Univ., X (1934-35), 46-48.

B6634 *King Henry V.* Ed. K. Schrey. Frankfurt a. M.: Diesterweg, 1938. Pp. 109.

B6635 *The Life of King Henry V.* French's Acting Eds. London: French, 1939.

B6636   *Henry V.* Ed. Ronald F. Fletcher. New Clarendon Shakespeare. Oxford and New York, 1941.

B6637   *The Life of King Henry the Fifth.* Ed. George Lyman Kittredge. Boston: Ginn and Co.,
        1945. Pp. 211.
            Rev: by Robert Adger Law, *MLN*, LXI (1946), 349-350.

B6638   *Henry V.* Ed. J. Dover Wilson. The New Shakespeare. Cambridge Univ. Press, 1947. Pp.
        lviii, 202. Republ. Cambridge Pocket Shakespeare, 1958.
            Rev: *TLS*, April 26, 1947, p. 203; ibid., June 21, p. 311; ibid., June 28, p. 323 (comment
        on a misprint in review of June 21); *N &Q*, 192 (1947), 219-220; by E. C. Pettet, *English*, VI,
        260-261; by Roy Walker, *Life and Letters*, LIV, 168-174; by B. R. Redman, *SRL*, Aug. 23,
        p. 33; by W. M. T. Dodds, *MLR*, XLII, 495-502; by F. C. Danchin, *LanM*, XLI, 298-299;
        by J. G. McManaway, *ShS*, I (1948), 129-130.

B6639   *The Life of King Henry V.* The Arden text ed. by Herbert Arthur Evans. With a general introd.
        by Mr. Evans and a special pref. note by Mark Van Doren. Ill. with paintings by Fritz Kredel
        based upon the film version of the play created by Laurence Olivier. New York: Limited
        Editions Club, 1951. Pp. xxxi, 157. Unlimited ed. of the same, New York: Heritage, 1951.

B6640   *The Life of Henry the Fifth.* Ed. R. J. Dorius. Yale Shakespeare. Rev. ed. New Haven:
        Yale Univ. Press, 1955. Pp. 166.
            Rev: *TLS*, Aug. 10, 1956, p. 480.

B6641   *The Life of King Henry the Fifth.* Ed. Dorothy Margaret Stuart and E. V. Davenport. London:
        Macmillan, 1957. Pp. xxvii, 158.

B6642   *The Life of King Henry the Fifth.* Ed. Louis B. Wright and Virginia Freund. Pelican Shake-
        speare. Baltimore: Penguin Books, 1957. Pp. 142.
            Rev: by Wallace A. Bacon, *QJS*, XLIII (1957), 308-309; by Wilbur Dunkel, *SQ*, IX (1958),
        416.

B6643   *King Henry the Fifth.* Ed. with commentary by G. G. Urwin. London English Literature
        Series. London: Univ. of London Press, 1958. Pp. 174.
            Rev: *TLS*, Sept. 19, 1958, p. 535.

B6644   *King Henry V.* Ed. J. H. Walter. Arden Ed. London: Methuen, 1954. Pp. xlvii, 167.
            Rev: *TLS*, March 19, 1954, p. 190; by L. H., *Dublin Magazine*, XXX, Oct.-Dec., p. 65;
        comment by David Hardman, *John o' London's Weekly*, LXIII, 414; by T. S. Dorsch, *YWES*,
        XXXV, 81; by J. Vallette, *MdF*, 321 (1954), 731-732; by T. M. Parrott, *JEGP*, LIV (1955),
        131-135; by C. G. Thayer, *Books Abroad*, XXIX, 99; by Wolfgang Clemen, *Archiv.*, 192
        (1955), 203-204; by Patrick Cruttwell, *EIC*, V, 382-390; by Hereward T. Price, *SQ*, VI,
        457-461; by Hermann Heuer, *SJ*, 91 (1955), 330-333; by C. Leech, *MLN*, LXX, 209-211;
        by E. A. J. Honigmann, *MLR*, L, 197; by Alice Walker, *RES*, NS, VI, 308-310; by E. J.
        West, *QJS*, XLI, 186-187; by R. Davril, *EA*, XI (1958), 53.

(c)   EMENDATIONS
i. General

B6645   Pollard, A. F. "A Shakespearean Pun?" *TLS*, April 3, 1937, p. 256.
        A possible reference in *Henry V* (Act V, prologue, I, 44) to Brooke's "Abridgement," famous
        legal textbook, first published in 1573/74: "Then Brook abridgement . . ."

B6646   Fijn van Draat, P. "A Solecism." *Neophil*, XXVI (1940/41), 36-41.

B6647   Price, Hereward T. " 'Like Himself'." [*Henry V*, I, Prol. 5.]. *RES*, XVI (1940), 178-181.
        J. M. Robertson's use of the phrase as a test of authorship.

B6648   Stearns, Monroe M. "Shakespeare's *Henry V* [II.iii]." *Expl.*, II (1943), No. 3.

B6649   LeComte, Edward S. "Shakspere, Guilpin, and Essex." *SAB*, XXIII (1948), 17-19.
        Gower's description of braggart camp followers in *Henry the Fifth*, III.vi. 72-88.

B6650   Holmes, Martin. "A Heraldic Allusion in *Henry V*." *N &Q*, 195 (1950), 333.

B6651   Wilkinson, Allen. "A Note on *Henry V*, Act. IV." *RES*, NS, I (1950), 345-346.

B6652   Maxwell, J. C. "*Henry V*, II.ii.103-104." *N &Q*, NS, I (1954), 195.

B6653   Walker, Alice. "Some Editorial Principles (with Special Reference to *Henry V*)." *SB*, VIII
        (1956), 95-111.

B6654   Blayney, Glenn H. "Dramatic Pointing in the Yorkshire Tragedy." *N &Q*, NS, IV (1957),
        191-192.

ii. Theobald's Emendation

B6655   Pearson, Hesketh, and Hugh Kingsmill. *This Blessed Plot.* London: Methuen, 1942. Pp. 214.
        Contains discussion of "A babbled of green fields."
            Rev: *TLS*, June 6, 1942, p. 286; by D. L. Murray, ibid., June 13, p. 295; comment by
        Hesketh Pearson, ibid., June 20, p. 309.

B6656   Bateson, F. W. "Editorial Commentary." *EIC*, V (1955), 91-95.
        Discusses critical implications of Theobald's emendation.

B6657   Hotson, Leslie. "Falstaff's Death and the Greenfield's." *TLS*, April 6, 1956, p. 212.
        Rejects Theobald's emendation.

B6658   Barker, Ernest. "The Death of Falstaff." *TLS*, April 13, 1956, p. 221.

Objects to B6657. See also Mr. Barker's letter of May 4, p. 269, wherein he deplores in Shakespeare study the "technique of the crossword puzzle mixed with the detective novel."

B6659 Young, N. "The Death of Falstaff." *TLS*, April 20, 1956, p. 237.
Answer to B6657.

B6660 Richmond, Oliffe. "The Death of Falstaff." *TLS*, April 27, 1956, p. 253.
On B6657.

B6661 Hulme, Hilda M. "Falstaff's Death: Shakespeare or Theobald." *N &Q*, NS, III (1956), 283-287.

B6662 Hulme, Hilda M. "The Table of Green Fields." *EIC*, VI (1956), 117-119.

B6663 Schanzer, Ernest. "The Table of Green Fields." *EIC*, VI (1956), 119-121.
Taking issue with Bateson B6656.

B6664 Tuckey, John S. "Table of Greene Fields' Explaines." *EIC*, VI (1956), 486-491.

B6665 Hulme, Hilda M., Peter Ure, and F. W. Bateson. "The Critical Forum: A Table of Green Fields." *EIC*, VII (1957), 222-226.

B6666 Eagle, Roderick L. "The Death of Falstaff." *N &Q*, NS, IV (1957), 240.

B6667 Schoeck, R. J. "The Death of Falstaff: Greenfields Once More." *Drama Critique*, I (1958), 27ff.

B6668 Gittings, Robert. "Falstaff and Sir Richard Grenville." *TLS*, May 9, 1958, p. 255.
Supports Leslie Hotson's argument for restoring the F reading "a Table of greene fields" (*TLS*, April 6, 1956; B6657). The discussion is continued in these letters in *TLS* by Mr. Hotson, E. M. W. Tillyard, and J. C. Maxwell, May 16, p. 269; by N. Young and Roy Walker, May 23, p. 283; by Mr. Hotson and Chalmers H. Davidson, May 30, p. 297; by Mr. Gittings, A. L. Rowse, and Hugh Ross Williamson, June 9, p. 313; by Mr. Maxwell, June 13, p. 329; by E. G. Coulson, June 20, p. 345; by Mr. Williamson, June 27, p. 361.

B6669 Fogel, Ephim G. "'A Table of Green Fields': A Defense of the Folio Reading." *SQ*, IX (1958), 485-492.

(2) LITERARY GENESIS AND ANALOGUES

B6670 Starnes, D. T. "More About the Prince Hal Legend." *PQ*, XV (1936), 358-366.

B6671 Grether, Emil. *Das Verhältnis von Shakespeares "Heinrich V" zu Sir Thomas Elyots "Governour."* DD, Marburg, 1938. Marburg: Bauer, 1938. Pp. 46.
Rev: by E. Mühlbach, *LZ*, 90 (1939), 963.

B6672 Watson, Sarah Ruth. "Shakespeare's Use of the *Arcadia*. An Example in *Henry V*." *N &Q*, 175 (1938), 364-365.
Rev: by J. E. Morris, *N &Q*, 175 (1938), 409.

B6673 Craig, Hardin. "Shakespeare's Development as a Dramatist in the Light of His Experience." *SP*, XXXIX (1942), 226-238.

B6674 Law, Robert Adger. "An Echo of Homer in *Henry the Fifth*?" *TxSE*, XXII (1942), 105-109.

B6675 Stewart, J. I. M. "King Cambyses's Vein [*1 Henry IV*, II. iv. 423-425]." *TLS*, May 26, 1945, p. 247.

B6676 Wilson, John Dover. "The Origins and Development of Shakespeare's *Henry IV*." *Library*, 4th Series, XXVI (1945), 2-16.

B6677 Walter, J. H. "'With Sir John In It'." *MLR*, XLI (1946), 237-245.

B6678 Brereton, J. Le Gay. "Shakespeare's Wild Irishman." *Writings on Elizabethan Drama*, Melbourne Univ. Press, 1948, pp. 91-92.

B6679 Jorgensen, Paul A. "The Courtship Scene in *Henry V*." *MLQ*, XI (1950), 180-188.

B6680 Wagner, Anthony R. "Shakespeare and the Agincourt Ennoblement." *N &Q*, 195 (1950), 105.
Points out that the full story, apparently utilized by Shakespeare, is found in Jean Juvénal de Ursins *Histoire de Charles VI* (an ed. in 1572).

B6681 Ashe, Dora Jean. *A Survey of Non Shakespearean Bad Quartos.* DD, University of Virginia, 1953. Pp. 286. Mic 54-1567. *DA*, XIV (1954), 1070. Publ. No. 7952.

B6682 Braddy, Haldeen. "The Flying Horse in *Henry V*." *SQ*, V (1954), 205-207.

B6683 Baldwin, T. W. "Perseus Purloins Pegasus." *Renaissance Studies in Honor of Hardin Craig*, Stanford Univ. Press, 1941, pp. 169-178; also *PQ*, XX (1941), 361-370.

B6684 Steadman, John M. "'Perseus upon Pegasus' and *Ovid Moralized*." *RES*, IX (1958), 407-410.
Continues from B6683.

B6685 Moore, John Robert. "Shakespeare's *Henry V* [II.iii.]." *Expl.*, I (1942-43), 61.
See comment by Monroe M. Stearns, ibid., II (1943-44), 19.

B6686 Lloyd, Roger. "Socrates and Falstaff." *Time and Tide*, Feb. 22, 1958, pp. 219-220.

B6687 Koller, Kathrine. "Falstaff and the Art of Dying." *MLN*, LX (1945), 383-386.

B6688 Adler, Alfred. "Falstaff's Holy Dying, Pagan as Well as Christian." *MLN*, LXI (1946), 72.

B6689 Jacob, Ernest Fraser. *Henry V and the Invasion of France.* London: Hodder and Stoughton, 1947. Pp. xiii, 207.
Rev: *TLS*, June 14, 1947, p. 291.

B6690 Somerset, R., Lord Raglan. *The Hero: A Study in Tradition, Myth, and Drama.* London: Watts, 1936. Republ. 1949. Pp. x, 310.
Character of historical *Henry V*, pp. 212-216.

B6691 Heist, William W. " 'Fulness of Bread'." *SQ*, III (1952), 140-142.

B6692 Parrott, T. M. "Fulness of Bread." *SQ*, III (1952), 379-381.

B6693 Harrison, G. B. "Distressful Bread." *SQ*, IV (1953), 105.

B6694 Smith, Warren D. "The *Henry V* Choruses in the First Folio." *JEGP*, LIII (1954), 38-57.

B6695 Law, Robert Adger. "The Choruses in *Henry the Fifth*." *TxSE*, XXXV (1956), 11-21.
See B6694.

B6696 Maughan, A. M. *Harry of Monmouth.* New York: William Sloane Associates, 1956. Pp. 440.
Rev: by Orville Prescott, *New York Times*, March 14, 1956, p. 31, Column 1; by P. Albert Duhamel, *NYTBR*, March 18, 1956, p. 38.

(3) USE OF LANGUAGE

B6697 Pollard, A. F. "A Shakespearean Pun?" *TLS*, April 3, 1937, p. 256.

B6698 Arnheim, Rudolf. "Psychological Notes on the Poetical Process." *Poets at Work.* New York: Harcourt Brace, 1948. Pp. ix, 186.
Discussions of imagery in *Henry V*, pp. 154-155.

(4) GENERAL CRITICISM OF THE PLAY

B6699 Traversi, D. A. *An Approach to Shakespeare.* London: Sands, Paladin Press, 1938. Pp. 152.
Second edition, revised and enlarged, New York: Doubleday, 1956. Pp. 304.
Rev: A8420.

B6700 Traversi, D. A. "*Henry V.*" *Scrutiny*, IX (1941), 352-374. Also in *The Importance of Scrutiny.* Ed. Eric Bentley. New York: Stewart, 1948, pp. 120-140.

B6701 Herzberg, M. J. "*Henry V*": *An Interpretation of the Play.* 1946. Pp. 16.

B6702 Blumert, Edythe. "Antechamber to Agincourt, a Study of Tempo in *Henry V.*" *West Virginia Univ. Bulletin: Philol. Papers*, VI (1949), 22-30.

B6703 Brereton, J. Le Gay. *Writings on Elizabethan Drama.* Collected by R. G. Howarth. Melbourne: Univ. Press, 1949. Pp. 115.
Includes a note on *Henry V*.

B6704 Borden, Arthur R. "*Henry V*": *Facts and Problems.* DD, Harvard University, 1950.

B6705 Berkelman, Robert. "Teaching *Henry V.*" *CE*, XIII (Nov., 1951), 94-99.

B6706 Gilbert, Allan. "Patriotism and Satire in *Henry V.*" Matthews and Emery, eds. *Studies in Shakespeare*, 1953, pp. 40-64.

B6707 Keirce, William F. "*Henry V.*" *Lectures on Four of Shakespeare's History Plays.* Carnegie Series in Engl. No. 1, 1953, pp. 53-69.

B6708 Maxwell, J. C. "Simple or Complex? Some Problems in the Interpretation of Shakespeare." *DUJ*, XLVI (1954), 112-113.

B6709 Merchant, W. M. "The Status and Person of Majesty." *SJ*, 90 (1954), 285-289.

B6710 Yano, Banri. "On Some Scenes in *Henry V.*" (In Japanese). *Studies in English Literature* (Tokyo), XXXII, No. 2 (1956).

B6711 Mendilow, A. A. "Falstaff's Death of a Sweat." *SQ*, IX (1958), 479-483.

B6712 Shaw, John. "The Minor Plot and *Henry V.*" *ShN*, VIII (1958), 2.
Abstract of paper delivered before the Northeast Ohio English Group.

(5) CHARACTERIZATION

B6713 Boughner, Daniel C. "Pistol and the Roaring Boys." *SAB*, XI (1936), 226-237.

B6714 Draper, J. W. "The Humor of Corporal Nym." *SAB*, XIII (1938), 131-138.

B6715 Gwin, Lois Lee. "*Henry V* and the Christian Prince Tradition." DD, University of Washington, 1939. Abstr. publ. in *Univ. of Washington Abstracts of Theses*, IV (1939), 125-126.

B6716 Smith, Herndon. *Some Aspects of the Low Character Groups of "Henry V."* DD, University of Washington, 1939. Abstr. publ. in *Univ. of Washington Abstracts of Theses*, IV (1939), 143-144.

B6717 Dangel, Anneliese. *Fähnrich Pistol und die Anfänge des Begriffes Rant.* DD, Leipzig, 1944. Pp. 118. Typewritten.

B6718 McCloskey, John C. "The Mirror of All Christian Kings." *SAB*, XIX (1944), 36-40.

B6719 Palmer, John. *Political Characters of Shakespeare.* London: Macmillan, 1945. Pp. xii, 335.
Rev: A6550a.

B6720 Lowe-Porter, H. T. "Henry V, Artist." *TLS*, Nov. 16, 1946, p. 563.

B6721 Jorgensen, Paul A. "Accidental Judgements, Casual Slaughters, and Purposes Mistook: Critical Reaction to Shakespeare's *Henry the Fifth*." *SAB*, XXII (1947), 51-61.
Upon criticism of Hazlitt, Palmer, G. B. Shaw, Dowden, John Masefield, Moulton, Bradley, Kittredge.

B6722   Hotson, Leslie. "Ancient Pistol." *YR*, XXXVIII (1948), 51-66. Also in *Shakespeare's Sonnets Dated, and Other Essays*. London: Rupert Hart-Davis; Toronto: Clarke, Irwin & Co., 1949. Pp. 244.
         Rev: C21.

B6723   Kris, E. "Prince Hal's Conflict." *Psychoanalytic Quarterly*, XVII (1948), 487-505. Also in *Psychoanalytic Explorations in Art*. New York: International Univ. Press, 1952. Pp. 358 plus 79 plates.

B6724   Draper, Charles L. [*sic*] "Falstaff's Bardolph." *Neophil*, XXXIII (1949), 222-226.

B6725   Jorgensen, Paul A. " 'My Name is Pistol Call'd'." *SQ*, I (1950), 73-75.

B6726   Empson, William. "Falstaff and Mr. Dover Wilson." *KR*, XV (1953), 213-262.

B6727   Greer, C. A. "Shakespeare and Prince Hal." *N & Q*, 198 (1953), 424-426.

B6728   Spivack, Bernard. "Falstaff and the Psychomachia." *SQ*, VIII (1957), 449-459.

(6)   MISCELLANEOUS ITEMS

B6729   Barrell, C. W. "*Henry V* Can Be Identified as Harry of Cornwall in Henslowe's Diary." *The Shakespeare Fellowship Quarterly*, VII (1946), 49-54.

B6730   White, D. M. "Shakespeare and Psychological Warfare." *The Public Opinion Quarterly*, XII (1948), 68-72.

B6731   Holmes, Martin. "A Heraldic Allusion in *Henry V*." *N & Q*, 195 (1950), 333.

B6732   Rowe, D. F. "Set Books: X. *Henry V*. Notes on the Method." *The Use of English*, Winter, 1957, pp. 106-110.

B6733   Steadman, John M. "Falstaff's 'Facies Hippocratica.' A Note on Shakespeare and Renaissance Medical Theory." *SN*, XXIX (1957), 130-135.

(7)   SUBSEQUENT HISTORY OF THE PLAY
(Other than productions after 1660)

B6734   Manheim, L. M. "The King in Dekker's *The Shoemakers Holiday*." *N & Q*, NS, IV (1957), 432-433.

JULIUS CAESAR (218;77)
(1)   THE TEXT
(a)   THE OLD TEXTS

B6735   Rossiter, A. P. "Line Division in *Julius Caesar*." *TLS*, July 29, 1939, p. 453.
         See letter by R. B. McKerrow, *TLS*, Aug. 19, 1939, p. 492.

B6736   Evans, G. Blakemore. "Shakespeare's *Julius Caesar*, a Seventeenth Century Manuscript." *JEGP*, XLI (1942), 401-417.
         A Restoration Copy in the Folger Lib. derives from 2nd Folio.

(b)   MODERN EDITIONS

B6737   "The Tragedy of Julius Caesar." With an Introd. and notes by H. de Groot. 2nd ed. Selections from English literature, 12. Groningen: P. Noordhoff, 1935. Pp. 132.

B6738   *Julius Caesar*. With Introd. and notes by P. Schultz. Münster: Aschendorf, 1936. Pp. 87.
         Rev: by A. Brandl, *Archiv*, 171 (1937), 120.

B6739   *Shakespeare's "Julius Caesar."* Interlinear edition prepared by George Coffin Taylor and Reed Smith. Boston: Ginn, 1936. Pp. xli, 155.
         Rev: by Samuel A. Tannenbaum, *SAB*, XI (1936), 252; by C. K. T., *QJS*, XXII, 685.

B6740   *Julius Caesar*. Ed. Hufford. New Pocket Classics. New York: Macmillan, 1937. Pp. 208.

B6741   *The Tragedy of Julius Caesar*. Ed. G. Skillan. London: French, 1937. Pp. 97, pl.
         Rev: by Alois Brandl, *Archiv*, 172 (1938), 248-249; by Elise Deckner, *Beiblatt*, XLIX, 114-115.

B6742   *Julius Caesar*. Ed. Max Draber. Leipzig: Quelle and Meyer, 1938. Pp. 69, 16. Republ. 1940.
         Rev: by Erich Thiele, *ZNU*, XXXIX (1940), 136.

B6743   *Julius Caesar. A Tragedy*. Bearb. von J. Kirchhoff. Schöninghs Engl. Lesebogen, 47. Paderborn: Schöningh, 1938. Pp. 48.

B6744   *Julius Caesar*. Ed. R. E. C. Houghton. New Clarendon Shakespeare. London: Oxford Univ. Press, 1938. Pp. 192.

B6745   *Julius Caesar*. Ed. Kurt Schrey. Frankfurt a. M.: Diesterweg, 1938. Pp. 97.
         Rev: by Bruno Engelhardt, *DNS*, XLVI (1938), 250; by Paul Scholz-Wülfing, *ZNU*, XXXVII, 195.

B6746   *The Tragedy of Julius Caesar*. Ed. George Lyman Kittredge. Boston: Ginn & Co., 1939. Pp. xx, 210.
         Rev: by William T. Hastings, *SRL*, Aug. 19, 1939, p. 13; *N & Q*, 176 (1939), 395-396; by C. J. Sisson, *MLN*, LV (1940), 145-147; by Robert Adger Law, *JEGP*, XXXIX, 578-581.

B6747   *Julius Caesar*. Ed. for reading and arranged for staging by Orson Welles and Roger Hill. Mercury Shakespeare. New York: Harper, 1939. Pp. 91.

B6748   *Julius Caesar.* Ed. by P. A. Gasper. London, 1940. Pp. 90.

B6749   *Julius Caesar.* Vollständige Ausg. mit Einl. u. Anm. Hrsg. von Emil Stein. Paderborn: Schöningh, 1941. Pp. 109.

B6750   *Julius Caesar.* Avec une Notice Biographique, une Notice Historique et Littéraire, des Notes Explicatives par H. Brigère. Classiques français et étrangers, 27. Paris: Ed. Diderot, 1947. Pp. 111.

B6751   *The Tragedy of Julius Caesar.* Berlin, Bielefeld: Cornelsen, 1949. Pp. 90.

B6752   *"Julius Caesar." A Tragedy.* Wörterverz. v. Ernst Barts. Berlin, Leipzig: Volk und Wissen, Teubner, 1949. Pp. 79, 48.

B6753   *Julius Caesar.* Ed. H. T. Price. Crofts Classics. New York: Appleton-Century-Crofts, 1950. Pp. xv, 79.

B6754   *Scenes from "Julius Caesar" and "Hamlet."* Ed. by Josef Raith. Munich: Hueber, 1949. Pp. 39.
      Rev: by H. Mannhart, *Leb. Fremdspr.*, I (1949), 352.

B6755   *Julius Caesar.* Ed. J. Dover Wilson. The New Shakespeare. Cambridge Univ. Press, 1949. Pp. xlvii, 219.
      Rev: *English*, VII (1949), 299-300; by Charlton Hinman, *MLN*, LXVI (1951), 71; by Frank Kermode, *RES*, NS, II, 166-168; by A. Koszul, *LanM*, XLV, 406-407; by J. G. McManaway, *ShS*, IV, 156-157; by L. Eckhoff, *ES*, XXXIII (1952), 77-78.

B6756   *Julius Caesar.* Anh. u. Wörterb. Bielefeld: Velhagen and Klasing, 1950. Pp. xiv, 97, 36, 369.

B6757   *Julius Caesar.* Ed. M. K. Shanmugan. Nillipuram: Little Flower & Co., 1950. Reissued in Madras, 1957.

B6758   *Julius Caesar.* Ed. D. R. Gupta. Chandausei: G. B. Bhargava & Sons, n.d. Pp. iv, 387.

B6759   *"Julius Caesar" and "Elizabeth the Queen."* Maxwell Anderson's. Ed. Helen E. Harding. Noble's Comparative Classics. New York: Noble, 1954. Pp. 338.

B6760   *Julius Caesar.* Ed. Tyrone Guthrie and G. B. Harrison. New Stratford Shakespeare. London: Harrap, 1954. Pp. 152.
      Rev: by Hermann Heuer, *SJ*, 91 (1955), 343-344.

B6761   *Julius Caesar.* Ingeleid, Geschiedkundig, Letterkundig en Taalkundig Toegelicht door R. M. S. van den Raevenbusch. Brugge: Desclée, De Brouwer, 1954. Pp. 115.

B6762   *Julius Caesar.* Ed. T. S. Dorsch. Arden Shakespeare. London: Methuen, 1955. Pp. lxxiv, 166.
      Rev: *TLS*, Dec. 2, 1955, p. 731; *Dublin Magazine*, XXXI (1956), 46; by Irving Ribner, *JEGP*, LV, 505-507; by Hermann Heuer, *SJ*, 92 (1956), 397-399; by Pat M. Ryan, Jr., *QJS*, XLII, 423-424; by J. G. Riewald, *LT*, p. 397; by J. Vallette, *MdF*, 326 (1956), 391; by S. F. Johnson, *SQ*, VIII (1957), 391-395; by J. G. McManaway, *ShS*, X, 152; by Alice Walker, *RES*, NS, IX (1958), 71-72; by R. Davril, *EA*, XI, 50; by G. A. Bonnard, *Erasmus*, XI, 43-46.

B6763   *The Merchant of Venice* and *Julius Caesar.* Being the text from the Oxford Shakespeare of the plays to be performed at the Stratford Shakespearean festival of 1955. With synopses of the plays and a note on *Oedipus Rex.* 2 vol. in 1. Toronto: Oxford Univ. Press, 1955.

B6764   *The Tragedy of Julius Caesar.* F. d. Schule bearb. v. Reinhold Arndt und Mitarb. v. Peter Browning. Notes. Dortmund: Lensing, 1958. Pp. 60, 12.

B6765   *Julius Caesar.* Ed. Francis Fergusson and Charles Jasper Sisson. Laurel Shakespeare. With a Modern Commentary by Philip Lawrence. New York: Dell Publishing Co., 1958. Pp. 188.

B6766   *Julius Caesar.* Ed. Louis B. Wright and Virginia A. LaMar. The Folger Library General Reader's Shakespeare. New York: Pocket Books, 1958. Pp. 136.

(c) EMENDATIONS

B6767   Tannenbaum, Samuel A. "Adding A Word to Shakspere's Vocabulary." *SAB*, XI (1936), 120-121.
      Would read *unstrengthed of malice* for *in strength of malice* of *Julius Caesar*, III. i. 196-199.

B6768   Deckner, Elise. "*Julius Caesar* II. i. 85." *Beiblatt*, LII (1941), 89-90.

B6769   Cole, Percival R. " 'The Most Unkindest'." *N&Q*, 183 (1942), 282.
      Argues against interpreting the phrase as a double superlative.

B6770   Wilson, J. Dover. "Ben Jonson and *Julius Caesar*." *ShS*, II (1949), 36-43.

B6771   Baldini, Gabriele. "Il Pudore di Bruto." *NA* (Rome), 86th year, Fasc. 1811 (Nov., 1951), 254-261.

B6772   Guidi, Augusto. " 'Creature' in Shakespeare." *N&Q*, 197 (1952), 443-444.
      Comment by W. H. Howse, p. 502. *Caesar* IV.i.34.

B6773   Nathan, Norman. "*Julius Caesar* and *The Shoemakers Holiday*." *MLR*, XLVIII (1953), 178-179.

B6774   Goldstein, Malcolm. "Pope, Sheffield, and Shakespeare's *Julius Caesar*." *MLN*, LXXI (1956), 8-10.

(2) LITERARY GENESIS AND ANALOGUES

B6775   *Shakespeare's Appian.* Ed. by Ernest Schanzer. A Selection from the Tudor Translation of Appian's *Civil Wars* (English Reprints Series). Liverpool Univ. Press, 1956. Pp. xxviii, 101.
      Rev: A4231.

B6776 Buchan, J. *Augustus.* Boston: Houghton Mifflin, 1937. Pp. 380.
       Rev: by M. Radin, *Books,* Nov. 21, 1937, p. 4x.
B6777 Williams, C. *Julius Caesar. Stories of Great Names.* London, 1937, pp. 29-65.
B6778 Morsbach, Lorenz. *Shakespeares Cäsarbild.* Halle, 1935.
       Rev: B6845.
B6779 Bush, Douglas. "*Julius Caesar* and Elyot's *Governour.*" *MLN,* LII (1937), 407-408.
B6780 Kranz, W. "Shakespeare und die Antike." *Eng. Studn.,* LXXIII (Nov., 1938), 33-35.
B6781 Staedler, E. "Die Klassischen Quellen der Antoniusrede in Shakespeares *Julius Caesar.*"
       N.Mon., x (1939), 235-245.
B6782 Smith, Marion B. *Marlowe's Imagery and the Marlowe Canon.* Univ. of Pennsylvania Press,
       1940. Pp. vii, 213.
       Chapter upon *Caesar.*
       Rev: B5321.
B6783 Jones, Robert E. "Brutus in Cicero and Shakespeare." *Classical Journal,* XXXVIII (1943),
       449-457.
B6784 Carrère, Félix Jean. *Le Théâtre de Thomas Kyd. Contribution à l'Etude du Drame Elizabéthain.*
       Thèse de Lettres, Paris, 1949. Toulouse: Edouard Privat, Editeur, 1951.
       Rev: A4979.
B6785 Nearing, Homer, Jr. "The Legend of Julius Caesar's British Conquest." *PMLA,* LXIV
       (1949), 889-929. Comments on Shak., pp. 927-928.
B6786 Wickert, Maria. "Antikes Gedankengut in Shakespeares *Julius Cäsar.*" *SJ,* 82/83 (1949),
       11-33.
B6787 Brewer, D. S. "Brutus' Crime: A Footnote to *Julius Caesar.*" *RES,* NS, III (1952), 51-54.
B6788 Schanzer, Ernest. "A Neglected Source of *Julius Caesar.*" *N &Q,* NS, I (1954), 196-197.
B6789 Rees, Joan. "*Julius Caesar*—An Earlier Play, and an Interpretation." *MLR,* L (1955), 135-141.
B6790 Barroll, John L., III. *Shakespeare and Roman History.* DD, Princeton University, 1956. Pp.
       675. Mic 57-996. *DA,* XVII (1957), 626. Publ. No. 20, 101.
       Ancient, Medieval and Renaissance views of the principals concerned.
       Caesar and *Antony* are only two plays discussed. Comparisons are made with other Cleopatra
       plays.
B6791 Maxwell, J. C. "*Julius Caesar* and Elyot's *Governour.*" *N &Q,* NS, III (1956), 147.
B6792 Honda, Akira. "Antonius to Antony." ["Antonius and Anthony"]. *Hosei Daigaku Bunga-
       kubu Kiyo.* Hosei Univ. Studies in English and American Literature, No. 3, 1958, pp. 1-15.
B6793 Ryan, Pat M., Jr. "Appian's *Civil Wars* Yet Again as Source for Antony's Oration." *QJS,*
       XLIV (1958), 72-73.

(3) USE OF LANGUAGE

B6794 Ewer, Bernard C. *Social Psychology.* New York: Macmillan Co., 1929.
       Julius Caesar, pp. 255-256, analyzes Antony's speech.
B6795 Lundholm, H. "Antony's Speech and the Psychology of Persuasion." *Character and Person-
       ality,* VI (1939), 293-305.
B6796 Rudolph, O. *Die Umschreibung der Einfachen Verben mit "to do" in Shakespeares "Julius Caesar."*
       DD, Marburg, 1939. Marburg/Lahn: Bauer, 1939. Pp. 86.
B6797 Siegloch, Arno. *Die Phonetischen Mittel der Deklamation bei W. J. Holloway in der Wiedergrabe
       der Leichenrede des Mark Anton (Shakespeare, "Julius Caesar"* III, ii). DD, Berlin, Humboldt
       Univ., 1939. Berlin: Bruyter, 1939. Pp. 26.
B6798 Azzalino, W. "Stilkundliche Betrachtung der Reden des Brutus und des Antonius in Shake-
       speares *Julius Caesar* (III.2)." *N. Mon.,* XI (1940), 249-271.
B6799 Zandvoort, R. W. "Brutus's Forum Speech in *Julius Caesar.*" *RES,* XVI (1940), 62-66.
B6800 Frye, Roland. "Rhetoric and Poetry in *Julius Caesar.*" *QJS,* XXXVII (1951), 41-48.
B6801 Bennett, Paul E. "The Statistical Measurement of a Stylistic Trait in *Julius Caesar* and *As You
       Like It.*" *SQ,* VIII (1957), 33-50.
B6802 Blau, Herbert. "Language and Structure in Poetic Drama." *MLQ,* XVIII (1957), 27-34.

(4) GENERAL CRITICISM OF THE PLAY

B6803 Larrick, N. "Mob Scenes in *Julius Caesar.*" *Virginia Teacher,* XVII (1936), 33-34.
B6804 Pongs, H. "Shakespeare und das Politische Drama." *DuV,* XXXVII, No. 3 (1936), 257-280.
B6805 Spiegler, C. G. "*Julius Caesar*: A Liberal Education." *High Points* (New York), XVIII (1936),
       25-34.
B6806 Spaeth, J. W., Jr. "Caesar's Friends and Enemies Among the Poets." *Classical Jour.,* XXXII
       (1937), 541-556.
B6807 Deutschbein, Max. "Die Tragik in Shakespeares *Julius Caesar.*" *Anglia,* LXII (1938), 306-320.
B6808 Draper, J. W. "Flattery, A Shakespearian Tragic Theme." *PQ,* XVII (1938), 240-250.
B6809 Van Doren, Mark. "Literature and Propaganda." *VQR,* XIV (1938), 203-208.

B6810   Knight, G. Wilson. *The Imperial Theme.* Further Interpretation of Shakespeare's Tragedies
        Including the Roman Plays. Oxford Univ. Press, 1939. Pp. 376.
        Rev: A8258.

B6811   Coles, Blanche. *Shakespeare Studies: "Julius Caesar."* New York: Smith, 1940. Pp. xii, 281.
        Rev: by H. N. Hillebrand, *MLN*, LVI (1941), 620-623.

B6812   Musgrove, S. *"Julius Caesar."* *A Lecture.* Sydney: Australian English Association, 1941.
        Pp. 26.

B6813   Heiseler, Bernt von. *Caesar. Tragödie.* Munich: Michael Beckstein, 1942. Pp. 122.
        Rev: by Hans J. Schlamp, *Europäische Literatur*, III (1944), Heft 3, p. 20.

B6814   Stewart, J. I. M. *"Julius Caesar* and *Macbeth.* Two Notes on Shakespearean Technique."
        MLR, XL (1945), 166-173.

B6815   Draper, John W. "The Speech-tempo of Brutus and Cassius." *Neophil*, XXX (1946), 184-186.

B6816   Ellis, Oliver C. de C. *Cleopatra in the Tide of Time.* London: Williams & Norgate, 1947.
        Pp. xv, 287. *Caesar*, pp. 135-146.
        Rev: B9407.

B6817   Granville-Barker, Harley. *Prefaces to Shakespeare.* 2 Vols. Princeton Univ. Press, 1946 1947.
        Rev: A8201.

B6818   Stegmeyer, Franz. *Europäische Profile. Essays.* Wiesbaden: Limes-Verlag, 1947. Pp. 186
        Caesar, pp. 32-43.

B6819   Kirschbaum, Leo. "Shakespeare's Stage Blood and Its Critical Significance." *PMLA*, LXIV
        (1949), 517-529.
        "Spectacular blood effects" in *Julius Caesar* "important for the full aesthetic richness of the
        play."

B6820   Connolly, Thomas F. "Shakespeare and the Double Man." *SQ*, I (1950), 30-35.

B6821   Felheim, Marvin. "The Problem of Time in *Julius Caesar.*" *HLQ*, XIII (1950), 399-405.

B6822   Barton, John. "Elizabethan Caesar." *ConR*, LXXIII (1951/52), 368.

B6823   Forster, E. M. *Two Cheers for Democracy.* London: Arnold, 1951. Pp. 371.
        Caesar, pp. 162-166. In the Harcourt Brace, New York edition (n.d.) the *Caesar* essay is
        pp. 154-158.
        Rev: A9087.

B6824   Raven, Simon. "Pomp and Circumstance." *ConR*, LXXIII (1951/52), 392-394.

B6825   Harris, William Oliver. *Honour and Ambition in Shakespeare, with Special Reference to Julius
        Caesar.* MA thesis, University of North Carolina, 1952. Abstr. publ. in *Univ. of North
        Carolina Record, Research in Progress*, Jan.-Dec., 1952, Grad. School Series No. 64, 1953, pp.
        114-115.

B6826   Dreizen, Lester. *Shakespeare: Mark-Antony and Mass Persuasion, A Study of Attitudes and Their
        Transformation.* Mesnil: Firmin-Ditot, 1953. Pp. viii, 64.

B6827   Knights, L. C. "Shakespeare and Political Wisdom: A Note on the Personalism of *Julius
        Caesar* and *Coriolanus.*" *SR*, LXI (1953), 43-55.

B6828   Breyer, Bernard R. "A New Look at *Julius Caesar.*" *Essays in Honor of Walter Clyde Curry.*
        Vanderbilt Univ. Press, 1954, pp. 161-180. Abstr. *ShN*, VI (1956), 5.

B6829   Foakes, R. A. "An Approach to *Julius Caesar.*" *SQ*, V (1954), 259-270.

B6830   Maxwell, J. C. "Simple or Complex? Some Problems in the Interpretation of Shakespeare."
        DUJ, June 1954, pp. 112-115.

B6831   Nathan, Norman. "Flavius Teases His Audience." *N&Q*, 199 (1954), 149-150.

B6832   Parsons, Howard. "Shakespeare's *Julius Caesar*: Dramatis Personae." *N&Q*, 199 (1954), 113.

B6833   Aldus, Paul J. "Analogical Probability in Shakespeare's Plays." *SQ*, VI (1955), 397-414.
        Comment by L. J. Mills and P. J. Aldus, VII (1956), 133-134.

B6834   Costa, Bruno. *La Tragedia di Giulio Cesare di William Shakespeare.* Rome: Ministero della
        Pubblica Istruzione. Quaderni didattici. Cineteca Scolastica Italiana, 1955. Pp. 28.

B6835   Marquard, N. J. "The Theme of Responsibility in *Julius Caesar.*" *Standpunte* (Amsterdam),
        IX (1955), 4-17.

B6836   Rubow, Paul V. *Shakespeares Ungdomsstykker.* The Royal Danish Scientifical Society: Histori-
        cal-Philosophical Informations, XXXIV, No. 5. Copenhagen: Munksgaard, 1955. Pp. 34.
        Shakespeare's early plays.

B6837   Schwamborn, Heinrich. "Brutus und Cassius, einige Betrachtungen zu *Julius Caesar.*" *NS*,
        NS, IV (1955), 24-32.

B6838   Knights, Lionel Charles. "Beyond Politics: An Aspect of Shakespeare's Relation to Tradition."
        Abstr. in *ShN*, VI (1956), p. 14.

B6839   Carson, R. A. G. "The Ides of March." *History Today*, VII (1957), 141-146.

B6840   Ribner, Irving. "Political Issues in *Julius Caesar.*" *JEGP*, LVI (1957), 10-22.

B6841   Bonjour, Adrien. *The Structure of "Julius Caesar."* With a Preface by Kenneth Muir. Liver-
        pool: Univ. Press, 1958. Pp. 81.

B6842 Brinkmann, Karl. *Erlauterungen zu Shakespeares "Julius Caesar."* Hollfeld-Obfr.: Bange, 1958. Pp. 80.

B6843 McFarland, T. "Antony and Octavius." *YR*, XLVIII (1958), 204-208.

B6844 Schwartz, Elias. "On the Quarrel Scene in *Julius Caesar*." *CE*, XIX (1958), 168-170.

(5) CHARACTERIZATION

B6845 Morsbach, Lorenz. *Shakespeares Cäsarbild.* Halle: Niemeyer, 1935.
Rev: by Swaen, *Museum*, XLIII (1935/36), Heft 10; by A. Gabele, *DL*, XXXIX (1936), 121; by Samuel A. Tannenbaum, *SAB*, XI, 58; by J. B. Leishman, *MLR*, XXXI, 467; by Tucker Brooke, *JEGP*, XXXV, 289-290; by Wolfgang Keller, *SJ*, LXXII, 144-145; by W. Wehe, *Bausteine z. dts. Nat. Theat.*, IV, p. 282; by Robert Adger Law, *MLN*, LII (1937), 526-530; by W. Fischer, *Beiblatt*, LI (1939), 12-13; by H. Mutschmann, *Lbl*, LXI (1940), 153-154.

B6846 Bramfitt, G. N. "The Tragedy of Cassius." *School*, XXIV (1936), 504-506.

B6847 Klein, David. "Has Cassius Been Misinterpreted?" *SAB*, XIV (1939), 27-36.

B6848 Messiaen, Pierre. "Qui Est le Héros de Jules César?" *Culture*, II (1939), 625-630.

B6849 Spiegelberger, W. "Shakespeares Caesarbild." *N. Mon.*, X (1940), 177-189.

B6850 Draper, John W. "Cassius and Brutus." *Bul. Hist. Medicine*, XIII (1943), 133-143.

B6851 Jones, Robert E. "Brutus in Cicero and Shakespeare." *Classical Journal*, XXXVIII (1943), 449-457.

B6852 Hunt, F. C. "Shakespeare's Delineation of the Passion of Anger." *Ba*, XXIX (1945), 135-141.

B6853 Palmer, John. *Political Characters of Shakespeare.* New York: Macmillan, 1945. Pp. xii, 335.
Rev: A6550a.

B6854 Hamilton, Roberta MacKenzie. *History of the Interpretation of Brutus, 1601-1948.* MA thesis, University of North Carolina, 1949. Abstr. publ. in *Univ. of North Carolina Record, Research in Progress*, Jan.-Dec., 1949, Grad. School Series No. 58. Pp. 119.

B6855 Stirling, Brents. " 'Or Else Were This a Savage Spectacle'." *PMLA*, LXVI (1951), 765-774. Reprinted in B5018 and in B4452.

B6855a Uhler, John Earle. "*Julius Caesar*—A Morality of Respublica." *Studies in Shakespeare.* Matthews and Emery, eds., 1953, pp. 96-106.

B6856 Brewer, D. S. "Brutus' Crime: A Footnote to *Julius Caesar*." *RES*, III (1952), 51-54.

B6857 Smith, Warren D. "The Duplicate Revelation of Portia's Death." *SQ*, IV (1953), 153-161.

B6858 Haywood, Richard M. "Shakespeare and the Old Roman." *CE*, XVI (1954-55), 98-101, 151.

B6859 Berkeley, David S. "On Oversimplifying Antony." *CE*, XVII (1955/56), 96-99.
Comment by Frank S. Hook, *CE*, XVII, 365-366. Answer by Berkeley, *CE*, XVIII, 286-287.

B6860 Feldman, Harold. "Unconscious Envy in Brutus." *American Imago*, IX (1952), 307-335.

B6861 Schanzer, Ernest. "The Problem of *Julius Caesar*." *SQ*, VI (1955), 297-308.

B6862 Schanzer, Ernest. "The Tragedy of Shakespeare's Brutus." *ELH*, XXII (1955), 1-15.

B6863 Schwamborn, Heinrich. "Brutus und Cassius. Einige Betrachtungen zu Shakespeares *Julius Caesar*." *NS*, NS, IV (1955), 24-32.

B6864 Blissett, William. "Lucan's Caesar and the Elizabethan Villain." *SP*, LIII (1956), 553-575. For Shak.'s *Caesar*, see pp. 569-570.

B6865 Flatter, Richard. "Julius Caesar—ein Tyrann?" In His *Triumph der Gnade. Shakespeare Essays.* Vienna, Munich: Kurt Desch, 1956, pp. 129-133.

B6866 Barroll, J. Leeds. "Antony and Pleasure." *JEGP*, LVII (1958), 708-720.

B6867 Evans, G. Blakemore. "The Problem of Brutus: An Eighteenth Century Solution." *Studies in Honor of T. W. Baldwin*, ed. by Don Cameron Allen, Univ. of Illinois Press, pp. 229-236.

B6868 Haines, Charles. *Two Men with Four Faces.* Milan: Ed. Cisalpino, 1957. Pp. 87.
"The Second: Brutus," pp. 55-85.

B6869 Ornstein, Robert. "Seneca and the Political Drama of *Julius Caesar* " *JEGP*, LVII (1958), 51-56.

(6) MISCELLANEOUS ITEMS

B6870 Rank, O. "Shakespeares Vaterkomplex." *Das Inzest-Motiv in Dichtung und Sage* Leipzig, 1912, pp. 204-233.

B6871 Burke, Kenneth. "Antony in Behalf of the Play." *Southern Rev.*, I (1935), 308-319. Reprinted in *The Philosophy of Literary Form*, Louisiana State Univ. Press, 1941; New York: Vintage Books, 1957.

B6872 Dodds, M. H. "*Julius Caesar* and the Duke of Guise." *N &Q*, 180 (1941), 276-279.

B6873 Schücking, Levin L. "*Über einige Nachbesserungen bei Shakespeare.* Leipzig: Hirzel, 1943. Pp. 66.

B6874 McDowell, John H. "Analyzing *Julius Caesar* for Modern Production." *QJS*, XXXI (1945), 303-314.

B6875 Charney, Maurice. "An Anachronism in *Julius Caesar*." *N &Q*, 198 (1953), 267.

B6876 Ferguson, J. Wilson. "The Iconography of the Kane Suetonius." *Princeton Univ. Library Chronicle*, XIX (1957), 34-45.

B6877 Morris, William Edgar. *The Seventeenth-Century English Funeral Sermon as a Literary Form.* DD, University of North Carolina, 1958.

(7) SUBSEQUENT HISTORY OF THE PLAY

(Other than productions after 1660)

B6878 Schanzer, Ernest. "Thomas Platter's Observations on the Elizabethan Stage." *N &Q*, NS, III (1956), 465-467.

B6879 Troubridge, Sir St. Vincent. "Oral Tradition in the Theatre." *Theatre Notebook*, V (July-Sept., 1951), 87-88.

AS YOU LIKE IT (222;79)

(1) TEXT

(a) MODERN EDITIONS

B6880 *As You Like It.* Ed. C. Boas. Scholar's Libr. London: Macmillan, 1936. Pp. 147.

B6881 *As You Like It.* Ed. Henry Norman Hudson and Others. Cameo Classics. New York: Grosset, 1936. Pp. 193.

B6882 *As You Like It.* Ed. Gaston. New Pocket Classics. New York: Macmillan, 1937. Pp. 243.

B6883 *As You Like It.* Ed. George Lyman Kittredge. Boston: Ginn and Company, 1939. Pp. xix, 205.
Rev: by William T. Hastings, *SRL*, Aug. 19, 1939, p. 13; by Robert Adger Law, *JEGP*, XXXIX (1940), 578-581.

B6884 *As You Like It.* New Clarendon Shakespeare. London, New York: Oxford Univ. Press, 1941. Pp. 190.

B6885 *As You Like It.* Ed. Sri P. A. Subrahmanya Ayyar. Jaffna, Ceylon: Kalaivani, 1948.

B6886 *As You Like It.* Ed. and Ill. George Skillan. New York: French, 1951. Pp. xii, 78.

B6887 *As You Like It.* Intro. by Peter Brook and Designs by Salvador Dali. London, 1953.
Rev: *TLS*, May 15, 1953, p. 322; by A. Koszul, *EA*, VII (1954), 324-325; by H. T. Price, *SQ*, V, 114-115.

B6888 *As You Like It.* Ed. H. J. Olendorf and H. Arguile. Cape Town: Maskew Miller, 1953. Pp. 155.

B6889 *As You Like It.* Ed. S. C. Burchell. Yale Shakespeare. New Haven: Yale Univ. Press, 1954. Pp. viii, 121.
Rev: by Helen Andrews Kaufman, *SQ*, VI (1955), 349-350; by Hermann Heuer, *SJ*, 91 (1955), 342-343; by C. J. Sisson, *MLR*, L, 196-197; *CE*, XVI, 258.

B6890 *As You Like It.* Ed. Alfred Harbage. Crofts Classics. New York: Appleton-Century-Crofts, 1954. Pp. xii, 83.

B6891 *As You Like It.* Ed. S. C. Sen Gupta. Calcutta: A. Mukherjee and Co., Ltd., 1952.

B6892 *As You Like It.* Ed. Sir Arthur Quiller-Couch and John Dover Wilson. Cambridge Pocket Shakespeare. Cambridge Univ. Press, 1957.
Rev: *N &Q*, NS, V (1958), 136.

(b) EMENDATIONS

B6893 Newdigate, B. H. "A Line in *As You Like It* [II. vii. 73]." *TLS*, Nov. 7, 1942, p. 550.

B6894 Darby, Robert H. "Christopher Marlowe's Second Death." *West Virginia Univ. Bull.: Philological Studies*, IX (1943), 81-85.
III. iii. 10-13.

B6895 Kökeritz, Helge. "Touchstone in Arden. *As You Like It*, II. iv. 16." *MLQ*, VII (1946), 61-63.

B6896 Jones, J. T. " 'What's That "Ducdame"?' (*As You Like It*, II. v. 60)." *MLN*, LXII (1947), 563-564.

B6897 Nearing, Homer, Jr. " 'The Penalty of Adam'." *MLN*, LXII (1947), 336-338.

(2) LITERARY GENESIS AND ANALOGUES

(a) GENERAL

B6898 Thaler, Alwin. "Shakespeare and *Everyman*." *TLS*, July 18, 1936, p. 600.

B6899 Thaler, Alwin. "Shakspere, Daniel, and *Everyman*." *PQ*, XV (1936), 217-218.

B6900 Dowlin, Cornell M. "Two Shakspere Parallels in Studley's Translation of Seneca's *Agamemnon*." *SAB*, XIV (1939), 256. See also "A Correction." *SAB*, XV (1940), 128.

B6901 Thaler, Alwin. *Shakespeare and Democracy.* Univ. Tennessee Press, 1941. Pp. xii, 312. Chap. XIII contains "A Note on *As You Like It*."
Rev: A1809.

B6902 Baird, Ruth Cates. "*As You Like It* and Its Source." *Essays in Honor of Walter Clyde Curry*. Vanderbilt Univ. Press, 1954, pp. 143-159. Abstr. in *ShN*, VI (1956), 5.

B6903 Felver, Charles S. "Robert Armin, Shakespeare's Source for Touchstone." *SQ*, VII (1956), 135-137.

B6904 Hiraoka, Tomokazu. "From *Rosalynde* to *As You Like It*." (In Japanese). *Toyama Daigaku Bungaku Kiyo* (Toyama, Japan), March 1956.

B6905 Onions, C. T. " 'Die and Live'." *RES*, VII (1956), 174-176.

B6906 Frankis, P. J. "The Testament of the Deer in Shakespeare." *N. Mitt.*, LIX (1958), 65-68.

B6907 Lees, F. N. "Shakespeare's *Love's Labor's Won*." *TLS*, March 28, 1958, p. 169.

(b) SEVEN AGES

B6908 Draper, John W. "Jacques' Seven Ages and Bartholomaeus Anglicus." *MLN*, LIV (1939), 273-276.

B6909 Gilbert, Allan H. "Jacques' Seven Ages and Censorinus." *MLN*, LV (1940), 103-105.

B6910 Allen, Don Cameron. "Jacques' Seven Ages and Pedro Mexía." *MLN*, LVI (1941), 601-603.

B6911 Wilcox, John. "Putting Jaques into *As You Like It*." *MLR*, XXXVI (1941), 388-394.

B6912 Bennett, Josephine W. "Jaques' Seven Ages." *SAB*, XVIII (1943), 168-174.

B6913 Chew, Samuel C. " 'This Strange Eventful History'." *AMS*, pp. 157-182.

B6914 Small, Samuel A. "The Iuventus Stage of Life." *Malone Festschrift*, 1949, pp. 235-238.

B6915 Bowers, R. H. "A Medieval Analogue to *As You Like It*, II. vii. 137-166." *SQ*, III (1952), 109-112.

B6916 Seronsy, Cecil C. "The Seven Ages of Man Again." *SQ*, IV (1953), 364-365.

(3) USE OF LANGUAGE

B6917 Draper, John W. "King James and Shakespeare's Literary Style." *Archiv*, 171 (1937), 36-48.

B6918 Lievsay, J. Leon. "Shakspere's 'Golden World' (*As You Like It*, I.i.127)." *SAB*, XIII (1938), 77-81.

B6919 Tannenbaum, Samuel A. "The Names in *As You Like It*." *SAB*, XV (1940), 255-256.

B6920 Marquardt, Hertha. "Der Englische Wortschatz als Spiegel Englischer Kultur." *GRM*, XXX (1942), 273-285. Shak., p. 279.

B6921 Bennett, Paul E. "The Statistical Measurement of a Stylistic Trait in *Julius Caesar* and *As You Like It*." *SQ*, VIII (1957), 33-50.

B6922 *Das Spiel von Celia und Rosalinde im Ardennerwald*. Aus Shakespeares Lustspiel *Wie es euch Gefällt*. Für d. Laienspiel Eingerichtet von Eva Ultsch. Kassel, Basel: Bärenreiter Verlag, 1953. Pp. 60.

B6923 Bernad, M. A. "Paradox of Shakespeare's Golden World." *Philippine Studies*, IV (1956), 441-458.

(4) GENERAL CRITICISM OF THE PLAY

B6924 Charlton, H. B. "Shakespeare's Comedies: The Consummation." *BJRL*, XXI (1937), 323-351.

B6925 Smith, James. "*As You Like It*." *Scrutiny*, IX (1940), 9-32. Also in Eric Bentley's *The Importance of Scrutiny*. New York: Stewart, 1948, pp. 99-120.

B6926 Barber, C. L. "The Use of Comedy in *As You Like It*." *PQ*, XXI (1942), 353-367.

B6927 Draper, John W. "The Tempo of Shakespeare's Speech." *ES*, XXVII (1946), 116-120.

B6928 Staebler, Warren. "Shakespeare's Play of Atonement." *SAB*, XXIV (1949), 91-105.

B6929 Cunningham, J. V. " 'Tragedy' in Shakespeare." *ELH*, XVII (1950), 36-46.

B6930 Hilpert, Heinz. "Etwas über *Wie es Euch Gefällt* (1948)." In his *Gedanken zum Theater*, Göttingen, 1951, pp. 147-149.

B6931 Jenkins, Harold. "*As You Like It*." *ShS*, VIII (1955), 40-51.

B6932 Shaw, John. "Fortune and Nature in *As You Like It*." *SQ*, VI (1955), 45-50.

B6933 Draper, R. P. "Shakespeare's Pastoral Comedy." *EA*, XI (1958), 1-17.

B6934 Schäfer, Dorothea. "Die Bedeutung des Rollenspiels in Shakespeares *Wie es Euch Gefällt*." *SJ*, 94 (1958), 151-174.

(5) CHARACTERIZATION

B6935 Fink, Z. S. "Jaques and the Malcontent Traveller." *PQ*, XIV (1935), 237-252.

B6936 Kobbe, Friedrich Karl. "Der Melancholische Jaques. Randbemerkungen zu Shakespeares *Wie es Euch Gefällt*." *DL*, XLI (1938/39), 105-107.

B6937 Bracy, William. *Jaques: A Study in Shakespearean Criticism*. MA thesis, University of North Carolina, 1939. Abstr. publ. in *Univ. of North Carolina Record, Research in Progress*, Grad. School Series No. 36, 1939, pp. 76-77.

B6938 Stoll, Elmer Edgar. "Jacques, and the Antiquaries." *MLN*, LIV (1939), 79-85.

B6939 Draper, John W. "Shakespeare's Orlando Innamorato." *MLQ*, II (1941), 179-184.

B6940   Plowman, Max. *The Right to Live.* Intro. by J. Middleton Murry. London: Dakers, 1942. "The Melancholy of Jacques," pp. 183-185.

B6941   Palmer, John. *Comic Characters of Shakespeare.* New York: Macmillan, 1946. Pp. 135. Rev: A6544.

B6942   Ritze, F. H. *Shakespeare's Men of Melancholy and His Malcontents.* MA thesis, Columbia University, 1947. Pp. 98.

B6943   Babb, Lawrence. "On the Nature of Elizabethan Psychological Literature." *AMS,* 1946, pp. 509-522.

B6944   Goldsmith, R. H. "Touchstone: Critic in Motley." *PMLA,* LXVIII (1953), 884-895.

B6945   Straumann, Heinrich. "Shakespeare und die Verblendete Mensch." *Neue Zürcher Zeitung* (Zurich), No. 1638, June, 1955.

(6) MISCELLANEOUS ITEMS

B6946   Draper, John W. "*As You Like It* and Belted Will Howard." *RES,* XII (1936), 440-444.

B6947   Brennecke, E., Jr. "Shakespeare's Musical Collaboration with Morley." *PMLA,* LIV (1939), 138-149.

B6948   Fellowes, Edmund H. " 'It Was a Lover and His Lass': Some Fresh Points of Criticism." *MLR,* XLI (1946), 202-206.

B6949   Koš, Erih. "Šekspir: *Kako vam Drago.*" [Shakespeare: *As You Like It.*]. *Književnost* (Belgrade), V, iv (1950), 381-383.

B6950   Brennecke, Ernest. " 'What Shall He Have That Killed the Deer?' A Note on Shakespeare's Lyric and Its Music." *Musical Times,* 93 (1952), 347-351.

B6951   Uhler, John Earle. *Morley's Canzonets for Two Voices.* Louisiana State Univ. Press, 1954. Pp. 17, Sigs. [A2]-D₄ + Sigs. [A2]-D₄.
        Includes facsimile reproductions of both cantus books and tenor book. Mentions Morley's probable authorship of music for "It was a lover and his lass."
        Rev: A6163a.

B6952   Bremer, Klaus. "*Wie Es Euch Gefällt* 1956." *Das neue Forum* (Darmstadt), V (1955/56), 267-272.

B6953   Auden, Wystan Hugh, and Chester Kallman. *An Elizabethan Song Book. Lute Songs, Madrigals and Rounds.* Music ed. by Noah Greenberg. London: Faber, 1957. Pp. xv, 240.

B6954   Stevens, Denis. *The Five Songs in Shakespeare's "As You Like It."* Adapted and Arranged from Sources Contemporary with the Play. London: Hinrichson, 1957.
        Rev: A6181.

(7) SUBSEQUENT HISTORY OF THE PLAY
(Other than productions after 1660)

B6955   Carson, William G. B. "*As You Like It* and the Stars: Nineteenth-Century Prompt Books." *QJS,* XLIII (1957), 117-127.

TWELFTH NIGHT (223;79)
(1) THE TEXT
(a) MODERN EDITIONS

B6956   *Twelfth Night.* Cameo Classics. New York: Grosset, 1937. Pp. 171.

B6957   *Twelfth Night.* New Clarendon Shakespeare. Ed. J. C. Dent. London: Oxford Univ. Press, 1938. Pp. 159.

B6958   *Twelfth Night.* Ed. for Reading and Arranged for Staging by Orson Welles and Roger Hill. Mercury Shakespeare. New York: Harper, 1939. Pp. 96.

B6959   *Twelfth Night.* Ed. George L. Kittredge. Boston: Ginn and Co., 1941. Pp. x, 190.

B6960   *Twelfth Night, or What You Will.* Turin: Gheroni, 1945. Pp. 64.

B6961   *Twelfth Night: or, What You Will.* Ed. Mark Eccles. Crofts Classics. New York: Crofts, 1948. Pp. vi, 87.

B6962   *Twelfth Night, or What You Will.* Lipsius & Tischers Neusprachl. Texte. Engl. Reihe 2. Kiel: Lipsius & Tischer, 1949. Pp. 93. Second edition: 1956. Pp. 90.
        Rev: by A. Geissler, *Leb. Fremdspr.,* II (1950), 93.

B6963   *Twelfth Night, or What You Will.* New Cambridge Shakespeare. Ed. for Syndics of Cambridge Univ. Press by John Dover Wilson. Cambridge Univ. Press, 1950. Pp. xxix, 193.

B6964   *Twelfth Night. The Play. A Critical Anthology.* Ed. Eric Bentley. New York: Prentice-Hall, 1951. Pp. xii, 774.
        Rev: by N. Balakian, *TAr,* XXXV (1951), 6, 8-9.

B6965   *Twelfth Night.* Ed. Tyrone Guthrie and G. B. Harrison. New Stratford Shakespeare. London: Harrap, 1954. Pp. 131.

B6966   *Twelfth Night or What You Will.* Ed. William P. Holden. Yale Shakespeare. New Haven: Yale Univ. Press, 1954. Pp. viii, 144.

Rev: by Helen Andrews Kaufman, *SQ*, VI (1955), 349-350; by Hermann Heuer, *SJ*, 91 (1955), 342-343; by C. J. Sisson, *MLR*, L, 196-197; *CE*, XVI, 258.

B6967   *Twelfth Night*. Text and Notes. Madras (India): Little Flower, 1957.

B6968   *Twelfth Night*, in *Eight Great Comedies*. Ed. Sylvan Barnet, Morton Berman, and William Burto. Mentor Book. New York: The New American Library of World Literature, Inc., 1958, pp. 107-172.

B6969   *Twelfth Night*. Ed. with Commentary by S. C. Boorman. London English Literature Series. Univ. of London Press, 1958. Pp. 160.
        Rev: *TLS*, Sept. 19, 1958, p. 535.

B6970   *Twelfth Night. Othello.* Ed. with Introd. and Notes by Alan Seymour Downer. New York: Rinehart, 1958. Pp. 186.

B6971   *Twelfth Night or What You Will.* With Notes and Introd. by Robin Marleyn. Leverkusen: Gottschalk, 1958. Pp. 100.

B6972   *Twelfth Night*. Ed. Charles Tyler Prouty. Pelican Shakespeare. Baltimore: Penguin Books, 1958. Pp. 121.

B6973   *Twelfth Night*. Ed. Sir Arthur Quiller-Couch and John Dover Wilson. Cambridge Pocket Shakespeare. Cambridge Univ. Press, 1958. Pp. 100.
        Rev: *The Humanist* (London), Dec., 1958, p. 26.

(b) EMENDATIONS

B6974   Chang, Y. Z. "Who and What Were the Cathayans?" *SP*, XXXIII (1936), 203-221.

B6975   Tilley, M. P., and J. K. Y. "Two Notes on Shakspere. I: Malvolio's Yellow Stockings and Cross-Garters; II: To Repent in Sack [*2 Henry IV*, I. ii. 222]." *SAB*, XII (1937), 54-56.

B6976   H., R. E. "Patience on a Monument." *N &Q*, 175 (1938), 441.

B6977   Armstrong, T. Percy. "Patience on a Monument." *N &Q*, 176 (1939), 10-11. See also letter by G. C. L., ibid. p. 11.

B6978   McCue, G. S. " 'Pistle' or 'Pistoll' in *Twelfth Night*." *N &Q*, 183 (1942), 345.

B6979   McCue, G. S. "Shakespeare's Use of 'Pistol'." *American Notes and Queries*, II (1942), 104.

B6980   Boughner, Daniel C. "Sir Toby's Cockatrice." *Italica*, XX (1943), 171-172.

B6981   Boas, Ralph P., and R. P. Boas, Jr. "Shakespeare's *Twelfth Night*, II. iii. 25-27." *Expl.*, III (1945), 29.

B6982   Chapman, Raymond. "The Youngest Wren." *TLS*, June 15, 1946, p. 283.
        Explains a passage in *Twelfth Night*, III. ii. 68, by analogy with a similar expression in Haywood's interlude, *Johan Johan*. See letters by M. R. Ruhl and C. Gwyn, *TLS*, June 29, 1946, p. 307.

B6983   Rattray, R. F. "Aguecake." *TLS*, Oct. 5, 1946, p. 479.
        Comment by W. W. Greg, "Aguecake," *TLS*, Oct. 12, 1946, p. 493; letter by R. F. Rattray, ibid., Oct. 19, p. 507.

B6984   Ruhl, M. R. "A Passage in *Twelfth Night*." *TLS*, June 29, 1946, p. 307.

B6985   Hotson, Leslie. "*Twelfth Night*." *TLS*, July 12, 1947, p. 351.
        See letter by J. Dover Wilson, *TLS*, July 26, 1947, p. 379.

B6986   Hotson, Leslie. "Sir Toby's 'Castiliano Vulgo'." *TLS*, Oct. 11, 1947, p. 521.

B6987   Pearce, T. M. "Shakespeare's *Twelfth Night*." II. v. 5-7." *Expl.*, VII (1948), 7, item 19.

B6988   Draper, John W. "Shakespeare and Abbas the Great." *PQ*, XXX (1951), 419-425.
        Sees in two references to "Sophy" (II. v. 161, III. iv. 266) a reflection of the travels to Persia of Sir Robert and Sir Anthony Sherley.

B6989   Boas, Louise S. "The Clown in *Twelfth Night*." *TLS*, Sept. 12, 1952, p. 597.

B6990   Cohen, Hennig. "Shakespeare's *Twelfth Night*, I. v. 128-130." *Expl.*, XIV (1955), item 12.

B6991   Camden, Carroll. "Three Notes on Shakespeare." *MLN*, LXXII (1957), 251-253.
        Twel., V. i. 224.

B6992   Holland, Norman N. "Cuckold or Counsellor in *Twelfth Night*, I. v. 56." *SQ*, VIII (1957), 127-129.

B6993   Hoepfner, Theodore C. "M.O.A.I.—*Twelfth Night*." *N &Q*, NS, V (1958), 193.
        Proposes that the initials stand for "Malevolus omnino amore sui infelix facitur."

B6994   Purcell, J. M. "*Twelfth Night*, II. iii. 27-28." *N &Q*, NS, V (1958), 375-376.

i. Lady of the Strachey

B6995   Morris, Joseph E. "*Twelfth Night*: The Lady of the Strachy." *N &Q*, 175 (1938), 347-348.
        See letter by H. Kendra Baker, *N &Q*, 175 (1938), 411.

B6996   Baker, H. Kendra. "*Twelfth Night*: 'The Lady of the Strachy'." *N &Q*, 176 (1939), 11-12.
        Letter by Rockingham, *N &Q*, 176 (1939), 249.

B6997   Welply, W. H. "The Lady of the Strachy." *N &Q*, 176 (1939), 48.
        On B6995 and B6996.

B6998   Sanders, Charles Richard. "William Strachey, the Virginia Colony and Shakespeare." *Virginia Magazine of History and Biography*, LVII (1949), 115-132.
Ref. to "Lady of the Strachey," p. 124.

B6999   Ashe, Geoffrey. "William Strachey." *N &Q*, 195 (1950), 508-511. Comment by R. L. Eagle and K. Muir, ibid., 196 (1951), 19-20; by H. H. Huxley, ibid., pp. 85-86.

(2)   LITERARY GENESIS AND ANALOGUES
i.   Italian Sources

B7000   Secchi, Nicolò. *Self-Interest*. Tr. William Reymes; ed. Helen Andrews Kaufman. Seattle: Univ. of Washington Press, 1955. Pp. xxix, 106.
Rev: A3526.

B7001   Gordon, D. J. "*Twelfth Night* and *Gli Ingannati*, a Note." *Bol. degli Studi Inglesi in Italia*, VII (1939), 17-27.

B7002   Snell, Otto. "Hier irren Shakespeare und Bandello." *Der Erbarzt. Beilage z. Dts. Ärzteblatt*, VI (1939), 71-72.
Rev: by F. Dx., *VB*(Mü), June 30, 1939.

B7003   George, J. "*Laelia* and *Twelfth Night*." *N &Q*, 194 (1949), 29-30.

B7004   de Chasca, Edmund V. "Early Editions of *Gl'Ingannati*: The Problem of Overlapping Dates." *MP*, L (1952), 79-87.

B7005   Kaufman, Helen Andrews. "Nicolò Secchi as a Source of *Twelfth Night*." *SQ*, V (1954), 271-280.
Secchi's two plays, *Gl'Inganni* and *L'Interesse*.

ii.   General

B7006   Garvin, K., H. W. Crundell, M. H. Dodds. "A Speculation About *Twelfth Night*." *N &Q*, 170 (1936), 326-328, 373, 442, 408-409.

B7007   Allen, Percy. "Montaigne and *Twelfth Night*." *TLS*, Sept. 18, 1937, p. 675.

B7008   Charlton, H. B. "Shakespeare's Comedies: The Consummation." *BJRL*, XXI (1937), 323-351.

B7009   "Actaeon: Myth and Moralising." *N &Q*, 175 (1938), 74-76.

B7010   Bellessort, A. "La Nuit des Rois." *Le Plaisir du Théâtre*. Paris: Perrin, 1939, pp. 110ff.

B7011   Thaler, Alwin. *Shakespeare and Democracy*. Univ. Tennessee Press, 1941. Pp. xii, 312.
Chap. VI. "The Original Malvolio?"
Rev: A1809.

B7012   Pyle, Fitzroy. "*Twelfth Night, King Lear* and *Arcadia*." *MLR*, XLIII (1948), 449-455.

B7013   Cauthen, I. B., Jr. "The Twelfth Day of December: *Twelfth Night*, II. iii. 91." *SB*, II (1949), 182-185.

B7014   Baldwin, T. W. "Shakspere's Aphthonian Man." *MLN*, LXV (1950), 111-112.

B7015   Chapman, Raymond. "The Fair-Haired Man: An Elizabethan Superstitution." *N &Q*, NS, II (1955), 332. Reply by W. H. W. Sabine, ibid., p. 547.

B7016   Muir, Kenneth. "The Sources of *Twelfth Night*." *N &Q*, NS, II (1955), 94.

B7017   Salingar, L. G. "Messaline in *Twelfth Night*." *TLS*, June 3, 1955, p. 301.

B7018   Filipović, Rudolf. "Shakespeareova Ilirija." ["Shakespeare's Illyria."] *Filologija* (Zagreb), I (1957), 123-138.

B7019   Akrigg, G. P. V. "*Twelfth Night* at the Middle Temple." *SQ*, IX (1958), 422-424.

B7020   Campbell, J. L. "Gaelic Folk Song." *TLS*, June 27, 1958, p. 361.
On the source of "Calen O Costure Me"; see also Kevin P. Neary, "Padraic Colum's Poems." *TLS*, May 23, 1958, p. 283, and J. Maclean's letter of May 9, same subject, i.e. Shak.'s source.

iii.   Hotson

B7021   Hotson, Leslie. *The First Night of "Twelfth Night."* London: Rupert Hart-Davis, 1954. Pp. 256.
Rev: *TLS*, Sept. 24, 1954, p. 607; by Robert Speaight, *Tablet*, 204 (1954), 403-404; by James G. McManaway, *NYTBR*, Dec. 12, p. 4; by G. Lambin, *LanM*, XLVIII, 542-543; by J. I. M. Stewart, *NstN*, XLVIII, 510-512; by R. Bennett, "Was the Play the Thing?" *Books of the Month*, LXIX, 22-23; *Listener*, LII, 1123; by J. Vallette, *MdF*, 322 (1954), 711-712; by H. B. Charlton, *MGW*, Oct. 7, p. 11; by C. V. Wedgwood, *Time and Tide*, Oct. 9, pp. 1344-45; by Ivor Brown, *Obs.*, Oct. 17, p. 9; *CE*, XVI (1955), 258; *VQR*, XXXI, xlii; by Alfred Harbage, *YR*, XLIV, 443-446; by M. St. Clare Byrne, *English*, X, 145-146; by Richard Moody, *QJS*, XLI, 318; by Aerol Arnold, *The Personalist*, XXXVI, 419-421; by George R. Kernodle, *ETJ*, VII, 262-263; by Rudolf Stamm, *SJ*, 91 (1955), 356-361; by M. St. Clare Byrne, *TN*, IX, No. 2, 46-52; by Gunnar Sjögren, *Dagens Nyheter* (Stockholm), Aug. 17; by Thomas Barbour, *Hudson Review*, VIII, 468-472; by J. S. Baxter, *QQ*, LXII, 274-276; by William T. Hastings, *SQ*, VI, 121-123, 128-129; "Clearing the Arena," *ShN*, V, 2; by F. Luft, *Der*

Monat, VIII (1956), Heft 90, pp. 79-82; by Gunnar Sjögren, *Sundsvalls Tidning*, Dec. 3, 1956; by F. David Hoeniger, *Canadian Forum*, XXXVI, 70-71; by R. C. Bald, *SQ*, VII, 246-248.

B7022 Empson, William. "The Elizabethan Stage." *TLS*, Dec. 10, 1954, p. 801.
Letter to the editor concerning Leslie Hotson's *The First Night of "Twelfth Night."* Acknowledged by Hotson, *TLS*, Jan. 7, 1955, p. 9.

B7023 Greg, W. W. "Twelfth Night." *TLS*, Dec. 31, 1954, p. 853.
Letter to the editor disputing a point in Leslie Hotson's *The First Night of "Twelfth Night."*

B7024 Hotson, Leslie. "The First Night of *Twelfth Night*." *TLS*, Jan. 21, 1955, p. 41.
A reply to B7023. Answered by Greg in *TLS*, Jan. 28, 1955, p. 57. Further comment by J. W. Lever on the Hotson-Greg dispute in *TLS*, Feb. 18, p. 105.

B7025 Dean-Smith, Margaret. "The First Night of *Twelfth Night*." *TLS*, Feb. 11, 1955, p. 89.
Agrees with Sir Walter Greg's objections to Hotson's dating of play.

B7026 Merion, Carslyn. "*Twelfth Night*." *TLS*, March 11, 1955, p. 149.
Questions, with reference to Hotson's book, whether we must assume that only one troupe of players performed before Elizabeth and Don Virginio Orsini on Twelfth Night, 1601.

B7027 Hotson, Leslie. "*Twelfth Night*." *TLS*, March 18, 1955, p. 165.
Letter answering Merion's suggestion that Queen Elizabeth sat through two plays on Twelfth Night, 1600-01. Answered by C. Merion, *TLS*, May 6, 1955, p. 237.

B7028 Hiscock, W. G. "Twelfth Day Fare, 1600-01." *TLS*, July 29, 1955, p. 429.
Reports discovery of bill of fare for the Twelfth Day dinner given by Queen Elizabeth to Don Virginio Orsini. No mention of *Twel*.

B7029 Saunders, J. W. "The Elizabethan Stage." *TLS*, Nov. 11, 1955, p. 680.
An objection to Hotson's arena staging.

B7030 Brown, Ivor. "The Orsini Story." In his *Theater* (London), 1954/55, pp. 66-71.

B7031 Bergman, Gösta M. "Världspremiären på Trettondagsafton." [The First Night of *Twelfth Night*.] *Teatern* (Norrköping), XXIII (1956), Heft 3, pp. 3-4.
On Leslie Hotson and the arena stage.

B7032 Race, Sydney. "The First Night of *Twelfth Night*." *N &Q*, II (1955), 52-55; III (1956), 423-424; comment ibid., K. B. Danks, "Dr. Hotson & Mr. Race." II, (1955), 316-317.

B7033 Dodds, Madeleine Hope. "The First Night of *Twelfth Night*." *N &Q*, NS, III (1956), 57-59.
Further remarks by G. R. Batho, ibid., p. 178.

B7034 Keen, Frances. "The First Night of *Twelfth Night*." *TLS*, Dec. 19, 1958, p. 737.
Makes a point on the dating of the Northumberland Manuscript on which Leslie Hotson based his claim. Because John Salusbury is mentioned in it as "Sir" and because Salusbury was not knighted until June, 1601, Hotson's conjectured date of 1600 is too early.

B7034a Sjögren, Gunnar. "Urpremiär på Trettondagsafton." [The First Night of *Twelfth Night*].
Var Othello neger och andra Shakespeareproblem? Stockholm: Natur och Kultur, 1958. Pp. 196.

iv. Love's Labor's Won

B7035 Chapman, Raymond. "*Twelfth Night* and the Swan Theatre." *N &Q*, 196 (1951), 468-470.

B7036 Baldwin, T. W. "Shakspere's *Love's Labor's Won*." New Evidence from the Account Books of an Elizabethan Bookseller. Carbondale: Southern Illinois Univ. Press, 1957. Pp. 52.
Rev: B8323.

(3) USE OF LANGUAGE

B7037 Williams, Charles. "The Use of the Second Person in *Twelfth Night*." *English*, IX (1952/53), 125-128.

B7038 Malone, Kemp. "Meaningful Fictive Names in English Literature." *Names* (*Journal of the American Name Society*), V (1957), 1-13.

B7039 Oyama, Toshiko. "The Language of Feste, The Clown." *Otsuka Festschrift*, 1958, pp. 379-393.

(4) GENERAL CRITICISM OF THE PLAY

B7040 Garvin, Katharine. "A Speculation about *Twelfth Night*." *N &Q*, 170 (1936), 326-328.
See letters by H. W. Crundell, *N &Q*, 170 (1936), 373; by M. H. Dodds, ibid., 170 (1936), 408-409; by Miss Garvin, ibid., 170 (1936), 442.

B7041 Tilley, M. P. "Malvolio's Yellow Stockings and Cross-Garters." *SAB*, XII (1937), 54-55.

B7042 Draper, John W. "Sir Toby's 'Cakes and Ale'." *ES*, XX (1938), 57-61.

B7043 Draper, John W. "Shakespeare's Illyria." *RES*, XVII (1941), 459-460.

B7044 Draper, John W. *The "Twelfth Night" of Shakespeare's Audience*. Stanford Univ. Press, 1949.
Pp. xiii, 271. London: Oxford Univ. Press, 1950. Pp. xiii, 280.
Rev: by R. Halsband, *SRL*, June 3, 1950, pp. 20-21; by H. Levin, *NYTBR*, March 26, pp. 7, 30; by D. Barrett, *N. Mitt.*, LI, 191-195; by Marcia L. Anderson, *South Atlantic Quar.*, XLIX, 552-553; by Roger Sharrock, *MLR*, XLVI (1951), 301; *TLS*, Feb. 9, p. 86; by Bertram Joseph, *RES*, NS, III (1952), 170-171; by S. B. Liljegren, *SN*, XXV (1953), 42-43; by G. A. Bonnard, *ES*, XXXIV, 175-178.

B7045   West, E. J. "Bradleyan Reprise: On the Fool in *Twelfth Night.*" *SAB*, XXIV (1949), 264-274.
B7046   Schröder, Rudolf Alexander. "Was Ihr Wollt." *Shakespeare-Tage*, Bochum, 1952, pp. 2-3.
B7047   Downer, Alan. "Feste's Night." *CE*, XIII (1952), 258-265.
B7048   Möhring, Hans. "Shakespeares Arbeit an Seinen Stücken. Einige Bemerkungen zu *Was Ihr Wollt.*" *Theater d. Zeit*, IX (1953), 26-29.
B7049   Crane, Milton. "*Twelfth Night* and Shakespearian Comedy." *SQ*, VI (1955), 1-8.
B7050   Schmidtbonn, Wilhelm. "*Was Ihr Wollt.*" *Das Festliche Haus*, (Cologne), 1955, pp. 118-122.
B7051   Summers, Joseph H. "The Masks of *Twelfth Night.*" *Univ. of Kansas City Review*, XXII (1955), 25-32.
B7052   Brittin, Norman A. "The *Twelfth Night* of Shakespeare and of Professor Draper." *SQ*, VII (1956), 211-216.
B7053   Hoskins, Frank L. "Misalliance: A Significant Theme in Tudor and Stuart Drama." *Renaissance Papers*, 1956, pp. 72-73.
B7054   Salingar, L. G. "The Design of *Twelfth Night.*" *SQ*, IX (1958), 117-139.

(5) CHARACTERIZATION

B7055   Draper, John W. "The Wooing of Olivia." *Neophil*, XXIII (1937), 37-46.
B7056   Draper, John W. "The Melancholy Duke Orsino." *Bull. Inst. Hist. Medicine*, VI (1938), 1020-29.
B7057   Draper, John W. "Et in Illyria Feste." *SAB*, XVI (1941), 220-228; ibid., XVII, 25-32.
B7058   McCullen, Joseph T., Jr. "Madness and Isolation of Character in Elizabethan and Early Stuart Drama." *SP*, XLVIII (1951), 206-218.
B7059   Barnet, Sylvan. "Charles Lamb and the Tragic Malvolio." *PQ*, XXXIII (1954), 177-188.
B7060   Calendoli, Giovanni. "Le Ambizioni Sbagliate della Dodicesima Notte." *La Fiera Letteraria*, No. 12, March 20, 1955, p. 7.
B7061   Summerskill, William H. J. "Aguecheek's Disease." *Lancet*, 269 (1955), 288ff.
        Comments by Rudolf Werner, "Shakespeare als Medizinischer Autor." *Medizin. Klinik*, L (1955), 1758.

(6) MISCELLANEOUS ITEMS
(a) GENERAL

B7062   Freeman, Bernice. "The Costumes of *Love's Labour's Lost*, *Twelfth Night*, and *The Tempest.*" *SAB*, XI (1936), 93-106.
B7063   Allen, Percy. "Montaigne and *Twelfth Night.*" *TLS*, Sept. 18, 1937, p. 675.
B7064   Wilson, J. D. Über Shakespeares *Twelfth Night*. Bericht über einen Vortrag in der Kaiser Wilhelm-Gesellschaft, Berlin. *DNS*, XLVII (1939), 307-308.
B7065   Walsh, Groesbeck, and Robert M. Pool. *Shakespeare's Knowledge of Twins and Twinning*. Fairfield, Alabama, 1940. (Reprinted from *Southern Medicine and Surgery*.)
B7066   Hotson, Leslie. "Manningham's 'Mid . . . .'." *TLS*, Sept. 9, 1949, p. 585.
B7067   Simonini, R. C., Jr. "The Pedant and Church in *Twelfth Night*, III. ii. 80." *MLN*, LXIV (1949), 513-515.
B7068   Chapman, Raymond. "*Twelfth Night* and the Swan Theatre." *N&Q*, Oct. 27, 1951, pp. 468-470.
B7069   Feldman, Abraham Bronson. "Dutch Theatrical Architecture in Elizabethan London." *N&Q*, 197 (1952), 444-446.
B7070   Southern, A. C. "The Elephant Inn." *TLS*, June 12, 1953, p. 381.
B7071   Race, Sydney. "Manningham's Diary: The Case for Re-examination." *N&Q*, 199 (1954), 380-383.
B7072   Watson, Sara Ruth. "The 'Mousetrap' Play in *Hamlet.*" *N&Q*, NS, II (1955), 477-478. Comments on *Twel.*
B7073   Ramage, David. "Sir Andrew Shakesface." *N&Q*, NS, III (1956), 508.
B7074   Sjögren, Gunnar. "Shakespeare och Trettondagsafton." ["Shakespeare and *Twelfth Night.*"] *Nerikes Allehanda* (Örebro), Nov. 9, 1956.

(b) MUSIC

B7075   Brennecke, E., Jr. "Shakespeare's Musical Collaboration with Morley." *PMLA*, LIV (1939), 138-149.
B7076   Moore, J. R. "Morley and 'O Mistress Mine'." *PMLA*, LIV (1939), 149-152.
B7077   Beck, Sydney. "The Case of 'O Mistress Mine'." *RN*, VI (1953), 19-23.
B7078   Long, John H. "Discussion of S. Beck's 'The Case of *O Mistress Mine*' (*RN*, VI, 19-23)." *RN*, VII (1954), 15-16.
        Refers to B7077.

B7079   Duckles, Vincent. "New Light on 'O Mistress Mine'." *RN*, VII (1955), 98-100.
         Refers to B7078.

B7080   Hollander, John. "Musica Mundana and *Twelfth Night.*" *Sound and Poetry, EIE, 1956.*
         New York: Columbia Univ. Press, 1957, pp. 55-82.

(7) SUBSEQUENT HISTORY OF THE PLAY
(Other than productions after 1660)

HAMLET (224;80)

B7081   Raven, Anton A. *Hamlet Bibliography and Reference Guide, 1877-1935.* Univ. of Chicago
         Press, 1936.
         Rev: A170.

(1) THE TEXT (224;80)
(a) OLD TEXTS
i. Reprints (224;80)

B7082   *Shakespeare's Hamlet. The First Quarto, 1603.* San Marino, California: The Henry E. Hunting-
         ton Library, 1953. Pp. 6, 66.
         Reissue of the facsimile which first appeared in 1931.
         Rev: by I. B. Cauthen, Jr., *SQ*, v (1954), 423.

B7083   *Shakespeare's Hamlet: The Second Quarto, 1604.* Reprod. in facsimile from the copy in the
         Huntington Lib. With an Intro. by Oscar James Campbell. San Marino, California: Hunting-
         ton Lib., 1938. Pp. 16. London: Milford, 1939.
         Rev: by E. E. Willoughby, *Lib. Quar.*, VIII (1938), 434; by Samuel A. Tannenbaum, *SAB*,
         XIII, 125-126; by H. de Groot, *ES*, XX, 237; by Clara (Longworth), Comtesse de Chambrun,
         EA, II, 456-457; *TLS*, May 14, p. 343; by R. B. McKerrow, *RES*, XV (1939), 96-97; by
         Baldwin Maxwell, *PQ*, XVIII, 91; by W. Fischer, *Beiblatt*, L, 98-99; *N &Q*, 176 (1939), 53-54;
         by Wolfgang Keller, *SJ*, LXXV, 148-149; by Peter Alexander, *MLR*, XXXV (1940), 234.

B7084   *The Tragedy of Hamlet: A Critical Edition of the Second Quarto, 1604, with Introduction and
         Textual Notes.* Ed. Thomas Marc Parrott and Hardin Craig. Princeton Univ. Press, 1938.
         Pp. viii, 247. London: Milford, 1937. Pp. x, 247.
         Rev: by Samuel A. Tannenbaum, *SAB*, XIII (1938), 189-190; *TLS*, Oct. 1, p. 631; *N &Q*,
         175 (1938), 484-485; by Baldwin Maxwell, *PQ*, XVIII, 88-91; by Wolfgang Keller, *SJ*, LXXV
         (1939), 146-148; by W. W. Greg, *RES*, XV, 208-213; by T. Pyles, *MLN*, LIV, 205-207; by
         L. L. Schücking, *Beiblatt*, LI (1940), 78-83; by Peter Alexander, *MLR*, XXXV, 232-234; by
         H. de Groot, *ES*, XXIII (1941), 112-115.

B7085   *Hamlet, First Quarto, 1603. Shakespeare Quarto Facsimile, 7.* With an Intro. Note by W. W.
         Greg. Shakespeare Assoc. London: Sidgwick & Jackson, 1951. Pp. 75.
         Reproduces B. M. copy of the 1603 Q.
         Rev: by J. G. McManaway, *SQ*, III (1952), 378; by F. C. Francis, *MLR*, XLVII, 572-573;
         by A. Koszul, *EA*, v, 242.

ii. Discussions (225;80)

B7086   Schücking, Levin L. *Zum Problem der Überlieferung des Hamlet-Textes.* Leipzig, 1931. In
         Ebisch and Schücking Supplement, p. 81.
         Rev: by Eduard Eckhardt, *Eng. Studn.*, LXXI (1936), 112-113.

B7087   Stoll, Elmer Edgar. "*Hamlet* and the *Spanish Tragedy*, Quartos I and II: A Protest." *MP*,
         XXXV (1937), 31-46.

B7088   Wilson, J. Dover. *The Manuscript of Shakespeare's "Hamlet" and the Problems of its Transmission.*
         Cambridge Univ. Press, 1934. 2 Vols.
         Rev: by L. C. Knights, *Criterion*, XIV (1934/35), 506-511; by E. Legouis, *RAA*, XII, 243-245;
         by P. M. Jack, *NYTBR*, Feb. 2, 1936, pp. 2, 24; by T. M. Parrott, *MLN*, LII (1937), 382-386;
         by W. Fischer, *DLZ*, LVIII, 781-783; by M. Deutschbein, *SJ*, LXXIII, 172-175; by N. B. Allen,
         SAB, XVI (1941), 154-165; by C. F. Tucker Brooke, "Soliloquy in a Shakespearean Cloister,"
         Essays on Shakespeare and Other Elizabethans, Yale Univ. Press, 1948, pp. 115-120 (first publ.
         YR, 1935).

B7089   Cairncross, A. S. *The Problem of Hamlet. A Solution.* London: Macmillan, 1936. Pp.
         xix, 205.
         Rev: B4916.

B7090   Handleman, Celia, and R. W. Babcock. " 'One Part Wisdom,' And Ever Two Parts—?"
         SAB, XI (1936), 191-225.
         Argues that Q2 and F1 of *Hamlet* are both cut or telescoped acting versions of Shakespeare's
         original play, which was probably in two parts.

B7091   Hart, Alfred. "The Vocabulary of the First Quarto of *Hamlet.*" *RES*, XII (1936), 18-30.

B7092   Allen, Percy. "The Date of *Hamlet.*" *TLS*, Jan. 2, 1937, p. 12.

B7093   Gray, Henry David. "The *Hamlet* First Quarto Pirate." *PQ*, XVI (1937), 394-401.

B7094   Kirschbaum, Leo. "The Date of Shakespeare's *Hamlet.*" *SP*, XXXIV (1937), 168-175.
         Concludes that Gabriel Harvey's marginalia cannot be used in dating *Hamlet.*

B7095   Tannenbaum, Samuel A. "Quarto 2." *SAB*, XIII (1938), 339-341.

B7096   Duthie, George Ian. *Elizabethan Pirated Dramas, with Special Reference to the "Bad" Quartos of "Hamlet," "Henry V," and "Romeo and Juliet": with an Appendix on the Problem of "The Taming of a Shrew."* DD, Edinburgh, 1939.

B7097   Lawrence, W. J. "The Folio Text of *Hamlet*." *TLS*, Dec. 30, 1939, p. 760.

B7098   Stainer, C. L. "Text of *Hamlet*." *TLS*, Jan. 6, 1940, p. 7.
On the folio text. Objects to various "inconsistencies" in folio text and suggests it is garbled.

B7099   Duthie, George Ian. *The "Bad" Quarto of "Hamlet."* Cambridge Univ. Press, 1941. Pp. xi, 279.
The author follows Chambers' opinion that all versions of *Hamlet* are derived from Quarto 2. He believes in the "pirate actor" theory.
Rev: by C. J. Sisson, *MLR*, XXXVI (1941), 404-407; *N &Q*, 180 (1941), 215-216; *TLS*, Feb. 22, 1941, p. 94; by Hazelton Spencer, *MLN*, LVII (1942), 223-225.

B7100   Shapin, Betty. "An Experiment in Memorial Reconstruction." *MLR*, XXXIX (1944), 9-17.
By reconstructing an unprinted modern play from the memory of one who acted a minor part in it, Miss Shapin obtained a text showing many of the characteristics of the first quarto of *Hamlet*. The experiment lends support to the conclusions of George I. Duthie, B7099.

B7101   Chambers, Sir E. K. *Shakespearean Gleanings.* Oxford Univ. Press, 1944. Chap. VIII: "The Date of *Hamlet*."
Rev: B4466.

B7102   Duthie, George Ian. (1) *Two Shakespeare Problems; (a) The "Bad" Quarto of "Hamlet," (b) "The Taming of a Shrew" and "The Taming of the Shrew"; (2) Shakespeare's "King Lear": A Critical Edition.* DD, Edinburgh, 1946.

B7103   Altman, George J. "Good Advice from the 'Bad' *Hamlet* Quarto." *ETJ*, II (Dec., 1950), 308-318.
Suggests that Q1 of *Hamlet*, as a report of an actual performance of the play, is, in many instances, a better guide to the staging of the play than either Q2 or the Folio.

B7104   Danks, K. B. " 'An Implication of Bibliographical Links'." *N &Q*, 195 (1950), 73-74.
Argues that because Q2 of *Hamlet* is related to Q1 by bibliographical links, Q2 text is related to the copy for Q1.

B7105   Jack, A. A. *Young Hamlet: A Conjectural Resolution of Some of the Difficulties in the Plotting of Shakespeare's Play.* Aberdeen Univ. Press, 1950. Pp. 176.
Rev: B7446.

B7106   Nosworthy, J. M. "Hamlet and the Player Who Could Not Keep Counsel." *ShS*, III (1950), 74-82.
The pirate responsible for Q1 was an actor who played, successively, Marcellus, Lucianus, and an Attendant Lord.

B7107   Walker, Alice. "The Textual Problem of *Hamlet*: A Reconsideration." *RES*, II (1951), 328-338.
Believes that to the end of Act 1, Q2 was printed from a corrected copy of Q1, and from the end of Act I, from a MS; that F was printed from a corrected copy of Q2; that probably a prompt book has the MS collated with Q2.

B7108   Danks, K. B. "*Hamlet*: The Problem of Copyright." *N &Q*, 197 (1952), 47-48.

B7109   Sidor, Krešimir. "Dvije verzije Shakespearova *Hamleta*." [Two Versions of Shakespeare's *Hamlet*.] *Hrvatsko Kolo* (Zagreb: Matica Hrvatska), V, Nos. 11-12, (1952), 697-701.
A dramaturgic analysis of the folio and quarto editions of the play.

B7110   Bowers, Fredson. "The Printing of *Hamlet*, Q2." With "Addendum." *SB*, VII (1955), 41-50; VIII (1956), 267-269.

B7111   Brown, John Russell. "The Compositors of *Hamlet* Q2 and *The Merchant of Venice*." *SB*, VII (1955), 17-40.

B7112   Jenkins, Harold. "The Relation Between the Second Quarto and the Folio Text of *Hamlet*." *SB*, VII (1955), 69-83.

B7113   Walker, Alice. "Collateral Substantive Texts (With Special Reference to *Hamlet*)." *SB*, VII (1955), 51-67.

B7114   Bowers, Fredson. "The Textual Relation of Q2 to Q1 *Hamlet* (I)." *SB*, VIII (1956), 39-66.

B7115   Honigmann, E. A. J. "The Date of *Hamlet*." *ShS*, IX (1956), 24-34.

(b) LATER EDITIONS (225;80)

B7116   Murry, J. M. "The 'New Temple' Edition of *Hamlet*." *Aryan Path*, VI (1935), 446-450.

B7117   *Hamlet.* The New Cambridge Shakespeare. Ed. J. Dover Wilson, 2nd ed. 1936. Cambridge Pocket Shakespeare. Cambridge Univ. Press, 1958. Pp. 169.
Rev: by L. L. Schücking, *Beiblatt*, XLVI (1935), 205-210; by L. C. Knights, *Criterion*, XIV (1934/35), 506-511; by R. Travers, *RAA*, XII, 245-248; by W. Keller, *SJ*, LXXI (1935), 114-115; by C. R. Baskervill, *MP*, XXXIII (1935/36), 201-202; by S. A. T., *SAB*, XI (1936), 185-186; by P. M. Jack, *NYTBR*, Feb. 2, 1936, pp. 2, 24; by Peter Alexander, *RES*, XII, 385-400; by Henry David Gray, *TLS*, Jan. 9, 1937, p. 28; by C. N. Menon, *MLR*, XXXII

(1937), 438-441; by T. Pyles, *ELH*, IV, 114-146; by W. Fischer, *DLZ*, LVIII, 783; by T. M. Parrott, *MLN*, LII, 382-386.

B7118   *Hamlet, Prince of Denmark. A Tragedy.* With an Intro. and Notes by H. de Groot. Third ed. Groningen: J. B. Wolters, 1936. Pp. 176. Fifth ed., 1947. Sixth ed., 1949. Seventh ed., 1951. Eighth ed., 1956.

B7119   *Hamlet.* Ed. Henry Norman Hudson and Others. Cameo Classics. New York: Grosset, 1936. Pp. 291.

B7120   *Hamlet.* Interlinear ed. prepared by George Coffin Taylor and Reed Smith. Boston: Ginn, 1936. Pp. xlix, 206.
      Rev: by Samuel A. Tannenbaum, *SAB*, XI (1936), 252.

B7121   *Hamlet.* Ed. George Lyman Kittredge. Boston: Ginn, 1939. Pp. xx, 334.
      Rev: by Robert Adger Law, *JEGP*, XXXIX (1940), 578-581.

B7122   Cancelled.

B7123   *Tragedies Old and New; Including Shakespeare's "Hamlet," Sophocles' "Elektra," O'Neill's "Beyond the Horizon."* New York: Noble & Noble, 1939. Pp. 492.
      Rev: by A. Tauber, *QJS*, XXV (1939), 505.

B7124   *Hamlet.* Ed. R. C. Bald. Crofts Classics. New York: Crofts, 1946. Pp. xiii, 114.

B7125   *Hamlet: With a Psycho-Analytic Study by Ernest Jones, M. D.* Drawings by F. Roberts Johnson. New York: Funk and Wagnalls; London: Vision Press, 1947. Pp. 180.
      Rev: A1298.

B7126   *Hamlet.* Ed. George Rylands. The New Clarendon Shakespeare. Oxford: Clarendon Press, 1947. Pp. 8, 256.
      Rev: *QJS*, XXXIV (1948), 108.

B7127   *Hamlet.* Pocket Classics. London: Burgess & Bowes, 1947. Pp. 136.

B7128   *Hamlet.* With Intro. and Notes by H. Oldendorf and H. Arguile. Cape Town: Maskew Miller, 1948. Pp. 211.

B7129   *Hamlet, Prince of Denmark.* Ed. Tarquinio Vallese. Naples: Pironti, 1948. Pp. xx, 120.

B7130   *The Tragedy of Hamlet.* Bielefeld: Cornelsen, 1948. Pp. 178.

B7131   *Hamlet.* Ed. J. J. Hogan. Malone Shakespeare. Dublin: Browne & Nolan, 1949. Pp. 251.

B7132   *Scenes from "Julius Caesar" and "Hamlet."* Ed. Josef Raith. Munich: Heuber, 1949. Pp. 39.
      Rev: B6754.

B7133   *Hamlet.* Ed. N. M. Kulkarni. Allahabad: Banaras, 1950. Pp. iv, 477.

B7134   *Hamlet.* With Linoleum cuts by Valenti Angelo. Mt. Vernon, New York: Peter Pauper Press, 1950. Pp. iv, 164.

B7135   *Hamlet.* As Arranged for the Stage of the Globe Theatre at the San Diego Exposition by Thomas Wood Stevens. New York: French, 1951. Pp. 85.

B7136   *Hamlet. Macbeth.* Third ed. Madrid: Aguilar, 1951. Pp. 540.

B7137   *The Revealment of Hamlet.* Ed. Alfred Stoner. New Orleans: Pelican, 1952. Pp. 153.

B7138   *Hamlet.* Commentary by Richard Burton, Illustrations by Roger Furse. London: Folio Society; New York: Philip C. Duschnes, 1954. Pp. 140.

B7139   *The Tragedy of Hamlet, Prince of Denmark.* Ed. Tucker Brooke and Jack Randall. Yale Shakespeare. Yale Univ. Press, 1957. Pp. 222. Oxford Univ. Press, 1957. Revised ed. paperback.
      Rev: *SatR*, Aug. 3, 1957, p. 28.

B7140   *The Tragedy of Hamlet, Prince of Denmark.* Ed. Willard Farnham. Pelican Shakespeare. Baltimore: Penguin Books, 1957. Pp. 176.

B7141   *Hamlet, Prince of Denmark.* In leicht gekürzter Form hrsg. u. m. Anm. u. e. Einl. vers. v. Stephan Hartmann. Second ed. Vienna: Österr. Bundesverl., 1957. Pp. 111.

B7142   *Hamlet* [and Six Other Plays]. New Simplified Shakespeare Series. Ed. Ian Stuart. Birmingham, Alabama: Vulcan Press, 1954; 1957. Pp. 273.
      Rev: by Robert Griswold, Jr., *SQ*, VIII (1957), 121.

B7143   *Hamlet.* Ed. Francis Fergusson and Charles Jasper Sisson. Laurel Shakespeare. With a Modern Commentary by Maurice Evans. New York: Dell Publishing Co., 1958. Pp. 255.

B7144   *Hamlet, Prince of Denmark.* Folger Lib. General Reader's Shakespeare. Ed. Louis Booker Wright and Virginia L. Freund, 1958.

(c) READINGS AND EMENDATIONS
i. Various Passages

B7145   Flatter, Richard. "Mad, Made and Maid." *TLS*, Oct. 6, 1945, p. 475; cf. Percy Walters, ibid., Nov. 10, p. 535; W. R. Dunstan, ibid., Nov. 3, p. 523; J. Nosworthy, ibid., Nov. 17, p. 547.

B7146   Trehern, E. M. "Notes on *Hamlet*." *MLR*, XL (1945), 213-216.
      (1) Hamlet's supposed earlier entry at II. ii. 159;
      (2) III. ii. 135: "Marry, this is miching mallecho: it means mischief."

B7147   Flatter, Richard. "Textual Notes: (a) The Two Pictures in *Hamlet*. (b) A Stage-Direction in *Hamlet*." *Shakespeare Quarterly* (London), I (1947), pp. 89-93.

B7148   Stewart, Charles D. "Four Shakespearean Cruxes." *CE*, IX (1948), 187-191. [III. iv. and IV. ii.]
See also B7312.

B7149   Orlando, Ruggero. "Amleto Esagerava." *Letteratura* (Florence), I, No. 3 (May-June, 1950).

B7150   Bowers, Fredson. "A Note on *Hamlet*, I. v. 33 and II. ii. 181." *SQ*, IV (1953), 51-56.

B7151   Carrington, Norman Thomas. *Hamlet*. Notes on chosen English texts series. London: Brodie, 1954. Pp. 88.

B7152   Cairncross, Andrew S. "Two Notes on *Hamlet*." *SQ*, IX (1958), 586-588.
III. iv. 169 and V. ii. 218-236.

ii.   Single Passages
(Arranged by Act and Scene)
aa.   Act I

B7153   Tannenbaum, Samuel A. " 'The Platform Where we Watched'." *SAB*, XIV (1939), 63-64.

B7154   Trench, W. F. "Shakespeare's Unfinished Sentences." *TLS*, July 25, 1936, p. 616.

B7155   Tannenbaum, Samuel A. "Shall a King Smite a King? *Hamlet*, I. i. 62-64." *PQ*, XV (1936), 307-310.

B7156   Jones, H. W. "*Hamlet*, I. i. 60-63." *N &Q*, 194 (1949), 535.

B7157   Parsons, Howard. "*Hamlet*, I. i. 60-63." *N &Q*, 195 (1950), 85-86.

B7158   Murphy, Mallie John. "Hamlet's Sledded Polack." *N &Q*, NS, III (1956), 509.
I. i. 60-63.

B7159   Deubel, Werner. "Von der Morgenröte." *DL*, XLIII (1940/41), 7.
I. i. 150.

B7160   Pearce, T. M. "*La Misa del Gallo* and Shakspere's 'Bird of Dawning'." *SAB*, XX (1945), 140-143.
Hamlet, I. i. 158-160.

B7161   Uhr, Leonard. "Hamlet's 'Coold Mother'." *N &Q*, NS, V (1958), 189-190.
Ham., I. ii. 77.

B7162   Maxwell, J. C. "Claudius and the Curse of Cain." *N &Q*, 194 (April, 1949), 142.
I. ii. 105.

B7163   Sylvester, William. "*Hamlet*, I. ii. 133." *N &Q*, NS, IV (1957), 223.

B7164   Crundell, H. W. " 'Discourse of Reason'." *N &Q*, 190 (1946), 84-85.
I. ii. 150.

B7165   Thaler, Alwin. "In My Mind's Eye, Horatio." *SQ*, VII (1956), 351-354.
I. ii. 185.

B7166   C., T. C. "Three Notes on Hamlet." *N &Q*, 175 (1938), 114.
Comment by H. Kendra Baker, ibid., p. 158; by Hibernicus, ibid., pp. 158-159.
I. ii. 185.

B7167   Carver, P. L. "The Source of the 'Mind's Eye'." *N &Q*, 175 (1938), 191.

B7168   Farrison, W. Edward. "Horatio's Report to Hamlet." *MLN*, LXXII (1957), 406-408.
I. ii. 186.

B7169   Deutschbein, Max. "O, that this too too solid flesh would melt. Eine Interpretation von *Hamlet* I. 2. 129ff." *SJ*, LXXIV (1938), 163-169.

B7170   Bowers, Fredson. "Hamlet's 'Sullied' or 'Solid' Flesh: A Bibliographical Case-History." *ShS*, IX (1956), 44-48.

B7171   Nathan, Norman. " 'Sallied' May Mean 'Sallied'." *N &Q*, NS, IV (1957), 279-280.

B7172   Kökeritz, Helge. "This Sullied Solid Flesh." *SN*, XXX (1958), 3-10.
A defense of emendation, and a reply to B7170.

B7173   David, R. W. "Sullied Flesh." *TLS*, Nov. 14, 1958, p. 657.

B7174   Tannenbaum, Samuel A. "Hamlet's Sect and Force." *SAB*, XV (1940), 125-126.
Hamlet, I. iii. 24-27, Q₂.

B7175   Savage, D. S. "A Word in *Hamlet*." *TLS*, May 5, 1950, p. 277.
Comment by O. G. W. Stallybrass, *TLS*, May 19, 1950, p. 309; by Clifford Bax, *TLS*, May 26, p. 325.
Suggests the reading, "Of each new-hatch'd, unfledged *comrage*," in *Hamlet*, I. iii.

B7176   Cripps, A. R. "A Difficult Line in *Hamlet*." *TLS*, Jan. 8, 1938, p. 28.
I. iii. precepts speech.

B7177   Tannenbaum, Samuel A. "Meddling with Shakspere's Text." *SAB*, XV (1940), 62-64.
On emendations of a passage in *Hamlet* (I. iii. 64-66, Furness).

B7178   Bronson, Bertrand H. " 'Costly Thy Habit,' &c." *SQ*, VII (1956), 280-281.
I. iii. 70.

B7179   Rockwell, K. A. "*Hamlet* I. iii. 74: 'Of a most select'." *N &Q*, NS, IV (1957), 64, 84.

B7180   Virtue, John. "Shakespeare's *Hamlet*, I. iii. 78-80." *Expl.*, XVI, ix (1958), No. 55.

B7181   Scott, Inez. "A *Hamlet* Emendation." *TLS*, Sept. 4, 1937, p. 640.
        I. iii. 108-109.

B7182   Leech, Clifford. "A 'Dram of Ease'." *TLS*, Jan. 11, 1936, p. 35.
        I. iv. 36.

B7183   Nosworthy, James M. " 'Dram of Eale'." *TLS*, March 21, 1936, p. 244.
        See letter by W. W. Greg, *TLS*, March 28, 1936, p. 278. *Hamlet*, I. iv. 36-38.

B7184   Crundell, H. W. "On Three Passages of Shakespeare." *N &Q*, 172 (1937), 331-332.
        Hamlet, I. iv.

B7185   Meyerstein, E. H. W. " 'The Dram of Eale' [*Hamlet*, I. iv. 38ff]." *TLS*, Nov. 10, 1945, p. 535.

B7186   Gordon, R. G. "The Crux in *Hamlet*." *TLS*, Dec. 11, 1948, p. 697.
        [I. iv. 36-38.]
        See the letter by Mr. R. W. Cruttwell, ibid., Dec. 18, 1948, p. 713.

B7187   Greg, W. W. "The Crux in *Hamlet*." *TLS*, Jan. 1, 1949, p. 9.
        Comment by John Buxton, *TLS*, Dec. 9, 1949, p. 809; continues from B7186. W. W. Greg
        inquires as to whether "noble" was ever used as a singular common noun. Buxton cites four
        examples of such use contemporaneous with *Hamlet*.

B7188   Savage, D. S. "An Alchemical Metaphor in *Hamlet*." *N &Q*, 197 (1952), 157-160.
        Would read the *eale* of "dram of eale . . . often dout," Q₂, I. iii. as *eisel*, vinegar.

B7189   Evans, G. Blakemore. "Thomas Nashe and the 'Dram of Eale'." *N &Q*, 198 (1953), 377-378.
        See note by R. L. Eagle, p. 545.

B7190   Allen, Glen O. " 'The Dram of Eale' Again." *N &Q*, NS, II (1955), 292-293.

B7191   Parsons, Howard. "The 'Dram of Eale'." *N &Q*, NS, II (1955), 409.
        On B7190.

B7192   Hart, Dominic. "Hamlet I. iv. 31-38." *N &Q*, NS, II (1955), 500.
        On B7190.

B7193   Greg, W. W. "*Hamlet* and *The Winter's Tale*." *TLS*, April 25, 1952, p. 281.
        Ham., I. v.

B7194   Evans, G. Blakemore. " 'My Tables, Meet It Is I Set It Down'." *MLR*, XLII (1947), 235-236.
        I. v. 107.

B7195   Visser, F. T. "To Note in Shakespeare's *Hamlet*, I. v. 178." *ES*, XXVI (1945), 142-144.

bb. Act II

B7196   Waldrun, John. " 'Machine': *Hamlet* II. ii. 124." *N &Q*, NS, I (1954), 515-516.

B7197   Hankins, John E. "Hamlet's 'god kissing carrion': A Theory of the Generation of Life."
        PMLA, LXIV (1949), 507-516.
        II. ii. 182.

B7198   Gibson, Evan K. " 'Conception is a Blessing'." *PMLA*, LXIV (1949), 1236-38.
        Comment on B7197.

B7199   Boyce, Benjamin. "Shakespeare's *Hamlet*, II. ii. 198-208." *Expl.*, VII (1948), item 2.

B7200   Bourland, Caroline B. "Of Men and Angels." *Essays Contributed in Honor of President William
        Allan Neilson*. Smith College Studies in Mod. Languages, XXI (1938), 6-9.
        II. ii. 290-300.

B7201   Kane, Robert J. "Hamlet's Apotheosis of Man—Its Punctuation." *RES*, XIV (1938), 67-68.

B7202   Knight, G. Wilson. "Like Angels." *TLS*, Oct. 26, 1946, p. 521.

B7202a "Shakespeare's Mind." *TLS*, Oct. 26, 1946, p. 521.

B7203   Bacon, Wallace A. "A Footnote to Mr. Harbage's *Hamlet*, II. ii. 306-324." *N &Q*, NS, II
        (1955), 475-477. Comment by B. R. Jerman, III (1956), 89.

B7204   Braddy, Haldeen. "I Know a Hawk from a Handsaw: *Hamlet*, II. ii. 360-361." *SAB*, XVI
        (1941), 29-32.

B7205   Kökeritz, Helge. "Five Shakespeare Notes." *RES*, XXIII (1947), 310-320.
        II. ii. 360-361.

B7206   Joseph, Bertram L. "Hamlet's Reference to Hawk and Handsaw (II. ii.)." *English*, VIII
        (1950/51), 47-48.

B7207   Cancelled.

B7208   Shaaber, M. A. "A Note on Hamlet's Abridgement." *SQ*, III (1952), 381-382.
        Glosses the word in II. ii. 438f. as "epitome."

B7209   Seaton, Ethel. " 'The Mobled Queene'." *TLS*, Aug. 30, 1947, p. 439.
        See the letters by Lindsay Scott, ibid., Sept. 6, 1947, p. 451; by Winifred Scott, idem; by
        R. W. Cruttwell, ibid., Sept. 13, 1947, p. 465.
        II. ii. 488.

B7210   M(abbott), T. O. " 'John-a-dreams'." *N &Q*, 181 (1941), 54.
        II. ii. 552.

cc. Act III

For Hamlet's soliloquy "To be or not,"
see numbers B7866-B7877 below.

B7211   Clair, John A. "Shakespeare's *Hamlet*, III. i. 92." *Expl.*, XIX, No. 5 (1955).
B7212   Madariaga, Salvador de. "*Hamlet*." *TLS*, June 5, 1948, p. 317.
        III. ii. 85-86.
B7213   Pyles, Thomas. "Ophelia's 'Nothing'." *MLN*, LXIV (1949), 322-323.
        III. ii. 124.
B7214   Reik, Theodor. "Shakespeare Visits a Psychoanalyst." *Complex*, VI (1941), 34-39.
        III. ii. 135.
B7215   Roberts, D. R. " 'Miching Mallico'." *TLS*, April 18, 1936, p. 336.
        III. ii. 136.
B7216   Hotson, Leslie. "Sables for Hamlet." *Time and Tide*, XXXIII (1952), 1266-67.
        III. ii. 138.
B7217   Ringler, William. "The Hobby Horse is Forgot." *SQ*, IV (1953), 485.
        III. ii. 143.
B7218   Mabbott, T. O. "*Hamlet:* 'Pajock'—on *Hamlet*, III. ii. 272." *N &Q*, 180 (1941), 258-259.
B7219   Smith, Roland M. "Hamlet Said 'Pajock'." *JEGP*, XLIV (1945), 292-295.
        See Samuel A. Tannenbaum, *SAB*, VII (1932), 127-130.
B7220   Tannebaum, Samuel A. "Claudius Not a Patchock." *SAB*, XX (1945), 156-159.
        III. ii. 272.
B7221   Nathan, Norman. "Horatio's 'You Might Have Rhymed'." *N &Q*, 198 (1953), 282-283.
        III. ii. 272.
B7222   Trienens, Roger J. "The Symbolic Cloud in *Hamlet*." *SQ*, V (1954), 211-213.
        III. ii. 368-375.
B7223   McManaway, James G., and William B. Van Lennep. "A *Hamlet* Emendation." *MLR*,
        XXXIV (1939), 68-70.
        III. ii. 396-397.
B7224   Parrott, Thomas Marc. "An Emendation of the Text of *Hamlet*." *SAB*, XII (1937), 44-48.
        III. iii. 5-7.
B7225   Tannenbaum, Samuel A. "A *Hamlet* Emendation." *SAB*, XII (1937), 64-66. On B7224.
        III. iii. 3-7.
B7226   Kurtze, Max. "Kritisches zur Bühnenanweisung im *Hamlet:* 'Lifts up the arras and dis-
        covers Polonius' (Akt III Szene IV)." *SJ*, 87/88 (1952), 43-47.
B7227   Tannenbaum, Samuel A. " 'That Monster Custom'." *PQ*, XV (1936), 401-405.
        Hamlet, III. iv. 161.
B7228   Hulme, Hilda. "Three Notes on the Pronunciation and Meaning of Shakespeare's Text."
        Neophil, 1957, pp. 275ff.
        III. iv. 169.

dd. Act IV

B7229   Culpin, A. E. "A Line in *Hamlet*." *TLS*, Nov. 15, 1947, p. 591.
        See the letter by W. W. Greg, ibid., Nov. 22, 1947, p. 603, and by William Bliss, ibid., Dec.
        13, 1947, p. 645.
        IV. iv. 18-20.
B7230   Madariaga, Salvador de. "A Passage in *Hamlet*." *TLS*, Aug. 31, 1946, p. 415.
        IV. iv. 23-30.
B7231   Norman, Sylva. "A Passage in *Hamlet*." *TLS*, Oct. 30, 1953, p. 393.
        See letter by John Middleton Murry, Nov. 6, 1953, p. 709.
        IV. iv. 53-56.
B7232   Brown, A. D. Fitton. "Two Points of Interpretation." *N &Q*, NS, IV (1957), 51.
        IV. iv. 53.
B7233   Copley, J. " 'They Say the Owle Was a Baker's Daughter' (*Hamlet*, IV. v. 40)." *N &Q*,
        NS, II (1955), 512-513.
B7234   Green, Andrew J. "Exit Horatio." *PQ*, XXX (1951), 220-221.
        IV. v. 75.
B7235   Morris, Harry. "Ophelia's 'Bonny Sweet Robin'." *PMLA*, LXXIII (1958), 601-603.
        IV. v. 187.
B7236   French, Joseph N. "*Hamlet*—An Emendation." *TLS*, June 21, 1957, p. 381.
        [IV. vii. 58.] See comment by W. W. Greg, "*Hamlet*, IV. vii. 58," *TLS*, June 28, 1957,
        p. 397.

ee. Act V

B7237   Schapiro, Meyer. " 'Cain's Jaw-Bone that Did the First Murder'." *Art Bul.*, XXIV (1942),

205-212. See letter by Ananda K. Coomaraswamy, ibid., XXIV, 383-384.
V. i. 83-87.

B7238 Pitcher, Seymour M. "Two Notes on Shakespeare." *PQ*, XXI (1942), 239-240.
V. i. 203.

B7239 Atthill, Robin. "Virgin Crants." *English*, VII (1949), 202-203.
V. i. 225.

B7240 Visser, F. T. "Two Remarkable Constructions in Shakespeare." *Neophil*, XXX (1946), 37-43.
V. i. 252 (Q₂).

B7241 Donovan, James L. "A Note on Hamlet's 'Not Shriving Time Allowed'." *N &Q*, NS, III (1956), 467-469.
V. ii. 47.

B7242 Cline, Ruth H. "A Note on *Hamlet*." *MLN*, LXVI (1951), 40.
V. ii. 193.

B7243 Morgan, Roberta. "Some Stoic Lines in *Hamlet* and the Problem of Interpretation." *PQ*, XX (1941), 549-558.
V. ii. 217-222.

B7244 Gibson, Martha Jane. " 'Fat' and 'Hot'." *American Speech*, XII (1937), 163.

B7245 Dickson, Arthur. " 'Fat' (*Hamlet* V. ii. 298)." *SQ*, II (1951), 171-172.

B7246 Maxwell, J. C. " 'Fat and Scant of Breath' Again." *ES*, XXXII (1951), 29-30.

B7247 Stoll, Elmer Edgar. "Not Fat or Thirty." *SQ*, II (1951), 295-301.
The Gravedigger's "thirty years" not meant to represent Hamlet's age: its coupling with Hamlet's birth-date one of Shakespeare's "factual inconsistencies." The Queen's description of Hamlet as "fat" a misprint for "hot."

B7248 Hotson, Leslie. "Hamlet Fat?" *Spectator*, May 30, 1952, p. 701.

B7249 Nowottny, Winifred M. T. "The Application of Textual Theory to Hamlet's Dying Words." *MLR*, LII (1957), 161-167.

(2) LITTERARY GENESIS (227;81)
(a) GENERAL WORKS ON GENESIS (227;81)

B7250 Simpson, P. *The Theme of Revenge in Elizabethean Tragedy*. Annual Shakespeare Lecture of British Academy. Oxford Univ. Press, 1935. Pp. 28.
Rev: by L. L. Schücking, *Beiblatt*, XLVII (1936), 75; by Mario Praz, *ES*, XVIII (1936), 177-181.

B7251 McMurray, Raymund Stanislaus. *Shakespeare's "Hamlet" Material*. MA thesis, Acadia (Canada), 1937.

B7251a Schücking, Levin L. "The *Spanish Tragedy* Additions: Acting and Reading Versions." *TLS*, June 12, 1937, p. 442.
Suggests some printed versions of plays were for publication only, not for acting. Comments upon graveyard scene in *Hamlet*.

B7252 Schick, J. *Corpus Hamleticum. Hamlet in Sage und Dichtung, Kunst und Musik*. 1 Abteilung. Bd. IV. 1. Teil. Leipzig, 1934.
Rev: by Erna Fischer, *Beiblatt*, XLVII (1936), 11-18.

B7252a Schick, J. *Corpus Hamleticum: Hamlet in Sage und Dichtung, Kunst und Musik*. 1, 5: *Die Scharfsinnsproben*. 2 Teil: *Von Vorderasien bis Germanien*. Leipzig: Harrassowitz, 1938. Pp. xii, 570.
Rev: by Alois Brandl, *Archiv*, 175 (1939), 249-250; by Wolfgang Keller, *SJ*, LXXV, 160-162; by Erna Fischer, *Beiblatt*, LI (1941), 219-223. The whole of this collection, the first part of which was published in 1912, is listed in Raven's bibliography (B7081), item 757.

B7253 Lawrence, William Witherle. "Hamlet's Sea Voyage." *PMLA*, LIX (1944), 45-70.
Comment by T. M. Parrott, "Hamlet's Sea Voyage—Bandits or Pirates? A Reply to Professor Lawrence." *SAB*, XIX (1944), 51-59.

B7254 Kudlinski, Tadeusz. *Dziedzictwo Zemstypolpowiesc* (*The Heritage of Revenge: A Semi-novel*). Wrocław-Warsaw: Ksiaznica-Atlas, 1948. Pp. 342.
In a semi-novelistic manner the author traces the evolution of the *Hamlet* Saga up to Shak. and sketches the story of *Hamlet* production on the Polish stage.

B7255 Jack, A. A. *Young Hamlet: A Conjectural Resolution of Some of the Difficulties in the Plotting of Shakespeare's Play*. Aberdeen Univ. Press, 1950. Pp. 176.
Rev: B7446.

B7256 Schulze, F. W. *Hamlet. Geschichtssubstanzen zwischen Rohstoff und Endform des Gedichts*. Halle (Saale): Max Niemeyer, 1956. Pp. 206.
Rev: by Hermann Heuer, *SJ*, 93 (1957), 262-264; by Hans Schnyder, *Archiv*, 194 (1957), 237; by J. Kleinstück, *NS*, VI, 294-295; by Adrien Bonjour, *DLZ*, LXXIX (1958), 128.

B7257 Cleeve, B. T. *The Development of the Hamlet Story*. DD, National University, Ireland, 1957.

(b) SOURCES AND RELATED MATERIAL
i. Saxo Grammaticus

B7258 Saxo Grammaticus. *Amlethus*. Hamburg: Gesellschaft der Bücherfreunde, 1949. Pp. 88. Latin text and German translation.
Rev: A3523.

B7259 Wales, Julia G. "Amleth's Shield: A Comment on the Pictorial Elements of the Hamlet Story." *Trans. of the Wisconsin Acad. of Sciences, Arts, and Letters*, xxx (1937), 303-312.

B7260 Schröder, F. R. "Der Ursprung der Hamletsage." *GRM*, xxvi (1938), 81-108.

B7261 Sperber, Hans. "The Conundrums in Saxo's Hamlet Episode." *PMLA*, LXIV (1949), 864-870.

B7262 Boberg, Inger Margrethe. "Saxo's Hamlet." *American-Scandinavian Review*, XLIV (1956), 50-56.

ii. The Ur-Hamlet

B7263 Stoll, Elmer Edgar. "*Hamlet* and *The Spanish Tragedy*, Quartos I and II: A Protest." *MP*, xxxv (1937), 31-46.

B7264 Stoll, Elmer Edgar. "*Hamlet* and *The Spanish Tragedy* Again." *MP*, xxxvii (1939), 173-186. Reiteration of views expressed in B7263.

B7265 Bowers, F. T. *Elizabethan Revenge Tragedy, 1587-1642*. Princeton Univ. Press, 1940. Pp. viii, 288. Section on Ur-Hamlet.
Rev: B4941.

B7266 Wilson, J. Dover, tr. "Nashe's 'Kyd in Aesop': A Danish Interpretation by V. Østerberg." *RES*, xviii (1942), 385-394.

B7267 Lawrence, William W. " 'Ophelia's Heritage': A Correction." *MLR*, xliv (1949), 236.

B7268 Law, Robert Adger. "Belleforest, Shakespeare, and Kyd." *AMS*, pp. 279-294.

B7269 Carrère, Félix Jean. *Le Théâtre de Thomas Kyd. Contribution à l'Etude du Drame Elizabéthain*. Thèse de Lettres, Paris, 1949. Toulouse: Edouard Privat, Editeur, 14, Rue des Arts, 1951.
Rev: A4979.

B7270 Maxwell, J. C. "*Hamlet*: An Echo of the *Ur-Hamlet*." *N&Q*, 197 (1952), 420.
Suggests that in III. iv. 209-210 of the play, Shak. is unconsciously influenced by an incident of his source-play.

B7271 Empson, William. "*Hamlet* When New." *SR*, LXI (1953), 15-42, 185-205.

B7272 Ratliff, John D. *The Kydian Revenge Play*. DD, Stanford University, 1955. Pp. 465. Mic A54-3472. *DA*, xiv (1954), 2338. Publ. No. 10,386.

B7273 Cleeve, B. T. "The Lost *Hamlet*." *Studies, Irish Quarterly Review*, xlvi (1957), 447-456.

B7274 Smith, John Harrington, Lois D. Pizer, and Edward K. Kaufman. "*Hamlet, Antonio's Revenge*, and the *Ur-Hamlet*." *SQ*, ix (1958), 493-498.

iii. The "Bestrafte Brudermord"

B7275 Knight, A. H. J. "*Der Bestrafte Brudermord* and *Hamlet*." *MLR*, xxxi (1936), 385-391.

B7276 Isaacs, J., ed. *William Poel's Prompt-Book of Fratricide Punished*. London, 1956.
Rev: B1826.

B7277 Freudenstein, Reinhold. *Der Bestrafte Brudermord: Shakespeares Hamlet auf der Wanderbühne des 17. Jahrhunderts*. DD, Marburg. Hamburg: Cram. de Gruyter, 1958. Pp. 130.

(c) FURTHER LITERARY RELATIONS OR SOURCES (229;82)
i. The Mousetrap

B7278 Bullough, G. " 'The Murder of Gonzago' a Probable Source for *Hamlet*." *MLR*, xxx (1935), 433-444.

B7279 Montgomerie, William. "Sporting Kid (The Solution of the 'Kidde in Aesop' Problem)." *Life and Letters Today*, xxxvi (1943), 18-24.

B7280 Evans, G. Blakemore. "Belleforest and the Gonzago Story: *Hamlet*, III. ii." *SAB*, xxiv (1949), 280-282.

B7281 Kuhl, E. P. "Hamlet's Mousetrap." *TLS*, July 8, 1949, p. 445.
Sees in Q₁'s "murder done in *Guyana*," a topical reference connected with Raleigh.
Comment by W. W. Greg, *TLS*, July 22, p. 473.

B7282 Montgomerie, William. "Lucianus, Nephew to the King." *N&Q*, ns, iii (1956), 149-151.

B7282a Montgomerie, William. "Provincial Roses." *N&Q*, ns, iii (1956), 361.

ii. General

B7283 Cameron, K. W. "Hamlet's Fourth Soliloquy and Samuel Ward." *SAB*, xi (1936), 59-60. On Irving Richard's "Meaning of Hamlet's Soliloquy," *PMLA*, XLVIII (1933), 741ff. Parallels to Richard's interpretation from Ward.

B7284 C., T. C. "Three Notes on Hamlet." *N&Q*, 175 (1938), 114.

B7284a Hibernicus. " 'The Mind's Eye'." *N&Q*, 175 (1938), 158-159.
Answer to B7284.

B7284b Baker, H. Kendra. "Notes on Hamlet." *N&Q*, 175 (1938), 158.
        More on B7284.

B7285   Cox, Ernest H. "Another Medieval Convention in Shakspere." *SAB*, XIII (1938), 67-72.
        Outlines the medieval and renaissance literary lineage of the *ubi sunt* formula which Hamlet
        employs in V. i. 231-239.

B7285a Cox, Ernest H. "Another Medieval Convention in Shakspere." *SAB*, XVI (1941), 249-253.
        The *ubi sunt* formula in *Hamlet*.

B7286   S., E. B. "A Polish Source for Shakespeare." *More Books*, XV (1940), 192.
        On the influence upon the conception of Polonius exerted by *The Counsellor*, 1598, a version
        of *De optimo senatore* by Laurentius Grimaldus Goslicius.

B7287   Baughan, Denver Ewing. "A Compliment to Sidney in *Hamlet*." *N&Q*, 177 (1939), 133-136.

B7288   Borgese, G. A. "The Dishonor of Honor: Francesco Giovanni Mauro to Sir John Falstaff."
        RR, XXXII (1941), 44-55.
        Tasso's influ. via Daniel, p. 50; *Ham.*, pp. 54-55.

B7289   Barnett, George L. " 'The Glass of Fashion and the Mould of Form' [*Hamlet*, III. i. 161]."
        N&Q, 185 (1943), 105.

B7290   M., A. "Hamlet Once More." *N&Q*, 184 (1943), 255, 282-283.
        Matthew Arnold on Shakespeare's thinking about Montaigne.

B7291   Matthes, Heinrich C. "Hamlet und Holger Danske." *Archiv*, 182 (1943), 103-107.

B7292   Montgomerie, William. "English Seneca." *Life and Letters Today*, XXXVI (1943), 25-28.
        Possible links between *Hamlet* and Seneca.

B7293   Deutschbein, Max. "Shakespeares Hamlet und Montaigne." *SJ*, 80/81 (1946), 70-107.

B7294   Barnett, George L. "Hamlet's Soliloquy." *MLQ*, VII (1946), 57-59.
        Analogous sentiments in Bodenham's *Belvedere*.

B7295   Evans, Dorothy Atkinson. "Some Notes on Shakespeare and *The Mirror of Knighthood*."
        SAB, XXI (1946), 161-167; XXII (1947), 62-68.

B7296   Hankins, John E. "Lear and the Psalmist." *MLN*, LXI (1946), 88-90.

B7297   Semper, I. J. " 'Yes, By St. Patrick'." *TLS*, Aug. 3, 1946, p. 367.
        Reference to Clarence Brownfield's suggestion that Holinshed is the source of Hamlet's
        phrase (*TLS*, May 25, 1946). Semper suggests Voragine's *Golden Legend*.

B7298   Seaton, Ethel. "Hamlet and Fortune." *TLS*, Nov. 1, 1947, p. 563.

B7299   Kan, A. H. "Plagiaat? (Hamlet en Catullus.)" *Hermeneus* (Zwolle), XX (1948), 24.

B7300   Boyce, Benjamin. "The Stoic *Consolatio* and Shakespeare." *PMLA*, LXIV (1949), 771-780.

B7301   Joseph, B. L. "Correspondence." *English*, VIII (1950), 47-48.
        Writes explaining Hamlet's references to the "handsaw"-*heronshaw* (cf. Joseph Hall's *Quo
        Vadis*), and to "French falconers;" suggests a source for his jingle on the stricken deer (Henry
        Petowe's *Hero and Leanders Further Fortunes*, London: 1598).

B7302   Braddy, Haldeen. "Shakespeare and Three Oriental Tales." *Midwest Folklore*, I (1951), 91-92.
        Early Oriental analogue to *Hamlet*, I. ii. 140.

B7303   Caldiero, Frank M. "The Source of Hamlet's 'What a Piece of Work is a Man!' " *N&Q*,
        196 (1951), 421-424.
        Finds the source of the speech in a hitherto unnoticed passage from the writings of Pico
        della Mirandola.

B7304   Harrison, Thomas P. "A Biblical Echo in *Hamlet*." *N&Q*, 196 (1951), 235.
        Hamlet, V. ii. 217-220, recalls *Habbakuk* ii:3.

B7305   Pazzini, Adalberto. "Shakespeare Lesse un Libro Anatomico Italiano?" *Osservatore Romano*,
        91, No. 44 (1951), 3.

B7306   Thompson, W. Lawrence. "*Hamlet* and Dante's *Paradiso*." *N&Q*, 196 (1951), 181-182.
        Finds an analogue in the cosmic imagery of Hamlet's speech in III. iv. 40-50 to that in the
        Paradiso XXVII, 19-30, 35-36, 109-111.

B7307   Walker, Roy. " 'The Upstart Crow'." *TLS*, August 10, 1951, p. 501. See also C. A. C. Davis,
        ibid., August 17, p. 517.

B7308   Bowers, Fredson. "The Pictures in *Hamlet* III. iv: A Possible Contemporary Reference."
        SQ, III (1952), 280-281.
        Sees a possible reflection of Hamlet's "Looke heere vpon this Picture, and on this" in the last
        scene of Thomas Dekker's *Satiromastix*, where Tucca displays and comments upon the two
        pictures he has brought in.

B7309   Heist, William W. " 'Fulness of Bread'." *SQ*, III (1952), 140-142.
        Shows the influence of a Biblical line on Shak.'s imagination.

B7310   Parrott, T. M. "Fulness of Bread." *SQ*, III (1952), 379-381.

B7311   Harrison, G. B. "Distressful Bread." *SQ*, IV (1953), 105.

B7312   Janson, H. W. *Apes and Ape Lore in the Middle Ages and the Renaissance*. Studies Warburg
        Inst., XX. Ed. H. Frankfort. London: Warburg Inst., 1952. Pp. 384; 57 pl.
            Rev: by W. S. Heckscher, *RN*, V (1952), 12-13; by Conway Zirkle, *Isis*, XLIV (1953), 79-80;
        by André Chastel, *Critique*, No. 75-76, Aug.-Sept., 1953, pp. 803-807.

B7313 Baldwin Peter, Brother, F. S. C. "*Hamlet* and *In Paradisum*." *SQ*, III (1952), 279-280.
Finds a similarity between the antiphon *In Paradisum* in the Roman Catholic services for the dead, and Horatio's lines in *Hamlet*, V. ii. 370-371.

B7314 Baldwin Peter, Brother, F. S. C. "*Hamlet* and *In Paradisum*." *SQ*, IV (1953), 209.
Corrects a statement in B7313.

B7315 Quinlan, Maurice J. "Shakespeare and the Catholic Burial Services." *SQ*, V (1954), 302-306.

B7316 Davenport, A. "Shakespeare and Nashe's *Pierce Penilesse*." *N &Q*, 198 (1953), 371-374.

B7317 Ratliff, John D. *The Kydian Revenge Play*. DD, Stanford University, 1955. Pp. 465. Mic A54-3472. *DA*, XIV (1954), 2338. Publ. No. 10,386.

B7318 Lambin, G. "Une Première Ebauche d'*Hamlet* (Mars, 1587)." *LanM*, XLIX (1955), 229-237.
Suggests that John Gordon's "Mânes d'Henri" addressed in 1587 to James VI, upon the execution of the queen, directly influ. Shak.'s *Hamlet* in his treatment of Gertrude.

B7319 McGlinchee, Claire. "Still Harping. . ." *SQ*, VI (1955), 362-364.
Suggests another likely source for Polonius' "precepts" speech in the advice given by Elder Knowell to his nephew Stephen in Jonson's *Every Man in His Humour*. (Act I, scene i), a play of whose cast Shak. was once a member.

B7320 Potts, Abbie Findlay. "Hamlet and Gloriana's Knights." *SQ*, VI (1955), 31-43.
The *Faerie Queene* is found useful in supplying "commentary on ethics and dramatic cruces" in Q_2 *Ham*. Parallels in situation, vocabulary, and imagery are noted.

B7321 Dwyer, J. J. "Did Shakespeare Read Dante?" *Tablet*, 206 (July 9, 1955), 33-34.

B7322 Semper, Msgr. I. J. "On the Dignity of Man." *Month*, 199 (1955), 292-301.
Hamlet's great lines on the dignity of man viewed as an ordered, phrase-by-phrase presentation of medieval Thomistic philosophy.

B7323 Muir, Kenneth. "Henry Swinburne and Shakespeare." *N &Q*, NS, IV (1957), 285-286.
Echoes in *Ham*. of Swinburne's *Briefe Treatise of Testaments and Last Willes*.

B7324 Turner, Paul. "True Madness: A Note on *Hamlet*, II. ii. 92-95." *N &Q*, NS, IV (1957), 194-196.
The lines in *Hamlet* may allude to a passage in Horace's third satire, book II, 83-94.

B7325 Potts, Abbie Findlay. *Shakespeare and "The Faerie Queene."* Cornell Univ. Press, 1958.
Pp. xii, 269.
Rev: A4819.

iii. Extra-literary Influences

B7326 Draper, John W. "King James and Shakespeare's Literary Style." *Archiv*, 171 (1937), 36-48.

B7327 Williams, Gwyn. "Correspondence." *RES*, XXI (1945), 147.

B7328 Bergsøe, Paul. *Den Virkelige Hamlet og Shakespeare*. Copenhagen: Sølling, 1949. Pp. 14.

B7328a Bergsøe, Paul. *The Real Hamlet, Shakespeare and Elsinore*. Copenhagen: Turistforeningen, 1950. Pp. 32.

B7329 LeComte, Edward S. "The Ending of *Hamlet* as a Farewell to Essex." *ELH*, XVII (1950), 87-114.

B7330 Savage, D. S. *Hamlet and the Pirates*. London: Eyre and Spottiswoode, 1950.
Rev: A2768.

B7331 Chwalewik, Witold. "Polska w Hamlecie." *Sprawozdania z czynności i posiedzań polskiej akademii umiejetności*, LII (1951), 313-316.
"Poland in *Hamlet*." See B7337.

B7332 Bowers, Fredson. "The Pictures in *Hamlet*, III. iv: A Possible Contemporary Reference." *SQ*, III (1952), 280-281.
Suggests that a scene in Dekker's *Satiromastix* comically alludes to the comparison of pictures in *Hamlet*, III. iv. 53 ff.

B7333 Rubow, Paul V. *Hamlet og Boghandlerne*. Det kongelige danske Videnskabernes Selskab. Historisk-filologiske Meddelelser, Vol. 32, No. 7. Copenhagen: Munksgaard, 1952. Pp. 14.

B7334 Hoepfner, Theodore C. "Hamlet and the Polonian Ambassador." *N &Q*, 198 (1953), 426.
Calls attention to Queen Elizabeth's answer to the Polish Ambassador, July 25, 1597, and its possible bearing upon *Hamlet*.

B7335 Lythe, S. G. E. "The Locale of *Hamlet*." *N &Q*, NS, I (1954), 111-112.

B7336 Chwalewik, Witold. "Z Motywów Polskich w *Hamlecie*." *Kwartalnik Neofilologiczny* (Warsaw), II (1955), 47-54.
On Polish motifs in *Hamlet*.

B7337 Chwalewik, Witold. *Polska W "Hamlecie."* Breslau: 1956. Pp. 121.
See B7331.
Rev: by Friedrich Kulleschitz, *SJ*, 94 (1958), 305-309.

B7338 Montgomerie, William. "Folk-Play and Ritual in *Hamlet*." *Folklore*, LXVII (1956), 214-227.

(3) USE OF LANGUAGE

B7339   Becker, Adolf. *Metrisch-textkritische Untersuchungen zu Shakespeares "Hamlet."* DD, Tübingen, 1920. Pp. xii, 78. Typewritten.

B7340   Sorensen, Frederick C. *Metre and Rhythm in English Prosody.* DD, Stanford University, 1938. Abstract publ. in *Abstracts of Dissertations*, Stanford Univ., XIII (1937-38), 50-51. His findings applied to first 2 scenes of *Hamlet.*

B7341   Groom, Bernard. "The Varieties of Style in *Hamlet.*" *Essays and Studies by Members of the English Association*, XXIV. Oxford: Clarendon Press, 1939, pp. 42-63.
        Rev: by Alb. Eichler, *Beiblatt*, LI (1940), 36.

B7342   Mahood, M. M. *Shakespeare's Word Play.* London: Methuen, 1956. Pp. 192. Chapter on *Ham.*
        Rev: A5815.

B7343   Armstrong, William A. "The Imagery of Hamlet." *Mitteilungsblatt d. Allg. Dt. Neuphilologenverbandes* (Berlin), X (1957), 70-73.

B7344   Donoghue, Denis. "Shakespeare's Rhetoric." *Studies, Irish Quarterly Review*, XLVII (1958), 431-440.

CRITICISM OF THE WHOLE PLAY (230;82)
(a) GENERAL

B7345   Symons, N. J. "Graveyard Scene in *Hamlet.*" *International Journal of Psycho-Analysis*, London, IX (1928), 96-119.

B7346   Chapman, J. A. *Hamlet.* Papers on Shakespeare, 1. Oxford Univ. Press, 1932. Pp. 39.
        Rev: *TLS*, Aug. 17, 1933, p. 551; *N &Q*, Jan. 21, p. 37; by L. Borinski, *Beiblatt*, XLIV (Apr.), 107-108; by H. N. Hillebrand, *MLN*, LI (1936), 458-463.

B7347   Brock, J. H. E. *The Dramatic Purpose of "Hamlet."* Cambridge: W. Heffer & Sons, 1935. Pp. viii, 48.

B7348   Conroy, J. P. "Shakespeare's Difficulty in Opening *Hamlet.*" *Catholic World*, 142 (1935), 192-196.

B7349   Heyse, Hans. *Idee und Existenz.* Hamburg: Hans. Verl. Anst., 1935. Pp. 363.
        Rev: by Herm. Pongs, *DuV*, XXXVII (1936), 389-390.

B7350   Schücking, L. L. *Der Sinn des "Hamlet." Kunstwerk—Handlung—Überlieferung.* Leipzig: Quelle & Meyer, 1936. Pp. viii, 132.
        Rev: by J. Speck, *Archiv*, 169 (1936), 99-100; by H. Pongs, *DuV*, XXXVII, 385-387; by W. Fischer, *Beiblatt*, XLVII, 103-105; by A. J. A. Waldock, *MLR*, XXXI, 567-568; by L. Stettner, *Neue Jahrbücher für Wissenschaft und Jugendbildung*, XII, 375; by H. C. Matthes, *Lbl*, LVII, 246-249; by T. Brooke, *JEGP*, XXXV, 149-150; by Frdr. Knorr, *DNL*, XXXVII, 536-538; by Aug. Kollmann, *DL*, XXXVIII (1935/36), 40; by J. B. Leishman, *RES*, XIII (1937), 91-92; *TAr*, XXI, 906-907; by O. Boerner, *NS*, XLV, 94-96; by R. A. Law, *MLN*, LII, 527; by Georges Connes, *RAA*, XIII, 434-435; by A. Koszul, *ES*, XX (1938), 127-129; by Albert Eichler, *Eng. Studn.*, LXXV (1941), 241-248.

B7351   Schücking, L. L. *The Meaning of "Hamlet."* Tr. of B7350 by Graham Rawson. Oxford Univ. Press, 1937. Pp. ix, 195.
        Rev: *TLS*, Sept. 11, 1937, p. 652; by Ronald Lewin, *NstN*, NS, XIV, 496-498; by W. J. Lawrence, *Spectator*, Sept. 24, pp. 514, 516; by E. H. W. Meyerstein, *London Mercury*, XXXVI, 581-582; *TAr*, XXI, 906-907; by P. Alexander, *RES*, XIV (1938), 339-341; by L. C. Knights, *Criterion*, XVII, 365-367; by A. Koszul, *ES*, XX, 128; by E. E. Stoll, *SJ*, LXXIV, 77-81; by Benjamin T. Spencer, *SR*, XLVII (1939), 119-129; by M. E. Prior, *MP*, XXXVIII (1940), 106-108.

B7352   Wilson, J. Dover. *What Happens in "Hamlet".* Cambridge Univ. Press, 1935. Second ed. Cambridge Univ. Press, 1937. Pp. xx, 342. Cambridge Univ. Press, 1951. Pp. xxii, 357.
        Rev: by R. Travers, *RAA*, XIII (1936), 241-243; by L. C. Knights, *Criterion*, XV, 529-532; by George Cookson, *English* I, 161-163; by R. W. Babcock, *SAB*, XI, 175-183; (see note Samuel A. Tannenbaum, ibid., XI, 185-187); by James Southall Wilson, *VQR*, XII, 636-640; by Wolfgang Keller, *SJ*, LXXII, 145-147; by E. Voris, *Silver Falcon* (New York: Hunter College) Dec., pp. 9-12; by Paul V. Rubow, *Tilskueren*, May, pp. 360-367; by L. L. Schücking, *Beiblatt*, XLVII, 141-144; by E. C. Dunn, *Atlantic Monthly*, May, "Bookshelf," p. 157; by P. M. Jack, *NYTBR*, Feb. 2, pp. 2, 24; by W. W. Greg, *MLR*, XXXI, 145-154; by Paul de Réal, *RUnBrux*, XLII (1936/37), 270-281; by T. M. Parrott, *MLN*, LII (1937), 382-386; by Paul Dottin, *Rev. de France*, I, 324-325; by Johannes Speck, *Archiv*, 171 (1937), 85-86; by W. Fischer, *DLZ*, LVIII, 786-788; by R. S. Knox, *UTQ*, VII (1938), 249-261; by Koszul, *ES*, XX, 127-128; by E. E. Stoll, *SJ*, LXXIV, 66-73; by Harold Child, *Essays and Reflections* (London), 1948, pp. 73-83; by G. Baldini, *Belfagor*, III, 49-50; by H. Heuer, *SJ*, 89 (1953), 233-234; by J. G. Weightman, *TS*, 154 (1953), 302-310.

B7353   Granville-Barker, Harley. "The Casting of *Hamlet.* A Fragment." *London Mercury*, XXXV (1936), 10-17.

B7354   Granville-Barker, Harley. *Prefaces to Shakespeare.* Series III (*Hamlet*). London: Sidgwick and Jackson, 1936. Pp. 339. Dramabooks Series. New York: Hill and Wang, 1957. Pp. 284. Included in B7354a.

Rev: by W. J. Lawrence, *Spectator*, Jan. 8, 1937, p. 56; *TLS*, Jan. 9, p. 25; by E. Martin Browne, *Criterion*, XVI, 735-739; by Robert M. Smith, *SAB*, XII, 159-172; by R. W. Babcock, ibid., XII, 173-179; by Georges Connes, *EA*, I, 330; by R. A. Scott-James, *London Mercury*, XXXV, 331-332; by Rosamond Gilder, *TAr*, XXI, 488-489; by W. Keller, *SJ*, LXXIII, 163-165; by O. Williams, *National Review*, 108 (1937), 386-394; by A. Koszul, *ES*, XX (1938), 129; by E. E. Stoll, *SJ*, LXXIV, 73-77; by R. S. Knox, *UTQ*, VII, 249-261; *ShN*, VII (1957), 22.

B7354a Granville-Barker, Harley. *Prefaces to Shakespeare*. 2 Vols. Princeton Univ. Press, 1946, 1947. Collection includes *Hamlet*.
Rev: A8201.

B7355 Lawrence, W. J. "Still Another *Hamlet* Problem." *Spectator*, Aug. 7, 1936, p. 243.

B7356 Pongs, H. "Shakespeare und das Politische Drama." *DuV*, XXXVII, No. 3 (1936), 257-280.

B7357 Price, H. T. "What Really Happened in *Hamlet*." *Contemporary* (Ann Arbor), 1936, pp. 6-7.

B7358 Strübe. "Über Hamlet." *Köln. Ztg.*, No. 546/547 (1936).

B7359 "The Triumph of Hamlet. Mr. Murry on the Shakespeare Man." *TLS*, Feb. 8, 1936, pp. 101-102.

B7360 Cancelled.

B7361 Cazamian, Louis. "Humour in *Hamlet*." *Rice Institute Pamphlet*, XXIV (1937), 214-228. Republished in *Essais en Deux Langues*, 1938.

B7362 Draper, John W. " 'My Switzers'." *MLR*, XXXII (1937), 585-588.

B7363 Fitzgerald, Gerald. *Shakespeare's "Hamlet": A Commentary*. MA thesis, Saint Joseph (Canada), 1937. Pp. 60.

B7364 Priess, M. "Das Hamlet-Problem." *Eng. Studn.*, LXXII (1937), 14-48.
Rev: by Th. Zeiger, *NS*, XLVI (1938), 34-35.

B7365 Weigelin, E. "Eine neue Hamleterklärung." *NS*, XLVI (1938), 353-355.
On B7364.

B7366 Raven, Anton A. "There Are More Things, Horatio." *SAB*, XII (1937), 236-245.

B7367 Wales, Julia Grace. "A Suggestion for a History of Shakespearean Criticism by Plays." *Trans. of the Wisconsin Acad. of Sciences, Arts, and Letters*, XXX (1937), 313-315.

B7368 Coles, Blanche. *Shakespeare Studies: "Hamlet".* New York: Smith, 1938. Pp. xii, 298.
Rev: by G. C. Taylor, *MLN*, LIV (1939), 233.

B7369 Gardner, Helen L. "Lawful Espials." *MLR*, XXXIII (1938), 345-355.
Overhearing in Shakespeare's plays with special reference to the Nunnery scene.

B7370 Gillard, Claire. *"Hamlet," A Study in Critical Method*. Thèse de la Licence, Univ. de Liège, 1938/39.

B7371 Heyn, W. *Hamlet, ich rufe dich: Die Losung des Hamlet-Problems*. Berlin: Deut. Verlagsgesellschaft, 1938. Pp. 151.
Rev: by W. Keller, *SJ*, LXXIV (1938), 184-185; by Wolfgang Keller, *ZNU*, XXXVII, 199-200; by Ernst Weigelin, *Beiblatt*, L (1939), 99-101; by Ernst Weigelin, *DDHS*, VI, 38; by C. F. W. Behl, *DL*, XLI (1938/39), 375-376; by H. Rüdiger, *Das Gymnasium*, L, 71.

B7372 Klein, Magdalene. "Shakespeares *Hamlet*." *NS*, XLVI (1938), 261-280.
Many past critics discussed.

B7373 Knox, R. S. "Shakespeare: A Diversity of Doctrine." *UTQ*, VII (1938), 249-261.
Discussion of recent attitudes, particularly of Wilson, Granville-Barker, and Murry.

B7374 Lawrence, W. J. "The Poisoned Chalice." *London Mercury*, XXXVII (1938), 527-531.
See letter by H. Granville-Barker, *London Mercury*, XXXVII (1938), 633.

B7375 Plowman, Max. "Some Values in *Hamlet*." *New Adelphi*, XIV (1938), 21-26, 76-83, 124-129. Also published in Max Plowman's *The Right to Live*, Intro. J. Middleton Murry. London: Dakers, 1942, pp. 131-163.

B7376 Adler, Alfred. *Social Interest: A Challenge to Mankind*. Tr. Linton and Vaughan. New York: Putnam, 1939.
Hamlet note pp. 106-107.

B7377 Bonjour, Adrien. "On Artistic Unity in *Hamlet*." *ES*, XXI (1939), 193-202.

B7378 Garde, Axel. "Hamlet i Generationernes Spejl Saerlig den Religiøse Hamlet." *Tilskueren* (Copenhagen), L, No. 1 (1939), 138-159.

B7378a Garde, Axel. *Hamlet i Generationernes Spejl. Et Essay*. Copenhagen: Gyldendal, 1946. Pp. 52.

B7379 Humphreys, Chad Noel Milliner. *Studies in "Hamlet".* MA thesis, Dalhousie, 1939. Pp. 178.

B7380 Knight, G. Wilson. *The Imperial Theme*. Further Interpretation of Shakespeare's Tragedies Including the Roman Plays. Oxford Univ. Press, 1939. Pp. 376.
Rev: A8258.

B7381 Künstler, G. A. "Der Dramatische Aufbau von Shakespeares *Hamlet*." *Z. f. Ästhetik u. allgem. Kunstwissensch.*, XXXII (1939), 46-86.

B7382 Morgan, Roberta. "The Philosophic Basis of Coleridge's *Hamlet* Criticism." *ELH*, VI (1939), 256-270.

B7383 Rubow, Paul V. "Hvad man mener om Hamlet." *Scrap Book*, 1939, pp. 121-131.

B7384 Glunz, H. H. *Der "Hamlet" Shakespeares*. Frankfurt a. M.: Vittorio Klostermann, 1940. Pp. 68.
Rev: by W. Fischer, *Beiblatt*, LI (1940), 84-85; see H. H. Glunz, "Der *Hamlet* Shakespeares." *FuF*, XVI, 335-357; by W. Kalthoff, *GA*, VII, 5; by R. W. Zandvoort, *ES*, XXII, Heft 4; by Wolfgang Keller, *SJ*, LXXVI, 209-211; by H. C. Matthes, *Archiv*, 180 (1941), 52-53; by Hans Marcus, *DLZ*, LXII, 212; by Paul Meissner, *GRM*, XXIX, 74; by Albert Eichler, *Eng. Studn.*, LXXV (1942), 243-248; by Ed. Eckhardt, *Lbl*, LXIII, 26-27.

B7385 Kirschbaum, Leo. "The Sequence of Scenes in *Hamlet*." *MLN*, LV (1940), 382-387.

B7386 Morozov, M. "Shakespeare's *Hamlet*." *The Young Guard* (USSR), 1940, pp. 5-6, 251-253.

B7387 Morozov, M. "Notes on *Hamlet*." *Theatre* (USSR), IV (1940), 45-52.

B7388 Doran, Madeleine. "That Undiscovered Country. A Problem Concerning the Use of the Supernatural in *Hamlet* and *Macbeth*." In *Renaissance Studies in Honor of Hardin Craig*. Stanford Univ. Press, 1941, pp. 221-235; also *PQ*, XX, 413-427.

B7389 Schücking, Levin L. "Die Kindertruppenstelle im *Hamlet*." *Archiv*, 179 (1940), 8-14.

B7390 Hankins, John Erskine. *The Character of Hamlet and Other Essays*. Univ. of North Carolina Press, 1941. Pp. xii, 264.
Rev: B7664.

B7391 Mathesius, V. "Shakespearův *Hamlet*." *Věda a Život*, VIII (1941), 11-18.
Shak.'s *Hamlet*: A Review of Problems in the Play.

B7392 Rubow, P. V. "Nyt om Hamlet." *Tilskueren* (Copenhagen), LIII, No. 1 (1941), 360-367.

B7393 Charlton, H. B. "*Hamlet*." *BJRL*, XXVI (1942), 265-286.
Based on a lecture given as the Spence Watson Memorial Lecture before the Newcastle-on-Tyne Literary and Philosophical Society, March 23, 1942.
See editorial note, *BJRL*, XXVI (1942), 240-241.

B7394 Niederstenbruch, A. "Einige Gedanken zur rassischen Betrachtung von Shakespeares *Hamlet*." *ZNU*, XLI (1942), 31-33.

B7395 Wales, Julia Grace. "Horatio's Commentary: A Study in the Warp and Woof of *Hamlet*." *SAB*, XVII (1942), 40-56.

B7396 Davis, Joe L. "Something of What Happens in *Hamlet*." *UTQ*, XII (1943), 426-434.
Views Hamlet as the cursed instrument of heaven in punishing regicide.

B7397 Shoemaker, F. "*Hamlet* Exemplifies the Modern Aesthetic Approach to World Literature." In *Aesthetic Experience and the Humanities*, New York: Columbia Univ. Press, 1943, pp. 192-227.
Rev: A8362.

B7398 Webster, M., S. Barr, M. Van Doren. "*Hamlet*." In *The New Invitation to Learning*, New York, 1942, pp. 44-58.

B7399 Barfield, Owen. "The Form of *Hamlet*." In *Romanticism Comes of Age*. London: Anthroposophical Soc., 1944, pp. 85-103.
On the "consciousness soul" in *Hamlet*.

B7400 Fairchild, Arthur H. R. *Shakespeare and the Tragic Theme*. Univ. Missouri Studies, XIX, No. 2. Univ. Missouri Press, 1944. Pp. 145.
Rev: A6853.

B7401 Lawrence, William Witherle. "Hamlet's Sea Voyage." *PMLA*, LIX (1944), 45-70.

B7402 Parrott, T. M. "Hamlet's Sea Voyage—Bandits or Pirates? A Reply to Professor Lawrence." *SAB*, XIX (1944), 51-59.
See B7401.

B7403 Stoll, Elmer Edgar. "Mainly Controversy: *Hamlet, Othello*." *PQ*, XXIV (1945), 289-316.
Partly on B7401.

B7404 Abe, Tomoji. "*Hamlet*." *World Literature* (Japan), No. 1, 1946.

B7405 Bøgholm, N. "The *Hamlet* Drama." *Orbis*, IV (1946), 157-228.

B7406 Craig, G. "Propos sur *Hamlet*." *Arts et Lettres*, 1946, pp. 210-217.

B7407 Orsini, Napoleone. "Amleto e l'Arte Drammatica." *Letteratura*, VIII (Jan.-Feb., 1946), 94-104.

B7408 Prym-von Becherer, Gisela. *Das Weltbild der Shakespearezeit mit besonderer Berücksichtigung von Shakespeares "Hamlet"*. DD, Marburg, 1946. Pp. xviii, 159, 8. Typewritten.

B7409 Ashe, Geoffrey. "Hamlet and Pyrrhus." *N &Q*, 192 (1947), 214-215.
Calls attention to the parallel between Pyrrhus and Hamlet, both seeking vengeance for the killing of their fathers.

B7410 Berry, Francis. "Young Fortinbras." *Life and Letters*, LII (1947), 94-103.
Fortinbras is foil to Hamlet; action in background and paralysis in foreground; both meet in Plain of Denmark Scene.

B7411 Beta Lambda. "Hamlet Miscellany." *Shakespeare Quarterly* (London), I (1947), 50-75.

B7412 Flint, Robert W. "The Tragedy of Hamlet." *Union Seminary Quarterly Review*, II, iii (1947), 20-25.
Suggests much scepticism in the times and in Shak. Discusses philos. views and religions. Declares the tragedies non-Christian.

B7413   Jaspers, Karl. *Von der Wahrheit.* Munich: Piper, 1947. Pp. xxiii, 1102.

B7414   Lawrence, William W. "Ophelia's Heritage." *MLR*, XLII (1947), 409-416.
Features in the earlier treatments of Ophelia (and the Elizabethan attitude towards madness) which help to explain her part in *Hamlet.*

B7415   McClure, Charles R. *Devices in English Plays of 1600-1607, with Particular Reference to "Hamlet."* DD, Indiana University, 1947.

B7416   McHugh, R. " 'Too Immoral for Any Stage'." *The Bell*, XV (Nov., 1947), 60-63.

B7417   Maugeri, Aldo. *Amleto, Studio Critico.* Messina: V. Ferrara Editore, 1947. Pp. 150.

B7418   Pons, C. "*Hamlet*: Introduction." *CS*, LXVIII (1947), 435-439.

B7419   Atthill, R. "*Hamlet.*" *The Wind and The Rain*, IV (1948), 240.

B7420   Bischoff, Dietrich. "*Hamlet.*" *Sammlung*, III (1948), 332-344.

B7421   Mueller, Gustav E. *Philosophy of Literature.* New York: Philosophical Soc., 1948. Pp. 226.
Rev: by V. B. Rhodenezert, *Dalhousie Rev.*, XXIX (1949), 210; by J. W. R. Purser, *MLR*, XLIV, 404-405.

B7422   Muir, Kenneth. "Portents in *Hamlet.*" *N &Q*, 193 (1948), 54-55.

B7423   González Ruiz, N. "Dos Ensayos Sobre Las Tragedias de Shakespeare." *Arbor* (Madrid), X (1948), 39-56.

B7424   Smelik, L. "Hamlet als Tragedie van het Recht." *Wending*, III (1948), 538-543.

B7425   Sullivan, Frank. "Hamlet's Hebona and Mercury Poisoning." *Los Angeles Tidings*, Dec. 31, 1948, p. 9.
Hydrargyrum, called mercury, was administered by ear as a poison.

B7426   Verkoren, L. "Iets over vorm en inhoud van Shakespeares Hamlet." *Neophil*, XXXI (1947), 69-75.

B7427   Bergsøe, P. *Den Virkelige Hamlet og Shakespeare.* Copenhagen, 1949. Pp. 15.

B7428   Flatter, Richard. *Hamlet's Father.* New Haven: Yale Univ. Press, 1949. Pp. viii, 206.
A study of many points in the play.
Rev: *TLS*, Sept. 9, 1949, p. 586; by John Whale, *Spectator*, Sept. 9, p. 336; by Nevill Coghill, ibid., Oct. 7, p. 464; *Dublin Mag.*, XXIV, 4, 39-40; by H. B. Charlton, *MGW*, Aug. 18, p. 12; by I. Ribner, *QJS*, XXXVI (1950), 422-423; by H. Smith, *YR*, XXXIX, 743-746; by E. E. Stoll, *SQ*, I, 36-43; by J. S. Wilson, *VQR*, XXVI, 318; by D. Bush, *NR*, April 24, 1950, p. 22; by Robert Halsband, *SRL*, Jan. 7, p. 18; by R. Lalou, *LanM*, XLIV, 121; by Hermann Heuer, *SJ*, 84/86 (1951), 256-257; by W. Clemen, *Archiv*, 189 (1952/53), 226; by H. Lüdeke, *ES*, XXXIV (1953), 38-40.

B7429   Graves, Robert. *The Common Asphodel: Collected Essays on Poetry, 1922-1949.* London: Hamish Hamilton, 1949. Pp. xii, 335.
Contains essay on *Hamlet.*
Rev: B4471.

B7430   Gregory, T. S. "I Hold You up a Glass." *Listener*, XLII, July 7, 1949, 19-21. W. Bliss, Raymond Chapman, A. R. Cripps, ibid., pp. 72-73; T. S. Gregory, ibid., pp. 109; W. Bliss and A. Gunner, ibid., p. 151.

B7431   Grün, Herbert. "Hamlet. Spočetje evropskega Individualizma" [Hamlet. The Beginning of European Individualism]. *Mladinska revija* (Ljubljana), V Nos. 3, 4-5 (1949), 131-134, 180-183.
Hamlet and *Sonnets* the keys to an understanding of Shak.

B7432   Hogrefe, Pearl. "Artistic Unity in *Hamlet.*" *SP*, XLVI (1949), 184-195.
Emphasizes III. iv.

B7433   Holmberg, A. Olle. *Inte Bara om Hamlet. Essäer.* Stockholm: Bonnier, 1949. Pp. 203.
Rev: by M. Gravier, *Etudes Germaniques*, VI (1951), 149.

B7434   Hondo, Masao. "A Study of *Hamlet.*" *The Literature* (Japan), No. 1, 1949.

B7435   Kindt, K. *Der Spieler Gottes, Shakespeares Hamlet als Christliches Welttheater.* Berlin-Spandau: Wichern Verlag, 1949. Pp. 153.
Rev: by W. Knevels, *TLZ*, LXXVI (1951), 114-116; by H. Heuer, *SJ*, 89 (1953), 234-235.

B7436   Langenfelt, Gösta. "The Geographical Position of Dansk(e), Danskin, Danskyn." *Studier i Modern Språkvetenskap*, XVII (1949), 62-70.

B7437   Macht, David I. "A Physiological and Pharmacological Appreciation of *Hamlet*, Act I, Scene 5, Lines 59-73." *Bul. Hist. Med.*, XXIII (1949), 186-194.
Notes that the drugs which come under consideration in connection with *hebenon* or *hebona* produce "marked shortening of coagulation time."

B7438   Penasco, S. A. "El Sentido de lo Trágico en *Hamlet.*" *Escritura* (Montevideo), III (1949), 104-122.

B7439   Smith, Robert M. "Current Fashions in *Hamlet* Criticism." *SAB*, XXIV (1949), 13-21.
See also the author's "Productions of *Hamlet*, 1930 to the Present," ibid., XXIV, 71-72.

B7439a   Stoll, Elmer Edgar. "A Spanish Hamlet." *MP*, XLVII (1949), 12-23.
A criticism of *Hamlet* criticism, with particular reference to B7697. See also B7439.

B7440 Tillyard, Eustace M. W. *Shakespeare's Problem Plays*. Univ. of Toronto Press, 1949; London:
Chatto & Windus, 1949. Pp. ix, 168.
Rev: B5222.

B7441 Connolly, Thomas F. "Shakespeare and the Double Man." *SQ*, I (1950), 30-35.

B7442 Cunningham, J. V. " 'Tragedy' in Shakespeare." *ELH*, XVII (1950), 36-46.

B7443 Eliot, Thomas Stearns. "*Hamlet*." In Eliot's *Ausgewählte Essays* (A8171), 1950, pp. 177-186.

B7444 Haydn, Hiram. *The Counter-Renaissance*. New York: Charles Scribner's Sons, 1950. Pp.
xvii, 705. *Hamlet* and *Lear*, pp. 619-671.
Rev: A3836.

B7445 Huhner, Max. *Shakespeare's Hamlet*. New York: Farrar, Straus; Toronto: Clarke, Irwin,
1950. Pp. xi, 163.
Rev: by Esther Cloudman Dunn, *NYTBR*, Aug. 13, 1950, p. 24; by Robert Halsband,
SRL, July 8, p. 17; by Albert H. Carter, *SQ*, II (1951), 139.

B7446 Jack A. A. *Young Hamlet: A Conjectural Resolution of Some of the Difficulties in the Plotting of
Shakespeare's Play*. Aberdeen Univ. Press, 1950. Pp. 176.
Rev: *TLS*, June 30, 1950, p. 410; by B. I. Evans, *MGW*, June 29, p. 12; *DUJ*, XII, 28-29;
by R. Walker, *English*, VIII, 144.

B7447 Meyers, Walter L. "Shakespeare's *Hamlet*." *Expl.*, IX, No. 2 (Nov. 1950).

B7448 Nakanishi, Shintaro. *An Introduction to Hamlet*. Tokyo: Kenkyusha, 1950. Pp. 226.

B7449 Smidt, Kristian. "Notes on *Hamlet*." *ES*, XXXI (1950), 136-141.
Comments on the Pyrrhus speech, Hamlet's interview with Ophelia, and the "suicide soliloquy."

B7450 Baiwir, Albert. "On *Hamlet* Again." *Revue des Langues Vivantes*, XVII (1951), 207ff.

B7451 Eliot, T. S. *Poetry and Drama*. Cambridge: Harvard Univ. Press, 1951. Pp. 44.
Contains numerous comments on Shak., including an analysis of the opening scene of *Ham*.
Rev: A5423.

B7452 Elliott, G. R. *Scourge and Minister: A Study of Hamlet as Tragedy of Revengefulness and Justice*.
Durham, North Carolina: Duke Univ. Press, Cambridge Univ. Press, 1951. Pp. xxxvi, 208.
Rev: by Harry Levin, *SQ*, II (1951), 259-260; *TLS*, Aug. 31, p. 550; by Henry Popkin,
TAr, May, p. 4; by A. P. Rossiter, *English*, IX (1952/53), 84; by R. A. Law, *SQ*, III (1952), 84.

B7453 James, D. G. *The Dream of Learning: An Essay on "The Advancement of Learning," "Hamlet"
and "King Lear."* Oxford: Clarendon Press, 1951. Pp. 126.
Rev: A3959.

B7454 Kalidasu, M. "*Hamlet*: A Tragedy of Environment." *Triveni* (Masulipatnam, India),
Oct., 1947.

B7455 Kulkarni, N. M. *Hamlet*. Introduction, Notes and Explanations. Allahabad: Students'
Friends, 1951. Text and full length study in English.

B7456 Nakanishi, Shintaro. "The Opening Scene of *Hamlet*." *The Rising Generation*, 97 (1951),
149-151.

B7457 Oppel, Horst. "Die Zeitgestaltung im *Hamlet*." *Jahrbuch für Aesthetik und Allgemeine
Kunstwissenschaft*. Ed. by Prof. Dr. H. Lützeler (Stuttgart), 1951, pp. 145-160.
Rev: by H. Heuer, *SJ*, 87/88 (1952), 259.

B7458 Paterson, John. "The Word in *Hamlet*." *SQ*, II (1951), 47-55.

B7459 Petančić, M. "Hamlet. William Shakespeare." *Program Narodnog Kazališta*, Osijek, 1951.
Pp. 15.

B7460 Rubow, Paul V. "Shakespeares Hamlet. Kritiske og Historiske Bidrag." In *Festschrift udg.
af Kôbenhavns Universitet i anledning af H. M. Kongens fødelsdag 11. marts 1951*. Copenhagen:
Univ., 1951. Pp. 80.

B7461 Waldock, A. J. A. *Sophocles the Dramatist*. Cambridge Univ. Press, 1951. Pp. x, 228.
Discusses some problems of Shakespearian criticism, and comments on *Hamlet*, *Macbeth*, and
Romeo and Juliet.
Rev: A8427.

B7462 Belinskij, Vissarion Grigorević. *Hamlet. Deutung und Darstellung*. Tr. by Albert Kloeckner.
Berlin: Henschel, 1952. Pp. 188.

B7462a Belinskij, Vissarion Grigorević. *Studija o Hamletu*. Tr. into Serbo-Croatian by Tankosava
Kašiković. Belgrade: Prosveta, 1953. Pp. 168.

B7463 Cazamian, Louis. *The Development of English Humor*. Duke Univ. Press, 1952. Pp. viii, 421.
Includes a long section on Shak.'s humor, divided into numerous parts.
Rev: B5186.

B7464 Craig, Hardin. "A Cutpurse of the Empire: On Shakespeare Cosmology." *A Tribute to
George Coffin Taylor*, Univ. North Carolina Press, 1952, pp. 3-16.

B7465 Frye, Roland Mushat. *The Accepted Ethics and Theology of Shakespeare's Audience as Utilized
by the Dramatist in Certain Representative Tragedies, with Particular Attention to Love and Marriage*. DD, Princeton University, 1952. Pp. 372. Mic A55-745. *DA*, XV, (1955), 581.
Publ. No. 10,901.
Rev: A2563.

B7466   Huhner, Max. *Shakespearean Studies and Other Essays.* With an Introd. by George S. Hellman. New York: Farrar Straus, 1952. Pp. 115.
"Polonius' Advice to Laertes," pp. 30-37; "Hamlet in Modern Dress," pp. 38-41.

B7467   Kubiak, Zygmunt. "Hamlet Czyli o Wielkościkultury." *Tygodnik Powszechny,* 1952, No. 19, pp. 1-2. See also ibid., Józef Marian Swiecicki. "Dwie Interpretacje," No. 24, pp. 4, 11; Maria Morstin-Górska. "Kryteria Moralności. Na. Marginesie Hamleta," No. 25, pp. 3-4.

B7468   Kurtze, Max. "Kritisches zur Bühnenanweisung im *Hamlet:* 'Lifts up the Arras and Discovers Polonius' (Akt III Szene IV)." *SJ,* 87/88 (1952), 43-47.

B7469   McCullen, J. T., Jr. "The Functions of Songs Aroused by Madness in Elizabethan Drama." In *A Tribute to George Coffin Taylor.* Ed. by Arnold Williams, 1952.

B7470   Röhrman, H. *Marlowe and Shakespeare: A Thematic Exposition of Some of Their Plays.* Arnhem: van Loghum Slaterus. Pp. x, 109.
Rev: A1023.

B7471   Schoff, Francis G. *Aspects of Shakespearean Criticism, 1914-1950: A Commentary Centered on British and American Criticism of Hamlet.* DD, University of Minnesota, 1952. Pp. 504. Mic A53-430. *DA,* XIII (1953), 230. Publ. No. 4877.

B7472   Schröder, Rudolf Alexander. "Shakespeares *Hamlet.*" *Dt. Beiträge,* II (1948), 14-33. Also published in Schröder: *Gesammelte Werke,* Vol. II, 1952, pp. 280-307.
Rev: by H. Heuer, *SJ,* 87/88 (1952), 261-262.

B7473   Stirling, Brents. "Theme and Character in *Hamlet.*" *MLQ,* XIII (1952), 323-332.

B7474   Swiecicki, Józef Marian. "*Hamlet*—Tragedia Zbezczeszczonych Wartości." *Przeglad Powszechny* (Warsaw), 1952, pp. 157-171.
Tragedy of desecrated valves.

B7475   Westfall, Alfred. "Why Did Shakespeare Send Hamlet to Wittenberg?" *Western Humanities Review,* VI (1952), 229-234.

B7476   Hallberg, P. "*Hamlet.*" *Edda,* LII (1952), 233-250.

B7477   Janaro, Richard Paul. "Dramatic Significance in *Hamlet.*" *Studies in Shakespeare.* Ed. by Matthews and Emery, 1953, pp. 107-115.

B7478   Jaspers, Karl. "*Hamlet.*" *Revue de Culture Européenne,* III, No. 5 (1953), 3-10.

B7479   Joseph, Bertram. *Conscience and the King: A Study of Hamlet.* London: Chatto and Windus, 1953. Pp. 175.
Rev: by H. B. Charlton, *MGW,* Sept. 24, 1953, pp. 10-11; *TLS,* Nov. 13, p. 720; by William Scawen, *Adelphi,* XXX, 86-88; by William Empson, *NstN,* Oct. 3, p. 380; by Ulick O'Connor, *Spectator,* 6543, Nov. 20, pp. 605-606; by F. S. Boas, *FortnR,* 1043 (1953), 352-353; by A. P. Rossiter, *ConR,* LXXV, 340-341; by J. Vallette, *MdF,* 319 (1953), 707-708; by Hermann Heuer, *SJ,* 90 (1954), 338-341; by Virgil K. Whitaker, *SQ,* VI (1955), 176-178; by Michel Poirier, *EA,* VIII, 258; by J. B. Fort, *EA,* VIII, 154.

B7480   Mack, Maynard. "The World of Hamlet." *YR,* XLI (1951-52), 502-523.
Also in Cleanth Brooks, *Tragic Themes in Western Literature.* New Haven: Yale Univ. Press, 1955, pp. 30-58.
Rev: by Joseph Remenyi, *Books Abroad,* XXX (1956), 91.

B7481   Paris, Jean. "Les Trois Mystères de *Hamlet.*" *Esprit,* XXI (Jan., 1953), 214-228. Comments by J. G. Weightman, "Edinburgh, Elsinore and Chelsea." *TC,* 154 (1953), 302-310.

B7482   Paris, Jean. *Hamlet ou les Personnages du Fils.* Paris: Editions du Seuil, 1953. Pp. 189.
Rev: by J. Vallette, *MdF,* 319 (1953), 708-709; by W. Empson, *NstN,* XLVI, 380; by L. Ch., *RHT,* I-II (1954), 97; by Frank Lehner, *Books Abroad,* XXVIII, 313; by T. S. Dorsch, *YWES,* XXXV, 99; by A. Koszul, *EA,* VIII (1955), 69-70; by Raymond Lenoir, *Rev. d'esthétique,* VIII, 328-331; by J. de Castro y Delgado, *Razón y Fe,* 152 (1955), 462-463.

B7483   Port, Elizabeth. *Die Motive in Shakespeares "Hamlet."* DD, Mainz, 1953. Pp. 190. Typewritten.

B7484   Cancelled.

B7485   Carrington, Norman Thomas. *Shakespeare: "Hamlet."* Notes on Chosen English Texts Series. London: Brodie, 1954. Pp. 88.

B7486   Coghill, Nevill. "Shakespeare as a Dramatist." *Talking of Shakespeare.* Ed. by John Garrett. London: Hodder & Stoughton & Max Reinhardt, 1954.

B7487   Crocker, Lester G. "*Hamlet, Don Quijote, La Vida es Sueño:* The Quest for Values." *PMLA,* LXIX (1954), 278-313.

B7488   Goodman, Paul. *The Structure of Literature.* Univ. of Chicago Press, 1954. Pp. vii, 282. Analyzes *Richard II, Hamlet, Henry IV.*
Rev: B5962.

B7489   Ornstein, Robert. *The Ethics of Jacobean Tragedy, A Study of the Influence of Renaissance Free Thought.* DD, University of Wisconsin, 1954. Abstr. published in *Summaries of Doctoral Dissertations,* 1953-54, XV. Madison: Univ. of Wisconsin Press, 1955, pp. 622-624.

B7490   Simonov, G. "Gamlet." *Ogonek* (Moscow), XXXIII (Sept., 1955), 20-21.

B7491   Stevenson, David L. "Objective Correlative for T. S. Eliot's *Hamlet.*" *JAAC,* XIII (1954), 69-79.

B7492   Williams, Raymond. *Drama in Performance*. Man and Society Series. Ed. by Lady Simon of Wythenshawe and Others. London: Frederick Muller, 1954. Pp. viii, 9-128. Chap. 4 on *Hamlet*.

B7493   Bowers, Fredson. "Hamlet as Minister and Scourge." *PMLA*, LXX (1955), 740-749.

B7494   Clair, John A. "Shakespeare's *Hamlet*, III. i. 92." *Expl.*, XIV (1955), 5.

B7495   Diekmann, Ernst. "Shakespeares *Hamlet*, Grundzüge einer Deutung." *NS*, X (1955), 456-468.

B7496   Ellison, Paul. "Reason to the Dane." *Studies in English* (Boston Univ.), I (1955), 20-37. The use of dialectic in *Hamlet*.

B7497   Marquard, N. J. "The Meaning of the Graveyard Scene in *Hamlet*." *Theoria*, VII (1955), 59-70.

B7498   Turovskaja, M. "Ešče o Gamlete." *Teatr* (Moscow), XVI, No. 9 (1955), 54-62.

B7499   Tuveson, Ernest. "Locke and the Dissolution of the Ego." *MP*, LII (1955), 159-174. Locke's influence upon *Hamlet* criticism, pp. 169-170.

B7500   Anikst, A. " 'Sein oder Nichtsein' unsres Hamlet." *Kunst und Literatur*, IV (1956), 41-60.

B7501   Byvanck, Willem Gertrud Cornelis. *Keur uit het Ongebundelde Werk*. Zwolle: Tjeenk Willink, 1956. Pp. 247. Includes a long introduction to *Hamlet* and tells how English play quartos were acquired by the Royal Library.

B7502   Condee, Ralph Waterbury. "The Pursuit of Hamlet." *ShN*, VI (1956), 10.

B7503   Flatter, Richard. "Hamlets Mutter." In Flatter's *Triumph der Gnade. Shakespeare Essays*. Vienna, Munich: Kurt Desch, 1956, pp. 84-103.

B7503a Flatter, Richard. "Die Sprache der Ophelia." In *Triumph der Gnade. Shakespeare Essays*. Vienna, Munich: Kurt Desch, 1956, p. 114.

B7503b Flatter, Richard. "Die Rede vom rauhen Pyrrhus." In Flatter's *Triumph der Gnade. Shakespeares Essays*. Vienna, Munich: Kurt Desch, 1956, pp. 115-116.

B7503c Flatter, Richard. "Einige Regiebemerkungen zu *Hamlet*." In Flatter's *Triumph der Gnade. Shakespeare Essays*, Vienna, Munich: Kurt Desch, 1956, pp. 104-113.

B7504   Foakes, R. A. "Hamlet and the Court of Elsinore." *ShS*, IX (1956), 35-43.

B7505   Jenkins, Harold. "How Many Gravediggers Has *Hamlet*?" *MLR*, LI (1956), 562-565.

B7506   Kitto, H. D. F. *Form and Meaning in Drama: A Study of Six Greek Plays and of "Hamlet"*. London: Methuen, 1956. Pp. ix, 341.
        Rev: by L. H., *Dublin Magazine*, XXXI, No. 4 (1956), 53-54; *QR*, 294 (1956), p. 528; *TLS*, Dec. 14, pp. 741-742 (comment by Roy Walker, Dec. 21, p. 765); *MdF*, Nov., p. 536; by Barbara P. McCarthy, *CR*, L, 62; by G. W. Horner, *ConR*, 190 (1956), 377-378; by Edward B. Partridge, *QJS*, XLIII (1957), 314-315; by Edwin B. Benjamin, *CE*, XIX, 89; by Hermann Heuer, *SJ*, 93 (1957), 255-258; by Roy Arthur Swanson, *Classical Journal*, LIII, 139-142; by A. José Axelrad, *EA*, X, 458-459; by J. M. Murry, *London Magazine*, March 4, 61-63; by Jonathan Tate, *RES*, IX (1958), 72-74; by Herbert Musurillo, S. J., *AJP*, LXXIX, 79-84; by William M. Calder, 3rd, *Classical Phil.*, LIII, 128-131.

B7507   Lehmann, Jakob, and Hermann Glaser. *Shakespeares "Hamlet." Ein Arbeitsheft zur Lektüre*. Bamberg, Wiesbaden: Bayer. Verl.-Anst., 1956. Pp. 51. A general discussion of the play followed by excerpts from famous German critics—Goethe, Schlegel, Grillparzer, Tieck, Heine, Nietzsche, Jaspers, etc.

B7508   Melchinger, Siegfried. "Antigone und Hamlet Bleiben. Der Formzerfall im Modernen Drama." *Wort und Wahrheit*, XI (1956), 210-220.

B7509   Schmitt, Carl. *Hamlet oder Hekuba. Der Einbruch der Zeit in das Spiel*. Düsseldorf: Diederichs, 1956. Pp. 72. The inroads of time in the play.
        Rev: *Spiegel*, X, No. 35 (1956), 41-42; by Albrecht B. Strauss, *Books Abroad*, XXXII (1958), 158.

B7510   Thayer, C. G. "*Hamlet*: Drama as Discovery and as Metaphor." *SN*, XXVIII (1956), 118-129.

B7511   Yoshida, Ken-ichi. "On Hamlet." (In Japanese.) *Bungei* (Tokyo), XII, No. 6, 1956.

B7512   Dobrev, Č. "Chamlet." *Septemvri* (Sofia), Sept. 10, 1957, pp. 177-182.

B7513   Driver, Tom Faw. *The Sense of History in Greek and Shakespearean Dramatic Form*. DD, Columbia University, 1957. Pp. 397. Mic 57-2807. *DA*, XVII (1957), 1748. Publ. No. 21,781.

B7514   Hoffmann, Klaus. "Der Maulwurf oder das Problem der Geister. Eine *Hamlet*-Studie." *Theater und Zeit* (Wuppertal), April 5, 1957/58, pp. 6-8.

B7515   Lüthi, Max. "Zwei *Hamlet*-Szenen als Spiegel des Shakespearen Dramas." *Schweizer Monatshefte*, XXXVI, (1956/57), 458-465.

B7516   McCollom, William G. "The Downfall of the Tragic Hero." *CE*, XIX (1957), 51-56. Hamlet and Antony used as illustrations in outlining four basic tragic patterns.

B7517   Morgan, George Alan. *Illustrations of the Critical Principles of E. E. Stoll*. DD, State University of Iowa, 1957. Pp. 224. Mic 57-4807. *DA*, XVII (1957), 3020. Publ. No. 23,772. The summary takes issue with Stoll's findings.

B7518   Murdoch, Walter. *Selected Essays*. London: Angus, 1957. Includes "Hamlet Revisited."

B7519   Shackford, Martha Hale. "Sources of Irony in Hamlet." In Shackford's *Shakespeare, Sophocles:*

Dramatic Modes, 1957, pp. 5-15.
Rev: B4489.

B7520 Siegel, Paul N. *Shakespearean Tragedy and the Elizabethan Compromise.* New York Univ. Press, 1957.
Chapter on *Ham.*
Rev: A1882.

B7521 West, Rebecca. *The Court and the Castle.* Yale Univ. Press, 1957. Pp. 319.
Rev: by Joseph Wood Krutch, *SatR*, Oct. 26, 1957, pp. 21-22; *Los Angeles Times*, Oct. 27, Part V, p. 7; *Time*, Nov. 11, pp. 126, 129; by Roger B. Dooley, *Catholic World*, Dec., pp. 233-234; by Anthony Bailey, *Commonweal*, Dec. 20, pp. 315-316; *Time*, Atl. ed., LXX, No. 20, 68-69; *Nineteenth Century Fiction*, XII (1958), 332-333; *TLS*, Aug. 8, p. 443; by Marjorie Bremner, *TC*, 164 (1958), 409-410; by John Wain, *London Magazine*, V, xii, 62-65; by J. Raymond, *NstN*, July 26, pp. 117-118; by Frank Kermode, *Spectator*, July 25, p. 146.

B7522 Brinkmann, Karl. *Erläuterungen zu Shakespeares "Hamlet, Prinz von Dänemark."* 6th ed. Wilhelm Königs Erläuterungen zu d. Klassikern. 39. Hollfeld/Ofr.: Bange, 1958. Pp. 84.

B7523 Farrison, Edward W. "Ophelia's Reply Concerning Her Father." *College Language Association Journal*, I (1958), 53-57.

B7524 Tomlinson, T. B. "Action and Soliloquy in *Macbeth.*" *EIC*, VIII (1958), 147-155.
Comments upon *Ham.* See B7524a.

B7524a Davies, Cecil W. "Action and Soliloquy in *Macbeth.*" *EIC*, VIII (1958), 451-453.
Opposes B7524.

B7525 Tykesson, Elisabeth. "Shakespeare-analysen i Goethes *Wilhelm Meister.*" *En Goethebok till Algot Werin.* Lund, 1958, pp. 59-75.
The *Ham.* analysis in *Wilhelm Meister*, Book 3, Chapter 8, with reference to contemporary scenic adaptations of *Ham.* by Ludwig Schröder.

(b) THE GHOST

B7526 Semper, I. J. "The Ghost in *Hamlet.*" *Catholic World*, 167 (1946), 510-517.

B7527 Battenhouse, Roy W. "The Ghost in *Hamlet*: A Catholic 'Lynchpin'?" *SP*, XLVIII (1951), 161-192.
Rev: by R. A. Law, *SQ*, III (1952), 85.

B7528 Semper, I. J. "The Ghost in *Hamlet*: Pagan or Christian?" *The Month*, NS, IX (1953), 222-234.
Contradicts Battenhouse, B7527.

B7529 West, Robert H. "King Hamlet's Ambiguous Ghost." *PMLA*, LXX (1955), 1107-1117.

B7529a Flatter, Richard. "Der Geist von Hamlets Vater." In Flatter's *Triumph der Gnade. Shakespeare Essays*, Vienna, Munich: Kurt Desch, 1956, pp. 116-119.

(c) THE FENCING MATCH

B7530 Gay, A. A. "The Fencing Match in *Hamlet.*" *RES*, XIII (1937), 326-329.

B7531 Mitchell, Lee. "The Fencing Scene in *Hamlet.*" *PQ*, XVI (1937), 71-73.

B7532 Tannenbaum, Samuel A. "Hamlet versus Laertes." *SAB*, XIV (1939), 127.

B7533 Guttman, Selma. "The Fencing Bout in *Hamlet.*" *SAB*, XIV (1939), 86-100.
See B7534.

B7534 Gilbert, Allan H. "The Fencing Match in *Hamlet.*" *SAB*, XVI (1941), 124-125.

B7535 Tannenbaum, Samuel A. "The Hamlet-Laertes Bout." *SAB*, XVI (1941), 60.
See letter by A. H. Gilbert, *SAB*, XVI, 124-125.

B7536 Jackson, James L. "The Exchange of Weapons in *Hamlet.*" *MLN*, LVII (1942), 50-55.

B7537 Müller-Steinhoff, Helmut. "Muss Hamlet Fechten Können?" *Theater d. Zeit*, May 13, 1958, pp. 63-64.

(5) CHARACTERIZATION (230;82)
(a) GENERAL

B7538 Steguweit, Heinz. "Yorick und Hamlet." *Die Bühne*, II (1936), 616.

B7538a Blyton, W. J. *We Are Observed: A Mirror of English Character.* London, 1937.
Rev: *TLS*, Feb. 5, 1938, p. 85.

B7539 Draper, John W. *The Hamlet of Shakespeare's Audience.* Duke Univ. Press, 1938. Pp. xi, 254.
Rev: by Georges Connes, *EA*, III (1939), 266-267; by John Wilcox, *SAB*, XIV, 122-126; by G. B. Harrison, *MLR*, XXXIV, 435; comment by J. W. Draper, *RES*, XV, 350-351; by Alois Brandl, *Archiv*, 175 (1939), 250; by L. L. Schücking, *RES*, XV, 350-351; by Wolfgang Keller, *SJ*, LXXV, 158-160; by F. Delattre, *RBPH*, XVIII, 545-547; by Robert Adger Law, *JEGP*, XXXIX (1940), 144-146; by E. Eckhardt, *Eng. Studn.*, LXXIV, 228-231; by H. de Groot, *ES*, XXIII, 89-90; by B. T. Spencer, "This Elizabethan Shakespeare," *SR*, XLIX (1941), 538-545.

B7540 Morsbach, Lorenz. *Shakespeares Dramatische Kunst und ihre Voraussetzungen. Mit e. Ausblick auf d. Hamlet-Tragödie.* Göttingen: Vanderhoek u. Ruprecht, 1940. Pp. 167.

Chap. IV. "Der Sinn der Hamlet-Tragödie. Die Charaktere der Hauptpersonen."

B7541 Schell, J. S. "Shakespeare's Gulls." *SAB*, xv (1940), 23-33.

B7542 Tannenbaum, Samuel A. "Hamlet Sr., Merchant or Knight." *SAB*, xv (1940), 60-62.

B7543 Mackenzie, William Roy. "Rosencrantz and Guildenstern." *Studies in Honor of Frederick W. Shipley*. Washington Univ. Press, 1942, pp. 221-243.
This is the only Shak. item in this collection.

B7544 Dean, Leonard F. "Shakespeare's Treatment of Conventional Ideas." *SR*, LII (1944), 414-423.

B7545 Ogilvie, V. "Three Characters in *Hamlet*." *Britain Today*, Oct. 1947, pp. 13-17.

B7546 Morozov, Mikhail M. "The Individualization of Shakespeare's Characters through Imagery." *ShS*, II (1949), 83-106.

B7547 Ehrenzweig, Anton. *The Psycho-Analysis of Artistic Vision and Hearing*. London: Routledge and Kegan Paul, 1953.

(b) SPECIFIC CHARACTERS
i. Claudius

B7548 Malleson, J. P. "Was King Claudius a Usurper?" *TLS*, Jan. 4, 1936, p. 15.
See letters by J. Dover Wilson, *TLS*, Jan. 11, 1936, p. 35; by G. M. Gathorne-Hardy, ibid., Jan. 18, p. 55; by J. P. Malleson and by J. Dover Wilson, ibid., Jan. 25, p. 75; see also B7599.

B7549 Beatty, J. M., Jr. "The King in *Hamlet*." *SAB*, XI (1936), 238-249.
See letter by Max Huhner, *SAB*, XII (1937), 130.

B7550 Cancelled.

B7551 Wales, Julia G. "Professor Beatty's Interpretation of Shakespeare." *Trans. of the Wisconsin Acad. of Sciences, Arts, and Letters*, XXXVI (1944), 441-458.

B7552 Maxwell, J. C. "Claudius and the Curse of Cain." *N &Q*, 194 (1949), 142.

B7553 McGregor, Herman S., Jr. *A History of the Criticism of the King in "Hamlet."* MA thesis, University of North Carolina, 1952. Abstr. publ. in *Univ. of North Carolina Record, Research in Progress*, Jan.-Dec., 1952, Grad. School Series, No. 64, 1953, p. 116.

B7554 Coe, Charles Norton. *Shakespeare's Villains*. New York: 1957.
Rev: A6796.

B7555 Major, John M. "The 'Letters Seal'd' in *Hamlet* and the Character of Claudius." *JEGP*, LVII (1958), 512-521.

ii. Gertrude

B7556 Smith, Robert M. "Hamlet and Gertrude, or The Conscience of the Queen." *SAB*, XI (1936), 84-92.

B7557 Heilbrun, Carolyn. "The Character of Hamlet's Mother." *SQ*, VIII (1957), 201-206.

iii. Polonius

B7558 Sleeth, C. R. "Shakespeare's Counsellors of State." *RAA*, XIII (1936), 97-113.

B7559 Gierasch, Walter. "Hamlet's Polonius, and Shakspeare's." *CE*, II (1941), 699-702.

B7559a Hudson, Hoyt Hopewell. "The Folly of Erasmus: An Essay." In Hopewell's edition of Erasmus' *Praise of Folly*, Princeton Univ. Press, 1941, pp. xi-xli.
Comments upon precepts speech, pp. xxvii-xxx.

B7560 Allen, N. B. "Polonius' Advice to Laertes." *SAB*, XVIII (1943), 187-190.

B7561 Tannenbaum, Samuel A. "Was Shakespeare a Botcher?" *SAB*, XVIII (1943), 191-192.
On B7560 and B7562.

B7562 Berkelman, Robert G. "Polonius as an Adviser." *CE*, IV (1943), 379-381.

B7563 Huhner, Max. "Polonius' Advice to Laertes." *SAB*, XIX (1944), 29-35.
Republished in his *Shakespearean Studies and Other Essays*, 1952.
On B7560 et seq.

B7564 Campbell, Lily B. "Polonius: The Tyrant's Ears." *AMS*, pp. 295-313.

B7565 Bennett, Josephine W. "Characterization in Polonius' Advice to Laertes." *SQ*, IV (1953), 3-9.
Polonius' speech, drawn from Isocrates, would strike the Eliz. audience as "a familiar and conventional set of wise saws . . . schoolboy wisdom. . ."

B7566 Bowers, R. H. "Polonius: Another Postscript." *SQ*, IV (1953), 362-363.
On B7565.

B7567 McGlinchee, Claire. " 'Still Harping. . . .' " *SQ*, VI (1955), 362-364.
Finds a parallel to Polonius' fatherly advice in Knowell's speech to Stephen his nephew (*Everyman In*, 1.1). On B7565.

B7568 Bennett, Josephine Waters. "These Few Precepts." *SQ*, VII (1956), 275-276.
On B7567.

B7569 Hunter, G. K. "Isocrates' Precepts and Polonius' Character." *SQ*, VIII (1957), 501-506.
On B7565.

B7570   Herbert, T. Walter. "Diversive Estimates of Polonius' Character: An Example of a Dramatic Technique." *Renaissance Papers*, 1957, pp. 82-86. Abstr. in *ShN*, VII (1957), 12.

B7571   Blum, Margaret Morton. "The *Fool* in 'The Love Song of J. Alfred Prufrock'." *MLN*, LXXII (1957), 424-426.

B7572   Wilson, Elkin Calhoun. "Polonius in the Round." *SQ*, IX (1958), 83-85.

B7573   Davis, O. B. "A Note on the Function of Polonius' Advice." *SQ*, IX (1958), 85-86.

iv. Ophelia

B7574   S., E. F. "The Insanity of Ophelia." *The Sketch*, London, April 26, 1905, p. 46.

B7575   Rahner, Rich. *Ophelia in Shakespeares "Hamlet."* Eine Psychologisch-Psychiatrische Studie. Leipzig: Xenien-Verlag, 1910.

B7576   Palmer, J. F. "Ophelia: A Short Study in Acute Delirious Mania." *The Medical Magazine* (London), XXI (1912), 448-453.

B7577   Draper, John W. "Ophelia's Crime of Felo De Se." *West Virginia Law Quar.*, XLII (1936), 228-234.

B7578   L., L. "Ophelia." *N &Q*, 177 (1939), 81; M. H. Dodds, ibid., pp. 212-213.

B7579   Tannenbaum, Samuel A. "Mistress Ophelia." *SAB*, XIV (1939), 252-254.

B7580   Corbin, John. "Ophelia Against Her Critics." *SRL*, Aug. 16, 1941, pp. 11-12.

B7581   Tannenbaum, Samuel A. "Ophelia Lies." *SAB*, XVI (1941), 215-219.

B7582   Foulds, Elizabeth. "Enter Ophelia, Distracted." *Life and Letters Today*, XXXVI (1943), 36-41.

B7583   Goddard, H. "In Ophelia's Closet." *YR*, XXXV (1946), 463-474.
        Argues that *Hamlet*, II. i, happens only in Ophelia's mind and is the first symptom of her lunacy.

B7584   Donaghy, J. Lyle. "Hamlet and Ophelia." *Dublin Magazine*, Jan.-March, 1949, pp. 29-32.

B7585   Nakano, Yoshio. "Ophelia's Death." *World News* (Japan), Nov., 1949.

B7586   Lever, J. W. "Three Notes on Shakespeare's Plants." *RES*, III (1952), 117-129.
        (3): Ophelia's words and actions with her flowers are "in keeping with her character, her good intentions, her abysmal ignorance of life."

B7587   Matsuura, Kaichi. "Ophelia Metamorphosed into Desdemona." *The Rising Generation*, 98 (1952), 50-51.

B7588   Craig, Hardin. "Hamlet and Ophelia." *The Written Word and Other Essays*. Chapel Hill: Univ. of North Carolina Press, 1953, pp. 32-48.

B7589   Patrick, J. Max. "The Problem of Ophelia." Matthews and Emery, eds., *Studies in Shakespeare*, 1953, pp. 139-144.

B7590   Geyer, Horst. *Dichter des Wahnsinns. Eine Untersuchung über die Dichterische Darstellbarkeit Seelischer Ausnahmezustände.* Göttingen: Musterschmidt, 1955. Pp. 322.
        Chapter 6, "Ein Psychogener Dämmerzustand. Shakespeares Ophelia," pp. 73-94; 269-282. Rev: A1375.

B7591   Goddard, Harold C. "Hamlet to Ophelia." *CE*, XVI (1955), 403-415.

B7592   Garey, Doris B. "Hamlet to Ophelia." *CE*, XVII (1955), 117-118.
        Comment on B7591.

B7593   Dührssen, Annemarie. "Lebensproblem und Daseinkrise bei Hamlet und Ophelia (Life Problems and Existential Crisis of Hamlet and Ophelia)." *Zeitschrift für Psychosomatische Medizin*, II (1956), 220-235, 295-311.

B7594   Kirschbaum, Leo. "Hamlet and Ophelia." *PQ*, XXXV (1956), 376-393.

B7595   Morris, Harry. "Ophelia's 'Bonny Sweet Robin'." *PMLA*, LXXIII (1958), 601-603.
        "Robin" appears to have been a phallic euphemism, and Ophelia's fragmentary song (IV. v. 187) helps signify that the prime cause of her madness was frustrated love, such as Polonius attributed to Hamlet.

v. Horatio

B7596   McDermott, L. "Horatio." *The Silver Falcon*. New York: Hunter College, Dec. 1936, pp. 13-15.

B7597   Druhman, Rev. Alvin W. *An Analysis of Four of the Level-of-Life Characters in Shakespeare's Tragedies.* DD, St. John's University, Brooklyn, 1952. Abstr. publ. in *Abstracts of Dissertations, 1951-1952*, Brooklyn: St. John's Univ., 1952, pp. 14-15.

B7598   Schoff, Francis G. "Horatio: A Shakespearian Confident." *SQ*, VII (1956), 53-57.

vi. Fortinbras

B7599   Wilson, J. Dover. "Prince Fortinbras." *TLS*, Sept. 26, 1936, p. 768; letters by H. W. Crundell, ibid., Oct. 3, p. 791; by J. P. Malleson, ibid., Oct. 10, p. 815; by J. D. Wilson, ibid., Oct. 17, p. 839; by A. Gomme, ibid., Oct. 31, p. 887. See also B7548.

B7600   Lawrence, William Witherle. "Hamlet and Fortinbras." *PMLA*, LXI (1946), 673-698.

B7601   Franzel, Emil. "Die Erscheinung des Fortinbras." *Die Lücke* (Waibstadt bei Heidelberg), VII (1948), 29-30.

B7602   Knoll, Robert E. *Fortinbras and His Character Type in Elizabethan Drama.* DD, University of Minnesota, 1950.

(6) ANALYSIS OF THE CHARACTER OF THE HERO (231;83)
(a) SURVEYS OF CRITICISM

B7603   Conklin, Paul S. *A History of "Hamlet" Criticism: Part I, 1601-1800.* DD, University of Minnesota, 1938. Abstr. publ. in *Summaries of PhD Theses*, Univ. of Minnesota, 1939, pp. 151-154.

B7604   Conklin, Paul S. *A History of "Hamlet" Criticism 1601-1821.* New York, 1947.
Rev: A7762.

B7605   Smith, Robert M. "An Agnostic Life of Shakespeare." *SAB*, XV (1940), 75-87.

B7606   Gutteling, J. F. C. "Modern *Hamlet*-Criticism." *Neophil*, XXV (1941), 276-285.
Reviews Jones (pp. 278-279) and finds him plausible. Examines Stoll and finds him wanting. Notices C. M. Lewis' *Genesis of Hamlet* (1907), A. J. A. Waldock's *Hamlet: A Study in Critical Method* (which he calls fine), Dover Wilson, and J. Draper.

B7607   Elling, Johnny. *Hamlet-skikkelsen i Forskjellig Lys* [*The Hamlet Figure in Various Lights*]. Oslo, 1943. Pp. 28.
Republished Oslo Univ. Press, 1957. Pp. 29.

B7608   Feibleman, James. "Theorien über *Hamlet*." *Die Amerikanische Rundschau*, IX (1946), 61-72.

B7609   Feibleman, James. "The Theory of *Hamlet*." *JHI*, VII (1946), 131-150.
Extended review of previous schools of criticism.

B7610   Gray, Henry David. "Some Methods of Approach to the Study of *Hamlet*." *SP*, XLV (1948), "No man can really know a past age with sufficient fulness and accuracy to say what that age was capable of thinking and of producing." —p. 207.

B7611   Klajn, Hugo. "Savremini Problemi u *Hamletu*" (Contemporary Problems in *Hamlet*). *Književnost* (Belgrade), IV (1949), 210-237.

B7612   Shoemaker, Lisle N. *The Whole History of "Hamlet."* DD, Western Reserve University, 1950. Abstr. publ. in Western Reserve Univ. *Bibliography of Published Research, 1948-50,* (?1953), pp. 140-142.

B7613   Williamson, C. C. H., ed. *Readings on the Character of Hamlet, 1661-1947.* London, 1950.
Rev: B7730.

B7614   Leech, Clifford. "Studies in *Hamlet*, 1901-1955." *ShS*, IX (1956), 1-15.

(b) HAMLET'S CHARACTER IN GENERAL

B7615   Régis, E. "Le Personnage d'Hamlet et son Interprétation par M_{me} Sarah Bernhardt." *Revue Philomatique de Bordeaux et du Sud-Ouest*, II (1899), 469-480. Also in *Revue de Psychologie Clinique et Thérapeutique* (Paris), III (1899), 336-344. Discussed in "La Folie d'Hamlet," *Le Gaulois*, Paris, Dec. 17, 1899.

B7616   Bettencourt-Ferreira, J. "La Folie au Théâtre. Quelques Considérations sur l'Etat Morbide Représenté dans *Hamlet*." *Revue de Psychologie Clinique et Thérapeutique* (Paris), IV (1900), 108-114.

B7617   Palmer, J. F. "Hamlet: A Study in Melancholia." *The Medical Magazine* (London), XX (1911), 396-411.

B7618   Oczeret, Herbert. "Das Hamlet-Problem und die Psychoanalyse." *Frankfurter Zeitung*, Frankfurt a. M., No. 65 (erstes Morgenblatt), March 6, 1914.

B7619   Mairet, P. "Hamlet der Neurotiker." *Internationale Zeitschrift für Individualpsychologie* (Leipzig), IX (1931), 424-437.

B7620   Linkenbach, Baldur. *Das Prinzip des Tragischen.* Munich: Einhorn-Verl., 1934. Pp. 110.
Ham., pp. 77-92.

B7621   Menninger, C. F. "Insanity of Hamlet." *Journal of Kansas Medical Society* (Topeka), XXXV (Sept., 1934), 334-338.
First delivered in 1890.

B7622   Stoll, E. E. *Hamlet the Man.* Eng. Assoc. Pamphlet No. 91. Oxford Univ. Press, 1935. Pp. 29.
Rev: by R. Travers, *RAA*, XIII (1936), 241-243; by A. J. A. Waldock, *MLR*, XXXI, 467-468; by Wolfgang Keller, *SJ*, LXXII, 147-148; by Robert Adger Law, *MLN*, LII (1937), 526-530.

B7623   Deutschbein, Max. "Macbeth und Hamlet." *Shakespeares "Macbeth" als Drama des Barock*, (A5525), pp. 117-128.

B7624   Flatter, R. *Hamlets Flucht in den Tod. Das Hamlet-Problem Neu Dargestellt und Gedeutet.* Vienna: Reichner, 1936. Pp. 88.

B7625   Frassati, Alfredo. *La Volontà in Amleto.* Bologna: Zanichelli, 1936. Pp. 151.
Rev: by J. Humphreys Whitfield, *English*, I (1937), 362.

B7626   Handleman, Celia, and R. W. Babcock. " 'One Part Wisdom,' and Ever Two Parts?" *SAB*, XI (1936), 191-225.

B7627 Kassner, R. "Über Shakespeare." *Corona*, VI (1936), 256-283, 408-423.

B7628 Kurlbaum-Siebert, M. "Hamlet Zwischen den Welten." *Das Deutsche Wort*, XII (1936), 278-284.

B7629 Meyer-Benfey, H. "Das Problem des Hamlet." *GRM*, XXIV (1936), 35-45.

B7630 Morgan, Mona. *Hamlet the Dane*. Philadelphia: Patterson White, 1936. Pp. 54.
       Rev: by S. A. T., *SAB*, XII (1937), 66.

B7631 Tannenbaum, Samuel A. "The Eavesdropping Hamlet." *SAB*, XI (1936), 185-186.

B7632 Weigelin, E. "Hamletstudien." 1934.
       In Ebisch and Schücking *Supplement*, p. 84.
       Rev: by von Grolmann, *DNL*, XXXVII (1936), 535-536.

B7633 Adler, Felix. "An Interpretation of *Hamlet*." *Standard*, XXIII (1937), 91-96.

B7634 Cairncross, A. S. "Hamlet Problems." *TLS*, Jan. 9, 1937, p. 28.

B7635 Draper, John W. "The Prince-Philosopher and Shakespeare's Hamlet." *West Virginia Univ. Studies*, Ser. III: Philological Papers. II (1937), 39-43.

B7636 Hiebel, Friedrich. "Das Licht des Neuzeitlichen Ichbewusstseins in Shakespeares Schaffen. I. 2: Hamlet." *Das Goetheanum*, XVI (1937), 20-21, 29-30.

B7637 Jensen, Johannes V. "Hamlets Karakter." *Politiken*, Feb. 19, 1937, pp. 12-13.

B7638 Keller, Wolfgang. "Hamlets Wunderliches Wesen." *NS*, XLV (1937), 1-16.

B7639 Lawrence, W. J. *Speeding Up Shakespeare*. Studies of the Bygone Theatre and Drama. London: Argonaut Press, 1937. Pp. 220.
       Rev: A7402.

B7640 Murry, J. M. (R. Kraushaar, tr.) "Shakespeares Ebenbild." *Die Neue Rundschau*, June 1937, pp. 604-620.

B7641 Stumpfe, Ortrud. "Der Protagonist der Gegenwart. Hamlet und Unsere Zeit." *DL*, XL (1937/38), 328-330.

B7642 Sampley, Arthur M. "Hamlets All." *SAB*, XII (1937), 41-43.

B7643 Weigelin, E. "Zum Problem des *Hamlet*." *SJ*, LXXIII (1937), 131-138.

B7644 Balmer, R. W. "Hamlet's Love and His Melancholy." *Adelphi*, XIV (1938), 308-311.

B7645 Frerking, J. "Hamlet und der Totengräber." *Deut. Zukunft*, VI (1938), 9.

B7646 Lea, F. A. "Hamlet Again." *Adelphi*, XIV (1938), 118-119.

B7647 Messiaen, Pierre. "Remarques sur Hamlet." *Revue de l'Enseignement des Langues Vivantes*, LV (1938), 447-458.

B7648 Spencer, Theodore. "Hamlet and the Nature of Reality." *ELH*, V (1938), 253-277.

B7649 "Great Individualists: Hamlet and Lincoln." *New York Times*, Oct. 22, 1938, p. 16.

B7650 Bassenge, Edmund. "Ist Hamlet Typus oder Individuum?" *SJ*, LXXV (1939), 127-133.

B7651 Bhattacharje, M. "Evolution of Hamlet's Personality." *Calcutta Review*, LXX (1939), 288-299.

B7652 Caldwell, J. R. "Hamlet: Dramatist." *Five Studies in Literature*. Ed. B. H. Bronson. Berkeley, California: Univ. of California Press; London: Cambridge Univ. Press, 1940. Pp. 153.

B7653 Draper, John W. "Hamlet's Melancholy." *Annals Medical Hist.*, NS, IX (1939), 142-147.
       Rev: by A. E. H. Swaen, *Neophil*, XXIV (1939), 153.

B7654 Huch, R. "Hamlet. Eine Studie." *DL*, XLI (1939), 475-478.

B7655 Levillier, Roberto. "Hamlet, el Resentido." *Nosotros*, Epoca 2a, IV (1939), 3-17.

B7656 Müller, Wolfgang. "Hamlet-Rätsel. Zur Religiösen Problematik Shakespeares." *Die Furche*, XXV (Berlin), (1939), 168-174.

B7657 Rubow, Paul V. "Prins Hamlet og hans Filosofi." *Scrap Book*, 1939, pp. 132-141.

B7658 Kalthoff, W. "Eine neue Hamlet-Interpretation." *GA*, VII (1940), 5.

B7659 Knights, L. C. "Prince Hamlet." *Scrutiny*, IX (1940), 148-160.

B7660 Sen, Taraknath. "Hamlet's Treatment of Ophelia in the Nunnery Scene." *MLR*, XXXV (1940), 145-152.

B7661 Stewart, C. D. "A Bit of Shakespeare Interpretation." *Wisconsin Magazine of History*, XXIII (1940), 272-280.

B7662 Stoll, Elmer Edgar. *Shakespeare and Other Masters*. Harvard Univ. Press, 1940. Pp. xv, 430.
       Rev: A8394.

B7663 Barzun, Jacques. "Hamlet's Politics." *SRL*, April 13, 1940, pp. 6-7, 14.

B7664 Hankins, John Erskine. *The Character of Hamlet and Other Essays*. Univ. of North Carolina Press, 1941. Pp. xii, 264.
       Rev: by Fredson Bowers, *MLN*, LVII (1942), 470-471; by Hardin Craig, *MLQ*, III, 125-126; by B. T. Spencer, "Shakespeare With and Without Tears," *SR*, L, 546-550; by G. I. Duthie, *RES*, XIX (1943), 79-80; by Alwin Thaler, *JEGP*, XLII, 275-277.

B7665 McCloskey, John C. "Hamlet's Quest of Certainty." *CE*, II (1941), 445-451.

B7666 Ross, John F. "Hamlet: Dramatist." *Five Studies in Literature: Univ. California Pubs. in Eng.*, VIII (1941), 55-72.

B7667   Shudofsky, M. Maurice. "Sarah Bernhardt on *Hamlet*." *CE*, III (1941), 293-295.

B7668   Deutschbein, Max. "Die Bedeutung von 'Mind' im 16. Jh. Eine Vor-Studie zu Shakespeares Hamlet." *Anglia*, LXVI (1942), 169-222.

B7669   Hudson, Arthur Palmer. "Romantic Apologiae for Hamlet's Treatment of Ophelia." *ELH*, IX (1942), 59-70.

B7670   Sampley, Arthur M. "Hamlet Among the Mechanists." *SAB*, XVII (1942), 134-149.
        Mainly an argument against Professor Stoll's interpretation of Hamlet's character.

B7671   Campbell, Oscar James. *Shakespeare's Satire.* Oxford Univ. Press, 1943. Pp. 227.
        "Hamlet and Other Malcontents," pp. 142-167.
        Rev: B5164.

B7672   Decreus, Juliette. "Forces Constructives dans Hamlet et dans La Princesse Maleine de Maeterlinck." *CL*, XI (1943), 5-8.

B7673   Lewis, C. S. *Hamlet: The Prince or the Poem?* Annual Shakespeare Lecture of the British Academy, 1942. London, 1943. Pp. 18. Also in *Proceedings of the British Academy*, XXVIII (1942).
        Rev: by W. W. Lawrence, *MLR*, XXXVIII (1943), 140-142; *N &Q*, 184 (1943), 269-270, 283-284; see also "Memorabilia," ibid., pp. 241-242; by W. H. J., "Shakespeare in Modern Dress," ibid., pp. 329-331; by E. G., "Costume in Hamlet," ibid., p. 374; by M. H. Dodds, ibid., 185 (1943), 323-324; by St. Vincent Troubridge, ibid., pp. 381-382; by Alfred Harbage, *MLN*, LIX (1944), 133.

B7674   Babb, Lawrence. "Hamlet, Melancholy, and the Devil" *MLN*, LIX (1944), 120-122.

B7675   Finlayson, Clarence. "Nuevamente en Torno al Hamlet." *Rev. de la Indias*, No. 61 (Jan., 1944), 394-407.

B7676   Arnold, Paul. "Raisons d'Hamlet." *Les Lettres*, I (1945), 114-124.

B7677   Donoso, A. C. "Hamlet: Estudio Literario." *Universidad de Antioquia*, XVIII (1945), 83-87.

B7678   Jaggard, W. "Hamlet's Character." *N &Q*, 188 (1945), 173-174.

B7679   Olybrius. "The Character of Hamlet." *N &Q*, 189 (1945), 130. See also *N &Q*, 188 (1944), 125.

B7680   Cancelled.

B7681   Auerbach, Erich. "Der Müde Prinz." In his *Mimesis*, Bern, 1946, pp. 298-319.

B7682   Auerbach, Erich. *Mimesis: The Representation of Reality in Western Literature.* Tr. Willard R. Trask. Princeton Univ. Press, 1953.
        "The Weary Prince," pp. 312-333, discusses mixture of comic and tragic in Shakespeare; study of fools and madmen, pp. 347-349.
        Rev: A6859a.

B7683   Castelain, M. "L'Enigme d'Hamlet." *Université de Poitiers, Mélanges Littéraires et Historiques Publiés à l'Occasion du Centenaire de Sa Restauration en 1845.* Paris: Belles-Lettres, 1946, pp. 20-36. Conclusion finds Shakespeare's private life in *Hamlet*.

B7684   Knights, L. C. *Explorations: Essays in Criticism, Mainly on the Literature of the Seventeenth Century.* London, 1946.
        Rev: A8269.

B7685   Tyler, P. "Hamlet as the Murdered Poet." *QR*, III (1946), 156-166.

B7686   Venable, Emerson. *The Hamlet Problem and Its Solution: An Interpretative Study.* Cincinnati: John G. Kidd & Son, 1946. Pp. 38. Republished Los Angeles: Oxford Press, Inc., 1954. Pp. 31.

B7687   Barrault, Jean-Louis. "*Hamlet*, Le Message de Shakespeare." *Conferencia*, November 15, 1947.

B7688   Draper, John W. "The Tempo of Hamlet's Role." *Rivista di Letterature Moderne*, II (1947), 194-203.

B7689   Fluchère, H. "Désmesure d'Hamlet." *CS*, LXVIII (1947), 456-460.

B7690   Ritze, F. H. *Shakespeare's Men of Melancholy and His Malcontents.* MS thesis, Columbia University, 1947. Pp. 98.

B7691   Simpson, R. R. "Wie Starb Hamlets Vater?" *Neue Auslese*, Oct. 2, 1947, pp. 75-78.
        From a London broadcast. Also published as "How Did Hamlet's Father Die?" *Listener*, April 17, 1946. Republished in Williamson's collection, B7730.

B7692   Weigelin, Ernst. "Hamlets Selbstbetrug." *SJ*, 82/83 (1948), 99-102.

B7693   Allen, D. C. "Hamlet and the Wages of Reason." *The Univ. of Chicago Magazine*, XLI, No. 11 (1948), 6-9, 21.

B7694   Babb, Lawrence. "On the Nature of Elizabethan Psychological Literature." *AMS*, pp. 509-522.

B7695   Danks, K. B. "Hamlet's Love-Letter." *N &Q*, 193 (1948), 266-268.

B7696   Dawson, Charles A. "Hamlet the Actor." *South Atlantic Quar.*, XLVII (1948), 522-533.

B7697   Madariaga, Salvador de. *On Hamlet.* London: Hollis and Carter, 1948. Pp. 130.
        Rev: *TLS*, July 3, 1948, p. 371; by Richard Flatter, "Hamlet." *TLS*, May 22, p. 289, objects to Mr. Madariaga's interpretation of *Hamlet*, III. ii. 856; see letter by Madariaga,

ibid., June 5, p. 317; by H. B. Charlton, *MGW*, June 3, p. 11; by Peter Fleming, *Spectator*, May 7, pp. 558-560; see the letters under "Sweet Prince?" by M. Judson and T. D. Lowe, *Spectator*, May 14, pp. 586-588; by G. W. Stonier, *NstN*, June 9, p. 503; by W. Weintraub, *Wiadomości* (London), No. 41; *Punch*, 214, 414-415; by J. Lequiller, *Le Monde*, May 29; by R. F. Laffray, *QR*, 581 (1949), 320-325; by J. D. Wilson, *MLR*, XLIV 390-397; by Robert Fricker, *ES*, XXX, 273-275; by J. Duncan Spaeth, *SAB*, XXIV, 75-78; by André Koszul, *LanM*, XLIV (1950), 422; by E. D., *N &Q*, 195, 538; by R. Flatter, *SJ*, 87/88 (1952), 244-246; by J. G. Weightman, "Edinburgh, Elsinore and Chelsea." *TC*, 154 (1953), 302-310.

B7698 Madariaga, Salvador de. *Hamlet in ny Belysning*. Tr. Gunnar Sjögren. Stockholm: Natur o. Kultur, 1951. Pp. 173.

B7699 "Hamlet by Moonshine." *Bulletin* (Sidney, Australia), LXIX (July 28, 1948), 2.
On B7697.

B7700 Bullett, G. "Madariaga on *Hamlet*." *The Literary Guide*, Nov. 1948, pp. 178-179.

B7701 Kingsmill, Hugh. "*Hamlet* Borgianised." *The New English Review*, XVII (1948), 83-86.
On B7697.

B7702 Stoll, E. E. "A Spanish Hamlet." *MP*, XLVII (1949), 12-23.
On B7697.

B7703 Moore, John R. "A Spanish Hamlet." *MLR*, XLV (1950), 512.
On B7697.

B7704 Wikland, Erik. "Hamlet—Karaktåren." *Edda*, LII (1952), 173-176.
On B7697.

B7705 Neri, Fernando. "La Prima Vita di Amleto." *Poesia nel Tempo*. Turin: Francesco de Silva, 1948, pp. 46-50.

B7706 Salter, F. M. "Shakespeare's Interpretation of Hamlet." *TRSC*, Sect. 2, Ser. 3, XLII (1948), 147-189.

B7707 Spencer, Theodore. "The Elizabethan Malcontent." *AMS*, pp. 523-535.

B7708 Walker, Roy. *The Time is Out of Joint: A Study of "Hamlet."* London: Andrew Dakers; New York: Universal Distributors, 1948. Pp. xv, 157.
Rev: by George Cookson, *English*, VII (1948), 82; by G. W. Stonier, *NstN*, June 9, p. 503; by Irving T. Richards, *SAB*, XXIV (1949), 73-75.

B7709 De Greef, Etienne. "La Névrose d'Hamlet." *Revue Nouvelle*, May 15, 1949, pp. 466-482.

B7710 Eliot, T. S. "Hamlet and His Problems." *Critiques and Essays in Criticism, 1920-1948*. New York: Ronald Press, 1949, pp. 384-388.

B7711 Houston, Percy H. "There's Nothing Either Good or Bad But Thinking Makes It So." *SAB*, XXIV (1949), 48-53.

B7712 McCanse, Ralph A. "Hamlet's Lack of Balance." *CE*, X (1949), 476-478.

B7713 McCarthy, Mary. "A Prince of Shreds and Patches." *Partisan Rev.*, XVI (1949), 82-84.

B7714 Mayo, Thomas F. "A World Fit for Hamlet." *Southwest Review*, XXXIV (1949), 350-356.

B7715 Millar, J. S. L. "The Significance of *Hamlet*." *Listener*, XLII (1949), 230-231.

B7716 Porena, M. "Le Ultime Parole di Amleto." *Rendiconti dell'Accademia Nazionale dei Lincei*. Cl. di Scienze Morali, Storiche e Filol., IV (1949), 497-501.

B7717 Raimondi, Giuseppe. "Un Pensiero sull'Amleto." *La Rassegna d'Italia* (Milan), IV (1949), 921-923.

B7718 Spaeth, J. Duncan. "Horatio's Hamlet." *SAB*, XXIV (1949), 37-47.

B7719 Chwalewik, Witwold. "Hamlet Jako Krytyk Teatru." *Polska Akademia Umiejętności*, LI (1950), 580-583.

B7720 Colberg, Klaus. "Hamlet Contra Hamlet Oder die Kunst aus Zweiter Hand." *Die neue Schau*, XI (1950), 105-106.
Comment by Marga Parzeller, ibid., p. 246.

B7721 Fergusson, Francis. *The Idea of a Theatre*. Princeton Univ. Press, 1949. Pp. x, 239.
Includes an essay on Hamlet; see the author's "*Hamlet*: The Analogy of Action," *Hudson Rev.*, II (1949), 165-210.
Rev: by Richard Gaines, *NYTBR*, Dec. 4, 1949, p. 30; by H. W. Wells, *SQ*, I (1950), 44-46; comment by James W. Andrews ("The Idea of a Theater: A Reply"), ibid., I, 185-188; further comment by H. W. Wells ("A Reply to James W. Andrews"), ibid., I, 189-190; by Marcia L. Anderson, *South Atlantic Quar.*, XLIX, 424-425; by A. S. Downer, *Hudson Rev.*, III, 145-151; by A. R. Thompson, *JAAC*, IX, 64; by K. Burke, *KR*, XII, 532-537; by J. H. McDowell, *QJS*, XXXVI, 266-267; by J. C. Lapp, *QQ*, LVII, 586-590; by Robert Halsband, *SRL*, Sept. 23, p. 33; by Garland Greever, *Personalist*, XXXII, 296-297; by Richard L. O'Connell, Jr., *Symposium*, V, 117-119; by James H. Miller, *New Mexico Quarterly*, XXI, 234-237; by Kenneth O. Hanson, *Western Review*, XV, 317-318; by H. C. Lancaster, *MLN*, LXV, 566; by Joseph Frank, *Partisan Review*, XVII, 743-748; by O. J. Campbell, *SQ*, II (1951), 109; by H. Heuer, *SJ*, 89 (1953), 216-217.

B7722 Godfrey, D. R. "The Player's Speech in *Hamlet*: A New Approach." *Neophil*, XXXIV (1950), 162-169.
Rev: by J. I. M. Stewart, *ShS*, V (1952), 133-134.

B7723 Van Lennep, C. *On Hamlet the Man.* The Hague: Printed by Drukkerij Trio, 1950. Pp. 64.

B7724 Levin, Harry. "An Explication of the Player's Speech: *Hamlet*, II. ii. 472-541." *KR*, xii (1950), 273-296.

B7725 Mahdi Ali Mirza. "Hamlet's Rôle as a Detective." *The Times of India* (Bombay), Oct., 1950.

B7726 Neilson, Francis. *Hamlet and Shakespeare.* New York, 1950.

B7727 Orlando, Ruggero. "Amleto Esagerava." *Letteratura* (Florence), I, No. 3 (1950).

B7728 Rubow, Paul V. *En Studie Bog [A Book of Studies].* Copenhagen: Gyldendal, 1950. Pp. 161. Includes two essays on *Hamlet*, pp. 89-98.

B7729 Utter, Robert Palfrey, Jr. "In Defense of Hamlet." *CE*, xii (1950), 138-144.

B7730 Williamson, C. C. H., ed. *Readings on the Character of Hamlet, 1661-1947.* London: Allen and Unwin, 1950. Pp. xiv, 783.
Rev: by Sir Desmond MacCarthy, *Sun. Times*, March 25, 1951, p. 3; *TLS*, April 6, p. 214; by H. B. C., *MGW*, April 19, p. 10; by T. C. Worsley, *NstN*, August 11, pp. 161-162; *Adelphi*, xxviii, 457-458; by Ivor Brown, *Obs.*, July 8, p. 7; by J. I. M. Stewart, *RES*, ns, iii (1952), 388-389; by H. Heuer, *SJ*, 87/88 (1952), 260; by Francis R. Johnson, *SQ*, iv (1953), 93-94.

B7731 Battenhouse, Roy W. "Hamlet's Apostrophe on Man: Clue to the Tragedy." *PMLA*, lxvi (1951), 1073-113.
Rev: by R. A. Law, *SQ*, iii (1952), 85.

B7732 Guinness, Alec. "My Idea of Hamlet." *Spectator*, 6419 (1951), 8.

B7733 Lion, Ferdinand. "*Hamlet.* Shakespeares Drama als Zeitensumme." *Der Monat*, iii (1951), Heft 6, 361-367.

B7734 McCullen, Joseph T., Jr. "Madness and the Isolation of Characters in Elizabethan and Early Stuart Drama." *SP*, xlviii (1951), 206-218.

B7735 Ordyński, Ryszard. "Hamlet—pulapka na . . . aktorów." *Teatr* (Warsaw), vi (1951), No. 11/12, 24-54.

B7736 Trehern, E. M. *More About Hamlet.* Cairo: Al Maaref Press, 1951.

B7737 Weigelin, Ernst. "Hamlets Unterredung mit seiner Mutter." *Neuphilologische Zeitschrift*, iii (1951), 261-266.

B7738 Banner, Friedrich. "Schicksal und Menschliche Tragik (Betrachtungen zum Hamletproblem)." *Neuphilologische Zeitschrift*, iv (1952), 365-369.

B7739 Fry, Christopher. "Letters to an Actor Playing Hamlet." *ShS*, v (1952), 58-61.

B7740 Hotson, Leslie. "Sables for Hamlet." *Time and Tide*, Nov. 1, 1952, pp. 1266-67.

B7741 Johnson, S. F. "The Regeneration of Hamlet: A Reply to E. M. W. Tillyard with a Counter-proposal." *SQ*, iii (1952), 187-207.

B7742 Josten, Walter. "Hamlets Natur und seine Rachepflicht." *Shakespeare-Tage* (Bochum), 1952, pp. 4-5.

B7743 Katz, Joseph. "Faith, Reason and Art." *American Scholar*, xxi (1952), 151-160. Comment by A. J. Levin, ibid., p. 363.

B7744 McKenzie, James. "A Shakespearean Interpretation [*Hamlet*, V. i. 311-315]." *N &Q*, 197 (1952), 160.

B7745 Schalla, Hans. "Was Ist Uns Hamlet?" *Shakespeare-Tage* (Bochum), 1952, p. 5.

B7746 Allen, Don Cameron. "Shakespeare's Hamlet." *Literary Masterpieces of the Western World.* Ed. Francis H. Horn. Baltimore: Johns Hopkins Press, 1953, pp. 148-163.

B7747 Empson, William. "*Hamlet* When New." *SR*, lxi (1953), 15-42, 185-205.

B7748 Javoršek, Jože. "Aktualnost Shakespearovega Hamleta" (Hamlet's Actuality). *Naša Sodobnost* (Ljubljana), I, 6 (1953).

B7749 Altick, Richard D. "*Hamlet* and the Odor of Mortality." *SQ*, v (1954), 167-176.

B7750 Chiaromonte, N. "Amleto al Naturale." *Il Mondo*, March 16, 1954.

B7751 Gérard, Albert. "Hamlet, ou le Mythe de l'Intellectuel." *Revue Nouvelle*, Jan. 1954, pp. 60-66.

B7752 Gradišnik, Fedor. "William Shakespeare: Hamlet." *Gledališni List* (Celje), iii (1954/55), 1-8.

B7753 Hartlaub, Gustav. "Hamlet und das Jenseits." *Euphorion, Zeitschrift für Literaturgeschichte* (Heidelberg), xlviii (1954), 435-447.

B7754 Hennings, Elsa. "*Hamlet,*" Shakespeares "*Faust*"-Tragödie. Bonn, 1954. Pp. 296.
Rev: A8574.

B7755 Hostos, Eugenio M. de "*Hamlet.*" *Estudio Crítico.* Buenos Aires: Ed. Inti, 1954.

B7756 Madariaga, Salvador de. "La Malinconia di Amleto." *La Fiera Letteraria*, May 30, 1954.

B7757 Mohrhenn, A. "Hamlet und die Verzweiflung." *Deutsche Rundschau*, lxxix (1953), 1056-71. Also in his *Lebendige Dichtung*, Heidelberg, 1956, pp. 66-93.

B7758 Withington, Robert. "Shakespeare, *Hamlet*, and Us." *South Atlantic Quarterly*, liii (1954), 379-383.

B7759 Alexander, Peter. *Hamlet: Father and Son.* Oxford: Clarendon Press, 1955. Pp. 189.
Rev: by E. C. Pettet, *English*, x (1954/55), 189-190; *NstN*, xlix (1955), 300-301; *ShN*,

v, 42; *TLS*, March 11, p. 147; by Kenneth Muir, *London Mag.*, II, No. 6 (1955), 104-106, 108; by Anthony Thwaite, *Spectator*, April 15, pp. 476, 478; by J. C. Trewin, *Books of the Month*, LXX, v, 9-22; by J. Crow, *Listener*, LIII, 543-545; by P. Benchettrit, *LanM*, XLIX, p. 272; by J. Vallette, *MdF*, 324 (1955), 532-533; by F. D. Hoeniger, *Canadian Forum*, Aug., p. 118; by Harry Levin, *SQ*, VII (1956), 104-107; by Hermann Heuer, *SJ*, 92 (1956), 374-376.

B7760   Eissler, K. R. "On *Hamlet*." *Samiksa* (Calcutta), VII (1955), 85-132, 155-202.

B7761   Grossman, L. "Problematika Gamleta." *Teatr* (Moscow), XVI, xi (1955), 113-124.

B7762   Highet, Gilbert. "Madness of Hamlet." *The Clerk of Oxenford*. London, New York: Oxford Univ. Press, 1954, pp. 142-148.

B7763   Lion, F. "Una Nuova Interpretazione dell'Amleto di Shakespeare." *Rivista di Studi Teatrali*, No. 7, 1953.

B7764   Bloch, Ernst. "Figuren der Grenzüberschreitung: Faust und Wette um den erfüllten Augenblick." *Sinn u. Form*, VIII (1956), 177-212.
          Hamlet, pp. 205-212.

B7765   Donovan, James L. "A Note on Hamlet's 'Not Shriving Time Allow'd'." *N &Q*, NS, III (1956), 467-469.

B7766   Johnson, Edgar. "*Hamlet*." *Great Moral Dilemmas*. Ed. Robert Morrison MacIver. New York: Harper, 1956. Pp. 189.
          Rev: *English Journal*, XLVI (1957), 588.

B7767   Muller, Herbert J. *The Spirit of Tragedy*. New York: Knopf, 1956. Pp. ix, 335.
          Hamlet, pp. 171-180.
          Rev: A6914.

B7768   Santayana, George. "*Hamlet*." *Obiter Scripta*. Ed. Buchler & Schwartz. New York: Scribner's, 1936, pp. 41-67. Republ. in Santayana's *Essays in Literary Criticism*. Ed. Irving Singer. New York: Scribner's, 1956, pp. 120-136.

B7769   Shepard, Warren V. "Hoisting the Enginer with His Own Petar." *SQ*, VII (1956), 281-285.

B7770   Sypher, Wylie. *Four Stages of Renaissance Style*. New York: Doubleday Anchor Books, 1956. Pp. 312.
          Rev: A5514.

B7771   Schadewaldt, Wolfgang. "Hamlet und sein Leid." *Das Neue Forum* (Darmstadt), VI (1956/57), 81-84.

B7772   Weil, Grete. "Stimmen zu Hamlet." *Das neue Forum* (Darmstadt), VI (1956/57), 85-92.

B7773   Zambrano, María. "Marco Aurelio y Hamlet." *Excelsior* (Mexico City), Aug. 4, 1957.

B7774   Fehrman, Carl. "Möten med Hamlet." [Confrontations with Hamlet.] *Svenska Dagbladet* (Stockholm), Aug. 4, 1958.

B7775   Hankiss, Elemer. "Neue Wege der Hamlet-Kritik." *SJ*, 94 (1958), 203-217.

B7776   Weidhorn, Manfred. "*Hamlet* and the Arts." *N &Q*, NS, V (1958), 52-53.

(c) MODERN PSYCHOLOGICAL APPROACHES

B7777   Freud, Sigmund. *The Interpretation of Dreams* (First Part). *The Standard Edition of the Complete Psychological Works*, IV, translated from the German under the General Editorship of James Strachey in Collaboration with Anna Freud. London: The Hogarth Press and The Institute of Psycho-Analysis, 1953. Freud's famous discussion of *Hamlet*, subsequently expanded by Ernest Jones, appears on pages 264-266.

B7778   Freud, Sigmund. "Psychopathic Characters on the Stage." Tr. by H. A. Bunker. *Psychoanalytic Quarterly*, XI (1942), 459-464. Also in *Standard Edition*, tr. by James Strachey, VII (1953), 305-310.

B7779   Lloyd, James Hendrie. "The So-called Œdipus-complex in Hamlet." *The Journal of the American Medical Association* (Chicago), LVI (1911), 1377-79.

B7780   Coriat, Isador H. *The Hysteria of Lady Macbeth*. New York: Moffat, Yard and Co., 1912. Pp. 94. 2nd edition, New York: Four Seas, 1921.
          Jones's Hamlet, pp. 26-28.

B7781   Rank, O. "Shakespeares Vaterkomplex." *Das Inzest-Motiv in Dichtung und Sage*, Leipzig, 1912, pp. 204-233.

B7782   Juliusburger, O. "Shakespeares Hamlet ein Sexualproblem." *Die neue Generation*, IX (1913).

B7783   MacCurdy, John T. "Concerning Hamlet and Orestes." *Journal of Abnormal Psychology*, XIII (1918), 250-260.

B7784   Delgado, Honorio F. "El Enigma Psicológico de Hamlet." *La Crónica Médica* (Lima), XXXVII (1920), 158-162.

B7785   Clutton-Brock, Arthur. *Shakespeare's "Hamlet."* London: Methuen, 1922.
          Rev: A1207.

B7786   Symons, Norman J. "The Graveyard Scene in *Hamlet*." *International Journal of Psycho-Analysis*, IX (Jan., 1928), 96-119.

B7787   Sharpe, Ella Freeman. "The Impatience of Hamlet." *International Journal of Psycho-Analysis*, x (1929), 270-279.
Same as: "Hamlets Ungeduld." *Internationale Zeitschrift für Individualpsychologie*, xv (1929), 329-339. Reprinted in B7827, pp. 203-213.

B7788   Rank, Otto. *Art and Artist*. Tr. by Charles F. Atkinson. New York: Knopf, 1932. Pp. xxvii, 431, xii.
Hamlet, pp. 284-285, 288, 292, 296, 333, 334, 420, 421, 423.

B7789   Bodkin, Maud. *Archetypal Patterns in Poetry*. Oxford Univ. Press, 1934. Pp. xiv, 340.
Hamlet and Oedipus considered, pp. 11-13; Hamlet and Lear, pp. 280-285.
Rev: A8096.

B7790   Ewing, Fayette C. *Hamlet: An Analytic and Psychologic Study*. Boston: Stratford Co., 1934. Pp. 32.

B7791   Granville-Barker, Harley. *Study of Drama*. Cambridge Univ. Press, 1934.
Section "(F) Freudianism in Literature," pp. 53-56, attacks Freud-Jones interpretation of *Hamlet*; calls it all "dirty nonsense." "I do not use the 'dirty' abusively, but to connote the more material side of our nature, which was formed, as we know, out of the dust of the earth." Subsequently he declares, "The artists' business is with spiritual tragedy . . . Let [the scientist] not—I most humbly suggest—try to imprison the spirit of man there, and range that among his specimens; neither let the artist betray his own ancient and honourable vocation by playing the jackal to such sacrilege."
Rev: A1233.

B7792   Sachs, Wulf. *Psychoanalysis: Its Meaning and Practical Applications*. London: Cassell, 1934.
Essay based on Jones's *Hamlet*, pp. 197-212.

B7793   Cazamian, Louis. "Humour in *Hamlet*." *Rice Institute Pamphlets*, xxiv (1937), 214-228. Also in *Essais en Deux Langues* (B4463), along with an essay entitled "La Psychanalyse et la Critique Littéraire."

B7794   Hinrichsen, O. "Is the Problem of Hamlet's Insanity Solved?" *Psychiatr.-Neurol.-Wochenschrift*, xxxix (1937), 36-40.

B7795   Oktski, Kenji. "Analytische Würdigung von Shakespeares *Hamlet*." *Tokyo Zeitschrift für Psychoanalyse*, 1938.

B7796   Reik, Theodor. "The Way of All Flesh." *From Thirty Years with Freud*. Tr. by Richard Winston. New York: Farrar and Rinehart, Inc., 1940, pp. 197-212.

B7797   Hendrick, Ives. *Facts and Theories of Psychoanalysis*. New York: Knopf, 1941.
Repeats Freud-Jones interpretation.

B7798   Wertham, Frederic. "The Matricidal Impulse; Critique of Freud's Interpretation of Hamlet." *Journal of Criminal Psychopathology*, ii (1941).

B7799   Wertham, Frederick. *Dark Legend*. New York: Duell, Sloan, and Pearce, 1941.
A case history of a boy comparable to the Jones interpretation of Hamlet, but differing in that Wertham's emphasis is on Hamlet's hostility to his mother.
Rev: by G. W. Stonier, *NstN*, xxxiv (1947), 454 (favorable); by Clifford Leech, *ShS*, ix (1956), 13.

B7800   Campbell, Oscar J. "What's the Matter with Hamlet?" *YR*, xxxii (1942), 309-322.
Critique of Freud-Jones view. Suggests Hamlet is the victim of cycles like those of a manic depressive which always give him the wrong emotion at the wrong time.

B7801   Stern, E. S., and W. H. Whiles. "Three Ganser States and *Hamlet*." *Journal of Mental Science*, 88 (1942), 134-141.
Ganser state: a psychotic patient, not knowing he's psychotic, feigns insanity.

B7802   Davie, T. M. "Hamlet's 'Madness'." *Journal of Mental Science*, 88 (1942), 449-450.
Answer to B7801.
Objections: 1. Hamlet is a literary character.
            2. A labeling explains nothing.
            3. Hamlet is not insane.

B7803   Bunker, H. Alden. "Mother-Murder in Myth and Legend." *Psychoanalytic Quarterly*, xiii (1944), 198-207.
Considers Hamlet more like Orestes than Oedipus. Murder of mother the result of repression; it equals incest.

B7804   Wittels, Fritz. "Psychoanalysis and Literature." *Psychoanalysis Today*. Ed. by Sandor Lorand. New York: International Universities Press, 1944, pp. 371-380. Supports Jones on *Hamlet*.

B7805   Brunot, Henriette. "*Hamlet* de Shakespeare, traduction d'André Gide." *Psyché*, i (1946), 229-232.
"L'explication psychanalytique d'Hamlet de Ernest Jones à propos de la création d'Hamlet par Jean-Louis Barrault. Cette explication est en effect une des meilleurs que l'on ait données." —Claude Dominique, B7812.

B7806   Lindbäck, Erland. "Hamlet i Psykoanalytisk Belysning." *Studier tillägnade Anton Blanck*, Dec. 29, 1946, pp. 61-79. Jonesian thesis.

B7807   Sypher, Wylie. "*Hamlet*: The Existential Madness." *Nation*, 162 (June 21, 1946), 750-751.
B7808   Tissi, Silvio. *Al Microscopio Psicanalitico. Pirandello, Ibsen, Shakespeare, Tolstoi, Shaw, Bourget, Gide*. 4th ed. Milan: Hoepli, 1946. Pp. xxx, 540.
B7809   *Hamlet: With a Psycho-Analytic Study by Ernest Jones, M. D.* Drawings by F. Roberts Johnson. New York: Funk and Wagnalls; London: Vision Press, 1947. Pp. 180.
         Rev: A1298.
B7810   Sachs, Wulf. *Black Hamlet*. Boston: Little, Brown, 1947. First published in 1937 in England. Tr. into French by H. Claireau. *Revue de Paris*, Feb. 15, 1939, pp. 39-69; Mar. 1, pp. 51-82; Mar. 15, pp. 336-373; Apr. 1, pp. 619-651. Cited in *ShS*, IX (1956), 13.
B7811   Cancelled.
B7812   Dominique, Claude. [A Review of the Olivier *Hamlet* Film.] *Psyché—Revue Internationale des Sciences de l'Homme et de Psychanalyse* (Paris, ed. by Mme. Maryse Choisy-Clouzet as the *Bulletin de la Ligue d'Hygiène Mentale*), III, Nos. 23-24 (Sept.-Oct., 1948), 1179-82.
B7813   Dupee, F. W. "Adjusting Hamlet." *Partisan Review*, xv (Oct., 1948), 1136-39.
         Review of B7809.
         Very unsympathetic both to Jones and to historical scholarship, but in itself rather trivial.
B7814   Jones, Ernest. "The Death of Hamlet's Father." *International Journal of Psycho-Analysis*, XXIX, Part III (Aug., 1949), 174-176.
         Also published in *Art & Psychoanalysis*. Ed. by Wm. Phillips. New York: Criterion Books, 1957, pp. 146-150.
         Rev: A1405.
B7815   K., H. "E. Jones' *Hamlet*: With a Psychoanalytical Study." *Punch*, 214 (Feb. 11, 1948), 128-129.
B7816   Lindner, Robert M. "The Equivalents of Matricide." *Psychoanalytic Quarterly*, XVII, No. 4 (1948), 453-470.
         Support for B7799 and B7803.
B7817   Sharpe, Ella M. "An Unfinished Paper on *Hamlet*." *International Journal of Psycho-Analysis*, XXIX (1948), Part II (May, 1949), 98-109. Reprinted in B7827, pp. 242-265.
B7818   Ashworth, John. "Olivier, Freud, and *Hamlet*." *Atlantic Monthly*, May, 1949, pp. 30-33.
B7819   Cardim, Luiz. *Os Problemas do Hamlet e as Suas Dificuldades Cénicas*. Lisbon, 1949. Pp. 125.
         Olivier's and film difficulties.
B7820   Jones, Ernest. *Hamlet and Oedipus*. London: Victor Gollancz, 1949. Pp. 166.
         A revised version of a psychoanalytical study first published in 1910.
         Rev: A1314. See also reviews of Olivier film, B3375-B3417.
B7821   Moloney, James Clark, and Laurence Rochelein. "A New Interpretation of *Hamlet*." *International Journal of Psycho-Analysis*, XXX (1949), 92-107.
B7822   Reik, Theodor. *Fragment of a Great Confession*. New York: Farrar, Straus, & Co., 1949.
         Hamlet's preoccupation with death, pp. 269-270.
B7823   Stearns, Marshall W. "*Hamlet* and Freud." *CE*, x (1949), 265-272.
         Comment by Robert Withington and Elliot M. Schrero, *CE*, x (1949), 475-476.
B7824   Stevenson, G. H. "Social Psychiatry and *Hamlet*." *TRSC* (Ottawa), XLIII, 3rd Series, (June, 1949), Section 2, pp. 143-151.
B7825   Wormhoudt, Arthur. *The Demon Lover*. New York: Exposition Press, 1949.
         Hamlet, pp. 7-8.
B7826   Rank, Otto. *Psychology and the Soul*. Tr. by William D. Turner, 1950.
         Hamlet, pp. 61-70.
B7827   Sharpe, Ella Freeman. *Collected Papers on Psycho-Analysis*. Ed. by Marjorie Brierley, pref. by Ernest Jones. International Psycho-Analytic Library, No. 36. London: Hogarth Press, 1950.
         Contains B7787 and B7817.
B7828   Slochower, Harry. "*Hamlet*: Myth of Renaissance Sensibility." *American Imago*, VII (1950), 197-238.
B7829   Trilling, Lionel. "Freud and Literature." *The Liberal Imagination*. New York: The Viking Press, 1950, pp. 34-57.
         Rev: A1334.
B7830   Klitscher, Hermann. "Über Sir Lawrence Oliviers *Hamlet*-Film." *Shakespeare-Studien, Festschrift für Heinrich Mutschmann*, pp. 107-114.
B7831   Hartwig, Theodor. *Hamlets Hemmungen. Psycholog. Studie*. Vienna: Cerny, 1952. Pp. 104.
B7832   Lüthi, Max. "Hamlet in der Gascogne." *SJ*, 87/88 (1952), 48-57.
B7833   Meltzer, J. "Some Psycho-Analytical Angles on Aspects of Shakespearean Drama." *Discussion* (South Africa), I, No. 6 (1952), 47-50.
B7834   Reik, Theodor. *The Secret Self*. New York: Farrar, Straus, and Young, 1952. Pp. 329.
         Psychoanalytic musings on *Hamlet*, among other subjects.
         Rev: A1356.
B7835   Donnelly, Mabel Collins. "Freud and Literary Criticism." *CE*, xv (Dec., 1953), 155-158.
         Benign toward Jones's interpretation of *Hamlet*.

B7836   Lucas, F. L. *Literature and Psychology.* London: Cassell, 1951. Pp. 340.
        Three essays on Hamlet, pp. 15-52.
        Rev: A1362.

B7837   Reik, Theodor. *The Haunting Melody.* New York: Farrar, Straus, and Young, 1953.
        Hamlet, p. 137.

B7838   MacCarthy, Desmond. *Theatre.* London: MacGibbon & Kee, 1954. Pp. vi, 191.
        Rev: *TLS*, Oct. 8, 1954, p. 643; *Listener*, LII, 635; by Anthony Hartley, *Spectator*, Oct. 1,
        pp. 410-411; *Thought*, xxx (1955), 320.

B7839   Strong, L. A. G. "Shakespeare and the Psychologists." *Talking of Shakespeare.* Ed. by
        John Garrett. London: Hodder & Stoughton & Max Reinhardt, 1954.
        Section VI discusses B7799.

B7840   Cancelled.

B7841   Lesser, Simon O. "Freud and *Hamlet* Again." *American Imago*, xii (1955), 207-220.
        An answer to B7818.

B7842   Müller-Hegemann, D. "Über die Beziehungen der Psychopathologie zur Literatur." *Psychia.
        Neurol. med. Psychol.* (Leipzig), v (1955), 341-346.

B7843   Dracoulides, N. N. "Tracé Psychoanalytique sur *Hamlet* de Shakespeare." *Psyché* (Paris),
        xi (1956), 129-155.

B7844   Frost, William. "Shakespeare His Own Granpaw." *CE*, xvii (1956), 219-222.

B7845   Hankins, John Erskine. "Hamlet and Oedipus Reconsidered." *ShN*, vi (1956), 11.

B7846   Kirschbaum, Leo. "Hamlet and Ophelia." *PQ*, xxxv (1956), 376-393.
        Critique of Freud-Jones view. Argues the play is a mystery that cannot be plucked out.

B7847   Kitto, H. D. F. *Form and Meaning in Drama: A Study of Six Greek Plays and of "Hamlet".*
        London, 1956. "Hamlet and the Oedipus," pp. 253-256.
        Rev: B7506.

B7848   Reik, Theodor. *The Search Within. The Inner Experiences of a Psychoanalyst.* Selections from
        the Works of T. Reik. New York: Grove Press, 1956. Pp. xi, 659.
        On *Ham.*, pp. 334-349. Parallels with a patient, p. 356.

B7849   Grotjahn, Martin. *Beyond Laughter.* New York: McGraw-Hill, 1957. Pp. 285.

B7850   Jones, Ernest. *The Life and Work of Sigmund Freud.* Vol. iii: The Last Phase, 1919-1939.
        New York: Basic Books, Inc., 1957. Pp. xvi, 537.
        Shak. criticism and theories of authorship, pp. 425-430.

B7851   Reed, Robert R., Jr. "Hamlet, the Pseudo-Procrastinator." *SQ*, ix (1958), 177-186.
See also items B7878, B7903, B7904, and section upon Olivier's *Hamlet* film, B3375-B3417.

(d) SPECIFIC ASPECTS OF HAMLET'S CHARACTER
i. His Name and Age (236;84)

B7852   Bayley, A. R. "Christian Name Hamnet." *N &Q*, 171 (1936), 428.

B7853   B., St. C. "Christian Name 'Hamnet'." *N &Q*, 172 (1937), 11.
        Continuation of B7852.

B7854   Jack, A. A. *Young Hamlet.* Aberdeen Univ. Press, 1950. Pp. xxx, 176.
        Rev: B7446.

B7855   Stoll, E. E. "Not Fat or Thirty." *SQ*, ii (1951), 295-301.

B7856   McKenzie, James. "Hamlet: A 'Youth'." *N &Q*, 197 (1952), 76.

B7857   Dymling, C. A. "Om Hamlets ålder." *Göteborgsstudier i litteraturhistoria tillägnade Sverker Ek*
        (Göteborg), 1954, pp. 26-54.

B7858   Dymling, Carl Anders. *Hamlet's Age.* Filologiskt arkiv, K. Vitterhets—historie—och antik-
        vitets—akademien. Stockholm, 1956. Pp. 37.

B7859   McKenzie, James J. "Hamlet's Age Again." *N &Q*, ns, iii (1956), 151-152.

B7860   Sjögren, Gunnar. *Var Othello Neger och Andra Shakespeare-problem?* Stockholm: Natur och
        Kultur, 1958. Pp. 196.
        Includes essay on Hamlet's age.

ii. The Antic Disposition

B7861   Finch, M. E. "Hamlet's 'Antic Disposition'." *N &Q*, 179 (1940), 62-63.

B7862   Thomas, Sidney. *The Antic Hamlet and Richard III.* DD, Columbia University, 1945. New
        York: King's Crown Press, 1943. Pp. 92.

B7863   Hunter, E. R. *Shakspere and Common Sense.* Boston, 1954.
        Two chapters on the "Antic Disposition."
        Rev: A971.

B7864   Doggett, Frank. "Shakespeare's *Hamlet*, II.ii.116-119." *Expl.*, Jan., 1958, No. 25.

B7865   Levin, Harry. "The Antic Disposition." *SJ*, 94 (1958), 175-190.

iii. The Third Soliloquy

B7866   Matthes, Heinrich Christoph. " 'Thus Conscience Does Make Cowards of Us All' (*Hamlet*, III.i)." *Anglia*, LX (1936), 181-196.

B7867   Allen, N. B. "Hamlet's 'To Be or Not To Be' Soliloquy." *SAB*, XIII (1938), 195-207.

B7868   Tannenbaum, Samuel A. " 'To Be or Not To Be'." *SAB*, XIV (1939), 62-63.

B7869   Deutschbein, Max. "Der Hamletmonolog 'To be or not to be'." *SJ*, 80/81 (1946), 31-69.

B7870   Chapman, Raymond. "Hamlet and Fortune." *TLS*, Oct. 25, 1947, p. 549.
Argues for the 1752 emendation of "slings" to "stings."

B7871   Brooke, C. F. Tucker. "Hamlet's Third Soliloquy." *Essays on Shakespeare and Other Elizabethans*, Yale Univ. Press, 1948, pp. 39-45.

B7872   Chwalewik, W. "To Be or Not To Be." *Proceedings of the Polish Academy of Sciences* (Krakow), L (1949), 291-294.

B7873   Lawrence, Gerald. "*Hamlet*." *TLS*, Aug. 12, 1949, p. 528.

B7874   Omand, Catherine D. "*Hamlet*." *TLS*, Aug. 26, 1949, p. 553.
Answers B7873.

B7875   Jordan, Hoover H. "Shakespeare's *Hamlet*, III.i.56-87." *Expl.*, VIII, No. 4 (1950), item 28.
See the note by W. L. Meyers, ibid., IX, No. 10 (1951).

B7876   Williams, Gwyn. " 'The Pale Cast of Thought'." *MLR*, XLV (1950), 216-218.
Hamlet's lines, III.i.85-86, embodying the metaphor of a cosmic mask.

B7877   Ube, Isamu. "Deliveries of the Hamlet Soliloquy. Act Three, Scene One." *Japan Science Review*, IX (1958), 82-87.

iv.   The Mousetrap (235;84)

B7878   Rank, Otto. "Das 'Schauspiel' in *Hamlet*." *Imago*, IV (1915), 41-51.
Develops Freud's idea; see Grinstein, B7903.

B7879   Gray, Henry David. "Hamlet Problems." *TLS*, Jan. 9, 1937, p. 28.

B7880   Roberts, Donald R. " 'Miching Mallico'." *TLS*, Apr. 18, 1936, p. 336.

B7881   Walker, Alice. " 'Miching Malicho' and the Play Scene in *Hamlet*." *MLR*, XXXI (1936), 513-517.

B7882   Palmer, F. G. "The Dumb-show in *Hamlet*." *New York Times*, Oct. 17, 1937, p. 2x.

B7883   Lawrence, William W. "Hamlet and the Mouse Trap." *PMLA*, LIV (1939), 709-735.

B7884   Tillyard, E. M. W. "The Dumb Show." *TLS*, April 15, 1939, p. 217.

B7885   Greg, W. W. "The Mouse-Trap—A Postscript." *MLR*, XXXV (1940), 8-10.

B7886   Nosworthy, J. M. "A Reading of the Play-Scene in *Hamlet*." *ES*, XXII (1940), 161-170.

B7886a   Stoll, Elmer Edgar. "Recent Elizabethan Criticism." *ELH*, VI (1939), 39-57.

B7887   Sisson, C. J. "The Mouse-Trap Again." *RES*, XVI (1940), 129-136.

B7888   Hart, Alfred. "Once More the Mouse-Trap." *RES*, XVII (1941), 11-20.

B7889   Kishimoto, G. S. "An Observation on the Play Scene in *Hamlet*." *Studies in English Literature* (Eng. Lit. Soc. Japan), XX (1941), 457-465.

B7890   Tannenbaum, Samuel A. "Hamlet and the Gonzago Murders." *SAB*, XVI (1941), 169-174.

B7891   Montgomerie, William. "Mirror for Magistrates. The Solution of the Mousetrap in *Hamlet*." *Life and Letters Today*, XXXIII (1942), 86-96.

B7892   Prior, Moody E. "The Play Scene in *Hamlet*." *ELH*, IX (1942), 188-197.

B7893   Walter, J. H. "The Dumb Show and the Mouse Trap." *MLR*, XXXIX (1944), 286-287.

B7894   Nosworthy, J. M. "The Structural Experiment in *Hamlet*." *RES*, XXII (1946), 282-288.

B7895   Flatter, Richard. "The Dumb Show in *Hamlet*." *Shakespeare Quarterly* (London), I (Summer, 1947), 26-49.
Suggests the dumb show was played on the upper stage, out of sight of king and queen seated in rear stage below, but visible to Ham. and Horatio leaning against the pillars.

B7896   Lambda, Beta. "Correspondence." *Shakespeare Quarterly* (London), I (Summer, 1947), 93-94.
Karl Immerman, director of theater in Düsseldorf from 1832 to 1837, anticipated staging of dumb show suggested by Dover Wilson, Granville-Barker, and Simpson.

B7897   Fiedler, Leslie A. "The Defense of the Illusion and the Creation of Myth: Device and Symbol in the Plays of Shakespeare." *EIE, 1948*. New York: Columbia Univ. Press, 1949, pp. 74-94.
Deals mainly with "the myth of the Cosmic Drama," esp. as seen in the play-within-the-play in *Hamlet*.

B7898   Flatter, Richard. *Hamlet's Father*. London, 1949.
Includes a staging proposal for the Mousetrap.
     Rev: B7428.

B7899   Flatter, Richard. "The Climax of the Play-Scene in *Hamlet*." *SJ*, 87/88 (1952), 26-42.

B7900   Green, Andrew J. "The Cunning of the Scene." *SQ*, IV (1953), 395-404.
The Pyrrhus passage, the advice to the players, and the play-within-the-play seen as strengthening the picture of Hamlet as a man of action.

B7901 Suneson, Bent. "Marlowe and the Dumb Show." *ES*, xxxv (1954), 242-253.
Deals mainly with Marlowe's *Edward II* but has references to the dumb show in *Hamlet*, II.iii.

B7902 Watson, Sara Ruth. "The 'Mousetrap' Play in *Hamlet*." *N &Q*, NS II (1955), 477-478.

B7903 Grinstein, Alexander. "The Dramatic Device: A Play-within-a-Play." *Journal of the American Psycho-Analytic Association*, IV (1956), 49-52.
The dream within a dream is compared to the play within a play as it occurs in *Hamlet*.

B7904 Wormhoudt, Arthur. *Hamlet's Mouse Trap*. A Psychoanalytical Study of the Drama. New York: Philosophical Library, Inc., 1956. Pp. 221.
Rev: by Carmen Rogers, *English Journal*, XLVI (1957), 371; *TAr*, June, p. 62; *ShN*, VII, 26; by Campbell Crockett, *JAAC*, XVI (1958), 403-405.

B7905 Müller, Dagobert. "Über die Schilderung einer Vergiftung in Shakespeares *Hamlet*." *Wissenschaftliche Zeitschrift der Humboldt-Universität zu Berlin: Gesellschafts- und Sprachwissenschaftliche Reihe*, VI (1956/57), 75-86.

B7906 Holland, Norman N. "The Dumb-Show Revisited." *N &Q*, NS, V (1958), 191.

v. Irresolution

B7907 Boswell, James. *London Journal, 1762-1763*. Ed. by Frederick A. Pottle. New York: McGraw-Hill, 1950. Pp. xxix, 370.
Reports "a most ingenious dissertation on the character of Hamlet" by Thomas Sheridan, in conversation with Boswell and others, April 6, 1763 (pp. 234-235). Probably the first recorded statement in detail of the theory of Hamlet as an irresolute intellectual, shrinking from an unwelcome task.

B7908 Young, Stark. "To Madame Frijsh." *NR*, 89 (1956), 146.
On the prayer scene and Hamlet's irresolution as portrayed by Leslie Howard and John Gielgud.

B7909 C., T. C. "*Hamlet*: Three Notes." *N &Q*, 155 (1938), 114-115.
See letters by H. Kendra Baker and Hibernicus, *N &Q*, 155 (1938), 158-159; by P. L. Carver and G. G. L., ibid., 155 (1938), 191.
Comments on the naturalness of Hamlet's irresolution.

B7910 Routh, C. R. N. "The Pyrrhus Speech in *Hamlet*." *TLS*, Aug. 5, 1944, p. 379.
Note letters by H. W. Crundell, *TLS*, Aug. 26, 1944, p. 415, and Nov. 23, 1935, p. 770.

B7911 Richard, P. M. "*Hamlet*, Tragédie de l'Indécision." *Le Magasin du Spectacle*, No. 7, Dec., 1946, pp. 27-34.

B7912 Bamborough, John. "The Missing Speech in *Hamlet*." *Listener*, XLII (July 14, 1949), 74-75.

B7913 Brillenburg-Wurth, G. "Droom en daad." *Horizon*, XII (1949), 17-21.

B7914 Detmold, George. "Hamlet's 'All But Blunted Purpose'." *SAB*, XXIV (1949), 23-36.

B7915 Wagenknecht, Edward. "The Perfect Revenge—Hamlet's Delay." *CE*, x (1949), 188-195.
Comment by Ralph A. McCanse, *CE*, x (1949), 476-478.

B7916 Lawlor, J. J. "The Tragic Conflict in *Hamlet*." *RES*, NS, I (1950), 97-113.
Rev: by J. I. M. Stewart, *ShS*, V (1952), 132-133.

B7917 Hutcheson, Harold R. "Hamlet's Delay." *ShN*, I (1951), 19.

B7918 Bonjour, Adrien. "*Hamlet* and the Phantom Clue." *ES*, xxxv (1954), 253-259.

B7919 Polanyi, Karl. "*Hamlet*." *YR*, XLIII (1954), 336-350.

(7) MISCELLANEOUS
(a) COSTUME

B7920 J., W. H. "Shakespeare in Modern Dress." *N &Q*, 184 (1943), 329-331.

B7921 G., E. "Costume in *Hamlet*." *N &Q*, 184 (1943), 374.

B7922 Dodds, M. H. "Costume in *Hamlet*." *N &Q*, 185 (1943), 323-324.

B7923 Troubridge, St. V. "Costume in *Hamlet*." *N &Q*, 185 (1943), 381-382.

B7924 Huhner, Max. "*Hamlet* in Modern Dress." *Shakespearean Studies and Other Essays*, New York, 1952, pp. 38-41.

B7925 Russell, D. A. "*Hamlet* Costumes from Garrick to Gielgud." *ShS*, IX (1956), 54-58.

B7925a Mander, Raymond, and Joe Mitchenson. "*Hamlet* Costumes: A Correction." *ShS*, XI (1958), 123-124.
Detailed corrections of factual errors appearing in B7925.

(b) SYMBOLISM (235;-)

B7926 Mandin, Louis. "Les Nouvelles Révélations sur *Hamlet* et Marie Stuart." *MdF*, 270 (1936), 652-658.

B7927 Lefranc, Abel. *A la Découverte de Shakespeare*. Vol. I. Paris: A. Michel, 1945. Pp. 600.
Rev: B4747.

B7928 Winstanley, Lilian. *Hamlet, Sohn der Maria Stuart.* Tr. by Anima Schmitt. Pfullingen: Neske, 1952. Pp. 171.
Rev: *Spiegel*, VI, No. 45 (1952), 26-27; by H. Heuer, *SJ*, 89 (1953), 235-238; by V. García Jebra, *Arbor* (Madrid), Feb., 1954.

(c) *HAMLET* AND OTHER SEVENTEENTH CENTURY WRITERS

B7929 McGinn, Donald Joseph. *Shakespeare's Influence on the Drama of his Age. Studies in "Hamlet."* New York: Appleton-Century; New Brunswick: Rutgers Univ. Press, 1938.
Rev: A8725.

B7930 O'Donnell, Norbert F. "Shakespeare, Marston, and the University: The Sources of Thomas Goffe's *Orestes.*" *SP*, L (1953), 476-484.

B7931 Madariaga, Salvador de. "*Hamlet* and Don Quixote." *Shakespeare Quarterly* (London), I (Summer, 1947), 22-25.

B7932 Turgenev, Ivan. *Hamlet en Don Quichote.* Uit het Russ. vert. en ingel. door Aleida G. Schot. Amsterdam: Meulenhoff, 1947. Pp. 48.

B7933 Irving, Thomas B. "Hamlet y Segismundo Ante la Vida." *Universidad de San Carlos* (Guatemala), No. 19, 1950, pp. 7-18.

(d) OTHERS

B7934 Seaton, Ethel. *Literary Relations of England and Scandinavia in the Seventeenth Century.* Oxford: Clarendon Press, 1935. Pp. 384.
Rev: A4630.

B7935 Allen, Percy. "Stage or Study?" *TLS*, Apr. 11, 1936, p. 316.
See letters by W. W. Greg, *TLS*, May 2, 1936, p. 379; reply by Mr. Allen, ibid., May 9, p. 400; by Levin L. Schücking, ibid., May 6, p. 420.
Allen argues against the traditional belief that Shakespeare considered his plays as stage plays only, and expresses a conviction that the great tragedies in uncut form were written for publication and, in particular, that Q₂ of *Hamlet* was intended not for stage presentation but "as a counterblast to, and protest against, the pirated Q₁."
Greg and Schücking concur.

B7935a "Stage or Study." *TLS*, Oct. 7, 1944, p. 487. Answered by H. S. Bennett, *TLS*, Oct. 14, p. 499.
Discussion of play length, audience, and Shakespearean intention.

B7936 Braumüller, W. "Shakespeares *Hamlet.*" *VB*(Mü), No. 23, 1936.

B7937 Fehr, Bernhard. "Hamlet vor der Praktischen Vernunft." *N. Zürch. Ztg.*, No. 1438, 1936.

B7938 Klein, M. "Shakespeares dramatisches Formgesetz in seiner Bedeutung für die Schule. Ein neuer Weg zu *Macbeth* und *Hamlet.*" *N. Mon.*, VI (1936), 487-498.

B7939 Dye, William S., Jr. "The Master Instructs his Puppets." *Essays in Honor of A. Howry Espenshade*, New York, 1937, pp. 46-71.
Observations growing out of Hamlet's instructions to the players.

B7940 Robertson, B. "Hamlet lived at Elsinore." *Travel*, LXVIII (1937), 15-17.

B7941 Sampley, A. M. "Hamlets All." *SAB*, XII (1937), 41-43.
The democracies in 1937 were Hamlet-like in their failure to act in the face of threatened destruction.

B7942 Innes, Michael [Pseud. for John Innes Mackintosh Stewart]. *Hamlet, Revenge!* London: Gollancz, 1938. Pp. 352.

B7943 Bellessort, A. *Le Plaisir du Théâtre.* Paris: Perrin, 1939. Pp. 292.
Part on *Hamlet*, pp. 95-102.

B7944 Glunz, H. H. "Das Problem des *Hamlet* Heute." *NS*, XLVII (1939), 356-370, 394-405, 639-646.

B7945 Hennion, Marion Garnett. "There's a Divinity that Shapes Our Ends." *Catholic World*, 150 (1940), 735-738.
Nothing about Shak.

B7946 "Aliens at Elsinore." *The London Times*, Apr. 3, 1943, p. 5.

B7947 Hartley, H. B. "Who Wrote Hamlet and Why?" *Peterborough Advertiser*, March 26, 1943.

B7948 Schücking, Levin Ldw. *Über einige Nachbesserungen bei Shakespeare. "Titus Andronicus," "Richard III," "Hamlet," "Julius Caesar," "Love's Labour's Lost."* Berichte über die Verhandlungen d. Sächs. Akad. d. Wiss. Phil. Kl., Band 95, Heft 1. Leipzig: Hirzel, 1943. Pp. 66.

B7949 Haggin, B. H. "Music for the Man Who Loves *Hamlet.*" *American Scholar*, XIII (1944), 162-170.

B7950 Eagle, R. L. "Shakespeare's Astronomy in *Hamlet.*" *N &Q*, 189 (1945), 43.

B7951 Tykesson, E. "Ynglingen Hamlet." Tykesson's *Tolv essayer*. Stockholm, 1945, pp. 203-210.

B7952 Krleža, Miroslav. "Hamlet iz Vesalove anatomije. Uz tristotridesetu obljetnicu Shakesperove smrti 23.IV.1616, 23.IV.1946" [Hamlet from Andreas Vesalius' Anatomy]. *Napriyed* (Zagreb), IV (1946), 17.

B7953 Semper, I. J. *Hamlet without Tears.* Dubuque, Iowa: Loras College Press, 1946. Pp. 107. From a Catholic point of view.
Rev: A1493.

B7954 Battenhouse, Henry Martin. "Shakespeare." *Poets of Christian Thought.* New York: Ronald, 1947, pp. 27-43.

B7955 Verkade, Eduard. *Uit het Dagboek van Horatio. Over Hamlet, prins van Denemarken.* Amsterdam: Van Campen, 1947. Pp. 135.

B7956 Hardenbrook, D. "Horatio and Dr. John H. Watson: A Literary Relationship." *Baker Street Journal,* III (1948), 358-360.

B7957 Candlin, E. Frank. "Hamlet's Successor." *Norseman,* 1949, pp. 348-355.

B7958 Arcturus, J. S. "Le Vrai Tombeau d'Hamlet." *France Illustration,* Feb. 6, 1950, p. 120.

B7959 Clemeshaw, Isabel B. "Literary Notes: *Hamlet.*" *Theosophical Forum,* XXVII (Oct., 1949), 612-619.
Comment by Madeline Clark, ibid., XXVIII (1950), 50.

B7960 Heppenstall, Rayner, and Michael Innes. *Three Tales of Hamlet.* London: Gollancz, 1950. Rev: B4069.

B7961 Norman, C. H. "Shakespeare and the Law." *TLS,* June 30, 1950, p. 412.
Comment by Donald Somervell, July 21, 1950, p. 453; reply by C. H. Norman, Aug. 4, 1950, p. 485.

B7962 Adler, Jacob H. "Origin of a Cliché? [neat but not gaudy]." *N &Q,* 196 (1951), 38-39; comment by G. H. Hatchman, p. 107.

B7963 Kemp, Lysander. "Understanding Hamlet." *CE,* XIII (1951), 9-13.
Comment by Demetrius Tarlton, and by George W. Feinstein, Dec., 1951, p. 163.

B7964 O'Connor, John J. "On the Authorship of the Ratsey Pamphlets." *PQ,* XXX (1951), 381-386. Contains a reference to Hamlet.

B7965 Pannenkowa, Irena. "Na Marginesie Teatralnych Wrażeń Hamleta." *Zycie i myśl,* Nos. 1/2, 1951, pp. 84-117.
Rev: by J. M. S., *Tygodnik powszechny,* No. 27, 1951, p. 7; reply by I. Pannenkowa, ibid., No. 23, 1952, pp. 6-7.

B7966 Ray, Sibnarayan. "*Hamlet.*" *Mysindia* (Bangalore), Jan. 1, 1951.

B7967 Savage, Derek Stanley. "Heraldry and Alchemy in Shakespeare's *Hamlet.*" *Univ. of Kansas City Rev.,* XVII (1951), 231-240.

B7968 Amrine, Michael. "The Scientist as Hamlet." *SatR,* Dec. 13, 1952, pp. 9-10, 34-36.

B7969 Gregor, Joseph. "Was Ist Uns Hamlet?" *SJ,* 87/88 (1952), 9-25.

B7970 Nehring, H. "Macbeth ein Bruder Hamlets?" *Neuphilologische Zeitschrift,* IV (1952), 361-364.

B7971 Robbins, William. "*Hamlet* as Allegory." *UTQ,* XXI (1952), 217-223.

B7972 Savage, D. S. "Alchemy in Shakespeare's *Hamlet*: An Essay in Creative Interpretation." *The Aryan Path,* XXXIII (Aug., 1952), 366-369.

B7973 Linneballe, Poul. "Hamlet and Kronborg." *Danish Foreign Office Jour.,* No. 8, 1953, pp. 19-23.

B7974 Vergani, O. "Pioggia per Amleto." *Corriere della Sera,* Sept. 7, 1953.

B7975 Bohannan, Laura. "'Miching Mallecho, That Means Witchcraft'." *London Magazine,* I (1954), 51-60.

B7976 Melchior, I. "Treasure Hunt Anyone?" *American Mercury,* LXXVIII (May, 1954), 111-114. Grave and the Shak.-Bacon controversy.

B7977 Starcke, Viggo. "Hamlet och jordfrågan." *Samtid och Framtid,* Feb., 1954, pp. 104-106. Hidden and unhidden references in *Hamlet* to the agricultural policy of the Elizabethan age.

B7978 Starcke, Viggo. "Hamlet og Jordspørgsmaalet." *Nationaltidende* (Copenhagen), Jan. 4, 1954. Essay on Hamlet's lines in the gravedigger scene concerning the question of land value.

B7979 "I Interviewed Hamlet." Intercepted over radio by Sergei Datlin, *News* (Moscow), No. 1, 1955, p. 17.
Hamlet answers political questions.

B7980 Alpers, B. "Russkij Gamlet." *Teatr* (Moscow), Aug. 16, 1955, pp. 65-80.

B7980a Anikst, Alexander. "Byt' ili ne byt' u nas Gamletu." *Teatr* (Moscow), XVI, iii (1955), 62-81.

B7981 Ochlopkov, N. "Iz Režisserskoj Eksplikacii Gamleta." *Teatr* (Moscow), Jan. 16, 1955, pp. 60-73.

B7982 Trewin, J. C. "A Walk in the Castle [*Hamlet*]." *Illustrated London News,* Dec. 24, 1955, p. 1112.

B7983 Grzegorczyk, P. "*Hamlet* w Nowym Spojrzeniu." *Twórczość* (Warsaw), June 6, 1956, pp. 172-175.

B7984 Juzovskij, Ju. "Gamlet i Drugie." *Teatr* (Moscow), XVII, ii (1956), 140-157.

B7985 Knorr, Friedrich. *Über Shakespeares "Hamlet."* Coburg, 1956. Pp. 66.
Offprint of "Donum autumnale II" Jahresgabe der Coburger Dienstagsgesellschaft.
Rev: by Hermann Heuer, *SJ,* 94 (1958), 278-279.

B7986   Schmitt, Carl. "*Hamlet* y Jacobo I de Inglaterra (Política y Literatura)." *Revista de Estudios Políticos*, LVI, No. 85 (1956), 59-91.

B7987   Brix, Hans. "Hamlet Sön af Kongen." *Berlingske Aften* (Copenhagen), 7/7 (1957).

B7988   White, C. F. "Hamlet in Jordan." *History Today*, VII (1957), 266.
        Letter protesting frequent misuse of "More honoured in the breach than the observance."

B7989   Withey, J. A. "Action in Life and in Drama." *ETJ*, X (1958), 233-236.

(8) STAGE PRODUCTIONS DURING
SHAKESPEARE'S LIFETIME

B7990   Barns, F. E. "The Original *Hamlet*." *Coronet*, III (1938), 95-98.

B7991   Jackson, Joan S. *An Analysis of Some Elizabethan and Some 20th Century Methods of Producing Shakespeare's "Hamlet."* MA thesis, McGill, 1943.

B7992   McManaway, J. G. "The Two Earliest Prompt Books of *Hamlet*." *Papers of the Bibliographical Society of America*, XLIII (1949), 288-320.
        Describes two prompt books (annotated copies of Q1676 and Q1683) prepared and used by John Ward c. 1740. Nature of the cuts in Restoration *Hamlet* probably Elizabethan. "A good ghost . . . and not too much of your damned poetry," simplified the characters and made it a play of action. The famous soliloquies and self-doubts were cut out, along with Hamlet's concern over his mother's sex life. John Ward was a grandparent of Sarah Siddons and John Philip Kemble.

B7993   Empson, William. "The Staging of *Hamlet*." *TLS*, Nov. 23, 1951, p. 749.
        Suggests that Shakespeare wanted to stage the closet scene on the balcony, but was overruled by his company.

B7994   Maxwell, J. C. "A Performance of *Hamlet*." *TLS*, Feb. 22, 1952, p. 141.
        Comment by F. S. Boas, Mar. 7, 1952, p. 173.
        Calls attention to Sydney Race's articles in *N &Q* on the Keeling Journal (to the effect that the performance of *Ham.* on board the *Dragon* in 1607 is probably a Collier forgery).

B7995   Reynolds, George F. "*Hamlet* at the Globe." *ShS*, IX (1956), 49-53.

(9) SUBSEQUENT HISTORY OF THE PLAY (237;85)
(a) PRODUCTIONS

B7996   Gielgud, John. "In the Margin." *TAr*, XXI (1937), 798-802.
        Some notes on *Hamlet* from Gielgud's forthcoming book, *The Hamlet Tradition. Some Notes on Costume, Scenery and Stage Business.*

B7997   Gilder, Rosamond. *John Gielgud's Hamlet.* Oxford Univ. Press, 1937. Pp. 234.
        Rev: B3219.

B7998   Hampden, John. "Without the Prince of Denmark." *TLS*, May 27, 1939, p. 313.
        See letter by Frederick Harker, *TLS*, May 27, 1939, p. 327. Traces "*Hamlet* without Hamlet" to 1775.
        Letter cites other cases of plays performed without the chief character.

B7999   Jackson, Joan S. *An Analysis of Some Elizabethan and Some 20th Century Methods of Producing Shakespeare's "Hamlet."* MA thesis, McGill, 1943.

B8000   Lambda, Beta. "Hamlet Miscellany." *Shakespeare Quarterly* (London), I (Summer, 1947), 50-75.
        Bygone actors and actresses in the role in London, Paris, Vienna, Weimar, 18th and 19th centuries. Goethe as producer of *Hamlet* and his conception of Ham.'s character.

B8000a Dent, Alan. *Hamlet, the Film and the Play.* World Film Publ., 1948.
        Rev: B3389.

B8001   McManaway, J. G. "The Two Earliest Prompt Books of *Hamlet*." *Papers of the Bibliographical Society of America*, XLIII (1949), 288-320.

B8002   *Hamlet, As Arranged for the Stage of the Globe Theatre at the San Diego Exposition.* Globe Theatre Version. Ed. by Thomas Wood Stevens. New York: Samuel French, 1952. Pp. 88.

B8003   Mander, R., and J. Mitchenson. *Hamlet Through the Ages: A Pictorial Record from 1709.* London: Rockliff, 1952. Second ed. New York: Macmillan, 1957.
        Arranged by Act & Scene; past stagings of any one are grouped. New ed. includes research and productions of *Ham.* through the 1955 season; 268 il.
        Rev: B1293.

B8004   Sutherland, W. O. S., Jr. "Polonius, Hamlet, and Lear in Aaron Hill's *Prompter*." *SP*, XLIX (1952), 605-618.
        Studies three essays by Hill and William Popple which appeared in 1735, and finds them to be "an early example of the transition from the theatrical to the literary criticism of character." The essays on Polonius and Hamlet anticipate the concerns of later critics.

B8005   Yoklavich, J. "Hamlet in Shammy Shoes." *SQ*, III (1952), 209-218.

B8006   Reardon, William Robert. *Banned in Boston: A Study of Theatrical Censorship in Boston from*

1630 to 1950. DD, Stanford University, 1953. Pp. 253. Mic A53-996. *DA*, XIII (1953), 609. Publication No. 5386.
From 1630 to 1900, 7 plays were banned; from 1901 to 1950, 67. *Ham.* in 1948.

B8007 Beck, Martha Ryan. *A Comparative Study of Prompt Copies of Hamlet Used by Garrick, Booth, and Irving.* DD, University of Michigan, 1956. Pp. 729. Mic 57-2269. *DA*, XVII (1957), 1412. Publication No. 21,144.

(b) COMPARISONS WITH MODERNS

B8008 Chakravarty, Amiya. *"The Dynasts" and the Post-war Age in Poetry.* Oxford Univ. Press, 1938. Comparison to Hardy.
Rev: "Hamlet and Napoleon," *TLS*, Dec. 31, 1938, p. 827.

B8009 Oppel, Horst. "Shakespeare und Kierkegaard." *SJ*, LXXVI (1940), 112-136.

B8010 Fowlie, Wallace. "Swann and Hamlet: A Note on the Contemporary Hero." *Partisan Review*, IX (1942), 195-202.

B8011 Petty, J. M. *A Study of "Winterset" Especially in the Light of "Hamlet."* MS thesis, Columbia University, 1948. Pp. 46.

B8012 Prior, Moody. "The Thought of *Hamlet* and the Modern Temper." *ELH*, XV (1948), 261-285.

B8013 Rougemont, Denis de. "Kierkegaard and Hamlet: Two Danish Princes." *The Anchor Review*, No. 1, 1955, pp. 109-127.
Adduces many curious details—notably those involving vocation— in which the religious ordeal of Søren Kierkegaard follows the tragic pattern of Hamlet.

B8014 Stavrou, Constantine N. P. "Hamlet as Existentialist." *ShN*, VII (1957), 13.

THE MERRY WIVES OF WINDSOR (217;76)
(1) THE TEXT
(a) OLD TEXTS
i. Reprints

B8015 *The Merry Wives of Windsor, 1602.* Shakespeare Quarto Facsimiles. London: Shakespeare Assoc. and Sidgwick & Jackson, 1939.
Rev: *TLS*, Dec. 2, 1939, p. 707; by B. M., *PQ*, XIX (1940), 413-414; by H. Sellers, *MLR*, XXXV, 235; by James G. McManaway, *MLN*, LV, 632-634; by D. C. Collins, *Jour. of the S. W. Essex Technical Coll.*, I (1941), 23-27.

ii. Discussions

B8016 Ogburn, Vincent H. "*The Merry Wives* Quarto, A Farce Interlude." *PMLA*, LVII (1942), 654-660.

B8017 White, David Manning. *The Textual History of "The Merry Wives of Windsor."* DD, State University of Iowa, 1942. Abstr. in Univ. of Iowa, *Abstracts and References*, III (1943), 262-268.

B8018 Hoppe, Harry R. "Borrowings from *Romeo and Juliet* in the 'Bad' Quarto of *The Merry Wives of Windsor.*" *RES*, XX (1944), 156-158.

B8019 E., S. Y. "A Shakespeare Manuscript?" *N &Q*, 189 (1945), 193.
Wm. Jaggard, ibid., p. 263, James G. McManaway, ibid., p. 284.

B8020 E., S. Y. "An Alleged Shakespeare Manuscript." *N &Q*, 191 (1946), 85; *N &Q*, 192 (1947), 218.
See correspondence in A451.

B8021 Bracy, William. *"The Merry Wives of Windsor": A Critical Study of Textual Transmission and Related Problems.* DD, University of North Carolina, 1950. Abstr. publ. in *Univ. of North Carolina Record, Research in Progress*, Jan.-Dec., 1949, Grad. School Series, No. 58, pp. 101-103.

B8022 Bracy, William. *"The Merry Wives of Windsor": The History and Transmission of Shakespeare's Text.* Columbia, Mo.: Univ. of Missouri Studies, XXV, No. 1 (1952). Pp. 154.
Rev: by Clifford Leech, *MLR*, XLVIII (1953), 333-335; by W. W. Greg, *SQ*, IV, 77-79; by H. Craig, *SQ*, IV, 119; by James G. McManaway, *ShS*, VI, 169; by Hermann Heuer, *SJ*, 89 (1953), 220.

B8023 Meadowcroft, James William Robert. *The Quarto of "The Merry Wives of Windsor"; A Critical Study.* MA thesis, McGill, 1952.

B8024 Brock, Elizabeth. *Shakespeare's "The Merry Wives of Windsor": A History of the Text from 1623 through 1821.* DD, University of Virginia, 1956. Pp. 623. Mic 57-1351. *DA*, XVII (1957), 847. Publication No. 20,349.
Discussion of all four folios, the 18th century editors, and the variorum editions of 1803 and 1821. Abstr. by Jack R. Brown, *ShN*, VIII (1958), 36.

B8025 Greer, C. A. "An Actor-Reporter in *The Merry Wives of Windsor.*" *N &Q*, NS, III (1956), 192-194.
Challenges the 1910 theory of Greg that the First Quarto is the result of the Actor-Host's imperfect memory; thinks the very nature of the discrepancies suggests Shak.'s own hasty adaptation of *The Jealous Comedy* to meet the 14-day deadline imposed by Queen Elizabeth. Later Shak. made an adaptation of his earlier one, "expanding it into what is now the Folio Version."

B8026 Clow, R. M. *Shakespeare's "Merry Wives of Windsor"*: *A Study of the 1602 Quarto and the 1623 Folio Texts*. DD, Stanford University, 1936. Pp. 364.

B8027 Cancelled.

(b) MODERN EDITIONS

B8028 *The Merry Wives of Windsor*. Milan: Uomo, 1945. Pp. 88.

B8029 *The Merry Wives of Windsor*. Ed. by Sir Arthur Quiller-Couch and John Dover Wilson. The New Shakespeare. Cambridge Univ. Press, 1955. A re-issue.

B8030 *The Merry Wives of Windsor*. Ed. by Beatrice White. Arden Shakespeare. London: Methuen, 1956.

B8031 *The Merry Wives of Windsor*. Acting Version by Romney Brent. New York: Hart Stenographic Bureau, 1958.

B8032 *The Merry Wives of Windsor*. Ed. by G. B. Harrison. Penguin Shakespeare. Harmondsworth: Penguin Books, 1957. Pp. 128.

(c) EMENDATIONS

B8033 Price, H. T. " 'To Leave on the Left'." *N &Q*, 171 (1936), 404.

B8034 R. " 'Ragged' a Monosyllable." *N &Q*, 173 (1937), 209. Cf. L. R. M. Strachan, ibid., 173 (1937), 246; J. E. Morris, ibid., p. 266.

B8035 Chang, Y. Z. "Who and What Were the Cathayans?" *SP*, xxxiii (1936), 203-221.
An examination of the term "Cataian" applied to Nym in the *Merry Wives of Windsor*.

B8036 Rook, W. Alan. "What the Good-Yere." [I.iv.130.] *TLS*, June 17, 1939, p. 358.
See letter by F. W. P. Hicks, *TLS*, June 24, 1939, p. 373.

B8037 Munro, John. "Some Matters Shakespearian." *TLS*, Sept. 13, 1947, p. 472; Oct. 11, p. 528; J. M. Nosworthy, ibid., Sept. 27, p. 497.

B8038 Kökeritz, Helge. "Five Shakespeare Notes." *RES*, xxiii (1947), 310-320.
Fourth note on *Merry Wives*, I.iii.50-56.

B8039 Parsons, Howard. *Emendations to Three of Shakespeare's Plays: "Merry Wives of Windsor," "Love's Labour's Lost," "Comedy of Errors."* London: Ettrick Press, 1953. Pp. 21.
Rev: B5636.

B8040 Montgomery, Roy F. "A Fair House Built on Another Man's Ground." *SQ*, v (1954), 207-208.

B8041 Walker, Alice. *"Merry Wives of Windsor, III.iii.176 ('Uncape')."* *RES*, ns, ix (1958), 173.

B8042 Williams, Gwyn. "The Cuckoo, the Welsh Ambassador." *MLR*, li (1956), 223-224.

(2) LITERARY GENESIS AND ANALOGUES

B8043 Crofts, J. E. V. *Shakespeare and the Post Horses. A New Study of "The Merry Wives of Windsor."* London: Arrowsmith, 1937. Pp. 237.
A general study dealing with text, sources (including symbolism and allusion), and dramatic structure.
Rev: *TLS*, Apr. 10, 1937, p. 277; *N &Q*, 172 (1937), 430-431; by F. S. Boas, *English*, i, 442-443; *London Mercury*, xxxv, 540; by R. B. Mowat, *Discovery*, xvii (1937), 244-245; by F. C. Danchin, *EA*, ii (1938), 44-45; by W. W. Greg, *RES*, xiv, 93-94; by Albert Eichler, *Beiblatt*, xlix, 104-108; by G. C. Taylor, *MLN*, liv (1939), 395-396; by Walt. Fischer, *DLZ*, lxii (1941), 402-405.

B8044 Crundell, H. W. "Two Notes on *The Merry Wives of Windsor*." *N &Q*, 173 (1937), 112-113.
Early stage history and influence on Etherege.

B8045 Seaton, Ethel. "Richard Galis and the Witches of Windsor." *Library*, 4th Series, xviii, 268-278.

B8046 Sewell, Sallie Wimberly. *The Relation of the "Merry Wives of Windsor" to Jonson's "Every Man in His Humour."* Master's thesis, University of North Carolina, 1939. Abstr. publ. in *University of North Carolina Record, Research in Progress*, Grad. School Series, No. 36, 1939, p. 82.

B8047 Sewell, Sallie. "The Relation Between *The Merry Wives of Windsor* and Jonson's *Every Man in His Humour*." *SAB*, xvi (1941), 175-189.

B8048 Bruce, Dorothy Hart. *"The Merry Wives and Two Brethren."* *SP*, xxxix (1942), 265-278.

B8049 Boughner, Daniel C. "Traditional Elements in Falstaff." *JEGP*, xliii (1944), 417-428.

B8050 Crundell, H. W. "Shakespeare and C. Swallow." *N &Q*, 189 (1945), 271-272.

B8051 White, David M. "An Explanation of the *Brook-Broome* Question in Shakespeare's *Merry Wives*." *PQ*, xxv (1946), 280-283.

B8052 Nosworthy, J. M. *"The Merry Wives of Windsor."* *TLS*, Sept. 27, 1947, p. 497.
Suggests that the play shows "reminiscences" of Henry Porter's work.

B8053 Thomas, S. G. "Source of *The Merry Wives of Windsor*." *TLS*, Oct. 11, 1947, p. 528.

B8054 Lindsay, J. "Shakespeare & Tom Thumb." *Life and Letters*, lviii (1948), 119-127.

B8055 Pendrill, Charles. "Bucklersbury." *National Rev.*, 130 (1948), 321-324.

B8056   Blair, Frederick G. "Shakespeare's Bear 'Sackerson'." *N &Q*, 198 (1953), 514-515.
The great Sackerson mentioned in *Merry Wives* (I.i.307-313) may have got his name from
John Sackerson, who owned four bears in 1583 when fire swept his town of Nantwich. See
B8083.

B8057   Starnes, DeWitt Talmage. "Acteon's Dogs." *Names*, III (1955), 19-25.
Dogs names in *Wives, Macb.*, probably from Golding's Ovid.

(3) USE OF LANGUAGE
(4) GENERAL CRITICISM OF THE PLAY

B8058   Haller, Eleanor J. "The Realism of the *Merry Wives*." *West Virginia Univ. Studies*, III: *Philological Papers*, Vol. II, 1937, pp. 32-38.

B8059   Divine, Hugh W. *A Study of Some of the Problems in the Falstaff Plays*. Master's thesis, Louisiana
State University, 1941. Abstr. in Louisiana State Univ. *Abstracts of Theses*, 1941, p. 51.

B8060   Schröder, Rudolf Alexander. "Das Menschenbild in Shakespeares *Sommernachtstraum*."
Zeitwende, XVIII (1946-47), 86-97, 172-183. Also published in Schröder's *Gesammelte Werke*,
Vol. II, 1952, pp. 248-280.

B8061   Schmidt, Karlernst. *Die Bühnenprobe als Lustspieltyp in der Englischen Literatur*. Halle: Niemeyer, 1952. Pp. 32.

B8062   Schröder, Rudolf Alexander. "*Die lustigen Weiber von Windsor*." *Gesammelte Werke*, Vol. II,
1952, pp. 337-343.

B8063   Schröder, Rudolf Alexander. "Ein Wort zu Shakespeares *Sommernachtstraum*." *Hamburgisches
Jahrbuch für Theater und Musik*, 1941. Ed. by Paul T. Hoffmann. Hamburg: Broschek &
Co., 1941, pp. 45-57. Also in Schröder's *Gesammelte Werke*, Vol. II, 1952, pp. 237-248.

(5) CHARACTERIZATION

B8064   Charlton, H. B. *Falstaff*. Manchester Univ. Press, 1935. Pp. 46. Reprint of article in *BJRL*,
XIX (1935), 46-89.
Rev: B6478.

B8065   Blyton, W. J. *We Are Observed: A Mirror of English Character*. London, 1937.
Rev: *TLS*, Feb. 5, 1938, p. 85.

B8066   Draper, J. W. "R. Shallow, esq., J. P." *N. Mitt.*, XXXVIII (1937), 257-269.

B8067   Draper, John W. "Falstaff and the Plautine Parasite." *Classical Jour.*, XXXIII (1938), 390-401.

B8068   Draper, John W. "The Humor of Corporal Nym." *SAB*, XIII (1938), 131-138.

B8069   Draper, J. W. "Falstaff's Robin and Other Pages." *SP*, XXXVI (1939), 476-490.

B8070   Wyneken, H. "Falstaff und Don Quichotte." *MNN*, No. 113, 1939.

B8071   Schell, J. S. "Shakespeare's Gulls." *SAB*, XV (1940), 23-33.

B8072   Stender, John L. "Master Doctor Caius." *Bul. Hist. Medicine*, VIII (1940), 133-138.

B8073   West, E. J. "On Master Slender." *CE*, VIII (1947), 228-230.

B8074   Draper, Charles L. [*Sic*] "Falstaff's Bardolph." *Neophil*, XXXIII (1949), 222-226.

B8075   Heath-Stubbs, John. "The Mythology of Falstaff." *Occult Observer* (London), I (1949), 21-30.

B8076   Hemingway, Samuel B. "On Behalf of that Falstaff." *SQ*, III (1952), 307-311.

B8077   Reik, Theodor. *The Secret Self*. New York: Farrar, Straus, and Young, 1952. Pp. 329.
Chapter V: "Comedy of Intrigue," pp. 63-75, on *Wives*.
Rev: A1356.

B8078   Greer, C. A. "Falstaff's Diminution of Wit." *N &Q*, 199 (1954), 468.

B8079   Wohlfarth, Paul. "Dr. Caius, a French Physician." *Sudhoffs Archiv f. Geschichte d. Med. u. d.
Naturwiss.*, XL (1956), 97-105.

(6) MISCELLANEOUS ITEMS

B8080   Cazamian, Louis. *The Development of English Humor*. Duke Univ. Press, 1952. Pp. viii, 421.
Falstaff, pp. 240-256.
Rev: B5186.

B8081   Schaller, Rudolf. "Meine Nachdichtung der *Lustigen Weiber von Windsor*." *Theater d. Zeit*,
VII, No. 18 (1952), 5-7.

B8082   Long, John H. "Another Masque for *The Merry Wives of Windsor*." *SQ*, III (1952), 39-43.

B8083   Keen, Alan. "Shakespeare's Northern Apprenticeship." *TLS*, Nov. 18, 1955, p. 689.
See also Keen's letter, *TLS*, Dec. 16, 1955, p. 761, in which he claims identification of the
famous bear Sackerson. See B8056.

(7) SUBSEQUENT HISTORY OF THE PLAY
(other than productions after 1660)

B8084   Crundell, H. W. "Two Notes on *The Merry Wives of Windsor*." *N &Q*, 173 (1937), 112-113.

The notes relate to the stage history of the play in the seventeenth century and indicate parallels in Etherege's *Love in a Tub*.

B8085	"Library Notes and News." *BJRL*, XXIX (1945), 22-23.
Includes "A Link with Shakespeare", pp. 22-23, announcing the exhibition of a 1619 edition of the *Merry Wives*, believed to have remained since its publication in Charlecote Park, the house of the Lucys'.

TROILUS AND CRESSIDA (239;85)
(1) THE TEXT

B8086	Tannenbaum, Samuel A., and D. R. *Shakespeare's "Troilus and Cressida": A Concise Bibliography*. New York, 601 W. 113th St., 1943. Pp. x, 44.

(a) OLD TEXTS
i. Reprints

B8087	Shakespeare, William. *Troilus and Cressida*. First Quarto, 1609. Shakespeare Quartos in Collotype Facsimile, No. 8. With Introd. note by W. W. Greg. London: For The Shakespeare Assoc., Sidgwick & Jackson, 1952. Unpaged.
Rev: *TLS*, Dec. 12, 1952, p. 826; by J. Vallette, *MdF*, 318 (1953), 340; by F. C. Francis, *MLR*, XLIX (1954), 392; by James G. McManaway, *ShS*, VII, 151-152.

ii. Discussions

B8088	Baldwin, T. W. "Shakespeare Facsimiles." *TLS*, May 6, 1939, p. 265.
B8089	Williams, Philip, Jr. *The 1609 Quarto of "Troilus and Cressida" and Its Relation to the Folio Text of 1623*. DD, University of Virginia, 1949. Abstr. publ. in *Abstracts of Dissertations*, Charlottesville: Univ. of Virginia, 1949.
B8090-B8189 Cancelled.
B8190	Williams, Philip, Jr. "The 'Second Issue' of *Troilus and Cressida*, 1609." *SB*, II (1949), 25-33.
B8191	Walker, Alice. "The Textual Problems of *Troilus and Cressida*." *MLR*, XLV (1950), 459-464.
B8192	Williams, Philip, Jr. "Shakespeare's *Troilus and Cressida*: The Relationship of Quarto and Folio." *SB*, III (1950), 131-143.
B8193	Greg, W. W. "The Printing of Shakespeare's *Troilus and Cressida* in the First Folio." *Papers of the Bibl. Soc. of Amer.*, XLV (1951), 273-282.
B8194	McManaway, James G. "Bibliography." *Literature and Science* (Proceedings of the Sixth Triennial Congress, Oxford, 1954), pp. 27-35. Oxford: Basil Blackwell, 1955. (For The International Federation for Modern Languages and Literatures).

(b) MODERN EDITIONS

B8195	*Troilus and Cressida*. Ed. Bonamy Dobrée. Warwick Shakespeare. London: Blackie, 1938. Pp. 172.
B8196	*Troilus and Cressida*. Ed. Harold N. Hillebrand and T. W. Baldwin. New Variorum Shakespeare. Philadelphia: Lippincott, 1953. Pp. xix, 613.
Rev: by M. A. Shaaber, *SQ*, IV (1953), 171-181; *TLS*, July 3, p. 428; by Kenneth Muir, *MLR*, XLIX (1954), 224-226; by R. A. Law, *JEGP*, LIII, 110-114; by Alice Walker, *RES*, NS, V, 288-291; *U. S. Quarterly Book Review*, X, 333; by Philip Williams, *South Atlantic Quarterly*, LIII, 272; by H. T. Price, *SQ*, V, 114; by James G. McManaway, *ShS*, VII, 149; by John Russell Brown, *MLN*, LXX (1955), 131-134; by Hermann Heuer, *SJ*, 91, (1955), 340-341.
B8197	*Troilus and Cressida*. Ed. Jackson J. Campbell. Yale Shakespeare. Yale Univ. Press, 1956.
Rev: *Essential Books*, April, 1956, p. 31; by C. G. Thayer, *Books Abroad*, Winter, 1957, p. 83; by Jiro Ozu, *SQ*, VIII, 242-243.
B8198	*The History of Troilus and Cressida*. Ed. Virgil K. Whitaker. Pelican Shakespeare. Baltimore: Penguin Books, 1958. Pp. 155.
Rev: *TLS*, Oct. 4, 1947, p. 511.
B8199	*Troilus and Cressida*. Ed. J. Dover Wilson and Alice Walker. The New Shakespeare. Cambridge Univ. Press, 1958. Pp. lvi, 254.
Rev: *ShN*, VIII (1958), 12; by Hermann Heuer, *SJ*, 94 (1958), 286-288; *N&Q*, NS, V, 503-504.

(c) EMENDATIONS

B8200	'Hibernicus'. "The Wallet of Oblivion in III. iii. 144." *N&Q*, 173 (1937), 227.
B8201	Starnes, D. T. "The Wallet of Oblivion." *N&Q*, 176 (1939), 29-30.
B8202	McCutchan, J. W. "Time's Wallet." *N&Q*, 192 (1947), 430-431. III. iii. 145.
B8203	Rossiter, A. P. "*Troilus and Cressida*." *TLS*, May 8, 1948, p. 261.
Suggests a rearrangement of last 25 lines of II. ii. and the reading *double-horned Spartan* for V. vii. 10-11.

B8204   Cunningham, J. V.   " 'Tragedy' in Shakespeare."   *ELH*, XVII (1950), 36-46.
V. ii. 153, 155.

B8205   Jones, Graham.   "The Goose in *Lear*."   *N &Q*, July 8, 1950, p. 295.
Relates *Lear*, II. ii. 88, to *Troilus and Cressida*, V. x. 55.

B8206   Megaw, Neill.   " 'Lines' as Surface Ripples ?"   *N &Q*, NS, III (1956), 315.

B8207   Reed, Victor B.   "*Troilus and Cressida*, IV. ii. 56."   *N. Mitt.*, LVII (1956), 128-132.

B8208   Thompson, Karl F.   "Cressid's Diet."   *N &Q*, NS, III (1956), 378-379.
Malone's 18th century gloss on V. ii. 181-185 in terms of the imagery of a love-feast is further
explained.

B8209   Halio, Jay Leon.   "*Traitor in All's Well and Troilus and Cressida*."   *MLN*, LXXII (1957), 408-409.
Lafew's use of "traitor" to mean both one guilty of treason and a harlot (*All's Well*, II.i.99)
clarifies Pindarus' epilogue "Oh traitours and bawdes. . ." (*Troilus and Cressida*, V.x.36-40).

B8210   Megaw, Neill.   "Shakespeare's *Troilus and Cressida*, I. iii. 354-356."   *Expl.*, XV, viii (1957),
item 52.

B8211   Hulme, Hilda M.   "Three Notes on the Pronunciation and Meaning of Shakespeare's Text."
Neophil, XLI (1958), 275-281; ibid., XLII, 212-215.
I. iii. 54.

B8212   Hulme, Hilda M.   "Three Notes: *Troilus and Cressida*, V. vii. 11; *Midsummer Night's Dream*,
II. i. 54; *Measure for Measure*, II. i. 39."   *JEGP*, LVII (1958), 721-725.

B8213   Thompson, Karl F.   "The Feast of Pride in *Troilus and Cressida*."   *N &Q*, NS, V (1958), 193-194.
In III. iii. 143, the Folio "feasting" is preferable to the Quarto "fasting," although both make
good sense.

(2)   LITERARY GENESIS AND ANALOGUES

B8214   Batchelder, Merrit C.   *The Elizabethan Elements in Shakespeare's "Troilus and Cressida."*   DD,
State University of Iowa, 1935.

B8215   Barker, E.   "A Shakespeare Discovery."   *Spectator*, 158 (1937), 615-616.
Troil. & Elyot's *Governour.*

B8216   Baldwin, T. W.   "Perseus Purloins Pegasus."   *PQ*, XX (1941), 361-370.

B8217   Sewell, Arthur.   "Notes on the Integrity of *Troilus and Cressida*."   *RES*, XIX (1943), 120-127.

B8218   Presson, Robert K.   Shakespeare's "*Troilus and Cressida*": *A Study of the Sources and Composition of the Play.*   DD, Harvard University, 1947.

B8219   Hotson, Leslie.   *Shakespeare's Sonnets Dated, and Other Essays.*   London: Rupert Hart-Davis;
Toronto: Clarke, Irwin & Co., 1949.   Pp. 244.
    Rev: C21.

B8220   Baldwin, T. W.   "Shakspere's Aphthonian Man."   *MLN*, LXV (1950), 111-112.
Points out that the pattern for praise in the grammar school Apthonius is reflected in *Troil.*,
I. ii. 274-278, and elsewhere.

B8221   Gilbert, Allan H.   " 'A Thousand Ships'."   *MLN*, LXVI (1951), 477-478.
II. ii. 81-82.

B8222   Arnold, Aerol.   "The Hector-Andromache Scene in Shakespeare's *Troilus and Cressida*."   *MLQ*,
XIV (1953), 335-340.

B8223   Jones, D. E.   *The Development of the Story of "Troilus and Cressida" as Reflecting the Change from
Medieval to Renaissance Sensibility.*   MA thesis, Wales, 1953.

B8224   Presson, Robert K.   Shakespeare's "*Troilus and Cressida*" *and the Legends of Troy.*   Univ. of
Wisconsin Press, 1953.   Pp. 176.
    Rev: by Jackson J. Campbell, *JEGP*, LIII (1954), 476-478; by H. T. Price, *SQ*, V, 111-112;
    by Ernst Th. Sehrt, *Anglia*, LXXII (1954-55), 458-459; by Philip Edwards, *MLR*, L (1955), 106;
    by John Russell Brown, *MLN*, LXX, 133-134; by John Arthos, *SQ*, VI, 103-104; by J. M.
    Nosworthy, *RES*, NS, VI, 195-196; by C. R. B. Combellack, *CL*, VII, 372-374; by René
    Pruvost, *EA*, IX (1956), 47-48; by Hermann Heuer, *SJ*, 92 (1956), 376-377.

B8225   Potts, Abbie Findlay.   "Cynthia's Revels, Poetaster, and *Troilus and Cressida*."   *SQ*, V (1954),
297-302.

B8226   Schlauch, Margaret.   "*Troilus i Kressyda* Szekspira i Chaucera-Jezyk Metaforyczny w Świetle
Przemiàn Społecznych."   *Kwartalnik Neofilologiczny* (Warsaw), I (1954), 3-20.

B8227   Legamn, G.   " 'Ever or Never'."   *N &Q*, NS, II (1955), 361.

B8228   Muir, Kenneth.   "Greene and *Troilus and Cressida*."   *N &Q*, NS, II (1955), 141-142.

B8229   Soellner, Rolf.   "The Troubled Fountain: Erasmus Formulates A Shakespearian Simile."
JEGP, LV (1956), 70-74.
Troil., III. iii. 310-315.

B8230   Mackay, Eleanor Maxine.   *The Clash and the Fusion of Medieval and Renaissance Elements in
Chaucer's "Troilus."*   DD, Emory University, 1958.   Pp. 650.   Mic 58-5161.   *DA*, XIX (1959),
2615.

(3)   USE OF LANGUAGE

B8231 Dayton, B. E. *Animal Similes & Metaphors in Shakespeare's Plays*. DD, University of Washington, 1937. Abstr. publ. in Univ. of Washington *Abstracts of Theses*, II (1937), 119-122.

B8232 Praz, Mario. *La Poesia Metafisica Inglese del Seicento: John Donne*. Rome, 1945.
Prints a series of lectures which constitute an abbreviated edition of the first part of the author's *Secentismo e Marinismo in Inghilterra* (1926), with two chapters added: one, a general short view of the *Secentismo* in Europe; the other, on the continuity of "metaphysical" elements from the days of Chaucer, with illustrations taken mainly from Chapman and from *Measure for Measure* and *Troilus*.
Rev: by Fr. A. Pompen, O.F.M., *ES*, XXVIII (1947), 50-52.

B8233 Ellis-Fermor, Una. "Some Functions of Verbal Music in Drama." *SJ*, 90 (1954), 37-48.

B8234 Munday, Mildred B. "Pejorative Patterns in Shakespeare's *Troilus and Cressida*." *Bucknell Rev.*, V (1955), 39-49.

B8235 Kramp, Karen. *Shakespeares "Troilus und Cressida." Eine Sprachlichstilistische Untersuchung*. DD, Freiburg i. Breisgau, 1957. Pp. 217. Typewritten.

B8236 Schmidt di Simoni, Karen. *Shakespeares "Troilus und Cressida." Eine Sprachlichstilistische Untersuchung*. DD, Freiburg i. Breisgau, 1957.

B8237 Berry, Francis. *Poets' Grammar*. London: Routledge and Kegan Paul, 1958. Pp. 190.
Section on tense in *Troil*.
Rev: A5230.

(4) GENERAL CRITICISM OF THE PLAY

B8238 Empson, W. *Some Versions of Pastoral*. London, 1935. Pp. 298.
Troil., pp. 34-42.

B8239 Sargeaunt, G. M. "*Troilus and Cressida*." *The Classical Spirit*, 1936, pp. 234-252.

B8240 Charlton, H. B. "Shakespeare's 'Dark Comedies'." *BJRL*, XXI (1937), 78-128.

B8241 Koszul, A. "*Troilus and Cressida*." *Bull. de la Faculté des Lettres de Strasbourg*, XV (1937), 167-172.

B8242 Lacy, E. W. *Justice in Shakespeare*. DD, Vanderbilt University, 1937. Abstr. publ. in *Abstract of Theses. Bull. of Vanderbilt Univ.*, XXXVII (1937), 42.

B8243 Campbell, Oscar J. *Comicall Satyre and Shakespeare's "Troilus and Cressida."* San Marino, California: The Henry E. Huntington Library, 1938. Pp. ix, 246.
Rev: A4913.

B8244 Traversi, D. A. "*Troilus and Cressida*." *Scrutiny*, VII (1938), 301-319.

B8245 Schmidt, W. "Die Wertlehre in *Troilus and Cressida*." *NS*, XLVII (1940), 181-188.

B8246 Deutschberger, Paul. "Shakspere on Degree: A Study in Backgrounds." *SAB*, XVII (1942), 200-207.

B8247 Spencer, Theodore. *Shakespeare and the Nature of Man*. Lowell Lectures, 1942. New York: Macmillan, 1942. Pp. xiii, 283.
Rev: A1044.

B8248 Ellis-Fermor, Una. *The Frontiers of Drama*. London: Methuen, 1945; New York: Oxford Univ. Press, 1946. Pp. vii, 154.
Chapter IV " 'Discord in the Spheres': The Universe of *Troilus and Cressida*."
Rev: A5941.

B8249 Merton, Stephen. "*The Tempest* and *Troilus and Cressida*." *CE*, VII (1945), 143-150.

B8250 Boas, G. "*Troilus and Cressida* and the Time Scheme." *New English Review*, XIII (1946), 529-535.

B8251 Clinton-Baddeley, V. C. "Shakespeare's Bitter War Play." *Radio Times*, Nov. 22, 1946.

B8252 Traversi, D. A. "Love and War in Shakespeare's *Troilus and Cressida*." *Essays in Love and Violence* (tr. by George Lamb of an issue of *Etudes Carmélitaines* in 1946 called *Amour et Violence*. Ed. by Father Bruno de Jésus-Marie). New York: Sheed & Ward, 1954. Pp. ix, 260.
Traversi's essay, pp. 35-49.

B8253 Pettigrew, Helen Purinton. "*Troilus and Cressida*: Shakespeare's Indictment of War." *West Virginia Univ. Bull.: Philological Papers*, V (1947), 34-48.

B8254 Brooke, C. F. Tucker. "Shakespeare's Study in Culture and Anarchy." *Essays on Shakespeare and Other Elizabethans*, Yale Univ. Press, 1948, pp. 71-77.

B8255 Evans, G. Blakemore. "Pandarus' House?: *Troilus and Cressida*, III. ii; IV. ii; IV. iv." *MLN*, LXII (1947), 33-35.

B8256 Patchell, Mary F. *The Palmerin Romances in Elizabethan Prose Fiction*. DD, Columbia University, 1946. *Columbia Univ. Stud. in Eng. and Comp. Lit.* No. 166. New York: Columbia Univ. Press, 1947. Pp. 154.
Shak., pp. 114-115.

B8257 Richards, I. A. "*Troilus and Cressida* and Plato." *Hudson Review*, I (1948), 362-376.

B8258 Wyneken, Hans. "*Troilus und Cressida*." *Dramaturg. Blätter*, II (1948), 140-142.

B8259 Tillyard, Eustace M. W. *Shakespeare's Problem Plays*. Univ. of Toronto Press, 1949; London:

Chatto and Windus, 1950. Pp. ix, 168.
Rev: A5222.

B8260 Baldwin, T. W. "Structural Analysis of *Troilus and Cressida*." *Heinrich Mutschmann Festschrift*, 1951, pp. 5-18.

B8261 Dunkel, Wilbur D. "Shakespeare's *Troilus*." *SQ*, II (1951), 331-334.

B8262 Duthie, G. I. *Shakespeare*. London: Hutchinson's Univ. Library, 1951. Pp. 206.
Rev: A8162.

B8263 James, D. G. *The Dream of Learning: An Essay on "The Advancement of Learning," "Hamlet" and "King Lear."* Oxford: Clarendon Press, 1951. Pp. 126.
Rev: A3959.

B8264 Kendall, Paul M. "Inaction and Ambivalence in *Troilus and Cressida*." *James Southall Wilson Festschrift*, 1952, pp. 131-145.

B8265 Knights, L. C. "*Troilus and Cressida* Again." *Scrutiny*, XVIII (1951), 144-157.

B8266 Presson, Robert K. "The Structural Use of a Traditional Theme in *Troilus and Cressida*." *PQ*, XXXI (1952), 180-188.

B8267 Röhrman, H. *Marlowe and Shakespeare: A Thematic Exposition of Some of Their Plays.* Arnhem: van Loghum Slaterus, 1952. Pp. x, 109.
Rev: A1023.

B8268 Arnold, Aerol. "The Hector-Andromache Scene in Shakespeare's *Troilus and Cressida*." MLQ, XIV (1953), 335-340.

B8269 Dickey, Franklin M. *Shakespeare's Presentation of Love in "Romeo and Juliet," "Antony and Cleopatra," "Troilus and Cressida."* DD, University of California, Los Angeles, 1954.
See B8287.

B8270 Heuer, Hermann. "*Troilus und Cressida* in Neuerer Sicht." *SJ*, 89 (1953), 106-127.
Rev: by H. T. Price, *SQ*, V (1954), 119.

B8271 Main, William W. *The Dramatic Context of Shakespeare's "Troilus and Cressida."* DD, University of North Carolina, 1954.

B8272 Meyer, George Wilbur. "Order Out of Chaos in Shakespeare's *Troilus and Cressida*." *Tulane Studies in English*, IV (1954), 45-56.

B8273 Nowottny, Winifred M. T. " 'Opinion' and 'Value' in *Troilus and Cressida*." *EIC*, IV (1954), 282-296.

B8274 Schlauch, Margaret. "*Troilus i Kressyda* Szekspira i Chaucera-Jezyk Metaforyczny w Świetle Przemiàn Społecznych." *Kwartalnik Neofilologiczny*, I (1954), 3-19.
Contrasts the two versions, stressing Shak.'s mercantile metaphors, in the light of social and economic change.

B8275 Schröder, R. A. "*Troilus and Cressida*." Eine Festrede des Präsidenten der Deutschen Shakespeare-Gesellschaft." *SJ*, 90 (1954), 11-36.

B8276 Kermode, Frank. "Opinion, Truth and Value." *EIC*, V (1955), 181-187.
Answer to B8273.

B8277 MacLure, Millar. "Shakespeare and the Lonely Dragon." *UTQ*, XXIV (1955), 109-120.
Comments upon Achilles.

B8278 Muir, Kenneth. "*Troilus and Cressida*." *ShS*, VIII (1955), 28-39.

B8279 Richards, I. A. *Speculative Instruments*. Univ. of Chicago Press, 1955. Pp. xii, 216.
Includes "*Troilus and Cressida* and Plato," pp. 198-213.
Rev: A8343.

B8280 Kaula, David Charles. *The Moral Vision of Shakespeare's "Troilus and Cressida."* DD, Indiana University, 1956. Pp. 262. Mic 56-3417. *DA*, XVI (1956), 2150. Publ. No. 17,963.

B8281 Lacy, Margaret Swanson. *The Jacobean Problem Play: A Study of Shakespeare's "Measure for Measure" and "Troilus and Cressida" in Relation to Selected Plays of Chapman, Dekker, and Marston.* DD, University of Wisconsin, 1956. Pp. 216. Mic 56-3019. *DA*, XVI (1956), 1899. Publ. No. 18,418.

B8282 Megaw, Neill. "The Sneaking Fellow: *Troilus and Cressida* I. ii. 246-249." *N &Q*, NS, III (1956), 469-470.

B8283 Muller, Herbert J. *The Spirit of Tragedy*. New York: Knopf, 1956. Pp. ix, 335.
Rev: A6914.

B8284 Muraoka, Isamu. "*Troilus and Cressida* of Shakespeare" (in Japanese). *Studies in English Literature* (Tokyo), XXXII, No. 2 (1956).

B8285 Scholz, Wilhelm von. *Das Drama: Wesen, Werden, Darstellung der Dramatischen Kunst.* Tübingen: Niemeyer, 1956. Pp. viii, 256. "*Troilus und Kressida* als szenische Aufgabe," pp. 227-234.

B8286 Chapman, John Jay. *The Selected Writings of John Jay Chapman.* Ed. with an Introd. by Jacques Barzun. New York: Farrar, Strauss and Cudahy, 1957. "*Troilus & Cressida*," pp. 268-276.
Rev: A9264.

B8287   Dickey, Franklin M. *Not Wisely but Too Well: Shakespeare's Love Tragedies.* San Marino California: The Huntington Library, 1957. Pp. ix, 205.
        Rev: A2562.

B8288   Swanston, Hamish F. G. "The Baroque Element in *Troilus and Cressida.*" *DUJ*, XIX (1957), 14-23.

B8289   Bradbrook, M. C. "What Shakespeare Did to Chaucer's *Troilus and Criseyde.*" *SQ*, IX (1958), 311-319.

B8290   Davis, E. "*Troilus and Cressida.*" *English Studies in Africa* (Johannesburg), I (1958), 10-26.

B8291   Knights, L. C. *Some Shakespearean Themes.* London: Chatto & Windus, 1959.
        Chapter on *Troil.*

B8292   Maurer, Wallace. "From Renaissance to Neo-Classic." *N &Q*, NS, V (1958), 287.
        Troil., I. iii. 119-124 and its equivalent in Dryden compared.

B8293   Morris, B. R. "Thomas Watson and *Troilus and Cressida.*" *N &Q*, NS, V (1958), 244-245.
        Poem 20 in Watson's *Superius. The first Sett, of Italian Madrigalls Englished* (1590) sees Troilus as the center of interest in the love tragedy.

(5) CHARACTERIZATION

B8294   Kenny, Hamill. "Shakespeare's Cressida." *Anglia*, LXI (1937), 163-176.

B8295   Lawrence, William Witherle. "Troilus, Cressida and Thersites." *MLR*, XXXVII (1942), 422-437.

B8296   Elton, William. "Shakespeare's Portrait of Ajax in *Troilus and Cressida.*" *PMLA*, LXIII (1948), 744-748.

B8297   Legouis, Pierre. "Troilus devant le Mariage." *LanM*, XLII (1948), fasc. A, A1-A13.

B8298   Negueloua, Lillian Mary. *The Literary Reputation of Shakespeare's Cressida.* MA thesis, University of North Carolina, 1948. Abstr. publ. in *Univ. of North Carolina Record, Research in Progress,* Grad. School Series No. 56, 1949, 224-225.

B8299   Dunkel, Wilbur D. "Shakespeare's Troilus." *SQ*, II (1951), 331-334.

B8300   Bowden, William R. "The Human Shakespeare and *Troilus and Cressida.*" *SQ*, VIII (1957), 167-177.

B8301   Eisenstein, Judith. "Thersites and the Abstraction." *Westwind*, Fall, 1957, pp. 17-19.
        Thersites, the disengaged skeptic, does not require a personal bias or social involvement for his bitterness.

(6) MISCELLANEOUS LITERATURE

B8302   Bellessort, A. "*Troilus and Cressida.*" *Le Plaisir du Théâtre.* Paris: Perrin, 1939, pp. 103-109.

B8303   Hibernicus. "The Wallet of Oblivion [*Troilus and Cressida*, III. iii. 144]." *N &Q*, 173 (1937), 227. See letter by Edward Bensly, ibid., p. 265.

B8304   Eagle, R. L. "Francis Bacon and *Troilus and Cressida.*" *N &Q*, 186 (1944), 275-276.

B8305   Reynolds, George F. "*Troilus and Cressida* on the Elizabethan Stage." *AMS*, pp. 229-238.

B8306   Kendall, Paul M. "Inaction and Ambivalence in *Troilus and Cressida.*" *James Southall Wilson Festschrift*, 1951, pp. 131-146.

B8307   Sternfeld, Frederick W. "*Troilus and Cressida*: Music for the Play." *EIE, 1952.* New York: Columbia Univ. Press, 1954, pp. 107-137.

B8308   Schröder, Rudolf Alexander. "*Troilus und Cressida.* Eine Festrede." *Merkur* (Stuttgart), IX (1955), 124-143.

(7) SUBSEQUENT HISTORY OF THE PLAY

B8309   Lill, James V. *Dryden's Adaptation from Milton, Shakespeare and Chaucer.* DD, University of Minnesota, 1954. Pp. 284. Mic A54-1780. *DA*, XIV (1954), 1214. Publ. No. 8462.

B8310   Shawe-Taylor, Desmond. "The Arts and Entertainment." *NstN*, Feb. 23, 1957, pp. 232-233.
        Sir William Walton's opera, *Troilus and Cressida.*

ALL'S WELL THAT ENDS WELL (241;86)
(1) THE TEXT
(a) MODERN EDITIONS

B8311   *All's Well That Ends Well.* Ed. G. B. Harrison. Penguin Shakespeare. London, 1955.
        Rev: *TLS*, Jan. 6, 1956, p. 10.

B8312   *All's Well That Ends Well.* Ed. Sir Arthur Quiller-Couch and John Dover Wilson. The New Shakespeare. Cambridge Univ. Press, 1955. Pp. 202.

B8313   *All's Well That Ends Well.* Ed. G. K. Hunter. The (New) Arden Shakespeare. London: Methuen; Cambridge, Mass.: Harvard Univ. Press, 1958.

(b) EMENDATIONS

LOVE'S LABOUR'S WON

B8314   Tannenbaum, Samuel A. "Removing a Scar from *All's Well* (IV. ii. 38-39)." *SAB*, XVIII (1943), 133-136.

B8315   Brooke, Tucker. " 'Men May Grope's in Such a Scarre' [*All's Well That Ends Well*, IV. ii. 38-39]." *MLN*, LVIII (1943), 426-428.

B8316   Koszul, A. "Some Notes on Shakespeare's Text." *ES*, XXXI (1950), 215-217.
          II. i. 110 (transposition of *honour* and *power*).

B8317   McKenzie, James. "A Shakespearean Emendation [*All's Well*, I. iii. 169-171]." *N &Q*, 197 (1952), 160.

B8318   Halio, Jay Leon. "*Traitor in All's Well and Troilus and Cressida*." *MLN*, LXXII (1957), 408-409.
          II. i. 97-101.

(2)   LITERARY GENESIS AND ANALOGUES

B8319   Crundell, H. W. "*All's Well That Ends Well*: The Episode of the King's Ring." *N &Q*, 180 (1941), 26-27.

B8320   Wright, H. G. "How Did Shakespeare Come to Know the Decameron?" *MLR*, L (1955), 45-48.

B8321   Wright, H. G. *Boccaccio in England, from Chaucer to Tennyson.* The Athlone Press: Univ. of London, 1957.
          Rev: A4487.

B8322   Chapman, Raymond. "*Twelfth Night* and the Swan Theatre." *N &Q*, 196 (1951), 468-470.

B8323   Baldwin, T. W. *Shakspere's "Love's Labor's Won."* New Evidence from the Account Books of an Elizabethan Bookseller. Southern Illinois Univ. Press, 1957. Pp. 50.
          Rev: *ShN*, VII (1957), 25; *TLS*, Feb. 21, 1958, p. 102; comment by F. N. Lees, March 3, p. 169; by W. W. Greg, *MLR*, LIII, 238-239; by R. C. Bald, *MP*, LV, 276-279; by George Hibbard, *N &Q*, NS, V, 276; by Giles E. Dawson, *JEGP*, LVII, 542-545; by Henry K. Zbiersky, *Kwartalnik Neofilologiczny*, V, 154-156; by J. A. Bryant, *SR*, LXVI, 325-326.

B8324   Cancelled.
See also *Troilus* Chapter in C21.

(3)   USE OF LANGUAGE

B8325   Ellis-Fermor, Una. "Some Functions of Verbal Music in Drama." *SJ*, 90 (1954), 37-48.

(4)   GENERAL CRITICISM OF THE PLAY

B8326   Charlton, H. B. "Shakespeare's 'Dark Comedies'." *BJRL*, XXI (1937), 78-128.

B8327   Pettigrew, Helen P. "The Young Count Rousillon." *West Virginia Univ. Bull.: Philological Studies*, IV (1943), 22-30.

B8328   Tillyard, Eustace M. W. *Shakespeare's Problem Plays.* Univ. of Toronto Press, 1949; London: Chatto & Windus, 1950. Pp. ix, 168.

B8329   Bradford, M. C. "Virtue Is the True Nobility. A Study of the Structure of *All's Well That Ends Well*." *RES*, NS, I (1950), 289-301.

B8330   Wilson, Harold S. "Dramatic Emphasis in *All's Well That Ends Well*." *HLQ*, XIII (1950), 217-240.

B8331   Leech, Clifford. "The Theme of Ambition in *All's Well That Ends Well*." *ELH*, XXI (1954), 17-29.

B8332   Arthos, John. "The Comedy of Generation." *EIC*, V (1955), 97-117.

B8333   Cunningham, Dolora. "Repentance and the Art of Living Well. The Tudor Interpretation of Penance, and its Relation to Dramatic Form in Comedy. With Analyses of *Love's Labour's Lost* and *All's Well That Ends Well* in Illustration." *Ashland Studies in Shakespeare*, 1955, pp. 4-18. (Mimeographed.)

B8334   Carter, Albert Howard. "In Defense of Bertram." *SQ*, VII (1956), 21-31.

B8335   Knight, G. Wilson. *The Sovereign Flower.* On Shakespeare as the Poet of Royalism together with Related Essays and Indexes [by Patricia M. Ball] to Earlier Volumes. London: Methuen, 1958. Pp. 324.
          Contains detailed analysis of *All's Well*.
          Rev: A1884.

(5)   CHARACTERIZATION

B8336   Legouis, Emile. "La Comtesse de Rousillon." *English*, I (1937), 399-404.

B8337   Vessie, P. R. "Interpretation of Shakespeare's Sex Play." *Medical Record*, 146 (1937), 14-16.

B8338   Pettigrew, Helen P. "The Young Count Lucien." *West Virginia Univ. Bulletin*, IV (Sept., 1943), 23-30.
          On Bertram.

B8339   Hannah, Barbara. "*All's Well That Ends Well*." *Studien z. analyt. Psychologie C. G. Jungs* (Zurich), II (1955), 344-363.

(6) MISCELLANEOUS ITEMS

B8340   Blayney, Glenn H.   "Wardship in English Drama (1600-1650)."   *SP*, LIII (1956), 470-484.

(7) SUBSEQUENT HISTORY OF THE PLAY
(Other than productions after 1660)

B8341   B., H. S.   "Helena in *All's Well That Ends Well*."   *N &Q*, 181 (1941), 75.
See letters by St. Vincent Troubridge, *N &Q*, 181 (1941), 109-110; by A. R. Bayley, ibid.,
p. 122; by Wm. Jaggard, ibid., p. 122.
Names of actresses playing the part of Helena.

MEASURE FOR MEASURE (240;86)
(1) THE TEXT
(a) MODERN EDITIONS

B8342   *Measure for Measure*.   Ed. Davis Harding.   Yale Shakespeare.   New Haven: Yale Univ.
Press, 1954.   Pp. 137.
   Rev: by F. E. Bowman, *South Atlantic Quarterly*, LIV (1955), 431-433; by Hermann Heuer,
SJ, 91 (1955), 342-343.

B8343   *Measure for Measure*.   Ed. G. B. Harrison.   Penguin Shakespeare.   London: Penguin Books,
1954.   Pp. 124.
   Rev: *TLS*, Aug. 27, 1954, p. 547; by Hermann Heuer, *SJ*, 91 (1955), 344-345.

B8344   *Measure for Measure*.   Ed. R. C. Bald.   Pelican Shakespeare.   Baltimore: Penguin Books,
1956.   Pp. 125.

B8345   *Measure for Measure*.   Edition avec Introduction, Traduction et Notes.   Ed. Michel Grivelet.
DD, Paris, 1956.   Thèse Complémentaire.   Typewritten.

B8346   *Measure for Measure*.   Ed. Sir Arthur Quiller-Couch and John Dover Wilson.   Cambridge
Pocket Shakespeare.   Cambridge Univ. Press, 1958.   Pp. 106.

(b) EMENDATIONS

B8347   Barrett, W. P.   "The Prenzie Angelo."   [*Measure for Measure*, III. i. 93].   *TLS*, Jan. 16, 1937,
p. 44.
See H. W. Crundell, "The Queazie Angelo."   *TLS*, April 23, 1938, p. 280.

B8348   Praz, Mario.   "All-Bridling Law."   [*Measure for Measure*, II. iv. 94].   *TLS*, Feb. 13, 1937,
p. 111.

B8349   Taylor, G.   "The Beetle and the Giant."   *TLS*, Oct. 20, 1945, p. 499.
Meas., III. i. 76-79.

B8350   Hotson, Leslie.   " 'The Prenzie, *Angelo* ?'."   *TLS*, Nov. 15, 1947, p. 603.
Gives evidence for believing *prenzie* (III. i. 94) to be Shakespeare's spelling of the Italian
prenze, 'prince,' and thus *prenzie gardes* (III. i. 97) = 'prince-robes.'
See the letter by Marie C. Stopes, ibid., Dec. 6, 1947, p. 629, deriving *prenzie* from *prenez*,
as used in fencing.

B8351   Pope, Elizabeth M.   "Shakespeare on Hell."   *SQ*, I (1950), 162-164.
Comment by T. W. Baldwin, ibid., I, 296.

B8352   Lascelles, Mary.   " 'Glassie Essence,' *Measure for Measure*, II. ii. 120."   *RES*, NS, II (1951),
140-142.

B8353   Siegel, Paul N.   "Angelo's Precise Guards."   *PQ*, XXIX (1950), 442-443.
III. i. 95-97.   See also B8436.

B8354   Shedd, Robert Gordon.   *The "Measure for Measure" of Shakespeare's 1604 Audience*.   DD,
University of Michigan, 1953.   Pp. 430.   Mic A53-1478.   *DA*, XIII (1953), 801.   Publ.
No. 5730.

B8355   Thaler, Alwin.   "The Devil's Crest' in *Measure for Measure*."   *SP*, L (1953), 189-195.
II. iv. 12-17.

B8356   Brewer, D. S.   "*Measure for Measure*, I. i. 3-9."   *N &Q*, NS, II (1955), 425.

B8367   Stevenson, David L.   "On Restoring Two Folio Readings in *Measure for Measure*."   *SQ*,
VII (1956), 450-453.
Two of Rowe's "corrections" (I. ii. 135-139 and II. i. 39) replaced by their original and
comprehensible readings.

B8358   Holland, Norman.   " 'Do' or 'Die' in *Measure for Measure*."   *N &Q*, NS, IV (1957), 52.

B8359   Drew, Philip.   "A Suggested Reading in *Measure for Measure*."   *SQ*, IX (1958), 202-204.
For two uses of *prenzie* (III. i. 94, 97) would read, respectively, *puisne* and *puny*.

B8360   Hulme, Hilda.   "Three Notes: *Troilus and Cressida*, V. vii. 11; *Midsummer Night's Dream*,
II. ii. 54; *Measure for Measure*, II. i. 39."   *JEGP*, LVII (1958), 721-725.

B8361   Winny, James.   "A Shakespeare Emendation."   *TLS*, April 18, 1958, p. 209.
II. i. 39-40.

(2) LITERARY GENESIS AND ANALOGUES

B8362   Izard, Thomas C. *George Whetstone, Mid-Elizabethan Gentleman of Letters.* DD, Columbia University, 1943. Columbia Univ. Studies in Engl. and Comp. Lit., 158. Columbia Univ. Press, 1942. Pp. viii, 297.
Promos & Cassandra, unacted 10-act play published 1578, a partial source for *Meas.*, pp. 52-74.
Rev: *TLS*, July 3, 1943, p. 322; by D. C. Allen, *JEGP*, XLII, 432-433; by F. S. Boas, *RES*, XIX, 413-416; by J. L. Lievsay, *MLQ*, V (1944), 237-239; by J. A. Gee, *MLN*, LIX, 143-145; by Jean Robertson, *MLR*, XXXIX, 73-75.

B8363   Ball, Robert H. "Cinthio's *Epitia* and *Measure for Measure.*" *George F. Reynolds Festschrift*, 1945, pp. 132-140.

B8364   Heine, Arthur. "The Influence of Environment." *SAB*, XX (1945), 77-81.
Southwark as a part of the setting in *Measure for Measure*.

B8365   Pope, Elizabeth Marie. "The Renaissance Background of *Measure for Measure.*" *ShS*, II (1949), 66-82.
Comment by G. Wilson Knight, *Scrutiny*, XVI (1949), 326-327.

B8366   Cook, Albert. "Metaphysical Poetry and *Measure for Measure.*" *Accent*, XIII (1953), 122-127.

B8367   Shedd, Robert Gordon. *The "Measure for Measure" of Shakespeare's 1604 Audience.* DD, University of Michigan, 1953. Pp. 430. Mic A53-1478. *DA*, XIII (1953), 801. Publ. No. 5730.
Section on sources.

B8368   Dwyer, J. J. "Did Shakespeare Read Dante?" *Tablet*, 206 (1955), 33-34.
Parallels in *Meas.*

B8369   Muir, Kenneth. "Shakespeare and Erasmus." *N&Q*, NS, III (1956), 424-425.
Proper names for *Meas.* may have been contracted while Shakespeare read the colloquy *Funus.*

B8370   Nathan, Norman. "The Marriage of Duke Vincentio and Isabella." *SQ*, VII (1956), 43-45.

B8371   Kaufman, Helen A. *"Trappolin Supposed a Prince* and *Measure for Measure.*" *MLQ*, XVIII (1957), 113-124.

B8372   Potts, Abbie Findlay. *Shakespeare and "The Faerie Queene."* Cornell Univ. Press, 1958. Pp. xii, 269.
Rev: A4819.

(3) USE OF LANGUAGE

B8373   Draper, John W. "King James and Shakespeare's Literary Style." *Archiv*, 171 (1937), 36-48.

B8374   Empson, William. "Sense in *Measure for Measure.*" *Southern Rev.*, IV (1938), 340-350.

B8375   Praz, Mario. *La Poesia Metafisica Inglese del Seicento*: *John Donne.* Rome, 1945.
Chapter on the continuity of "metaphysical" elements from the days of Chaucer, with illustrations taken mainly from Chapman and from *Measure for Measure* and *Troilus.*
Rev: B8232.

B8376   Empson, William. *The Structure of Complex Words.* London: Chatto & Windus, 1951. Pp. 449.
Rev: A5136.

B8377   Dupont, Victor. "Etude des Images dans le Premier Acte de *Measure for Measure.*" *Annales de la Faculté des Lettres de Toulouse*, December 1952, pp. 129-148.

(4) GENERAL CRITICISM OF THE PLAY

B8378   Draper, J. W. "Political Themes in Shakespeare's Later Plays." *JEGP*, XXXV (1936), 61-93.

B8379   Chambers, R. W. *The Jacobean Shakespeare and "Measure for Measure."* Annual Shakespeare Lecture of the British Academy, 1937; Oxford Univ. Press, 1938. Pp. 60.
Rev: A8129.

B8380   Charlton, H. B. "Shakespeare's 'Dark Comedies'." *BJRL*, XXI (1937), 78-128.

B8381   Grewe, W. "Die Gnade." *Dt. Volkstum*, XVIII (1936), 31-36.

B8382   Loewer, K. *"Mass für Mass."* *Die Christliche Welt*, LI (1937), 605-607.

B8383   Reimer, Christian Josef. *Der Begriff der Gnade in Shakespeares "Measure for Measure."* DD, Marburg, 1937. Düren: Reimer, 1937. Pp. xi, 110.

B8384   Belgion, Montgomery. "The Measure of Kafka." *Criterion*, XVIII (1938), 1-28.
Meas., pp. 18-28.

B8385   *Studies in the Comic.* By B. H. Bronson, J. R. Caldwell, W. H. Durham, B. H. Lehman, Gordon McKenzie and J. F. Ross. *Univ. of California Publications in English*, VIII, No. 2. Berkeley: Univ. of California Press, 1941. Pp. iv, 155-298.
Essay on *Measure for Measure*.

B8386   Bradbrook, M. C. "Authority, Truth and Justice in *Measure for Measure.*" *RES*, XVIII (1942), 385-399.

B8387   Knights, L. C. "The Ambiguity of *Measure for Measure.*" *Scrutiny*, X (1942), 222-233. Also in *The Importance of Scrutiny*. Ed. Eric Bentley. New York: Stewart, 1948, pp. 141-150.

B8388   Leavis, F. R. "The Greatness of *Measure for Measure.*" *Scrutiny*, X (1942), 234-247. Also in

The Importance of Scrutiny. Ed. Eric Bentley. New York: Stewart, 1948, pp. 150-162. Answer to B8387. See also B8404.

B8389   Traversi, D. A. *"Measure for Measure."* Scrutiny, X (1942), 40-58.

B8390   Battenhouse, Roy W. *"Measure for Measure* and Christian Doctrine of the Atonement." *PMLA*, LXI (1946), 1029-59.

B8391   Sitwell, Edith. "A Note on *Measure for Measure.*" *Nineteenth Century*, 140 (1946), 131-135.

B8392   Maxwell, J. C. *"Measure for Measure*: A Footnote to Recent Criticiam." *Downside Rev.*, LXV (1947), 45-59.

B8393   West, E. J. "Dramatist at the Crossroads (A Suggestion Concerning *Measure for Measure*)." *SAB*, XXII (1947), 136-141.

B8394   Hafele, Melanie. *Gnade und Recht bei Shakespeare, Besonders Untersucht an "Mass für Mass," dem "Kaufman von Venedig" und "Sturm."* DD, Innsbruck, 1949. Pp. 129. Typewritten.

B8395   Schröder, Rudolf Alexander. *"Mass für Mass, 1949."* Also in his *Gesammelte Werke*, B4486.

B8396   Tillyard, Eustace M. W. *Shakespeare's Problem Plays.* Univ. of Toronto Press, 1949; London: Chatto & Windus, 1950. Pp. ix, 168.
        Rev: B5222.

B8397   Leech, Clifford. "The 'Meaning' of *Measure for Measure.*" *ShS*, III (1950), 66-73.
        Objects to "historical" approaches. Declares the play contains "a passionate sympathy with the unfortunate and hard-pressed."

B8398   Simpson, Lucie. "The Sex Bias of *Measure for Measure.*" *The Secondary Heroes of Shakespeare and Other Essays.* London: Kingswood Press, 1950, pp. 41-50.

B8399   Smith, Robert M. "Interpretations of *Measure for Measure.*" *SQ*, I (1950), 208-218.

B8400   Sypher, Wylie. "Shakespeare as Casuist: *Measure for Measure.*" *SR*, LVIII (1950), 262-280.

B8401   Harding, Davis P. "Elizabethan Betrothals and *Measure for Measure.*" *JEGP*, XLIX (1950), 139-158.

B8402   Krieger, Murray. *"Measure for Measure* and Elizabethan Comedy." *PMLA*, LXVI (1951), 775-784.

B8403   Fergusson, Francis. "Philosophy and Theatre in *Measure for Measure.*" *KR*, XIV (1952), 103-120. Translated as "Filosofia e teatralità in *Measure for Measure*" in *Rivista di Studi Teatrali*, I (1952), 28-40.

B8404   Leavis, F. R. *The Common Pursuit.* New York: George W. Stewart, 1952. Pp. 307. Contains B8388.

B8405   Draper, John W. "Patterns of Tempo in *Measure for Measure.*" *West Virginia Univ. Philol. Papers*, IX (1953), 11-19.

B8406   Goldschmidt, Werner. "Problemas de Justicia en *Medida por Medida* de Shakespeare." *Revista de Estudios Políticos* (Madrid), No. 72 (1953), 3-22.

B8407   Lascelles, Mary. *Shakespeare's "Measure for Measure."* Athlone Press, 1953. Pp. xii, 172.
        Rev: by John Crow, *Listener*, Oct. 8, 1953, pp. 607-608; ibid., p. 865; by J. D. Wilson, ibid., pp. 777, 953; by William Scawen, *Adelphi*, XXX, 86-88; by Donald Davie, *NstN*, Oct. 24, p. 496; by Bonamy Dobrée, *Spectator*, Nov. 20, pp. 595-596; by H. T. Price, *SQ*, V (1954), 111; by A. P. Rossiter, *ConR*, LXXV, 340-341; *TLS*, Feb. 19, p. 122; by Harold Jenkins, *RES*, V, 409-411; by G. Lambin, *LanM*, XLVIII, 85; by Roy Walker, *The Aryan Path*, XXV, 178-179; by Harold S. Wilson, *SQ*, VI (1955), 172-174; by Ernst Th. Sehrt, *SJ*, 91 (1955), 348-350.

B8408   Siegel, Paul N. *"Measure for Measure:* The Significance of the Title." *SQ*, IV (1953), 317-320.

B8409   Wilson, Harold S. "Action and Symbol in *Measure for Measure* and *The Tempest.*" *SQ*, IV (1953), 375-384.

B8410   Harrison, John L. "The Convention of 'Heart and Tongue' and the Meaning of *Measure for Measure.*" *SQ*, V (1954), 1-10.

B8411   Radbruch, Gustav. *"Mass für Mass."* Radbruch's *Gestalten und Gedanken.* Stuttgart: Koehler, 1954, pp. 41-48.

B8412   Coghill, Nevill. "Comic Form in *Measure for Measure.*" *ShS*, VIII (1955), 14-26.

B8413   Čulić, Čiro. "Shakespeareova *Mjera za Mjeru* u Izvedbi Splitskoz Narodnog Kazališta." *Mogućnosti* (Split), VII (1955), 555-558.

B8414   Fort, J. -B. "Les Problèmes de *Measure for Measure.*" *EA*, VIII (1955), 326-329.

B8415   Knorr, Friedrich. *Shakespeares "Mass für Mass."* Jahresgabe der Coburger Dienstagsgesellschaft. Coburg, 1955. Pp. 45.

B8416   Pavić, Milorad. "Jedan Šekspirov motiv kod Vojislava J. Ilića." *Prilozi za Književnost, Jezik, Istoriju i Folklore* (Belgrade), 1955, pp. 3-4.

B8417   Lacy, Margaret Swanson. *The Jacobean Problem Play: A Study of Shakespeare's "Measure for Measure" and "Troilus and Cressida" in Relation to Selected Plays of Chapman, Dekker, and Marston.* DD, University of Wisconsin, 1956. Pp. 216. Mic 56-3019. *DA*, XVI (1956), 1899. Publ. No. 18,418.

B8418   Millet, Stanton. "The Structure of *Measure for Measure.*" *Boston Univ. Studies in English*, II (1956), 207-217.

B8419 Smith, Donald George. *Studies in Shakespeare's "Measure for Measure."* DD, Duke University, 1956.

B8420 Stevenson, David L. "Design and Structure in *Measure for Measure*: A New Appraisal." *ELH*, XXIII (1956), 256-278.

B8421 Fergusson, Francis. *The Human Image in Dramatic Literature.* Doubleday Anchor Books. New York: Doubleday & Company, 1957. Pp. xx, 217.
Part II. Shak., pp. 115-157, includes "*Macbeth* as The Imitation of an Action," "*Measure for Measure*," and "Two Comedies" (*Errors* and *Much*).

B8422 Ornstein, Robert. "The Human Comedy: *Measure for Measure.*" *Univ. of Kansas City Review*, XXIV (1957), 15-22.

B8423 Hennings, Elsa. "Shakespeares *Mass für Mass.*" Veröffentlichungen d. Universitäts-Gesellschaft Hamburg, No. 11. Hamburg: Univ.-Ges., 1958. Pp. 23.

B8424 Lawrence, William W. "*Measure for Measure* and Lucio." *SQ*, IX (1958), 443-453.

B8425 Mikkelson, Robert S. "To Catch a Saint: Angelo in *Measure for Measure.*" *Western Humanities Review*, XIII (1958), 261-275.

B8426 Slack, Robert C. "Shakespeare's *Measure for Measure.*" *Carnegie Magazine*, XXXII (Mar., 1958), 86-89. Also in *Shakespeare: Lectures on Five Plays.* Carnegie Institute of Technology, Department of English, 1958, pp. 19-35.

(5) CHARACTERIZATION

B8427 Kronacher, B. "Shakespeares Bild von der Frau." *Die Deutsche Höhere Schule*, II (1935), No. 23.

B8428 Sleeth, C. R. "Shakespeare's Counsellors of State." *RAA*, XIII (1936), 97-113.

B8429 Vessie, P. R. "Psychiatry Catches up with Shakespeare." *Medical Record*, 144 (1936), 141-145.

B8430 Lawson, Reginald. "Lucio in *Measure for Measure.*" *ES*, XIX (1937), 259-264.
"Drawn in detail from contemporary life."

B8431 Durham, W. H. "What Art Thou Angelo?" *Studies in the Comic, Univ. of California Publications in Eng.*, VIII, No. 2 (1941), 155-174.

B8432 Pushkin, A. S. "Notes on Shylock, Angelo, and Falstaff." Tr. Albert Siegel. *SAB*, XVI (1941), 120-121.

B8433 Dawson, Ann. *Changing Conceptions of Isabella.* MA thesis, University of North Carolina, 1942. Abstr. publ. in *Univ. of North Carolina Record, Research in Progress*, Grad. School Series No. 42, 1942, p. 79.

B8434 Sachs, Hanns. "The Measure in *Measure for Measure.*" *The Creative Unconscious*, Cambridge, Massachusetts: Sci-Art, 1942, pp. 63-99.

B8435 Dodds, W. M. T. "The Character of Angelo in *Measure for Measure.*" *MLR*, XLI (1946), 246-255.

B8436 McGinn, Donald. "The Precise Angelo." *AMS*, pp. 129-139.

B8437 Maxwell, J. C. "Creon and Angelo: A Parallel Study." *Greece & Rome*, XVII (1949), 32-36.

B8438 Gibian, George. "*Measure for Measure* and Pushkin's *Angelo.*" *PMLA*, LXVI (1951), 426-431.

B8439 Baldini, Gabriele. "Atti Pigri e Corte Parole. Un Belacqua Shakespeariano." *Belfagor* (Florence), VIII, No. 3 (1955), 324-330.

B8440 Nagarajan, S. "A Note on the Duke in *Measure for Measure.*" *Half-Yearly Journal of the Mysore Univ.*, XIII (1953), 1-9.

B8441 Daiches, David. *Critical Approaches to Literature.* London: Longmans, 1956. Pp. ix, 404. *Meas.*, pp. 348-355.
Rev: A1381.

B8442 Flatter, Richard. "Angelo in *Mass für Mass.*" In his *Triumph der Gnade. Shakespeare Essays.* Vienna and Munich: Kurt Desch, 1956, pp. 137-138.

B8443 Coe, Charles Norton. *Shakespeare's Villains.* New York, 1957.
Rev: A6796.

(6) MISCELLANEOUS ITEMS

B8444 Beaujon, E., and R. Junod. "*Mesure pour Mesure*, ou le petit Shakespeare et le grand Piachaud." *Essai de Littérature et de Mensuration Comparée.* Genève, 1941.

B8445 Sypher, Wylie. *Four Stages of Renaissance Style.* New York: Doubleday Anchor Books, 1956. Pp. 312. *Meas.* passim.
Rev: A5514.

(7) SUBSEQUENT HISTORY OF THE PLAY
(Other than productions after 1660)

OTHELLO (246;87)

B8446 Tannenbaum, Samuel A. *Shakespeare's "Othello": A Concise Bibliography.* New York: The Author, 1943. Pp. x, 132.

(1) THE TEXT

(a) OLD TEXTS
i. Reprints

B8447   *Othello: Paralleldruck der ersten Quarto und der ersten Folio mit Lesarten der zweiten Quarto.* Hsg.
von M. M. Arnold Schröer. Englisch-Textbibliotek, Heft XIV. Heidelberg: Carl Winter,
Universitätsverlag, 1949. Pp. xvi, 212.
Reproduces the "diplomatic reprint" of 1909, with slight abridgement of the introduction and
with correction of errors from the earlier list of errata.
Rev: by Charlton Hinman, *JEGP*, XLVIII (1949), 439; by W. H., *Archiv*, 186 (1949), 160;
by H. Marcus, *DLZ*, LXXI (1950), 496-497; by Walter Hübner, *Neuphilologische Zeitschrift*,
III (1951), 301.

ii. Discussions

B8448   Kies, Paul P. "On the Dating of *Othello* and *Lear.*" *Research Studies of the State College of
Washington*, III, No. 2 (1936), 72-73.

B8449   Hinman, Charlton. "Principles Governing the Use of Variant Spellings as Evidence of
Alternate Setting by Two Compositors." *Library*, XXI (1940), 78-94.
The principles proposed are based on a study of the variant spellings of *The Sun's Darling* (1656)
and *Othello* (1622).

B8450   Hinman, Charlton Joseph Kadio. *The Printing of the First Quarto of "Othello."* DD, University
of Virginia, 1941. Abstr. publ. in *Abstracts of Dissertations*, Charlottesville: Univ. of Virginia,
1941, pp. 5-8.

B8451   Hinman, Charlton. "A Proof Sheet in the First Folio of Shakespeare." *Library*, NS, XXIII
(1943), 101-107; 3 pl.
Explanation of "hell gnaw his bones" crux.

B8452   Walpole, V. " 'And Cassio High in Oath' (*Othello*, II. iii. 227)." *MLR*, XL (1945), 47-48.

B8453   Hinman, Charlton. "The 'Copy' for the Second Quarto of *Othello* (1630)." *AMS*, pp. 373-389.

B8454   Muir, Kenneth. "Folio Sophistications in *Othello.*" *N &Q*, 197 (1952), 335-336.

B8455   Walker, Alice. "The 1622 Quarto and the First Folio Texts of *Othello.*" *ShS*, V (1952), 16-24.

B8456   Scott, R. I. *A Study of the First Quarto and First Folio Editions of Shakespeare's "Othello."* B. Litt.
thesis, Glasgow, 1956.

B8457   Rosenberg, Marvin. "On the Dating of *Othello.*" *ES*, XXXIX (1958), 72-74.

(b) MODERN EDITIONS

B8458   *Othello.* Ed. Henry Norman Hudson and Others. Cameo Classics. New York: Grosset,
1936. Pp. 240.

B8459   *Othello. Text, Glossary, Notes.* Ed. M. Morozov. English text. Moscow, 1936. Pp. 183.

B8460   *Othello.* Ed. G. Skillan. London: French, 1936. Pp. 94.
Rev: by A. Brandl, *Archiv*, 170 (1936), 141; by Elise Deckner, *Beiblatt*, XLVIII (1937), 99-
100.

B8461   *The Tragedy of Othello, the Moor of Venice.* Ed. George L. Kittredge. Boston: Ginn, 1941.
Pp. xi, 265.

B8462   *Othello.* Paris: Aubier, 1942.

B8463   *Othello, the Moor of Venice.* Ed. Mark Eccles. Crofts Classics. New York: Crofts, 1946.
Pp. xi, 113.

B8464   *Othello.* Ed. Tarquinio Vallese. Naples: Pironti, 1948. Pp. xx, 105.

B8465   *Othello.* Bearbeitung von Friedrich von Schiller. In Schiller's *Werke.* Nationalausg. Band
XIV. Weimar: Böhlau, 1949, pp. 147-264; 343-377.
Rev: by W. Stroedel, *SJ*, 91 (1955), 368.

B8466   *Othello. The Play. A Critical Anthology.* Ed. Eric Bentley. New York: Prentice-Hall, 1951.
Pp. xii, 774.
Rev: B6964.

B8467   *Othello.* London: Folio Society, 1955. Pp. 128.

B8468   *Othello.* Ed. S. C. Sen Gupta. Calcutta: A. Mukerjee and Co., Ltd., n.d.

B8469   *Othello.* Introd., Paraphrase, Word Meaning and Notes, by Shiv Kumar. Delhi, India:
Chand, 1956.

B8470   *The Tragedy of Othello, the Moor of Venice.* Ed. Tucker Brooke and Lawrence Mason. Yale
Shakespeare. Yale Univ. Press, 1957. Pp. 188. Revised ed. (paperback).
Rev: *SatR*, Aug. 3, 1957, p. 28.

B8471   Cancelled.

B8472   *Othello.* Ed. Alice Walker and John Dover Wilson. The New Shakespeare. Cambridge Univ.
Press, 1957. Pp. lxi, 246.
Rev: *N &Q*, NS, IV (1957), 228-229; *TN*, XI, 148; *ShN*, VII, 14; by Hermann Heuer, *SJ*,
93 (1957), 270-271; by J. Vallette, *MdF*, 330 (1957), 160; by Peter Ure, *DUJ*, XLIX, 129-133;
by L. L. Schücking, *Anglia*, LXXV, 468-471; by Kenneth Muir, *SQ*, IX (1958), 197-200;
by Peter Alexander, *RES*, NS, IX, 188-193.

B8473   *The Tragedy of Othello, the Moor of Venice.* Ed. Louis B. Wright and Virginia L. Freund. New York: Pocket Books, 1957. Pp. xxxviii, 128, with 128 unnumbered note pages facing the text. Second title in the Folger Library General Reader's Shak. series.
  Rev: by Hubert Heffner, *ETJ*, IX (1957), 359-360; by C. N. Coe, *CE*, XIX, 275; *ShN*, VIII (1958), 3.

B8474   *The Tragedy of Othello the Moor of Venice.* Ed. Gerald Eades Bentley. Pelican Shakespeare. Baltimore: Penguin Books, 1958. Pp. 154.

B8475   *Twelfth Night. Othello.* Ed. with an Introd. and Notes by Alan Seymour Downer. New York: Rinehart, 1958. Pp. 186.

B8476   *Othello.* Ed. M. R. Ridley. Arden Shakespeare. London: Methuen, 1958. Pp. lxx, 246. A re-edited edition, based mainly on Q (1622). Much of the Introd. is devoted to the relationship between Q and F_1.
  Rev: *TLS*, Feb. 14, 1958, p. 89; by W. Bridges-Adams, *Drama*, Summer, pp. 39, 41; *English*, XII, 76; *ShN*, VIII, 38; by Hermann Heuer, *SJ*, 94 (1958), 291-292; *Dublin Magazine*, April-June, pp. 48-49; *N&Q*, NS, V, 501-502.

(c) EMENDATIONS

B8477   Dunlap, A. R. "What Purgative?" *MLN*, LIV (1939), 92-94.

B8478   Mandin, Louis. "Etude Shakespearienne: Le Mystère de la Perle et du Judéen." *MdF*, March 1, 1939, pp. 257-292; April 1, pp. 238-243; May 1, pp. 736-741. See B8479.

B8479   Messiaen, Pierre. "A Propos d'*Othello*." *MdF*, April 1, 1939, pp. 237-238; May 1, pp. 733-735.

B8480   Tannenbaum, Samuel A. "Cassio's Hopes." *PQ*, XVIII (1939), 316-318.

B8481   Kahin, Helen A. "A Note on *Othello*, II. i. 110-113." *MLQ*, I (1940), 475-479.

B8482   Muir, Kenneth. "Latin Derivatives in English Verse." *TLS*, March 13, 1943, p. 127.

B8483   Hunter, Grace. "Notes on Othello's 'Base Indian'." *SAB*, XIX (1944), 26-28.

B8484   Lewis, C. S. "*Othello*." *TLS*, June 19, 1948, p. 345. I. iii. 95.

B8485   Nieman, Fraser. "Shakespeare's *Othello*, IV. ii. 47-53." *Expl.*, VI (1948), Item 54.

B8486   Anderson, Viola H. "Othello and Peregrina, 'Richer Than All His Tribe'." *MLN*, LXIV (1949), 415-417.

B8487   Brunner, Karl. " 'It is a Sword of Spain, the Isebrookes Temper' (*Othello*, V. ii. 253)." *Shakespeare-Studien, Festschrift für Heinrich Mutschmann*, pp. 19-20.

B8488   Stoll, E. E. " 'Keep up Your Bright Swords'." *SQ*, III (1952), 388.

B8489   "Clogged Up." *John o' London's Weekly*, LXIII (1954), 278. Request for information on the meaning of "clogs" in Brabantio's speech, Act I.

B8490   Dorsch, T. S. "This Poor Trash of Venice." *SQ*, VI (1955), 359-360.

B8491   Hoepfner, Theodore C. "An Othello Gloss." *N&Q*, NS, III (1956), 470. V. ii. 258.

B8492   Brown, A. D. Fitton. "Two Points of Interpretation." *N&Q*, NS, IV (1957), 51. V. ii. 198-200.

B8493   Ivy, Geoffrey S. "Othello and the Rose-Lip'd Cherubin: An Old Reading Restored." *SQ*, IX (1958), 208-212. IV. ii. 63-65.

(2) LITERARY GENESIS AND ANALOGUES

B8494   Stroup, Thomas B. "Shakespeare's Use of a Travel-Book Commonplace." *PQ*, XVII (1938), 351-358.

B8495   Meyerstein, E. H. W. "Othello and C. Furius Cresinus." *TLS*, Feb. 7, 1942, p. 72.

B8496   Stoll, Elmer E. "Source and Motive in *Macbeth* and *Othello*." *RES*, XIX (1943), 25-32.

B8497   Draper, John W. "Shakespeare and the Doge of Venice." *JEGP*, XLVI (1947), 75-81.

B8498   Allen, Ned B. "The Source of *Othello*." *Delaware Notes*, 21st ser. (1948), 71-96.

B8499   Dzhivelegov, A. K. "*Othello*. K voprosu o proiskhozhdenii tragedii." ["*Othello*. On the Question of the Origin of the Tragedy."] V sb. *Ezhegodnik in-ta istorii iskusstv.* Akademiia nauk SSSR. [In anthology, *Annual of the Institute of the History of the Arts.* Academy of Sciences of the USSR], II (1948), 165-188.

B8500   Maugeri, Aldo. "Otello e la Storia del Capitano Moro." *Anglica*, II (1948), iii, 1-39.

B8501   Camden, Carroll. "Iago on Women." *JEGP*, XLVIII (1949), 57-71. Places Iago's speeches (II. ii. 101-161) in their tradition.

B8502   Bradbrook, M. C. "*Lucrece* and *Othello*." *TLS*, Oct. 27, 1950, p. 677.

B8503   Babcock, C. Merton. "An Analogue for the Name Othello." *N&Q*, 196 (1951), 515.

B8504   Braddy, Haldeen. "Shakespeare and Three Oriental Tales." *Midwest Folklore*, I (1951), 91-92. I. ii. 167-168.

B8505   Chester, Allan G. "John Soowthern's *Pandora* and *Othello* II. i. 184." *MLN*, LXVI (1951), 481-482.

B8506   Eagle, R. L. "Sources of *Othello*." *N&Q*, 196 (1951), 546.

B8507   Muir, Kenneth. "Shakespeare and Florio." *N &Q*, 197 (1952), 493-495.

B8508   Muir, Kenneth. "Holland's Pliny and *Othello*." *N &Q*, 198 (1953), 513-514.

B8509   Spencer, Terence. "Three Shakespearian Notes." *MLR*, XLIX (1954), 46-51.
(3) The number of contemporary references suggests that the description of the Pontic Sea (*Othello*, III. iii. 453-456) is a bit of local color known to travellers which did not necessarily have Pliny as its source.

B8510   Muir, Kenneth. "Shakespeare and Lewkenor." *RES*, VII (1956), 182-183.

B8511   Brocker, Harriet Durkee. *The Influence of "Othello" in Jacobean and Caroline Drama*. DD, University of Minnesota, 1957. Pp. 349. Mic 57-3223. *DA*, XVII (1957), 2006. Publ. No. 22,444.

B8512   Spivack, Bernard. *Shakespeare and the Allegory of Evil*. Columbia Univ. Press, 1958. Pp. ix, 508.
       Rev: A4951.

(3) USE OF LANGUAGE

B8513   Nottrott, Marianne. *Der Formale Gebrauch des Epithetons in Shakespeares Dramen "Othello", "King Lear," "Macbeth" und "Coriolanus."* DD, Leipzig, 1922. Pp. vi, 254. Handwritten. Publ. in *Jahrbuch der Philosophischen Fakultät Leipzig*, I (1923).

B8514   Yeo, Emsley Lewis. *The Characterization of Othello and Iago in the Light of Comparative Idiom*. MA thesis, British Columbia, 1930. Pp. 117.

B8515   Empson, William. "The Best Policy." *Life and Letters*, XIV (1937), 37-45.
Forty-eight uses of the word "honesty" in *Othello*.

B8516   Hinman, Charlton. " 'Nether' and 'Neither' in the Seventeenth Century." *MLN*, LXIII (1948), 333-335.

B8517   Morozov, Mikhail M. "The Individualization of Shakespeare's Characters through Imagery." *ShS*, II (1949), 83-106.

B8518   Allen, Don Cameron. "Three Notes on Donne's Poetry with a Side Glance at *Othello*." *MLN*, LXV (1950), 102-106.

B8519   Empson, William. *The Structure of Complex Words*. London: Chatto and Windus, 1951. Pp. 449.
       Rev: A5136.

B8520   Draper, John W. "Patterns of Style in *Othello*." *West Virginia Univ. Philol. Papers*, VIII (1951), 32-39.

B8521   Heilman, Robert B. "More Fair Than Black: Light and Dark in *Othello*." *EIC*, I (1951), 315-335.

B8522   Bethell, S. L. "Shakespeare's Imagery: The Diabolic Images in *Othello*." *ShS*, V (1952), 62-80.

B8523   Heilman, Robert B. "Dr. Iago and His Potions." *VQR*, XXVIII (1952), 568-584.

B8524   Money, John. "Othello's 'It is the cause . . .' An Analysis." *ShS*, VI (1953), 94-105.

B8525   Muir, Kenneth. "Freedom and Slavery in *Othello*." *N &Q*, NS, I (1954), 20-21.

B8526   Nishida, Kunio. "On the Imagery of *Othello*" (in Japanese). *Kanazawa English Studies* (Kanazawa Univ.) Jan., 1956.

B8527   Tazawa, Keito. "On the Imagery in *Othello*" (in Japanese). *Kyoto Joshidai English Studies* (Kyoto), May, 1956.

B8528   Donoghue, Denis. "Shakespeare's Rhetoric." *Studies, Irish Quarterly Review*, XLVII (1958), 431-440.

B8529   Nash, Walter. "Paired Words in *Othello*: Shakespeare's Use of a Stylistic Device." *ES*, XXXIX (1958), 62-67.

B8530   Gerritsen, Johan. "More Paired Words in *Othello*." *ES*, XXXIX (1958), 212-214.
On B8529.

B8531   Nash, Walter. "Postscript." *ES*, XXXIX (1958), 214-216.
On B8530.

B8532   Smith, Philip A. "Othello's Diction." *SQ*, IX (1958), 428-430.

B8533   Webb, Henry J. " 'Rude am I in my Speech'." *ES*, XXXIX (1958), 67-72.

(4) GENERAL CRITICISM OF THE PLAY

B8534   Sedgewick, G. G. *Of Irony, Especially in Drama*. Univ. of Toronto Studies, No. 10. Univ. of Toronto Press, 1935. Pp. 150. Republ. 1949.
Includes a chapter on *Othello*.
       Rev: A5617-18.

B8535   Stoll, Elmer Edgar. "Another *Othello* Too Modern." *AMS*, pp. 351-371.
On B8534.

B8536   Wales, Julia G. "Elaboration of Setting in *Othello* and the Emphasis of the Tragedy." *Trans. of the Wisconsin Acad. of Sciences, Arts, and Letters*, XXIX (1935), 319-340.

B8537   Stoll, E. E. "Tartuffe and the 'Optique du Théâtre'." *RAA* (Feb., 1936), 193-213.

B8538 Legouis, E., and L. Cazamian. "A Propos d'une Critique de E. E. Stoll." *RAA* (Feb., 1936), 214-218.

B8539 Elliott, G. R. "*Othello* as a Love-Tragedy." *American Review*, VIII (1937), 257-288.

B8540 Evans, M. S. "Free-will in the Drama." *Personalist*, XVIII (1937), 273-291.

B8541 Lacy, E. W. *Justice in Shakespeare.* DD, Vanderbilt University, 1937. Abstr. in *Bull. of Vanderbilt Univ.*, XXXVII (1937), 42.

B8542 Leavis, F. R. "Diabolic Intellect and the Noble Hero: A Note on *Othello*." *Scrutiny*, VI (1937), 259-283. Reprinted in *The Common Pursuit.* New York: George W. Stewart, 1952. Pp. 307.

B8543 Schücking, L. L. "Der neue Othello." *Brunner Festschrift. Wiener Beiträge zur Englischen Philologie*, LXV (1957), 191-200.

B8544 "Un'Interpretazione razzista dell'*Otello*." *La difesa della Razza* (Rome), III (1939/40 [?]), 30

B8545 Baine, Rodney M. "The Sagittary: A Note on *Othello*." *SAB*, XIV (1939), 226-231.

B8546 Hübscher, Arthur. "Aufgaben der Shakespeare-Regie. Zu einem Gespräch mit Alexander Golling: Das *Othello*-Problem." *MNN*, April 28, 1940, No. 119.

B8547 Miller, Donald C. "Iago and the Problem of Time." *ES*, XXII (1940), 97-115.

B8548 Stoll, Elmer Edgar. *Shakespeare and Other Masters.* Harvard Univ. Press, 1940. Pp. xv, 430.
Rev: A8394.

B8549 Valency, Maurice J. *The Tragedies of Herod and Mariamne.* DD, Columbia University, 1940. Columbia Univ. Studies in Eng. and Compt. Lit., 145. Columbia Univ. Press, 1940. Pp. xi, 304.
Occasional comments upon *Oth.*
Rev: *N&Q*, 178 (1940), 378; by H. T. E. Perry, *MLN*, LVI (1941), 151-152; by H. A. Pochmann, *Monatshefte*, XXXIII, 190; by T. M. Campbell, *GR*, XVI, 312-316; by R. P. Rosenberg, *GQ*, XV (1942), 114-116.

B8550 Gordon, George. *Shakespearian Comedy and Other Studies.* Ed. Sir Edmund Chambers. Oxford Univ. Press, 1944. Pp. 168.
Othello, pp. 95-115.
Rev: B5165.

B8551 Putney, R. "What 'Praise to Give?' Jonson *vs.* Stoll." *PQ*, XXIII (1944), 307-319.

B8552 Withington, Robert. "Shakespeare and Race Prejudice." *Elizabethan Studies and Other Essays: In Honor of George F. Reynolds*, pp. 172-184.

B8553 Babcock, R. W. "A Preface to *Othello*." *SAB*, XXI (1946), 108-115.

B8554 Draper, John W. "Changes in the Tempo of Desdemona's Speech." *Anglica*, I (1946), 149-153.

B8555 Granville-Barker, Harley. *Othello.* Prefaces to Shakespeare. Fourth Series. London: Sidgwick & Jackson, 1946. Pp. 223. Paperback ed., Princeton Univ. Press, 1958. Pp. 149.
Rev: by N. Orsini, *Anglica*, I (1946), 217-221; "Study and Stage," *TLS*, June 8, p. 271; by George Rylands, *NstN*, Mar. 30, p. 231; by H. B. Charlton, *MGW*, LIV, 100; by R. W. Babcock, *SAB*, XXI, 108-115; by Allardyce Nicoll, *RES*, XXIII (1947), 69-70; by A. Koszul, *LanM*, XLIII (1949), 65; by S. Gorley Putt, *ES*, XXXI (1950), 143-144.

B8556 Granville-Barker, Harley. *Prefaces to Shakespeare.* 2 Vols. Princeton Univ. Press, 1946, 1947. Combined edition of the Prefaces.
Rev: A8201.

B8557 Stoll, Elmer Edgar. "Mainly Controversy: *Hamlet, Othello*." *PQ*, XXIV (1945), 289-316. Answers to B8551 and B8641, among others.

B8558 Draper, John W. "Patterns of Tempo and Humor in *Othello*." *ES*, XXVIII (1947), 65-74.

B8559 Draper, J. W. "Shakespeare and the Doge of Venice." *JEGP*, XLVI (1947), 75-81.

B8560 Draper, John W. "Speech-Tempo in Act I of *Othello*." *West Virginia Univ. Bull.: Philological Papers*, V (1947), 49-58.

B8561 Prior, Moody E. "Character in Relation to Action in *Othello*." *MP*, XLIV (1947), 225-237.

B8562 Stoll, E. E. "A New 'Reading' of *Othello*." *MP*, XLV (1948), 208-210.
On B8561.

B8563 Prior, Moody E. " 'A "New" Reading of *Othello*.' A Reply to Mr. Stoll." *MP*, XLV (1948), 270-272.
On B8562.

B8564 Charlton, H. B. "Shakespeare's *Othello*." *BJRL*, XXXI (1948), 28-53.

B8565 Foligno, Cesare. *Sussidi alla Interpretazione con Riferimenti all' Othello Shakespeareano e Altre Opere.* Naples: Pironti, 1948. Pp. 92.

B8566 Stanislavski, K. S. *Rejisserkii Plan "Othello."* Leningrad: State Publishing House, 1944. Pp. 392. Tr. Helen Nowak as *Stanislavski Produces "Othello."* London: Bles, 1948. Pp. 244.
Rev: A9938.

B8567 Bonnard, Georges. "Are Othello and Desdemona Innocent or Guilty?" *ES*, XXX (1949), 175-186.

B8568   Wilcox, John. "Othello's Crucial Moment." *SAB*, XXIV (1949), 181-192.

B8569   Connolly, Thomas F. "Shakespeare and the Double Man." *SQ*, I (1950), 30-35.

B8570   Flatter, Richard. *The Moor of Venice*. London: William Heinemann, 1950. Pp. x, 225.
        Rev: *TLS*, May 5, 1950, p. 278; by J. I. M. Stewart, *NstN*, April 15, p. 434; by L. H.,
        Dublin Mag., XXV iii, 54-56; by Hermann Heuer, *SJ*, 84/86 (1951), 258.

B8571   Haydn, Hiram. *The Counter-Renaissance*. New York, 1950.
        Rev: A3836.

B8572   Jorgensen, Paul A. "*Honesty* in *Othello*." *SP*, XLVII (1950), 557-567.

B8573   Thaler, Alwin. "Delayed Exposition in Shakespeare." *SQ*, I (1950), 140-145.

B8574   Traversi, Derek. "*Othello*." *The Wind and the Rain*, VI (1950), 248-268.

B8575   Burke, Kenneth. "*Othello*: An Essay to Illustrate A Method." *Hudson Review*, IV (1951),
        165-203.

B8576   Rosenberg, Marvin. "*Othello*": A Critical Study. DD, University of California, Berkeley,
        1951.

B8577   Battenhouse, Roy W. "Shakespeare and the Tragedy of Our Time." *Theology Today*, VIII
        (1952), 518-534.

B8578   Carrère, F. "La Conception Shakespearienne du Tragique et le Drame d'Othello." *Annales
        de la Faculté des Lettres de Toulouse*, I (1952), 77-85.

B8579   Draper, John W. *The "Othello" of Shakespeare's Audience*. Paris: Didier, 1952. Pp. 246.
        Rev: by S. B. Liljegren, *SN*, XXV (1953), 180-181; by Price, *N. Mitt.*, LIV, Heft 3/4;
        by John E. Hankins, *SQ*, V (1954), 91-92.

B8580   Grabowsky, Adolf. "Der Emporkömmling. Studien zu Shakespeares *Othello*." *Unsere
        Schule* (Hannover), VII (1952), 520-526.

B8581   Muir, Kenneth. "Double Time in *Othello*." *N &Q*, 197 (1952), 76-77.

B8582   Nowottny, Winifred M. T. "Justice and Love in *Othello*." *UTQ*, XXI (1952), 330-344.

B8583   Poirier, Michel. "Le 'Double Temps' dans *Othello*." *EA*, V (1952), 107-116.

B8584   Wilson, Edward M. "*Othello*, a Tragedy of Honour." *Listener*, June 5, 1952, pp. 926-927.
        Comment by Janet Spens, June 19, ibid., p. 1007.

B8585   Brennecke, Ernest. " 'Nay, That's Not Next': The Significance of Desdemona's 'Willow
        Song'." *SQ*, IV (1953), 35-38.

B8586   Carrère, F. "Deux Motifs sur l'*Othello* de Shakespeare: le Monologue—l'Amour et la Jalousie."
        Littératures (Annales Publiées par la Faculté des Lettres de Toulouse), II (1953), 16-30.

B8587   Elliott, G. R. *Flaming Minister: A Study of "Othello" as Tragedy of Love and Hate*. Duke Univ.
        Press, 1953. Pp. xxxvi, 245.
        Rev: by William Empson, *KR*, XVI (1954), 163-166 (reply by Elliott, XVI, 335-336); by
        Kenneth Muir, *MLN*, LXIX, 433-435; by R. A. Foakes, *English*, X, 20; *Listener*, LI, 937; by
        L. H., *Dublin Mag.*, XXX (April-June), 55-56; by J. -B. Fort, *EA*, VII, 230; by Clifford Leech,
        SQ, V, 88-90 (correspondence from Elliott and Leech in *SQ*, V, 214); by E. J. West, *QJS*, XL,
        212-213; by G. K. Hunter, *RES*, NS, VI (1955), 82-83; by Helen C. White, *JEGP*, LV (1956),
        645-647; *ShN*, VII (1957), 40.

B8588   Howarth, R. G. *The Tragedy of "Othello."* Sydney, N. S. W., 1953. Pp. 16.

B8589   Speaight, Robert. "Réflexions sur *Othello*." *MdF*, No. 1079 (July, 1953), 478-493.

B8590   Siegel, Paul N. "The Damnation of *Othello*." *PMLA*, LXVIII (1953), 1068-78.

B8591   Siegel, Paul. "The Damnation of *Othello*: An Addendum." *PMLA*, LXXI (1956), 279-280.

B8592   Hubler, Edward. "The Damnation of *Othello*: Some Limitations on the Christian View of the
        Play." *SQ*, IX (1958), 295-300.
        See commentary by Harold S. Wilson, ibid., pp. 307-310.

B8593   Siegel, Paul N. "Correspondence." *SQ*, IX (1958), 433-435.
        Answer to B8592.

B8594   Stoll, E. E. "Slander in Drama." *SQ*, IV (1953), 433-450.

B8595   Wilson, Edward M. "Family Honour in the Plays of Shakespeare's Predecessors and Con-
        temporaries." *Essays and Studies*, NS, VI (1953), 19-40.

B8596   Axelrad, A. José. "Un Point de Droit Elizabéthain sur la Scène Dramatique." *Revue du Nord*,
        XXXVI (1954), 195-200.

B8597   Rosenberg, Marvin. "A Sceptical Look at Sceptical Criticism." *PQ*, XXXIII (1954), 66-77.

B8598   Zeisler, Ernest B. "*Othello*": Time Enigma and Color Problems. Chicago: Alexander J. Isaacs,
        1954. Pp. 60.
        Rev: by Philip Butcher, *SQ*, VI (1955), 191.

B8599   Allen, N. B. "Who Stole the Handkerchief?" *N &Q*, NS, II (1955), 292.

B8600   Gardner, Helen. *The Noble Moor*. Annual Shakespeare Lecture, 1955. *Proceedings of the
        British Academy, 1955*, XLI (1955), 189-205. Oxford Univ. Press, 1956.
        Rev: A956.

B8601 Heilman, Robert B. "Wit and Witchcraft: Thematic Form in *Othello.*" *Arizona Quarterly*, XII (1956), 5-16.

B8602 Pearce, Thomas W. "Wit and Wisdom in Mr. Heilman's *Othello.*" *ShN*, VIII (1958), 42.

B8603 McPeek, James A. S. "The 'Arts Inhibited' and the Meaning of *Othello.*" *Boston Univ. Studies in Eng.*, I (1955), 129-147.

B8604 Ribner, Irving. "*Othello* and the Pattern of Shakespearean Tragedy." *Tulane Studies in Eng.*, V (1955), 69-82.

B8605 Rudolf, Branko. "Othello v Mariboru 1954. Othellov Problem." *Nova Obzorja* (Maribor), I (1955), 57-64.

B8606 De Villiers, Jacob. "The Tragedy of *Othello.*" *Theoria*, VII (1955), 71-78.

B8607 Flatter, Richard. "*Rodrigo*" and "*Der Doppeltriumph des Othello.*" In his *Triumph der Gnade. Shakespeare Essays.* Vienna and Munich: Kurt Desch, 1956, pp. 125-129.

B8608 Heilman, Robert B. "Approach to *Othello.*" *SR*, LXIV (1956), 98-116.

B8609 Heilman, Robert B. *Magic in the Web: Action and Language in "Othello."* Univ. of Kentucky Press, 1956. Pp. 316.
   Rev: *Essential Books*, June, 1956, p. 35; *Dublin Mag.*, XXXI, No. 4, 62-64; *VQR*, XXXII, cxii-cxiv; by Robert A. Law, *Southwest Review*, XLI, 390-391; by D. B. Dodson, *JEGP*, LVI (1957), 276-278; by Winifred M. T. Nowottny, *MLR*, LII, 586-587; by W. Gordon Zeeveld, *SQ*, VIII, 538-540; by H. C. Kiefer, *Arizona Quar.*, XIII, 266-268; by John Arthos, *MLN*, LXXII, 439-442; by G. B. Harrison, *SatR*, Aug. 3, p. 17; by J. A. Bryant, Jr., *SR*, LXV, 152-160; by Hardin Craig, *Expl.*, Jan., 4; by John Robert Moore, *MLQ*, XVIII, 267-268; by G. K. Hunter, *EIC*, VIII (1958), 106-110; *ShN*, VIII, 12; by Charles Norton Coe, *CE*, XX, 99; by A. A., *Personalist*, XXXIX, 93-95.

B8610 Siegel, Paul N. *Shakespearian Tragedy and the Elizabethan Compromise.* New York: New York Univ. Press, 1956.
   Rev: A1882.

B8611 Sproule, Albert Frederick. "A Time Scheme for *Othello.*" *SQ*, VII (1956), 217-226.

B8612 Arnold, Aerol. "The Function of Brabantio in *Othello.*" *SQ*, VIII (1957), 51-56.

B8613 Auden, W. H. "The Dyer's Hand: Poetry and the Poetic Process." *The Anchor Review*, No. 2 (1957), pp. 255-301.
   Includes section called "Othello's Final Speech."

B8614 Cutts, John P. "A Reconsideration of the Willow Song." *Jour. American Musicological Soc.*, X (1957), 14-24.

B8615 Herbert, Carolyn. "Comic Elements in *Othello.*" *Renaissance Papers*, 1957, pp. 32-38. Abstr. in *ShN*, VII (1957), 12.

B8616 Langbaum, Robert. *The Poetry of Experience: The Dramatic Monologue in Modern Literary Tradition.* New York: Random House, 1957. Pp. 246.
   Othello, pp. 163-170.
   Rev: A6512.

B8617 Morgan, George Alan. *Illustrations of the Critical Principles of E. E. Stoll.* DD, Iowa State University, 1957. Pp. 224. Mic 57-4807. *DA*, XVII (1957), 3020. Publ. No. 23,772.
   "Illustrated" from *Ham.*, *Oth.*, and *Macb.* The summary takes issue with Stoll's findings.

B8618 Ross, Lawrence J. *The Shakespearean "Othello," A Critical Exposition on Historical Evidence.* DD, Princeton University, 1957.

B8619 Shackford, Martha Hale. "Discovery, Recognition, Reversal in *King Oedipus* and *Othello.*" In Shackford's *Shakespeare, Sophocles: Dramatic Modes*, 1957, pp. 29-37.
   Rev: B4489.

B8620 Clare Immaculate, Sister. "The Problem of Suffering in Shakespeare's *Othello.*" *Catholic Educator*, XXVII (1957), 178-180.

B8621 Arthos, John. "The Fall of Othello." *SQ*, IX (1958), 93-104.

B8622 Burckhardt, Carl J. *Bildnisse.* Frankfurt: S. Fischer, 1958.
   Contains essay on *Othello*.

B8623 Penlington, Norman. "The Terrible Sickness in Shakespeare's *Othello.*" *Motive* (Nashville), Jan. 1958, pp. 14-15, 30-32.

(5) CHARACTERIZATION
(a) GENERAL

B8624 Tannenbaum, Samuel A. "The Wronged Iago." *SAB*, XII (1937), 57-62.

B8625 Stoll, Elmer Edgar. "Shakespeare Forbears." *MLN*, LIV (1939), 332-337.

B8626 Raymond, William O. "Motivation and Character Portrayal in *Othello.*" *UTQ*, XVII (1947), 80-96.

B8627 Babb, Lawrence. "On the Nature of Elizabethan Psychological Literature." *AMS*, pp. 509-522.

B8628 Bonnard, G. "Are Othello and Desdemona Innocent or Guilty?" *ES*, XXX (1949), 175-184.

B8629   Jordan, Hoover H. "Dramatic Illusion in *Othello*." *SQ*, I (1950), 146-152.

B8630   Lucas, F. L. *Literature and Psychology*. London: Cassell, 1951. Pp. 340.
        Oth., pp. 72-76.
        Rev: A1362.

B8631   Webb, Henry J. "The Military Background in *Othello*." *PQ*, xxx (1951), 40-52.

B8632   Moore, John Robert. "Othello, Iago, and Cassio as Soldiers." *PQ*, xxxi (1952), 189-194.
        Against B8631.

B8633   MacCarthy, Desmond. *Theatre*. London: MacGibbon & Kee, 1954. Pp. vi, 191.
        Rev: B7838.

(b) MORE SPECIFIC
i. Othello

B8634   Prentiss, E. *A Study of the Inferiority Feeling in "Othello."* MA thesis, University of Oregon,
        1925.

B8635   Cavalli, E. *La Gelosia di Otello*. Loano: Tip. G. Olocco, 1934. Pp. 24.

B8636   Clerk, Piers. "*Othello*." *English Rev.*, LXIV (1937), 403-404.

B8637   Baldensperger, Fernand. "Was Othello an Ethiopian?" In *Harvard Studies and Notes in
        Philol. and Lit.*, xx (1937), Harvard Univ. Press, 1938, pp. 3-14.

B8638   Fairchild, Arthur H. R. *Shakespeare and the Tragic Theme*. Univ. Missouri Studies, xix,
        No. 2. Univ. Missouri Press, 1944. Pp. 145.
        Rev: A6853.

B8639   Kirschbaum, Leo. "The Modern Othello." *ELH*, xi (1944), 283-296.

B8640   Stoll, Elmer Edgar. "An Othello All-too Modern." *ELH*, xiii (1946), 46-58.
        Against B8639.

B8641   Stirling, Brents. "Psychology in *Othello*." *SAB*, xix (1944), 135-144.
        Rebuttal of Professor Stoll's view that Othello's actions are not psychologically motivated.

B8642   Withington, R. "Othello Not a Negro." *New York Times Magazine*, Feb. 20, 1944, p. 2.

B8643   Aubin, R. A. " 'Black as the Moor of Venice'." *TLS*, July 13, 1946, p. 331.

B8644   Nicholson, Catherine. *The History of the Criticism of the Character Othello*. MA thesis, Univer-
        sity of North Carolina, 1945. Abstr. publ. in *Univ. of North Carolina Record, Research in Prog-
        ress*, Grad. School Series No. 50, 1946, pp. 159.

B8645   Alden, Barbara. *Differences in the Conception of Othello's Character as Seen in the Performances
        of Three Important Nineteenth-Century Actors on the American Stage—Edwin Forrest, Edwin Booth,
        Tommaso Salvini*. DD, University of Chicago, 1950.

B8646   Duthie, G. I. *Shakespeare*. London: Hutchinson's Univ. Library, 1951. Pp. 206.
        First Chap. attacks Stoll's view of *Oth.* in *Art & Artifice*, A8390.
        Rev: A8162.

B8647   Di Pilato, Sergio. "Otello o della Gelosia." *Archivio Penale*, July-August, 1951, fasc. vii-viii.

B8648   Kliger, Samuel. "Othello: The Man of Judgment." *MP*, xlviii (1951), 221-224.

B8649   Cohen, Hennig. "Shakespeare's *Merchant of Venice* II. vii. 78-99." *SQ*, II (1951), 79.
        The Moor a symbol of the Devil to an Eliz. audience.

B8650   Butcher, Philip. "Othello's Racial Identity." *SQ*, III (1952), 243-247.

B8651   Wilson, Arthur H. "Othello's Racial Identity." *SQ*, IV (1953), 209.
        Comments on B8650.

B8652   Feldman, Abraham B. "Othello's Obsessions." *American Imago*, IX (1952), 147-164.

B8653   Meltzer, J. "Some Psycho-Analytical Angles on Aspects of Shakespearean Drama." *Dis-
        cussion* (South Africa), I, No. 6 (1952), 47-50.

B8654   Dzieduszycki, Wojciech. "Maur czy Murzyn? (Otello Shakespearea)." *Teatr* (Warsaw),
        No. 2 (1953), 22.

B8655   Geyer, Horst. *Dichter des Wahnsinns. Eine Untersuchung über die Dichterische Darstellbarkeit
        Seelischer Ausnahmezustände*. Göttingen: Musterschmidt, 1955. Pp. 322.
        Chapter II, "Eifersuchtswahn. Shakespeares Leontes und Othello," pp. 178-196, 282-295.
        Rev: A1375.

B8656   Feldman, A. Bronson. "The Yellow Malady: Short Studies of Five Tragedies of Jealousy."
        Literature and Psychology, VI (1956), 38-52.

B8657   Natanson, W. "Psychologiczne Problemy Otella." *Teatr* (Warsaw), XI, No. 8 (1956), 13-14.

B8658   Cancelled.

B8659   Gérard, Albert. " 'Egregiously an Ass': The Dark Side of the Moor. A View of Othello's
        Mind." *ShS*, x (1957), 98-106.

B8660   Harris, Bernard. "A Portrait of a Moor." *ShS*, xi (1958), 89-97.

B8661   Sjögren, Gunnar. *Var Othello Neger och Andra Shakespeareproblem*. Stockholm: Natur och
        Kultur, 1958. Pp. 196.

ii. Desdemona

B8662   Matsuura, Kaichi. "Ophelia Metamorphosed into Desdemona." *The Rising Generation*, 98 (1952), 50-51.

B8663   Reik, Theodor. *The Secret Self.* New York: Farrar, Straus, and Young, 1952. Pp. 329. Desdemona, pp. 57-62.
Rev: A1356.

iii. Brabantio

B8664   Draper, John W. "Signior Brabantio, Plaintiff." *ES*, XXII (1940), 193-198.

B8665   Draper, John W. "Signior Brabantio's Humor." *Bul. Hist. Med.*, XVIII (1945), 539-543.

iv. Iago

B8666   Brock, J. H. E. *Iago and Some Shakespearean Villains.* Cambridge: W. Heffer & Sons, 1937. Pp. viii, 48.
Rev: A1245.

B8667   Bridie, J. "Mr. Olivier's Iago." *NstN*, XV (1938), 405.
"We are shown a vital and intelligent man with a diseased and perverted sexual 'make-up' . . . His pathetic rationalizations and uncontrolled bursts of smutty talk were the expression of his conflict . . . It was drawn from a real man, and the picture is horrifyingly accurate."

B8668   Draper, John W. "The Jealousy of Iago." *Neophil*, XXV (1939), 50-60.

B8669   Goll, A. Tr. Moritzen. "Iago, the Criminal Type." *Journal of Criminal Law and Criminology*, XXX (1939), 35-51.

B8670   Meyerstein, E. H. W. "Iago's Age." *TLS*, March 23, 1940, p. 147.

B8671   McCloskey, John C. "The Motivation of Iago." *CE*, III (1941), 25-30.

B8672   Bowman, Thomas D. "A Further Study in the Characterization and Motivation of Iago." *CE*, IV (1943), 460-469.

B8673   Moore, John Robert. "The Character of Iago." *Studies in Honor of A. H. R. Fairchild*, pp. 37-46.

B8674   Thomas, Mary Olive. *A Study of the Criticism of Iago.* MA thesis, University of North Carolina, 1944. Abstr. publ. in *Univ. of North Carolina Record, Research in Progress*, Grad. School Series No. 50, 1946, pp. 163.

B8675   Ritze, F. H. *Shakespeare's Men of Melancholy and His Malcontents.* MS thesis, Columbia University, 1947. Pp. 98.

B8676   Brooke, C. F. Tucker. "The Romantic Iago." In *Essays on Shakespeare and Other Elizabethans*, Yale Univ. Press, 1948, pp. 46-56.

B8677   Spencer, Theodore. "The Elizabethan Malcontent." *AMS*, pp. 523-535.

B8678   Stoll, Elmer Edgar. "Iago Not a Malcontent." *JEGP*, LI (1952), 163-167.
Answer to B8677.

B8679   Sprague, Arthur Colby. "Edwin Booth's Iago: A Study of a Great Shakespearean Actor." *TAr*, 1948, pp. 7-17.

B8680   Bonfanti, Giosuè. "Spiritualità di Jago." *La Rassegna d'Italia*, IV (1949), 190-194.

B8681   Jorgensen, Paul A. "*Honesty* in *Othello*." *SP*, XLVII (1950), 557-567.

B8682   Rand, Frank P. "The Over Garrulous Iago." *SQ*, I (1950), 155-161.

B8683   Wangh, Martin. "*Othello:* The Tragedy of Iago." *Psychoanalytic Quarterly*, XIX (1950), 202-212.

B8684   Muir, Kenneth. "The Jealousy of Iago." *English Miscellany*, ed. by Mario Praz (Rome: Edizioni di Storia e Letteratura), II (1952), 65-83.

B8685   Russo, Luigi. "L'Onesto Iago." *Belfagor* (Messina-Florence), Sept. 30, 1952, pp. 584-586.

B8686   Heilman, Robert B. "The Economics of Iago and Others." *PMLA*, LXVIII (1953), 555-571.
Rev: by H. T. Price, *SQ*, V (1954), 125-126.

B8687   Weisinger, Herbert. "Iago's Iago." *The Univ. of Kansas City Review*, XX (1953), 83-90.

B8688   Henderson, Archibald, Jr. *Family of Mercutio.* DD, Columbia University, 1954. Pp. 270. Mic A54-2044. *DA*, XIV (1954), 1395. Publ. No. 8684.
Includes a chapter on *Othello*.

B8689   "An *Othello* Problem." *Birmingham* (England) *Post*, March 30, 1955.

B8690   Hoepfner, Theodore C. "Iago's Nationality." *N &Q*, NS, II (1955), 14-15.

B8691   Rosenberg, Marvin. "In Defense of Iago." *SQ*, VI (1955), 145-158.

B8692   Strix. "Iago and Others." *Spectator*, 6676 (1956), 789.

B8693   Coe, Charles Norton. *Shakespeare's Villains.* New York: Bookman Associates, 1957. Pp. 76.
Rev: A6796.

B8694   Quijano, Margarita. *La Celestina y Otelo.* University of Mexico, 1957. Pp. 180.

B8695   Faggett, Harry L.   "The State of Venice Versus Shakespeare's Iago."   *College Language Association Journal*, I (1958), 106-108.
B8696   Gérard, Albert.   "Alack, Poor Iago!   Intellect and Action in *Othello*."   *SJ*, 94 (1958), 218-232.
B8697   Spivack, Bernard.   *Allegory of Evil*.   DD, Columbia University, 1953.   Revised and published as *Shakespeare and the Allegory of Evil*, New York: Columbia Univ. Press, 1958.
        Rev: A4951.

v.   Emilia

B8698   Morris, Amos R.   " 'I Thought So Then'."   *Papers of the Michigan Acad. of Science, Arts, and Letters*, XXV (1939), 573-578.
B8699   Bowman, Thomas D.   "In Defense of Emilia."   *SAB*, XXII (1947), 99-104.
B8700   Smith, Fred M.   "Shylock on the Rights of the Jews and Emilia on the Rights of Women."   *West Virginia Univ. Bulletin.   Philological Papers*, V (1947), 32-33.

vi.   Cassio

B8701   Glen, Enid.   "Cassio the Puritan."   *N &Q*, 172 (1937), 43-44.
B8702   Draper, John W.   "The Choleric Cassio."   *Bull. Hist. Medicine*, VII (1939), 583-594.

(b)   SYMBOLISM

B8703   Feldman, A. Bronson.   "Othello in Reality."   *American Imago*, XI (1954), 147-179.
        The author of *Oth.* was Edward de Vere, Earl of Oxford.

(7)   MISCELLANEOUS ITEMS

B8704   Klajn, Hugo.   "Otela danas."   (*Othello* today).   *Naša Književnost* (Belgrade), II (1947), 138-150.
B8705   Clemeshaw, Isabel B.   "Literary Notes: *Othello*."   *Theosophical Forum*, XXVIII (1950), 116-120.
B8706   Simpson, Lucie.   "The Temperance Note in *Othello* and *Macbeth*."   In *The Secondary Heroes of Shakespeare and Other Essays*, pp. 105-108.
B8707   Babcock, C. Merton.   "An Analogue for the Name Othello."   *N &Q*, 196 (1951), 515.
B8708   Frye, Roland Mushat.   *The Accepted Ethics and Theology of Shakespeare's Audience as Utilized by the Dramatist in Certain Representative Tragedies, with Particular Attention to Love and Marriage*.   DD, Princeton University, 1952.   Pp. 372.   Mic A55-745.   *DA*, XV (1955), 581.   Publ. No. 10,901.
        Rev: A2563.
B8709   Garçon, Maurice, ed.   *Plaidoyers Chimériques*.   Paris: Fayard, 1954.
        Selections from Shak.'s famous declaimers or legal defendants, as the "romantique Antony" and "le More de Venise."
        Rev: B4170.
B8710   Gombač, Branko.   "Današnji Othello.   Odlomki Predavanja."   *Celjski Gledališki List* (Celje), No. 1 (1955/56).
B8711   Moravec, Dušan.   "Shakespeare pri Slovencih.   Odlomki iz Obširne Razprave."   *Celjski Gledališki List* (Celje), No. 1 (1955/56), 1-7.
B8712   Gallagher, Ligera Cécile.   *Shakespeare and the Aristotelian Ethical Tradition*.   DD, Stanford, University, 1956.   Pp. 338.   Mic 56-3017.   *DA*, XVI (1956), 1898.   Publ. No. 17,720.
        Chapt. VIII on *Othello* and *Lear*.
B8713   Sypher, Wylie.   *Four Stages of Renaissance Style*.   New York: Doubleday Anchor Books, 1956.   Pp. 312.
        Rev: A5514.
B8714   Seng, Peter J.   "The Earliest Known Music for Desdemona's 'Willow Song'."   *SQ*, IX (1958), 419-420.

(8)   SUBSEQUENT HISTORY OF THE PLAY
(Other than productions after 1660)

B8715   Tillotson, Geoffrey.   "*Othello* and *The Alchemist* at Oxford in 1610."   *Essays in Criticism and Research*, Cambridge Univ. Press, 1942, pp. 41-48.
        Previously published in *TLS*, 1933.
B8716   Alden, Barbara.   *The History and Interpretation of Shakespeare's "Othello" on the American Stage*.   DD, University of Chicago, 1942.
B8717   Robeson, Paul.   "Some Reflections on *Othello* and the Nature of Our Time."   *Amer. Scholar*, XIV (1945), 392-393.
        Based on his performance and his reaction to it.
B8718   Goldstone, Richard H.   "Experiments with Audio-Visual Aids: I. In Teaching Shakespeare."   *CE*, XIII (1952), 319-322.
B8719   Kernan, Joseph.   "Verdi's *Otello*, or Shakespeare Explained."   *Hudson Review*, VI (1953), 266-277.

B8720 Rosenberg, Marvin. "The 'Refinement' of *Othello* in the Eighteenth Century British Theatre."
       SP, LI (1954), 75-94.
B8721 "Dark Mystery: *Othello*." *Musical America*, Aug., 1956, p. 17.
B8722 Brocker, Harrier Durkee. *The Influence of "Othello" in Jacobean and Caroline Drama*. DD,
       University of Minnesota, 1957. Pp. 349. Mic 57-3223. *DA*, XVII (1957), 2006. Publ.
       No. 22,444.

                              KING LEAR (242;86)

B8723 Tannenbaum, Samuel A. *Shakespeare's "King Lear": A Concise Bibliography*. Elizabethan
       Bibliographies, No. 16. New York: Author, 1940. Pp. 112.

                           (1) THE TEXT
                             (a) OLD TEXTS
                                i. Reprints

B8724 *King Lear*. Parallel Texts of the Q₁ and the F₁. Ed. for the Use of University Classes by
       Wilh. Viëtor. 3rd ed. Shakespeare Reprints. Marburg: Elwert, 1937. Pp. iv, 178.
B8725 *King Lear, 1608* (Pied Bull Quarto). *Shakespeare Quarto Facsimiles*. London: Shakespeare
       Assoc. and Sidgwick & Jackson, 1939.
       Rev: *TLS*, Dec. 2, 1939, p. 707; by B. M., *PQ*, XIX (1940), 413-414; by H. Sellers, *MLR*,
       XXXV, 235; by James G. McManaway, *MLN*, LV, 632-634.

                                ii. Discussions

B8726 Dam, B. A. P. van. *The Text of Shakespeare's "Lear."* Materials for the Study of the Old
       English Drama, No. 10. Ed. H. DeVocht. Louvain: Uystpruyst, 1935. Pp. 110.
       Rev: by R. W. Zandvoort, *ES*, XVIII (1935), 48; by Wolfgang Keller, SJ, LXXII (1936),
       148-149; by Madeleine Doran, *MP*, XXXIV (1937), 430-433; by Robert Adger Law, *JEGP*,
       XXXVI, 275-276; by H. Craig, *MLN*, LIII (1938), 204-207.
B8727 Cairncross, A. S. *The Problem of Hamlet. A Solution*. London: Macmillan, 1936. Pp. xix, 205.
       Lear as the source of *Leir*.
       Rev: B4916.
B8728 Greg, W. W. "*King Lear*—Mislineation and Stenography." *Library*, NS, XVII (1936), 172-183.
B8729 Kies, Paul P. "On the Dating of *Othello* and *Lear*." *Research Studies of the State College of
       Washington*, III, No. 2 (1936), 72-73.
B8730 Stössel, Oskar. *Stenographische Studien zu Shakespeares "King Lear."* DD, Munich, 1937. Pp. 80.
B8731 Kirschbaum, Leo. "How Jane Bell Came to Print the Third Quarto of Shakespeare's *King
       Lear*." *PQ* XVII (1938), 308-311.
B8732 Greg, W. W. "The Date of *King Lear* and Shakespeare's Use of Earlier Versions of the Story."
       Library, XX (1939), 377-400.
B8733 Greg, W. W. *The Variants in the First Quarto of "King Lear."* London, Oxford Univ. Press
       for the Bibliographical Society, 1940 (for 1939). Pp. 192.
       Rev: *TLS*, Nov. 16, 1940, p. 584; by Leo Kirschbaum, *MLN*, LVI, 624-626; by J. G. McManaway, *MLR*, XXXVII (1942), 86-88.
B8734 Greg, W. W. "The Staging of *King Lear*." *RES*, XVI (1940), 300-303.
B8735 Kirschbaum, Leo. "The True Text of *King Lear*." *SAB*, XVI (1941), 140-153.
B8736 Kirschbaum, Leo. *The True Text of "King Lear."* Johns Hopkins Press, 1945. Pp. ix, 81.
       Rev: A2945.
B8737 Duthie, George Ian. (*1*) *Two Shakespeare Problems; (a) The "Bad" Quarto of "Hamlet,"
       (b) "The Taming of a Shrew" and "The Taming of the Shrew"; (2) Shakespeare's "King Lear":
       A Critical Edition*. DD, Edinburgh, 1946.
B8738 Greg, W. W. "The Staging of *King Lear*." *RES*, XXII (1946), 229.
       Revises his opinion to accept Mr. John Berryman's view that act and scene division in the
       Folio is not "original" and may be the work of the Folio editor.
B8739 Small, S. A. "The *King Lear* Quarto." *SAB*, XXI (1946), 177-180.
B8740 Bowers, Fredson. "An Examination of the Method of Proof Correction in *Lear*." *Library*,
       II (1947), 20-44.
B8741 Bowers, Fredson. "Elizabethan Proofing." *AMS*, pp. 571-586.
B8742 Williams, Philip, Jr. "The Compositor of the 'Pied Bull' *Lear*." *Papers Bibl. Soc. Univ.
       Virginia*, I (1948-49), 59-68.
B8743 Williams, George W. "A Note on *King Lear*, III. ii. 1-3." *SB*, II (1949), 175-182.
B8744 Duthie, G. I. *Elizabethan Shorthand and the First Quarto of "King Lear."* Oxford, 1950.
       Rev: A2758.
B8745 Muir, Kenneth. "A Test for Shakespeare Variants." *N &Q*, 195 (1950), 513-514.
       II. i. 76.
B8746 Cauthen, Irby B., Jr. *Shakespeare's "King Lear": An Investigation of Compositor Habits in the

First Folio and Their Relation to the Text. DD, University of Virginia, 1951. Abstr. publ. in *Abstracts of Dissertations,* Charlottesville: Univ. of Virginia, 1951, pp. 13-18.

B8747 Cauthen, I. B., Jr. "Compositor Determination in the First Folio *King Lear.*" *SB,* V (1952-53), 73-80.

B8748 Walker, Alice. *"King Lear*—the 1608 Quarto." *MLR,* XLVII (1952), 376-378.

B8749 Williams, Philip. "Two Problems in the Folio Text of *King Lear.*" *SQ,* IV (1953), 451-460.

B8750 Cairncross, Andrew S. "The Quartos and the Folio Text of *King Lear.*" *RES,* NS, VI (1955), 252-258.

B8751 Walton, J. K. *The Copy for the Folio Text of "Richard III."* With a Note on the Copy for the Folio Text of *King Lear.* Monograph Series, No. 1. Auckland University College, New Zealand: The Pilgrim Press, 1955. Pp. 164.
Rev: A3301.

B8752 Brown, John Russel. "A Proof-sheet from Nicholas Okes' Printing-shop." *SB,* XI (1958). 228-231.

(b) MODERN EDITIONS

B8753 *The Tragedy of King Lear.* Ed. George L. Kittredge. Boston, 1940. Pp. xiv, 264.

B8754 *King Lear.* Ed. Joseph Kirchhoff. New Ed. Paderborn: Schöningh, 1946. Pp. 48.

B8755 *King Lear.* Ed. Tarquinio Vallese. Naples: Pironti, 1948. Pp. xx, 106.

B8756 *King Lear.* Ed. R. C. Bald. Crofts Classics. New York: Appleton-Century-Crofts, 1949. Pp. xii, 115.

B8757 *Shakespeare's "King Lear": A Critical Edition.* Ed. George Ian Duthie. Oxford: Blackwell; New York: Macmillan, 1949. Pp. ix, 425.
Rev: by W. W. Greg, *MLR,* XLIV (1949), 397-400; *N &Q,* 194 (1949), 263; by J. B. Fort, *LanM,* XLIV (1950), 415-417; by Harry R. Hoppe, *MLN,* LXVI (1951), 337-338; by Fredson Bowers, *MLQ,* XII, 363-364; by Leo Kirschbaum, *RES,* NS, II, 168-173; by Robert Fricker, *ES,* XXXIV (1953), 178-181; *Studier i Modern Språkvetenskap* (Stockholm), XLVI, 110-112.

B8758 *King Lear.* Ed. Kenneth Muir. Arden Ed. London: Methuen, 1952. Pp. lxv, 256. Republ. 1957. Pp. lxiv, 258.
Rev: *TLS,* Oct. 31, 1952, p. 709; comments by John W. Harvey, ibid., Nov. 14, p. 743; by Kenneth Muir, ibid., Nov. 21, p. 761; by O. H. T. Dudley and John W. Harvey, ibid., Dec. 5, p. 797; by Louise F. W. Eickhoff and J. Lloyd, ibid., Dec. 12, p. 819; by F. W. Bateson, *EIC,* III (1953), 124; by Alice Walker, *RES,* IV, 376-377; by Fredson Bowers, *SQ,* IV, 471-477; by T. M. Parrott, *JEGP,* LII, 409-416; *The Listener,* May 14, pp. 901, 903; by J. Vallette, *MdF,* 318 (1953), 340; by A. Koszul, *EA,* VII (1954), 325-326; by James G. McManaway, *ShS,* VII, 149-150; by R. W. Zandvoort, *ES,* XXXVI (1955), 83-85; by Patrick Cruttwell, *EIC,* V, 382-390; by L. L. Schücking, *Anglia,* LXXIV (1956/57), 373-380; *N &Q,* V (1958), 501-502; by H. Heuer, *SJ,* 94 (1958), 291-292.

B8759 *King Lear.* Introd. by Donald Wolfit, with Designs in Colour by Noguchi. London: Folio Society, 1956. Pp. 128.
Illustrations are reproductions of the designs for the sets and costumes of the recent European tour of the Shak. Memorial Theatre Company.

B8760 *King Lear. Eight Great Tragedies.* Eds. Sylvan Barnet, Morton Berman, and William Burto. New York: Mentor, 1957, pp. 133-227.

B8761 *The Tragedy of King Lear.* Eds. Tucker Brooke and William Lyon Phelps. Yale Shakespeare. Yale Univ. Press, Oxford Univ. Press, 1947. Pp. 222. Yale Univ. Press, 1957. Pp. 202.
Rev: *SatR,* Aug. 3, 1957, p. 28.

B8762 *King Lear.* Ed. with an Introd. and Notes by F. E. Budd. Scholar's Library. London: Macmillan, 1957. Pp. xxv, 186.

B8763 *King Lear.* Ed. by R. E. C. Houghton. New Clarendon Shakespeare Series. Oxford: Clarendon Press, 1957. Pp. 256.
Rev: by Gerald Kahan, *Players Magazine,* XXXIV (1958), 10.

B8764 *King Lear.* Ed. S. Krishnamurthi. Madras (India): Little Flower, 1957. Pp. 496.

B8765 *King Lear.* Eds. Louis B. Wright and Virginia L. Freund. New York: Pocket Books, 1957. Pp. xliii, 125.
First title in the Folger Library General Reader's Shakespeare series.
Rev: *ShN,* VII (1957), 4; by Hubert Heffner, *ETJ,* IX 359-360; *SCN,* XV, 24; *ShN,* VIII (1958), 3; by Charles Norton Coe, *CE,* XIX, 189.

B8766 *The Tragedy of King Lear.* Ed. Alfred Harbage. Pelican Shakespeare. Baltimore: Penguin Books, 1958. Pp. 180.

B8767 Jazayery, Mohammed Ali, and Robert Adger Law. "Three Texts of *King Lear*: Their Differences." *TxSE,* XXXII (1953 [pub. 1954]), 14-24.
Compares the Globe, Neilson, and Kittredge texts.

(c) EMENDATIONS

B8768 Cuningham, Henry. "*King Lear,* III. vii. 65." *TLS,* March 19, 1938, p. 188.

B8769   Sledd, James. "Hause and Slaves in *King Lear*." *MLN*, LV (1940), 594-596.
        II. iv. 75-77; IV. i. 68-70.

B8770   Tannenbaum, Samuel A. "An Emendation in *King Lear*." *SAB*, XVI (1941), 58-59.
        I. ii. 21.

B8771   Cancelled.

B8772   Brown, B. Goulding, "*King Lear*, IV. iii. 29-32." *TLS*, Dec. 23, 1944, p. 619.

B8773   Moses, S. W. "*King Lear*, IV. iii. 29-32." *TLS*, Feb. 24, 1945, p. 91.

B8774   Heilman, R. B. "Shakespeare's *King Lear*, IV. vi. 169." *Expl.*, VI, ii (1947), item 10.

B8775   Camden, Carroll. "The Suffocation of the Mother." *MLN*, LXIII (1948), 390-393.
        II. iv. 56-58; V. iii. 309.

B8776   Stewart, Charles D. "Four Shakespearean Cruxes." *CE*, IX (1948), 187-191.
        "Eat no fish," "Heaven's benediction," and the last words of the Fool in *King Lear*.

B8777   Owen, W. J. B. " 'A Dogge, So Bade in Office'." *N&Q*, 194 (1949), 141-142.
        IV. vi. 164.

B8778   Muir, Kenneth. "*King Lear*, IV. i. 10." *TLS*, June 3, 1949, p. 365.
        See letters by William Bliss, ibid., June 24, 1949, p. 413; by Richard Flatter, ibid., July 22,
        p. 473.

B8779   Jones, Graham. "The Goose in *Lear*." *N&Q*, 195 (1950), 295.

B8780   Muir, Kenneth. "*King Lear*, II. iv. 170." *N&Q*, 196 (1951), 170.

B8781   Empson, W. " 'This' a Good Block'." *TLS*, Dec. 19, 1952, p. 837.

B8781a Muir, Kenneth. "This' a Good Block." *TLS*, Jan. 30, 1953, p. 73.

B8782   Hoepfner, Theodore C. "Sessa!" *N&Q*, 197 (1952), 502.

B8783   Davenport, A. "Notes on *King Lear*." *N&Q*, 198, No. 1 (1953), 20-22.
        II. i. 56; II. iv. 89; III. iv. 85ff; III. vi. 9ff; IV. i. 10.

B8784   Parrott, T. M. " 'God's' or 'gods' ' in *King Lear*, V. iii. 17." *SQ* IV (1953), 427-432.

B8785   Anderson, D. M. "A Conjecture on *King Lear*, IV. ii. 57." *N&Q*, 199, No. 8 (1954), 331.

B8786   Hoepfner, Theodore C. " 'We That Are Young'." *N&Q*, NS, I (1954), 110.

B8787   Craik, T. W. "Cordelia as 'Last and Least' of Lear's Daughters." *N&Q*, NS, III (1956), 11.

B8788   Heninger, S. K., Jr. "Shakespeare's *King Lear*, III. ii. 1-9." *Expl.*, XV, No. 1 (Oct., 1956), 1.

B8789   McKenzie, James J. "Edgar's 'Persian Attire'." *N&Q*, NS, III (1956), 98-99.

B8790   Bradbrook, F. W. "Shylock and King Lear." *N&Q*, NS, IV (1957), 142-143.

B8791   Camden, Carroll. "Three Notes on Shakespeare." *MLN*, LXXII (1957), 251-253.
        IV. ii. 39.

B8792   Hulme, Hilda. "Three Shakespearian Glosses." *N&Q*, NS, IV (1957), 237-238.
        IV. vi. 81.

B8793   Musgrove, S. "*King Lear*, I. i. 170 ('To come betwixt our sentence/sentences and our
        power')." *RES*, NS, VIII (1957), 170-171.

B8794   Cauthen, I. B., Jr. " 'The Foule Flibbertigibbet,' *King Lear*, III. iv. 113, IV. i. 60." *N&Q*,
        NS, V (1958), 98-99.

B8795   Major, John M. "Shakespeare's *King Lear*, IV. ii. 62." *Expl.*, XVII, ii (1958), item 13.

B8796   Seronsy, Cecil C. "Shakespeare's *King Lear*, I. i. 159-163." *Expl.*, XVII, iii (1958), item 21.

B8797   Spevack, Marvin. "Shakespeare's *King Lear*, IV. iv. 152." *Expl.*, XVII, i (1958), item 4.

(2) LITERARY GENESIS AND ANALOGUES

B8798   Atkinson, Dorothy F. "*King Lear*—Another Contemporary Account." *ELH*, III (1936),
        63-66.

B8799   Merrifield, F. de G. "Background to *King Lear*." *TLS*, March 7, 1936, p. 204.

B8800   Draper, John W. "The Occasion of *King Lear*." *SP*, XXXIV (1937), 176-185.

B8801   Kranz, W. "Shakespeare und die Antike." *Eng. Studn.* LXXIII (1938), 35-38.

B8802   Henderson, W. B. Drayton. "Montaigne's *Apologie of Raymond Sebond*, and *King Lear*."
        SAB, XIV (1939), 209-225; ibid., XV (1940), 40-56.

B8803   Wells, William. "The Authorship of *King Leir*." *N&Q*, 177 (1939), 434-438.

B8804   Greg, W. W. "The Date of *King Lear* and Shakespeare's Use of Earlier Versions of the
        Story." *Library*, XX (1940), 377-400.

B8805   Greg, W. W. "Shakespeare and *King Leir*." *TLS*, March 9, 1940, p. 124.

B8806   Taylor, George Coffin. "Two Notes on Shakespeare." *Renaissance Studies in Honor of Hardin
        Craig*, 1941, pp. 179-184; also in *PQ*, XX (1941), 371-376.
        The first is "Shakespeare and the Prognostications, *King Lear*, I. ii. 111-145."

B8807   Greer, Howard Kelley. "*King Lear*." MA thesis, Dalhousie, 1943. Pp. 154.
        Sources, date, variants, stage history, critical opinions.

B8808   Parr, Johnstone. "A Note on the 'Late Eclipses' in *King Lear*, I. ii. 98ff. ." *SAB*, XX (1945),
        46-48.

B8809   Berryman, John. "Shakespeare's Greek." *TLS*, March 13, 1946, p. 151.

B8810   Fox, Gladys. *Studies in the Composition of Shakespeare's "King Lear," "Macbeth" and "Cymbeline."* DD, Univ. of Texas, 1946.

B8811   Hammer, J. "Note sur l'Histoire du Roi Lear dans Geoffrey de Monmouth." *Latomus*, 1946, pp. 299-301.

B8812   Hankins, John E. "Lear and the Psalmist." *MLN*, LXI (1946), 88-90.

B8813   Smith, Roland M. "King Lear and the Merlin Tradition." *MLQ*, VII (1946), 153-174.

B8814   Lange, Günther. *Der Autor des Vorshakespeareschen Chronikspieles vom König Leir.* DD, Erlangen 1947. Pp. 278. Typewritten.

B8815   Pyle, Fitzroy. *"Twelfth Night, King Lear* and *Arcadia."* *MLR*, XLIII (1948), 449-455.

B8816   Rubow, Paul V. *Shakespeare og hans Samtidige.* Copenhagen: Gyldendal, 1948. Pp. 155. Contains essay on *Leir.*
        Rev: C74.

B8817   Armstrong, William A. *"King Lear* and Sidney's *Arcadia."* *TLS*, Oct. 24, 1949, p. 665. See the letter by Fitzroy Pyle, ibid., Nov. 11, 1949, p. 33.

B8818   Carrère, Félix Jean. *Le Théâtre de Thomas Kyd. Contribution à l'Etude du Drame Elizabéthain.* Thèse de Lettres, Paris, 1949. Publ. Toulouse: Edouard Privat, Editeur, 14, Rue des Arts, 1951.
        Rev: A4979.

B8819   Fischer, Walther P. *"King Lear* at Tuebingen: Johannes Nauclerus and Geoffrey of Monmouth." *Philologica: The Malone Anniversary Studies.* Eds. T. A. Kirby and H. B. Woolf. Baltimore: The Johns Hopkins Press, 1949, pp. 208-227.

B8820   Hewitt, Douglas. "The Very Pompes of the Divell—Popular and Folk Elements in Elizabethan and Jacobean Drama." *RES*, XXV (1949), 10-23.
        Includes a discussion of parallels between *King Lear* and certain folk ceremonies.

B8821   Ashe, Geoffrey. "William Strachey." *N &Q*, 195 (1950), 508-511.
        Replies by R. L. Eagle, ibid., 196 (1951), p. 19; by Kenneth Muir, ibid., pp. 19-20; by Herbert H. Huxley, ibid., pp. 85-86.

B8822   Law, Robert A. "Holinshed's Leir Story and Shakespeare's." *SP*, XLVII (1950), 42-50.

B8823   Muir, Kenneth, and John F. Danby. *"Arcadia* and *King Lear."* *N &Q*, 195 (1950), 49-51.

B8824   Muir, Kenneth. "Samuel Harsnett and *King Lear."* *RES*, II (1951), 11-21.
        Offers a full collection of passages from *A Declaration of Egregious Popish Impostures* which may have echoes in *Lear.*

B8825   Muir, Kenneth. "Shakespeare and Harsnett." *N &Q*, 197 (1952), 555-556.

B8826   Isham, Sir Gyles. "The Prototypes of King Lear and His Daughters." *N &Q*, NS, I (1954), 150-151.

B8827   Ribner, Irving. "Sidney's *Arcadia* and the Structure of *King Lear."* *SN*, XXIV (1952), 63-68.

B8828   Salter, K. W. *"Lear* and the Morality Tradition." *N &Q*, 199, No. 3 (1954), 109-110.

B8829   Law, Robert Adger. " 'Genouestan Gawles' and 'Red-Shanks'." *1953 Proceedings, Texas Publs. of the Conference of College of English*, 1955, pp. 6-9.

B8830   Muir, Kenneth. *"King Lear,* IV. 6." *N &Q*, NS, II (1955), 15.

B8831   Taylor, E. M. M. "Lear's Philosopher." *SQ*, VI (1955), 364-365.

B8832   Musgrove, S. "The Nomenclature of *King Lear."* *RES*, NS, VII (1956), 294-298.

B8833   Ekeblad, Inga-Stina. *"King Lear* and *Selimus."* *N &Q*, NS, IV (1957), 193-194.

B8834   Goldsmith, Robert Hillis. "Did Shakespeare Use the Old Timon Comedy?" *SQ*, IX (1958), 31-38.
        No single borrowing, but a network of approximate resemblances, suggests that Shak. used the MS *Timon* not only for *Tim.* but also for *Lear.*

B8835   Law, Robert Adger. *"King Leir* and *King Lear*: An Examination of the Two Plays." *Studies in Honor of T. W. Baldwin*, 1958, pp. 112-124.

B8836   McNeal, Thomas H. "Shakespeare's Cruel Queens." *HLQ*, XXII (1958), 41-50.

(3) USE OF LANGUAGE

B8837   Nottrott, Marianne. *Der Formale Gebrauch des Epithetons in Shakespeares Dramen "Othello," "King Lear," "Macbeth" und "Coriolanus."* DD, Leipzig, 1922. Pp. vi, 254. Handwritten. Publ. *Jahrbuch der Philosophischen Fakultät Leipzig,* I (1923).

B8838   Dayton, B. E. *Animal Similes and Metaphors in Shakespeare's Plays.* DD, University of Washington, 1937. Abstr. publ. in *Abstracts of Theses*, Univ. of Washington, II (1937), 119-122.

B8839   Gill, W. W. "Pronunciation of 'Daughter'." *N &Q*, 177 (1939), 15.

B8840   Orsini, N. "La Coscienza della Lingua nel Rinascimento: Shakespeare." *Anglica*, I (1946), 200-203.

B8841   Heilman, Robert B. "The Times' Plague: The Sight Pattern in *King Lear."* *Quar. Rev. of Literature*, IV (1947), 77-91.

B8842   Heilman, R. B. "Poor Naked Wretches and Proud Array: The Clothes Pattern in *King Lear*."
        Western Review (Lawrence), XII (Autumn, 1947), 5-15.

B8843   Sitwell, Edith. "*King Lear*." *Atlantic Monthly*, May, 1950, pp. 57-62.

B8844   Empson, William. *The Structure of Complex Words*. London: Chatto & Windus, 1951.
        Pp. 449.
        Includes extended critical remarks on *Lear*.
        Rev: A5136.

B8845   Williams, George W. "The Poetry of the Storm in *King Lear*." *SQ*, II (1951), 57-71.
        An extended analysis of the poetic and dramatic significance of Lear's speech, III. ii. 1-9.

B8846   Greenfield, Thelma Nelson. "The Clothing Motif in *King Lear*." *SQ*, V (1954), 281-286.

B8847   Blackmur, R. P. "The Language of Silence: A Citation." *SR*, LXIII (1955), 382-404.

B8848   Provost, George Foster. *The Techniques of Characterization and Dramatic Imagery in "Richard II"
        and "King Lear*." DD, Louisiana State University, 1955. Pp. 274. Mic 55-280. *DA*, XV
        (1955), 1616. Publ. No. 12,525.

(4) GENERAL CRITICISM OF THE PLAY

B8849   Freud, S. "The Theme of the Three Caskets." *Collected Papers*, International Psycho-Analytic
        Library. London: Hogarth Press, IV, 1950, pp. 244-256. Also in Standard Edition, XII, 1958,
        pp. 289-301. First publ. in 1913 in *Imago*.

B8850   Ten Holder, Klemens. "Erinnerung an einen Sprachlehrer der das Tragische in *König Lear*
        seinen Schülern Erläuterte." *Das Wort in der Zeit*, III (1935/36), 738-747.
        Comment by K. A. Horst, ibid., pp. 1141-1144.

B8851   Fijn van Draat, P. "*Koning Lear* in een Nieuw Licht." *Haagsch Maandblad*, No. 2, 1936,
        pp. 523-533.

B8852   Kassner, R. "Über Shakespeare." *Corona*, VI (1936), 256-283, 408-423.

B8853   Pongs, H. "Shakespeare und das Politische Drama." *DuV*, XXXVII, No. 3 (1936), 257-280.

B8854   Lacy, E. W. *Justice in Shakespeare*. DD, Vanderbilt University, 1937. Abstr. publ. in *Bull.
        of Vanderbilt Univ.*, XXXVII (1937), 42.

B8855   Gurland, Ingeborg. *Das Gestaltungsgesetz von Shakespeares "König Lear*" (Versuch einer Deu-
        tung). DD, Bonn, 1938. Pp. 99. Publ. Würzburg: Triltsch, 1938. Pp. 99.

B8856   Graham, Paul G. "Hebbel's Study of *King Lear*." *Essays Contributed in Honor of President
        William Allan Neilson*. Smith College Studies in Modern Languages, Vol. 21. Northampton,
        Massachusetts: Dept. of Modern Languages of Smith College, 1939. Pp. vii, 269.

B8857   Myers, H. A. "Dramatic Poetry and Values." *English Journal*, XXVIII (1939), 356-364.

B8858   Nosworthy, J. M. "*King Lear*—The Moral Aspect." *ES*, XXI (1939), 260-268.

B8859   Perkinson, Richard H. " 'Is This the Promised End?' " *Eng. Studn.*, LXXIII (1939), 202-211.

B8860   Rathkey, W. A. " 'Vex Not His Ghost'." *English*, II (1939), 355-361.

B8861   Turel, A. "*King Lear*." Bachofen-Freud: *Zur Emanzipation d. Mannes vom Reich d. Mütter*.
        Bern: H. Huber, 1939, pp. 61-74.

B8862   Greg, W. W. "Time, Place, and Politics in *King Lear*." *MLR*, XXXV (1940), 431-446.

B8863   Taylor, G. C. "Two Notes on Shakespeare." *PQ*, XX (1941), 371-376.

B8864   M. Angeline Cahill, Sister. *Tragic Effect and Poetic Justice Theoretically and in "King Lear"
        "Twixt Two Extremes of Passion, Joy and Grief*." DD, Boston College, 1942.

B8865   Watkins, W. B. C. "The Two Techniques in *King Lear*." *RES*, XVIII (1942), 1-26.
        The two techniques: psychological realism and symbolical stylization.

B8866   Perkinson, Richard H. "Shakespeare's Revision of the Lear Story and the Structure of *King
        Lear*." *PQ*, XXII (1943), 315-329.

B8867   Gordon, George. *Shakespearian Comedy and Other Studies*. Ed. Sir Edmund Chambers.
        Oxford Univ. Press, 1944. Pp. 168.
        Contains essay on *Lear*, pp. 116-128.
        Rev: B5165.

B8868   Hazen, A. T. "Shakespeare's *King Lear*, IV. i." *Expl.*, II, ii (1943), item 10.
        See comment by Monroe M. Stearns, idem.
        Answers query of R. K. J., ibid., I (1942-43), Q38, about motivation for Edgar's concealing
        his identity from Gloucester.

B8868a Arms, G. W., et al. "Shakespeare's *King Lear*, v. iii." *Expl.*, III, iii (1944), item 21.
        See B8871.

B8869   Spencer, Benjamin T. "*King Lear*: A Prophetic Tragedy." *CE*, V (1944), 302-308.

B8870   Danby, John F. "The Fool in *King Lear*." *DUJ*, XXXVIII (1945), 17-24.

B8871   Hankins, John E. "Shakespeare's *King Lear*, V, iii." *Expl.*, III, vi (1945), item 48.
        Answers B8868a.

B8872   Kernodle, George R. "The Symphonic Form of *King Lear*." *Elizabethan Studies and Other
        Essays: In Honor of George F. Reynolds*, 1945, pp. 185-191.

B8873	Stewart, J. I. M. "The Blinding of Gloster." *RES*, XXI (1945), 264-270.

B8874	Parr, Johnstone. "Edmund's Nativity." *SAB*, XXI (1946), 181-185.

B8875	Seelye, Mary-Averett. *Nature in "King Lear" as a Basis for the Unity of Action.* MA thesis, University of North Carolina, 1944. Abstr. publ. in *University of North Carolina Record, Research in Progress*, Grad. School Series No. 50, 1946, pp. 160-161.

B8876	Bickersteth, Geoffrey L. *The Golden World of "King Lear."* Annual Shakespeare Lecture of the British Academy, 1946. *Proceedings of the British Academy*, XXXII, 147-171. Oxford Univ. Press, 1947. Pp. 27.
	Rev: *TLS*, May 17, 1947, p. 243; *Spectator*, Aug. 15, p. 218; by F. T. Prince, *RES*, XXIV, 251-252; by J. M. S. Tompkins, *MLR*, XLIII (1948), 293.

B8877	Chapman, J. A. *"King Lear." Nineteenth Century*, 142 (1947), 95-100.
	Observations upon the play and upon Bradley's criticism.

B8878	Draper, John W. "Patterns of Humor and Tempo in *King Lear." Bul. Hist. Medicine*, XXI (1947), 390-401.

B8879	Granville-Barker, Harley. *Prefaces to Shakespeare.* 2 Vols. Princeton Univ. Press, 1946, 1947.
	Rev: A8201.

B8880	Heilman, Robert B. "The Two Natures in *King Lear." Accent*, VIII (1947), 51-59.

B8881	Hobday, C. H. "The Social Background of *King Lear." Modern Quarterly Miscellany*, No. I, 1947, pp. 37-56.

B8882	Lloyd, Roger. "The Rack of This Tough World." *QR*, 285 (1947), 530-540.

B8883	Muir, Edwin. *The Politics of King Lear.* The Seventh W. P. Ker Memorial Lecture. Glasgow Univ. Pub. No. 72. Glasgow: Jackson, Son & Co., 1947. Pp. 24.
	Also publ. in Muir's *Essays on Literature and Society.* London: Hogarth Press, 1949.
	Rev: A1830.

B8883a	"Shakespeare's Politics." *TLS*, Dec. 4, 1948, p. 681.
	On B8883.

B8884	Adams, John C. "The Original Staging of *King Lear." AMS*, pp. 315-335.

B8885	Backer, Franz der. "Over *Koning Lear." Miscellanea J. Gessler.* Deurne: Anvers, 1948, pp. 141-145.

B8886	Brooke, C. F. Tucker. *"King Lear* on the Stage." *Essays on Shakespeare and Other Elizabethans*, Yale Univ. Press, 1948, pp. 57-70.

B8887	Campbell, O. J. "The Salvation of Lear." *ELH*, XV (1948), 93-109.

B8888	Danby, John F. *"King Lear* and Christian Patience." *CamJ*, I (1948), 305-320.

B8889	Fort, J. B. "La Signification de *King Lear." LanM*, XLII (1948), fasc. A, A38-A40.

B8890	Heilman, Robert B. "The Lear World." *EIE, 1948.* New York: Columbia Univ. Press, 1949, pp. 29-57.

B8891	Heilman, Robert B. "The Unity of *King Lear." SR*, LVI (1948), 58-68. Republ. in *Critiques and Essays in Criticism, 1920-1948.* New York: Ronald Press, 1949, pp. 154-161.

B8892	Heilman, Robert B. *This Great Stage: Image and Structure in "King Lear."* Louisiana State Univ. Press, 1948. Pp. xi, 339.
	Rev: by J. C. Maxwell, *Spectator*, Nov. 26, 1948, p. 708; by A. Harbage, *MLN*, LXIV (1949), 357-358; by R. W. Babcock, *South Atlantic Quar.*, XLVIII, 301-303; by H. T. Price, *MLQ*, X, 239-240; by O. J. Campbell, *JEGP*, XLVIII, 405-408; by William Empson, *KR*, XI, 342-354; by R. A. Law, *Southwest Rev.*, XXXVI, 100-101; by Philip Edwards, *MLR*, XLIV, 264-265; by R. S. Knox, *UTQ*, XIX, 93-95; by Robert Fricker, *ES*, XXX, 276-277; by R. W. Babcock, *SAB*, XXIV, 123-131; by R. G. Cox, *Scrutiny*, XVI, 71-74; by F. Brantley, *Furioso*, IV (Fall, 1949), 100-104; by James Southall Wilson, *VQR*, XXVI (1950), 316-320; by Horst Frenz, *CE*, XII (1951), 301-302; by G. I. Duthie, *RES*, NS, II, 78-81; by Wolfgang Clemen, *SJ*, 87/88 (1952), 69-86.

B8893	Keast, W. R. "Imagery and Meaning in the Interpretation of *King Lear." MP*, XLVII (1949), 45-64. Also publ. as "The 'New Criticism' and *King Lear." Critics and Criticism, Ancient and Modern.* Univ. of Chicago Press, 1952, pp. 108-137.
	An important review article criticizing the basic assumptions and the method of "New Critics," with particular reference to B8892.

B8894	Renner, Ida. *Der Ordnungsgedanke bei Shakespeare mit Besonderem Hinblick auf "King Lear."* DD, Münster, 1948. Pp. 114. Typewritten.

B8895	Schomerus, H. *Heillose Welt: Betrachtungen zu Shakespeares "King Lear."* Hamburg: Reich und Heidrich, 1948. Pp. 46.

B8896	Danby, John F. *Shakespeare's Doctrine of Nature: A Study of "King Lear."* London: Faber and Faber, 1949. Pp. 234.
	Comment by G. Wilson Knight, *Scrutiny*, XVI (1949), 325.
	Rev: A934.

B8897	Empson, William. "Fool in *Lear." SR*, LVII (1949), 177-214.

B8898	Van Heiseler, Bernt. "Shakespeares *König Lear." Zeitwende* (Munich), XX (1949), 930-931.

B8899   Lothian, John M. *"King Lear": A Tragic Reading of Life.* Toronto: Clarke, Irwin & Co., 1949. Pp. 109.
        Rev: by F. D. Hoeniger, *Canadian Forum*, July, 1949; *Winnipeg Free Press*, June 18; *TLS*, Feb. 17, 1950, p. 110; *UTQ*, XIX, 304-305; by Kenneth Muir, *RES*, NS, II (1951), 405.

B8900   Young, G. M. *"King Lear." TLS*, Sept. 30, 1949, p. 633.
        Notes that the stocking of Kent in II accords with the dicipline observed in a great house of the time.

B8901   Connolly, Thomas F. "Shakespeare and the Double Man." *SQ*, I (1950), 30-35.

B8902   Haydn, Hiram. *The Counter-Renaissance.* New York: Charles Scribner's Sons, 1950. Pp. xvii, 705. *Ham.* and *Lear*, pp. 619-671.
        Rev: A3836.

B8903   Kralj, Vladimir. "William Shakespeare: *Kralj Lear." Novi Svet* (Ljubljana), V (1950), 63-69.

B8904   Watkins, W. B. C. *Shakespeare and Spenser.* Princeton Univ. Press, 1950. Pp. ix, 339.
        Rev: A8549.

B8905   Bodkin, Maud. *Studies of Type-Images in Poetry, Religion, and Philosophy.* New York: Oxford Univ. Press, 1951.
        Lear as child; also as archetype of man in his godlike kingly role, p. 138.

B8906   Isenberg, Arnold. "Cordelia Absent." *SQ* II (1951), 185-194.

B8907   James, D. G. *The Dream of Learning: An Essay on "The Advancement of Learning," "Hamlet" and "King Lear."* Oxford: Clarendon Press, 1951. Pp. 126.
        Rev: A3959.

B8908   Maclean, Norman. "Episode, Scene, Speech, and Word: The Madness of Lear." *Journal of General Education*, V (1951), 186-201. Also publ. in *Critics and Criticism, Ancient and Modern.* Univ. of Chicago Press, 1952, pp. 595-615.
        Rev: by N. Frye, *SQ*, V (1954), 80.

B8909   Sisson, C. J. "Elizabethan Life in Public Records." *The Listener*, June 21, 1951, pp. 998-999.
        Calls attention to a case resembling the plot of *Lear.*

B8910   Bergemann, Otto. *Der Dramatische Aufbau von Shakespeares "King Lear."* DD, Marburg, 1952. Pp. 183. Typewritten.

B8911   Danby, John F. *Poets on Fortune's Hill: Studies in Sidney, Shakespeare, Beaumont and Fletcher.* London: Faber and Faber, 1952. Pp. 212.
        Contains "*King Lear* and Christian Patience: A Culmination," pp. 108-127.
        Rev: A8156.

B8912   Dunn, E. Catherine. "The Storm in *King Lear." SQ*, III (1952), 329-333.

B8913   Frye, Roland Mushat. *The Accepted Ethics and Theology of Shakespeare's Audience as Utilized by the Dramatist in Certain Representative Tragedies, with Particular Attention to Love and Marriage.* DD, Princeton University, 1952. Pp. 372. Mic A55-745. *DA*, XV (1955), 581. Publ. No. 10,901.
        Rev: A2563.

B8914   Harvey, John W. "Lear and Cordelia." *TLS*, Nov. 14, 1952, p. 743.
        Comment by Kenneth Muir, *TLS*, Nov. 21, 1952, p. 761; by O. H. T. Dudley, *ibid.*, Dec. 5, p. 797. Reply to Prof. Muir by John W. Harvey, *ibid.*, Dec. 5, p. 797. Further comment by Louise F. W. Eickhoff and J. Lloyd, *ibid.*, Dec. 12, p. 819.

B8915   Martey, Herbert. "Shakespeare's *King Lear*, IV. vi. 1-80." *Expl.*, XI, ii (1952), item 10.

B8916   Price, Alan. "The Blinding of Gloucester." *N &Q*, 197 (1952), 313-314.

B8917   Traversi, D. A. *"King Lear* (I)." *Scrutiny*, XIX (1952), 43-64. Part II, pp. 126-142; Part III, pp. 206-230.

B8918   Kaneda, Tamayo. " 'Patience' in *King Lear." Essays and Studies in British and American Literature* (Tokyo Woman's Christian College), II, No. 1 (Summer, 1954), 1-26 (In English).

B8919   Parr, Johnstone. *Tamburlaine's Malady.* Univ. of Alabama Press, 1953. Pp. 158.
        Contains two chapters on *Lear*: "The 'Late Eclipses' in *King Lear*," pp. 70-79, and "Edmund's Birth Under Ursa Major," pp. 80-84.
        Rev: A2148.

B8920   Rinehart, Keith. "The Moral Background of *King Lear." The Univ. of Kansas City Review*, XX (1953), 223-228.

B8921   Bergemann, Otto. "Zum Aufbau von *King Lear." SJ*, 90 (1954), 191-209.

B8922   Ornstein, Robert. *The Ethics of Jacobean Tragedy, a Study of the Influence of Renaissance Free Thought.* DD, University of Wisconsin, 1954. Abstr. publ. in *Summaries of Doctoral Dissertations*, 1953-54, Vol. 15, Madison: Univ. of Wisconsin Press, 1955, pp. 622-624.

B8923   Raphael, D. Daiches. "Tragedy and Religion." *Listener*, LII (1954), 360-361.
        See also letters to the editor, *Listener*, LII, 403-404, and LII, 529.
        Lear may fit Christian ethics, but it cannot fit Christian theology.

B8924   Rosier, James L. "The Lex Aeterna and *King Lear." JEGP*, LIII (1954), 574-580.

B8925   Rubow, Paul V. *"King Lear." Klassiske og moderne Studier* (Copenhagen), 1954, pp. 52-56.

B8926　Siegel, Paul N. "Adversity and the Miracle of Love in *King Lear.*" *SQ*, VI (1955), 325-336.

B8927　Smith, Gerald. "A Note on the Death of Lear." *MLN*, LXX (1955), 403-404.

B8928　Thaler, Alwin. "The Gods and God in *King Lear.*" *Renaissance Papers, 1955* (Univ. of South Carolina), 1955, pp. 32-39.

B8929　Clay, James H. "A New Theory of Tragedy: A Description and Evaluation." *ETJ*, VIII (1956), 295-305.
On the basis of Susanne Langer's theory of "symbolic transformation" in *Feeling and Form* (1953), *Lear* is analyzed with particular attention to the Life-Death dichotomy.

B8930　Gallagher, Ligera Cécile. *Shakespeare and the Aristotelian Ethical Tradition.* DD, Stanford University, 1956. Pp. 338. Mic 56-3017. *DA*, XVI (1956), 1898. Publ. No. 17,720.
Chapter VIII, "Aristotelian Norms in *Othello* and *King Lear*," pp. 263-313.

B8931　Knights, Lionel Charles. "The Grounds of Literary Criticism." *Neophil*, XL (1956), 207-215.

B8932　Knights, L. C. "Shakespeare: *King Lear* and the Great Tragedies." In Boris Ford's *The Age of Shakespeare*, Pelican Book Guide to Engl. Lit., II, 1956, pp. 228-256.

B8933　Lüthi, Max. "*König Lear.*" *Sammlung*, XI (1956), 552-561.

B8934　Matsumoto, Kan. "An Essay on *King Lear*" (in Japanese). *Studies in Eng. Lit. and Language* (Hiroshima), III, No. 2, 1956.

B8935　Muller, Herbert J. *The Spirit of Tragedy.* New York: Knopf, 1956. Pp. ix, 335.
Lear, pp. 185-193.
Rev: A6914.

B8936　Reik, Theodor. *The Search Within. The Inner Experiences of a Psychoanalyst. Selections from the Works of T. Reik.* New York: Grove Press, 1956. Pp. xi, 659.
On *Lear*, pp. 452-453.

B8937　Ribner, Irving. "Shakespeare and Legendary History: *Lear* and *Cymbeline.*" *SQ*, VII (1956), 47-52.

B8938　Vančura, Zdeněk. "Přednáška Dr. A. Kettla v Shakespearovské komisi CSAV." *Časopis pro Moderní Filologii* (Prague), XXXVIII, No. 5 (1956), 300-301.
Professor Vančura reviews a lecture on *Lear* given by Dr. Arnold Kettle of the Univ. of Leeds at the Shakespearian Commission of the Czechoslovak Academy of Sciences.

B8939　Zandvoort, R. W. "*King Lear*: The Scholars and Critics." *Mededelingen der Koninklijke Nederlandse Academie van Wetenschappen, afd. Letterkunde.* Amsterdam: N. V. Noord-Hollandsche Uitgevers Maatschappij, NR, XIX, No. 7 (1956), 229-244.
Rev: by M. Poirier, *EA*, X (1957), 55; by P. Fison, *SN*, XXIX, 104-105; by H. Reinhold, *Anglia*, LXXV (1957/1958) 462-463; by T. Riese, *Archiv*, 194 (1958), 338.

B8940　Flanagan, Sarah Patricia. *A Reinterpretation of "King Lear."* DD, Brown University, 1957. Pp. 166. Mic 58-4321. *DA*, XVIII (1958), 581. Publ. No. 23,435.

B8941　Kimura, Keiko. "A Study of *King Lear.*" *Essays and Studies in British and American Literature*, Tokyo Woman's Christian College, V, No. 1 (Summer, 1957), 1-28 (in English).

B8942　Morris, Ivor. "Cordelia and Lear." *SQ*, VIII (1957), 141-158.

B8943　Musgrove, S. *Shakespeare and Jonson.* Bulletin No. 51, English Series, No. 9. Aukland Univ. College, 1957. Pp. 55.
No. II. "Tragical Mirth: *King Lear* and *Volpone.*"
Rev: A623.

B8944　Nowottny, Winifred M. T. "Lear's Questions." *ShS*, X (1957), 90-97.

B8945　Siegel, Paul N. *Shakespearean Tragedy and the Elizabethan Compromise.* New York Univ. Press, 1957.
Contains a chapter on *Lear.*
Rev: A1882.

B8946　Barish, Jonas A., and Marshall Waingrow. " 'Service' in *King Lear.*" *SQ*, IX (1958), 347-355.

B8947　Brinkmann, Karl. *Erläuterungen zu Shakespeares "König Lear."* Newly edited. Wilhelm Königs Erläuterungen zu den Klassikern, 65. Hollfeld/Ofr.: Bange, 1958. Pp. 84.

B8948　Elton, William. "*King Lear*" and the Gods: Shakespeare's Tragedy and Renaissance Religious Thought.* DD, Ohio State University, 1958.

B8949　French, Carolyn Schorr. "*King Lear*": Poem or Play?* DD, Stanford University, 1958. Pp. 327. Mic 58-3603. *DA*, XIX (1958), 796-797.

B8950　Frost, William. "Shakespeare's Rituals and the Opening of *King Lear.*" *Hudson Review*, X (1958), 577-585.

B8951　Phialas, Peter G. "Renaissance Conference." *South Atlantic Bulletin*, XXIV (1958), 9-11.
Includes notices of the reading of papers on Sex and Pessimism in *King Lear* by Robert J. West.

B8952　Ribner, Irving. "The Gods Are Just: A Reading of *King Lear.*" *The Tulane Drama Review*, II (1958), 34-54.

B8953　Rosati, Salvatore. *Il Giro della Ruota. Saggio su "King Lear" di Shakespeare.* Florence: Le Monnier, 1958. Pp. 249.

B8954　Knights, L. C. *Some Shakespearean Themes.* Chatto & Windus, 1959.

Chapter on *Lear*.
Rev: A8270.

(5) CHARACTERIZATION

B8955 Pauncz, Arpad. "Der Learkomplex, die Kehrseite des Oedipuskomplexes." *Zeitschrift für die Gesamte Neurologie und Psychiatrie*, 143 (1933), 294-332.

B8956 Pauncz, Arpad. "The Concept of Adult Libido and the Lear Complex." *American Journal of Psychotherapy*, v (April, 1951).

B8957 Pauncz, Arpad. "Psychopathology of Shakespeare's *King Lear*: Exemplification of the Lear Complex (A New Interpretation)." *American Imago*, IX (1952), 57-78.

B8958 Pauncz, Arpad. "The Lear Complex in World Literature." *American Imago*, XI (1954), 51-83.

B8959 Bransom, James S. H. *The Tragedy of King Lear*. Oxford: B. Blackwell, 1934.

B8960 Fijn van Draat, P. "King Lear and His Daughters." *Eng. Studn.*, LXX (1936), 352-357.

B8961 Law, Robert Adger. "Waterish Burgundy." *SP*, XXXIII (1936), 222-227.

B8962 Sleeth, C. R. "Shakespeare's Counsellors of State." *RAA*, XIII (1936), 97-113.

B8963 Brock, J. H. E. *Iago and Some Shakespearean Villains*. Cambridge: W. Heffer & Sons, 1937. Pp. viii, 48.
Rev: A1245.

B8964 Fijn van Draat, P. "*King Lear*." *Anglia*, LXI (1937), 177-185.

B8965 Schücking, L. L. "Goneril." *NS*, XLV (1937), 413.

B8966 Walker, Albert L. "Convention in Shakespeare's Description of Emotion." *PQ*, XVII (1938), 26-66.

B8967 Fijn van Draat, P. "If Cordelia . . . A Fantasy on What Might Have Been." *Anglia*, LXIII (1939), 135-143.

B8968 Draper, John W. "The Old Age of King Lear." *JEGP*, XXXIX (1940), 527-540.

B8969 Hazen, A. T. "Shakespeare's *King Lear*, IV. i." *Expl.*, II (1943), No. 2, item 10.
Comment also by Monroe M. Stearns.

B8970 Sims, Ruth E. "The Green Old Age of Falstaff." *Bul. Hist. Medicine*, XIII (1943), 144-157.

B8971 Abenheimer, K. M. "On Narcissism—Including an Analysis of Shakespeare's *King Lear*." *British Journal of Medical Psychology*, XX (1945), 322-329.
On Lear as child.

B8972 Draper, John W. "Shakespeare's Attitude Toward Old Age." *Jour. Gerontology*, I (1946), 118-126.
"In short, the depiction of Lear's senility is Shakespeare's own," p. 124.

B8973 Parr, Johnstone. "Edmund's Nativity in *King Lear*." *SAB*, XXI (1946), 181-185.

B8974 Pritchett, Frances G. *The History of the Interpretation of Cordelia in English and American Literary Criticism, 1710 to 1940*. MA thesis, University of North Carolina, 1944. Abstr. publ. in *Univ. of North Carolina Record, Research in Progress*, Grad. School Series No. 50, 1946, pp. 159-160.

B8975 Sharpe, Ella Freeman. "From *King Lear* to *The Tempest*." *International Journal of Psycho-Analysis*, XXVII (1946). Repr. in her *Collected Papers on Psycho-Analysis*. Ed. Marjorie Brierley, Pref. by Ernest Jones. International Psycho-Analytic Library No. 36. London: Hogarth Press, 1950, pp. 214-241.

B8976 Orwell, George. "King Lear, Tolstoy and the Fool." *Polemic*, 1947, pp. 2-17. Repr. in his *Shooting an Elephant and Other Essays*. New York, 1950, pp. 32-52. Also in *The Orwell Reader*. New York: Harcourt-Brace, 1956, pp. 300-315.

B8977 Ribner, Irving. "*King Lear*": *A Study in Shakespearean Character Criticism*. MA thesis, University of North Carolina, 1947. Abstr. publ. in *Univ. of North Carolina Record, Research in Progress*, Grad. School Series No. 56, 1949, pp. 227-228.

B8978 Ribner, Irving. "Lear's Madness in the Nineteenth Century." *SAB*, XXII (1947), 117-129.

B8979 Kirschbaum, Leo. "A Detail in *King Lear*." *RES*, XXV (1949), 153-154.

B8980 Maxwell, J. C. "The Technique of Invocation in *King Lear*." *MLR*, XLV (1950), 142-147.

B8981 Trilling, Lionel. "Freud and Literature." *The Liberal Imagination*. New York: The Viking Press, 1950, pp. 34-57.
Rev: A1334.

B8982 Flatter, Richard. "Sigmund Freud on Shakespeare." *SQ*, II (1951), 368-369.
Transcribes brief letter from Freud on Lear's mental state.

B8983 Lucas, F. L. *Literature and Psychology*. London: Cassell, 1951. Pp. 340. Republ. as an Ann Arbor Paperback. Univ. of Michigan Press, 1957. Pp. 340. *Lear*, pp. 62-78.
Rev: A1362.

B8984 McCullen, Joseph T., Jr. "Madness and Isolation of Character in Elizabethan and Early Stuart Drama." *SP*, XLVIII (1951), 206-218.

B8985 Druhman, Rev. Alvin W. *An Analysis of Four of the Level-of-life Characters in Shakespeare's Tragedies*. DD, St. John's University, 1952. Abstr. publ. in *Abstracts of Dissertations, 1951-1952*, Brooklyn: St. John's Univ., 1952, pp. 14-15.

B8986 Eickhoff, Louise F. W. "Lear and Cordelia." *TLS*, Dec. 12, 1952, p. 819.
       See letters by O. H. T. Dudley and John W. Harvey, *TLS*, Dec. 5, 1952, p. 797; J. Lloyd, ibid.,
       Dec. 12, p. 819.

B8987 Meltzer, J. "Some Psycho-Analytical Angles on Aspects of Shakespearean Drama." *Discussion* (South Africa), I, No. 6 (1952), 47-50.
       Discusses the heroes in *Oth.*, *Lear*, *Macb.*, and *Ham.* as types of Freudian inversion and masochism.

B8988 Smith, R. M. "A Good Word for Oswald." *A Tribute to George Coffin Taylor*, 1952, pp. 62-66.

B8989 Sutherland, W. O. S., Jr. "Polonius, Hamlet, and Lear in Aaron Hill's *Prompter*." *SP*, XLIX (1952), 605-618.

B8990 Poethen, Wilhelm. "Die Gestalt der Cordelia in Shakespeares *König Lear*." *Wirkendes Wort*, V (1954/55), 285-292.

B8991 Donnelly, John. "Incest, Ingratitude, and Insanity." *Psychoanalytic Review*, XL (1955), 149-155.

B8992 Geyer, Horst. *Dichter des Wahnsinns. Eine Untersuchung über die dichterische Darstellbarkeit seelischer Ausnahmezustände.* Göttingen: Musterschmidt, 1955. Pp. 322.
       Chap. 14: "Altersschwachsinn. Shakespeares *Lear*," pp. 234-256, 295-310.
       Rev: A1375.

B8993 Provost, George Foster. *The Techniques of Characterization and Dramatic Imagery in "Richard II" and "King Lear."* DD, Louisiana State University, 1955. Pp. 274. Mic 55-280. *DA*, XV (1955), 1616. Publ. No. 12,525.

B8994 Straumann, Heinrich. "Shakespeare und der Verblendete Mensch." *Neue Zürcher Zeitung* (Zurich), No. 1638, June 19, 1955.
       Links between *Lear*, *AYL*, and *Dream*.

B8995 Coe, Charles Norton. *Shakespeare's Villains.* New York: 1957.
       Rev: A6796.

B8996 Kahn, Sholom J. " 'Enter Lear Mad'." *SQ*, VIII (1957), 311-329.

B8997 Kirschbaum, Leo. "Banquo and Edgar: Character or Function." *EIC*, VII (1957), 1-21.
       See comments by Christopher Gillie, ibid., pp. 322-324, by A. S. Knowland, ibid., pp. 325-330, and by Peter Ure, ibid., pp. 457-459.

B8998 Wright, Celeste Turner. "The Queen's Husband: Some Renaissance Views." *Studies in English*, III (1957), 133-138.

B8999 Goldsmith, Robert Hillis. "Plain, Blunt Englishman." *Renaissance Papers*, 1957, pp. 94-99. Abstr. in *ShN*, VII (1957), 12.
       On Kent in *Lear*: his dramatic antecedents and the function of his bluntness in the play.

(6) MISCELLANEOUS ITEMS

B9000 Darby, Robert H. "Astrology in Shakespeare's *Lear*." *ES*, XX (1938), 250-257.

B9001 Tannenbaum, Samuel A. "Editorial Notes and Comments." *SAB*, XIV, (1939).
       Contains "The Classic Players and King Lear," pp. 127-128.

B9002 Greer, Howard Kelley. "*King Lear*." MA thesis, Dalhousie, 1943. Pp. 154.
       Sources, date, variants, stage history, critical opinions.

B9003 Fairchild, Arthur H. R. *Shakespeare and the Tragic Theme.* Univ. Missouri Studies, XIX, No. 2. Univ. Missouri Press, 1944. Pp. 145.
       Part I, 3. "Social Institutions in Lear."
       Rev: A6853.

B9004 Kane, Robert J. "Tolstoy, Goethe, and *King Lear*." *SAB*, XXI (1946), 159-160.

B9005 Lebesque, M. "Devant *King Lear*." *Le Magasin du Spectacle*, No. 7, Dec. 1946, pp. 63-71.

B9006 Milne, Evander. "On the Death of Cordelia." *English*, VI (1947), 244-248.
       Notes on treatment of Cordelia in its sources, and by N. Tate; Addison's, Johnson's views; decline of Tate's version; discussion of significance of the play, which is seen to be in the cosmic injustice suffered by Cordelia.

B9007 Adams, John C. "The Original Staging of *King Lear*." *AMS*, pp. 315-335.

B9008 Bald, R. C. " 'Thou, Nature, Art My Goddess': Edmund and Renaissance Free-Thought." *AMS*, pp. 337-349.

B9009 Walker, Roy. "Swinburne, Tolstoy, and *King Lear*." *English*, VII (1949), 282-284.
       Swinburne praised it for its spiritual democracy and its socialism. Furness's excerpts are inadequate because it was inaccessible to him. Tolstoi ill-informed.

B9010 Fort, Joseph B. "Quelques Problèmes Shakespeariens: L'Homme, Le Texte, La 'Sagesse Pourpre'." *LanM*, Nov. 1950, pp. 38-41.

B9011 Grün, Herbert. "*Kralj Lear*. Meditacije pred Premiero." [*King Lear*. Meditations before the First Performance.] *Mladinska Revija* (Ljubljana), V, Nos. 4-5 (1950), pp. 220-224.

B9012 Clemeshaw, Isabel B. "Literary Notes: *King Lear*." *Theosophical Forum*, XXIX (1951), 31-38.
       "Transmigration of the Life Atoms was common knowledge in England among the best educated from Chaucer's time . . ."

B9013   Bogdanović, Milan. *"Kralj Lir."* *Almanah-Poezija-Proza*, 1952, pp. 49-52.

B9014   Hugo, Howard E. "The Madman of the Heath and the Madwoman of Chaillot." *Chrysalis* (Boston), v, Nos. 3-4 (1952), 3-11.

B9015   Legouis, Emile. *"La Terre de Zola et le Roi Lear."* *RLC*, XXVII (1953), 417-427.

B9016   Abrams, M. H. "Belief and Suspension of Disbelief." *Literature and Belief. EIE, 1957* (1958), 1-30.

B9017   Brøgger, Niels Christian. "Det er vi som er Kong Lear." ["We are King Lear"]. *Vinduet* (Oslo), XI (1957), 75-80.

B9018   Jaffa, Harry V. "The Limits of Politics: An Interpretation of *King Lear*, Act I, Scene I." *Amer. Pol. Sci. Rev.*, LI (1957), 405-427.

B9019   Schechter, Abraham. *"King Lear"*: *Warning or Prophecy?* 32-43 Ninetieth Street, East Elmhurst 69, New York: The Author, 1957.
        Rev: *Dublin Magazine*, Jan.-March, 1957, pp. 55-56.

B9020   Seng, Peter J. "An Early Tune for the Fool's Song in *King Lear*." *SQ*, IX (1958), 583-584.

(7)   SUBSEQUENT HISTORY OF THE PLAY
(Other than specific productions after 1660)

B9021   Drews, Wolfgang. *"König Lear" auf der Deutschen Bühne bis zur Gegenwart.* Berlin, 1932.
        Rev: A9432.

B9022   Kidd, Catherine Elizabeth. *The Stage Performance of "King Lear"*: *A Critical Review.* MA thesis, Queen's (Canada), 1935. Pp. 109.
        Shak.'s purposes in *Lear*, original conditions of performance, subsequent stage history.

B9023   Derrick, Leland Eugene. *The Stage History of "King Lear."* DD, University of Texas, 1940.

B9024   Baxter, Beverley. *First Nights and Noises Off.* London: Hutchinson, 1949. Pp. 239.
        A worldly and cheerfully amateur discussion of *Lear* in the theater.
        Rev: *TLS*, June 17, 1949, p. 399.

B9025   Platt, P. *Le Roi Lear en France.* MA thesis, Edinburg, 1955.

B9026   Lief, Leonard. *The Fortunes of King Lear: 1605-1838."* DD, Syracuse University, 1953. Pp. 291. Abstr. publ. in *ShN*, VI (1956), 22.

B9027   Schulz, Max F. *"King Lear*: A Box-Office Maverick Among Shakespearian Tragedies on the London Stage, 1700-01 to 1749-50." *Tulane Studies in English*, VII (1957), 83-90.

MACBETH (247:88)
(1)   THE TEXT

B9028   Tannenbaum, Samuel A. *Shakespeare's "Macbeth": A Concise Bibliography.* New York: The Compiler, 1939. Pp. x, 166.

(a)   OLD TEXTS

B9029   Cairncross, A. S. *The Problem of Hamlet. A Solution.* London: Macmillan, 1936. Pp. xix, 205. Dates *Macbeth* early.
        Rev: B4916.

B9030   Clarkson, Paul S., and Clyde T. Warren. "Copyhold Tenure and *Macbeth*, III. ii. 38." *MLN*, LV (1940), 483-493.

B9031   Stunz, Arthur N. "The Date of *Macbeth*." *ELH*, IX (1942), 95-105.

B9032   Nosworthy, J. M. "The Bleeding Captain Scene in *Macbeth*." *RES*, XXII (1946), 126-130.

B9032a Nosworthy, J. M. *"Macbeth* at the Globe." *Library*, II (1947), 108-118.

B9033   Sullivan, Frank. *"Macbeth*, Middleton's *Witch* and *Macbeth* Again." *Los Angeles Tidings*, Sept. 24, 1948, p. 6.
        Dates *The Witch* 1609, and the received text of *Macbeth* after that.

B9034   Flatter, Richard. " 'True Originall Copies' Shakespeare's Plays—Outline of a New Conception." *Proc. Leeds Philos. and Lit. Soc., Lit. & Hist. Sec.* VIII, Pt. 1 (1952), 31-42.
        Reply to criticis of A5944, with further examples.

B9035   Amneus, Daniel A. *A Textual Study of "Macbeth."* DD, University of Southern California, 1953.

B9036   Gierow, K. R. "När skrevs Macbeth?" [When was *Macbeth* written?]. *Svenska Dagbladet* (Stockholm), March 2, 1955.

B9037   Danks, K. B. "Is F_1 *Macbeth* a Reconstructed Text?" *N &Q*, NS, IV (1957), 516-519.

(b)   MODERN EDITIONS
i.   The More Important Texts

B9038   *Macbeth.* Interlinear ed. prepared by George Coffin Taylor and Reed Smith. Boston: Ginn, 1936. Pp. xlvii, 144.
        Rev: by Samuel A. Tannenbaum, *SAB*, XI (1936), 252; by C. K. T., *QJS*, XXII, 685.

B9039   *Macbeth*. Ed. W. D. Sargeaunt. London: Heath, Cranton, 1937.
        Rev: *QR*, 268 (1937), 369-370.
B9040   *Macbeth*. Ed. Bernard Groom. (New) Clarendon Shakespeare. London and New York:
        Oxford Univ. Press, 1939. Pp. 191.
B9041   *Macbeth*. Ed. George Lyman Kittredge. Boston: Ginn & Company, 1939. Pp. xx, 254.
        Rev: by William T. Hastings, *SRL*, Aug. 19, 1939, p. 13; *N &Q*, 176 (1939), 395-396;
        by C. J. Sisson, *MLN*, LV (1940), 145-147; by Robert Adger Law, *JEGP*, XXXIX, 578-581.
B9042   *Macbeth*. Ed. George Lyman Kittredge. Illustrated by Salvador Dali. New York: Double-
        day, 1946. Pp. 125.
        Rev: by Wolcott Gibbs, *NYTBR*, Dec. 15, 1946, p. 6.
B9043   Cancelled.
B9044   *Macbeth*. Ed. J. Dover Wilson. The New Shakespeare. Cambridge: Cambridge Univ.
        Press, 1947. Pp. lxxxiv, 186.
        Rev: *TLS*, Oct. 25, 1947, p. 554; by J. Hampden, *Britain Today*, 142 (Feb., 1948), 45;
        by F. C. Danchin, *LanM*, XLII, 181-182; by J. M. S. Tompkins, *MLR*, XLIII, 527-528; by
        J. M. Nosworthy, *Life & Letters*, LVI, 256-259; by George Cookson, *English*, VII, 27-28;
        by Kenneth Muir, *RES*, XXIV, 328-329; *N &Q*, 193 (1948), 43-44; by B. R. Redman, *SRL*,
        March 20, p. 38; by P. V. Rubow, *ES*, XXIX, 115-116; by J. G. McManaway, *ShS*, II (1949),
        145-148; by Charlton Hinman, *MLN*, LXIV, 69; by Richard Flatter, *MP*, XLIX (1951),
        124-132; see reply by Wilson, ibid., pp. 274-275; by Richard Flatter, *SJ*, 87/88 (1952),
        221-223.
B9045   *Macbeth*. Ed. John Dover Wilson. Cambridge Pocket Shakespeare. Cambridge Univ.
        Press, 1958. Pp. 100.
B9046   *Macbeth*. Ed. Wolfgang Keller. Cologne: Schaffstein, 1948. Pp. 88.
B9047   *Macbeth*. Ed. Tarquinio Vallese. Naples: Pironti, 1948. Pp. xx, 73.
B9048   *Macbeth*. Ed. M. A. Shaaber. Crofts Classics. New York: Appleton-Century-Crofts, 1949.
        Pp. xii, 79.
B9049   *The Tragedy of Macbeth*. Intro. by Sir Lewis Casson. Designs by Michael Ayrton. London:
        Folio Soc., 1951. Pp. 111.
B9050   *Macbeth*. Ed. Tyrone Guthrie and G. B. Harrison. New Stratford Shakespeare. London:
        Harrap, 1954. Pp. 147.
B9051   *Macbeth*. Ed. Alfred Harbage. Pelican Shakespeare. Baltimore: Penguin Books, 1956.
        Pp. 114.
        Rev: by Alice Griffin, *TAr*, April, 1957, p. 62; *ShN*, VII, 4; by John Russell Brown, *SQ*,
        VIII, 550-551; by Hermann Heuer, *SJ*, 93 (1957), 272-273; by Wallace A. Bacon, *QJS*,
        XLIII, 308-309; by Sears Jayne, *CE*, XX (1958), 101-102. (All these reviews, except the last,
        cover other 1956 volumes of the Pelican Shak.)
B9052   *Macbeth*. Ed. S. C. Sen Gupta. Annotated plays of Shakespeare. Calcutta: A Mukherjee
        and Co., Ltd., 1956.
B9053   *Macbeth*. Ed. Kenneth Muir. Arden Shakespeare. London: Methuen, 1957. Pp. lxxiv,
        201. First publ. 1951.
        Eighth ed. reprinted with minor corrections and new appendix.
        Rev: by R. W. Zandvoort, *ES*, XXXII (1951), 262-264; by Walter Hübner, *Neuphilologische
        Zeitschrift*, III, 438-440; *TLS*, May 11, p. 295; by J. Isaacs, *The Listener*, April 26, p. 680;
        by H. B. C., *MGW*, April 19, p. 10; *Adelphi*, XXVII, 359-361; *National & Eng. Rev.*, 137
        (1951), 58-59; by A. P. Rossiter, *CamR*, 73 (1951), 205-206; by Virgil B. Heltzel, *SQ*, III
        (1952), 126-127; by J. Dover Wilson, *RES*, III, 71-75; *TLS*, Oct. 31, p. 701; by H. Heuer,
        SJ, 87/88 (1952), 254-255; by R. A. Law, *SQ*, III, 83; by F. W. Bateson, *EIC*, III (1953),
        124; by Richard Flatter, *SJ*, 89 (1953), 207-212; by T. M. Parrott, *JEGP*, LIII (1954), 107-
        109; by E. J. West, *QJS*, XL, 213; by Patrick Cruttwell, *EIC*, V (1955), 383-387.
B9054   *Macbeth*. Ed. G. C. Rosser. The London English Literature Series. Univ. of London Press,
        1957. Pp. 158.
        Rev: *TLS*, Oct. 11, 1957, p. 615.
B9055   *The Tragedy of Macbeth*. Ed. Eugene M. Waith. Yale Shakespeare. Rev. ed. Yale Univ.
        Press, 1954. Pp. 138. Revised ed., paperback, 1957.
        Rev: by Kenneth Muir, *SQ*, VI (1955), 348-349; by Hermann Heuer, *SJ*, 91 (1955), 342-
        343; by C. J. Sisson, *MLR*, L, 196-197; *CE*, XVI, 258; *SatR*, Aug. 3, 1957, p. 28.
B9056   *Macbeth*. Ed. Bernard Lott. New Swan Shakespeare. London: Longmans, 1958. Pp.
        x, 246.
        Rev: by G. Schad, *NS*, VII (1958), 585.

ii. Trade Editions

B9057   *Macbeth*. Ed. Henry Norman Hudson and Others. Cameo Classics. New York: Grosset,
        1936. Pp. 190.
B9058   *Macbeth*. Short ed. by Karl Arns. Schöninghs Engl. Lesebogen, 54. Paderborn: Schöningh,
        1937. Pp. 61.
        Rev: by Fiedler, *Archiv*, 173 (1938), 115.

B9059 *Macbeth.* Ed. M. Castelain. Paris, 1937. Pp. xiv, 164.

B9060 *Macbeth.* With Introd. and Notes ed. by Gustav Hagemann. Aschendorffs Moderne Aus-landsbücherei. Münster: Aschendorff, 1937. Pp. 86, 28.
Rev: by Arth. Szogs, *Beiblatt*, XLIX (1938), 254; by Paul Scholz-Wülfing, *ZNU*, XXXVII, 195.

B9061 *Macbeth.* Ed. Max Draber. Anmerkungen. Leipzig: Quelle & Meyer, 1940. Pp. 65, 20.
Rev: by Erich Thiele, *ZNU*, XXXIX (1940), 136.

B9062 *Macbeth.* Ed. F. L. Sack. Glossary. Bern: Francke, 1941. Pp. 88, 21.

B9063 *Macbeth.* Eds. O. Welles and R. Hill. New York: Harper, 1941.

B9064 *Macbeth.* Ill. by Salvador Dali. New York: Doubleday, 1946; London: Low, 1947. Pp. 125.

B9065 *Macbeth.* Pocket Classics. London: Burgess & Bowes, 1947. Pp. 88.

B9066 *Macbeth.* Im Sinne d. Lehrpläne d. Unterrichtsmin. u. d. Richtlinien d. Arbeitsgem. d. Anglisten hrsg. v. Stephan Hartmann. Vienna: Österr. Bundesverl., 1948. Pp. 88. 2nd ed., 1954. 3rd, 1958.

B9067 *Macbeth.* Foreword by Gottfried Ippisch. Kleine Humboldt-Bibl. 8. Vienna: Humboldt-Verlag, 1948. Pp. 104.

B9068 *Macbeth.* Mit Anm. Oberursel: Kompass-Verlag, 1949. Pp. 120.
The first of Fritz Hummel's *Shakespeare Readers.*

B9069 *The Tragedy of Macbeth.* Cornelsen Fremdsprachenreihe, 64. 2nd ed. Berlin, Bielefeld: Cornelsen, 1949. Pp. 117.

B9070 *Macbeth.* Ed. Fritz Brather. M. Anh. u. Wörterb. Engl. Authors, 14. Bielefeld: Velhagen & Klasing, 1950. Pp. ix, 93, 44, 35.
Rev: by H. Mannhart, *Leb. Fremdspr.*, III (1951), 221.

B9071 *Macbeth.* Complete text. Ed. Lili Burger. Braunsche Schulbücherei. Textausg. Reihe 3, 9. Karlsruhe: Braun, 1950. Pp. xv, 142.

B9072 *The Tragedy of Macbeth.* Eds. Friedrich Hackenberg and Elsa Brause. M. Anm. u. Wörterverz. Die Brücke. Reihe A, 3. Bremen: Dorn, 1950. Pp. 102, 31.

B9073 *Macbeth.* Ed. P. A. ter Weer. 2nd ed. Stories and Sketches. 41. Zwolle: Tjeenk Willink, 1950. Pp. 86, 53.

B9074 *Hamlet. Macbeth.* 3rd ed. Madrid: Aguilar, 1951. Pp. 540.

B9075 *Macbeth.* (With Eugene O'Neill's *The Emperor Jones.*) Eds. Benjamin Alexander Heydrick and Alfred Arundel May. Noble's Comparative Classics. New York: Noble, 1952. Pp. 276.
The Tragedie of Macbeth. First Folio text with Illustrations by Mary Grabhorn. San Francisco, Grabhorn Press, 1952.
Rev: by Ben Ray Redman, *SatR*, Dec. 1952, p. 23.

B9076-77 Cancelled.

B9078 *Macbeth.* Ill. de 20 eaux-fortes Originales Gravées par Marcel Gromaire. Paris: Ed. Verve, 1958.

(c) EMENDATIONS

B9079 Eckels, R. P. "Wolf's Tooth." *N &Q*, 171 (1936), 158-159.

B9080 Morris, Joseph E. "The Fatal Bellman" [*Macbeth*, I. i]. *N &Q*, 171 (1936), 404-405.
Further comments by Edward Bensly, ibid., p. 443, and C. A. Bradford, ibid., p. 457.

B9081 Franz, W. "Zu *Macbeth* III. i." In *Beitr. z. Geschichte, Literatur und Sprachkunde, vornehmlich Württembergs.* Hrsg. v. H. Bihl. Tübingen: Mohr, 1938, pp. 254-256.

B9082 Long, Wm. Stapelton. "Communication. [Meaning of the passage at the beginning of Act II:] 'How goes the night, boy?' " *SAB*, XIII (1938), 191.

B9083 Dunlap, A. R. "What Purgative Drug?" [*Macbeth*, V. iii. 556.] *MLN*, LIV (1939), 92-94.

B9084 C., T. C. " 'A Summer's Cloud'." *N &Q*, 177 (1939), 99; M. H. Dodds, ibid., 212.

B9085 Thorson, P. "A Note on *Macbeth* [I. ii. 59-62]." *ES*, XXI (1939), 73-75.

B9086 Thompson, D'Arcy W. "The Winds and the Churches: An Emendation in *Macbeth*." *N &Q*, 179 (1940), 118.

B9087 Alspach, Russell K. " 'Making the Green One Red' [*Macbeth*, II. ii. 64]." *SAB*, XVI (1941), 166-168.

B9088 Sullivan, Frank. "Cyme, A Purgative Drug [*Macbeth*, V. iii. 55-56]." *MLN*, LVI (1941), 263-264.

B9089 Eliason, Norman E. "Shakespeare's Purgative Drug *Cyme* [*Macbeth*, V. iii. 55]." *MLN*, LVII (1942), 663-665.

B9090 Smith, Roland M. "Macbeth's *Cyme* Once More." *MLN*, LX (1945), 33-38.

B9091 Anderson, Ruth L. " 'The Foot of Motion'." *SAB*, XXII (1947), 81-83. II. iii. 130-131.

B9092 Bald, R. C. "Macbeth's 'Baby of a Girl'." *SAB*, XXIV (1949), 220-222.

B9093 Donner, H. W. "De Dödas Uppror. Ett omtvistat Textställe i *Macbeth* (IV. i. 97). Sättryck ur Hyllningsskrift tillägnad Rolf Pipping på hans sextioårsdag den I Juin 1949." *Acta Academiae Aboensis Humaniora*, XVIII (1949), 83-95. Also publ. separately: Åbo: Åbo Akademi,

1949. Pp. 13. See B9094 on same passage.
Rev: by J. M. Nosworthy, *RES*, II (1951), 298.

B9094 Donner, H. W. " 'Rebellious Dead'." *TLS*, Sept. 28, 1949, p. 617.
See the letter by J. Dover Wilson, ibid., Sept. 30, 1949, p. 633.

B9095 Hoepfner, Theodore C. "Shakespeare's *Macbeth*, I. vii. 1-28." *Expl.*, VII, No. 5 (1949), item 34.

B9096 Fatout, Paul. "Shakespeare's *Macbeth*, II. ii. 40." *Expl.*, IX (1950), no. 22.

B9097 Cossons, Judith. "*Macbeth*, I. vii. [6.]" *N &Q*, 196 (1951), 368.

B9098 Harris, B. Kingston. "Martlets in *Macbeth*." *TLS*, March 16, 1951, p. 165.
See letter by C. W. Scott-Giles, ibid., April 13, 1951, p. 229.

B9099 Parsons, Howard. "Shakespeare Emendations." *N &Q*, 196 (1951), 27-29.
Concerns five passages in Act I of *Macbeth*: ii. 25ff., ii. 56ff., iii. 48ff., iii. 142ff., and v. 14ff.

B9100 Empson, William. "Dover Wilson on *Macbeth*." *KR*, XIV (1952), 84-102.

B9101 Baldini, Gabriele. "Shakespeariana: di una lezione poco nota in *Macbeth*, V. v. 23, secondo in Folio." *Convivium* (Turin), No. 6 (1952), 896-904.

B9102 Parsons, Howard. "*Macbeth*: Some Emendations." *N &Q*, 197 (1952), 403.
I. v. 43; IV. i. 145; I. vii. 61; II. i. 56.

B9103 Maxwell, J. C. "The Punctuation of *Macbeth*, I. i. 1-2." *RES*, IV (1953), 356-358.

B9104 Parsons, Howard. "*Macbeth* Conjectures." *N &Q*, 198 (1953), 54-55, 464-466.
III. i. 18; III. ii. 27; III. ii. 46; III. iv. 100; IV. i. 79; IV. i. 111; IV. ii. 17; V. iv. 10; V. viii. 27.

B9105 Schoff, F. G. "Shakespeare's 'Fair is Foul'." *N &Q*, NS, I (1954), 241-242.

B9106 Wheelwright, Philip. "Philosophy of the Threshold." *SR*, LXI (1953), 56-75.

B9107 Danks, K. B. "Macbeth and the Word 'Strange'." *N &Q*, NS, I (1954), 425.

B9108 Parsons, Howard. "*Macbeth*: Emendations." *N &Q*, NS, I (1954), 331-333.
IV. i. 79; IV. i. 111; IV. ii. 17; V. iv. 10; V. viii. 27.

B9109 Boyle, Robert R., S.J. "The Imagery of *Macbeth*, I. vii. 21-28." *MLQ*, XVI (1955), 130-136.

B9110 Frye, Roland Mushat. " 'Out, Out, Brief Candle,' and the Jacobean Understanding." *N &Q*, NS, II (1955), 143-145.

B9111 Starnes, DeWitt Talmage. "Acteon's Dogs." *Names*, III (1955), 19-25.

B9112 Maxwell, J. C. "*Macbeth* IV. iii. 107." *MLR*, LI (1956), 73.

B9113 Wain, John, ed. *Interpretations*. London: Routledge, 1956.
Comment by Graham Martin on I. vii. 1-28, pp. 17-30.
Rev: B4441.

B9114 Schanzer, Ernest. "Four Notes on *Macbeth*." *MLR*, LII (1957), 223-227.
I. vii. 64-68; III. i. 60-63; III. iv. 121-125; III. v. 23-29.

(2) LITERARY GENESIS AND ANALOGUES

B9115 Middleton, Thomas. *The Witch*. Eds. Walter Wilson Greg and Frank Percy Wilson. London: Malone Soc., 1948. Pp. xv, 94, 4 facs.

B9116 Bestian, Hans. "Shakespeares *Macbeth* und sein Politischer Hintergrund." *Gelbe Hefte*, XII (1935/36), 370-374.

B9117 Brandl, A. "Zur Vorgeschichte der Weird Sisters im *Macbeth*." *Forschungen und Charakteristiken* (Berlin), 1936, pp. 82-97.
First published 1921, in *Festgabe für Felix Liebermann*.

B9118 Fletcher, B. J. *Shakespeare's Use of Holinshed's Chronicles in "Richard III," "Richard II," "Henry IV," and "Macbeth."* DD, University of Texas, 1937.

B9119 Draper, John W. "Historic Local Colour in *Macbeth*." *Revue Belge de Phil. et d'Hist.*, XVII (1938), 43-52.

B9120 Draper, John W. "*Macbeth* as a Compliment to James I." *Eng. Studn.*, LXXII (1938), 207-220.

B9121 Dowlin, Cornell M. "Two Shakspere Parallels in Studley's Translation of Seneca's *Agamemnon*." *SAB*, XIV (1939), 256. See also "A Correction," *SAB*, XV (1940), 128.

B9122 Hadas, Moses. "Clytemnestra in Elizabethan Dress." *Classical Weekly*, XXXII (1939), 255-256.

B9123 Stunz, Arthur N. *The Contemporary Setting of "Macbeth."* DD, State University of Iowa, 1940.

B9124 Thaler, Alwin. *Shakespeare and Democracy*. Univ. Tennessee Press, 1941. Pp. xii, 312.
Chap. IV. The "Lost Scenes" of *Macbeth*.
Rev: A1809.

B9125 Calhoun, Howell V. "James I and the Witch Scenes in *Macbeth*." *SAB*, XVII (1942), 184-189.

B9126 Heuer, H. "Shakespeares Verhältnis zu König Jacob I." *Anglia*, LXVI (1942), 223-227.

B9127 Stoll, Elmer E. "Source and Motive in *Macbeth* and *Othello*." *RES*, XIX (1943), 25-32.

B9128 Fox, Gladys. *Studies in the Composition of Shakespeare's "King Lear," "Macbeth" and "Cymbeline."* DD, University of Texas, 1946.

B9129 Paul, Henry N. "The First Performance of *Macbeth*." *SAB*, XXII (1947), 149-154.

B9130   Maxwell, J. C. "Montaigne and *Macbeth.*" *MLR*, XLIII (1948), 77-78.
B9131   Muir, Kenneth. "*Macbeth* and *Sophonisba.*" *TLS*, Oct. 9, 1948, p. 569.
        See letters by D. S. Bland, ibid., Oct. 16, 1948, p. 583; by Kenneth Muir, ibid., Oct. 23, p. 597.
B9132   Nosworthy, J. M. "The Hecate Scenes in *Macbeth.*" *RES*, XXIV (1948), 138-139.
B9133   Nosworthy, J. M. "Shakespeare and the Siwards." *RES*, XXIV (1948), 139-141.
B9134   Paul, Henry N. "The Imperial Theme in *Macbeth.*" *AMS*, pp. 253-268.
B9135   Bland, D. S. "*Macbeth* and the 'Battle of Otterburn'." *N&Q*, 194 (1949), 335-336.
B9136   Boyce, Benjamin. "The Stoic *Consolatio* and Shakespeare." *PMLA*, LXIV (1949), 771-780.
B9137   Muir, Kenneth. "A Borrowing from Seneca." *N&Q*, 194 (1949), 214-216.
B9138   Muir, Kenneth. "Shakespeare and Dante." *N&Q*, 194 (1949), 333.
B9139   Ure, Peter. "*Macbeth* and Warner's *Albion's England.*" *N&Q*, 194 (1949), 232-233.
B9140   Elton, William. "Timothy Bright and Shakespeare's Seeds of Nature." *MLN*, LXV (1950), 196-197.
B9141   Craig, Hardin. "Morality Plays and Elizabethan Drama." *SQ*, I (1950), 64-72.
B9142   Lees, F. N. "A Biblical Connotation in *Macbeth.*" *N&Q*, 195 (1950), 534.
B9143   Paul, Henry N. *The Royal Play of "Macbeth": When, Why, and How It Was Written by Shakespeare.* New York: Macmillan, 1950. Pp. 438.
        Rev: by R. C. Bald, *SQ*, II (1951), 257-259; by H. S. Wilson, *UTQ*, XXI, 83-88; by O. J. Campbell, *SRL*, June 9, pp. 17, 40; by O. J. Campbell, *SQ*, II, 104; by George R. Kernodle, *QJS*, XXXVII, 238-239; by J. Dover Wilson, *NR*, March 12, pp. 19-20; by Esther Cloudman Dunn, *NYTBR*, Jan. 28, p. 20; by Henry Popkin, *TAr*, May, p. 4; *Listener*, XLVII (1952), 275-277; by J. Dover Wilson, *RES*, III, 386-388; by Richard Flatter, *SJ*, 87/88 (1952), 240-241.
B9144   Atherton, J. S. "Shakespeare's Latin, Two Notes." *N&Q*, 196 (1951), 337.
B9145   Bradbrook, M. C. "The Sources of *Macbeth.*" *ShS*, IV (1951), 35-47.
B9146   Campbell, Lily B. "Political Ideas in *Macbeth* IV. iii." *SQ*, II (1951), 281-286.
B9147   Law, Robert Adger. "The Composition of *Macbeth* with Reference to Holinshed." *TxSE*, XXXI (1952), 35-41.
B9148   Davenport, A. "Shakespeare and Nashe's *Pierce Penilesse.*" *N&Q*, 198 (1953), 371-374.
B9149   Nathan, Norman. "Duncan, Macbeth, and Jeremiah." *N&Q*, NS, I (1954), 243.
B9150   Bache, William B. " 'The Murder of Old Cole': A Possible Source for *Macbeth.*" *SQ*, VI (1955), 358-359.
B9151   Danks, K. B. "Shakespeare and 'Equivocator' Etc." *N&Q*, NS, II (1955), 289-292.
B9152   Gierow, K. R. "Pa spar i en Mordaffar" (Tracking a Murder Case). *Svenska Dagbladet* (Stockholm), Mar. 18, 1955.
B9153   Jack, Jane H. "Macbeth, King James, and the Bible." *ELH*, XXII (1955), 173-193.
B9154   Maxwell, J. C. "The Relation of *Macbeth* to *Sophonisba.*" *N&Q*, NS, II (1955), 373-374.
B9155   Muir, Kenneth. "Buchanan, Leslie and *Macbeth.*" *N&Q*, NS, II (1955), 511-512.
B9156   Nørgaard, Holger. "The Bleeding Captain Scene in *Macbeth* and Daniel's *Cleopatra.*" *RES*, NS, VI (1955), 395-396.
B9157   Sheppard, Sir John Tresidder. "*Agamemnon* and *Macbeth.*" *Proc. of the Royal Institution of Great Britain*, 160 (1955), 560-569.
B9158   Muir, Kenneth. "Seneca and Shakespeare." *N&Q*, NS, III (1956), 243-244.
B9159   Adam, R. J. "The Real Macbeth: King of Scots, 1040-1054." *History Today*, VII (1957), 381-387.
B9160   Christ, Henry I. "*Macbeth* and the Faust Legend." *English Journal*, XLVI (1957), 212-213.
B9161   Flatter, Richard. "Who Wrote the Hecate-Scene?" *SJ*, 93 (1957), 196-210.
B9162   Cutts, John P. "Who Wrote the Hecate-Scene?" *SJ*, 94 (1958), 200-202.
        On B9161.
B9163   Jacquot, Jean. "Les études Shakespeariennes. Problèmes et méthodes: l'Exemple de *Macbeth.*" *La Mise en Scène des Œuvres du Passé. Études Réunies et Presentées par Jean Jacquot et André Veinstein.* Entretiens d'Arras 1956. Paris: Centre Nat. de la Recherche Scientifique, 1957, pp. 177-209.
B9164   Barker, Richard Hindry. *Thomas Middleton.* New York: Columbia Univ. Press, 1958. Pp. ix, 216.
        Rev: A4901.
B9165   McNeal, Thomas H. "Shakespeare's Cruel Queens." *HLQ*, XXII (1958), 41-50.

(3)   USE OF LANGUAGE

B9166   Nottrott, Marianne. *Der Formale Gebrauch des Epithetons in Shakespeares Dramen "Othello," "King Lear," "Macbeth" und "Coriolanus."* DD, Leipzig, 1922. Pp. vi, 254. Handwritten. Publ. in *Jahrbuch der Philosophischen Fakultät Leipzig,* I (1923).

B9167   Garrett, J. "Drama and the Poet's Tongue." *Nineteenth Century*, 119 (1936), 350-360.

B9168   Draper, John W. "King James and Shakespeare's Literary Style." *Archiv*, 171 (1937), 36-48.

B9169   Franz, Wilhelm. "Zu der Sprache von Shakespeares *Macbeth* (Akt IV)." *Anglia*, LXV (1941), 87-100.

B9170   Brooks, Cleanth. *The Well Wrought Urn: Studies in the Structure of Poetry*. New York: Reynal & Hitchcock, 1947. Pp. xi, 270.
         Rev: A8116.

B9171   Morozov, Mikhail M. "The Individualization of Shakespeare's Characters Through Imagery." *ShS*, II (1949), 83-106.

B9172   Muir, Kenneth. "The Uncomic Pun." *CamJ*, III (1950), 472-485.

B9173   Sitwell, Edith. "*Macbeth*." *Atlantic Monthly*, April 1950, pp. 43-48.

B9174   Schmetz, Lotte. "Die Charakterisierung der Personen durch die Sprache in *Macbeth*." *SJ*, 84/86 (1951), 97-113.

B9175   Kantak, V. Y. "The Imagery of *Macbeth*." *Journal of the Maharaja Sayaji Rao University of Baroda*, II (Mar., 1953), 41-57.

B9176   Babcock, Weston. "Macbeth's 'Cream-Fac'd Loone'." *SQ*, IV (1953), 199-202.

B9177   Burrell, Margaret D. "*Macbeth*: A Study in Paradox." *SJ*, 90 (1954), 167-190.

B9178   Stamm, Rudolf. *Shakespeare's Word-Scenery*. With Some Remarks on Stage History and the Interpretation of His Plays. Veröffentlichungen der Handels-Hochschule St. Gallen, Reihe B, Heft 10. Zürich u. St. Gallen: Polygraphischer Verlag, 1954. Pp. 34.
         Rev: A5603.

B9179   Mahood, M. M. *Shakespeare's Word Play*. London: Methuen, 1956.
         Chapter on *Macbeth*.
         Rev: A5815.

B9180   Lawlor, John. "Mind and Hand: Some Reflections on the Study of Shakespeare's Imagery." *SQ*, VIII (1957), 179-193.

B9181   Berry, Francis. *Poets' Grammar*. London: Routledge and Kegan Paul, 1958. Pp. 190.
         Rev: A5230.

(4) GENERAL CRITICISM OF THE PLAY

B9182   De Quincey, Thomas. "On the Knocking at the Gate in *Macbeth*." *TAr*, XXXIII, No. 2 (1949), 26.

B9183   Sachs, Hanns. "Aesthetics and Psychology of the Artist." *International Journal of Psycho-Analysis*, II (1921), 98-100.

B9184   Jekels, L. "Shakespeares *Macbeth*." *Imago*, V (1917-1919), 170.

B9185   Jekels, Ludwig. "The Riddle of Shakespeare's *Macbeth*." *Psychoanalytic Review*, XXX (1943), 361-385. Repr. in Jekels, *Selected Papers*, New York and London, 1953.

B9186   Jekels, Ludwig. "The Problem of the Duplicated Expression of Psychic Themes." *International Journal of Psycho-Analysis*, XIV (July, 1933), 300-309. Repr. in *Selected Papers*, New York and London, 1953.

B9187   Draper, J. W. "Political Themes in Shakespeare's Later Plays." *JEGP*, XXXV (1936), 61-93.

B9188   Kassner, R. "Über Shakespeare." *Corona*, VI (1936), 256-283, 408-423.

B9189   Pongs, H. "Shakespeare und das Politische Drama." *DuV*, XXXVII, No. 3 (1936), 257-280.

B9190   Baird, David. "Some Doubtful Points in *Macbeth*." *N&Q*, 173 (1937), 224.

B9191   Curry, Walter Clyde. *Shakespeare's Philosophical Patterns*. Louisiana State Univ. Press, 1937. Pp. xii, 244.
         Rev: A931.

B9192   Evans, M. S. "Free-will in the Drama." *Personalist*, XVIII (1937), 273-291.

B9193   Hunter, Edwin R. "*Macbeth* as a Morality." *SAB*, XII (1937), 217-235. Repr. in *Shakespeare and Common Sense*. Boston: Christopher, 1954.
         Rev: A971.

B9194   Lacy, E. W. *Justice in Shakespeare*. Master's thesis, Vanderbilt University, 1937. Abstr. publ. in *Bull. of Vanderbilt Univ.*, XXXVII (1937), 42.

B9195   Sargeaunt, W. D. "*Macbeth*": *A New Interpretation of the Text of Shakespeare's Play*. London: Heath Cranton, Ltd., 1937. Pp. 208.
         Rev: by Richard David, *London Mercury*, XXXV (1937), 529; by J. W. Draper, *MLR*, XXXII 661; by F. C. Danchin, *EA*, I, 329.

B9196   Waldock, A. J. A. [Henry] *James, Joyce and Others*. London: Williams and Norgate, 1937. Pp. 133.
         Includes a study of *Macbeth*.
         Rev: by H. W. Häusermann, *Eng. Studn.*, LXXIV (1940/41), 382.

B9197   Coles, Blanche. *Shakespeare Studies: "Macbeth."* New York: Smith, 1938. Pp. viii, 289.
         Rev: by G. C. Taylor, *MLN*, LIV (1939), 233; by Robert Adger Law, *JEGP*, XXXIX (1940), 144-146; by T. W. Baldwin, *MLN*, LV, 458-459.

B9198 Stunz, Arthur M. *The Contemporary Setting of "Macbeth."* DD, State University of Iowa, 1939. Abstr. publ. in [Univ. of Iowa] *Programs Announcing Candidates for Higher Degrees* . . . , [no pagination]. *Univ. of Iowa Studies*, NS, No. 378.

B9199 Kellett, E. E. *"Macbeth* and Satan." *London Quar. and Holborn Rev.*, July, 1939, pp. 289-299.

B9200 Knight, G. Wilson. *The Imperial Theme.* Further Interpretation of Shakespeare's Tragedies including the Roman Plays. Oxford Univ. Press, 1939. Pp. 376.
  Rev: A8258.

B9201 Milne, W. S. "Shakespeare: Script Writer." *Canadian Forum*, XIX (1939), 252.

B9202 Niederstenbruch, Alex. "Shakespeares *Macbeth* in Moderner Unterrichtlicher Behandlung." *Der Deutsche Erzieher. Beil: Niedersächs. Erzieher* (Gau Südhannover-Braunschweig), VII (1939), 274-276.

B9203 Perazzi, Vincenzo. "Una Nota al *Macbeth.*" *Studi Inglesi*, Jan., 1939.

B9204 Plowman, Max. "Notes on *Macbeth.*" *Adelphi*, XV (1939), 238-242, 287-291. Repr. in Plowman's *The Right to Live*, Intro. J. Middleton Murry. London: Dakers, 1942, pp. 164-176.

B9205 Z. "The Witches' Brew in *Macbeth.*" *N &Q*, 178 (1939), 352.

B9206 Bajocchi, Fedele. *"Macbeth,* I. ii." *TLS*, March 23, 1940, p. 147.

B9207 Giordano-Orsini, G. N. *"Macbeth.*" *TLS*, April 6, 1940, p. 171.
  On B9206.

B9208 Williams, Edwin E. *Tragedy of Destiny. Oedipus Tyrannus, Macbeth, Athalie.* Cambridge, 1940. Pp. 35.
  Rev: by G. M. Harper, Jr., *Class. Week.*, XXXV (1941), 9-10.

B9209 Spender, Stephen. "Time, Violence and *Macbeth.*" *Penguin New Writing*, III (1940-41), 115-120.

B9210 Vogel, Walter. "Shakespeares *Macbeth.*" *ZDB*, XVII (1941), 83-90.

B9211 Doran, Madeleine. "That Undiscovered Country. A Problem Concerning the Use of the Supernatural in *Hamlet* and *Macbeth.*" *Renaissance Studies in Honor of Hardin Craig*, Stanford Univ. Press, 1941, pp. 221-235; also *PQ*, XX (1941), 413-427.

B9212 Franz, W. "Shakespeares Kulturkampf im *Macbeth:* Formen und Verwendung der Equivocation." *ZNU*, XLI (1942), 119-123.

B9212a Franz, W. "Shakespeares Kulturkampf im *Macbeth.* 1. Der Kulturgeschichtliche Unter- und Hintergrund. 2. Die Pulverschwörung vom 5. Nov. 1605." *ZNU*, XLI (1942), 172-178.

B9212b Heuer, Hermann. "Zur Deutung von Shakespeares *Macbeth.*" *ZNU*, XLI (1942), 201-209.
  On B9212 and B9212a.

B9213 Stewart, J. I. M. *"Julius Caesar* and *Macbeth.* Two Notes on Shakespearean Technique." *MLR*, XL (1945), 166-173.

B9214 Fairchild, Arthur H. R. *Shakespeare and the Tragic Theme.* Univ. Missouri Studies, XIX, No. 2. Univ. Missouri Press, 1944. Pp. 145.
  Rev: A6853.

B9215 McCloskey, John C. "Why Not Fleance?" *SAB*, XX (1945), 118-120.

B9216 Masefield, John. *A Macbeth Production.* London: Heinemann, 1945; New York, 1946. Pp. 64.
  Rev: A9069.

B9217 Smith, Fred Manning. "The Relation of *Macbeth* to *Richard the Third.*" *PMLA*, LX (1945), 1003-20.

B9218 Knights, L. C. *Explorations: Essays in Criticism, Mainly on the Literature of the Seventeenth Century.* London, 1946.
  1. "How Many Children Had Lady Macbeth?"
  Rev: A8269.

B9219 Weilgart, Wolfgang J. *"Macbeth": Demon and Bourgeois.* New Orleans, 1946.

B9220 Broszinski, Hans. "Christian Reality in *Macbeth.*" *Theology*, L (1947).

B9221 Draper, John W. "Patterns of Humor and Tempo in *Macbeth.*" *Neophil*, XXXI (1947), 202-207.

B9222 Gardner, Helen. "Milton's 'Satan' and the Theme of Damnation in Elizabethan Tragedy." *Essays and Studies*, NS, I (1948), 46-66.

B9223 Spargo, John Webster. "The Knocking at the Gate in *Macbeth:* An Essay in Interpretation." *AMS*, pp. 269-277.

B9224 Knight, George Wilson. *Christ and Nietzsche.* London: Staples Press, 1949. Pp. 244.
  Rev: A1508.

B9225 Knight, G. Wilson. "The Milk of Concord: An Essay on Life-Themes in *Macbeth.*" *Critiques and Essays in Criticism, 1920-1948.* New York: Ronald Press, 1949, pp. 119-140.

B9226 Walker, Roy. *The Time Is Free: A Study of "Macbeth."* London: Dakers, 1949. Pp. xvii, 234.
  Rev: *TLS*, Sept. 9, 1949, p. 582; by H. B. Charlton, *MGW*, Aug. 18, p. 12; by Una Ellis-Fermor, *NstN*, XXXVIII, 311-312; by J. S. Wilson, *VQR*, XXVI (1950), 317-318; by R. H., *SRL*, April 1, p. 16; by H. Levin, *NYTBR*, March 26, pp. 7, 30.

B9227   Brock, F. H. Cecil. "Oedipus, *Macbeth* and the Christian Tradition." *ConR*, March, 1950, pp. 176-181.

B9228   Connolly, Thomas F. "Shakespeare and the Double Man." *SQ*, I (1950), 30-35.

B9229   Haydn, Hiram. *The Counter-Renaissance*. New York, 1950.
       Rev: A3836.

B9230   Waith, Eugene M. "Manhood and Valor in Two Shakespearean Tragedies." *ELH*, XVII (1950), 262-272.

B9231   Campbell, Lily B. "Political Ideas in *Macbeth* IV. iii." *SQ*, II (1951), 281-286.

B9232   Draper, John W. "Scene-Tempo in *Macbeth*." *Shakespeare-Studien, Festschrift für Heinrich Mutschmann*. Marburg: Verlag N. G. Elwert, 1951, pp. 56-63.

B9233   Flatter, Richard. "The Dumb-Show in *Macbeth*." *TLS*, March 23, 1951, p. 181.
       Comment by Peter Ure, ibid., April 6, p. 213; by C. B. Purdom, ibid., April 20, p. 245.

B9234   Waldock, A. J. A. *Sophocles the Dramatist*. Cambridge Univ. Press, 1951. Pp. x, 228.
       Rev: A8427.

B9235   Zandvoort, R. W. "Dramatic Motivation in *Macbeth*." *LanM*, March/April, 1951, pp. 62-72. Repr. in R. W. Zandvoort, *Collected Papers* (1954), pp. 63-75.

B9236   Battenhouse, Roy W. "Shakespeare and the Tragedy of Our Time." *Theology Today*, VIII (1952), 518-534.

B9237   Boyd, Catharine B. "The Isolation of Antigone and Lady Macbeth." *Classical Jour.*, XLVII (1952), 174-177, 203.

B9238   Empson, William. "Dover Wilson on *Macbeth*." *KR*, XIV (1952), 84-102.

B9239   Fergusson, Francis. "*Macbeth* as the Imitation of an Action." *EIE, 1951*, Columbia Univ. Press, 1952, pp. 31-43. Repr. in Francis Fergusson, *The Human Image in Dramatic Literature*, Doubleday Anchor Books. New York: Doubleday & Company, 1957. Pp. xx, 217.
       Rev: by W. H. Clemen, *SQ*, V (1954), 188-189.

B9240   Frye, Roland Mushat. "*Macbeth* and the Powers of Darkness." *Emory Univ. Quar.*, VIII (1952), 164-174.

B9241   Neilson, Francis. *A Study of "Macbeth" for the Stage*. Mineola, New York: Davenport Press, 1952. Pp. 135.
       Rev: *TLS*, Oct. 3, 1952, p. 650.

B9242   Röhrman, H. *Marlowe and Shakespeare: A Thematic Exposition of Some of Their Plays*. Arnhem: van Loghum Slaterus, 1952. Pp. x, 109.
       Rev: A1023.

B9243   Zandvoort, R. W. *Shakespeare in de Twintigste Eeuw*. Groningen: J. B. Wolters, 1952. Pp. 19.
       Rev: A365.

B9244   Craig, Hardin. "These Juggling Fiends: On the Meaning of *Macbeth*." *The Written Word and Other Essays*, Univ. of North Carolina Press, 1953, pp. 49-61.

B9245   Fiocco, Achille. "I Rischi del *Macbeth*." *La Fiera Letteraria*, No. 10 (March 8, 1953), p. 8.

B9246   Ribner, Irving. "Political Doctrine in *Macbeth*." *SQ*, IV (1953), 202-205.

B9247   Stirling, Brents. "The Unity of *Macbeth*." *SQ*, IV (1953), 385-394.

B9248   Walker, Roy. "Macbeth's Entrance." *TLS*, Aug. 21, 1953, p. 535.

B9249   Burrell, Margaret D. "*Macbeth*: A Study in Paradox." *SJ*, 90 (1954), 167-190.

B9250   Purdom, C. B. "Who Was the Third Murderer in *Macbeth*:" *The Shakespeare Stage*, Nos. 6-7 (1954), 49-53.

B9251   Waith, Eugene M. "*Macbeth*: Interpretation versus Adaptation." In *Shakespeare: Of an Age and for All Time*. The Yale Shakespeare Festival Lectures, 1954, 103-122.

B9252   Arnold, Aerol. "The Recapitulation Dream in *Richard III* and *Macbeth*." *SQ*, VI (1955), 51-62.

B9253   Braun, Felix. "Über *Macbeth*. Eine Ansprache." *Die Eisblume*. Salzburg, 1955, pp. 84-91.

B9254   Gierow, K. R. "Macbeths Son." *Svenska Dagbladet* (Stockholm), March 7, 1955.

B9255   Higashi, Tosiko. "On *Macbeth*." In *Essays and Studies in British and American Literature*, Tokyo Woman's Christian College, III, i (Autumn, 1955), 1-26 (in English).

B9256   Reed, R. R., Jr. "The Fatal Elizabethan Sisters in *Macbeth*." *N &Q*, NS, II (1955), 425-427.

B9257   Siegel, Paul N. "Echoes of the Bible Story in *Macbeth*." *N &Q*, NS, II (1955), 142-143.

B9258   Speaight, Robert. "Nature and Grace in *Macbeth*." In *Essays by Diverse Hands, Being the Transactions of the Royal Society of Literature*, NS, XXVII (1955), 89-109.

B9259   Zacharias, Gerhard P. "*Macbeth* in Uns." *Das neue Forum* (Darmstadt), V (1955/56), 113-114.

B9260   Brinkmann, Karl. *Erläuterungen zu Shakespeares "Macbeth"*. 7th ed. Wilhelm Königs Erläuterungen zu d. Klassikern, 45. Hollfeld/Ofr.: Bange, 1956. Pp. 72.

B9261   Knights, L. C. "On the Background of Shakespeare's Use of Nature in *Macbeth*." *SR*, LXIV (1956), 207-217.

B9262   Landauer, Gustav. "*Macbeth*—ein Dämonisch Auserwählter." *Blätter d. Dt. Theaters in Göttingen*, VII, Heft 112 (1956/57), 202-203.

B9263   Nagarajan, S. "A Note on Banquo." *SQ*, VII (1956), 371-376.

B9264   Pack, Robert. "*Macbeth:* The Anatomy of Loss." *YR*, XLV (1956), 533-548.

B9265   Santayana, George. "Tragic Philosophy." In *Essays in Literary Criticism*, Introd. by Irving Singer. New York: Scribner's, 1956, pp. 266-277.

B9266   Stroedel, Wolfgang. "Shakespeares Entwicklung von *Romeo und Julia* zu *Macbeth*." *ZAA*, II (1956), 137-148.

B9267   West, Robert H. "Night's Black Agents in *Macbeth*." In *Renaissance Papers 1956*, Columbia, South Carolina, 1957, pp. 17-24.

B9268   Winters, Yvor. "Problems for the Modern Critic of Literature." *Hudson Review*, IX (1956), 325-386.

B9269   Auden, W. H. "The Dyer's Hand: Poetry and the Poetic Process." *The Anchor Review*, No. 2 (1957), 255-301.
Includes section on "*Oedipus Rex* and *Macbeth*."

B9270   Morgan, George Alan. *Illustrations of the Critical Principles of E. E. Stoll*. DD, State University of Iowa, 1957. Pp. 224. Mic 57-4807. *DA*, XVII (1957), 3020. Publ. No. 23, 772.

B9271   Siegel, Paul N. *Shakespearean Tragedy and the Elizabethan Compromise*. New York Univ. Press, 1957. Chapter on *Macbeth*.
Rev: A1882.

B9272   Carrington, Norman T. *Shakespeare: Macbeth*. Rev. ed. London: Brodie, 1958. Pp. 72.

B9273   Dean, Leonard F. "*Macbeth* and Modern Criticism." *Eng. Jour.*, XLVII (1958), 57-67.

B9274   Elliott, G. R. *Dramatic Providence in "Macbeth": A Study of Shakespeare's Tragic Theme of Humanity and Grace*. Princeton Univ. Press, 1958. Pp. xvi, 234.
Rev: by H. Rogers, *Eng. Jour.*, XLVII (1958), 527; by D. A. Sears, *ShN*, VIII, 38; by Julia Gray, *Canadian Modern Language Review*, XV, 56; by Robert Adger Law, *Southwest Rev.*, XLVIII, 178-179; by Philip Leon, *Hibbert Jour.*, LVII, 90-92; *NstN*, Nov. 29, pp. 772-773

B9275   Jeffreys, M. D. W. "The Weird Sisters in *Macbeth*." *English Studies in Africa* (Johannesburg), I (1958), 43-54.

B9276   Rosier, James Louis. *The Chain of Sin and Privation in Elizabethan Literature*. DD, Stanford University, 1958. Pp. 240. Mic 58-4326. *DA*, XVIII (1958), 583. Publ. No. 25,387.

B9277   Tomlinson, T. B. "Action and Soliloquy in *Macbeth*." *EIC*, VIII (1958), 147-155.
Cf. comment by Cecil W. Davies, ibid., pp. 451-453.

B9278   Knights, L. C. *Some Shakespearean Themes*. London: Chatto & Windus, 1959.

(5) CHARACTERIZATION

B9279   Palmer, J. F. "*Macbeth:* A Study in Monomania." *The Medical Magazine* (London), XIX (1910), 577-584.

B9280   Sadger, I. *Über Nachtwandeln und Mondsucht*. Eine Medizinisch-literarische Studie. Leipzig and Vienna: F. Deuticke, 1914. Tr. by Louise Brink as *Sleep Walking and Moon Walking*. A medico-literary study. New York and Washington: Nervous and Mental Disease Publishing Co., 1920.
"*Macbeth* von Shakespeare," pp. 143-169 of German ed.

B9281   Coriat, I. H. "Psychoanalyse der Lady Macbeth." *Zentralbl. f. Psa.*, IV (1914), 384.

B9282   Coriat, Isador H. *The Hysteria of Lady Macbeth*. New York: Moffat, Yard and Co., 1912. Pp. 94. 2nd ed. New York: Four Seas, 1921.

B9283   Mallinckrodt, Frieda. "Zur Psychoanalyse der Lady Macbeth." *Int. Zeitschrift für Psa.*, IV (Aug. 1914), 612-613.

B9284   Freud, S. "Einige Charaktertypen aus der Psychoanalyt. Arbeit." *Imago*, IV (1916), 317 and *Sammlg. kl. Schr. z. Neur.*, IV (1918), 521-522. Tr. by E. Colburn Mayne as "Some Character-Types Met with in Psycho-Analytic Work." *Collected Papers*, IV, 323-333. Also in the Standard Edition of the *Complete Psychological Works*, tr. James Strachey and Others, XIV (1957), 309-333.

B9285   Freud, S. "Contributions to the Psychology of Love." *Collected Papers*, IV, Chap. XI, 192-202. [Macduff, p. 201.] Also in the Standard Edition of the *Complete Psychological Works*, tr. by James Strachey and Others, XI, London: Hogarth Press, 1957, pp. 165-175. [Macduff, p. 173.]

B9286   Goll, A. "Macbeth and the Lady as Criminal Types." Tr. J. Moritzen. *Journal of Criminal Law and Criminology*, XXIX (1939), 645-667.

B9287   Goll, A. "Lady Macbeth as a Criminal Type." Tr. J. Moritzen. *Case and Comment*, XLV (July, 1939), 5-11.

B9288   MacDowell, David Archibald. *The History of the Interpretation of Lady Macbeth in English and American Literary Criticism, 1747-1939*. MA thesis, University of North Carolina, 1939. Abstr. publ. in *Univ. of North Carolina Record, Research in Progress*, Grad. School Series No. 36, 1939, p. 81.

B9289   Buck-Marchand, Eva. "*Macbeth*, eine Charakteranalyse." *SJ*, LXXVII (1941), 49-73.

B9290   Draper, John W. "The 'Gracious Duncan'." *MLR*, XXXVI (1941), 495-499.

B9291 Draper, John W. "Lady Macbeth." *Psychoanalytic Rev.*, XXVIII (1941), 479-486.

B9292 Draper, John W. "*Macbeth*, 'Infirme of Purpose'." *Bul. Hist. Medicine*, X (1941), 16-26.

B9293 Lynch, James J. "Macduff, Not Macbeth." *MLN*, LVI (1941), 603-604. See note by H.[azelton] S.[pencer], ibid., pp. 604.

B9294 Armstrong, W. A. "The Elizabethan Conception of the Tyrant." *RES*, XXII (1946), 161-181.

B9295 Henneberger, Olive. "Banquo, Loyal Subject." *CE*, VIII (1946), 18-22.

B9296 Westbrook, Perry D. "A Note on *Macbeth*, Act II, Scene I." *CE*, VII (1946), 219-220.

B9297 Arthos, John. "The Naive Imagination and the Destruction of Macbeth." *ELH*, XIV (1947), 114-126.

B9298 Bossler, Robert. "Was Macbeth a Victim of Battle Fatigue?" *CE*, VIII (1947), 436-438.

B9299 Röling, B. V. A. *De Criminologische Betekenis van Shakespeares "Macbeth."* Nijmegen: Dekker & Van de Vegt, 1947. Pp. xvi, 143.

B9300 Traz, R. de. "Lady Macbeth." *Revue de Paris*, LIV (1947), 25-38.

B9301 Waith, Eugene M. "Manhood and Valor in Two Shakespearian Tragedies." *ELH*, XVII (1950), 262-273.

B9302 Schmetz, Lotte. "Die Charakterisierung der Personen durch die Sprache in *Macbeth*." *SJ*, 84/86 (1948-50), 97-113.

B9303 Stein, Arnold. "*Macbeth* and Word-Magic." *SR*, LIX (1951), 271-284.

B9304 Boyd, Catharine B. "The Isolation of Antigone and Lady Macbeth." *Classical Journal*, XLVII (1952), 174-177, 203.

B9305 Meltzer, J. "Some Psycho-Analytical Angles on Aspects of Shakespearean Drama." *Discussion* (South Africa), I, No. 6 (1952), 47-50.

B9306 Parsons, A. E. "Macbeth's Vision." *TLS*, Oct. 24, 1952, p. 700.

B9307 Lucas, F. L. *Literature and Psychology.* London: Cassell, 1951. Pp. 340. Rev: A1362.

B9308 Kocher, Paul H. "Lady Macbeth and the Doctor." *SQ*, V (1954), 341-349.

B9309 Brugger, Ilse. *El Porter de Shakespeare y el Pförtner de Schiller.* Buenos Aires, 1955.

B9310 Frye, Roland M. "Macbeth's Usurping Wife." *RN*, VIII (1955), 102-105.

B9311 Gogoleva, Elena. "My Conception of Lady Macbeth." *News* (Moscow), No. 19 (Oct. 1, 1955), 29.

B9312 Klajn, Hugo. "Dobra Ledi Magbet — ili 'Arhiveštica'?" *Savremenik* (Belgrade), I (1955), 320-324.

B9313 Coe, Charles Norton. *Shakespeare's Villains.* New York, 1957. Rev: A6796.

B9314 Kirschbaum, Leo. "Banquo and Edgar: Character or Function?" *EIC*, VII (1957), 1-21. See comments by Christopher Gillie, ibid., pp. 322-324, A. S. Knowland, ibid., pp. 325-330, and Peter Ure, ibid., pp. 457-459.

(6) MISCELLANEOUS ITEMS

B9315 Rank, O. "Shakespeares Vaterkomplex." *Das Inzest-Motiv in Dichtung und Sage.* Leipzig, 1912, pp. 204-233.

B9316 Deutschbein, Max. *Shakespeares "Macbeth" als Drama des Barock.* Leipzig: Quelle and Meyer, 1936. Pp. 130. Rev: A5525.

B9317 Klein, M. "Shakespeares Dramatisches Formgesetz in Seiner Bedeutung für die Schule. Ein neuer Weg zu *Macbeth* und *Hamlet*." *N. Mon.*, VI (1936), 487-498.

B9318 Strout, Alan L. " 'How Far is't Call'd to Forres?'" *N &Q*, 176 (1939), 330.

B9319 Pinto, V. de Sola. "Shakespeare and the Dictators." *Essays by Divers Hands.* Transactions Royal Soc. Lit., XXI, ed. by Walter de la Mare. Oxford Univ. Press, 1945, pp. 82-102.

B9320 Masefield, John. *A "Macbeth" Production.* London: Heineman, 1945; New York: Macmillan, 1946. Pp. 64. Rev: A9069.

B9321 Clemeshaw, Isabel B. "Literary Notes: *Macbeth*." *Theosophical Forum*, XXVIII (1950), 291-297.

B9322 Simpson, Lucie. "The Temperance Note in *Othello* and *Macbeth*." *The Secondary Heroes of Shakespeare and Other Essays.* London: Kingswood Press, 1950, pp. 105-108.

B9323 Akerhielm, H. "*Macbeth*-Problem." *Teatern* (Stockholm), XIX, Heft 2 (1952), 3-4, 12.

B9324 Nehring, H. "Macbeth ein Bruder Hamlets?" *Neuphilologische Zeitschrift*, IV (1952), 361-364.

B9325 Prema, B. S. "Lady Macbeth and Clytemnestra." *The Literary Criterion* (India), I (1952).

B9326 Witte, W. "Time in *Wallenstein* and *Macbeth*." *Aberdeen Univ. Review*, XXXIV (1952), 217-224.

B9327 Driver, Tom Faw. *The Sense of History in Greek and Shakespearean Dramatic Form.* DD, Columbia University, 1957. Pp. 397. Mic 57-2807. *DA*, XVII (1957), 1748. Publ. No. 21,781.

B9328   Syrkin, Marie. "Youth and Lady Macduff." *The Use of English*, VIII (1957), 257-261.
        See B9328a.

B9328a Herman, G. "Macduff's Boy: A Reply to Professor Syrkin." *The Use of English*, IX (1957),
        40-42.

B9329   *Map of Scotland Illustrating Macbeth*. Educational Illustrators, 40 West Lincoln, Westerville,
        Ohio, 1957.
            Rev: *Eng. Jour.*, XLVI (1957), 595.

B9330   Loomis, Edward Alleyn. "Master of the Tiger." *SQ*, VII (1956), 457.

B9331   Louis, Sister. "Macbeth, Deliverer and Destroyer of a Kingdom." *Catholic Scholarly Jour-
        nal*, LVI (1956), 293-294.

(7) SUBSEQUENT HISTORY OF THE PLAY
(other than productions after 1660)

B9332   Baird, David. *The Thane of Cawdor. A Detective Study of "Macbeth."* New York: Oxford
        Univ. Press, 1937. Pp. xii, 105.
            Rev: B4132.

B9333   B., W. G. "*Macbeth* at Windsor in 1829." *N &Q*, 195 (1950), 473.

B9334   Purdom, C. B. *The Crosby Hall Macbeth*. London: Dent, for the Shakespeare Stage Society,
        1951.

B9335   Spencer, Christopher. *The Problems of Davenant's Text of Shakespeare's "Macbeth" Together
        with a Typed Facsimile of the Yale Manuscript*. DD, Yale University, 1955.

B9336   Cutts, John P. "The Original Music to Middleton's *The Witch*." *SQ*, VII (1956), 203-209.

B9337   Tucker, Susie I. "Johnson and Lady Macbeth." *N &Q*, NS, III (1956), 210-211.

B9338   Falkenberg, Hans-Geert. "Zur Entstehungs- und Bühnengeschichte von Shakespeares
        Macbeth." *Blätter d. Deutschen Theaters in Göttingen*, No. 112 (1956/57), 209-212.

TIMON OF ATHENS (252;90)
(1) THE TEXT
(a) MODERN EDITIONS

B9339   *The Life of Timon of Athens*. Ed. G. B. Harrison. Penguin Shakespeare. London: Penguin
        Books, 1956. Pp. 126.
            Rev: *TLS*, Oct. 19, 1956, p. 623.

B9340   *Timon of Athens*. Ed. J. C. Maxwell. The New Shakespeare. Cambridge Univ. Press, 1957.
        Pp. lvi, 190.
            Rev: by H. J. Oliver, *SQ*, IX (1958), 406-407; *ShN*, VIII, 12; by Hermann Heuer, *SJ*, 94
            (1958), 285-286; *N &Q*, NS, V, 503-504.

B9341   *Timon of Athens*. Ed. H. J. Oliver. The New Arden Shakespeare. London: Methuen;
        Cambridge, Mass.: Harvard Univ. Press, 1958.

(b) EMENDATIONS

B9342   Tannenbaum, Samuel A. "Farewell to 'Vllorxa' [*Timon of Athens*, III. iv. 112]." *SAB*, XI
        (1936), 41-45.

B9343   Hippoclides. "My Foot." *N &Q*, 176 (1939), 426; C. Wanklyn, ibid., 177 (1939), 34.

B9344   Kökeritz, Helge. "Five Shakespeare Notes." *RES*, XXIII (1947), 310-320.
        III. iv. 305-310.

B9345   Tidwell, James N. "Shakespeare's 'Wappen'd Widow'." *N &Q*, 195 (1950), 139-140.
        Interprets the phrase in *Timon*, IV. iii. 38, to mean "wanton widow."

B9346   Pyle, Fitzroy. "Hostilius: *Timon of Athens*, III. ii. 70." *N &Q*, 197 (1952), 48-49.

B9347   Spencer, Terence. "Shakespeare Learns the Value of Money: The Dramatist at Work on
        Timon of Athens." *ShS*, VI (1953), 75-78.

(2) LITERARY GENESIS AND ANALOGUES

B9348   Bond, R. W. "Lucian and Boiardo in *Timon*." *Studia Otiosa*, pp. 75-105.
            Rev: B4459.

B9349   B., A. "An Echo of the 'Paragone' in Shakespeare." *Jour. Warburg Inst.*, II (1939), 260-262.

B9350   Kocher, Paul H. "*Timon of Athens*, Act V, Scene V, 3." *SAB*, XIV (1939), 239-242.
        Argues for Shak.'s authorship of the scene on evidence of parallel passages.

B9351   Haug, Ralph A. "The Authorship of *Timon of Athens*." *SAB*, XV (1940), 227-248.

B9352   Ashe, Geoffrey. "William Strachey." *N &Q*, 195 (1950), 508-511.
        Replies by R. L. Eagle, ibid., 196 (1951), p. 19; Kenneth Muir, ibid., pp. 19-20; Herbert H.
        Huxley, ibid., pp. 85-86.

B9353   Bonnard, Georges. "Note sur les Sources de *Timon of Athens*." *EA*, VII (1954), 59-69.

B9354   Maxwell, J. C. "William Painter's Use of Mexía." *N &Q*, 199 (1954), 16.

B9355 Goldsmith, Robert Hillis. "Did Shakespeare Use the Old Timon Comedy?" *SQ*, IX (1958), 31-38.

(3) USE OF LANGUAGE

B9356 Empson, William. "Timon's Dog." *Life and Letters*, XV, No. 6 (1937), 108-115. Reprinted in William Empson and George Garrett, *Shakespeare Survey*. London: Brendin, 1937. Pp. 63. Rev: A204.

B9357 Farnham, Willard. "The Beast Theme in Shakespeare's *Timon*." In *Essays and Studies by Members of the Department of English*, Univ. of California, Univ. California Pubs. Eng., Vol. XIV. Univ. California Press, 1943, pp. 49-56.

B9358 Kökeritz, Helge. "Five Shakespeare Notes." *RES*, XXIII (1947), 310-320. II. A Pun in *Timon*.

B9359 Empson, William. *The Structure of Complex Words*. London: Chatto & Windus, 1951. Pp. 449. Rev: A5136.

(4) GENERAL CRITICISM OF THE PLAY

B9360 Ellis-Fermor, Una. "*Timon of Athens*. An Unfinished Play." *RES*, XVIII (1942), 270-283.

B9361 Kemp, Robert. "En Relisant *Timon d'Athènes*." *Le Temps*, April, 1942, pp. 4-5.

B9362 Anderson, Ruth L. "Excessive Goodness a Tragic Fault." *SAB*, XIX (1944), 85-96.

B9363 Collins, A. S. "*Timon of Athens*: A Reconsideration." *RES*, XXII (1946), 96-108.

B9364 Knight, G. Wilson. "Timon of Athens." *RES*, XXII (1946), 325.

B9365 Morstin, L. H. [*Timon*] *Teatr Miesoceznik* (Poland), No. 4-5 (1946).

B9366 Muir, Kenneth. "*Timon of Athens* and the Cash-Nexus." *Modern Quarterly Miscellany*, No. 1, 1946.

B9367 Pettet, E. C. "*Timon of Athens*: The Disruption of Feudal Morality." *RES*, XXIII (1947), 321-336.

B9368 Draper, John W. "Patterns of Tempo in Shakespeare's *Timon*." *SAB*, XXIII (1948), 188-194.

B9369 Maxwell, J. C. "Timon of Athens." *Scrutiny*, XV (1948), 195-208.

B9370 Knight, George Wilson. *Christ and Nietzsche*. London: Staples Press, 1949. Pp. 244. Rev: A1508.

B9371 Muir, Kenneth. "In Defence of Timon's Poet." *EIC*, III (1953), 120-121. See also B9379.

B9372 Merchant, W. M. "*Timon* and the Conceit of Art." *SQ*, VI (1955), 249-257.

B9373 Draper, R. P. "*Timon of Athens*." *SQ*, VIII (1957), 195-200.

(5) CHARACTERIZATION

B9374 Dees. "Timon von Athen, Drama von Shakespeare, nach Psychopathologischen Gesichtspunkten erklärt." *Zeitschrift für die gesamte Neurologie und Psychiatrie* (Berlin and Leipzig), XXVIII (1915), 50-64.

B9375 Woods, Andrew H. "Syphilis in Shakespeare's Tragedy of *Timon of Athens*." *The American Journal of Psychiatry* (Baltimore), 91 (1934), 95-107.

B9376 Draper, John W. "The Psychology of Shakespeare's Timon." *MLR*, XXXV (1940), 521-525.

B9377 Campbell, Oscar James. *Shakespeare's Satire*. Oxford Univ. Press, 1943. Pp. 227. Rev: B5164.

B9378 Ritze, F. H. *Shakespeare's Men of Melancholy and His Malcontents*. MS thesis, Columbia University, 1947. Pp. 98.

(6) MISCELLANEOUS ITEMS

B9379 Thomson, Patricia. "The Literature of Patronage, 1580-1630." *EIC*, II (1952), 267-284.

(7) SUBSEQUENT HISTORY OF THE PLAY
(Other than productions after 1660.)

ANTONY AND CLEOPATRA (250;90)
(1) THE TEXT
(a) OLD TEXTS

B9380 Maxwell, J. C. "Shakespeare's Manuscript of *Antony and Cleopatra*." *N &Q*, 196 (1951), 337.

B9381 Thomas, Mary Olive. "The Repetitions in Antony's Death Scene." *SQ*, IX (1958), 153-157.

B9382 Galloway, David. " 'I am Dying, Egypt, Dying': Folio Repetitions and the Editors." *N &Q*, NS, V (1958), 330-335.

(b) MODERN EDITIONS

B9383 *The Tragedy of Antony and Cleopatra.* Ed. George Lyman Kittredge. Boston: Ginn, 1941.
       Pp. xii, 236.

B9384 *The Tragedy of Antony and Cleopatra.* Ed. Theodore Spencer. Crofts Classics. New York:
       Crofts, 1948. Pp. ix, 115.

B9385 *Antony and Cleopatra.* Ed. J. Dover Wilson. The New Shakespeare. Cambridge Univ. Press,
       1950. Pp. xlvii, 262.
           Rev: *TLS*, Dec. 29, 1950, p. 830; by A. P. Rossiter, *CR*, LXXII, 590, 592; by J. B. Fort,
       LanM, XLV (1951), 406; by Baldwin Maxwell, *MLR*, XLVI, 480-482; *N&Q*, 196 (1951),
       87-88; by Elkin C. Wilson, *SQ*, II, 265-267; by R. A., *Time and Tide*, Jan. 6, p. 20; by Roy
       Walker, *English*, VIII, 255; by H. Nørgaard, *ES*, XXXIII (1952), 28-30; by R. C. Bald, *MLN*,
       LXVII, 499; by M. R. Ridley, *RES*, III, 281-283.

B9386 *Tragedy of Antony and Cleopatra.* Introd. by Sir Laurence Olivier, design for costumes and
       scenery by Audrey Cruddas & Roger Furse. London: Folio Society; New York: Dodd,
       Mead, 1952. Pp. 134.
           Rev: B3151.

B9387 *Antony and Cleopatra.* Ed. T. Henshaw. London: Ginn, 1953. Pp. xc, 250.

B9388 *Antony and Cleopatra.* Ed. M. R. Ridley, based on the ed. of R. H. Chase. Arden Ed. London:
       Methuen, 1954. Pp. lvi, 285.
           Rev: *Dublin Mag.*, XXX (Oct.-Dec., 1954), 65-66; *Adelphi*, XXX, 381-382; *TLS*, June 4, p.
       367; by T. S. Dorsch, *YWES*, XXXV, 80; *CE*, XVI (1955), 258; by Patrick Cruttwell, *EIC*,
       V, 382; by T. M. Parrott, *JEGP*, LIV, 128-129; by J. R. Brown, *MLR*, L, 197-199; by E. J.
       West, *QJS*, XLI, 186-187; *MdF*, 323 (1955), 518-519; by Elkin C. Wilson, *SQ*, VI, 337-339;
       by Alice Walker, *RES*, NS, VI, 415-417; by Hermann Heuer, *SJ*, 91 (1955), 333-336; by
       Wolfgang Clemen, *Archiv*, 192 (1955), 203-204.

B9389 *The Tragedy of Antony and Cleopatra.* Ed. P. G. Phialas. Yale Shakespeare. Rev. Ed. New
       Haven: Yale Univ. Press, 1955. Pp. 171.
           Rev: *Essential Books*, Dec., 1955, p. 26; *TLS*, Feb. 3, 1956, p. 75; by Irving Ribner, *SQ*,
       VIII (1957), 240-241.

(c) EMENDATIONS

B9390 Bronson, B. H. "Arme-gaunt." [*Antony and Cleopatra*, I. v. 48] *TLS*, Oct. 8, 1938, p. 644.
       See letter by D. E. Yates, *TLS*, Oct. 22, 1938, p. 678.

B9391 Cook, Albert. "Shakespeare's *Antony and Cleopatra*, V. ii. 338-341." *Expl.*, VI (1947), 9.

B9392 Eagle, R. L. "Estridge." *N&Q*, 196 (1951), 369. Comment by H. W. Crundell, ibid., p.
       437, and K. R. Webb, ibid., p. 482.
       III. xiii. 197.

B9393 Wheelwright, Philip. "Philosophy of the Threshold." *SR*, LXI (1953), 56-75.

B9394 Nathan, Norman. "*Antony and Cleopatra:* IV. vii. 6-10." *N&Q*, NS, II (1955), 293-294.

B9395 Purcell, J. M. "*Antony and Cleopatra*, I. i. 42-43." *N&Q*, NS, V (1958), 187-188.

B9396 Smith, Constance I. "A Further Note on *Antony and Cleopatra*, I. i. 42-43." *N&Q*, NS,
       V (1958), 371.
       On B9395.

(2) LITERARY GENESIS AND ANALOGUES
(a) ANCIENT SOURCES

B9397 Westbrook, Perry D. "Horace's Influence on Shakespeare's *Antony and Cleopatra*." *PMLA*,
       LXII (1947), 392-398.

B9398 Nyland, Waino S. "Pompey as the Mythical Lover of Cleopatra." *MLN*, LXIV (1949),
       515-516.

B9399 Barroll, John L., III. *Shakespeare and Roman History.* DD, Princeton University, 1956. Pp.
       675. Mic 57-996. *DA*, XVII (1957), 626. Publ. No. 20,101.

B9400 Norman, Arthur M. Z. "Source Material in *Antony and Cleopatra*." *N&Q*, NS, III (1956),
       59-61.

B9401 Schanzer, Ernest, ed. *Shakespeare's Appian.* A Selection from the Tudor translation of Ap-
       pian's *Civil Wars* (English Reprints Series). Liverpool Univ. Press, 1956. Pp. xxviii, 101.
           Rev: A4231.

B9402 Thomas, Mary Olive. *Plutarch in "Antony and Cleopatra."* DD, Duke University, 1956.

B9403 Honda, Akira. "Antonius to Antony" ("Antonius and Anthony"). *Hōsei Daigaku Bunga-
       kubu Kiyo* (Hosei Univ. Studies in Engl and American Lit.), No. 3 (1958), pp. 1-15.

B9404 Seaton, Ethel. "*Antony and Cleopatra* and the *Book of Revelation.*" *RES*, XXII (1946), 219-224.

B9405 Lindsay, J. "*Antony and Cleopatra* and the *Book of Revelation.*" *RES*, XXIII (1947), 66.

(b) CONTEMPORANEOUS SOURCES

B9406 Traub, Walter. *Auffassung und Gestaltung der Cleopatra in der Englischen Literatur.* DD,
       Tübingen, 1937. Würzburg: Triltsch, 1937. Pp. 108.

Rev: by W. Mann, *Beiblatt*, L (1939), 201-202; by Margarete Rösler, *Eng. Studn.*, LXXIV (1940), 233-235; by W. Keller, *SJ*, LXXVI, 212.

B9407   Ellis, Oliver C. de C. *Cleopatra in the Tide of Time.* London: Williams & Norgate, 1947. Pp. xv, 287.
Discusses the Cleopatra of antiquity and the Cleopatras of Shaw and Shak.
Rev: by P. H.-W., *MGW*, May 1, 1947, p. 11.

B9408   Jorgensen, Paul A. "Enobarbus' Broken Heart and *The Estate of English Fugitives.*" *PQ*, XXX (1951), 387-392.

B9409   Ribner, Irving. "Shakespeare and Peele: The Death of Cleopatra." *N &Q*, 197 (1952), 244-246.
Comment by John D. Reeves, ibid., pp. 441-442; by Holger Nørgaard, ibid., pp. 442-443.

B9410   Aboul-Enein, A. M. *Cleopatra in French and English Drama from Yodelle to Shakespeare.* DD, Trinity College, Dublin, 1954.

B9411   Bradbrook, F. W. "Thomas Nashe and Shakespeare." *N &Q*, 199 (1954), 470.

B9412   Harrison, Thomas P. "Shakespeare and Marlowe's *Dido, Queen of Carthage.*" *TxSE*, XXXV (1956), 57-63.

B9413   Schanzer, Ernest. "*Antony and Cleopatra* and the Countess of Pembroke's *Antonius.*" *N &Q*, NS, III (1956), 152-154.

i. Daniel

B9414   Schütze, Johannes. "Daniels *Cleopatra* und Shakespeare." *Eng. Studn.*, LXXI (1936), 58-72.

B9415   Dennett, Drayton N. *Samuel Daniel's "Tragedy of Cleopatra": A Critical Edition with Introduction and Notes.* DD, Cornell University, 1951.

B9416   Leavenworth, Russell E. *Daniel's "Cleopatra": A Critical Study.* DD, University of Colorado, 1953. Abstr. publ. in "Abstracts of Theses for Higher Degrees, 1953," in *Univ. of Colorado Studies*, XXIX (April, 1954), 26-27.

B9417   Rees, Joan. "An Elizabethan Eyewitness of *Antony and Cleopatra?*" *ShS*, VI (1953), 91-93.

B9418   Nørgaard, Holger. "Shakespeare and Daniel's *Letter from Octavia.*" *N &Q*, NS, II (1955), 56-57.

B9419   Norman, Arthur M. Z. "Daniel's *The Tragedie of Cleopatra* and *Antony and Cleopatra.*" *SQ*, IX (1958), 11-18.

(c) MODERN ACCOUNTS

B9420   Lindsay, J. *Marc Antony: His World and His Contemporaries.* London: Routledge, 1936; New York: E. P. Dutton & Co., 1937. Pp. xii, 330.
Rev: by M. Radin, *NYHTBR*, Dec. 5, 1937, p. 40x.

B9421   Ludwig, E. *Cleopatra: The Story of a Queen.* Tr. B. Miall. New York: The Viking Press, 1937. Pp. 342.
Rev: by R. L. Duffus, *NYTBR*, Dec. 5, 1937, p. 9: *TLS*, Dec. 11, p. 940.

(3) USE OF LANGUAGE

B9422   Binder, Rudolf. *Der Dramatische Rhythmus in Shakespeares "Antonius und Cleopatra."* DD, Tübingen, 1939. Pp. 183. Würzburg-Aumühle: Triltsch, 1939. Pp. 176.
Rev: by W. Kalthoff, *Beiblatt*, LI (1940), 108-111; by W. Keller, *SJ*, LXXVI, 210-212; by E. Eckhardt, *Eng. Studn.*, LXXIV, 231-233; by Walter Jacobi, *Archiv*, 178 (1941), 40; by Eva Buck-Marchand, *N. Mitt.*, XLII, 87-94; by Pet. W. Biesterfeldt, *Anzeiger für dts. Altertum*, LX, 42-44; by R. Fricker, *ES*, XXV (1943), 113-115.

B9423   Griffith, Hubert. "Antony, Cleopatra, and Others." *New English Review*, XIV (1947), 162-165.

B9424   Mahood, M. M. "The Fatal Cleopatra: Shakespeare and the Pun." *EIC*, I (1951), 193-207.

B9425   "Shakespeare's Roman Plays: And Other Subjects." *ShN*, VI (1956), 4, 14, 20.

B9426   Charney, Maurice. "Shakespeare's Antony: A Study of Image Themes." *SP*, LIV (1957), 149-161.

B9427   Spencer, Benjamin T. "*Antony and Cleopatra* and the Paradoxical Metaphor." *SQ*, IX (1958), 373-378.

(4) GENERAL CRITICISM OF THE PLAY

B9428   Leavis, F. R. "*Antony and Cleopatra* and *All For Love:* A Critical Exercise." *Scrutiny*, V (1936), 158-169.

B9429   Wilcox, John. "Love in *Antony and Cleopatra.*" *Papers of the Michigan Academy of Science, Arts, and Letters*, XXI (1936), 531-544.

B9430   Rosenblatt, L. M. *Literature as Exploration.* New York, 1938. Pp. xiv, 340.

B9431   Missenharter, H. "*Antonius und Kleopatra.*" *DL*, XLI (1938/39), 422.

B9432   Knight, G. Wilson. *The Imperial Theme.* Further Interpretation of Shakespeare's Tragedies Including the Roman Plays. Oxford Univ. Press, 1939. Pp. 376.
Rev: A8258.

B9433 Lyman, Dean B. "Janus in Alexandria: A Discussion of *Antony and Cleopatra*." *SR*, XLVIII (1940), 86-104.

B9434 Cairns, H., A. Tate, M. Van Doren. *Invitation to Learning*. New York: Random House, 1941. Section on *Antony and Cleopatra*, pp. 200-212.

B9435 Cecil, Lord David. *Antony and Cleopatra*. The W. P. Ker Memorial Lecture for 1943. Glasgow: Jackson, 1944.
Also in Cecil, *Poets and Story-Tellers*, London, 1949, pp. 3-24.

B9436 Gaillard, P. "*Antony and Cleopatra*." *La Pensée* (July, 1945), pp. 112-114.

B9437 Draper, John W. "Speech-tempo and Humor in Shakespeare's Antony." *Bul. Inst. Hist. Medicine*, XX (1946), 426-432.

B9438 Granville-Barker, Harley. *Prefaces to Shakespeare*. 2 Vols. Princeton Univ. Press, 1946, 1947.
Rev: A8201.

B9439 Wimsatt, W. K., Jr. "Poetry and Morals." *Thought*, XXIII (1948), 281-299.
Antony and Cleopatra, pp. 293-298.

B9440 Danby, John F. "The Shakespearean Dialectic: An Aspect of *Antony and Cleopatra*." *Scrutiny*, XVI (1949), 196-213.

B9440a Knights, L. C. "On the Tragedy of *Antony and Cleopatra*." *Scrutiny*, XVI (1949), 318-323.
Comment on B9440, ibid., pp. 323-325; by J. F. Danby, ibid., pp. 326-327.

B9441 Schwalb, Harry M. "Shakespeare's *Antony and Cleopatra*, I. ii. 1-5." *Expl.*, VIII (1950), No. 53.

B9442 Waith, Eugene M. "Manhood and Valor in Two Shakespearean Tragedies." *ELH*, XVII (1950), 262-272.

B9443 Croce, Benedetto. "Shakespeare I. Persona Pratica e Persona Poetica. II. La Tragedia della Volontà (*Antonio e Cleopatra*)." In Croce's *Filosofia—Poesia—Storia*. Naples: Ricciardi, 1951, pp. 788-801.

B9444 Blanco, Julio Enrico. "Las Pruebas del Alter Ego en D'Annunzio y en Shakespeare." *Ideas y Valores* (Bogota), No. 6 (1952).

B9445 Danby, John F. *Poets on Fortune's Hill: Studies in Sidney, Shakespeare, Beaumont and Fletcher*. London: Faber and Faber, 1952. Pp. 212.
Rev: A8156.

B9446 Pearce, T. M. "Shakespeare's *Antony and Cleopatra*, V. ii. 243-359." *Expl.*, XII (1953), item 17.

B9447 Walker, Roy. "*Antony and Cleopatra*." *TLS*, May 29, 1953, p. 349.

B9448 Dickey, Franklin M. *Shakespeare's Presentation of Love in "Romeo and Juliet," "Antony and Cleopatra," and "Troilus and Cressida."* DD, University of California, 1954. Pp. 359. Abstr. publ. in *ShN*, VI (1956), 30.

B9449 Dickey, Franklin M. *Not Wisely but Too Well: Shakespeare's Love Tragedies*. San Marino, California: The Huntington Library, 1957. Pp. ix, 205.
Rev: A2562.

B9450 Pearson, Norman Holmes. "*Antony and Cleopatra*." *Shakespeare: Of an Age and for all Time*. The Yale Shakespeare Festival Lectures, 1954, pp. 125-147.

B9451 Schanzer, Ernest. "A Plot Chain in *Antony and Cleopatra*." *N &Q*, NS, I (1954), 379-380.

B9452 Williams, Raymond. *Drama in Performance*. Man and Society Series. Ed. Lady Simon of Wythenshawe and Others. London: Frederick Muller, 1954. Pp. viii, 128. Chap. 3 on *Antony and Cleopatra*.

B9453 Aldus, Paul J. "Analogical Probability in Shakespeare's Plays." *SQ*, VI (1955), 397-414.
Comment by L. J. Mills and answer by P. J. Aldus, *SQ*, VII (1956), 133-134.

B9454 MacLure, Millar. "Shakespeare and the Lonely Dragon." *UTQ*, XXIV (1955), 109-120.
Includes comments on *Antony*.

B9455 Obertello, Alfredo. "La Morte di Cleopatra in Shakespeare." *Vita e Pensiero* (Milan), XXXVIII (1955), 696-699.

B9456 Beauchamp, Virginia Walcott. *Dramatic Treatment of "Antony and Cleopatra" in the Sixteenth and Seventeenth Centuries: Variations in Dramatic Form Upon a Single Theme*. DD, University of Chicago, 1956.

B9457 Rohrmoser, Günter. "*Antonius und Cleopatra*." *Shakespeare-Tage 1956* (Bochum), pp. 1-6.

B9458 Stempel, Daniel. "The Transmigration of the Crocodile." *SQ*, VII (1956), 59-72.

B9459 Barnet, Sylvan. "Recognition and Reversal in *Antony and Cleopatra*." *SQ*, VIII (1957), 331-334.

B9460 Bowling, Lawrence E. "Duality in the Minor Characters in *Antony*." *CE*, XVIII (1957), 251-255.

B9461 Fischer, Hermann. *Interpretationskommentar zu Shakespeares "Antonius und Cleopatra."* DD, Munich, 1957. Pp. xi, 81. Handwritten.

B9462 McCollom, William G. "The Downfall of the Tragic Hero." *CE*, XIX (1957), 51-56.

B9463 Ruppel, K. H. "*Antonius und Cleopatra*. Werkgestalt und Bühnenerscheinung." *SJ*, 93 (1957), 186-195.

B9464 Warner, Alan. "A Note on *Antony and Cleopatra*." *English* XI (1957), 139-144.

B9465   Barroll, J. Leeds. "Scarrus and the Scarred Soldier." *HLQ*, XXII (1958), 31-39.

B9466   McFarland, Thomas. "Antony and Octavius." *YR*, XLVIII (1958), 204-228.

B9467   Siegel, Paul N. "Foreshadowings of Cleopatra's Death." *N &Q*, NS, V (1958), 386-387.

B9468   Wright, Austin. "*Antony and Cleopatra.*" *Shakespeare: Lectures on Five Plays*, Carnegie Institute of Technology, Department of English (1958), pp. 37-51.

B9469   Knights, L. C. *Some Shakespearean Themes*. London: Chatto & Windus, 1959. Chapter on *Antony and Cleopatra*.

(5) CHARACTERIZATION

B9470   Bradford, Gamaliel. *Elizabethan Women*. Ed. Harold Ogden White. Boston: Houghton Mifflin, 1936. Pp. 243. Chap. X: "The Serpent of Old Nile: A Study of the Cleopatra Tragedy."
         Rev: A2478.

B9471   Hodgson, G. "Enobarbus, the Enigma." *Church Quarterly Rev.*, 122 (1936), 88-99.

B9472   Soreson, C. " 'Whom Everything Becomes'." *The Silver Falcon*, New York: Hunter College, 1936, pp. 21-24.

B9473   Boas, G. "The Influence of the Boy-actor in Shakespeare's Plays." *ConR*, 152 (1937), 69-77.

B9474   Buck, Eva. "Cleopatra, eine Charakterdeutung: Zur Interpretation von Shakespeares *Antony and Cleopatra.*" *SJ*, LXXIV (1938), 101-122.

B9475   Tourneur, Z. "Le nez de Cléopâtre." *MdF*, XLIX (1938), 344-357.

B9476   Urban, Wilhelm. *Die Dämonische Persönlichkeit des Antonius in Shakespeares "Antony and Cleopatra.*" DD, Marburg, 1940. Pp. v, 64.

B9477   Kirschbaum, Leo. "Shakespere's Cleopatra." *SAB*, XIX (1944), 161-171.

B9478   Griffiths, G. S. "*Antony and Cleopatra.*" *Essays and Studies by Members of the English Assoc.*, XXXI, 1945. Coll. by V. de Sola Pinto. Oxford: Clarendon Press, 1946, pp. 34-67.

B9479   Hillemann, Felix. *Shakespeares Kleopatra (in "Antony and Cleopatra"). Ein Entwurf ihrer Problemeinheit*. DD, Marburg, 1946. Pp. vi, 59.

B9480   Wilson, Elkin Calhoun. "Shakespeare's Enobarbus." *AMS*, pp. 391-408.

B9481   Bacon, Wallace A. "The Suicide of Antony in *Antony and Cleopatra*, Act IV, Scene xiv." *SAB*, XXIV (1949), 193-202.

B9482   Glover, Allison. *A Survey of Shakespeare's Cleopatra*. MA thesis, University of North Carolina, 1948. Abstr. Publ. in *Univ. of North Carolina Record, Research in Progress*, Grad. School Series No. 56, 1949, pp. 207.

B9483   Berkeley, David S. "Antony, Cleopatra, and Proculeius." *N &Q*, 195 (1950), 534-535.

B9484   Simpson, Lucie. "Shakespeare's Cleopatra." *The Secondary Heroes of Shakespeare and Other Essays*. London: Kingswood Press, 1950, pp. 27-37.

B9485   Phillips, Allen C. *A Critical History of Marc Antony (in Shakespeare's "Antony and Cleopatra")*. MA thesis, University of North Carolina, 1951. Abstr. publ. in *Univ. of North Carolina Record, Research in Progress*, Grad. School Series No. 62, 1951, p. 126.

B9486   Druhman, Rev. Alvin W. *An Analysis of Four of the Level-of-Life Characters in Shakespeare's Tragedies*. DD, St. John's University, 1952. Abstr. publ. in *Abstracts of Dissertations, 1951-1952*, Brooklyn: St. John's Univ., 1952, pp. 14-15.
         Horatio, Enobarbus, Kent, and Menenius Agrippa.

B9487   Berkeley, David S. "The Crux of *Antony and Cleopatra.*" *Bull. Oklahoma A. & M. Coll.*, L (1953), 1-13.

B9488   Henderson, Archibald, Jr. *Family of Mercutio*. DD, Columbia University, 1954. Pp. 270. Mic A54-2044. *DA*, XIV (1954), 1395. Publ. No. 8684.

B9489   Berkeley, David. "On Oversimplifying Antony." *CE*, XVII (1955), 96-99.
         Comment by Frank S. Hook, *CE*, XVII, 365-366. Berkeley's "Rejoinder," *CE*, XVIII, 286-287.

B9490   Cunningham, Dolora G. "The Characterization of Shakespeare's Cleopatra." *SQ*, VI (1955), 9-17.

B9491   Donno, Elizabeth Story. "Cleopatra Again." *SQ*, VII (1956), 227-233.
         On B9490.

B9492   Hayashi, Shigeko. "*Antony and Cleopatra.*" *Studies in English and American Literature* (Tokyo Christian Woman's Univ.), IV, No. 1 (1956).

B9493   Nosworthy, James M. "Symbol and Character in *Antony and Cleopatra.*" *ShN*, VII (1957), 4.

B9494   Stull, Joseph S. "Cleopatra's Magnanimity: the Dismissal of the Messenger." *SQ*, VII (1956), 73-78.

B9495   Bowman, Thomas D. "Antony and the 'Lass Unparalleled'." *ShN*, VII (1957), 47.

B9496   Barroll, J. Leeds. "Antony and Pleasure." *JEGP*, LVII (1958), 708-720.

(6) MISCELLANEOUS ITEMS

B9497   Jenkin, Bernard. "*Antony and Cleopatra:* Some Suggestions on the Monument Scenes." *RES*, XXI (1945), 1-14.

B9498 Camden, Carroll. "Elizabethan Chiromancy." *MLN*, LXII (1947), 1-7.

B9499 Brown, Ivor. "The Two Cleopatras." *TAr*, XXXV (Dec., 1951), 10-11, 71.

B9500 Cancelled.

B9501 Garçon, Maurice, ed. *Plaidoyers Chimériques*. Paris: Fayard, 1954. Pp. 169.
Rev: B4170.

B9502 Brown, Ivor. *Dark Ladies*. London: Collins, 1956. Pp. 320.
"Cleopatra," pp. 160-252.
Rev: B4162.

(7) SUBSEQUENT HISTORY OF THE PLAY
(Other than productions after 1660)

B9503 Wallerstein, Ruth. "Dryden and the Analysis of Shakespeare's Techniques." *RES*, XIX (1943), 165-185.

B9504 Lill, James V. *Dryden's Adaptation from Milton, Shakespeare and Chaucer*. DD, University of Minnesota, 1954. Pp. 284. Mic A54-1780. *DA*, XIV (1954), 1214. Publ. No. 8462.

B9505 Hilpert, Heinz. "*Antonius und Cleopatra*—Heute." *Blätter d. Deutschen Theaters in Göttingen* (Göttingen), Heft 89 (1955-1956).

CORIOLANUS (251;90)
(1) THE TEXT
(a) OLD TEXTS

B9506 Harrison, G. B. "A Note on *Coriolanus*." *AMS*, pp. 239-252.

B9507 Gilman, Albert. *Textual and Critical Problems in Shakespeare's "Coriolanus."* DD, University of Michigan, 1954. Pp. 271. Mic A54-969. *DA*, XIV (1954), 673-674. Publ. No. 7652.

(b) MODERN EDITIONS

B9508 *The Tragedy of Coriolanus*. Ed. Dr. Geo. Kohlmann. Frankf. a/M.: Diesterweg, 1939. Pp. 147.

B9509 *The Tragedy of Coriolanus*. Harmondsworth: Penguin Books, 1947. Pp. 158.
Rev: *TLS*, Oct. 4, 1947, p. 511.

B9510 *Scenes from "Coriolanus."* Ed. Josef Raith. Huebers Fremdsprachl. Texte, 10. Munich: Hueber, 1949. Pp. 31.

B9511 *Coriolanus*. Ed. B. H. Kemball-Cook. New Clarendon Shakespeare Series. Oxford, 1954. Pp. 254.
Rev: by Robert H. Goldsmith, *SQ*, VI (1955), 471; *ShN*, V, 22.

B9512 *Coriolanus*. Ed. Harry Levin. Pelican Shakespeare. Baltimore: Penguin Books, 1956. Pp. 164.

B9513 *Coriolanus*. Ed. V. de Sola Pinto. London: Macmillan, 1957. Pp. xxi, 197.

B9514 *Coriolanus*. Ed. John Dover Wilson. Cambridge Pocket Shakespeare. Cambridge Univ. Press, 1958. Pp. 159.

(c) EMENDATIONS

B9515 Crundell, H. W. "On Three Passages of Shakespeare." *N&Q*, 172 (1937), 331-332.
Cor., IV. vii. 31-57.

B9516 King, A. H. "Notes on *Coriolanus*." *ES*, XIX (1937), 13-20.

B9517 Visser, F. Th. "Two Remarkable Constructions in Shakespeare." *Neophil*, XXX (1946), 37-43.
Cor., IV. vi. 35.

B9518 Roussel, L. "Shakespeare's Greek." *TLS*, Feb. 2, 1946, p. 55. Comments by D. Koffler, ibid., p. 91 and p. 115; by R. L. Eagle, ibid., p. 127.

B9519 Berryman, John. "Shakespeare's Greek." *TLS*, March 13, 1946, p. 151.

B9520 Quincey, A. de "Shakespeare's Greek." *TLS*, April 27, 1946, p. 199.

B9521 Eardley-Wilmot, H. "*Coriolanus*." *TLS*, Oct. 13, 1950, p. 645.
Comment by A. P. Rossiter, ibid., Oct. 20, p. 661.
III. i. 304-306.

B9522 Hunter, G. K. "Shakespeare's Hydra." *N&Q*, 198 (1953), 100-101.
III. i. 89-99.

B9523 Maxwell, J. C. "Menenius' Fable." *N&Q*, 198 (1953), 329.
I. i. 134.

B9524 Hulme, Hilda. "Three Notes on the Pronunciation and Meanings of Shakespeare's Text: *Let him be made an Ouerture for th' Warres (Coriolanus*, I. ix. 46); *And either the deuill, or throwe him out (Hamlet*, III. iv. 169); *A whole Armado of conuicted saile (King John*, III. iv. 2)." *Neophil*, XLI (1957), 275-281.

B9525 Purcell, J. M. "Shakespeare's *Coriolanus*, III. i. 101." *Expl.*, XV, vi (1957), item 36.

(2) LITERARY GENESIS AND ANALOGUES

B9526   Scott, John A. "An Unnoticed Homeric Phrase in Shakespeare." [*Coriolanus*, IV. vi. 144.] *Classical Philology*, XXXIII (1938), 414.

B9527   Heuer, Hermann. "Shakespeare und Plutarch. Studien zu Wertwelt und Lebensgefühl im *Coriolanus*." *Anglia*, LXII (1938), 321-346.

B9528   Elton, William. "Two Shakesperian Parallels." *SAB*, XXII (1947), 115-116. *Cor.*, I. i. 95-159.

B9529   Lees, F. N. "*Coriolanus*, Aristotle, and Bacon." *RES*, NS, I (1950), 114-125.

B9530   Muir, Kenneth. "Menenius's Fable." *N &Q*, 198 (1953), 240-242. See letter by J. C. Maxwell, ibid., p. 329.

B9531   Heuer, Hermann. "From Plutarch to Shakespeare: A Study of *Coriolanus*." *ShS*, X (1957), 50-59. Abstr. in *ShN*, VI (1956), 20.

(3) USE OF LANGUAGE

B9532   Nottrott, Marianne. *Der Formale Gebrauch des Epithetons in Shakespeares Dramen "Othello," "King Lear," "Macbeth" und "Coriolanus."* DD, Leipzig, 1922. Pp. vi, 254. Handwritten. Publ. *Jahrbuch der Philosophischen Fakultät Leipzig*, I (1923).

B9533   Burre, H. "Coriolan und Menenius in Sprachlich-Stilistischer Deutung." *ZNU*, XXXVI (1937), 162-169.

B9534   Traversi, D. A. "*Coriolanus*." *Scrutiny*, VI (1937), 43-58.

B9535   Traversi, D. A. "*Coriolanus*." *Critiques and Essays in Criticism, 1920-1948.* New York: Ronald Press, 1949, pp. 141-153.

B9536   Granville-Barker, Harley. "Verse and Speech in *Coriolanus*." *RES*, XXIII (1947), 1-15.

B9537   Maxwell, J. C. "Animal Imagery in *Coriolanus*." *MLR*, XLII (1947), 417-421.

B9538   Ellis-Fermor, Una. "Some Functions of Verbal Music in Drama." *SJ*, 90 (1954), 37-48.

B9539   Dean, Leonard F. "Voice and Deed in *Coriolanus*." *Univ. of Kansas City Review*, XXI (1955), 177-184.

B9540   Charney, Maurice. "The Dramatic Use of Imagery in Shakespeare's *Coriolanus*." *ELH*, XXIII (1956), 183-193.

B9541   M. Clarita Felhoelter, Sister, O. S. U. *Proverbialism in "Coriolanus".* DD, Catholic University of America, 1956. Abstracted by Jack R. Brown, *ShN*, VII (1957), 12.

B9542   Heerwagen, H. "Shakespeares *Coriolanus* als Beitrag zur Führerfrage." *Politische Erziehung Monatsschr. d. NS.-Lehrerbundes, Gauverb. Sachsen.* Beilage: Die Höhere Schule, 1936, pp. 241-247.

(4) GENERAL CRITICISM OF THE PLAY

B9543   Pongs, H. "Shakespeare und das Politische Drama." *DuV*, XXXVII (1936), 257-280.

B9544   Zucker, A. E. "Ibsen, Hettner, *Coriolanus*, *Brand*." *MLN*, LI (1936), 99-106.

B9545   Lacy, E. W. *Justice in Shakespeare.* DD, Vanderbilt University, 1937. Abstr. publ. in *Bull. of Vanderbilt Univ.*, XXXVII (1937), 42.

B9546   Rieschel, H. "Das Tragische Geschehen im *Coriolanus*." *Junge Geisteswissenschaft. Arbeiten junger Göttinger Germanisten. Festgabe zur 200-Jahrfeier der Georgia Augusta.* Göttingen: Turm Verlag, 1937, pp. 21-22.

B9547   Hodgson, G. "*Coriolanus* and Shakespeare's Tragic Course." *The Church Quarterly Review*, 117 (1938), 292-303.

B9548   Knight, G. Wilson. *The Imperial Theme.* Further Interpretation of Shakespeare's Tragedies including the Roman Plays. Oxford Univ. Press, 1939. Pp. 376.
            Rev: A8258.

B9549   Krieger, H. "Shakespeares *Coriolan* und Wir." *NS*, XLVII (1939), 131-147.
            "Gewiss hat Nietzsches Philosophie der grossen Personlichkeit im Führergedanken des Nationalsozialismus weitgehende Parallelen. . . Coriolan ähnelt in vielen dem Herrenmenschen Nietzschescher Prägung aber aus ganz anderen Boden, und darauf kann bei der Durchnahme in der Klasse gar nicht nachdrücklich genug hingewiesen werden. Dann wird die Antwort auf die Frage: Shakespeares Coriolan und wir auch zugleich eine Antwort werden auf die Frage: Nietzsche und Wir." See B9572 and B9578.

B9550   Salter, C. H. "Poetry and Politics." *Poetry Review*, XXX (1939), 345-361.

B9551   Palmer, John. *Political Characters of Shakespeare.* London: Macmillan, 1945. Pp. xii, 335.
            Rev: A6550a.

B9552   Granville-Barker, Harley. *Prefaces to Shakespeare.* 2 Vols. Princeton Univ. Press, 1946, 1947. Vol. II includes B9553.
            Rev: A8201.

B9553   Granville-Barker, Harley. "*Coriolanus*." *Prefaces to Shakespeare.* Fifth Series. London: Sidgwick & Jackson, 1948. Pp. viii, 195.
            Rev: by H. B. Charlton, *MGW*, March 4, 1948, p. 11; by George Rylands, *NstN*, Feb. 21, p. 157; by Desmond MacCarthy, *Sun. Times*, Feb. 22, p. 3 and ibid., Feb. 29, p. 3; *TLS*,

April 3, p. 194; *TLS*, Feb. 12, 1949, p. 107; by Robert M. Smith, *SAB*, xxiv, 291-293; by
J. Vallette, *MdF*, 305 (1949), 535-537.

B9554   Kirschbaum, Leo. "Shakespeare's Stage Blood and Its Critical Significance." *PMLA*, LXIV
(1949), 517-529.

B9555   Shanker, Sidney. "Some Clues for *Coriolanus*." *SAB*, xxiv (1949), 209-213.
The play considered in relation to the grain riots of 1607-1608. The poor died in the streets in
lots up to 16 for want of bread. The worst riots were in Warwickshire in 1607. See B9598.

B9556   Murry, John Middleton. *John Clare and Other Studies*. London: Nevill, 1950. Pp. 252.
Cor., pp. 222-245.

B9557   Pettet, E. C. "*Coriolanus* and the Midlands Insurrection of 1607." *ShS*, III (1950), 34-42.

B9558   Honig, Edwin. "*Sejanus* and *Coriolanus*: A Study in Alienation." *MLQ*, XII (1951), 407-421.

B9559   Lehman, Alan D. *The Coriolanus Story Through the Ages*. DD, State University of Iowa, 1951.

B9560   Knights, L. C. "Shakespeare and Political Wisdom: A Note on the Personalism of *Julius
Caesar* and *Coriolanus*." *SR*, LXI (1953), 43-55.

B9561   Rosati, Salvatore. "Il *Coriolano* di Shakespeare." *Nuova Antologia* (Rome), No. 1856 (1953),
427-444.

B9562   Gilman, Albert. *Textual and Critical Problems in Shakespeare's "Coriolanus."* DD, University
of Michigan, 1954. Pp. 271. Mic A54-969. *DA*, XIV (1954), 673-674. Publ. No. 7652.

B9563   Knights, Lionel Charles. *Poetry, Politics and the English Tradition*. London: Chatto & Windus,
1954. Pp. 32.

B9564   Enright, D. J. "*Coriolanus*: Tragedy or Debate?" *EIC*, IV (1954), 1-19. Repr. in Enright's
The Apothecary's Shop. London: Secker & Warburg, 1957, pp. 32-53.

B9565   Michel, Laurence. "Yardsticks for Tragedy." *EIC*, V (1955), 81-88.
Partly on B9564.

B9566   MacLure, Millar. "Shakespeare and the Lonely Dragon." *UTQ*, xxiv (1955), 109-120.

B9567   Brittin, Norman A. "Coriolanus, Alceste, and Dramatic Genres." *PMLA*, LXXI (1956),
799-807.

B9568   Carrington, Norman Thomas. *Shakespeare: "Coriolanus."* Notes on Chosen English Texts.
London: Brodie, 1956. Pp. 105.

B9569   Knights, Lionel Charles. "Beyond Politics: An Aspect of Shakespeare's Relation to Tradition." Abstr. of a lecture. *ShN*, VI (1956), 14.

B9570   Hofling, Charles K. "An Interpretation of Shakespeare's *Coriolanus*." *American Imago*, XIV
(1957), 407-435.

B9571   Vecchi, V. "*Coriolan*, Fuori della Confusione." *Il Dramma* (Turin) No. 255 (1957).

B9572   Dort, Bernard. "*Coriolan*, Pièce Fasciste?" *Théâtre Populaire* (Paris), No. 29 (1958). See
also B9548 and B9578.

B9573   Habart, Michel. "Clés pour *Coriolan*." *Europe* (Paris) No. 347 (1958), 103-113.

B9574   Sen, Sailendra Kumar. "What Happens in *Coriolanus*." *SQ*, IX (1958), 331-345.

B9575   Knights, L. C. *Some Shakespearean Themes*. London: Chatto & Windus, 1959.

(5) CHARACTERIZATION

B9576   Towne, Jackson Edmund. "A Psychoanalytic Study of Shakespeare's *Coriolanus*." *Psychoanalytic Review*, VIII (1921), 84-91.

B9577   Glen, Enid. "A Note on *Coriolanus*." *N &Q*, 174 (1938), 347.

B9578   Heuer, Hermann. "Shakespeare und Plutarch: Studien zu Wertwelt und Lebensgefühl im
Coriolanus." *Anglia*, LXII (1938), 321-346.
"Die Charakterdiagnose führt zum 'Charakterproblem.' Der Charakter tritt in das Dämmerlicht
der Spekulation, er gehört einem Raume dunkler metaphysischer Verbundenheit mit an.
Germanisch-nordische Welt metaphysischer Daseinsdeutung öffnet ihre Tore." See also
B9549 and B9572.

B9579   Draper, John W. "Shakespeare's *Coriolanus*: A Study in Renaissance Psychology." *West
Virginia Univ. Bull.*, Sept., 1939, pp. 22-36.

B9580   Brown, D. " 'My Gracious Silence!' " *SAB*, xv (1940), 55-56.

B9581   Goll, A. "*Coriolan*, Shakespeare's Tragedy." *Gads Danske Magasin* (Copenhagen) XXVIII
(1939), 333-368.

B9582   Franke, Hans. "Vier Arten des heldischen Menschen. Zur Dramaturgie des Charakters."
Dts. Dramaturgie, Zs. für die Probleme der Darstellenden Künste, I (1942), 107-110.

B9583   Campbell, Oscar James. *Shakespeare's Satire*. Oxford Univ. Press, 1943. Pp. 227.
Rev: B5164.

B9584   Burns, Winifred. "The Character of Marcius Coriolanus." *Poet Lore*, LII (1946), 31-48

B9585   Trilling, Lionel. "Freud and Literature." *Horizon*, XVI (1947), 182-200. Also in *The Liberal
Imagination*, New York: The Viking Press, 1950, pp. 34-57.
Suggests *Cor.* deals with Oedipus motive. See B9576.
Rev: A1334.

B9586   Harrison, G. B. "A Note on *Coriolanus*." *AMS*, pp. 239-252.

B9587   Jorgensen, Paul A. "Shakespeare's *Coriolanus*: Elizabethan Soldier." *PMLA*, LXIV (1949), 221-235.

B9588   Schartle, Patty McFarland. *Aristocratic "Coriolanus": A Study in Shakespearean Criticism*. MA thesis, University of North Carolina, 1946. Abstr. publ. in *Univ. of North Carolina Record, Research in Progress*, Grad. School Series No. 56, 1949, pp. 228.

B9589   Druhman, Rev. Alvin W. *An Analysis of Four of the Level-of-life Characters in Shakespeare's Tragedies*. DD, St. John's University, 1952. Abstr. publ. in *Abstracts of Dissertations, 1951-1952*, Brooklyn: St. John's Univ., 1952, pp. 14-15.

B9590   Ribner, Irving. "The Tragedy of *Coriolanus*." *ES*, XXXIV (1953), 1-9.

B9591   Muir, Kenneth. "In Defence of the Tribunes." *EIC*, IV (1954), 331-333. Defends the behavior of the Tribunes in *Coriolanus*.

B9592   Browning, I. R. "Coriolanus: Boy of Tears." *EIC*, V (1955), 18-31.

B9593   Oliver, H. J. "Coriolanus as Stage Hero." *ShN*, VI (1956), 4. Abstr. of lecture.

B9594   Heuer, Hermann. "From Plutarch to Shakespeare: A Study of *Coriolanus*." *ShS*, X (1957), 50-59.

(6) MISCELLANEOUS ITEMS

B9595   Rank, O. "Shakespeares Vaterkomplex." *Das Inzest-Motiv in Dichtung und Sage*, Leipzig, 1912, pp. 204-233.

B9596   Bellessort, A. *Le Plaisir du Théâtre*. Paris: Perrin, 1939. Pp. 292. *Cor.*, pp. 88-94.

B9597   "Aeschylus and Shakespeare." *Ba*, XXX (1946), 45-46.

B9598   *Transactions of the Leicestershire Archaeological Society*, XXIII, Pt. 11, 1947. Bowling Green St., Leicester: W. Thornley, 1948. Pp. xl, 135-339.
Includes, i.a., transcriptions of the Leicestershire returns of the inquiry into depopulation which followed the suppression (1607) of the peasant rising at Cotesbach and Hillmorten. See B9555.

B9598a   Gould, J. D. "The Inquisition of Depopulation of 1607 in Lincolnshire." *EHR*, LXVII (1952), 392-395.

B9599   Minor, Worthington. "Shakespeare for the Millions." *TAr*, June 1951, pp. 58, 94.

B9600   Johnson, S. F. "Shakespeare Without Ear—The Protest of a Professor." *TAr*, Oct. 1951, pp. 38-39.

(7) SUBSEQUENT HISTORY OF THE PLAY
(Other than productions after 1660)

B9601   Chabrier, Victor. "*Coriolan* aux Nuits de Bendor." *CS*, No. 337 (October 1956). n.p. (B₁ recto).

B9602   Lemarchand, Jacques. "*Coriolan* à la Comédie Française." *NRF*, V (1957), No. 49, 128-132.

CYMBELINE (254;91)
(1) THE TEXT (254;91)
(a) MODERN EDITIONS

B9603   *Cymbeline*. Ed. G. Boas. Scholar's Libr. London: Macmillan, 1936.

B9604   *Cymbeline*. Ed. J. M. Nosworthy. Arden Ed. London: Methuen, 1955. Pp. lxxxiv, 224.
Rev: by Kenneth Muir, *London Mag.*, II, No. 6 (1955), 104-106, 108; by C. G. Thayer, *Books Abroad*, XXIX, 471; by Patrick Cruttwell, *EIC*, V, 382-390; *Dublin Mag.*, XXXI, No. 2, 45; by Hermann Heuer, *SJ*, 91 (1955), 337-340; *Adelphi*, XXXI, No. 3, 310-311; by W. M. T. Nowottny, *MLR*, L, 327-330; *TLS*, March 4, p. 139; *English*, X, 157; *The Statesman* (Delhi and Calcutta), May 8, p. 15; by J. Vallette, *MdF*, 324 (1955), 530-531; by C. Devlin, *Month*, NS, XIV, 110-111; by Pat M. Ryan, Jr., *QJS*, XLII (1956), 84-86; by Moody E. Prior, *SQ*, VII, 111-113; by Augusto Guidi, *Idea* (Rome), VIII, No. 24 (June 10), 4; by James G. McManaway, *ShS*, IX, 151-152; by G. Bullough, *RES*, VIII (1957), 432-434; by Edward Hubler, *JEGP*, LVI, 269-274.

B9605   *The Tragedy of Cymbeline*. Ed. G. B. Harrison. Penguin Shakespeare. Harmondsworth: Penguin Books, 1957. Pp. 160.
Rev: *TLS*, June 21, 1957, (p. 387).

(b) EMENDATIONS

B9606   Cuningham, Henry. "*Cymbeline*, III. v. 70-74." *TLS*, Nov. 13, 1937, p. 871.

B9607   Johnston, Mary. "*Cymbeline*, III. v. 70-74." *TLS*, Jan. 22, 1938, p. 60.

B9608   Tannenbaum, Samuel A. "The Jay of Italy." [*Cymbeline*, III. iv. 51.] *SAB*, XII (1937), 193-194.

B9609   Onions, C. T. " 'Sit' versus 'Fit'." *TLS*, June 21, 1941, p. 299.

B9610   Munro, John. "Some Matters Shakespearian." *TLS*, Sept 27, 1947, p. 500.

B9611   Kôkeritz, Helge. "A Biblical Echo in *Cymbeline*." *RES*, XXIII (1947), 313-314.

B9612   Main, W. W. "Shakespeare's 'Fear No More the Heat o' th' Sun'." *Expl.*, IX, v (1951), item 36.

B9612a Nolan, Edward F. "Shakespeare's *Fear No More the Heat o' th' Sun*." *Expl.*, XI, i (1952), item 4.

B9613   Phillips, George L. "Shakespeare's 'Fear No More the Heat o' th' Sun'." *Expl.* XII, i (1953), item 2.

B9614   Wheelwright, Philip. "Philosophy of the Threshold." *SR*, LXI (1953), 56-75.

B9615   Duncan-Jones, E. E. " 'Forlorn' in *Cymbeline* and *I Henry VI*." *N &Q*, NS, IV (1957), 64.

(2) LITERARY GENESIS AND ANALOGUES

B9616   Knight, G. Wilson. "The Vision of Jupiter in *Cymbeline*." *TLS*, Nov. 21, 1936, p. 958.

B9617   Evans, Dorothy Atkinson. "Some Notes on Shakespeare and *The Mirror of Knighthood*." *SAB*, XXI (1946), 161-167; XXII (1947), 62-68.

B9618   Fox, Gladys. *Studies in the Composition of Shakespeare's "King Lear," "Macbeth" and "Cymbeline."* DD, University of Texas, 1946.

B9619   Koenig, V. Frederic. "A New Perspective on the Wager Cycle." *MP*, XLIV (1946), 76-83.

B9620   Nosworthy, J. M. "The Sources of the Wager Plot in *Cymbeline*." *N &Q*, 197 (1952), 93-96.

B9621   Kane, Robert J. " 'Richard du Champ' in *Cymbeline*." *SQ*, IV (1953), 206-207.

B9622   Wright, H. G. "How Did Shakespeare Come to Know the *Decameron?*" *MLR*, L (1955), 45-48.

B9623   Nitze, William A. "On the Derivation of Old French Enygeus (Welsh *Innogen*, Shakespeare *Imogen*)." *Zs. f. Franz. Sprache u. Lit.*, LXVI (1956), 40-42.

B9624   Hoeniger, F. David. "Two Notes on *Cymbeline*." *SQ*, VIII (1957), 132-133.

B9625   Matthews, C. M. "The True *Cymbeline*." *History Today*, VII (1957), 755-759.

B9626   Wright, H. G. *Boccaccio in England, from Chaucer to Tennyson*. The Athlone Press: Univ. of London, 1957.
        Rev: A4487.

(3) USE OF LANGUAGE

B9627   Stephenson, A. A. "The Significance of *Cymbeline*." *Scrutiny*, X (1942), 329-338.

B9628   Leavis, F. R. "The Criticism of Shakespeare's Late Plays: A Caveat." *Scrutiny*, X (1942), 339-345.
        In part answer to B9627.

B9629   Nosworthy, J. M. "The Integrity of Shakespeare: Illustrated from *Cymbeline*." *ShS*, VIII (1955), 52-56.

(4) GENERAL CRITICISM OF THE PLAY

B9630   Bond, R. W. "The Puzzle of *Cymbeline*." *Studia Otiosa*, 1938, pp. 69-74.

B9631   Tillyard, E. M. W. *Shakespeare's Last Plays*. London: Chatto & Windus, 1938. Pp. 85.
        Rev: B5233.

B9632   Tinkler, F. C. "*Cymbeline*." *Scrutiny*, VII (1938), 5-19.

B9633   Kemp, Robert. "En Relisant *Cymbeline*." *Le Temps*, March, 1942, pp. 28-29.

B9634   Russev, Russi. "Kum Paralelizma u Shakespeare: *Burya* i *Cymbeline*." [*The Tempest* and *Cymbeline*: A Study in Shakespeare Parallelism.] *Godšinik na Sofiiskiya Universitet, Istoriko-filologičeski Fakultet (Annuaire de l'Université de Sofia, Faculté Historico-philologique)*, XLI (1945), 1-8.

B9635   Granville-Barker, Harley. *Prefaces to Shakespeare*. 2 Vol. Princeton Univ. Press, 1946, 1947.
        Rev: A8201.

B9636   Knight, G. Wilson. *The Crown of Life: Interpretation of Shakespeare's Final Plays*. Oxford Univ. Press, 1947. Pp. viii, 9-336.
        Rev: B5241.

B9637   Wilson, Harold S. "*Philaster* and *Cymbeline*." *EIE, 1951*, pp. 146-167.
        Rev: A8790.

B9638   Swander, Homer D. *The Design of "Cymbeline."* DD, University of Michigan, 1953. Pp. 244. Mic A53-1499. *DA*, XIII (1953), 814. Publ. No. 5744.

B9639   Carrington, Norman Thomas. "*Cymbeline*." Notes on Chosen Engl. Texts. London: Brodie, 1954. Pp. 79.

B9640   Fischer, Walther. "Shakespeares Späte Romanzen." *SJ*, 91 (1955), 7-24.

B9641   Guidi, Augusto. "Il *Cymbeline* di Shakespeare." *Idea*, No. 22 (May 22, 1955), 1.

B9642   Ribner, Irving. "Shakespeare and Legendary History: *Lear* and *Cymbeline*." *SQ*, VII (1956), 47-52.

B9643   Brockbank, J. P. "History and Histrionics in *Cymbeline.*" *ShS*, XI (1958), 42-49.

B9644   Stamm, Rudolf. "George Bernard Shaw and Shakespeare's *Cymbeline.*" *Baldwin Festschrift*, 1958, pp. 254-266.

B9645   Stoltzenberg, Gisela Freiin v. "Shakespeares *Cymbeline:* Versuch zur Deutung." *GRM*, VIII (1958), 46-64.

B9646   Woodruff, Neal, Jr. "*Cymbeline.*" *Shakespeare: Lectures on Five Plays.* Carnegie Institute of Technology, Department of English, 1958, pp. 53-69.

(5) CHARACTERIZATION

B9647   Brock, J. H. E. *Iago and Some Shakespearean Villains.* Cambridge: W. Heffer & Sons, 1937. Pp. viii, 48.
        Rev: A1245.

B9648   Schell, J. S. "Shakespeare's Gulls." *SAB*, XV (1940), 23-33.

B9649   Camden, Carroll. "The Elizabethan Imogen." *The Rice Institute Pamphlet*, XXXVIII (1951), 1-17.

B9650   Smith, Warren D. "Cloten with Caius Lucius." *SP*, XLIX (1952), 185-194.

B9651   Behrens, Ralph. "On Possible Inconsistencies in Two Character Portrayals in *Cymbeline.*" *N &Q*, NS, III (1956), 379-380.

B9652   Wright, Celeste Turner. "The Queen's Husband: Some Renaissance Views." *Studies in English*, III (1957), 133-138.

(6) MISCELLANEOUS ITEMS

B9653   Sachs, Hanns. "*The Tempest.*" *International Journal of Psycho-Analysis*, IV (1923), 43-88. Comments on *Cym.* also.

B9654   Thewlis, G. A. "An Unpublished Contemporary Setting of 'Hark, Hark!' " *Music and Letters*, XXII (1941), 32-35.

B9655   Evans, Willa McClung. "Shakespeare's 'Harke, Harke, Ye Larke'." *PMLA*, LX (1945), 95-101.
        Discusses Bodleian MS version of this song.

(7) SUBSEQUENT HISTORY OF THE PLAY
(Other than productions after 1660)

B9656   Shaw, Bernard. *Cymbeline Refinished.* A Variation on Shakespeare's Ending. In Shaw's *Geneva, Cymbeline Refinished and Good King Charles.* London: Constable, 1946, pp. 133-150. Also in *London Mercury*, XXXVII (1938), 373-389.

B9657   Worsley, Thomas C. "G. B. S. and *Cymbeline.*" *NstN*, XXXVIII (July 2, 1949), 11.

B9658   West, E. J. "Shaw, Shakespeare, and *Cymbeline.*" *Theatre Annual*, VIII (1950), 7-24.

THE WINTER'S TALE (255;91)
(1) THE TEXT
(a) OLD TEXTS

B9659   Bullard, J. E., and W. M. Fox. "*The Winter's Tale.*" *TLS*, March 14, 1952, p. 189.
        Suggests that the play was written and acted with a last act different from that printed in F_1.

(b) MODERN EDITIONS

B9660   "*The Winter's Tale.*" Texte Anglais. Les Classiques Pour Tous, 537. Paris: A. Hatier, 1934. Pp. 79.

B9661   *The Winter's Tale.* Harmondsworth: Penguin Books, 1947. Pp. 142.
        Rev: *TLS*, Oct. 4, 1947, p. 511.

B9662   *The Winter's Tale.* Ed. Baldwin Maxwell. Pelican Shakespeare. Baltimore: Penguin Books, 1956. Pp. 140.
        Rev: B9051.

B9663   *The Winter's Tale.* Ed. J. H. P. Pafford. Arden Shakespeare. London: Methuen, 1956.

B9664   *The Winter's Tale.* Ed. S. L. Bethell. New Clarendon Shakespeare. Oxford, 1956.
        Rev: by J. H. P. Pafford, *RES*, NS, IX (1958), 117-118; by Sears Jayne, *CE*, XX, 101-102; by Glenn H. Blayney, *SQ*, IX, 580-581.

(c) EMENDATIONS

B9665   Rashbrook, R. F. "*The Winter's Tale.*" *N &Q*, 192 (1947), 520-521.
        V. i. 58-60.

B9666   Greg, W. W. "*Hamlet* and *The Winter's Tale.*" *TLS*, April 25, 1952, p. 281.

B9667   Pafford, J. H. P. "The Unmarried Primrose." *N &Q*, NS, I (1954), 37.

(2) LITERARY GENESIS AND ANALOGUES

B9668   Taylor, George C. "Hermione's Statue Again (Shakspere's Return to Bandello)." *SAB*, XIII (1938), 82-86.

B9669   Hastings, William T. "The Ancestry of Autolycus." *SAB*, XV (1940), 253.

B9670   Hughes, Merritt Y. "A Classical vs. a Social Approach to Shakspere's Autolycus." *SAB*, XV (1940), 219-226.

B9671   Elton, William. "Two Shakespeare Parallels." *SAB*, XXII (1947), 115-116. *Winter's Tale*, IV. iv. 215-227, 309-317 with *The Four P. P.*

B9672   Bullard, J. E., and W. M. Fox. "*The Winter's Tale.*" *TLS*, March 14, 1952, p. 189. Comment by C. B. Purdom, *TLS*, March 21, 1952, p. 205; by Richard Flatter, April 4, p. 237; by W. W. Greg, April 25, p. 281; by E. P. Kuhl, May 9, p. 313.

B9673   Janson, H. W. *Apes and Ape Lore in the Middle Ages and the Renaissance.* Stud. Warburg Inst., XX. London: Warburg Inst., 1952. Pp. 384; 57 pl.
        Rev: B7312.

B9674   Bryant, J. A., Jr. "Shakespeare's Allegory: *The Winter's Tale.*" *SR*, LXIII (1955), 202-222.

B9675   Honigmann, E. A. J. "Secondary Sources of *The Winter's Tale.*" *PQ*, XXXIV (1955), 27-38.

B9676   Künstler, Ernst. "Julio Romano im Wintermärchen." *SJ*, 92 (1956), 291-298.

(3) USE OF LANGUAGE

B9677   Griffin, William J. "Names in *The Winter's Tale.*" *TLS*, June 6, 1936, p. 480.

B9678   Allen, P. "Names in *The Winter's Tale.*" *TLS*, July 18, 1936, p. 600.

B9679   Mahood, M. M. *Shakespeare's Word Play.* London: Methuen, 1956. Chapter on *Winter's Tale*.
        Rev: A5815.

B9680   Berry, Francis. *Poets' Grammar.* London: Routledge and Kegan Paul, 1958. Pp. 190.
        Rev: A5230.

(4) GENERAL CRITICISM OF THE PLAY

B9681   Tinkler, F. C. "*The Winter's Tale.*" *Scrutiny*, V (1937), 344-364.

B9682   Tillyard, E. M. W. *Shakespeare's Last Plays.* London: Chatto & Windus, 1938. Pp. 85.
        Rev: B5233.

B9683   Bethell, Samuel Leslie. "*The Winter's Tale*": *A Study.* London: Staples Press, 1947. Pp. 128.
        Rev: by J. H. P. Pafford, *RES*, XXIV (1948), 329-330; by J. H. Walter, *MLR*, XLIII, 414-415; by L. Reynolds, *The Bell*, XV, 64-66; *TLS*, Feb. 12, 1949, p. 107.

B9684   Knight, G. Wilson. *The Crown of Life: Interpretation of Shakespeare's Final Plays.* Oxford Univ. Press, 1947. Pp. viii, 9-336.
        Rev: B5241.

B9685   Hoeniger, F. David. "The Meaning of *The Winter's Tale.*" *UTQ*, XX (1950), 11-26.

B9686   Bonjour, Adrien. "The Final Scene of *The Winter's Tale.*" *ES*, XXXIII (1952), 193-208.

B9687   Kuhl, E. P. "*The Winter's Tale.*" *TLS*, May 9, 1952, p. 313.

B9688   Fischer, Walther. "Shakespeares Späte Romanzen." *SJ*, 91 (1955), 7-24.

B9689   Carrington, Norman Thomas. *Shakespeare: "The Winter's Tale."* Notes on Chosen English Texts Series. London: Brodie, 1956. Pp. 80.

B9690   Luserke, Martin. *Pan—Apollon—Prospero. "Ein Mittsommernachtstraum," "Die Winterssage" und "Der Sturm."* Zur Dramaturgie von Shakespeare-Spielen. Hamburg, 1957.

B9691   Nathan, Norman. "Widowers and Their Wife's Funeral." *N &Q*, NS, IV (1957), 458.

B9692   Coghill, Nevill. "Six Points of Stage-Craft in *The Winter's Tale.*" *ShS*, XI (1958), 31-41.

(5) CHARACTERIZATION

B9693   Brandl, A. "Das Söhnchen des Leontes." In Brandl's *Forschungen und Charakteristiken* (Berlin), 1936, pp. 173-174. First publ. in *Blätter des Dts. Theaters*, IV, No. 50.

B9694   Sleeth, C. R. "Shakespeare's Counsellors of State." *RAA*, XIII (1936), 97-113.

B9695   Dodds, M. H. "The Age of Shakespeare's Characters." *N &Q*, 177 (1939), 197.

B9696   White, Christine. "A Biography of Autolycus." *SAB*, XIV (1939), 158-168.

B9697   Siegel, Paul N. "Leontes a Jealous Tyrant." *RES*, NS, I (1950), 302-307.

B9698   Simpson, Lucie. "Paulina in *The Winter's Tale.*" *The Secondary Heroes of Shakespeare and Other Essays.* London: Kingswood Press, 1950, pp. 119-128.

B9699   Trienens, Roger J. "The Inception of Leontes' Jealousy in *The Winter's Tale.*" *SQ*, IV (1953), 321-326.

B9700   Geyer, Horst. *Dichter des Wahnsinns. Eine Untersuchung über die Dichterische Darstellbarkeit Seelischer Ausnahmezustände.* Göttingen: Musterschmidt, 1955. Chapter 11. "Eifersuchts-wahn. Shakespeares Leontes und Othello," pp. 178-196; 282-295.
        Rev: A1375.

(6) MISCELLANEOUS ITEMS

B9701 Sachs, Hanns. "*The Tempest.*" *International Journal of Psycho-Analysis*, IV (1923), 43-88.
Comments on *Winter's Tale* also.

B9702 Baughan, Denver Ewing. "Shakespeare's Probable Confusion of the Two Romanoes."
JEGP, XXXVI (1937), 35-39.

B9703 Eagle, R. L. "The Oracle in *The Winter's Tale.*" *N &Q*, 180 (1941), 135.

B9704 Wilson, Harold S. " 'Nature and Art' in *Winter's Tale* (IV. iv. 86ff)." *SAB*, XVIII (1943),
114-120.

B9705 Chase, Stanley P., and George H. Quinby. "A Prologue for *The Winter's Tale*, Acts IV and V."
SAB, XX (1945), 134-139.

B9706 Spencer, Terence. "Shakespeare's Isle of Delphos." *MLR*, XLVII (1952), 199-202.

B9707 Arnold, P. "Esotérisme du *Conte d'Hiver.*" *MdF*, 318 (July, 1953), 494-512.

B9708 Künstler, Ernst. "Böhmen am Meer." *SJ*, 91 (1955), 212-216.

B9709 Cutts, John P. "An Unpublished Contemporary Setting of a Shakespeare Song." *ShS*, IX
(1956), 86-89.

B9710 Driver, Tom Faw. *The Sense of History in Greek and Shakespearean Dramatic Form.* DD,
Columbia University, 1957. Pp. 397. Mic 57-2807. *DA*, XVII (1957), 1748. Publ. No. 21,781.

B9711 Truesdale, Calvin William. *English Pastoral Verse From Spenser to Marvell: A Critical Revalua-
tion.* DD, University of Washington, 1956. Pp. 342. Mic 57-1737. *DA*, XVII (1957), 1087.
Publ. No. 20,402.
Abstract mentions *Winter's Tale.*

(7) SUBSEQUENT HISTORY OF THE PLAY
(Other than productions after 1660)

B9712 Legouis, Pierre. "La Mort de Cléomène. Sujet de Tragédie au XVIe Siècle." *LanM*, XLV
(1951), 121-134.
Starts with *Winter's Tale* and continues through Dryden.

THE TEMPEST (256;92)
(1) THE TEXT
(a) MODERN EDITIONS

B9713 *The Tempest.* Ed. George Lyman Kittredge. Boston: Ginn, 1939. Pp. xxi, 173.
Rev: by William T. Hastings, *SRL*, Aug. 19, 1939, p. 13; by Robert Adger Law, *JEGP*,
XXXIX (1940), 578-581.

B9714 *The Tempest.* Ed. J. B. Sutherland. New Clarendon Shakespeare. London, New York:
Oxford Univ. Press, 1939.
Rev: by Max Priess, *Eng. Studn.*, LXXV (1942/43), 361-363.

B9715 "*Tempest.*" Ed. P. A. Gasper. London, 1940. Pp. 88.

B9716 *The Tempest: A Comedy.* Ed. Alfred Harbage. Crofts Classics. New York: Crofts, 1946.
Pp. xi, 84.

B9717 *The Tempest.* With 29 Drawings by Willy Baumeister. 500 Numbered and Signed Copies.
Stuttgart: Hatje, 1946/47. Pp. 85.

B9718 *The Tempest.* Ed. Frank Kermode. Arden Shakespeare. London: Methuen, 1954. Pp.
lxxxviii, 167. Revised ed., London: Methuen; Cambridge, Massachusetts: Harvard Univ.
Press, 1958.
Rev: *TLS*, July 23, 1954, p. 478; by David Hardman, *John o' London's Weekly*, LXIII, 772;
by L. H., *Dublin Magazine*, Oct.-Dec., p. 66; by John Crow, *Listener*, LII, 975-977; by J.
Vallette, *MdF*, 322 (1954), 366; by T. S. Dorsch, *YWES*, XXXV, 81-82; *QR*, 293 (1955),
131-132; by Wolfgang Clemen, *Archiv*, 192 (1955), 203-204; by Patrick Cruttwell, *EIC*, V,
382-390; by Hermann Heuer, *SJ*, 91 (1955), 336-337; by W. M. T. Nowottny, *MLR*, L,
327-330; *CE*, XVI, 258; *The Statesman* (Delhi and Calcutta), Aug. 22, p. 4; by Alice Walker,
RES, NS, VII (1956), 75-77; by Pat M. Ryan, Jr., *QJS*, XLII, 84-86; by T. M. Parrott, *JEGP*,
LV, 149-156; by Harry R. Hoppe, *SQ*, VII, 261-263; by James G. McManaway, *ShS*, IX, 151.

B9719 *The Tempest.* Ed. David Horne. Yale Shakespeare. Yale Univ. Press, 1955.

B9720 *The Tempest.* Ed. V. H. Kulkarni. With Complete Paraphrase Printed Opposite to the Text.
Bombay: Booksellers' Publ. Co., 1955. Pp. 278.

B9721 *The Tempest.* Ed. S. C. Sen Gupta. Calcutta: A. Mukherjee and Co., Ltd., n.d. (1955?).

B9722 *The Tempest: A Comedy.* Ed. and Illustrated by George Skillan. London: S. French, 1955.
Pp. xii, 74.

B9723 *The Tempest.* Introduction and Notes by H. J. Oldendorf and H. Arguile. Cape Town:
Maskew Miller, 1956. Pp. v, 178.

B9724 *The Tempest.* Ed. Northrop Frye. The Pelican Shakspeare. Baltimore: Penguin Books, 1958.
Rev: by W. A. Bacon, *QJS*, XLIII (1957), 308-309; by W. Dunkel, *SQ*, IX (1958), 416; by
S. Jayne, *CE*, XX (1958/59), 101-102.

(b) EMENDATIONS

B9725 Garvin, K. " 'Most Busy Lest'." *TLS*, April 25, 1936, p. 356.

B9726 Allen, Harold B. "Shakespeare's *Lay Her A-Hold*." *MLN*, LII (1937), 96-100.

B9727 Hippoclides. "My Foot." *N &Q*, 176 (1939), 426; C. Wanklyn, ibid., 177 (1939), 34.

B9728 King, A. H. "Some Notes on Shakespeare's *Tempest*." *ES*, XXII (1940), 70-74.

B9729 Rhodes, F. "The Flower to Make Cold Nymphs Chaste Crowns." *N &Q*, 180 (1941), 226.

B9730 Boas, Ralph P. "Shakespeare's *The Tempest*, V. i. 181-184." *Expl.*, II, i (1943), item 3.

B9731 Disher, M. Willson. " 'Most Busie Lest, When I Doe It' [*Tempest*, III. i. 15]." *TLS*, May 8,
       1943, p. 228. See also W. H. Moore, *TLS*, May 15, 1943, p. 235; M. W. Disher, *TLS*, May 22,
       p. 247.
       See B9733.

B9732 Harrison, Thomas P., Sr. "A Note on *The Tempest*: A Sequel." *MLN*, LVIII (1943), 422-426.

B9733 Bacon, Percy. " 'Most Busie Lest, When I Doe It'." *TLS*, Feb. 19, 1944, p. 91.
       See reply by Willson Disher, *TLS*, April 15, 1944, p. 192. Matter of B9731 reopened.

B9734 Kökeritz, Helge. "Thy Pole-Clipt Vineyard, *The Tempest*, IV. i. 68." *MLR*, XXXIX (1944),
       178-179.

B9735 Flatter, Richard. "Mad, Made, and Maid [*I Henry IV*, II. iv. 547ff]." *TLS*, Oct. 6, 1945,
       p. 475. *The Tempest*, I. ii. 424.

B9736 Harrison, Thomas P., Sr. "The 'Broom-groves' in *The Tempest* [IV. i. 66]." *SAB*, XX (1945),
       39-45.

B9737 Shaaber, M. A. " 'A Living Drollery' (*Tempest*, III. iii. 21)." *MLN*, LX (1945), 387-391.

B9738 Simpson, Percy. "The Supposed Crux in *The Tempest*." *RES*, XXII (1946), 225-226.
       On "Most Busie Lest, When I Doe It."

B9739 Bacon, Wallace A. "A Note on *The Tempest*, IV. i." *N &Q*, 192 (1947), 343-344.

B9740 Jones, H. W. "*The Tempest*, III. i. 13-17." *N &Q*, 195 (1950), 293-294.

B9741 Parsons, Howard. "Shakespeare's *Tempest*: An Emendation." *N &Q*, 194 (1949), 121-122, 303.
       I. ii. 100; V. i. 6.

B9742 Parsons, Howard. "Shakespeare's *Tempest*: A Further Emendation." *N &Q*, 194 (1949), 424.
       III. i. 9.

B9743 Parsons, Howard. "Further Emendation in *The Tempest*." *N &Q*, 195 (1950), 74-75, 294-295.
       See the letters by J. B. Whitmore, ibid., p. 195; by H. Parsons, ibid., pp. 261, 369.
       Concerns IV. i. 64 (Mr. Whitmore objects; rejoinder by Mr. Parsons); IV. i. 127, 179; V. i. 34.

B9744 Parsons, Howard. "Further Emendations in *The Tempest*." *N &Q*, 196 (1951), 54-55.
       Concerns III. iii. 73ff.; V. i. 95ff.; V. i. 141.

B9745 Cairncross, Andrew S. "*The Tempest*, III. i. 15, and *Romeo and Juliet*, I. i. 121-128." *SQ*, VII
       (1956), 448-450.

B9746 Berry, Francis. "Shakespeare's Directive to the Player of Caliban." *N &Q*, NS, IV (1957), 27.
       Preference for the original spelling of "yee" in *Temp.*, I. ii. 320.

B9747 Fox, C. A. O. "A Crux in *The Tempest*." *N &Q*, NS, IV (1957), 515-516.

B9748 Kermode, Frank. "A Crux in *The Tempest*." *TLS*, Nov. 29, 1957, p. 728.
       For F₁ reading (III. i. 16) "Most busie lest, when i doe it," proposes "Most busilest when I
       doe it." See letter by H. W. Jones (*TLS*, Dec. 6, p. 739), affirming that he had reached the
       same conclusion in *N &Q*, July 8, 1950.

B9749 Weidhorn, Manfred. "A Possible Textual Corruption in *The Tempest*." *N &Q*, NS, IV (1957),
       335.
       The lines assigned to Stephano in *Temp.*, III. ii. 14-16, should be assigned to Trinculo.

(2) LITERARY GENESIS AND ANALOGUES

B9750 Jourdain, Silvester. *A Discovery of the Barmudas Otherwise Called the Isle of Divels* (1610). Introd.
       by Joseph Q. Adams. Scholars' Facsimiles and Reprints, Third Ser., New York, 1940.

B9751 Sachs, Hanns. "*The Tempest*." *International Journal of Psycho-Analysis*, IV (1923), 43-88.

B9752 Grégoire, Henri. "L'Origine Bulgare de la *Tempête* de Shakespeare." *Actes du 4e Congrès
       Internat. d'Etudes Byzantines*. I, *Jzvestija na Bulgarskija Archeologičeski Institut*, T. 9., (1935),
       pp. 81-97. Shorter version publ. as "Source Byzantino-Bulgare de la *Tempête* de Shakespeare."
       Byzantion, IX (1934), 787-792. Abstr. publ. as "On the Source of the *Tempest* of Shakespeare."
       Comptes Rendus de l'Acc. des Inscr. et Belles-Lettr., 1935, pp. 66-67.

B9752a Grégoire, Henri. "The Bulgarian Origins of *The Tempest* of Shakespeare." *SP*, XXXVII (1940),
       236-256.

B9753 Howarth, R. G. *Shakespeare's "Tempest."* A Public Lecture Delivered for the Australian
       English Assoc., Oct. 1, 1936. Sydney: Australian English Assoc., 1936. Pp. 55. Revised
       and abridged, 1947.
          Rev: *TLS*, Oct. 9, 1937, p. 737; by Albert Eichler, *Eng. Studn.*, LXXII (1938), 406-407; by
       V. de Sola Pinto, *English*, II, 116; by Robert Withington, *MLN*, LIII, 619-623.

B9754   Currey, R. N. "Jonson and *The Tempest.*" *N &Q*, 192 (1947), 468.
Report of B9753.

B9755   Golding, L. T. *An Elizabethan Puritan*: *A. Golding*. New York: R. R. Smith, 1937. Pp. xii, 276.

B9756   Thompson, James Westfall. "A Note on *The Tempest.*" *MLN*, LII (1937), 200-201.

B9757   Hankins, John E. "Caliban the Bestial Man." *PMLA*, LXII (1947), 793-801.

B9758   Heine, Arthur. "The Influence of Environment." *SAB*, XX (1945), 77-81.
Southwark as a part of the setting in *The Tempest*.

B9759   Evans, Dorothy Atkinson. "Some Notes on Shakespeare and *The Mirror of Knighthood.*" *SAB*, XXI (1946), 161-167; ibid., XXII (1947), 62-68.

B9760   McPeek, James A. S. "The Genesis of Caliban." *PQ*, XXV (1946), 378-381.

B9761   Nosworthy, J. M. "The Narrative Sources of *The Tempest.*" *RES*, XXIV (1948), 281-294.

B9762   Wilson, Winifred Graham. "A Discovery of the Barmudas." *Life and Letters*, LVI (1948), 97-106.

B9763   Graves, Robert. "The Sources of *The Tempest.*" In Graves's *The Common Asphodel*. London, 1949, pp. 27-49.

B9764   Sanders, Charles Richard. "William Strachey, the Virginia Colony and Shakespeare." *Virginia Magazine of History and Biography*, LVII (1949), 115-132.

B9765   Waterston, G. Chychele. "Shakespeare and Montaigne: A Footnote to *The Tempest.*" *RR*, XL (1949), 165-172.
". . . not only does the commonwealth passage resemble the words of Montaigne, but . . . the passage selected by Shak. is one which epitomizes that part of M.'s philosophy which must have made the deepest impression upon Shak.'s age: his attack upon kingship and his desire to 'execute all things by contraries,' contrary, that is, to the hierarchy of the universe which was accepted at that time," p. 167.

B9766   Ashe, Geoffrey. "William Strachey." *N &Q*, 195 (1950), 508-511.
Replies by R. L. Eagle, ibid., 196 (1951), 19; Kenneth Muir, ibid., 19-20; Herbert H. Huxley, ibid., 85-86.

B9767   Johnson, W. Stacy. "Folklore Elements in *The Tempest.*" *Midwest Folklore*, I (1951), 223-228.

B9768   Johnson, W. Stacy. "The Genesis of Ariel." *SQ*, II (1951), 205-210.

B9769   Livermore, Ann. "Gil Vicente and Shakespeare." *Book Handbook*, II (1951), 1-12. Portuguese version, "Gil Vicente e Shakespeare." *Revista da Fac. de Letras* (Univ. de Lisbon), XVII, i (1951).

B9770   Hodgen, Margaret T. "Montaigne and Shakespeare Again." *HLQ*, XVI (1952), 23-42.

B9771   Macht, David I. "Biblical Allusions in Shakespeare's *The Tempest* in the Light of Hebrew Exegesis." *The Jewish Forum*, Aug., 1956, pp. 3-5.

B9772   Hart, Jeffrey P. "Prospero and Faustus." *Boston Univ. Studies in Eng.*, II (1956), 197-206.

B9773   Allen, William. "Atlantic Surprise: Cuttyhunk." *Travel*, June, 1957, p. 60.

(3) USE OF LANGUAGE

B9774   Trench, W. F. "Shakespeare's Unfinished Sentences." *TLS*, April 4, 1936, p. 300.
See letters by J. M. Nosworthy, *TLS*, March 21, 1936, p. 244, and April 25, p. 356; by Katharine Garvin, "Most Busy Lest" [*Tempest*, III. i. 15], ibid., April 25, p. 356; by Mr. Trench, ibid., May 2, p. 379, and July 25, p. 616.

B9775   Atkinson, A. D. " 'Full Fathom Five'." *N &Q*, 194 (1949), 465-468; 493-495.

B9776   Traversi, Derek. "*The Tempest.*" *Scrutiny*, XVI (1949), 127-157.

B9777   Heuer, Hermann. "Traumwelt und Wirklichkeit in der Sprache des *Tempest.*" *SJ*, 90 (1954), 210-228.

B9778   Berry, Francis. *Poets' Grammar*. London: Routledge and Kegan Paul, 1958. Pp. 190.
Rev: A5230.

(4) GENERAL CRITICISM OF THE PLAY

B9779   von Winterstein, Alfred Freiherr. "Zur Psychoanalyse des Reisens." *Imago*, I (1912), 497.

B9780   Sachs, Hanns. "*Der Sturm.*" *Imago*, V (1916), 203.

B9781   Allen, L. H. "The Hypnosis Scene in *The Tempest.*" *Australasian Journal of Psychology and Philosophy*, IV (1926), 110-118.

B9782   Wagner, Emma Brockway. *Shakespeare's "The Tempest": An Allegorical Interpretation*. Ed. from MS and Notes by H. R. Orr. Yellow Springs (Ohio): Antioch Press, 1935. Pp. viii, 133.

B9783   Wilson, J. Dover. *The Meaning of "The Tempest."* Newcastle-upon-Tyne: Lit. and Phil. Soc., 1936. Pp. 23.

B9784   Curry, Walter Clyde. *Shakespeare's Philosophical Patterns*. Louisiana State Univ. Press, 1937. Pp. xii, 244.
Rev: A931.

B9785   Ewen, C. L'Estrange. "A Criticism of *The Tempest* Wreck Scene." London: The Author, 1937.

B9786   Messiaen, Pierre. *"La Tempête* de Shakespeare." *Revue de l'Enseignement des Langues Vivantes,*
        LIV (1937), 11-15, 63-67.

B9787   Adams, John C. "The Staging of *The Tempest,* III. iii." *RES,* XIV (1938), 404-419.

B9788   Tillyard, E. M. W. *Shakespeare's Last Plays.* London: Chatto & Windus, 1938. Pp. 85.
        Rev: B5233.

B9789   Reik, Theodor. "The Way of all Flesh." *From Thirty Years with Freud.* Tr. by Richard
        Winston. New York: Farrar and Rinehart, Inc., 1940, pp. 197-212.
        Discusses death in *Hamlet* and *The Tempest.*

B9790   Stoll, Elmer Edgar. *Shakespeare and Other Masters.* Harvard Univ. Press, 1940. Pp. xv, 430.
        Rev: A8394.

B9791   Kemp, Robert. "En Relisant *La Tempête.*" *Le Temps,* March, 1942, pp. 21-22.

B9792   Prager, H. *"Der Sturm.* Musik der Menschlichkeit." *Philosophia* (Belgrade), III (1942?),
        382-401.

B9793   Sachs, Hanns. "The Unconscious in Shakespeare's *Tempest,* Analytical Considerations."
        The Creative Unconscious. Cambridge (Massachusetts): Sci-Art, 1942, pp. 289-323. 2nd ed.,
        1951.

B9794   Auden, W. H. "The Sea and the Mirror." *For the Time Being.* New York: Random House,
        1944.
        Rev: *NYTBR,* Sept. 17, 1944, p. 4.

B9795   Chambers, Sir E. K. *Shakespearean Gleanings.* Oxford Univ. Press, 1944.
        Contains "The Integrity of *The Tempest.*"
        Rev: B4466.

B9796   Gordon, George. *Shakespearian Comedy and Other Studies.* Ed. Sir Edmund Chambers. Oxford
        Univ. Press, 1944. Pp. 168.
        Rev: B5165.

B9797   Campbell, Oscar. "Miss Webster and *The Tempest.*" *Amer. Scholar,* XIV (1945), 271-281.

B9798   Merton, Stephen. *"The Tempest* and *Troilus and Cressida.*" *CE,* VII (1945), 143-150.

B9799   Russev, Russi. "Kum Paralelizma u Shakespeare: *Burya* i *Cymbeline.*" [*The Tempest* and
        Cymbeline: A Study in Shakespeare Parallelism.] *Godišnik na Sofiiskiya Universitet, Istoriko-
        filologičeski Fakultet (Annuaire de l'Université de Sofia, Faculté Historico-philologique),* XLI (1945), 1-8.

B9800   Abenheimer, K. M. "Shakespeare's *Tempest.* A Psychological Analysis." *Psychoanalytic
        Review,* XXXIII (1946), 399-415.

B9801   Munro, J. *"The Tempest.*" *New English Review,* XII (1946), 61-69.

B9802   Sharpe, Ella Freeman. "From *King Lear* to *The Tempest.*" *International Journal of Psycho-
        Analysis,* XXVII (1946). Repr. in her *Collected Papers on Psycho-Analysis.* London: Hogarth
        Press, 1950, pp. 214-241.

B9803   Braun, H. "Zu Shakespeares Sturm." *Das Goldene Tor,* II (1947), 245-255.

B9804   Friedrich, H. E. "Caliban und das Drama." *Prisma,* I (1947), Heft 7, 1-3.

B9805   Grolman, Adolf von. "Shakespeare. Der Sturm." In Grolman's *Europ. Dichterprofile.*
        Düsseldorf, 1947, pp. 21-35.

B9806   Knight, G. Wilson. *The Crown of Life: Interpretation of Shakespeare's Final Plays.* Oxford Univ.
        Press, 1947. Pp. viii, 9-336.
        Rev: B5241.

B9807   Winters, Robert Hunter. "A Student's Guide to *The Tempest.*" Sydney: Metropolitan
        Business College, 1947. Pp. 100.

B9808   Hafele, Melanie. *Gnade und Recht bei Shakespeare, Besonders Untersucht an "Mass für Mass,"
        dem "Kaufmann von Venedig," und "Sturm."* DD, Innsbruck, 1949. Pp. 129. Typewritten.

B9809   Krzyżanowski, Juliusz. "Arielowe ú Pienie." *Obdicie ze Sprawozdán Polskiej Akademii Umiej,*
        I, No. 8 (1949).

B9810   Traversi, Derek. *"The Tempest.*" *Scrutiny,* XVI (1949), 127-157.

B9811   Mitchell, Lee. "Two Notes on *The Tempest.*" *Educational Theatre Jour.,* II (1950), 228-234.

B9812   Reeg, Ludwig. *Shakespeare und die Weltordnung.* Stuttgart: Schröder, 1950. Pp. 151.

B9813   Bowling, Lawrence E. "The Theme of Natural Order in *The Tempest.*" *CE,* XII (1951), 203-209.

B9814   Draper, John W. "Humor and Tempo in *The Tempest.*" *N. Mitt.,* LII (1951), 205-217.

B9815   Sansom, Clive. *"The Tempest.*" *TLS,* Sept. 28, 1951, p. 613.
        Comment by Gwynneth Bowen, *TLS,* Oct. 5, 1951, p. 629.

B9816   Brower, Reuben Arthur. "The Heresy of Plot." *EIE, 1951,* pp. 44-69.

B9816a Brower, Reuben Arthur. "The Mirror of Analogy: *The Tempest.*" In Brower's *The Fields of
        Light: An Experiment in Critical Reading.* New York: Oxford Univ. Press, 1951, pp. 95-122.
        See also pp. 13-15 and 213-215.
        Rev: by R. Mayhead, *Scrutiny,* XIX (1952/53), 65-67.

B9817   Dobrée, Bonamy. *"The Tempest.*" *Essays and Studies,* NS, V (1952), 13-25.
        Rev: by Arnold Edinborough, *SQ,* VII (1956), 121-122.

B9818   Schröder, Rudolf Alexander. "Über Shakespeares Sturm." *Zeitwende,* XVIII (1946/47), 700-
        719. Also in Schröder's *Gesammelte Werke,* II (1952), 307-333.

B9819   Craig, Hardin. "Prospero's Renunciation." *ShN*, III (1953), 13.

B9820   Speaight, Robert. "Nature and Grace in *The Tempest*." *Dublin Review*, No. 459 (1953), 28-51.

B9821   Wilson, Harold S. "Action and Symbol in *Measure for Measure* and *The Tempest*." *SQ*, IV (1953), 375-384.

B9822   Heuschele, Otto. "Shakespeares Abschied. Gedanken über den *Sturm*." *Die neue Schau*, XV (1954), 147-148.

B9823   Knox, Bernard. "*The Tempest* and the Ancient Comic Tradition." *English Stage Comedy*. *EIE*, *1954*, pp. 52-73. See also *VQR*, XXXI (1955), 73-89, and comment, *CE*, XVI (1955), 455.
          Rev: *TLS*, Nov. 4, 1955, p. 652; by B. Dobrée, *SQ*, VII (1956), 424.

B9824   Oppel, Horst. "Die Gonzalo-Utopie in Shakespeares *Sturm*." *DVLG*, XXVIII (1954), 194-220.

B9825   Fischer, Walther. "Shakespeares Späte Romanzen." *SJ*, 91 (1955), 7-24.

B9826   Gillie, Christopher. "*The Tempest*." *The Use of English*, VII (1955), 37-41.

B9827   Speaight, Robert. *Nature in Shakespearean Tragedy*. London: Hollis and Carter, 1955. Pp. viii, 179.
          Rev: A1035.

B9828   Stroedel, Wolfgang. "Shakespeares *Sturm*." *Shakespeare-Tage* (Bochum), 1955, pp. 8-13. See also *Prisma* (Bochum), 1954/55, pp. 121-125.

B9829   Hoeniger, F. D. "Prospero's Storm and Miracle." *SQ*, VII (1956), 33-38.

B9830   Neilson, Frances (Rhadamanthus, pseudonym). *Shakespeare and the "Tempest."* New Hampshire: Richard R. Smith, 1956. Pp. 181.
          Rev: by Robert Adger Law, *SQ*, IX (1958), 412-413.

B9831   Neilson, Francis. "Shakespeare and *The Tempest*." *American Journal of Economics and Sociology*, XV (1956), 425-436; ibid., XVI (1957), 89-103; 177-193; 309-326; 421-429; ibid., XVII (1958), 321-327; 421-429.

B9832   Lowenthal, Leo. *Literature and the Image of Man: Sociological Studies of the European Drama and Novel, 1600-1900*. Boston: Beacon Press, 1957.
          Chap. III, pp. 57-97, on *The Tempest*.
          Rev: A1404.

B9833   Luserke, Martin. *Pan—Apollon—Prospero. "Ein Mittsommernachtstraum," "Die Winterssage," und "Der Sturm." Zur Dramaturgie von Shakespeare-Spielen*. Hamburg, 1957.

B9834   Summersgill, Travis. "Structural Parallels in *Eastward Ho* and *The Tempest*." *Bucknell Rev.*, April 6, 1957, pp. 24-28.

B9835   Hart, John A. "*The Tempest*." *Shakespeare: Lectures on Five Plays*. Carnegie Institute of Technology, Department of English, 1958, pp. 71-83.

B9836   Kirschbaum, Leo. "*The Tempest*—Apologetics or Spectacle?" Abstr. publ. in "Eighth International Conference at Stratford." *ShN*, VIII (1958), 4.

B9837   Lambin, G. "L'Île de Prospero ou les Faux Prodiges." *LanM*, LII (1958), 37-44.

B9838   Sisson, C. J. "The Magic of Prospero." *ShS*, XI (1958), 70-77.

B9839   Smith, Irwin. "Ariel as Ceres." *SQ*, IX (1958), 430-432.

(5)   CHARACTERIZATION

B9840   Eisler, Robert. "Der Fisch als Sexualsymbol." *Imago*, III (1914), 165-196.

B9841   Garrett, George. "That Four-Flusher Prospero." *Life and Letters Today*, XVI (1937), 21-35. Also in *Shakespeare Survey*. Eds. William Empson and George Garrett. London: Brendin, 1937. Pp. 68.

B9842   Koszul, A. "Ariel." *ES*, XIX (1937), 200-204.

B9843   Wile, Ira S. "Love at First Sight as Manifest in *The Tempest*." *American Journal of Orthopsychiatry*, VIII (1938), 341-356.

B9844   Dodds, M. H. "The Age of Shakespeare's Characters." *N&Q*, 177 (1939), 197.

B9845   McCloskey, John C. "Caliban, Savage Clown." *CE*, I (1940), 354-357.

B9846   Hankins, John E. "Caliban the Bestial Man." *PMLA*, LXII (1947), 793-801.

B9847   Schede, W. M. "Prospero. Versuch einer Deutung." *Das Goldene Tor*, II (1947), 238-244.

B9848   Cochran, Ruth Maidee. *Prospero: A Study in Shakespeare Character Criticism*. MA thesis, University of North Carolina, 1948. Abstr. publ. in *Univ. of North Carolina Record, Research in Progress*, Grad. School Series No. 56, 1949, pp. 204.

B9849   Ruegg, August. "Caliban und Miranda." *SJ*, 89 (1953), 128-131.

B9850   Durrant, G. H. "Prospero's Wisdom." *Theoria*, VII (1955), 50-58.

B9851   Bloch, Ernst. "Figuren der Grenzüberschreitung: Faust und Wette um den erfüllten Augenblick." *Sinn u. Form*, VIII (1956), 177-212. "Prospero, Grundlose Freude," pp. 205-212.

B9852   Goldsmith, Robert Hillis. "The Wild Man on the English Stage." *MLR*, LIII (1958), 481-491.

(6)   MISCELLANEOUS ITEMS

B9853   Sachs, Hanns. "Aesthetics and Psychology of the Artist." *International Journal of Psycho-Analysis*, II (1921), 98-100.

B9854   Curry, Walter Clyde. "Sacerdotal Science in Shakespeare's *The Tempest.*" *Archiv*, 168 (1935), 25-36 and 185-196.

B9855   Freeman, Bernice. "The Costumes of *Love's Labour's Lost, Twelfth Night,* and *The Tempest.*" *SAB*, xi (1936), 93-106.

B9856   Koszul, A. "*Tempest*: Bibliographie Choisie et Programme d'Etude." *Bull. de la Faculté des Lettres de Strasbourg*, xiv (1936), 251-260.

B9857   Still, Colin. *The Timeless Theme: A Critical Theory Formulated and Applied.* London: Nicholson & Watson, 1936. Pp. x, 244.
        Part II "An Interpretation of Shak.'s *Tempest,*" pp. 127-244.
        Rev: by Desmond Hawkins, *Spectator*, July 10, 1936, p. 70.

B9858   Morley, Christopher. "Shakespeare and Ivory Bomb Shelters." *SRL*, xxxiv (April 26, 1941), 3-4, 17-18.

B9859   Einstein, Alfred. "Mozart und Shakespeare's *Tempest.*" *Monatshefte*, xxxvi (1944), 43-48.

B9860   Moss, Arnold. "We are Such Stuff. . ." *TAr*, xxix (1945), 407-408.

B9861   Hartlaub, Gustav Friedrich. *Prospero und Faust. Ein Beitr. z. Problem d. Schwarzen u. Weissen Magie.* Shakespeare-Schriften, 3. Dortmund: Schwalvenberg, 1948. Pp. 32.
        Rev: A8566.

B9862   Carrère, Félix. "Le Surnaturel dans *La Tempête.*" *LanM*, July, Aug., 1950, pp. 252-257.

B9863   Polak, A. Laurence. "*The Tempest* and *The Magic Flute.*" *English*, ix (1952), 2-7.

B9864   Saito, Kinuko. "A Note on *The Tempest*—The Utopian Notion in Shakespeare." *Essays and Studies in British and American Literature*, Tokyo Woman's Christian College, i, i (Spring, 1954), 35-43 (In English).

B9865   Solem, Delmar. "Some Elizabethan Game Scenes." *ETJ*, Oct., 1954, pp. 15-21.

B9866   Truesdale, Calvin William. *English Pastoral Verse from Spenser to Marvell: A Critical Revaluation.* DD, University of Washington, 1956. Pp. 342. Mic 57-1737. *DA*, xvii (1957), 1087. Publ. No. 20,402.

B9867   Cutts, John P. "Music and the Supernatural in *The Tempest*: A Study in Interpretation." *Music and Letters*, xxxix (1958), 347-358.

(7) SYMBOLISM

B9868   Wilson, J. Dover. "The Meaning of *The Tempest.*" Newcastle-upon-Tyne: Literary and Philosophical Soc., 1936. Pp. 23.
        Rev: by C. J. Sisson, *MLR*, xxxii (1937), 332.

B9869   Bowen, G. *Shakespeare's Farewell.* Inglethorpe, Buxton, Derbyshire: The Author, 1951. Pp. 20.

(8) SUBSEQUENT HISTORY OF THE PLAY
(Other than productions after 1660)

B9870   Iacuzzi, Alfred. "The Naive Theme in *The Tempest* as a Link Between Thomas Shadwell and Ramón de la Cruz." *MLN*, lii (1937), 252-256.

B9871   Ward, Charles E. "*The Tempest*: A Restoration Opera Problem." *ELH*, xiii (1946), 119-130.

B9872   Milton, William M. "*Tempest* in a Teapot." *ELH*, xiv (1947), 207-218.

B9873   Babler, O. F. "Shakespeare's *Tempest* as an Opera." *N &Q*, 196 (1951), 30-31.

B9874   McManaway, James G., ed. "Songs and Masques in *The Tempest* (c. 1674)." Theatre Miscellany, No. 14. *Six Pieces Connected with the Seventeenth-Century Stage.* Oxford: Basil Blackwell for the Luttrell Society, 1953, pp. 69-96.
        Rev: by Harold Jenkins, *RES*, ns, vi (1955), 86-88.

B9875   Haywood, Charles. "The Songs and Masque in the *New Tempest*: An Incident in the Battle of the Two Theatres, 1674." *HLQ*, xix (1955), 39-56.
        Reports the discovery, in the Huntington Library, of this second English libretto, supporting the hypothesis of James G. McManaway, B9874.

B9876   Mannoni, O. *Prospero and Caliban: A Study of the Psychology of Colonization.* London: Methuen, 1956.
        Rev: *QR*, 610 (1956), 526.

KING HENRY VIII (259;92)
(1) TEXT
(a) OLD TEXTS

B9877   Foakes, R. A. "On the First Folio Text of *Henry VIII.*" *SB*, x (1958), 55-60.

(b) MODERN EDITIONS

B9878   *King Henry VIII.* Ed. M. St. Clare Byrne. Scholar's Libr. London: Macmillan, 1937. Pp. 205.

B9879   *King Henry VIII.* Ed. R. A. Foakes. Arden Shakespeare. London: Methuen, 1957. Pp. lxv, 215.
        Rev: *TLS*, May 17, 1957, p. 300; *SCN*, xv, 24; *N &Q*, ns, iv, 362-363; by Pat M. Ryan, Jr.,

QJS, XLIII, 312; by Hermann Heuer, *SJ*, 93 (1957), 269-270; by J. Vallette, *MdF*, 330 (1957), 710-711; *Dublin Mag.*, July-Sept., pp. 69-70; by Harold S. Wilson, *MLN*, LXXIII (1958), 292-294; by Franklin B. Williams, Jr., *MLR*, LIII, 237-238; by Baldwin Maxwell, *SQ*, IX, 400-402; *ShN*, VIII, 38; by Peter Ure, *DUJ*, L, 90-94; by Maurice Charney, *Hist. Mag. Prot. Episc. Church*, XXVII, 172-173; by G. A. Bonnard, *Erasmus*, XI, 43-46; by J. A. Bryant, *SR*, LXVI, 325.

B9880   *Henry the Eighth.* Ed. G. B. Harrison. Penguin Shakespeare. Harmondsworth: Penguin Books, 1958. Pp. 155.
         Rev: *TLS*, Feb. 21, 1958, p. 107.

(c) EMENDATIONS

B9881   Rossiter, A. P. "A Passage in *Henry VIII.*" *TLS*, July 15, 1949, p. 459.
         Maintains that I. i. 72ff. needs no emendation.

(2) LITERARY GENESIS AND ANALOGUES

B9882   Maxwell, Baldwin. *Studies in Beaumont, Fletcher, and Massinger.* Univ. North Carolina Press. 1939.
         Rev: A4866.

B9883   Wiley, Paul L. "Renaissance Exploitation of Cavendish's *Life of Wolsey.*" *SP*, XLIII (1946), 121-146.

B9884   Kermode, Frank. "What is Shakespeare's *Henry VIII* About?" *DUJ*, XL (1947), 48-55.

B9885   Partridge, A. C. *The Problem of "Henry VIII" Re-opened.* Cambridge: Bowes & Bowes, 1949. Pp. 35.
         Rev: *TLS*, Jan. 13, 1950, p. 23; by R. Walker, *English*, VIII, 144; by David L. Patrick, *SQ*, II (1951), 139-141; by Frank Kermode, *RES*, NS, II, 273-274; by R. Flatter, *SJ*, 87/88 (1952), 233.

B9886   Steiner, F. George. "A Note on Cavendish's *Life of Cardinal Wolsey.*" *English*, IX (1952/53), 51-54.

B9887   Koebner, Richard. " 'The Imperial Crown of This Realm': Henry VIII, Constantine the Great, and Polydore Vergil." *Bul. Inst. Hist. Research* (London Univ.), XXVI (1953), 29-52.

B9888   Oras, Ants. " 'Extra Monosyllables' in *Henry VIII* and the Problem of Authorship." *JEGP*, LII (1953), 198-213.

B9889   Beecham, Sir Thomas. *John Fletcher.* Romanes Lecture. Oxford: Clarendon Press, 1956. Pp. 23.

B9890   Ferguson, Charles W. *Naked to Mine Enemies.* New York: Little, Brown, 1957. Pp. 543.
         Rev: by Garrett Mattingly, *SatR*, L (Feb. 15, 1958), 24, 43; *TLS*, Nov. 21, p. 667; by Eric McDermott, *Catholic Historical Review*, XLIV, 178-179; by J. H. Hexter, *Nation*, June 21, pp. 567-568; by Crane Brinton, *NYHTBR*, Jan. 19, p. 1; by James McConica, *QQ*, LXV, 525-526; by H. C. Porter, *Canadian Forum*, XXXVIII, 21-22; by Christopher Hill, *Spectator*, Dec. 5, pp. 824-825; by Henry Drury Noyes, C.S.P., *Catholic World*, 187 (1958), 74-75; by A. L. Rowse, *NYTBR*, Jan. 19, pp. 1, 14.

B9891   Law, Robert Adger. "Holinshed and *Henry the Eighth.*" *TxSE*, XXXVI (1957), 1-11.

B9892   McManaway, James G. "A Casual Recollection of Holinshed?" *N&Q*, NS, IV (1957), 371.

(3) USE OF LANGUAGE

(4) GENERAL CRITICISM OF THE PLAY

B9893   Knight, G. Wilson. "A Note on *Henry VIII.*" *Criterion*, XV (1936), 228-236.

B9894   Wiley, Paul Luzon. *Wolsey's Career in Renaissance English Literature.* DD, Stanford University, 1944. Abstr. publ. in Stanford Univ. *Abstracts of Dissertations*, XIX (1943-44), 23-28.

B9895   Kermode, Frank. "What is Shakespeare's *Henry VIII* About?" *DUJ*, XL (1947), 48-55.

B9896   Knight, G. Wilson. *The Crown of Life: Interpretation of Shakespeare's Final Plays.* Oxford Univ. Press, 1947. Pp. viii, 9-336.
         Rev: B5241.

B9897   Parker, A. A. "Henry VIII in Shakespeare and Calderón. An Appreciation of *La Cisma de Ingalaterra.*" *MLR*, XLIII (1948), 327-352.

B9898   Waith, Eugene M. *The Pattern of Tragicomedy in Beaumont and Fletcher.* Yale Studies Eng., 120. Yale Univ. Press, 1952. Pp. xiv, 212.
         "*Henry VIII* and More Historical Tragedies," pp. 117-132.
         Rev: A6894.

(5) CHARACTERIZATION

B9899   Oman, C. W. C. "The Personality of Henry VIII." *QR*, 269 (1937), 88-104.

B9900   Walleser, Joseph G. "Staging a Tertiary." *Franciscan Studies*, XXV (1944), 63-78.

(6) MISCELLANEOUS ITEMS

B9901 Hackett, F. *Queen Anne Boleyn: A Novel.* New York: Doubleday, Doran and Co., 1939.
Rev: by H. Gorman, *NYTBR*, Sept. 24, 1939, p. 9.

B9902 Richey, Dorothy. "The Dance in *Henry VIII*: A Production Problem." *Bull. of Furman Univ.*, xxxv, iii (1952), 1-11.

(7) SUBSEQUENT HISTORY OF THE PLAY
(Other than productions after 1660)

PERICLES (260;92)
(1) THE TEXT
(a) OLD TEXTS

B9903 Edwards, Philip. "An Approach to the Problem of *Pericles.*" *ShS*, v (1952), 25-49.
Rev: by J. G. McManaway, *ShS*, vi (1953), 164-165.

(b) MODERN EDITIONS

B9904 *Pericles, Prince of Tyre.* Ed. J. C. Maxwell. The New Shakespeare. Cambridge Univ. Press, 1956. Pp. xli, 209.
Rev: *TLS*, Oct. 26, 1956, p. 639; *ShN*, vi, 42; *N &Q*, ns, iii, 550-551; by R. A. Foakes, *English*, xi (1957), 150-151; *SCN*, xv, 14; by James G. McManaway, *MLR*, lii, 583-584; by Philip Edwards, *SQ*, viii, 535-538; by Hermann Heuer, *SJ*, 93 (1957), 271-272; by J. Jacquot, *RHT*, ix, 196-197; by C. Leech, *DUJ*, xlix, 133-134; by Arthur Brown, *RES*, ns, ix (1958), 313-314.

B9905 *Pericles.* Ed. G. B. Harrison. Penguin Shakespeare. Harmondsworth: Penguin Books, 1958. Pp. 121.
Rev: *TLS*, Oct. 24, 1958, p. 614; by H. Heuer, *SJ*, 94 (1958), 295-296; by J. G. Riewald, *LT*, 194 (1958), 305.

(c) EMENDATIONS

B9906 Tannenbaum, Samuel A. "A Passage in *Pericles.* [IV. i. 4-6.]" *SAB*, xii (1937), 190-191.

B9907 Lloyd, Bertram. " 'Portage' in *Pericles.*" *N &Q*, 182 (1942), 342-343.

B9908 Long, John H. "Laying the Ghosts in *Pericles.*" *SQ*, vii (1956), 39-42.
"Exorcises" the dancing ladies of III. iii as a bit of non-Shak. stage business introduced by Malone and found still in recent editions.

(2) LITERARY GENESIS AND ANALOGUES

B9909 Grismer, R. L., & E. Atkins. *The Book of Apollonius Translated into English Verse.* Minneapolis, Minnesota: Univ. of Minnesota Press, 1936. Pp. xx, 114.

B9910 Wilkins, George. *The Painfull Adventures of Pericles, Prince of Tyre.* Ed. Kenneth Muir. Univ. Liverpool Press, 1953. Pp. xv, 120.
Rev: A3525.

B9911 Hastings, William T. "Exit George Wilkins?" *SAB*, xi (1936), 67-83.

B9912 Millenkovich-Morold, Max. "*Perikles, Fürst von Tyrus.* Eine Neuheit des Wiener Burgtheaters. Ein gutes Theaterstück, Wahrscheinlich von Shakespeare Gelungener Versuch." *VB*, xix (1937), 11.

B9913 Dickson, George B. "The Identity of George Wilkins." *SAB*, xiv (1939), 195-208.

B9914 Hastings, William T. "Shakespeare's Part in *Pericles.*" *SAB*, xiv (1939), 67-85.

B9915 Craig, Hardin. "Shakespeare's Development as a Dramatist in the Light of His Experience." *SP*, xxxix (1942), 226-238.

B9916 Munro, John. "Some Matters Shakespearian." *TLS*, Oct. 11, 1947, p. 528.

B9917 Craig, Hardin. "*Pericles* and *The Painfull Adventures.*" *SP*, xlv (1948), 600-605.

B9918 Parrott, Thomas Marc. "*Pericles*: The Play and the Novel." *SAB*, xxiii (1948), 105-113.

B9919 Muir, Kenneth. "The Problem of *Pericles.*" *ES*, xxx (1948), 65-83.

B9920 Elton, William. "*Pericles*: A New Source or Analogue." *JEGP*, xlviii (1949), 138-139.

B9921 Waith, Eugene M. "*Pericles* and Seneca the Elder." *JEGP*, l (1951), 180-183.

B9922 Seiler, Grace E. *Shakespeare's Part in "Pericles."* DD, University of Missouri, 1951. Pp. 329. *DA*, xii (1952), 309-310. Publ. No. 2694.

B9923 Kane, Robert J. "A Passage in *Pericles.*" *MLN*, lxviii (1953), 483-484.

B9924 Evans, Bertrand. "The Poem of *Pericles.*" *The Image of the Work, Essays in Criticism* by B. H. Lehman and Others. Berkeley and Los Angeles: Univ. of California Press, 1955, pp. 35-56.

B9925 Goolden, P. "Antiochus's Riddle in Gower and Shakespeare." *RES*, ns, vi (1955), 245-251.

B9926 García Lora, José. "Péricles y Apolonio." *Insula* (Madrid), No. 111 (March 15, 1955), Supl., pp. 1-2.

B9927 Gesner, Carol. *The Greek Romance Materials in the Plays of Shakespeare.* DD, Louisiana State University, 1956. Pp. 352. Mic 56-3435. *DA*, xvi (1956), 2162. Publ. No. 17,442.

B9928　Nathan, Norman. *"Pericles* and *Jonah." N &Q,* NS, III (1956), 10-11.

B9929　Guidi, Augusto. "Le fasi del *Pericles." Studi in Onore di Pietro Silva.* Ed. by the Facoltà di Magistero of Rome Univ. Florence: F. Le Monnier, 1957, pp. 107-117.

B9930　Muir, Kenneth. "A Mexican Marina." *ES,* XXXIX (1958), 74-75.

(3)　USE OF LANGUAGE

B9931　Smith, G. "The Tennis-Ball of Fortune." *N &Q,* 190 (1946), 202-203.

(4)　GENERAL CRITICISM OF THE PLAY

B9932　Knight, G. Wilson. *The Crown of Life*: *Interpretation of Shakespeare's Final Plays.* Oxford Univ. Press, 1947. Pp. viii, 9-336.
　　　　Rev: B5241.

B9933　Muir, Kenneth. *"Pericles,* II. v." *N &Q,* 193 (1948), 362.

B9934　Craig, Hardin. *"Pericles, Prince of Tyre." Hunt Festschrift,* 1948, pp. 1-14.

B9935　Tompkins, J. M. S. "Why *Pericles?" RES,* NS, III (1952), 315-324.

B9936　Arthos, John. *"Pericles, Prince of Tyre*: A Study in the Dramatic Use of Romantic Narrative." *SQ,* IV (1953), 257-270.

B9937　Fischer, Walther. "Shakespeares Späte Romanzen." *SJ,* 91 (1955), 7-24.

(5)　CHARACTERIZATION

(6)　MISCELLANEOUS ITEMS

B9938　Feldman, A. Bronson. "Imaginary Incest." *The American Imago,* XII (1955), 117-155.

(7)　SUBSEQUENT HISTORY OF THE PLAY
(Other than productions after 1660)

III.　SHAKESPEARE'S POEMS (262;93)
1.　SHAKESPEARE'S POEMS IN GENERAL (262;93)
a.　EDITIONS OF THE POEMS
(SOMETIMES INCLUDING SONNETS) (262;93)

B9939　*The Lyrics and Shorter Poems.* London: Chatto & Windus, 1937. Pp. 58.

B9940　Cancelled.

B9941　*Poems: "Venus and Adonis," "Lucrece," "The Passionate Pilgrim," "The Phoenix and the Turtle," "A Lover's Complaint."* Ed. Hyder E. Rollins. *The New Variorum Ed.* Philadelphia: Lippincott, 1938. Pp. xvii, 667.
　　　　Rev: by Samuel A. Tannenbaum, *SAB,* XIII (1938), 128; by W. W. L., *SRL,* June 18, p. 20; by A. B., *Archiv,* 174 (1938), 262-263; *TLS,* Dec. 24, p. 817; by Wolfgang Keller, *SJ,* LXXV (1939), 142-143; by L. L. Schücking, *Beiblatt,* L, 97-98; by R. A. Law, *MLN,* LIV, 138-140; by Alwin Thaler, *JEGP,* XXXVIII, 450-455; by C. J. Sisson, *MLR,* XXXIV, 259-260; by G. G. Loane, "Notes on Shakespeare's Poems: New Variorum Editions," *N &Q,* 173 (1940), 188-189; by E. A. Strathmann, *MLQ,* II (1941), 319-320.

B9942　*Under the Greenwood Tree.* Songs from the Plays. Selected by Julia Louise Reynolds. New York: Oxford, 1940. Pp. 51.

B9942a　*Songs from Shakespeare.* Illus. by Geoffrey Tory. Limit. ed. Mt. Vernon, New York: Peter Pauper Press, 1941. Pp. 64.

B9943　*All the Love Poems.* Decorations by Eric Gill. London: Sylvan Press, 1947. Pp. 166.

B9944　*Shakespeare's Earliest Poems, in Approximately Chronological Order.* Ed. A. W. Titherley. Winchester: Warren, 1953. Pp. viii, 78.

B9945　*The Complete Sonnets, Songs and Poems of William Shakespeare.* Ed. Henry W. Simon. New York: Pocket Books, 1954. Pp. 333.

B9946　*The Love Poems and Sonnets of William Shakespeare.* New York, 1957. London: Bailey and Swinfen, 1957. Pp. 160.
　　　　Rev: *TLS,* March 21, 1958, p. 158.

B9947　*Love Poems and Sonnets of William Shakespeare.* New York: Doubleday, 1957.

b.　ANTHOLOGIES CONTAINING REPRINTINGS

B9948　Hamer, Enid. *The English Sonnet: An Anthology.* Ed. with Introd. and Notes. London: Methuen, 1936. Pp. 250.
　　　　Rev: *N &Q,* 170 (1936), 90; *Cornhill Mag.,* 153 (1936), 380.

B9949　Black, Matthew Wilson. *Elizabethan and Seventeenth Century Lyrics.* An Anthology Based to Some Extent on Two Anthologies of Felix E. Schelling; for Students. Philadelphia: Lippincott, 1938. Pp. 635.

B9950　Harrison, George Bagshawe. *A Book of English Poetry*: *Chaucer to Rossetti.* New York: Penguin Books, 1939. Pp. 244.

B9951   Auden, W. H., and N. H. Pearson, eds. *Poets of the English Language.* 5 Vols. New York:
         Viking Press, 1951. London: Eyre and Spottiswoode, 1952.
         Various poems by Shak., Vol. II, pp. 154-291.
             Rev: *TLS*, May 25, 1951, p. 328; by David Daiches, *SRL*, Feb. 10, pp. 15-16; by Dudley
             Fitts, *Amer. Scholar*, XX, 250, 252; by C. F. B., *Dalhousie Rev.*, XXXI, 1, xxxiv-v; by Dudley
             Fitts, *NYTBR*, July 1, p. 5; *Listener*, XLVIII (1952), 473; by M. Willy, *English*, IX (1952/53),
             146-147.

B9952   Muir, Kenneth. *Elizabethan Lyrics.* A Critical Anthology. London: Harrap, 1952.
         Various sonnets and poems, pp. 61-62, 99-105, 139-140; 190-192.
             Rev: *Listener*, XLIX (1953), 983; *NstN*, XLV, 242; by H. Heuer, *SJ*, 90 (1954), 335; by
             M. Poirier, *EA*, VII, 117.

B9953   Roberts, Denys Kilham. *The Centuries' Poetry.* 1. Chaucer to Shakespeare. London: Penguin
         Books, 1953.
         Shak., pp. 134-154.

B9954   Herrington, H. W. *English Masterpieces 700-1800.* London: Owen, 1957.
         "Songs from the Plays. Sonnets," pp. 317-341.

B9955   Hampden, John, ed. *Great Poems from Shakespeare to Gerard Manley Hopkins.* Univ. of London
         Press, 1958. Pp. 256. Second ed.
             Rev: *TLS*, Sept. 5, 1958, p. 503.

c. STUDIES OF THE POEMS AND/OR POEMS AND SONNETS (263;93)

B9956   Reimer, Hans. *Der Vers in Shakespeares Nichtdramatischen Werken.* DD, Bonn, 1908. Pp. 60.

B9957   Lucas, Wilfrid Irvine, M. A. *Die Epischen Dichtungen Shakespeares in Deutschland.* DD, Heidel-
         berg, 1934. Pp. 113.

B9958   Hinkle, George H. *Shakespeare's Poems of 1640.* DD, Stanford University, 1937. Abstr. publ.
         in *Abstracts of Dissertations, 1936-37*, Stanford Univ., 1937, pp. 41-46.

B9959   Drinkwater, John. *English Poetry: An Unfinished History.* Preface by St. John Ervine. London:
         Methuen, 1938. Pp. 227.
         Venus, pp. 92-94; *Sonnet 30*, p. 137.
             Rev: A9085.

B9960   Berringer, Ralph W. *The Reaction in the Poetry of 1595-1620 Against Elizabethan Conventionalism.*
         DD, Brown University, 1941.

B9961   Hunt, James Clay. *The Beginnings of the Neo-Classic Movement in Elizabethan Poetry.* DD,
         Johns Hopkins University, 1941.

B9962   Swan, Marshall W. S. "Shakespeare's 'Poems': The First Three Boston Editions." *Papers
         Bibl. Soc. Amer.*, XXXVI (1942), 27-36.

B9963   Wade, James Edgar. *Medieval Rhetoric in Shakespeare.* DD, St. Louis University, 1942. Pp.
         185. Mic A44-671, *Mcf Ab*, V (1944), 72. Publ. No. 613.
         Chap. III "Ornamental Rhetoric in *Venus & Adonis*," pp. 39-87. Chap. IV "Ornamental
         Rhetoric in *The Rape of Lucrece*," pp. 88-130.

B9964   Chambers, Sir Edmund K. *Sources for a Biography of Shakespeare.* Oxford: Clarendon Press,
         1946. Pp. 80.
             Rev: A395.

B9965   Mackenzie, Barbara A. *Shakespeare's Sonnets: Their Relation to His Life.* Cape Town: Maskew
         Miller, 1946. Pp. x, 82.
             Rev: *English*, VI (1946), 153; by Harold Jenkins, *MLR*, XLII (1947), 261-262; by R. M.
             Smith, *JEGP*, XLVI, 218; by C. Hinman, *MLN*, LXIII (1948), 213-214; by Mario Praz, *ES*,
             XXIX, 53-58.

B9966   Brooke, C. F. Tucker. "Willobie's *Avisa*." *Essays in Honor of Albert Feuillerat*, Yale Romanic
         Studies, XXII, Yale Univ. Press, 1943. Also in *Essays on Shakespeare and Other Elizabethans*,
         Yale Univ. Press, 1948, pp. 167-178.

B9967   Halliday, F. E. *Shakespeare and His Critics.* London: Gerald Duckworth & Co., 1949.
         Pp. 522.
             Rev: A8596.

B9968   Baldwin, T. W. *On the Literary Genetics of Shakspere's Poems and Sonnets.* Urbana: Univ. of
         Illinois Press, 1950. Pp. xi, 399.
             Rev: A4170.

B9969   Simpson, Lucie. "The Principle of Beauty in Shakespeare's Poetry." *The Secondary Heroes of
         Shakespeare and Other Essays.* London: Kingswood Press, 1950, pp. 73-76.

B9970   Watkins, W. B. C. *Shakespeare and Spenser.* Princeton Univ. Press, 1950. Pp. ix, 339.
             Rev: A8549.

B9971   Smith, Hallet. *Elizabethan Poetry.* Harvard Univ. Press, 1952. Pp. viii, 355.
             Rev: A8369.

B9972   James, Wilfred P. *The Life and Work of Richard Barnfield: A Critical Study.* DD, Northwestern
         University, 1952. Abstr. publ. in Northwestern Univ. *Summaries of Doctoral Dissertations, 1952*,
         Vol. 20, Chicago and Evanston, 1953, pp. 14-18.

B9973   Lloyd, Roger. "Love and Charity and Shakespeare." *MGW*, Feb. 16, 1956, p. 6.

B9974   Keen, Frances. *Phoenix: An Inquiry into the Poems of Robert Chester's "Love's Martyr" (1601) and the "Phoenix Nest" (1593), in Relation to Shakespeare's "Sonnets" and "A Lover's Complaint."* London: Author, (Broadsheet), 1957.

B9975   Rousselot, Jean. "Shakespeare poète ou le Théâtre Intérieur." *Cahiers de la Compagnie Madeleine Renaud—Jean-Louis Barrault* (Paris), No. 17 (1957), 115-124.

2. THE SONNETS (263;93)

B9976   Tannenbaum, Samuel A. *Shakespeare's Sonnets.* Elizabethan Bibliographies, 10. New York: The Author, 1940. Pp. xii, 88.

a. EDITIONS (263;93)
(1) OF 1609 AND 1640
(a) FACSIMILES

B9977   *Sonnets.* Neuer before imprinted; at London, by G. Eld for T. T. and are to be solde by Iohn Wright, dwelling at Christ Church Gate, 1609. For the Facsimile Text Soc. Columbia Univ. Press, 1936. Pp. 76.

B9978   *Shakespeare's Sonnets.* Printed after the Praetorius Facsimile ed. from the copy of the First Quarto, 1609, in the British Museum. Limited autographed ed. Lexington: Anvil Press, 1956. Pp. 85.

(b) DISCUSSIONS

B9979   Eagle, R. L. "The Headpiece on Shakespeare's Sonnets, 1609." *N &Q*, 192 (1947), 38.

B9980   Carter, Albert Howard. "The Punctuation of Shakespeare's *Sonnets* of 1609." *AMS*, pp. 409-428.

B9981   *Thorpe's Edition of Shakespeare's "Sonnets 1609."* An Explanatory Introd. by C. Longworth de Chambrun. With Text Transcription. Aldington, Kent: Hand & Flower Press, 1950. Pp. 135.
        Rev: *TLS*, Dec. 29, 1950, p. 830; by J. G. McManaway, *SQ*, II (1951), 366; by Ivor Brown, *Obs.*, April 22, p. 7; by L. Bonnerot, *EA*, V (1952), 75-76.

B9982   Smith, Hallett. " 'No Cloudy Stuffe to Puzzell Intellect': A Testimonial Misapplied to Shakespeare." *SQ*, I (1950), 18-21.
    John Benson's prefatory remarks to 1640 edition of *Poems* plagiarized from testimonial poem to Joseph Rutter by Thomas May, in 1635 volume published by Benson.

(2) MODERN EDITIONS

B9983   *Sonnets.* Arranged by G. W. Phillips. Oxford: B. Blackwell, 1934. Pp. viii, 163.

B9984   *Sonnets.* Ed. Tucker Brooke, with Introd. and Notes. Oxford Univ. Press, 1936. Pp. x, 375.
        Rev: by Rosamond Gilder, *TAr*, XXI (1937), 330-331; by W. Keller, *SJ*, LXXIII, 153; *TLS*, May 14, 1938, p. 334; by M. D. Clubb, *MLN*, LIII, 201-204; by H. Lüdeke, *ES*, XXII (1939), 151-155; by G. Bullough, *MLR*, XXXIV, 591-593; by W. Fischer, *DLZ*, LXII (1941), 589-591.

B9985   *Sonnets.* Ed. Henry Norman Hudson and Others. Cameo Classics. New York: Grosset, 1936. Pp. 166.

B9986   *Sonnets.* Mt. Vernon, New York: Peter Pauper Press, 1936. Pp. 80.

B9987   Bray, Denys. *Shakespeare's Sonnet Sequence.* London, 1938.
        Rev: C44.

B9988   *The Sonnets of William Shakespeare and Henry Wriothesley, third Earl of Southampton, Together with A Lover's Complaint and The Phoenix and Turtle.* Ed., with an Intro. by Walter Thomson. Oxford: Blackwell, 1938. Pp. 199.
        Rev: by Clara (Longworth), Comtesse de Chambrun, *EA*, II (1938), 396-397; *TLS*, May 14, p. 334; *London Mercury*, XXXVIII, 292-293; by W. J. Lawrence, *Spectator*, May 6, p. 818; see letter by Mr. Thomson, ibid., May 20, p. 916; by H. B. Charlton, *MGW*, May 20, p. 394; by Samuel A. Tannenbaum, *SAB*, XIII, 188-189; by J. A. Chapman, *Poetry Rev.*, XXIX, 473-475; by T. C. K., *Birmingham Post*, May 17; by V. H. R., *Country Life*, May 28; by W. Thomson, *Spectator*, May 20, p. 916; *The Scotsman*, May 23; by W. B. Kempling, *Stratford Herald*, May 20; by S. Jeffrey, *Liverpool Echo*, April 26; by O. E., *Liverpool Daily Post*, May 18; by C. D. F., *Evening Express*, April 28; by R. Lynd, *News Chronicle*, May 20; by I. Brown, *Obs.*, May 20; by H. B. Charlton, *Manchester Guardian*, May 13; by W. E. W., *Hawick Express*, April 5; *The Nottingham Guardian*, June 23; *The Madras Mail*, June 11; by F. S. Boas, *Drama*, XVI, 151-152; by J. B. Leishman, *RES*, XV (1939), 93-96; by G. Bullough, *MLR*, XXXIV, 591-593; by T. Brooke, *MLN*, LIV, 630; by Eduard Eckhardt, *Eng. Studn.*, LXXIV (1940), 124-125; by Elise Deckner, *Beiblatt*, LIII (1941), 57-59; by Wolfgang Keller, *SJ*, LXXVII, 195-196.

B9989   Withers, C., ed. *Shakespeare's Sonnets. Penguin Book of Sonnets*, 1943, pp. 3-80.

B9990   *Sonnets.* Paris: Ed. Charbot, 1944.

B9991   *Sonnets.* A Variorum Edition. Ed. Hyder E. Rollins. 2 Vols. Philadelphia: Lippincott, 1944.
        Pp. xx, 404; viii, 532.
            Rev: by R. S. Hillyer, *NYTBR*, Oct. 1, 1944, pp. 7, 29; by Samuel A. Tannenbaum, *SAB*,
            XIX, 190; by S. C. Chew, *NYHTBR*, Dec. 17, p. 10; by G. E. Bentley, *CE*, VII (1945), 118;
            by F. T. Prince, *RES*, NS, I (1950), 255-258.

B9992   *Sonnets for a Dark Beauty.* Basel: H. R. Linder, 1945. Pp. 58.

B9993   *The Sonnets of William Shakespeare.* Oxford: Shakespeare Head Press, 1945. Pp. 77.

B9994   *Shakespeare's Sonnets.* Ed. by Barbara A. Mackenzie. Cape Town: Maskew Miller, 1946.
        Pp. x, 82.
            Rev: by Roland M. Smith, *JEGP*, XLVI (1947), 218.

B9995   *The Sonnets.* Ed. Seán Jennett. London: Grey Walls Press, 1948. Pp. 228.
            Rev: *TLS*, May 20, 1949, p. 326.

B9996   *The Sonnets.* Decorative Head-pieces by Reynolds Stone. Folio Soc. Ill. Classics. London:
        Cassell, 1948. Pp. 160. New York: Duschnes, 1957. Pp. 160.

B9997   *Sonnets.* Cornelsen-Fremdsprachenreihe, 66. Berlin, Bielefeld: Cornelsen, 1948. Pp. 79.

B9998   *Sonnets.* Bussum: Kroonder, 1948. Pp. 83.

B9999   *The Sonnets and A Lover's Complaint.* Ed. George Bagshawe Harrison. London: Penguin
        Books, 1949. Pp. 128.

B10000 *The Sonnets.* Illustrated by Steven Spurrier. Leigh-on-Sea: F. Lewis, 1950. Pp. 154.
            Rev: *TLS*, Dec. 29, 1950, p. 830.

C1   *Sonnets.* Ed. Hyder E. Rollins. Crofts Classics Edition. New York: Appleton-Century-
        Crofts, 1951.

C2   *Forty Sonnets. The Poet's Own Drama.* Deutsche Nachdichtungen von Hans Mühlestein.
        Zurich: Fretz & Wasmuth, 1952. Pp. 26.

C3   *The Complete Sonnets, Songs and Poems of William Shakespeare.* Ed. Henry W. Simon. New York:
        Pocket Books, 1954. Pp. 333.

C4   *The Complete Sonnets of William Shakespeare.* Sylvanus Editions. London: Sylvan Press, 1955.
        Pp. 76.
            Rev: *TLS*, Feb. 10, 1956, p. 86; by Hermann Heuer, *SJ*, 92 (1956), 378-379.

C5   Strong, L. A. G. *The Body's Imperfection.* London: Methuen, 1957. Pp. 164.

C5a   *Sonnets to a Dark Lady and Others.* Mount Vernon, New York: Peter Pauper Press, 1958.
        Pp. 31.

C6   *Sonnets.* Ed. L. Fox. Corman House Series. London: Jarrold, 1958. Pp. 168.

b. STUDIES (265;94)

(1) THE ENGLISH SONNET GENERALLY

C7   Vaganay, Hugues. "Sonnets Elizabéthains." *RLC*, XIV (1934), 333-337.
            Rev: by J. G. Scott-Espiner, *RLC*, XV (1935), 107-109.

C8   Kelley, Tracy R. *Studies in the Development of the Prosody of the Elizabethan Sonnet.* DD, Uni-
        versity of California, 1937.

C9   John, Lisle Cecil. *The Elizabethan Sonnet Sequences: Studies in Conventional Conceits.* Columbia
        Univ. Studies in Eng. and Comparative Lit., 133. New York: Columbia Univ. Press, 1938.
        Pp. x, 278.
            Rev: by H. E. Rollins, *MLN*, LIV (1939), 315-316; by Kathleen Tillotson, *RES*, XV,
            348-350; by G. Bullough, *MLR*, XXXIV, 635-636; *N &Q*, 176 (1939), 198; by Elise Deckner,
            Beiblatt, LI (1940), 94-95.

C10   Michelagnoli, A. *Il Sonetto nella Letteratura Inglese.* Padua: Cedam, 1938. Pp. 131.

C11   Mitchell, Charles B. *The English Sonnet in the Seventeenth Century, Especially after Milton.* DD,
        Harvard University, 1939. Abstr. publ. in Harvard Univ. *Summaries of Theses, 1939*, Cambridge,
        1942, pp. 239-243.

C12   Yates, Frances. "The Emblematic Conceit in Giordano Bruno's *De Gli Eroici Furori* and in the
        Elizabethan Sonnet Sequences." *JWCI*, VI (1944), 101-121.

C13   Siegel, Paul N. "The Petrarchan Sonneteers and Neo-Platonic Love." *SP*, XLII (1945),
        164-182.

C14   Smith, Hallett. *Elizabethan Poetry: A Study in Conventions, Meaning, and Expression.* Harvard
        Univ. Press, 1953. Pp. xii, 355.
        Chap. III "The Sonnets," pp. 131-193.
            Rev: A8369.

C15   Lewis, Clive Staples. *English Literature in the Sixteenth Century Excluding Drama.* Oxford
        History of English Literature, 3. Oxford: Clarendon Press, 1954. Pp. vii, 696.
        Shak.'s poetry, pp. 498-509; 670-672.
            Rev: A8051.

C16   Potter, James L. *The Development of Sonnet-patterns in the Sixteenth Century.* DD, Harvard
        University, 1954.

C17   Mönch, Walter. *Das Sonett, Gestalt und Geschichte*. Heidelberg: F. H. Kerle, 1955. Pp. 341.
      Rev: by Hermann Heuer, *SJ*, 91 (1955), 327-328; *TLS*, Sept. 2, p. 506; by A. Closs, *DLZ*,
      LXXVII (1956), 421-422; by F. M. Wassermann, *JEGP*, LV, 318-321.

C18   Lever, J. W. *The Elizabethan Love Sonnet*. London: Methuen, 1956. Pp. 282.
      Rev: *TLS*, April 6, 1956, p. 206; *Dublin Magazine*, XXXI, No. 2, 45-46; by Hermann Heuer,
      SJ, 92 (1956), 379-381; by John Holloway, *Spectator*, March 23, p. 384; by Lisle John, *RN*,
      IX, 201-206; *Listener*, LV, 259, 261; by J. Vallette, *MdF*, 327 (1956), 528-530; by Clifford
      Leech, *DUJ*, XLIX (1957), 38-40; by J. R., *RES*, VIII, 429-432; by J. B. Leishman, *MLR*, LII,
      251-256; by Brita Tigerschiöld, *Göteborgs Handels— & Sjöfartstidning*, Jan.; by K. Muir,
      ShS, X, 141; by Aerol Arnold, *Personalist*, XXXIX (1958), 311-312.

(2)   SHAKESPEARE'S SONNETS
(a)   DATE

C19   Darby, Robert H. "The Date of Some Shakespeare Sonnets." *SJ*, LXXV (1939), 135-138.

C20   Hotson, Leslie. "When Shakespeare Wrote the Sonnets." *Atlantic Monthly*, Dec., 1949,
      pp. 61-67.
      Discussion, ibid., Feb., 1950, pp. 17-19. See C21.

C21   Hotson, Leslie. *Shakespeare's Sonnets Dated, and Other Essays*. London: Rupert Hart-Davis;
      Toronto: Clarke, Irwin & Co., 1949. Pp. 244.
      Rev: *Listener*, XLII (1949), 917; by George Rylands, *Spectator*, Dec. 9, p. 824; by Edward
      Hubler, *SQ*, I (1950), 78-83; *TLS*, Feb. 10, p. 88; by G. Lambin, *LanM*, March-April, p. 123;
      by Samuel C. Chew, *NYHTBR*, April 2; comment by Hugh R. Williamson and Peter
      Leyland, *TLS*, Feb. 17, p. 105; by F. E. Halliday, Feb. 24, p. 121; by John Sparrow, March 3,
      p. 137; by Christopher Lloyd, March 10, p. 153; by C. H. Hobday, March 24, p. 185; by
      C. L. de Chambrun, March 31, p. 201; by I. A. Shapiro, April 21, p. 245; reply by Leslie
      Hotson, June 2, p. 348; comment by Arthur J. Perrett, June 16, p. 373; by Michael Lewis
      and Catherine W. Scotland, June 23, p. 389; by F. S. Boas, July 7, p. 421; by G. Wilson
      Knight, July 14, p. 437; by Robert Halsband, *SRL*, April 1, p. 16; by Douglas Bush, *NR*,
      April 24, pp. 21-22; by Hallett Smith, *YR*, XXXIX, 743-746; by A. L. Rowse, *Sun. Times*,
      Jan. 15, p. 3; by Alfred Harbage, "Dating Shakespeare's Sonnets," *SQ*, I, 57-63; by R. F.
      Rattray, *Spectator*, 6337 (1950), 78; *CE*, XI, 470; by F. S. Boas, *English*, VIII, 32-33; by E.
      Neis, *Leb. Fremdspr.*, III (1951), 367-368; by O. J. Campbell, *SQ*, II, 104-105; by J. G. Mc-
      Manaway, *ShS*, IV, 153-156; by F. T. Prince, *RES*, II, 271-272; by Elkin C. Wilson, *RN*, IV,
      6-8; by R. Fricker, *SJ*, 87/88 (1952), 201-202.

C22   Hotson, Leslie. "More Light on Shakespeare's Sonnets." *SQ*, II (1951), 111-118.

C23   Bateson, F. W. "Elementary My Dear Hotson! A Caveat for Literary Detectives." *EIC*, I
      (1951), 81-88.
      See letter by I. A. Shapiro, ibid., p. 192. Argues against Hotson's theory of an early date for
      the Sonnets, and finds his topical interpretations at variance with the style and structure of
      the poems.

C24   Chambrun, Clara Longworth de "Une Critique de la Critique: Mr. Leslie Hotson et la Date des
      Sonnets de Shakespeare." *EA*, V (1952), 44-49.

C25   Nosworthy, J. M. "All too Short a Date: Internal Evidence in Shakespeare's Sonnets." *EIC*,
      II (1952), 311-324.
      Questions the early dates given by Dr. Hotson to sonnets CVII, CXXIII, and CXXIV; finds
      evidence in parallels in vocabulary between the sonnets and plays for later dates, 1600-1606.

C26   Stone, Walter B. "Shakespeare and the Sad Augurs." *JEGP*, LII (1953), 457-479.
      Takes issue with Leslie Hotson over the dating of sonnet CVII.

C27   Michel, Laurence. "Shakespeare's *Sonnet CVII*." *JEGP*, LIV (1955), 301-305.
      Comments on Leslie Hotson's dating.

(b)   SOURCES AND PARALLELS

C28   Baym, Max I. "Recurrent Poetic Theme." *SAB*, XII (1937), 155-158.
      Additional illustrations, ibid., Oct., p. 258.

C29   Hutton, James. "Analogues of Shakespeare's Sonnets 153-154: Contributions to the History
      of a Theme." *MP*, XXXVIII (1941), 385-403.

C30   Davenport, A. "Seed of a Shakespeare Sonnet." *N &Q*, 182 (1942), 242-244.

C31   Valente, Pier Luigi. "Petrarca e Shakespeare." *Studi Petrarcheschi* (Accad. Petrarca di Lettere,
      Arti e Scienze di Arezzo), I (1948), 195-201.

C32   Starnes, D. T. "Shakespeare's *Sonnet 60*: Analogues." *N &Q*, 194 (1949), 454.

C33   West, Bill C. *Anti-Petrarchism: A Study of the Reaction Against the Courtly Tradition in English
      Love Poetry from Wyatt to Donne*. DD, Northwestern University, 1950. Abstr. publ. in *Sum-
      maries of Doctoral Dissertations, 1950*, Vol. 18, Chicago & Evanston: Northwestern Univ.,
      1951, pp. 35-37.

C34   Disher, M. Willson. "The Trend of Shakespeare's Thought." *TLS*, Oct. 20, 27, Nov. 3, 1950,
      pp. 668, 684, 700.
      See the letters "The Rival Poet" by J. M. Murry, ibid., Nov. 17, p. 727; by A. S. Cairncross,

ibid., Dec. 1, p. 767; by Lynette Feasey, ibid., Dec. 8, p. 785. Mr. Disher argues that Sidney's *Arcadia* fixed Shak.'s belief while *"Astrophel and Stella* moulded its form."

C35   Valente, Pier Luigi. "Quesiti nell'Interpretazione Italiana dei *Sonetti* Shakespeariani." *Studi Petrarcheschi* (Accad. Petrarca di Lettere, Arti e Scienze di Arezzo), III (1950), 171-182.

C36   D., A. "Shakespeare's *Sonnets.*" *N &Q*, 196 (1951), 5-6.

C37   Bradner, Leicester. "From Petrarch to Shakespeare." *The Renaissance: A Symposium*, Feb. 8-10, 1952. New York: Metropolitan Museum of Art, 1953, pp. 63-78.

C38   Peterson, Douglas L. "A Probable Source for Shakespeare's *Sonnet CXXIX.*" *SQ*, V (1954), 381-384.

C39   Wilkinson, L. P. "Shakespeare and Horace." *TLS*, May 6, 1955, p. 237.
Influence of Horace's Epode XI on Shak.'s Sonnet 104.

C40   Fox, Charles A. O. "Thomas Lodge and Shakespeare." *N &Q*, NS, III (1956), 190.
Sonnet 129.

C41   Bludau, Diethild. "Sonettstruktur bei Samuel Daniel." *SJ*, 94 (1958), 63-89.

C42   Schaar, Claes. "Shakespeare's *Sonnets L-LI* and Tebaldeo's *Sonnet CVII.*" *ES*, XXXVIII (1957), 208-209.

(c) ARRANGEMENT

C43   Brooke, Tucker, ed. *Shakespeare's Sonnets.* New York: Oxford Univ. Press, 1936. Pp. 353.
Rev: B9984.

C44   Bray, Denys. *Shakespeare's Sonnet Sequence.* London, 1938.
Full text of the sonnets in a new order is given (first proposed 1925; modified by C. Tucker Brooke in his edition of 1936), based on continuity of sense, word-articulations, and rhyme links.
Rev: *TLS*, Dec. 17, 1938, p. 806; by Kathleen Tillotson, *RES*, XV (1939), 346-348; by Wolfgang Keller, *SJ*, LXXV, 162-163.

C45   Golding, N. L. *A Survey of the Proposed Arrangements of the Sonnets.* MS thesis, Columbia University, 1948. Pp. 78.

C46   *Thorpe's Edition of Shakespeare's "Sonnets, 1609."* An Explanatory Introduction by C. Long-worth de Chambrun. Aldington, Kent: Hand and Flower Press, 1950.
Rev: B9981.

(d) GENERAL CRITICISM

C47   Rinaker, Clarissa. "Some Unconscious Factors in the Sonnet as a Poetic Form." *International Journal of Psycho-Analysis*, XII (1931), 167-187.

C48   Rank, Otto. *Art and Artist.* Tr. Charles Francis Atkinson. New York: Alfred A. Knopf, 1932. Pp. xlix, 431.
Sonnets, pp. 55-58.

C49   Adnès, André. *Shakespeare et la Folie: Etude Médico-Psychologique.* DD, Paris, 1935. Paris: Librairie Maloine, 1936.
Addenda on the sonnets, pp. 281-289.
Rev: A1237.

C50   Neri, Ferdinando. *"Alla Ricerca di Shakespeare"* and *"I Sonnetti."* *Saggi di Letteratura Italiana, Francese e Inglese.* Naples: Loffredo, 1936, pp. 245-250, 251-256.

C51   Young, H. McClure. *The Sonnets of Shakespeare: A Psycho-Sexual Analysis.* Menasha: Wisconsin, 1936.
Rev: by C. J. Sisson, *MLR*, XXXII (1937), 659-660; *ES*, XIX, 143; *TLS*, May 14, 1938, p. 334; see letter, Alfred Douglas, ibid., May 21, p. 353; by H. T. Price, *JEGP*, XXXVII, 432; by Elise Deckner, *Beiblatt*, XLIX, 116.

C52   Iwakura, Tomahide. "Psychosexuale Analyse von Shakespeares *Sonetten.*" *Tokyo Zeitschrift für Psychoanalyse*, VI (May 1938).
A translation into Japanese of Chap. II of C51.

C53   Empson, W. *Some Versions of Pastoral.* London, 1935. Publ. in U.S.A. as *English Pastoral Poetry.* New York: Norton, 1938. Pp. 298.
Sonnets, pp. 89-101.
Rev: B5290.

C54   Mills, L. J. *One Soul in Bodies Twain: Friendship in Tudor and Stuart Drama.* Bloomington, Indiana: Principia Press, 1937. Pp. x, 470.
Rev: A6290.

C55   Muir, Kenneth, and Sean O'Loughlin. *The Voyage to Illyria.* A New Study of Shakespeare. London: Methuen, 1937. Pp. 242.
Rev: A8307.

C56   Ransom, John C. "Shakespeare at Sonnets." *Southern Review*, III (1937), 531-553.

C57   Wells, Henry W. "A New Preface to Shakespeare's *Sonnets.*" *SAB*, XII (1937), 118-129.

C58   "The Problem of the *Sonnets:* Fresh Interpretations." *TLS*, May 14, 1938, p. 334.

See "Lord Douglas, Shakespeare and Will Hughes," ibid., May 21, p. 353; ibid., May 28, p. 370.

C58a   Rang, Florens Christian. "Shakespeare der Christ. Eine Deutung der Sonette." *Die Schild-genossen* (Rothenfels), XVII (1938), 55-72.
See C94.

C59   Ransom, John Crowe. *The World's Body.* New York: Scribner's, 1938. Pp. xiv, 350.
Rev: by Michael Roberts, *Criterion*, XVIII (1938), 152-154; by F. A. Pottle, *YR*, XXVIII, 183-185; by C. Arnavon, *EA*, III (1939), 180-181.

C60   Traversi, D. A. *An Approach to Shakespeare.* London: Sands, Paladin Press, 1938. Pp. 152. Second ed. revised and enlarged, New York: Doubleday, 1956. Pp. 304.
Rev: A8420.

C61   Deutschbein, Max. "Die Politischen *Sonette* Shakespeares." *SJ*, LXXVI (1940), 161-188.

C61a   Boerner, Oskar. "Zur Frage der Politischen Sonette Shakespeares." *Archiv*, 180 (1941), 9-18. On C61.

C62   Deutschbein, Max. "Shakespeares Persönliche und Literarische Sonette. I." *SJ*, LXXVII (1941), 151-188. "Shakespeares Persönliche und Literarische Sonette. II." *SJ*, LXXVIII/LXXIX (1943), 105-127.

C63   Chapman, J. A. "Marching Song." *Essays and Studies*, XXVIII (1942), 13-21.

C64   Cellini, B. *Vita e Arti nei Sonetti di Shakespeare.* Col Testo dei Sonetti Riordinati e Commentati. Rome: Tumminelli, 1943. Pp. vii, 396.
Rev: by Mario Praz, *ES*, XXIX (1948), 53-58.

C65   Reul, P. de. "Introduction aux sonnets de Shakespeare." *Acad. Royale de Belgique. Bul. de la Classe des Lettres et des Sciences Morales et Politiques*, XXIX (1943), 104ff.

C66   Stocker, A. *Des Hommes Qui Racontent leur Ame.* St. Maurice, Suisse: Editions St. Augustin, 1943.
Contains an essay entitled "La Prière du Grand Will—Etude Psychologique de Quelques Sonnets de Shakespeare."

C67   Anspacher, L. K. *Shakespeare as Poet and Lover and the Enigma of the Sonnets.* New York: Island Press, 1944. Pp. vi, 56.

C68   Chambers, Sir E. K. *Shakespearean Gleanings.* Oxford Univ. Press, 1944.
Contains three essays on the sonnets: 10. "The Order of the Sonnets," 11. "The 'Youth' of the Sonnets," and 12. "The 'Mortal Moon' Sonnet."
Rev: B4466.

C69   Shakespeare, William. *Les Sonnets de Shakespeare.* Essai d'Interprétation Poétique Française et Introd. par André Prudhommeau. Porrentruy: Aux Portes de France, 1945. Pp. iv, 113.

C70   Bray, Denys. "Difficult Passages in the Sonnets Reexamined." *N &Q*, 190 (1946), 200-202; 191 (1947), 92-95.

C71   Knights, L. C. *Explorations: Essays in Criticism, Mainly on the Literature of the Seventeenth Century.* London, 1946.
Contains essay on the sonnets.
Rev: A8269.

C72   Norman, C. "Shakespeares Sonnette: Eine Studie." *Die Amerikanische Rundschau*, XVI (Dec., 1947), 32-43.

C73   Rubow, P. V. "Shakespeare's Sonnets." *Orbis*, IV (1947), 2-44.

C74   Rubow, Paul V. *Shakespeare og hans Samtidige.* Copenhagen: Gyldendal, 1948. Pp. 155.
Contains discussion of the sonnets.
Rev: by P. Krüger, *Orbis*, VII (1949), 310-312; by Hans Brix, *Analyser og Problemer*, VI (1950), 316-322.

C75   Sitwell, Edith. *A Notebook on William Shakespeare.* New York, London: Macmillan, 1948. Pp. xii, 233.
Rev: A8365.

C76   Berkelman, Robert. "The Drama in Shakespeare's Sonnets." *CE*, X (1948), 138-141.

C77   Engel, Werner. *Veränderlichkeit—Vergänglichkeit—Tod in Shakespeares "Sonetten."* DD, Marburg, 1949. Pp. 107. Typewritten.

C78   Grün, Herbert. *"Hamlet.* Spočetie Evropskega Individualizma" [*Hamlet.* The Beginning of European Individualism]. *Mladinska Revija* (Ljubljana), V (1949), 3, 4-5, 131-134, 180-183. *Hamlet* and *Sonnets* the keys to an understanding of Shak.

C79   Viswanathan, K. "Falstaff and the Sonnets." *Triveni* (Madras), XX (1949), 569-573.

C80   Appel, Louis D. *The Concept of Fame in Tudor and Stuart Literature.* DD, Northwestern University, 1949. Abstr. publ. in *Summaries of Doctoral Dissertations*, 1949, XVII (1950), 9-13.

C81   Emde Boas, Conrad van. "The Connection Between Shakespeare's Sonnets and His 'Travesti-Double' Plays." *International Journal of Sexology*, Nov., 1950.

C82   Shackford, Martha Hale. *The Eternitie of Poetrie.* Natick, Massachusetts: The Suburban Press, 1950. Section on sonnets, 1-126, pp. 15-26.

C83   Emde Boas, C. van. *Shakespeare's Sonnetten en Hun Verband met de "Travesti-Double" Spelen. Een Medesch-Psychologische Studie.* Amsterdam, 1951. Pp. 520.
       Rev: A870.

C84   Flatter, Richard. "Zur Frage der Shakespeare-Sonette." *Das Antiquariat,* VII (1951), No. 21-24, pp. 86-87.

C85   Hubler, Edward. *The Sense of Shakespeare's Sonnets.* Princeton Univ. Press, 1952. Pp. x, 170.
       Rev: by Herschel Baker, *SQ,* III (1952), 374-375; by S. F. Johnson, *ShN,* II, 39; by P. Chamaillard, *EA,* V, 243-244; by G. B. Harrison, *SatR,* June 14, pp. 28-29; by F. Cudworth Flint, *RN,* V, 57-58; *TLS,* March 6, 1953, p. 151; by Philip Williams, *South Atlantic Quar.,* LII, 490; by William H. Davenport, *Personalist,* XXXIV, 203; by Ernest A. Strathmann, *JEGP,* LII, 531-542; by Sandford Salyer, *Books Abroad,* XXVII, 82; by G. Bullough, *MLN,* LXIX (1954), 514-516; by A. José Axelrad, *RLC,* XXVIII (1955), 496-497; by H. Lüdeke, *ES,* XXXVIII (1957), 79-82.

C86   Matthews, G. M. "Sex and the Sonnet." *EIC,* II (1952), 119-137.
       See comment by Paul N. Siegel, ibid., pp. 465-468.

C87   Berryman, John. "Shakespeare at Thirty." *Hudson Review,* VI (1953), 175-203.

C88   Cruttwell, Patrick. "A Reading of the *Sonnets.*" *Hudson Review,* V (1952/53), 554-570.

C89   Cruttwell, Patrick. *The Shakespearean Moment.* London: Chatto and Windus, 1953. Pp. 256.
       Rev: B5257.

C90   Fell, K. *The Background, Content and Style of Shakespeare's "Sonnets."* MA thesis, Sheffield Univ., 1953.

C91   Highet, Gilbert. "The Autobiography of Shakespeare." *People, Places, and Books.* New York, 1953, pp. 86-93.
       Rev: *TLS,* Jan. 21, 1955, p. 38.

C92   Hunter, G. K. "The Dramatic Technique of Shakespeare's Sonnets." *EIC,* III (1953), 152-164.

C93   Knight, G. Wilson. *The Mutual Flame: An Interpretation of Shakespeare's Sonnets.* London: Methuen, 1955. Pp. xi, 233.
       Rev: *TLS,* May 20, 1955, p. 268; by John Heath-Stubbs, *Time and Tide,* XXXVI, 534; by E. C. Pettet, *English,* x, 189; *Dublin Magazine,* NS, XXXI (July-Sept.), 79-80; by George Freedley, *Library Journal,* 80 (1955), 1714; by David Daiches, *Manchester Guardian,* March 25, p. 9; and in *MGW,* March 31, p. 10; by John Jones, *NstN,* XLIX, 478; by C. G. Martin, *EIC,* V, 398-404; *The Statesman* (Delhi and Calcutta), May 8, p. 15; by Roy Walker, *The Aryan Path* (Bombay), XXVI, 317; by Christopher Devlin, *The Month,* NS, XIV, 372-374; by Gunnar Sjögren, *Dagens Nyheter* (Stockholm), Aug. 17; by Kenneth Muir, *London Mag.,* II, No. 6, 104-106, 108; *Listener,* LIII, 1167; by J. Vallette, *MDF,* 324 (1955), 531-532; by J. P. Curgenven, *Litera,* II, 126-128; by Hyder E. Rollins, *SQ,* VII (1956), 107-108; by Wallace A. Bacon, *QJS,* XLII, 201-202; by Hermann Heuer, *SJ,* 92 (1956), 381-383; by John Hollander, *KR,* XVIII, 659-663; by Michel Poirier, *EA,* IX, 255-256; by L. C. Knights, *RES,* NS, VIII (1957), 302-304.

C94   Rang, Florens Christian. *Shakespeare der Christ. Eine Deutung der Sonette.* Ed. Bernhard Rang. Darmstadt: Veröffentlichungen der Deutschen Akademie für Sprache und Dichtung. Heidelberg: L. Schneider, 1954. Pp. 205. See C58a.
       Rev: by Hermann Heuer, *SJ,* 92 (1956), 383-384; by H. Schnyder, *Archiv,* 193 (1957), 332.

C95   Schoff, F. G. "Shakespeare's 'Fair is Foul'." *N &Q,* 199 (1954), 241-242.

C96   Tigerschiöld, Brita. "Dödsperspektivet i en Grupp Shakespearesonetter." *Ord och Bild,* No. 9 (1954), 553-561.

C97   Guttmann, Bernhard. "Shakespeare im Selbstgesprach." In Guttmann's *Das alte Ohr.* Frankfurt a.M., 1955, pp. 123-139.

C98   Jouve, Pierre Jean. "Sonnets de Shakespeare." *MdF,* 324 (1955), 5-16.
       See note ibid., August, 1955, p. 724.

C99   Wellington, James Ellis. *An Analysis of the Carpe Diem Theme in Seventeenth-Century English Poetry (1590-1700).* DD, Florida State University, Tallahassee, 1956. Pp. 471. Mic 56-3901. *DA,* XVI (1956), 2450. Publ. No. 17,033.
       Chap. IV "Persuasions to Marry," pp. 214-266. Shak's sonnets, pp. 238-240.

C100   Landry, Hilton James. *Readings in Shakespeare's Sonnets.* DD, Harvard University, 1958.

C101   Knights, L. C. *Some Shakespearean Themes.* London: Chatto & Windus, 1959.
       Chapter on Sonnets.

i. Language

C102   Schmidt, Wolfgang. "Sinnesänderung und Bildvertiefung in Shakespeares *Sonnetten.*" *Anglia,* LXII (1938), 286-305.

C103   Skinner, B. F. "The Alliteration in Shakespeare's Sonnets: A Study in Literary Behavior." *Psychological Record,* III (1939), 186-192.
       Answered by E. E. Stoll, *MLN,* LIV (1939), 388-390.

C104   Mizener, Arthur. "The Structure of Figurative Language in Shakespeare's Sonnets." *Southern Rev.,* V (1940), 730-747.

C105   Pratt, Marjory Bates. *Formal Designs from Ten Shakespeare Sonnets.* New Brunswick, New Jersey: Author, 1940.
C106   Herbert, T. Walter. "Shakespeare's Word-Play on *Tombe.*" *MLN,* LXIV (1949), 235-241.
C106a   Louthan, Doniphan. "The 'Tome—Tomb' Pun in Renaissance England." *PQ,* XXIX (1950), 375-380.
C107   Goldsmith, Ulrich K. "Words Out of a Hat? Alliteration and Assonance in Shakespeare's Sonnets." *JEGP,* XLIX (1950), 33-48.
C108   Schmidt-Hidding, Wolfgang. "Shakespeares Stilkritik in den *Sonetten.*" *Heinrich Mutschmann Festschrift,* 1951, pp. 119-126.
C109   Nowottny, Winifred M. T. "Formal Elements in Shakespeare's Sonnets: Sonnets I-VI." *EIC,* II (1952), 76-84.
C110   Masson, David I. "Free Phonetic Patterns in Shakespeare's Sonnets." *Neophil,* XXXVIII (1954), 277-289.
C111   Mahood, M. M. *Shakespeare's Word Play.* London: Methuen, 1957.
        Chapter on the Sonnets.
            Rev: A5815.

ii. Grammar

C112   Archer, C. " 'Thou' and 'You' in the Sonnets." *TLS,* June 27, 1936, p. 544.
C113   Abend, Murray. "Two Unique Gender Forms in the Shakespeare Sonnets." *N &Q,* 195 (1950), 325.
C114   Berry, Francis. " 'Thou' and 'You' in Shakespeare's Sonnets." *EIC,* VIII (1958), 138-146.
        See Thomas Finkenstaedt. "Pronouns in Poetry," ibid., pp. 456-457.
C115   Berry, Francis. *Poets' Grammar.* London: Routledge and Kegan Paul, 1958. Pp. 190.
            Rev: A5230.

(e) SPECIFIC SONNETS
(Arranged by number of sonnet discussed)

C116   Elmen, Paul. "Shakespeare's Gentle Hours." *SQ,* IV (1953), 301-309.
        Sonnet 5.
C117   Banks, Theodore H. "Shakespeare's *Sonnet No. 8.*" *MLN,* LXIII (1948), 541-542.
C118   Herbert, T. Walter. "Sound and Sense in Two Shakespeare Sonnets." *Tenn. Studies in Lit.,* III (1958), 43-52.
        Examines Sonnets 12 and 30.
C119   Tannenbaum, Samuel A. "Sonnet 20 Interpreted." *SAB,* XIII (1938), 188.
C120   Fowler, Clayton V. *Shakespeare's "Sonnet 24" in the Light of Contemporary Art Theory.* DD, State University of Iowa, 1952.
C121   Zahniser, Howard. "Lake Solitude Sermon." *Nature,* 1958, pp. 452-453.
        Sonnet 30.
C122   Cancelled.
C123   Piper, H. W. "Shakespeare's Thirty-first Sonnet." *TLS,* April 13, 1951, p. 229.
C124   Clarkson, Paul S., and Clyde T. Warren. "Pleading and Practice in Shakespeare's Sonnet 46." *MLN,* LXII (1947), 102-110.
C125   Davenport, A. "Shakespeare's Sonnet 51 Again." *N &Q,* 198 (1953), 15-16.
C126   Hussey, R. "Shakespeare and Gower." *N &Q,* 180 (1941), 386.
        Sonnet 64.
C127   Caldwell, James R. "States of Mind: States of Consciousness." *EIC,* IV (1954), 168-179.
        Sonnet 64.
C128   Reeves, James. *The Critical Sense.* London: Heinemann, 1956.
        Section Shak., pp. 105-107. Sonnet 65.
            Rev: by Howard Sergeant, *English,* XI (1956), 112.
C129   Lumiansky, R. M. "Shakespeare's Sonnet 73." *Expl.,* VI (1948), item 55.
C130   Noland, Edward F. "Shakespeare's Sonnet 73." *Expl.,* VII (1948), item 13.
C131   Bateson, F. W. "The Function of Criticism at the Present Time." *EIC,* III (1953), 1-27.
        Discusses Empson's analysis of Sonnet 73.
        Comment by W. Empson, reply to F. W. Bateson, further comment by W. Empson, *EIC,* III (1953), 357-363.
C132   Wheeler, Charles B., and F. W. Bateson. "Bare Ruined Choirs." *EIC,* IV (1954), 224-226.
        See also C131.
C133   Moore, Carlisle. "Shakespeare's Sonnets 71-74." *Expl.,* VIII (1949), item 2.
C134   Debeljak, Anton. "Shakespearov Sonet 97 Pojasnjen." [Shakespeare's Sonnet 97 Explained] *Novi Svet* (Ljubljana), VI (1951), 382-384.
C135   Murry, John Middleton. *John Clare and Other Studies.* London: Nevill, 1950. Pp. 252.
        Sonnet 107, pp. 246-252.

C136   Kenyon, John S. "Shakespeare, Sonnet CXI, 12." *MLN*, LX (1945), 357-358.
C137   Louthan, Doniphan. "Sonnet 113." *TLS*, July 6, 1951, p. 421.
C138   MacLeish, Archibald. "The Proper Pose of Poetry." *SatR*, March 5, 1955, pp. 11-12, 47-49. Sonnet 116.
C139   Burckhardt, Sigurd. "The Poet as Fool and Priest." *ELH*, XXIII (1956), 279-298. Sonnet 116, pp. 289-298.
C140   Fox, Charles Overbury. "Shakespeare's Sonnet 126, Lines 1 and 2." *N&Q*, 197 (1952), 134-135.
C141   Thompson, Karl F. "Shakespeare's Sonnet 129." *Expl.*, VII (1949), item 27.
C142   Johnson, C. W. M. "Shakespeare's Sonnet 129." *Expl.*, VII (1949), item 41.
C143   McNeal, Thomas H. "Studies in the Greene-Shakespeare Relationship." *SAB*, XV (1940), 210-218. Sonnet 130.
C144   Herbert, T. Walker. "Shakespeare's Sonnet 142." *Expl.*, XIII (1955), item 38.
C145   Smith, Gordon Ross. "A Note on Shakespeare's Sonnet 143." *American Imago*, XIV (1957), 33-36.
C146   Stauffer, D. A. "Critical Principles and Sonnet 146." *American Scholar*, XII (1942), 52-62.
C147   Fox, Charles A. O. "Shakespeare's Sonnet 146." *N&Q*, NS, I (1954), 83.
C148   Parsons, Howard. "Shakespeare's Sonnet 146." *N&Q*, NS, II (1955), 97.
C149   Clarke, Robert F. "An Emendation of Sonnet 146." *ShN*, VIII (1958), 11.
C150   Bray, Denys. "Sonnet 149." *TLS*, July 4, 1942, p. 331.

(f) IDENTITY OF THE PRINCIPAL FIGURES

C151   Disher, M. Willson. "The Trend of Shakespeare's Thought." *TLS*, Oct. 20, 27, Nov. 3, 1950, pp. 668, 684, 700.
       See the letters "The Rival Poet" by J. M. Murry, ibid., Nov. 17, 1950, p. 727; by A. S. Cairncross, ibid., Dec. 1, p. 767; by Lynette Feasey, ibid., Dec. 8, p. 785; by Lawrence Durrell, ibid., Jan. 5, 1951, p. 7; by C. Longworth de Chambrun, ibid., Feb. 2, p. 69.

i. Mr. W. H.

C152   Nisbet, Ulric. *The Onlie Begetter*. London: Longmans, 1936. Pp. 112.
       Rev: *TLS*, May 16, 1936, p. 414; *N&Q*, 170 (1936), 413-414; by H. B. Charlton, *MGW*, June 19, p. 495; *QR*, 267 (1936), 185-186; *Cornhill Mag.*, 154 (1936), 125; by Tucker Brooke, *SRL*, Aug. 22, p. 11; by John Hayward, *NstN*, NS, XI, 780; by P. M. Jack, *NYTBR*, Aug. 2, p. 2; by William Empson, *Life and Letters Today*, XV (1937), 201; see letters by A. W. Baldwin, *TLS*, June 12, p. 447; by Norman G. Brett-James, ibid., June 19, p. 464.
C153   Hinman, C. "The Pronunciation of 'Wriothesly'." *TLS*, Oct. 2, 1937, p. 715.
       Comment by A. F. Pollard, *TLS*, Oct. 9, 1937, p. 735.
C154   Douglas, Lord Alfred. "Shakespeare and Will Hughes." *TLS*, May 21, 1938, p. 353.
       Rev: A689.
C155   Shield, H. A. "Links with Shakespeare. VI." *N&Q*, 195 (1950), 205-206.
C156   Jouve, Pierre Jean. "Sur Les Sonnets de W. S." *La Revue de Paris*, LXII (1955), 112-119.
       Commented on by M. P., *La Revue de Paris*, LXII (Oct., 1955), 173.
C157   Taylor, Dick, Jr. "The Third Earl of Pembroke As a Patron of Poetry." *Tulane Studies in English*, V (1955), 41-67.
C158   Williams, Franklin B., Jr. "An Initiation Into Initials." *SB*, IX (1957), 163-178.
C159   Pohl, Frederick J. "On the Identity of 'Mr. W. H.'." *ShN*, VIII (1958), 43.
C160   Wilde, Oscar. *The Portrait of Mr. W. H.* The Greatly Enlarged Version Prepared by the Author after the Appearance of the Story in 1889, but not Published; ed. with an Intro. by Vyvyan Holland. London: Methuen 1958. Pp. iii-xv, 90.
       Rev: A9063.

ii. The Dark Lady

C161   Angell, P. K. "Light on the Dark Lady: A Study of Some Elizabethan Libels." *PMLA*, LII (1937), 652-674.
C162   Angell, Pauline K., and T. W. Baldwin. " 'Light on the Dark Lady'." *PMLA*, LV (1940), 598-602.
C163   Tromöhlen, R. "Wer War Shakespeares Dunkle Dame?" *Chemnitzer Tageblatt und Anzeiger*, April 23, 1939.
C164   Gray, Cecil G. "Mary Fitton and Sir Richard Leveson." *N&Q*, 197 (1952), 74-75.
C165   Shield, H. A. "Links with Shakespeare, IX." *N&Q*, 197 (1952), 156-157.
C166   O'Neal, Cothburn. *The Dark Lady*. New York: Crown, 1953. Pp. 313.
       Rev: *SatR*, Jan. 8, 1954, pp. 34; *Time*, Sept. 9, p. 106; by M. Crane, *SQ*, VI (1955), 355.

C167   Moeller, Kristian Langdal. "Shakespeare og den Mørke Dame." [Shakespeare and the Dark
       Lady] *Aarhus Stiftstidende* (Aarhus, Denmark), May 22, 1954.
C168   Munro, John. "Dark Ladies of Literature." *ConR*, No. 1060, 185 (1954), 227-231.
C169   Hope-Wallace, Philip. "In the Basket." *Listener*, Oct. 6, 1955, p. 569.
       See Hope-Wallace's similar notice in *Time and Tide*, XXXVI (1955), 968.
C170   Brown, Ivor. *Dark Ladies*. London: Collins, 1956. Pp. 320.
       "Shak.'s Dark Lady," pp. 253-309.
           Rev: B4162.

iii.   The Rival Poet

C171   Murry, John Middleton. "Chapman the Rival Poet." *TLS*, June 4, 1938, pp. 385-386.
       See letters by G. G. Loane and Alfred Douglas, *TLS*, June 11, 1938, p. 402.
C172   Gray, Henry David. "Shakespeare's Rival Poet." *JEGP*, XLVII (1948), 365-373.
C173   Schrickx, W. "De Probabiliteit der Shakespearewetenschap met een Poging tot Analyse van
       het 'Rival Poet' sonnet." *Tijdschrift voor Levende Talen*, XVI (1950), 393-404. *Revue des Langues
       Vivantes*, XVI (1950), 393-404.

iv.   The Youth

C174   Chambers, E. K. "The 'Youth' of Shakespeare's Sonnets." *RES*, XXI (1945), 331.

(g)   INFLUENCE

C175   Kahn, Ludwig W. *Shakespeares Sonnette in Deutschland: Versuch einer Literarischen Typologie*.
       Bern and Leipzig, 1935.
           Rev: A9435.
C176   Sanderlin, George. "The Repute of Shakespeare's Sonnets in the Early Nineteenth Century."
       MLN, LIV (1939), 462-466.
C177   Schoen-René, Otto Eugene. *Shakespeare's Sonnets in Germany, 1787-1939*. DD, Harvard
       University, 1942. Abstr. publ. in *Summaries of PhD Theses, 1942*, Cambridge: Harvard Univ.
       Press, 1946, pp. 284-287.
C178   Ehrentreich, Alfred. "Das 'Englische' Sonett und die Deutsche Lyrik." *Neuphilologische
       Zeitschrift*, II (1950), 38-44, 403-404.
C179   McNeal, Thomas H. "*Every Man Out of His Humour* and Shakespeare's *Sonnets*." *N &Q*, 197
       (1952), 376.
C180   Hübner, Hans. *Sonette in Deutscher Sprache und Italienischer Versform*. Rostock: C. Hinstorff,
       1956. Pp. 196.
C181   Lever, Julius Walter. "Chapman and Shakespeare." *N &Q*, NS, V (1958), 99-100.

(h)   MISCELLANEOUS

C182   Evans, W. McC. "Lawes' Version of Shakespeare's Sonnet 116." *PMLA*, LI (1936), 120-122.
C183   Ross, William. *The Story of Anne Whately and William Shaxpere*. London: Holmes, 1940.
       Pp. 231.
       That Anne Whately wrote the sonnets.
C184   Flatter, Richard. "Sigmund Freud on Shakespeare." *SQ*, II (1951), 368-369.
C185   Feldman, A. Bronson. "The Confessions of William Shakespeare." *American Imago*, X (1953),
       113-116.
C186   Phillips, Gerald William. *Shakespeare's Sonnets*. Addressed to Members of the Shakespeare
       Fellowship. Cambridge: Published privately for the author and distributed by Heffer, 1954.
       Pp. 23.
C187   Kaplan, Milton. "Retarding Shakespeare." *Harper's Magazine*, Jan., 1956, pp. 37-38.
C188   *Sonety Shekspira*. Desiat Sonetov Shekspira. Moscow, 1957. Pp. 37.
       Musical settings for Shak.'s Sonnets.

3.   SHAKESPEARE'S EPIC POEMS (269-94)
a.   GENERAL TREATISES (269;-)

C189   Bond, R. W. "The Art of Narrative Poetry." *Studia Otiosa*, 1938, pp. 1-17.
C190   Wade, James Edgar. *Medieval Rhetoric in Shakespeare*. DD, St. Louis University, 1942. Pp.
       185. *Mic* A44-671. *Mcf Ab*, V (1944), 72. Publ. No. 613.
       Chap. III. "Ornamental Rhetoric in *Venus & Adonis*," pp. 39-87. Chap. IV. "Ornamental
       Rhetoric in *The Rape of Lucrece*," pp. 88-130.
C191   Zocca, Louis R. *Elizabethan Narrative Poetry*. Rutgers Univ. Press, 1950. Pp. xii, 306.
           Rev: *N &Q*, 195 (1950), 527; by Robert A. Law, *SQ*, II (1951), 136-137; by Louis L. Martz,
           YR, XL, 562-565; by Allan H. Gilbert, *South Atlantic Quar.*, L, 286-287; by Sears Jayne, *MP*,
           L (1952), 143-144; by Virgil B. Heltzel, *MLN*, LXVII, 479-481.

C192   Head, E. A. *The Ovidian Mythological Verse Romance in England During the Early Seventeenth Century*. MA thesis, University of London, 1953.

C193   Smith, Hallett. *Elizabethan Poetry: A Study in Conventions, Meaning, and Expression*. Harvard Univ. Press, 1953. Pp. xii, 355.
        Rev: A8369.

C194   Colbrunn, Ethel B. *The Simile as a Stylistic Device in Elizabethan Narrative Poetry: An Analytical and Comparative Study*. DD, University of Florida, 1954. Pp. 315. Mic A54-3073. *DA*, XIV (1954), 2065. Publ. No. 9541.

C195   Miller, Paul W. "The Elizabethan Minor Epic." *SP*, LV (1958), 31-38.
        Considers so-called Ovidian poems like *Hero and Leander* as epyllia. See Walter Allen, Jr., "The Non-Existent Classical Epyllion." *SP*, LV (1958), 515-518, who denies the existence of the epyllion as a literary genre.

b. VENUS AND ADONIS (269;94)
(1) EDITIONS (269;-)

C196   Loane, G. G. "Notes on Shakespeare's Poems: New Variorum Edition." *N &Q*, 178 (1940), 188-189.

C197   *Venus and Adonis*. Designed and Drawn by Peter Rudland. London: W. H. Allen, 1948. Pp. 87.

C198   *Venus and Adonis*. Ill. by J. Yunge-Bateman. London: Winchester Publ., 1948. Pp. 87.

C199   *Venus and Adonis*. With Marlowe's *Hero and Leander*. Due Poemetti Elisabettiani. Ed. Gabriele Baldini. Collezione Fenice Diretta da Attilio Bertolucci, Edizione fuori serie, No. 20. Parma: Ugo Guanda Editore, 1952. Pp. xx, 199.

C200   *Venus and Adonis*. With Illustrations by Rockwell Kent. Rochester, New York: The Printing House of Leo Hart, 1956.

(2) STUDIES (269;94)

C201   Hotson, Leslie. "An Elizabethan Madman: Publication of *Venus and Adonis*." *The Times* (London), April 21, 1939, p. 19.

C201a   Hotson, Leslie. *Shakespeare's Sonnets Dated, and Other Essays*. London: Rupert Hart-Davis; Toronto: Clarke, Irwin & Co., 1949. Pp. 244.
        Rev: C21.

C202   Putney, Rufus. "*Venus and Adonis*: Amour with Humor." *PQ*, XX (1941), 533-548.

C203   Price, Hereward T. "Function of Imagery in *Venus and Adonis*." *Papers Michigan Acad. Science, Arts, and Letters*, XXXI (1945), 275-297.

C204   Hatto, A. T. "*Venus and Adonis*—and the Boar." *MLR*, XLI (1946), 353-361.

C205   Schaus, Hermann. "The Relationship of *Comus* to *Leander* and *Venus and Adonis*." *TxSE*, XXV (1945-46), 129-141.

C206   Jackson, William A. "The Lamport Hall—Brittwell Court Books." *AMS*, 1948, pp. 587-599.

C207   D., A. "Weever, Ovid and Shakespeare." *N &Q*, 194 (1949), 524-525.
        Picus and Circe episode in *Metamorphoses* as source of passages in *Venus and Adonis*.

C208   Webster, Peter Dow. "A Critical Fantasy or Fugue." *American Imago*, VI (1949), 297-309.

C209   Bartlett, Phyllis. "Ovid's 'Banquet of Sense'?" *N &Q*, 197 (1952), 46-47.

C210   Miller, Robert P. "Venus, Adonis, and the Horses." *ELH*, XIX (1952), 249-264.

C211   Putney, Rufus. "Venus Agonistes." *Univ. Colo. Studies, Lang. & Lit. Ser.* No. 4 (1953), 52-66.

C212   Partridge, A. C. "Shakespeare's Orthography in *Venus and Adonis* and Some Early Quartos." *ShS*, VII (1954), 35-47.

C213   Thayer, C. G. "Ben Jonson, Markham, and Shakespeare." *N &Q*, NS, I (1954), 469-470.

C214   Miller, Robert P. *The Double Hunt of Love: A Study of Shakespeare's "Venus and Adonis" as a Christian Mythological Narrative*. DD, Princeton University, 1955. Pp. 587. Mic A54-3471. *DA*, XIV (1954), 2338. Publ. No. 9436.

C215   Cross, K. Gustav. "'Balm' in Donne and Shakespeare: Ironic Intention in *The Extasie*." *MLN*, LXXI (1956), 480-482.

C216   Dickey, Franklin M. *Not Wisely but Too Well: Shakespeare's Love Tragedies*. San Marino, California: The Huntington Library, 1957. Pp. ix, 205.
        While not discounting the nobility of much love in Shak., this study attempts to right the balance in favor of the non-romantic view, taking quite seriously the stated opinions of Elizabethan poets, moralists, and literary critics.
        Rev: A2562.

c. THE RAPE OF LUCRECE (270;95)
(1) EDITIONS (270;-)
(a) SHAKESPEARE'S POEM

C217   *The Rape of Lucrece*. Illus. by J. Yunge-Bateman. London: Winchester Publ., 1948. Pp. 116.
        Rev: by J. W., *MGW*, July 15, 1948, p. 11.

(b) RELATED CONTEMPORANEOUS POEMS

C218   Middleton, Thomas. *The Ghost of Lucrece*. Reprod. in facsimile from the unique copy in the Folger Shakespeare Library, with an intro. and ed. text by Joseph Quincy Adams. New York: Scribner's, 1937. Pp. xxxiii, 43.
    Rev: *TLS*, March 12, 1938, p. 176; by Robert Withington, *MLN*, LIII, 619-623; by W. W. Greg, *Library*, NS, XIX, 120-121. See also James G. McManaway, "Fortune's Wheel," *TLS*, April 16, p. 264; by C. J. Sisson, *MLR*, XXXIV, 261-262.

C219   Heywood, Thomas. *The Rape of Lucrece*. Ed. Allan Holaday. Illinois Studies in Language and Lit., 34, 3. Urbana: Univ. of Illinois Press, 1950. Pp. ix, 185.
    Rev: by J. G. McManaway, *JEGP*, L (1951), 266-268; by A. Koszul, *LanM*, XLV, 268; by P. Edwards, *MLR*, XLVI, 483-484; by M. A. Shaaber, *MLN*, LXVII (1952), 564-567; by A. M. Clark, *RES*, NS, III, 285-289.

C220   Shaaber, M. A. "*The First Rape of Faire Hellen* by John Trussell." *SQ*, VIII (1957), 407-448.

(2) STUDIES (270;95)

C221   Galinsky, H. *Der Lukretia-Stoff in der Weltliteratur*. Breslin, 1932.
    Rev: by Wolfgang Keller, *SJ*, LXXII (1936), 149-150; by Eb. Semrau, *ZDP*, LX (1935), 91-94.

C222   Croce, Benedetto. "Intorno a Lucrezia nella Poesia e nella Casista Morale." *La Critica*, XXXV (1937), 146-152.

C223   Kuhl, E. P. "Shakespeare's *Rape of Lucrece*." *Renaissance Studies in Honor of Hardin Craig*, pp. 160-168; also *PQ*, XX, 352-360.

C224   Duncan, Ronald. "How *The Rape of Lucrece* Became an Opera." *Shakespeare Quarterly* (London), I (1947), 95-100.

C225   Bradbrook, M. C. "Lucrece and Othello." *TLS*, Oct. 27, 1950, p. 677.

C226   Tolbert, James M. *Shakespeare's "Lucrece": Its Antecedents, Sources and Composition*. DD, University of Texas, 1950.

C227   Tolbert, James M. "The Argument of Shakespeare's *Lucrece*: Its Sources and Authorship." *TxSE*, XXIX (1950), 77-90.

C228   Hunter, G. K. "A Source for Shakespeare's *Lucrece*?" *N &Q*, 197 (1952), 46.

C229   Oppel, Horst. "Das Bild des Brennenden Troja in Shakespeares *Rape of Lucrece*." *SJ*, 87/88 (1952), 69-86.

C230   Tolbert, James M. "A Source of Shakespeare's *Lucrece*." *N &Q*, 198 (1953), 14-15.

C231   Muir, Kenneth. "Shakespeare and Erasmus." *N &Q*, NS, III (1956), 424-425.

C232   Oppel, Horst. "Shakespeares *Rape of Lucrece*." *Shakespeare-Tage* (Bochum), 1956, pp. 10-14.

C233   Dickey, Franklin M. *Not Wisely but Too Well: Shakespeare's Love Tragedies*. San Marino, California: The Huntington Library, 1957. Pp. ix, 205.
    Rev: A2562.

C234   Parish, John E. "Another Pun on Will." *N &Q*, NS, IV (1957), 147.

4. SHAKESPEARE'S LYRIC POEMS (270;95)
a. A LOVER'S COMPLAINT (270;95)
b. THE PASSIONATE PILGRIM (270;-)
(1) EDITIONS

C235   *The Passionate Pilgrim*. Intro. by J. Q. Adams. Folger Shakespeare Lib. Pubs. New York: Scribner's, 1939. Pp. lxiii, 27.
    Rev: by W. W. Greg, *MLN*, LV (1940), 462-464; by Samuel A. Tannenbaum, *SAB*, XV, 128.

C236   *The Passionate Pilgrim*. 3rd. Ed. 1612, Reproduced in Facsimile from the Copy in the Folger Shakespeare Library. Intro. by Hyder Edward Rollins. New York: Scribner's, 1940. Pp. xlii, 137.
    Rev: by E. A. Strathmann, *MLQ*, II (1941), 319-320; by T. Brooke, *MLN*, LVII (1942), 378-379.

(2) STUDIES

C237   Carter, Albert Howard. "On the Use of Details of Spelling, Punctuation, and Typography to Determine the Dependence of Editions." *SP*, XLIV (1947), 497-503.

C238   Kökeritz, Helge. "Five Shakespeare Notes." *RES*, XXIII (1947), 310-320.
Applies the "linguistic approach" to *The Passionate Pilgrim*, II. 13-14.

C239   Johnson, Francis R. "Printers' 'Copy Books' and the Black Market in the Elizabethan Book Trade." *Library*, 5th Series, I (1947), 97-105.

C240   Bond, William H. "The Cornwallis-Lyson's Manuscript and the Poems of John Bentley." *AMS*, 1948, pp. 683-693.

C241   Jackson, William A. "The Lamport Hall—Brittwell Court Books." *AMS*, 1948, pp. 587-599.

C242   Izon, John. "Bartholomew Griffin and Sir Thomas Lucy." *TLS*, April 19, 1958, p. 245.

C243   Cutts, John P.   "Two Hitherto Unpublished Settings of Sonnets from *The Passionate Pilgrim*."
        SQ, IX (1958), 588-590.

c.   THE PHOENIX AND THE TURTLE (270;95)
(1) EDITIONS

C244   *The Phoenix and Turtle*.   Ed. Bernard H. Newdigate.   The Shakespeare Head Quartos, VII.
        Oxford: Blackwell, 1937.   Pp. 31.
        Rev: *TLS*, Sept. 25, 1937, p. 691; *N &Q*, 173 (1937), 250-251; by J. B. Leishman, *RES*,
        XIV (1938), 341-343.

C245   *The Phoenix and Turtle*.   Ed. with an Intro. by Gerald Bullett.   London: Pear Tree Press, 1938.
        Pp. 15.
        Rev: *TLS*, May 14, 1938, p. 334.

C246   *The Phoenix and the Turtle*.   Il. by L. Gischia.   Paris: R. Mortier, 1944.

(2) STUDIES

C247   Newdigate, B. H.   "*The Phoenix and Turtle*: Was Lady Bedford the Phoenix?"   *TLS*, Oct. 24,
        1936, p. 862.
        See letters by Mr. Newdigate, *TLS*, Nov. 28, p. 996; by W. B. Kempling, ibid., Dec. 5, p. 1016;
        by R. W. Short, ibid., Feb. 13, 1937, p. 111; by B. H. Newdigate, ibid., Feb. 20, p. 131.

C248   Chambrun, Clara Longworth, Comtesse de.   *Shakespeare Rediscovered by Means of Public Records,
        Secret Reports and Private Correspondence Newly Set Forth as Evidence on His Life and Work*.   Preface
        by G. B. Harrison.   New York: Scribner's, 1938.   Pp. xii, 323.
        Rev: A509.

C249   Hubaux, J., and M. Leroy.   *Le Mythe du Phénix*.   Paris: E. Droz, 1939.   Pp. 268.

C250   D., W. P.   "*The Phoenix and the Turtle*."   *N &Q*, 179 (1940), 408; B. H. Newdigate, G. Catalini
        and Wm. Jaggard, ibid., pp. 459-460.

C251   Jaggard, Wm.   "*The Phoenix and the Turtle*: Translation of Pliny."   *N &Q*, 180 (1941), 51.

C252   Cooper, M.   "Phoenixities."   *TLS*, April 26, 1941, p. 203; May 24, p. 251.

C252a   Baldwin, T. W.   "Phoenixities."   *TLS*, June 14, 1941, p. 287.

C253   Sitwell, Osbert.   " 'The Sole Arabian Tree'."   *TLS*, April 26, 1941, pp. 199, 206.
        See editorial comment, *TLS*, April 26, 1941, p. 203; letters by Malcolm Letts, ibid., May 3,
        p. 215; C. H. Wilkinson, ibid., May 3, pp. 215, 216; Margaret Cooper, ibid., May 24, p. 251;
        T. W. Baldwin, ibid., June 14, p. 287.

C254   "*The Phoenix and the Turtle*."   *TLS*, July 19, 1941, p. 347.

C255   Benham, Sir Gurney.   "*The Phoenix and the Turtle*."   *TLS*, July 19, 1941, p. 352; July 26, p. 364;
        letter by Mr. Sitwell, ibid., July 26, p. 351.

C256   Thompson, D. W.   "*Phoenix and the Turtle*."   *TLS*, Aug. 16, 1941, p. 397.

C257   Guthrie, W. N.   "*The Phoenix and the Turtle*: A Liberal Plea for Symbolic Orthodoxy."
        Anglican Theological Review, XXVI (1944), 10-13.

C258   Shahani, Ranjee G.   "*The Phoenix and the Turtle*."   *N &Q*, 191 (1946), 99-101; ibid., pp.
        120-123.

C259   Chwalewik, Witwold.   "Poemat Szekspira o 'Feniksie i Gołebiu'."   *Polska Akademia Umiejet-
        nósci*, LI (1950), 348-352.

C260   Verstegen, Hubertus Hendrikus.   *Het Phoenix-Motief*.   Bijdrage tot de Studie van de Human-
        istische visie op de Vorst.   DD, Nijmegan Roonis-Katholieke Universiteit, 1950.

C261   Harrison, Thomas P.   "*Love's Martyr*, by Robert Chester: A New Interpretation."   *TxSE*,
        XXX (1951), 66-85.
        Rev: *SQ*, IV (1953), 353.

C262   Cunningham, J. V.   " 'Essence' and *The Phoenix and Turtle*."   *ELH*, XIX (1952), 265-276.

C263   Green, Charles H.   *The Sources of "Love's Martyr," by Robert Chester*.   DD, University of Texas,
        1952.

C264   Knight, G. Wilson.   *The Mutual Flame: An Interpretation of Shakespeare's Sonnets*.   London:
        Methuen, 1954.
        Rev: C93.

C265   Parker, Marion Hope.   *The Slave of Life*.   London: Chatto and Windus, 1954.   Pp. 264.
        Rev: A1532.

C266   Rang, Florens Christian.   *Shakespeare der Christ*.   *Eine Deutung der Sonette*.   Ed. Bernhard Rang.
        Darmstadt, 1954.   Pp. 205.
        "The Phoenix and the Turtle," pp. 194-200.
        Rev: C94.

C267   Straumann, Heinrich.   *Phönix und Taube*.   Zur Interpretation von Shakespeares Gedankenwelt.
        Zurich: Artemis Verlag, 1953.   Pp. 63.
        Rev: by A. Koszul, *EA*, VII (1954), 321; by C. J. Sisson, *MLR*, XLIX, 542; by Rolf Soellner,
        JEGP, LIII, 239-240; by Hermann Heuer, *SJ*, 90 (1954), 342-343; by E. Th. Sehrt, *Anglia*,
        LXXII, 487-488; by H. Oppel, *NS*, III, 43-45; by W. Clemen, *Archiv*, 191 (1954), 95-96; by
        Hereward T. Price, *SQ*, VI (1955), 181-183; by Holger Nørgaard, *ES*, XXXVII (1956), 83.

C268   Alvarez, A. "How to Read a Poem (III). Shakespeare's *The Phoenix and the Turtle.*" *Mandrake*, II (1955-56), 395-408.

C268a   Alvarez, A. "Shakespeare: *The Phoenix and the Turtle.*" *Interpretations.* Ed. John Wain. London: Routledge & Kegan Paul, 1955. Pp. 1-16.
        Rev: B4441.

C269   Bates, Ronald. "Shakespeare's *The Phoenix and the Turtle.*" *SQ*, VI (1955), 19-30.

C270   Bradbrook, M. C. "*The Phoenix and the Turtle.*" *SQ*, VI (1955), 356-358.

C271   Ong, Walter J. "Metaphor and the Twinned Vision." *SR*, LXIII (1955), 193-201.

C272   Matchett, William Henry. *These Dead Birds: "The Phoenix and the Turtle.*" DD, Harvard University, 1957.

C273   Matchett, William H. "The Entry into English of 'Analysis' and 'Pathos'." *N&Q*, NS, IV (1957), 242-243.

C274   Richards, I. A. "The Sense of Poetry: Shakespeare's *The Phoenix and the Turtle.*" *Daedalus*, 87, iii (1958), 86-94.

IV. THE SHAKESPEARE APOCRYPHA (271;95)
1. THE SHAKESPEARE APOCRYPHA IN GENERAL (271;95)
a. EDITIONS (271;-)

C275   Parks, Edd Winfeld. "Simms's Edition of the Shakespeare Apocrypha." Eds. Matthews and Emery, *Studies in Shakespeare*, 1953, pp. 30-39.

b. STUDIES (272;96)

C276   Castle, E. "Theobalds *Double Falsehood* und *The History of Cardenio* von Fletcher und Shakespeare." *Archiv*, 169 (1936), 182-199.

C277   Adams, Joseph Quincy. "Hill's List of Early Plays in Manuscript." *Library*, XX (1939), 71-90.

C278   Cadwalader, John. "Theobald's Alleged Shakespeare Manuscript." *MLN*, LV (1940), 108-109.

C279   Harbage, Alfred. "Elizabethan-Restoration Palimpsest." *MLR*, XXXV (1940), 287-319.

C280   Bentley, Gerald Eades. *The Jacobean and Caroline Stage: Dramatic Companies and Players.* 2 Vols. Oxford: Clarendon Press, 1941. Pp. xx, 342; 343-748.
        Rev: *N&Q*, 180 (1941), 323-324; by Ivor Brown, *MGW*, April 18, p. 297; *TLS*, June 14, p. 288; by Bonamy Dobrée, *Spectator*, May 30, p. 588; by F. S. Boas, *English*, III, 222-223; by St. John Irvine, *FortnR*, No. 893, NS, 197-198; by Allardyce Nicoll, *JEGP*, XLI (1942), 239-240; by H. S., *MLN*, LVII, 321-322; by C. J. Sisson, *MLR*, XXXVII, 88-91; by G. F. Reynolds, *MP*, XXXIX, 431-432; by Alice Walker, *Library*, NS, XXII, 177-178; by K. M. Lea, *RES*, XVIII, 491-496; by Rosamond Gilder, *TAr*, XXVI, 140; by J. G. McManaway, *MLQ*, IV (1943), 245-247.

C281   Bentley, Gerald Eades. *The Jacobean and Caroline Stage: Plays and Playwrights.* New York: Oxford, Univ. Press. Vols. III-V, 1956.
        Rev: by R. Walker, *TC*, 160 (1956), 90-92; *TLS*, Nov. 9, p. 688; by Anthony Hartley, *Spectator*, Feb. 3, p. 163; by C. J. Sisson, *MLR*, LII (1957), 257-258; by Godfrey Davies, *EHR*, LXXII, 323-325; by G. B. Harrison, *MLN*, LXXII, 444-446; by Allardyce Nicoll, *JEGP*, LVI, 486-487; by James G. McManaway, *SQ*, VIII, 397-398; by R. C. Bald, *Library*, XII, 283-285; by P. F. Barum, *South Atlantic Quar.*, LVI, 266-267; *ShN*, VIII (1958), 3 (including Vols. I-II, 1941); by Harold Jenkins, *RES*, NS, IX, 196-202.

C282   Adams, Henry H. *English Domestic, or Homiletic Tragedy, 1575 to 1642; Being an Account of the Development of the Tragedy of the Common Man Showing its Great Dependence on Religious Morality, Illustrated with Striking Examples of the Interposition of Providence for the Amendment of Men's Manners.* DD, Columbia University, 1944. Columbia Univ. Studies in Engl. and Comp. Lit, 159. New York: Columbia Univ. Press, 1944. Pp. 228.
        Rev: by Sister Emmanuel Collins. *Catholic Hist. Rev.*, XXX (1944), 356; by Roy W. Battenhouse, *Church Hist.*, XIII, 231-232; by E. Ayers Taylor, *MLQ*, VI (1945), 102-104; by Willard Farnham, *MLN*, LX, 278-280; by Ernest Bernbaum, *Rev. Religion*, IX, 213-214; by R. H. Perkinson, *Thought*, XX, 550-551.

C283   Krzyżanowski, J. "Some Conjectural Remarks on Elizabethan Dramatists." *N&Q*, 192 (1947), 276-277.
        A miscellany of proposed readings: Arden of F., Yorkshire T., Fair Em, Two Noble K., and Others.

C284   Halliday, F. E. *Shakespeare and His Criticis.* London: Gerald Duckworth & Co., 1949. Pp. 522.
        Rev: A8596.

C285   Lyman, Dean B. "Apocryphal Plays of the University Wits." *English Studies in Honor of James Southall Wilson.* Ed. Fredson Bowers, Charlottesville, 1951, pp. 211-221.

C286   Ashe, Dora Jean. *A Survey of Non-Shakespearean Bad Quartos.* DD, University of Virginia, 1953. Pp. 286. Mic 54-1567. *DA*, XIV (1954), 1070. Publ. No. 7952.

C287   Kesler, Charlotte Ruth. *The Importance of the Comic Tradition of English Drama in the Interpretation of Marlowe's "Doctor Faustus."* DD, University of Missouri, 1954. Pp. 258. Mic 55-234.

DA, xv (1955), 1387. Publ. No. 9183.
Aprocrypha *passim*.

C288   Maxwell, Baldwin. *Studies in the Shakespeare Apocrypha.* New York: Columbia Univ. Press, 1956. Pp. 272.
Discusses the provenance of four plays: *The Yorkshire Tragedy, The Puritan Locrine,* and *Thomas Lord Cromwell.*
Rev: *Essential Books,* Feb., 1956, p. 22; *SCN,* xiv, 4; *N &Q,* ns, iii, 506, 552; by I. B. Cauthen, Jr., *CE,* xviii (1957), 292; by Samuel Schoenbaum, *JEGP,* lvi, 278-281; by F. David Hoeniger, *SQ,* viii, 236-237; *VQR,* xxxiii, xlv; by G. K. Hunter, *MLR,* lii, 587-588; by M. A. Shaaber, *MLN,* lxxii, 290-292; by J. M. Nosworthy, *RES,* ns, ix (1958), 434-436; by Hermann Heuer, *SJ,* 94 (1958), 293-294.

C289   Muir, Kenneth. *"Cardenio."* *EA,* xi (1958), 202-209.
A search for Shak. echoes in *Double Falsehood,* a play prepared for the stage by Theobald from an earlier play, *Cardenio,* believed by Theobald to be by Fletcher and Shak.

2. THE INDIVIDUAL PLAYS (272;96)
a. ARDEN OF FEVERSHAM (272;96)
(1) EDITIONS

C290   McIlwaith, A. K., ed. *Five Elizabethan Tragedies.* Oxford Univ. Press, 1938. Pp. 398. (Includes *Arden*).
Rev: by Reinald Hoops, *Eng. Studn.,* lxxiii (1938), 91; by W. Fischer, *Beiblatt,* l (1939), 114; by T. W. Baldwin, *MLN,* lv (1940), 458.

(2) STUDIES

C291   Oliphant, E. H. C. *"Arden of Feversham."* *TLS,* Jan. 18, 1936, p. 55.
See letter by V. Scholderer, *TLS,* Feb. 1, 1936, p. 96.

C292   Taylor, Rupert. "A Tentative Chronology of Marlowe's and Some Other Elizabethan Plays." *PMLA,* li (1936), 643-688.

C293   Boas, F. S. *Christopher Marlowe: A Biographical and Critical Study.* Oxford: Clarendon Press, 1940. Pp. 347.
Rev: A4867.

C294   Gillet, Louis. "Arden de Feversham." *Le Théâtre Elizabéthain.* Paris: Les Cahiers du Sud, 1940, pp. 197-207.

C295   Smith, Marion B. *Marlowe's Imagery and the Marlowe Canon.* Univ. of Pennsylvania Press, 1940. Pp. vii, 213.
Rev: B5321.

C296   Greg, W. W. "Shakespeare and *Arden of Feversham.*" *RES,* xxi (1945), 134-136.

C297   Zanco, Aurelio. *Shakespeare in Russia e Altri Saggi.* Turin-Genoa, 1945. Pp. 200.
Rev: A9787.

C298   Rubow, Paul V. *Shakespeare og hans Samtidige.* Copenhagen: Gyldendal, 1948. Pp. 155.
Essay on *Arden.*
Rev: C74.

C299   Baldini, Gabriele. "Un Apocrifo Shakespeariano: *Arden of Feversham.*" *Annali della Scuola Normale Superiore di Pisa* (Florence), Serie *II,* xviii (1949), 93-107.

C300   Carrère, Félix Jean. *Le Théâtre de Thomas Kyd. Contribution à l'Étude du Drame Élizabéthain.* Thèse de Lettres, Paris, 1949. Toulouse: Edouard Privat, 1951. Pp. 128.
Rev: A4979.

C301   Carrère, Félix Jean. *Arden de Feversham.* Thèse de Lettres Complémentaire, Paris, 1949.

C301a   Carrère, Félix. *Arden de Feversham.* Étude Critique, Traduction et Notes. Paris: Aubier, 1950. Pp. 245.

C302   Nosworthy, J. M. "The Southouse Text of *Arden of Feversham.*" *Library,* v (1950), 113-129.

C303   Wadsworth, Frank Whittemore. *The White Devil, An Historical and Critical Study.* DD, Princeton University, 1951. Pp. 416. Mic A55-1111. *DA,* xv (1955), 832. Publ. No. 11,051. Includes discussion of *Arden.*

C304   Legouis, Pierre. "The Epistolary Past in English." *N &Q,* 198 (1953), 111-112.

C305   Blayney, Glenn H. *"Arden of Feversham*—An Early Reference." *N &Q,* ns, ii (1955), 336.

C306   Chapman, Raymond. *"Arden of Feversham*: Its Interest Today." *English,* xi (1956), 15-17.

C307   Wentersdorf, Karl P. "The 'Fence of Trouble' Crux in *Arden of Feversham.*" *N &Q,* ns, iv (1957), 160-161.
Notes the references to muddy springs as symptoms of disorder in *Ham.* and *Shrew.*

b. LOCRINE (273;-)

C308   Muir, Kenneth. *"Locrine* and *Selimus."* *TLS,* Aug. 12, 1944, p. 391.
In *Selimus* every apparent borrowing from Spenser's *Complaints* is a real borrowing from *Locrine,* whose author uses Spenser as a source.

C309   Smith, G. "The Tennis-Ball of Fortune." *N &Q*, 190 (1946), 202-203.

c. KING EDWARD III (273;96)

C310   Crundell, H. W. "Drayton and *Edward III*." *N &Q*, 176 (1939), 258-260.
Letters by Kathleen Tillotson, *N &Q*, 176 (1939), 318-319; by Mr. Crundell, ibid., pp. 356-357.

C311   Reese, Gertrude C. "The Question of the Succession in Elizabethan Drama." *TxSE*, XXII (1942), 59-85.
Discussion, i. a., of *Edward III*.

C312   Bartley, J. O. "The Development of a Stock Character: The Stage Scotsman; The Stage Welshman (to 1800)." *MLR*, XXXVIII (1943), 279-288.

C313   Craig, M. R. *The Technique of the Chronicle Play*. MS thesis, Columbia University, 1947. Pp. 79.
Includes *Edward III* in the discussion.

C314   Muir, Kenneth. "A Reconsideration of *Edward III*." *ShS*, VI (1953), 39-48.
Finds that the vocabulary and imagery of the play support the theory of Shak.'s authorship, especially of the Countess scenes. Suggests that Shak. may have revised play by another dramatist.

C315   Dobson, Willis Boring. "*Edward the Third*": *A Study of its Composition in Relation to its Sources*.
DD, University of Texas, 1956. Pp. xxxiv, 456. Abstracted by Jack R. Brown, *ShN*, VII (1957), 19.

d. MUCEDORUS (274;-)

C316   Ramondt, Marie. "Vondel, Mucedorus en Pieter Breughel." *De Nieuwe Taalgids*, XLIII (1951), 10-12.

C317   Kirschbaum, L. "Texts of *Mucedorus*." *MLR*, L (1955), 1-5.
Reply by W. W. Greg, *MLR*, L (1955), 322. Argues that *Mucedorus* is a bad quarto, and that "the extant text can tell us only about the taste of the *reading* public"—and not about the author, the dramatic company, or the theatre public. Questions the stage vogue of the play, and declares the attribution of "primitive" qualities to the Eliz. stage comes from the assumption that "bad" quartos are accurate texts.

e. SIR JOHN OLDCASTLE (274;-)

C318   Adkins, Mary Grace Muse. "Sixteenth-Century Religious and Political Implications in *Sir John Oldcastle*." *TxSE*, XXII (1942), 86-104.

C319   Wilson, John Dover. "The Origins and Development of Shakespeare's *Henry IV*." *Library*, 4th Series, XXVI (1945), 2-16.

C320   Oliver, Leslie M. "Sir John Oldcastle: Legend or Literature?" *Library*, 5th Series, I (1947), 179-183.

C321   Fiehler, Rudolph. "Sir John Oldcastle Reconsidered." *Concordia Theological Monthly*, XXVIII (1957), 579-594.

f. THE LIFE AND DEATH OF THOMAS LORD CROMWELL (275;-)

g. THE LONDON PRODIGAL (275;96)

C322   *Le Prodigue de Londres*. Adapt. par Henri Ghéon selon la Version d'Ernest Kamnitzer. Paris: Impr. Artistique, 1947. Pp. xiii, 206.

C323   Maxwell, Baldwin. "Conjectures on *The London Prodigal*." *Studies in Honor of T. W. Baldwin*, 1958, pp. 171-184.

h. A YORKSHIRE TRAGEDY (275;96)

C324   Friedlaender, Marc. "Some Problems of *A Yorkshire Tragedy*." *SP*, XXXV (1938), 238-253.

C325   Pellegrini, Giuliano. "Note sulla *Yorkshire Tragedy*." *Convivium* (Turin), 1950, pp. 206-215.
Also in Pellegrini's *Barocco Inglese*. Messina, Florence: D'Anna, 1953, pp. 223-235.
Rev: A5536.

C326   *Una Tragedia Nella Contea di York* (English and Italian). Florence: Sansoni, 1952. Pp. 90.

C327   Blayney, Glenn H. "Massinger's Reference to the Calverley Story." *N &Q*, NS, I (1954), 17-18.
Massinger's *Guardian* (written before Nov., 1633) may allude to the tragedy of Walter Calverley as shown in one or both of *The Miseries of Inforst Marriage* and *A Yorkshire Tragedie*; the reference may indicate that Massinger regarded the treatment of the theme of wardship and marriage as central in his play.

C328   Blayney, Glenn H. "Variants in Q_1 of *A Yorkshire Tragedy*." *Library*, XI (1956), 262-267.
Presents and suggests the importance of the textual variants of the known extant copies of Q_1, not noted in Tucker Brooke's ed. in *The Shakespeare Apocrypha*.

C329   Blayney, Glenn H. "Dramatic Pointing in the *Yorkshire Tragedy*." *N &Q*, IV (1957), 191-192.

C330   Blayney, Glenn H. "Wilkins's Revisions in *The Miseries of Inforst Mariage*." *JEGP*, LVI (1957), 23-41.

i. FAIR EM (275;96)

C331 Thaler, Alwin. *Shakespeare and Democracy.* Univ. Tennessee Press, 1941. Pp. xii, 312.
Chap. VII. "*Faire Em* in Lancashire."
Rev: A1809.

j. THE TWO NOBLE KINSMEN (275;97)
(1) TEXT (275;-)

C332 Waller, Frederick O. *A Critical, Oldspelling Edition of "The Two Noble Kinsmen."* DD, University of Chicago, 1958. Microfilm No. 5423 PR. Dept. of Photographic Reproduction, Univ. of Chicago, 1957.

(2) STUDIES (275;97)

C333 Hart, Alfred. "Shakespeare and the Vocabulary of *The Two Noble Kinsmen.*" *Shakespeare and the Homilies, and Other Pieces of Research into the Elizabethan Drama.* Melbourne Univ. Press, 1934.
Rev: A4649.

C334 Spencer, Theodore. "*The Two Noble Kinsmen.*" *MP*, XXXVI (1939), 255-276.

C335 Agate, James. *Brief Chronicles, a Survey of the Plays of Shakespeare and the Elizabethans in Actual Performance.* London: J. Cape, 1943. Pp. 311.
Includes a piece on Shak.'s share in *Two Noble K.*

C336 Kökeritz, Helge. "The Beast-Eating Clown, *The Two Noble Kinsmen*, III. v. 131." *MLN*, LXI (1946), 532-535.

C337 Waggoner, George R. *The School of Honor, Warfare and the Elizabethan Gentleman.* DD, University of Wisconsin, 1948. Abstr. publ. in *Summaries of Doctoral Dissertations, 1947-49*, Vol. 10, Madison: Univ. of Wisconsin Press, 1950, pp. 624-626.
Section on *TNK.*

C338 Mincoff, M. "The Authorship of *The Two Noble Kinsmen.*" *ES*, XXXIII (1952), 97-115.

C339 Oras, Ants. " 'Extra Monosyllables' in *Henry VIII* and the Problem of Authorship." *JEGP*, LII (1953), 198-213.
Rev: by H. T. Price, *SQ*, V (1954), 126-127.

C340 Muir, Kenneth. "The Kite-Cluster in *The Two Noble Kinsmen.*" *N &Q*, NS, I (1954), 52-53.
The appearance of the cluster of images associated with *kite* and *pie* supports the attribution of the opening scene to Shak.

C341 Muir, Kenneth. "Shakespeare's Hand in *The Two Noble Kinsmen.*" *ShS*, XI (1958), 50-59.

C342 Waller, Frederick O. "Printer's Copy for *The Two Noble Kinsmen.*" *SB*, XI (1958), 61-84.

k. THE BIRTH OF MERLIN (276;-)

l. THE BOOK OF SIR THOMAS MORE (277;97)

C343 Tannenbaum, Samuel A. *Antony Mundy. Including the Play of Sir Thomas Moore (A Concise Bibliography).* Elizabethan Bibliographies, No. 27. New York: Samuel A. Tannenbaum, 1942. Pp. viii, 36.

(1) TEXT (277;-)

C344 *Sir Thomas More: An Anonymous Play of the Sixteenth Century Ascribed in Part to Shakespeare.* Ed. John Shirley. Canterbury: Goulden, 1938.
Rev: *TLS*, Jan. 28, 1939, p. 62.

C345 "The 'Shakespearian' Additions in *The Booke of Sir Thomas More.*" Ed. R. C. Bald. *ShS*, II (1949), 62-65.

C346 Black, Ben W. *The Book of Sir Thomas More: A Critical Edition.* DD, University of Michigan, 1953. Pp. 568. Mic A53-2025. *DA*, XIII (1953), 1182. Publ. No. 5639.

(2) STUDIES (277;97)

C347 Chambrun, Clara Longworth, Comtesse de. *Shakespeare Rediscovered by Means of Public Records, Secret Reports and Private Correspondence Newly Set Forth as Evidence on His Life and Work.* Preface by G. B. Harrison. New York: Scribner's, 1938. Pp. xii, 323.
Rev: A509.

C348 Cancelled.

C349 Crundell, H. W. "Shakespeare and the Play of *More.*" *TLS*, May 20, 1939, pp. 297-298.

C350 Chambers, R. W. "Shakespeare and *More.*" *TLS*, June 3, 1939, p. 327.

C351 Eagle, R. L. "The Date and Authorship of the MS Play *Sir Thomas More.*" *N &Q*, 177 (1939), 78.
See letters by H. W. Crundell, *N &Q*, 177 (1939), 120-121; by C. T. Onions, ibid., 177 (1939), p. 158.

C352   Deutschberger, Paul. "Shakspere and *Sir Thomas Moore.*" *SAB*, XVIII (1943), 75-91, 99-108, 156-167.
        The status of the question regarding Shak.'s alleged authorship of three pages of *The Booke of Sir Thomas Moore.*

C353   Krämer, Hildegard. *Zur Verfasserschaft der Aufruhrszene im Anonymen Drama "Sir Thomas Moore."* DD, Leipzig, 1944. Pp. 157. Typewritten.

C354   E., S. Y. "A Shakespeare MS?" *N &Q*, 189 (1945), 193; Wm. Jaggard, ibid., p. 263; James G. McManaway, ibid., p. 284; W. Jaggard, ibid., 190 (1946), p. 65.

C355   Flatter, Richard. "Eine Szene in Shakespeares Handschrift." *Neue Auslese*, II (1947), No. 6, 61-66. Comment, *Neues Abendland*, III (1948), 59.

C356   Jenkins, Harold. "Readings in the Manuscript of *Sir Thomas More.*" *MLR*, XLIII (1948), 512-514.
        An item overlooked in the previous Bibl.

C357   Bald, R. C. "*The Booke of Sir Thomas More* and Its Problems." *ShS*, II (1949), 44-61.
        A fresh treatment of the entire problem. Dates work in 1600-1 and accepts Shak. as author of additions in Hand D.

C358   Carrère, Félix Jean. *Le Théâtre de Thomas Kyd. Contribution à l'Etude du Drame Elizabéthain.* Thèse de Lettres, Paris, 1949. Publ. Toulouse: Edouard Privat, 1951.
            Rev: A4979.

C359   Stirling, Brents. *The Populace in Shakespeare.* Columbia Univ. Press, 1949. Pp. 203.
        Contains an analysis of the "Shak." scenes of *Sir Thomas More*. Stirling "finds these completely at variance in concept with anything in the dramatist's acknowledged work."—*YWES*.

C360   Maas, P. "Henry Finch and Shakespeare." *RES*, NS, IV (1953), 142.
        Parallels passages from a 1593 speech by Finch, and from Scene vi (in Hand D) of *The Booke of Sir Thomas Moore.*

C361   Nosworthy, J. M. "Shakespeare and *Sir Thomas More.*" *RES*, NS, VI (1955), 12-25.
        Argues that the problem of authorship of additions is inseparable from the problem of date. Vocabulary, phrase, and ideas of Addition II and III point to Shak.'s authorship in 1601-2.

C362   Shapiro, I. A. "The Significance of a Date." *ShS*, VIII (1955), 100-105.
        By correcting the reading of the date on the MS of Mundy's *John a Kent* from 1596 to 1590, suggests that *Sir Thomas More*, and other Elizabethan plays, must be redated—suggests, in fact, that our knowledge of dramatic chronology in the 1580's must be precarious if it can be upset by the redating of a single play.

C363   Nosworthy, J. M. "Hand B in *Sir Thomas More.*" *Library*, XI (1956), 47-50.
        Upon comparison with the script in *The Captives*, Hand B apparently is not Heywood's; nor does it belong to any other Elizabethan dramatist whose handwriting is known.

C364   Wilson, J. Dover. "The New Way with Shakespeare's Texts: An Introduction for Lay Readers. III. In Sight of Shakespeare's Manuscripts." *ShS*, IX (1956), 69-80.
        Analyzes the significance of scholarly discoveries concerning Shak.'s hand in *Sir Thomas More.*
            Rev: by Jacques Vallette, *MdF*, June, 1956, p. 365.

m. THE PURITAN

C365   Izeutschler, Artur. *Das Drama "The Puritan."* DD, Breslau, 1909. Pp. ix, 59.

V.   UNCLASSIFIED ITEMS
        1. THESES

C366   Connor, M. E. *Romance in Elizabethan Drama.* Master's thesis, University of New Zealand, 1926.

C367   Hewitt, Barnard W. *The Theatre and the Graphic Arts.* DD, Cornell University, 1936.

C368   Russell, Fielding D. *Six Tragedies by Aaron Hill.* DD, George Washington University, 1948.

C369   Redfern, Richard K. *A Study of Act-Structure in Drama.* DD, Cornell University, 1950.

C370   Sloca, Charles. *The Dramatic Conflict.* DD, Cornell University, 1950.

C371   Wu, Chi-hwei. *Elements of Conflict in Elizabethan Tragedy.* DD, Cornell University, 1951.

C372   Fowler, Frank C. *Modern American Dramatization.* DD, Columbia University, 1953.

C373   Ahmed El Tayib. *The Drama in Arabic from 1848 to 1950.* DD, University of London, 1954.

C374   Hansen, Edwin R. *Space in the Theatre: Its Use and Significance.* DD, Cornell University, 1954.

C375   Morris, T. G. *Stuart Overture.* DD, National University of Ireland, 1954.

C376   Smith, Herbert L. *The Presentational Theater and Drama.* DD, Cornell University, 1954.

C377   Bruckshaw, M. M. *Nature in Seventeenth Century English Poetry.* DD, University of Manchester, 1955.

C378   Schlichte, Franz. *Die Zustände Leidenschaftlichen Aussersichseins im Werk William Shakespeares.* DD, Tübingen, 1957.

2. OTHERS

C379 Bauer, W. "Von Shakespeares Gestalten und Welt." *Berliner Tagebl.*, 1935, No. 510.

C380 Laaths, E. "Shakespeares Dichterisches Theater." *Düsseldorfer Nachr.*, 1935, No. 545.

C381 Horst, Karl August. "Zu Klemens ten Holders 'Erinnerungen an einen Sprachlehrer'." *Das Wort in der Zeit* (Regensburg), III (1935/36), 1141-1144.

C382 Lawrence, W. J. "How Shakespeare Was Marred." *Birmingham Mail*, Sept. 1936.

C383 Luserke, Martin. "Landnahme und Weiterfahrt." *DNL*, XXXVII (1936), 313-321.

C384 Rauhut, F. "Der *Sponsus*." *Roman. Forsch.*, I (1936), 21-50.

C385 Ruutz-Rees, C. "Flower Garlands of Poets: Milton, Shakespeare, Spenser, Marot, Sannazaro." *Mélanges Abel Lefranc*. Paris: Droz, 1936, pp. 75-90.

C386 Steinböhmer, Gustav. "Shakespeare und kein Ende." *MNN*, 1936, No. 39.

C387 Vietta, Egon. "*Hamlet*." *Köln. Ztg.*, 1936, No. 439/40.

C388 "Shakespeare und Das Englische Nationaltheater." *Rhein.-Westfäl. Ztg.* (Essen), Oct. 12, 1937.

C389 Belloni-Filippi, F. "Minima Shakespeariana." *Annali della Reale Scuola Norm. Sup. di Pisa. Lettere, Storia e Filosofia.* Ser. II, IV (1937?), 183-190.

C390 Dam, B. A. P. van. "100 Regele van Shakespeare." *Jaarboek van de Maatschapij der Nederlandsche Letterkunde te Leiden*, 1937/38, pp. 89-114.

C391 Haacke, Wilmont. "Ein Wort zur Shakespeare-Debatte." *Ostdeutsche Monatsheft*, XVII (1936/37), 648.

C392 Hughes, W. R. "They All Wrote Plays." *Blackwood's Magazine*, 252 (1937), 70-84.

C393 Morando, F. E. "Intorno allo Shakespeare." *Studi di Letteratura e di Storia.* Florence: La Nuova Italia, 1937, pp. 70-88.

C394 Schlösser, Rainer. "Shakespeare—die Vollendung." *VB*, October 12, 1937.

C395 Stieber, H. "Ein neuer Sommernachstraum." *LNN*, Feb. 25, 1937.

C396 Veth, C. "Een Nederlands boek over Shakespeare." *De Socialistische Gids* (Amsterdam), XXIII (1937/38?) 344-349.

C397 Boillet, A. "Ebauche d'une Explication de Shakespeare." *Revue de l'Enseignement des Langues Vivantes*, LV (1938), 214-217.

C398 "Das Geheimnis um Shakespeare." *Neue Augsburger Ztg.*, April 9, 1938.

C399 Henriot, E. "L'Affaire Shakespeare." *Le Temps*, March 1, 1938.

C400 Huch, R. "Das Rätsel Shakespeare." *Deutsches Volkstum*, XX, 2 (1938), 80-87.

C401 Kroepelin, H. "Wie hat Shakespeare Ausgesehen?" *VB*(B), Nov. 7, 1938, No. 316.

C402 Ludwig, O. "Shakespeare." *Freiburger Theaterblätter.* 1937/38, p. 85.

C403 "Der Streit um die 'Sieben' Shakespeares." *Germania* (Berlin), Oct. 27, 1938.

C404 Wagner, G. "Shakespeares Kranz." *Kölnische Volksztg.*, Aug. 27, 1938.

C405 Winter, J. "War Shakespeare—Shakespeare." *Danziger Neueste Nachrichten*, Dec. 23, 1938.

C406 "Shakespeare on Czechoslovakia." *Christian Century*, LV (1938), 1288-89.

C407 "Reverence for Shakespeare." *AglGR*, II (1938), 189.

C408 Cancelled.

C409 Cremer, L. "Pole der Shakespeare-Deutung." *Kölnische Ztg.*, Dec. 24, 1939.

C410 Morton Fullerton, W. "Shakespeare Revit." *Journal des Débats*, July 26, 1939.

C411 Medefind, H. "Das Geheimnis von Westminister. Wird Man dem Rätsel Shakespeare auf die Spur Kommen?" *Berliner Ill. Ztg.*, XLVIII (1939), No. 11.

C412 Medefind, H. "Shakespeare mit Stratforder Augen: Eine Neue Stellungnahme zu einer Alten Literarischen Streitfrage." *Hamburger Tagebl.*, 1939, No. 217.

C413 Millot, H. "Shakespeare à Paris." *Revue des Jeunes*, XXX, No. 5, Aug. 10, 1939.

C414 Münch, R. "Immer Noch Rätsel um Shakespeare?" *Chemnitzer Tageblatt u. Anzeiger*, April 23, 1939.

C415 Rivière, P. L. "Affaire Shakespeare." *Revue des Travaux de l'Académie des Sciences Morales et Politiques.* 3rd Ser., 98 (1938/39?), 314-334.

C416 Wachter, Ernst. "Ist Shakespeare ein Deckname?" *Hamburger Tageblatt*, (1939), No. 168.

C417 Wehner, Carl. "Eine Neue, Interessante Shakespeare-Theorie." *Neue Leipziger Ztg.*, Feb. 16, 1939.

C418 Winter, J. W. "Fünfzehnmal Shakespeare." *Schlesische Ztg.* (Breslau), July 11, 1939.

C419 Feldkeller, P. "Das Erbe Shakespeare." *Dts. Allg. Ztg.*, April 25, 1940.

C420 Hofmüller, Rudolf. "Um den Sommernachtstraum." *VB*(Mü), No. 356, Dec. 21, 1940.

C421 Klingsor, Francis. "*Richard III*." *Beaux Arts, Chronique des Arts* . . . (Paris), LXXII, No. 47 (1940), 7f.

C422 Møller, N. "Et Shakespeare-Find." *Tilskueren* (Copenhagen), XLIX, ii, 219-224.

C423 Steguweit, Heinz. "Shakespeare war im Bilde." *Volk und Welt*, II (1940), 12-14.

C424 Thorndike, Russell. *A Wanderer with Shakespeare*. London: Rich and Cowan, 1940. Pp. 381.

C425 Ernst, Paul. "Zwei Arten von Dramen (1915)." *VB*(Mü), March 14, 1941, No. 73.

C426 Hering, Gerhard F. "Jünglinge. Aus einer Folge von Shakespeare-Studien." *Köln. Zeitung*, 1941, Nos. 260-261.

C427 Hering, Gerhard F. "Natur und Kunst. Aus Einer Folge von Shakespeare-Studien." *Köln. Zeitung*, 1941, Nos. 232-233.

C428 Kölli, Joseph Georg. "Shakespeare Problematisch Gesehen." *Volk im Werden*, LX (1941), 1-8.

C429 Packard, F. R. "Fig Leaves for Shakespeare and Michel Montaigne." *Proceedings of the Charaka Club*, 1941, pp. 31-44.

C430 Rusch, H. "Schöpfer der Weltliteratur." *Westfälische Landeszeitung*, Rote Erde, No. 110, 1941.

C431 Cancelled.

C432 Florentiis, G. de. "Shakespeare ai Saggi X." *Sapere* (Milan), VI (1941/42?), 67.

C433 Lanzisera, Francesco. *Elisabeth, Marlowe, Shakespeare*. Bari: Soc. Ed. Tipogr., 1942. Pp. xiii, 274.

C434 Ihering, Herbert. *Regie*. Berlin: Hans von Hugo Vlg., 1943. Pp. 104.

C435 Jacobs, Wilhelm. "Dionysisches und Dramatisches." *Deutsche Dramaturgie*, II (1943), 131-133.

C436 Miles, Josephine. "Some Major Poetic Words." *Essays and Studies by Members of the Department of English, Univ. of California*. Univ. California Pubs. Eng., XIV. Univ. California Press, 1943, pp. 233-239.

C437 Maugeri, Aldo. *Il Dramma Elisabettiano*. Parts I, II, III. 3 Vols. Messina: V. Ferrara, 1944, 1945, 1946.

C438 Hewitt, Barnard. "The Elizabethan Theatre." *Dramatics*, XVIII (Nov., 1945), 3-5.

C439 Lannes, R. "Les Spectacles de Paris." *Fontaine*, VIII (1945), 386-389.

C440 Massey, G. "Shakespeare." (12 lines). *The Shakespeare Fellowship Quarterly*, VII (1946), 19.

C441 Morozov, Mikhail Mikhailovich. "330 Godina od Sekspirove Smrti." [330th Anniversary of Shak.'s death.] Preveo Dobriša Cesarić. *Republika* (Zagreb), II (1946), 654-657.

C442 Bell, A. F. G. "Shakespeare." *Cervantes*. Norman, Oklahoma: Univ. of Oklahoma Press, 1947.

C443 Buckinx, W. "Shakespeare in His Own Dress." *Revue des Langues Vivantes*, XIII (1947), 72-74.

C444 Foster, W., and H. Bryant, eds. *The Gateway to Shakespeare*. Sydney, 1947. Pp. 159.

C445 Glaglin, B. S. *Journey Through Shakespeare*. (Mimeographed by M. O'Dwyer) Hollywood, 1947.

C446 Strodthoff, Emil. "Shakespeare und kein Ende." *Neues Europa*, II (1947), 18, 25-29.

C447 Altrocchi, Rudolph. "How to Shake Hands with Shakespeare." *Catholic World*, 167 (1948), 116-121.

C448 Brooke, Charles Frederick Tucker, and Nathaniel B. Paradise. *English Drama 1580-1642*. New York: D. C. Heath, 1933; London: Harrap, 1948. Pp. 1044.
Texts of plays. None by Shak. No Shak. Apocrypha.

C449 Sanín Cano, Baldomero. "Cervantes: Un Vínculo Inmortal de dos Pueblos." Calderón Caballero, Eduardo: *Cervantes en Colombia* (Madrid), 1948, pp. 241-250.

C450 Foligno, Cesare. *Personaggi Shakespeareani*. Naples: Pironti, 1948. Pp. 127.

C451 Guttmann, W. "Ein Sommernachtstraum." *Öesterreichische Rundschau*, III (1948), 299-301.

C451a Helsztyiński, Stanisław. *Od Szekspira do Joyce'a*. Warsaw: Stanisław Cuzrowski, 1948. Pp. 325.

C452 Melcer, Wanda. "Szekspir na Półmisku." *Odrodzenie* (Warsaw), No. 28 (1948), 7.

C453 Branchi, E. C. *Escursioni Letterarie da Londra a Firenze*. Le Fonti Italiane della Letteratura Inglese. Santiago de Chile: Pubblicazioni del Collegio Italiano, 1949. Pp. 51.

C454 Crewe, Elsie. *Who Wrote Shakespeare?* Cape Town: Maskew Miller, 1949. Pp. 49.

C455 Figueiredo, Fidelino de. "Shakespeare e Garrett." *Boletín de la Academia Argentina de Letras*, XVIII (Oct.-Dec., 1949), 485-549.

C456 Florquin, J. "Shakespeareana." *Dietsche Warande en Belfort*, 1949, pp. 186-187.

C457 Honda, Akira. *A Study of Shakespeare*. Kobundo, 1949.

C458 Janssen, J. "Een Toneelscherm bij Shakespeare." *LT*, 1949, pp. 48-49.
Comment by H. de Groot, ibid., pp. 49-50.

C459 McGregor, J. S. I., ed. *Notes on Shakespeares Plays*. No. 1. Cape Town: Juta, 1949. Pp. 32.

C460 Reinhardt, Heinz. "Shakespeare und die Atomwissenschaft." *Die Pforte* (Urach), II (1949-50), 23-24, 849-855.

C461 Sikelianos, A. "*La Tempête* de Shakespeare." *Revue Anglo-Hellénique*, III (1949).

C462 Viswanathan, K. "Falstaff and the *Sonnets*." *Triveni* (Masulapatam, Andhra), June, 1949.

C463 "Zu Shakespeares *Hamlet*." *Deutschunterricht*, April 2, 1949, pp. 33-45.

C464 Beckmann, Heinz. "Im Spiegel Shakespeares." *Rhein. Merkur*, V (1950), No. 19, p. 6.

C465 Godwin, Edward F., and Stephani Allfree Godwin. *The Greenwood Tree. A Portrait of William Shakespeare*. Ill. New York: Dutton, 1950. Pp. 178.

C466 Manggold, Walter. "Der Wahre Shakespeare? Zu Shakespeare-Bildern." *Die Erzählung* (Konstanz), IV (1950), 8.

C467 Sanvic, Romain. "L'Obsession du Théâtre." *Beaux-Arts*, Dec. 22, 1950.

C468 Cancelled.

C469 Vodák, Jindrich. *Shakespeare Kritikuv Breviár*. Vodák: Kritické dilo. 4. Prague: Melantrich, 1950. Pp. 677.

C470 Kapitan, Hans. *Glimpses of Shakespeare*. Engl. Lesehefte. Horn: Berger, 1951. Pp. 64.

C471 Koffka, Friedrich. "Seitenlicht auf Shakespeare." *Deutsche Rundschau*, LXXVII (1951), 1099-1102.

C472 Meyer, Justus. "Nieuwe Sensatie Rond Shakespeare." *Groene Amsterdammer*, April 14, 1951.

C473 Roberts, Daisy Oke. *Shakespeare and Co., Unlimited*, by Shakespeare and Co. Boreham Wood (Herts): Roberts, 1951. Pp. 104.

C474 Šaula, Dorte. "Shakespearova Komedija *Na Tri Kralja* [*Twelfth Night*]." *Studentski List* (Zagreb), VII (1951), 20.

C475 Scharff, Erich. "Shakespeares *Was Ihr Wollt*." *Die Volksbühne, Blätter für Kunst und Volkskultur* (Hamburg), I (1951), No. 1.

C476 Bodmer, Martin. "Zum Thema Shakespeare." *Neue Schweizer Rundschau*, XX (1952), 173-175.

C477 Ertugrul, Muhsin. "Ne Isterseniz" ["What you will"]. *Kucük Sahne* (Oct., 1952), p. 7.

C478 Hatcher, Harlan. "The Pure Flame." *PMLA*, LXVII (1952), 67-70.

C479 Janzon, A. "Ur Mörkret Kring Shakespeare." *Bonniers-Litterära Magasin*, XXI (1952), 193-197.

C480 Obertello, A. "Tempo Elisabettiano e Realtà Storica." *Acme*, V (1952), 163-166.

C481 Lebesque, Morvan. "Shakespeare s'appelait Shakespeare." *Théâtre Populaire*, Sept.-Oct., 1953, pp. 26-41.

C482 Monsey, Derek. "Un Grande Avvenimento a Stratford-on-Avon." *Idea* (Rome), June 14, 1953, p. 5.

C483 Chwalewik, Witold. "Z Problemów Szekspirowskich: Świat Jako Teatr." *Kwartalnik Neofilologiczny* (Warsaw), I (1954), 21-27.

C483a Connes, Georges. "Le Mystère Shakespeare." *Letterature Moderne*, LXVIII (1954), 76.

C484 Jones, Margo. "Shakespeare in the Round." *World Theatre*, III, i (1954), 29.

C485 Rubow, Paul V. "Shakespeare's *Julius Caesar*." *Berlingske Aften* (Copenhagen), Aug. 24, 25, 1954.

C486 Valogne, Cathérine. *Jean Vilar*. Paris: Pr. Littéraires de France, 1954. Pp. 60.
        Rev: by R. M. Moudouès, *RHT*, VI (1954), 315.

C487 Westecker, Wilhelm. "Shakespeare im Schwarzen Revier." *Christ und Welt*, April 29, 1954, p. 6.

C488 Ahlberg, Alf. "Stackars William Shakespeare." *Dala-Demokraten*, IV (1955), 8; *Smålands Folkblad*, VI (1955), 8; *Norrländska Socialdemokraten*, XII (1955), 8.

C489 Engberg, Jytte. "Om Shakespeare." *Dansk Udsyn* (Copenhagen), XXXV (1955), 243-255.

C490 Fyton, F. "Shakespeare Recitations Saved the Bank." *Times of India* (Bombay), Jan. 23, 1955, p. 7.

C491 Gerber, Richard. "Zum Tragödienstil der Shakespeare-Zeit." *Neue Zürcher Ztg.*, Fernausg., No. 165, June 18, 1955, pp. 8, 10.

C492 Koskenniemi, I. "Tutkimuksia Shakespearean Kuvakielessä." *Valvoja* (Helsinki), 1955, No. 5.

C493 Kruuse, Jens. "De Leger Alvor i Illyrien." *Jyllandsposten* (Aarhus, Denmark), June 30, 1955.

C494 Kruuse, Jens. "Mellem Himmel og Jord." *Jyllandsposten* (Aarhus, Denmark), July 28, 1955.

C495 Moritz, Sven. "Shakespeare's *En Skaersommernatsdröm*." *Aalborg-Amtstidende* (Aalborg, Denmark), April 18, 1955.

C496 Omkarananda, Swami. *Shakespeare on Sivananda*. Rishakesh: Divine Life Society, Yoga Vedanta Forest Univ., n.d. (1955?). Pp. 66.
        Rev: B118.

C497 Przywara, Erich. "Shakespearesch." *Die Besinnung* (Nürnberg), X (1955), 318-334.

C498 Rubow, Paul V. "Shakespeare-Overleveringen." *Berlingske Aften* (Copenhagen), Sept. 8, 1955.

C499 Sörensen, Poul. "Det Menneskelige Umenneske." *Politiken* (Copenhagen), Feb. 11, 1955.

C500 Stroedel, Wolfgang. "*Komödie der Irrungen*." *Prisma* (Bochum), 1955/56, pp. 109-112.

C501 Vries, Theun de. "Anon, Sir! Begegnung mit William Shakespeare." *Sinn u. Form*, VII (1955), 594-608.

C502   Bodmer, Martin. "Zum Thema Shakespeare." *Variationen zum Thema Weltliteratur.* Frankfort a.M.: Suhrkamp, 1956, pp. 208-211.

C503   Gerhardt, Mia I. "Tragedie en Drama." *LT*, 1956, pp. 276-289.

C504   Hansen-Skovmoes, Jörgen. "Nöglen til Shakespeare." *Kristeligt Dagblad* (Copenhagen), Jan. 18, 1956.

C505   Ingram, William. "Shakespeare in a Temple of Bacchus." *Plays and Players*, Nov. 1956, p. 7.

C506   Lewalter, Christian E. "Warum Eigentlich Nicht Shakespeare? Einiges Grundsätzliche zu Überflüssigen Scharfsinnsübungen." *Die Zeit*, XI, 1956, No. 10, p. 7.

C507   Little, Hubert V. *The Gospel According to Shakespeare.* Published by author. 138 East Dulwich Grove, London, S.E. 22, 1956. Pp. 24.

C508   Marcus, Aage. "Sid Ned, Sid Ned hos Shakespeare." *Politiken* (Copenhagen), Jan. 12, 1956.

C509   Patterson, H. Temple. "Apparition de Shakespeare dans 'Notre Dame de Paris'." *Vie et Langage*, No. 57 (Dec., 1956).

C510   Stephenson, A. A. "Tales of Hoffman Irk the English." *America*, June 30, 1956, pp. 325-326.

C511   Trilling, Ossia. "Hven Myrdede William Shakespeare?" *Det Danske Magasin* (Copenhagen), IV (1956), 174-179.

C512   *Der Grosse Brockhaus.* Wiesbaden, Bd. 10, 1956, pp. 675-679.

C513   *Der Grosse Herder.* Freiburg i. Br., Bd 8, 1956, pp. 677-681.

C514   Vianu, Tudor. "Shakespeare Si Antropologia Renasterii." *Teatrul* (Bucharest), No. 1, 1956.

C515   Zamfirescu, I. "Observatii Asupra Unei Traduceri din Dramaturgia Clasica Engleza." *Limba Romina* (Bucharest), April 5, 1956, pp. 85-94.

C516   Friis, Niels. " 'En Skaersommernatsdröm' i Sit Rette Element." *Fyns Stiftstidende* (Odense Denmark), July 2, 1957.

C517   Hicks, Eric. "Thames-side Theatrical Traditions." *P.L.A. Monthly*, Jan. 1957, pp. 24-27.

C518   Moore, J. M. "Rare and Glorious Hamlet." *Canadian Commentator*, July 1957, p. 3.

C519   Moritz, Sven. "Shakespeare's 'Trold Kan Taemmes'." *Aalborg-Amstidende* (Aalborg, Denmark), March 26, 1957.

C520   Ritzau, Tue. "William Shakespeare og Drejebogen." *Aarhus Stiftstidende* (Aarhus, Denmark), June 27, 1957.

C521   Sörensen, Aage. "Kobmanden i Venedig." *Fyns Tidende* (Odense, Denmark), March 16, 1955.

C522   Baeckström, Tord. "Shakespeare med och utan Fernissa." *Göteborgs Handelstidning* (Göteborg), July 14, 1958.

C523   Chauvet, Victor. *Manzoni-Stendhal-Hugo e altri Saggi su Classici e Romantici.* A cura di Carlo Cordié. Catania: Università di Catania, 1958.

C524   Elling, Christian. "Shakespeare og Nogle Kreaturer." *Berlingske Aften* (Copenhagen) March 25, 1958.

C525   Mary Faith, Sister. "Scripture from the Billboards: Face of Falstaff." *America*, May 10, 1958, pp. 194-195.

C526   Langenfelt, Gösta. "Når Shakespeare var 'Ociviliserad'." *Sundsvalls Tidning* (Sundsvall), July 3, 1958.

C527   Nielsen, Johs. "Shakespeare For Alle Og. I. Alle Lande." *Söro Amtstidende*, Oct. 4, 1958.